The Hutchinson Chronology of World History

Volume IV

The Modern World

1901–1998

THE HUTCHINSON CHRONOLOGY OF WORLD HISTORY

Other volumes in the series:

The Ancient and Medieval World
Prehistory–AD 1491

The Expanding World
1492–1775

The Changing World
1776–1900

THE HUTCHINSON CHRONOLOGY OF WORLD HISTORY

VOLUME IV

The Modern World

1901–1998

Neville Williams

Helicon

Copyright © Helicon Publishing Limited 1999
This is an extensively revised and updated edition of the
Chronology of the Modern World 1763–1992 by Neville Williams
originally published in 1966.

This edition published 1999

Helicon Publishing Ltd
42 Hythe Bridge Street
Oxford OX1 2EP
England

e-mail: admin@helicon.co.uk
Web site: www.helicon.co.uk

Printed and bound by DeAgostini, Novara, Italy

ISBN 1-85986-284-5

British Library Cataloging in Publication Data

A catalog record of this book is available from the British Library.

Papers used by Helicon Publishing Ltd are natural recyclable
products made from wood grown in sustainable forests. The
manufacturing processes of both raw material and paper conform
to the environmental regulations of the country of origin.

Photo credits: U.S.A. Army Corps *c.*1930, © SuperStock.

Contents

Preface

The new *Hutchinson Chronology of World History* has over 70,000 entries. *The Modern World* is the most detailed and comprehensive overview of the modern world available in one volume. It begins as President McKinley's death in the USA propels Teddy Roosevelt into office, and Queen Victoria dies in the UK. During the same year instant coffee is invented, the Chicago White Sox win the first American League championship, and students and workers riot throughout Russia in protest against repression of political activity. It ends as 1998 draws to a close a century racked with The Great Depression and two World Wars, but marked by phenomenal strides forward in all aspects of human endeavor.

Order of Entries

The Modern World is arranged in strict chronological sequence by year, month, and day. Within each year, the entries have been carefully grouped into four main categories and 25 subcategories. Subcategories are arranged alphabetically within each main category.

Politics, Government, and Economics
   Business and Economics
   Colonization
   Human Rights
   Politics and Government
Science, Technology, and Medicine
   Agriculture
   Computing
   Ecology
   Exploration
   Health and Medicine
   Math
   Science
   Technology
   Transportation

Arts and Ideas
   Architecture
   Arts
   Film
   Literature and Language
   Music
   Theatre and Dance
   Thought and Scholarship
Society
   Education
   Everyday Life
   Media and Communication
   Religion
   Sports

Whether you are looking for a specific fact, tracing events over a period of time, or reading for pure enjoyment, the date coupled with the categories, subcategoires, and indexes will help you find your way around.

Special Features

Special mini-chronologies provide at-a-glance information about important people, topics, or events. They have been designed to provide an overview of an event or development in a concise, easy-to-read format. For a more extensive study of the subject, the mini-chronologies provide guidelines to the dates of numerous related entries in the body of the *Chronology*. Birth and death dates of noteworthy people can be found at the end of each year in tinted boxes. Where available, birth announcements include the year of death in parentheses, e.g. (–1997), and death entries conclude with the age at death, e.g. (80).

Indexes

An extensive Main Index includes virtually every name, title, place, event, and subject appearing in the *Chronology*. The volume's vast coverage of works of art, literature, music, dance, film, theater, and scholarship can be searched using the titles index.

Special Features

Contributors and Acknowledgements

Consultant Editors
T. C. W. Blanning, *Professor of Modern European History, University of Cambridge, and Fellow of Sidney Sussex College, Cambridge, U.K.*
David Feldman, *Birkbeck College, University of London, U.K.*
Roy Porter, *Wellcome Institute for the History of Medicine, London, U.K.*
Bruce Schulman, *Professor of History, Boston University, U.S.A.*
Alison Scott, *Head, Popular Culture Library and Associate Professor of Popular Culture, Bowling Green State University, Ohio, U.S.A.*
John Sutherland, *Lord Northcliffe Professor of Modern English Literature, University College London, U.K.*

Contributing Editors
Duncan Anderson M.A., D.Phil.
Edward Barratt B.A.
Tallis Barker D.Phil., A.R.C.M.
Andrew Colquhoun B.Sc., M.A.
Sara Coombs M.A.
David Gould
Jonathan M. Hansen Ph.D.
Simon Harratt M.A., Ph.D.
John Haywood Ph.D.
Chris Holdsworth M.A., Ph.D.
Nicola Matthews B.A.
Tracy Miller
Chris Murray
Malgorzata Nawrocka-Colquhoun D.Phil.
Robert Peberdy
David Petts
Benedict Ramos
Adrian Room M.A., Dip.Ed., F.R.G.S.
Jon Rowe Ph.D.
Harold Sawdon
Christopher M. Scribner Ph.D.
Martha Y. Scribner M.A.
Harry Sidebottom M.A., D.Phil.
Giles Sparrow M.Sc.
Joe Staines B.A.
Matthew Steggle M.A., D.Phil.
Steve Williams Ph.D.

Editorial Director
Hilary McGlynn

Managing Editor
Katie Emblen

Project Manager
Susan Mendelsohn

Editors
Rachel Beckett
Chris Clark
Susan Cuthbert
Denise Dresner
Jo Linzey
Mark McGuinness
Richard Martin
Rachel Minay
Amy Myers
Kate O'Leary
Clare Ramos
Lisa Sullivan
John Wright
Karen Young

Index
Martin Hargreaves
  Indexing Services

Electronic Publishing Manager
Nick Andrews

Database Editor
Louise Richmond

Senior Technical Editor
Graham Bennett

Technical Editor
Claire Lishman

Production Director
Tony Ballsdon

Art and Design Manager
Terence Caven

Typesetting and Page Layout
Mendip Communications Ltd,
Frome, Somerset

1901

POLITICS, GOVERNMENT, AND ECONOMICS

Business and Economics

- Sir William Henry Wills forms the Imperial Tobacco Co. in Britain, which, through later mergers, will become W. D. & H. O. Wills.
- Swedish immigrant John W. Nordstrom opens a shoe store in Seattle, Washington, which will grow into the retail store, Nordstroms.
- The shah of Persia grants an oil concession of over 1.2 million sq km/480,000 sq mi to the New Zealand gold prospector William Knox D'Arcy.

FEBRUARY

2   J. P. Morgan buys Andrew Carnegie's steel companies for $250 million, forming the U.S. Steel Corporation, the first U.S. corporation to have assets exceeding $1 billion.

MAY

- A contest to control the assets of the Northern Pacific Railroad sparks a panic on Wall Street.

Colonization

MAY

- The U.S. Supreme Court decrees the former Spanish colonies, Puerto Rico and the Philippines, to be U.S. protectorates.

JULY

20   Morocco grants the control of its frontier police to France, and recognizes greater French influence in its affairs.

SEPTEMBER

25   The Ashanti Kingdom is annexed to Britain's Gold Coast Colony (modern Ghana) following the suppression of several revolts there.

Human Rights

- The new Alabama state constitution features literacy laws and grandfather clauses designed to deprive black Americans of the vote. The grandfather clause exempts from literacy requirements persons who were eligible to vote on January 1, 1867, or their descendants, thus excluding former slaves, who had not been given the right to vote by that date. The constitution comes into effect in 1903.

September 1901–20   About 280,000 people emigrate from Anatolia (modern Turkey) and 350,000 people emigrate from Greece in response to persecution by the Ottoman government.

Politics and Government

- The British viceroy in India, George Curzon, establishes the North-West Frontier as a buffer zone between Punjab and Afghanistan.
- The final Pendleton Act creates the U.S. career civil service. The Pendleton Acts concerned federal employment based on merit and not political affiliation.

JANUARY

1   Horatio, Lord Kitchener, launches two major offensives against Boer forces in South Africa. To combat the guerrilla actions of the Boer troops, he extends the British "scorched earth" policy.

1   The Commonwealth of Australia comes into being, with the federalist and protectionist Edmund Barton as prime minister.

22   Queen Victoria of Great Britain dies after a brief illness, with Kaiser Wilhelm II of Germany at her side. The prince of Wales accedes to the throne as Edward VII on the same day.

FEBRUARY

- Students and workers riot in major cities throughout Russia over the repression of political activity. As a result, many provinces are placed under martial law.

7   The Italian government, led by Giuseppe Saracco, is overthrown for its feeble response toward striking dockers in Genoa, Italy.

8   On receiving Russia's conditions for withdrawing its troops from Manchuria, China appeals to the other major powers and gains support from Britain, Japan, and Germany. Russia's demands include the granting of a monopoly of trade concessions in Manchuria, Mongolia, and Chinese Central Asia.

23   Britain and Germany sign an agreement over the boundary between German East Africa and Nyasaland (modern Tanzania and Malawi), following an improvement in relations.

27   The Russian minister of education, M. Bogoljepoff, is wounded by an ex-student of Moscow University seeking to avenge the repression of student political activity.

28   The Boer leader Louis Botha meets the British representative Lord Kitchener at Middelburg, South Africa, for peace talks.

MARCH

- Through a combination of cunning and treachery, U.S. Army troops apprehend Philippine resistance leader, Emilio Aguinaldo, in Isabela, Luzon.
2 An amendment to an act of Congress provides for the United States to withdraw its troops from Cuba when Cuba has established a republican form of government and has entered into other stipulations. The United States will retain supervision over Cuba's foreign policy and will acquire sites there for naval stations.
2 The U.S. Congress adopts two amendments to the Army Appropriations Bill of 1901 providing for U.S. intervention abroad. The Platt amendment, named for Connecticut senator Orville H. Platt, authorizes U.S. intervention in Cuba in the case of political, economic, or social upheaval. A separate amendment by J. C. Spooner calls for civil government in the Philippines.
4 U.S. president William McKinley is inaugurated for his second term of office in Washington, D.C.
15 In the German Reichstag (parliament), the chancellor, Prince Bernhard von Bülow, declares that the 1900 British–German Yangzi Agreement on trade with China did not apply to Manchuria. As a result, the London discussions on the possibility of creating a British–German–Japanese bloc against Russia end abruptly.
16 Peace negotiations between the British and the Boers break down when the British government continues to refuse an amnesty for Boer rebels in the Cape and Natal.

APRIL

- With its leader, Emilio Aguinaldo, in U.S. custody, the Philippine Independence Movement disintegrates, bringing an end to the U.S.-Filipino War.
2 Following protests from Britain and Japan, China refuses to sign a convention with Russia giving it control of Manchuria, and on April 6 Russia drops its demands.

MAY

7–14 A state of siege is declared in Barcelona, Spain, following rioting by anarchists and republicans.
20 U.S. military rule in Cuba ends.

JUNE

6 A Moroccan mission to Paris, France, London, England, and Berlin, Germany, seeks a British–German pact on Morocco as a counterweight to French influence there.
12 A new Cuban constitution is agreed, reserving U.S. rights that effectively make the country a U.S. protectorate.

JULY

- The Socialist Party of America is formed in Indianapolis, Indiana, from a merger of Eugene V. Debs's Social Democracy and the Victor Berger wing of the Socialist Labor Party.
1 The anticlerical Association Law is promulgated in France. This demands the compulsory regulation of all religious congregations and associations, and the dissolution of those not authorized by the state.
4 Civil government replaces military rule in the Philippines with William Taft as governor-general. He proclaims an amnesty for rebels who take the oath of allegiance to the United States.
7 The Liberal government in the Netherlands is replaced by a government of Calvinists and Catholics led by Dr.

Abraham Kuyper, following an election in which the Liberals were split on suffrage reform.
16 A Liberal ministry is formed under Dr. Johan Deutzer in Denmark, following elections that end an era of Conservative government.
20 Following the breakdown of Anglo-German talks on an alliance to preserve China from Russian domination, negotiations begin in London, England, for a British–Japanese alliance.

AUGUST

7 Horatio, Lord Kitchener, issues a proclamation in South Africa to the effect that leaders of Boer forces who do not surrender by September 15 will be permanently banished from South Africa. It also states that the property of other combatants who do not surrender will be used to cover the cost of maintaining their families.

SEPTEMBER

2 Speaking on the topic of diplomacy, President Theodore Roosevelt vows to "speak softly and carry a big stick," meaning that the United States will not hesitate to use force in international affairs in order to achieve its desires.
6 The anarchist Leon Czolgosz shoots the U.S. president William McKinley at a reception in Buffalo, New York. McKinley dies on September 14 and Vice President Theodore Roosevelt is sworn in as president. Aged 42, Roosevelt is the youngest man yet to hold the U.S. presidency.
7 The Peace of Beijing formally ends the Boxer Rising in China. Under the agreement, China is to pay an indemnity to the European powers, lower tariffs on imports, and accept a strengthening of European protection of its representatives and interests.
9 Boer raiders invade Natal and Cape Colony.
9 The visit to France of the Russian czar, Nicholas II, provokes antimilitarist demonstrations.
14 President William McKinley dies eight days after being shot by anarchist Leon Czolgosz at the Pan-American Exposition in Buffalo, New York. McKinley is succeeded by Vice President Theodore Roosevelt, who becomes the nation's youngest chief executive.

OCTOBER

16 President Theodore Roosevelt creates great controversy by inviting black American educationist Booker T. Washington to the White House.
16 The Japanese minister to Britain, Tadasu Hayashi, reopens British–Japanese negotiations for an alliance against Russia, in London, England.
25 The British colonial secretary, Joseph Chamberlain, makes an anti-German speech at Edinburgh, Scotland. This leads to a breakdown in negotiations for a British–German alliance on December 27.
29 The anarchist Leon Czolgosz is executed in the electric chair in New York, New York, for the murder of President William McKinley.

NOVEMBER

9 The Ottoman sultan Abdul Hamid II accepts a French ultimatum to stop interference with French interests in Anatolia (modern Turkey).
18 A second Hay–Pauncefote Convention between the United States and Great Britain provides for the United

States to construct a canal across the Isthmus of Panama. The canal zone will be under U.S. jurisdiction.

25–December 4 Prince Hirobumi Ito of Japan visits St. Petersburg, Russia, seeking Russian agreement to Japanese claims to influence in Korea, which is traditionally a Chinese fiefdom.

DECEMBER

2 The U.S. Supreme Court rules that inhabitants of Puerto Rico and other U.S. overseas territories are U.S. nationals, not citizens, and the U.S. Constitution applies only in territories incorporated by the U.S. Congress.

7 Britain and Italy sign an agreement settling the frontier between Anglo-Egyptian Sudan and the Italian possession of Eritrea.

7 Japan drops negotiations with Russia, deciding instead to conclude an alliance with Britain.

25 The Boer armies under General Christiaan De Wet achieve their last notable victory over the British in the South African Boer War, at Tweefontein.

31 Tomás Estrada Palma is elected in the Cuban presidential election, and is inaugurated on May 20, 1902.

SCIENCE, TECHNOLOGY, AND MEDICINE

Ecology

JANUARY

10 Prospector Anthony F. Lucas strikes oil at the Spindletop claim outside Beaumont, Texas, the largest oil field in the United States. This inaugurates the Texas oil boom.

MAY

3 A fire in Jacksonville, Florida, burns 1,700 buildings, leaving 10,000 people homeless and causing more than $11 million in property damage.

Health and Medicine

c. 1901 British soldiers are immunized against typhoid fever during the Boer War.

- Dutch physician Gerrit Grijns demonstrates that beriberi is caused by a nutritional deficiency of vitamin B1.
- German bacteriologist Emil von Behring receives the first Nobel Prize for Physiology or Medicine for his work on serum therapy, especially its application against diphtheria.
- Japanese-born U.S. biochemist Jokichi Takamine first synthesizes the heart stimulant adrenaline (epinephrine) from the suprarenal gland. It is the first pure hormone to be synthesized from natural sources.
- Miller Reese Hutchinson patents the first electric hearing aid, the Acousticon, in the United States.
- U.S. oil magnate John Rockefeller founds the Rockefeller Institute for Medical Research in New York, New York. It becomes the Rockefeller Institute in 1958.

FEBRUARY

- The U.S. Congress creates the Army Nurse Corps under the authority of the U.S. Army.
- The U.S. Congress establishes the U.S. Army Dental Corps, to safeguard dental hygiene in the military.

Science

- British chemist George Davis publishes the first textbook on chemical engineering.
- Dutch chemist Jacobus van't Hoff receives the first Nobel Prize for Chemistry for his discovery of the laws of chemical dynamics and osmotic pressure.
- English biochemist Frederick Gowland Hopkins isolates the amino acid tryptophan.
- French physicist Antoine-Henri Becquerel reports the first radiation burn. It is caused by a sample of radium carried in his waistcoat pocket and leads to the use of radium for medical purposes.
- German chemist Adolf Windaus discovers ergosterol, a chemical precursor of vitamin D that is converted to vitamin D by ultraviolet light.
- German chemist Wilhelm Normann discovers a process for hardening liquid fats to prevent them from turning rancid.
- German engineer Carl von Linde separates liquid oxygen from liquid air. It leads to the widespread use of oxygen in industry.
- German physicist Wilhelm Röntgen receives the first Nobel Prize for Physics for his discovery of X-rays.

Technology

- Dutch biologist Samuel Schouten describes a method of isolating a single bacterium in the field of a high-powered microscope.
- U.S. electrical engineer Peter Cooper Hewitt invents the mercury vapor lamp.

DECEMBER

12 Italian physicist Guglielmo Marconi, in St. John's, Newfoundland, Canada, receives the letter "S" in Morse code, from Poldhu, Cornwall, England. It is the first transmission of a radio signal across the Atlantic Ocean, a distance of 3,200 km/2,000 mi, and it inaugurates the development of radio communication.

Transportation

- Austrian engineer Wilhelm Kress builds the first airplane that has a framework of steel tubing. It fails to fly, crashing on its first test.
- German car manufacturer Daimler-Motoren-Gesellschaft introduces the Mercedes, which is named for the daughter of Emil Jellinek, the Austrian consul in Nice, France, a major investor in the company.
- Henry E. Huntington incorporates the Pacific Railroad Company in the United States and starts building a network of electric interurban lines around Los Angeles, California. By 1913 the system reaches 42 incorporated cities, the development having initiated a building boom.
- The first driving school, the Liver Motor Car Depot and School of Automobilism opens in Birkenhead, England.

- The first motorcycle with a gasoline engine is built in Britain.
- The Imperial Canal in California is opened. It diverts water from the Colorado River into the Imperial Valley where it is used for irrigation.
- The mass production of cars in Detroit, Michigan, begins when U.S. car manufacturer Ransom Eli Olds produces the three-horsepower Oldsmobile buggy. The first car with a curved dash, it is also the first to be made using assembly line techniques and the first commercially successful car in the United States.
- U.S. company S. H. Davis develops the first car odometer.
- U.S. engineer Simon Lake builds the 18-m/60-ft long submarine *Protector*. It is purchased by the Russian navy.
- U.S. inventors Charles Hart and Charles Parr introduce the Hart-Parr tractor, the first commercially successful tractor with an internal combustion engine

DECEMBER

26 The Uganda Railroad opens in Kenya between Mombasa and Lake Victoria, allowing the resources around the lake to be developed. It never reaches Uganda but stops at the lake.

ARTS AND IDEAS

Architecture

- The Horniman Museum in London, England, designed by the English architect Charles Harrison Townsend, is completed.
- The Scottish architect Charles Rennie Mackintosh designs the interior and furnishings for the Ingram Street Tea Rooms in Glasgow, Scotland. His work is one of the finest expressions of art nouveau design in Britain.

Arts

- The French artist Paul Gauguin paints *The Gold in their Bodies*.
- The Norwegian artist Edvard Munch paints *Girls on the Bridge*.
- The Spanish artist Pablo Picasso paints *Self-Portrait*, which marks the beginning of his Blue Period, and *Child Holding a Dove*.
- The U.S. artist Everett Shinn paints *Early Morning, Paris*.
- The U.S. artist Maurice Prendergast paints *The East River*.

Film

c. 1901 Traveling showmen show movies in fairs around the United States and Europe, an important factor in their quickly gaining popularity.
- The movie *Fire!*, directed by James Williamson, is released in Britain.

Literature and Language

- Black American educationist, Booker T. Washington, publishes his autobiography, *Up From Slavery*.
- The Australian writer Miles Franklin publishes her novel *My Brilliant Career*, widely seen as one of the first wholly Australian novels.
- The English writer and novelist Samuel Butler publishes *Erewhon Revisited*, a sequel to his satirical novel *Erewhon* published in 1872.
- The English writer Hall Caine publishes his novel *The Eternal City*.
- The English writer H. G. Wells publishes his novel *The First Men in the Moon*.
- The English writer Rudyard Kipling publishes his novel *Kim*.
- The English writer Thomas Hardy publishes *Poems of the Past and Present*.
- The first Nobel Prize for Literature is awarded, to the French poet Sully Prudhomme.
- The French writer Colette and her husband Henri Gauthier-Villars publish their novel *Claudine à Paris/Claudine in Paris*. The second of the "Claudine" novels, it is published under his pseudonym, Willy.
- The German writer Thomas Mann publishes his novel *Buddenbrooks*.
- The Swedish writer Selma Lagerlöf publishes her novel *Jerusalem*, which establishes her as the leading novelist of her age.
- The U.S. philosopher Josiah Royce publishes *The World and the Individual*.
- The U.S. writer Frank Norris publishes *The Octopus*, his first novel.
- The U.S. writer Henry James publishes his novel *The Sacred Fount*.

Music

- "Ragtime" music, an African-American musical style characterized by a syncopated beat, is popular in the United States, but the American Federation of Musicians condemns it because of its association with black Americans and "low dives" and recommends that its members refrain from playing it.
- The English composer Edward Elgar completes his orchestral works *Cockaigne* and *Pomp and Circumstance* marches (Nos. 1 and 2).
- The French composer Gabriel Fauré completes his orchestral suite *Pelléas et Mélisande/Pelléas and Mélisande*.
- The French composer Maurice Ravel completes his piano work *Jeux d'eau/Fountains*.
- The opera *Manru*, by the Polish composer Ignacy Jan Paderewski, is first performed in Dresden, Germany.
- The opera *Much Ado About Nothing*, by the Irish composer Charles Villiers Stanford, is first performed in London, England. It is based on Shakespeare's play.
- The opera *Rusalka*, by the Czech composer Antonín Dvořák, is first performed, in Prague, Bohemia. It premieres in Chicago, United States, in 1935 and in London, England, in 1950.
- The Romanian composer George Enescu completes his *Romanian Rhapsodies*.

- The Russian composer Sergey Rachmaninov completes his Piano Concerto No. 2.
- The U.S. composer Charles Ives completes his Symphony No. 2 and his chamber work *From the Steeples and the Mountains.*
- The U.S. composer John Philip Sousa completes his march *The Invincible Eagle.*
- U.S. songwriter Carrie Jacobs-Bond writes the song "I Love You Truly."
- U.S. songwriter Porter Steele writes the song "High Society."

Theater and Dance

- The Irish writer George Bernard Shaw publishes his play *Caesar and Cleopatra*, which is first performed in 1906 in Berlin, Germany.
- The play *Tri sestry/Three Sisters*, by the Russian writer Anton Chekhov, is first performed in Moscow, Russia.

BIRTHS & DEATHS

JANUARY

12 Kurt Jooss, German dancer, choreographer, and teacher who worked in England during the Hitler regime, born in Wasseralfingen, Germany (–1979).

16 Fulgencio Batistá y Zaldívar, Cuban soldier and dictator 1933–44 and 1952–59, born in Banes, Cuba (–1973).

16 Laura Riding, U.S. prose writer and poet and a member of the Fugitive Group of poets, born in New York, New York (–1991).

22 Victoria, Queen of the United Kingdom of Great Britain and Ireland 1837–1901, empress of India 1876–1901, dies in Osborne, near Cowes, Isle of Wight (80).

27 Giuseppe Fortunino Francesco Verdi, Italian operatic composer, dies in Milan, Italy (87).

FEBRUARY

1 Clark Gable, U.S. film star, born in Cadiz, Ohio (–1960).

20 Louis Isadore Kahn, Estonian-born U.S. architect, born in Osel, Russian Estonia (–1974).

27 Marino Marini, Italian portrait sculptor, born in Pistoia, Italy (–1980).

28 Linus Pauling, U.S. chemist who won the Nobel Prize for Chemistry in 1954 for his discoveries concerning chemical bonding, and the Nobel Peace Prize (1962) for crusading against the use of nuclear weapons, born in Portland, Oregon (–1994).

MARCH

4 Charles Goren, U.S. bridge player and columnist, born in Philadelphia, Pennsylvania (–1991).

13 Benjamin Harrison, 23rd president of the United States (1889–93), a Republican, dies in Indianapolis, Indiana (67).

27 Eisaku Sato, prime minister of Japan 1964–72, born in Tabuse, Japan (–1975).

APRIL

29 Hirohito, Emperor of Japan 1927–89, born in Tokyo, Japan (–1989).

MAY

7 Gary Cooper, U.S. actor, born in Helena, Montana (–1961).

23 Edward Rubbra, English composer and pianist, born in Northampton, England (–1986).

JUNE

6 Achmed Sukarno, leader of Indonesia's independence movement and the country's first president 1949–66, born in Surabaja, Java, Dutch East Indies (–1970).

13 Tage Erlander, Prime Minister of Sweden (1946–69) responsible for turning Sweden into a welfare state, born in Ransäter, Sweden (–1985).

JULY

28 Rudy Vallee, U.S. singer popular in the 1920s and 1930s, born in Island Pond, Virginia (–1986).

31 Jean Dubuffet, French painter and sculptor, the founder of Art Brut ("raw art"), born in Le Havre, France (–1985).

AUGUST

8 Ernest Orlando Lawrence, U.S. physicist who invented the cyclotron particle accelerator, born in Canton, South Dakota (–1958).

SEPTEMBER

8 Hendrik Frensch Verwoerd, Prime Minister of South Africa 1958–66, who created the Bantu Homelands and took South Africa out of the Commonwealth, born in Amsterdam, the Netherlands (–1966).

9 Henri de Toulouse-Lautrec, French artist who depicted the personalities of Parisian night life, dies in Malromé, France (36).

19 Joseph Pasternak, U.S. film producer, born in Szilagy-Somlyo, Austria-Hungary (–1991).

29 Enrico Fermi, Italian-born U.S. physicist who was responsible for overseeing the first nuclear chain reaction, born in Rome, Italy (–1954).

OCTOBER

10 Alberto Giacometti, Swiss painter and sculptor, born in Borgonovo, Switzerland (–1966).

NOVEMBER

3 André Malraux, French novelist, art historian and statesman, born in Paris, France (–1976).

7 Li Hunag-Chang, leading 19th-century Chinese statesman who attempted to modernize China, dies in China (78).

17 Joyce Wethered, English golfer who dominated English ladies' golf in the early 1920s, born in Brook, Surrey, England (–1997).

17 Lee Strasberg, U.S. actor and artistic director of the Actors Studio from 1948, born in Budzanow, Poland, Austria-Hungary (–1982).

18 George Gallup, U.S. pollster who began the first public opinion polls, born in Jefferson, Iowa (–1984).

DECEMBER

5 Walt Disney, U.S. motion-picture producer and creator of Mickey Mouse, Donald Duck, and other characters, born in Chicago, Illinois (–1966).

5 Werner Heisenberg, German physicist and philosopher who introduced the uncertainty principle into quantum mechanics, born in Würzburg, Germany (–1976).

16 Margaret Mead, U.S. anthropologist, born in Philadelphia, Pennsylvania (–1978).

20 Robert Jemison Van de Graaff, U.S. physicist who invented the high electric-voltage Van de Graaff generator, born in Tuscaloosa, Alabama (–1967).

27 Marlene Dietrich, German-born U.S. motion-picture actress, born in Berlin, Germany (–1992).

Thought and Scholarship

- Belgian writer Maurice Maeterlinck publishes *La Vie des abeilles/The Life of the Bee*, a blend of science and philosophy.
- English jurist and statesman James Bryce publishes *Studies in History and Jurisprudence*.
- German philosopher Edmund Husserl publishes *Logische Untersuchungen/Logical Investigations*.

AUGUST

8 The British Academy for the Promotion of Historical, Philosophical and Philological Studies is founded in London, England.

SOCIETY

Education

- The U.S. Army War College opens in Washington, D.C.
- The U.S. College Entrance Examination Board offers the nation's first college entrance examinations.

MARCH

- Scottish-born U.S. billionaire steel magnate Andrew Carnegie donates $5.2 million to help launch the branch system of the New York Public Library.

Everyday Life

- Frank Hornby develops the children's building kit Meccano in Britain.
- The Japanese-born U.S. chemist Satori Kato creates the first soluble instant coffee.

- The Scottish engineer Hubert Cecil Booth invents the first practical upright electric vacuum cleaner for domestic use.

DECEMBER

10 King Charles XV of Sweden awards the first Nobel prizes, funded by the legacy of the Swedish industrialist Alfred Nobel.

Media and Communication

- The eugenics journal *Biometrika* is founded.

Sports

c. 1901 The Ling Association (an association of physical training teachers) in Britain draws up a code of rules for netball, which was introduced from the United States in 1895 as a version of basketball suitable for women.
- In major league baseball, the Chicago White Sox are the first champions of the inaugural American League.

JANUARY

8–11 The American Bowling Congress stages the first National Bowling Championships in Chicago.

AUGUST

5 Peter O'Connor of Ireland establishes a new world long-jump record in Dublin of 7.61 m/24 ft 11¾ in; the record stands until 1921 when Edwin Gourdin of the United States jumps 7.69 m/25 ft 3 in.

OCTOBER

- The U.S. jockey Lester Reiff, champion jockey in 1900, has his license to ride in Britain withdrawn by the British Jockey Club for "throwing" (deliberately losing) a race.

1902

POLITICS, GOVERNMENT, AND ECONOMICS

Business and Economics

- Entrepreneur Cyrus McCormack founds International Harvester from four U.S. harvester makers.
- Entrepreneur James Cash Penney, lays the foundation for retail giant J. C. Penney Co. by opening the Golden Rule in Kemmerer, Wyoming.

- New York tobacco importer Gustav Eckmeyer helps Philip Morris of London, England, to establish a U.S. branch of the company, the New York Philip Morris Corporation.
- The Minnesota Mining and Manufacturing (3M) company is founded in the United States.
- The Texas Oil Company (Texaco) is founded in the United States.
- The U.S. pharmacist Caleb Bradham establishes Pepsi-Cola in New Bern, North Carolina.

MAY

14 Portugal, having declared itself bankrupt, wins the agreement of foreign bondholders to a reduction in its debts.

Anglo–Boer Wars (1899–1902)

1899

OCTOBER

12 A Boer ultimatum demanding Britain stop sending troops to southern Africa expires and the Second Anglo-Boer War begins.

30 Boer general Piet Joubert wins the battle of Nicholson's Nek, against a British force under Sir George White.

NOVEMBER

1 The town of Ladysmith, Natal, center of British operations, is besieged by Boer forces under General Piet Joubert.

DECEMBER

10 A British force is defeated by Boer irregulars at Stromberg.

11 The British forces led by Lord Methuen are repulsed by General Piet Cronje at Magersfontein, Orange Free State, and on December 15 the "Black Week" ends with Boer general Louis Botha repulsing the British forces under General Redvers Buller at Colenso.

12 Canadian and Australian volunteers land in southern Africa to assist Britain in the struggle against the Boers.

1900

JANUARY

10 Following four months of Boer advances, Field Marshal Frederick, Lord Roberts ("Bobs") lands in southern Africa as the new commander in chief of the British army, with Horatio, Lord Kitchener, as chief of staff.

25 In the Battle of Spion Kop, a Boer army forces the British troops under General Sir Redvers Buller to retreat with heavy losses.

FEBRUARY

15 A British army under General Sir John French relieves Kimberley, Northern Cape Province, which has been under siege by a Boer force since October 15, 1899.

27 The Boer commander Piet Cronje and his army surrender to General John French, at Paardeberg, Orange Free State, having been besieged there since their defeat of February 18.

28 General Sir Redvers Buller relieves the town of Ladysmith in Natal, which has been besieged by a Boer force since October 30, 1899.

MARCH

13 Field Marshal Frederick, Lord Roberts, captures Bloemfontein, capital of the Orange Free State.

MAY

17–18 British forces under General Sir Redvers Buller relieve the town of Mafeking, following a seven-month siege by a Boer force.

31 British troops under Field Marshal Frederick, Lord Roberts and General Sir Redvers Buller occupy Johannesburg and the Rand.

JUNE

5 British troops capture Pretoria.

AUGUST

14 The British armies commanded by Field Marshal Frederick, Lord Roberts, and General Sir Redvers Buller unite at Vlakfontein.

27 A Boer army under the command of Louis Botha is defeated by a British force at Bergendal.

SEPTEMBER

3 Field Marshal Frederick, Lord Roberts, formally proclaims the annexation of the Transvaal by Great Britain.

11 Paul Kruger crosses from Transvaal into Portuguese Southeast Africa following defeat in the Second Anglo-Boer War, and subsequently leaves for Europe.

OCTOBER

24 Paul Kruger, seeking assistance in Europe against the British, is denied an audience by Kaiser Wilhelm II of Germany.

NOVEMBER

11 Following British conquests, the Boer forces under General Christiaan De Wet resort to guerrilla tactics, raiding communications and British outposts. Horatio, Lord Kitchener, orders that women and children related to Boer combatants be interred in concentration camps, and extends the "scorched earth" policy started by Field Marshal Frederick, Lord Roberts, destroying Boer farms.

1901

JANUARY

1 Horatio, Lord Kitchener, launches two major offensives against Boer forces. To combat the guerrilla actions of the Boer troops, he continues the British "scorched earth" policy.

FEBRUARY

28 The Boer leader Louis Botha meets the British representative Lord Kitchener at Middelburg, South Africa, for peace talks.

MARCH

16 Peace negotiations between the British and the Boers break down when the British government continues to refuse an amnesty for Boer rebels in the Cape and Natal.

AUGUST

7 Horatio, Lord Kitchener, issues a proclamation to the effect that leaders of Boer forces who do not surrender by September 15 will be permanently banished from South Africa. It also states that the property of other combatants who do not surrender will be used to cover the cost of maintaining their families.

DECEMBER

25 The Boer armies under General Christiaan De Wet achieve their last notable victory over the British, at Tweefontein.

1902

APRIL

12 British general Horatio, Lord Kitchener, meets with Boer leaders in Pretoria, Transvaal, to discuss peace proposals.

MAY

31 The Peace of Vereeniging ends the South African Boer War, in which 5,774 British troops were killed as a result of the conflict and 16,000 through disease, while 4,000 Boers were killed. The Boer people accept British sovereignty, but are promised self-government in the Orange River Colony and the Transvaal, and £3 million for restocking their farms.

OCTOBER

16   The United Mine Workers Union ends the anthracite coal miners' strike in the United States when President Theodore Roosevelt threatens to work anthracite mines with federal troops and mine owners agree to the appointment of an arbitration commission to investigate miners' claims.

Colonization

SEPTEMBER

27   Part of Uganda is transferred to British East Africa, inaugurating white settlement of the East African uplands.

Politics and Government

- President Theodore Roosevelt appoints the scholar Oliver Wendell Holmes, Jr., to the U.S. Supreme Court.
- Russian populists meeting in Switzerland decide to form a Socialist Revolutionary Party.

JANUARY

7   Following the suppression of the Boxer Rising, the Chinese imperial court returns to Beijing, China, and begins a program of extensive reforms.

15   Italian aircraft drop leaflets in Libya, offering the Arabs food and money if they surrender.

30   Britain qualifies its isolationist foreign policy by signing a treaty with Japan to safeguard their common interests in China and Korea. Under the terms of the treaty, in the event of Britain or Japan being at war with a foreign power in East Asia, the other will maintain strict neutrality, but shall assist its ally if a second foreign power should join the first.

FEBRUARY

2   The Italian government prevents a general strike by calling up all eligible railroad workers into the army.

6   A French agreement with Ethiopia that France will subsidize the Djibouti–Addis Ababa railroad provokes protests from Britain and Italy.

MARCH

- In his State of the Union address, President Theodore Roosevelt asserts a need to protect the United States's natural resources.
- President Theodore Roosevelt enforces the Sherman Antitrust Act (1890) to prosecute J. P. Morgan's Northern Securities Company for unlawful restraint of trade.
- U.S. Congress creates the Census Bureau.

20   A Franco–Russian declaration acknowledges the terms of the British–Japanese alliance of January 30, but reserves the right for them to safeguard their own interests.

APRIL

- U.S. Congress extends the Chinese Exclusion Act (1882) to prohibit the immigration of Chinese workers from the Philippines.

8   A Russo–Chinese Manchurian Convention is signed. This allows for the gradual evacuation of Russian troops from Manchuria, accompanied by the guarantee of Russian interests there.

12   Following successful actions in South Africa against Boer forces during February and March, the British general Horatio, Lord Kitchener, meets with Boer leaders in Pretoria, Transvaal, to discuss peace proposals.

15   Britain signs a treaty with Ethiopia, defining the border between Ethiopia and the Sudan at a considerable distance from the River Nile.

15   The Russian minister of the interior, Dmitry Sipyagin, is assassinated by an ex-student.

MAY

- Cuba gains independence from the United States.

16   King Alfonso XIII of Spain is enthroned on his sixteenth birthday, ending his minority and rule by regent.

31   The Peace of Vereeniging ends the South African Boer War, in which 5,774 British troops were killed as a result of the conflict and 16,000 through disease, while 4,000 Boers were killed. The Boer people accept British sovereignty, but are promised self-government in the Orange River Colony and the Transvaal, and £3 million for restocking their farms.

JUNE

3   The French prime minister, René Waldeck-Rousseau, resigns following Radical electoral gains, and is succeeded by the Radical Emile Combes, who directs a vigorous anticlerical policy.

17   The U.S. Congress passes the Newlands Reclamation Act. It leads to the development of irrigation and hydroelectric projects in the western states.

28   The Triple Alliance (originally agreed in 1882) of Germany, Austria, and Italy is renewed for six years.

28   The U.S. Congress passes the Isthmian Canal Act, which authorizes the U.S. president to purchase the rights of the French Panama Company, and to acquire perpetual control of the canal zone from Colombia.

JULY

- U.S. militiamen quell a riot of coal miners at Shenandoah, Pennsylvania. The riot began after operators used replacement workers to fill jobs vacated by striking miners.

1   The U.S. Congress passes the Philippines Government Act, making the Philippines a U.S. territory. It creates a bicameral (two-chamber) legislature, but retains a U.S. right of veto under a civil governor. The first governor, William Howard Taft, takes office July 4.

11   Robert Cecil, Lord Salisbury, retires as British prime minister, and is immediately succeeded by his nephew Arthur Balfour.

AUGUST

9   The coronation of King Edward VII and Queen Alexandra takes place in Westminster Abbey, London, England.

SEPTEMBER

5   A British–Chinese commercial treaty is agreed, allowing the free movement of goods (excluding salt and opium) across China, following payment of an import tax.

NOVEMBER

- In U.S. Congressional elections, Republicans retain majorities in the House (208–178) and Senate (57–33).

1   A Franco-Italian *entente* is agreed, in which Italy assures France of its neutrality if France is attacked.

8   Spain holds back from signing an agreement with France on Morocco, fearing to antagonize Britain.

13 Persia concludes a favorable tariff agreement with Russia, which discriminates against British goods.

DECEMBER

18 An education act brings elementary and secondary education under local council control in Great Britain.

19 Germany and Britain seize the Venezuelan navy and are joined by Italy in a blockade of Venezuelan ports, in protest at Cipriano Castro's refusal to meet claims for injuries caused during his revolution of 1899.

SCIENCE, TECHNOLOGY, AND MEDICINE

Ecology

- The Santa Maria volcano in Guatemala erupts violently, killing 6,000.
- The U.S. Congress establishes Crater Lake National Park from 649 sq km/160,290 acres of Oregon wilderness. It encompasses the 589 m/1,932 ft deep Crater Lake.

MAY

8 Mt. Pelée volcano in Martinique erupts. All but one of the port of Saint-Pierre's 30,000 inhabitants are killed by the force of the eruption. The survivor is protected by the thick walls of his prison cell.

Health and Medicine

- British bacteriologist Ronald Ross receives the Nobel Prize for Physiology or Medicine for showing how malaria is transmitted via the mosquito.
- British physiologists William Bayliss and Ernest Starling establish the role of hormones by discovering that a substance, which they call secretin, is released into the bloodstream by cells in the duodenum. Once there, it stimulates the secretion of digestive juices by the pancreas.
- French physiologist Charles Richet discovers cases of acute sensitivity to antidiphtheria serum, which he calls "anaphylaxis." His work leads to a greater understanding of problems of asthma, hay fever, and other allergic reactions.
- The coronation of the British king Edward VII is postponed because of his appendicitis. British surgeon Frederick Treves performs abdominal surgery, draining the king's appendix. Thereafter appendectomy becomes accepted medical practice.
- The International Sanitary Bureau is established by 21 countries in North and South America. It becomes the Pan-American Health Organization in 1949.
- U.S. pathologist Eugene Lindsay Opie publishes *Diseases of the Pancreas*, in which he associates the degenerative changes in the islets of Langerhans with diabetes.
- U.S. surgeon Harvey Williams Cushing publishes *The Pituitary Body and its Disorders*, which investigates the pituitary gland and its relationship to various diseases.

Math

- U.S. physicist J. Willard Gibbs publishes *Elementary Principles of Statistical Mechanics*, in which he develops the mathematics of statistical mechanics.

Science

- Austrian chemist Richard Zsigmondy invents the ultramicroscope, which is used to study colloids.
- British physicist Oliver Heaviside and U.S. electrical engineer Arthur Kennelly independently predict the existence of a conducting layer in the atmosphere that reflects radio waves.
- Canadian-born U.S. physicist Reginald Fessenden discovers the heterodyne principle whereby high-frequency radio signals are converted to lower frequency signals that are easier to control and amplify. It leads to the superheterodyne principle essential in modern radio and television.
- Dutch physicists Hendrik Lorentz and Pieter Zeeman share the Nobel Prize for Physics for their researches into the influence of magnetism upon radiation phenomena.
- English Egyptologist Howard Carter discovers the tombs of Egyptian pharaohs Hatshepsut and Thutmose IV in the Valley of the Kings.
- French chemist Auguste Verneuil develops a method of making artificial rubies and sapphires, which are important for making watches and clocks.
- French engineer and chemist Georges Claude develops a method of producing liquefied air in quantity.
- German chemist Emil Fischer is awarded the Nobel Prize for Chemistry for his synthesis of sugars and purines.
- German chemist Friedrich Ostwald patents the industrially important process of producing nitric acid by the catalytic oxidation of ammonia.
- German chemists Emil Fischer and Franz Hofmeister discover that proteins are polypeptides consisting of amino acids.
- Italian physicist Guglielmo Marconi discovers that radio waves are transmitted further at night than during the day because they are affected by changes in the atmosphere (actually by a layer of ionized gas in the ionosphere).
- New Zealand-born British physicist Ernest Rutherford and British physicist Frederick Soddy discover thorium X and publish *The Cause and Nature of Radioactivity*, which outlines the theory that radioactivity involves the disintegration of atoms of one element into atoms of another.
- Scottish physicist William Thomson proposes a model of the atom in which electrons are embedded in a sphere of positive charge.
- Scottish-born U.S. billionaire steel magnate Andrew Carnegie founds the Carnegie Institute for Scientific Research in Washington, D.C.
- The American Anthropological Association is founded and begins publication of the journal *American Anthropologist*.
- U.S. chemist, Arthur D. Little, patents rayon, an artificial fiber made from cellulose.

May 1902–04   U.S. geneticist Walter Sutton and the German zoologist Theodor Boveri found the chromosomal theory of inheritance when they show that cell division is connected with heredity.

Technology

- Italian physicist Guglielmo Marconi patents the magnetic detector, which detects the arrival of a telephone signal, thus improving the efficiency of communications.
- The Blickensderfer Electric, the first effective electric typewriter, is launched in Britain. Commercial success is limited, however, by the lack of mains electricity in most offices.
- The Dow Chemical Company begins the commercial manufacture of synthetic indigo in the United States.
- The first armored vehicle is exhibited in London, England.
- The Fuller (Flatiron) skyscraper in New York, New York, famous for its triangular shape, designed by U.S. architects Daniel Hudson Burnham and John Wellborn Root, is completed. It is the tallest building in the world at 87 m/286 ft.
- The U.S. printing company Sackett-Williams installs the first air-conditioning system to regulate both temperature and humidity.

Transportation

- An underground railroad opens in Berlin, Germany.
- English aeronautics engineer Frederick William Lanchester invents the disc brake.
- French aeronautical engineers Paul and Pierre Lebaudy build *La Jaune*, the first successful semirigid airship.
- French engineer Louis Renault develops drum brakes.
- German engineer G. Honold invents the Bosch spark plug.
- Italy begins to convert its railroads to electricity: the first country to do so.
- Scottish-born U.S. car manufacturer Alexander Winton sets a land speed record of one mile in 52.2 seconds in his race car *Bullet No.1*, at Daytona Beach, Florida. He is the first person to drive a mile in under a minute.
- The 132 m/433 ft long German ship *Preusseb* is launched. It is the largest sailing ship in the world and has five steel masts.
- The British firm of Thorpe and Salter manufacture the first car speedometers; they have a scale of 0–35 mph (0–55 kph).

MARCH
- Nine automobile clubs create the American Automobile Association (AAA) in Chicago, Illinois, to provide an emergency road service to motorists.

JUNE
15   The New York Central Railroad completes its run from New York, New York, to Chicago, Illinois, in a record time, 20 hours.

SEPTEMBER
1–October 31   U.S. aviators Orville and Wilbur Wright fly more than 1,000 test flights, some more than 180 m/600 ft, in their third glider, their first successful one, at Kitty Hawk, North Carolina.

3   While visiting Pittsfield, Massachusetts, President Theodore Roosevelt's coach collides with a trolley car. The accident kills one of the president's bodyguards but the president escapes injury.

ARTS AND IDEAS

Architecture

- Deanery Gardens, a house in the village of Sonning, Berkshire, England, designed by the English architect Edwin Lutyens, is completed. It is one of the finest works to emerge from the Arts and Crafts Movement.
- The report of the federal McMillan Commission in the United States calls for the reconstruction of Washington, D.C., including a pedestrian mall from the White House to the Lincoln Memorial.

JULY
14   The bell tower in St. Mark's Square, Venice, Italy, collapses suddenly and unexpectedly.

DECEMBER
10   The Aswan Dam on the River Nile in Egypt is officially opened, having been started in 1898. The largest dam in the world, it is 2,142 m/7,027 ft long and has 180 sluices.

Arts

c. 1902   The Norwegian artist Edvard Munch paints *Summer Night on the River Bank*.
- Art nouveau, as displayed in the architecture of Gaudí, Tiffany lamps, and Lalique jewelry, is very popular. A major exhibition is held in Paris, France.
- The French artist Claude Oscar Monet paints *Waterloo Bridge*.
- The French artist Paul Gauguin paints *Horsemen on the Beach*.
- The German artist Max Liebermann paints *The Parrot's Walk at the Amsterdam Zoo*.
- The photography society, the Photo-Secession, is formed in New York, New York, the intention being to establish photography as a fine art. Outstanding members include Alfred Stieglitz, Edward Steichen, and Gertrude Käsebier. A gallery is opened in 1905; the group exhibits for the last time in 1910, but their journal *Camera Work* continues until 1917.
- The Spanish artist Pablo Picasso paints *Woman with a Scarf*.
- The U.S. artist Robert Henri paints *West 57th Street, New York*.

Film

- Charles Pathé opens a movie studio at Vincennes, Paris, France, and designs a movie camera that will be an industry standard for 20 years.
- The movie *Le Voyage dans la lune/Trip to the Moon*, directed by Georges Méliès, is released in France. It is a fantasy featuring Méliès's hallmark trick photography, such as the use of slow motion, fade out, and double

exposure. In the same year he films a studio reconstruction of Edward VII's coronation, which is completed before the actual event takes place.

- The movie *The Victims of Alcoholism*, produced by Ferdinand Zecca, is released in France.

Literature and Language

- British writer Beatrix Potter publishes the classic children's book *The Tale of Peter Rabbit*.
- The Belgian writer Emile Verhaeren publishes his poetry collection *Les Forces tumultueuses/The Tumultuous Forces*.
- The English writer and politician Charles Masterman publishes *The Heart of Empire*.
- The English writer Hilaire Belloc publishes his travel book *The Path to Rome*.
- The English writer John Masefield publishes his poetry collection *Salt Water Ballads*.
- The English writer Rudyard Kipling publishes his collection of children's tales *Just So Stories*.
- The French writer André Gide publishes his novel *L'Immoraliste/The Immoralist*.
- The Indian writer Rabindranath Tagore publishes his novel *Binodini*.
- The Nobel Prize for Literature is awarded to the German historian Theodor Mommsen.
- The Polish-born English writer Joseph Conrad publishes his story collection *Youth: A Narrative and Two Other Stories*, which includes one of his best-known works, *The Heart of Darkness*.
- The Russian anarchist Peter Alekseyevich Kropotkin publishes his political tract *Mutual Aid*, written in English and published in England.
- The Scottish writer Arthur Conan Doyle publishes *The Hound of the Baskervilles*, one of the best-known Sherlock Holmes novels.
- The U.S. National Education Association adopts simplified spellings for words such as altho, thru, catalog, program, thoro, and tho. Some of the changes become permanent, others fail to catch on.
- The U.S. writer Ellen Glasgow publishes her novel *The Battle-Ground*.
- The U.S. writer Helen Keller publishes *The Story of My Life*, in which she describes how, though deaf and blind since infancy, she was taught to read and write by her companion, Anne Mansfield Sullivan.
- The U.S. writer Henry James publishes his novel *The Wings of the Dove*.
- The U.S. writer Jack London publishes his first novel, *A Daughter of the Snows*.
- The U.S. writer Owen Wister writes *The Virginian*, a Western novel set in Wyoming, with a preface by U.S. president Theodore Roosevelt.

Music

- Harry von Tilzer writes the song "In the Sweet Bye and Bye."
- Hughie Cannon writes the song "Bill Bailey, Won't You Please Come Home?"
- The Austrian composer Gustav Mahler completes his Symphony No. 5.

- The Danish composer Carl Nielsen completes his Symphony No. 2, *De Fire Temperamenter/Four Temperaments*.
- The English composer Edward Elgar completes his choral work *Coronation Ode* for the coronation of King Edward VII. The best-known section is the finale, *Land of Hope and Glory*, adapted from March No. 1 of his *Pomp and Circumstance*. The words are taken from a poem by the English writer A. C. Benson.
- The Finnish composer Jean Sibelius completes his Symphony No. 2.
- The opera *Adriana Lecouvreur*, by the Italian composer Francesco Cilea, is first performed in Milan, Italy.
- The opera *Le Jongleur de Notre Dame/Our Lady's Juggler*, by the French composer Jules Massenet, is first performed in Monte Carlo.
- The opera *Pelléas et Mélisande/Pelléas and Mélisande*, by the French composer Claude Debussy, is first performed in Paris, France. It is based on a play by the Belgian writer Maurice Maeterlinck performed in 1893.
- The opera *Saul og David/Saul and David* by the Danish composer Carl Nielsen is first performed, in Copenhagen, Denmark.
- The operetta *Merrie England*, by the English composer Edward German, is first performed in London, England.
- The U.S. composer Edward MacDowell completes his *New England Idylls* for piano.
- The U.S. composer Scott Joplin writes the ragtime tune "The Entertainer."
- U.S. lyricist George Evans and U.S. composer Ren Shields write the song "In the Good Old Summertime."

Theater and Dance

- The play *Cathleen ni Houlihan*, by the Irish writers W. B. Yeats and Lady Gregory, is first performed in Dublin, Ireland.
- The play *Der Erdgeist/The Earth Spirit*, by the German dramatist Frank Wedekind, is first performed in Berlin, Germany.
- The play *Mrs Warren's Profession*, by the Irish writer George Bernard Shaw, is first performed, in New Haven, Connecticut. It was written in 1893 and published in 1898.
- The play *Na dne/The Lower Depths*, by the Russian writer Maxim Gorky, is first performed in Moscow, Russia.
- The play *The Admirable Crichton*, by the Scottish writer J. M. Barrie, is first performed, at the Duke of York's Theatre in London, England.
- The play *The Girl with Green Eyes*, by the U.S. dramatist Clyde Fitchis, is first performed, in New York, New York.

Thought and Scholarship

- English economist John Atkinson Hobson publishes *Imperialism*.
- English geographer and politician Halford John Mackinder publishes *Britain and the British Seas*.
- English historian Charles Oman publishes the first volume of his *A History of the Peninsular War, 1807–14*. The last volume appears in 1930.

- German economist Werner Sombart publishes *Der moderne Kapitalismus/Modern Capitalism*.
- Russian revolutionary leader Vladimir Ilyich Lenin publishes *Chto Dielat?/What Is To Be Done?*, one of the central works of Soviet communism.
- Scottish historian James Gairdner publishes *History of the English Church in the Sixteenth Century from Henry VIII to Mary*.
- The English historian Albert Frederick Pollard publishes *Henry VIII*.
- The French linguists Jules Gilliéron and Edmond Edmont publish the first part of their *L'Atlas linguistique de la France/Linguistic Atlas of France*. The last part appears in 1910.
- The Italian philosopher Benedetto Croce publishes *Estetica come scienza dell'espressione e linguistica generale/Aesthetics as the Science of Expression and General Linguistics*.
- U.S. historian Abbott Lawrence Lowell publishes *The Influence of Party upon Legislation in England and America*.
- U.S. philosopher William James publishes *Varieties of Religious Experience: Two Supposed Objections to the Doctrine*.
- U.S. social reformer Jane Addams publishes *Democracy and Social Ethics*.
- U.S. statesman Thomas Woodrow Wilson publishes his five-volume *History of the American People*.

SOCIETY

Everyday Life

- A Russian immigrant toy-store owner, in New York, New York, Morris Mitchom creates the teddy bear, inspired by Clifford Berryman's cartoon of U.S. president Theodore "Teddy" Roosevelt refusing to shoot a bear cub.
- A survey in the United States finds that the average wage for female store clerks in Boston, Massachusetts, is only between $5 and $6 per week.
- Australian stationer J. A. Birchall invents the notepad, a bound collection of paper rather than loose sheets.
- British inventor John Ransome constructs the first successful gasoline-powered lawn mower.
- Fish and chips becomes more popular in Britain as advances in refrigeration and the railroad network allow cheap and quick delivery of fish to inland areas, resulting in an inexpensive and tasty meal. Fish and chip shops are credited with dramatically increasing the protein intake of the working class.
- Frank Clarke launches the first automatic tea-maker, in Britain.
- The first electric hair dryers are introduced.
- The U.S. Army changes its uniform colors from blue to olive drab. The Spanish-American War proved blue to be too inviting a target.
- The U.S. carpenter Pearl B. Wait creates the dessert Jell-O.
- The U.S. company Binney and Smith launch Crayola crayons.

- The U.S. Envelope Co. launches envelopes with windows, invented by Americus F. Callahan.

MAY

- Pennsylvania coal miners strike after operators reject the offer of United Mine Workers president, John Mitchell, to arbitrate. The union sought a 20% wage increase and an eight-hour day. On October 16, the United Mine Workers Union ends the anthracite coal miners' strike in the United States when President Theodore Roosevelt threatens to work anthracite mines with federal troops and mine owners agree to the appointment of an arbitration commission to investigate miners' claims.
12–October 13   Coal miners strike in Pennsylvania, United States, for higher wages and improved conditions.

Media and Communication

- *McClure's* magazine publishes articles exposing corruption in U.S. cities, and attacks large companies.
- Irish-born U.S. inventor John Gregg publishes *Gregg Shorthand*, which outlines his shorthand system.

Sports

- Scottish golfer Alex Herd's victory in the British Open golf championship popularizes use of the Haskell golf ball, developed by the U.S. dentist Dr. Coburn Haskell; the ball uses a core of elastic thread, rather than of gutta percha, enabling players to hit it longer distances.
- The English filly Sceptre, owned by U.S. gambler Bob Sievier, wins four of the five English horse-racing classics: the 1,000 and 2,000 Guineas, the Oaks, and the St. Leger.
May 1902–03   Henry Lunn, the English founder of the Lunn travel agency business, pioneers skiing holidays and skiing races through the Public Schools Alpine Sports Club.

JANUARY

1   In college football, Michigan beats Stanford 49–0 to win the inaugural Tournament of Roses game at Pasadena, California (from 1923 officially known as the Rose Bowl). The game is not played again until 1916, after which it becomes an annual fixture.

JULY

17   The Baltimore Americans of baseball's American League are unable to field a team for a game against St. Louis after their star players are poached by the National League, as part of a continuing battle between the established National League and its new rival.

BIRTHS & DEATHS

JANUARY

4   John Alex McCone, U.S. industrialist and head of the Central Intelligence Agency (CIA) 1961–65, born in San Francisco, California (–1991).

FEBRUARY

4   Charles Lindbergh, U.S. aviator, the first person to fly solo nonstop across the Atlantic, born in Detroit, Michigan (–1974).

10   Walter Brattan, U.S. physicist who shared the Nobel Prize for Physics in 1956 for the development of the transistor, born in Ammoy, China.

11   Arne Jacobsen, Danish architect and designer, born in Copenhagen, Denmark (–1971).

17   Marian Anderson, U.S. contralto, born in Philadelphia, Pennsylvania (–1993).

20   Ansel Adams, U.S. landscape photographer and technical innovator, born in San Francisco, California (–1984).

27   John Steinbeck, U.S. novelist who wrote *The Grapes of Wrath*, born in Salinas, California (–1968).

MARCH

2   Edward U. Condon, U.S. physicist who used quantum mechanics to understand the atom and its nucleus, born in Alamogordo, New Mexico (–1974).

9   Edward Durell Stone, U.S. architect who designed modern buildings around the world, born in Fayetteville, Arkansas (–1978).

17   Bobby Jones, U.S. amateur golfer, the first person to win the Grand Slam (the British and U.S. Amateur and Open Championships), born in Atlanta, Georgia (–1971).

26   Cecil Rhodes, English financier, prime minister of Cape Colony 1890–96, and philanthropist who established the Rhodes scholarships at Oxford University, England, dies in Muizenberg, Cape Colony (48).

29   William Walton, English composer of orchestral music, born in Oldham, Lancashire, England (–1983).

APRIL

14   Menachem Mendel Schneerson, Russian-born U.S. rabbi, leader in 1950 of the Lubavitch right-wing orthodox Judaic movement, born in Nikolayev, Russia (now Ukraine) (–1994).

MAY

10   David O. Selznick, U.S. film director, born in Pittsburgh, Pennsylvania (–1965).

15   Richard Daly, mayor of Chicago 1955–76, born in Chicago, Illinois (–1976).

21   Marcel Lajos Breuer, U.S. architect, born in Pécs, Austria-Hungary (–1981).

22   Maurice Griffiths, English yacht designer and author, editor of *Yachting Monthly* 1927–67, born in London, England (–1997).

JUNE

15   Erik (Homburger) Erikson, German-born U.S. psychoanalytic theorist who coined the phrase "identity crisis," born in Frankfurt am Main, Germany (–1994).

16   Barbara McClintock, U.S. geneticist who discovered the phenomenon of crossing over of segments of chromosomes during meiosis, born in Hartford, Connecticut (–1992).

16   George Gaylord Simpson, U.S. paleontologist who contributed to evolutionary theory, born in Tucson, Arizona (–1984).

18   Samuel Butler, English novelist, dies in London, England (66).

19   Guy Lombardo, Canadian-born U.S. dance band leader known for hosting New Year's Eve celebrations on radio and television, born in London, Ontario, Canada (–1977).

26   William P. Lear, U.S. industrialist, known for his Lear business jets, born in Hannibal, Missouri (–1978).

28   Richard Rodgers, U.S. composer and songwriter of musical comedy who had a long partnership with Oscar Hammerstein, born in New York, New York (–1979).

JULY

4   Meyer Lansky, U.S. crime syndicate boss, born in Grodno, Russia (now Lithuania) (–1983).

28   Karl Raimund Popper, Austrian-born English philosopher who argued that only one exception was needed to prove a hypothesis false, born in Vienna, Austria (–1994).

AUGUST

6   Dutch Schultz (real name Arthur Flegenheimer), gangster and bootlegger, born in the Bronx, New York (–1935).

8   Paul Adrien Maurice Dirac, English physicist, author of the complete theoretical formulation of quantum mechanics, born in Bristol, England (–1984).

13   Felix Wankel, German engineer who designed a revolutionary rotary internal combustion engine known as the Wankel engine, born in Lahr, Germany (–1988).

18   Leona Baumgartner, U.S. doctor and government official noted for her promotion of health care, born in Chicago, Illinois (–1991).

19   Ogden Nash, U.S. poet and editor, born in Rye, New York (–1971).

22   Leni Riefenstahl, German film producer and director known for her films extolling the Nazi movement in Germany, born in Berlin, Germany.

24   Fernand Braudel, French historian, born in Lunéville, France (–1985).

SEPTEMBER

5   Rudolf Virchow, German pathologist who pioneered the use of cell theory to explain disease, dies in Berlin (80).

6   Frederick Augustus Abel, English chemist who invented cordite, dies in Westminster, London, England (75).

21   Edward Evans-Pritchard, English anthropologist known for his studies of religion among African peoples, born in Crowborough, East Sussex, England (–1973).

29   Emile Zola, French novelist and critic who founded the Naturalist movement, dies in Paris, France (62).

OCTOBER

5   Ray Kroc, U.S. restaurateur who founded McDonald's fast-food hamburger restaurants, born in Chicago, Illinois (–1984).

NOVEMBER

9   John (Norris) McArthur, Scottish malariologist and microscopist who develops the McArthur microscope, a cigarette pack-size light microscope, born in Glasgow, Scotland (–1996).

17   Eugene Paul Wigner, Hungarian-born U.S. physicist who introduces the notion of parity, or symmetry theory, into nuclear physics, born in Budapest, Austria-Hungary (–1995).

22   Walter Reed, U.S. Army surgeon who proved that yellow fever is transmitted by mosquito, dies in Washington, D.C. (51).

29   Carlo Levi, Italian writer and painter who began a trend toward social realism in Italian literature, born in Turin, Italy (–1975).

DECEMBER

4   Charles Henry Dow, U.S. financial journalist who established the Dow–Jones average, dies in Brooklyn, New York (51).

13   Talcott Parsons, U.S. sociologist, born in Colorado Springs, Colorado (–1979).

23   Frederick Temple, English educational reformer and archbishop of Canterbury 1896–1902, dies in London, England (81).

1903

POLITICS, GOVERNMENT, AND ECONOMICS

Business and Economics

- A tariff is introduced in New Zealand, which favors British goods.
- Several electrical companies in Germany unite to found the Telefunken Company.
- The Krupp metalworking industries are founded in the Ruhr region of Germany.
- The U.S. confectioner Milton Hershey establishes a factory and subsidized housing for workers at Derry Church, Pennsylvania. The town is soon renamed Hershey.
- U.S. chemist Caleb Bradham trademarks the name Pepsi-Cola.
- U.S. engineer Frederick Winslow Taylor publishes *Shop Management*, which helps to establish the "scientific management" of work forces.

MARCH

21 The Anthracite Coal Strike Commission, which held hearings on the grievances of U.S. anthracite coal miners (who held a strike in 1902), releases its report. Contract miners are awarded a pay increase of 10% and a shorter working day, and employers may not discriminate against union members, but mine owners refuse to recognize the United Mine Workers' Union.

JUNE

- Henry Ford combines with John and Horace Dodge and nine others to establish the Ford Motor Company in Detroit, Michigan, making the city the "motor capital" of the world.

NOVEMBER

11 A commission in the British colony of Transvaal favors the use of immigrant Chinese labor in the Rand mines. This is subsequently sanctioned by the British prime minister, Arthur Balfour.

Colonization

MARCH

15 British forces under Colonel Morland complete the conquest of northern Nigeria by taking the key Nigerian town of Sokoto from the emir of Kano.

Human Rights

FEBRUARY

2 A report by the British consul Roger Casement reveals the atrocious treatment of African and Indian laborers in the Belgian Congo by white traders. A British government commission confirms the findings.

Politics and Government

- President Theodore Roosevelt appoints jurist William R. Day to the U.S. Supreme Court.
- The Union of Liberation is founded in Russia with the support of members of the professions, to agitate for a liberal constitution.
- The U.S. state of Wisconsin institutes primary elections to enable voters to choose election candidates.
- U.S. antitrust laws are reinforced.

JANUARY

1 The emperor of India, King Edward VII of Great Britain, holds a coronation *durbar* (court) in Delhi, India, to celebrate his accession as king of Great Britain and emperor of India. Most Indian rulers attend, together with 40,000 troops and 173,000 visitors. Celebrations continue until January 8.
22 The United States and Columbia sign the Hay-Herrán Treaty, which provides the United States with a 99-year lease over the prospective Panama Canal zone. The treaty passes the U.S. Senate on March 17, but the Columbian Senate rejects it on August 12.

FEBRUARY

- President Theodore Roosevelt signs legislation creating the Department of Commerce and Labor, the ninth Cabinet Office.
- The Supreme Court, in *Champion v. Ames*, upholds the right of the federal government to prohibit the sale of lottery tickets through the U.S. mail.
- The U.S. Congress passes the Elkins Act, amending the Interstate Commerce Act of 1887. The new legislation prohibits railroad companies from deviating from published rate tables.
2 Russia and Austria call for a program of reforms for the Ottoman province of Macedonia, which has been destabilized by conflict between its constituent ethnic groups.
2 The British colonial secretary, Joseph Chamberlain, visits South Africa to direct British policy toward conciliation with the Boer people.
13 Germany, Britain, and Italy lift their blockade of Venezuela (imposed in December 1902) when The Hague tribunal appoints a commission to investigate

their claims for damages incurred in the 1899 revolution in Venezuela.

APRIL

- The U.S. Supreme Court, in *Giles v. Harris*, upholds an Alabama law disenfranchising black voters.
4 Britain and France withhold support for Germany's construction of a railroad to Baghdad, Iraq, fearing a threat to their interests in the Near East.
7 King Alexander of Serbia suspends the constitution in order to deal with pro-Russian agitators.

MAY

1 The U.S. state of New Hampshire issues liquor licenses, thereby ending a 48-year total prohibition of alcohol.
1–4 King Edward VII of Great Britain visits Paris, France, beginning an improvement in Anglo-French relations.
15 The British foreign secretary, Lord Lansdowne, declares that Britain will resist the establishment of a fortified base in the Persian Gulf by any power, in response to Russian activity in the region.

JUNE

10 The autocratic king Alexander I of Serbia and his wife, Queen Draga, are murdered by disaffected soldiers.

JULY

6–9 The French president Emile Loubet and his foreign minister Théophile Delcassé visit London, England, and begin conversations leading to the *Entente Cordiale* between the two countries.
20 Following the death of Pope Leo XIII, Giuseppe Sarto is elected Pope Pius X.

AUGUST

2 A rising begins against Turkish rule in the Ottoman province of Macedonia, principally among the Albanian and Bulgarian people there.
12 Japan protests to Russia over the latter's failure to evacuate the Chinese province of Manchuria, which has been occupied by Russian troops since 1901.
14 The Irish Land Purchase Act is passed in Britain, making it easier for tenants to purchase land, and establishing an Irish Land Commission to collect annuities from tenants rather than rent.
29 The Russian finance minister, Count Sergei Witte, is dismissed following opposition to his autocratic style and agricultural reforms. His dismissal is seen as a victory for the faction favoring Russian expansion in Manchuria and Korea.

SEPTEMBER

16 Emperor Franz Josef of Austria's aim to bring Hungarian regiments into a unified army system provokes Magyar opposition.

OCTOBER

2–3 The European powers approve an Austro-Russian agreement at Mürzsteg, Austria, which states that their advisors are to assist the Ottoman inspector general in Macedonia, Hilmi Pasha.
10 Anglo-Russian talks break down through Russian unwillingness to negotiate over its interests in Persia.
20 The Alaskan frontier dispute is settled by a three-power commission, the British representative giving the casting vote in favor of the United States, which embitters Canada.

31 A group of U.S. and Panamanian partisans stage a rebellion in Colombia near the site of the proposed Panama canal. The U.S. Navy prevents the Colombian military from entering the area. Three days later the Republic of Panama is declared.

NOVEMBER

3 A group of Panamanian partisans, backed by the United States, proclaims the Republic of Panama independent from Colombia, three days after a rebellion near the site of the proposed Panama Canal.
17 The Russian Social Democratic Party splits into the Mensheviks ("minority"), led by Grigory Plekhanov, and the Bolsheviks ("majority"), led by Vladimir Ilyich Lenin, at their London congress. The latter group favors a violent seizure of power.
17 Under the Treaty of Petropolis, Bolivia cedes territory to Brazil in return for a rail and water outlet to the east.
19 The Hay-Bunau-Varilla Treaty is signed between the newly-proclaimed Republic of Panama and the United States. It grants the United States the right to build and operate a canal through Panama in return for $10 million plus an annual fee of $250,000.

SCIENCE, TECHNOLOGY, AND MEDICINE

Ecology

- Prospectors strike oil in Oklahoma territory on land belonging to the Osage Indians.
- The U.S. Congress creates Wind Cave National Park from 113 sq km/28,000 acres of South Dakota's Black Hills region to protect its limestone caverns and herds of buffalo.
- The U.S. president Theodore Roosevelt establishes the first U.S. national wildlife refuge on Pelican Island, off the east coast of Florida. By 1929, 87 federal refuges will be established.

MAY

31 The flooding Kansas, Missouri, and Des Moines rivers kill more than 200 people and leave 8,000 others without homes.

Exploration

- Russian scientist Konstantin Eduardovich Tsiolkovsky writes "Investigations of Space by Means of Rockets," in which he outlines the use of liquid-propelled rockets to escape the earth's gravity.

Health and Medicine

- Danish physician Niels Ryberg Finsen receives the Nobel Prize for Physiology or Medicine for his treatment of skin diseases, especially lupus vulgaris, with concentrated light radiation.

- Dutch physiologist Willem Einthoven invents the string galvanometer (electrocardiograph), which measures and records the tiny electrical impulses produced by contractions of the heart muscle. He uses it to diagnose different types of heart disease.
- German surgeon Georg Clems Perthes discovers that X-rays inhibit the growth of cancerous tumors and suggests they be used as a treatment.
- In New York, New York, a cook called Mary Mallon—"Typhoid Mary"—is discovered to be a carrier of typhoid, unwittingly carrying and spreading the disease through handling food.
- Millionaire Henry Phipps founds the Phipps Institute for the Study, Treatment, and Prevention of Tuberculosis in Philadelphia, Pennsylvania.
- Polish surgeon Johannes von Mikulicz-Radecki performs the first operation to remove a cancerous portion of the colon.
- The German company A. G. Bayer launches Veronal, the first sleeping pill.

Science

- French physicists Antoine-Henri Becquerel and Pierre and Marie Curie share the Nobel Prize for Physics for their discovery of radioactivity. Curie is the first woman to win a Nobel prize.
- New Zealand-born British physicist Ernest Rutherford discovers that a beam of alpha particles is deflected by electric and magnetic fields. From the direction of deflection he is able to prove that they have a positive charge and from their velocity he determines the ratio of their charge to their mass. He also names the high-frequency electromagnetic radiation escaping from the nuclei of atoms as gamma rays.
- Scottish chemist William Ramsay shows that helium is produced during the radioactive decay of radium—an important discovery for the understanding of nuclear reactions.
- Scottish physicist Charles Thomson Rees Wilson develops the sensitive electroscope, which is used to detect the electric charge of ionizing radiation.
- Swedish chemist Svante Arrhenius receives the Nobel Prize for Chemistry for his theory of electrolytic dissociation.
- The Prix Goncourt is launched in France, a literary award funded by the legacy of French writer Edmond de Goncourt.

Technology

- Danish engineer Valdemar Poulsen patents an arc generator for producing continuous radio waves; an important step in the development of radio broadcasting.
- Texaco (the Texas Company) sinks its first major oil well, in Texas.
- The 16-story Ingalls Building in Cincinnati, Ohio, is completed. It is the first skyscraper built of reinforced concrete.
- The first commercially effective gasoline turbine is built in Paris, France. It operates with an efficiency of only 3%.

- The Springfield Armoury, Massachusetts, introduces the Springfield Model 1903 rifle. It proves to be the world's most reliable and accurate rifle.
- The Telegraphone, the first magnetic recorder, is launched in the United States. It is initially intended for office uses such as recording telephone messages and dictation. Though limited in scope, its technology forms the basis of current telephone answering machines.
- U.S. inventor Michael Owens automates his bottle-making machine permitting the mass production of bottles and lightbulbs, and stimulating the spread of electric lighting.
- William Harley teams up with Arthur, Walter, and William Davidson to produce the first Harley-Davidson motorcycles.

JANUARY

1   San Francisco, California, is linked by undersea cable to Honolulu, Hawaii.

JULY

4   Honolulu, the United States, and Manila in the Philippines are linked by undersea cable. U.S. president Theodore Roosevelt inaugurates transpacific communications by sending a message around the world via San Francisco, Honolulu, and Manila. It takes 12 minutes.

Transportation

- The Williamsburg Bridge, New York, New York, opens. It is the first suspension bridge to use steel towers instead of masonry ones.
- U.S. aeronautical engineer Charles Manley builds a lightweight highly efficient internal combustion engine. Weighing 85 kg/187 lb it produces over 50 horsepower and can run for 10 consecutive hours. It is used in the first airplanes.

MARCH

- U.S. aviators Orville and Wilbur Wright apply for a patent for the first practical glider that can be controlled.

MAY

23–July 26   U.S. drivers H. Nelson Jackson and Sewall K. Crocker make the first automobile drive across the United States, from San Francisco, California, to New York, New York, in their 20-horsepower Winton.

AUGUST

8   U.S. astronomer and physicist Samuel Pierpont Langley achieves the first flight of a heavier-than-air vehicle powered by a gasoline engine. It is uncrewed and flies 300 m/1,000 ft in 27 seconds.

SEPTEMBER

1   The first car license plates in the United States are issued in Massachusetts; other states soon follow.

DECEMBER

8   U.S. astronomer and physicist Samuel Pierpont Langley attempts his first manned flight. His plane, with a wing span of 13 m/40 ft, weighing only 386 kg/850 lb (including pilot), and powered by U.S. aeronautical engineer Charles Manley's engine, snags on takeoff and plunges into the Potomac River just nine days before the Wright brothers make their first successful flight. It is

reconstructed several years later and successfully flown by U.S. aviator Glenn Curtiss.

17 U.S. aviator Orville Wright makes the first successful flight in an airplane with a gasoline engine at Kitty Hawk, North Carolina, covering 37 m/120 ft in a flight lasting just 12 seconds. During the day, Orville and his brother Wilbur make a number of flights, the longest covering 260 m/852 ft and lasting 59 seconds.

ARTS AND IDEAS

Architecture

- Hill House in Helensburgh, Scotland, designed by the Scottish architect Charles Rennie Mackintosh, is completed.
- The Convalescent Home at Purkersdorf, near Vienna, Austria, designed by the Austrian architect Josef Hoffmann, is completed.
- The Spanish architect Antonio Gaudí begins work on upper transept of the Sagrada Familia Church in Barcelona, Spain. He began work on the church in 1884.

Arts

- The French artist Henri Matisse sculpts *Serf*.
- The U.S. artist Everett Shinn paints *The Laundress*.
- The National Art Collections Fund is formed in Britain to raise money to prevent works of art leaving the country.

Film

- The movie *La Vie d'un joueur/The Life of a Gambler*, produced by Ferdinand Zecca, is released in France.
- The movie *The Great Train Robbery*, directed by Edwin S. Porter, is released in the United States, starring G. M. Anderson. It is remarkable for its innovations in editing and for being the first significant Western in movie history.
- The movie *The Melomaniac*, directed by George Méliès, is released in France.
- The movie *The Passion Play* is produced in the United States; its running time is 36 minutes, one of the longest-running movies to date, about seven times the typical length.

Literature and Language

- A donation from the U.S. newspaper publisher Joseph Pulitzer is used to found the Columbia University Graduate School of Journalism, in New York, New York, and the Pulitzer prizes, awarded annually for outstanding achievement in journalism, letters, and music.
- Kate Douglas Wiggin publishes the children's classic *Rebecca of Sunnybrook Farm*.
- The English writer George Gissing publishes his novel *The Private Papers of Henry Rycroft*.

- The English writer John Morley publishes his biography *Life of Gladstone*.
- The first volumes of the 39-volume complete *Works of John Ruskin* are published, edited by the English scholars E. T. Cook and A. D. D. Wedderburn. The last volumes appear in 1912.
- The German writer Thomas Mann publishes his short novel *Tonio Kröger*.
- The satirical novel *The Way of All Flesh*, by the English writer Samuel Butler, is published posthumously.
- The U.S. cowboy and writer Andy Adams publishes his novel *The Log of a Cowboy*.
- The U.S. writer Frank Norris publishes his novel *The Pit*, and his essay collection *Responsibilities of the Novelist and Other Essays*.
- The U.S. writer Frank Norris publishes his short-story collection *A Deal in Wheat*.
- The U.S. writer Henry James publishes his novel *The Ambassadors* and the story "The Beast in the Jungle."
- The U.S. writer Jack London publishes his novel *The Call of the Wild*.
- The U.S. writer Mary Austin publishes *The Land of Little Rain*, a description of life on the deserts of New Mexico.
- The U.S. writer Willa Cather publishes her poetry collection *April Twilights*.
- The Nobel Prize for Literature is awarded to the Norwegian novelist and poet Bjørnstjerne Bjørnson.

Music

- Australian songwriter Marie Cowan adapts an old Scottish song to create "Waltzing Mathilda," with lyrics, based on a traditional Australian ballad, by Australian composer Andrew Peterson.
- The Austrian composer Arnold Schoenberg completes his orchestral work *Pelleas und Melisande/Pelleas and Melisande*.
- The French composer Claude Debussy completes his piano work *Estampes/Engravings*.
- The French composer Erik Satie completes his piano work *Trois Morceaux en forme de poire/Three Pieces in the Form of a Pear*.
- The French composer Vincent d'Indy completes his Symphony No. 2.
- The French composer Maurice Ravel completes his String Quartet in F.
- The German composer Richard Strauss completes his orchestral work *Symphonica Domestica*.
- The opera *Siberia*, by the Italian composer Umberto Giordano, is first performed in Milan, Italy.
- The opera *Tiefland/Lowland*, by the Scottish-born German composer Eugen d'Albert, is first performed in Prague, Bohemia.
- The Russian composer Sergey Rachmaninov completes his piano *Preludes* (Opus 23).
- The Swedish composer Hugo Alfvén completes his orchestral rhapsody *Midsommarvaka/Midsummer's Vigil*.
- U.S. composers Henry W. Armstrong and Richard H. Gerard write the song "You're the Flower of My Heart, Sweet Adeline."

Theater and Dance

- English scholar and critic Edmund Kerchever Chambers publishes *The Medieval Stage*.
- The play *In the Shadow of the Glen*, by the Irish writer John Millington Synge, is first performed in Dublin, Ireland.
- The play *The Hour-Glass*, by the Irish writers W. B. Yeats and Lady Gregory, is first performed in Dublin, Ireland.

JANUARY
20 The musical *The Wizard of Oz*, with music by A. Baldwin Sloane and Paul Tietjens, is performed for the first time, at the Majestic Theater, New York, New York. It is based on the book by Frank L. Baum, who also writes the lyrics.

OCTOBER
13 The musical *Babes in Toyland*, with music by Victor Herbert and lyrics by Glen MacDonough, is performed for the first time at the Majestic Theater in New York, New York. Songs include "Babes in Toyland" and "March of the Toys."

DECEMBER
16 The Majestic Theater in New York, New York, hires its first female ushers.
30 A fire at the Iroquois Theater in Chicago, Illinois, during an Eddie Foy performance, kills 588 people. The public outcry helps lead to the passage of theater safety codes in many U.S. cities.

Thought and Scholarship

- Black American civil-rights proponent W. E. B. Du Bois publishes *The Souls of Black Folk*.
- English jurist William Searle Holdsworth publishes the first volume of his *History of English Law*. The final volume (he died in 1944, so the work had to be completed by others) appears in 1972.
- English philosopher G. E. Moore publishes his influential study of ethics *Principia Ethica/Principles of Ethics*.

- German archeologist Max Uhle publishes *Pachacamac*, an account of his excavations at the site of Pachacamac on the coast of Peru, South America.
- Russian physiologist Ivan Pavlov describes learning by conditioning. He trains dogs to expect food when they hear a bell and eventually they salivate every time the bell rings.
- U.S. writer and feminist Charlotte Perkins Gilman publishes *The Home: Its Work and Influence*.

SOCIETY

Education

- The University of Puerto Rico opens in Rio Piedras.

Everyday Life

- U.S. manufacturer King C. Gillette patents disposable safety razor blades.

APRIL
4 The Dutch government uses troops to end railroad and dock strikes.

Media and Communication

- Italian philosopher Benedetto Croce founds the journal *La Critica* to reinvigorate Italian thought. He edits it until 1943.

MARCH
29 A regular news service is set up on the Marconi wireless between London, England, and New York, New York.

Sports

- In baseball, a vitriolic dispute between the American League and the National League, largely over poaching

---

BIRTHS & DEATHS

- Andrey Nikolayevich Kolmogorov, Russian mathematician who developed some basic postulates of probability theory, born in Tambov, Russia (–1987).
- George Orwell (Eric Arthur Blair), English novelist who wrote *Animal Farm* and *Nineteen Eighty-Four*, born in Motihari, Bengal, India (–1950).

JANUARY
11 Alan Paton, South African novelist who publicized the problems of apartheid in *Cry, the Beloved Country*, born in Pietermaritzburg, Natal, South Africa (–1988).

27 John Crew Eccles, Australian physiologist who discovered how nerve impulses are chemically transmitted, born in Melbourne, Australia.

FEBRUARY
21 Anaïs Nin, French-born U.S. novelist and diarist influenced by the surrealists and psychology, born in Neuilly, France (–1977).
22 Hugo Wolf, Austrian composer, dies in Vienna, Austria (42).
26 Richard Jordan Gatling, U.S. inventor of the Gatling machine gun, dies in New York, New York (84).

MARCH
11 Lawrence Welk, U.S. bandleader and accordion player, born in Strasburg, North Dakota (–1992).
24 Adolf Butenandt, German biochemist who discovered the sex hormones estrone, androsterone, and progesterone, born in Bremerhaven-Lehe, Germany (–1995).

APRIL
12 Jan Tinbergen, Dutch economist who, with Ragnar Frisch, received the first Nobel Prize for Economics for developing econometrics, born in The Hague, the Netherlands (–1994).

APRIL

19 Eliot Ness, U.S. law enforcement officer, head of the "Untouchables" (a special squad of supposedly incorruptible officers), born in Chicago, Illinois (–1957).

28 Josiah Willard Gibbs, U.S. theoretical physicist, dies in New Haven, Connecticut (64).

MAY

2 Dr. Benjamin Spock, U.S. pediatrician, who wrote *Common Sense Book of Baby and Child Care*, born in New Haven, Connecticut (–1998).

8 Paul Gauguin, French Postimpressionist painter, dies in Atuona, Hiva Oa, Marquesas Islands, French Polynesia (54).

12 Wilfred Hyde White, English actor, born in Bourton-on-the-Water, Gloucestershire, England (–1991).

29 Bob Hope, U.S. actor and entertainer, born in Eltham, near London, England.

JUNE

6 Aram Khachaturian, Russian composer, born in Tiflis (modern Tbilisi), Georgia, Russian Empire (–1978).

13 Harold Edward "Red" Grange, U.S. football player, born in Forksville, Pennsylvania (–1991).

19 Lou Gehrig, U.S. professional baseball player, born in New York, New York (–1941).

23 John Dillinger, U.S. bank robber, born in Indianapolis, Indiana (–1934).

JULY

2 Alec Douglas-Home, Baron Home of the Hirsel, prime minister of Britain 1963–64, a Conservative, born in London, England (–1995).

2 Olaf V of Norway, Norwegian monarch (1957–91), born at Appleton House, near Sandringham, Norfolk, England (–1991).

14 Irving Stone, U.S. author of biographical novels such as *The Agony and the Ecstasy* about Michelangelo, born in San Francisco (–1989).

17 James Whistler, U.S.-born artist active in London, dies in London, England (67).

20 Pope Leo XIII, Italian pope 1878–1903, dies in Rome, Italy (92).

AUGUST

1 Calamity Jane (Martha Jane Cannary Burke), U.S.

frontierswoman, dies in Terry, near Deadwood, South Dakota (51).

7 Louis Leakey, Kenyan archeologist and anthropologist who discovered fossil hominids in Olduvai Gorge, Kenya, born in Kabete, Kenya (–1972).

22 Lord Salisbury (Robert Arthur Talbot Gascoyne-Cecil), British prime minister 1885–86, 1886–92, and 1895–1902, a Conservative, dies in Hatfield, Hertfordshire, England (73).

24 Graham Sutherland, English painter known for his surrealist landscapes and his portraits, born in London, England (–1980).

28 Bruno Bettelheim, Austrian-U.S. psychologist noted for his treatment of emotionally disturbed children, born in Vienna, Austria (–1990).

28 Frederick Law Olmsted, U.S. landscape architect who designed Central Park in New York, New York, dies in Brookline, Massachusetts (80).

SEPTEMBER

13 Claudette Colbert, U.S. actress, born in Paris, France (–1996).

15 Roy Acuff, U.S. country and western singer, born in Maynardsville, Tennessee (–1992).

25 Marc Rothko, Russian-born U.S. abstract expressionist painter, born in Dvinsk, Russia (now Daugavpils in Latvia) (–1970).

29 Greer Garson, U.S. actress, born in County Down, Ireland (–1996).

OCTOBER

4 Ernst Kaltenbrunner, Austrian Nazi, head of the Austrian SS, born in Ried im Innkreis, Austria-Hungary (–1946).

6 Ernest Thomas Sinton Walton, Irish physicist who with John Cockcroft developed the first particle accelerator and shared the Nobel Prize for Physics in 1951, born in Dungarvan, Ireland (–1995).

22 George Wells Beadle, U.S. biochemist who received the Nobel Prize for Physiology or Medicine in 1958 for demonstrating that genes control enzyme structure, born in Wahoo, Nebraska (–1989).

22 William Edward Hartpole Lecky, Irish historian, dies in London, England (65).

28 Evelyn Waugh, English satirical novelist, born in London, England (–1966).

29 Mary Bancroft, U.S. spy during World War II, born in Cambridge, Massachusetts (–1997).

31 Joan Robinson, English economist who continued the development of the Keynesian economic theory, born in Camberley, Surrey, England (–1983).

NOVEMBER

1 Theodor Mommsen, German historian, dies in Charlottenburg, near Berlin, Germany (85).

3 Walker Evans, U.S. photographer best known for his photographs of rural U.S. southerners during the Great Depression, born in St. Louis, Missouri (–1975).

27 Lars Onsager, Norwegian-born U.S. chemist who developed a general theory of irreversible processes, born in Kristiania, Norway (–1976).

DECEMBER

3 John von Neumann, Hungarian-born U.S. mathematician who worked in quantum physics, logic, and computer science, born in Budapest, Austria-Hungary (–1957).

4 A(lfred) L(eslie) Rowse, British historian, born in Tregonissey, Cornwall, England (–1997).

8 Herbert Spencer, English sociologist and philosopher who believed in the primacy of the individual over society, dies in Brighton, Sussex, England (83).

10 Mary Norton, English writer of children's stories who created the Borrowers, born in London, England (1992).

13 Camille Pissaro, French impressionist painter, dies in Paris, France (72).

13 Carlos García Montoya, Spanish guitarist noted for his flamenco music, born in Madrid, Spain (–1993).

13 John Egerton Christmas Piper, English painter, printmaker, and designer known for his dramatic views of landscape and architecture, born in Epsom, Surrey, England (–1992).

17 Erskine Caldwell, U.S. author whose works depicted the poverty of farmers during the Depression, born in Coweta County, Georgia (–1987).

19 George Snell, U.S. immunologist who discovered the histocompatibility gene complex, making tissue transplant more feasible, born in Brookline, Massachusetts (–1996).

players, comes to an end when both leagues recognize each other as equals. Rules are drawn up on player and franchise movement, and a joint national commission is organized to govern baseball.

- Ohio emerges as a center for professional football in the United States with Massillon and Canton the top teams.
- The British tennis player Hugh Doherty becomes the first overseas player to win the men's singles title at the U.S. lawn tennis championships held at the Casino, Newport, Rhode Island.

March, 1903–04 In card playing, auction bridge is devised as a variation of bridge whist in Britain and the United States.

JULY

1–19 The Tour de France cycling race is run for the first time, organized by Henri Desgrange, editor of the French cycling magazine *L'Auto*. Twenty-one of the 60 entrants finish the 2,428-km/1,509-mi race, with Maurice Garin of France the winner.

OCTOBER

1–13 The World Series, between the winners of the American League and the National League, is inaugurated in the United States. The first title is won by the Boston Red Sox of the American League, who beat the National League's Pittsburgh Pirates by five games to three.

24 Lou Dillon becomes the first trotting horse to break two minutes for the mile, at Memphis, Tennessee.

1904

POLITICS, GOVERNMENT, AND ECONOMICS

Business and Economics

APRIL

23 The United States acquires the property of the French Panama Canal Company when the Panama Canal zone is transferred at a meeting in Paris, France.

MAY

4 Henry Royce and Charles Rolls start manufacturing and selling cars under the name Rolls-Royce in Britain.

OCTOBER

19 James Buchanan Duke merges his tobacco companies Consolidated Tobacco and American & Continental to form the American Tobacco Company.

DECEMBER

- U.S. industrialist Charles M. Schwab establishes the Bethlehem Steel Corporation in Bethlehem, Pennsylvania, as a rival to J. P. Morgan's company, U.S. Steel.

Human Rights

- U.S. progressive reformers establish the National Child Labor Committee.

December 1904–05 Anti-Jewish pogroms take place

across Russia, but the authorities take little preventative action.

Politics and Government

- Canada passes a protectionist tariff.
- Sir John Fisher is made first sea lord of Great Britain, and begins building bigger, better-armed warships that revolutionize sea warfare.

JANUARY

- The U.S. Supreme Court rules that Puerto Rican citizens, though not U.S. citizens, cannot be refused admission to the United States.

FEBRUARY

- President Theodore Roosevelt appoints the Panama Canal Commission to oversee construction of the project.

8–9 The Russo-Japanese War starts when the Japanese fleet makes a surprise attack on the Russian squadron at Port Arthur (the Russian treaty port in northeastern China) without a declaration of war, and damages two battleships and a cruiser.

10 Japan declares war on Russia, aiming to end Russian influence in Manchuria and to secure Japanese rights in Korea.

17 Korea signs a treaty with Japan, virtually making it a Japanese protectorate.

MARCH

11 The Army Bill is passed in Hungary, despite Magyar obstruction, and incorporates Hungary's forces into those of Austria.

14 The U.S. Supreme Court finds J. P. Morgan's Northern Securities Company in violation of the Sherman

Antitrust Act (1890) by its attempts to merge railroad interests and orders the company dissolved.

APRIL

4   John Christian Watson becomes the world's first Labor prime minister, in Australia.

8   The *Entente Cordiale* settles British–French differences in Morocco, Egypt, and the Newfoundland fishery, and Britain recognizes the Suez Canal Convention and surrenders its claim to Madagascar.

24–27   The French president Emile Loubet and his foreign minister Théophile Delcassé visit King Victor Emmanuel III of Italy. The papacy expresses annoyance at the visit.

MAY

- The Panama Canal Commission appoints John Findley Wallace as chief engineer of the canal construction project.

- The Socialist Party of America nominates Eugene V. Debs for president and Benjamin Hanford for vice president.

1   The Japanese army attacks and defeats the Russian army at Xinyizhou in the Russo-Japanese War.

17   The French ambassador at the Vatican is recalled to Paris, France.

26   At the Battle of Nanshan, Japanese forces under General Yasukata Oku are victorious and cut off the Russian garrison in Port Arthur, China, from other Russian land forces in Manchuria.

JUNE

- Republicans nominate Pennsylvania physician, Silas C. Swallow, for president, and Indiana businessman, Charles W. Fairbanks, for vice president.

JULY

- Democrats nominate New York judge Alton B. Parker for president and West Virginian politician Henry G. Davis for vice president.

7   As part of a movement to end clerical influence in France, a law is passed forbidding religious teaching.

7   Rafael Reyes becomes dictator in Colombia and begins an attempt to reorganize the country's finances.

28   Germany signs commercial treaties with Belgium, Switzerland, Sweden, and Austria-Hungary.

28   Vyacheslav Plehve, the hard-line Russian minister of the interior, is assassinated.

AUGUST

25–September 3   The Japanese forces under Field Marshal Iwao Oyama defeat the Russian troops led by General Alexei Kuropatkin at Liaoyang, China, in the Russo-Japanese War.

SEPTEMBER

7   At the culmination of a British expedition to Lhasa, Tibet, Colonel Francis Younghusband forces a treaty on Tibet, under which its ruler, the Dalai Lama, will not be able concede territory to a foreign power without British consent.

OCTOBER

3   France and Spain sign a treaty preserving the independence of Morocco, but include secret clauses

Russo–Japanese War (1904–05)

1904

FEBRUARY

8–9   The Russo-Japanese War starts when the Japanese fleet makes a surprise attack on the Russian squadron at Port Arthur (the Russian treaty port in northeastern China) without a declaration of war, and damages two battleships and a cruiser.

10   Japan declares war on Russia, aiming to end Russian influence in Manchuria and to secure Japanese rights in Korea.

MAY

1   The Japanese army attacks and defeats the Russian army at Xinyizhou.

26   At the Battle of Nanshan, Japanese forces under General Yasukata Oku are victorious and cut off the Russian garrison in Port Arthur, China, from other Russian land forces in Manchuria.

AUGUST

25–September 3   The Japanese forces under Field Marshal Iwao Oyama defeat the Russian troops led by General Alexei Kuropatkin at Liaoyang, China.

OCTOBER

21   The Russian Baltic fleet, bound for the Far East via the Cape of Good Hope, fires on British trawlers in the Dogger Bank area of the North Sea, believing them to be

Japanese torpedo boats. One vessel sinks, provoking a wave of indignation in Britain.

1905

JANUARY

2   The Russian commander of Port Arthur, General Anatoli Steseł, surrenders the port to Japanese forces under General Maresuke Nogi.

FEBRUARY

20–March 9   The Japanese forces under Field Marshal Iwao Oyama overcome a Russian force under General Alexei Kuropatkin, and capture the city of Mukden (Shenyang), a key point for the control of Manchuria.

MAY

27–29   During the Battle of Tsushima in the Tsushima Strait between Korea and Japan, the Japanese fleet under Vice Admiral Heirachiro Togo sinks two-thirds of the recently-arrived Russian Baltic fleet commanded by Admiral Zinovi Rozhdestvenski.

SEPTEMBER

6   Although Russia has now built up massive forces in Manchuria, internal unrest dictates that she negotiate a peace with Japan. The treaty signed at Portsmouth, New Hampshire, on September 6 recognized that Korea was in Japan's sphere of influence, but neither power was allowed a predominant position in Manchuria. Thus were sown the seeds of later conflict.

aimed at its ultimate partition between the two countries.

3   Members of the Herero and Hottentot people rebel in German South West Africa.

10 Italian socialists, discredited by the recent wave of strike action, lose heavily in the Italian elections.

20 Bolivia and Chile settle their territorial differences over disputed mineral-rich provinces by treaty.

21 The Russian Baltic fleet, bound for the Far East via the Cape of Good Hope, fires on British trawlers in the Dogger Bank area of the North Sea, believing them to be Japanese torpedo boats. One vessel sinks, provoking a wave of indignation in Britain.

28 Following the Dogger Bank incident in which the Russian fleet mistakenly sank a British trawler, Czar Nicholas II of Russia agrees to refer the question of compensation to The Hague international commission.

NOVEMBER

8   In the U.S. presidential election, President Theodore Roosevelt (Republican) defeats Alton B. Parker (Democrat) with 336 electoral votes to Parker's 140. In the popular vote Roosevelt polls 7,623,486 votes and Parker 5,077,911. In the Congressional elections, the Republicans maintain majorities in the House (250–136) and Senate (57–33).

11 The Zemstvo (local government) congress at St. Petersburg, Russia, demands a republican constitution and civil liberties.

23 German–Russian negotiations for an alliance (begun on October 27) break down through Russia's unwillingness to sign before consulting France.

DECEMBER

•   In a foreign-policy statement, President Theodore Roosevelt delineates the Roosevelt Corollary to the Monroe Doctrine: the United States reserves the right to intervene in Western Hemisphere nations plagued by "wrongdoing or impotence."

2   Members of the British Parliament representing Ulster, Ireland, form an organization (known as the Ulster Unionist Council from March 1905) which favors the preservation of British rule in Ulster.

10 A nationalist anti-Austrian ministry takes office in Serbia, led by Nicola Pašić.

SCIENCE, TECHNOLOGY, AND MEDICINE

Ecology

•   A typhoon drowns nearly 5,000 in the Mekong Delta, French Indochina.

•   The fungus *Endothis parasitica* is imported into the United States from Japan and rapidly begins to destroy the American Chestnut *Castanea dentata*, which is soon virtually wiped out on the continent.

FEBRUARY

7   Fire consumes more than 1,300 buildings in the business section of the city of Baltimore, Maryland, burning for 30 hours and causing an estimated $80 million damage.

APRIL

19 Over 20 acres of downtown Toronto, Ontario, Canada are destroyed by fire. The damage is an estimated $10,000 and 6,000 people are unemployed as a result.

Health and Medicine

•   Russian physiologist Ivan Pavlov receives the Nobel Prize for Physiology or Medicine for his work on the physiology of digestion.

•   The National Association for the Study and Prevention of Tuberculosis is established in the United States. It founds tuberculosis clinics throughout the country where patients can receive free examination and treatment.

•   U.S. Army surgeon William Gorgas introduces mosquito control in the Panama Canal Zone and within two years effectively eradicates yellow fever and malaria.

Science

•   English chemist Frederic Kipping pioneers the development of silicones, organic compounds of silicon.

•   English physicist Charles Glover Barkla demonstrates that each element can be made to emit X-rays of a characteristic frequency.

•   English physicist John Fleming patents the diode valve, which allows electricity to flow in only one direction. It is an essential development in the evolution of television.

•   English physicist John William Strutt, Baron Rayleigh, receives the Nobel Prize for Physics for his discovery of argon.

•   German engineer Christian Hülsmeyer patents the first primitive radar system.

•   Japanese physicist Hantaro Nagaoka proposes a model of the atom in which the electrons are located in an outer ring and orbit the positive charge which is located in a central nucleus. The model is ignored because it is thought the electrons would fall into the nucleus.

•   New Zealand-born British physicist Ernest Rutherford publishes *Radio-Activity*, summarizing his work on the subject and pointing out that radioactivity produces more heat than other chemical reactions.

•   Nicotine is first synthesized.

•   Scottish chemist William Ramsay receives the Nobel Prize for Chemistry for his involvement in the discovery of inert gases in air and their locations in the periodic table.

•   Spanish physiologist Santiago Ramón y Cajal demonstrates that the neuron is the basis of the nervous system.

•   U.S. archeologist Edward Thompson begins excavating the ancient Mayan city of Chichén Itzá.

•   U.S. chemist Bertram Borden Boltwood discovers the radioactive element ionium, now called thorium-230.

SEPTEMBER

•   In a lecture at St. Louis, Missouri, French mathematician Jules-Henri Poincaré proposes a theory of relativity to explain Michelson and Morley's failed experiment to determine the velocity of the earth.

Technology

- Italian inventor Giovanni Conti installs the first geothermal electric generating station at Larderello, Italy.
- Searchlights are first used in the Russo-Japanese war.
- The Eastern Lithographic Co. uses the first offset-litho printing press in the United States.
- U.S. engineer Charles Franklin Kettering invents the first electric cash register.
- U.S. printer Ira Rubel accidentally discovers offset printing.

MAY
3   U.S. inventor George Parker patents a pen with a lever to fill the ink barrel.

Transportation

- The Austro-Daimler company builds the first turreted armored cars, in Germany.
- The British ship *Baltic* enters service. It is the largest ship in the world at 221 m/726 ft.
- The paddle-wheeler *General Slocum* catches fire on the Hudson River, New York, New York; over 1,000 die.
- The Trans-Siberian Railway, begun in 1891, is completed, linking Moscow and Vladivostok. It opens up Siberia to exploitation, settlement, and industrialization.

MARCH
8   The Hudson and Manhattan Railway Company completes construction of the first tunnel under the Hudson River, New York, New York.

MAY
23 Competition between shipping lines introduces a new cheap steerage rate, which encourages migration from Europe to the United States.

JUNE
28 The Danish steam ship *Norge* sinks off the coast of Scotland; 620 die.

SEPTEMBER
20 U.S. aviators Wilbur and Orville Wright are the first to fly a full circle in their flying machine.

OCTOBER
27 The first section of the subway system in New York, New York, opens, with electric trains running from City Hall to 145th Street, with fares of five cents. The first underground system in the United States, it becomes the largest in the world.

ARTS AND IDEAS

Architecture

- The Larkin Building, designed by U.S. architect Frank Lloyd Wright, is completed in Buffalo, New York (destroyed in 1940).

- The metal arches over the entrances to the Metro stations, designed by the French architect Hector Guimard, are completed in Paris, France. Their elaborate ironwork is one of the leading examples of the art nouveau style.
- The Stock Exchange, designed by the U.S. architect George B. Post, is completed in New York, New York.

Arts

- The French artist Henri Matisse paints *Luxe, Calme et Volupté/Luxury, Calm and Voluptuousness*.
- The French artist Henri Rousseau paints *The Wedding*.
- The French artist Odilon Redon paints *Portrait of Gauguin*.
- The Scottish architect Charles Rennie Mackintosh designs the interior and furnishings for the Willow Tea Rooms, Glasgow, Scotland.
- The Scottish photographer James Craig Annan takes *Stirling Castle*.
- The Spanish artist Pablo Picasso paints *Woman Ironing*.
- The U.S. artist Robert Henri paints *Portrait of George Luks*.
- The U.S. photographer Edward Steichen takes *The Flatiron*.

Film

- The Cinema Moderno opens in Rome, the first purpose-built movie theater in Italy.

Literature and Language

- The English naturalist and writer William Henry Hudson publishes his novel *Green Mansions*.
- The English scholar and writer M. R. James publishes *Ghost Stories of an Antiquary*.
- The English writer Baron Corvo publishes his autobiographical fantasy *Hadrian the Seventh*.
- The English writer G. K. Chesterton publishes his novel *The Napoleon of Notting Hill*.
- The French writer Romain Rolland publishes the first part of his multipart novel *Jean-Christophe*. The work is completed in 1912.
- The German writer Hermann Hesse publishes his first novel, *Peter Camenzind*.
- The Italian writer Luigi Pirandello publishes his novel *Il fu Mattia Pascal/The Late Mattia Pascal*.
- The Polish-born English writer Joseph Conrad publishes his novel *Nostromo*.
- The U.S. writer Ellen Glasgow publishes her novel *The Deliverance*.
- The U.S. writer Henry James publishes his novel *The Golden Bowl*.
- The U.S. writer Jack London publishes his novel *The Sea-Wolf*.
- The U.S. writer O. Henry publishes the short-story collection *Cabbages and Kings*.
- U.S. journalist Lincoln Steffens publishes *The Shame of the Cities*, a collection of articles on urban reform which pinpoint public apathy, rather than boss corruption, as the cause of urban problems. His work came to be

identified with what would later be termed "muckraking."

Music

- Axel Christensen publishes *Instruction Book No. 1 for Rag-Time*, a popular book that teaches the rudiments of ragtime music in 20 lessons.
- The Austrian composer Gustav Mahler completes his song cycle *Kindertotenlieder/Songs of the Death of Children*.
- The English composer Edward Elgar completes his orchestral work *In the South*.
- The French composer Claude Debussy completes his piano work *L'Ile joyeuse/The Island of Joy*.
- The French composer Florent Schmitt completes his *Psalm 47* for voice and orchestra.
- The German company International Talking Machine Co. launches the first double-sided records in Germany and Britain.
- The opera *Jenůfa*, by the Czech composer Leoš Janáček, is first performed in Brno. It premieres in New York, New York, in 1935, and in London, England, in 1956.
- The opera *Koanga*, by the English composer Frederick Delius, is first performed in Elberfield, Germany. It premieres in London, England, in 1935.
- The opera *Madame Butterfly*, by the Italian composer Giacomo Puccini, is first performed in Milan, Italy. It premieres in London, England, in 1905, and in New York, New York, in 1907.
- The song "Home on the Range," with lyrics by Bruce Higley and music by Daniel E. Kelly (revised by William Goodwin), is published.
- U.S. songwriter Hughie Cannon writes the song "Frankie and Johnny."

Theater and Dance

- The Abbey Theatre opens in Dublin, Ireland. The intention of its directors—the writers W. B. Yeats, John Millington Synge, and Lady Gregory—is to "create a National Irish theatre."
- The children's play *Peter Pan, or The Boy Who Would Not Grow Up*, by the Scottish writer J. M. Barrie, is first performed, at the Duke of York's Theatre in London, England.
- The play *Die Büchse der Pandora/Pandora's Box*, by the German dramatist Frank Wedekind, is first performed in Nuremberg, Germany.
- The play *Riders to the Sea*, by the Irish writer John Millington Synge, is first performed in Dublin, Ireland.
- The play *Vishnovy sad/The Cherry Orchard*, by the Russian writer Anton Chekhov, is first performed in Moscow, Russia.

NOVEMBER

17 George M. Cohan produces the musical *Little Johnny Jones*, featuring the songs "Give My Regards to Broadway" and "The Yankee Doodle Boy," at the Liberty Theater, New York, New York.

Thought and Scholarship

- Austrian psychoanalyst Sigmund Freud publishes *Zur Psychopathologie des Alltagslebens/The Psychopathology of Everyday Life*.
- British psychologist Charles Spearman publishes "General Intelligence, Objectively Determined and Measured," in which he is the first to apply statistical correlation methods to human mental abilities. He does so in an attempt to demonstrate general fundamental laws of psychology.
- English archeologist William Flinders Petrie publishes *Methods and Aims in Archaeology*.
- English historian George Macaulay Trevelyan publishes *England under the Stuarts*.
- English social philosopher Leonard Trelawney Hobhouse publishes *Democracy and Reaction*.
- Lithuanian-born U.S. art historian Bernard Berenson publishes *Drawings of the Florentine Painters*.
- The Nobel Prize for Literature is awarded to the French poet Frédéric Mistral, and to the Spanish dramatist José Echegaray y Eizaguirre.
- U.S. historian Henry Brooks Adams privately publishes his historical study *Mont St. Michel and Chartres: A Study of 13th Century Unity*.
- U.S. psychologist Granville Stanley Hall publishes *Adolescence*, in which he suggests that mental growth occurs in evolutionary stages.

BIRTHS & DEATHS

JANUARY

9 George Melitonovich Balanchine, U.S. choreographer, born in St. Petersburg, Russia (–1983).

18 Cary Grant, British-born U.S. film actor, born in Bristol, England (–1986).

FEBRUARY

1 S(idney) J(oseph) Perelman, U.S. humorist who wrote film scripts for the Marx Brothers and shared an Academy Award for the script of *Around the World in Eighty Days*, born in Brooklyn, New York (–1979).

3 Luigi Dallapiccola, Italian composer of atonal choral and orchestral works, born in Pisino, Istria (now Pazin, Croatia) (–1975).

21 Alexey Nikolaievich Kosygin, Soviet statesman and premier of the Soviet Union 1964–80, born in St. Petersburg, Russia (–1980).

22 Peter Hurd, U.S. artist and book illustrator whose work includes *The Last of the Mohicans* (1926), born in Roswell, New Mexico Territory (–1984).

23 William L(awrence) Shirer, U.S. journalist and historian, commentator for the Columbia Broadcasting System (CBS), and author of *The Rise and Fall of the Third Reich: A History of Nazi Germany*, born in Chicago, Illinois (–1993).

27 James T. Farrell, U.S. novelist, short-story writer, and critic, born in Chicago, Illinois (–1979).

29 Jimmy Dorsey, U.S. big-band leader and jazz musician, born in Shenandoah, Pennsylvania (–1957).

MARCH

1 Glenn Miller, U.S. composer, trombonist and big-band leader, born in Clarinda, Iowa (–1944).

2 Dr. Seuss (pseudonym of Theodore Seuss Geisel), U.S. writer of children's books, born in Springfield, Massachusetts (–1991).

5 Karl Rahner, German Jesuit priest, Roman Catholic theologian, and philosopher, born in Breisgau, Baden, Germany (–1984).

20 B(urrhus) F(rederic) Skinner, U.S. psychologist who developed behaviorist psychology, born in Susquehanna, Pennsylvania (–1990).

APRIL

15 Arshile Gorky, Armenian-born U.S. painter of the abstract expressionist school, born in Khorkom Vari, Turkish Armenia (–1948).

22 J. Robert Oppenheimer, U.S. theoretical physicist and director of the Los Alamos laboratory that built the first atomic bomb, born in New York, New York (–1967).

24 Willem de Kooning, Dutch-born U.S. abstract expressionist painter, born in Rotterdam, the Netherlands.

27 Cecil Day-Lewis, Irish poet, British poet laureate after 1968, born in Ballintogher, County Sligo, Ireland (–1972).

30 George Robert Stibitz, U.S. mathematician who developed the first binary calculator (one of the first digital computers), born in York, Pennsylvania (–1995).

MAY

1 Antonín Dvořák, Czech composer who is known for the influence of folk music in his works, dies in Prague, Bohemia (now the Czech Republic) (62).

2 (Harry Lillis) "Bing" Crosby, U.S. actor and singer, born in Tacoma, Washington (–1977).

8 Eadweard Muybridge, English-born U.S. photographer who made the first photographic studies of motion, dies in Kingston upon Thames, Surrey, England (74).

10 Henry Morton Stanley, Welsh-born British–U.S. newspaper correspondent and explorer who rescued David Livingstone in the Congo, dies in London, England (63).

11 Salvador Dalí, Spanish surrealist painter who also designed furniture, jewelry, and stage and film sets, born in Figueras, Spain (–1989).

20 Margery Allingham, English writer who created the detective Albert Campion, born in London, England (–1966).

21 Thomas "Fats" Waller, U.S. jazz pianist and composer, born in New York, New York (–1943).

30 Solly Zuckerman, South African-born British zoologist who did extensive research on primates, born in Cape Town, South Africa (–1993).

JUNE

2 Johnny Weissmuller, U.S. freestyle Olympic swimmer and film actor best known for his role as Tarzan, born in Friedorf, near Timişoara, Romania (–1984).

JULY

2 Anton Chekhov, Russian writer and dramatist known for his mastery of the short story, dies in Badenweiler, Germany (44).

2 René Lacoste, French tennis player, born (–1996).

3 Theodor Herzl, Austrian Zionist who promoted an international effort to establish a Jewish homeland, dies in Edlach, Austria (44).

5 Ernst Mayr, German-born U.S. biologist and population geneticist, born in Kempten, Germany.

12 Pablo Neruda, Chilean poet, diplomat, and Marxist, born in Parral, Chile (–1973).

14 Paul Kruger, South African statesman who founded the Afrikaaner nation and was instrumental in initiating the Second Anglo-Boer War, dies in Clarens, Switzerland (79).

24 Richard B. Morris, U.S. historian of the Colonial period and the American Revolution, born in New York, New York (–1989).

AUGUST

7 Ralphe Bunche, U.S. diplomat who successfully negotiated the Arab–Israeli peace agreement (1949), for which he won the Nobel Peace Prize (1950), born in Detroit, Michigan (–1971).

9 Friedrich Ratzel, German geographer and ethnologist, dies in Ammerland, Germany (59).

21 Count (William) Basie, U.S. pianist and big-band leader, born in Red Bank, New Jersey (–1984).

22 Deng Xiaoping, Chinese communist leader 1980–97, born in Szechwan Province, China (–1997).

26 Christopher Isherwood, English-born U.S. novelist and playwright, born in High Lane, Cheshire, England (–1986).

SEPTEMBER

4 Julian Hill, U.S. chemist who discovered nylon, born in St. Louis, Missouri (–1996).

21 Chief Joseph, Nez Percé Native American chief who led his people on a 1,600-km/1,000-mi journey to escape the U.S. Army, dies in Colville Reservation, Washington (about 64).

22 Joseph Valachi, U.S. gangster who became the first person to reveal the history, membership, and inner workings of the Mafia crime organization, born in New York, New York (–1971).

OCTOBER

1 Otto Frisch, Austrian-born physicist who described the process of nuclear fission, born in Vienna, Austria (–1979).

1 Vladimir Horowitz, Russian-born U.S. pianist, born in Kiev, Russia (–1989).

2 Graham Greene, English novelist, born in Berkhamsted, Hertfordshire, England (–1991).

NOVEMBER

1 Laura La Plante, U.S. silent film actress, born in St. Louis, Missouri (–1996).

8 Norman Adrian de Bruyne, English inventor and aircraft designer, designer of the Snark monoplane, born in Chile (–1997).

11 Alger Hiss, U.S. diplomat and liberal Democrat who was convicted in 1950 of being a Soviet spy, born in Baltimore, Maryland (–1996).

16 Nnamdi Azikiwe, first president of Nigeria 1963–66, born in Zungeru, Nigeria (–1996).

17 Isamu Noguchi, U.S. sculptor of organic abstract shapes, born in Los Angeles, California (–1988).

DECEMBER

10 Antonin Novotný, Czechoslovakian president 1957–68, deposed because of his Stalinist beliefs and policies, born in Letnany, near Prague, Bohemia (now Czech Republic) (–1975).

18 George Stevens, U.S. film director who won Oscars for *A Place in the Sun* and *Giant*, and also directed *Shane*, born in Oakland, California (–1975).

SOCIETY

Education

- The Deutsches Museum opens in Munich, Germany. Conceived by German electrical engineer Oskar von Miller, it is the world's first teaching museum. Visitors learn the scientific principles of technological innovations by operating the exhibits. It serves as the model for subsequent science museums.

MAY
- Helen Keller, deaf and blind, graduates magna cum laude from Radcliffe College.

Everyday Life

- Dr. George Wander markets Ovaltine, originally under the name of Ovomaltine, in Switzerland.
- The Danish postmaster Einar Holböll creates Christmas seals, to raise funds for a tuberculosis campaign.
- The St. Louis International Exposition in the United States opens one year late to honor Thomas Jefferson and commemorate the Louisiana Purchase. It popularizes the hamburger and the edible ice-cream cone in the United States.
- Thermos flasks become popular in the United States.
- Thomas Sullivan invents the tea bag in the United States.

APRIL
- Scottish-born U.S. billionaire steel magnate, Andrew Carnegie, donates $5 million to establish a so-called hero fund, to award individuals, or their survivors, who imperil their lives while saving others.

JULY
- Textile workers strike for higher wages in Fall River, Massachusetts. The strike ends January 8, 1905, when mill operators meet the strikers' demands.

SEPTEMBER
9 A general strike takes place in Italy, culminating in violent incidents in Milan, Italy.

Media and Communication

- CDQ is adopted as the radio distress signal. It signifies "All stations—urgent."
- Newspaper tycoon William Randolph Hearst founds the *Boston American* in the United States.

Sports

- Charles W. Follis of the United States becomes the first black professional player in American football when he signs for the Shelby Blues.
- The World Series is canceled due to a dispute between the president of the American League, Ban Johnson, and the manager of the National League champions New York Giants, John McGraw, over the latter's defection a year earlier from the Baltimore Americans, of the American League team.
- The first U.S. national ski championships are held at Ishpeming, Michigan, by the recently formed National Ski Association.
- The U.S. president Theodore Roosevelt starts a vogue for the Japanese martial art jujitsu, after he receives regular training for it in the White House.

JANUARY
12 The U.S. car manufacturer Henry Ford, a year after setting up the Ford Motor Company, sets an unofficial new world land-speed record of 147.04 kph/91.37 mph on ice on Lake St. Clair, near Detroit, United States.

MAY
5 The U.S. baseball player Denton T. "Cy" Young of the Boston Red Sox achieves the first perfect pitching game under modern rules, against the Philadelphia A's.
21 The Fédération Internationale de Football Association (FIFA), a world governing body for soccer, is founded in France, without British support.

JUNE
- The first American Power Boat Association (APBA) Gold Cup power boat race is run on the Hudson River, New York. The winning boat is *Standard* driven by the U.S. driver Carl Riotte at an average speed of 37.272 kph/23.160 mph.
3 The U.S. golfer Walter J. Travis wins the British Amateur Golf Championship at Sandwich, Kent, England.

JULY
July–November Jai alai, or pelota, is introduced to the United States at the St. Louis World Fair.
1–November 23 The 3rd Olympic Games are held in St. Louis, Missouri, to coincide with the World Fair. Most of the competitors come from the United States; sports such as cycling attract no foreign entrants at all, although the general standard of the games is high. U.S. athletes Joseph Stadler, in the standing high jump, and George Poage, in the 200 meters and 400 meters hurdles, become the first black competitors to win Olympic medals.

1905

POLITICS, GOVERNMENT, AND ECONOMICS

Colonization

- The viceroy of British-ruled India, Lord Curzon, divides Bengal into east and west sections and unites Muslim East Bengal with Assam, provoking enormous opposition from nationalists.

Human Rights

APRIL

- In an article in *Ladies' Home Journal*, former U.S. president Grover Cleveland claims that woman do not need to vote because men have greater intelligence.

JULY

- W. E. B. Du Bois calls a meeting of black American civil-rights leaders in Niagara Falls, Ontario, to issue a collective demand for full citizenship rights for black Americans. The so-called Niagara Movement becomes the foundation for the National Association of Colored People (NAACP), founded in 1909.

NOVEMBER

11   King Leopold II of Belgium is excused in the report published by the commission of inquiry into atrocities in the Congo Free State.

Politics and Government

- President Theodore Roosevelt creates the Bureau of Forestry, a branch of the U.S. Department of Agriculture. Congress assigns the new bureau the task of safeguarding the nation's newly designated National Forests.
- Sun Zhong Shan organizes the Combined League Society of Chinese to work for the expulsion of Manchu rulers and administrators from China.
- The Oriental Exclusion League, with more than 78,000 members, begins a campaign in the western states of the United States to end Japanese immigration.
- The Russian government receives 60,000 peasant petitions requesting reform.
- The state of New York investigates insurance houses following charges of corrupt practice.

JANUARY

- The U.S. Supreme Court, in *Swift v. United States*, finds the Beef Trust to have violated the Sherman Antitrust Act (1890) and orders its dissolution.
- The United States and the Dominican Republic sign a protocol, never ratified, making the United States the guarantor of the Dominican Republic's economic and territorial integrity.

1   Louis Botha forms *Het Volk* (The People), a Boer organization with the purpose of agitating for responsible government in British-ruled Transvaal.

2   The Russian commander of Port Arthur, China, General Anatoli Stesël, surrenders the port to Japanese forces under General Maresuke Nogi.

22   Guards outside the Winter Palace in St. Petersburg, Russia, fire on a procession of workers and their families led by the priest Father Gapon, who is carrying a petition to Czar Nicholas II. Over 100 people are killed, and the day becomes known as "Bloody Sunday." Strikes break out across Russia in protest.

FEBRUARY

- The U.S. Supreme Court, in *Jacobson v. Massachusetts*, rules compulsory state vaccination laws to be constitutional.

4   Terrorists in Russia assassinate the czar's uncle Grand Duke Sergei.

20–March 9   The Japanese forces under Field Marshal Iwao Oyama overcome a Russian force under General Alexei Kuropatkin, and capture the city of Mukden (Shenyang), a key point for the control of Manchuria.

MARCH

- Theodore Roosevelt is inaugurated to his first full term as president.

3   Czar Nicholas II of Russia responds to recent protests by promising to undertake religious and other reforms and to call a consultative assembly.

21   Britain and Persia sign an agreement to try to counter Russian plans to extend its influence in the Near East.

30   Greeks in Crete revolt against Turkish rule.

31   The visit of Emperor Wilhelm II of Germany to Tangier, Morocco, sets off the "First Moroccan Crisis," being seen as a test of the British–French convention of 1904 which arranged for French predominance in Morocco.

APRIL

- The U.S. Supreme Court, in *Lochner v. New York*, strikes down a New York state law limiting working hours.

25   Britain grants a constitution to Transvaal, but it is considered inadequate by the Transvaal leader Louis Botha.

30 British–French military conversations, in response to the threat of war with Germany over Morocco, improve relations between the two countries.

MAY

1–5 The French prime minister, Maurice Rouvier, fails to settle the dispute with Germany over Morocco, and Germany insists on an international conference.

8 The Russian Union of Unions is formed, led by Paul Miliukov, combining various liberal elements demanding parliamentary institutions.

17 Britain tacitly proposes joint action with France against Germany over the Moroccan question.

27–29 During the Battle of Tsushima in the Tsushima Strait between Korea and Japan, the Japanese fleet under Vice Admiral Heirachiro Togo sinks two-thirds of the recently-arrived Russian Baltic fleet commanded by Admiral Zinovi Rozhdestvenski.

JUNE

6 Théophile Delcassé, French foreign minister since 1898, is forced to resign as a condition imposed by Germany for negotiating over the Moroccan question.

7 The Norwegian Störting (parliament) decides on the separation of Norway from Sweden.

28 Following a mutiny by sailors on the Russian battleship *Potemkin* at Odessa, Russia, unrest spreads throughout the Russian navy.

JULY

7 China boycotts U.S. goods in protest at U.S. restrictions on immigration into and visits to the United States by Chinese citizens.

8 France, assured of British support against unreasonable demands by Germany, agrees to a conference on Morocco.

23–August 4 Emperor Wilhelm II of Germany and Czar Nicholas II of Russia sign the Treaty of Björkö promising mutual aid in Europe.

25 U.S. interests begin construction on the Panama Canal. The French effort was abandoned in 1889.

AUGUST

8 The Maji Maji people rise against colonial rule in German East Africa.

12 The British–Japanese alliance is renewed for ten years.

American Civil Rights (1905–92)

1905

July U.S. civil rights leader W. E. B. Du Bois calls a meeting of black American civil-rights leaders in Niagara Falls, Ontario, to issue a collective demand for full citizenship rights for black Americans. The so-called Niagara Movement becomes the foundation for the National Association of Colored People (NAACP), founded in 1909.

1909

June The National Association for the Advancement of Colored People (NAACP) is formally established in New York, New York, as the National Committee for the Advancement of the Negro.

1917

July 2–5 A race riot erupts in East St. Louis, Missouri, where alienated white workers rampage through black neighborhoods killing any black American in sight. "Official" figures list 39 black and 8 white people killed, but W. E. B. Du Bois insists that as many as 125 people died.

1921

August A revived Ku Klux Klan causes havoc throughout the South, beating and harassing black Americans and white sympathizers.

1931

April 9 Nine black American youths are convicted of having raped two white women on a train outside Paint Rock, Alabama, on March 25. Eight of the so-called Scottsboro Boys are sentenced to death; one, the youngest, receives a life sentence. Over the next four years, the U.S. Supreme Court will twice overturn the convictions of the Scottsboro Boys, whose sentences will eventually be commuted to life in prison.

1939

• In the case *Gaines v. Canada*, the U.S. Supreme Court rules that "separate but equal" must mean that facilities are of equal standard for black and white.

1944

April The U.S. Supreme Court, in the case *Smith v. Allwright*, rules that the citizen's right to vote cannot be withdrawn because of color.

1948

July 30 The U.S. armed forces are desegregated by order of President Harry S. Truman.

1952

• U.S. civil-rights activist Malcolm X joins the Nation of Islam, after serving six years in prison.

1954

May The U.S. Supreme Court, in *Brown v. Board of Education*, overturns the *Plessy v. Ferguson* decision of 1896 and declares separate but equal schools to be unconstitutional.

1955

November The U.S. Supreme Court orders the desegregation of public parks and recreation facilities.

December U.S. seamstress and social activist Rosa Parks is arrested after refusing to relinquish her seat to a white man on a bus in Montgomery, Alabama. Her arrest galvanizes the U.S. civil-rights movement.

1957

• U.S. civil-rights leader Martin Luther King, Jr., helps establish the Southern Christian Leadership Conference, an organization devoted to ending discrimination nonviolently.

September President Dwight D. Eisenhower calls out 1,000 U.S. paratroops to enforce the desegregation of Central High School in Little Rock, Arkansas.

19 In response to political unrest, Czar Nicholas II of Russia issues an "imperial manifesto," which proposes to create an imperial duma (parliament), elected on a limited franchise and with only deliberative (not law-making) powers.

SEPTEMBER

1 The provinces of Alberta and Saskatchewan are formed in Canada.

5 The Treaty of Portsmouth (New Hampshire) is mediated by the U.S. president Theodore Roosevelt and ends the Russo-Japanese War. Russia is to cede Port Arthur and the Guangdong Peninsula in China, evacuate Manchuria and half of Sakhalin Island (in the Sea of Okhotsk off the coast of Russia), and recognize Japan's interests in Korea. Japan gives up its demand for an indemnity.

24 The Swedish Riksdag (parliament) agrees to Norway's demand for independence.

28 Germany agrees with France to call a conference on Morocco.

OCTOBER

14–30 A strike breaks out across Russia for political reform.

26 Delegates of strike committees in St. Petersburg, Russia, form the first workers' soviet (council).

26 Under a treaty of separation between Norway and Sweden, King Oscar II of Norway and Sweden abdicates the Norwegian crown.

30 Czar Nicholas II of Russia issues the "October Manifesto," capitulating to demands for the duma (parliament) to have legislative powers and a wider franchise for its election, and civil liberties.

NOVEMBER

16 The reformer Count Sergei Witte is appointed prime minister of Russia.

17 Japan forces the emperor of Korea to sign a treaty, which gives control of Korea's foreign policy to Japan through a resident-general.

18 Prince Charles of Denmark is elected King Haakon VII of Norway following Norway's independence from Sweden.

1963

April 12 Police in Birmingham, Alabama, arrest and jail Martin Luther King for his role in desegregation protests in that city. While incarcerated, King pens his famous "Letter from a Birmingham Jail."

June President John F. Kennedy challenges Congress to enact major civil rights legislation, mandating, among other things, an end to the segregation of all public facilities—even those privately owned.

June U.S. civil-rights leader Medgar Evers is assassinated outside his home in Jackson, Mississippi. President John F. Kennedy condemns the killing. Evers is buried at Arlington National Cemetery.

June 11 After Alabama governor George C. Wallace refuses to permit two black students, Vivian Malone and James Hood, to enter the state university, the National Guard, summoned by President John F. Kennedy, ushers the students into the school buildings, desegregating the campus.

August 28 Two hundred thousand black Americans take part in the March on Washington, a peaceful demonstration for civil rights in Washington, D.C. They are addressed by Martin Luther King, who proclaims, with the Lincoln Memorial as a backdrop, "I have a dream that my four little children will one day live in a nation where they will not be judged by the color of their skin but by the content of their character."

1964

October Martin Luther King wins the Nobel Peace Prize.

1965

February 21 Radical black leader Malcolm X is shot dead at the Audubon Ballroom, New York, New York.

1967

July A race riot erupts in Newark, New Jersey, after police beat a black man stopped for a traffic violation. It takes the National Guard five days to restore order; 26 people die,

1,300 are injured, and millions of dollars worth of property is destroyed. Cambridge, Maryland, erupts in racial animosity, following a speech by H. Rap Brown, chairman of the Student Nonviolent Coordinating Committee. Brown is later arrested for inciting the violence. Detroit, Michigan, erupts in riots; the National Guard restores order, but not before 43 people die and an estimated $200 million worth of property is destroyed, making this the worst race riot in U.S. history.

October U.S. civil-rights lawyer Thurgood Marshall is sworn in as the nation's first black Supreme Court justice.

1968

April 4 Martin Luther King is assassinated in Memphis, Tennessee, by a sniper later identified as escaped convict James Earl Ray. King's assassination sparks a week of rioting in black ghettos throughout the nation. Ray is arrested in London, England, on June 8 and promptly extradited to the United States.

1984

January 17 The Commission on Civil Rights in the United States votes to discontinue the use of numerical quotas in the promotion of black Americans.

1986

January 20 Martin Luther King Day is observed for the first time.

1991

March 3 A nationwide outcry follows the televising in the United States of video footage showing the black motorist Rodney King being beaten by four white policeman in Los Angeles, California.

1992

April 29 Four white policemen in Los Angeles, California, are acquitted of beating Rodney King; between April 30 and May 3, 58 people die in riots and looting which break out in protest at the acquittals.

23   The British Liberal Party leader, Sir Henry Campbell-Bannerman, makes a speech in Stirling, Scotland, advocating Home Rule for Ireland "by installments."

DECEMBER

4   The British Conservative prime minister, Arthur Balfour, resigns because of the split in the party between protectionists and free-traders.

5   Sir Henry Campbell-Bannerman forms a Liberal ministry in Great Britain with Sir Edward Grey as foreign secretary, Herbert Asquith as chancellor of the Exchequer, and Richard Haldane as war secretary.

12   A revolution begins in Persia against the corrupt rule of Shah Mohammed Ali.

12   King Nicholas of Montenegro grants a constitution creating parliamentary institutions.

22–January 1, 1906   An insurrection of workers in Moscow, Russia, is bloodily repressed.

SCIENCE, TECHNOLOGY, AND MEDICINE

Agriculture

- The International Institute of Agriculture is founded in Rome, Italy; it is the precursor of the Food and Agriculture Organization (FAO) designed to protect farmers from market fluctuations.
- U.S. president Theodore Roosevelt, an ardent hunter, establishes the Wichita Mountains Refuge for big game in Oklahoma territory.

Ecology

- The Colorado River floods destroying the Imperial Canal and creating the 775 sq-km/330 sq-mi inland Salton Sea in California.
- The world's largest deposit of nickel begins to be mined at Copper Cliff-Sudbury, Ontario, Canada.
- U.S. conservationists combine with nature lovers to found the National Audubon Society.
- U.S. president Theodore Roosevelt creates the U.S. Forest Service and establishes millions of acres of additional forest reserves.

APRIL

4   Jammu and Kashmir in India experience an earthquake estimated to measure 8.6 on the Richter scale; 19,000 die.

Health and Medicine

c. 1905   English biochemist Frederick Gowland Hopkins shows that the amino acid tryptophan and other essential amino acids cannot be manufactured from other nutrients but must be supplied in the diet.

- Austrian surgeon E. Zirm performs the first cornea transplant.

- French surgeon Alexis Carrel develops techniques for suturing severed blood vessels, in the United States. It opens up the possibility of organ transplants.
- German bacteriologist Robert Koch receives the Nobel Prize for Physiology or Medicine for his work on tuberculosis.
- German surgeon Friedrich Voelcker, in one of the first diagnostic uses of X-rays, introduces a radio-opaque substance into the kidney to study the urinary tract.
- German surgeon Heinrich Braun introduces the local anesthetic Novocaine (procaine hydrochloride) into clinical use in the United States as a substitute for cocaine.
- German zoologist Fritz Schaudinn and dermatologist Erich Hoffmann isolate the microorganism that causes syphilis, *Spirochaeta pallida* (later called *Treponema pallidum*).
- Scottish physiologist John Scott Haldane discovers that breathing is regulated by the concentration of carbon dioxide in the blood affecting the respiratory center of the brain.
- The last outbreak of yellow fever in the United States is reported in New Orleans.
- The world's first major epidemic of poliomyelitis occurs in Sweden.
- U.S. surgeon George Washington Crile develops the direct linkage method of blood transfusion, where donor and recipient are linked up to each other.

Science

c. 1905   English chemist John William Strutt, Baron Rayleigh, invents the radium clock.

- Danish botanist Wilhelm Johannsen introduces the terms "genotype" and "phenotype" to explain how genetically identical plants differ in external characteristics.
- English physiologist Ernest Starling coins the word "hormone" (from Greek *hormon* "impel") to describe chemicals that stimulate an organ from a distance.
- German chemist Adolf von Baeyer receives the Nobel Prize for Chemistry for his discovery and work with indigo and other hydroaromatic dyes.
- German chemist Otto Hahn discovers the radioisotope radiothorium.
- German physicist Albert Einstein develops his special theory of relativity in a series of four papers in Switzerland. In "On the Motion—Required by the Molecular Kinetic Theory of Heat—of Small Particles Suspended in a Stationary Liquid" he explains Brownian motion. In "On a Heuristic Viewpoint Concerning the Production and Transformation of Light" he explains the photoelectric effect by proposing that light consists of photons and also exhibits wavelike properties. In "On the Electrodynamics of Moving Bodies" he proposes that space and time are one and that time and motion are relative to the observer. In "Does the Inertia of a Body Depend on its Energy Content?" he argues that mass and energy are equivalent, which can be expressed by the formula $E=mc^2$.
- German physicist Philipp Lenard receives the Nobel Prize for Physics for his work on cathode rays.

- Scottish physicist William Thomson proposes a model of the atom in which positive and negatively charged spheres alternate.
- Swiss chemist Jacques Brandenberger invents cellophane.
- U.S. astronomer Percival Lowell, after a study of the gravitation of Uranus, predicts the existence of the planet Pluto.
- U.S. chemist Bertram Boltwood suggests that lead is the final decay product of uranium.

April 1905–07 Danish astronomer Ejnar Hertzsprung discovers that there is a relationship between the color and absolute brightness of stars and classifies them according to this relationship. The relationship is used to determine the distances of stars and forms the basis of theories of stellar evolution.

Technology

c. 1905 German inventor Richard Fiedler develops two flame throwers. The first, which is small enough to be carried by one person, throws a flame 18 m/20 ft; the second throws a flame 36 m/40 ft. They are first used in combat in 1915.

c. 1905 Italian physicist Guglielmo Marconi patents the horizontal directional aerial, which improves the efficiency of radio communication.

- German engineer Hans Holzwarth invents the gas-explosion turbine, in which the exhaust of an explosion of gas drives the turbine.

Transportation

- *McClure's* magazine begins serialization of journalist Ray Stannard Baker's *The Railroads on Trial*, which makes the case for railroad regulation.
- British engineer Frederick Simms patents car bumpers in Britain, after designing a pneumatic bumper for the 20 HP Simms-Wellbeck.
- French firm Renault Frères introduces the first motor taxi cabs, in Paris, France.
- The French navy builds the *Aigrette*, the first diesel-powered submarine.
- The Germany navy builds its first submarine, the *Unterseeboot No 1* ("Submarine No. 1"). It is 42-m/139-ft long and powered by an oil engine on the surface and an electric engine when submerged.
- There are 77,988 automobiles registered in the United States, up from 300 in 1895.
- U.S. aviators Glenn Curtiss and Thomas Scott Baldwin produce the U.S. Army's first aircraft, the SC-1 airship.
- U.S. racing driver Arthur Macdonald sets a land speed record of 167.44 kph/104.651 mph at Daytona Beach, Florida.

NOVEMBER

8 The Chicago and North Western's Overland Limited railroad, which links Chicago, Illinois, and California, introduces the first electric lamps on a railroad car.

ARTS AND IDEAS

Architecture

- The Telephone Company Building in Helsinki, Finland, designed by the Finnish architect Lars Sonck, is completed.

Arts

- The expressionist art group Die Brücke ("The Bridge") is formed in Dresden, Germany. The group includes the artists Ernst Kirchner and Karl Schmidt-Rottluff. It is dissolved in 1913.
- The French art critic Louis Vauxcelles coins the name *Les Fauves* ("The Wild Beasts") for the group of French artists led by Henri Matisse.
- The French artist André Derain paints *Fishing Port, Collioure*.
- The French artist Aristide Maillol sculpts *The Mediterranean*.
- The French artist Henri Rousseau paints *The Hungry Lion*.
- The French artist Henri Matisse paints *Portrait of Madame Matisse (The Green Line)*.
- The French artist Paul Cézanne paints *The Great Bathers*.
- The Spanish artist Pablo Picasso paints *Acrobat and Young Harlequin* and *Boy with Pipe*.
- The U.S. artist George B Luks paints *Spieler/Players*.
- The U.S. artist John Singer Sargeant paints *The Marlborough Family*.
- The U.S. artist William Glackens paints *Chez Mouquin*.
- The U.S. photographer Alfred Stieglitz opens his Little Gallery of the Photo-Secession at 291–293 Fifth Avenue in New York, New York. Later known simply as "291," the gallery shows photographs, paintings, and sculpture, becoming one of the most influential galleries in the development of modern U.S. art.

Film

- *La presa di Roma/The Capture of Rome*, directed by Filoteo Alberini, is released in Italy, the first Italian movie with a fictional plot.
- Italian filmmakers Filoteo Alberini and Dante Santoni establish the Cinés movie studio in Italy.
- The movie *Rescued by Rover*, directed by Lewis Fitzhamon, is released in Britain, starring Cecil Hepworth.
- The movie *The Life of Charles Peace*, directed by British actor and director William Hagger, is released. He also stars in it.
- The first nickelodeon movie theater opens in Pittsburgh, Pennsylvania; thousands open in the next few years. For five cents, people get to see a 20-30 minute movie.

Literature and Language

- *De Profundis/Out of the Depths*, a testament written in prison by the Irish writer Oscar Wilde, is published posthumously.
- The English writer E. M. Forster publishes his novel *Where Angels Fear to Tread*.
- The English writer G. K. Chesterton publishes his collection of short stories *The Club of Queer Trades*.
- The English writer H. G. Wells publishes his novel *Kipps: The Story of a Simple Soul*.
- The German poet Rainer Maria Rilke publishes *Das Stundenbuch/Poems from the Book of Hours*.
- The Nicaraguan writer Rubén Darío publishes his poetry collection *Cantos de vida y esperanza/Songs of Life and Hope*.
- The Scottish writer Arthur Conan Doyle publishes his story collection *The Return of Sherlock Holmes*.
- The U.S. writer Edith Wharton publishes her novel *House of Mirth*.
- The U.S. writer Jack London publishes his novel *White Fang*.
- The U.S. writer Thomas Dixon publishes his novel *The Clansman*, which advocates white supremacy. It is adapted in the movie *The Birth of a Nation* 1915 by D. W. Griffith.
- The U.S. writer Willa Cather publishes her short-story collection *The Troll Garden*.

Music

- A popular song in the United States is "Everybody Works But Father."
- Scottish entertainer Harry Lauder writes the song "I Love a Lassie."
- The Austrian composer Anton Webern completes his String Quartet (in one movement).
- The Austrian composer Gustav Mahler completes his Symphony No. 6, which he revises in 1908, and his Symphony No. 7, which he revises in 1909.
- The Czech composer Leoš Janáček completes his piano work *Sonata 1:x:1905 (A street scene; Z ulice)*.
- The English composer Edward Elgar completes his *Introduction and Allegro for Strings*.
- The French composer Claude Debussy completes his piano work *Images I* and his orchestral work *La Mer/ The Sea*.
- The French composer Maurice Ravel completes his chamber work *Introduction and Allegro* and his piano work *Miroirs/Mirrors*.
- The Norwegian composer Edvard Grieg completes his *Moods* for piano (Opus 73).
- The opera *Salome*, by the German composer Richard Strauss, is first performed in Dresden, Germany.
- The operetta *Die lustige Witwe/The Merry Widow*, by the Austro-Hungarian composer Franz Lehár, is first performed in Vienna, Austria.
- U.S. composers Gus Edwards and Vincent Bryan write the song "In My Merry Oldsmobile."

Theater and Dance

- Harvard University in Cambridge, Massachusetts, begins 47 Workshop, at which George P. Baker teaches playwriting and provides a laboratory for experimental productions.
- The Aldwych Theatre opens in London, England.
- The English actor and director Gordon Craig publishes his influential study of drama *The Art of the Theatre*.
- The exotic dancer Mata Hari makes her debut in Paris, France. During World War I, she is discovered to be a German spy.
- The play *Dödsdansen/The Dance of Death*, by the Swedish writer August Strindberg, is first performed, in Cologne, Germany.
- The play *Elga*, by the German dramatist Gerhart Hauptmann, is first performed in Berlin, Germany.
- The play *The Girl of the Golden West*, by the U.S. dramatist David Belasco, is first performed, in New York, New York.
- The play *The Squaw Man*, by the U.S. dramatist Edward Milton Royle, is first performed in New York, New York.
- The play *The Voysey Inheritance*, by the English dramatist Harley Granville-Barker, is first performed in London, England.
- The play *The Well of the Saints*, by the Irish dramatist John Millington Synge, is first performed in Dublin, Ireland.
- The play *Triplepatte*, by the French dramatist Tristram Bernard, is first performed, in Paris, France.
- The plays *Major Barbara* and *Man and Superman*, by the Irish dramatist George Bernard Shaw, are first performed at the Royal Court Theatre in London, England.

Thought and Scholarship

- Austrian psychoanalyst Sigmund Freud publishes *Drei Abhandlungen zur Sexualtheorie/Three Contributions to the Theory of Sexuality*, in which he suggests that children have sexual urges toward their parents, and *Der Witz und seine Beziehung zum Unbewussten/Jokes and their Relation to the Unconscious*.
- Austrian scientist and philosopher Ernst Mach publishes *Erkenntnis und Irrtum/Knowledge and Error*.
- French journalist and critic Charles Maurras publishes his collection of essays *L'Avenir de l'intelligence/The Future of Intelligence*.
- French psychologists Alfred Binet, Victor Henri, and Theodore Simon introduce the first intelligence test for children.
- Russian revolutionary leader Vladimir Ilyich Lenin publishes *Dve taktiti/Two Tactics*.
- Scottish writer Andrew Lang publishes *John Knox and the Reformation*.
- Spanish-born U.S. philosopher and writer George Santayana publishes *The Life of Reason*.
- The Nobel Prize for Literature is awarded to the Polish novelist Henryk Sienkiewicz.

BIRTHS & DEATHS

JANUARY

3 Dante Giacosa, Italian car designer who creates the Fiat 500 or "Topolino" ("Little Mouse"), which sold over four million between 1936 and 1975, born in Rome, Italy (–1996).

8 Carl G. Hempel, German philosopher of science, a member of the Vienna circle of logical positivists, born in Oranienburg, Germany (–1997).

21 Christian Dior, French fashion designer, born in Granville, France (–1957).

25 Elias Canetti, Bulgarian-born English novelist and playwright who won the Nobel Prize for Literature in 1981, born in Ruse, Bulgaria (–1994).

FEBRUARY

1 Emilio Segré, Italian physicist who discovered the antiproton, born in Tivoli, Italy (–1989).

2 Ayn Rand, Russian-born U.S. novelist and philosopher known for her novels *The Fountainhead* and *Atlas Shrugged*, born in St. Petersburg, Russia (–1982).

6 Władysław Gomułka, Polish politician and Communist Party leader 1943–48 and 1956–70, born near Krosno, Poland (–1982).

9 Adolf Menzel, German painter, dies in Berlin, Germany (89).

15 Harold Arlen, U.S. popular composer and songwriter, born in Buffalo, New York (–1986).

15 Lewis Wallace, Union general during the American Civil War and author of *Ben-Hur*, dies in Crawfordsville, Indiana (77).

MARCH

15 Meyer Guggenheim, Swiss-born U.S. industrialist who built up the largest mining corporation in the United States, dies in Palm Beach, Florida (77).

24 Jules Verne, French author who pioneered modern science fiction writing, dies in Amiens, France (77).

26 Viktor E. Frankl, Austrian psychiatrist and psychotherapist, author of *Man's Search for Meaning* based on his experience in a Nazi concentration camp, born in Vienna, Austria (–1997).

28 Pandro (Samuel) Berman, U.S. film producer, known especially for films starring Ginger Rogers and Fred Astaire, born in Pittsburgh, Pennsylvania (–1996).

APRIL

2 Serge Lifar, Russian-born French dancer and choreographer, ballet master of the Paris Opéra Ballet, born in Kiev, Russia (now Ukraine) (–1986).

9 James William Fulbright, U.S. senator who initiated the Fulbright scholarship to encourage international exchange of students, born in Sumner, Missouri.

24 Robert Penn Warren, U.S. novelist and poet, the only U.S. writer to win Pulitzer prizes for fiction and poetry, and the first poet laureate in the United States (1986), born in Guthrie, Kentucky (–1989).

MAY

14 Nikolay Aleksandrovich Tikhonov, Soviet prime minister (chair of the Council of Ministers) 1980–85, born in Kharkov, Russia (now Ukraine) (–1997).

16 Henry Fonda, U.S. actor of stage and film, born in Grand Island, Nebraska (–1982).

24 Mikhail Sholokhov, Russian novelist and short-story writer, born in Veshenskaya, Russia (–1984).

JUNE

13 Adolphus "Doc" Cheatham, U.S. jazz trumpeter, born in Nashville, Tennessee (–1997).

21 Jean-Paul Sartre, French existentialist philosopher, novelist, and playwright, born in Paris, France (–1980).

JULY

1 John Hay, U.S. secretary of state (1898–1905) who was responsible for the "Open Door Policy" with regard to China, dies in Newbury, New Hampshire (66).

29 Clara Bow, U.S. silent film star, born in Brooklyn, New York (–1965).

29 Dag Hammarskjöld, Swedish statesman and second secretary-general of the United Nations (1953–61), born in Jönköping, Sweden (–1961).

AUGUST

2 Myrna Loy, U.S. actress, born in Raidersburg, Montana (–1993).

21 Friz Freleng, U.S. animator, best known for the characters Sylvester and Tweety and Speedy Gonzalez, born in Kansas City, Missouri (–1995).

SEPTEMBER

3 Carl David Anderson, U.S. physicist who discovered the positron, the first particle of antimatter, born in New York, New York (–1991).

5 Arthur Koestler, Hungarian-born British novelist and critic, born in Budapest, Austria-Hungary (–1983).

18 Agnes George DeMille, U.S. choreographer, born in New York, New York (–1993).

18 Greta Garbo, Swedish-born U.S. film star of the 1920s and 1930s, then a legendary recluse after 1941, born in Stockholm, Sweden (–1990).

24 Severo Ochoa, Spanish biologist who first synthesized RNA, born in Luarca, Spain (–1993).

28 Max Schmeling, German boxer who became the first European to win the world heavyweight boxing championship (1930), born in Klein Lucknow, Germany.

30 Nevill Francis Mott, English physicist who researched the electronic properties of metals, semiconductors, and noncrystalline materials, winner of the Nobel Prize for Physics in 1977, born in Leeds, England (–1996).

OCTOBER

6 Helen Wills, U.S. tennis player, who dominated women's tennis in the late 1920s and 1930s, winning Wimbledon eight times, born in Berkeley, California.

15 C(harles) P(ercy) Snow, English novelist, scientist, and government administrator and advisor, born in Leicester, England (–1980).

18 Félix Houphouët-Boigny, first president of the independent Republic of Ivory Coast 1960–93, born in Yamoussoukro, Ivory Coast (–1993).

22 Karl Jansky, U.S. engineer, who initiated the science of radio astronomy with his discovery of extraterrestrial sources of radio waves, born in Norman, Oklahoma (–1950).

DECEMBER

21 Anthony Dymoke Powell, English novelist, born in London, England.

24 Howard Hughes, reclusive U.S. manufacturer, aviator, and film producer, born in Houston, Texas (–1976).

28 Earl "Fatha" Hines, U.S. bandleader known as "the father of modern jazz piano," born in Duquesne, Pennsylvania (–1983).

31 Jule (Julius Kerwin) Styne, English-born U.S. composer of songs, mainly for musicals and films, born in London, England (–1994).

SOCIETY

Education

- Italian educator Maria Montessori publishes *Manuale di pedagogica scientifica/Manual of Scientific Pedagogy*.
- Scottish-born U.S. billionaire steel magnate Andrew Carnegie, provides $10 million to establish the Carnegie Foundation for the Advancement of Teaching.

Everyday Life

- B. W. Johnson Soap Co. launches Palmolive soap in the United States.
- U.S. food manufacturer H. J. Heinz begins to sell canned baked beans in the north of England, focusing his marketing on working-class women.
- Charles Fey develops the Liberty Bell, the first slot-machine, in the United States. It is manufactured by the Mills Novelty Co., which introduces fruit symbols to represent the fruit gum "prizes," as a means of getting around antigambling laws in some states.
- Cigarette makers in the United States introduce the first testimonials by stars of the entertainment industry, including movie star "Fatty" Arbuckle.
- L. C. Smith and Brothers begin selling typewriters in the United States. The company will become the largest manufacturer of typewriters in the world.
- The first dial telephones are introduced in the United States.
- The Italian immigrant Gennaro Lombardi introduces pizza at his restaurant in New York, New York.
- The population density in the slums of New York, New York, reaches 1,000 persons an acre, higher than in Bombay, India.
- The U.S. company Chapman & Skinner launches the first portable electric vacuum cleaner for domestic use.
- The U.S. drinks company Coca-Cola changes some of the ingredients of its drink, replacing cocaine with caffeine.

JULY

- U.S. proponents of industrial unionism, meeting in Chicago, form the Industrial Workers of the World (IWW). Its radical policies will clash noticeably with those of the conservative, craft-based organization, the American Federation of Labor (AFL).

DECEMBER

23 The first British beauty contest, the "Blond and Brunette Beauty Show," takes place in Newcastle upon Tyne.

Media and Communication

- The entertainment publication *Variety* is launched in the United States.

Sports

- Eighteen players are killed and 154 seriously injured during the American football season; the U.S. president Franklin D. Roosevelt threatens to ban the sport unless action is taken to curb the violence.
- The first Australasian lawn tennis championships are held in Melbourne (from 1927 they become known as the Australian Championships).

JULY

8 May G. Sutton of the United States becomes the first overseas player to win a title at the Wimbledon lawn tennis championships in London, England, when she wins the women's singles.

SEPTEMBER

22 U.S. golfer Willie Anderson becomes the first player to win the U.S. Open golf championship three years in a row, an unsurpassed achievement.

OCTOBER

- The U.S. pacer Dan Patch breaks the mile pacing record for the third year in succession, at the Red Mile, Lexington, Kentucky. His time of 1 minute $55\frac{1}{4}$ seconds is not surpassed until 1938.

DECEMBER

28 The Intercollegiate Athletic Association of the United States (later the National Collegiate Athletic Association or NCAA) is founded in New York, New York.

1906

POLITICS, GOVERNMENT, AND ECONOMICS

Business and Economics

- A crisis hits the French wine industry as prices decline.
- Amedeo Obici and Mario Peruzzi start the Planters Nut and Chocolate Company in Wilkes-Barres, Pennsylvania.

MARCH

16 Japan's railroads are nationalized in its continuing process of modernization.

Human Rights

- Aga Khan III founds the All India Muslim League to campaign for Muslim rights.

JUNE

24 Czar Nicholas II of Russia grants universal suffrage in response to popular demand.

OCTOBER

- A universal suffrage bill is introduced in Austria-Hungary.
23 Women suffragists demonstrate in the outer lobby of the British House of Commons. Ten of the demonstrators are charged the following day, and sent to prison.

Politics and Government

- President Theodore Roosevelt appoints jurist William H. Moody to the U.S. Supreme Court.
- The British Trade Disputes Act reverses the Taff Vale judgment of 1901. Peaceful picketing is now allowed and unions are immune from claims for damage caused by strikes.
- The first municipal reference bureau in the United States is established in New York, New York, to study local financial operations.
- The Marine Insurance Act codifies English common law on the subject of marine insurance, while other legislation reforms conditions in the merchant navy.
- The U.S. Antiquities Act permits the president to reserve federal lands for the protection of objects of scientific, prehistoric, or historic interest.
- The U.S. National Forests Commission is established.

- Theodore Roosevelt becomes the first U.S. citizen to be awarded the Nobel Peace Prize, for his work in helping end the Russo-Japanese war.

JANUARY

1 Helmuth von Moltke, nephew of the victor of the Franco-Prussian War of 1870–71, becomes chief of the German general staff.
10 Britain and France conduct military and naval discussions over concerns about Germany's actions in Morocco.
12 The Liberal Party, committed to sweeping social reforms, wins a massive victory in the British general election. The Liberals take 377 seats with a majority of 84 over all parties, the Unionists winning 157 seats, the Irish Nationalists 83, and Labour 53. Sir Henry Campbell-Bannerman forms a government.
16–April 7 The Algeciras conference of the European powers (Britain, France, Germany, Russia, and Austria-Hungary), meets to discuss Franco-German rivalry over Morocco. It places Morocco under joint Franco-Spanish control, an embarrassing defeat for Germany.
17 The radical Clément Fallières, the candidate of the Left, is elected president of France.

FEBRUARY

11 Pope Pius X issues an encyclical *Vehementer nos*, which condemns the French separation of church and state as an insult to God.

MARCH

- The U.S. Supreme Court, in *Hale v. Henkel*, upholds antitrust legislation compelling witnesses to testify against their employers.
10 An explosion at the Courrières mine near Lens, France, kills about 1,800 miners.

APRIL

- The New York state assembly adopts some of the earliest legislation designed to reform the life insurance industry.
4 Elections for Russia's first duma (parliament) give half of the seats to the liberal Kadet Party, and an overall majority to the liberals and left wing representatives.
5 Kaiser Wilhelm II of Germany dismisses Count Friedrich Holstein (a key advisor in the foreign ministry), ending fear of a war with France over Morocco.
8 The Act of Algeciras is signed, ending the Moroccan crisis. It gives France and Spain chief control in Morocco under a Swiss inspector, and respects the sultan's authority.

MAY

5 Count Sergei Witte is replaced as Russian prime minister by the conservative Ivan Goremykin, when Czar Nicholas II feels threatened by Witte's increasing personal power.

5   The Ottoman Empire yields to British pressure over Egypt's frontier with Palestine, having previously claimed the Sinai peninsula.

6   Czar Nicholas II promulgates the Fundamental Law of the Russian Empire, reaffirming autocratic rule.

8   The U.S. Congress permits Alaska to elect a delegate to Congress (the first delegate will arrive on December 3).

9   The Chinese government decides to take over the administration of the Imperial Customs Service, which has been run since 1863 by the U.S. inspector-general, Robert Hart.

10   The first duma (parliament) meets in Russia, resulting in deadlock when the Kadet Party criticises the Fundamental Laws.

11   Alexander Isvolsky, who favors cooperation with the duma (parliament), becomes Russian foreign secretary.

19   João Franco becomes prime minister of Portugal with dictatorial powers, following conflict between the king and liberals.

30   Giovanni Giolitti forms a coalition ministry in Italy, charged with dealing with strikes and unrest in southern Italy. The arrangement will continue until December 1909.

JUNE

- The U.S. Congress passes the Railroad Rate Act (or Hepburn Act), authorizing the Interstate Commerce Commission to set interstate shipping rates.
- U.S. Congress passes the Pure Food and Drug Act, prohibiting the distribution of contaminated food and drugs; and the Meat Inspection Act, authorizing the federal government to police the beef packaging industry.

5   The third German Navy Bill provides for increases in the size and number of German battleships, in response to the launch of Britain's HMS *Dreadnought*.

6   The reformer Peter Stolypin becomes prime minister of Russia.

25   U.S. architect Stanford White is shot dead by Harry K. Thaw, the husband of White's former mistress, Evelyn Nesbit, in the rooftop restaurant of Madison Square Garden, New York, New York. Evelyn Nesbit was the model for the statue of Diana mounted on the roof of Madison Square Garden. The murder and the later trial become one of the most sensational cases of the decade.

JULY

3   The Russian government publishes plans for the distribution of state lands while refusing to divide private estates.

4   Britain, France, and Italy guarantee the independence of Ethiopia.

12   Following a high profile campaign to release the French army officer Alfred Dreyfus, the guilty verdict returned against him in September 1899 for treason is formally annulled.

21   On the dissolution of the recalcitrant Russian duma (parliament) by the czar, the Kadet Party relocates to Finland and issues the "Vyborg Manifesto," calling on the Russian people to refuse to pay taxes.

22   The pardoned Jewish French army officer Alfred Dreyfus is reinstated into the French army and is awarded the *Légion d'Honneur* (Legion of Honor).

AUGUST

8   A British–Chinese convention agrees that Britain will not interfere in events in Tibet, and China will prevent others from doing so.

13   A race riot erupts in Brownsville, Texas, after troops from a black American infantry battalion allegedly kill a white bartender and wound a police lieutenant in what becomes known as the Brownsville Raid.

15   Kaiser Wilhelm II of Germany holds talks with King Edward VII of Great Britain at Kronberg, Germany, with a view to slowing the naval race. The talks fail to show results.

23   A liberal revolt begins in Cuba, protesting against the fraudulent activities of President Tomás Palma's government. President Palma requests U.S. intervention and mediators U.S. war secretary, William Howard Taft, and Robert Bacon arrive on September 25; Taft commands the Cuban government for 13 days.

SEPTEMBER

20   A Chinese imperial edict orders an end to the use of opium within ten years.

22   A race riot in Atlanta, Georgia, leaves 18 black Americans and two white policemen dead, and scores injured. The riot was sparked by reports of alleged assaults on white women by black men.

29   Following the resignation of President Palma of Cuba, the United States declares a provisional government in Cuba until order is restored.

NOVEMBER

- Despite a lack of incriminating evidence, President Theodore Roosevelt discharges without honor 167 out of 170 members of the black American infantry battalion implicated in the Brownsville (Texas) Raid on August 13.
- In U.S. Congressional elections, the Republicans maintain majorities in the House (222–164) and Senate (61–31).
- Theodore Roosevelt becomes the first sitting U.S. president to travel abroad. The president visited the Panama Canal, returning November 26.

22   The Russian prime minister, Peter Stolypin, introduces agrarian reforms in Russia, empowering peasants to claim their share of communal land as private property.

DECEMBER

- Oscar S. Straus becomes the first Jew to hold a cabinet level appointment in the United States, when President Theodore Roosevelt appoints him secretary of Department of Commerce and Labor.

6   Britain grants self-government to Transvaal and Orange River Colony following agitation for autonomy there.

13   As a result of a revolt of the Center Party, the German Reichstag (parliament) opposes granting expenses for colonial wars. Chancellor Bernhard von Bülow dissolves the Reichstag.

SCIENCE, TECHNOLOGY, AND MEDICINE

Agriculture

- The Florida Everglades begin to be drained to convert the area to agricultural use.

Ecology

- Mesa Verde National Park, Colorado, is established. It contains hundreds of prehistoric cliff dwellings, some 1,300 years old.
- U.S. president Theodore Roosevelt establishes Devil's Tower National Monument in Devil's Tower, Wyoming. This 264-m/865-ft-high rock spire measures 305 m/1,000 ft in diameter at its base and 84 m/275 ft in diameter at its top.

APRIL

18 San Francisco, California is hit at 5:13 a.m by the worst earthquake in U.S. history, estimated to measure 8.3 on the Richter scale. The quake ruptures water and gas lines and ignites a fire that burns for three days, destroying 28,000 buildings, around two-thirds of the city, and causing $350–400 million in damages. 2,500 people are killed and 250,000 are left homeless.

AUGUST

16 A violent earthquake in Chile destroys parts of Santiago, Valparaíso, and between 40 and 50 smaller towns. It is estimated to measure 8.6 on the Richter scale; 20,000 die.

SEPTEMBER

18 A typhoon hits Hong Kong, killing about 10,000 people.

Health and Medicine

- Belgian bacteriologists Jules Bordet and Octave Gengou discover the bacterium responsible for whooping cough, *Bordetella pertussis*.
- English biochemist Frederick Gowland Hopkins suggests that necessary "accessory factors" (vitamins) are contained in foods in addition to carbohydrates, fats, minerals, and water.
- English neurophysiologist Charles Scott Sherrington publishes *The Integrative Action of the Nervous System*, in which he classifies sense organs into three main groups: exteroceptive (sight, smell, hearing, and touch), interoceptive (taste), and proprioceptive (interior receptors that control balance and breathing and so on).
- German bacteriologist August von Wassermann develops the Wassermann test for syphilis.
- Italian physiologist Camillo Golgi and Spanish histologist Santiago Ramón y Cajal share the Nobel Prize for Physiology or Medicine for their work on the structure of the nervous system.

- The term "allergy" is coined by Austrian physician Clemens Freiherr von Pirquet.
- U.S. surgeon John Murphy devises the first artificial joints. They are first used in the hip of an arthritic patient.

Math

- Russian mathematician Andrey Andreyevich Markov studies random processes that are subsequently known as Markov chains.

Science

- British biochemists Arthur Harden and William Young discover catalysis among enzymes.
- English biologist William Bateson introduces the term "genetics."
- English physicist Frederick Soddy discovers that ionium and radiothorium are chemically indistinguishable variants of thorium but have different radioactive properties. He later calls them isotopes.
- English physicist J. J. Thomson receives the Nobel Prize for Physics for his theoretical and experimental investigations on the conduction of electricity by gases.
- French chemist Ferdinand-Frédéric Moissan receives the Nobel Prize for Chemistry for his discovery of fluorine and for the introduction of the Moissan electric furnace.
- German physicist Walther Herman Nernst formulates the third law of thermodynamics, which states that matter tends toward random motion and that energy tends to dissipate at a temperature above absolute zero (–273.12°C/–350°F).
- Irish geologist Richard Oldham proves that the earth has a molten core, by studying seismic waves.
- Russian botanist Mikhail Semyonovich Tsvet develops chromatography for separating plant pigments.
- The asteroid Achilles is discovered by German astronomer Max Wolf. It is the first of approximately 1,000 asteroids known as Trojan planets that form an equilateral triangle with Jupiter and the sun—an example of the solution to the three-body-problem in astronomy, it revolves around the sun in the Lagrangian point of Jupiter's orbit.
- U.S. astronomer Percival Lowell publishes *Mars and its Canals*, in which he argues that the canal-like markings on Mars are irrigation canals built by intelligent creatures.
- U.S. physicist Frederick Gardner Cottrell develops the first practical electrostatic precipitator for removing impurities from the air.

September 1906–08   Excavations by German and Turkish scholars at Boghazköy in Anatolia (modern Turkey) reveal that the city was ancient Hattusas, capital of the Hittites.

Technology

- Miller Reese Hutchinson patents the electric loudspeaker in the United States.
- The first oil hydraulic system is used on the U.S. warship *Virginia* to raise and lower its guns.

DECEMBER

- Private inventor Reginald A. Fessenden transmits what is believed to be the world's first radio broadcast from his home in Branch Rock, Massachusetts.

Transportation

- Brazilian-born French aviator Alberto Santos-Dumont makes the first successful powered flight in an airplane in Europe. He flies 220 m/780 ft in 21 seconds.
- English motorbike manufacturer Wilbur Gunn forms the Lagonda Motor Co. Ltd.
- German inventor Ferdinand, Graf von Zeppelin, receives a commission from the German government for a fleet of lighter-than-air ships after he makes a 24-hour flight.
- The International Motor Car Exhibition is held at Olympia in London, England.
- The Simplon Tunnel between Switzerland and Italy, is opened. Begun in 1898, and with a length of 19.8 km/12.3 mi, it is the longest railroad tunnel in the world.
- U.S. inventors Francis and Freelan Stanley build a steam car that sets the world land speed record for the fastest mile at 28.2 seconds, which corresponds to a speed of 205.4 kph/127.66 mph.

FEBRUARY

10 The British battleship HMS *Dreadnought* is launched at Portsmouth, England. Its massive armament (10 30-cm/12-in guns and 24 12-pounder guns) makes all other warships obsolete and its name becomes a generic term for battleships with large-calibre armament.

ARTS AND IDEAS

Architecture

- The Post Office Savings Bank in Vienna, Austria, designed by the Austrian architect Otto Wagner, is completed.
- The Unity Temple Church in Oak Park, Chicago, Illinois, is completed. It is designed by the U.S. architect Frank Lloyd Wright. His application of abstract forms devoid of ornament is made possible by the use of concrete.

Arts

- The English artist Laura Knight paints *The Beach*.
- The French artist André Derain paints *The Port of London*.
- The French artist Georges Rouault paints *At the Mirror*.
- The French artist Henri Matisse paints *The Gypsy*.
- The French artist Paul Cézanne paints *Mont Sainte-Victoire*, one of several pictures by him of this mountain.
- The French artist Pierre Auguste Renoir paints *Nude (After the Bath)*.
- The German artist Paula Modersohn-Becker paints *Old Poorhouse Woman with Glass Bottle and Poppy*.

- The Italian artist Medardo Rosso sculpts *Ecce Puer/Behold the Boy*.
- The Spanish artist Pablo Picasso paints *Composition: Peasants* and *Portrait of Gertrude Stein*.
- The U.S. artist Arthur B. Davies paints *Unicorns*.
- The U.S. artist Everett Shinn paints *Theater Box*.

Film

- Background music is regularly composed for movies in Italy. Romolo Bacchini is among the first composers to write for this medium.
- Eugène Lauste patents the first sound-on-film process in Britain, though it is not yet suitable for speech. His attempts at later commercial exploitation of it are thwarted by the war.
- George Albert Smith of the Charles Urban Trading Co. develops Kinemacolour, the first commercially successful color process for film: it uses two color filters and two reels of film.
- The Biograph 14th Street movie studio opens in New York, New York.
- The Cinéma Omnia Pathé opens in Paris, France, the first purpose-built movie theater in the world.
- The first animated cartoons are made in the United States and Britain.
- The first ever feature-length movie is produced, *The Story of the Kelly Gang*, in Australia. It is directed by Charles Tait, and stars Elizabeth Tait and an uncredited actor as Ned Kelly.
- U.S. movie director James Stuart Blackton produces *Humorous Phases of Funny Faces*, the first animated cartoon.

Literature and Language

- British publisher Joseph Dent begins publishing the "Everyman's Library," inexpensive editions of important literary works.
- The Austrian writer Robert Musil publishes his novel *Die Verwirrungen des Zöglings/Young Törless*.
- The English lexicographers Henry Watson Fowler and Frank George Fowler publish *The King's English*.
- The English statesman and writer Winston Churchill publishes a biography of his father, *Lord Randolph Churchill*.
- The English writer John Galsworthy publishes *The Man of Property*, the first novel in his sequence of novels and stories *The Forsyte Saga*. The final volume appears in 1922.
- The English writer Rudyard Kipling publishes his collection of children's stories *Puck of Pook's Hill*.
- The Hungarian writer Endre Ady publishes *Uj versek/New Poems*.
- The Japanese writer Natsume Soseki publishes his novel *Kusa makura/The Three-Cornered World*.
- The U.S. journalist Upton Sinclair publishes his novel *The Jungle*, a controversial book that exposes the conditions in the Chicago stockyards. As a direct result Congress passes laws to improve conditions in slaughterhouses.
- The U.S. writer Joel Chandler Harris, creator of Br'er Rabbit, publishes *Uncle Remus and Br'er Rabbit*.

- The U.S. writer O. Henry publishes his short-story collection *The Four Million*.

Music

- The Alsatian-born U.S. composer Charles Martin Loeffler completes his orchestral work *A Pagan Poem*.
- The Austrian composer Arnold Schoenberg completes his *Kammersymphonie/Chamber Symphony* No. 1.
- The Czech composer Josef Suk completes his Symphony No. 2, *Asrael*.
- The English composer Samuel Coleridge-Taylor completes his orchestral work *Symphonic Variations on an African Air*.
- The French composer Maurice Ravel completes his song cycle *Histoires naturelles/Natural Histories*, settings of poems by the French writer Jules Renard, and his *Cinq Mélodies populaires grecques/Five Popular Greek Melodies* for voice and orchestra.
- The John Gabel Automatic Entertainer, the first selective disc-playing jukebox, is introduced in the United States.
- The opera *Francesca da Rimini* by the Russian composer Sergey Rachmaninov is first performed, in Moscow, Russia. He also completes his *15 Songs* (Opus 26), the best known of which is "K detyam"/"To the Children."
- The opera *Maskarade* by the Danish composer Carl Nielsen is first performed, in Copenhagen, Denmark.
- The opera *The Wreckers*, by the English composer Ethel Smyth, is first performed, in Leipzig, Germany. It premieres in London, England, in 1909.
- The U.S. composer Charles Ives completes his orchestral work *Central Park in the Dark in the Good Old Summertime*.
- U.S. composers Charles A. Zimmerman and Alfred H. Miles write the song "Anchors Aweigh."
- U.S. inventor Thaddeus Cahill develops the teleharmonium, the first musical instrument to generate sound electrically.
- U.S. ragtime pianist "Jelly Roll" Morton writes "The King Porter Stomp," one of his many compositions that give Scott Joplin's ragtime style a heavy beat.

Theater and Dance

- Audiences in New York, New York, flock to see Ruth St. Denis's exotic dances, including so-called Hindoo dances.
- The play *Brewster's Millions*, by the U.S. dramatists Winchell Smith and Byron Ongley, is first performed, in New York, New York.
- The play *The Doctor's Dilemma*, by the Irish dramatist George Bernard Shaw, is first performed at the Royal Court Theatre in London, England.
- The play *The Great Divide*, by the U.S. dramatist William Vaughan Moody, is first performed in New York, New York.
- The play *The Silver Box*, by the English writer John Galsworthy, is first performed in London, England.
- The play *Waste*, by the English dramatist Harley Granville-Barker, is first performed in London, England.
- Theatres in New York, New York, feature six different George Bernard Shaw plays: *Caesar and Cleopatra*; *Arms and the Man*; *Man and Superman*; *John Bull's Other Island*; *Mrs Warren's Profession*; and *Major Barbara*.

FEBRUARY

12 The musical *George Washington, Jr.*, with songs by George M. Cohan, is performed for the first time, at the Knickerbocker Theater, New York, New York.

Thought and Scholarship

- *Lectures on Modern History* by the English historian Lord Acton is published posthumously.
- English economists and social historians Stanley and Beatrice Webb publish the first volume of their nine-volume *English Local Government*. The final volume appears in 1929.
- English historian Charles Oman publishes *The Great Revolt of 1381*.
- Italian philosopher Giovanni Papini publishes *Il crepuscolo dei filosofi/The Twilight of the Philosophies*.
- The Nobel Prize for Literature is awarded to the Italian poet Giosue Carducci.
- U.S. writer Mark Twain anonymously publishes his essay "What is a Man?" as a pamphlet. It was read at a meeting of the Monday Club (a literary society) in Hartford, Connecticut, in February 1883.

SOCIETY

Everyday Life

- A telephone directory inquiries service is introduced in New York, New York.
- British chemical company Lever Bros. introduces Lux Flakes, a detergent for delicate fabrics.
- G. W. Maxwell introduces the milk carton in the United States.
- German hairdresser Karl Ludwig Nessler introduces the permanent wave for hair styling in Britain. Because of the expense and awkwardness of the process, it will not really catch on until he moves to the United States, where the bob is popular.
- Malcolm Mackinnon begins commercial production of the whiskey liqueur Drambuie in Scotland.
- U.S. cartoonist Thomas ("Tad") Aloysius Dorgan names the "hot dog" with a sketch of a dachshund inside a bread roll.

Media and Communication

- The Victor Talking Machine Co. introduces the Victrola, a record player with the phonograph horn encased in a cabinet.

MARCH

- In a speech at the Gridiron Club in Washington, D.C., President Theodore Roosevelt coins the term "Muckraker," criticizing investigative journalists who engaged in the "literature of exposure."

BIRTHS & DEATHS

c. 1906   Faisal Ibn Abd al-Aziz, King of Saudi Arabia (1964–75), born in Riyadh, Arabia (–1975).

- Hastings Kamuzu Banda, prime minister of Nyasaland (now Malawi) 1964–66, first president of Malawi 1966–94, born near Kasungu, British Central Africa Protectorate (now Malawi) (–1997).

JANUARY
3   William Wilson Morgan, U.S. astronomer who discovered the spiral structure of the Milky Way, born in Bethseda, Tennessee (–1994).

13   Aleksandr Stepanovich Popov, Russian physicist and electrical engineer who invented the radio independently of Marconi, dies in St. Petersburg, Russia (46).

15   Aristotle Onassis, Greek shipping magnate whose second wife was Jacqueline Kennedy, born in Smyrna, Anatolia (modern Turkey) (–1975).

16   Marshall Field, U.S. founder of Field's department stores, dies in New York, New York (71).

FEBRUARY
4   Clyde William Tombaugh, U.S. astronomer who discovered Pluto, born in Streator, Illinois (–1997).

4   Dietrich Bonhoeffer, German Protestant theologian, born in Breslau, Prussia (now Wrocław, Poland) (–1945).

8   Chester F. Carlson, U.S. physicist who invented xerography, born in Seattle, Washington (–1968).

9   Gwen Catley, English soprano, born in London, England (–1996).

27   Samuel Pierpont Langley, U.S. aeronautics pioneer who built the first heavier-than-air flying machine, dies in Aiken, South Carolina (71).

28   "Bugsy" Siegel, U.S. gangster who began the development of gambling in Las Vegas, born in Brooklyn, New York (–1947).

MARCH
9   David Smith, U.S. sculptor known for his welded metal forms, born in Decatur, Indiana (–1965).

13   Susan B(rownell) Anthony, U.S. suffragist whose work eventually led to women's suffrage in the United States (1920), dies in Rochester, New York (85).

19   Adolf Eichmann, German Nazi war criminal, born in Solingen, Germany (–1962).

25   A(lan) J(ohn) P(ercivale) Taylor, English historian, journalist, and lecturer, born in Birkdale, Lancashire, England (–1990).

25   Jean Sablon, French singer popular in the United States and Europe during the 1930s, born in Nogent-sur-Marne, France (–1994).

APRIL
11   James Anthony Bailey, one of the originators of the Barnum and Bailey Circus, dies in Mt. Vernon, New York (58).

13   Samuel Beckett, Irish writer and winner of the Nobel Prize for Literature in 1969, born in Foxrock, Ireland (–1989).

19   Pierre Curie, French physicist who, with his wife Marie Curie, discovered radium and polonium, is run over and killed by a horse in Paris, France (46).

28   Kurt Gödel, Austrian-born U.S. mathematician and logician, born in Brünn, Austria-Hungary (now Brno, Czech Republic) (–1978).

MAY
6   Richmond Alexander Lattimore, U.S. poet and scholar, translator of Homer's *Iliad* and *Odyssey*, born in Paotingfu, China (–1984).

23   Henrik Ibsen, Norwegian poet and playwright whose works include *Peer Gynt* (1867) and *A Doll's House* (1879), dies in Christiania (now Oslo), Norway (78).

JUNE
3   Josephine Baker, U.S. singer and dancer who took Paris, France, by storm in the 1920s, born in St. Louis, Missouri (–1975).

19   Ernst Boris Chain, German-born British biochemist who isolated and conducted trials of penicillin, born in Berlin, Germany (–1979).

JULY
2   Hans Albrecht Bethe, German-born U.S. physicist who received the Nobel Prize for Physics in 1967 for elucidating the forces governing the structure of atomic nuclei, born in Strasbourg, Germany.

8   Philip Johnson, U.S. architect of the International School, born in Cleveland, Ohio.

22   Russell Sage, U.S. philanthropist who financed much of the U.S. railroad system, dies in Lawrence Beach, Long Island, New York (79).

AUGUST
17   Marcello Caetano, prime minister of Portugal 1968–74, born in Lisbon, Portugal (–1980).

26   Albert Bruce Sabin, Polish-born U.S. physician who developed an oral vaccine for poliomyelitis, born in Białystok, Poland (–1993).

SEPTEMBER
5   Ludwig Eduard Boltzmann, Austrian physicist who developed the science of statistical mechanics, dies in Duino, Italy (62).

17   Junius Richard Jayawardene, prime minister of Sri Lanka in 1977 and first president 1978–88, born in Colombo, Ceylon (now Sri Lanka) (–1996).

25   Dmitry Shostakovich, Russian composer, born in St. Petersburg, Russia (–1975).

27   William Empson, English poet and literary critic who had a major influence on 20th-century literary criticism, born in Howden, Yorkshire (now Humberside), England (–1984).

OCTOBER
9   Joseph Farwell Glidden, U.S. inventor, dies in De Kalb, Illinois (93).

9   Léopold Senghor, Senegalese poet and president of Senegal 1960–80, born in Joal, Senegal.

22   Paul Cézanne, French Postimpressionist painter whose work led to the development of cubism, dies in Aix-en-Provence, France (67).

23   Gertrude Ederle, U.S. swimmer who was the first woman to swim the English Channel (1926), born in New York, New York.

NOVEMBER
2   Luchino Visconti, Italian film, theater, and opera director, born in Milan, Italy (–1976).

9   Arthur Randolph, German-born U.S. rocket scientist, chief coordinator of the Saturn project which sent a man to the moon, born (–1996).

14   Louise Brooks, U.S. film star of the silent era, born in Cherryvale, Kansas (–1985).

DECEMBER
2   Peter C. Goldmark, Hungarian-born U.S. inventor of the long-playing record and the first practical color television, born in Budapest, Austria-Hungary (–1977).

9   Grace Hopper, U.S. computer scientist who creates the first compiler and helps invent the computer language COBOL, born in New York, New York (–1992).

13   Laurens van der Post, South African-born English author and explorer, born in Philippolis, Orange Free State (now South Africa) (–1996).

19   Leonid Brezhnev, Soviet statesman, First Secretary of the Soviet Communist Party 1964–82, born in Kamenskoye, Russia (–1982).

DECEMBER

24 Canadian-born U.S. physicist Reginald Fessenden makes the first wireless transmission of speech and music from Brant Rock, Massachusetts, using amplitude modification. He broadcasts music, a poem, and a talk, all heard by ships' radio operators.

Sports

- Alessandro Cagno of Italy, in an Itala, wins at the Macedonie circuit in Sicily in the first Targa Florio motor race.
- The American Turf Association is founded by U.S. colonel Matt Winn with the aim of reviving horse racing in the United States where corruption, doping, and betting scandals have led to the closure of hundreds of race tracks and the exodus of many of the best trainers, jockeys, and owners to Europe.
- The U.S. Intercollegiate Athletic Association redrafts the rules of American football. The forward pass is legalized for the first time and, following a large number of fatalities in the previous season, a number of dangerous plays are eliminated.

FEBRUARY

23 Tommy Burns of Canada defeats defending champion Marvin Hart of the United States in 20 rounds at Los Angeles, United States, to win the World Heavyweight Boxing Championship.

APRIL

22–May 2 The Interim (or Intercalated) Olympic Games are held in Athens, Greece, attended by 826 competitors, 6 of whom are women, from 20 nations. France wins 15 gold medals; the United States, 12; Greece and Britain, 8 each; Italy, 7; Switzerland, 5; and Germany and Norway, 4 each.

JUNE

26–27 The Hungarian driver Ferenc Szisz, in a Renault, wins the French Grand Prix at Le Mans. This is regarded as the first ever motor-racing Grand Prix.

1907

POLITICS, GOVERNMENT, AND ECONOMICS

Business and Economics

- A reorganization at Guffey Oil produces the Gulf Oil Company.
- Atlanta businessman A. L. Neiman joins his brother-in-law, Herbert Marcus, to found the clothes store Neiman–Marcus in Dallas, Texas.
- Entrepreneur Frank Sherman Washburn establishes the fertilizer producer American Cyanamid Co. in Niagara Falls, Ontario.
- The French chemist Eugène Schueller forms the L'Oréal beauty product company.
- The Royal Dutch Shell Oil Company is formed from a merger of Royal Dutch Oil and Britain's Shell Transport and Trading Company.

Colonization

MAY

23 A legislative council is created to represent Europeans in the Portuguese colony of Mozambique.

Human Rights

JANUARY

26 Following a long campaign for reform, a bill that extends suffrage to all males aged 24 or over is passed in Austria.

JUNE

14 Female suffrage is introduced in Norway.

OCTOBER

10 Demonstrations and strikes are held in support of full adult suffrage at the opening of parliament in Budapest, Austria-Hungary.

Politics and Government

- Des Moines, capital of the U.S. state of Iowa, adopts the "city manager" form of government pioneered in Galveston, Texas, in 1900, in which commissioners run the municipal government.
- Over 1.25 million immigrants arrive in the U.S., an all-time record.
- The city government of New Haven, Connecticut, becomes the first city authority in the United States to establish a planning department. Chicago, Illinois, follows suit in 1909.
- William D. Haywood, president of the Western Miners Union and cofounder of the International Workers of the World (IWW), is acquitted of the murder of former

Idaho governor Frank Steunenberg. Haywood had been arrested on false evidence, making his a cause célèbre among labor activists.

JANUARY

- The U.S. Congress passes legislation prohibiting corporate campaign contributions to candidates in federal elections.

FEBRUARY

- President Theodore Roosevelt signs the Immigration Act of 1907, authorizing the president to restrict Japanese immigration.
- The U.S. and Dominican Republic sign a treaty, authorizing the United States to serve as the Dominican Republic's international fiscal agent and guarantor.
- U.S. Congress passes the General Appropriations Act, raising the salaries of Cabinet officers, the vice president, and the speaker of the House of Representatives to $12,000, and senators and representatives to $7,500.
19 War breaks out between Honduras, Nicaragua, and El Salvador when Nicaraguan president José Santos Zelaya tries to use force to create a Central American confederation under his leadership. The conflict continues until December.

MARCH

- Fulfilling his promise to intervene in Western Hemisphere nations plagued by economic and political upheaval, President Theodore Roosevelt sends U.S. Marines to Honduras to protect U.S. property during an episode of political upheaval.
- President Theodore Roosevelt issues an executive order prohibiting the immigration of Japanese workers to the United States.
- President Theodore Roosevelt creates the Inland Waterways Commission to monitor the environmental impact of the nation's commercial waterways on surrounding forests.
3 A peasant revolt breaks out in the Romanian province of Moldavia and is violently suppressed, ending in April.
5 A second duma (parliament) meets in Russia, elections having introduced further polarization between the Right and the Left.

APRIL

8 A British–French convention confirms the independence of Siam (modern Thailand).
21 Irish political clubs merge to form the Sinn Féin League.

MAY

14 Sweden adopts proportional representation for elections to both chambers of its parliament, and introduces universal adult suffrage for its second chamber.
16 Britain, France, and Spain sign the Pact of Cartagena to counter German designs on the Balearic and Canary Islands.

JUNE

10 France and Japan make an agreement to preserve the "open door" (equal trading rights) with China.
15–October 18 A peace conference of the great powers is held at The Hague in the Netherlands. Originally called at the suggestion of the U.S. president Theodore Roosevelt in 1904, it was postponed because of the Russo-Japanese War. It now fails in its attempt to stop the arms race, but makes progress in promoting the

voluntary arbitration of disputes, despite German opposition.

JULY

1 A revised constitution for the newly-autonomous British Orange River Colony is promulgated in Bloemfontein.
7 The Triple Alliance between Germany, Austria, and Italy is renewed for six years.
20 Kojong, the emperor of Korea, abdicates under pressure from Japan.
25 Japan declares in a treaty that Korea is its protectorate. Korea also agrees a convention giving Japan control over its government through Japanese vice ministers in its major departments. Japan has controlled Korea's foreign policy since 1905.
30 A Russo-Japanese agreement on China secretly establishes a demarcation line for their interests in Manchuria.
30 Elections for the first assembly in the Philippines return 32 Nationalists, 20 Independents, and 16 Progressives.

AUGUST

3 Kaiser Wilhelm II of Germany and Czar Nicholas II of Russia meet at Swinemünde (now Świnoujście, Poland) to discuss the proposed Baghdad Railroad. Kaiser Wilhelm agrees not to make an anti-Russian agreement with Britain.
4 The French fleet bombards Casablanca, Morocco, following antiforeign disturbances there.
31 Britain and Russia sign a convention on Persia, Afghanistan, and Tibet, establishing zones of influence and removing obstacles toward an alignment of Russia with Britain and France against the Central Powers (Germany, Austria-Hungary, and Italy).

SEPTEMBER

17 The U.S. state of Georgia and the Oklahoma territory prohibit the sale and consumption of alcohol.
21 Hereros rebelling in German South West Africa since 1904 are finally suppressed.
26 New Zealand becomes known as the Dominion of New Zealand, reflecting its autonomous status within the British Empire.

NOVEMBER

14 The third duma (parliament) meets in Russia, having been elected on a restricted franchise and having increased conservative representation.
16 Oklahoma is admitted to the Union as the 46th U.S. state.

DECEMBER

6 The frontier between the British possessions of Uganda and East Africa is redefined.
7 The first congress of the Egyptian nationalist movement meets under the leadership of Mustafa Kemal.
8 Following the death of King Oskar II, Gustavus V succeeds as king of Sweden (–1950).
12 The leading Bolshevik, Vladimir Ilyich Lenin, flees Russia for the second time. He will not return until 1917.
15 The shah of Persia, Mohammed Ali, imprisons his liberal prime minister, Nasir-ul Muk, leading to a successful rising for his reinstatement.
16 A fleet of 16 battleships, known as the "Great White Fleet," departs on a round-the-world tour to demonstrate the military might of the United States, returning on February 22, 1909.

SCIENCE, TECHNOLOGY, AND MEDICINE

Ecology

- Etosha National Park, one of the world's largest game reserves, covering 22,270 sq km/8,598 sq mi, and Namib Desert National Park (23,400 sq km/9,035 sq mi), containing the only desert in southern Africa, are established in South West Africa (Namibia).
- Jasper National Park, British Columbia, Canada, is established. It contains the Columbia ice field, the largest glacier in North America south of the Arctic Circle.
- U.S. president Theodore Roosevelt adds 64,750 sq km/16 million acres of forest in five states to the nation's national forest preserve.
- President Theodore Roosevelt's chief forester, Gifford Pinchot, first applies the term "conservation" to U.S. environmental policy. In Pinchot's lexicon, conservation means employing "foresight, prudence, thrift and intelligence in dealing with public matters ... [for] national efficiency."

JANUARY
14 An earthquake in Jamaica badly damages Kingston and kills between 700 and 800 people.

NOVEMBER
9 The largest diamond found to date, the Cullinan Diamond, weighing approximately 3,106 carats, is presented by the South African province of Transvaal to King Edward VII of Britain.

DECEMBER
5 An explosion kills 361 miners in Monongah, West Virginia, in one of the worst mining disasters in U.S. history.
19 Less than two weeks after a devastating coal mine explosion in West Virginia, a blast in Jacobs Creek, Pennsylvania, claims the lives of 239 more people.

Health and Medicine

- Austrian physician Clemens Freiherr von Pirquet devises a skin test for diagnosing tuberculosis.
- British researcher Hendry Fraser shows that people living on a polished rice diet in Malaysia develop beriberi, whereas those eating brown rice do not. This finding leads to the discovery of vitamins.
- Bubonic plague kills 1.3 million in India.
- English biochemists Frederick Gowland Hopkins and Walter Fletcher show that working muscle accumulates lactic acid, which leads to a greater understanding of the chemistry of muscular contraction.
- French physician Charles Laveranin receives the Nobel Prize for Physiology or Medicine for his work on the role played by protozoa in causing diseases.
- U.S. zoologist Granville Ross Harrison develops the first successful animal tissue cultures; they prove vital in cancer research.

Science

- Austrian chemist Carl von Welsbach and French chemist Georges Urbain independently discover the rare-earth element lutetium (atomic no. 71).
- English anthropologist and eugenicist Francis Galton founds the English Eugenics Society.
- French physicist Pierre-Ernest Weiss develops the domain theory of ferromagnetism, which suggests that in a ferromagnet, such as loadstone, there are regions, or domains, where the molecules are all magnetized in the same direction.
- German chemist Eduard Büchner receives the Nobel Prize for Chemistry for his work on enzymes.
- German chemist Emil Fischer publishes *Researches on the Chemistry of Proteins*, in which he describes the synthesis of amino acid chains in proteins.
- German scientists Richard Anschütz and Max Schuler perfect the gyrocompass, which always points to true north.
- Scottish physiologist John Scott Haldane develops a stage-decompression method that permits deep-sea divers to ascend safely.
- The Heidelberg jaw is discovered in a sand pit at Mauer, Germany. Belonging to *Homo erectus*, it is the oldest European hominid fossil discovered to date and thought to be 400,000 years old.
- U.S. chemist Bertram Boltwood uses the ratio of lead and uranium in some rocks to determine their age. He estimates his samples to be 410 million to 2.2 billion years old.
- U.S. physicist Albert Michelson receives the Nobel Prize for Physics for his optical precision instruments and his spectroscopic and meteorological investigations.

Technology

- Arc welding, using modern electrodes, is introduced.
- British painter Samuel Simon develops the silk-screen printing process in Manchester, England.
- French engineer Edourd Belin, improving on the work of German inventor Arthur Korn in developing telephotography, invents a device that allows him to make the first long-distance transmission of a photograph, Paris–Lyon–Bordeaux. It is used in Europe to transmit news photographs.
- French inventor Auguste Lumière develops an improved process for color reproduction through autochrome plates.
- German inventor Arthur Korn further develops telephotography. He transmits a photograph of French president Armand Fallières between Munich and Berlin.
- Russian scientist Boris Rosing experiments with the Nipkow disc (a rotating disc used to scan pictures) and suggests that cathode-ray tubes and fluorescent screens could be used as receivers for television, or "electric vision" pictures.
- The Rectigraph Co. launches the first photocopier, the Rectigraph, in the United States.
- U.S. electrical engineers Edward Hewlett and Harold Buck develop the first suspension insulators, which make possible the transmission of voltages over 100,000 volts.

- U.S. inventor Charles Krumm devises a prototype teletypewriter.
- U.S. physicist Lee De Forest invents the "audion tube," a triode vacuum tube with a third electrode, shaped like a grid, between the cathode and anode, that controls the flow of electrons and permits the amplification of sound. It is an essential element in the development of radio, radar, television, and computers.

Transportation

- French aviator Louis Blériot builds the first successful monoplane. Two years later he flies it across the English Channel helping to establish the design.
- Italian engineers Vincenzo Lancia and Claudio Fogolin begin building cars: their business will develop into the Lancia car company.
- Philadelphia's subway system opens.
- The first metered taxicabs in the United States that are powered by gasoline appear in New York, New York. They appear in most U.S. cities soon afterwards.

FEBRUARY

12 The passenger steamer *Larchmont* sinks in the Long Island Sound off New York, New York, killing 131 people.

MARCH

29 A train derails near Colton, California, killing 26 people and leaving approximately 100 others injured.

SEPTEMBER

- The British luxury liner *Lusitania* is completed. At 241 m/790 ft long it is the largest ship in the world.

NOVEMBER

13 French engineer Paul Cornu constructs a helicopter and achieves a vertical flight of a few seconds, but is unable to control it.

ARTS AND IDEAS

Architecture

- The Customs House, designed by the U.S. architect Cass Gilbert, is completed in New York, New York.
- The Hochzeitsturm (Wedding Tower) at Darmstadt, Germany, designed by the Austrian architect Joseph Maria Olbricht, is completed.

Arts

- At the art gallery Salon d'Automne in Paris, France, there is retrospective of the works of the French artist Paul Cézanne. The exhibition has an important impact on the development of 20th-century art.
- The French artist André Derain paints *Blackfriars Bridge*.
- The French artist Henri Rousseau paints *The Snake Charmer*.
- The French artist Henri Matisse paints *Blue Nude*.

- The Irish artist William Orpen paints *Portrait of the Honourable Percy Wyndham*.
- The Norwegian artist Edvard Munch paints *Amor and Psyche*.
- The Romanian artist Constantin Brancusi sculpts *The Kiss*.
- The Spanish artist Pablo Picasso paints *Les Demoiselles d'Avignon/The Women of Avignon*, one of the central works of 20th-century art.
- The U.S. artist George Wesley Bellows paints *Stag at Sharkey's*, and *Forty-Two Kids*.
- The U.S. artist George B. Luks paints *The Wrestlers*.
- The U.S. artist John Sloan paints *The Wake of the Ferry II*.
- The U.S. artist Robert Henri paints *Eva Green*.
- The U.S. photographer Alfred Stieglitz expands his "291" art gallery on Fifth Avenue in New York, New York, and shows works by Henri Matisse, Francis Picabia, Constantin Brancusi, Pablo Picasso, and others. In the same year Stieglitz takes *Steerage*.
- The U.S. photographer Edward Steichen takes *Steeplechase Day, Paris*.
- The U.S. photographers Alfred Stieglitz and Clarence White take *Miss Thompson*.
- The Welsh artist Augustus John paints *Portrait of W. B. Yeats*.

Film

c. 1907 In the early days of cinema, actors are not credited by name on movies. For example, Florence Lawrence was known only as "the Biograph Girl." Production companies are keen to keep salaries down and the actors are often only too happy to retain their anonymity, as cinema is still regarded as marginal to their main careers.

- *Salaviinan Polttajat/Bootleggers*, made by Louis Sparre and Teuvo Puro, is released in Finland, the first Finnish movie with a fictional plot.
- The cinema is becoming a very popular pastime in the United States and Europe, especially among the working classes.
- The movie *20,000 Leagues Under the Sea*, directed by Georges Méliès, is released in France.
- The French Lumière brothers develop the Autochrome system, which makes color photography in natural colors viable.
- The U.S. movie pioneer Thomas Edison signs an exclusive agreement with George Eastman of the Eastman Kodak Co. for the sole supply of cinema film.

Literature and Language

- Henry Vallienne publishes *Kastele de Prelongo/The Castle of Prelongue*, the first novel in Esperanto.
- The English writer and critic Edmund Gosse publishes his autobiography, *Father and Son*.
- The English writer E. M. Forster publishes his novel *The Longest Journey*.
- The English writer Robert William Service publishes his verse collection *Songs of a Sourdough*, which features the character Dangerous Dan McGrew.

- The first volume of the *Letters of Queen Victoria*, edited by the English scholars A. C. Benson and Viscount Esher, is published. The last volume will appear in 1932.
- The first volume of the *Cambridge History of English Literature* is published. The last volume will appear in 1927.
- The German poet Rainer Maria Rilke publishes *Neue Gedichte/New Poems*.
- The Polish-born English writer Joseph Conrad publishes his novel *The Secret Agent*.
- The Russian writer Maxim Gorky publishes his novel *Mat/Mother*.
- The U.S. historian Henry Brooks Adams privately publishes his autobiography, *The Education of Henry Adams: A Study of 20th Century Multiplicity*.
- The U.S. writer Jack London publishes his novels *The Road* and *The Iron Heel*.
- The U.S. writer O. Henry publishes his short-story collection *The Trimmed Lamp*.
- The U.S. writer Sara Teasdale publishes her poetry collection *Sonnets to Duse and Other Poems*.

Music

- The Austrian composer Gustav Mahler completes his Symphony No. 8.
- The English folk song collector Cecil Sharp publishes *English Folk Songs: Some Conclusions*.
- The Finnish composer Jean Sibelius completes his Symphony No. 3.
- The French composer Maurice Ravel completes his orchestral work *Rhapsodie espagnole/Spanish Rhapsody* and his *Vocalise en forme d'Habañera/Vocalise in the Form of a Habañera* for voice and piano.
- The opera *Ariane et Barbe-Bleue/Ariane and Bluebeard*, by the French composer Paul Dukas, is first performed in Paris, France.
- The opera *Romeo und Julia auf dem Dorfe/A Village Romeo and Juliet*, by the English composer Frederick Delius, is first performed in Berlin, Germany.
- The operetta *Die Dollarprinzessin/The Dollar Princess*, by the Austrian composer Leo Fall, is first performed in Vienna, Austria.
- The Russian composer Sergey Rachmaninov completes his Symphony No. 2 and his Piano Sonata No. 1.
- The Russian composer Igor Stravinsky completes his Symphony No. 1.
- The U.S. composer Charles Ives completes his piano work *Five Take-Offs: Seen and Unseen, Rough and Ready, Song Without (Good) Words, Scene Episode, Bad Resolutions and Good.*
- U.S. composer John W. Bratton writes the song "The Teddy Bears' Picnic."

Theater and Dance

- The play *Ett drömspel/A Dream Play*, by the Swedish writer August Strindberg, is first performed in Stockholm, Sweden.
- The play *Playboy of the Western World*, by the Irish dramatist John Millington Synge, is first performed at the Abbey Theatre in Dublin, Ireland. Its depiction of Irish life offended many in the audience and fights break out at several performances.
- The play *The Rising of the Mood*, by the Irish writer Lady Gregory, is first performed in Dublin, Ireland.

JUNE
13 The musical *The Honeymooners*, with songs by George M. Cohan, who also features in the show, is performed for the first time, at the Aerial Garden, New York, New York.

JULY
8 *Follies of 1907*, a spectacular music and dance show, is first performed at the Jardin de Paris, New York, New York. It is produced by Florenz Ziegfeld and is the first of the *Ziegfeld Follies*.

DECEMBER
3 The musical *The Talk of the Town*, with songs by George M. Cohan, is performed for the first time, at the Knickerbocker Theater, New York, New York.

Thought and Scholarship

- Czech orientalist Bedřich Hrozný publishes the key to the translation of Hittite documents in the scholarly journal *Proceedings of the German Oriental Society*.
- French philosopher Henri Bergson publishes *L'Evolution créatrice/Creative Evolution*.
- The Nobel Prize for Literature is awarded to the British novelist and poet Rudyard Kipling.
- U.S. anthropologist Edward Curtis publishes the first volume of his 20-volume *North Native American*, a vast photographic record of every aspect of Native American life. He worked on the projects until 1930.
- U.S. philosopher William James publishes *Pragmatism: A New Way for Some Old Ways of Thinking*.
- U.S. sociologist William Isaac Thomas publishes *Sex and Society*, the first scientific study on the subject.

SOCIETY

Education

- The Russell Sage Foundation is founded, becoming the oldest surviving U.S. research institute in modern times.
- The University of California at Riverside opens.
- The University of Hawaii opens in Honolulu.
- The University of Saskatchewan opens in Saskatoon.

JUNE
- Dropsie College for Hebrew and Cognate Learning opens in Philadelphia, Pennsylvania.

Everyday Life

- British tobacconist Alfred Dunhill opens his world-famous tobacco store in London, England.
- More than 338,000 Austro-Hungarian immigrants arrive in the United States.

BIRTHS & DEATHS

JANUARY

11 Pierre Mendès-France, French socialist politician, premier of France 1954–55, born in Paris, France (–1982).

20 Manfred von Ardenne, German scientist and inventor of the high definition electron microscope, born in Hamburg, Germany (–1997).

20 Roy (Roland) Welensky, Rhodesian politician instrumental in the creation of the Federation of Rhodesia and Nyasaland (1953), and prime minister 1956–63, born in Salisbury, Southern Rhodesia (now Harare, Zimbabwe) (–1991).

FEBRUARY

2 Dmitry Mendeleyev, Russian chemist who developed the periodic table of elements, dies in St. Petersburg, Russia (72).

3 James Michener, U.S. author, born in New York, New York (–1997).

11 William Jaird Levitt, U.S. architect who pioneered the use of mass-produced single-dwelling houses for U.S. servicemen returning from World War II, born in New York, New York (–1994).

15 Cesar Romero, U.S. actor, born in New York, New York (–1994).

20 Henri Moissan, French chemist who developed the electric arc furnace for preparing new substances, dies in Paris, France (54).

21 W(ystan) H(ugh) Auden, English-born U.S. poet, born in York, Yorkshire (now North Yorkshire), England (–1973).

MARCH

9 Mircea Eliade, Romanian-born U.S. religious scholar, born in Bucharest, Romania (–1986).

18 J(ohn) Z(achary) Young, English zoologist who contributed to knowledge of nerve structure and function through his discovery and study of the giant nerve fibers in squids, born in Bristol, England (–1997).

23 Daniel Bovet, Swiss physiologist who pioneered research into antihistamine drugs, born in Neuchâtel, Switzerland (–1992).

APRIL

14 François Duvalier (known as "Papa Doc"), president of Haiti (1957–71) who ruled through terror and corruption, born in Port-au-Prince, Haiti (–1971).

15 Nikolaas Tinbergen, Dutch zoologist and ethologist, born in The Hague, the Netherlands (–1988).

29 Fred Zinnemann, Austrian-born U.S. film producer, who produced *High Noon* and *Oklahoma*, born in Vienna, Austria (–1997).

MAY

4 Lincoln Kirstein, founder and general director of the New York City Ballet, born in Rochester, New York (–1996).

12 Joris Karl Huysmans, French novelist, dies in Paris, France (59).

12 Katharine Hepburn, U.S. stage and motion picture actress, born in Hartford, Connecticut.

12 Leslie Charteris, British-born U.S. author who created Simon Templar ("the Saint"), is born in Singapore (–1993).

13 Daphne du Maurier, English gothic novelist whose works include *Rebecca* and *The Birds*, born in London, England (–1989).

22 Laurence Olivier, English stage and film actor, director, and producer, born in Dorking, Surrey, England (–1989).

25 U Nu, prime minister of the Union of Burma 1948–58 and 1960–62, born in Wakema, Burma (now Myanmar) (–1995).

26 John Wayne, U.S. star of westerns and war films, born in Winterset, Iowa (–1979).

JUNE

1 Frank Whittle, English engineer who developed the jet engine, born in Coventry, Warwickshire, England (–).

15 William Le Baron Jenny, U.S. civil engineer and architect who, in Chicago, Illinois, built the first skyscraper, dies in Los Angeles, California (74).

17 Charles Eames, U.S. furniture designer and architect, born in St. Louis, Missouri (–1978).

20 Lillian Hellman, U.S. dramatist and screenwriter who opposed injustice and exploitation, born in New Orleans, Louisiana (–1984).

23 James Edward Meade, English Keynesian economist who shared the Nobel Prize for Economics in 1977 for his work on trade and capital movements, born in Swanage, England (–1995).

25 Hans Jensen, German physicist who, with Maria Goeppert-Mayer and Eugene P. Wagner, proposed the shell theory of the atom, born in Hamburg, Germany (–1974).

JULY

7 Robert Heinlein, U.S. science-fiction writer, born in Butler, Missouri (–1988).

29 Melvin Belli, U.S. trial lawyer known for defending the common people against large corporations, born in Sonora, California (88).

AUGUST

3 Augustus St.-Gaudens, U.S. sculptor, dies in Cornish, New Hampshire (59).

3 Gerard Ernest Geisel, president of Brazil 1974–79, born in Rio Grande de Sul, Brazil (–1996).

30 John Mauchly, U.S. physicist and engineer who, with John P. Eckert, built ENIAC, the first electronic computer, born in Cincinnati, Ohio (–1980).

SEPTEMBER

4 Edvard Grieg, Norwegian nationalist composer, dies in Bergen, Norway (64).

17 Warren Burger, Chief Justice of the U.S. Supreme Court 1969–86, born in St. Paul, Minnesota (–1995).

18 Edwin McMillan, U.S. nuclear physicist who discovered neptunium and plutonium, born in Redondo Beach, California (–1991).

OCTOBER

2 Alexander Robertus Todd, Scottish organic chemist, winner of the Nobel Prize for Chemistry in 1957 for synthesizing nucleotides, which make up DNA and RNA, born in Glasgow, Scotland (–1997).

22 Jimmie Foxx, U.S. baseball player who became the second person to hit over 500 runs (after Babe Ruth), born in Sudlersville, Maryland (–1967).

30 Sol Tax, U.S. anthropologist, born in Chicago, Illinois (–1995).

NOVEMBER

16 Burgess Meredith, U.S. actor, born in Cleveland, Ohio (–1997).

19 Jack Schaeffer, U.S. novelist best known for his book *Shane*, born in Cleveland, Ohio (–1991).

28 Alberto Moravia, Italian existentialist novelist and short-story writer, born in Rome, Italy (–1990).

DECEMBER

5 Lin Biao, Chinese field commander of the Red Army, born in Huang-kang, Hupeh province, China (–1971).

15 Oscar Niemeyer, Brazilian architect who designed the government buildings in Brasília, born in Rio de Janeiro, Brazil.

17 William Thomson (Lord Kelvin), Scottish physicist who developed the absolute temperature scale, dies in Netherhall near Largs, Ayrshire, Scotland (84).

25 Cab Calloway, U.S. entertainer and big-band leader, born in Rochester, New York (–1994).

- The Hamburg zoo is opened; it is the first to use moated enclosures.
- The Hurley Machine Corporation launches the Thor, the first self-contained electric washing machine, in the United States, designed by Alva J. Fisher.
- The U.S. company General Electric launches a more efficient light bulb, replacing the usual carbon filament with tungsten.
- The U.S. Hoover Suction-Sweeping Co. launches the first effective portable vacuum cleaner for domestic use. It is designed by James M. Spangler.
- There is increasing concern in the United States at the depressing effect the presence of new immigrants, who are less literate and often unskilled workers, is having on wages.
- U.S. cartoonist Harry Fisher creates Mutt and Jeff, the first serialized comic strip to feature regular characters.

MAY

1   May Day labor demonstrations take place in many European capitals, including a general strike in Warsaw, Poland.

JUNE

6   British chemical company Lever Bros launches Persil, the first ever household detergent, in Germany.

Media and Communication

- A wireless telegraphy service is established between the United States and Ireland.

- Lee De Forest of the De Forest Radio Telephone Co. begins the first regular experimental radio broadcasts in the United States, in New York, New York. These are for entertainment, and consist mainly of music.
- U.S. media tycoon William Randolph Hearst founds the International News Service press agency to supply news for his newspaper group.

Religion

SEPTEMBER

8   Pope Pius X issues an encyclical *Pascendi gregis*, which condemns the modernist movement in the Roman Catholic Church.

Sports

- The first International Horse Show is staged at Olympia, London, England.

JUNE

10–August 10   Prince Scipione Borghese of Italy, driving an Itala, wins the motor race from Beijing, China, to Paris, France, the first ever long-distance motor rally.

17   The world's first specialized motor-racing circuit is opened in Britain at Brooklands, near Weybridge, Surrey.

21   Arnaud Massy of France becomes the first overseas player to win the British Open golf championship, at Hoylake, northwest England.

1908

POLITICS, GOVERNMENT, AND ECONOMICS

Business and Economics

- The U.S. entrepreneur Howard Robard Hughes establishes Hughes Tool Co. in Houston, Texas; the company provides drilling equipment for the nation's oil industry.
- The Hungarian–American pharmacist Max Kiss founds the laxative manufacturing company Ex-Lax in the United States.
- The International Convention on Copyright is held in Berlin, Germany, extending copyright to musical and cinematic works, and establishing a period of 50 years

after the author's death during which copyright remains active.

SEPTEMBER

14   William C. Durant of the Buick Motor Company forms the General Motors Company in Detroit, Michigan, as the basis for establishing a conglomerate of car-building companies.

Colonization

AUGUST

20   King Leopold II of Belgium transfers the Congo to Belgium, having previously exploited it through a private company.

OCTOBER

6   Austria annexes Bosnia and Herzegovina from the Ottoman Empire, by decree.

Human Rights

JANUARY

- The Sullivan Ordinance in New York, New York, prohibits women from smoking in public places.
- 10 Socialist-organized demonstrations take place throughout Germany, demanding universal suffrage in Prussia, which still has a three-class voting system.

JULY

- 7 A Pan-Slavic conference takes place in Prague (now in the Czech Republic), where the Czechs resurrect the movement for Slavic recognition.

Politics and Government

- Arthur Hyne is convicted of bigamy in Britain, after marrying and deserting five wives since 1905. He is also thought to be wanted in the United States for similar offenses.
- Staunton, Virginia, devises the "municipal manager" system of government. The mayor and council hire a general manager to control the town administration and give the manager freedom to appoint subordinates. The model is adopted by other cities.
- The American Bar Association adopts an ethics code.
- The states of Mississippi, North Carolina, and Tennessee adopt prohibition.

JANUARY

- The U.S. Supreme Court, in *Adair v. United States*, upholds the dismissal of a railroad employee for his union membership.
- 6 The brother of Sultan Abdul Aziz of Morocco, Mulai Hafid, rebels following protests at European interference in Moroccan affairs and is proclaimed sultan at Fez, Morocco.
- 27 The Austrian foreign minister, Count Alois Aehrenthal, announces that the Austrian government will build a railroad toward Thessaloníki (English Salonika), Greece, to extend facilities for trade and to widen Austro-Hungarian influence.

FEBRUARY

- The *Muller v. Oregon* case upholds the right of a U.S. state to regulate the maximum hours of work for women on health grounds. The Supreme Court bases its decision on a brief that includes sociological data, written by Massachusetts jurist Louis D. Brandeis.
- The U.S. Supreme Court, in *Loewe v. Lawlor*, decrees labor boycotts an unfair restraint of trade.
- 1 King Carlos I of Portugal and the crown prince are murdered in Lisbon, Portugal, by republicans, and Prince Manuel becomes King Manuel II (–1910).

MARCH

- 4 A fire in a primary school at Collingwood near Cleveland, Ohio, kills 180 children and 9 teachers.

APRIL

- Towns and cities throughout the state of Massachusetts adopt prohibition ordinances. In Worcester alone, the closing of 76 saloons leaves 2,000 people out of work.
- 6 The British prime minister, Sir Henry Campbell-Bannerman, resigns because of ill health.

- 8 Herbert Asquith becomes British prime minister, with radical member of Parliament David Lloyd George as chancellor of the Exchequer.

MAY

- The U.S. Socialist Party nominates Eugene V. Debs for president and New York printer Benjamin Hanford for vice president.
- U.S. Congress passes legislation establishing guidelines for child labor in Washington, D.C.
- 5 The Australian government is defeated in a confidence vote, and a Labor government takes office under Andrew Fisher.
- 22 The United States increases the number of members in the Philippine commission (the nominated upper house of the legislature) to nine, including four Filipinos.

JUNE

- President Theodore Roosevelt appoints a 57-member National Commission for the Conservation of Natural Resources. The Commission will be directed by Gifford Pinchot, who first applied the term "conservation" to the environment.
- Republicans nominate former war secretary, William Howard Taft, for president and New York businessman, James S. Sherman, for vice president.
- 9 King Edward VII of Great Britain visits Russia and meets Czar Nicholas II at Reval (Tallinn) in Estonia, where the czar agrees to the introduction of extensive reforms in the troubled Ottoman province of Macedonia.
- 14 The fourth German Navy Bill authorizes expenditure on four further capital ships, continuing Germany's expansion of its maritime capability.
- 23 In a Russian-backed counterrevolutionary coup, Shah Mohammed Ali overthrows the Persian constitution of December 1906.
- 23 The United States severs diplomatic relations with Venezuela when Cipriano Castro refuses to compensate U.S. citizens for injuries incurred in his revolution of 1899.

JULY

- A revolt begins in Tabriz, Persia, against Shah Mohammed Ali's coup.
- Democrats nominate Nebraska politician William Jennings Bryan for president and Indiana politician John W. Kern for vice president.
- 6 Young Turk nationalists under Niazi Bey stage a revolt at Resina in Macedonia. The government troops, sent to quell the rising, desert.
- 24 Following the revolt of the Young Turk nationalists in Macedonia, the Ottoman sultan Abdul Hamid II restores the Ottoman constitution of 1876.
- 26 The U.S. Bureau of Investigation is founded as part of the Justice Department. It is renamed the Federal Bureau of Investigation (FBI) on July 1, 1935.

AUGUST

- 13 King Edward VII of Great Britain meets Emperor Franz Joseph of Austria-Hungary at Ischl, Austria, and attempts to persuade him to put pressure on Germany to halt the naval arms race.
- 23 Germany initiates the Baltic Convention (Germany, Sweden, Denmark, and Russia) and the North Sea Convention (Britain, Germany, Denmark, France, and

the Netherlands) in order to guarantee the status quo on the shores of the two seas, and to prevent destabilization following the granting of Norwegian independence.

23 Mulai Hafid, the new sultan of Morocco, defeats Sultan Abdul Aziz at Marrakesh, Morocco.

SEPTEMBER

9 The Sinn Féin League of Ireland becomes simply Sinn Féin.

16 The foreign ministers of Austria and Russia, Count Alois Aehrenthal and Alexander Izvolsky, hold the Buchlau conference. Austria undertakes not to oppose the opening of the Dardanelles to Russian warships and Russia agrees to Austria's proposed annexation of Bosnia and Herzegovina.

25 The "Casablanca incident," in which German deserters from the French Foreign Legion are taken by force from a German consular official, heightens Franco-German tension.

26 Germany agrees to support Russian plans to have the Dardanelles reopened to its warships, in return for Russian backing in its dispute with Britain over the building of the Baghdad Railroad.

OCTOBER

5 King Ferdinand I of Bulgaria declares Bulgaria's independence from the Ottoman Empire and assumes the title of czar.

7 In response to events in Bulgaria and Bosnia and Herzegovina, the Ottoman possession of Crete announces its union with Greece.

9–14 The Russian foreign minister Alexander Izvolsky visits London, England, to try to enlist British support for Russian plans to have the Dardanelles opened to Russian warships. This was forbidden by the Treaty of Berlin of 1878.

10 The Australian parliament agrees to the establishment of a new federal capital at Canberra, near Sydney.

12 A South African constitutional convention meets at Durban, Natal, to discuss a proposed union of the British colonies of South Africa.

27 The British *Daily Telegraph* publishes remarks by Kaiser Wilhelm II of Germany in which he states that the German people are hostile to Britain, though he remains a friend. The statement arouses strong feelings in Germany against Britain, and also against the Kaiser for making policy pronouncements without consulting the German chancellor.

NOVEMBER

• Americans elect William Howard Taft as president and James S. Sherman as vice president. In Congressional elections, Republicans retain majorities in the House (219–172) and the Senate (61–32).

10–11 The German Reichstag (parliament) debates the *Daily Telegraph* interview, further embittering British–German relations.

14 A Liberal victory in the Cuban elections leads to the election of José Gómez as president (–1913).

14 Emperor Guangxu of China dies, to be followed on November 15 by the Dowager Empress Cixi. P'u-i becomes emperor, with the reactionary Prince Ch'un as regent.

DECEMBER

• The U.S. Supreme Court upholds the prison sentences of American Federation of Labor (AFL) president, Samuel Gompers, and two assistants.

2 An abortive Czech revolt against Austrian rule breaks out in Bohemia.

4 The European powers begin an abortive conference, with a view to regulating the conditions of naval warfare.

17 The first session of the Ottoman parliament opens with a large Young Turk nationalist majority.

SCIENCE, TECHNOLOGY, AND MEDICINE

Ecology

• Kaziranga National Park, Assam, India is established; it serves as a refuge for the Indian rhinoceros.

• U.S. president Theodore Roosevelt creates Muir Woods National Monument from 2 sq km/500 acres of redwood forest in Marin County, California.

• U.S. president Theodore Roosevelt creates Grand Canyon National Monument in Arizona.

APRIL

12 10,000 are left homeless and $10 million of property is destroyed when the city of Chelsea, Massachusetts, goes up in flames.

MAY

13 44 state and territorial governors attend an environmental conservation conference, convened by President Theodore Roosevelt, at the White House in Washington, D.C.

JUNE

30 An aerial explosion equivalent to 10–15 megatons of TNT flattens approximately 2,000 sq km/1,243 mi of forest near the Tunguska River, Siberia, Russian Empire. No meteorite fragments are discovered but it is thought to have been a fragment of a comet disintegrating in the atmosphere.

DECEMBER

28 An earthquake hits the region of the Strait of Messina, between Sicily and South Calabria, Italy, estimated to measure 7.5 on the Richter scale. The towns of Messina in Sicily and Reggio di Calabria on the mainland are the worst hit, and are both devastated, with Reggio di Calabria suffering a tidal wave following the earthquake. Estimates of the death toll vary between 75,000 and 200,000, most deaths occurring in the two towns. It is Europe's worst earthquake.

Health and Medicine

• The Nobel Prize for Physiology or Medicine is awarded jointly to Russian biologist Ilya Ilyich Mechnikov and German scientist Paul Ehrlich for their work on immunity.

- The U.S. Navy establishes the Nurse Corps, with Esther Hasson as its first superintendent.
- U.S. pathologist Howard Taylor Ricketts discovers that Rocky Mountain spotted fever is caused by the microorganism *Rickettsia rickettsi*, which is transmitted by the bite of a certain tick, found particularly on cattle and sheep.

Math

- English mathematician Godfrey Hardy and German physician Wilhelm Weinberg establish the mathematical basis for population genetics.
- German mathematician Ernst Zermelo publishes *Untersuchungen über die Grundlagen der Mengenlehre/Investigations on the Foundations of Set Theory*, which forms the basis of modern set theory.

Science

- After nine years' endeavor Massachusetts chemist, Carl M. Wheaton, informs the U.S. Army that he has developed a formula for poison gas.
- Dutch physicist Heike Kamerlingh-Onnes liquefies helium at 4.2 K (–268.95°C/–117°F).
- French physicist Gabriel Lippmann receives the Nobel Prize for Physics for his method of reproducing colors photographically based on the phenomenon of interference.
- German chemist Fritz Haber invents a process for synthesizing ammonia from nitrogen and hydrogen. Commercial production begins in 1909.
- German physicist Hans Geiger and New Zealand-born British physicist Ernest Rutherford develop the Geiger counter, which counts individual alpha particles emitted by radioactive substances.
- Japanese chemist Kikunae Ikeda isolates monosodium glutamate (MSG) from seaweed.
- New Zealand-born British physicist Ernest Rutherford and his student Thomas Royds prove that the alpha particle is the helium atom.
- New Zealand-born British physicist Ernest Rutherford is awarded the Nobel Prize for Chemistry for his investigations concerning the disintegration of elements and the chemistry of radioactive substances.
- U.S. astronomer George Ellery Hale discovers that sunspots have magnetic fields.
- U.S. physicist Percy Williams Bridgman invents equipment that can create atmospheric pressures of 100,000 atmospheres (later 400,000) creating a new field of investigation.

Technology

- Belgian-born U.S. chemist Leo H. Baekeland invents the plastic Bakelite: its insulating and malleable properties, combined with the fact that it does not bend when heated, ensures it has many uses.
- Scottish electrical engineer A. Campbell Swinton proposes that cathode-ray tubes be used for both television camera and receiver.
- Swiss chemist Jacques Brandenberger creates cellophane, which becomes invaluable in food packaging.

- U.S. engineer William Coolidge develops a process of making tungsten ductile enough to be drawn. It substantially improves electric lights.

OCTOBER

12 An international conference on electrical units and standards opens in London, England, involving representatives of 18 countries.

Transportation

- A road race is held from New York, New York, to Paris, France, via Vladivostok, Russia: the winner, George Schuster from the United States, completes the course in 169 days.
- French aviator Henri Farman invents the aileron, which permits lateral control of aircraft. It is used on all subsequent airplanes.
- French aviators Henri and Maurice Farman complete a circular flight of 1.6 km/1 mi, the first circular flight in Europe.
- German-born U.S. inventor Emil Berliner designs an internal combustion engine that is light and serves as the prototype for subsequent aircraft motors.
- The subway system in New York, New York, is expanded, as two further lines are opened.

JUNE

- The steamship *Lusitania* travels from Queenstown, Ireland, to New York, New York, in 4 days, 15 hours—a new transatlantic record.

AUGUST

8 U.S. aviator Wilbur Wright flies his plane the *Flyer* at Le Mans, France, providing impetus to the European aviation industry.

12 U.S. car manufacturer Henry Ford of the Ford Motor Company introduces the Model T. Inexpensive (sold for $850), easy to maintain, and mass-produced after 1913, it revolutionizes transportation.

SEPTEMBER

- U.S. aviator Wilbur Wright stays in the air over Le Mans, France for 1 hr 31 min 25 sec—a new record. The flight covers 61 miles.
- U.S. Signal Corps lieutenant, Thomas W. Selfridge, becomes the first person killed in a plane crash, when he and Orville Wright plummet from the sky in Wright's airplane at Fort Meyer, Virginia.

1 The 1,320-km/820-mi Hejaz Railroad between Damascus, Syria, and Mecca and Medina, Arabia, is completed. It serves to strengthen the Ottoman Empire's control of the area and to bring pilgrims to Mecca.

OCTOBER

12 A meeting of the International Road Congress opens in Paris, France, and attracts representatives of 29 countries.

DECEMBER

31 U.S. aviator Wilbur Wright covers a distance of 124 km/77.5 mi in 2 hr 20 min, setting a world endurance record.

ARTS AND IDEAS

Architecture

- The Austrian architect Adolf Loos publishes his book *Ornament und Verbrechen/Ornament and Crime* which has a major impact on architecture and design.
- The Robie House, designed by the U.S. architect Frank Lloyd Wright, is completed in Chicago, Illinois. Here Wright creates a new, distinctively American form of domestic architecture—the "prairie house"—in which both the design and materials of the building form an integral part of the landscape.
- The Singer Building, designed by the U.S. architect Ernest Flagg, is completed in New York, New York.

Arts

- *c. 1908* The English artist Walter Richard Sickert paints *The Camden Town Murder, or What Shall We Do for the Rent?*
- *c. 1908* The U.S. artist Maurice Prendergast paints *East Boston Ferry.*
- The French artist Auguste Rodin sculpts *Cathedral.*
- The French artist Georges Braque paints the cubist landscape *Trees at L'Estaques*, one of a series painted at L'Estaques in France.
- The French artist Henri Matisse paints *Harmony in Red* and sculpts *The Back, I.*
- The French artist Henri Rousseau paints *Football Players.*
- The French artist Maurice de Vlaminck paints *The Red Trees.*
- The French artist Pierre Auguste Renoir paints *Portrait of Ambroise Vollard.*
- The French artist Pierre Bonnard paints *Nude Standing Against the Light.*
- The Romanian artist Constantin Brancusi sculpts the first of several versions of his work *Mademoiselle Pogany.*
- The Russian artist Wassily Kandinsky paints *Blue Mountain.*
- The U.S. artist Arthur Dove paints *The Lobster.*
- The U.S. artist John Sloan paints *South Street Bathers.*
- The U.S. artist Robert Henri paints *Portrait of Jessica Penn in Black.*

Film

- *Dr Jekyll and Mr Hyde*, produced by the U.S. Selig Polyscope Co. and starring Richard Mansfield, is released in the United States, the first horror movie.
- *Stenka Razin*, directed by Vladimir Romachkov, is the first significant Russian movie to be released.
- A movie of William Shakespeare's *Romeo and Juliet* is released in the USA, directed by J. Stuart Blackton, and starring Florence Lawrence and Paul Panzer.
- Desperate to protect his position in the development of cinematic technology, U.S. inventor Thomas Edison organizes a deal with his main competitors to pool their patents and to discourage other companies'

development. Their techniques are extreme, and the organization—the Motion Pictures Patents Company—is later judged to be restrictive of trade.
- Filming of *The Count of Monte Cristo* is completed near Los Angeles, California; in the next few years, more filmmakers are attracted to California by the low costs and reliable climate.
- French singer Maurice Chevalier begins his movie career with an appearance in the silent short feature *Top Crédule.*
- The movie *The Adventures of Dollie* is released in the United States, the first directed by the pioneer U.S. filmmaker D. W. Griffith. Later in the same year, his movie *The Curtain Pole* is released in the United States, starring Linda Arvidson and Mack Sennett.
- The movie *Tosca* is released, starring Sarah Bernhardt, based on the play by Victorien Sardou (1887).
- The Film d'Art company is formed in France, representing a collaboration between the movie industry, La Comédie Française, and the Académie Française.
- The French movie company Pathé Frères introduce rental contractual obligations, forbidding exhibitors from rerenting, selling or copying the films they distribute.

DECEMBER

24 New York mayor, George B. McClellan, revokes the licenses of some 550 movie theater operators, pledging to restore their licenses on the condition that they refrain from Sunday viewings and showing immoral movies.

Literature and Language

- L. M. Montgomery publishes the classic children's novel *Anne of Green Gables.*
- The American Academy of Arts and Letters admits its first female member: poet Julia Ward Howe.
- The Boston, Massachusetts, Watch and Ward Society launches a successful censorship campaign against author Elinor Glyn's novel *Three Weeks* which tells the story of a love affair.
- The English writer Arnold Bennett publishes his novel *The Old Wives' Tale.*
- The English writer E. M. Forster publishes his novel *A Room With a View.*
- The English writer G. K. Chesterton publishes his novel *The Man Who Was Thursday: A Nightmare.*
- The French writer Anatole France publishes his satirical novel *L'Ile des pingouins/Penguin Island.*
- The Scottish writer Kenneth Grahame publishes his children's novel *The Wind in the Willows.*
- The U.S. writer Jack London publishes his short story "To Build a Fire" in *Century Magazine.*
- The U.S. writer Upton Sinclair publishes his novels *The Moneychangers* and *The Metropolis.*
- The Welsh writer W. H. Davies publishes *Autobiography of a Super Tramp.*

Music

- The Austrian composer and conductor Gustav Mahler makes his debut at the New York Metropolitan Opera.

- The Austrian composer Anton Webern completes his orchestral work *Passacaglia* (Opus 1).
- The Austrian composer Alban Berg completes his Piano Sonata.
- The English composer Edward Elgar completes his Symphony No. 1.
- The French composer Claude Debussy completes his six piano pieces *Children's Corner*, which includes *Golliwog's Cake Walk*.
- The French composer Maurice Ravel completes his piano work *Gaspard de la nuit/Gaspard of the Night*.
- The operetta *Der tapfere Soldat/The Chocolate Soldier*, by the Austrian composer Oscar Straus, is first performed, at the Theater-an-der-Wien, Vienna, Austria. It is based on the play *Arms and the Man* by the Irish writer G. B. Shaw.
- The Russian composer Alexander Scriabin completes his orchestral work *Poema ekstasa/Poem of Ecstasy*.
- The U.S. composer Charles Ives completes his orchestral work *The Unanswered Question, or A Contemplation of a Serious Matter*.
- U.S. songwriters Albert von Tilzer and Jack Norworth write the song "Take Me Out to the Ball Game."
- U.S. songwriters Nora Bayes and Jack Norworth write the song "Shine on, Harvest Moon."

Theater and Dance

- The play *L'Oiseau bleu/The Blue Bird*, by the Belgian writer Maurice Maeterlinck, is first performed, in Moscow, Russia.
- The play *Spöksonaten/The Ghost Sonata*, by the Swedish writer August Strindberg, is first performed, in Stockholm, Sweden.
- The play *What Every Woman Knows*, by the Scottish writer J. M. Barrie, is first performed in London, England.

Thought and Scholarship

- British-born U.S. psychologist William McDougall publishes *An Introduction to Social Psychology*, founding the school of social psychology.
- English colonial administrator Evelyn Baring, Earl of Cromer, publishes *Modern Egypt*.
- English jurist Frederic William Maitland's *The Constitutional History of England* is published posthumously.
- English political psychologist Graham Wallas publishes *Human Nature in Politics*.
- French archeologist Joseph Déchelette publishes the first volume of his *Manuel d'archéologie préhistorique, celtique et gallo-romaine/Manual of Prehistoric, Celtic, and Gallo-Roman Archeology*. The final volumes (completed by Albert Grenier) appear in 1934.
- French social philosopher Georges Sorel publishes *Réflexions sur la violence/Reflections on Violence*.
- The Nobel Prize for Literature is awarded to the German philosopher Rudolf Eucken.
- U.S. historian Abbott Lawrence Lowell publishes *The Government of England*.

- U.S. philosopher Josiah Royce publishes *The Philosophy of Loyalty*.
- U.S. statesman Thomas Woodrow Wilson publishes his *Constitutional Government in the United States*.

SOCIETY

Education

- The University of Alberta opens in Edmonton, Canada.
- The University of California opens at Davis, near Sacramento.
- The University of Missouri establishes the first journalism school in the United States.
- The University of the Philippines opens in Manila.

Everyday Life

- A study shows that 35% of German immigrants to the United States receive money or passenger tickets from relatives already in the United States.
- Monosodium glutamate is identified in Japan as a taste enhancer.
- Narrow skirts without petticoats, net stockings, and boned collars are popular styles in the United States.
- Smith Richardson relaunches Vicks VapoRub in the United States, with the slogan "Rub it on, sniff it in, it's good for you, it's made by Presbyterians."
- The electric toaster is introduced in the United States.
- The German company Rowenta launches the first commercial electric iron.
- The U.S. Eck Dynamo & Electric Co. produces the first oscillating electric fan.
- The U.S. Public Cup Vendor Co. develops an effective disposable paper drinking cup.

MAY

10 Mother's Day becomes institutionalized in Grafton, West Virginia, at the instigation of Anna Jarvis, in memory of her own mother. By next year, every state will celebrate Mother's Day on the second Sunday in May.

JULY

24 In Canada, near Quebec city, the Plains of Abraham (scene of British general James Wolfe's victory over the French in 1759) are dedicated as a national monument.

OCTOBER

1 Postage for mail from the United States to Great Britain is raised from 1 cent to 2 cents.

Media and Communication

- Mary Baker Eddy founds the *Christian Science Monitor* in Boston, Massachusetts.
- The English writer and critic Ford Madox Ford founds the literary journal *The English Review* in Britain.
- The Morse code for SOS is formally introduced as the international distress signal - three dashes, three dots, and three dashes.

BIRTHS & DEATHS

JANUARY

9   Simone de Beauvoir, French existentialist writer, philosopher, and feminist, born in Paris, France (–1986).

15 Edward Teller, Hungarian-born U.S. physicist who directed the development of the first hydrogen bomb, born in Budapest, Austria-Hungary.

18 Jacob Bronowski, Polish-born English mathematician and writer, born in Łódź, Poland (–1974).

22 Lev Davidovich Landau, Soviet physicist, born in Baku, Azerbaijan, Russian Empire (–1968).

26 Stephane Grapelli, French jazz musician and violinist, born in Paris, France (–1997).

FEBRUARY

6   Amintore Fanfani, prime minister of Italy five times during the 1950s, early 1960s, and early 1980s, born in Pieve Santo Stefano, Italy.

17 Geronimo, Apache Native American chief who fought the U.S. military during the 1870s and early 1880s, dies in Fort Sill, Oklahoma (78).

MARCH

5   Rex Harrison, English actor of stage and screen, born in Huyton, Lancashire, England (–1990).

6   Lou Costello (Louis Francis Cristillo), U.S. comedian, born in Paterson, New Jersey (–1959).

14 Maurice Merleau-Ponty, French phenomenologist philosopher, born in Rochefort, France (–1961).

23 Joan Crawford, U.S. motion picture actress, born in San Antonio, Texas (–1977).

25 David Lean, English film director who directed *The Bridge on the River Kwai*, *Lawrence of Arabia*, and *Dr Zhivago*, born in Croydon, Surrey, England (–1991).

31 Don Ameche (real name Dominic Felix Amici), U.S. actor, born in Kenosha, Wisconsin (–1993).

APRIL

5   Bette Davis, U.S. film actress, born in Lowell, Massachusetts (–1989).

5   Herbert von Karajan, Austrian orchestra and opera conductor, born in Salzburg, Austria (–1989).

22 Henry Campbell-Bannerman, British prime minister 1905–8, a Liberal, dies in London, England (71).

MAY

20 James Stewart, U.S. actor, born in Indiana, Pennsylvania (–1997).

23 John Bardeen, U.S. physicist who shared two Nobel Prizes for Physics, one for inventing the transistor (1956) and one for developing a theory of superconductivity (1972), born in Madison, Wisconsin (–1991).

26 Robert Morley, English actor and playwright, born Semley, Wiltshire, England (–1992).

28 Ian Fleming, English writer who created James Bond, secret agent OO7, born in London, England (–1964).

30 Hannes Alfvén, Swedish astrophysicist who shared the Nobel Prize for Physics in 1970 for his role in founding plasma physics, born in Norrköping, Sweden.

30 Hannes Olof Gösta Alfvén, Swedish astrophysicist who made fundamental contributions to the field of magnetohydrodynamics (MHD) and helped found plasma physics, born in Norrköping, Sweden (–1995).

JUNE

9   Luis Kutner, U.S. human rights activist who created Amnesty International, born in Chicago, Illinois (–1993).

21 Nikolay Rimsky-Korsakov, Russian composer, dies in Lyubensk, Russia (64).

24 Stephen Grover Cleveland, 22nd (1885–89) and 24th (1893–97) president of the United States, a Democrat, dies in Princeton, New Jersey (71).

JULY

2   Jean Sinclair, South African activist, founder of the antiapartheid Black Sash movement, born in Germiston, near Johannesburg, South Africa (–1996).

2   Thurgood Marshall, first black member of the U.S. Supreme Court, born in Baltimore, Maryland (–1993).

3   Joel Chandler Harris, U.S. author, creator of "Uncle Remus," dies in Atlanta, Georgia (59).

8   Nelson Rockefeller, vice president of the United States 1974–77 and governor of New York 1959–73, born in Bar Harbor, Maine (–1979).

22 Amy Vanderbilt, U.S. author of *Amy Vanderbilt's Complete Book of Etiquette* born in New York, New York (–1974).

26 Salvador Allende, Marxist president of Chile (1970–73), born in Valparaíso, Chile (–1973).

AUGUST

20 Kingsley Davis, U.S. sociologist who coined the terms "zero population growth" and "population explosion," born in Tuxedo, Texas.

22 Henri Cartier-Bresson, French photographer who helped establish photojournalism, born in Chanteloup, France.

25 Henri Becquerel, French physicist who discovered radioactivity, dies in Le Croisic, France (55).

27 Lyndon Baines Johnson, 36th president of the United States 1963–69, a Democrat, born in Gillespie County, Texas (–1973).

28 Roger Tory Peterson, U.S. ornithologist, known in Britain as the author of *A Field Guide to the Birds of Britain and Europe*, born in Jamestown, New York (–1996).

30 Lé Fini, French surrealist painter, born in Buenos Aires, Argentina (–1996).

31 William Saroyan, U.S. Pulitzer prizewinning playwright and novelist, born in Fresno, California (–1981).

OCTOBER

9   Jacques Tati, French film actor and director known for his comic pantomime acting, born in Pecq, France (–1982).

15 John Kenneth Galbraith, Canadian-born U.S. economist known for his liberal ideas, born in Iona Station, Ontario, Canada.

16 Enver Hoxha, Albanian prime minister (1946–54) and First Secretary of the Albanian Communist Party (1954–85), born in Gjirokastër, Albania (–1985).

24 Tuzo Wilson, Canadian geophysicist who developed the science of plate tectonics, born in Ottawa, Ontario, Canada (–1993).

NOVEMBER

14 Joe (Joseph Raymond) McCarthy, U.S. senator, who initiated an era of "McCarthyism" by making unsubstantiated claims of communist subversion about high-ranking government officials during the 1950s, born in Appleton, Wisconsin (–1957).

28 Claude Lévi-Strauss, French structuralist anthropologist, born in Brussels, Belgium.

DECEMBER

10 Olivier Messiaen, French composer and organist, born in Avignon, France (–1992).

11 Elliott Carter, U.S. composer who twice won the Pulitzer Prize for Music (1960 and 1973), born in New York, New York.

17 Willard Frank Libby, U.S. chemist who discovered the technique of radioactive carbon dating, born in Grand Valley, Colorado (–1980).

22 Giacomo Manzù, Italian sculptor, born in Bergamo, Italy (–1991).

28 Lew Ayres, U.S. actor, born in Minneapolis, Minnesota (–1996).

Religion

- Pope Pius X declares that the United States is no longer a missionary area.

NOVEMBER

- The Gideon Society, an interdenominational Christian society, begins distributing Bibles in hotel rooms in the United States.

Sports

- Colonel Matt Winn, founder of the American Turf Association, sets up a pari-mutuel betting system, which becomes the only legal betting medium in U.S. racing.

APRIL

27 The 4th Olympic Games open in London, England, attended by 2,305 competitors, 36 of whom are women, from 22 nations. Most events, including swimming, are staged at a new stadium at White City with capacity for 68,000 spectators.

JULY

- At the Olympic Games in London, England, John Taylor becomes the first black American to win an Olympic gold medal when he helps the United States to victory in the medley relay.

24 The U.S. runner Johnny Hayes wins the marathon at the Olympic Games in London, England. Dorando Pietri of Italy is first over the finishing line but he is disqualified for receiving help from officials after collapsing on the final stadium lap. In sympathy he is awarded a special gold cup by Queen Alexandra.

AUGUST

25 The first American Trotting Derby is held at Readville, Massachusetts. It is the first harness race in the United States to reach the $50,000 mark in prize money.

OCTOBER

31 The 4th Olympic Games close in London, England. Britain wins 56 gold medals; the United States, 23; Sweden, 8; France, 5; and Germany, Austria-Hungary, and Canada, 3 each.

DECEMBER

26 Jack Johnson of the United States becomes the first black fighter to win the World Heavyweight Boxing Championship, beating the defending champion, Tommy Burns of Canada, in 14 rounds in Sydney, Australia.

1909

POLITICS, GOVERNMENT, AND ECONOMICS

Business and Economics

- Filene's Automatic Bargain Basement retail store opens in Boston, Massachusetts.
- The Anglo-Persian Oil Company is formed when the British government buys William Knox D'Arcy's oil concession in Persia, which was granted by the shah of Persia in 1901.
- The U.S. food company Kraft, Inc. is founded as a wholesale cheese delivery company by James L. Kraft.

AUGUST

- The Philadelphia Mint issues the Lincoln penny, designed by sculptor Victor D. Brenner.

Human Rights

JANUARY

- U.S. reformers William English Walling, Mary White Ovington, and Dr. Henry Moskowitz meet in Walling's apartment in New York, New York, to discuss the formation of the National Association of Colored People (NAACP).

MARCH

25 Press censorship is imposed in Egypt to control the nationalists there.

JUNE

- The National Association for the Advancement of Colored People (NAACP) is formally established in New York, New York, as the National Committee for the Advancement of the Negro.

Politics and Government

- Mahatma Gandhi launches the Hind Swaraj or Indian Home Rule movement.
- The British security agencies MI5 and MI6 are founded in response to fears of German espionage.

- The International Office of Public Health is established in Paris, France. It is the ancestor of the World Health Organization (WHO).
- U.S. Congress establishes a zoning ordinance in Washington, D.C., prohibiting private construction of buildings exceeding 40m/130 feet high.

JANUARY

- President William Howard Taft recalls U.S. troops from Cuba. U.S. forces had occupied Cuba since September 1906.
1   The dismissal of Yuan Shikai and (on October 4) Chang Chih-Tung from Chinese government posts places the administration exclusively in Manchu hands.

FEBRUARY

- The United States's "Great White Fleet" of battleships and destroyers returns to Hampton Roads, Virginia, after circumnavigating the globe on a display mission.
8   Germany recognizes France's special interests in Morocco in return for economic concessions.
13   The grand vizier of the Ottoman Empire, Kiamil Pasha, is forced to resign by the Turkish nationalists, who now dominate the Ottoman parliament.
21   King Ferdinand I of Bulgaria visits Russia to obtain financial aid toward an indemnity required by the Ottoman Empire in exchange for Bulgarian independence.
26   The Ottoman Empire recognizes Austria's annexation of Bosnia and Herzegovina, and is paid compensation.

MARCH

2   The European powers intervene to prevent a Serbo-Austrian war over the disputed territory of Bosnia and Herzegovina.
4   William Howard Taft is inaugurated 27th president of the United States. Violent snowstorms and winds cause the transfer of the ceremony from outside the Capitol to the Senate chamber, and trains carrying 30,000 guests are held up in the snow.
12   British alarm at the growth of the German navy leads to the passage of a naval bill in which Britain declares that it will build two more battleships than Germany every year.
31   Serbia accepts the Austrian annexation of Bosnia-Herzegovina following the loss of Russian support (Russia is unprepared for war).

APRIL

- Approximately 30,000 Armenian civilians are massacred by Islamic extremists.
9   The European powers recognize Austria-Hungary's annexation of Bosnia and Herzegovina.
13   An army counterrevolution begins in Constantinople (modern Istanbul), Ottoman Empire, against the rule of the Young Turks, following agitation by the Islamic Mohammedan Union.
13   The Ottoman Empire recognizes Bulgarian independence.
19   The Ottoman army captures Constantinople from the First Army Corps, which has been in revolt since April 13.
27   The Young Turks depose the Ottoman sultan Abdul Hamid II because of his sympathy for the attempted counterrevolution. He is succeeded by his brother Mohammed V (–1918).

MAY

5   The Greek army forms a military league to press the government for much-needed reform of the armed forces and civil administration.
25   The British Parliament's Indian Councils Act gives greater powers to legislative councils, most of whose members are to be directly elected, and ensures the appointment of an Indian representative to the viceroy's executive council.

JULY

- The U.S. Senate submits the Sixteenth Amendment, providing for an income tax, to the states.
12   Forces led by Ali Kuli Khan, revolting against the reactionary shah of Persia, capture Tehran, Persia.
14   Bernhard von Bülow resigns as German chancellor because of disagreements with Kaiser Wilhelm II and the naval program, and is succeeded by Theobald von Bethmann Hollweg.
16   Mohammed Ali, shah of Persia, is deposed by the proliberal Bakhtiari chief, Ali Kuli Khan, in favor of Sultan Ahmad Shah, aged 12.
24   Following the resignation of Georges Clemenceau in reaction to turbulence over his antistrike measures, the more moderate Aristide Briand forms a government in France.
28–September 26   A state of siege is declared in Barcelona, Spain, as strikes and riots break out throughout Catalonia in protest at conscription for the war in Morocco.

AUGUST

- The U.S. president William Howard Taft signs the Payne-Aldrich tariff, which retains high duties on foreign imports.

OCTOBER

13   Francisco Ferrer Guardia, leader of militant anticlericals in Spain, is executed following recent unrest.
21   A Liberal ministry under Segismundo Moret comes to power in Spain as King Alfonso XIII attempts to defuse public discontent.
24   Following the recent upheavals in the Balkan states, Russia and Italy sign the "Racconigi agreement," with a view to preserving the status quo in the region.
25   Prince Ito of Japan, the former Japanese resident in Korea, is assassinated by a Korean nationalist in Harbin, Manchuria.

NOVEMBER

- President William Howard Taft orders U.S. warships to Nicaragua, after Nicaraguan dictator José Santos Zelaya executes several hundred revolutionaries, including two Americans.
11   Germany and Britain discuss the control of the controversial Baghdad Railroad, continuing the debate into December.

DECEMBER

- Nicaraguan dictator, José Santos Zelaya, steps down, partly due to pressure brought to bear by U.S. armed forces, who have been supporting the Nicaraguan rebels.
2   The Italian prime minister Giovanni Giolitti resigns and Baron Sidney Sonnino forms a government of moderates.

12 Civil war breaks out in Honduras between the supporters of President Miguel Dávila and ex-president Manuel Bonilla, and continues until 1911.

17 Following the death of King Leopold II of Belgium, Albert I succeeds as king (–1934).

19 Juan Gómez seizes power in Venezuela, becoming dictator.

SCIENCE, TECHNOLOGY, AND MEDICINE

Ecology

- The U.S. Congress creates the National Bison Refuge outside Moise, Montana.

JULY

30 Earthquakes cause a huge amount of damage in Mexico, destroying the city of Acapulco.

AUGUST

- Seattle, Washington, hosts the first National Conservation Congress, representing 37 states.

SEPTEMBER

- President William Howard Taft declares 12,140 sq km/3 million acres of Western lands to be off-limits to private development.

NOVEMBER

13 An explosion and fire in a coal mine at Cherry, Illinois, kills about 250 miners.

Health and Medicine

- French bacteriologist Charles-Jules-Henri Nicolle discovers that typhus is transmitted by the body louse.
- Swiss physiologist Emil Kocher receives the Nobel Prize for Physiology or Medicine for his work on the physiology, pathology, and surgery of the thyroid gland.
- Walter Reed Army Medical Center opens in Washington, D.C.

Math

- French mathematician Jules Henri Poincaré publishes *Science et méthode/Science and Method*.

Science

- Croatian physicist Andrija Mohorovičić discovers the Mohorovičić discontinuity in the earth's crust. Located about 30 km/18 mi below the surface, it forms the boundary between the crust and the mantle.
- Danish biochemist Søren Sørensen devises the pH scale for measuring acidity and alkalinity.
- Danish botanist Wilhelm Ludvig Johannsen introduces the term "gene."
- Dutch physicist Hendrik Lorentz publishes *The Theory of Electrons and its Applications to the Phenomena of Light and Radiant Heat*, in which he unifies the theories of electricity in terms of electrons.

- English astronomer John Evershed discovers that gases radiate from the centers of sunspots.
- English biologist William Bateson publishes *Mendel's Principles of Genetics*, which introduces Mendelian genetics to the English-speaking world.
- German botanist Carl Correns shows that certain hereditary characteristics of plants are determined by factors in the cytoplasm of the female sex cell. It is the first example of non-Mendelian heredity.
- German chemist Friedrich Ostwald wins the Nobel Prize for Chemistry for his work on catalysis, chemical, equilibrium, and reaction velocities.
- German chemist Karl Hofmann produces synthetic rubber from butadiene.
- German physicist Albert Einstein introduces his idea that light exhibits both wave and particle characteristics.
- Russian-born U.S. chemist Phoebus Levene discovers D-ribose, the five-carbon sugar that forms the basis of RNA.

Technology

- French chemist Edouard Bénédictus patents safety glass, which does not shatter when broken.
- German physicist Karl Braun and Italian physicist Guglielmo Marconi share the Nobel Prize for Physics for their development of wireless telegraphy.
- U.S. firm Corona introduces the portable typewriter.

Transportation

- Brazilian-born French aviator Alberto Santos-Dumont makes "Demoiselle" and "Grasshopper" monoplanes. They are the forerunners of the modern light airplane.
- The Anonima Lombarda Fabbrica Automobila company is formed in Milan, Italy. Following a move to Rome, this will become the Alfa-Romeo car company.
- U.S. inventor Elmer Ambrose Sperry uses a gyroscope to construct the first automatic pilot for airplanes.

November 1909–10   Russian engineer Igor Sikorsky builds two 25-horsepower helicopters. Both manage to achieve lift-off but Sikorsky is unable to control them.

JULY

- The U.S. Army's first airplane, *Airplane No. 1*, is bought from the Wright brothers. Wilbur Wright establishes the U.S. Army's first flying school.

25 French aviator Louis Blériot crosses the English Channel by monoplane in 37 minutes from Le Boraques, France, to Dover, England.

ARTS AND IDEAS

Architecture

- The AEG Turbine Factory in Berlin, Germany, designed by the German architect Peter Behrens, is completed. It is one of the first steel and glass buildings.

- The David B. Gamble House, designed by the U.S. architects Charles Sumner Greene and Henry Mather Greene, is completed in Pasadena, California.
- The School of Art, designed by the Scottish architect Charles Rennie Mackintosh, is completed in Glasgow, Scotland. It is one of the most original art nouveau buildings in Britain.
- The Tietz Department Store in Düsseldorf, Germany, designed by the Austrian architect Joseph Maria Olbricht, is completed.

Arts

- The American Federation of Arts, a nonprofit visual arts society which organizes traveling exhibitions, is founded.
- The Dutch-born English artist Lawrence Alma-Tadema paints *A Favourite Custom*.
- The French artist Auguste Rodin sculpts *Bust of Gustav Mahler* and *Torso of a Young Woman*.
- The French artist Georges Braque paints *Violin and Palette*.
- The German artist Emil Nolde paints *The Last Supper*.
- The Italian artist Gino Severini paints *The Boulevard*.
- The Italian writer and publicist Filippo Tommaso Marinetti publishes "First Futurist Manifesto" in the French newspaper *Le Figaro*. This launches the Futurist movement in the visual arts.
- The Norwegian artist Edvard Munch paints *Self-Portrait in Blue Suit*.
- The Russian artist Wassily Kandinsky paints *Mountain*.
- The Spanish artist Pablo Picasso sculpts *Woman's Head*.
- The U.S. artist George B. Luks paints *Roundhouses at Highbridge*.
- The Victoria and Albert Museum in South Kensington, London, England, is opened. Its collection of arts and crafts is one of the finest in the world.
- U.S. sociologist Lewis Hein takes *Carrying-In Boy*, one of the best-known images of a range of his photographs, to highlight the working conditions of the U.S. poor.

MARCH
- The U.S. Congress passes a new copyright law, effective July 1, extending copyright protection to authors, artists, and playwrights.

Film

- *Gertie the Dinosaur*, one of the first animated movies, is released in the United States. It features more than 10,000 drawings, by the U.S. cartoonist Winsor Mackay, who works for the *New York American*.
- The documentary *The Ranch Life in the Great Southwest* is released in the United States, directed by Francis Boggs.
- The movie *Friends* is released, starring Lionel Barrymore and directed by D. W. Griffith.
- The movie *The Death of Ivan the Terrible*, directed by Vassili Goncharov, is released in Russia.
- The movie *The Lonely Villa*, directed by D. W. Griffith, is released in the United States.
- The French movie executive Charles Pathé aims to counter the virtual monopoly of the Eastman Kodak Co. in the manufacture of film by building a factory in Vincennes, France, to produce his own film stock.

- The French movie company Pathé Frères introduce the *Pathé-Journal*, a weekly movie newsreel. It is the first generally distributed newsreel.
- U.S. movie director D. W. Griffith works with Canadian-born child actress Gladys Smith, and helps transform her into Mary Pickford, one of the first great movie stars, who comes to be known as "America's Sweetheart." Their first movie together is *The Violin Maker of Cremona* (1909).

MARCH
- The National Board of Censorship of Motion Pictures is founded in the United States. There is no classification system for movies—they are either approved or cuts are recommended.

Literature and Language

- Journalist Herbert Croly, publishes *The Promise of American Life*, outlining a progressive political agenda.
- The English writer H. G. Wells publishes his novel *Tono-Bungay*.
- The French writer André Gide publishes his novel *La Porte Etroite/Strait is the Gate*.
- The French writer Guillaume Apollinaire publishes his poetry collection *L'Enchanteur pourrissant/The Rotting Magician*.
- The Swiss writer Robert Walser publishes his novel *Jakob von Gunten*.
- The U.S. writer Ellen Glasgow publishes her novel *The Romance of a Plain Man*.
- The U.S. writer Ezra Pound publishes his poetry collections *Personae* and *Exultations*.
- The U.S. writer Gertrude Stein publishes her prose work *Three Lives*.
- The U.S. writer Jack London publishes his autobiographical novel *Martin Eden*.
- The U.S. writer Vachel Lindsay publishes his poetry collection *The Tramp's Excuse*.

Music

- U.S. musical instrument manufacturers build 177,000 pianos.
- The Austrian composer Arnold Schoenberg completes his work for voice and orchestra *Erwartung/Expectation*.
- The Austrian composer Gustav Mahler completes his song-symphony *Das Lied von der Erde/The Song of the Earth*, set to poems translated from Chinese.
- The English composer Ralph Vaughan Williams completes his song cycle, *On Wenlock Edge*, inspired by the poems of A. E. Housman, and his Symphony No. 1, *A Sea Symphony*.
- The English composer Arnold Bax completes his orchestral work *In the Faery Hills*.
- The Finnish composer Jean Sibelius completes his string quartet *Voces Intimae/Friendly Voices*.
- The Hungarian composer Béla Bartók completes his String Quartet No. 1.
- The Italian composer Ferruccio Busoni completes his orchestral work *Berceuse élégiaque/Elegiac Berceuse*.
- The opera *Elektra/Electra*, by the German composer Richard Strauss, is first performed in Dresden, Germany.

It premieres both in New York, New York, and in London, England, in 1910.

- The opera *Zolotoy petushok/The Golden Cockerel*, by the Russian composer Nikolay Rimsky-Korsakov, is first performed in Moscow, Russia.
- The Russian composer Sergey Rachmaninov completes his symphonic poem *Ostrov myortvykh/Isle of the Dead*, inspired by an 1880 painting by the Swiss artist Arnold Böcklin, and his Piano Concerto No. 3.
- The Spanish composer Isaac Albéniz completes his piano suite *Iberia*. It is published in four volumes.
- The U.S. composer Charles Ives completes his *Studies* for piano, including *The Anti-Abolitionist Riots* and *Baseball Take-Off*, and his Piano Sonata No. 1.
- U.S. composer Bennett Scott and U.S. lyricist A. J. Mills write the song "Ship Ahoy," also known as "All the Nice Girls Love a Sailor."
- U.S. songwriters Eddie Newton and T. Lawrence Weibert write the song "Casey Jones."
- U.S. songwriters Gus Edwards and Edward Madden write the song "By the Light of the Silvery Moon."
- U.S. songwriters Joseph E. Howard and Frank R. Adams write the song "I Wonder Who's Kissing Her Now."
- W. C. Handy writes the song "Memphis Blues," originally intended to be an electioneering song called "Mr. Crump" for Memphis mayoral candidate E. H "Boss" Crump.

Theater and Dance

- The English writer D. H. Lawrence writes his play *A Collier's Friday Night*. It is first performed in 1965 at the Royal Court Theatre in London, England.
- The play *Strife*, by the English writer John Galsworthy, is first performed in London, England.
- The play *The City*, by the U.S. dramatist Clyde Fitch, is first performed in New York, New York.
- The Russian impressario Sergei Diaghilev presents a season of Russian opera and ballet in Paris, France. It is from this initiative that the Ballets Russes develops.

SEPTEMBER

4 The play *The Fortune Hunter*, by the U.S. dramatist Winchell Smith, is first performed, in New York, New York.

Thought and Scholarship

- English economist John Atkinson Hobson publishes *The Crisis of Liberalism*.
- Italian philosopher Benedetto Croce publishes *Logica come scienza del concetto puro/Logic as the Science of Pure Concept*.
- Russian revolutionary leader Vladimir Ilyich Lenin publishes *Materializm i empiriokrititsizm/Materialism and Empiric Criticism*.
- The Nobel Prize for Literature is awarded to the Swedish novelist Selma Lagerlöf.
- U.S. philosopher William James publishes *The Meaning of Truth: A Sequel to "Pragmatism"*.

SOCIETY

Education

- Reed College opens in Portland, Oregon.

Everyday Life

- Americans consume more than 30 million gallons of ice cream.
- The Austrian Count von Welsbach invents the first gasoline-fueled, wheel-driven cigarette lighter.
- The British confectioner William Cadbury publishes *Labour in Portuguese West Africa*, advocating a boycott on Portuguese cocoa because of the terrible working conditions there.
- The increasing cost of living in the United States is resulting in people having smaller families.
- The U.S. firm General Electric introduces the first electric toaster.

MARCH

15 The U.S. businessman H. G. Selfridge opens the first modern department store in Britain, Selfridge's in London, England, using the slogan, "All your shopping under one roof."

APRIL

4 Postal workers strike in Paris, France, over the right of civil servants to affiliate with the Confédération Générale du Travail (Labor Union Association), continuing until May.

AUGUST

4 A general strike is called in Sweden over wages and working conditions.

NOVEMBER

- 20,000 U.S. members of the International Ladies' Garment Workers Union strike for higher wages and better working conditions.

Religion

- Russian and Polish Jews set up the first kibbutz, Degania, at Lake Kinnaret, Tiberias, in Palestine.

Sports

- A commission set up by sports goods manufacturer A. G. Spalding to investigate the origins of baseball asserts that the game is of U.S. origin, not, as it had been claimed, derived from the English game of rounders, and that it was founded by Abner Doubleday in 1839 at Cooperstown, New York. However, a pamphlet written by a librarian from the New York Public Library finds a reference to "baseball" in a children's book published in England in 1744 and twice reprinted in the United States in the 18th century, and other evidence, exposes what becomes known as the "Doubleday myth."
- Luigi Ganna of Italy wins the first Giro d'Italia (Tour of Italy) bicycle stage race. Forty-nine of the 127 starters complete the 2,448-km/1,521-mi course.

BIRTHS & DEATHS

c. 1909   Sundance Kid (nickname of Harry Longarbaugh), U.S. train and bank robber, dies near San Vicente, Bolivia (about 39).

JANUARY

3   Victor Borge, Danish-born U.S. entertainer, born in Copenhagen, Denmark.

6   George Dixon, U.S. bantamweight boxer and the first black person to win a boxing championship, dies in New York, New York (38).

14   Joseph Losey, U.S. film director, born in La Crosse, Wisconsin (–1984).

22   U Thant, Burmese educator and civil servant, secretary-general of the United Nations 1961–71, born in Pantanaw, Burma (now Myanmar) (–1974).

FEBRUARY

9   Dean Rusk, U.S. secretary of state under Kennedy and Johnson, born in Cherokee county, Georgia (–1994).

11   Joseph L(eo) Mankiewicz, U.S. filmmaker, born in Wilkes Barre, Pennsylvania (–1993).

MARCH

1   David Niven, English film actor, novelist, and author of popular anecdotal memoirs, born in Kirriemuir, Angus, Scotland (–1983).

4   Harry Helmsley, U.S. property tycoon who buys the Empire State Building in 1961, born in New York, New York (–1997).

19   Otto John, German secret agent who is involved in the plot to kill Hitler, born in Marburg, Germany (–1997).

24   Clyde Barrow, U.S. bank robber along with Bonnie Parker, born in Telico, Texas (–1934).

28   Nelson Algren, U.S. novelist and travel writer whose best-known novel *The Man with the Golden Arm* (1949) won the National Book Award and was filmed in 1956, born in Detroit, Michigan (–1981).

APRIL

5   Albert R. Broccoli, U.S. film producer who produced the James Bond films, born in New York, New York (–1996).

10   Algernon Charles Swinburne, English poet and critic, dies in Putney, London, England (71).

15   Arthur Tracy, Royal biographer who writes biographies of the queen, queen mother, prince of Wales, and others, under the pen name Helen Cathcart, born in London, England (–1997).

21   Rollo Reece May, U.S. psychologist who pioneered existential psychology, born in Ada, Ohio (–1994).

30   Juliana, Queen of the Netherlands (1948–80), born in The Hague, the Netherlands.

MAY

1   Kate Smith, U.S. singer known for singing "God Bless America," born in Greenville, Virginia (–1986).

7   Edwin Herbert Land, U.S. physicist who developed the Polaroid camera, an instantaneous one-step process for developing and printing photographs, born in Bridgeport Connecticut (–1991).

9   Gordon Bunshaft, U.S. architect who introduced the International Style to corporate architecture, born in Buffalo, New York (–1990).

15   James Mason, English film actor who often portrayed villains, born in Huddersfield, Yorkshire, England (–1984).

16   Luigi Viloresi, Italian race car driver, born in Milan, Italy (–1997).

18   Fred (Frederick John) Perry, English lawn-tennis player who dominated men's singles tennis in the mid-1930s and was the last Briton to win the men's singles at Wimbledon, in 1936, born in Stockport, Cheshire, England (–1995).

30   Benny Goodman, U.S. jazz and classical clarinetist and orchestra leader in the Swing era of the 1930s and 1940s, born in Chicago, Illinois (–1986).

JUNE

6   Isaiah Berlin, Latvian-born British political philosopher, born in Riga, Latvia (–1997).

7   Jessica Tandy, British-born U.S. actress, is born in London, England (–1994).

14   Burl Ives, U.S. actor and folk singer, born in Hunt, Illinois (–1995).

20   Errol Flynn, Australian-born U.S. actor known for his swashbuckling films, born in Hobart, Tasmania, Australia (–1959).

24   William Penny, British physicist who developed Britain's first atomic bomb, born in Gibraltar (–1991).

JULY

11   Simon Newcomb, Canadian-born U.S. astronomer and mathematician who constructed tables giving the daily positions of celestial bodies, dies in Washington, D.C. (74).

13   Prince Souphanouvong, leader of the Laotian guerrilla organization Pathet Lao (Land of the Lao) and first president of the Republic of Laos, 1975–86, born in Luang Prabang, Laos (–1995).

18   Andrey Andreyevich Gromyko, Soviet foreign minister (1957–85) and president (1985–88), born in Starye Gromyki, Russia (–1989).

AUGUST

10   (Clarence) Leo Fender, U.S. guitarmaker who creates the solid-body electric guitar, born in Anaheim, California (–1991).

13   A(rthur) H(ilary) Armstrong, English classical scholar, born (–1997).

SEPTEMBER

9   Jane Baxter (originally Feodora Katherine Alice Forde), English film and stage actress, born in Bremen, Germany (–1996).

21   Kwame Nkrumah, West African nationalist politician, the first prime minister of independent Ghana, then president 1957–66, born in Nkroful, Gold Coast (–1972).

OCTOBER

4   Zhang Zhidong, Chinese reformer who tried to modernize China, dies in China (72).

9   Donald Coggan, archbishop of Canterbury 1974–80, born in London, England.

13   Herbert Lawrence Block ("Herblock"), U.S. cartoonist who won a Pulitzer prize in 1942, 1954, and 1979, born in Chicago, Illinois.

26   Ito Hirobumi, premier of Japan (1885–88, 1892–96, 1898, and 1900–01) who helped to modernize Japan, is assassinated in Harbin, Manchuria, China (68).

26   Oliver O. Howard, Union general in the American Civil War, dies in Burlington, Vermont (78).

28   Francis Bacon, Irish-born English artist known for his macabre paintings, born in Dublin, Ireland (–1992).

DECEMBER

14   Edward L. Tatum, U.S. biochemist, pioneer in the field of molecular genetics, born in Boulder, Colorado (–1975).

- The Grey Cup is donated by the governor-general of Canada, Lord Grey, for the annual winner of the Rugby Football Championship of Canada. It is not until 1954 that the cup is awarded to the winner of the Canadian Football Championship.

JUNE

1–29 The first transcontinental automobile race, for the Guggenheim Trophy, held between New York, New York, and Seattle, Washington, is won by a Ford.

AUGUST

23 The U.S. newspaper proprietor James Gordon Bennett organizes the world's first aviation meeting at Reims, France, the centerpiece of which is the competition for the Gordon Bennett International Aviation Cup.

1910

POLITICS, GOVERNMENT, AND ECONOMICS

Business and Economics

- Nebraska entrepreneur Joyce Clyde Hall enters the greetings card business, laying the foundation for Hallmark, Inc., the most successful greetings cards manufacturer in the world.
- The Japanese engineer Namihei Odaira founds Hitachi Ltd., initially manufacturing electrical industrial machinery.
- The U.S. firm Fisher Brothers build the first enclosed car bodies—for Cadillac.
- U.S. entrepreneur A. C. Fuller incorporates the Fuller Brush Co.

JANUARY

- U.S. entrepreneur, Benjamin Biscoe, founds the United States Motor Company to compete with General Motors.

Colonization

JANUARY

15 Gabon is reorganized into new administrative districts as French Equatorial Africa.

AUGUST

22 Japan formally annexes Korea, having already secured political and military control of the Chinese fiefdom.

Human Rights

- Bert Williams is the first black American entertainer to receive equal billing with whites on Broadway when he joins the *Ziegfeld Follies*.

FEBRUARY

28 The last Chinese laborers leave the Rand diamond mines in South Africa, the slave-like conditions of their employment having created a furor throughout the British Empire.

APRIL

- The National Association for the Advancement of Colored People begins publishing its monthly journal *Crisis*, in the United States.

MAY

27 The Prussian diet (assembly) rejects an attempt to introduce a limited reform of suffrage.

Politics and Government

- The Royal Canadian Navy is formed.
- The U.S. Immigration Commission recommends restricting the immigration of unskilled workers.
- U.S. physician Dr. Hawley Harvey Crippen murders his second wife, Cora Turner, and dissects and buries her body at their home in London, England. Crippen plans to escape to Canada with his mistress and former secretary Ethel Le Neve, but is caught on board the SS *Montrose* after the suspicious captain contacts Scotland Yard (the first use of radio in catching criminals). Crippen is tried and hanged.

JANUARY

1 The Military League in Greece forces the Greek parliament and the king to summon a national assembly to undertake revision of the 1864 constitution. The Cretan Eleutherios Venizelos acts for the League in negotiations with political leaders.

FEBRUARY

20 Boutros Ghali, the first native prime minister of Egypt and a Christian Copt, is shot dead by a Muslim nationalist student.

22 A constitution for Bosnia and Herzegovina extends Austro-Hungarian civil rights to it, and establishes a diet and a presidency which is to be rotated annually between Serb, Croat, and Muslim delegates.

MARCH

- President William Howard Taft sends 20,000 U.S. troops to the U.S.–Mexican border to prevent the Mexican revolution from spilling over onto U.S. territory.
- The U.S. Congress amends the Immigration Act of 1907. The new law adds criminals, paupers, anarchists, and the sick to the list of unwanted immigrants.
- 3   Luigi Luzzatti succeeds Baron Sidney Sonnino as Italian prime minister when the government is defeated over the awarding of shipping contracts.
- 19 The "Insurgent" Republicans in the U.S. House of Representatives, in a revolt against the Speaker "Czar" Joe Cannon, reduce the Speaker's customary power to appoint members of committees and control business, by rejecting a nominee to the Rules Committee and passing legislation providing for the election of the House Rules Comittee.
- 31 The Military League in Greece proclaims its dissolution in return for the convocation of a national assembly.

APRIL

- President William Howard Taft appoints New York governor, Charles Evans Hughes, to the U.S. Supreme Court.
- 4   A revolt in the Ottoman possession of Albania is suppressed by the Ottoman army.
- 27 Louis Botha and James Hertzog found the South African Party, which advocates the union of the South African colonies.

MAY

- 6   King Edward VII of Great Britain and Ireland dies at Buckingham Palace, London, England, after a brief illness, and is succeeded by George V.
- 14 A British–Belgian agreement assigns the west shore of Lake Albert to the Belgian Congo.
- 21 French forces advancing through Morocco occupy Fez.
- 24 The pro-British Leander Starr Jameson founds the Unionist Party in South Africa, which supports continuing links between South Africa and the British Empire.

JUNE

- The U.S. Congress passes the Mann-Elkins Act which brings telephone and telegraph traffic under federal jurisdiction as interstate commerce.
- The U.S. Senate authorizes the territories of Arizona and New Mexico to adopt state constitutions and governments in preparation for statehood.
- U.S. Congress passes the Mann White Slave Traffic Act which bans the interstate transportation or national importation of women destined for prostitution.

JULY

- 1   By an act of the British Parliament the Union of South Africa becomes a dominion, an independent country remaining within the British Empire.
- 4   Russia and Japan agree to maintain the status quo in Manchuria and Korea.

AUGUST

- 8   An Austro-Hungarian commercial treaty with Serbia partially repairs relations between the two countries following their dispute over Bosnia and Herzegovina.
- 21 The Greek National Assembly meets for the first time.

28 Montenegro is proclaimed a kingdom independent of the Ottoman Empire under Nicholas I.

31 Former president Theodore Roosevelt delineates his New Nationalism at a speech in Osawatomie, Kansas, advocating tariff revision and greater federal control of working conditions. Roosevelt is apparently positioning himself for another run for the presidency in 1912.

SEPTEMBER

7   The International Court of Arbitration at The Hague, the Netherlands, settles the dispute between Britain and the United States over the Newfoundland fisheries, which was referred to the court in October 1906.

15 The South African Party wins the first South African elections and Louis Botha becomes prime minister.

OCTOBER

4   King Manuel II of Portugal flees to England as revolution breaks out in Lisbon, Portugal.

5   Portugal is proclaimed a republic under Theophila Braga, following the deposition of King Manuel II.

18 The nationalist Eleutherios Venizelos becomes prime minister of Greece and begins financial reforms.

NOVEMBER

- An amendment to the Washington state constitution provides for women's suffrage.
- In U.S. Congressional elections, Democrats attain their first majority in the House (228–162), since 1894. Republicans retained a 51–41 majority.
- 4–5 Czar Nicholas II of Russia meets German Kaiser Wilhelm II at Potsdam, Germany, and agrees to drop his opposition to the Baghdad Railroad on condition that Russia is given a free hand in northern Persia.

DECEMBER

11 The supporters of the Greek prime minister Eleutherios Venizelos win 300 seats out of the available 364 in the elections for the national assembly in Greece.

12 In the British general election the Liberals win 272 seats, Labour win 42 seats, the Irish Nationalists win 84, and the Unionists 272. This gives a majority of 126 seats for a Parliament Bill and Home Rule, an increase of 4 since the January election.

23 The Liberal prime minister of Spain, José Canalejas, encourages the passing of a law banning the founding of religious orders without government permission.

SCIENCE, TECHNOLOGY, AND MEDICINE

Ecology

- Glacier National Park, Montana, is established. Covering 4,102 sq km/1,584 sq mi it contains several active glaciers.
- Rainbow Bridge National Park, Utah, is established; it contains a salmon-pink sandstone bridge 94 m/309 ft high, the largest natural bridge in the world.
- The U.S. Congress creates Glacier National Park from more than a 4,047 sq km/1 million acres of Montana wilderness.

APRIL

23 A cold snap in the Midwest destroys $30 million in crops and property.

Health and Medicine

- German bacteriologist Paul Ehrlich discovers "Salvarsan," the first specific antibacterial agent. It is used to treat syphilis.
- German biochemist Albrecht Kossel receives the Nobel Prize for Physiology or Medicine for his work on proteins, including the nucleic substances.
- The first health centers in the United States open in Pittsburgh and Wilkes-Barre, Pennsylvania. Others open soon afterwards in New York, New York (1913), Boston, Massachusetts (1916), and Philadelphia, Pennsylvania (1916).
- U.S. educator and physician Abraham Flexner publishes *Medical Education in the United States and Canada*. Based on a survey of 155 medical colleges in the United States and Canada, it reports that medical education is totally inadequate compared to Europe, with the exception of Johns Hopkins University in Baltimore, Maryland. It results in over $600 million being spent to improve medical education over the next few years.
- U.S. physician James Herrick is the first to describe the genetic disease sickle-cell anemia.

Science

- Dutch physicist Johannes van der Waals receives the Nobel Prize for Physics for his work on the equation of state for gases and liquids.
- English physicist J. J. Thomson discovers the proton.
- Polish-born French chemist Marie Curie publishes *Treatise on Radiography*, outlining her ideas about radioactivity.
- French chemists Marie Curie and A. Diebierne isolate radium.
- French engineer and chemist Georges Claude proposes that liquid oxygen be used for smelting iron. It is not adopted until the late 1940s.
- German chemist Otto Wallach receives the Nobel Prize for Chemistry for alicyclic compounds.
- German physicist Wolfgang Gaede develops the molecular vacuum pump, which can generate a vacuum of 0.00001 mm of mercury.
- Swedish physicist Nils Dalén designs an automatic sun valve to regulate a gaslight by the action of sunlight, turning it off at sunrise and on at sunset. It gains widespread use in uncrewed lighthouses and buoys.
- French physicist Georges Claude develops neon lighting when he discovers that the gas emits light when an electric current is passed through it. As it is initially only possible to produce red lighting, its potential is mainly restricted to advertising.
- U.S. geneticist Thomas Hunt Morgan discovers that certain inherited characteristics of the fruit fly *Drosophila melanogaster* are sex linked. He later argues that because all sex-related characteristics are inherited together they are linearly arranged on the X-chromosome.

MAY

19 Halley's comet—which comes near the earth roughly every 75 years—returns, with the earth passing through the comet's tail. In the United States, it is regarded by some as announcing the end of the world. "Comet Pills," allegedly an antidote to the poisonous gases thought to be in the comet's tail, also sell well.

Technology

- French chemist Louis Dufay makes an additive-color film using tiny red, green, and blue elements under the photographic emulsion.
- German chemical company Bayer manufactures synthetic rubber, developed by German chemist Karl Hofmann.
- Swedish firm Svenska Kullager Fabriken (SKF) (Swedish Ball Bearing Factory) produces the first roller bearings.
- The British company Bowden Co. creates the cycle dynamo.

JUNE

30 U.S. aviator Glenn Curtiss experiments with the first bombs dropped from an aircraft—dummies that he drops on a ship.

Transportation

- Part of the Magdeburg–Halle mainline railroad in Germany is electrified.
- Swiss railroads are nationalized.
- The Grande Semaine d'Aviation is held at Reims, France. It is the first great aviation meet.

OCTOBER

22–31 A new altitude record of 2,960 m/9,700 ft and speed record of 98 kph/68 mph are set at the air show at Belmont Park, New York, New York.

NOVEMBER

14 U.S. pilot Eugene Ely is the first person to take off from a ship—from a platform constructed on the cruiser *Birmingham*.

ARTS AND IDEAS

Architecture

- Manhattan Bridge in New York, New York, is opened.
- The Casa Milá, an apartment block in Barcelona, Spain, designed by the Spanish architect Antonio Gaudí, is completed.
- The Steiner House in Vienna, Austria, designed by the Austrian architect Adolf Loos, is completed.

Arts

c. 1910 The U.S. artist Albert Pinkham Ryder paints *The Race Track (Death on a Pale Horse)*.

c. 1910   The U.S. artist Arthur B. Carles paints *L'Eglise*.

- The exhibition "Manet and the Postimpressionists" is held at the Grafton Galleries in London, England. Organized by the English art critic Roger Fry (who coined the term "postimpressionist"), it has a major impact on the development of British art.
- The French artist Fernand Léger paints *Nudes in the Forest*.
- The French artist Georges Braque paints *Violin and Pitcher*.
- The French artist Henri Matisse paints *The Dance*.
- The French artist Henri Rousseau paints *The Dream*.
- The French artist Odilon Redon paints *Portrait of Mademoiselle Violette Heymann*.
- The French artist Robert Delaunay paints *The Eiffel Tower*, the first of a series on this subject.
- The German artist Erich Heckel paints *Franzi with Doll*.
- The German artist Ernst Kirchner paints *Nude Behind a Curtain*.
- The Italian artist Umberto Boccioni paints *Riot in the Galleria* and *The City Rises*.
- The Russian artist Kasimir Malevich paints *The Woodcutter*.
- The Spanish artist Pablo Picasso paints *Portrait of Ambroise Vollard* and *Portrait of D. H. Kahnweiler*.
- The Swiss-born French artist Félix Vallotton paints *Nude on a Red Carpet*.
- The U.S. artist Abraham Walkowitz paints *Bathers*.
- The U.S. artist John Marin paints *Brooklyn Bridge*.
- The U.S. artist Maurice Prendergast paints *Central Park*.
- The U.S. artist William Glackens paints *Nude with Apple*.

Film

- As the studios recognize the drawing power of actors such as Florence Lawrence, movies start to be sold on the strength of the names of the stars.
- Nickelodeons attract some 20% of the population each week in the United States.
- The Cinematograph Act is passed in Britain, aiming to establish safety measures in movie theaters, where the highly flammable film poses a constant risk.
- The movie *Broncho Billy's Redemption* is released in the United States by Essanay Company, starring G. M. Anderson.
- The movie *Frankenstein*, an adaptation of the novel by Mary Shelley, written and directed by J. Searle Dawley, is released in the United States by Edison Studios, starring Charles Ogle.
- The movie *In Neighbouring Kingdoms*, is released, starring John Bunny.
- The movie *The Abyss*, directed by Peter Urban Gad, is released in Denmark, starring Asta Nielsen.
- The movie *Werther*, directed by Henri Pouctal, is released in France. Based on the work by Goethe, it stars André Brulé.
- The French movie company Pathé Frères introduce the *Pathé-Gazette*, a weekly movie newsreel, in Britain and the United States.
- The Gaumont-Palace opens in Paris, France, the first of the great "picture palaces" and one of the first movie

theaters with facilities to give continuous showing of multireel movies.

JULY
2   Fire destroys the Vitagraph studios, along with many negatives, in New York, New York.
20   The Christian Endeavor Society of Missouri launches a crusade to ban movies showing kissing between unmarried couples.

Literature and Language

- The English writer Arnold Bennett publishes *Clayhanger*, the first volume of his Clayhanger trilogy.
- The English writer E. M. Forster publishes his novel *Howards End*.
- The English writer Henry Newbolt publishes his collection of verse, *Songs of the Fleet*.
- The English writer H. G. Wells publishes his novel *The History of Mr Polly*.
- The French writer Charles Péguy publishes his long poem *Le Mystère de la charité de Jeanne d'Arc/The Mystery of the Charity of St. Joan of Arc*.
- The French writer Paul Claudel publishes his poetry collection *Cinq grandes odes/Five Great Odes*.
- The German writer Gerhart Hauptmann publishes his novel *Der Narr in Christo Emanuel Quint/The Fool in Christ Emanuel Quinto*.
- The German writer Hermann Hesse publishes his novel *Gertrud*.
- The German writer Rainer Maria Rilke publishes his novel *Die Aufzeichnungen des Malte Laurids Brigge/The Notebooks of Malte Laurids Brigge*.
- The Indian writer Rabindranath Tagore publishes his Bengali poetry collection *Gitanjali/Song Offering*.
- The Japanese writer Junichiro Tanizaki publishes his short story "Shisei"/"Tattoo."
- The U.S. writer Edwin Arlington Robinson publishes his poetry collection *The Town down the River*, which includes one of his best-known poems, "Miniver Cheevy."
- The U.S. writer O. Henry publishes his short-story collection *Strictly Business*.

Music

- The Austrian composer Alban Berg completes his String Quartet (Opus 3).
- The Austrian composer Anton Webern completes his *6 Stücke/6 Pieces* for orchestra (Opus 6).
- The Austrian composer Gustav Mahler completes his Symphony No. 9.
- The Danish composer Carl Nielsen completes his *Ved en ung kunstners baare/At the Bier of a Young Artist* for string quartet.
- The English composer Ralph Vaughan Williams completes his orchestral work *Fantasia on a Theme of Thomas Tallis*.
- The English composer Samuel Coleridge-Taylor completes his *Petite Suite de Concert*.
- The French composer Claude Debussy completes his piano work *Préludes I* for piano.
- The French composer Maurice Ravel completes his orchestral work *Pavane pour une infante défunte/Pavan*

for a Dead Infanta, based on a piano work of 1899, and his work for two pianos *Ma Mère l'oye/Mother Goose*, which he orchestrates in 1911 and turns into a ballet in 1912.

- The Italian composer Ferruccio Busoni completes his piano work *Fantasia contrappuntistica/Contrapuntal Fantasia*, based on keyboard works by Bach.
- The opera *Königskinder/The King's Children* by the German composer Engelbert Humperdinck is first performed, at the Metropolitan opera House, New York, New York.
- The opera *La fanciulla del West/The Girl of the Golden West* by the Italian composer Giacomo Puccini is first performed in New York, New York.
- The revised version of the opera *Königskinder/The King's Children*, by the German composer Engelbert Humperdinck, is first performed in New York, New York.
- The Russian composer Alexander Scriabin completes his symphonic poem *Prometheus – The Poem of Fire*.
- The Russian composer Sergey Rachmaninov completes his choral work *Liturgy of St. John Chrysostom* and his piano *Preludes* (Opus 32).
- U.S. songwriter Shelton Brooks writes the song "Some of These Days."
- U.S. songwriters Leo Friedman and Beth Slater Whitson write the song "Let Me Call You Sweetheart."

July 1910–11 The U.S. band conductor and composer John Philip Sousa and his band go on a world tour.

Theater and Dance

- The ballet *The Firebird*, by the Russian composer Igor Stravinsky and the Russian choreographer Mikhail Fokine, is first performed in Paris, France, under the Russian impressario Sergei Diaghilev.
- The English writer Thomas Hardy publishes the complete version of his verse drama *The Dynasts, A Drama of the Napoleonic Wars*.
- The Palladium Theatre opens in London, England. It will be popularly known as the London Palladium.
- The play *Deirdre of the Sorrows*, by the Irish writer John Millington Synge, is first performed in Dublin, Ireland.
- The play *Get-Rich-Quick Wallingford*, by U.S. dramatist and songwriter George M. Cohan, which satirizes Americans' fixation with fame and money, is first performed, in New York, New York.
- The play *Justice*, by the English writer John Galsworthy, is first performed in London, England.
- The play *The Madras House*, by the English actor and dramatist Harley Granville-Barker, is first performed in London, England.
- The tango dance craze catches on in the United States.

NOVEMBER

7 The musical *Naughty Marietta*, with music by Irish-born U.S. composer Victor Herbert and lyrics by Rida Johnson Young, is performed for the first time, at the New York Theater, New York, New York. Songs include "Ah, Sweet Mystery of Life."

Thought and Scholarship

- A booklet entitled *The Fundamentals: A Testimony to the Truth* gives birth to the modern Christian fundamentalist movement in the United States. The fundamentals are the Virgin birth, accuracy of Scriptures, the physical resurrection of Jesus Christ, vicarious atonement, and the second coming of Jesus Christ.
- English philosophers Bertrand Russell and Alfred North Whitehead publish the first volume of their three-volume *Principia Mathematica/Principles of Mathematics*. The last volume appears in 1913.
- English writer and pacifist Norman Angell publishes *The Great Illusion: A Study of the Relation of Military Power in Nations to their Economic and Social Advantage*.
- Italian educator Maria Montessori publishes *Antropologia pedagogica/Pedagogic Anthropology*.
- Scottish-born U.S. steel magnate Andrew Carnegie founds the Carnegie Endowment for International Peace, to conduct research into international law, economics, and history in order to advance international understanding.
- Swedish archeologist Gerhard de Geer publishes *A Geochronology of the Last 12,000 Years*, setting out his influential system for dating rock strata.
- The Nobel Prize for Literature is awarded to the German poet, novelist, and dramatist Paul von Heyse.
- U.S. archeologist Charles Pickering Bowditch publishes *The Numeration, Calendar Systems and Astronomical Knowledge of the Mayas*, a groundbreaking study of Mayan civilization.
- U.S. philosopher John Dewey publishes *How We Think*.
- U.S. philosopher William James publishes his essay "The Moral Equivalent of War."
- U.S. social reformer Jane Addams publishes *Twenty Years At Hull House*.

SOCIETY

Education

- Bowling Green State University opens in Bowling Green, Ohio.
- Kent State University opens in Kent, Ohio.

FEBRUARY

6 U.S. educator Dr. Luther Halsey Gulick and his wife Charlotte create the Camp Fire Girls of America.

6 U.S. illustrator Daniel ("Uncle Dan") Carter Beard establishes the Boy Scouts of America, based on a British prototype founded two years earlier.

Everyday Life

- 32,077,000 Americans live on farms, according to the U.S. Census Bureau.
- Elizabeth Arden opens her first beauty store, in New York, New York. She will later expand to create a chain of stores and a very successful range of cosmetics.

- English manufacturer Alfred Cohn launches the Cona coffee-maker in Britain.
- Gimbel's department store opens in New York, New York.
- Less than half the population over 25 in the United States has a high school education and just 4% are college graduates.
- Louis Diat, the chef at the Ritz-Carlton, New York, New York, invents vichyssoise soup.

- The British clothing company Burberry introduces the trench coat. Its name is acquired during the First World War, when a version for army officers is created.
- The German company Jas Ravenol Gesellschaft launches domestic bathroom scales.
- The synthetic fabric rayon is used in Germany for stockings, the first garment to be manufactured from it.
- The U.S. Census lists the population at 91,972,266.
- The U.S. company Hamilton Beach Manufacturing Co. launches the first electric food mixer.
- There are 2,600 daily newspapers in the United States.

BIRTHS & DEATHS

FEBRUARY
9 Jacques L. Monod, French biochemist who with Jacob François discovered regulator genes, born in Paris, France (–1976).
11 Carmine Galante, organized crime leader in New York, New York, for over 30 years, born in New York, New York (–1979).
13 William B. Shockley, U.S. physicist who was instrumental in the development of the transistor, born in London, England (–1989).

MARCH
9 Samuel Barber, U.S. composer, born in West Chester, Pennsylvania (–1981).
12 Masayoshi Ohira, Japanese prime minister 1978–80, born in Toyohama, Japan (–1980).
23 Akira Kurosawa, Japanese film director, born in Tokyo, Japan (–1998).
27 Ai Qing, Chinese poet, born in Zheihang province, China (–1996).

APRIL
11 Marshall Antonio de Spínola, president of Portugal whose book *Portugal and the Future*, published in 1974, sparks the revolution against the dictatorship which brings him to power and eventually restores democracy, born in Estremoz, Portugal (–1996).
21 Mark Twain (pseudonym of Samuel Langhorne Clemens), U.S. author who created the characters Tom Sawyer and Huckleberry Finn, dies in Redding, Connecticut (74).
26 Tomoyuki Tanaki, Japanese film producer, creator of the movie monster Godzilla, born in Osaka, Japan (–1997).

MAY
6 Edward VII, King of Great Britain and Ireland 1901–10, dies in London, England (68).
12 Dorothy Hodgkin (born Dorothy Crowfoot), English chemist who determined the structure of vitamin B12, born in Cairo, Egypt (–1994).

27 Robert Koch, German physician who discovered the bacilli responsible for tuberculosis and cholera, and founded the science of bacteriology, dies in Baden-Baden, Germany (66).
29 Mily Alexseyevich Balakirev, Russian composer, dies in St. Petersburg, Russia (73).
31 Elizabeth Blackwell, first woman to receive a medical degree in the U.S., dies in Hastings, Sussex, England (89).

JUNE
5 O. Henry (pen name of William Sydney Porter), U.S. short-story writer and novelist, dies in New York, New York (47).
11 Jacques Cousteau, French oceanographer who invented the aqualung, born in St-André-de-Cubzac, France (–1997).
22 Conrad Zuse, German engineer who built Z3, the first program-controlled binary digital computer, born in Berlin, Germany (–1995).
23 Jean Anouilh, French playwright, born in Bordeaux, France (–1987).

JULY
5 Robert K. Merton, U.S. sociologist, born in Philadelphia, Pennsylvania.
12 Charles Stewart Rolls, English motorist and aviator, joint founder of the Rolls-Royce company, dies in a flying accident (the first British pilot to do so), in Bournemouth, Hampshire, England (32).
14 William Hanna, U.S. animator and creator, with Joseph Barbera, of the cartoon characters Tom and Jerry and the Flintstones, born in Melrose, New Mexico.

AUGUST
13 Florence Nightingale, "Lady of the Lamp," English nurse who was in charge of nursing the British troops during the Crimean War and who established nursing as a profession for women, dies in London, England (90).

20 Eero Saarinen, Finnish-born U.S. architect, born in Kirkkonummi, Finland (–1961).
26 William James, U.S. pragmatist philosopher and functionalist psychologist, dies in Chocorua, New Hampshire (68).
27 Mother Teresa (born Agnes Gonxha Bojaxhiu), Albanian-born Indian ascetic who founded the Order of the Missionaries of Charity, devoted to helping the poor, born in Yugoslavia of Albanian parents (–1997).

SEPTEMBER
2 Henri Rousseau, French painter, dies in Paris, France (66).
29 Winslow Homer, U.S. artist noted for his seascapes, dies in Prouts Neck, Maine (74).

OCTOBER
19 Subrahmanyan Chandrasekhar, Indian-born U.S. astrophysicist who made pioneering studies of the structure and evolution of stars and shared the Nobel Prize for Physics in 1983 with U.S. astrophysicist William Alfred Fowler for his work on the origin of chemical elements, born in Lahore, India (now Pakistan), (–1995).
23 Chulalongkorn, King of Siam (1868–1910) whose modernizing reforms prevented Thailand from becoming a European colony, dies in Bangkok, Siam (now Thailand) (57).
29 A(lfred) J(ules) Ayer, English philosopher and the major proponent of logical positivism, born in London, England (–1989).

NOVEMBER
20 Lev Nikolayevich ("Leo") Tolstoy, Russian author best known for *War and Peace* and *Anna Karenina*, dies in Astapovo, Russia (82).

DECEMBER
3 Mary Baker Eddy, founder of the Christian Science movement, dies in Chestnut Hill, Massachusetts (89).

JUNE
- Residents of Spokane, Washington, celebrate the first Father's Day.

OCTOBER
10 Aristide Briand averts a general strike in France by threatening to enlist strikers into the army.

Media and Communication

- Italian physicist Guglielmo Marconi, in Buenos Aires, Argentina, receives radio messages from Clifden, Ireland, a record distance of about 9,650 km/6,000 mi.
- Kits for building a radio go on sale in the United States.
- The De Forest Radio Telephone Co. makes the first ever outside broadcast in the United States. It features operatic tenor Enrico Caruso, broadcast from the Metropolitan Opera House in New York, New York.

DECEMBER
- The *Miami Herald* begins publication.

Sports

- Roller-skating becomes a popular pastime in the United States and Britain.
- The first aviation meeting in the United States, held in Los Angeles, attracts crowds of up to 50,000.
- The National Hockey Association, a professional ice-hockey league, is founded in Montreal, Canada.

MARCH
3 The U.S. driver Barney Oldfield, sets a new land speed record of 212 kph/131 mph over 1.6 km/1 mi at Daytona Beach, Florida, in a "Blitzen Benz."

JUNE
30 The New Zealand tennis player Tony Wilding wins the first of four successive men's singles titles at the Wimbledon lawn tennis championships in London, England.

JULY
4 The black American boxer Jack Johnson retains the world heavyweight title, beating the former champion Jim Jeffries of the United States in 15 rounds in Reno, Nevada, United States. Disturbances arising from Johnson's victory lead to the deaths of ten people in seven U.S. cities, and a movie of the fight is not shown in many cities for fear of triggering race riots.

SEPTEMBER
10 The inaugural Pendleton Round-Up rodeo is staged in Oregon.

DECEMBER
29 The Intercollegiate Athletic Association of the United States is renamed the National Collegiate Athletic Association (NCCA).

Religion

MAY
26 Pope Pius X issues an encyclical *Editio saepe*, which angers German Protestants because of its derogatory comments about Martin Luther and the Reformation.

JUNE
11 Following representations from Prussia, Pope Pius X expresses regret about the anti-Lutheran comments he made in his recent encyclical, and orders German bishops to stop its circulation in Germany.

1911

POLITICS, GOVERNMENT, AND ECONOMICS

Business and Economics

- Camillo Olivetti, designer and manufacturer of the first Italian typewriter, founds the Olivetti company in Italy. It will go on to become a leading manufacturer of computer hardware.
- Former General Motors president, William C. Durant, founds Chevrolet Motor Co.

JANUARY
7 The Carnegie Trust Company of New York, New York, is closed by the state supervisor of banks.

FEBRUARY
10 Persia appoints the U.S. financier W. Morgan Shuster to reorganize its finances.
28 The Australian Labor prime minister, Andrew Fisher, plans to nationalize the country's monopolies.

MAY
15 The U.S. Supreme Court orders the dissolution of the Standard Oil Company.

OCTOBER
23 The U.S. Ford Motor Company establishes its first factory in Britain, at Trafford in Manchester, England.

NOVEMBER

- Scottish-born U.S. billionaire steel magnate Andrew Carnegie endows the Carnegie Corporation with an initial investment of $125 million.

Human Rights

APRIL

30 Portuguese women get the vote.

NOVEMBER

21 British suffragists (campaigners for the female vote) riot in Whitehall, London, England.

Politics and Government

- An investigation into corruption in the U.S. state of Ohio reveals that a quarter of the electorate sold their votes.
- President William Howard Taft appoints jurist Edward D. White as Chief Justice of the U.S. Supreme Court, and jurist Willis Van Devanter and judge Joseph R. Lamar to the Court.
- The Cooperative League is founded in the United States. It is a research institute interested in public policy, which will be renamed the Twentieth Century Fund in 1919.

JANUARY

- Wisconsin senator Robert M. La Follette establishes the National Progressive Republican League to promote democratic reform.
17 An anarchist attempts to assassinate Prime Minister Aristide Briand in the French Chamber of Deputies.
20 Ecuador refuses to submit its dispute with Peru to The Hague Tribunal in the Netherlands.
24 Twenty-four Japanese anarchists are executed in Tokyo, Japan, for conspiring to assassinate the emperor.
25 During the Mexican civil war, the U.S. cavalry is sent to preserve the neutrality of Rio Grande, and to guard U.S. territory against Mexican insurgents.

FEBRUARY

21 The United States and Japan sign a commercial treaty at Washington, D.C.
22 The Canadian parliament resolves to preserve its union with the British Empire, while controlling its own fiscal policy.
23 The French Chamber of Deputies votes to build two battleships, against a background of increasing tension with Germany.
27 The French prime minister, Aristide Briand, resigns due to lack of support from the Left over his treatment of the unions.

MARCH

17 A female deputy is elected to the Norwegian Störting (parliament).
18 The Italian prime minister, Luigi Luzzatti, resigns following opposition to an electoral reform bill.
26 One hundred and twenty-six suffragists are tried in Britain and sentenced to between three and six months in prison for criminal damage following a demonstration.

APRIL

April–June A revolt in the Ottoman province of Albania is put down by Ottoman troops.
3 Great Britain and Japan sign a commercial treaty, which reduces the tariff on textiles and products imported into Japan.
4 The U.S. Congress meets in extraordinary sessions to deal with the reciprocity agreement with Canada (ratified by the Senate on July 22).
13 The U.S. House of Representatives votes in favor of the direct election of senators.
21 The Portuguese church and state are officially separated by the government there.

MAY

- The U.S. Supreme Court upholds the federal jurisdiction over U.S. forest reserves.
- The U.S. Supreme Court, in *New Jersey v. United States*, finds the John D. Rockefeller's Standard Oil Company to be in violation of the Sherman Antitrust Act (1890) and orders the company's dissolution into 34 companies.
- The U.S. Supreme Court finds the American Tobacco Company to be in violation of the Sherman Antitrust Act (1890) and orders the company's dissolution.
4 The British chancellor of the Exchequer, David Lloyd George, introduces the National Insurance Bill, which establishes the principle of using compulsory contributions from employees, employers, and a state fund for the payment of sickness and unemployment benefit.
23 Russia warns the Ottoman Empire to withdraw its troops from Montenegro's frontier. Albanian citizens have been crossing the frontier into Montenegro, fleeing from Ottoman troops putting down their revolt.
25 The veteran president of Mexico, Porfirio Díaz, resigns following rural unrest led by Francisco Madero.
26 The German Reichstag (parliament) grants the French territory of Alsace-Lorraine (seized following the Franco-Prussian war of 1870–71) its own legislature and a large measure of autonomy.

JUNE

11 A revised Greek constitution is promulgated, which establishes the use of "purified literary language" in official and ecclesiastical documents. This provokes riots in favor of popular Greek.
13 The Christian socialists are defeated in Austrian elections.
22 The coronation of King George V of Great Britain takes place in Westminster Abbey, London, England.
27 Joseph Caillaux forms a ministry in France on the resignation of Ernest Monis following opposition from the unions.
28 Japan signs a commercial treaty with France.

JULY

1 The German gunboat *Panther* arrives in Agadir, Morocco, allegedly to protect German interests threatened by French involvement in Morocco, and sparks an international crisis.
10 Russia notifies Germany of its support for France in the Moroccan crisis.
13 The British–Japanese alliance is renewed for four years.

26   The U.S. president William Taft signs the Reciprocity Bill with Canada.

AUGUST

*   U.S. President William Taft vetoes Arizona statehood, arguing that the state's constitution jeopardized the principle of an independent judiciary by permitting the recalling of judges.
3   Great Britain, the United States, and France sign treaties providing for the arbitration of their disputes by a neutral judge.
10   The British House of Commons votes for the first time to pay members of Parliament (£400 per year), to facilitate the election of members from all classes.
18   Portugal's constituent assembly adopts a Liberal constitution.
21   Kaiser Wilhelm II of Germany speaks at Hamburg, Germany, on Germany's "place in the sun," a colonial empire which he intends to have the navy secure.
21   The *Mona Lisa* by Leonardo da Vinci is stolen from the Louvre museum, Paris, France. It is recovered in 1913.

SEPTEMBER

11   An attempt to repeal the prohibition laws of the U.S. state of Maine is defeated.
14   The Russian prime minister, Peter Stolypin, is assassinated by a revolutionary, and on September 19 the moderate Vladimir Kokovtsov is appointed prime minister.
21   The Liberals are defeated in the Canadian general election, having stood for reciprocity of tariffs with the United States. The reciprocity agreement is later annulled.
23   Fifty thousand people demonstrate in Belfast, Ireland, against Home Rule for Ireland.
29   Italy, wanting to conquer the Ottoman territory of Libya as a counterweight to French influence in Morocco, declares war on the Ottoman Empire.
29   The first Swedish election under the proportional representation system takes place.

OCTOBER

10   Robert K. Borden forms a Conservative ministry in Canada following victory in the recent election.
11   A revolution breaks out in Szechwan, central China, against the government and foreign intervention in China.
26   A revolutionary Chinese republic is proclaimed by revolutionaries contesting the rule of the Manchu emperors.

NOVEMBER

4   A convention ends the "Agadir crisis" in Morocco, when Germany allows France a free hand in Morocco in return for territory in the Congo.
5   Italy annexes Tripolitania, Cyrenaica, and Libya from the Ottoman Empire.
5   Russia issues an ultimatum to Persia to dismiss its U.S. financial advisor W. Morgan Schuster.
6   The revolutionary leader Francisco Madero is unopposed in his election as president of Mexico.
25   Chinese revolutionaries bomb Nanjing, China.
26   Italian forces score a decisive victory in Tripoli in their invasion of Libya.

DECEMBER

*   At President William Howard Taft's request, the U.S. Congress annuls the U.S.–Russian treaty of 1832 in protest at Russia's refusal to honor U.S. passports held by Jews and clergymen of certain denominations.
*   In a letter to William B. Howland, former president Theodore Roosevelt announces that he will run for president in 1912.
7   A Chinese edict abolishes pigtails, and orders reform of the calendar.
12   King George V of Great Britain holds a Delhi *durbar* (court), a celebration of his coronation as emperor of India.
29   Sun Zhong Shan is elected president of the United Provinces of China by a revolutionary assembly in Nanjing, China.

SCIENCE, TECHNOLOGY, AND MEDICINE

Agriculture

*   Famine in Russia affects 30 million.

Ecology

*   The U.S. Bureau of Reclamation completes work on the Roosevelt Dam on Arizona's Salt River. The project is designed to provide water for irrigation.

SEPTEMBER

*   The Chang Jiang River in China floods creating a lake covering 7,250sq km/2,800 sq mi. An estimated 100,000 people die.

Health and Medicine

*   Swiss psychologist Eugene Bleuler publishes *Dementia Praecox, oder Gruppe der Schizophrenien/Dementia Praecox, or the Group of Schizophrenias*, in which he suggests that dementia praecox is not a single disease but a group of mental disorders that he calls schizophrenia, and which he describes as splitting of the personality.
*   U.S. neurologist Walter Cannon publishes *Mechanical Factors of Digestion*, which describes his work using X-rays to study digestion.
*   U.S. physicians George McCoy and Charles Chapin first describe the infectious disease tularemia among ground squirrels in Tulare, California. Affecting primarily wild mammals, especially rabbits, it can be passed to humans.

Science

*   Austrian physicist Victor Francis Hess discovers cosmic radiation using crewed balloons.

- Dutch physicist Heike Kamerlingh-Onnes discovers superconductivity, the characteristic of a substance to display zero electrical resistance when cooled to just above absolute zero.
- Polish-born French chemist Marie Curie receives the Nobel Prize for Chemistry for her discovery of radium and polonium, and the isolation and study of radium.
- German physicist Albert Einstein calculates the deflection of light caused by the sun's gravitational field.
- German physicist Wilhelm Wien receives the Nobel Prize for Physics for his laws regarding the radiation of heat by blackbodies.
- New Zealand-born British physicist Ernest Rutherford proposes the concept of the nuclear atom, in which the mass of the atom is concentrated in a nucleus occupying one ten-thousandth of the space of the atom and which has a positive charge balanced by surrounding electrons.
- New Zealand-born British physicist Ernest Rutherford and English physicist Frederick Soddy devise a method for the "transmutation" of the elements, producing a simpler atom from a complex one.
- German-born U.S. anthropologist Franz Boas publishes *The Mind of Primitive Man*, which discusses his ideas on race and refutes racist theories.
- U.S. physicist Robert Millikan measures the electric charge on a single electron in his oil-drop experiment, in which the upward force of the electric charge on an oil droplet precisely counters the known downward gravitational force acting on it.

July

24 U.S. archeologist Hiram Bingham discovers the Inca city of Machu Picchu in Peru. Excavation begins the following year.

Technology

- Steam-powered shovels are first used in strip-mining for coal in the United States at the Mission field in Illinois.
- U.S. inventor Isaac Newton Lewis patents the Lewis machine gun. Its light recoil makes it ideal for use in airplanes and it is widely used by the allied forces during World War I.
- U.S. inventor Willis Haviland Carrier publishes "Rational Psychometric Formulae," which presents the theoretical basis of air conditioning.

December

- An Italian pilot drops four grenades on two Ottoman targets during the Italo-Ottoman war; it is the first aerial bombardment and the first time an airplane has been used as an instrument of war.

Transportation

- The British liner *Olympic* is launched. At 272 m/892 ft long it is the largest ship in the world.
- The Buenos Aires–Valparaíso Railroad (between Argentina and Chile) is completed.
- The German firm Wiencziers manufactures the first airplane with a retractable undercarriage; it is not generally adopted until the 1940s.
- The last horse-drawn omnibus in London, England, goes out of service.

January

18 U.S. pilot Eugene Ely lands his Curtiss biplane on an improvised flight deck on the battleship *Pennsylvania*, then turns around and takes off. He thus demonstrates the feasibility of aircraft carriers.

February

17 U.S. aviator Glenn Curtiss makes the first successful take off and landing on water in the first sea plane, the *Flying Fish*.

April

- French aviator Louis Paulhan flies from London, England, to Manchester, England, a distance of 293 km/183 mi in 4 hr 2 min, claiming a £10,000 prize from the London newspaper *Daily Mail*.

September

7–November 5 U.S. aviator Calbraith P. Rodgers makes the first transcontinental flight when he flies from Sheepshead Bay, New York, to Pasadena, California, in 82 hours 4 minutes. He does it in 68 hops and crashes 15 times.

ARTS AND IDEAS

Architecture

- Pennsylvania Station, designed by the U.S. architects Charles Follen McKim, William Rutherford Mead, and Stanford White, is completed in New York, New York.
- St. Jude's Church in Hampstead, London, England, is completed. It is designed by the English architect Edward Lutyens.
- The Fagus Shoe Factory in Alfeld-an-der-Leine, Germany, designed by the German architects Walter Gropius and Adolph Meyer, is completed. It is one of the earliest examples of the International Style.
- The New York Public Library in New York, New York, designed by the U.S. architects John Merven Carrère and Thomas Hastings, is completed.

Arts

c. 1911 The U.S. artist Patrick Henry Bruce paints *Still Life (Flower Pot and Bananas)*.
- The expressionist art group *Der Blaue Reiter* ("The Blue Rider") is founded in Munich, Germany. Leading figures include the Russian artist Wassily Kandinsky and the German artists Franz Marc, August Macke, and Gabriele Münter.
- The French artist Georges Braque paints *The Portuguese*, the first work on which he uses stencilled letters.
- The French artist Henri Matisse paints *The Red Studio* and *The Blue Window*.
- The French photographer Jacques Henri Lartigue takes *Avenue du Bois de Boulogne*.
- The Italian artist Amedeo Modigliani sculpts *Head*.
- The Italian artist Carlo Carrà paints *Funeral of the Anarchist Galli*.

- The Russian artist Wassily Kandinsky paints *Improvisation 21a* and *Composition IV*. It is at this time, in a series of paintings called *Compositions* and *Improvisations*, that Kandinsky develops his own form of abstract art.
- The Russian-born artist Marc Chagall paints *I and My Village*.
- The Spanish artist Juan Gris paints *Man in a Café*.
- The Spanish artist Pablo Picasso paints *The Accordionist*.
- The U.S. artist John Singer Sargent paints *Portrait of the Artist's Niece Rose Marie Ormond*.

Film

- David Horsley establishes the first movie studio in Hollywood, California, the Nestor Studio. Fifteen movie companies are also established within the year.
- The animated movie *Pinocchio*, directed by Cesare Antamoro, is released.
- The British movie-going public sees news footage of British explorer Captain Robert Scott's South Pole expedition, shot by cameraman Herbert G. Ponting.
- The movie *La Dame aux camélias/The Lady of the Camellias*, directed by Henri Pouctal and Paul Capellani, is released in France, starring Sarah Bernhardt.
- The movie *The Lonedale Operator*, directed by D. W. Griffith, is released in the United States, starring Blanche Sweet.
- The first Wurlitzer movie theater organs are introduced in New York, New York.

Literature and Language

- The English lexicographers Henry Watson and Frank George Fowler publish their *Concise Oxford Dictionary of Current English*.
- The English writer Arnold Bennett publishes *Hilda Lessways*, the second volume of his Clayhanger trilogy, and his novel *The Card*.
- The English writer D. H. Lawrence publishes his novel *The White Peacock*.
- The English writer G. K. Chesterton publishes his collection of detective stories *The Innocence of Father Brown*.
- The English writer Hugh Walpole publishes his novel *Mr Perrin and Mr Traill*.
- The English writer H. G. Wells publishes his novel *The New Machiavelli*.
- The English writer John Masefield publishes his poetry collection *The Everlasting Mercy*.
- The English writer Max Beerbohm publishes his novel *Zuleika Dobson*.
- The English writer Norman Douglas publishes his travel book *Siren Land*.
- The English writer Rupert Brooke publishes *Poems*.
- The English-born U.S. writer Frances Hodgson Burnett publishes her children's novel *The Secret Garden*.
- The French writer Jules Romains publishes his novel *Mort de quelqu'un/The Death of a Nobody*.

- The New Zealand writer Katherine Mansfield publishes her collection of short stories *In a German Pension*.
- The Polish-born English writer Joseph Conrad publishes his novel *Under Western Eyes*.
- The Scottish writer Saki publishes his collection of short stories *The Chronicles of Clovis*.
- The U.S. writer Ambrose Bierce publishes his collection of satirical definitions *The Devil's Dictionary*.
- The U.S. writer Edith Wharton publishes her tale *Ethan Frome*.
- The U.S. writer Theodore Dreiser publishes his novel *Jennie Gerhardt*.

Music

- British songwriter R. P. Weston writes the song "I'm 'Enry the Eighth I Am."
- Scottish entertainer Harry Lauder and English songwriter Gerald Grafton write the song "A Wee Doch-an-Doris." Harry Lauder writes the song "Roamin' in the Gloamin'."
- The Austrian composer Arnold Schoenberg completes his *Gurrelieder* for soloists, chorus, and orchestra.
- The Danish composer Carl Nielsen completes his Symphony No. 3, the *Sinfonia espansiva/Expansive Symphony*.
- The English composer Edward Elgar completes his Symphony No. 2.
- The English composer Frank Bridge completes his orchestral suite *The Sea*.
- The English composer Frederick Delius completes his orchestral work *Summer Night on the River*, one of his *Two Mood Pictures*.
- The Finnish composer Jean Sibelius completes his Symphony No. 4.
- The French composer Maurice Ravel completes his orchestral work *Daphnis et Chloé/Daphnis and Chloe Suite No. 1*, his orchestral work *Ma Mère l'oye/Mother Goose*, based on a piano work of 1910, and his piano work *Valses nobles et sentimentales/Noble and Sentimental Waltzes*, which he orchestrates in 1912.
- The opera *Conchita*, by the Italian composer Riccardo Zandonai, is first performed in Milan, Italy.
- The opera *Der Rosenkavalier/The Cavalier of the Rose*, by the German composer Richard Strauss, is first performed in Dresden, Germany. It premieres in both London, England, and New York, New York, in 1913.
- The opera *Il segreto di Susanna/Susanna's Secret*, by the Italian composer Ermanno Wolf-Ferrari, is first performed in Munich, Germany.
- The opera *L'Heure espagnole/The Spanish Hour*, by the French composer Maurice Ravel, is first performed in Paris, France.
- The Russian composer Sergey Rachmaninov completes his piano *Etudes tableaux* (Opus 33).
- The Russian composer Igor Stravinsky completes his *Firebird Suite*, based on his ballet *The Firebird*. A second version appears in 1919, and a third in 1945.
- The Spanish composer Enrique Granados completes his piano suite *Goyescas*.
- The U.S. composer Charles Ives completes his Symphony No. 3, *The Camp Meeting*, and his orchestral

works *The Gong on the Hook and Ladder (Fireman's Parade on Main Street)* and *Tone Roads No. 1.*

- U.S. composer Erne Burnett and U.S. lyricists Maybelle E. Watson and George A. Norton write the song "My Melancholy Baby."
- U.S. composer Irving Berlin writes the song "Alexander's Ragtime Band," which will make ragtime widely popular, and the song "Everybody's Doin' It."
- U.S. songwriters Nathaniel Davis Ayer and Seymour Brown write the song "O, You Beautiful Doll."

Theater and Dance

- The ballet *Le Martyre de St.-Sébastien/The Martydrom of St. Sebastian*, by the Italian writer Gabriele D'Annunzio, the French composer Claude Debussy, and the Russian choreographer Ida Lvovna Rubinstein, is first performed, in Paris, France.
- The ballet *Petrushka*, by the Russian composer Igor Stravinsky and Russian choreographer Mikhail Fokin, is first performed in Paris, France, under the Russian impresario Sergei Diaghilev.
- The play *Die Ratten/The Rats*, by the German dramatist Gerhart Hauptmann, is first performed in Berlin, Germany.
- The play *Jedermann/Everyman*, by the Austrian dramatist Hugo von Hofmannsthal, is first performed in Berlin, Germany.

APRIL

19 The play *Kismet*, by U.S. dramatist Edward Knoblock, a tale of intrigue set in Baghdad, is first performed, at the Knickerbocker Theater in New York, New York.

Thought and Scholarship

- Australian ethnologist Grafton Elliot Smith publishes *The Ancient Egyptians.*
- Austrian-born U.S. economist Joseph Schumpeter publishes *Theory of Economic Development.*
- English economist John Atkinson Hobson publishes *The Science of Wealth.*
- English social historians John Lawrence and Barbara Hammond publish *The Village Labourer.*
- German philosopher Hans Vaihinger publishes *Die Philosophie des Als Ob/The Philosophy of "As If."*
- The Nobel Prize for Literature is awarded to the Belgian dramatist Maurice Maeterlinck.
- U.S. anthropologist Franz Boas publishes *The Mind of Primitive Man.*
- U.S. economist Irving Fisher publishes *The Purchasing Power of Money.*
- U.S. engineer Frederick Winslow Taylor publishes *The Principles of Scientific Management.*

Everyday Life

- Swedish physiologist Allvar Gullstrand receives the Nobel Prize for Physiology or Medicine for his work on the dioptrics of the eye.

April 1911–14   82,500 Mexicans emigrate to the United States.

MARCH

10 Clocks are put back by 9 minutes and 21 seconds at midnight in France and Algeria, making Greenwich time the standard.

25 A fire at the Triangle Shirtwaist Company in New York, New York, kills 146 people, mostly young women. Some escape doors had been locked by the management to control the labor force.

APRIL

- 11,745 immigrants pass through Ellis Island in New York, New York, an all-time record.

JUNE

14 British seamen begin a strike for better wages.

24 Shipping magnates meeting in Southampton, England, concede higher wages and overtime rates in order to end the seamen's dispute.

Sports

- The first Monte Carlo Rally motor race is won by Henri Rougier of France in a Turcat-Mery.
- The U.S. baseball player Denton T. "Cy" Young retires from major league competition. The 511 games won during his career, most of them with the Boston Red Sox, remains an all-time major league pitching record.

MAY

30 The Indianapolis 500 motor race is run for the first time in the United States; the winner is U.S. driver Ray Harroun, driving a Marmon Wasp.

JUNE

17 The U.S. tennis player Hazel Hotchkiss (later Hazel Wightman) wins the women's singles at the U.S. lawn tennis championships at the Philadelphia Cricket Club, Pennsylvania, for the third year in succession.

24 The U.S. golfer Johnny McDermott, at the age of 19, becomes the youngest winner of the U.S. Open golf championship, at the Chicago Golf Club, Wheaton, Illinois.

NOVEMBER

11 Carlisle Indian School, led by the future U.S. Olympic track and field star Jim Thorpe, create one of the biggest upsets in college football history when they defeat Harvard 18–15.

SOCIETY

Education

- Southern Methodist University opens in Dallas, Texas.

BIRTHS & DEATHS

- Bonnie Parker, U.S. bank robber with Clyde Barrow, is born in Rowena, Texas (–1934).
- Joseph Barbera, U.S. animator and creator with William Hanna of the cartoon characters Tom and Jerry, Scooby Doo, and the Flintstones, born in New York, New York.

JANUARY

16 Dizzy Dean (Jay Hanna Dean), U.S. professional baseball player and baseball commentator, born in Lucas, Arkansas (–1974).

17 Francis Galton, English anthropologist and eugenicist, dies in Grayshott House, Haslemere, Surrey, England (88).

30 Roy Eldridge, U.S. jazz trumpeter popular in the 1940s, born in Pittsburgh, Pennsylvania (–1989).

FEBRUARY

6 Ronald Reagan, 40th president of the United States 1981–89, a Republican, born in Tampico, Illinois.

13 Jean Muir, U.S. actress, born in Missouri (–1996).

MARCH

3 Jean Harlow, U.S. actress and sex symbol, born in Kansas City, Missouri (–1937).

16 Josef Mengele, the "Angel of Death," Nazi doctor who managed the gas chambers at Auschwitz extermination camp and conducted experiments on inmates, born in Günzburg, Germany (–1979).

26 Tennessee Williams (Thomas Lanier Williams), U.S. dramatist, most of whose plays are set in the Deep South, born in Columbus, Mississippi (–1983).

APRIL

8 Melvin Calvin, U.S. chemist, winner of the Nobel Prize for Chemistry in 1961 for discovering the chemical nature of photosynthesis, born in St. Paul, Minnesota (–1997).

MAY

18 Gustav Mahler, Austrian composer, dies in Vienna, Austria (50).

24 U Ne Win, head of state of Burma 1961–82, born in Paungdale, Burma (now Myanmar).

27 Hubert Humphrey, Democrat politician, 38th vice president of the United States (1965–69) and senator from Minnesota (1949–65 and 1971–78), born in Wallace, South Dakota (–1978).

27 Vincent Price, U.S. actor noted for his horror thrillers, born in St. Louis, Missouri (–1993).

29 William Schwenk Gilbert, English playwright known for his works produced with Arthur Seymour Sullivan, dies in Harrow Weald, Middlesex, England (74).

JUNE

9 Carry Nation, U.S. temperance militant who attacked bars with a hatchet, dies in Leavenworth, Kansas (64).

13 Luis W. Alvarez, U.S. physicist who received the Nobel Prize for Physics in 1968 for his discovery of several subatomic particles, born in San Francisco, California (–1988).

24 Juan Manuel Fangio, Argentine race-car driver who wins the drivers' world championship a record five times 1951–57, born in Balcarce, Argentina (–1995).

JULY

5 Georges Pompidou, French statesman, premier of France 1962–68 and president of the Fifth French Republic 1969–74, born in Montboudif, France (–1974).

16 Ginger Rogers, U.S. dancer and actress, partner of Fred Astaire, born in Independence, Missouri (–1995).

21 Marshall McLuhan, Canadian communications scholar who was convinced of the power of television and electronic media over the written word, born in Edmonton, Alberta, Canada (–1980).

AUGUST

6 Lucille Ball, U.S. actress, star of the television series I Love Lucy, born in Jamestown, New York (–1989).

9 William Alfred Fowler, U.S. astrophysicist who worked on the life cycle of stars and shared the Nobel Prize for Physics in 1983 with Indian-born U.S. astrophysicist Subrahmanyan Chandrasekhar for his work on the origin of chemical elements, born in Pittsburgh, Pennsylvania (–1995).

12 Samuel Fuller, U.S. film director, born in Worcester, Massachusetts (–1997).

16 Ernst Friedrich Schumacher, German-born British economist, government advisor, born in Bonn, Germany (–1977).

17 Mikhail Botvinnik, Russian chess player, world champion 1948–57,

1958–60, and 1961–63, born in St. Petersburg, Russia (–1995).

29 John Charnley, English orthopedic surgeon who developed the technique of hip replacement, born in Bury, Lancashire, England (–1982).

SEPTEMBER

9 William Golding, English novelist whose works include Lord of the Flies (1954), born in St. Columb Minor, Cornwall, England (–1993).

13 Bill Munro, U.S. bluegrass musician, born near Rosine, Kentucky (–1996).

16 Edward Whymper, English mountaineer who was the first to climb the Matterhorn, dies in Chamonix, France (71).

24 Konstantin Ustinovich Chernenko, president of the Soviet Union 1984–85, born in Bolshaya Tes, Siberia, Russian Empire (–1985).

OCTOBER

1 Wilhelm Dilthey, German philosopher who developed hermeneutics—a philosophy of the humanities and social sciences, dies in Seis am Schlern, Austria-Hungary (77).

19 Bob Jones, Jr., U.S. fundamentalist preacher and president of Bob Jones University, born.

24 Clarence M. Kelly, U.S. director of the Federal Bureau of Investigation (FBI) 1973–77, born in Kansas City, Missouri (–1997).

26 Mahalia Jackson, U.S. gospel singer, born in New Orleans, Louisiana (–1972).

29 Joseph Pulitzer, U.S. newspaper editor and publisher who established the Pulitzer prizes, dies in Charleston, South Carolina (64).

NOVEMBER

2 Odysseus Elytis (pen name of Odysseus Alepoudhelis), Greek poet, winner of the Nobel Prize for Literature in 1979, born in Heraklion, Crete (now in Greece), (–1996).

DECEMBER

22 Grote Reber, U.S. astronomer who built the first radio telescope, born in Wheaton, Illinois.

23 Niels Kaj Jerne, British–Danish immunologist who theorized that the body has an immense variety of antibodies that are activated when needed, born in London, England (–1994).

1912

POLITICS, GOVERNMENT, AND ECONOMICS

Business and Economics

- Maine sportsman-entrepreneur, Leon Leonwood Bean, establishes the retail store L. L. Bean, Inc., in Freeport Maine.
- The consumer price index is established in the United States to provide a guide for setting cost of living adjustments for U.S. wages.
- The U.S. National Biscuit Co. introduces the Oreo cookie.

SEPTEMBER
6 The British Labour Union Congress votes against incorporating the different trades within an industry into a single union.
23 The Chinese government declines a loan from the European powers for the development of China, in favor of a loan from Birch, Crisp, and Company of London, England.

NOVEMBER
27 A run on savings banks begins in central and eastern Europe, because of instability caused by the Balkan War.

Human Rights

MARCH
28 The British House of Commons rejects a women's franchise bill.

JUNE
25 The Labour member of Parliament George Lansbury protests in the British House of Commons against the forcible feeding of imprisoned suffragists on hunger strike.
29 The right to vote is widened in Italy, now amounting to almost universal suffrage.

Politics and Government

- An amendment to the 1909 U.S. Copyright Act grants copyright in photoplays and other motion pictures.
- Massachusetts enacts the nation's first minimum wage law for child and female labor.
- President William Howard Taft appoints jurist Mahlon Pitney to the U.S. Supreme Court.

- The U.S. Congress amends the Pure Food and Drug Law of 1906, prohibiting drug producers from issuing overblown claims of a drug's therapeutic effect.
- The U.S. Underwood–Simmons Act lowers tariffs, especially on raw materials.
- U.S. Congress passes a new Homestead Act, reducing the residency requirement for homesteaders from five to three years.

JANUARY
- President William Howard Taft sends U.S. troops into Tientsin in China to protect U.S. interests jeopardized by the outbreak of civil war.
1 Elections to the German Reichstag (parliament) leave the Socialist Party in the strongest position.
6 New Mexico is admitted to the Union as the 47th U.S. state.
10 The French prime minister, Joseph Caillaux, resigns following a ministerial crisis, and on January 14 Raymond Poincaré forms a cabinet.

FEBRUARY
- President William Howard Taft sends U.S. marines to Honduras to protect U.S. commercial interests during a period of political upheaval.
3 Plans for an extensive naval building program are introduced to the Japanese imperial diet.
6 The revolutionary Nanjing assembly of China endorses premier Yuan Shikai's proposals for constitutional reform.
8 The British secretary for war, Lord Haldane, visits Berlin, Germany, and offers British support for German colonial ambitions in return for an end to the naval arms race. Germany rejects the offer.
12 P'u-i, the last Manchu emperor of China, abdicates, and China becomes a republic under provisional president Sun Zhong Shan.
14 Arizona is admitted to the Union as the 48th U.S. state.
27 A German women's congress opens in Berlin, Germany.

MARCH
- The U.S. Justice Department launches a successful antitrust suit against the Union Pacific railroad company, which had acquired a controlling interest in the Southern Pacific railroad.
8 A new German naval bill increases the planned size of the German navy, making provision for a third squadron.
9 The European powers ask Italy to state the terms on which it would accept arbitration to end its war with the Ottoman Empire.
13 Bulgaria and Serbia sign a treaty of alliance in preparation for a war with the Ottoman Empire.
14 The U.S. president, William Howard Taft, forbids the shipment of arms to Mexico, where the government faces rebellion.

First Balkan War (1912–13)

1912

AUGUST

14 As a pretext for war, Bulgaria demands autonomy for Macedonia from the Ottoman Empire.

SEPTEMBER

30 Bulgarian and Serbian armies mobilize for war against the Ottoman Empire, seeking to eliminate Ottoman power in the Balkans.

OCTOBER

8 Montenegro declares war on the Ottoman Empire.

18 The Ottoman Empire declares war on Bulgaria and Serbia.

NOVEMBER

3 The Ottoman Empire asks the European powers to intervene to end its war with Serbia, Bulgaria, and Montenegro.

9 Ottoman forces surrender to a Greek force at Thessaloníki (Salonika), Macedonia, in the First Balkan War.

15–18 Serbia defeats the Ottoman Empire at the battle of Monastir, Macedonia.

21 The Ottoman Empire declares that the peace terms of their enemy, the Balkan allies, are unacceptable.

DECEMBER

3 An armistice is agreed between the Ottoman Empire, Bulgaria, Serbia, and Montenegro, ending the fighting in the First Balkan War in spite of a Greek abstention.

1913

JANUARY

2 The Ottoman garrison on the island of Chios surrenders to Greek troops.

6 The London peace conference between the Ottoman Empire and the Balkan states is suspended when the Ottoman Empire refuses to cede Adrianople, Crete, and the Aegean Islands.

18 A Greco-Ottoman naval battle is fought off the Aegean island of Tenedos.

FEBRUARY

3 Bulgaria renews war with the Ottoman Empire following the breakdown of the London peace conference.

MARCH

14 The Balkan allies accept the mediation of the European powers in a settlement of the war with the Ottoman Empire.

26 A Bulgarian force takes Adrianople from the Ottoman Empire.

31 The Ottoman Empire accepts the peace recommendations of the European powers.

APRIL

16 The Ottoman Empire signs an armistice, ending its war with Bulgaria.

MAY

30 A peace treaty between the Ottoman Empire and the Balkan states is signed in London, England, ending the First Balkan War.

---

19 The U.S. Excise Bill is introduced, which taxes net income from business sources.

30 Sultan Abdul Hamid II of Morocco signs a treaty making Morocco a French protectorate.

APRIL

9 Canada and the West Indies sign an agreement on mutual tariff reductions.

11 The British prime minister, Herbert Asquith, introduces a bill in Parliament to grant Home Rule for Ireland.

18–May 1 The Ottoman Empire closes the Dardanelles to shipping in response to the threat of an Italian invasion.

20 The U.S. House of Representatives resolves that the election expenses of presidential and vice presidential candidates should be published.

MAY

• The Taft administration orders U.S. steamships to provide lifeboats for all passengers in the wake of the *Titanic* tragedy.

• The U.S. Socialist Party nominates Eugene V. Debs for president and Emil Seidelm, mayor of Milwaukee, Wisconsin, for vice president.

4 Italy occupies the Ottoman Dodecanese Islands.

22 Count Stephen Tisza, leader of the Hungarian National Party of Work, is elected president of the Hungarian chamber. Socialists call a strike in support of universal male suffrage and riots occur in Budapest, Austria-Hungary.

22 The German Reichstag (parliament) is adjourned following socialist attacks on Kaiser Wilhelm II of Germany.

29 Greece and Bulgaria sign a treaty of alliance in preparation for a war with the Ottoman Empire.

JUNE

• Political turmoil in Cuba prompts President William Howard Taft to dispatch U.S. marines to the island nation.

2 The clericals win the Belgian elections, which were fought over the question of educational policy.

19 U.S. Congress passes legislation granting federal workers an eight-hour day.

22 The former U.S. president Theodore Roosevelt founds the Progressive "Bull Moose" Republican Party at the Republican convention in Chicago, Illinois.

22 William Howard Taft is nominated as the Republican presidential candidate and James S. Sherman as vice presidential candidate at a convention at Chicago, Illinois.

JULY

2 New Jersey governor Woodrow Wilson is nominated as the Democratic presidential candidate and Thomas R. Marshall as the vice presidential candidate, at the Democratic Party convention in Baltimore, Maryland.

9 Following the electoral victory in New Zealand of the new Reform Party over the Liberals, Thomas Mackenzie resigns and William Massey forms a ministry.
18 Tewfik Pasha becomes grand vizier of Persia, following the fall of Said Pasha's ministry.
30 The Japanese emperor, Meiji, dies and is succeeded by Yoshihito.

AUGUST

- For the third time in one year, President William Howard Taft dispatches U.S. marines to a neighboring country to protect U.S. commercial interests from political tumult. This time the country is Nicaragua, where the marines will remain until 1933.
- President William Howard Taft signs the Panama Canal Act which provides toll rebates for U.S. shipping. The act outrages European nations, who accuse the United States of violating the Hay-Pauncefote Treaty of 1901.
2 The U.S. Senate resolves to extend the Monroe doctrine (opposing the influence of outside powers in the United States) to foreign corporations holding territory on the American continent.
5 A convention of the Progressive Republican Party in Chicago, Illinois, nominates former president Theodore Roosevelt as its U.S. presidential candidate and California governor Hiram Johnson as vice presidential candidate.
5–16 The French prime minister and foreign secretary Raymond Poincaré visit Russia to coordinate policy following recent events in the Balkans.
7 A Russo-Japanese agreement delineates the two countries' spheres of influence in the Chinese territories of Mongolia and Manchuria.
14 As a pretext for war, Bulgaria demands autonomy for Macedonia from the Ottoman Empire.
17 Britain issues a diplomatic note to restrain China from sending a military expedition to Tibet.
17 Britain protests to the United States that the Panama Canal rates infringe the Hay-Pauncefote treaty of November 1901.
19 Britain accepts a project for reform in Macedonia, which was suggested by the Austrian foreign minister Count Leopold von Berchtold.

SEPTEMBER

13 Revolution breaks out in the Dominican Republic.
18 Anti-Home Rule demonstrations are organized at Enniskillen in northern Ireland, by the Ulster Unionist and British member of Parliament Edward Carson.
28 Thousands of Unionist opponents of Home Rule in northern Ireland sign the "Solemn League and Covenant," pledging themselves to resist Home Rule.
29 British and French forces pacify demonstrations for independence on the Ottoman island of Samos following the forced withdrawal of Ottoman troops on September 4.
30 Bulgarian and Serbian armies mobilize for war against the Ottoman Empire, seeking to eliminate Ottoman power in the Balkans.

OCTOBER

- The New York state assembly outlaws the 54-hour work week.
8 Montenegro declares war on the Ottoman Empire.

12 The Ottoman Empire declines to undertake reforms in Macedonia, despite the insistence of the European powers.
14 New York malcontent, John Schrank, shoots Progressive Party candidate, Theodore Roosevelt, in the chest from close range. Wounded but undeterred, Roosevelt delivers a scheduled speech before seeking medical treatment.
18 Italy and the Ottoman Empire sign a peace treaty at Lausanne, Switzerland, by which Tripoli and Cyrenaica are granted autonomy under Italian suzerainty, and Italy restores the Dodecanese Islands to the Ottoman Empire.
18 The Ottoman Empire declares war on Bulgaria and Serbia.

NOVEMBER

3 The Ottoman Empire asks the European powers to intervene to end its war with Serbia, Bulgaria, and Montenegro.
5 The Democrat Woodrow Wilson wins the U.S. presidential election with 435 electoral votes, while the Progressive candidate, Theodore Roosevelt, wins 88 votes, and the residing Republican president, William Howard Taft, wins 8. In the popular vote Wilson receives 6,293,454 votes, Roosevelt 4,119,538, and Taft 3,484,980. Democrats attain majorities in both the House (2911–127) and Senate (51–44).
9 Ottoman forces surrender to a Greek force at Thessaloníki (Salonika), Macedonia, in the First Balkan War.
11 Following animosity over territorial disputes, Chile resumes diplomatic relations with Peru after a break of 30 months.
12 The Liberal Spanish prime minister, José Canalejas, is assassinated.
15–18 Serbia defeats the Ottoman Empire at the battle of Monastir, Macedonia, in the first of the Balkan wars.
21 The Ottoman Empire declares that the peace terms of the Balkan allies with whom the Empire is at war are unacceptable.

DECEMBER

- Former U.S. secretary of state, Elihu Root, wins the Nobel Peace Prize for his work at the Carnegie Endowment for International Peace.
2 The U.S. Supreme Court orders the dissolution of the Union Pacific and Southern Pacific railroads merger.
3 An armistice is agreed between the Ottoman Empire, Bulgaria, Serbia, and Montenegro, ending the fighting in the Balkan War in spite of a Greek abstention.
14 Louis Botha resigns as South African prime minister, and forms a new cabinet on December 20 without General James Hertzog, who has made inflammatory comments on loosening the ties between South Africa and Britain.
19 The Japanese prime minister, Matsukata, resigns following the resignation of the minister for war. Prince Katsura forms a cabinet.
20 At the London peace conference between the Ottoman Empire and the Balkan states, the ambassadors of the European powers accept the principle of Albanian autonomy, providing Serbia has canal access to the Adriatic Sea.

SCIENCE, TECHNOLOGY, AND MEDICINE

Health and Medicine

- English biochemist Frederick Gowland Hopkins publishes the results of his experiments that prove that "accessory substances" (vitamins) are essential for health and growth and that their absence may lead to diseases such as scurvy or beriberi. In the same year, Polish-born U.S. biochemist Casimir Funk discovers that pigeons fed on rice polishings can be cured of beriberi, and suggests that the absence of a vital nitrogen-containing substance known as an amone causes such diseases. He calls these substances "vitamines."
- English physiologist Ernest Starling publishes *Principles of Human Physiology*, which is still an international standard text on physiology.
- French surgeon Alexis Carrel receives the Nobel Prize for Physiology or Medicine for his work on vascular suture and the transplant of blood vessels and organs.
- French surgeon Théodore Tuffier performs the first successful operation on the aortic valve of the heart.
- U.S. entomologist Leland Ossian Howard publishes *The House Fly, Disease Carrier*, in which he identifies the common housefly as a major carrier of disease.
- U.S. physician James Herrick is the first to describe a coronary thrombosis—a blood clot in the coronary artery that causes damage to the heart (heart attack).

Science

- French chemists Victor Grignard and Paul Sabatier share the Nobel Prize for Chemistry: Grignard for his discovery of Grignard reagent, and Sabatier for the catalytic hydrogenation of organic compounds.
- German meteorologist Alfred Wegener suggests the idea of continental drift and proposes the existence of a supercontinent (Pangaea) in the distant past.
- German physicist Max von Laue demonstrates that crystals are composed of regular, repeated arrays of atoms by studying the patterns in which they diffract X-rays. It is the beginning of X-ray crystallography.
- Scottish physicist Charles Thomson Rees Wilson perfects the cloud chamber, which detects ion trails since water molecules condense on ions. It is used to study radioactivity, X-rays, cosmic rays, and other nuclear phenomena.
- Swedish physicist Nils Dalén receives the Nobel Prize for Physics for his invention of automatic regulators for use in gas lights for lighthouses and buoys.
- U.S. astronomer Edward Barnard discovers Barnard's star. Second nearest star to the sun, it displays the greatest movement of any star relative to others.
- U.S. astronomer Henrietta Swan Leavitt establishes a relationship between the period and luminosity of Cepheid variable stars (stars which pulsate and vary regularly in brightness). The relationship is later used to calculate interstellar and intergalactic distances.

- U.S. chemist Irving Langmuir discovers that filling tungsten-filament light bulbs with inert gases greatly prolongs their life—because it eliminates the evaporation of the tungsten.

December 1912–14 British archeologist Leonard Woolley and English adventurer T. E. Lawrence excavate the ancient Syrian city of Carchemish.

December 1912–25 U.S. astronomer Vesto Slipher measures the radial velocities of spiral nebulae by examining small changes in the Doppler effect which suggest that they must be external to our galaxy. His work is later built on by U.S. astronomer Edwin Hubble to show that the universe is expanding.

JUNE

- English amateur archeologist Charles Dawson discovers a human skull with an ape-like jaw, the fossil remains of Piltdown man *Eoanthropus dawsoni*, in a gravel pit in Piltdown, southeast England. In 1953 they are discovered to be a hoax.

Technology

- British metallurgist Henry Brearley invents a type of stainless steel, an alloy of steel and chrome.
- U.S. inventor Edwin Armstrong devises a regenerative, or positive feedback circuit in which part of the high-frequency radio signal is fed back into the tuning circuit, amplifying it a thousand-fold.
- U.S. physicist Lee De Forest links three Audion tubes together to amplify high-frequency radio signals, an essential development for the subsequent improvement of radio and television.

Transportation

c. 1912 Paraffin and acetylene lights and bulb horns on cars begin to be rapidly replaced by electric lights and horns.

- Norway is the first country to introduce compulsory third-party insurance for car owners.
- The Danish ship *Selandia* is launched; it is the first diesel-powered steamship.
- The first regular air service, between Berlin and Friedrichshafen in Germany, is established, using the airships *Victoria*, *Luise*, and *Hansa*.
- The Madeira–Mamoro railroad is completed, in Brazil. It is 408 km/255 mi long and bypasses 19 waterfalls on the Madeira River, thus linking the upper and lower reaches of the river and allowing the exploitation of the Amazon's rubber trees. Disease and attacks by hostile Amazonians have claimed over 6,000 lives in its construction.
- U.S. engineer Charles Kettering develops the first effective electric starter-motor for cars. It is first introduced on Cadillacs.

MARCH

1 U.S. Army officer Albert Berry is the first person to use a parachute for jumping from a moving aircraft.

APRIL

14–15 The British luxury liner *Titanic*, carrying 2,224 people on its maiden transatlantic voyage, hits an iceberg 640 km/400 mi off the coast of Newfoundland

and sinks causing the deaths of 1,513. One of the largest ships afloat (269 m/882 ft), it has a double-hulled bottom and is considered unsinkable. The accident leads to the first international convention for safety at sea, held in London, England, the following year, which draws up safety standards.

SEPTEMBER

28 The Japanese ship *KicheMaru* sinks off the Japanese coast and 1,000 die.

ARTS AND IDEAS

Architecture

- The Christian Science Building in Berkeley, California, designed by the U.S. architect Bernard Ralph Maybeck, is completed.
- The Hôtel Guimard in Paris, France, designed by the French architect Hector Guimard, is completed.

APRIL

25 The new bell tower in St. Mark's Square, Venice, Italy, is inaugurated.

Arts

c. 1912 The U.S. artist William Glackens paints *29 Washington Square*.
- The English artist George Frampton sculpts *Peter Pan*, which is set up in Kensington Gardens, London, England.
- The French artist Auguste Rodin sculpts *Nijinsky*.
- The French artist Georges Braque creates the first *papiers-collés* (paintings that incorporate pieces of paper), exemplified by works such as *Fruit Dish and Glass*.
- The French artist Marcel Duchamp paints *Nude Descending a Staircase, No 2*.
- The French artist Robert Delaunay begins painting the series *Simultaneous Windows*.
- The French artists Albert Gleizes and Jean Metzinger publish their influential study *Du Cubisme/Cubism*.
- The German artist Emil Nolde paints *The Missionary*.
- The German artist Ernst Kirchner paints *Striding into the Sea*.
- The Italian artist Giacomo Balla paints *Dog on a Leash* and *Girl Running on a Balcony*.
- The Italian artist Giorgio de Chirico paints *Melancholy*.
- The Italian artist Gino Severini paints *Blue Dancer*.
- The Italian artist Luigi Russolo paints *Music*.
- The Italian artist Umberto Boccioni paints *Materia* and sculpts *Development of a Bottle in Space*.
- The Russian artist Mikhail Larionov paints *Rayonnist Landscape*.
- The Russian artist Wassily Kandinsky publishes *Über das Geistige in der Kunst/On the Spiritual in Art*, one of the first attempts to provide a theoretical basis for abstract art.
- The Spanish artist Juan Gris paints *Homage to Picasso*.

- The Spanish artist Pablo Picasso creates one of the first collages (a picture incorporating ready-made images) with the painting *Still Life with Chair Caning*.
- The U.S. artist John Marin paints *St Paul's, Lower Manhattan*.
- The U.S. artist John Sloan paints *Six O'Clock*.
- The U.S. artist Marguerite Thompson Zorach paints *Windy Day in the Sierras* and *Man Among Redwoods*.
- The U.S.-born English artist Jacob Epstein sculpts *Tomb of Oscar Wilde* for the Père Lachaise Cemetery in Paris, France.

Film

- Four movies directed by D. W. Griffith are released in the United States: *An Unseen Enemy*, starring sisters Lillian and Dorothy Gish; *Her First Biscuit*, starring Mary Pickford; *The New York Hat*, starring Lillian Gish and Lionel Barrymore; and *Voice of a Million*.
- London, England, has 400 movie theaters, up from 90 in 1909; in the United States, 5 million people visit the movies daily.
- Mack Sennett founds the Keystone studio in the United States, to make comedy movies.
- The Edison movie studio produces the first movie with sound. It is a 15-minute musical based on nursery rhymes in which the sound is roughly synchronized on a phonograph with the image.
- The movie *Bout-de-Zan*, directed by Louis Feuillade, is released in France.
- The movie *L'Homme nu/The Naked Man*, directed by St. Raime, is released in France.
- The movie *Queen Elizabeth*, directed by Louis Mercanton, is released in France, starring Sarah Bernhardt.
- The movie *Quo Vadis?/Where Are You Going?*, directed by Enrico Guazzoni, is released in Italy, based on the book by Henryk Sienkiewicz, and achieves success worldwide, particularly in the United States.
- The movie *The Black Masks*, directed by Mauritz Stiller, is released in Sweden, starring Victor Sjöström.
- The first awards for feature-length movies take place at the International Exhibition in Turin, Italy.

Literature and Language

- According to *Life* magazine, popular slang phrases in the United States include "floozy," "beat it," "it's a cinch," "peachy," "nutty," and "getting your goat."
- Franciscan friars in Arizona compile and publish the first Navajo dictionary.
- The black American poet-historian James Weldon Johnson anonymously publishes *The Autobiography of an Ex-Colored Man*.
- The English writer and artist Isaac Rosenberg publishes his poetry collection *Night and Day*.
- The English writer Compton Mackenzie publishes his novel *Carnival*.
- The English writer Ethel M. Dell publishes her romantic novel *The Way of an Eagle*.
- The English writer E. C. Bentley publishes his detective novel *Trent's Last Case*.

- The English writer Hilaire Belloc publishes his novel *The Green Overcoat*.
- The English writer Lytton Strachey publishes *Landmarks in French Literature*.
- The English writer Max Beerbohm publishes his collection of short stories *A Christmas Garland*.
- The German writer Thomas Mann publishes his novella *Der Tod in Venedig/Death in Venice*.
- The Polish-born English writer Joseph Conrad publishes his novel *Chance* in serial form in the *New York Herald*. It is published as a book in 1914.
- The Scottish writer Saki publishes his novel *The Unbearable Bassington*.
- The Scottish writer Arthur Conan Doyle publishes his novel *The Lost World*.
- The U.S. immigrant Mary Antin publishes *The Promised Land*.
- The U.S. writer Amy Lowell publishes her poetry collection *A Dome of Many-Colored Glass*.
- The U.S. writer Edith Wharton publishes her novel *The Reef*.
- The U.S. writer Theodore Dreiser publishes his novel *The Financier*.

Music

- The Austrian composer Alban Berg completes his *Altenberglieder/Altenberg Songs* for voice and orchestra.
- The Austrian composer Arnold Schoenberg completes his *Pierrot lunaire/Moonstruck Pierrot*, settings of poems by the French poet Albert Giraud for spoken voice (or Sprechstimme) and chamber ensemble.
- The English composer Frederick Delius completes his orchestral work *On Hearing the First Cuckoo in Spring*, one of his *Two Mood Pictures*.
- The French composer Claude Debussy completes his *Syrinx* for solo flute and his orchestral work *Images*.
- The French composer Maurice Ravel completes his orchestral work *Daphnis et Chloé/Daphnis and Chloe* Suite No. 2 and his orchestral work *Valses nobles et sentimentales/Noble and Sentimental Waltzes*, based on a piano work of 1911.
- The opera *Ariadne auf Naxos/Ariadne on Naxos* by the German composer Richard Strauss is first performed, in Stuttgart, Germany.
- The opera *Mona*, by the U.S. composer Horatio Parker, is first performed in New York, New York.
- The Russian composer Sergey Rachmaninov completes his *14 Songs* (Opus 34), the best known of which is "Vocalise," which he revises in 1915.
- The U.S. composer Charles Griffes completes his *Three Tone Pictures* for piano.
- The U.S. composer Charles Ives completes his choral works *Three Harvest Home Chorales* and *Lincoln The Great Commoner*.
- U.S. songwriters Percy Wenrich and Edward Madden write the song "Moonlight Bay."

DECEMBER

23 The revue *Hullo, Ragtime* is first performed, at the Hippodrome in London, England, encouraging the craze for ragtime songs.

Theater and Dance

- The ballet *Daphnis et Chloé/Daphnis and Chloe*, by the French composer Maurice Ravel and the Russian choreographer Mikhail Fokin, is first performed in Paris, France, under the Russian impresario Sergei Diaghilev. The sets and costumes are by the Russian artist Léon Bakst.
- The ballet *L'Après-midi d'un faune/The Afternoon of a Faun*, by the French composer Claude Debussy and the Russian dancer Vaslav Nijinsky, is first performed in Paris, France, under the Russian impresario Sergei Diaghilev. The sets and costumes are by the Russian artist Léon Bakst and Nijinsky dances the central role.
- The ballet *Ma Mère l'oye/Mother Goose* is first performed, in Paris, France. The music is by the French composer Maurice Ravel, with choreography by the French choreographer Léo Staats.
- The play *He and She*, by Rachel Crothers, about a woman trying to balance her family and her career, is first performed, in New York, New York.
- The play *L'Annonce faite à Marie/Tidings Brought to Mary*, by the French writer Paul Claudel, is first performed in Paris, France.
- The play *La Marquess Rosalinda/The Marchioness Rosalinda*, by the Spanish dramatist Ramón del Valle-Inclán, is first performed in Madrid, Spain.
- The play *Tod und Teufel/Death and Damnation*, by the German dramatist Frank Wedekind, is first performed in Berlin, Germany.

Thought and Scholarship

- Czech psychologist Max Wertheimer and German psychologists Kurt Koffka and Wolfgang Köhler develop Gestalt psychology, which endeavors to explain psychological phenomena holistically.
- English philosopher George Edward Moore publishes *Ethics*.
- English philosopher Bertrand Russell publishes *The Problems of Philosophy*.
- French historian Elie Halévy publishes the first volume of his *Histoire du peuple anglais au XIXe siècle/A History of the English People in the Nineteenth Century*. The last volume appears in 1932.
- French sociologist Emile Durkheim publishes *Les Formes élémentaires de la vie religieuse/The Elementary Forms of the Religious Life*, dealing with totemic systems in which he argues that society is the personification of God.
- The Nobel Prize for Literature is awarded to the German dramatist Gerhart Hauptmann.
- U.S. historian James Harvey Robinson publishes *The New History*, which argues that history ought to reflect the totality of the human experience, not just its political or economic aspects.

SOCIETY

Education

- Italian educationist, Maria Montessori, introduces the Montessori teaching method in Rome, Italy.
- Rice University opens in Houston, Texas, as Rice Institute.
- The University of California opens at San Diego, California.

Everyday Life

- German-American delicatessen owner Richard Hellmann introduces Hellmann's mayonnaise, the first ready-made mayonnaise, in the United States.
- The Associated Advertising Clubs of America adopt a voluntary truth in advertising code meant to forestall federal legislative action.

JANUARY
- The International Workers of the World (IWW) orchestrates a successful textile strike in Lawrence, Massachusetts, gaining national recognition.

FEBRUARY
22 The Girl Scouts of America has its beginning in the Girl Guides, created by Daisy Gordon, in Savannah, Georgia.

Media and Communication

- Herbert Croly publishes the *New Republic* in the United States.
- The *Farm Journal* holds the first national public opinion poll in the United States, to predict the presidential election result.
- The Federal Telegraph Company in the United States opens a radio telegraph service between San Francisco, California, and the island of Honolulu.
- The socialist paper *Pravda* ("Truth") is founded in Russia.
- The U.S. writer and editor Harriet Monroe founds *Poetry*, the first U.S. periodical devoted exclusively to verse.

February 1912–14 Benito Mussolini, journalist and future fascist leader, edits the Milan socialist paper *Avanti* ("Forwards") in Italy.

AUGUST
13 Congestion of the airwaves causes the U.S. Congress to pass the Radio Act, requiring operators to obtain a license from the Department of Commerce and Labor.

Religion

- German Protestant theologian Ernst Troeltsch publishes *The Social Teaching of the Christian Churches*, an influential study of the relationship between church and the state. It is translated into English in 1931.

Sports

APRIL
20 A crowd of nearly 30,000 people watches the Boston Red Sox defeat the New York Highlanders 7–6 in the opening baseball game at their new stadium, Fenway Park, in Boston, Massachusetts.

MAY
5 The 5th Olympic Games open in Stockholm, Sweden, attended by 2,547 competitors, 57 of whom are women, from 28 nations. Women's swimming events are introduced. In athletics, running events are timed electronically for the first time. The equestrian three-day event is introduced as an Olympic sport.

JULY
17 The International Amateur Athletic Federation (IAAF), the world governing body for track and field, is formed in Stockholm, Sweden, with 17 founder members.
22 The 5th Olympic Games close in Stockholm, Sweden. The United States wins 25 gold medals; Sweden, 24; Britain, 10; Finland, 9; France, 7; and Germany, 5. The stars of the games are Hannes Kolehmainen of Finland who wins the 5,000, 10,000, and 12,000 meter cross-country events and Jim Thorpe of the United States who wins the pentathlon and decathlon.

AUGUST
26 Maurice McLoughlin of the United States wins the men's singles at the U.S. lawn tennis championships at the Casino, Newport, Rhode Island. For the first time there is no Challenge Round, so the preceding year's champion has to play through the tournament.

OCTOBER
8–16 The Boston Red Sox defeat the New York Giants by four games to three in baseball's World Series.

BIRTHS & DEATHS

- Otto Ernst Remer, German Nazi security chief during World War II, born in Marbella, Spain (–1997).

JANUARY

1 Kim Philby, British intelligence officer and Soviet spy, born in Amabala, India.

6 Danny Thomas, U.S. comedian, born in Deerfield, Michigan (–1991).

15 Michel Debré, prime minister of France 1959–62, born in Paris, France (–1996).

19 Leonard Vitalyvich Kantorovich, Soviet economist who applied the technique of linear programming to improve economic forecasting, born in St. Petersburg, Russia (–1986).

21 Konrad Bloch, German-born U.S. biochemist who shared the Nobel Prize for Physiology or Medicine in 1964 with Feodor Lynen for discovering how acetic acid molecules form cholesterol, born in Neisse, Germany.

FEBRUARY

2 Burton Lane, Broadway and Hollywood composer, born in New York, New York (–1997).

10 Joseph Lister, English surgeon who founded antiseptic medicine, dies in Walmer, Kent, England (84).

MARCH

12 Robert Falcon Scott, British naval officer and explorer who tried to reach the South Pole, dies in Antarctica (43).

19 Adolf Galland, German air ace of World War II who commanded the Luftwaffe (German air force), born in Westerhult, Germany (–1996).

23 Werner von Braun, German rocket engineer who was also involved in the exploration of space in Germany and the United States, born in Wirsitz, Germany (–1977).

27 James Callaghan, British prime minister 1976–79, a Labour politician, born in Portsmouth, Hampshire, England (–1997).

28 Kazuo Taoka, Japanese crime boss who headed the 10,000-member Yamaguchi-gumi crime organization, born in Sanshomura, Japan (–1981).

APRIL

8 Sonja Henie, Norwegian-born U.S. figure skater and world amateur champion for ten successive years (1927–36), born in Christiania (now Oslo), Norway (–1969).

12 Clara Barton, U.S. schoolteacher who founded the U.S. Red Cross, dies in Glen Echo, Maryland (90).

15 Kim Il Sung, Korean dictator 1948–94, born near Pyongyang, Korea (now North Korea) (–1994).

19 Glenn T. Seaborg, U.S. nuclear chemist who discovered several elements heavier than uranium, born in Ishpeming, Michigan.

MAY

14 August Strindberg, Swedish playwright and novelist who developed expressionist drama, dies in Stockholm, Sweden (63).

27 Sam Snead, U.S. golfer, born in Hot Springs, Virginia.

28 Patrick White, Australian novelist and playwright, born in London, England (–1990).

30 Julius Axelrod, U.S. biochemist who received the Nobel Prize for Physiology or Medicine in 1970 for his discovery of the enzyme that breaks down neurotransmitters, born in New York, New York.

30 Wilbur Wright, U.S. pioneer of aviation, who, with his brother Orville, was the first to achieve sustained powered flight, dies in Dayton, Ohio (45).

JUNE

23 Alan Mathison Turing, English mathematician who pioneered computer theory and computer processes, born in London, England (–1954).

JULY

14 Northrop Frye, Canadian literary critic, born in Sherbrooke, Quebec, Canada (–1991).

14 Woody Guthrie, U.S. folk singer and songwriter, born in Okemah, Oklahoma (–1967).

17 Henri Poincaré, French mathematician, theoretical astronomer, and philosopher of science, dies in Paris, France (58).

20 Andrew Lang, Scottish collector of fairy tales, dies in Banchory, Aberdeenshire, Scotland (67).

31 Milton Friedman, U.S. *laissez-faire* economist, born in Brooklyn, New York.

AUGUST

13 Jules Massenet, French operatic composer, dies in Paris, France (70).

13 Salvador Edward Luria, Italian-born U.S. physician who received the Nobel Prize for Physiology or Medicine (1969) for his work on bacteriophages, born in Turin, Italy (–1991).

13 William Benjamin Hogan, U.S. golfer, born in Dublin, Texas.

20 William Booth, English preacher who founded the Salvation Army, dies in London, England (83).

23 Gene Kelly, U.S. actor and dancer, born in Pittsburgh, Pennsylvania (–1997).

25 Erich Honecker, German communist politician, leader of East Germany 1971–89, born in Neunkirchen, Germany (–1994).

30 Edward Purcell, U.S. physicist who shared the Nobel Prize for Physics with Felix Bloch in 1952 for his work on nuclear magnetic resonance (NMR), born (–1997).

SEPTEMBER

1 The English composer Samuel Coleridge-Taylor dies (37).

5 John Milton Cage, U.S. composer, born in Los Angeles, California (–1992).

29 Michelangelo Antonioni, Italian film director, born in Ferrara, Italy.

OCTOBER

10 Charles Madge, British sociologist who organized the Mass Observation project to measure public opinion, born in Johannesburg, South Africa (–1996).

17 John Paul I, Roman Catholic pope (1978), born in Forno di Canale, Italy (–1978).

21 Georg Solti, Hungarian-born British conductor, music director at the Royal Opera House, London, 1961–71, and director of the Chicago Symphony Orchestra, 1969–91, born in Budapest, Austria-Hungary (–1997).

26 Donald Siegel, U.S. film director, born in Chicago, Illinois (–1991).

NOVEMBER

26 Eric Sevareid, U.S. radio and television newscaster, born in Velva, North Dakota (–1992).

26 Eugène Ionesco, Romanian-born French dramatist who inspired the Theater of the Absurd, born in Slatina, Romania (–1994).

DECEMBER

1 Minoru Yamasaki, U.S. architect, designer of New York's World Trade Center, born in Seattle, Washington (–1986).

12 Henry Armstrong, U.S. boxer who simultaneously held the featherweight, welterweight, and lightweight championships (1937–39), born in Columbus, Mississippi (–1988).

19 Tip (Thomas Philip) O'Neill, U.S. speaker of the U.S. House of Representatives (1977–86), born in Cambridge, Massachusetts (–1994).

1913

POLITICS, GOVERNMENT, AND ECONOMICS

Business and Economics

- Cleveland, Ohio, candy manufacturer Clarence Crane introduces the Life Saver.
- R. J. Reynolds tobacco company introduces Camel cigarettes in the United States. Supported by a huge advertising campaign, they become the best-selling brand in five years.
- The United States's manufacturing output exceeds the combined output of France, Germany, and Britain.

JANUARY
- Speaking before the Chicago Commercial Club, President Woodrow Wilson vows to end business monopolies.

FEBRUARY
- The U.S. House Committee on Banking and Currency reports alarmingly that the nation is in the grip of a "money trust" whose machinations imperil U.S. democracy.

OCTOBER
- Henry Ford introduces the assembly line process, reducing the time required to produce a Model T car from 12.5 to 1.5 hours.

Colonization

DECEMBER
14   Greece formally annexes Crete from the Ottoman Empire.

Human Rights

- Jamaican civil-rights leader, Marcus Moziah Garvey, founds the Universal Negro Improvement Association in Kingston, Jamaica.

JANUARY
28   Suffragists demonstrate in London, England, following the withdrawal, on January 27, of a franchise bill to which an amendment for female suffrage might have been added.

MARCH
3   On the eve of the inauguration of the U.S. president, 5,000 suffragists led by Alice Paul parade down Pennsylvania Avenue in Washington, D.C., demanding female suffrage. They receive a hostile response and about 40 people are wounded in the clash, which is finally halted by cavalry troops from nearby Fort Meyer.

APRIL
3   Militant suffragist Emmeline Pankhurst is imprisoned in Britain for inciting persons to place explosives outside the house of the chancellor of the Exchequer, David Lloyd George.

MAY
6   The British House of Commons rejects a women's franchise bill.

JUNE
4   The British suffragist Emily Davidson is killed when she runs under the king's horse at the Derby.

Politics and Government

- Judge Archibald of the U.S. federal commercial court is found guilty of corruption.
- U.S. Congress authorizes the construction of California's Hetch Hetchy Dam, despite opposition from environmental activists.

JANUARY
2   The Ottoman garrison on the island of Chios surrenders to Greek troops in the First Balkan War.
5   Gottlieb von Jagow becomes German foreign minister (–1916).
6   The London peace conference between the Ottoman Empire and the Balkan states is suspended when the Ottoman Empire refuses to cede Adrianople, Crete, and the Aegean Islands.
17   Raymond Poincaré is elected president of France (–1920).
18   A Greco-Ottoman naval battle is fought off the Aegean island of Tenedos.
21   The moderate Aristide Briand succeeds Raymond Poincaré as prime minister of France.

FEBRUARY
- President William Howard Taft vetoes immigration legislation that would impose an English literacy test on prospective immigrants.
- The U.S. Supreme Court upholds the Mann White Slave Traffic Act (1910), which prohibits interstate commerce in women destined for prostitution.
3   Bulgaria renews war with the Ottoman Empire following the breakdown of the London peace conference, hostilities continuing until April 16.

8   Part of the Mexican army rebels and frees the ex-prime minister Felix Díaz and General Fernando Reyes.

13   A Franco-U.S. agreement extends the 1908 arbitration convention for five years.

18   The commander of the Mexican army, Victoriano Huerta, joins the rebel Mexican soldiers and forces President Francisco Madero to resign. He subsequently declares himself president, and civil war ensues.

23   Francisco Madero, the deposed president of Mexico, is murdered.

25   The 16th amendment to the U.S. Constitution takes effect, empowering the U.S. Congress to collect income tax.

MARCH

- The U.S. Congress divides the Department of Commerce and Labor into two distinct cabinet offices.
- U.S. Congress creates the Board of Mediation and Conciliation to settle labor disputes.

4   Woodrow Wilson is inaugurated as the 28th president of the United States.

11   A British–German agreement defines the frontier between Nigeria and Cameroon (under British and German rule respectively).

14   The Balkan allies accept the mediation of the European powers in a settlement of the war with the Ottoman Empire.

18   King George I of Greece is assassinated in newly occupied Thessaloníki (Salonika) by a drunken Greek, Alexandros Skinas.

18   The French senate rejects Aristide Briand's plan for proportional representation, and Briand resigns as prime minister.

26   A Bulgarian force takes Adrianople from the Ottoman Empire.

28   The Belgian Army Bill introduces universal military service to safeguard its neutrality in wartime.

31   The Ottoman Empire accepts the peace recommendations of the European powers.

APRIL

8   Following a break of 112 years, the U.S. president Woodrow Wilson resumes the delivery, in person, of the "State of the Union" address to Congress. He urges Congress to adopt legislation reducing the nation's tariffs.

8   The first parliament of the new Chinese republic meets.

16   The Ottoman Empire signs an armistice, ending its war with Bulgaria.

MAY

- California governor, Hiram Johnson, signs the Webb Alien Land-Holding Bill, which prohibits Japanese immigrants from owning land in California. The legislation provokes an outcry from the government of Japan, as well as from President Woodrow Wilson.
- President Woodrow Wilson officially recognizes the Republic of China, currently embroiled in civil war against the communists.

6   King Nicholas of Montenegro yields the Ottoman town of Scutari (held by Montenegro since 1912) to the European powers until an Albanian government is created in December.

30   A peace treaty between the Ottoman Empire and the Balkan states is signed in London, England, ending the First Balkan War.

30   The Canadian senate rejects a naval bill which provides for high expenditure on ships for the imperial navy.

31   The 17th amendment to the U.S. Constitution, transferring the election of senators from state legislators to a popular vote, becomes law.

JUNE

- Union and Confederate war veterans converge on Gettysburg, Pennsylvania, to commemorate the 50th anniversary of the battle.

10   The U.S. Supreme Court rules that states have the right to fix interstate rail rates.

15   Count Stephen Tisza, already very influential in Hungarian politics, becomes prime minister there.

26   Bulgaria signs a defensive treaty with Austria-Hungary.

29   The Second Balkan War begins when Bulgaria attacks Serbian and Greek positions.

30   The German Reichstag (parliament) passes a bill to fund an increase of 117,000 men in the size of the German army, giving the army a complement of 870,000 men.

JULY

7   The British House of Commons passes the Irish Home Rule Bill, but it is rejected on July 15 by the House of Lords.

10   Russia joins the Second Balkan War, opening hostilities against Bulgaria.

Second Balkan War (1913)

1913

JUNE

29   The Second Balkan War begins when Bulgaria attacks Serbian and Greek positions.

JULY

10   Rumania joins the Second Balkan War, opening hostilities against Bulgaria.

12   The Ottoman Empire enters the Second Balkan War, and on July 20 recaptures Adrianople from Bulgaria.

30   The Balkan states sign an armistice in Bucharest, Romania, ending the Second Balkan War.

AUGUST

10   The Balkan states sign a peace treaty in Bucharest, Romania, in which Serbia and Greece retain the areas of Macedonia they have taken from Bulgaria.

SEPTEMBER

18   A Bulgarian–Ottoman treaty settles the frontier in Thrace, leaving Adrianople under Ottoman rule.

NOVEMBER

13   A Greek–Ottoman peace treaty following the Second Balkan War allows Greece to absorb Crete and all the Aegean islands except Tenedos, Imbros, and the Dodecanese.

12 A meeting of 150,000 Ulstermen at Craigavon, Ireland, pledges to resist Home Rule for Ireland, by force if necessary.

12 The Ottoman Empire enters the Second Balkan War, and on July 20 recaptures Adrianople from Bulgaria.

23 A rebellion breaks out in Yangtzi Valley and southern China against the rule of Yuan Shikai.

30 The Balkan states sign an armistice in Bucharest, Romania, ending the Second Balkan War.

AUGUST

• Jewish factory superintendent Leo Moses Frank is convicted and sentenced to death for the murder, in April, of employee Mary Phagan in Atlanta, Georgia. The evidence against him is extremely weak and his case becomes a cause célèbre among U.S. intellectuals.

• President Woodrow Wilson adopts a policy of "watchful waiting" following a military coup in Mexico lead by General Victoriano Huerta.

7 In response to the German army bill of June 30, a French army bill increases compulsory military service to three years.

10 The Balkan states sign a peace treaty in Bucharest, Romania, in which Serbia and Greece retain the areas of Macedonia they have taken from Bulgaria.

SEPTEMBER

3 The revolutionary city of Nanjing, China, falls to the forces of the Chinese ruler Yuan Shikai.

16 Japan sends a naval flotilla to the River Yangtzi following China's failure to honor the reparations agreement made after the Sino-Japanese War of 1894–95.

18 A Bulgarian–Ottoman treaty settles the frontier in Thrace, leaving Adrianople under Ottoman rule.

24 Unionists in northern Ireland appoint their own provisional government to take power when the Irish Home Rule Bill takes effect.

OCTOBER

• At the push of a button in Washington, D.C., President Woodrow Wilson detonates an explosion at the Gamboa Dike in Panama, completing construction on the Panama canal.

• The U.S. president Woodrow Wilson signs the Underwood-Simmons Tariff Act, the biggest change in tariffs since the mid-19th century, which reduces or removes duties on some 958 items.

6 Yuan Shikai is elected president of the Chinese republic.

17 Serbian troops invade Albania following Albanian raids into disputed Serbian territory.

21 A royalist uprising in Portugal is suppressed by the government.

27 The Conservatives return to power in Spain following a split in the Liberal Party in the aftermath of the assassination of José Canalejas.

28 Britain, France, and Germany withhold recognition of Victoriano Huerta's government in Mexico until the United States decides its policy toward it.

NOVEMBER

1 The Triple Alliance of Germany, Austria-Hungary, and Italy agrees a naval convention.

3 The United States demands the withdrawal of General Victoriano Huerta from Mexico.

4 Premier Yuan Shikai of China purges the parliament of revolutionary Guomindang party members.

5 A joint declaration by Russia and China recognizes the autonomy of Outer Mongolia under Chinese suzerainty.

6 Mahatma Gandhi, leader of the Indian Passive Resistance Movement, is arrested.

11 Premier Yuan Shikai outlaws the revolutionary Guomindang party, seeking to make himself sole ruler of China.

11 The German general Otto Liman von Sanders is appointed a high commander of the Ottoman army in Constantinople, Anatolia (modern Istanbul, Turkey), while heading a German military mission appointed to improve the Ottoman army.

13 A Greek–Ottoman peace treaty following the Second Balkan War allows Greece to absorb Crete and all the Aegean islands except Tenedos, Imbros, and the Dodecanese.

17 The first vessel passes through the Panama Canal.

20 The "Zabern incident," in which a German officer in Alsace-Lorraine insults Alsatian recruits, raises tension in Franco-German relations.

DECEMBER

13 Britain and France send a diplomatic note to the Ottoman Empire, warning it against becoming too closely involved with Germany.

23 The U.S. Congress passes the Glass-Owen Currency Act (Federal Reserve Bank Act), establishing a Federal Reserve Board with power over monetary policy and 12 district Federal Reserve banks, and creating the nation's first central banking system since the dissolution of the Second Bank of the United States in the 1830s.

SCIENCE, TECHNOLOGY, AND MEDICINE

Ecology

• U.S. Congress passes legislation to protect migratory game and insect-eating birds.

MARCH

21–6 Ohio's Miami River overflows its banks, devastating the city of Dayton and surrounding areas. The flood kills 400 people and causes an estimated $100 million damage.

AUGUST

• The Keokuk Dam on the Mississippi River, the world's largest hydroelectric dam, becomes operational. Spanning the towns of Keokuk, Iowa, and Hamilton, Illinois, the dam is intended to control flooding and promote irrigation as well as produce electricity.

OCTOBER

• Torrential rain inundates Texas, causing some 500 deaths and causing an estimated $50 million damage.

Health and Medicine

- 1,192 people in Mississippi die from pellagra, a disease caused by deficiency in nicotinic acid (one of the B vitamins), common when the staple food is corn.
- Drinking water is sterilized by ultraviolet rays in Manila, Philippines.
- French physiologist Charles Richet receives the Nobel Prize for Physiology or Medicine for his discovery of anaphylaxis.
- German bacteriologist Emil von Behring introduces a toxin–antitoxin vaccine against diphtheria.
- Hungarian-born U.S. pathologist Bela Schick devises the "Schick" skin test for immunity from diphtheria.
- The American Cancer Society is founded to support research into cancer.
- The American College of Surgeons is founded.
- The British Army begins to immunize its troops against typhoid. Almost all are immunized during World War I, which is the first war in which more British soldiers die in combat than from infection and disease.
- U.S. physiologist John Abel invents the first artificial kidney.

Math

- English mathematician and philosopher Bertrand Russell publishes the final volume of *Principia Mathematica/ Principles of Mathematics* in collaboration with another English mathematician and philosopher, Alfred North Whitehead. They attempt to derive the whole of mathematics from a logical foundation.

Science

- Danish astronomer Ejnar Hertzsprung introduces a luminosity scale of Cepheid variable stars to measure their distance.
- Danish physicist Niels Bohr proposes that electrons orbit the atomic nucleus in fixed orbits thus upholding New Zealand-born British physicist Ernest Rutherford's model proposed in 1911.
- Dutch physicist Heike Kamerlingh-Onnes receives the Nobel Prize for Physics for his investigations on the properties of matter at low temperatures and the production of liquid helium.
- English geologist Arthur Holmes uses radioactivity to date rocks, establishing that the earth is 4.6 billion years old.
- English physicist Frederick Soddy coins the term "isotope" (from the Greek *isos*, "equal," and *topos*, "place") to describe atoms of the same chemical element but with different atomic numbers.
- English physicist Henry Moseley equates the atomic number of an atom with the positive charge on its nucleus, and shows that the characteristics of an element depend on its atomic number, not its atomic weight. He draws up the periodic table, based on atomic numbers, that is in use today.
- English physicist J. J. Thomson develops a mass spectrometer, called a parabola spectrograph. A beam of charged ions is deflected by a magnetic field to produce parabolic curves on a photographic plate.

- English physicist J. J. Thomson discovers neon-22, an isotope of neon. It is the first isotope of a nonradioactive element to be discovered.
- English physicists William and Lawrence Bragg develop X-ray crystallography by establishing that the orderly arrangement of atoms in crystals displays interference and diffraction patterns. They also demonstrate the wave nature of X-rays.
- French physicist Charles Fabry discovers the ozone layer in the upper atmosphere.
- German biochemists Leonor Michaelis and Maude Menten develop a mathematical equation describing the rate of enzyme-catalyzed reactions.
- German chemist Friedrich Bergius publishes *The Use of High Pressure in Chemical Actions* in which he describes his process of converting coal at high pressure to produce gasoline.
- German chemist Fritz Haber develops a process for nitrogen fixation from air.
- German chemist Richard Willstätter determines the composition of chlorophyll.
- German physicist Albert Einstein formulates the law of photochemical equivalence, which states that for every quantum of radiation absorbed by a substance one molecule reacts.
- German physicist Johannes Stark discovers that an electric field splits the spectral lines of hydrogen.
- German physicists Hans Geiger and Ernst Marsden prove, by scattering experiments, that New Zealand-born British physicist Ernest Rutherford's model of the nuclear atom (proposed 1911) is correct.
- Swiss chemist Alfred Werner receives the Nobel Prize for Chemistry for his work on the bonding of atoms within molecules.
- U.S. astronomer Henry Russell shows that there is a correlation between a star's brightness and its spectrum. The correlation is important in determining stellar distances.
- U.S. biochemist Elmer Verner McCollum isolates vitamin A.
- U.S. chemists K. Fajans and O. H. Göhring discover the short-lived variety of the radioactive element protactinium (protactinium-234).
- U.S. physicist Albert Munsell develops the Munsell color scheme, which defines colors according to their hue (wavelength), value (brightness), and chroma (purity).

Technology

- German inventor Oskar Barnak devises the first 35-mm camera. It is not commercialized until 1924.
- The first stainless steel is cast in Britain, by Harry Brearley in Sheffield.
- The Woolworth building, designed by U.S. architect Cass Gilbert, is completed in New York, New York. At 232 m/791 ft high, it is the tallest building in the world.
- U.S. chemist William Burton patents a thermal cracking process whereby the less volatile fractions of petroleum are distilled and then chemically converted into gasoline. It doubles the yield of gasoline from crude oil.

JULY

15 German engineer Franz Schneider patents a synchronizing machine gun that shoots through the propellers of airplanes. The prototype is lost, however.

Transportation

- British firm Vickers introduce the Experimental Fighting Biplane No. 1. It is the first plane to have a machine gun mounted on it.
- The German liner *Imperator* enters service. It is the largest ship in the world at 280 m/919 ft long.
- The subway system in Buenos Aires, Argentina, is completed: the first in South America.
- The Transcontinental Railroad in Canada is used for the first time by a train; it is carrying grain.
- The world's first diesel-electric locomotives begin running in Sweden.

JANUARY

11 The last horse-drawn omnibus in Paris, France, ceases operation.

ARTS AND IDEAS

Architecture

- Grand Central Station, designed by the U.S. architects Charles Reed and Allen Stem, is completed in New York, New York.
- Texans restore the Alamo, a site of a battle in Texas's fight for independence from Mexico, to its original appearance as a mission and dedicate it as a historic landmark. U.S. president Woodrow Wilson creates the Alamo National Monument in San Antonio, Texas.
- The Jahrhunderthalle in Breslau, Prussia (now Wrocław, Poland) is completed. Built of reinforced concrete, it is designed by the German architect Max Berg.
- The Woolworth Building, designed by the U.S. architect Cass Gilbert, is completed in New York, New York. With 60 floors, it will be world's highest skyscraper until 1931.

Arts

- c. 1913 The English artist Walter Richard Sickert paints *Ennui*.
- In Britain, the artists Harold Gilman, Walter Sickert, and Wyndham Lewis form the London Group, exhibiting for the first time in 1914.
- The French artist Fernand Léger paints *Contrast of Forms*.
- The French artist Henri Matisse paints *Portrait of Madame Matisse* and sculpts *The Back, II*.
- The French artist Marcel Duchamp creates *Bicycle Wheel*. The first "assisted readymade," it consists of a bicycle wheel fastened on top of a stool.
- The French artist Pierre Bonnard paints *Dining Room in the Country*.

- The French writer Guillaume Apollinaire publishes *Les Peintres cubistes/The Cubist Painters*.
- The German artist Ludwig Kirchner paints *Berlin Street Scene*.
- The German artist Wilhelm Lehmbruck sculpts *Ascending Youth*.
- The International Exhibition of Modern Art is held in New York, New York. Known as the "Armory Show," it proves to be a controversial exhibition of postimpressionist and cubist art, widely criticized as decadent. The exhibition plays an important role in introducing modern European art to the United States.
- The Italian artist Amadeo Modigliani paints *Portrait of Paul Alexandre*.
- The Italian artist Giocomo Balla paints *Abstract Speed*.
- The Italian artist Giorgio de Chirico paints *The Uncertainty of the Poet*.
- The Italian artist Umberto Boccioni sculpts *Unique Forms of Continuity in Space*.
- The Russian artist Kasimir Malevich paints *The Black Cross*.
- The Russian artist Natalia Goncharova paints *The Laundry* and *The Cyclist*.
- The Russian artist Wassily Kandinsky paints *Improvisation 31 – Sea Battle*.
- The Spanish artist Pablo Picasso paints *Man with a Guitar*.
- The U.S. artist Ernest Lawson paints *Spring Night, Harlem River*.
- The U.S. artist George Bellows paints *Cliff Dwellers*.
- The U.S. artist Joseph Stella paints *Battle of Lights, Coney Island*.
- The U.S. artist Samuel Halpert paints *Brooklyn Bridge*.
- The U.S. photographer Alvin Langdon Coburn publishes *Men of Mark*, portraits of leading British and Irish figures such as George Bernard Shaw and George Meredith.

DECEMBER

- Leonardo da Vinci's *Mona Lisa*, missing since 1911, is recovered; the thief, Vincenzo Perugia, claims he was retaliating against France for taking Italian art works from Italy.

Film

- A movie of Shakespeare's *Hamlet*, directed by Cecil Hepworth, is released in Britain, starring Johnson Forbes-Robertson.
- British actor Charlie Chaplin makes 35 movies for U.S. movie producer Mack Sennett in this year.
- The movie *Arizona*, produced by the All Star Feature Corporation and starring Cyril Scott, is released in the United States, the first feature-length Western.
- The movie *Barney Oldfield's Race for Life*, directed by Mack Sennett, is released in the United States. He also stars in it with Mabel Normand.
- The movie *East Lynne*, directed by Bert Haldane, is released in Britain.
- The movie *Fantômas*, directed by Louis Feuillade, is released in France.
- The movie *The Sea Wolf*, directed by Hobart Bosworth, is released in the United States.

- The movie *The Student of Prague*, directed by Stellan Rye, is released in Germany.
- The movie *The Squaw Man*, directed by Cecil B. De Mille, is released in the United States. The first full-length feature movie to be shot on location in California, it stars Dustin Farnum.
- The movie *Traffic in Souls*, directed by George Loane Tucker, is released in the United States, starring Matt Moore, Jane Gail, and Ethel Grandin.
- The first movies made by the Warner brothers are released in the United States, and the Fox and Universal film companies are formed.
- U.S. movie producer Mack Sennett makes comic actor Roscoe "Fatty" Arbuckle one of his Keystone Kops, a group of slapstick comedians, dressed in ill-fitting policemen's uniforms, who are stock characters in Sennett comedies.

APRIL

9   The Danish Statens Arkiv—a national movie archive—is established in Copenhagen.

Literature and Language

- Robert Bridges becomes poet laureate in England, a position he holds until 1930.
- The English writer Compton Mackenzie publishes the first part of his novel *Sinister Street*. The second part appears in 1914.
- The English writer D. H. Lawrence publishes his novel *Sons and Lovers*.
- The French writer Alain-Fournier publishes his novel *Le Grand meaulnes/The Lost Domain*.
- The French writer Marcel Proust publishes *Du Côté de chez Swann/Swann's Way*. This is the first volume of his multivolume novel *A la recherche du temps perdu/ Remembrance of Things Past*.
- The Russian writer Osip Mandelstam publishes his poetry collection *Kamen/Stone*.
- The U.S. writer Edith Wharton publishes her novel *The Custom of the Country*.
- The U.S. writer Eleanor Porter publishes her children's novel *Polyanna*.
- The U.S. writer Ellen Glasgow publishes her novel *Virginia*.
- The U.S. writer Henry James publishes his first book of autobiography *A Small Boy and Others*.
- The U.S. writer Jack London publishes his memoirs *John Barleycorn*.
- The U.S. writer Robert Frost publishes his poetry collection *A Boy's Will* in England.
- The U.S. writer Willa Cather publishes her novel *O Pioneers!*
- U.S. historian Charles Beard publishes *An Economic Interpretation of the Constitution of the United States*.

Music

- English songwriter C. W. Murphy writes the song "Hold Your Hand Out, Naughty Boy."
- Kenneth J. Alford (pen name of English bandsman Frederick Joseph Ricketts) writes the march "Colonel Bogey."

- The Austrian composer Anton Webern completes his *Bagatelles* for string quartet (Opus 9), *5 Stücke/Five Pieces* for orchestra (Opus 10) and *6 Bagatelles* for string quartet (Opus 11).
- The English composer George Butterworth completes his symphonic rhapsody *A Shropshire Lad*, inspired by the poems of A. E. Housman.
- The English composer Ivor Gurney completes his song settings *Five Elizabethan Songs*.
- The English composer Ralph Vaughan Williams completes his Symphony No. 2, *A London Symphony*.
- The English composer Gustav Holst completes his orchestral work *St Paul's Suite*.
- The English composer Arnold Bax completes his orchestral work *The Garden of Fand*.
- The English musicologist and author Edward Joseph Dent publishes *Mozart's Operas: A Critical Study*.
- The French composer Claude Debussy completes his piano work *Préludes II*.
- The French composer Maurice Ravel completes his song cycle *Poèmes de Stéphane Mallarmé*, settings of poems by the French writer Stéphane Mallarmé for voice and chamber orchestra.
- The Hungarian composer Ernst von Dohnányi completes his *Variations on a Nursery Song*.
- The Italian composer Ferruccio Busoni completes his *Indianische Fantasie/Indian Fantasy* for piano and orchestra.
- The opera *L'amore dei tre re/The Love of the Three Kings*, by the Italian composer Italo Montemezzi, is first performed in Milan, Italy.
- The opera *Pénélope/Penelope* by the French composer Gabriel Fauré is first performed, in Monte Carlo, Monaco.
- The Russian composer Sergey Rachmaninov completes his choral work *The Bells*, and his Piano Sonata No. 2, which he revises in 1931.
- The U.S. composer Charles Ives completes his work *New England Holidays* for orchestra and chorus, which includes *Decoration Day*. He also completes his choral work *Walt Whitman*.
- U.S. Salvation Army member George Bennard writes the hymn "The Old Rugged Cross."
- U.S. songwriters Chris Smith and James Henry Burris write the song "Ballin' the Jack."
- U.S. songwriters James V. Monaco and Joe McCarthy write the song "You Made Me Love You (I Didn't Want to Do It)."

Theater and Dance

- The ballet *Jeux/Games*, by the French composer Claude Debussy and the Russian dancer Vaslav Nijinsky, is first performed in Paris, France, under the Russian impresario Sergei Diaghilev. The sets and costumes are by the Russian artist Léon Bakst and Nijinsky dances the central role.
- The ballet *Le Sacre du printemps/The Rite of Spring*, by the Russian composer Igor Stravinsky and the Russian dancer Vaslav Nijinsky, is first performed, in Paris, France, under the Russian impresario Sergei Diaghilev. Nijinsky dances the central role. Audiences riot, judging the work to be crude and offensive.

- The fox-trot dance becomes popular in the United States, and later spreads to Europe.
- The Palace Theater opens on Broadway in New York, New York.
- The play *Androcles and the Lion*, by the Irish writer George Bernard Shaw, is first performed at the St. James's Theatre in London, England. A German version of the play was previously performed in Berlin in 1912.
- The play *Romance*, by the U.S. dramatist Edward Sheldon, is first performed, in New York, New York.

FEBRUARY

3   The musical *The Sunshine Girl*, with music by John L. Golden and lyrics by Joseph Cawthorne, is performed for the first time, at the Knickerbocker Theater, New York, New York.

Thought and Scholarship

- Austrian psychoanalyst Sigmund Freud publishes *Totem und Tabu/Totem and Taboo.*
- German philosopher and sociologist Max Scheler publishes *Der Formalismus in der Ethik und die materiale Werkethik/Formalism in Ethics and the Material Work Ethic.*
- German philosopher Edmund Husserl publishes *Ideen zu einer reinen Phänomenologie und phänomenologischen Philosophie/Ideas: General Introduction to Pure Phenomenology.* He also publishes *Cartesian Meditations*, which is translated into English in 1931. One of his major works, it becomes a central text of phenomenology.
- Irish writer Lady Gregory publishes *Our Irish Theatre.*
- Spanish writer and philosopher Miguel de Unamuno publishes *Del sentimiento trágico de la vida en los hombres y en los pueblos/The Tragic Sense of Life in Men and Peoples.*
- The English historian George Peabody Gooch publishes *History and Historians of the Nineteenth Century.*
- The Nobel Prize for Literature is awarded to the Indian poet Rabindranath Tagore.
- U.S. historian Charles Austin Beard publishes *An Economic Interpretation of the Constitution of the United States.*
- U.S. political journalist Walter Lippmann publishes *Preface to Politics.*
- U.S. psychologist John Watson publishes the article "Psychology as a Behaviorist Views It," in which he introduces the behaviorist school of psychology that advocates that psychology should concern itself with objectively observable actions.

SOCIETY

Everyday Life

- Coco Chanel's boutique at Deauville, France, leads a trend toward more casual fashions in women's dress.
- Liggett & Myers introduces Chesterfield cigarettes in the United States.

- Milton B. Loel of the Brillo Manufacturing Corporation launches Brillo pads in the United States.
- The first domestic refrigerators appear on the market in the United States and Germany.
- The French designer Coco Chanel introduces sportswear for women.
- The United Mine Workers union strikes at John D. Rockefeller's Colorado Fuel and Iron Company to protest against unsafe working conditions. Violence erupts when two mines are set on fire; 27 strikers are killed.
- The U.S. company Formica Insulation Co. launches formica.
- The U.S. Postal Service establishes Parcel Post, the package delivery system.

JANUARY

January–March   Garment workers strike in New York, New York, demanding higher wages, shorter hours, and the recognition of their union. The strike ends on March 12, after the workers' grievances are largely met. The strike spreads to Boston, Massachusetts, from February into April. It ends there on April 21, after workers receive increased pay, shorter hours, and union recognition.

FEBRUARY

- The International Workers of the World (IWW) launches an unsuccessful strike of silk workers in Patterson, New Jersey. Local businessmen and politicians had vowed to resist the union's demands for shorter hours and union recognition.

MAY

14   Standard Oil founder John D. Rockefeller provides $100 million to establish the Rockefeller Foundation in New York, New York, "to promote the well-being of mankind."

Media and Communication

- The Eiffel Tower Radio Station in Paris, France, begins broadcasting regular time signals.
- U.S. engineer Frederick Kolster devises a direction finder or radio-compass and installs transmitters on the coast of New Jersey.

JULY

- *Billboard* magazine is the first publication in the United States to print a weekly chart of best-selling popular songs.

DECEMBER

21   The *New York World* newspaper prints the first modern crossword puzzle in the United States, devised by Arthur Wynne.

Sports

- The German firm Neufeldt and Kuhnke introduce an armored diving suit with ball-and-socket joints.

FEBRUARY

5   Fights between Caucasian and black American boxers in New York, New York, are banned by the New York State Athletic Commission in the United States.

BIRTHS & DEATHS

JANUARY

9 Richard M(ilhous) Nixon, 37th president of the United States 1969–74, a Republican, the first president to resign, born in Yorba Linda, California (–1994).

10 Gustáv Husák, president of Czechoslovakia (now the Czech and Slovak Republics) 1975–89, born in Dúbravka, Slovakia (now the Slovak Republic) (–1991).

19 Minnesota Fats (adopted name of Rudolf Walter Wanderone), U.S. pool player, born (–1996).

FEBRUARY

3 Mary Leakey, English-born Kenyan anthropologist, born in London, England (–1996).

14 Jimmy Hoffa, U.S. labor leader, president of the International Brotherhood of Teamsters (1957–71), born in Brazil, Indiana (–1975).

22 Ferdinand de Saussure, Swiss linguist whose ideas about the structure of language laid the foundation of modern linguistics, dies in Geneva, Switzerland (55).

22 Francisco Madero, Mexican revolutionary and president of Mexico 1911–13 who overthrew the dictator Porfirio Díaz, is assassinated in Mexico City (39).

27 Paul Ricoeur, French philosopher, born in Valence, France.

MARCH

26 Paul Erdös, Hungarian mathematician, born in Budapest, Hungary (–1996).

31 J(ohn) P(ierpont) Morgan, U.S. financier, dies in Rome, Italy (75).

APRIL

27 Philip Hauge Abelson, U.S. physicist who developed the gas diffusion method of separating isotopes of uranium and, with U.S. physicist Edward M. McMillan, discovered neptunium (1940), born in Tacoma, Washington.

MAY

6 Stewart Granger (born James Lablache), English-U.S. film actor, born in London, England (–1993).

16 Woody Herman, U.S. clarinetist, saxophonist, band leader, and vocalist, born in Milwaukee, Wisconsin (–1987).

19 Janjiva Reddy, president of India 1977–82, born in Hyderabad, India (–1996).

26 Peter Wilton Cushing, English actor known for his roles of Dracula,

Frankenstein, and Dr. Who, born in Kenley, Surrey, England (–1994).

JUNE

11 Vince Lombardi, U.S. football coach who led the Green Bay Packers to five NFL championships, born in Brooklyn, New York (–1970).

29 Tony Zale (originally Anton Florian Zaleski), U.S. world middle weight boxing champion 1940–48, born in Gary, Indiana (–1997).

JULY

14 Gerald Ford, 38th president of the United States (1974–77), a Republican, born in Omaha, Nebraska.

18 Red Skelton, U.S. radio and television comedian, born in Vincennes, Indiana.

AUGUST

10 Wolfgang Paul, German nuclear physicist who developed the ion trap, or "Paul trap," used to store single atoms long enough to make accurate spectroscopic measurements on single atoms, born in Lorenzkirch, Germany (–1993).

13 August Bebel, German socialist who founded the German Social Democratic Party, dies in Passugg, Switzerland (73).

13 Makarios III, Cypriot archbishop, leader in the struggle for union with Greece, and president of the Independent Republic of Cyprus 1959–77, born in Pano Panaiya, Paphos, Cyprus (–1977).

16 Menachem Begin, prime minister of Israel 1977–83, born in Brest-Litovsk, Russia (–1992).

20 Roger Wolcott Sperry, U.S. neurologist who elucidated the functions of different parts of the human brain, born in Hartford, Connecticut (–1994).

28 (William) Robertson Davies, Canadian novelist known for his Deptford trilogy, born in Thamesville, Ontario, Canada (–1995).

28 Terence Reese, English bridge player and author, born (–1996).

31 Bernard Lovell, English radio astronomer who founded the Jodrell Bank experimental station, born in Oldland Common, Gloucestershire, England.

SEPTEMBER

12 Jesse Owens, black U.S. track and field athlete who won four gold

medals at the 1936 Olympics in Berlin, born in Danville, Alabama (–1980).

28 Alice Marble, U.S. tennis player who dominated women's singles and doubles tennis during the late 1930s, born in Plumes County, California (–1990).

29 Rudolf Diesel, German engineer who invented the diesel engine, drowns when he falls overboard on a steamer traveling to London, England (56).

OCTOBER

22 Bao Dai, last emperor of Vietnam 1927–55, born in Hué, Vietnam (–1997).

23 Edwin Klebs, German physician who, with Friedrich Löffler, discovered the diphtheria bacillus, dies in Bern, Switzerland (79).

25 Klaus Barbie, German Nazi war criminal known as the "Butcher of Lyon," born in Bad Godesburg, Germany (–1991).

NOVEMBER

2 Burt Lancaster, U.S. film actor, born in New York, New York (–1994).

5 Vivien Leigh, English actress, born in Darjeeling, India (–1967).

7 Alfred Russel Wallace, Welsh naturalist who developed a theory of evolution by natural selection independently of Charles Darwin, dies in Bradstone, Dorset, England (90).

22 Albert Camus, French novelist who received the Nobel Prize for Literature in 1957, born in Mondovi, Algeria (–1960).

22 Benjamin Britten, English composer, born in Lowestoft, Suffolk, England (–1976).

DECEMBER

7 Montogomery Ward, U.S. merchant who introduced the mail-order method of selling, dies in Highland Park, Illinois (69).

12 Menelik II, King of the Ethiopian kingdom of Shewa 1865–69 and emperor of Ethiopia 1889–1913, dies in Addis Ababa, Ethiopia (69).

13 Archie Moore, U.S. boxer, world light-heavyweight champion 1952–62, born in Benoit, Mississippi.

18 Willy Brandt, chancellor of the Federal Republic of Germany (West Germany) 1969–74, born in Lübeck, Germany (–1992).

MAY

30   Jules Goux of France, in a Peugeot, becomes the first foreign winner of the Indianapolis 500 motor race.

JUNE

7   Hudson Stuck, an Episcopalian clergyman, becomes the first person to reach the summit of Mt. McKinley in Alaska, the highest mountain in North America (6,194 m/20,320 ft).

23–July 4   Women's doubles and mixed doubles events are held for the first time at the Wimbledon lawn tennis championships in London, England.

SEPTEMBER

20   Francis Ouimet, a store clerk from Boston, United States, becomes the first amateur golfer to win the U.S. Open golf championship, at the Country Club, Brookline, Massachusetts.

OCTOBER

20   The International Lawn Tennis Federation is established in Paris, France. It replaces the English Lawn Tennis Association as the world governing body for the game.

NOVEMBER

1   Notre Dame, led by Knute Rockne and Gus Dorais, defeat the Army 35–13 in the first U.S. college football game between the two teams.

1914

POLITICS, GOVERNMENT, AND ECONOMICS

Business and Economics

- According to the National Negro Business League there are 40,000 businesses owned by black Americans in the United States.
- New York entrepreneur Charles E. Merrill enters the brokerage business, laying the seed for the brokerage firm Merrill Lynch.

AUGUST

1–January 4, 1915   Following the outbreak of war in Europe, the London stock market in England closes.

Colonization

JANUARY

1   Northern and southern Nigeria are amalgamated as the British Colony and Protectorate of Nigeria.

NOVEMBER

5   Britain annexes Ottoman Cyprus, which has been occupied by Britain since June 1878.

Human Rights

MAY

6   The Women's Enfranchisement Bill is defeated in the British House of Lords.

Politics and Government

- President Woodrow Wilson appoints scholar James C. McReynolds to the U.S. Supreme Court.
- The Harrison Narcotic Act restricts the availability of powerful drugs such as heroin in the United States.

JANUARY

8   Gaston Calmette, editor of the French newspaper *Le Figaro*, makes charges of financial malpractice against Joseph Caillaux, the French minister of finance.

8   The German general Otto Liman von Sanders is made inspector-general of the Ottoman army, and relinquishes command of the German First Army Corps in order to mollify Britain, France, and Russia.

11   Yuan Shikai extends his power in China, dissolving parliament and governing alone.

27   President Oreste of Haiti abdicates during a revolt, and U.S. marines are sent in to preserve order. General Zamon is elected president on February 8.

MARCH

8   The Monarchist Party wins the Spanish elections.

14   An Ottoman–Serbian peace treaty establishes the rights of Muslims now living in Serbian-controlled areas.

16   Mme. Caillaux assassinates Gaston Calmette, editor of the French newspaper *Le Figaro*, in retaliation for his smear campaign against her husband, Joseph Caillaux, the French finance minister.

20   The "Curragh incident" or "mutiny" takes place when General Hubert Gough and 58 other British cavalry officers stationed at Curragh near Dublin, Ireland, indicate that they would resign if the army were ordered to take action in northern Ireland to enforce Home Rule.

APRIL

- In response to the U.S. incursion in Mexico, Mexico severs diplomatic relations with the United States.

April–July Argentina, Brazil, and Chile—the ABC Powers—offer to mediate in the U.S.-Mexican conflict. President Woodrow Wilson accepts the offer, but the crisis dissolves after Mexican president Victoriano Huerta resigns from office on July 15.

1 A civil government is established in the Panama Canal Zone.

6 Catalonia, Spain, is awarded limited self-government.

10 U.S. sailors buying gasoline in Tampico, Mexico, are temporarily arrested by Mexican troops. Following their release, President Victoriano Huerta of Mexico refuses a U.S. request for Mexican guns to salute the U.S. flag.

22 Four U.S. marines die and twenty are wounded in a punitive U.S. assault on the Mexican port of Veracruz, initiated after a group of U.S. marines were briefly detained on April 10.

May

• U.S. Congress adopts a resolution formally decreeing Mother's Day the second Sunday in June.

20 Argentina, Brazil, and Chile arbitrate in the dispute between the United States and Mexico, at the Niagara Falls on the border of the United States and Canada.

25 The British House of Commons passes the Irish Home Rule Bill.

June

11 Delegates at the Niagara Falls approve a new Mexican government in negotiations to reach a peace agreement between the United States and Mexico, which eventually will be signed on June 24.

13 Greece annexes the Aegean islands of Chios and Mytilene (Lesbos), which were formerly Ottoman possessions.

13 René Viviani forms a ministry in France following a crisis over the introduction of the military three-year service bill.

15 A British–German agreement settles the dispute over the Baghdad Railroad, when Germany agrees not to build a route south of Baghdad, Iraq, and promises to respect British interests.

23 The British prime minister, Herbert Asquith, introduces a further compromise on Ulster, Ireland, into the House of Lords, allowing it to secede from the proposed Irish parliament for an unlimited period.

28 Archduke Franz Ferdinand of Austria-Hungary and his wife are assassinated at Sarajevo, Bosnia, by Gavrilo Princip, an 18-year-old Bosnian Serb student linked with the Serbian nationalist society "the Black Hand."

July

6 Germany issues the "blank check", promising support to Austria-Hungary in any action it chooses to take against Serbia over the assassination of Archduke Ferdinand.

8 The British House of Lords considers an amending bill to allow for the temporary exclusion of parts of northern Ireland from Home Rule, but they vote to exclude northern Ireland permanently, and thus create deadlock over the Home Rule issue.

10 The provisional government in Ulster, northern Ireland, reaffirms Ulster's determination to resist Home Rule.

14 Following the assassination of Archduke Ferdinand, the Austrian crown council decides on war with Serbia.

16 An announcement is made that President Victoriano Huerta of Mexico has gone into exile and has been replaced by Carbajal as provisional president. In August Carbajal also flees the country.

20–29 President Raymond Poincaré and Prime Minister René Viviani of France visit Russia, and agree to ask for British help in stopping Austria making war with Serbia.

23 Austria-Hungary, suspecting Serbian involvement in the assassination of Archduke Franz Ferdinand, issues an ultimatum to Serbia, which contains deliberately unreasonable demands.

25 Serbia replies to the Austro-Hungarian ultimatum and promises to comply with most of its points, though it has already mobilized its army.

26 The British prime minister, Sir Edward Grey, proposes a four-power mediation of the Balkan crisis.

26 Troops clash with Irish nationalists involved in gunrunning, in Dublin, Ireland.

28 Austria-Hungary declares war on Serbia.

30 Russia orders the general mobilization of its armies in response to the Austro-Hungarian declaration of war on Serbia.

31 Germany issues an ultimatum which gives Russia 12 hours in which to stop the mobilization of its army. Meanwhile, Austria-Hungary mobilizes its army.

31 The leading French socialist Jean Jaurès is murdered in Paris, France, following fears that he might paralyze the French war effort with a call for a general strike.

August

1 Germany declares war on Russia.

2 A secret German–Ottoman treaty of alliance is signed at Constantinople, Anatolia (modern Turkey).

2 Germany occupies Luxembourg and sends an ultimatum to Belgium demanding the free passage of German troops.

3 Germany declares war on France.

3 Italy declares its neutrality in the European conflict.

4 Britain declares war on Germany and establishes a naval blockade of the North Sea, the Channel, and the Mediterranean Sea in order to cut supplies to the Central Powers.

4 Germany declares war on Belgium and invades Belgium and France.

4 The U.S. president, Woodrow Wilson, proclaims U.S. neutrality in the European war.

5 The German Second Army under General Otto von Emmich reaches Liège, Belgium, where it is resisted by Belgian defenders (until August 16).

6 Austria-Hungary declares war on Russia.

6 Serbia and Montenegro declare war on Germany.

7 Spain declares its neutrality in the European war, but secretly communicates that it is sympathetic to France.

7–17 Troops of the British Expeditionary Force land in France to resist the German invasion.

8 Britain and France occupy the German protectorate of Togoland (modern Togo and the Volta region of Ghana).

8 The Defence of the Realm Act is passed in Britain, conferring emergency powers on the government.

10 The German cruisers *Breslau* and *Goeben* elude British ships in the Mediterranean Sea and enter the Black Sea, where they are purchased by the Ottoman Empire to replace ships seized by Britain.

12 Britain declares war on Austria-Hungary.

12 France declares war on Austria-Hungary.

14 Russia promises autonomy to Russian Poland in return for Polish aid in the war.

14–25 French troops trying to invade Germany are thrown back in the "battle of the frontiers" on the Western Front.

15 Japan issues an ultimatum to Germany demanding the evacuation of the German treaty port of Qingdao in northern China, and the withdrawal of the German fleet from the Far East.

20 A constitutionalist army, led by General Carranza, occupies Mexico City, Mexico.

20 Advancing Russian forces under General Paul Rennenkampf defeat German troops under General Friedrich von Prittwitz at the battle of Gumbinnen in East Prussia.

20 German troops under General Alexander von Kluck occupy Brussels, Belgium.

21 The British government orders the raising of the first "new army" of volunteers.

22 Following Russian advances in East Prussia, retired General Paul von Hindenburg is appointed commander of the German Eighth Army there.

23 At the Battle of Mons in Belgium, British troops under Sir John French are thrown back in confusion by the German First Army, led by General Alexander von Kluck.

23 Japan declares war on Germany.

24 Advancing Russian troops score another victory over German forces at Frankenau, East Prussia.

24–September 5 British, Belgian, and French troops retreat from Mons, Belgium, in the face of a rapid German advance.

26 The British general Horace Smith-Dorien fights a delaying action at the battle of Le Cateau, France, on the Western Front, giving the rest of the British Army time to retreat.

26–30 German forces defeat the Russian armies at the Battle of Tannenberg (now Grunwald, Poland) in East Prussia, and halt the Russian advance in the region.

26–September 2 Austrian troops under General Moritz von Auffenberg defeat a Russian force under General Alexei Brusilov at Zamość-Komarów, Poland.

27 German General Liman von Sanders is appointed commander in chief of the Ottoman army.

27 The political parties in France declare a *Union Sacrée* ("Sacred Union", or coalition government), with a reconstructed cabinet under René Viviani, and the appointment of General Joseph Galliéni as governor of Paris, France.

28 Austria-Hungary declares war on Belgium.

28 British cruisers commanded by Admiral Sir David Beatty raid the Heligoland Bight in the North Sea, sinking three German ships.

30 German troops take Amiens, France, on the Western Front during World War I.

31–September 2 General Alexander von Kluck leads his advancing German troops to the east of Paris, France, rather than encircling it from the west as envisioned in the "Schlieffen Plan" (devised in 1905).

SEPTEMBER

- The U.S. president Woodrow Wilson signs the U.S. Federal Trade Commission Act, establishing the Federal Trade Commission to prevent unfair competition in commerce.

1 The name of the city of St. Petersburg is changed to a more Russian one, becoming Petrograd.

2 The French government moves from Paris to Bordeaux in the face of the German advance.

3 German troops cross the River Marne on the Western Front of World War I.

5 France, Russia, and Britain make the Pact of London, each agreeing not to make a separate peace with the Central Powers.

5–10 In the First Battle of the Marne on the Western Front of World War I, the armies led by General Joseph Joffre halt the German advance on Paris, France.

6–15 At the First Battle of the Masurian Lakes in East Prussia, German forces drive back the occupying Russian troops.

8–12 At the Battle of Lemburg, Russian troops force Austro-Hungarian forces out of East Galicia, having captured the city in Austria-Hungary on September 3.

10–13 German troops fall back from the River Marne and straighten their line along the River Aisne, their advance having been halted by the French army.

14 Allied forces reoccupy Reims, France, as German forces pull back and adjust their lines.

14 Eric von Falkenhayn succeeds Helmuth von Moltke as German commander in chief, when von Moltke retires following the failure of the "Schlieffen Plan."

15 German troops in German New Guinea capitulate to a British force.

15 U.S. troops withdraw from the port of Veracruz, Mexico, which they have occupied since April 22.

15–18 At the Battle of the Aisne on the Western Front of World War I, the Allied forces attack the German line, and the first trenches are dug.

15–November 24 The "race to the sea" takes place as Allied and German forces move northward trying to outflank one other. This establishes the basic line of the Western Front, stretching from the North Sea through Belgium and France to Switzerland.

18 General Paul von Hindenburg is appointed to command all German armies in the East when General Friedrich von Prittwitz retires following defeats by Russian troops.

18 The Home Rule and Welsh Church Disestablishment Acts receive royal assent in Britain, but are immediately suspended for the duration of the war.

22 The German cruiser *Emden* bombards Madras, India.

22 The German submarine *U-9* sinks HMS *Cressy* and two other British cruisers in the North Sea.

27 Duala, capital of the German Cameroon, surrenders to British and French forces.

27 Russian troops cross the Carpathian Mountains and invade Austria-Hungary.

28–October 31 German and Austrian forces attack Russian troops south of Warsaw, Poland, in the First Battle of Warsaw, but are driven back.

OCTOBER

- The Clayton Antitrust Act is passed by the U.S. Congress. It strengthens U.S. law against monopolist company policies, and excludes unions and agricultural cooperatives from anticombination laws. It also

World War I (1914–18)

1914

JULY

28   Following the assassination of Archduke Ferdinand (June 28), the Austrian crown council decides on war with Serbia.

30   Russia orders the general mobilization of its armies in response to the Austro-Hungarian declaration of war on Serbia.

31   Germany issues an ultimatum which gives Russia 12 hours in which to stop the mobilization of its army. Meanwhile, Austria-Hungary mobilizes its army.

AUGUST

1   Germany declares war on Russia.

3   In accordance with the Schlieffen Plan, a grand strategic scheme designed to obviate the need to fight simultaneously on two fronts, Germany declares war on France and invades Belgium, thereby precipitating a British declaration of war (August 4) and the despatch of a British Expeditionary Force to the continent (August 7–17).

5–20   German forces sweep through Belgium, occupying Brussels (August 20).

14–25   French troops trying to invade Germany are thrown back in the "battle of the frontiers".

23–September 5   British, Belgian, and French troops retreat from Mons, Belgium, in the face of a rapid German advance, the British fighting a delaying action at Le Cateau, France (August 26). By September 3, the Germans have crossed the Marne to the east of Paris.

26–31   Having fallen back before Russian advances into East Prussia, German forces under General Paul von Hindenberg counterattack and envelop the enemy in the Battle of Tannenberg, inflicting 125,000 casualties for the loss of only 15,000.

SEPTEMBER

2   In the face of the German advance, the French government moves from Paris to Bordeaux, returning only when the line has been stabilised (November 18).

15–November 24   The "race to the sea" takes place as Allied and German forces move northward trying to outflank one other. This establishes the basic line of the Western Front, stretching from the North Sea through Belgium and France to Switzerland.

OCTOBER

29–November 5   Following secret negotiations with the Central Powers, Turkish warships bombard Russian Black Sea ports, leading Britain and France to declare war on the Turkish Empire (November 5).

NOVEMBER

1–December 8   Attempting to trap the German Pacific squadron, a British force loses two cruisers in the Battle of Coronel off the coast of Chile (November 1). The German squadron, sailing into the South Atlantic, attempts to attack Port Stanley, but is annihilated by British battlecruisers in the Battle of the Falkland Islands (December 8). Meanwhile, after a successful career destroying Allied merchantmen, the German cruiser *Emden* has been sunk by the Australian cruiser *Sydney* in a battle off the Cocos Islands in the Indian Ocean (November 9).

1915

JANUARY

19   The first German Zeppelin airship raid is carried out over Britain, targeting East Anglian ports.

FEBRUARY

3   The German army uses poison gas at Bolimów (Bolimov), Poland, on the Eastern Front. It is the first time that they have used poison gas on a significant scale.

4–10   The German declaration of the establishment of a submarine blockade around Britain from February 18 elicits from the United States a warning that Germany will be held responsible for any attacks on U.S. ships or citizens.

16–30   French offensives against the German trenches in Champagne are repelled with heavy losses.

19–March 18   Following Russian appeals for assistance on their Caucasus front (January 2), British and French ships bombard Turkish forts at the entrance to the Dardanelles (February 19), and make an unsuccessful attempt to fight their way to Istanbul (March 18).

MARCH

10   At the Battle of Neuve Chapelle in northeastern France, British and Indian forces break German lines and capture the village of Neuve Chapelle, but are unable to exploit their victory.

22   After a siege of 194 days, Russian forces take Przemyśl, a key strategic point between the Pripet Marshes and the Carpathian Mountains, in the Polish area of northeastern Austria-Hungary.

APRIL

22–May 25   Supporting a major offensive against the British-held Ypres salient in Belgium, the Germans employ poison gas on the Western Front for the first time.

24   Following the massacre of some 120,000 Turks by Armenians in eastern Anatolia (December 1914), the Turks begin the deportation and massacre of the Armenians. Some 1.75 million people are driven across the Mesopotamian desert, over a million of them dying in the process.

25   Allied landings take place on the Gallipoli Peninsula in the Dardanelles under the command of Sir Ian Hamilton. British and French forces land at Cape Helles, and Australian and New Zealander Army Corps (ANZACS) at Anzac Cove. Initiated because of the stalemate on the Western Front, their aim is to knock the Ottoman Empire out of the war and assist the Russian effort against Germany on the Eastern Front, but the Allies meet stiff resistance from the Ottoman army commanded by Mustafa Kemal and the German general Otto Liman von Sanders.

MAY

7   A German submarine sinks the British liner *Lusitania* off the south coast of Ireland, killing 1,198 passengers and crew, including 114 U.S. citizens.

23   Italy declares war on Austria-Hungary.

JUNE

1   German Zeppelin airships make their first raid on London.

3–September 18   The German recapture of Przemyśl collapses the Russian front, enabling a series of spectacular advances. German and Austro-Hungarian forces take Lemberg (June 23), Warsaw (August 7), Brest Litovsk (August 23), and Vilna (modern Vilnius, Lithuania) (September 18).

23–July 7   The Italian offensive across the Isonzo river into Austrian-controlled territory suffers massive losses. The Italians renew this offensive ten more times : July 18–August 30, 1915; October 18–November 3, 1915; November 10–December 10, 1915; February 15–March 17, 1916; August 6–17, 1916; September 14–18, 1916; October 9–12, 1916; October 31–November 4, 1916; May 12–June 8, 1917; August 17–September 12, 1917. In all of these offensives, which become known as the First–Eleventh Battles of the Isonzo, the Italian army suffers heavy casualties for very little gain.

JULY

9   The surrender of German forces in South West Africa to South African General Botha marks the end of the first stage of the conquest of the German colonial empire. In the preceding 11 months the Germans have surrendered Samoa to New Zealand, New Guinea to Australia, Tsingtau to Japan, and Togo to forces from British West Africa. A small detachment holds out in Cameroons until February 8, 1916, at which time only the forces of von Lettow Vorbeck in Tanganyika remain in the field. In one of the most successful guerrilla campaigns of all time, von Lettow Vorbeck will continue to outmaneuver pursuing British forces until the armistice in 1918.

AUGUST

30   Following protests from the United States, Germany orders its submarines and ships to warn enemy passenger vessels before sinking them.

SEPTEMBER

5   Czar Nicholas II of Russia takes personal command of the Russian armies, replacing Grand Duke Nicholas after the defeats of the summer.

25–November 4   In a renewed offensive in the Artois region in northeastern France, and in Champagne in the southeast, French forces attack the German line, while the British, using gas for the first time, attack the line at Loos on November 4. Casualties are heavy and gains are small.

28   Advancing up the Tigris in Mesopotamia, British forces under Major General Charles Townshend capture Kut-al-Imara from the Ottoman army.

OCTOBER

5   The Allies land troops at Thessaloníki (Salonika) in neutral Greece, to aid Serbia against impending attack by the Central Powers.

6–January 17   Austro-Hungarian troops under General August von Mackensen renew their invasion of Serbia, capturing Belgrade on October 9. Bulgaria joins the attack on October 14, forcing the heavily outnumbered Serbs to retreat across the Albanian mountains to the Adriatic (January 17, 1916).

13   The largest Zeppelin raid of the European war takes place over London.

DECEMBER

7   Following their defeat in the battle of Ctesiphon (November 22), British and Indian troops retreat to Kut-al-Imara where they are besieged by the Turks.

18–January 9, 1916   In a highly successful evacuation, Allied troops withdraw from the Gallipoli Peninsula following the failure of the Dardanelles campaign.

1916

FEBRUARY

21–December 18   German and Allied troops meet in the Battle of Verdun in France, the German commander Eric von Falkenhayn planning to sap French reserves in a battle of attrition. By the end of the battle each side has lost about 400,000 men.

MARCH

15   Germany begins a second campaign of unrestricted submarine warfare.

20   The Allies launch an air attack against the German submarine base at Zeebrugge, Belgium.

24   A German submarine sinks the passenger ship *Sussex* without warning. The victims include U.S. citizens.

26   The Allies agree on the partition of the Ottoman Empire in the event of victory. Russia will receive Armenia, Kurdistan, and part of Anatolia, while Britain and France will gain spheres of influence in Arabia.

APRIL

20   A German submarine lands the Irish nationalist Roger Casement in Ireland to lead an Irish rising, but he is arrested on April 24 and executed on August 3 for high treason.

20   Germany suspends unrestricted submarine warfare because of U.S. protests over the sinking of the *Sussex*.

29   The Ottoman army recaptures the Mesopotamian city of Kut-al-Imara from the occupying British forces, following a siege dating from December 7, 1915. Ten thousand prisoners are taken.

MAY

9   The "Sykes–Picot Agreement" between Britain and France establishes their intended postwar spheres of influence in the Middle East.

31–June 1   The British and German surface fleets clash in the Battle of Jutland in the North Sea, their one major conflict of the war. The British fleet under Admiral Sir John Jellicoe loses a greater number of ships, but succeeds in reaffirming its naval dominance. The German fleet will remain in harbor for the rest of the war.

JUNE

4–August 20   The Russian armies commanded by General Alexei Brusilov mount the Brusilov Offensive, pushing the Austro-Hungarian line south of the Russian Pripet Marshes, but the attack is blunted by German reinforcements.

5   A British-supported Arab revolt against Ottoman rule in the Hejaz region begins at Medina (in modern Saudi Arabia).

5   Ottoman forces led by Enver Pasha in Persia begin a counteroffensive against the advancing Russian troops, but are defeated at Erzinjan, Armenia, on July 25.

World War I (1914–18) *continued*

JULY

1–November 18 French and British troops mount the Battle of the Somme in France, a massive offensive which gains 8 km/5 mi of territory. The British Army suffers 60,000 casualties (including 20,000 dead) on the first day, while the whole campaign results in over 620,000 British and French casualties and about 450,000 German casualties.

AUGUST

4–January 9, 1917 British forces drive back Ottoman troops in a battle near Romani, Egypt.

17–September 18 A Bulgarian and German force attacks the Allied enclave around Thessaloníki (Salonika), Greece, at the Battle of Florina.

27 Romania joins the Allies and declares war on Austria-Hungary.

28 A Russian force begins an invasion of Austro-Hungarian Transylvania.

29 Following victories on the Eastern Front, Field Marshal Paul von Hindenburg is appointed German chief of the general staff (with Eric Ludendorff as quartermaster general) in sucession to Eric von Falkenhayn, whose strategy at Verdun, France, is not working.

31 The German government accepts the "Hindenburg Plan" for militarization of the German war economy.

SEPTEMBER

6 The Central Powers establish a Supreme War Council, increasing German influence in the dispirited Austro-Hungarian armed forces.

15 The first tanks are used by the British Army during the Somme offensive on the Western Front in France.

27 General Eric von Falkenhayn leads a successful Austro-German invasion of Romania, which continues until January 1917.

OCTOBER

10–December 12 Allied troops under French general Maurice Sarrail begin an offensive against the Bulgarian and German army at Thessaloníki (Salonika), taking Monastir in Macedonia on November 9. Meanwhile on October 1, the pro-Central Power government of Greece accepts the Allies' ultimatum of October 10, which requires the country to hand over its fleet.

NOVEMBER

5 The Central Powers proclaim the Kingdom of Poland, setting up a council of state under their influence.

DECEMBER

• The "turnip winter" in Central Europe sees food shortages caused by the Allied naval blockade and a high mortality rate among the civilian population.

12 Germany, having decisively defeated Romania, sends a peace note to the Allies indicating that the Central Powers are prepared to negotiate. On December 30 a reply is sent via the U.S. ambassador in Paris.

13 Robert Nivelle is appointed commander in chief of the French armies in northern and northeastern France, replacing the unsuccessful General Joffre, who is appointed technical advisor to the government.

1917

FEBRUARY

1 Germany announces its return to a policy of unrestricted submarine warfare in order to cut off the supplies sent to the Allies from the British Empire and the United States.

12 President Wilson refuses to reopen negotiations with Germany until it abandons its policy of unrestricted submarine warfare.

24 British forces under Sir Frederick Maude recapture Kut-al-Imara, Mesopotamia, from the Ottoman army, and advance along the River Tigris.

26 President Wilson, without the authority of Congress, orders the arming of U.S. merchant ships in the face of Germany's resumption of unrestricted submarine warfare. Such a measure ordinarily requires Senate approval, but the president maintains that the U.S. Justice Department has sanctioned the move.

MARCH

1 The publication in the United States of the "Zimmermann telegram" causes outrage. The telegram is a message from the German foreign minister Arthur Zimmermann to the German ambassador in Mexico City, Mexico, which states that if war breaks out between Germany and the United States, the ambassador is to propose an alliance with Mexico and support Mexico's reacquisition of territory lost to the United States in 1848.

4–April 5 German troops withdraw to the specially constructed "Hindenburg Line", a defensive system on the Western Front.

11 In the Mesopotamian campaign, British forces capture Baghdad from the Ottoman army.

APRIL

• German submarines sink 875,000 tons of Allied shipping, mostly British.

6 The United States declares war on Germany. Cuba follows suit the following day.

9–May 4 At the Battle of Arras on the Western Front, the British Third Army advances 6.5 km/4 mi.

16–May 9 The French commander General Robert Nivelle launches the "Chemin des Dames" offensive (or Second Battle of the Aisne) along the River Aisne. The French forces make tiny advances at heavy cost.

17 The first in a wave of French army mutinies occurs on the Western Front in protest at the "Chemin des Dames" offensive. A more serious mutiny begins on April 29, and such mutinies continue until August 1917, ending the French army's capacity to mount offensives.

JUNE

7–14 British forces straighten the Ypres salient at the Battle of Messines Ridge in southeastern Belgium, in preparation for a major offensive.

13 The first part of the American Expeditionary Force, commanded by General John J. Pershing, departs for France.

18–July 13 The Russian minister of war, Alexander Kerensky, launches the Kerensky Offensive on the Eastern Front with a series of attacks against the German armies, which are quickly repulsed with heavy Russian losses.

JULY

6   An Arab force takes Aqaba, in the Hejaz region, from an Ottoman force.

31–November 6   The Third Battle of Ypres (the Battle of Passchendaele) takes place on the Western Front. British forces in Belgium advance about 13 km/8 mi, but at a heavy cost in casualties.

SEPTEMBER

1–5 A German offensive led by General Oscar von Hutier on the Eastern Front leads to the occupation of Riga (now in Latvia) on the River Dvina after Russian troops under General Lavr Kornilov are defeated at the Battle of Riga.

29–October 1   German aircraft attack London on successive nights.

OCTOBER

24–December 26   At the Battle of Caporetto, Italy (now Kobarid, Slovenia), the Austro-Hungarian and German forces under General Otto von Below break the Italian line and advance 16 km/10 mi. French and British troops are sent to help the Italians (November 3) and eventually the advance of the Central Power forces is brought to a stop on the Piave River.

31–November 16   With a dramatic charge by the Australian Light Horse breaking the Turkish line at Beersheba in Palestine on October 31, British forces led by General Edmund Allenby take Gaza on November 7, and advance to capture Jaffa on November 16.

NOVEMBER

7   The Allied conference at Rapallo in northwestern Italy decides on a Supreme Allied War Council (which first meets on December 1 at Versailles, France).

20–December 7   The Battle of Cambrai takes place in northeastern France and is the first major battle involving tanks. A British tank force breaks the German line at Cambrai, but their success is not exploited.

DECEMBER

9   A British force led by General Sir Edmund Allenby captures Jerusalem from the Ottoman army.

20   German and Russian delegates begin peace negotiations at Brest-Litovsk, Russia.

1918

MARCH

21–April 5   The German army launches a spring offensive on the Western Front with the Second Battle of the Somme, and advances 64 km/40 mi toward Paris.

23–August 9   Massive German guns shell Paris, France.

APRIL

9–29   The German army launches its second major operation of the year in the Lys offensive on the Western Front.

21   The German air ace Manfred von Richthofen (the "Red Baron") is shot down and killed, either by Canadian pilot Roy Brown or by ground fire.

22–23   British ships raid Zeebrugge, Belgium, blocking the entrance to Bruges Canal and the German submarine base there.

MAY

10   The British cruiser *Vindictive* is sunk deliberately in an unsuccessful attempt to block the entrance to the German submarine base at Ostend, Belgium.

JUNE

9–13   A German offensive near Compiègne, France, is repulsed by French and U.S. troops.

15–23   In the Battle of the Piave, Italy, Austro-Hungarian troops cross the River Piave to attack the Italian line, but are resisted.

JULY

18   Allied forces begin a counteroffensive against the German armies on the Western Front, following the cessation of the German spring offensive.

AUGUST

8–11   Concentrated en masse for the first time and supported by more than 400 British tanks, Australian and Canadian divisions smash through the German line before Amiens and advance more than 12 miles, taking more than 30,000 German prisoners. A badly shaken Ludendorff, realizing that defeat is now inevitable, refers to August 8 as "the black day of the German army."

SEPTEMBER

•   One million two hundred thousand U.S. troops participate in the Battle of the Meuse-Argonne, two rivers in northeast France. The Americans cut the Sedan-Mézières railroad, a crucial German supply line, in early November.

2   Following recent defeats, German troops again retreat to the "Hindenburg Line."

15–24   An Allied (French, British, Italian, and Serbian) offensive makes large gains at the Battle of Monastir on the Macedonian front, leading to Bulgaria signing an armistice on September 30.

18   A British offensive begins in Palestine when troops under Sir Edmund Allenby defeat an Ottoman force at the Battle of Megiddo, the British advancing and taking Damascus, Syria, on October 1.

OCTOBER

5   A note from the new German chancellor Prince Max of Baden is sent to the United States, via Switzerland, asking for assistance in brokering a European peace treaty, suggesting an armistice based on President Wilson's "fourteen points."

18   Lille, France, is liberated by British troops.

20   Germany and Austria-Hungary agree to the peace terms of President Wilson, including the stipulation that their troops should retreat to their own territory before an armistice is signed, and Wilson relays this message to the Allies. Germany suspends submarine warfare.

24–November 4   The Battle of Vittorio Veneto on the Italian front leads to the collapse of the Austro-Hungarian army. On October 27 Austro-Hungary asks Italy for an armistice.

27–30   Following General Eric Ludendorff's resignation as quartermaster general of the German army (October 27), the sailors of the German fleet refuse to obey Admiral Franz von Hipper's orders to sail on a suicide mission in the North Sea (October 30).

30–November 1   The Allies sign an armistice with the Ottoman Empire on the warship *Agamemnon* at the port of Mudros on the Greek island of Lemnos in the Aegean Sea. Forty-eight hours later British and French forces occupy Constantinople.

NOVEMBER

8   A German armistice commission meets the Allied delegation, headed by the French marshal Ferdinand Foch, in a railroad carriage in Compiègne, France. An armistice is agreed, to be effective from November 11.

strengthens unions by forbidding the issue of injunctions against unions without notice.

1 The Ottoman Empire closes the Dardanelles to shipping.

4 Austria launches an offensive against invading Russian forces and drives them out of the Carpathian Mountains.

9 Antwerp, Belgium, surrenders to German troops under General Hans von Beseler on the Western Front.

13 General Christiaan De Wet leads a Boer rebellion against the British in South Africa.

16 The first Canadian troops sent to fight against Germany on the Western Front land in England.

17 The first units of the Australian Expeditionary Force leave for France.

18–30 At the Battle of Yser in Belgium, Allied troops prevent German forces from reaching the Channel ports.

29 Ottoman warships bombard the Russian ports of Odessa and Sevastopol.

30–November 24 German troops attempt to break the Allied line on the Western Front, in the First Battle of Ypres, Belgium.

31 A congress in Mexico deposes General Carranza and elects General Carlos Gutiérrez as provisional president.

NOVEMBER

1 At the naval Battle of Coronel (west of Chile), a German squadron under Vice Admiral Maximilian von Spee sinks two ships of a British naval force under Sir Christopher Cradock.

2 Russia declares war on the Ottoman Empire.

3 In U.S. Congressional elections, Democrats manage to retain majorities in the House (230–196) and Senate (56–40), although the Republicans make huge gains.

5 France and Britain declare war on the Ottoman Empire.

7 Anglo-Indian forces land and oppose an Ottoman army in Mesopotamia.

9 The German cruiser *Emden* is sunk by HMS *Sydney* off the Cocos Islands in the Indian Ocean.

14 Sultan Mehmet V of the Ottoman Empire proclaims a *Jihad* ("Holy War") against the British Empire.

18 German forces break the Russian line at Kutno, Poland, on the Eastern Front of World War I.

18 The French government starts to transfer back to Paris, France, from Bordeaux, the war having stabilized along the line of the Western Front.

21 Anglo-Indian troops occupy the Ottoman city of Basra in Mesopotamia.

23 The British navy bombards German-held Zeebrugge in Belgium.

DECEMBER

2 Advancing Austrian forces take the Serbian capital of Belgrade.

5–17 Austrian troops defeat the Russian armies at the Battle of Limanowa on the Eastern Front, but fail to break the Russian lines in front of Kraków, Poland.

6 German forces take the Polish city of Łódź from the Russian army on the Eastern Front.

8 In the Battle of the Falkland Islands, a British naval force under Vice Admiral Sir Frederick Sturdee destroys Vice Admiral Maximilian von Spee's German East Asia Squadron.

17 A British protectorate is proclaimed in Egypt, and on December 18 Khedive Abbas II is deposed and succeeded by Prince Husein Kemel.

21 Germany makes its first air raid on Britain, bombing the towns on the south coast of England.

22–January 18, 1915 The Ottoman army makes unsuccessful attacks on Russian forces in the Caucasus region.

26 The German government assumes control of food supplies and allocations in Germany.

SCIENCE, TECHNOLOGY, AND MEDICINE

Agriculture

MAY

8 The Smith-Lever Act is passed in the United States. It provides for training farmers in improved practices and the establishment of the national 4-H club that provides agricultural training for youth.

Ecology

MAY

30 Mt. Lassen in California erupts without warning. It erupts again on May 19, 1915, and a further 150 eruptions follow until 1919.

SEPTEMBER

1 The last passenger pigeon dies in the Cincinnati zoo, Ohio.

Health and Medicine

- Austrian otologist Robert Bárány receives the Nobel Prize for Physiology or Medicine for his work on the physiology and pathology of the vestibular apparatus.

Science

- British astronomer John Franklin publishes the Franklin-Adams Charts, the first photographic star charts of the entire sky.

- English astrophysicist Arthur Eddington, publishes *Stellar Movement and the Structure of the Universe*, in which he theorizes that spiral nebulae are galaxies similar to the Milky Way.

- German archeologist Robert Koldewey publishes *The Excavations in Babylon*, which describe his excavations and reveals that the Babylon of the Bible exists.

- German biochemist Fritz Albert Lepmann explains the role of adenosine triphosphate (ATP) as the carrier of chemical energy from the oxidation of food to the energy consumption processes in the cells.

- German chemist Dr. von Tappen creates tear gas in Germany. It is used in 1915 against the Russians at Bolimów (Bolimov), Poland.

- German physicist Max von Laue receives the Nobel Prize for Physics for his discovery of the diffraction of X-rays by crystals.

- German physicists James Franck and Gustav Hertz provide the first experimental evidence for the existence of discrete energy states in atoms and thus verify Danish physicist Niels Bohr's atomic model.
- German-born U.S. geologist Beno Gutenberg discovers the discontinuity that marks the boundary between the earth's lower mantle and outer core, about 2,800 km/1,750 mi below the surface.
- Polish–American biochemist Casimir Funk isolates vitamin B, a vital discovery in the treatment of beriberi.
- U.S. biochemist Edward Kendall isolates the hormone thyroxine from the thyroid gland. It regulates metabolism by stimulating all cells to consume oxygen.
- U.S. chemist Theodore Richards is awarded the Nobel Prize for Chemistry for his accurate determination of the atomic masses of many elements.
- U.S. physicist Robert Millikan demonstrates that radiation shows some of the properties of particles—a verification of Einstein's photoelectric effect.

Technology

- English embryologist John Graham Kerr advocates camouflaging ships with countershading and strongly contrasting patches.

Transportation

- The 81.3-km/50.5-mi Houston Ship Canal is completed; it gives Houston, Texas, access to the Gulf of Mexico.
- The first U.S. battleships, the *New York* and *Texas*, are launched.

September 1914–15   U.S. aeronautical engineers Jerome Hunsaker and Donald Douglas build the first wind tunnel.

September 1914–18   During World War I, the motorcycle gains in popularity for sending dispatches.

APRIL

7   The Canadian Grand Trunk Pacific Railroad is completed.

MAY

29   The Canadian ship *Empress of Ireland* sinks with the loss of 1,023 lives after colliding with a Norwegian freighter in the Gulf of St. Lawrence.

JULY

- The Cape Cod Canal, connecting Cape Cod Bay and Buzzards Bay, opens to boat traffic.

AUGUST

15   The Panama Canal opens to traffic. One of the world's greatest engineering feats, it is 81.6 km/50.7 mi long and saves 12,800 km/8,000 mi on the trip around South America. It cost $366,650,000 and around six thousand workers died during its construction.

SEPTEMBER

15   The British Royal Flying Corps begins to use aerial photography for determining German positions.

ARTS AND IDEAS

Architecture

- The Italian architect Antonio Sant'Elia exhibits his futuristic city design project *Città nuova (Milano 2000)/ The New City (Milan 2000)* in Milan, Italy.
- The Model Factory and Office Building at the Werkbund Exhibition in Cologne, Germany, designed by the German architects Walter Gropius and Adolph Meyer, is completed.
- The Park Güell, a fantastical housing estate on the edge of Barcelona, Spain, designed by the Spanish architect Antonio Gaudí, is completed.
- The railroad station in Helsinki, Finland, designed by the Finnish architect Eliel Saarinen, is completed.
- The Swiss-born French architect Le Corbusier develops his concept of the Maison Domino—mass-produced housing units to be arranged to suit the requirements of a specific site.

Arts

- The English writer and artist Wyndham Lewis paints *Workshop*.
- The French artist Francis Picabia paints *I See Again in Memory My Dear Udnie*.
- The French artist Georges Braque paints *Glass, Bottle and Newspaper*.
- The French artist Henri Gaudier-Brzeska sculpts *Hieratic Head of Ezra Pound*.
- The French artist Henri Matisse paints *The Goldfish Bowl*.
- The French artist Marcel Duchamp creates *Bottle Rack*. The first true "ready made" (or everyday, manufactured object presented as an art work), it is, simply, a mass-produced bottle rack.
- The French artist Raymond Duchamp-Villon sculpts *Horse*.
- The French artist Roger de la Fresnaye paints *Sitting Man, or the Architect*.
- The German artist Ernst Barlach sculpts *The Avenger*.
- The German artist Ernst Kirchner paints *Nude Woman, Sitting with her Legs Crossed*.
- The Italian artist Carlo Carrà creates the collage *Words-in-Freedom: Interventionist Demonstration*.
- The Italian artist Giorgio de Chirico paints *The Enigma of a Day* and *Portrait of Guillaume Apollinaire*.
- The Lithuanian artist Jacques Lipchitz sculpts *Sailor with Guitar*.
- The Romanian artist Constantin Brancusi sculpts *Little French Girl*.
- The Russian artist Kasimir Malevich paints *The Aviator*.
- The Russian artist Marc Chagall paints *The Jew in Pink*.
- The Russian artist Wassily Kandinsky paints *Fugue*.
- The Spanish artist Pablo Picasso sculpts *Glass of Absinthe*.
- The U.S. artist Andrew Dasburg paints *Floral Still Life*.
- The U.S. artist Arthur Dove paints *Nature Symbolized, No 2*.
- The U.S. artist Marsden Hartley paints *Portrait of a German Officer*.

- The U.S.-born English artist Jacob Epstein sculpts *Rock Drill*.
- The vorticist art group (strongly influenced by Italian Futurism) is formed in London, England. Its leading figure is the English writer and artist Wyndham Lewis, who launches the short-lived journal *Blast*.

Film

- For the first time, U.S. movies make more money in France than home-produced movies.
- The movie *Anna Karenina*, directed by Vladimir Gardine and based on the novel by Leo Tolstoy, is released in Russia.
- The movie *Cabiria*, directed by Giovanni Pastrone, is released in Italy, and achieves considerable success worldwide.
- The movie *Judith of Bethulia*, directed by D. W. Griffith, is released in the United States, starring Blanche Sweet, Henry B. Walthall, and Mae Marsh. Griffith's movie *The Battle of Elderbush Gulch* is also released in the United States.
- The movie *The Typhoon* is released, directed by Reginald Barker and starring Japanese-born U.S. actor Sessue Hayakawa.
- The movie *The Virginian*, directed by Cecil B. De Mille, is released in the United States, starring Dustin Farnum and Winifred Kingston.
- The movie *Tillie's Punctured Romance*, directed by Mack Sennett, is released in the United States, starring Marie Dressler, Fatty Arbuckle, Charlie Chaplin, and Mabel Normand.

MAY

4   *Caught in the Rain* is released in the United States, the first movie to be written and directed entirely by Charlie Chaplin.

Literature and Language

- *The Single Hound*, a selection of the poems by the U.S. writer Emily Dickinson, is published posthumously.
- The English writer and critic Austin Dobson publishes *Eighteenth-Century Studies*.
- The English writer Compton Mackenzie publishes the second part of his novel *Sinister Street*. The first part appeared in 1913.
- The English writer Henry Newbolt publishes his verse collection *Drake's Drum and other Songs of the Sea*.
- The English writer Robert Tressell publishes his novel *The Ragged Trousered Philanthropist*.
- The German writer Hermann Hesse publishes his novel *Rosshalde*.
- The Irish writer George Moore publishes *Hail and Farewell*, three volumes of memoirs.
- The Irish writer James Joyce publishes his collection of short stories *Dubliners*. The stories were written between 1904 and 1907.
- The Irish writer W. B. Yeats publishes his poetry collection *Responsibilities*.
- The Japanese writer Natsume Soseki publishes his novel *Kokoro*.
- The Spanish writer and philosopher Miguel de Unamuno publishes his novel *Niebla/Mist*.

- The U.S. writer Amy Lowell publishes her poetry collection *Sword Blades and Poppy Seeds*.
- The U.S. writer and editor Harriet Monroe publishes her poetry collection *You and I*.
- The U.S. writer Booth Tarkington publishes his novel *Penrod*.
- The U.S. writer Conrad Aiken publishes his poetry collection *Earth Triumphant and Other Tales in Verse*.
- The U.S. writer Gertrude Stein publishes her poetry collection *Tender Buttons: Objects, Food, Rooms*.
- The U.S. writer Henry James publishes his second book of autobiography *Notes of a Son and Brother*.
- The U.S. writer Robert Frost publishes his poetry collection *North of Boston*, in England. It contains some of his best-known poems including "The Death of the Hired Man" and "Mending Wall."
- The U.S. writer Theodore Dreiser publishes his novel *The Titan*.
- The U.S. writer Vachel Lindsay publishes his poetry collection *The Congo and Other Poems*.
- U.S. journalist Walter Lippmann publishes *Drift and Mastery*.
- U.S. legal scholar Louis Brandeis publishes *Other People's Money*, an attack on the abuses of the banking and finance industry.
- U.S. novelist Edgar Rice Burroughs publishes *Tarzan of the Apes*.

Music

- English songwriters David Ivor Davies and Lena Ford write the song "Keep the Home Fires Burning."
- The Austrian composer Alban Berg completes his *3 Stücke/3 Pieces for Orchestra* (Opus 6).
- The English composer Ralph Vaughan Williams completes his romance for violin and orchestra *The Lark Ascending*.
- The opera *Francesca da Rimini*, by the Italian composer Riccardo Zandonai, is first performed in Turin, Italy. It is based on a text by the Italian writer Gabriele D'Annunzio.
- The opera *Mârouf, savetier du Caire/Mârouf, the Cobbler of Cairo*, by the French composer Henri Rabaud, is first performed in Paris, France.
- The opera *The Immortal Hour* by the English composer Rutland Boughton is first performed, at Glastonbury, England.
- The U.S. composer Charles Ives completes his *Orchestral Set No. 1*, *Three Places in New England* and his choral work *General William Booth Enters into Heaven*.
- U.S. composer W. C. Handy writes the song "St. Louis Blues."

FEBRUARY

13   A group of composers founds the American Society of Composers, Authors, and Publishers in New York, New York.

Theater and Dance

- The ballet *Die Josephslegende/The Story of Joseph*, by the German composer Richard Strauss and the Russian choreographer Mikhail Fokin, is first performed in Paris, France, under the Russian impresario Sergei Diaghilev. The sets and costumes are by the Russian artist Léon Bakst.

- The play *Pygmalion*, by the Irish writer George Bernard Shaw, is first performed at His Majesty's Theatre in London, England. A German version was previously performed in Vienna, Austria, in 1913.

Thought and Scholarship

- British philosopher Francis Herbert Bradley publishes *Essays on Truth and Reality*.
- English philosopher Charlie Dunbar Broad publishes *Perception, Physics, and Reality*.
- English philosopher E. F. Carritt publishes *Theory of Beauty*.
- The Nobel Prize for Literature is not awarded this year.
- The Spanish philosopher José Ortega y Gasset publishes *Meditaciones del Quijote/Meditations on Quixote*.
- U.S. psychologist John Broadus Watson publishes *Behaviour: An Introduction to Comparative Psychology*, in which he advocates the use of animal subjects in psychological studies.

SOCIETY

Everyday Life

- c. 1914 Soldiers fighting in World War I find wristwatches a practical option, even though they had previously been considered effeminate.
- Charles Pajeau receives a patent for his Tinkertoys, a popular children's game that allows participants to build structures with the game pieces, in the United States.
- Mary Phelps Jacob patents the modern elasticated backless bra in the United States. She sells rights to the U.S. corset company Warner, which begins production.
- Swede Josef Jonsson invents aluminum foil tops for milk bottles.
- The Crescent Washing Machine, the first domestic electric dishwasher, is launched in the United States.
- The U.S. Post Office censors the novel *The Woman Rebel* by U.S. social reformer Margaret Sanger, because it discusses birth control.
- There is an outcry over the "Copperfield Affair" in the United States: when the governor of Virginia sends his secretary to administer the boom town of Copperfield, she closes all the saloons within 80 minutes of arrival.
- U.S. automobile-manufacturer Henry Ford doubles the wages of his employees in a move to offset the boredom of working on an assembly line.
- Wrigley's launches Doublemint chewing gum in the United States.

Media and Communication

- Journalist and future fascist leader Benito Mussolini founds the newspaper *Il Popolo d'Italia* ("The People of Italy") in Italy.

- The first issue of the literary journal *The Little Review* is published in Chicago, Illinois, edited by Margaret C. Anderson. Appearing until 1929, it publishes work by T. S. Eliot, Ezra Pound, W. B. Yeats, Wallace Stevens, Sherwood Anderson, James Joyce, and Amy Lowell, among many others.

February 1914–18 Radio is used extensively for the first time in warfare communication.

MARCH

19 The *Times Literary Supplement* is published as a separate periodical in Britain; it had formerly been part of the newspaper.

NOVEMBER

- The first issue of the U.S. journal *The New Republic* is published in New York, New York, edited by Herbert Croly.

Religion

SEPTEMBER

3 Following the death of Pope Pius X on August 20, the Italian clergyman Giacomo Della Chiesa is elected Pope Benedict XV.

Sports

- The Stanley Cup, originally donated to the Canadian Amateur Hockey Association in 1893, is awarded to the winner of a play-off between the ice-hockey champions of the eastern professional National Hockey Association (NHA) and the western professional Pacific Coast Hockey Association (PCHA). The NHA's Toronto Blueshirts are the winners.
- Yale University's new football stadium, the Yale Bowl, with capacity for 61,000 spectators, opens in New Haven, Connecticut.

MARCH

21 At the inaugural U.S. figure skating championships the men's individual event is won by the Canadian star Norman Scott and the women's individual event is won by Theresa Weld of the United States.

JUNE

- The British golfer Harry Vardon wins a sixth British Open golf title, at Prestwick, Scotland; his achievement remains unsurpassed.

JULY

4 The Harvard eight become the first U.S. winners of the Grand Challenge Cup for rowing at the Henley Regatta in England.

AUGUST

21 The U.S. golfer Walter Hagen, aged 21, wins the U.S. Open at the Midlothian Country Club, Blue Island, Illinois.

BIRTHS & DEATHS

- Jiang Qing, third wife of the Chinese leader Mao Zedong, a member of the Gang of Four and influential in promoting China's Cultural Revolution, born in Zhucheng, Shandong Province, China (–1991).

JANUARY
9 Gypsy Rose Lee, U.S. striptease artist and entertainer, born in Seattle, Washington (–1970).

FEBRUARY
5 Alan Hodgkin, British physiologist who discovered how nerve impulses are transmitted chemically, born in Banbury, Oxfordshire, England.
5 William S(eward) Burroughs, U.S. writer noted for his experimental methods, black humor, explicit homo-eroticism, and apocalyptic vision, author of *Naked Lunch*, born in St. Louis, Missouri (–1997).

MARCH
1 Ralph Waldo Ellison, black U.S. novelist, author of *Invisible Man*, published in 1952, born in Oklahoma City, Oklahoma (–1994).
12 George Westinghouse, U.S. industrialist who was responsible for the use of alternating current rather than direct current in the United States, dies in New York, New York (–1914).
25 Frédéric Mistral, French poet, dies in Maillane, France (83).
28 Edmund S(ixtus) Muskie, U.S. Democrat politician, the first Democratic senator from Maine (1959) and secretary of state under U.S. president Jimmy Carter, born in Rumford, Maine (–1996).

APRIL
2 Alec Guinness, English stage and screen actor, born in London, England.
4 Marguerite Duras, French writer, dramatist, and filmmaker, born in Gia Dinh, Cochin-China (now Vietnam) (–1996).
19 Charles Sanders Peirce, U.S. logician and philosopher who advocated pragmatism, dies near Milford, Pennsylvania (74).

MAY
5 Tyrone Power, U.S. actor known for his adventure roles, born in Cincinnati, Ohio (–1958).
13 Joe Louis, black U.S. world heavyweight champion boxer 1937–49, born in Lexington, Alabama (–1981).
15 Tenzing Norgay, Nepalese sherpa who, with Edmund Hillary, was the first person to reach the summit of Mt. Everest, born in Solo Khumbu, Nepal (–1986).
18 Boris Christoff, Bulgarian bass singer known for his interpretation of Verdi and for his Russian operas, born in Plovdiv, Bulgaria (–1993).
18 Pierre Balmain, French couturier and founder of the House of Balmain fashion house, born in St.-Jean-de-Maurienne, France (–1982).
19 Max Perutz, Austrian-born British biochemist, who analyzed the structure of the hemoglobin molecule, born in Vienna, Austria.
27 Joseph Wilson Swan, English physicist who invented an early electric light bulb, dies in Warlingham, Surrey, England (85).

JUNE
15 Yuri Vladimirovich Andropov, Soviet leader 1982–84 and head of the KGB 1967–82, born in Nagutskoye, Russia (–1982).
26 Laurie Lee, English writer, author of *Cider with Rosie*, born in Stroud, Gloucestershire (–1997).
28 Franz Ferdinand, Austrian archduke whose death sparked World War I, is assassinated in Sarajevo, Bosnia (now Bosnia-Herzegovina) (50).

JULY
8 Billy (William Clarence) Eckstine (originally Eckstein), U.S. jazz singer, bandleader, and trumpet player, born in Pittsburgh, Pennsylvania (–1993).
31 Jean Léon Jaurès, French socialist leader who united various socialist groups into one Socialist Party, is assassinated in Paris, France (54).

AUGUST
20 Pope Pius X, Italian pope 1903–14, dies in Rome, Italy (79).
26 Julio Cortázar, Argentine writer, born in Brussels, Belgium (–1984).

SEPTEMBER
3 Dixie Lee Ray, U.S. zoologist who popularized science, born in Tacoma, Washington (–1994).
7 James Alfred Van Allen, U.S. physicist who discovered the magnetosphere, two zones of intense radiation encircling the earth, born in Mt Pleasant, Iowa.
28 Richard Warren Sears, U.S. mail-order merchant who developed the large retail company Sears, Roebuck, dies in Waukesha, Wisconsin (50).

OCTOBER
1 Daniel J(oseph) Boorstin, U.S. social historian and librarian of Congress (1975–87), born in Atlanta, Georgia.
6 Thor Heyerdahl, Danish explorer who made several oceanic voyages on rafts to demonstrate the possibility of ancient contacts between distant peoples, born in Larvik, Norway.
17 Jerry Siegel, creator of Superman and other comic-book characters, born in Cleveland, Ohio (–1996).
25 John Berryman, U.S. poet, born in McAlester, Oklahoma (–1972).
26 Jackie Coogan, U.S. silent film and television actor who was Hollywood's first major child star, born in Los Angeles, California (–1984).
27 Dylan Thomas, Welsh poet, born in Swansea, Glamorgan, Wales (–1953).
28 Jonas Salk, U.S. physician who developed the first effective vaccine against poliomyelitis, born in New York, New York (–1995).
28 Richard Laurence Millington Synge, English biochemist who, with Archer J. P. Martin, developed partition chromatography, born in Liverpool, England (–1994).

NOVEMBER
5 August Weismann, German biologist, one of the founders of genetics who developed a "germ plasm" theory of inheritance, dies in Freiburg im Breisgau, Germany (80).
7 Eddie Chapman, English safecraker and double agent who carried out sabotage missions for the Germans during World War II, born in Sunderland, England (–1997).
14 Frederick, Lord Roberts, British field marshal during the Afghan War (1878–80), and the South African War (1899–1902), dies in St.-Omer, France (82).
20 Marchese di Barsento Pucci, Italian fashion designer whose brightly colored designs were popular in the mid-1950s to mid-1960s, born in Naples, Italy (–1992).
25 Joe DiMaggio (Joseph Paul DiMaggio), U.S. baseball player, born in Martinez, California.

DECEMBER
10 Dorothy Lamour, U.S. actress, born in New Orleans, Louisiana (–1996).
24 Dorothy Hyson, U.S. film and stage actress, born in Chicago, Illinois (–1996).

1915

POLITICS, GOVERNMENT, AND ECONOMICS

Business and Economics

SEPTEMBER

25 The United States lends $500 million to Britain and France to help fund their war effort.

DECEMBER

• The millionth Model T rolls off the Ford Motor Company's assembly line in Detroit, Michigan.

Colonization

NOVEMBER

12 Britain annexes the Gilbert and Ellice Islands (modern Tuvalu and Kiribati) in the Pacific Ocean, converting the protectorate into a colony.

Human Rights

JANUARY

12 The U.S. House of Representatives defeats a proposal for women's suffrage.

NOVEMBER

• The Ku Klux Klan, a racist society that originated in the 1860s, is revived by William Joseph Simmons near Atlanta, Georgia, dedicated to "white supremacy" and "Americanism." Within six years it attracts a membership of nearly 100,000.

Politics and Government

• German industrialist Walter Rathenau organizes a government *Kriegsrohstoffabteilung/War Raw Materials Department* or KRA, which establishes corporations to oversee the supply of raw materials to industry and to procure extra supplies where necessary.

• Outbreaks of tetanus in the trenches are controlled through serum injections.

JANUARY

• The U.S. Supreme Court strikes down a Kansas law prohibiting discrimination against union workers.

2 Russia appeals to Britain to mount an operation in the Caucasus region to relieve pressure from the Ottoman army.

8–February 5 Heavy fighting takes place in the Bassée Canal and Soissons area of France on the Western Front, resulting in small German gains.

13 South African troops occupy Swakopmund in German South West Africa.

18 Japan delivers a secret ultimatum of 21 demands to China, including mineral and railroad rights in the Shandong Peninsula and leases in Manchuria, with a view to increasing Japanese influence in China at the expense of other powers.

19 The first German Zeppelin airship raid is carried out over Britain, targeting East Anglian ports.

23 Heavy fighting takes place in the Carpathian Mountains between Russian and Austro-Hungarian forces, continuing until mid-April.

24 In the Battle of Dogger Bank in the North Sea, a British force under Admiral Sir David Beatty sinks the German cruiser *Blücher*.

28 The U.S. president Woodrow Wilson vetoes an immigration bill which includes a literacy test for immigrants.

FEBRUARY

3 A British force under General Charles Townshend starts an advance toward Baghdad along the River Tigris in Mesopotamia.

3 The German army uses poison gas at Bolimów (Bolimov), Poland, on the Eastern Front. It is the first time that they have used poison gas on a significant scale.

4 German-trained Ottoman troops under Djemal Pasha fail in their attack on the British-controlled Suez Canal in Egypt.

4 Germany declares the establishment of a submarine blockade around Britain from February 18, and declares that any foreign vessel found in the area will be considered a legitimate target.

4 The British Foreign Office announces that any vessel carrying grain to Germany will be seized.

7–21 In the Winter Battle of Masuria on the Eastern Front, the German and Austro-Hungarian armies force the Russian troops to retreat.

10 The United States announces that Germany will be held responsible for any attacks on U.S. ships or citizens.

16–30 French forces bombard and unsuccessfully attack German troops in Champagne, France, on the Western Front.

17 German forces recapture Memel (modern Klaipeda in Lithuania) from the Russian army on the Eastern Front.

19 British and French fleets bombard Ottoman forts at the entrance to the Dardanelles.

23 Britain seizes the Ottoman-held Aegean island of Lemnos as a base for its operations in the Dardanelles.

23 The Nevada assembly adopts legislation enabling individuals to attain a divorce after only six months' residence in the state.

MARCH

• U.S. Congress passes the La Follette Seaman's Act, designed to improve the life of merchant seamen.

6 The Greek prime minister Eleutherios Venizelos resigns over the failure of King Constantine to aid the Allies against the Ottoman Empire. Demetrios Gournaris forms a government in his place.

10–13 At the Battle of Neuve Chapelle in northeastern France, British and Indian forces break German lines and capture the village of Neuve Chapelle, but are unable to exploit their victory.

18 British and French ships under the British admiral John de Robeck attempt to push through the Dardanelles but are repulsed by Ottoman gun batteries and mines.

21 German Zeppelin airships make a bombing raid on Paris, France.

22 Russian forces take Przemyśl in the Polish area of northeastern Austria-Hungary (a key strategic point in the Carpathian Mountains) after a siege of 194 days.

APRIL

11 A British force under General Sir John Nixon repulses an Ottoman attack on Basra in Mesopotamia.

22 German troops use poison gas released from cylinders for the first time, at Langemarck near Ypres, Belgium.

22–May 25 At the Second Battle of Ypres, Belgium, a German counteroffensive pushes the Western Front in southwestern Belgium forward by 5 km/3 mi.

24 The wartime deportation and massacre of Armenians accused of collaborating with the Allies begins in the Ottoman Empire. 1.75 million people are driven across the Mesopotamian desert, over a million of them dying in the process.

25 Allied landings take place on the Gallipoli Peninsula in the Dardanelles under the command of Sir Ian Hamilton. British and French forces land at Cape Helles, and Australian and New Zealander Army Corps (ANZACS) forces at Anzac Cove. Deployed because of the stalemate on the Western Front, their aim is to knock the Ottoman Empire out of the war and assist the Russian effort against Germany on the Eastern Front, but the Allies meet stiff resistance from the Ottoman army commanded by Mustafa Kemal and the German general Otto Liman von Sanders.

26 A German offensive begins in Courland (modern Latvia) and, on April 27, in Lithuania.

26 Britain, France, and Italy make the secret Treaty of London, under which Italy will join the war in return for land and reparations from Germany and Austria-Hungary when the war ends.

MAY

• Germany responds to the U.S. demand for reparations for the sinking of the *Lusitania* by insisting that it acted in self-defense: the ship was loaded with contraband of war.

• In a letter to the U.S. secretary of state William Jennings Bryan, the British government maintains that the *Lusitania* was not armed when sunk by a German submarine.

1 The U.S. vessel *Gulflight* is sunk without warning by a German submarine.

2–September 19 An Austro-German offensive begins in Galicia (northeastern Austria-Hungary) with the Battle of Gorlice-Tarnów, breaking the Russian lines.

3 Italy denounces its Triple Alliance with Germany and Austria-Hungary (renewed in December 1912) following its secret alliance with Britain and France.

7 A German submarine sinks the British liner *Lusitania* off the south coast of Ireland, killing 1,198 passengers and crew, including 114 U.S. citizens.

9–10 British forces make an unsuccessful push in northeastern France at the Battle of Aubers Ridge.

9–June 18 At the Second Battle of Artois in France, the French armies under General Henri Pétain push forward in northeastern France, but gain little ground in spite of diversionary British attacks.

12 South African troops under Louis Botha occupy Windhoek, capital of German South West Africa.

13 President Woodrow Wilson demands that Germany pay reparations for the 114 U.S. lives lost aboard the British liner *Lusitania*, sunk six days before.

14 A liberal insurrection in Portugal overthrows the military ruler, General Pimenta de Castro.

15–25 British and Canadian forces conduct an unsuccessful offensive at the Battle of Festubert in northeastern France.

23 Italy declares war on Austria-Hungary and seizes several areas of land belonging to it.

25 China accepts the Japanese ultimatum of January 18.

29 Theophilo Braga is elected president of Portugal.

JUNE

• A New Jersey District Court exonerates John D. Rockefeller's United States Steel Corporation of antitrust violation.

• The U.S. president Woodrow Wilson dispatches a second note to Germany warning it to refrain from attacking unarmed passenger ships and merchant vessels.

1 German Zeppelin airships make their first raid on London, England.

3 An Allied conference opens in Paris, France, to establish cooperation in the economic aspects of the war.

3 The Russian southern front collapses when German forces recapture Przemyśl, Poland.

9 The U.S. secretary of state William Jennings Bryan resigns after President Woodrow Wilson refuses to concede that the *Lusitania* had indeed been transporting war munitions. The president feared that such an acknowledgment would weaken the United States's moral position. On June 23 Robert Lansing is appointed to the position.

9–11 Anti-German riots break out in Moscow, Russia, quickly developing into an attack on western Europeans in general.

23 German and Austro-Hungarian forces take Lemberg in northeastern Austria-Hungary from the Russian army.

23 The German Social Democratic Party issues a manifesto asking for a peace to be negotiated.

23–July 7 The First Battle of the Isonzo takes place when an Italian army under General Luigi Cadorna tries to force bridgeheads on the River Isonzo at Gorizia and

Tolmino in Italy, an area held by Austrian forces led by Archduke Eugene.

JULY

- Germany responds to President Woodrow Wilson's second *Lusitania* note, pledging not to attack unarmed, neutral shipping.
- In a third *Lusitania* note, President Woodrow Wilson warns Germany that the United States would view any further violations of U.S. sovereignty as deliberate provocation.
- The New York Court of Appeals upholds a state workmen's compensation law signed the previous May.
- The U.S. secret service acquires a notebook belonging to German-American physician Heinrich F. Albert which implicates members of the German consular and embassy staffs, along with several prominent German-Americans, in a German espionage ring.

1   Germany and Austria-Hungary launch their second major offensive of the year on the Eastern Front.

2–3   German national Erich Muenter, a professor at Cornell University, detonates a bomb in the U.S. Capitol, destroying the Senate reception room. The next day Muenter shoots billionaire J. P. Morgan, Jr., at Glen Cove, Long Island, allegedly for his role in lobbying the U.S. government to adopt munitions contracts with Britain. Muenter commits suicide on July 6.

9   German forces in South West Africa surrender to the South African Louis Botha.

12   The German government takes control of the German coal industry.

18–August 30   Italian and Austro-Hungarian forces meet in the Second Battle of the Isonzo in Italy.

27   Revolution breaks out in Haiti and President Vilbrun Guillaume Sam is killed by a mob.

28   President Woodrow Wilson dispatches U.S. troops to Haiti following the assassination of the Haitian president Vilbrun Guillaume Sam the previous day.

AUGUST

- A mob in Atlanta, Georgia, lynches the Jewish factory superintendent, Leo Moses Frank, convicted of murdering Mary Phagan, an employee, in April 1913.
- Washington, D.C., plays host to a meeting of Latin American representatives, called to promote an end to the civil war in Mexico.

4–7   German troops under General Max von Gallwitz take Warsaw in Russian Poland.

6   Allied troops under Sir Frederick Stopford land at Suvla Bay, Gallipoli, in the Dardanelles, in an unsuccessful attempt to outflank the Ottoman forces pinning down the Allied troops at Cape Helles and Anzac Cove.

6   Bernadino Machado is elected president of Portugal.

12   William Massey's government in New Zealand is reconstituted with Liberal Party members as a wartime coalition National Ministry.

20   On the Eastern Front, Germany takes the key fortress of Novogeorgievsk on the river Vistula, 35 km/21 mi northwest of Warsaw, from Russian forces.

21   Italy declares war on the Ottoman Empire.

25   An advancing German army captures Brest-Litovsk in Russian Poland.

30   Following protests from the United States, Germany orders its submarines and ships to warn enemy passenger vessels before sinking them.

SEPTEMBER

September, 1915–February 1916   The United States and Haiti sign a treaty, ratified February 28, 1916, making Haiti a U.S. protectorate.

5   Czar Nicholas II of Russia takes personal command of the Russian armies, replacing Grand Duke Nicholas after the defeats of the summer.

6   Bulgaria signs military alliances with Germany and the Ottoman Empire in preparation for an attack on its neighbor, Serbia.

6–16   Russian forces check the advance of the Austro-Hungarian army at Tarnopol, Russia.

9   Russian forces halt the German offensive at the Battle of Dvinsk on the Eastern Front.

9   The United States asks Austria to recall its ambassador, and on October 5 he leaves New York, New York.

18   German forces under General Max von Gallwitz capture Vilna (modern Vilnius, Lithuania) from the Russians, marking the furthest extent of the German advance in 1915.

18   Germany undertakes to withdraw its submarines from the English Channel and western approaches in order to reduce the danger to U.S. ships.

25–October 15   At the Third Battle of Artois, French forces attack the German line in northeastern France and in Champagne to the southeast, while a British force, using gas for the first time, attacks the line at Loos on November 4. Only small gains are made.

28   British forces under Major General Charles Townshend, advancing along the River Tigris in Mesopotamia, capture Kut-al-Imara from the Ottoman army.

OCTOBER

5   The Allies land troops at Thessaloníki (Salonika) in neutral Greece, to aid Serbia against impending attack by the Central Powers.

6–November 20   Austro-Hungarian troops under General August von Mackensen renew their invasion of Serbia, capturing Belgrade on October 9.

9   A conference of Latin American states recognizes Venustiano Carranza as chief of the de facto government in Mexico.

12   Following the invasion of Serbia by the Central Powers, the Allies declare that they will assist Serbia under the terms of the Bucharest Treaty of August 10, 1913.

12   Greece refuses a Serbian appeal for aid against invasion by the Central Powers, under the terms of the Serbo-Greek treaty of 1913.

12   The German authorities in Brussels, Belgium, execute British nurse Edith Cavell for harboring British and French prisoners and aiding escapees.

13   The French foreign minister, Théophile Delcassé, resigns in protest at the sending of Allied troops to Thessaloníki (Salonika), Greece.

13   The largest Zeppelin raid of the European war takes place over London, England.

14   Bulgaria enters the war on the side of the Central Powers.

15   Britain declares war on Bulgaria following its entry into the war against Serbia. France does likewise on October 16, and Russia and Italy on October 19.

16   Sir Charles Munro replaces Sir Ian Hamilton as commander of the Allied Dardanelles expedition, and plans are drawn up for an evacuation.

18–November 3 The Third Battle of the Isonzo takes place, the Italian army making small gains of territory against the opposing Austro-Hungarian forces.

19 Japan becomes a signatory to the Treaty of London of April 26, undertaking not to make a separate peace with the Central Powers.

19 President Woodrow Wilson recognizes General Venustiano Carranza as president of Mexico.

20 The success of James Hertzog's Nationalist Party in the South African elections leaves the South African Party government in a minority.

27 Andrew Fisher resigns as Australian prime minister to become high commissioner in London, England. He is succeeded as prime minister by William Hughes.

28 René Viviani resigns as prime minister of France and is replaced on October 29 by the former prime minister Aristide Briand.

NOVEMBER

- The U.S. Supreme Court rules as unconstitutional an Arizona law requiring businesses to maintain an employee pool of at least 80% native-born Americans.

5 Chinese princes vote for the establishment of a monarchy, with Premier Yuan Shikai as emperor.

6 Sophocles Skouloudis forms a government in Greece which favors the Allies.

7 40,000 men protest in Chicago against a city ordinance closing saloons on Sunday.

8 Greece declares itself a benevolent neutral in the European war, but favors the Allies.

10–December 10 The Fourth Battle of the Isonzo is fought in Italy, with neither the Italian nor the Austro-Hungarian forces gaining ground.

13 Following the failure of the Gallipoli campaign in the Ottoman Empire, the first lord of the Admiralty, Winston Churchill, resigns from the British Cabinet.

14 The Senussi tribe of western Egypt rises against British rule.

21 Italy makes an agreement with the Allies not to make a separate peace with the Central Powers.

22–December 4 In the Battle of Ctesiphon, Ottoman troops force the British invaders of Mesopotamia back to Kut-al-Imara, Mesopotamia.

DECEMBER

- President Woodrow Wilson marries Edith Bolling Galt in Washington, D.C.
- The controversial Ford Peace Ship, chartered by automobile magnate Henry Ford, departs for Europe on what will prove to be a futile peace mission.

4 The state of Georgia grants the Ku Klux Klan a new charter, signaling the reemergence of the white supremacist group.

7 Ottoman troops begin the siege of British forces at Kut-al-Imara in Mesopotamia.

18–19 In a highly successful evacuation, Allied troops withdraw from Suvla Bay and Anzac Cove on the Gallipoli Peninsula following the failure of the Dardanelles campaign.

21 William Robertson, a proponent in Britain of concentrated attacks on the Western Front, becomes chief of the imperial general staff.

28 The British Cabinet agrees on the principle of making military service compulsory.

SCIENCE, TECHNOLOGY, AND MEDICINE

Ecology

JANUARY

- The U.S. Congress establishes Rocky Mountain National Park from 1,060 sq km/262,000 acres of Colorado wilderness. It contains more than 100 peaks over 3,000 m/10,000 ft.

13 The town of Avezzano, Italy, is destroyed by an earthquake estimated to measure 7.5 on the Richter scale; over 32,000 people are killed.

AUGUST

16 Galveston, Texas, is hit by one of the worst hurricanes of the century. It causes over $50 million in damage, but because a sea wall was built after the 1900 hurricane only 275 people are killed.

Health and Medicine

- French surgeon Alexis Carrel and British chemist Henry Dakin independently treat battle wounds with antiseptic irrigations, now known as the Carrel–Dakin method.
- Japanese chemists Katsusaboro Yamagiwa and Koichi Ichikawa identify coal tar as a carcinogen—the first to be discovered.
- New Zealand-born British surgeon Harold Delf Gillies develops plastic surgery when he treats war casualties at Sidcup, Kent.
- The German company Bayer introduces aspirin in tablet form.
- U.S. microbiologist Simon Flexner isolates the dysentery bacillus *Shigella dysenteriae*.

August 1915–16 Austrian psychologist Sigmund Freud writes *A General Introduction to Psychoanalysis*, in which he outlines his psychoanalytic theory.

JUNE

June–August A typhus epidemic in Serbia kills 150,000 people.

Science

- English physicists William and Lawrence Bragg win the Nobel Prize for Physics for their work showing that the atomic structure of crystals can be analyzed from the diffraction patterns of X-rays.
- German chemist Richard Willstätter receives the Nobel Prize for Chemistry for research into plant pigments, especially chlorophyll.
- Scottish astronomer Robert Innes discovers Proxima Centauri. The closest star to the sun, it is 4.4 light-years away.
- U.S. geneticists Thomas Hunt Morgan, Alfred Sturtevant, Calvin Bridges, and Hermann Muller publish *The Mechanism of Mendelian Heredity*, which outlines their work on the fruit fly *Drosophila melanogaster* demonstrating that genes can be mapped on chromosomes.

June 1915–16   English naturalist Archibald Thorburn publishes *British Birds*, which describes and catalogs the birds in Britain.

Technology

- Automatic leveling is introduced on elevators precisely to position elevators at the floor; it takes over from the operators when the elevator approaches the floor.
- Dutch airman Anthony Fokker develops a gear system that synchronizes a machine gun with the propellers of airplanes so that it shoots through them. It gives Germany air superiority during World War I.
- U.S. blacksmith August Freuhauf invents the tractor trailer.
- U.S. firm Corning Glass Works introduces the heat- and chemical-resistant glass "Pyrex," which expands only one-third as much as ordinary glass. It is used for ovenware, industrial equipment, and laboratory apparatus.
- U.S. physicist Manson Benedicks discovers that a germanium crystal can convert alternating current to direct current. It leads to the development of the microchip.

JANUARY
- Germany uses chlorine gas against the Russians. It is the first use of chemical warfare, but it has little effect. On April 22, however, they use it at the Battle of Ypres to rout French and Canadian troops.

MAY
24   The U.S. inventor Thomas Alva Edison announces that he has invented the telescribe, which records telephone conversations.

SEPTEMBER
- The armored car division of the British Royal Naval Air Service introduce "Little Willie," the first purpose-built tank. A second model, "Big Willie," is introduced shortly afterwards.

Transportation

- Leipzig railroad station, the largest in Europe, is completed in Germany.
- Russian engineer Igor Sikorsky builds a 16-passenger biplane. Passengers are in an enclosed cabin and the airplane is powered by four 100-horsepower Mercedes engines. It is the first multiengine airplane.
- The German aircraft designer Hugo Junkers constructs the J-1 Blechesel monoplane, the first all-metal airplane.
- The Tunkhannock Creek Viaduct, Pennsylvania, is completed. The longest reinforced concrete bridge in the United States, it is 724 m/2,375 ft long.
- The U.S. Sperry company develop a gyrostabilizer to reduce the rolling of ships.

September 1915–16   Britain launches the Queen Elizabeth class battleships. They travel at 25 knots.

JANUARY
18   A train derails and plunges into a gorge in Guadalajara, Mexico, killing 600 people.

MARCH
3   U.S. Congress establishes the National Advisory Committee for Aeronautics, to conduct research on aeronautics.

JULY
24   The passenger steamboat *Eastland* capsizes at her berth at a pier in Chicago, Illinois, killing 852 people.

OCTOBER
27   U.S. pilot Oscar A. Brindley sets a new seaplane flight record when he flies 870 km/544 mi along the California coast.

DECEMBER
18   British firm Hadley-Page test-flies the HP 0/100, the first purpose-built bomber.

ARTS AND IDEAS

Architecture

- Palais Stoclet in Brussels, Belgium, designed by the Belgian architect Josef Hoffmann, is completed. Its interior decoration includes mosaics by the Austrian artist Gustav Klimt.

Arts

- The German art historian Heinrich Wölfflin publishes *Kunstgeschichtliche Grundbegriffe/Principles of Art History*.
- The English artist Walter Richard Sickert paints *Brighton Pierrots*.
- The English writer and artist Wyndham Lewis paints *The Crowd*.
- The French artist Francis Picabia paints *Very Rare Picture on the Earth*.
- The German artist Otto Dix paints *Self-Portrait as Soldier*.
- The Italian artist Amedeo Modigliani paints *Portrait of Raymond Radiguet* and *Portrait of Beatrice Hastings*.
- The Italian artist Gino Severini paints *Armoured Train*.
- The Norwegian artist Edvard Munch completes his series of frescoes for the assembly hall of Oslo University in Norway.
- The Polish-born U.S. artist Elie Nadelman sculpts *Man in the Open Air*.
- The Russian artist Alexander Archipenko sculpts *Woman Combing her Hair*.
- The Russian artist Kasimir Malevich paints *Suprematist Composition: Black Square*.
- The Russian artist Lyubov Popova paints *The Philosopher*.
- The Russian artist Marc Chagall paints *The Birthday*.
- The Russian artist Vladimir Tatlin creates his sculpture *Counter-Corner Relief*.
- The Spanish artist Pablo Picasso paints *Harlequin*.
- The U.S. artist Max Weber paints *Rush Hour, New York*, and *Chinese Restaurant*.

- The U.S. artist Morgan Russell paints *Synchromie Cosmique*.

Film

- Dr. Herbert Kalmus develops the Technicolor film process in the United States. It will not be commercially viable until the 1930s.
- The movie *A Fool There Was*, directed by Frank Powell, is released in the United States, starring Theda Bara.
- The movie *A Welsh Singer* is released, starring Edith Evans.
- The movie *Carmen*, directed by Cecil B. de Mille, is released in the United States, starring Wallace Reed and Geraldine Farrar. De Mille's movie *The Cheat* is also released in the United States, starring Fannie Ward and Sessue Hayakawa.
- The movie *Fatty and Mabel's Simple Life*, directed by Roscoe "Fatty" Arbuckle, is released in the United States. He also stars in it with Mabel Normand.
- The movie *Just Nuts*, directed by Harold Lloyd, is released in the United States. He also stars in it.
- The movie *The Lamb*, directed by Christy Cabanne, is released in the United States, starring Douglas Fairbanks.
- The movie *The Tramp*, directed by Charlie Chaplin, is released in the United States. He also stars in it, with Edna Purviance.
- The word "fans" comes into general use in the United States and Britain, to describe regular movie-goers.
- U.S. actress Audrey Munson becomes the first person to appear nude in a mainstream movie, in U.S. director George Foster Platt's *Inspiration*.

December 1915–16 The French director Louis Feuillade releases his movie serial *Les Vampires/The Vampires* in France.

FEBRUARY

8 The movie *Birth of a Nation*, directed by D. W. Griffith, is released in the United States. An influential and commercially successful silent movie, it stars Lillian Gish, Mae Marsh, and Henry B. Walthall. Its epic scope and innovative cinematic techniques are, however, marred by racism, which includes a sympathetic portrayal of the Ku Klux Klan.

Literature and Language

- Birth control advocate, Margaret Sanger, is convicted in New York state of propagating literature "contrary not only to the law of the state, but to the law of God." The offending literature is Sanger's book, *Family Limitation*.
- Literary critic Van Wyck Brooks publishes *America's Coming-of-Age* which concerns the Puritan heritage and its effects on American literature.
- The Bohemian-born German writer Franz Kafka publishes his novella *Die Verwandlung/Metamorphosis*.
- The English writer Arnold Bennett publishes *These Twain*, the third volume of his Clayhanger trilogy.
- The English writer and artist Isaac Rosenberg publishes his poetry collection *Youth*.
- The English writer Dorothy Richardson publishes her novel *Pointed Roofs*, the first volume of her *Pilgrimage* series. The last volume appears in 1938.

- The English writer D. H. Lawrence publishes his novel *The Rainbow*.
- The English writer Ford Madox Ford publishes his novella *The Good Soldier*.
- The English writer Norman Douglas publishes his travel book *Old Calabria*.
- The English writer Rupert Brooke publishes his poetry collection *1914 and Other Poems*.
- The English writer Somerset Maugham publishes his novel *Of Human Bondage*.
- The English writer Virginia Woolf publishes her first novel, *The Voyage Out*.
- The Polish-born English writer Joseph Conrad publishes his novel *Victory*.
- The Scottish writer John Buchan publishes his adventure novel *The Thirty-Nine Steps*.
- The U.S. writer Edgar Lee Masters publishes his poetry collection *The Spoon River Anthology*.
- The U.S. writer Sara Teasdale publishes her poetry collection *Rivers to the Sea*.
- The U.S. writer Theodore Dreiser publishes his autobiographical novel *The 'Genius'*.
- The U.S. writer Willa Cather publishes her novel *The Song of the Lark*.

Music

- English songwriter Felix Powell and his brother George Asaf (pen name of George Henry Powell) write the song "Pack Up Your Troubles in Your Old Kit Bag."
- The Austrian composer Alexander Zemlinsky completes his String Quartet No. 2.
- The English composer Albert Ketèlbey completes his orchestral work *In a Monastery Garden*.
- The Finnish composer Jean Sibelius completes the first version of his Symphony No. 5.
- The French composer Claude Debussy completes his two sets of *Etudes* for piano.
- The French composer Gabriel Fauré completes his song cycle *Le Jardin clos/The Enclosed Garden*.
- The German composer Max(imilian) Reger completes his orchestral work *Variations and Fugue on a Theme of Beethoven*.
- The German composer Richard Strauss completes his tone poem *Alpensinfonie/Alpine Symphony*.
- The Italian composer Ferruccio Busoni completes his *Indianische Tagebuch/Indian Diary* Book I (for piano), and Book II (for orchestra).
- The operetta *Die Csárdásfürstin/The Gypsy Princess*, by the Hungarian composer Emmerich (Imre) Kálmán, is first performed in Vienna, Austria.
- The U.S. composer Charles Ives completes his *Orchestral Set No. 2* and his Piano Sonata No. 2, *Concord Massachusetts 1840–1860*, which includes solos for viola and flute.
- The U.S. composer John Alden Carpenter completes his orchestral suite *Adventures of a Perambulator*.
- U.S. composer "Jelly Roll" Morton publishes the song "Jelly Roll Blues" (written in 1905).

Theater and Dance

FEBRUARY

- The Neighborhood Playhouse opens off Broadway on Grand Street in New York, New York. Designed to show experimental theater, the playhouse also leads to the formation of the Washington Square Players, a modern theater group.

Thought and Scholarship

- Australian ethnologist Grafton Elliot Smith publishes *The Migrations of Early Culture*.
- English philosopher Bernard Bosanquet publishes *Three Lectures on Aesthetics*.
- The Nobel Prize for Literature is awarded to the French novelist Romain Rolland.

- U.S. economist, Horace Kallen, publishes his two-part essay "Democracy versus the Melting Pot," in which he advances an ideal of cultural pluralism.
- U.S. historian Carl Lotus Becker publishes *The Beginnings of the American People*.
- U.S. historian Charles Austin Beard publishes *The Economic Origins of Jeffersonian Democracy*.
- U.S. journalist Lynn Haines publishes *Your Congress*.

SOCIETY

Education

- Emory University is chartered in Atlanta, Georgia, United States.
- The University of British Columbia opens in Vancouver, Canada.

BIRTHS & DEATHS

JANUARY

14 Richard Condon, U.S. thriller writer, author of *The Manchurian Candidate* (1959), and *Prizzi's Honor* (1982), born in New York, New York (–1996).

24 Robert Motherwell, U.S. abstract expressionist painter, born in Aberdeen, Washington (–1991).

31 Gary Moore, U.S. television quiz show host and entertainer, born in Baltimore, Maryland (–1993).

31 Thomas Merton, French-born U.S. Roman Catholic monk and spiritual writer, born in Prades, France (–1968).

FEBRUARY

5 Robert Hofstadter, U.S. physicist who discovered the structure of protons and neutrons, born in New York, New York (–1990).

28 Zero Mostel, U.S. theater and film actor, born in New York, New York (–1977).

MARCH

15 Joseph Mitsuo Kitagawa, Japanese-born U.S. theologian, born in Osaka, Japan (–1992).

20 Sviatoslav Richter, Russian concert pianist, one of the 20th century's greatest pianists, born in Zhitomir, Ukraine, Russian Empire (–1997).

21 Frederick Winslow Taylor, U.S. inventor and engineer who revolutionized modern industry through his time management studies, dies in Philadelphia, Pennsylvania (59).

APRIL

2 Paul Touvier, French war criminal known as the "Hangman of Lyons"

who escaped custody for 40 years, born in Lyons, France (–1996).

7 Billie Holiday (real name Eleanora Fagan), U.S. jazz singer, born in Baltimore, Maryland (–1959).

27 Alexander Scriabin, Russian composer, dies in Moscow, Russia (53).

MAY

6 Orson Welles, U.S. film actor, director, producer, and writer, best known for *Citizen Kane*, born in Kenosha, Wisconsin (–1985).

10 Monica (Enid) Dickens, English novelist, born in London, England (–1992).

20 Moshe Dayan, Israeli soldier who directed Israel's armed forces during the Six-Day War (1967), born in Degania, Palestine (now Israel) (–1981).

JUNE

10 Saul Bellow, Canadian-born U.S. writer who won the Nobel Prize for Literature in 1976, born in Lachine, Canada.

18 Red Adair, U.S. oil-well firefighter who capped all the oil-well fires in Kuwait after the Gulf War (1991), born in Houston, Texas.

JULY

28 Charles Hard Townes, U.S. physicist who invented the maser (microwave amplification by stimulated emission of radiation), born in Greenville, South Carolina.

AUGUST

20 Paul Ehrlich, German medical researcher who discovered the first effective treatment for syphilis, dies

in Bad Homburg von der Höhe, Germany (61).

29 Ingrid Bergman, Swedish actress, born in Stockholm, Sweden (–1982).

SEPTEMBER

9 A(lbert) G(oodwill) Spalding, U.S. baseball player and sporting goods manufacturer, dies in Point Loma, California (65).

OCTOBER

15 Yitzhak Shamir, prime minister of Israel 1983–84 and 1986–92 born in Ruzinoy, Poland, Russian Empire.

17 Arthur Miller, U.S. playwright, born in New York, New York.

NOVEMBER

12 Roland Barthes, French intellectual and critic, born in Cherbourg, France (–1980).

14 Booker T. Washington, U.S. educator and black American spokesman between 1895 and 1915, dies in Tuskegee, Alabama (59).

25 Augusto Pinochet, Chilean president 1973–89, and military dictator, born.

DECEMBER

12 Frank Sinatra, U.S. singer and actor, born in Hoboken, New Jersey.

13 John Vorster, prime minister of South Africa 1966–78 and president 1978–79, born in Jamestown, Cape Province, Union of South Africa (–1986).

Everyday Life

- J. L. Kraft and Bros launches Kraft processed cheese in the United States, initially selling it in tins.
- The alcoholic drink absinthe, which contains thuzone, a toxic chemical found in wormwood that is believed to cause convulsions, hallucinations, and mental deterioration, is made illegal in France.
- The U.S. cereal company Kellogg's launches Bran Flakes.
- The U.S. vice president Thomas R. Marshall coins a popular phrase, "what this country really needs is a good five cent cigar," after presiding over another interminably dull debate in the U.S. Senate.
- U.S. researchers Eugene C. Sullivan and William C. Taylor at the Corning Glass Works create Pyrex, a heatproof and shockproof kitchenware.

JANUARY

25 A transcontinental telephone service is inaugurated by the Scottish-born U.S. inventor Alexander Graham Bell, in San Francisco, California, when he says to his former employee Thomas Watson in New York, New York, "Mr. Watson, come here, I want you," repeating the first telephone conversation Bell had when he invented the telephone in 1876.

FEBRUARY

- The Panama-Pacific International Exposition opens in San Francisco, California.

Media and Communication

- The first transatlantic radio telephony transmission is made—from Arlington, Virginia, to the Eiffel Tower, Paris, France.

JULY

27 Direct radio communication begins between the United States and Japan.

Sports

- The former Olympic track and field and college football star Jim Thorpe signs for the Canton Bulldogs of the professional Ohio League Championship.
- The U.S. baseball player Ty Cobb of the Detroit Tigers sets a major league record of 96 stolen bases in one season. His record is not surpassed until 1962, when Maury Wills of the Los Angeles Dodgers steals 104.
- Wexford beats Kerry in the All-Ireland Gaelic Football final, the first of four consecutive victories.

APRIL

15 The U.S. boxer Jess Willard, known as "the Great White Hope," wins the world heavyweight title, knocking out the defending champion, black American Jack Johnson, in the 26th round of their fight in Havana, Cuba.

MAY

6 At the Polo Grounds, New York, New York, Babe Ruth, a left-handed pitcher for the Boston Red Sox, hits his first-ever home run in major league baseball. He is not converted to an outfielder until he moves to the New York Yankees in 1920.

8 Regret, ridden by the U.S. jockey Joe Notter, becomes the first filly to win the Kentucky Derby horse race.

AUGUST

31 The British boxer Ted "Kid" Lewis defeats the U.S. boxer Jack Britton on points in Boston, Massachusetts, to become the undisputed world welterweight boxing champion.

1916

POLITICS, GOVERNMENT, AND ECONOMICS

Business and Economics

- Polish-born U.S. entrepreneur Nathan Handwerker opens a frankfurter stand in Coney Island, New York, that will blossom into the hot dog emporium Nathan's Famous.
- The American Tobacco Co. introduces Lucky Strike brand cigarettes.

- The Boeing aircraft company is founded by timber merchant William E. Boeing in Seattle, Washington.
- The Converse shoe company of Massachusetts introduces the Converse basketball shoe, one of the nation's first brand-name sneakers.
- The U.S. shoe manufacturer United States Rubber Co. introduces the sneaker brand U.S. Keds.

Human Rights

- The Jamaican civil-rights activist Marcus Moziah Garvey arrives in New York, New York, where he establishes a new command post for his Universal Negro Improvement Association.

NOVEMBER

7   Montana voters make Jeanette Rankin the first woman to be elected to the U.S. House of Representatives.

Politics and Government

- Despite the huge success of the recruiting campaign of 1915, conscription is introduced in Britain with supervision from the new Ministry of National Service.
- The clocks are put forward by one hour in Germany in order to save energy for the war effort by reducing the need for artificial illumination.
- The Institute for Government Research is founded in the United States.
- The Rural Credits Act is introduced in the United States.
- The states of Michigan, Montana, Nebraska, South Dakota, and Utah adopt prohibition, making 24 states dry.
- The United States establishes a shipping board.
- Zoning laws are enacted in New York, New York, to control development in the city.

JANUARY

- In yet another note to the U.S. president Woodrow Wilson about submarine warfare, Germany pledges to comply unequivocally with international law.
- The U.S. president Woodrow Wilson appoints the legal scholar Louis D. Brandeis to the U.S. Supreme Court. Confirmed June 1, Brandeis becomes the first Jewish Associated Judge to serve on the High Court.

8–9 Allied forces are withdrawn from Cape Helles on the Gallipoli Peninsula in the Ottoman Empire, completing the evacuation of troops from the Dardanelles.

8–17 Austro-Hungarian forces attack Montenegro, and the Serbian army flees to Corfu.

11–September 5 General Nicolay Yudenich leads a Russian offensive against the Ottoman Empire, south of the Caucasus region.

16   Supporters of the Mexican rebel Francisco "Pancho" Villa kill 16 U.S. citizens near Chihuahua in northern Mexico.

24   The U.S. Supreme Court rules that income tax law is constitutional in *Brushaber v. Union Pacific Railroad Co.*

FEBRUARY

- The South Carolina assembly adopts legislation raising the mandatory age for child industrial labor from 12 to 14.

2   The conservative Boris Stürmer becomes Russian prime minister, replacing the elderly Ivan Goremykin.

14   The Allies guarantee Belgium a place at the peace conference.

15–March 17 The Fifth Battle of the Isonzo takes place in Italy between Italian and Austro-Hungarian forces, but results in little change in the status quo.

16   Russian troops under General Nikolai Yudenich, advancing south of the Caucasus region, capture Erzurum in northeastern Anatolia (modern Turkey).

18   The last German garrison in the Cameroons surrenders to the British general Sir Charles Dobell.

21–December 18 German and Allied troops meet in the Battle of Verdun in France, the German commander Eric von Falkenhayn planning to sap French reserves in a battle of attrition. By the end of the battle each side has lost about 400,000 men.

25   During the Battle of Verdun on the Western Front, German troops take Fort Douaumont, France.

MARCH

- Events in Europe and Mexico prompt the U.S. Senate to adopt a resolution calling up all U.S. military reserves.

2   The Russian armies capture Bitlis in southeastern Anatolia (modern Turkey). It will be reconquered by Ottoman forces on August 8.

9   Germany declares war on Portugal when German ships are seized in Portuguese harbors at the request of Britain.

9   The Mexican revolutionary Francisco "Pancho" Villa and 1,500 followers raid the town of Columbus, New Mexico, killing 19 U.S. citizens. Apparently, Villa intended to punish the United States for President Woodrow Wilson's recognition of General Venustiano Carranza as president of Mexico. U.S. troops relieve the border town, pushing Villa back into Mexico.

13   Germany relaxes its rules governing the sinking of ships, allowing that submarines can sink British vessels around Britain if they appear not to be passenger ships.

15   A U.S. punitive expedition under the command of General John J. Pershing is sent into Mexico to pursue the Mexican revolutionary Francisco "Pancho" Villa.

15   Germany begins a second campaign of unrestricted submarine warfare.

15   The German secretary of state for the navy Alfred von Tirpitz resigns over Germany's reluctance to use its surface fleet.

20   The Allies launch an air attack against the German submarine base at Zeebrugge, Belgium.

24   A German submarine sinks the passenger ship *Sussex* without warning. The victims include U.S. citizens.

26   The Allies agree on the partition of the Ottoman Empire in the event of victory. Russia will receive Armenia, Kurdistan, and part of Anatolia, while Britain and France will gain spheres of influence in Arabia.

APRIL

17   Russian troops capture Trebizond in northeastern Anatolia (modern Turkey).

18   President Woodrow Wilson admonishes Germany that he will sever U.S.-German relations if German submarines attack one more passenger liner carrying U.S. citizens.

20   A German submarine lands the Irish nationalist Roger Casement in Ireland to lead an Irish rising, but he is arrested on April 24 and executed on August 3 for high treason.

20   Germany suspends unrestricted submarine warfare because of U.S. protests over the sinking of the *Sussex*.

24   The British fishing ports of Lowestoft and Yarmouth are shelled by German warships.

24–May 1 With the support of Sinn Féin, members of the Irish Republican Brotherhood take part in the "Easter Rising" in Dublin, Ireland, in an attempt to end British rule in Ireland. The rising is suppressed by British forces after heavy fighting, and its leaders (including Patrick Pearse and James Connolly) are executed.

29   The Ottoman army recaptures the Mesopotamian city of Kut-al-Imara from the occupying British forces,

following a siege dating from December 7, 1915. 10,000 prisoners are taken.

MAY

- Germany responds to President Woodrow Wilson's warning of April 18, pledging not to attack merchant vessels without affording passengers a chance to escape.
- New York governor Charles S. Whitman vetoes legislation authorizing movie censorship.
- President Woodrow Wilson dispatches U.S. marines to Santo Domingo to quell civil unrest. The United States occupies the country until 1924.
- The U.S. president Woodrow Wilson signs the Harrison Drug Act, requiring pharmaceutical stores to maintain an inventory file with the Internal Revenue Service. In June, the U.S. Supreme Court authorizes the prosecution of opium retailers.
8   ANZAC troops (from Australia and New Zealand) arrive in France to fight on the Western Front.
9   The "Sykes–Picot Agreement" between Britain and France establishes their intended postwar spheres of influence in the Middle East.
15–June 3   Austro-Hungarian troops under General Franz Conrad mount the Asiago offensive near Verona, Italy, but make few gains.
31–June 1   The British and German surface fleets clash in the Battle of Jutland in the North Sea, their one major conflict of the war. The British fleet under Admiral Sir John Jellicoe loses a greater number of ships, but succeeds in reaffirming its naval dominance. The German fleet will remain in harbor for the rest of the war.

JUNE

- After U.S. troops reenter Mexico, Mexican authorities warn that the U.S. force will be attacked unless they are withdrawn.
- Mexico warns the U.S. general John J. Pershing to halt his pursuit of the Mexican revolutionary Francisco "Pancho" Villa.
- President Woodrow Wilson signs legislation incorporating the Boy Scouts of America.
- U.S. Congress passes the National Defense Act, increasing the number of U.S. Army personnel to 175,000 and U.S. National Guard personnel to 450,000.
- U.S. secretary of state Robert Lansing informs Mexico that U.S. troops will not withdraw from the border region until it is secure from banditry.
4–August 20   The Russian armies commanded by General Alexei Brusilov mount the Brusilov Offensive, pushing the Austro-Hungarian line south of the Russian Pripet Marshes, but the attack is blunted by German reinforcements.
5   A British-supported Arab revolt against Ottoman rule in the Hejaz region begins at Medina (in modern Saudi Arabia).
5   Ottoman forces led by Enver Pasha in Persia begin a counteroffensive against the advancing Russian troops.
6   British and French armies blockade Greece, suspecting that King Constantine is in league with the Central Powers, and only relent when the Greek army is stood down on June 22.
6   The autocratic president of China, Yuan Shikai, dies.

7   During the Battle of Verdun on the Western Front, German troops take Fort Vaux, France.
7   Grand Sheriff Hussein of Mecca revolts against the Ottoman Empire.
10   The Republican convention in the United States nominates Supreme Court associate judge Charles E. Hughes as its presidential candidate and Indiana politician Charles Warren Fairbanks as its vice presidential candidate.
13   Jan Smuts, commander in chief of Allied troops, captures Wilhelmsthal in German East Africa (now Tanzania).
15   The Democratic convention at St. Louis, Missouri, nominates President Woodrow Wilson as its presidential candidate and Vice President Thomas R. Marshall as its vice presidential candidate.
17   Following the fall of Antonio Salandra on June 11, Paolo Boselli forms a coalition government in Italy, which includes Catholics and Reformist Socialists. Boselli has championed the Allied cause since the start of the war.
18   Russian troops recapture Czernowitz (now Chernovtsy in Ukraine) from the Austria-Hungarians during the Brusilov offensive.
21   Mexican troops attack U.S. forces at Carrizal, Mexico, near the U.S.-Mexican border. The United States suffers 17 casualties, the Mexicans 38.
23   During the Battle of Verdun on the Western Front, German troops take Fort Thiaumont, France.
23   The Convention of Ulster Nationalists agrees to an amendment to exclude Ulster from Irish rule under the Government of Ireland Act.
25   Czar Nicholas of Russia orders the conscription of Kazakhs and Kirghiz. As they have been traditionally exempt from military service, their conscription leads to the outbreak of civil disorder and the deaths of 100,000 people.
26   The former U.S. president Theodore Roosevelt declines nomination as the Progressive Republican presidential candidate.

JULY

- A bomb rips through a Preparedness Day parade in San Francisco, California, killing 10 and wounding 40. Labor leaders Tom Mooney and Warren K. Billings are arrested and later convicted for the killings. Both will be exonerated in 1939.
- The United States accuses Germany of sabotage after a munitions depot explodes on Toms River Island, New Jersey.
- The United States and Mexico agree to submit their differences to arbitration.
1–November 18   French and British troops mount the Battle of the Somme in France, a massive offensive which gains 8 km/5 mi of territory. The British Army suffers 60,000 casualties (including 20,000 dead) on the first day, while the whole campaign results in over 620,000 British and French casualties and about 450,000 German casualties.
11   President Woodrow Wilson signs the Shackleford Good Roads Bill (Federal Highway Act), which provides $5 million in matching funds to promote highway construction in the states.
25   Russian troops under General Nicolay Yudenich inflict a heavy defeat on an Ottoman force at Erzinjan, Armenia.

25 The Russian foreign minister, Sergei Sazonov, is dismissed, his position having been undermined by conservative factions at the Russian court.

26 U.S.–British relations deteriorate when the United States protests after Britain publishes a list of 80 U.S. firms blacklisted for allegedly violating Britain's "trading with the enemy" act by trading with the Central Powers.

AUGUST

• U.S. Congress creates the National Park Service within the Department of the Interior to administer the nation's growing network of federal parks.

4 The Danish government agrees to sell the West Indian Virgin Islands to the United States, though the treaty is opposed in Denmark. The matter is put to a referendum, and on December 14 the sale is approved.

4–January 9, 1917 British forces drive back Ottoman troops in a battle near Rumani, Egypt.

6–17 At the Sixth Battle of the Isonzo in Italy, Italian forces advance and take Gorizia from Austro-Hungarian troops.

17–September 18 A Bulgarian and German force attacks the Allied enclave around Thessaloníki (Salonika), Greece, at the Battle of Florina.

19 A British naval force damages the German battleship *Westfalen* in the North Sea; a German naval force bombards the English coast.

24 Russian troops under General Nicolay Yudenich take Bitlis and Mush, Armenia, from an Ottoman force.

27 Romania joins the Allies and declares war on Austria-Hungary.

28 A Russian force begins an invasion of Austro-Hungarian Transylvania on the Eastern Front.

28 Italy declares war on Germany.

29 Following victories on the Eastern Front, Field Marshal Paul von Hindenburg is appointed German chief of the general staff (with Eric Ludendorff as quartermaster general) in sucession to Eric von Falkenhayn, whose strategy at Verdun, France, is not working.

30 The Ottoman Empire declares war on Romania.

31 The German government accepts the "Hindenburg Plan" for militarization of the German war economy.

SEPTEMBER

• The U.S. president Woodrow Wilson signs the Adamson Eight-Hour Act, providing railroad workers with an eight-hour day.

• U.S. Congress passes a Workmen's Compensation Act, protecting some 500,000 federal workers in the event of disabling injury.

• U.S. Congress passes the Owen-Keating Act, prohibiting the interstate shipment of goods on which children under 14 years have worked, or on which children between the ages of 14 and 16 years have worked for more than 8 hours.

1 Bulgaria declares war on Romania.

4 Allied troops under the South African general Jan Smuts take Dar es Salaam, the capital of German East Africa (now Tanzania).

6 The Central Powers establish a Supreme War Council, increasing German influence in the dispirited Austro-Hungarian armed forces.

14–18 At the Seventh Battle of the Isonzo in Italy, the Italian army makes small gains against the Austro-Hungarian forces.

27 General Eric von Falkenhayn leads a successful Austro-German counteroffensive in Romania, which continues until January 1917.

OCTOBER

• Less than a month before President Woodrow Wilson will be reelected on the platform "He kept us out of war," the president concedes in Cincinnati, Ohio, that neutrality in "modern war" is impossible.

9 The former Greek prime minister Eleutherios Venizelos arrives in Thessaloníki (Salonika), Greece, to establish a provisional government supportive of the Allies.

9–12 The Eighth Battle of the Isonzo takes place in Italy, the Italian forces making small gains.

10–December 12 Allied troops under the French general Maurice Sarrail begin an offensive against the Bulgarian and German army at Thessaloníki (Salonika), Greece.

11 Greece accepts the Allies' ultimatum of October 10, which requires Greece to hand over its fleet.

19 A Franco-British conference at Boulogne, France, recognizes the provisional Greek government at Thessaloníki (Salonika), Greece, under the former Greek prime minister Eleutherios Venizelos, which is supportive of the Allies.

21 The conservative Austrian prime minister Count Carl Stürgkh is assassinated by Friedrich, son of the Austrian socialist Victor Adler.

24–November 5 French forces launch an offensive to the east of Verdun, France.

28–February 10, 1917 The German authorities in occupied Belgium forcibly deport 60,000 Belgian civilians to work in Germany.

29 Sheriff Hussein of Mecca is proclaimed king of the Arabs.

31–November 4 The Ninth Battle of the Isonzo is fought in Italy, the Italian army gaining very little from the Austro-Hungarian forces.

NOVEMBER

2 During the Battle of Verdun on the Western Front, French forces retake Forts Douaumont and Vaux from the German armies.

5 The Central Powers proclaim the Kingdom of Poland, setting up a council of state under their influence.

7 The Democrat Woodrow Wilson is reelected U.S. president with 277 electoral votes, while the Republican Charles E. Hughes wins 254 votes. In the popular vote Wilson polls 9,129,606, Hughes 8,538,221, and A. L. Benson 585,113. In the Congressional elections, Democrats retain majorities in the House (216–210) and Senate (53–42).

13 Cardinal Mercier, archbishop of Malines, Belgium, protests against the deportation of Belgian civilians to Germany for forced labor.

19 Allied troops under the French general Maurice Sarrail take Monastir, Macedonia, from German–Bulgarian forces.

21 Arthur Zimmermann becomes German foreign minister following the resignation of Gottlieb von Jagow, who is opposed to unrestricted submarine warfare.

24 A U.S.–Mexican protocol is signed at Atlantic City, New Jersey, but on December 18 President Carranza of Mexico refuses to ratify it.

25   Germany's air forces are established as a separate military division.

DECEMBER

- The "turnip winter" in Central Europe sees food shortages caused by the Allied naval blockade and a high mortality rate among the civilian population.

1   A combined army consisting of an Austrian force led by General August von Mackensen and German troops under General Eric von Falkenhayn defeats the Romanian army of General Alexandru Averescu at Argesul, outside Bucharest, Romania.

4   A "patriotic service law" in Germany provides for the conscription of civilians into jobs in the war economy.

6–November 30, 1918   Eric von Falkenhayn's German army occupies Bucharest, Romania.

7   David Lloyd George is appointed British prime minister and forms a coalition government. On December 10 he forms a war cabinet, including the Conservatives Arthur Balfour, Andrew Bonar Law, Lord Curzon, and Lord Milner, and the Labour leader Arthur Henderson.

8   The Allies begin a blockade of Greece, demanding the withdrawal of its troops from Thessaly. Greece has declared itself neutral in the conflict, but is suspected of favoring the Central Powers.

12   Aristide Briand forms a French war ministry along similar lines to the arrangement in Britain, appointing five leading political figures to the administration.

12   Germany, having decisively defeated Romania, sends a peace note to the Allies indicating that the Central Powers are prepared to negotiate. On December 30 a reply is sent via the U.S. ambassador in Paris, France.

12   The U.S. Senate passes its Immigration Bill, with an amended literacy test clause designed to meet Japanese criticism.

13   Robert Nivelle is appointed commander in chief of the French armies in northern and northeastern France, replacing the unsuccessful General Joffre, who is appointed technical advisor to the government.

14   The Allies, mindful of the possibility of neutral Greece aiding the Central Powers in the Balkans, send an ultimatum to Greece demanding the withdrawal of its forces from Thessaly. The ultimatum is accepted on December 15.

15   Britain recognizes the Kingdom of Hejaz in Arabia, with Hussein as its leader.

15–17   A French offensive begins between the River Meuse and the Woëvre Plain.

20   The U.S. president Woodrow Wilson issues a "peace note" to the belligerents in the European war, asking them to state their terms for negotiating and for avoiding war in the future.

30   A group of nobles murders Rasputin, the "debauched holy man" who holds considerable influence over Tsarina Alexandra, in Petrograd, Russia.

SCIENCE, TECHNOLOGY, AND MEDICINE

Agriculture

- The Japanese beetle (*Popillia japonica*) is accidentally imported into the United States from Japan, in the soil of imported plants. A major pest, it thrives on over 200 different species.

Ecology

- The U.S. Congress creates Hawaii Volcanoes National Park from some 890 sq km/356 sq mi acres of volcanic terrain on the island of Hawaii. It contains the active volcanoes Mauan Loa and Kilauea.
- The U.S. Congress creates the Lassen Volcanic National Park from 433 sq km/107,000 acres in California.

JANUARY

14   The sea floods the Netherlands; 10,000 people die.

AUGUST

- The United States and Canada sign a treaty by which they agree to protecting insect-eating migratory birds.

Health and Medicine

- An epidemic of poliomyelitis sweeps the United States; 6,000 people die, including 2,000 in New York, New York.
- Swiss psychiatrist Eugene Bleuler publishes *Lehrbuch der Psychiatrie/Textbook of Psychiatry*, which becomes a standard text on the subject.

OCTOBER

- U.S. birth control advocates Margaret Sanger, Fania Mindell, and Ethel Burne open the nation's first birth control clinic in Brooklyn, New York. The clinic is raided by the police and Sanger is jailed for five days.

Science

- Dutch chemist Peter Debye demonstrates that the powdered form of a substance can be used instead of its crystal form for the X-ray study of its crystal structure.
- German astronomer Karl Schwarzschild offers a solution to Einstein's gravitational field equations which predicts the existence of black holes, collapsed stellar bodies.
- German physicist Albert Einstein publishes *The Foundation of the General Theory of Relativity*, in which he postulates that space is a curved field modified locally by the existence of mass and that this can be demonstrated by observing the deflection of starlight around the sun during a total eclipse. This replaces previous Newtonian ideas which invoke a force of gravity. Einstein also derives the basic equations for the exchange of energy between matter and radiation.

- Russian-born British chemist and politician Chaim Weizmann develops a method of extracting acetone from corn, to be used to make the explosive cordite.
- The journal *Genetics* is founded in the United States by the Genetics Society of America.
- The U.S. National Academy of Sciences establishes the National Research Council to coordinate the scientific activities of scientists in industry, government, and universities.
- U.S. chemist Gilbert Lewis states a new valence theory, in which electrons are shared between atoms.
- U.S. engineer William David Coolidge patents an X-ray tube that can produce highly predictable amounts of radiation. It serves as the prototype of the modern X-ray tube.

Technology

- A passive form of sonar is developed in the United States and Britain to detect submarines. It consists of a microphone towed behind ships.
- British scientist Herbert Jackson succeeds in making optical glasses of the same standard as those of the Zeiss works at Jena, Germany.
- Captain Peter Nissen designs the Nissen hut in France.
- Officials in New York, New York, revise the building code to allow skyscrapers of unlimited height.

SEPTEMBER

15 The first military tanks are used by the British Army during the Somme offensive on the Western Front in France.

Transportation

- German company Anschütz installs the first automatic pilot for ships, in a Danish passenger liner.
- German engineers build Gotha biplanes. Among the first bombers, they have a wingspan of 27 m/90 ft, can carry a 909 kg/2,000 lb bomb load, and have a range of 480 km/300 mi.
- Mechanically operated windshield wipers are introduced in the United States. The electric variety will not appear until 1923.
- Of all cars sold in the United States, a third are made by Henry Ford. Thanks to his success he is able to keep lowering the cost of his Model T.
- The first artificial horizon for aircraft is introduced by the U.S. Sperry Company. Consisting of a three-frame gyroscope, it indicates side-to-side motion (roll), fore-and-aft motion (pitch), and altitude.
- U.S. engineer Henry Marmon introduces the high-priced "Marmon," the first car to have an aluminum engine.

FEBRUARY

26 The French cruiser *Provence* is sunk by a German submarine in the Mediterranean Sea; 3,100 people are killed.

AUGUST

29 The Chinese steamship *Hsin Yu* sinks off the coast of China; 1,000 die.

ARTS AND IDEAS

Architecture

- The Villa Schwob in Le Chaux-de-Fonds, Switzerland, designed by the Swiss-born French architect Le Corbusier, is completed. It is one of the first houses to be built of reinforced concrete.
- The Walter L. Dodge House in Los Angeles, California, designed by the U.S. architect Irving Gill, is completed.

Arts

- The Dada movement (producing iconoclastic "antiart" works) emerges in Zürich in Switzerland, its leading figures including the Romanian writer Tristan Tzara and the French artist Hans Arp. It lasts until the early 1920s, when it is absorbed by surrealism.
- The English artist Christopher Nevinson paints *Troops Resting*.
- The English artist Mark Gertler paints *The Merry-Go-Round*.
- The French artist Henri Matisse paints *Piano Lesson* and sculpts *The Back, III*.
- The German artist Georg Grosz paints *Metropolis*.
- The Italian artist Amedeo Modigliani paints *Portrait of Max Jacob*.
- The Italian artist Giorgio Morandi paints *Still Life*.
- The Italian artist Mario Sironi paints *The Cyclist*.
- The Lithuanian artist Jacques Lipchitz sculpts *Man with a Guitar*.
- The Russian artist Kasimir Malevich paints *Suprematist Composition*.
- The Spanish artist Pablo Picasso designs curtains for *Parade*, a play by Jean Cocteau first performed in Paris, France, in 1917. The design marks a return to classicism.
- The U.S. artist Man Ray paints *The Rope Dancer Accompanies Herself with her Shadows*.
- The U.S. photographer Alvin Langdon Coburn takes *Ezra Pound Vortograph*.
- The U.S. photographer Paul Strand takes *The White Fence* and *Blind Woman*.

Film

- The movie *Civilization*, directed by Thomas H. Ince, is released in the United States, starring Enid Markey, Howard Hickman, and J. Barney Sherry. Also, his movie *Hell's Hinges* is released in the United States, starring William S. Hart.
- The movie *Intolerance*, directed by D. W. Griffith, is released in the United States, starring Lillian Gish, Robert Harron, Mae Marsh, and Constance Talmadge.
- The movie *Love and Journalism*, directed by Finnish filmmaker Mauritz Stiller, is released in Germany.
- The movie *The Aryan*, directed by Reginald Barker, is released in the United States, starring William S. Hart.
- The movie *War Brides*, directed by Herbert Brenon, is released, starring Alla Nazimova.

- The movie serial *Judex/Judge*, directed by Louis Feuillade, is released in France, starring René Cresté, Musidora, Yvette Andreyor, and Louis Leubas.
- The French comic actor Max Linder moves to the United States to replace Charlie Chaplin at the Essanay studio, and makes a series of comedy movies.
- The Italian poet Emilio Filippo Tommaso Marinetti publishes a manifesto entitled *The Futuristic Cinema*.

September 1916–20 The importation of U.S. movies is prohibited in Germany. After the ban is lifted the showing of U.S. movies is still restricted, because of the high costs of importing them.

Literature and Language

- Officials in New York, New York, censor Theodore Dreiser's novel *The "Genius"* (1915), the story of a gifted, but morally weak, artist.
- The Bohemian-born German writer Franz Kafka publishes his short story "Das Urteil"/"The Judgment."
- The English writer H. G. Wells publishes his novel *Mr Britling Sees It Through*.
- The Irish writer George Moore publishes his novel *The Brook Kerith*.
- The Irish writer James Joyce publishes his novel *Portrait of the Artist as a Young Man*. It has already been published serially in the English literary journal *The Egoist* during 1914 and 1915.
- The Italian writer Giuseppe Ungaretti publishes his poetry collection *Il porto sepolto/The Buried Port*.
- The novel *The Mysterious Stranger*, by the U.S. writer Mark Twain, is published posthumously.
- The Scottish writer John Buchan publishes his novel *Greenmantle*.
- The Spanish writer Vicente Blasco Ibáñez publishes his novel *Los cuatro jinetes del Apocalipsis/The Four Horsemen of the Apocalypse*.
- The Swiss linguist Ferdinand de Saussure's lectures are published posthumously in the collection *Cours de linguistique générale/Course in General Linguistics*. This work is regarded as founding the linguistic discipline of structuralism.
- The U.S. writer Booth Tarkington publishes his novel *Seventeen*.
- The U.S. writer Carl Sandburg publishes his poetry collection *Chicago Poems*.
- The U.S. writer Edwin Arlington Robinson publishes his poetry collection *The Man Against the Sky*.
- The U.S. writer Ezra Pound publishes his poetry collection *Lustra*.
- The U.S. writer Hilda Doolittle Aldington publishes her poetry collection *Sea Garden* under the pseudonym H. D.
- The U.S. writer Robert Frost publishes his poetry collection *Mountain Interval*.
- The U.S. writer Sherwood Anderson publishes *Windy McPhersons's Son*, his first published novel.
- The U.S. writer Theodore Dreiser publishes his first book of autobiography, *A Hoosier Holiday*.

Music

- The Danish composer Carl Nielsen completes his Symphony No. 4, *Det Uudslukkelige/The Inextinguishable*.
- The English composer Gustav Holst completes his orchestral suite *The Planets*.
- The English composer Hubert Parry completes his *Jerusalem*, inspired by the poetry of William Blake.
- The French composer Gabriel Fauré completes his Violin Sonata No. 2.
- The Italian composer Ottorino Respighi completes his orchestral work *Fontane di Roma/The Fountains of Rome*.
- The revised version of the opera *Ariadne auf Naxos/Ariadne on Naxos* by the German composer Richard Strauss is first performed, in Vienna, Austria.
- The Spanish composer Manuel de Falla completes his orchestral work *Noches en los jardines de España/Nights in the Gardens of Spain*.
- The term "jazz" emerges, for syncopated, improvisational, highly rhythmic music originating in black communities in the southern United States.
- The U.S. composer Charles Ives completes his Symphony No. 4.
- The U.S. composer Charles Griffes completes his *Four Roman Sketches* for piano.
- U.S. composer Spencer Williams and U.S. lyricist Roger Graham write the song "I Ain't Got Nobody."
- U.S.-born British composer Nat Ayer and English lyricist Clifford Grey write the song "If You Were the Only Girl in the World."

Theater and Dance

- The comedy *Hobson's Choice*, by the English writer Harold Brighouse, is first performed in London, England.
- The play *A Kiss for Cinderella*, by the Scottish writer J. M. Barrie, is first performed in London, England.
- The play *Bound East for Cardiff*, by the U.S. dramatist Eugene O'Neill, is first performed, in New York, New York.

AUGUST

31 The musical *Chu Chin Chow*, based on a book by Oscar Asche and with music by Frederick Norton, is first performed, at His Majesty's Theatre, London, England; it is seen by many British soldiers on leave, and has a run of 2,238 performances, a record not exceeded until the 1950s.

Thought and Scholarship

- British neurologist Frederick Mott develops the theory of shell-shock.
- English essayist Goldsworthy Lowes Dickinson publishes *The European Anarchy*.
- Italian philosopher Giovanni Gentile publishes *Teoria generale dello spirito come atto puro/General Theory of the Spirit as Pure Act*.
- Swiss psychologist Carl Gustav Jung publishes *Wandlungen und Symbole der Libido/Psychology of the*

Unconscious, in which he develops the concept of the collective unconscious.

- The English writer and critic Arthur Quiller-Couch publishes *The Art of Writing*.
- The Nobel Prize for Literature is awarded to the Swedish poet Verner von Heidenstam.
- U.S. cultural critic Madison Grant publishes *The Passing of the Great Race*, a lament against the nation's increasing ethnic and racial heterogeneity.
- U.S. cultural critic Randolph Bourne publishes the essay "Trans-National America," advancing an ideal of cultural pluralism.
- U.S. psychologist Lewis Madison Terman publishes *The Measurement of Intelligence*, in which he introduces the

Stanford–Binet intelligence quotient (IQ) test. The test considers both chronological age as well as mental age so that an average person of any age has an IQ of 100.

SOCIETY

Education

- The Massachusetts Institute of Technology assumes its current location on the Cambridge, Massachusetts, side of the Charles River, opposite the city of Boston.

BIRTHS & DEATHS

JANUARY
12 P. W. Botha, prime minister of South Africa 1978–84 and first president 1984–89, born in Paul Roux, South Africa.

FEBRUARY
12 Richard Dedekind, German mathematician who gave an arithmetic definition to irrational numbers, dies in Brunswick, Germany (84).
19 Ernst Mach, Austrian physicist and philosopher who established the principles of supersonics, dies in Haar, Germany (78).
28 Henry James, U.S.-born British novelist and playwright, dies in Chelsea, London, England (72).

MARCH
4 Hans Jürgen Eysenck, German psychologist whose theory that intelligence is almost entirely inherited and can be only slightly modified by education arouses controversy, born in Berlin, Germany (–1997).
10 Pamela Mason, English-born U.S. author and actress, born in London, England (–1996).
11 Harold Wilson, Labour prime minister of Britain 1964–70 and 1974–76, born in Huddersfield, Yorkshire, England (–1995).
15 Prudence Napier, English primatologist, born in Liverpool, England (–1997).

APRIL
22 Yehudi Menuhin, U.S.-born British violin virtuoso, born in New York, New York.
28 Ferruccio Lamborghini, Italian automobile manufacturer noted for his luxury sports cars, born in Cento, Italy (–1993).

MAY
6 Ross Hunter (originally Martin Fuss), U.S. film producer who

produced *Pillow Talk* (1959), and *Airport* (1970), born in Cleveland, Ohio (–1996).
21 Harold Robbins, U.S. author of popular novels including *The Carpetbaggers*, *Stiletto*, and *The Betsy*, born in New York, New York (–1997).
30 John Singleton Mosby, U.S. Confederate guerrilla during the American Civil War, dies in Washington, D.C. (83).

JUNE
5 Horatio Herbert Kitchener, British field marshal who conquered Sudan, was commander in chief during the Boer War, and who, as secretary of state for war, organized the British armed forces at the start of World War I, dies at sea near the Orkney Islands, Scotland (66).
8 Francis Crick, English biophysicist who, with James Watson, determined the structure of deoxyribonucleic acid (DNA), born in Northampton, England.
24 John Anthony Ciardi, U.S. poet, critic, translator, and author of *How Does a Poem Mean?*, born in Boston, Massachusetts (–1986).
25 Thomas Eakins, U.S. realist painter, dies in Philadelphia, Pennsylvania (71).

JULY
1 Olivia de Havilland, U.S. actress, born in Tokyo, Japan.
9 Edward Heath, prime minister of Britain 1970–74, a Conservative, born in Broadstairs, Kent, England.
16 Elie Metchnikoff, Russian zoologist who discovered the process of phagocytosis, dies in Paris, France (71).
23 William Ramsay, Scottish chemist who discovered the noble gases neon, argon, krypton, and xenon, dies in High Wycombe, Buckinghamshire, England (63).

AUGUST
9 Peter (Maurice) Wright, English secret intelligence agent, author of *Spycatcher: The Candid Autobiography of a Senior Intelligence Officer*, born in Chesterfield, Derbyshire, England (–1995).

OCTOBER
3 James Herriot (pen name of James Alfred Wight), English author and veterinary surgeon, born in Scotland (–1995).
4 Kenneth Wood, English electrical engineer, inventor of the Kenwood electric mixer, born in Lewisham, England (–1997).
26 François Mitterrand, Socialist president of France 1981–96, born in Jarnac, France (–1996).

NOVEMBER
14 H(ugh) H(ector) Munro ("Saki"), Scottish writer, is killed in action near Beaumont-Hamel, France (45).
21 Franz Joseph, emperor of Austria 1848–1916 and king of Hungary 1867–1916, who created the Austro–Hungarian Empire, dies in Schloss Schönbrunn near Vienna, Austria (86).
22 Jack London (pseudonym of John Griffith Chaney), U.S. novelist and short-story writer, dies in Glen Ellen, California (40).
23 Charles Booth, English sociologist who was one of the first to apply statistics to social problems, dies in Whitwick, Leicestershire, England (76).

DECEMBER
30 Grigory Yefimovich Rasputin, Siberian peasant and mystic who influenced the Russian czar Nicholas II and tsarina Alexandra, is murdered in Petrograd, Russia (about 54).

Family Planning (1916–97)

1916

October U.S. birth control advocates Margaret Sanger, Fania Mindell, and Ethel Burne open the nation's first birth control clinic in Brooklyn, New York. The clinic is raided by the police and Sanger is jailed for five days.

c. 1936

- Home remedies used to terminate pregnancies rely on solutions of water, Lysol, carbolic soap, iodine, and turpentine. The bark of the American slippery elm tree, rolled and inserted in the cervix, is also used to abort the fetus.

1938

- British chemist Charles Dodds creates the first synthetic estrogen and Schering Pharmaceutical chemists create an estrogen contraceptive pill.
- Margaret Sanger helps establish the Birth Control Federation of America, later called the International Planned Parenthood Federation.

1940

- The First Lady of the United States, Eleanor Roosevelt, publicly endorses birth control.

1954

- U.S. scientists Gregory G. Pincus, Hudson Hoagland, and Min-Cheh Chang, of the Worcester Foundation, develop an oral contraceptive using the hormone norethisterone.

1961

- U.S. physician Jack Lippes introduces the first intrauterine device (IUD) for birth control.

1971

- An IUD called the Dalkon Shield is introduced in the United States; 4 million are sold before infections, miscarriages, and birth defects are linked to the device and it is removed from the market.

1973

January 21 In the case Roe v. Wade, the U.S. Supreme Court rules that state restrictions on abortion are unconstitutional and that a woman has the right to an abortion within the first six months of pregnancy. This provokes militant anti-abortion protests.

1976

September The U.S. House of Representatives approves the Hyde Amendment to the Health, Education and Welfare appropriations bill. It prohibits the use of federal funds for abortion except in cases where the life of the mother is in jeopardy.

1978

July 25 Louise Brown is born at Oldham Hospital, London, England; she is the first "test tube" baby. Having been unable to remove a blockage from her mother's Fallopian tube, gynecologist Patrick Steptoe and physiologist Robert Edwards removed an egg from the mother's ovary, fertilized it with her husband's sperm, and reimplanted it in her uterus.

1981

- Strict population controls in China that limit families to one child lead to an increase in female infanticide.

1983

- A referendum in the Republic of Ireland results in a two-to-one majority for continuing the existing legal ban on abortion in the national constitution.

1987

- The case of Baby M., the child of a surrogate birth agreement in the United States, raises ethical issues when her custody is contested by her natural mother Mary Beth Whitehead and the couple who paid for the surrogacy, William and Elizabeth Stern. On March 31, the New Jersey judge rules that Whitehead has no parental rights. Surrogacy, not covered by existing laws, is becoming increasingly common. Full custody of the baby is given to William Stern.
- January 16 KRON television in San Francisco, California, shows the first advertisements promoting the use of condoms for safe sex.

1989

April 9 About 300,000 pro-abortion activists march in Washington, D.C., to protest against U.S. government plans to tighten up abortion laws.

1990

December 10 The U.S. Food and Drug Administration approves the highly effective Norplant contraceptive invented by Rockefeller Foundation researcher Sheldon Segal. Already in use in 14 other countries, it is implanted under the skin of the arm and slowly releases progesterone over a 15-year period.

1992

- The U.S. company Pharmacal launches Femidom, a female condom originally developed for use in the Third World.

1996

- The rate of growth in world population declines for the first time since the flu epidemic at the end of World War I, and includes all African countries for the first time. The decline is due to the greater availability of contraceptives, more family planning centers, better education of girls, and a growing recognition that children cost money.

1997

November 19 The first septuplets to be successfully delivered alive are born in Des Moines, Iowa, to Kenny and Bobbi McCaughey, who had been taking fertility drugs.

- The U.S. philanthropist Margaret Olivia Slocum Sage establishes Russell Sage College for Women in Troy, New York.
- U.S. philosopher John Dewey publishes *Democracy and Education*, arguing that in a democracy educationists must equip individuals with the capacity to pursue indefinitely their own self-education.

APRIL

- The Board of Education in New York, New York, rejects a proposal to introduce military training in public schools.

Everyday Life

- Coca-Cola launches its distinctively shaped bottle.
- George Jung of the Hong Kong Noodle Co. devises fortune cookies in the United States.
- Northam Warren introduces Cutex, the first liquid nail polish, in the United States.
- Ransomes, Sims & Jeffries Ltd. launches the first electric lawn mower in Britain.
- The Austrian War Dog Institute and the German Association for Serving Dogs begin training dogs as guides for the blind.

JANUARY

- U.S. steelworkers conclude a strike in East Youngstown, Ohio, after winning a 10% wage increase.

MARCH

17–April 4 Workers strike in the munitions factories along the River Clyde in Scotland.

Media and Communication

- Canadian entrepreneur William Beaverbrook founds his British newspaper publishing empire with the acquisition of the *Daily Express*.
- The American Radio and Research Corporation makes regular broadcasts two or three times a week.
- The newspaper *El Universal* is launched in Mexico.
- The socialist newspaper *Le Populaire* is launched in France.
- U.S. entrepreneur David Sarnoff proposes the "radio music box," a commercial radio receiver, and envisions one in every home.

Sports

- The 6th Olympic Games, scheduled to take place in Berlin, Germany, are canceled because of World War I.

FEBRUARY

- The Professional Golfer's Association of America is founded, in New York, New York.

APRIL

1 The Amateur Athletic Union holds the first U.S. national women's swimming championships.

OCTOBER

7–12 The Boston Red Sox of the American League defeat the Brooklyn Dodgers of the National League by four games to one in baseball's World Series.

14 Jim Barnes of Philadelphia, Pennsylvania, wins the inaugural United States Professional Golfers' Association (U.S. PGA) championship, at the Siwanoy Country Club, Bronxville, New York.

1917

POLITICS, GOVERNMENT, AND ECONOMICS

Business and Economics

- Frank and Lee Eldas Phillips of Bartlesville, Oklahoma, found Phillips Petroleum.
- The car manufacturer Bayrische Motoren Werke (Bavarian Motor Works or BMW) is founded in Germany.

APRIL

- Cotton climbs to 21.25 cents per 0.45 kg/1 lb on the New York Stock Exchange, its highest level since the American Civil War.
- Wheat prices soar to over $2 per bushel in anticipation of war with Germany.

Human Rights

JULY

2–5 A race riot erupts in East St. Louis, Missouri, where alienated white workers rampage through black neighborhoods killing any black American in sight. "Official" figures list 39 black and 8 white people killed, but civil-rights leader W. E. B. Du Bois insists that as many as 125 people have died.

AUGUST

- Ten U.S. suffragists are arrested outside the White House in Washington, D.C.

NOVEMBER

- New York state adopts women's suffrage.

Politics and Government

- In settling the *Bunting v. Oregon* case, the U.S. Supreme Court overrules the 1905 decision of *Lochner v. New York* and upholds a state law which regulates hours on health grounds.
- The U.S. government establishes several agencies to regulate its war effort, including the War Industries Board under financier Bernard M. Baruch for the coordination of war production (started in July 1917 and reorganized in March 1918), the Food Administration under Herbert Hoover for boosting the production and export of food, and the Fuel Administration for increasing coal and oil production.

November 1917–19 The Committee on Public Information, the U.S. government's wartime information agency, distributes more than one million patriotic posters and publications.

JANUARY

- The German ambassador to the United States Count Johann-Heinrich von Bernstorff informs the United States that Germany will resume unrestricted submarine warfare against neutral, as well as belligerent, ships.
- The U.S. president Woodrow Wilson issues his "Peace Without Victory" speech, introducing his notion of a world federation committed to preserving peace.
- The U.S. president Woodrow Wilson recalls general John J. Pershing from Mexico, after months of futile searching for the Mexican revolutionary Francisco "Pancho" Villa.
- U.S. clergyman Paul Smith spearheads a drive to rid the city of San Francisco, California, of prostitution. By the end of the month some 200 prostitution houses have been shut down.

1 The Ottoman Empire denounces the Treaty of Paris of 1856 and the Treaty of Berlin of 1878, which defined Ottoman territories.

FEBRUARY

- The U.S. Congress passes an Immigration Act over President Woodrow Wilson's veto. The act imposes a literacy test and bars most Asian immigrants.
- U.S. Congress passes the Smith–Hughes Act, creating the Federal Board for Vocational Training. The Board will provide states with matching funds to promote industrial education.

1 Germany announces its return to a policy of unrestricted submarine warfare in order to cut off the supplies sent to the Allies from the British Empire and the United States.

3 A German submarine sinks the U.S. liner *Housatonic* off the coast of Sicily, after giving the crew one hour's warning, leading the United States to break off diplomatic relations with Germany.

12 The U.S. president Woodrow Wilson refuses to reopen negotiations with Germany until it abandons its policy of unrestricted submarine warfare.

17 Supporters of the Australian prime minister, William Hughes, form a coalition government with the Liberals (known as the Commonwealth War Government).

24 British forces under Sir Frederick Maude recapture Kut-al-Imara, Mesopotamia, from the Ottoman army, and advance along the River Tigris.

26 The U.S. president Woodrow Wilson, without the authority of Congress, orders the arming of U.S. merchant ships in the face of Germany's resumption of unrestricted submarine warfare. Such a measure ordinarily requires Senate approval, but the president maintains that the U.S. Justice Department has sanctioned the move.

MARCH

- At the request of the Wilson administration, railroad managers grant workers an eight-hour day. The move is intended to prevent disruption of U.S. communication lines in the event of war.
- The U.S. president Woodrow Wilson is inaugurated for a second term.
- The U.S. Senate adopts a closure rule, whereby the majority party may terminate a debate, but not before each senator is afforded one hour of speaking time. The move comes in response to a prolonged filibuster by eleven senators opposed to the arming of merchant ships.
- U.S. Congress passes legislation authorizing a tax of between 20% and 60% on corporate profits exceeding 7% to 9% of capital. This is the first such excess profits tax in U.S. history.

1 The publication in the United States of the "Zimmermann telegram" causes outrage. The telegram is a message from the German foreign minister Arthur Zimmermann to the German ambassador in Mexico City, Mexico, which states that if war breaks out between Germany and the United States, the ambassador is to propose an alliance with Mexico and support Mexico's reacquisition of territory lost to the United States in 1848.

2 U.S. Congress passes the Jones Act (or Organic Act), making the island of Puerto Rico a U.S. territory and conferring U.S. citizenship upon its inhabitants.

4–April 5 German troops withdraw to the specially constructed "Hindenburg Line" on the Western Front. The line is a defensive system in which weak points found in the previous front line have been avoided.

8 U.S. marines land at Santiago, Cuba, at the request of the civil government there.

8–15 The "February Revolution" takes place in Russia, striking workers being joined on March 10 by soldiers. On March 14 the duma (parliament) establishes a provisional government headed by Prince George Lvov. The revolution is called the "February Revolution" on the basis of the old Julian calendar, under which the revolution takes place in the period February 23–March 2.

11 In the Mesopotamian campaign, British forces led by Sir Frederick Maude capture Baghdad from the Ottoman army.

15 Czar Nicholas II of Russia abdicates the throne on behalf of both himself and his son. His brother Grand Duke Michael refuses the throne on March 16, thereby ending the rule of the Romanov dynasty.

17–18 British troops capture Bapaume and Péronne in France.

19 The French prime minister, Aristide Briand, resigns over the continued stalemate in the war. Alexandre Ribot forms a cabinet.

26–27 British troops under General Sir Charles Dobell defeat the Ottoman army in Gaza, Palestine, but retreat before exploiting their victory.

30 The Russian provisional government guarantees the independence of Poland.

31 The United States finally acquires the West Indian Virgin Islands from Denmark, which it requires in order to prevent German acquisition and to protect the Panama Canal.

APRIL

- German submarines sink 875,000 tons of Allied shipping, mostly British.
- The U.S. president Woodrow Wilson creates the Committee on Public Information, a propaganda agency, headed by journalist George Creel.

2 The U.S. president Woodrow Wilson calls a special session of the U.S. Congress to debate a declaration of war against Germany, telling Congress, "The world must be made safe for democracy." The Senate votes 82–6 to declare war on Germany and the House of Representatives votes 373–50 in favor.

6 The United States declares war on Germany.

7 Cuba declares war on Germany.

7 In an attempt to maintain Prussia's support in the war, Kaiser Wilhelm II of Germany promises an end to the three-class voting system there once the war is over.

9–14 Canadian troops mount an offensive along the Vimy Ridge on the Western Front and succeed in taking it.

9–May 4 At the Battle of Arras on the Western Front, the British Third Army advances 6.5 km/4 mi.

16 Food strikes take place in Berlin, Germany, in protest at shortages.

16 The Russian Bolshevik leader Vladimir Ilyich Lenin arrives in Petrograd, Russia, having traveled (with German assistance) from Switzerland via Germany, Sweden, and Finland.

16–May 9 The French commander General Robert Nivelle launches the "Chemin des Dames" offensive (or Second Battle of the Aisne) along the River Aisne. The French forces make tiny advances at heavy cost.

17 The first in a wave of French army mutinies occurs on the Western Front in protest at the "Chemin des Dames" offensive. A more serious mutiny begins on April 29, and such mutinies continue until August 1917, ending the French army's capacity to mount offensives.

17 The Russian Bolshevik leader Vladimir Ilyich Lenin publishes his "April Theses," calling for a transfer of power to the soviets (councils), land to the peasants, and immediate peace.

18–19 At the Second Battle of Gaza in Palestine, the Ottoman army, with German support, repulses the attacks of Sir Archibald Murray's British troops.

20 The United States severs relations with the Ottoman Empire.

24 The U.S. president Woodrow Wilson signs the Liberty Loan Act authorizing the Treasury to issue a public subscription for $2 billion of so-called Liberty Bonds for

Russian Revolution (1917)

1917

MARCH

8–15 The "February Revolution" takes place in Russia, soldiers joining striking workers on March 10. On March 14 the duma (parliament) establishes a provisional government headed by Prince George Lvov. The revolution is called the "February Revolution" on the basis of the old Julian calendar, under which the revolution takes place in the period February 23–March 2.

APRIL

16 The Russian Bolshevik leader Vladimir Ilyich Lenin arrives in Petrograd, Russia, having traveled (with German assistance) from Switzerland via Germany, Sweden, and Finland.

JUNE

24 The Russian Black Sea fleet mutinies at Sevastopol.

JULY

16–17 During mass demonstrations in Petrograd, known as the "July Days," the provisional government is undermined, but an attempted Bolshevik rising fails after details emerge of the dealings between the Bolshevik leader Lenin and Germany, who had helped him return to Russia.

SEPTEMBER

9–14 General Lavr Kornilov attempts a counterrevolutionary coup but is prevented from reaching Petrograd by Bolshevik rail workers. Kornilov is later arrested.

NOVEMBER

6 In the "October Revolution", Lenin and the Bolsheviks seize the Winter Palace in Petrograd, overthrowing the provisional government on November 7 and 8. The revolution is named for the date on which it commences under the old Julian calendar (October 24).

7 At a meeting of the all-Russian congress of soviets (councils) in Petrograd, most Mensheviks and other socialists walk out, leaving the Bolsheviks in control. Vladimir Ilyich Lenin forms the Council of People's Commissars (composed of Bolsheviks) as the new government.

8 Lenin becomes chairman of the Council of People's Comissars, and Leon Trotsky is appointed prime minister.

10–12 Provisional government troops retake the Kremlin in Moscow from the Bolsheviks.

15 The Bolsheviks take Moscow after overcoming resistance from provisional government troops.

the war. Offered to the public on May 2, it is oversubscribed by half by June 15.

28 Henri Pétain, the French hero of the Verdun action, is promoted to the position of chief of the general staff.

MAY

- The U.S. Congress passes the Selective Service Act, requiring all men between the ages of 21 and 30 to register for the draft.

5 The British foreign secretary Arthur Balfour becomes the first non-U.S. speaker to address the U.S. House of Representatives.

12–June 8 In the Tenth Battle of the Isonzo in Italy, the Italian army under General Luigi Cadorna makes some advances against the Austro-Hungarian forces, but at a huge cost of life.

15 Following the mutinies in response to the costly "Chemin des Dames" offensive, General Robert Nivelle is dismissed as commander in chief of the French army and is replaced by Henri Pétain, who is renowned for using his troops sparingly. Ferdinand Foch replaces Pétain as chief of the general staff.

18 Prince George Lvov reforms the cabinet of the Russian provisional government with representation by socialists, and Alexander Kerensky becomes minister of war.

22 The conservative Hungarian prime minister Count Stephen Tisza resigns in protest at the decree of the new Austro-Hungarian emperor Karl for suffrage reform in Austria-Hungary.

23 President Li Yuan-Hung of China dismisses the reactionary prime minister Tuan Ch'i-jui, provoking a rising of military governors.

JUNE

2 Following the sinking of Brazilian ships by German submarines, Brazil revokes its neutrality and seizes German ships.

3 Albania proclaims its independence, under the protection of Italy.

7–14 British forces straighten the Ypres salient at the Battle of Messines Ridge in southeastern Belgium, in preparation for a major offensive.

10 Riots break out in Dublin, Ireland, in support of those imprisoned after the "Easter Rising" of 1916.

10–26 Italian troops attack Austro-Hungarian forces in the Trentino region of Italy.

12 Following threats of invasion from the Allies, the pro-German King Constantine I of Greece abdicates in favor of his second son, Alexander (–1920).

13 The first part of the American Expeditionary Force, commanded by General John J. Pershing, departs for France.

14 A U.S. mission under Senator Elihu Root arrives in Petrograd, Russia, to encourage continued Russian participation in the war.

15 The British government grants an amnesty to those imprisoned after the 1916 "Easter Rising" in Dublin, Ireland.

15 The Espionage Act is passed in the United States, allowing people to be fined or imprisoned for hindering the war effort.

16–July 7 The first all-Russian congress of workers' and soldiers' soviets (councils) is held in Petrograd, Russia.

18–July 13 The Russian minister of war, Alexander

Kerensky, launches the Kerensky Offensive on the Eastern Front with a series of attacks against the German armies; the offensive is quickly repulsed with heavy Russian losses.

24 The Russian Black Sea fleet mutinies at Sevastopol, Russia.

26 The pro-Allies head of the Greek provisional government Eleutherios Venizelos travels across Greece from Thessaloníki (Salonika) to Athens to become prime minister.

29 Greece declares war on the Central Powers.

JULY

- 15,000 black American men, women, and children march silently down Fifth Avenue in New York, New York, in an effort to force a response from President Woodrow Wilson to the East St. Louis race riot of July 2–5. One banner reads, "Mr. President, Why Not Make America Safe For Democracy?"

- In a gesture laden with symbolism, U.S. Army colonel, Charles E. Stanton, visits the tomb of the French nobleman Marquis de Lafayette on American Independence Day, remarking famously, "Lafayette, we are here."

- The U.S. House of Representatives passes legislation appropriating money for an air force program.

1 Rebels restore the Manchu dynasty in China.

1 The Russian commander General Alexei Brusilov launches a major offensive against Austria-Hungary in Galicia.

6 An Arab force takes Aqaba, in the Hejaz region, from an Ottoman force.

12 The reactionary Tuan Ch'i-jui resumes the Chinese premiership.

14 Theobald von Bethmann Hollweg resigns as German chancellor because of opposition from the conservative army high command, and is succeeded by George Michaelis.

16–17 During mass demonstrations in Petrograd, Russia, known as the "July Days," the provisional government is undermined, but an attempted Bolshevik rising fails after details emerge of the dealings between the Bolshevik leader Vladimir Ilyich Lenin and Germany, who had helped him return to Russia.

17 The Bolshevik attempt to seize power in Petrograd, Russia, is ended by leaks of Vladimir Ilyich Lenin's dealings with the Germans (in an attempt to arrange his return to Russia from exile).

18 Feng Kuo-Chang, an ally of premier Tuan Ch'i-jui, becomes president, having taken Beijing, China, from rebel forces.

19 The SPD, Center Party, and Progressives in the German Reichstag (parliament) combine to pass a motion demanding peace with no annexations or indemnities.

19 Zeppelin airships attack English industrial areas.

19–August 4 In the Battle of East Galicia on the Eastern Front, a counteroffensive by German and Austro-Hungarian forces pushes back the Russian line.

21 Alexander Kerensky replaces Prince George Lvov as Russian prime minister.

25 A convention of different Irish interests meets in Dublin, Ireland, to seek a program for self-government, but is weakened by the absence of Sinn Féin and by Ulster Unionist intransigence.

27 Representatives of the Serb, Croat, and Slovene people make the "Corfu Declaration," demanding an independent state.

31–November 6 The Third Battle of Ypres (the Battle of Passchendaele) takes place on the Western Front. British forces in Belgium advance about 13 km/8 mi, but at a heavy cost in casualties.

AUGUST

1 Richard von Kühlmann succeeds Arthur Zimmermann as German foreign minister, Zimmermann having been discredited by the "Zimmermann telegram" to the German ambassador in Mexico.

3 Left wing sailors mutiny at the German naval base of Wilhelmshaven.

3 The Russian army retakes Czernowitz in East Galicia (now Chernovtsy in the Ukraine) on the Eastern Front.

10 Catalan activists demand the creation of a representative body to investigate Catalonia's claims to autonomy.

14 China declares war on Germany and Austria-Hungary.

14 Pope Benedict XV makes an unsuccessful attempt to bring about peace in the European conflict.

17–September 12 At the Eleventh Battle of the Isonzo in Italy the Italian forces make minor advances.

20–December 15 The second Battle of Verdun begins as the French armies attempt to relieve pressure on the British forces in Flanders.

25–28 In an attempt to increase support for the Russian provisional government, Alexander Kerensky holds a state conference in Moscow, Russia.

SEPTEMBER

• Federal agents raid offices of the International Workers of the World (IWW), which has been accused of obstructing the U.S. war effort. IWW leader William D. Haywood is arrested along with ten others.

1–5 A German offensive led by General Oscar von Hutier on the Eastern Front, leads to the occupation of Riga (now in Latvia) on the River Dvina after Russian troops under General Lavr Kornilov are defeated at the Battle of Riga.

9 The Guomindang party under Sun Zhong Shan organizes its own provisional government in China, based in Guangzhou.

9–14 General Lavr Kornilov attempts a counterrevolutionary coup but is prevented from reaching Petrograd, Russia, by Bolshevik railroadmen. Kornilov is later arrested.

12 Paul Painlevé forms a French cabinet following the fall of Alexandre Ribot.

14 The Russian prime minister, Alexander Kerensky, declares a republic in Russia.

29–October 1 German aircraft attack London, England, on successive nights.

OCTOBER

• U.S. Congress sponsors a second Liberty Loan drive, this time authorizing the distribution of bonds worth $3 billion.

10 The Petrograd soviet (council) in Russia elects the Bolshevik Leon Trotsky as chairman.

15 Afro-German troops under Paul von Lettow-Warbeck inflict heavy casualties on an Allied force at the Battle of Maiwa in East Africa.

15 The Dutch dancer Mata Hari is executed in France after being convicted of spying for Germany.

24–December 26 At the Battle of Caporetto, Italy (now Kobarid, Slovenia), the Austro-Hungarian and German forces under General Otto von Below break the Italian line and advance 16 km/10 mi. The Italian army regroups along the River Piave.

25 Under the direction of the Bolshevik Leon Trotsky, the Petrograd soviet (council) sets up a committee to plan the overthrow of the provisional government.

28 Vittorio Orlando becomes Italian prime minister following the major military defeat at Caporetto, and establishes a *Unione Sacra* coalition government which keeps Italy in the war.

NOVEMBER

• The U.S. 42nd Division arrives in France. With troops from every state in the Union, it is known as the "Rainbow" Division.

• Three U.S. soldiers die, five are wounded, and twelve go missing in fighting along the Western Front in the first U.S. troop engagement in World War I.

1 Count Georg von Hertling succeeds George Michaelis as German chancellor when the latter fails to quell the propeace lobby.

2 The British foreign secretary, Arthur Balfour, issues the "Balfour declaration" on Palestine, in which he favors the establishment of a national home for the Jewish people without prejudice to non-Jewish communities.

3 French and British troops are sent to help the Italian army, which has been broken by a German–Austrian advance which smashed through the front line of the Isonzo line at Caporetto. The Allies set up a blocking defensive line to stop Italy from being overrun and taken out of the war.

6 Canadian and British troops capture Passchendaele Ridge in southwestern Belgium.

6 The "October Revolution" takes place in Russia, Vladimir Ilyich Lenin and the Bolsheviks seizing the Winter Palace in Petrograd, Russia, on 7 and November 8 and overthrowing the provisional government. The revolution is named for the date on which it commences under the old Julian calendar (October 24).

7 At a meeting of the all-Russian congress of soviets (councils) in Petrograd, Russia, most Mensheviks and other socialists walk out, leaving the Bolsheviks in control. Vladimir Ilyich Lenin forms a council of people's commissars (composed of Bolsheviks) as the new government.

7 British forces led by General Sir Edmund Allenby take Gaza, Palestine, from the Ottoman army.

7 The Allied conference at Rapallo in northwestern Italy decides on a Supreme Allied War Council (which first meets on December 1 at Versailles, France).

8 Vladimir Ilyich Lenin becomes chairman of the Council of People's Comissars (effectively the government of Russia) and Leon Trotsky is appointed prime minister following the "October Revolution" in Russia.

10–12 Provisional government troops retake the Kremlin in Moscow, Russia, from the Bolsheviks.

15 The Bolsheviks take Moscow, Russia, after overcoming resistance from provisional government troops.

16 British forces under Sir Edmund Allenby take Jaffa, Palestine, from the Ottoman army.

16 Paul Painlevé falls as prime minister of France amid fears of French capitulation in the European war, and

the aggressive Georges Clemenceau ("the tiger") forms a cabinet.

20 The Ukraine proclaims itself a republic, independent of Russia.

20–December 7 The Battle of Cambrai takes place in northeastern France and is the first major battle involving tanks. A British tank force breaks the German line at Cambrai, but its success is not exploited.

26 The Russian Bolshevik government offers an armistice to Germany and Austria.

28 Estonia proclaims its independence from Russia.

DECEMBER

• The Russian VSNKh, or the Supreme Council of National Economy, is created by the Bolsheviks to run the economy.

• The U.S. Congress submits the 18th Amendment, introducing Prohibition, to the states.

1 Paul von Lettow-Warbeck's Afro-German troops continue their guerrilla warfare into Portuguese East Africa.

5 German and Russian delegates sign an armistice at Brest-Litovsk (in modern Belarus).

5 The Bolsheviks abolish the Russian legal system and establish revolutionary tribunals as instruments of control.

5 The pro-German General Sidonio Paes of Portugal overthrows the government and installs himself as dictator.

6 Finland declares itself a republic, independent from Russia.

7 The United States declares war on Austria-Hungary.

8 Bolshevik rule is established in Estonia under the communist leader Jaan Anvelt; it lasts only until the German occupation of the country in February 1918.

9 A British force led by General Sir Edmund Allenby captures Jerusalem from the Ottoman army.

9 Romania signs an armistice with the Central Powers at Focsani, Romania.

10 An Italian force torpedoes the Austrian battleship *Wien* in Trieste, Italy.

17 Following the Unionist's victory in the Canadian elections, Robert Borden becomes Canadian prime minister.

20 German and Russian delegates begin peace negotiations at Brest-Litovsk, Russia (now Belarus).

20 Vladimir Ilyich Lenin establishes the Cheka (the Bolshevik secret police force) to deal with opposition to the regime.

26 The Bolsheviks establish a government in Kharkov in the Ukraine to rival the established Ukrainian rada (council) in Kiev.

27 The Bolshevik government in Russia allows workers' committees to supervise businesses, and nationalizes banks.

28 The Bessarabia region proclaims its independence from Russia, calling itself the Moldavian Republic (modern Moldova).

28 The U.S. government takes control of U.S. railroads.

SCIENCE, TECHNOLOGY, AND MEDICINE

Agriculture

• U.S. researcher Donald Jones discovers the "double cross" technique of hybridizing corn; four inbred lines, instead of two, are crossbred.

Ecology

• Mt. McKinley National Park (now Denali National Park) in Alaska is established; it encompasses Mt. McKinley, the highest mountain in North America. Covering 24,419 sq km/9,428 sq mi, it is the largest national park in the United States.

Health and Medicine

• New Zealand-born British plastic surgeon Harold Delf Gillies introduces the pedicle skin graft, where skin and subcutaneous tissue from one part of the body is used to replace damaged skin in another area.

December 1917–20 An epidemic of typhus in Russia kills nearly 3 million.

Science

• Dutch astronomer Willem de Sitter shows that Einstein's theory of general relativity implies that the universe must be expanding.

• English physicist Charles Glover Barkla receives the Nobel Prize for Physics for his discovery of the characteristic X-ray radiation of the elements.

• Langley Field Research Center is established in Virginia. It quickly becomes the world's leading aeronautical research center.

• The 2.5-m/100-in Hooker reflecting telescope is installed at Mt. Wilson Observatory, California. It is the world's largest reflecting telescope to date.

• The radioactive element protactinium-231 is independently discovered by three research groups (Otto Hahn and Lise Meitner in Germany; Kasimir Fajans in the United States; and Frederick Soddy, John Cranston, and Alexander Fleck in Britain).

• U.S. astronomer Harlow Shapley determines that the sun is situated about 30,000 light-years from the central plane of the Galaxy.

Technology

• The German army introduces poisonous mustard gas, which causes blistering in the lungs. It is used extensively by both sides the following year.

• The U.S. inventor Edwin Armstrong invents the superheterodyne radio circuit. It allows easy tuning of weak radio waves, which it also amplifies. Its design ᵃ

becomes the basis of radar, television, and all amplitude modulation (AM) radios.

- U.S. inventor Daniel McFarlan Moore develops the neon gas-discharge lamp, which allows light intensity in television receivers to be modulated by varying the electrical input.
- U.S. inventor Elmer Sperry devises the "aerial torpedo," a pilotless airplane with an explosive charge. The forerunner of the cruise missile, it uses gyroscopes and an automatic control to fly to its target.

Transportation

- French aviator Louis-Charles Bréguet develops the "gyroplane," a forerunner of the helicopter.
- French aviators Maurice and Henri Farman stimulate commercial aviation with the introduction of the "Goliath," the first long-distance passenger plane.
- The trans-Australian railroad (started in 1912) is completed.
- There are 4,842,139 motor vehicles registered in the United States, including more than 435,000 trucks, over half of world total.

JANUARY
28 A train wreck in Tshura, Romania, kills 500 people.

OCTOBER
21 The U.S. military produces the first "Liberty" airplane engine. It has 12 cylinders.

DECEMBER
6 Much of Halifax, Nova Scotia, Canada, is destroyed, and nearly 2,000 people killed when the Norwegian ship *Imo* hits the French ship *Mont Blanc*, which is loaded with more than 6,000 metric tons of explosives.
12 A passenger train is derailed at Modane, France, killing 543 people. It is Europe's worst train wreck to date.

ARTS AND IDEAS

Architecture

MARCH
- The Hell Gate Railroad Bridge, across East River in New York, New York, opens. Designed by the Austrian-born U.S. architect Gustav Lindenthal, it is the longest steel arch in the world (298 m/977 ft).

Arts

- Following the Bolshevik Revolution in Russia, all art collections are nationalized, all art academies are closed, and modernist art is officially patronized by the new regime.
- The Dutch artist Piet Mondrian launches the *De Stijl* magazine in the Netherlands, which gives its name to a style of art and design characterized by basic forms and primary colors.

- The Dutch artist Theo van Doesburg paints *Cow*.
- The English artist L. S. Lowry paints *Coming from the Mill*.
- The French artist Fernand Léger paints *Game of Cards*.
- The French artist Hans Arp creates *Collage with Squares Arranged According to the Laws of Chance* and sculpts *Forest*.
- The French artist Pierre Auguste Renoir sculpts *The Washerwoman*.
- The French writer Guillaume Apollinaire coins the term "surrealist," which he uses to describe the costumes and stage designs by the Spanish artist Pablo Picasso for the ballet *Parade* performed in Paris, France, by the Ballets Russes in 1917. During the year, Picasso also paints *Portrait of Olga in an Armchair*.
- The Italian artist Amedeo Modigliani paints *Portrait of Jacques and Bertha Lipchitz* and *Reclining Nude*.
- The Italian artist Giorgio de Chirico paints *Disquieting Muses*.
- The Russian artist Marc Chagall paints *Self-Portrait with a Glass of Wine*.
- The U.S. artist Abraham Walkowitz paints *New York*.
- The U.S. artist Charles Burchfield paints *Church Bells Ringing, Rainy Winter Night*, and *Noontide in Late May*.
- The U.S. artist Charles Demuth paints *Trees and Barns, Bermuda*.
- The U.S. artist Georgia O'Keeffe paints *Evening Star III*.
- The U.S. artist Stanton Macdonald-Wright paints *Abstraction on Spectrum (Organization 5)*.

Film

- As a result of the United States's entry into the war, U.S. director D. W. Griffith's movie *Intolerance* is held to be inappropriate and is no longer shown. Severe losses for the producer and distributor result.
- Dr. Herbert Kalmus makes the first successful use of the Technicolor film process, which he invented in 1915. *The Gulf Between* is the first technicolor movie.
- Moviegoing is becoming a more popular pastime among the middle classes in the United States and in Europe with the advent of better-quality movies and the need for diversion during the war.
- The movie *Raffles, The Amateur Cracksman* is released, based on the novel by E. W. Hornung, starring John Barrymore, and directed by George Irving.
- The movie *Rebecca of Sunnybrook Farm*, directed by Marshall Neilan, is released in the United States. Based on the novel by Kate Douglas Wiggins, it stars Mary Pickford.
- The movie *Terje Vigen/A Man There Was*, directed by Victor Sjöström, is released in Sweden. Sjöström also stars in it. His movie *The Girl from Stormycroft* is also released in Sweden.
- The movie *The Butcher Boy*, directed by Roscoe "Fatty" Arbuckle, is released in the United States, starring Buster Keaton.
- The movie *The Poor Little Rich Girl*, directed by French filmmaker Maurice Tourneur, is released in the United States, starring Mary Pickford.

- The movie *The Right to Life*, directed by Abel Gance, is released in France, starring Paul Vermoyal, Léon Mathot, and Andrée Brabant.
- The movie *The Silent Man*, directed by William S. Hart, is released in the United States. Hart also stars in it.
- The movie *Thomas Graal's Best Picture*, directed by Finnish filmmaker Mauritz Stiller, is released in Germany.
- The movies *Easy Street*, *The Cure*, and *The Immigrant*, all directed by Charlie Chaplin, are released in the United States. Chaplin also stars in them alongside Edna Purviance.
- The French army shows movies to troops at the front to help promote morale.
- The German government recognizes movies as a powerful means of influencing the people. It takes control of the German movie industry, establishing a unifying organization, Universum Film Aktien Gesellschaft (Universal Motion Picture Joint-Stock Company).

Literature and Language

- Pulitzer Prizes are first awarded, by Columbia University, New York, New York, made possible by a donation from the U.S. newspaper publisher Joseph Pulitzer in 1903.
- The *World Book* encyclopedia is first published in the United States; it becomes the world's biggest-selling encyclopedia.
- The Australian writer Henry Handel Richardson publishes her novel *Australia Felix*, the first part of her trilogy *The Fortunes of Richard Mahony*.
- The Czech orientalist Bedřich Hrozný publishes *Die Sprache der Hethiter/The Hittite Language*.
- The English writer Alec Waugh publishes his novel *The Loom of Youth*.
- The English writer Frank Swinnerton publishes his novel *Nocturne*.
- The English writer Mary Webb publishes her novel *Gone to Earth*.
- The English writer P. G. Wodehouse publishes *The Man with Two Left Feet*, a collection of stories in which his comic characters Jeeves and Wooster first appear.
- The English writer Ronald Firbank publishes his novel *Caprice*.
- The English writer Robert Graves publishes his poetry collection *Fairies and Fusiliers*.
- The English writer Thomas Hardy publishes his poetry collection *Moments of Vision and Miscellaneous Verses*.
- The first Pulitzer Prize for Biography is awarded, to Laura Elizabeth Richards and Maude Howe Elliott, with Florence Howe Hall, for *Julia Ward Howe*.
- The first Pulitzer Prize for History is awarded, to Jean Jules Jusserand, for *With Americans of Past and Present Days*.
- The French writer Paul Valéry publishes his long poem *La Jeune Parque/The Young Fate*.
- The Irish writer W. B. Yeats publishes his poetry collection *The Wild Swans at Coole*, which includes "An Irish Airman Foresees his Death."
- The Norwegian writer Knut Hamsun publishes his novel *Markens grøde/Growth of the Soil*.

- The Scottish writer Norman Douglas publishes his novel *South Wind*.
- The Spanish poet Juan Ramón Jiménez publishes his poetry collection *Diario de un poeta recién casado/Diary of a Newly Married Poet*.
- The term "pie in the sky" enters the U.S. lexicon. It comes from the labor movement, when workers note that after a life of eating hay, they would have their pie in the sky.
- The U.S. writer Amy Lowell publishes her critical study *Tendencies in Modern American Poetry*.
- The U.S. writer Edna St. Vincent Millay publishes her poetry collection *Renascence and Other Poems*.
- The U.S. writer Sara Teasdale publishes her poetry collection *Love Songs*.
- The U.S. writer Vachel Lindsay publishes his poetry collection *The Chinese Nightingale and Other Poems*.

Music

- George W. Meyer, Edgar Leslie, and E. Ray Goetz write the song "For Me and My Gal."
- Inspired by Stephen Foster's 1851 song "Old Folks at Home," U.S. composers George Gershwin and Irving Caesar write "Swanee."
- Storyville, the area of New Orleans, Louisiana, where prostitution was licensed and jazz flourished, is closed down. Some jazz musicians move to Chicago, Illinois, and other cities.
- The English composer Arnold Bax completes his orchestral work *Tintagel*.
- The French composer Claude Debussy completes his *Violin Sonata*.
- The French composer Maurice Ravel completes his piano work *Le Tombeau de Couperin/The Tomb of Couperin*, which he orchestrates in 1919.
- The opera *Arlecchino/Harlequin* by the Italian composer Ferruccio Busoni is first performed, in Zürich, Switzerland.
- The opera *La Rondine/The Swallow* by the Italian composer Giacomo Puccini is first performed, in Monte Carlo, Monaco.
- The opera *Palestrina* by the German composer Hans Pfitzner is first performed, in Munich, Germany.
- The Original Dixieland Jazz Band, an all-white quintet from New Orleans, Louisiana, takes jazz to New York, New York, for the first time and makes the first jazz record with the Victor Talking Machine Company. It includes the song "Original Dixieland One-Step."
- The Russian composer Sergey Prokofiev completes his Symphony No. 1, the *Classical Symphony*.
- The Russian composer Sergey Rachmaninov completes his piano *Etudes tableaux* (Opus 39).
- The U.S. composer Charles Griffes completes his orchestral work *The Pleasure Dome of Kubla Khan*, inspired by a poem by the English writer Samuel Taylor Coleridge. Griffes has based the work on a piano piece he wrote in 1912.
- The U.S. songwriter George M. Cohan writes the song "Over There," to inspire U.S. soldiers on their way to the fighting in Europe.

OCTOBER

27   The Russian-born violinist Jascha Heifetz makes his
debut in the United States at Carnegie Hall, New York,
New York, aged 16.

Theater and Dance

- The ballet *Parade* is first performed, in Paris, France, by
the Ballets Russes under the Russian impresario Sergei
Diaghilev. The story is by the French writer Jean
Cocteau, music by the French composer Eric Satie,
costumes and stage designs by the Spanish artist Pablo
Picasso, and choreography by the Russian
choreographer Léonide Massine.
- The play *Les Mamelles de Tirésias/The Breasts of
Tiresias*, by the French writer Guillaume Apollinaire is
first performed, in Paris, France.
- The plays *Dear Brutus* and *Seven Women*, by the
Scottish writer J. M. Barrie are first performed, in
London, England.
- The plays *In the Zone* and *The Long Voyage Home*, by
the U.S. dramatist Eugene O'Neill, are first performed,
in New York, New York.

FEBRUARY

20   The musical *Oh, Boy!*, with lyrics by P. G. Wodehouse
and music by Jerome Kern, is first performed, at the
Princess Theater, New York, New York.

Thought and Scholarship

- English social historians John Lawrence and Barbara
Hammond publish *The Town Labourer, 1760–1832*.
- Italian philosopher Benedetto Croce publishes *Teoria e
storia della storiografia/History: Its Theory and Practice*.
- Russian revolutionary leader Vladimir Ilyich Lenin
publishes *Imperializm, kak novieishii etap kapitalizma/
Imperialism: The Last Stage of Capitalism*.
- The Nobel Prize for Literature is awarded to the Danish
novelists Karl Gjellerup and Henrik Pontoppidan.

SOCIETY

Education

- The University of Alaska opens as Alaska Agricultural
College and School of Mines in the town of College,
Alaska.

JULY

4   The U.S. military opens the nation's first flight training
field at Rantoul, Illinois.

Everyday Life

- The need for British women to cut their hair short for
war work in the factories leads to a fashion for the bob.
- The U.S. inventor Clarence Birdseye develops a rapid
freezing method of preserving food that also preserves
its flavor.
- The U.S. population exceeds 100 million.
- U.S. tobacco manufacturers supply troops at the front
with free cigarettes to help calm their nerves.

NOVEMBER

18   Federal war ration officials in the United States declare
that electric signs must be shut off on Thursdays and
Sundays in order to save energy.

Media and Communication

- Following the Bolshevik Revolution in Russia, *Pravda*
("Truth") becomes the leading newspaper, as the
mouthpiece of the Bolshevik (Communist) Party;
Izvestiya ("News") is also founded.

Sports

- In Canadian ice hockey, the National Hockey
Association is disbanded and is replaced by the National
Hockey League, founded in Montreal, Canada,
November.
- The first national body for women's athletics is founded
in France.
- The national governing body for equestrian sports in the
United States, the American Horse Shows Association
(AHSA), is founded by Reginald Vanderbilt.

November 1917–18   Volleyball, invented in the United
States in the 1890s, is introduced to Europe by U.S.
troops toward the end of World War I.

SEPTEMBER

30–October 14   The first official South American
Championship for soccer (from 1975 known as the
Copa América) is won by the host country, Uruguay.

BIRTHS & DEATHS

JANUARY

2 Edward Burnett Tylor, English anthropologist, founder of cultural anthropology in Britain, dies in Wellington, Somerset, England (84).

10 William F. Cody ("Buffalo Bill"), U.S. buffalo hunter and Wild West showman, dies in Denver, Colorado (70).

16 George Dewey, U.S. naval commander who defeated the Spanish in Manila harbor during the Spanish–American War, permitting the United States to acquire the Philippines, dies in Washington, D.C. (79).

18 Oscar Lowenstein, English theater and film producer, born in Hackney, London, England (–1997).

24 Ernest Borgnine, U.S. actor, born in Hamden, Connecticut.

29 Evelyn Baring, Lord Cromer, who, as British ambassador to Egypt (1883–1907), had a significant influence on Egypt's development, dies in London, England (75).

FEBRUARY

25 Anthony Burgess (pen name of Anthony John Burgess Wilson), English novelist and critic, born in Manchester, England (–1993).

MARCH

1 Frances Rose ("Dinah") Shore, U.S. singer, born in Winchester, Tennessee (–1994).

1 Robert Lowell, U.S. poet, born in Boston, Massachusetts (–1977).

8 Ferdinand (Adolf August Heinrich) Graf von Zeppelin, German builder of rigid dirigible airships, dies in Charlottenburg, near Berlin, Germany (78).

24 John Kendrew, English biochemist who, with Max Perutz, received the Nobel Prize for Chemistry in 1962 for determining the structure of myoglobin, born in Oxford, England (–1997).

31 Emil Behring, German bacteriologist who founded the science of immunology and received the first Nobel Prize for Physiology or Medicine in 1901, dies in Marburg, Germany (63).

APRIL

1 Scott Joplin, U.S. composer and pianist known as the "King of Ragtime," dies in New York, New York (48).

10 Robert Burns Woodward, U.S. chemist who first synthesized chlorophyll, tetracycline, cholesterol, cortisone, vitamin B_{12}, and other complex organic substances, born in Boston, Massachusetts (–1979).

22 Sidney Robert Nolan, Australian artist known particularly for his paintings of the Australian outback and Australian folklore, born in Melbourne, Australia (–1992).

28 Jack Kirby, U.S. comic book artist who created over 400 characters including Spiderman, the Incredible Hulk, and Captain America, born in New York, New York (–1994).

MAY

c. 8 Sonny Liston, U.S. world heavyweight boxing champion 1962–64, born in St. Francis County, Arkansas (–1970).

19 Beva Ann Lockwood, U.S. lawyer, U.S. presidential candidate 1884, and first woman to practice law before the U.S. Supreme Court, dies in Washington, D.C. (86).

21 Raymond Burr, Canadian actor known for his roles as the detectives Perry Mason and Ironside, is born in New Westminster, British Columbia, Canada (–1993).

29 John F. Kennedy, 35th president of the United States 1961–63, a Democrat, born in Brookline, Massachusetts (–1963).

JUNE

17 Dean Martin, U.S. singer and actor, born in Steubenville, Ohio (–1995).

AUGUST

6 Robert (Charles Duran) Mitchum, U.S. film actor, born in Bridgeport, Connecticut (–1997).

20 Adolph von Baeyer, German chemist who discovered the structure of indigo for which he received the Nobel Prize for Chemistry in 1905, dies in Starnberg, near Munich, Germany (81).

SEPTEMBER

11 Ferdinand Marcos, corrupt and authoritarian Philippine head of state 1966–86, born in Sarrat, Philippines (–1989).

14 Park Chung Hee, president of South Korea 1963–79, whose policies were responsible for South Korea's rapid economic expansion, born in Taegu region, Korea (–1979).

20 Fernando Rey, Spanish actor, born in La Coruña, Spain (–1994).

27 Edgar Degas, French artist known for his paintings, drawings, and bronzes of the human figure in motion, dies in Paris, France (83).

OCTOBER

15 Arthur Schlesinger, Jr., U.S. writer and educator, born in Columbus, Ohio.

15 Mata Hari (Gertrud Margarete Zelle), Dutch dancer and spy, is shot by the French as a suspected spy (41).

21 "Dizzy" Gillespie (John Birks Gillespie), U.S. trumpet player and bandleader who originated the "bebop" style of jazz, born in Cheraw, South Carolina (–1993).

27 Oliver Tambo, president of the African National Congress (ANC) 1969–91, born in Bizana, near Johannesburg, South Africa (–1993).

NOVEMBER

11 Liloukalani, first Hawaiian queen and last reigning sovereign of Hawaii 1891–95, dies in Honolulu, Hawaii (79).

15 Emile Durkheim, French sociologist and founder of sociology, dies in Paris, France (59).

17 Auguste Rodin, French sculptor renowned for his realistic treatment of the human figure, dies in Meudon, France (77).

19 Indira Gandhi, prime minister of India 1966–77 and 1980–84, born in Allahabad, India (–1984).

26 Leander Starr Jameson, British statesman who, with Cecil Rhodes, tried to unite southern Africa under British rule, dies in London, England (64).

DECEMBER

9 (Leo) James Rainwater, U.S. physicist whose work concerned atomic nuclei, born in Council, Idaho (–1986).

16 Arthur C. Clarke, English writer of science fiction, born in Minehead, Somerset, England.

16 Frank Gotch, U.S. professional wrestler, who won 154 of his 160 matches, dies (39).

21 Heinrich Böll, German poet, novelist, short-story writer, and translator, born in Cologne, Germany (–1985).

1918

POLITICS, GOVERNMENT, AND ECONOMICS

Business and Economics

- The Kimberly & Clark Co. of Neenah, Wisconsin, produces the first sanitary napkin using Celucotton, a product originally developed for hospital bandages. Celucotton sanitary napkins will be sold under the new name Kotex in 1921.

NOVEMBER
15 German labor unions and employers form the *Zentralarbeitsgemeinschaft* ("Central Working Council") in order to establish cooperation in labor policy.

Human Rights

- In the face of increasing suspicion in wartime, many German-Americans play down their origins and try to integrate themselves into U.S. life more inconspicuously.

JANUARY
- The U.S. House of Representatives passes a women's suffrage amendment, but it is rejected by the U.S. Senate.

MARCH
- Female suffrage is granted in Canada.

APRIL
21 Universal suffrage is granted in Denmark.

SEPTEMBER
- The U.S. president Woodrow Wilson exhorts Congress to adopt a women's suffrage amendment, calling the measure a vital necessity of war.

Politics and Government

- Australia introduces the "alternative vote" system of proportional representation in elections.
- In *Hammer v. Dagenhout*, the U.S. Supreme Court strikes down a federal statute against child labor on the grounds that Congress has power over interstate commerce, but not manufacturing.
- Mississippi becomes the last state in the Union to adopt a mandatory school attendance law.

- The United States makes propaganda radio broadcasts to German troops, in an attempt to provoke insurrection.

JANUARY
1 Members of the extreme left wing Spartacists found the German Communist Party.
4 Joseph Caillaux, former prime minister of France, is arrested and imprisoned on suspicion of planning a coup and seeking a premature peace. In April 1920 he is sentenced to imprisonment.
5 The British prime minister, David Lloyd George, outlines Britain's war aims, which include the realization of the national aspirations of the peoples of Europe and Arabia and the establishment of an international body to prevent war in the future.
8 In a message to the U.S. Congress, President Woodrow Wilson propounds "fourteen points" for a peace settlement, including the principles of national self-determination, free trade, open diplomacy, and the founding of a league of nations.
18 The Russian Constituent Assembly opens in Petrograd, Russia, with a majority for the peasant-supported Socialist Revolutionaries.
20 The German battleship *Breslau* is sunk by a mine near the Dardanelles after making a sortie in the Mediterranean Sea.
26 The left wing of the Social Democratic Party in Finland seizes control in Helsinki, Finland, and proclaims the Finnish Workers' Socialist Republic.
26 The U.S. food administrator Herbert Hoover urges Americans to refrain from eating meat one day a week, from wheat two days, and from pork for three days in order to conserve food during wartime.
27 Russia denounces the British–Russian treaty of 1907 on the Near East, which created an *entente* between the two countries.
28 Bolshevik troops occupy Helsinki, Finland.
28 The Bolsheviks in Russia issue a decree founding the Red Army.
31 Russia adopts the "new style" Gregorian calendar, replacing the Julian calendar which lags the former by 11 days.

FEBRUARY
10 The Bolsheviks, unwilling to accept German peace terms but recognizing Russia's inability to continue the war, adopt Leon Trotsky's strategy of passive noncooperation, "no war, no peace."
16 Lithuania proclaims its independence from Russia.
18 Bolshevik troops capture Kiev in the Ukraine from White nationalists.
18 Germany resumes military operations against Russia after peace talks at Brest-Litovsk (now in Belarus), break down.

Russian Civil War (1918–20)

1918

JANUARY

28 Bolshevik troops occupy Helsinki, Finland.

FEBRUARY

18 Bolshevik troops capture Kiev in the Ukraine from White nationalists.

MARCH

3 A British force lands in Murmansk, Russia, to aid anti-Bolshevik forces and keep Russia in the war against Germany.

MAY

13 A Bolshevik decree in Russia declares war on *kulaks* (wealthier peasants) in an attempt to supply the cities with grain.

AUGUST

30 The Left Socialist revolutionary Fanny Kaplan shoots and seriously wounds Vladimir Ilyich Lenin in Russia. Her actions unleash a wave of Bolshevik terror.

NOVEMBER

18 Admiral Alexander Kolchak establishes an anti-Bolshevik dictatorial regime at Omsk, Russia.

DECEMBER

18 Allied forces under French command land at Odessa and other ports in the Ukraine to assist anticommunist forces in the civil war in Russia.

24 Admiral Alexander Kolchak's White Russian force takes Perm, Siberia, in its advance against the Bolsheviks.

1919

JANUARY

4 The Red Army takes Riga, Latvia, as the Russian communists attempt to reconquer the Baltic states.

25 The Red Army retakes Yekaterinburg in an offensive against Admiral Alexander Kolchak's White forces.

FEBRUARY

3–9 General Anton Denikin's White Russian army routs the Bolsheviks in the Caucasus region.

6 The Red Army captures Kiev, Ukraine.

APRIL

8 The Allies are driven out of their base at Odessa, Ukraine, by the Red Army.

19 Polish forces recapture the disputed city of Vilna (modern Vilnius), Lithuania, from the Red Army and begin to advance into Belarus.

28 The Red Army begins a counteroffensive against the White forces in Siberia under Admiral Kolchak.

JUNE

9 The Red Army takes Ufa in Siberia from White forces.

SEPTEMBER

2 The White Army takes Kiev, Ukraine, from the communists.

30–October 12 British troops are withdrawn from Archangel, Russia (September 30), and from Murmansk, Russia, which are subsequently occupied by the Red Army.

OCTOBER

13 The White Army captures Orel, southwest of Moscow, but is soon driven out by the Red Army.

22 The Red Army defeats an advancing White force under General Nikolay Yudenich near Petrograd.

NOVEMBER

14 The Red Army takes Omsk from the forces of Admiral Kolchak and pushes them back into Siberia.

DECEMBER

13 The Red Army captures the Ukrainian city of Kharkov from White forces.

17 The Red Army expels White forces from Kiev.

1920

JANUARY

5 Polish and Latvian troops capture Dvinsk (now Daugavpils in Latvia) from the Bolsheviks.

8 The Red Army defeats a White army under Admiral Alexander Kolchak at Krasnoyarsk in south-central Siberia. Kolchak is executed by the Bolsheviks on February 7.

FEBRUARY

8 The Red Army captures Odessa in the Ukraine from White forces.

MARCH

27 The Red Army takes Novorossiisk on the Black Sea, precipitating the collapse of Anton Denikin's White Army. General Peter Wrangel takes command of White operations.

APRIL

28 The Red Army takes Baku (now in Azerbaijan) the Caucasus, from General Peter Wrangel's White Army.

JULY

6 Britain evacuates Batumi in Georgia to avoid a clash with Red Army troops advancing through the Caucasus region.

NOVEMBER

14 The Russian Red Army takes Sevastopol in the Crimea. With the evacuation of General Peter Wrangel's White forces to Constantinople, Anatolia (modern Turkey), the civil war in Russia is effectively over, with the communists victorious.

21 Australian troops take the ancient city of Jericho in Palestine from the Ottoman army.

MARCH

- The rate at which British vessels are sunk by German submarines falls to an average of 330,000 tons per month in the first quarter of the year, well below the 600,000 tons which would cause major shortages.
- The U.S. president Woodrow Wilson creates the Distinguished Service Medal for "exceptionally meritorious service" in the armed forces.
1 German forces take Kiev in the Ukraine from the Bolsheviks, and on March 4 take Narva in Estonia.
3 A British force lands in Murmansk, Russia, to aid anti-Bolshevik forces and keep Russia in the war against Germany.
3 Russia and the Central Powers sign the Treaty of Brest-Litovsk, in which Russia cedes the Baltic Provinces and Russian Poland, and recognizes the independence of Finland and the Ukraine. The Ottoman Empire takes the former Russian districts of Kars, Ardahan, and Batum.
3 The Bolsheviks move the Russian capital from Petrograd to Moscow, in order to distance it from the German army.
12 Ottoman forces occupy Erzurum in Azerbaijan (–14th May), expanding into the Caucasus region following the withdrawal of Russian interests.
21–April 5 The German army launches a spring offensive on the Western Front with the Second Battle of the Somme, and advances 64 km/40 mi toward Paris, France.
23–August 9 Massive German guns shell Paris, France, from 120 km/75 mi away.
26 France and Britain make an agreement at Doullens, France, in the first step toward giving Ferdinand Foch overall command of the French and British armies.

APRIL

- The U.S. Congress authorizes a third Liberty Loan Drive of $3 billion.
3 German troops led by General Colmar von der Goltz land in Finland to oppose the communist takeover there.
4 Japanese troops advance into Siberia in an attempt to exploit Russia's internal disorder by seizing territory.
8–10 The Rome Congress of Oppressed Nationalities announces the aspirations of Czechs and Slovaks, Romanians, Poles, and peoples from the Yugoslavia area to form their own nation states.
9–29 The German army launches the second of its major operations of the year in the Lys offensive on the Western Front.
13 Following the withdrawal of Bolshevik troops from Helsinki, Finland, an occupying German force moves in.
14 The Allies agree that U.S. troops will fight as a single army under the command of General John Pershing, but all armies will be nominally under the supreme command of the French marshal Ferdinand Foch.
19 Alfred Milner becomes the British war secretary, replacing Lord Derby who is opposed to a joint Allied command structure.
21 The German air ace Manfred von Richthofen (the "Red Baron") is shot down and killed, either by Canadian pilot Roy Brown or by ground fire.
22–23 British ships raid Zeebrugge, Belgium, blocking the entrance to Bruges Canal and the German submarine base there.
30 The Finnish communists are decisively defeated by their White opponents at the Battle of Vyborg.

MAY

- President Woodrow Wilson signs the Sedition Act, prohibiting conduct harmful to the U.S. war effort.
- The U.S. government orchestrates the merger of the Adams, American, Wells-Fargo, and Southern Express railroad companies into the American Railroad Express Company. The move is intended to expedite shipment of war materials.
- U.S. war secretary Newton D. Baker stipulates that conscientious objectors may perform farm work rather than military service.
1 German troops occupy the Ukrainian city of Sevastopol in the Crimea, taking possession of territory claimed by Germany under the Treaty of Brest-Litovsk.
5–19 Allied forces mount an unsuccessful attempt to break through on the Macedonian front.
7 Romania signs the Peace of Bucharest with Germany and Austria-Hungary. Romania is allowed to annex Bessarabia (modern-day Moldova), though Russia refuses to recognize the annexation.
10 The British cruiser *Vindictive* is sunk deliberately in an unsuccessful attempt to block the entrance to the German submarine base at Ostend, Belgium.
13 A Bolshevik decree in Russia declares war on *kulaks* (wealthier peasants) in an attempt to supply the cities with grain.
14 The U.S. Overman Act empowers the U.S. president to reorganize executive departments.
18 British aircraft make bombing raids on Germany.
18 Eamon De Valera and other Sinn Féin leaders are arrested for alleged collaboration with Germany.
26 Georgia proclaims independence from Russia.
27 A German offensive on the Western Front is stopped by U.S. troops at Château-Thierry, France.
29 German forces capture Soissons and Reims in France.

JUNE

- The U.S. Socialist leader Eugene V. Debs is arrested for violating the Espionage Act in a speech at Canton, Ohio in mid-June.
- The United States loses nearly 8,000 men in a prolonged but successful engagement with German forces at Belleau Wood in France.
9–13 A German offensive near Compiègne, France, is repulsed by French and U.S. troops.
15–23 In the Battle of the Piave, Italy, Austro-Hungarian troops cross the River Piave to attack the Italian line, but are resisted.
17 Food riots break out in Vienna, Austria.
25 Czech soldiers in Siberia, who were originally captured by the imperial Russian army, revolt. They seize the Trans-Siberian Railway in their attempt to reach Vladivostok, Russia.
25 The British government announces the abandonment of conscription in Ireland.
28 The Bolshevik government in Russia decrees the nationalization of heavy industry.

JULY

- Former U.S. president Theodore Roosevelt's youngest son, Quentin, is killed in a dogfight over France.

- The U.S. food administrator Herbert Hoover rations sugar to 0.9 kgs/2 lbs per person per month and urges people to cut back on consumption of other foods.
6 The German ambassador to Russia, Count von Mirbach, is assassinated by a Left Socialist Revolutionary.
6 The Montagu–Chelmsford Report on the constitution of India is published. The report advocates that Indian ministers be given charge of aspects of provincial government.
10 Russia adopts a new constitution as the basic document of the new Russian Soviet Federated Socialist Republic (RSFSR).
15–18 Some 250,000 U.S. troops figure prominently in the Allies' successful Aisne–Marne offensive, halting a German advance at the Second Battle of the Marne River, northeast of Paris, France.
16 The ex-czar Nicholas II and his family are executed by the Bolsheviks at Yekaterinburg in Russia.
18 Allied forces begin a counteroffensive against the German armies on the Western Front, following the cessation of the German spring offensive.
22 Allied forces cross the River Marne in France.
26 The Czech legion takes Yekaterinburg, Russia, from the Bolsheviks.

AUGUST

- The U.S. War Industries Board suspends civilian automobile production, effective January 1, 1919, as part of the war mobilization effort.
- U.S. troops help launch a major offensive against German forces along the Somme River in northern France.
1–2 British forces land at Archangel and Murmansk, Russia, to support anti-Bolshevik forces.
2 French forces recapture Soissons, France.
3 A British force lands at Vladivostok, Russia, beginning a joint effort with France and the United States to prevent Japanese aggrandizement in Siberia.
8–11 The Battle of Amiens is fought on the Western Front, British forces breaking the German line to such an extent that August 8 becomes known as "the black day of the German army."
15 The United States and communist Russia sever diplomatic relations.
30 The Left Socialist revolutionary Fanny Kaplan shoots and seriously wounds Vladimir Ilyich Lenin in Russia. Her actions unleash a wave of Bolshevik terror.
31 British forces take Péronne, France.

SEPTEMBER

- 1,200,000 U.S. troops participate in the Battle of the Meuse-Argonne, two rivers in northeast France. The Americans cut the Sedan-Mézières railroad, a crucial German supply line in early November.
- The U.S. secretary of war Newton D. Baker suspends the baseball season for the duration of the war.
2 Following recent defeats, German troops again retreat to the "Hindenburg Line," a series of highly fortified defensive emplacements constructed along the Franco-Belgian border since September 1916.
10 Muslims riot in Calcutta in British-ruled India.
12–13 At the Battle of St-Mihiel in northeast France, the U.S. First Army under General John Pershing captures the St-Mihiel salient and takes an estimated 15,000 German soldiers prisoner.
14 Austria-Hungary makes a peace offer, which the Allies refuse on September 20.
14 The leading U.S. socialist Eugene V. Debs is sentenced to 10 years in prison for violating the Espionage Act in a speech in Canton, Ohio, the previous June. On March 10, 1919, the Supreme Court will uphold the conviction.
15–24 An Allied (French, British, Italian, and Serbian) offensive makes large gains at the Battle of Monastir on the Macedonian front.
18 A British offensive begins in Palestine when troops under Sir Edmund Allenby defeat an Ottoman force at the Battle of Megiddo.
22 Ottoman resistance in Palestine collapses under British pressure.
29 Belgian troops capture Dixmude, Belgium.
29 The German quartermaster general, General Eric Ludendorff, and the commander in chief, Paul von Hindenburg, advocate that Germany should become a constitutional monarchy and approach the Allies for an armistice.
30 Bulgaria signs an armistice with the Allies.
30 The German chancellor, Count George von Hertling, resigns in order to facilitate the appointment of a liberal government to make peace with the Allies.

OCTOBER

1 British and Arab forces occupy Damascus, Syria.
1 French forces take St. Quentin, France.
4 The liberal Prince Max of Baden is appointed German chancellor to negotiate for peace with the Allies.
5 A note from the new German chancellor Prince Max of Baden is sent to the United States, via Switzerland, asking for assistance in brokering a European peace treaty, suggesting an armistice based on the U.S. president Woodrow Wilson's "fourteen points."
7 A French naval force occupies the formerly Ottoman-held Beirut in Lebanon.
9 British forces take Cambrai and Le Cateau in France.
12 The U.S. president Woodrow Wilson replies to the German chancellor Prince Max of Baden's note of October 5, telling him that peace will be brokered by military authorities. Further, the president maintains, Germany must cease its aggression and banish autocratic government as a condition of peace.
14 The Ottoman Empire sends a message to the U.S. president Woodrow Wilson, proposing an armistice.
18 Belgian troops recapture Zeebrugge and (on October 19) Bruges, Belgium.
18 Lille, France, falls to British troops.
20 Germany and Austria-Hungary agree to the peace terms of the U.S. president Woodrow Wilson, including the stipulation that their troops should retreat to their own territory before an armistice is signed, and Wilson relays this message to the Allies.
20 Germany suspends submarine warfare.
21 Czechoslovakia is proclaimed an independent republic in the Czech city of Prague.
24–November 4 The Battle of Vittorio Veneto on the Italian front leads to the collapse of the Austro-Hungarian army.
27 Austria-Hungary asks Italy for an armistice.

27 General Eric Ludendorff resigns as quartermaster general of the German army and is replaced by General Wilhelm von Gröner.

30 A mutiny of German sailors takes place at Kiel, Germany, when they refuse Admiral Franz von Hipper's orders to sail on a suicide mission in the North Sea.

30 The Allies sign an armistice with the Ottoman Empire on the warship *Agamemnon* at the port of Mudros on the Greek island of Lemnos in the Aegean Sea.

31 The former Hungarian prime minister Count Stephen Tisza is assassinated by leftist rebels who hold him responsible for Hungary's involvement in the war.

NOVEMBER

• Newspapers in New York, New York, mistakenly declare the signing of an armistice with Germany, sparking joyous celebration.

• The U.S. president Woodrow Wilson announces that he will attend the Paris Peace Conference.

• The U.S. president Woodrow Wilson signs the Wartime Prohibition Act, banning the domestic manufacture and sale of alcoholic beverages.

1 British and French forces occupy the Ottoman capital of Constantinople.

2 Riots break out in Vienna, Austria, and Budapest, Austria-Hungary.

3 A Polish republic is proclaimed in Warsaw, Poland, by the Russian-sponsored regency council.

3 Riots spread across Germany from the north German port of Kiel, and workers' and soldiers' soviets (revolutionary councils) or *Räte* are established.

3 The Allies sign an armistice with Austria-Hungary, which is to come into force on November 4.

5 In U.S. Congressional elections Republicans regain majorities in the House (240–190) and Senate (49–47).

6 U.S. troops occupy Sedan in France.

7 A republic is proclaimed in Bavaria, Germany, by the socialist Kurt Eisner.

8 A German armistice commission meets the Allied delegation, headed by the French marshal Ferdinand Foch, in a railroad carriage in Compiègne, France. An armistice is agreed, to be effective from November 11.

9 The Social Democrat Philip Scheidemann preempts the proclamation of a communist republic in Germany by declaring a republic himself. Friedrich Ebert replaces Prince Max as chancellor and, on November 10, Kaiser Wilhelm II of Germany flees to the Netherlands.

10 Friedrich Ebert's government in Germany receives the support of the armed forces and of the workers' and soldiers' councils of Berlin, Germany.

11 The armistice between the Allies and Germany comes into force from 11 a.m.

12 Austria proclaims itself a republic following Austria-Hungary's defeat in World War II and the demands of the Empire's subject nationalities for independence.

12 Emperor Charles I abdicates in Austria and, on November 13, in Austria-Hungary.

13 The nationalist Wafd Party is established in Egypt, initially to provide a delegation of Egyptians to attend the Paris Peace Conference.

13 The Russian government annuls the harsh Treaty of Brest-Litovsk, signed with Germany in March following the defeat of Germany by the Western allies in World War II.

14 Tomáš Masaryk Garrigue is elected president of Czechoslovakia.

16 Hungary proclaims itself a republic independent of the Austro-Hungarian Empire.

18 A national council proclaims the independence of Latvia.

18 Admiral Alexander Kolchak establishes an anti-Bolshevik dictatorial regime at Omsk, Russia.

18 German troops evacuate France.

19 Friedrich Ebert (now chairman of the Council of People's Commissars) persuades the Congress of Soldiers' and Workers' Councils in Berlin, Germany, to agree to elections for a national assembly. The elections will be held on January 19, 1919.

20 The German navy surrenders its submarines at Harwich on the east coast of England, to be followed on November 21 by the surrender of its surface fleet at the Firth of Forth, Scotland.

22 The Red Army takes Narva, Estonia, in an attempt to reconquer the newly independent Baltic states.

23 Radical sailors in Berlin, Germany, occupy the chancellery and take Friedrich Ebert prisoner. He is rescued on November 24 by soldiers from Potsdam, Germany.

25 German troops led by Paul von Lettow-Warbeck in northern Rhodesia surrender.

26 The national assembly in Montenegro proclaims the deposition of King Nicholas and the union of Montenegro with Serbia.

30 Iceland becomes a sovereign state, independent of Denmark but under the same monarch.

DECEMBER

1 A convention of Romanians in the Hungarian region of Transylvania proclaims its union with Romania. On December 2 a provisional government is established.

1 The Allies begin their occupation of Germany.

4 A national council proclaims the formation of the Kingdom of Serbs, Croats, and Slovenes, with Alexander I (son of King Peter of Serbia) as prince-regent. The country will be renamed Yugoslavia in 1929.

14 In the British general election, the victorious wartime coalition wins a majority of 249. The coalition Conservatives take 335 seats, the coalition Liberals 133, and the coalition Labour candidates 10, giving the coalition a total of 478 seats, while the Irish Unionists win 25 seats, the Irish Nationalists 7, the Conservatives 23, the Liberals 28, Labour 63, Sinn Féin 73, and others 10.

14 Sidonio Paes, the dictatorial president of Portugal, is assassinated. Democracy is subsequently restored.

18 Allied forces under French command land at Odessa and other ports in the Ukraine to assist anticommunist forces in the civil war in Russia.

20 A conference of workers' and soldiers' delegates in Berlin, Germany, demands the nationalization of industries.

24 Admiral Alexander Kolchak's White Russian force takes Perm, Siberia, in its advance against the Bolsheviks.

27 Polish forces occupy Posen (modern Poznań, Poland), which they claim from Germany.

28 The extremist Independent Socialists withdraw from the government in Berlin, Germany, leaving Friedrich Ebert and his majority socialists free to suppress revolutionary forces.

SCIENCE, TECHNOLOGY, AND MEDICINE

Ecology

- Katmai National Park, Alaska, is established; it contains active volcanoes.

Health and Medicine

- English pharmacologist Edward Mellanby discovers that a vitamin (vitamin D) in cod-liver oil cures rickets.
- Scottish geneticist Ronald Fisher shows that both genes and environmental factors affect an individual's behavior.
- The epidemic of Spanish influenza in the United States leads to the rationing of Vicks VapoRub because of the increase in demand.
- U.S. physician Walter Dandy studies the internal structure of the brain by injecting air into the ventricles of the brain to provide contrast for X-rays.

December 1918–19 A worldwide pandemic of Spanish influenza (so called because of its particular virulence in Spain) or *Encephalitis lethargica* (sleeping sickness) kills over 20 million people, more than were killed during the conflicts of the First World War. The movement of the armed forces at the end of the war promotes its spread.

OCTOBER
- The U.S. influenza epidemic that will claim nearly half a million lives peaks, impeding war mobilization and sparking widespread apprehension.

Science

- English astrophysicist Arthur Eddington publishes *Report on the Relativity Theory of Gravitation*, which is the first explanation of Einstein's theory of relativity in English.
- German chemist Fritz Haber receives the Nobel Prize for Chemistry for the synthesis of ammonia from its elements, nitrogen and hydrogen.
- German physicist Max Planck receives the Nobel Prize for Physics for his discovery of energy quanta.
- U.S. astronomer Harlow Shapley estimates the size of the Milky Way (70,000 light-years in diameter).

Technology

c. 1918 Swiss chemists Henry and Camille Dreyfus develop cellulose acetate, which is used as a textile fiber and for photographic film.
- The Anti-Submarine Detection Investigation Device (ASDIC) is developed by British and U.S. naval scientists. An active sonar system, it uses the echo of a pulsed sound to detect submarines.
- The British armed forces introduce the Medium A tank. Weighing only 12,700 kg/14 tons and traveling at 13 kph/8 mph with a range of 125 km/80 mi, it is lighter and faster than previous tanks.
- The Krupp Armaments factory in Germany makes "Big Bertha." The biggest piece of artillery in the world, it has a range of 122 km/76 mi and is used to shell Paris, France, in March. The long range is achieved by firing the shells 19 km/12 mi into the stratosphere, where drag is minimal. The previous long-range limit was 35 km/22 mi.
- The U.S. engineer Charles Kettering develops a guided missile carrying a 90-kg/200-lb explosive charge. It is propeller-driven, and a gyroscope and barometer maintain its pitch, direction, and altitude. The number of revolutions of the propeller is used to determine distance.
- U.S. inventor Elmer Sperry develops a searchlight six times brighter than any other previous lights.
- U.S. inventor John Moses Browning introduces the Browning automatic rifle; it is adopted by the U.S. Army as a light machine gun.
- U.S. inventor Robert Hutchings Goddard patents a shoulder-type rocket launcher. It is the forerunner of the "bazooka."
- The French introduce the Renault F. T. tank. Designed primarily as a support for infantry, it is light and slow. Its design serves as the prototype for other tanks.

Transportation

- Three-color traffic lights are installed in New York, New York.

JUNE
22 Two trains crash head-on in Tennessee, killing 99 people.

SEPTEMBER
- The Royal Navy launches the first aircraft carrier, the *Argus*. A converted merchant ship, it has a flight deck measuring 170.7 m/560 ft and a hangar that can house 20 airplanes.

NOVEMBER
2 In a subway accident in New York, New York, 97 people die when a train jumps the track, the worst underground accident to date. The accident occurs while supervisors have assumed workers' duties during a strike.

ARTS AND IDEAS

Architecture

- The Quebec Railroad Bridge over the St. Lawrence River at Quebec City, Quebec, Canada, is completed. It is the longest cantilever bridge in the world at 549 m/1,801 ft.
- The Hallidie Building, designed by the U.S. architect Willis Polk, is completed in San Francisco, California. This is one of the first examples of the modern "curtain wall," a continuous wall of steel and glass that is hung on the building's frame.

Arts

- French artist Amédée Ozenfant and the Swiss architect Le Corbusier publish *Après le Cubisme/After Cubism*, a manifesto on "Purism."
- The English artist Eric Gill sculpts *Stations of the Cross* for Westminster Cathedral in London, England.
- The English artist Paul Nash paints *We Are Making a New World*.
- The French artist Amédée Ozenfant paints *Bottle, Pipe and Books*.
- The French artist Fernand Léger paints *Factories*.
- The Italian artist Amedeo Modigliani paints *Portrait of Léopold Zborowski*.
- The Russian artist Alexander Rodchenko paints *Black on Black*.
- The Russian artist Kasimir Malevich paints *Suprematist Composition: White on White*.
- The Swiss artist Paul Klee paints *Gartenplan/Plan of a Garden*.
- The U.S. artist Charles Burchfield paints *The First Hepaticas*.

Film

- The movie *Carmen*, directed by Ernst Lubitsch, is released in Germany. Based on the novel by Prosper Merimée, it stars Pola Negri.
- The movie *Hearts of the World*, directed by D. W. Griffith, is released in the United States. Made with British finance to inspire sympathy in the United States for the war effort, it stars Lillian Gish and Robert Harron.
- The movie *Hell Bent*, directed by Jack Ford, is released in the United States, starring Harry Carey.
- The movie *La Dixième Symphonie/The Tenth Symphony*, directed by Abel Gance, is released in France.
- The movie *Shoulder Arms*, directed by Charlie Chaplin, is released in the United States. Chaplin also stars in it with Edna Purviance.
- The movie *Tarzan of the Apes* is released. Based on the book by Edgar Rice Burroughs, it stars Elmo Lincoln and is directed by Scott Sidney.
- The movie *The Eyes of the Mummy*, directed by Fritz Lang, is released in Germany.
- The movie *The Outlaw and his Wife*, directed by Victor Sjöström, is released in Sweden. Sjöström also stars in it with Edith Erastoff.
- The movie studios Louis B. Mayer Pictures and Warner Bros are founded in the United States.

Literature and Language

- The *Collected Poems* of the English writer Rupert Brooke (who died while on military service in 1915) are published posthumously.
- The *Poems* of the English Victorian writer Gerard Manley Hopkins are published posthumously.
- The English churchman William Ralph Inge publishes *The Philosophy of Plotinus*.
- The English poet and translator Arthur Waley publishes *A Hundred and Seventy Chinese Poems*.

- The English writer and artist Percy Wyndham Lewis publishes his novel *Tarr*.
- The English writer Lytton Strachey publishes his biographical studies *Eminent Victorians*.
- The English writer Siegfried Sassoon publishes his poetry collection *Counter Attack*.
- The English writer William Henry Hudson publishes his autobiography *Far Away and Long Ago*.
- The Irish writer Rebecca West publishes her novella *The Return of the Soldier*.
- The Peruvian writer César Vallejo publishes his poetry collection *Los heraldos negros/The Black Heralds*.
- The Pulitzer Prize for Biography is awarded to William C. Bruce for *Benjamin Franklin, Self-Revealed* and the Pulitzer Prize for Fiction is awarded for the first time, to Ernest Poole for *His Family*. A special Pulitzer Prize for Poetry, made possible by a gift from the Poetry Society, is awarded to Sara Teasdale for *Love Songs*.
- The Russian poet Alexander Blok publishes his poem "Dvenadtsat"/"The Twelve."
- The U.S. writer Booth Tarkington publishes his novel *The Magnificent Ambersons*.
- The U.S. writer Conrad Aiken publishes his poetry collection *The Charnel Rose*.
- The U.S. writer Sherwood Anderson publishes his poetry collection *Mid-American Chants*.
- The U.S. writer Theodore Dreiser publishes his short-story collection *Free and Other Stories*.

Music

c. 1918 The U.S. composer Charles Griffes completes his *Two Sketches Based on Indian Themes* for string quartet.
- Irving Berlin writes the unofficial national anthem "God Bless America" while serving in the American Expeditionary Force.
- The Australian composer Percy Grainger completes his setting of English folk songs, *Country Gardens*.
- The Czech composer Leoš Janáček completes his orchestral rhapsody *Taras Bulba*.
- The French composer Germaine Tailleferre completes her String Quartet.
- The French composer Camille St.-Saëns completes his String Quartet No. 2.
- The Jazz Boys is the first U.S. jazz band to visit Britain.
- The opera *A Kékszakállù herceg vára/Duke Bluebeard's Castle* by the Hungarian composer Béla Bartók is first performed, in Budapest, Hungary. It was written in 1911.
- The opera *Die Gezeichneten/The Signified* by the Austrian composer Franz Schreker is first performed, in Frankfurt am Main, Germany.
- The set of three brief operas *Il trittico/The Triptych* by the Italian composer Giacomo Puccini is first performed, in New York, New York. The individual titles are *Il Fabarro*, *Suor Angelica*, and *Gianni Schicchi*.
- U.S. jazz quintet the Original Dixieland Jazz Band records "Tiger Rag."
- U.S. songwriters Henry Creamer and Turner Layton write the song "After You're Gone."

Theater and Dance

- The first Pulitzer Prize for Drama is awarded, to Jesse L. Williams for *Why Marry?*
- The play *Abraham Lincoln*, by the English writer John Drinkwater, is first performed, in Birmingham, England.
- The Yiddish Art Theater is founded by the Russian-born U.S. actor Maurice Schwartz in New York, New York.

AUGUST

26 The play *Lightnin'*, by Winchell Smith and Frank Bacon, is first performed, at the Gaiety Theater in New York, New York.

OCTOBER

4 The musical *Sometime*, with songs by Bohemian-born U.S. composer Rudolf Friml, and starring Mae West, opens at the Shubert Theater, New York, New York.

BIRTHS & DEATHS

JANUARY

6 Georg Cantor, Russian mathematician who established set theory, dies in Halle, Germany (72).

15 Gamal Abdel Nasser, prime minister of Egypt 1954–56 and then president 1956–70, born in Alexandria, Egypt (–1970).

26 Nicolae Ceauşescu, president of the Socialist Republic of Romania 1967–89, born in Scorniceşti, Romania (–1989).

FEBRUARY

4 Ida Lupino, British-born U.S. actress, director, and screen writer, born in London, England (–1995).

6 Gustav Klimt, Austrian painter, dies in Vienna, Austria (57).

11 Michael Balfour, English actor, born in Kent, England (–1997).

12 Julian Seymour Schwinger, U.S. quantum physicist whose research concerned the behavior of charged particles in electrical fields, winner of the Nobel Prize for Physics in 1965, born in New York, New York (–1994).

25 Barney Ewell, U.S. sprinter who dominated the sport in the mid 1940s, born in Lancaster, Pennsylvania (–1996).

25 Robert ("Bobby") Riggs, U.S. tennis player, born in Los Angeles, California (–1995).

MARCH

3 Arthur Kornberg, U.S. biochemist who discovered how the DNA molecule replicates itself, born in Brooklyn, New York, New York.

6 John Redmond, Irish Nationalist Party leader, dies in London, England (61).

9 Frank Wedekind, German actor and dramatist, dies in Munich, Germany (53).

9 Mickey Spillane, U.S. novelist known for his detective stories, born in Brooklyn, New York, New York.

15 Janet Leach, English potter, born in Grand Saline, Texas (–1997).

25 Claude Debussy, French composer, dies in Paris, France (55).

27 Henry Adams, U.S. historian and author, known for his autobiography *The Education of Henry Adams: A Study of 20th Century Multiplicity*, dies in Washington, D.C. (80).

APRIL

21 Manfred, Freiherr von Richthofen (the "Red Baron"), German aviator and leading ace during World War I, is shot down and killed in Vaux-sur-Somme, France (26).

25 Ella Fitzgerald, U.S. jazz singer, born in Newport News, Virginia (–1996).

MAY

4 Kakuei Tanaka, Japanese businessman and prime minister of Japan 1972–74, born in Kariwa, Japan (–1993).

11 Richard Feynman, U.S. theoretical physicist in the field of quantum electrodynamics, born in New York, New York (–1988).

12 Julius Rosenberg, U.S. spy, born in New York, New York (–1953).

16 Juan Pérez Rulfo, Mexican writer, a founder of the "magic realism" school of writing, born in Sayula, Mexico (–1986).

30 Georgy Valentinovich Plekhanov, founder of the Marxist movement in Russia, dies in Terioki, Finland (61).

JULY

14 Ingmar Bergman, Swedish film director, born in Uppsala, Sweden.

16 Nicholas II, Czar of Russia 1895–1917, is executed along with his family in Yekaterinburg, Russia (50).

16 Alexandra Fyodorovna, consort of the Russian emperor Nicholas II, whose misrule while he was at war helped lead to the Russian Revolution, is executed in Yekaterinburg, Russia (46).

18 Nelson Mandela, South African nationalist, political prisoner, and president from 1994, born in Umtata, Cape of Good Hope, South Africa.

AUGUST

25 Leonard Bernstein, U.S. conductor, born in Lawrence, Massachusetts (–1990).

31 Alan Jay Lerner, U.S. lyricist who collaborated with Frederick Loewe for many years writing Broadway musicals, born in New York, New York (–1986).

SEPTEMBER

17 Chaim Herzog, president of Israel 1983–93, born in Belfast, Ireland (–1997).

27 Martin Ryle, English radioastronomer who developed a revolutionary radio telescope system that enabled weak radio sources to be located, born in Brighton, Sussex, England (–1984).

OCTOBER

17 Rita Hayworth, U.S. motion picture actress, born in Brooklyn, New York, New York (–1987).

NOVEMBER

4 Wilfred Owen, English poet noted for his war poems, is killed in action in France (25).

7 Billy Graham, U.S. evangelist, born in Charlotte, North Carolina.

9 Spiro T(heodore) Agnew, the first U.S. vice president (1969–73) to resign under duress, born in Baltimore, Maryland (–1996).

DECEMBER

2 Edmond Rostand, French dramatist who wrote *Cyrano de Bergerac*, dies in Paris, France (50).

11 Alexander Solzhenitsyn, Russian novelist and historian, born in Kislovodosk, Russia.

21 Kurt Waldheim, Secretary General of the United Nations 1972–81 and president of Austria 1986–92, born in Andrä-Wördern, Austria.

23 Helmut Schmidt, chancellor of West Germany 1974–82, born in Hamburg, Germany.

25 Anwar Sadat, Egyptian president 1970–81, born in Mit Abu al-Kum al-Minufiyah governate, Egypt (–1981).

Thought and Scholarship

- German historian Oswald Spengler publishes the first volume of his *Der Untergang des Abendlandes/The Decline of the West*. The second volume appears in 1922.
- German philosopher Moritz Schlick publishes *Allgemeine Erkenntnislehre/General Theory of Knowledge*.
- Russian revolutionary leader Vladimir Ilyich Lenin publishes *Gosudarstvo i revoliutsiia/The State and Revolution*.
- The Nobel Prize for Literature is not awarded this year.
- The Pulitzer Prize for History is awarded to James Ford Rhodes for *A History of the Civil War, 1861–1865*.
- U.S. historian Carl L. Becker publishes *The Eve of the Revolution*.
- U.S. historian Ulrich Bonnell Phillips publishes *American Negro Slavery*.
- U.S. psychologist Robert Woodworth publishes *Dynamic Psychology*, in which he explains behavior by synthesizing theories of perception, learning, motivation, and thinking.

SOCIETY

Everyday Life

- Daylight Saving time is introduced in the United States.
- In a wartime reaction against German culture, sauerkraut is renamed "liberty cabbage" in the United States.
- The birth-control pioneer Dr. Marie Stopes publishes the controversial book *Married Love*, a manual on sex, marriage, and contraception, in Britain.
- The U.S. cartoonist John Gruelle creates the Raggedy Ann doll character in stories and drawings. It is quickly merchandized.
- The U.S. inventor Charles Strite patents the pop-up toaster, which is initially used in restaurants.

JANUARY
16 A general strike takes place in Vienna, Austria, in protest at food shortages following a cut in the flour ration.

28–February 3 A strike takes place in Berlin, Germany, following shortages.

MARCH
11 Austrian civilian aircraft begin the first regular airmail service, from Vienna to Lemberg (modern Lvov, Ukraine).

MAY
- The U.S. Post Office releases the first domestic airmail stamps, worth 6, 16, and 24 cents.
15 The U.S. Post Office begins using planes to deliver mail between Washington, D.C., and New York, New York.

AUGUST
17 Airmail stickers for letters, labeled "Par avion," go on sale in France.

OCTOBER
21 Margaret Owen of New York, New York, sets a typewriting speed record when in a competition she types 170 words in one minute with no errors.

Media and Communication

FEBRUARY
8 The U.S. military periodical *Stars and Stripes* is published.

SEPTEMBER
- The Marconi long-wave radio station at Caernarvon, Wales, sends a radiotelegraph message to Australia, a distance of 17,700 km/11,000 mi.

Religion

- 45 Lutheran synods in the United States merge to form the United Lutheran Church.

Sports

- The U.S. inventors Alexander Graham Bell and Casey Baldwin build a hydrofoil that sets a water speed record of 60 knots.

SEPTEMBER
5–11 The Boston Red Sox defeat the Chicago Cubs by four games to two in baseball's World Series. It is the Boston Red Sox's third World Series in four years.

1919

POLITICS, GOVERNMENT, AND ECONOMICS

Business and Economics

- Ernest Oppenheimer founds the Anglo-American Corporation of South Africa in order to exploit the Witwatersrand goldfield.
- The U.S. entrepreneur Conrad Nicholson Hilton buys the Mobley Hotel in Crisco, Texas, the first in his hotel chain.

MARCH

9 The Canadian Grand Trunk Pacific Railroad goes bankrupt. It is nationalized in 1920.

NOVEMBER

2–9 United Mine Workers in the bituminous coal industry go on strike, but are forced back to work a week later by a wartime injunction which is still in effect.

Colonization

NOVEMBER

21 The Allied Supreme Council gives Poland a mandate over East Galicia, a region disputed with Czechoslovakia.

Human Rights

MAY

9 Universal suffrage is granted in Belgium.
26 Female suffrage is granted in Sweden.

AUGUST

9 Universal suffrage is granted in the Netherlands.

NOVEMBER

28 In Britain, Lady Nancy Astor is elected in a by-election and becomes the first woman member of Parliament to take her seat.

Politics and Government

- Germany establishes a Ministry of Economics.
- In the U.S. Supreme Court, the *Schenck v. USA* case establishes the "clear and present danger" test for the restriction of free speech.

JANUARY

- The 18th Amendment to the U.S. Constitution, prohibiting the manufacture, sale, and distribution of alcoholic beverages, becomes law.
3 The U.S. politician Herbert Hoover becomes director-general of the Commission for Relief and Reconstruction of Europe.
4 The Red Army takes Riga, Latvia, as the Russian communists attempt to reconquer the Baltic states.
5 The German Workers' Party (later the National Socialist German Workers' Party) is formed in Munich, Germany. On September 12 Adolf Hitler will attend for the first time.
5–15 A communist (Spartacist) revolt takes place in Berlin, Germany.
10 The British Army takes over the administration of the Baghdad Railroad from the German authorities.
10–February 4 A Bolshevik-inspired soviet republic is established in Bremen in northwestern Germany.
15 Volunteer soldiers suppress the Spartacist rising in Berlin, Germany, and the Spartacist leaders Karl Liebknecht and Rosa Luxemburg are arrested and shot.
17 Józef Piłsudski becomes president of Poland, and Ignacy Jan Paderewski becomes prime minister of the coalition government there. Paderewski resigns on December 7.
18 The Paris Peace Conference opens in France under the chairmanship of the French president, Georges Clemenceau.
19 Elections are held for the German national assembly, the Social Democrats and the Center Party taking the largest proportions of the vote with 38% and 20% respectively.
21 Sinn Féin members elected to the British Westminster Parliament meet in Dublin, Ireland, as a constituent assembly for Ireland (the Dáil Eireann). They proclaim an Irish republic and elect a president (Eamon de Valera), electing ministers on April 5. Meanwhile, the Irish Republican Army (IRA) attacks British authorities in Ireland.
22 Czech forces occupy the Teschen area (now Cieszyn in southwestern Poland) to press their claim to that part of Silesia.
25 The Paris Peace Conference in France adopts the principle of founding a League of Nations.
25 The Red Army retakes Yekaterinburg, Russia, in an offensive against Admiral Alexander Kolchak's White forces.
29 Czechoslovakian forces defeat Polish troops in a clash in the disputed Carpathian region.

FEBRUARY

- The U.S. Congress creates the Navy Distinguished Service Medal, to honor meritorious service in the war.

3 An international socialist conference in Bern, Switzerland, distances its democratically inclined members from communism.

3–9 General Anton Denikin's White Russian army routs the Bolsheviks in the Caucasus region.

6 A German national assembly convenes at Weimar, Germany, and on February 11 elects Friedrich Ebert as president of Germany. Philip Scheidemann forms a ministry of Social Democrat and Center Party members on February 12.

6 The Red Army captures Kiev, Ukraine, in the civil war in Russia.

14 The U.S. president Woodrow Wilson lays the draft League of Nations covenant before the Paris Peace Conference in France. It will be adopted on March 25.

20 Habibullah, the pro-British emir of Afghanistan, is murdered by nationalists.

28 Senator H. C. Lodge of the United States begins a campaign against the League of Nations.

MARCH

• Representatives from 1,000 units of the American Expeditionary Force establish the American Legion veterans organization in Paris, France.

• The U.S. Supreme Court upholds the conviction of Socialist leader Eugene V. Debs for violating the Espionage Act in a speech at Canton, Ohio in June 1918.

2 The Communist Third International (Comintern) is founded to encourage world revolution. The debate over affiliation to this body will mark the split between socialist and communist movements and parties.

3 The eighth congress of the Bolsheviks renames them the Russian Communist Party and establishes the Political Bureau ("Politburo"), Organization Bureau, and Secretariat.

8 Nationalist riots break out in Cairo, Egypt, when British authorities deport the nationalist leader Saad Zaghlul to Malta in order to prevent him attending the Paris Peace Conference in France.

12 The Austrian constitution declares Austria part of the German Republic, to be known as "German Austria."

16 The socialist Karl Renner is appointed chancellor of Austria.

19 A Spartacist (German communist) rising in the Ruhr region of Germany is put down by troops.

21 A soviet government is formed in Budapest, Hungary, under the revolutionary leader Béla Kun.

23 Benito Mussolini founds the Fasci d'Italiani di Combattimento, an Italian fascist movement.

28 Hungary declares war on Czechoslovakia over disputed areas of Slovakia.

APRIL

4 The Philippines demand independence from the United States.

4–May 1 A soviet republic is established in Bavaria, Germany, by communists, following a radicalization of politics in the wake of the assassination of Kurt Eisner.

8 The Allies are driven out of their base at Odessa, Ukraine, by the Red Army.

10 Romania invades Hungary to prevent it attempting to retake disputed Transylvania.

13 Gurkha troops of the British Army fire on a protesting crowd in northern India in what becomes known as the "Amritsar Massacre," killing 379 people and wounding over 1,200 more.

19 Polish forces recapture the disputed city of Vilna (modern Vilnius), Lithuania, from the Red Army and begin to advance into Belarus.

28 Germany's delegates arrive at the Paris Peace Conference in France to be informed of the Allies' peace terms.

28 The Red Army in Russia begins a counteroffensive against the White forces in Siberia under Admiral Kolchak.

29 The Dodecanese Islands vote to return to Greece, having been under Italian rule since 1912.

30 The Paris Peace Conference grants the German concession in the Shandong peninsula of China to Japan, and China abandons the talks.

MAY

• Violence erupts at May Day rallies throughout the United States, as antiradical vigilantes confront workers emboldened by the events of the Russian Revolution.

1 Bavarian government troops capture Munich, Germany, from the communists, ending the rule of the soviet.

3 War begins between British India and Afghanistan following Afghanistan's demand for complete independence. On August 8 a peace will be agreed at Rawalpindi (now in Pakistan), conceding independence.

4 Riots break out in Beijing and other Chinese cities following the news that the Paris Peace Conference has confirmed Japanese holdings in China.

7 At the Paris Peace Conference in France, the Allies present their terms to Germany without giving opportunity for negotiation. The Rhineland is to be demilitarized and semioccupied for between 5 and 15 years, reparations are to be paid, limits will be placed on the size of Germany's armed forces, and it is to accept a "war guilt" clause acknowledging responsibility for starting the European War. Germany's colonies are also disposed of, assigning German East Africa to Britain as a mandated territory of the League of Nations, and German South West Africa as a mandate under the administration of South Africa.

15 With Allied support and the protection of Allied ships, a Greek force occupies Smyrna (modern Izmir in Turkey) to further its territorial claims in the region.

28 Armenia declares its independence from Anatolia (modern Turkey).

29 Germany's delegates make counterproposals to the Paris Peace Conference in France.

30 At the Paris Peace Conference in France, Britain agrees to the transfer of part of German South West Africa to Belgium.

JUNE

6 Finland declares war on Bolshevik Russia following a territorial dispute over the Karelian isthmus.

9 The Russian Red Army takes Ufa in Siberia from White forces.

10 Austria protests against the terms of the Paris Peace Conference.

19 Mustafa Kemal and other Turkish nationalist leaders sign the Amasia Protocol, declaring their determination to resist the Allies' plans to partition the Turkish Empire and to resist the sultan's cooperation with the Allies.

20 The German chancellor, Philip Scheidemann, resigns in opposition to the Treaty of Versailles, which dictates pace terms unfavorable to Germany. The Social Democrat Gustav Bauer forms a cabinet comprising Social Democrats, Center Party delegates, and Democrats on June 21.

21 Francesco Nitti becomes prime minister of Italy following the fall of Vittorio Orlando on June 19.

21 German sailors scuttle the "Grand Fleet" in Scapa Flow, the British naval base in the Orkney Islands where the fleet has been quartered since the end of World War I, to prevent it falling into Allied hands following the signing of the Treaty of Versailles.

22 The German national assembly at Weimar, Germany, authorizes the signature of the Treaty of Versailles.

28 Britain and the United States guarantee French security in the event of an unprovoked German attack, though the U.S. Senate later refuses to ratify the treaty.

28 German representatives sign the peace treaty ending the 1914–18 war in the Hall of Mirrors of the Palace of Versailles near Paris, France (for terms, see May 7).

JULY

• A race riot erupts in Washington, D.C., where recently returned white soldiers rampage through black neighborhoods, attacking inhabitants at random. Chicago, Illinois, explodes in racial conflagration after white bathers attack a black swimmer for straying onto a segregated lake-front beach. Before order is restored 23 blacks and 15 whites are killed.

• In what might be described as the most significant nonevent of the mounting "Red Scare" (fear of a communist revolt), police forces throughout the United States brace for a radical insurrection that never materializes.

• The U.S. president Woodrow Wilson submits the Treaty of Versailles and League of Nations covenant to the U.S. Senate.

• The U.S. State Department lifts the ban on trade with Germany.

4 President José Pardo of Peru is overthrown and is succeeded by the reforming Augusto Leguía on August 24.

12 A modification of French electoral law makes it more difficult for a government to obtain a parliamentary majority.

12 Britain and France authorize the resumption of commercial relations with Germany following the signing of the Treaty of Versailles.

12 The Unionist British member of Parliament Edward Carson demands the repeal of the 1914 Home Rule for Ireland Bill, and threatens to call out the Ulster Volunteers to oppose it.

23 A congress of Turkish nationalists convenes at Erzurum, Anatolia (modern Turkey), under the leadership of Mustafa Kemal, to resist the Allied dismemberment of Anatolia. A second congress will be held on September 4.

31 The German national assembly promulgates the "Weimar constitution," establishing proportional representation and giving the president powers to govern by decree in a national emergency.

AUGUST

1 The Hungarian socialist regime under Béla Kun falls in the face of the advance of the Romanian army.

4–November 14 The Romanian army occupies Budapest, Hungary, in support of Romania's claim to the disputed territory of Transylvania.

5 William Mackenzie King is elected leader of the Canadian Liberal Party.

6 Archduke Joseph becomes "state governor" of Hungary, but resigns on August 23 at the demand of the Allies.

9 Britain and Persia make an agreement at Tehran, Persia, to preserve the integrity of Persia.

25 The wartime coalition government in New Zealand breaks up, though William Massey remains prime minister of a Reform Party government.

SEPTEMBER

• Catching the spirit of the mounting "Red Scare," U.S. president Woodrow Wilson decries "the poison of disorder, the poison of revolt, the poison of chaos" that is forcing its way "into the veins of this free people."

• Despite evidence of mounting physical and psychological exhaustion, the U.S. president Woodrow Wilson departs on a nationwide campaign to win ratification of the Treaty of Versailles.

1 The U.S. Socialist Party, meeting in Chicago, Illinois, splits into factions, including a Communist Party and a Communist Labor Party. The latter adopts the platform of the Third International (Comintern).

2 General Anton Denikin's White Russian army takes Kiev, Ukraine, from the communists.

10 Austria signs a treaty of peace with the Allies at St.-Germain-en-Laye near Paris, France, in which Austria recognizes the independence of Poland, Czechoslovakia, Hungary, and the Kingdom of the Serbs, Croats, and Slovenes, and agrees not to ally with Germany. Its name subsequently changes from German Austria to the Republic of Austria.

12 The poet and nationalist Gabriele d'Annunzio leads an unofficial Italian army to seize the northern Adriatic port of Fiume (now Rijeka, Croatia) before it is incorporated into the Kingdom of the Serbs, Croats, and Slovenes.

15 China officially terminates its war with Germany, having not signed the Treaty of Versailles in protest at the transfer of German concessions and colonies to Japan.

25 The Paris Peace Conference grants Norway sovereignty over the island of Spitsbergen in the Arctic Ocean.

25 The U.S. president Woodrow Wilson suffers a breakdown in Denver, Colorado, while on a national speaking tour in aid of securing Senate ratification of the Treaty of Versailles.

27 The League of Nations refers the Polish-Czech dispute over Upper Silesia to a plebiscite.

30 British troops are withdrawn from Archangel, Russia, which is subsequently occupied by the Red Army.

OCTOBER

2 Three weeks into a nationwide campaign to secure Senate ratification of the Treaty of Versailles, President Woodrow Wilson suffers a stroke in Wichita, Kansas, after suffering a breakdown in Denver, Colorado, on September 25.

7 Sir Edmund Allenby becomes British high commissioner in Egypt.

10 A referendum in Luxembourg returns a vote in favor of the monarchy and economic union with France.
12 British troops withdraw from Murmansk, Russia.
13 General Anton Denikin's White Russian army captures Orel, southwest of Moscow, Russia, but is soon driven out by the Red Army.
22 The Bolshevik Red Army defeats an advancing White force under General Nikolay Yudenich near Petrograd, Russia.
27 The U.S. president Woodrow Wilson vetoes the Volstead Prohibition Enforcement Bill, but the House of Representatives and the Senate overturn his veto.

NOVEMBER

• The U.S. House of Representatives unseats Wisconsin Socialist Victor Berger for his allegedly incendiary socialist views.
• The U.S. Supreme Court, in *Abrams v. USA*, upholds the imminent deportation of Russian nationals opposed to U.S. intervention in Russia. Writing in dissent, justice Oliver Wendell Holmes, Jr., cautions against abridging free speech in all but the most exigent circumstances.
7 The Allied Supreme Council demands the withdrawal of Romanian troops from Hungary.
11 For the first time in Britain, a two minutes' silence is observed in memory of war victims, at 11a.m.
14 Romanian troops evacuate Hungary, having occupied it since April.
14 The Bolshevik Red Army takes Omsk, Russia, from the forces of Admiral Kolchak and pushes them back into Siberia.
19 In a 55–39 vote the U.S. Senate rejects the Treaty of Versailles, leaving the United States outside the League of Nations.
20 German troops are forced to evacuate Latvia and Lithuania under the terms of the Treaty of Versailles.
25 Sinn Féin is outlawed in Ireland as a criminal organization.
27 The Peace of Neuilly formally ends the war between the Allies and Bulgaria, with Bulgaria recognizing the independence of the Kingdom of the Serbs, Croats, and Slovenes and agreeing to pay reparations.

DECEMBER

5 The Kingdom of the Serbs, Croats, and Slovenes agrees to peace treaties with Austria and Bulgaria.
9 U.S. delegates leave the Paris Peace Conference, France.
13 The Red Army captures the Ukrainian city of Kharkov from the White forces of General Anton Denikin.
17 The Red Army expels Anton Denikin's White forces from Kiev, Russia.
20 The U.S. House of Representatives moves to curtail immigration.

SCIENCE, TECHNOLOGY, AND MEDICINE

Agriculture

c. 1919 Crop dusting begins in the United States, using World War I surplus airplanes.

• Japanese-American farmers in California own more than 18,000 hectares/45,000 acres of land and produce about 10% of the state's vegetables.

Ecology

• Grand Canyon National Park, Arizona, is established. Covering 4,931 sq km/1,904 sq mi, it preserves 160 km/100 mi of the Grand Canyon.
• Mt. Kelud in Java erupts violently. Volcanic ash mixes with 38 million cu m/50 million cu yd of water in the lake of the volcano's crater, producing mud flows that kill 5,100 people.
• Norwegian meteorologists Vilhelm and Jakob Bjerknes introduce the term "front" in meteorology (after the military front), which describes the transition zone between two masses of air differing in density and temperature.
• The U.S. Congress creates Lafayette National Park on Mt. Desert Island, Maine, a 2,000 hectare/5,000 acre gift from U.S. oil magnate John D. Rockefeller. The park will be renamed Acadia National Park in 1929.
• Zion National Park, Utah, is established; it contains deep canyons, high cliffs, and evidence of prehistoric humans.

Exploration

• U.S. inventor Robert Hutching Goddard publishes "A Method of Reaching Extreme Altitudes," which outlines the use of rockets as a means to reach the moon.

Health and Medicine

• Belgian bacteriologist Jules Bordet receives the Nobel Prize for Physiology or Medicine for his discoveries relating to immunity.
• U.S. photography entrepreneur George Eastman founds the Eastman School of Medicine and Dentistry at the University of Rochester, New York.
• U.S. physician Louise Pearce develops tryparsamide, a synthetic drug used in the treatment of sleeping sickness.

Math

• English philosopher Bertrand Russell publishes *Introduction to Mathematical Philosophy*.

Science

• Austrian zoologist Karl von Frisch discovers that bees communicate the location of nectar through wagging body movements and rhythmic dances.
• English physicist Francis Aston builds the first mass-spectrograph, which allows him to separate ions or isotopes of the same element.
• English physicist Francis Aston confirms that the element neon consists of two isotopes of different masses. Their relative abundances explain the observed atomic weight of 20.25.

- German physicist Johannes Stark receives the Nobel Prize for Physics for showing that an electric field splits the spectral lines of hydrogen and for predicting that high-velocity rays of positive ions will demonstrate the Doppler effect.
- New Zealand-born British physicist Ernest Rutherford splits the atom by bombarding a nitrogen nucleus with alpha particles, discovering that it ejects hydrogen nuclei (protons). It is the first artificial disintegration of an element and inaugurates the development of nuclear energy.
- The International Astronomical Union (IAU) is founded to promote international cooperation in astronomy.
- The Society of Antiquaries of London, England, begins excavations at Stonehenge, England.
- U.S. astronomer William Pickering predicts the existence and location of the planet Pluto.

MAY

29 English astrophysicist Arthur Eddington and others observe the total eclipse of the sun on Príncipe Island (West Africa), and discover that the sun's gravity bends the light from the stars beyond the edge of the eclipsed sun, thus confirming Albert Einstein's theory of relativity.

Technology

- Dutch inventor Hugo Koch discovers the rotor concept for deciphering coded messages; it develops into the German Enigma cipher machine.
- John Rawlings develops the Rawlplug, a wall-fixing for screws, in Britain.
- The U.S. Navy develops the Hayes sonic depth finder. It consists of a device that generates sound waves and receives their echo from the ocean floor. A timing device indicates the depth of the water.
- U.S. car manufacturer Elwood Haynes patents a nonrusting stainless steel.

Transportation

- André Citroën launches the Citroën car in France.
- German aircraft designer Hugo Junkers builds the J-13, the first all-metal transport airplane.
- The airline KLM (Koninklijkje Luchtvaart Maatschappij voor Nederland an Kolonien/Royal Dutch Air Transportation Service for the Netherlands and the Colonies) is founded in the Netherlands.
- The British ship *Hermes* is launched. It is the first purpose-built aircraft carrier.
- U.S. inventor Henry Berliner makes the first successful helicopter flight.
- W. O. Bentley launches the Bentley car in Britain.

FEBRUARY

25 Oregon is the first U.S. state to impose a state tax on gasoline.

MAY

16–27 A U.S. Navy Curtiss-4 is the first airplane to cross the Atlantic Ocean. Piloted by Lieutenant Commander Albert C. Read, it flies from the United States to England via Newfoundland, the Azores, and Portugal.

JUNE

14–15 British aviators John Alcock and Arthur Whitten Brown fly, in a Vickers-Vimy twin-engined biplane, from Newfoundland to Ireland in 16 hr 12 min, winning the £10,000 prize offered by the *Daily Mail* for the first nonstop transatlantic flight.

JULY

2–13 The British dirigible *R-34* makes the first round-trip Atlantic crossing, flying from New York, New York, to London, England, and back.

SEPTEMBER

10 The "Avus" autobahn opens in Berlin, Germany. The world's first controlled access highway, it is 10 km/6.2 mi long.

18 U.S. pilot Roland Rohls sets a world altitude record of 10,643 m/34,919 ft, in a Curtiss "Wasp."

NOVEMBER

12–December 10 Australian aviators Ross and Keith Macpherson-Smith fly from London, England, to Darwin, Australia, in a Vickers-Vimy twin-engine biplane with two passengers. It is the first flight from England to Australia.

ARTS AND IDEAS

Architecture

- The Bauhaus school of design, architecture, and crafts is founded in Weimar, Germany, by the German architect Walter Gropius. It is transferred to Dessau in 1926.
- The Spaarndammerbuurt housing complex in Amsterdam, the Netherlands, designed by the Dutch architect Michel de Klerk, is completed.

Arts

- German artist Hannah Hoch creates the photomontage *Schnitt mit dem Küchenmesser (durch die letzte Weimarer Bierbuche-Epoche Deutschlands)/Cut With The Kitchen Knife (Through the Last Weimar Beer Belly Cultural Epoch)*.
- The English artist Alfred Munnings paints *Zennor Hill*.
- The English artist Stanley Spencer paints *Travoys Arriving with Wounded at a Dressing Station at Smol, Macedonia*.
- The French artist Fernand Léger paints *Men in the City*.
- The French artist Marcel Duchamp creates the work *L H O O Q*, a reproduction of the painting *Mona Lisa*, on which he has painted a moustache.
- The German artist Ernst Barlach sculpts *Veiled Beggar Woman*.
- The Italian artist Amedeo Modigliani paints *Portrait of Jeanne Hébuterne in a Sash* and *Self-Portrait*.
- The Russian artist El Lissitzky creates the poster *Beat the Whites with the Red Wedge*.
- The U.S. artist Georgia O'Keeffe paints *Black Spot, No 2*.

Film

- Charlie Chaplin, D. W. Griffith, Mary Pickford, and Douglas Fairbanks found the movie studio United Artists.
- The movie *Blind Husbands*, directed by Erich von Stroheim, is released in Austria. Von Stroheim also stars in it. Also his movie *The Devil's Pass Key* is released in Austria, starring Una Trevelyan and Sam De Grasse.
- The movie *Broken Blossoms*, directed by D. W. Griffith, is released in the United States, starring Lillian Gish and Richard Barthelmess.
- The movie *Don't Change Your Husband*, directed by Cecil B. De Mille, is released in the United States, starring Gloria Swanson. His movie *Male and Female*, starring Gloria Swanson, Bebe Daniels, and Thomas Meighan, is also released in the United States.
- The movie *J'Accuse/I Accuse*, directed by Abel Gance, is released in France, starring Romuald Joubé. Gance remakes the film in 1937.
- The movie *Madame Dubarry* or *Passion*, directed by Ernst Lubitsch, is released in Germany, starring Pola Negri.
- The movie *Sunnyside*, directed by Charlie Chaplin, is released in the United States. Chaplin also stars in it with Edna Purviance.
- The movie *The Cabinet of Dr Caligari*, directed by Robert Wiene, is released in Germany, starring Wener Krauss and Conrad Veidt.
- The movie *The Spiders*, directed by Fritz Lang, is released in Germany.
- The movie *Tih-Minh*, directed by Louis Feuillade, is released in France.
- The State School of Cinematography is established in Moscow, Russia, the first movie school in the world.
- The U.S. director D. W. Griffith's movie *Intolerance*, released in 1916, is at last shown in France, but in a heavily cut form, because of its allegedly biased representation of French history.

FEBRUARY

26 The French Directors' Union decides to ban the screening of German and Austrian movies in France for 15 years in view of the recent war.

AUGUST

- Russian leader Vladimir Ilyich Lenin nationalizes Russia's movie industry.

Literature and Language

- The Bohemian-born German writer Franz Kafka publishes his collection of tales *Ein Landarzt/The Country Doctor*.
- The English writer Daisy Ashford publishes her novel *The Young Visiters*, written in 1890 when she was nine.
- The English writer Somerset Maugham publishes his novel *The Moon and Sixpence*.
- The French writer André Gide publishes his novella *La Symphonie pastorale/The Pastoral Symphony*.
- The French writer Marcel Proust publishes *A l'ombre des jeunes filles en fleurs/Within a Budding Grove*, the second volume of his multivolume novel *A la recherche du temps perdu/Remembrance of Things Past*.

- The German writer Hermann Hesse publishes his novel *Demian*.
- The Italian writer Giuseppe Ungaretti publishes his poetry collection *Allegria di naufragi/Happy Shipwrecks*.
- The Japanese writer Toson Shimazaki publishes his novel *Shinsei/A New Life*.
- The Pulitzer Prize for Biography is posthumously awarded to Henry Adams for his autobiography *The Education of Henry Adams: A Study of 20th Century Multiplicity* and the Prize for Fiction is awarded to Booth Tarkington for *The Magnificent Ambersons*. Special Pulitzer Prizes for Poetry, made possible by a gift from the Poetry Society, are awarded to Carl Sandburg for *Corn Huskers* and Margaret Widdemer for *Old Road to Paradise*.
- The U.S. journalist H. L. Mencken publishes *The American Language*.
- The U.S. writer James Branch Cabell publishes his novel *Jurgen*.
- The U.S. writer Sherwood Anderson publishes his short-story collection *Winesburg, Ohio*.
- The U.S.-born English writer T. S. Eliot publishes his poetry collection *Poems*, which includes "Gerontion."

Music

- Paul Whiteman forms his jazz orchestra, in San Francisco, California.
- The Czech composer Leoš Janáček completes his song cycle *Zápisník zmizelého/Diary of a One Who Disappeared*.
- The French composer Gabriel Fauré completes his orchestral suite *Masques et bergamasques*.
- The French composer Maurice Ravel completes his orchestral suite *Le Tombeau de Couperin/The Tomb of Couperin*, based on a piano work of 1917.
- The French composer Germaine Tailleferre completes her *Piano Concerto*.
- The opera *Die Frau ohne Schatten/The Woman without a Shadow* by the German composer Richard Strauss is first performed, in Vienna, Austria.
- The operetta *Monsieur Beaucaire* by the French composer André Messager is first performed, in Birmingham, England.
- The Swedish composer Hugo Alfvén completes his Symphony No. 4.
- The U.S. composer Aaron Copland completes his piano work *The Cat and the Mouse*.
- The U.S. composer Charles Griffes completes his orchestral work *The White Peacock*.
- The U.S. composer Irving Berlin writes the song "A Pretty Girl is Like a Melody."

APRIL

7 The Original Dixieland Jazz Band makes its debut in London, England, and its song "Tiger Rag" becomes very popular.

Theater and Dance

- The ballet *Le Tricorn/The Three-Cornered Hat* is first performed, in Paris, France, by the Ballets Russes under the Russian impresario Sergei Diaghilev. The music is by the Spanish composer Manuel de Falla, costumes and stage designs by the Spanish artist Pablo Picasso, and choreography by the Russian choreographer Léonide Massine.

- The play *The Exiles*, by the Irish writer James Joyce, is first performed, in Munich, Germany. It is first performed in English in 1926, in London, England.
- The Pulitzer Prize for Drama is not awarded this year.

APRIL

9 The play *The Jest*, by U.S. dramatist Edward Shelton, is first performed, at the Plymouth Theater in New York, New York.

AUGUST

- Stage actors strike throughout the United States in order to win recognition of the Actors' Equity Association.

Thought and Scholarship

- Dutch historian Johan Huizinga publishes *Herfsttijd der middeleeuwen/The Waning of the Middle Ages*.
- English economist John Maynard Keynes publishes *The Economic Consequences of the Peace*.
- English philosopher Alfred North Whitehead publishes *Enquiry Concerning the Principles of Natural Knowledge*.
- English social historians John Lawrence and Barbara Hammond publish *The Skilled Labourer, 1760–1832*.
- English writer Leonard Woolf publishes *Empire and Commerce in Africa: A Study in Economic Imperialism*.
- French philosopher Etienne Gilson publishes *Le Thomisme: Introduction au système de St. Thomas d'Aquin/The Philosophy of St. Thomas Aquinas*.
- German historian Frederick Meinecke publishes *Weltbürgertum und Nationalstaat/Cosmopolitanism and the National State*.
- German historian Oswald Spengler publishes his *Prussentum und Sozialismus/Prussianism and Socialism*.
- German philosopher Moritz Schlick publishes *Raum und Zeit in der gegenwärtigen Physik/Space and Time in Contemporary Physics*.
- German political thinker Karl Johann Kautsky publishes *Die Diktatur des Proletariats/The Dictatorship of the Proletariat*.
- The Nobel Prize for Literature is awarded to the Swiss poet and novelist Carl Spitteler.
- The Pulitzer Prize for History is not awarded this year.
- U.S. journalist John Reed publishes *Ten Days that Shook the World*, his account of the Russian Revolution.
- U.S. psychologist John Broadus Watson publishes *Psychology from the Standpoint of a Behaviourist*, in which he promotes the use of conditioning in behavioral research.

SOCIETY

Education

- The Carnegie Endowment for International Peace creates the Institute for International Education to promote student exchange.
- The University of California opens a campus at Los Angeles (UCLA).

Everyday Life

- The Australian cartoonist Otto Messmer and the U.S. animator Pat Sullivan create the animated cartoon character Felix the Cat.
- The first international fair of Dada art and literature is held, in Berlin, Germany.
- The first regular international civilian airmail service is set up between London, England, and Paris, France, by French aviators Maurice and Henri Farman. It is initially too expensive to catch on.
- The U.S. company Kellogg's launches the high-fiber cereal All-Bran.
- The U.S. inventor George B. Hansburg invents the pogo stick.

MAY

1–June 15 A mass strike is organized in Winnipeg, Canada.

JULY

1 A daily airmail service begins between New York, New York, and Chicago, Illinois.

SEPTEMBER

- A policemen's strike in Boston, Massachusetts, leads to widespread looting and prompts Massachusetts governor Calvin Coolidge to deny the "right to strike against the public safety by anybody, anywhere, at anytime."
- Steelworkers strike in Garry, Indiana, to compel United States Steel officials to recognize their union. By the year's end the strike remains unresolved.

OCTOBER

13 Dock workers strike in New York, New York.

Media and Communication

- *The Thrill Book* is launched, the first science-fiction magazine in the United States.
- The first radio station in Britain is established at Chelmsford, Essex. Using a 6 kW transmitter, two half-hour speech and music programs are broadcast daily. They are banned the following year for fear of commercialization.
- The General Electric Company creates the Radio Corporation of America (RCA), to take over the American Marconi Company in the United States.

JUNE

- The tabloid newspaper the *New York Daily News* is first published in New York, New York.

NOVEMBER

5 The Dutch radio station PCGG begins regular scheduled broadcasts from The Hague. It is the first European station to broadcast internationally, with programs being picked up in Britain and France, and has a specially designed weekly program transmitted in English, French, and Dutch.

Religion

- German theologian Karl Barth publishes *Der Römerbrief/The Epistle to the Romans*.

NOVEMBER

11 Pope Benedict XV ends the Roman Catholic Church's condemnation of Italians who take part in politics.

BIRTHS & DEATHS

JANUARY

1 J. D. Salinger U.S. novelist, author of *Catcher in the Rye*, born in New York, New York.

6 Theodore ("Teddy") Roosevelt, 26th president of the United States 1901–09, a Republican, dies in Oyster Bay, New York (60).

11 Eva Gabor, Hungarian-born U.S. actress, born in Budapest, Hungary (–1995).

14 Giulio Andreotti, Italian premier 1972–73, 1976–79, and 1989–92, born in Rome, Italy.

15 Karl Liebknecht, German Social Democrat who cofounded the Spartacus League which evolved into the German Communist Party, shot in Berlin, Germany (47).

31 Jackie Robinson, U.S. baseball player, the first black player in the major leagues, born in Cairo, Georgia (–1972).

FEBRUARY

5 Andreas Papandreou, premier of Greece 1981–89, 1993–96, born in Chios, Greece (–1996).

13 Tennessee Ernie Ford, U.S. country and western singer, born in Bristol, Tennessee (–1991).

17 Wilfrid Laurier, prime minister of Canada 1896–1911, a Liberal, dies in Ottawa, Ontario, Canada (77).

21 Kurt Eisner, German socialist leader, prime minister of Bavaria 1918–19, who organized the revolution that overthrew the Bavarian monarchy (1918), is assassinated in Munich, Germany, by the right wing nobleman Count Anton Arco-Valley (51).

MARCH

17 Nat "King" Cole, U.S. jazz and popular singer, born in Montgomery, Alabama (–1965).

APRIL

4 William Crookes, English physicist who discovered the element thallium, dies in London, England (86).

8 Ian Smith, first prime minister of Southern Rhodesia 1964–79 who proclaimed Rhodesia independent in 1965, born in Selukwe, Rhodesia.

9 John Presper Eckert, Jr., U.S. engineer who, with John W. Mauchley, invented ENIAC (Electronic Numerical Integrator and Calculator), the first electronic digital computer, born in Philadelphia, Pennsylvania (–1993).

10 Emiliano Zapata, Mexican revolutionary who led a guerrilla force during the Mexican Revolution, is ambushed and shot in Morelos, Mexico (39).

MAY

3 Pete Seeger, U.S. folk singer, born in New York, New York.

7 Eva Perón, unofficial Argentine political leader and wife of Juan Perón, born in Los Todos, Argentina (–1952).

JUNE

30 John William Strutt, Baron Rayleigh, English physicist who experimented in optics and microscopy, and (with William Ramsay) discovered and isolated the element argon, dies in Witham, Essex, England (76).

JULY

7 William Moses Kunstler, U.S. lawyer, known for representing radical groups including the Black Panthers and the Chicago Seven, born in New York, New York (–1995).

15 Emil Fischer, German chemist who investigated purines and sugars, dies in Berlin, Germany (66).

15 Iris Murdoch, Anglo-Irish novelist, born in Dublin, Ireland.

20 Edmund Hillary, New Zealand mountaineer who, with Nepalese sherpa Tenzing Norgay, was the first person to reach the summit of Mt. Everest (1953), born in Auckland, New Zealand.

AUGUST

9 Ernst Haeckel, German zoologist and evolutionist who believed that ontogeny recapitulates phylogeny, dies in Jena, Germany (85).

11 Andrew Carnegie, U.S. steel magnate and philanthropist, dies in Lenox, Massachusetts (83).

25 George Wallace, governor of Alabama, vehement opponent of racial integration, born in Clio, Alabama (–1998).

27 Louis Botha, first prime minister of South Africa (1910–19), dies in Pretoria, South Africa (56).

28 Godfrey Hounsfield, English electrical engineer who developed computerized axial tomography (CAT), born in Newark, Nottinghamshire, England.

SEPTEMBER

27 Adelina Patti (Adela Juana Patti), Italian soprano, dies in Craig-y-Nos Castle, Brecknockshire, Wales (76).

OCTOBER

18 Pierre Trudeau, prime minister of Canada 1969–79, 1980–84, a Liberal, born in Montreal, Quebec, Canada.

22 Doris Lessing, British writer, born in Kermanshah, Iran.

26 Muhammad Reza Shah Pahlavi, Shah of Iran 1941–79, born in Tehran, Persia (–1980).

NOVEMBER

29 Pearl Primus, U.S. dancer, choreographer, and dance teacher who pioneered an awareness and understanding of the black American tradition in dance, born in Trinidad (–1994).

DECEMBER

3 Pierre-Auguste Renoir, French impressionist painter, dies in Cannes, France (78).

18 John William Alcock, English aviator who made the first transatlantic flight (1919), dies in Cottévrard, France, when his plane crashes (27).

29 William Osler, Canadian physician who transformed medical training in North America by emphasizing clinical experience, dies in Oxford, England (70).

Sports

- An influenza epidemic leads to the abandonment of the Stanley Cup ice-hockey finals between the Montreal Canadiens and the Seattle Metropolitans.
- The world's first commercial greyhound race track with a mechanical hare is opened in Emeryville, California.

MAY

10–June 11 Sir Barton, ridden by U.S. jockey Johnny Loftus, wins the Kentucky Derby, Preakness, and Belmont Stakes to become the first horse to win the U.S. Triple Crown (though the term "triple crown" is not applied to this feat until 1930).

JULY

4 The U.S. boxer Jack Dempsey, the "Manassa Mauler," wins the world heavyweight title, beating fellow U.S. boxer Jess Willard in three rounds at Toledo, Ohio.
5 The French tennis player Suzanne Lenglen wins the first of five consecutive women's singles titles at the Wimbledon lawn tennis championships in London, England.

OCTOBER

1–9 The Chicago White Sox lose the U.S. World Series to the Cincinnati Reds by five games to three. Eight Sox players ("the Black Sox") are subsequently banned for life from major league baseball for conspiracy to "throw" the series, but an attempt to have them committed for fraud collapses when they are acquitted on a technicality.

1920

POLITICS, GOVERNMENT, AND ECONOMICS

Business and Economics

- A combination of a deflationary budget and a rise in the bank rate halts the economic boom in Britain, causing prices and output to fall steeply, while unemployment rises to over one million and remains there for the entire inter-war period. The U.S. economy also suffers a sharp slump.
- Italian-American entrepreneur Charles Ponzi creates a considerable stir in U.S. investment circles by promising Bostonians between 50% and 100% on their investment in three months or less with a program for using international reply coupons to make large profits. By mid-year, Ponzi's suspect investment program has caught the attention of the local district attorney; by the end of the year, it has precipitated the failure of six banks and defrauded over 20,000 investors of over $10 million. No money was in fact invested.
- Puerto Rican sugar traders Sosthenes and Hernand Behn create International Telephone and Telegraph (ITT) for the Puerto Rican and Cuban telephone and telegraph market.
- Qantas (Queensland and Northern Territories Aerial Services) Airways Ltd. is founded in Australia.

- The Curtiss Candy Company of Chicago, Illinois, introduces the Baby Ruth candy bar, named for the daughter of former president Grover Cleveland.
- The Suzuki Motor Co. is founded in Japan.
- Youngstown, Ohio, confectioner Harry Burt launches the Good Humor ice cream bar.

AUGUST

31 Half a million Italian steel and engineering workers begin occupying their factories and running them themselves following a lock out by employers. Prime Minister Giolitti intervenes and forces the owners to make concessions.

Colonization

MAY

5 Britain is awarded a mandate over Iraq by the Supreme Council of the Paris Peace Conference deciding terms for the end of World War II.

JULY

23 Britain annexes its East African Protectorate as Kenya Colony (a crown colony).
25 France occupies Damascus, Syria, in support of its mandate to govern, and King Feisal leaves the country.

DECEMBER

23 A Franco-British convention agrees the boundaries of Syria and Palestine.

Human Rights

- Four years after its foundation, Marcus Moziah Garvey's Universal Negro Improvement Association has taken root in most major U.S. cities, as Garvey accelerates his "back to Africa" movement.

- The U.S. suffragist Carrie Chapman Catt creates the League of Women Voters, providing newly enfranchised women with reliable, unbiased electoral information.
- U.S. social reformers Upton Sinclair, Jane Addams, Helen Keller, and Norman Thomas, among others, form the American Civil Liberties Union to protect Americans' civil liberties amid a climate of political reaction.

MAY

28 Jewish emancipation is granted in Romania.

AUGUST

- The 19th Amendment to the U.S. Constitution, granting women's suffrage, becomes law.

OCTOBER

30 The Ku Klux Klan parades in Jacksonville, Florida, indicating the group's prominence in the South as well as the Midwest.

Politics and Government

- A system of works councils is established in Germany, giving workers a share in the management of businesses.
- Following the establishment of the League of Nations, numerous countries become members, including Argentina (January 13), Switzerland (February 13), Norway (March 5), Denmark (March 8), the Netherlands (March 10), Austria (December 3), Bulgaria, Costa Rica, Finland, and Latvia (December 16), and Albania (December 17).
- Greek forces, encouraged by the British prime minister David Lloyd George, begin an offensive against the increasingly popular Turkish Nationalists of Mustapha Kemal. By July 9 the Greeks have occupied Bursa in western Anatolia (modern Turkey).
- The former French prime minister Joseph Caillaux is sentenced to three years in prison for trying to come to an arrangement with Germany during the European War.
- The Naval Research Laboratory, the world's first military research institution, is established in the United States.
- The Royal Institute of International Affairs (Chatham House) is founded in London, England.

JANUARY

2 The British government reinforces the Royal Irish Constabulary with ex-soldiers known as "Black and Tans" because of their temporary uniforms. They adopt a policy of reprisals for terrorist attacks, gaining a reputation for brutality. They are withdrawn after the truce of December 1921.

5 Polish and Latvian troops capture Dvinsk (now Daugavpils in Latvia) from the Bolsheviks.

8 In the Russian Civil War, the Red Army defeats a White army under Admiral Alexander Kolchak at Krasnoyarsk in south-central Siberia. Kolchak is executed by the Bolsheviks on February 7.

10 Plebiscites begin in the cantons of Eupen, Malmédy, and St. Vith, small territories along the German-Belgian border. Inhabited by Walloon and French speakers, these areas had been under Prussian/German rule from

1815 but were reassigned to Belgium in the Treaty of Versailles. Voting ends on July 23, with majorities favoring continued union with Belgium.

10 Ratification of the Treaty of Versailles brings the League of Nations into existence, with 29 initial members (out of 32 Allied signatories to the Versailles Treaty; the exceptions are the United States, China, Ecuador, and Nicaragua). The League has been created to adjudicate disputes between countries and generally to keep international peace.

10 The Supreme Allied Council transfers the border towns of Eupen and Malmédy from Germany to Belgium, a move which will be ratified by plebiscites later in the year.

16 The League of Nations' Council meets for the first time, in Paris, France.

16 The U.S. Senate votes against joining the League of Nations.

17 Paul Deschanel is elected president of France following Georges Clemenceau's fall over accusations that the Treaty of Versailles is too lenient. Deschanel takes office on February 18.

23 The government of the Netherlands rejects the demand of the Supreme Allied War Council that the former ruler of Germany, ex-Kaiser Wilhelm II, should be handed over for trial. Wilhelm continues to live in the Netherlands until his death in 1941.

28 The new Turkish parliament, with a nationalist majority, issues the Pact of Ankara, which affirms the integrity of Turkish territory based on the resolutions of the nationalist congresses of 1919.

FEBRUARY

2 In a treaty signed at Tartu in Estonia, the Bolsheviks recognize the independence of Estonia and renounce all claims to Russian sovereignty over the Baltic state.

8 The Red Army captures Odessa in the Ukraine from White Russian forces.

10 Under the terms of the Treaty of Versailles, a plebiscite is held in the northern zone of Schleswig (part of Germany inhabited by Danes). The result favors unification with Denmark. On March 14, voters in the middle zone vote in favor of remaining part of Germany.

13 Following differences with President Woodrow Wilson, Robert Lansing resigns as U.S. secretary of state at Wilson's request. On February 25 Wilson appoints Bainbridge Colby as secretary of state.

15 The Allies take over the important port of Memel (modern Klaipeda) in Lithuania, in response to conflict in the Baltic states.

26 In accordance with the Treaty of Versailles, the League of Nations takes over the Saar area between France and Germany; France takes control of the Saar's coal deposits.

27 The Allies, principally France and Britain, make preparations for a peace settlement with Anatolia (modern Turkey). They announce that Anatolia will retain Constantinople (modern Istanbul), but that the Dardanelles straits, linking the Mediterranean and the Black Sea, will be under international control.

28 A new Hungarian constitution is adopted, reflecting Hungary's status as an independent nation since the breakup of the Austro-Hungarian empire.

29   A constitution is adopted in Czechoslovakia, a new nation formed from the former provinces of Bohemia, Moravia, and Slovakia after the breakup of the Austro-Hungarian empire.

MARCH

1   The military commander in chief Admiral Miklós Horthy is elected regent of Hungary, pending a possible restoration of the Habsburg monarchy.

1   The U.S. Esch–Cummins Act returns railroads to private ownership and management.

10   The Ulster Unionist Council votes to accept the British Parliament's Government of Ireland Bill, partitioning Ireland into two states, north and south, each with its own Home Rule parliament.

11   A national congress in Syria proclaims Feisal (third son of King Hussein of the Hejaz) king of an independent Syria.

13–17   The "Kapp Putsch" takes place in Germany, the government fleeing when U.S.-born German journalist Wolfgang Kapp and his right-wing military supporters seize Berlin, Germany. However, a general strike prevents the conspirators from establishing their authority.

16   In response to growing nationalist agitation, Allied forces surround Constantinople, Anatolia (modern Istanbul, Turkey), and arrest and deport leading nationalists. The sultan of Anatolia closes the parliament.

27   Following the "Kapp Putsch" in Germany, Gustav Bauer resigns as German chancellor and is succeeded by Hermann Müller (also a Social Democrat).

27   The Red Army takes Novorossiisk on the Black Sea, precipitating the collapse of Anton Denikin's White Russian army. General Peter Wrangel takes command of White operations.

APRIL

•   A revolt against President Venustiano Carranza breaks out in Mexico, provoked by his attempt to force through the election of his nominee as his successor.

•   Five robbers murder a paymaster and guard at a shoe factory in South Braintree, Massachusetts, making off with $15,000. The U.S. anarchists Nicola Sacco and Bartolomeo Vanzetti are arrested for the murder on May 5.

6   German troops suppress a rebellion in the demilitarized Ruhr area.

6–May 17   In a countermeasure to the action of German troops in suppressing a rebellion in the Ruhr demilitarized area, French troops occupy Frankfurt, Darmstadt, and Hanau, Germany.

23   A new Turkish assembly opens at Ankara, Anatolia (modern Turkey), which elects the nationalist Mustafa Kemal as its president and proclaims a new constitution, the Law of Fundamental Organization.

25–October 12   A Polish offensive is launched under Józef Piłsudski, which aims to capture the Ukraine. The action begins the Polish–Russian War.

28   The Red Army takes Baku, the Caucasus, from General Peter Wrangel's White army.

30   Conscription, introduced as a wartime measure in 1916, is abolished in Britain.

MAY

•   President Woodrow Wilson issues an executive order protecting members of the Communist Labor Party from deportation.

5   The Treaty of Berlin ends the war between Germany and Latvia and recognizes Latvian independence.

7   During the Polish–Russian War, Polish and Ukrainian forces enter Kiev in the Ukraine, but are driven out by Bolshevik forces on June 11.

20   President Venustiano Carranza of Mexico is assassinated. In response the U.S. government suspends diplomatic relations with Mexico. Adolfo de la Huerta takes office as provisional president of Mexico.

27   President Woodrow Wilson of the United States vetoes the Knox peace resolution which would formally have terminated the state of war between the United States and Germany.

27   The Russian trade delegate Leonid Krassin arrives in London, England, in a first step to reestablishing vital trade links between Russia and Britain.

JUNE

•   The U.S. Congress passes the Merchant Marine Act, authorizing the sale of government ships to merchant shipping companies.

4   The Allies (principally France and Britain) agree the Treaty of Trianon with Hungary. It removes various territories from Hungary, imposes limits on Hungary's armed forces, and requires Hungary to pay reparations for damage inflicted by Austro-Hungarian forces during the war.

6   The first German elections since the signing of the Treaty of Versailles produce a swing away from the Social Democrats and the Center Party toward extremist parties.

11   The Red Army takes Kiev, Ukraine, from the Polish army in the continuation of the Polish–Russian War.

12   The Republican convention in Chicago, Illinois, nominates Ohio senator Warren G. Harding for president and Massachusetts governor Calvin Coolidge for vice president.

21   Konstantin Fehrenbach of the German Center Party becomes chancellor of Germany, his coalition government of Social Democrats and Center Party members being joined by members of the People's Party.

22   Greece, with the support of Britain, invades Anatolia (modern Turkey) in order to force it to accept the peace dictated by the Allies.

25   The Hague in the Netherlands is selected as the seat of the League of Nations' International Court of Justice.

JULY

1   The Canadian prime minister Robert Borden resigns because of ill health. He is succeded July 10 by Arthur Meighen.

5   Following a plebiscite held on February 10, northern Schleswig is transferred from German to Danish sovereignty.

5   The Democratic convention in San Francisco, California, nominates Ohio governor James M. Cox for president and assistant navy secretary Franklin D. Roosevelt for vice president.

5–16   The Allies and Germany meet at the Spa Conference in Belgium to discuss reparations, and fix a schedule for the payment for war damages (primarily to France, Britain, Belgium, and Italy).

6   Britain evacuates Batumi in Georgia to avoid a clash with Red Army troops advancing through the Caucasus region.

11   A plebiscite is held in East and West Prussia: a 97% majority of the inhabitants vote to remain in Germany rather than accept Polish sovereignty.

12   Russia and Lithuania sign a peace treaty in Moscow, Russia, under which Russia recognizes Lithuania's independence.

15   The Red Army takes Vilna (modern Vilnius), Lithuania, from the Polish army in a further stage of the Polish–Russian War.

21   King Feisal of Syria recognizes the French mandate over Syria.

23–August 31   Rioting in Belfast, Ireland, by Sinn Féin supporters and Unionists leaves around 30 people dead.

24   The Treaty of St. Germain-en-Laye between the Allies (principally Britain and France) and Austria (signed September 19, 1919) comes into force.

25   Greek forces under King Alexander of Greece occupy Adrianople, Anatolia (modern Turkey), during the Greek-Turkish war.

27   Russian forces take Pinsk and invade Poland, opening a new phase of the Polish–Russian War.

28   The Teschen (Cieszyn) Agreement, which divides the territory disputed between Czechoslovakia and Poland, is signed in Paris, France.

AUGUST

8   Russia, with its forces advancing on Warsaw, Poland, rejects proposals for an armistice with Poland.

10   Greece and Italy agree a treaty assigning the Dodecanese islands (except Rhodes) in the southeast Aegean Sea to Greece. Sovereignty over Rhodes is to be determined by a plebiscite after 15 years.

10   The Allies, Romania, Czechoslovakia, and Poland sign the New States Treaty, while Romania, Czechoslovakia, and the Kingdom of the Serbs, Croats, and Slovenes sign the Frontier Treaty.

10   The Treaty of Sèvres is signed, ending the war between the Ottoman Empire and the Allies. Under the terms of the agreement the Empire is broken up. Mesopotamia and Palestine become British mandates and Syria becomes a French mandate. Part of eastern Thrace, Smyrna (modern Izmir), and other territory is awarded to Greece, Rhodes is awarded to Italy, the Hejaz region becomes independent, and the Dardanelles are internationalized.

11   Russia and Latvia sign the Riga Treaty, in which Russia recognizes Latvia's independence.

14   The Kingdom of the Serbs, Croats, and Slovenes and Czechoslovakia make an alliance (and are joined in 1921 by Romania) to form the "Little Entente," a defensive measure against Hungarian revanchism (a policy aimed at regaining lost territories).

14–16   Polish forces under Józef Piłsudski defeat the advancing Russian troops led by Mikhail Tukhachevski at Warsaw, Poland.

18   The Milner–Zaghlul agreement is made following discussions between Lord Alfred Milner for Britain and the Egyptian nationalist leader, Saad Zaghlul. Britain agrees in principle to recognizing the independence of

Egypt, provided that the two countries make a close alliance.

19   Polish forces, counterattacking after their victory at Warsaw, enter Brest-Litovsk in western Russia, during the Polish–Russian War.

SEPTEMBER

•   Terrorists target the office of the U.S. banking magnate J. P. Morgan on Wall Street in New York, New York, detonating a bomb that kills 30 people, injures 200, and causes an estimated $2 million damage.

5   Alvaro Obregón is elected president of Mexico and takes office on December 1.

7   France and Belgium agree a military convention under which they will cooperate in any international action.

10   Negotiations between Russia and Britain are suspended following an alleged Russian attempt to subsidize the British newspaper the *Daily Herald*.

23   Alexandre Millerand succeeds Paul Deschanel as president of France, the latter having resigned on September 15 because of ill health.

OCTOBER

1   A new constitution is adopted in Austria, an independent state since the breakup of the Austro-Hungarian Empire.

9   Advancing Polish forces annex the disputed city of Vilna (modern Vilnius) from Lithuania, which laid siege to it following the Red Army's withdrawal on August 24.

10   A plebiscite in the former Habsburg duchy of Carinthia favors joining Austria.

12   Russia and Poland sign a peace treaty to end their war, at Tartu, Estonia, signing a full treaty on March 18, 1921.

20   France and Anatolia (modern Turkey) sign the Treaty of Ankara.

20   The United States and China sign a tariff treaty.

24   Terence MacSwiney, the Republican mayor of Cork, Ireland, dies in a hunger strike.

27   Poland signs a treaty with Danzig (modern Gdańsk in Poland), making it a free city under the Treaty of Versailles.

27   The League of Nations' headquarters are moved to Geneva, Switzerland.

NOVEMBER

2   The Republican Warren G. Harding wins the U.S. presidential election with 404 electoral votes, the Democrat James M. Cox taking 127 votes. In the popular vote Harding wins 16,152,200 votes, Cox wins 9,147,353, and the socialist Eugene V. Debs (in prison) takes 919,799. In Congressional elections, Republicans retain majorities in the House (301–131) and Senate (59–37).

12   Under the Treaty of Rapallo, Italy gains Istria but cedes Dalmatia to the Kingdom of the Serbs, Croats, and Slovenes. The city of Fiume (now Rijeka, Croatia) is to be independent.

14   The general election in Greece results in a crushing defeat for the supporters of the prime minister Eleutherios Venizelos. Popular opinion is unsupportive of the war with Anatolia (modern Turkey).

14   The Russian Red Army takes Sevastopol in the Crimea. With the evacuation of General Peter Wrangel's White forces to Constantinople, Anatolia (modern Turkey), the civil war in Russia is effectively over, with the communists victorious.

15 Danzig (modern Gdańsk in Poland) is proclaimed a free city under the terms of the Treaty of Versailles. In early December its constitutional assembly is proclaimed the city parliament. Close commercial ties with Poland are confirmed.

17 Following the death of King Alexander, dowager Queen Olga becomes regent of Greece.

21 Members of the Irish Republican Army (IRA) kill 11 British officers on "Bloody Sunday" in Dublin, Ireland. Later the same day, British irregular policemen (the "Black and Tans") fire into a soccer crowd, killing 12.

28 Eighteen policemen are ambushed and killed by the Irish Republican Army (IRA) in County Cork, Ireland.

DECEMBER

2 Following the Turkish attack on Armenia, the Treaty of Alexandropol is concluded and Armenia cedes territory to Anatolia (modern Turkey).

5 A plebiscite in Greece following the death of King Alexander favors the return of the former king, Constantine, who abdicated under Allied pressure in 1917. On December 19 he returns to Greece.

9 Michael Hainisch is elected first president of Austria.

10 The former U.S. president Woodrow Wilson and the former French prime minister Léon Bourgeois are awarded the Nobel Peace Prize for their work in creating the League of Nations.

12 Martial law is imposed in Cork, Ireland, following Irish Republican Army (IRA) attacks on the authorities.

15–22 An international conference meets in Brussels, Belgium, to discuss German reparations.

23 The British Parliament passes the Government of Ireland Bill, by which Southern Ireland (26 counties) and Northern Ireland (6 counties) are each to have their own parliaments.

27 Italian troops force the revolutionary nationalist Gabriele D'Annunzio and his troops out of Fiume, Italy (now Rijeka, Croatia).

30 A conference of the French Socialist Party at Tours, France, votes for membership in the Third International (Comintern), and the party becomes the French Communist Party. A minority, led by Léon Blum, secede to form a new French Socialist Party.

SCIENCE, TECHNOLOGY, AND MEDICINE

Agriculture

• The British Agricultural Act establishes price supports for farm produce in response to an agricultural depression.

Ecology

• Forest coverage in the United States reaches a historic low point.

December, 1920–1921 Drought in northern China results in 500,000 deaths.

DECEMBER

16 Kansu province, China, experiences an earthquake estimated to measure 8.5 on the Richter scale; over 200,000 die.

Health and Medicine

• U.S. pathologist George Whipple discovers that feeding liver to dogs restores their hemoglobin levels. It leads to liver treatment for pernicious anemia.

Science

• Belgian-born U.S. chemist Julius Nieuwland discovers that acetylene molecules can be polymerized to form a rubber-like substance.

• Danish physicist Niels Bohr introduces the correspondence principle, which relates the motion of particles to the radiation emitted.

• Danish physiologist Schack Krogh receives the Nobel Prize for Physiology or Medicine for his discovery of the capillary motor regulating mechanism.

• English physicist Frederick Soddy suggests that isotopes can be used to determine geological age.

• French physicist Charles Guillaume receives the Nobel Prize for Physics for his discovery of anomalies in alloys and the discovery of the nickle-steel alloy Invar.

• German astronomer Walter Baade discovers the asteroid Hidalgo, which is unusual in that its orbit is tilted out of the plane of the solar system by 43°.

• German chemist Walther Nernst receives the Nobel Prize for Chemistry for work on thermochemistry.

• New Zealand-born British physicist Ernest Rutherford recognizes the hydrogen nucleus as the fundamental particle and names it the "proton."

• Russian botanist Nikolay Ivanovich Vavilov states that a plant's place of origin is the region where its greatest diversity is found. He identifies 12 world centers of plant origin.

• U.S. physicist Albert Michelson, using a stellar interferometer, measures the diameter of the star Betelgeuse to be 386,160,000 km/241,350,000 mi, which is about 300 times the diameter of the sun. It is the first time an accurate measurement of the size of a star other than the sun has been made.

Technology

• Austrian inventor Viktor Kaplan develops a turbine with variable-angle blades that match the angle of the water for a given flow, thus improving their efficiency.

• The U.S. inventor James Smathers pioneers the electric typewriter as an office machine.

DECEMBER

• U.S. gunsmith John Thompson patents the submachine gun. Popular with gangsters during prohibition, it is called the "Tommy gun" and is adopted by the U.S. Army in 1928.

Transportation

c. 1920 Commercial passenger flights between major cities, especially in the United States and Europe, begin.
- The British ship SS *Victoria* is the first ocean liner to have a radio telephone.
- There are 253,000 miles of railroad track in the United States.

December
22 A train wreck in Petrograd, Russia, kills 212.

ARTS AND IDEAS

Arts

- Soviet leader Joseph Stalin's disapproval of the avant-garde leads to the departure of many artists from Russia. Kasimir Malevich and Vladimir Tatlin remain.
- The Austrian artist and writer Raoul Hausmann creates the photomontage *The Art Critic*.
- The English art critic Roger Fry publishes *Vision and Design*, a collection of essays.
- The English potter Bernard Leach establishes the Leach Pottery at St. Ives in Cornwall, England.
- The French artist Fernand Léger paints *The Mechanic*.
- The French photographer Jacques Henri Lartigue takes *Bibi at the Restaurant d'Eden Roc, Cap d'Antibes*.
- The German artist Ernst Barlach sculpts *The Refugee*.
- The Italian artist Mario Sironi paints *The White Horse and the Pier*.
- The Russian artist Naum Gabo creates *Kinetic Sculpture* and sculpts *Head of a Woman*.
- The Russian artists Antoine Pevsner and Naum Gabo, brothers, issue the *Realist Manifesto*, containing the principles of constructivism, a movement in abstract art which influences later art and architecture.
- The Spanish artist Juan Gris paints *Guitar, Book, and Newspaper*.
- The Spanish artist Pablo Picasso paints *Seated Woman*.
- The U.S. artist Jo Davidson sculpts *Portrait of Gertrude Stein*.

Film

- The movie *Anna Boleyn*, directed by Ernst Lubitsch, is released in Germany.
- The movie *Blade af Satan's Bog/Leaves from Satan's Book*, directed by Carl Dreyer, is released in Denmark.
- The movie *Dr Jekyll and Mr Hyde*, directed by John S. Robertson, is released in the United States. Based on the novel by Robert Louis Stevenson, it stars John Barrymore.
- The movie *Erotikon*, directed by Finnish filmmaker Mauritz Stiller, is released in Germany.
- The movie *The Golem*, directed by Paul Wegener and Carl Boese, is released in Germany.
- The movie *The Love Flower*, directed by D. W. Griffith, is released in the United States, starring Richard Barthelmess and Carol Dempster. Also his movie *Way Down East* is released in the United States, starring Lillian Gish and Richard Barthelmess.
- The movie *The Mark of Zorro*, directed by Fred Niblo, is released in the United States, starring Douglas Fairbanks.
- The movie *The Round Up*, directed by George Melford, is released in the United States, starring Roscoe "Fatty" Arbuckle.
- The movie *The Saphead*, directed by Winchell Smith, is released in the United States, starring Buster Keaton.

Literature and Language

- The *Collected Poems* of the English poet Wilfred Owen (killed in World War I) are published posthumously, edited by Siegfried Sassoon.
- The English writer Agatha Christie publishes *The Mysterious Affair at Styles*. Her first novel, it introduces her Belgian detective Hercule Poirot.
- The English writer John Galsworthy publishes *In Chancery*, the second novel in his sequence of novels and stories *The Forsyte Saga*. The first volume, *The Man of Property*, appeared in 1906.
- The English writer Rose Macaulay publishes her novel *Potterism*.
- The French writer Colette publishes her novel *Chéri/Darling*.
- The French writer Marcel Proust publishes *Le Côté de Guermantes/The Guermantes Way*, the third volume of his multivolume novel *A la recherche du temps perdu/Remembrance of Things Past*. The English translation is published in 1925.
- The New Zealand writer Katherine Mansfield publishes her collection of short stories *Bliss*, which includes the story "Prelude."
- The Norwegian writer Sigrid Undset publishes her novel *Kransen/The Bridal Wreath*, the first volume of her trilogy *Kristin Lavransdatter*.
- The Pulitzer Prize for Biography is awarded to Albert J. Beveridge for *The Life of John Marshall*. The Pulitzer Prize for Fiction is not awarded this year.
- The term "smoke-filled room" enters the U.S. political lexicon when, at the Republican National Convention in Chicago, Illinois, Harry Daugherty, Warren G. Harding's campaign manager, uses it to describe his prediction of where and how the Republican candidate for president would be chosen.
- The U.S. novelist Sinclair Lewis publishes *Main Street*, a critique of the parochialism and hypocrisy of small-town United States.
- The U.S. writer Carl Sandburg publishes his poetry collection *Smoke and Steel*.
- The U.S. writer Conrad Aiken publishes his poetry collection *The House of Dust*.
- The U.S. writer Edna St. Vincent Millay publishes her poetry collection *A Few Figs from Thistles*. The line "My candle burns at both ends" becomes a catch phrase of the 1920s.
- The U.S. writer F. Scott Fitzgerald publishes his first novel, *This Side of Paradise*.
- The U.S. writer John Dos Passos publishes *One Man's Initiation – 1917*, his first novel.

- The U.S. writer Sara Teasdale publishes her poetry collection *Flame and Shadow*.
- The U.S. writer Sherwood Anderson publishes his novel *Poor White*.
- The U.S. writer Upton Sinclair publishes his novel *100%: The Story of a Patriot*.
- The U.S. writer Willa Cather publishes her short-story collection *Youth and Bright Medusa*, which contains one of her best-known stories, "Paul's Case."
- The U.S. writer William Carlos Williams publishes his poetry collection *Kora in Hell*.
- The U.S.-born English writer T. S. Eliot publishes *The Sacred Wood*, essays on literature in which he introduces his influential critical concepts "objective correlative" and "dissociation of sensibility."

Music

- A group of five French and one Swiss avant-garde French composers are dubbed "Les Six" by the French music critic Henri Collet. They are: Darius Milhaud, Francis Poulenc, Louis Durey, Germaine Tailleferre, Georges Auric, and Arthur Honegger.
- Popular songs in the United States include "Margie," "Avalon," and "Whispering."
- The French composer Maurice Ravel completes his orchestral work *La Valse/The Waltz*. It is turned into a ballet in 1929. He also completes his chamber work *Le Tombeau de Claude Debussy/The Tomb of Claude Debussy*.
- The French composers Maurice Yvain and Jacques-Charles write the song "Mon Homme"/"My Man."
- The opera *Die tote Stadt/The Dead City*, by the Austrian composer Erich Korngold, is first performed, simultaneously in Hamburg and Cologne, Germany.
- The opera *Výlety páně Broučkovy/The Excursions of Mr. Brouček* by the Czech composer Leoš Janáček is first performed, in Prague, Czechoslovakia.
- The Russian composer Igor Stravinsky completes his *Concertino* for string quartet.
- The U.S. composer Charles Ives completes his choral work *An Election, or November 2, 1920*.
- U.S. songwriters Albert von Tilzer and Neville Fleeson write the song "I'll Be With You In Apple Blossom Time."

DECEMBER

10 The U.S. singer Mamie Smith is the first black singer to make a record. "Crazy Blues," written by Perry Bradford, sells over one million copies in six months.

Theater and Dance

- Polish-born English dancer Marie Rambert founds the Rambert School of Ballet in London, England, leading to the establishment of the Marie Rambert Dancers in 1926.
- The play *Der Dibuk/The Dybbuk*, by the Russian writer Ansky is first performed, in Warsaw, Poland. It becomes a classic of Yiddish theater.
- The play *East of Suez*, by the English writer W. Somerset Maugham, is first performed, in London, England.

- The play *The Emperor Jones*, by the U.S. dramatist Eugene O'Neill, is first performed, in New York, New York.
- The play *The Skin Game*, by the English writer John Galsworthy, is first performed, in London, England.
- The Pulitzer Prize for Drama is awarded to Eugene O'Neill for *Beyond the Horizon*.
- The surrealistic pantomime *Le Boeuf sur le toit/The Ox on the Roof*, by the French composer Darius Milhaud and the French writer Jean Cocteau, is first performed, in Paris, France. The designs are by the French artists Raoul Dufy and Guy-Pierre Fauconnet.

Thought and Scholarship

- Australian philosopher Samuel Alexander publishes *Space, Time, and Deity*.
- Austrian psychologist Sigmund Freud writes *Beyond the Pleasure Principle*, in which he argues that the goal of instincts is to return to an earlier state.
- English philosopher Alfred North Whitehead publishes *The Concept of Nature*.
- English writer H. G. Wells publishes *The Outline of History*.
- German sociologist Max Weber publishes his influential *Die Protestantische Ethik und der Geist des Kapitalismus/The Protestant Ethic and the Spirit of Capitalism*.
- German writer Ernst Jünger publishes *In Stahlgewittern/The Storm of Steel*, a reflection on the consequences of World War I.
- Spanish-born U.S. writer and philosopher George Santayana publishes *Character and Opinion in the United States*.
- The Nobel Prize for Literature is awarded to the Norwegian novelist Knut Hamsun.
- The Pulitzer Prize for History is awarded to Justin H. Smith for *The War with Mexico*.
- The U.S. philosopher John Dewey publishes *Reconstruction in Philosophy*, in which he advocates replacing the metaphysical search for timeless truths with a pragmatic hunt for truths derived empirically.
- U.S. historian Carl L. Becker publishes *The United States: An Experiment in Democracy*.
- U.S. historian Frederick Jackson Turner publishes *The Frontier in American History*.
- U.S. jurist Oliver Wendell Holmes publishes *Collected Legal Papers*.

SOCIETY

Education

- Clark University in Worcester, Massachusetts, establishes the nation's first graduate program in geography.

JANUARY

- The New York State education commissioner Frank B. Gibbert warns public school teachers that membership in the Communist Party will constitute grounds for dismissal.

Everyday Life

c. 1920   Joseph Krieger manufactures the first commercially available tea bags, in San Francisco, California. Originally intended for caterers, they soon become popular with housewives.

- Abortion is legalized in Russia.
- Abortion is made illegal in France, to increase the population which has dropped because of World War I.

- Frei-Sonnenland, the first nudist camp, opens at Motzener See in Germany.
- Jersey Standard Oil creates antifreeze in the United States.
- The average life expectancy in the United States is 54 years, up from 49 years in 1901.
- The U.S. Census lists the population at 105,710,620. The Census also reveals that illiteracy has reached a new low of 6%, down from 7.7% in 1910, and 20% in 1870.

BIRTHS & DEATHS

JANUARY

2   Isaac Asimov, U.S. science fiction writer, born in Petrovichi, Russia (−1992).

4   Benito Pérez Galdós, Spanish novelist, dies in Madrid, Spain (76).

4   William Colby, director of the Central Intelligence Agency (CIA) 1973–76, born in St. Paul, Minnesota (−1996).

6   Sun Myung Moon, Korean evangelist who established the Unification Church, born in Pyungan Buk-do, Korea.

19   Javier Pérez de Cuellar, Peruvian diplomat and fifth secretary-general of the United Nations, born in Lima, Peru.

20   Federico Fellini, Italian film director, born in Rimini, Italy (−1993).

24   Amedeo Modigliani, Italian painter and sculptor, dies in Paris, France (35).

FEBRUARY

8   Lana Turner, U.S. actress, born in Wallace, Idaho (−1995).

11   Farouk I, King of Egypt 1936–52, born in Cairo, Egypt (−1965).

20   Robert Edwin Peary, U.S. explorer who was the first to reach the North Pole, dies in Washington, D.C. (63).

MARCH

11   Nicolaas Bloembergen, Dutch-born U.S. physicist, who shared the Nobel Prize for Physics (1981) with Arthur Leonard Schawlow for the development of laser spectroscopy, born in Dordrecht, the Netherlands.

20   Pamela Harriman, U.S. ambassador to France 1993–97, fundraiser for President Bill Clinton, courtesan, and daughter-in-law of Winston Churchill, born in Minterne Magna, Dorset, England (−1997).

MAY

3   Sugar Ray Robinson, U.S. professional boxer, six times world champion, born in Detroit, Michigan (−1989).

11   William Dean Howells, U.S. novelist, dies in New York, New York (83).

18   John Paul II, pope from 1978, the first non-Italian pope in 456 years, born in Wadowice, Poland.

21   Howard L. Bachrach, U.S. biochemist, who was the first to purify the polio virus, born in Faribault, Minnesota.

JUNE

- Amus Tutola, Nigerian novelist, author of *The Palm-Wine Drinkard* (1952), born in Abeokuta, Nigeria (−1997).

7   Georges Marchais, French politician, secretary-general of the French Communist Party 1972–94, born (−1997).

14   Max Weber, German sociologist and political economist, who developed the idea of the "Protestant Ethic," which relates Protestantism to capitalism, dies in Munich, Germany (56).

17   François Jacob, French biologist, who, with Jacques Monod, discovered regulator genes, born in Nancy, France.

20   Dmitry Iosifovich Ivanofsky, Russian microbiologist, who discovered viruses, dies in Rostov-na-Donu, Russia (55).

JULY

5   Max Klinger, German painter and sculptor, dies near Naumberg, Germany (63).

10   Owen Chamberlain, U.S. physicist, who, with Emilio Segré, discovered the antiproton (1955), born in San Francisco, California.

24   Bella Abzug (born Savitsky), U.S. lawyer and politician and one of the key figures in the modern feminist movement, born in the Bronx, New York.

AUGUST

1   Bal Gangadhar Tilak, Indian mathematician, philosopher, and militant nationalist, a leader of the

Indian independence movement, dies in Bombay, India (63).

16   Joseph Norman Lockyer, English astronomer who discovered the element helium, dies in Salcombe Regis, Devon, England (83).

22   Ray Bradbury, U.S. science fiction writer, born in Waukegan, Illinois.

29   Charlie "Yardbird" or "Bird" Parker, U.S. saxophonist, composer and bandleader, born in Kansas City, Kansas, (−1955).

31   Wilhelm Wundt, German psychologist, the founder of experimental psychology, dies in Grossbothen, Germany (88).

SEPTEMBER

24   Peter Carl Fabergé, Russian goldsmith and jewelry designer, dies in exile in Lausanne, Switzerland (74).

29   Peter Dennis Mitchell, English chemist who received the Nobel Prize for Chemistry in 1978 for work on the conservation of energy by plants during respiration and photosynthesis, born in Mitcham, Surrey, England (−1992).

OCTOBER

- Louis Ducos du Hauron, French physicist who invented the first practical method of color photography, dies in Agen, France (83).

10   Thelonius Monk, U.S. jazz pianist and composer, born in Rocky Mountain, North Carolina (−1982).

22   Timothy Leary, U.S. writer and psychologist who advised the world to "turn on, tune in, and drop out," born in Springfield, Massachusetts (−1996).

25   King Alexander of Greece dies.

NOVEMBER

21   Stan Musial ("Stan the Man"), U.S. baseball player, born in Donora, Pennsylvania.

- U.S. barman Fernand L. Petior, of Harry's New York Bar, creates the Bloody Mary cocktail, originally named the Bucket of Blood.

JANUARY

16 Prohibition (the ban on manufacturing, selling, or transporting alcohol) begins in the United States, leading to an increase in the sales of soft drinks and coffee and a thriving bootleg and homebrew industry.

SEPTEMBER

7 The first "Miss America" beauty competition is held in Atlantic City, New Jersey; the winner is Miss Margaret Gorman.

8 Transcontinental airmail begins in the United States.

DECEMBER

- The Amalgamated Clothing Workers of America strike against clothing manufacturers in eastern cities for the purpose of winning union recognition.

Media and Communication

- Canada's first radio broadcasts begin from Montreal.
- The U.S. radio station 8MK Detroit, in Michigan, is the first to broadcast news bulletins.

December 1920–22 Between 1920 and 1922, 570 radio stations are licensed in the United States.

NOVEMBER

2 The Westinghouse Company establishes the world's first commercial radio station, KDKA, in East Pittsburgh, Pennsylvania, run by the U.S. engineer Frank Conrad, inaugurating national radio broadcasting in the United States. The first broadcast is of the presidential election returns.

Sports

- The International Greyhound Association is founded at Tulsa, Oklahoma, by the U.S. pioneers of modern greyhound racing, Oliver Patrick Smith and George Sawyer.
- The Negro National League, a professional baseball league, is founded in the United States.

- The U.S. thoroughbred racehorse Man O'War wins 11 out of 11 races in one season and sets a season record of $166,140 in winnings.

JANUARY

5 The New York Yankees purchase the U.S. baseball player Babe Ruth from the Boston Red Sox for $125,000.

APRIL

20–September 12 The 7th Olympic Games are held in Antwerp, Belgium, attended by 2,668 competitors, 71 of whom are women, from 29 nations; in the aftermath of World War I, Germany, Austria, Hungary, and Anatolia (modern Turkey) are not invited. The Olympic oath and flag are introduced. The United States wins 41 gold medals; Sweden, 19; Finland, 15; Britain, 14; and Belgium, Norway, and Italy, 13 each.

JUNE

4 The U.S. sculler John B. Kelly is refused entry to the Henley Regatta, England, because it is deemed that his job as a bricklayer gives him an unfair advantage in competition with "gentlemen." He goes on to win two gold medals for rowing at the Antwerp Olympic Games.

JULY

3 Bill Tilden of the United States wins the first of two successive men's singles titles at the Wimbledon lawn tennis championships in London, England.

9–16 In the first Davis Cup Challenge Round since 1913, the United States team of tennis players led by Bill Tilden and Bill Johnston defeats Australia 5–0.

25 Philippe Thys of Belgium becomes the first cyclist to win the Tour de France three times.

SEPTEMBER

17 A new professional American football league, the American Professional Football Association, the forerunner of the National Football League, is formed at Canton, Ohio. It comprises 10 teams (soon extended to 14).

OCTOBER

- Comrade, ridden by British jockey Frank Bullock, wins the inaugural Prix de l'Arc de Triomphe horse race at Longchamp, Paris, France.

1921

POLITICS, GOVERNMENT, AND ECONOMICS

Business and Economics

- President Warren G. Harding imposes duties on foreign beef and agriculture in order to buoy up the United States's glutted markets.
- The Johnson & Johnson corporation of New Brunswick, New Jersey, introduces the Band Aid adhesive bandage.
- The U.S. economy enters a postwar recession, precipitating layoffs, wage cuts, and labor unrest throughout U.S. industry.

MARCH
16 A British–Russian trade agreement is made by a British trade mission visiting Moscow.

JULY
- In the face of a postwar recession, the U.S. Railroad Labor Board authorizes a 12% wage cut.

AUGUST
- As the postwar depression tightens its grip, the U.S. Labor Department estimates that nearly six million Americans are unemployed.

DECEMBER
15 In response to the world depression, Australia erects tariff barriers to protect its industries.

Human Rights

JUNE
20 Oklahoma representative Alice Robertson becomes the first woman to preside over the U.S. Congress, when she occupies the chair in the House of Representatives for 30 minutes.

Politics and Government

- Five million people die in a famine in the Volga region of Russia, a consequence of Bolshevik food requisitioning policies and drought.
- Soviet Russia establishes its first concentration camp at Archangel.
- The German political leader Adolf Hitler is elected "unlimited chairman" of the National Socialist German

Workers' (Nazi) party. The same year the party adopts the swastika as its emblem.
- The Port Authority of New York and New Jersey is established.
- The U.S. Congress creates the General Accounting Office as a branch of Congress, charging it with policing federal spending.
- The U.S. Federal Highway Act gives grants of 50% from the federal government for road construction.
- The U.S. Interior Department secretary Albert B. Fall secretly leases the Teapot Dome naval oil reserves to private oil speculators, triggering the series of events that will become known as the Teapot Dome scandal.
- Widespread disorder occurs in India resulting from demands for home rule and Hindu–Muslim rivalry.

JANUARY
1 Greek troops begin an offensive into Anatolia (modern Turkey) in the Greek–Turkish War.
3 The U.S. Supreme Court upholds the prosecution of labor unions under the provision of the Sherman Antitrust Act: unions can be found in restraint of trade as well as businesses.
13–22 A general congress of the Italian Socialist Party in Livorno, Italy, results in the formation of a separate Communist Party.
16 The moderate French Republican politician Aristide Briand forms a government in France.
24–29 A conference of the World War I allies meets in Paris, France, to discuss Germany's reparation payments.

FEBRUARY
2 The Russian Red Army invades Georgia following its defeat of General Peter Wrangel's White Russian army (in 1920).
4 The Irish politician James Craig is elected Ulster Unionist leader, in succession to Edward Carson.
8 Jan C. Smuts's South African Party wins 76 seats in the South African elections, against 47 for the Nationalists and 10 for Labor.
19 France and Russia sign a treaty with one another for mutual assistance should either be attacked, inspired by concern at a potential revival of German power.
21 The nationalist army officer Reza Khan stages a coup in Persia (modern Iran).
21–March 14 A London conference of the Allies and representatives of the Turkish sultan's government and the nationalist government in Ankara, Anatolia (modern Turkey), fails to reach a settlement of Greek territorial claims in Anatolia.
25 A Bolshevik government is established in the republic of Georgia.
26–28 Russia signs treaties with Persia (modern Iran) and, on February 28, with Afghanistan.

27   Riots take place between communists and fascists in Florence, Italy, during a period of widespread political violence.

28–March 17   A mutiny of sailors begins at Kronstadt naval base near Petrograd, Russia, in opposition to the communist government's harsh policies; it is put down by troops.

MARCH

•   The U.S. secretary of state Charles Evans Hughes informs his Russian counterpart that the United States will never normalize trade relations with a communist Russia.

1   Anatolia (modern Turkey) signs a treaty of alliance with Afghanistan.

3   France and Romania sign an offensive–defensive treaty.

4   Warren G. Harding, a Republican, is inaugurated as the 29th president of the United States.

5   The United States warns Costa Rica and Panama to settle their frontier dispute by arbitration.

7   The ex-emperor of Austria and king of Hungary, Charles, attempts a coup in Hungary but is rejected by the national assembly because of fear of an Allied invasion to oppose his return.

8–September 30   French troops occupy Düsseldorf and other towns in the Ruhr, Germany, because of Germany's failure to make a preliminary reparations payment (compensation for World War I damages).

9   France agrees to leave Cilicia in southeast Anatolia (modern Turkey) in response to nationalist attacks.

9   France signs a defensive treaty with Poland, part of an attempt to create a buffer zone around Germany.

15   Rwanda, East Africa, is ceded to Britain by Belgium.

17   At the 10th Congress of the Russian Communist Party, the Russian leader Vladimir Ilyich Lenin introduces his New Economic Policy, which restores some private business and freedom of trade; the forcible requisition of grain has led to famine and revolts.

18   The Treaty of Riga between Russia and Poland delineates their common frontier.

20   A plebiscite is held in Upper Silesia (part of prewar Germany) to decide if it should be part of Poland or Germany; 63% vote for incorporation with Germany.

23   Germany announces that it will be unable to pay the £600 million due on May 1 as reparations for World War I.

24   A British Reparation Recovery Act imposes a 50% duty on German goods following Germany's failure to begin reparation payments for World War I (the duty is reduced to 26% on May 20).

24   Communist riots break out in Hamburg, Germany.

25   The United States refuses Russia's request to resume trading.

APRIL

•   The U.S. congressman Andrew Volstead proposes legislation banning the sale of beer, even for medicinal purposes.

2   A Bolshevik government is established in the republic of Armenia.

2   In the Greek–Turkish War, Turkish troops under Ismet Pasha halt the Greek advance at Inönö and the Greek army withdraws.

12   The U.S. president Warren G. Harding declares that the United States can play no part in the League of Nations.

14   The conservative Count Stephen Bethlen becomes prime minister of Hungary.

23   Through a Czechoslovak-Romanian alliance, Romania joins the "Little Entente" (a defensive alliance of eastern European nations).

24   Germany unsuccessfully asks the United States to mediate in the controversy over its payment of World War I reparations.

24   The northern Adriatic port of Fiume (now Rijeka, Croatia), disputed between Italy and the Kingdom of the Serbs, Croats, and Slovenes, votes to become a free city.

24   The war crimes court in Leipzig, Germany, acquits the German general Erich von Ludendorff of breaches of the laws of war.

27   The Allied Reparations Commission fixes the amount Germany has to pay in compensation for World War I at 132,000 million gold marks (£6,650 million/$33,000 million).

MAY

2   French troops are mobilized for a full-scale occupation of the Ruhr area of Germany, should Germany refuse to accept the amount of World War I reparations payments demanded by the Allies.

4   The German chancellor Konstantin Fehrenbach's government resigns in protest at the size of the World War I reparations payment demanded by Britain and France.

5   The Allied Supreme Council warns Germany that failure to accept the amount of reparations demanded for World War I damage by May 12 will lead to occupation of the Ruhr area of Germany.

6   A peace treaty is signed between Germany and the communist government of Russia, formally ending hostilities between them.

10   Following a German cabinet crisis, Karl Wirth of the Catholic Center Party becomes chancellor.

11   The German Reichstag (parliament) votes to accept the Allies' ultimatum on reparations for World War I damages.

13   In elections to the Irish parliament no contests are held, because of the prevailing guerrilla war between Irish nationalists and the British; 124 Sinn Féin and 4 Unionists (representing Dublin University) are returned unopposed.

15   The state legislature in New York passes a law allowing a state commissioner to censor dance styles.

15   Thirty-five fascists are returned at the elections in Italy.

20   Germany and China resume diplomatic relations.

24   In elections to the Northern Ireland parliament, the Unionists win 40 seats, the Nationalists 6, and Sinn Féin 6.

28   Following discussions between the British government and Sultan Ahmed Fuad I of Egypt, and the formation of a new Egyptian government, nationalists riot in Alexandria, Egypt.

28   France resumes diplomatic relations with the Vatican (they were severed in 1904).

28   The German chancellor Karl Wirth appoints the industrialist Walter Rathenau as minister for reconstruction (including responsibility for World War I reparations).

JUNE

- U.S. Congress creates the Bureau of the Budget and the office of comptroller general within the U.S. Treasury Department.

5   An agreement is reached on control of the disputed port of Fiume (Rijeka) between Italy and the Kingdom of the Serbs, Croats, and Slovenes.

7   An alliance is made between Romania and the Kingdom of the Serbs, Croats, and Slovenes, completing Romania's entry into the "Little Entente" (a defensive alliance of eastern European nations).

7   The new parliament of Northern Ireland opens in Belfast, with the Ulster Unionist leader James Craig as its first prime minister.

7   The United States refuses to recognize the Mexican government until international obligations are honored.

19 The powers agree to mediate between Anatolia (modern Turkey) and Greece to end the war between them.

25 Greece refuses the offer made by the powers on June 19 to mediate between Anatolia (modern Turkey) and Greece to end the war between them.

26 The Italian prime minister Giovanni Giolitti resigns because of failures in his foreign policy; he is succeeded by Ivanoe Bonomi.

27 A treaty is signed between Afghanistan and Persia (modern Iran).

30 The U.S. president Warren G. Harding appoints former president William Taft as chief justice of the U.S. Supreme Court.

JULY

- A joint resolution of the U.S. Congress formally ends the state of war with Germany.

7   The Chinese Communist Party is founded in Shanghai, China.

9   The Irish nationalist leader Eamon de Valera, on behalf of the self-declared Irish Republic, agrees a truce with the British authorities (fighting ends two days later).

14–21   At a conference in London, England, attended by the British prime minister David Lloyd George, the Ulster Unionist leader James Craig, and the Irish nationalist leader Eamon de Valera, de Valera rejects dominion status for Ireland.

16 In the Greek–Turkish War, Greek troops under King Constantine resume the invasion of Anatolia and press toward the River Sakkaria.

16 War trials begin in Leipzig, Germany, before a German supreme court.

21 Spanish troops under General Fernandez Silvestre waging a campaign against the Riffians in Morocco are defeated by troops led by Abd al-Karim; 12,000 are killed.

23 A convention is signed which internationalizes the River Danube (with effect from June 30, 1922).

25 Belgium and Luxembourg sign a 50-year economic pact.

28 Following resistance to a proposed plebiscite in the disputed area of southern Silesia, the Allied powers decide to divide the area between Poland and Czechoslovakia.

AUGUST

- A revived Ku Klux Klan causes havoc throughout the South, beating and harassing black Americans and their white sympathizers.

11 The United States invites world powers to a conference in Washington, D.C., on the Far East and the limitation of armaments.

12 Following conflict between Poles and Germans in Silesia, the Allied Supreme Council refers the question of the assignment of Upper Silesia to the League of Nations.

16 King Peter I of the Kingdom of the Serbs, Croats, and Slovenes dies; he is succeeded by his son, Alexander I.

16 The Sinn Féin members elected to the Irish parliament in May meet in Dublin and constitute themselves as a second Dáil Eireann; they appoint representatives (led by Arthur Griffith and Michael Collins) to negotiate with Britain on full Irish independence.

23 Faisal (the former king of Syria) is crowned as King Faisal I in the British mandate of Iraq following a plebiscite in his favor.

24 The United States signs a peace treaty with Austria.

24–September 16   At the Battle of the Sakkaria River in the Greek–Turkish War, the Turks, commanded by Mustafa Kemal Pasha (later known as Atatürk), prevent Greek forces from reaching Ankara, Anatolia (modern Turkey); the Greeks subsequently retreat.

25 The United States signs a peace treaty with Germany.

26 Mathias Erzberger, former German finance minister, signatory of the Armistice, and supporter of republican democracy in Germany, is assassinated by a nationalist gang while on holiday in the Black Forest, Germany.

29 The United States signs a peace treaty with Hungary.

29–December 16   A state of emergency is proclaimed in Germany in the face of economic crisis.

SEPTEMBER

15 Guatemala, Honduras, and El Salvador agree to form a Republic of Central America (with its capital at Tegucigalpa, Honduras).

22 States admitted to the League of Nations include Estonia and Lithuania.

OCTOBER

6   France and Germany sign an agreement for the supply of World War I reparations in kind because of Germany's financial crisis.

12 The Council of the League of Nations awards 3,400 sq km/1,300 sq mi of Upper Silesia, including most of the coal mines and steelworks, to Poland. The rest is awarded to Germany.

13 A treaty is signed in Kars, Anatolia (modern Turkey), between Russia, the Caucasian republics, and the Turkish government in Ankara.

19–20   A revolution in Lisbon, Portugal, forces the prime minister to resign; the following day Manuel Coelho forms a government.

20 A Franco-Turkish agreement is signed in Ankara, Anatolia (modern Turkey), recognizing the nationalist Ankara government.

25–November 10   Poland and Germany reluctantly accept the division of Upper Silesia determined by the Council of the League of Nations on October 12.

29 The ex-emperor of Austria and king of Hungary, Charles, is expelled from Hungary following the failure of a second attempted coup.

NOVEMBER

1   Otto Braun, a Socialist, forms a ministry in Prussia.

4   The Japanese prime minister Takashi Hara is murdered at Tokyo railroad station by a right-wing extremist.

5   A treaty of alliance is signed between the communist governments of Mongolia and Russia following the defeat of anticommunist White Russian forces under Roman von Ungern-Sternberg.

9   A meeting of the European powers fixes Albania's borders as those of 1913.

11   The Unknown Soldier, whose body has been lying in state in the Capitol rotunda in Washington, D.C., is buried at Arlington National Ceremony, Virginia, as a memorial to all other unidentified U.S. soldiers killed in World War I.

12–February 6, 1922   The Washington Naval Conference on the Limitation of Naval Armaments is held in Washington, D.C. Convinced that naval armament represents the gravest threat to world peace, the United States proposes to drastically reduce its naval tonnage if other nations reciprocate.

DECEMBER

- President Warren G. Harding commutes the prison sentence of Eugene V. Debs and 23 others convicted of espionage during World War I.
- The U.S. Supreme Court, in *Truax v. Corrigan*, rules unconstitutional an Arizona law which prohibits picketing.

6   The British government and representatives of the Dáil Eireann sign the Anglo-Irish Treaty providing for an independent southern Ireland with dominion status (within the British Empire).

7   The United States and Austria resume diplomatic relations.

13   The United States, Britain, France, and Japan sign a treaty at the Washington Conference, agreeing to respect each other's possessions in the Pacific.

14   In a plebiscite held in Ödenburg (Sopron) in western Hungary, 65% vote for union with Hungary rather than with Czechoslovakia.

15   Germany applies for a moratorium on World War I reparations payments because of its financial weakness.

16   The British Parliament ratifies the Anglo-Irish Treaty signed on December 6. In Ireland the nationalist leader Eamon de Valera, a signatory to the treaty, repudiates it, demanding full independence.

21   Russia and Anatolia (modern Turkey) form an alliance.

27   Italy and Russia sign a commercial agreement.

27   Peru receives a new liberal constitution.

29   Following the defeat of the Conservatives in the Canadian general election, the Liberal leader William Mackenzie King is appointed prime minister and governs with support from the Progressives.

29   The United States, Britain, France, Italy, and Japan sign a treaty at the Washington Conference, agreeing to limit naval armaments.

SCIENCE, TECHNOLOGY, AND MEDICINE

Agriculture

- U.S. botanist Edward Murray East develops a high-yield hybrid corn.

December 1921–30   Tractors begin to replace draft animals on farms, especially in the United States.

Ecology

- The U.S. Congress grants U.S. oil producers a tax break of 27.5%, designed to promote the discovery and exploitation of new oil reserves.
- Ujong-kulon Nature Reserve is established in Java, Indonesia; it contains the last natural forest in Java and is a refuge for the Javanese tiger and Javanese rhinoceros.
- U.S. Congress creates Hot Springs National Park on 14 sq km/5.6 sq mi in Arkansas.
- U.S. forester Benton MacKaye proposes the creation of a 3,219 km/2,000 mi Appalachian Trail, stretching from Maine to Georgia.

JUNE

- The rampaging Arkansas River virtually razes the town of Pueblo, Colorado, killing some 1,500 people and causing an estimated $25 million damage.

Health and Medicine

- A cholera epidemic in India claims 500,000 lives.
- Canadian microbiologist Félix-Hubert D'Hérelle publishes *Le Bactériophage, son rôle dans l'immunité/ The Bacteriophage, Its Role in Immunity*, in which he describes the discovery of bacteriophages, viruses that infect bacteria.
- Canadian physiologists Frederick Banting, Charles Best, and John James MacLeod isolate insulin. A diabetic patient in Toronto, Canada, receives the first insulin injection.
- French physician Jean Athanese Sicard uses a radiopaque iodine substance to X-ray the internal structure of the spinal column. He studies the bronchial tube the next year.
- Iodized salt is introduced in the United States as a preventative against thyroid disease.
- Scottish bacteriologist Alexander Fleming discovers the antibacterial enzyme lysozyme, which is found in tears and saliva.
- Swiss psychiatrist Hermann Rorschach publishes *Psychodiagnostik/Psychodiagnostics*, in which he introduces the Rorschach ink-blot test for personality.
- The death rate in the United States is 1,163.9 per 100,000 population, compared with 1,755 in 1900.

MARCH

6   A study released in the United States states that 5,361 people died from cancer in 1920, a 6% increase from 1919.

Science

- British archeologist John Marshall discovers the Harappa village in the Indus valley (in modern Pakistan), pushing the Indian subcontinent's history back to 3500 BC.
- Dutch elm disease, caused by the fungus *Ceratocystis ulmi* and spread by bark beetles, is first described in the Netherlands. A serious disease of elm trees, it is thought to have come from Asia after World War I.
- English physical chemist Frederick Soddy receives the Nobel Prize for Chemistry for his work on radioactive substances, especially isotopes.
- English physicist Patrick Stuart Blackett uses cloud-chamber photographs of atomic nuclei bombarded with alpha particles to show how they are disintegrated.
- German physicist Albert Einstein receives the Nobel Prize for Physics for his work on the photoelectric effect.
- German physicist Max Born develops a mathematical description of the first law of thermodynamics.
- Norwegian meteorologist Vilhelm Bjerknes publishes *On the Dynamics of the Circular Vortex with Applications to the Atmosphere and to Atmospheric Vortex and Wave Motion*, in which he summarizes his work on the movement of air masses and weather forecasting.
- Swedish archeologist Johan Gunnar Andersson discovers a cave at Yangshao in Hunan, northern China, which provides evidence of the first Neolithic culture in China, the Yangshao culture (5000–3000 BC).
- The fossil remains of Rhodesian man (Kabwe man), who is thought to have lived 50,000 years ago, are discovered at Broken Hill, Northern Rhodesia (modern Zambia). The almost complete skull shows traits similar to the skulls both modern humans and Neanderthals. The fossil is classified as an extinct subspecies of modern humans, *Homo sapiens rhodesiensis*.
- U.S. chemist Thomas Midgley discovers that tetraethyl lead added to gasoline prevents knock.
- U.S. medical student John Larson invents the lie detector or polygraph, so-called because it simultaneously records blood pressure, pulse, and respiration, which are affected by a person's emotional state.

Technology

- The first transatlantic phototransmission is made between Annapolis, Maryland, and La Malmaison, France, using French engineer Edourd Belin's "Belino."
- U.S. physicist Albert Hull invents the magnetron, an oscillator that generates microwaves.

March 1921–30 Advances in pipeline technology make the transmission of natural gas over long distances practical for the first time.

Transportation

FEBRUARY

19 The U.S. Red Cross announces that 20,000 children die in automobile accidents each year.

23 A U.S. airmail plane sets a record time for a flight from San Francisco, California, to New York, New York, of 2,600 miles in 33 hrs 20 min.

JULY

- U.S. Army general William ("Billy") Mitchell highlights the superiority of air power over naval power by sinking the former German battleship *Ostfriesland* in a demonstration of concentrated bombing off Hampton Roads, Virginia.

SEPTEMBER

5 U.S. Army officer James Doolittle flies 2,094 miles from San Diego, California, to Jacksonville, Florida, in 22 hrs 30 min with just one stop, a new record.

ARTS AND IDEAS

Architecture

- The Einstein Tower in Potsdam, Germany, designed by the German architect Erich Mendelssohn, is completed, one of the finest examples of expressionist architecture.

Arts

- The Belgian artist Georges Vantongerloo sculpts *Construction in Volume Relations*.
- The Dutch artist Piet Mondrian paints *Composition with Red, Yellow, Blue, and Black*.
- The English artist Stanley Spencer paints *Christ's Entry into Jerusalem*.
- The French artist Amédée Ozenfant paints *Still Life with a Glass of Red Wine*.
- The French artist Fernand Léger paints *Landscape with Figures*.
- The French artist Georges Braque paints *Still Life with Guitar*.
- The French artist Henri Matisse paints *Odalisque with Red Culottes* and *Interior at Nice*.
- The French artist Marcel Duchamp creates *Why Not Sneeze, Rose Sélavy?*, a Dadaist sculpture consisting of a small bird cage filled with marble cubes.
- The German artist Max Ernst paints *The Elephant Celebes*.
- The Russian artist Alexander Rodchenko sculpts *Suspended Composition*.
- The Spanish artist Pablo Picasso paints *Three Musicians*.
- The Swiss artist Paul Klee paints *The Fish*.
- The U.S. artist Charles Demuth paints *Incense of a New Church*.
- The U.S. artist Stuart Davis paints *Lucky Strike*.

Film

- In Germany this year 600 movies are produced.
- The movie *Destiny*, directed by Fritz Lang, is released in Germany, starring Lil Dagover, Rudolph Klein-Rogge, Bernhard Götzke, and Walter Janssen.
- The movie *Dream Street*, directed by D. W. Griffith, is released in the United States, starring Tyrone Power, Sr., Ralph Graves, and Carol Dempster. It is the first to

feature some singing and dialogue, supplied on synchronized records.

- The movie *Innocent*, directed by Maurice Elvey, is released in Britain, starring Basil Rathbone.
- The movie *L'Atlantide/The Queen of Atlantis*, also released as *Missing Husbands*, directed by Jacques Feyder, is released in France, starring Jean Angelo, Stacia Napierkowska, and Georges Melchior.
- The movie *Nosferatu*, based on *Dracula* by Bram Stoker, directed by F. W. Murnau, is released in Germany, starring Max Schreck, Gustav von Wangenheim, Greta Schröder, and Alexander Granach. Also released in Germany is his movie *The Haunted Castle*.
- The movie *The Affairs of Anatole*, directed by Cecil B. De Mille, is released in the United States, starring Wallace Reid and Gloria Swanson.
- The movie *The Four Horsemen of the Apocalypse*, directed by Rex Ingram, is released in the United States, starring Rudolph Valentino and Alice Terry.
- The movie *The Haunted Castle*, directed by F. W. Murnau, is released in Germany.
- The movie *The Kid*, directed by Charlie Chaplin, is released in the United States. Chaplin also stars in it along with Jackie Coogan.
- The movie *The Mountain Cat*, directed by Ernst Lubitsch, is released in Germany.
- The movie *The Sheik*, directed by George Melford, is released in the United States, starring Rudolph Valentino and Agnes Ayres.
- The movie *The Three Musketeers*, directed by Henri Diamant-Berger, is released in France. Based on the novel by Alexandre Dumas, it stars Aimé Simon-Girard.
- The movie *The Three Musketeers*, directed by Fred Niblo, is released in the United States. Based on the novel by Alexandre Dumas, it stars Douglas Fairbanks.
- The movie *Une Brute/A Beast*, directed by Daniel Bompard, is released in France, starring André Noix.
- The U.S. movie comedian, writer, and director Roscoe "Fatty" Arbuckle is arrested after a death at a party; although he is acquitted of rape and murder, his career never recovers.

Literature and Language

- The Czech writer Jaroslav Hašek publishes the first volume of his satirical novel *Osudy dobrého vojáka Švejka za světové války/The Good Soldier Schweik*. The last volume appears in 1923.
- The English writer Aldous Huxley publishes his novel *Crome Yellow*.
- The English writer D. H. Lawrence publishes his novel *Women in Love*. It was privately published in the United States in 1920.
- The English writer John Galsworthy publishes *To Let*, the third novel in his sequence of novels and stories *The Forsyte Saga*. The first volume, *The Man of Property*, appeared in 1906.
- The English writer Lytton Strachey publishes his biography *Queen Victoria*.

- The English writer Rose Macaulay publishes her novel *Dangerous Ages*.
- The French writer Marcel Proust publishes *Sodome et Gomorrhe/Cities of the Plain*, the fourth volume of his multivolume novel *A la recherche du temps perdu/ Remembrance of Things Past*.
- The Irish writer George Moore publishes his novel *Héloïse and Abelard*.
- The Irish writer W. B. Yeats publishes his poetry collection *Michael Robartes and the Dancer*, which includes "Easter 1916" and "The Second Coming."
- The Italian writer Italo Svevo publishes his novel *La coscienza di Zeno/The Confessions of Zeno*.
- The Italian writer Umberto Saba publishes his poetry collection *Il Canzoniere/Songbook*.
- The Italian-born English writer Raphael Sabatini publishes his novel *Scaramouche*.
- The Norwegian writer Sigrid Undset publishes her novel *Husfrue/The Mistress of Husaby*, the second volume of her trilogy *Kristin Lavransdatter*.
- The Pulitzer Prize for Biography is awarded to Edward Bok for *The Americanization of Edward Bok* and the Prize for Fiction is awarded to Edith Wharton for *The Age of Innocence*.
- The U.S. writer Booth Tarkington publishes his novel *Alice Adams*.
- The U.S. writer Edwin Arlington Robinson publishes his *Collected Poems*, which includes "Mr. Flood's Party."
- The U.S. writer H. D. publishes her poetry collection *Hymen*.
- The U.S. writer John Dos Passos publishes his World War I novel *Three Soldiers*.
- The U.S. writer Sherwood Anderson publishes his short-story collection *The Triumph of the Egg*.
- The U.S. writer William Carlos Williams publishes his poetry collection *Sour Grapes*.

Music

- The English composer John Ireland completes his symphonic rhapsody *Mai-Dun*.
- The English composer Peter Warlock completes his song cycle *The Curlew*, settings of poems by the Irish writer W. B. Yeats, accompanied by string quartet and winds.
- The English composer William Walton completes his "entertainment" *Façade* for voices and chamber ensemble. It consists of settings of poems by the English writer Edith Sitwell.
- The French composer Germaine Tailleferre completes her Violin Sonata No. 1.
- The opera *Il piccolo Marat/The Little Marat* by the Italian composer Pietro Mascagni is first performed, in Rome, Italy.
- The opera *Kát'a Kabanová/Katya Kabanova* by the Czech composer Leoš Janáček is first performed, in Brno, Czechoslovakia.
- The opera *Love for Three Oranges* by the Russian composer Sergey Prokofiev is first performed, in Chicago, Illinois.
- The Swiss composer Arthur Honegger completes his dramatic psalm *Le Roi David/King David*.

Theater and Dance

- The ballet *Les Mariés de la Tour Eiffel/The Newlyweds of the Eiffel Tower* is first performed, in Paris, France. The music is by the French composer Darius Milhaud, the choreography by the Swedish dancer Jean Börlin, and the story by the French writer Jean Cocteau.
- The play *Anna Christie*, by the U.S. dramatist Eugene O'Neill is first performed, in New York, New York.
- The play *Le Pêcheur d'ombres/The Fisher of Shadows*, by the French dramatist Jean Sarment, is first performed, in Paris, France.
- The play *R U R: Rossum's Universal Robots*, by the Czech writer Karel Čapek, is first performed, in Prague, Czechoslovakia. It popularizes the word "robot," from the Czech word "*robota*," meaning "compulsory labor."
- The play *Sei personaggi in cerca d'autore/Six Characters in Search of an Author*, by the Italian writer Luigi Pirandello, is first performed, in Rome, Italy.
- The play *Ze života hmyzu/The Insect Play*, by the Czech writers Karel and Josef Čapek (brothers) is first performed, in Prague, Czechoslovakia.
- The Pulitzer Prize for Drama is awarded to Zona Gale for *Lulu Bett*.

Thought and Scholarship

- Dutch-born U.S. historian Henrik Willem Van Loon publishes *The Story of Mankind*.
- English archeologist Arthur Evans publishes the first volume of *The Palace of Minos at Knossos*. The final volume appears in 1935.
- English archeologist Osbert Crawford publishes *Man and his Past*, a pioneering study of prehistory by means of aerial photography.
- English philosopher John McTaggart publishes *The Nature of Existence*.
- English philosopher Bertrand Russell publishes *The Analysis of Mind*.
- Swiss psychologist Carl Jung publishes *Psychologische Typen/Psychological Types*, in which he differentiates two personality types: extroverted and introverted.
- The international writers' organization PEN (an acronym for poets, playwrights, editors, essayists and novelists) is founded in London, England.
- The Nobel Prize for Literature is awarded to the French novelist Anatole France.
- The Pulitzer Prize for History is awarded to William Sowden Sims and Burton J. Hendrick for *The Victory at Sea*.
- U.S. historian Albert Weinberg publishes *Manifest Destiny: A Study of National Expansionism in American History*.
- U.S. jurist Roscoe Pound publishes *The Spirit of the Common Law*.
- U.S. psychologist Robert Woodworth's book *Psychology* becomes the standard psychology text book.

APRIL

- New York officials fine physician William Jay Robinson $250 for publishing Marie C. Stopes's censored book, *Love in Marriage*.

SOCIETY

Everyday Life

- Pennsylvania potato farmer Earl V. Wise introduces the Wise potato chip.
- The first wholly automatic telephone dialing service is introduced, in Omaha, Nebraska.
- The Kimberly & Clark Co. of Neenah, Wisconsin, begins to sell its Celucotton sanitary napkins under the new name Kotex.
- The shimmy becomes a popular dance in the United States.
- The state of Missouri has experienced a 100% increase in divorces since 1896.
- U.S. hemlines rise appreciably in what some cultural arbiters construe to be evidence of the U.S. woman's new-found liberation. Women's fashions include knee-length skirts.

JANUARY

- The U.S. Census Bureau reports that 51% of Americans live in cities and towns with populations over 2,500.

MAY

5 Chanel No. 5 perfume, created by perfumer Ernst Beaux, is launched.
19 The University of Chicago announces that the average college graduate earns $5,762 per year after ten years of work.

JULY

19 A study in the United States states that there are 8 million working women in the United States, of which 1.9 million are married.

SEPTEMBER

30 20,000 businesses have failed in the United States since the start of the year.

NOVEMBER

2 The U.S. birth control advocates Margaret Sanger and Mary Ware Dennett establish the American Birth Control League.
5 The U.S. president Warren G. Harding declares Armistice Day (November 11, the date of the end of World War I in 1918) a national holiday.

Media and Communication

- Radio broadcasting begins in Australia, at Melbourne.
- The *Deutsche Allgemeine* newspaper is launched in Germany.

Sports

- Frenchwoman Alice Milliat founds the Fédération Sportive Féminine Internationale (FSFI), which campaigned for the inclusion of track and field events for women at the Olympics and also organized women's athletics meetings, holding its own *Jeux Olympiques* (Olympic Games) in Paris, France, in 1922; in Göteborg,

Sweden, in 1926; and in Prague, Czechoslovakia, in 1930.

- The 27-year reign of the German chess player Emanuel Lasker as world champion is brought to an end when he is defeated 9–5 by José Capablanca of Cuba, in Havana, Cuba.

- The Chicago Staleys, led by the U.S. player-coach George Halas, win the second American Professional Football Association championship. The following year they are renamed the Chicago Bears.

- The Ottawa Senators defeat the Vancouver Millionaires by three games to two to win hockey's Stanley Cup.

- The U.S. baseball player Babe Ruth hits a major league season record of 59 home runs for the New York Yankees, beating his own record set the previous season.

MAY

- The Fédération Equestre Internationale (FIE), the first international ruling body for equestrian sport, is founded in Brussels, Belgium, with eight founder nations.

BIRTHS & DEATHS

JANUARY

1   César (adopted name of César Baldaccini), French sculptor, many of whose works consist of crushed cars, born in Marseilles, France.

18   Bruce Woodcock, British heavyweight boxing champion 1945–50, born (–1997).

19   Patricia Highsmith, U.S. crime novelist, creator of the psychopathic murderer Tom Ripley, born in Fort Worth, Texas (–1995).

FEBRUARY

8   Peter Kropotkin, Russian revolutionary, dies in Dmitrov, near Moscow, Russia (78).

22   Jean-Bédel Bokassa, ruler of the Central African Republic 1965–79, born near Bangui, French colony of Oubangui-Chari (now Central African Republic) (–1996).

MARCH

2   Robert Simpson, English composer, principally of symphonies and string quartets, born in Leamington Spa, Warwickshire, England (–1997).

21   Jack Clayton, English film director, known especially for his films *Room at the Top* and *The Innocents*, born (–1995).

25   Simone Signoret, French dramatic actress of stage and film, born in Wiesbaden, Germany (–1985).

28   Dirk Bogarde, English actor, born in Hampstead, London, England.

APRIL

16   Peter Ustinov, British actor, director, playwright, novelist and screenwriter, born in London, England.

MAY

2   Satyajit Ray, Indian film director, born in Calcutta, India (–1992).

12   Joseph Beuys, German sculptor, born in Düsseldorf, Germany (–1986).

21   Andrey Dimitriyevich Sakharov, Soviet nuclear physicist and outspoken supporter of human rights and civil liberties, born in Moscow, Russia (–1989).

JUNE

2   Alexander Salking, U.S. film producer of *Superman*, born in the free city of Danzig (modern Gdańsk in Poland) (–1997).

8   Thojib Suharto, Indonesian army officer and politician, president of Indonesia 1968–98, born in Kemusu Argamulja, Indonesia.

10   Philip, Duke of Edinburgh, husband of Queen Elizabeth II of Great Britain and Northern Ireland, born in Corfu, Greece.

14   Eric Laithwaite, English electrical engineer who built the first magnetically-levitating high-speed train, born at Atherton, Yorkshire, England (–1997).

JULY

13   Gabriel Lippmann, French physicist who produced the first color photographic plate, dies at sea on route from Canada to France (75).

14   Geoffrey Wilkinson, English inorganic chemist who conducted pioneering work on the organometallic compounds of the transition metals, born in Todmorden, Yorkshire, England (–1996).

18   John Glenn, U.S. astronaut and politician, the first U.S. astronaut to orbit the earth, born in Cambridge, Ohio.

31   Whitney M. Young, U.S. civil-rights leader, who fought for equal opportunities for blacks in industry and government service, born in Lincoln Ridge, Kentucky (–1971).

AUGUST

2   Enrico Caruso, Italian operatic tenor and the first leading musician to record his voice, dies in Naples, Italy (48).

11   Alex (Palmer) Haley, U.S. author best known for his Pulitzer prizewinning book *Roots: The Saga of an American Family* (1976; prize 1977), born in Ithaca, New York (–1992).

19   Gene Roddenberry, U.S. writer and film and television producer who created *Star Trek*, born in El Paso, Texas (–1991).

SEPTEMBER

25   Robert David Muldoon, New Zealand prime minister 1975–84, born in Auckland, New Zealand (–1992).

27   Engelbert Humperdinck, German operatic composer known best for *Hansel and Gretel* (1893), dies in Neusterlitz, Germany (67).

OCTOBER

13   Yves Montand, Italian-born French singer and actor, born in Monsummano Alto, Italy (–1991).

17   George Mackay Brown, Scottish poet, born in Stromness, Orkney Islands, Scotland (–1996).

25   Bat Masterson (nickname of William Barclay Masterson), Canadian-born U.S. lawman, sportswriter, and, saloon keeper, dies in New York, New York (67).

NOVEMBER

5   Antoinette Brown Blackwell, U.S. Congregationalist and Unitarian minister, the first woman minister in the U.S., dies in Elizabeth, New Jersey (96).

6   James Jones, U.S. writer, author of the novel *From Here to Eternity*, born in Robinson, Illinois (–1977).

9   Viktor Ivanovich Chukarin, Soviet gymnast, winner of 11 gold medals in the 1952 and 1956 Olympics, born in Krasnoarmeyskoye, Ukraine, Russia (–1984).

27   Alexander Dubček, Czechoslovak communist leader 1968–69 whose liberal policies led to the Soviet occupation of Czechoslovakia (now the Czech and Slovak Republics), born in Uhrovec, Slovakia (–1992).

DECEMBER

16   Camille St.-Saëns, French composer whose work includes *Samson et Dalila*, and *Carnaval des animaux/Carnival of the Animals*, dies in Algiers (86).

25 Teams from Britain, France, Italy, Switzerland, and Norway compete in Monte Carlo, Monaco, in the first-ever international track and field athletics meeting outside the Olympic Games.

JUNE

17–18 The first National Collegiate Athletic Association track and field championships are held at Stagg Field, University of Chicago, Illinois.

25 Jock Hutchison becomes the first U.S. golfer to win the British Open golf championship, at St. Andrews, Scotland.

JULY

2 In the first-ever boxing match to gross over a million dollars, more than 80,000 people in a purpose-built wooden stadium in Jersey City, United States, watch the defending U.S. champion Jack Dempsey knock out

George Carpentier of France in four rounds to retain his world heavyweight boxing title.

OCTOBER

5–13 The first radio coverage of the World Series between the New York Giants and the New York Yankees is broadcast, in bulletins, by the WJZ radio station in Newark, New Jersey, and at the Electrical Show, a trade show in New York, New York.

5–13 The New York Yankees reach the World Series for the first time. However, they are beaten five games to three by city rivals, the New York Giants.

DECEMBER

• The Football Association in England bans women's matches from taking place at the grounds of clubs under its control. Women's football is not fully recognized by the Football Association until the 1970s.

◆

1922

POLITICS, GOVERNMENT, AND ECONOMICS

Business and Economics

• The U.S. Federal Reserve Board establishes a system to transmit securities electronically which avoids the problems associated with physical transfer.

AUGUST

• The value of the German mark, already severely weakened, begins to fall rapidly, from 162 to over 7,000 to the U.S. dollar.

Colonization

JULY

20–24 The Council of the League of Nations approves mandates for the former German colonies of Togoland (now Togo) and the Cameroons to France and Britain, and Tanganyika (now Tanzania) and Palestine to Britain.

Human Rights

FEBRUARY

• The U.S. Supreme Court upholds the 19th Amendment, granting suffrage to women.

SEPTEMBER

• U.S. President Warren G. Harding signs the Cable Act, granting married women citizenship status independent of their spouses.

Politics and Government

• U.S. President Warren G. Harding appoints the former Utah senator George Sutherland and the Minnesota lawyer Pierce Butler to the U.S. Supreme Court.

• The United Evangelical Church merges with the Evangelical Association to form the Evangelical Church in the United States.

• The United States sets up the "Prohibition Navy" to prevent widespread liquor smuggling.

JANUARY

7 The Dáil Eireann ratifies the 1921 Anglo-Irish Treaty by 64 votes to 57, bringing the Irish Free State into existence.

9 Following the Dáil Eireann's ratification of the 1921 Anglo-Irish Treaty, Eamon de Valera resigns as president of the self-proclaimed Irish Republic.

10 Arthur Griffith replaces Eamon de Valera as president of the self-proclaimed Irish Republic.

13 During a conference in Cannes, France, Britain and France agree to postpone Germany's payment of World War I reparations.

15 Raymond Poincaré forms a ministry in France dedicated to the extraction of World War I reparations from Germany (following Aristide Briand's resignation on January 12).

15 The Irish Sinn Féin leader Michael Collins becomes the first prime minister of the Irish Free State (now the Republic of Ireland) and forms a provisional government.

26 The legislative council of British Southern Rhodesia (now Zimbabwe) accepts a draft constitution conferring limited self-government.

31 The Jewish industrialist Walther Rathenau is appointed German foreign minister.

FEBRUARY

• U.S. Congress passes the Capper–Volstead Act, relieving agricultural cooperatives of antitrust liability.

1 The Washington Conference in the United States approves treaties restricting submarine warfare and the use of poison gas.

4 At the Washington Conference in the United States, Japan agrees to restore the Shandong peninsula to China, retaining some mining and commercial interests.

9–25 The resignation of the Italian prime minister Ivanoe Bonomi produces a crisis; Luigi Facta agrees to form a government on February 25.

11 A nine-power Treaty of Washington, brokered by the U.S. secretary of state Charles Evans Hughes, is signed securing China's independence and maintaining the "open door" for international trade with China.

15 The Permanent Court of International Justice set up by the League of Nations holds its first session at The Hague in the Netherlands.

28 The British government announces its acceptance of Egypt's wish to become an independent state, but states that Britain will retain considerable influence.

MARCH

1 Sweden and Russia sign a trade agreement.

6 The United States prohibits the export of arms to China.

10 Martial law is introduced in South Africa following violence during the miners' strike against the employment of blacks; 10,000 miners are arrested.

12 The communist republics of Georgia, Armenia, and Azerbaijan combine to form the Transcaucasian Socialist Republic.

15 A modified World War I reparations agreement—for Germany to pay with raw materials—is signed by France and Germany (approved by the Allied Reparations Commission on March 31).

15 Sultan Ahmed Fuad I of Egypt assumes the title of king as Fuad I, and Sudan comes under joint British–Egyptian sovereignty.

15 The Irish nationalist leader Eamon de Valera organizes a Republican Society demanding full independence for Ireland, to fight the Pro-Treaty Party (Cumann na nGaedheal) which supports the 1921 Anglo-Irish Treaty.

17 The Baltic states and Poland sign a convention to remain neutral should another state be attacked.

18 Mahatma Gandhi, the leader of the Indian Home Rule movement, is sentenced to six years' imprisonment for civil disobedience.

20 U.S. president Warren G. Harding orders the return of U.S. troops from the Rhineland, Germany.

24 An Allied conference in Paris, France, recommends that the warring Greeks and Turks should seek an armistice; the Turks, however, will only make peace if Greece evacuates Anatolia.

APRIL

• Wyoming senator John B. Kendrick launches the Teapot Dome investigation, having discovered that the interior secretary Albert B. Fall has leased oil reserves set aside for the U.S. Navy to private oil producers.

1 The ex-emperor of Austria and king of Hungary, Charles, dies on the island of Madeira.

7 Britain concedes drilling rights in Palestine to the U.S. Standard Oil Company.

10–May 19 An economic conference of the European powers is held in Genoa, Italy, breaking down over France's demand that communist Russia honor the former imperial government's debts.

14 Antitreaty rebels seize the Four Courts, Dublin, from the government of the Irish Free State.

16 By the Rapallo Treaty between Germany and Russia, Germany recognizes Russia as "a great power" and both sides waive World War I reparations claims; the treaty leads to the resumption of diplomatic and trade relations and to cooperation between the two countries' armies.

MAY

• U.S. President Warren G. Harding signs legislation creating the Federal Narcotics Control Board.

• The Lincoln Memorial is dedicated in Washington, D.C.

10 By the Genoa Convention, Russia agrees to respect Catholic rights and the Vatican drops claims relating to church property lost during the 1917 Russian Revolution.

15 Germany cedes the disputed territory of Upper Silesia to Poland.

24 Italy signs a commercial treaty with Russia.

26 The Russian leader Vladimir Ilyich Lenin suffers a stroke.

31 The Allied Reparations Commission grants Germany a year-long moratorium on its World War I reparations payments because of its financial difficulties.

JUNE

5 The U.S. Congress presents the Medal of Congress to the people of Verdun, France, honoring their resistance in World War I.

10 The bankers' committee of the Allied Reparations Commission decides not to recommend an international loan for German reconstruction.

16 Elections in the Irish Free State (now the Republic of Ireland) give a majority to the Pro-Treaty (Anglo-Irish Treaty) candidates (58, against 35 anti-Treaty Republicans); anti-Treaty Republicans continue to oppose the new government, with the Irish Republican Army (IRA) taking large areas under its control.

18–July 19 A Kurdish revolt for independence breaks out on the Iraqi-Turkish border.

22 Two Irishmen in London, England, murder Field Marshal Henry Wilson, an advocate of the British reconquest of Ireland; the British government demands the restoration of order in the Irish Free State (now the Republic of Ireland).

24 The Jewish German foreign minister Walther Rathenau is murdered by anti-Semitic nationalists.

26 Following an international fall in confidence in the German economy in the aftermath of the German foreign minister Walter Rathenau's assassination, an emergency decree is passed in an attempt to protect it.

28–30 Anti-Treaty (Anglo-Irish Treaty) republicans seize the assistant chief of staff of the Irish army, General Ginger O'Connell, in Dublin in the Irish Free State (now the Republic of Ireland) and hold him hostage in the Four Courts building; the Irish army besieges the building and the rebel forces present surrender. Fighting continues in the rest of Dublin.

28–July 5 Heavy fighting continues in Dublin, in the Irish Free State (now the Republic of Ireland), between the army and anti-Treaty (Anglo-Irish Treaty) rebels.

JULY

8 Chile and Peru agree to submit their dispute over the Tacna and Arica territories (on the border between the two countries) to arbitration.

20 Government troops in the Irish Free State (now the Republic of Ireland) capture Limerick and Waterford from nationalist anti-Treaty (Anglo-Irish Treaty) rebels.

29 The Allied powers issue an ultimatum forbidding Greek occupation of Constantinople (modern Istanbul) in the Greek–Turkish War.

31 A general strike begins in Italy, in protest against the weakness of the state's opposition to fascist agitation.

AUGUST

1 Britain, France, and Italy warn Greece against the attempted occupation of Palestine in the Greek–Turkish War.

1 The Balfour Note is circulated to the Allies, stating that Britain would only expect to recover from its European debtors the sum owed by Britain to the United States, thus placing responsibility for the collection of war debts on the United States.

3–8 Fighting between fascists and socialists takes place in Italian cities; the fascists take Milan on August 4.

11 Free State Irish government troops capture the city of Cork from anti-Treaty (Anglo-Irish Treaty) republican forces.

12 Arthur Griffith, president of the Dáil of the Irish Free State (now the Republic of Ireland), dies suddenly of a brain hemorrhage and the prime minister Michael Collins steps into his position for 10 days.

22 Michael Collins, the prime minister of the provisional government of the Irish Free State (now the Republic of Ireland), is killed by a republican ambush in west Cork.

24 The Arab Congress at Nablus, Palestine, rejects the League of Nations' granting of a British mandate over Palestine.

30 In the Greek–Turkish War, the Ankara Turks (nationalists) defeat the Greeks at the Battle of Afyon in Anatolia (modern Turkey).

31 An alliance is made between Czechoslovakia and the Kingdom of the Serbs, Croats, and Slovenes.

31 The Allied Reparations Commission adopts a Belgian proposal for Germany's World War I reparations payments to be made in installments by treasury bills rather than hard currency, because of Germany's financial crisis.

SEPTEMBER

• U.S. Congress passes the Fordney–McCumber Tariff Act, restoring tariffs to their 1909 levels and authorizing the president to adjust the tariff by as much as 50% on individual items.

• U.S. Congress passes the Grain Futures Act, designed to prevent the speculation that precipitated a collapse of grain prices in 1920.

9 In the Greek–Turkish War, the Turks take the city of Smyrna from the Greeks; many Greek inhabitants are massacred.

9 The Dáil of the Irish Free State (now the Republic of Ireland) meets under heavy guard; it elects William Cosgrave as president to replace the deceased Arthur Griffith.

11 Britain's mandate over Palestine is formally proclaimed, while Arabs declare a day of mourning.

13 France and Poland sign a ten-year military convention.

16 A British force lands at Chanak on the Dardanelles to oppose the Turkish nationalists' advance on the Dardanelles in the Greek–Turkish War.

18 Hungary is admitted to the League of Nations, the first of the defeated Central Powers of World War I to be admitted.

23 With the Turkish nationalist army now advancing on the Dardanelles, the Allies invite the Ankara (Turkish nationalist) government to a peace conference.

27 King Constantine I of Greece abdicates for the second time, following a rising of the ex-prime minister Eleutherios Venizelos's supporters, and is succeeded by his son George II.

30 Conscription of all 20-year-old males is introduced in Russia.

OCTOBER

• The Georgia governor Thomas W. Hardwick names Mrs. W. H. Felton to fill the Senate vacancy created by the death of Thomas E. Watson, making Felton the first woman to serve in the U.S. Senate.

4 Austria receives an international loan to finance its postwar reconstruction.

10 The formal British mandate over Iraq is ended and an alliance between the two is concluded.

13 The Armistice of Mudania is signed, ending the Greek–Turkish War and formalizing relations between the Allies and the Turkish nationalist government in Ankara; the Allies allow Turkish troops to enter Constantinople (modern Istanbul).

19 Following the "Chanak Crisis" of September–October (when the British prime minister David Lloyd George reinforced British troops at Chanak on the Dardanelles and threatened Turkey), the Conservatives withdraw from the coalition government in Britain and David Lloyd George resigns as prime minister.

23 Andrew Bonar Law forms a Conservative government in Britain after the resignation of David Lloyd George over the "Chanak Crisis" of September–October.

24 At the opening of the Fascist Congress in Naples, Italy, the fascist leader Benito Mussolini demands participation in the government.

24 The Dáil adopts a constitution for the Irish Free State (now the Republic of Ireland), which provides for a governor-general to represent the British crown.

24 The socialist Friedrich Ebert is reelected president of Germany.

27 A referendum in the British colony of Southern Rhodesia (modern Zimbabwe) votes against joining the Union of South Africa.

27 The Italian cabinet offers its resignation in the face of mounting fascist power, but it is not accepted by King Victor Emmanuel III.

28 The fascists in Italy begin the "March on Rome" to bring down the government.

31 The Italian fascist leader Benito Mussolini forms a government of liberals, nationalists, and fascists at King Victor Emmanuel III's request.

NOVEMBER

1 The Turkish nationalist leader Mustafa Kemal Pasha (later known as Atatürk) proclaims Turkey a republic and the sultanate abolished.

2–7 A Berlin conference of monetary experts discussing ways of stabilizing German finances fails to reach any agreement.

7 In U.S. Congressional elections, Republicans retain majorities in the House (225–205) and Senate (51–43).

9–11 At a London Conference, Britain offers to cancel German World War I reparations but France refuses.

17 Following the victory of the Turkish nationalists in the Greek–Turkish War, the caliph (and former sultan) of Turkey, Muhammad VI, leaves the country and is declared deposed; his successor, Prince Abd ul-Mejid, renounces the sultanate (political leadership) and holds only the caliphate (religious leadership).

17 In the British general election, the Conservatives win 345 seats, Labour 142, David Lloyd George's Liberals 62, and Herbert Asquith's Liberals 54.

17 The Far Eastern Republic votes for union with Russia, following the defeat of White Russian forces previously active in the region.

20 A conference opens in Lausanne, Switzerland, to conclude peace between Greece and Turkey.

22 The industrialist Wilhelm Cuno succeeds Karl Wirth as German chancellor following his resignation (on November 4).

24 The leading republican Erskine Childers is executed in the Irish Free State (now the Republic of Ireland) for possession of a firearm.

25 The Italian parliament grants the fascist leader Benito Mussolini temporary emergency powers to force through reforms.

28 Six Greek former ministers and generals are executed for Greece's defeat in the Greek–Turkish War.

DECEMBER

1 President Józef Piłsudski of Poland resigns to become chief of the army.

3 Ahmed Bey Zogu, leader of the Yugoslav Party, becomes Albanian prime minister.

6 The Dáil of the Irish Free State (now the Republic of Ireland) and the British Parliament ratify the 1921 Anglo-Irish Treaty; Tim Healy is appointed the British governor-general in Ireland.

7 The Northern Ireland parliament votes against inclusion in the Irish Free State (now the Republic of Ireland) and remains instead a part of Britain.

15 A Franco-Canadian trade agreement establishes mutual tariff reductions.

15 The Russian leader Vladimir Ilyich Lenin suffers a second stroke and dictates his "Testament," detailing the strengths and weaknesses of his potential successors and harshly criticizing both Joseph Stalin and Leon Trotsky.

17 The last British troops leave the Irish Free State (now the Republic of Ireland) following its acceptance of dominion status.

26 The Allied Reparations Commission, against Britain's vote, declares that Germany has made a voluntary default in its World War I reparations payments and is therefore liable to punitive action.

30 The Union of Soviet Socialist Republics (USSR) is established through the confederation of Russia, Belarus, the Ukraine, and the Transcaucasian Federation.

SCIENCE, TECHNOLOGY, AND MEDICINE

Agriculture

- U.S. farmer-entrepreneur Thomas Meredith launches the periodical *Better Homes and Gardens* in the United States.

Ecology

- British meteorologist Lewis Fry Richardson publishes *Weather Prediction by Numerical Process*, in which he applies the first mathematical techniques to weather forecasting.
- Wood Buffalo National Park, Alberta, Canada, is established. The largest national park in the world, covering 44,800 sq km/17,300 sq mi, it contains the only remaining free-ranging buffalo herds.

Exploration

MAY

12 A twenty-ton meteorite lands in a field near Blackstone, Virginia, leaving a 46 sq m/500 sq ft hole in the ground.

Health and Medicine

- English biochemist Frederick Gowland Hopkins isolates glutathione and demonstrates its vital role in the cell's utilization of oxygen.
- English physiologist Archibald Hill and German physiologist Otto Fritz Meyerhof share the Nobel Prize for Physiology or Medicine, Hill for his discovery relating to the production of heat in the muscle and Meyerhof for his discovery of the fixed relationship between the consumption of oxygen and the metabolism of lactic acid in the muscle.
- French surgeon Alexis Carrel discovers white blood cells (leukocytes).

Math

- Polish mathematician Stefan Banach begins his work on a development of vector spaces, an important tool in general analysis.

Science

- British archeologist Leonard Woolley begins excavating the ancient Sumerian city of Ur in Iraq (completed 1934).
- Danish physicist Niels Bohr receives the Nobel Prize for Physics for his investigation of the structure of atoms and the radiation emanating from them.
- English physicist Francis Aston receives the Nobel Prize for Chemistry for pioneering the mass spectrometry of isotopes of radioactive elements and enunciating the whole-number rule.
- English physicist Patrick Maynard Blackett undertakes experiments on the transmutation of elements.
- German chemist Hermann Staudinger coins the word "macromolecule" to describe the chain of isoprene units that make up rubber.
- Polish-born British anthropologist Bronislaw Malinowski publishes *Argonauts of the Western Pacific*, which establishes fieldwork and participant observation as the primary methodology in anthropology.
- The first ionamide dyes are prepared.
- U.S. chemist Herbert McLean Evans discovers vitamin E.
- U.S. physicist Arthur Holly Compton discovers that X-rays scattered by an atom have a shift in frequency. He explains the phenomenon, known as the Compton effect, by treating the X-rays as a stream of particles, thus confirming the wave–particle idea of light.

NOVEMBER
4 The English archeologist Howard Carter discovers the tomb of Pharaoh Tutankhamen in Luxor, Egypt, the only ancient Egyptian pharaoh's tomb discovered complete with grave goods.

Technology

- British horologist John Harwood invents the self-winding wrist-watch.
- Italian physicist Guglielmo Marconi suggests that radio waves may be used to detect moving objects. The U.S. Naval Research Laboratory tests the idea and detects a ship moving between the receiver and transmitter. It is the first example of a sophisticated radar system.
- Oil is discovered in Venezuela.
- Production of the Austin Seven, the first British mass-produced car, begins in Cowley, Oxfordshire.

OCTOBER
14 The Bell Telephone Company installs the first mechanical switchboard system in New York, New York. The exchange is called "Pennsylvania."

Transportation

- The first car radio is installed in Britain by the Italian physicist and inventor Guglielmo Marconi.

- The U.S. Fageol Safety Coach Company of Oakland, California, builds the first true bus. It has an extra-long wheelbase, wide-tread tires, a front-mounted engine, and a lower frame.
- U.S. firm Deusenberg Automobile and Motor Company introduces the Model A Deusenberg, the first U.S. car with hydraulic brakes.

MARCH
- The U.S. ship *Langley* enters service. A converted collier, it is the nation's first aircraft carrier.

OCTOBER
18 U.S. Army officer William Mitchell sets an air speed record of 356.74 kph/222.96 mph.

DECEMBER
- The Japanese ship *Hosyo* enters service. It is Japan's first purpose-built aircraft carrier.

ARTS AND IDEAS

Architecture

- The Amstellaan housing complex in Amsterdam, the Netherlands, designed by the Dutch architect Michel de Klerk, is completed.
- The Swiss architect Le Corbusier designs his project Ville Contemporaine, a total plan for a city built on rigorously logical principles.

Arts

- English art critic Clive Bell publishes *Since Cézanne*.
- New Zealand cartoonist David Low publishes *Lloyd George and Co*, a book of political cartoons.
- The Lincoln Memorial, designed by the U.S. architect Henry Bacon, is completed in Washington, D.C.
- The Romanian artist Constantin Brancusi sculpts *The Fish* and *Torso of a Young Man*.
- The Russian artist Kasimir Malevich sculpts *Suprematist Architecton No 3*.
- The Spanish artist Joan Miró paints *The Farm*.
- The Spanish artist Pablo Picasso paints *Paul as Harlequin*.
- The U.S. artist and photographer Man Ray takes *Violon, d'Ingres/Violin, by Ingres*.
- The U.S. artist Gerald Murphy paints *Villa America*.
- The U.S. artist John Marin paints *Maine Islands*.
- The U.S. artist John Sloan paints *The City from Greenwich Village*.

Film

- The documentary *Nanook of the North*, directed by Robert Flaherty, is released in Britain.
- The fascist government in Italy gives support to the Italian movie industry in an attempt to reduce the influence of U.S. culture in the country.
- The movie *Blood and Sand*, directed by Fred Niblo, is released in the United States, starring Rudolph Valentino and Nita Naldi.

- The movie *Dr Mabuse* or *The Gambler*, directed by Fritz Lang, is released in Germany, starring Rudolph Klein-Rogge, Alfred Abel, and Gertrude Welcker.
- The movie *Foolish Wives*, directed by Austrian filmmaker Erich von Stroheim, is released in the United States. Von Stroheim also stars in it along with Mae Busch, Maud George, and Cesare Gravina.
- The movie *Häxan* or *Witchcraft Through the Ages*, directed by Benjamin Christiansen, is released in Sweden, starring Oscar Stribolt, Clara Pontoppidan, and Karen Winther.
- The movie *La Femme de Nulle Part/The Woman of No Account*, directed by Louis Delluc, is released in France, starring Eve Francis, Roger Karl, and Gine Avril.
- The movie *Orphans of the Storm*, directed by D. W. Griffith, is released in the United States, starring sisters Lillian Gish and Dorothy Gish.
- The movie *Robin Hood*, directed by Alan Dwan, is released in the United States, starring Douglas Fairbanks.
- The movie *Storm on the Mountain*, directed by Julien Duvivier, is released in France, starring Gaston Jacquet and Lotte Loring.
- The movie *The Loves of Pharaoh*, directed by Ernst Lubitsch, is released in Germany, starring Emil Jannings. In addition, when shown in Paris, France, his movie *Madame Dubarry* incites unrest, as right-wing groups criticize foreign portrayals of French history.

FEBRUARY
- U.S. Postmaster-General Will Hays is appointed by major Hollywood movie studios to head Motion Pictures and Producers of America, an organization that is founded in an effort to improve the image of the movie industry. It soon becomes known as the Hays office.

Literature and Language

- The English writer Charles Edward Montague publishes *Disenchantment*, a series of essays based on his experiences in World War I.
- The English writer D. H. Lawrence publishes his novel *Aaron's Rod*.
- The English writer David Garnett publishes his novel *Lady into Fox*.
- The English writer Hugh Walpole publishes his novel *The Cathedral*.
- The English writer Henry Williamson publishes his novel *Dandelion Days*.
- The English writer May Sinclair publishes her novel *Life and Death of Harriett Frean*.
- The English writer Richmal Crompton publishes her collection of short stories *Just – William*, the first of a series of children's books featuring the archetypal English schoolboy William.
- The English writer Virginia Woolf publishes her novel *Jacob's Room*.
- The French writer François Mauriac publishes his novel *Le Baiser au lépreux/The Kiss of the Leper*.
- The French writer Paul Valéry publishes his poetry collection *Charmes ou poèmes/Charms or Poems*, which includes his poem "Le Cimetière marin"/"Graveyard by the Sea."

- The French writer Roger Martin du Gard publishes *Le Cahier gris/The Grey Notebook*, the first volume of his *Les Thibault/The Thibault Family* cycle of novels. The last volume will appear in 1940.
- The Irish writer James Joyce publishes his novel *Ulysses* in Paris, France.
- The literary review *The Criterion* is first published in Britain, founded and edited by the U.S.-born English writer T. S. Eliot. Appearing until 1939, it publishes works by W. H. Auden, Ezra Pound, D. H. Lawrence, Eliot, Stephen Spender, and others.
- The New Zealand writer Katherine Mansfield publishes her collection of short stories *The Garden Party and Other Stories*.
- The Norwegian writer Sigrid Undset publishes her novel *Korset/The Cross*, the third volume of her trilogy *Kristin Lavransdatter*.
- The Peruvian writer César Vallejo publishes his poetry collection *Trilce*.
- The Pulitzer Prize for Biography is awarded to Hamlin Garland for *A Daughter of the Middle Border*, the Prize for Fiction is awarded to Booth Tarkington for *Alice Adams*, and the Prize for Poetry is awarded to Edwin Arlington Robinson for *Collected Poems*.
- The Scottish writer John Buchan publishes his novel *Huntingtower*.
- The U.S. writer Carl Sandburg publishes his poetry stories *Rootabaga Stories*.
- The U.S. writer Carl Van Vechten publishes his novel *Peter Whiffle*.
- The U.S. writer e e cummings publishes *The Enormous Room*, an account of his time in a French prison during World War I.
- The U.S. writer F. Scott Fitzgerald publishes his story collection *Tales of the Jazz Age*, which includes "The Diamond as Big as the Ritz."
- The U.S. writer Sinclair Lewis publishes his novel *Babbitt*.
- The U.S. writer Theodore Dreiser publishes his second book of autobiography, *A Book about Myself*.
- The U.S. writer Willa Cather publishes her World War I novel *One of Ours*.
- U.S. Post Office officials destroy 500 copies of the Irish writer James Joyce's novel *Ulysses*, imported from France, which has been condemned as obscene.
- U.S.-born English writer T. S. Eliot publishes his long poem "The Waste Land" in *The Criterion*.

Music

- Popular songs in the United States include "Song of Love," "April Showers," "My Man," and "Rose of the Rio Grande."
- The Danish composer Carl Nielsen completes his Symphony No. 5.
- The English composer Arthur Bliss completes his *Colour Symphony*.
- The English composer Ralph Vaughan Williams completes *A Pastoral Symphony*.
- The French composer Maurice Ravel completes his Sonata for Violin and Cello.
- The French composer Jacques Ibert completes his orchestral suite *Escales/Ports of Call*.

- The French-born U.S. composer Edgard Varèse completes his orchestral work *Amériques/Americas*.
- The U.S. composer George Antheil completes his *Airplane Sonata*.
- The white jazz group New Orleans Rhythm Kings is formed in Chicago, Illinois.
- U.S. cornetist, bandleader, and composer Joe "King" Oliver leads his Creole Jazz Band at Lincoln Gardens, Chicago, Illinois.
- U.S. musician Ben Pollack leads the band at the Venice Ballroom, Los Angeles, California.
- Young Viennese musicians found the International Society for Contemporary Music (ISCM) in Salzburg, Austria, under the direction of the British musicologist Edward Dent. The festival is to be held each year at a different center.

AUGUST
- The Paul Whiteman Orchestra, a symphonic jazz group, records "Three O'Clock in the Morning" at the Victor Studios in Camden, New Jersey.

SEPTEMBER
9   John Carson, U.S. fiddler, performs on the WSB station in Atlanta, Georgia. He is one of the first country musicians to be heard on radio.

Theater and Dance

- The play *Abie's Irish Rose*, by the U.S. dramatist Anne Nichols, is first performed, in New York, New York. It runs for 2,327 performances, a record at that time.
- The play *Back to Methuselah*, by the Irish writer George Bernard Shaw, is first performed, at the Garrick Theater in New York, New York.
- The play *Enrico IV/Henry IV*, by the Italian writer Luigi Pirandello, is first performed, in Rome, Italy.
- The play *Le Cocu magnifique/The Magnificent Cuckold*, by the Belgian dramatist Fernand Crommelynck, is performed at the Meyerhold Theater in Moscow, Russia. The sets, by the Russian artist Liubov Popova, make the production one of the major expressions of constructivism in the theater.
- The play *The Cat and the Canary*, by the U.S. dramatist John Willard, is first performed, in New York, New York.
- The play *The Hairy Ape*, by the U.S. dramatist Eugene O'Neill is first performed, at the Provincetown Playhouse in New York, New York.
- The play *Trommeln in der Nacht/Drums in the Night*, by the German writer Bertolt Brecht, is first performed, in Munich, Germany.
- The play *Věc Makropoulos/The Makropoulos Affair*, by the Czech writer Karel Čapek, is first performed, in Prague, Czechoslovakia. The Czech composer Leoš Janáček turns it into an opera in 1926.
- The Pulitzer Prize for Drama is awarded to Eugene O'Neill for *Anna Christie*.

Thought and Scholarship

- Austrian philosopher Ludwig Wittgenstein publishes *Tractatus Logico-Philosophicus/Tract on Logic and Philosophy*, a classic of 20th-century philosophy that analyzes the relationship between reality and language.

- German historian Oswald Spengler publishes the second volume of his *Der Untergang des Abendlandes/The Decline of the West*. The first volume appeared in 1918.
- Indian scholar Surendra Nath Dasgupta publishes the first volume of his five-volume *History of Indian Philosophy*. The final volume appears in 1955.
- The Nobel Prize for Literature is awarded to the Spanish dramatist Jacinto Benavente y Martínez.
- The Pulitzer Prize for History is awarded to James Truslow Adams for *The Founding of New England*.
- U.S. historian Carl L. Becker publishes *The Declaration of Independence*.
- U.S. jurist Roscoe Pound publishes *Introduction to the Philosophy of Law*.
- U.S. philosopher John Dewey publishes *Human Nature and Conduct*.
- U.S. political journalist Walter Lippmann publishes *Public Opinion*.

SOCIETY

Education

- The Institute of Economics is founded in the United States.

Everyday Life

- Americans use 14.2 million postage stamps, compared with 3.9 million in 1900.
- The U.S. magazine *Vanity Fair* employs the term "flapper" to denote an independent young woman who does not conform to traditional notions of femininity, dresses in a provocative manner, and smokes. Clara Bow, in the 1927 movie *It*, is subsequently seen as the embodiment of the flapper.

JANUARY
10   A strike begins in the Rand gold mines of South Africa, protesting at the employment of blacks.

FEBRUARY
- Workers strike at the Amoskeag textile mill in Manchester, New Hampshire, after management announces plans to cut pay by 20% while increasing the working week from 48 to 52 hours.

Media and Communication

- AT&T begin "toll broadcasting" in the United States, which offers the opportunity to broadcast to the U.S. public by radio, by establishing the WEAF station in New York, New York. The commercial advertising potential is quickly seen, and on August 28, WEAF radio station broadcasts the first radio advertisement: a real estate firm buys ten minutes to extol its new housing development in the borough of Queens.

- Long-distance telephone lines are used to connect a radio station in New York, New York, with one in Chicago, Illinois, that is broadcasting the action of a football game. It is the beginning of network broadcasting.
- The first commercial radio telephone service between New York, New York, and London, England, opens.

FEBRUARY

5   U.S. publishers DeWitt Wallace and his wife Lila Acheson Wallace publish the first issue of the *Reader's Digest* magazine in Greenwich Village, New York, New York.

14   Radio station 2MT, near Chelmsford, England, is the first commercial radio station in Britain to begin authorized broadcasts.

OCTOBER

4–8 The WJZ radio station in Newark, New Jersey, broadcasts the first radio play-by-play coverage of the World Series, between the New York Giants and the New York Yankees. Grantland Rice, a sportswriter, broadcasts the games from the Polo Grounds in New York, New York.

NOVEMBER

14   Following a governmental decision that radio broadcasting should come within the control of the Post Office, the British Broadcasting Company (BBC), under its general manager John Reith, makes its first broadcast, on station 2LO in London, England.

Religion

- The Russian leader Vladimir Ilyich Lenin steps up the communist government's campaign against organized religion.

FEBRUARY

6   Following the death of Pope Benedict XV on January 22, the Italian clergyman Ambrogio Damiano Achille Ratti is elected Pope Pius XI.

Football (1905–96)

1905
- Eighteen players are killed and 154 seriously injured during the football season; U.S. president Franklin D. Roosevelt threatens to ban the sport unless action is taken to curb the violence.

1906
- The U.S. Intercollegiate Athletic Association redrafts the rules of football. The forward pass is legalized for the first time and, following a large number of fatalities in the previous season, a number of dangerous plays are eliminated.

1920
September 17   A new professional football league, the American Professional Football Association, the forerunner of the National Football League, is formed at Canton, Ohio. It comprises 10 teams (soon extended to 14).

1922
- The American Professional Football Association is renamed the National Football League.

1933
July 8   The National Football League (NFL) is split into Eastern and Western divisions, with the winners meeting to decide the championship.

1935
- Jay Berwanger of Chicago, Illinois, wins the inaugural DAC Trophy presented by the Downtown Athletic Club of New York to the outstanding college football player east of the Mississippi. The following year the award is renamed the Heisman Trophy and college players from the whole of the United States are eligible to win it.
May 19   The draft system is introduced into football: the team at the bottom of the NFL is allowed first choice of players graduating from college, starting in the 1936 season.

1936
- A rival to the NFL, the second to call itself The American Football League, is formed. The Boston Shamrocks are its first champions.

1939
January 15   The New York Giants defeat the Pro-All Stars 13–10 at Wrigley Field, Los Angeles, California, in the inaugural Pro Bowl game.

1943
April   The wearing of helmets is made compulsory in the NFL.

1950
January 20   Unlimited free substitution, adopted in 1943, but withdrawn three years later, is restored, paving the way for the modern system of specialization in offense and defense in pro football.
March 3   Following the merger of the All-America Football Conference (AAFC) and the NFL, the American and National Divisions are created to replace the NFL's Eastern and Western Divisions.

1960
- The American Football League (AFL) is formed to challenge the NFL.

1963
September 7   The Pro Football Hall of Fame, established by the NFL in honor of famous players, is dedicated in Canton, Ohio.

1966
June 8   The mounting rivalry between the AFL and the NFL is ended when the two bodies agree to merge. The merger will not be fully effective until 1970, but from 1967 a common draft of college players will take place and a Super Bowl game between the champions of each league will be inaugurated.

SEPTEMBER

12 The U.S. Protestant Episcopal Church changes its marriage ceremony, deleting the word "obey" from the vows.

Sports

- Molla Bjursted Mallory, who emigrated to the United States from Norway in 1914, wins the her seventh women's singles title in eight years at the U.S. lawn tennis championships at Germantown Cricket Club, Philadelphia, Pennsylvania.
- The 20-year-old U.S. golfer Gene Sarazen wins the U.S. Open and U.S. Professional Golfers' Association (PGA) championships.
- The All England Lawn Tennis and Croquet Club moves from Worple Road, Wimbledon, London, England, to new premises in nearby Church Road. The newly built Centre Court has 9,989 seats and standing room for 3,600 spectators.

- The American Professional Football Association is renamed the National Football League.
- The British Alpine skiing pioneer Arnold Lunn invents the modern slalom event at Mürren, Switzerland.
- The Chicago Staleys, last year's winners of the American Professional Football Association championship, are renamed the Chicago Bears.
- The Toronto St. Pats (who become known as the Toronto Maple Leafs from 1926) defeat the Vancouver Millionaires by three games to two to win hockey's Stanley Cup.

MARCH

5 The inaugural Vasaloppet 90-km/56-mi cross-country skiing race between Mora and Sälen is staged in Sweden.

APRIL

11 A boxing match between the U.S. fighters Johnny Dundee and Johnny Ray at Motor Square, Pittsburgh, United States, is the first sporting event to be broadcast on the radio.

1967

January 15 The first Super Bowl is held; the Green Bay Packers beat the Kansas City Chiefs 35–10 before 61,496 spectators in Los Angeles, California.

1970

- Professional football is reorganized into two "conferences," the National Football Conference (NFC) and the American Football Conference (AFC), each with 13 teams and 3 divisions.

1972

- The Dallas Cowboys become the first football team to introduce professional cheerleaders.

1974

April 25 The introduction of sudden-death overtime in preseason and regular season games is one of several changes made by the National Football League (NFL) to make the game more exciting.

1980

January 20 The Pittsburgh Steelers defeat the Los Angeles Rams 31–19 in Super Bowl XIV before a record crowd of 103,985 in Pasadena, California, to become the first team to win four Super Bowls.

1982

September 20–November 22 The football season is interrupted by a players' strike lasting 57 days. The dispute is settled by a Collective Bargaining Agreement which establishes a minimum salary for players and introduces severance pay to help those moving to other careers.

1983

July 17 The Michigan Panthers defeat the Philadelphia Stars 24–22 in Denver, Colorado, to win the inaugural United States Football League (USFL) championship, set up as a rival to the NFL.

1984

December Eric Dickerson of the Los Angeles Rams sets new game and season professional records for rushing 215 yards and 2,105 yards respectively.

1986

August 4 The USFL announces that it is canceling its 1986 season, six days after winning just one dollar in a $1.69 billion antitrust law suit against the NFL.

September 7 Instant video replays operated by an extra official are used for the first time in the NFL to decide disputed plays in certain situations.

1990

January 28 The San Francisco 49ers defeat the Denver Broncos 55–10 in Super Bowl XXIV in New Orleans, Louisiana, to match the Pittsburgh Steelers' achievement of four Super Bowls. It is the first time that a football team has scored over 50 points in the Super Bowl.

1995

- Emmitt Smith of the Dallas Cowboys scores 25 touchdowns, surpassing the National Football League all-time season record of 24 set by John Riggins of the Washington Redskins in 1983.

1996

November 10 The Miami Dolphins quarterback Dan Marino becomes the first player in the history of the NFL to reach a career passing mark of 50,000 yards.

BIRTHS & DEATHS

c. 1922 Fahd ibn Abd al-Aziz, King of Saudi Arabia from 1982, born in Riyadh, Arabia.

JANUARY

5 Ernest Shackleton, British explorer, who tried to reach the South Pole, dies in Grytviken, South Georgia, Russia (47).

9 Har Gobind Khorana, Indian-born U.S. biochemist who in 1970 cloned the first gene (a yeast gene), born in Raipur, India.

9 Sékou Touré, first president of the Republic of Guinea 1958–84, born in Faranah, French Guinea (–1984).

22 Benedict XV, pope 1914–22, dies in Rome (67).

FEBRUARY

1 Yamagata Aritomo, Japanese soldier and statesman, first prime minister of Japan 1889–91 and again 1898–1900, responsible for turning Japan into a military power, dies in Tokyo, Japan (83).

MARCH

• Julius Nyerere, first prime minister of independent Tanganyika 1961 and president of Tanzania 1965–85, born in Butiama, Tanganyika.

1 Yitzhak Rabin, prime minister of Israel 1974–77 and 1992–95, born in Jerusalem (–1995).

12 Jack Kerouac, U.S. poet, novelist, and leader of the Beat movement, born in Lowell, Massachusetts (–1969).

APRIL

2 Hermann Rorschach, Swiss psychiatrist who developed the inkblot test that bears his name, dies in Herisau, Switzerland (37).

12 Tiny Tim (originally Herbert Kauhry), U.S. singer known for his song "Tiptoe Through the Tulips," born in New York, New York (–1996).

13 John Braine, English author of *Room at the Top* (1957), one of the "Angry Young Men," born in Bradford, Yorkshire (now West Yorkshire), England (–1986).

16 Kingsley Amis, English writer, born in London, England (–1995).

22 Charlie Mingus, U.S. jazz composer, bassist, pianist, and bandleader, born in Nogales, Arizona (–1979).

MAY

7 John Henry Patterson, U.S. manufacturer who developed the cash register and founded the National Cash Register Company (NCR), dies near Philadelphia, Pennsylvania (77).

18 Alphonse Laveran, French physician who discovered the malaria parasite, dies in Paris, France (76).

31 Denholm Elliott, English actor, born in London, England (–1992).

JUNE

3 Alain Resnais, French film director, born in Vannes, France.

6 Lilian Russell, U.S. actress and singer, dies in Pittsburgh, Pennsylvania (70).

10 Judy Garland, U.S. singer and actress, born in Grand Rapids, Michigan (–1969).

JULY

7 Pierre Cardin, French fashion designer, born in Venice, Italy.

12 Michael Ventris, English cryptographer who deciphered the Minoan Linear B script, showing it to be an early form of Greek, born in Wheathampstead, Hertfordshire, England (–1956).

15 Bruce Merrifield, U.S. biochemist who discovered how to synthesize polypeptide chains in any predetermined order, born in Fort Worth, Texas.

19 George S. McGovern, U.S. senator and Democratic candidate for the U.S. presidency (1972), born in Avon, South Dakota.

22 Jokichi Takamine, Japanese biochemist who isolated adrenaline (epinephrine), the first hormone to be isolated from natural sources, dies in New York, New York (67).

28 Jacques Piccard, Swiss engineer and physicist who, with his father, designed the bathyscaph for deep sea exploration, born in Brussels, Belgium.

AUGUST

2 Alexander Graham Bell, Scottish-born U.S. scientist who invented the telephone, dies in Beinn Bhreagh, Cape Breton Island, Nova Scotia, Canada (75).

4 Enver Pasha, Ottoman general who was largely responsible for the Ottoman Empire entering World War I on the side of Germany, dies in Baldzhuan, Turkestan (40).

8 Rudi Gernrich, U.S. avant-garde fashion designer, born in Vienna, Austria.

9 Philip Larkin, English poet, born in Coventry, England (–1985).

12 Arthur Griffith, Irish journalist and nationalist, founder of Sinn Féin 1905 and president of the Irish Republic 1922, dies in Dublin, Ireland (60).

14 Alfred Harmsworth, Viscount Northcliffe, British newspaper publisher, dies in London, England (57).

SEPTEMBER

7 William Stewart Halsted, U.S. surgeon who established the first surgical school in the United States at Johns Hopkins University, Baltimore, dies in Baltimore, Maryland (69).

10 Bernard Bailyn, U.S. historian, born in Hartford, Connecticut.

17 Agostinho Neto, Angolan poet, physician, and first president of the People's Republic of Angola 1975–79, born in Icolo e Bengo, Angola (–1979).

OCTOBER

24 George Cadbury, English businessman who developed the Cadbury Brothers chocolate-manufacturing firm, dies in Birmingham, Warwickshire, England (83).

31 Norodom Sihanouk, King of Cambodia 1941–55, prime minister 1955–60, head of state 1960–70, 1975–76, president 1991–93, and king again from 1993, born in Phnom Penh, Cambodia.

NOVEMBER

3 Charles Bronson, U.S. actor, born in Ehrenfield, Pennsylvania.

8 Christiaan Barnard, South African surgeon, who performed the first successful heart transplant, born in Beaufort West, South Africa.

11 Kurt Vonnegut, Jr., U.S. novelist, born in Indianapolis, Indiana.

14 Boutros Boutros-Ghali, Egyptian politician and secretary-general of the United Nations 1992–96, born in Cairo, Egypt.

18 Marcel Proust, French novelist who wrote *A la recherche du temps perdu/Remembrance of Things Past* (1913–27), dies in Paris, France (51).

19 Stanley Keith Runcorn, English geophysicist who discovered that the earth's magnetic field undergoes periodic reversals, born in Southport, Lancashire, England (–1995).

26 Charles Schulz, U.S. cartoon artist who created "Peanuts," born in Minneapolis, Minnesota.

DECEMBER

8 Lucian Freud, German-born British artist known for his nudes, born in Berlin, Germany.

14 Nikolay Gennadievich Basov, Russian physicist who created the first quantum generation maser, born in Leningrad, Soviet Union.

JULY

9   The U.S. freestyle swimmer Johnny Weissmuller becomes the first person to swim the 100 meters in less than a minute, in Alameda, California.

AUGUST

28   The Monza Autodrome automobile racing track is opened near Milan, Italy.

29   The first Walker Cup match is held between the amateur golfers of the United States and Britain and Ireland at Long Island, New York; the United States wins 8–4.

OCTOBER

4–8 The New York Giants defeat the New York Yankees by four games to one to win the U.S. World Series for the second successive year.

NOVEMBER

•   The British home secretary, William Bridgeman, prohibits a boxing match between Battling Siki of Senegal and the British fighter Joe Beckett on the grounds that it is undesirable for a "colored" man to fight a "white" man.

1923

POLITICS, GOVERNMENT, AND ECONOMICS

Business and Economics

•   Chicago taxicab operator John D. Hertz founds Hertz Drive-Ur-Self System, the precursor of Hertz Rent-A-Car.
•   The Chicago marketing consultant Arthur Charles Nielsen establishes the research firm A. C. Nielsen Co.
•   U.S. entrepreneur Eugene F. McDonald founds Zenith Radio in Chicago, Illinois.

AUGUST

•   U.S. Steel greets evidence of a recovering economy by reducing its working day from 12 to 8 hours.

SEPTEMBER

15   Germany's bank rate is raised to 90% in response to hyperinflation.

NOVEMBER

15   The value of the German mark drops to rate of 4,200,000 million to the U.S. dollar; the government introduces a new currency, the rentenmark, to replace the mark.

Colonization

OCTOBER

1   Southern Rhodesia becomes a self-governing British colony.

Human Rights

•   The U.S. women's rights proponent Alice Paul presents a draft of an Equal Rights Amendment to delegates of the National Woman's Party at its annual convention in Seneca Falls, New York.
•   U.S. writer and feminist Charlotte Perkins Gilman publishes *His Religion and Hers: A Study of the Faith of our Fathers and the Work of our Mothers.*

OCTOBER

16   The New York State Court of Appeals upholds a literacy test for new voters.

Politics and Government

•   Interpol, the international police coordination body, is founded at a conference in Vienna, Austria.
•   President Warren G. Harding appoints the lawyer Edward T. Sanford to the U.S. Supreme Court.
•   A Soviet forced-labor camp is established on the Solvetsky Islands, northwest of Archangel, USSR.
•   The Health Organization of the League of Nations is established; it is the precursor of the World Health Organization (WHO).

JANUARY

•   President Warren G. Harding orders home the remaining U.S. occupation forces in Germany.
9   Germany is declared to have defaulted on its deliveries of coal, to be paid as World War I reparations to France and Britain.
10   The disputed Baltic port of Memel (now Klaipeda, Lithuania), under protective Allied occupation, is seized by Lithuanian forces.
11   Because of Germany's failure to meet World War I reparations payments, French and Belgian troops occupy the Ruhr, Germany; its inhabitants respond with passive resistance and sabotage.
14   Fascist squads are formed into a militia in Italy.

31 Britain agrees a schedule for paying off its World War I debt to the United States.

FEBRUARY

2   The Australian prime minister William Hughes is forced to resign following defeat in the elections; Stanley Bruce forms a coalition ministry from the Nationalist and Country Parties.

2   The Central American Republics sign a treaty of amity in Washington, D.C.

10 Turkey signs a treaty of alliance with Afghanistan.

16 A conference of European ambassadors assigns the disputed Baltic port of Memel (Klaipeda) to Lithuania.

MARCH

3   The U.S. Senate rejects a proposal to join the International Court of Justice.

4   In the Teapot Dome scandal in the United States, the secretary of the interior Albert B. Fall resigns as a Senate committee investigates alleged unlawful leasing of government oil reserves and other matters.

5   The states of Montana and Nevada grant the nation's first old-age pensions.

10 The Soviet leader Vladimir Ilyich Lenin suffers a third stroke and is paralyzed.

14 The Allies recognize Vilna (modern Vilnius) which is disputed with Lithuania, and East Galicia (most of which is in the Ukraine today) which is disputed with Czechoslovakia, as Polish.

21 Austen Chamberlain is elected leader of the British Conservative Party.

21 Bulgaria agrees World War I reparations payments to the Allies.

21 The U.S. secretary of state Charles Evans Hughes declares that the United States will not recognize the Union of Soviet Socialist Republics (USSR) unless it acknowledges foreign debts and restores alien property.

27 A Romanian constitution abolishes the three-class voting system and introduces a secret ballot.

APRIL

9   A liberal fundamental law passed in Afghanistan establishes the basis for modernization of the country.

9   In *Adkins v. Children's Hospital*, the U.S. Supreme Court rules unconstitutional a law guaranteeing a minimum wage for women and children.

19 The Egyptian constitution is formally promulgated, establishing parliamentary government.

26 Mexico recognizes oil concessions granted before 1917. The constitution of 1917 had severely disrupted the rights of oil lease-owners.

27 The Irish nationalist leader Eamon de Valera suspends the anti-Treaty (Anglo-Irish Treaty) republicans' guerrilla operations for peace talks with the Irish Republic under President William Cosgrove, following significant losses of personnel.

MAY

4   The New York state assembly repeals a Prohibition enforcement act, leaving federal officials responsible for enforcing Prohibition.

8   Britain sends a diplomatic note to the USSR objecting to the dissemination of anti-British propaganda.

10 Vatslav Vorovski, the Soviet delegate at the conference in Lausanne, Switzerland, to conclude peace between Greece and Turkey, is murdered by a Swiss anticommunist, Maurice Conradi.

24 The Irish nationalist leader Eamon de Valera calls off the guerrilla war, suspended since April 27, of the anti-Treaty (Anglo-Irish Treaty) republicans who have been fighting for full independence for Ireland because of high losses of men.

25 Britain, France, Italy, and Belgium agree to reimburse the United States for the cost of the U.S. Army of the Rhine in an attempt to keep U.S. troops in Europe.

26 Emir Abdullah ibn Hussein (second son of King Hussein of the Hejaz) is proclaimed ruler of Transjordan (modern Jordan), which becomes an autonomous state under a British mandate.

JUNE

9   A coup in Bulgaria by discontented army officers leads to the fall of the prime minister Alexander Stambolisky (he is assassinated on June 15).

10 A Swiss-Liechtenstein customs union is agreed.

15 Opposition deputies withdraw from the chamber of deputies in Italy when it becomes clear that the kidnapped Socialist deputy Giacomo has been murdered (this withdrawal is known as the "Aventine Secession").

19 The British prime minister Stanley Baldwin and the U.S. secretary of state Andrew Mellon sign a formal British–U.S. convention on the repayment of Britain's World War I debt to the United States.

26 A commercial treaty between Germany and Estonia is signed.

JULY

6   The Union of Soviet Socialist Republics (USSR), with a new constitution, formally comes into existence.

24 By the Treaty of Lausanne between Greece, Turkey, and the Allies, ending the Greek–Turkish War, Greece agrees to give up Eastern Thrace and the islands of Imbros and Tenedos.

AUGUST

2   The U.S. president Warren G. Harding dies suddenly of an embolism in San Francisco, California; he is succeeded on August 3 by Vice President Calvin Coolidge. Harding is buried August 10 in Marion, Ohio.

6   Following the resignation of Wilhelm Cuno, Gustav Stresemann is appointed German chancellor and foreign minister and forms a grand coalition of parties.

10–13 Strikes and riots take place in Germany in protest at the government's failure to deal effectively with the economic crisis.

15 Irish Free State (now Republic of Ireland) troops arrest the anti-Treaty nationalist leader Eamon de Valera (he is imprisoned until July 1924).

27 In the Irish Free State elections, the Pro-Treaty Party (Cumann na nGaedheal, in support of the 1921 Anglo-Irish Treaty) wins 63 seats, the anti-Treaty Republicans 44.

31 Following the murder (on August 27) of General Enrico Tellini, an Italian helping to fix the course of the Greek–Albanian frontier, the Italian leader Benito Mussolini demands reparation from Greece and bombards and occupies Corfu town.

SEPTEMBER

3   Greece appeals to the League of Nations over Italy's occupation of Corfu town.

10 The Irish Free State (now the Republic of Ireland) is admitted to the League of Nations.

13 The Spanish soldier and politician Miguel Primo de Rivera becomes dictator in Spain (ruling under King Alfonso XIII) after a coup.

15 Oklahoma governor John Calloway Walton places his state under martial law to curb Ku Klux Klan terrorist activity.

26 The German chancellor Gustav Stresemann calls for an end to passive resistance to the French and Belgian occupation of the Ruhr (France is making the region work with imported labor while Germany's economy disintegrates).

26–28 A communist revolt in Bulgaria is suppressed.

27 A state of emergency is declared in Germany, under Article 48 of the constitution, in response to its financial crisis and political violence resulting from it.

27 Italy ends its occupation of Corfu town.

28 Ethiopia is admitted to the League of Nations.

OCTOBER

• The U.S. Senate subcommittee investigating the Teapot Dome oil leases holds its first meeting.

13 Ankara becomes the capital of modern Turkey, succeeding the Ottoman capital of Constantinople (modern Istanbul).

21 France recognizes and encourages the separatist government established in the Rhineland Palatinate of Germany.

26–November 8 The Imperial Conference in London, England, recognizes the right of the Dominions (Australia, New Zealand, Canada, and South Africa) to make treaties with foreign powers.

29 The Turkish nationalist leader Mustafa Kemal Pasha (later known as Atatürk) is elected president of Turkey.

NOVEMBER

8–9 In the "Munich Putsch," the German Nazi leader Adolf Hitler and his National Socialist German Workers' (Nazi) Party attempt a coup to overthrow the Bavarian government in Munich, Germany.

14 The Italian parliament passes an election law whereby the party that wins the greatest number of votes receives two-thirds of the seats.

15 The acquittal in Switzerland of the anticommunist Maurice Conradi of the charge of assassinating the Soviet diplomat Vatslav Vorovski in May increases tension between the two countries.

23 The German chancellor Gustav Stresemann fails to win a vote of confidence for changes to his government and resigns.

29 The Allied Reparations Commission appoints two committees of experts under the U.S. Republican politician Charles Dawes and British Liberal politician Reginald McKenna, to investigate the German economy.

DECEMBER

December–April 1924 Adolfo de la Huerta attempts a rising against the Mexican government.

1 Wilhelm Marx of the Center Party manages to form a new coalition government and becomes chancellor of Germany.

6 In his second annual address to Congress, U.S. President Calvin Coolidge promises to enforce Prohibition and comply with the rulings of the World Court.

6 In the British general election the Conservatives, standing on a platform of using a protective tariff to relieve unemployment, lose heavily.

8 The United States signs a treaty of friendship and commerce with Germany.

18 Britain, France, and Spain sign a convention on the Moroccan port of Tangier and a small surrounding enclave, establishing it as a neutral zone under French and Spanish influence.

19 King George II leaves Greece at the request of the ruling revolutionary committee.

SCIENCE, TECHNOLOGY, AND MEDICINE

Agriculture

• A locust swarm 480 km/300 mi by 62.5 km/100 mi destroys crops in Montana.

December 1923–32 The Zuider Zee drainage program is constructed in the Netherlands; it consists of a 30 km/19 mi long dam, as well as pumping stations, dikes, sluices, and locks. Funds for the scheme were granted in 1918.

Ecology

SEPTEMBER

1 Tokyo and Yokohama, Japan, are destroyed by an earthquake estimated to measure 8.3 on the Richter scale; 140,000 die.

Health and Medicine

• Canadian physicians Frederick Banting and John MacLeod receive the Nobel Prize for Physiology or Medicine for their discovery of insulin.

• French bacteriologists Albert Calmette and Camille Guérin develop the tuberculosis vaccine, known as Bacillus Calmette-Guérin (BCG), and use it to vaccinate newborns at a hospital in Paris, France.

• French bacteriologist Gaston Ramon improves the diphtheria vaccine, making it the most effective of all vaccines.

• U.S. neurologist Walter Cannon publishes *Traumatic Shock*, which describes his work on hemorrhagic and traumatic shock.

• U.S. pathologist Eugene Opie shows that tuberculosis is spread by contact. Until this time its mode of transmission has been unknown.

• U.S. physicians George and Gladys Dick isolate the microorganism responsible for scarlet fever (*Streptococcus pyogenes*) and develop an antitoxin.

MAY

• New York federal District Court judge John C. Knox upholds prescriptions for medicinal whiskey.

Math

• German mathematician Hermann Oberth publishes *Die Rakete zu den Planetenräumen/The Rocket into*

Interplanetary Space, a treatise on space flight in which he is the first to provide the mathematics of how to achieve escape velocity.

Science

- Austrian chemist Fritz Pregl receives the Nobel Prize for Chemistry for the microanalysis of organic substances.
- Danish chemist Johannes Brønsted and British chemist Thomas Martin Lowry simultaneously and independently introduce the idea that an acid tends to lose a proton and a base tends to gain a proton.
- Dutch chemist Peter Debye and German chemist Erich Hückel demonstrate that the disassociation of positive and negative ions of salts in solution is complete and not partial.
- Dutch physicist Dirk Coster and the Hungarian physicist Georg von Hevesy discover the element hafnium (atomic no. 72).
- German-born British physicist Frederick Lindemann investigates the size of meteors and the temperature of the upper atmosphere.
- U.S. physicist Albert Michelson determines the speed of light to be 299,798 km per sec/187,374 mi per sec.
- U.S. physicist Robert Millikan receives the Nobel Prize for Physics for his work on the elementary charge of electricity and on the photoelectric effect.

JANUARY

- U.S. politician William Jennings Bryan sparks a nationwide debate about evolution by denouncing Darwin's theory as "infidelity masquerading under the name of science" in a speech to ministers at St. Paul, Minnesota.

Technology

- British metallurgist John Tytus invents continuous hot-strip rolling of steel.
- The first seismic prospecting takes place in the United States when geologists use seismometers to discover an oil field.
- The Russian-born U.S. engineer Vladimir Zworykin develops the iconoscope in the United States, an image-scanner that can produce electronic signals for reconstitution on the screen of a cathode-ray tube—the basis of television.
- U.S. physicist Lee De Forest develops Phonofilm, a system of recording and reproducing sound on film. Although he demonstrates it in theaters, movie producers show little interest.

NOVEMBER

6 Colonel Jacob Schick receives the first patent for an electric razor.

Transportation

- Spanish inventor Juan de la Cierva Codorniu flies the first autogyro. He solves the problem of control by using individually articulated rotor blades. His design establishes the principles of subsequent helicopters.
- The Canadian government merges the Grand Trunk and Intercolonial railroads with bankrupt local lines to form the Canadian National Railways.

- There are more than 13 million passenger automobiles in the United States.

MAY

2–3 U.S. Army pilots make the first nonstop transcontinental flight from New York, New York, to San Diego, California.

JULY

15 The Russian Volunteer Air Fleet begins service in the USSR; it develops into the national airline Aeroflot (1932).

OCTOBER

- The U.S. airship *Shenandoah* makes its first flight. It is the first rigid airship to be filled with helium rather than hydrogen.

ARTS AND IDEAS

Architecture

- Swiss architect Le Corbusier publishes his influential collection of essays *Vers une architecture/Towards a New Architecture*.
- The Bridge of St. Pierre-du-Vauvray in France, designed by the French architect Eugène Freyssinet, is completed.

Arts

- The French artist Marcel Duchamp completes his sculpture *The Large Glass* (*The Bride Stripped Bare by her Bachelors, Even*).
- The German artist Max Beckmann paints *Self-Portrait with Cigarette*.
- The German artist Max Ernst paints *Pietà, or Revolution by Night*.
- The German artist Rudolf Belling sculpts *Sculpture 23*.
- The Mexican artist Diego Rivera paints the mural *Creation* in the National Preparatory School in Mexico City, Mexico.
- The Romanian artist Constantin Brancusi sculpts *Bird in Space*.
- The Russian artist Marc Chagall paints *The Green Violinist*.
- The Russian artist Naum Gabo (Naum Neemia Pevsner) sculpts *Column*.
- The Spanish artist Joan Miró paints *The Tilled Field*.
- The Spanish artist Pablo Picasso paints *The Race* and *Harlequin and Mirror*.
- The U.S. artist and photographer Man Ray creates *Rayograph*, one of a series of experiments with light-sensitive paper.
- The U.S. artist Marsden Hartley paints *Landscape, New Mexico*.

Film

- Harry, Albert, Sam, and Jack L. Warner found the movie company Warner Bros in the United States. Their studio was established in 1918.

- The fascist government in Italy adopts stricter controls over the film industry, affecting the content of movies both while in production and once complete.
- The movie *Cyrano de Bergerac*, directed by Italian filmmaker Augusto Genina, is released in France. Based on the play by Edmond Rostand, it stars Pierre Magnier and Linda Moglia.
- The movie *Das alte Gesetz/The Ancient Law*, directed by E. A. Dupont and starring Ewald André, is released in Germany.
- The movie *La Roue/The Wheel*, by the French director Abel Gance, is released, starring Séverin-Mars, Ivy Close, and Gabriel de Gavrone.
- The movie *Raskolnikov*, directed by Robert Wiene, is released in Germany. An adaptation of the novel *Crime and Punishment* by Fyodor Mikhailovich Dostoyevsky, it stars Grigory Khmara, Mikhail Tarkhanov, Pavel Pavlov, and Vera Toma.
- The movie *Rosita*, directed by German filmmaker Ernst Lubitsch, is released in the United States, starring Mary Pickford.
- The movie *Safety Last*, directed by Sam Taylor, is released in the United States, starring Harold Lloyd. It features Lloyd's best-known scene, in which he hangs from a clock face.
- The movie *Scaramouche*, directed by Rex Ingram, is released in the United States, starring Ramon Navarro and Alice Terry.
- The movie *The Atonement of Gösta Berling*, directed by Finnish filmmaker Mauritz Stiller, is released in Sweden. Based on the novel by Selma Lagerlöf, it stars Greta Garbo and Lars Hanson.
- The movie *The Covered Wagon*, directed by James Cruze, is released in the United States, starring J. Warren Kerrigan, Lois Wilson, and Alan Hale.
- The movie *The Hunchback of Notre Dame*, directed by Wallace Worsley, is released in the United States. Based on the novel by Victor Hugo, it stars Lon Chaney, Norman Kerry, and Patsy Ruth Miller.
- The movie *The Ten Commandments*, directed by Cecil B. De Mille, is released in the United States, starring Theodore Roberts, Richard Dix, Rod la Roque, Edythe Chapman, Beatrice Joy, and Nita Naldi. It costs $1.5 million to produce, making it the most expensive movie to date.
- The movie *The White Sister*, directed by Henry King, is released in the United States, starring Ronald Colman and Lillian Gish.

Literature and Language

- The English critics I. A. Richards and C. K. Ogden publish *The Meaning of Meaning*.
- The English writer D. H. Lawrence publishes his critical work *Studies in Classic American Literature*.
- The English writer D. H. Lawrence publishes his novel *Kangaroo*.
- The English writer Dorothy L. Sayers publishes *Whose Body?*, her first novel, which introduces the character Lord Peter Wimsey.
- The English writer P. G. Wodehouse publishes his novel *Leave it to Psmith*.

- The French writer Colette publishes her novel *Le Blé en herbe/The Ripening Seed*.
- The German writer Rainer Maria Rilke publishes his *Duineser Elegien/Duino Elegies*, and his poetry cycle *Die Sonette an Orpheus/Sonnets to Orpheus*.
- The Lebanese-born U.S. writer and mystic Khalil Gibran publishes *The Prophet*, a collection of prose poems.
- The Pulitzer Prize for Biography is awarded to Burton J. Hendrick for *The Life and Letters of Walter Hines Page*, the Pulitzer Prize for Fiction is awarded to Willa Cather for *One of Ours*, and the Prize for Poetry is awarded to Edna St. Vincent Millay for *The Ballad of the Harp-Weaver and Other Poems*.
- The Scottish scholar William Paton Ker publishes *The Art of Poetry*.
- The U.S. dissident Emma Goldman writes *My Disillusionment in Russia*.
- The U.S. writer e e cummings publishes his first poetry collection, *Tulips and Chimneys*.
- The U.S. writer Robert Frost publishes his poetry collection *New Hampshire*.
- The U.S. writer Sherwood Anderson publishes his short-story collection *Horses and Men*.
- The U.S. writer Wallace Stevens publishes *Harmonium*, his first book of poems.
- The U.S. writer Willa Cather publishes her novel *A Lost Lady*.
- The U.S. writer William Carlos Williams publishes his poetry collection *Spring and All*, which includes "The Red Wheelbarrow."

Music

- "Hillbilly" music becomes popular in the United States, including John Carson's "The Old Hen Cackled and the Rooster's Going to Crow."
- Popular songs in the United States include "Yes, We Have No Bananas," "Sonny Boy," and "Linger Awhile."
- The Cotton Club opens in Harlem, New York, New York, providing black American music and entertainment for a white audience.
- The Czech composer Leoš Janáček completes his String Quartet No. 1, the *Kreutzer Sonata*, inspired by a story by the Russian writer Leo Tolstoy.
- The French-born U.S. composer Edgard Varèse completes his orchestral works *Hyperprism* and *Octandre*.
- The Hungarian composer Zoltán Kodály completes his *Psalmus Hungaricus/Hungarian Psalm* for chorus and orchestra.
- The Swiss composer Arthur Honegger completes his orchestral work *Pacific 231*.

Theater and Dance

- The ballet *La Création du monde/The Creation of the World* is first performed, in Paris, France. The music is by the French composer Darius Milhaud, the choreography by the Swedish dancer Jean Börlin, and the story by the Swiss writer Blaise Cendrars. The French artist Fernand Léger designed the costumes and scenery.

- The ballet *Les Noces/The Wedding* is first performed, by Sergei Diaghilev's Ballets Russes in Paris, France. The music is by the Russian composer Igor Stravinsky, the choreography by the Russian dancer Vaslav Nijinsky, and the costumes and sets by the Russian artist Natalia Goncharova.
- The Nobel Prize for Literature is awarded to the Irish poet and dramatist W. B. Yeats.
- The play *Der deutsche Hinkemann/Hinkmann*, by the German dramatist Ernst Toller, is first performed, in Leipzig, Germany.
- The play *Die Maschinenstürmer/The Machine Wreckers*, by the German dramatist Ernst Toller, is first performed, in Berlin, Germany.
- The play *Icebound*, by the U.S. dramatist Owen Davis, is first performed, in New York, New York.
- The play *Shadow of a Gunman*, by the Irish dramatist Sean O'Casey, is first performed, at the Abbey Theatre in Dublin, Ireland.
- The play *The Adding Machine*, by the U.S. dramatist Elmer Rice is first performed, in New York, New York.
- The Pulitzer Prize for Drama is awarded to Owen Davis for *Icebound*.

MAY

23 A jury in New York, New York, convicts the producer and cast of the Apollo Theater production *God of Vengeance* of immoral behavior.

OCTOBER

29 The revue *Runnin' Wild*, is performed for the first time, at the Colonial Theater, New York, New York. It includes "Charleston" by Cecil Mack and James P. Johnson, which launches a dance craze.

Thought and Scholarship

- *Chance, Love, and Logic: Philosophical Essays by the Late Charles S. Pierce* is published posthumously, edited by the U.S. philosopher Morris R. Cohen. Though one of the most important U.S. philosophers of the 19th century, Pierce published very little during his lifetime.
- Austrian psychiatrist Sigmund Freud publishes *The Ego and the Id*, in which he elaborates his division of the mind into the id, ego, and superego.
- Austrian theologian Martin Buber publishes *Ich und Du/I and Thou*.
- English economist Alfred Marshall publishes *Money, Credit and Commerce*.
- English scholar Edmund Kerchever Chambers publishes *The Elizabethan Stage*.
- English statesman and writer Winston Churchill publishes the first volume of his historical study *The World Crisis, 1911–1914*. The final volume will appear in 1929.
- German philosopher and sociologist Max Scheler publishes *Die Sinngesetze des emotionalen Lebens: Wesen und Formen der Sympathie/The Nature of Sympathy*.
- German philosopher Ernst Cassirer publishes the first volume of his *Philosophie der symbolischen Formen/The Philosophy of Symbolic Forms*. The final volume appears in 1929.
- German political philosopher Karl Korsch publishes *Marxismus und Philosophie/Marxism and Philosophy*.

- Hungarian cultural philosopher György Lukács publishes *Geschichte und Klassenbewusstein: Studien über marxistische Dialektik/History and Class Consciousness: Studies in Marxist Dialectic*.
- The Pulitzer Prize for History is awarded to Charles Warren for *The Supreme Court in United States History*.

SOCIETY

Education

- Texas Tech University opens in Lubbock, Texas.
- The Daytona Normal and Industrial Institute for Negro Girls merges with the Cookman Institute for Men at Jacksonville to form the Bethune–Cookman College in Daytona, Florida.

Everyday Life

- Long shawls are a popular fashion accessory for women in the United States, and hemlines are about 25 cm/10 in off the floor.
- The Charleston and the Foxtrot emerge as popular dances in the United States.
- The U.S. confectioner Forrest Mars invents the Milky Way chocolate bar.

Media and Communication

- Supporters of the Nazi Party in Germany acquire the *Völkischer Beobachter* newspaper to serve as Hitler's mouthpiece.
- The Italian physicist Guglielmo Marconi begins shortwave radio communication when he transmits signals from Poldhu, Cornwall, using a one-kilowatt transmitter. The signals are received 2,250 km/1,400 mi away and are clearer than longwave signals received a few hundred miles away, from a transmitter in Caernarvon, Wales, using a 100-kilowatt transmitter.
- The U.S. publisher Frank Ernest Gannett establishes the Gannet news syndicate in Rochester, New York.

MARCH

3 U.S. editor Henry A. Luce and U.S. publisher Briton Hadden found the weekly news magazine *Time* in New York, New York.

DECEMBER

6 U.S. president Calvin Coolidge's second annual message to Congress is the first official presidential address to be broadcast on radio.

Religion

- Canadian evangelist Aimée Semple McPherson founds the International Church of the Foursquare Gospel in Los Angeles, California. The movement is based around the four roles of Jesus Christ, as Savior, Baptiser, Healer, and Coming King, as well as other aspects associated with Christian fundamentalism, such as faith-healing. The church achieves success partly due to McPherson's skill in publicity and flamboyant character.

Sports

- The first short-track speedway motorcycle races are staged by Johnnie Hoskins at the West Maitland Agricultural Show, New South Wales, Australia. Hoskins later introduces the sport to Britain.
- The inaugural Wightman Cup match between the women tennis players of Britain and the United States is played at Forest Hills, New York. The United States wins, 7–0.

APRIL

18 Yankee Stadium, the new home of the New York Yankees baseball team, dubbed "the house that Ruth built," is opened in New York, New York, before a 74,000 capacity crowd.

28 The English Football Association (FA) Cup final is held at Wembley Stadium, London, England, for the first time. An estimated 200,000 spectators see Bolton Wanderers beat West Ham United 2–0.

MAY

26–27 The French drivers André Lagache and René Leonard, in a 3-liter Chenard and Walcker "Sport," win the inaugural Le Mans 24-hour motor race in France. They drive 2,210 km/1,373 mi at an average speed of 92 kph/57.2 mph.

BIRTHS & DEATHS

JANUARY

1 Wee Willie Keeler, U.S. baseball player, dies in Brooklyn, New York (50).

6 Norman E. Kirk, New Zealand prime minister 1972–74 who opposed French nuclear testing in the Pacific, born in Waimate, New Zealand (–1974).

31 Norman Mailer, U.S. novelist, born in Long Branch, New Jersey.

FEBRUARY

1 Ernst Troeltsch, German theologian and philosopher, dies in Berlin, Germany (57).

9 Norman E. Shumway, U.S. surgeon who performed the first heart transplant in the United States, born in Kalamazoo, Michigan.

10 Wilhelm Röntgen, German physicist who discovered X-rays, dies in Munich, Germany (77).

13 Charles (Chuck) E. Yeager, U.S. test pilot, the first person to break the sound barrier, born in Myra, West Virginia.

22 Théophile Delcassé, French foreign minister 1898–1905 and 1914–15, who was responsible for arranging European alliances prior to World War I, dies in Nice, France (70).

MARCH

22 Marcel Marceau, French mime artist, born in Strasbourg, France.

26 Sarah Bernhardt, French actress, dies in Paris, France (77).

27 Shusako Endo, Japanese novelist, born in Tokyo, Japan (–1996).

APRIL

17 Harry Reasoner, U.S. broadcast journalist, born in Dakota City, Iowa (–1991).

25 Albert King, influential U.S. blues guitarist and singer, born in Indianola, Mississippi (–1992).

MAY

1 Joseph Heller, U.S. novelist known best for *Catch 22* (1961), born in Brooklyn, New York.

27 Henry A. Kissinger, German-born U.S. presidential advisor on foreign affairs, born in Fürth, Germany.

28 György Ligeti, Hungarian composer known for his experimental approach to composition, born in Dicsöszentmarton, Hungary.

28 N(andamuri) T(arako) Rama Roa, Indian politician and film star who portrayed mythological characters, born (–1996).

31 Rainier III, 31st hereditary ruler of Monaco 1949–, born in Monaco.

JUNE

20 Francisco "Pancho" Villa, Mexican revolutionary who fought against the regimes of Porfirio Díaz and Victoriano Huerto, is assassinated at his ranch in Parral, Mexico (44).

JULY

6 Wojciech Jaruzelski, Polish general, prime minister 1981–85 and president of Poland 1985–90, who imposed martial law (1981–83) in an attempt to quash the Solidarity movement, born in Kurów, Poland.

AUGUST

2 Warren G. Harding, 29th president of the United States 1921–23, a Republican, dies in San Francisco, California (57).

8 Jimmy Witherspoon, U.S. blues singer, born in Gurdon, Arkansas (–1997).

16 Shimon Peres, Israeli socialist politician responsible for the country's defense policy during the 1950s, 1960s, and 1970s, and prime minister 1984–86 and 1995–96, born in Wołożyn, Poland.

SEPTEMBER

1 Rocky Marciano (Rocco Francis Marchegiano), U.S. world heavyweight boxer 1952–56, born in Brockton, Massachusetts (–1969).

9 D. Carlton Gadjusek, U.S. physician who discovered that certain neurological disorders are caused by slow-acting viruses, born in Yonkers, New York.

16 Lee Kuan Yew, prime minister of Singapore 1959–90, born in Singapore.

17 Hank Williams, U.S. country music singer and guitarist, born in Georgiana, Alabama (–1953).

OCTOBER

23 Roy Lichtenstein, U.S. painter, born in New York, New York.

26 Charles Proteus Steinmetz, German-born U.S. electrical engineer and politician who developed the mathematics of alternating circuits, dies in Schenectady, New York (57).

30 Andrew Bonar Law, British Conservative politician, prime minister 1922–23, dies in London, England (65).

NOVEMBER

18 Alan B. Shepard, Jr., first U.S. astronaut to travel in space, born in East Derry, New Hampshire (–1998).

DECEMBER

2 Maria Callas (Maria Cecilia Sophia Anna Kalogeropoulos), U.S. operatic soprano, born in New York, New York (–1977).

5 Maurice Barrès, influential French writer and politician, dies in Paris, France (61).

27 Gustav Eiffel, French civil engineer who built the Eiffel Tower for the Paris Exhibition 1867, dies in Paris, France (90).

AUGUST

18   The 17-year-old U.S. tennis player Helen Wills defeats Molla Bjurstedt Mallory of the United States to win the women's singles title at the U.S. lawn tennis championships at Forest Hills, New York.

SEPTEMBER

29   The first Amateur Athletic Union (AAU) track and field meeting for women is held at Newark, New Jersey.

OCTOBER

6   U.S. Army officer Al Williams, flying a Curtiss Racer at the Pulitzer Trophy Contest in St. Louis, Missouri, sets a new air speed record of 392.28 kph/243.76 mph.

10–15   The New York Yankees win their first-ever World Series, beating the New York Giants by four games to two.

20   Zev, the winner of the U.S. horse-racing Kentucky Derby, beats Papyrus, the winner of the English Epsom Derby, by five lengths at Belmont Park, New York, New York.

1924

POLITICS, GOVERNMENT, AND ECONOMICS

Business and Economics

- Dean Witter brokers are founded on Wall Street, New York, New York.
- Imperial Airways is founded. It is one of the pioneers of intercontinental air travel.
- The Chicago physician Jules C. Stein establishes the recording label Music Corporation of America (MCA).
- The German firm Leitz introduces the Leica camera, the first commercially produced camera that takes 35-mm film.
- The U.S. cereal maker Washburn, Crosby Co. (later General Mills) introduces Wheaties, supposedly the "breakfast of champions."
- The U.S. clothing salesman Barney Pressman establishes the men's apparel store Barney's, in lower Manhattan, New York, New York.
- The U.S. Computing-Tabulating-Recording Company is renamed International Business Machines (IBM).
- U.S. retailers Bernard F. Gimbel and Horace Saks open the department store Saks Fifth Avenue in midtown Manhattan, New York, New York.

AUGUST

30   The German Reichsbank becomes independent of the government and introduces a new mark, following the complete devaluation of the old one by hyperinflation.

NOVEMBER

- The U.S. retail emporium R. H. Macy Co. sponsors the first Macy's Thanksgiving Day parade down Fifth Avenue from Central Park in New York, New York.

Human Rights

NOVEMBER

1   A riot in Niles, Ohio, sparked off by a Ku Klux Klan rally, leaves 12 people injured.

Politics and Government

- J. Edgar Hoover is appointed acting director of the Bureau of Investigation (later the Federal Bureau of Investigation, FBI) in the United States.
- Owens Valley, California, becomes the site of violent clashes between state militiamen and local farmers loath to see the valley's precious water supply being funneled to the city of Los Angeles.

JANUARY

11   The former Greek prime minister Eleutherios Venizelos accepts the premiership of the Greek national assembly.

21   A congress of the Guomindang (Chinese National People's Party) admits communists to the party and welcomes Soviet advisers.

21   The Soviet leader Vladimir Ilyich Lenin dies, initiating a struggle for the leadership of the USSR.

22   Following the defeat of the Conservatives in the general election (December 1923), the British prime minister Stanley Baldwin resigns.

23   A convention is signed between the United States and Britain permitting U.S. seizure and inspection of ships thought to be infringing Prohibition; British ships are, however, permitted to enter and leave U.S. ports carrying liquor.

23   Ramsay MacDonald forms the first Labour government in Britain (without an overall majority), with Philip Snowden as chancellor of the Exchequer.

24   Nonfascist labor unions are abolished in Italy.

25   A French-Czechoslovak alliance is formed; France wishes to create a defensive ring around Germany.

27 The Kingdom of the Serbs, Croats, and Slovenes signs a treaty with Italy, recognizing the port of Fiume (Rijeka, now in Croatia) as an Italian possession.

28 Following the Nationalists' victory in the Egyptian elections, Saad Zaghlul forms a government.

31 The independent republic in the Rhineland seeking secession from Germany collapses through lack of support.

FEBRUARY

1 The British Labour government formally recognizes the USSR.

3 The Greek prime minister Eleutherios Venizelos resigns.

4 Mahatma Gandhi, the leader of the Indian Home Rule movement, is released from his six-year prison sentence for civil disobedience.

4 Twenty-two policemen are killed in a nationalist-led peasant revolt in Chauri Chaura, United Provinces, India.

18 The U.S. Navy secretary Edwin Denby is forced to resign through connection with the Teapot Dome oil leases scandal, in which interior secretary Albert B. Fall secretly leased the Teapot Dome oil reserves, which belonged to the navy, to private oil speculators.

19 Shah Ahmad of Persia (modern Iran) is deposed by the nationalist army officer Reza Khan.

23 Britain reduces the reparation recovery duties on German goods to 5%, in view of Germany's economic crisis.

31 The separatist movement in the Rhineland, Germany, collapses following the fall of the independent republican government January 31.

MARCH

3 Germany signs a treaty of friendship with Turkey.

3 The Turkish national assembly expels the Ottoman dynasty and abolishes the caliphate and other religious institutions.

9 Italy annexes the independent port of Fiume (Rijeka, now in Croatia) but abandons its claims to the Dalmatian coast of the Kingdom of the Serbs, Croats, and Slovenes.

25 Greece is proclaimed a republic (confirmed by plebiscite on April 13; Admiral Pavlos Koundouriotis becomes president).

31 The U.S. Supreme Court overturns an Oregon law compelling young children to attend public grammar schools.

APRIL

1 Following the failed 1923 "Munich Putsch," the German Nazi leader Adolf Hitler is sentenced to five years' imprisonment (he is released on December 20). While in prison he dictates his political manifesto *Mein Kampf/My Struggle*.

6 In the general election in Italy, the fascists win 65% of the vote following the widespread intimidation of voters.

9 Committees under the U.S. financier Charles Dawes and British politician Reginald McKenna make reports on the World War I reparations issue; the Dawes Plan reduces Germany's debt to 1 million gold marks.

11 The Social Democrats under Theodor Stauning form a government in Denmark after winning 55 seats to the Liberals' 44, Radicals' 20, and Conservatives' 28.

14 A British–Soviet conference opens in London, England, to discuss economic cooperation.

20 A new, more democratic, constitution is adopted in Turkey; tithes are abolished and military service shortened.

MAY

- U.S. Congress passes the Soldiers' Bonus Bill over President Calvin Coolidge's veto. The bill allocates $2 billion to provide veterans with prepaid 20-year annuities.

- U.S. Congress passes the Johnson–Reed Immigration Act, setting the annual immigration quota at 2% of the U.S. population (based on the 1890 census) from any given country. Exceptions are Japanese immigrants, who are totally excluded, and immigrants from Canada and Latin America, for whom there are no limits.

4 In elections to the German Reichstag (parliament), the Conservative Nationalists (with 95 seats) and communists (62 seats) strengthen their position against the Social Democrats (100 seats) and Center Party (65 seats); the National Socialist German Workers' (Nazi) Party enters the Reichstag for the first time with 32 seats.

10 The Northern Ireland government refuses to appoint a representative to the Irish boundary conference in London, England; the British government appoints a commissioner on Northern Ireland's behalf.

11 In French elections the national bloc is defeated by the left cartel and the prime minister Raymond Poincaré resigns.

26 The government of Wilhelm Marx in Germany resigns on the breakdown of negotiations for a coalition.

31 China recognizes the USSR and in return the USSR relinquishes some disputed tsarist territory to China.

JUNE

- A U.S. federal grand jury charges the interior secretary Albert B. Fall and oil producers Harry Sinclair, Edward L. Doheny, and Edward L. Doheny, Jr., with bribery and conspiracy in the Teapot Dome oil lease scandal.

- U.S. Congress submits a Constitutional amendment prohibiting child labor to the states. The amendment will not become law.

6 A World Power Conference is held at Wembley, London, England, to discuss the standardization of power supplies.

10 Giacomo Matteotti, an Italian Socialist deputy who has attacked Benito Mussolini's fascist government, is abducted and subsequently murdered.

10 President Alexandre Millerand of France resigns following allegations that he has sided with the political right rather than remaining neutral.

10 The Republican Convention at Cleveland, Ohio, nominates President Calvin Coolidge for the U.S. presidency and Chicago banker Charles Dawes for the vice presidency.

13 The moderate Gaston Doumergue is elected president of France, succeeding Alexandre Millerand, who has resigned.

15 Edouard Herriot becomes prime minister of France.

24 The Democrat Convention in New York, New York, nominates West Virginia lawyer John W. Davis for president and Nebraska governor Charles W. Bryan for vice president.

25 Britain states that it will not leave the Sudan, despite Egyptian demands for complete evacuation.

30 James Hertzog, the Nationalist Party leader, forms a ministry in South Africa, with Labor support, following the defeat of Jan Smuts's South African Party in elections.

JULY

• The Conference for Progressive Political Action nominates Wisconsin senator, Robert M. La Follette, for president and Montana senator, Burton K. Wheeler, for vice president. La Follette will win 16% of the popular vote in the November election.

10 A liberal and representative constitution is promulgated in the British protectorate of Iraq.

11–15 Rioting takes place between Hindus and Muslims in Delhi, India.

16 The Dawes Plan for reducing Germany's reparations payments is approved at a conference in London, England.

21 New York teenagers Nathan Leopold and Richard Loeb are sentenced to life imprisonment for the kidnapping and murder of Bobby Franks. The two friends had committed the murder to see what the experience would be like.

AUGUST

16 French delegates at the London conference on World War I reparations agree to evacuate the Ruhr, Germany, within a year.

29–September 1 The German Reichstag (parliament) approves the Dawes Plan for World War I reparations and the plan comes into force on September 1.

SEPTEMBER

5 A military junta takes power in Chile.

20 Britain takes its dispute over the city of Mosul in Iraq (claimed by Turkey) to the League of Nations.

25–October 3 The Egyptian prime minister Saad Zaghlul visits Britain to discuss Egypt's demand for sovereignty over the Sudan, which is rejected by the British prime minister Ramsay MacDonald.

27 Following an election, Plutarco Calles is declared president of Mexico. He takes office October 1.

29 Germany states the terms on which it will join the League of Nations, including a permanent seat on the Council.

OCTOBER

2 The League of Nations adopts the Geneva Protocol for the peaceful settlement of international disputes, making arbitration between rival nations compulsory.

3 King Hussein abdicates the throne of the Arabian kingdom of Hejaz in favor of his son Ali, following popular opposition to his rule.

9 The British Parliament is dissolved following the defeat of the Labour government on the question of prosecuting John Campbell, acting editor of the *Workers' Weekly*, for inciting soldiers to mutiny rather than be used to break strikes.

10 An international loan to Germany to help finance postwar reconstruction is arranged in London, England.

25 The British newspaper the *Daily Mail* publishes the "Zinoviev Letter," a document inciting revolutionary activity in the army and Ireland, which is said to be from Grigory Zinoviev, chairman of the External Committee of the Comintern (the Soviet-controlled

Communist International). It is later proved to be a forgery.

28 France formally recognizes the USSR.

29 The Conservatives win the British general election with 415 seats against Labour's 151 and the Liberals' 44 seats.

NOVEMBER

4 Ramsay MacDonald resigns as British prime minister following Labour's electoral defeat; a week later Stanley Baldwin forms a Conservative government with Austen Chamberlain as foreign secretary and Winston Churchill as chancellor of the Exchequer.

4 The Republican candidate Calvin Coolidge wins the U.S. presidential election with 382 electoral votes over John W. Davis, Democrat, with 136 votes, and Robert M. LaFollette, Progressive, with 13; the popular vote is Coolidge 15,725,016, Davis 8,386,503, and LaFollette, 4,822,856. Republicans maintain majorities in the House (247–183) and Senate (56–39).

18 The evacuation of the Ruhr area of Germany by French troops is completed (the Ruhr having been occupied in 1923 because of Germany's default in payment of World War I reparations).

19 Sir Lee Stack, the British governor of the Sudan, is murdered in Cairo, Egypt, by nationalists, leading Britain to demand the withdrawal of Egyptian forces from the Sudan.

21 The British prime minister Stanley Baldwin informs the USSR that Britain will not proceed with treaties negotiated by the former Labour government (following publication of the "Zinoviev Letter" on October 25).

30 The Belgian troops are withdrawn from the Ruhr, Germany, following the ending of the policy of forcibly extracting World War I reparations from Germany.

30 The Egyptian prime minister Saad Zaghlul accepts most of the British demands following the assassination of Lee Stack, the British governor of the Sudan, on November 19.

DECEMBER

2 Britain and Germany sign a commercial treaty.

7 In the German elections the communists (with 45 seats) lose ground to the Social Democrats (131 seats); the Conservative Nationalists (103 seats) improve their strength while the Nazi Party slumps to 14 seats; the Center Party has 69 seats.

15–January 15, 1925 A cabinet crisis occurs in Germany following inconclusive elections to the Reichstag (parliament).

20 The League of Nations takes over Hungary's finances to hasten postwar reconstruction.

24 Albania is proclaimed a republic, with Ahmed Bey Zogu as president.

SCIENCE, TECHNOLOGY, AND MEDICINE

Ecology

- The Gila Wilderness Area is created within the Gila National Forest, New Mexico, United States; this is the first unmodified area to be set aside for recreational use.
- The Long Island State Park Commission president Robert Moses creates Jones Beech State Park in New York.
- U.S. Congress passes the Oil Pollution Act, prohibiting oil producers from polluting the environment.

Health and Medicine

- Dutch physiologist Willem Einthoven receives the Nobel Prize for Physiology or Medicine for his discovery of the electrical properties of the heart through the electrocardiograph.
- U.S. physicians George and Gladys Dick develop a skin test for scarlet fever—the "Dick" test.

Science

- Australian-born South African anthropologist Raymond Dart discovers the skull of an early hominid at Tuang, Botswana, which he calls *Australopithecus africanus*. It is now believed to be one of the oldest human ancestors.
- Czech chemist Jaroslav Heyrovský develops the polarograph, used for electrochemical analysis.
- English physicist Edward Appleton discovers that radio emissions are reflected by an ionized layer of the atmosphere.
- English physiologist Ernest Starling finds that bicarbonates, chlorides, glucose, and water excreted by the kidney are reabsorbed by the glomeruli at the lower end of the kidney tubules.
- French physicist Louis de Broglie argues that particles can also behave as waves, laying the foundations for wave mechanics. He demonstrates that a beam of electrons has a wave motion with a short wavelength. The discovery permits the development of the electron microscope.
- Swedish physicist Karl Manne Siegbahn receives the Nobel Prize for Physics for his research in the field of X-ray spectroscopy.
- U.S. astronomer Edwin Hubble demonstrates that certain Cepheid variable stars are several hundred thousand light-years away and thus outside the Milky Way galaxy. The nebulae they are found in are the first galaxies to be discovered that are proved to be independent of the Milky Way.

MAY
21 The U.S. Presbyterian General Assembly, meeting in San Antonio, Texas, repudiates the theory of evolution.

Technology

- The Russian-born U.S. engineer Vladimir Zworykin patents the kinescope television receiver. It develops into the modern television picture tube.
- The Scottish engineer John Logie Baird produces televised images in outline.

MAY
12 The Brooklyn Edison Corporation opens the world's largest electricity generating plant with steam-powered turbines, in New York, New York.

NOVEMBER
30 The Radio Corporation of America demonstrates the radio transmission of photographs when it sends an image from London, England, to New York, New York, in around 20 minutes.

Transportation

- German inventor Anton Flettner develops the rotor ship, which uses rotating cylinders instead of sails, after he discovers that the pressure of the wind is greater on a cylinder than on a sail.
- German-born U.S. engineer Grover Loening builds the first amphibious airplane, which operates on land as well as water.
- The prices of Ford automobiles have declined from $950 for a Model T in 1909 to $290.
- The Schwandbach Bridge in Switzerland is completed. Designed by Swiss engineer Robert Maillart, it is the first reinforced-concrete arched bridge with a curved roadway.
- U.S. engineer William Price develops the first U.S. diesel-electric locomotive, for the Central Railroad of New Jersey.

APRIL
6–September 28 Two U.S. Army Douglas "World Cruisers," *New Orleans* and *Chicago*, make the first around-the-world flight, a distance of 42,152 km/26,345mi. Two other planes go missing.

MAY
21 U.S. Army pilot J. A. Macready sets a new altitude record of 10,741 m/35,239 ft.

JUNE
15 The Ford Motor Company announces the production of its 10 millionth automobile.

ARTS AND IDEAS

Architecture

- The airship hangars at Orly near Paris, France, designed by the French engineer Eugène Freyssinet, are completed. They are the first giant structures to be built in reinforced concrete.
- The American Radiator Building, designed by the U.S. architect Raymond Mathewson Hood, is completed in New York, New York.

- The Chile-Haus in Hamburg, Germany, designed by the German architect Fritz Höger, is completed.
- The Schröder House in Utrecht, the Netherlands, designed by the Dutch architect Gerrit Rietveld, is completed.

Arts

- French writer André Breton publishes his *Manifeste du surréalisme/Surrealist Manifesto*.
- Spanish artist Juan Gris lectures at the Sorbonne in Paris, France, on *Possibilités de la Peinture/On the Possibilities of Painting*.
- The German artist Kurt Schwitters creates his *Merz 32* collage.
- The German photographer Kurt Hielscher publishes *Deutschland: Baukunst und Landschaft/Germany: Architecture and Landscape*, a photograph album.
- The Italian artist Mario Sironi paints *The Pupil*.
- The Spanish artist Joan Miró paints *Harlequin's Carnival*.
- The U.S. artist Arthur Dove creates the collage *Portrait of Ralph Dusenberry*.
- The U.S. artist George Bellows paints *Dempsey and Firpo*.
- The U.S. artist Gerald Murphy paints *Razor*.
- The U.S. artist Stuart Davis paints *Odol*.
- The U.S. photographer Edward Weston takes *Guadalupe Marin de Rivera*.
- The Welsh artist Gwen John paints *The Convalescent*.

Film

- *Alice's Day at the Sea*, a mixture of cartoon and live action, is released in the United States, the first in Walt Disney's *Alice in Cartoonland* series.
- Columbia Pictures is founded in the United States.
- Movie production for the year in Italy stands at just 10% of its level in 1920. Mussolini attempts to revivify the industry in the name of Italian fascism.
- The movie *Aelita*, directed by Yakov Protazanov, is released in the USSR. Based on the novel by Lev Nikolayevich ("Leo") Tolstoy, it stars Yulia Solntseva, Nikolai Batalov, and Igor Ilinsky.
- The movie *Die Nibelungen/The Nibelungs*, directed by Fritz Lang, is released in Germany, starring Paul Richter, Margarethe Schön, and Hanna Ralph.
- The movie *Forbidden Fruit*, directed by German filmmaker Ernst Lubitsch, is released in the United States, starring Pola Negri, Rod la Rocque, and Adolphe Menjou.
- The movie *Girl Shy*, directed by Fred Newmeyer, is released in the United States, starring Harold Lloyd and Jobyna Ralston.
- The movie *Greed*, directed by Austrian filmmaker Erich von Stroheim, is released in the United States, starring Gibson Gowland, Zasu Pitts, Jean Hersholt, and Chester Conklin.
- The movie *He Who Gets Slapped*, directed by Swedish filmmaker Victor Seastrom, is released in the United States, starring Lon Chaney, Norma Shearer, and John Gilbert.

- The movie *Mikaël*, directed by Carl Theodor Dreyer, is released in Denmark. It features an appearance by the Austrian psychoanalyst Sigmund Freud.
- The movie *Sherlock Junior*, directed by Buster Keaton, is released in the United States. Keaton also stars in it.
- The movie *Strike*, directed by Sergey Eisenstein, is released in the USSR, starring Grigory Alexandrov, Maxim Strauch, and Mikhail Gomarov.
- The movie *The Extraordinary Adventures of Mr West in the Land of the Bolsheviks*, directed by Lev Kuleshov, is released in the USSR.
- The movie *The Iron Horse*, directed by John Ford, is released in the United States, starring George O'Brien, Madge Bellamy, Cyril Chadwick, and Fred Kohler.
- The movie *The Last Laugh*, directed by F. W. Murnau, is released in Germany, starring Emil Jannings.
- The movie *The Navigator*, directed by Donald Crisp, is released in the United States, starring Buster Keaton and Kathryn McGuire.
- The movie *The Thief of Baghdad*, directed by Raoul Walsh, is released in the United States, starring Douglas Fairbanks and Snitz Edwards.
- The movie *Waxworks*, directed by Paul Leni, is released in Germany, starring William Dieterle, Emil Jannings, Conrad Veidt, and Werner Krauss.
- The movie company Metro-Goldwyn-Mayer, a merger of the Metro and the Goldwyn studios, with the addition of Louis M. Mayer Productions, is formed, thanks to negotiations by Marcus Loews, president of Loew's Inc., a theater company. Louis Mayer becomes head of the studio, a position he holds for three decades.
- U.S. inventor and radio engineer Lee DeForest invents the Phonofilm system, which records sound optically on film.

Literature and Language

- *Autobiography*, by the U.S. writer Mark Twain, is published posthumously.
- The Chilean writer Pablo Neruda publishes *Veinte poemas de amor y una canción desesperada/Twenty Love Poems and a Song of Despair*.
- The English critic I. A. Richards publishes *The Principles of Literary Criticism*.
- The English writer A. A. Milne publishes his collection of children's verse *When We Were Very Young*.
- The English writer David Garnett publishes his novel *A Man in the Zoo*.
- The English writer E. M. Forster publishes his novel *A Passage to India*.
- The English writer Edgar Wallace publishes his novel *Room 13*.
- The English writer Ford Madox Ford publishes his novel *Some Do Not*, the first part of his four-part cycle *Parade's End*.
- The English writer John Galsworthy publishes his novel *The White Monkey*.
- The English writer Mary Webb publishes her novel *Precious Bane*.
- The English writer Margaret Kennedy publishes her novel *The Constant Nymph*.
- The French writer St-John Perse publishes his epic poem *Anabase/Anabasis*.

- The German writer Thomas Mann publishes his novel *Der Zauberberg/The Magic Mountain*.
- The novella *Billy Budd* by the U.S. writer Herman Melville is published posthumously. It was written in 1891.
- The Pulitzer Prize for Biography is awarded to Michael Pupin for *From Immigrant to Inventor*, the Prize for Fiction is awarded to Margaret Wilson for *The Able McLaughlins*, and the Prize for Poetry is awarded to Robert Frost for *New Hampshire*.
- The Russian director and actor Konstantin Sergeyevich Stanislavsky publishes *My Life in Art*, written in English.
- The U.S. writer and editor Harriet Monroe publishes her poetry collection *The Difference and Other Poems*.
- The U.S. writer Edna Ferber publishes her novel *So Big*.
- The U.S. writer H. D. publishes her poetry collection *Heliodora and Other Poems*.
- The U.S. writer Robinson Jeffers publishes his poetry collection *Tamar and Other Poems*.

Music

c. 1924 The U.S. composer Charles Ives completes his piano fantasy *Celestial Railroad*, arranged from the second movement of his Symphony No. 4.
- Philadelphia philanthropist Mary Louise Curtis Bok establishes the Curtis Institute for Music in Philadelphia, Pennsylvania.
- The Czech composer Leoš Janáček completes his chamber suite *Mládí/Youth* for wind sextet. His opera *Příhody lišky bystroušky/The Cunning Little Vixen* is first performed, in Brno, Czechoslovakia.
- The Italian composer Ottorino Respighi completes his orchestral work *Pini di Roma/The Pines of Rome*.
- The Juilliard Graduate School is founded in New York, New York, using an endowment from U.S. businessman Augustus D. Juilliard. In 1926 it will be combined with the Institute of Musical Art, founded in 1905, to form the Juilliard School of Music.
- The light opera *Rose Marie* is first performed, at the Imperial Theater in New York, New York, featuring the works of composer Rudolph Friml.
- The opera *Intermezzo* by the German composer Richard Strauss is first performed, in Dresden, Germany.
- The opera *Zwingburg/Dungeon Castle* by the Austrian composer Ernst Krenek is first performed, in Berlin, Germany.
- The operetta *Gräfin Maritza/Countess Maritza* by the Hungarian composer Emmerich (Imre) Kálmán is first performed, in Vienna, Austria.
- The operetta *The Student Prince* by the Hungarian-born composer Sigmund Romberg is first performed, in New York, New York.
- The Russian composer Sergey Prokofiev completes his Symphony No. 2.
- The Russian composer Igor Stravinsky completes his Piano Sonata.
- The U.S. composer Aaron Copland completes his Symphony No. 1 for organ. He completes his Symphony No. 1 without organ in 1928.

- The U.S. composer George Gershwin completes his orchestral work *Rhapsody in Blue*.

Theater and Dance

- The ballet *Les Biches/The Does* is first performed, in Monte Carlo, Monaco, by Sergei Diaghilev's Ballets Russes. The music is by the French composer Francis Poulenc, the choreography by the Russian dancer Vaslav Nijinsky, and the costumes and sets by the French artist Marie Laurencin.
- The French artist Fernand Léger makes his movie *Ballet mécanique/Mechanical Ballet*.
- The play *Ciasuno a suo modo/Each in his Own Way*, by the Italian writer Luigi Pirandello, is first performed, in Milan, Italy.
- The play *Desire under the Elms*, by the U.S. dramatist Eugene O'Neill, is first performed, at the Greenwich Village Theater in New York, New York. *All God's Chillun Got Wings* receives also its first performance in the same year.
- The play *Juno and the Paycock*, by the Irish dramatist Sean O'Casey, is first performed, at the Abbey Theatre in Dublin, Ireland.
- The play *The Vortex*, by the English writer and performer Noël Coward, is first performed, in London, England.
- The play *What Price Glory?*, by the U.S. writers Maxwell Anderson and Laurence Stallings, is first performed, in New York, New York.
- The Pulitzer Prize for Drama is awarded to Hatcher Hughes for *Hell-Bent for Heaven*.
- The U.S. composer George Antheil completes his *Ballet mécanique/Mechanical Ballet*, scored for airplane propellers, anvils, motor horns, and several musical instruments.

OCTOBER

14 The Russian ballet dancer Anna Pavlova begins a farewell tour in New York, New York.

DECEMBER

1 The musical *Lady Be Good!*, with music and lyrics by George and Ira Gershwin, is performed for the first time, at Liberty Theater, New York, New York. It features the songs "The Man I Love" and "Fascinating Rhythm."

Thought and Scholarship

- English historian Eileen Power publishes *Medieval People*.
- English philosopher Robin George Collingwood publishes *Speculum mentis/Mirror of the Mind*.
- The French philosopher Léon Brunschvicg publishes *Le Génie de Pascal/The Genius of Pascal*.
- The Nobel Prize for Literature is awarded to the Polish novelist Władysław Reymont.
- The Pulitzer Prize for History is awarded to Charles Howard McIlwain for *The American Revolution: A Constitutional Interpretation*.
- U.S. archeologist Alfred Vincent Kidder publishes *An Introduction to the Study of South-Western Archaeology*.

- U.S. architect Louis Harry Sullivan publishes his *Kindergarten Chats on Architecture, Education and Democracy*.
- U.S. jurist Roscoe Pound publishes *Law and Morals*.

SOCIETY

Education

- The Robert Brookings Graduate School of Economics and Government is founded in Washington, D.C.
- Trinity College in Durham, North Carolina, becomes Duke University after American Tobacco president

BIRTHS & DEATHS

JANUARY

6 Earl Scruggs, U.S. bluegrass musician who popularized the banjo, born in Flint Hill, North Carolina.

21 Aristoteles ("Telly") Savalas, U.S. actor known for his role as the New York police lieutenant Kojak, born in Garden City, New York (–1994).

21 Vladimir Ilyich Lenin, founder of the Russian Communist Party, leader of the Russian Revolution, and head of the Soviet Union 1917–24, dies in Gorky, near Moscow, USSR (53).

FEBRUARY

3 (Thomas) Woodrow Wilson, 28th president of the United States 1913–21, a Democrat, dies in Washington, D.C. (67).

20 Sidney Poitier, U.S. actor and film director, born in Miami, Florida.

21 Robert Mugabe, first prime minister of Zimbabwe from 1980 and president from 1987, born in Kutama, Southern Rhodesia.

23 Allan Macleod Cormack, South African-born U.S. physicist who shared the Nobel Prize for Physiology or Medicine in 1979 for his development of computerized axial tomography (CAT), a new medical diagnostic technique, born in Johannesburg, South Africa.

MARCH

27 Sarah Vaughn, U.S. jazz vocalist, born in Newark, New Jersey.

APRIL

3 Marlon Brando, U.S. actor, born in Omaha, Nebraska.

14 Louis Sullivan, U.S. architect who designed some of the first skyscrapers, dies in Chicago, Illinois (67).

16 Henry Mancini, U.S. composer noted for his film scores, born in Cleveland, Ohio (–1994).

28 Kenneth Kaunda, president of Zambia 1964–91, born in Lubwa, Northern Rhodesia.

MAY

29 Paul Cambon, French ambassador to Britain 1898–1920 who was

responsible for the "Entente Cordiale" in 1904 between Britain and France, dies in Paris, France (81).

JUNE

1 Paula Hinton, English ballerina, born in Ilford, England (–1996).

3 Franz Kafka, Bohemian-born German writer, dies in Kierling, near Vienna, Austria (40).

12 George Herbert Walker Bush, 41st president of the United States 1989–93, a Republican, born in Greenwich, Connecticut.

18 George Mikan, U.S. basketball player, born in Joliet, Illinois.

19 General Andres Rodriguez, president of Paraguay 1989–93 who overthrew the Paraguayan dictator Alfredo Stroessner and restored the country to democracy, born in Borja, Paraguay (–1997).

AUGUST

2 James Baldwin, U.S. novelist, born in New York, New York (–1987).

3 Joseph Conrad (pen name of Józef Teodor Konrad Korzeniowski), Polish-born British novelist whose works include *Heart of Darkness, Nostromo,* and *Chance,* dies in Canterbury, Kent, England (66).

12 Mohammad Zia-ul-Haq, president of Pakistan 1978–88, who had his predecessor, Lulfiqar Ali Bhutto, executed, born in Jullundur, Punjab (–1988).

15 Robert (Oxton) Bolt, English historical dramatist and screenwriter who wrote *A Man for All Seasons* (1960), *Lawrence of Arabia* (1962), and *Dr Zhivago* (1965), born near Manchester, England (–1995).

SEPTEMBER

16 Lauren Bacall (Betty Joan Perske), U.S. actress, born in New York, New York.

18 Francis Herbert Bradley, English idealist philosopher, dies in Oxford, England (78).

28 Marcello Mastroianni, Italian film star, born in Fontana Liri, Italy (–1996).

30 Truman Capote, U.S. playwright and novelist, born in New Orleans, Louisiana (–1984).

OCTOBER

1 Jimmy Carter, 39th president of the United States 1977–81, a Democrat, born in Plains, Georgia.

3 Harvey Kuntzman, U.S. cartoonist who created Alfred E. Neuman, and *Mad* magazine, born in New York, New York (–1993).

10 James Clavell, Australian-born U.S. novelist, born in Sydney, Australia (–1994).

12 Anatole France (pen name of Jacque-Anatole-François Thibault), French writer and winner of the Nobel Prize for Literature in 1921, dies in St.-Cyr-sur-Loire, France (80).

NOVEMBER

9 Henry Cabot Lodge, U.S. Republican senator 1893–1924, dies in Cambridge, Massachusetts (74).

10 Dion O'Bannion, Chicago bootlegger and crime boss, is murdered by agents of Al Capone in Chicago, Illinois (32).

23 Colin Macmillan Turnbull, English anthropologist known for his work among the pygmies, born in Harrow, England (–1994).

29 Giacomo Puccini, Italian operatic composer, dies in Brussels, Belgium (66).

DECEMBER

10 Michael Manly, prime minister of Jamaica 1972–80, and 1989–92, born in St. Andrew, Jamaica (–1997).

13 Samuel Gompers, long-serving president of the American Federation of Labor, dies (74).

28 Milton Obote, first prime minister from 1962 and president 1966–71 and 1980–85 of the independent state of Uganda, born in Akoroko village, Lango, Uganda.

James Buchanan Duke donates $47 million to the school.
- U.S. educationist Franklin Bobbit publishes *How to Make a Curriculum*.

Everyday Life

- Clarence Birdseye founds the General Sea Foods Co. in the United States to undertake the preparation and sale of frozen fish.
- The World War I hospital bandage maker Kimberly & Clark introduces the disposable handkerchiefs that will become known as Kleenex.

OCTOBER

5 *Little Orphan Annie*, a comic strip that chronicles the life of a plucky orphan girl, by U.S. cartoonist Harold Lincoln Gray, debuts in the *New York Daily News*.

Media and Communication

- Columbia University in New York, New York, introduces educational radio broadcasting.
- The New York newspaper moguls Gordon Bennett and Horace Greeley join forces to create the *Herald Tribune*.
- The U.S. firm Zenith produces the first portable radio. Weighing 6.6kg/14.6 lb and costing $230, it is the size of a suitcase.
- Two million radio sets are in use in the United States.
- William Randolph Hearst founds the *Daily Mirror* tabloid newspaper in New York, New York; Bernard Macfadden's tabloid, the *Daily Graphic*, follows. In New York's "war of the tabs," the two papers battle with the *Daily News* for readers.

Sports

- Roger Hornsby of the St. Louis Cardinals bats at .424, a season record in modern major league baseball.
- The Fédération Internationale de Ski (FIS) or International Ski Federation is founded, in Stockholm, Sweden. It succeeds the International Ski Commission, founded in Oslo, Norway, in 1910, as the sport's governing body.
- The first motocross (or scrambling) off-road motorcycle race is held, at Camberley, Surrey, England.
- The inaugural Hart Memorial Trophy, awarded to the most valuable hockey player in the National Hockey

League, is won by Frank Nighbor of the Ottawa Senators.
- The Kansas City Monarchs of the Negro National League defeat the Philadelphia Hillbillies of the Eastern Colored League by five games to four in the first "Colored World Series."

JANUARY

25 The 1st Winter Olympic Games open at Chamonix, France, attended by 258 competitors, 13 of whom are women, from 16 nations. Norway and Finland win 4 gold medals each; Austria, 2; and the United States, Switzerland, Canada, and Sweden, 1 each. Clas Thunberg of Finland wins five speed-skating medals, including three golds.

MAY

4–July 27 The 8th Olympic Games are held in Paris, France, attended by 3,092 competitors, 136 of whom are women, from 44 countries. The United States wins 45 gold medals; Finland, 14; France, 13; Britain, 9; and Italy, 8. The star of the games is Paavo Nurmi of Finland who wins gold medals in the 1,500 meters, 5,000 meters, 3,000 meters team race, and 10,000 meters individual and team cross-country events. Harold Abrahams of Britain is the first European to win the 100 meters.

17 Black Gold, ridden by John Mooney, wins the 50th annual Kentucky Derby horse race.

JULY

5 The victory of the French tennis player Jean Borotra, "the Bounding Basque," is the first of six consecutive men's singles titles won by French players at the Wimbledon lawn tennis championships in London, England.

OCTOBER

4–10 The Washington Senators defeat the New York Giants by four games to three to win the World Series.

18 Harold "Red" Grange of the University of Illinois scores 4 touchdowns in the first 12 minutes in a game of football against the University of Michigan. He scores a 5th touchdown later in the game and throws 1 touchdown pass. In all he carries the ball 15 times for 402 yards.

NOVEMBER

1 The Boston Bruins become the first U.S. professional hockey team to join the National Hockey League.

1925

POLITICS, GOVERNMENT, AND ECONOMICS

Business and Economics

- A reorganization of the Maxwell Motor Company results in the founding of the Chrysler Corporation.

APRIL

- The New York banking firm Dillon, Read & Company buys Dodge automobile company for $146 million, a record transaction.
28 Britain returns sterling to the gold standard (linking the value of the pound to the Bank of England's gold reserves) at the prewar level of U.S. $4.86, an act deemed necessary by politicians to maintain London, England, as an international center of finance, but which leads to increasing difficulties for British industry.

OCTOBER

- The unparalleled real estate speculation in the state of Florida reaches its zenith.

Colonization

MAY

1 Cyprus is declared a British crown colony (having been occupied in 1914).

Human Rights

- The U.S. anatomist Florence Sabin becomes the first woman member of the American Academy of Sciences.

JANUARY

5 Nellie Taylor Ross is inaugurated governor of Wyoming, elected to complete her deceased husband William B. Ross's term of office. She is the first female governor in U.S. history.

MARCH

2 Universal suffrage is granted in Japan.

AUGUST

8 An estimated 40,000 Ku Klux Klan members march down Pennsylvania Avenue in Washington, D.C., providing unmistakable evidence of the Klan's reemergence.

Politics and Government

- New laws passed by the fascists in Italy provide for the reduction of the king's prerogative, the dismissal of civil servants who frustrate government policy, and the appointment of a governor of Rome.
- The Italian-American gangster Al "Scarface" Capone assumes command of the underworld operations ring in Chicago, Illinois, of bootlegger Johny Torrio. Capone emerges as the most legendary mob figure in U.S. history.
- The Mexican government requires oil companies to replace ownership of oil fields with 50-year leases.
- Turkmenistan and Uzbekistan become Soviet Socialist Republics.

JANUARY

- In an oft-repeated, often vilified remark, President Calvin Coolidge assures the Society of American Newspaper Editors that "the business of America is business."
1 Christiania, the Norwegian capital, resumes the name of Oslo (abandoned in 1624).
1 The mandated territories of Damascus and Aleppo are united by France to form the state of Syria.
3 The Italian fascist leader Benito Mussolini announces that he will make himself dictator.
11 F. B. Kellogg is appointed U.S. secretary of state, following the resignation of Charles Hughes from the post.
15 The German politician Hans Luther, an independent, succeeds Wilhelm Marx of the Center Party as German chancellor, with Gustav Stresemann as foreign minister.
16 Leon Trotsky, outmaneuvered by Joseph Stalin in his battle for the leadership of the USSR, is dismissed from the chairmanship of the Revolutionary Military Council.
20 A Soviet–Japanese convention is signed, establishing diplomatic relations and the basis for future cooperation.
29 The former prime minister David Lloyd George succeeds the retiring Herbert Asquith, Lord Oxford, as Liberal Party leader in Britain.

FEBRUARY

February–April A revolt of Kurds in Turkey is put down by the Turkish president Mustafa Kemal Pasha (later known as Atatürk).
2 The anticlerical French government closes its embassy at the Vatican.
14 France gives up its special rights in Siam (modern Thailand) by a treaty with Japan.

MARCH

- President Calvin Coolidge is inaugurated to his first full term as president of the United States.

- The U.S. Senate ratifies the Isle of Pines Treaty, granting the Isle of Pines to Cuba.
9   The U.S. president Calvin Coolidge arbitrates in the Chilean-Peruvian dispute over the Tacna and Arica border territories.
12   Britain refuses to sign the Geneva Protocol of October 2, 1924 for the peaceful settlement of international disputes. Britain and its dominions were wary of Japanese intentions to use the treaty to protest against restrictions on Japanese immigration introduced by Canada, Australia, and New Zealand.

APRIL

3   The Netherlands and Belgium sign a convention on the navigation of the River Scheldt, a long-term source of friction between the two countries.
4   Japan evacuates the island of Sakhalin (occupied in 1905 and 1918) under the terms of its convention with the USSR, signed on January 20.
16   Macedonian terrorists detonate a bomb in Sophia Cathedral, Bulgaria, killing 123 people.
17   Paul Painlevé becomes prime minister of France, following the resignation of Edouard Herriot on April 10 after it becomes known that the government has printed more money than is allowed.
18   An attempted military coup in Lisbon, Portugal, is quickly put down.
25   The former military leader Paul von Hindenburg is elected president of Germany, having entered the contest only in the second ballot; he wins 48.5% of the popular vote against 45.2% for Wilhelm Marx of the Center Party.

MAY

4–June 17   A conference in Geneva, Switzerland, discusses the regulation of arms traffic and passes a convention prohibiting the use of poison gas in war.
20   The homicide rate in New York, New York, is reported at 387 per year.
23   An immigration act is passed in Australia, giving the government power to stop designated groups from entering the country.
30   Joseph Coates of the Reform Party becomes prime minister of New Zealand, following the death of William Massey on May 10.
30   The shooting of Chinese students by police in the British colony of Shanghai combined with other incidents in the city of Guangzhou provokes a Chinese boycott of British goods.

JUNE

- The U.S. Supreme Court, in *Gitlow v. New York*, upholds the conviction of left-winger Benjamin Gitlow on the grounds that his rhetoric constituted "the language of direct incitement."
8   Britain and France accept Germany's proposals of February 9 for a security pact to guarantee Franco-German and Belgian-German boundaries.
26   General Theodoros Pangalos seizes power in a coup in Athens, Greece.

JULY

7   The South African Senate rejects a bill to restrict the use of black and Indian labor in the mining industry.
10–21   The celebrated Scopes monkey trial is held in Dayton, Tennessee. The case pits liberal lawyer Clarence

Darrow against politician and fundamentalist William Jennings Bryan in the case of a schoolteacher, John T. Scopes, arrested in May for teaching the theory of evolution, which is contrary to state law. Scopes is convicted and fined $100, but this is waived on a technical point.
13   French troops begin to evacuate the Rhineland, Germany.
16   The first elected parliament of Iraq opens in Baghdad.
18   The Treaty of Nettuno between Italy and the Kingdom of the Serbs, Croats, and Slovenes settles disputes over Dalmatia.
26   France and Spain agree to take common action against the Riff revolt led by Abd al-Karim in Morocco.

AUGUST

15   Norway formally annexes the island of Spitsbergen, the largest island of the Svalbard archipelago in the Arctic Ocean.
18   The United States makes an agreement with Belgium on World War I debts.
28   Britain resumes diplomatic relations with Mexico after a break of eight years.
29   An amnesty is granted in Germany for Wolfgang Kapp and other promonarchical conspirators who mounted the "Kapp Putsch" of March 1920.

SEPTEMBER

24   The French general Henri Pétain takes command of French troops in Morocco after the resignation of General Louis Lyautey on the grounds of ill health.

OCTOBER

5–16   The Locarno Conference in Switzerland drafts a treaty by which Britain, France, Belgium, Italy, and Germany guarantee Germany's western borders, and draws up lesser mutual assistance treaties to stabilize Germany's eastern borders.
10   The Greek army invades Bulgaria in a frontier dispute; Bulgaria appeals to the League of Nations.
12   Germany and the USSR sign a commercial treaty.
18–20   Following uprisings in Syria, the French fleet bombards the capital, Damascus.
19   Italy completes the occupation of Italian Somaliland in east Africa (part of present-day Somalia), making it a protectorate.
29   The Conservatives win seats in the Canadian elections but the prime minister William Mackenzie King continues to lead the Liberal government with the support of the Progressives.
31   The nationalist army officer Reza Khan declares the absent shah of Persia (modern Iran) deposed.

NOVEMBER

- Voters in New York, New York, elect James ("Jimmy") J. Walker to a first term as mayor. Walker's immense popularity will be tarnished by political scandal, and he will resign from office on September 1, 1932.
12   The United States reaches an agreement with Italy on World War I debts.
18   A customs conference of 13 nations in Beijing, China, agrees that China will be free to set its own tariffs.
22   The representative for the Irish Free State (now the Republic of Ireland) on the Irish boundary commission, Eoin MacNeill, resigns because the Free State does not accept the commission's draft treaty.

27 The French socialist politician Aristide Briand forms the first of three successive ministries in France.

DECEMBER

1 British troops evacuate Cologne, Germany, as part of the ending of the postwar Allied occupation of Germany.

1 The Locarno treaties guaranteeing Germany's western borders are signed in London, England.

3 The existing boundary between the Irish Free State (now the Republic of Ireland) and Northern Ireland is confirmed; the same agreement relieves the Free State of its share of British national debt and transfers the powers relating to Northern Ireland to the Northern Irish government.

5–January 20, 1926 A cabinet crisis ensues in Germany when the chancellor Hans Luther resigns; he resumes his post and reforms his cabinet when President Paul von Hindenburg threatens to rule by decree.

6 Italy agrees a settlement of the disputed border area around Cyrenaica, Libya.

12 The U.S. colonel and aviation pioneer William ("Billy") Mitchell is found guilty of insubordination by court martial after having accused the U.S. War and Navy Departments of incompetence.

13 The nationalist army officer Reza Khan becomes shah of Persia (modern Iran).

15 Greece agrees to the penalties imposed by the League of Nations over its invasion of Bulgaria.

16 The League of Nations settles the disputed possession of the city of Mosul in favor of Iraq.

17 The USSR signs a defensive alliance with Turkey.

SCIENCE, TECHNOLOGY, AND MEDICINE

Agriculture

- The U.S. Census Bureau reports that there are 75,000 fewer farms in the United States than in 1920.

Ecology

- Virunga National Park is established in the Belgian Congo (in modern Zaire). It includes active and extinct volcanoes, gorillas, and a population of pygmies.

MARCH

18 Thousands of people are injured and 689 killed when a tornado, the worst in U.S. history to date, passes through Missouri, Illinois, and Indiana.

Exploration

- U.S. inventor Robert Hutchings Goddard conducts a static test of a liquid-propelled rocket.

Health and Medicine

- Canadian pathologist James Collip obtains an extract from the parathyroid gland for treating tetanus.
- Kansas physician Charles F. Menninger establishes the Menninger Clinic in Topeka, Kansas. The clinic will treat mentally incapacitated patients with a new "total-environment" approach.
- The United States's foremost medical societies endorse birth control, due to the tireless lobbying efforts of obstetrician Robert L. Dickinson.

Math

- English geneticist Ronald Fisher publishes *Statistical Methods for Research Workers*, in which he demonstrates experimental techniques and statistical methods to be used in biology.

Science

- Austrian chemist Richard Zsigmondy receives the Nobel Prize for Chemistry for his work on colloids.
- Austrian physicist Wolfgang Pauli discovers the exclusion principle, which accounts for the chemical properties of the elements.
- English astrophysicist Arthur Eddington publishes *Internal Constitution of the Stars*, in which he shows that the luminosity of a star is a function of its mass.
- French anthropologist Marcel Mauss publishes *Essai sur le don/The Gift*, a comparative study relating forms of exchange to social structure.
- German chemists Ida and Walter Noddack and Otto Berg discover the rare metallic element rhenium (atomic no. 75).
- German physicists James Franck and Gustav Hertz receive the Nobel Prize for Physics for their discovery of the laws governing the impact of an electron upon an atom.
- Swedish astronomer Bertil Lindblad discovers that the Milky Way rotates around its center. One rotation takes 210 million years.
- The U.S. Navy develops a pulse modulation technique to measure the distance above the earth of the ionizing layer in the atmosphere.
- U.S. astronomer Heber Curtis and Swedish astronomer Knut Lundmark contend that spiral nebulae are galaxies similar to the Milky Way.
- U.S. geneticists Thomas Hunt Morgan, Alfred Sturtevant, and Calvin Blackman Bridges publish the results of their genetic experiments with the fruit fly *Drosophila melanogaster*, showing that genes can be mapped onto chromosomes.
- U.S. pathologist George Whipple demonstrates that iron is the most important factor involved in the formation of red blood cells.

Technology

c. 1925 The British armed forces introduce "tankettes," small light tanks without turrets designed for a two-person crew.

c. 1925 U.S. chemist Thomas Midgley discovers Freon-12 (dichlorodifluoromethane), a chlorofluorocarbon (CFC) used in refrigeration.
- Bell Laboratories is founded in New Brunswick, New Jersey, by AT&T to conduct research into telecommunications.
- Chromium electroplating is introduced in the United States. It is used to coat machine parts because of its low friction properties, and also in the auto industry because of chromium's ability to retain its brightness indefinitely.
- German-born U.S. inventor Emil Berliner patents an acoustic tile. It is used in concert halls and large auditoriums.
- The Russian-born U.S. engineer Vladimir Zworykin files a patent for an all-electronic color television system (granted 1928).
- The Scottish electrical engineer John Logie Baird transmits the first television images of recognizable human faces.
- The British armed forces introduce the Independent tank, which has five turrets and serves as the prototype for subsequent tanks.

Transportation

- The Bronx River Parkway is opened in New York, New York. It is 15 km/24 mi long and is the first controlled-access road in the United States.
- The first headlights with two beam levels are introduced.
- The first motel in the United States opens in California.
March 1925–31 The George Washington Bridge between Manhattan and New Jersey is constructed. The longest suspension bridge built to date, its main span is 1,067m/3,500 ft long, nearly twice that of the previous longest span.

JUNE
6   The U.S. Chrysler Motor Company releases its first car, at a price of $1,500.

ARTS AND IDEAS

Architecture

- The Swiss architect Le Corbusier publishes *Urbanisme/The City of Tomorrow and Its Planning*.
- The Tribune Tower, designed by the U.S. architects John Mean Howells and Raymond Mathewson Hood, is completed in Chicago, Illinois. Though a successful use of modern materials and technology, this classic of the golden age of the skyscraper has ornately Gothic decoration.
- The Tristan Tzara House in Paris, France, designed by the Austrian architect Adolf Loos, is completed.
- The Wrigley Building, designed by the U.S. firm Graham, Anderson, Probst and White, is completed in Chicago, Illinois.

Arts

- An international exposition of decorative arts—the Exposition Internationale des Arts Décoratifs et Industriels Modernes—is held in Paris, France, and gives rise to the term "art deco."
- The first surrealist exhibition is held, at the Galerie Pierre in Paris, France.
- The French artist André Masson creates *Automatic Drawing*.
- The French photographer Jean Eugène Auguste Atget takes *Avenue des Gobelins*, one of his many street scenes.
- The German artist Otto Dix paints *Three Prostitutes on the Street*.
- The Russian artist Chaim Soutine paints *Carcass of Beef*.
- The Russian artist Naum Gabo sculpts *Construction in Space with Balance on Two Points*.
- The Spanish artist Pablo Picasso paints *Three Dancers*.
- The U.S. artist Edward Hopper paints *House by the Railroad*.
- The U.S. photographer Imogen Cunningham takes *Magnolia Blossom*.

DECEMBER
6   The trustees of John Simon Guggenheim establish the John Simon Guggenheim Foundation to promote art and scholarship.

Film

- Georges-Michel Coissac publishes *L'Histoire du cinématographe/History of the Cinema*, the first history of movie making.
- The movie *Ben Hur*, directed by Fred Niblo, is released in the United States, starring Ramon Navarro, Francis X. Bushman, Carmel Myers, May McAvoy, and Betty Bronson. It is based on the 1880 novel *Ben Hur* by U.S. soldier, diplomat, and writer Lew Wallace.
- The movie *Gribiche*, directed by Jacques Feyder and starring Françoise Rosay, is released in Belgium.
- The movie *Joyless Street*, directed by Czech filmmaker G. W. Pabst, is released in Germany, starring Greta Garbo (in her last role in a European movie), Asta Nielsen, and Werner Krauss.
- The movie *Madame Sans-Gêne/Woman of Leisure*, directed by Léonce Perret, is released in France, starring Gloria Swanson, Charles de Roche, and Emile Drain.
- The movie *The Battleship Potemkin*, directed by Sergey Eisenstein, is released in the USSR, starring Alexander Antonov, Grigory Alexandrov, and Vladimir Barsky.
- The movie *The Big Parade*, directed by King Vidor, is released in the United States, starring John Gilbert, Renee Adoree, and Hobart Bosworth.
- The movie *The Death Ray*, directed by Lev Kuleshov, is released in the USSR.
- The movie *The Gold Rush*, directed by Charlie Chaplin, is released in the United States. Chaplin also stars in it.
- The movie *The Merry Widow*, directed by Austrian filmmaker Erich von Stroheim, is released in the United States, starring Mae Murray, John Gilbert, Ron D'Arcy, and Tully Marshall.

- The movie *The Phantom of the Opera*, directed by Rupert Julian, is released in the United States. Based on the novel by Gaston Leroux, it stars Lon Chaney, Mary Philbin, Norman Kerry, and Gibson Gowland.
- The movie *The Unholy Three*, directed by Tod Browning, is released in the United States, starring Lon Chaney, Harry Earles, Victor McLaglen, and Mae Busch.
- The French physicist Henri Chrétien invents the anamorphic objective lens, which contracts images vertically, permitting wide-screen movies. It is ignored until the 1950s when it becomes known as CinemaScope.

OCTOBER

13 The movie *The Pony Express*, directed by James Cruze, is released in the United States, starring Billy Compson and Wallace Beery.

Literature and Language

- Black American poet Alain Locke publishes *The New Negro*, an anthology of the literature of the Harlem Renaissance.
- The Australian writer Henry Handel Richardson publishes her novel *The Way Home*, the second part of her trilogy *The Fortunes of Richard Mahony*.
- The black American writer Countee Cullen publishes his poetry collection *Color*, which includes "Yet Do I Marvel."
- The English critic I. A. Richards publishes *Science and Poetry*.
- The English writer Aldous Huxley publishes his novel *Those Barren Leaves*.
- The English writer Ford Madox Ford publishes his novel *No More Parades*, the second part of his four-part cycle *Parade's End*.
- The English writer Ivy Compton-Burnett publishes her novel *Pastors and Masters*.
- The English writer P. G. Wodehouse publishes his novel *Carry on Jeeves*.
- The English writer Virginia Woolf publishes her novel *Mrs Dalloway* and *The Common Reader*, a collection of essays.
- The English writer William Gerhardie publishes his novel *The Polyglots*.
- The French writer Jules Supervielle publishes his poetry collection *Gravitations*.
- The German writer Lion Feuchtwanger publishes his novel *Jud Süss/Jew Süss*.
- The Irish writer Liam O'Flaherty publishes his novel *The Informer*.
- The Italian writer Eugenio Montale publishes his poetry collection *Ossi di seppia/Cuttlefish Bones*.
- The novel *Der Prozess/The Trial* by the Bohemian-born German writer Franz Kafka is published posthumously.
- The Pulitzer Prize for Biography is awarded to M. A. DeWolfe Howe for *Barrett Wendell and his Letters*, the Prize for Fiction is awarded to Edna Ferber for *So Big*, and the Prize for Poetry is awarded to Edwin Arlington Robinson for *The Man Who Died Twice*.
- The Russian writer Boris Pasternak publishes his story "Detstvo Lyuvers"/"The Childhood of Luvers."

- The U.S. writer Anita Loos publishes her novel *Gentlemen Prefer Blondes*.
- The U.S. writer e e cummings publishes his poetry collections *XLI Poems* and *&*.
- The U.S. writer Edith Wharton publishes her critical study *The Writing of Fiction*.
- The U.S. writer Edwin DuBose Heyward publishes his novel *Porgy*. He and his wife turn it into a play in 1927, and it is used as the basis of the opera *Porgy and Bess* in 1935.
- The U.S. writer Ellen Glasgow publishes her novel *The Barren Ground*.
- The U.S. writer Ernest Hemingway publishes his story collection *In Our Time*.
- The U.S. writer F. Scott Fitzgerald publishes his novel *The Great Gatsby*.
- The U.S. writer Gertrude Stein publishes her novel *The Making of Americans: Being a History of a Family's Progress*, a work she completed in 1911.
- The U.S. writer John Dos Passos publishes his novel *Manhattan Transfer*.
- The U.S. writer Sherwood Anderson publishes his novel *Dark Laughter*.
- The U.S. writer Sinclair Lewis publishes his novel *Arrowsmith*.
- The U.S. writer Willa Cather publishes her novel *The Professor's House*.
- The U.S. writer William Carlos Williams publishes *In the American Grain*, a collection of biographical essays.
- The U.S.-born English writer T. S. Eliot publishes his poem "The Hollow Men."

Music

- Black American singer Paul Robeson gives his first recital of "Negro spirituals" in New York, New York, then tours Europe.
- In the United States, the regular broadcasting of country music from Nashville, Tennessee, starts with the *National Barn Dance* country variety program and the *Grand Ole Opry* radio show.
- Popular songs in the United States include "Show Me the Way to Go Home," "Collegiate," and "Thanks for the Buggy Ride."
- The Danish composer Carl Nielsen completes his Symphony No. 6, the *Sinfonia semplice/Simple Symphony*.
- The French-born U.S. composer Edgard Varèse completes his orchestral work *Intégrales*.
- The opera *Doktor Faust/Doctor Faust* by the Italian composer Ferruccio Busoni is first performed, posthumously, in Dresden, Germany.
- The opera *L'Enfant et les sortilèges/The Spellbound Child*, a "lyrical fantasy" by the French composer Maurice Ravel, is first performed, in Monte Carlo, Monaco. The story is by the French writer Colette, the choreography by the Russian choreographer George Balanchine.
- The opera *Wozzeck* by the Austrian composer Alban Berg is first performed, in Berlin, Germany. It is based on the play *Woyzeck*, published in 1836 by the German writer Georg Büchner.

- The Russian composer Dmitry Shostakovich completes his Symphony No. 1.
- The Russian composer Igor Stravinsky completes his Piano Serenade.
- The U.S. composer Aaron Copland completes his choral work *The House on the Hill* and his orchestral work *Music for the Theater*.
- The U.S. composer George Gershwin completes his Piano Concerto.
- The U.S. industrialist Henry Ford starts a drive against jazz by organizing a series of folk dances.
- The U.S. jazz trumpeter, singer, and composer Louis "Satchmo" Armstrong begins recording with his group, The Hot Five, in Chicago, Illinois.

Theater and Dance

- The ballet *Les Matelots/Sailors* is first performed by the Ballets Russes under the Russian impresario Sergei Diaghilev in London, England. The music is by the French composer Georges Auric, the choreography by the Russian choreographer Léonide Massine.
- The Goodman Theater Center of the Art Institute of Chicago is founded, in Chicago, Illinois.
- The play *Hay Fever*, by the English writer and performer Noël Coward, is first performed, in London, England.
- The play *The Last of Mrs Cheyney*, by the English dramatist Frederick Lonsdale, is first performed, in London, England.
- The play *Veland*, by the German dramatist Gerhart Hauptmann is first performed, in Hamburg, Germany.
- The Pulitzer Prize for Drama is awarded to Sidney Howard for *They Knew What They Wanted*.

Thought and Scholarship

- Australian archeologist Vere Gordon Childe publishes *The Dawn of European Civilization*.
- Belgian historian Henri Pirenne publishes *Medieval Cities*, lectures he gave at Princeton University in New Jersey.
- Canadian-born English newspaper owner and politician Max Beaverbrook publishes *Politicians and the Press*.
- English philosopher Charlie Dunbar Broad publishes *The Mind and its Place in Nature*.
- English philosopher and mathematician Alfred North Whitehead publishes *Science and the Modern World*, in which he discusses the growth, success, and impact of "scientific materialism," the idea that nature consists solely of matter and energy.
- English political scientist Harold Laski publishes *A Grammar of Politics*.
- The German political leader Adolf Hitler publishes *Mein Kampf/My Struggle*, his political manifesto.
- The Nobel Prize for Literature is awarded to the Irish dramatist George Bernard Shaw.
- The Pulitzer Prize for History is awarded to Frederic L. Paxton for *A History of the American Frontier, 1763–1893*.
- U.S. psychologist Arnold Gesell publishes *The Mental Growth of the Pre-School Child*.

SOCIETY

Education

- Bennington College for Women opens in Bennington, Vermont.
- The University of Miami opens in Coral Gables, Florida.
- U.S. Zionist Judah Leon Magnes founds Hebrew University in Jerusalem.

OCTOBER

16 The Texas State Textbook Board bans the theory of evolution from the public school curriculum.

Everyday Life

- Prest-Air Devices Company of Long Island, New York, manufactures the first dry ice for commercial sale.
- The card game of contract bridge is developed by the U.S. railroad heir and yachtsman Harold S. Vanderbilt while on a cruise. By the early 1930s it will virtually replace auction bridge.
- The flapper dress, which features a drop waist, becomes a popular women's style in the United States.
- The U.S. soap manufacturer Lever Brothers launches Lux soap.
- U.S. food manufacturer Clarence Birdseye's General Seafoods Company extends its deep-freezing process to precooked foods.

APRIL

3 The right to strike is abolished in Italy by the fascist government.

AUGUST

- The U.S. publisher A. Philip Randolph establishes the Brotherhood of Sleeping Car Porters, a labor union for black trainmen, in New York, New York.

Media and Communication

- New York publisher A. Philip Randolph introduces *The Messenger*, a monthly periodical of black American politics and culture.

FEBRUARY

21 The first issue of the magazine *New Yorker*, featuring fiction, humor, and cartoons, appears in the United States, edited by Harold Ross.

MARCH

22 Tokyo Shibaura, Japan's first radio station, begins broadcasting in Tokyo.

APRIL

- The European Broadcasting Union (UIR) is established as a forum for handling broadcasting issues affecting Europe.

JULY

10 The Tass (Telegrafnoe Agentsvo Sovetskogo Soyuza) press agency is founded in the USSR.

BIRTHS & DEATHS

c. 1925 Idi Amin (dada Oumee), president of Uganda 1971–79, who tortured and murdered between 100,000 and 300,000 Ugandans during his presidency, born in Koboko, Uganda.

JANUARY

7 Gerald (Malcolm) Durrell, English naturalist, writer, and zoo curator, born in Jamshedpur, India (–1995).

21 Benny Hill, English comedian who wrote and starred in the television show *The Benny Hill Show* (1955–88), born in Southampton, Hampshire, England (–1992).

24 Joseph Rowntree, English industrial reformer and philanthropist, dies in York, England (88).

26 Paul Newman, U.S. actor and film director, born in Cleveland, Ohio.

FEBRUARY

4 Robert Koldewey, German architect and archeologist who excavated Babylon, dies in Berlin, Germany (69).

20 Robert Altman, U.S. film director, born in Kansas City, Missouri.

21 Sam Peckinpah, U.S. film director and screenwriter known for his violent westerns, born in Fresno, California (–1984).

28 Friedrich Ebert, German Social Democrat, president of the Weimar Republic 1919–25, dies in Berlin, Germany (54).

MARCH

7 Georgy Yevgenyevich Lvov, Russian social reformer and head of the first Russian provisional government after the Russian Revolution in 1917, dies in Paris, France (63).

7 Richard Vernon, English actor, born in Reading, England (–1997).

12 Sun Zhong Shan (Sun Yat-Sen), leader of the Chinese Nationalist Party (Guomindang) which overthrew the Manchu dynasty, first president of the Republic of China 1911–12, and de facto ruler 1923–25, dies in Beijing, China (58).

14 John (Barrington) Wain, English poet and novelist, one of the "Angry Young Men," born in Stoke-on-Trent, Staffordshire, England (–1994).

20 John D. Ehrlichman, U.S. presidential assistant to Richard M. Nixon who was deeply involved in the Watergate scandal, born in Tacoma, Washington.

26 Pierre Boulez, French composer, born in Montbrison, France.

APRIL

3 Tony (Anthony Wedgwood) Benn, outspoken British Labour politician, born in London, England.

15 John Singer Sargent, U.S. painter, dies in London, England (69).

MAY

13 Alfred Milner, British colonial administrator whose policies and attitudes were instrumental in beginning the Boer War 1899–1902, dies at Sturry Court, near Canterbury, England (71).

14 H. Rider Haggard, English novelist, dies in London, England (68).

19 Malcolm X, U.S. black militant leader, born in Omaha, Nebraska (–1965).

23 Joshua Lederberg, U.S. geneticist who discovered mechanisms of genetic recombination in bacteria, born in Montclair, New Jersey.

JUNE

18 Robert M. La Follette, U.S. senator 1906–25, leader of the Progressive Movement, dies in Washington, D.C. (70).

JULY

1 Erik Satie, French composer, dies in Paris, France (59).

2 Patrice Lumumba, first elected president of the Democratic Republic of the Congo (modern Zaire) 1960, born in Onalua, Belgian Congo (–1961).

26 Gottlob Frege, German mathematician who founded mathematical logic, dies in Bad Kleinen, Germany (76).

26 William Jennings Bryan, U.S. lawyer, three-time Democratic presidential candidate, and prosecuting attorney in the Scopes trial (against Tennessee schoolteacher John T. Scopes for teaching Darwinism), dies in Dayton, Tennessee (65).

28 Baruch S. Blumberg, U.S. physician who discovered the antigen that causes antibody production to Hepatitis B, born in New York, New York.

AUGUST

18 Brian Aldiss, English science-fiction writer, born in East Dereham, Norfolk, England.

SEPTEMBER

7 Laura Ashley, Welsh fashion designer, born in Merthyr Tydfil, Glamorgan, Wales (–1985).

8 Peter Sellers, English radio, television, and film comedian who became famous in *The Goon Show*, and as Inspector Clouseau in the *Pink Panther* films, born in Southsea, Hampshire, England (–1980).

16 B. B. King, U.S. blues guitarist, born in Itta Bena, Mississippi.

16 Charles James Haughey, prime minister of Ireland 1979–81, 1982, and 1987–92, born at Castlebar, County Mayo, Ireland.

28 Seymour Cray, U.S. computer designer who built the first super computers, born in Colorado Springs, Colorado (–1996).

29 Léon Bourgeois, French prime minister 1895–96, recipient of the Nobel Peace Prize in 1920, dies near Epernay, France (74).

OCTOBER

3 Gore Vidal, U.S. novelist, playwright, and essayist, born in West Point, New Hampshire.

8 Andrey Sinyavsky, Russian novelist and dissident, born in Moscow, Russia (–1997).

13 Margaret Thatcher, prime minister of Britain 1979–90, a Conservative, born in Grantham, Lincolnshire, England.

18 Melina Mercouri, Greek actress and politician, born in Athens, Greece (–1994).

22 Robert Rauschenberg, U.S. painter and graphic artist, born in Port Arthur, Texas.

23 Johnny Carson, host of the *Tonight Show*, born in Corning, Iowa.

24 Luciano Berio, Italian composer, born in Oneglia, Italy.

NOVEMBER

10 Richard Burton (adopted name of Richard Walter Jenkins), Welsh actor, born in Pontrhydyfen, Wales (–1984).

20 Robert Kennedy, U.S. attorney general and presidential advisor, born in Brookline, Massachusetts (–1968).

DECEMBER

23 Pierre (Eugène) Bérégovoy, prime minister of France 1992–93, born in Déville-les-Rouen, France (–1993).

Religion

MAY

- The Florida legislature passes a law mandating daily Bible readings in public schools.

JULY

18–June 6, 1927 An insurrection of Druses (members of a religious sect) against French rule takes place in Syria.

Sports

- The Fastnet Race for yachts is inaugurated in Britain. Competitors sail from the Isle of Wight, off southern England, round the Scilly Isles, then to the Fastnet rock off southwest Ireland, and back to Plymouth, England, a distance of around 968 km/605 mi.
- The French tennis championships in Paris, France, inaugurated in 1891, become an international open event (the French Open). Nevertheless, the French players René Lacoste and Suzanne Lenglen respectively win the men's and women's singles titles.

- The University of Illinois star running back Harold "Red" Grange signs for the Chicago Bears for $100,000. The fame he has acquired in college football greatly raises the profile of professional football.
- The U.S. waterskiing pioneer Ralph Samuelson builds the first water-ski jump, on Lake Pepin in Minnesota.
- The Victoria Jaguars defeat the Montreal Canadiens by three games to one to win hockey's Stanley Cup.

MAY

30 The U.S. driver Peter DePaulo, in a Duesenberg, becomes the first driver to win the Indianapolis 500 motor race at an average speed of over 160 kph/100 mph.

SEPTEMBER

19 The U.S. tennis player Bill Tilden wins the men's singles title at the U.S. lawn tennis championships at Forest Hills, New York, for the sixth year in succession.

OCTOBER

7–15 The Pittsburgh Pirates defeat the Washington Senators by four games to three to win the World Series.

1926

POLITICS, GOVERNMENT, AND ECONOMICS

Business and Economics

- The U.S. industrialist Henry Ford introduces the 40-hour work week to the consternation of his peers and the applause of labor advocates.
- Trans World Airlines opens under the name Western Air Express.

AUGUST

10 Following the devaluation of the French franc, a sinking fund is established to pay off the national debt. France returns to the gold standard, linking the value of the franc to the nation's gold reserves.

Human Rights

- The American Eugenics Society is founded in the United States. It advocates the idea that the upper classes possess a superior genetic endowment, which justifies their wealth and social position.

Politics and Government

- A new constitution for Lebanon (a French mandate) seeks to balance the different communities in government by providing for a Maronite president, a Sunni Muslim prime minister, and a Shiite Muslim speaker of the chamber.
- A New York State district court upholds a one-hour release time for religious worship in New York public schools.
- Benjamin Cardozo becomes chief justice of the New York Court of Appeals, where he revives the justices' contribution to the development of law.
- The British legation in Beijing, China, declares Britain's sympathy with the Chinese nationalist movement (the Guomindang).
- The fascist government in Italy undertakes (in theory at least) a "corporatist" reorganization of industry with the declaration of 13 state-controlled corporations and the establishment of the National Council of Corporations. Workers are to be represented by fascist labor syndicates.
- U.S. Congress passes the Railway Labor Act, creating a mediation board to settle railroad disputes.

JANUARY

3 General Theodoros Pangalos assumes dictatorial powers in Greece.

4   A moderate ministry under Andrew Liapchev takes office in Bulgaria, offering an amnesty to all political prisoners except communists.

8   Following conquests in Arabia and the abdication of Hussein ibn Ali (October 5, 1924), Ibn Saud is proclaimed king of the Hejaz in Mecca.

14–30   Denmark, Sweden, Norway, and Finland make a series of agreements for the peaceful settlement of disputes.

FEBRUARY

• President Calvin Coolidge signs a Revenue Act, reducing income taxes, surtaxes, and automobile taxes.

2   Tension grows between Italy and Austria over the Germanization of the South Tirol, which has a large Italian population.

10   Germany applies for admission to the League of Nations.

17   A modern law code is adopted in Turkey, based on the Swiss code (rather than Islamic principles); polygamy is prohibited.

MARCH

11   Eamon de Valera resigns as leader of Sinn Féin, which has repudiated his decision to enter the Irish Dáil.

17   Brazil and Spain block Germany's admission to the League of Nations, protesting against the plan to give Germany a seat on the Council (which they believe they should have instead).

26   Romania and Poland form an alliance.

APRIL

• The United States and France reach an agreement by which the United States cancels 60% of France's war debt in exchange for a French promise to repay the United States some $4 billion by 1988.

7   The first of several attempts to assassinate the Italian fascist leader Benito Mussolini is made by the Irishwoman Violet Gibson.

14   General Theodoros Pangalos is elected president of Greece, having assumed dictatorial powers on January 3.

22   Persia (modern Iran), Turkey, and Afghanistan sign a treaty of mutual security.

24   A treaty of friendship and neutrality is signed between Germany and the USSR in Berlin, Germany.

MAY

2   The U.S. president Calvin Coolidge dispatches U.S. marines to Nicaragua following a coup by Nicaraguan general Augusto Cesar Sandino. U.S. forces depart Nicaragua on June 5.

8   During the revolt of the Druses in Syria, the French fleet bombards the capital Damascus.

10   Wincenty Witos, leader of the Peasants' Party, forms a government in Poland.

12   The German chancellor Hans Luther resigns.

12–15   The chief of the Polish army Józef Piłsudski and army units march on the Polish capital Warsaw and seize power. President Wojciechowski and Prime Minister Wincenty Witos resign on May 15; the speaker of parliament becomes acting president.

16   The Irish nationalist Eamon de Valera founds the Fianna Fáil ("Soldiers of Destiny") party in the Irish Free State (now the Republic of Ireland) to put up republican candidates for election to the Dáil (parliament).

18–26   A preparatory disarmament conference organized by the League of Nations meets, attended by the United States but not the USSR.

20   The U.S. president Calvin Coolidge signs the Civilian Aviation Act, creating the Bureau of Air Commerce to oversee the nation's civil aviation.

23   France proclaims the Lebanon (part of the territory mandated to it by the League of Nations) a republic.

26   The Riff revolt against the French and Spanish invaders in Morocco ends with the Berber leader Abd-al-Karim's surrender to France.

28   General Manuel de Oliveira Gomes da Costa leads a coup in Portugal and deposes President Bernardino Machado.

31   The Polish parliament elects Józef Piłsudski as president, but he refuses to take office.

JUNE

1   Ignacy Mościcki is elected president of Poland.

5   A British–Turkish agreement on the city of Mosul is signed, with most of the area assigned to Iraq in accordance with League of Nations' award of December 1925.

7   A Liberal ministry under Karl Ekman replaces the Socialist government in Sweden.

10   Spain announces its withdrawal from the League of Nations in protest against Germany joining, but later rescinds its decision.

26   The McNary–Haugen Bill for a tariff on agricultural products is defeated in the U.S. Senate.

28   William Mackenzie King resigns as Canadian prime minister as a result of customs scandals; Arthur Meighen forms a Liberal government.

JULY

• The U.S. Congress creates the Army Air Corps.

• U.S. Congress establishes the Distinguished Flying Cross to reward meritorious service in the U.S. Air Corps.

1   A British–Portuguese agreement defines the boundary between South West Africa (modern Namibia) and Angola.

9   The insurgent Portuguese general Manuel de Oliveira Gomes da Costa is overthrown by General Antonio Oscar de Fragoso Carmona.

15   The French government of Aristide Briand falls because of a financial crisis.

23   Raymond Poincaré becomes prime minister of a National Union ministry in France, a coalition formed to deal with the current financial crisis.

26   The Philippines legislature calls for a plebiscite on independence from the United States, which is vetoed by the governor.

28   Following a Belgian financial crisis the Belgian franc is devalued and King Albert I is given dictatorial powers for six months.

28   The United States and Panama form an alliance to protect the Panama Canal in wartime.

30   A treaty between Albania, Greece, and the Kingdom of the Serbs, Croats, and Slovenes recognizes Albania's frontiers.

31   Afghanistan signs a nonaggression pact with the USSR.

AUGUST

7   Fascist Italy signs a treaty of friendship with dictatorially governed Spain.

17 Greece signs a treaty of friendship with the Kingdom of the Serbs, Croats, and Slovenes.

SEPTEMBER

1 Civil marriage becomes compulsory in Turkey.
2 Italy agrees a treaty with the Yemen (the start of Italy's attempt to dominate the east coast of the Red Sea).
6 The Guomindang Chinese nationalist forces led by Jiang Jie Shi reach Hankou at the confluence of the Han and

the Chang Jiang rivers; Hankou becomes the Guomindang capital.
8 Germany is admitted to the League of Nations.
11 Spain leaves the League of Nations following the admission of Germany on September 8. Spain had announced its withdrawal earlier in the year in protest, but had later rescinded the decision.
17 An Italian-Romanian treaty of friendship is signed; Italy wants to extend its influence through southeastern

Chinese Civil War (1926–49)

Phase One, 1926–36

1926

September 6 The Guomindang Chinese nationalist forces led by Jiang Jie Shi (Chiang Kai-shek) reach Hankou at the confluence of the Han and the Chang Jiang rivers; Hankou becomes the Guomindang capital.

1927

March 24 Guomindang nationalists take the city of Nanjing on the lower Chang Jiang River.

May 27 Japan intervenes on the Shandong Peninsula, China, to block the advance of Guomindang nationalists on the Chinese capital Beijing.

September 19 A communist rising in China led by Mao Zedong is put down by Guomindang nationalists.

1928

May 3–11 Clashes between Guomindang nationalists and Japanese troops take place at Jinan in northeastern China, after which Japan reoccupies part of the Shandong Peninsula.

June 8 The Guomindang nationalists capture Beijing.

1931

September 9 The Canton rebel government mounts a military offensive toward the Chinese capital of Nanjing.

1934

October 15 The Long March of the Chinese communists begins, led by Mao Zedong and others. Driven out by a Nationalist offensive, some 100,000 people leave the Jiangxi Soviet in southern China and march 9,600 km/6,000 mi to the province of Shaanxi in the extreme northwest, where the survivors set up a new communist revolutionary base.

1936

August 11 Jiang Jie Shi, head of the ruling Nationalist Party (Guomindang) in China, enters the port of Canton for the first time since 1926, strengthening his hold on the south.

December 12–26 At Sian in northern China, Jiang Jie Shi is held in "protective custody" by dissident generals until he agrees to an armistice with the communists so that China can concentrate on facing the threat from Japan. Though there continue to be numerous clashes between communist and Nationalist forces, there are no major actions until after Japan's capitulation to the Allies in August 1945.

Phase Two, 1945–49

1945

August 8 The United States attempts to mediate when conflict breaks out in China between the Nationalist government and the communists.

October 11 A breakdown of negotiations in China between the president Jiang Jie Shi and the communist leader Mao Zedong leads to fighting between nationalists and communists for the control of Manchuria.

1946

January 10 A truce is signed between Chinese nationalists and communists, which holds until April 14.

February 25 Chinese nationalists and communists agree to merge their armies following the mediation of the U.S. secretary of state, General George C. Marshall, but their failure to keep the agreement leads to renewed civil war.

1947

January 29 The United States abandons efforts at mediation.

March 19 Nationalist forces capture the communist capital of Yan'an.

1948

November 11 Communist forces complete the conquest of Manchuria from the nationalists. Massive forces then fight for Suzhou, which is captured in early January 1949.

1949

January 10 The communist army under Zhu De in China captures the city of Xuzhou from the nationalists, exposing the nationalists' capital at Nanjing to a new offensive.

January 15 Communist forces capture the city of Tianjin in northeast China from the nationalists.

January 22 Jiang Jie Shi resigns the presidency of China following successive setbacks for the Nationalist forces in the civil war.

April 24 Communist forces in China capture Nanjing, the nationalist capital.

May 23 Chinese communist forces resume their offensive to drive nationalist forces off the mainland.

July 16 Chinese nationalists organize a Supreme Council, under the former president Jiang Jie Shi, which begins to evacuate its military forces to the island of Formosa (now Taiwan) after a succession of defeats by communist forces.

August 5 The United States ends its aid to the nationalist side, recognizing that the Nationalist Guomindang (KMT) party is deeply corrupt and the war against the communists unwinnable.

Europe so that it can challenge the boundaries fixed by the 1919 Treaty of Versailles.

18 Poland signs a treaty of friendship with the Kingdom of the Serbs, Croats, and Slovenes.

25 Following the defeat of the Conservatives in the House of Commons and in a general election, William Mackenzie King forms another Liberal ministry in Canada.

25 The fascist Italian government begins a campaign against the Mafia in Sicily.

OCTOBER

• The U.S. Supreme Court rules that the U.S. president may remove Cabinet members from office without Senate consent, thus overturning an 1876 law.

2 The military leader Józef Piłsudski becomes prime minister of Poland.

10 A National Peasant Party is founded in Romania under Julius Maniu, former leader of the pro-Romanian Transylvanian nationalist movement in Hungary.

15 Ignaz Seipel, Christian Socialist, forms a ministry in Austria, replacing Rudolf Ramek.

19 Leon Trotsky and Grigory Zinoviev are expelled from the Politburo of the Communist Party in the USSR, having been defeated by Joseph Stalin on the question of whether to continue Vladimir Ilyich Lenin's New Economic Policy.

19–November 18   An Imperial Conference in London, England, decides that Britain and the Dominions (Australia, New Zealand, Canada, and South Africa) are autonomous communities, equal in status.

NOVEMBER

• In U.S. Congressional elections, the Republicans retain majorities in the House (237–195) and Senate (49–46).

November 1926–July 1927   An unsuccessful communist revolt takes place in Java, Dutch East Indies (later Indonesia).

8 The British Parliament appoints a commission under Lord Simon to examine the working of the 1919 Government of India Act, following disturbances in India.

10 Vincent Massey becomes the first Canadian minister in Washington, D.C.

11 The Italian Socialist, Republican, and Communist parties are dissolved and the abstaining antifascist deputies are declared to have forfeited their parliamentary seats.

11 The upper parliamentary house, representing the landed aristocracy, is reestablished in Hungary.

27 The Treaty of Tirana is agreed between Italy and Albania; Italy recognizes the status quo, but rapidly turns Albania into a virtual protectorate.

DECEMBER

• The U.S. vice president Charles G. Dawes shares the Nobel Peace Prize with Britain's Sir Austen Chamberlain. Dawes is honored for the Dawes Plan (1924), which provided for the restructuring of German debt.

15 Following minor losses by the Social Democrats and Radicals in a general election in Denmark, the Liberals form a government under Thomas Madsen-Mygdal, but the Social Democrats remain the largest single party.

25 Emperor Yoshihito of Japan dies and is succeeded by his son Hirohito.

SCIENCE, TECHNOLOGY, AND MEDICINE

Ecology

JULY

10 Lightning starts a fire at an ammunition depot in Lake Denmark, New Jersey, killing 31 people and causing $93 million in property damage.

SEPTEMBER

18 A hurricane sweeps across Mississippi, Alabama, and Florida, killing 372 people and injuring more than 6,000 others.

Exploration

• The Scott Polar Research Institute is opened in Cambridge, England, to conduct Antarctic research.

MAY

9 U.S. explorers Floyd Bennett and Richard Evelyn Byrd fly over the North Pole in a trimotor Fokker named *Josephine Ford*.

11–14 U.S. explorer Lincoln Ellsworth and Norwegian explorers Umberto Nobile and Roald Amundsen cross the North Pole from Spitsbergen to Alaska, in a dirigible, the *Norge*. They are the first to do so.

Health and Medicine

• Danish physiologist Johannes Fibiger receives the Nobel Prize for Physiology or Medicine for his discovery of the parasite *Spiroptera carcinoma*, which allows the first controlled induction of cancer in laboratory animals.

• U.S. physicians George Richards Minot and William Parry Murphy use raw-liver extract for treating the previously fatal disease pernicious anemia.

May 1926–30   A smallpox epidemic in India claims 500,000 lives.

Science

• A stone spearhead is discovered embedded in the ribcage of an extinct bison at Folsom, New Mexico. It is the first discovery in the Americas of artificial artifacts in association with the bones of extinct mammalian forms, and is also the first discovery of the Folsom culture complex, which thrived about 10,000 BC.

• Austrian physicist Erwin Schrödinger develops wave mechanics.

• Austrian-born U.S. physicist Joseph Goldberger isolates vitamins B and B2.

• Dutch chemist Peter Debye proposes a method of obtaining temperatures a fraction of a degree above absolute zero by removing their magnetic field. Canadian-born U.S. scientist William Giauque independently proposes the same idea the following year.

- Dutch physicist Willem Keesom solidifies helium.
- French physicist Jean Perrin receives the Nobel Prize for Physics for his work on the discontinuous structure of matter, and especially for his discovery of sedimentation equilibrium.
- German chemist Hermann Staudinger shows that plastics consist of small molecules (monomers) that form long chainlike structures (polymers) and that they do so through chemical interaction and not by simple aggregation.
- Swedish chemist Theodor Svedberg receives the Nobel Prize for Chemistry for his investigation of dispersed systems.
- U.S. biochemist Elmer McCollum isolates vitamin D and uses it to successfully treat rickets.
- U.S. biochemist James Sumner crystallizes the enzyme urease. It is the first enzyme to be crystallized. Sumner's achievement demonstrates that enzymes are proteins.
- U.S. geneticist Thomas Hunt Morgan publishes *The Theory of the Gene*, in which he demonstrates that the gene will form the foundation of all future genetic research.
- U.S. physiologist John Jacob Abel isolates and crystallizes insulin.

Technology

- Cemented tungsten-carbide cutting tools, known as Widia, are first introduced in Germany. Almost as hard as diamond, they can operate at cutting speeds much higher than high-speed steel.
- The Scottish electrical engineer John Logie Baird transmits pictures of moving objects over telephone lines between London, England, and Glasgow, Scotland. The first demonstration of true television, the images are 30-line silhouettes.
- U.S. engineer John Garand patents the Garand semiautomatic, or M1 rifle. It becomes standard issue for the U.S. armed forces in 1938, and over 5 million are made.

MARCH

- AT&T demonstrates the first transatlantic telephone conversation between New York, New York, and London, England.
- 16 U.S. inventor Robert Hutchings Goddard achieves the first flight of a liquid-propelled rocket, at Auburn, Michigan. It reaches an altitude of 12 m/41 ft.

Transportation

- U.S. inventor Francis Davis installs the first power-steering on a Pierce-Arrow runabout, although it does not become commercially available until the 1950s.

JANUARY

- U.S. philanthropist Daniel Guggenheim establishes the Daniel Guggenheim Fund for the Promotion of Aeronautics. Begun with $3 million, its aim is to promote education and research into aeronautics and to further the aeronautic industry.

MARCH

3 British aviator Alan Cobham flies from Croydon, England, to Cape Town in South Africa and back to explore the possibilities of long-distance air routes.

AUGUST

19 A train derailment in Hanover, Germany, results in 248 deaths.

ARTS AND IDEAS

Architecture

- Gledstone Hall in Yorkshire, England, designed by the English architect Edwin Lutyens, is completed.
- New Ways, a house in Northampton, England, designed by the German architect Paul Behrens, is completed.
- The Bauhaus school of design, architecture, and crafts, founded by the German architect Walter Gropius, is transferred from Weimar to Dessau in Germany. The purpose-built complex in Dessau was designed by Gropius.
- The Benjamin Franklin Bridge over the Delaware River, Philadelphia, designed by Polish-born U.S. architect Ralph Modjeski, is completed. It is the longest suspension bridge in the world to date (533 m/1,748 ft).
- The Grundtvig Church in Copenhagen, Denmark, designed by the Danish architect Peder Vilhelm Jensen Klint, is completed.

Arts

c. 1926   The Russian artist Chaim Soutine paints *Pageboy at Maximus*.
- The Armenian-born U.S. artist Arshile Gorky paints *Artist and Mother*, a theme he is to return to several times.
- The Belgian artist René Magritte paints *The Murderer Threatened*.
- The English artist L. S. Lowry paints *An Accident*.
- The English artist Stanley Spencer paints *The Resurrection, Cookham*.
- The German artist George Grosz paints *Pillars of Society*.
- The German artist Otto Dix paints *The Poet Ivan von Lucken* and *The Journalist*.
- The Hungarian photographer André Kertész takes *On the Quais, Paris*.
- The Russian artist Antoine Pevsner sculpts *Torso*.
- The Spanish artist Joan Miró paints *Person Throwing a Stone at a Bird*.
- The Spanish artist Salvador Dalí creates his *Lobster Telephone* sculpture.
- The Swiss artist Alberto Giacometti sculpts *Spoon Woman*.
- The U.S. artist Charles Burchfield paints *Sulphurous Evening*.
- The U.S. artist Edward Hopper paints *Sunday*.
- The U.S. artist Georgia O'Keeffe paints *Black Iris*.
- The U.S. artist Walter Kuhn paints *Dressing Room*.
- The U.S. photographer Paul Strand takes *Toadstool and Grasses*.

Film

- The movie *A Page of Madness*, directed by Teinosuke Kinugasa, is released in Japan.
- The movie *Don Juan*, directed by Alan Crosland, is released in the United States, starring John Barrymore and Mary Astor. It is the first film to use Vitaphone sound (a sound-on-disc system), featuring music and sound effects, but no dialogue.
- The movie *Faust*, directed by F. W. Murnau, is released in Germany, starring Emil Jannings, Gosta Ekman, and Camilla Horn.
- The movie *Flesh and the Devil*, directed by Clarence Brown, is released in the United States, starring Greta Garbo and John Gilbert.
- The movie *La Bohème/The Bohemian Girl*, directed by King Vidor, is released in the United States, starring Lillian Gish and Erich von Stroheim.
- The movie *Mantrap*, directed by Victor Fleming, is released in the United States, starring Clara Bow.
- The movie *Mat/Mother*, directed by Vsevolod Pudovkin, is released in the USSR. Adapted from a work by Maxim Gorky, it stars Vera Baranovskaya and Nikolai Batalov.
- The movie *Metropolis*, directed by Fritz Lang, is released in Germany, starring Brigitte Helm, Alfred Abel, Gustav Frölich, Rudolf Klein-Rogge, and Fritz Rasp.
- The movie *Secrets of a Soul*, directed by Czech filmmaker G. W. Pabst, is released in Germany, starring Wener Krauss, Jack Trevor, Ruth Weyher, and Pavel Pavlov.
- The movie *The Black Pirate*, directed by Albert Parker, is released in the United States, starring Douglas Fairbanks. It is the first movie in two-tone Technicolor.
- The movie *The General*, directed by Buster Keaton, is released in the United States. Keaton also stars in it.
- The movie *The Lodger*, directed by Alfred Hitchcock, is released in Britain, starring Ivor Novello.
- The movie *The Scarlet Letter*, directed by Swedish filmmaker Victor Seastrom, is released in the United States. Based on the novel by Nathaniel Hawthorne, it stars Lillian Gish and Lars Hanson.
- The movie *Tramp Tramp Tramp*, directed by Frank Capra, is released in the United States, starring Harry Langdon, Joan Crawford, and Alec B. Francis.
- The U.S. movie studio Warner Brothers adds a recorded "canned" musical score and sound effects to feature movies.
- The U.S. research company Bell Laboratories issues the first synchronous sound motion picture system.

Literature and Language

- A Gutenberg Bible, a complete extant copy of the first book printed from moveable type, is sold in New York, New York, for $106,000.
- The English economist and social historian Beatrice Webb publishes her autobiography *My Apprenticeship*.
- The English soldier and writer T. E. Lawrence ("Lawrence of Arabia") publishes *Seven Pillars of Wisdom*, an account of his war exploits in the Middle East during World War I.
- The English writer A. A. Milne publishes his children's story book *Winnie-the-Pooh*.
- The English writer D. H. Lawrence publishes his novel *The Plumed Serpent*.
- The English writer Ford Madox Ford publishes his novel *A Man Could Stand Up*, the third part of his four-part cycle *Parade's End*.
- The English writer Ronald Firbank publishes his novel *Concerning the Eccentricities of Cardinal Pirelli*.
- The French writer Georges Bernanos publishes his novel *Sous le soleil de Satan/Under the Sun of Satan*.
- The Japanese writer Yasunari Kawabata publishes his novel *Izu no odoriko/The Izu Dancer*.
- The literary journal *Voorslug* is founded by the South African writers Roy Campbell and William Plomer.
- The novel *Das Schloss/The Castle* by the Bohemian-born German writer Franz Kafka is published posthumously.
- The Pulitzer Prize for Biography is awarded to Harvey Cushing for *The Life of Sir William Osler* and the Prize for Fiction is awarded to Sinclair Lewis for *Arrowsmith* who refuses it, saying that accepting awards makes writers less independent. The Pulitzer Prize for Poetry is awarded to Amy Lowell for *What's O'Clock?*
- The Russian writer Isaak Babel publishes his story collection *Konarmiya/Red Cavalry*.
- The Russian-born U.S. writer Vladimir Nabokov publishes *Mashenka/Mary*, his first novel.
- The Scottish writer Hugh MacDiarmid publishes his poetry collection *A Drunk Man Looks at the Thistle*.
- The U.S. writer Carl Sandburg publishes his biography *Abraham Lincoln: The Prairie Years*.
- The U.S. writer Carl Van Vechten publishes his novel *Nigger Heaven*, a controversial attempt by a white American to enter fully into the minds of black American characters.
- The U.S. writer Dorothy Parker publishes her poetry collection *Enough Rope*.
- The U.S. writer e e cummings publishes his poetry collection *is 5*.
- The U.S. writer Edna Ferber publishes her novel *Show Boat*.
- The U.S. writer Ellen Glasgow publishes her novel *The Romantic Comedians*.
- The U.S. writer Ernest Hemingway publishes his novel *The Sun Also Rises*, which is published as *Fiesta* in Britain. He also publishes his novel *The Torrents of Spring*.
- The U.S. writer Hart Crane publishes his poetry collection *White Buildings*, which includes "For the Marriage of Faustus and Helen."
- The U.S. writer Langston Hughes publishes his poetry collection *The Weary Blues*, which includes "Dream Variation."
- The U.S. writer Sara Teasdale publishes her poetry collection *Dark of the Moon*.
- The U.S. writer Thornton Wilder publishes his novel *The Cabala*.
- The U.S. writer Vachel Lindsay publishes his poetry collection *Going-to-the Stars*.
- The U.S. writer William Faulkner publishes *Soldiers' Pay*, his first published novel.

APRIL

- U.S. advertising executive Harry Scherman founds the first book club in the world, the Book-of-the-Month Club, in the United States.

Music

- Popular songs in the United States include "Bye Bye Blackbird," "The Desert Song," "Blue Room," and "Play Gypsy."
- The Austrian composer Alban Berg completes his *Lyric Suite* for string quartet.
- The Czech composer Leoš Janáček completes his *M'sa glagolskaja/Glagolitic Mass*. His opera *Věc Makropoulos/The Makropoulos Affair* is first performed, in Brno, Czechoslovakia. It is based on the play *Věc Makropulos* by Karel Čapek, first performed in 1922.
- The magazine *Melody Maker* is founded in Britain: it plays an important role in promoting the spread of jazz in the country.
- The opera *A csodálatos mandarin/The Miraculous Mandarin* by the Hungarian composer Béla Bartók is first performed, in Cologne, Germany.
- The opera *Cardillac* by the German composer Paul Hindemith is first performed, in Dresden, Germany.
- The opera *Háry János* by the Hungarian composer Zoltán Kodály is first performed, in Budapest, Hungary.
- The opera *Król Roger/King Roger* by the Polish composer Karol Szymanowski is first performed, in Warsaw, Poland.
- The opera *Turandot* by the Italian composer Giacomo Puccini is first performed, in Milan, Italy. Puccini died during its composition, and it was completed by Franco Alfano.
- The Russian composer Sergey Rachmaninov completes his Piano Concerto No. 4, which he revises in 1941.
- The Russian composer Dmitry Shostakovich completes his Piano Sonata No. 1.
- The Swiss-born U.S. composer Ernest Bloch completes his symphonic poem *America*.
- The U.S. composer Aaron Copland completes his Piano Concerto.
- U.S. pianist and jazz composer "Jelly Roll" Morton forms his band, the Red Hot Peppers, to record for the Victor label.

Theater and Dance

- The farce *Rookery Nook*, by the English dramatist Ben Travers, is first performed, in London, England.
- The play *In Abraham's Bosom*, by the U.S. dramatist Paul Eliot Green, is first performed, in New York, New York.
- The play *The Great God Brown*, by the U.S. writer Eugene O'Neill, is first performed, in New York, New York.
- The play *The Plough and the Stars*, by the Irish dramatist Sean O'Casey, is first performed, at the Abbey Theatre in Dublin, Ireland.
- The Pulitzer Prize for Drama is awarded to George Kelly for *Craig's Wife*.

- The Russian director and actor Konstantin Stanislavsky publishes *An Actor Prepares*, which is translated into English in 1948.
- The Shakespeare Memorial Theatre in Stratford-upon-Avon, England, is destroyed in a fire.

SEPTEMBER

11 The first *Blackbirds* revue takes place in London, England, at the London Pavilion.

NOVEMBER

30 The musical *The Desert Song*, with music by Sigmund Romberg and lyrics by Otto Harbach and others, is first performed, at the Casino Theater, New York, New York.

Thought and Scholarship

- English historian George Macaulay Trevelyan publishes his *History of England*.
- German philosopher and sociologist Max Scheler publishes *Die Wissensformen und die Gesellschaft/Forms of Knowledge and Society*.
- The English historian Richard Henry Tawney publishes *Religion and the Rise of Capitalism: A Historical Study*.
- The Nobel Prize for Literature is awarded to the Italian novelist Grazia Deledda.
- The Pulitzer Prize for History is awarded to Edward Channing for *The History of the United States*.
- U.S. cultural critic H. L. Mencken publishes *Notes on Democracy*, an indictment of U.S. conformity.
- U.S. historian Charles Austin Beard publishes *The Supreme Court and the Constitution*.
- U.S. historian James Garfield Randall publishes *Constitutional Problems under Lincoln*.
- U.S. political scientist Leonard D. White publishes *Introduction to the Study of Public Administration*.

SOCIETY

Education

- Long Island University opens in Brooklyn, New York.
- Sarah Lawrence College is founded in Bronxville, New York.
- The U.S. philanthropist Julius Rosenwald establishes the Museum of Science and Technology in Chicago, Illinois.

FEBRUARY

- The school board of Atlanta, Georgia, bans teaching of the theory of evolution in the city's public schools.

Everyday Life

- Charles Atlas (real name Angelo Siciliano) opens a gymnasium in New York to promote his body-building techniques. As this proves to be successful, he will expand it into a lucrative mail-order business.
- The German avant-garde furniture company Thonet launches the first tubular steel chair, designed by the German architect Ludwig Mies van der Rohe.

MAY

3–12 A general strike in Britain in support of the striking coal miners paralyzes the country.

JULY

5 Subway workers in New York, New York, launch a successful strike for better pay and shorter hours.

Media and Communication

• The National Broadcasting Company (NBC) purchases the WEAF station as the basis for establishing a national network of radio stations in the United States, offering a mixture of sponsored and public-service programs.

JULY

• Following concern about the control of radio in Britain, the British Broadcasting Company (BBC) is incorporated by royal charter (effective from January 1, 1927). As a public body, it is run by a crown-appointed chairman and governors and financed by a license fee.

OCTOBER

• The U.S. demagogue Charles Edward Coughlin, begins the first in a long series of radio broadcasts from Detroit, Michigan, for the radio station WJR.

NOVEMBER

• The television pioneer David Sarnoff establishes the National Broadcasting Company (NBC).

BIRTHS & DEATHS

JANUARY

14 Peter Winch, English philosopher, author of *The Idea of a Social Science* 1958, born (–1997).

29 Abdus Salam, Pakistani theoretical physicist, joint winner with Steven Weinberg and Sheldon Glashow of the Nobel Prize for Physics in 1979 for their work on unified theory, born in Jhang, Pakistan (–1996).

FEBRUARY

2 Valéry Giscard d'Estaing, president of France 1974–81, born in Koblenz, Germany.

8 William Bateson, English biologist who founded the science of genetics, dies in London, England (64).

21 Heike Kamerlingh Onnes, Dutch physicist who discovered superconductivity, dies in Leiden, Netherlands (72).

APRIL

6 Ian Paisley, Northern Irish protestant leader of the Ulster Unionist Party, born in Armagh, Northern Ireland.

21 Elizabeth II, Queen of Great Britain and Northern Ireland from 1952, born in London, England.

MAY

16 Mehmed VI, last sultan of the Ottoman Empire 1918–22, dies in San Remo, Italy (65).

23 Joe (Yoseel Masheel) Slovo, South African lawyer and politician, general secretary of the South African Communist Party 1987–91 and one of the most influential figures in the African National Congress (ANC), born in Obelai, Lithuania (–1995).

25 Miles Davis, U.S. jazz trumpeter and bandleader, born in Alton, Illinois (–1991).

JUNE

1 Marilyn Monroe, U.S. actress and sex symbol, born in Los Angeles, California (–1962).

3 Allen Ginsberg, U.S. poet and political activist, born in Newark, New Jersey (–1997).

10 Antonio Gaudí, Spanish architect known for his free-flowing forms and rich colors, dies in Barcelona, Spain (73).

13 Jérôme-Jean-Louis-Marie Lejeune, French geneticist who discovered the first chromosomal abnormality (trisomy 21, responsible for Down's syndrome), born in Montrouge, France (–1994).

29 Sheikh Jabu al-Ahmad al-Jaber al-Sabah, Emir of Kuwait from 1977, born.

JULY

2 Emile Coué, French pharmacist who introduced the phrase "Every day and in every way, I am becoming better and better" into psychotherapy, dies in Nancy, France (69).

12 Gertrude Bell, English writer and administrator who helped establish the Hashimite dynasty in Baghdad, dies in Baghdad, Iraq (57).

AUGUST

13 Fidel Castro, Cuban communist revolutionary and leader of Cuba from 1959, born near Birán, Cuba.

23 Rudolph Valentino, Italian-born U.S. silent film star, known as the "Great Lover," dies in New York, New York (31).

SEPTEMBER

21 Donald A. Glasser, U.S. physicist who invented the bubble chamber, born in Cleveland, Ohio.

OCTOBER

8 César Milstein, Argentine immunologist who codeveloped monoclonal antibodies, born in Bahía Blanca, Argentina.

15 Michel Foucault, French structuralist philosopher, born in Poitiers, France (–1984).

18 Chuck Berry, U.S. singer and guitarist and one of the first rock and roll stars, born in St. Louis, Missouri.

18 Klaus Kinski, German actor, born in Zoppot, near the free city of Danzig (now Sopot near Gdańsk in Poland) (–1991).

20 Eugene Debs, U.S. labor leader and five-time presidential candidate for the Socialist Party, dies in Elmhurst, Illinois (70).

22 Harry Greb, U.S. professional boxer who lost only 7 of 94 bouts between 1913 and 1926, dies in New York, New York (32).

27 H(arry) R(obbins) Haldeman, U.S. businessman and chief of staff to Richard M. Nixon 1969–73, crucially involved in the Watergate cover-up, born in Los Angeles, California (–1993).

31 Harry Houdini (Erich Weiss), U.S. conjurer and escape artist, dies in Detroit, Michigan (52).

DECEMBER

5 Claude Monet, French impressionist painter, dies in Giverny, France (87).

10 Nikola Pašić, prime minister of Serbia 1891–92, 1904–05, 1906–08, 1909–11, 1912–18, and prime minister of the Kingdom of the Serbs, Croats, and Slovenes (later Yugoslavia) 1918, 1921–24 and 1924–26, dies in Belgrade, Serbia (81).

29 Rainer Maria Rilke, Austro-German poet, dies in Valmont, Switzerland (51).

Religion

- English philosopher Alfred North Whitehead publishes *Religion in the Making*.

MAY

18 Canadian evangelist Aimée Semple McPherson, founder of the International Church of the Foursquare Gospel, disappears while swimming in the Pacific Ocean. She reappears a month later, claiming she had been kidnapped, but inconsistencies in her story cause dissatisfaction with her leadership in the church.

JUNE

- The Chicago cardinal, John Bonzano, presides over the Catholic Church's first international Eucharistic Congress at Chicago, Illinois.

JULY

- Pope Pius XI consecrates the Sanctuary of Our Lady of Victory in Lackawanna, New York, as a basilica.

Sports

- The British car and motorboat racing driver Henry O'Neal de Hane Segrave sets a land-speed record of 245.15 kph/152.33 mph.
- The Montreal Maroons defeat the Victoria Cougars by three games to one to win hockey's Stanley Cup.
- The U.S. court tennis player Jay Gould, who has held the U.S. amateur title since 1906 without losing a set, retires from singles play.

APRIL

25 The American Association of University Professors calls for collegians to be limited to one year of playing football; the group claims that the sport promotes dishonesty and neglect of academic work.

JUNE

- The French tennis player Suzanne Lenglen ends her amateur career after walking out of the Wimbledon tennis championships in London, England, over a dispute with the All England Lawn Tennis and Croquet Club. Since winning her first Wimbledon title in 1919, she has lost only one singles match anywhere in the world.

AUGUST

8 Gertrude Ederle of the United States becomes the first woman to swim the English Channel, completing the 56 km/35 mi crossing from Cape Nez, France, to Dover, England, in 14 hrs, 31 min, a new world record for a man or a woman.

30 Guy McKinney, driven by Nat Ray, wins the inaugural Hambletonian Stakes trotting race at Syracuse, New York.

SEPTEMBER

11 The U.S. men's tennis team, led by Bill Tilden and Bill Johnson, defeats France in Philadelphia, Pennsylvania, to win the Davis Cup for lawn tennis for the seventh year in succession.

23 The U.S. boxer Gene Tunney outpoints fellow U.S. boxer Jack Dempsey to win the world heavyweight boxing title in Philadelphia, Pennsylvania.

OCTOBER

2–10 The St. Louis Cardinals defeat the New York Yankees by four games to three in baseball's World Series.

9 The first professional lawn tennis tournament is held at the recently rebuilt Madison Square Garden, New York, with Suzanne Lenglen of France as the star attraction.

DECEMBER

- The International Table Tennis Federation is formed and the first world championships are held in the Memorial Hall, Farringdon Street, London, England. Hungary wins every title.

♦

1927

POLITICS, GOVERNMENT, AND ECONOMICS

Business and Economics

- Massachusetts becomes the first U.S. state to introduce a compulsory car insurance fund.
- Pan American and Eastern airlines are founded in the United States.

- The Florida land boom collapses after excessive speculation and some outright fraud.
- The U.S. Continental Baking Co. introduces Wonder Bread.

Politics and Government

- The U.S. Supreme Court rules that illegal income is taxable, thus furnishing prosecutors with an instrument to combat U.S. gangsters.

JANUARY

29 A German cabinet crisis is resolved with Wilhelm Marx of the Center Party becoming chancellor.

31 The inter-Allied military control of Germany, in force since the end of World War I, ends.

FEBRUARY

3–13 A revolt in Portugal against the military dictatorship of General Antonio Carmona is defeated.
18 The United States establishes direct diplomatic relations with Canada (not via Britain).

MARCH

24 The Guomindang Chinese nationalists take the city of Nanjing on the lower Chang Jiang River.

APRIL

5 A treaty of friendship is signed between Italy and Hungary.
12 Following the arrival of Guomindang forces in Shanghai, east China, their leader Jiang Jie Shi and conservatives start purging communists and other leftist elements from the Guomindang (Chinese National People's Party).
15 The USSR and Switzerland resume diplomatic relations, broken off in the aftermath of the assassination of the Soviet delegate Vatslav Vorovski in Lausanne, Switzerland (May 10, 1923).
17 A bank crisis in Japan forces the resignation of Reijiro Wakatsuki's government.
21 A labor charter is issued in Italy, embodying the principles of fascist corporatism.

MAY

2–23 An economic conference is held in Geneva, Switzerland, attended by 52 nations, including the USSR.
4 The U.S. secretary of state Henry Stimson brings together factions in Nicaragua; the United States is asked to supervise elections.
9 The new Parliament House in Canberra, Australia, is opened.
20 By the Treaty of Jiddah, Britain recognizes the independent rule of Ibn Saud in the Arabian kingdom of Hejaz.
27 Japan intervenes on the Shandong Peninsula, China, to block the advance of the Guomindang Chinese nationalists on the Chinese capital Beijing.
27 Tomáš Garrigue Masaryk is reelected president of Czechoslovakia.

JUNE

3 A new republican constitution is promulgated in Greece following the overthrow of the military dictator Theodoros Pangalos.
6 Albania and the Kingdom of the Serbs, Croats, and Slovenes break off diplomatic relations following frontier incidents.
6 The Druse revolt against French rule in Syria is finally ended.
9 Elections in the Irish Free State (now the Republic of Ireland) produce a deadlock: Cumann na nGaedheal, 47 seats; Fianna Fáil, 44; Labour, 22; Farmers' Union, 11; National League, 8; Republicans, 5; others, 16.
20–August 4 Britain, the United States, and Japan confer in Washington, D.C., on naval disarmament, but fail to reach agreement.

JULY

July, 1927–October Unrest flares in Samoa (modern Western Samoa) until October, when German property holders are expelled.
10 The assassination of the Irish government minister Kevin O'Higgins provokes fresh denunciations of the tactics of Irish republicans in the Irish Free State (now the Republic of Ireland).
15–16 Socialist riots and a general strike in Vienna, Austria, follow the acquittal of nationalists for political murders.
27 Belgium and Portugal make territorial adjustments in the Congo (modern Zaire).

AUGUST

• The U.S. president Calvin Coolidge surprises political pundits by announcing that he will not seek reelection next year.
7 The International Peace Bridge between the United States and Canada is opened.
8 A new criminal code is published in Italy, reintroducing the death penalty, abolishing trial by jury, and introducing new punishments.
11 The Irish government passes a Public Safety Act in the wake of the assassination of the Irish government minister Kevin O'Higgins, clamping down on terrorist societies.
12 Having agreed to swear an oath of allegiance to the Dáil of the Irish Free State (now the Republic of Ireland), the Fianna Fáil leader Eamon de Valera and other anti-Treaty (Anglo-Irish Treaty) republicans agree to take up their seats in the Dáil.
22 The Allied military control of Hungary, in force from the end of World War I, is ended.
23 Following the death of the prime minister Saad Zaghlul, Nahas Pasha becomes the leader of the Wafd nationalist party in Egypt.
23 The execution of the Italian immigrant anarchists Nicola Sacco and Bartolomeo Vanzetti for murder during a robbery in 1920 causes an outcry in the United States because of the slim evidence against them. (Posthumous pardons are awarded by Michael Dukakis, governor of Massachusetts, in 1977).

SEPTEMBER

2 The Turkish president Mustafa Kemal Pasha (later known as Atatürk) is empowered to nominate all candidates in the elections, giving his People's Party a monopoly.
15 In the second general election of the year in the Irish Free State (now the Republic of Ireland), Cumann na nGaedheal with 62 seats fails to win a clear majority over Fianna Fáil (57 seats) and other parties (Labour, 13; Farmers' Union, 6; National League, 2; others, 13); William Cosgrave forms a new ministry in October with support from the Farmers' Union and independents.
16 President Paul von Hindenburg of Germany, dedicating the Tannenberg memorial, repudiates Germany's responsibility for World War I, contravening article 231 of the Treaty of Versailles.
19 A communist rising in China led by Mao Zedong is put down by the Guomindang nationalist forces of Jiang Jie Shi.

OCTOBER

- The U.S. Supreme Court nullifies the Mammoth Oil Company's lease of the notorious Teapot Dome oil fields, conferred by former interior secretary Albert B. Fall in 1921.
- 1   The USSR and Persia (modern Iran) sign a nonaggression pact.
- 17   The first Labour government is formed in Norway by Christopher Hornsrud, following a general election in which Labour won 59 seats, the Conservatives 30, the Liberals 30, and the Farmers' Party 26.

NOVEMBER

- 11   A treaty of friendship is signed between France and the Kingdom of the Serbs, Croats, and Slovenes.
- 14   In Soviet leader Joseph Stalin's decisive victory over his rivals, Leon Trotsky and Grigory Zinoviev are expelled from the Soviet Communist Party.
- 15   Canada is elected to a seat on the Council of the League of Nations.
- 22   In reply to the treaty between France and the Kingdom of the Serbs, Croats, and Slovenes, Albania signs a defensive alliance with Italy.
- 22   Persia (modern Iran) claims the Bahrain Islands in the Persian Gulf following the discovery of oil beneath them.
- 30–December 3   At a meeting of the Preparatory Commission on Disarmament in Geneva, Switzerland, Maxim Litvinov, the USSR's commissar for foreign affairs, proposes immediate disarmament, but this is rejected as a "communist trick."

DECEMBER

- 14   Britain recognizes Iraq's independence and promises to support its application for membership in the League of Nations in 1932.
- 14   China and the USSR break off diplomatic relations following an attempted communist coup in Guangzhou.
- 27   The expulsion of Leon Trotsky and Grigory Zinoviev from the Soviet Communist Party by Soviet leader Joseph Stalin on November 14 is confirmed by the 15th Party Congress.

SCIENCE, TECHNOLOGY, AND MEDICINE

Ecology

- An earthquake in Kansu, China, kills nearly 100,000 people.
- Nan Shan in China experiences an earthquake estimated to measure 8.0 on the Richter scale; 40,000 people die.
- The Hugoton natural gas field is discovered in Kansas. It is the largest natural gas field in the United States and has reserves estimated at 1.99 trillion cubic meters.
- The Kirkuk oil field is discovered in northeastern Iraq.

APRIL

- The flooding Mississippi River overflows onto 16,000 sq km/6250 sq mi, leaving 600,000 people without homes for weeks and causing $300 million in property damage.

SEPTEMBER

- 29   A tornado sweeps through St. Louis, Missouri, killing 87 people and causing $50 million in property damage.

Exploration

- The Verein für Raumschiffahrt (Society for Space Travel) is founded in Germany for rocket experimentation.

Health and Medicine

- Austrian neurophysiologist Manfred Sakel introduces insulin shock-therapy to treat schizophrenia.
- Austrian-born U.S. immunologist Karl Landsteiner discovers the M and N blood groups.
- German psychiatrist Julius Wagner-Jauregg receives the Nobel Prize for Physiology or Medicine for his discovery of the therapeutic value of malaria inoculation in the treatment of paralysis caused by mental deterioration.
- New York governor Franklin D. Roosevelt establishes the Georgia Warm Springs Foundation for the treatment of polio, a condition from which he suffers himself.
- Portuguese physician António Egas Moniz is the first to use radiopaque substances to study the blood vessels in the brain.
- The Food, Drug, and Insecticide Association (later the Food and Drug Administration, or FDA) is created, in the United States.
- U.S. scientists Philip Drinker and Louis Shaw invent the iron lung, a mechanical respiration device

JULY

- 29   Bellevue Hospital in New York, New York, installs an electric respirator, a device designed to offset respiratory failure designed by Harvard University physicians Philip Drinker and Louis Shaw.

Science

- Belgian astronomer Georges Lemaître proposes that the universe was created by an explosion of energy and matter from a "primaeval atom"—the beginning of the big bang theory.
- British archeologist Leonard Woolley makes important discoveries at the site of the ancient Sumerian city of Ur (now in Iraq).
- Canadian anthropologist Davidson Black discovers the first specimens of "Beijing man" (*Sinanthropous pekinensis*), a species of *Homo erectus* believed to be 300,000 to 400,000 years old, at Choukoutien, China.
- German biochemist Heinrich Wieland receives the Nobel Prize for Chemistry for his research into the constitution of bile acids and related substances.
- German physicist Werner Heisenberg propounds the "uncertainty principle" in quantum physics, which states that it is impossible to simultaneously determine the position and momentum of an atom. It explains why Newtonian mechanics is inapplicable at the atomic level.
- German physicists Walter Heitler and Fritz London discover that quantum mechanics can explain chemical bonding.

- The International Temperature Scale is adopted by countries subscribing to the International Bureau of Weights and Measures.
- U.S. astronomer Edwin Hubble shows that galaxies are receding and that the further away they are, the faster they are receding.
- U.S. geneticist Hermann Muller uses X-rays to cause mutations in the fruit fly. It permits a greater understanding of the mechanisms of variation.
- U.S. physicist Arthur Holly Compton and Scottish physicist Charles Thomson Rees Wilson share the Nobel Prize for Physics: Compton for his discovery of the change in wavelength in diffused X-rays, and Wilson for his method of making the paths of electrically charged particles visible by condensation of vapor.
- U.S. physicist Clinton Davisson and, independently, English physicist George Paget Thomson show that electrons can be diffracted.

Technology

- German metallurgist Siegfried Junghans develops a process for continuous casting of nonferrous metal.
- The U.S. inventor Philo Taylor Farnsworth transmits a 60-line image of a dollar sign and takes out one of the first patents on television.

July 1927–31 There are at least ten major natural gas pipelines built in the United States.

APRIL

7 The American Telephone and Telegraph company (AT&T)'s president Walter Gifford gives the first demonstration of television in the United States, in the auditorium of Bell Laboratories. The image and voice of U.S. commerce secretary Herbert Hoover is transmitted from Washington, D.C., to New York, New York.

Transportation

- Tokyo's subway system opens in Japan.

MAY

20–21 U.S. aviator Charles Lindbergh, in his single-engine aircraft *Spirit of St Louis*, flies from New York, New York, to Paris, France, the first nonstop solo transatlantic flight. He arrives at Le Bourget Airfield, outside Paris, at 10:24 p.m., 33 hr 29 min after departing Roosevelt Field, Long Island.

JULY

4 U.S. Navy pilot C. C. Champion sets a new world altitude record of 11,581 m/37,995 ft.

NOVEMBER

6 U.S. Navy officer A. J. Williams sets a new world airspeed record of 516.2 kph/322.6 mph.

12 The New York–New Jersey Holland Tunnel under the Hudson River, New York, New York, opens. The world's longest (1,600 m/5,400 ft) vehicular tunnel, it solves the problem of noxious fumes from car exhausts by employing huge ventilator fans. It is the nation's first underwater automobile tunnel.

DECEMBER

1 The Ford Motor Company launches its new Model A at the Waldorf-Astoria Hotel in New York, New York; the car has a back order of 50,000.

ARTS AND IDEAS

Architecture

- The Housing Estate at Hoek van Holland, designed by the Dutch architect J. J. P. Oud, is completed in the Netherlands.
- The U.S. architect Richard Buckminster Fuller develops the "Dymaxion" house, a prefabricated, self-sufficient house that costs as much as a car.

Arts

- The English artist L. S. Lowry paints *Coming out of School*.
- The English artist Walter Richard Sickert paints *Lazarus Breaks his Fast: Self-Portrait*.
- The French artist Fernand Léger paints *Woman Holding a Vase*.
- The French photographer Claude Cahun takes *Self-Portrait, 1927*.
- The German artist Ernst Barlach sculpts *Güstrow Angel*.
- The Italian artist Giorgio de Chirico paints *Furniture in a Valley*.
- The U.S. artist Charles Demuth paints *My Egypt*.
- The U.S. artist Edward Hopper paints *Drug Store*.
- The U.S. artist Georgia O'Keeffe paints *Red Hills and the Sun*.
- The U.S. artist Hugo Robus sculpts *Woman Combing her Hair*.
- The U.S. artist Stuart Davis paints *Egg Beater, Number 2*.
- The U.S. photographer Edward Weston takes *Shell*.
- The U.S. photographer Ansel Adams takes *Monolith, the face of Half Dome, Yosemite Valley, California*.
- The U.S.-born English artist Jacob Epstein sculpts *Madonna and Child* and *Bust of Paul Robeson*.
- Work begins on Mt. Rushmore in South Dakota, which when complete will include the likenesses of U.S. presidents George Washington, Thomas Jefferson, Abraham Lincoln, and Theodore Roosevelt.

Film

- Five hundred feature movies are produced in U.S. movie studios.
- Grauman's Chinese Theater opens in Hollywood, California. Built in flamboyant style, it is typical of movie production companies' increasingly ambitious moves into movie theater ownership.
- The Academy of Motion Picture Arts and Sciences is formed in the United States for the purpose of bestowing annual awards to encourage the development of cinematic art and technique.
- The movie *An Italian Straw Hat*, directed by René Clair, is released in France, starring Albert Préjean, Olga Tschekowa, Marise Maia, and Alice Tissot.
- The movie *It*, directed by Clarence Badger, is released in the United States, starring Clara Bow and Antonio Moreno.

- The movie *King of Kings*, directed by Cecil B. De Mille, is released in the United States, starring H. B. Warner, Jacqueline Logan, Joseph Schildkraut, and Ernest Torrence.
- The movie *Long Pants*, directed by Frank Capra, is released in the United States, starring Harry Langdon.
- The movie *Napoleon*, directed by Abel Gance, is released in France, starring Albert Dieudonné, Antonin Artaud, and Pierre Batcheff.
- The movie *October*, directed by Sergey Eisenstein, is released in the USSR.
- The movie *Seventh Heaven*, directed by Frank Borzage, is released in the United States, starring Janet Gaynor and Charles Farrell.
- The movie *Sunrise*, directed by German filmmaker F. W. Murnau, is released in the United States, starring Janet Gaynor, George O'Brien, and Margaret Livingston.
- The movie *The End of St Petersburg*, directed by V. I. Pudovkin, is released in the USSR.
- The movie *The Kiss of Mary Pickford*, directed by Sergei Komarov, is released in the USSR.
- The movie *The Temptress*, directed by Finnish filmmaker Mauritz Stiller and U.S. filmmaker Fred Niblo, is released in the United States, starring Greta Garbo, Antonio Moreno, and Lionel Barrymore.
- The movie *Underworld*, directed by Austrian filmmaker Josef von Sternberg, is released in the United States, starring George Bancroft, Evelyn Brent, Clive Brook, and Larry Semon.
- The movie *Wings*, directed by William Wellman, is released in the United States, starring Charles Buddy Rogers, Richard Arlen, and Clara Bow.
- The movie *Zvenigora*, directed by Alexander Dovzhenko, is released in the USSR.
- The impressionist documentary *Berlin, Symphony of a Great City*, directed by Walter Ruttman, is released in Germany.
- The Museum of Photography and Cinematography opens in Paris, France.
- The U.S. motion picture executive William Fox produces the *Movietone News* newsreel. It is the first commercially successful sound film combining narration and picture.

OCTOBER

6   The movie *The Jazz Singer*, directed by Alan Crosland and produced by the movie company Warner Brothers, is released in the United States. It is the first feature-length movie with spoken dialogue, and it stars Al Jolson, May McAvoy, and Warner Oland. All U.S. movie studios convert to sound within two years.

DECEMBER

13 The movie *Bed and Sofa*, directed by Abram Room, is released in the USSR, commissioned to commemorate the 10th anniversary of the Russian Revolution.

Literature and Language

- The Austrian writer Joseph Roth publishes his novel *Die Flucht ohne Ende/Flight without End*.
- The English writer E. M. Forster publishes his critical work *Aspects of the Novel*, first delivered as Clark lectures at Cambridge University, England.
- The English writer Henry Williamson publishes his nonfiction animal story *Tarka the Otter*.

- The English writer Hilaire Belloc publishes his biography *Cromwell*.
- The English writer Robert Graves publishes *Poems, 1914–1926*.
- The English writer Rosamund Lehmann publishes her novel *Dusty Answer*.
- The English writer Radclyffe Hall publishes her novel *The Well of Loneliness*, a controversially frank account of lesbian love.
- The English writer T. F. Powys publishes his novel *Mr Weston's Good Wine*.
- The English writer Virginia Woolf publishes her novel *To the Lighthouse*.
- The Free Library of Philadelphia, Pennsylvania, opens to the public.
- The German writer Hermann Hesse publishes his novel *Der Steppenwolf/Steppenwolf*.
- The novel *Amerika/America* by the Bohemian-born German writer Franz Kafka is published posthumously.
- The Pulitzer Prize for Biography is awarded to Emory Holloway for *Whitman: An Interpretation in Narrative*, the Prize for Fiction is awarded to Lewis Bromfield for *Early Autumn*, and the Prize for Poetry is awarded to Leonora Speyer for *Fiddler's Farewell*.
- The U.S. literary historian Vernon Louis Parrington publishes the first volume of his three-volume *Main Currents in American Thought: An Interpretation of Literature from the Beginning to 1920*. The last volume appears in 1930.
- The U.S. writer Ernest Hemingway publishes his story collection *Men Without Women*.
- The U.S. writer Langston Hughes publishes his poetry collection *Fine Clothes to the Jew*.
- The U.S. writer Robinson Jeffers publishes his poetry collection *The Women at Point Sur*.
- The U.S. writer Sinclair Lewis publishes his novel *Elmer Gantry*.
- The U.S. writer Thornton Wilder publishes his novel *The Bridge of San Luis Rey*.
- The U.S. writer Upton Sinclair publishes his novel *Oil!*
- The U.S.-born English writer T. S. Eliot publishes his poem "Journey of the Magi."

Music

- Popular songs in the United States include "Ol' Man River," "Let a Smile Be Your Umbrella," "Blue Skies," and "Tree in the Park."
- The Austrian composer Arnold Schoenberg completes his String Quartet No. 3 (Opus 30).
- The English composer Havergal Brian completes his *Gothic Symphony*. Scored for four brass bands, an orchestra of 180 players, and a choir, it is not performed until 1961.
- The English composer Constant Lambert completes *The Rio Grande* for chorus and orchestra.
- The French-born U.S. composer Edgard Varèse completes his orchestral work *Arcana*.
- The opera *Jonny spielt auf/Jonny Strikes Up* by the Austrian composer Ernst Krenek is first performed, in Leipzig, Germany.

- The opera *Švanda dudák/Schwanda the Bagpiper* by the Czech composer Jaromír Weinberger is first performed, in Prague, Czechoslovakia.
- The opera-oratorio *Oedipus Rex* by the Russian composer Igor Stravinsky is first performed, in Paris, France. The libretto is by the French writer Jean Cocteau.
- The Russian composer Dmitry Shostakovich completes his Symphony No. 2, the *October*.
- The U.S. AMI Corporation introduces the first commercially successful jukebox.
- The U.S. composer Charles Ives completes his *Orchestral Set No. 3*.

Theater and Dance

- The ballet *Krasny mak/The Red Poppy* by the Russian composer Reinhold Glière and the Russian choreographers Lev Alexandrovich Lashchilin and Vassili Dimitrievich Tikhomirov, is first performed, in Moscow, USSR.
- The farce *Thark*, by the English dramatist Ben Travers, is first performed, in London, England.
- The play *Saturday's Children*, by the U.S. dramatist Maxwell Anderson, is first performed, in New York, New York.
- The Pulitzer Prize for Drama is awarded to Paul Green for *In Abraham's Bosom*.

MAY

23 The pioneering black American musical *Shuffle Along*, with lyrics and music by Eubie Blake and Noble Sissle, is performed for the first time, at the 63rd Street Music Hall, New York, New York.

AUGUST

19 The musical *Strike Up the Band*, with lyrics by George S. Kaufman and music by George Gershwin, is first performed in Long Branch, New Jersey.

NOVEMBER

27 The musical *Show Boat*, with lyrics by Oscar Hammerstein and music by Jerome Kern, is first performed, at the Ziegfeld Theater, New York, New York. The songs featured include "Can't Help Lovin' that Man" and "Ol' Man River."

Thought and Scholarship

- English philosopher Bertrand Russell publishes *The Analysis of Matter*.
- French writer and philosopher Gabriel Marcel publishes his *Journal métaphysique/Metaphysical Journal*.
- German philosopher Martin Heidegger publishes his central work *Sein und Zeit/Being and Time*.
- The French essayist and critic Julien Benda publishes *La Trahison des clercs/The Treason of the Intellectuals*.
- The Nobel Prize for Literature is awarded to the French philosopher Henri Bergson.
- The Pulitzer Prize for History is awarded to Samuel Flagg Bemis for *Pinckney's Treaty*.
- The U.S. Institute for Government Research, Institute of Economics, and Robert Brookings Graduate School of Economics and Government are merged to form the Brookings Institution.

- The U.S. philosopher John Dewey publishes *The Public and its Problems*, in which he defends U.S. democracy from disillusioned critics.
- U.S. historians Charles Austin Beard and Mary Ritter Beard publish their *Rise of American Civilization*.

SOCIETY

Everyday Life

JANUARY

7 A transatlantic telephone service begins between London, England, and New York, New York, provided by the American Telephone and Telegraph company (AT&T).

Media and Communication

- The radio company United Independent Broadcasters Inc. is founded in the United States. It will become the Columbia Broadcasting System (CBS) in 1928.
- The U.S. Congress passes the Radio Act. It establishes the Federal Communications Commission (FCC), which regulates radio broadcasters.

Sports

- Abraham M. Saperstein, a Jewish immigrant from Chicago, Illinois, founds the Harlem Globetrotters in the United States, a black professional exhibition basketball team.
- Howie Morenz of the Montréal Canadiens becomes the first National Hockey League hockey player to score over 50 points in a season.
- The Ottawa Senators defeat the Boston Bruins by two games to none to win the first Stanley Cup held as a play-off exclusively between National Hockey League teams, following the demise of the Pacific Coast Hockey Association in 1924 and the Western Hockey League in 1927.

MARCH

26–27 The Italian drivers Ferdinando Minoia and Giuseppe Morandi, in an OM, win the inaugural *Mille Miglia* ("Thousand Miles") motor race from Brescia to Rome and back, in Italy.

29 The British driver Henry Segrave establishes a new world land-speed record of 327.96 kph/203.79 mph in a 1,000 hp Sunbeam, at Daytona Beach, Florida. He is the first person to set a land-speed record in excess of 200 mph.

JUNE

3–4 The first Ryder Cup match between the professional golfers of the United States and Great Britain is held at Worcester, Massachusetts. The U.S. team wins 9–2.

JULY

2 The U.S. tennis player Helen Wills (later Helen Moody) wins the first of eight ladies' singles titles at the

New Food Products (1904–98)

1904
- The St. Louis exposition popularizes the hamburger and the edible ice-cream cone in the United States.

1905
- Italian immigrant Gennaro Lombardi introduces pizza at his restaurant in New York, New York.

1912
- German–American delicatessen owner Richard Hellmann introduces Hellmann's mayonnaise, the first ready-made mayonnaise, in the United States.
- The U.S. National Cookie Co. introduces the Oreo cookie.

1913
- Cleveland, Ohio, candy manufacturer Clarence Crane introduces the Life Saver.

1927
- The U.S. Continental Baking Co. introduces Wonder Bread.

1928
December   U.S. entrepreneur Frank H. Fleer introduces the first bubble gum, Dubble Bubble, in Philadelphia, Pennsylvania.

1933
- Ruth Wakefield creates the Toll House Cookie, the definitive chocolate chip cookie.

1937
- Spam, made from pork shoulder and ham, is first marketed by George A. Hormel & Co. in Minnesota. It becomes the world's best-selling canned meat. Its name is a contraction of "spiced ham."

1940
- Colonel Sanders concocts his special recipe for Kentucky Fried Chicken.
- Richard and Maurice McDonald of Glendora, California, sell their first hamburger at a drive-in movie theater. They will go on to establish the McDonalds fast food chain in 1948.
- U.S. soldiers enjoy the first M&M candies, produced for the military by Mars, Inc.

1942
- The Kellogg corporation introduces Raisin Bran, offering Americans a way of dodging the government's wartime sugar rationing.

1948
- The Baskin–Robbins ice cream chain is started when Burton "Butch" Baskins and Irvine Robbins merge their ice cream parlors. They soon start to franchise the name.

1949
- Charles Lubin launches his Sara Lee bakery line in Chicago, Illinois, with his first product, the Sara Lee cheesecake.

1961
- The Coca-Cola Company launches "Sprite," a lemon-lime flavoured carbonated soft drink, as a competitor to "7 Up" (produced by the company 7 Up).
- U.S. ice-cream manufacturer Reuben Mattus creates a range of high-quality ice creams and invents a name which will suggest richness and a European origin— Häagen-Dazs.

1964
- The U.S. food company Kellogg introduces Pop-Tarts.

1965
- The artificial sweetener aspartame is launched in the United States, marketed under the name of Nutra-Sweet.

1975
- Philip Morris launches Miller Lite, the first light beer, in the United States.

1978
May 5   The first Ben and Jerry's ice-cream store is opened by Ben Cohen and Jerry Greenfield in Burlington, Vermont. They specialize in "superpremium" ice-cream and attempt to pursue a progressive social agenda as part of their business practice.

1982
- The Coca-Cola Company launches Diet Coke.

1985
April 23   The Coca-Cola Company replaces its established recipe with a sweeter version, called New Coke, aimed at younger consumers, in the United States. Following protests, it has to reinstate the old formula under the Classic name.

1991
- The "coffee culture" emerges in Seattle, Washington, personified, in part, by the national success of the Seattle-based purveyors of gourmet coffee, Starbuck's.

1998
February 10   U.S. food company Frito-Lay begins selling fat-free potato chips made with olestra, a synthetic fat substitute produced by U.S. company Procter and Gamble.

Wimbledon lawn tennis championships in London, England. Full seeding for all five events at the championships is introduced.

AUGUST

25 U.S. coach George Bresnahan invents starting blocks for track and field racing.

SEPTEMBER

• The Russian émigré Alexandre Alekhine defeats José Capablanca of Cuba 18.5–15.5 in Buenos Aires, Argentina, to become world chess champion.

30 The U.S. baseball player Babe Ruth of the New York Yankees sets a major league record of 60 home runs in a season. The record stands until 1961 when Roger Maris, also of the Yankees, hits 61, from 7 more games.

OCTOBER

5–8 The New York Yankees defeat the Pittsburgh Pirates by four games to none, to win the World Series.

NOVEMBER

5 The U.S. golfer Walter Hagen wins the U.S. Professional Golfers Association (PGA) Championship for an unprecedented fourth successive year.

BIRTHS & DEATHS

JANUARY

17 Marcus Samuel, businessman, philanthropist and cofounder of Shell Transport and Trading Company, later Shell Oil, dies in London, England (73).

30 Olof Palme, Swedish prime minister 1969–76 and 1982–86, born in Stockholm, Sweden (–1986).

FEBRUARY

6 Gerard Kitchen O'Neill, U.S. physicist who developed the colliding beam storage-ring particle accelerator, born in New York, New York (–1992).

19 Georg Brandes, Danish literary critic, dies in Copenhagen, Denmark (85).

MARCH

1 Harry Bellafonte, U.S. singer, born in New York, New York.

31 Cesar Estrada Chavez, U.S. migrant farm worker who established the National Farm Workers Association in 1962, born in Yuma, Arizona (–1993).

31 K'ang Yu-wei, Chinese social reformer, dies in Tsingtao, Shantung province, China (69).

APRIL

6 Gerry (Gerald) Mulligan, U.S. jazz saxophonist, arranger, and composer, born in Queens Village, Long Island, New York (–1996).

18 Li Ta-chao, Chinese scholar and cofounder of the Chinese Communist Party, dies in Beijing, China (38).

MAY

6 Hudson Maxim, U.S. inventor and manufacturer of explosives, dies in Landing Post Office, New Jersey (73).

JUNE

1 John Bagnell Bury, Irish classical historian, dies in Rome, Italy (65).

JULY

3 Ken Russell, English director whose films are designed to shock their audience, born in Southampton, England.

4 Neil Simon, U.S. playwright, born in New York, New York.

14 John Chancellor, U.S. television journalist, born in Chicago, Illinois (–1996).

AUGUST

4 Eugène Atget, French photographer known for his photographs of everyday life in Paris, dies in Paris, France (70).

6 Andy Warhol, U.S. artist and filmmaker, a leading exponent of pop art in the 1960s, born in Pittsburgh, Pennsylvania (–1987).

23 Saad Zaghlul, Egyptian statesman, leader of the nationalist movement that gained Egypt's independence, dies in Cairo, Egypt (66).

25 Althea Gibson, black U.S. tennis player who dominated women's singles tennis during the late 1950s, born in Silver, South Carolina.

SEPTEMBER

14 Isadora Duncan, U.S. interpretative dancer, dies in Nice, France (50).

29 Willem Einthoven, Dutch physiologist who developed the electrocardiograph, dies in Leiden, the Netherlands (67).

OCTOBER

2 Svante Arrhenius, Swedish chemist who received the Nobel Prize for Chemistry in 1903 for his discovery that certain substances dissociate in water into ions, dies in Stockholm, Sweden (68).

13 Turgut Özal, prime minister of Turkey 1983–89, president 1989–93, born in Malatya, Turkey (–1993).

DECEMBER

5 Bhumibol Adulyadej, King of Thailand from 1946, born in Cambridge, Massachusetts.

20 Kim Young Sam, South Korean president from 1993, born in Kyongsang province, Korea.

1928

POLITICS, GOVERNMENT, AND ECONOMICS

Business and Economics

- Italy adopts the gold standard, directly relating the value of the lira to its gold reserves.
- The Cable and Wireless Corporation is formed in the United States.
- The Michigan food purveyor Daniel F. Gerber begins distribution of Gerber baby food.
- The U.S. Swift Packing Co. affiliate, E. K. Pond, introduces Peter Pan Peanut Butter.

JUNE

24 The French franc is again devalued to make the national debt easier to pay as France's economic difficulties continue.

DECEMBER

- The U.S. entrepreneur Frank H. Fleer introduces the first bubble gum, Dubble Bubble, in Philadelphia, Pennsylvania.

Human Rights

MAY

12 An Italian law abolishes female suffrage, reduces the electorate from 10 million to 3 million, and arranges for 400 government candidates to be accepted or rejected *en bloc*.

JULY

2 Women's suffrage rights are extended in Britain to become equal with those of men.

NOVEMBER

- In the wake of a presidential election in which Democrat presidential candidate Alfred E. Smith became the target of anti-Catholic bigotry, U.S. civil-rights activists establish the National Conference of Christians and Jews.

Politics and Government

- A new law in Italy reorganizes the membership in the government: the 13 state corporations are to submit candidates' names to the Grand Council of Fascism, which then finalizes the lists and submits them to the electorate for ratification or rejection.
- Mass strikes hit India for the first time.
- The British War Office abolishes the use of the lance as a weapon of war.
- The League of Nations attempts to create a full system of legal arbitration of international relations questions in the General Act for the Peaceful Settlement of International Disputes.

JANUARY

13 The Allied military control of Bulgaria is abolished.

14 The first Conservative administration in Latvia is formed under Peteris Jurasevskis.

29 A treaty between Germany and Lithuania provides for arbitration over the disputed Baltic port of Memel (now Klaipeda).

FEBRUARY

20 Transjordan (modern Jordan) becomes independent under the British mandate.

21 The fascist militia is incorporated into the Italian army.

MARCH

16 The nationalist leader Nahas Pasha is appointed prime minister of Egypt.

25 General Antonio Carmona is elected president of Portugal.

APRIL

6 In arbitration of a dispute between the United States and the Netherlands, Palmas Island, near the Philippines, is awarded to the Netherlands.

13 The U.S. secretary of state Frank B. Kellogg submits a plan for renunciation of war to the Locarno powers (Britain, France, Belgium, Italy, and Germany).

21 The French foreign minister Aristide Briand proposes a draft treaty for outlawing war.

22 The National Union government of Raymond Poincaré continues in power after inconclusive elections in France.

27 The reforming Portuguese academic Antonio de Oliveira Salazar is given wide powers as minister of finance to address Portugal's economic problems.

29 A British ultimatum forces Egypt to give up a bill to provide for freedom of public meetings.

MAY

- U.S. Congress passes a Flood Control Act, authorizing the construction of levées on the banks of the Mississippi River.
- U.S. Congress passes the Jones-White Merchant Marine Act, granting subsidies to U.S. shipping.

3–11 Clashes between Guomindang Chinese nationalists and Japanese troops take place at Jinan in northeastern China, after which Japan reoccupies part of the Shandong Peninsula.

20 In the German elections, the Social Democrats increase their number of seats from 131 to 153 and are the largest party, but without an overall majority; the Center Party has 62 seats, the communists 54, the German National People's Party 73, the German People's Party 45, and the Nazis 12.

JUNE

- Democrats nominate New York governor Alfred E. Smith for president and Arkansas senator Joseph T. Robinson for vice president.
- Republicans nominate the U.S. commerce secretary Herbert Hoover for president and Charles Curtis for vice president.

8 The Guomindang Chinese nationalists capture the Chinese capital Beijing (though the Guomindang and now Chinese capital remains at Nanjing).

9 France convenes a constituent assembly in its mandate Syria; it has a nationalist majority.

27 Kazimierz Bartel replaces Józef Piłsudski as prime minister of Poland (though Piłsudski remains minister of defense).

28 Hermann Müller, Social Democrat, is appointed German chancellor (following the resignation of Wilhelm Marx's ministry on June 13).

JULY

3 Following his return to Greece in March, the veteran politician Eleutherios Venizelos is again appointed prime minister.

17 Alvaro Obregón, the newly elected president of Mexico, is assassinated before taking office; the congress appoints Emilio Portes Gil as his successor.

19 King Fuad I stages a coup in Egypt, where parliament is dissolved and the constitution suspended; the king rules by decree.

AUGUST

2 Italy signs a 20-year treaty of friendship with Ethiopia.

8 The Croats withdraw from the parliament of the Kingdom of the Serbs, Croats, and Slovenes and establish a separatist assembly in Zagreb, following the assassination of their leader Stjepan Radić.

19 A general election in Greece produces a victory for the Liberal Party supporters of Prime Minister Eleutherios Venizelos.

27 The Kellogg–Briand Pact (drawn up by the U.S. secretary of state F. B. Kellogg and the French foreign minister Aristide Briand), outlawing war and providing for the pacific settlement of disputes, is signed in Paris, France, by 15 states, including the United States.

28 An all-party conference in Lucknow, India, votes for dominion status for India within the British Empire; however, two days later, radical members form the Independence of India League.

SEPTEMBER

1 Albania is proclaimed a kingdom and President Ahmed Bey Zogu is elected as King Zog.

10 The Argentine chamber of deputies votes to revoke oil concessions (the senate adjourns before considering the matter).

11 A Portuguese treaty with South Africa regulates the problems of transport and labor recruitment from its colonies to South Africa.

23 Italy signs a treaty of friendship with Greece.

26 An act of the League of Nations Assembly, embodying the Kellogg–Briand Pact of August 27, is signed by 23 nations, in Geneva, Switzerland.

OCTOBER

- On the campaign trail Republican presidential nominee Herbert Hoover maintains that the United States stands "nearer the final triumph over poverty than ever before in the history of any land"—words that will come back to haunt him as president in little over a year.

1 The Soviet leader Joseph Stalin ends the New Economic Policy and introduces state-directed economic planning and distribution, the development of industry, and collectivization of agriculture, in accordance with the first Five-Year Plan.

2 Arvid Lindman forms a Conservative ministry in Sweden following a general election in which the Social Democrats win 40 seats, the Prohibitionist Liberals 28, the Liberals 4, the Conservatives 73, the Agrarian Party 27, and the communists 8.

4–16 A plebiscite in Germany against building new battleships fails.

6 The nationalist leader Jiang Jie Shi is elected president of China, the Guomindang (Chinese National People's Party) having secured control of nearly all the country.

7 The modernizing Ras (prince) Tafari becomes negus (king) of Ethiopia on the death of Hapta Giorgis. He retains the position of regent and heir apparent to the empress Zauditu.

7 The Republican candidate Herbert Hoover wins the U.S. presidential election with 444 electoral votes against Alfred E. Smith, Democrat, with 87; the popular vote is Hoover, 21,391,381; Smith, 15,016,443; and Norman Thomas (Socialist), 267,835. In U.S. Congressional elections, Republicans retain majorities in the House (267–167) and Senate (56–39).

8 Police raid twenty speakeasies in New York, New York, in an effort to crack down on illegal liquor sales.

NOVEMBER

9 The Peasant Party leader Julius Maniu becomes prime minister of Romania.

14 In elections in New Zealand, the United (Liberal) Party under Joseph Ward wins 25 seats, the Reform Party 25, and Labor 19.

DECEMBER

5 Wilhelm Miklas is elected president of Austria, in succession to Michael Hainisch.

6 War breaks out between Bolivia and Paraguay.

12 The arrest of Voitech Tuka, a Slovak deputy, for irredentist agitation in favor of Hungary raises tension within Czechoslovakia.

12 The Peasants' Party wins the first free elections to be held in Romania.

20 Britain recognizes the Guomindang nationalist government under Jiang Jie Shi in Nanjing, China.

22 A committee under the U.S. financier Owen D. Young is appointed to examine the World War I reparations question.

SCIENCE, TECHNOLOGY, AND MEDICINE

Ecology

- U.S. Congress creates Bryce Canyon National Park from 146 sq km/36,000 acres of Utah desert.
- December, 1928–1929 Drought-induced famine kills nearly 3 million in northern China.

MARCH

- 13 A dam burst in the Santa Clara River Valley, California, kills 450 people.

SEPTEMBER

- 10–16 Over 1,800 people die when Lake Okeechobee in Florida overflows during a hurricane.

Health and Medicine

- Dutch radiologist Ziedes de Plantes develops a moving X-ray technique that maintains a single plane of a patent's body in focus. It is the forerunner of the CAT (computerized axial tomography) scan.
- English bacteriologist Fred Griffith discovers that the virulence of pneumococci bacteria (responsible for pneumonia) depends on the presence of an envelope of polysaccharides (sugar units) surrounding the bacteria cells.
- French physiologist Charles Nicolle receives the Nobel Prize for Physiology or Medicine for his work on typhus.
- Greek-born U.S. physician George Papanicolaou develops the Pap smear to test for uterine cancers.
- Scottish bacteriologist Alexander Fleming discovers penicillin when he notices that the mold *Penicillium notatum*, which has invaded a culture of staphylococci, inhibits the bacteria's growth.

Science

- c. 1928 English mathematician and physicist James Hopwood Jeans proposes the steady-state hypothesis, which states that the universe is constantly expanding and maintaining a constant average density through the continuous creation of new matter.
- Boron carbide, the hardest artificial substance known, is synthesized.
- British physicist Owen Willans Richardson receives the Nobel Prize for Physics for his work on the thermionic phenomenon and especially for the discovery of Richardson's law.
- Chinese archeologist Li Chi, under the auspices of the Academia Sinica, begins the first excavations of An-Yang, the capital of the Shang dynasty (1384–1111 BC).
- English physicist Paul Dirac describes the electron by four wave equations. The equations imply that the electron must spin on its axis and that negative states of matter must exist.
- English physiologists Edgar Douglas Adrian and Charles Sherrington publish *The Basis of Sensation*, which discusses how the nerves transmit messages to and from the brain.
- German biochemist Adolf Windaus receives the Nobel Prize for Chemistry for his work on the constitution of sterols and related vitamins.
- Germany physicist Rolf Wideröe develops the resonance linear accelerator, which he uses to accelerate potassium and sodium to an energy of 710 keV to split the lithium atom.
- It is discovered that Neptune's moon Triton rotates in the retrograde direction, that is, opposite that of Neptune's spin.
- Russian physicist George Gamow shows that the atom can be split using low-energy ions. It stimulates the development of particle accelerators.
- Russian physicist George Gamow and U.S. physicists R. W. Gurney and Edward Condon explain the relationship between the half-life of a radioactive element and the energy emitted by the alpha particle.
- The German organizations Deutsche Orientgesellschaft and Deutsches Archäologisches Institut begin excavations of the Sumerian city of Uruk.
- U.S. anthropologist Margaret Mead publishes *Coming of Age in Samoa*, in which she demonstrates that adolescence is not universally stressful.
- U.S. biochemist Charles King and Hungarian biochemist Albert Szent-Györgyi, independently discover vitamin C.

Technology

- German firm Franke and Heidecke introduce the Rolleiflex camera. It is the first twin-lens reflex camera and has one lens that acts as a viewfinder and another that transmits the image to the film.
- Polyvinyl chloride (PVC) is developed, simultaneously, by the U.S. companies Carbide and Carbon Corporation and Du Pont and the German firm I. G. Farben.
- U.S. inventor Laurens Hammond perfects his electric clock.

FEBRUARY

- 4 The first demonstration of color television is given at the Dominion Hotel, London, England, on a 9 ft by 12 ft screen, by John Logie Baird.

DECEMBER

- U.S. Congress passes the Boulder Dam Project Act, authorizing construction of a hydroelectric power facility in Boulder, Colorado. The act will serve as precedent for future federal government-sponsored resource management initiatives.

Transportation

- A transcontinental bus service is introduced in the United States by the U.S. firm Pioneer Yelloway, which runs a bus from California to New York, New York.
- British aviators Charles Kingsford-Smith and Charles Ulm are the first to fly across the mid-Pacific by air—from Oakland California, to Brisbane, Australia, via Honolulu and Fiji.
- The airship *Graf Zeppelin* completes the transatlantic flight from Friedrichshafen in Germany to New Jersey, United States, in 4 days 15½ hours.

- The New York Central Railroad inaugurates the use of two-way radio to communicate between train driver and controller.

FEBRUARY
- British aviator Bert Hinkler makes the first solo flight from London, England, to Australia.
- Lady Mary Heath flies solo from Cape Town in South Africa to London, England.

MARCH
15 German car manufacturer Fritz von Opel tests the *Opel-Rak 1*, the world's first rocket-propelled car.

APRIL
12 German aviators Hermann Köhl and James Fitzmaurice, Baron Gunther, Hunefield, make the first east–west transatlantic flight, in a Junkers W-33 monoplane from Ireland, to Labrador, Newfoundland, Canada.

MAY
28 The Chrysler Motor Company and Dodge Brothers, Inc. in the United States merge to become what will be the nation's third largest automobile manufacturer, behind Ford and General Motors.

JUNE
17–18 U.S. aviator Amelia Earhart is the first woman to cross the Atlantic (as a passenger) in an airplane.

SEPTEMBER
- The German airship *Graf Zeppelin* is launched and in October begins the first transatlantic air service.

DECEMBER
- Washington, D.C., is host to the International Civil Aeronautics Conference, called to celebrate the 25th anniversary of motor-powered aviation.

ARTS AND IDEAS

Architecture

- The British Embassy in Washington, D.C., designed by the English architect Edwin Lutyens, is completed.
- The city library in Stockholm, Sweden, designed by the Swedish architect Erik Gunnar Asplund, is completed.
- The Philip Lovell House, designed by the Austrian-born U.S. architect Richard Neutra, is completed in Los Angeles, California.

Arts

- English art historian Kenneth Clark publishes *The Gothic Revival*.
- English historian George Gordon Coulton publishes *Art and the Reformation*.
- The Belgian artist René Magritte paints *Threatening Weather*.
- The Brazilian artist Tarsila do Amaral paints *Abaporu*.
- The French artist Henri Matisse paints *Seated Odalisque*.
- The German artist Max Ernst paints *The Virgin Spanking the Infant Jesus Before Three Witnesses*.

- The German artist Max Beckmann paints *Black Lilies*.
- The Italian artist Arturo Martini sculpts *Monument to the Italian Pioneers of America*.
- The Italian photographer Tina Modotti takes *Tehuantepec Woman*.
- The Polish artist Tamara de Łempicka paints *Portrait of Tadeusz de Łempicki*.
- The Russian artist Alexander Rodchenko takes the photograph *At the Telephone*.
- The Russian artist Wassily Kandinsky paints *The Great Gate of Kiev*.
- The Spanish artist Joan Miró paints *Dutch Interior I*.
- The U.S. artist Alexander Calder sculpts *The Hostess*.
- The U.S. artist Charles Demuth paints *I Saw the Figure 5 in Gold*, his response to a poem by the U.S. writer William Carlos Williams.
- The U.S. artist John Steuart Curry paints *Baptism in Kansas*.
- The U.S. artist Kenneth Hayes Miller paints *The Shopper*.

Film

c. 1928 Production of movies with sound is crude because of the technical restriction imposed on the movements of the actors; location shooting also becomes rarer. Post-dubbed sound is adopted as a solution. These restrictions mean that production of small-scale comedies and musicals is favoured.
- Motion pictures with sound are dismissed as a fad and their quality criticized by many, including French inventor Louis-Jean Lumière, the creator of the first movie projector.
- The documentary *The Man with the Movie Camera*, directed by Dziga Vertov, is released in the USSR.
- The movie *Crossways*, directed by Teinosuke Kinugasa, is released in Japan.
- The movie *L'Argent/Money*, directed by Marcel L'Herbier, is released in France.
- The movie *La Petite Marchande d'Allumettes/The Little Matchgirl*, by the French directors Jean Renoir and Jean Tedesco, and starring Amy Wells, is released.
- The movie *Les Nouveaux Messieurs/The New Gentlemen*, directed by Jacques Feyder, is released in France, starring Albert Préjean, Gaby Morlay, and Henri Roussel.
- The movie *Storm over Asia*, directed by V. I. Potemkin, is released in the USSR, starring I. Inkizhinov, V. Inkizhinov, and A. Dedintsev.
- The movie *The Circus*, directed by Charlie Chaplin, is released in the United States. He also stars in it, along with Merna Kennedy.
- The movie *The Docks of New York*, directed by Austrian filmmaker Josef von Sternberg, is released in the United States, starring George Bancroft and Betty Compson. Also released in the United States is his film *The Last Command*, starring Emil Jannings, William Powell, and Evelyn Brent.
- The movie *The Fall of the House of Usher*, directed by French filmmaker Jean Epstein and Spanish filmmaker Luis Buñuel, is released. Based on the story by Edgar Allan Poe, it stars Marguerite Gance, Jean Debucourt, and Charles Lamy.

- The movie *The Passion of Joan of Arc*, directed by Danish filmmaker Carl Theodor Dreyer, is released in France, starring Renée Falconetti.
- The movie *The Seashell and the Clergyman*, directed by Germaine Dziga, is released. It is regarded as the first surrealist movie.
- The movie *The Way of All Flesh*, directed by Victor Fleming, is released in the United States, starring Emil Jannings, Belle Bennett, and Phyllis Haver.
- The movie *The Wind*, directed by Swedish filmmaker Victor Seastrom, is released in the United States, starring Lillian Gish and Lars Hanson.
- The movie *Un Chien Andalou/An Andalusian Dog*, directed by Luis Buñuel, is released in Spain. It is written by Buñuel and the surrealist painter Salvador Dalí, and also stars them, along with Simone Mareuil, Pierre Batcheff, and Jaime Miravilles.
- The musical *The Singing Fool*, directed by Lloyd Bacon, is released in the United States. One of the earliest pictures with spoken dialogue, it stars Al Jolson.
- The Quota Act (The Cinematograph Films Act 1927) in Britain requires an increase in the number of movies made each year in Britain, with an initial target of 7.5%, rising to 20% by 1938. The intention was to keep the British movie industry alive in the face of U.S. competition.
- The U.S. company Western Electric develops a sound-on-film system with greater flexibility than Vitaphone (a sound-on-disc system), which has proved expensive and difficult to transport.
- The Walt Disney cartoon *Steamboat Willie* is released in the United States, starring Mickey Mouse, the first animated movie with sound.

Literature and Language

- The Australian writer Martin à Beckett Boyd publishes *Montforts*.
- The English writer Aldous Huxley publishes his novel *Point Counter Point*.
- The English writer Christopher Isherwood publishes *All the Conspirators*, his first novel.
- The English writer D. H. Lawrence publishes his novel *Lady Chatterley's Lover* privately in Florence, Italy. Thought obscene, the full text is not published until 1959 in the United States, and 1960 in Britain.
- The English writer Evelyn Waugh publishes his novel *Decline and Fall*.
- The English writer Ford Madox Ford publishes his novel *Last Post*, the final part of his four-part cycle *Parade's End*.
- The English writer Somerset Maugham publishes his novel *Ashenden, or The British Agent*.
- The English writer Siegfried Sassoon publishes his autobiographical novel *Memoirs of a Foxhunting Man*, part of the Sherston trilogy.
- The English writer Virginia Woolf publishes her novel *Orlando*.
- The final volume of the *Oxford English Dictionary* is published. The first volume appeared in 1884.
- The first volume of the *Dictionary of American Biography* is published, edited by Allen Johnson, financed by *The New York Times*, and published under

the auspices of the American Council of Learned Societies. The last volume of this 20-volume edition appears in 1936.
- The French writer André Breton publishes his novel *Nadja*.
- The Irish writer W. B. Yeats publishes his poetry collection *The Tower*, which includes "Sailing to Byzantium" and "Among School Children."
- The Northwestern University anthropologist Melville Jean Herskovits publishes *American Negro: A Study in Racial Crossings*, which maintains that black Americans possess a discrete culture within the confines of the nation's larger Anglo-Saxon culture.
- The Pulitzer Prize for Biography is awarded to Charles Edward Russell for *The American Orchestra and Theodore Thomas*, the Prize for Fiction is awarded to Thornton Wilder for *The Bridge of the San Luis Rey*, and the Prize for Poetry is awarded to Edwin Arlington Robinson for *Tristram*.
- The Russian-born U.S. writer Vladimir Nabokov publishes his novel *Korol, dama, valet/King, Queen, Knave*.
- The Spanish writer Federico García Lorca publishes his poetry collection *Romancero gitano/Gypsy Ballads*.
- The U.S. writer Archibald MacLeish publishes his poetry collection *The Hamlet of A. MacLeish*.
- The U.S. writer Carl Sandburg publishes his poetry collection *Good Morning, America*.
- The U.S. writer Dorothy Parker publishes her poetry collection *Sunset Gun*.
- The U.S. writer Stephen Vincent Benét publishes his epic poem about the American Civil War, *John Brown's Body*, which wins the Pulitzer Prize for Poetry in 1929.
- The U.S. writer Upton Sinclair publishes his novel *Boston*, which is based on the controversial trial of the two U.S. anarchists Nicola Sacco and Bartolomeo Vanzetti, who were executed in 1927.

Music

- Clarence "Pine Top" Smith records "Pine Top's Boogie-Woogie" in the United States, considered the earliest commercial use of the term "boogie-woogie."
- Popular songs in the United States include "Making Whoopee," "Silver Moon," and "Am I Blue?"
- The Austrian composer Arnold Schoenberg completes his orchestral *Variations* (Opus 31).
- The Austrian composer Anton Webern completes his Symphony (Opus 21) for chamber orchestra.
- The Czech composer Leoš Janáček completes his String Quartet No. 2, *Listy důvěrné/Intimate Letters*.
- The Hungarian composer Béla Bartók completes his String Quartet 4.
- The opera *Die ägyptische Helena/The Egyptian Helena* by the German composer Richard Strauss is first performed, in Dresden, Germany.
- The opera *Die Dreigroschenoper/The Threepenny Opera* by the German composer Kurt Weill is first performed, in Berlin, Germany. It is a modern interpretation of John Gay's *The Beggar's Opera* of 1728, with material by the German writer Bertolt Brecht.

- The opera *Fra Gherardo/Brother Gerard* by the Italian composer Ildebrando Pizzetti is first performed, in Milan, Italy.
- The Swiss composer Arthur Honegger completes his orchestral work *Rugby*.
- The U.S. composer Aaron Copland completes his Symphony No. 1. He completed his Symphony for Organ and Orchestra in 1925.
- The U.S. composer George Gershwin completes his orchestral work *An American in Paris*.
- The U.S. singer and actor Al Jolson records the songs "Sonny Boy" and "There's a Rainbow Around My Shoulder."
- U.S. jazz pianist, composer, and bandleader Earl "Fatha" Hines founds his first band, in Chicago, Illinois.

Theater and Dance

- The ballet *Boléro* by the French composer Maurice Ravel and the Russian dancer Bronislava Fominitshna Nijinska, is first performed, in Paris, France.
- The play *Kvadratura kruga/Squaring the Circle*, by the Russian dramatist Valentin Katayev, is first performed, in Moscow, USSR.
- The play *Strange Interlude*, by the U.S. dramatist Eugene O'Neill, is first performed, at the John Golden Theater in New York, New York.
- The play *The Front Page*, by the U.S. journalists Ben Hecht and Charles MacArthur, is first performed, in New York, New York.
- The play *Topaze*, by the French writer Marcel Pagnol, is first performed, in Paris, France.
- The Pulitzer Prize for Drama is awarded to Eugene O'Neill for *Strange Interlude*.

BIRTHS & DEATHS

JANUARY
5 Walter F. Mondale, vice president of the United States 1977–81, born in Ceylon, Minnesota.
5 Zulfikar Ali Bhutto, Pakistani president 1971–73 and prime minister 1973–77, born near Larkana, Sind, India (now Pakistan) (–1979).
11 Thomas Hardy, English novelist and poet, dies in Dorchester, Dorset, England (87).
21 George Washington Goethals, U.S. Army engineer who supervised the construction of the Panama Canal 1907–14, dies in New York, New York (69).
25 Eduard Amvrosiyevich Shevardnadze, Georgian politician, foreign affairs minister of the USSR 1985–91, head of state of Georgia 1992–95, president of Georgia from 1995, born in Mamati, Georgia, USSR.
29 Douglas Haig, Earl Haig, British field marshal who commanded the British forces in France during most of World War I, dies in London, England (66).

FEBRUARY
15 Herbert Henry Asquith, British prime minister 1908–16, a Liberal, dies in Sutton Courtenay, England (75).

MARCH
12 Edward Franklin Albee III, U.S. playwright, born in Washington, D.C.
19 Hans Küng, Swiss Roman Catholic theologian, born in Sursee, Switzerland.
31 Gordie Howe, Canadian-born U.S. ice hockey player, born in Floral, Saskatchewan, Canada.

APRIL
6 James Dewey Watson, U.S. geneticist who, with Francis Crick, discovered the molecular structure of deoxyribonucleic acid (DNA), born in Chicago, Illinois.
10 Stanley John Weyman, English writer of historical romance, dies in Ruthin, Clwyd, Wales (72).
23 Shirley Temple, U.S. diplomat and child star of the 1930s, born in Santa Monica, California.

MAY
4 Hosni Mubarak, president of Egypt from 1981, born in al-Minufiyah governorate, Egypt.
9 Pancho Gonzales, U.S. tennis player who dominated U.S. singles tennis during the 1950s, born in Los Angeles, California (–1995).
26 Jack Kevorkian, U.S. physician known for assisting terminally ill patients to commit suicide, born in Pontiac, Michigan.

JUNE
5 Tony (Cecil Antonio) Richardson, English director and producer who helped establish the English Stage Company 1955 at the Royal Court Theatre in London, born in Shipley, Yorkshire, England (–1991).
14 Che (Ernesto) Guevara, Cuban and South American communist guerrilla, born in Rosario, Argentina (–1967).
14 Emmeline Pankhurst, militant English suffragette, dies in London, England (69).
18 Roald Amundsen, Norwegian explorer who was the first person to reach the South Pole, dies in the Arctic Ocean sometime after this date (he disappeared on this day;

the exact date of his death is not known), while trying to rescue the Italian explorer Umberto Nobile (55).

JULY
9 Vince Edwards (originally Vincent Edward Zoino), U.S. television and film actor, known for his role as Dr. Ben Casey, born in New York, New York (–1996).
21 Ellen Terry, English actress popular in both Britain and the United States, dies in Small Hythe, Kent, England (81).
26 Stanley Kubrick, U.S. film director, born in New York, New York.

AUGUST
12 Leoš Janáček, Czech operatic composer whose music was intimately connected with the inflections of his native tongue, dies in Ostrava, Czechoslovakia (now the Czech Republic) (74).
27 Mangosuthu Gatsha Buthelezei, known as Chief Buthelezei, Zulu leader and politician, born in Mahlabatini, South Africa.

OCTOBER
1 George Peppard, U.S. film actor, born in Detroit, Michigan (–1994).
6 Hafez al-Assad, Ba'athist party premier of Syria from 1971, born in Qardaha, Syria.

NOVEMBER
22 Pat(ricia) Rosemary Koechlin-Smythe, UK international showjumper, born in Barnes, London, England (67).

DECEMBER
7 Noam Chomsky, U.S. linguist and founder of the school of linguistic analysis known as transformational grammar, born in Philadelphia, Pennsylvania.

- The U.S. singer Paul Robeson sings "Ol' Man River" in the British production of *Show Boat*, by Oscar Hammerstein and Jerome Kern.

Thought and Scholarship

- German philosopher and sociologist Max Scheler publishes *Die Stellung des Menschen im Kosmos/The Place of Man in the Universe.*
- German philosopher Edmund Husserl publishes the second volume of his *Ideen zu einer reinen Phänomenologie und phänomenologischen Philosophie/ Ideas: General Introduction to Pure Phenomenology.* The first volume appeared in 1913.
- German philosopher Rudolf Carnap publishes *Der logische Aufbau der Welt/The Logical Structure of the World* and *Scheinproblem in der Philosophie/Pseudo-Problems in Philosophy.*
- German theologian Karl Barth publishes *Die Theologie und die Kirche/Theology and the Church.*
- Irish writer George Bernard Shaw publishes his political tract *The Intelligent Woman's Guide to Socialism and Capitalism.*
- The Nobel Prize for Literature is awarded to the Norwegian novelist Sigrid Undset.
- The Pulitzer Prize for History is awarded to Vernon Louis Parrington for *Main Currents in American Thought: An Interpretation of Literature from the Beginning to 1920.*
- U.S. psychologist Arnold Gesell publishes *Infancy and Human Growth* in which he asserts that motor, language, personal, and social skills are hereditary.

SOCIETY

Everyday Life

- The first homogenized peanut butter, Peter Pan Peanut Butter, is produced by Swift Packing Company in the United States.
- The overproduction of coffee causes a price slump and economic crisis in Brazil.

NOVEMBER
6   The *New York Times* mounts an animated electric sign wrapped around its building in Times Square, New York, New York, in order to show election returns.

Media and Communication

- The U.S. entrepreneur David Sarnoff establishes a National Broadcasting Corporation (NBC) television station to conduct research.

MAY
11   The WGY station of Schenectady, New York, transmits the first program of scheduled television broadcasts.

Religion

APRIL
9   Islam is disestablished as the state religion of Turkey.

Sports

- The first Spartakiade workers' sports festival is held in Moscow, USSR, as an alternative to the "bourgeois" Olympic Games being held in Amsterdam, the Netherlands. Over 4,000 athletes, including around 600 from outside the Soviet Union, take part.
- The French tennis player Henri Cochet defeats fellow French player René Lacoste to win the men's singles title at the French Open tennis championships, at the newly built Stade Roland Garros in Paris, France.
- Track and field events for women are introduced at the 1928 Olympics in Amsterdam, in large part due to agitation from the Fédération Sportive Féminine Internationale (FSFI).

FEBRUARY
11–19   The 2nd Winter Olympic Games are held in St. Moritz, Switzerland, attended by 464 competitors, 26 of whom are women, from 25 nations. Norway wins 6 gold medals and the United States, Sweden, and Finland win 1 each. Sonja Henie of Norway, aged 15, wins the first of three successive figure skating gold medals. Canada wins the ice hockey without conceding a goal.

APRIL
5–14   The New York Rangers defeat the Montreal Canadiens by three games to two to become the first U.S. team to win the National Hockey League Stanley Cup.

MAY
17–August 12   The 9th Olympic Games are held in Amsterdam, the Netherlands, attended by 3,014 competitors, 290 of whom are women, from 46 nations. Women's track and field events are held for the first time. The United States wins 22 gold medals; Germany, 10; Finland, 8; Sweden, Italy, and Switzerland, 7 each; and France and the Netherlands, 6 each. Percy Williams of Canada wins both the 100 meters and 200 meters sprints.

OCTOBER
4–9   The New York Yankees win their second consecutive World Series, defeating the St. Louis Cardinals by four games to none.

1929

POLITICS, GOVERNMENT, AND ECONOMICS

Business and Economics

- A merger of several U.S. milling companies results in the creation of General Mills in Minneapolis, Minnesota. General Mills becomes the world's largest milling company.
- Illinois engineer Paul Vincent Galvin introduces the Motorola car.
- Indiana entrepreneur Donald F. Duncan introduces the yo-yo from the Philippines into the United States.
- The multinational household products firm Unilever is formed by the merger of British and Dutch firms.
- The U.S. food retail companies Postum and Birdseye merge to form General Foods.

SEPTEMBER

19 Share values on the Wall Street stock exchange, New York, New York, reach their highest point in a "bull" market.

19 The Wall Street Dow Jones Industrial Average in the United States reaches an index high of 381, compared to 88 in 1924. The U.S. Common Stock Prices Index also reaches a high of 190.3, compared to the 1926 base of 100.

OCTOBER

24–29 Share values crash on the Wall Street stock market, New York, New York, starting with "Black Thursday" and continuing (after closure of the market from noon on October 24 until October 28) on "Black Monday" (October 28) and "Black Tuesday" (October 29). Widespread panic results in the trading of some 16.4 million shares, a new record. The episode triggers still more panic in the days and weeks ahead, ultimately precipitating the Depression.

30 U.S. loans to Europe, on which postwar recovery have been based, are withdrawn following the Wall Street crash.

NOVEMBER

13 The Bank for International Settlements is founded in Basel, Switzerland, to deal with Germany's World War I reparation payments under the Young Plan.

Politics and Government

- Tajikistan becomes a separate constituent republic within the USSR.
- The Migratory Bird Conservation Act in the United States provides authority and funds for the establishment of refuges for migrating birds.
- The National Revolutionary Party (PNR) is founded in Mexico (renamed the Party of the Mexican Revolution in 1938 and the Institutional Revolutionary Party in 1946).

JANUARY

- The U.S. Senate ratifies the Kellogg-Briand Peace Pact, which renounces war as an instrument of foreign policy.

5 An inter-American treaty of arbitration, analogous to the Kellogg–Briand Pact of August 27, 1928, is signed in Washington, D.C.

5 King Alexander I suppresses the constitution of the Kingdom of the Serbs, Croats, and Slovenes and establishes a royal dictatorship.

14 Emir Amanullah flees from Afghanistan following opposition to his radical reforms.

21 The Croat party in the Kingdom of the Serbs, Croats, and Slovenes is dissolved following King Alexander's establishment of a dictatorship.

31 Leon Trotsky, having lost the contest to succeed Vladimir Ilyich Lenin as Soviet leader to Joseph Stalin, is expelled from the USSR.

FEBRUARY

6 Germany accepts the Kellogg–Briand Pact of August 27, 1928, renouncing war.

9 The Litvinov Protocol, or Eastern Pact, between the USSR, Estonia, Latvia, Poland, and Romania renounces war, providing instead for the peaceful resolution of disputes.

11 The Lateran Treaties recognize the pope's sovereignty over the Vatican, bringing the Vatican City State into being, and ending the hiatus in Italian relations with the Vatican that had existed since Italian unification in 1870.

14 In the "St. Valentine's Day Massacre" in Chicago, Illinois, gangsters dressed as policemen, working for Al Capone, gun down seven members of the gang led by George "Bugsy" Moran.

27 Turkey signs the Litvinov Protocol of February 9, renouncing war.

MARCH

- Herbert Hoover is inaugurated 31st president of the United States.

6 A Bulgarian–Turkish treaty promising neutrality and the arbitration of disputes is signed.

17 The Spanish government closes Madrid University to stifle student agitation.

24 The fascists "win" single-party elections in Italy.

27 A pact of friendship is made between Greece and the Kingdom of the Serbs, Croats, and Slovenes.

28 A new constitution in Ecuador ends the military regime of Isidro Ayora (head of state since 1926).

APRIL

3   Persia (modern Iran) signs the antiwar Litvinov Protocol of February 9.

24 The Social Democrats win 61 seats in the general election in Denmark; the Liberals win 43 seats, the Conservatives 24, and the Radicals 16. Theodor Stauning remains prime minister of a Liberal–Radical coalition.

30 The Christian Socialist Ernst Streeruwitz is appointed chancellor of Austria.

MAY

• The U.S. Supreme Court upholds the so-called pocket veto, by which the president may halt legislation simply by ignoring it.

1–3 Three days of clashes between communist demonstrators and police in Berlin, Germany, leave 250 people dead or injured.

16 The Greek senate, abolished in 1862, is reconstituted in the hope of stabilizing the republican regime.

20 Japan evacuates the Shandong Peninsula, China.

26 In the Belgian general election, the Catholic parties win 77 seats, the Workers' Party 70, the Liberals 78, and the Flemish Nationalists 11.

30 In the British general election, the first held under universal adult suffrage, Labour wins 287 seats, the Conservatives 260, the Liberals 59, and others 9.

JUNE

3   A settlement is reached in the Arica–Tacna border territory dispute (originated in 1910), by which Chile is awarded Arica, Peru gains Tacna, and Bolivia acquires railroad rights.

5   Ramsay MacDonald forms a Labour government in Britain, with Arthur Henderson as foreign secretary, Philip Snowden as chancellor of the Exchequer, and John Clynes as home secretary.

7   The Young Committee reviewing German World War I reparations payments recommends that Germany should pay annuities (secured on a mortgage of German railroads) to an international bank until 1988, thus greatly easing the burden of repayments.

27 The German Reichstag (parliament) repeals the Protection of the Republic Act.

27 The Turkish president Mustafa Kemal Pasha (later known as Atatürk) acts to suppress the dissemination of communist propaganda.

JULY

2   The Giichi Tanaka ministry in Japan is succeeded by a government formed by Yuko Hamaguchi following the army's refusal to punish officers responsible for the assassination of the Chinese warlord Zhang Zuolin.

27 Raymond Poincaré resigns because of ill health and Aristide Briand again becomes prime minister of France.

AUGUST

6–13 At the Reparations Conference in The Hague in the Netherlands, Germany accepts the Young Plan for German World War I reparations; in return, the Allies agree to evacuate the Rhineland by June 1930.

8   Arab attacks on Jews in Palestine follow disputes over Jewish use of the Wailing Wall, Jerusalem.

8   Ibn Saud, King of Hejaz and Sultan of Nejd, signs a treaty of friendship with Turkey.

11 Iraq and Persia (modern Iran) sign a treaty of friendship.

24 Ibn Saud, King of Hejaz and Sultan of Nejd, signs a treaty of friendship with Persia (modern Iran).

SEPTEMBER

5   The French prime minister Aristide Briand proposes a European federal union to the League of Nations, with no result.

12 The Italian leader Benito Mussolini's son-in-law Count Dino Grandi is appointed Italian foreign minister.

14 The United States joins the International Court of Justice.

16 A peace treaty is signed between Bolivia and Paraguay.

26 Johann Schober forms a ministry in Austria, supported by Christian Socialists and Nationalists, with a program for restoring order following political clashes.

OCTOBER

• Former U.S. interior secretary Albert B. Fall is convicted of accepting a bribe in the Teapot Dome oil leasing scandal. Fall is fined $100,000 and sentenced to one year in prison.

• The British prime minister Ramsay MacDonald becomes the first of his office to address the U.S. Congress. He speaks on the subject of global security.

3   Britain resumes relations with the USSR, having broken them off in 1927 following disputes over alleged communist subversion.

3   Julius Curtius is appointed German foreign minister on Gustav Stresemann's death.

3   The name of the Kingdom of the Serbs, Croats, and Slovenes is changed to Yugoslavia as part of King Alexander I's attempts to end ethnic divisions within the country.

12 The Labor Party wins the Australian elections.

16 The modernizing general Muhammad Nadir becomes king of Afghanistan, following a period of political unrest.

21 A general election in Egypt results in victory for the Wafd nationalist party.

22 Following the success of the Labor Party in the Australian elections on October 12, James H. Scullin forms a government.

NOVEMBER

17 The "Right Opposition" led by Nikolai Bukharin is expelled from the Communist Party of the USSR by the Soviet leader Joseph Stalin.

DECEMBER

12 A round-table conference on dominion status for Indian leaders takes place between the viceroy, Lord Irwin, and Indian party leaders.

12 China announces that all foreign concessions based on "unequal treaties" with the former imperial government will end on January 1, 1930 (but implementation is postponed).

22 A referendum in Germany upholds the adoption of the Young Plan for German World War I reparations despite opposition from the Nationalists.

22 By the Khabarovsk Protocol between the USSR and China, China is to deal with the activities of anti-Soviet "White" Russian bands based in Manchuria and a conference is to be held to settle other issues.

SCIENCE, TECHNOLOGY, AND MEDICINE

Agriculture

JUNE

- The U.S. president Herbert Hoover signs the Agricultural Marketing Act, creating a Federal Farm Board to monitor and adjust agricultural prices.

Ecology

- Regulation L-20 is introduced in the United States, permitting the heads of national forests to set aside wilderness areas for recreational use. By 1939 some 72 areas have been designated.

Exploration

NOVEMBER

28–29 U.S. explorer Richard Byrd and a crew of three fly over the South Pole.

Health and Medicine

- English biochemist Frederick Gowland Hopkins and Dutch biochemist Christiaan Eijkman share the Nobel Prize for Physiology or Medicine; Hopkins for his discovery of growth-stimulating vitamins and Eijkman for his discovery of the antineuritic vitamin B1.
- German physician Werner Forssmann develops the technique of cardiac catheterization, in which a flexible tube is threaded through the veins of the arm into the heart, by experimenting on himself. The technique permits surgeons to observe the coronary arteries, inject radiopaque dyes, and surgically correct heart problems.
- German psychiatrist Hans Berger invents the electroencephalograph, which measures and records brain wave patterns.
- U.S. physician Samuel Levine discovers a connection between hypertension (high blood pressure) and heart disease.

Science

- *The Universe Around Us* is published by English physicist James Hopwood Jeans and helps to popularize astronomy.

- Belgian-born U.S. chemist Julius Nieuwland and the U.S. DuPont corporation introduce the synthetic rubber neoprene.
- British neurologist Edgar Douglas Adrian, using an ultra-sensitive galvanometer, is able to follow a single impulse in a single nerve fiber. It aids understanding of the physical basis of sensation.
- By studying the magnetism of rocks, the Japanese geologist Motonori Matuyama shows that the earth's magnetic field periodically reverses direction.
- English archeologist Charles Leonard Woolley publishes *Ur of the Chaldees*.
- English biochemist Arthur Harden and German chemist Hans von Euler-Chelpin share the Nobel Prize for Chemistry for their investigations of the fermentation of sugars and fermentative enzymes.
- English philosopher Alfred North Whitehead publishes *Process and Reality: An Essay in Cosmology*.
- French engineer and chemist Georges Claude demonstrates that the temperature difference between the upper and lower depths of the ocean can be used to generate electricity.
- French physicist Louis de Broglie receives the Nobel Prize for Physics for his discovery of the wave nature of electrons.
- German biochemist Adolf Butenandt and, simultaneously and independently, U.S. biochemist Edward Doisy isolate the hormone estrone, which is involved in the growth and development of females.
- German physicist Albert Einstein publishes *Unitary Field Theory*, in which he attempts to explain the various atomic forces by a single theory.
- Irish physicist Ernest Walton and English physicist Douglas Cockcroft develop the first particle accelerator.
- Russian-born U.S. chemist Phoebus Levene discovers 2-deoxyribose, the five-carbon sugar that forms the basis of deoxyribonucleic acid (DNA).
- Russian-born U.S. physicist George Gamow, U.S. physicist R. Atkinson, and German physicist F. Houtermans suggest that thermonuclear processes are the source of solar energy.
- U.S. astronomer Edwin Hubble publishes Hubble's Law, which states that the ratio of the speed of a galaxy to its distance from Earth is a constant (now known as Hubble's constant).
- U.S. astronomer Henry Russell publishes "Stellar Evolution," in which he suggests that stars begin as huge cool red bodies, shrink to become hot yellow stars and then hot white and blue dwarfs, and then shrink to become cool red stars.
- German mathematician Hermann Julius Oberth publishes *Wege zur Raumschiffahrt/Ways to Spaceflight*, which discusses ion rockets and electric propulsion.

Technology

- French chemist Eugéne Houdry develops the Houdry process of cracking crude oil to obtain gasoline.
- The "Vacublitz" photoflash bulb is invented in Germany. It consists of a vacuum lamp filled with

oxygen and a knot of fine magnesium or aluminum fibers that is ignited by an electric current.

- The automobile industry tops U.S. manufacturing for the first time in terms of the overall value of goods manufactured; 2,798,737 passenger cars are produced in 1929.
- The U.S. engineer Frank Gray patents a method of transmitting two or more signals over the same channel. It permits the development of color television where the colors are transmitted separately but simultaneously.
- U.S. firm Kodak introduces 16-mm color film for amateur use.
- U.S. inventors Joseph Horton and Warren Marrison apply the oscillations of the quartz crystal to timekeeping. Because the crystals oscillate at 100,000 hertz, they greatly improve the accuracy of clocks, gaining or losing only about one second every ten years.

JUNE

27 Scientists at Bell Laboratories in New Jersey demonstrate the transmission of moving color images; 50 lines are scanned at 17.7 frames per second. Among the pictures they show are the U.S. flag, the Union Jack, and a bouquet of roses.

Transportation

- Pan American Airways Corporation inaugurates the first airline service to South America using Sikorsky S-38 and S-40 amphibious aircraft.
- The first electric fuel gauges appear on cars.
- The International Safety of Life at Sea Convention is drawn up; it establishes minimum standards for the construction of passenger ships and the provision of life-saving and radio equipment.
- The Warsaw Convention establishes the rules for the air carriage of goods across international boundaries.
- U.S. automobile manufacturer Errett Lobban Cord introduces the Cord L-29, the first commercially successful front-wheel-drive car.

June 1929–30 The German ships *Bremen* and *Europa* are launched. They are the first ships with a bulbous bow, which provides them with greater buoyancy and maneuverability.

JUNE

- Delta Air Service, eventually Delta Air Lines, begins a passenger service between Dallas, Texas, and Jackson, Mississippi.

AUGUST

- The *Graf Zeppelin* airship flies 34,600 km/21,500 mi around the world in 21 days.

SEPTEMBER

24 U.S. Army officer James Doolittle takes off, flies a predetermined course and lands relying solely on his instruments. It is the first "blind" flight.

30 German car manufacturer Fritz von Opel test-pilots the first rocket-powered aircraft, a glider with a gunpowder rocket attached.

ARTS AND IDEAS

Architecture

- The German Pavilion at the International Exhibition in Barcelona, Spain, designed by the German architect Ludwig Mies van der Rohe, is completed.
- The Library at Viipuri, Finland, designed by the Finnish architect Alvar Aalto, is completed.
- The United States now has 377 skyscrapers with more than 20 stories.

Arts

- The German artist Max Ernst completes *La Femme 100 Têtes/Woman with a 100 Heads*, a picture book of collages.
- The Belgian artist René Magritte paints *The Treachery of Images (Ceci n'est pas une pipe/This is not a Pipe)* and *On the Threshold of Liberty*.
- The Dutch artist Piet Mondrian paints *Composition with Yellow and Blue*.
- The English artist Henry Moore sculpts *Mask*.
- The German artist Christian Schad paints *Agosta the Pigeon Chested Man and Rasha the Black Dove*.
- The German photographer August Sander publishes his photo album *Antlitz der Zeit/Face of our Time*. Beginning in 1910, Sander tried to create a comprehensive "man of the 20th century" series, photographing a wide range of Germans in their everyday occupations. One of the best-known images is *The Pastry Cook* 1928.
- The Hungarian photographer André Kertész takes *Breton Girls*.
- The Italian photographer Tina Modotti takes *Hands of the Puppeteer*.
- The Museum of Modern Art (MOMA) opens in New York, New York, with exhibitions of works by Paul Cézanne, Paul Gauguin, Georges Seurat, and Vincent van Gogh.
- The Spanish artist Pablo Picasso paints *Nude in an Armchair*.
- The Swiss artist Paul Klee draws *Fool in a Trance* with one continuous line.
- The U.S. artist Arthur Dove paints *Fog Horns*.
- The U.S. artist Charles Sheeler paints *Upper Deck*.
- The U.S. artist John Steuart Curry paints *Tornado over Kansas*.

Film

c. 1929 European countries such as France and Hungary set up quotas for home movie production in an attempt to protect the domestic film industry and to reduce the influence of U.S. culture.

- *Skeleton Dance* is released in the United States, the first of Walt Disney's *Silly Symphony* series of animations set to music.
- Hollywood studios have 116 sound recording machines in use, compared with just 16 the previous year.

- The 1928–29 Academy Awards take place. Best Actor: Waner Baxter, for *In Old Arizona*; Best Actress: Mary Pickford, for *Coquette*; Best Picture: *Broadway Melody*, directed by Harry Beaumont; Best Director: Frank Lloyd, for *The Divine Lady*.
- The average Hollywood studio movie costs $200,000 to produce.
- The movie *Arsenal*, directed by Alexander Dovzhenko, is released in the USSR, starring Semyon Svanshenko, A. Buchma, and M. Nademsky.
- The movie *Blackmail*, directed by Alfred Hitchcock, is released in Britain. The first British movie with spoken dialogue throughout, it stars Anny Ondra, Sara Allgood, John Longden, and Charles Paton.
- The movie *Fragment of an Empire*, directed by Friedrich Ermler, is released in the USSR, starring Fyodor Nikitin, Yakov Gudkin, and Ludmila Semyonova.
- The movie *Hallelujah*, directed by King Vidor, is released in the United States. The first feature-length movie with an all-black cast, it stars Daniel Hayes, Nina Mae McKinney, and William Fontaine.
- The movie *Madame X*, directed by Lionel Barrymore, is released in the United States, starring Ruth Chatterton and Raymond Hackett.
- The movie *Pandora's Box*, directed by Czech filmmaker G. W. Pabst, is released in Germany. An adaptation of the Franz Wedekind play *Lulu*, it stars Louise Brooks, Fritz Kortner, Franz Lederer, and Gustav Diessl.
- The movie *The Cocoanuts*, directed by F. Robert Florey, is released in the United States. Based on the stage play of the same name, it stars the four Marx Brothers in their first feature, with songs by Irving Berlin.
- The movie *The General Line* or *The Old and the New*, directed by Sergey Eisenstein, is released in the USSR, starring Marta Lapkina.
- The movie *The Mysterious Dr. Fu Manchu*, directed by Rowland V. Lee, is released in the United States, starring Warner Oland, Jean Arthur, Neil Hamilton, and O. P. Heggie. It is based on the novels and stories by English author Sax Rohmer (pen name of Arthur Sarsfield Wade).
- The movie *The New Babylon*, directed by Grigory Kozintsev, is released in the USSR, starring Elena Kuzmina and Leonid Trauberg.
- The movie *The Virginian*, directed by Victor Fleming, is released in the United States, starring Gary Cooper, William Huston, and Richard Arlen.
- The movie *The Wild Party*, directed by Dorothy Arzner, is released in the United States, starring Fredric March and Clara Bow.
- The movie musical *On with the Show*, directed by Alan Crosland, is released in the United States. The first musical movie in color, it stars Betty Compson and Joe E. Brown.
- The movie musical *Broadway Melody*, directed by Harry Beaumont, is released in the United States, starring Bessie Love, Anita Page, and Charles King. In addition to the title song, it features "You Were Meant For Me."
- The movie musical *Rio Rita*, directed by Luther Reed, is released in the United States, starring Bebe Daniels and John Boles.
- The U.S. firm Grandeur Films makes the first 70-mm movies which give a wider field of view.

- U.S. jazz singer Bessie Smith makes the short two-reel movie of *St Louis Blues*, which is suppressed for "bad taste" because of its realism.

MAY

16 The U.S. Academy of Motion Picture Arts and Sciences presents its first awards, the gold-plated statuettes, later known as "Oscars." The first ceremony, in Los Angeles, California, covers the years 1927 and 1928. Best Actor: Emil Jannings, for *The Last Command* and *The Way of All Flesh*; Best Actress: Janet Gaynor, for *Seventh Heaven*, *Street Angel*, and *Sunrise*; Best Picture: *Wings*, directed by William Wellman; Best Director: Frank Borzage, for *Seventh Heaven*.

OCTOBER

2 The movie *Disraeli*, based on the play by Louis N. Packer, is released by Warner Brothers, starring George Arliss.

Literature and Language

- The Australian writer Henry Handel Richardson publishes her novel *Ultima Thule*, the third part of her trilogy *The Fortunes of Richard Mahony*.
- The black American writer Countee Cullen publishes his poetry collection *The Black Christ and Other Poems*.
- The British playwright and novelist Sir James Barrie donates the rights to his play *Peter Pan* to the Hospital for Sick Children, Great Ormond Street, London, England.
- The English historian Albert Frederick Pollard publishes *Wolsey*.
- The English literary critic Lord David Cecil publishes *The Stricken Deer*, a study of the English poet William Cowper.
- The English writer Henry Green publishes his novel *Living*.
- The English writer Ivy Compton-Burnett publishes her novel *Brothers and Sisters*.
- The English writer John Cowper Powys publishes his novel *Wolf Solent*.
- The English writer J. B. Priestley publishes his novel *The Good Companions*.
- The English writer Robert Bridges publishes his long poem *The Testament of Beauty*.
- The English writer Robert Graves publishes *Goodbye to All That*, his memoirs of World War I.
- The English writer Richard Hughes publishes his novel *A High Wind in Jamaica*, which is published in the United States as *The Innocent Voyage*.
- The English writer Virginia Woolf publishes *A Room of One's Own*, a collection of essays.
- The first issue of the surrealist review *Documents* is published in France, edited by the French writer Georges Bataille.
- The French writer Antoine Marie Roger de St.-Exupéry publishes his novel *Courrier-Sud/Southern Mail*.
- The French writer, filmmaker, and artist Jean Cocteau publishes his novel *Les Enfants terribles/The Incorrigible Children*.
- The German writer Alfred Döblin publishes his novel *Berlin Alexanderplatz*.

- The German writer Erich Remarque publishes his novel *Im Westen nichts Neues/All Quiet on the Western Front*.
- The Italian writer Alberto Moravia publishes his novel *Gli indifferenti/The Time of Indifference*.
- The Japanese writer Junichiro Tanizaki publishes his novel *Tade kuu mushi/Some Prefer Nettles*.
- The Pulitzer Prize for Biography is awarded to Burton J. Hendrick for *The Training of an American: The Earlier Life and Letters of Walter Hines Page*, the Prize for Fiction is awarded to Julia M. Peterkin for *Scarlet Sister Mary*, and the Prize for Poetry is awarded to Stephen Vincent Benét for *John Brown's Body*.
- The Spanish writer Federico García Lorca writes his poems *Poeta en Nueva York/Poet in New York*, which are published posthumously in 1940.
- The U.S. humorist S. J. Perelman publishes *Dawn Ginsbergh's Revenge*, a collection of sketches and cartoons.
- The U.S. humorists James Thurber and E. B. White publish *Is Sex Necessary?*
- The U.S. writer and critic Edmund Wilson publishes his novel *I Thought of Daisy*.
- The U.S. writer Conrad Aiken publishes *Selected Poems* and his poetry collection *Prelude*.
- The U.S. writer Dashiell Hammett publishes *Red Harvest*, his first novel, first serialized in *Black Mask* magazine.
- The U.S. writer Edith Wharton publishes her novel *Hudson River Bracketed*.
- The U.S. writer Ernest Hemingway publishes his novel *A Farewell to Arms*.
- The U.S. writer H. D. publishes her poetry collection *Red Roses for Bronze*.
- The U.S. writer Sinclair Lewis publishes his novel *Dodsworth*.
- The U.S. writer Thomas Wolfe publishes his novel *Look Homeward, Angel*.
- The U.S. writer Vachel Lindsay publishes his poetry collection *Every Soul is a Circus*.
- The U.S. writer William Faulkner publishes his novels *Sartoris* and *The Sound and the Fury*.

Music

- In the United States, the pianist "Fats" Waller emerges as a leading jazz performer and composer.
- Milton Ager, American composer of popular music, and Jack Yellen write the song "Happy Days Are Here Again."
- The English composer Arnold Bax completes his Symphony No. 3.
- The English composer Eric Coates completes his orchestral suite *From Meadow to Mayfair*.
- The operetta *Das Land des Lächelns/The Land of Smiles* by the Austrian composer Franz Lehár is first performed, in Berlin, Germany.
- U.S. composer Hoagy Carmichael and U.S. lyricist Mitchell Parish write the song "Stardust."

Theater and Dance

- The all-black revue *Hot Chocolate* is first staged, at Connie's Inn, Harlem, New York, New York. The show includes "Ain't Misbehavin" and "What Did I Do To Be So Black and Blue?" by "Fats" Waller.
- The ballet *La Valse/The Waltz* by the French composer Maurice Ravel, with choreography by the Russian dancer Vaslav Nijinsky, is first performed, in Monte Carlo, Monaco. Ravel based the score on an orchestral work of 1920.
- The play *Amphitryon 38*, by the French writer Jean Giraudoux is first performed, in Paris, France.
- The play *Journey's End*, by the English dramatist R. C. Sherriff, is first performed, at the Savoy Theatre in London, England. It becomes a classic depiction of World War I.
- The play *Street Scene*, by the U.S. dramatist Elmer Rice, is first performed, in New York, New York.
- The play *The Apple Cart*, by the Irish writer George Bernard Shaw, is first performed, in Warsaw, Poland.
- The play *The Silver Tassle*, by the Irish writer Sean O'Casey, is first performed, in London, England.
- The Pulitzer Prize for Drama is awarded to Elmer Rice for *Street Scene*.

NOVEMBER

27 The musical *Fifty Million Frenchmen*, with lyrics and music by Cole Porter, is first performed, at the Lyric Theater, New York, New York. It is his first major success.

Thought and Scholarship

- German philosopher Martin Heidegger publishes *Was ist Metaphysik?/What is Metaphysics?*
- Robert and Helen Lynd publish *Middletown: A Study in Contemporary American Culture*, a study of the social behavior in the putative middle-American town of Muncie, Indiana.
- Spanish philosopher José Ortega y Gasset publishes *La rebelión de las masas/The Revolt of the Masses*.
- The Nobel Prize for Literature is awarded to the German novelist Thomas Mann.
- The Pulitzer Prize for History is awarded to Fred Albert Shannon for *The Organization and Administration of the Union Army, 1861–1865*.
- The Spanish writer Salvador de Madariaga publishes *Ingleses, franceses, españoles/Englishmen, Frenchmen and Spaniards*, a study of national types.
- U.S. historian Ulrich Bonnell Phillips publishes *Life and Labor in the Old South*.

SOCIETY

Everyday Life

- Dorothy H. W. Eustis of Nashville, Tennessee, establishes the first class to train guide dogs for the blind, based on the German use of trained dogs to help war veterans.

- Membership in labor unions in the United States declines to 3,442,600, down from 5,000,000 in 1921.
- Unemployment in Britain reaches 12.2% of the work force, with particular concentrations in areas dominated by the stagnant traditional industries of coal, textiles, shipbuilding, and iron and steel manufacturing.

APRIL

15 Police in New York, New York, raid the Birth Control Clinical Research Center, founded by Margaret Sanger, and arrest several doctors and nurses for providing birth control information and devices, which is illegal. The action is apparently undertaken at the urging of local Daughters of the American Revolution. A judge later throws the case out of court in May, saying the raid limited the doctors' right to practice medicine.

Media and Communication

- *The Listener*, a magazine reprinting talks from BBC radio programs, is launched in Britain.
- NBC begins operating the first public television broadcasting station in the United States; 60 lines are scanned at 20 frames per second.

April 1929–35 Experimental television broadcasting begins in England.

SEPTEMBER

- The periodical *Business Week* is published in New York, New York.

Religion

JULY

25 Pope Pius XI, no longer a "a voluntary prisoner" following the Lateran Treaty (of February 11),

BIRTHS & DEATHS

- Babrak Karmal, prime minister and then president of Afghanistan 1979–86, who was installed as the new head of state with Soviet support, born in Kabul, Afghanistan (–1996).

JANUARY

13 Wyatt Earp, U.S. law officer and gunslinger, dies in Los Angeles, California (80).

15 Martin Luther King, Jr., U.S. Baptist minister and civil-rights leader, born in Atlanta, Georgia (–1968).

FEBRUARY

15 Graham Hill, English race-car driver, winner of the Grand Prix World Championship in 1962 and 1968, born in London, England (–1975).

MARCH

20 Ferdinand Foch, marshal of France and commander of the Allied forces at the end of World War I, dies in Paris, France (77).

23 Roger Bannister, English athlete and the first person to a run a mile in under four minute, born in Harrow, Middlesex, England.

APRIL

4 Carl Friedrich Benz, German engineer who built the first practical car, dies in Mannheim, Germany (84).

6 André Previn, German-born U.S. pianist, composer, and conductor, born in Berlin, Germany.

MAY

2 Edouard Balladur, prime minister of France 1993–95, born in Izmir, Turkey.

4 Audrey Hepburn (born Edda van Heemstra Hepburn-Ruston), U.S. motion picture actress, born in Brussels, Belgium (–1993).

21 Archibald Philip Primrose, Lord Rosebery, British prime minister 1894–95, a Liberal, dies in Epsom, Surrey, England (82).

JUNE

10 Edward O. Wilson, U.S. biologist who pioneered the field of sociobiology, born in Birmingham, Alabama.

12 Anne Frank, German Jew whose diary written while hiding from the Nazis has been translated into over 30 languages, born in Frankfurt am Main, Germany (–1945).

18 Jürgen Habermas, German philosopher, born in Düsseldorf, Germany.

JULY

14 Baldwin Spencer, English anthropologist who worked with the Australian aborigines, dies on an expedition in Tierra del Fuego, Argentina (69).

15 Hugo von Hofmannsthal, Austrian poet and dramatist, dies in Vienna, Austria (55).

28 Jacqueline Bouvier Kennedy Onassis, wife of President John F. Kennedy, born in East Hampton, New York (–1994).

AUGUST

3 Thorstein Veblen, U.S. economist and social scientist, dies near Menlo Park, California (71).

19 Sergey Diaghilev, Russian arts promoter who did much to revive ballet in Europe, dies in Venice, Italy (57).

24 Yassir Arafat, Palestinian nationalist politician and president of the Palestine Liberation Organization (PLO) from 1969, born in Jerusalem, in the British mandate of Palestine.

SEPTEMBER

10 Arnold Palmer, U.S. golfer, born in Youngstown, Pennsylvania.

15 Murray Gell-Mann, U.S. physicist who presented the first classification scheme for subatomic particles, born in New York, New York.

17 Stirling Moss, English automobile racing driver, born in London, England.

OCTOBER

3 Gustav Stresemann, chancellor of Germany 1923, and foreign minister 1923, 1924–29, dies in Berlin, Germany (51).

22 Lev Yashin, Soviet soccer player who was goalkeeper for the USSR throughout the 1950s and 1960s, born in the USSR (–1990).

NOVEMBER

12 Grace Patricia Kelly, U.S. film actress and wife of Prince Rainier III of Monaco, born in Philadelphia, Pennsylvania (–1982).

24 Georges Clemenceau, French journalist and prime minister 1917–20 who helped draft the Treaty of Versailles (1919), dies in Paris, France (88).

DECEMBER

9 Bob Hawke, Australian Labor prime minister 1983–91, born in Bordertown, South Australia.

10 Franz Rosenzweig, German Jewish Existentialist theologian, dies in Frankfurt am Main, Germany (42).

13 Christopher Plummer, Canadian actor, born in Toronto, Ontario, Canada.

28 Terry Sawchuck, Canadian-U.S. ice hockey goalkeeper, born in Winnipeg, Manitoba, Canada (–1970).

leaves the Vatican, the first pope to do so since 1870.

Sports

- The Green Bay Packers, led by U.S. coach Curly Lambeau, win the National Football League in the United States without losing a game, the first of three consecutive titles.

MARCH

28–29 The Boston Bruins defeat the New York Rangers by two games to none to win the National Hockey League Stanley Cup for the first time.

OCTOBER

8–14 The Philadelphia Athletics defeat the Chicago Cubs by four games to one to win the World Series.

NOVEMBER

3 The Providence Steam Rollers from Rhode Island host the Chicago Cardinals in the first floodlit National Football League game.

1930

POLITICS, GOVERNMENT, AND ECONOMICS

Business and Economics

- Boeing Transport merges with National Air Transport to form United Airlines.
- Connecticut entrepreneur Jacob Schick establishes Schick Dry Shaver, Inc. in Stamford, Connecticut.
- Michigan industrialist Errett Cord founds American Airlines under the name American Airways. It reorganizes and integrates its routes in 1934.
- The German firm I. G. Faberindustrie begins the production of polystyrene.
- The Pan-Am airline merges with a smaller company and becomes the largest airline company in the United States.
- The U.S. Common Stock Prices Index declines to 149.8, against the September 1929 figure of 190.3; in 1932, at the height of the Depression, the Index will reach a low of 48.6, against a 1926 base of 100.

APRIL

30 A national insurance program is set up in France incorporating payments from workers, employers, and the state.

MAY

2 The Dunning tariff is introduced in Canada, imposing high duties but giving Britain preferential treatment.

DECEMBER

- The Bank of the United States closes its doors in New York, New York. Sixty local branches serving an estimated 40,000 depositors, also close.

Human Rights

- *c.* 1930 It becomes socially acceptable for women to wear trousers when playing golf or riding a horse.
- Chen Li, who became China's first female major general and led communist troops against nationalist forces, survives the Long March to Shensi.
- The first school for midwives is established in Egypt. Its graduates are ostracized until authorities assure society that the midwives have legitimate medical training.
- Women in French Indochina form the Anticolonialist Women's Association to fight for independence and reunification.

MAY

19 White women are enfranchised in South Africa.

Politics and Government

- Following the replacement of Arabic script by the Latin alphabet, the Turkish government orders the post office to return all mail not bearing the new spellings of place-names.
- France begins construction of the Maginot Line defense system along the French-German border.

JANUARY

1 Following the victory of the Wafd nationalist party in the general election, the party leader Nahas Pasha forms a Wafd ministry in Egypt.

1 The Indian National Congress decides to demand complete independence for India from Britain, rather than accept dominion status within the British Empire.

5 The Soviet leader Joseph Stalin's farm collectivization program progresses in the USSR.

20 Bulgarian reparations payable to the World War I Allies are greatly reduced by an agreement made in The Hague, the Netherlands.

21 A conference on naval disarmament opens in London, England, with delegates from Britain, the United States, France, Italy, and Japan.

23 Wilhelm Frick is appointed minister for the interior and education in Thuringia, Germany, the first Nazi Party member to become a minister in a state government.

28–30 The Spanish dictator Primo de Rivera resigns following the army's withdrawal of its support, and the Liberal general Dámaso Berenguer forms a ministry (January 30) pledged to a restoration of democracy.

FEBRUARY

• Chicago police raid an extensive bootlegging ring, arresting 158 people.

• President Herbert Hoover appoints former U.S. secretary of state Charles Evans Hughes chief justice of the U.S. Supreme Court.

2 The U.S. president Herbert Hoover of the United States sends a commission to Haiti to prepare for the end of the U.S. occupation; it persuades President Borno to resign.

6 A treaty of friendship is signed between Austria and Italy.

18–24 A tariff conference, organized by the League of Nations, takes place in Geneva, Switzerland, to little effect.

MARCH

• A joint U.S.-League of Nations report accuses Liberia of perpetuating the institution of slavery.

• Oil producer Edward L. Doheny is acquitted in a federal court of bribing former interior secretary Albert B. Fall in the Teapot Dome oil leasing scandal.

12 A customs agreement is made between China and Japan, whereby Japan recognizes China's autonomy in setting tariffs (ratified in May).

12–April 6 The Indian nationalist leader Mahatma Gandhi opens a civil disobedience campaign in India with his "Salt March" (a march from Ahmedabad, Gujarat, to Dandi on the coast where, on April 6, Gandhi seizes salt to protest at the levying of salt tax on poor people).

27 The German government under Hermann Müller resigns because the Social Democrats oppose cuts in unemployment benefit planned as a money-saving measure.

28 The city of Constantinople, Turkey, is renamed Istanbul. Adrianople is renamed Edirne, and Smyrna becomes Izmir.

30 Heinrich Brüning, leader of the Center Party, forms a coalition of the right in Germany, replacing the Social Democrats, but without a majority in the Reichstag (parliament).

31 A revolt begins in Ethiopia, led by the empress Zauditu's brother Ras Gugsa.

APRIL

3 Ras Tafari, regent of Ethiopia, becomes emperor on the death of Empress Zauditu; he assumes the name Haile Selassie ("Might of the Trinity").

22 The United States, Britain, France, Italy, and Japan end the London Conference (held since January 21), signing a treaty on naval disarmament, regulating submarine warfare and limiting aircraft carriers.

30 Italy announces a naval program to build 29 new vessels.

MAY

• The U.S. Senate confirms President Herbert Hoover's nomination of jurist Owen J. Roberts to the U.S. Supreme Court but rejects his nomination of judge John R. Parker.

• The U.S. Supreme Court rules that the purchase of alcohol does not violate prohibition.

5 A liberal opposition party is founded in Turkey by Ali Fethi Bey, favoring greater ties with the West.

5 The Indian nationalist leader Mahatma Gandhi is arrested following disorder in India.

8 Talks in London, England, between Britain and Egypt regarding the government of the Sudan break down without agreement.

11 A conference of Chinese and Soviet representatives opens in Moscow, USSR, to deal with outstanding problems between the two countries.

22 France makes Syria a republic with its own constitution.

24 The Italian leader Benito Mussolini, aiming to extend Italian territory and influence, calls for a revision of the 1919 Treaty of Versailles.

28 George Forbes becomes prime minister of the United Party ministry in New Zealand, following the resignation of Joseph Ward on May 15 due to ill health.

JUNE

8 Crown Prince Carol, strongly supported by the army and the peasantry, is elected king of Romania as Carol II by the national assembly, which sets aside his son Michael, king since 1927.

17 The U.S. president Herbert Hoover signs the Smoot–Hawley Tariff Act, raising duties on some 890 agricultural and manufactured items.

21 Following the resignation of the Wafd government in Egypt (after King Fuad I blocked the government's attempt to limit his powers), Ismail Sidky Pasha is appointed prime minister.

30 A 20-year treaty is signed between Britain and Iraq, establishing close cooperation between them before Iraq becomes independent (1932).

30 The last Allied troops leave the Rhineland, Germany, in accordance with the agreement made at the Reparations Conference in The Hague, the Netherlands, in 1929.

JULY

• The U.S. president Herbert Hoover signs the Veterans Administration Act, creating the Veterans Administration.

• The U.S. Senate ratifies the London Naval Treaty, by which the United States, Britain, and Japan extend a moratorium on the construction of capital ships.

7 An uprising of Kurds demanding autonomy takes place on the Persian-Turkish frontier.

16 The German president Paul von Hindenburg authorizes the German budget by decree under Article 48 of the constitution, following the refusal of the Reichstag (parliament) to pass the budget because of the cuts it makes in government expenditure.

21 Maxim Litvinov becomes the Soviet foreign minister.

28 The Conservatives win the Canadian general election with 137 seats; Labor wins 91 and other parties win 17.

30 The (neofascist) National Union Party is founded in Portugal.

AUGUST

6   Following the general election victory of the Conservatives in July, the Liberal leader William Mackenzie King resigns as prime minister of Canada; he is succeeded by the Conservative leader Richard B. Bennett.

12   Persian and Turkish troops begin an offensive action against Kurdish rebels.

17   The Pact of San Sebastián is made between Spanish republicans and supporters of Catalan autonomy: autonomy is to be granted to Catalonia if a Spanish republic is created.

25   Following the outbreak of center-left mass protests in Poland, Józef Piłsudski forms a ministry (parliament is dissolved on August 30; 70 opposition members are arrested and imprisoned in September).

25–27   Following a revolt by an army garrison, a military junta takes power in Peru and forces Augusto Leguía to resign the presidency. Colonel Luis Sánchez Cerro, leader of the original revolt, becomes president on August 27 after marching on the capital Lima.

SEPTEMBER

• In the face of mounting unemployment, the U.S. State Department orders a complete halt to immigration.

6   Demonstrations by crowds in Buenos Aires and a revolt by the army force President Hipólito Irigoyen of Argentina to resign; General José Uriburu is appointed president.

8–22   Special sessions of the Canadian parliament enact emergency laws to deal with the depression caused by the 1929 Wall Street stock market crash.

14   In the German elections the Social Democrats win 143 seats and the communists 77, but the National Socialists (Nazis), denouncing the 1919 Treaty of Versailles, gain 107 seats (the Center Party has 68 seats, the National People's Party 41, and others 137).

15   The removal of press censorship in Spain brings independent demands for the establishment of a republic.

OCTOBER

1   Britain restores the naval base of Weihaiwei to China (it was leased by Britain in 1898).

1–November 14   At an Imperial Conference in London, England, Britain rejects a Canadian proposal for a preferential tariff to help exports of wheat produced by the Dominions (Australia, New Zealand, South Africa, and Canada).

4   Following a Liberal revolt in Brazil, martial law is declared in three provinces by President Luis Sánchez Cerro to prevent the accession of the president-elect Dr. Júlio Prestes.

5–12   A conference of Balkan powers is held in Athens, Greece; this is the origin of the Balkan Entente (leading to the pact of February 1934).

10   A national assembly is elected in Haiti, which elects Sténio Joseph Vincent as president.

14   An attempted fascist coup is resisted in Finland.

20   The White Paper on Palestine prepared by the secretary for the colonies Sidney Webb, Lord Passfield, is published in Britain, stressing the need to tackle the problem of shortage of land for Arab farmers. The proposed policy threatens the expansion of the Jewish homeland in Palestine and is denounced by Zionists.

22   King Fuad I of Egypt announces changes to the constitution: the king is to nominate the majority of senate members and the chamber is to be elected by an indirect system.

23   Military leaders force President Luis Sánchez Cerro of Brazil to resign.

30   A treaty between Turkey and Greece is signed in Ankara, Turkey, recognizes the status quo following a settlement of the compensation claims of the populations exchanged after the Greek–Turkish War.

NOVEMBER

• In U.S. Congressional elections, Republicans retain a slim majority in the Senate (48–47), but surrender leadership of the House (220–214).

• The U.S. diplomat Frank B. Kellogg wins the Nobel Peace Prize for his work in brokering the Kellogg-Briand Peace Pact of 1928.

2   Haile Selassie is formally crowned as emperor of Ethiopia.

4   Dr. Getúlio Vargas is installed as temporary president of Brazil.

11   Repressive legislation is passed in Finland against communism.

12–January 19, 1931   A round-table conference on granting India dominion status is held in London, England (without representatives of the Indian Congress Party, who demand complete independence).

14   A Japanese nationalist attempts to assassinate Prime Minister Hamaguchi of Japan for his support of the London Naval Treaty of April 22.

16   In a general election in Poland, the nonparty bloc of government supporters wins 44.7% of the votes.

DECEMBER

• U.S. Congress passes legislation allocating $116 million for public works projects designed to help relieve unemployment spawned by the Depression.

3   Otto Ender, Christian Socialist, forms a ministry in Austria after the defeat of extremist parties in elections preceded by political violence.

4   Józef Piłsudski resigns as prime minister of Poland but remains minister of defense.

9   The Preparatory Commission on Disarmament adopts a draft convention for discussions at the League of Nations Conference in February 1932, but Germany and the USSR reject it.

12   The last Allied troops leave the industrial district of the Saar, a part of Germany held by the League of Nations since World War I.

15   An abortive military uprising against the Spanish government by the garrison at Jaca in northeastern Spain is put down and martial law is imposed.

23   A dervish (religious mendicant) uprising begins in Turkey.

30   The Scandinavian states and the Netherlands, Belgium, and Luxembourg sign the Oslo agreements promising not to raise tariffs without prior consultation.

SCIENCE, TECHNOLOGY, AND MEDICINE

Ecology

- Dutch elm disease is introduced into the United States on elm burl logs used in the furniture industry. The fungus kills over 13 million trees by 1970.
- Great Smokey Mountains National Park, North Carolina and Tennessee, is established. It contains parts of the Appalachian mountains, the oldest in the world.
- U.S. Congress creates Carlsbad Caverns National Park in southern New Mexico. It contains the world's largest system of caves.

October

21 An explosion in a coal mine at Aachen, Germany, kills 262 people.
25 An explosion in a Saar coal mine, Germany, kills about 100 people.

December

- Hundreds of people fall ill and 60 die during a four-day fog in the industrialized Meuse Valley in Belgium. It is the first recorded air pollution disaster.

Exploration

- U.S. anthropologist Margaret Mead publishes *Growing Up in New Guinea*.
- December 1930–31 English diplomat Bertram Thomas, minister to the sultan of Muscat, crosses the "Empty Quarter" of the Arabian desert.

Health and Medicine

- Austrian-born U.S. immunologist Karl Landsteiner receives the Nobel Prize for Physiology or Medicine for his discovery of the major blood groups.
- U.S. physician Karl Menninger publishes *The Human Mind*, in which he argues that psychiatry is a science and that mentally ill people differ from normal people only in degree.

Science

- Dutch chemist Peter Debye investigates the structure of molecules with X-rays, providing information about the arrangement of atoms in molecules and the distances between atoms.
- English archeologist Charles Leonard Woolley publishes *The Sumerians*.
- English geneticist Ronald Fisher publishes *The Genetical Theory of Natural Selection* in which he synthesizes Mendelian genetics and Darwinian evolution.
- German biochemist Hans Fischer of Germany receives the Nobel Prize for Chemistry for his analysis and synthesis of hemin and for his chlorophyll research.
- Indian physicist Chandrasekhara Venkata Raman receives the Nobel Prize for Physics for his work on the scattering of light and for the Raman effect.

- Swedish biochemist Arne Tiselius invents electrophoresis, a method of separating proteins in suspension based on their electrical charge.
- Swiss biochemist Paul Karrer formulates the structure of betacarotene, the precursor to vitamin A.
- Swiss-born U.S. astronomer Robert Trumpler discovers the existence of intergalactic material that reduces the apparent brightness of distant stars.
- The Woods Hole Oceanographic Institution is established in Massachusetts.
- U.S. biochemist Edward Doisy crystallizes the hormone estriol, the first estrogen hormone to be crystallized.
- U.S. biochemist John Northrop crystallizes pepsin and trypsin, demonstrating that they are proteins.

February

18 U.S. astronomer Clyde Tombaugh, at the Lowell Observatory, Arizona, discovers the ninth planet, Pluto.

Technology

- c. 1930 Explosion seismology—the study of seismic waves caused by explosions—is used by the oil industry to explore for oil in the United States.
- A researcher at the U.S. Naval Research Laboratory, using an experimental transmitter and receiver, notices that the received signal increases when a plane passes between them. It helps lead to the development of radar.
- British chemist William Chalmers invents acrylic plastic or Plexiglas™.
- German chemist J. W. Reppe makes artificial fabrics from an acetylene base.
- German optician Bernhard Schmidt develops the Schmidt telescope, which is free from spherical aberration.
- The Chrysler Building in New York, New York, designed by the U.S. architect William Van Alen, is completed. The decoration of its upper floors makes it one of the most conspicuous examples of art deco style. With 77 stories and a height of 319.4 m/1,048 ft it is, for a brief period, the tallest building in the world.
- U.S. electrical engineer Vannevar Bush builds the differential analyzer. The first analog computer, it is used to solve differential equations. It is the forerunner of modern computers.
- U.S. researchers at the Dunlop Rubber Corporation, E. A. Murphy and W. H. Chapman, invent foam rubber.
- February 1930–36 The Boulder Dam (renamed Hoover Dam in 1947) on the Colorado River (on the border of Arizona and Nevada) is constructed to provide hydroelectricity. The dam is 221 m/726 ft high and 379 m/1,244 ft wide, and the lake behind the dam, Lake Mead, is 185 km/115 mi long, making it the largest artificial lake in the United States.
- February 1930–41 U.S. inventor Robert H. Goddard conducts extensive tests of liquid-propellant rockets at his New Mexico ranch.

March

- The former president Calvin Coolidge presides at the dedication of the Coolidge Dam, named for him, in Arizona.

Transportation

- English inventor Frank Whittle patents a turbo-jet engine. It is later used on the first jet airplane.
- French civil engineer Eugène Freyssinet completes the Plougastel Bridge at Brest, France. It is the largest reinforced-concrete bridge built to date, with three 187 m/612 ft spans.
- The Turkestan–Siberia railroad in the USSR is completed.

MAY

May 1930–July   British aviator Charles Kingsford-Smith, piloting the *Southern Cross*, makes the first solo around-the-world flight.

JUNE

11   The first bathysphere, a spherical steel craft for undersea exploration, built by U.S. zoologist William Beebe and U.S. engineer Otis Baron, descends to 435 m/1,428 ft.

JULY

4   U.S. Navy pilot Apollo Soucek sets a world altitude record of 13,157 m/43,166 ft.
16   Trans World Airlines (TWA) is founded through the amalgamation of Western Air Express and Transcontinental Air Transport.

SEPTEMBER

3   U.S. inventor Thomas Edison installs an experimental electric passenger train on the Lakawanna Railroad in New Jersey.

ARTS AND IDEAS

Architecture

- The Daily News Building in New York, New York, designed by the U.S. architect Raymond Mathewson Hood, is completed.

Arts

c. 1930   The U.S. artist Patrick Henry Bruce paints *Still Life*.
- The English photographer Cecil Beaton publishes *Book of Beauty*, photographs of English high society.
- The French artist Henri Matisse sculpts *The Back IV*.
- The Hungarian artist László Moholy-Nagy sculpts *Light-Space Modulator*.
- The Mexican artist Diego Rivera paints the mural *The Conquest of Mexico* in the Palacio de Cortès in Cuernavaca, Mexico.
- The Russian artist Marc Chagall paints *Lovers in the Lilacs*.
- The Soviet artist Isaak Brodsky paints *Lenin at the Smolny Institute*, which becomes one of the best-known images of Lenin. The work is a celebrated example of Soviet Socialist realism.
- The Spanish artist Joan Miró paints *Painting*.
- The Spanish artist Pablo Picasso paints *Seated Bather*.

- The Swiss artist Alberto Giacometti sculpts *Suspended Ball*.
- The Swiss artist Paul Klee paints *Prophet*.
- The U.S. artist Charles Sheeler paints *American Landscape*.
- The U.S. artist Edward Hopper paints *Early Sunday Morning*.
- The U.S. artist Grant Wood paints *American Gothic*, which becomes an icon of U.S. life, and *Stone City, Iowa*.
- The U.S.-born English artist Jacob Epstein completes his carving *Genesis*, which is widely condemned as obscene.

Film

- A wider movie screen, the Vitascope screen, is introduced by producers and theaters.
- Movie-going in the United States peaks in this year, with the advent of sound. However, movie production costs have doubled.
- The movie *All Quiet on the Western Front*, directed by Russian-born filmmaker Lewis Milestone, is released in the United States. Based on the novel by Erich Maria Remarque, it stars Lew Ayres, Louis Wolheim, Slim Summerville, John Wray, Raymond Griffith, Russell Gleason, and Ben Alexander.
- The 1929–30 Academy Awards take place. Best Actor: George Arliss, for *Disraeli*; Best Actress: Norma Shearer, for *The Divorcee*; Best Picture: *All Quiet on the Western Front*, directed by Lewis Milestone; Best Director: Lewis Milestone, for *All Quiet on the Western Front*.
- The Austrian National Library sets up a movie archive.
- The documentary *A propos de Nice/About Nice*, directed by Jean Vigo, is released in France.
- The movie *Anna Christie*, directed by Clarence Brown, is released in the United States, starring Charles Bickford and Greta Garbo, in her first speaking role.
- The movie *Earth*, directed by Alexander Dovzhenko, is released in the USSR, starring Semyon Svanshenko, Stephen Shkurat, and Mikola Nademsky.
- The movie *Hell's Angels*, directed by Howard Hughes, is released in the United States, starring Ben Lyon and James Hall.
- The movie *Journey's End*, directed by James Whale, is released in Britain, starring Colin Clive, Ian MacLaren, and David Manners.
- The movie *L'Age D'Or/The Golden Age*, directed by Luis Buñuel, is released in Spain, starring Gaston Modot, Lya Lys, and Max Ernst.
- The movie *La Fin du Monde/The End of the World*, directed by Abel Gance, is released in France. He also stars in it, along with Colete Darfeuil, Sylvia Grenade, and Victor Francen.
- The movie *Morocco*, directed by Austrian filmmaker Josef von Sternberg, is released in the United States, starring Marlene Dietrich, Gary Cooper, and Adolphe Menjou. It starts a fashion for trousers as everyday wear for women. His movie *The Blue Angel* is also released in the United States, starring Marlene Dietrich and Emil Jannings.
- The movie *Murder*, directed by Alfred Hitchcock, is released in Britain, starring Herbert Marshall and Norah Baring.

- The movie *Sous les Toits de Paris/Under the Roofs of Paris*, directed by René Clair, is released in France, starring Albet Préjean, Pola Illery, Gaston Modot, and Edmond Gréville.
- The movie *The Big House*, directed by George Hill, is released in the United States, starring Chester Morris, Wallace Beery, Robert Montgomery, and Lewis Stone.
- The movie *The Big Trail*, directed by Raoul Walsh, is released in the United States, starring John Wayne, Marguerite Churchill, and El Brendel.
- The movie *The Dawn Patrol*, directed by Howard Hawks, is released in the United States, starring Richard Barthelmess and Douglas Fairbanks, Jr.
- The movie *The Love Parade*, directed by German filmmaker Ernst Lubitsch, is released in the United States, starring Maurice Chevalier and Jeanette MacDonald.
- The movie musical *Whoopee!*, directed by Thornton Freeland, is released in the United States, starring Eddie Cantor.
- The Guomindang in China develops rules for movie censorship.
- The Motion Pictures Producers and Distributors of America, better known under president Will Hays as the Hays Office, adopts the Motion Picture Production Code, a self-regulatory code to give guidance on content issues in movies, especially sex and religion.

Literature and Language

- John Masefield becomes poet laureate in England, a position he holds until 1967.
- Laura Elizabeth Ingalls Wilder publishes *Little House on the Prairie*.
- The Austrian writer Robert Musil publishes the first part of his novel *Der Mann ohne Eigenschaften/The Man Without Qualities*. The final part appears in 1943.
- The English artist and writer Percy Wyndham Lewis publishes his satirical novel *The Apes of God*.
- The English writer Agatha Christie publishes her novel *Murder at the Vicarage*, which introduces her amateur detective Miss Jane Marple.
- The English writer and literary critic William Empson publishes his critical work *Seven Types of Ambiguity*.
- The English writer Evelyn Waugh publishes his novel *Vile Bodies*.
- The English writer Somerset Maugham publishes his novel *Cakes and Ale*.
- The English-born U.S. writer W. H. Auden publishes *Poems*.
- The German writer Hermann Hesse publishes his novel *Narziss und Goldmund/Narcissus and Goldmund*.
- The Italian writer Salvatore Quasimodo publishes his poetry collection *Acque e terre/Water and Land*.
- The Norwegian writer Sigrid Undset publishes her novel *Den braendende busk/The Burning Bush*.
- The Portuguese writer José Maria Ferreira de Castro publishes his novel *A selva/The Jungle*.
- The Pulitzer Prize for Biography is awarded to Marquis James for *The Raven: A Biography of Sam Houston*, the Prize for Fiction is awarded to Oliver La Farge for *Laughing Boy*, and the Prize for Poetry is awarded to Conrad Aiken for *Selected Poems*.

- The Russian revolutionary leader Leon Trotsky publishes *Moia zizhn: opyt avtobiografii/Autobiography*.
- The U.S. writer Carl Van Vechten publishes his collection of short stories *Feathers*.
- The U.S. writer Conrad Aiken publishes his poetry collection *Selected Poems*.
- The U.S. writer Dashiell Hammett publishes his novel *The Maltese Falcon*, a classic of U.S. hard-boiled detective fiction.
- The U.S. writer Hart Crane publishes his epic poem *The Bridge*.
- The U.S. writer John Dos Passos publishes his novel *42nd Parallel*.
- The U.S. writer Katherine Anne Porter publishes her short-story collection *Flowering Judas*.
- The U.S. writer Langston Hughes publishes his novel *Not Without Laughter*.
- The U.S. writer Robert Frost publishes *Collected Poems*.
- The U.S. writer Thornton Wilder publishes his novel *The Woman of Andros*.
- The U.S. writer William Faulkner publishes his novel *As I Lay Dying*.
- The U.S.-born English writer T. S. Eliot publishes his poem sequence *Ash Wednesday*.
- The Welsh writer E. M. Delafield publishes *Diary of a Provincial Lady*.
- The West Indian writer Jean Rhys publishes her novel *After Leaving Mr Mackenzie*.
- U.S. writer James Weldon Johnson publishes *Black Manhattan*, a study of black American life.

September 1930–35 The Hittite hieroglyphic is substantially deciphered. It provides information about the early Indo-European sound system.

Music

- German movie actress Marlene Dietrich records the song "Falling in Love Again," written by English songwriters Sammy Lerner and Friedrich Hollander.
- The English composer Kaikhosru Shapurji Sorabji completes his piano work *Opus clavicembalisticum/Work for the Clavicembalo* which lasts nearly three hours.
- The French composer Jacques Ibert completes his orchestral work *Divertissement*.
- The French composer Albert Roussel completes his Symphony No. 3.
- The French composer Maurice Ravel completes his Piano Concerto for left hand.
- The opera *Aufstieg und Fall der Stadt Mahagonny/The Rise and Fall of the City of Mahagonny* by the German composer Kurt Weill and the German writer Bertolt Brecht is first performed, in Leipzig, Germany.
- The opera *Christophe Colomb/Christopher Columbus* by the French composer Darius Milhaud is first performed, in Berlin, Germany. The libretto is by the French writer Paul Claudel.
- The opera *Nos/The Nose* by the Russian composer Dmitry Shostakovich is first performed, in Leningrad (now St. Petersburg), USSR.
- The opera *Z mrtvého domu/From the House of the Dead* by the Czech composer Leoš Janáček is first

performed, in Brno, Czechoslovakia. It is based on a novel by the Russian writer Fyodor Dostoyevsky.

- The Russian composer Igor Stravinsky completes his *Symphony of Psalms* for chorus and orchestra.

Theater and Dance

- The ballet *Zolotoy vek/The Age of Gold*, by the Russian composer Dmitry Shostakovich, is first performed, in Leningrad (now St. Petersburg), USSR. The choreography is by the Russian dancer Semyon Kaplan.
- The musical *White Horse Inn*, with music and lyrics by Ralph Benatzky and Robert Stolz, is performed for the first time.
- The play *Banya/The Bathhouse*, by the Russian writer Vladimir Mayakovsky, is first performed, in Leningrad (now St. Petersburg), USSR.
- The play *Camo tu mi vuoi/As You Desire Me*, by the Italian writer Luigi Pirandello, is first performed, in Milan, Italy.
- The play *La zapatera prodigiosa/The Shoemaker's Amazing Wife*, by the Spanish writer Federico García Lorca, is first performed, in Madrid, Spain.
- The play *Private Lives*, by the English writer and performer Noël Coward, is first performed, at the Phoenix Theatre in London, England.
- The play *The Anatomist*, by the Scottish dramatist James Bridie, is first performed, in Edinburgh, Scotland.
- The play *The Barrets of Wimpole Street*, by the Dutch-born English dramatist Rudolph Besier, is first performed, at the Malvern Festival in Great Malvern, England. Based on the relationship between the poets Elizabeth Barrett and Robert Browning, it becomes very popular.
- The play *The Green Pastures*, by the U.S. dramatist Marc Connelly, is first performed, in New York, New York.
- The Pulitzer Prize for Drama is awarded to Marc Connelly for *The Green Pastures*.

OCTOBER

14 The musical *Girl Crazy*, with lyrics by Ira Gershwin and music by George Gershwin, is first performed, at the Alvin Theater, New York, New York.

Thought and Scholarship

- English economist J. M. Keynes publishes his *Treatise on Money*.
- English historian George Gordon Coulton publishes *The Medieval Scene*.
- English political scientist Harold Laski publishes *Liberty and the Modern State*.
- English social historians John Lawrence and Barbara Hammond publish *The Age of the Chartists*.
- German philosopher Moritz Schlick publishes *Fragen der Ethik/Problems of Ethics*.
- German political thinker Alfred Rosenberg publishes *Der Mythus des 20 Jahrhunderts/The Myth of the 20th Century*, one of the most influential expressions of Nazi doctrine.
- Russian revolutionary leader Leon Trotsky publishes *Permanentnaia revoliutsiia/The Permanent Revolution*.

- The literary anthology *I'll Take My Stand: The South and the Agrarian Tradition* is published by "Twelve Southerners," who include the writers John Crowe Ransom, Donald Davidson, and Allen Tate. It sets out the concept of "regionalism."
- The Nobel Prize for Literature is awarded to the U.S. novelist Sinclair Lewis.
- The Pulitzer Prize for History is awarded to Claude H. Van Tyne for *The War of Independence*.
- U.S. jurist Jerome Frank publishes *Law and the Modern Mind*.
- U.S. philosopher and historian Arthur Oncken Lovejoy publishes *The Revolt Against Dualism*.

SOCIETY

Education

- New Jersey philanthropist Louis Bamberger and his sister Mrs. Felix Fuld endow the Institute for Advanced Study in Princeton, New Jersey.
- U.S. historian Harry Elmer Barnes publishes *Education versus Enlightenment*.

Everyday Life

- In the face of widespread unemployment, the International Apple Shippers Union grants apples on credit to an estimated 6,000 unemployed men, who turn up as apple peddlers on New York street corners by November.
- Mussolini's regime outlaws the distribution of birth control information and abortions, but half a million abortions continue to be carried out in Italy every year.
- Pope Pius XI condemns contraception, but allows the use of the rhythm method for birth control.
- The U.S. census lists the U.S. population at 122,775,046. Illiteracy has dropped from 6% to 4.3% since 1920.
- Unemployment in Britain at the end of 1930 nears double the 1928 total; by spring 1931 almost 25% of the British work force is unemployed.
- Unemployment in the United States passes a total of 4 million as the Depression continues to hit industries and markets worldwide.

APRIL

- Fire kills 318 inmates at the Ohio State Penitentiary in Columbus. The jailhouse is nearly 200% over capacity.

Media and Communication

- Media tycoon William Randolph Hearst owns 33 newspapers in the United States, with a total circulation of 11 million.

JANUARY

7 A picture telegraphy service between Britain and Germany is opened.

MARCH

- A television set is installed in 10 Downing Street, London, England, the official home of Prime Minister Ramsay MacDonald.

DECEMBER

29 Radio Luxembourg is authorized to begin broadcasting by the government of Luxembourg.

Religion

AUGUST

- Lutheran synods from Buffalo, New York, Toledo, Ohio, and Iowa merge to form the American Lutheran Church.

Sports

- The Fédération Internationale de Ski (FIS), after years of opposition, adopts the British Alpine skiing pioneer Arnold Lunn's rules for downhill and slalom skiing.
- The U.S. golfer Bobby Jones wins the inaugural James E. Sullivan Memorial Award, given by the Amateur Athletic Union to the amateur athlete who has done most during the year to advance the cause of sportsmanship.

APRIL

19 Clarence DeMar of Melrose, Massachusetts, wins the Boston Marathon for the seventh time, 21 years after his first victory.

BIRTHS & DEATHS

- Károly Grósz, prime minister of Hungary 1987–90, born in Miskolic, Hungary (–1996).

JANUARY

20 Edwin Eugene ("Buzz") Aldrin, U.S. astronaut who was the second person to walk on the moon, born in Montclair, New Jersey.

23 Derek Walcott, St. Lucia poet and playwright, born in Castries, St. Lucia.

30 Gene Hackman, U.S. actor who won Academy Awards in *The French Connection* and *The Unforgiven*, born in San Bernadino, California.

MARCH

2 D(avid) H(erbert) Lawrence, English poet and novelist, author of the controversial *Lady Chatterley's Lover*, dies in Vence, near Antibes, France (45).

6 Alfred von Tirpitz, German admiral who built up the German navy prior to World War I, dies in Ebenhausen, near Munich, Germany (80).

8 William Howard Taft, 27th president of the United States 1909–13, a Republican, dies in Washington, D.C. (72).

16 Primo de Rivera, Spanish general, dictator of Spain 1923–30, dies in Paris, France (60).

19 Arthur James Balfour, British prime minister 1902–05, a Conservative, dies in Woking, Surrey, England (81).

22 Stephen Sondheim, U.S. composer and lyricist of Broadway musicals, born in New York, New York.

APRIL

3 Helmut Kohl, chancellor of Germany 1982–98, born in Ludwigshafen-am-Rhein, Germany.

MAY

13 Fridtjof Nansen, Norwegian explorer, oceanographer, and statesman, dies in Lysaker, near Oslo, Norway (68).

15 Jasper Johns, U.S. pop art artist, born in Augusta, Georgia.

31 Clint Eastwood, U.S. actor, director, and producer, star of many westerns, born in San Francisco, California.

JUNE

9 Ben Abruzzo, U.S. balloonist, the first to cross the Atlantic in a balloon, born in Rockfort, Illinois (–1985).

10 Adolf von Harnack, Estonian-born German theologian and church historian, dies in Berlin, Germany (79).

13 Henry Segrave, U.S.-born British car and motor-boat racer who set three world land speed records, dies on Lake Windermere, Westmorland, England, when his boat crashes at over 160 kph/100 mph (33).

16 Elmer Ambrose Sperry, U.S. inventor who developed the gyroscopic compass and stabilizers now used in most guidance and stabilizing systems, dies in Brooklyn, New York, New York (69).

27 H. Ross Perot, U.S. computer systems billionaire who ran for the U.S. presidency in 1992, born in Texarkana, Texas.

JULY

7 Arthur Conan Doyle, Scottish novelist who created the detective Sherlock Holmes, dies in Crowborough, Sussex, England (71).

15 Jacques Derrida, French deconstructionist philosopher, born in El Biar, Algeria.

AUGUST

1 Pierre Bourdieu, French sociologist who developed a theory of practice, born in Denguin, France.

5 Neil Armstrong, U.S. astronaut and the first person to set foot on the moon (1969), born in Wapakoneta, Ohio.

8 Fred MacMurray, U.S. actor born in Kankakee, Illinois (–1991).

12 George Soros, Hungarian investment banker, born in Budapest, Hungary.

15 Tom Mboya, Kenyan political leader, born near Nairobi, Kenya (–1969).

26 Lon Chaney, U.S. actor known for his grotesque characterizations, dies in Los Angeles, California (47).

SEPTEMBER

7 Baudouin I, King of the Belgians 1951–93, born in Stuyvenberg castle, near Brussels, Belgium (–1993).

23 Ray Charles, U.S. pianist, singer, and composer, born in Albany, Georgia.

OCTOBER

8 Toru Takemitsu, Japanese composer, born in Tokyo, Japan (–1996).

14 Mobutu Sese Seko, President of Zaire 1965–97, born in Lisala, Congo (now Zaire) (–1997).

15 Herbert Henry Dow, U.S. chemist who established the Dow Chemical Company in 1887, dies in Rochester, Minnesota (64).

NOVEMBER

5 Christiaan Eijkman, Dutch physiologist whose discovery that beriberi is caused by a nutritional deficiency led to the discovery of vitamins, dies in Utrecht, the Netherlands (71).

14 Elisabeth Frink, English sculptor known for her rugged, naturalistic bronzes based on human and animal forms, born in Thurlow, Surrey, England (–1993).

DECEMBER

3 Jean-Luc Godard, French film director, born in Paris, France.

MAY

31–September 27 Bobby Jones of the United States wins four national golf championships in one year: the U.S. and British Opens and the U.S. and British Amateur Championships. Following this unique achievement he retires from competitive golf.

JUNE

12 The German boxer Max Schmeling wins the world heavyweight title at the Yankee Stadium, New York, New York, when the U.S. boxer Jack Sharkey is disqualified for a low punch.

13 At Lake Windermere, Westmorland, England, car and motorboat racing driver Henry Segrave sets a water speed record of 158.01 kph/98.76 mph. He is fatally injured shortly after setting the record when his boat hits a floating log.

JULY

5 Bill Tilden of the United States wins his third men's singles title at the Wimbledon lawn tennis championships in London, England, breaking the continuous run of French winners of the event since 1923.

13–30 The first soccer World Cup is held in Uruguay; 11 nations take part in the event, which is won by the host nation, beating Argentina 4–2 in the final in Montevideo before a crowd of 93,000. British teams are unable to participate, having withdrawn from the Fédération Internationale de Football Association (FIFA) in 1928.

SEPTEMBER

13–17 The U.S. yacht *Enterprise*, owned and skippered by Harold Vanderbilt, successfully defends the America's Cup trophy against the British challenger *Shamrock V*, owned by Thomas Lipton, winning the series 4–0. It is Lipton's fifth and final attempt to win the trophy.

1931

POLITICS, GOVERNMENT, AND ECONOMICS

Business and Economics

- Modest first-quarter increases in production and employment convince some economists that the U.S. economy is recovering. However, the European banking collapse in the spring precipitates a global credit crisis, inspiring a new wave of liquidations.
- Some 2,294 U.S. banks (with deposits worth roughly $1.7 billion) close their doors, up from 1,352 banks the year before.

MARCH

31 Swissair is formed.

MAY

11 The bankruptcy of the Creditanstalt, Austria's most influential bank, triggers the collapse of banks throughout central Europe.

JUNE

16 The Bank of England advances money to Austria following the collapse of the Austrian bank Creditanstalt, but France withholds its support.

JULY

13 The bankruptcy of the German Danatbank leads to the closure of all German banks until August 5.

AUGUST

1 France and the United States make a joint loan to Britain as the worldwide economic crisis continues to hit it particularly hard.

19 France grants a loan to Hungary in response to the banking crisis in Central Europe.

19 The Layton–Wiggin report calls for a six-month extension of foreign credit to Germany.

SEPTEMBER

21 Britain abandons the gold standard (the linking of the value of sterling to the Bank of England's gold reserves), signaling its willingness to take economic decisions without regard to international finance.

DECEMBER

8–January 1, 1932 Departing from his *laissez-faire* philosophy, the U.S. president, Herbert Hoover, asks Congress to create the Reconstruction Finance Corporation (RFC). Capitalized in January at $2 billion, the RFC will lend money to banks, railroads, insurance companies, and building and loan associations.

11 Japan abandons the gold standard.

Colonization

- An International Colonial Exhibition is held in Paris, France.

JANUARY

26 The Indian nationalist leader Mahatma Gandhi is released from imprisonment in India for his protest against British government policy so that he can attend the Round Table Conference on Indian constitutional reform in London, England.

MARCH

4 Under the terms of the Delhi pact between the Indian nationalist leader Mahatma Gandhi and the British viceroy of India, Lord Irwin, the civil disobedience campaign organized by the Indian National Congress is suspended. The Congress Party promises to participate in the Round Table Conference on Indian constitutional reform in London, England, and political prisoners are released.

JULY

10 Norway's annexation of East Greenland provokes a protest by Denmark. The matter is referred to the League of Nations.

SEPTEMBER

7–December 1 A second Round Table Conference on India is held in London, England, with the participation of the Indian nationalist leader Mahatma Gandhi, but fails to reach agreement on the representation of religious minorities.

DECEMBER

12 The British Parliament passes the Statute of Westminster, establishing the equality of Britain and its dominions of Canada, Australia, New Zealand, Ireland, and Newfoundland.

Human Rights

- Suffrage is granted to women in Chile, Spain, and Portugal.

Politics and Government

- The Australian politician Joseph Lyons forms the United Australia Party from the former Nationalist Party and Labor dissidents.
- The British Commonwealth of Nations is founded, reflecting the autonomy and equality of status of the Dominions (Australia, New Zealand, South Africa, and Canada) with Britain.
- The Chinese communist leader Mao Zedong establishes the Chinese Soviet Republic (Jianxi Soviet) in southeast China. Many of its social policies will be applied to the entire country after the communist takeover in 1949.
- The Massachusetts state legislature requests repeal of the Prohibition amendment to the U.S. Constitution, under which alcohol is illegal.

JANUARY

12 The Allied military control committee, set up in Germany, Britain, and France to administer German reparations payments after World War I, is dissolved.

27 Center-right senator Pierre Laval becomes prime minister of France.

FEBRUARY

14 General Fernando Berenguer resigns as prime minister of Spain but serves as minister of war under his successor, Admiral Juan Bautista Aznar-Cabañas.

MARCH

15 The Peasant Party (Polskie Stronnictwo Ludowe, PSL) is founded in Poland by Wincenty Witos to represent Poland's many small farmers and agricultural workers.

21 Austria and Germany agree to create a customs union. When France, Italy, and Czechoslovakia protest, the issue is referred to the League of Nations and the International Court of Justice.

26 A friendship treaty is signed between Iraq and Transjordan.

APRIL

9 In the Scottsboro case, nine black American youths are convicted of having raped two white women on a train outside Paint Rock, Alabama, on March 25. Eight of the so-called Scottsboro Boys are sentenced to death; one, the youngest, receives a life sentence. Over the next four years, the U.S. Supreme Court will twice overturn the convictions of the Scottsboro Boys, whose sentences will eventually be commuted to life in prison.

14 Following municipal elections in Spain, Niceto Alcalá Zamora, leader of a revolutionary committee in Madrid, successfully demands the abdication of Alfonso XIII. Alcalá Zamora becomes president of a provisional government.

22 A treaty of friendship is signed between Egypt and Iraq, the first pact between Egypt and another Arab state.

MAY

5 A People's Convention meets in Nanjing, China. On May 12, it adopts a constitution, due to come into effect on June 1.

5 Following the forced abdication of Alfonso XIII, many Spanish churches are burned, the clergy are attacked, and the primate, Cardinal Pedro Segura, is expelled.

8 The Farmers' Party (Bondepartiet), led by Peter Kolstad, forms a government in Norway.

13 Radical senator Paul Doumer is elected president of France.

15 Pope Pius XI issues the encyclical "Quadragesimo anno," condemning attempts to upset the social order.

28 Rebel members of the Nationalist Party (Guomindang) in China establish another government in Canton.

JUNE

15 The USSR and Poland sign a treaty of friendship and commerce.

20 U.S. president Herbert Hoover proposes a moratorium on World War I reparations payments and inter-Allied debts in response to the worldwide economic depression; a London protocol is drawn up to formalize the moratorium.

21 The Christian Socialist leader, Karl Buresch, becomes prime minister in Austria.

24 The USSR and Afghanistan sign a renewed treaty of neutrality and nonaggression.

28 Left-wing parties win a large majority in the Spanish general election.

JULY

9 The German Nazi leader, Adolf Hitler, and Alfred Hugenberg of the German National Peoples' Party agree

Sino-Japanese War (1931–40)

1931

September 18 Japanese troops occupy Mukden (now Shenyang), northeast China, and, joined by reinforcements, begin to expand throughout north Manchuria.

1932

January 7 The U.S. secretary of state, Henry Stimson, sends notes to China and Japan opposing Japanese aggression in Manchuria, China, and stating that the United States will not recognize gains made by armed force.

January 28 Japanese forces capture the port of Shanghai, but are driven out by the Chinese on March 3.

March 9 The Japanese state republic of Manchukuo is proclaimed in Manchuria, with the former Manchu emperor Xuantong (Pui) made "chief executive," then emperor.

May 15 Inukai Tsuyoshi, Prime Minister of Japan, is assassinated by young naval officers following his attempt to halt military activities against China.

October 2 The Lytton Commission, set up by the League of Nations to investigate Japan's 1931 invasion of Manchuria, recognizes Japan's special transport and economic interests in the region and recommends an autonomous state under Chinese sovereignty but Japanese control.

December 9 Japanese forces capture the city of Jehol (Chengde), northeast China, and then continue southward.

1933

May 31 An armistice is signed between China and Japan, under the terms of which Japanese invasion forces in China are to withdraw to the north of the Great Wall.

1937

July 7 A conflict between Chinese and Japanese troops near the Marco Polo Bridge outside the city of Beijing leads to the Japanese invasion of northeast China.

July 28–29 Japanese forces seize the cities of Beijing (July 28) and Tianjin (July 29) in northeast China.

August 8–November 11 Japanese forces launch an amphibious assault on the port of Shanghai, on the east coast of China.

November 11 Japanese troops capture Shanghai.

December 5–13 Japanese troops take the Chinese city of Nanjing. Their victory is followed by the "rape of Nanjing," when around a quarter of a million Chinese are killed.

December 24 Japanese forces capture the Chinese city of Hangzhou, southwest of the port of Shanghai.

1938

January 10 Japanese forces enter the port of Qingdao in northeast China.

March 1–24 Japanese forces advance southward from the city of Jinan in north China, but are blocked by a large Chinese army at Taierzhuang and forced to withdraw.

March 28 Japan installs a puppet government in Nanjing.

April 1–May 20 A Japanese force again advances southward from Jinan, while another Japanese army advances northward from Nanjing. They meet at Xuzhou on May 20.

May 12 Germany recognizes Manchukuo, the Japanese puppet state established in Manchuria.

June 1–July 1 Japanese forces advance west from Suchow, China. They take Kaifeng on June 6, but as they approach Zhengzhou the Chinese break dykes on the Huang (Yellow) River, halting their advance.

August 1 Japanese forces advance southwest from Suchow.

September 27 The League of Nations pronounces Japan to be the aggressor in China.

October 2 Japan withdraws from the League of Nations in protest at its identification by the League as the aggressor in the Sino-Japanese war.

October 10 The Japanese capture the city of Hankow, the seat of Jiang Jie Shi's (Chiang Kai-shek's) Chinese government before it moved to the port of Chongqing in the southwest.

October 25 Japanese troops take the port of Guangzhou in south China.

1939

February 10 Japanese troops occupy the Chinese island of Hainan in the South China Sea and other Chinese ports.

September 14 Japanese troops advance south toward the port of Changsha, but are repulsed. This ends Japanese expansion in central China until 1944.

November 15 Japanese forces invade southern China and capture Nanning, cutting the railroad between Hanoi in Vietnam and Changsha in southeast China.

1940

June 25 Japan demands that war supplies to China through French Indochina should be halted, and that a Japanese mission should be allowed to enter the country to verify the closure of the railroad lines concerned.

October 18 Britain reopens the Burma Road supply route, previously closed under diplomatic pressure from the Japanese, enabling supplies for Jiang Jie Shi's nationalist forces against Japan to get through.

1941

July 1–26 In an attempt to constrict further China's supply lines Japanese forces occupy southern Indo-China. The United States responds by freezing all Japanese assets, an action soon followed by Great Britain and the Netherlands government in exile. This has the effect of cutting off Japan's supplies of oil. Japan is now faced with a dilemma—to agree to American demands, which include withdrawing not only from Indo-China but China as well, or to go to war. On December 7, the Sino-Japanese War becomes part of the Second World War.

to cooperate in an attempt to overthrow the government.

26 Colonel Carlos Ibáñez del Campo resigns as president of Chile owing to popular opposition to his repressive regime and the failure of his economic policies in the face of the worldwide depression, and flees to exile in Argentina.

AUGUST

28 The International Court of Justice at The Hague, in the Netherlands, rules that the proposed customs union between Germany and Austria contravenes the Geneva Protocols of October 14, 1922.

SEPTEMBER

9   The Canton rebel government mounts a military offensive toward the Chinese capital of Nanjing.

10 Riots break out in London, England, and Glasgow, Scotland, when the British government attempts to implement expenditure cuts, as recommended by the May Committee to balance the British budget.

12 Mexico is admitted to the League of Nations.

13 The Heimwehr (an extreme-right paramilitary organization) unsuccessfully attempts a coup in Austria, under the fascist leader Dr. Walther Pfrimer.

15 Naval crews mutiny at Invergordon, Scotland, over pay cuts made as part of the British government's austerity measures.

18 Japanese troops occupy Mukden (now Shenyang), northeast China, and, joined by reinforcements, begin to expand throughout north Manchuria.

18 The United and Reform parties form a coalition in New Zealand under the premiership of George Forbes.

OCTOBER

14 Following Niceto Alcalá Zamora's resignation over the anticlerical nature of the proposed new Spanish constitution, Manuel Azaña of the Left Republicans becomes president of the provisional government.

16 U.S. delegates attend the League of Nations council to discuss Japanese aggression in Manchuria, China.

17 The Chicago, Illinois, gangster Al "Scarface" Capone is sentenced in the United States to 11 years in prison for tax evasion.

20 The Protection of the Republic law comes into force in Spain.

27 In the British general election, the National Government wins 554 seats, against the opposition's 61. Oswald Mosley's New Party fails to win a seat.

DECEMBER

9   A republican constitution is proclaimed in Spain, following the revolution of April 1931.

16 Niceto Alcalá Zamora, leader of the Liberal Republican Right, is elected president of Spain, and the left-wing Manuel Azaña is appointed prime minister.

SCIENCE, TECHNOLOGY, AND MEDICINE

Agriculture

- The United States becomes self-sufficient in potash used for fertilizer.

Ecology

- A typhoon causes the Chang Jiang River in China to flood 104,000 sq km/40,000 sq mi. It is followed by widespread famine.
- Kalahari Gemsbock National Park is created in the Cape of Good Hope, South Africa.
- Victoria Falls National Park is created in Rhodesia (modern Zimbabwe).

AUGUST

- One of the worst floods in history occurs when the Huang Ho River, China, overflows its banks; 3.7 million people die.

Exploration

- U.S. explorer Lincoln Ellsworth explores the Arctic Ocean.

Health and Medicine

c. 1931 Cryogenic surgery begins to be used to correct retinal separation.

- German physiologist Otto Warburg receives the Nobel Prize for Physiology or Medicine for his work on respiratory enzymes.
- The U.S. Public Health Service warns that air pollution from cars, factories, homes, and steam engines is a serious health hazard.
- U.S. biologist Ernest Goodpasture grows viruses in eggs, making possible the production of vaccines for such viral diseases as polio.

Math

- Austrian mathematician Kurt Gödel publishes "Gödel's proof", which questions the possibility of establishing dependable axioms in mathematics, showing that any formula strong enough to include the laws of arithmetic is either incomplete or inconsistent. The proof is contained in *Über formal unentscheidbare Sätze der Principia Mathematica und verwandter Systeme/On Formally Undecidable Propositions in Principia Mathematica and Related Systems*, which proves that in any mathematical system such as arithmetic, there are statements that cannot be proved true or false.

Science

- German biochemist Adolf Butenandt isolates the male sex hormone androgen.
- German chemists Karl Bosch and Friedrich Bergius share the Nobel Prize for Chemistry for their development of chemical high-pressure methods.
- U.S. chemist Harold C. Urey and atomic physicist J. Washburn discover that electrolyzed water is denser than ordinary water, leading to the discovery of deuterium ("heavy hydrogen").
- U.S. engineer Karl Jansky discovers that the interference in telephone communications is caused by radio emissions from the Milky Way. He thus begins the development of radio astronomy.
- U.S. physicists Ernest Lawrence and M. Stanley Livingston build a cyclotron, particle accelerator.

Technology

- Belgian-U.S. chemist Julius A. Nieuwland invents "Neoprene," a synthetic rubber.
- British chemicals company Imperial Chemical Industries (ICI) produces gasoline from coal.
- British inventor Isaac Shoenberg begins the development of a practical television broadcast system under the auspices of a television research group established by the British company Electric and Musical Industries (EMI).
- French engineer G. J. M. Darrieus patents a two-bladed vertical axis windmill; a 30m/100 ft prototype is erected at Yalta, USSR.
- Photographic engineer William Goodman develops the first exposure meter for photographers; it can be used to translate brightness levels into camera aperture settings.
- The American Telephone and Telegraph company (AT&T) develops teletypewriters, later known as telex machines.
- U.S. corporation Du Pont introduces Freon, a chlorofluorocarbon (CFC), as an aerosol propellant and refrigerant; it begins to replace ammonia in refrigerators.
- U.S. scientist Harold Edgerton invents the electronic flash, for use in photography.
- *c.* 1931–*c.* 1940 The development of facsimile machines is furthered with the discovery of a dry chemical copying process.

November

- RCA-Victor in the United States releases Beethoven's Fifth Symphony as the first long-playing record (33⅓ RPM compared to 78).
- 21 The American Telephone and Telegraph Company (AT&T) introduces the first telex service.

Transportation

- A subway system is opened in the Japanese city of Kyoto.
- Aeronautical engineer Irmgard Lotz develops a formula for calculating the effect of an airplane's wingspan, regardless of the shape of the wing, on the wing's lifting force.
- The B-9 bomber, the progenitor of all modern combat airplanes, is produced by the Boeing Aircraft Company in the United States; it is the first twin-engine, all-metal bomber with retractable landing gear.
- The Bayonne bridge, linking Staten Island, New York, and New Jersey, opens in the United States; it is the world's longest steel arch bridge, with a span of 510 m/1,683 ft.
- U.S. aviators Clyde Pangborn and Hugh Herndon fly nonstop across the Pacific from Sabishiro, Japan, to Wenatchee, Washington, in 41 hours.

November 1931–32 French theologian and scientist Teilhard de Chardin makes one of the longest overland expeditions by car to date when he travels 13,000 km/8,000 mi from Beirut, Lebanon, to Beijing, China, to make geological studies in central Asia. The trip is financed by André Citroën.

c. 1931–*c.* 1940 Airplanes undergo radical changes; they become streamlined, are made almost entirely of metal, acquire controllable-pitch propellers, have air-cooled engines and retractable landing gear, and passengers and crew are protected in soundproofed and insulated cabins.

c. 1931–*c.* 1940 Autogyros, rotary-winged aircraft, create a wave of interest in the early 1930s but virtually disappear by 1940, replaced by the helicopter.

c. 1931–*c.* 1940 Balloon-tires, hydraulic brakes, automatic transmissions, and self-starting engines begin to appear in U.S.-made vehicles.

c. 1931–*c.* 1940 The aircraft carrier is developed in the U.S., Japanese, and British navies from a naval auxiliary into a capital ship capable of launching and recovering repeated airborne attacks on enemy targets.

May

- Swiss physicist Auguste Piccard ascends to 15,781 m/51,774 ft in a pressurized gondola suspended from a balloon. The following year he reaches 16,201 m/53,152 ft.

June

23–July 1 U.S. aviators Wiley Post and Harold Gatty make the first flight around the world, covering 24,898 km/15,474 mi in 8 days 16 hr.

July

1 The Benguela–Katanga railroad opens in southern Africa, completing the first trans-African railroad.

October

24 The George Washington Bridge, linking New York to New Jersey, opens to traffic.

ARTS AND IDEAS

Architecture

- In India, the Viceroy's House in New Delhi, designed by the English architect Edwin Lutyens, is completed.
- The McGraw Hill Building, designed by U.S. architect Raymond Hood, is completed in New York, New York. It is one of the first skyscrapers designed in the International Style.

APRIL

30   The Empire State Building is completed in New York, New York. Its designers are the architectural firm of Shreve, Lamb, and Harmon. It has 102 floors and soon becomes a symbol of the city. At 381m/1,250 ft, it remains the highest building in the world until 1972.

Arts

- In the United States, the Mexican artist José Clemente Orozco completes murals in the New School for Social Research in New York, New York.
- The Dutch artist Piet Mondrian paints *Composition with Two Lines*.
- The English artist Barbara Hepworth sculpts *Figure in Sycamore*.
- The English artist Eric Gill completes his sculpture *Prospero and Ariel*, which is on the wall of Broadcasting House in London, England.
- The Romanian artist Constantin Brancusi sculpts the last of several versions of his work *Mademoiselle Pogany*.
- The Russian artist Wassily Kandinsky paints *Rows of Signs*.
- The Spanish artist Pablo Picasso paints *Figures by the Sea*, sculpts *Construction*, and sculpts *Woman's Head* in metal, including some kitchen utensils.
- The Spanish artist Salvador Dalí paints *The Persistence of Memory*, one of his best-known works.
- The U.S. artist Edward Hopper paints *Route 6, Eastham*.
- The U.S. artist Peter Blume paints *South of Scranton*.
- The U.S. artist Thomas Hart Benton paints the mural *American Today* for the New School of Social Research, in New York, New York.
- U.S. photographer Edward Weston takes *Cabbage Leaf*.
- U.S. photographer Paul Strand takes *Church, Ranchos de Taos, New Mexico*.

Film

- *The Champ* is released in the United States, starring Wallace Beery and Jackie Cooper and directed by King Vidor.
- Movie censors in Germany authorize the showing of *All Quiet on the Western Front*, despite opposition from the German parliament and the Hitler Youth movement.
- The 1930–31 Academy Awards take place. Best Actor: Lionel Barrymore, for *A Free Soul*; Best Actress: Marie Dressler, for *Min and Bill*; Best Picture: *Cimarron*, directed by Wesley Ruggles; Best Director: Norman Taurog, for *Skippy*.
- The Depression prompts a change in movie exhibition and in an attempt to improve business U.S. movie theaters begin to show double features, involving the screening of two feature movies, a newsreel, and a cartoon, all for the price of a single movie. The double feature is so successful that it remains the standard mode of exhibition until 1940.
- The movie *A Nous la Liberté/Freedom is Ours*, a satire on industrialization that influenced Charles Chaplin's *Modern Times* of 1936, is released in France, directed by René Clair. Also released is Clair's musical movie *Le Million/The Million*, starring Annabella, René Lefèvre, and Paul Olivier.
- The movie *An American Tragedy*, directed by the Austrian-born filmmaker Josef von Sternberg, is released in the United States, starring Phillips Holmes and Sylvia Sidney.
- The movie *City Lights*, directed by and starring Charlie Chaplin, in which the Little Tramp falls for a blind flower girl, is released in the United States. The cast also includes Virginia Cherrill, Florence Lee, and Harry Myers.
- The movie *La Chienne*, directed by Jean Renoir, is released in France, starring Michel Simon.
- The movie *Le Bal/The Ball*, directed by Wilhelm Thiele, is released in France, starring Danielle Darrieux, André Lefaur, and Germaine Dermoz.
- The movie *M*, directed by Austrian-born filmmaker Fritz Lang, is released in Germany, the tale of a sociopathic child killer played by Hungarian-born actor Peter Lorre.
- The movie *Marius*, directed by the Hungarian-born filmmaker Alexander Korda, is released in France. The first in a trilogy written by Marcel Pagnol, it stars Raimu, Pierre Fresnay, and Orane Demazis.
- The movie *Monkey Business*, directed by Norman Z. McLeod, is released in the United States, starring the Marx Brothers.
- The movie *One Night*, directed by Gustav Molander, is released in Sweden, starring Uno Henning and Björn Berglund.
- The movie *Platinum Blonde*, directed by Frank Capra, is released in the United States, starring Jean Harlow, Loretta Young, and Robert Williams.
- The movie *Tabu*, directed by German filmmaker F. W. Murnau and U.S. filmmaker Robert Flaherty, is released in the United States. It tells the story of the life of a Tahitian pearl fisherman.
- The movie of *The Threepenny Opera*, based on the play by Bertolt Brecht and adapted from *The Beggar's Opera* by John Gay, is released in Germany. It is directed by leading German-based filmmaker G. W. Pabst.
- The releases of the movies *Dracula*, directed by the U.S. director Tod Browning, and *Frankenstein*, directed by the English filmmaker James Whale, signal the start of a popular 1930s series of horror movies in the United States. *Dracula* is based on the novel by Bram Stoker and stars Bela Lugosi; *Frankenstein* is based on the novel by Mary Shelley and stars Colin Clive, with Boris Karloff as the monster.
- The U.S. movie industry responds to the economic depression by producing movies which are more daring in content, such as *Tarnished Lady*, directed by U.S. filmmaker George Cukor, and *The Public Enemy*, directed by U.S. filmmaker William A. Wellman.
- There are reports of a crisis in the movie industry in the United States, arising from too few new releases to meet demand and the high costs of sound production.

April 1931–34   In England, Ealing Studios are rebuilt for Basil Dean's Associated Talking Pictures, on the site of the original studios of 1902 (disused since the 1920s).

Literature and Language

- In France, the Romanian poet Tristan Tzara publishes his long surrealist poem *L'Homme approximatif/The Approximate Man*.
- T. S. Stribling writes *The Forge*, the first of a trilogy about the Vaiden family of Alabama.
- The Belgian-born French crime writer Georges Simenon publishes his first Maigret novel, *Pietr-le-Letton/The Case of Peter the Lett*.
- The English writer Anthony Powell publishes his novel *Afternoon Men*.
- The English writer Ivy Compton-Burnett publishes her novel *Men and Wives*.
- The English writer Lytton Strachey publishes *Portraits in Miniature*, a series of biographical essays.
- The English writer Vita Sackville-West publishes her novel *All Passion Spent*.
- The English writer Virginia Woolf publishes her novel *The Waves*.
- The French writer and aviator Antoine Marie Roger de St-Exupéry publishes his second novel *Vol de nuit/Night Flight*.
- The French writer Georges Bernanos publishes the political pamphlets *La Grande peur des bien-pensants/The Great Fear of Right-Thinking People*. A leading Catholic, Bernanos is here attacking the spiritual bankruptcy of the middle classes.
- The Greek writer George Seferis publishes his poetry collection *I strofi/Turning Point*.
- The Irish novelist James Hanley publishes *Men in Darkness: Five Stories* and the novel *Boy*—fiction that draws strongly on his experiences as a seaman. *Boy* is briefly banned because it is considered obscene.
- The Nobel Prize for Literature is awarded to the Swedish poet Erik Axel Karlfeldt.
- The Pulitzer Prize for Biography is awarded to Henry James for *Charles W. Eliot*. Margaret Ayer Barnes receives the Prize for Fiction for her *Years of Grace*, and the Prize for Poetry is awarded to Robert Frost for *Collected Poems*.
- The U.S. literary critic and writer Edmund Wilson publishes *Axel's Castle*, a study of Symbolist literature.
- The U.S. writer Damon Runyon publishes *Guys and Dolls*, a collection of stories about New York gamblers and sportsmen written in colorful slang.
- The U.S. writer Dorothy Parker publishes her poetry collection *Death and Taxes*.
- The U.S. writer Langston Hughes publishes his poetry collection *The Negro Mother and Other Dramatic Recitals*.
- The U.S. writer Pearl Buck publishes her novel *The Good Earth*. A story about peasant life in China, it becomes the best-selling novel in the United States for two years. She receives a Pulitzer prize for it in 1932 and it contributes to her winning the Nobel Prize for Literature in 1938.
- The U.S. writer Theodore Dreiser publishes his third book of autobiography *Dawn*.
- The U.S. writer Wallace Stevens reissues (with a few additions) his first poetry collection *Harmonium*, which was originally published in 1923.
- The U.S. writer Willa Cather publishes her novel *Shadows on the Rock*.
- The U.S. writer William Faulkner publishes his novel *Sanctuary*. Despite its subject matter—rape, murder, and a lynching—it is the first of his novels to achieve popular success.

DECEMBER

22 In Rome, Italy, a fire in the Vatican Library destroys about 15,000 books.

Music

- In London, England, the theater manager Lilian Baylis reopens Sadler's Wells Theatre as a venue for opera and ballet.
- In the USSR, the music of the Russian composer Sergey Rachmaninov is banned as "decadent."
- The English composer William Walton completes his dramatic cantata *Belshazzar's Feast*.
- The French composer Maurice Ravel completes his Piano Concerto in G.
- The French-born U.S. composer Edgar Varèse completes *Ionisation*. Aggressively modern, this is a work for percussion and siren.
- The Hungarian composer Béla Bartók completes his Piano Concerto No. 2 and his *Transylvanian Dances*.
- The opera *Matka/Mother* by the Czech composer Alois Hába opens in Munich, Germany.

MARCH

3 The U.S. Senate makes the song "The Star-Spangled Banner," written in 1814 by the U.S. writer Francis Scott Key, the national anthem of the United States.

Theater and Dance

- In England, singer and comedian George Formby, Jr., presents his own variety show, which leads to numerous movies and hit records in the 1930s and 1940s.
- The ballet *Bacchus et Ariane* is first performed, in Paris, France. The music is by the French composer Albert Roussel, the choreography by the Russian-born French choreographer Serge Lifar, and the costumes and sets by the Italian artist Giorgio de Chirico.
- The ballet *Bolt/The Bolt*, by the Russian composer Dmitry Shostakovich, is first performed, in Leningrad (St. Petersburg), Russia. The choreography is by the Russian dancer Fyodor Lopokov.
- The musical *Of Thee I Sing*, with lyrics by Ira Gershwin and music by George Gershwin, opens at the Music Box Theater in New York, New York.
- The play *Cavalcade*, by the English playwright Noël Coward, is first performed, at the Drury Lane Theatre in London, England. A panorama of British life from the turn of the century, it becomes very popular.
- The play *Mourning Becomes Electra*, by the U.S. writer Eugene O'Neill, is first performed, in the Guild Theater in New York, New York. Set in Puritan New England, it is a retelling of the ancient Greek trilogy the *Oresteia*, by Aeschylus.
- The play *Noé/Noah*, by the French writer André Obey, is first performed, in Paris, France.
- The Polish composer Karol Szymanowski completes his ballet *Harnasie*.

- The Pulitzer Prize for Drama is awarded to Susan Glaspell for *Alison's House*.

Thought and Scholarship

- British economists Norman Angell and Harold Wright publish *Can Governments Cure Unemployment?*
- English historian Herbert Butterfield publishes *The Whig Interpretation of History*, a widely influential attack on the belief in inevitable progress in the course of history.
- English historian Richard Henry Tawney publishes *Equality*.
- Spanish-born U.S. philosopher and writer George Santayana publishes *The Genteel Tradition at Bay*.
- The English historian Arthur Bryant publishes his biography *King Charles II*.
- The Pulitzer Prize for History is awarded to Bernadotte E. Schmitt for *The Coming of the War: 1914*.
- The U.S. social reformer Jane Addams and U.S. educator Nicholas M. Butler share the Nobel Peace Prize.

- U.S. historians Samuel Eliot Morison and Henry Steele Commager publish *The Growth of the American Republic*.
- U.S. philosopher John Dewey publishes *Philosophy and Civilization*.

SOCIETY

Education

- English educationist Susan Isaacs publishes *Social Development in Young Children* in the UK.
- In London, England, the Courtauld Institute for the study of the history of art, a part of London University, is founded.

BIRTHS & DEATHS

JANUARY

3 Joseph Joffre, commander in chief of the French forces in World War I, dies in Paris, France (78).

5 Alvin Ailey, U.S. choreographer who formed the Alvin Ailey American Dance Theater, born in Rogers, Texas.

6 E(dgar) L(awrence) Doctorow, U.S. novelist and playwright, born in New York, New York.

15 Thomas Hoving, U.S. art historian and director of New York's Metropolitan Museum of Art 1966–77, born in New York, New York.

23 Anna Pavlova, Russian ballerina, dies in The Hague, Netherlands (49).

25 Stikkan "Stig" Anderson, Swedish manager and producer of the pop group Abba, born in Hova, Sweden (–1997).

27 Mordecai Richler, Canadian novelist and short story writer, born in Montreal, Canada.

FEBRUARY

1 Boris Yeltsin, Russian politician who was a prime force in the establishment of a new Commonwealth of Independent States to replace the USSR, born in Sverdlovsk (now Yekaterinburg), Russia.

18 Toni Morrison (pen name of Chloe Anthony Wofford), novelist, born in Lorain, Ohio.

23 Nellie Melba, Australian soprano, dies in Sydney, Australia (72).

MARCH

2 Mikhail Gorbachev, Russian politician, president of USSR 1990–91 during the downfall of communism and the breakup of the Soviet Union, born in Stavropol Kray, Russia.

2 Tom (Thomas Kennerly) Wolfe, U.S. novelist and journalist, born in Richmond, Virginia.

4 Alice Rivlin, U.S. economist who served as chief economic analyst during President Bill Clinton's first term, born in Philadelphia, Pennsylvania.

25 Ida Wells-Barnett, civil-rights activist and newspaper editor, dies in Chicago (68).

APRIL

26 George Herbert Mead, U.S. pragmatist philosopher, dies in Chicago, Illinois (68).

MAY

3 Aldo Rossi, Italian architect, born in Milan, Italy (–1997).

6 Willie Mays, black U.S. professional baseball player, born in Westfield, Alabama.

9 Albert Abraham Michelson, German-born U.S. physicist who established the speed of light, dies in Pasadena, California (78).

JULY

8 Roone Arledge, U.S. television executive who led both the news and sports divisions at ABC, born in New York, New York.

SEPTEMBER

10 William Goldman, leading U.S. screenwriter and twice an Academy Award winner, born in Chicago, Illinois.

24 John Michael Geoffrey Mannington Adams, Labor prime minister of Barbados 1976–85, born in Barbados (–1985).

OCTOBER

4 Richard Rorty, U.S. philosopher, educator, and critic, born in New York, New York.

7 Desmond Tutu, South African Anglican bishop, a vigorous opponent of apartheid, born in Klerksdorp, South Africa.

18 Thomas Alva Edison, prolific U.S. inventor who invented the light bulb, phonograph, and motion picture projector, dies in West Orange, New Jersey (84).

20 Mickey Mantle, U.S. professional baseball player, born in Spavinaw, Oklahoma.

NOVEMBER

18 Roberto Gouzieta, chief executive officer of Coca-Cola, born in Havana, Cuba.

DECEMBER

25 Uzo Egonu, Nigerian painter and printmaker, born in Onitsha, Nigeria (–1996).

26 Melvil Dewey, U.S. librarian who introduced the Dewey Decimal System of cataloging books, dies in Lake Placid, Florida (80).

Everyday Life

- 4,745 divorce decrees are handed down in Reno, Nevada, the divorce capital of the world.
- Alfred Mosher Butts of Rhinebeck, New York, invents the word game Scrabble under the name Criss-Cross. The first sets do not go on sale until 1946, under the name Lexico. Two years later the name Scrabble is adopted.
- In the United States, unemployment figures reach 8 million.
- In the United States, union membership declines to 3.3 million, down from a high of 5 million in 1920.
- Nearly 7 million Americans are unemployed, up from approximately 4 million in 1930. Meanwhile investments continue to plunge, from $10 billion in 1929 to $3 billion this year.
- Selected population figures (in millions): China 410; India 338; USSR 168; United States 122; Japan 75; Germany 64; Great Britain 46; France 42.

MARCH

18 Schick Dry Shaver Inc. in Stamford, Connecticut, markets the first electric shavers.

Media and Communication

FEBRUARY

12 Pope Pius XI makes the first papal broadcast on Vatican radio.
27 Walter Lippmann joins the *New York Herald Tribune* and begins his nationally-syndicated column that influences U.S. public opinion.

MARCH

6 Capitalizing on its comic-strip popularity, *Little Orphan Annie* is launched as a radio show in the United States, sponsored by the makers of Ovaltine.

Religion

- English historian Norman Hepburn Baynes publishes *Constantine the Great and the Christian Church*.
- Swedish Lutheran theologian Gustaf Emmanuel Hildebrand Aulén publishes one of his best-known works, *Christus Victor/Christ Victorious*, an interpretation of Christ's death.

Sports

- Hubert Opperman of Australia wins the 1,200 km Paris–Brest–Paris cycle race, the longest single race in the world, in a new record time of 49 hours, 21 minutes.
- In the United States, the University of Southern California, with a record of ten wins and one loss, wins the national college football championship.
- The Green Bay Packers win the National Football League (NFL) championship title for the third consecutive season.

FEBRUARY

17 A baseball game played at the Tozuka Baseball Ground, Tokyo, Japan is the first sporting event to be televised. It is transmitted by closed circuit television to the Electrical Laboratory at Waseda University. Seven months later a school match at the Tozuka ground is publicly televised.

MARCH

21 U.S. national figure skating champions are: Maribel Vinson; Roger Turner; Beatriz Loughran and Sherwin Badger, pairs.

APRIL

3–14 The Montreal Canadiens defeat the Chicago Black Hawks three games to two to win the National Hockey League (NHL) championship.
23 Tony Canzoneri of the United States knocks out British boxer Jack "Kid" Berg in a world junior-lightweight title bout in Cleveland, Ohio. Canzoneri had previously held titles at featherweight and lightweight.

MAY

30 U.S. racing driver Louis Schneider wins the 19th annual Indianapolis 500 auto race, with an average speed of 97 mph.

JUNE

23 Lili de Alvarez of Spain appears on the Centre Court at the Wimbledon tennis championships in England wearing a trousered frock. Her opponent, Joan Lycett, of Great Britain, also breaks with tradition by becoming the first woman to play on the Centre Court without stockings.
30–July 26 In cycling, French rider Antonin Magne wins the Tour de France. It is the last Tour de France over 5,000 km.

JULY

4 At the Wimbledon tennis championships in England, 20-year-old U.S. tennis player Sidney Wood, Jr., becomes the youngest ever men's singles champion.
6 U.S. golfer Billy Burke wins the U.S. Open golf tournament, defeating George Von Elm after two 36-hole playoffs.

AUGUST

20 The U.S. Lawn Tennis Association champions are U.S. tennis players Helen Wills Moody and Ellsworth Vines, Jr.
25 The first ever televised boxing match goes out from the Columbia Broadcasting System (CBS) Studios in New York, New York.

OCTOBER

1–10 The St. Louis Cardinals beat the Philadelphia A's by four games to three in the World Series.

1932

POLITICS, GOVERNMENT, AND ECONOMICS

Business and Economics

- The U.S. economy deteriorates. In one year unemployment rises from 7 to 13 million, as the nation's industrial output drops to less than half its 1929 level. Twenty-one thousand Americans commit suicide.

MARCH

12 The Swedish "match king," Ivar Kreuger, commits suicide in Paris, France, and his national and international business empire collapses.

JUNE

30 Interest rates in Britain fall to 2%, starting a seven-year period of low rates.

DECEMBER

27 South Africa abandons the gold standard.

Colonization

JULY

21–August 20 An Imperial Conference in Ottawa, Canada, proposes the creation of a closed economic trading area for countries within the British Empire, but completely free trade within the empire is rejected.

OCTOBER

3 Britain terminates its mandate over Iraq, and it is admitted to the League of Nations as an independent state.

Human Rights

- In Vienna, the first all-woman orchestra performs its first concert.
- Mary Dewson, leader of the National Consumers' League, organizes the Reporter Plan in the United States for women to inform communities around the country about President Franklin D. Roosevelt's "New Deal" legislation.
- The French Senate denies women's suffrage for the third time.
- Women in Brazil gain the vote.
- Women in Thailand win the right to vote and to hold public office.

SEPTEMBER

20 The nationalist leader Mahatma Gandhi begins a fast in prison in India to protest against the treatment of the Harijans (untouchables).

Politics and Government

- The infamous couple Bonnie Parker and Clyde Barrow commit a series of robberies and kill fifteen people throughout the South and Midwest United States.

JANUARY

- A communist revolt in El Salvador is suppressed with great loss of life.
4 Following the return of the nationalist leader Mahatma Gandhi to India from the second Round Table Conference in London, England, and the revival of civil disobedience, the Indian government is granted emergency powers for six months. The Indian National Congress is declared illegal and Gandhi is arrested.
4 Japanese troops occupying Manchuria reach the eastern end of the Great Wall of China.
7 Chancellor Heinrich Brüning declares that Germany cannot, and will not, resume reparations payments to Britain, France, and the United States, currently subject to a moratorium.
7 The U.S. secretary of state, Henry Stimson, sends notes to China and Japan opposing Japanese aggression in Manchuria, China, and stating that the United States will not recognize gains made by armed force.
12 Oliver Wendell Holmes retires as associate justice of the U.S. Supreme Court, to be succeeded by Benjamin Cardozo.
21 The USSR and Finland sign a three-year nonaggression pact.
22 The Reconstruction Finance Corporation is established in the United States to provide financial aid for firms in difficulty.
28 Japanese forces capture the port of Shanghai in China.

FEBRUARY

2 Sixty nations, including the United States and the USSR, attend the Geneva Disarmament Conference, at which a French proposal for an armed force under international control is opposed by Germany.
6 A pro-German coup is effected in Klaipeda (formerly Memel), Lithuania; the leader, Herbert Boettcher, is arrested on the orders of the Nationalist Union leader and virtual dictator, Antanas Smetona.
7 Under the terms of the Convention of Oslo, the Scandinavian countries, Belgium, and the Netherlands commit themselves to mutual economic cooperation.
8 Bulgaria renounces further reparations payments to the Allies.

9   The Army Comrades Association (the future National Guard, or "Blueshirts"), is founded in the Irish Free State.

16   The Fianna Fáil party, led by Éamon de Valera, wins the general election in the Irish Free State

16   The French senate, dissatisfied with failures in French foreign and economic policies, overthrows the government of Pierre Laval.

20   The right winger André Tardieu becomes prime minister of France for the third time.

27   The Federal Reserve System is reorganized in the United States with the aim of stabilizing the economy by regulating the national banking system.

29–March 3   The government in Finland quells an armed uprising of the Lapua Movement, a fascist faction opposed to the Finnish Communist Party.

MARCH

1   The baby son of U.S. aviator Charles Lindbergh and Anne Morrow Lindbergh is kidnapped from the couple's home in Hopewell, New Jersey. Bruno Hauptmann, a German-born carpenter and petty criminal, is executed for the child's murder on April 3, 1936.

1   The Import Duties Act comes into force in Britain, effectively ending 80 years of free trade.

3   Chinese forces drive the Japanese invaders from the port of Shanghai.

3   In a sign of declining labor–management relations, police kill four demonstrators and wound scores of others at the Ford Motor Company in Dearborn, Michigan.

3   The Norris–La Guardia Act in the United States restricts the use of injunctions in labor disputes and forbids management from discriminating against union members.

3   The U.S. Congress submits the Twentieth amendment to the states for ratification. It stipulates that Congress shall be called into session on January 3 and the president and vice president inaugurated on January 20.

9   The Dáil (lower house of the legislature) elects Éamon de Valera as president of the executive council (prime minister) in the Irish Free State.

9   The Japanese state republic of Manchukuo is proclaimed in Manchuria, China, with the former Manchu emperor Xuantong (Pui) made "chief executive," then emperor.

13   In the German presidential election, the conservative former field marshal Paul von Hindenburg receives 18.6 million votes (49.6%) against the Nazi leader Adolf Hitler's 11.3 million (30.1%), falling just short of the necessary absolute majority.

APRIL

10   Paul von Hindenburg is reelected German president on the second ballot.

24   Nazis in Germany gain election victories in Prussia, Bavaria, Württemberg, and Hamburg. In Prussia, the Nazi Party becomes the largest single party in the state parliament.

MAY

6   The French president, Paul Doumer, is assassinated by a White Russian anarchist, Paul Gorgonlov.

8   Left-wing parties emerge from the second round of the French elections with a gain of about 100 seats; the right-wing prime minister André Tardieu resigns on May 10.

10   The moderate conservative Albert Lebrun succeeds Paul Doumer as French president.

15   Inukai Tsuyoshi, Prime Minister of Japan, is assassinated by young naval officers following his attempt to halt military activities against China.

19   In the Irish Free State, the Dáil (lower house) votes for the abolition of the oath of loyalty to the British crown, but opposition in the senate prevents its enactment.

20   The Austrian chancellor, Engelbert Dollfuss, forms a Conservative coalition led by the Christian Social Party.

30   The German chancellor, Heinrich Brüning, resigns following an intrigue against him initiated by the president, Paul von Hindenburg.

JUNE

2   Franz von Papen, expelled from the Center Party on becoming chancellor, forms a nonparty "cabinet of barons" in Germany.

4   The Radical-Socialist Edouard Herriot becomes prime minister in France for the third time.

6–18   A military revolt in Chile establishes the socialist Carlos Dávila as president.

13   Britain and France sign a pact of friendship at Lausanne, Switzerland.

15   The Chaco War between Bolivia and Paraguay begins, with Bolivians attacking Paraguayan positions in the disputed border territory of Chaco Boreal.

16   A ban on Nazi storm troopers in Germany, in force since April, is lifted by the government.

16–July 9   At the Lausanne reparations conference, in Switzerland, Germany accepts a proposal for a final conditional payment of 3,000 million Reichsmarks to Britain, France, and the United States.

24   A constitutional monarchy is established in Siam (modern Thailand) following a bloodless coup led by a young lawyer, Pridi Phanomyong, in which the king, Rama VII, was held captive until he granted Western, liberal reforms.

JULY

2   In his acceptance speech at the Democratic National Convention, the presidential nominee Franklin D. Roosevelt calls for a "new deal for the American people."

5   President Antonio Carmona of Portugal appoints the authoritarian Antonio de Oliveira Salazar as prime minister.

7   The scope of the U.S. Reconstruction Finance Corporation, established on January 22, is broadened to include financing for state and local public works.

9–October 2   A revolt of federalists in São Paulo, Brazil, against the centralizing government of Getúlio Vargas is unsuccessful.

15   The League of Nations grants Austria a large loan on the condition that it renounces *Anschluss* ("Annexation," union with Germany) for 30 years.

18   In Belgium, French becomes official language of Walloon provinces, Flemish the language of Flanders.

18   Turkey is admitted to the League of Nations.

20   Following lawlessness in Prussia, the German chancellor, Franz von Papen, dismisses the prime minister, Otto Braun, together with his ministerial colleagues.

25 The USSR and Poland sign a mutual nonaggression pact.
28 U.S. World War I veterans petitioning the administration of President Herbert Hoover in Washington, D.C., for payment of bonuses are dispersed by armed forces.
31 The Nazis win 230 seats in the election to the German Reichstag (lower legislative house). The Social Democrats gain 133, the Center 75, the communists 89, the National People's Party 37, and others 44. The result is a stalemate, since neither Nazis nor Social Democrats will enter a coalition.

AUGUST

10 A revolt in Seville, Spain, led by the right-wing general José Sanjurjo, is suppressed.
13 The Nazi leader, Adolf Hitler, refuses President Paul von Hindenburg's request that he serve as German vice chancellor under Franz von Papen.

SEPTEMBER

1 A Peruvian military force enters Leticia in Colombia, seeking to recover the strategic Amazon port, which had been awarded to Colombia under the 1922 treaty between the two states.
9 A military coup ousts President Carlos Dávila in Chile.
9 The northeast region of Catalonia is granted autonomy in Spain, with its own flag, language, and parliament.
14 Germany temporarily (until December) withdraws from the Geneva Disarmament Conference, demanding that it be allowed armaments equal to those of other powers.
14 The Belgian government gains special powers to handle the financial crisis afflicting the country as a result of the worldwide economic depression.
15 Legislation is passed in Spain providing for the expropriation of landed estates, which are to be administered by an Institute of Agrarian Reform.

OCTOBER

1 The authoritarian Gyula Gömbös becomes prime minister in Hungary following the resignation of Count Julius Károlyi.
2 The Lytton Commission, set up by the League of Nations to investigate Japan's 1931 invasion of Manchuria, China, recognizes Japan's special transport and economic interests in the region and recommends an autonomous state under Chinese sovereignty but Japanese control.
31 The Greek liberal prime minister, Eleutherios Venizelos, resigns following his party's defeat in the general election.

NOVEMBER

4 In Greece, the Royalist Panayiotis Tsaldaris is elected prime minister.
6 Further elections to the German Reichstag (parliament), after the inconclusive elections of July 31, produce another deadlock, with some communist gains from Nazis.
8 Franklin D. Roosevelt wins the U.S. presidential election in a Democratic landslide, with 472 electoral votes to the Republican Herbert Hoover's 59 votes. In the House of Representatives, Democrats pick up 90 seats for a 310–117 majority; in the Senate, Democrats gain 13 seats for a majority of 60–35.

14 Croats and Serbian democrats in Yugoslavia demand a new constitution to replace the royal dictatorship of Alexander I.
17 Franz von Papen resigns as German chancellor to permit a new coalition to be formed after the elections.
19–24 At President Paul von Hindenburg's invitation, the Nazi leader, Adolf Hitler, attempts to form a coalition commanding a majority in the German parliament, but fails.
29 France and the USSR sign a nonaggression pact.
29 Persia annuls the 1901 agreement allowing the Anglo–Persian Oil Company to exploit oil reserves of the D'Arcy Concession area of Persia.

DECEMBER

4 General Kurt von Schleicher becomes chancellor in Germany, attempting to conciliate the center and the left.
9 Japanese forces capture the city of Jehol (Chengde), northeast China.
11 Britain, France, Germany, and Italy sign the "No Force Declaration," renouncing the use of force for settling differences.
12 The conservative liberal Arturo Alessandri Palma is reelected president of Chile.
16 The National Union (the ruling nationalist party) in Lithuania adopts a fascist program.
18 The Radical-Socialist Edouard Herriot resigns as prime minister of France following the refusal of the Chamber of Deputies to pay the latest installment of the country's war debts to the United States. Joseph Paul-Boncour succeeds him.
28 The U.S. Congress passes a resolution against the cancellation of Germany's war debt.

SCIENCE, TECHNOLOGY, AND MEDICINE

Agriculture

• Balloon-tires are produced for farm tractors.
December 1932–34 Soviet leader Joseph Stalin collectivizes farms and seizes grain and livestock in the Ukraine and Caucasus regions, starting a famine; an estimated 5 million people die.

Ecology

• Waterton-Glacier International Peace Park, straddling the U.S.-Canadian border, opens.

NOVEMBER

9 Cuba is hit by a severe hurricane; the storm surge kills 2,500 people.

DECEMBER

25 An earthquake measuring 7.6 on the Richter scale kills 70,000 people in Gansu province, China.

Exploration

- A German-U.S. expedition led by mountaineer Willy Merkl attempting to scale the Nanga Parbat massif in the Punjab Himalayas (now in Pakistan) fails to reach the summit.

Health and Medicine

- British physiologists Edgar Adrian and Charles Sherrington share the Nobel Prize for Physiology or Medicine for their discoveries regarding the action of neurons.
- English physician Cecily Williams describes the protein-deficiency disease kwashiorkor.
- German chemist Gerhard Domagk discovers that the red azo dye Prontosil can control streptococcal infections in mice. This is the first antibacterial sulfonamide drug ("sulfa drug").
- In the United States, 26 states have passed compulsory sterilization laws for those described as "morons, mental defectives, epileptics, illiterates, paupers, unemployables, criminals, prostitutes, and dope fiends."
- The Benzedrine Inhaler is marketed as a decongestant and as a treatment for hyperkinetic children; because it contains amphetamine, it is also soon abused as "speed."
- U.S. physiologist Armand Quick introduces a test to measure the clotting ability of blood—the Quick test.

JUNE
June–October   Over 4,000 people die from cholera in New York, New York.

Science

- British physicist James Chadwick discovers the neutron, an important discovery in the development of nuclear reactors.
- British physicists John D. Cockcroft and Ernest Walker develop a high-voltage particle accelerator, which they use to split lithium atoms.
- English archeologist Cyril Fox publishes *The Personality of Britain*.
- German physicist Werner Heisenberg receives the Nobel Prize for Physics for his formulation of the indeterminancy principle in quantum mechanics.
- German-born British biochemist Hans Krebs discovers the urea cycle, in which ammonia is turned into urea in mammals.
- The shape memory effect is discovered by U.S. chemical engineers L. C. Change and T. A. Read in a gold and cadmium alloy; if the alloy is bent it returns to its original shape when heated.
- U.S. anthropologist George Edward Lewis discovers the jaw of a Miocene ape *Ramapithecus* in the Siwalik Hills of India. Living about 8–15 million years ago, it is thought to be the oldest human ancestor.
- U.S. chemist Irving Langmuir receives the Nobel Prize for Chemistry for his work on surface chemistry.
- U.S. scientist Carl David Anderson, while analyzing cosmic rays, discovers positive electrons ("positrons"), the first form of antimatter to be discovered.

- Vitamin C (ascorbic acid) is isolated by the U.S. medical researcher Charles Glen King in the United States.

Technology

- German physicist and engineer Wernher von Braun begins work on rocket development.
- Pioneering radar equipment at the U.S. Naval Research Laboratory is able to detect aircraft 80 km/50 mi away from its transmitter, but unable to locate them.
- The double-deck elevator is first introduced; it services two floors simultaneously.
- The largest hydroelectric power station in Europe is built at Zaporozhye on the River Dnieper, USSR; it produces 560 megawatts of electricity.
- The Radio Corporation of America (RCA) demonstrates the first all-electronic television system; it operates on a 120-line scan.
- The U.S. corporation Technicolor develops a special camera in which three separate films, registering red, green, and blue, are exposed simultaneously.
- U.S. inventor Edwin Land invents the synthetic light polarizer in which all light rays are aligned in the same plane. It comes on the market in 1935.
- The Martin B-10 bomber is introduced in the U.S. armed forces. Capable of flying at 340 kph/213 mph, the B-10 also features other improvements over the Boeing B-9, including an enclosed cockpit and an internal weapons bay for its 1,030 kg/2,260 lb bomb load.

Transportation

- A streamlined diesel-electric train is introduced in Germany; it runs on the Berlin-to-Hamburg line at an average speed of 124 kph/77 mph.
- An automatic pilot is introduced on civilian aircraft.
- The Cologne–Bonn autobahn, one of the world's first highways, is opened in Germany.
- The Welland Canal in the United States opens after being rebuilt; it connects lakes Erie and Huron.
- U.S. car manufacturer Ford introduces the V-8 engine.
- U.S. car sales drop to around 1 million, from more than 5 million in 1929.

June 1932–37   The Moscow–Volga canal is constructed giving Moscow access to the River Volga.

MAY
20–21   U.S. aviator Amelia Earhart flies from Newfoundland, Canada, to Londonderry, Northern Ireland, in 13.5 hr, the first woman to make a solo flight across the Atlantic.

SEPTEMBER
10   The subway system in New York, New York, is expanded with the opening of the independent subway system.

ARTS AND IDEAS

Architecture

- An exhibition at the Museum of Modern Art (MOMA), New York, New York, "The International Style: Architecture since 1920," helps to identify the International Style as the dominant style of modern architecture. The influential catalog, *The International Style: Architecture Since 1922*, was written by the U.S. architects Philip Johnson and Henry-Russell Hitchcock.
- In England, work begins on the Liverpool Metropolitan Cathedral to plans by Edwin Lutyens. These plans are later abandoned, though Lutyens' crypt was incorporated into the final building.
- The Philadelphia Savings Fund Building in Philadelphia, Pennsylvania, designed by the U.S. architects George Howe and William Lescaze, is completed.
- The Stadium in Florence, Italy, designed by the Italian architect Pier Luigi Nervi, is completed.

MARCH

18 Sydney Harbour Bridge opens in Australia; with a main span of 500 m/1,650 ft, it is one of the world's longest steel-arch bridges.

Arts

- French photographer Henri Cartier-Bresson takes *Brussels*.
- German artist John Heartfield creates the anti-Hitler photomontage *Adolf, der Übermensch: Schlukt Gold und redet Blech/Adolf, the Superman, Swallows Gold and Spouts Rubbish*.
- In the United States, the Mexican artist José Clemente Orozco paints the mural *Prometheus* at Pomona College in Claremont, California.
- The English artist Henry Moore sculpts *Composition*.
- The English artist L. S. Lowry paints *The Empty House*.
- The English engineer George Carwardine designs the *Anglepoise Lamp*.
- The French artist Georges Rouault paints *Christ Mocked*.
- The French-born U.S. artist Gaston Lachaise sculpts *Standing Woman*.
- The Italian surrealist artist and writer Alberto Savinio (the brother of Giorgio de Chirico) paints *Annunciation*.
- The Mexican artist Frida Kahlo paints *My Birth*.
- The Russian artist Kazimir Malevich, the originator of a form of abstract painting known as suprematism, paints *The Red House*.
- The Spanish artist Julio González sculpts *Maternity*.
- The Spanish artist Pablo Picasso paints *Girl Before a Mirror*, *Woman Lying Down*, and *Nude in an Armchair*.
- The Swiss artist Alberto Giacometti completes *The Palace at 4 am*, an early (and uncharacteristic) sculpture which reflects the influence of surrealism, and sculpts *Woman with her Throat Cut*.
- The Swiss artist Paul Klee paints *Ad Parnassum/To Parnassus*.

- The U.S. artist Ben Shahn completes his 23 paintings of the Sacco and Vanzetti trial.
- The U.S. artist Charles Ephraim Burchfield paints *The Old Farmhouse*.
- The U.S. artist Georgia O'Keeffe paints *White Canadian Barn No.2*.
- The U.S. artist Grant Wood paints *Daughters of the Revolution*.
- The U.S. artist Man Ray completes his painting *Observatory Time – The Lovers*.
- The U.S. artist Stuart Davis paints *Landscape with Garage Lights*.
- U.S. sculptor Alexander Calder creates his *Mobiles* (sculptures moved by engines or air currents), soon followed by *Stabiles* which do not move.

Film

- *Freaks* is released, directed by U.S. filmmaker Tod Browning and featuring an array of real-life sideshow "attractions." The movie is extensively edited in the United States and is banned in the UK for 30 years.
- *Scarface* is released in the United States. Directed by Howard Hawks, produced by Howard Hughes, and starring Paul Muni, the movie is a thinly veiled life-story of Chicago-based gangster Al Capone.
- The 1931–32 Academy Awards take place. Best Actor (jointly): Wallace Beery, for *The Champ*, and Fredric March, for *Dr Jekyll and Mr Hyde*; Best Actress: Helen Hayes, for *The Sin of Madelon Claudet*; Best Picture: *Grand Hotel*, directed by Edmund Goulding; Best Director: Frank Borzage, for *Bad Girl*.
- The movie *Blonde Venus*, directed by Austrian-born filmmaker Josef von Sternberg, is released in the United States, starring Marlene Dietrich, Herbert Marshall, and Cary Grant.
- The movie *Boudu sauvé des eaux/Boudu Saved from Drowning*, directed by Jean Renoir, is released in France, an ironic dissection of middle-class values starring Michel Simon, Charles Grandval, and Marcelle Hainia.
- The movie *Das Blaue Licht/The Blue Light*, directed by Leni Riefenstahl, is released in Germany. She also stars in it.
- The movie *Dr Jekyll and Mr Hyde*, directed by Russian-born filmmaker Rouben Mamoulian, is released in the United States, based on the novel by Robert Louis Stevenson and starring Fredric March.
- The movie *Fanny*, directed by Marc Allégret, is released in France. The second in a trilogy by Marcel Pagnol, it stars Raimu, Pierre Fresnay, Fernand Charpin, and Orane Demazis.
- The movie *Grand Hotel*, directed by Edmund Goulding, is released in the United States. Its all-star cast includes Greta Garbo, Lionel Barrymore, Joan Crawford, and Wallace Beery.
- The movie *I Am a Fugitive from a Chain Gang*, directed by Mervyn LeRoy, is released in the United States, starring Paul Muni.
- The movie *I Was Born, But...*, directed by Yasujiro Ozu, is released in Japan, starring Mitsuko Yoshikawa.
- The movie *One Hour With You*, directed by German filmmaker Ernst Lubitsch, is released in the United

States, starring Maurice Chevalier and Jeanette MacDonald.

- The movie *Shanghai Express*, directed by Austrian-born filmmaker Josef von Sternberg, is released in the United States, starring Marlene Dietrich and Clive Brook.
- The movie *Tarzan the Ape Man*, directed by W. S. Van Dyke, is released in the United States. The first Tarzan talkie, it stars the former Olympic swimmer Johnny Weissmuller as Tarzan.
- The movie *Vampyr*, a dreamlike, visually striking adaptation of Joseph Sheridan Le Fanu's book *Carmilla* directed by Danish filmmaker Carl Theodor Dreyer, is released. It is filmed in German, French, and English versions.
- The Venice Film Festival—The International Exhibition of Cinematographic Art—is inaugurated.

Literature and Language

- An expurgated version of D. H. Lawrence's *Lady Chatterley's Lover* (published in 1928) is published in London, England.
- German writer Hans Fallada publishes *Kleiner Mann, was nun?/Little Man, What Now?*, a novel focusing on German social problems. It receives international acclaim.
- The Belgian surrealist writer and artist Henri Michaux publishes *Un Barbare en Asie/A Barbarian in Asia*, a vivid account of his travels in Asia.
- The British novelist Evelyn Waugh publishes his satire on colonialism, *Black Mischief*.
- The English literary critic Frank Raymond Leavis publishes his *New Bearings in English Poetry*. A widely influential work that champions such modern writers as Ezra Pound, T. S. Eliot and W. B. Yeats, it helps to bring about a major revision of the English poetic tradition.
- The English literary critic Queenie Dorothy Leavis publishes *Fiction and the Reading Public*, which traces the history of the relationship between popular and high-brow literature. With her husband F. R. Leavis, she launches the influential Cambridge-based literary journal *Scrutiny*.
- The English writer Aldous Huxley publishes his novel *Brave New World*, which presents a nightmarish vision of a utopia based on science and technology.
- The English writer Charles Morgan publishes his novel *The Fountain*.
- The English writer Graham Greene publishes his fourth novel, *Stamboul Train*.
- The English writer Rosamund Lehmann publishes her novel *Invitation to the Waltz*.
- The English writer Stella Gibbons publishes *Cold Comfort Farm*, a satirical novel of rural life that becomes very popular after being publicly praised by the politician Stanley Baldwin.
- The English-born U.S. writer W. H. Auden publishes *The Orators*, an early collection of poetry.
- The first edition of *The Oxford Companion to English Literature*, edited by Paul Harvey, is published.
- The French Catholic writer François Mauriac publishes *Le Noeud de Vipères/A Nest of Vipers*, one of his finest novels.

- The French writer Jules Romains publishes *Les Hommes de bonne volonté/Men of Good Will*, the first volume of an epic 27-volume novel sequence.
- The French writer Louis-Ferdinand Céline publishes his novel *Voyage au bout de la nuit/Journey to the End of the Night*. A grimly realistic account of his experiences as a doctor among the poor, written in a strikingly original style, it wins international acclaim.
- The German writer Hermann Broch publishes his trilogy of novels *Die Schlafwandler/The Sleepwalkers*, a depiction of European society from the late 19th century to the end of World War I.
- The Irish writer George Bernard Shaw publishes *The Adventures of the Black Girl in Her Search for God*.
- The Nobel Prize for Literature is awarded to the British novelist John Galsworthy.
- The Pulitzer Prize for Biography is awarded to Henry Pringle for *Theodore Roosevelt*. Pearl Buck receives the Prize for Fiction for *The Good Earth*, and the Prize for Poetry goes to George Dillon for *The Flowering Stone*.
- The Russian writer Boris Pasternak publishes his poetry collection *Vtoroe rozhdenie/Second Birth*.
- The Scottish writer Lewis Grassic Gibbon publishes *Sunset Song*, the first novel in his *A Scots Quair* trilogy.
- The U.S. writer Edith Wharton completes her novel *The Gods Arrive*.
- The U.S. writer Ellen Glasgow publishes her novel *The Sheltered Life*.
- The U.S. writer Ernest Hemingway publishes *Death in the Afternoon*, a study of bullfighting.
- The U.S. writer Erskine Caldwell publishes his novel *Tobacco Road*, which establishes his reputation and becomes a best seller. In 1933, dramatized by Jack Kirkland, it will run on Broadway for more than 3,000 performances.
- The U.S. writer James Thomas Farrell publishes his novel *Young Lonigan*, the first part of the *Studs Lonigan* trilogy, a grimly realistic depiction of life in Chicago's poor districts.
- The U.S. writer John Dos Passos publishes his novel *1919*, the second part of his monumental trilogy *USA*.
- The U.S. writer William Faulkner publishes his novel *Light in August*, the seventh of his novels set in his fictional Yoknapatawpha County.
- The Welsh novelist John Cowper Powys publishes his novel *A Glastonbury Romance*.

Music

- In the United States, the song "Brother, Can You Spare a Dime?," written by Jay Gourlay and sung by Bing Crosby, becomes popular. Its lyrics reflect the consequences of the Depression.
- The Austrian composer Arnold Schoenberg completes the first two acts of his opera *Moses und Aaron*. The third act is often spoken (as Schoenberg said it should be) though it is sometimes set to music from the first two acts.
- The English actor, writer, and composer Noël Coward publishes what will become his best-known song, "Mad Dogs and Englishmen." It is said to have been conceived in 1930.

- The English composer Benjamin Britten completes his *Sinfonietta* Opus 1.
- The English conductor Thomas Beecham founds the London Philharmonic Orchestra and becomes the principal conductor at Covent Garden.
- The Romanian composer George Enescu completes his opera *Oedipe/Oedipus*.
- The Russian composer Nikolay Myaskovsky completes his Symphony No. 12.
- The Russian composer Dmitry Shostakovich completes his *Hamlet* suite.
- The Russian composer Sergey Prokofiev completes his Piano Concerto No. 5.
- The U.S. bandleader Tommy Dorsey's "I'm Getting Sentimental Over You" becomes a hit.
- The U.S. composer George Gershwin completes his *Cuban Overture*.
- The U.S. jazz musician Louis Armstrong appears in Britain for the first time, including a concert at the London Palladium.

Theater and Dance

- The play *Dangerous Corner*, by the English writer J. B. Priestley, is first performed, in London, England.
- The Pulitzer Prize for Drama is awarded to George Kaufman and Morris Ryskind for *Of Thee I Sing*.
- The Shakespeare Memorial Theatre is opened at Stratford-upon-Avon, England.

NOVEMBER

29 The musical *Gay Divorcée*, with music and lyrics by Cole Porter, opens at the Ethel Barrymore Theater in New York, New York.

DECEMBER

27 The 6,200-seat Radio City Musical Hall opens in New York, New York.

Thought and Scholarship

- *The Epic of America* by the U.S. historian James Truslow Adams is the best-selling nonfiction title in the United States.
- Dutch historian Pieter Geyl publishes his multivolume *The Revolt of the Netherlands*.
- Finnish social philosopher Edvard Westermarck publishes his *Ethical Relativity*.
- French Catholic philosopher Jacques Maritain publishes *Les Degrés du savoir/The Degrees of Knowledge*.
- French philosopher Henri Bergson publishes *Les Deux Sources de la morale et de la religion/The Two Sources of Morality and Religion*, which analyzes the role of morality and religion in society.
- German philosopher Karl Jaspers publishes his three-volume *Philosophie/Philosophy*, in which he expounds his own distinctive form of existentialism.
- Russian revolutionary leader Leon Trotsky publishes his 3-volume *History of the Russian Revolution*.
- The English writer James Louis Garvin publishes the first volume of *The Life of Joseph Chamberlain*.
- The Pulitzer Prize for History is awarded to John J. Pershing for *My Experience in the World War*.
- U.S. economists A. A. Berle and G. C. Means publish *The Modern Corporation and Private Property*.

- U.S. historian Carl Becker publishes *The Heavenly City of the Eighteenth-Century Philosophers*.
- U.S. Protestant theologian Reinhold Niebuhr publishes *Moral Man and Immoral Society*, in which he argues that the church ought to take an active role in social reform.
- U.S. social psychologist George Herbert Mead publishes *The Philosophy of the Present*. Mead's interest in how individuals give meaning to their worlds gave rise to the sociological discipline of symbolic interactionism.

SOCIETY

Everyday Life

- Big Bear Super Market, the first discount self-serve grocery, opens in New Jersey.

MAY

5–July 7 The first of some 15,000 "Bonus Marchers" arrive in Washington, D.C. These unemployed veterans from across the U.S. demand that Congress fulfill a pledge to let them borrow from federally sponsored insurance policies. After a stalemate extends into the summer, the Hoover administration dislodges the veterans by force in late July.

AUGUST

2 In Slough, England, Forrest Mars launches the Mars Bar: this product will form the basis of the Mars confectionery empire.

NOVEMBER

11 The Tomb of the Unknown Soldier is dedicated at Arlington National Cemetery outside of Washington, D.C.

Media and Communication

JUNE

27 In the United States, Ted Husing of the Central Broadcasting Service (CBS) carries out the first vox pop interviews with delegates at the Democratic Convention in Chicago, Illinois.

AUGUST

22–September 10 In collaboration with Baird Company, the British Broadcasting Corporation (BBC) begins the first regular television service, with transmissions between 11 a.m. and 11:30 p.m.

OCTOBER

3 *The Times* introduces the Times New Roman font, in the UK. Designed by Stanley Morrison, it will become the most widely used font for newspapers and magazines.

11 The Democratic Party gives the first party political television broadcast, in New York, New York.

DECEMBER

25 King George V of Britain makes the first Christmas broadcast by a British head of state.

Religion

- Austrian Jewish theologian Martin Buber publishes *Köningtum Gottes/The Kingship of God.*
- In Britain, Wesleyan Methodists, Primitive Methodists, and the United Methodist Church form the Methodist Church of Great Britain and Ireland.
- Swiss Protestant theologian Karl Barth publishes the first volume of *Die Kirchliche Dogmatic/Church Dogmatics.*

MARCH

29–April 6 Jewish athletes from 20 countries participate in the inaugural World Maccabiah Games in Tel Aviv.

JUNE

- The Catholic Eucharistic Congress is held in Ireland for the first time, coinciding with celebrations of the 1,500th anniversary of the arrival of St. Patrick.

Sports

- Mildred "Babe" Didrikson wins the U.S. women's Amateur Athletic Union team title for her club, Employers' Casualty of Dallas. She enters eight out of ten events and wins the 80 m hurdles, the long jump, javelin, shot, and baseball throwing, and is equal first in the high jump.
- Undefeated University of Southern California wins its second consecutive national college football championship.

FEBRUARY

4–15 The 3rd Winter Olympic Games are held at Lake Placid, New York, in the United States. The hosts win 22 gold medals; Germany, 10; Finland, 8; Sweden, Italy, and Switzerland, 7 each. Sonja Henie of Norway wins her second successive gold medal in the figure skating, which is held indoors for the first time. Canada wins its fourth successive ice hockey title, thanks to a superior goal average, after three periods of overtime in the final game against the United States.

APRIL

5–9 The Toronto Maple Leafs beat the New York Rangers in three games to win the National Hockey League (NHL) championship.

MAY

21 The first Curtis Cup match between the women golfers of the United States and those of Great Britain and Ireland is held at Wentworth, Surrey, England; the U.S. team wins 5½–3½.

BIRTHS & DEATHS

JANUARY

5 Chuck Noll, who coached the Pittsburgh Steelers to four Super Bowl championships, born in Cleveland, Ohio.

6 Julius Ronsenwald, heir to Sears fortune and philanthropist of U.S. education, dies in Chicago (69).

7 André Maginot, French statesman, dies in Paris, France (54).

FEBRUARY

6 François Truffaut, French, director, screenwriter, and actor born in Paris, France (–1984).

10 Edgar Wallace, English novelist, playwright, and journalist, known for his detective stories, dies in Hollywood, California (57).

18 Miloš Forman, award-winning U.S. film director, screenwriter, and producer, born in Caslav, Czechoslovakia.

22 Edward Kennedy, U.S. politician and senator from Massachusetts, born in Boston, Massachusetts.

26 Johnny Cash, U.S. country music singer known for his black attire and his songs of despair, born in Kingsland, Arkansas.

27 Elizabeth Taylor, winner of two Academy Awards for best film actress, born in London, England.

MARCH

6 John Philip Sousa, U.S. bandmaster and composer of military marches, dies in Reading, Pennsylvania (77).

7 Aristide Briand, French statesman, premier of France 11 times, dies in Paris, France (69).

14 George Eastman, U.S. inventor, manufacturer, and philanthropist who introduced the Kodak camera, dies in Rochester, New York (77).

18 John Updike, U.S. novelist, short story writer, and poet, born in Shillington, Pennsylvania.

21 Walter Gilbert, U.S. molecular biologist in the field of DNA, born in Boston, Massachusetts.

APRIL

4 Anthony Perkins, U.S. actor, born in New York, New York (–1992).

14 Loretta Lynn, U.S. country music singer whose life inspired the movie *The Coal Miner's Daughter*, born in Butcher Hollow, Kentucky.

JUNE

7 William Williams Keen, the first brain surgeon in the United States, dies in Philadelphia, Pennsylvania (95).

11 Athol Fugard, South African dramatist, actor, and director, born in Middleburg, South Africa.

JULY

22 Florenz Ziegfeld, U.S. theatrical producer known for his Ziegfeld Follies, dies in Hollywood, California (63).

22 Reginald Aubrey Fessenden, Canadian-U.S. pioneer of long-distance radio broadcasts, dies in Hamilton, Bermuda (65).

29 Nancy Landon Kassebaum, daughter of presidential candidate Alf Landon and senator from Kansas, born in Topeka, Kansas.

AUGUST

17 V(idiadhar) S(urajprasad) Naipaul, Trinidadian-British writer of novels and nonfiction, born in Trinidad.

SEPTEMBER

16 Ronald Ross, British bacteriologist who discovered that malaria is transmitted by mosquitos, dies in Putney Heath, London, England (75).

OCTOBER

27 Sylvia Plath, U.S. poet and novelist, born in Boston, Massachusetts (–1963).

30 Louis Malle, French film director, born in Thumeries, France.

NOVEMBER

29 Jacques Chirac, French politician, prime minister 1974–76 and 1986–88 and president from 1995, born in Paris, France.

DECEMBER

14 Charlie Rich, U.S. country singer, born in Colt, Arkansas (–1995).

JUNE

21 Jack Sharkey of the United States outpoints Max Schmeling of Germany in 15 rounds in Long Island, New York, to win the world heavyweight boxing title.

25 U.S. golfer Gene Sarazen wins the U.S. Open golf championship.

JULY

1–2 At the Wimbledon tennis championships in England, Helen Wills Moody of the United States wins the women's championship, and Ellsworth Vines, Jr., of the United States captures the men's title.

6–31 In cycling, André Leducq of France wins the Tour de France for the second time in three years.

30–August 14 The 10th Olympic Games are held in Los Angeles, California. The United States wins 16 gold medals; Italy, 12; France, 10; Sweden, 9; Japan, 7; Hungary, 6; Finland, 5. National flags and the three-tiered victory stand are used in medal ceremonies for the first time; photo-finish equipment is first used in track events. The games are attended by 1.25 million spectators. Mildred "Babe" Didrikson of the United States wins a gold medal in the javelin and the 80 m hurdles, and a silver medal in the high jump. Kusuo Kitamura of Japan, aged 14 years and 309 days, wins the men's 1,500-meters freestyle swimming gold medal.

U.S. athlete Eddie Tolan wins the men's 100-m and 200-m gold medals.

31 In tennis, the French Davis Cup team defeats the United States by three matches to two to win its sixth successive title.

AUGUST

21–September 3 The U.S. Lawn Tennis Association competition takes place. U.S. tennis players Helen Hull Jacobs and Ellsworth Vines, Jr., are the champions.

SEPTEMBER

28–October 2 The New York Yankees defeat the Chicago Cubs four games to none in the World Series.

OCTOBER

13 Kid Chocolate of the United States knocks out countryman Lew Feldman in the 12th round of the featherweight championship fight in New York, New York.

DECEMBER

18 The Chicago Bears beat the Portsmouth Spartans 9–0 in the first-ever play-off game in professional football history after the two sides finished the regular season in equal first place. The game takes place indoors at the Chicago Stadium in Illinois because of heavy snow.

1933

POLITICS, GOVERNMENT, AND ECONOMICS

Business and Economics

APRIL

19 The U.S. president Franklin D. Roosevelt removes the U.S. dollar from the gold standard, allowing U.S. economic problems to be addressed without reference to international financial cooperation.

25 Canada abandons the gold standard.

JUNE

6 The Glass–Steagall Act in the United States creates the Federal Deposit Insurance Corporation (FDIC) and directs banks to separate securities investments from commercial banking.

6 The National Industrial Recovery Act in the United States calls on business to set and maintain reasonable price, wage, and competition standards in return for relief from antitrust regulation. The act also authorizes workers to organize and negotiate on their own behalf.

12–July 27 Sixty-four countries attend the World Monetary and Economic Conference in London, England, but fail to reach agreement on how to achieve currency stabilization.

AUGUST

30 Air France is founded.

Colonization

JUNE

13 Australia claims one third of the land area of Antarctica.

Human Rights

APRIL

1 The official persecution of the Jews in Germany begins, with a national boycott of Jewish stores, businesses, and professionals.

Politics and Government

- Germany introduces a four-year plan (the Schacht Plan) to abolish unemployment by expanding public works.
- Social legislation under President Franklin D. Roosevelt's New Deal in the United States extends government involvement in social provision.
- The Confederation of Autonomous Right Wing Groups (CEDA) wins 115 seats in the Spanish general election; the next largest party is the Radicals with 102.
- German Nazis open Ravensbrück, the first concentration camp for women.
- The U.S. president Franklin D. Roosevelt appoints John Collier, secretary of the Indian Defense Association, Commissioner of Indian Affairs. A champion of Native American civil rights, Collier works to reverse the cultural havoc wreaked by the Dawes Severalty Act of 1887.

JANUARY

2   Anarchists and syndicalists revolt in Barcelona, Spain, in pursuit of a radical anarcho-syndicalist program.

13 The U.S. Congress votes for independence for the U.S.-held Philippines, after a transition period.

16 Eleutherios Venizelos becomes prime minister of Greece after his republican opposition forces the royalist Pannyiotis Tsaldaris to resign. (Tsaldaris is later restored.)

22 The USSR launches its second five-year plan, envisioning the continued growth of heavy industry and increased production of consumer goods.

23 The Twentieth amendment to the U.S. Constitution advances the inauguration date of presidents to January 20, with senators and representatives taking office on January 3.

24 The prime minister Éamon de Valera's Fianna Fáil party retains a majority of one in the Irish Free State general election.

28 The German president, Paul von Hindenburg, dismisses Kurt von Schleicher as chancellor after his failure to obtain a governing majority in the Reichstag (parliament).

30 The German president, Paul von Hindenburg, appoints the Nazi leader, Adolf Hitler, as chancellor. His cabinet includes only two other Nazis, Hermann Goering and Wilhelm Frick. Franz von Papen is vice chancellor and Constantin von Neurath foreign minister.

31 The Radical Edouard Daladier becomes prime minister of France.

FEBRUARY

2   The U.S. Congress sends the 21st amendment, repealing Prohibition, to the states.

15 A gunman attempts to assassinate the U.S. president-elect, Franklin D. Roosevelt.

16 The Little Entente (the defense agreement between Czechoslovakia, Romania, and Yugoslavia) is reorganized following threats of German domination.

23–March 12 Japanese forces advance southwest from Manchuria, China, into the city of Jehol (Chengde), northeast of the Great Wall of China, and then continue southward.

24 The League of Nations adopts the findings of the Lytton Commission, set up to investigate the Japanese invasion of Manchuria, China, that both parties are guilty. Japan rejects the findings.

27 The Reichstag, seat of the German parliament, is set on fire.

28 German chancellor Adolf Hitler persuades president Paul von Hindenburg to issue a "decree for the protection of people and state." It suppresses civil liberties and freedom of the press in the wake of the Reichstag fire and allows the Nazis to arrest thousands of their opponents.

MARCH

4   Franklin D. Roosevelt is inaugurated as 32nd president of the United States. He declares that "the only thing we have to fear is fear itself." Cordell Hull is appointed secretary of state.

5   President Franklin D. Roosevelt summons the U.S. Congress to Washington, D.C., for a special session on March 9, and closes all banks from March 6 to 9.

5   The Nazis win a large majority of 288 seats in the German general election.

6   A Republican coup in Greece led by Nicholas Plastiras briefly deposes the royalist prime minister Panayiotis Tsaldaris. He is restored on March 10.

7   The Austrian chancellor, Engelbert Dollfuss, suspends parliament after political polarization makes democratic government impossible: he rules by decree while a new constitution is drawn up.

9–June 16 The U.S. Congress begins a special session to deal with economic and social problems, granting President Franklin D. Roosevelt control over gold and silver bullion and foreign exchange. It passes 15 major bills during the "Hundred Days."

12 President Roosevelt holds the first "fireside chat" by radio with the U.S. people, to encourage support for the New Deal.

16 At the League of Nations Disarmament Conference in Geneva, Switzerland, Britain's plan for a reduction in the size of armies fails when Germany insists that storm troopers should not form part of the total.

19 The Italian fascist prime minister Benito Mussolini proposes a four-year pact with Britain, France, and Germany.

20 The first Nazi concentration camp is created at Dachau, near Munich, Germany.

23 An enabling bill is passed by the Nazi-dominated Reichstag (parliament) in Germany giving the chancellor, Adolf Hitler, full dictatorial powers.

26 A new constitution, known as the "Estado Novo" is drawn up in Portugal, establishing a dictatorial government under the president, Sidónio Pais.

27 Japan announces that it will leave the League of Nations as from 1935, in response to League attempts to contain Japanese expansion in China.

30 The South African prime minister, J. B. M. Hertzog, forms a coalition with the deputy prime minister, Jan Smuts, against extreme nationalists.

31 German chancellor Adolf Hitler uses the enabling bill to dissolve provincial diets and replace the deputies with a Nazi majority. Communists are excluded.

APRIL

5   The International Court at The Hague in the Netherlands rules that Greenland is a Danish possession, thus dismissing Norway's claim to it.

7 Chancellor Adolf Hitler creates Reich governors for the German provinces and arms them with dictatorial powers.

26 Hermann Goering, German minister of the interior for Prussia in Adolf Hitler's Nazi-dominated government, forms the *Geheime Staatspolizei* (Gestapo, or secret state police) from the former Prussian police.

27 The dispute over Persia's annulment of the Anglo-Persian Oil Company's concession in Persia is settled with a new agreement.

30 President Sáncho Cerro of Peru is assassinated and succeeded by Oscar Benevides.

MAY

5 The U.S. Congress creates the Tennessee Valley Authority, a regional revitalization program affecting eight southern states, which aims to control flooding, produce electric power, and improve agriculture along the Tennessee River and its tributaries.

5 The U.S. Congress passes the Federal Emergency Relief Act. Under the leadership of the New York social worker Harry L. Hopkins, the Emergency Relief Administration provides states with cash to assist the unemployed.

7 The Spanish republican government nationalizes church property and closes church schools.

10 Paraguay formally declares war on Bolivia in the Chaco War over the disputed border territory of Chaco Boreal.

17 In the South African elections, the National Coalition led by J. B. M. Hertzog and Jan Smuts wins 138 seats and the nationalist Opposition 12.

28 The Nazis win elections in the free city of Danzig (now Gdańsk, Poland).

31 An armistice is signed between China and Japan, under the terms of which Japanese invasion forces in China are to withdraw to the north of the Great Wall.

JUNE

2 The German chancellor, Adolf Hitler, forms a new government, with increased Nazi representation.

6 The Rome Pact is initialed, binding France, Britain, Germany, and Italy to support the Covenant of the League of Nations, the Locarno treaties, and the Kellogg–Briand Pact.

13–June 1, 1936 Congress creates the Home Owners Loan Corporation, which in its three-year existence will provide Americans with loans for one million mortgages.

15 Britain makes a token final payment to the United States for World War I debts.

19 The Austrian chancellor, Engelbert Dollfuss, leader of the "Fatherland Front," dissolves the Austrian Nazi Party, but Nazi agitation continues.

20 A military coup in Siam (modern Thailand), led by Colonel Phya Bahol Sena, forces the reconstitution of the parliamentary assembly.

JULY

3 The USSR and other Eastern European countries sign the London Convention defining aggression.

14 All political parties other than the National Socialist (Nazi) Party are banned in Germany.

AUGUST

5 Poland signs an agreement with the free city of Danzig (now Gdańsk), guaranteeing a proportion of Polish

trade to the port in return for favorable treatment of Poles living in the city.

12 President Gerardo Machado of Cuba is forced into exile by the army, led by Fulgencio Batista and supported by the United States.

22 The National Guard ("Blueshirts") is declared illegal in the Irish Free State.

SEPTEMBER

14 Greece and Turkey agree to a ten-year nonaggression pact.

OCTOBER

10 There is increasing unrest in Palestine against Jewish immigration from Germany.

14 Germany withdraws from the League of Nations and its disarmament conference.

16 The Labor Party wins the Norwegian general election, but Johan Mowinckel's Liberal cabinet remains in power.

23 The Radical leader Albert Sarraut becomes prime minister of France.

25 The Labour Party overturns a government majority of 14,000 in the East Fulham by-election, in London, England. This is widely interpreted as a vote in favor of pacifism and against the means test (the evaluation of people's income to decide whether they qualify for state aid).

NOVEMBER

8 King Nadir Shah of Afghanistan is assassinated and succeeded by his son Mohammed Zahir Shah.

12 In the German general election, 92% of electors are recorded as voting for Nazi candidates, with 96% of the electorate turning out to vote.

16 Brazil's provisional president, Getúlio Vargas, gains dictatorial powers.

17 The United States officially recognizes the USSR, and resumes trade.

22 The Radical Camille Chautemps is reelected prime minister of France.

DECEMBER

9–19 An uprising of anarchists and syndicalists against the republican government erupts in Spain.

12 Jews in Palestine protest at immigration restrictions imposed by the British authorities because of the flood of Jewish refugees from Germany and Palestinian Arab hostility toward them.

15 A black American released by a court in Tennessee, United States, is lynched by a white mob.

18 Newfoundland loses its status as a British dominion owing to mismanagement of economic affairs; its constitution is suspended and its government surrenders control to a commission nominated by the British Treasury.

29 The Romanian prime minister, Ion Duca, is assassinated by members of the fascist Iron Guard. He is succeeded by authoritarian Gheorghe Tatarescu.

SCIENCE, TECHNOLOGY, AND MEDICINE

Agriculture

- Hybrid corn (Golden Cross Bantam) begins to be planted on a large scale in the United States. In 1933, 1% of total corn acreage is planted in hybrid corn; in 1939, 15%; 1946, 69%; and 1960, 96%. Average yield per acre increases from 23 bushels in 1933 to 83 bushels by 1980.

MAY

5   The Agricultural Adjustment Act in the United States rewards farmers for uprooting crops in order to curtail overproduction.

NOVEMBER

11–13   A dust storm blows topsoil from South Dakota as far east as New York State; the U.S. Department of Agriculture sets up a Soil Erosion Service to teach farmers tilling methods that minimize erosion.

Ecology

AUGUST

- A massive forest fire in Oregon, later known as the "Tillamook Burn," advances along an 30-km/18-mi front and destroys 12 billion board-feet of virgin timber.

NOVEMBER

2   Death Valley National Park is created to preserve its unique flora and fauna and geological features; it contains the lowest point on land in the western hemisphere and covers 7,800 sq km/3,000 sq mi.

Exploration

- Muslim convert H. St. John Philby crosses Arabia's "Empty Quarter," discovering natural lakes formed in the craters from a meteor impact in the middle of the desert.

November 1933–34   British soldier Wilfred Thesiger explores the Danakil Desert of Ethiopia on an unaccompanied expedition.

November 1933–34   U.S. naval officer and explorer Richard Byrd explores the region of Antarctica now called "Byrd Land," establishing a permanent base on the Ross Ice Shelf.

Health and Medicine

- An unidentified disease kills 50,000 people in China.
- British biochemist Ernest Kennaway discovers that hydrocarbons produced from incomplete combustion, and found in cigarette smoke, car exhausts, and air pollution, can cause cancer in test animals. These are the first chemical carcinogens to be isolated.
- British physician Grantley Dick-Read advocates relaxation exercises and courses on childbirth for expectant mothers in his book *Natural Childbirth*; his ideas become popular in the 1950s.
- Physician Evarts Graham removes a cancerous lung; this is the first time such an operation is performed.
- U.S. biologist George Wald demonstrates that vitamin A is important in preventing night blindness.
- U.S. microbiologist Thomas Francis, Jr., isolates the virus responsible for influenza A.
- U.S. physiologist Thomas Hunt Morgan receives the Nobel Prize for Physiology or Medicine for his work on heredity and chromosomes.
- Viennese neurophysiologist Manfred Sakel uses insulin shock therapy to treat schizophrenic patients.

Science

- Austrian-born German organic chemist R. Kuhn, Hungarian-born U.S. biochemist A. von Szent-Györgyi, and J. Wagner-Jauregg discover vitamin B2 (riboflavin), in Hungary.
- British geneticist John B. S. Haldane popularizes evolution with the publication of *The Causes of Evolution*.
- British physicist Arthur Stanley Eddington publishes *The Expanding Universe*, in which he lays out his theory that the universe is constantly increasing in size.
- Canadian biologist Ludwig von Bertalanffy writes *Theoretical Biology* in which he attempts to develop a common methodological approach to all sciences based on the tenets of organismic biology.
- English physicist Paul Dirac and Austrian physicist Erwin Schrödinger share the Nobel Prize for Physics for their work on wave mechanics in quantum mechanics.
- German physicists Walter Meissner and R. Ochensfeld discover that superconducting materials expel their magnetic fields when cooled to superconducting temperatures—the Meissner effect.
- High-intensity mercury vapor lights are introduced.
- Polish biochemist Tadeus Reichstein synthesizes vitamin C (ascorbic acid), in Switzerland, and Swiss biochemist Paul Karrer establishes the structure of vitamin A (retinol).
- The Steinheim skull is discovered by the River Murr in Germany. Classified as an early subspecies of *Homo sapiens*, it leads to the rejection of the theory that Neanderthal humans were in the line of descent leading to *Homo sapiens*.
- U.S. astronomer Walter Baade suggests that supernovas develop into neutron stars after exploding.
- U.S. physician Ralph Minton introduces the general anesthetic cyclopropane; it represents the first improvement over nitrous oxide and ether.
- U.S. scientist Carl David Anderson succeeds in producing positrons by gamma irradiation.

Technology

- British company Imperial Chemical Industries (ICI) makes the first commercially produced synthetic detergent.
- French civil engineer Eugène Freyssinet builds the Gare Maritime (harbor station) at Le Havre, France, the first building to be made of prestressed concrete.

- German engineer Ernst August Friedrich Ruska builds the first electron microscope; it has a magnification power of 12,000.
- German scientist Ida Noddack reveals research demonstrating nuclear fission.
- Soviet engineer Sergei Korolev builds a liquid-propellant rocket that reaches an altitude of 4.8 km/3 mi.
- The British Marconiphone Company makes the first all-metal radio valve.
- U.S. inventor Paul Galvin and the U.S. Army Corps of Engineers develop portable two-way radios or "walkie-talkies."
- U.S. inventor Philo Farnsworth develops electronic television.

SEPTEMBER

8 Work begins on the Grand Coulee Dam across the Columbia River; it is the largest concrete structure ever built.

Transportation

c. 1933 Railroads in the United States begin to face increasing competition from trucks.
- A subway system is opened in the Japanese city of Osaka.
- Aluminum alloys are used in the construction of bridges for the first time.
- Dutch serviceman Jan Wickers invents the snorkel—a telescopic tube to supply fresh air to the diesel engines of submerged submarines. The Dutch navy begins using them in 1936 and the German navy in 1940.
- Railroad rail segments are welded together for the first time.
- Soviet scientists G. Profkoviet, F. N. Birnbaum, and K. D. Godunow reach a height of 18,495m/60,680 ft in a hot-air balloon.
- The Italian liner *Rex* crosses the Atlantic from Cherbourg, France, to New York, New York, in 4 days, 13 hours, 58 minutes, setting a new transatlantic record.
- U.S. engineer Buckminster Fuller makes the "Dymaxion" car. The first streamlined three-wheeled car, it can accelerate to 190 kph/120mph, complete a 180° turn within its own length, and carry 12 passengers. Designed to maximize gain from the minimum of energy input, it is never put into production.

JUNE

1 The Douglas Company DC-1 airliner makes its first flight from Santa Monica, California. During the flight it loses power in both engines. Power is regained on the descent and it is discovered that the carburetors have been installed backward. The plane has variable speed propellers and can fly at 241kph/150 mph and carry 12 passengers.

22 The Illinois Waterway opens; it links the Great Lakes with the Gulf of Mexico via the Mississippi River.

JULY

15–22 U.S. aviator Wiley Post makes the first solo flight around the world, in 7 days 18 hr 49 min.

ARTS AND IDEAS

Architecture

- Nazi authorities close the Bauhaus design school in Berlin, Germany, considering the modern art it advocates "degenerate."
- The Cité de Refuge, a Salvation Army hostel in Paris, France, designed by the Swiss architect Le Corbusier, is completed.
- The Convalescent Home in Paimio, Finland, designed by the Finnish architect Alvar Aalto, is completed.
- The Danish architect and designer Arne Jacobsen designs the Bellavista Housing Estate at Klampenborg, near Copenhagen. It is his first major work.
- The Penguin Pool of London Zoo, designed by the Russian-born English architect Berthold Lubetkin, is completed in London, England.

Arts

- British art critic and writer Herbert Read publishes *Art Now*, a defense of developments in modern art.
- French photographer Henri Cartier-Bresson takes *Seville*.
- The English artist Stanley Spencer paints *Sarah Tubb and the Angels*.
- The French artist Fernand Léger paints *Marie the Acrobat*.
- The French artist Pierre Bonnard paints *Nude at the Mirror*.
- The German artist Max Beckmann paints his triptych *Departure*.
- The Hungarian-born French photographer Brassaï publishes *Paris du Nuit/Paris by Night*, which contains many of his best-known images of life in Paris during the 1920s and early 1930s.
- The Mexican artist Diego Rivera completes murals in the Rockefeller Center, New York, New York. They are soon destroyed because they contain a portrait of the Soviet leader Lenin.
- The Spanish artist Joan Miró paints *Painting*.
- The Swiss artist Paul Klee paints *Von der Liste Grestrichen*, a noted self-portrait.
- The U.S. artist Thomas Hart Benton completes his mural *The Social History of the State of Indiana* for the Indiana state building at the World's Fair in Chicago, Illinois.
- Throughout the New Deal, U.S. government agencies hire more than 2,500 artists and 1,000 architects.

Film

- *Zéro de conduite*, directed by influential filmmaker Jean Vigo, is released in France, starring Jean Dasté, Louis Lefèvre, and Gilbert Pruchon.
- In Britain, the British Film Institute is established to develop knowledge about the movies.
- The backstage musical gains popularity with the release in the United States of such movies as *Gold Diggers of 1933*, directed by Mervyn LeRoy, and *42nd Street* and

Footlight Parade, both directed by Lloyd Bacon. All three movies feature the work of choreographer and filmmaker Busby Berkeley.

- The British government ceases to fund the Empire Marketing Board, the center of documentary filmmaking in England. The General Post Office (GPO) takes over funding, and renames it the GPO Film Unit.
- The movie *Cavalcade*, directed by Frank Lloyd, is released in the UK. Based on a play by Noël Coward, it stars Clive Brook and Diana Wynyard.
- The movie *Dinner at Eight*, directed by George Cukor, is released in the United States. It stars Marie Dressler, John Barrymore, Lionel Barrymore, Billie Burke, Wallace Beery, and Jean Harlow.
- The movie *Duck Soup*, directed by Leo McCarey, is released in the United States, starring the Marx brothers.
- The movie *King Kong*, directed by U.S. filmmakers Merian C. Cooper and Ernest B. Shoedsack and starring Robert Armstrong and Fay Wray, signals a major advance in special effects and animation. The monster in the movie is created by the animator Willis O'Brien, using stop-motion animation.
- The movie *Little Women*, directed by George Cukor, is released in the United States. Based on the novel by Louisa May Alcott, it stars Katharine Hepburn, Paul Lukas, Joan Bennett, Frances Dee, Jean Parker, and Spring Byington.
- The movie *She Done Him Wrong*, directed by Lowell Sherman, is released in the United States. Based on Mae West's play *Diamond Lil*, it stars Mae West and Cary Grant.
- The movie *The Invisible Man*, adapted from the H. G. Wells novel, is released in the United States. It stars Claude Rains in his first leading role, and is directed by James Whale.
- The movie *The Private Life of Henry VIII*, directed by Hungarian-born filmmaker Alexander Korda, is released in the UK, starring Charles Laughton, Elsa Lanchester, Robert Donat, Merle Oberon, and Binnie Barnes.
- The movie *The Testament of Dr Mabuse*, directed by Fritz Lang, is released in Germany starring Rudolph Klein-Rogge, Otto Wenicke, and Gustav Diesl. The German censors prevent it being shown, and Fritz Lang leaves Germany shortly afterwards.
- The musical movie *Flying Down to Rio*, directed by Thornton Freeland, is released in the United States, starring Dolores del Rio, Gene Raymond, Raul Roulien, Ginger Rogers, and Fred Astaire.

JUNE

6 Josef Goebbels, the German Minister of Information and Propaganda, authorizes legislation to exclude Jews and foreigners from involvement in movie production. As the Nazis increase their control over the movie industry, a number of noted Germans involved in movie production, notably Fritz Lang, Erich Pommer, Leontine Sagan, and Max Ophüls, leave the country.

Literature and Language

- *The Complete Works of Geoffrey Chaucer*, edited by F. N. Robinson, is published.
- 8.1 million books are published in the United States.

- Hervey Allen's historical romance *Anthony Adverse* is the best-selling novel in the United States.
- The *Shorter Oxford English Dictionary* is published for the first time.
- The English author Dorothy Leigh Sayers publishes her novel *Murder Must Advertise*.
- The English poet Stephen Spender publishes his *Poems*.
- The English scholar Helen Waddell publishes her novel *Peter Abelard*, based on the life of a medieval philosopher.
- The English writer Antonia White publishes her first novel, *Frost in May*.
- The English writer George Orwell publishes *Down and Out in Paris and London*, an account of his experience of working among the poor and dispossessed.
- The English writer H. G. Wells publishes his science-fiction "prophecy" *The Shape of Things to Come*, an attack on fascism.
- The English writer James Hilton publishes *Lost Horizon*, a popular novel that describes the discovery of Shangri-La, a utopian society hidden in the Himalayas.
- The English writer Walter Greenwood publishes *Love on the Dole*, an account of a family living through the Depression.
- The French writer André Malraux publishes his novel *La Condition humaine/Man's Estate*.
- The French writer Louis Aragon publishes his novel *Les Cloches de Bâle/The Bells of Basel*.
- The French writer Raymond Queneau publishes his novel *Le Chiendent/The Bark Tree*.
- The German writer Thomas Mann publishes *Die Geschichten Jaakobs/The Tales of Jacob*, the first volume of *Joseph und seine Brüder/Joseph and his Brothers*, the final volume of which will appear in 1943.
- The Nobel Prize for Literature is awarded to the Russian novelist Ivan Bunin.
- The Polish-born U.S. logician Alfred Tarski publishes *Der Wahrheitsbegriff in den Formalisierten Sprachen/The Concept of Truth in Formalized Languages*.
- The Pulitzer Prize for Fiction is awarded to T. S. Striblin for *The Store*. Allan Nevins wins the Prize for Biography for *Grover Cleveland*, and the Prize for Poetry is awarded to Archibald MacLeish for *Conquistador*.
- The Scottish writer Lewis Grassic Gibbon publishes *Cloud Howe*, the second novel in his *A Scots Quair* trilogy.
- The U.S. District Court in New York, New York, rules that the banned novel *Ulysses* by the Irish writer James Joyce, published in Paris, France, in 1922, is not obscene and can be published in the United States.
- The U.S. humorist James Thurber publishes *My Life and Hard Times*, a collection of short stories.
- The U.S. writer Erskine Caldwell publishes *God's Little Acre*, set in the agriculturally depressed South. Following on the success of *Tobacco Road*, published in 1932, it becomes a best seller, after various censorship trials.
- The U.S. writer Gertrude Stein publishes *The Autobiography of Alice B. Toklas*, her autobiography.
- The U.S. writer Nathanael West publishes his novel *Miss Lonelyhearts*, a bitter satire on U.S. life.
- The U.S. writer Sherwood Anderson publishes his short-story collection *Death in the Woods and Other Stories*.

- The U.S.-born English writer T. S. Eliot publishes *The Use of Poetry and the Use of Criticism* (his Charles Eliot Norton lectures at Harvard University).
- The Welsh writer John Cowper Powys publishes his novel *Weymouth Sands*.

June 1933–38 The English statesman and writer Winston Churchill publishes *Marlborough: His Life and Times*.

June 1933–45 The French writer Georges Duhamel publishes his ten-volume novel cycle *Chronique des Pasquier/The Pasquier Chronicles*.

Music

- Duke Ellington's orchestra plays in Britain for the first time.
- The Austrian composer Franz Schmidt completes his Symphony No. 4 in C major.
- The English composer Benjamin Britten completes his choral work *A Boy was Born* and *A Simple Symphony*, Opus 2.
- The French composer Olivier Messiaen completes his orchestral work *The Ascension*.
- The German composer Kurt Weill writes his ballet *The Seven Deadly Sins* in seven scenes with songs for soprano and male chorus.
- The Hungarian composer Béla Bartók completes his *Hungarian Sketches*.
- The Hungarian composer Zoltán Kodály completes his orchestral suite *Dances of Galánta*.
- The Italian composer Mario Castelnuovo-Tedesco completes his Violin Concerto No. 2.
- The opera *Arabella* by the German composer Richard Strauss is first performed, in Dresden, Germany.
- The Russian composer Dmitry Shostakovich completes his Piano Concerto No. 1.
- The U.S. composer Aaron Copland completes his Symphony No. 2, the *Short Symphony*.
- U.S. inventor Franklin V. Hunt improves the sound quality of records by introducing lateral engraving.

Theater and Dance

- The Pulitzer Prize for Drama is awarded to Maxwell Anderson for *Both Your Houses*.
- The Spanish writer Federico García Lorca completes his play *Bodas de sangre/Blood Wedding*.

Thought and Scholarship

- Austrian psychoanalyst Wilhelm Reich publishes *Massenpsychologie des Faschismus/The Mass Psychology of Fascism*.
- English churchman Ernest William Barnes publishes *Scientific Theory and Religion*.
- English churchman William Ralph Inge publishes *God and the Astronomers*.
- English economist John Maynard Keynes publishes *The Means to Prosperity*.
- English philosopher Alfred North Whitehead publishes *Adventures of Ideas*.

- Swedish churchman Nathan Söderblom publishes *The Living God* (originally delivered as his "Gifford Lectures").
- Swiss psychoanalyst Carl Gustav Jung publishes *Modern Man in Search of a Soul*.
- The 16-volume *Geschichte der Päpste seit dem Ausgang des Mittelalters/History of the Popes from the Close of the Middle Ages* by the German historian Ludwig Pastor is completed after his death in 1928. He published the first volume in 1886.
- The English writer Norman Angell publishes *The Great Illusion, 1933*. A follow-up to his *The Great Illusion*, published in 1910, it argues that war does not have positive economic consequences, even for the victors. He is awarded the Nobel Peace Prize in 1933.
- The Irish critic of French literature Enid Starkie publishes her classic study *Baudelaire*.
- The Pulitzer Prize for History is awarded to Frederick Jackson Turner for *The Significance of Sections in American History*.

SOCIETY

Education

- U.S. educator Isaac Leon Kandel publishes *Comparative Education*.

Everyday Life

- America's largest union, the American Federation of Labor (AFL), endorses the five-day work week and six-hour work day.
- In the United States, Prohibition ends, although controls remain in some states; an estimated 1.4 billion gallons of illegal alcohol have been consumed. The boom in sales of soft drinks ends, and grape sales are also hit, as home wine-making declines in popularity.
- Ruth Wakefield creates the Toll House Cookie, the definitive chocolate chip cookie.
- The average life expectancy in the United States is 59 years, as opposed to 49 years in 1900.
- The Borden Company introduces the first vitamin D-fortified milk in the United States.
- The German birth rate begins to increase, as a result of Adolf Hitler's economic incentives to "Aryan" Germans to have children.

MARCH

3 The U.S. Civilian Conservation Corps is established to relieve unemployment during the Depression by employing young men in conservation projects, until 1942. A work force of 3 million plants 2 billion trees, builds flood barriers, fights forest fires, and maintains forest roads.

MAY

2 Labor unions are suppressed by the Nazi government in Germany.

OCTOBER

23 Lyons opens its "Corner House" fast-food restaurant with seats for 2,000 in London, England.

Media and Communication

- In Germany, Adolf Hitler persuades President Paul Hindenburg to use presidential emergency powers to suspend or close down several hundred newspapers.
- In Paris, France, the first issue of *Minotaure*, a surrealist review, is published. Its editors include André Breton, Marcel Duchamp, and Paul Eluard.
- The U.S. magazine *Good Housekeeping* is the first such publication to accept advertisements for sanitary towels.
- U.S. engineer Edwin Armstrong patents frequency modulation (FM) in radio, which eliminates static.

Religion

JULY
- The Lutheran churches in Germany are formed into the German Evangelical Church League. On September 27, the national synod elects the pro-Nazi Ludwig Müller as Reich bishop. Opponents rally around the German pastor Martin Niemöller and form the anti-Nazi Confessional Church.
9 The Vatican and the German government initial a new concordat, defining the position of the Roman Catholic Church in Germany.

Sports

- Arlington Park in Chicago, Illinois, is the first horse track to use a totalizer, an electrical machine that prints and issues betting tickets and also tabulates and displays the race results.

- In golf, Great Britain regains the Ryder Cup from the United States at Southport, Lancashire, in England, when Britain's Syd Easterbrook defeats Densmore Shute, winning the concluding singles match at the final hole to seal a 6½–5½ victory.
- The newly formed Amateur Softball Association of America organizes the first national softball championships for both men and women, in Chicago, Illinois.

FEBRUARY
26 The United States, represented by the Boston Olympics club, wins the world amateur ice hockey championship for the first time.

MARCH
18 U.S. national figure skating champions are Maribel Vinson and Roger Turner. Maribel Vinson and George Hill win the pairs.

APRIL
4–13 The New York Rangers beat the Toronto Maple Leafs three games to one to win the National Hockey League (NHL) championship.

MAY
30 U.S. racing driver Louis Meyer wins the Indianapolis 500.

JUNE
5 Peggy Scriven becomes the first British player to win a singles title at the French tennis championships in Paris.
10 U.S. golfer Johnny Goodman wins the U.S. Open golf championship.

BIRTHS & DEATHS

- Tuzo Itami, Japanese movie director, born in Kyoto, Japan (–1997).

JANUARY
5 Calvin Coolidge, 30th president of the United States 1923–29, a Republican, dies in Northampton, Massachusetts (60).
25 Corazon Aquino, president of the Philippines, born in Tarlac, Philippines.

FEBRUARY
6 Leslie Crowther, English comedian, born in Nottingham, England (–1996).
18 James Corbett (Gentleman Jim), U.S. world heavyweight boxing champion, dies in New York, New York (66).

MARCH
14 Quincy Jones, U.S. musician, composer, and movie producer, born in Chicago, Illinois.
19 Philip Roth, U.S. novelist and short story writer, born in Newark, New Jersey.

APRIL
15 Elizabeth Montgomery, U.S. actress known for her role in the television

program *Bewitched*, born in Beverly Hills, California (–1995).
22 Frederick Henry Royce, English industrialist, joint founder of the Rolls-Royce company, dies in West Wittering, Sussex, England (60).
26 Arno Penzias, German-born U.S. radio astronomer, born in Munich, Germany.
26 Carol Burnett, U.S. comedian who had her own long-running TV variety show 1966–77, born in San Antonio, Texas.

MAY
11 Louis Farrakhan, U.S. religious leader who heads the Nation of Islam, born in New York, New York.

JULY
8 Anthony Hope (Hawkins), English author best known for his *Prisoner of Zenda*, dies in Walton-on-the-Hill, Surrey (69).

SEPTEMBER
1 Conway Twitty, U.S. country music singer, born in Friars Point, Mississippi (–1993).
8 Faisal I, King of Iraq 1921–33 and promoter of pan-Arab nationalism, dies in Bern, Switzerland (48).

25 Ring Lardner, U.S. short story writer and satirist, previously a sportswriter, dies in East Hampton, New York (48).

NOVEMBER
19 Larry King, popular radio and television interviewer, born in New York, New York.

DECEMBER
4 Stefan George, German lyric poet, dies in Minusio, near Locarno, Switzerland (65).
6 Henryk Górecki, Polish composer, born in Czernica, Poland.
21 Knud Johan Victor Rasmussen, Danish explorer and ethnologist who studied the Inuit tribes across the Arctic, dies in Gentofts, Denmark (54).
23 Akihito, emperor of Japan from 1989, son of the Emperor Hirohito, born in Tokyo, Japan.

27–July 23 Georges Speicher of France wins the Tour de France cycle race.

29 Primo Carnera of Italy knocks out Jack Sharkey of the United States in the sixth round of their fight in Long Island, New York, to win the world heavyweight boxing title.

JULY

6 At Comiskey Park, Chicago, Illinois, before a crowd of 49,200, the American League defeats the National League 4–2 in the first annual All-Star baseball game.

8 The National Football League (NFL) is split into Eastern and Western divisions, with the winners meeting to decide the championship.

8 U.S. tennis player Helen Wills Moody wins the women's championship at the Wimbledon tennis championships in England; Jack Crawford is the men's champion.

28–30 In tennis, Great Britain defeats France by three matches to two in Paris, France, to win the Davis Cup for the first time since 1912.

SEPTEMBER

10 Fred Perry becomes the first British tennis player to win the U.S. Lawn Tennis Association Championship men's singles since the 1903 victory of Hugh Doherty. Helen Hull Jacobs of the United States retains her title as women's champion.

OCTOBER

3–7 The New York Giants of the National League defeat the Washington Senators of the American League four games to one in the World Series.

DECEMBER

17 The Chicago Bears of the Western Division defeat the New York Giants of the Eastern Division 23–21 to win the inaugural National Football League (NFL) championship game.

1934

POLITICS, GOVERNMENT, AND ECONOMICS

Business and Economics

- The Louisiana senator Huey Long announces his "Share Our Wealth" campaign, calling for taxation of the rich and handouts for the poor.
- The U.S. economy shows signs of rebounding: about 4 million unemployed workers find jobs, the number of business failures declines, and corporate profits rise. However, farm income remains at half its 1929 level and food shortages abound.

JANUARY

1 The U.S. president, Franklin D. Roosevelt, estimates that the cost of the national recovery program will approach $10.5 million by the middle of 1935.

MARCH

13 Signaling confidence in the economy, the U.S. automobile manufacturer Henry Ford reinstates the $5.00-a-day minimum wage for two-thirds of his work force.

Colonization

- France completes the pacification of the hinterland of French Morocco, finally ending the resistance of the peoples of the interior to French colonial rule. Anticolonial resistance after 1934 is concentrated in the cities.

MARCH

3 The French high commissioner in Syria dismisses the cabinet and suspends parliament for seven months.

APRIL

7 The nationalist leader Mahatma Gandhi suspends the civil disobedience campaign in India.

AUGUST

6 U.S. marines withdraw from Haiti after 19 years of military occupation.

Human Rights

- Elijah Muhammad (originally Poole) becomes head of the Nation of Islam (Black Muslims) in Detroit, Michigan, following the disappearance of its former leader, Wallace Fard.
- The Fraternal Council of Negro Churches is established in the United States with the intention of campaigning for social change.
- U.S. writer James Weldon Johnson publishes *Negro Americans, What Now?*, challenging black Americans to develop an independent social philosophy.

DECEMBER

14   Women are given the vote in Turkey.

Politics and Government

- Special commissioners, all Nazis, are placed in charge of state governments in Germany, and state parliaments are abolished.
- The Bank Secrecy Act is passed in Switzerland to ensure the confidentiality of customers' accounts.
- The Nazi government develops a plan for labor regulation and a reduction of the German reliance on foreign trade. Unemployment in Germany falls rapidly.
- The U.S. Prison Bureau acquires the island of Alcatraz in San Francisco Bay as a site for a new federal prison.
- Using powers granted to him by the Gold Reserve Act, the U.S. president Franklin D. Roosevelt devalues the dollar to 59.06% of its last official gold value.

JANUARY

1   The Turkish government launches a five-year plan to expand the textile, metal, paper, chemical, and other industries.

8   The French financier Alexandre Stavisky, accused of issuing fraudulent bonds, is found dead. The government's attempt to hush up the affair results in a popular charge of corruption.

14   Elections in the autonomous region of Catalonia are won by the left, while elsewhere in Spain the right predominates.

26   Germany signs a ten-year nonaggression pact with Poland.

30   The Radical Edouard Daladier forms a second coalition government in France.

31   The Federal Farm Mortgage Corporation is established in the United States to take over farm mortgages and stem foreclosures during the economic depression.

FEBRUARY

1–16   Political parties are forcibly dissolved in Austria except for Chancellor Engelbert Dollfuss's Fatherland Front.

2   The second five-year plan, launched on January 22, 1933, is adopted by the 17th Party Congress in the USSR.

6–7   Riots break out in Paris, France, in protest against the financial corruption implied by the Stavisky affair, following his death on January 8.

8   The former Radical president, Gaston Doumergue, is called on to form a new government in France, but his plans for an all-party coalition are unsuccessful.

9   Greece, Turkey, Romania, and Yugoslavia form the Balkan Entente as a counterpart to the Little Entente (Czechoslovakia, Romania, and Yugoslavia), with the aim of preventing attack by another Balkan state.

15   The Civil Works Emergency Relief Act becomes law in the United States, extending the scope of New Deal relief and work relief provision through civil works projects during the economic depression.

16   Britain and Russia sign a trade agreement.

17   King Albert I of Belgium is killed in a climbing accident. He is succeeded by his son, Leopold III.

21   The former guerrilla leader in Nicaragua, César Sandino, is assassinated by the National Guard under Anastasio Somoza.

MARCH

15   Premier Karlis Ulmanis becomes dictator in Latvia after suspending parliament in response to an alleged communist plot.

16   German chancellor Adolf Hitler announces the creation of an army of half a million soldiers, in direct contravention of the Treaty of Versailles.

16–17   Protocols are signed in Rome between Italy, Austria, and Hungary to form a Danubian bloc against the Little Entente (Czechoslovakia, Romania, and Yugoslavia).

24   The U.S. Tydings–McDuffie Act declares the independence of the Philippines from the United States from 1945.

APRIL

4   Heinrich Himmler, as head of the SS (*Schutzstaffel*, Nazi elite corps), is appointed assistant chief of the Gestapo (secret state police) in Prussia.

4   Socialists lead a strike in Barcelona, Spain, taking advantage of the victory of moderate Left parties in Catalan regional elections in January and increasing tensions with the coalition government in Madrid.

7   The 1932 nonaggression pact between the USSR and Finland is extended for ten years.

MAY

19   Fascists in Bulgaria seize power in collaboration with King Boris.

24   Colombia and Peru agree to continue discussions over the disputed port of Leticia in Colombia.

JUNE

5   Jan Smuts's South African Party merges with J. B. M. Hertzog's Nationalist Party. Daniel Malan leaves the government and forms the Purified National Party in opposition.

6   The Indian Reorganization Act in the United States encourages Native American self-government, promotes the study of Native American culture, creates a Court of Indian Affairs, and ends the policy of dividing Native American lands into individual parcels.

6   The Securities and Exchange Commission is formed in the United States. Its aim is to oversee acts of Congress that regulate the securities market and so prevent the recurrence of the abuses of the 1920s and the 1929 Wall Street crash.

6   The U.S. Congress establishes the Federal Communications Commission (FCC) to regulate telegraph, cable, and radio traffic.

6   The U.S. Congress passes the Reciprocal Trade Agreement Act. It authorizes the president to conclude trade agreements with individual nations, thereby annulling the 1930 Smoot–Hawley tariff.

8   Oswald Mosley, leader of the British Union of Fascists, addresses a mass meeting of the party at Olympia, London, England.

9–10   The USSR renews relations with Czechoslovakia (June 9) and Romania (June 10) in the light of the perceived German threat in Eastern Europe.

11   The Geneva Disarmament Conference ends in failure, rejecting the proposal of the USSR to turn it into a "permanent periodically convening peace conference."

12   Political parties are banned in Bulgaria as part of a conservative backlash against a perceived communist threat.

12   The South African Status Bill grants the Cape Parliament the right to secede from the British Commonwealth.

14–15   A meeting in Venice, Italy, between the German chancellor, Adolf Hitler, and the Italian prime minister, Benito Mussolini, fails to improve mutual relations because of divergent interests in the Danube valley.

19   The U.S. Silver Purchase Act authorizes the purchase by the government of silver to provide partial backing for the dollar.

20   Britain and Italy exchange diplomatic notes defining the frontier between the Anglo-Egyptian territory of Sudan and the Italian colony of Libya.

23   Following a six-week war, Saudi Arabia and the Yemen sign a peace agreement.

30   The German chancellor, Adolf Hitler, purges the SA (*Sturmabteilung*, storm troopers or "Brownshirts") of dozens of its top leaders in the "Night of the Long Knives." Those murdered by Heinrich Himmler's SS (*Schutzstaffel*, Nazi elite corps) as potential rivals to Hitler include the SA head Ernst Röhm and the former chancellor Kurt von Schleicher.

JULY

2   General Lázaro Cárdenas, of the reformist wing of the ruling National Revolutionary Party, is elected president of Mexico.

7   Admiral Keisuke Okada becomes prime minister of a largely nonpartisan government in Japan.

12   Belgium bans uniformed political parties in an attempt to limit Nazi influence.

16   A new constitution in Brazil gives the central government greater powers while reducing the powers of the president.

19   The acting British prime minister, Stanley Baldwin, announces an increase in the size of the Royal Air Force as a modest armament boost in response to reports of growing German air power.

22   FBI agents kill the notorious bank-robber John Dillinger in Chicago, Illinois.

25   Engelbert Dollfuss, leader of the Fatherland Front, chancellor, and effective fascist dictator of Austria, is assassinated by the Nazis in an attempted coup.

30   The "Fatherland Front" politician Kurt von Schuschnigg is appointed Austrian chancellor following the assassination of Engelbert Dollfuss by the Nazis.

AUGUST

2   The German president, Paul von Hindenburg, dies. The presidency is merged with the chancellorship and all members of the armed forces take an oath of loyalty to Adolf Hitler personally as Führer ("Leader").

19   A referendum is held in Germany on the vesting of sole executive power in Adolf Hitler as Führer; 89.9% of voters approve the change.

SEPTEMBER

9   Fascist and antifascist demonstrations are held in Hyde Park, London, England.

12   The Baltic states (Estonia, Latvia, and Lithuania) sign a Treaty of Understanding and Cooperation (known as the "Baltic Entente") in Geneva, Switzerland.

15   The German-born U.S. carpenter and burglar Bruno Hauptmann is arrested in New York, New York, and charged with kidnapping the baby son of aviator Charles Lindbergh and Anne Morrow Lindbergh in 1932.

15   The United Australia Party, founded by Joseph Lyons in 1931, wins the largest number of seats in the Australian general election.

18   The USSR is admitted to the League of Nations.

OCTOBER

2   The Royal Indian Navy is founded, replacing the former Royal Indian Marine.

4   Alejandro Lerroux forms a second center-right coalition government in Spain. A left-wing uprising of miners in Asturias and a separatist rising in Catalonia the following day are brutally suppressed.

9   King Alexander I of Yugoslavia is assassinated by a Croatian separatist agent during a visit to France. He is succeeded by his 11-year-old son, Peter II.

15   The Long March of the Chinese communists begins, led by Mao Zedong and others. Driven out by a Nationalist offensive, some 100,000 people leave the Jiangxi Soviet in southern China and march 9,600 km/6,000 mi to the province of Shaanxi in the extreme northwest, where the survivors set up a new communist revolutionary base.

23–December 19   Discussions on naval disarmament are held in London, England, between delegates from Japan, the United States, and Britain.

24   Mahatma Gandhi, leader of the Indian nationalist Congress Party, resigns, disillusioned by its use of nonviolent disobedience as a political expedient, rather than a fundamental principle. He devotes himself to a constructive program of "social and economic uplift" in rural India.

30   The Greek–Turkish Commission, established in 1923, is dissolved.

NOVEMBER

3   The French high commissioner in Syria suspends parliament indefinitely.

7   Joseph Lyons's United Australia Party forms a coalition government with the Country Party.

8   Ex-president Gaston Doumergue resigns as prime minister of France because of opposition to his plans for constitutional reform and for an all-party coalition, the Union Nationale. He is succeeded by Pierre-Etienne Flandin, leading a new, broad coalition government.

11   In the U.S. congressional elections, the Democrats retain their majorities in the Senate and the House of Representatives. In the Senate, Democrats win 69 seats, Republicans 25, and others 2; in the House, Democrats 322, Republicans 103, and others 10.

11   The Moroccan nationalist movement is founded, to campaign for independence from France and Spain.

14   The British government announces a plan for depressed areas, providing modest funds and two commissioners for the promotion of economic development and social improvement.

30   King Fuad suspends the constitution in Egypt following riots by supporters of the nationalist Wafd party.

DECEMBER

•   Daniel Salamanca, the president of Bolivia, is overthrown in a military coup, following Paraguayan victories in the Chaco War.

1   Sergey Kirov, Party leader in Leningrad and a senior communist leader in the USSR, is assassinated, probably with the connivance of the Soviet leader Joseph Stalin.

The assassination marks the beginning of the Great Purge (1934–38).

5   Clashes between Italian and Ethiopian troops break out on the frontier between Ethiopia (Abyssinia) and Italian Somaliland.

16   A right-wing confederation of parties in Spain known as the Confederación Español de Derechas Autónomas (CEDA) gains seats in elections. However, president Alcalá Zamora makes the moderate Republican Alejandro Lerroux prime minister instead of CEDA's anti-republican José Maria Gil Robles.

16   General elections are held in Portugal, but under the authoritarian regime of Antonio de Oliveira Salazar no opposition parties are allowed to put forward candidates.

29   Japan formally denounces the Washington treaties of 1922 and 1930, indicating its opposition to the limits these treaties impose on the sizes of navies in the Pacific.

SCIENCE, TECHNOLOGY, AND MEDICINE

Agriculture

- President Lazaro Cárdenas of Mexico redistributes 162,000 sq km/62,500 sq mi of land to peasants as part of the country's agrarian revolution.

December 1934–36 Drought continues in the United States, drastically reducing crop yields.

December 1934–37 Germany begins to increase domestic food production. By the end of this period, 90% of the food it consumes is produced within the country.

December 1934–54 Wild horses in the Midwest United States are systematically killed to preserve rangeland. By 1952 there are only about 33,000 left.

Ecology

- Ecuador makes part of the Galápagos Islands a wildlife sanctuary to protect its unique flora and fauna. It is extended in 1959 and in 1968 becomes the Parque Nacional Galápagos.
- To preserve the last remaining stand of southern primeval hardwood forest in the United States, the Great Smoky Mountains National Park in North Carolina is created; it covers 209 sq km/81 sq mi.

May

- As the drought in the U.S. dust bowl enters its second year, about 270 billion kg/300 million tons of topsoil from 40 million hectares/100 million acres in Kansas, Texas, Colorado, and Oklahoma is blown into the Atlantic causing large-scale migration to California and other states.

June

28   To control grazing and erosion of the western grasslands, the U.S. Congress passes the Taylor Grazing Act.

September

21   One of the most powerful typhoons in history (1,800 km/1,120 mi across) hits Japan; nearly 50,000 homes are destroyed and over 3,000 people are killed.

Exploration

- A German expedition led by mountaineer Willy Merkl attempting to scale the Nanga Parbat massif in the Punjab Himalayas (now in Pakistan) again fails to reach the summit. Merkl and other members of the team lose their lives in the attempt.

August

18   U.S. explorers and biologists William Beebe and Otis Baron descend in a bathysphere to a record 923 m/3,028 ft in the Atlantic off Bermuda.

Health and Medicine

- German biochemist Adolph Butenandt isolates the female sex hormone progesterone.
- Norwegian biochemist Asbjörn Fölling discovers the genetic metabolic defect phenylketonuria, which can cause retardation; his discovery stimulates research in biochemical genetics and the development of screening tests for carriers of deleterious genes.
- Quinacrine is introduced as a more effective treatment of malaria than quinine.
- U.S. physiologists George Minot, William Murphy, and George Whipple share the Nobel Prize for Physiology or Medicine for their work on liver therapy to counter anemia.

Science

c. 1934 Italian physicist Enrico Fermi bombards uranium with neutrons and discovers the phenomenon of atomic fission, the basic principle of atomic bombs and nuclear power.

- French archeologist Abbé Henri Breuil publishes *L'Evolution de l'art pariétal dans les cavernes et abris ornées de France/The Evolution of Rock Art in the Caves of France*. Breuil is one of the first to record and interpret the prehistoric cave art of Europe.
- French physicists Frédéric and Irène Joliot-Curie bombard boron, aluminum, and magnesium with alpha particles and obtain radioactive isotopes of nitrogen, phosphorus, and aluminum—elements that are not normally radioactive. They are the first radioactive elements to be prepared artificially.
- Italian physicist Enrico Fermi suggests that neutrons and protons are the same fundamental particles in two different quantum states.
- Russian physicist Pavel Cherenkov discovers that light is emitted when particles pass through liquids or transparent solids faster than the speed of light in the same medium. The phenomenon becomes known as "Cherenkov radiation."
- U.S. anthropologist Ruth Benedict initiates the development of cultural psychology in *Patterns of Culture*, which describes cultures in terms of personality types.

- U.S. chemist Harold Urey receives the Nobel Prize for Chemistry for discovering heavy hydrogen.

Technology

- A new tungsten filament is invented that provides a light 20% more efficient than existing filaments; the new light bulbs become commercially available in the United States in 1937.
- Chemist Robert Boyer exhibits plastic parts for cars, made from soy beans.
- Freeze-dried coffee is manufactured in Switzerland; this is the first application of the freeze-drying technique.
- German physicist and engineer Wernher von Braun successfully launches the A2 series of rockets. Powered by alcohol and liquid oxygen, they reach a height of 2.4 km/1.5 mi.
- Phthalocyanine dyes are developed—metal derivative dyes that are brilliant blue to green.
- The Hungarian photographer André Kertész publishes *Paris vu par André Kertész/Paris through the Eyes of André Kertész*, a photograph album that contains his best-known images of Paris.
- The Panzer IV tank is designed in Germany; it has a 75mm gun and is intended to spearhead the new armored (Panzer) divisions.
- The refrigerator is redesigned by Raymond Loewy for Sears Roebuck and Co. With aluminum shelves, it causes a sensation in France at the 1937 Paris International Exhibit. His designs influence the subsequent design of all kitchen appliances.
- U.S. clock maker Laurens Hammond patents the Hammond organ; the world's first pipeless organ, it leads to the development of other electrically amplified instruments.
- U.S. organic chemist Wallace Hume Carothers invents nylon, the first synthetic polymer fiber to be commercially produced in 1938.

August 1934–39 Fluorescent lights are under development by General Electric in 1939; they are far more energy-efficient than incandescent lights.

MARCH

20 German scientist Rudolf Kuhnold, using a 700-watt transmitter on 600 megacycles plus a receiver, succeeds in receiving echoes bounced off a battleship anchored 550 m/1,800 ft away. It is the first practical demonstration of radar.

JULY

14 An oil pipeline from Mosul, Iraq, to Tripoli, Lebanon, is opened.

Transportation

- American Airlines is created out of the existing American Airways, Inc.
- English inventor Percy Shaw develops the "cat's eye," a reflective device to make road markings more visible at night; the first cat's eyes are laid in Bradford, Yorkshire, England.
- French car manufacturer Citroën introduces the only front-wheel drive vehicle of its time, the Citroën 7.

- U.S. entrepreneur Walter T. Varney founds Varney Airlines in Denver, Colorado; its name is changed to Continental Airlines in 1937.
- U.S. motor manufacturer Chrysler introduces the Chrysler Airflow, the first streamlined car and the first car with overdrive and a one-piece curved windshield.

JANUARY

30 A Soviet balloon, *Osoaviakhim*, ascends 20.8 km/13 mi into the stratosphere.

FEBRUARY

3 Deutsche Lufthansa start the first regular transatlantic airmail service, completing the journey from Berlin, Germany, to Buenos Aires, Argentina, in four days.

MARCH

26 The Road Traffic Act introduces driving tests in the UK.

MAY

26 The end of the steam era begins in the United States with the start of the Burlington Zephyr train service which uses streamlined diesel engines to pull passenger trains between Chicago, Illinois, and Denver, Colorado, at an average speed of 124.9 kph/77.6 mph.

JUNE

- In London, England, 60 official pedestrian crossing places are established on roads.

SEPTEMBER

26 The luxury liner SS *Queen Mary* is launched in Scotland for the British Cunard Company. It has four screw propellers and is 310.7 m/1,019.5 ft long.

ARTS AND IDEAS

Architecture

- Battersea Power Station, designed by Giles Scott, is completed, in London, England.

Arts

- Hungarian artist and photographer Lászlo Moholy-Nagy takes *Stockholm*.
- The Belgian artist René Magritte paints *The Human Condition* and *Le Viol/The Rape*.
- The English artist Edward Burra paints *Harlem*.
- The French artist Jean Arp sculpts *Pagoda Fruit*.
- The German artist Max Ernst creates *Une Semaine de bonté/A Week of Goodness*, a series of collages made up of old engravings.
- The German artist Max Beckmann paints *The Man in Darkness*.
- The Russian-born French artist Marc Chagall paints *Bella in Green*.
- The Spanish artist Pablo Picasso engraves illustrations for an edition of the ancient Greek *Lysistrata*, by Aristophanes.
- The Swiss artist Paul Klee paints *Fear*.
- The U.S. artist Archibald Motley, Jr., paints *Black Belt*.

- The U.S. artist Jacob Lawrence paints *Girl in a Red Dress*.
- The U.S. artist Reginald Marsh paints *Negroes on Rockaway Beach*.

Film

- *It Happened One Night*, a romantic comedy directed by Frank Capra and starring Clark Gable and Claudette Colbert, makes Academy Award history by winning awards in all five major categories (best picture, actor, actress, director, and screenplay).
- The movie *David Copperfield*, directed by George Cukor, is released in the United States. Based on the novel by Charles Dickens, it stars Frank Lawton, with W. C. Fields as Mr. Micawber.
- The movie *L'Atalante*, directed by French filmmaker Jean Vigo shortly before he dies of leukemia at the age of 29, is released in France. It stars Jean Dasté, Dita Parlo, Michel Simon, and Giles Margarites.
- The movie *Madame Bovary*, directed by Jean Renoir, is released in France. Based on the novel by Gustav Flaubert, it stars Valentine Tessier and Pierre Renoir.
- The movie *Of Human Bondage*, directed by John Cromwell, is released in the United States. Based on the story by W. Somerset Maugham, it stars Bette Davis.
- The movie *The Orient Express* directed by Paul Martin is released, based on the novel *Stamboul Train* by Graham Greene.
- The movie *Twentieth Century*, directed by Howard Hawks, is released in the United States, starring John Barrymore and Carole Lombard.
- The musical movie *The Gay Divorcée*, directed by Mark Sandrich, is released in the United States, starring Fred Astaire and Ginger Rogers.
- The German Minister of Information and Propaganda, Josef Goebbels, introduces The Film of the Nation Prize. Its aim is effectively to reward production of propaganda in the movies.
- U.S. actors William Powell and Myrna Loy make one of their many screen outings together in *The Thin Man*, directed by W. S. Van Dyke. The movie, an adaptation of Dashiell Hammett's novel of the same title, initiates a popular, long-running cycle of Thin Man movies.
- U.S. comic W. C. Fields stars in *It's A Gift*, directed by Norman Z. McLeod.

JUNE
9 Walt Disney releases the animated cartoon *The Wise Little Hen*, the first cartoon starring Donald Duck.

Literature and Language

- The Australian writer Eleanor Dark publishes her novel *Prelude to Christopher*.
- The English crime writer Agatha Christie publishes her novel *Murder on the Orient Express*.
- The English novelist Evelyn Waugh publishes his satirical novel *A Handful of Dust*.
- The English novelist James Hilton publishes his sentimental novel about a school teacher, *Goodbye, Mr Chips*. It becomes a best seller in the United States.
- The English writer Alphonse James Albert Symons publishes *The Quest for Corvo*, a biography of the eccentric Frederick Rolfe.
- The English writer Dorothy Leigh Sayers publishes her crime novel *The Nine Tailors*.
- The English writer George Orwell publishes his novel *Burmese Days*.
- The English writer Harold Nicolson publishes his biography *Curzon, the Last Phase*.
- The English writer H. G. Wells publishes his *Experiment in Autobiography*.
- The English writer Robert Graves publishes *I, Claudius* and *Claudius the God*, novels set in ancient Rome.
- The first Congress of Soviet Writers is held, under the new doctrine of Socialist Realism; this doctrine becomes the basis of the official fiction style of the USSR.
- The French surrealist writer Louis Aragon publishes the poem "Hourra l'Oural."
- The French writer Henry de Montherlant publishes his novel *Les Célibataires/The Bachelors*.
- The German philosopher Rudolf Carnap publishes *Logische Syntax der Sprache/The Logical Syntax of Language*.
- The Nobel Prize for Literature is awarded to the Italian dramatist Luigi Pirandello.
- The novel *And Quiet Flows the Don* by the Russian writer Mikhail Sholokhov is published in English. The first part of a two-part English translation, it comprises the first two volumes of the four-volume epic *Tikhy Don/The Silent Don*, which began appearing in the Soviet Union in 1928.
- The Pulitzer Prize for Biography is awarded to Tyler Dennett for *John Hay*, the Prize for Fiction is awarded to Caroline Miller for *Lamb in His Bosom*, and the Pulitzer Prize for Poetry is awarded to Robert Hillyer for *Collected Verse*.
- The Scottish writer Lewis Grassic Gibbon publishes *Grey Granite*, the final novel in his *A Scots Quair* trilogy.
- The Scottish writer Edwin Muir publishes his poetry collection *Variations on a Time Theme*.
- The U.S. poet William Carlos Williams publishes *Collected Poems, 1922–1931*.
- The U.S. writer Dashiell Hammett publishes his detective novel *The Thin Man*.
- The U.S. writer Edna St. Vincent Millay publishes her poetry collection *Wine from These Grapes*.
- The U.S. writer F. Scott Fitzgerald publishes his fourth novel, *Tender is the Night*. Because it is heavily criticized, he prepares a revised version.
- The U.S. writer Henry Roth publishes his novel *Call it Sleep*.
- The U.S. writer Irving Stone publishes his novel *Lust for Life*, based on the life of the painter Vincent van Gogh.
- The U.S. writer James M. Cain publishes his novel *The Postman Always Rings Twice*, a violent melodrama that quickly becomes a best seller.
- The U.S. writer John Henry O'Hara publishes his novel *Appointment in Samarra*.
- The U.S. writer William Saroyan publishes *The Daring Young Man on the Flying Trapeze*, a collection of short stories that establishes his reputation.
- The U.S. writer Zora Neale Hurston publishes her novel *Jonah's Gourd Vine*.

- The U.S.-born English writer T. S. Eliot publishes *After Strange Gods*, essays that see literature in terms of Christian belief.
- The Welsh novelist John Cowper Powys publishes his highly original *Autobiography*.
- While living in Paris, France, the U.S. writer Henry Miller publishes his novel *Tropic of Cancer*, which is controversial because of its sexual explicitness.

Music

- Belgian jazz guitarist Django Reinhardt and French violinist Stéphane Grappelli form the Quintette du Hot Club de France in Paris, France.
- The English composer and critic Constant Lambert publishes *Music, Ho!*, a highly individual account of contemporary music.
- The English composer Benjamin Britten completes his choral work *Te Deum*.
- The French composer Jacques Ibert completes his Flute Concerto.
- The German composer Paul Hindemith completes the symphonic version of *Mathis der Maler/Matthias the Painter*.
- The Glyndebourne Opera Festival is founded by the English teacher and musician John Christie and his wife, soprano Audrey Mildmay, at his own country estate in Glyndebourne, Sussex.
- The Hungarian composer Béla Bartók completes his String Quartet No. 5.
- The opera *The Lady Macbeth of the Mtsensk District* by the Russian composer Dmitry Shostakovich is first performed, in Leningrad (now St. Petersburg), Russia.
- The Russian composer Sergey Rachmaninov completes his *Rhapsody on a Theme of Paganini*.
- The Russian composer Dmitry Shostakovich completes his *Suite for Jazz Orchestra No. 1*.
- The Russian composer Sergey Prokofiev completes his *Lieutenant Kijé* suite.

Theater and Dance

- The English writer Laurence Housman publishes *Victoria Regina*, a series of short plays about Queen Victoria. The performance of them is banned because they are considered disrespectful.
- The musical *Anything Goes*, with lyrics by Guy Bolton and P. G. Wodehouse, and music by Cole Porter, is first performed, in New York.
- The musical *Blue Mountain Melody*, by Charles Zwar, is staged at the Theatre Royal in Sydney, Australia.
- The play *Eden End*, by the English writer J. B. Priestley, is first performed, in London, England.
- The play *La Machine infernale/The Infernal Machine*, an adaptation of the Oedipus myth by the French writer Jean Cocteau, is first performed, in Paris, France.
- The play *Within the Gates*, by the Irish writer Sean O'Casey is first performed, in London, England.
- The Pulitzer Prize for Drama is awarded to Sidney Kingsley for *Men in White*.
- The Spanish writer Federico García Lorca completes his play *Yerma*.

NOVEMBER

21 The year's smash Broadway play *Anything Goes* opens. It is a musical comedy featuring music by Cole Porter.

Thought and Scholarship

- Austrian-born English philosopher Karl Popper publishes *Logik der Forschung/The Logic of Scientific Discovery*.
- English churchman William Temple publishes *Nature, Man and God*.
- English historian Arnold Toynbee publishes the first volume of his monumental 12-volume *A Study of History*. The last volume will appear in 1961.
- English historian John Ernest Neale publishes *Queen Elizabeth*, which is awarded the James Tait Black Memorial Prize.
- English philosopher Bertrand Russell publishes *Freedom and Civilization*.
- French philosopher Maurice-Edouard Blondel publishes *La Pensée/Thought*.
- German economist Werner Sombart publishes *Deutscher Sozialismus/German Socialism*, translated as *A New Social Philosophy* in 1937. It is an early defense of German National Socialism.
- Swiss Protestant theologian Karl Barth publishes *Nein! Antwort an Emil Brunner/No! (A Response to Emil Brunner)*.
- The first volume of the *Oxford History of England*, edited by G. N. Clark, is published. The last volume will be published in 1965.
- The Pulitzer Prize for History is awarded to Herbert Agar for *The People's Choice*.
- The two-volume *Early Victorian England*, edited by the English historian George Malcolm Young, is published.
- U.S. social philosopher Lewis Mumford publishes *Technics and Civilization*. His aim is to reveal the possible dehumanizing consequences of the unthinking use of technology.

SOCIETY

Everyday Life

FEBRUARY

12–13 A general strike is called in France in protest at the danger posed by the rise of fascism.

APRIL

18 The first launderette opens in Fort Worth, Texas. It charges by the hour.

MAY

28 The Dionne quintuplets, the world's first quintuplets to survive, are born in Canada.

JULY

- In New York, New York, the American Foundation for the Blind issues the first "talking book," a collection of Americana.

16   The first general strike in the United States takes place in San Francisco, California, with workers out in sympathy with the striking members of the International Longshoreman's Association.

NOVEMBER

26   Family names are made obligatory in Turkey from January 1, 1935, and titles are abolished; the Grand National Assembly gives President Mustafa Kemal the name Atatürk, "Father of the Turks."

DECEMBER

8   A regular airmail service from London, England, to Australia is inaugurated.

Media and Communication

- 1,929 daily newspapers in the United States have a circulation of 36.7 million.

Religion

- In the United States the "radio priest" Father Charles E. Coughlin founds the National Union for Social Justice and attracts 5 million members.
- Japanese Buddhist scholar Daisetsu Teitaro Suzuki publishes *An Introduction to Zen Buddhism*.

JANUARY

7–21 Billy Sunday, an evangelist, holds a two-week long revival in New York, New York, his first trip there since 1917.

BIRTHS & DEATHS

JANUARY

29   Fritz Haber, German chemist who discovered a method of producing ammonia cheaply, dies in Basel, Switzerland (65).

FEBRUARY

5   William Morris Davis, U.S. geographer, geologist, and meteorologist who pioneered the science of geomorphology, dies in Pasadena, California (83).

23   César Sandino, Nicaraguan guerrilla leader, is shot at the presidential palace in Managua, Nicaragua (about 41).

23   Edward Elgar, English composer, dies in Worcester, England (76).

MARCH

9   Yuri Alekseyevich Gagarin, Soviet cosmonaut and the first person to travel in space, born near Gzhatsk, Russia (–1968).

20   Eric Hebborn, English art forger, born in London, England (–1996).

27   Arthur Mitchell, U.S. ballet dancer, born in New York, New York.

APRIL

3   Jane Goodall, English anthropologist and author, best known for her studies of chimpanzee behavior, born in London, England.

24   Shirley MacLaine, U.S. actress, born in Richmond, Virginia.

MAY

19   Jim Lehrer, U.S. television broadcast journalist, born in Wichita, Kansas.

23   U.S. bank robber Bonnie Parker is killed by police in a roadside ambush near Gibsland, Louisiana (22).

23   U.S. bank robber Clyde Barrow is killed by police in a roadside ambush near Gibsland, Louisiana (25).

25   Gustav Holst, English composer, author of the suite *The Planets*, dies in London, England (59).

JUNE

9   Jackie Mason, U.S. stage and television comedian, born in Sheboygan, Wisconsin.

10   Frederick Delius, English composer, dies in Grez-sur-Loing, France (71).

JULY

1   Sydney Pollack, U.S. director and producer, born in Lafayette, Indiana.

4   Hayyim Nahman Bialik, leading Hebrew poet, dies in Vienna, Austria (61).

4   Marie Curie (born Skłodowska), Polish-born French physicist who, with her husband Pierre Curie, discovered polonium and radium, and who won the Nobel Prize for Physics in 1903 and for Chemistry in 1911, dies near Sallanches, France (66).

9   Michael Graves, U.S. postmodernist architect, born in Indianapolis, Indiana.

13   Wole Soyinka, Nigerian poet, novelist, playwright, and critic, born near Abeokuta, Nigeria.

AUGUST

2   Paul von Hindenburg, German field marshal, president of the Weimar Republic 1925–34, dies in Neudeck, Germany (87).

22   H. Norman Schwarzkopf, U.S. army officer, supreme commander of "Operation Desert Storm" during the Gulf War (1991), born in Trenton, New Jersey.

SEPTEMBER

17   Maureen Connolly, U.S. tennis player, born in San Diego, California (–1969).

20   Sophia Loren, Italian film actress, born in Rome, Italy.

24   Manfred Wörner, German defense minister who was secretary-general of NATO 1988–94, born in Stuttgart, Germany (–1994).

OCTOBER

15   Raymond Poincaré, French statesman, prime minister 1912 and president of the Third Republic during World War I, dies in Paris, France (74).

17   Santiago Ramón y Cajal, Spanish histologist who, with Camillo Golgi, established that the neuron is the basic unit of the nervous system, dies in Madrid, Spain (82).

NOVEMBER

9   Carl Sagan, U.S. astronomer and author who designed the plaque on the Pioneer space probe, born in New York, New York (–1996).

16   Carl von Linde, German engineer who developed a process of liquefying gases and laid the foundation of the science of refrigeration, dies in Munich, Germany (92).

24   Alfred Schnittke, Russian composer and writer on Russian music, born in Engels, near Saratov, in the USSR (–1998).

DECEMBER

10   Howard Martin Temin, U.S. virologist who, with Renato Dulbecco and David Baltimore, discovered reverse transcriptase, born in Philadelphia, Pennsylvania (–1994).

MAY

- German Protestant leaders meet at the Synod of Barmen to organize resistance to Nazism. They produce the Barmen Declaration, which affirms basic Christian doctrines and condemns attempts to accommodate Christianity to Nazism. More synods are held until 1937.

Sports

- Beattie Feathers of the Chicago Bears becomes the first football player to rush for 1,000 yards in a single season.
- British tennis player Fred Perry wins the men's singles titles at Wimbledon, the U.S., and the Australian championhips.
- Two undefeated teams, the University of Minnesota and the University of Alabama, share the college football national championship.

MARCH

- The first U.S. Masters (later to become the fourth major golfing championship) is held in at the Augusta National Golf Club in Augusta, Georgia; the winner is Horton Smith of the United States.
- 10 U.S. national figure skating champions are: Suzanne Davis; Roger Turner; Grace Madden and James Madden, pairs.

APRIL

- 3–10 The Chicago Black Hawks win the National Hockey League (NHL) championship, beating the Detroit Red Wings three games to one.

MAY

- 27–June 10 The second soccer World Cup is held in Italy; Italy wins the trophy, beating Czechoslovakia 2–1 in the final in Rome, before a crowd of 55,000.
- 30 U.S. racing driver Bill Cummings wins the Indianapolis 500.

JUNE

- 9 U.S. golfer Olin Dutra beats Gene Sarazen by one stroke to win the U.S. Open golf championship.
- 14 U.S. boxer Max Baer knocks out Primo Carnera of Italy in the 11th round of their world heavyweight title fight in Long Island, New York, in front of a crowd of 48,495.
- 25–30 English golfer Henry Cotton wins the British Open at the Royal St. George's course at Sandwich, in Kent, England.

JULY

- Walter Lindrum of Australia successfully defends his billiards world championship in Melbourne, Australia. He retains it unchallenged until he retires in 1950.
- 3–29 In cycling, French rider Antonin Magne wins the Tour de France for the second time.

AUGUST

- 19–September 12 At the U.S. Lawn Tennis Association championships, Helen Hull Jacobs of the United States wins the women's division, and Fred Perry of the UK captures the men's title.

SEPTEMBER

- 8–9 In athletics, the inaugural European Championships for men are held in Turin, Italy. Separate women's championships are inaugurated in 1938, and women participate jointly from 1946.
- 17–25 In the America's Cup, the U.S. yacht *Rainbow*, skippered by Harold Vanderbilt, defeats the British challenger, Thomas Sopwith's *Endeavour*, by four races to two.

OCTOBER

- 3–9 The St. Louis Cardinals defeat the Detroit Tigers four games to three in the U.S. World Series.

DECEMBER

- 9 The New York Giants beat the Chicago Bears 30–13 at the Polo Grounds, New York, in the U.S. National Football League (NFL) championship game.

1935

POLITICS, GOVERNMENT, AND ECONOMICS

Colonization

SEPTEMBER
10 An assembly of white settlers in Kenya denounces British colonial policy and advocates closer union with Uganda and Tanganyika.

NOVEMBER
15 The commonwealth of the Philippines is inaugurated as largely self-governing, with Manuel Quezon as president. Douglas MacArthur of the U.S. Army is appointed to reorganize the defense forces.

DECEMBER
12 Wafd nationalists in Egypt demand the restoration of the 1923 constitution, after repeated breakdowns in negotiations with Britain for full Egyptian independence.

Human Rights

• The black American writer and reformer William Edward Burghardt Du Bois publishes *Black Reconstruction*, advocating full racial equality.
• The National Association for the Advancement of Colored People appoints the black American lawyer Charles Hamilton Houston as its special counsel. Houston resolves to fight school segregation all the way to the U.S. Supreme Court.

MARCH
19–21 Riots break out in New York, New York, after police are accused of the brutal treatment of a black American arrested for shoplifting.

Politics and Government

• In a second round of New Deal legislation in the United States, President Franklin D. Roosevelt establishes the Resettlement Administration, to help owners and tenants move to better land; the Works Progress Administration, to provide work for the unemployed; and the Rural Electrification Administration, to raise the standard of rural living by equipping farms with electric power.
• Persia changes its name to Iran ("land of the Aryans").

• Soviet Muslims are prohibited by the communist government from visiting Mecca.

JANUARY
• The Canadian Conservative prime minister, Richard Bennett, announces a New Deal for Canada to combat the effects of the Great Depression.
1 A constitutional convention is elected in the Philippines. The U.S. president Franklin D. Roosevelt subsequently confirms that the proposed constitution conforms with the 1934 Tydings–McDuffie Act, granting independence from the United States from 1945.
7 France and Italy sign the Agreement of Marseille, under which France makes a number of concessions concerning colonial possessions in Africa in an effort to promote a united Franco-Italian front against Germany.
15–17 Grigory Zinoviev, Lev Kamenev, and other former leading communists in the USSR are tried and imprisoned for "moral complicity" in the assassination of party leader Sergey Kirov in December 1934, beginning the "Great Terror", or purge of the Communist Party.

FEBRUARY
1–3 A British–French conference is held in London, England, to discuss Germany's rearmament.
22 Italian troops depart for East Africa, in preparation for their invasion of Ethiopia (Abyssinia).
28 The Irish Free State makes the import and sale of contraceptives illegal.

MARCH
1 The district of Saarland, administered by the French under the League of Nations since 1919, is restored to Germany.
1 The former Greek prime minister Eleutherios Venizelos leads a rebel group attempting to prevent the restoration of the monarchy. The attempt fails and he flees to France.
2 King Rama VII of Siam abdicates and is succeeded by his nephew Rama VIII.
3 New York State authorizes blood tests as evidence in criminal and civil law cases.
16 Germany repudiates the disarmament clauses of the 1919 Treaty of Versailles and the Führer Adolf Hitler reintroduces general military conscription.
20 The Labor Party forms a government in Norway with Johan Nygaardsvold as prime minister.
25 Paul van Zeeland forms a government of National Unity in Belgium and devalues the Belgian franc.

APRIL
1 The U.S. Supreme Court overturns the convictions of the "Scottsboro Nine" (a group of black youths accused in 1931 of raping two white women), ruling that the state of Alabama had always excluded blacks from juries.

11–14 The prime ministers of Italy, France, and Britain, conferring in Stresa, Italy, protest against German rearmament and agree to act jointly against Germany, forming what becomes known as the Stresa Front.

23 The Polish president, Ignacy Mościcki, approves a new constitution.

MAY

2 France and the USSR sign a five-year mutual aid treaty.

5 The U.S. Congress creates the Works Progress Administration (WPA). Capitalized at $5 billion, the WPA employs more than 2 million people on a diverse array of projects ranging from theater productions to the cutting of hiking trails.

5 The U.S. president Franklin D. Roosevelt establishes the Rural Electrification Administration to bring electricity to isolated communities and farms.

16 The USSR and Czechoslovakia sign a mutual aid pact.

19 The Sudeten German (Nazi) Party in Czechoslovakia wins 44 out of 300 seats in the parliamentary elections, making it the second largest party.

27 In the case *Schechter Poultry Corporation v. US*, the U.S. Supreme Court declares sections of the National Industrial Recovery Act unconstitutional because its regulation of hours and wages delegates legislative power from Congress to the executive.

31 The French prime minister, the centrist Pierre Flandin, resigns after the Bank of France blocks his attempt to extend deflationary policies.

JUNE

3 Croatians boycott the Yugoslav parliament.

4 Center-right senator Pierre Laval is reelected prime minister of France.

7 The Conservative Stanley Baldwin succeeds Ramsay MacDonald as prime minister of Britain, heading a National Government. Sir John Simon is home secretary, and Samuel Hoare is foreign secretary.

9 The Populists (Monarchists) win 243 seats in the Greek general election, which the Republican Party boycotts.

12 A truce is arranged in the Chaco War between Paraguay and Bolivia, in which about 100,000 lives have been lost.

18 Britain and Germany make an agreement by which Germany undertakes that its navy will not exceed a third of the tonnage of Britain's Royal Navy. Britain's independent negotiation of the agreement fatally undermines the unity of the Stresa Front (formed in April 1935).

JULY

4 Austria, encouraged by the Italian prime minister, Benito Mussolini, abolishes the anti-Habsburg laws and restores some imperial property.

7 The National Labor Relations Act (Wagner Act) in the United States recognizes labor and management as equal partners. The act outlaws company unions, sanctions collective bargaining, and safeguards union members from discrimination; it creates a National Labor Relations Board to manage union elections and settle labor disputes.

13 The USSR and the United States sign a trade pact.

25–August 20 The Comintern (Third International) holds its seventh and last congress in the USSR, declaring that its prime objective is the defeat of fascism, which communists of all countries are urged to combat in "popular fronts."

27 The French government is granted emergency powers to curtail government spending as part of a deflationary policy against the worldwide economic depression.

AUGUST

2 The British Parliament passes the Government of India Act. It reforms the governmental system, separates Burma and Aden from India, grants provincial governments greater autonomy, and creates a central legislature in Delhi (effective from April 1, 1937).

14 The Social Security Act is enacted in the United States. It provides for old-age pensions, help for the disabled, and unemployment assistance (from 1942), paid for by contributions rather than from tax revenues. The act also provides states with matching grants to help them care for dependent mothers and children.

SEPTEMBER

15 The German Führer Adolf Hitler announces the racist "Nuremberg Laws" against Jews at the Nazi Party Nuremberg rally. Legislation will define Jews, ban them from professions, and forbid their marriage or sexual relations with non-Jews.

OCTOBER

3 Italy invades Ethiopia (Abyssinia), aiming to extend Italian territory in East Africa.

7 Following Italy's invasion of Ethiopia, the League of Nations Council denounces Italy as an aggressor.

7–17 The Austrian chancellor, Kurt von Schuschnigg, in collaboration with his vice chancellor, Prince von Starhemberg, contrives a bloodless coup against Emil Fey, minister of the interior, and his Nazi allies.

14 The Liberal Party wins an overwhelming victory in the Canadian general election, with 173 seats to the Conservatives' 40.

19 The League of Nations imposes sanctions against Italy, in response to the Italian invasion of Ethiopia (Abyssinia).

23 William L. Mackenzie King is appointed prime minister of Canada.

NOVEMBER

3 Socialist groups in France merge as the Socialist and Republican Union under Léon Blum. The new party subsequently joins with the Radical Socialists and communists to found a Popular Front.

4 Germany and Poland sign an economic agreement.

5 The Slovak politician Milan Hodža, leader of the Agrarian Party, becomes prime minister of Czechoslovakia.

7 The treaties between the USSR and Turkey are extended for ten years.

14 The Conservative party prospers in the British general election, winning 388 seats; its leader, Stanley Baldwin, forms a National Government.

15 Canada and the United States sign a reciprocal trade agreement.

27 The New Zealand general election results in victory for the Labor party.

29 Michael Joseph Savage becomes New Zealand's first Labor prime minister.

DECEMBER

1   Jiang Jie Shi is elected chairman of the Guomindang (Nationalist Party) Executive Council, so becoming virtual ruler of China.

12   The City Housing Authority in New York, New York, opens the first U.S. public housing project on the Lower East Side.

13   Eduard Beneš succeeds Tomáš Masaryk Garrigue as president of Czechoslovakia.

18   Samuel Hoare resigns as British foreign secretary following criticism of the Hoare–Laval Plan for the partition of Ethiopian territory between Ethiopia and Italy.

18   Venezuela's dictatorial president Juan Gómez dies and is succeeded by general Eleazar Contreras.

SCIENCE, TECHNOLOGY, AND MEDICINE

Agriculture

- A combine harvester designed to be operated by one person is developed in the United States.

Ecology

c. 1935   Airplanes begin to be used for weather reporting.

- Shenandoah National Park is created in Virginia's Blue Ridge Mountains; it covers 78 sq km/30 sq mi.
- The U.S. Weather Bureau establishes hurricane forecasting centers.
- Windstorms bring further devastation to the dust bowl area of the Midwest in the United States.

MAY

31   An earthquake measuring 7.5 on the Richter scale kills an estimated 50,000 people in Quetta, India.

SEPTEMBER

2–3   A hurricane kills 408 people in the Florida Keys—more than half the population at the time—and destroys the stone causeway that supports the Overseas Railroad.

Exploration

- Jim Jarratt, diving 100 m/330 ft in an armored suit called the "Iron Man," locates the wreck of the *Lusitania* off the coast of Ireland.

NOVEMBER

- U.S. explorer Lincoln Ellsworth flies from the Weddell Sea to the Ross Sea to become the first person to fly successfully across Antarctica.

Health and Medicine

- German chemist Gerhard Domagk uses Prontosil to cure a streptococcal infection in his youngest daughter; this is the first use of a sulfa drug on a human.

- German physiologist Hans Spemann receives the Nobel Prize for Physiology or Medicine for his work on the organizer effect in embryos.

JUNE

6   Recovering U.S. alcoholics Bill Wilson and Dr. Robert H. Smith found Alcoholics Anonymous in New York, New York.

OCTOBER

- British inventor A. Edwin Stevens builds the first wearable hearing aid; it weighs 0.9 kg/2 lb.

Math

- U.S. mathematician Alonzo Church invents lambda calculus, a mathematical method for representing mechanical computations.

Science

- Austrian zoologist Konrad Lorenz founds the discipline of ethology by describing the learning behavior of young ducklings; visual and auditory stimuli from the parent object cause them to "imprint" on the parent.
- Canadian scientist William Giauque cools liquid helium to 0.0004°C/0.0002°F above absolute zero.
- English physicist James Chadwick receives the Nobel Prize for Physics for his discovery of the neutron.
- French physicists Frédéric and Irène Joliot-Curie share the Nobel Prize for Chemistry for their synthesis of new radioactive elements.
- Japanese physicist Hideki Yukawa proposes the existence of a new particle, the meson, to explain nuclear forces.
- Swiss chemist Paul Karrer synthesizes vitamin B_2 (riboflavin), for which he wins a Nobel prize in 1937.
- U.S. anthropologist Margaret Mead publishes *Sex and Temperament*, which examines the social expectations of men and women in three societies.
- U.S. anthropologist Ruth Benedict publishes *Zuni Mythology*.
- U.S. biochemist Edward Calvin Kendall isolates the steroid hormone cortisone from the adrenal cortex.
- U.S. biochemist Wendell Meredith Stanley shows that viruses are not submicroscopic organisms but are proteinaceous in nature.
- U.S. seismologist Charles Richter introduces the Richter scale for measuring the magnitude of earthquakes at their epicentre.

Technology

- British physicist Robert Watson-Watt builds radar equipment that can detect aircraft up to 64 km/40 mi away.
- Chemists working for the British company Imperial Chemical Industries (ICI) polymerize ethylene to make polyethylene, the first true plastic.
- Construction of the first commercial electron microscope begins in England.
- Gas turbine engines, which aid in the development of jet engines, are patented in Germany and England.

- The magnetophone, the first tape recorder to use plastic tape, is developed by AEG in Berlin, Germany.
- U.S. inventor Robert H. Goddard launches a liquid-propelled rocket faster than the speed of sound.

October 1935–39 U.S. physicists Russel H. and Sigurd Fergus Varian develop the klystron, a thermionic electron tube capable of generating microwaves. Used in radar receivers, its power output proves to be too low to be used in radar transmitters.

APRIL

15 U.S. scientists Leopold Godowsky and Leopold Mannes announce the development of "Kodachrome," the first commercially available color film.

Transportation

- Length of railroad that is in operation: United States 409,244 km/254,347 mi; Great Britain 100,566 km/62,502 mi; USSR 84,773 km/52,687 mi; Germany 43,794 km/27,218 mi; France 42,767 km/26,580 mi.
- Oklahoma City becomes the first city in the world to have parking meters installed.
- The Boeing B-17 bomber, known as the "Flying Fortress," makes a test flight; it goes into production in 1937 for the U.S. armed forces.
- The Toyoda Automatic Loom Works in Japan makes the first prototype Toyota car.
- U.S. car manufacturer General Motors begins making diesel locomotives.
- U.S. servicemen A. W. Stevens and O. A. Anderson set an altitude record of 22,066 m/72,395 ft in a balloon.

JANUARY

- U.S. aviator Amelia Earhart is the first person to fly from Hawaii to California.

14 The Lower Zambezi railroad bridge in Mozambique, the longest in the world (until December 1935), is opened to traffic.

MARCH

23 The USSR sells the Chinese Eastern Railroad to the Japanese puppet state of Manchukuo in China.

MAY

- The Metropol subway opens in Moscow, Russia, with 8.8 km/5.5 mi of track.

30–June 3 The French vessel SS *Normandie* crosses the Atlantic in a record time of 4 days 3 hr 2 min; it uses a turboelectric drive.

SEPTEMBER

12 U.S. multimillionaire Howard Hughes sets the world's airspeed record of 567.23 kph/352.46 mph, in an airplane of his own design.

NOVEMBER

22 Pan American Airways' *China Clipper* starts a trans-Pacific airmail service from California in the United States to Manila in the Philippines.

DECEMBER

6 Trans World Airways uses air hostesses on its 14-seat airplanes.

ARTS AND IDEAS

Architecture

DECEMBER

10 The Huey P. Long Bridge at Metairie, Louisiana, is completed. At 7.1 km/4.4 mi long, it is the longest railroad bridge in the world.

Arts

- In the United States, the Federal Art Project (part of the Works Progress Administration) employs thousands of artists, including Arshile Gorky, Jackson Pollock, and Ben Shahn, for public works. The artists are paid from the federal payroll.
- Polish-born French artist Hans Bellmer creates *The Doll*, ten tinted photographs.
- The English artist Ben Nicholson, one of the leading advocates of abstract art in Britain, sculpts *White Relief*.
- The English artist Barbara Hepworth sculpts *Three Forms*.
- The English artist Henry Moore sculpts *Family*.
- The English artist Stanley Spencer paints *St. Francis and the Birds*.
- The German artist Kurt Schwitters leaves incomplete his first *Merzbau*, a room in a house in Hanover, Germany, which he has filled with constructions made of discarded materials.
- The Italian artist Mario Sironi paints the mural *Italy between the Arts and Sciences*.
- The Polish-born French artist Balthus paints *The Street*.
- The Spanish artist Pablo Picasso completes his *Minotaurmachy* etchings.
- The Spanish artist Salvador Dalí paints *Suburbs of the Paranoiac-Critical Town*.
- The U.S. artist Jackson Pollock paints *Going West*.
- The U.S.-born English artist Jacob Epstein sculpts *Ecce Homo/Behold the Man*.
- U.S. photographer Alfred Eisenstaedt takes *Feet of an Ethiopian Soldier*.
- U.S. photographer Alfred Stieglitz takes *Portrait of Dorothy Norman*.

Film

- *A Midsummer Night's Dream*, adapted from Shakespeare's play, directed by the Austrian-born director Max Reinhardt and the German-born director William Dieterle, is released in the United States. It stars U.S. actors James Cagney, Mickey Rooney, and Dick Powell.
- The 1932–33 Academy Awards take place. Best Actor: Charles Laughton, for *The Private Life of Henry VIII*; Best Actress: Katharine Hepburn, for *Morning Glory*; Best Picture: *Cavalcade*, directed by Frank Lloyd; Best Director: Frank Lloyd, for *Cavalcade*.
- Attendance at U.S. movie theaters averages 8 million per week.

- The movie *A Night at the Opera*, directed by Sam Wood, is released in the United States, starring the Marx Brothers.
- The movie *Becky Sharp*, directed by Russian-born U.S. filmmaker Rouben Mamoulian, is released in the United States, the first feature-length movie to be shot using Technicolor. Based on William Thackeray's novel *Vanity Fair*, it stars Miriam Hopkins and Cedric Hardwicke.
- The movie *Dangerous*, directed by Alfred E. Green, is released in the United States, starring Bette Davis.
- The movie *Les Misérables*, directed by Polish filmmaker Richard Boleslavsky, is released in the United States. Based on the novel by Victor Hugo, it stars Fredric March, Charles Laughton, Cedric Hardwicke, and Rochelle Hudson.
- The movie *Magnificent Obsession*, directed by John M. Stahl, is released in the United States, starring Irene Dunne and Robert Taylor.
- The movie *Mutiny on the Bounty*, directed by Frank Lloyd, is released in the United States, starring Clark Gable and Charles Laughton.
- The movie *The Informer*, directed by John Ford, is released in the United States, starring Victor McLaglen.
- The movie *The Scarlet Pimpernel*, directed by Hungarian filmmaker Alexander Korda, is released in the UK. Based on the novel by Baroness Orczy, it stars Leslie Howard and Merle Oberon.
- The movie *The Thirty-Nine Steps*, directed by Alfred Hitchcock, is released in the UK. Based on the novel by John Buchan, it stars Robert Donat and Madeleine Carroll.
- The musical movie *Top Hat*, directed by Mark Sandrich, is released in the United States, starring Fred Astaire and Ginger Rogers.
- The first International Film Festival in Eastern Europe is held in Moscow.
- The name "Oscar" is adopted for the Academy Awards.
- The witty horror movie *Bride of Frankenstein* is released in the United States, directed by the English filmmaker James Whale and starring Colin Clive, Boris Karloff, and Elsa Lanchester.

FEBRUARY

4 The first national movie archive, the Reichsfilmsarchiv, is founded in Germany.

Literature and Language

- In the United States, the Federal Writers' Project (part of the Works Progress Administration) is inaugurated, finding work for writers. The project creates more than 1,000 books and pamphlets, its greatest achievement being the American Guide series. Those who work on the project include Saul Bellow, Nelson Algren, Conrad Aiken, and Richard Wright.
- Publisher Victor Gollancz founds the world's first book club, the Left Book Club, in London, England. Its first publication is in May 1936.
- The 15th edition of the *Brockhaus Enzyklopädie/Brockhaus Encyclopedia*, the leading German encyclopedia, is published. It is published as *Der grosse Brockhaus/The Large Brockhaus*, the name Brockhaus being used for the first time. The first parts were published in 1796.
- The Bulgarian writer Elias Canetti publishes the novel *Die Blendung/The Blinding* in German. It will be translated in 1946 as *Auto-Da-Fé* in Britain and *The Tower of Babel* in the United States.
- The English art critic and writer Herbert Read publishes his fantasy novel *The Green Child*.
- The English comic writer P. G. Wodehouse publishes his novel *Blandings Castle*.
- The English writer Cecil Day Lewis publishes his poetry collection *A Time to Dance*.
- The English writer Christopher Isherwood publishes his novel *Mr Norris Changes Trains*. It is published in the United States as *The Last of Mr Norris*.
- The English writer Edward Frederic Benson publishes the comic novel *Mapp and Lucia*.
- The English writer Graham Greene publishes his novel *England Made Me*.
- The English writer Ivy Compton-Burnett publishes her novel *A House and its Head*.
- The English writer Walter de la Mare publishes *Poems, 1919–34*.
- The French writer André Malraux publishes his novel *Le Temps du mépris/Days of Contempt*.
- The Japanese writer Toson Shimazaki publishes his novel *Yoake mae/Before the Dawn*.
- The Nobel Prize for Literature is not awarded this year.
- The Polish-born German novelist Ben Traven publishes *The Treasure of the Sierra Madre*, a novel written in German in 1927 as *Der Schatz der Sierra Madre*.
- The Pulitzer Prize for Biography is awarded to Douglas Freeman for *R E Lee*, the Prize for Fiction is awarded to Josephine Johnson for *Now in November*, and the Prize for Poetry is awarded to Audrey Wurdemann for *Bright Ambush*.
- The Spanish-born U.S. philosopher and writer George Santayana publishes his novel *The Last Puritan: A Memoir in the Form of a Novel*.
- The U.S. novelist Ernest Hemingway publishes his novel *The Green Hills of Africa*.
- The U.S. novelist Lloyd C. Douglas's *Green Light* is the best-selling novel in the United States.
- The U.S. writer John Steinbeck publishes his novel of Northern California working-class life, *Tortilla Flat*, which establishes his reputation.
- The U.S. writer Sinclair Lewis publishes *It Can't Happen Here*, a novel warning of the possibility of a fascist takeover of the United States.
- The U.S. writer Thomas Wolfe publishes *Of Time and the River: A Legend of Man's Hunger in His Youth*.
- The U.S. writer Wallace Stevens publishes his poetry collection *Ideas of Order*.
- The U.S. writer Willa Cather publishes her novel *Lucy Gayheart*.
- The U.S.-born English poet T. S. Eliot publishes "Burnt Norton," the first part of his *Four Quartets*.
- Under the pseudonym of T. E. Shaw, the English soldier and writer T. E. Lawrence ("Lawrence of Arabia") publishes his translation of Homer's *Odyssey*.

Music

- In the UK, the first recordings by the dance band of Victor Silvester are made.
- The Austrian composer Alban Berg completes his Violin Concerto.
- The band of jazz musician Count Basie becomes famous through performances at the Famous Door Club, New York, New York.
- The British Ministry of Labour effectively bans U.S. jazz musicians by stipulating that they can only play in Britain if there are reciprocal arrangements with the American Federation of Musicians. As a result, few foreign jazz musicians will play in Britain over the next 20 years.
- The English composer Ralph Vaughan Williams completes his Symphony No. 4 in F minor and his choral suite *Five Tudor Portraits*. His *Fantasia on Greensleeves* (taken from his 1928 opera *Sir John in Love*) is arranged for strings and harp by Ralph Greaves.
- The English composer William Walton completes his Symphony No. 1.
- The first Gibson electro-acoustic guitar is manufactured, in the United States.
- The jazz musician Artie Shaw creates his first band, in the United States.
- The opera *Die Schweigsame Frau/The Silent Woman* by the German composer Richard Strauss is first performed, in Dresden, Germany.
- The opera *Porgy and Bess* by the U.S. composer George Gershwin is first performed, in New York, New York, and Boston, Massachusetts.
- The operetta *Glamorous Night* by the Welsh composer Ivor Novello is first performed, in London, England.
- The Russian composer Sergey Prokofiev completes his Violin Concerto No. 2.
- The Swiss composer Arthur Honegger completes his oratorio *Jeanne d' Arc au bûcher/Joan of Arc at the Stake*.
- The tune "Good Morning to All" is published as "Happy Birthday to You," in the United States. The words are by Patty Smith Hill, the music by Mildred J. Hill.
- The U.S.-born violinist Yehudi Menuhin makes his first world tour, accompanied by his sister Hephzibah Menuhin.

February 1935–39 The English musicologist Donald Tovey publishes his six-volume *Essays in Musical Analysis*.

OCTOBER
- German radio bans jazz of black or Jewish origin.

Theater and Dance

- In the United States, the Federal Theater Project (part of the Works Progress Administration) is inaugurated to create work for actors, writers, directors, and designers. About a thousand productions are mounted.
- The English-born U.S. writers W. H. Auden and Christopher Isherwood publish their play *The Dog Beneath the Skin*.

- The New York Drama Critics' Circle is founded.
- The play *La Guerre de troie n'aura pas lieu/Tiger at the Gates*, by the French writer Jean Giraudoux, is first performed, in Paris, France.
- The play *Night Must Fall*, by the Welsh writer Emlyn Williams, is first performed, in London, England.
- The play *Waiting for Lefty*, by the U.S. writer Clifford Odets is first performed, at the Civic Theater in New York, New York. It becomes one of the best-known examples of U.S. proletarian drama.
- The Pulitzer Prize for Drama is awarded to Zoë Akins for *The Old Maid*.
- The verse play *Murder in the Cathedral*, by the U.S.-born English writer T. S. Eliot, is first performed, in Canterbury Cathedral, England.

Thought and Scholarship

- English economists and social reformers Sidney and Beatrice Webb publish *Soviet Communism: A New Civilisation?*
- English historian George Dangerfield publishes *The Strange Death of Liberal England*.
- English historian Herbert Albert Laurens Fisher publishes his three-volume *A History of Europe*.
- German philosopher Karl Jaspers publishes *Vernuft und Existenz/Reason and Existence*.
- New Zealand historian Ronald Syme publishes *The Roman Revolution*, a study of Roman politics that brings a new objectivity to the subject.
- The Pulitzer Prize for History is awarded to Charles McLean Andrews for *The Colonial Period of American History*.
- U.S. historian Carl Lotus Becker publishes *Everyman His Own Historian: Essays on History and Politics*.

SOCIETY

Everyday Life

- Despite emigration and a falling birth rate, overpopulation causes concern in Japan: the population has effectively doubled in size since 1872 and stands at more than 70 million.
- There are 17.4 million telephones in the United States; 32% of homes have telephones.
- U.S. businesses spend $1.7 billion on advertising: $762 million in newspapers; $136 million in magazines; and $112 million on radio.

FEBRUARY
28 French labor unions recognize the right of women to take up regular employment.

APRIL
- The first chain letter, sent under the name of the Prosperity Club, circulates in Denver, Colorado.

NOVEMBER
11 John L. Lewis, president of the United Mine Workers in the United States, deserts the craft-based American Federation of Labor to form the Committee for

Industrial Organization (CIO; from 1938, the Congress of Industrial Organizations). Seven other unions follow in the same year.
28 The Miles quads of St. Neots, England, are the first quadruplets to survive infancy.

Media and Communication

- Regular television broadcasting begins in Germany; images are based on a 180-line scan.
- U.S. pollster George Gallup founds the American Institute of Public Opinion. Using statistical techniques he successfully predicts the reelection of President Roosevelt the following year, while the larger but less scientific effort of the *Literary Digest* forecasts his defeat—the magazine does not recover.

MARCH
25 After inviting discussion in the press, the British Broadcasting Corporation (BBC) officially adopts the name "televiewer" for the members of its audience; this is soon shortened to "viewer."

APRIL
20 In the United States, the world's first radio ratings show, *Your Lucky Strike Hit Parade* starts, featuring the 15 most popular songs of the week.

NOVEMBER
- *The New York Times* begins putting its archive of back issues on to microfilm.

Religion

- The Swiss Protestant theologian Karl Barth publishes *Credo*.

Sports

- In cycling, the first Vuelta a España (Tour of Spain) is won by Gustave Deloor of Belgium.
- In the United States, the University of Minnesota and the Southern Methodist University share the college football national championship.
- Jay Berwanger of Chicago, Illinois, wins the inaugural DAC Trophy presented by the Downtown Athletic Club

BIRTHS & DEATHS

JANUARY
4 Floyd Patterson, U.S. professional boxer, born in Waco, North Carolina.
8 Elvis Presley, U.S. rock and roll singer, whose great success changed U.S. popular culture, born in Tupelo, Mississippi (–1977).
16 Ma Barker, U.S. criminal who robbed banks in Oklahoma with her sons, dies in Oklawaha, Florida (52).
19 Zia ur-Rahman, president of Bangladesh 1975–81 and founder of the Bangladesh National Party, born (–1981).

MARCH
6 Oliver Wendell Holmes, U.S. legal historian and philosopher, justice of the U.S. Supreme Court, dies in Washington, D.C. (93).
15 Jimmy Swaggart, U.S. Pentecostal minister who had a popular religious TV show before becoming embroiled in a sex scandal, born in Ferriday, Louisiana.

MAY
11 Doug McClure, U.S. actor, born in Glendale, California (–1995).
12 Józef Piłsudski, Polish revolutionary and statesman, first president 1918–22 of the newly independent Poland, dies in Warsaw, Poland (67).
17 Paul Dukas, French composer best known for *The Sorcerer's Apprentice*, dies in Paris, France (69).

19 T(homas) E(dward) Lawrence ("Lawrence of Arabia"), British scholar, military strategist, and author, dies in Clouds Hill, Dorset, England (46).
21 Jane Addams, U.S. social reformer and Nobel Peace Prize winner in 1931, dies in Chicago, Illinois (74).

JUNE
13 Christo (born Christo Javacheff), Bulgarian sculptor of controversial outdoor works, born in Gabrovo, Bulgaria.
21 Françoise Sagan, French novelist and dramatist, born in Carjac, France.
25 Larry Kramer, U.S. writer and AIDS activist, born in Bridgeport, Connecticut.

JULY
3 André-Gustave Citroën, French engineer who established one of the largest car manufacturing firms in Europe, dies in Paris, France (57).

AUGUST
15 Wiley Post, U.S. aviator who made the first solo flight around the world, is killed when his plane crashes near Point Barrow, Alaska (35).
15 Will Rogers, U.S. actor and humorist, is killed in a plane crash near Point Barrow, Alaska (55).

SEPTEMBER
10 Huey Long, U.S. senator and governor of Louisiana, known for his autocratic style, assassinated in Baton Rouge, Louisiana (42).

16 Carl André, U.S. sculptor, born in Quincy, Massachusetts.
19 Konstantin Eduardovich Tsiolkovsky, Russian aeronautics and astronautics scientist who pioneered rocket and space travel research, dies in Kaluga, Russia (78).

OCTOBER
12 Luciano Pavarotti, Italian tenor and opera singer, born in Modena, Italy.
23 "Dutch" Schultz, gangster and bootlegger in New York, New York, is gunned down in Newark, New Jersey, by gunmen of rival crime bosses (33).
23 Charles Demuth, U.S. painter, dies in Lancaster, Pennsylvania (51).
24 Henri Pirenne, Belgian educator and scholar, dies in Eccle, near Brussels, Belgium (72).

NOVEMBER
16 Elizabeth Drew, U.S. political journalist, born in Cincinnati, Ohio.

DECEMBER
1 Woody Allen, U.S. film director, screenwriter, actor, and author, born in Brooklyn, New York.
14 Lee, Remick, U.S. film and television actress, born in Quincy, Massachusetts (–1991).
24 Alban Berg, Austrian composer, dies in Vienna, Austria (50).

of New York to the outstanding college football player east of the Mississippi. The following year the award is renamed the Heisman Trophy and college players from the whole of the United States are eligible to win it.

- The U.S. women's tennis team defeats the British team 9–3 in the Wightman Cup at Ridgewood, New Jersey. Great Britain does not regain the cup for another 22 years.

- U.S. golfer Gene Sarazen wins the Masters at Augusta, Georgia, after a play-off. He becomes the first golfer to have won all four majors during his career.

JANUARY

- In college football, Tulane wins the inaugural Sugar Bowl and Bucknell wins the first Orange Bowl.

FEBRUARY

9 U.S. national figure skating champions are: Maribel Vinson; Robin Lee; Maribel Vinson and George Hill, pairs.

APRIL

4–9 The Montreal Maroons beat the Toronto Maple Leafs in three games to win the National Hockey League (NHL) championship.

MAY

4–June 8 Omaha, ridden by Willie Saunders, wins the Kentucky Derby, the Preakness Stakes, and the Belmont Stakes, becoming only the third horse to win the American Triple Crown.

19 The draft system is introduced into American football: the team at the bottom of the National Football League (NFL) is allowed first choice of players graduating from college, starting in the 1936 season.

24 At Crosley Field in Cincinnati, Ohio, 20,000 fans watch the Cincinnati Reds beat the Philadelphia Phillies in major league baseball's first night game.

25 In less than an hour at the Big Ten Championships held at Ann Arbor, Michigan, U.S. athlete Jesse Owens, of Ohio State University, breaks the world record in the long jump, the 220 yards, the 220-yard hurdles, and equals the record for the 100 yards. His jump of 8.13 m/26 ft 8¼in is the first ever over 8 meters and is not bettered until 1960.

30 U.S. racing driver Kelly Petillo of Los Angeles, California, wins the Indianapolis 500.

JUNE

8 U.S. golfer Sam Parks, Jr., wins the U.S. Open golf championship.

13 James Braddock of the United States outpoints fellow U.S. boxer Max Baer over 15 rounds to win the world heavyweight boxing title in Long Island, New York.

JULY

4–28 Belgian cyclist Romain Maes leads the Tour de France from start to finish.

6 For the seventh time, U.S. tennis player Helen Wills Moody wins the women's singles title at the Wimbledon tennis championships in England.

AUGUST

15 The first U.S. national skeet shooting championships are held in Cleveland, Ohio.

SEPTEMBER

3 British driver Malcolm Campbell drives *Bluebird* at 484.5 kph/301.1 mph at the Bonneville Salt Flats in Utah, United States; he sets a new land speed record.

11 U.S. tennis player Helen Hull Jacobs garners her fourth straight title at the U.S. Lawn Tennis Association championships; Wilmer Allison of the United States wins the men's division.

OCTOBER

2–7 The Detroit Tigers defeat the Chicago Cubs four games to two to win their first World Series.

DECEMBER

7 The National Convention of the U.S. Amateur Athletic Union decides, by 61 votes to 55, not to withdraw from the Olympic Games in Germany. The German government's discriminatory attitude against Jewish athletes, it is argued, is in violation of Olympic rules.

15 The Detroit Lions defeat the New York Giants 26–7 in the National Football League (NFL) championship game in Detroit, Michigan.

16 The Russian-born French chess world champion Alexander Alekhine loses his title to Max Euwe of the Netherlands, by 15½ to 14½.

1936

POLITICS, GOVERNMENT, AND ECONOMICS

Business and Economics

- English economist John Maynard Keynes publishes *General Theory of Employment, Interest, and Money*, proposing that recession can be prevented if the government sponsors a full employment policy. It has a profound effect on economic thinking and government economic strategy worldwide.
- Farm prices and automobile production rise in the United States, but 8 million Americans remain unemployed.
- The A&P chain of supermarkets opens for business in the United States.
- The Reserve Bank of New Zealand is nationalized.

JUNE

12 A strike by 300,000 workers results in social reforms in France, including a 40-hour working week and paid holiday.

SEPTEMBER

27 France, Switzerland, and the Netherlands abandon the gold standard.

OCTOBER

2 France devalues the franc.
5 Italy devalues the lira.

Human Rights

- A system of maternity welfare is established in the USSR, including child care and financial support for women.

OCTOBER

12 Oswald Mosley, head of the British Union of Fascists, leads an anti-Jewish march along Mile End Road, in a Jewish district of London, England. It is confronted by a left-wing counterdemonstration (the "Battle of Cable Street"), and Mosley is seriously injured in the ensuing violence.

Politics and Government

- Armenia, Azerbaijan, Georgia, and Kazakhstan are incorporated as republics of the USSR.

- In Moscow, Russia, the government revokes a 1920 law legalizing abortion, and introduces restrictions on the availability of abortion.
- In the case *US v. Curtiss-Wright Export Corporation*, the U.S. Supreme Court, upholding an arms embargo, rules that the federal government's powers of external sovereignty do not depend on affirmative statements in the constitution.
- The black American educator Mary McLeod Bethune, president of the National Council of Negro Women, is appointed director of the Division of Negro Affairs of the National Youth Administration in the United States.

JANUARY

6 In the case *U.S. v. Butler*, the U.S. Supreme Court declares unconstitutional the tax on food processing in the Agricultural Adjustment Act of 1933.
6–March 25 The London naval conference resumes, six years after the conclusion of the London Naval Treaty. Japan withdraws on January 15 because other countries refuse to accept its demand for parity with the United States and Britain on the upper limit on naval strength in the Pacific.
23 Pierre Laval resigns as prime minister of France following attacks on the Hoare–Laval Plan of December 9, 1935. A new government is formed by Albert Sarraut.

FEBRUARY

- In a rare legal triumph for the Roosevelt administration, the U.S. Supreme Court rules in the case *Ashwander v. Tennessee Valley Authority (TVA)* that the TVA may sell surplus hydroelectric power.
16 The Popular Front coalition of left-wing parties wins 256 seats in the Spanish election, against 165 for the right and 52 for the center. Manuel Azaña again becomes prime minister and reestablishes the constitution of 1931.
17 A trade pact between Britain and Ireland ends the dispute between the two states over import duties imposed by Britain.
26 The Japanese finance minister, Takahashi Korekiyo, is killed in a military revolt in Tokyo. Okada Keisuke resigns as prime minister and is succeeded by Hirota Koki.
29 The U.S. president, Franklin D. Roosevelt, signs the Soil Conservation and Domestic Allotment Act to replace the unconstitutional Agricultural Adjustment Act. The new act rewards farmers for growing soil-enhancing crops.

MARCH

3 The British defense budget rises from £122 million to £158 million to increase the Fleet Air Arm, add 250 aircraft for home defense, and provide four new infantry battalions.
7 German troops occupy the demilitarized zone of the Rhineland, violating the 1919 Treaty of Versailles.

Spanish Civil War (1936–39)

1936

JULY

18 The right-wing Spanish general Francisco Franco leads an army mutiny in Morocco against the Spanish Republican government. Other mutinies break out on the Spanish mainland, marking the start of the Spanish Civil War.

24 Spanish Nationalists establish a committee of national defense under General Emilio Mola at Burgos, north of Madrid.

AUGUST

4 General Franco's Nationalist army captures Badajoz in the southwest, enabling antigovernment forces in the north and south to combine.

SEPTEMBER

9–17 In a conference in London, England, 27 countries join a nonintervention committee charged with preventing the supply of armaments to Spain and the intervention of foreign forces there.

NOVEMBER

6 The Spanish Nationalist siege of Madrid begins. The Republican defenders under General José Miaja are joined by members of the International Brigades (foreign volunteer fighters recruited by the Comintern). The Republican government moves to Valencia on the east coast.

18 Germany and Italy recognize General Franco's rebel Nationalist government.

1937

FEBRUARY

8 Spanish Nationalist forces under General Gonzalo Queipo de Llano take the Republican-held city of Málaga in the south of the country, with Italian military aid.

MARCH

8–18 Italian tanks and troops supporting the Nationalists advance on Republican-held Madrid and are dispersed by Soviet dive-bombers.

18 The Italian Legion is defeated at Brihuega (near Madrid) by Republican and International Brigade forces, checking the Nationalists' threat to Madrid.

APRIL

1 Spanish Nationalist forces launch a major offensive against Republican-held areas in the north of the country.

19 The Falange, the Carlists, and other right-wing factions in Spain are forcibly merged into the Falange Española Tradicionalista de las Juntas de Ofensiva Nacional Sindicalista ("Traditional Spanish Phalanx of the Juntas of the National Syndicalist Offensive"), under the leadership of General Franco.

26 Guernica, the historic Basque capital in northern Spain, is heavily bombed by aircraft of the German Condor Legion supporting the Spanish Nationalist rebels.

MAY

3–10 Anarchists and Syndicalists revolt against the increasingly authoritarian and communist-dominated wartime policies of the Republican government, in Barcelona, northeast Spain. The revolt is put down by government troops, causing a crisis in the government.

JUNE

19 Nationalist forces capture Bilbao, the capital of the pro-Republican Basque region in the northwest of the country, after an 80-day siege.

23 Germany and Italy withdraw from the committee formed in September 1936 to prevent foreign intervention in the Spanish Civil War.

AUGUST

25 Spanish Nationalist forces capture the north-coast port of Santander as their offensive against Republican areas in the north continues.

OCTOBER

1 General Franco assumes the formal leadership of the Nationalists in Spain and outlines the main policies to be followed by a Nationalist government.

21 Spanish Nationalist forces take Gijón, the last major town in the pro-Republican north of the country.

28 The Spanish Republican government moves from Valencia to Barcelona on the northeast coast as Nationalist offensives begin in the southeast.

NOVEMBER

28 Nationalist forces, with help from Italy, begin a naval blockade of the Spanish coast to prevent arms supplies to the remaining Republican areas of the country.

DECEMBER

14 Republican forces launch an offensive against Nationalist positions in Aragon.

1938

JANUARY

9 Republican troops capture the city of Teruel from Nationalist forces.

FEBRUARY

22 Spanish Nationalist forces recapture the city of Teruel and advance toward the Mediterranean.

APRIL

3 Nationalist troops capture the city of Lérida, west of Barcelona, from Republican forces.

15 Nationalist forces take the town of Vinaroz on the Mediterranean coast, separating the Republican troops in Catalonia from those in southeast Spain.

OCTOBER

29 Belgium withdraws from the committee formed in September 1935 to prevent foreign intervention in the Spanish Civil War.

DECEMBER

23 Nationalist forces launch an offensive in the autonomous Spanish region of Catalonia, with the aim of capturing the Republican stronghold of Barcelona.

1939

JANUARY

26 Nationalist forces, assisted by Italian troops, take Barcelona.

FEBRUARY

27 Britain and France recognize General Franco's Nationalist government in Spain.

MARCH

28–29 Madrid surrenders to the Spanish Nationalists, after a siege of almost two and a half years. The remaining Republican areas capitulate on March 29, ending the Spanish Civil War.

12 The USSR and Mongolia sign a mutual aid treaty.

13 Thomas Inskip is appointed as Britain's first minister for the coordination of defense.

23 Italy, Austria, and Hungary pledge that none of the three will discuss trade and navigation rights on the River Danube without consulting the other two.

25 Britain, the United States, and France sign the London Naval Treaty, which defines categories of ship, permitted tonnages, and gun sizes, and requires advance notification of building programs.

29 In the German elections 99% of the electorate vote for the official National Socialist (Nazi) Party candidates.

APRIL

1 Austria reintroduces conscription, thus repudiating its obligations under the 1919 Treaty of St. Germain.

3 German-born U.S. carpenter and burglar Bruno Hauptmann, convicted for kidnapping and murder of the baby son of the aviator Charles Lindbergh and Anne Morrow Lindbergh in 1932, is executed in Trenton, New Jersey.

10 The Spanish parliament dismisses the president, Niceto Alcalá Zamora of the Liberal Republican Right, following left-wing gains in the elections.

13 General Ioannis Metaxas is appointed prime minister of Greece by King George II.

15–November 11 Serious Arab unrest breaks out in Palestine over Jewish immigration from Nazi Germany. Jews are murdered and Jewish property attacked.

28 King Fuad of Egypt dies. He is succeeded by his 16-year-old son, Farouk.

MAY

2 A general election in Egypt results in victory for the Wafd nationalists. Nahhas Pasha becomes prime minister for the third time.

3 Left-wing parties supporting the Popular Front win 376 seats in the French general election, against 147 for the Socialists.

5 Italian forces occupy the Ethiopian capital, Addis Ababa, thereby ending the war caused by their invasion.

9 Italy formally annexes Ethiopia (Abyssinia), having occupied the capital, Addis Ababa, on May 5.

10 Manuel Azaña of the Republican Left succeeds Niceto Alcalá Zamora as president of Spain.

21 The Austrian chancellor, Kurt von Schuschnigg, becomes leader of the Fatherland Front, the only permitted political party.

24 The Rexists (fascists) win 21 seats, more than 10% of the chamber, in the Belgian general elections.

JUNE

• The Democratic Party renominates Franklin D. Roosevelt and John Nance Garner for U.S. president and vice president respectively.

• The Republican Party nominates Alfred M. Landon, the governor of Kansas, for U.S. president and Colonel Frank Knox of Illinois for vice president.

4 The Popular Front leader, Léon Blum, becomes the first Socialist and Jewish prime minister of France.

9 Count Galeazzo Ciano, Mussolini's son-in-law, is appointed Italian foreign minister.

17 The Canadian supreme court nullifies most of the New Deal legislation of Richard Bennett's 1935 government.

18 The Irish Republican Army (IRA) is again declared illegal in the Irish Free State, and the movement goes underground.

20 The U.S. Congress passes the Robinson–Patman Act, forbidding price discrimination on the part of manufacturers.

23 The British Opposition leader, Clement Attlee, moves a vote of censure in the House of Commons on Stanley Baldwin's government for pursuing a weak and dangerous foreign policy. His motion is defeated by 384 votes to 170.

24 The Belgian prime minister, Paul van Zeeland, proposes a radical program of social reform.

JULY

11 An Austrian–German convention, following negotiations between Austrian chancellor Kurt von Schuschnigg and German chancellor Adolf Hitler, acknowledges the independence of Austria.

17 The munitions industry is nationalized in France by Léon Blum's Popular Front government.

18 The right-wing Spanish general Francisco Franco leads an army mutiny in Morocco against the Spanish Republican government. Other mutinies break out on the Spanish mainland, marking the start of the Spanish Civil War.

20 Under the terms of the Montreux Convention, Turkey recovers its sovereignty over the Dardanelles and the Bosporus straits.

24 Spanish Nationalists establish a committee of national defense under General Emilio Mola at Burgos, north of Madrid.

AUGUST

2 France proposes a policy of nonintervention in the Spanish Civil War to Britain.

4 In the Spanish Civil War, General Franco's Nationalist army captures Badajoz in the southwest, enabling antigovernment forces in the north and south to combine.

4 Martial law is proclaimed by the Greek dictator Ioannis Metaxas (the so-called "Regime of 4th August") in order to preempt a general strike.

11 Jiang Jie Shi, head of the ruling Nationalist Party (Guomindang) in China, enters the port of Canton for the first time since 1926, strengthening his hold on the south.

24 Germany introduces a compulsory two-year period of military service following the German government's decision to begin rearming in 1935. Both acts violate the Treaty of Versailles of 1919.

26 A treaty of alliance is signed between Britain and Egypt. To last for 20 years, it gives Britain the right to station troops in the Suez Canal region and use Alexandria as a naval base.

26 Britain signs a treaty with Egypt recognizing the latter's sovereignty and independence, and pledging mutual defense and a 20-year alliance.

SEPTEMBER

• Japan makes secret demands of China for the employment of Japanese officials in the Chinese government and the formation of a united front against communists.

9 France signs a treaty of friendship with Syria, by which its mandate is to end in 1939.

9–17 In a conference on the Spanish Civil War in London, England, 27 countries join a nonintervention committee charged with preventing the supply of armaments to Spain and the intervention of foreign forces there.

10   The German propaganda minister, Joseph Goebbels, accuses Czechoslovakia of harboring Soviet aircraft.

OCTOBER

• Troops are called up in Austria, following the reintroduction of conscription in April.

1   The Nationalist rebels against the government of Spain appoint General Francisco Franco as chief of state in their provisional government.

1   The USSR accedes to the London Naval Treaty of March 25 establishing internationally agreed limits to the size of fleets.

5–11   Britain's first woman Labour member of Parliament, Ellen Wilkinson, leads a "hunger march" of workers from Jarrow in northeast England to London as a protest against unemployment following the closure of local shipyards.

6   The British Labour Party conference rejects the Communist Party's application for affiliation.

10   The Austrian chancellor, Kurt von Schuschnigg, dissolves the Heimwehr (fascist home defense force) and incorporates it in the Fatherland Front, which he leads.

14   Alarmed at the German occupation of the Rhineland, Belgium renounces its military alliance with France.

22   Martial law is proclaimed in Belgium to combat unrest caused by the increasingly popular and powerful Rexists (fascists).

28   Unions collectivize agriculture and industry in the republican areas of Spain and ban Christian worship.

NOVEMBER

1   Following the visit to Berlin, Germany, of the Italian foreign minister Count Galeazzo Ciano, Italy's prime minister Benito Mussolini proclaims the Rome–Berlin axis, an alliance between Nazi Germany and fascist Italy.

6   The Spanish Nationalist siege of Madrid begins. The Republican defenders under General José Miaja are joined by members of the International Brigades (foreign volunteer fighters recruited by the Comintern). The Republican government moves to Valencia on the east coast.

13   France signs a treaty of friendship with Lebanon, by which its mandate will end in 1939.

14   Germany denounces the clauses of the 1919 Treaty of Versailles that relate to the internationalization of its waterways.

16   Edward VIII, King of Great Britain and Northern Ireland, confides to Stanley Baldwin, Britain's prime minister, that he plans to marry Mrs. Wallis Simpson, a divorced U.S. citizen. Baldwin warns that the marriage would offend public opinion and damage the prestige of the throne.

18   Germany and Italy recognize General Francisco Franco's rebel Nationalist government in Spain.

23   An expropriation law in Mexico empowers the government to seize private property.

25   Germany and Japan sign an anti-Comintern pact and agree to work together against international communism. Germany also recognizes Japan's regime in Manchuria, China.

DECEMBER

1–16   A Pan-American peace conference is held in Buenos Aires, Argentina, at the request of President Franklin D. Roosevelt of the United States.

5   A new constitution is drawn up in the USSR under the Soviet leader, Joseph Stalin. It rearranges national political boundaries and creates the bicameral Supreme Soviet.

11   Edward VIII abdicates as king of Great Britain and Northern Ireland following his refusal to give up the idea of marriage to the U.S. divorcée Wallis Simpson.

12   The Constitution (amendment) Act in the Irish Free State removes the king from membership in the Irish parliament and deprives the British governor-general of most of his functions.

12   The Duke of York, younger brother of Edward VIII, succeeds to the British throne as George VI, following Edward's abdication on December 11.

12   The former king Edward VIII of Great Britain and Northern Ireland, who abdicated on December 11, 1936, is created Duke of Windsor.

SCIENCE, TECHNOLOGY, AND MEDICINE

Ecology

• Japan creates Fuji-Hakone-Izu National Park on the slopes of Mt. Fuji.

• The radio meteorograph (radiosonde) is developed by the U.S. Weather Service; it transmits information on temperature, humidity, and barometric pressure from uncrewed balloons. A network of stations is also inaugurated.

Health and Medicine

c. 1936   Home remedies used to terminate pregnancies include solutions of water, Lysol, carbolic soap, iodine, and turpentine. The bark of the American slippery elm tree, rolled and inserted in the cervix, is also used to abort the fetus.

• British physiologist Henry Dale and German physiologist Otto Loewi share the Nobel Prize for Physiology or Medicine for their work on the chemical transmission of nerve impulses.

• Plexiglas lenses, the first plastic contact lenses, are manufactured in Germany by I. G. Farben.

• Rates of maternal mortality begin to drop in the United States because of antibiotics and better trained physicians; they continue to decline sharply for the next 20 years.

• U.S. chemists Ernest Volviler and Donalee Tabern develop sodium pentothal ("truth serum"), which is used as an anesthetic.

• U.S. medical researchers Houston Merritt and Tracy Putnam develop the anticonvulsant heart drug dilantin.

Math

- British mathematician Alan Turing supplies the theoretical basis for digital computers by describing a machine, now known as the Turing machine, capable of universal rather than special-purpose problem solving.

Science

- Australian archeologist V. Gordon Childe—one of the most influential of his generation—publishes *Man Makes Himself*.
- Austrian physicist Victor Hess shares the Nobel Prize for Physics with U.S. physicist Carl Anderson; Hess for discovering cosmic radiation and Anderson for discovering the positron.
- Danish seismologist Inge Lehmann postulates the existence of a solid inner core of the earth from the study of seismic waves.
- Dutch chemist Peter Debye receives the Nobel Prize for Chemistry for his work on X-ray diffraction of gases.
- English archeologist Grahame Clark publishes *The Mesolithic Settlement of Northern Europe*.
- Fossil remains of *Pithecanthropus* (now *Homo erectus*) found in Java indicate that *Homo erectus* lived in the area 500,000–1 million years ago.
- U.S. anthropologist Ralph Linton publishes *The Study of Man*, drawing together theories from anthropology, psychology, and sociology.
- U.S. archeologist Andrew E. Douglass develops dendrochronology; a dating system based on the measurement of growth rings in trees.
- U.S. chemist Robert Runnels Williams synthesizes vitamin B_1 (thiamine).
- U.S. physicist Carl D. Anderson discovers the muon, an electron-like particle over 200 times more massive than an electron.
- U.S. physicists George Gamow and Edward Teller develop the theory of beta decay—the nuclear process of electron emission.
- Vitamin E is obtained in pure form by U.S. biochemists Herbert Evans and Oliver and Gladys Emerson.

Technology

c. 1936 Catalytic cracking, a chemical process in which long-chain hydrocarbon molecules are broken down into smaller ones, is introduced to produce gasoline from low-grade crude oil by the U.S. Sun Oil Company and Socony-Vacuum Company.

- The Magnetophon Company demonstrates the Magnetophon at the Berlin Radio Fair, Germany; it is the first tape recorder to use plastic tape. The German head of state Adolf Hitler uses it to tape his speeches, which sound live over the radio because of the absence of noise.

APRIL
- U.S. scientists produce a workable radar with a range of 4 km/2.5 mi. By the end of the year this is extended to 11 km/7 mi.

Transportation

- Austrian car manufacturer Daimler-Benz introduces the first diesel-powered car.
- The *Wupperthal*, the first diesel-electric vessel, is launched in Germany.
- The Fiat Topolino is developed in Italy as a "people's car" similar to the Volkswagen Beetle.
- U.S. aircraft manufacturer Douglas introduces the 21-passenger DC-3, one of the most successful commercial aircraft ever built (10,000 are produced by 1945). Powered by two 1200-horsepower engines, it reaches speeds of 300 kph/186 mph.
- U.S. inventor Carl C. Magee patents the first parking meter.

FEBRUARY
- Adolf Hitler commissions Ferdinand Porsche to design a "people's car" and the Volkswagen Beetle is born.

MARCH
5 British Royal Air Force (RAF) captain J. Summers test flies the prototype Spitfire fighter designed by Reginald Joseph Mitchell. Nearly 20,000 are produced during World War II and reach speeds of 740 kph/460 mph.

MAY
6 The German rigid airship *Hindenburg* makes its maiden voyage from Stuttgart, Germany, to New York, New York. It is 245 m/804 ft long and can carry 1,000 passengers.

JUNE
26 German engineer Heinrich Focke tests flies a helicopter, the Fa-61; it has vertical ascent and descent capabilities, can hover, and can fly forward or backward by changing the angle of the rotor.

ARTS AND IDEAS

Architecture

- A bridge at Aue, Germany, is the first constructed with prestressed concrete.
- The Highpoint Flats II, in Highgate, London, England, designed by the architectural group Tecton, are completed. Tecton, whose members include Berthold Lubetkin and Denys Lasdun, has brought the International Style to Britain. The group also designed the Finsbury Health Centre, London, England, completed in the same year.
- Impington Village College, near Cambridge, England, designed by the English architect Edwin Maxwell Fry and the German architect Walter Gropius, is completed. They also complete the Film Studios, Denham, in Buckinghamshire, England. Fry and Gropius are among the leading exponents of the International Style in Britain.
- The German architect Erich Mendolsohn and the Russian architect Serge Chermayeff design the De la Warr Pavilion in Bexhill-on-Sea, Sussex, England, and No. 6 Old Church Street in Chelsea, London, England.

Arts

- Hungarian-born U.S. photographer Frank Capa takes *Death of a Loyalist* (also known as *Moment of Death*), one of the best-known images of the Spanish Civil War.
- The "Cubism and Abstract Art" and the "Fantastic Art, Dada, and Surrealism" exhibitions are held at the Museum of Modern Art (MOMA) in New York, New York.
- The Armenian-born U.S. artist Arshile Gorky paints *Organization*.
- The Dutch artist Piet Mondrian paints *Composition in Red and Blue*.
- The English artist Laura Knight paints *Ballet*.
- The English artist Leonora Carrington paints *The Inn of the Dawn Horse (Self-Portrait)*.
- The English artist Stanley Spencer paints *Self-Portrait with Patricia Preece*.
- The English artist Walter Richard Sickert paints *HM King Edward VIII*.
- The Federal Art Project of the Works Progress Administration (WPA) in the United States employs about 5,000 artists in 44 states.
- The First International surrealist Exhibition opens, in London, England.
- The German artist Käthe Kollwitz sculpts *Mother and Child, or Pietà*.
- The German artist Max Beckmann paints *Adam and Eve*.
- The German Artist Max Ernst paints *The Entire City*.
- The German-born English art historian Nikolaus Pevsner publishes *Pioneers of the Modern Movement*.
- The Mexican artist Diego Rivera paints the mural *Mexico Today, Mexico Tomorrow*, part of his cycle of murals in the National Palace of Mexico City, Mexico.
- The Mexican artist José Clemente Orozco paints the mural *The Four Ages of Man* in the Hospicio Cabañas in Guadalajara, Mexico.
- The Spanish artist Joan Miró creates *Object*, an assemblage.
- The Spanish artist Salvador Dalí paints *Giraffe in Flames*.
- The Swiss artist Meret Oppenheim creates *Object (Fur Tea Cup)*. A fur-lined tea cup, it becomes one of the most familiar images of surrealism.
- The U.S. artist Joseph Cornell creates his assemblage sculpture *Soap Bubble Set*.

Film

- Movie censorship guidelines in fascist Italy discourage the portrayal of women as anything but virgins, wives, or mothers. The Pope expresses concern about the moral influence of motion pictures.
- French social reforms give workers increased recreation time: this results in a growth in the popularity of motion pictures.
- German filmmaker Leni Riefenstahl, one of the leading women directors in motion picture history, directs *Olympia* (released 1938–39). It is a stylized two-part movie documenting the Berlin Olympic Games, and is recognized as one of the landmarks of Nazi moviemaking.

- Pare Lorentz completes the documentary *The Plow That Broke the Plains*, about the agricultural depression, for a New Deal agency. He completes *The River*, about the Mississippi River, in 1936.
- The 1935 Academy Awards take place. Best Actor: Victor McLaglen, for *The Informer*; Best Actress: Bette Davis, for *Dangerous*; Best Picture: *Mutiny on the Bounty*, directed by Frank Lloyd; Best Director: John Ford, for *The Informer*.
- The movie *Anthony Adverse* directed by U.S. filmmaker Mervyn LeRoy is released. Based on the novel by Hervey Allen, it stars Fredric March, Olivia de Havilland, and Claude Rains.
- The movie *As You Like It*, directed by Hungarian-born German director Paul Czinner, is released in the UK. Based on Shakespeare's play, it stars Laurence Olivier, Elisabeth Bergner, Sophie Stewart, and Leon Quatermaine, and features music by William Walton. This is Olivier's first Shakespearean performance on screen.
- The movie *Camille* is released in the United States, directed by George Cukor and starring Swedish-born actress Greta Garbo.
- The movie *César*, directed and written by Marcel Pagnol, is released in France, starring Raimu, Orane Demazis, Pierre Fresnay, and Fernand Charpin. It is the third installment in a trilogy of movies to be adapted from Pagnol's own screenplays, following *Marius*, directed by Hungarian filmmaker Alexander Korda, and *Fanny*, directed by Swiss filmmaker Marc Allégret.
- The movie *Flash Gordon* is released in the United States. Based on the comic-strip hero created by Alex Raymond and directed by Frederick Stephani, it and its many sequels star Buster Crabbe and Charles Middleton.
- The movie *Fury*, directed by Austrian-born filmmaker Fritz Lang, is released in the United States, his first U.S. movie. It stars Sylvia Sidney and Spencer Tracy.
- The movie *Le Roman d'un tricheur/The Story of a Cheat*, directed by Sacha Guitry, is released in France. He also stars in it, along with Marguerite Moreno and Serge Grave.
- The movie *Modern Times*, directed by British filmmaker Charlie Chaplin, is released, the last of the great silent movies. He also stars in it, along with Paulette Goddard.
- The movie *Mr Deeds Goes to Town*, directed by Frank Capra, is released in the United States, starring Gary Cooper, Jean Arthur, Raymond Walburn, and Lionel Stander.
- The movie *The Charge of the Light Brigade*, directed by the Hungarian-born filmmaker Michael Curtiz, is released in the United States, starring Errol Flynn and Olivia de Havilland.
- The movie *The Great Ziegfeld*, directed by Robert Z. Leonard, is released in the United States, starring William Powell, Luise Rainer, and Myrna Loy.
- The movie *The Trail of the Lonesome Pine*, directed by Henry Hathaway, is released in the United States. The first movie to contain location shooting in color, it stars Fred MacMurray, Sylvia Sidney, and Henry Fonda.
- The movie *These Three*, directed by German-born U.S. filmmaker William Wyler, is released. Adapted by Lillian Hellman from her play *The Children's Hour*, it stars Merle Oberon, Miriam Hopkins, Joel McCrea, and

- Bonita Granville. The movie is remade by the same director under this latter title in 1962.
- The movie *Things to Come*, directed by William Cameron Menzies, is released in the UK. Based on H. G. Wells's novel *The Shape of Things to Come*, it stars Raymond Massey, Edward Chapman, and Ralph Richardson.
- The movie *Une Partie de Campagne/A Day in the Country*, directed by Jean Renoir, is filmed in France, although not released until 1946. It is based on a story by Guy de Maupassant. However, Renoir's movies *Le Crime de Monsieur Lange/The Crime of Monsieur Lange* and the Communist Party-funded documentary *La Vie est à nous/The People of France* are released in France.
- The movie industry has its most prosperous year, completing 500 feature-length motion pictures, most in black and white although Technicolor has been invented.
- The rejection of German movies abroad, because of the unpalatably high propaganda content, leads to a crisis in the German movie industry.
- The U.S. movie star Shirley Temple, aged eight, signs a five-year contract for $1,000 per week.
- U.S. performers Fred Astaire and Ginger Rogers star in *Swing Time*, directed by George Stevens. It is considered one of the most accomplished of the many movies on which the couple collaborated.

Literature and Language

- *Illusion and Reality*, an influential Marxist interpretation of literature by the English writer Christopher Caudwell is published posthumously.
- *The Concise Oxford Dictionary of English Place-Names* is published, edited by Eilert Ekwall.
- *The Oxford Book of Modern Verse, 1892–1935* is published, edited by the Irish poet W. B. Yeats.
- In Britain, the writers John and Rosamund Lehmann (brother and sister) begin editing *New Writing*, an international literary journal that is to play a role in supporting working-class writers, and in introducing European literature to English readers.
- The Australian writer Miles Franklin publishes her novel *All that Swagger*, praised for its depiction of life in the outback.
- The British publisher Allen Lane founds Penguin Books, starting a revolution in publishing—the creation of inexpensive paperbacks.
- The English novelist Rebecca West publishes her novel *The Thinking Reed*.
- The English writer and critic Cyril Connolly publishes his novel of decadent life in the South of France, *The Rock Pool*.
- The English writer and critic C. S. Lewis publishes *The Allegory of Love*, a study of medieval literature. It is awarded the Hawthornden Prize the same year.
- The English writer Aldous Huxley publishes his novel *Eyeless in Gaza*.
- The English writer George Orwell publishes his novel *Keep the Aspidistra Flying*.
- The English writer Siegfried Sassoon publishes his autobiographical novel trilogy, *Sherston's Progress*.
- The English writer W. H. Auden publishes his poetry collection *Look, Stranger!* and writes the verse commentary for the General Post Office documentary *Night Mail*, directed by Harry Watt and Basil Wright.
- The English writer Winifred Holtby publishes her novel *South Riding*.
- The French Catholic writer Georges Bernanos publishes *Journal d'un curé de compagne/Journal of a Country Priest*, perhaps his finest novel.
- The French writer Henry de Montherlant publishes the first volume of his four-volume novel cycle *Les jeunes filles/The Girls*.
- The Nobel Prize for Literature is awarded to the U.S. dramatist Eugene O'Neill.
- The Pulitzer Prize for Biography is awarded to Ralph B. Perry for *The Thought and Character of William James*, the Pulitzer Prize for Fiction is awarded to H. L. Davis for *Honey in the Horn*, and the Prize for Poetry is awarded to Robert Coffin for *Strange Holiness*.
- The Russian-born U.S. writer Vladimir Nabokov publishes his novel *Otchayaniye/Despair*.
- The U.S. writer Carl Sandburg publishes his poetry collection *The People, Yes*.
- The U.S. writer John Dos Passos publishes *The Big Money*, the final part of his trilogy *USA*.
- The U.S. writer Willa Cather publishes her collection of essays *Not Under Forty*.
- The U.S. writer William Faulkner publishes his novel *Absalom, Absalom!*
- The Welsh writer Dylan Thomas publishes his poetry collection *Twenty-five Poems*.
- U.S. writer Margaret Mitchell publishes her novel *Gone with the Wind*, which becomes one of the best-selling novels of the 20th century.
- While living and working in Paris, France, the U.S. writer Djuna Barnes publishes her novel *Nightwood*.

Music

- In the United States, the band leader and broadcaster Benny Goodman is labeled "The King of Swing."
- The Austrian composer Arnold Schoenberg completes his Violin Concerto (Opus 36) and his String Quartet No. 4 (Opus 37).
- The English composer Ralph Vaughan Williams completes his cantata *Dona nobis pacem/Grant us Peace*.
- The English composer Benjamin Britten writes the incidental music for the documentary *Night Mail*, and completes his *Three Divertimenti* for string quartet.
- The French composer Olivier Messiaen completes his song cycle *Poèmes pour Mi/Poems for Mi*.
- The French-born U.S. composer Edgard Varèse completes his *Density 21.5* for solo flute.
- The German composer and conductor Berthold Goldschmidt completes his *Ciaconna Sinfonica*. He settled in England in 1935.
- The Hungarian composer Béla Bartók completes his *Music for Strings, Percussion and Celesta*.
- The Hungarian composer Zoltán Kodály completes his *Ode to Ferencz Liszt* for chorus.
- The opera *Giulio Cesare/Julius Caesar* by the Italian composer Gian Francesco Malipiero is first performed, in Genoa, Italy.

- The Russian composer Sergey Rachmaninov completes his Symphony No. 3.
- The song "Pennies From Heaven" becomes popular in both the United States and Britain. The music is by the U.S. musician Arthur Johnston, the words by Johnny Burke.
- The U.S. jazz clarinettist Woody Herman takes over Isham Jones's band, which is renamed "The Band That Plays the Blues."

Theater and Dance

- The comedy *French Without Tears*, by the English writer Terence Rattigan opens at the Criterion Theatre in London, England, establishing his reputation.
- The French writer Armand Salacrou completes *L'Inconnue d'Arras/The Unknown Woman of Arras*.
- The musical *On Your Toes*, with lyrics by Lorenz Hart and music by Richard Rodgers, is first performed, in New York, New York.
- The Pulitzer Prize for Drama is awarded to Robert Sherwood for *Idiot's Delight*.
- The Spanish writer Federico García Lorca completes his play *La casa de Bernarda Alba/The House of Bernarda Alba*.

Thought and Scholarship

- English historian and journalist Robert Charles Kirkwood Ensor publishes *England, 1870–1914*.
- English historian George Malcolm Young publishes *Victorian England: Portrait of an Age*.
- English Sanskrit scholar Arthur Berriedale Keith publishes *A Constitutional History of India, 1600–1935*.
- German philosopher Edmund Husserl publishes his last work, *Die Krisis der europäischen Wissenschaften und die transzendetale Phänomenologie/The Crisis of European Sciences and Transcendental Phenomenology*.
- German-born U.S. logician Rudolf Carnap publishes the essay "Testability and Meaning" in the journal *Philosophy of Science*.
- The English philosopher A. J. Ayer publishes *Language, Truth, and Logic*. A brilliant exposition of logical positivism, its claim that the statements of morality and religion are, literally, "meaningless," makes it the most controversial British philosophical work of the period.
- The exiled Russian revolutionary Leon Trotsky publishes *The Revolution Betrayed*.
- The Pulitzer Prize for History is awarded to Andrew C. McLaughlin for *The Constitutional History of the United States*.
- U.S. philosopher Arthur O. Lovejoy publishes *The Great Chain of Being*.
- U.S. philosopher Sidney Hook publishes *From Hegel to Marx*, an influential exposition of Marxism.
- U.S. scholar Van Wyck Brooks publishes his history *The Flowering of New England*, which receives a Pulitzer prize in 1937.

SOCIETY

Everyday Life

- 38% of families in the United States live below the poverty line designated by the government.
- Earl Haas patents tampons and commercial production begins at Tampax, Inc. in New Brunswick, New Jersey.
- G. H. Bass of Wilton, Maine, sells Bass Weejuns, the first loafers, so named because they follow a Norwegian design. They cost $12 and are only available for men; a version for women is introduced in 1937.
- In Slough, England, the confectionery company Mars introduces Maltesers.
- Populations (in millions) include: China, 422; India, 360; USSR, 173; United States, 127; Japan, 89; Germany, 70; Great Britain, 47; France, 44.
- Stanley Tools in Sheffield, England, produces the Stanley knife, a tool originally designed for cutting fibreboard.
- The American Federation of Labor grants a charter to the Brotherhood of Sleeping Car Porters, a union of black workers.
- The American Optical Society produces Polarized sunglasses, developed by Edwin Land of Boston, Massachusetts.
- The New Zealand government legislates for a five-day working week.
- The Nutone Co. in Cincinnati, Ohio, begins manufacturing electric chimes for doors, designed by J. Ralph Corbett.
- The self-help book *How to Win Friends and Influence People* by Dale Carnegie is published. It will sell more copies than any other nonfiction title apart from the Bible.
- U.S. author Irma S. Rombauer publishes *The Joy of Cooking*, a seminal text in U.S. culinary art.

FEBRUARY

14 The United Rubber Workers of America union holds the first sit-in strike, when members who have been laid off occupy one of the Goodyear Tire Company plants in Akron, Ohio.

MARCH

25 In Germany, the first public videophone service, to be used by Aryans only, starts in Berlin and Leipzig.

DECEMBER

December, 1936–February 1937 General Motors (GM) workers stage a series of "sit-down" strikes to win recognition of the new United Auto Workers union (UAW) in the U.S. After UAW and GM officials reach an agreement in February, sit-down strikes proliferate across the U.S.

3 In the UK, the press, after a period of self-restraint, breaks the news of King Edward's intention to marry Mrs. Wallis Simpson.

Media and Communication

- A picturephone service between Berlin, Nuremberg, Leipzig, and Hamburg is developed in Germany.

Scanned at 180 lines, images are transmitted over coaxial cables.
- Henry Luce, publisher of *Time* and *Fortune*, publishes the weekly picture magazine, *Life*, in the United States.
- In the United States the Gallup poll successfully predicts the reelection of President Roosevelt.
- The British Broadcasting Corporation (BBC) begins the first public television broadcasts; the system used has 405-line pictures.
- The Canadian Broadcasting Corporation is founded.
- The first Japanese fashion magazine is launched by novelist Ghiyu Uno.
- U.S. pollster George Gallup founds the British Institute of Public Opinion.

OCTOBER

25–March 26, 1939 In Berlin, Germany, Heinz Goedecke presents *You Ask – We Play*, the world's first radio request show.

NOVEMBER

2 The British Broadcasting Corporation (BBC) starts the world's first public high-definition television service from its transmitter at Alexandra Palace, London, England, using Logie Baird's mechanical system and EMI's electronic system.

Religion

- The English churchman Michael Ramsey, archbishop of Canterbury 1961–74, publishes *The Gospel and the Catholic Church*.

Sports

c. 1936 Trampolining is developed in the United States by the diving champion and acrobat Goerge Nissen, of Iowa.
- A rival to the National Football League (NFL), the second to call itself The American Football League, is formed. The Boston Shamrocks are its first champions.

JANUARY

29 Ty Cobb, Walter Johnson, Christy Mathewson, Babe Ruth, and Honus Wagner become the first members to be elected to the Baseball Hall of Fame.

BIRTHS & DEATHS

JANUARY

10 Robert Woodrow Wilson, U.S. radio astronomer, born in Houston, Texas.

18 Rudyard Kipling, English novelist, short story writer, and poet, dies in London, England (70).

20 George V, king of the United Kingdom 1910–36, dies at Sandringham, Norfolk, England (70).

FEBRUARY

8 Charles Curtis, U.S. Republican politician and vice president under Herbert Hoover 1929–33, dies in Washington, D.C. (76).

19 Billy Mitchell, U.S. Army officer who recommended establishing a separate U.S. air force, dies in New York, New York (56).

21 Barbara Jordan, U.S. Democratic congresswoman, first black woman from the South to be elected to Congress (1971) born in Houston, Texas (–1996).

27 Ivan Petrovich Pavlov, Russian physiologist who developed the idea of conditioned reflex through his work on salivating dogs, dies in Leningrad (now St. Petersburg), Russia (86).

MARCH

6 Marion S. Barry, Jr., U.S. civil-rights activist and mayor of Washington, D.C., born in Itta Benna, Mississippi.

18 Eleutherios Venizelos, Greek politician, prime minister of Greece 1910–15, 1917, 1924, and 1928–30, dies in Paris, France (71).

18 F(rederik) W(illem) de Klerk, South African politician, president of South Africa 1989–94, who ended the apartheid system, born in Johannesburg, South Africa.

APRIL

18 Ottorino Respighi, Italian composer, dies in Rome, Italy (57).

MAY

8 Oswald Spengler, German philosopher, dies in Munich, Germany (55).

12 Frank Stella, U.S. painter, born in Malden, Massachusetts.

JUNE

11 Julius Arthur Nieuwland, Belgian-born U.S. chemist who developed neoprene, the first synthetic rubber, dies in Washington, D.C. (58).

14 G(ilbert) K(eith) Chesterton, English author, poet, essayist, and critic, dies in Beaconsfield, Buckinghamshire, England (62).

18 Maxim Gorky, Russian novelist and short story writer, dies in the USSR (68).

JULY

10 Herbert Boyer, U.S. scientist who carried out work with DNA, born in Pittsburgh, Pennsylvania.

23 Donald Scott Drysdale, U.S. baseball player and sports broadcaster, born in Van Nuys, California (–1993).

29 Elizabeth Dole, high-ranking official in several Republican administrations and president of the U.S. Red Cross, born in Salisbury, North Carolina.

AUGUST

2 Louis Blériot, French aviator and the first person to fly across the English Channel, dies in Paris, France (64).

OCTOBER

3 John Heisman, U.S. American football coach who introduced a number of innovations to the game, dies in New York, New York (66).

5 Václav Havel, Czech dissident playwright and poet, president of Czechoslovakia in 1989, president of the newly formed Czech Republic in 1992, born in Prague, Czechoslovakia.

31 Michael Landon, U.S. actor and director known for his roles in *Little House on the Prairie* and *Bonanza*, born in Forest Hills, New York (–1991).

DECEMBER

2 John Ringling, U.S. impresario, who managed the Ringling Brothers circus, dies in New York, New York (70).

10 Luigi Pirandello, Italian playwright, novelist, and short story writer, dies in Rome, Italy (69).

15 Muhammad Farah Aidid, Somali soldier and politician who drove the Somali president, Siad Barre, from office in 1991, born in Belet Huen, Somalia (–1996).

FEBRUARY

6–16 The 4th Olympic Winter Games are held at Garmisch-Partenkirchen, Germany. Norway wins 7 gold medals; Germany, 3, and the United States, 2. Alpine skiing is included for the first time. Sonja Henie of Norway wins her third successive figure skating title. Norwegian Birger Ruud wins his second ski jump title in a row and also the Alpine downhill gold medal.

13 U.S. national figure skating champions are: Maribel Vinson; Robin Lee; Maribel Vinson and George Hill, pairs; Marjorie Parker and Joseph Savage, dance.

MARCH

• At the World Table Tennis Championships in Prague, Czechoslovakia, the match between Michael Haguaneur of France and Dvoboj Marin of Romania lasts over seven hours.

23–24 A National Hockey League game between the Montreal Maroons and the Detroit Red Wings remains scoreless until 2:20 am when, after two hours', 56 minutes' and 30 seconds' play, Montreal's Mud Brunteau finally beats the Detroit goalie.

APRIL

5–11 The Detroit Red Wings defeat the Toronto Maple Leafs three games to one to win the National Hockey League (NHL) Stanley Cup (the trophy given to the league's champion).

MAY

30 Driving an average speed of 174 kph/109 mph, U.S. racing driver Louis Meyer wins the Indianapolis 500.

JUNE

6 U.S. Open golf champion Tony Manero shoots a record low 282 at the 72-hole tournament.

19 U.S. boxer Joe Louis, the "Brown Bomber," loses to Max Schmeling of Germany in the 12th round of their nontitle fight at Yankee Stadium, New York, New York.

22–July 3 English tennis player Fred Perry wins his third consecutive Wimbledon men's singles title.

JULY

7–August 2 Sylvère Maes of Belgium wins the Tour de France cycle race.

28 The Great Britain tennis team defeats Australia by three matches to two to win the Davis Cup for the fourth consecutive year.

AUGUST

• At the Olympic Games in Berlin, Germany, Jack Lovelock of New Zealand wins the men's 1,500-meter title in a world record time of 3 minutes 47.8 seconds.

1–16 The 11th Olympic Games are held in Berlin, Germany. Germany wins 33 gold medals; the United States, 24; Hungary, 10; Italy, 8; Finland and France, 7 each; Sweden and Holland, 6 each; Japan, 5. The U.S. black American athlete Jesse Owens wins 4 gold medals, in the 100 meters, the 200 meters, the long jump, and the 4 × 100-meter relay. Jack Lovelock of New Zealand wins the 1,500 meters title in a world-record time of 3 minutes 47.8 seconds. A selection of highlights is shown live and viewed by an estimated 150,000 people in the public viewing rooms in Berlin.

6 At the Olympic Games in Berlin, Germany, Naoto Tajima of Japan achieves the first ever 16-m/52-ft triple jump.

12 At the Olympic Games in Berlin, Germany, Marjorie Gestring of the United States becomes the youngest-ever individual Olympic champion when she wins the women's springboard diving title at the age of 13 years 268 days.

SEPTEMBER

12 Alice Marble of the United States and Fred Perry of Great Britain win the U.S. Lawn Tennis Association championships.

30–October 6 The New York Yankees defeat the New York Giants four games to two in the World Series.

NOVEMBER

15 Germany and Italy draw 2–2 in Berlin, Germany, in the first soccer match to be televised live.

DECEMBER

13 The Green Bay Packers defeat the Boston Redskins 21–6 in the National Football League (NFL) championship game at the Polo Grounds, New York, New York.

1937

POLITICS, GOVERNMENT, AND ECONOMICS

Business and Economics

- After recovering over the past four years, the U.S. economy recedes in the fall. National income falls by 13%, production of durable goods by 50%, and profits by 78%. Unemployment rises.
- Henry Ford employs a "service department" of 600 armed men to discourage workers' moves toward unionization in the United States.
- Howard Johnson, unable to get financial backing for his own restaurant chain, sets up the first chain of franchised restaurants, "Howard Johnson's." The first restaurant, in Cambridge, Massachusetts, features 28 flavors of ice cream refrigerated under a bright orange roof.

Colonization

MARCH
18 The Committee of the All-India Congress Party votes to accept invitations to form provincial governments provided that Britain's colonial governors undertake not to use special powers.

JULY
7 A British royal commission on Palestine proposes an end to the British mandate and the partition of the country into a British area, a Jewish state, and an Arab area joined with Transjordan.

Human Rights

- The U.S. president makes William Hastie, attorney for the National Association for the Advancement of Colored People, the nation's first black American federal judge.

MAY
23 The Matrimonial Causes Act, introduced by the author, lawyer, and politician A. P. Herbert, gives women equality with men in divorce proceedings in England and Wales.

JULY
1 The German pastor and preacher Martin Niemöller is arrested by the Gestapo (secret police) for his opposition to the German Führer and Nazism. He is tried in February 1938, when he is acquitted, then rearrested and sent to a concentration camp.

Politics and Government

- A German court rules that the state may remove children from homes that do not teach Nazi ideology.
- Japanese troops rape and murder over 10,000 women during the march into Nanjing, China. The Imperial Army authorizes "comfort girl" battalions of women and children to satisfy the soldiers' sexual urges.

JANUARY
1 The Public Order Act comes into force in Britain. It proscribes political uniforms and permits the police to ban processions if there is a threat of disorder.
2 Britain and Italy sign an agreement affirming free passage of shipping in the Mediterranean.
6 The U.S. president renews the Neutrality Act forbidding U.S. shipments of arms to Spain in the light of the civil war there.
9 The former Soviet communist leader and theorist Leon Trotsky seeks asylum in Mexico after living in exile in France and Norway.
12 The British government begins the production of gas masks for civilians at a factory in Blackburn, England.
14 The Unity Campaign is formed in Britain by the communists, the Independent Labour Party, and the Socialist League with the aim of opposing rearmament and transforming the Labor movement.
15 Under German pressure, the Austrian government declares an amnesty for Nazis accused of attempting to overthrow the government in pursuit of closer Austrian ties with Germany.
20 The U.S. president Franklin D. Roosevelt is inaugurated for a second term.
23–30 Karl Radek and other leading Soviet communists are accused of participating in a Trotskyite conspiracy to dismember the USSR. Radek confesses his guilt to the fabricated charge and he and three others are sentenced to ten years in prison. The rest are executed.
24 Bulgaria and Yugoslavia sign a treaty of permanent peace.

FEBRUARY
- The All-India Congress Party is the most successful party in the Indian elections.
February–July The U.S. president Franklin D. Roosevelt sparks a "court-packing" controversy by introducing legislation (the Judicial Procedures Reform Act) that would enable him to appoint younger judges to the federal courts when older judges did not resign within six months of their 70th birthday. The Senate kills the legislation on July 14.

8 Spanish Nationalist forces under General Gonzalo Queipo de Llano take the Republican-held city of Málaga in the south of the country, with Italian military aid.

14 The Austrian chancellor, Kurt von Schuschnigg, reserves the initiative to organize any restoration of the Habsburg monarchy.

20 Paraguay withdraws from the League of Nations, following its adoption of a fascistic regime in 1936.

27 France creates a ministry of defense, extends the Maginot Line (fortification system along the German frontier), and nationalizes the Schneider–Creusot arms factory—all in response to the increased threat of war with Nazi Germany.

MARCH

- In the first of several decisions favorable to the Roosevelt administration, the U.S. Supreme Court upholds a minimum wage law for women in the case *West Coast Hotel v. Parrish*.
- The North Carolina Board of Health opens a contraceptive clinic in the state capital, Raleigh.

1 The Supreme Court Retirement Act in the United States allows the Court's judges to retire at 70 on full pay. President Franklin D. Roosevelt also proposes that if judges over 70 refuse to retire, the president can appoint extra judges. Strong opposition in Congress forces him to withdraw the proposal in July.

8–18 In the Spanish Civil War, Italian tanks and troops supporting the Nationalists advance on Republican-held Madrid, Spain, and are dispersed by Soviet dive-bombers.

16 The Italian prime minister visits the Italian colony of Libya.

18 The Italian Legion, fighting for the Spanish Nationalists, is defeated at Brihuega (near Madrid) by Republican and International Brigade forces, checking the Nationalists' threat to Madrid.

18 The oil industry is nationalized in Mexico and the National Petroleum Corporation is established to administer oil-producing lands.

25 Italy and Yugoslavia sign the Belgrade Pact of mutual aid for five years.

APRIL

- The U.S. Supreme Court, in the case *National Labor Relations Board v. Jones and Laughlin Steel*, upholds the controversial collective bargaining provisions of the 1935 National Labor Relations Act.

1 Spanish Nationalist forces launch a major offensive against Republican-held areas in the north of the country.

1 The Indian constitution comes into force. Because British colonial provincial governors refuse to give formal undertakings not to use special powers, the All-India Congress Party refuses to form governments.

2 The South African government prohibits political activity by foreigners in its mandated territory of South West Africa (now Namibia).

19 The Falange, the Carlists, and other right-wing factions in Spain are forcibly merged into the Falange Española Tradicionalista de las Juntas de Ofensiva Nacional Sindicalista ("Traditional Spanish Phalanx of the Juntas of the National Syndicalist Offensive"), under the leadership of General Francisco Franco.

22 The Austrian chancellor, Kurt von Schuschnigg, meets the Italian prime minister in Venice, Italy.

26 Guernica, the historic Basque capital in northern Spain, is heavily bombed by aircraft of the German Condor Legion supporting the Spanish Nationalist rebels.

MAY

- The U.S. Supreme Court upholds the 1935 Social Security Act in the case *Steward Machine Company v. Davis and Helvering*.

3–10 Anarchists and Syndicalists revolt against the increasingly authoritarian and communist-dominated wartime policies of the Republican government, in Barcelona, northeast Spain. The revolt is put down by government troops, causing a crisis in the government.

8 The Montreux Convention abolishes the Capitulations in Egypt, removing the right of foreign powers to protect non-Muslim inhabitants as if under separate jurisdictions.

12 George VI is crowned king of Great Britain and Northern Ireland in Westminster Abbey, London, England. He is the first monarch to appear on television, when the coronation procession is filmed by the British Broadcasting Corporation (BBC).

15 A Muslim uprising in protest of the dictatorship of King Zog in Albania is suppressed within a few days.

26 Egypt joins the League of Nations.

28 Stanley Baldwin retires as British prime minister. Neville Chamberlain forms a National Government, with Sir John Simon as chancellor of the Exchequer and Anthony Eden as foreign secretary.

28 The senate of the Irish Free State is abolished following a motion moved by Éamon de Valera, as the first step in a constitutional change toward full Irish independence from Britain.

JUNE

- Several prominent military leaders are tried, convicted, and shot in the USSR for collaboration with Germany as part of a massive purge of the Soviet armed forces.

1 Prince Konoe Fumimaro becomes prime minister of Japan, with Koki Hirota as foreign minister.

3 The Duke of Windsor, formerly King Edward VIII of Great Britain and Northern Ireland, marries Mrs. Wallis Simpson in France.

14 The Dáil (lower house) approves Prime Minister Éamon de Valera's constitution in the Irish Free State. It changes the name of the country to Eire, abolishes the office of the British governor-general, and provides for a new form of senate and a president.

19 Spanish Nationalist forces under General Fidel Dánila capture Bilbao, the capital of the pro-Republican Basque region in the northwest of the country, after an 80-day siege.

21 Léon Blum resigns as prime minister of France when the Senate refuses his demands for emergency fiscal powers. Camille Chautemps forms a Radical–Socialist ministry as his second term in office.

23 Germany and Italy withdraw from the nonintervention committee formed in September 1936 to prevent foreign intervention in the Spanish Civil War.

JULY

- The U.S. Congress passes the Bankhead-Jones Farm Tenancy Act that creates the Farm Security Administration (FSA). Against congressional opposition, the FSA works to promote land ownership, collective farming, and sanitation among migrant farm communities.

1   Éamon de Valera again becomes prime minister in Ireland, following an election in which the Fianna Fáil party win 69 seats and the Fine Gael 48.

7   A conflict between Chinese and Japanese troops near the Marco Polo Bridge outside the city of Beijing leads to the Japanese invasion of northeast China.

8   Afghanistan, Iran, Iraq, and Turkey sign a nonaggression pact.

17 Agreements limiting naval power are signed between Britain, Germany, and the USSR.

28–29 Japanese forces seize the cities of Beijing (July 28) and Tianjin (July 29) in northeast China.

AUGUST

•   The U.S. president signs the Marijuana Traffic Act, outlawing the possession and sale of marijuana.

4   The United States and the USSR sign a trade pact.

8–November 11 Japanese forces launch an amphibious assault on the port of Shanghai, on the east coast of China.

12 The Iraqi dictator General Bake Sidqi is assassinated by a Kurdish nationalist.

14 The Canadian prime minister announces the establishment of a commission to reexamine the structure of the confederation of Canadian provinces.

25 Spanish Nationalist forces capture the north-coast port of Santander as their offensive against Republican areas in the north continues.

SEPTEMBER

3   The National Council of Labour in Britain declares that another war in Europe is not inevitable and supports Britain's role in the League of Nations.

15 The National Housing Act (Wagner–Steagall Act) creates the U.S. Housing Authority, to make housing for people on low incomes more affordable and to spur rural and urban construction.

25–28 The Italian prime minister visits Berlin, Germany, to confer with the German Führer Adolf Hitler.

26 Arabs in Palestine murder the British district commissioner for Galilee.

OCTOBER

•   President Franklin D. Roosevelt of the United States speaks out in favor of collective sanctions against aggressor nations.

1   General Francisco Franco assumes the formal leadership of the Nationalists in Spain and outlines the main policies to be followed by a Nationalist government.

13 Germany guarantees the inviolability of Belgian territory.

16 Fascist groups in Hungary form a National Socialist Party.

17 Pro-German riots break out in the German-populated Sudetenland area of Czechoslovakia.

21 Spanish Nationalist forces take Gijón, the last major town in the pro-Republican north of the country.

23 The Labor Party is defeated in the Australian elections by the United Australia and Country parties.

24 Paul van Zeeland, the prime minister of Belgium, resigns on charges of corruption. He is succeeded by Paul Janson, a Liberal.

28 The Spanish Republican government moves from Valencia to Barcelona on the northeast coast as Nationalist offensives begin in the southeast.

NOVEMBER

3–24 A Brussels conference of Allied powers discusses the Sino-Japanese War, provoked by the Japanese aggression from 1931.

6   Italy joins the German–Japanese Anti-Comintern Pact against international communism.

10 The Brazilian president Getúlio Vargas organizes a coup that annuls the 1934 constitution and sets up the totalitarian Estado Novo (New State).

11 Japanese troops capture the Chinese east coast port of Shanghai.

15 An extraordinary session of the U.S. Congress opens to promote a legislative program.

17–21 Britain's lord privy seal pays a visit to the German Führer with the aim of securing a peaceful settlement of the problem of pro-German agitation in the Sudetenland area of Czechoslovakia.

24 Walther Funk replaces Dr. Hjalmar Schacht as German minister of economics.

28 Nationalist forces, with help from Italy, begin a naval blockade of the Spanish coast to prevent arms supplies to the remaining Republican areas of the country.

29 German members from the Sudetenland area leave the Czech parliament following a ban on political meetings.

DECEMBER

•   U.S.–Japanese relations deteriorate after Japanese planes sink the U.S. gunboat *Panay* off the coast of China. Tensions ease after Japan apologizes and promises restitution on December 14.

5–13 Japanese troops take the Chinese city of Nanjing. Their victory is followed by the "rape of Nanjing," when around a quarter of a million Chinese are killed.

11 Italy withdraws from the League of Nations.

14 Political parties are banned in Brazil under the totalitarian regime of President Getúlio Vargas.

14 Spanish Republican forces launch an offensive against Nationalist positions in Aragon, northeastern Spain.

24 Japanese forces capture the Chinese city of Hangzhou, southwest of the port of Shanghai.

28 The anti-Semite Octavian Goga becomes prime minister in Romania, after the fall of Gheorge Tatarescu. He is dismissed a few weeks later.

29 The new Irish constitution comes into force and the Irish Free State becomes Eire.

30 The Liberal Constitution Party forms a government in Egypt.

SCIENCE, TECHNOLOGY, AND MEDICINE

Agriculture

•   U.S. spinach growers erect a statue to Popeye in honor of his achievements in boosting the image of their product.

- U.S. wheat crops are attacked by black stem rust, but the drought that has plagued the Midwest for the past four years ends.

Computing

December 1937–39   U.S. mathematician and physicist John V. Atanasoff invents an electromechanical digital computer for solving systems of linear equations. It uses punched cards and is the first electronic calculator using electronic vacuum tubes.

Ecology

- Steps are taken to preserve wildlife in the United States by taxing hunting weapons and ammunition under the Federal Aid to Wildlife Restoration Act.

JANUARY

January–February   The Ohio, Mississippi, and Allegheny rivers overflow their banks causing major floods in the Midwest United States; a million people are left homeless and damage is estimated at $300 million.

MARCH

18   A school fire in New London, Texas, kills 294 students and teachers.

OCTOBER

31   Sphinx Rock meteorological station in Bernese Oberland, Switzerland, is opened.

Health and Medicine

- British biochemist Walter Haworth receives the Nobel Prize for Chemistry for his work on carbohydrates and vitamin C.
- British biochemists W. Ewins and H. Phillips synthesize sulfapyridine, the second sulfa drug.
- French microbiologist Max Theiler develops a vaccine against yellow fever; it is the first antiviral vaccine.
- French surgeon Alexis Carrel develops an artificial heart.
- Medical chemists D. A. Scott and A. M. Fisher in Toronto, Canada successfully use zinc protamine insulin to treat diabetes, reducing the need for diet therapy.
- Spanish physician José Trutta Raspall develops a closed-plaster method of treating compound bone fractures.
- U.S. biochemist Conrad Arnold Elvehjem finds that vitamin B_3 (niacin) prevents pellagra, a vitamin deficiency disease.
- U.S. psychiatrist Karen Horney publishes *The Neurotic Personality of Our Times*.
- U.S. psychologist and educator Edward Lee Thorndike publishes *The Teaching of Controversial Subjects*.

Math

- U.S. mathematician Georges Stibitz builds the first binary circuit that can add two binary numbers based on Boolean algebra. Consisting of batteries, lights, and wires, it is instrumental in the development of subsequent electromechanical computers.

Science

- Austrian astronomer Marietta Blau examines cosmic radiation using a photographic plate.
- Austrian zoologist Konrad Lorenz becomes editor of the *Zeitschrift für Tierpsychologie/Journal of Animal Psychology*, published by the newly formed German Society for Animal Psychology. His work as editor plays a major role in founding the discipline of ethology.
- Crystalline vitamin A and vitamin K concentrate are obtained.
- German-born British biochemist Hans Krebs describes the citric acid cycle in cells, which converts sugars, fats, and proteins into carbon dioxide, water, and energy—the "Krebs cycle."
- Hungarian physiologist Albert Szent-Györgyi receives the Nobel Prize for Physiology or Medicine for his work on biological combustion.
- Italian-born U.S. physicists Emilio Segrè and Carlo Perrier discover technetium (atomic no. 43)—the first artificial element.
- The Human Relations Area Files (HRAF) are started at Yale University in New Haven, Connecticut. By quantifying ethnographic data from hundreds of societies they enable statistical cross-cultural analysis.
- U.S. physicist Clinton Davisson shares the Nobel Prize for Physics with English physicist George Paget Thomson for their experiments on the interference phenomenon in crystals.

Technology

- A rocket research facility is established at Peenemünde, northern Germany.
- British inventor Alec Reeves develops a system in which analog sound is transformed into electrical impulses and a receiver transforms them back into an analog signal—the basis of digital recording.
- Nylon, developed by W. H. Carothers, is patented by the U.S. chemicals company Du Pont and is commercially available the following year in the form of toothbrush bristles; nylon stockings become widely available in the United States in May 1940.
- Polystyrene becomes commercially available; it resists attack by acids, alkalis, and many solvents, is an excellent insulator, and does not absorb water; it is used to make household appliances and toys.
- The first automatic machine for molding plastics is invented.
- The synthetic polyurethane is patented in Germany; it is used in a range of products from clothing to furniture.
- The U.S. photographer Margaret Bourke-White and the U.S. writer Erskine Caldwell publish *You Have Seen Their Faces*, a record of rural poverty during the Great Depression.
- The USSR establishes a navigation and communications station on an ice floe near the North Pole. In June, two Soviet planes use the base as a navigation aid to make nonstop flights from Moscow to Oregon and Washington.
- The Waring Blender, the first food processor, appears in the United States; it is not used extensively in the home until 1947.

- U.S. astronomer Grote Reber builds the first radio telescope. It has a parabolic reflector 9.4 m/31 ft in diameter and begins service in Wheaton, Illinois.
- Xerography, an electrostatic copying process, is pioneered in the United States by electrical engineer Chester Carlson; it becomes commercially available in 1950.

October 1937–53 The Delaware Aqueduct is constructed. The first stage, completed in 1944, supplies water to New York, New York, from the Delaware River and at 136 km/85 mi long is the longest tunnel in the world. When the last stage is completed it has a total length of 169 km/105 mi.

APRIL

12 English engineer Frank Whittle tests the first prototype jet engine. A similar engine is developed in Germany at the same time.

MAY

12 The first worldwide radio broadcast transmits the coronation of King George VI of Britain to the ears of U.S. listeners.

Transportation

- British Imperial Airways and U.S. Pan American Airways operate experimental flight services between Bermuda and New York, New York.
- Mass production of the Volkswagen Beetle begins in Germany.
- The Junkers JU-87 "Stuka" dive-bomber enters service in the German air force.
- The La Roche-Guyon Bridge is completed in France. With a span of 161 m/528 ft, it is the longest overhead-arch bridge to date.
- U.S. vehicle manufacturer Oldsmobile introduces cars with automatic transmissions.

JANUARY

19 U.S. multimillionaire Howard Hughes reduces the transatlantic flight time to 7 hr 28 min.

MAY

6 The giant German airship *Hindenburg* explodes in the United States as it attempts to moor at Lakehurst Naval Station, New Jersey; 36 people are killed.

10–23 A bus strike takes place in London, England.

27 The Golden Gate Bridge in San Francisco, California, opens; it is the longest suspension bridge to date at 1,965 m/6,450 ft.

DECEMBER

22 The Lincoln Tunnel under the Hudson River opens, connecting New York, New York, and Weehawken, New Jersey.

ARTS AND IDEAS

Architecture

- The U.S. architect Frank Lloyd Wright publishes *An Organic Architecture: The Architecture of Democracy*.

Arts

c. 1937 The U.S. artist Sargent Claude Johnson sculpts *Mask*.

- In London, England, the artists William Coldstream, Victor Pasmore, and others found the Euston Road Group. Rejecting the current trends of surrealism and abstraction, they advocate a return to naturalism.
- Nazi authorities hold an exhibition entitled "Entartete Kunst"/"Degenerate Art" in Munich, Germany. The artists whose works are on display include Kandinsky, Picasso, Chagall, van Gogh, Beckmann, and Matisse. Nearby, the authorities endorse an exhibition of approved art, German and very traditional in style.
- The Austrian artist Oskar Kokoschka paints *Portrait of a "Degenerate Artist"*, a self-portrait.
- The English artist Barbara Hepworth sculpts *Conicoid: Sphere and Hollow*.
- The French artist Georges Braque paints *Woman with a Mandolin*.
- The French artist Jean Fautrier paints *Head*.
- The French artist Pierre Bonnard paints *Nude in the Bath*, one of many pictures on a theme for which he becomes famous.
- The Spanish artist Julio González sculpts *Montserrat*.
- The Spanish artist Pablo Picasso paints *Woman Weeping*. He also paints *Guernica*, inspired by the bombing of the Basque town of Guernica during the Spanish Civil War. One of his best-known works, it becomes a powerful symbol of the horrors of war.
- The Spanish artist Salvador Dalí paints *Sleep* and the *The Metamorphosis of Narcissus*.
- At the International Exhibition held in Paris, France, the French artist Fernand Léger and his students exhibit *Le Transport des Forces*. The Spanish artist Pablo Picasso exhibits his *Guernica*. Léger designs sets for the play *Naissance d'une Cité*.
- The U.S. artist David Smith sculpts *Interior*.
- The U.S. artist Georgia O'Keeffe paints *From the Faraway Nearby*.
- The U.S. artist Jackson Pollock paints *Flame*.
- The U.S. artist John B. Flannagan sculpts *Jonah and the Whale*.
- U.S. photographer Alfred Eisenstaedt takes *Nurses Attending a Lecture*.

Film

- French director Jean Renoir's *La Grande Illusion/The Great Illusion* is released. A pacifist movie set in a German prisoner-of-war camp during World War I, it will be acclaimed as a classic of world cinema. The movie stars Jean Gabin, Pierre Fresnay, and Erich von Stroheim.
- In France, the "Prix Louis Delluc" is founded, to be awarded to the best French movie each year.
- In the United States, 98% of all movies have gained the approval of the Hays Office's Production Code Administration, established to enforce a fairly rigid system of movie censorship.
- The 1936 Academy Awards take place. Best Actor: Paul Muni, for *The Story of Louis Pasteur*; Best Supporting Actor: Walter Brennan, for *Come and Get It*; Best

Actress: Luise Rainer, for *The Great Zeigfeld*; Best Supporting Actress: Gale Sondergaard, for *Anthony Adverse*; Best Picture: *The Great Zeigfeld*, directed by Robert Z. Leonard; Best Director: Frank Capra, for *Mr Deeds Goes to Town*.

- The animated character Bugs Bunny makes his debut in the Warner Bros production *Porky's Hare Hunt*, released in the United States, although it will take a few years before his looks and character become settled.
- The movie *A Day at the Races*, starring the Marx Brothers, is released in the United States. It is directed by Sam Wood.
- The movie *A Star is Born*, directed by William A. Wellman, is released in the United States, starring Janet Gaynor and Fredric March.
- The movie *Captains Courageous*, directed by Victor Fleming, is released in the United States, based on the novel by Rudyard Kipling and starring Spencer Tracy and Lionel Barrymore.
- The movie *Fire Over England*, directed by U.S. filmmaker William K. Howard, is released in the UK. A historical depiction of England's fight against the Spanish Armada, it stars Flora Robson, Laurence Olivier, Leslie Banks, Vivien Leigh, and Raymond Massey.
- The movie *Lost Horizon*, directed by Frank Capra, is released. Based on a novel by James Hilton, it stars Ronald Colman, H. B. Warner, Thomas Mitchell, Edward Everett Horton, and Sam Jaffe.
- The movie *Pépé Le Moko* is released in France, directed by Julien Duvivier. It is a classic of French Poetic Realism, a cycle of movies that anticipates the U.S. *film noir* movement.
- The movie *Stella Dallas*, directed by King Vidor, is released in the United States, starring Barbara Stanwyck and John Boles.
- The movie *The Awful Truth*, directed by Leo McCarey, is released in the United States. A classic example of zany sophisticated 1930s comedies, it stars Cary Grant and Irene Dunne.
- The movie *The Edge of the World* is released in the UK. Filmed on the remote Scottish island of Foula, it serves as British director Michael Powell's "calling card" to the British movie industry after serving a lengthy apprenticeship making "quota quickies."
- The movie *The Good Earth*, directed by Sidney Franklin, is released in the United States. Based on the novel by Pearl S. Buck, it stars Paul Muni and Luise Rainer.
- The movie *The Life of Emile Zola*, directed by German filmmaker William Dieterle, is released in the United States, starring Paul Muni.
- The movie *The Prisoner of Zenda* is released in the United States, produced by David O. Selznick and directed by John Cromwell. Based on the novel by Anthony Hope, it stars Ronald Colman, Mary Astor, and Douglas Fairbanks, Jr.
- The movie *The Stage Door* is released in the United States. It stars Katherine Hepburn and Ginger Rogers, and is directed by Gregory La Cava.
- The movie *They Won't Forget* is released in the United States. It is directed by Mervyn LeRoy and stars Claude Rains, Gloria Dickson, Edward Norris, Elisha Cook, Jr., and Lana Turner.

- The movie industry in the United States attracts three-quarters of all spending on leisure and entertainment.
- Walt Disney's *Snow White and the Seven Dwarfs* is released in the United States. It is the first feature-length animated movie.

APRIL

28 The Cinecittà Studios in Rome, Italy, open, the largest movie studios in Europe. Mussolini has encouraged the project, appreciating the value of cinema as propaganda. The motto above the studio gates reads "The cinematograph is the strongest weapon."

Literature and Language

- The Danish writer Karen Blixen (Isak Dinesen) publishes *Den Afrikanske Farm/The African Farm*, which she translates into English the same year as *Out of Africa*.
- The English writer Charles Williams publishes his novel *Descent into Hell*.
- The English writer C. S. Forester publishes *The Happy Return*, the first novel in his popular "Hornblower" series, set on an English warship during the Napoleonic wars.
- The English writer David Jones publishes *In Parenthesis*, an account of World War I in prose and verse.
- The English writer George Orwell publishes *The Road to Wigan Pier*, an account of his visits to working-class areas in Lancashire, England.
- The English writer Ivy Compton-Burnett publishes her novel *Daughters and Sons*.
- The English writer J. R. R. Tolkien publishes his fantasy novel *The Hobbit*.
- The English writer Rudyard Kipling publishes *Something of Myself*, a volume of his autobiography.
- The English writer Rex Warner publishes his novel *The Wild Goose Chase*.
- The English writer Stevie Smith publishes her poetry collection *A Good Time Was Had By All*.
- The English writer Virginia Woolf publishes her novel *The Years*.
- The English writer Wyndham Lewis publishes the memoirs *Blasting and Bombardiering*.
- The French philosopher and writer Jean-Paul Sartre publishes his novel *Nausée/Nausea*. It becomes one of the classics of the philosophy of Existentialism.
- The French writer André Malraux publishes his novel *L'Espoir/Days of Hope*, set in the Spanish Civil War.
- The French writer Georges Bernanos publishes his novel *Mouchette*.
- The Hungarian-born English writer Arthur Koestler publishes *Spanish Testament*, an account of his experiences in the Spanish Civil War. It is republished in 1942 as *Dialogue with Death*.
- The Irish writer Oliver St. John Gogarty publishes his memoirs *As I Was Going Down Sackville Street*.
- The Japanese writer Yasunari Kawabata publishes his novel *Yukiguni/The Snow Country*.
- The Nobel Prize for Literature is awarded to the French novelist Roger Martin du Gard.
- The Persian writer Sadiq Hidayat publishes his novel *Bufikur/The Blind Owl*.

- The Polish writer Witold Gombrowicz publishes his novel *Ferdydurke*.
- The Pulitzer Prize for Biography is awarded to Allan Nevins for *Hamilton Fish: The Inner History of the Great Administration*, the Pulitzer Prize for Fiction is awarded to Margaret Mitchell for *Gone with the Wind*, and the Prize for Poetry is awarded to Robert Frost for *A Further Range*.
- The Scottish writer A. J. Cronin publishes his novel about medical life, *The Citadel*.
- The U.S. writer Allen Tate publishes his *Selected Poems*.
- The U.S. writer Ernest Hemingway publishes his novel *To Have and Have Not*.
- The U.S. writer John Steinbeck publishes his novella *Of Mice and Men*.
- The U.S. writer Leonard Q. Ross publishes *The Education of H*Y*M*A*N K*A*P*L*A*N*, humorous sketches of immigrants attending night school in New York, New York.
- The U.S. writer Wallace Stevens publishes his poetry collection *The Man with the Blue Guitar*.
- The U.S. writer Zora Neale Hurston publishes her novel *Their Eyes Were Watching God*, a classic of black American literature.

Music

- "Sweet Leilani," sung by the U.S. crooner Bing Crosby, becomes the first of his million-selling records.
- The English composer Benjamin Britten completes his *Variations on a Theme by Frank Bridge* and *On This Island*, settings of five poems by W. H. Auden.
- The English composer William Walton writes *In Honour of the City of London* for chorus and orchestra.
- The German composer Carl Orff completes his *Carmina Burana, cantiones profanae/Carmina Burana, Secular Songs*.
- The German composer Hans Eisler completes his *Lenin Requiem*, with words by the German writer Bertolt Brecht.
- The Italian composer Alfredo Casella completes his *Concerto for Orchestra*.
- The opera *Lucrezia* by the Italian composer Ottorino Respighi is first performed, in Milan, Italy.
- The opera *Lulu* by the Austrian composer Alban Berg is first performed, in Zürich, Switzerland. It was left unfinished at his death in 1935. The first complete performance, with the last act completed by the Austrian composer Friedrich Cerha, will be given in Paris, France, in 1979.
- The Polish pianist Artur Rubinstein tours the United States to great acclaim.
- The Russian composer Dmitry Shostakovich completes his Symphony No. 5 in D minor, *A Soviet Artist's Reply to Just Criticism*. It was written in response to severe criticism of Shostakovich (inspired by the Soviet leader Joseph Stalin) that appeared in the official newspaper *Pravda*.
- The Russian composer Sergey Prokofiev completes his *Cantata on the 20th Anniversary of the October Revolution*.
- U.S. folk singer Woody Guthrie stars in the radio show *Here Come Woody and Lefty Lou* on KFVD in Los Angeles, California.

Theater and Dance

- *The Cradle Will Rock*, a controversial left-wing musical drama by Marc Blitzstein, opens at the Venice Theater in New York, New York, after protests had forced the cancellation of performances elsewhere.
- The ballet *Jeu de Cartes/Card Game*, by the Russian composer Igor Stravinsky, is first performed, in New York, New York. The choreography is by the Russian choreographer George Balanchine.
- The musical *Me and My Girl*, with lyrics by L. Arthur Rose and Douglas Furber and music by Noël Gay, is first performed, in London, England. It includes the famous song-and-dance routine "The Lambeth Walk."
- The play *Electre/Electra*, by the French writer Jean Giraudoux, is first performed, in Paris, France.
- The play *Time and the Conways*, by the English writer J. B. Priestley, is first performed, in London, England.
- The Pulitzer Prize for Drama is awarded to George Kaufman, Moss Hart, and Ira Gershwin for *You Can't Take It With You*.
- The verse play *The Ascent of F6*, by the English-born U.S. writers W. H. Auden and Christopher Isherwood, is first performed, at the Mercury Theatre in London, England. It was published in 1936.

Thought and Scholarship

- *Mahomet et Charlemagne/Mohammed and Charlemagne* by the Belgian historian Henri Pirenne is published posthumously.
- English businessman and social reformer Seebohm Rowntree publishes *The Human Needs of Labour*.
- The Pulitzer Prize for History is awarded to Van Wyck Brooks for *The Flowering of New England*.
- U.S. historian Charles Austin Beard publishes *The Making of American Civilization*.
- U.S. philosopher Charles Morris publishes *Logical Positivism, Pragmatism, and Scientific Empiricism*.
- U.S. philosopher Charles Hartshorne publishes *Beyond Humanism: Essays in the New Philosophy of Nature*.
- U.S. political journalist Walter Lippmann publishes *The Good Society*. The book marks his move away from his earlier liberalism.
- U.S. sociologist Talcott Parsons publishes *The Structure of Social Action*.

JULY
12 The 26th International Conference on "Church, Community, and State" is held in Oxford, England.

SOCIETY

Education

- The German ministry of education decrees that all educational institutions should "educate German youth for membership in the racial community and full commitment to the Führer."

JULY

8 English philanthropist Lord Nuffield offers Oxford University £900,000 for the foundation of a college specializing in social studies.

Everyday Life

- An artificial sweetener without saccharine's bitter aftertaste, sodium cyclamate, is discovered by Michael Sveda in the United States. It is subsequently discovered to be carcinogenic and is banned.
- Britain's first frozen foods are produced by Wisbech Produce Canners Limited. The first product is asparagus.
- Current consumption of petroleum products (in millions of barrels; motor fuel in parentheses): United States, 1,167 (517); USSR, 158 (24); UK, 85 (43); France, 50 (25); Canada, 43 (21); Germany, 43 (20); Japan, 34 (10).
- Current oil production (in millions of barrels): United States, 1,277; USSR, 196; Venezuela, 182; Iran, 73;

Romania, 53; Dutch East Indies, 50; Mexico, 46.
- Dunlop Latex Development Laboratories in Birmingham, England, begin manufacturing foam rubber carpet underlay.
- Grand Mufti of Islam issues a fatwa permitting Muslims to use contraceptives when both parties agree.
- In the United States, Levi Strauss modifies the design of its jeans as teachers complain that the uncovered rivets are scratching seats.
- Spam, made from pork shoulder and ham, is first marketed by George A. Hormel & Co. in Minnesota. It becomes the world's best-selling tinned meat. Its name is a contraction of "spiced ham."
- The Hobart Manufacturing Co. in the United States markets an electric coffee grinder for use in the domestic kitchen, which costs $12.75.
- The Swiss confectionery company Nestlé introduces the Milky Bar, the first chocolate bar made from white chocolate.
- Three million refrigerators are produced in the United States.

BIRTHS & DEATHS

JANUARY
31 Philip Glass, U.S. composer, born in Baltimore, Maryland.

MARCH
6 Rudolf Otto, German theologian, philosopher, and historian, dies in Marburg, Germany (67).
30 Warren Beatty, U.S. actor, director, and producer, born in Richmond, Virginia.

APRIL
22 Jack Nicholson, U.S. actor, screenwriter, and director, born in Neptune, New Jersey.
27 Antonio Gramsci, Italian politician and intellectual who founded the Italian Communist Party, dies in Rome, Italy (46).

MAY
8 Thomas Pynchon, U.S. novelist, born in Glen Cove, Long Island, New York.
12 Beryl Burton, English cyclist, five-time world 3,000 meter pursuit champion and two-time road racing champion, born in Leeds, England (–1996).
23 John D(avison) Rockefeller, U.S. industrialist who founded Standard Oil, and philanthropist who founded the Rockefeller Foundation, dies in Ormond Beach, Florida (97).
28 Alfred Adler, Austrian psychiatrist who introduced the idea of the inferiority complex, dies in Aberdeen, Scotland (66).

JUNE
7 Jean Harlow, U.S. actress and sex symbol, dies in Los Angeles, California (26).

19 J(ames) M(atthew) Barrie, Scottish dramatist and novelist, author of *Peter Pan*, dies in London, England (77).
24 Anita Desai, Indian novelist, born in Mussoorie, India.

JULY
2 Amelia Earhart, U.S. aviator, the first woman to fly across the Atlantic alone, disappears near Howland Island, Central Pacific Ocean (38).
3 Tom Stoppard, Czech-born British playwright, born in Zlín, Czechoslovakia.
9 David Hockney, English painter, photographer, printmaker, and stage designer, born in Bradford, Yorkshire, England.
11 George Gershwin, U.S. composer and songwriter for Broadway musicals, dies in Hollywood, California (38).
20 Guglielmo Marconi, Italian physicist and inventor of radio, dies in Rome, Italy (63).

AUGUST
8 Dustin Hoffman, U.S. actor, star of the 1967 film *The Graduate*, born in Los Angeles, California.
11 Edith Wharton, U.S. author, dies in St-Brice-sous-Forêt, France (75).
18 Robert Redford, U.S. actor, producer, and director, born in Santa Monica, California.
26 Andrew W. Mellon, U.S. secretary of the treasury 1921–32 and philanthropist, dies in Southampton, New York (82).

SEPTEMBER
2 Pierre, Baron de Coubertin, French administrator who was responsible for the revival of the Olympic Games and who served as the first president of the International Olympic Committee 1896–1925, dies in Geneva, Switzerland (64).
14 Tomáš Masaryk Garrigue, founder and first president of the state of Czechoslovakia 1918–35, dies in Lany, Czechoslovakia (87).

OCTOBER
19 Ernest Rutherford, New Zealand-born British physicist and investigator of radioactivity, dies in Cambridge, England (66).
31 Ralph Connor (Charles William Gordon), Canadian author and Presbyterian minister, dies in Winnipeg, Manitoba, Canada (77).

NOVEMBER
9 Ramsay MacDonald, British politician, first Labour Party prime minister of Britain 1924, prime minister again in 1929, and in a coalition government 1931–35, dies at sea (71).

DECEMBER
20 Erich Ludendorff, German field marshal in World War I, dies in Munich, Germany (72).
21 Frank Billings Kellogg, U.S. secretary of state 1925–29, dies in St. Paul, Minnesota (80).
28 Maurice Ravel, French composer, author of *Boléro*, dies in Paris, France (62).

MARCH

1   United Steel Workers union is recognized by United States Steel, the industry's largest company.

JUNE

- The introduction of the shopping cart, which replaced smaller, hand-held bags and was devised by Sylvan N. Goldman in Oklahoma City, Oklahoma, revolutionizes grocery shopping in the United States.

JULY

1   The 999 emergency telephone number for police, fire, and ambulance services is introduced in the UK.

Media and Communication

- *Newsweek* begins publication in the United States. The magazine is created by the merging of *Today* and *News-Week*.
- In Richmond, Virginia, Irv Abeloff presents the first phone-in radio program, *Telephone Interviews*. Radio legislation does not permit callers to appear live, and so all calls are recorded.
- In the UK, the *Morning Post* is absorbed into the *Daily Telegraph*, to form the *Daily Telegraph and Morning Post*.
- The British Institute of Public Opinion is founded by George Gallup to introduce his polling method from the United States into Britain.
- The National Broadcasting Company (NBC) makes regular experimental television broadcasts in the United States.

MAY

6   Herbert Morrison conducts the first coast-to-coast radio program, reporting the Hindenburg fire in Lakehurst, New Jersey. The dirigible exploded when a spark ignited its hydrogen during the aircraft's mooring.

OCTOBER

1   *Women's Day*, a women's service magazine distributed by a grocery store chain in the United States, is first published.

Religion

- Russian Orthodox theologian Sergey Nikolayevich Bulgakov publishes *Wisdom of God*.
- The Holy Synod of the Ecumenical Patriarch grants autocephalic status to the Albanian Orthodox Church, which enables it to be governed by its own synod.
- U.S. theologian Reinhold Niebuhr publishes *Beyond Tragedy: Essays on the Christian Interpretation of History*.

Sports

- Sportswriters crown Texas Christian University as college football's national champions.
- The National Basketball League, a fully professional basketball league, is formed in the United States.

JANUARY

1   Texas Christian University defeats Marquette 16–6 in the inaugural Cotton Bowl, in Dallas, Texas.

20 Sportswriters elect second baseman Napoleon Lajoie; outfielder Tris Speaker; pitcher Cy Young; and managers Connie Mack and John McGraw into baseball's Hall of Fame.

FEBRUARY

3–6   The United States wins both the men's and women's team titles at the world table tennis championships in Baden-Baden, Germany.

13 U.S. national figure skating champions are: Maribel Vinson; Robin Lee; Maribel Vinson and George Hill, pairs; Nettie Prantel and Harold Hartshorne, dance.

APRIL

6–15   The Detroit Red Wings win the National Hockey League (NHL) Stanley Cup by beating the New York Rangers three games to two.

MAY

31 Racing driver Wilbur Shaw wins his hometown race, the Indianapolis 500.

JUNE

12 U.S. golfer Ralph Guldahl wins the U.S. Open golf championship.

21 The Wimbledon tennis championships are televised for the first time in the UK.

22 Joe Louis of the United States wins the world heavyweight boxing title by knocking out James Braddock of the United States in the eighth round in Chicago, Illinois.

30–July 25   Roger Lapébie of France wins the Tour de France cycle race.

JULY

10 At Carnoustie, Scotland, English golfer Henry Cotton wins the British Open for the second time in four years.

24–27   On the Centre Court at Wimbledon, England, the U.S. tennis team wins the Davis Cup for the first time since 1926, beating the holders, Great Britain, by four matches to one.

31–August 5   In the America's Cup, the U.S. yacht *Ranger*, skippered by Harold Vanderbilt, defeats the British challenger, Thomas Sopwith's *Endeavour II*, by four races to none.

AUGUST

- English runner Sydney Wooderson breaks the world mile record with a time of 4 min 06.4 sec.

SEPTEMBER

11 Don Budge of the United States and Anita Lizana of Chile win titles at the U.S. Lawn Tennis Association championships. Budge becomes the first person to win three titles at Wimbledon: the men's singles, men's doubles, and mixed doubles.

OCTOBER

6–10   The New York Yankees defeat the New York Giants four games to one to win the World Series.

DECEMBER

- Russian-born chess player Alexander Alekhine of France becomes the first player to regain the world chess championship when he defeats the holder, Max Euwe of the Netherlands, 17½–12 ½.

12 The Redskins, in their first season after moving to Washington, D.C., from Boston, Massachusetts, defeat the Chicago Bears 28–21 in the National Football League (NFL) championship game.

1938

POLITICS, GOVERNMENT, AND ECONOMICS

Business and Economics

- The Hewlett-Packard company is founded in Palo Alto, California, by electrical engineers William Hewlett and David Packard, to manufacture electrical and electronic equipment.
- The U.S. aircraft manufacturer John Knudsen Northrop creates the Northrop Aircraft company.
- The U.S. aircraft manufacturer James Smith McDonnell, Jr., creates the McDonnell Aircraft corporation.
- The U.S. recession persists, with nearly 6 million Americans unemployed. The Dow Jones Industrial Average sinks to 98.95, down from 194.40 in early 1937. By the end of the year, the market will rebound to 158.41.

MARCH

29   The U.S. airline company Eastern Airlines is founded by World War I ace Edward V. Rickenbacker and associates.

Colonization

JANUARY

4   Britain postpones its program for the partition of Palestine (under British mandate) and appoints a commission under Sir John Woodhead to study boundaries. The commission is boycotted by the Arabs.

OCTOBER

25   The Italian colony and former Ottoman state of Libya, occupied by Italian forces after World War I, is declared to be part of Italy.

Human Rights

- Women are permitted to hold all government posts in Norway.

MAY

5   The House Un-American Activities Committee (or Dies Committee) is established in the United States to uncover Nazi infiltration, but it begins to persecute purported communists.

JULY

15   Massachusetts essayist Ralph Waldo Emerson delivers his "Divinity School Address" to the senior class of Divinity College, Harvard, Massachusetts. Emerson exhorts his young listeners to forsake dogmatic Christianity for individually-derived moral revelation.

NOVEMBER

9–10   Following the assassination of a Nazi diplomat in Paris, France, the Nazis organize a night of violence in Germany against Jews and their property. The assault is known as Kristallnacht ("crystal night"), because of the litter of broken glass.

DECEMBER

- The U.S. Supreme Court, in the case *Missouri ex rel. Gaines v. Canada, Registrar of the University, et al.*, insists that states must provide education for all their students regardless of race.

Politics and Government

- Japanese and German aggression overseas forces the United States to review its policy of isolationism.
- The Emergency Relief Appropriations Act in the United States allocates extra funds for the creation of public works programs.
- The Temporary National Economic Commission investigates the power of monopolies in the United States.
- The U.S. president Franklin D. Roosevelt appoints Stanley F. Reed, ex-Attorney General, to the U.S. Supreme Court.

JANUARY

- The Chamber of Deputies in Italy is replaced by the Chamber of Fasces and Corporations, part of the fascist reorganization of the Italian state.
- The Indiana representative Louis Ludlow sponsors a resolution calling for a national referendum on the question of whether the United States should declare war on Germany. The Ludlow Resolution is tabled to committee.

January–May   The U.S. president asks Congress to expand the U.S. navy. Congress responds by passing the Naval Expansion Act of 1938, which allocates $1 billion to increase naval tonnage over the next ten years.

9   Republican troops capture the city of Teruel, in eastern Spain, from Nationalist forces.

10   Japanese forces enter the port of Qingdao in northeast China.

14   The Socialists leave the French cabinet; the prime minister, Camille Chautemps, reorganizes his government as a Radical ministry.

FEBRUARY

- The U.S. president Franklin D. Roosevelt signs a second Agricultural Adjustment Act, designed to ease the economic plight of U.S. farmers.
4   The German war minister and Wehrmacht (army) commander, Field Marshal Werner von Blomberg, resigns following a personal domestic scandal. The Führer formally declares himself commander with Wilhelm Keitel as chief of staff. Joachim von Ribbentrop is appointed foreign minister.
12   The Austrian chancellor Kurt von Schuschnigg visits the German Führer in Berchtesgaden, Germany. He is requested to appoint the Nazi sympathizer Arthur Seyss-Inquart minister of the interior and security and to release imprisoned Austrian Nazis.
16   Imprisoned Austrian Nazis are released by the Austrian government at the request of the German Führer Adolf Hitler.
18   The French Chamber cancels the Labor code.
20   The British foreign minister Anthony Eden resigns in protest at Prime Minister Neville Chamberlain's policy of appeasement of Nazi Germany and fascist Italy.
21–22   The British Conservative politician Winston Churchill leads a House of Commons revolt against Prime Minister Neville Chamberlain's policy of appeasement of Nazi Germany and fascist Italy. On February 22, 25 members of the administration vote against the government in a censure motion.
22   Spanish Nationalist forces recapture the city of Teruel, eastern Spain, and advance toward the Mediterranean.

MARCH

1–24   Japanese forces advance southward from the city of Jinan in north China, but are blocked by a large Chinese army at Taierzhuang and forced to withdraw.
2–14   The former leading communist Nikolai Bukharin and other political leaders are put on trial in the USSR. Bukharin is falsely accused of counterrevolutionary activities and espionage, found guilty, and shot on March 14.
9   The Austrian chancellor Kurt von Schuschnigg announces a referendum to be held on March 12 on whether Austria should remain independent.
12   German troops are ordered to invade Austria to prevent a vote for continued independence in the referendum proposed by the Austrian chancellor Kurt von Schuschnigg; the referendum is called off before they enter Austrian territory.
13   Austria is declared part of the German Reich, after the cancellation of a proposed referendum on unity with Germany (*Anschluss* or "Annexation").
13   Léon Blum succeeds Camille Chautemps as prime minister of France and continues his Popular Front ministry.
19   Lithuania capitulates to Poland's demands and reopens the frontier between the two countries.
28   Japan installs a puppet government in the Chinese city of Nanjing.

APRIL

1–May 20   A Japanese force again advances southward from Jinan, China, while another Japanese army advances northward from Nanjing. They meet at Xuzhou on May 20.

3   Spanish Nationalist troops capture the city of Lérida, west of Barcelona, from Republican forces.
10   The radical Socialist Edouard Daladier becomes prime minister of France, supported by the former premier Léon Blum.
15   Spanish Nationalist forces take the town of Vinaroz on the Mediterranean coast, separating the Republican troops in Catalonia from those in southeast Spain.
16   In an attempt to move fascist Italy away from German influence, the British prime minister Neville Chamberlain agrees to recognize Italian supremacy in Ethiopia. Italy in turn undertakes to withdraw its troops from the Spanish Civil War.
17   Almost 200 members of the fascist Iron Guard in Romania are arrested following the discovery of a plot against the government. The Iron Guard leader, Corneliu Codreanu, is sentenced to ten years in prison.
24   Konrad Henlein, leader of the Sudeten Germans in Czechoslovakia, unsuccessfully demands autonomy for the Sudetenland.
25   A British three-year agreement with Eire (Ireland) settles outstanding disputes on British use of Irish ports, finance, and trade.
27   Greece and Turkey sign a treaty of friendship.

MAY

3–9   The German Führer, Adolf Hitler, visits the Italian prime minister in Rome, Italy.
4   Douglas Hyde, a Protestant, is elected the first president of Eire (Ireland), holding the powers of the former governor-general but not representing the British monarch.
12   Germany recognizes Manchukuo, the Japanese puppet state established in Manchuria, China, in 1932.
13   Paul Spaak becomes Belgium's first Socialist prime minister.
18   J. B. M. Hertzog's United Party is confirmed in power in the South African elections.

JUNE

- The U.S. Congress passes the Wheeler–Lea Act to regulate food, drugs, and cosmetics.
1–July 1   Japanese forces advance west from Suchow, China. They take Kaifeng on June 6, but as they approach Zhengzhou the Chinese break dykes on the Huang (Yellow) River, halting their advance.
14   The Fair Labor Standards Act (Wages and Hours Act) is signed in the United States. It establishes a minimum wage of 25 cents an hour, rising to 40 cents within seven years, and a maximum working week of 44 hours, reducing to 42 in the second year, and 40 thereafter.
17   The Fianna Fáil party wins 77 seats in the Irish general election, against 61 to the opposition Fine Gael.

JULY

11–August 11   Soviet troops clash with Japanese forces on the border of the Japanese puppet state of Manchukuo (Manchuria), China.
21   A peace treaty is agreed between the South American countries of Paraguay and Bolivia, ending the dispute over the Chaco Boreal border territory. Paraguay retains at least three-quarters of the territory.
31   Bulgaria signs a nonaggression pact with Greece and other powers of the Balkan Entente (Turkey, Romania, and Yugoslavia).

AUGUST

1   Japanese forces advance southwest from Suchow, China.

3   British envoy Lord Runciman arrives in Prague, Czechoslovakia, to mediate between the Czech government and the Sudeten Germans living in Czechoslovakia.

12 Germany mobilizes its armed forces in response to international tensions over the fate of the German-populated Sudetenland region of Czechoslovakia.

21–23 The Little Entente (Czechoslovakia, Romania, and Yugoslavia) recognizes the right of Hungary to rearm.

SEPTEMBER

7   The Sudeten Germans in Czechoslovakia break off relations with the Czech government following clashes in the region.

15 The British prime minister visits the German Führer in Berchtesgaden, Germany. Hitler states his determination to annex the Sudetenland in Czechoslovakia.

16 British envoy Lord Runciman's main recommendations on Czechoslovakia are reported to the British cabinet. He advocates transfer of the Sudetenland (the area inhabited by Germans) to Germany without a referendum.

18–21 Britain and France make proposals for the Czechs to accept Germany's terms over the transfer of the Sudetenland to Germany. This is rejected by the Czechs on September 20, but accepted on September 21.

22 Milan Hodža's cabinet resigns in Czechoslovakia in protest at international proposals for the German annexation of the Sudetenland.

22 The British prime minister visits the German Führer in Bad Godesberg, Germany. Hitler proposes immediate military occupation by Germany of the Sudetenland (home of the Sudeten Germans) in Czechoslovakia. Chamberlain seeks British, French, and Czech agreement for Hitler's plan.

26 France partially mobilizes its armed forces in response to the political crisis in the Sudetenland, Czechoslovakia.

26 Gas-masks are issued to civilians in Britain.

27 Britain's Royal Navy is mobilized in response to tension between Britain and Germany over the Sudetenland, Czechoslovakia.

27 The League of Nations pronounces Japan to be the aggressor in China, where the Sino-Japanese War continues.

29 Poland demands that Czechoslovakia cede the largely Polish-populated Teschen (Cieszyn) region of north central Czechoslovakia, disputed since the end of World War I.

30 The Munich Agreement is signed in Munich, Germany, by the British prime minister, the French prime minister, the German Führer, and the Italian prime minister. It permits Germany to annex the Sudetenland in western Czechoslovakia. Chamberlain returns to London, England, speaking of "peace with honour" and "peace in our time."

OCTOBER

1   Britain's first lord of the admiralty resigns in protest at the Munich Agreement, which approves Germany's annexation of the Sudetenland in Czechoslovakia.

1   The League of Nations separates its covenant from the Treaty of Versailles, in which it was originally contained, the Treaty of Versailles having become a dead letter with the end of reparations and German expansionism.

1–10 Following the signing of the Munich Agreement, Germany occupies the Sudetenland in western Czechoslovakia with the approval of Britain, France, and Italy.

2   Japan withdraws from the League of Nations in protest at its identification by the League as the aggressor in the Sino-Japanese war.

4   The Popular Front government falls in France when the socialists and communists abstain from a vote of confidence because they are opposed to government economic policy (particularly the devaluation of the franc).

5   The president of Czechoslovakia, Eduard Beneš, resigns as a result of the German annexation of the Sudetenland.

6   Czechoslovakia grants autonomy to the province of Slovakia, as specified by the Munich Agreement.

6   Italy's Grand Fascist Council passes anti-Semitic legislation. Jews are to be excluded from public activities, such as journalism, and are to cede property to the state.

8   Czechoslovakia grants autonomy to the region of Ruthenia, as specified by the Munich Agreement.

10 The Japanese capture the city of Hankow, the seat of Jiang Jie Shi's Chinese government before it moved to the port of Chongqing in the southwest.

25 Japanese troops take the port of Guangzhou in south China.

29 Belgium withdraws from the nonintervention committee formed in September 1935 to prevent foreign intervention in the Spanish Civil War.

NOVEMBER

•   In U.S. congressional elections, the Democrats retain a 69–23 majority over Republicans in the Senate and a 261–164 majority in the House of Representatives.

2   Hungary annexes the Czechoslovak province of southern Slovakia, another ethnically-mixed area disputed since the end of World War I.

26 A declaration of friendship between the USSR and Poland renews their nonaggression pact of 1934.

30 Corneliu Codreanu, the leader of the fascist Iron Guard in Romania, and 13 other members are garrotted and shot, supposedly while attempting to escape from prison.

30 Emil Hácha, an advocate of appeasement and cooperation with Germany, is elected president of Czechoslovakia.

30 Speeches in the Italian parliament claim Nice and Corsica in France for Italy.

DECEMBER

1   Britain establishes a national register for war service in response to the threat of war with Germany.

6   France and Germany sign a pact confirming the inviolability of their existing frontiers.

17 Italy denounces its 1935 agreement with France following disputes over the French possessions of Corsica and Tunisia.

23 Nationalist forces launch an offensive in the autonomous Spanish region of Catalonia, with the aim of capturing the Republican stronghold of Barcelona.

26 A Pan-American conference makes the Declaration of Peru against all foreign intervention in political events in the American continent.
28 Iraq severs its relations with France.

SCIENCE, TECHNOLOGY, AND MEDICINE

Agriculture

- The self-propelled combine harvester is introduced on farms in the United States.

Computing

- U.S. engineer Thomas Ross develops a mechanical mouse that can find its way around a maze by trial and error; it is the first machine that can learn from experience.

Ecology

- The U.S. Congress creates Olympic National Park, protecting 363 sq km/140 sq mi of rainforest in the Pacific Northwest of the United States.
- The U.S. Congress establishes Olympic National Park on the Olympic peninsula in the state of Washington. The park incorporates nearly a million acres of rainforest.

SEPTEMBER

21–22 The worst hurricane in 100 years hits New England. High winds, storm surges, and river flooding kill 682 people, cause over $400 million damage in property, destroy 2 billion trees, and permanently alter the coastline from New Jersey to Massachusetts.

Health and Medicine

- Belgian physiologist Corneillie Heymans receives the Nobel Prize for Physiology or Medicine for discovering the role of aortic and sinus mechanisms in the regulation of respiration.
- British chemist Charles Dodds creates the first synthetic estrogen, and Schering Pharmaceutical chemists create an estrogen contraceptive pill.
- Electroconvulsive therapy (ECT) or shock therapy, for treating depression and schizophrenia, is developed by Italian doctors Ugo Cerletti and Lucio Bini.
- The stainless steel artificial hip replacement is invented by British surgeon Philip Wiles.

JUNE

27 The Food, Drug, and Cosmetics Act comes into force in the United States. It requires ingredients to be listed on food product labels.

SEPTEMBER

- Du Pont markets the first nylon toothbrush, Dr. West's Miracle Tuft Toothbrush, in Arlington, New Jersey.

Science

- German chemist Richard Kuhn wins the Nobel Prize for Chemistry for his work on vitamins; he is unable to receive it until 1945.
- German physicists Lise Meitner, Otto Hahn, and Fritz Strassmann repeat Fermi's experiments and conclude that bombarding uranium atoms with neutrons splits the atom and releases huge amounts of energy by the conversion of some of the mass of the uranium atom into energy.
- Italian physicist Enrico Fermi receives the Nobel Prize for Physics for the artificial production of elements through neutron irradiation.
- The Soviet physicist Pyotr Kapitza discovers that liquid helium exhibits superfluidity, the ability to flow over its containment vessel without friction, when cooled below 2.18K/–270.97°C.

September 1938–40 Five independent researchers isolate and synthesize vitamin B_6 in Germany.

DECEMBER

- A coelacanth, an ancient fish assumed to be extinct, is discovered in the Indian Ocean.

Technology

- A scanning electron microscope is demonstrated by German physicist Manfred von Ardenne.
- French scientist Georges Valensi patents a method that allows color images to be transmitted and received on both color and black and white televisions.
- German astronomer and rocket engineer Wernher von Braun produces a rocket that can travel 18 km/11 mi.
- German inventor Konrad Zuse constructs the first binary calculator using a binary code (Boolean algebra); it is the first working computer.
- German scientists at AGFA discover the diffusion-transfer process for making photographic prints; it becomes the basis of the Polaroid process.
- Hungarian inventor Ladislao Biró patents his ballpoint pen: a few more technical refinements and it becomes a mass-market success.
- Katherine Burr Blodgett invents nonreflecting glass in the United States, which is used by General Electric in camera lenses, picture frames, and store windows.
- Polyvinyl acetate, the water-insoluble resin in latex paints and adhesives, is developed.
- Super Kodak Six-20, available at a price of $225 in the United States, is the first camera which has fully automatic exposure.
- The Cryovac deep-freezing method is introduced by the U.S. company Dewey & Almy, to preserve foods.
- The English photographer Bill Brandt publishes *A Night in London*, a photograph album.
- The Garand or M1 semiautomatic rifle is adopted by the U.S. army; more than 5 million are issued.
- The horizontal resolution of television pictures is doubled with the development of a sideband filter by U.S. electrical engineer George Harold Brown.
- The polyamide plastic Perlon (similar to nylon in the United States) is discovered in Germany by chemist P. Schlack.

- The U.S. photographer Walker Evans publishes *American Photographs*, a photograph album that contains some of the best-known images of the United States during the 1930s. Typical is *American Legionnaire, Bethlehem, Pennsylvania, November 1935*.
- U.S. corporation Owens-Illinois and Corning Ware introduce fiberglass.

FEBRUARY

4 John Logie Baird gives a demonstration of a higher definition color television system which he calls "Telechrome" at the Dominion Theatre in London, England.

APRIL

1 GEC and Westinghouse both begin the commercial production of fluorescent lamps in the United States, which cost $1.50–2.00.

6 U.S. chemist Roy Plunkett discovers the stable and slippery substance polytetrafluoroethylene (PTFE) (a synthetic resin), marketed by Du Pont as Teflon. The most slippery substance known, it becomes commercially available in 1947–48 and is used for electrical insulation and to produce nonstick coatings; it is marketed in Britain as Fluon.

OCTOBER

22 In the United States, Chester Carlson produces the first example of xerography ("dry writing"), which is to develop into modern photocopying.

Transportation

c. 1938 The success of diesel locomotives inhibits further growth and development of electrification in the United States.

- France nationalizes all railroads still privately owned.
- The Mittelland Canal is completed in Germany; it gives the city of Berlin water access to the North Sea and the Baltic.
- The radio altimeter is invented by U.S. pilot Royden Sanders.

MAY

26 The German head of state Adolf Hitler opens the first Volkswagen car factory, in Wolfsburg, Germany, for the production of mass-market cars. Only a few are made before production is changed due to the war. Over 15 million Volkswagens, or "people's cars", are made by 1972.

JUNE

23 The Civil Aeronautics Authority is established in the United States; two years later it becomes a licensing and regulatory agency.

JULY

10–14 U.S. businessman Howard Hughes flies around the world in 3 days 19 hours and 17 minutes in the monoplane *New York World Fair*, having covered 24,800 km/15,500 mi.

SEPTEMBER

27 The luxury liner *Queen Elizabeth* is launched in Scotland for the British Cunard line; at 314 m/1,031 ft it is the world's largest ocean liner.

ARTS AND IDEAS

Arts

- French photographer Henri Cartier-Bresson takes *Sunday, Bank of the Marne*.
- Polish-born U.S. photographer Weegee takes *Untitled (Woman Being Pulled Away from a Dying Man)*.
- The Belgian artist Paul Delvaux paints *The Call of the Night*.
- The English artist Eric Gill carves a relief for the League of Nations Building in Geneva, Switzerland.
- The English artist Paul Nash paints *Landscape from a Dream*.
- The German artist Max Beckmann paints *Birds' Hell*.
- The Russian-born French artist Marc Chagall paints *White Crucifixion*.
- The Spanish artist Pablo Picasso paints *Portrait of Maïa with a Doll*.
- The Spanish painter Joan Miró paints *Head of a Woman*.
- The Swiss artist Kurt Seligmann creates *Ultra-Furniture*, a stool supported by three mannequin legs.
- The Welsh artist Augustus John paints the portrait *Dylan Thomas*.

September 1938–39 The Mexican artist José Clemente Orozco completes his cycle of murals in the Guadalajara orphanage, a dramatic depiction of Mexican history.

Film

- Movie attendance stands at 80 million people a week in the United States.
- The 1937 Academy Awards take place. Best Actor: Spencer Tracy, for *Captains Courageous*; Best Supporting Actor: Joseph Schildkraut, for *The Life of Emile Zola*; Best Actress: Luise Rainer, for *The Good Earth*; Best Supporting Actress: Alice Brady, for *In Old Chicago*; Best Picture: *The Life of Emile Zola*, directed by William Dieterle; Best Director: Leo McCarey, for *The Awful Truth*.
- The annual quota regulations for British movies are adjusted to permit more U.S. investment in high-budget productions.
- The movie *Alexander Nevsky* is released in the Soviet Union, directed by Sergey Eisenstein and with music by Sergey Prokofiev. Set during a 13th-century German invasion of Russia, the movie is intended as a propaganda piece, alluding to Nazi activity in contemporary Europe.
- The movie *Angels with Dirty Faces*, directed by Michael Curtiz, is released in the United States. It stars James Cagney, Pat O'Brien, and Humphrey Bogart.
- The movie *Bringing Up Baby* is released in the United States, directed by Howard Hawks and starring Cary Grant and Katherine Hepburn.
- The movie *Dawn Patrol*, directed by Edmund Goulding, is released in the United States, starring Errol Flynn, Basil Rathbone, and David Niven.
- The movie *Hôtel du Nord*, directed by Marcel Carné, is released in France. The cast includes Jean-Pierre Aumont, Annabella, Louis Jouvet, and Arletty.

- The movie *Jezebel*, directed by William Wyler, is released in the United States, starring Bette Davis. It marks Davis's return to Hollywood after Warner Brothers successfully sues her for breach of contract.
- The movie *La Bête Humaine/The Human Beast*, directed by Jean Renoir, is released in France, based on the novel by Emile Zola and starring Jean Gabin and Simone Simon.
- The movie *La Femme du Boulanger/The Baker's Wife*, directed by Marcel Pagnol, is released in France, starring Raimu and Ginette Leclerc.
- The movie *Le Quai des brumes/Port of Shadows*, directed by Marcel Carné, is released in France, starring Jean Gabin, Michèle Morgan, Michel Simon, and Pierre Brasseur.
- The movie *Pygmalion*, directed by Anthony Asquith and Leslie Howard, is released in the UK. Based on the play by George Bernard Shaw, it stars Howard as Professor Higgins and Wendy Hiller as Eliza Doolittle.
- The movie *The Adventures of Robin Hood,* directed by William Keighley and Michael Curtiz, is released in the United States, starring Errol Flynn, Melville Cooper, and Olivia de Havilland.
- The movie *The Childhood of Maxim Gorky*, directed by Mark Donskoi, is released in the USSR, starring Alexei Lyarsky. The first of a trilogy about the life of the writer Gorky based on his memoirs, it is followed by *Out in the World* and *My Universities*.
- The movie *The Citadel* directed by King Vidor, is released in Britain, based on the novel by A. J. Cronin, and with an all-star cast featuring Robet Donat and Rosalind Russell.
- The movie *The Lady Vanishes*, directed by Alfred Hitchcock, is released. Adapted from the novel by Daphne du Maurier, it stars Margaret Lockwood and Michael Redgrave.
- The movie *You Can't Take It With You*, directed by Frank Capra, is released in the United States, starring Jean Arthur, Lionel Barrymore, and James Stewart.
- The Italian movie industry is under centralized government control.
- The Japanese government imposes controls on the movie industry, requiring movies to present a positive image of contemporary events.

Literature and Language

- *The Oxford Book of Light Verse* is published, edited by W. H. Auden.
- Selections from the diaries of the English clergyman Francis Kilvert, written in the second half of the 19th century, are published for the first time. A second selection will appear in 1940.
- The Anglo-Irish writer Elizabeth Bowen publishes her novel *The Death of the Heart*.
- The Chinese author Lin Yutang's *The Importance of Living* is the best-selling nonfiction title of the year in the United States.
- The English writer and critic Cyril Connolly publishes *Enemies of Promise*, literary essays which include an autobiographical sketch.
- The English writer Cecil Day Lewis publishes his poetry collection *Overtures to Death*.

- The English writer Daphne du Maurier publishes her highly successful romantic melodrama *Rebecca*.
- The English writer Evelyn Waugh publishes his satirical novel *Scoop*.
- The English writer Graham Greene publishes his novel *Brighton Rock*.
- The English writer George Orwell publishes *Homage to Catalonia*, an account of his experiences in the Spanish Civil War.
- The English writer Lawrence Durrell publishes his novel *The Black Book: An Agon* in Paris, France. Because of its strong language and eroticism it will not be published in the United States until 1960.
- The English writer Robert Graves publishes his *Collected Poems 1914–1938*, and his novel *Count Belisarius*.
- The English writer Richard Hughes publishes his novel *In Hazard*.
- The English writer Somerset Maugham publishes his autobiographical *The Summing-Up*.
- The Irish writer Samuel Beckett publishes his first novel, *Murphy*.
- The Nigerian writer Daniel Fagunwa publishes *Ogboju Ode Ninu Igbo Irunmale/The Forest of a Thousand Demons*, the first full-length novel in Yoruba. His fiction draws heavily on traditional tales of gods, demons, and sorcery.
- The novel *The Buccaneers*, by the U.S. writer Edith Wharton, is published posthumously.
- The Pulitzer Prize for Biography is awarded to Odell Shepard for *Pedlar's Progress: The Life of Bronson Alcott*, and to Marquis James for *Andrew Jackson*, the Pulitzer Prize for Fiction is awarded to J. P. Marquand for *The Late George Apley*, and the Prize for Poetry is awarded to Marya Zaturenska for *Cold Morning Sky*.
- The Russian-born U.S. writer Vladimir Nabokov publishes his novel *Priglasheniye na kazn/Invitation to a Beheading*.
- The U.S. crime writer Rex Stout publishes *Too Many Cooks*, a novel featuring his detective hero Nero Wolfe.
- The U.S. philosopher Charles Morris publishes *Foundations of a Theory of Signs*.
- The U.S. writer Allen Tate publishes his novel *The Fathers*.
- The U.S. writer and critic Edmund Wilson publishes *The Triple Thinkers*, a work of criticism.
- The U.S. writer e e cummings publishes *Collected Poems*.
- The U.S. writer Ernest Hemingway publishes *The Fifth Column and the First Forty-Nine Stories*.
- The U.S. writer Laura Riding publishes her *Collected Poems*.
- The U.S. writer Marjorie Kinnan Rawlings's *The Yearling*, the story of a stray deer, is the best-selling novel in the United States.
- The U.S. writer William Faulkner publishes his novel *The Unvanquished*.

NOVEMBER

- The U.S. novelist Pearl S. Buck is awarded the Nobel Prize for Literature for her novels, including *The Good Earth*.

Music

- In the United States, Glenn Miller forms his second band, which achieves great popularity with "Moonlight Serenade" and other hits. The band will split in 1942.
- The Australian composer Arthur Benjamin completes his *Jamaican Pieces*. The second, "Jamaican Rumba," is one of the first pieces of European music to incorporate rhythms of the Rumba, a Cuban dance.
- The Austrian composer Anton Webern completes his String Quartet, Opus 28.
- The English composer Ralph Vaughan Williams completes his *Serenade to Music*.
- The English composer Benjamin Britten completes his Piano Concerto, Opus 13.
- The Hungarian composer Béla Bartók completes his Violin Concerto No. 2.
- The opera *Le Diable boiteux/The Lame Devil* by the French composer Jean Françaix is first performed, in Paris, France.
- The opera *Mathis der Maler/Matthias the Painter* by the German composer Paul Hindemith is first performed, in Zürich, Switzerland.
- The plight of hard-pressed laborers is given poignant expression as the U.S. folk singer Woody Guthrie canvasses the nation's back alleys and dusty roadways for inspiration.
- The Russian composer Igor Stravinsky completes his orchestral work *Dumbarton Oaks*.
- The Russian composer Dmitry Shostakovich completes his *Suite for Jazz Orchestra No. 2* and his String Quartet No. 1.
- The U.S. composer Samuel Barber writes his *Adagio for Strings*, which he has adapted from his String Quartet of 1936.
- Two operas by the German composer Richard Strauss are first performed in Germany: in Munich, *Friedenstag/Day of Peace*; and in Dresden, *Daphne*.

JANUARY
- The Benny Goodman Band gives a highly acclaimed jazz concert at Carnegie Hall, in New York, New York.

Theater and Dance

- The ballet *Billy the Kid* is first performed, in the Civic Opera House in Chicago, Illinois. The score is by the U.S. composer Aaron Copland, the choreography by the U.S. choreographer Eugene Loring.
- The ballet *Romeo i Dzhulyetta/Romeo and Juliet*, by the Russian composer Sergey Prokofiev, is first performed, in Brno, USSR. The choreography is by the Czech choreographer Ivo Váňa Psoda.
- The French artist Henri Matisse designs costumes and settings for *Rouge et noir/Scarlet and Black*, a ballet choreographed by Léonide Massine and performed in 1939 by Serge Diaghilev's Ballet Russe of Monte Carlo.
- The French writer and actor Antonin Artaud publishes *Le Théâtre et son double/The Theater and Its Double* in which he proposes a "theater of cruelty."
- The play *Le Bal des voleurs/Thieves' Carnival*, by the French writer Jean Anouilh, is first performed, in Paris, France.
- The play *Les Parents terribles/The Terrible Parents*, by the French writer Jean Cocteau, is first performed, in Paris, France.
- The play *Our Town*, a classic of small-town U.S. life by the U.S. writer Thornton Wilder, is first performed, at the Henry Miller Theater in New York, New York.
- The play *The Corn is Green*, by the Welsh writer Emlyn Williams, is first performed, in England.
- The Pulitzer Prize for Drama is awarded to Thornton Wilder for *Our Town*.

Thought and Scholarship

- *Studies in a Dying Culture*, by the English writer Christopher Caudwell, is published posthumously.
- Dutch historian Johan Huizinga publishes *Homo Ludens*, which analyzes the role of play in human culture.
- English historians George Douglas Howard Cole and Raymond Williams Postgate publish *The Common People, 1746–1938*.
- English scientist and writer Lancelot Hogben publishes *Science for the Citizen*.
- English statesman David Lloyd George publishes *The Truth about the Peace Treaties*.
- French philosopher Gaston Bachelard publishes *La Psychoanalyse du feu/The Psychoanalysis of Fire*.
- French sociologist Raymond Aron publishes *Introduction à la philosophie de l'histoire/Introduction to the Philosophy of History*.
- German philosopher of science Hans Reichenbach publishes *Experience and Prediction*.
- Swiss psychotherapist Carl Gustav Jung publishes *Psychology and Religion*, based on the Terry Lectures he gave this year.
- The Pulitzer Prize for History is awarded to Paul Herman Buck for *The Road to Reunion, 1865–1900*.
- U.S. critic Lewis Mumford traces the cultural impact of urbanization in *The Culture of Cities*.
- Welsh historian Llewellyn Woodward publishes *The Age of Reform, 1815–1870*.

SOCIETY

Education

- President Roosevelt's Advisory Committee on Education recommends that the U.S. federal government should be given powers to relieve the unsatisfactory state of education in the United States.
- The U.S. philosopher John Dewey publishes *The Theory of Inquiry* and *Experience in Education*, groundbreaking texts in the field of learning theory.

Everyday Life

- Amount of coal being produced (in million metric tons): UK, 230; Germany, (including Saar) 153; USSR, 150; France, 46.

- At his restaurant in Beverly Hills, California, Laurence L. Frank produces the first baked potatoes with toppings, which include cheese and bacon.
- Beton Toys in Carlstadt, New Jersey, begins to manufacture plastic toy soldiers.
- During 1938, there are 32,000 automobile-related deaths in the United States, one-third involving pedestrians.
- Immigration to Great Britain: 504,527. Emigration from Great Britain: 1,609,847 British and 491,176 foreign.
- In Santa Monica, California, Joseph F. Friedman invents the flexible drinking straw by incorporating a corrugated component.
- In the UK, the Amulree Committee report recommends the extension to most workers of a week's paid annual holiday, on grounds of social justice and industrial efficiency.
- Number of private cars in use (in millions): United States, 19; UK, 1.7; Germany (including Austria), 1.3; Italy, 1.1; France, 0.8.
- Superman appears in *Action Comics*, in the United States. Cartoonists Jerry Siegel and Joseph Shuster created the super-hero character while still in high school.
- The Fair Labor Standard Act is passed in the United States, limiting working hours and confirming statutory minimum wage and overtime rates.
- The most popular dance in the United States is the Lambeth Walk.
- The Swiss food company Nestlé produces instant coffee in response to a coffee surplus in Brazil.
- The U.S. birth-control advocate Margaret Sanger helps establish the Birth Control Federation of America, later called the International Planned Parenthood Federation.

BIRTHS & DEATHS

- Moshoeshoe II, king of Lesotho 1966–96 who leads the country to independence, born in Mokhotlong, Lesotho (–1996).

JANUARY
5 Juan Carlos, king of Spain from 1975 on the death of Franco, born in Rome, Italy.
21 Wolfman Jack, popular radio disk jockey, born in New York, New York.

FEBRUARY
16 John Corigliano, U.S. composer, born in New York, New York.
21 George Ellery Hale, U.S. astronomer who developed the Hale telescope at Mt. Palomar, California, dies in Pasadena, California (69).

MARCH
1 Gabriele D'Annunzio, Italian poet, novelist, dramatist, military, and political leader, dies in the Gardone Riviera, on Lake Garda, Italy (75).
7 David Baltimore, U.S. virologist, born in New York, New York.
13 Clarence Darrow, U.S. criminal lawyer who defended the Tennessee school teacher John T. Scopes when he was charged with teaching the theory of evolution, dies in Chicago, Illinois (80).
17 Rudolf Hametovich Nureyev, Russian ballet dancer, born near Irkutsk, USSR (–1993).
28 Edward Mandell House, U.S. advisor to President Woodrow Wilson, dies in New York, New York (79).

APRIL
4 A. Bart(lett) Giamatti, president of Yale University and commissioner of Major League Baseball, born in Boston, Massachusetts.

21 Muhammad Iqbal, Indian poet and philosopher who campaigned for the establishment of a separate Muslim state (later realized as Pakistan), dies in Lahore, Punjab (60).
27 Edmund Husserl, German philosopher, founder of phenomenology, dies in Freiburg im Breislau, Germany (79).

JUNE
15 Ernst Ludwig Kirchner, German expressionist painter, dies near Davos, Switzerland (58).
16 Joyce Carol Oates, U.S. author, poet, and playwright, born in Lockport, New York.
26 James Weldon Johnson, poet, diplomat, and anthologist of black culture, dies in Wiscasset, Maine (67).

JULY
4 Suzanne Lenglen, French tennis player who dominated women's singles tennis between 1919 and 1926, dies in Paris, France (39).
9 Benjamin Cardozo, Justice of U.S. Supreme Court, dies in Port Chester, New York (68).
14 Jerry Rubin, U.S. political activist during the Vietnam era, born in Cincinnati, Ohio (–1994).

AUGUST
7 Konstantin Stanislavsky, Russian actor, director and producer who founded the Moscow Arts Theater, dies in Moscow, USSR (75).
9 Rod Laver, Australian tennis player, born in Rockhampton, Queensland, Australia.

SEPTEMBER
13 Samuel Alexander, British philosopher, dies in Manchester, England (79).

15 Thomas Wolfe, U.S. writer, dies in Baltimore, Maryland (37).

OCTOBER
13 Elzie Segar, U.S. cartoonist who created Popeye, dies in Santa Monica, California (43).
15 Fela Anikulapo Kuti, Nigerian singer, songwriter, and musician, proponent of African nationalism and ethnic identity, born in Abeokuta, Nigeria (–1997).
17 Evel Knievel, U.S. daredevil and stunt man, born in Butte, Montana.

NOVEMBER
10 (Mustafa) Kemal Atatürk, Turkish soldier, statesman, and reformer, founder and first president of the Republic of Turkey 1923–38, dies in Istanbul, Turkey (57).
11 "Typhoid Mary" (nickname of Mary Mallon), U.S. cook and a carrier of typhoid who caused several outbreaks of the disease in the New York City area during the early 1900s, dies in North Boulder Island, New York (about 68).
17 Gordon Lightfoot, Canadian musician and balladeer, born in Orillia, Canada.
28 William McDougall, British-born U.S. psychologist who laid the foundation of social psychology, dies in Durham, South Carolina (67).

DECEMBER
15 Karel Čapek, Czech novelist and playwright, dies in Prague, Czechoslovakia (48).
18 Chas Chendley, bass guitarist with the rock group The Animals, born in Heaton, Newcastle upon Tyne, England (57).

JULY

- In the UK, the British Social Hygiene Council provides a marriage guidance service, with appointed counselors.

OCTOBER

- William Green, President of the American Federation of Labor, extends an olive branch to members of the rival Committee for Industrial Organization (soon to be the Congress of Industrial Organizations, or CIO).

NOVEMBER

- The Committee for Industrial Organization changes its name to the Congress of Industrial Organizations at its annual meeting in Pittsburgh, Pennsylvania. John L. Lewis remains the group's president.

Media and Communication

- Edward Hulton founds the illustrated news magazine *Picture Post*, in the UK.
- Following the union of Germany and Austria, many established Austrian newspapers are suppressed.
- The first panel games on British television appear, *Spelling Bee* and *General Knowledge Bee*.
- U.S. journalist Frank Luther Mott publishes *A History of American Magazines*.

JANUARY

3   The British Broadcasting Corporation (BBC) External Service launches the Arabic Service with the first-ever foreign-language broadcast.

JULY

- Experimental television transmissions begin in the USSR.

AUGUST

22   The first Promenade Concert to be televised is broadcast by the British Broadcasting Corporation (BBC) from the Queen's Hall in England.

SEPTEMBER

30   The British Broadcasting Corporation (BBC) broadcasts Neville Chamberlain's return to Britain from Munich, Germany, waving Adolf Hitler's guarantee of peace.

OCTOBER

30   The U.S. actor Orson Welles broadcasts H. G. Wells's *The War of the Worlds*, convincing a credulous U.S. radio audience that Martians have landed and are engaging in war with humans.

Religion

- The Dutch theologian Hendrik Kraemer publishes *The Christian Message in a Non-Christian World*.

Sports

- Donald Budge of the United States becomes the first tennis player to achieve the Grand Slam, holding all four major tournaments (Wimbledon and the U.S., French, and Australian championships) simultaneously.
- In college basketball, the inaugural National Invitational Tournament is won by Temple, who defeat Colorado 60–36 in the final at Madison Square Garden, New York, New York.

- The Agricultural and Mechanical College of Texas wins the college football national championship.

FEBRUARY

26   U.S. national figure skating champions are: Joan Tozzer; Robin Lee; Joan Tozzer and Bernard Fox, pairs; Nettie Prantel and Harold Hartshorne, dance.

APRIL

5–12   The National Hockey League (NHL) Stanley Cup goes to the Chicago Black Hawks, who beat the Toronto Maple Leafs three games to one.

MAY

14   On the advice of the Football Association and the British Ambassador, the English team give the Nazi salute during the playing of "Deutschland über Alles" before an international soccer match with Germany in Berlin, Germany. England win the game 6–3.

30   Racing driver Floyd Roberts of California wins the Indianapolis 500.

JUNE

3–4   Great Britain and Ireland win the Walker Cup golf trophy for the first time, beating the United States 7½–4½ at St. Andrews, Scotland.

4–19   The third soccer World Cup is held in France; Italy retains the trophy, beating Hungary 4–2 in the final in Paris before a crowd of 55,000.

11   U.S. golfer Ralph Guldahl wins his second consecutive U.S. Open golf championship.

JULY

2   Helen Wills Moody of the United States wins her eighth singles title at the Wimbledon tennis championships in London, England.

5–31   Gino Bartali of Italy wins the Tour de France cycle race.

AUGUST

17   U.S. boxer Henry "Homicide Hank" Armstrong becomes the first boxer to hold three world professional titles simultaneously: featherweight, welterweight, and lightweight.

SEPTEMBER

17   U.S. tennis players Alice Marble and Don Budge win the U.S. Lawn Tennis championships.

OCTOBER

5–9   In baseball, the New York Yankees become the first team to win three consecutive World Series, defeating the Chicago Cubs by four games to none.

DECEMBER

- Starting blocks in athletics are recognized by the International Amateur Athletic Federation.

11   The New York Giants defeat the Green Bay Packers 27–17 in the National Football League (NFL) championship game in New York, New York.

1939

POLITICS, GOVERNMENT, AND ECONOMICS

Business and Economics

- Italian automobile manufacturer Enzo Ferrari founds his car company, the Auto Avio Construzione.
- The British company Imperial Chemical Industries (ICI) begins the commercial production of polythene.
- The outbreak of war in Europe and subsequent increases in U.S. defense spending propel the U.S. economy out of recession.
- The Tokyo Shibaura Electric Company (Toshiba) is founded in Japan.
- The U.S. tycoon Howard Hughes acquires a controlling interest in Transcontinental and Western Airlines (TWA).

MAY
- In a sign of labor's increasing bargaining power in the United States, the United Mine Workers' union secures a favorable contract after halting the processing of soft coal.
16 The U.S. Department of Agriculture distributes the nation's first food stamps to the poor in Rochester, New York. The plan is copied by more than 100 U.S. cities in the next two years. Discontinued in 1943, the food stamp program will begin anew in 1964.

OCTOBER
- BMI (Broadcast Music, Inc.) opens for business in the United States, offering radio networks an alternative to the ASCAP (American Society of Composers, Authors, and Publishers) radio monopoly.

NOVEMBER
24 British businessman John Charles Reith merges Imperial Airways with British Airways to form the British Overseas Airways Corporation (BOAC).

Colonization

JANUARY
1 The French prime minister visits Algeria, Tunisia, and Corsica to affirm the integrity of the French Empire.

MAY
23 The British Parliament approves a plan for an independent Palestine (currently under British mandate) by 1949. This is subsequently denounced by Jews and Arabs in Palestine.

Human Rights

- German Jewish refugees on the SS *St Louis* are turned back by U.S. authorities at Havana, Cuba. They are eventually accepted by European countries, but many are captured by the Nazis in 1940.
- Women gain the right to vote in the Philippines.

OCTOBER
10 The deportation of Polish Jews to the Lublin ghetto begins.

Politics and Government

- British secret service officer Frederick Winterbotham sets up the "Ultra" project in Bletchley Park, Buckinghamshire, England, 80 km/50 mi north of London, to decode the German "Enigma" ciphers.
- In the case *Gaines v. Canada*, the U.S. Supreme Court rules that "separate but equal" must mean that facilities are of equal standard for black and white.
- The evacuation of around 650,000 children from London to rural England begins. Some 1.5 million people in total will move to the country for part of the war.
- The Hatch Act in the United States restricts political activities by civil servants.
- The U.S. Attorney General, Frank Murphy, establishes, at the bidding of President Franklin D. Roosevelt, a Civil Rights Division in the U.S. Department of Justice.
- The U.S. president appoints Felix Frankfurter, law professor and trusted advisor, and William O. Douglas, formerly of the Securities and Exchange Commission, to the U.S. Supreme Court.
October 1939–45 The airplane's military role increases dramatically during World War II, as it is being used as military transport and as a strategic and combat weapon.

JANUARY
4 President Franklin D. Roosevelt asks Congress for $552 million for defense funding in the United States.
10 The British prime minister and the foreign secretary visit Rome for talks with the Italian prime minister.
21 The German Führer dismisses Hjalmar Schacht as president of the Reichsbank for opposing his rearmament expenditure. He replaces him with Walther Funk, minister of economics.
26 Nationalist forces, assisted by Italian troops, take the city of Barcelona, the last major stronghold of the Republican government in northeastern Spain.

FEBRUARY
- The U.S. Supreme Court declares the sit-down strike unconstitutional.

10 Japanese troops occupy the Chinese island of Hainan in the South China Sea and other Chinese ports.

27 Britain and France recognize General Francisco Franco's Nationalist government in Spain.

MARCH

6 On secret German orders, the Czech government dismisses the autonomous government of Ruthenia, in order to foment nationalist feeling in the province.

9 On secret German orders, the Czech government dismisses the autonomous government of Slovakia, in order to foment nationalist feeling in the province.

14 Responding to pressure from the German Führer, the former Slovak prime minister Jozef Tiso proclaims Slovakia's independence from Czechoslovakia and appeals to Germany for protection.

15 German troops occupy Bohemia and Moravia in Czechoslovakia. The German Führer makes a triumphal entry into Prague, the Czech capital, the same evening. The regions become a German protectorate under Konstantin von Neurath.

16 The Czech province of Slovakia is placed under German "protection," while Hungary annexes Ruthenia, formerly part of Czechoslovakia.

17 French prime minister Edouard Daladier is granted wide powers by the French parliament to step up rearmament in response to Germany's dismemberment of Czechoslovakia.

20 The U.S. government recalls its ambassador from Berlin, Germany, in protest at the German dismemberment of Czechoslovakia.

21 Germany demands the free city of Danzig (now Gdańsk) from Poland and the routes through the "Polish Corridor" that give Poland access to the Baltic Sea. Poland rejects the demands.

22 Germany annexes the city of Memel (now Klaipeda) from Lithuania and forces Lithuania to sign a treaty of acceptance.

28 The German Führer denounces Germany's nonaggression pact of January 1934 with Poland.

28–29 Madrid surrenders to the Spanish Nationalists, after a siege of almost two and a half years. The remaining Republican areas capitulate on March 29, ending the Spanish Civil War.

31 Britain and France pledge to support Poland in any attack on Polish independence. On April 6 a pact is signed by all three governments confirming the pledge.

APRIL

1 The United States recognizes General Francisco Franco's Nationalist government in Spain.

7 Italy invades and occupies Albania. The Albanian king, Ahmed Bey Zogu, flees to Greece.

7 Spain joins Germany, Italy, and Japan in the Anti-Comintern Pact, against international communism.

11 Hungary withdraws from the League of Nations.

13 Britain and France guarantee the independence of Romania and Greece.

15 The U.S. president asks the German Führer Adolf Hitler and Italian prime minister Benito Mussolini for assurances that they will not attack 31 named states.

18 The USSR proposes a triple alliance with Britain and France.

24 Robert Menzies succeeds the late Joseph Lyons as prime minister of Australia, also taking over as leader of the United Australia Party.

27 Conscription for men aged 20–21 is introduced in Britain.

28 The German Führer denounces the 1935 British–German naval agreement and repeats his demands of March 21 for Polish cessation of Danzig (now Gdańsk) and the Polish Corridor to Germany.

MAY

3 Vyacheslav Molotov replaces Maxim Litvinov as commissar of foreign affairs in the USSR.

8 Spain withdraws from the League of Nations.

11 Siam changes its name to Thailand.

12 Britain and Turkey sign a pact of mutual assistance.

17 Sweden, Norway, and Finland reject Germany's offer of nonaggression pacts, but Denmark, Estonia, and Latvia accept.

22 The German Führer, Adolf Hitler, and Italian prime minister, Benito Mussolini sign a ten-year political and military alliance, the "Pact of Steel."

JUNE

14 Japanese forces blockade the British concession (an area under British colonial administration) at Tianjin, northeast China.

JULY

• The U.S. president creates the Federal Works Agency, an umbrella organization that subsumes the Public Building, Public Roads, Public Works, and Works Progress and Administrations, along with the U.S. Housing Authority.

9 The British Conservative politician Winston Churchill urges Britain to make a military alliance with the USSR.

16 The United States denounces its 1911 trade pact with Japan because of Japan's continuing aggression in China.

AUGUST

• The U.S. Congress passes the Hatch Act, prohibiting federal employees from participating in political election campaigns.

• U.S. newspapers trumpet news of a probable Hitler–Stalin nonaggression pact in Europe.

5 A British military mission leaves for Moscow, to discuss a possible treaty against Germany.

18 The USSR and Germany sign a commercial agreement.

23 The British prime minister warns the German Führer that Britain will stand by Poland and pleads for the settlement of German claims on the free city of Danzig (now Gdańsk).

23 The USSR and Germany sign a nonaggression agreement. Secret protocols provide for the partition of Poland and for the USSR to operate freely in the Baltic states, Finland, and the Romanian province of Bessarabia.

24 The British Parliament passes the Emergency Powers Bill in a single day, enabling the government to maintain public safety and wage war by order in council.

25 Britain and Poland sign a treaty of mutual assistance in London, England.

26–31 The French and British governments negotiate secretly through Birger Dahlerus, a Swedish businessman (and openly through the British ambassador in Berlin, Germany, Sir Arthur Henderson) with the German Führer Adolf Hitler to prevent war in Europe through further territorial concessions to Germany.

30 The evacuation of children from Paris begins as France prepares for war.

31 The Supreme Soviet of the USSR ratifies the nonaggression pact of August 23 with Germany.

SEPTEMBER

- The U.S. president summons Congress into special session in response to the outbreak of war in Europe, and urges repeal of the arms embargo mandated by the 1937 Neutrality Act.

- Thirty Americans perish after the British passenger vessel *Athenia* is sunk by a torpedo from a German U-boat at the start of World War II. The event prompts the U.S. secretary of state Cordell Hull to discourage Americans from traveling abroad.

1 Germany invades Poland and annexes the free city of Danzig (now Gdańsk). Italy declares its neutrality.

3 Britain and France declare war on Germany when it fails to respond to ultimatums following the German invasion of Poland. Australia and New Zealand also declare war on Germany.

3 The British prime minister forms a war cabinet, with Winston Churchill as First Lord of the Admiralty.

4–5 A government motion proposing neutrality in the European war (the early stages of World War II) is defeated in South Africa. The prime minister, J. B. M. Hertzog, resigns. A coalition government is formed by Jan Smuts of the United Party on September 5.

7–10 German forces overrun the Polish territories of Pomerania and Silesia. By September 10, Germany has control in western Poland.

13 The French prime minister Edouard Daladier reforms his government, himself becoming foreign secretary.

14 Japanese troops advance south toward the Chinese port of Changsha, but are repulsed. This ends Japanese expansion in central China until 1944.

17 Invading German forces reach the city of Brest-Litovsk, on the Polish border with the USSR.

17 President Ignacy Mościcki of Poland flees from the German and Soviet invasion to Romania, where he is interned.

17 Red Army troops from the USSR invade Poland from the east, to effect the secretly agreed partition of Poland with Germany.

17 The British aircraft carrier HMS *Courageous* is torpedoed by the German U-boat U 29 southwest of Ireland, with the loss of 514 crew.

19 Britain's Royal Air Force begins to drop propaganda leaflets over Germany.

21 The Romanian prime minister Armand Calinescu is assassinated by the fascist Iron Guard.

27 Poland's capital, Warsaw, surrenders after three days of German bombardment.

28 The USSR signs a mutual aid pact with Estonia. Its terms permit the deployment of Soviet troops there.

29 Most units of the Polish army surrender to Germany and the USSR, who sign a treaty formalizing the partitioning of Poland.

30 Władysław Raczkiewicz succeeds Ignacy Mościcki as president of Poland. General Władysław Sikorski forms a Polish government in exile in Paris, France.

OCTOBER

- The U.S. president Franklin Roosevelt closes U.S. waters to belligerent submarines.

3 The United States declares its neutrality in the European war.

5 The USSR signs a military pact with Latvia, allowing Soviet troops to be stationed there.

6 Peace overtures made by the German Führer Adolf Hitler to Britain and France are summarily rejected.

8 Germany incorporates western Poland into the German Reich.

10 The USSR signs a pact with Lithuania allowing Soviet troops to be stationed on Lithuanian territory (and in effect reducing the Baltic state to a Soviet colony). The city of Vilna (now Vilnius), formerly in Poland but taken by the USSR on September 28, is returned to Lithuania.

14 The German U-boat U 47, captained by Günther Prien, torpedoes the British battleship HMS *Royal Oak* inside the Royal Navy anchorage at Scapa Flow, northern Scotland.

NOVEMBER

- Heeding President Franklin D. Roosevelt's request, the U.S. Congress passes the Neutrality Act of 1939, repealing the 1937 ban on arms exports.

1 Germany formally annexes western Poland into the German Reich.

2 The USSR formally annexes eastern Poland into the Soviet Union.

4 U.S. president Franklin D. Roosevelt signs a bill enabling belligerents in the war in Europe to buy arms in the United States on a "cash and carry" basis, provided that such arms are carried in their own ships. Britain's naval blockade of German trade ensures that only Britain and France are able to take advantage of this provision.

7 King Leopold III of Belgium and Queen Wilhelmina of the Netherlands approach King George VI of Britain to advocate peace with Germany.

8 Two British Secret Service officers are kidnapped by a German SS (*Schutzstaffel*, Nazi elite corps) team operating clandestinely in Venlo, in the Netherlands.

15 Japanese forces invade southern China and capture Nanning, cutting the railroad between Hanoi in Vietnam and Changsha in southeast China.

18 German U-boats lay magnetic mines that sink 60,000 metric tons of shipping off the east coast of England in a single week.

30 The USSR invades Finland, with its main offensive to the north of Lake Ladoga. Finland responds by declaring war on the USSR.

DECEMBER

13–17 The British heavy cruiser *Exeter* and light cruiser *Ajax*, and the New Zealand light cruiser *Achilles* engage the German "pocket battleship" *Graf Spee* in the Battle of the Rio de la Plata (River Plate) in South America. It ends with the scuttling of the German warship off Montevideo, Uruguay.

14 The USSR is expelled from the League of Nations following the outbreak of the Russo-Finnish war.

World War II (1939–45)

1939

SEPTEMBER

1–17 Striking from East Prussia and recently occupied Slovakia, German forces push deep into Poland, smashing the organisation of Polish armies and isolating Warsaw.

3–4 The British and French Empires, a potentially massive combination covering one third of the world's land surface and encompassing one quarter of the world's population, go to war with Germany.

17 The USSR invades Poland from the east, to effect a secretly agreed partition of Poland with Germany.

17–December 17 German U-boats sink the British carrier *Courageous* on September 17, and the battleship *Royal Oak* at anchor in Scapa Flow on October 14, but after a sea chase British cruisers trap the German pocket battleship *Graf Spee* in Montevideo harbour, inducing her captain to scuttle her in the River Plate on December 17.

27–October 5 Surrounded and under heavy bombardment, Warsaw surrenders on September 27, followed eight days later by the last organised Polish army.

NOVEMBER

30–March 12, 1940 The USSR's invasion of Finland meets fierce resistance, but the Soviets eventually gain the upper hand in February 1940 through sheer weight of numbers. Finland is forced to sign an armistice and cede territory north of Leningrad.

1940

APRIL

9 German troops invade Denmark and Norway, occupying major ports and cities in Norway.

10–13 Several naval battles are fought between British and German forces off the port of Narvik in northern Norway; ten German destroyers (from a total of twenty) are sunk. Their loss, added to the loss of three (out of eight) cruisers in the invasion of Norway itself severely weakens the German navy's offensive capability.

MAY

10–14 German forces invade the Netherlands, Belgium, and Luxembourg.

14 The Dutch army surrenders to the invading German forces after a heavy air attack devastates the port of Rotterdam.

23 German forces of Army Group A commanded by General Gerd von Rundstedt pierce the French defenses near Sedan, northeast France, and drive west for the English Channel, dividing the Allied (British and French) forces into two and cutting off the main concentration of British and French armor in Belgium and the Netherlands.

26–June 4 Over 338,000 British, French, and Belgian troops are evacuated from Dunkirk, France, to England by an unprecedented armada of small British boats, following the German encirclement of Allied forces in northeastern France.

28 The Belgian army surrenders to the invading German forces. King Leopold III is taken prisoner.

JUNE

9 A cease-fire in German-occupied Norway is declared at midnight. King Haakon VII flees to Britain.

10 German occupying forces in France cross the River Seine at Rouen. The French government leaves Paris for Bordeaux.

10 Italy declares war on France and Britain.

13 British prime minister Winston Churchill visits the French prime minister Paul Reynaud in Tours, France, to argue that any French effort to secure a separate peace with Germany would contravene the terms of the Anglo-French alliance, and to support France's further appeal to the United States for support.

14 Invading German troops enter Paris.

22 France signs an armistice with Germany and is divided into two zones. The Germans occupy northern and southwestern France, and a so-called autonomous "Vichy" French state is to control the remaining third of the country.

28 Britain recognizes General Charles de Gaulle as leader of the Free French organization of French exiles.

JULY

3 Britain's Royal Navy destroys most of the French fleet at Mers el-Kebir, Algeria, to prevent them being commandeered by the Germans.

10–August 18 Bomber and fighter aircraft of the German *Luftwaffe* (air force) attack shipping convoys in British waters and English ports, in the first phase of the Battle of Britain.

AUGUST

13 The German *Luftwaffe* (air force) makes 1,786 sorties in the Battle of Britain, against 975 by the British Royal Air Force. It is known as "Adler Tag" (Eagle Day), the most intense 24 hours of the Battle of Britain, and marks the beginning of "Adlerangraft" (Eagle War), a two-week attack on RAF Fighter Command's aircraft, airfields, and installations.

23 An all-night German bombing raid on London begins the period of intense bombing known as the "Blitz."

SEPTEMBER

15–16 The Italian 10th Army in Libya, under General Mario Berti, advance into Egypt, reaching the coastal town of Sidi Barrani.

23–25 British and Free French forces fail in an attempt to occupy Dakar, the capital of Senegal, a French territory loyal to Vichy France.

OCTOBER

28 Italy demands the cession of strategic points in Greece but Greece rejects the demands. An Italian invasion from Albania follows.

NOVEMBER

11–12 Twenty-one British Swordfish naval torpedo-bombers from the aircraft carrier HMS *Illustrious* attack and cripple the Italian fleet at Taranto, southeast Italy, severally damaging the battleships *Conte di Cavour*, *Littorio*, and *Caio Duilio*.

14–15 German aircraft bomb Coventry, England, killing 380 people and injuring 865, and destroying the city center, the cathedral, and twelve armaments factories.

DECEMBER

9 Operation "Compass" begins in North Africa. The British Eighth Army under General Sir Archibald Wavell advances from Egypt into Libya, crossing the border on December 15.

1941

JANUARY

- President Roosevelt signals the end to U.S. isolationism, announcing a lend–lease policy to furnish the Allies in World War II with arms and other commodities.

MARCH

24 German and Italian forces commanded by the German general Erwin Rommel take El Algheila in Libya from the British 8th Army, the start of an offensive that will clear British troops from all of Libya apart from the besieged coastal town of Tobruk.

28 The British cruisers *Orion*, *Ajax*, *Gloucester*, and *Perth* intercept an Italian squadron off Cape Matapan, southern Greece. The Italian cruisers *Zara*, *Pola*, and *Fiume* are sunk, and the battleship *Vittorio Veneto* is damaged.

APRIL

5–8 British forces in Italian-controlled Ethiopia take the capital, Addis Ababa, after heavy fighting and, on April 8, the port of Massawa in Eritrea.

6 German, Italian, and Bulgarian forces invade Yugoslavia, and German forces attack the Metaxas Line, Greece's main system of defenses.

21 The Greek army surrenders to the invading German forces; the last British forces are evacuated from mainland Greece on April 28.

MAY

20–30 In Operation *Merkur* (Mercury), German airborne and parachute forces shatter the resistance of the British, Commonwealth, and Greek garrison in Greece, which retreats to the south side of the island and is evacuated to Egypt.

24–27 Attempting to break out into the North Atlantic the German battleship *Bismarck* sinks the British battle cruiser HMS *Hood*, but is herself trapped and sunk by overwhelming British naval forces.

JUNE

22–September 26 In Operation Barbarossa, the largest land offensive yet seen, three million German soldiers strike deep into the unprepared USSR, taking more than four million prisoners in vast encirclements. The last of these encirclements, that of Kiev between August 21 and September 26, produces 665,000 prisoners, the largest number ever taken outside of a general capitulation. In newly occupied areas, SS *Einsatzgruppen* (special action detachments) begin the large-scale extermination of members of the Communist Party and Jews.

JULY

12 Britain and the USSR sign an agreement of mutual aid as part of a general Allied coalition against Germany.

23 Following Japan's demand for military and naval bases in Indochina, Britain and the United States freeze Japanese assets.

AUGUST

25–September 17 Soviet and British forces invade Iran, following the shah's refusal to reduce the number of resident Germans.

OCTOBER

1–December 5 Although exhausted by the advances of the summer, German forces launch Operation Tycoon, the drive on Moscow. The beginning of the autumn rains on October 9, and the early onset of winter in mid November, at times slows the German advance to a crawl, but by December 4 the Germans, although by now suffering severe logistic problems, are in the outer suburbs of the Soviet capital.

31 A series of clashes between neutral American destroyers and German U-boats culminates in the torpedoing of the U.S. destroyer *Reuben James*, which sinks with the loss of 115 of ther crew.

DECEMBER

5–January 5, 1942 Soviet armies of the Northwest, Volkhov, and Kalinin fronts, reinforced by units from Siberia, launch a counteroffensive north and south of Moscow to relieve pressure from the German Army Group Center's advance on the Soviet capital.

7 Japanese naval aircraft make a surprise air attack on the U.S. naval base at Pearl Harbor, Hawaii, destroying or damaging eight battleships, and killing 2,330 personnel. The following day the U.S. Congress, hitherto riven by isolationist sentiment, votes overwhelmingly for war. Two days later, honoring the Axis pact, Germany and Italy declare war on the United States.

8–May 6, 1942 The Japanese conduct a relentless offensive, sinking two British capital ships off the eastern coast of Malaya on December 10, and overrunning Hong Kong on December 24, Maila on January 2, Kuala Lumpur on January 10, Singapore on February 15, Batavia (Djakarta) and Rangoon on March 9, and Mandaly on April 30. On May 6 the last American outpost, the fortress island of Corregidor in Manila Bay, is overrun, by which time the Japanese have defeated a third of a million European, American, and colonial troops, and taken control of a vast area stretching from the borders of India to the Central Pacific.

World War II (1939–45) *continued*

16   German forces of Army Group Center, on the Moscow front, begin to retreat before Marshal Georgy Zhukov's Soviet counterattack.

22–January 14, 1942   At the Arcadia Conference in Washington, D.C., President Roosevelt and Prime Minister Churchill establish a joint Chiefs of Staff committee to plan a war strategy.

26   German forces of Army Group Center retreat from Kaluga, southwest of Moscow, as the Soviet counteroffensive continues.

1942

JANUARY

20   At the Wannsee Conference in Germany, which is chaired by Reinhard Heydrich, head of the Nazi secret police, Nazi officials discuss "the final solution" of "the Jewish question" (in effect, the annihilation of European Jewry).

FEBRUARY

• President Roosevelt issues Executive Order 9066, sanctioning the internment of Japanese-Americans living along the west coast.

APRIL

4   Continuous raids by the German and Italian air forces on the British base of Malta threaten British convoys to Egypt and hamper Allied attempts to disrupt Axis convoy routes to Libya.

18   A U.S. strike force of 16 B-25 bombers under Brig. Gen. James Doolittle bomb Tokyo, Yokohama, and other Japanese cities.

18–July 29   German forces of Army Group South advance into eastern Ukraine, aiming to capture the oil fields in the Caucasus.

23–30   In the Baedeker raids, named for the German tourist guidebooks, German aircraft bomb Exeter, Bath, and other historic cities in Britain in reprisal for British raids on Cologne and Lübeck.

MAY

May–November 1943   Japan constructs the Kwai Railroad between Bangkok in Siam (modern Thailand) and Moulmein in Burma (now Myanmar). Over 15,000 Allied prisoners of war and 90,000 native laborers die during its construction.

4–8   U.S. naval forces narrowly succeed in preventing a Japanese attempt to take the Allied base at Port Moresby, Papua, in the first great carrier battle of the Pacific War, the Battle of the Coral Sea.

5   British troops successfully invade the Vichy French territory of Madagascar.

27–July 4   German and Italian forces under Erwin Rommel outflank the British at Gazala, Libya, take the important port of Tobruk on June 21, and are only brought to a halt at El Alamein.

30–31   The first British "thousand bomber" raid is launched against the city of Cologne, Germany.

JUNE

3–6   U.S. carrier planes sink the Japanese aircraft carriers *Hiryu*, *Soryu*, *Kaga*, and *Akagi* for the loss of the U.S. carrier *Yorktown* in the Battle of Midway, off Midway Island in the Pacific. The naval balance in the Pacific war swings in favor of the Allies.

10   The German Gestapo (secret police) destroys the village of Lidiče, Czechoslovakia, in reprisal for the killing of Reinhard Heydrich, the Nazi "protector" of Bohemia and Moravia, by Czech resistance fighters; 198 men are shot, 184 women sent to the Ravensbrück concentration camp, and 98 children deported.

JULY

1   "Ash Wednesday" in Cairo, so called because of the dense clouds of burning paper which float above the city as British headquarter's units, expecting Rommel's imminent arrival, burn their documents.

28   Units of the German Army Group South retake the Soviet port of Rostov-on-Don. The newly-organized Army Group A overruns the northern Caucasus, reaching Grozny and Ordzhonikidze by November.

AUGUST

19   Canadian and British forces raid the port of Dieppe in northeast France. The operation is a disaster, and casualties include 3,367 Canadians killed, wounded, or taken prisoner.

30   Rommel launches his final attempt to break the British 8th Army's Alamein line and take Egypt, leading to the Battle of Alam Halfa. The 8th Army, superior in armor, halts the German advance by September 2.

SEPTEMBER

13–February 2, 1943   The German 6th Army under General Paulus fights its way into the city of Stalingrad (now Volgograd) on the Volga but becomes bogged down in house-to-house fighting against tenacious Soviet resistance. On November 19, Soviet forces launch counterattacks to the west of Stalingrad, which four days later successfully encircle Paulus's forces. The failure of a breakthrough attempt by forces under Erich von Manstein on December 12, and the inability of the *Luftwaffe* to deliver sufficient supplies by air, dooms the garrison to lingering starvation in freezing termperatures. The last German forces, some 40,000 in the north of the city, surrender on February 2, bringing total German casualties to 160,000 dead and wounded, and 107,000 prisoners.

OCTOBER

23–February 4, 1943   In a grinding 12-day battle (October 23–November 4), the British 8th Army under General Bernard Montgomery breaks through Erwin Rommel's German and Italian forces at El Alamein, and in an unrelenting pursuit of the retreating Axis army, reaches the Tunisian border, 1,500 miles to the west, on February 4, 1943.

24–26 Two U.S. aircraft carrier task forces engage the Japanese South Seas fleet under Vice-Admiral Nobutaki Kondo off the Santa Cruz Islands, near Guadalcanal. The Japanese aircraft carriers *Zuiho* and *Shokaku* are damaged, but the U.S. carrier *Hornet* is sunk, leaving the damaged *Enterprise* the only operational Allied aircraft carrier in the Pacific.

NOVEMBER

8 British and U.S. forces land in Vichy French-held Morocco and Algeria (Operation "Torch"), and advance swiftly toward Tunisia.

11 Hitler orders the German occupation of Vichy France.

1943

FEBRUARY

8 Soviet troops recapture the city of Kursk, USSR, from German forces in a general advance after the German defeat at Stalingrad.

9 Organized Japanese resistance to U.S. forces on the island of Guadalcanal comes to an end.

14–May 7 Despite a brilliant counterattack at the Kasserine Pass against American forces advancing into Tunisia from the west, Rommel's army is pushed out of the Mareth Line on the Tunisian-Libyan frontier by a British 8th Army attack on March 28, and is penned up in Tunis and Bizerta, where its last elements surrender on May 7.

14–April 24 British and Gurkha troops under Brigadier Orde Wingate (the "Chindits") leave the city of Imphal in India on a sabotage mission in Burma behind Japanese lines.

25 Following a decision made at the Casablanca Conference, British and U.S. military aircraft begin round-the-clock bombing of Germany.

MARCH

15 A German counterattack masterminded by General Erich von Manstein throws back the Soviet advance into the Don basin; General Paul Hauser's SS Panzer Corps recaptures the city of Kharkov.

MAY

11 A U.S. force retakes the island of Attu in the Aleutian Islands, off Alaska, from the Japanese.

16 British bombers attack three dams in the Ruhr industrial region of Germany in Operation Chastise, using the rotating bouncing bombs designed by the British aeronautical engineer Barnes Wallis. Two dams are breached.

JULY

1–November 25 U.S. troops recapture islands in the Solomon Islands from the Japanese in Phase One of Operation Cartwheel.

5 German forces of Army Group Center and Army Group South mount their last major offensive on the Eastern Front against well-prepared Soviet positions north and

south of a huge salient around Kursk, USSR. It is the largest tank battle in history, and fatally weakens German forces on the Eastern Front.

10 U.S. and British forces land in German-occupied Sicily, beginning the Allied liberation of western Europe.

25–September 15 Following secret negotiations with the Allies, King Victor Emmanuel III of Italy dismisses Benito Mussolini and has him imprisoned in a hotel on top of Gran Sasso, a 6,000-foot-high mountain peak, on July 25. German commandos, landing gliders on the hotel's tennis court, rescue Mussolini on September 12, and fly him to Salò on Lake Garda, where he establishes a new Facist regime (September 15).

AUGUST

14–24 At the Quadrant Conference of Allied leaders in Quebec, Canada, Roosevelt and Churchill agree a plan to defeat Germany before Japan and to aim for an invasion of France in May 1944.

SEPTEMBER

3 Allied forces land in mainland Italy; an armistice is signed between the Allies and the Italian government of Marshal Pietro Badoglio on the same day.

NOVEMBER

November–March, 1944 The British Royal Air Force mount a series of 16 heavy night raids on Berlin in the "Battle of Berlin." They cause heavy damage, but nearly 600 bombers are lost.

20 U.S. Army and Marine forces land on the Japanese-held Tarawa atoll, in the Gilbert archipelago in the Pacific. Amtracs (Amphibious Landing Vehicles, Tracked) are used for the first time directly in the assault, rather than for resupply, but U.S. casualties are severe in taking the island.

DECEMBER

24–May 5, 1944 The Soviet army, having recaptured two-thirds of the Soviet territory occupied by the Germans, launches an offensive in Ukraine.

1944

JANUARY

14 Soviet forces launch an offensive aimed at breaking the German siege of the city of Leningrad (now St. Petersburg).

22 U.S. and British troops land at Anzio, southeast of Rome, Italy, in an attempt to outflank the German Gustav Line. The beachhead is quickly sealed off by German forces.

24–May 18 After many failed British, Free French, and American attempts to break the German Gustav Line at Monte Cassino in Italy, a Polish division finally succeeds on May 18. This allows Allied forces in the Anzio bridgehead to break out.

World War II (1939–45) *continued*

27 Soviet forces clear German troops from the Leningrad–Moscow railroad line, ending the German siege of Leningrad after 900 days and over 1 million civilian deaths from starvation and enemy action.

FEBRUARY

20–27 During "Big Week," a combined U.S.–British air assault on German aircraft-making capability, 18,874 metric tons/20,799 tons of bombs are dropped on selected targets in Germany.

MARCH

6 U.S. bombers begin daylight air attacks on Berlin; the attacks are made possible by equipping the U.S. P-51 "Mustang" fighters with long-range capabilities as an escort for the bombers.

29–June 22 Japanese troops under Lt. Gen. Renyu Mutaguchi invade India from Burma (now Myanmar) and besiege the city of Imphal in Assam, held by Allied forces under General William Slim.

JUNE

4 The U.S. 5th Army under General Mark Clark enters Rome.

6–August 21 In Operation Overlord, the largest amphibious operation in history, 4,000 ships and 1,000 transport aircraft and gliders land seven Allied divisions on the coast of Normandy in northwestern France, in the face of determined German opposition. Although the landing and the build-up are successful, with the British establishing artificial harbors (Mulberries) and the Americans capturing Cherbourg on June 27, the difficult terrain and the skill of the German defenders delay an Allied breakout until August 1. General George Patton's American 3rd Army swings south east and then north, trapping more than 50,000 German defenders in an enormous pocket around Falaise, on August 21.

10 In a reprisal against Resistance attacks, German SS troops in the village of Oradour-sur-Glane, south-central France, herd men into barns and women and children into the church and burn all the buildings, killing 642 civilians.

13 Germany launches the first V1 (*Vergeltungswaffen*, "retribution weapon") pilotless flying-bombs from mainland Europe against London, in retaliation against Allied bombing of German cities.

15–July 9 U.S. forces capture the island of Saipan in the Mariana Islands from the Japanese.

22–July 28 In Operation Bagration, the largest Soviet offensive to date, Soviet army groups strike into the southern and northern flanks of German Army Group Centre, and, meeting at Minsk on July 3, encircle more than a half-million Axis soldiers. Soviet forces reach Brest-Litovsk on the 1939 Soviet-German frontier on July 28.

JULY

20 An abortive assassination attempt is made on Hitler in his Rastenburg headquarters. The planter of the bomb, Count Claus von Stauffenberg, is shot the same evening.

AUGUST

1–October 2 Polish resistance forces in Warsaw under General Tadeusz Bór-Komorowski (commander in chief of the Polish Home Army) rebel against the German occupation, but Soviet forces outside the city fail to assist them and the Soviet government bans the use of airfields to fly in supplies from the west.

14 In Operation Anvil, later renamed Dragoon, Allied forces land on the south French coast between the ports of Toulon and Cannes and push 32 km/20 mi inland on the first day, against weak German opposition.

24 U.S. units enter Paris following the liberation of the city from German occupation, and a French unit is allowed to lead the procession into the city the following day.

SEPTEMBER

3 British troops enter Brussels, the Belgian capital.

8 The first German V2 (*Vergeltungswaffen*, "retribution weapon") rocket is fired, against London.

11–16 At the Octagon Conference in Quebec, President Roosevelt and Prime Minister Churchill approve plans for the Allied advance into Germany, the establishment of occupation zones after Germany's defeat in World War II, and the deindustrialization of Germany as proposed by the Morgenthau Plan.

17–28 In Operation Market Garden in the Netherlands, U.S. airborne troops land at Eindhoven and Nijmegen to seize bridges over the rivers Maas, Waal, and Rhine (Market), while British troops land at Arnhem on the Rhine to open a route to the Ruhr region in Germany (Garden). The landing at Arnhem is a disaster.

25 Hitler calls up all remaining males between 16 and 60 in Germany for service in the *Volkssturm*, a home defense force, to defend Germany against Allied invasion.

OCTOBER

14 Rommel chooses to commit suicide rather than face a court martial and ignominy for his family following disclosure of his implication in the bomb plot of July 20 against Hitler.

20–December 31 American forces under General Douglas MacArthur land on the island of Leyte in the Philippines, fulfilling the general's promise "I shall return", made when he was forced to leave the islands early in 1942. In the Battle of Leyte Gulf, the largest naval battle ever fought, three Japanese task forces attempt to destroy the landing force, but are virtually annihilated (October 24–25). American ground forces advance against fanatical opposition and the island is not secured until the end of the year.

30–February 13, 1945 Armies of the Soviet 2nd and 3rd Ukrainian fronts besiege Budapest, but the German defenders maintain their hold on the city.

NOVEMBER

24 B-29 bombers from the airbase on the island of Saipan in the Pacific make the first U.S. raid on Tokyo since the Doolittle raid of April 1942.

DECEMBER

18–January 12, 1945 In the Battle of the Bulge, 27 German divisions launch a massive blow through the heavily wooded Ardennes, intending to cross the Meuse, swing north, and split the American and British fronts. Advancing more than 40 miles, the Germans are stopped just short of the Meuse, in part because of their failure to take a vital road junction at Bastogne. Beginning on December 26, American counterattacks push the Germans back to their start lines, and complete this on January 12.

1945

JANUARY

9 U.S. forces land on the shores of the Lingayen Gulf on the island of Luzon in the Philippines.

12–February 2 In the Vistula–Oder Operation, two Soviet army groups clear Poland of German forces, Soviet advance guards reaching the Oder only 70 miles from Berlin at the end of January, and are prevented from advancing further only by a sudden thaw on February 2, which turns Poland into a quagmire and sends the Oder into spate.

20 The garrison of German troops in Budapest surrender to the besieging armies of the Soviet 2nd and 3rd Ukrainian fronts.

22 The Burma Road is reopened by the Allies for the supply of munitions to China.

27 Soviet forces reach the Auschwitz (Oświęcim) concentration camp in Poland.

FEBRUARY

3–March 3 U.S. forces begin their liberation of Japanese-occupied Manila, which results in the destruction of the city and 100,000 civilian casualties.

4–11 At the Yalta Conference in the Crimea, Roosevelt, Churchill, and Stalin plan for the division of postwar Germany into four occupied zones, with four zones in Berlin.

8–March 21 Operation Veritable opens the Allies' Rhineland campaign. Canadian and British forces begin a drive south from Nijmegen in the Netherlands to capture land between the Rhine and Maas rivers and so clear German troops from the west bank of the Upper Rhine.

13–15 British and U.S. aircraft bomb the city of Dresden in eastern Germany, ostensibly to disrupt the transfer of German troops to the Soviet front. Over 60,000 people are killed, and the city's historic center is destroyed.

19–March 24 U.S. marines capture the Japanese island of Iwo Jima after fierce fighting, which results in over 21,000 U.S. casualties.

MARCH

7–25 Moving up the Rhine, U.S. troops manage to capture the Ludendorff railroad bridge at Remagen, south of the city of Bonn. The main crossings take place on March 22–23, U.S. forces crossing at Oppenheim, and British and Canadian forces crossing at Rees and Wesel. On March 25, U.S. forces break out of their bridgeheads south of the Ruhr.

20 British and Indian troops recapture Mandalay in Burma (now Myanmar) from the occupying Japanese forces.

APRIL

1–June 22 U.S. forces capture Okinawa, the largest of the Japanese Ryukyu Islands. There are 49,151 U.S. and 110,000 Japanese casualties.

5 The USSR denounces its neutrality pact with Japan of April 13, 1941.

9 An Allied offensive across northern Italy begins, under the British field marshal Harold Alexander.

10 U.S. troops take the city of Hanover, but German forces resist an attack on Bremen.

11 U.S. troops in Germany reach the River Elbe near Wittenberge, northwest of Berlin.

13 Vienna falls to Soviet troops.

16 Soviet forces in Germany launch an offensive from their bridgehead on the River Oder toward Berlin.

25 U.S. and Soviet troops in Germany link up at Torgau on the River Elbe, cutting Germany in half.

29 German forces in Italy surrender to the Allies.

30 With Soviet troops only a few streets away, Adolf Hitler and Eva Braun retire to the Führer's study deep in the command bunker in Berlin and commit suicide. Two days later the remnants of German forces in Berlin surrender.

MAY

2 British forces in Germany reach the port of Lübeck, southeast of the Jutland peninsula, aiming to prevent the Soviet occupation of Denmark.

3 British and Indian forces capture Rangoon in Burma (now Myanmar) from the occupying Japanese forces.

4 All German forces under arms in northwest Germany surrender to Allied forces under Field Marshal Sir Bernard Montgomery.

8 General Alfred Jodl signs the official surrender of Germany in World War II in Reims, France, at 2:41 a.m., in the presence of U.S. general Dwight D. Eisenhower and other Allied officers. May 8 is celebrated as V.E. (Victory in Europe) Day in western Europe and the United States.

JULY

16 The first atomic explosion occurs when the nuclear device code-named "Trinity" is exploded near Alamogordo, New Mexico.

AUGUST

6 The U.S. B-29 bomber *Enola Gay* drops an atomic bomb on Hiroshima, Japan, destroying two-thirds of the city.

8 The USSR declares war on Japan and invades Japanese-occupied Manchuria, China.

9 The U.S. B-29 bomber *Bock's Car* drops an atomic bomb on Nagasaki, Japan, destroying half the city.

12 Soviet forces occupy Japanese-held northern Korea, the island of Sakhalin, and the Kuril Islands.

14 The Japanese emperor Hirohito proclaims Japan's acceptance of the Allies' terms for ending World War II in the Pacific and urges his people to accept the surrender.

SEPTEMBER

2 Japan signs its capitulation on board the U.S.S. *Missouri*, marking the end of World War II.

28 Meat rationing is introduced in Britain as part of the war effort; rationing of butter and sugar follow on January 8, 1940.

SCIENCE, TECHNOLOGY, AND MEDICINE

Agriculture

- U.S. crops are plagued by the Japanese beetle (*Popillia japonica*), which was introduced into the United States about 1916.

Ecology

- Major earthquakes in Chile kill thousands of people.
- The northern provinces of China are hit by floods which kill 200,000 people.

JANUARY

24 Approximately 30,000 people die in an earthquake in Concepción, Chile; it measures 8.3 on the Richter scale.

DECEMBER

27 Erzincan, Turkey is hit by an earthquake measuring 7.9 on the Richter scale. The city is leveled and nearly 50,000 people are killed.

Health and Medicine

- A rabies epidemic among bats, foxes, dogs, cows, and other mammals breaks out in Poland and spreads across Europe at about 40 km/25 mi per year.
- German chemist Gerhard Domagk receives the Nobel Prize for Physiology or Medicine for his work on Prontosil's antibacterial effect.
- German physician F. H. Müller first links smoking with lung cancer, in a study entitled *Tabakmissbrauch und Lungencarcinom/Tobacco Abuse and Lung Cancer*.
- Sulfathiazole, the third sulfa drug, is created. It is the most widely used sulfa drug in the fight against bacteria until the discovery of penicillin.
- U.S. microbiologist René J. Dubos is the first to search systematically for, and discover, natural antibiotics. He looks for soil bacteria that kill other bacteria and discovers the antibiotics gramicidin and tyrocidine.

Science

- French physicist Marguerite Perey discovers the alkali metal francium (atomic no. 87).
- French physicists Frédéric Joliot and Irène Curie-Joliot demonstrate the possibility of a chain reaction when they split uranium nuclei.
- German biochemist Adolf Butenandt shares the Nobel Prize for Chemistry with Swiss chemist Leopold Ruzicka, Butenandt for his work on sexual hormones and Ruzicka for his work on polymethelenes; Butenandt declines the prize.

- German physicists Hans Bethe and Carl von Weizsäcker propose that nuclear fusion of hydrogen is the source of a star's energy.
- Powder metallurgy, the manufacture of metal objects from powder rather than molten metal, is introduced.
- U.S. anthropologist Margaret Mead publishes *From the South Seas: Studies in Adolescence and Sexuality in Primitive Societies*.
- U.S. biochemist Edward Adelbert Doisy analyzes the structure of vitamin K and synthesizes it.
- U.S. chemist Linus Pauling consolidates his theory of the chemical bond in *The Nature of the Chemical Bond, and the Structure of Molecules and Crystals*.
- U.S. geophysicist Walter Maurice Elsasser formulates the "dynamo model" of the earth, which proposes that eddy currents in the earth's molten iron core cause its magnetism.

Technology

- Eastman Kodak in Rochester, New York, produces the first camera with synchronized flash for amateur use.
- Polyethylene becomes commercially available and is first used in radar equipment.
- The New York banker Oliver Sachs hands the U.S. president, Franklin D. Roosevelt, a letter from the physicist-émigrés Albert Einstein and Leo Szilard, warning that Germany possesses nuclear fission capability and urging the administration to undertake the creation of an atomic bomb. Roosevelt sets up an Advisory Committee on Uranium that leads to the establishment of the Manhattan Project (1942).
- The orthicon camera tube is developed in the United States; it produces better pictures than the iconoscope tube and is capable of responding to very low light levels, making it suitable for studio productions.
- The Parker Dam on the Colorado River, 249 km/155 mi downstream from Boulder Dam, is completed. It is an integral part of the Colorado River Aqueduct System that taps a billion gallons of water from the river each day, lifts it nearly 400 m/1,300 ft, and transports it across the desert to Los Angeles, California.
- The T-34 tank is developed by Soviet armaments designers Mikhail Koshkin, Alexander Morozov, and Nikolai Kucherenko; it goes into production in 1941. Fast, well-armored, and with a 76 mm gun, it becomes one of the decisive weapons of World War II.
- U.S. inventor Edwin Armstrong constructs the first FM radio transmitter station.
- U.S. physicist Ernest Lawrence receives the Nobel Prize for Physics for inventing the cyclotron.

c. 1939–*c.* 1945 Germany begins experimenting with launching rockets from submarines.

APRIL

- The pressure cooker, introduced at the World's Fair by National Presto Industries, drastically reduces cooking times.
- U.S. physicists Georges Stibitz and Samuel B. Williams of Bell Laboratories build a computer consisting of over 400 relays connected to teletype machine for input and output of data, thus introducing the idea of operating a

computer via a terminal. Called a Complex Number Calculator, it is demonstrated on January 8, 1940.

Transportation

- A streamlined diesel train achieves 212.8 kph/133.6 mph between Hamburg and Berlin, Germany.
- Air services operate regularly between France, Germany, and Italy, and Africa and South America.
- Bullet-proof windshields and armor plating, to protect the pilot from behind, become standard on new fighter aircraft.
- German pilot Ewald Rohlfs sets an altitude record of 3,565 m/11,700 ft in a Foch-Achgelis helicopter.
- Small refrigerators are installed in the ventilation systems of some cars to provide air conditioning.
- Soviet aircraft designer Sergey Vladimirovich Ilyushin designs the Il-2 Stormovik armored ground-attack aircraft. Mass production begins in March 1941.
- The Messerschmitt Me 109 fighter aircraft sets a world speed record of 774 kph/481 mph in Germany.

April 1939–40   Variable-pitch propellers are installed in the UK on Royal Air Force (RAF) Hurricane and Spitfire fighters, improving takeoff and cruising.

c. 1939–c. 1945   In Japan, I-400 class submarines are built. Over 122 m/400 ft long and with a hangar that can accommodate three float planes, they are the largest conventional powered submarines ever built.

JANUARY

- The Trans-Iranian Railroad opens; it links the Caspian Sea to the Persian Gulf.

MAY

20 Pan-American Airways begin regular commercial flights between the United States and Europe.

JUNE

28 Pan-American Airways' *Yankee Clipper* flies from Port Washington, New York, to Marseille, France, inaugurating the first commercial transatlantic air passenger service.

AUGUST

27 The Heinkel He 178 makes a test flight in Germany, achieving a speed of 500 kph/360 mph; it is the first jet airplane to fly.

SEPTEMBER

14 The first effective helicopter, the VS-300, designed by Ukranian-born U.S. engineer Igor Sikorsky, makes its first test flight.

ARTS AND IDEAS

Architecture

- The Factory and Workers' Housing in Sumila, Finland, designed by the Finnish architect Alvar Aalto, is completed.
- The Rockefeller Center in New York, New York, designed by U.S. architectural firm Reinhard and

Hofmeister (with help from the U.S. architects Harvey Wiley Corbett and Raymond Hood), is completed.
- The U.S. architect Frank Lloyd Wright publishes *The Architecture of Democracy*.
- Two major designs by the U.S. architect Frank Lloyd Wright are completed in the United States: the Kaufman House, "Falling Water," in Bear Run, Pennsylvania; and the Johnson Wax Factory (with umbrella columns), in Racine, Wisconsin.

Arts

c. 1939   The English artist Leonora Carrington paints her *Portrait of Max Ernst*.

- The Belgian artist René Magritte paints *Train Transfixed*.
- The English artist Graham Sutherland paints *Entrance to a Lane*.
- The English writer and artist Percy Wyndham Lewis paints *Portrait of Ezra Pound*.
- The Mexican artist David Siqueiros paints the mural *Portrait of the Bourgeoisie* in the Electricians Union Headquarters in Mexico City, Mexico.
- The Mexican artist Frida Kahlo paints *The Two Fridas* and *The Dream*.
- The Solomon R. Guggenheim Foundation Museum of Non-Objective Painting opens in New York, New York.
- The Spanish artist Pablo Picasso paints *Night Fishing at Antibes* and *Cat Devouring a Bird*.
- The Swiss artist Paul Klee paints *La Belle Jardinière/The Beautiful Gardener*.
- The U.S. artist Ben Shahn paints *Hard Ball*.
- The U.S. artist John Sloan paints the mural *The First Mail Arrives at Bronxville, 1846* for the Bronxville Post Office in New York.
- The U.S. artist Joseph Stella paints *Brooklyn Bridge*.
- The U.S. artist Marsden Hartley paints *Sustained Comedy – Portrait of an Object*.
- The U.S. artist Reginald Marsh paints *Ten Shots, Ten Cents*.
- The U.S. naive artist "Grandma Moses" becomes famous overnight from the "Unknown American Painters" Exhibition at the Museum of Modern Art in New York, New York.
- U.S. photographer Dorothea Lange and the U.S. economist Paul Taylor publish *An American Exodus: A Record of the Human Erosion*, a survey of poverty in California during the Depression. It contains one of Lange's best-known images, *Migrant Mother*.

Film

- As the threat of war increases, the French authorities tighten up the censorship of movies, radio programs, and printed materials.
- Following Goebbels's effectual nationalization of the German movie industry, state-controlled movie companies are responsible for around 60% of movie production.
- The 1938 Academy Awards take place. Best Actor: Spencer Tracy, for *Boys Town*; Best Supporting Actor: Walter Brennan, for *Kentucky*; Best Actress: Bette Davis, for *Jezebel*; Best Supporting Actress: Fay Bainter, for

Jezebel; Best Picture: *You Can't Take It With You*, directed by Frank Capra; Best Director: Frank Capra, for *You Can't Take It With You.*

- The classic Western *Stagecoach*, directed by John Ford, is released in the United States, starring John Wayne, Claire Trevor, Thomas Mitchell, and George Bancroft. Ford's movie *Young Mr Lincoln*, starring Henry Fonda, is also released in the United States.
- The movie *Derrière la façade/Behind the Façade*, directed by Yves Mirade and Georges Lacombe, is released in France, starring Lucien Baroux, Jacques Baumer, and Jules Berry.
- The movie *Gone With the Wind*, directed by Victor Fleming (with George Cukor and Sam Wood), is released in the United States, premiering in Atlanta, Georgia. Based on the novel by Margaret Mitchell, it stars Vivien Leigh and Clark Gable. One of the most commercially successful movies of all time, it is 222 minutes long and wins eight Academy Awards.
- The movie *Goodbye Mr Chips*, directed by Sam Wood, is released in the United States. Based on the book by James Hilton, it stars Robert Donat and Greer Garson.
- The movie *Jamaica Inn*, directed by Alfred Hitchcock, is released in the UK. Based on the novel by Daphne du Maurier, and starring Charles Laughton and Maureen O'Hara, it is Hitchcock's last movie in Britain until *Frenzy* in 1972.
- The movie *La Règle du jeu/The Rules of the Game*, directed by Jean Renoir, is released in France, starring Marcel Dalio, Nora Gregor, Jean Renoir, Mila Parély, Julien Carette, Gaston Modot, and Roland Toutain.
- The movie *Le Jour se lève/Daybreak*, directed by Marcel Carné, is released in France, starring Jean Gabin.
- The movie *Mr Smith Goes to Washington*, directed by Frank Capra, is released in the United States, starring James Stewart, Claude Rains, Jean Arthur, Thomas Mitchell, and Edward Arnold.
- The movie *Nintotchka*, directed by German filmmaker Ernst Lubitsch, is released in the United States, starring Greta Garbo. A musical remake, *Silk Stockings*, directed by Rouben Mamoulian and starring Fred Astaire and Cyd Charisse, is released in the United States in 1957.
- The movie *Only Angels Have Wings*, directed by Howard Hawks, is released in the United States, starring Cary Grant and Jean Arthur.
- The movie *The Hunchback of Notre Dame*, directed by German filmmaker William Dieterle, is released in the United States. Based on the novel by Victor Hugo, it stars Charles Laughton, Cedric Hardwicke, and Maureen O'Hara.
- The movie *The Roaring Twenties* is released in the United States. It is directed by Raoul Walsh and Anatole Litvak, and stars James Cagney, Humphrey Bogart, and Priscilla Lane.
- The movie *The Stars Look Down*, adapted from the novel by A. J. Cronin, is released in the UK. It is directed by Carol Reed and stars Michael Redgrave and Margaret Lockwood.
- The movie *Wuthering Heights*, directed by William Wyler, is released in the United States. Based on the novel by Emily Brontë, it stars Laurence Olivier and Merle Oberon.
- The movie musical *The Wizard of Oz*, directed by Victor Fleming and King Vidor, is released in the United

States. Based on the novel by Frank L. Baum, it stars Judy Garland, Frank Morgan, Ray Bolger, Jack Haley, Bert Lahr, and Margaret Hamilton.
- The movies *The Hound of the Baskervilles*, directed by Sidney Lanfield, and *The Adventures of Sherlock Holmes*, directed by Alfred Weker, are released in the United States. Both star Basil Rathbone as the English detective Holmes, with Nigel Bruce as his sidekick Dr. Watson.
- The propaganda movie *Lion Has Wings*, directed by Michael Powell with Brian Desmond-Hurst and Adrian Brunel, is released in Britain. The movie employs a "docudrama" technique and exemplifies the British movie industry's efforts to support the government's war effort.
- There are 2,012 movies produced world-wide; 483 of these are produced in the United States.

September 1939–44 The Committee for the Liberation of the Cinema is active in France in anti-Nazi resistance throughout the war.

Literature and Language

- *These Are Our Lives*, a collection of autobiographies produced under the auspices of the Works Progress Administration, is published in the United States.
- Living in Paris, France, the U.S. writer Henry Miller publishes his novel *Tropic of Capricorn* in France. Considered obscene, it is not published in the United States until 1961.
- The Belgian writer Marguerite Yourcenar publishes her novel *Le Coup de grâce*.
- The English crime writer Eric Ambler publishes his novel *The Mask of Dimitrios*.
- The English novelist Joyce Cary publishes his novel *Mister Johnson*.
- The English novelist C. S. Forester publishes his adventure novel *Captain Hornblower RN*.
- The English novelist T. H. White publishes his Arthurian fantasy *The Sword in the Stone*.
- The English writer Agatha Christie publishes her crime novel *Ten Little Niggers*.
- The English writer Christopher Isherwood publishes his novel *Goodbye to Berlin*.
- The English writer Flora Thompson publishes *Lark Rise*, the first of three popular books in which she depicts life in an English village.
- The English writer Graham Greene publishes his espionage "entertainment," *The Confidential Agent*.
- The English writer Geoffrey Household publishes his adventure novel *Rogue Male*.
- The English writer Patrick Hamilton publishes *Hangover Square*.
- The English writer P. G. Wodehouse publishes his comic novel *The Code of the Woosters*.
- The English writer Rumer Godden publishes her novel *Black Narcissus*. A melodrama set in a convent in the Himalayas, it becomes a best seller.
- The French writer André Gide publishes his *Journal 1885–1939*.
- The German writer Ernst Jünger publishes his novel *Auf den Marmorklippen/On the Marble Cliffs*.

- The German writer Thomas Mann publishes his novel *Lotte in Weimar*.
- The Irish dramatist Sean O'Casey publishes *I Knock at the Door*, the first volume of his autobiography.
- The Irish writer Flann O'Brien publishes his novel *At Swim-Two-Birds*.
- The Irish writer James Joyce publishes the final version of his novel *Finnegan's Wake* (parts had appeared as early as 1928).
- The Nobel Prize for Literature is awarded to the Finnish novelist Frans Eemil Sillanpää.
- The Pulitzer Prize for Biography is awarded to Carl Van Doren for *Benjamin Franklin*, the Pulitzer Prize for Fiction is awarded to Marjorie K. Rawlings for *The Yearling*, and the Prize for Poetry is awarded to John Gould Fletcher for *Selected Poems*.
- The Russian-born French writer Nathalie Sarraute publishes her experimental work of fiction *Tropismes/Tropisms*.
- The unfinished novel *The Web and the Rock* by the U.S. writer Thomas Wolfe is published posthumously.
- The U.S. crime writer Raymond Chandler publishes his classic novel *The Big Sleep*, the first of his novels to feature his detective Philip Marlowe.
- The U.S. humorist James Thurber publishes his story "The Secret Life of Walter Mitty" in *New Yorker* magazine. In 1942 it is published in the collection *My World – And Welcome to It*.
- The U.S. semanticist Samuel Ichiye Hayakawa publishes *Language in Action*.
- The U.S. writer and humorist Dorothy Parker publishes *Here Lies*, a collection of short stories.
- The U.S. writer Carl Sandburg publishes the last volume of his six-volume biography *Abraham Lincoln*, the first volume of which appeared in 1926.
- The U.S. writer James Agee and the U.S. photographer Walker Evans publish *Let Us Now Praise Famous Men*, a vivid depiction in words and images of the hardships endured in the southern states during the Depression.
- The U.S. writer John Steinbeck publishes his novel *The Grapes of Wrath*, a vivid account of the Depression in California.
- The U.S.-born English writer T. S. Eliot publishes *Old Possum's Book of Practical Cats*, a collection of humorous verse for children.
- The Welsh novelist Richard Llewellyn publishes his novel *How Green Was My Valley*, a story of a Welsh mining community. In 1940 it is the best-selling novel of the year in the United States.

Music

- Americans buy 45 million "popular" music records and 5 million "classical" records.
- The Austrian composer Arnold Schoenberg completes his revisions of his Chamber Symphony No. 2.
- The black American singer Marian Anderson sings at the Lincoln Memorial (invited by President Roosevelt) after the Daughters of the American Revolution refused to permit a concert booking for her at their Constitution Hall in Washington, D.C. Anderson is also the first black singer to sing at the New York Metropolitan Opera House (1955).

- The English composer William Walton completes his Violin Concerto.
- The English composer Elisabeth Lutyens completes her orchestral work *Three Pieces*.
- The English musicologist Donald Tovey publishes the last volume of his six-volume *Essays in Musical Analysis*. The first volume appeared in 1935.
- The Hungarian composer Béla Bartók completes his String Quartet No. 6.
- The Hungarian composer Zoltán Kodály completes his orchestral work *Variations on a Hungarian Folk Song, the Peacock*.
- The Russian composer Dmitry Shostakovich completes his Symphony No. 6.
- The Russian composer Sergey Prokofiev completes his *Seven Songs*, Opus 79, and his score for the opera *The Duenna (Betrothal in a Monastery)*.
- The Spanish composer Joaquín Rodrigo completes his *Concierto de Aranjuez* for guitar and orchestra.

Theater and Dance

- The German writer Bertolt Brecht completes his play *Leben des Galilei/The Life of Galileo*. It will first be performed in 1943, in Zürich, Switzerland.
- The play *The Little Foxes*, by the U.S. dramatist Lillian Hellman, is first performed, at the National Theater in New York, New York.
- The play *The Philadelphia Story*, by the U.S. writer Philip Barry, is first performed, at the Shubert Theater in New York, New York.
- The Pulitzer Prize for Drama is awarded to Robert Sherwood for *Abe Lincoln in Illinois*.
- The verse play *The Family Reunion*, by the U.S.-born English writer T. S. Eliot, is first performed, in London, England.

Thought and Scholarship

- *Erfahrung und Urteil/Experience and Judgment* by the German philosopher Edmund Husserl is published posthumously.
- English historian Edward Hallett Carr publishes *The Twenty Years' Crisis*.
- English political philosopher Michael Oakeshott publishes *The Social and Political Doctrines of Contemporary Europe*.
- French historian Marc Bloch publishes *La Société féodale/Feudal Society*.
- French writer Antoine Marie Roger de St.-Exupéry publishes *Terre des hommes/Wind, Sand and Stars*, a series of reflections of life.
- Latvian-born English philosopher Isaiah Berlin publishes *Karl Marx*.
- The Pontifical Institute of Medieval Studies in Toronto, Canada, publishes *Mediaeval Studies*.
- The Pulitzer Prize for History is awarded to Frank Luther Mott for *A History of American Magazines*.
- The revivalist Oxford Group, set up in England by the U.S. evangelist Frank Buchman, takes the name "Moral Rearmament."
- U.S. historian R. R. Palmer publishes *Catholics and Unbelievers in Eighteenth-Century France*.

- U.S. philosopher Brand Blanshard publishes *The Nature of Thought*.
- U.S. philosopher John Dewey publishes *Freedom and Culture*.
- U.S. psychiatrist Karen Horney publishes *New Ways in Psycho-Analysis*.
- U.S.-born English writer T. S. Eliot publishes his essay "The Idea of a Christian Society."

SOCIETY

Education

- Dorothy Garrod becomes the first woman to receive a professorship at Cambridge University, England. She serves as professor of archeology until 1952.
- Education in the United States, formerly overseen by a bureau in the Department of the Interior, becomes the responsibility of the Federal Security Agency.

Everyday Life

- For the first time Thanksgiving Day is celebrated on the fourth rather than the last Thursday in November in the United States, in order to guarantee a longer Christmas shopping period.
- The character of Batman is created in the United States by Bob Kane and appears in *Detective Comics*. His sidekick Robin joins him shortly afterwards.

- The first precooked frozen meals are marketed by General Foods in the United States under the Birds Eye label.
- The world fair in San Francisco, California, opens.
- Warner Brothers' designer Leona Gross Lax in the United States develops the concept of bra cup-sizing.

FEBRUARY

- The British government begins to build air-raid shelters in areas likely to be bombed in wartime.

APRIL

30 The World's Fair in Queens, New York, New York, is the biggest international exhibition ever, featuring international technical, business, and cultural displays: Germany is notably absent.

MAY

16 Rochester, New York, begins a food-stamp plan to distribute surplus food to the poor, a plan copied by more than 100 U.S. cities in the next two years.

SEPTEMBER

3 The Citizens' Advice Bureaux program is launched in the UK with the opening of 200 offices.

OCTOBER

- Nylon stockings are sold for the first time in the United States. They prove an instant success and by May 1940 are marketed by a range of manufacturers. However, nylon production is shortly to be taken up with military requirements.

Media and Communication

- After the German annexation of Czechoslovakia and the invasion of Poland, the free press is closed down in both countries.

BIRTHS & DEATHS

JANUARY

2 Jim Bakker, U.S. televangelist who had a popular television show with his wife Tammy Faye and was later imprisoned for fraud, born in Muskegon, Michigan.

28 W(illiam) B(utler) Yeats, Irish poet, dramatist, and nationalist, dies in Roquebrune-Cap-Martin, France (73).

FEBRUARY

4 Edward Sapir, German-born U.S. linguist and anthropologist, dies in New Haven, Connecticut (55).

10 Pope Pius XI 1922–39 dies in Rome, Italy (81).

MARCH

20 Brian Mulroney, Canadian Conservative politician, prime minister 1984–93, born in Baie Comeau, Québec, Canada.

31 Zviad Gamsakhurdia, anticommunist prime minister 1989–91 and then president of Georgia 1991–92, born in Tbilisi, Soviet Georgia (–1993).

APRIL

7 Francis Ford Coppola, U.S. film director, writer, and producer, born in Detroit, Michigan.

7 The Australian prime minister, Joseph Lyons, dies.

MAY

13 Stanisław Leśniewski, Polish mathematician and logician, dies in Warsaw, Poland (53).

26 Al Unser, U.S. race-car driver and Indianapolis 500 champion, born in Albuquerque, New Mexico.

JUNE

25 Harold Melvin, lead singer of the 1950s group the Blue Notes, born in Philadelphia, Pennsylvania (–1997).

AUGUST

17 Luther Allison, U.S. guitarist, singer and composer, born in Widener, Arkansas (–1997).

SEPTEMBER

17 Ethel M. Dell (Savage), popular novelist, dies in Hereford, England (58).

23 Sigmund Freud, Austrian neurologist, founder of psychoanalysis, dies in London, England (83).

OCTOBER

23 Zane Grey, U.S. author of western novels, dies in Altadena, California (67).

NOVEMBER

18 Margaret (Eleanor) Atwood, Canadian novelist, poet, short-story writer, and critic, born in Ottawa, Ontario, Canada.

28 James A. Naismith Canadian-born U.S. physical education director who invented the game of basketball, dies in Lawrence, Kansas (78).

DECEMBER

12 Douglas Fairbanks, Sr., U.S. star of early films, dies in Santa Monica, California (56).

23 Anthony Fokker, Dutch airman and aircraft manufacturer, dies in New York, New York (49).

- FM radio receivers go on sale in the United States.
- Many countries (mainly in Europe) start foreign-language broadcasts, including Vatican Radio.
- The Radio Corporation of America (RCA) develops the first experimental television sets in the United States.
- William C. Huebner introduces the photosetting of type.

APRIL

- Germany begins overseas broadcasts in English. After the outbreak of war in September, an upper-class voice on the service is nicknamed "Lord Haw-Haw" by British journalist Jonah Barrington.
1   In England, the Oxford–Cambridge Boat Race is televised for the first time.
1   The women's fashion magazine *Glamour* begins publication.
30 The National Broadcasting Corporation (NBC) makes the first public demonstration of television in the United States with President Roosevelt opening the New York World's Fair. The broadcast is seen by 1,000 people. Later in the year, NBC begins broadcasting for two hours a week. The Columbia Broadcasting System (CBS) also starts to broadcast.

AUGUST

26 The world's first regular advertisements on television are read live by the commentator in the interval of a baseball game in the United States.

SEPTEMBER

1   The British Broadcasting Corporation (BBC) stops television broadcasting in the UK for the duration of the war in the middle of a Mickey Mouse movie. Service is resumed in 1946.

Religion

- The German Catholic theologian Karl Rahner publishes *Geist in Welt/Spirit in the World*.

MARCH

2   Following the death of Pope Pius XI on February 10, Eugenio Pacelli is elected pope and takes the name Pius XII.

MAY

10 The Methodist Episcopal Church, Methodist Episcopal Church, South, and Methodist Protestant Church combine in the United States to form the Methodist Church. This reunification take place after 109 years of division, a split caused between churches in the North and South over slavery.

Sports

- Little League Baseball is founded in Williamsport, Pennsylvania, by George and Bert Bebble and Carl Stotz.
- Minnesota is college football's national champion.
- The inaugural U.S. national water-ski championships are held by the recently formed American Water Ski Association.

JANUARY

15 The New York Giants defeat the Pro-All Stars 13–10 at Wrigley Field, Los Angeles, California, in the inaugural Pro Bowl game.

21 U.S. national figure skating champions are: Joan Tozzer; Robin Lee; Joan Tozzer and Bernard Lee, pairs; Sandy MacDonald and Harold Hartshorne, dance.
24 Second baseman Eddie Collins, outfielder Wee Willie Keeler, and first baseman George Sisler are elected to baseball's Hall of Fame.

APRIL

6–16 The Boston Bruins defeat the Toronto Maple Leafs four games to one to win the National Hockey League (NHL) Stanley Cup.

MAY

2   Five players and an owner from an earlier era are elected to baseball's Hall of Fame. They are: Cap Anson, William Cummings, Charles Radbourne, Albert Spaulding, and Charles Comiskey.
2   U.S. baseball player Lou Gehrig withdraws from the lineup after making 2,130 consecutive appearances for the New York Yankees, a sequence that stands as a major league record until 1995.
16 The Philadelphia A's play the Cleveland Indians in the American League's first-ever night baseball game.
30 Racing driver Wilbur Shaw wins the Indianapolis 500. In the same race, Floyd Roberts, the defending champion, dies in a crash.

JUNE

12 The National Baseball Hall of Fame and Museum is dedicated at Cooperstown, New York.
12 U.S. golfer Byron Nelson wins the U.S. Open golf championship.
26–July 8 U.S. tennis player Bobby Riggs wins the men's singles, men's doubles, and mixed doubles titles on his first and only appearance at Wimbledon, England. His partner in the mixed doubles, fellow U.S. player Alice Marble, also wins the women's singles and doubles.

JULY

10–30 Sylvère Maes of Belgium wins the Tour de France cycle race for the second time.

AUGUST

19 British automobile racing driver Malcolm Campbell breaks the world water-speed record for the third time in two years with a speed of 228.1 kph/141.7 mph on Coniston Water, Lancashire, in England.
23 British automobile racing driver John Cobb breaks the world land-speed record at Bonneville Salt Flats, Utah, reaching a speed of 595.02 kph/369.74 mph in his Railton Mobil Special.

SEPTEMBER

30 A college football game between Fordham University and Waynesburg College at Randall's Island, New York, is the first-ever football game to be televised.

OCTOBER

4–8 The New York Yankees defeat the Cincinnati Reds four games to none to win their fourth consecutive World Series.
9–30 In the space of only 21 days, U.S. boxer Henry Armstrong competes in five welterweight world title fights and wins them all.

DECEMBER

10 The Green Bay Packers defeat the New York Giants 27–0 in the National Football League (NFL) championship game at Milwaukee, Wisconsin.

1940

POLITICS, GOVERNMENT, AND ECONOMICS

Business and Economics

- Richard and Maurice McDonald of Glendora, California, sell their first hamburger at a drive-in. They will go on to establish the McDonalds fast food chain in 1948.
- Social security payments start in the United States. The first check is for $22.54.
- U.S. soldiers enjoy the first M&M candies, produced for the military by Mars, Inc.

Colonization

AUGUST

8 The Indian Congress Party rejects the British viceroy's invitation to serve on a War Advisory Council.

Human Rights

- U.S. anthropologist Ruth Benedict publishes *Race: Science and Politics*, an attack on racism.

Politics and Government

- "V" begins to be used among the Allies as a symbol for Victory.
- President Franklin D. Roosevelt establishes the National Defence Advisory Commission in the United States, and with the Canadian prime minister, William L. Mackenzie King, creates the Permanent Joint Board of Defense to protect North America against attack.
- The Export Control Act is passed in the United States to conserve resources as war spreads in Asia and Europe.
- The U.S. president appoints former Attorney General Frank Murphy to the U.S. Supreme Court.
- U.S. journalist Dorothy Thompson makes a national tour of the United States, urging support for U.S. intervention in the European war.

JANUARY

- The "Barlow Report" urges the establishment of a National Industries Board to encourage the dispersal of industry throughout the UK.

21 Winston Churchill, the British First Lord of the Admiralty, advises neutral states in Europe to side with Britain before they become the object of German aggression in World War II.

FEBRUARY

1 After unexpected initial reverses in the Russo-Finnish war, the USSR launches attacks on the Karelian Isthmus.

11 In the Russo-Finnish war, the USSR attacks the Mannerheim Line (the line of forts forming Finland's southern defensive barrier across the Karelian Isthmus).

26 The U.S. Air Defense Command is created to coordinate the country's air defenses.

MARCH

4 In the Russo-Finnish war, Soviet forces capture the port of Vyborg in Finland.

12 The Russo-Finnish war ends. Finland signs a peace treaty with the USSR, ceding the Karelian Isthmus, the shores of Lake Ladoga, the city of Viborg, and the Hango naval base. About 200,000 Finns are evicted from the area.

20 The French prime minister Edouard Daladier resigns. He is succeeded by the minister of finance, Paul Reynaud.

28 Britain and France agree not to conclude a separate peace with Germany in World War II.

APRIL

- Britain sets up the MAUD Committee, headed by the British physicist George Thomson, to examine the possibility of developing an atomic bomb.

3 In Winston Churchill's war cabinet in Britain, Lord Woolton is appointed minister of food and Lord Beaverbrook minister of aircraft production.

9 German troops invade Denmark and Norway, occupying major ports and cities in the latter.

10–13 Several naval battles are fought between British and German forces off the port of Narvik in northern Norway; ten German destroyers (from a total of twenty) are sunk. Their loss, added to the loss of three (out of eight) cruisers in the invasion of Norway itself severely weakens the German navy's offensive capability.

14–17 British forces land at Namsos (April 14), and Åndalsnes (April 17), Norway, to assist the Norwegians against the invading German forces. Units from Åndalsnes reach the city of Lillehamer (May 21) before withdrawing.

15 British cryptographers in the Ultra project at Bletchley Park, Buckinghamshire, England, begin to crack the cipher used for encoding military messages sent using the German Enigma machine after the Royal Navy recovers an Enigma signal book from a captured German minelayer.

MAY

10 German armored forces begin to break through French and British defensive positions into northern France.

10 The British prime minister Neville Chamberlain resigns following criticism for the failure of the British military expedition to Norway. Winston Churchill forms a coalition government, with Lord Halifax foreign secretary and Labour members Clement Attlee as Lord Privy Seal, Albert Alexander as First Lord of the Admiralty, and Ernest Bevin as minister of labour.

10–14 German forces invade the Netherlands, Belgium, and Luxembourg.

13 Winston Churchill makes his "blood, toil, tears, and sweat" speech in the British House of Commons, boosting public morale and rallying confidence in his leadership during World War II.

14 Recruiting begins for the Local Defence Volunteers (later the Home Guard) in Britain.

14 The Dutch army surrenders to the invading German forces after a heavy air attack devastates the port of Rotterdam.

22 Germany and Romania sign an agreement under which Romania will supply oil to Germany.

22 The British Parliament grants the war government wide emergency powers.

23 German forces of Army Group A commanded by General Gerd von Rundstedt pierce the French defenses near Sedan, northeast France, and drive west for the English Channel, dividing the Allied (British and French) forces into two and cutting off the main concentration of British and French armor in Belgium and the Netherlands.

23 The German Führer Adolf Hitler orders the German armies in Belgium and France to halt their advance. The advance resumes two days later.

26–June 4 Over 338,000 British, French, and Belgian troops are evacuated from Dunkirk, France to England by an unprecedented armada of small British boats, following the German encirclement of Allied forces in northeastern France.

28 The Belgian army surrenders to the invading German forces. King Leopold III is taken prisoner.

30 The former British Labour member of Parliament, Sir Stafford Cripps, is appointed British ambassador to the USSR, initially to organize trade relationships.

JUNE

• The Republicans nominate Wendell L. Willkie, a former Indiana utility executive, and Charles L. McNary for U.S. president and vice president respectively.

• The U.S. Congress passes the Alien Registration Act (Smith Act), requiring the registration of aliens. The act also forbids membership in organizations advocating the overthrow of the U.S. government.

9 A cease-fire in German-occupied Norway is declared at midnight. King Haakon VII flees to Britain.

9–13 German troops in Norway proceed to the port of Narvik in the north.

10 German occupying forces in France cross the River Seine at Rouen. The French government leaves Paris for Bordeaux.

10 Italy declares war on France and Britain.

13 The British prime minister Winston Churchill visits the French prime minister Paul Reynaud in Tours, France,

to argue that any French effort to secure a separate peace with Germany would contravene the terms of the Anglo-French alliance, and to support France's further appeal to the United States for support.

14 Invading German troops enter Paris, France.

14 The French government, fleeing from the German occupying forces, arrives in the city of Bordeaux.

15 The United States rejects France's renewed appeal (May 13) for help against the German invasion.

15–17 The USSR occupies the Baltic states of Estonia, Latvia, and Lithuania, formally incorporating them into the USSR in August.

16 The British prime minister Winston Churchill offers France union with Britain as a means to continue the war against Germany after the defeat of France, but the French reject the proposal. The French prime minister Paul Reynaud resigns when an armistice with Germany is proposed, and is succeeded as head of state by Marshal Philippe Pétain.

17 The French head of state Marshal Philippe Pétain, seeing the French army defeated, negotiates an armistice with Germany. General Charles de Gaulle refuses to accept this arrangement and flees to Britain to lead the Free French, who continue the fight against Germany.

22 France signs an armistice with Germany and is divided into two zones. The Germans occupy northern and southwestern France, and a so-called autonomous "Vichy" French state is to control the remaining third of the country.

24 An armistice is signed between France (in collaboration with Germany) and Italy, and includes the withdrawal of French colonies from the war.

25 Japan demands that war supplies to China through French Indochina should be halted, and that a Japanese mission should be allowed to enter the country to verify the closure of the railroad lines concerned.

26–28 The USSR demands Bessarabia and Bukovina from Romania. Romania requests German support for rejection of the demand, but the German Führer refuses. Romania cedes the territories on June 27 and they are occupied by Soviet troops on June 28.

28 Britain recognizes General Charles de Gaulle as leader of the Free French organization of French exiles during the German occupation of France in World War II.

30 German forces occupy Britain's Channel Islands, indefensible from Britain after the fall of mainland France.

JULY

• Political parties are dissolved in Japan and are replaced by the Imperial Rule Association.

• The Democrats renominate Franklin D. Roosevelt for U.S. president. Former agriculture secretary Henry A. Wallace rounds out the ticket.

• The Local Defence Volunteers in the UK are reformed as the "Home Guard."

3 Britain's Royal Navy destroys most of the French fleet at Mers el-Kebir, Algeria, to prevent them being commandeered by the Germans.

5 France's Vichy government breaks off relations with Britain.

5 U.S. president Franklin D. Roosevelt bans the shipment of strategic materials to Japan.

9 Romania places itself under German protection.

10–August 18 Bomber and fighter aircraft of the German Luftwaffe (air force) attack shipping convoys in British waters and English ports, in the first phase of the Battle of Britain.

11–12 Marshal Philippe Pétain becomes president of Vichy France, a regime collaborating with Germany to administer central and southern France. Pierre Laval is appointed vice president on July 12.

18 Britain agrees to close the Burma Road, cutting off military supplies to China, in return for Japanese agreement to discuss peace terms with the Chinese Nationalist government.

21 Britain recognizes the Czechoslovak National Committee in London, England, as a provisional government during World War II.

22 Britain creates the Special Operations Executive (SOE), to oversee and coordinate clandestine operations in German-occupied Europe.

22 Prince Konoe Fumimaro is reappointed prime minister in Japan. He declares that Japan's aim is to establish a "New Order in greater East Asia."

22–September 24 The French-administered New Hebrides (now Vanuatu) join the Free French movement (July 22). By September 24 many French territories, apart from those in North Africa, do likewise.

AUGUST

3 Italian armed forces advance from Ethiopia into British Somaliland.

5 Britain signs an agreement recognizing the Polish government of General Władysław Sikorski in exile in London, England.

7 Britain signs an agreement with the Free French organization of French exiles under Charles de Gaulle in London, England.

13 The German Luftwaffe (air force) makes 1,786 sorties in the Battle of Britain, against 975 by the British Royal Air Force. It is known as "Adler Tag" (Eagle Day), the most intense 24 hours of the Battle of Britain, and marks the beginning of "Adlerangraft" (Eagle War), a two-week attack on RAF Fighter Command's aircraft, airfields, and installations.

14 The British Tizard Committee visits the United States and hands over technical information on the cavity magnetron, radar, proximity fuses, jet propulsion, and atomic research.

23 An all-night German bombing raid on London, England, begins the period of intense bombing known as the "Blitz."

SEPTEMBER

- A government edict in Japan orders the establishment of community councils and neighborhood associations to motivate people in support of the war effort.
- Britain loses 160,000 metric tons of shipping to World War II enemy action.
- German long-range artillery based in France shells Dover and areas of southeast England.

3 The United States sells 50 veteran destroyers to Britain for use by the Royal Navy in World War II in return for a 99-year rent-free lease of bases in Newfoundland and the Caribbean.

4 Ion Antonescu becomes prime minister of Romania and establishes a fascist dictatorship. King Carol II abdicates

in favor of his son, Michael, and flees to Switzerland with his mistress, Magda Lupescu.

15–16 The Italian 10th Army in Libya, under General Mario Berti, advance into Egypt, reaching the coastal town of Sidi Barrani.

16 The Selective Training and Service Act provides for men aged 21–35 to be called up for 12 months' military training in the United States.

22 Japanese troops are granted air and military bases around Hanoi in French Indochina (now Vietnam).

23–25 British and Free French forces fail in an attempt to occupy Dakar, the capital of Senegal, a French territory loyal to Vichy France.

24 The George Cross is instituted in Britain, primarily to reward civilian acts of the greatest heroism and courage in circumstances of extreme danger.

25 King Haakon of Norway is deposed, and Vidkun Quisling, leader of the Norwegian Nazi Party, is appointed prime minister by the German Reichscommissioner in Norway.

27 Germany, Italy, and Japan sign the Tripartite Pact in Berlin, Germany, pledging mutual military and economic cooperation.

OCTOBER

3 Neville Chamberlain retires from the British government through ill health and is succeeded by Sir John Anderson. Kingsley Wood becomes chancellor of the Exchequer and Ernest Bevin minister of labor.

4 The German Führer Adolf Hitler meets the Italian prime minister Benito Mussolini in the Brenner Pass in the Alps for consultations.

7 German troops enter Romania by agreement and take control of the oil fields.

12 The German Führer Adolf Hitler postpones Operation "Sea Lion," the planned amphibious invasion of Britain. The German Luftwaffe (air force) switches its attacks from military installations to London, England, and other cities.

18 Britain reopens the Burma Road supply route, previously closed under diplomatic pressure from the Japanese, enabling supplies for Jiang Jie Shi's nationalist forces war against Japan to get through.

23 The German Führer Adolf Hitler meets General Francisco Franco of Spain at Hendaye, France, and offers him Gibraltar and parts of North Africa in exchange for his support. Franco declines the offer.

24 The 40-hour work week, declared by Congress in a 1938 law, goes into effect in the United States.

28 Italy demands the cession of strategic points in Greece but Greece rejects the demands. An Italian invasion from Albania follows.

NOVEMBER

- Franklin D. Roosevelt is reelected U.S. president for an unprecedented third term, with 449 Democratic electoral votes to the Republican Wendell Willkie's 82. The Democrats retain a 66–28 majority over the Republicans in the Senate and a 268–162 majority in the House of Representatives.

3 A small detachment from Britain's Royal Air Force lands at Suda Bay, Crete, to support the Greek resistance to Italy's invasion.

11–12 Twenty-one British Swordfish naval torpedo-bombers from the aircraft carrier HMS *Illustrious* attack and cripple the Italian fleet at Taranto, southeast Italy, severally damaging the battleships *Conte di Cavour*, *Littorio*, and *Caio Duilio*.

12–14 The Soviet foreign minister, Vyacheslav Molotov, visits Berlin, Germany, for discussions with the German Führer Adolf Hitler and his foreign secretary, Joachim von Ribbentrop.

14–15 German aircraft bomb Coventry, England, killing 380 people and injuring 865, and destroying the city center, the cathedral, and twelve armaments factories.

16 Following the German bombing of Coventry, England, Britain's Royal Air force retaliates with a raid on the German city of Hamburg.

18 Airborne radar used by Britain's Royal Air Force (RAF) in the Atlantic detects a German U-boat for the first time.

20 Hungary endorses the German–Italian–Japanese Tripartite Pact of September 27.

20 The United States and Britain sign an agreement for the partial standardization of weapons and the pooling of technical knowledge during World War II.

23 Romania endorses the German–Italian–Japanese Tripartite Pact of September 27.

DECEMBER

9 Operation "Compass" begins in North Africa. The British Eighth Army under General Sir Archibald Wavell advances from Egypt into Libya, crossing the border on December 15.

SCIENCE, TECHNOLOGY, AND MEDICINE

Agriculture

- Chemists at British company Imperial Chemical Industries (ICI) discover that certain plant hormones can be used as selective herbicides.

Ecology

c. 1940 Information from uncrewed weather balloons indicates that columns of warm air rise more than 1.6 km/1 mi above the earth and winds form layers in the lower atmosphere, often blowing in different directions.

- Odzala National Park is created in the Congo; several groups of Pygmy people live in the park.
- The British government creates Serengeti National Park in Tanganyika (modern Tanzania); it covers an area of 14,763 sq km/5,700 sq mi and provides a refuge for the rare black rhinoceros.
- The U.S. Congress establishes the 218-sq-km/84-sq-mi Isle Royale National Park in the United States on the largest island in Lake Superior, which has a large moose population.
- The U.S. Fish and Wildlife Service is established to conserve, protect, and enhance fish and wildlife and their habitats.

Health and Medicine

- The first blood bank is opened by U.S. surgeon Charles R. Drew.
- The globulin, albumin, and fibrin fractions in blood are separated by U.S. scientist Edwin J. Cohn. Albumin is used to treat shock, globulin to prevent infection, and fibrin to stop hemorrhaging.
- U.S. microbiologist Thomas Francis, Jr. isolates the virus responsible for influenza B.

AUGUST

24 Australian pathologist Howard Florey and German-born British biochemist Ernst Chain develop penicillin, in Oxford, England, for general clinical use as an antibiotic, announcing their results in *The Lancet*.

Science

- Australian archeologist V. Gordon Childe publishes *Prehistoric Communities of the British Isles*.
- Austrian-born U.S. immunologist Karl Landsteiner and U.S. physician and immunohematologist Alexander Wiener discover the rhesus (Rh) factor in blood, in the United States.
- Belgian astronomer Marcel Gilles Jozef Minnaert publishes *Photometric Atlas of the Solar Spectrum*, a standard reference text providing measurements of the absorption lines from 3,332 angstroms to 8,771 angstroms.
- Canadian biochemist Martin Kamen discovers carbon-14. It becomes a vital tool in dating archeological remains.
- The Rockefeller Foundation grants funds to the University of California, to build a giant cyclotron (a type of particle accelerator), under the direction of U.S. physicist Ernst Orlando Lawrence.
- U.S. physicist J. R. Dunning leads a research team that uses a gaseous diffusion technique to isolate uranium-235 from uranium-238. Because uranium-235 readily undergoes fission into two atoms, and in doing so releases large amounts of energy, it is used for fueling nuclear reactors.
- U.S. physicists Edwin McMillan and Philip Abelson synthesize the first transuranic element, neptunium (element 93), by bombarding uranium with neutrons at the cyclotron at Berkeley, California.
- U.S. physicists Emilio Segrè, Dale Corson, and K. R. Mackenzie discover the radioactive element astatine (atomic no. 85).
- U.S. physicists Glenn T. Seaborg, Joseph W. Kennedy, and Archer C. Wahl discover plutonium (atomic no. 94).
- U.S. physiologist Herbert M. Evans uses radioactive iodine to prove that iodine is used by the thyroid gland.

SEPTEMBER

12 Schoolboys discover Paleolithic paintings and engravings in a cave at Lascaux, France.

Technology

- British chemist J. T. Dickson invents Dacron (Terylene in the United Kingdom); a polyester fiber made from terephthalic acid and ethylene glycol, it is more heat-resistant than nylon and more wear-resistant than rayon. The first yarn is made from the fiber the following year.

- British scientists John Turon Randall and Henry Albert Boot develop the cavity magnetron, which could generate high power at high frequencies (20,000 watts at 3,000 megahertz), making centimetric radar practical for the first time. The resulting smaller radar antennae make airborne radar a practicality.
- Carson Smith, president of Consolidation Coal, and U.S. engineer Harold Silver develop a continuous coal-digging machine that revolutionizes the coal-mining industry; it can dig a series of vertical sections 46 cm/18 in deep and bore a tunnel up to 4.5 m/18 ft wide.
- Freeze-drying of food is used for the first time in the United States.
- German inventor Konrad Zuse builds a computer, using telephone relays as its mechanical circuits.
- German technicians H. J. von Braunmühl and W. Weber add high-frequency bias to magnetic plastic tape, thereby improving the quality of sound recording.
- The first synthetic rubber tires are made commercially available by U.S. rubber manufacturer B. F. Goodrich.
- U.S. physicist Donald W. Kerst directs the construction of the first betatron, a device that accelerates beta particles to high velocities in a circular path.
- Ventilation fans for drying crops in barns are first used, in the United States.

APRIL

- The first Würzburg radar system (model A) enters service with the German armed forces. It is able to locate incoming aircraft, but not accurate enough to control antiaircraft fire.
1 The Radio Corporation of America (RCA) demonstrates an electron microscope that can magnify up to 100,000 diameters.

MAY

- Nylon stockings are marketed in the United States by a range of manufacturers and prove an instant success; however, nylon production is shortly to be taken up with military requirements.

SEPTEMBER

11 U.S. computer pioneers George Stibitz and Samuel Williams use a teletype in Dartmouth College, New Hampshire, to operate a complex number computer in New York, New York.

NOVEMBER

7 The Tacoma Narrows Bridge over Puget Sound in Washington state collapses four months after its opening. A landmark failure in engineering history, the bridge is vulnerable to aerodynamic forces. High winds cause it to oscillate until it is ripped from its moorings; its collapse stimulates rethinking of future bridge design.

Transportation

- German scientist Helmuth Walter begins to develop a prototype submarine, the V-80. It uses a turbine that runs on oxygen generated from hydrogen peroxide, allowing the submarine to travel submerged at up to 20 knots for over 5 hours.

- Number of private cars being used (in millions): United States, 32.4; UK, 2.4; France, 2.3; Canada, 1.4.
- The Mikoyan MIG-1 fighter plane enters service with the Soviet air force.
- U.S. engineers J. H. "Dutch" Kindelberger and John Atwood design and build a prototype of the P-51 Mustang fighter plane; it takes them only 127 days.

JULY

- The Civil Aeronautics Board is established in the United States to regulate airline safety and economics.
8 Transcontinental & Western Air's *Stratoliner* enters service. It is the first commercial flight with a pressurized cabin.

OCTOBER

1 The first modern limited-access toll highway in the United States, the Pennsylvania Turnpike, officially opens. It creates an economic boom along its route and heralds a new era in transportation in the United States. Other states begin constructing highways soon afterwards.

NOVEMBER

- U.S. engineer Karl Pabst designs the jeep (the name comes from the initials GP—general purpose). The Willys Corporation begins production for the U.S. army the following year.

DECEMBER

- The first part of the Los Angeles freeway system, the Arroyo Seco Parkway, opens in California.

ARTS AND IDEAS

Architecture

- The Chapel of Florida Southern College, designed by the U.S. architect Frank Lloyd Wright, is completed.

Arts

- Following the Nazi occupation of France, many artists flee Paris, France. The Spanish artist Pablo Picasso remains, protected by his prestige, but he is forbidden to exhibit or sell.
- The Dutch-born U.S. artist Willem de Kooning paints *Seated Woman*.
- The English artist John Piper paints *St Mary le Port, Bristol*.
- The German artist Max Ernst paints *The Robing of the Bride*.
- The Mexican artist Frida Kahlo paints *Self-Portrait with Cropped Hair*.
- The official war artists Edward Ardizzone, Muirhead Bone, Henry Lamb, John Nash, Paul Nash, Eric Ravilious, and Stanley Spencer are appointed in Britain.
- The Russian artist Wassily Kandinsky paints *Sky Blue*.
- The Spanish artist Pablo Picasso paints *Woman Dressing Her Hair*.
- The Swiss artist Paul Klee paints *Death and Fire*.

- The U.S. artist Alice Neel paints *T.B., Harlem*.
- The U.S. artist Edward Hopper paints *Gas*.
- The U.S. artist Jacob Lawrence paints *Harriet Tubman Worked as a Water Girl to Cotton Pickers; She Also Worked at Plowing, Carting, and Hauling Logs*.
- The U.S. artist John Steuart Curry completes his mural *The Tragic Prelude* in the Kansas State Capitol in Topeka, Kansas.

Film

- In occupied territories, the German authorities reopen the movie theaters in order to show German propaganda. However, they also take over movie censorship. All movies subsequently need German approval before they can be shown.
- The 1939 Academy Awards take place. Best Actor: Robert Donat, for *Goodbye Mr Chips*; Best Supporting Actor: Thomas Mitchell, for *Stagecoach*; Best Actress: Vivien Leigh, for *Gone with the Wind*; Best Supporting Actress: Hattie McDaniel (the first black woman to win an Oscar), for *Gone With the Wind*; Best Picture: *Gone With the Wind*, directed by Victor Fleming; Best Director: Victor Fleming, for *Gone With the Wind*.
- The movie *Dance, Girl, Dance*, directed by Dorothy Arzner, is released in the United States, starring Maureen O'Hara and Lucille Ball.
- The movie *Rebecca*, based on the novel by Daphné du Maurier is released in the United States. It stars Joan Fontaine, Laurence Olivier, George Sanders, and Judith Anderson, and is English director Alfred Hitchcock's first Hollywood movie.
- The movie *The Bank Dick* is released in the United States, starring W. C. Fields and directed by Eddie Cline.
- The movie *The Grapes of Wrath*, adapted from the novel by John Steinbeck, is released in the United States. It is directed by John Ford and stars Henry Fonda, Jane Darwell, and John Carradine.
- The movie *The Great Dictator*, directed by British filmmaker Charlie Chaplin, is released. He also stars in it. A critique of fascism, it is his first movie with spoken dialogue.
- The movie *The Philadelphia Story*, directed by George Cukor, is released in the United States, starring Cary Grant, Katharine Hepburn, and James Stewart. It is based on the play by Philip Barry.
- The movie *The Road to Singapore*, directed by Victor Schertzinger, is released in the United States. It is the first of the very popular *Road* series, and stars Bing Crosby, Bob Hope, and Dorothy Lamour.
- The movie *The Thief of Bagdad* is released, produced by Alexander Korda, and directed by Michael Power and Ludwig Berger. An epic production, begun in the UK and completed in the United States after the outbreak of World War II, the movie features Academy Award-winning Technicolor photography, special effects, and art direction, and stars Conrad Veidt and Sabu.
- The movie *The Westerner*, directed by William Wyler, is released in the United States, starring Gary Cooper, Walter Brennan, and Doris Davenport.
- The movies *The Great McGinty* and *Christmas in July*, both directed by Preston Sturges, are released in the United States. They are his first two movies as a director. Both showcase his skill at social satire,

previously evident in his writing work for other filmmakers.
- The screwball comedy *His Girl Friday*, adapted from the play *The Front Page* by Ben Hecht and Charles MacArthur, is released in the United States. It is directed by Howard Hawks and stars Cary Grant, Rosalind Russell, and Ralph Bellamy.
- U.S. animators William Hanna and Joseph Barbera create the cartoon duo Tom (a cat) and Jerry (a mouse), who appear in their first cartoon *Puss Gets the Boot*.
- Walt Disney releases the feature-length animation *Fantasia*. The classical music score includes Dukas's *The Sorcerer's Apprentice*. They also release the animated movie *Pinocchio* in the United States.

OCTOBER

10 At the World's Fair in New York, New York, the first "Smellie" movie, *My Dream*, is featured. Its smells include flowers, gasoline, and smoked meat.

Literature and Language

- 11,328 new books are published in the United States, including William Faulkner's *The Hamlet*, the first novel in a trilogy about the Snopes family.
- A book about Britain at war, *Mrs Miniver*, by the English writer Jan Struther, is a huge success in the United States.
- The *Cambridge Bibliography of English Literature* is published, edited by F. W. Bateson.
- The Australian writer Christina Stead publishes her novel *The Man Who Loved Children*.
- The English writer C. P. Snow publishes his novel *Strangers and Brothers*, the first volume in a series of the same title.
- The English writer Graham Greene publishes his novel *The Power and the Glory*.
- The Hungarian-born English writer Arthur Koestler publishes *Darkness at Noon*, set in Russia during the Stalinist purges of the 1930s.
- The Italian writer Dino Buzzati publishes his novel *Il desertodei tartari/Tartar Steppe*.
- The Nobel Prize for Literature is not awarded this year.
- The Pulitzer Prize for Biography is awarded to Ray Stannard Baker for *Woodrow Wilson: Life and Letters*, the Pulitzer Prize for Fiction is awarded to John Steinbeck for *The Grapes of Wrath*, and Prize for Poetry is awarded to Mark Van Doren for *Collected Poems*.
- The U.S. crime writer Raymond Chandler publishes his novel *Farewell, My Lovely*.
- The U.S. novelist Richard Wright publishes *Native Son*, the story of a black American encounter with crime and punishment.
- The U.S. writer Carson McCullers publishes her novel *The Heart is a Lonely Hunter*.
- The U.S. writer Ernest Hemingway publishes his novel *For Whom the Bell Tolls*, set during the Spanish Civil War.
- The U.S. writer Robert Hayden publishes his poetry collection *Heart-Shape in the Dust*.
- The U.S. writer Upton Sinclair publishes his novel *World's End*.
- The U.S. writer Walter van Tilburg Clark publishes his novel *The Ox-Bow Incident*. Based on a lynching, the

story brings considerable psychological and moral depth to a Wild West novel.

- The U.S. writer Willa Cather publishes her novel *Sapphira and the Slave Girl*.
- The U.S. writer William Saroyan publishes his short-story collection *My Name is Aram*.
- The U.S.-born English poet T. S. Eliot publishes *East Coker*, which is later part of *Four Quartets*, published in 1943.
- The Welsh writer Dylan Thomas publishes *Portrait of the Artist as a Young Dog*, a largely autobiographical account of a boy's childhood in Wales.
- The Welsh writer Howard Spring publishes his novel *Fame is the Spur*.

Music

- In the United States, the U.S. jazz musician Stan Kenton sets up the Stan Kenton Band.
- The Armenian composer Aram Khachaturian completes his Violin Concerto in D minor.
- The Austrian composer Anton Webern completes his *Variations for Orchestra*, Opus 30.
- The English composer Benjamin Britten completes his *Sinfonia da Requiem/Requiem Symphony*, Opus 20, and his song cycle *Seven Sonnets of Michelangelo*.
- The pianist Myra Hess organizes lunchtime concerts at the National Gallery in London, England. They popularize classical music and help to improve morale during the war.
- The Russian composer Sergey Prokofiev completes his Piano Sonata No. 6 in A minor.

JULY

20 The world's first record chart appears in the U.S. magazine *Billboard*.

Theater and Dance

- The English composer William Walton completes his score for the ballet *The Wise Virgins*. It is a transcription from Bach.
- The play *The Fifth Column*, by the U.S. writer Ernest Hemingway, published in 1938, is adapted for stage by Benjamin Glazer. Its theme is the Spanish Civil War.
- The Pulitzer Prize for Drama is awarded to William Saroyan for *The Time of Your Life*. He refuses the award.

Thought and Scholarship

- English monk Dom David Knowles publishes *The Monastic Order in England, 943–1216*.
- English philosopher A. J. Ayer publishes *The Foundation of Empirical Knowledge*.
- English philosopher Bertrand Russell publishes *An Inquiry into Meaning and Truth*.
- English political scientist Harold Joseph Laski publishes *The American Presidency: An Interpretation*.
- French philosopher Gaston Bachelard publishes *Le Philosophie du non/The Philosophy of No*.
- Hungarian-born German sociologist Karl Mannheim publishes *Man and Society in an Age of Social*

Reconstruction, a pioneering work on the "sociology of knowledge."

- Russian-born U.S. sociologist Mirra Komarovsky publishes *The Unemployed Man and His Family*.
- Scottish historian Denis William Brogan publishes *The Development of Modern France, 1870–1939*.
- The English writer George Orwell publishes *Inside the Whale*, a collection of essays.
- The Pulitzer Prize for History is awarded to Carl Sandburg for *Abraham Lincoln: The War Years*.
- U.S. scholar Van Wyck Brooks publishes his history *New England: Indian Summer*.
- U.S. statistician George Horace Gallup publishes *The Pulse of Democracy: The Public Opinion and How It Works*. In 1939 he founded the Audience Research Institute, in Princeton, New Jersey. His work will provide the basis of modern opinion polls.
- U.S. writer and critic Edmund Wilson publishes *To the Finland Station*, a study of the thinkers who helped to create the Russian Revolution.

SOCIETY

Education

- English educator Fred Clarke publishes *Education and Social Change*, a work that will have a profound influence on the development of education in postwar Britain.
- Hunter College opens on the Upper East Side of New York, New York.

JANUARY

12 The Office of Education in the United States is authorized to provide "short intensive courses of college grade, designed to meet the shortage of engineers in activities essential to national defense."

MARCH

March–April Education officials in New York, New York, block the appointment of the British libertarian philosopher Bertrand Russell to a professorship at City College. Russell's iconoclastic view of marriage proves offensive to many New Yorkers, though not to officials at Harvard who offer Russell a position.

Everyday Life

- 45% of the students enrolled in fifth grade eight years earlier graduate from high school in the United States.
- About 4% of blacks and 14% of whites have completed four years of high school in the United States.
- Illiteracy in the United States reaches an all-time low; 4.2% of the population are illiterate, a drop from 4.3% in 1930 and 15.8% in 1870.
- In the United States, about 5% of whites and about 1% of blacks have completed four years of college.
- In the United States, Colonel Sanders concocts his special recipe for Kentucky Fried Chicken.
- Norman Breakey, a Canadian, invents the paint roller.

- Rationing of basic foods begins in the UK, with bacon, butter, and sugar among the first items.
- Remington in Ilion, New York, produces an electric shaver for women.
- The First Lady of the United States, Eleanor Roosevelt, publicly endorses birth control.
- The jewelers Tiffany & Co., New York, New York, becomes the first store to be fully air-conditioned.
- The new census lists the U.S. population at 131,669,275, and the center of population is Indiana. The average life expectancy in the United States is 64 years.
- The population of the world is estimated at 2.229 billion.
- The populations figures for the United Kingdom are (in millions): England 39.2; Wales 2.5; Scotland 4.9; Ireland/Northern Ireland 1.3.
- There are 264,000 divorces in the United States and 8,396 in Great Britain.
- U.S. consumers spend $22 billion on food, beverages, and tobacco (31%); $9 billion on clothes (13%); $20 billion on housing and household operations (28%); $3 billion on medical care (4%); and $4 billion on recreation (5%).
- U.S. unemployment stands at 8 million: this represents 14.6% of the population.

March 1940–44   A large-scale migration of people from rural areas of the United States to the cities creates major urban problems.

March 1940–49   Immigration into the United States for the period 1940–49 stands at 856,608.

JUNE

30   Mrs. Dale Messick's cartoon character Brenda Starr debuts in the *Chicago Tribune*.

JULY

- Free milk is provided in the UK for mothers and children.

NOVEMBER

- There are 3.3 million telephones and 8.9 million radios in use in the UK.

Media and Communication

- In Britain, the British Broadcasting Corporation (BBC) launches the radio series *Sincerely Yours*, starring Vera Lynn, who popularizes the songs "We'll Meet Again" and "White Cliffs Of Dover."
- The Columbia Broadcasting System (CBS) demonstrates its color-television system, making the world's first broadcast in color from the Chrysler Building, New York, New York. The system is based on a three-color rotating disk developed by U.S. engineer Peter Goldmark.
- There are 23 television stations in the United States by mid-year.

BIRTHS & DEATHS

JANUARY

14   Julian Bond, U.S. civil-rights activist and scholar, born in Nashville, Tennessee.

21   Jack Nicklaus, U.S. golfer, born in Columbus, Ohio.

FEBRUARY

6   Tom Brokaw, U.S. television newscaster, born in Webster, South Dakota.

MARCH

9   Raul Julia, U.S. film actor, born in San Juan, Puerto Rico (–1994).

16   Bernardo Bertolucci, Italian film director, born in Parma, Italy.

16   Selma Lagerlöf, Swedish novelist, dies in Mårbacka, Sweden (81).

MAY

7   Angela Carter, English author of *The Magic Toyshop* (1967), *Nights at the Circus* (1984), and *Wise Children* (1991), born in Eastbourne, East Sussex, England (–1992).

24   Joseph Brodsky, Russian poet, winner of the Nobel Prize for Literature in 1987, born in Leningrad (now St. Petersburg), Russia (–1996).

JUNE

5   Orlando Patterson, Jamaican sociologist and scholar of race and slavery, born in Westmoreland, Jamaica.

10   Marcus Garvey, Afro-Caribbean leader of Back to Africa and the United Negro Improvement Association in the 1920s, dies in London, England (62).

22   Wladimir Köppen, German meteorologist who mapped the climatic zones of the earth, dies in Graz, Austria (93).

23   Wilma Glodean Rudolph, U.S. track and field athlete who, at the 1960 Olympics, became the first U.S. woman to win three gold medals at a single Olympics, born in Clarksville, Tennessee (–1994).

29   Paul Klee, Swiss Abstract artist, dies in Muralto-Locarno, Switzerland (60).

AUGUST

18   Walter Percy Chrysler, U.S. automobile manufacturer, dies in Great Neck, New York (65).

21   Leon Trotsky (adopted name of Lev Davidovitch Bronstein), communist theorist and activist, and a leader in Russia's October Revolution of 1917, is assassinated in Coyaocán, near Mexico City, Mexico (61).

30   J(oseph) J(ohn) Thomson, English physicist, discoverer of the electron, dies in Cambridge, England (83).

SEPTEMBER

15   Merlin Olsen, U.S. football player who was elected to the Hall of Fame and later became a television star, born in Logan, Utah.

OCTOBER

9   John Lennon, English pop singer and songwriter, one of the Beatles, born in Liverpool, England (–1980).

14   Cliff Richard, English pop singer who also appeared in several film musicals, born in Lucknow, India.

23   Pelé (Edson Arantes do Nascimento), Brazilian soccer player, born in Três Corações, Brazil.

NOVEMBER

9   Neville Chamberlain, British prime minister 1937–40, a Conservative, dies in Heckfield, England (71).

DECEMBER

21   F. Scott Fitzgerald, U.S. novelist and short-story writer, dies in Hollywood, California (44).

21   Frank (Francis Vincent) Zappa, U.S. rock musician and composer, born in Baltimore, Maryland (–1993).

November 1940–43   Germany continues making broadcasts and takes over the Eiffel Tower transmitter in Paris after the invasion of France.

Religion

- There are 21.4 million Catholics, 7.3 million Methodists, 5.1 million Southern Baptists, 2.1 million Episcopalians, and 1.9 million Presbyterians in the United States.

FEBRUARY

22   The 14th Dalai Lama, Bstan'-dzin-rgya-mtsho, is inaugurated as spiritual leader of Tibetan Buddhists.

Sports

- During the year, 8.5 million Americans attend horse races, where they bet more than $408.5 million.
- Minnesota is college football's national champion for the second consecutive year.

FEBRUARY

10   U.S. national figure skating champions are: Joan Tozzer; Eugene Turner; Joan Tozzer and Bernard Fox, pairs; Harold Hartshorne and Sandy MacDonald, dance.

25   An ice hockey game between the New York Rangers and the Montreal Canadiens at Madison Square Garden, New York, New York, is the first ice hockey game to be televised. It is transmitted by the W2XBS broadcasting company, who three days later televise basketball for the first time when they cover a game between Fordham University and the University of Pittsburgh, also at Madison Square Garden.

MARCH

15   The 12th Olympic Games, due to be held in Tokyo, Japan, are canceled because of World War II.

APRIL

2–13   The New York Rangers win the National Hockey League (NHL) Stanley Cup, defeating the Toronto Maple Leafs in six games.

MAY

30   For the second consecutive year and third overall, U.S. racing driver Wilbur Shaw, in a Boyle special, wins the Indianapolis 500 in Indianapolis, Indiana.

JUNE

9   U.S. golfer W. Lawson Little wins the U.S. Open golf championship.

12   Pont L'Eveque, ridden by Sam Wragg, wins the Epsom Derby, which is held at Newmarket, England, instead of Epsom, because of the war.

SEPTEMBER

9   U.S. tennis player Alice Marble wins her third consecutive singles title at the U.S. Championships.

OCTOBER

- The Cincinnati Reds defeat the Detroit Tigers four games to three to win their first World Series since 1919.

4   Henry Armstrong loses his welterweight world title on points to fellow U.S. boxer Fritzie Zivic.

11   A German bomb strikes the roof of the Centre Court at Wimbledon, England, causing extensive damage. The court is not restored to its prewar capacity until 1949.

DECEMBER

8   The Chicago Bears beat the Washington Redskins by a record score of 73–0 in the U.S. National Football League (NFL) championship game.

1941

POLITICS, GOVERNMENT, AND ECONOMICS

Business and Economics

- The U.S. investment firm of Merrill Lynch Pierce Fenner & Beane is established when Merrill Lynch Pierce merges with Fenner & Beane.

MARCH

- The U.S. Congress allocates $7 billion in lend–lease assistance for the Allies during World War II.

JUNE

- The U.S. president Franklin D. Roosevelt freezes German and Italian assets in the United States.

JULY

23   Following Japan's demand for military and naval bases in Indochina, Britain and the United States freeze Japanese assets.

Human Rights

- Women in Panama gain the right to vote on the same basis as men.

JUNE

25   President Franklin D. Roosevelt establishes the Fair Employment Practices Commission in the United States to investigate alleged discrimination on the basis of color, race, national origin, or creed.

AUGUST

14   The British prime minister Winston Churchill and the U.S. president Franklin D. Roosevelt meet at the Placentia Bay conference on board the U.S. cruiser *Augusta*. They sign the Atlantic Charter, condemning territorial changes and affirming human rights, which subsequently becomes the basis of the United Nations (UN) Declaration of Human Rights.

DECEMBER

8   The use of gas in the so-called "final solution" to the Jewish problem begins when 2,300 Polish Jews are gassed at Chełmno, western Poland.

Politics and Government

- One thousand three hundred and sixty Soviet heavy industrial plants are moved further east to continue production after the German invasion of the USSR.
- President Franklin D. Roosevelt appoints Harlan Stone chief justice of the U.S. Supreme Court and appoints South Carolina politician James F. Byrne and adviser Robert N. Jackson to the Court.
- The United Service Organization (USO) is formed in the United States to organize entertainments for Allied soldiers by performers such as Bob Hope and Bing Crosby.
- The U.S. president Franklin D. Roosevelt announces an embargo of iron and gasoline to Japan and freezes Japanese assets.

JANUARY

- The U.S. president Franklin D. Roosevelt establishes the Office of Production Management to oversee defense contracting during World War II, and sends Congress a $17.5 billion budget proposal, two-thirds of it earmarked for national defense.
- The U.S. president Franklin D. Roosevelt is inaugurated for a third term.
22   The Italian-held port of Tobruk, Libya, falls to British forces under Lieutenant-General Richard O'Connor during World War II.

MARCH

- The U.S. president Franklin D. Roosevelt creates the National Defense Mediation Board to arbitrate differences in the armament industries.
1   Bulgaria signs the Tripartite Pact of September 27, 1940, allying itself with the Axis powers (Germany, Italy, and Japan).
4   The first British commando raid takes place, on the Lofoten Islands off German-occupied Norway.
7   British troops begin disembarking in Greece to counter possible German expansion into the Balkans.
7   The British Western Desert Force under General Sir Richard O'Connor invade Italian-controlled Ethiopia.

11   President Franklin D. Roosevelt signs the Lend-Lease Bill in the United States. It gives the president authority to aid any nation whose defense is regarded as vital to the United States and to accept repayment. This signals the end of U.S. isolationism.
19   The German Luftwaffe (air force) resumes air raids on London, England, having suspended them while attacks were made on the Royal Air Force's installations.
24   German and Italian forces commanded by the German general Erwin Rommel take El Algheila in Libya from the British 8th Army, the start of an offensive that will clear British troops from all of Libya apart from the besieged coastal town of Tobruk.
24   The USSR undertakes to support Turkey if it becomes the victim of aggression.
25   Yugoslavia joins the Tripartite Pact of September 27, 1940, becoming an ally of Germany, Italy, Japan, and Bulgaria (which joined on March 1).
27   Prince Paul, Regent of Yugoslavia, is deposed in a coup organized by air force officers exploiting the unpopularity of adherence to the Tripartite Pact between the Axis powers (Germany, Italy, and Japan).
28   The British cruisers *Orion*, *Ajax*, *Gloucester*, and *Perth* intercept an Italian squadron off Cape Matapan, southern Greece. The Italian cruisers *Zara*, *Pola*, and *Fiume* are sunk, and the battleship *Vittorio Veneto* is damaged.

APRIL

- The U.S. president Franklin D. Roosevelt creates the Office of Price Administration and Civilian Supply to monitor inflation.
5   The USSR signs a treaty of friendship and nonaggression with Yugoslavia in the event of a German invasion, but relations are broken off when Germany invades Yugoslavia the following day.
5–8   British forces in Italian-controlled Ethiopia take the capital, Addis Ababa, after heavy fighting and, on April 8, the port of Massawa in Eritrea.
6   German, Italian, and Bulgarian forces invade Yugoslavia, and German forces attack the Metaxas Line, Greece's main system of defenses.
10   The Yugoslav province of Croatia declares its independence following the invasion of Yugoslavia by Germany, Italy, and Bulgaria.
11   German bombers attack aircraft factories near Coventry, England.
13   The USSR signs a neutrality pact with Japan.
17   Yugoslavia formally surrenders to the invading German forces.
21   The Greek army surrenders to the invading German forces; the last British forces are evacuated from mainland Greece on April 28.
25   The German-Italian offensive commanded by Erwin Rommel against the British in Libya reaches the Egyptian frontier.

MAY

- Germany's invasion of Greece and Yugoslavia inspires the U.S. president, Franklin D. Roosevelt, to declare a national emergency. The declaration is designed to clear the way for extraordinary legislation.

6 Joseph Stalin, general secretary of the Soviet Communist Party, appoints himself chair of the Council of People's Commissars (head of government in the USSR).

10 German aircraft drop hundreds of incendiary bombs on London, England, destroying the British Parliament's House of Commons building at Westminster.

10 Rudolf Hess, deputy leader of the Nazi Party in Germany, secretly flies to Scotland with peace proposals, but is treated as a prisoner of war.

12 Admiral François Darlan, Vice President of Vichy France, meets the German Führer Adolf Hitler for discussions. They agree to the "Paris Protocols," by which Vichy grants Germany military facilities in Syria, Tunisia, and French West Africa in return for reduction in the "occupation costs" levied on France.

18 Bulgaria annexes the Greek and Yugoslav parts of Macedonia.

20 German airborne and paratroop forces begin Operation *Merkur* (Mercury), the invasion of the Greek island of Crete, which is garrisoned by British and New Zealand forces evacuated from mainland Greece.

20 President Roosevelt moves Thanksgiving to the last Thursday of November, ending a two-year experiment in which it was the fourth Thursday of the month.

24 The German battleship *Bismarck* sinks the British battle cruiser HMS *Hood* off Greenland, while seeking to break through to the Atlantic to attack Allied merchant shipping.

24–30 The anti-British government in Iraq collapses. The prime minister, Rashid Ali, and others flee abroad.

27 The German battleship *Bismarck*, on its first and only sortie into the Atlantic, is sunk, after a long hunt, by units of Britain's Royal Navy west of Brest, France.

29–31 British and allied forces evacuate the port of Iráklion, Crete, and withdraw to Egypt, leaving the Greek island of Crete under German occupation.

JUNE

• The U.S. State Department shuts down German consulates and bans Nazi propaganda groups in the United States.

1 Clothes are rationed in the UK and "utility" clothing and furniture are introduced.

22 Operation Barbarossa, the German invasion of the USSR, begins.

25 Following Germany's invasion of the USSR, Finland declares that it is at war with the USSR.

27 British Broadcasting Corporation (BBC) broadcasts urge occupied countries to use the Morse code symbol for V (for Victory), 3 dots and a dash, and to whistle the first four notes of Beethoven's Fifth Symphony in the company of Nazis as a gesture of defiance.

27 Hungary declares war on the USSR, following the German invasion of Soviet territory.

28 German forces of Army Group North and Army Group Center occupy the city of Minsk in the western USSR, surrounding 27 Soviet divisions in pockets around Białystok, Volkhovysk, and to the west of Minsk.

28 U.S. president Franklin D. Roosevelt creates an Office of Scientific Research and Development.

30 The State Committee of Defense, under Joseph Stalin, is established in the USSR as the supreme wartime organ of government.

JULY

6 After heavy defeats in Poland, the Baltic States, and the western USSR, Soviet troops attempt to halt the German advance at the "Stalin Line," on the prewar frontier with Poland.

10 German forces of Army Group North begin their advance on the city of Leningrad (now St. Petersburg) in the USSR, but fail to capture it.

12 Britain and the USSR sign an agreement of mutual aid as part of a general Allied coalition against Germany.

24 Japanese troops begin the occupation of central and southern Indochina.

25 German forces of Army Group North capture Tallinn, the former Estonian capital, in the USSR.

29 Romania reoccupies the territories of Bessarabia and Bukovina, which it had ceded to the USSR in June 1940.

AUGUST

• Examination of air photographs shows that Royal Air Force (RAF) bombers rarely hit their targets; this accelerates British research into radar navigation systems.

• The U.S. president Franklin D. Roosevelt extends the Selective Service Act. Enlistment terms will not exceed 30 months, but the peacetime limit of 900,000 men in the U.S. armed forces becomes void.

12 Britain and the USSR sign a trade agreement.

25–September 17 Soviet and British forces invade Iran, following the shah's refusal to reduce the number of resident Germans.

SEPTEMBER

• The U.S. Congress enacts sweeping tax increases to defray the cost of wartime expenses.

• The U.S. president Franklin D. Roosevelt announces that German and Italian vessels in U.S. waters will be subject to attack.

9 In response to the German invasion of the USSR, the British Communist Party launches a campaign in Britain in favor of the rapid opening of a second military front against Germany in Europe.

20 German forces capture Kiev, the Ukrainian capital in the USSR, after Panzer (armored) divisions commanded by Heinz Guderian move south from Smolensk to take the Soviet defenses from behind.

21 The first "Liberty Ship" is launched in the United States in a bid to redress the heavy losses of merchant ships carrying supplies to Britain; 2,610 of these emergency freighters are ultimately produced, many in a record time of ten days.

24 The Allied conference in London, England, endorses the Atlantic Charter signed by the British prime minister Winston Churchill and the U.S. president Franklin D. Roosevelt on August 14.

OCTOBER

• As German U-boats fix their sights on American ships, the U.S. destroyer *Kearny* is hit off Iceland.

• The U.S. Congress allocates another $6 billion in lend–lease aid to the Allies during World War II.

1 German forces of Army Group Center advance from the city of Smolensk toward Moscow, the Soviet capital.

3 The German Second Panzer Army captures the city of Orel, south of Moscow, in the USSR.

13   Britain's Royal Air Force bombs the German city of Nuremberg.

15   As German forces approach the Soviet capital, Moscow, the Soviet government is transferred to Kuybyshev on the River Volga. The Soviet leader, Joseph Stalin, stays in Moscow.

16   German forces of Army Group South capture the Soviet port of Odessa in the Crimea.

16   Prince Konoe Fumimaro resigns as prime minister of Japan and is succeeded by General Hideki Tojo.

24   The German Army Group South captures Kharkov, the second largest city in the Ukraine.

25   The first phase of the German Army Group Center's offensive against the Soviet capital, Moscow, fails as Red Army resistance stiffens.

31   A German U-boat torpedoes and sinks the U.S. destroyer *Reuben James*, killing 115 of the crew.

NOVEMBER

3   Units of the German Army Group Center capture the city of Kursk, USSR.

13   The British aircraft carrier *Ark Royal* is torpedoed by the German U-boat (submarine) U81 off Gibraltar; it sinks the following day, severely weakening the British Mediterranean Fleet.

13   The U.S. Congress votes to amend the Neutrality Act, allowing U.S. merchant ships to be armed and to enter war zones.

16   The second phase of the German Army Group Center's offensive against the Soviet capital, Moscow, begins. After initial successes, the German advance is paralyzed by severe cold.

27–29   Soviet armies in the Southern Ukraine under Marshal Semyon Timoshenko counterattack the German Army Group South's advanced positions at Rostov-on-Don, forcing them to evacuate the port on November 29.

DECEMBER

•   Admiral H. E. Kimmel, commander of the U.S. Pacific Fleet, is dismissed after having been caught off guard by the Japanese at Pearl Harbor, Hawaii, on December 7. He is replaced by Chester W. Nimitz.

•   The U.S. Congress allocates another $10 billion of lend–lease assistance to the Allies during World War II.

•   The U.S. Congress declares war on Germany and Italy.

5   Britain declares war on Finland, Hungary, and Romania when they refuse to withdraw from supporting Germany's war against the USSR.

5   The British foreign secretary, Anthony Eden, visits Moscow to discuss the military situation with the Soviet leader, Joseph Stalin, and the Soviet foreign secretary, Vyacheslav Molotov.

5–January 5, 1942   Soviet armies of the Northwest, Volkhov, and Kalinin fronts, reinforced by units from Siberia, launch a counteroffensive north and south of Moscow to relieve pressure from the German Army Group Center's advance on the Soviet capital.

7   Howell Forgy, a naval chaplain based at Pearl Harbor, utters the phrase "praise the Lord and pass the ammunition," which becomes a popular war-time saying.

7   Japanese naval aircraft make a surprise air attack on the U.S. naval base at Pearl Harbor, Hawaii. Four

battleships and 140 aircraft are destroyed and 2,330 troops killed.

8   Japanese forces attack Wake Island and Guam, U.S. possessions in the Pacific Ocean, and occupy the islands.

8   Responding to the Japanese attack on Pearl Harbor in Hawaii, the U.S. president Franklin D. Roosevelt declares December 7 "a date which shall live in infamy." Meanwhile the Senate and House declare war on Japan and the president promptly signs the order.

9–10   Japanese aircraft sink the British battleship *Prince of Wales* and battlecruiser *Repulse* off the east coast of Malaya, leaving the Allies with no active battleship in the Pacific and severely weakening the defenses of Singapore.

16   German forces of Army Group Center, on the Moscow front, begin to retreat before Marshal Georgy Zhukov's Soviet counterattack.

19   The German army commander in chief, Field Marshal Walther von Brauchitsch, is removed from command by the Führer, Adolf Hitler, following the failure of Army group Center's offensive against the Soviet capital, Moscow.

20   President Roosevelt signs the Draft Act, which calls for all men 18 to 64 to register and all men 20 to 44 to be eligible for active duty.

22–January 14, 1942   At the Arcadia Conference in Washington, D.C., President Franklin D. Roosevelt and British prime minister Winston Churchill establish a joint Chiefs of Staff committee to plan a war strategy.

25   The British Chinese territory of Hong Kong surrenders to Japanese forces.

26   German forces of Army Group Center retreat from Kaluga, southwest of Moscow, as the Soviet counteroffensive continues.

SCIENCE, TECHNOLOGY, AND MEDICINE

Agriculture

•   Stem rust destroys nearly half of Mexico's wheat harvest.

December 1941–43   Greece, Poland, and Yugoslavia experience famine as Germany blocks the shipment of wheat from the Ukraine and north Caucasus; about 450,000 people die, including over 40,000 in Warsaw, Poland.

Computing

•   German mathematician Konrad Zuse develops a type of digital computer using binary codes, while working on ballistics. The machine has no memory capacity.

Ecology

DECEMBER

14 Huaráz, Peru, is inundated by flood after a landslide; 3,000 people perish.

Health and Medicine

- Canadian-U.S. surgeon Charles B. Huges discovers that progesterone can control prostate cancer.
- U.S. chemist Richard O. Roblin discovers sulfadiazine; it becomes the most widely used sulfa drug.

Science

- Norton and Loring use X-ray diffraction to demonstrate that Hooke's law of elasticity is due to the spaces in a solid's crystal structure.
- Pilots flying westward over the Pacific discover "jet streams"—air currents with speeds up to 500 kph/310 mph.
- The Society of Applied Anthropology is founded in the United States to study the effects of rapid industrial change on people.
- U.S. physicists Glenn Theodore Seaborg and Edwin McMillan synthesize plutonium (element 94).

Technology

c. 1941 Etched circuits are developed during the decade; electronic connection patterns are etched on metallic foil which is then attached to an insulating substrate; the leads of miniature components are then inserted through holes in the substrate and soldered in place.

- British researchers develop polyester.
- J. R. Whinfield and J. T. Dickson of Calico Printers' Association invent Terylene in England; after the war, it is marketed in the United States as Dacron.
- The proximity fuse, which senses when a target is close enough to be damaged, is developed. It increases the effectiveness of artillery and is first used by the Allies in the Battle of the Bulge in 1944.
- U.S. design engineers Beauchamp E. Smith and Palmer C. Putnam build a windmill with two blades on Grandpa's Knob near Rutland, Vermont with a tip-to-tip diameter of 53.3 m/175 ft; one of the most efficient windmills to date, it produces 1,250 kw of electricity.

JANUARY

1 Five hundred and twenty-five lines becomes the standard for television broadcasting in the United States.

DECEMBER

6 The "Manhattan Project" starts in Chicago, Illinois, and Los Angeles, California, before being concentrated at Los Alamos in 1943 under the direction of U.S. physicist Julius Robert Oppenheimer. Its aim is to develop an atomic bomb.

Transportation

- "Big Boy," the biggest steam locomotive ever built at 547 metric tons/604 tons, 40 m/132 ft, and 7,000 horsepower, goes into service for the Union Pacific Railroad company in the United States; 25 are built.
- The first diesel freight locomotives in the United States begin service between Chicago, Illinois, and California.
- U.S. car manufacturer Ford builds the first car with an all-plastic body.

MAY

6 Ukrainian-born U.S. engineer Igor Sikorsky stays aloft for a record 1 hr 32 sec, in an improved helicopter.

DECEMBER

30 There are 38.8 million private cars in the United States and 2.2 million in Great Britain.

ARTS AND IDEAS

Architecture

- The Swiss architectural theorist Sigfried Gidion publishes *Space, Time, and Architecture* (in English).

Arts

- In the United States, Gutzon Borglum, creator of the Mt. Rushmore Memorial (portraits of presidents Washington, Jefferson, Roosevelt, and Lincoln carved into a mountain) dies. His son, Lincoln, completes the work the same year.
- In the United States, the National Gallery of Art opens in Washington, D.C. The buildings were funded by the late Andrew W. Mellon, and the collection was based around Mellon's personal art collection, donated in 1937.
- The English artist Henry Moore begins drawing people huddled in the Underground (subway) during the London Blitz.
- The English artist Paul Nash paints *Totes Meer/Dead Sea*.
- The French artist Francis Gruber paints *Homage to Jacques Callot*, a symbol of French resistance to Nazi occupation.
- The Italian artist Renato Guttuso paints *Crucifixion*, an attack on fascism.
- The Spanish artist Joan Miró completes his series of paintings *Constellations*.
- The U.S. artist Marsden Hartley paints *Fishermen's Last Supper*.
- U.S. photographer Ansel Adams takes *Moonrise, Hernandez*.

Film

- Hollywood stars Barbara Stanwyck and Gary Cooper feature in *Meet John Doe*, directed by Frank Capra.
- In the United States, the comedy *Here Comes Mr Jordan*, starring Robert Montgomery and Claude Rains, is released in the United States. It is directed by Alexander Hall.

- The 1940 Academy Awards take place. Best Actor: James Stewart, for *The Philadelphia Story*; Best Supporting Actor: Walter Brennan, for *The Westerner*; Best Actress: Ginger Rogers, for *Kitty Foyle*; Best Supporting Actress: Jane Darwell, for *The Grapes of Wrath*; Best Picture: *Rebecca*, directed by Alfred Hitchcock; Best Director: John Ford, for *The Grapes of Wrath*.
- The movie *49th Parallel* is released in the UK. It is directed by Michael Powell and cowritten and adapted from a story by Emeric Pressburger. It stars Eric Portman, Laurence Olivier, Anton Walbrook, Leslie Howard, and Raymond Massey, and features music by Ralph Vaughan Williams.
- The movie *Citizen Kane*, directed by Orson Welles, is released in the United States. He also cowrites and stars in it, with Joseph Cotten, Dorothy Comingore, and Everett Sloane. The U.S. millionaire William Randolph Hearst threatens to sue the makers, regarding the movie as personally defamatory.
- The movie *High Sierra* is released in the United States. It is directed by Raoul Walsh, scripted by John Huston and W. R. Burnett, and stars Humphrey Bogart and Ida Lupino.
- The movie *How Green Was My Valley*, directed by John Ford, is released in the United States. Based on the novel by Richard Llewellyn, it stars Walter Pidgeon, Maureen O'Hara, and Roddy McDowall.
- The movie *Jew Süss*, directed by Veit Harlan, is released in Germany. A notorious travesty of an earlier movie of the same name, this is an example of German anti-Semitic propaganda at its most repellent. It stars Ferdinand Marian, Werner Krauss, Heinrich George, and Kristina Söderbaum.
- The movie *Kipps* (*The Remarkable Mr Kipps* in the United States), directed by Carol Reed, is released in the UK. Based on the novel by H. G. Wells, it stars Michael Redgrave, Phyllis Calvert, Diana Wynyard, and Arthur Riscoe.
- The movie *Love on the Dole* directed by British filmmaker John Baxter is released. Based on the novel by Walter Greenwood, it stars Deborah Kerr, Clifford Evans, and George Carney.
- The movie *Sergeant York*, directed by Howard Hawks, is released in the United States, starring Gary Cooper.
- The movie *Sullivan's Travels*, directed by Preston Sturges, is released in the United States. It stars Joel McCrea as an idealistic movie director. His movie *The Lady Eve*, starring Barbara Stanwyck and Henry Fonda, is also released in the United States.
- The movie *Suspicion*, directed by Alfred Hitchcock, is released in the United States, starring Joan Fontaine.
- The movie *The Big Store*, directed by Charles Riesner, is released in the United States, starring the Marx Brothers.
- The movie *The Little Foxes*, directed by William Wyler, is released in the United States. Based on the play by Lillian Hellman, it stars Bette Davis.
- The movie *The Maltese Falcon*, directed by John Huston, is released in the United States. Based on the novel by Dashiell Hammett, it stars Humphrey Bogart, Mary Astor, Sydney Greenstreet, Peter Lorre and Elisha Cook, Jr.

- Walt Disney releases the cartoon animated movie *Dumbo* in the United States.

Literature and Language

- *The Last Tycoon*, an unfinished novel by the U.S. writer F. Scott Fitzgerald, is published posthumously.
- *The Oxford Dictionary of Quotations* is published for the first time.
- The Austrian writer Franz Werfel publishes his novel *Das Lied von Bernadette/The Song of Bernadette*.
- The complete version of English writer Rudyard Kipling's autobiographical *Something to Myself* is published posthumously.
- The English novelist A. J. Cronin's *The Keys of the Kingdom* is the best-selling novel of the year in the United States. *Berlin Diary*, by William L. Shirer, is the best-selling nonfiction title.
- The English writer Ivy Compton-Burnett publishes her novel *Parents and Children*.
- The English writer Joyce Cary publishes his novel *Herself Surprised*.
- The English writer Rex Warner publishes his allegorical novel *The Aerodrome*.
- The English writer Virginia Woolf publishes her last novel *Between the Acts*.
- The English writer W. H. Auden publishes his poetry collection *The Double Man* (published in Britain as *New Year Letter*).
- The French writer Louis Aragon publishes the poetry collection *Le Crève-Coeur/Heart Break*.
- The Irish writer Flann O'Brien publishes his Gaelic novel *An Béal Bocht/The Poor Mouth*. An English translation appears in 1973.
- The New Zealand writer Allen Curnow publishes his poetry collection *Island and Time*.
- The Nobel Prize for Literature is not awarded this year.
- The Pulitzer Prize for Biography is awarded to Ola Elizabeth Winslow for *Jonathan Edwards*, and the Prize for Poetry goes to Leonard Bacon for *Sunderland Capture*. The Pulitzer Prize for Fiction is not awarded this year.
- The Russian writer Ilya Ehrenburg publishes his novel *Padeniye Parizha/The Fall of Paris*.
- The Russian-born U.S. novelist Vladimir Nabokov publishes *The Real Life of Sebastian Knight*, his first novel in English.
- The U.S. writer and critic Edmund Wilson publishes his critical work *The Wound and the Bow*.
- The U.S. writer Carson McCullers publishes her novel *Reflections in a Golden Eye*.
- The U.S. writer Eudora Welty publishes *A Curtain of Green*, a collection of short stories that includes "Why I Live at the P.O."
- The U.S. writer J. P. Marquand publishes his novel *H.M. Pulham, Esquire*.
- The U.S.-born English writer T. S. Eliot publishes *The Dry Salvages*, the second part of *The Four Quartets*, which is published in 1943.

MAY

31 In Germany, Roman type replaces Gothic.

Music

- English concert pianist Myra Hess is named Dame Commander of the British Empire.
- In the United States, William Benton acquires and expands the Muzak Company, which provides piped music to public places.
- The English composer Richard Addinsell writes *Warsaw Concerto*, music for the movie *Dangerous Moonlight*.
- The English composer Michael Tippett completes his choral work *A Child of Our Time*.
- The folk group the Almanac Singers—Pete Seeger, Lee Hayes, and Millard Lampell—are joined by Woody Guthrie, in the United States.
- The French composer Olivier Messiaen completes his *Quartet for the End of Time*, written while he is in a German prisoner-of-war camp.
- The Hungarian-born U.S. musicologist and critic Paul Henry Lang publishes *Music in Western Civilization*.
- The Italian composer Luigi Dallapiccola completes his *Canti di prigioniera/Songs of Imprisonment* for chorus and orchestra.
- The Russian composer Dmitry Shostakovich completes his Symphony No. 7 during the siege of Leningrad by German forces. Dedicated to the defenders of the city, it becomes known as the *Leningrad* Symphony. It is first performed in Kuibyshev in the USSR in 1942.
- The Russian composer Sergey Prokofiev completes his *Suite 1941*.

Theater and Dance

- The play *Le Desir attrapé par la queue/Desire Caught by the Tail*, by the Spanish artist Pablo Picasso, is first performed, informally, in Paris, France. It is performed (read) in his studio by friends such as Jean-Paul Sartre and Raymond Queneau. Written in 1941, it is a surrealistic response to the privations of the German occupation.
- The play *Mutter Courage und ihre Kinder/Mother Courage and her Children*, by the German writer Bertolt Brecht, is first performed, in Zürich, Switzerland.
- The Pulitzer Prize for Drama is awarded to Robert Sherwood for *There Shall Be No Night*.
- The Russian composer Dmitry Shostakovich leaves incomplete his opera *The Gamblers*, based on the play *Igroki/The Gamblers*, by Nikolai Gogol (1832).
- The song "London Pride" by the English writer and actor Noël Coward becomes popular. His play *Blithe Spirit* is first performed.
- The U.S. writer Eugene O'Neill completes one of his best-known plays, *Long Day's Journey into Night*. It will not open until 1956.

Thought and Scholarship

- English businessman and social reformer Benjamin Seebohm Rowntree publishes *Poverty and Progress: A Second Social Survey of York*.
- English historian A. L. Rowse publishes *Tudor Cornwall*.
- English historian A. J. P. Taylor publishes *The Habsburg Monarchy, 1815–1918*.

- English historian Eileen Power publishes *The Wool Trade in English Medieval History*.
- French philosopher Etienne Gilson publishes *God and Philosophy*, lectures delivered at Yale University in New Haven, Connecticut.
- German-born U.S. political philosopher Herbert Marcuse publishes *Reason and Revolution*.
- German-born U.S. psychologist Erich Fromm publishes *Escape from Freedom*.
- The first volume of the *Cambridge Economic History of Europe* is published.
- The Pulitzer Prize for History is awarded to Marcus Lee Hansen for *The Atlantic Migration, 1607–1860*.
- U.S. historian Oscar Handlin publishes *Boston's Immigrants, 1790–1865*.

SOCIETY

Everyday Life

- About 20% of German women belong to the Nazi Women's Association.
- Sanger's Circus in the UK, founded in 1820, closes down.
- Selected population figures (in millions) are: China 450; India 389; USSR 182; United States 131; Germany, including Austria, Slovakia, West Poland, etc., 110; Japan 105; Great Britain 47; Brazil 41; France 40.
- The General Mills corporation introduces the breakfast cereal Cheerios in the United States.
- The UK government introduces "double summer time," with clocks running two hours ahead of Greenwich Mean Time.
- Unemployment is virtually eliminated in the UK.

FEBRUARY

- The U.S. Supreme Court upholds the Federal Wage and Hour Law banning the employment of children under 16 in mining and manufacturing and under 18 in other hazardous occupations.
- 26 The Congress of Industrial Organizations (CIO) calls a strike at the Bethlehem Steel plants over a government-established wage and price formula. The newly established U.S. Office of Production Management settles the strike during the month, favoring the CIO.

APRIL

- In a sign of organized labor's mounting influence in the United States, the Ford Motor Company enters into a contract with the Congress of Industrial Organizations (CIO) after a nine-day strike by 85,000 workers at Ford's River Rouge factory in Detroit, Michigan. It accepts worker unionization and recognizes the United Auto Workers (UAW).
- Rice-rationing is introduced in Japan.
- The U.S. aviator Charles A. Lindbergh, U.S. publishing mogul Robert R. McCormick, and Sears chairman, Robert E. Wood, establish the America First Committee, an isolationist organization committed to halting the United States's apparent slide toward war.

MAY

- The U.S. vehicle manufacturer General Motors raises wages ten cents per hour to stave off strikes.

OCTOBER

3 U.S. chemists Lyle D. Goodhue and W. N. Sullivan patent the aerosol container.

DECEMBER

- In the United States, food prices are 61% above prewar levels.
- The American Federation of Labor announces a no-strike policy and initiates a rapprochement with the Congress of Industrial Organizations (CIO). A week later, delegates to an industry–labor conference pledge to avoid strikes and lockouts and to submit grievances to a War Labor Board.
9 The National Service Bill in the UK lowers the age of call-up to 18½ and renders single women aged 20–30 liable to military service.

Media and Communication

- Marshall Field founds the *Chicago Sun*, which is later published as a tabloid (from 1947).

JANUARY

1 The Columbia Broadcasting System (CBS) begins regular television broadcasting (in competition with NBC).
21 The British communist paper, the *Daily Worker*, is suppressed.

JULY

1 Financed by corporate sponsorship, the National Broadcasting Corporation (NBC) and the Columbia Broadcasting System (CBS) start transmitting 15 hours of broadcasts, including sports and cartoons, from New York, New York.

Religion

- The German Catholic theologian Karl Rahner publishes *Hörer des Wortes/Hearers of the Word*.

BIRTHS & DEATHS

JANUARY

5 Henri Bergson, French philosopher, dies in Paris, France (81).

8 Amy Johnson, English pioneer aviator who flew solo from London, England, to Darwin, Australia, disappears over the Thames Estuary, England (38).

8 Robert Baden-Powell, British soldier, founder of the Boy Scouts and Girl Guides, dies in Nyeri, Kenya (83).

11 Emanuel Lasker, German chess master, world champion 1894–1920, dies in New York, New York (72).

13 James Joyce, Irish novelist and poet, dies in Zürich, Switzerland (58).

21 Richie Havens, U.S. folk and rock musician, born in New York, New York.

FEBRUARY

14 Paul Tsongas, U.S. Democratic presidential candidate in 1992, born (–1997).

21 Frederick Grant Banting, Canadian physician who, with Charles H. Best, discovered insulin, dies in Newfoundland, Canada (49).

MARCH

8 Sherwood Anderson, U.S. novelist and short-story writer, dies in Colón, Panama (65).

28 Virginia Woolf, English author and critic, dies near Rodmell, Sussex, England (59).

APRIL

11 Ellen Goodman, U.S. newspaper and magazine columnist and Pulitzer prizewinner, born in Newton, Massachusetts.

30 Edwin S. Porter, U.S. pioneer filmmaker who introduced dramatic editing, dies in New York, New York (69).

MAY

18 Werner Sombart, German historical economist, dies in Berlin, Germany (78).

24 Robert Zimmerman (Bob Dylan), U.S. singer and songwriter, known for his "protest songs" of the 1960s, born in Duluth, Minnesota.

JUNE

2 Lou Gehrig, U.S. professional baseball player, dies in New York, New York (37).

4 Kaiser Wilhelm II, German emperor and king of Prussia 1888–1918, dies in Doorn, the Netherlands (82).

6 Louis Chevrolet, U.S. automobile designer, dies in Detroit, Michigan (62).

22 Ed Bradley, U.S. television news reporter who appears on *60 Minutes*, born in Philadelphia, Pennsylvania.

27 Krzysztof Kieślowski, Polish film director and screenwriter, born in Warsaw, Poland (–1996).

29 Ignacy Jan Paderewski, Polish pianist, composer, and statesman, prime minister of Poland in 1919, dies in New York, New York (80).

JULY

1 Twyla Tharp, U.S. dancer and choreographer, born in Portland, Indiana.

AUGUST

7 Rabindranath Tagore, Indian poet, also a composer and painter, dies in Calcutta, India (80).

29 Slobodan Milošević, president of Serbia 1989–, thought to be responsible for much of the ethnic conflict in Yugoslavia, born in Pozarevac, Czechoslovakia.

SEPTEMBER

9 Kim Casali, English cartoonist, creator of the series "Love is...," and also the first woman in England to conceive her husband's baby by artificial insemination after his death, born in New Zealand (–1997).

10 Stephen Jay Gould, U.S. paleontologist and prizewinning author, born in New York, New York.

OCTOBER

5 Louis Brandeis, influential U.S. lawyer and first Jewish Supreme Court Justice, dies in Washington, D.C. (84).

10 Kenule ("Ken") Saro-Wiwa, Nigerian author and environmental activist, born in Bori, near Port Harcourt, Nigeria (–1995).

NOVEMBER

18 Walther Hermann Nernst, German scientist who formulated the third law of thermodynamics, dies in Muskau, Germany (77).

- The German Protestant theologian Rudolf Bultmann publishes *New Testament and Mythology*.
- The U.S. theologian Reinhold Niebuhr publishes the first volume of *The Nature and Destiny of Man*. The second volume will appear in 1943.

Sports

- Ohio State becomes college football's national champion.

APRIL

6–12 The Boston Bruins beat the Detroit Red Wings to win the National Hockey League (NHL) Stanley Cup.

26–June 17 U.S. athlete Les Steers breaks the world high jump record three times, clearing 2.10 m, 2.105 m, and then 2.11 m.

MAY

15–July 16 In baseball, Joe DiMaggio of the New York Yankees hits safely in a major league record 56 consecutive games.

JUNE

7 U.S. golfer Craig Wood wins the U.S. Open golf championship, which because of World War II will not be played again until 1946.

JULY

- Whirlaway, ridden by Eddie Arcaro, wins the Kentucky Derby, Preakness Stakes, and Belmont Stakes to become the fifth horse to win the American Triple Crown.

OCTOBER

1–6 The New York Yankees defeat the Brooklyn Dodgers four games to one in the World Series.

DECEMBER

21 The Chicago Bears retain the National Football League (NFL) Championship defeating the New York Giants 37–9 in Chicago, Illinois.

1942

POLITICS, GOVERNMENT, AND ECONOMICS

Business and Economics

OCTOBER

- Bell Aircraft Corporation of California tests the first U.S. jet airplane.

Colonization

AUGUST

8 The Indian Congress Party passes a motion calling on the British to "quit India" immediately.

Human Rights

- Students from the University of Chicago, in Illinois, establish the Congress of Racial Equality. The organization applies the Indian nationalist leader Mahatma Gandhi's strategy of passive resistance at sit-ins designed to end racial segregation. James L. Farmer is appointed national chair.

JANUARY

20 At the Wannsee Conference in Germany, which is chaired by Reinhard Heydrich, head of the Nazi secret police, Nazi officials discuss "the final solution" of "the Jewish question" (in effect, the annihilation of European Jewry).

JULY

7 In a break with tradition, St. Peter's Cathedral in Rome, Italy allows women without stockings to enter.

Politics and Government

- Germany begins the manufacture of Tabun nerve gas. Around 15,000 tons are produced and stockpiled.
- The U.S. president Franklin D. Roosevelt establishes an Office of Economic Stabilization to monitor U.S. wages, salaries, and prices.
- The U.S. Supreme Court rules Nevada divorces binding in other states.
- Tire and gasoline rationing are introduced to conserve rubber in the United States.

July 1942–45 During the war, U.S. women are recruited on a large scale for the war effort; between 1942 and 1945 the number of working women increases by 50%.

JANUARY

- Japanese troops seize Manila, the capital of the Philippines, forcing the U.S. general Douglas MacArthur to retreat to the Battan peninsula on the island of Luzon.

- The U.S. Office of Production Management bans retail sales of new cars and passenger trucks to shift the focus of the auto industry to the production of military vehicles.
- The U.S. president Franklin D. Roosevelt submits a $59 billion budget to Congress; $52 million is devoted to military expenditures. He also signs the Price Control Bill, authorizing the Office of Price Administration to fix U.S. prices.

January–March   Delegates to an Inter-American Conference in Rio de Janeiro, Brazil, sever relations with the Axis nations and establish an Inter-American Defense Board (in March).

11   Japanese forces advancing through Malaya capture the capital, Kuala Lumpur.

20–March 8   Japanese forces cross Thailand and invade Burma, capturing the city of Rangoon on March 8.

23   A Japanese force captures Rabaul, the chief town on the island of New Britain in the Pacific Ocean, as part of an attempt to outflank Allied positions in New Guinea.

FEBRUARY

- The U.S. president Franklin D. Roosevelt issues Executive Order 9066, sanctioning the internment of Japanese-Americans living along the west coast.

1   British forces withdraw to the naval base of Singapore after a series of defeats by Japanese forces on the Malayan peninsula

1–March 4   U.S. carrier aircraft attack Japanese bases on the Marshall, Gilbert, Wake, and Marcus islands in the Pacific Ocean.

9   Clocks in the United States turn ahead one hour for daylight saving time, where they will remain for the duration of World War II.

11–12   The German battlecruisers *Scharnhorst* and *Gneisenau* break out of Brest harbor in western France and through the English Channel to their German base, protected from British air and naval attack by bad weather and by electronic countermeasures against British radar.

15   The strategic British colony and naval base of Singapore surrenders to Japanese forces, together with over 70,000 British and Commonwealth soldiers and airmen. British prime minister Winston Churchill later describes the event as "the worst disaster and largest capitulation in British history."

19   Japanese planes bomb Darwin in north Australia.

27–28   Two Japanese cruiser groups escorting a Japanese invasion fleet bound for Java destroy an Allied cruiser squadron under the Dutch rear admiral Karel Doorman in the Battle of the Java Sea. The Dutch cruisers *De Ruyter* and *Java*, the British cruiser *Exeter*, the Australian cruiser *Perth*, the U.S. cruiser *Houston*, and all but four escorting destroyers are sunk.

28   Japanese forces land on the island of Java in the Netherlands East Indies.

MARCH

23   Japanese forces occupy northern Sumatra in the Netherlands East Indies and the Andaman and Nicobar Islands in the Indian Ocean.

28   British aircraft bomb the port of Lübeck, north Germany, destroying most of the medieval city.

30–April 30   Japanese forces advance northward through Burma (now Myanmar), inflicting a series of defeats on British and Colonial forces.

APRIL

- Japanese forces overrun Burma (now Myanmar), seize the town of Lashio near Mandalay, and close the Burma Road, the main supply route for China's war effort running from Lashio, Burma, to Kunming, China.

4   Continuous raids by the German and Italian air forces on the British base of Malta threaten British convoys to Egypt and hamper Allied attempts to disrupt Axis convoy routes to Libya.

9   U.S. and Filipino forces in the Philippines holding out against the Japanese on the Bataan Peninsula surrender. About 70,000 prisoners are taken on a forced march, only 54,000 reaching the destination camp.

15   King George VI of Britain awards the George Cross to the people of Malta for their fortitude under German and Italian bombardment.

18   A U.S. strike force of 16 B-25 bombers under Brig. Gen. James Doolittle bomb Tokyo, Yokohama, and other Japanese cities.

18   Pierre Laval becomes president and minister for foreign affairs and the interior in Vichy France.

18–July 29   German forces of Army Group South advance into eastern Ukraine, aiming to capture the oil fields in the Caucasus.

23–30   In the Baedeker raids, named for the German tourist guidebooks, German aircraft bomb Exeter, Bath, and other historic cities in Britain in reprisal for British raids on Cologne and Lübeck.

28   A nighttime blackout goes into effect along a 15-mile strip of the United States's Atlantic coast.

28   The U.S. Office of Production Management (OPA), given the power to fix all prices except farm produce, stabilizes rents in 301 communities, affecting 86 million Americans.

MAY

- The U.S. president Franklin D. Roosevelt orders sugar rationing.

May 1942–November 1943   Japan constructs the Kwai Railroad between Bangkok in Siam (modern Thailand) and Moulmein in Burma (now Myanmar). Over 15,000 Allied prisoners of war and 90,000 native laborers die during its construction.

1   Japanese forces in Burma (now Myanmar) take Mandalay, while the British and colonial forces withdraw along the Chindwin Valley to India.

4–8 U.S. naval forces narrowly succeed in preventing a Japanese attempt to take the Allied base at Port Moresby, Papua, in the first great carrier battle of the Pacific War, the Battle of the Coral Sea.

5   British troops successfully invade the Vichy French territory of Madagascar.

6   U.S. and Filipino forces on the island of Corregidor in the Philippines surrender to the Japanese.

14   In the United States, women's military involvement in the war begins when Congress founds WAAC (Women's Auxiliary Army Corps).

27   The Nazi "protector" of Bohemia and Moravia, Reinhard Heydrich, is shot in Prague, Czechoslovakia, by Czech resistance fighters.

27–September 5   The German and Italian forces under Erwin Rommel outflank the defensive position of the

British 8th Army under General Sir Neil Ritchie at Gazala, Libya, inflicting a severe defeat.

30–31 The first British "thousand bomber" raid is launched against the city of Cologne, Germany.

JUNE

• The U.S. president Franklin D. Roosevelt creates the Office of War Information to monitor news and broadcast propaganda.

3–6 U.S. carrier planes sink the Japanese aircraft carriers *Hiryu*, *Soryu*, *Kaga*, and *Akagi* for the loss of the U.S. carrier *Yorktown* in the Battle of Midway, off Midway Island in the Pacific. The naval balance in the Pacific war swings in favor of the Allies.

5 Japanese forces seize Attu, an island in the U.S. Aleutian chain in the north Pacific, off Alaska.

10 The German Gestapo (secret police) destroys the village of Lidiče, Czechoslovakia, in reprisal for the killing of Reinhard Heydrich, the Nazi "protector" of Bohemia and Moravia, by Czech resistance fighters; 198 men are shot, 184 women sent to the Ravensbrück concentration camp, and 98 children deported.

17 The U.S. Army sponsors *Yank* magazine.

17–21 The U.S. president Franklin D. Roosevelt and the British prime minister Winston Churchill meet at the Washington Conference to discuss war production and military strategy for World War II.

21 German and Italian forces under the German general Erwin Rommel retake the port of Tobruk in Libya from the British 8th Army. British forces retreat eastward to positions at Mersa Matruh, and Sir Claude Auchinleck succeeds Sir Neil Ritchie as 8th Army commander on June 25.

JULY

• The U.S. Congress approves the creation of Women Accepted for Voluntary Emergency Service (WAVES) to bolster U.S. naval reserves.

1–4 The British 8th Army under General Claude Auchinleck halts the advance of German troops under Field Marshal Erwin Rommel into British-held Egypt at the First Battle of El Alamein.

7 Japanese troops deploying through the Solomon Islands in the Pacific land on the island of Guadalcanal.

21–January 22, 1943 Japanese troops land in New Guinea in the Pacific and advance through the interior of the island toward the Allied base at Port Moresby, Papua.

26 British aircraft bomb the German city of Hamburg.

28 Units of the German Army Group South retake the Soviet port of Rostov-on-Don. The newly-organized Army Group A overruns the northern Caucasus, reaching Grozny and Ordzhonikidze by November.

AUGUST

• The U.S. marine lieutenant colonel Evans F. Carlson leads a successful raid on a Japanese radio station on Makin Island in the occupied Gilbert Islands. "Carlson's Raiders" are celebrated for their daring.

13 General Bernard Montgomery is appointed commander of Britain's 8th Army in North Africa.

19 Canadian and British forces raid the port of Dieppe in northeast France. The operation is a disaster, and casualties include 3,367 Canadians killed, wounded, or taken prisoner.

30 German field marshal Erwin Rommel launches his final attempt to break the British 8th Army's Alamein line

and take Egypt, leading to the Battle of Alam Halfa. The 8th Army, superior in armor, halts the German advance by September 2.

SEPTEMBER

13–February 2, 1943 Units of the German 6th Army and 4th Panzer Army (Army Group B) reach the outskirts of the city of Stalingrad (now Volgograd), on the Volga; resistance of the Soviet 64th and 62nd armies is tenacious.

OCTOBER

3 The U.S. Congress empowers the Office of Price Administration to impose a freeze on prices, wages, and rents.

23 The British 8th Army begins its successful offensive against German and Italian positions at El Alamein, Egypt.

24–26 Two U.S. aircraft carrier task forces engage the Japanese South Seas fleet under Vice Admiral Nobutaki Kondo off the Santa Cruz Islands, near Guadalcanal. The Japanese aircraft carriers *Zuiho* and *Shokaku* are damaged, but the U.S. carrier *Hornet* is sunk, leaving the damaged *Enterprise* the only operational Allied aircraft carrier in the Pacific.

NOVEMBER

• In the U.S. congressional elections, the Democrats retain a 58–37 majority in the Senate and a 218–208 majority in the House of Representatives.

• The U.S. Congress authorizes the creation of Semper Paratus Always Ready Service (SPARS), a female reserve of the Coast Guard.

• The U.S. president Franklin D. Roosevelt orders coffee rationing.

4 German and Italian forces under the German general Erwin Rommel retreat westward in North Africa, pursued by the British.

8 British and U.S. forces land in Vichy French-held Morocco and Algeria (Operation "Torch"), and advance swiftly toward Tunisia.

11 The German Führer Adolf Hitler orders the German occupation of Vichy France.

11 The U.S. general Dwight D. Eisenhower recognizes Admiral François Darlan as French chief of state in North Africa, arousing the indignation of the British government.

13 Advance units of the British 8th Army enter the port of Tobruk, Libya, as German and Italian forces retreat westward.

19–23 A Soviet counteroffensive at the city of Stalingrad (now Volgograd) surrounds the besieging German 6th army, commanded by Friedrich von Paulus.

DECEMBER

12–23 Units of the German 4th Panzer Army under Field-Marshal Erich von Manstein attempt unsuccessfully to relieve the trapped German 6th Army of General Friedrich von Paulus at Stalingrad.

24 Admiral François Darlan, Vichy French Chief of State in French North Africa, is assassinated in Algiers by an anti-Vichy agent.

SCIENCE, TECHNOLOGY, AND MEDICINE

Agriculture

- Fungus destroys the rice crop near Bombay, India; 1.6 million people die of starvation.
- Vegetables become scarce and nearly 40% of all U.S. vegetables are grown in "Victory Gardens."

Ecology

- About 40,000 people die in a cyclone near Chittagong, India.

OCTOBER

16   A hurricane in Bengal, India, kills over 40,000 people.

NOVEMBER

28   The Coconut Grove, a nightclub in Boston, Massachusetts, burns, killing 487 people. It is the worst single fire in the modern era.

Health and Medicine

- Canadian anesthiologists H. R. Griffith and E. Johnson use curare to produce muscular paralysis during surgery.
- French physician André Loubatière leads the development of oral drugs for diabetics with his discovery that sulfa drugs lower blood sugar levels.
- Grantly Dick-Read publishes *Revelation of Childbirth*, an extension of his 1933 work *Natural Childbirth*.

Science

- Archeologists discover the "Mildenhall Treasure," a collection of Roman silver tableware and other objects dating from the 4th century AD, near the Mildenhall airbase in east England.
- Australian archeologist V. Gordon Childe publishes *What Happened in History*.
- German philosopher of science Hans Reichenbach publishes *Philosophy Foundations of Quantum Mechanics*.
- Radar operators in the British army detect, for the first time, radio emissions from the sun.
- U.S. astronomer Grote Reber makes the first radio maps of the sky, locating individual radio sources.

Technology

- A loran (long-range navigation) system, where location is determined by noting time differences in the reception of synchronized pulses from "master and slave" transmitting stations, begins operation for the first time along the east coast of North America.
- Magnetic tape is invented in the United States.
- The Grand Coulee Dam on the Columbia River in the United States is completed; at 167.6 m/550 ft high and 1,271.9 m/4,173 ft long, it is world's largest concrete structure.

- The United States begins producing the M4 Sherman tank with a 75 mm gun; nearly 50,000 are built by 1944.
- c. 1942   The installation of radar equipment begins on U.S., British, and German submarines.
- Mass production of the Ilyushin IL-2 "Stornovik" dive bomber and ground-attack aircraft begins in the USSR; over 36,000 are produced during the war.
- The Lockheed P-38 "Lightning" enters active service with the U.S. Air Force; it becomes the principal U.S. fighter escort.

JANUARY

- The U.S. president Franklin D. Roosevelt establishes the War Production Board (WPB) to oversee the refitting of U.S. industry for arms production and to monitor military contracting. The WPB replaces the Office of Production Management.

6   U.S. scientist William Hewlett patents the variable frequency oscillation generator, or audio oscillator, which generates high-quality audio frequencies.

OCTOBER

3   The V2 rocket, the ancestor of modern space rockets, is first launched, in Germany; weighing 40 tons it is 12 m/40 ft long, burns an alcohol-liquid oxygen mixture, can reach a distance of 200 km/125 mi, a height of 97 km/60 mi, and travels at 5,300kph/3,300 mph.

DECEMBER

2   Italian physicist Enrico Fermi and his colleagues at the University of Chicago, Illinois, use thin layers of uranium oxide and graphite to create the first nuclear pile and initiate a controlled chain-reaction—the first nuclear reactor.

Transportation

FEBRUARY

10   The last automobile is produced in the United States until 1945; car manufacturers gear up to produce tanks, aircraft, and other equipment for the war effort.

MARCH

March–November   The Alaska Highway is built from Dawson Creek, British Columbia, Canada, to Fairbanks, Alaska; 2,451 km/1,523 mi long, it is completed by U.S. army engineers in less than nine months.

MAY

- Seventeen eastern U.S. states begin rationing gasoline to 11.4 l/3 gal a week for discretionary driving.

JULY

- The German Messerschmidt Me 262 makes its first flight; it is the first operational jet airplane.
- U.S. internal improvements proceed apace as President Franklin D. Roosevelt authorizes $93 million for a canal to be built connecting Florida's Gulf and Atlantic coasts.

SEPTEMBER

- The Boeing B-29 "Superfortess" bomber makes its first flight; some 2,180 subsequently serve with the U.S. Army Air Force.

OCTOBER

1   The Bell XP-59A makes a test flight at Muroc Lake, California; it is the first U.S. jet to fly.

NOVEMBER

- The Alcan International Highway, linking Alaska and Alberta, Canada, opens to traffic.

ARTS AND IDEAS

Architecture

- Camp David, the U.S. presidential retreat in Thrumount, Maryland, is completed after three years' construction work.
- The German-born English art historian Nikolaus Pevsner publishes *An Outline of European Architecture*.
- The U.S. architect Frank Lloyd Wright draws up designs for the Guggenheim Museum, New York, which will be completed in 1959.

Arts

- The English artist Paul David Bomberg paints *Underground Bomb Store*.
- The exhibition "Artists Aid Russia" is held at Hertford House, London, England.
- The French artist Georges Braque paints *Kitchen Table*.
- The French artist Jean Fautrier paints *Great Tragic Head*.
- The French artist Yves Tanguy paints *Infinite Divisibility*.
- The German artist Max Ernst paints *Europe after the Rain*.
- The Norwegian artist Edvard Münch paints *Self-Portrait Between the Clock and the Bed*.
- The Spanish artist Pablo Picasso paints *Woman with a Hat in the Shape of a Fish*.
- The U.S. artist Edward Hopper paints *Nighthawks*.
- U.S. photographer Gordon Parks takes *American Gothic, Washington, D.C.*

Film

- Hollywood filmmakers work with censors to make movies to inspire and support the war effort, such as *Desperate Journey*, directed by Raoul Walsh, and *Mrs Miniver*, directed by William Wyler and starring Greer Garson, Walter Pidgeon, and Teresa Wright. The latter is adapted from the 1940 novel by English writer Jan Struther.
- Mark Sandrich's musical movie *Holiday Inn* is released, starring Bing Crosby and Fred Astaire. It features the song "White Christmas" by the composer Irving Berlin, sung by Bing Crosby.
- The 1941 Academy Awards take place. Best Actor: Gary Cooper, for *Sergeant York*; Best Actress: Joan Fontaine, for *Suspicion*; Best Supporting Actress: Mary Astor, for *The Great Lie*; Best Picture: *How Green Was My Valley*, directed by John Ford; Best Director: John Ford, for *How Green Was My Valley*.
- The annual quota regulations for British movies are suspended.

- The comedy duo of Bud Abbott and Lou Costello are the nation's top box office draw, followed by Clark Gable, Gary Cooper, and Mickey Rooney.
- The movie *Casablanca*, directed by Michael Curtiz, is released in the United States. It stars Ingrid Bergman, Humphrey Bogart, Paul Henreid, Claude Rains, Peter Lorre, Dooley Wilson, and Sydney Greenstreet.
- The movie *I Married a Witch*, directed by French filmmaker René Clair, is released in the United States, starring Fredric March and Veronica Lake.
- The movie *In Which We Serve*, directed by David Lean and Noël Coward, is released in the UK. Noël Coward wrote, produced, and scored the movie; he also stars in it, along with Bernard Miles, John Mills, Richard Attenborough, and Celia Johnson.
- The movie *Les Visiteurs du soir/The Devil's Envoy*, directed by Marcel Carné, is released in France, starring Alain Cluny, Arletty, and Jules Berry.
- The movie *Now, Voyager*, starring Bette Davis, is released in the United States. It is directed by Irving Rapper.
- The movie *Ossessione/Obsession*, directed by Luchino Visconti, is released in Italy. Based on James M. Cain's novel *The Postman Always Rings Twice*, it stars Massimo Girotti, Clara Calamai, and Elio Marcuzzo. It is seized by the fascist authorities.
- The movie *The Cat People*, directed by Jacques Tourneur, is released in the United States, starring Simone Simon, Kent Smith, and Tom Conway.
- The movie *The First of the Few* (*Spitfire* in the United States), directed by Leslie Howard, is released in the UK. He also stars in it, along with David Niven and Rosamund John.
- The movie *The Magnificent Ambersons*, directed by Orson Welles, is released in the United States, starring Joseph Cotten, Dolores Costello, Agnes Moorehead, and Tim Holt. Desperate for box office success, the movie company RKO edit the movie beyond recognition in Welles's absence, cutting over 40 minutes. No copy of the original is kept.
- The movie *This Above All*, directed by Russian filmmaker Anatole Litvak, is released in the United States, starring Tyrone Power and Joan Fontaine.
- The movie *To Be or Not to Be*, directed by Ernst Lubitsch, is released in the United States, starring Jack Benny, Carole Lombard, and Robert Stack.
- The movie *Woman of the Year*, directed by George Stevens, is released in the United States. It stars Spencer Tracy and Katharine Hepburn.
- The movie *Yankee Doodle Dandy*, directed by Michael Curtiz, is released in the United States, starring James Cagney, Joan Leslie, Walter Huston, and Rosemary de Camp.
- The occupying German authorities in France ban Jews and foreigners from involvement in movie production, even under pseudonyms. The showing of English and U.S. movies is also prohibited.
- Twentieth Century Fox insure the legs of movie star and war pin-up girl Betty Grable with Lloyds of London for $1 million.
- U.S. actors Alan Ladd and Veronica Lake costar in *This Gun for Hire*, directed by Frank Tuttle, and *The Glass Key*, directed by Stuart Heisler.

Literature and Language

- The Algerian-born French writer Albert Camus publishes his novel *L'Etranger/The Outsider*.
- The Chinese leader Mao Zedong publishes *Talks at the Yenan Forum on Art and Literature*, setting out the role of the arts in China's revolutionary struggle.
- The English writer and scholar C. S. Lewis publishes *The Screwtape Letters*, a popular discussion of Christian belief.
- The English writer Enid Blyton publishes the first of her *Famous Five* children's novels.
- The English writer Evelyn Waugh publishes his novel *Put Out More Flags*.
- The English writer Stephen Spender publishes his poetry collection *Ruins and Visions*.
- The French writer Antoine Marie Roger de St.-Exupéry publishes his autobiographical *Pilote de Guerre/Flight to Arras*.
- The French writer Paul Eluard publishes his poetry collection *Poésie et vérité/Poetry and Truth*.
- The Irish writer Patrick Kavanagh publishes his major poem "The Great Hunger."
- The Nobel Prize for Literature is not awarded this year.
- The Pulitzer Prize for Biography is awarded to Forrest Wilson for *Crusader in Crinoline*, the Pulitzer Prize for Fiction is awarded to Ellen Glasgow for *In This Our Life*, and the Prize for Poetry is awarded to William Rose Benét for *The Dust Which is God*.
- The Spanish writer Camilo José Cela publishes his novel *La Familia de Pascual Duarte/The Family of Pascal Duarte*. Its bitterness reflects the aftermath of the Spanish Civil War.
- The U.S. novelist Lloyd C. Douglas's melodramatic novel about the crucifixion, *The Robe*, is published and in 1943 becomes the best-selling novel of the year in the United States.
- The U.S. writer Eudora Welty publishes her novel *The Robber Bridegroom*.
- The U.S. writer John Steinbeck publishes *The Moon is Down*, a novel about Norwegian resistance to German occupation.
- The U.S. writer Mary McCarthy publishes her first novel, *The Company She Keeps*.
- The U.S. writer Wallace Stevens publishes two collections of poetry: *Notes towards a Supreme Fiction* and *Parts of a World*.
- The U.S.-born English writer T. S. Eliot publishes *Little Gidding*, the last part of his *Four Quartets*, which is published in 1943.

Music

- In the United States, the U.S. jazz musician Lionel Hampton founds the Hampton Big Band.
- The Austrian composer Arnold Schoenberg completes his Piano Concerto, Opus 42.
- The English composer Benjamin Britten completes his *Hymn to St Cecilia*.
- The English composer Gerald Finzi completes his songs *Let Us Garlands Bring*, settings of Shakespeare.
- The opera *Capriccio* by the German composer Richard Strauss is first performed, in Munich, Germany.

- The Russian composer Dmitry Shostakovich completes his Piano Sonata No. 2.
- The U.S. bandleader Glenn Miller dissolves his own band to direct the American Air Force Band.
- The U.S. composer Aaron Copland completes his *Lincoln Portrait*, for speaker and orchestra; his score for the ballet *Rodeo*; and his *Fanfare for the Common Man*.
- The U.S. composer Henry Cowell completes his Symphony No. 3, the *Gaelic*.
- The U.S. composer John Cage completes his String Quartet.
- The U.S. singer Frank Sinatra makes his first stage appearance in New York, New York.

FEBRUARY
- In the United States, the Radio Corporation of America (RCA) presents the Glenn Miller orchestra with a gold record to mark sales of 1.2 million records of *Chattanooga Choo Choo*. It was probably the first presentation of a "gold disc" for sales of more than one million.

Theater and Dance

- The Armenian composer Aram Khachaturian completes his score for the ballet *Gayaneh*.
- The play *Flare Path*, by the English writer Terence Rattigan, is first performed, in London, England. It is based on his war experiences in the Royal Air Force.
- The play *Red Roses For Me*, by the Irish writer Sean O'Casey, is first performed, in Dublin, Ireland.
- The play *The Skin of our Teeth*, by the U.S. writer Thornton Wilder, is first performed, at the Plymouth Theater in New York, New York.
- The Pulitzer Prize for Drama is not awarded this year.

Thought and Scholarship

- Austrian-born U.S. economist Joseph Aois Schumpeter publishes *Capitalism, Socialism and Democracy*.
- English historian E. H. Carr publishes *Conditions of Peace*.
- English historian George Macaulay Trevelyan publishes *English Social History*.
- English philosopher R. G. Collingwood publishes *The New Leviathan*.
- The Pulitzer Prize for History is awarded to Margaret Leech for *Reveille in Washington*.
- U.S. philosopher Susanne Langer publishes *Philosophy in a New Key*.
- West Indian politician Eric Eustace Williams (the first prime minister of Trinidad and Tobago, 1962–81) publishes *The Negro in the Caribbean*.

SOCIETY

Education

- Carleton University opens in Ottawa, Ontario, Canada.

- Fairfield University opens in Fairfield, Connecticut.

Everyday Life

- A group of university academics in Oxford, England, concerned at the plight of children in occupied Greece, form the aid agency OXFAM (Oxford Committee for Famine Relief). They are headed by the classicist Gilbert Murray.
- Maxwell House instant coffee first appears as part of soldiers' "K rations." It is produced by General Foods of Hoboken, New Jersey, who will market the coffee to civilians after World War II.
- The Kellogg corporation introduces Raisin Bran, offering Americans a way of dodging the government's wartime sugar rationing.
- The T-shirt is produced, designed specifically for the U.S. Navy to allow freedom of movement and to absorb sweat.

MARCH

17 The American Federation of Labor (AFL) and Congress of Industrial Organizations (CIO) announce a joint no-strike agreement, supplanting the AFL's unilateral pledge of December 1941.
17 The two largest unions in the United States, the American Federation of Labor (AFL) and the Congress of Industrial Organizations (CIO), agree to a no-strike truce.

Media and Communication

- In Chicago, Illinois, John H. Johnson publishes the monthly *Negro Digest*.
- The *Evening Post* in New York, New York, becomes the tabloid *New York Post*.
- The U.S. government introduces press censorship and some publications are suppressed.

BIRTHS & DEATHS

- Moamer al-Khaddhafi, Libyan leader, ardent Arab nationalist and Muslim fundamentalist, born near Surt, Libya.

JANUARY
1 "Country Joe" McDonald, U.S. folk singer and anti-Vietnam War activist, born in El Monte, California.
8 Stephen Hawking, English theoretical physicist known for his theory of expanding black holes, born in Oxford, England.
17 Muhammad Ali (Cassius Clay), U.S. professional boxer, born in Louisville, Kentucky.
22 Walter Sickert, English painter, most important of the English impressionists, dies in Bath, Somerset, England (81).
31 Derek Jarman, British filmmaker of innovative and controversial films, born in Northwood, England (–1994).

FEBRUARY
9 Carole King, U.S. singer-songwriter whose album *Tapestry* is one of the best-selling records of all time, born in New York, New York.
12 Grant Wood, U.S. painter of "American Gothic" and stylized landscapes of the rural Midwest, dies in Iowa City, Iowa (49).

MARCH
28 Neil Kinnock, British politician, leader of the Labour Party 1983–92, born in Tredegar, Monmouthshire, Wales.

APRIL
24 Barbra Streisand, U.S. singer, actress, and director, born in Brooklyn, New York, New York.

24 Lucy Maude Montgomery, Canadian romantic novelist, dies in Toronto, Canada (67).

MAY
16 Bronislaw Malinowski, Polish-born British anthropologist who founded social anthropology in Britain, dies in New Haven, Connecticut (58).
27 Ch'en Tu-hsiu, Chinese revolutionary who founded the Chinese Communist Party, dies in Chiangching, China (62).
29 John Barrymore, U.S. actor in the early "talkies," dies in Hollywood, California (60).

JUNE
9 Ossie Clark (originally Raymond Clarke), English fashion designer, born in Liverpool, England (–1996).
18 Paul McCartney, English musician who was a member of The Beatles, born in Liverpool, England.
28 Chris (Martin Thembisile) Hani, South African communist and antiapartheid activist, leader of the military wing of the African National Congress (ANC) 1987–93, born in Colim Vaba, Transvaal, South Africa (–1993).

JULY
13 Harrison Ford, U.S. actor in many popular adventure films, born in Chicago, Illinois.
28 William Flinders Petrie, British archeologist and Egyptologist who developed a method of dating cultures by comparing pottery fragments, dies in Jerusalem, Palestine (89).

SEPTEMBER
5 Werner Herzog, German film director, producer, and writer, born in Munich, Germany.
16 James Jeans, English physicist and writer who believed that matter is continuously created in the universe, dies in Dorking, Surrey, England (69).

OCTOBER
23 Michael Crichton, popular U.S. author who has had several books made into films and television shows, born in Chicago, Illinois.

NOVEMBER
2 Shere Hite, U.S. author and researcher about human sexual behavior, born in St. Joseph, Missouri.
5 George M. Cohan, U.S. actor, playwright, composer, director, and producer, dies in New York, New York (64).
17 Martin Scorsese, U.S. film writer and director, born in Flushing, Long Island.
21 James Barry Munnik Hertzog, South African soldier and statesman, president of the Union of South Africa 1924–39, dies in Pretoria, South Africa (76).
27 Jimi Hendrix, U.S. rock singer and influential guitarist, born in Seattle, Washington (–1970).

DECEMBER
22 Franz Boaz, U.S. anthropologist, the founder of relativist anthropology in the United States, dies in New York, New York (84).

FEBRUARY

15 The first *New York Times* crossword puzzle appears.

APRIL

• The U.S. attorney general bans (Father) Charles E. Coughlin's periodical *Social Justice* from the U.S. mail for its apparent fascist sympathy.

21 *ITMA (It's That Man Again)*, starring Tommy Handley, is broadcast by the British Broadcasting Corporation (BBC) as the first royal command performance of a radio program.

NOVEMBER

2 *Stars and Stripes*, a daily paper for U.S. troops in Europe, is published from the office of *The Times* in London, England.

Religion

• English churchman William Temple is appointed as archbishop of Canterbury, England, and publishes *Christianity and the Social Order*.

• The British Council of Churches is inaugurated with a service in St. Paul's Cathedral, London, England. The preacher is the newly appointed archbishop of Canterbury, William Temple.

Sports

• Ohio State is college football's national champion for the second consecutive year.

JANUARY

9 In his 20th defense of his heavyweight boxing title, U.S. boxer Joe Louis knocks out his U.S. opponent Buddy Baer in the second round.

FEBRUARY

21 U.S. national figure skating champions are: Jane Sullivan; Bobby Specht; Doris Schubach and Walter Noffke, pairs; Edith Whetstone and Alfred Richards, dance.

APRIL

4–18 The Toronto Maple Leafs win the last four games after losing the first three games to the Detroit Red Wings and capture the National Hockey League (NHL) Stanley Cup.

MAY

23 U.S. pole-vaulter Cornelius Warmerdam establishes a new world record of 4.75 m/15 ft 7 in at Modesto, California. Ten months later he jumps 4.79 m/15 ft 8.5 in indoors, which remains the highest vault using a bamboo pole.

31 U.S. golfer Sam Snead wins the U.S. Professional Golf Association tournament at the Sea View course, in Atlantic City, New Jersey, to record his first victory in a major.

JULY

1–11 Gunder Hägg of Sweden sets 10 world track records over a period of 82 days, including a new mile record time of 4 min 6.2 sec.

8 The Office of Defense Transportation in the United States prohibits all automobile and motorcycle racing until the end of the war in order to save rubber.

AUGUST

7 Manual Ortiz of the United States wins the world bantamweight title when he beats fellow U.S. fighter Lou Salica on points over 12 rounds in Hollywood, California.

SEPTEMBER

6–7 U.S. tennis players Fred Schroeder and Pauline Betz win singles titles at the U.S. Lawn Tennis Association championships.

30–October 5 The St. Louis Cardinals defeat the New York Yankees four games to one in the World Series.

NOVEMBER

7 In cycling, Fausto Coppi of Italy sets a new one-hour world record of 45.871 km/28.503 miles, beating the existing mark, set in 1937 by Maurice Archambaud of France, by 0.031 km.

DECEMBER

13 The Chicago Bears, without coach George Halas, who joined the U.S. Navy in midseason, lose the National Football League (NFL) championship game 14–6 to the Washingon Redskins.

1943

POLITICS, GOVERNMENT, AND ECONOMICS

Business and Economics

NOVEMBER

1 The United Mine Workers withdraw from the Congress of Industrial Organizations (CIO).

Human Rights

FEBRUARY

16 German authorities execute resistance fighter Dr. Mildred Harnack-Fish, who helped arrange the escape of dissidents and Jews.

APRIL

19 The rebellion of Warsaw Jews against the Nazis begins.

MAY

8 The rebellion of Warsaw Jews against the Nazis is put down. Around 14,000 have died, and the 7,000 survivors are sent to the death camp at Treblinka, Poland.

AUGUST

1 A race riot in Harlem, a black neighborhood in New York, New York, leads to the death of 5 people and $5 million in property damage.

Politics and Government

• Americans recycle rubber, metal, paper, silk, nylon, tin cans, and fat.
• Judge Samuel I. Rosenman is appointed the first full-time writer of speeches and messages for the U.S. president.
• Meat rationing is introduced in the United States.
• The U.S. president Franklin D. Roosevelt appoints jurist Wiley B. Rutledge to the U.S. Supreme Court.

JANUARY

• The U.S. Supreme Court finds the American Medical Association guilty of violating antitrust laws for thwarting cooperative health organizations.
2 The German Army Group A begins its withdrawal from the Caucasus.
14–24 A conference is held at Casablanca in newly

liberated Morocco between British prime minister Winston Churchill and U.S. president Franklin Roosevelt. They agree to increase bombing of Germany and mount an invasion of Sicily to exploit Allied success in North Africa. They also demand the unconditional surrender of the Axis powers.

18 The German Luftwaffe (air force) renews its air attacks on London, England.

18–June 16 Japan deploys submarines off the east coast of Australia.

27 The civil conscription of women in Germany begins.

31 The German 6th Army, commanded by Friedrich von Paulus, surrenders at Stalingrad (now Volgograd) in the USSR, to the Soviet armies encircling it. Over 200,000 Germans are killed and captured in a major blow for the Third Reich.

FEBRUARY

• The administration of U.S. president Franklin D. Roosevelt introduces shoe rationing. Civilians may buy no more than three pairs of shoes a year.
• The U.S. Congress authorizes the Marine Corps to establish a female unit.
8 Soviet troops recapture the city of Kursk, USSR, from German forces in a general advance after the German defeat at Stalingrad.
9 Organized Japanese resistance to U.S. forces on the island of Guadalcanal in the Solomon Islands comes to an end.
14 Soviet armies advancing after their victory at Stalingrad recapture the port of Rostov-on-Don.
14–April 24 British and Gurkha troops under Brigadier Orde Wingate (the "Chindits") leave the city of Imphal in India on a sabotage mission in Burma behind Japanese lines.
25 Following a decision made at the Casablanca Conference, British and U.S. military aircraft begin round-the-clock bombing of Germany.

MARCH

• The administration of U.S. president Franklin D. Roosevelt orders the rationing of canned food, followed by the rationing of meat, fat, and cheese at the end of the month.
• U.S. bombers rout the Japanese navy and air force in the Battle of the Bismark Sea in the Pacific.
7–11 The British repulse heavy Axis (German and Italian) counterattacks in Tunisia.
15 A German counterattack masterminded by General Erich von Manstein throws back the Soviet advance into the Don basin; General Paul Hauser's SS (*Schutzstaffel*) Panzer Corps recaptures the city of Kharkov.
20–28 British 8th Army forces advancing westward attack the Axis (German and Italian) Mareth Line in Tunisia, breaking it on March 28.

APRIL

- The U.S. War Manpower Commission prohibits 27 million essential workers from quitting their jobs.
- 4 British and U.S. bombers make heavy raids on the Ruhr industrial region in Germany.
- 6–8 Axis (German and Italian) forces under the German general Erwin Rommel retreat northward from Gabes Gap in Tunisia, enabling the U.S. forces from Algeria and the British 8th Army from Libya to link up on April 8.
- 13 The Germans announce the discovery of mass graves of 4,443 Polish officers at Katyn near Smolensk in the USSR. The Soviet authorities deny having executed the officers as prisoners.
- 25 The USSR breaks off diplomatic relations with General Władysław Sikorski's Polish government in London, England, claiming he had falsely blamed the USSR for the massacre of Polish officers at Katyn in the USSR.

MAY

- The U.S. Congress listens as the visiting British prime minister Winston Churchill predicts the defeat of Japan after the downfall of the German dictator Adolf Hitler.
- The U.S. government assumes control of soft coal mines, after striking miners ignore an order to return to work.
- U.S. troops capture the port of Bizerta while the British take the capital, Tunis, completing the Allied conquest of Tunisia.
- 5 President Franklin D. Roosevelt creates an Office of War Mobilization (OWM) in the United States to coordinate government defense agencies. The former Supreme Court chief justice James F. Byrnes becomes the OWM's president.
- 11 A U.S. force retakes the island of Attu in the Aleutian Islands, off Alaska, from the Japanese.
- 16 British bombers attack three dams in the Ruhr industrial region of Germany in Operation Chastise, using the rotating bouncing bombs designed by the British aeronautical engineer Barnes Wallis. Two dams are breached.
- 22 The Soviet leader, Joseph Stalin, dissolves the Third Communist International (Comintern) to allay fears of communist subversion among the other Allies.
- 27 The clandestine National Resistance Council under Jean Moulin is created in France to coordinate the noncommunist resistance groups.

JUNE

- 9 The U.S. Congress approves the "Pay-As-You-Go" program by which employers deduct income tax from salaries and wages.
- 14 In the case *West Virginia Board of Education v. Barnette*, the U.S. Supreme Court rules that compulsory saluting of the flag is unconstitutional, reversing an earlier ruling.

JULY

- 1–November 25 U.S. troops recapture islands in the Solomon Islands from the Japanese in Phase One of Operation Cartwheel.
- 5 German forces of Army Group Center and Army Group South mount their last major offensive on the Eastern Front against well-prepared Soviet positions north and south of a huge salient around Kursk, USSR. It is the

largest tank battle in history, and fatally weakens German forces on the Eastern Front.
- 10 U.S. and British forces land in German-occupied Sicily, beginning the Allied liberation of western Europe.
- 20 The German Führer Adolf Hitler orders German forces in the USSR to mount no further offensives on the eastern front.
- 25 King Victor Emmanuel III of Italy dismisses Benito Mussolini as prime minister and appoints Marshal Pietro Badoglio in his place.

AUGUST

- 1 A strong force of 177 U.S. Consolidated B-24 Liberator bombers of the U.S. 9th Air Force raids oil installations at Ploeşti, in German-dominated Romania; 50 bombers are lost during the long flight over well-defended enemy territory.
- 5 Soviet counteroffensives against German positions around Orel and Belgorod (north and south of the Kursk salient in the USSR) end German attempts to break through the Soviet defenses.
- 14–24 At the Quadrant Conference of Allied leaders in Quebec, Canada, the U.S. president Franklin D. Roosevelt and the British prime minister Winston Churchill agree a plan to defeat Germany before Japan and to aim for an invasion of France in May 1944.
- 23 The Soviet army recaptures the city of Kharkov in the USSR from the Germans.
- 24 The United States and Britain grant limited recognition to the French Committee of National Liberation, based in Algiers, the capital of Algeria.
- 25 U.S. troops complete the reconquest of New Georgia in the Solomon Islands from the Japanese.

SEPTEMBER

- 3 Allied (British and U.S.) forces land in mainland Italy; an armistice is signed between the Allies and the Italian government of Marshal Pietro Badoglio, the successor to the deposed dictator Benito Mussolini, on the same day.
- 12 German commandos free the former Italian prime minister Benito Mussolini from prison in the Abruzzi Mountains, Italy, in Operation Oak, and he escapes to Munich, Germany.
- 15 The former Italian prime minister Benito Mussolini establishes a new republican fascist government at Salò on Lake Garda, Italy.
- 25 The Soviet army recaptures the city of Smolensk.

OCTOBER

- 18–30 The Moscow Conference of Allied foreign ministers decides to establish the European Advisory Commission to provide a forum for U.S., British, and Soviet consultation on the future of Europe.

NOVEMBER

- November 1943–March 1944 The British Royal Air Force mount a series of 16 heavy night raids on Berlin, Germany, the "Battle of Berlin." They cause severe damage, but nearly 600 bombers are lost.
- 6 The Soviet army recaptures the city of Kiev.
- 20 U.S. Army and Marine forces land on the Japanese-held Tarawa atoll, in the Gilbert archipelago in the Pacific. Amtracs (Amphibious Landing Vehicles, Tracked) are used for the first time directly in the assault, rather than

for resupply, but U.S. casualties are severe in taking the island.

28–December 1   At the Tehran Conference in Iran, President Franklin D. Roosevelt of the United States and Prime Minister Winston Churchill of Britain outline to the Soviet leader, Joseph Stalin, the plan for an invasion of German-occupied France in 1944.

December

- The U.S. president Franklin D. Roosevelt orders that the railroads be seized to prevent a nationwide railroad strike.
- 1   Gas rationing begins in the United States.
- 12   The USSR and Czechoslovakia sign a treaty for postwar cooperation.
- 17   U.S. president Franklin D. Roosevelt signs the repeal of the Chinese Exclusion Act of 1882, granting Chinese people resident in the United States the right to naturalization and permitting immigration of 105 Chinese citizens a year.
- 24–May 5, 1944   The Soviet army, having recaptured two-thirds of the Soviet territory occupied by the Germans, launches an offensive in Ukraine.

SCIENCE, TECHNOLOGY, AND MEDICINE

Agriculture

- Between 35,000 and 50,000 people die from famine in Rwanda.
- Rinderpest, a cattle disease, kills most of the livestock in Burma (modern Myanmar), resulting in a poor rice harvest as animals do most of the heavy agricultural work.
- The Rockefeller Foundation and the government of Mexico enter into a cooperative research program that by 1956 doubles the per-acre yield of wheat in Mexico through the introduction of new varieties.
- The worst rice crop for 50 years in Japan leads to deprivation.

December 1943–44   In Bengal, India, 1.5 million people die from starvation because they are unable to buy rice; during a severe famine, the price has been driven up by speculators.

Computing

- Colossus, the first electronic computer and code-breaker, is developed at Bletchley Park, England, to break German codes. Designed by Thomas Flowers, M. H. A. Newman, and English mathematician Alan Turing, it has 1,500 vacuum tubes and is the first all-electronic calculating device.

Ecology

February

20   In central Mexico, the volcano Paricutín emerges from a cornfield; eruptions continue until 1952.

Health and Medicine

- c. 1943   Dutch physician Wilhelm Kolff secretly invents a kidney dialysis machine in the German-occupied Netherlands to filter poisonous wastes in the blood; he saves the lives of Dutch partisans.
- A nutritional study reports that only one-quarter of the U.S. population has a healthy diet.
- A polio epidemic erupts in the United States, killing 1,151 people and crippling many more.
- Danish biochemist Henrik Dam and U.S. chemist Edward Doisy receive the Nobel Prize for Physiology or Medicine for their work on vitamin K.
- Nearly 75% of the bread produced in the United States is fortified with iron and vitamin B.
- Penicillin is successfully applied to treat chronic diseases.
- Sulfones are shown to be partially successful in treating leprosy.
- The U.S. medical establishment recognizes the "pap" smear (named for Greek-born U.S. physician George Nicholas Papanicolaou) for detecting cervical cancer. In 20 years cervical cancer drops from the first to the third most common cause of death among U.S. women.
- U.S. biologist Selman A. Waksman discovers the antibiotic streptomycin, which is used as a treatment for tuberculosis; he coins the term "antibiotic."
- U.S. chemist Russell Marker begins development of an oral contraceptive, tapping the Mexican barbasco plant as a source for the hormone progesterone.
- U.S. psychologists Arnold L. Gesell and Frances Ilg publish *The Infant and Child in the Culture of Today* and argue that infants should be given greater autonomy.

Science

- Albert Hoffman, a Swiss research chemist, discovers the hallucinogenic properties of the drug LSD when he accidentally swallows some.
- English archeologist Mortimer Wheeler is appointed Director-General of Antiquities in India. His work in India over the next four years includes major excavations at Mohenjo Daro and Harappa, leading centers of the Indus Valley civilization.
- Hungarian chemist Georg de Hevesy receives the Nobel Prize for Chemistry for the use of isotopes as tracers.
- U.S. physicist Otto Stern receives the Nobel Prize for Physics for his discovery of the magnetic moment of the proton.

Technology

- Chemists develop silicone rubber, the first inorganic "rubber." Chemically stable, silicones make good electrical insulation, waterproof coatings for fabric, and components for aircraft and cars.

- Electrical-discharge machining (EDM) is introduced; it is a new process of cutting steel that uses electrical spark discharges to manufacture machine tools.
- French oceanographer Jacques Cousteau invents the aqualung (or self-contained underwater breathing apparatus, "scuba"), the first fully automatic compressed-air breathing apparatus. It allows him to dive to a depth of 64 m/210 ft.
- Improved sonars and depth charges are introduced on Allied naval escorts; they are immediately effective against German U-boats (submarines).
- In Switzerland, Buhrle & Co. develop the first telephone answering machine, which is then manufactured under the name of Ipsophone.
- The 7.92-mm "Kurz" round and the assault rifle MP-44 are developed for the German armed forces, improving the range and accuracy of submachine guns.
- The Panzer V (Panther) medium tank, armed with a high-velocity 75mm gun, is introduced in German Panzer (armored) divisions.
- U.S. physicists John V. Atanasoff and Clifford Berry build the Atanasoff–Berry computer; designed to solve linear equations, it uses vacuum tubes and stored programs.

JULY
- The world's longest oil pipeline is completed in Longview, Texas. Dubbed the "Big Inch," the pipeline extends 2,018 km/1,254 mi from Texas oil fields to refineries on the east coast of the United States.

Transportation

OCTOBER
16 In Illinois, Chicago's first subway opens; it is 8 km/5 mi long.

ARTS AND IDEAS

Architecture

- In Brazil, the casino, club, and Church of St. Francis in Pampulha, Belo Horizonte, designed by the Brazilian architect Oscar Niemeyer, are completed.
- The Jefferson Memorial, in honor of Thomas Jefferson, the third president of the United States, is dedicated in Washington, D.C.

JANUARY
- Construction ends on the Pentagon, the office of the U.S. military, in Arlington, Virginia.

Arts

c. 1943 The Armenian-born U.S. artist Arshile Gorky paints *Garden in Sochi*.

- German-born U.S. art historian Erwin Panofsky publishes *The Life and Art of Albrecht Dürer*.
- The Chilean artist Matta paints *Vertu Noir/Black Virtue*.
- The Cuban artist Wilfredo Lam paints *The Jungle*.
- The Dutch artist Piet Mondrian completes his painting *Broadway Boogie-Woogie*.
- The English artist Henry Moore sculpts *Madonna and Child*.
- The English artist Paul Nash paints *Vernal Equinox*.
- The French artist Henri Laurens sculpts *Woman and Bird*.
- The French artist Jean Dubuffet paints *Metro*.
- The Spanish artist Pablo Picasso creates *Bull's Head*, using the seat and handlebars of a bicycle.
- The U.S. artist Jackson Pollock paints *The She-Wolf*.

Film

- Domestic movie production in France flourishes during German occupation, though overtly political themes are banned.
- The *Motion Picture Herald* in the United States lists the results of a public opinion poll on movies. The public want them to be more entertaining and distracting, with fewer war themes.
- The 1942 Academy Awards take place. Best Actor: James Cagney, for *Yankee Doodle Dandy*; Best Supporting Actor: Van Heflin, for *Johnny Eager*; Best Actress: Greer Garson, for *Mrs Miniver*; Best Supporting Actress: Teresa Wright, for *Mrs Miniver*; Best Picture: *Mrs Miniver*, directed by William Wyler; Best Director: William Wyler, for *Mrs Miniver*.
- The movie *For Whom the Bell Tolls*, based on the novel by Ernest Hemingway, is released in the United States. It is directed by Sam Wood and stars Gary Cooper and Ingrid Bergman.
- The movie *Heaven Can Wait*, directed by Ernst Lubitsch, is released in the United States. A comedy of manners, it stars Don Ameche, Gene Tierney, and Charles Coburn, and features Laird Cregar as an affable Satan.
- The movie *I Walked with a Zombie* is released in the United States. It is produced by Val Lewton and directed by Jacques Tourneur, and stars Frances Dee, James Ellison, and Tom Conway.
- The movie *Ivan the Terrible, Part I*, directed by Latvian-born Soviet director Sergey Eisenstein, is released in the USSR. It features a score by Russian composer Sergey Prokofiev and stars Nikolai Cherkassov, Ludmilla Tselitovskaya, and Serafima Birman. It is criticized in Russia for allegedly reducing great historical themes to the banal and petty.
- The movie *Lassie Come Home*, directed by Fred M. Wilcox, is released in the United States, starring Roddy McDowall, Elizabeth Taylor, and a male dog called Pal as Lassie.
- The movie *Münchausen*, directed by Josef von Baky, is released in Germany. Produced on the orders of the Nazi head of propaganda Josef Goebbels, it stars Hans Albers, Wilhelm Bendow, and Michael Bohnen.
- The movie *Shadow of a Doubt*, about a serial killer who murders widows, is released in the United States. It stars

Joseph Cotten and Teresa Wright and is directed by Alfred Hitchcock.

- The movie *Stage-Door Canteen*, directed by Frank Borzage, is released in the United States. Depicting how New York stars entertain the troops, its extensive cast includes Cheryl Walker, Lou McCallister, and Judith Anderson.
- The movie *The Gentle Sex*, directed by Leslie Howard and Maurice Elvey, is released in the UK, starring Rosamund John, Joan Greenwood, Joan Gates, Jean Gillie, Lilli Palmer, Joyce Howard, and Barbara Waring.
- The movie *The Human Comedy*, directed by Clarence Brown, is released in the United States. Based on the novel by William Saroyan, it stars Mickey Rooney.
- The movie *The Life and Death of Colonel Blimp*, starring Roger Livesey, Deborah Kerr, and Anton Walbrook, is released in the UK. It is written, produced, and directed by Michael Powell and Emeric Pressburger.
- The movie *The Ox-Bow Incident*, directed by William Wellman, is released in the United States, starring Henry Fonda and Dana Andrews. It is based on the novel by Walter van Tilburg Clark.
- The movie *The Outlaw*, directed by Howard Hughes, is released in the United States, starring Jack Beutel and Jane Russell. The director's ardent focus on Jane Russell's chest throughout the movie causes a six-year censorship wrangle.
- The movie *The Song of Bernadette*, directed by Henry King, is released in the United States, starring Jennifer Jones.
- The movie *Vredens Dag/Day of Wrath*, directed by Carl Theodor Dreyer, is released in Denmark, a powerful, visually striking drama about witchcraft.
- The movie musical *Girl Crazy*, directed by Norman Taurog, is released in the United States. It features music and lyrics by George and Ira Gershwin, and stars Mickey Rooney and Judy Garland.
- The thriller *Le Corbeau/The Raven* is released in France, directed by Henri-Georges Clouzot. It stars Pierre Fresnay, Pierre Larquey, and Ginette Leclerc. Produced with German funding in occupied France, it is regarded by French authorities after the war as a work of anti-French propaganda.
- When fascism is overthrown, the Italian movie industry is producing about 120 movies a year.

Literature and Language

- The Algerian-born French writer Albert Camus publishes his influential philosophical study *Le Mythe de Sisyphe/The Myth of Sisyphus*.
- The Austrian writer Robert Musil publishes the last part of his three-part novel *Der Mann ohne Eigenschaften/ The Man without Qualities*. The first part appeared in 1930.
- The English writer Denton Welch publishes his novel *Maiden Voyage*.
- The English writer Henry Green publishes his novel *Caught*.
- The first issue of the British literary magazine *New Writing and Daylight*, edited by the English writer John Lehmann, is published.

- The French writer Antoine Marie Roger de St.-Exupéry publishes his children's story *Le Petit Prince/The Little Prince*.
- The French writer Romain Rolland publishes his two-volume biography *Péguy*.
- The German writer Hermann Hesse publishes his novel *Das Glasperlenspiel/The Glass Bead Game*.
- The Nobel Prize for Literature is not awarded this year.
- The Pilgrim Trust in Britain purchases Sir Isaac Newton's library. The trust was created in 1930 by the U.S. philanthropist Edward S. Harkness for the preservation of Britain's cultural heritage.
- The Pulitzer Prize for Biography is awarded to Samuel Eliot Morison for *Christopher Columbus: Admiral of the Ocean Sea*. The Pulitzer Prize for Fiction is awarded to Upton Sinclair for *Dragon's Teeth*, and the Prize for Poetry is awarded to Robert Frost for *A Witness Tree*.
- The Russian-born U.S. writer Ayn Rand publishes her novel *The Fountainhead*.
- The U.S. novelist William Saroyan publishes *The Human Comedy*.
- The U.S. writer Jane Bowles publishes her novel *Two Serious Ladies*.

Music

- The English composer Ralph Vaughan Williams completes his Symphony No. 5.
- The English composer Geoffrey Bush completes his *Divertimenti* for strings.
- The French composer Francis Poulenc completes his Violin Sonata.
- The Hungarian composer Béla Bartók completes his Concerto for Orchestra.
- The New York City Opera is founded as part of the New York City Center of Music and Drama. Its musical director is Laszlo Halász. The first production, in February 1944, is *Tosca*.
- The Russian composer Dmitry Shostakovich completes his Symphony No. 8.
- The U.S. blues singer Muddy Waters starts his singing career in Chicago, Illinois. He was discovered by folk singer Alan Lomax on a plantation in 1941.
- The U.S. jazz pianist Art Tatum founds his famous trio with Slam Stewart and Tiny Grimes. The trio will play together until 1956.

NOVEMBER

14 The U.S. composer and conductor Leonard Bernstein makes his public debut as conductor of the New York Philharmonic Orchestra, deputizing at short notice for Bruno Walter.

Theater and Dance

- On Broadway in New York, New York, the musical *Carmen Jones* (adapted from Bizet's *Carmen*), with a new libretto by Oscar Hammerstein, is first performed. It features an all-black cast.
- The play *Les mouches/The Flies*, by the French writer and philosopher Jean-Paul Sartre, is first performed, in Paris, France.
- The Pulitzer Prize for Drama is awarded to Thornton Wilder for *The Skin of Our Teeth*.

- The revue *Sweet and Low*, starring Hermione Gingold, opens in London, England.
- Two plays by the German writer Bertolt Brecht are first performed in Zürich, Switzerland: *Der gute Mensch von Setzuan/The Good Person of Setzuan* and *Leben des Galilei/The Life of Galileo*.

MARCH

- The musical *Oklahoma*, with music by Richard Rodgers and Oscar Hammerstein, is first performed, in New York, New York.

Thought and Scholarship

- English historian Frank Merry Stenton publishes *Anglo-Saxon England*, part of the *Oxford History of England* series.
- English historian James Matthew Thompson publishes *The French Revolution*.
- English political scientist Harold Laski publishes *Reflections on the Revolution of Our Times*.
- French writer and philosopher Jean-Paul Sartre publishes *L'être et le néant/Being and Nothingness*. His most important philosophical work, it becomes a central text of the philosophy of Existentialism.
- Hungarian-born German sociologist Karl Mannheim publishes *Diagnosis of Our Time: Wartime Essays of a Sociologist*.
- Scottish historian Denis William Brogan publishes *The English People: Impressions and Observations*.
- The English literary historian E. M. W. Tillyard publishes *The Elizabethan World Picture*.
- The Pulitzer Prize for History is awarded to Esther Forbes for *Paul Revere in the World He Lived In*.
- U.S. political journalist Walter Lippmann publishes *Foreign Policy: Shield of the Republic*.

SOCIETY

Education

- French philosopher Jacques Maritain publishes *Education at the Crossroads*.
- In Britain, Winston Churchill, with support from U.S. president Franklin D. Roosevelt, appoints a committee to study ways of extending the use of Basic English (devised by the linguist Charles Kay Ogden and supported by the dramatist George Bernard Shaw).
- The Barlow Report in Britain recommends that British universities double their output of scientists.

Everyday Life

- All-America Comics launch a new cartoon starring Wonder Woman, a female version of Superman.
- Jive, a faster, more danceable version of jazz, emerges as a popular musical style.
- Joe Sheridan, a chef in a hotel at Limerick Airport in Ireland, creates the Irish coffee to help passengers ward off the cold.

- Nationwide salvage drives in the United States collect 255,513 tons of tin cans, 6 million tons of waste paper, and 26 million tons of iron and steel scrap.
- The jitterbug is the year's dance craze.
- The U.S. women's fashion industry sees World War II in Europe as an opportunity to go its own way, emphasizing rectilinear lines and appropriate simplicity.
- The zoot suit, an oversized one-button jacket with wide lapels and padded shoulders, and baggy pants that are tight at the ankles, remains the hip style for men in the United States.

MAY

- The United Mine Workers union, formerly of the Congress of Industrial Organizations, begs membership in the American Federation of Labor.
- 5 The U.S. Post Office begins postal zone numbers in 178 cities in order to speed delivery.

JUNE

- 20–22 Race riots break out in Detroit, Michigan, caused by the migration of 300,000 black Americans to the city for war industry jobs, leading to 35 deaths and injuring 600 people. Rioting also occurs in other U.S. cities.

DECEMBER

- A system of balloting National Service boys to provide extra manpower in coal mines is introduced in the UK. In 1944–45, 21,000 ballotees, popularly known as "Bevin boys," after Ernest Bevin, Minister of Labour, worked in the mines.

Media and Communication

- Edward Noble, the millionaire U.S. creator of Life Savers candy, establishes the American Broadcasting Company (ABC) from the former National Broadcasting Company (NBC) Blue Network.

Religion

- Archbishop Suhard of Paris, France, founds the worker-priest movement, which attempts to integrate priests into society by having them live and work alongside their parishioners.
- Bertrand Griffin is appointed Roman Catholic archbishop of Westminster, London, England, as successor to Cardinal Arthur Hinsley.
- The English monk Dom Gregory Dix publishes *The Shape of the Liturgy*.
- The Papal Encyclical *Divino Afflante Spiritu* sets out the official Roman Catholic approach to biblical scholarship.

Sports

- New York Giants relief pitcher Ace Adams sets a record by pitching in 70 games during the season.
- Sportswriters crown Notre Dame college football's national champions.
- Swedish middle distance runner Arne Andersson reduces the world mile record set by his compatriot Gunder Hägg by 2 seconds to 4 min 2.6 sec.

MARCH

8   U.S. national figure skating champions are: Gretchen Morrill; Arthur Vaughn; Doris Schubach and Walter Noffke, pairs; Marcella May and James Lochead, Jr., dance.

APRIL

• In the United States, the wearing of helmets is made compulsory in the National Football League (NFL).

1–8 The Detroit Red Wings beat the Boston Bruins four games to zero to win the National Hockey League (NHL) Stanley Cup.

27 Judy Johnson makes her debut as the first professional woman jockey in a steeplechase race at the Pimlico Racetrack, Baltimore, Maryland. She has been granted a license by the Maryland Jockey Club because of the shortage of male jockeys resulting from their enlistment to the armed forces.

MAY

1–June 5   Count Fleet, ridden by Johnny Longden, wins the Kentucky Derby, Preakness Stakes, and Belmont Stakes to become the sixth horse to win the American Triple Crown.

OCTOBER

5–11   The New York Yankees defeat the St. Louis Cardinals four games to one in the World Series.

DECEMBER

26 The Chicago Bears defeat the Washington Redskins 41–21 in Chicago, Illinois, to win the National Football League (NFL) Championship for the third time in four years.

BIRTHS & DEATHS

JANUARY

5   George Washington Carver, U.S. agricultural chemist who transformed agriculture in the U.S. southwest by developing over 300 products from peanuts, dies in Tuskegee, Alabama (82).

7   Nikola Tesla, Croatian-born U.S. electrical engineer who discovered the rotating magnetic field and invented a polyphase system of alternating current, dies in New York, New York (86).

FEBRUARY

11 Mary Quant, English fashion designer associated with miniskirts and "hot pants," born in London, England.

14 David Hilbert, German mathematician, dies in Göttingen, Germany (81).

MARCH

9   Bobbie Fischer, U.S. World Champion chess master, born in Chicago, Illinois.

13 John Pierpont Morgan, Jr., U.S. banker, dies in Boca Grande, Florida (75).

13 Stephen Vincent Benét, U.S. poet and novelist, dies in New York, New York (44).

22 George Benson, U.S. jazz guitarist, born in Pittsburgh, Pennsylvania.

28 Sergey Vasilevich Rachmaninov, Russian composer and piano virtuoso, dies in Beverly Hills, California (69).

29 John Major, British politician, Conservative prime minister on the resignation of Margaret Thatcher in 1990, then again 1992–97, born in London, England.

APRIL

18 Yamamoto Isoroku, Japanese naval officer who planned and carried out the attack on Pearl Harbor in 1941, is shot down over the Solomon Islands (59).

JUNE

26 Karl Landsteiner, Austrian-born U.S. immunologist who discovered blood groups, dies in New York, New York (75).

JULY

4   Władysław Sikorski, Polish soldier and statesman, leader of Poland's goverment-in-exile during World War II, is killed in an airplane crash at Gibraltar during a tour of inspection of Polish troops in the Mediterranean (62).

10 Arthur Ashe, U.S. tennis player and the first black man to win a major men's singles championship, born in Richmond, Virginia (–1993).

SEPTEMBER

2   Marsden Hartley, U.S. modernist painter, dies in Ellsworth, Maine (66).

5   Aleš Hrdlička, U.S. anthropologist who hypothesized that Native Americans migrated from Asia, dies in Washington, D.C. (74).

29 Lech Wałęsa, Polish labor activist and statesman, president of Poland 1990–95, born in Popowo, Poland.

OCTOBER

12 Max Wertheimer, Czech psychologist who cofounded Gestalt psychology, dies in New Rochelle, New York (63).

31 Max Reinhardt, Austrian-born U.S. theatrical director who helped found the Salzburg Festival, dies in New York, New York (70).

NOVEMBER

5   Sam Shepard, U.S. playwright of allegorical, surrealistic plays, born in Fort Sheridan, Illinois.

22 Billie Jean King, U.S. women's tennis player, born in Long Beach, California.

26 Charles Roberts, Canadian nationalist poet, editor, and novelist, dies in Toronto, Canada (83).

DECEMBER

15 "Fats" Waller, U.S. jazz pianist and composer, dies in Kansas City, Missouri (39).

22 Beatrix Potter, English writer of children's books, who created Peter Rabbit, Mrs. Tiggy Winkle, and other characters, dies in Sawrey, Lancashire, England (77).

31 John Denver (born John Deutschendorf), U.S. country singer and songwriter, born (–1997).

1944

POLITICS, GOVERNMENT, AND ECONOMICS

Business and Economics

- Family Allowance is introduced in the UK: it is a state payment to mothers for each child.

1944–58　The English historian John Harold Clapham publishes his three-volume *The Bank of England: A History*.

AUGUST
- In a sign of military optimism, the War Production Board authorizes the production of consumer goods in the United States.

Human Rights

- Following the German occupation of Hungary, about 400,000 Hungarian Jews are rounded up and sent to concentration camps.
- In the case *Smith v. Allwright*, the U.S. Supreme Court rules that whites-only primary elections are unconstitutional.
- The French provisional (wartime) government gives women the vote and allows them to sit in parliament.
- West Indian politician Eric Eustace Williams (the first prime minister of Trinidad and Tobago, 1962–81) publishes *Capitalism and Slavery*.

APRIL
- The U.S. Supreme Court, in the case *Smith v. Allwright*, rules that the citizen's right to vote cannot be deprived because of color.

MAY
26　There are street riots in Damascus after the Syrian government permits women to remove their veils in public.

NOVEMBER
7　Adam Clayton Powell, Jr., is elected as the first black congressman of New York, New York.

Politics and Government

- Amphibious tanks capable of making their way ashore from an invasion fleet are developed in the UK; they take part in the Normandy landings in June.

- The Soviet leader Joseph Stalin acts to reestablish communist rule in the USSR's non-Russian European regions. Using the pretext that various ethnic groups have collaborated with the Germans, he orders mass deportations and annuls autonomous regions.

JANUARY
- The U.S. president Franklin D. Roosevelt submits a $70 billion budget to Congress, more than one-third less than the previous year's budget.
14　Soviet forces launch an offensive aimed at breaking the German siege of the city of Leningrad (now St. Petersburg).
22　U.S. and British troops land at Anzio, southeast of Rome, Italy, in an attempt to outflank the German Gustav Line. The beachhead is quickly sealed off by German forces.
24–February 12　The British X Corps, the U.S. II Corps, and the French Corps attempt unsuccessfully to break the German Gustav Line at Monte Cassino in Italy; the German 10th Army, under General Heinrich von Vietinghoff, recovers all the positions gained by the Allied attack.
27　Soviet forces clear German troops from the Leningrad–Moscow railroad line, ending the German siege of Leningrad after 900 days and over 1 million civilian deaths from starvation and enemy action.

FEBRUARY
1–7　U.S. forces recapture the Kwajalein atoll in the Pacific from the Japanese, after heavy fighting.
15–17　U.S. and British troops make a second attack on the German Gustav Line at Monte Cassino in Italy, bombing and destroying the historic monastery.
17–21　U.S. forces capture the Pacific atoll of Eniwetok from the Japanese in World War II.
19–26　German aircraft make their heaviest raids (known as the "Little Blitz") on London, England, since May 1941.
20　Saboteurs blow up a ferry on Lake Tinnsjo, Norway, destroying Germany's entire supply of "heavy water" (for use in atomic research).
20–27　During "Big Week," a combined U.S.–UK air assault on German aircraft-making capability, 18,874 metric tons/20,799 tons of bombs are dropped on selected targets in Germany.

MARCH
6　U.S. bombers begin daylight air attacks on the German capital, Berlin; the attacks are made possible by equipping the U.S. P-51 "Mustang" fighters with long-range capabilities as an escort for the bombers.
10　A Provisional National Liberation Committee is formed from resistance groups in Greece.
15　U.S., British, and New Zealand forces launch a third attack on Monte Cassino, Italy, in an attempt to break the German Gustav Line.

17 Soviet forces cross the River Dniester in the southern Ukraine.

19 Germany sends troops to occupy Hungary after learning of its secret preliminary peace negotiations with the Allies.

24 Seventy-six Royal Air Force (RAF) officers escape from Sagan prisoner of war camp in Poland. Three make it to England; the rest are recaptured, and 50 are shot on orders from the German chancellor Adolf Hitler.

29–June 22 Japanese troops under Lt. Gen. Renyu Mutaguchi invade India from Burma and besiege the city of Imphal in Assam, held by Allied forces under General William Slim.

APRIL

- During April, the Allies drop 80,975 metric tons/82,279 tons of bombs on Germany and occupied Europe, as they establish increasing air superiority prior to D-Day.
- The U.S. government seizes the Montgomery Ward mail order distribution plant in Chicago, Illinois, after the chairman, Sewell Avery, reneges on a Congress of Industrial Organizations (CIO) contract mandated by the War Labor Board.
- The U.S. House of Representatives extends its Lend–Lease provision of armaments to other Allied states until June 1945.

2 Soviet forces in southern Ukraine advance across the border into Romania.

11–18 Soviet forces clear all of the Crimea, apart from the port of Sevastopol, of German troops.

22–August 5 U.S. troops land at Aitape and Hollandia (now Jayapura), New Guinea, but take until August 5 to defeat the Japanese in occupation.

MAY

- The U.S. Communist Party disbands after its convention in New York, New York.
- The U.S. government calls an end to meat rationing.

1 Spain makes an agreement with Britain to reduce its exports of wolfram (tungsten) ore to Germany, thus further hindering German armaments production.

9 German forces evacuate the port of Sevastopol in the Crimea, USSR.

11–18 Allied forces finally break through the German Gustav Line at Monte Cassino, Italy, with Polish troops storming the monastery on May 18. The German defeat enables Allied troops at Anzio to break out of the beachhead, and clears the way to Rome.

JUNE

- The Republicans nominate New York governor Thomas E. Dewey for U.S. president and Ohio governor John W. Bricker for vice president.
- The U.S. Supreme Court rules that insurance companies, because they engage in interstate commerce, are subject to the Sherman Antitrust Act.

3 The French Committee of National Liberation, based in Algiers, renames itself the Provisional Government of the French Republic.

4 The U.S. 5th Army under General Mark Clark enters Rome, Italy.

6 D-day marks the start of Operation Overlord. Allied forces (British, U.S., and Canadian) land on five beaches in Normandy, northwest France, against heavy German opposition.

10 In a reprisal against Resistance attacks, German SS (*Schutzstaffel*, Nazi elite corps) troops in the village of Oradour-sur-Glane, south-central France, herd men into barns and women and children into the church and burn all the buildings, killing 642 civilians.

10 Soviet forces begin an offensive against Finland, allied to Nazi Germany.

13 Germany launches the first V1 (*Vergeltungswaffen*, "retribution weapon") pilotless flying-bombs from mainland Europe against London, England, in retaliation against Allied bombing of German cities.

13–30 U.S. troops take the Cotentin peninsula in Normandy, northwest France, capturing the port of Cherbourg on June 27.

15–July 9 U.S. forces capture the island of Saipan in the Mariana Islands from the Japanese.

22 The U.S. president Franklin D. Roosevelt signs the Servicemen's Readjustment Act, also known as the GI Bill of Rights. The act guarantees veterans a wide range of benefits, including money for college tuition and low-cost home mortgages.

22–August 23 Soviet forces in Belarus mount a huge offensive (Operation Bagration) against the German Army Group Center.

26 Armies of the Soviet 3rd Belarussian Front enter the city of Vitebsk as Operation Bagration gathers pace; large numbers of German troops are captured.

JULY

- The Democrats nominate Franklin D. Roosevelt for reelection as U.S. president and Missouri senator Harry S. Truman for vice president.

1–22 The Bretton Woods Conference in New Hampshire draws up financial plans for the postwar world after the expected defeat of Germany and Japan.

3 Armies of the Soviet 2nd and 3rd Belarussian Fronts recapture the city of Minsk from the occupying German forces, during Operation Bagration.

4 The Soviet advance against the German Army Group Center reaches the 1939 Polish–USSR border.

9 Allied forces (principally British and Canadian) capture the city of Caen in Normandy, northwest France, after heavy fighting and the almost complete demolition of the city by Allied bombers.

18 General Hideki Tojo is forced to resign as prime minister of Japan following the loss of the Pacific island of Saipan to U.S. forces. He is succeeded by General Kuniaki Koiso.

20 An abortive assassination attempt is made on the German Führer Adolf Hitler in his Rastenburg headquarters. The planter of the bomb, Count Claus von Stauffenberg, is shot the same evening.

22 Armies of the Soviet 1st Belarussian Front reach the city of Lublin in Poland, where the Soviet puppet Polish Committee for National Liberation is established and declares itself the executive authority of the country.

28 Armies of the Soviet 1st Belarussian Front recapture the city of Brest-Litovsk (now Brest), on the Polish-Soviet border, concluding Operation Bagration. The huge Soviet offensive has virtually destroyed German field marshal Ernst Busch's Army Group Center.

AUGUST

1–October 2 Polish resistance forces in Warsaw under General Tadeusz Bór-Komorowski (commander in chief of the Polish Home Army) rebel against the German occupation, but Soviet forces outside the city fail to assist them and the Soviet government bans the use of airfields to fly in supplies from the west.

4   South African troops take the city of Florence in Italy from the occupying German forces.

14 In Operation Dragoon, Allied forces land on the south French coast between the ports of Toulon and Cannes and push 32 km/20 mi inland on the first day, against weak German opposition.

17 Canadian troops capture the town of Falaise in eastern Normandy, northwest France. U.S. forces simultaneously break through the German defenses in western Normandy, and sweep northeastward behind the German positions.

20 U.S. troops cross the River Seine at Nantes, northwest France, after breaking through German defensive positions in Normandy.

21 Allied troops encircle a large concentration of German armored forces to the south of the town of Falaise, northwest France, as U.S. forces link up with the steady British and Canadian advance southward. Some 50,000 Germans are captured.

21–October 7 At the Dumbarton Oaks Conference in Washington, D.C., China, the USSR, the United States, and Britain draw up proposals for a new world organization, the future United Nations.

23 A coup led by King Michael of Romania overthrows Ion Antonescu's pro-German government and seeks an armistice with the USSR.

24 U.S. units enter Paris, France, following the liberation of the city from German occupation, and a French unit is allowed to lead the procession into the city the following day.

28 The provisional government of France is transferred from Algiers, Algeria, to Paris, France.

31 Soviet forces enter Bucharest, the Romanian capital.

SEPTEMBER

1   Britain's Royal Air force and Yugoslav partisans launch Operation Ratweek in Yugoslavia, attacking roads and railroads to prevent the occupying Germans from withdrawing.

3   British troops enter Brussels, the Belgian capital.

4   A cease-fire is called between Finnish and Soviet forces on the Finnish front.

4   British forces capture the port of Antwerp in Belgium.

5   The USSR declares war on Bulgaria. Bulgaria declares war on Germany, its former ally, and requests an armistice with the USSR.

6   The Soviet-supported Polish Committee for National Liberation decrees the expropriation of farms with more than 50 ha/123.5 acres of arable land or over 10 ha/247 acres.

10 The French provisional government abolishes the Vichy legislature.

10 U.S. troops enter the Duchy of Luxembourg.

11 U.S. troops cross from Luxembourg into Germany near the city of Trier.

11–16 At the Octagon Conference in Quebec, Canada, the U.S. president Franklin D. Roosevelt and the British prime minister Winston Churchill approve plans for the Allied advance into Germany, the establishment of occupation zones after Germany's defeat in World War

II, and the deindustrialization of Germany as proposed by the Morgenthau Plan.

12 Romania signs an armistice with the USSR, the United States, and Britain.

17–28 In Operation Market Garden in the Netherlands, U.S. airborne troops land at Eindhoven and Nijmegen to seize bridges over the rivers Maas, Waal, and Rhine (Market), while British troops land at Arnhem on the Rhine to open a route to the Ruhr region in Germany (Garden). The landing at Arnhem is a disaster.

19 Finland signs an armistice with the USSR.

24 Resistance forces in France are integrated into the French army.

25 The German Führer Adolf Hitler calls up all remaining males between 16 and 60 in Germany for service in the *Volkssturm*, a home defense force, to defend Germany against Allied invasion.

28 Canadian troops liberate the port of Calais in northern France.

29 Soviet forces invade German-occupied Yugoslavia.

OCTOBER

2   The Warsaw uprising in Poland against the German occupation ends when the insurgents surrender to the Germans after savage fighting. Around 250,000 of its inhabitants have been killed and the city is virtually destroyed.

4   British troops land in German-occupied Greece.

6   Soviet forces enter Czechoslovakia.

8   King Farouk of Egypt dismisses the nationalist Wafd government led by Nahhas Pasha.

9–19 At the Moscow Conference in the USSR, the British prime minister, Winston Churchill, Averell Harriman (Special Envoy of the U.S. president Franklin D. Roosevelt), and the Soviet leader, Joseph Stalin, discuss military plans.

14 British troops in Greece liberate the capital, Athens, from the occupying German forces.

14 The German field marshal Erwin Rommel chooses to commit suicide rather than face a court martial and ignominy for his family following disclosure of his implication in the bomb plot of July 20 against Adolf Hitler.

17 German troops in Hungary abduct the acting regent of Hungary, Admiral Miklós Horthy, following his attempt on October 15 to conclude a separate peace with the Allies.

20 General Douglas MacArthur of the United States, forced to evacuate the islands on March 12, 1942, fulfills his celebrated promise to return to the Philippines.

20 Soviet and Yugoslav troops capture Belgrade, the Yugoslav capital, from the occupying German forces.

20–December 31 U.S. troops retake the island of Leyte in the Philippines from the Japanese.

22 The United States, the USSR, and Britain recognize General Charles de Gaulle's provisional wartime government of France, based in Paris.

24–25 U.S. ships cripple the Japanese fleet in the Battle of Leyte Gulf, enabling U.S. forces to invade the Philippines.

28 The new government in Bulgaria signs an armistice with the Allies.

30–February 13, 1945 Armies of the Soviet 2nd and 3rd Ukrainian fronts besieges the Hungarian capital,

Budapest, but the German defenders maintain their hold on the city.

NOVEMBER

- The Democrat Franklin D. Roosevelt defeats the Republican challenger Thomas E. Dewey in the U.S. presidential election to win a record fourth term. Roosevelt receives 432 electoral votes to Dewey's 99. In the U.S. congressional elections, the Democrats retain a 56–38 majority in the Senate and a 242–190 majority in the House of Representatives.
- 11 British and Greek forces complete the liberation of Greece from German occupation, and the communist-controlled resistance organization EAM-ELAS (National Liberation Front and National Popular Liberation Army) virtually overruns the country.
- 12 British bombers sink the last German battleship, *Tirpitz*, in the Tromsö fjord, Norway, enabling Britain's large ships to be released for service in the Pacific.
- 24 Allied forces capture the city of Strasbourg, in eastern France, from the occupying German troops.
- 24 B-29 bombers from the airbase on the island of Saipan in the Pacific make the first U.S. raid on the Japanese capital, Tokyo, since the Doolittle raid of April 1942.

DECEMBER

- The U.S. Congress creates a new military rank: general of the army (or five-star general). It bestows the honor on Henry "Hap" Arnold, Dwight D. Eisenhower, Douglas MacArthur, and George C. Marshall.
- 3 Police action against demonstrations by EAM-ELAS (the communist-controlled resistance organization) in Athens raises criticisms of British policy in Greece following its liberation from German occupation.
- 5 Allied forces capture the city of Ravenna in Italy from the occupying German troops.
- 16 German forces launch the Battle of the Bulge, or Ardennes offensive, against the Allies in the Ardennes, a wooded plateau in Luxembourg and Belgium. It is the last major German offensive of World War II
- 17–18 The U.S. War Department revokes the order of 1942 excluding Japanese Americans from the Pacific coastal areas of the United States. The next day the Supreme Court rules that the War Relocation Authority has no legal power to detain loyal U.S. citizens.
- 18 Northern Burma is cleared of Japanese forces by a British and Indian Army offensive.
- 22 A provisional Hungarian government, based in the city of Debrecen, is formed under Soviet supervision; the Hungarian capital, Budapest, remains under German occupation.
- 26 In the Battle of the Bulge in Belgium, U.S. forces relieve the town of Bastogne, freeing U.S. troops who had been trapped there by the German offensive.

SCIENCE, TECHNOLOGY, AND MEDICINE

Agriculture

- Soybean production begins to increase in the United States as new uses for the beans are discovered.

Ecology

- Hurricanes in the Atlantic and Pacific are hunted by U.S. military flight crews as part of the joint Weather Bureau and armed services project.
- Kosciusko National Park is created in New South Wales, Australia, around Mt. Kosciusko (Australia's highest mountain).
- The U.S. Congress incorporates 286,617 ha/708,221 acres along the Rio Grande River in Texas into Big Bend National Park.

JULY

- 6 A fire at the Ringling Bros. and Barnum & Bailey Circus in Hartford, Connecticut, kills 167 spectators.

OCTOBER

- 13–21 Cuba and the eastern U.S. states are struck by a hurricane that kills hundreds of people.

Health and Medicine

- Freudian analyst Helene Deutsch publishes *The Psychology of Women*, which provides a theoretical basis for the theory that a woman's mental and emotional core lies in her reproductive organs.
- Swiss pharmacologist Daniel Bovet discovers pyrilamine, the first antihistamine.
- The first eye bank is established in New York, New York.
- U.S. physiologists Joseph Erlanger and Herbert S. Glasser share the Nobel Prize for Physiology or Medicine for their researches on nerve fibers.

NOVEMBER

- 9 U.S. physicians Alfred Blalock and Helen Taussig successfully operate on "blue" babies, correcting the heart defect that prevents enough blood getting into the lungs.

Math

MAY

- Hungarian-born U.S. mathematician John von Neumann and the German-born U.S. economist Oskar Morgenstern publish *Theory of Games and Economic Behavior*. Games theory is important in the study of economics, biology, and sociology.

Science

- British chemists Archer J. P. Martin and Richard L. M. Synge separate amino acids by using a solvent in a column of silica gel. The beginnings of partition chromatography, the technique leads to further advances in chemical, medical, and biological research.

- Dutch astronomer Hendrik van de Hulst predicts that cosmic hydrogen will emit line radiation at 21 cm/8.26 in.
- German chemist Otto Hahn receives the Nobel Prize for Chemistry for his discovery of nuclear fission.
- Swiss psychologist Carl Gustav Jung publishes *Psychology and Alchemy*, in which he argues that religion is part of the historic process necessary for the development of consciousness.
- The electromagnetic method of enrichment separation of uranium isotopes U-235 and U-238 is performed in a mass-spectrometer.
- The role of deoxyribonucleic acid (DNA) in genetic inheritance is first demonstrated by U.S. bacteriologist Oswald Avery, U.S. biologist Colin MacLeod, and U.S. biologist Maclyn McCarthy; it opens the door to the elucidation of the genetic code.
- The statutes of the Royal Society in London, England, are amended to permit the admission of women as fellows.
- The well-preserved body of a man who died by strangulation in the 1st century BC (the so-called Tollund man) is found in a peat bog near Viborg, Denmark.
- U.S. chemist Glenn T. Seaborg and his associates discover Americium (element 95) and Curium (element 96).
- U.S. chemist Robert Burns Woodward synthesizes quinine.
- U.S. physicist Isidor Rabi receives the Nobel Prize for Physics for his discovery of the resonance method for registering the magnetic properties of atomic nuclei.

Technology

- A second atomic pile is built at Clinton, Tennessee, as part of the Manhattan project for manufacturing plutonium for an atomic bomb.
- The 41,700-kg/46-ton Josef Stalin 2 heavy tank, armed with a 122mm gun, is introduced in the Soviet armed forces.
- The 61,670-kg/68-ton Tiger II ("King Tiger") heavy tank is introduced in some German Panzer (armored) divisions; it is the heaviest tank of World War II.
- The Pilot's Universal Sighting System (PUSS) is developed; it permits the automatic sighting of guns, rockets, bombs, and torpedoes.
- The U.S. Eastman Kodak company produces Kodacolor, a color negative film which makes it possible to take color pictures with a reasonably cheap camera.
- U.S. mathematician Howard Aitken builds the Harvard University Mark I, or Automatic Sequence Controlled Calculator. The first program-controlled computer, it is 15 m/50 ft long and 2.4 m/8 ft high, and its operations are controlled by a sequence of instruction codes on punched paper that operate electromechanical switches. Simple multiplication takes 4 sec and division 11 sec.

SEPTEMBER
8   The first German V2 (*Vergeltungswaffen*, "retribution weapon") rocket is fired, against London, England. Before the end of the war in Europe, 1,115 are launched

against Britain, 1,341 against Antwerp (Belgium), 65 against Brussels (Belgium), 98 against Liège (Belgium), 15 against Paris (France), 5 against Luxembourg, and 11 against the bridge over the River Rhine at Remagen.

Transportation

- The first modern helicopter, the VS 36 A, is built by U.S.-Russian aircraft designer Igor Sikorsky; it has adjustable pitch rotor blades and an enclosed cockpit.

JANUARY
- The federal government restores U.S. railroads to their owners after averting a railroad strike.

SEPTEMBER
8   The first nonstop transatlantic flight, from London, England, to Canada, is made.

NOVEMBER
29 The Federal Highway Act is passed in the United States; it establishes a national system of highways.

ARTS AND IDEAS

Arts

- In Paris, France, following the city's liberation from German occupation, the Salon d'Automne is renamed Salon de la Libération, with a special gallery for Picasso's works. This is the first official recognition accorded to him in France.
- The Armenian-born U.S. artist Arshile Gorky paints *Water of the Flowery Mill*.
- The Belgian artist Paul Delvaux paints *Sleeping Venus*.
- The Dutch-born U.S. artist Willem de Kooning paints *Pink Lady*.
- The English artist Barbara Hepworth sculpts *Wood and Strings*.
- The English artist Ivon Hitchens paints *Hazel Wood*.
- The French artist Francis Gruber paints *Job*.
- The French artist Jean René Bazaine paints *La Messe de L'homme Armé/Mass of the Armed Man*.
- The French artist Jean Dubuffet paints *Vue de Paris – Le Petit Commerce/View of Paris—Small Traders*.
- The German-born U.S. artist Hans Hofmann paints *Effervescence*.
- The Irish-born British artist Francis Bacon paints *Three Studies for Figures at the Base of a Crucifixion*.
- The Mexican artist Diego Rivera completes his set of "portable" murals for the National Institute of Cardiology in Mexico City, Mexico.
- The Spanish artist Pablo Picasso sculpts *Man with a Sheep*.
- The U.S. artist Clyfford Still paints *No. 1*.

JUNE
6   Hungarian-born U.S. photographer Frank Capa photographs the D-Day Landings on the beaches of Normandy in France during World War II.

Film

- In the UK, English filmmakers Michael Powell and Emeric Pressburger produce, write, and direct the movie *A Canterbury Tale*.
- Ingrid Bergman gives an Academy Award-winning performance in the Hollywood production of *Gaslight*. It is directed by George Cukor and is based on Patrick Hamilton's play *Angel Street*.
- The 1943 Academy Awards take place. Best Actor: Paul Lukas, for *Watch on the Rhine*; Best Supporting Actor: Charles Coburn, for *The More the Merrier*; Best Actress: Jennifer Jones, for *The Song of Bernadette*; Best Supporting Actress: Katina Paxinou, for *For Whom the Bell Tolls*; Best Picture: *Casablanca*, directed by Michael Curtiz; Best Director: Michael Curtiz, for *Casablanca*.
- The movie *Arsenic and Old Lace*, directed by Frank Capra, is released in the United States, starring Cary Grant, Josephine Hull, Jean Adair, and Priscilla Lane.
- The movie *Double Indemnity*, directed by Billy Wilder, is released in the United States. Based on the novel by James M. Cain and adapted for the screen by Raymond Chandler, it stars Fred MacMurray, Barbara Stanwyck, and Edward G. Robinson, and becomes a landmark movie in the evolution of the U.S. *film noir* movement. Other *film noirs* this year include *Laura*, directed by Otto Preminger, and starring Dana Andrews, Gene Tierney, and Clifton Webb; *Murder My Sweet* (also known as *Farewell, My Lovely*), directed by Edward Dmytryk; *Phantom Lady*, directed by Robert Siodmak; and *When Strangers Marry* (also known as *Betrayed*), directed by William Castle.
- The movie *Frenzy/Torment*, directed by Alf Sjöberg, is released in Sweden. With a screenplay by Ingmar Bergman, it stars Stig Jarrel, Alf Kjellin, and Mai Zetterling.
- The movie *Going My Way*, directed by Leo McCarey, is released in the United States, starring Bing Crosby and Barry Fitzgerald.
- The movie *Jane Eyre* is released in the United States. It is directed by Robert Stevenson and stars Orson Welles and Joan Fontaine.
- The movie *Lifeboat*, directed by Alfred Hitchcock, is released in the United States. Based on a story by John Steinbeck, it stars Tallulah Bankhead, Walter Slezak, and William Bendix.
- The movie *Maria Candelaria*, directed by Emilio Fernandez, is released in Mexico, starring Dolores Del Rio and Pedro Armendariz.
- The movie *The Miracle of Morgan's Creek*, directed by Preston Sturges, is released in the United States, starring Betty Hutton, Eddie Bracken, William Demarest, and Diana Lynn.
- The movie *The Mask of Dimitrios* directed by Jean Negulesco is released in the United States. Based on the novel by Eric Ambler, it stars Peter Lorre and Sydney Greenstreet.
- The movie *The Way Ahead* (*The Immortal Battalion* in the United States), directed by Carol Reed, is released in the UK, starring David Niven, Stanley Holloway, Raymond Huntley, and William Hartnell.
- The movie *The White Cliffs of Dover*, directed by Clarence Brown, is released in the United States, starring Irene Dunne, Alan Marshall, Frank Morgan, May Whitty, and Roddy McDowall.
- The movie *This Happy Breed*, directed by David Lean, is released in the UK. Based on the play by Noël Coward, it stars Robert Newton, Celia Johnson, Stanley Holloway, and John Mills.
- The movie *To Have and Have Not*, directed by Howard Hawks, is released in the United States. Based on the novel by Ernest Hemingway, it stars Humphrey Bogart and Lauren Bacall.
- The Hollywood musical *Meet Me in St Louis* is released. It is directed by Vincente Minnelli, and stars Judy Garland, Tom Drake, Mary Astor, Leon Ames, and Margaret O'Brien.
- The U.S. movie industry takes in more than $1.5 billion at the box office during the year.

Literature and Language

- English writer and critic Cyril Connolly publishes *The Unquiet Grave*, a collection of observations and aphorisms. They have previously appeared under the pen name "Palinurus."
- German philosopher Ernst Cassirer publishes *An Essay on Man: An Introduction to Human Culture*.
- The Argentinean writer Jorge Luis Borges publishes *Fictions*.
- The Australian writer Christina Stead publishes her novel *For Love Alone*.
- The Belgian writer Henri Michaux publishes his poetry collection *L'Espace du dedans/The Space Within*.
- The English novelist Joyce Cary publishes his novel *The Horse's Mouth*.
- The English novelist Rosamund Lehmann publishes her novel *The Ballad and the Source*.
- The English writer Aldous Huxley publishes his novel *Time Must Have a Stop*.
- The English writer H. E. Bates publishes his novel *Fair Stood the Wind for France*.
- The English writer Ivy Compton-Burnett publishes her novel *Elders and Betters*.
- The English writer L. P. Hartley publishes his novel *The Shrimp and the Anemone*, the first part of his *Eustace and Hilda* trilogy.
- The English writer Somerset Maugham publishes his novel *The Razor's Edge*.
- The French writer Jean Genet publishes his first novel *Notre Dame des fleurs/Our Lady of the Flowers*, written in prison.
- The French writer Paul Eluard publishes his poetry collection *Au rendez-vous allemand/German Rendezvous*.
- The French writer Pierre-Jean Jouve publishes his poetry collection *La Vierge de Paris/The Virgin of Paris*.
- The Italian writer Alberto Moravia publishes his novel *Agustino*, later translated as *Two Adolescents*.
- The Nobel Prize for Literature is awarded to the Danish novelist Johannes Vilhelm Jensen.
- The Pulitzer Prize for Biography is awarded to Carleton Mabee for *The American Leonardo: The Life of Samuel F. B. Morse*. The Pulitzer Prize for Fiction is awarded to Martin Flavin for *Journey in the Dark*, and the Prize for

Poetry is awarded to Stephen Vincent Benét for *Western Star*.

- The U.S. novelist Lillian Smith's novel of racial prejudice in the southern United States, *Strange Fruit*, is the best-selling work of fiction in the United States. War correspondent Ernie Pyle's *Brave Men* is the top-selling nonfiction title.
- The U.S. poet Karl Shapiro publishes *V-Letter and Other Poems*. It wins a Pulitzer prize in 1945.
- The U.S. writer Charles Reginald Jackson publishes his novel *The Lost Weekend*, a controversial study of alcoholism.
- The U.S. writer John Hersey publishes *A Bell for Adano*, a novel about the U.S. occupation of an Italian town. It receives a Pulitzer prize in 1945.
- The U.S. writer Saul Bellow publishes his novel *Dangling Man*.

Music

- A dress rehearsal of the opera *Die Liebe der Danae/Danae's Love* by the German composer Richard Strauss is held in Salzburg, Austria. It is not until 1952 that it is performed.
- In the Soviet Union, the "Internationale" is replaced as the national anthem by a patriotic song.
- The Austrian composer Viktor Ullmann completes his opera *Der Kaiser von Atlantis/The Emperor of Atlantis*, written in Theresienstadt concentration camp. He is killed the same year. It is first performed in Amsterdam, the Netherlands, in 1975.
- The Brazilian composer Heitor Villa-Lobos completes his *Bachianas Brasiliera*, nine pieces combining elements of Bach and Brazilian music. The first was written in 1930.
- The British bandleader Ted Heath founds the Ted Heath Band. Their first tour of the United States will be in 1956.
- The conductor Sir Henry Wood conducts his last Promenade Concert at the Albert Hall in London, England.
- The French composer Olivier Messiaen completes his work for piano *Vingt Regards sur l'Enfant Jésus/Twenty Looks at the Infant Jesus*.
- The Russian composer Sergey Prokofiev completes his Symphony No. 5.
- The Russian composer Igor Stravinsky completes his cantata *Babel*.
- The Russian composer Dmitry Shostakovich completes his String Quartet No. 2.
- The Swiss composer Frank Martin completes his oratorio *In Terra Pax/Peace on Earth*.
- The U.S. composer and conductor Leonard Bernstein completes his Symphony No. 1, *Jeremiah*.
- The U.S. composer Roy Harris completes his Symphony No. 6, *Gettysburg Address*.
- The U.S. composer Virgil Thomson completes his *Suite (Portraits) Nos. 1 and 2*.
- The U.S. jazz promoter Norman Granz stages a jazz concert at the Philharmonic Hall in Los Angeles, California, the first in the series "Jazz at the Philharmonic." The series continues in various cities until 1967.

- U.S. record company Capitol Records starts recording in Nashville, Tennessee. Their studios will be built in 1950.

JANUARY

17 The New York Metropolitan Opera House holds its first jazz concert.

Theater and Dance

- The ballet *Fancy Free* is first performed, at the Metropolitan Opera House in New York, New York. The score is by U.S. composer Leonard Bernstein, the choreography by the U.S. choreographer Jerome Robbins. It is so successful it is turned into a musical, *On the Town* with lyrics by Betty Comden and Adolph Green, and music by Leonard Bernstein.
- The ballet *Miracle in the Gorbals* is first performed, in London, England. The score is by the English composer Arthur Bliss, the choreography by the Australian choreographer Robert Helpmann.
- The play *Huis Clos/In Camera* (in the United States *No Exit*), by the French writer and philosopher Jean-Paul Sartre, is first performed, in Paris, France. It contains the famous line "hell is other people."
- The play *Le Malentendu/Cross Purpose*, by the Algerian-born French writer Albert Camus, is first performed, in Paris, France.
- The Pulitzer Prize for Drama is not awarded this year, though there is a special award for the best musical play, which is given to Richard Rodgers and Oscar Hammerstein for *Oklahoma!*
- The revue *Sweeter and Lower*, with music by Charles Zwar and Geoffrey Wright, opens in London, England, starring Hermione Gingold.
- The U.S. composer Aaron Copland completes his score for the ballet *Appalachian Spring*, with choreography by Martha Graham. It is first performed the same year in Washington, D.C.

Thought and Scholarship

- Austrian-born English economist Friedrich von Hayek publishes *The Road to Serfdom*.
- English economist William Beveridge publishes *Full Employment in a Free Society*.
- English historian Benedict Humphrey Sumner publishes his *Survey of Russian History*.
- Swedish sociologist Gunnar Myrdal publishes *An American Dilemma: The Negro Problem and Modern Democracy*. It is a path-breaking study of U.S. race relations.
- The Pulitzer Prize for History is awarded to Merle Curti for *The Growth of American Thought*.
- The U.S. philosopher Charles Stevenson publishes *Ethics and Language*.
- The U.S. philosopher Morris R. Cohen publishes *Preface to Logic*.
- U.S. social philosopher Lewis Mumford publishes *The Condition of Man*.

SOCIETY

Education

- The University of California at Santa Barbara opens.

Everyday Life

- Cartoonist Bill Maudlin creates Willie and Joe, a pair of combat-weary GIs, for the U.S. armed services newspaper; George Baker creates Sad Sack, a similar character.
- The United Fruit Company introduces the Chiquita banana in the United States, along with an accompanying marketing jingle.

AUGUST

14 Production of consumer goods, such as vacuum cleaners and stoves, resumes in the United States.

Media and Communication

- In France, only four prewar national newspapers—those that refused to collaborate with the occupying German authorities—are allowed to resume publication.
- The *Al-Akhbar* newspaper is founded in Cairo, Egypt.
- The French news agency Agence France-Presse is established, taking over the assets of the older Agence Havas.
- The U.S. publisher Walter H. Annenberg creates *Seventeen* magazine, a periodical for young women.

AUGUST

1 British newspaper *The Times* begins publishing an "Air Edition" on India paper.

DECEMBER

19 *Le Monde*, an independent newspaper, succeeds the prewar *Le Temps* in France.

Religion

- The ecumenical community at Taizé, near Cluny, France, is founded by brother Roger Schutz of the Protestant French Reformed Church. The aim is to foster Christian unity.
- The English churchman William Temple (archbishop of Canterbury 1942–44) publishes *The Church Looks Forward*.
- The Russian theologian Vladimir Lossky publishes *The Mystical Theology of the Eastern Church*.

Sports

- Army wins college football's national championship in the United States.

BIRTHS & DEATHS

JANUARY

1 Edwin Lutyens, English architect who planned the city of New Delhi, India, dies in London, England (75).

6 Ida Tarbell, U.S. journalist who helped popularize the muckraking style in the early 20th century, dies in Bethel, Connecticut (86).

12 Joe Frazier, U.S. heavyweight boxing champion, born in Beaufort, South Carolina.

18 Paul Keating, Australian politician, Labor prime minister from 1991, on the resignation of Robert Hawke, born in Sydney, Australia.

23 Edvard Munch, Norwegian painter of psychological subjects such as *The Scream*, dies in Ekely, near Oslo, Norway (80).

28 John Tavener, English composer, born in London, England.

FEBRUARY

1 Piet Mondrian, Dutch Abstract painter, dies in New York, New York (71).

9 Alice Walker, U.S. novelist, author of *The Color Purple* (1983), born in Eatonton, Georgia.

23 Leo Hendrik Baekeland, U.S. inventor who invented Bakelite, dies in Beacon, New York (80).

MARCH

28 Stephen Leacock, Canadian humorist and economist, dies in Toronto, Canada (74).

MAY

14 George Lucas, U.S. film director and producer, born in Modesto, California.

JUNE

16 Marc Bloch, French historian, dies near Lyon, France (57).

25 Gary David Goldberg, U.S. television producer who created hits such as *Family Ties*, born in New York, New York.

JULY

26 Reza Shah Pahlavi, shah of Iran 1925–41, dies in Johannesburg, South Africa (68).

AUGUST

1 Manuel Quezon, Filipino independence leader and first president of the Philippine Commonwealth 1935–44, dies in Saranac Lake, New York (65).

19 Henry Wood, English conductor, founder of the Promenade Concerts (the "Proms") in 1895, dies in Hitchin, Hertfordshire, England (75).

20 Rajiv Gandhi, prime minister of India 1984–91, born in Bombay, India (–1991).

SEPTEMBER

19 Brian Epstein, the Beatles' manager, born in Liverpool, England (–1967).

OCTOBER

14 Erwin Rommel, German field marshal who commanded the Afrika Korps during World War II, commits suicide in Herrlingen, near Urm, Germany to avoid being prosecuted for his part in the attempt to assassinate Hitler (52).

NOVEMBER

12 George David Birkhoff, U.S. mathematician, dies in Cambridge, Massachusetts (60).

22 Arthur Stanley Eddington, English astronomer, mathematician, and physicist, dies in Cambridge, England (61).

DECEMBER

13 Wassily Kandinsky, Russian-born artist, founder of abstract art, dies in Neuilly-sur-Seine, France (77).

16 Glenn Miller, U.S. composer, trombonist and big-band leader, dies in an airplane crash en route from London, England to Paris, France (40).

30 Romain Rolland, French novelist and dramatist, dies in Vézelay, France (78).

- U.S. golfer Byron Nelson, the top winner on the professional golf circuit, earns $37,967 during the year.
- U.S. swimmer Ann Curtis becomes the first woman to win the James E. Sullivan Memorial Award. Since 1930 the award has been presented annually by the U.S. Amateur Athletic Union to the country's outstanding amateur athlete.

JANUARY

27 The 13th Olympic Games, due to take place in London, England, are not held because of World War II.

APRIL

4–13 The Montreal Canadiens win the National Hockey League (NHL) Stanley Cup four games to zero over the Chicago Black Hawks.

JUNE

10 Joe Nuxhall, aged 15, becomes the youngest-ever major league baseball player when he makes his debut for the Cinncinnati Reds against the St. Louis Cardinals.

AUGUST

- U.S. golfer Bob Hamilton wins the United States Professional Golf Association tournament at the Manito course, in Spokane, Washington. It is the only one of the four majors to take place.

SEPTEMBER

3 U.S. tennis players Frank A. Parker and Pauline Betz win singles titles at the U.S. Lawn Tennis Association championships.

OCTOBER

4–9 The St. Louis Cardinals defeat the St. Louis Browns four games to two in the World Series.

DECEMBER

17 The Green Bay Packers defeat the New York Giants 14–7 in the National Football League (NFL) championship game in New York, New York.

1945

POLITICS, GOVERNMENT, AND ECONOMICS

Business and Economics

- The *Greater London Plan, 1944* is published in Britain and becomes known as the "Abercrombie Report" after its author Sir Leslie Abercrombie. It depicts postwar London, England, as a set of concentric circles with different economic activities and population densities.
- The U.S. gross national product (GNP) is $215 billion, up two-thirds from 1939.
- The U.S. hotelier Conrad Hilton opens the first Hilton Hotel in Chicago, Illinois.

Colonization

SEPTEMBER

20–23 The All-India Congress Committee under Mahatma Gandhi and Pandit Nehru rejects the British proposals for self-government and calls on Britain to "quit India."

23 Egypt demands the revision of the 1936 British–Egyptian treaty, the end of Britain's military presence in Egypt, and the return of the Sudan from British rule.

Human Rights

JULY

- New York State creates a Commission Against Discrimination to combat racial discrimination in the workplace.

DECEMBER

15 The Japanese parliament, under pressure from Allied occupation forces, grants women voting rights.

Politics and Government

- Christian Democratic parties are founded in the Allied-occupied zones of Germany.
- Members of the wartime administration are tried in Bulgaria, and all the leading members of the government are executed.
- The French government nationalizes the Bank of France and other private banks, Air France, and the Renault car company.
- The U.S. president Harry S. Truman appoints Harold H. Burton to the U.S. Supreme Court.
- William Joyce, the Nazi propagandist known as "Lord Haw-Haw," is captured and convicted in the UK of treason; he is hanged on January 3, 1946.

JANUARY

- The U.S. private Eddie Slovik becomes the first U.S. soldier to be executed for desertion since the Civil War (1861–65).

1 The Soviet-sponsored Lublin Committee proclaims itself Poland's provisional government.

1–3 U.S. forces capture the island of Mindoro in the Philippines from the occupying Japanese troops.

3 The British 14th Army begins a new offensive in Burma, aimed at clearing Japanese forces from the remainder of the country.

8 A general election in Egypt, boycotted by the Wafd nationalists, results in a majority for Ahmad Mahir, the prime minister.

9 U.S. forces land on the shores of the Lingayen Gulf on the island of Luzon in the Philippines.

11 The communists agree to a truce in the civil war in newly-liberated Greece.

12 Soviet forces in Poland launch an offensive from the River Vistula, aiming to reach the River Oder and press toward Berlin, Germany.

15 The U.S. president Franklin D. Roosevelt orders a nationwide "dim-out" to conserve precious fuel reserves.

17 Soviet forces in Poland liberate the capital, Warsaw, from the occupying German forces.

19 Soviet forces in Poland liberate the city of Kraków from the occupying German forces.

20 German troops in Budapest, Hungary, surrender to the besieging armies of the Soviet 2nd and 3rd Ukrainian fronts.

20 The provisional Hungarian government under General Bela Miklós, in the city of Debrecen, concludes an armistice with the Allies.

22 Advancing Soviet troops cross the River Oder near the town of Oppeln in Germany (now Opole in Poland).

22 The Burma Road is reopened by the Allies for the supply of munitions to China.

23 Soviet forces in Poland liberate the town of Tilsit (later Sovetsk in Russia) from the occupying German forces.

27 Soviet forces reach the Auschwitz Oświęcim concentration camp in Poland.

FEBRUARY

3 U.S. forces begin their siege of Japanese-occupied Manila, the capital of the Philippines.

4 U.S. bombers make a low-level attack on the port of Kobe, Japan, using incendiary bombs. Their success leads to similar attacks on other Japanese cities.

4–11 At the Yalta Conference in the Crimea, USSR, the U.S. president, Franklin D. Roosevelt, the British prime minister, Winston Churchill, and the Soviet leader, Joseph Stalin, plan for the division of postwar Germany into four occupied zones, with four zones in Berlin, the capital.

8–March 21 Operation Veritable opens the Allies' Rhineland campaign. Canadian and British forces begin a drive south from Nijmegen in the Netherlands to capture land between the Rhine and Maas rivers and so clear German troops from the west bank of the Upper Rhine.

13–15 British and U.S. aircraft bomb the city of Dresden in eastern Germany, ostensibly to disrupt the transfer of German troops to the Soviet front. Over 60,000 people are killed and the city's historic center is destroyed.

19–March 24 U.S. marines capture the Japanese island of Iwo Jima after fierce fighting, which results in over 21,000 U.S. casualties.

24 Ahmad Mahir, prime minister of Egypt, is assassinated after announcing Egypt's declaration of war on Germany.

26 The administration of U.S. president Franklin D. Roosevelt enacts a midnight curfew on amusement parks to conserve fuel.

28 The U.S. general Douglas MacArthur enters Manila, the capital of the Philippines, three years after being forced out by the Japanese.

MARCH

• The U.S. president Franklin D. Roosevelt, negotiating reciprocal trade agreements, asks Congress for authority to reduce the tariff rate by as much as 50%.

6 Petru Groza is appointed prime minister of Romania under Soviet pressure, and forms a pro-Soviet government.

7 U.S. troops in Germany capture the Ludendorff railroad bridge at Remagen, south of the city of Bonn. One hundred troops cross the River Rhine in the evening.

20 British and Indian troops recapture Mandalay in Burma (now Myanmar) from the occupying Japanese forces.

22 The League of Arab States (Arab League) is founded by a treaty signed in Cairo, Egypt.

22 U.S. troops in Germany cross the River Rhine at Oppenheim, between Mainz and Mannheim, and secure bridgeheads on the German side of the river.

23 British and Canadian troops in Germany cross the River Rhine at Rees and Wesel, near the German–Netherlands border, in a successful culmination of Operation Veritable.

25 U.S. troops in Germany break out of their Rhine bridgeheads to the south of the Ruhr industrial region.

29 Soviet forces enter Austria.

30 Soviet forces in Poland liberate the port of Danzig (now Gdańsk, Poland) from the occupying Germans.

APRIL

• The administration of U.S. president Harry S. Truman cuts sugar rations by an additional 25%.

1–June 22 U.S. forces capture Okinawa, the largest of the Japanese Ryukyu Islands. There are 49,151 U.S. and 110,00 Japanese casualties.

2 German test pilot Hannah Reitsch flies high-ranking officers into Berlin, Germany, eluding the Allied forces that surround the city.

3 President Edvard Beneš of Czechoslovakia reestablishes a government in his native land, with the Socialist Zdenek Fierlinger as prime minister, Jan Masaryk as foreign minister, and the communist Václav Nosek as interior minister.

5 The USSR denounces its neutrality pact with Japan of April 13, 1941.

9 An Allied offensive across northern Italy begins, under the British field marshal Harold Alexander.

9 The leading German anti-Nazi pastor Dietrich Bonhoeffer is hanged by the Nazi authorities; he has been held in prison since April 5, 1943.

10 U.S. troops take the city of Hanover in northern Germany, but German forces resist an attack on Bremen.

11 U.S. troops in Germany reach the River Elbe near Wittenberge, northwest of the capital, Berlin.

12 Franklin Delano Roosevelt, president of the United States, dies and is succeeded by Vice President Harry S. Truman.
13 Soviet forces liberate the Austrian capital, Vienna, from the occupying German troops, and establish a provisional government of Social Democrats, Social Christians, and communists, with Karl Renner as prime minister.
16 Soviet forces in Germany launch an offensive from their bridgehead on the River Oder toward the capital, Berlin.
25 The United Nations Conference on International Organization (UNCIO) in San Francisco, California, attended by representatives of 50 nations, drafts the Charter of the United Nations.
25 U.S. and Soviet troops in Germany link up at Torgau on the River Elbe.
28 Benito Mussolini, the Italian prime minister, is shot by the Italian Resistance in Dongo, Italy. His mistress Clara Petacci and members of his entourage are also shot.
29 German forces in Italy surrender to the Allies.
29 The German Führer Adolf Hitler marries his mistress, Eva Braun, in their Berlin bunker.
30 Adolf Hitler, dictator of Germany 1933–45, commits suicide in his bunker in Berlin, Germany. He and his wife, Eva Braun, take poison.

MAY

• The U.S. president Harry S. Truman lifts the "dim-out" mandated on January 15. The next day he ends the midnight entertainment curfew enacted on February 26.
2 British forces in Germany reach the port of Lübeck, southeast of the Jutland peninsula, aiming to prevent the Soviet occupation of Denmark.
2 The German capital, Berlin, surrenders to Soviet forces.
3 British and Indian forces capture Rangoon in Burma (now Myanmar) from the occupying Japanese forces.
4 All German forces under arms in Germany surrender to Allied forces under Field Marshal Sir Bernard Montgomery.
8 General Alfred Jodl signs the official surrender of Germany in World War II in Reims, France, at 2:41 a.m., in the presence of U.S. general Dwight D. Eisenhower and other Allied officers. May 8 is celebrated as VE (Victory in Europe) Day in western Europe and the United States.
9 German troops in Prague, the Czech capital, surrender to Soviet forces.
9 VE (Victory in Europe) Day, following the German surrender to the Allies on May 8, is celebrated in the USSR.

JUNE

• The U.S. House of Representatives extends the Office of Price Administration by an additional year.
5 Following the German surrender, the Allied Control Council proclaims its control of Germany, and its authority over the definition of Germany's territories and borders.
6 The Reestablishment and Employment Act in Australia provides for the demobilization of armed forces and war workers.
9 The USSR forms the Soviet Military Administration in the eastern part of Germany, following the German surrender.
10 José Bustamante becomes president of Peru.

11 The Liberals under William L. Mackenzie King win the Canadian general election with 125 seats, against the Conservatives' 67.
18 The Czechoslovak government under Zdenek Fierlinger, based in Košice, orders the expulsion of all Germans and Magyars who had not been antifascists during World War II.
26 Sean O'Kelly becomes president of Eire (Ireland) on the retirement of Douglas Hyde.
27 The U.S. Federal Communications Commission (FCC) allocates thirteen channels for commercial television broadcasting.
28 A Polish Government of National Unity is formed, comprising 16 ministers from the old provisional government and 5 new ministers. Edward Osóbka-Morawski is prime minister.

JULY

• The U.S. Communist Party is restored.
• The U.S. Senate ratifies the United Nations Charter by a vote of 89 to 2.
3 Following the German surrender, the United States, Britain, and France occupy zones in the German capital of Berlin, while Soviet forces occupy a zone in the east of the city.
5 The Australian prime minister, John Curtin, dies (60).
5 The U.S. general Douglas MacArthur announces the liberation of the Philippines from the Japanese.
5 The United States and Britain recognize the new post-World War II government in Poland, withdrawing recognition from the government-in-exile in London, England.
7 The USSR establishes five *Länder* (states) in its zone of eastern Germany.
12 Labor politician Joseph Chifley succeeds the late John Curtin as prime minister of Australia.
17–August 2 At the Potsdam Conference in Germany, the Soviet leader Joseph Stalin, the U.S. president Harry S. Truman, and the British prime minister (first Winston Churchill, then Clement Attlee after the Labour election victory of July 26) organize the occupation of Germany following its surrender in World War II.
26 In the Soviet zone of Germany, all banks are closed and inhabitants are ordered to hand over gold and silver currency, foreign bank notes, and valuables.
26 Labour wins a landslide victory in the British general election, with 393 seats against the Conservatives' 199. Clement Attlee becomes prime minister, Ernest Bevin foreign secretary, and Hugh Dalton chancellor of the Exchequer.

AUGUST

• The U.S. president Harry S. Truman suspends many wartime restraints and reinstitutes the civilian economy. The rationing of shoes, meat, butter, and rubber draws to a close.
• The U.S. president Harry S. Truman signs the McMahan Act establishing the Atomic Energy Commission.
• The War Manpower Commission eases restrictions on workers' autonomy in the United States.
6 The U.S. B-29 bomber *Enola Gay* drops an atomic bomb on Hiroshima, Japan, destroying two-thirds of the city.

8 The United States attempts to mediate when conflict breaks out in China between the Nationalist government (Guomindang) and the communists.

8 The USSR declares war on Japan and invades Japanese-occupied Manchuria, China.

9 The U.S. B-29 bomber *Bock's Car* drops an atomic bomb on Nagasaki, Japan, destroying half the city.

12 Soviet forces occupy Japanese-held northern Korea, the island of Sakhalin, and the Kuril Islands.

13 The World Zionist Congress demands the admission of 1 million Jews to Palestine.

14 The Japanese emperor Hirohito proclaims Japan's acceptance of the Allies' terms for ending World War II in the Pacific and urges his people to accept the surrender.

14 The USSR signs a treaty with Nationalist China, recognizing the independence of Outer Mongolia.

15 General Henri-Philippe Pétain, the chief of state of Vichy France, is condemned to death for treason. The sentence is immediately commuted to life imprisonment.

15 Rationing of gasoline and fuel oil in the United States comes to an end.

16 The USSR and Poland sign a treaty demarcating the new post-World War II Soviet–Polish frontier.

17 Indonesian leaders proclaim their country's independence from Dutch rule, but this is rejected by the Netherlands.

19 The Vietminh (Vietnam Independence League) seize power from the Japanese in French Indochina and force Emperor Bao Dai to abdicate.

24 The U.S. President Harry S. Truman orders the cessation of the Lend-Lease system (launched on March 11, 1941), which has cost the United States $49.1 billion.

28 Japanese forces in Burma (now Myanmar) formally surrender to the Allies in Rangoon.

28 The first advance units of the U.S. armed forces land on the Japanese mainland to secure the surrender of Japan. Combat troops of the U.S. Army and Navy arrive in Japan on August 30.

SEPTEMBER

2 Ho Chi Minh, leader of the Vietminh (Vietnam Independence League), proclaims the independent Democratic Republic of Vietnam, but the French refuse to recognize it.

2 Japan signs its capitulation on board the USS *Missouri*, marking the end of World War II.

6 Communist-influenced nationalists in Korea proclaim the Korean People's Republic.

Nuclear Disarmament (1945–95)

1945

July 16 The first atomic explosion occurs when the nuclear device code-named "Trinity" is exploded near Alamogordo, New Mexico. On August 6 and August 9 similar devices are dropped on Hiroshima and Nagasaki, Japan.

1946

August 1 The U.S. Atomic Energy Commission is established; its goal is to control nuclear weapon development and to direct research and development into peaceful uses of nuclear energy.

1958

April Atomic scientist Edward Teller tells a U.S. Senate subcommittee that ending nuclear testing would subject the nation to grave peril.

1959

August In an effort to encourage the USSR and Britain to curb nuclear testing, the United States extends a unilateral ban on testing to December 31.

1962

January 29 The three-power (United States, USSR, and Britain) Conference on the Discontinuance of Nuclear Weapon Tests, which has met 353 times at Geneva, Switzerland, since October 31, 1958, finally collapses.

August At resumed nuclear disarmament talks in Geneva, the USSR rejects a U.S. and British proposal to ban nuclear tests and submit the issue of compliance to international inspection.

1963

January The Soviet Union walks away from informal nuclear test ban talks held in New York, New York, after two weeks of negotiations.

February Following the Soviet Union's abandonment of informal nuclear test ban discussions a week earlier, the U.S. proceeds with underground nuclear testing.

August 5 The United States, USSR, and Britain sign a nuclear test ban treaty, which is subsequently signed by 96 states, but not France.

October 7 The United States and USSR sign a limited nuclear test ban treaty, effective October 10. President John F. Kennedy ratifies the recent nuclear test ban treaty with the Soviet Union by authorizing the sale of 4 million metric tons of wheat to the USSR.

1965

August 17 With the war in southeast Asia escalating, Soviet negotiators ridicule a U.S. nuclear nonproliferation proposal before the UN Disarmament Committee in Geneva. The committee disbands two days later.

1967

January 27 A treaty banning nuclear weapons from outer space is signed by 60 countries, including the United States and USSR. It will be effective from October 10.

1969

November 24 The United States and USSR ratify a nuclear nonproliferation treaty.

1971

• Greenpeace, the environmental campaign organization, is founded to protest against U.S. nuclear testing at Amchitka Island, Alaska.

1979

June 15–18 A summit meeting in Vienna, Austria, between the U.S. and Soviet presidents Jimmy Carter and Leonid Brezhnev, ends with the signing of the SALT II treaty limiting nuclear weapons between the two countries.

10 Vidkun Quisling, Norwegian fascist leader and collaborator with Nazi Germany during World War II, is sentenced to death for treason.

12 The USSR creates a central administration for its zone of post-World War II Germany under the chairmanship of Marshal Georgy Zhukov.

27 Elections for the Central Legislative Assembly are held in India; most seats are won by the Congress Party or its rival, the Muslim League.

OCTOBER

• The Food and Agriculture Organization (FAO) is established, the first of the UN's specialized agencies. Its objective is to eliminate hunger and improve nutrition worldwide.

9 Admiral Pierre Laval, the prime minister of Vichy France, is sentenced to death for treason.

11 A breakdown of negotiations in China between the president Jiang Jie Shi and the communist leader Mao Zedong leads to fighting between nationalists and communists for the control of Manchuria.

15 The Labor and Dominion parties in South Africa withdraw from the coalition government, leaving Jan Smuts prime minister of a United Party ministry.

20 Egypt, Iraq, Syria, and Lebanon warn the United States that the creation of a Jewish state in Palestine will lead to war.

21 The elections for the French constituent assembly show a swing to the left, with the communists winning 148 seats and socialists 134, against 141 for the Popular Republican Movement (MRP).

24 The Czechoslovak government of Zdenek Fierlinger, based in Košice, nationalizes the country's key industries and banks.

24 The United Nations, with headquarters in New York, New York, comes into formal existence on the ratification of its Charter by 29 nations.

25 The Brazilian army forces President Getúlio Vargas to resign.

30 The Social Democrats emerge as the strongest single party in elections in Denmark, but Erik Eriksen forms a coalition of Liberals and Conservatives.

NOVEMBER

• Former U.S. secretary of state Cordell Hull wins the Nobel Peace Prize for his work in helping to establish the United Nations.

• The U.S. Congress cuts taxes by $6 billion.

1980–95

1981

October 24 One hundred and fifty thousand people attend a CND (Campaign for Nuclear Disarmament) rally in London, England.

November 18 U.S. president Ronald Reagan offers to cancel the deployment of Cruise and Pershing missiles in Europe if the USSR dismantles medium-range nuclear missiles targeted on western Europe.

1982

June 12 Approximately 550,000 protesters against nuclear arms march though New York, New York.

1983

January 27 U.S.–Soviet arms reduction talks resume in Geneva, Switzerland, with the USSR proposing a nuclear-free zone for central Europe.

1984

December 15 Soviet Politburo member Mikhail Gorbachev visits London, England, and states that the USSR is willing to negotiate large reductions in nuclear weapons. The British prime minister Margaret Thatcher declares "I like Mr. Gorbachev. We can do business together."

1986

January 25 Soviet head of state Mikhail Gorbachev proposes a 15-year timetable for the elimination of all nuclear weapons.

1987

February 28 Mikhail Gorbachev proposes a separate agreement abolishing intermediate-range nuclear weapons in Europe and drops the USSR's insistence on the curtailment of the U.S. Star Wars program.

March 2–4 Proposals from both the United States and the USSR on the limitation or abolition of medium-range nuclear missiles in Europe are tabled at the Geneva arms talks in Switzerland.

April 10 Mikhail Gorbachev announces that the USSR is prepared to negotiate on short- as well as intermediate-range nuclear missiles.

June 4 The West German Bundestag (parliament) endorses the U.S.–Soviet plan to eliminate medium-range nuclear missiles from Europe.

July 22 Mikhail Gorbachev offers to dismantle all short- and medium-range nuclear missiles in the USSR.

December 7–10 At a U.S.–Soviet summit in Washington, D.C., U.S. president Ronald Reagan and Soviet leader Mikhail Gorbachev agree to eliminate intermediate-range nuclear forces.

1988

June 1 Ronald Reagan and Mikhail Gorbachev sign an intermediate-range nuclear forces treaty in Moscow.

1991

July 31 U.S. president George Bush and Mikhail Gorbachev sign the Strategic Arms Reduction Treaty (START) to reduce their arsenals of long-range nuclear weapons by a third.

1993

January 3 George Bush and Russian president Boris Yeltsin sign the second Strategic Arms Reduction Treaty (START II), committing the United States and Russia to dismantling two-thirds of their nuclear warheads.

1995

May 12 A Review and Extension Conference of Parties to the 1968 Treaty on Nonproliferation of Nuclear Weapons, in New York, New York, ends with agreement to extend the treaty indefinitely.

4   The Smallholders' Party wins the general election in Hungary with 60% of the vote, against only 17% for the communists.

10   A Central Planning Office is established in Poland to direct the future development of the Polish economy.

10   Enver Hoxha's communist-dominated government in Albania is recognized by the Western powers.

11   Marshal Josip Broz Tito's National Front wins elections to the constituent assembly in Yugoslavia.

13   General Charles de Gaulle is elected president of France's post-World War II provisional government in Paris.

16   The United Nations Educational, Scientific, and Cultural Organization (UNESCO) is set up, with its headquarters in Paris, France. It comes into operation in November 1946.

18   Iranian government troops sent to quell a communist rising in Azerbaijan province, Iran, are stopped by Soviet forces at the town of Kazvin.

18   Prime Minister Antonio Salazar's National Union Party wins a Portuguese general election, which is boycotted by the opposition.

18   The communist-dominated Fatherland Front wins an election in Bulgaria.

20   The Allied Control Council, the body officially charged with governing post-World War II Germany, approves a plan to transfer 6.6 million Germans from Austria, Hungary, and Poland to Germany pending a peace settlement.

20   The trials of 24 leading Nazis opens before the Allied International Military Tribunal in Nuremberg, Germany. The Tribunal rules that an individual's obedience to orders is an insufficient defense for crimes committed against humanity. The trials continues until August 31, 1946.

23   All rationing stops in the United States, with the exception of sugar. Food remains scarce everywhere else and the black market continues to exist throughout Europe.

25   The People's Party wins the Austrian elections.

29   The Federal Republic of Yugoslavia is proclaimed, under Marshal Josip Broz Tito, leader of the communist resistance against Germany during World War II.

DECEMBER

•   The National Wage Stabilization Board supplants the National War Labor Board in the United States.

2   Eurico Dutra is elected president of Brazil with the support of the Social Democrats.

6   The United States makes a loan of $3.75 billion to Britain to help postwar economic recovery.

20   Karl Renner, of the Austrian Social Democratic Party, is unanimously elected president of Austria.

SCIENCE, TECHNOLOGY, AND MEDICINE

Agriculture

•   The chemical herbicides 2,4-D, 2,4,5,-T and IPC are introduced; they herald a new era in chemical weed control as their high toxicity permits them to be used in dosages as low as one or two pounds per acre.

•   Working in Japan, U.S. geneticist Samuel G. Salmon discovers Norin 10, a semidwarf wheat variety which grows quickly, responds well to fertilizer, does not fall over from the weight of the grains, and when crossed with disease-resistant strains in the United States results in a wheat strain that increases wheat harvests by more than 60% in India and Pakistan.

Ecology

•   The lowest barometric pressure on record to date, 64.9 cm/25.55 in, is recorded in the eye of a typhoon near Okinawa, Japan.

SEPTEMBER

•   The Makurazaki typhoon destroys over 60,000 homes and kills over 3,000 people in Japan.

Health and Medicine

c. 1945   The first effective vaccine against influenza is developed.

•   Grand Rapids, Michigan, begins adding fluoride to its water to help prevent tooth decay; other cities in the United States soon follow.

•   Scottish biochemist Alexander Fleming, German-born British biochemist Ernst Chain, and Australian pathologist Howard Florey share the Nobel Prize for Physiology or Medicine for their discovery of penicillin.

•   The antihistamine Benadryl (diphenydramine), used to control hay fever, is discovered in the United States.

•   U.S. physician Alton Ochsner points to the relationship between cigarette smoking and lung cancer.

Science

•   Austrian physicist Wolfgang Pauli receives the Nobel Prize for Physics for his discovery of the exclusion principle.

•   Finnish chemist Artturi Virtanen receives the Nobel Prize for Chemistry for his invention of a method of preserving fodder.

•   Hungarian astronomer Z. Bay and the U.S. Army Signal Corps Laboratory receive radar echoes from the moon.

•   Hungarian scientist Lajos Jánossy investigates cosmic radiation.

•   Single-stage sounding rockets, reaching speeds of 4,800–8,000 kph/3,000–5,000 mph, and a maximum altitude of 160 km/100 mi, are launched carrying instrumentation to gather information about the upper atmosphere.

- U.S. anthropologist Ralph Linton publishes *Cultural Background of Personality*, which advances the idea that basic personality types are formed from common elements within a culture.
- U.S. chemists mix gasoline and the aluminum salt of naphthenic and palmitic acids to produce the jellied incendiary napalm.
- U.S. physicist Edwin M. McMillan and Soviet physicist V. I. Veksler (1943) independently describe the principle of phase stability. By removing an apparent limitation on the energy of particle accelerators for protons, it makes possible the construction of magnetic-resonance accelerators, or synchrotrons. Synchrocyclotrons are soon built at the University of California and in England.

Technology

- A nuclear reactor using natural uranium and heavy water as both coolant and moderator (a material that slows down the fission process) begins operating at Chalk River, Ontario, Canada; a second reactor starts operation two years later.
- English author Arthur C. Clarke writes an article entitled "Extra-Terrestrial Relays" which proposes geosynchronous satellites that can relay radio and television signals worldwide; they are developed 20 years later.
- Germany introduces the Type XXI U-boat (submarine). Provided with extra battery capacity and a snorkel to allow the charging of batteries by diesel engine while submerged, the Type XXI is able to operate submerged for up to four days, and to operate at twice the depth of other submarines; it is the most advanced submarine made during World War II.
- The eidophor is invented; it can project television pictures on screens up to 10 m/33 ft square.
- The White Sands rocket testing ground in New Mexico, United States, is established.

FEBRUARY

- German attempts to perfect a manned, rocket-powered, vertically-launched interceptor fighter suffer a severe setback with the death of the test pilot, Lothar Siebert, in the unsuccessful launch of a Natter fighter developed by Bachem AG.

MAY

- The U.S. government reduces military aircraft production by one-third.
- The War Production Board sanctions the production of 73 more consumer goods in the United States.

JULY

16 The first atomic explosion occurs when the nuclear device code-named "Trinity" is exploded near Alamogordo, New Mexico. On August 6 and August 9 similar devices are dropped on Hiroshima and Nagasaki, Japan.

OCTOBER

8 In Waltham, Massachusetts, Percy LeBaron Spencer patents the first microwave oven, which is used in restaurants and institutions.

Transportation

- A British Gloster Meteor jet airplane sets a new world air speed record of 975 kph/606 mph. The modified British Gloster Meteor fighter becomes the first turboprop airplane to fly.
- British aircraft manufacturer Rolls-Royce develops the afterburner for jet engines; a second combustion chamber at the rear of the engine into which additional fuel is injected, it increases thrust for takeoff and supersonic flight.
- The full-tracked and fully enclosed M-44 armored personnel carrier is introduced in the U.S. armed forces; it carries 27 men.
- The Pershing M-26 heavy tank, armed with a 90 mm gun, is introduced in U.S. armored divisions.
- Total lengths of operational railroad in use in selected countries are: United States, 386,411 km/240,156 mi; USSR, 84,773 km/52,687 mi; Great Britain, 81,343 km/50,555 mi; France, 11,102 km/6,900 mi.

ARTS AND IDEAS

Arts

- French photographer Henri Cartier-Bresson takes *The Deported Return*.
- The Arts Council of Great Britain is established to encourage performance in the arts.
- The Belgian artist René Magritte illustrates an edition of the prose poems *Chants de Maldoror* by the French writer Count Lautréamont.
- The English artist Graham Sutherland paints *Thorn Trees*.
- The English artist L. S. Lowry paints *VE Day*.
- The French artist Balthus paints *Les Beaux Jours/The Beautiful Days*.
- The French artist Henri Matisse paints *The Romanian Blouse*.
- The French artist Jean Dubuffet paints *Wall with Inscriptions*.
- The French artist Jean Fautrier exhibits *Otages/Hostages* in Paris, France—a series of paintings done during the German occupation of France.
- The French artist Wols paints *Drunken Boat*.
- The Spanish artist Pablo Picasso paints *The Charnel House*.
- The U.S. artist Alexander Calder creates the mobile *Red Pyramid*.
- The U.S. artist David Smith sculpts his *Pillar of Sunday* series.
- U.S. photographer Alfred Eisenstaedt takes *The Kiss (V-J Day)*.
- U.S. photographer Joe Rosenthal takes *Marines Raising the American Flag on Iwo Jima, 1945*.
- U.S. photographer Lee Miller takes *Captures Prison Guards, Buchenwald*.

October 1945–55 English art historian Ernest William Tristram publishes his three-volume *English Medieval Wall-Painting*.

Film

- A movie of Shakespeare's *Henry V*, directed by English actor Laurence Olivier, is released. He also stars in it.
- The 1944 Academy Awards take place. Best Actor: Bing Crosby, for *Going My Way*; Best Supporting Actor: Barry Fitzgerald, for *Going My Way*; Best Actress: Ingrid Bergman, for *Gaslight*; Best Supporting Actress: Ethel Barrymore, for *None But the Lonely Heart*; Best Picture: *Going My Way*, directed by Leo McCarey; Best Director: Leo McCarey, for *Going My Way*.
- The Allies effectively dismantle the production and distribution infrastructure of the movie industry in Germany.
- The doom-laden *film noir*, *Detour*, directed by Edgar G. Ulmer, is released in the United States.
- The movie *A Tree Grows in Brooklyn*, directed by Elia Kazan, is released in the United States, starring Peggy Ann Garner, James Dunn, Dorothy McGuire, Joan Blondell, and Lloyd Nolan.
- The movie *Blithe Spirit*, directed by David Lean, is released in Britain, adapted from the Noël Coward play, and starring Rex Harrison. Also released is Lean's movie *Brief Encounter*, written by Noël Coward and starring Trevor Howard and Celia Johnson. It memorably features Rachmaninov's Piano Concerto No. 2.
- The movie *Boule-de-suif*, directed by Christian-Jaque, is released in France. Based on a story by Guy de Maupassant, it stars Micheline Presle.
- The movie *Les Enfants du Paradis*, directed by Marcel Carné, is released, starring Arletty, Jean-Louis Barrault, and Pierre Brasseur. Filmed in France during the German occupation, its treatment of passion and sacrifice embody the French spirit in wartime.
- The movie *Mildred Pierce* is released in the United States. It is directed by Michael Curtiz and stars Joan Crawford.
- The movie *National Velvet*, directed by Clarence Brown, is released in the United States. Based on the novel by Enid Bagnold, it stars Mickey Rooney, Elizabeth Taylor, and Anne Revere.
- The movie *Roma, città aperta/Rome, Open City*, directed by Roberto Rossellini, is released in Italy. Dealing with the Italian underground movement against the Nazis near the end of World War II, it stars Aldo Fabrizzi, Anna Magnani, Marcello Pagliero, and Maria Michi.
- The movie *Spellbound*, directed by Alfred Hitchcock, is released in the United States, starring Gregory Peck and Ingrid Bergman.
- The movie *The Corn is Green*, directed by Jon Amiel, is released in the United States. Based on the play by Emlyn Williams, it stars Bette Davis, John Dall, and Rosalind Ivan.
- The movie *The Lost Weekend*, directed by Billy Wilder, is released. Based on the 1944 novel of the same name by Charles Reginald Jackson, and focusing on the social problems caused by alcoholism, it stars Ray Miland, Jane Wyman, and Philip Terry.
- The movie *The Naughty Nineties*, directed by Jean Yarborough, is released in the United States. It stars the comedy duo Bud Abbott and Lou Costello and features their most famous dialogue "Who's on First?"
- The movie *The Southerner*, directed by French filmmaker Jean Renoir, is released in the United States, starring Zachary Scott, Betty Field, and Beulah Bondi.
- The movie *The Wicked Lady*, directed by Leslie Arliss, is released in the UK, starring Margaret Lockwood and James Mason. Some scenes have to be reshot for the U.S. market, because too much cleavage is shown.
- The movie musical *Anchors Aweigh*, directed by George Sidney, is released in the United States, starring Gene Kelly and Frank Sinatra.

Literature and Language

- In France, the Prix Goncourt for literature is awarded to a woman for the first time. The recipient is the Russian-born writer Else Triolet for her novel *Le premier accroc coûte 200 francs/The First Tear Costs 200 Francs*.
- The Bosnian writer Ivo Andrić publishes his novel *Na Drini ćuprija/The Bridge on the Drina*.
- The English novelist Evelyn Waugh publishes his novel about the Catholic English aristocracy, *Brideshead Revisited*.
- The English writer Denton Welch publishes his novel *In Youth is Pleasure*.
- The English writer George Orwell publishes his novel *Animal Farm*, a satire directed against Stalinist Russia in particular, and totalitarianism in general.
- The English writer Henry Green publishes his novel *Loving*.
- The English writer W. H. Auden, settled in the United States, publishes *For the Time Being*, a Christmas oratorio.
- The French writer and philosopher Jean-Paul Sartre publishes his novels *L'Age de raison/The Age of Reason* and *Le Sursis/The Reprieve*. They form the first two parts of his novel sequence *Les Chemins de la liberté/The Roads to Freedom*.
- The German musicologist Alfred Einstein (the cousin of the physicist Albert Einstein) publishes *Mozart: His Character, His Work*.
- The German writer Herman Broch publishes his novel *Der Tod des Vergil/The Death of Vergil*.
- The Italian writer Carlo Levi publishes *Cristo si èfermato ad Eboli/Christ Stopped at Eboli*, a lyrical account of his political exile in southern Italy.
- The Nobel Prize for Literature is awarded to the Chilean poet Gabriela Mistral.
- The Norwegian writer Cora Sandel publishes her novel *Kranes Konditori/Krane's Café*.
- The Pulitzer Prize for Biography is awarded to Russel B. Nye for *George Bancroft: Brahmin Rebel*, the Pulitzer Prize for Fiction is awarded to John Hersey for *A Bell for Adano*, and the Pulitzer Prize for Poetry is awarded to Karl Shapiro for *V-Letter and Other Poems*.
- The U.S. novelist Kathleen Winsor's *Forever Amber*, a historical romance, is the best-selling fiction title in the United States.
- The U.S. writer Chester Himes publishes his novel *If He Hollers Let Him Go*.
- The U.S. writer John Steinbeck publishes his novel *Cannery Row*.
- The U.S. writer Richard Wright publishes the novel *Black Boy*, a powerful, if somewhat apocryphal, account of his childhood in rural Mississippi.

Music

c. 1945   In the United States, bluegrass music, based on
   hillbilly music, becomes popular through performances
   by Bill Monroe's Bluegrass Boys.
- The Czech composer Bohuslav Martinů completes his
  Symphony No. 4 and his Cello Concerto No. 2.
- The energetic "Bebop" jazz style, pioneered by Charlie
  "Bird" Parker and others, sweeps the United States.
- The English composer Benjamin Britten completes his
  Nine Holy Sonnets of John Donne for piano and voice.
- The first recorded music album sales chart is released, in
  the United States.
- The opera Peter Grimes by the English composer
  Benjamin Britten is first performed, at the Sadler's Wells
  Theatre in London, England.
- The French composer Darius Milhaud completes his
  Kaddisch, for voice and orchestra, and his Elégie/Elegy
  for piano and cello.
- The French composer Olivier Messiaen completes his
  vocal work Harawi, chant d'amour et de mort/Harawi,
  Song of Love and Death.
- The German composer Richard Strauss completes his
  orchestral work Metamorphosen/Metamorphoses.
- The Hungarian composer Béla Bartók completes his
  Piano Concerto No. 3.
- The Russian composer Sergey Prokofiev completes his
  Violin Sonata No. 1.
- The Russian composer Dmitry Shostakovich completes
  his Symphony No. 9.
- The Russian composer Igor Stravinsky completes his
  Symphony in Three Movements.
- The U.S. jazz musician Dizzy Gillespie records
  "Groovin' High."
- The U.S. singer Perry Como records "Till the End of
  Time."

Theater and Dance

- The musical Carousel, by Richard Rodgers and Oscar
  Hammerstein, is first performed, at the Majestic Theater
  in New York, New York.
- The play La Folle de Chaillot/The Mad Woman of
  Chaillot, by the French dramatist Jean Giraudoux, is
  first performed, in Paris, France.
- The play The Glass Menagerie, by the U.S. writer
  Tennessee Williams, is first performed, at the Plymouth
  Theater in New York, New York.
- The Pulitzer Prize for Drama is awarded to Mary Chase
  for Harvey.
- The U.S. writer Robert Frost publishes Masque of
  Reason, a verse play.

Thought and Scholarship

- Austrian-born English philosopher Karl Popper
  publishes The Open Society and its Enemies.
- English historian A. J. P. Taylor publishes The Course of
  German History: A Survey of the Development of
  Germany since 1815.

- English philosopher Bertrand Russell publishes History
  of Western Philosophy, which becomes an unexpected
  best seller both in Britain and in the United States.
- English writer H. G. Wells publishes his work of
  nonfiction Mind at the End of its Tether, which gives a
  pessimistic assessment of the future.
- French philosopher Maurice Merleau-Ponty publishes
  Phénoménologie de la perception/Phenomenology of
  Perception.
- Hungarian-born English writer Arthur Koestler
  publishes The Yogi and the Commissar and Other
  Essays.
- The Pulitzer Prize for History is awarded to Stephen
  Bonsal for Unfinished Business.

SOCIETY

Education

- The Roosevelt College opens in Chicago, Illinois, as the
  Thomas Jefferson College.
- The University of Calgary opens in Calgary, Alberta,
  Canada.

Everyday Life

- "Coke" becomes a registered trademark of the Coca-
  Cola Company in the United States.
- Frozen orange juice becomes available in the United
  States.
- Swanson frozen chicken and turkey arrives on the
  shelves in U.S. supermarkets.
- The Medal of Freedom is founded in the United States
  to reward outstanding civilian endeavor.
- There are 27.8 million telephones in the United States,
  or one telephone for every five people. 45% of homes
  have telephones.
- U.S. chemist Earl W. Tupper invents a range of sealable
  plastic bowls and containers—Tupperware—that will be
  sold through Tupperware parties in the home.
- U.S. inventor Forest Gill of Kansas invents car stickers:
  among the first are VISIT... and VOTE FOR...

FEBRUARY
6   The World Labor Union Conference opens in London,
    England, organized by British Labor Union Congress
    and attended by representatives from Allied and neutral
    countries.

OCTOBER
29   Ballpoint pens are a great commercial success when they
     go on sale in New York, New York.

NOVEMBER
21–March 13, 1946   United Auto Workers at the General
    Motors plant in Detroit strike for 113 days before
    gaining better wages and benefits; the strike is the first
    sign of postwar labor trouble.

Media and Communication

- After a delay caused by the war, television broadcasting in the United States begins on a regular basis.
- In Germany, the occupying powers publish several newspapers, including *Die Neue Zeitung* in Munich, the *Tägliche Rundschau* in Berlin, and *Die Welt* in Hamburg; these titles continue after the end of the occupation.

- Macy's Thanksgiving Parade in the United States is televised for the first time.
- Publisher John H. Johnson founds the illustrated monthly magazine *Ebony*, aimed at black Americans. This will form the basis of a very successful publishing empire.
- The British Broadcasting Corporation (BBC) extends its range of radio programs with the establishment of the Home Service and the Light Program.

BIRTHS & DEATHS

JANUARY

9 Frank Biondi, U.S. cable television executive, born in Livingston, New Jersey.

26 Jacqueline du Pré, English virtuoso cellist, born in Oxford, England (−1987).

FEBRUARY

1 Johan Huizinga, Dutch historian, dies in De Steeg, the Netherlands (72).

6 Bob Marley, Jamaican singer whose band The Wailers popularized reggae music, born in Kingston, Jamaica.

MARCH

- Anne Frank, German Jew whose diary written while hiding from the Nazis has been translated into over 30 languages, dies in Bergen-Belsen concentration camp near Hanover, Germany (15).

26 David Lloyd George, Welsh Liberal politician, British prime minister 1916–22, dies in Ty-newydd, Caernarvonshire, Wales (82).

APRIL

11 Frederick John Dealtry Lugard, British soldier and colonial administrator, high commissioner of Nigeria 1900–06, and governor-general of Nigeria 1912–19, dies in Abinger, Surrey, England (87).

12 Franklin Delano Roosevelt, U.S. statesman, 32nd president of the United States 1933–45 (reelected three times), a Democrat, dies in Warm Springs, Georgia (63).

18 Ernie Pyle, U.S. reporter who won a Pulitzer prize for his coverage of World War II, dies in fighting in Okinawa, Japan (44).

22 Käthe Kollwitz, German graphic artist and sculptor, dies in Dresden, Germany (77).

27 August Wilson, U.S. playwright, born in Pittsburgh, Pennsylvania.

28 Benito Mussolini, Italian prime minister 1922–43, first of Europe's fascist dictators, shot by the Italian Resistance in Dongo, Italy (61).

30 Adolf Hitler, German fascist leader of the National Socialist (Nazi) Party, dictator of Germany 1933–45, commits suicide in his bunker in Berlin, Germany (56).

30 Annie Dillard, U.S. poet and essayist on nature, and journalist on ecological subjects, born in Pittsburgh, Pennsylvania.

MAY

1 Joseph Goebbels, German Nazi leader and minister of propaganda under Adolf Hitler, commits suicide (47).

23 Heinrich Himmler, German Nazi leader, head of the SS, and organizer of the Nazi death camps, commits suicide after being captured in Lüneberg, Germany (44).

JUNE

7 Kitaro Nishida, Japanese philosopher who attempted to integrate Western philosophy with Japanese spiritual traditions, dies in Kamakura, Japan (76).

23 Simon Lake, U.S. engineer who built the *Argonaut*, the first submarine to operate in the open ocean, dies in Bridgeport, Connecticut (78).

JULY

19 Heinrich Wölfflin, Swiss historian and writer on aesthetics, dies in Basel, Switzerland (81).

20 Paul Valéry, French poet, essayist, and critic, dies in Paris, France (74).

AUGUST

10 Robert Goddard, U.S. astronautics pioneer who developed modern rockets used for launching spacecraft, dies in Baltimore, Maryland (62).

SEPTEMBER

15 Anton Webern, Austrian composer, dies in Mittersill, near Salzburg, Austria (61).

15 Jessye Norman, U.S. soprano, born in Augusta, Georgia.

26 Béla Bartók, Hungarian-born composer and pianist, dies in New York, New York (64).

OCTOBER

13 Milton Snavely Hershey, U.S. manufacturer who founded the Hershey Chocolate Corporation, dies in Hershey, Pennsylvania (88).

15 Pierre Laval, French politician, leader of the collaboration Vichy government during World War II, is executed for treason in Paris, France (62).

24 Vidkun Quisling, Norwegian fascist army officer who collaborated with the Germans during World War I, and whose name has become synonymous with "traitor," is executed for treason in Akershus Forress, Oslo, Norway (58).

30 Henry Winkler, U.S. actor who played the Fonz on *Happy Days*, born in New York, New York.

NOVEMBER

20 Francis William Aston, English physicist who developed the mass spectrograph, dies in Cambridge, England (68).

DECEMBER

4 Thomas Hunt Morgan, U.S. zoologist and geneticist who carried out work on heredity, dies in Pasadena, California (79).

16 Fumimaro Konoe, prime minister of Japan 1937–39 and 1940–41, commits suicide in Tokyo, Japan (53).

16 Giovanni Agnelli, Italian industrialist who founded the Fiat automobile company and supplied the Italian military with its war machines during both world wars, dies in Turin, Italy (80).

21 George S. Patton, U.S. general during World War II, is killed in a road traffic accident in Heidelberg, Germany (60).

28 Theodore Dreiser, U.S. novelist of the Naturalist school, dies in Hollywood, California (74).

- The first high-fidelity record player in the world, the Decca Piccadilly, is produced in the UK; the first hi-fi recordings were made the previous year.

OCTOBER

14   Portuguese prime minister Antonio Salazar reimposes press censorship, despite having permitted opposition parties to be formed.

Religion

- An important collection of Coptic Gnostic manuscripts is discovered at Nag Hammadi, in Egypt.
- Austrian Jewish theologian Martin Buber publishes *For the Sake of Heaven*.
- Pope Pius XII condemns the atomic bombing of Hiroshima and Nagasaki, Japan.
- The Allied Control Commission in Japan orders the disestablishment of State Shinto (state rites conducted by the emperor), to be replaced by Shrine Shinto (private practices of the imperial family).

APRIL

19   In England, following the death of Archbishop Temple, Geoffrey Fisher becomes archbishop of Canterbury. He will hold the post until 1961.

Sports

- Army is college football's national champion for the second consecutive year.
- The first Sydney to Hobart yacht race is held in Australia.

JANUARY

26   The heirs of Jacob Ruppert sell the New York Yankees to a syndicate headed by Lawrence MacPhail for $2.8 million.

MARCH

2–5 U.S. national figure skating champions are: Gretchen Merrill; Donna Pospisil and Jean Pierre Brunet, pairs; Kathy Williams and Robert Swenning, dance. There is no men's competition.

APRIL

6–22   The Toronto Maple Leafs beat the Detroit Red Wings in a seventh game to win the National Hockey League (NHL) Stanley Cup.

24   The owners of U.S. baseball teams name former Kentucky senator Albert "B. Happy" Chandler as commissioner of the sport.

JUNE

- At the Wimbledon tennis championships in England, the United States defeats the British Empire 4–1 in a charity tennis match before 6,000 spectators on No. 1 Court.

JULY

15   U.S. golfer Byron Nelson wins his fifth major at the United States Professional Golf Association tournament at the Morraine Club in Dayton, Ohio.

17   Swedish runner Gunder Hägg breaks the world mile record set in 1944 by his great rival Arne Andersson with a time of 4 min 1.4 sec. However, later in the year both runners are suspended from international amateur competition for allegedly taking money.

SEPTEMBER

2   At the U.S. Lawn Tennis Association championships, U.S. tennis player Frank A. Parker retains his title as men's champion, and U.S. tennis player Sarah Cooke wins the women's title.

OCTOBER

3–10   The Detroit Tigers defeat the Chicago Cubs four games to three in the World Series.

DECEMBER

16   The Cleveland Rams defeat the Washington Redskins 15–14 in Cleveland to win their first National Football League (NFL) Championship.

1946

POLITICS, GOVERNMENT, AND ECONOMICS

Business and Economics

- Hyperinflation in Hungary is the highest in history, resulting in the printing of a 100-trillion-pengö note.
- Procter & Gamble introduces Tide, the first commercially available domestic detergent to wash clothes.
- The Exchange National Bank in Chicago, Illinois, becomes the first drive-in bank.
- The first completely automated production lines are introduced at the Ford Motor Company in the United States.

JANUARY
- The American Federation of Labor readmits the United Mine Workers union.

Colonization

FEBRUARY
2 The British government sends a mission to India to discuss the country's future constitution with political leaders.

MARCH
6 France recognizes Vietnam as a democratic republic within the Indochinese federation.
10 British and French troops begin to withdraw from Lebanon; despite promising autonomy for Lebanon in 1936 and during World War II, France is only compelled to withdraw by popular protest.
22 Britain recognizes the independence of Transjordan, a British League of Nations mandate since the end of World War I.

JULY
- The U.S. president Harry S. Truman proclaims the independence of the Philippines from the United States.
22 Zionist terrorists, intent on forcing Britain to set up a Jewish state in Palestine, blow up part of the King David Hotel in Jerusalem containing British government and military offices, killing 91 people.

SEPTEMBER
2 The Congress Party forms a provisional government in India, with Jawaharlal Nehru elected vice president to the viceroy, Lord Wavell.

NOVEMBER
23 A French cruiser bombards the port of Haiphong in northeast Vietnam, killing almost 6,000 people, in retaliation for attacks by Vietnamese communists on French garrisons in the country. The incident leads to the Vietnamese war for independence.

DECEMBER
9 The Indian constituent assembly meets to discuss independence from Britain, but is boycotted by the Muslim League.
19 The French Indochina War (for Vietnamese independence) begins, and Ho Chi Minh, the leader of the Vietminh (Vietnam Independence League), seeks refuge in a remote area of north Vietnam.

Human Rights

- Mexican women gain the right to vote on the same basis as men.
- The authorities in the city of Bombay in India remove official discrimination against the Harijans ("untouchables").
- The Cultural Relaxation Center (COC) in the Netherlands is the first cultural facility in the world established for homosexuals.
- The French constitution recognizes women's equality in most political areas.
- Women are granted a statutory right to equal pay in France.
- Women gain the vote in Italy.

JULY
5 An anti-Jewish pogrom is mounted by Poles in the city of Kielce, Poland.

SEPTEMBER
18 Archbishop Stefinać of Croatia is imprisoned in Yugoslavia as part of a communist clampdown on the church.

NOVEMBER
6 A royal commission in Britain favors equal pay for women.

Politics and Government

- Heavy industry is nationalized in Austria.
- The Christian Social Union (CSU) is founded as a political party in Bavaria, Germany.
- The International Court of Justice is established in The Hague, the Netherlands, as the judicial body of the United Nations (UN).
- The United Nations (UN) establishes the International Refugee Organization (IRO) to take over the refugee

work of the United Nations Relief and Rehabilitation Administration (UNRRA).

- The U.S. general Douglas MacArthur purges militarists in Japan, after the end of World War II.
- The U.S. president Harry S. Truman names legal scholar Frederick M. Vinson chief justice of the U.S. Supreme Court.
- Verdicts of the International Military Tribunal at Nuremberg, Germany, establish that individuals can be guilty of war crimes and punished for crimes against international law.

JANUARY

1   Polish industrial enterprises employing more than 50 workers per shift are nationalized, as are all former German businesses in Poland.

7   The Western powers recognize the Austrian Republic within its 1937 frontiers, though the country remains occupied jointly by Britain, France, the United States, and the USSR.

10 A truce is signed in the Chinese Civil War between nationalists and communists, which holds until April 14.

10 The first session of the United Nations (UN) General Assembly opens in London, England, with Belgium's foreign minister, Paul Spaak, as president.

11 Albania's constituent assembly proclaims the country a people's republic.

20 Charles de Gaulle resigns the presidency of the post-World War II French provisional government when he is frustrated by the parliamentary system in the implementation of his plans for postwar reconstruction.

31 A new constitution in Yugoslavia creates six constituent republics, all subordinate to the central authority: Serbia, Montenegro, Croatia, Slovenia, Bosnia-Herzegovina, and Macedonia.

FEBRUARY

- In an effort to curtail labor unrest in the United States, President Harry S. Truman announces a plan to raise wages by one-third in order to match the increased cost of living over the previous five years. In the same month, he restores the Office of Economic Stabilization to monitor inflation.
- The U.S. Congress publicly commits itself to full employment.

1   Hungary is proclaimed a republic, with Zoltán Tildy, leader of the Smallholders' Party, as president.

1   The Norwegian Labor politician Trygve Lie is elected the first secretary-general of the United Nations (UN), serving until 1952.

2   The U.S. military government in southern Korea establishes the Representative Democratic Council, chaired by Syngman Rhee, while Kim Il Sung becomes head of a Soviet-established government in the north of the country.

13 The 1927 Trades Disputes Act, outlawing general and sympathetic strikes, is repealed in Britain.

17 The Christian Socialists win the Belgian elections, but the position of the monarchy hampers the formation of a coalition.

24 The army officer Juan Perón is elected president of Argentina, with 69% of the popular vote.

25 Nationalists and communists in China agree to merge their armies following the mediation of the U.S. secretary of state, General George C. Marshall, but their failure to keep the agreement leads to renewed civil war.

MARCH

1   The British government nationalizes the Bank of England.

5   The former British prime minister Winston Churchill, in a speech in Fulton, Missouri, declares that "from Stettin in the Baltic to Trieste in the Adriatic an iron curtain has descended across the [European] Continent," marking the start of the Cold War.

15 The USSR adopts its fourth five-year plan. Its main aim is to restore industry in the area devastated during World War II.

19 The Council of Ministers, with Joseph Stalin as chair, replaces the Council of People's Commissars as the ruling executive in the USSR.

26 The Allied Control Council, the body officially charged with governing post-World War II Germany, limits the level of German production.

29 A new constitution in the Gold Coast (now Ghana) grants Africans a majority in the legislative council.

APRIL

5   The USSR agrees, under pressure from the Western Allies, to withdraw troops from Iran on the promise of reforms in the Iranian province of Azerbaijan.

10 Results in the Japanese election favor the moderate parties.

18 The League of Nations dissolves itself, its function having been taken over by the United Nations (UN).

19 The United States recognizes the communist republic of Yugoslavia under Marshal Josip Broz Tito.

22 Social Democrats merge with the communists in the Soviet zone of post-World War II Germany to form the Socialist Unity Party of Germany (SED).

27 The International Military Tribunal for the Far East opens its war crimes trial in Tokyo, Japan. It continues until November 12, 1948, indicting Hideki Tōjō, the former prime minister, and 27 associates.

29 The British–U.S. committee sent to report on the situation in Palestine advises against the partition of the British mandate into Jewish and Arab areas.

MAY

- The U.S. Congress extends the Selective Service Act in the face of Soviet muscle-flexing in Europe.

5   Civil war breaks out in Greece between the British-backed monarchists and the communists supported by Albania, Bulgaria, and Yugoslavia.

5   The draft of a new constitution in France, abolishing the upper chamber (the Senate), is rejected by a referendum.

9   King Victor Emmanuel III of Italy abdicates in favor of his son, Umberto II.

17 Ion Antonescu, Romania's fascist dictator in World War II, is sentenced to death by the Communist People's Court. He is executed on June 1.

20 The British House of Commons passes a bill to nationalize the coal mines.

25 Abdullah Ibn Hussein is crowned king of Transjordan.

26 The Communist Party wins a majority in the general election in Czechoslovakia.

30   The Catholic People's Party wins the general election in the Netherlands, with Joseph Beel forming a new coalition.

JUNE

1   The autonomous Republic of Cochin-China is set up under a French puppet government in an attempt to frustrate moves toward full independence.

2   A referendum in Italy produces a majority in favor of a republic.

2   Britain and the United States restore military bases in the Azores islands in the Atlantic to Portugal, having used them during World War II.

2   In the French constituent assembly election, the Popular Republican Movement (MRP) wins 160 seats, against the communists with 146 and socialists with 115.

3   The South African parliament passes the Asiatic Land Tenure and Indian Representation Bill, an important step in the creation of apartheid.

3   The U.S. Supreme Court rules that black segregation on interstate buses is unconstitutional.

6   The United States organizes state elections in its zone in post-World War II Germany and state governments are formed.

14   King Umberto II and his male heirs are permanently banished from Italy after the popular vote for a republican constitution.

19   Georges Bidault of the Popular Republican Movement (MRP) is elected president of the French post-World War II provisional government.

24   Fred Vinson is appointed chief justice of the U.S. Supreme Court.

27   Foreign ministers of the United States, Britain, France, and the USSR agree that the Dodecanese Islands, Italian since World War I, should pass from Italy to Greece.

28   Enrico de Nicola is elected president of Italy.

28   Widespread dismissals for incompetence are made among Soviet industrial staff.

30   A referendum in Poland favors a single-house assembly and wide nationalization.

JULY

•   The U.S. joins the United Nations Educational, Scientific, and Cultural Organization (UNESCO).

3   The communist leader Klement Gottwald becomes prime minister of Czechoslovakia.

4   The Republic of the Philippines is proclaimed, with Manuel Roxas as its first president.

7   At a conference on the future of Indochina hosted by the French at Fontainebleau, near Paris, Ho Chi Minh, the leader of the Vietminh (Vietnam Independence League), walks out.

7   The election of Miguel Alemán, a civilian, as president of Mexico leads to closer links with the United States.

15   A Canadian commission reports on Soviet espionage.

15   President Harry S. Truman of the United States signs a $3.75 billion bill of credit for Britain, to assist economic recovery after World War II.

29–October 15   A conference of the 21 nations that had opposed the Axis powers (Germany, Italy, and Japan) in World War II meets in Paris, France, to draft peace treaties.

AUGUST

13   The Indian Claims Commission is created in the United States to receive petitions for land claims from Native Americans.

20   The Allied Control Council, the body officially charged with governing post-World War II Germany, disbands the German army.

SEPTEMBER

1   A referendum in Greece restores the monarchy.

6   The U.S. secretary of state, James F. Byrnes, in a speech in Stuttgart, Germany, urges German cooperation with the United States in the post-World War II era.

8   A referendum in Bulgaria votes the monarchy out of existence, and the nine-year-old king, Simeon II, goes into exile with his mother, Queen Ioanna.

9–December 12   A conference on Palestine is held in London, England, but is boycotted by Zionists.

28   King George II returns to Greece from exile during the German occupation in World War II.

OCTOBER

•   The U.S. president Harry S. Truman announces an end to price controls on meat.

1   The International Military Tribunal at Nuremberg, Germany, announces its verdict on Nazi war criminals: Joachim von Ribbentrop, Hermann Goering, and ten other leading Nazis (including Martin Bormann, tried *in absentia*) are sentenced to death, and Rudolf Hess, Walter Funk, and Erich Raeder to life imprisonment. Four others receive long sentences, but Hjalmar Schacht, Franz von Papen, and Hans Fritzsche are acquitted.

5   Tage Erlander, a Social Democrat, becomes prime minister of Sweden on the death of Per Hansson.

10   The Representative Democratic Council in southern Korea is replaced by an interim legislative assembly.

10   The USSR organizes elections to state councils in its zone in post-World War II Germany.

13   Thailand accepts the verdict of the United Nations (UN) that territory must be returned to Indochina.

13   The French constituent assembly adopts a revised constitution, but many deputies abstain from voting.

15   The former leading Nazi and head of the Luftwaffe (German air force) Hermann Goering, awaiting execution for war crimes, commits suicide in Nuremberg Prison, Germany, by taking poison.

16   Ten of the defendants at the Nuremberg trial for Nazi war criminals in Germany are hanged in the prison gymnasium by the U.S. hangman John C. Woods.

23   The United Nations (UN) General Assembly meets for the first time in New York, New York; previous meetings had been in London, England.

27   Following a general election in Bulgaria, a Fatherland Front government is formed by the communist Georgi Dimitrov.

NOVEMBER

•   The U.S. congressional elections mark a decisive political shift, as the Republicans attain a 51–45 majority in the Senate and a 245–188 majority in the House of Representatives.

•   The U.S. president Harry S. Truman announces an end to wage and price controls, except in the cases of rent, sugar, and rice.

4   China and the United States sign a treaty of friendship and commerce.
10   Communists win 166 seats in the elections to the French National Assembly, against 158 for the Popular Republican Movement (MRP) and 90 for the Socialists, resulting in a political deadlock.
11   The United Nations Educational, Scientific, and Cultural Organization (UNESCO), with its headquarters in Paris, France, comes into operation.
19   Communists hold key positions in the left-wing government formed by Petru Groza after elections in Romania.
27   The Labor Party retains power in the New Zealand elections with a win of 42 seats, against 38 for the National Party.

DECEMBER
- John D. Rockefeller, Jr., son of the U.S. oil magnate and philanthropist, donates $8.5 million to the United Nations (UN) to enable the organization to erect permanent headquarters in New York, New York.
- The U.S. president Harry S. Truman lifts price controls, initiating spiraling inflation.
2   The U.S. secretary of state, James F. Byrnes, and the British foreign secretary, Ernest Bevin, agree to the economic union of the U.S. and British occupation zones in post-World War II Germany.
5   New York, New York, is chosen as the site for the permanent headquarters of the United Nations (UN).
11   The United Nations (UN) bars Spain from membership because of its right-wing Phalangist government's links with the prewar German and Italian regimes.
14   The United Nations (UN) rejects South Africa's proposal for the incorporation of South West Africa (now Namibia) into South Africa.
16   Léon Blum forms a Socialist "caretaker" government in France.
24   The Fourth Republic is declared in France when a new constitution is narrowly ratified by a referendum.
30   The United Nations (UN) Atomic Energy Commission approves the U.S. plan for the control of nuclear weapons.
31   The U.S. president Harry S. Truman proclaims an official end to hostilities, but maintains the state of emergency announced by his predecessor.

SCIENCE, TECHNOLOGY, AND MEDICINE

Agriculture

OCTOBER
- Land reform in Japan dispossesses absentee landlords, converting tenants into owners; within four years two-thirds of the land has changed ownership.

Ecology

- An unparalleled outbreak of red tide (excessive amounts of phytoplankton in the water) devastates fishing stocks in the Gulf of Mexico.
- The first cloud-seeding experiments are conducted in the United States in an attempt to produce rain.
- The Williamson diamond mine in Tanganyika (now Tanzania) is found to have the largest diamond reserves in the world.

APRIL
1   An earthquake in the Aleutian Trench creates a tsunami 13.7 m/45 ft high; 5 hours later it kills 173 people in Hawaii. The U.S. Coast Guard and Geodetic Survey establish an underwater earthquake warning system following the tsunami.

AUGUST
1   The U.S. Atomic Energy Commission is established; its goal is to control nuclear weapon development and to direct research and development into peaceful uses of nuclear energy.

DECEMBER
7   In the worst hotel fire in U.S. history, 127 die in a blaze at Winecoff Hotel in Atlanta, Georgia.

Exploration

December 1946–47   U.S. naval officer Richard Byrd mounts an expedition to the South Pole.
December 1946–48   British soldier and explorer Wilfred Thesiger completes a double crossing of the Arabian desert's "Empty Quarter."

Health and Medicine

- Carbon-13, an isotope of carbon, is discovered; it is used to cure metabolic diseases.
- Penicillin is synthesized by U.S. chemist Vincent du Vigneaud.
- The anti-inflammatory drug cortisone is synthesized.
- U.S. biologists Max Delbrück and Alfred D. Hershey discover recombinant DNA (deoxyribonucleic acid) when they observe that genetic material from different viruses can combine to create new viruses.

Science

- Cygnus A, the first radio galaxy, and the most powerful cosmic source of radio waves, is discovered.
- English physicists Edward Appleton and Donald Hay discover that sunspots emit radio waves.
- Russian physicist Igor Kurchatov creates the first Soviet atomic chain reaction.
- The Japanese Union of Scientists and Engineers (JUSE) is established; its aim is to revive Japanese industry by improving the quality of products.
- The magnetic north pole is discovered to be 400 km/250 mi north of the charted position.
- UK physicist Edward Appleton discovers the "Appleton" layer in the ionosphere, which reflects radio waves; it makes long-range radio communication possible and also aids the development of radar.

- U.S. anthropologist Ruth Benedict publishes *The Chrysanthemum and the Sword*, a study of Japanese culture that influences U.S.–Japanese relations.
- U.S. biochemist Hermann Muller receives the Nobel Prize for Physiology or Medicine for his work on X-ray-induced mutations.
- U.S. chemists John Northrop, Wendell Stanley, and James Sumner share the Nobel Prize for Chemistry for their work on enzymes.
- U.S. geneticists Joshua Lederberg and Edward Lawrie Tatum pioneer the field of bacterial genetics with their discovery that sexual reproduction occurs in the bacterium *Escherichia coli*.
- U.S. physicist Percy Bridgman receives the Nobel Prize for Physics for his work on high pressure physics.
- U.S. physicists Edward Mills Purcell and Felix Bloch independently discover nuclear magnetic resonance, which is used to study the structure of pure metals and composites.

Technology

- A liquid polysulfide polymer is found in the United States to be the ideal rocket propellant as it bonds to the walls of the rocket as well as acting as a fuel.
- British scientist Maurice Wilkes writes the first assembly language—a mnemonic code using alphabetic symbols which translates instructions into computer machine language.
- ENIAC (acronym for "Electronic Numerical Integrator, Analyzer, and Calculator"), the first general purpose, fully electronic digital computer, is completed at the University of Pennsylvania for use in military research. It uses 18,000 vacuum tubes instead of mechanical relays, and can make 4,500 calculations a second. It is 24 m/80 ft long and is built by electrical engineers John Presper Eckert and John Mauchly, with input from John Atanasoff.
- Kuwait becomes the largest oil-producing country in the Middle East.
- Microwave relay stations are introduced in the United States for long-distance telephone communication; the first is set up between Boston, Massachusetts, and New York, New York. Eliminating the need for long-distance trunk lines, they form the basis of cellular telephones.
- Mobile telephones are introduced.
- The British Fairey Aviation Company constructs a pilotless radio-controlled rocket missile.
- The Decca Navigator is developed; a radio navigational aid with a range of between 160–480 km/100–300 mi, it permits a ship to locate its position with great accuracy.
- The first zoom lens is introduced.
- The U.S. corporation Westinghouse introduces the front-loading washing machine.
- The U.S. Fender Guitar Company manufactures the first electric guitar.
- The USSR's first nuclear reactor begins operation.
- U.S. camera manufacturer Eastman Kodak introduces "Ektachrome," the first color film that can be developed by the photographer.
- U.S. researchers Ross Gunn and Philip Abelson, at the U.S. Naval Research Laboratory in Washington, D.C., begin research into the feasibility of nuclear reactors as a source of energy for submarines.

December 1946–48 Swiss physicist Auguste Piccard constructs the bathyscaph *FNRS 2*, a navigable diving vessel designed for deep descent into the ocean.

JULY
- The U.S. carries out atomic bomb tests at Bikini Atoll in the Marshall Islands in the Pacific Ocean.

Transportation

- Cars are permitted to operate on the island of Bermuda for the first time.
- U.S. corporation Douglas Aircraft introduces the DC-6; it can fly at up to 483 kph/300 mph and carry 70 passengers.
- Vespa scooters are brought onto the Italian market by Enrico Piaggio as a cheap form of transportation. Vespa means "wasp" in Italian and refers to the noisiness of the engines.

MAY
- A railroad strike in the United States prompts President Harry S. Truman to seize control of the railroads. His action precipitates a settlement.

ARTS AND IDEAS

Architecture

- The ranch house, a one-story design, becomes the most popular style in the United States's growing suburbs.

Arts

- A conference on "Industrial Design as a New Profession" is held at the Museum of Modern Art (MOMA) in New York, New York.
- The English artist Barbara Hepworth sculpts *Pelagos*.
- The English artist Graham Sutherland paints *Crucifixion*.
- The English artist Stanley Spencer paints *Shipbuilding on the Clyde: Furnaces*.
- The French artist Germaine Richter sculpts *The Bat-Man*.
- The German artist Wols paints *Composition V*.
- The Spanish artist Pablo Picasso founds a pottery at Vallauris, in the south of France.
- The U.S. artist Barnett Newman paints *Pagan Void*.
- The U.S. artist Clyfford Still paints *Painting 1946 – H (Indian Red and Black)*.
- The U.S. artist Isamu Goguchi sculpts *Humpty Dumpty*.
- The U.S. artist Mark Rothko paints *Sacrifice*.
- U.S. art historian John Rewald publishes *The History of Impressionism*.

Film

- After an abortive start in 1939, the Cannes Film Festival in France is fully inaugurated.

- In France, the Centre National du Cinéma Français is established.
- The 1945 Academy Awards take place. Best Actor: Ray Milland, for *The Lost Weekend*; Best Supporting Actor: James Dunn, for *A Tree Grows in Brooklyn*; Best Actress: Joan Crawford, for *Mildred Pierce*; Best Supporting Actress: Anne Revere, for *National Velvet*; Best Picture: *The Lost Weekend*, directed by Billy Wilder; Best Director: Billy Wilder, for *The Lost Weekend*.
- The espionage thriller *Notorious* is released in the United States. It is directed by Alfred Hitchcock, scripted by Ben Hecht, and stars Cary Grant, Ingrid Bergman, and Claude Rains.
- The movie *A Matter of Life and Death* (titled *Stairway to Heaven* in the United States) is released in the UK. It is written, produced, and directed by Michael Powell and Emeric Pressburger, and stars David Niven, Kim Hunter, and Roger Livesey.
- The movie *Gilda*, directed by Charles Vidor, is released in the United States, starring Rita Hayworth in a role which proves her to be Hollywood's leading sex symbol.
- The movie *Great Expectations*, directed by David Lean, is released in the UK. Based on the novel by Charles Dickens, it stars John Mills, Bernard Miles, Finlay Currie, Martita Hunt, Valerie Hobson, and Jean Simmons.
- The movie *It's a Wonderful Life*, directed by Frank Capra, is released in the United States, starring James Stewart, Henry Travers, Donna Reed, and Lionel Barrymore.
- The movie *La Belle et la Bête/Beauty and the Beast* is released in France. It is directed by Jean Cocteau and stars Jean Marais and Josette Day.
- The movie *La Symphonie pastorale/Pastoral Symphony*, directed by Jean Delannoy, is released in France. Based on the novel by André Gide, it stars Pierre Blanchar and Michèle Morgan.
- The movie *Les Portes de la Nuit/Gates of the Night* is released in France, directed by Marcel Carné, and starring Pierre Brasseur, Yves Montand, and Nathalie Nattier.
- The movie *My Darling Clementine*, directed by John Ford, is released in the United States. Heralding the golden period of the Western, it stars Henry Fonda, Victor Mature, Walter Brennan, and Linda Darnell.
- The movie *Paisà*, directed by Roberto Rossellini, is released in Italy, starring William Tubbs, Gar Moor, and Maria Michi.
- The movie *Sciuscia/Shoeshine*, directed by Vittorio De Sica, is released in Italy, starring Franco Interlenghi and Rinaldo Smordoni.
- The movie *The Best Years of Our Lives*, directed by William Wyler, is released in the United States. Focusing on the difficulties of reintegration for returning soldiers, it stars Fredric March, Myrna Loy, Teresa Wright, and Dana Andrews.
- The movie *The Big Sleep*, directed by Howard Hawks, is released in the United States. Based on the novel by Raymond Chandler and adapted for the screen by William Faulkner, Jules Furthman, and Leigh Brackett, it stars Humphrey Bogart, as Philip Marlowe, and Lauren Bacall.
- The movie *The Killers*, directed by Robert Siodmak, is released in the United States, starring Burt Lancaster, Edmond O'Brien, and Ava Gardner.
- The movie *The Postman Always Rings Twice*, directed by Tay Garnett, is released in the United States. Based on the novel by James M. Cain, it stars Lana Turner, John Garfield, and Cecil Kelloway.
- The movie *The Razor's Edge*, directed by Edmund Goulding, is released in the United States. Based on the novel by W. Somerset Maugham, it stars Tyrone Power, Gene Tierney, and Clifton Webb.
- The movie *The Yearling*, directed by Clarence Brown, is released in the United States. Based on the novel by Marjorie Kinnan Rawlings, it stars Gregory Peck and Claude Jarman, Jr.
- The melodramatic Western *Duel in the Sun* is released in the United States. It is produced by David O. Selznick, directed by King Vidor, and stars Jennifer Jones, Gregory Peck, and Joseph Cotten.

Literature and Language

- The English novelist Daphne du Maurier's *The King's General* is the best-selling novel in the United States.
- The English scholar E. V. Rieu publishes his translation of Homer's *Odyssey*.
- The English writer L. P. Hartley publishes his novel *The Sixth Heaven*, the second part of his *Eustace and Hilda* trilogy, published in 1947.
- The English writer Mervyn Peake publishes his fantasy novel *Titus Groan*.
- The English writer Philip Larkin publishes his novel *Jill*.
- The French poet Jacques Prévert publishes his poetry collection *Paroles/Words*.
- The French writer André Gide publishes his *Journal, 1939–42*.
- The French writer Jean Genet publishes his novel *Miracle de la Rose/Miracle of the Rose*.
- The Greek writer Nikos Kazantzakis publishes his novel *Víos kai politía tou Aléxi Zormá/Zorba the Greek*.
- The Guatemalan writer Miguel Angel Asturias publishes his novel *El señor Presidente/The President*.
- The Indian mystic Paramahamsa Yogananda publishes *Autobiography of a Yogi*.
- The Nobel Prize for Literature is awarded to the German novelist Herman Hesse.
- The Pulitzer Prize for Biography is awarded to Linnie Marsh Wolfe for *Son of the Wilderness: The Life of John Muir*. The Prizes for Fiction and Poetry are not awarded this year.
- The U.S. author Kathleen Winsor's novel *Forever Amber* is cleared of charges of violating Massachusetts obscenity laws.
- The U.S. novelist and academic Robert Penn Warren's novel *All the King's Men*, based on the career of Louisiana governor Huey Long, is published.
- The U.S. writer Carson McCullers publishes her novel *The Member of the Wedding*.
- The U.S. writer Eudora Welty publishes her novel *Delta Wedding*.
- The U.S. writer Gore Vidal publishes his first novel, *Williwaw*.

- The U.S. writer Robert Lowell publishes his poetry collection *Lord Weary's Castle*, which wins a Pulitzer prize in 1947.
- The Welsh writer Dylan Thomas publishes his poetry collection *Deaths and Entrances*.
- U.S. critic and writer Edmund Wilson publishes a collection of short stories, *Memoirs of Hecate County*, provoking outrage among sexual conservatives.

OCTOBER

24 In Britain, King George VI opens the New Bodleian Library in Oxford, England.

Music

- The Austrian composer Arnold Schoenberg completes his String Trio, Opus 45.
- The English composer Lennox Berkeley completes his *Five de la Mare Songs*.
- The English composer Benjamin Britten completes his *Young Person's Guide to the Orchestra (Variations and Fugue on a Theme of Purcell)*.
- The French singer Edith Piaf records "La Vie en rose."
- The opera *The Telephone*, by the Italian-born U.S. composer Gian Carlo Menotti, is first performed, in New York, New York.
- The Russian composer Dmitry Shostakovich completes his String Quartet No. 3.
- The Swiss composer Arthur Honegger completes his Symphony No. 4 *Deliciae basiliensis*.
- The U.S. composer Aaron Copland completes his Symphony No. 3.
- The U.S. composer Elliot Carter completes his *Elegy* for string orchestra.

Theater and Dance

- The ballet *Cave of the Heart* by the U.S. dancer and choreographer Martha Graham, music by U.S. composer Samuel Barber, is first performed, at Columbia University, New York, New York. It is later known as *Medea*.
- The French writer Jean Cocteau writes the story for the ballet *Le Jeune Homme et la mort/The Young Man and Death*.
- The musical *Annie Get Your Gun*, with words and music by Irving Berlin, is first performed in New York, New York. One of its best-known songs is "There's No Business Like Show Business."
- The musical *Street Scene*, by the German composer Kurt Weill, is first performed, in Philadelphia, Pennsylvania. It opens in New York, New York, in 1947.
- The play *An Inspector Calls*, by the English writer J. B. Priestley, is first performed, in London, England.
- The play *The Iceman Cometh*, by the U.S. writer Eugene O'Neill, is first performed, at the Martin Beck Theater in New York, New York.
- The play *The Winslow Boy*, by the English writer Terence Rattigan, is first performed, at the Lyric Theatre in London, England.
- The Pulitzer Prize for Drama is awarded to Russel Crouse and Howard Lindsay for *State of the Union*.
- Two plays by the French writer and philosopher Jean-Paul Sartre are first performed, in Paris, France: *Morts sans sépulture/Men Without Shadows*; and *Laputain respectueuse/The Respectable Prostitute*.

Thought and Scholarship

- English art historian John Summerson publishes *Georgian London*.
- English philosopher R. G. Collingwood publishes *The Idea of History*.
- French writer and philosopher Jean-Paul Sartre publishes *L'Existentialisme est un humanisme/Existentialism and Humanism*.
- German historian Frederick Meinecke publishes *Die deutsche Katastrophe/The German Catastrophe*, a reflection on the rise of National Socialism and Germany's responsibility for the war.
- German philosopher Ernst Cassirer publishes *The Myth of the State*.
- Hungarian-born English scientist and social philosopher Michael Polanyi publishes *Science, Faith, and Society*.
- The British scholar George F. Black publishes *The Surnames of Scotland: Their Origin, Meaning and History*.
- The Pulitzer Prize for History is awarded to Arthur M. Schlesinger, Jr., for *The Age of Jackson*.
- U.S. historian Charles A. Beard publishes *American Foreign Policy in the Making, 1932–40*.
- U.S. writer John Hersey publishes *Hiroshima*, a classic account of the atomic bomb explosion over the city, filling an entire issue of *New Yorker* magazine.

SOCIETY

Education

- Claremont–McKenna College opens in Claremont, California.
- Official support is given to child-centered teaching methods in experimental *classes nouvelles* ("new classes") in France.
- The Australian federal government's Commonwealth Office of Education is established to manage the education systems of the six Australian states.
- The Fulbright scholarships are instituted in the United States to enable U.S. citizens to study abroad and people from abroad to study in the United States.

Everyday Life

- Achille Gaggia invents the espresso coffee machine in Italy.
- Following his wartime research into timing mechanisms for bombs, Joakim Lehmkuhl of Waterbury Watch Co. introduces the Timex watch in the United States.
- Housing shortages and consumer frustration lead to high inflation and wage demands in the United States.
- K. Hattori & Co. launches Seiko watches, in Japan.
- Selected population figures (in millions): China 455; India 311; USSR 194; United States 140; Japan 73; West

Germany 48; Italy 47; Britain 46; Brazil 45; France 40; Spain 27; Poland 24; Korea 24; Mexico 22; East Germany 18; Egypt 17.

- The city of Las Vegas, Nevada, begins its ascent toward notoriety when Benjamin "Bugsy" Siegel erects the Flamingo Hotel.
- The Estée Lauder beauty products empire is launched with Estée Lauder's first sales to Saks, New York, New York.
- The postwar baby boom begins in the United States. Some 3,411,000 babies are born this year, up from 2,858,000 the previous year. High birth rates continue into the 1960s.
- The report produced by the Reith Committee in the UK leads to the founding of New Towns as growth points in Britain, with Stevenage the first New Town to be built.
- U.S. pediatrician Benjamin Spock publishes *The Common Sense Book of Baby and Child Care*. The book becomes an unexpected best seller and a generation of children is raised according to its permissive guidelines of parental understanding and flexibility.

JANUARY

9–20 Over a period of two weeks, telephone mechanics, electrical and machine workers, meat industry workers, and steelworkers go on strike for higher wages in the United States. They want a larger share of war-induced prosperity. 116 million working days are lost.

MAY

- Soldiers occupy U.S. soft coal mines to end a mining strike.

JULY

5 French designer Louis Réard launches the bikini, naming it after the nuclear-test site Bikini Atoll.

NOVEMBER

- The U.S. social reformer Emily Greene Balch and the U.S. religious leader and social worker John Raleigh Mott share the Nobel Peace Prize.

November–December Members of the United Mine Workers union in the United States, under John L. Lewis, flout a federal court injunction and strike against soft coal operators. After being fined $3.5 million, the strikers return to work in early December.

DECEMBER

- Nylon stockings, the first commercial nylon goods to be manufactured in Britain, go on sale in London, England.

Media and Communication

- The Asociación Interamericana de Radiodifusión (AIR) is founded.
- The first broadcast by the British Broadcasting Corporation (BBC) of Alistair Cooke's *Letter from America* takes place in the UK.
- The press agency Allgemeiner Deutscher Nachrichtendienst is founded in the Soviet zone of Germany.

JUNE

1 Television licenses are introduced in the UK: around 7,500 are sold, at a cost of £2 each.

JULY

12 Pius XII becomes the first pope to appear on television when the Radio Corporation of America (RCA) broadcasts a papal address from the Vatican.

SEPTEMBER

- After starting out as a free periodical, *Family Circle* is sold as a monthly magazine in the United States at a price of 5 cents.

Religion

- In England, the International Christian Conference, held in Cambridge, aims at closer relations between Protestant and Orthodox Churches.

JANUARY

- In Japan, Emperor Hirohito repudiates the doctrine of the emperor's divinity.

JULY

- The Italian-born Roman Catholic nun Mother Frances Xavier Cabrini (1850–1917), founder of the Missionary Sisters of the Sacred Heart of Jesus, is the first U.S. citizen to be canonized.

NOVEMBER

- The Evangelical Church and the Church of the United Brethren of Christ unite in the United States to form the Evangelical United Brethren Church.

Sports

- At St. Andrews, Scotland, U.S. golfer Sam Snead wins the first British Open to be held since 1939. He is the first U.S. golfer to win the British Open since 1933.
- Sportswriters vote Notre Dame college football's national champion in the United States.
- The National Football League (NFL) champions, the Rams, are given permission to move to Los Angeles, California, from Cleveland, Ohio.

JANUARY

1 In American football, quarterback Bobby Layne leads the University of Texas to a 40–27 victory over Missouri in the Cotton Bowl, playing a role in every point that his team scores.

4 The All-America Football Conference is established to challenge the National Football League; rivalry persists until the Conference folds in 1949.

MARCH

2–3 U.S. national figure skating champions are: Gretchen Merrill; Dick Button; Donna Pospisil and Jean Pierre Brunet, pairs; Anne Davies and Carelton Hoffner, dance.

30–April 9 The Montreal Canadiens defeat the Boston Bruins to win the National Hockey League (NHL) Stanley Cup.

APRIL

20 Stylianos Kyriakides of Greece wins the 50th annual Boston Marathon in a time of 2 hr 29 min 27 sec.

23 Eleven new members are elected to baseball's Hall of Fame, including the members of the Chicago Cubs' famous double-play combination, Joseph Tinker, John Evers, and Frank Chance.

MAY

30 Racing driver George Robson of Los Angeles, California, wins the Indianapolis 500.

JUNE

14–15 The U.S. women's tennis team beats Britain 7–0 in the Wightman Cup, without losing a set.

16 U.S. golfer Lloyd Mangrum wins the U.S. Open golf championship.

JULY

6 U.S. tennis player Pauline Betz wins the women's singles title at the Wimbledon tennis championships in England.

AUGUST

29–September 1 The inaugural U.S. Women's Open Golf Championship at Spokane, Washington is won by Patty Berg of the United States.

SEPTEMBER

8 U.S. tennis players Pauline Betz and Jack Kramer win titles at the U.S. Lawn Tennis Association championships.

OCTOBER

3–15 In baseball, the St. Louis Cardinals defeat the Brooklyn Dodgers in the first regular season pennant play-off in major league history, after both sides finish with identical 96-58 records in the National League. The Cardinals then defeat the Boston Red Sox four games to three in the World Series.

BIRTHS & DEATHS

JANUARY

19 Dolly Parton, U.S. country music singer and actress, born in Sevierville, Tennessee.

29 Harry Hopkins, U.S. administrator and Franklin D. Roosevelt's personal advisor during World War II, dies in New York, New York (55).

MARCH

8 Frederick William Lanchester, English automobile manufacturer who built the first British automobile powered by an internal combustion engine, dies in Birmingham, Warwickshire (77).

12 Roger Schank, U.S. computer scientist, born in New York, New York.

APRIL

1 Ronnie Lene, English pop singer, songwriter, and founder of the Small Faces, born in Plaistow, London, England (–1997).

17 Georges Jean Franz Köhler, German immunologist who helped revolutionize medical research through the development of monoclonal antibodies, born in Munich, Germany (–1995).

21 John Maynard Keynes, English economist concerned with the causes and solutions of long-term unemployment, dies in Firle, Scotland (60).

MAY

11 Robert Jarvik, U.S. physician and medical researcher who invented an artificial heart, born in Midland, Michigan.

31 Rainer Werner Fassbinder, German film and theater director, writer, and actor, born in Bad Wörishofen, Germany (–1982).

JUNE

3 Mikhail Ivanovich Kalinin, head of state of the Soviet Union 1919–46, dies in Moscow, USSR (70).

8 Gerhart Hauptmann, German poet, playwright, and novelist, dies in Agnetendorf, Germany (83).

10 Jack Johnson, U.S. boxer and the first black person to win the world heavyweight boxing championship (1908–15), dies in Raleigh, North Carolina (68).

14 John Logie Baird, Scottish engineer who was the first to televise moving pictures, dies in Bexhill-on-Sea, Sussex, England (57).

23 William S. Hart, U.S. silent film actor known for his Westerns, dies in Newhall, California (75).

JULY

13 Alfred Stieglitz, U.S. photographer who advocated photography as an art form, dies in New York, New York (82).

29 Gertrude Stein, U.S. avant-garde writer and eccentric, dies in Paris, France (72).

AUGUST

13 H(erbert) G(eorge) Wells, English novelist, sociologist, and historian, who wrote *The Time Machine*, *The War of the Worlds*, and *The Invisible Man*, dies in London, England (70).

19 William Clinton, U.S. Democratic politician, 42nd president of the United States from 1993, born in Hope, Arkansas.

SEPTEMBER

5 Freddie Mercury, lead singer and songwriter of the British rock group Queen, born in Zanzibar (–1991).

OCTOBER

4 Barney Oldfield, U.S. automobile racing driver who set several world speed records in the early 1900s, dies in Beverly Hills, California (68).

16 Alfred Jodl, German general who was head of Germany's armed forces operations staff and helped plan most of the country's military operations in World War II, is executed for war crimes in Nuremberg, Germany (56).

16 Ernst Kaltenbrunner, Austrian Nazi, head of the Austrian SS, is hanged in Nuremberg, Germany, for war crimes (43).

16 Joachim von Ribbentop, German Nazi foreign minister who negotiated Germany's treaties prior to World War II, is executed for war crimes in Nuremberg, Germany (53).

16 Wilhelm Keitel, German field marshal who was head of the German armed forces high command during World War II, is hanged in Nuremberg, Germany, for war crimes (64).

NOVEMBER

23 Arthur Dove, U.S. painter, an early exponent of abstract expressionism, dies in Huntington, New York (66).

25 Henry Morgenthau, U.S. banker and diplomat, dies in New York, New York (90).

DECEMBER

10 Damon Runyon, U.S. short story writer and journalist, dies in New York, New York (62).

25 W. C. Fields (adopted name of William Claude Dukenfield), U.S. comic actor and screenwriter, dies in Pasadena, California (66).

DECEMBER

15   The Chicago Bears defeat the New York Giants 24–14 in the National Football League (NFL) championship game in New York, New York.

20   U.S. boxer Sugar Ray Robinson outpoints Tommy Bell (also of the United States) to win the world welterweight title at Madison Square Gardens, New York, New York.

26   In tennis, the United States defeats Australia five to zero to regain the Davis Cup, which Australia has held since 1939.

1947

POLITICS, GOVERNMENT, AND ECONOMICS

Business and Economics

- Ingvar Kamprad founds the Swedish furniture company IKEA.
- Masaru Ibuka and Akio Morita start the Sony Corporation, in Japan.

FEBRUARY

17   A fuel crisis strikes Britain forcing a reduction in the size of newspapers and curtailment of magazine publication (with further reductions on July 21).

JUNE

June–July   The federal government releases control of U.S. coal mines seized in 1946 to forestall strikes. A wage increase granted on July 7 prevents another work stoppage.

DECEMBER

16   The USSR devalues its currency in response to inflation caused by an increase of money in circulation during World War II.

Colonization

JANUARY

1   Britain grants Nigeria a modified form of self-government.

21   Jan Smuts, Prime Minister of South Africa, refuses to place South West Africa (now Namibia) under United Nations (UN) trusteeship.

FEBRUARY

7   The British proposal for dividing Palestine into Arab and Jewish zones administered as a trusteeship is rejected by the Arabs and Jews.

20   The British government announces its intention to transfer power in India to the Indians no later than June 1948.

MARCH

23   Lord Wavell resigns as British viceroy of India. He is succeeded by Lord Mountbatten, who consults local leaders and announces that Muslim-dominated areas must become a separate independent state.

29–July 7   Nationalists in Madagascar revolt against French rule.

JUNE

17   The constituent assembly in Burma (now Myanmar) resolves for independence from Britain.

JULY

20   Dutch troops launch a "police action" against the independence movement in the Netherlands East Indies and succeed in establishing control over Dutch estates in the interior of the main islands.

DECEMBER

30   Conflict in the state of Kashmir between Indian government troops and Muslim Pathan tribesmen is referred to the United Nations (UN).

Human Rights

- The Commission on Civil Rights is appointed in the United States.

MAY

5   The Japanese parliament adopts an equal-rights amendment that bans discrimination by sex and gives women the power to bring lawsuits charging bias.

SEPTEMBER

9   Women in Argentina gain the right to vote thanks to the efforts of First Lady Eva Perón.

Politics and Government

- Australia, New Zealand, the United States, Britain, and France found the South Pacific Commission to coordinate social and economic development in the South Pacific.
- India is partitioned by the British authorities into the separate, independent states of India (predominantly Hindu in religion) and Pakistan (predominantly

Muslim). The partition leads to massacres and widespread disorder, especially in the divided provinces of Bengal and Punjab.

- The 1944 Servicemen's Readjustment Act (or GI Bill of Rights) spurs more than 1 million veterans to enrol in U.S. colleges.
- The General Agreement on Tariffs and Trade (GATT) is founded in Geneva, Switzerland, to promote trade between nations, especially by negotiating lower tariffs.
- The Presidential Succession Act establishes the order of succession to the U.S. presidency between elections, with the vice president first, then the speaker of the House of Representatives.
- The U.S. Supreme Court, in the case *Friedman v. Schwellenback*, declines to review a case involving the firing of a civil servant for disloyalty.
- Yugoslavia launches a five-year plan to collectivize half the country's agricultural land and develop industry.

JANUARY

7 General George C. Marshall succeeds James F. Byrnes as U.S. secretary of state.

16 Vincent Auriol is elected president of France.

22 The Socialist Paul Ramadier forms a coalition government in France on Léon Blum's resignation.

26 Egypt breaks off diplomatic relations with Britain when the British government revises the 1936 Anglo-Egyptian treaty and states that it will prepare the Sudan for self-government.

29 The United States abandons efforts at mediation in the civil war between Chinese nationalists and communists.

FEBRUARY

1 Alcide de Gasperi forms a new government in Italy, consisting of Christian Democrats, communists, and Left Socialists.

10 By a treaty signed in Paris, France, Italy loses the Dodecanese Islands to Greece and border territories to France and Yugoslavia; Romania loses Bessarabia and North Bukovina to the USSR but regains Transylvania; Bulgaria retains South Dobrudja; Hungary regains its 1938 frontiers; and Finland cedes Petsamo (now Pechenga) to the USSR.

21 The British government informs the United States that it cannot afford to keep troops in Greece to prevent a communist takeover, and will withdraw them by the end of March.

MARCH

- The U.S. Congress sends the Twenty-second Amendment, limiting the president to two terms in office, to the states.

1 The Allied Control Council, the body officially charged with governing post-World War II Germany, formally abolishes the state of Prussia, as a "promoter of militarism and reaction in Germany."

3 Nikolai Bulganin replaces Joseph Stalin as Soviet defense minister, with the rank of marshal of the Soviet Union.

3 The U.S. government introduces security and loyalty checks on its employees, following several leaks of government papers.

4 Britain and France sign a treaty of alliance.

10–April 24 A conference of foreign ministers in Moscow, USSR, fails through disagreement between the West and the USSR over the future of post-World War II Germany, currently jointly occupied by Britain, France, the United States, and the USSR.

12 The U.S. president Harry S. Truman announces a plan (the Truman Doctrine) to give aid to Greece, which is threatened by communist insurrection, and to Turkey, which is under pressure from Soviet expansion.

19 Chinese Nationalist forces capture the communist capital of Yan'an.

19 Paul Spaak forms a coalition government of Catholics and Socialists in Belgium.

APRIL

2 Britain refers the question of partitioning Palestine into Jewish and Arab zones to the United Nations (UN).

2 The United Nations (UN) Security Council appoints the United States as trustee for the Pacific islands formerly under Japanese mandate.

4 Britain organizes elections in its occupation zone in post-World War II Germany, and state governments are formed.

14 Charles de Gaulle in France organizes the Rassemblement du Peuple Français (RPF, or Gaullists) to rally the noncommunists to unity and reform.

18 Jozef Tiso, the former president of Slovakia under German domination in World War II, is executed for treason and crimes against humanity.

MAY

3 Japan introduces a new constitution, with the approval of the diet (legislative assembly), the emperor, and the people by means of a referendum, in which women vote for the first time.

5 France organizes elections in its occupation zone in post-World War II Germany, and state governments are formed.

5 Serious strikes break out in France following the dismissal of communist ministers from the coalition government of Paul Ramadier.

29 Ferenc Nagy, Prime Minister of Hungary, resigns following his indictment for crimes against the state. He is succeeded by Lajos Dinnyés, also of the Smallholders' Party.

31 Alcide de Gasperi forms a government of Christian Socialists and Independents in Italy.

JUNE

5 The U.S. secretary of state, General George C. Marshall, calls for a European Recovery Program (the Marshall Plan) funded by the United States, to forestall the emergence of communist governments throughout the continent.

11 Sugar rationing comes to an end in the United States.

23 The U.S. Congress passes the Taft–Hartley Act over President Harry S. Truman's veto. It prohibits the use of union funds for political purposes, outlaws the closed shop (where all employees at a place of work or within a section belong to a single labor union), and strengthens the government's hand in strikes and lockouts.

JULY

- The U.S. president Harry S. Truman signs the Presidential Succession Act. The act stipulates that, in the event of the death or incapacitation of both the president and vice president, the Speaker of the House and then the president of the Senate should be next in line for the post.

6   Spain passes a bill of succession to restore the monarchy on the death or resignation of the Spanish dictator, General Francisco Franco.

12–15   Sixteen West European nations meet in Paris, France, to discuss the U.S. Marshall Plan for European economic recovery.

26   The National Security Act in the United States establishes the National Security Council (NSC) to advise the president on domestic, foreign, and military policies related to national security. The act makes the U.S. Air Force an independent branch of the U.S. military, combines all branches of the military under one secretary of defense, and creates the Central Intelligence Agency (CIA).

28   The National Peasant Party is dissolved in Romania by the communist government.

AUGUST

1   The United Nations (UN) Security Council calls for a cease-fire in the Netherlands East Indies, where there is fighting between members of the independence movement and the Dutch colonialists.

8   Hungary launches a three-year plan to nationalize banking, industry, mining, and most trades.

15   British rule in India ends after 163 years and the two new independent countries of India and Pakistan are established. Jawaharlal Nehru becomes prime minister of India, and Mohammed Ali Jinnah governor-general of Pakistan, with Liaquat Ali Khan as prime minister.

31   The Communist Party makes substantial gains in a general election in Hungary.

SEPTEMBER

2   The South American republics sign a treaty of mutual assistance in Rio de Janeiro, Brazil.

14   Poland denounces its 1925 concordat with the Roman Catholic Church, following communist victories in the January elections.

26   D. S. Senanayake becomes the first prime minister of Ceylon.

30   Pakistan and the Yemen are admitted to the United Nations (UN).

OCTOBER

5   The Cominform (Communist Information Bureau) is founded in Poland to coordinate the activities of the European communist parties.

10   Muslim Pathan tribesmen invade the Indian state of Kashmir in response to the decision of the state's Hindu raja (princely ruler) to accede to India. Indian troops intervene to assist the raja.

19–26   Charles de Gaulle's RPF party (Rassemblement du Peuple Français) becomes the strongest group in the French municipal elections, winning 38.7% of the vote.

21   The United Nations (UN) General Assembly calls on Greece and the Balkan powers to settle their regional disputes by peaceful means.

29   Belgium, the Netherlands, and Luxembourg ratify a customs union (Benelux), effective from November 1.

NOVEMBER

• Ten Hollywood artists (the "Hollywood Ten") are blacklisted by U.S. industry executives and held in contempt of Congress for not cooperating with the House Un-American Activities Committee in its investigation of communist infiltration.

13   The Social Democrats under Hans Hedtoft form a minority cabinet in Denmark.

14   The United Nations (UN) General Assembly adopts a resolution requiring elections to be held throughout Korea under a UN temporary commission on Korea.

19   Paul Ramadier resigns as prime minister of France following widespread opposition and strikes in protest at his harsh deflationary policy.

20   The wedding of Princess Elizabeth and Philip Mountbatten takes place in Westminster Abbey, London, England.

23   Robert Schuman of the Popular Republican Movement (MRP) in France forms a government supported by Socialists.

25–December 16   A meeting in London, England, of the "Big Four" powers (Britain, the United States, France, and the USSR) to discuss the future of post-World War II Germany fails through the USSR's demands for reparations.

27   Banks are nationalized in Australia.

29   The United Nations (UN) adopts a plan for the partition of Palestine into Jewish and Arab zones, with Jerusalem under UN trusteeship, sparking fights between Jews and Arabs in Palestine.

DECEMBER

• The U.S. Congress, at the request of President Harry S. Truman, allocates $540 million to aid France, Italy, and Austria to assist in reconstruction in the aftermath of World War II.

14   The Democratic Action candidate, Rómulo Gallegos, is elected president of Venezuela.

19   Romania and Yugoslavia sign a treaty of friendship.

22   A new constitution in Italy centralizes the government and provides for a popularly elected senate.

27   The Greek government outlaws the Communist Party and the communist-controlled National Liberation Front (EAM) in response to their attempts to seize power.

30   King Michael of Romania abdicates under pressure from the pro-Soviet government.

SCIENCE, TECHNOLOGY, AND MEDICINE

Ecology

• Everglades National Park is established in Florida.

• Millions of fish and shellfish are killed on Florida's west coast by the worst red tide (excessive amounts of phytoplankton in the water) in U.S. history.

• The U.S. Congress incorporates 566,580 ha/1.4 million acres of Florida wetlands into the Everglades National Park.

• U.S. meteorologist Irving Langmuir carries out the first hurricane-seeding experiment; 91 kg/200 lb of dry ice is distributed in a storm.

Exploration

- In an attempt to demonstrate that the Pacific could have been peopled from South America, the Norwegian anthropologist Thor Heyerdahl spends 101 days on his balsa raft *Kon-Tiki*, covering 6,900 km/4,300 mi of Pacific Ocean.

Health and Medicine

- DDT-resistant strains of the housefly are reported in Italy. Soon afterwards DDT-resistant mosquitoes are also discovered.
- The "Bataan experiment" in the Philippines demonstrates that rice enriched with vitamins and iron reduces the incidence of beriberi by up to 90%.
- The poliomyelitis virus is isolated by U.S. physician Jonas E. Salk.
- U.S. optician Kevin Touchy introduces the corneal contact lens, which covers only the cornea and floats on a film of tears.
- U.S. physiologists Carl F. Cori and Gerty T. Cori, and Argentine physiologist Bernardo Houssay share the Nobel Prize for Physiology or Medicine for their work on the role of the pituitary hormone in sugar metabolism.

Science

- British physicists Cecil Frank Powell and G. P. S. Occhialini discover the pion (or pi-meson) subatomic particle.
- British scientist Patrick M. S. Blackett advances the theory that all massive rotating bodies are magnetic.
- English physicist Edward Appleton receives the Nobel Prize for Physics for his discovery of the Appleton layer in the atmosphere.
- English physiologists Alan Hodgkin and Andrew Huxley insert microelectrodes into the giant nerve fibers of the squid *Loligo forbesi* to discover the chemical and electrical properties of the transmission of nerve impulses.
- Scottish chemist Robert Robertson receives the Nobel Prize for Chemistry for his work on alkaloids.
- The Dead Sea Scrolls are discovered by shepherd boys in a cave near the Dead Sea in Palestine; stored in earthen jars, the Hebrew manuscripts date from the mid-3rd century BC to AD 68.
- U.S. chemists J. A. Marinsky, E. L. Glendenin, and C. D. Coryell discover Promethium (atomic no. 61); it is the last rare element to be discovered.
- U.S. educator and agricultural chemist Karl Paul Link develops the rat poison warfarin; an anticoagulant, it causes rats to bleed to death.
- U.S. physicist Willard Libby develops carbon-14 dating.
- Vitamin A is synthesized.

Technology

- Epoxy glue is developed.
- The AK-47 assault rifle is developed in the USSR; it becomes the standard rifle in most communist armies.
- The American Standards Association standardizes photographic film speeds in the United States by introducing ASA ratings.
- The Massachusetts-based Raytheon Co. introduces the first commercial microwave oven.
- The printed circuit board is developed by British scientist John Sargrove. Because the layout of wiring is planned, it greatly simplifies the production of radio and television.
- The reflecting microscope is developed.
- The United States launches its first guided missile from a submarine.
- U.S. inventor Edwin Land causes a revolution in photography when he develops the "Polaroid Land Camera," a camera that develops and prints photographs in 60 seconds; it goes on sale on November 26 the following year.
- U.S. physicist William W. Hansen constructs the first traveling-wave linear accelerator of electrons based on microwave technology at Stanford University in Palo Alto, California.
- U.S.-Hungarian mathematician John Von Neumann introduces the idea of a stored program computer, in which both instruction codes and data are stored.

AUGUST

- Britain's first atomic pile, at Harwell, Oxfordshire, comes into operation.
- 11 Construction of the first nuclear generating station in the United States starts at Brookhaven, New York.

Transportation

- A U.S. Douglas C-54 transport plane is the first airplane to cross the Atlantic relying solely on automatic pilot.
- The B. F. Goodrich corporation introduces tubeless automobile tires in the U.S.
- The North American Aviation Inc.'s F-86 is tested; it becomes the first U.S. jet fighter.
- The U.S. Boeing Corporation's B-47 Stratojet makes its test flight.
- U.S. industrial designer Raymond Loewy designs the Studebaker; its streamlined shape influences all subsequent car design.
- U.S. tire manufacturer B. F. Goodrich introduces tubeless tires that seal themselves when punctured; they become standard in the 1950s.

JUNE

17–20 The first round-the-world airline service is introduced by Pan-American Airways, flying a Lockheed Constellation.

AUGUST

- U.S. aviator William Odum flies around the world in 73 hr 5 min 11 sec, setting a new world record.

OCTOBER

14 U.S. test pilot Major Charles "Chuck" Yeager becomes the first person to fly faster than the speed of sound; he does it in a Bell X-1 rocket plane which reaches Mach 1.06 (1,207 kph/750 mph)

NOVEMBER

2   U.S. millionaire Howard Hughes's eight-engine wooden seaplane *Spruce Goose* makes a 1.6-km/1-mi flight at an altitude of 21.3 m/70 ft. Weighing 127 metric tons/140 tons and with a wingspan of 97.5 m/320 ft, it is the largest aircraft ever built. It never flies again.

ARTS AND IDEAS

Architecture

- The Equitable Life Assurance Building in Portland, Oregon, designed by the Italian-born U.S. architect Pietro Belluschi, is completed.
- The Kaufmann Desert House, Palm Springs, California, designed by the Austrian-born U.S. architect Richard Neutra, is completed.
- The Marcel Breuer House in New Canaan, Connecticut, designed by the Hungarian-born U.S. architect Marcel Breuer, is completed.
- The Promontory Apartments, designed by the German architect Ludwig Mies van der Rohe, are completed in Chicago, Illinois.
- The Unitarian Church in Madison, Wisconsin, designed by the U.S. architect Frank Lloyd Wright, is completed.

OCTOBER

- Abraham Levitt & Sons builds Levittown on Long Island, New York, for war veterans; this starts the trend toward mass suburbanization in the United States.

Arts

- In Britain, the cleaning of Rembrandt's *Woman Bathing* and other pictures in the National Gallery provokes controversy on the principles of cleaning major works of art.
- The Armenian-born artist Arshile Gorky paints *The Betrothal II.*
- The Belgian artist René Magritte paints *Philosophy of the Boudoir.*
- The English artist Ben Nicholson paints *November 11, 1947 (Mousehole).*
- The English artist Victor Pasmore paints *The Park.*
- The French artist Jean Helion paints *A Rebours.*
- The French artist Jean Dubuffet paints *Will to Power.*
- The German artist Max Ernst paints *Head of a Man Fascinated by the Flight of a Non-Euclidean Fly.*
- The Italian artist Marino Marini sculpts *Horseman.* The theme of horse and rider will occupy him throughout his career.
- The Swiss artist Alberto Giacometti sculpts *Man Pointing*, one of the earliest of the tall, thin sculptures for which he becomes known.
- The U.S. artist Arshile Gorky paints *Agony.*
- The U.S. artist David Smith sculpts *The Royal Bird.*
- The U.S. artist Jackson Pollock paints *Cathedral.* This is one of the earliest examples of his characteristic drip-and-splash style of abstract expressionism.
- The U.S. artist William Baziotes paints *The Dwarf.*

Film

- A movie of Shakespeare's *Macbeth*, directed by Orson Welles, is released in the United States. Welles also stars in it.
- The 1946 Academy Awards take place. Best Actor: Fredric March, for *The Best Years of Our Lives*; Best Supporting Actor: Harold Russell, for *The Best Years of Our Lives*; Best Actress: Olivia de Havilland, for *To Each His Own*; Best Supporting Actress: Anne Baxter, for *The Razor's Edge*; Best Picture: *The Best Years of Our Lives*, directed by William Wyler; Best Director: William Wyler, for *The Best Years of Our Lives.*
- The movie *Black Narcissus*, directed by Michael Powell and Emeric Pressburger, is released in the UK, starring Deborah Kerr, David Farrar, and Sabu. It is based on the novel by Rumer Godden.
- The movie *Brighton Rock*, directed by John Boulting, is released in the UK. Based on the novel of the same name by Graham Greene, it stars Richard Attenborough, Hermione Baddeley, and Harcourt Williams.
- The movie *Crossfire*, directed by Edward Dmytryk, is released in the United States. Typical in style of the *films noirs* made in Hollywood after the end of the war, it stars Robert Young, Robert Mitchum, Robert Ryan, and Gloria Grahame.
- The movie *Gentleman's Agreement*, directed by Elia Kazan, is released in the United States, starring Gregory Peck, Dorothy McGuire, and John Garfield.
- The movie *It Always Rains on Sundays*, directed by Robert Hamer, is released in the UK, starring Googie Withers, John McCallum, and Jack Warner.
- The movie *La Terra Trema/The Earth Trembles*, directed by Luchino Visconti, is released in Italy. The cast is made up of the inhabitants of Aci Trezza in Sicily.
- The movie *Le Diable au corps/Devil in the Flesh*, directed by Claude Autant-Lara, is released. Based on a novel by Raymond Radiguet, it stars Gérard Philipe and Micheline Presle.
- The movie *Le Silence est d'or/Silence is Golden* or *Man About Town*, directed by René Clair, is released in France, starring Maurice Chevalier, François Perier, and Marcelle Derrien.
- The movie *Les Maudits/The Damned*, directed by René Clément, is released in France, starring Dalio, Henri Vidal, Michel Auclair, and Florence Marly.
- The movie *Life With Father*, directed by Michael Curtiz, is released in the United States, starring William Powell and Irene Dunne.
- The movie *Miracle on 34th Street*, by director George Seaton, is released in the United States.
- The movie *Monsieur Verdoux*, directed by British filmmaker Charlie Chaplin, is released in the United States. He also stars in it with Martha Raye and Isobel Elsom.
- The movie *Odd Man Out*, directed by Carol Reed, is released in the UK, starring James Mason, Robert Newton, Kathleen Ryan, and F. J. McCormick.
- The movie *Out of the Past*, directed by French filmmaker Jacques Tourneur and based on Geoffrey Homes's novel *Build My Gallows High*, is released in the United States. It stars Robert Mitchum, Jane Greer, and Kirk Douglas.

- The movie *Quai des Orfèvres/Goldsmith's Quay*, directed by Henri-Georges Clouzot, is released in France, starring Louis Jouvet, Bernard Blier, and Suzy Delair.
- The movie *T-Men*, directed by Anthony Mann, is released in the United States. A *film noir* classic, it features stunning black-and-white cinematography by John Alton.
- The movie *The Fugitive*, directed by John Ford, is released in the United States. Based on Graham Greene's novel *The Power and the Glory*, it stars Henry Fonda, Dolores Del Rio, and Pedro Armendariz.
- The movie *The Ghost and Mrs Muir*, starring Gene Tierney and Rex Harrison, is released in the United States. It is directed by Joseph L. Mankiewicz.
- The movie *The Secret Life of Walter Mitty*, directed by Norman Z. McLeod, is released in the United States, starring Danny Kaye, Virginia Mayo, Ann Rutherford, Florence Bates, and Fay Bainter.

October 1947–57 Weekly attendance at U.S. movie theaters decreases by 50% during this period, with the spread of television.

NOVEMBER

25 Prompted by the House Un-American Activities Committee (HUAC) hearings, which are intended to expose alleged communists working in Hollywood, the U.S. movie industry blacklists a number of writers and producers.

Literature and Language

- *Het Achterhuis/The Diary of Anne Frank*, the diary of a Jewish girl who lived in hiding in Amsterdam, the Netherlands, and later died in Bergen-Belsen concentration camp, is published.
- The Algerian-born French writer Albert Camus publishes his novel *La Peste/The Plague*.
- The English poet and novelist Philip Larkin publishes his novel *A Girl in Winter*.
- The English poet Robert Graves publishes his study of literature and mythology, *The White Goddess*.
- The English poet W. H. Auden (who took U.S. citizenship in 1946) publishes his long poem *The Age of Anxiety: A Baroque Eclogue*. It wins a Pulitzer prize in 1948.
- The English writer L. P. Hartley publishes his novel *Eustace and Hilda*, the last volume in the *Eustace and Hilda* trilogy.
- The English writer Malcolm Lowry publishes his finest novel *Under the Volcano*.
- The French writer Jean Genet publishes two novels: *Querelle de Brest/Querelle of Brest* and *Pompes funèbres/Funeral Rites*.
- The French writer St.-John Perse publishes his poetry collection *Vents/Winds*.
- The German writer Thomas Mann publishes his novel *Doktor Faustus*.
- The Italian novelist Alberto Moravia publishes his novel *La Romana/The Woman of Rome*.
- The Italian writer Italo Calvino publishes his novel *Il sentiero del nidi di rango/The Path to the Nest of Spiders*.

- The Italian writer Primo Levi publishes *Se questo è un uomo/If This is a Man*, an account of his experiences in a concentration camp.
- The Japanese writer Osamu Dazai publishes his novel *Shayo/The Setting Sun*. Its note of pessimism reflects the postwar mood of Japan.
- The Martinique writer Aimé Césaire publishes *Cahier d'un retour au pays natal/Return to My Native Land*.
- The Nobel Prize for Literature is awarded to the French novelist André Gide.
- The Pulitzer Prize for Biography is awarded to William Allen White for *Autobiography*, the Pulitzer Prize for Poetry is awarded to Robert Lowell for *Lord Weary's Castle*, and the Pulitzer Prize for Fiction is awarded to Robert Penn Warren for *All The King's Men*.
- The Scottish writer Compton Mackenzie publishes his comic novel *Whisky Galore*.
- The U.S. writer Richard Wilbur publishes his poetry collection *The Beautiful Changes*.
- The U.S. writer Saul Bellow publishes his novel *The Victim*.

Music

- Capitol Records first uses tape for recordings, in the United States.
- In Italy, the U.S. opera singer Maria Callas makes her debut in Verona.
- In Scotland, the Edinburgh Festival of Music and Drama is founded.
- The Austrian composer Arnold Schoenberg completes his vocal work *A Survivor from Warsaw*, for speaker, male chorus, and orchestra.
- The comic opera *Albert Herring* by the English composer Benjamin Britten is first performed, at Glyndebourne, England. Britten also completes *A Charm of Lullabies* for voice and piano.
- The English composer Lennox Berkeley completes his *Stabat Mater*.
- The French composer Francis Poulenc completes his *Sinfonietta*.
- The German conductor Wilhelm Furtwängler withdraws as conductor of the Chicago Symphony Orchestra over claims that he had Nazi sympathies during the war.
- The opera *Dantons Tod/Danton's Death* by the Austrian composer Gottfried von Einem is first performed, in Salzburg, Austria. It is based on the play by Georg Büchner, written in 1835.
- The opera *The Taras Family* by the Russian composer Dmitri Kabalevsky is first performed, in Leningrad (St. Petersburg).
- The opera *The Mother of Us All* by the U.S. composer Virgil Thomson is first performed, at Columbia University in New York, New York. The libretto is by the U.S. writer Gertrude Stein.
- The Polish composer Witold Lutosławski completes his Symphony No. 1.
- The Russian composer Sergey Prokofiev completes the first version of his score for the opera *War and Peace*.
- U.S. gospel singer Mahalia Jackson records "Move On Up a Little Higher," one of her seven gospel records to sell more than a million copies.

Theater and Dance

- The American Theater Wing establishes the Tony Awards to honor outstanding Broadway productions and the people involved in them.
- The directors Elia Kazan and Lee Strasberg found the Actors' Studio in New York, New York. Their intention is to propagate the "Method," principles of experimental, introspective acting.
- The musical *Brigadoon*, by Alan Jay Lerner and Frederick Loewe, is first performed, in New York, New York.
- The musical *Finian's Rainbow*, with lyrics by Edgar Harburg and Fred Sady, and music by Burton Lane, is first performed, in New York, New York.
- The play *All My Sons*, by the U.S. writer Arthur Miller, is first performed, at the Coronet Theater in New York, New York.
- The play *L'Invitation au château/Ring Around the Moon*, by the French writer Jean Anouilh, is first performed, in Paris, France.
- The Pulitzer Prize for Drama is not awarded this year.

DECEMBER
- The play *A Streetcar Named Desire*, by the U.S. writer Tennessee Williams, is first performed, in New York, New York, directed by Elia Kazan and starring Marlon Brando.

Thought and Scholarship

- *La Pesanteur et la Grâce/Gravity and Grace* by the French philosopher and mystic Simone Weil is published posthumously.
- *Lettere del carcere/Prison Notebooks* by the Italian political thinker Antonio Gramsci is published posthumously.
- English economist William Beveridge publishes his *Report on Social Insurance and Allied Services*. The work of Beveridge is to provide the foundation of the welfare society in the postwar years.
- English historian George Douglas Howard Cole publishes *The Intelligent Man's Guide to the Post-War World*.
- English historian Hugh Trevor-Roper publishes *The Last Days of Hitler*.
- English historian Maurice Powicke publishes *King Henry III and the Lord Edward*.
- English historians Ronald McCallum and Alison Readman publish *The British General Election of 1945*.
- English politician Leo Amery publishes *Thoughts on the Constitution*.
- English scholar Heathcote William Garrod publishes *Scholarship: Its Meaning and Value*.
- German philosopher of science Hans Reichenbach publishes *Elements of Symbolic Logic*.
- German philosophers Theodor Adorno and Max Horkheimer publish *Dialektik der Aufklärung/Dialectic of Enlightenment*.
- The German-born U.S. logician Rudolf Carnap publishes *Meaning and Necessity: A Study in Semantics and Modal Logic*.
- The Pulitzer Prize for History is awarded to James Phinney Baxter for *Scientists Against Time*.

- U.S. journalist John Gunther publishes *Inside USA*.
- U.S. philosopher C. I. Lewis publishes *An Analysis of Knowledge and Valuation*.
- U.S. political journalist Walter Lippmann publishes *The Cold War*.

JULY
- U.S. State Department official George F. Kennan, writing under the pseudonym "X," introduces the concept of "containment" in the July issue of *Foreign Policy*.

SOCIETY

Education

- The Fundamental Law on Education reshapes the Japanese school system along U.S. lines.

DECEMBER
6 Cambridge University, England, votes to admit women to membership and degree courses.

Everyday Life

- Colgate–Palmolive–Peet launches the cleaning fluid Ajax, in the United States.
- Half of all Americans profess belief in UFOs (unidentified flying objects).
- In the United States, 18% of white males and 16% of white females finish four years of high school; the corresponding figures for blacks are 8% and 9%.
- In the United States, 5.4% of white men and 3.7% of white women complete four years of college; the corresponding figures for blacks are 2.3% and 2.6%.
- Kenneth Wood designs the Kenwood Chef, the first food processor, in Woking, England.
- Reddi-Wip Inc. markets whipped cream in an aerosol can, the first food to be produced in this way, in the United States.
- Reynolds Metals introduces an aluminum foil for use in the kitchen, in Louisville, Kentucky.
- The first microwave ovens go on sale, in the United States, but the public are slow to buy them.
- The first recorded sighting of an unidentified flying object (UFO) is made in the sky over Kansas, by Kenneth Arnold.
- The Marriage Guidance Council is set up in Sheffield, England, specifically to help couples adjust to changing roles after the war.

FEBRUARY
12 Designer Christian Dior introduces his New Look, which lowers skirt lengths to 12 inches off the floor, pads bras, unpads shoulders, and adds hats.

APRIL
21 The first airport duty-free store is opened at Shannon Airport in Eire.

DECEMBER
- The United Mine Workers union withdraws once more from the American Federation of Labor.

Media and Communication

- 38 U.S. magazines have circulations of more than one million; a distinction no magazine reached in 1900.
- In Germany, the news magazine *Der Spiegel* is published.
- U.S. airline Pan-American Airways launches *The Clipper*, the first in-flight magazine.

OCTOBER

5   U.S. president Harry S. Truman makes the first presidential address to the nation on television.

DECEMBER

27–September 30, 1960   *Howdy Doody*, a children's program starring Bob Smith and his marionette Howdy Doody, appears on U.S. television.

Religion

- Religious denominations in the United States (in millions): Roman Catholics, 25.2; Baptists, 15; Methodists, 10.3; Lutherans, 5.2; Episcopalians, 2.1; Mormons, 1.
- The Church of South India is inaugurated by the union of Anglicans, Methodists, and the South Indian United Church.

Sports

- At Bonneville Salt Flats, Utah, British racing driver John Cobb extends his world land-speed record from 595.02 kph/369.74 mph, set in 1939, to 634.37 kph/394.19 mph. On one of the two runs necessary for the record, he becomes the first person to exceed 400 mph on land, attaining a speed of 648.7 kph/403.1 mph.
- Notre Dame is college football's national champion for the second consecutive year.
- The British jockey Gordon Richards rides 269 winners in the flat race season, breaking his own record of 259 winners set in 1933.
- The National Association of Stock-Car Auto Racing (NASCAR) is formed in Daytona, Florida, by Bill France.
- The Philadelphia Warriors win the inaugural Basketball Association of America (BAA) professional championship.
- Williamsport, Pennsylvania, defeat Lock Haven, Pennsylvania, 16–7 in the inaugural Little League Baseball World Series.

MARCH

9   U.S. national figure skating champions are: Gretchen Merrill; Dick Button; Yvonne Sherman and Robert Swenning, pairs; Lois Waring and Walter Bainbridge, dance.

BIRTHS & DEATHS

- Sayid Mohammad Najibullah, communist president of Afghanistan 1986–92, born in Paktia, Afghanistan (–1996).

JANUARY

25   Al Capone, U.S. gangster, dies in Miami Beach, Florida (48).

FEBRUARY

4   Dan (J. Danforth) Quayle, U.S. Republican politician, vice president under George Bush 1989–93, born in Indianapolis, Indiana.

MARCH

6   Rob Reiner, U.S. actor and movie director, born in New York, New York.

9   Carrie Chapman Catt, U.S. feminist leader whose activities led to women's suffrage in the United States in 1920, dies in New Rochelle, New York (88).

18   Will C. Durant, U.S. founder of General Motors, dies in New York, New York (85).

APRIL

7   Henry Ford, U.S. industrialist who developed the mass-production of cheap Ford cars, dies in Dearborn, Michigan (82).

12   David Letterman, U.S. television talk-show host, born in Indianapolis, Indiana.

16   Kareem Abdul-Jabbar (Lew Alcindor), U.S. basketball player, born in New York, New York.

24   Willa Cather, U.S. novelist, dies in New York, New York (73).

MAY

3   Doug Henning, Canadian magician, born in Fort Gary, Manitoba, Canada.

16   Frederick Gowland Hopkins, British biochemist who discovered vitamins, dies in Cambridge, England (85).

JUNE

19   Salman Rushdie, Indian-born British novelist, whose controversial book *The Satanic Verses* outraged many Muslims, born in Bombay, India.

20   "Bugsy" Siegel (nickname of Benjamin Siegel), U.S. gangster who initiated development of gambling in Las Vegas, is gunned down in his home in Beverly Hills, California (39).

AUGUST

21   Ettore Bugatti, Italian designer of racing and luxury cars, dies in Paris, France (65).

29   James Simon Wallis Hunt, English race-car driver, winner of the 1976 Formula 1 Grand Prix, born in London, England (–1993).

OCTOBER

4   Max Planck, German theoretical physicist who was the originator of quantum theory, dies in Göttingen, Germany (89).

NOVEMBER

29   Petra Kelly, German political activist, cofounder of the Green Party, born in Günzburg, West Germany (–1992).

30   David Mamet, U.S. playwright, filmmaker, director, and adaptor, born in Flossmoor, Illinois.

DECEMBER

1   Godfrey Harold Hardy, English mathematician whose work with prime number theory had applications in genetics, dies in Cambridge, England (70).

14   Stanley Baldwin, British Conservative politician, prime minister 1923–24, 1924–29, and 1935–37, dies in Astley, Lancashire, England (80).

30   Alfred North Whitehead, English mathematician and philosopher who collaborated with Betrand Russell, dies in Cambridge, Massachusetts (86).

APRIL

8–19 The National Hockey League (NHL) Stanley Cup goes to the Toronto Maple Leafs, who beat the Montreal Canadiens four games to two.

15 Jackie Robinson becomes the first black American player in major league baseball since Moses Fleetwood Walker in 1884 when he plays for the Brooklyn Dodgers against the Boston Braves. Five days earlier Robinson joined the Dodgers from the Montreal Royals of the International League.

MAY

30 Racing driver Mauri Rose of Chicago, Illinois wins the Indianapolis 500.

JUNE

12 Golfer Mildred "Babe" Zaharias (formerly Didrikson) becomes the first U.S.-born woman to win the British Women's Amateur Championship.

15 Lew Worsham wins the U.S. Open golf championship, beating Sam Snead by one stroke in an eighteen-hole playoff.

25–July 20 In cycling, French rider Jean Robic wins the first Tour de France to be held since 1939. He is the first winner to go into the final stage of the tour without having led the race.

JULY

4 U.S. tennis player Margaret Osborne wins the women's singles title at the Wimbledon tennis championships in England.

7–September 14 Jack Kramer of the United States wins the men's singles at Wimbledon and the U.S. Lawn Tennis Association Championships.

16 Rocky Graziano wins the world middleweight boxing title from Tony Zale in Chicago, Illinois. The fight grosses $422,918, a new record for an indoor fight.

21 Baseball's Hall of Fame inducts 15 new members, including Carl Hubbell, Lefty Grove, Mickey Cochrane, and Frankie Frisch.

SEPTEMBER

14 U.S. tennis player Louise Brough wins the women's singles title at the U.S. Lawn Tennis Association championships.

30–October 6 In baseball, the New York Yankees defeat the Brooklyn Dodgers four games to three to win their 11th World Series.

NOVEMBER

1–2 In golf, the U.S. Ryder Cup team defeat the British team by a record score of 11–1 at Portland, Oregon.

DECEMBER

28 The Chicago Cardinals defeat the Philadelphia Eagles 28–21 to win their first National Football League (NFL) championship title.

1948

POLITICS, GOVERNMENT, AND ECONOMICS

Business and Economics

JANUARY

1 The Benelux Customs Union comes into effect, creating a free-trade zone between Belgium, the Netherlands, and Luxembourg. It is a significant step toward closer European integration.

MAY

• In a sign of improved labor–management relations in one sector of the U.S. economy, General Motors grants an automatic cost-of-living adjustment to 265,000 workers.

Colonization

JANUARY

17 The Netherlands signs a truce with the insurgent Indonesian independence movement.

FEBRUARY

4 Ceylon becomes a self-governing British dominion.

MAY

15 The British mandate in Palestine ends, and the Jewish authorities proclaim the new state of Israel, with David Ben-Gurion as prime minister. Egypt, Transjordan, Iraq, and Syria invade Israel and occupy areas in the south and east.

DECEMBER

18 Following a breakdown in negotiations, the Dutch renew their offensive against the independence movement in the Netherlands East Indies and capture provisional president Sukarno's republican government.

Human Rights

- Belgian women gain the vote.
- The U.S. Supreme Court invalidates restrictive covenants that prevent the inhabitants of exclusive districts from selling their houses to blacks.
- Women are permitted to hold all judicial offices in France.

JANUARY

12 In the case *Sipeul v. Board of Regents*, the U.S. Supreme Court rules that black applicants must be admitted to whites-only law schools unless equivalent black law tuition is provided.

JULY

30 The U.S. armed forces are desegregated by order of President Harry S. Truman.

NOVEMBER

2 Margaret Chase Smith is elected the first woman senator in the United States.

DECEMBER

9–10 The United Nations (UN) General Assembly adopts a convention on the prevention and punishment of genocide, and the Universal Declaration of Human Rights.

Politics and Government

- All Commonwealth citizens qualify for British passports by the passing of the British Citizenship Act.
- By the Displaced Persons Act, Congress permits some 400,000 homeless people to settle in the United States.
- Polish-born English criminologist Leon Radzinowicz publishes the first volume of *A History of English Criminal Law and its Administration, from 1750*. The last volume, written with Roger Hood, appears in 1986.
- South African socialite Helen Beatrice May Joseph helps found the Congress of Democrats, the white wing of the African National Congress (ANC).
- The government completes the nationalization of finance, industry, and commerce in Romania.
- The Protestant churches and Jewish community in Hungary accept compensation payments for their educational establishments and recognize the authority of the state. The Roman Catholic Church, under Cardinal József Mindszenty, refuses to accept a similar arrangement and its schools are forcibly nationalized.
- The railroads, electricity industry, and gas industry are nationalized in Britain.
- The RAND (Research and Development) Corporation, a U.S. "think-tank," is established in Santa Monica, California.
- The United Nations (UN) General Assembly adopts the Universal Declaration of Human Rights.
- The World Health Organization (WHO) is established, with its headquarters in Geneva, Switzerland; its aim is to improve world health conditions.

JANUARY

- The U.S. Congress gives funding to the *Voice of America* radio broadcasts to foreign countries.
1 The General Agreement on Tariffs and Trade (GATT), founded to promote trade between nations, especially by negotiating lower tariffs, comes into effect.

4 Burma (now Myanmar) achieves independence from Britain and becomes a republic.
7 The United States and Britain expand the German council running their occupation zones in post-World War II Germany, thus increasing German participation in the administration of western Germany.

FEBRUARY

2 The United States and Italy sign a ten-year treaty of friendship and commerce.
20 Twelve anticommunist government ministers resign in Czechoslovakia in protest at increasing communist influence in the police force.
25 President Eduard Beneš of Czechoslovakia bows to communist pressure to accept an all-communist cabinet, although Jan Masaryk remains foreign minister.

MARCH

2 The communist government of Czechoslovakia subordinates the autonomous province of Slovakia to rule from Prague.
8 In the case *McCollum v. Board of Education*, the U.S. Supreme Court rules that school prayer violates the constitutional separation of church and state in the United States.
10 Czechoslovakia's foreign minister, Jan Masaryk, is found dead in the capital, Prague; murder by communist agents is suspected.
16 A United Nations (UN) Palestine commission reports that it cannot implement partition into Arab and Jewish areas because of local opposition.
17 France, Belgium, the Netherlands, Luxembourg, and Britain sign the Brussels Treaty for a 50-year alliance against armed attack in Europe, with economic, social, and military cooperation.
20 Soviet delegates walk out of a meeting of the Allied Control Council, the body officially charged with governing post-World War II Germany, claiming they were snubbed when secret talks were held in London, England, to discuss the future of Germany.
26 A customs union is concluded between France and Italy.
29 The Nationalist leader Jiang Jie Shi, reelected president of China by the Nanjing assembly, is granted dictatorial powers.
31 The U.S. Congress passes the Marshall Aid Act, contributing $5.3 billion for European recovery after World War II.

APRIL

- The U.S. Congress overrides a presidential veto to enact the Income Tax Reduction Act.
- The U.S. Congress passes the Foreign Assistance Act implementing the Marshall Plan to provide economic aid to postwar Europe.
1 The USSR begins to disrupt traffic between the Western-occupied sectors of Berlin and the western zones of Germany, though outright blockade does not begin until June 24.
4 The Indian government passes legislation for the state to develop key sectors of industry where it has been neglected by private enterprise.
6 The USSR agrees to a treaty of mutual assistance with Finland.
13 The Romanian constitution is remodeled on Soviet lines.
16 Countries participating in the U.S.-funded European Recovery Program (the Marshall Plan, to assist

economic recovery after World War II) meet in Paris, France, and set up the Organization for European Economic Cooperation (OEEC).

18 The Christian Democrats win an absolute majority in the Italian elections, with 305 out of 574 seats.

30 The Organization of American States (OAS) is founded at the 9th Pan-American Conference, in Bogotá, Colombia.

MAY

• The U.S. Supreme Court, in the case *Shelley v. Kramer*, rules that the federal government has no authority to uphold private discrimination.

7 A meeting is held in The Hague, the Netherlands, of a movement for European unity under Winston Churchill, former prime minister of Britain.

9 The constituent assembly of Czechoslovakia accepts a new constitution for a "People's Democracy," but President Eduard Beneš refuses to sign it.

10 Elections are held in southern Korea under the supervision of the United Nations (UN) Temporary Commission, but the Commission is denied entry to Soviet-occupied northern Korea by the USSR.

11 The Liberal economist and journalist Luigi Einaudi is elected president of Italy.

16 Chaim Weizmann becomes president of the newly proclaimed Jewish state of Israel.

26 Jan Smuts's coalition of United and Labor Parties is defeated in the South African election by the Nationalists and the Afrikaner Party, who advocate a social policy of apartheid.

31 The National Assembly meets in southern Korea and elects Syngman Rhee as its chair.

JUNE

• The Republicans nominate New York governor Thomas E. Dewey for U.S. president and California governor Earl Warren for vice president.

• The U.S. president Harry S. Truman signs the Displaced Persons Bill, admitting 205,000 uprooted Europeans into the United States.

3 Daniel Malan, leader of the National Party, becomes prime minister of South Africa and forms a government of Afrikaners.

7 President Beneš of Czechoslovakia resigns, following his refusal to accept the proposed new communist-style constitution.

7 The United States, Britain, France, Belgium, the Netherlands, and Luxembourg agree a plan for the development of the U.S., British, and French occupation zones of post-World War II Germany, to include a constituent assembly and a federal government.

11 The United Nations (UN) mediator, the Swedish Count Folke Bernadotte, obtains a cease-fire in the fighting between Arabs and Jews in Israel for four weeks.

14 The communist prime minister Klement Gottwald succeeds Eduard Beneš as president of Czechoslovakia and ratifies the new constitution.

14 The Social Democrats merge with the communists in Hungary to form the Hungarian Workers' Party.

19 The U.S. Selective Service Act requires men aged 19–25 to register for military duty and provides for 19-year-olds to be called up.

20 A currency reform is implemented in Western Germany, unifying the U.S., British, and French zones.

24 The USSR blockades road and rail traffic between the German city of Berlin and the West, in response to the currency reform of June 20 in the Western zones of Germany. The blockade forces the Western powers to organize a massive airlift to bring in supplies for the U.S., British, and French zones of Berlin, which continues until September 30, 1949.

28 Yugoslavia is expelled from the Cominform (Communist Information Bureau) for its hostility to the USSR.

JULY

• A federal grand jury indicts 12 Communist Party leaders for urging the overthrow of the U.S. government.

• The Democrats nominate Harry S. Truman for U.S. president and Kentucky senator Alben W. Barkley for vice president.

7 An amnesty is proclaimed in the Philippines, but the communist-led Peasants' Party rebels refuse to comply with its terms.

10 The Provisional People's Committee adopts a draft constitution for North Korea.

18 A second truce is agreed in Israel after renewed fighting between Arabs and Jews over claims to land, but fighting continues and the Jews extend their territory.

29 Marshal Josip Broz Tito denies the Cominform (Communist Information Bureau) charges of hostility to the USSR and is given a vote of confidence by the Yugoslav Communist Party, which is later purged of Cominform supporters.

30 Zoltán Tildy resigns as president of Hungary following the arrest of his son-in-law for treason.

30–August 18 A conference of ten nations meets in Belgrade, Yugoslavia, to consider the future of the River Danube. Despite the protests of the United States, Britain, and France, the USSR is left in effective control of half the river's length, in violation of the convention of 1921.

AUGUST

• The U.S. Congress passes the Anti-Inflation Act to curb buying on credit.

2 Árpád Szakasits succeeds Zoltán Tildy as president of Hungary.

6 Willem Drees is elected prime minister of the Netherlands and forms a coalition of his own Party of Labor and the Catholic People's Party.

15 The Republic of Korea is proclaimed in the city of Seoul, ending the U.S. military administration of World War II in southern Korea.

25 The USSR breaks off diplomatic relations with the United States, alleging that it had kidnapped two visiting Soviet teachers. The United States claims that the teachers had chosen to stay in the United States.

SEPTEMBER

3 Władysław Gomułka, the Polish Workers' Party leader, resigns, accused of "nationalist deviation." He is replaced by Bolesław Bierut.

4 Queen Wilhelmina of the Netherlands abdicates for health reasons. Two days later she is succeeded by her daughter Juliana.

9 The Supreme People's Assembly in North Korea proclaims the Democratic People's Republic of Korea, with Pyongyang as its capital, and claims authority over

the entire country of Korea. The prime minister is Kim Il Sung.

10 Henri Queuille, a Radical, forms a government in France, with the Republican People's Movement (MRP) leader Robert Schuman as foreign minister.

17 Count Folke Bernadotte, the Swedish United Nations (UN) mediator in Israel, is assassinated by Jewish extremists. He is succeeded by his deputy, Ralph Bunche of the United States.

17 The independent state of Hyderabad, in southern India, surrenders to Indian forces and agrees to join the Indian Union.

18 Indonesian communists set up a Soviet government on the island of Java, but are forced to withdraw by Dutch troops.

OCTOBER

7   A Democratic–Liberal government is formed in Japan by Yoshida Shigeru.

24 In a speech to a U.S. Senate committee, Bernard Baruch popularizes the phrase "Cold War."

25 The USSR vetoes the proposal by the nonpermanent members of the United Nations Security Council to end the Soviet blockade of Berlin, Germany, which prevents road and rail access from the West.

29 A military junta under General Manuel Odría ends José Bustamante's government in Peru.

NOVEMBER

•   The Democratic candidate Harry S. Truman wins the U.S. presidential election. In the congressional elections the Democrats reclaim majorities in the House of Representatives (263–171) and in the Senate (54–42).

7   Charles de Gaulle's RPF (Rassemblement du Peuple Français) gains a large number of seats in the French elections for the Council of the Republic.

11 Chinese communist forces complete the conquest of Manchuria from the Nationalists. Massive forces then fight for Suzhou, which is captured in early January 1949.

12 The main Japanese war crimes trial ends in Tokyo. The former prime minister during World War II, Hideki Tōjō, and six others are sentenced to death; 16 receive life imprisonment, and two are given lesser sentences.

15 William L. Mackenzie King, prime minister of Canada, resigns and retires, to be succeeded by Louis St. Laurent.

DECEMBER

•   The former U.S. State Department official Alger Hiss is indicted for lying to a federal grand jury about alleged espionage activity.

1   The Arab Congress in Jericho proclaims Abdullah ibn Hussein of Transjordan king of Palestine.

5   Ernst Reuter, an anticommunist Social Democrat, is elected mayor of West Berlin, Germany.

12 The United Nations (UN) General Assembly recognizes the government in Seoul, South Korea, as the lawful government of Korea and recommends that occupying powers remaining in the country after World War II should withdraw.

15 The Polish Workers' Party and Polish Socialist Party merge to form the Polish United Workers' Party, led by Bolesław Bierut.

25 The USSR claims to have withdrawn its forces from northern Korea, in response to the United Nations (UN) General Assembly recommendation of December 12.

27 The refusal of Roman Catholics in Hungary to make concessions to the government leads to the arrest of the Roman Catholic leader, Cardinal Mindszenty.

28 Nokrashy Pasha, the prime minister of Egypt, is assassinated by the terrorist Muslim Brotherhood organization.

28 The United States, Britain, France, Belgium, the Netherlands, and Luxembourg establish an International Ruhr Authority to administer the Ruhr industrial area of post-World War II Germany.

SCIENCE, TECHNOLOGY, AND MEDICINE

Agriculture

•   U.S. zoologist Fairfield Osborne writes *Our Plundered Planet*, warning of the dangers posed by the insecticide DDT.

Computing

•   A magnetic drum for storage of computer data is introduced; data are recorded on magnetic tape on a rapidly spinning drum.

•   Manchester University in Manchester, England, demonstrates a computer with a simple memory, which permits some software development. The stored-program electronic computer, Mark I, designed by Tom Kilburn, is the first to use Von Neumann architecture and stores data in a type of cathode ray tube (Williams tube).

Ecology

•   Stirling Range National Park is created in Western Australia.

•   Sulfur from the Donora steel mill in Pennsylvania combines with moisture in the air to form a sulfuric acid fog that affects over 5,000 nearby residents and kills 22 people.

•   The Fresh Kills landfill site on Staten Island, New York, opens. By the 1990s its volume will exceed that of the Great Wall of China, making it the largest artificial structure on Earth.

•   Tsavo National Park is created in Kenya; it offers a refuge for the black rhinoceros.

JUNE

•   More than 3,500 people are killed by flooding in Fujian province, China.

Exploration

•   English explorer Wilfred Thesiger crosses the Arabian desert and penetrates the Oman steppes.

- The Norwegian anthropologist Thor Heyerdahl publishes *The Kon-Tiki Expedition*.

Health and Medicine

- Abortion is freely available in Japan, where overpopulation continues to be a problem. The population stands now at about 80 million.
- Caranamide, a penicillin by-product, is found to be an effective treatment of gout.
- Dramamine, an antihistamine used to counter travel sickness, is invented.
- Swiss physiologist Walter Hess describes using fine electrodes to stimulate or destroy specific regions of the brain in cats and dogs; it allows him to discover the role played by various parts of the brain.
- The antibiotic aureomycin is discovered by U.S. botanist Benjamin M. Duggar.
- The antibiotic Nystatin is discovered. It is the first safe fungicide and is used to treat fungal infections as well as to restore books and paintings attacked by fungus.
- U.S. chemist Edward Kendall and U.S. physician Philip Hench discover that cortisone can successfully treat rheumatoid arthritis.
- Using penicillin to prevent bacterial infection, U.S. microbiologists John F. Enders, Thomas H. Weller, and Frederick C. Robbins grow the mumps virus in test tubes; the technique is later used to propagate the polio virus, leading to a vaccine.

Math

- U.S. mathematician Claude Elwood Shannon invents information theory, a mathematical treatment of information that has important applications in computer science and communications.

Science

- *The Military and Political Consequences of Atomic Energy* by the English scientist P. M. S. Blackett argues that an independent nuclear deterrent is beyond Britain's means. Blackett—awarded the Nobel Prize for Physics in 1948—is excluded from government advisory circles for more than a decade.
- *Proconsul africanus* is discovered by Kenyan anthropologist Louis S. B. Leakey in Kenya. It is a Miocene ape that is a possible ancestor of both apes and monkeys.
- Austrian-born British mathematician Hermann Bondi and Austrian astronomer Thomas Gold publish *The Steady State Theory of the Expanding Universe* in which they argue that the universe is constantly expanding, but maintaining a constant density through the continual creation of new stars and galaxies at a rate equal to the rate at which old ones become unobservable because of their increasing distance.
- British anthropologist Arthur Keith publishes *A New Theory of Human Evolution*, in which he emphasizes competition as a major factor in human evolution and argues that racial prejudice is inborn.

- British biochemist Dorothy Hodgkin analyzes the complex structure of vitamin B_{12} and makes the first X-ray photographs of it.
- English anthropologist Mary Leakey discovers the 1.7 million-year-old skeleton of a primitive ape in Africa.
- English physicist Patrick Blackett receives the Nobel Prize for Physics for his work in nuclear physics and cosmic radiation.
- Hungarian-British physicist Dennis Gabor invents holography, the production of three-dimensional images.
- Scottish geneticist Charlotte Auerbach's studies begin the science of chemogenetics.
- Soviet biologist Trofim D. Lysenko outlaws orthodox genetics in favor of "Michurin" genetics in the USSR. Purges of geneticists (and assertions that, for example, wheat plants can produce rye seeds) obstruct agricultural development.
- Swedish chemist Arne Tiselius receives the Nobel Prize for Chemistry for his work on electrophoresis and serum proteins.
- Swiss biochemist Paul Müller receives the Nobel Prize for Physiology or Medicine for his work on the properties of DDT.
- U.S. architect Buckminster Fuller builds the first sizeable geodesic dome at Black Mountain College, North Carolina.
- U.S. astronomer G. P. Kuiper discovers and photographs Miranda, the fifth moon of Uranus.
- U.S. biologist Alfred Mirsky discovers ribonucleic acid (RNA) in chromosomes.
- U.S. biologist Alfred Charles Kinsey publishes *Sexual Behavior of the Human Male*, "the Kinsey Report"; it indicates that many sexual acts thought to be abnormal are very common and should be considered normal. It becomes a controversial best seller.
- U.S. chemist Karl Folkers and British chemist Alexander Todd isolate vitamin B_{12}.
- U.S. physicists George Gamow and Ralph Alpher develop the "Big Bang" theory of the origins of the universe, which says that a primeval thermonuclear explosion led to the universe expanding rapidly from a highly compressed original state.
- U.S. physicists Richard Feynman and Julian S. Schwinger, and Japanese physicist Shin'ichiro Tomonaga, independently develop quantum electrodynamics, the theory that accounts for the interactions between radiation, electrons, and positrons.

Technology

- France's first natural uranium reactor at Fontenay-aux-Roses goes into operation; it is moderated by heavy-water.
- Israeli army major Uziel Gal develops the Uzi submachine gun.
- Nippon Kogaku K. K. in Japan introduces the Nikon camera to compete with the German Leica.
- The "Joy Ripper" revolutionizes coal mining; it is the first continuous miner, applicable in the room and pillar method.
- The first atomic clock is installed at the National Bureau of Standards, Washington, D.C.; it is based on the

oscillation of the ammonia molecule and operates using the natural vibrations of atoms. It is extremely accurate, with an error margin of 2 seconds in every 2 million years.

- The first solar-heated house is built by U.S. architect Eleanor Raymond and engineer Maria Telkes in Dover, Maine.
- The gun on the British Centurion heavy tank is upgraded from 76 mm to 83.4 mm and fires newly developed high velocity armor-piercing ammunition.
- The X-ray reflection microscope is developed by U.S. physicists Paul Kirkpatrik and Albert Baez.
- Two small nuclear reactors are built in the UK for research purposes.
- U.S. mathematician Norbert Wiener publishes *Cybernetics*, summarizing the field of information control, particularly for application in machines such as computers.
- U.S. physicists John Bardeen, William Bradley Shockley, and Walter Brattain develop the transistor in research at Bell Telephone Laboratories in the United States. A solid-state mechanism for generating, amplifying, and controlling electrical impulses, it revolutionizes the electronics industry by enabling the miniaturization of computers, radios and televisions, as well as the development of guided missiles.

JUNE

3 The 5-m/200-in Hale reflector telescope is installed at Mt. Palomar Observatory, California; it remains the world's largest and most powerful telescope until 1974.

Transportation

- Radial tires are introduced by the French tire manufacturer Michelin.
- The Consolidated B-36 bomber is introduced in the U.S. Air Force. With a range of 16,000 km/10,000 mi, it is the first intercontinental bomber.
- The first cars fitted with air-conditioning come into production.
- The first four-wheel-drive Land Rovers are sold in the UK.
- The Soviet air force introduces the Ilyushin IL-28 jet bomber.
- Transfer machines for manufacturing engine blocks are introduced in car plants; transferring the block along a series of workstations, they perform hundreds of tooling operations in a few minutes, considerably improving the quality of car engines and accelerating their production.
- Work begins on the design of an atomic airplane in the United States, under the auspices of the Atomic Energy Commission.

MAY

10 To avert a national rail strike, the U.S. president Harry S. Truman orders the U.S. army to operate all railroads.

JULY

12 Six British Royal Air Force (RAF) de Havilland Vampires are the first jet aircraft to fly across the Atlantic.

31 Idlewild International Airport in New York, New York, is officially opened; it is the largest airport in the world.

ARTS AND IDEAS

Architecture

- The Exhibition Hall in Turin, Italy, designed by the Italian architect Pier Luigi Nervi, is constructed. It is a single-roof structure made of undulating prefabricated concrete.
- The Swiss architectural theorist Sigfried Gidion publishes *Mechanization Takes Command* (in English).

Arts

- British photographer Bill Brandt publishes *Camera in London*, a book of his photographs.
- The Argentinian-born artist Léonor Fini paints *Portrait of Genet*.
- The English artist Henry Moore sculpts *Family Group*, to be set up in Stevenage New Town, England.
- The French artist Bernard Buffet paints *Absinthe Drinker*.
- The French artist Germaine Richier sculpts *Storm Man*.
- The German artist Max Ernst paints *The Temptation of St Anthony*.
- The Russian-born French artist Nicolas de Staël paints *Marathon*.
- The U.S. artist Andrew Wyeth paints *Christina's World*.
- The U.S. artist Barnett Newman paints *Onement I* and becomes one of the leading figures in the development of color field painting.
- The U.S. artist Ben Shahn paints *Miners' Wives*.
- The U.S. artist Jackson Pollock paints *Composition No. 1*.

Film

- A movie of Shakespeare's *Hamlet*, directed by Laurence Olivier, is released in the UK. He also stars in it, along with Eileen Herlie, Basil Sydney, Jean Simmons, and Felix Aylmer.
- In the UK, Michael Powell and Emeric Pressburger write, direct, and produce *The Red Shoes*. A stylish fusion of narrative filmmaking and ballet, it stars Moira Shearer, Anton Walbrook, and Marius Goring.
- The *film noir Force of Evil* is released in the United States, starring John Garfield. It is the first movie to be directed by Abraham Polonsky, who is blacklisted in 1951.
- The 1947 Academy Awards take place. Best Actor: Ronald Colman, for *A Double Life*; Best Supporting Actor: Edmund Gwenn, for *Miracle on 34th Street*; Best Actress: Loretta Young, for *The Farmer's Daughter*; Best Supporting Actress: Celeste Holm, for *Gentleman's Agreement*; Best Picture: *Gentlemen's Agreement*, directed by Elia Kazan; Best Director: Elia Kazan, for *Gentlemen's Agreement*.
- The movie *A Double Life*, directed by George Cukor, is released in the United States, starring Ronald Colman and Shelley Winters.
- The movie *Abbott and Costello Meet Frankenstein*, directed by Charles Barton, is released in the United

States, starring the comedy duo Bud Abbott and Lou Costello, Lon Chaney, Jr., and Bela Lugosi.

- The movie *Fort Apache*, directed by John Ford, is released in the United States, starring Henry Fonda, John Wayne, and Shirley Temple.
- The movie *Germany Year Zero*, directed by Roberto Rossellini, is released, starring Edmund Moeschke, Ernst Pittschau, Franz Krüger, and Ingetraud Hintze.
- The movie *Key Largo*, directed by John Huston, is released in the United States, starring Humphrey Bogart, Lauren Bacall, and Edward G. Robinson. Another Huston movie *The Treasure of the Sierra Madre* is also released in the United States. It stars his father Walter Huston, Humphrey Bogart, and Tim Holt.
- The movie *L'Amore*, directed by Roberto Rossellini, is released. Consisting of two short movies, *The Human Voice* and *The Miracle*, it stars Anna Magnani and Federico Fellini.
- The movie *Ladri di Biciclette/Bicycle Thieves*, directed by Vittori De Sica, is released in Italy, starring Lamberto Maggiorani and Enzo Staiola.
- The movie *Letter from an Unknown Woman* is released in the United States, directed by Max Ophuls and starring Joan Fontaine and Louis Jourdan.
- The movie *Monsieur Vincent*, directed by Maurice Cloche, is released in France, starring Pierre Fresnay.
- The movie *Red River*, directed by Howard Hawks, is released in the United States, starring John Wayne, Montgomery Clift, Joanne Drun, and Walter Brennan.
- The movie *Riso Amaro/Bitter Rice*, directed by Giuseppe De Santi, is released in Italy, starring Silvana Mangano and Raf Vallone.
- The movie *State of the Union*, directed by Frank Capra, is released in the United States, starring Spencer Tracy and Katharine Hepburn.
- The movie *The Fallen Idol*, directed by Carol Reed, is released in the UK. Based on the Graham Greene story "The Basement Room," it stars Ralph Richardson.
- The movie *The Lady from Shanghai*, directed by Orson Welles, is released in the United States. He also stars in it, along with Rita Hayworth, Everett Sloane, and Glenn Anders.
- The movie *The Naked City*, directed by U.S.-born French filmmaker Jules Dassin, is released in the United States, starring Barry Fitzgerald, Don Taylor, and Howard Duff.
- The movie *The Pearl*, directed by Emilio Fernandez, is released in Mexico. Based on the novel by John Steinbeck, it stars Pedro Armendariz, Maria Elena Marques, and Alfonso Bedoya.
- The movie *The Three Musketeers*, directed by George Sidney, is released in the United States, starring Gene Kelly.
- The movie *Whisky Galore* (known in the United States as *Tight Little Island*), directed by Alexander Mackendrick, is released in Britain. A classic Ealing movie, it is based on the novel by Compton Mackenzie and stars Basil Radford, Joan Greenwood, Gordon Jackson, and James Robertson Justice.
- The movie *Yoidore Tenshi/Drunken Angel*, directed by Akira Kurosawa, is released in Japan, starring Takashi Shimura, Tishiro Mifune, and Reizaburo Yamamoto.
- The movie musical *Easter Parade*, directed by Charles Walters, is released in the United States. It features music and lyrics by Irving Berlin and stars Fred Astaire and Judy Garland.

Literature and Language

- In the Soviet Union, Andrei Zhdanov, Stalin's cultural spokesperson, launches a series of outspoken attacks on writers, artists, and composers who are not faithfully following the principle of Socialist Realism.
- The Australian writer Patrick White publishes his novel *The Aunt's Story*.
- The Belgian-born French writer Georges Simenon publishes his autobiographical novel *Pedigree*.
- The English literary critic F. R. Leavis publishes his study of English fiction, *The Great Tradition*.
- The English writer Evelyn Waugh publishes his satirical novel about the U.S. funerary industry, *The Loved One*.
- The English writer Graham Greene publishes his novel *The Heart of the Matter*.
- The English writer Harold Acton publishes *Memoirs of An Aesthete*.
- The English writer Henry Green publishes his novel *Concluding*.
- The Nobel Prize for Literature is awarded to the U.S.-born English poet and critic T. S. Eliot.
- The Pulitzer Prize for Biography is awarded to Margaret Clapp for *Forgotten First Citizen: John Bigelow*, the Pulitzer Prize for Poetry is awarded to W. H. Auden for *The Age of Anxiety*, and the Pulitzer Prize for Fiction is awarded to James A. Michener for *Tales of the South Pacific*.
- The Romanian-born German poet Paul Celan publishes his poetry collection *Der Sand aus den Urnen/The Sand from the Urns*.
- The Russian-born French writer Nathalie Sarraute publishes her novel *Portrait d'un inconnu/Portrait of an Unknown Man*.
- The South African writer Alan Paton publishes *Cry, the Beloved Country*, a novel which brings international attention to apartheid in South Africa.
- The U.S. monk Thomas Merton publishes *Seven Storey Mountain*, an autobiography published in Britain as *Elected Silence*.
- The U.S. novelist Lloyd C. Douglas's novel about St. Peter, *The Big Fisherman*, is the best-selling fiction title in the United States. The best-selling nonfiction title is Dwight D. Eisenhower's *Crusade in Europe*.
- The U.S. writer Carl Sandburg publishes his historical novel *Remembrance Rock*, which covers the history of America from the landing at Plymouth Rock to the mid-20th century.
- The U.S. writer Ezra Pound publishes his poems *The Pisan Cantos*, sections of the *Cantos* Pound has been working on since 1915.
- The U.S. writer Gore Vidal publishes his novel *The City and the Pillar*. Its treatment of the main character's homosexuality makes it controversial.
- The U.S. writer Irwin Shaw publishes his novel *The Young Lions*.
- The U.S. writer Norman Mailer publishes *The Naked and the Dead*. A novel depicting the lives of U.S. soldiers in the Second World War, it quickly becomes a best seller.

- The U.S. writer Robert Penn Warren publishes his short-story collection *Circus in the Attic*, which includes the story "Blackberry Winter."
- The U.S. writer Thornton Wilder publishes his novel *The Ides of March*.
- The U.S. writer Truman Capote publishes his first novel *Other Voices, Other Rooms*.
- The U.S. writer William Faulkner publishes his novel *Intruder in the Dust*.

Music

- The British composer Benjamin Britten founds Aldeburgh Festival, an annual music festival held in the village of Aldeburgh in Suffolk, east England.
- The English composer Elisabeth Lutyens completes her *Nine Songs*, settings of poems by the English writer Stevie Smith.
- The English conductor Sir Malcolm Sargent becomes chief conductor of the Promenade Concerts, held annually in the Albert Hall in London, England.
- The French composer Olivier Messiaen completes his *Turangalîla Symphony* and his vocal work *5 Rechants*.
- The French composer Francis Poulenc completes his *Calligrammes*, settings of poems by the French poet Guillaume Apollinaire.
- The German composer Richard Strauss completes his *Vier letzte Lieder/Four Last Songs*.
- The jazz musician Humphrey Lyttelton forms a band, in Britain.
- The Russian composer Dmitry Shostakovich completes his Violin Concerto No. 1.
- The U.S. jazz singer Duke Ellington is given permission to play in Britain. He is the first U.S. jazz musician to appear in Britain since World War II.
- The U.S. jazz singer Ella Fitzgerald records "My Happiness."

JUNE
- The U.S. Columbia Record Company releases the first long-playing record (LP), invented by U.S. engineer Peter Carl Goldmark. By 1950 the playing speed of 33.3 revolutions per minute is established. With grooves only 0.076 mm/0.003 in wide as opposed to 0.25 mm/0.01 in for the old 78-rpm records, the equivalent of six 78-rpm records can now be compressed onto one LP.

Theater and Dance

- In New York, New York, the musical *Kiss Me, Kate*, with lyrics by Bella and Samuel Spewack, and music by Cole Porter, is first performed. It is based on William Shakespeare's *Taming of the Shrew*.
- The ballet *Orpheus*, by the Russian composer Igor Stravinsky, is first performed, in New York, New York. The choreography is by the Russian choreographer George Balanchine.
- The play *L'Etat de siege/State of Siege*, by the Algerian-born French writer Albert Camus, is first performed, in Paris, France.
- The play *Les Bonnes/The Maids*, by the French writer Jean Genet, is first performed, in Paris, France.

- The play *Les Mains sales/Dirty Hands*, by the French writer and philosopher Jean-Paul Sartre, is first performed, in Paris, France.
- The play *Light Up the Sky*, by the U.S. writer Moss Hart, is first performed, in New York, New York.
- The play *The Browning Version*, by the English writer Terence Rattigan, is first performed, in London, England.
- The Pulitzer Prize for Drama is awarded to the U.S. dramatist Tennessee Williams for *A Streetcar Named Desire*.
- The romantic comedy *The Lady's Not for Burning*, by the English writer Christopher Fry, is first performed, in the Arts Theatre, London, England.
- The three biggest hits on Broadway are the musical comedy revues *Lend an Ear*, *Make Mine Manhattan*, and *Inside USA*. All three feature the comedienne Bea Lillie.

Thought and Scholarship

- English historian Arnold Hugh Martin Jones publishes *Constantine and the Conversion of Europe*.
- English historian Lewis Bernstein Namier publishes *Diplomatic Prelude, 1938–9*.
- English historian Thomas Southcliffe Ashton publishes *The Industrial Revolution, 1760–1830*.
- English philosopher Bertrand Russell publishes *Human Knowledge: Its Scope and Limits*.
- The Pulitzer Prize for History is awarded to Bernard DeVoto for *Across the Wide Missouri*.
- The U.S. theologian Paul Tillich publishes *The Shaking of the Foundations*.
- U.S.-born English writer T. S. Eliot publishes his critical study *Notes Towards the Definition of Culture*.
June 1948–53 English statesman and writer Winston Churchill publishes his five-volume history of World War II, *The Gathering Storm*.

SOCIETY

Education

- Brandeis University opens in Waltham, Massachusetts.
- St. Antony's College is founded at Oxford University, England.
- The Institute of Advanced Legal Studies is founded in London, England.
- The University of Nottingham is founded in England.

Everyday Life

- Bread rationing in Britain comes to an end.
- Chicago's Armour and Co. introduces Dial, the first deodorant soap in the United States.
- In the United States, Campbell Soup Co. introduce "V-8," a cocktail of eight vegetable juices, including tomato, carrot, and celery.
- In the United States, the Baskin–Robbins ice cream chain is started when Burton "Butch" Baskins and Irvine

Robbins merge their ice cream parlors. They soon start to franchise the name.
- The British solicitor's clerk Anthony Pratt develops the board game Cluedo. It is later marketed in the United States under the name Clue.
- The U.S. photographic company Polaroid introduces the Land Camera, which produces its own prints within a minute.
- U.S. sales of oregano increase over the next decade in response to the demand created by returning GIs, who have experienced Italian cuisine while in Europe.

MARCH
15–April 12 Over 200,000 U.S. coal miners strike for more generous pension benefits. They return to work on April 12 after the United Mine Workers union president, John L. Lewis, reaches an agreement with mine operators.

JUNE
- The American John Grimek wins the first Mr. Universe contest.
8 The *Empire Windrush* sets sail for Britain from Kingston, Jamaica, with 492 emigrants on board, marking the start of immigration to Britain from the West Indies.

DECEMBER
- In the United States, the McDonald brothers open the first McDonald's when they convert their drive-in to a self-service hamburger restaurant. They grant Ray Kroc all franchise rights 12 years later, which begins the expansion that will make it the world's largest fast-food company.

Media and Communication

- In the United States, Marshall Field combines the newspapers the *Chicago Sun* and the *Times* to form the *Sun-Times*.
- New programs in the United States include *Candid Camera* and *Hopalong Cassidy* (the first Western series).
- One million homes have television sets in the United States, compared to 5,000 in 1945.
- The American Broadcasting Company (ABC) installs the first reel-to-reel tape recorders in its studio.
- The weekly news magazine *US News and World Report* is launched, to compete with *Time* and *Newsweek*.

APRIL
21 *Hamlet*, produced by George More O'Ferrall and broadcast by the British Broadcasting Corporation (BBC), wins the TV Society's Silver Medal, the first television award to be made.

JUNE
20 The variety program *The Toast of the Town*, which later becomes *The Ed Sullivan Show*, is broadcast on U.S. television by the Columbia Broadcasting System (CBS). Performers who appear on the program include Elvis Presley, Albert Schweitzer, Irving Berlin, Hedy Lamarr, Walt Disney, Fred Astaire, and the Beatles.

SEPTEMBER
15 An international conference to determine the redistribution of wavelengths takes place.

21–June 5, 1956 The comedy program *The Milton Berle Show* appears on U.S. television under various titles. Known as "Mr. Television," Berle becomes one of television's first superstars.

Religion

- Albanian missionary Agnes Bojaxhiu, better known as Mother Teresa, forms the Missionaries of Charity in Calcutta, India.
- The English churchman George Kennedy Allen Bell publishes *Christian Unity: The Anglican Position*.
- The English churchman William Ralph Inge publishes *Mysticism in Religion*.
- The Evangelical Church is formed in Germany by the Lutheran, Reformed, and United churches.
- The World Jewish Congress is held at Montreux in Switzerland.
December 1948–55 The German Protestant theologian Rudolph Bultmann publishes his multivolume *Kerygma und Mythos/Kerygma and Myth*.

Sports

- A new form of bicycle racing called keirin, in which the riders are paced around a track by a motorcycle before an all-out sprint, is developed in Japan.
- At Muirfield, Scotland, English golfer Henry Cotton wins the British Open for the third time, eleven years after his last victory.
- Gino Bartali of Italy wins the Tour de France cycle race, ten years after his last victory.
- Mikhail Botvinnik of the USSR wins a tournament to decide the world chess championship, which had been left vacant since the death in 1946 of the last holder, Alexander Alekhine.
- The Cleveland Browns win their third consecutive All-America Football Conference (AAFC) title.
- U.S. sportswriters vote the University of Michigan college football's national champion.

JANUARY
30–February 8 The 5th Winter Olympic Games are held at St. Moritz, Switzerland. Norway and Sweden each win four gold medals; Switzerland and the United States, three each; France and Canada, two each. Henri Oreiller of France wins gold medals in the men's downhill and men's Alpine combination and a bronze in the men's slalom. Alpine skier Gretchen Fraser of the United States becomes the first non-European to win a skiing medal.

FEBRUARY
13 U.S. figure skater Dick Button wins the men's title at the world figure skating championships, the first victory ever by a U.S. man.

APRIL
3 U.S. national figure skating champions are: Gretchen Merrill; Dick Button; Karol and Peter Kennedy, pairs; Lois Waring and Walter Bainbridge, Jr., dance.
7–14 The Toronto Maple Leafs win their second straight National Hockey League (NHL) Stanley Cup, beating the Detroit Red Wings in four games.

MAY

1–June 12 Citation, ridden by Eddie Arcaro, wins the Kentucky Derby, the Preakness Stakes, and the Belmont Stakes to become the eighth horse to win the American Triple Crown. Arcaro becomes the first jockey to ride two Triple Crown winners, having won with Whirlaway in 1941.

31 U.S. racing driver Mauri Rose wins his second consecutive Indianapolis 500.

JUNE

12 U.S. golfer Ben Hogan wins the U.S. Open at the Riviera Country Club in Los Angeles, California, with a championship record of 276, five strokes less than the previous best hit, by Ralph Gruldahl in 1937.

JULY

2 At the Wimbledon tennis championships in England, Robert Falkenburg of the United States wins the men's singles, and Louise Brough of the United States wins the singles, doubles, and mixed doubles titles.

6 British boxer Freddie Mills wins the world light-heavyweight title when he outpoints the defending champion, Gus Lesnevich of the United States, over 15 rounds of their bout in London, England.

29 To coincide with the opening day of the Olympic Games in London, England, the inaugural national Stoke Mandeville Games, the forerunner of the Paralympics for disabled athletes, are held at Stoke Mandeville hospital, Buckinghamshire, England.

29–August 14 The 14th Olympic Games are held in London, England. The United States wins 38 gold medals; Sweden, 16; France and Hungary, 10 each; Italy and Finland, 8 each; Turkey and Czechoslovakia, 6 each; Switzerland, Denmark, and the Netherlands, 5 each.

AUGUST

• At the Olympic Games in London, England, 30-year-old mother of two Fanny Blankers-Koen of the Netherlands wins gold medals in the 100 meters, 200 meters, 80-meter hurdles, and the 4 × 100-meter relay.

• At the Olympic Games in London, England, U.S. athlete Bob Mathias becomes the youngest ever male athlete to receive an individual track and field gold medal when he wins the decathlon title at the age of 17 years 263 days.

15 U.S. golfer Mildred "Babe" Didrikson Zaharias wins the U.S. Women's Open golf tournament.

SEPTEMBER

19 The U.S. Lawn Tennis Association championship singles winners are U.S. tennis players Ricardo ("Pancho") Gonzales and Margaret du Pont.

OCTOBER

2 In automobile racing, Luigi Villoresi, driving a Maserati, wins the first Silverstone British Grand Prix.

BIRTHS & DEATHS

JANUARY

8 Kurt Schwitters, German dada artist and poet, dies in Little Langdale, Westmorland, England (60).

28 Mikhail Baryshnikov, Soviet-born U.S. ballet dancer, choreographer, and actor, born in Riga, Latvia, USSR.

30 Mahatma Gandhi (honorific name of Mohandas Karamchand Gandhi), leader of the nationalist movement to free India from British rule, assassinated in Delhi, India (78).

30 Orville Wright, U.S. pioneer of aviation who, with his brother Wilbur, was the first to achieve sustained powered flight, dies in Dayton, Ohio (76).

FEBRUARY

• Sergey Mikhaylovich Eisenstein, Russian film director, dies in Moscow, USSR (50).

23 John Robert Gregg, Irish-born U.S. inventor who developed the shorthand system named for him, dies in New York, New York (80).

MARCH

22 Andrew Lloyd Webber, English composer of popular musicals with lyricist Tim Rice, born in London, England.

31 Al Gore, Jr., U.S. politician, senator from Tennessee and vice president of the United States, born in Washington, D.C.

JULY

15 John J. Pershing, U.S. Army general, commander of the U.S. Expeditionary Force in Europe during World War I, dies in Washington, D.C. (87).

21 Arshile Gorky, Armenian-born U.S. painter of the abstract expressionist school, dies in Sherman, Connecticut (44).

23 D(avid) W(ark) Griffith, U.S. pioneer of filmmaking, dies in Hollywood, California (73).

AUGUST

16 (George Herman) "Babe" Ruth, U.S. professional baseball player, dies in New York, New York (53).

27 Charles Evans Hughes, U.S. politician who was Chief Justice of the Supreme Court and governor of New York, dies in Osterville, Massachusetts (86).

SEPTEMBER

3 Eduard Beneš, Bohemian statesman and president 1935–38, 1941–45 in exile, and 1946–48, one of the founders of the state of Czechoslovakia, born in Kozlany,

Bohemia, dies in Sezimovo Ustí, Czechoslovakia (65).

11 Muhammad Ali Jinnah, Indian/Pakistani Muslim politician, founder and first premier of Pakistan 1947–48, dies in Karachi, Pakistan (71).

17 Ruth Benedict, U.S. cultural anthropologist best known for her research on the ethnology of Native Americans, dies in New York, New York (60).

OCTOBER

4 Arthur Whitten Brown, British aviator who, with John W. Alcock, was the first person to fly nonstop across the Atlantic in 1919, dies in Swansea, Wales (62).

NOVEMBER

14 Charles Philip Arthur George, British heir to the throne, eldest child of Queen Elizabeth II and Prince Philip, born in Buckingham Palace, London, England.

DECEMBER

23 Hideki Tōjō, prime minister of Japan during most of World War II (1941–44), is executed in Tokyo, Japan, for war crimes (63).

31 Malcolm Campbell, British car and motorboat speed record holder, dies in Reigate, Surrey, England (63).

6–11   The Cleveland Indians defeat the Boston Braves four games to two to win their first World Series since 1920.

DECEMBER

19   In the lowest scoring National Football League (NFL) championship game ever, the Philadelphia Eagles defeat the Chicago Cardinals 7–0 in Philadelphia, Pennsylvania.

1949

POLITICS, GOVERNMENT, AND ECONOMICS

Business and Economics

MAY

- The American Federation of Labor (AFL) refuses to readmit the United Mine Workers union.

JULY

18   A new agreement for the supply of oil is signed between Iran and the Anglo-Iranian Oil Company, but is later rejected by the Iranian assembly.

SEPTEMBER

18   Britain devalues the pound by 30.5% from $4.03 to $2.80. The Federal Republic of Germany, Belgium, and Italy also devalue their currencies.

Colonization

MARCH

31   Newfoundland becomes the tenth province of Canada.

JUNE

2   The former British mandate of Transjordan is renamed the Hashemite Kingdom of Jordan.

14   The Vietnamese state is established by the French, with Saigon (now Ho Chi Minh City) as its capital, but conflict with the Vietminh (Vietnam Independence League) continues.

Human Rights

- Social legislation in South Africa begins to implement apartheid, suspending the automatic granting of citizenship to Commonwealth immigrants after five years, outlawing marriage between Europeans and non-Europeans, and banning sexual intercourse between Europeans and coloreds. The Population Registration Act starts the process of defining people as white, colored, or African.
- The French writer and philosopher Simone de Beauvoir publishes *Le Deuxième Sexe/The Second Sex*, a classic of feminist literature.
- The Italian movie director Pier Paolo Pasolini is expelled from the Communist Party because of his homosexuality.

MAY

14   The United Nations (UN) General Assembly invites India, Pakistan, and South Africa to discuss alleged discrimination against the Indian races in South Africa.

Politics and Government

- Eleven communists are convicted in the United States under the Smith Act of 1940 for advocating the forcible overthrow of the government.
- Gaston Eyskens, a Christian Socialist, forms a coalition government in Belgium with Liberal support.
- The U.S. Congress establishes the General Service Administration to manage government property.
- The U.S. president Harry S. Truman appoints the jurists Sherman Minton and Tom C. Clark to the U.S. Supreme Court.

JANUARY

- The U.S. Justice Department files an antitrust suit against the American Telephone and Telegraph company (AT&T). The suit aims to split the parent company from its manufacturing subsidiary, Western Electric.
- The U.S. Supreme Court rules that states may outlaw the closed shop (where all employees at a place of work or within a section belong to a single labor union).

1   Czechoslovakia launches a "five-year plan," a state-directed initiative to develop the economy.

7   Dean Acheson succeeds General George C. Marshall as U.S. secretary of state.

10   The communist army under Zhu De in China captures the city of Xuzhou from the Nationalists, exposing the Nationalists' capital at Nanjing to a new offensive.

15   Communist forces capture the city of Tianjin in northeast China from the Nationalists.

20   Making his inaugural address, President Harry S. Truman of the United States announces his Fair Deal: a

liberal domestic reform program that extends social security, raises the minimum wage, and increases public housing legislation. He also announces a four-point program that includes economic aid for underdeveloped countries.

20 The United Nations (UN) Security Council calls for the end of hostilities between the alliance of Karen tribesmen demanding independence (and their communist temporary allies) and the Burmese government.

22 Jiang Jie Shi resigns the presidency of China following successive setbacks for the Nationalist forces in the civil war.

25 The Council for Mutual Economic Assistance (Comecon) is formed in Moscow to further economic cooperation between the USSR and its satellites (Bulgaria, Czechoslovakia, Hungary, Poland, Romania, and Albania, with Yugoslavia as an associated member).

FEBRUARY

• The Hoover Commission on Organization of the Executive Branch of the Government recommends trimming the executive office of the U.S. government.

16 The Knesset, a single-chamber parliament, is established in the new state of Israel.

24 Israel agrees to an armistice with Egypt, following the invasion of southeastern Israel by Egypt, Lebanon, Transjordan, and Syria in protest against Israeli territorial claims.

MARCH

3 Israel agrees to an armistice with Lebanon, following the Lebanese invasion (with Egypt, Transjordan, and Syria) of southeastern Israel in protest against Israeli territorial claims.

4 Andrei Vyshinsky replaces Vyacheslav Molotov as Soviet foreign minister.

13 Belgium, the Netherlands, and Luxembourg agree to implement full economic union as soon as possible.

26 France and Italy agree to implement full economic union as soon as possible.

APRIL

3 Israel agrees to an armistice with Transjordan, following the Transjordanian invasion (with Egypt, Lebanon, and Syria) of southeastern Israel in protest against Israeli territorial claims.

4 The North Atlantic Treaty Organization (NATO) is founded to provide mutual support against the Soviet military presence in eastern Europe. The treaty is signed by the United States, Canada, Britain, France, Luxembourg, Belgium, the Netherlands, Italy, Portugal, Denmark, Iceland, and Norway.

9 In its first decision, the United Nations (UN) International Court of Justice holds Albania responsible for incidents in the Corfu Straits in 1946 and awards damages to Britain.

10 The United States, Britain, and France announce a new statute for their occupation zones in post-World War II Germany. The French zone is to be merged with the U.S. and British zones and a new West German state created with full self-government except for certain reserved matters.

18 Eire is formally proclaimed the Republic of Ireland and leaves the Commonwealth.

19 A U.S. foreign assistance bill authorizes $5.43 billion for the European Recovery Program (Marshall Plan), to assist economic recovery after World War II.

24 Communist forces in China capture Nanjing, the Nationalist capital.

MAY

May–November The former U.S. State Department official Alger Hiss goes on trial for perjury in New York, New York. After his jury is deadlocked on July 8, a retrial begins on November 17.

5 The Council of Europe is established in London, England, by Belgium, Denmark, France, Britain, Ireland, Italy, Luxembourg, the Netherlands, Norway, and Sweden, who undertake to promote European unity, protect human rights, and advance economic progress.

8 The Basic Law of the German Federal Republic (West Germany) restores the control of education to the *Länder* (states).

11 Israel is admitted to the United Nations (UN).

12 The Berlin airlift bringing supplies into West Berlin, Germany (blockaded by the USSR from June 1948) ends after 277,264 flights when the USSR allows normal land communications to resume.

12 The Far Eastern Commission terminates Japan's World War II reparation payments in order to aid the country's recovery.

23 Chinese communist forces, commanded by Zhu De, resume their offensive to drive Nationalist forces off the mainland.

23 The Federal Republic of Germany (West Germany) comes into being, with Bonn as its capital. West Berlin is excluded from the new state but associated with it.

30 A People's Congress in the Soviet zone of post-World War II Germany adopts a new constitution, providing for a People's Chamber and a Chamber of States.

JUNE

2 The British Parliament passes the Ireland Bill, which recognizes Ireland's independence but declares the special relationship of Irish citizens to the United Kingdom and reaffirms the position of Northern Ireland within the United Kingdom.

16 The communist government in Hungary begins a purge of government officials.

27 The Liberals under Louis St. Laurent win a large majority in the Canadian general election, with 193 seats against the Conservatives' 41.

29 The United States completes the withdrawal of its occupying forces from southern Korea after World War II.

JULY

• The U.S. Congress passes a Housing Act to clear slums and promote affordable housing.

• The U.S. Senate ratifies the North Atlantic Treaty for the collective defense of the major West European and North American states against the perceived threat of the USSR by a vote of 82–13.

7 Alger Hiss, a former senior officer of the U.S. State Department, is suspected of involvement in a communist espionage ring and tried for perjury. The trial ends in a hung jury and a retrial is ordered.

7 The former emperor of Vietnam, Bao Dai, returns to Vietnam as chief of state, at the invitation of the French.

13 Pope Pius XII's "Apostolica Acta" condemns those who support communism.

16 Chinese Nationalists organize a Supreme Council, under the former president Jiang Jie Shi, which begins to evacuate its military forces to the island of Formosa (now Taiwan) after a succession of defeats by communist forces in the civil war.

20 Israel and Syria agree an armistice, following Syria's invasion (with Egypt, Lebanon, and Transjordan) of southeastern Israel in protest against Israeli territorial claims.

29 The United Nations (UN) Atomic Energy Commission suspends meetings until a broader basis for agreement among its members is reached.

AUGUST

5   The United States ends its aid to the Nationalist side in the Chinese Civil War, recognizing that the Nationalist Guomindang (KMT) party is corrupt and the war against the communists unwinnable.

10 The Christian Socialists and Liberals form a coalition government under the Christian Socialist leader Gaston Eyskens in Belgium.

11 The U.S. War Department is retitled the Department of Defense.

14 In West Germany's first general election, the Christian Democrats under Konrad Adenauer win 139 seats, the Social Democrats 131, and the Free Democrats 52.

18 Hungary adopts a new constitution on Soviet lines and becomes a People's Republic.

SEPTEMBER

2   The United Nations (UN) Commission warns of the danger of war in Korea between the communist, Soviet-supported North and the U.S.-supported South.

12 Theodor Heuss, a Free Democrat, is elected president of West Germany, and Konrad Adenauer, the Christian Democratic leader, becomes chancellor. Adenauer forms a government of Christian Democrats, Free Democrats, and the German Party.

21 An Allied High Commission, headquartered in Bonn and consisting of representatives from Britain, France, and the United States, replaces the post-World War II Allied military government in West Germany.

OCTOBER

1   China's communist leader Mao Zedong proclaims the establishment of a People's Republic, with its government based in Beijing and with Zhou Enlai as prime minister and foreign minister.

6   President Harry S. Truman of the United States signs the Mutual Defense Assistance Act for the provision of military aid to NATO countries.

7   The Soviet-occupied zone of Germany (East Germany) is proclaimed a Democratic Republic.

11 Wilhelm Pieck is elected president of East Germany and Otto Grotewohl prime minister.

15 Chinese communist forces capture the Nationalist-held port of Canton.

16 The civil war in Greece between the monarchists and the rebel communists (ELAS) ends with the defeat of the rebels.

28 Georges Bidault forms a coalition government in France following Henri Queuille's resignation over a financial crisis.

NOVEMBER

11–13 The Polish United Workers' Party is purged of members with Titoist (pro-Yugoslav communist) leanings.

21 The United Nations (UN) General Assembly votes for the ultimate independence of Italy's former colonies.

24 The Allied High Commission, overseeing the western Allied occupation of Germany, makes further economic concessions to West Germany on its accession to the International Ruhr Authority.

26 India adopts a constitution as a federal republic within the Commonwealth, to come into force on January 26, 1950.

DECEMBER

5   The United Nations (UN) General Assembly requires member states to submit information on their armaments and armed forces.

8   Chinese Nationalists, driven by communist military forces from the mainland, declare Taipei on the island of Formosa (Taiwan) to be the capital of the Republic of China.

8   The United Nations (UN) calls on its members to recognize the political independence of communist China.

14 Israel moves its capital from Tel Aviv to Jerusalem, ignoring the United Nations (UN) resolution for the internationalization of Jerusalem.

15 West Germany becomes a full member of the U.S.-funded European Recovery Program (Marshall Plan).

17 Robert Menzies becomes prime minister of a Liberal–Country Party coalition in Australia.

27 An Indonesian republic, known as the "United States of Indonesia," is established, comprising all the former Netherlands East Indies territories except western New Guinea and having a nominal union with the Netherlands.

SCIENCE, TECHNOLOGY, AND MEDICINE

Ecology

- Nearly 20 million people are left homeless in China as a result of floods.
- Saudi Arabia grants a 60-year concession to Getty Oil of the United States, controlled by company president John Paul Getty.

AUGUST

5   Nearly 6,000 people die in an earthquake measuring 6.8 on the Richter scale in Pelileo, Ecuador.

Health and Medicine

- British biochemist Dorothy Hodgkin works out the chemical structure of penicillin.
- Indian physician Jal Vakil discovers that the powdered root of *Rauwolfia serpentina* (Resperine) is effective in the treatment of high blood pressure. U.S. physician

Robert W. Wilkins begins using it to treat hypertension the following year.

- Lithium is first used to treat mental patients.
- Swiss physiologist Walter Rudolf Hess and Portuguese physiologist António Egs Moniz share the Nobel Prize for Physiology or Medicine; Hess for his work on the function of the middle brain and Moniz for the value of leucotomy in psychosis.
- The antibiotic chloramphenicol (Chloromycetin) is introduced; it is the first effective treatment for typhoid fever.
- The antibiotic tetracycline is discovered.
- U.S. biologist Selman A. Waksman isolates the antibiotic neomycin.
- U.S. researchers synthesize adrenocorticotropic hormone (ACTH) which the pituitary gland secrets to stimulate the adrenal glands.

FEBRUARY

- The American Medical Association endorses a voluntary health insurance plan.

Science

- Excavation of the Temple of Inscriptions at the Mayan city of Palenque in Mexico reveals a pyramid, skeletons, and funerary goods, demonstrating that Mayan pyramids were funerary buildings.
- French anthropologist Claude Lévi Strauss publishes *Elementary Structures of Kinship*, which examines kinship in the light of the incest taboo.
- Japanese physicist Yukawa Hideki receives the Nobel Prize for Physics for his prediction of the existence of mesons.
- The Chinese Academy of Sciences is founded in Shanghai.
- The U.S. anthropologist Margaret Mead publishes *Male and Female*.
- U.S. astronomer Walter Baade discovers the close approach asteroid Icarus; except for comets, it has the most eccentric orbit of any body in the solar system, and passes closest to the sun (45 million km/28 million mi).
- U.S. chemist Glenn T. Seaborg and his team discover Berkelium (atomic no. 97).
- U.S. chemist William Giauque receives the Nobel Prize for Chemistry for his work on the behavior of substances at extremely low temperatures.

Technology

- EDSAC (acronym for Electronic, Delay, Storage, Automatic, Calculator) is constructed at Cambridge University, England; one of the first stored-program computers, it uses 3,000 vacuum tubes and is nearly six times faster than other computers; data are stored in mercury delay lines.
- French scientist Felix Trombe builds an experimental solar furnace using a paraboloid mirror to concentrate sunlight; it has an output of 50 kW.
- German engineer S. Junghans develops continuous casting in steel manufacture.
- Swiss engineer Georges de Mestral invents velcro after getting the idea from the burs that stick to his socks. The name is formed from the first letters of velvet and crochet.

- The Intertype Fotosetter Photographic Line Composing Machine is introduced in the United States; it is the first typesetting machine that does not use metal type.
- The United States launches a guided missile to a height of 400 km/250 mi—the highest altitude achieved to date.
- The United States tests the first multistage rocket.
- U.S. engineer John W. Mauchly develops the Short Code, the first high-level programming language, which allows computers to recognize two-digit mathematical codes.

AUGUST

- BINAC (acronym for binary automatic computer) is built by U.S. scientists John W. Mauchly and John Presper Eckert. It is the first electronic stored-program computer to store data on magnetic tape.
- 29   The USSR tests its first atomic bomb.

Transportation

- U.S. automobile production attains its 1929 production level of 5.1 million cars.

FEBRUARY

- The U.S. automobile company General Motors voluntarily reduces prices on all cars and trucks.
- 27–March 2   The U.S. B-50 bomber *Lucky Lady II* is the first airplane to fly nonstop around the world, refueling in midair and completing 37,734 km/23,452 mi in 94 hr 1 min.

JUNE

- A strike by British dock workers closes ports.

OCTOBER

- 6   U.S. engineer M. B. Taylor builds the Aerocar Model I or "flying automobile;" it logs over 5,000 hours flying time and travels over 320,000 km/200,000 mi on roads.

ARTS AND IDEAS

Architecture

- In the United States, the Johnson House (the "Glass" house), in New Canaan, Connecticut, designed by the U.S. architect Philip Johnson, is completed.
- In the United States, the Research Tower for S. C. Johnson & Son, in Wisconsin, designed by the U.S. architect Frank Lloyd Wright, is completed.
- The Eames House in Santa Monica, California, designed by the architect and designer Charles Eames, is completed. It is a prefabricated building, the doors and windows ordered from a manufacturer's catalog.
- The Hall of Residence at the Massachussetts Institute of Technology (MIT) in Cambridge, Massachusetts, designed by the Finnish architect Alvar Aalto, is completed.

Arts

- *Life* magazine features the U.S. artist Jackson Pollock and asks "Jackson Pollock: Is he the greatest living painter in the U.S.?"

- English art historian Kenneth Clark publishes *Landscape into Art*.
- In Paris, France, the French artist Jean Dubuffet organizes the exhibition "L'Art Brut Préféré aux Arts Culturels/Raw Art is Preferred to Cultural Art." The works exhibited include paintings from patients in psychiatric hospitals. Dubuffet is the originator of "Art Brut."
- The Argentinean artist Lucio Fontana exhibits his *Ambiente Spaziale a Luce Nera/Spatial Room at Luce Nera* in Milan, Italy. It is a work which, using space and lights, anticipates the "environments" developed during the 1960s.
- The Danish artist Karel Appel paints *Questioning Children*.
- The Dutch-born U.S. artist Willem de Kooning paints *Asheville* and *Covenant*.
- The English artist Graham Sutherland paints the portrait *Somerset Maugham*.
- The English artist L. S. Lowry paints *The Cripples*.
- The French artist Georges Braque paints *Atelier II*, one of the *Ateliers/Studios* series he paints between the late 1940s and 1956.
- The French artist Henri Matisse creates *The Tree of Life*, a maquette for stained glass for the Chapel of the Rosary of the Dominican Nuns in Vence, France.
- The German artist Wols paints *Bird*.
- The German-born U.S. artist Josef Albers begins the *Homage to the Square* series, continuing it until his death in 1976.
- The Italian artist Marino Marini sculpts *Horse and Rider*, a theme he returns to many times.
- The U.S. artist Alexander Calder sculpts *International Mobile*.
- The U.S. artist Robert Motherwell begins his series *Elegy to the Spanish Republic*.
- The U.S.-born English artist Jacob Epstein sculpts *Lazarus*.

Film

- The 1948 Academy Awards take place. Best Actor: Laurence Olivier, for *Hamlet*; Best Supporting Actor: Walter Huston, for *The Treasure of the Sierra Madre*; Best Actress: Jane Wyman, for *Johnny Belinda*; Best Supporting Actress: Claire Trevor, for *Key Largo*; Best Picture: *Hamlet*, directed by Laurence Olivier; Best Director: John Huston, for *Key Largo*.
- The movie *Adam's Rib*, directed by George Cukor, is released in the United States, starring Spencer Tracy, Katharine Hepburn, and Judy Holliday.
- The movie *All the King's Men*, directed by Robert Rossen, is released in the United States, starring Broderick Crawford, John Ireland, Mercedes McCambridge, and Joanne Dru. It is based on the novel by Robert Penn Warren.
- The movie *Champion*, directed by Mark Robson, is released in the United States, starring Kirk Douglas, Arthur Kennedy, and Marilyn Maxwell.
- The movie *Jour de Fête/Holiday*, directed by Jacques Tati, is released in France. Tati also stars in it.

- The movie *Kind Hearts and Coronets*, directed by Robert Hamer, is released in the UK, starring Dennis Price and Alec Guinness.
- The movie *Les Enfants terribles/The Incorrigible Children*, directed by Jean-Pierre Melville, is released in France. Based on the book by Jean Cocteau, it stars Nicole Stéphane, Edouard Dermith, Renée Cosima, and Jacques Bernard.
- The movie *Manèges/The Wanton*, directed by Yves Allégret, is released in France, starring Simone Signoret, Bernard Blier, Frank Villard, and Jane Marken.
- The movie *Manon*, directed by Henri-Georges Clouzot, is released in France, starring Michel Auclair and Cécile Aubry.
- The movie *Passport to Pimlico*, directed by Henry Cornelius, is released in the UK, starring Stanley Holloway, Margaret Rutherford, and Basil Radford.
- The movie *She Wore a Yellow Ribbon*, directed by John Ford, is released in the United States, starring John Wayne.
- The movie *The Heiress*, directed by William Wyler, is released in the United States. Based on the Henry James novel *Washington Square*, it stars Olivia de Havilland, Ralph Richardson, and Montgomery Clift.
- The movie *The Third Man*, directed by Carol Reed, is released in the UK, starring Joseph Cotten, Trevor Howard, Orson Welles, and Alida Valli, and featuring the music of Anton Karas on the zither.
- The movie *To Joy*, directed by Ingmar Bergman, is released in Sweden, starring Maj-Britt Nilsson, Stig Olin, and Victor Sjöström.
- The movie *White Heat*, directed by Raoul Walsh, is released in the United States, starring James Cagney, Edmond O'Brien, and Margaret Wycherly.
- The movie musical *On the Town*, directed by Gene Kelly, is released in the United States. He also stars in it, along with Frank Sinatra and Jules Munshin.

NOVEMBER

4 The influential *film noir* road movie *They Live by Night*, directed by Nicholas Ray, is released in the United States.

Literature and Language

- The Bible is published in Basic English, a simplified form of English developed in the 1920s by the English linguist Charles Kay Ogden.
- The British writer Louis MacNeice publishes his *Collected Poems 1925–1948*.
- The English writer Charles Morgan publishes his novel *The River Line*, which is dramatized in 1952.
- The English writer Enid Blyton publishes the first of her *Noddy* children's books.
- The English writer George Orwell publishes his novel *Nineteen Eighty-Four*, a darkly pessimistic vision of the future.
- The English writer H. E. Bates publishes *The Jacaranda Tree*.
- The English writer Nancy Mitford publishes her novel *Love in a Cold Climate*.
- The Finnish writer Mika Waltari's *The Egyptian* is the best-selling novel in the United States.

- The French writer and philosopher Jean-Paul Sartre publishes his novel *La Mort dans l'âme/Iron in the Soul*. It forms the third part of his novel sequence *Les Chemins de la liberté/The Roads to Freedom*.
- The French writer Jean Genet publishes his autobiographical novel *Journal du voleur/The Thief's Journal*.
- The Irish writer Elizabeth Bowen publishes her novel *The Heat of the Day*.
- The Italian writer Cesare Pavese publishes his novel *Il carcere/The Prisoner*.
- The Japanese writer Yukio Mishima publishes his autobiographical novel *Kamen no kokuhaku/ Confessions of a Mask*.
- The New Zealand writer Frank Sargeson publishes his novel *I Saw in My Dreams*.
- The Nobel Prize for Literature is awarded to the U.S. novelist William Faulkner.
- The Pulitzer Prize for Biography is awarded to Robert E. Sherwood for *Roosevelt and Hopkins*, the Pulitzer Prize for Poetry is awarded to Peter Viereck for *Terror and Decorum*, and the Pulitzer Prize for Fiction is awarded to James Gould Cozzens for *Guard of Honor*.
- The Russian philosopher Nicholai Berdyaev publishes *Dream and Reality: An Essay in Autobiography*.
- The U.S. writer Gwendolyn Brooks publishes her poetry collection *Annie Allen*, for which she wins a Pulitzer prize, the first black poet to do so.
- The U.S. writer Paul Bowles publishes his novel *The Sheltering Sky*.

Music

- In the United States, *Billboard* magazine introduces the term "Rhythm and Blues," a description for the current rage of black music, and begins a Country and Western chart.
- In the United States, RCA releases the first single record at the playing speed of 45 revolutions per minute.
- The English composer Gerald Finzi completes his *Clarinet Concerto*.
- The French composer Jacques Ibert completes his orchestral work *Symphonie concertante*.
- The opera *Il Cordovano* by the Italian composer Goffredo Petrassi is first performed, in Milan, Italy.
- The opera *Regina* by the U.S. composer Marc Blitzstein is first performed, in New York, New York. It is based on the play *The Little Foxes* by the U.S. writer Lillian Hellman.
- The Russian composer Sergey Prokofiev completes his Cello Sonata.
- The Russian composer Dmitry Shostakovich completes his String Quartet No. 4.
- The U.S. folk group The Weavers is founded. It is disbanded for political reasons in 1952, and then restarted in 1955.
- The U.S. jazz musician Sidney Bechet records "Les oignons"/"Onions."
- Works by Rodger and Hammerstein, Irving Berlin, and Cole Porter are among the year's most popular songs.

Theater and Dance

- In New York, New York, the musical *South Pacific*, with lyrics by Oscar Hammerstein and music by Richard Rodgers, is first performed.
- In the United States, the Shakespeare Festival is inaugurated in Balboa Park, San Diego, California.
- The ballet *The Age of Anxiety*, by U.S. choreographer Jerome Robbins and U.S. composer Leonard Bernstein, is first performed, in New York, New York. It is based on a poem of that title by W. H. Auden.
- The German writer Bertolt Brecht and the Austrian actress Helene Weigel found the Berliner Ensemble at the Theater am Schiffbauerdamm in East Berlin, Germany.
- The musical *Gentlemen Prefer Blondes*, with lyrics by Leo Robin and music by Jule Styne, is first performed, in New York, New York.
- The play *Cock-a Doodle Dandy*, by the Irish writer Sean O'Casey, is first performed, at the Abbey Theatre in Dublin, Ireland.
- The play *Death of a Salesman*, by the U.S. writer Arthur Miller, is first performed, in New York, New York.
- The Pulitzer Prize for Drama is awarded to Arthur Miller for *Death of a Salesman*.
- The U.S. writer Maxwell Anderson writes *Lost in the Stars*, an adaptation for stage of the novel *Cry, the Beloved Country* by the South African writer Alan Paton.
- The verse play *The Cocktail Party*, by the U.S.-born English writer T. S. Eliot, is first performed, at the Edinburgh Festival in Scotland.

Thought and Scholarship

- *Apologie pour le métier d'historien/The Historian's Craft* by the French historian Marc Bloch is published posthumously.
- *L'Enracinement/The Need for Roots* by the French philosopher and mystic Simone Weil is published posthumously.
- English historian John Ernest Neale publishes *The Elizabethan House of Commons*.
- English philosopher Gilbert Ryle publishes *The Concept of Mind*.
- English theologian Eric Lionel Mascall publishes *Existence and Analogy*.
- French historian Fernand Braudel publishes *La mediterrané et le monde mediterranéen à l'epoque de Philippe II/The Mediterranean and the Mediterranean World in the Age of Philip II*.
- Mexican writer Octavio Paz publishes *El laberinto de la soledad/The Labyrinth of Solitude*, an influential study of Mexican history and culture.
- Scottish diplomat and soldier Fitzroy Maclean publishes *Eastern Approaches*.
- The Pulitzer Prize for History is awarded to Roy Franklin Nichols for *The Disruption of American Democracy*.
- The U.S. philosopher Max Black publishes *Language and Philosophy: Studies in Method*.

SOCIETY

Education

- Following the communists' victory in the Chinese civil war between communists and nationalists, the Common Program establishes the right of all citizens to education and the responsibility of the state to provide it.
- In the United States, the Harvard Graduate Center in Cambridge, Massachusetts, designed by the German architect Walter Gropius, is completed.
- The Teachers' Registration Council is abolished in England and Wales, having failed to register more than half of the profession since its inception in 1912.
- The University College of North Staffordshire (from 1962 Keele University) in England is granted a charter to award its own degrees.

OCTOBER
9   Harvard Law School announces that it will enrol women.

Everyday Life

- Adolf Dassler designs the prototype training shoe, which is sold in Germany by Addas (which later changes its name to Adidas).
- Ballpoint pens become established in the United States, with sales exceeding those of fountain pens for the first time.
- Charles Lubin launches his Sara Lee bakery line in Chicago, Illinois, with his first product, the Sara Lee cheesecake.
- Cole & Son in Islington, London, England, introduce coordinated wallpaper and fabric into Britain from France.
- General Foods and Pillsbury launch the first prepared cake mixes in the United States.
- Meat, sugar, and dairy produce are still scarce in the UK, and sales are restricted.
- The children's novelty "Silly Putty" is invented in the United States by James Wright of General Electric when a chemical process goes wrong. It is sold through bookstores for $1.
- The United Nations International Children's Emergency Fund (UNICEF) issues the first charity Christmas card, based on a design by the seven-year-old Czechoslovakian girl Jitka Samkova.
- Unemployment in the United States rises to 5.9% from 3.8% the previous year.

FEBRUARY
1   Clothes rationing ends in the UK.

APRIL
9   In the United States, the first telethon is presented by Milton Berle in aid of cancer research. It runs for 14 hours and raises more than $1 million.

MAY
9   The first self-service launderette in Britain opens in London, England, with Bendix Home Appliances Ltd. supplying the fully automatic washing machines.

JUNE
27–August 15   A coal strike in Australia ends only after emergency legislation authorizes troops to work the mines.

AUGUST
- The Grand Army of the Republic, a Civil War veterans' organization, encamps for the 83rd and final time.
3   The U.S. Congress designates June 14 as Flag Day.

OCTOBER
- The U.S. Congress raises the minimum wage from 40 to 75 cents.
1–November 11   A nationwide strike by 500,000 steelworkers leads to a new pension plan.

Media and Communication

- *Paris-Match*, an illustrated news magazine, begins publication in France.
- Funded mainly by the U.S. Central Intelligence Agency, Radio Free Europe begins broadcasting to the Eastern bloc from its base in Munich, Germany.
- The press agency Deutsche Presse-Agentur is founded in Hamburg, Germany.

JANUARY
17   The Columbia Broadcasting System (CBS) shows *The Goldbergs*, the first situation comedy on television.
25   Awards for television are inaugurated in the United States: the first Emmy awards are presented by Walter O'Keefe in Hollywood, California.

MAY
- EMI sets up the first permanent closed-circuit television system in Britain, in Guy's Hospital in London, England.

SEPTEMBER
15–September 12, 1957   *The Lone Ranger*, a U.S. Western children's series about a masked man and his loyal Native American friend, Tonto, begins on television, starring Clayton Moore, Jay Silverheels, Chuck Courtney, and Ralph Littlefield. Scriptwriters are instructed that the hero always uses perfect grammar, doesn't smoke or drink, and never shoots to kill.

Religion

- The German Protestant theologian Rudolph Bultmann publishes *Primitive Christianity in its Contemporary Setting*.

Sports

- In cycling, Fausto Coppi of Italy wins both the Tour de France and the Giro d'Italia.
- U.S. sportswriters vote Notre Dame as college football's national champions. It is the seventh time they have been so honored, and the fourth under coach Frank Leahy, who resigns in 1953.

FEBRUARY
17   U.S. figure skater Dick Button is the men's world figure skating champion for the second consecutive year.

22 George Mikan of the Minneapolis Lakers establishes a National Basketball Association (NBA) individual points scoring record, with 48 points in a game against the New York Knicks.

MARCH

1   After 25 successful title defenses, the U.S. boxer Joe Louis retires as world heavyweight champion.
13 U.S. national figure skating champions are: Yvonne Sherman; Dick Button; Karol and Peter Kennedy, pairs; Lois Waring and Walter Bainbridge, dance.

APRIL

8–16 In ice hockey, the Toronto Maple Leafs defeat the Detroit Red Wings in four straight games to win the Stanley Cup for the third consecutive year.

MAY

4   Seventeen members of the Torino (Turin) soccer team, which is on the verge of winning its fifth consecutive Italian League Championship, are killed in a plane crash at Superga, on the outskirts of Turin, in Italy.
30 Indianapolis 500 winner Bill Holland drives a record average speed of 121.327 mph.

JUNE

11 Carey Middlecoff wins the U.S. Open golf tournament, beating Sam Snead who won the Masters and the PGA titles earlier the same year.
22 Ezzard Charles of the United States outpoints fellow U.S. boxer Jersey Joe Walcott, also of the United States, over 15 rounds in Chicago, Illinois, to win the vacant world heavyweight title in New York, New York.

JULY

1   Ted Schroeder of the United States wins the men's singles at the Wimbledon tennis tournament in London, England. He is the first champion to be presented with his trophy on the Centre Court. Louise Brough of the United States wins the women's singles.

AUGUST

3   In the United States, the Basketball Association of America merges with the National Basketball League to form the National Basketball Association (NBA).
28 In tennis, the U.S. team defeats the Australian team for the fourth consecutive year in the Davis Cup Challenge Round.

SEPTEMBER

5   U.S. tennis players Pancho Gonzales and Margaret du Pont are the singles champions at the U.S. Lawn Tennis Association championships for the second consecutive year.

OCTOBER

5–9 The New York Yankees defeat the Brooklyn Dodgers four games to one in the World Series.

DECEMBER

8   The Amateur Fencers League of America votes to admit players "regardless of color or race."
11 The Cleveland Browns win their fourth consecutive All-America Football Conference (AAFC) title two days after it is announced that they will join the National Football League (NFL), along with San Francisco and Baltimore, in 1950.
18 The Philadelphia Eagles defeat the Los Angeles Rams 14–0 to win their second successive National Football League (NFL) title.

BIRTHS & DEATHS

JANUARY

1   Pablo Gaviria Escobar, Colombian drug dealer, racketeer, and politician, born in Río Negro, Colombia (–1993).
8   Wolfgang Puck, Austrian chef and restaurant owner who popularized California-style cuisine, born in St. Veit, Austria.

FEBRUARY

22 Félix d'Hérelle, French-Canadian microbiologist who discovered the bacteriophage, a virus that infects bacteria, dies in Paris, France (75).

MAY

6   Maurice Maeterlinck, Belgian Symbolist poet and playwright, dies in Nice, France (86).

JUNE

5   Ken Follett, British author of best-selling thrillers and historical novels, born in Cardiff, Wales.

AUGUST

9   Edward Lee Thorndike, U.S. psychologist and animal behaviorist who developed the theory of connectionism which states that behavioral responses are due to neural connections resulting from trial and error, dies in Montrose, New York (74).
16 Margaret Mitchell, U.S. author of *Gone with the Wind*, dies in Atlanta, Georgia (49).

SEPTEMBER

7   José Clemente Orozco, Mexican painter of murals, dies in Mexico City, Mexico (65).
8   Richard Strauss, German composer, dies in Garmisch-Partenkirchen, Germany (85).
23 Bruce Springsteen, U.S. rock singer, songwriter, and guitarist, born in Freehold, New Jersey.

OCTOBER

2   Annie Leibovitz, U.S. photographer, born in Westbury, Connecticut.
5   Brian Connolly, British singer with the pop group Sweet, born in Hamilton, Scotland (–1997).
31 Edward R. Stettinius, U.S. secretary of state and industrialist who helped to establish the United Nations (UN), dies in Greenwich, Connecticut (49).

DECEMBER

2   John Akii-Bua, Ugandan Olympic hurdler, born in Lira, Uganda (–1997).

1950

POLITICS, GOVERNMENT, AND ECONOMICS

Business and Economics

- Diners Club cards, introduced in the United States, become the first credit cards. Initially issued by lawyer Frank X. McNamara to around 200 members for use in 27 restaurants in the New York, New York, area, the program gains popularity and quickly spreads.

SEPTEMBER

19 The European Payments Union (EPU) is established to manage and settle trade deficits and surpluses between 15 countries, including the whole of the sterling area (the area where the British pound is used).

Colonization

- Denmark annuls its 1918 Act of Union with Iceland.

APRIL

1 Italian Somaliland, occupied by British troops from 1941 to 1949, becomes a United Nations (UN) trust territory under Italian administration, but most of modern Somalia (British Somaliland) continues as a British protectorate until 1960.

Human Rights

- The Council of Europe produces the European Convention on Human Rights, providing for a European Court of Human Rights and a commission to enforce the convention.
- Women in India gain the right to vote on the same basis as men.

SEPTEMBER

7 As a result of a government decree in Hungary, most religious orders are dissolved, their buildings closed, and their members evicted.

Politics and Government

- Hungary launches a five-year plan with the aim of developing heavy industry.
- The Celler–Kefauver Act in the United States makes horizontal mergers between companies in the same industry illegal.

- The International Law Commission submits its formulation of the "Nuremberg principles" on war crimes, crimes against peace, and crimes against humanity to the United Nations (UN) General Assembly.
- The Kefauver Committee investigates the extent of organized crime in the United States.
- The Korean War, between North Korea, supported by communist China, and South Korea, supported by the United Nations (UN), leads to tax rises and a burst of inflation in Western countries.
- The United Nations (UN) headquarters, designed by the U.S. architect Wallace K. Harrison and others, is completed in New York, New York.
- The U.S. cartoonist "Herblock" coins the term "McCarthyism" for unsubstantiated accusations made against political opponents, based on the communist witch-hunts of U.S. senator Joe McCarthy.
- The U.S. Congress passes the Internal Security (McCarran) Bill, which requires the registration of communist organizations and forbids the employment of communists in defense companies.

JANUARY

3 The nationalist Wafd party wins an overwhelming majority in the Egyptian elections, ending five years of government by minority administrations.

5 The Greek prime minister, Alexander Diomedes, resigns.

6 A Franco–German parliamentary conference opens in Basel, Switzerland, to discuss the two countries' economic and political relations within the framework of a united Europe.

6 Britain formally recognizes communist China under Mao Zedong.

7 John Theotokis, a Populist, becomes Greek prime minister and heads a caretaker government.

9 A conference of Commonwealth foreign ministers in Colombo, Ceylon (now Sri Lanka), draws up plans for cooperation in the economic development of Asiatic states.

12 Capital punishment is reintroduced in the USSR.

12 Mustafa an-Nahhas Pasha forms a nationalist Wafd government in Egypt that includes all those ministers dismissed in 1944.

13 The United Nations (UN) Security Council rejects the motion of the USSR that the representatives of Nationalist China (Formosa) should be removed. Soviet delegates then boycott the UN until August 1.

25 In a retrial, the former U.S. State Department official Alger Hiss is convicted of perjury in the United States for concealing his membership in the Communist Party. Four days later he is sentenced to two concurrent five-year prison terms.

26 India is proclaimed a republic, with Rajendra Prasad, a supporter of the late nationalist leader Mahatma Gandhi, as its first president.
27 Alcide de Gasperi forms a new coalition of Christian Democrats, Democratic Socialists, and Republicans in Italy following the resignation of the Democratic Socialist government in November 1949 and the withdrawal of Liberal support.
27 Bilateral agreements for defense aid are signed in Washington, D.C., between the United States and, individually, Britain, France, Belgium, the Netherlands, Luxembourg, Norway, Denmark, and Italy.
29 The South African government's racial policy provokes riots in the city of Johannesburg.
30 Britain, Norway, Denmark, and Sweden sign an agreement for economic cooperation.
31 U.S. president Harry S. Truman instructs the Atomic Energy Commission to proceed with the development of a thermonuclear or hydrogen bomb—a far more powerful atomic weapon than those dropped on Japan.

FEBRUARY

1 Vlko Chervenkov becomes communist prime minister of Bulgaria on the death of Vasil Kolarov.
9 U.S. Senator Joseph McCarthy claims that there are 205 communists in the U.S. State Department.
13 The heads of U.S. missions in 14 Asian countries meet in Bangkok, Thailand, to discuss U.S. support for moves toward independence.
14 The USSR and communist China sign a 30-year treaty of friendship, alliance, and mutual aid.
20 The United States severs diplomatic relations with Bulgaria when Bulgaria refuses to withdraw a charge that Donald Heath, a U.S. minister, had been involved with Traicho Kostov, a former senior communist executed in 1949.

MARCH

1 Jiang Jie Shi resumes the presidency of Nationalist China.
1 The German atomic scientist Klaus Fuchs is sentenced to 14 years' imprisonment in Britain for betraying atomic secrets to Soviet agents. His evidence is used to incriminate Harry Gold, his contact in the United States, and the U.S. spies Julius and Ethel Rosenberg.
3 The French government signs agreements with the government of the German *Land* (state) of Saarland, confirming the latter's autonomy in legislative, administrative, and juridical matters, but reserving control over foreign policy and security in the post-World War II era.
8 Klimenti Voroshilov, marshal of the USSR, announces that the USSR possesses the atomic bomb.
12 A referendum in Belgium narrowly supports the return of King Leopold III from the exile to which he had been forced by allegations of collaboration with the occupying Germans during World War II.
16 Dean Acheson, the U.S. secretary of state, makes a speech suggesting ways in which the USSR could end the Cold War (the political tension between the USSR and Eastern Europe, and the United States and Western Europe).
18 The Belgian government resigns because of disagreement over the return of King Leopold III from exile.

21 West German chancellor Konrad Adenauer advocates economic union between West Germany and France.

APRIL

8 India and Pakistan sign the Delhi Pact, under which each country commits itself to upholding the rights of its minority populations.
11 Following the USSR's shooting down of a U.S. Flying Fortress bomber on April 8, the USSR states that the aircraft had entered Soviet air space in Latvia.
27 The Communist Party is outlawed in Australia.

MAY

1 Polygamy, infanticide, and child marriage are banned in the People's Republic of China.
9 The Schuman Plan is announced in France for the creation of a single authority to control the production of steel and coal in France and West Germany, with membership then opened to other countries.
11 The foreign ministers of Britain, France, and the United States confer in London, England, on the future of Germany in the post-World War II era.
22 The Chinese communist government offers Tibet regional autonomy if it will adopt the communist system.

JUNE

5 President Harry S. Truman of the United States signs a bill providing foreign aid of $3,121 million, including funds for the European Recovery Program (Marshall Plan).
6 Trygve Lie, the Norwegian secretary-general of the United Nations (UN), announces a 20-year peace program, envisioning more regular meetings of foreign ministers, the creation of a permanent UN military force, the admission of new members to the UN, and greater aid for poorer countries.
15 West Germany is admitted to the Council of Europe.
24 The French prime minister, Georges Bidault, resigns after his government is defeated in a vote on a technical issue.
25 Communist North Korean forces invade South Korea, with several armies advancing southward.
27 President Harry S. Truman of the United States orders U.S. air and naval forces in eastern Asia to resist North Korean aggression against South Korea and sends reinforcements to the South.
28 North Korean forces capture Seoul, the capital of South Korea, destroying most of the South Korean army.

JULY

1 The first United Nations (UN) forces arrive at Pusan in the South Korean peninsula.
7 The United Nations (UN) Security Council instructs the United States to appoint a supreme commander of the UN forces in Korea. The U.S. general Douglas MacArthur is appointed on July 8.
11 René Pleven forms a French government, which includes Guy Mollet and other Socialists.
19 President Harry S. Truman of the United States sends a message to Congress urging a vast military budget. His aim is to give the United States a worldwide capability for action against communist insurgency, and is given added urgency by the war in Korea.

Korean War (1950–53)

1950

JUNE

25　Communist North Korean forces invade South Korea, with several armies advancing southward.

27　President Harry S. Truman orders U.S. air and naval forces in eastern Asia to resist North Korean aggression against South Korea and sends reinforcements to the South.

28　North Korean forces capture Seoul, the capital of South Korea, destroying most of the South Korean army.

JULY

1　The first United Nations forces arrive at Pusan in the South Korean peninsula.

8　The U.S. general Douglas MacArthur is appointed commander of the United Nations forces in Korea.

SEPTEMBER

15　U.S. forces acting for the United Nations make a surprise amphibious landing in South Korea at Inchon, west of Seoul, causing the North Korean forces to panic and retreat.

OCTOBER

1　South Korean and United Nations forces, moving north, cross the 38th parallel, the border line between North and South Korea.

20　United Nations forces capture the North Korean capital, Pyongyang.

NOVEMBER

24　United Nations forces launch an offensive into northeast Korea.

26　Chinese troops enter the Korean War, obliging United Nations forces to retreat south from the Manchurian border.

DECEMBER

27　China refuses a United Nations appeal for a cease-fire in the Korean War.

1951

JANUARY

1　North Korean and Chinese forces break United Nations lines on the 38th parallel and, on January 4, take Seoul.

25–February 10　United Nations forces under General Matthew Ridgway launch a counteroffensive against Chinese and North Korean troops.

MARCH

7–31　United Nations forces move northward to the 38th parallel, recapturing Seoul March 14: General MacArthur advocates extending the war into China, using atomic bombs.

APRIL

11　The U.S. president Harry S. Truman relieves General Douglas MacArthur of command of the United Nations forces in Korea, because of his public advocacy of war with China. He is succeeded by Ridgway.

22–25　In bitter fighting along the Imjin river, the British 29th Brigade, including the Gloucestershire Regiment and the 3rd Battalion Royal Australian Regiment, stops a massive Communist offensive and prevents the collapse of the United Nations front.

MAY

14–20　Chinese armies launch an offensive along most of the front in central Korea, forcing back the United Nations forces.

JUNE

23　Soviet representative to the United Nations Yakov Malik calls for a cease-fire and armistice talks in the Korean War. Truce negotiations begin at Kaesong, Korea, on July 8, but break down on August 23.

OCTOBER

25　Negotiations for an armistice in the Korean War are renewed at Panmunjom, Korea.

NOVEMBER

14　The United States alleges that North Koreans have murdered 5,970 United Nations prisoners and about 250,000 Korean civilians during the Korean War.

DECEMBER

27　Talks for an armistice in the Korean War fail.

1952

MARCH

4　The Chinese communist government accuses U.S. forces in Korea of using germ warfare.

MAY

20　Serious rioting breaks out among communist prisoners of war at the Koje Island prison camp in South Korea.

JUNE

23　The U.S. Air Force bombs hydroelectric plants in North Korea.

1953

MARCH

5　The death of Soviet leader Joseph Stalin enables more moderate elements in Moscow to press the need for compromise on the North Korean leadership.

APRIL

11　The United Nations forces and their communist opponents arrange for an exchange of prisoners.

JUNE

18　South Korea releases 27,000 noncommunist North Korean prisoners.

JULY

27　Delegates from the United Nations, North Korea, and China sign an armistice at Panmunjom, ending the Korean War. The U.S. has suffered 137,051 casualties, of whom 25,604 were killed, 103,492 were wounded, and 7,955 are missing.

20 The U.S. Senate accepts a committee report denying Senator Joseph McCarthy's charge that communists had infiltrated the State Department.

22–23 King Leopold III returns to Belgium after six years in exile. Socialist demonstrations in Brussels on July 23–24 protest against his return.

AUGUST

1 King Leopold III of Belgium abdicates in favor of his son, Prince Baudouin, who acts as head of state from August 11 to July 17, 1951, when he is crowned king.

1 The Soviet diplomat Yakov Malik chairs a meeting of the United Nations (UN) Security Council, ending the Soviet boycott that began in January over the proposed removal of representatives of Nationalist China.

4 After the start of fighting in Korea, the U.S. Army calls up 21,000 enlisted reservists for 21 months' duty.

11 At the meeting of the Consultative Assembly of the Council of Europe in Strasbourg, France, Winston Churchill, former prime minister of Britain, supports a motion calling for the creation of a European army. The motion is passed by 89 votes to 5.

15 Paul van Zeeland forms a Christian Socialist government in Belgium.

17 A centralized state organization in the new Indonesian Republic replaces the federal system structure of the former Netherlands East Indies.

SEPTEMBER

1 North Korean forces attack across the Naktong River at the southeast end of the South Korean peninsula.

4 A new constitution in Syria curtails the powers of the president.

15 The United States proposes West German rearmament to counter the threat of Soviet expansion; France opposes the proposal.

15 U.S. forces acting for the United Nations (UN) make a surprise amphibious landing in South Korea at Inchon, west of Seoul, causing the North Korean forces to panic and retreat.

22 U.S. diplomat Ralph Bunche wins the Nobel Peace Prize for his work in negotiating the Arab–Israeli truce in 1949.

26 United Nations (UN) forces recapture Seoul, the South Korean capital, from the North Koreans.

28 The newly independent Republic of Indonesia is admitted to the United Nations.

29 General Douglas MacArthur of the United States is authorized to organize the advance of United Nations (UN) forces into North Korea.

OCTOBER

1 South Korean and United Nations (UN) forces, moving north, cross the 38th parallel, the border line between North and South Korea.

4 Turkey agrees to cooperate with NATO defense plans for the Mediterranean.

7 Dean Acheson, the U.S. secretary of state, proposes that if the United Nations Security Council is unable to adopt a course of action against an act of aggression, the General Assembly should recommend a course of action. His plan is adopted on October 19.

10 West Germany's Christian Democratic parties unite as the Christian Democratic Union (CDU).

15 The East German elections result in a 99.6% vote in favor of the communist-dominated National Front.

20 United Nations (UN) forces capture the North Korean capital, Pyongyang.

21 Chinese forces occupy the independent area of Tibet, with the irregular Tibetan military forces accepting defeat.

21 Soviet bloc representatives chaired by the Soviet foreign minister Vyacheslav Molotov meet in Prague, Czechoslovakia, to discuss the future of Germany in the post-World War II era.

24 The French prime minister René Pleven proposes a plan (the Pleven Plan) for the creation of a European army, the European Defense Community.

26 The Danish prime minister, Hans Hedtoft, resigns following a general election. He is succeeded by his finance minister, Erik Eriksen, who forms a coalition of his own Liberal Agrarian Party and the Conservatives.

26 The United Nations (UN) Security Council passes a resolution demanding the withdrawal of North Korean forces from South Korea.

30 Nationalists seeking independence from the United States rebel in Puerto Rico.

NOVEMBER

• In the U.S. congressional elections the Democrats retain slim majorities in the House of Representatives (235–199) and in the Senate (49–47).

1 Two Puerto Rican nationalists attempt to assassinate the U.S. president Harry S. Truman in Washington, D.C.

3 French forces withdraw from the frontier of northern Vietnam.

4 The United Nations (UN) General Assembly revokes the 1946 resolutions on Spain. These had barred Spain from UN membership and recommended that members should not maintain diplomatic relationships with Spain.

5 Douglas MacArthur, the United Nations (UN) commander in Korea, reports the massing of Chinese troops in North Korea.

18 The Consultative Assembly of the Council of Europe hears a speech by Robert Schuman, the French foreign minister, supporting the Pleven Plan for the establishment of a European army, the European Defense Community.

24 United Nations (UN) forces launch an offensive into northeast Korea.

26 Chinese troops enter the Korean War, obliging United Nations (UN) forces to retreat south from the Manchurian border.

27 Delegates of China's communist government attend the United Nations (UN) as observers.

28 Poland and East Germany proclaim the Oder–Neisse line as the frontier between the two countries, giving Poland territorial gains in the west to compensate for territory lost to the USSR at the end of World War II.

30 Tibet appeals to the United Nations (UN) against Chinese aggression.

DECEMBER

8 President Harry S. Truman bans U.S. trade with the People's Republic of China following China's entry into the Korean War.

13 Aid to Britain under the U.S.-funded Marshall Plan (European Recovery Program) ceases.

13 South Africa refuses to place South West Africa (now Namibia) under United Nations (UN) trusteeship after

the UN rejection of a South African application to annex the former mandated territory.

16 A state of emergency is proclaimed in the United States following the setbacks of United Nations forces in the Korean War.

19 A meeting of the North Atlantic Council, NATO's governing body, agrees to create an integrated defense force under the supreme command of U.S. general Dwight D. Eisenhower.

23 Vietnam becomes a sovereign state within the French Union.

27 China refuses a United Nations (UN) appeal for a cease-fire in the Korean War.

27 The United States and Spain resume diplomatic relations.

28 Chinese forces, advancing south, cross the 38th parallel into South Korea.

SCIENCE, TECHNOLOGY, AND MEDICINE

Agriculture

c. 1950 The production of fertilizers and pesticides begins to increase dramatically.

- A new agrarian reform law in China, emphasizing the use of chemical fertilizers and farm machinery, results in a rise in agricultural production.
- The first embryos are transplanted in cattle.
- U.S. crops are ravaged by insects; $4 billion worth are destroyed.

Computing

- EDVAC (Electronic, Discrete, Variable, Automatic Computer) is constructed at Princeton University in Princeton, New Jersey. Its instructions, or programs, are stored within the computer in numerical form.
- Hungarian-U.S. mathematician John von Neumann makes the first 24-hour weather forecast using a computer.

Ecology

- Kafue National Park is established in Zambia as a refuge for the black rhinoceros.

AUGUST

15 An earthquake measuring 8.6 on the Richter scale kills 1,500 people in Assam, India.

Exploration

- A French expedition mounts the first successful ascent of Mt. Annapurna in Nepal.
- Cape Canaveral, Florida, is established as a rocket assembly and launching facility.

Health and Medicine

- Americans spend $120 billion for health care services.
- Manual heart massage is used for the first time to save a patient.
- Sales of antihistamines in the United States reach $100,000,000.
- The tranquilizer Miltown (meprobamate) is introduced to treat insomnia and neurotic disorders.
- U.S. biochemists Philip S. Hench and Edward C. Kendall and Swiss physiologist Tadeusz Reichstein share the Nobel Prize for Physiology or Medicine for their research on adrenal cortex hormones.

Math

- Russian mathematician Andrey Nikolaevich Kolmogorov presents the first formal treatment of probability in *Foundations of the Theory of Probability*.

Science

- British physicist Louis Essen develops a new means of calculating the velocity of light by measuring the speed of radio waves in a vacuum.
- Dutch astronomer Jan Hendrik Oort proposes that comets originate in a vast cloud of bodies (the "Oort cloud") that orbits the sun at a distance of about one light-year.
- English archeologist Brian Hope-Taylor excavates remains of a large Anglo-Saxon hall at Yeavering, Northumberland, England.
- English physicist Cecil Powell receives the Nobel Prize for Physics for his work on mesons and for his photographic methods of studying nuclear processes.
- German chemists Otto Diels and Kurt Alder share the Nobel Prize for Chemistry for their discovery of diene synthesis.
- The U.S. Atomic Energy Commission separates plutonium from pitchblende concentrates.
- U.S. chemist Glenn T. Seaborg and his colleagues at the University of California discover Californium (atomic no. 98).

Technology

- A coaxial telephone cable with submerged repeaters is laid between Miami, Florida, and Havana, Cuba; its success paves the way for transatlantic cables.
- Community Antenna Television (CATV) is introduced in the United States. The first cable television, it provides television for areas with poor reception.
- Dr. Yoshiro Nakamata of the Imperial University, Tokyo, Japan, develops the floppy disk and licenses it to International Business Machines (IBM).
- Otis Elevators introduce the first elevators with self-operating doors, in Dallas, Texas.
- The black, rotary-dial, desk telephone is introduced.
- The first gas turbine engines are installed on trucks.
- The first Xerox photocopying machine is produced by the Haloid Company (later to become the Xerox Corporation) in Rochester, New York.

- The Semi-Automatic Ground Environment (SAGE) system is set up by the U.S. Air Force to provide early warning of an enemy attack. It consists of a dozen computer centers throughout Canada and the United States, which continuously process data from many radar units and other sources.
- The synthetic fiber Orlon is introduced by the U.S. corporation Du Pont.
- The vidicon television camera tube, the first to make use of the phenomenon of photoconductivity, and to be suitable for portable cameras, is introduced.
- Three-quarters of U.S. farms now have electricity.
- U.S. camera manufacturer Polaroid introduces a camera that automatically selects the shutter speed.

Transportation

c. 1950 Fuel injection is introduced by Mercedes-Benz in its racing models; it soon becomes popular in passenger vehicles.
- A jet-propelled pilotless aircraft is constructed in Australia.
- A subway system is opened in Stockholm, Sweden.
- In London, England, Horizon becomes the first air charter company.
- The *Mistral* electric passenger train enters service in France. It covers the 1,088-km/676-mi Paris–Nice trip in 9 hr 8 min, and runs on welded track with polished seams.
- U.S. automobile company General Motors reports a net income of $656,434,232 for the previous year.

AUGUST
- U.S. president Harry S. Truman orders the railroads to be seized to prevent a strike scheduled for August 28.

ARTS AND IDEAS

Architecture

- The Farnsworth House in Fox River, Illinois, designed by the German architect Ludwig Mies van der Rohe, is completed.
- The Olivetti Building in Ivrea, Italy, designed by the Italian architects Luigi Figini and Gino Pollini, is completed.

Arts

- Austrian-born English art historian E. H. Gombrich publishes *The Story of Art*, which becomes an unexpected best seller.
- The U.S. photographer Ansel Adams publishes his photography album *Portfolio Two: The National Parks*.
- The Canadian artist Armand Flint paints *The Queen and Sherbourne*.
- The Danish artist Asger Jorn paints *Entry of Churchill into Copenhagen*.
- The French art critic Michel Tapié coins the term Art Informel ("informal art") to denote the European

expressionist style running parallel with abstract expressionism in the United States.
- The French artist Germaine Richier sculpts *Christ* for the church at Assy, France. An outcry over the figure's stark and agonized appearance forces it to be removed.
- The French artist Jean Dubuffet paints *Sang et Feu (Corps de Dames)/Blood and Fire (Women's Bodies)*.
- The German-born U.S. artist Hans Hofmann paints *Magenta and Blue*.
- The Italian artist Emilio Vedova paints *Concentration Camp*.
- The Russian-born artist Serge Poliakoff paints *Abstract Composition*, one of a series of abstract works begun in the late 1930s.
- The Spanish artist Pablo Picasso sculpts *The She-Goat*.
- The Swiss artist Alberto Giacometti sculpts *Tall Forest*.
- The U.S. artist Clyfford Still paints *1950-A, No. 2*.
- The U.S. artist David Smith sculpts *Blackburn, Song on an Irish Blacksmith*.
- The U.S. artist Franz Kline paints *Chief*.
- The U.S. artist Jackson Pollock paints *Autumn Rhythm: No. 30*.
- The U.S. artist Mark Rothko paints *Number One*.
- U.S. photographer Ansel Adams takes *White Branches, Lake Mono, California*.

Film

- The 1949 Academy Awards take place. Best Actor: Broderick Crawford, for *All the King's Men*; Best Supporting Actor: Dean Jagger, for *Twelve O'Clock High*; Best Actress: Olivia de Havilland, for *The Heiress*; Best Supporting Actress: Mercedes McCambridge, for *All the King's Men*; Best Picture: *All the King's Men*, directed by Robert Rossen; Best Director: Joseph L. Mankiewicz, for *A Letter to Three Wives*.
- The movie *All About Eve*, directed by Joseph L. Mankiewicz, is released in the United States, starring Bette Davis, George Sanders, Anne Baxter, and Celeste Holm.
- The movie *Father of the Bride*, directed by Vincente Minelli, is released in the United States, starring Spencer Tracy, Joan Bennett, and Elizabeth Taylor.
- The movie *Harvey*, directed by Henry Koster, is released in the United States, starring James Stewart.
- The movie *In a Lonely Place*, directed by Nicholas Ray, is released in the United States, starring Humphrey Bogart, Gloria Grahame, and Frank Lovejoy.
- The movie *La Beauté du diable/Beauty and the Devil*, directed by René Clair, is released in France, starring Michel Simon, Gérard Philipe, and Raymond Cordy.
- The movie *La Ronde*, directed by Max Ophuls, is released in France, starring Anton Walbrook, Simone Simon, and Simone Signoret.
- The movie *Le Journal d'un curé de campagne/Diary of a Country Priest*, directed by Robert Bresson, is released in France. Based on the novel by Georges Bernanos, it stars Claude Laydu and Jean Riveyre.
- The movie *Los Olvidados/The Young and the Damned*, directed by Spanish filmmaker Luis Buñuel, is released in Mexico, starring Alfonso Mejia, Miguel Inclán, Estela Inda, and Roberto Cobo.

- The movie *Miss Julie*, directed by Alf Sjöberg, is released in Sweden, starring Anita Björk and Ulf Palme.
- The movie *Orphée/Orpheus*, directed by Jean Cocteau, is released in France, starring Jean Marais, François Perier, and Maria Casarès.
- The movie *Rio Grande*, directed by John Ford, is released in the United States, starring John Wayne, Maureen O'Hara, and Ben Johnson.
- The movie *Sommarlek/Summer Interlude*, directed by Ingmar Bergman, is released in Sweden, starring Maj-Britt Nilsson, Birger Malmsten, and Alf Kjellin.
- The movie *Stromboli*, directed by Roberto Rossellini, is released in Italy, starring Ingrid Bergman and Mario Vitale.
- The movie *Sunset Boulevard*, directed by Billy Wilder, is released in the United States, starring Gloria Swanson, Wiliam Holden, and Erich von Stroheim.
- The movie *The Asphalt Jungle*, directed by John Huston, is released in the United States, starring Sterling Hayden, Louis Calhern, and Sam Jaffe.
- The movie *The Blue Lamp*, directed by Basil Dearden, is released in the UK, starring Dirk Bogarde and Jack Warner.
- The movie *The Winslow Boy*, directed by Anthony Asquith, is released in the UK, starring Robert Donat, Cedric Hardwicke, Margaret Leighton, and Frank Lawton.
- The movie *The Wooden Horse*, directed by Jack Lee, is released in the UK. Based on the novel *The Tunnel Escape* by Eric Williams, it stars Leo Genn, David Tomlinson, and Anthony Steel.
- The movie musical *Annie Get Your Gun*, directed by George Sidney, is released in the United States. It features music and lyrics by Irving Berlin, and stars Betty Hutton, Howard Keel, and Edward Arnold.
- The intricately structured movie *Rashomon*, directed by Akira Kurosawa, is released in Japan, starring Toshiro Mifune, Machiko Kyo, and Masayuki Mori. It wins the Grand Prix at the Venice International Film Festival the following year, helping to create a market for Japanese movies in the West.
- The United States has some 16,000 of the world's estimated 70,000 movie theaters. The U.S. figure includes more than 4,000 drive-ins.
- There is no Cannes Film Festival this year as the festival moves from September to the spring.

Literature and Language

- *Boswell's London Journal, 1762–3* is published, edited by the English scholar F. A. Pottle.
- *Geiriadur Prifysgol Cymru/A Dictionary of the Welsh Language* is published.
- The best-selling cookbook in the United States is *Betty Crocker's Picture Cookbook*.
- The Chilean writer Pablo Neruda publishes his *Canto General/General Song*, a series of poems that give an epic account of the history of South America.
- The English classical scholar Maurice Bowra publishes his critical work *The Romantic Imagination*.
- The English historian Cecil Woodham-Smith publishes *Florence Nightingale*.

- The English scholar E. V. Rieu publishes his translation of Homer's *The Iliad*.
- The English writer Angus Wilson publishes *Such Darling Dodos*, a collection of short stories.
- The English writer C. P. Snow publishes his novel *The Masters*.
- The English writer C. S. Lewis publishes his novel *The Lion, the Witch and the Wardrobe*, the first volume of *The Chronicles of Narnia*.
- The English writer Doris Lessing publishes her novel *The Grass is Singing*.
- The English writer Henry Green publishes his novel *Nothing*.
- The English writer Mervyn Peake publishes his fantasy novel *Gormenghast*.
- The English writer Nevil Shute publishes his novel *A Town Like Alice*.
- The English writer W. H. Auden publishes his *Collected Shorter Poems*.
- The French writer Julien Green publishes his novel *Moira*.
- The French writer Marguerite Duras publishes her novel *Un Barrage contre le Pacifique/The Sea of Troubles*.
- The Greco-Armenian mystic G. I. Gurdjieff publishes *Beelzebub's Tales to his Grandson*.
- The Indian poet and mystic Sri Aurobindo publishes *Savitri: A Legend and a Symbol*, the longest verse epic in English.
- The Italian writer Cesare Pavese publishes his novel *La luna e ifalò/The Moon and Bonfire*.
- The Nobel Prize for Literature is awarded to the English philosopher Bertrand Russell.
- The Polish-born U.S. writer Isaac Bashevis Singer publishes his novel *The Family Moskat*.
- The Pulitzer Prize for Biography is awarded to Samuel Flagg Bemis for *John Quincy Adams and the Foundations of American Foreign Policy*, the Pulitzer Prize for Poetry is awarded to Gwendolyn Brooks for *Annie Allen*, and the Pulitzer Prize for Fiction is awarded to A. B. Guthrie, Jr., for *The Way West*.
- The Swedish writer Stig Dagerman publishes *Nattenslekar/The Games of Night*, a collection of short stories.
- The U.S. novelist Henry Morton Robinson's *The Cardinal* is the best-selling novel in the United States.
- The U.S. scientist Norbert Wiener, a leading figure in the development of cybernetics (robot systems) publishes *The Human Uses of Human Beings*, a warning against the dangers of modern science.
- The U.S. writer Carl Sandburg publishes his *Collected Poems*.
- The U.S. writer Ernest Hemingway publishes his novel *Across the River and into the Trees*.
- The U.S. writer Ezra Pound publishes his *Letters, 1907–41*.
- The U.S. writer J. D. Salinger publishes his short story "For Esme—With Love and Squalor" in the *New Yorker* magazine.
- The U.S. writer Ray Bradbury publishes his science-fiction novel *The Martian Chronicles*.

Music

- The English composer Lennox Berkeley completes his *Sinfonietta*.
- The German composer Paul Hindemith writes *A Composer's World: Horizons and Limitations*, based on a series of lectures he gave at Harvard University, Cambridge, Massachusetts.
- The Mexican composer Carlos Chávez completes his Violin Concerto.
- The Mexican composer Julián Carrillo completes his orchestral work *Horizontes*.
- The opera *Job* by the Italian composer Luigi Dallapiccola is first performed, in Rome, Italy.
- The opera *Wat Tyler* by the English composer Alan Bush is first performed, in Leipzig, Germany.
- The U.S. composer John Cage completes his vocal work *The Wonderful Widow of Eighteen Springs*; and *In the Name of the Holocaust* for "prepared piano" (that is, a piano that has had various objects placed on its wires).
- The U.S. singer Fats Domino records the song "The Fat Man".

APRIL

4   Dresden's Mozart Girls Choir seeks protection as political refugees in West Berlin, Germany.

AUGUST

19–November 11   The U.S. folk group Weavers releases the single "Goodnight Irene," a song by black American folk singer Leadbelly. It remains at number one on Billboard's weekly hit list for 12 weeks.

Theater and Dance

- The musical *Call Me Madam*, by the Russian-born U.S. songwriter Irving Berlin, is first performed, at the Imperial Theater in New York, New York.
- The musical *Guys and Dolls*, by Frank Loesser and Abe Burrows, is first performed, in New York, New York. It is taken from the collection of stories by the U.S. writer Damon Runyon.
- The play *Bell, Book and Candle*, by the U.S. writer John Van Druten, is first performed, in New York, New York.
- The play *La Cantatrice chauve/The Bald Soprano*, by the Romanian-born French writer Eugène Ionesco, is first performed, in Paris, France.
- The play *Les Justes/The Just Assassins*, by the Algerian-born French writer Albert Camus, is first performed, in Paris, France.
- The Pulitzer Prize for Drama is awarded to Richard Rodgers, Oscar Hammerstein, and Joshua Logan for the musical *South Pacific*.
- The verse play *Venus Observed*, by the English writer Christopher Fry, is first performed, at the St. James's Theatre in London, England.

Thought and Scholarship

- Austrian-U.S. psychologist Bruno Bettelheim's book *Love is not Enough* outlines his work with severely disturbed children; his methods are later applied in the study of normal children.
- English historian A. L. Rowse publishes *The England of Elizabeth*.
- English historian E. H. Carr publishes the first volume of his 14-volume *History of Soviet Russia*. The last volume will be published in 1978.
- English historian Richard Morris Titmuss publishes *Problems of Social Policy*.
- English historian Stanley Thomas Bindoff publishes *Tudor England*.
- English philosopher Stephen Toulmin publishes *An Examination of the Place of Reason in Ethics*.
- German-born U.S. logician Rudolf Carnap publishes *Logical Foundations of Probability*.
- The English statesman Richard Crossman edits *The God That Failed: Six Studies in Communism*. The contributors are Louis Fischer, André Gide, Arthur Koestler, Ignazio Silone, Stephen Spender, and Richard Wright.
- The English theologian Ronald A. Knox publishes *Enthusiasm*.
- The Pulitzer Prize for History is awarded to Oliver W. Larkin for *Art and Life in America*.
- U.S. historian Henry Steele Commager publishes *The American Mind: An Interpretation of American Thought and Character since the 1880s*.
- U.S. sociologists David Riesman, Jr., Reuel Denney, and Nathan Glazer publish *The Lonely Crowd*. This analysis of the changing character of U.S. society becomes an important part of the intellectual debate of the 1950s and 1960s.

SOCIETY

Everyday Life

- 11 million books are published in the United States.
- 2% of 40,000 Japanese college students are women.
- A special tax and coloring restrictions on margarine are lifted at federal level in the United States.
- Club Med opens its first holiday village. Set up in Majorca, Spain, it consists of tents supplied from U.S. army surplus and caters mainly for water-polo players.
- General Food introduces Minute Rice.
- Illiteracy in the United States sinks to 3.2%, down from 4.2% in 1940.
- In the United States, the annual divorce rate is 385,000; in Great Britain, it stands at 32,516.
- In the United States, the lowest fifth of the population earns 4.5% of all income; the second fifth, 11.9%; the third fifth, 23.4%; the fourth fifth, 23.4%; and the highest fifth, 42.8%.
- Life expectancy for men and women in India is 32 compared to 66 and 71 in the United States.
- No-smear lipstick is introduced in the United States.
- Population figures for the United Kingdom (in millions): England 41.1; Wales 2.5; Scotland 5.2; Ireland/Northern Ireland 1.4.
- Selected population figures for cities (in millions): London, England 8.3; New York, New York 7.8; Tokyo, Japan 5.3; Moscow, Russia 4.1; Chicago, Illinois

3.6; Shanghai, China 3.6; Calcutta, India 3.5; Berlin, Germany 3.3.

- Smokey the Bear survives a forest fire in the United States to become an emblem of National Park fire safety.
- The 1,772 daily newspapers in the United States (1,450 evening newspapers and 322 morning papers) have a circulation of 53.8 million; 46 million homes receive the 466 newspapers printed on Sunday.
- The average family income in the United States is $3,319; $3,455 for whites and $1,869 for blacks and other minorities.
- The average weekly industrial wage in the United States rises to $60.53.
- The mambo, a Cuban dance, becomes a craze in the United States.
- The population of the world is estimated at 2,516 million.
- The U.S. Census lists the population at 150,697,361, and the center of the nation's population moves westward into Illinois.
- There are 27.8 million Catholics, 8.9 million Methodists, 7 million Southern Baptists, 5 million Jews, 2.5 million Episcopalians, and 2.4 million Presbyterians in the United States.
- There are 43 million telephones in the United States and 60% of homes have telephones.
- U.S. businesses spend $5.7 billion on advertising: $2.1 billion in newspapers; $605 million on radio; $515 in magazines; and $171 million on television.
- U.S. consumers spend $58 billion on food, beverages, and tobacco (30%); $24 billion on clothes (12%); $50 billion on housing and household operations (26%); $9 billion on medical care (5%); and $11 billion on recreation (6%).

August 1950–59   The number of people in the United States who live in the suburbs increases by 44% in the 1950s.

FEBRUARY

18   In the United States, telephone direct-dialing becomes possible between New York and New Jersey.

MARCH

1   The rationing of all foods except sugar ends in West Germany.

23   The U.S. Labor Department announces that in the past decade wages have risen 130% but buying power has increased only 35%.

APRIL

11–16   Dock workers go on strike in London, England.

MAY

23   The Treaty of Detroit is signed in the United States as a five-year agreement between General Motors and the United Auto Workers to deliver high wages and industrial harmony.

NOVEMBER

13–16   In Bermuda, the United States wins the inaugural World Bridge Championship.

Media and Communication

- A new European Broadcasting Union is formed, representing mainly countries in Western Europe.

- Americans read 6,960 different magazines and journals.
- Millionaire U.S. industrialist, aviator, and movie producer Howard Hughes becomes a recluse.
- New television programs in the United States include *Your Show of Shows* with Sid Caesar and *What's My Line?*

FEBRUARY

23   For the first time, British election returns are televised.

OCTOBER

2   In the United States, Charles Schulz's comic strip *Peanuts*, starring Charlie Brown, Snoopy, and friends, appears in newspapers for the first time.

3–September 22, 1953   The dramatic series *Beulah* appears on U.S. television. It is the first dramatic series on U.S. television to star an African American: Ethel Waters appears as the title character until April 1952 when she is replaced by Louise Beavers. Other stars include William Post, Jr., David Bruce, Dooley Wilson, and Butterfly McQueen.

11   The Federal Communications Commission gives the Columbia Broadcasting System (CBS) the license to broadcast in color.

28–September 10, 1964   *The Jack Benny Program* appears on U.S. television. Benny, who has been popular on radio, relies on his character as a violin-playing skinflint and a fine supporting cast (including Eddie Anderson, Don Wilson, Dennis Day, Mel Blanc, Mary Livingstone, and Frank Nelson) to create a program that blends elements of variety and situation comedy.

Religion

- Pope Pius XII issues the encyclical *Humani Generis*, which argues against existentialism and "erroneous" scientific theories.
- The *Journal of Ecclesiastical History* is first issued.
- The Chinese book *I Ching*, one of the classics of Confucianism, is published in a translation by Richard Wilhelm.
- The Macedonian Orthodox Church is separated from the Serbian patriarchate in Yugoslavia.
- The National Council of Churches of Christ is established in the United States.
- The U.S. Scientologist L. Ron Hubbard publishes *Dianetics: The Modern Science of Mental Health*.

NOVEMBER

1   In *Munificentissimus Deus/Most Munificent God*, Pope Pius XII promulgates the dogma of the bodily Assumption of the Virgin Mary.

Sports

- Argentina wins the first world men's basketball championship, in Buenos Aires.
- In baseball, Connie Mack retires after 50 years as manager of the Philadelphia A's.
- Oklahoma, coached by Bud Wilkinson, wins the college football national championship with a record of ten wins and no losses.
- South African golfer Bobby Locke wins the British Open for the second successive year.
- The first cyclo-cross world championship title is won by French rider Jean Robic.

JANUARY

20 Unlimited free substitution, adopted in 1943, but withdrawn three years later, is restored, paving the way for the modern system of specialization in offense and defense in pro football.

FEBRUARY

8 Sportswriters in the United States name Man O' War, who won 20 of his 21 starts, as the horse of the half-century.

MARCH

3 Following the merger of the All-America Football Conference (AAFC) and the National Football League (NFL), the American and National Divisions are created to replace the NFL's Eastern and Western Divisions.

7 U.S. figure skater Dick Button of the United States wins his third consecutive world figure skating championship.

24 U.S. national figure skating champions are: Yvonne Sherman; Dick Button; Karol and Peter Kennedy, pairs; Lois Waring and Michael McGean, dance.

APRIL

8–23 In the United States, the Minneapolis Lakers defeat the Syracuse Nationals by four games to two to win the inaugural National Basketball Association (NBA) championship.

11–23 The Detroit Red Wings beat the New York Rangers four games to three, to win the National Hockey League (NHL) Stanley Cup.

MAY

12 The American Bowling Congress, after court action, revokes its 34-year-old rule limiting participation in its annual tournament to "the white male race."

31 In Johannesburg, South Africa, U.S. boxer Manual Ortiz loses his world bantamweight title to Vic Toweel of South Africa. Ortiz had won 20 of his 21 world title fights since being crowned champion in 1942.

31 U.S. racing driver Johnny Parsons wins the Indianapolis 500 with an average speed of 200 kph/124 mph.

JUNE

• Stanley Sayres of the United States breaks Donald Campbell's 11-year-old world water speed record, setting a speed of 258.014 kph/160.330 mph in his boat Slo-Mo-Ahun IV.

2–July 16 Uruguay beats the host side Brazil 2–1 in the final of the fourth football World Cup in Rio de Janeiro, Brazil, witnessed by 199,854 spectators at the Maracana Stadium in Rio de Janeiro. England, the British representatives in the finals, lose 1–0 to the United States in one of the biggest upsets in the history of the competition.

10 U.S. golfer Ben Hogan wins the second U.S. Open after a playoff at the Merion Cricket Club in Ardmore, Pennsylvania.

JULY

7–8 At the Wimbledon tennis championships in London, England, Budge Patty of the United States wins the men's title and Louise Brough of the United States wins the women's singles and doubles, and the mixed doubles for the second consecutive year.

13–August 7 In cycling, Ferdi Kübler becomes the first Swiss rider to win the Tour de France.

AUGUST

• In the United States, the National Hot Rod Association (NHRA) is founded to govern the growing sport of drag racing.

20–22 The record times for swimming the English Channel are broken. Florence Chadwick of the United States

BIRTHS & DEATHS

JANUARY

9 Alec Jeffreys, British biochemist working with DNA who discovered "genetic fingerprinting," born in Oxford, England.

21 George Orwell, English novelist who wrote *Animal Farm* and *Nineteen Eighty-Four*, dies in London, England (46).

FEBRUARY

1 Karl Jansky, U.S. engineer, inaugurator of the science of radio astronomy, dies in Red Bank, New Jersey (44).

10 Marcel Mauss, French anthropologist who examined the relationship between social structure and forms of exchange, dies in Paris, France (77).

10 Mark Spitz, U.S. swimmer who won a record seven gold medals at the 1972 Olympics, born in Modesto, California.

MARCH

1 Edgar Rice Burroughs, U.S. novelist, creator of Tarzan, dies in Encino, California (74).

1 Heinrich Mann, German novelist and essayist, dies in Santa Monica, California (78).

5 Eugene Fodor, U.S. violinist, born in Denver, Colorado.

30 Léon Blum, French politician, first socialist president of France 1936–37, dies in Jouy-en-Josas, France (77).

APRIL

3 Kurt Weill, German composer of popular satirical opera, dies in New York, New York (50).

8 Vaslav Nijinsky, Russian-born ballet dancer and choreographer, dies in London, England (60).

28 Jay Leno, U.S. comedian and host of the *Tonight Show*, born in New Rochelle, New York.

JULY

2 William Mackenzie King, Canadian statesman, Labor prime minister 1921–26, 1926–30, and 1935–48, dies in Kingsmere, Quebec, Canada (75).

SEPTEMBER

1 Jan Christian Smuts, South African soldier and statesman, prime minister 1919–24 and 1939–48, dies in Irene, near Pretoria, South Africa (80).

OCTOBER

2 Al Jolson (adopted name of Asa Yoelson), U.S. popular singer and comedian, star of *The Jazz Singer* (1927), the first feature film with synchronized speech and music, dies in San Francisco, California (64).

31 John (Franklin) Candy, Canadian comedian, born in Newmarket, Ontario, Canada (–1994).

NOVEMBER

2 George Bernard Shaw, Irish dramatist, literary critic, and socialist propagandist, dies in Ayot St. Lawrence, Hertfordshire, England (94).

swims across in 13 hours and 20 minutes, breaking Trudy Ederle's 1926 record by over an hour (August 20). Then Hassan Abd el-Rehim of Egypt makes the crossing in 10 hours 50 minutes, 15 minutes inside the 1926 record of Georges Michel.

SEPTEMBER

5   In tennis, Louise Brough and Margaret du Pont win their ninth successive women's doubles title in the U.S. championships, and du Pont wins her third successive singles title. Arthur Larsen wins the men's singles title.

27 In the United States, Joe Louis fails in his attempt to regain the world heavyweight boxing title that he relinquished on his retirement in 1949, when he loses on

points to defending champion Ezzard Charles in New York, New York.

OCTOBER

4–7 The New York Yankees defeat the Philadelphia Phillies 4–0 in the World Series.

DECEMBER

24 The Cleveland Browns defeat the Los Angeles Rams 30–28 in the National Football League (NFL) championship game in Cleveland, Ohio.

1951

POLITICS, GOVERNMENT, AND ECONOMICS

Business and Economics

JANUARY
* The U.S. Federal Reserve Board raises the margin requirement for stock purchases from 50% to 70%.

MAY
15 AT&T announces that it is the first corporation to have more than 1 million stockholders.

AUGUST
18 A U.S. Commerce Department survey states that the average salary is $1,436, an increase of $116 from the previous year.

OCTOBER
10 The Bell Telephone Company of New Jersey introduces the first U.S. transcontinental telephone service, between Englewood, New Jersey and Alameda, California.

Human Rights

* Wisconsin senator Joseph McCarthy accuses former secretary of state George C. Marshall of being a communist agent, as part of McCarthy's continuing campaign, begun the previous year, to show that the country is under the threat of foreign subversion. McCarthy has yet to show any evidence, but despite this, and attacks on him by other senators and congressmen, he pursues the campaign.

DECEMBER
* Harry T. Moore, the state secretary of the National Association for the Advancement of Colored People (NAACP), and his wife Harriet are murdered when a bomb rips through their house in the town of Mims, Florida. No arrests are made.

Politics and Government

* The United Nations Secretariat Building in New York, New York, designed by U.S. architect Wallace Harrison and others, is completed.

JANUARY
* The U.S. National Production Authority announces a 30-day moratorium on commercial construction, effective February 15. It is designed to conserve resources necessary for defense contracting required by the Korean War.
1   In the Korean War, North Korean and Chinese forces break United Nations (UN) lines on the 38th parallel and, on January 4, take Seoul, capital of South Korea.
25–February 10 In the Korean War, United Nations (UN) forces under General Matthew Ridgway launch a counteroffensive against the Chinese and North Korean troops.
28 Shah Mohammed Reza Pahlavi of Iran orders his land to be sold to the peasantry.

FEBRUARY
* The 22nd Amendment limits U.S. presidents to two terms in office. If a vice president succeeds to office and serves more than half his predecessor's term, the vice president may only serve one additional term.
February–April U.S. labor representatives withdraw from government agencies to protest against the Truman administration's mobilization program for the Korean

War. On April 17 labor is granted representation on the National Advisory Board on Mobilization Policy; labor's boycott of defense agencies ends two weeks later.

15 A conference opens in Paris, France, to discuss the formation of the proposed European Defense Community and Army (along the lines of the Pleven Plan of 1950).

19 Dr. Muhammad Mossadegh, chairman of the oil commission of the Iranian Majlis (parliament), proposes that the (British owned) oil industry in Iran should be nationalized.

21 A communist-sponsored World Peace Council opens in East Berlin, Germany.

28 René Pleven's French coalition government falls over the issue of electoral reform.

MARCH

2 Reports emerge that the Czechoslovak Communist Party is undergoing an internal purge.

5–June 21 The deputy foreign ministers of Britain, France, the United States, and the USSR meet in Paris, France, to prepare an agenda for a future conference, but disagreement over disarmament hampers progress.

7 General Ali Razmara, prime minister of Iran, is assassinated by a militant nationalist.

7–31 In the Korean War, United Nations (UN) forces move northward to the 38th parallel, recapturing the South Korean capital of Seoul March 14: the UN commander General Douglas MacArthur advocates extending the war into China, using atomic bombs.

10 Henri Queuille forms a ministry in France, ending a cabinet crisis.

20 An oil nationalization bill in Iran becomes law, leading to a dispute with Britain. Under the 1933 Oil Convention, the concession to the Anglo-Iranian Oil Company should not be altered unilaterally and disputes should be referred to arbitration.

29 The Chinese government rejects the United Nations (UN) commander Douglas MacArthur's offer of truce discussions in the Korean War. On March 31 India urges the signing of a truce, followed by Britain on April 2.

30–April 5 A federal judge in New York, New York, finds Ethel and Julius Rosenberg guilty of passing atomic weapons secrets to the Soviets; the Rosenbergs are sentenced to death on April 5.

APRIL

• Before a joint session of the U.S. Congress, retired general Douglas MacArthur defends his advocacy of war with China and proclaims his military career over, declaring "Old soldiers never die, they simply fade away."

11 The U.S. president Harry S. Truman relieves General Douglas MacArthur of command of the United Nations (UN) forces in Korea, because of his public advocacy of war with China. He is succeeded by General Matthew Ridgway.

22–25 A defensive action by United Nations (UN) troops in the Korean War halts a Chinese and North Korean offensive north of the 38th parallel.

28 Following a fortnight of rioting in Abadan, Iran, the shah of Iran appoints the nationalist Dr. Muhammad Mossadegh as prime minister.

MAY

14–20 In the Korean War, Chinese armies launch an offensive along most of the front in central Korea, forcing back the United Nations (UN) forces.

JUNE

• The U.S. Congress extends the Selective Service Act to July 1, 1955. The new legislation lowers the draft age to 18.5, extends enlistment terms to two years, and inaugurates universal military training.

3 The Indian Socialist Party organizes a mammoth demonstration in Delhi, India, in protest at the government's food and housing policies.

13 Following the general election in the Republic of Ireland on May 30, the prime minister, Dr. John Costello, is not reelected by the Dáil (the lower chamber of the Irish parliament), and Éamon de Valera returns to power as head of a coalition government.

17 In elections for the French National Assembly the Gaullists win 107 seats, the communists 97, the socialists 94, the Conservatives 87, the Popular Republicans 82, and the Radical Socialists 77.

23 Soviet representative to the UN Jacob Malik calls for a cease-fire and armistice talks in the Korean War. Truce negotiations begin at Kaesong, Korea, on July 8, but break down on August 23.

JULY

• The New York State Court of Appeals upholds release time for religious studies in the state's public schools.

3 India complains to the United Nations (UN) Security Council that Pakistan has violated a cease-fire agreement in Kashmir.

5 In the dispute between Iran and Britain over oil nationalization in Iran, the International Court of Justice issues an interim order, which is rejected by Iran. On July 15 the U.S. president Harry S. Truman sends the U.S. diplomat Averell Harriman to Iran to urge a compromise settlement.

10 The commanders of the opposing sides in the Korean War reopen armistice negotiations.

20 King Abdullah of Jordan is assassinated in Jerusalem and is succeeded by his son Talal, who is proclaimed king on September 6.

AUGUST

5 A "World Youth Festival," a mammoth communist youth rally, opens in East Berlin, Germany.

5 General Matthew Ridgway, the supreme commander of the United Nations (UN) forces in Korea, breaks off armistice talks, charging communist North Korea with violating cease-fire arrangements.

7 The U.S. Congress rejects a Soviet proposal for an agreement on arms and atomic weapons, advising it to honor existing obligations first.

11 A French ministerial crisis following the elections on June 17 ends with René Pleven forming a coalition of the center parties.

SEPTEMBER

1 The United States, Australia, and New Zealand sign the Pacific Security Agreement (also known as the ANZUS Pact), in San Francisco, California, providing for mutual assistance if any signatory power is attacked.

8 Representatives of 49 powers sign a peace treaty with Japan, ending hostilities from World War II, in San

Francisco, California. The USSR and its satellites boycott the final session of the peace conference.

10 The foreign ministers of the United States, Britain, and France discuss plans to use West German troops in the army of the North Atlantic Treaty Organization (NATO).

13 Following attempts by the Arab League to tighten their economic blockade of Israel, the United Nations (UN) Conciliatory Commission begins negotiations with Israeli and Arab delegates aimed at improving relations in the Middle East. The talks break down on November 21.

OCTOBER

- President Harry S. Truman signs the Mutual Security Act of 1951. The act allocates nearly $7.5 billion in foreign aid.
- President Harry S. Truman proclaims the U.S. state of war with Germany officially over.

9   The Israeli socialist statesman David Ben-Gurion ends eight months of ministerial crisis in Israel by forming a coalition government.

12 Britain's dispute with Iran over Iranian oil nationalization is placed before the United Nations (UN) Security Council.

16 The prime minister of Pakistan Liaquat Ali Khan is assassinated by an Afghan nationalist. Civil disorder follows.

25 Negotiations for an armistice in the Korean War are renewed at Panmunjom, Korea.

27 The veteran British Conservative Party leader Winston Churchill forms a government, with Anthony Eden as foreign secretary and R. A. "Rab" Butler as chancellor of the Exchequer.

NOVEMBER

8   The U.S. secretary of state Dean Acheson presents disarmament proposals to the United Nations (UN) General Assembly, which are countered by the USSR with a rival plan.

10 France, Britain, the United States, and Turkey announce a security program for the Near East.

11 Senior military officers stage a coup in Thailand and restore the constitution of 1932. Luang Pibul Songgram remains prime minister.

14 The United States alleges that North Koreans have murdered 5,970 United Nations (UN) prisoners and about 250,000 Korean civilians during the Korean War.

16 Egypt offers to let the future of Sudan be decided by a plebiscite under United Nations (UN) supervision.

29 The Syrian army, led by the chief of staff, Adib Shishkali, mounts a coup in Syria.

DECEMBER

6   East and West Germany agree to send representatives to the United Nations (UN) to discuss the holding of free elections in Germany, but the USSR opposes the project.

13 The French National Assembly ratifies the Schuman Plan, which places the French and West German coal, iron, and steel industries under a common authority to which other European nations might accede, by 377 votes to 233.

19 The Soviet foreign minister Marshal Andrey Vyshinsky demands that the United Nations (UN) require the United States to revoke its Mutual Security Act.

20 Greece is elected to the United Nations (UN) Security Council after 19 ballots, in preference to Belarus, which had been nominated by the USSR.

24 Libya (an Italian colony 1911–42, and under British military administration since then) becomes an independent federation under King Idris I, previously emir of Cyrenaica, a region of eastern Libya. This follows a resolution of the United Nations (UN) General Assembly of November 21, 1949, that Libya should become independent, and makes Libya the first independent state to be created by the UN.

27 Talks for an armistice in the Korean War fail.

30 A public announcement is made in Paris, France, at a meeting of the foreign, finance, and defense ministers of France, Italy, Luxembourg, Belgium, the Netherlands, and West Germany, that the proposed European defense force is to be called the European Defense Community, and that it is envisioned that one day the Community will be replaced by a more powerful federal body.

SCIENCE, TECHNOLOGY, AND MEDICINE

Agriculture

- Infectious myxomatosis, which is endemic in South America, is introduced into Australia to reduce the rabbit population. Over 99% of the rabbits are eliminated.

December 1951–60 Echo sounders begin to be installed on fishing vessels to locate schools of fish.

Computing

- U.S. computer scientist Grace Hopper develops the first compiler. It translates programmers' codes into the binary machine codes used by computers.

JUNE

- U.S. engineers John Mauchly and John Eckert build UNIVAC 1 (Universal Automated Computer), the first commercially available electronic digital computer, in Philadelphia, Pennsylvania. Built for the U.S. Bureau of the Census by the Remington Rand corporation, it uses vacuum tubes, is the first to handle both numeric and alphabetical information easily, has a memory of 1.5 kilobytes, and is the first to store data on magnetic tape.

Ecology

JANUARY

18–21 Mt. Larmington erupts in New Guinea, killing 3,000 people.

JULY

2–19 Kansas and Missouri are flooded, leaving 41 dead, 200,000 homeless, and causing over $1 billion in property damage.

Exploration

SEPTEMBER

20 The U.S. Air Force makes the first successful recovery of animals from a rocket flight when a monkey and 11 mice are recovered from a flight to an altitude of 72,000 m/236,000 ft.

Health and Medicine

- South African physician Max Theiler receives the Nobel Prize for Physiology or Medicine for his development of a successful vaccine for yellow fever.

September 1951–60 Screening for cervical cancer becomes routine in the United States and Europe.

Science

- English physicist John Cockcroft and Irish physicist Ernest Walton share the Nobel Prize for Physics for their work on the transmutation of atomic nuclei by artificially accelerated atomic particles.
- Polish-born English scientist Jacob Bronowski publishes *Science and Common Sense*.
- U.S. astronomer Gerard Kuiper proposes the existence of a ring of small, icy bodies orbiting the sun beyond Pluto, thought to be the source of comets. They are discovered in the 1990s and it is named the Kuiper belt.
- U.S. biochemist Robert Woodward synthesizes cortisone.
- U.S. chemists Edwin McMillan and Glenn Seaborg receive the Nobel Prize for Chemistry for their discovery of and research on transuranic elements.
- U.S. chemists Linus Pauling and Robert Corey establish the helical or spiral structure of proteins.
- U.S. physicist Edward Purcell discovers line radiation (radiation emitted at only one specific wavelength) at 21 cm/8 in emitted by hydrogen in space. It allows the distribution of hydrogen clouds in galaxies and the speed of the Milky Way's rotation to be determined.

SEPTEMBER

14 The "close-approach" asteroid Geographos is discovered by astronomers at the Mt. Palomar Observatory in California.

Technology

- A Dutch–Norwegian joint atomic energy research establishment opens at Hjeller, near Oslo, Norway.
- The U.S. Army first tests the antiaircraft Nike-Ajax missile. It is 6 m/21 ft long and has a range of 40 km/25 mi.
- Two plutonium-production reactors, the first full-scale nuclear reactors in the UK, go into operation at Windscale (known as Sellafield from 1973) in Cumbria, England.
- U.S. researchers Fred Joyner and Harry Coover discover the adhesive power of cyanoacrylate—"superglue."

FEBRUARY

- The U.S. Langley Research Center tests a jet-thrust device attached to a person's feet.

DECEMBER

12 The first power station in the United States to produce electricity from atomic energy begins operating at Arco, Idaho. Built by the U.S. Department of Energy's Idaho National Engineering Laboratory and known as experimental breeder reactor No. 1 (EBR-I), it is built to demonstrate the feasibility of nuclear power. It generates 300 kW.

Transportation

- For the first time air passenger-miles (10,679,281,000) exceeds total passenger-miles in railroad cars (10,224,714,000) in the United States.
- U.S. automotive firm Chrysler installs the first power steering in 10,000 of its Crown Imperials.
- U.S. engineer Charles Franklin Kettering invents a revolutionary high-compression car engine.

JUNE

11 U.S. Navy pilot William Bridgeman sets the airplane speed and altitude records in a Navy D-558-II Douglas Sky-rocket, achieving a speed of over 1,920 kph/1,200 mph and an altitude estimated at 21,336 m/70,000 ft.

NOVEMBER

5 State authorities open 82 km/51 mi of the New Jersey Turnpike, a toll road that will eventually stretch 190 km/118 mi across the entire state of New Jersey, connecting to other state highways at both ends.

ARTS AND IDEAS

Architecture

- Lake Shore Drive Apartments, in Chicago, Illinois, designed by the German architect Ludwig Mies van der Rohe, are completed.

Arts

- French photographer Robert Doisneau takes *Down and Out in Paris*.
- The English artist Kenneth Armitage sculpts *People in a Wind*.
- The English artist Peter Lanyon paints *Porthleven*.
- The exhibition "L'Ecole de Paris 1900–1950" is held at the Royal Academy in London, England, presenting a survey of progressive French painting.
- The French artist Henri Matisse paints *Blue Nude I*.
- The French writer André Malraux publishes *Les Voix de silence/The Voices of Silence*, a study of art.
- The German-born English artist Lucian Freud paints *Interior Near Paddington*.
- The Italian artist Lucio Fontana creates *Neon Structure*.
- The Spanish artist Pablo Picasso paints *The Korean Massacres* and sculpts *Baboon and Baby*.
- The U.S. artist Barnett Newman paints *Vir Heroicus Sublimis/Sublime Heroic Man*.

- The U.S. artist David Smith sculpts *Hudson River Landscape*.
- The U.S. artist Jackson Pollock paints *Echo no. 25*.

Film

- A movie of Shakespeare's *Othello*, directed by Orson Welles, is released in the United States. Welles also stars in it.
- At the Cannes Film Festival in France, the Palme d'Or is awarded jointly to *Miracola a Milano/Miracle in Milan*, directed by Vittorio de Sica and *Miss Julie*, directed by Alf Sjöberg.
- The movie *A Place in the Sun*, directed by George Stevens, is released in the United States. Based on the novel *An American Tragedy* by Theodore Dreiser, it stars Montgomery Clift, Elizabeth Taylor, and Shelley Winters.
- The movie *A Streetcar Named Desire*, directed by Turkish-born filmmaker Elia Kazan, is released in the United States. Based on the play by Tennessee Williams, it stars Vivien Leigh, Marlon Brando, and Karl Malden.
- The movie *An Outcast of the Islands*, directed by Carol Reed, is released in Britain. Based on the novel by Joseph Conrad, it stars Trevor Howard, Ralph Richardson, and Kerima.
- The movie *Bedtime for Bonzo*, directed by Frederick de Cordova, is released in the United States, starring the U.S. actor Ronald Reagan (subsequently governor of California and U.S. president).
- The movie *Miracola a Milan/Miracle in Milan*, directed by Vittorio de Sica, is released in Italy, starring Francesco Golisano, Brunella Bova, Emma Gramatica, and Paolo Stoppa.
- The movie *Strangers on a Train*, directed by the English filmmaker Alfred Hitchcock, is released in the United States, starring Farley Granger, Robert Walker, and Ruth Roman.
- The movie *The African Queen*, directed by John Huston, is released in the United States. Based on the book by C. S. Forester, it stars Humphrey Bogart, Katharine Hepburn, and Robert Morley. Also Huston's movie *The Red Badge of Courage* is released in the United States. It is based on the novel by Stephen Crane and it stars Audie Murphy.
- The movie *The Day the Earth Stood Still*, directed by Robert Wise, is released in the United States, starring Michael Rennie and Patricia Neal.
- The movie *The Man in the White Suit*, directed by U.S. filmmaker Alexander Mackendrick, is released in Britain, starring Alec Guinness and Joan Greenwood.
- The movie musical *An American in Paris*, directed by Vincente Minnelli, is released in the United States. With music and lyrics by George and Ira Gershwin, it stars Gene Kelly, Leslie Caron, Oscar Levant, and Nina Foch.
- The horror movie *The Thing from Another World* (known in the United States as *The Thing*), directed by Christian Nyby, is released in the United States. Based on the short story "Who Goes There?" by John D. Campbell, it stars Kenneth Tobey, Margaret Sheridan, Robert Cornthwaite, Douglas Spencer, and James Arness.

JANUARY

1   The British Board of Film Censors introduces the "X" classification, to identify movies unsuitable for those under 16.

APRIL

16   The 1950 Academy Awards take place. Best Actor: José Ferrer, for *Cyrano de Bergerac*; Best Supporting Actor: George Sanders, for *All About Eve*; Best Actress: Judy Holliday, for *Born Yesterday*; Best Supporting Actress: Josephine Hull, for *Harvey*; Best Picture: *All About Eve*, directed by Joseph L. Mankiewicz; Best Director: Joseph L. Mankiewicz, for *All About Eve*.

Literature and Language

- The *Collected Poems* of the English writer Keith Douglas (who was killed in World War II) are published posthumously.
- The Belgian writer Marguerite Yourcenar publishes her novel *Mémoirs d'Hadrien/Memoirs of Hadrian*.
- The English writer Arthur C. Clarke publishes his short story "The Sentinel," which is filmed in 1968 as *2001: A Space Odyssey*.
- The English writer Anthony Powell publishes *A Question of Upbringing*, the first of 12 volumes in the sequence *A Dance to the Music of Time*. The final volume appears in 1975.
- The English writer C. S. Lewis publishes his novel *Prince Caspian*, the second volume of *The Chronicles of Narnia*.
- The English writer Graham Greene publishes his novel *The End of the Affair*.
- The English writer John Wyndham publishes his novel *The Day of the Triffids*.
- The English writer Nicholas Monsarrat publishes his novel *The Cruel Sea*.
- The English writer T. H. White publishes his nonfiction animal story *Goshawk*.
- The German writer Heinrich Böll publishes his novel *Wo warst du Adam?/Adam, Where Art Thou?*
- The Irish writer Samuel Beckett publishes his novels *Malone meurt/Malone Dies* and *Molloy* in French (the English versions appear in 1956 and in 1955 respectively).
- The Italian writer Alberto Moravia publishes his novel *Il conformiste/The Conformist*.
- The Japanese writer Shohei Ooka publishes his novel *Nobi/Fires on the Plain*, a Japanese account of World War II.
- The New Zealand writer Janet Frame publishes her story collection *Lagoon and Other Stories*.
- The Nobel Prize for Literature is awarded to the Swedish novelist and dramatist Pär Lagerkvist.
- The Pulitzer Prize for Biography is awarded to Margaret Louise Coit for *John C. Calhoun: American Portrait*, the Pulitzer Prize for Poetry is awarded to Carl Sandburg for *Complete Poems*, and the Pulitzer Prize for Fiction is awarded to Conrad Richter for *The Town*.
- The Russian-born U.S. writer Isaac Asimov publishes *Foundation*, the first novel in his science fiction *Foundation Trilogy*.
- The Russian-born U.S. writer Vladimir Nabokov publishes his autobiography *Speak, Memory*.

- The Spanish writer Camilo José Cela publishes his novel *La colmena/The Hive*.
- The U.S. writer Carson McCullers publishes her novella *The Ballad of the Sad Café*.
- The U.S. writer Herman Wouk publishes his novel *The Caine Mutiny*.
- The U.S. writer J. D. Salinger publishes his novel *The Catcher in the Rye*.
- The U.S. writer James Jones publishes his novel *From Here to Eternity*.
- The U.S. writer Marianne Moore publishes her *Collected Poems*.
- The U.S. writer Ray Bradbury publishes his novel *The Illustrated Man*.
- The U.S. writer Truman Capote publishes his novel *The Grass Harp*.
- The U.S. writer William Faulkner publishes his novel *Requiem for a Nun*.
- The U.S. writer William Styron publishes his novel *Lie Down in Darkness*.

Music

- More than 190 million record albums are bought in the United States.
- The British-based Mantovani Orchestra releases the instrumental single "Charmaine," arranged by Mantovani.
- The Dave Brubeck jazz quartet is founded in the United States.
- The English composer Michael Tippett completes his song cycle *The Heart's Assurance*, settings of poems by the British poets Alun Lewis and Sidney Keyes.
- The opera *Amahl and the Night Visitors* by the Italian-born U.S. composer Gian Carlo Menotti is first performed, on National Broadcasting Corporation (NBC) television in the United States.
- The opera *Billy Budd* by the English composer Benjamin Britten is first performed, at Covent Garden in London, England. It is based on a novella by the U.S. writer Herman Melville.
- The opera *The Rake's Progress* by the Russian composer Igor Stravinsky is first performed, in Venice, Italy. Inspired by engravings by the English artist William Hogarth, the text is by the English-born U.S. writer W. H. Auden.
- The Russian composer Dmitry Shostakovich completes his *Twenty-Four Preludes and Fugues* for piano (Opus 87).
- The U.S. composer Elliott Carter completes his String Quartet No. 1.
- The U.S. pop singer Johnnie Ray releases the single "Cry."
- The U.S. singer Tony Bennett releases the single "Because of You."

Theater and Dance

- The play *Graf Öderland/Count Oderland*, by the Swiss writer Max Frisch, is first performed, in Zürich, Switzerland.
- The play *I am a Camera*, dramatized by the U.S. dramatist John Van Druten from stories by the English-born U.S. writer Christopher Isherwood, is first performed, in New York, New York. It forms the basis of the musical *Cabaret* in 1966.
- The play *La Leçon/The Lesson*, by the Romanian-born French dramatist Eugène Ionesco, is first performed, in Paris, France.
- The play *Le Diable et le Bon Dieu/Lucifer and the Lord*, by the French writer and philosopher Jean-Paul Sartre, is first performed, in Paris, France.
- The play *The Autumn Garden*, by the U.S. writer Lillian Hellman, is first performed, in New York, New York.
- The play *The Love of Four Colonels*, by the Russian-born English writer and actor Peter Ustinov, is first performed, in London, England.
- The play *The Rose Tattoo*, by the U.S. dramatist Tennessee Williams, is first performed, in New York, New York.
- The Pulitzer Prize for Drama is not awarded this year.
- The verse play *A Sleep of Prisoners*, by the English dramatist Christopher Fry, is first performed, in Oxford, England.

MARCH
25 The 1950–51 Tony Awards take place. Best Actor: Claude Rains; Best Actress: Uta Hagen; Best Play: *The Rose Tattoo*; Best Musical: *Guys and Dolls*.

MAY
29 The musical *The King and I*, with lyrics by Oscar Hammerstein and music by Richard Rodgers, is first performed, at the St. James Theater, New York, New York.

NOVEMBER
12 The musical *Paint Your Wagon*, with lyrics by Alan Jay Lerner and music by Frederick Loewe, is first performed, at the Shubert Theater, New York, New York.

Thought and Scholarship

- Algerian-born writer Albert Camus publishes his philosophical study *L'Homme révolté/The Rebel*.
- Austrian-born U.S. economist Joseph Alois Schumpeter publishes *Imperialism and Social Classes*.
- English historian Stephen Runciman publishes the first part of his *History of the Crusades*. The final part appears in 1958.
- German philosopher Hans Reichenbach publishes *The Rise of Scientific Philosophy*.
- German-born U.S. philosopher Hannah Arendt publishes *The Origins of Totalitarianism*.
- Hungarian-born English philosopher Michael Polanyi publishes *The Logic of Liberty: Reflections and Rejoinders*.
- The Canadian communications theorist Marshall McLuhan publishes *The Mechanical Bride*.
- The Pulitzer Prize for History is awarded to Carlyle Buley for *The Old Northwest: Pioneer Period 1815–1840*.
- U.S. historian C. Vann Woodward publishes *The Origins of the New South, 1877–1913*.
- U.S. historian Dumas Malone publishes *Jefferson and the Rights of Man*.
- U.S. journalist William F. Buckley publishes *God and Man at Yale: The Superstition of Academic Freedom*.

- U.S. philosopher Nelson Goodman publishes *The Structure of Appearance*.
- U.S. psychologist Carl Rogers publishes *Client-Centered Therapy*.

SOCIETY

Education

AUGUST

23 Ninety cadets are expelled from the United States Military Academy at West Point, New York, for cheating on examinations.

Everyday Life

- More women are working than during World War II (when women had to take over many jobs because of men joining the army) in the United States.
- The Crazy Horse Saloon strip-tease bar opens in Paris, France, the first such establishment in postwar Europe.
- There are 12,000 trade associations, representing various businesses, in the United States.
- U.S. book publishers sell 231 million paperback reprints.

MARCH

21 U.S. armed forces personnel reach a total of 2.9 million, more than double the strength of the previous year, before the outbreak of the Korean War.

APRIL

28 The U.S. Office of Price Stabilization sets a price ceiling on beef.

DECEMBER

16 A study finds that on an average weekend 1.2 million bagels are consumed in New York, New York.

Media and Communication

- The first issue of the journal *History Today* is published in the UK.
- The radio series *Amos 'n' Andy* is adapted for television in the United States, starring black American actors Alvin Childress and Spencer William, Jr.

December 1951–52 *Joyce Jordan, MD*, a weekly program about a woman doctor, runs for one season on ABC radio.

December 1951–57 *Superman*, a U.S. children's television series based on the D.C. Comics character about the double life of Clark Kent, a mild-mannered newspaper reporter and superhero, begins, starring George Reeves, Phyllis Coates (later Noel Neil), Jack Larson, and John Hamilton.

JANUARY

23 The 1950–51 Emmy Awards for television are held. Best Dramatic Show: *Pulitzer Prize Playhouse*; Best Variety Show: *The Alan Young Show*; Best Actor: Alan Young; Best Actress: Gertrude Berg.

JUNE

23 A study in the United States reports that there are 107 television stations operating in 63 cities reaching 62% of the U.S. population.

25 The U.S. communications company Columbia Broadcasting System (CBS) begins experimental broadcasts of color television along the northeastern seaboard of the United States, even though the U.S. public owns no color television sets. They are abandoned after a few months for lack of interest and because black-and-white sets cannot receive the signals. The technology has taken CBS 11 years and $5 million to create.

SEPTEMBER

September 1951–September 1986 *Search for Tomorrow*, a long-running daytime serial drama, appears on U.S. television.

4 Ninety-four U.S. television stations carry the nation's first transcontinental TV broadcast using a new coaxial cable, President Harry S. Truman's address to delegates of the Japanese Peace Treaty Conference in San Francisco, California.

30–August 29, 1971 *The Red Skelton Show* appears on U.S. television, featuring sketch comedy based on Skelton's characters such as Freddie the Freeloader, Clem Kadiddlehopper, Sheriff Deadeye, Cauliflower McPugg, and San Fernando Red.

OCTOBER

5–June 30, 1954 *Mark Saber Mystery Theater* (also titled *Inspector Mark Saber and Homicide Squad*) appears on U.S. television, a crime series featuring a British police inspector working in the United States.

15–June 24, 1957 *I Love Lucy*, U.S. television's first smash hit situation comedy, is shown, starring Lucille Ball, Desi Arnaz, Vivian Vance, and William Frawley.

NOVEMBER

2 "Dennis the Menace," a cartoon created by Henry King "Hank" Ketchum, makes its first appearance in U.S. newspapers.

Sports

- The first world parachuting championships take place at Lesce-Bled in Yugoslavia (now in Slovenia).
- The inaugural American Bowling Congress Masters Bowling Tournament is won by Lee Jouglard of Detroit, at St. Paul, Minnesota.
- The International Amateur Athletic Federation establishes a series of area championships: the Asian Games, first held in New Delhi, India; the Pan-American Games, first held in Buenos Aires, Argentina; and the Mediterranean Games, first held in Alexandria, Egypt.

MARCH

27 The University of Kentucky, coached by Adolph Rupp, wins the National Collegiate Athletic Association (NCAA) basketball championship.

MAY

24 The Oxford and Cambridge University Boat Race on the River Thames, England, is postponed after the Oxford boat sinks; Cambridge wins by 12 lengths when the race is rerun two days later.

JULY

10 In one of the greatest upsets in boxing history, Randolph Turpin of Great Britain outpoints the defending champion, Sugar Ray Robinson of the United States, to win the world middleweight boxing title at Earl's Court, London, England.

14 The U.S. thoroughbred Citation, ridden by U.S. jockey Steve Brooks, wins the Hollywood Gold Cup at Inglewood, California, to become the first horse to earn $1 million in prize money.

18 The U.S. boxer Jersey Joe Walcott knocks out the defending champion, fellow U.S. boxer Ezzard Charles, in the seventh round to win the world heavyweight boxing title fight in Pittsburgh, Pennsylvania, United States.

SEPTEMBER

12 Sugar Ray Robinson of the United States regains the world middleweight boxing title from Randolph Turpin of Great Britain at the Polo Grounds in New York, New York, which Turpin won just 64 days earlier in one of the greatest upsets in boxing history.

28 The U.S. footballer Norm van Brocklin passes a record 506.5 m/554 yds for the Los Angeles Rams against the New York Yankees in a National Football League (NFL) match.

OCTOBER

4–10 The New York Yankees defeat the New York Giants by four games to two in the World Series.

DECEMBER

23 The Los Angeles Rams defeat the Cleveland Browns 24–17 in the National Football League (NFL) Championship Game, which is televised coast to coast for the first time.

BIRTHS & DEATHS

- Bertie Ahern, Irish prime minister, born in Dublin, Ireland.

JANUARY

10 Sinclair Lewis, U.S. novelist and social critic, dies near Rome, Italy (65).

27 Carl Mannerheim, Finnish military leader who defended Finland from the Soviet Union during World War II and who was the country's first president 1944–46, dies in Lausanne, Switzerland (83).

30 Ferdinand Porsche, Austrian automotive engineer who designed the Volkswagen car, dies in Stuttgart, West Germany (75).

FEBRUARY

19 André Gide, French writer and humanist, dies in Paris, France (81).

APRIL

23 Charles Dawes, U.S. vice president 1925–29 who developed the "Dawes Plan" for organizing Germany's war reparations after World War I, dies in Evanston, Illinois (85).

29 Ludwig Wittgenstein, Austrian-born British philosopher, one of the most influential in the 20th century, dies in Cambridge, England (62).

MAY

23 Anatoly Yevgenyevich Karpov, Soviet chess master who dominated international chess from the mid-1970s to the mid-1980s, born in Zlatoust, Russia.

29 Fanny Bryce, U.S. comedienne, dies in Los Angeles, California (59).

JULY

13 Arnold Schoenberg, Austrian composer who developed a new "atonal" method of musical composition, dies in Los Angeles, California (76).

23 Henri Philippe Pétain, French general during World War I, dies in prison in Île d'Yeu, France (95).

AUGUST

14 William Randolph Hearst, U.S. newspaper publisher, dies in Beverley Hills, California (88).

SEPTEMBER

1 Nicu Ceauşescu, son of Romanian dictator Nicolae Ceauşescu, noted for his sadistic practices and his excesses of alcohol, drugs, and sex, born in Romania (–1996).

OCTOBER

6 W(ill) K(eith) Kellogg, U.S. industrialist who founded the W. K. Kellogg Company to manufacture breakfast cereals, dies in Battle Creek, Michigan (91).

DECEMBER

31 Maksim Maksimovich Litvinov, Soviet diplomat, dies in Moscow, USSR (75).

1952

POLITICS, GOVERNMENT, AND ECONOMICS

Business and Economics

- General Dynamics incorporates in New York, New York. It then merges with its parent company, Electric Boat Company, established in 1899.
- The U.S. builder Kemmons Wilson opens his first motel, the first Holiday Inn, in Memphis, Tennessee. A partnership with Wallace E. Johnson formed in 1953 will result in the development of the Holiday Inn chain.

Colonization

JANUARY

14 The French protectorate of Tunisia appeals, unsuccessfully, to the United Nations (UN) Security Council for permission to state its case for autonomy.

Human Rights

- U.S. civil-rights activist Malcolm X joins the Nation of Islam, after serving six years in prison.

MARCH

3 The Florida Supreme Court upholds the Miami Springs Country Club's rule that allows black Americans to play golf on Mondays only.

Politics and Government

- The West German *Länder* (states) of Baden, Württemberg-Baden, and Württemberg-Hohenzollern are merged to form Baden-Württemberg.

JANUARY

7 René Pleven's ministry in France falls after plans to reorganize nationalized industries and social services are defeated. On January 22 the Radical Edgar Faure forms a coalition government.
11 The United Nations (UN) establishes a disarmament commission.
15 The United States, Britain, and France submit a draft treaty to the USSR, proposing that Austria (occupied by the Allies since 1945) should become an independent democratic state with the frontiers of January 1, 1938, but the USSR rejects the treaty in August.
18–27 Anti-British riots take place in Egypt, which end with King Farouk's dismissal of the prime minister Mustafa an-Nahas Pasha and the appointment of the nationalist Ali Maher Pasha in his place.
24 Vincent Massey becomes the first Canadian to be appointed governor-general of Canada, a post previously always filled by a Briton.
26 Representatives of France, Italy, Luxembourg, Belgium, Netherlands, and West Germany, meeting in Paris, France, agree the outlines of an army to be established under the proposed European Defense Community.

FEBRUARY

6 King George VI of Great Britain and Northern Ireland dies, and is succeeded by his daughter Queen Elizabeth II, who is on a visit to Kenya at the time (proclaimed on February 8).
20–25 A North Atlantic Treaty Organization (NATO) Council, meeting in Lisbon, Portugal, approves the establishment of the proposed European Defense Community; members agree to provide 50 divisions for NATO service by December.
26 The British prime minister Winston Churchill announces that Britain has produced its own atomic bomb. The first successful test of the new weapon takes place on October 2 over the Monte Bello Islands in the Pacific Ocean.
29 Edgar Faure's ministry in France resigns after failing to obtain the National Assembly's assent to tax increases; on March 11 the Conservative Antoine Pinay forms a cabinet with some Gaullist support.

MARCH

- The U.S. Supreme Court rules that public schools may exclude teachers thought to be subversive.
1 Ali Maher Pasha resigns as prime minister of Egypt against a background of difficulties in Egypt's relations with Britain, and is succeeded by Ahmed Nagib al Hilaly.
1 In India's first national elections Pandit Nehru's Congress Party wins 364 of 489 seats in the National Assembly.
4 The Chinese communist government accuses U.S. forces in Korea of using germ warfare.
10 Fulgencio Batista (in exile since 1944) overthrows the Cuban government of President Prio Socarras.
10 The USSR proposes a four-power conference on the unification and rearmament of Germany. The Western powers reply, on March 23, that free elections would be a prerequisite, that Germany should not be empowered to rearm, and that its boundaries, as settled by the Potsdam Conference of 1945, would be subject to revision.

20 The Supreme Court of South Africa holds that the apartheid legislation of Daniel Malan's government, which is designed to enforce racial segregation, is unconstitutional.

21 The prime minister of Ceylon (now Sri Lanka), Don Stephen Senanayake, is thrown from his horse and, on March 22, dies. He is succeeded on March 26 by his son Dudley Senanayake.

30 Anti-French riots take place in Tangier, French Morocco.

APRIL

10 The USSR proposes that all-German elections be held under a four-power commission, instead of under United Nations (UN) supervision, and rejects the West's demands that Germany's frontiers should be revised.

22 The South African prime minister Daniel Malan introduces a bill to make the South African parliament a high court, in order to prevent the supreme court from invalidating apartheid legislation.

28 Dwight D. Eisenhower is relieved of his post as Supreme Allied Commander in Europe of North Atlantic Treaty Organization (NATO) forces at his own request and is succeeded by General Matthew Ridgway (who is succeeded in Korea by General Mark Clark).

28 Japan signs a treaty with Nationalist China, formally ending World War II in the Pacific Ocean.

MAY

- The Truman administration announces that the U.S. possesses a 75-ton atomic cannon.

20 Serious rioting breaks out among communist prisoners of war at the Koje Island prison camp in South Korea.

27–31 The foreign ministers of France, Italy, Luxembourg, Belgium, the Netherlands, and West Germany sign a series of agreements in Paris, France, establishing a European Defense Community (EDC), with reciprocal guarantees between the North Atlantic Treaty Organization (NATO) and the EDC.

28 Communist demonstrations take place in Paris, France.

JUNE

- As the Korean War continues, the U.S. Congress extends wage and rent controls and defense industry prioritizing.

- The U.S. Congress passes the McCarran–Walter Immigration and Nationality Act over President Harry S. Truman's veto. The act ends the ban on Asian and African immigrants, while upholding the quota system of the Johnson–Reed Act (1924).

- The U.S. Supreme Court, in *Youngstown v. Sawyer*, declares President Harry S. Truman's seizure of the nation's steel industry of April to be unconstitutional.

1 The United National Party under Dudley Senanayake, acting prime minister since the death of his father Don Stephen Senanayake on March 22, wins the national elections in Ceylon (now Sri Lanka).

23 The U.S. Air Force bombs hydroelectric plants in North Korea.

JULY

- Democrats nominate Illinois governor Adlai E. Stevenson for president and Alabama senator John J. Sparkman for vice president.

- President Harry S. Truman signs a GI Bill of Rights providing benefits to veterans of the Korean War.

- Republicans nominate General Dwight D. Eisenhower for president and Senator Richard M. Nixon for vice president.

- The Truman administration lifts price controls on meats and vegetables.

1 The Schuman Plan, which creates a European Coal and Steel Community (ECSC), comes into force.

17 The Iranian prime minister, Muhammad Mossadegh, is replaced with the pro-Western Ahmad Ghavam.

22 Following riots in Tehran, Iran, the nationalist leader Dr. Muhammad Mossadegh is reappointed prime minister, and on August 11 the Iranian parliament votes to give him emergency powers for six months.

23 General Muhammad Naguib Bey overthrows King Farouk and seizes power in Egypt.

24 India makes an agreement with the head of the government of the disputed province of Kashmir, agreeing union with India but preserving Kashmir's status.

24 King Farouk of Egypt abdicates in favor of his infant son Fuad following General Muhammad Naguib Bey's coup.

AUGUST

4–September 25 A conference of the Pacific Council (Australia, New Zealand, and the United States), is held in Honolulu under the Pacific Security Treaty of September 1951.

11 The Jordanian parliament ends the reign of King Talal because of his chronic schizophrenia. His son Hussein, educated in England at Harrow and Sandhurst, is proclaimed king.

14 Mátyás Rákosi, secretary of the Hungarian Workers' Party, is appointed prime minister of Hungary following the resignation of István Dobi.

17–September 22 A large Chinese mission, led by premier Zhou Enlai, visits the USSR.

23 The Arab League Security Pact of 1950 comes into force following ratification by its member states.

SEPTEMBER

1 The Labor politician William Drees reforms his coalition in the Netherlands following a general election.

10 The first meeting of the assembly of the European Coal and Steel Community (ECSC) opens and, on September 11, elects Paul-Henri Spaak as its president.

11 The United Nations (UN) settlement devised for the former Italian colony of Eritrea (that is, a federation with Ethiopia) is ratified by Emperor Haile Selassie of Ethiopia. Eritrea is to have autonomy in domestic affairs.

18 Finland completes reparation payments due to the USSR under the Paris Treaty of 1947, ending hostilities between them.

24 A revised constitution in Romania disenfranchises all citizens except members of the Workers' Party and their associates.

30 The Council of Europe adopts the plan of the British foreign secretary Anthony Eden, that creates a framework by which the Council may incorporate the European Coal and Steel Community (ECSC) and the European Defense Community (EDC).

OCTOBER

- In the U.S. presidential campaign, Republican nominee Dwight D. Eisenhower promises to bring the Korean War to a speedy and honorable end if elected president.
1 In its first postwar elections, Japan elects a Liberal government under Shigeru Yoshida.
2 The Chinese government holds an "Asia and Pacific Peace Conference" in Beijing, China, with delegates from 37 countries.
3 The USSR demands that the United States recall George Kennan, the U.S. ambassador in Moscow, for his comments made in Germany about the "icy cold" isolation of Western diplomats in Moscow. The United States repudiates Soviet complaints, but Kennan does not resume his post.
5 The 19th Congress of the Communist Party opens in the USSR, the first congress since 1939. The next day it adopts directives for the Fifth Five-Year Plan; the plan envisions an increase in industrial production by 1955 of 70% over 1950 production and large increases in agricultural output.
13 Egypt reaches agreement with Sudan, ending their dispute over the use of the waters of the River Nile.
20 Britain proclaims a state of emergency in its colony of Kenya because of Mau Mau nationalist disturbances, and about 200 leading members of the Kenya African Union (the political party led by future president Jomo Kenyatta, the alleged leader of the Mau Mau movement) are arrested.
22 The Anglo-Egyptian Sudan becomes self-governing.

NOVEMBER

- Americans elect Dwight D. Eisenhower as president in a landslide victory. In the Congressional elections, the Republican party regains control of the House (221–211) and Senate (48–47).
- To fulfill a campaign promise, president-elect Eisenhower visits U.S. front-line positions in Korea.
10 The secretary-general of the United Nations (UN), Trygve Lie, makes a surprise announcement of his resignation, hoping, in view of Soviet opposition to his reappointment, that it will enable the five permanent members of the Security Council to cooperate.
11 Rudolf Slansky (the former secretary of the Czech Communist Party), Vladimir Clementis (the former foreign minister), and 11 others (all Jews) are tried in Czechoslovakia for "Titoism." All but three are hanged on December 2.
14 Control of the Moroccan port of Tangier is restored to Morocco following abrogation of the U.S., French, and British joint rule there, this having been established in 1945.
16 Field Marshal Alexandros Papagos forms a government in Greece following the success of his conservative Greek Rally Party in the elections.
20 Following the first general election held in Poland October 26 under the new constitution, the communist Bolesław Bierut is elected prime minister by the Sejm (the Polish assembly).

DECEMBER

3 The United Nations (UN) General Assembly adopts an Indian proposal calling for an armistice in the Korean War.
7 Anti-French riots take place in French Morocco.

8 Following the death of the president of Israel Chaim Weizmann on November 9, Itzhak Ben-Zvi takes his place.
10 General Muhammad Naguib, the revolutionary leader of Egypt, abolishes the 1923 constitution.
12 A communist world conference is held in Vienna, Austria.
15 China rejects an Indian plan for an armistice in the Korean War.
23 The French prime minister Antoine Pinay resigns following the growth of dissension within his government and opposition to his fiscal policies (by the end of the year the 1953 budget had not been voted on).

SCIENCE, TECHNOLOGY, AND MEDICINE

Agriculture

- Rabbits infected with myxomatosis are introduced into France to control the rabbit population.

Ecology

- Murchison National Park (later renamed Kabarega National Park) is established in Uganda; it contains the Murchison Falls on the Nile.
- Norwegian-U.S. meteorologist Jacob Bjerknes discovers that centers of low pressure, or cyclones, develop at the fronts that separate different air masses. It leads to improved weather forecasting. He is also the first to use photographs, taken from high-altitude rockets, as a tool in weather analysis and forecasting.
- U.S. meteorologists establish the first weather station in the Arctic, at Ice Island T-3.

DECEMBER

- Smog hits London, England: weather conditions and industrial and domestic pollution combine to produce a haze of toxic pollutants, which limit visibility to a few feet. It lasts for three weeks, and over 4,000, mostly elderly, people die from respiratory problems caused by poor air quality. The disaster leads to antipollution legislation.

Health and Medicine

- British doctor Douglas Bevis develops amniocentesis, a diagnostic test on the fetus.
- Danish surgeon K. Hamburger performs the first successful sex-change operation. George Jorgensen becomes Christine Jorgensen.
- French psychiatrist Jean Delay introduces the synthetic tranquilizer chlorpromazine as a treatment for psychosis.
- G. D. Searle laboratories in the United States make a contraceptive tablet of phosphorated hesperidin.

- More than 50,000 people are stricken by a poliomyelitis epidemic in the United States; 3,300 people die and thousands more are left disabled.
- The antimicrobial drug Isoniazid is introduced as a treatment against tuberculosis.
- U.S. physician Jonas E. Salk tests a vaccine against poliomyelitis using killed viruses.
- U.S. physician Robert Wilkins isolates the first tranquilizer, reserpine, from the roots of the tropical plant *Rauwolfa serpentia*.
- U.S. physician Virginia Apgar introduces the Apgar score for estimating the health of newborns. It takes into account pulse, respiration, muscle tone, color, and reflexes, and is quickly adopted in hospitals throughout the world.
- U.S. physiologist Selman Waksman receives the Nobel Prize for Physiology or Medicine for his discovery of streptomycin, the first antibiotic effective against tuberculosis.
- U.S. surgeon John Floyd Lewis reduces the body temperature of his heart patients to slow the heart down and reduce the need for oxygen while he operates.
- U.S. surgeon Samuel Rosen performs the first surgery on the inner ear using an operating microscope.

MARCH

8 An artificial heart keeps a patient alive for 80 minutes at the Pennsylvania Hospital, Philadelphia, United States.

DECEMBER

29 The U.S. Sonotone Corporation introduces the first transistorized hearing aid.

Science

- Austrian zoologist Konrad Lorenz publishes *King Solomon's Ring*, in which he argues that natural selection works on behavioral as well as physical characteristics.
- British anthropologist Arnold Radcliffe-Brown publishes *Structure and Function in Primitive Society*, in which he develops the school of structural-functionalism where society is seen as analogous to an organism, the various parts acting to maintain its structure.
- English biophysicist Rosalind Franklin uses X-ray diffraction to study the structure of DNA. She suggests that its sugar-phosphate backbone is on the outside—an important clue that leads to the elucidation of the structure of DNA the following year.
- U.S. biologists Alfred Day Hershey and Martha Chase use radioactive tracers to show that bacteriophages infect bacteria with DNA and not protein.
- U.S. chemist Albert Ghiorso and colleagues at the University of California, Berkeley, discover the radioactive elements einsteinium (atomic no. 99) and fermium (atomic no. 100) in the radioactive debris collected by drone airplanes flown through the radioactive cloud from a hydrogen bomb explosion in the Pacific. They are named for the German physicist Albert Einstein and the U.S. physicist Enrico Fermi.
- U.S. nuclear physicist Donald Glaser develops the bubble chamber to observe the behavior of subatomic particles. It uses a superheated liquid instead of a vapor to track particles.

- U.S. physicists Felix Bloch and Edward Mills Purcell are jointly awarded the Nobel Prize for Physics for their development of nuclear magnetic resonance in solids.

Technology

- c. 1952 Radioisotopes begin to be used extensively in scientific research, medicine, and industry; Britain becomes the chief exporter of isotopes.
- A method of converting iron to steel, known as the basic oxygen process, is developed in Linz and Donawitz, Austria. By blowing a supersonic jet of oxygen over the surface of the molten material the nitrogen content is reduced, producing a better quality steel. It replaces the Bessemer process.
- English chemists Archer Martin and Richard Synge receive the Nobel Prize for Chemistry for their invention of partition chromatography.
- The Associated Press news agency in the United States uses the first overseas teleprinter link.
- The first numerical-control machine tool is demonstrated at the Massachusetts Institute of Technology, Massachusetts. The machine is controlled by symbols and numbers and represents the beginning of robotics.
- The first proton synchrotron linear accelerator to exceed energies greater than 1 GeV, the Cosmotron at Brookhaven, New York, begins operating, initially at 2.3 GeV.
- The French photographer Henri Cartier-Bresson publishes *Images à la Sauvette/The Decisive Moment*, an influential album of photographs that contains his ideas on photography.
- The Japanese Asahi Optical Company introduces the Asahiflex 1, the world's first single-lens reflex camera.
- The Japanese firm Sony introduces the transistor radio.
- U.S. astronomers Horace Babcock and Harold Babcock develop the solar magnetograph, a device for making detailed measurements of the sun's magnetic field.
- U.S. physicists L. Courant and H. S. Snyder increase the power of particle accelerators without increasing their size by the technique of alternating-gradient focusing, which allows magnets only 1/100 of their previous size to be used.

OCTOBER

2 The UK tests its first atomic bomb in Monte Bello Islands, northwest Australia.
25 A hydroelectric power station and dam are opened at Donzère-Mondragon in the Rhône Valley of France. The project is part of a larger program to produce 25% of France's electricity in the Rhône Valley.

NOVEMBER

1 The United States explodes the first thermonuclear fusion device, or hydrogen bomb, at Eniwetok island in the Marshall Islands, although this is not revealed until February 1954.
11 The world's first videotape machine is demonstrated by U.S. inventors Wayne Johnson and John Multin.

Transportation

- The Volga–Don Shipping Canal is completed in the USSR. The 101-km/63-mi canal links the Volga and the

Don rivers permitting ships in the Caspian Sea to reach the Baltic.

APRIL

26 The U.S. ships *Hobson* and *Wasp* collide in the mid-Atlantic; 176 people die.

MAY

2 BOAC's De Havilland Comet inaugurates jet-powered passenger aircraft service with the first scheduled commercial flight, from London, England, to Johannesburg, South Africa.

3 A USAF Douglas C-47 "ski-and-wheel" airplane makes the first successful landing at the North Pole.

JULY

3 The U.S. passenger liner *United States* is launched and sets a new transatlantic speed record of 3 days 10 hr 40 min. Designed by U.S. naval architect William Gibbs, it can sail at 80 kph/50 mph and can be quickly converted to a troop carrier.

31 Two U.S. Air Force Sikorsky H-19s make the first transatlantic helicopter flight.

ARTS AND IDEAS

Architecture

- The Lever House, on Park Avenue in New York, New York, designed by the U.S. architectural firm of Skidmore, Owings, and Merrill, is completed.
- The Town Hall in Säynätsalo, Finland, designed by the Finnish architect Alvar Aalto, is completed.
- The Unité d'Habitation, an influential housing complex in Marseille, France, designed by the Swiss-born French architect Le Corbusier, is completed.

Arts

- English writer and art critic Herbert Read publishes *The Philosophy of Modern Art*.
- The Dutch-born U.S. artist Willem de Kooning paints *Woman with Lipstick*.
- The English artist Carel Weight paints *The Visitor*.
- The English artist Edward Burra paints *John Deth*.
- The English artist Henry Moore sculpts *King and Queen*.
- The French artist Henri Matisse paints *The Swimming Pool*.
- The Italian artist Alberto Burri creates his collage *Sack*, the first of his *Sacchi/Sack* series.
- The Spanish artist Pablo Picasso paints *War* and *Peace*.
- The U.S. artist Helen Frankenthaler paints *Mountains and Sea*.
- The U.S. artist Jackson Pollock paints *Convergence*.
- The U.S. artist Robert Rauschenberg paints *Black Painting*.
- The U.S. artist Sam Francis paints *St Honoré*.

Film

- Natural Vision, the first true three-dimensional motion-picture process, is invented in the United States. Movies,

which are exposed using a twin-lens camera, are dyed red and green and projected by two synchronized projectors. Viewers wear polarized lenses, one tinted red and the other green, to view the movie in 3-D. The first 3-D movie in Natural Vision is *Bwana Devil*, directed by Arch Obler and starring Robert Stack and Barbara Britton.

- The English movie director and star Charlie Chaplin leaves the United States after allegations that he has connections with subversive causes. When he is informed that his reentry would be challenged, he announces that he will never return, and settles in Vevey, Switzerland.
- The movie *Don't Bother to Knock*, directed by Roy Baker, is released in the United States, starring Marilyn Monroe and Richard Widmark.
- The movie *Casque D'Or* or *Golden Marie*, directed by Jacques Becker, is released in France, starring Simone Signoret and Serge Reggiani.
- The movie *Due Soldi de Speranza/Two Cents Worth of Hope*, directed by Renato Castellani, is released in Italy, starring Vincenzo Musolino, Maria Fiore, and Filumena Russo. In the same year, it receives, jointly with Orwelle's *Othello*, the Palme d'Or at the Cannes Film Festival in France.
- The movie *El/He*, directed by Luis Buñuel, is released in Spain, starring Arturo de Cordova, Delia Garces, Luis Beristain, and Aurora Walker.
- The movie *High Noon*, directed by Fred Zinnemann, is released in the United States, starring Gary Cooper and Grace Kelly.
- The movie *Ikiru*, directed by Akira Kurosawa, is released in Japan, starring Takashi Shimura, Nobuo Kaneko, and Kyoko Seki.
- The movie *Jeux Interdits/Forbidden Games*, directed by René Clement, is released in France, starring Brigitte Fosey, Georges Poujouly, and Amédée.
- The movie *Le Plaisir/Pleasure*, directed by the German filmmaker Max Ophuls, is released in France. Based on three stories by Guy de Maupassant, the stars include Claude Dauphin, Ginette Leclerc, Jean Gabin, and Simone Simon.
- The movie *Limelight*, directed by Charlie Chaplin, is released in Britain. Chaplin also stars in it along with Claire Bloom.
- The movie *Macao*, directed by the Austrian-born filmmaker Josef von Sternberg, is released in the United States, starring Robert Mitchum, Jane Russell, and William Bendix.
- The movie *Moulin Rouge*, directed by John Huston, is released in the United States. A fictionalized biography of the French artist Toulouse-Lautrec, it stars José Ferrer.
- The movie *Summer With Monika*, directed by Ingmar Bergman, is released in Sweden, starring Harriet Andersson and Lars Ekborg.
- The movie *The Bad and the Beautiful*, directed by Vincente Minnelli, is released in the United States, starring Kirk Douglas, Lana Turner, and Walter Pidgeon.
- The movie *The Greatest Show on Earth*, directed by Cecil B. De Mille, is released in the United States, starring Betty Hutton, Cornel Wilde, James Stewart, Charlton Heston, and Dorothy Lamour.

- The movie *The Quiet Man*, directed by John Ford, is released in the United States, starring John Wayne and Maureen O'Hara.
- The movie *The Sound Barrier*, directed by David Lean, is released in Britain, starring Ralph Richardson, Nigel Patrick, and Ann Todd.
- The movie *This is Cinerama* is released in the United States, the first movie shot in Cinerama. The technique, developed by U.S. photographer Fred Waller, involves three synchronized projectors, each projecting one-third of the movie image onto a wide, curved screen to give a field of view of 70–80°.
- The movie musical *Singin' in the Rain*, directed by Gene Kelly, is released in the United States. Kelly also stars in it with Donald O'Connor and Debbie Reynolds.

APRIL

14 The 1951 Academy Awards take place. Best Actor: Humphrey Bogart, for *The African Queen*; Best Supporting Actor: Karl Malden, for *A Streetcar Named Desire*; Best Actress: Vivien Leigh, for *A Streetcar Named Desire*; Best Supporting Actress: Kim Hunter, for *A Streetcar Named Desire*; Best Picture: *An American in Paris*, directed by Vincente Minelli; Best Director: George Stevens, for *A Place in the Sun*.

Literature and Language

- The English literary critic F. R. Leavis publishes his collection of essays *The Common Pursuit*.
- The English writer Angus Wilson publishes his novel *Hemlock and After*.
- The English writer Anthony Powell publishes *A Buyer's Market*, the second novel of his 12-volume sequence *A Dance to the Music of Time*.
- The English writer C. S. Lewis publishes his novel *The Voyage of the Dawn Treader*, the third volume of *The Chronicles of Narnia*.
- The English writer Doris Lessing publishes her novel *Martha Quest*.
- The English writer Evelyn Waugh publishes his novel *Men at Arms*, the first part of the *Sword of Honour* trilogy.
- The Hungarian-born English writer Arthur Koestler publishes *The Arrow in the Blue*, a volume of autobiography.
- The Japanese writer Yasunari Kawabata publishes his novel *Sembazuru/Thousand Cranes*.
- The Nobel Prize for Literature is awarded to the French novelist François Mauriac.
- The Pulitzer Prize for Biography is awarded to Merlo J. Pusey for *Charles Evans Hughes*, the Pulitzer Prize for Poetry is awarded to Marianne Moore for *Collected Poems*, and the Pulitzer Prize for Fiction is awarded to Herman Wouk for *The Caine Mutiny*.
- The Romanian-born German poet Paul Celan publishes his poetry collection *Mohn und Gedächtnis/Poppy and Memory*.
- The Russian-born U.S. writer Isaac Asimov publishes *Foundation and Empire*, the second novel in his science fiction *Foundation Trilogy*.
- The South African writer and traveler Laurens van der Post publishes his travel book *Venture to the Interior*.

- The U.S. writer Bernard Malamud publishes his allegorical novel about baseball *The Natural*.
- The U.S. writer Ernest Hemingway publishes his novella *The Old Man and the Sea*.
- The U.S. writer Flannery O'Connor publishes her novel *Wise Blood*.
- The U.S. writer Frank O'Hara publishes his poetry collection *A City Winter*.
- The U.S. writer John Steinbeck publishes his novel *East of Eden*.
- The U.S. writer Mary McCarthy publishes her novel *The Groves of Academe*.
- The U.S. writer Paul Bowles publishes his novel *Let It Come Down*.
- The U.S. writer Peter De Vries publishes his short-story collection *No, But I Saw the Movie*.
- The U.S. writer Ralph Ellison publishes his novel *Invisible Man*, which is based on the premise that U.S. society ignores black people.
- The Welsh writer Dylan Thomas publishes his poetry collection *In Country Sleep*.

Music

- English composer Elisabeth Lutyens completes her motet *Excerpta – Logico Philosopici/Logical Philosophical Excepts*, settings of texts by the Austrian philosopher Ludwig Wittgenstein.
- The English composer Ralph Vaughan Williams completes his orchestral work *Sinfonia Antarctica/ Antarctic Symphony*.
- The German-born U.S. composer Lukas Foss completes *A Parable of Death* for voice and orchestra.
- The opera *Boulevard Solitude*, by the German composer Hans Werner Henze, is first performed, in Hannover, Germany.
- The opera *Trouble in Tahiti*, by the U.S. conductor and composer Leonard Bernstein, is first performed, at Brandeis University, Waltham, Massachusetts.
- The Russian composer Igor Stravinsky completes his *Cantata* for voices and chorus, settings of anonymous English poems.
- The U.S. composer Aaron Copland publishes *Music and Imagination*.
- The U.S. composer John Cage creates *4' 33'*, a piece for piano that consist of a pianist sitting silently at a piano for 4 minutes and 33 seconds.
- The U.S. composer Ned Rorem completes his choral work *The Mild Mother*.
- The U.S. composer Otto Luening completes his electronic work *Fantasy in Space*.
- The U.S. disc jockey Alan Freed plays black American music on his radio program *Moondog's Rock 'n' Roll Party* on the Cleveland, Ohio, station WJW, and popularizes the term "rock 'n' roll."

NOVEMBER

14 The popular music magazine *New Musical Express* publishes Britain's first pop singles chart.

DECEMBER

17 The U.S. soprano Dorothy Maynor sings at the Daughters of the American Revolution (DAR)'s Constitution Hall in Washington, D.C., making her the first black person to sing there since 1939, breaking a

formal ban that went into effect when the DAR refused to let Marian Anderson sing at their headquarters.

Theater and Dance

- The play *Deep Blue Sea*, by the English dramatist Terence Rattigan, is first performed, in London, England.
- The play *Dial 'M' for Murder*, by the English dramatist Frederick Knott, is first performed, in London, England.
- The play *Die Ehe des Herrn Mississippi/The Marriage of Mr. Mississippi*, by the Swiss writer Friedrich Dürrenmatt, is first performed, in Munich, Germany.
- The play *Les Chaises/The Chairs*, by the Romanian-born French dramatist Eugène Ionesco, is first performed, in Paris, France.
- The play *The Mousetrap*, by the English writer Agatha Christie, is first performed, in London, England.
- The play *The Seven Year Itch*, by the U.S. dramatist George Axelrod, is first performed, in New York, New York.
- The Pulitzer Prize for Drama is awarded to Joseph Kramm for *The Shrike*.

MARCH

30   The 1951–52 Tony Awards take place. Best Actor: José Ferrer; Best Actress: Julie Harris; Best Play: *The Fourposter*; Best Musical: *The King and I*.

Thought and Scholarship

- English historian Alan Bullock publishes *Hitler: A Study in Tyranny*.
- English philosopher John Wisdom publishes *Other Minds*.
- English philosopher R. M. Hare publishes *The Language of Morals*.
- The Pulitzer Prize for History is awarded to Oscar Handlin for *The Uprooted*.

SOCIETY

Everyday Life

- Employment reaches a record high of 62,500,000 in the United States.
- Kellogg's Sugar Frosted Flakes are sold in U.S. grocery stores; 29% of their contents is sugar.
- U.S. clergyman Norman Vincent Peale publishes *The Power of Positive Thinking*, which sells more than 2 million copies that year.
- Wayfarer sunglasses, based on a military model, become commercially available.

APRIL

- President Harry S. Truman seizes U.S. steel mills in an attempt to prevent a strike, but the Supreme Court finds his order illegal on June 2. On June 23 the Congress of Industrial Organization's (CIO) steel workers begin a 53-day strike.

JUNE

30   A Brookings Institute study finds that 6.5 million Americans own stock, and that 75% of stockholders earn less than $10,000 a year after taxes.

Media and Communication

- *The National Enquirer*, founded in 1926, is taken over by U.S. publisher Generoso Pope, Jr., who, by emphasizing celebrity news and gossip, will reach 4 million in weekly circulation by 1975.
- The long-running U.S. television dance show *Bandstand* begins, on WFIL-TV in Philadelphia, Pennsylvania.
- There are 17 million television sets in U.S. homes, up from around 7 million in 1950.

JANUARY

7–April 24, 1959   *Arthur Godfrey Time*, a 60-minute, Monday–Thursday variety program, appears on U.S. television. Godfrey is simultaneously appearing in the programs *Arthur Godfrey and His Friends* and *Arthur Godfrey and His Ukulele*, making him the most visible star on U.S. television.

16   *Today*, a daily morning program featuring news and interviews, begins on U.S. television, with Dave Garroway as host. It remains in production.

FEBRUARY

18   The 1951–52 Emmy Awards for television are held. Best Dramatic Show: *Studio One*; Best Comedy Show: *Red Skelton*; Best Actor: Sid Caesar; Best Actress: Imogene Coca.

MAY

- *Mad*, a comic magazine edited by Harvey Kurtzman and published by William Gaines, begins publication.

JULY

3–June 12, 1955   The situation comedy *Mr Peepers* appears on U.S. television. Starring Wally Cox, Tony Randall, Harvey Weskitt, Georgann Johnson, Patricia Benoit, Jack Warden, and Sylvia Field, it is described by *TV Guide* as "close to being the perfect TV show."

SEPTEMBER

20–September 12, 1970   *The Jackie Gleason Show*, featuring song, dance, and sketch comedy, appears on U.S. television. The sketches about the life of the bus driver Ralph Kramden (Gleason), his wife Alice (Audrey Meadows), and his friends Ed (Art Carney) and Trixie Norton (Joyce Randolph), take on a life of their own as *The Honeymooners*.

23   Vice presidential candidate Richard M. Nixon delivers the "Checkers" speech, in which he defends himself against charges of accepting illegal gifts from supporters.

OCTOBER

1–September 10, 1961   The TV program *This Is Your Life* appears on U.S. television. A special guest is brought to the studio by a ruse and events from his or her past are relived by friends and relatives who are in on the trick. Celebrity guests include Lowell Thomas, Stan Laurel, and Oliver Hardy.

3–September 3, 1966   The situation comedy *The Adventures of Ozzie and Harriet* appears on U.S. television; the longest-running situation comedy to date, it stars the Nelson family, Ozzie, Harriet, David, and Ricky.

NOVEMBER

3–October 1, 1953 *City Hospital*, one of the first television programs to use doctors as main characters and medical issues as the main subject themes, has a two-season run on television in the United States, starring Melville Ruick.

Sports

- Horse racing is the most popular spectator sport, attended by 45.9 million Americans. In contrast, about 40.9 million people attend baseball games.
- During the year more than 26 million Americans attend horse races, where they bet $1.9 billion.
- The butterfly stroke, developed by U.S. swimmers in the 1930s and used in breaststroke races, is recognized and regulated as a separate stroke by the Fédération Internationale de Natation Amateur (International Swimming Federation, or FINA).
- The first official ice-dancing world championships, in Paris, France, are won by Jean Westwood and Lawrence Demmy of Great Britain.
- The introduction of automatic pinspotters for tenpin bowling and their approval by the American Bowling Congress helps increase the popularity of the game in the United States.
- The Italian race-car driver Alberto Ascari, competing in a Ferrari, wins the World Drivers' Championship; he wins six of this year's seven Grand Prix races.

JANUARY

19 The U.S. Professional Golfers Association (PGA) approves the participation of black Americans in its golf tournaments.

FEBRUARY

14–25 The 6th Winter Olympic Games take place in Oslo, Norway; 694 competitors (including 109 women) from 30 countries compete in 22 events. The host country wins 7 gold medals; the United States, 4; Finland and West Germany, 3 each; and Austria, 2. Stein Eriksen of Norway wins the Giant Slalom to become the first Scandinavian to win an Alpine skiing event. Dick Button of the United States retains his figure-skating title.

29 Dick Button of the United States wins the men's world figure-skating title for the fifth successive year, in Paris, France.

MAY

3 The U.S. jockey Eddie Arcaro, riding Hill Gail, wins a record fifth Kentucky Derby and Hill Gail's trainer, Ben Jones, achieves a record sixth victory in the race.

JULY

- At the Olympic Games in Helsinki, Finland, Bob Mathias of the United States retains his decathlon title and fellow U.S. athlete Harrison Dillard, who won the 100 meters at the 1948 Games, wins gold medals in the 110-meter hurdles and the sprint relay. Horace Ashenfelter wins the 3,000-meters steeplechase, the United States's first long-distance Olympic track title since 1908.
- At the Olympic Games in Helsinki, Finland, Viktor Chukarin of the Soviet Union wins four gold medals and two silver medals in the men's gymnastics.
- At the Olympic Games in Helsinki, Finland, Marjorie Jackson of Australia sets world records in winning the women's 100 meters and 200 meters gold medals.

19 The 15th Olympic Games open in Helsinki, Finland, attended by 4,925 competitors, including 518 women, from 69 countries. The Soviet Union and Israel compete at the Games for the first time.

20–27 At the Olympic Games in Helsinki, Finland, the Czech athlete Emil Zatopek wins the 5,000 meters, the

BIRTHS & DEATHS

FEBRUARY

6 George VI, King of Great Britain and Northern Ireland 1936–52, dies at Sandringham, Norfolk, England (56).

MARCH

4 Charles Scott Sherrington, English physiologist who laid the foundation for understanding the functioning of the nervous system, dies in Eastbourne, Sussex, England (94).

MAY

6 Maria Montessori, Italian educator, dies in Noordwijk aan Zee, the Netherlands (81).

8 William Fox, Hollywood motion picture magnate who founded Twentieth Century Fox studios, dies in New York, New York (73).

JUNE

1 John Dewey, U.S. philosopher and one of the main founders of pragmatism, dies in New York, New York (92).

20 Vikram Seth, Indian novelist who wrote *A Suitable Boy*, born in Calcutta, India.

JULY

1 Daniel Edward (Dan) Ackroyd, Canadian-born U.S. comedy actor, born in Ottawa, Ontario.

15 Johnny Thunders, U.S. rock guitarist, singer, and songwriter, born in New York, New York (–1991).

26 Eva Perón, unofficial Argentine political leader and wife of Juan Perón, dies in Buenos Aires, Argentina (33).

SEPTEMBER

2 Jimmy Connors, U.S. tennis player who dominated international tennis during the 1970s, born in East St. Louis, Illinois.

26 George Santayana, Spanish-born U.S. philosopher and poet, dies in Rome, Italy (88).

OCTOBER

14 Nikolay Yefimovich Andrianov, Russian gymnast who won gold medals in the 1972, 1976, and 1980 Olympics, born.

NOVEMBER

9 Chaim Weizmann, first president of Israel 1949–52, dies in Rehovot, Israel (77).

20 Benedetto Croce, Italian historian and philosopher who championed the idea of unrestricted freedom, dies in Naples, Italy (86).

10,000 meters, and the marathon. His wife, Dana, wins a gold medal in the javelin.

AUGUST

3   The 15th Olympic Games close in Helsinki, Finland. The United States wins 40 gold medals; the Soviet Union, 22; Hungary, 16; Sweden, 12; Italy, 8; Czechoslovakia, 7; and France, Australia, and Finland, 6 each. Britain comes away with only 1 gold medal.

3   The U.S. athletics administrator Avery Brundage, the president of the U.S. Olympic Committee since 1928, is appointed president of the International Olympic Committee.

SEPTEMBER

23   The U.S. boxer Rocky Marciano knocks out the defending champion, Jersey Joe Walcott of the United States, in the 12th round of their fight in Philadelphia, United States, to win the world heavyweight boxing title. This is Marciano's 43rd consecutive victory as a professional.

OCTOBER

5   British speedboat driver John Cobb is killed establishing a water speed record of 332.9 kph/206.89 mph at Loch Ness, Scotland.

1953

POLITICS, GOVERNMENT, AND ECONOMICS

Business and Economics

- Commercial construction increases by 43% over the previous year in the United States.
- IBM introduces its first computer, the IBM 701, which competes with Remington Rand's UNIVAC. It has a memory of 4 kilobytes.
- The Ford Foundation endows the $15 million Fund for the Republic, designed to promote intellectual freedom.
- The U.S. federal budget deficit reaches a new peacetime high of $9.4 billion.

JUNE

- The U.S. Steelworkers of America reaches a new contract with United States Steel Corporation. The contract raises hourly wages by 8.5 cents per hour and hourly benefits by 0.5 cents per hour.

DECEMBER

9   The General Electric Corporation announces plans to fire all communist employees.

Colonization

JANUARY

1   The Maldive Islands become independent under British protection. The new president, Amin Didi, plays center forward in a ceremonial soccer match.

NOVEMBER

2   The Constituent Assembly in Pakistan decides to declare the country a republic, within the British Commonwealth, as the "Islamic Republic of Pakistan."

Human Rights

JUNE

10–19   A bus boycott in Baton Rouge, Louisiana, results in an amendment of the rules requiring blacks to sit at the back of buses; it is the first major action of the modern civil-rights movement.

DECEMBER

- U.S. scientist J. Robert Oppenheimer, who led the Manhattan Project to create an atomic bomb during World War II, is charged with having communist sympathies. His security clearance is revoked the following year, even though he is cleared of disloyalty charges.

Politics and Government

- Former U.S. secretary of state George C. Marshall, founder of the Marshall Plan, wins the Nobel Peace Prize.
- In countries belonging to the European Coal and Steel Community (ECSC), namely France, Italy, Luxembourg, Belgium, the Netherlands, and West Germany, a common market for coal and iron ore comes into operation on February 10, for scrap on March 15, and for steel on May 1.
- President Dwight D. Eisenhower appoints former California governor, Earl Warren, as Chief Justice of the U.S. Supreme Court.
- The Chinese First Five-Year Plan is inaugurated, aiming to achieve rapid industrialization (with assistance from the USSR) and to collectivize agriculture.

JANUARY

- A New York federal judge convicts 13 Communist Party leaders of conspiring to overthrow the U.S. government.
- Two days before relinquishing office, the U.S. president Harry S. Truman declares offshore oil deposits a national reserve.
1 Representatives of the British government and of the British protectorates of Northern Rhodesia, Southern Rhodesia, and Nyasaland (respectively modern Zambia, Zimbabwe, and Malawi) meet in a conference in London, England, to discuss the proposed creation of an autonomous federation to handle external affairs, defense, and currency in the protectorates.
5–9 The British prime minister Winston Churchill visits the U.S. president-elect Dwight D. Eisenhower for discussions.
6 An Asian socialist conference opens in Rangoon, Burma (now Yangon in Myanmar).
7 The Radical René Mayer forms a government in France, ending a cabinet crisis.
8 Riots break out in Karachi, Pakistan, followed by others elsewhere in the country, reflecting difficult economic conditions and dissatisfaction with the government.
12 The Yugoslav National Assembly adopts a new constitution and, on January 14, Marshal Tito is elected first president of the Yugoslav Republic.
14 A consultative assembly of the Council of Europe meets in Strasbourg, France, to draft a constitution for a European Political Community (adopted on February 10).
16 Egyptian premier Muhammad Naguib dissolves all political parties in Egypt.
21 An electoral reform bill in Italy, aimed at strengthening the parliamentary system by providing bonus seats in the chamber for any party or alliance that wins over 50% of votes, passes the chamber, with communists abstaining. The bill is passed by the senate on March 29.
31 The Soviet newspaper *Pravda* alleges a "Doctors Plot" to kill political figures, beginning a purge of Jews in the USSR.

FEBRUARY

- The U.S. Office of Defense Mobilization renews rationing of steel, copper, and aluminum.
1 Communist Vietminh insurgents renew their offensive against government forces in Laos.
6 The U.S. government lifts all salary and wage controls as well as most controls on the prices of consumer goods.
10 General Muhammad Naguib Bey is voted dictatorial powers in Egypt for a period of three years.
12 A British–Egyptian agreement on the Sudan is announced, providing for a transitional period of self-government for the Sudan, followed by self-determination.
12 The USSR severs relations with Israel following the bombing of the Soviet embassy in Tel Aviv, Israel.
24 A Public Safety Act is passed in South Africa to give the government the power to declare a state of emergency and rule by decree, in an effort to combat civil rights movements.
24 Foreign ministers of member countries of the European Defense Community (EDC) hold a conference in Rome, Italy.

28 A treaty of friendship is signed by Greece, Turkey, and Yugoslavia.

MARCH

- The U.S. Office of Price Stabilization formally announces an end to all price controls, after many were removed on February 6.
- U.S. secretary of state, John Foster Dulles, proclaims publicly that Stalin's death heralds brighter prospects for world peace.
5 The Soviet leader Joseph Stalin dies and, on March 6, Georgi Malenkov, designated by Stalin, succeeds as chairman of the council of ministers.
16 President Tito of Yugoslavia makes a state visit to Britain.
19 The West German Bundestag (the legislative assembly) approves the Bonn and Paris agreements establishing a European Defense Community (EDC).
26 Mau Mau nationalists, a mainly Kikuyu terrorist group dedicated to driving European settlers from Kenya, kill 150 members of the Kikuyu people loyal to the Kenyan government, at Lari in the Rift Valley.
30 Denmark adopts a new constitution, abolishing the upper house and reducing the voting age to 23.
31 Dag Hammarskjöld of Sweden is elected secretary-general of the United Nations (UN) by the Security Council in succession to Trygve Lie. On April 7 the election is ratified by the General Assembly.

APRIL

- The U.S. Congress establishes the Department of Health, Education, and Welfare (HEW).
- The U.S. Justice Department orders the U.S. Communist Party to register as an organization controlled and directed by foreigners.
2 Following elections in Austria, Julius Raab of the People's Party succeeds Dr. Leopold Figl as chancellor and forms a coalition government of People's Party members and Socialists, similar to the preceding government.
6 The West German chancellor Konrad Adenauer visits New York, New York, and, on May 14, visits London, England.
8 Following a massacre of 150 Kikuyu people loyal to the Kenyan government by Mau Mau terrorosts (a Kikuyu nationalist group), at Lari in the Rift Valley, in the British colony of Kenya on March 26, Jomo Kenyatta and five others are convicted of organizing terrorism.
11 The United Nations (UN) forces and their communist opponents arrange for an exchange of prisoners in the Korean War.
15 The South African National Party under Daniel Malan, committed to racial segregation, secures a clear majority in South African elections.
17 Ghulam Mohammed, the governor-general of Pakistan, dismisses the government of Khwaja Nazimuddin and appoints the Muslim League leader Mohammed Ali as prime minister in order to deal with growing economic and social problems.
21 The Danish premier Erik Eriksen resigns following gains for the Social Democratic Party in the Danish elections.
30 The first general election to be held under the new constitution in British Guiana (now Guyana) is won by the left-wing People's Progressive Party led by Cheddi Jagan.

MAY

12 General Aldred Gruenther of the United States is appointed Supreme Allied Commander in Europe of North Atlantic Treaty Organization (NATO) forces.

20 France signs an agreement with the former German industrial region of the Saar, giving it autonomy but establishing economic union with France.

21 René Mayer resigns as prime minister of France following defeat on a vote of confidence; his resignation is followed by the longest interregnum of the fourth republic (–June 26).

28–September 30, 1954 The U.S. government discharges 3,002 employees it considers to be security risks because of alleged connections with communists.

JUNE

7 In the Italian elections, the prime minister Alcide de Gasperi's Christian Democratic coalition wins seats from the socialists and communists.

8 The nationalist Kenya African Union is banned by the Kenyan government following unrest.

17 A strike in East Berlin on June 16 turns into a rising against East Germany's communist government; in the afternoon the Soviet commandant of Berlin proclaims a state of emergency and Soviet military forces put down the rising.

18 A republic is proclaimed in Egypt, with General Muhammad Naguib Bey as president and prime minister, and Colonel Gamal Abdel Nasser as deputy prime minister and minister of the interior.

18 South Korea releases 27,000 noncommunist North Korean prisoners of the Korean War.

19 Ethel and Julius Rosenberg, having been convicted of spying on April 5, 1951, are executed at Sing Sing prison in Ossining, New York.

26 The French Independent (Right) politician Joseph Laniel ends a cabinet crisis by forming a government in France.

JULY

2 Following the loss of a Fianna Fáil seat in a by-election in the Republic of Ireland, Prime Minister Éamon de Valera calls a vote of confidence, and wins by 73 votes to 71.

4 Mátyás Rákosi is removed as prime minister of Hungary, and is replaced by the more moderate Imre Nagy.

9 Lavrenti Beria, the Soviet minister of internal affairs, is arrested (and shot on December 23); his Politburo rivals for leadership of the USSR fear his potential power.

10 Two parties opposed to Prime Minister Daniel Malan's apartheid racial policies are launched in South Africa; they are Alan Paton's Liberal Party and the Federal Union Party.

10–14 U.S., British, and French foreign ministers meet in Washington, D.C., to discuss the reunification of Germany and the occupation of Austria.

12 The dictatorial Brigadier Adib Shishkali is elected president of Syria, having seized power in October 1951.

15 Britain proposes a four-power conference on Germany, involving the United States, USSR, and France.

15 The Kenyan supreme court quashes Mau Mau leader Jomo Kenyatta's conviction for terrorist activities, though the conviction is upheld on September 22 by the East African court of appeal.

20 The USSR and Israel resume diplomatic relations (broken off on February 12).

26 Fidel Castro leads an attempt to overthrow the Batista government of Cuba. Castro is imprisoned, but is released under amnesty in 1955 and goes to Mexico.

27 Delegates from the United Nations, North Korea, and China sign an armistice at Panmunjom, ending the Korean War.

27 Delegates from the United Nations, North Korea, and China sign an armistice at Panmunjom, ending the Korean War. The U.S. has suffered 137,051 casualties, of whom 25,604 were killed, 103,492 were wounded, and 7,955 are missing.

28 The new Italian coalition government of Alcide de Gasperi is defeated in the chamber, and the economist Giuseppe Pella forms a government of Christian Democrats on August 15.

AUGUST

• U.S. president Dwight D. Eisenhower proposes to extend social security to 10.5 million Americans left without its protection.

• U.S. president Dwight D. Eisenhower signs the Refugee Relief Act to admit 214,000 more refugees than current legislation allows for.

• The U.S. Congress creates the Foreign Operations Administration to oversee all foreign aid programs.

8 A mutual defense treaty is agreed by the United States and South Korea following the end of the Korean War.

10 The Canadian Liberal Party under Louis Saint Laurent retains power following a general election in Canada. The Liberals take 171 seats, the Progressive Conservatives 51, and others 43.

13 The shah of Iran attempts to appoint General Fazollah Zahedi as prime minister but, on August 16, flees when the nationalist leader Muhammad Mossadegh refuses to step down.

14 France deposes the sultan of Morocco Sidi Mohammed and, on August 21, replaces him with Sidi Mohammed ben Arafa.

19 The Iranian army retakes Tehran, Iran, from the rebellious Iranian prime minister Muhammad Mossadegh, who is later sentenced to three years in prison for treason.

23 The USSR cancels reparations owed by East Germany for losses caused in World War II.

24 The Kenyan government calls on Mau Mau nationalist terrorists to surrender.

30 Hungary and Yugoslavia resume relations following the solution of a border dispute.

SEPTEMBER

• U.S. secretary of labor Martin P. Durkin resigns to protest against President Dwight D. Eisenhower's refusal to amend the Taft–Hartley Act (1946), which restricts labor's right to strike.

6 Chancellor Konrad Adenauer's Christian Democratic Union wins a West German general election with 243 seats, while the Social Democrats win 151, the Free Democrats 48, and others 45.

12 Nikita Khrushchev is appointed first secretary of the central committee of the Soviet Communist Party.

12 The U.S. senator from Massachusetts and future president John Fitzgerald Kennedy marries Jacqueline Lee Bouvier, in Newport, Rhode Island, United States.

26 The primate of Poland Cardinal Stefan Wyszyński is arrested by the communist authorities.

27 A U.S.–Japanese agreement allows Japan, disarmed in 1945, to contribute to its own security by establishing a national defense force.

30 Following the first Danish general election under the new constitution, on September 22, in which the Social Democrats won the largest number of seats, their leader, Hans Hedtoft, forms a minority government.

OCTOBER

6 Fearing the establishment of communism in British Guiana (now Guyana) by the People's Progressive Party, Britain sends troops and, on October 9, the constitution is suspended and the governor rules under a state of emergency.

8 The United States and Britain decide to hand over the administration of Zone A of the disputed port of Trieste to Italy, and on October 11 Marshall Tito of Yugoslavia threatens to invade Zone A in support of his country's claim to Trieste.

9 Adib Shishkali's Arab Liberation movement "wins" one-party Syrian elections.

12 The Norwegian Labor Party wins a majority in the Norwegian elections, and Oscar Torp remains prime minister.

12 The prime minister of Ceylon (now Sri Lanka), Dudley Senanayake, retires; Sir John Kotalawala forms a ministry.

23 The federal constitution of the Central African Federation (North and South Rhodesia and Nyasaland, now Zambia, Zimbabwe, and Malawi respectively) comes into force.

26 The United States publishes a report on alleged communist outrages in the Korean War.

NOVEMBER

8 The dictator Antonio de Oliveira Salazar's National Unity Party wins all the seats in the Portuguese elections, its opponents having withdrawn in protest at his rule.

17 A nonparty government is formed in Finland under the governor of the Bank of Finland, Sakari Tuomioja.

20 Vietminh guerrillas besiege French troops garrisoning the village of Dien Bien Phu in Vietnam, a sovereign state within the French Union.

30 The British government announces that it has withdrawn its recognition of the kabaka of Buganda, the traditional ruler of the British colony of Uganda, following his demands for independence; the governor of Uganda orders Kabaka Mutesa II to be deported.

DECEMBER

4–7 The U.S. president Dwight D. Eisenhower, the British prime minister Winston Churchill, the French prime minister Joseph Laniel, and their foreign ministers meet in Bermuda for talks on the future of Germany and Austria.

5 Britain and Iran resume diplomatic relations, pledging to find a negotiated settlement to their dispute over Iran's nationalization of its oil industry.

7 David Ben-Gurion resigns as Israeli prime minister after prolonged tension in his coalition government, and is succeeded on December 9 by Moshe Sharett.

8 In his "Atoms for Peace" speech, the U.S. president Dwight D. Eisenhower proposes to the United Nations (UN) General Assembly the establishment of an

International Atomic Energy Agency (IAEA) to monitor the spread of atomic technology for peaceful purposes.

18 Following elections, Godfrey Huggins of the Federal Party forms a ministry in the newly created Central African Federation of North and South Rhodesia and Nyasaland.

23 René Coty is elected president of France.

SCIENCE, TECHNOLOGY, AND MEDICINE

Agriculture

- Infectious myxomatosis is introduced from continental Europe to Britain, killing millions of rabbits.

Computing

- IBM introduces the IBM 650, the first computer to be produced in large numbers. It has a memory of 10 kilobytes.
- U.S. electrical engineer Jay Wright Forrester develops ferrite core memory for computers, which becomes commonly used in second-generation computers.

Ecology

- The U.S. Congress creates Cape Hatteras National Seashore, the first national seashore, in North Carolina.

FEBRUARY

1 Large parts of the coastal areas of the Netherlands are flooded when dikes break during a storm in the North Sea; 1,800 people drown and 100,000 are left homeless.

MAY

11 Tornadoes sweep through Waco and San Angelo, Texas, killing 124 people.

JUNE

8 A tornado blows through Ohio and southern Michigan, killing 139 people.

Health and Medicine

- *Reader's Digest* magazine warns about the harmful effects of smoking in an article entitled "Cancer by the Carton."
- The first woman to be impregnated with frozen sperm is impregnated at the University of Iowa Medical School.
- The World Health Organization, in a successful campaign to wipe out typhus in Afghanistan, dusts nearly 350,000 people and 20,000 houses with pesticides.
- University of Minnesota scientist Ancel Keys suggests that coronary heart disease may be related to diets high in animal fats.
- U.S. physiologist Fritz Lipmann and German-born British physiologist Hans Krebs share the Nobel Prize for Physiology or Medicine: Krebs for his discovery of

the citric acid cycle; and Lipmann for his discovery of coenzyme A and its importance in metabolism.
- U.S. physiologists Eugene Aserinsky and Nathaniel Kleitman discover the rapid eye movements (REM) that characterize a very active period of sleep. It causes a revolution in the understanding of sleep processes since it is at odds with the prevailing concept of sleep as quiet.
- U.S. scientist David D. Peebles invents nonfat dry milk.

FEBRUARY
- A presidential commission on the U.S. healthcare system endorses a voluntary program of health insurance financed by federal, state, and local money.

MAY
6   U.S. physician John Gibbon performs the first successful open-heart operation. He uses a heart–lung machine to oxygenate the blood during the operation.

DECEMBER
3   Scientists at the University of Iowa announce that they have induced pregnancy using deep-frozen sperm, a process previously used to inseminate cattle.

Science

- An international laboratory for nuclear research is opened at Meyrin, near Geneva, Switzerland.
- British biochemists Archer Martin and A. T. James develop gas chromatography, a technique for separating the elements of a gaseous compound through differential absorption in a permeable solid.
- Dutch physicist Frits Zernike receives the Nobel Prize for Physics for his development of phase contrast microscopy and for his invention of the phase contrast microscope.
- English biochemist Frederick Sanger determines the structure of the insulin molecule. The largest protein molecule to have its chemical structure determined to date, it is essential in laboratory synthesis.
- German chemist Hermann Staudinger receives the Nobel Prize for Chemistry for his discoveries in macromolecular chemistry.
- U.S. biochemist Stanley Lloyd Miller shows that amino acids can be formed when simulated lightning is passed through containers of water, methane, ammonia, and hydrogen—conditions under which life may have arisen.
- U.S. geophysicist William Ewing announces that there is a crack, or rift, running along the middle of the Mid-Atlantic Ridge.
- U.S. physicist Murray Gell-Mann introduces the concept of "strangeness," a property of subatomic particles, to explain their behavior.

APRIL
25   English molecular biologist Francis Crick and U.S. biologist James Watson announce the discovery of the double helix structure of DNA, the basic material of heredity. They also theorize that if the strands are separated then each can form the template for the synthesis of an identical DNA molecule. It is perhaps the most important discovery in biology.

SEPTEMBER
21   British anthropologists J. S. Weiner, Kenneth Oakely, and Wilfred Le Gros Clark expose the fossil remains of

Piltdown Man, "found" in Piltdown, southern England, in 1912, as a forgery.

Technology

c. 1953   The Soviet army introduces the T-54 heavy tank armed with a 100-mm gun; it becomes the communist bloc's standard tank.
- German chemist Karl Ziegler discovers a chemical catalyst that permits polyethylene plastics to be produced at atmospheric pressure. Previous methods require pressures of 30,000 lb per sq in.
- The first intermediate-range ballistic missile (IRBM) is launched by the United States.
- The National Television Systems Committee (NTSC) develops a color television system compatible with current black and white television sets. Two images are transmitted simultaneously, one carrying the color and the other information about brightness and detail. It forms the basis of other color systems worldwide.
- The TRAPIL oil pipeline, Europe's first, is completed in France. It runs from the lower Seine region to Paris.
- The U.S. military announces the development of the first nuclear artillery weapon, a gun weighing 77,000 kg/85 tons, which fires a 280-mm/11-in calibre projectile.

MARCH
- The U.S. Navy announces that it is producing a jet-propelled guided missile system.

MAY
- The U.S. Army tests the first atomic artillery shell in the Nevada desert.

AUGUST
1   The U.S. bathyscaph *Trieste* is launched. Later in the year it dives to a record 3,150 m/10,300 ft.
12   The USSR explodes its first hydrogen bomb at a secret location.

DECEMBER
- U.S. physicist Charles Townes develops the maser (microwave amplification by stimulated emission of radiation), a device that produces and amplifies microwave radiation. It is used to amplify microwave signals from satellites and is a precursor of the laser.

Transportation

- Radial ply tires are introduced by Michelin in France and Pirelli in Italy.
- The Ford Popular, the world's cheapest four-cylinder automobile, is launched in Britain.

MARCH
3   A Canadian jet crashes at Karachi, Pakistan, killing 11 people; it is the first commercial passenger jet to crash.

APRIL
18   A BOAC Vickers Viscount is the first turboprop airplane to enter scheduled service, in the UK.

MAY
2   A British Comet jet airliner crashes near Calcutta, India, killing all 43 people on board.
18   U.S. pilot Jacqueline Cochran, in an F-86, becomes the first woman to fly faster than the speed of sound.

18 A U.S. Air France jet crashes near Tokyo, Japan, killing 129 people.

SEPTEMBER
1 The first aerial refueling of a jet aircraft by a jet tanker takes place—a B-47 Stratojet by a KB-47B.

NOVEMBER
20 U.S. pilot Scott Crossfield, in a D-558-II jet airplane, establishes an air speed record of 2,124.8 kph/ 1,328 mph at Edwards Air Force Base, California—the first Mach 2 flight (2.01).

DECEMBER
- U.S. Air Force major Charles ("Chuck") E. Yeager sets a new air-speed record of 2,640 kph/1,650 mph, over twice the speed of sound, in a Bell X-1A.

ARTS AND IDEAS

Architecture

- The Yale University Art Gallery, in New Haven, Connecticut, designed by the U.S. architects Louis Kahn and Donald Orr, is completed.

Arts

- The English art historian Anthony Blunt publishes *Art and Architecture in France 1500–1700*.
- The French artist Germaine Richier sculpts *The Bullfighter*.
- The French artist Henri Matisse creates his collage *The Snail*.
- The Institute of Contemporary Art, in London, England, holds an international sculpture competition on the theme *The Unknown Political Prisoner*, which is won by the English artist Reg Butler.
- The Irish-born British artist Francis Bacon paints *Study After Velàzquez: Pope Innocent X*.
- The Russian-born French artist Nicolas de Staël paints *Agricento*.
- The U.S. artist Alice Neel paints *Last Sickness*.
- The U.S. artist Ellsworth Kelly paints *Black, Two Whites*.
- The U.S. artist Jackson Pollock paints *Blue Poles (Number 11)*.
- The U.S. artist Larry Rivers paints *Washington Crossing the Delaware*.
- The U.S. artist Mark Tobey paints *Edge of August*.

Film

- The movie *From Here to Eternity*, directed by Fred Zinnemann, is released in the United States. Based on the novel by James Jones, it stars Burt Lancaster, Frank Sinatra, and Deborah Kerr.
- The movie *I Vitelloni/Spivs*, directed by Federico Fellini, is released in Italy, starring Franco Fabrizi, Franco Interlenghi, Eleonora Ruffo, and Albert Sordi.

- The movie *Jigokumon/Gate of Hell*, directed by Teinosuke Kinugasa, is released in Japan, starring Machiko Kyo, Kazuo Hasegawa, and Isao Yamagata.
- The movie *La Salaire de la Peur/Wages of Fear*, directed by Henri-Georges Clouzot, is released in France, starring Yves Montand, Folco Lulli, Charles Vanel, and Peter Van Eyck. It receives the Palme d'Or at the Cannes Film Festival in France.
- The movie *Les Vacances de Monsieur Hulo/Mr. Hulot's Holiday*, directed by Jacques Tati, is released in France. Tati also stars in it.
- The movie *Roman Holiday*, directed by William Wyler, is released in the United States, starring Gregory Peck and Audrey Hepburn.
- The movie *Shane*, directed by George Stevens, is released in the United States. Based on the novel by Jack Schaeffer, it stars Alan Ladd and Jean Arthur.
- The movie *Stalag 17*, directed by Billy Wilder, is released in the United States, starring William Holden, Don Taylor, Otto Preminger, and Robert Strauss.
- The movie *The Big Heat*, directed by German filmmaker Fritz Lang, is released in the United States, starring Glenn Ford and Gloria Grahame.
- The movie *The Cruel Sea*, directed by Charles Frend, is released in Britain. Based on the novel by Nicholas Monsarrat, it stars Jack Hawkins, Donald Sinden, Stanely Baker, John Stratton, and Denholm Elliott.
- The movie *The Robe*, directed by Henry Koster and produced by Twentieth Century Fox, is released in the United States, starring Richard Burton, Jean Simmons, Michael Rennie, and Victor Mature. It is the first feature-length movie made in CinemaScope, a technique by which a wide picture is squeezed onto a 35-mm film by a special lens, and then expanded onto a wide screen with a special projector. The technique was invented in 1925 but ignored.
- The movie *Tokyo Story*, directed by Yasujiro Ozu, is released in Japan, starring Chishu Ryu and Chieko Higashiyama.
- The movie *Ugetsu Monogatari/Tales of Moonlight and Rain*, directed by Kenji Mizoguchi, is released in Japan. It is based on the book by Ueda Akinari and stars Masayuki Mori and Michiko Kyo.
- The movie *Where Chimneys Are Seen*, directed by Heinosuke Gosho, is released in Japan.
- The movie musical *Gentlemen Prefer Blondes*, directed by Howard Hawks, is released in the United States. Based on the novel by Anita Loos, it stars Jane Russell and Marilyn Monroe, and features the song "Diamonds Are a Girl's Best Friend."
- The science-fiction movie *The Beast from 20,000 Fathoms*, directed by Eugene Lourie, is released in the United States. Featuring animation effects by Ray Harryhausen and based on the short story "The Foghorn" by Ray Bradbury, it stars Paul Christian, Paula Raymond, and Cecil Kellaway.
- Walt Disney releases the animated movie *Peter Pan*, based on the play by J. M. Barrie, in the United States.

APRIL

13 The 1952 Academy Awards take place. Best Actor: Gary Cooper, for *High Noon*; Best Supporting Actor: Anthony Quinn, for *Viva Zapata!*; Best Actress: Shirley Booth, for *Come Back Little Sheba*; Best Supporting

Actress: Gloria Grahame, for *The Bad and the Beautiful*; Best Picture: *The Greatest Show on Earth*, directed by Cecil B. De Mille; Best Director: John Ford, for *The Quiet Man*.

Literature and Language

- The English writer C. S. Lewis publishes his novel *The Silver Chair*, the fourth volume of *The Chronicles of Narnia*.
- The English writer Elizabeth Jennings publishes *Poems*.
- The English writer Ian Fleming publishes *Casino Royale*, the first James Bond thriller.
- The English writer John Wain publishes his novel *Hurry on Down* (published in the United States as *Born in Captivity*), one of the earliest "Angry Young Man" works.
- The English writer L. P. Hartley publishes his novel *The Go-Between*.
- The English writer Rosamund Lehmann publishes her novel *The Echoing Grove*.
- The French cultural critic Roland Barthes publishes *Le Degré zéro de l'écriture/Writing Degree Zero*, a critical text of structuralist literary theory.
- The French writer Alain Robbe-Grillet publishes his novel *Les Gommes/The Erasers*.
- The German writer Heinrich Böll publishes his novel *Und sagte kein einziges Wort/Acquainted with the Night*.
- The Guinean writer Camara Laye publishes his autobiographical novel *L'Enfant Noir/The African Child* (published in the United States as *The Dark Child*).
- The Irish writer Samuel Beckett publishes his novel *L'Innommable/The Unnamable* in French. The English version appears in 1958. He also publishes his novel *Watt*.
- The Irish-born English writer and philosopher Iris Murdoch publishes *Sartre: Romantic Rationalist*.
- The Nobel Prize for Literature is awarded to the English writer and politician Winston Churchill.
- The Polish writer Czesław Miłosz publishes his collection of essays *Zniewolony umysł/The Captive Mind*.
- The Pulitzer Prize for Biography is awarded to David J. Mays for *Edmund Pendleton, 1721–1803*, the Pulitzer Prize for Poetry is awarded to Archibald MacLeish for *Collected Poems, 1917–1952*, and the Pulitzer Prize for Fiction is awarded to Ernest Hemingway for *The Old Man and the Sea*.
- The Russian-born U.S. writer Isaac Asimov publishes *Second Foundation*, the third novel in his science fiction *Foundation Trilogy*.
- The U.S. writer and critic Leon Edel publishes the first volume of his five-volume biography *Henry James*. The final volume appears in 1970.
- The U.S. writer Charles Olson publishes his poetry collection *In Cold Thicket, in Thicket*.
- The U.S. writer James Baldwin publishes his autobiographical first novel *Go Tell It On The Mountain*.
- The U.S. writer Ray Bradbury publishes his novel *Fahrenheit 451*.

- The U.S. writer Raymond Chandler publishes his novel *The Long Goodbye*.
- The U.S. writer Richard Wright publishes his novel *The Outsider*.
- The U.S. writer Saul Bellow publishes his novel *The Adventures of Augie March*.
- The U.S. writer Theodore Roethke publishes his Pulitzer prizewinning poetry collection *The Waking*.
- The U.S. writer William Burroughs publishes his novel *Junkie: Confessions of an Unredeemed Drug Addict*.

Music

- Popular songs in the United States include "I Believe" and "I'm Walking Behind You."
- The Czech composer Bohuslav Martinů completes his Symphony No. 6, the *Fantaisies Symphoniques/ Symphonic Fantasies*.
- The English composer Michael Tippett completes his *Fantasia Concertante on a Theme by Corelli* for strings and his orchestral work *Ritual Dances from the Midsummer Marriage*.
- The English composer Elisabeth Lutyens completes her *Three Songs*, settings of poems by the Welsh writer Dylan Thomas.
- The French composer Jean Françaix completes his Symphony No. 2.
- The German composer Bernd Zimmermann completes his orchestral work *Contrasts*.
- The opera *Abstrakte Oper No. 1/Abstract Opera No. 1*, by the German composer Boris Blacher, is first performed, in Mannheim, Germany.
- The opera *Der Prozess/The Trial*, by the German composer Gottfried von Einem, is first performed, in Salzburg, Austria. It is based on the novel *The Trial* by the Czech-born German writer Franz Kafka.
- The opera *Gloriana*, by the English composer Benjamin Britten, is first performed, at Covent Garden in London, England.
- The Polish composer Tadeusz Baird completes his Concerto for Orchestra.
- The Russian composer Dmitry Shostakovich completes his Symphony No. 10 and his String Quartet No. 5.
- The U.S. singer Marty Robbins releases the single "Singin' the Blues."
- The U.S. singer Patti Page releases the single "Doggie in the Window."

Theater and Dance

- The play *Tea and Sympathy*, by the U.S. dramatist Robert Anderson, is first performed, in New York, New York.
- The play *Don Juan, oder die Liebe zur Geometrie/Don Juan, or the Love of Geometry*, by the Swiss writer Max Frisch, is first performed, in Berlin, Germany.
- The play *En attendant Godot/Waiting for Godot*, by the Irish writer Samuel Beckett, is first performed, in Paris, France.

- The play *The Confidential Clerk*, by the U.S.-born English writer T. S. Eliot, is first performed, at the Edinburgh Festival in Scotland.
- The play *The Crucible*, by the U.S. dramatist Arthur Miller, is first performed, at the Martin Beck Theater in New York, New York.
- The play *Under Milk Wood*, by the Welsh writer Dylan Thomas is first performed, at Harvard University, Cambridge, Massachusetts. It is written for radio, and is broadcast by the British Broadcasting Corporation (BBC) the following year, narrated by Richard Burton.
- The Pulitzer Prize for Drama is awarded to William Inge for *Picnic*.

FEBRUARY

25 The musical *Wonderful Town*, with lyrics by Betty Comden and Adolph Green and music by Leonard Bernstein, is first performed, at the Winter Garden Theater, New York, New York.

MARCH

29 The 1952–53 Tony Awards take place. Best Actor: Tom Ewell; Best Actress: Shirley Booth; Best Play: *The Crucible*; Best Musical: *Wonderful Town*.

APRIL

14 The musical *The Boy Friend*, with lyrics and music by Sandy Wilson, is first performed, at the Players' Theatre, London, England. It features the song "I Could Be Happy With You."

DECEMBER

3 The musical *Kismet*, with lyrics by Charles Lederer and Luther Davis and using music by Alexander (Aleksandr) Borodin, is first performed, at the Ziegfeld Theater, New York, New York. It features the hit song "Stranger in Paradise."

Thought and Scholarship

- *Philosophical Investigations* by the Austrian philosopher Ludwig Wittgenstein is published posthumously. This work (which marks a complete break with his early philosophy) has a profound impact on Anglo-American philosophy.
- British cryptographer Michael Ventris publishes "Evidence for Greek Dialect in the Mycenaean Archives," in which he announces his decipherment (1952) of the Minoan Linear B script, an ancient form of Greek written between 1500 and 1200 BC.
- English historian G. R. Elton publishes *The Tudor Revolution in Government*.
- German philosopher Martin Heidegger publishes *Einführung in die Metaphysik/An Introduction to Metaphysics*.
- German-born English psychologist Hans Eysenck publishes his anti-Freudian *The Uses and Abuses of Psychology*.
- The Pulitzer Prize for History is awarded to George Dangerfield for *The Era of Good Feelings*.
- U.S. economist Walt W. Rostow publishes *The Process of Economic Growth*.
- U.S. historians Edmund S. Morgan and Helen Morgan publish *The Stamp Act Crisis*.

- U.S. philosopher Willard V. Quine publishes *From a Logical Point of View: Nine Logico-Philosophical Essays*.
- U.S. psychologist B. F. Skinner publishes *Science and Human Behavior*.

SOCIETY

Everyday Life

- U.S. zoologist Alfred Kinsey publishes *Sexual Behavior of the Human Female*. Based on interviews with thousands of women, it indicates a wide range of sexual behavior.

JULY

4 An international confederation of free labor unions meets in Stockholm, Sweden.

AUGUST

6 Following the announcement of a change in the retirement age for public workers, widespread strikes begin in France, continuing into late August.

OCTOBER

30 A general strike takes place in Austria, in protest against its continued occupation by the wartime Allies.

DECEMBER

- "TV dinners," precooked frozen dinners, are introduced by the food processing company C. A. Swanson of Omaha, Nebraska.

Media and Communication

- The *Indian Express* is published, and achieves the highest circulation of any English-language newspaper in India.

JANUARY

20 Dwight D. Eisenhower is inaugurated as 34th president of the United States. The ceremony is broadcast throughout the country on television for the first time.

FEBRUARY

1 Nippon Hoso Kyokai (NHK), the Japan Broadcasting Corporation, begins broadcasting its first television programs, the first in Japan.
11 The 1952–53 Emmy Awards for television are held. Best Dramatic Show: *US Steel Hour*; Best Actor: Donald O'Connor; Best Actress: Eve Arden.

APRIL

3 The first issue of *TV Guide* is issued, by U.S. publisher Walter Annenberg.

JUNE

2 The coronation of Queen Elizabeth II is watched on televisions in homes and public places, such as church halls, by an estimated 20 million viewers in Britain. The event also stimulates the purchase of television sets.
25 The Columbia Broadcasting System (CBS) begins the first regular television broadcasts in color, in the United States.

OCTOBER

22 The first television broadcasts are made in the Philippines.

DECEMBER

- Hugh Hefner publishes the soft porn magazine *Playboy* in the United States. Its mixture of serious journalism, erotic fiction, and the nude feature "Playmate of the Month" proves successful.

Religion

- L. Ron Hubbard founds the Church of Scientology in Washington, D.C.

JULY

22 At a religious gathering at Yankee Stadium in the Bronx, New York, New York, the Jehovah's Witnesses baptize 4,640 babies.

Sports

- Argentina wins the first World Cup men's professional golf competition, known at this time as the Canada Cup, in Montreal, Canada.
- In the first major league baseball franchise shift for 50 years, the Boston Braves of the National League move to Milwaukee, Wisconsin.
- The first Pan-Arab Games, organized by the Arab League, are held.
- The Spanish showjumper Francisco Goyoago, riding Quorum, wins the inaugural world championship showjumping title in Paris, France.
- The U.S. lawn tennis player Maureen "Little Mo" Connolly, aged 18, becomes the first woman to achieve the Grand Slam, winning the singles titles at the Australian, French, Wimbledon, and U.S. championships within the same calendar year.

APRIL

April–July The U.S. golfer Ben Hogan wins the U.S. Masters, the U.S. Open, and the British Open to become the first player to win three majors in a single year; he is unable to compete in the year's fourth major event, the U.S. Professional Golfers Association (PGA) tournament, because the date clashes with that of the British Open.

MAY

23–June 13 Native Dancer, ridden by Eric Guerin, wins the Preakness Stakes and Belmont Stakes horse races in the United States. Earlier he had come second to Dark Star in the Kentucky Derby, the only defeat of his 22-race career.

29 Edmund Hilary from New Zealand and Sherpa Norkey Tenzing from Nepal, as part of John Hunt's British expedition, complete the first successful ascent of Mt. Everest, the world's highest mountain (8,848 m/ 29,028 ft) in the Himalayas, Nepal.

JUNE

13 The U.S. golfer Ben Hogan wins an unprecedented fourth U.S. Open championship.

SEPTEMBER

30–October 5 The New York Yankees defeat the Brooklyn Dodgers by four games to two to become the first baseball team to win the World Series five times in succession.

DECEMBER

27 In the National Football League (NFL) Championship Game in Detroit, Michigan, the Detroit Tigers defeat the Cleveland Browns 17–16 to record their second successive victory over the Browns.

BIRTHS & DEATHS

JANUARY

1 Hank Williams, U.S. country music singer and guitarist, dies in Oak Hill, West Virginia (29).

FEBRUARY

24 Gerd von Rundstedt, German field marshall during World War II, dies in Hannover, West Germany (77).

MARCH

5 Joseph Stalin (adopted name, Russian for steel, of Josef Vissarionovich Dzhugashvili), secretary-general of the Communist Party of the Soviet Union 1922–53 and premier 1941–53, dies in Moscow, USSR (73).

5 Sergey Sergeyivich Prokofiev, Russian composer, dies in Moscow, USSR (61).

28 Jim Thorpe, U.S. professional football and baseball player, Olympic gold medallist in the pentathlon and decathlon, dies in Lomita, California (66).

MAY

6 Tony (Antony Charles Lynton) Blair, British prime minister from 1997, a Labour politician, is born in Edinburgh, Scotland.

JUNE

5 Bill Tilden, U.S. tennis player who dominated the sport during the early 1920s, dies in Hollywood, California (60).

21 Benazir Bhutto, prime minister of Pakistan 1988–90 and from 1993, born in Karachi, Pakistan.

JULY

15 Jean-Bertrand Aristide, the first elected president of Haiti, is born in Port Salut, Haiti.

SEPTEMBER

28 Edwin Powell Hubble, U.S. astronomer who provided the first proof that the universe is expanding, dies in San Marino, California (63).

OCTOBER

3 Arnold Bax, English composer, dies in Cork, Ireland (69).

NOVEMBER

3 Roseanne Barr, U.S. comedienne, born in Salt Lake City, Utah.

9 Dylan Thomas, Welsh poet, dies in New York, New York (39).

9 Ibn Saud, Arabian tribal and Muslim leader who founded the modern state of Saudi Arabia in 1932 and began to exploit its oil resources, dies in Aṭ Ṭāif, Saudi Arabia (about 73).

27 Eugene O'Neill, U.S. dramatist, dies in Boston, Massachusetts (65).

DECEMBER

8 Kim Basinger, U.S. actress, born in Athens, Georgia.

19 Robert Andrews Millikan, U.S. physicist who developed a method of determining the electric charge on a single electron, dies in San Marino, California (85).

1954

POLITICS, GOVERNMENT, AND ECONOMICS

Business and Economics

- The fuel giant Tenneco opens under the name Cumberland Corporation.
- The U.S. Gross National Product (GNP) reaches a new high of $365 billion.

JANUARY

19   U.S. automobile company General Motors announces a $1 billion expansion program.

JUNE

- The United Steelworkers of America and United States Steel Corporation agree to a two-year contract that gives workers a schedule of wage increases and increased insurance and pension benefits.

NOVEMBER

23   The 50 millionth car produced by U.S. automobile manufacturer General Motors is rolled off the company's assembly plant in Flint, Michigan. The car is a gold-painted Chevrolet sport coupé.

Human Rights

APRIL

22–June 17   The McCarthy "witch-hunts" reach their peak as Wisconsin senator Joseph McCarthy, chairman of the Senate Permanent Investigations Subcommittee, alleges that a communist spy ring is active at the U.S. Army Signal Corps headquarters at Fort Monmouth, New Jersey. During the hearings, which are televised across the country, McCarthy accuses the Army secretary of deliberately concealing evidence. McCarthy's conduct turns public opinion against him.

MAY

18   The European Convention on Human Rights comes into force.

Politics and Government

- A new constitution in the British protectorate of Nigeria establishes the Federation of Nigeria, comprising northern, eastern, and western regions, the Southern Cameroons (a United Nations Trust territory), and the Federal Territory of Lagos.

- The U.S. Congress passes the new Atomic Energy Act, which permits nuclear reactors to be privately owned and licensed.

JANUARY

- Chinese military attacks on the Nationalist Chinese-held islands of Quemoy and Matsu in the Taiwan Strait raise international tension.
- In a speech before the U.S. Congress, President Dwight D. Eisenhower endorses revision of the Taft–Hartley Act (1946), which restricts labor's right to strike.
- The U.S. Senate authorizes construction of the St. Lawrence Seaway, designed to connect the Great Lakes to the Atlantic Ocean.

5   Giuseppe Pella resigns as Italian prime minister and, on January 18, Amintore Fanfani forms a ministry of Christian Democrats.

8–15   British Commonwealth finance ministers meet at Sydney, Australia, under the Australian prime minister Robert Menzies, to consolidate the economic progress of the sterling area and the Commonwealth.

24   Moshe Sharett forms a new coalition government in Israel.

25–February 18   The foreign ministers of the United States, USSR, Britain, and France meet in Berlin, Germany, but the USSR rejects the West's proposal for the reunification of Germany through free elections.

30   Amintore Fanfani resigns as Italian prime minister after losing a vote of confidence.

FEBRUARY

- The United States announces that it detonated the world's first hydrogen bomb at Eniwetok Atoll in the Marshall Islands two years before.

10   Mario Scelba forms an Italian coalition government of Christian Democrats, Social Democrats, and Liberals, with parliamentary support from Republicans.

23   Britain announces its intention to turn the protectorate of Uganda into a self-governing state, without recognizing the authority of the kabaka of Buganda; in Uganda, supporters of the kabaka bring a legal action claiming that Britain's withdrawal of recognition of the kabaka in November 1953 was illegal.

25   Deputy prime minister Colonel Gamal Abdel Nasser seizes power in Egypt as prime minister, but on February 27 the British-appointed General Mohammed Neguib Bey, recently resigned as president and prime minister, resumes his position after demands by civilian and military groups.

25   President Adib Shishkali of Syria flees following an army revolt. On March 1 Sabri el Assali forms a government.

MARCH

- The U.S. Atomic Energy Commission announces plans to build the nation's first atomic power plant, in Pittsburgh, Pennsylvania.

- The U.S. House of Representatives approves a 50% cut in federal luxury taxes.
1   Lolita Lebron, a Puerto Rican nationalist, enters the chamber of the U.S. House of Representatives and fires eight shots that wound five U.S. congressmen, none fatally.
1   The United States tests a hydrogen bomb in the Marshall Islands in the Pacific Ocean. The bomb is over 500 times more powerful than the bomb dropped on Hiroshima, Japan, in 1945, giving the United States the technology to produce a bomb capable of razing any of the world's largest cities.
4   Following the death of President Amin Didi in January, the sultanate is restored in the Maldive Islands, with Amir Mohammed Didi as sultan.
8   The United States and Japan sign a mutual defense agreement that allows Japan to rearm itself in a limited and gradual way.
9   The Center and Right make gains in the Finnish elections and, on May 5, Ralph Törngren, leader of the Swedish People's Party, forms a coalition government with the Social Democratic Party and the Agrarian Party.
13–May 7   Communist Vietminh guerrillas launch a large-scale assault on the French forces besieged at Dien Bien Phu, Vietnam.
23   Israel withdraws from the United Nations (UN) Mixed Armistice Commission, which is attempting to negotiate a settlement of its disputes with Syria, Egypt, and Jordan, complaining of its ineffectiveness.

APRIL

- The U.S. Congress authorizes the establishment of the U.S. Air Force Academy. On June 24, Air Force secretary Harold E. Talbot announces that it will be built in Colorado Springs.
12   Dr. Cheddi Jagan, former prime minister and leader of the People's Progressive Party of British Guiana (now Guyana), is sentenced to six months in prison for violating an order restricting his movements.
12   In Belgian elections, the Christian Socialists lose their absolute majority to the Socialists and Liberals, and on April 22 the Socialist Achille van Acker forms a coalition government.
13   Diplomat Vladimir Petrov of the Soviet embassy in Canberra, Australia, is granted asylum in Australia, and reveals the existence of a spy network there.
16   The U.S. president Dwight D. Eisenhower pledges U.S. support to the six countries intending to form the European Defense Community (EDC): France, Italy, Luxembourg, Belgium, the Netherlands, and West Germany.
17   Colonel Gamal Abdel Nasser officially becomes prime minister and military governor of Egypt, following a failed attempt to seize power on February 25.
21   The shah of Iran reappoints General Fazlo'llah Zahedi as prime minister.
23   The USSR breaks off relations with Australia following its refusal to return the defector Vladimir Petrov.
26–July 21   An international conference is held in Geneva, Switzerland, to try to resolve the problems of Korea and Indochina.
28   India signs a commercial and cultural agreement with China.

28   The prime ministers of India, Pakistan, Burma (now Myanmar), Indonesia, and Ceylon confer at Colombo, Ceylon (now Sri Lanka).

MAY

- The U.S. Senate defeats an amendment that would reduce the voting age to 18.
- The U.S. Supreme Court, in *Brown v. Board of Education*, overturns the *Plessy v. Ferguson* decision of 1896 and declares "separate but equal" schools to be unconstitutional.
- The U.S. Supreme Court upholds the Internal Security Act of 1950, which provides for the deportation of aliens holding membership in the Communist Party.
7   The Vietminh siege of French forces at Dien Bien Phu in North Vietnam ends with the surrender of 10,000 French troops; 5,000 more French troops are dead and the defeat effectively ends French power in Indochina.
18   In a general election in the Republic of Ireland, Fianna Fáil wins 65 seats, Fine Gael 50, and Labour 19.
29   In the Australian general election, Robert Menzies' coalition of Liberal and Country parties is reelected with a slightly reduced majority (the Liberals win 47 seats, the Country Party 17, and Labor 57).
29   Thailand complains to the United Nations (UN) Security Council that communists in Indochina threaten its security.
31   A state of emergency is declared in the Buganda region of Uganda following unrest.
31   President Tito of Yugoslavia visits Greece.

JUNE

2   Following the election in the Republic of Ireland in May, John Costello (Fine Gael) replaces Éamon de Valera as prime minister and forms a coalition government.
12   The French government is defeated in the national assembly after the defeat of the French army by Viet Minh forces at Dien Bien Phu, Vietnam.
15   The proindependence Convention People's Party wins the elections in the British colony of Gold Coast (now Ghana) and, on June 21, Dr. Kwame Nkrumah forms a government.
18   The Radical Pierre Mendès-France becomes prime minister of France.
29   Following the meeting of the U.S. president Dwight D. Eisenhower and the British prime minister Winston Churchill in Washington, D.C., the Potomac Charter, a six-point affirmation of Western policy toward the communist world, is issued.

JULY

- U.S. senator Ralph E. Flanders of Vermont introduces a resolution of censure against colleague Joseph McCarthy for conduct unbecoming a senator.
2   French forces evacuate the southern part of the Red River Delta, Indochina.
3   Marilyn Sheppard, the 31-year-old pregnant wife of an osteopath, is murdered in her home in Bay Village, Ohio. Her husband, Samuel H. ("Dr. Sam") Sheppard, claims that "a bushy-haired man" killed his wife and knocked him unconscious. Despite his protestations, Sheppard is arrested for murder. The case becomes the inspiration for the U.S. television program *The Fugitive* (1963–67).
17   Finland and the USSR sign a trade pact.

17 The Free Democrat Theodor Heuss is reelected president of West Germany.

20 An armistice ending the fighting in Indochina is signed in Geneva, Switzerland. Under the terms of the agreement France is to evacuate North Vietnam, while the communists are to evacuate South Vietnam, Cambodia, and Laos. France also undertakes to respect the independence of Cambodia, Laos, and Vietnam, and the communist leader Ho Chi Minh is to form a government in North Vietnam.

23 The settlement ending the war in Indochina is approved by the French national assembly.

AUGUST

5 Iran and a consortium of eight foreign companies announce an agreement for the production and export of oil, resolving the British–Iranian oil crisis.

11 The Netherlands–Indonesian Union agreed in 1947 is dissolved.

19 Fearing a vote against the European Defense Community (EDC) Treaty of May 1952, the French government submits a revised treaty to its cosignatories, but the draft is rejected on August 22.

23 Greece, Yugoslavia, and Turkey sign a treaty of mutual assistance.

30 The French parliament votes against ratification of the 1952 treaty establishing the European Defense Community (EDC), which is destroyed by the decision.

SEPTEMBER

• The U.S. president Dwight D. Eisenhower signs the Espionage and Sabotage Act. It mandates the death penalty for spying in peacetime and eliminates the statute of limitations on these crimes.

8 The South-East Asian Defense Treaty (for mutual defense) and Pacific Charter are signed in Manila, Philippines, by the United States, Australia, New Zealand, Pakistan, Thailand, the Philippines, Britain, and France. The treaty establishes SEATO, the South-East Asia Treaty Organization, based in Bangkok, Thailand.

15–28 The All-China People's Congress meets for the first time, in Beijing, China. It adopts a new constitution for China on September 20 and, on September 27, it elects Mao Zedong as chairman, Zhu De as vice chairman, and Zhou Enlai as prime minister.

OCTOBER

3 A nine-power conference in London, England, on European unity, agrees that West Germany should enter the North Atlantic Treaty Organization (NATO).

5 The United States, Britain, Italy, and Yugoslavia agree that the disputed port of Trieste should be divided into Italian and Yugoslav zones, thus ending the dispute.

8 Communist forces occupy Hanoi, North Vietnam, following the signing of the Geneva settlement of July 20.

19 Colonel Gamal Abdel Nasser, prime minister of Egypt, signs a British–Egyptian agreement that terminates the treaty of alliance of 1936. British troops are to withdraw from the Suez Canal zone, but Britain reserves the right to intervene if the canal is threatened. The agreement comes into force from December 6.

23 The United States, Britain, France, and the USSR agree, in Paris, France, to end the occupation of Germany. A further nine-power agreement, not including the USSR, is signed, permitting Italy and Germany to join the Western European Union established under the Brussels Treaty of 1948.

24 A state of emergency is declared in Pakistan by the governor-general following economic and social unrest.

26 France and West Germany sign an economic and cultural agreement.

30–November 1 An insurrection is mounted in Algeria, with over 60 attacks on French police and troops. The rebels call themselves the Front for National Liberation (FLN) and demand the establishment of an independent Algeria.

NOVEMBER

• In U.S. Congressional elections, Democrats regain majorities in the House (232–203) and Senate (48–47).

2 Fulgencio Batista is elected Cuban president with no opposition, his opponent Ramon Grau San Martin having withdrawn, alleging election rigging.

4 The Ugandan high court supports the legality of the British colonial government withdrawing recognition of the kabaka (king) of Buganda, following seccessionist moves by the Ugandan province.

5 Burma (now Myanmar) signs a peace treaty ending hostilities with Japan dating from World War II.

13 Successes for the Social Credit Party in the New Zealand elections reduce the National Party's majority, but Sidney Holland remains prime minister.

14 President Muhammad Naguib Bey of Egypt is deposed and, on November 18, prime minister Colonel Gamal Abdel Nasser becomes head of state.

29 A conference of representatives of Soviet satellite states opens in Moscow, USSR; it is also attended by observers from communist China.

DECEMBER

1 The United States signs a mutual security pact with Nationalist China (Formosa, now Taiwan).

2 The Nationalist Johannes Strijdom forms a ministry in South Africa following the retirement of Daniel Malan.

2 The U.S. Senate votes by 67 to 22 to censure Wisconsin senator Joseph McCarthy on charges of misconduct, after public opinion has turned against his accusations of subversive activity in the government and army.

12 France sends 20,000 troops to Algeria in response to the October 30 attempt to stage a nationalist insurrection.

14 Supporters for the union (Enosis) of the British colony of Cyprus and Greece riot in Athens, Greece. During 1954, George Grivas's National Organization of Cypriot Fighters (EOKA) has emerged as a pro-Enosis terrorist organization.

17 President Tito of Yugoslavia visits Delhi, India.

20 The USSR threatens to annul its alliance treaty with Britain of May 1942 if the Paris agreement of October 23 (allowing Germany to join the Western European Union) is ratified.

21 Samuel H. ("Dr. Sam") Sheppard is convicted of the second-degree murder of his wife Marilyn, and is sentenced to life in prison, after a trial in Cleveland, Ohio, that is later characterized as filled with "prejudicial publicity" and having a "carnival atmosphere." The verdict is overturned in 1966.

29 Vietnam, Laos, and Cambodia all become independent under a treaty with France.

SCIENCE, TECHNOLOGY, AND MEDICINE

Agriculture

- U.S. entomologist Edward Knipling air-drops thousands of sterilized male screwworm flies over the Caribbean island of Curaçao in an effort to control the pest. The insect is wiped out within six months and the test is followed by two successful experiments in the United States.

Computing

- The UNIVAC 1103A computer is introduced in the UK. It is the first commercial computer to have a magnetic-core memory and is 50 times faster than UNIVAC I, introduced in 1951.

Ecology

JULY

31 A study in the United States finds that automobiles contribute 80% of the pollution in the greater Los Angeles community, in California.

AUGUST

1 The Chang Jiang River floods in China, killing 40,000 people and forcing 10 million to leave their homes.

SEPTEMBER

1 Hurricane Carol strikes Long Island, New York, killing 68 people and causing $50 million of property damage.

OCTOBER

- A U.S. Aerobee rocket takes the first picture of a complete hurricane, at an altitude of 160 km/100 mi off the Texas Gulf coast.

15 Hurricane Hazel smashes into the northern U.S. and Canadian seaboard, killing 348 people.

Exploration

FEBRUARY

15 The French bathyscaph *FNRS 3* descends to a record 4,000 m/13,000 ft in the Atlantic Ocean off Senegal.

Health and Medicine

- The synthetic tranquilizer chlorpromazine, developed in France in 1952, is introduced in the United States as Thorazine and used to treat schizophrenia.
- The U.S. National Cancer Institute suggests a link between smoking and lung cancer.
- U.S. scientists Gregory G. Pincus, Hudson Hoagland, and Min-Cheh Chang, of the Worcester Foundation, develop an oral contraceptive using the hormone norethisterone.
- U.S. virologists John Enders, Thomas Weller, and Frederick Robbins are jointly awarded the Nobel Prize

for Physiology or Medicine for their cultivation of poliomyelitis viruses in various types of tissue.

FEBRUARY

- U.S. physician Jonas E. Salk, developer of the poliomyelitis vaccine, inoculates children against polio in Pittsburgh, Pennsylvania.

DECEMBER

23 U.S. surgeon Peter Brent performs the first successful kidney transplant, at Brigham Hospital, Boston, Massachusetts. The donor is the patient's identical twin.

Science

- English archeologist Mortimer Wheeler publishes *The Indus Civilization*.
- Italian chemist Giulio Natta polymerizes propylene to obtain polypropylene.
- Russian-born U.S. cosmologist George Gamow suggests that the genetic code consists of the order of nucleotide triplets in the DNA molecule.
- UK physicist Max Born and German physicist Walther Bothe share the Nobel Prize for Physics: Born for his research in quantum mechanics, especially his statistical interpretation of the wave function, and Bothe for his invention of the coincidence method.
- U.S. biochemist Robert Burns Woodward synthesizes the poison strychnine, and lysergic acid, the basis of LSD (lysergic acid diethylamide).
- U.S. chemist Linus Pauling receives the Nobel Prize for Chemistry for his discoveries concerning the nature of chemical bonds.

MAY

21 The Central Observatory of the Soviet Academy of Sciences, near Leningrad (now St. Petersburg), USSR, opens.

Technology

- A direct current (DC) submarine cable is installed between the Swedish island of Gotland and the Swedish mainland, 97 km/60 mi away. Operating at 100,000 volts, and carrying 20,000 kilowatts of power, it uses newly developed high-voltage mercury-arc rectifiers and is the first high-voltage DC transmission line. It stimulates further research into DC, and later in the year power from the hydroelectric station at Harsprånget, 35 km/22 mi north of the Arctic circle, is transmitted to southern Sweden, over 960 km/600 mi away using the first high-voltage transmission line to use bundle conductors. It carries 380,000 volts and its success raises the possibility of transmitting even higher voltages.
- Guidance systems have been miniaturized and refined to the point where they can be used to guide intercontinental ballistic missiles (ICBMs) accurately to targets 8,000 km/5,000 mi away.
- The basic oxygen process for producing steel, developed in Austria in 1952, is introduced into the United States by the McLouth Steel Company.
- The British Parliament establishes the Atomic Energy Authority to develop civilian applications of nuclear power.
- The first volume of the five-volume *The History of Technology*, edited by the English historian of science

Charles Singer and others, is published. The last part appears in 1958.

- The silicon transistor is developed by Texas Instruments engineer Gordon Teal. Cheaper and more resistant to higher temperatures than germanium, the development of silicon transistors stimulates the growth of solid state components in computers, airplanes, and missiles.
- The U.S. Bell Telephone Laboratories develops the solar battery, an array of photovoltaic cells capable of converting the sun's radiation into electricity. It is especially suited for generating power in space.

JANUARY

21 The first nuclear-powered submarine, the *Nautilus*, is launched by the United States at Groton, Connecticut. It is also the largest submarine, at 97 m/319 ft long.

JUNE

27 The world's first commercial nuclear power generating station begins producing electricity at Obninsk outside Moscow, USSR. It generates five megawatts of electricity.

JULY

25 The U.S. Naval Research Laboratory makes use of the moon as a communications satellite by bouncing voice messages off it.

Transportation

- An atomic-powered railroad locomotive is designed at the University of Utah, Salt Lake City, Utah.
- British Comet jet airliners crash near Elba (January 10, killing 35 people) and Messina (April 9, killing 21 people); the jets are grounded and metal fatigue in a section of the cabin roof is thought to be the cause of the crashes (announced on October 19).
- The first vertical take off and landing (VTOL) aircraft, known as the "flying bedstead," is developed in the UK.
- The Scenecruiser bus is introduced in the United States for long-distance routes. It has toilet facilities, plus an upper level for viewing.
- The subway system opens in Toronto, Canada.
- U.S. entrepreneur Malcolm Maclean initiates the use of containers to ship goods between New York, New York, and Houston, Texas. The idea catches on rapidly throughout the world.
- West German car manufacturing company Daimler-Benz introduces the Mercedes 300 SL, the first car to have a fuel injection system.

JANUARY

1 Flashing directional indicator lights are made compulsory on cars in Britain.

JUNE

4 U.S. Air Force pilot Major Arthur Murray, in the X-1A research airplane, achieves a record altitude of slightly over 27,432 m/90,000 ft.
24 New York State Thruway is opened, a 894-km/559-mi long highway stretching from New York, New York, to Buffalo, New York.

JULY

- President Dwight D. Eisenhower announces a plan to modernize the nation's highways, its cost to be borne by both state and federal government.

15 The Boeing 707 four-engine jet passenger aircraft makes its first test flight at Seattle, Washington. Capable of carrying 179 passengers, it becomes the standard long-range passenger aircraft. It is officially launched on July 17.

SEPTEMBER

26 The Japanese ferry *Toya maru* overturns during a typhoon in Hakodate Bay, killing 700 people.

OCTOBER

- The U.S. Air Force begins production of the first supersonic bomber, the B-58.
4 British Overseas Airways (BOAC) begins operating the world's first transatlantic jet service, between London, England and New York, New York, using a British de Havilland Comet 4.
17 U.S. pilot Billy Wester establishes a world helicopter altitude record of 7,468 m/24,500 ft, at Bridgeport, Connecticut, in a Sikorsky XH-39.

DECEMBER

- The aircraft carrier USS *Forestal* is launched at Newport News, Virginia. Weighing 59,650 tons, it is the largest warship ever built.

ARTS AND IDEAS

Architecture

- The English architectural historian John Harvey publishes *English Medieval Architecture: A Biographical Dictionary down to 1550*.
- The English architectural historian Howard Colvin publishes *A Biographical Dictionary of English Architects, 1660–1840*.
- The Manufacturers Trust Bank in New York, New York, designed by the U.S. architectural firm of Skidmore, Owings, and Merrill, is completed.

Arts

- The English artist Barbara Hepworth sculpts *Two figures, Menhirs*.
- The English artist Graham Sutherland paints *Portrait of Winston Churchill*, which is later destroyed by Churchill's wife, who disliked it.
- The English artist Henry Moore sculpts *Internal and External Forms*.
- The English artist Kenneth Armitage sculpts *Seated Group Listening to Music*.
- The French-U.S. artist Grace Hartigan paints *Grand Street Brides*.
- The German-born U.S. art theorist Rudolf Arnheim publishes *Art and Visual Perception*.
- The Irish-born British artist Francis Bacon paints *Head Surrounded by Sides of Beef*.
- The Polish-born French artist Balthus paints *Le Passage du Commerce Saint André/Saint André Commercial Street*.
- The Spanish artist Pablo Picasso paints *Portrait of Sylvette in a Green Armchair*.
- The U.S. artist Ad Reinhardt paints *Abstract Painting, Black*.

- The U.S. artist Joseph Cornell creates his assemblage sculpture *Untitled (Ostend)*.
- The U.S. artist Mark Rothko paints *Untitled: Yellow, Orange, Red on Orange*.
- The U.S. artist Robert Rauschenberg paints *Pink Door*.
- The U.S. artist Robert Motherwell paints *Elegy to the Spanish Republic No. 34*.

Film

- At the Cannes Film Festival in France, the Palme d'Or is awarded to *Jigokumon/Gate of Hell*, directed by Teinosuke Kinugasa.
- The movie *Pokolenie/A Generation*, directed by Andrzej Wajda, is released in Poland, starring Tadeusz Łomnicki, Urszula Modrzyńska, and Roman Polański.
- The movie *East of Eden*, directed by Elia Kazan, is released in the United States. Based on the novel by John Steinbeck, it stars Raymond Massey and, in his first major role, James Dean. Another Kazan movie *On the Waterfront* is released in the United States, starring Marlon Brando, Rod Steiger, Lee J. Cobb, and Eve Marie Saint.
- The movie *Executive Suite*, directed by Robert Wise, is released in the United States, starring Fredric March, Barbara Stanwyck, William Holden, and June Allyson.
- The movie *Genevieve*, directed by Henry Cornelius, is released in Britain, starring Kenneth More, Dinah Sheridan, John Gregson, and Kay Kendall. It is the first British movie to be shot in Technicolor.
- The movie *La Strada/The Road*, directed by Federico Fellini, is released in Italy, starring Giulietta Masina and Anthony Quinn.
- The movie *Les Diaboliques/The She-Devils*, directed by Henri-Georges Clouzot, is released in France, starring Simone Signoret, Vera Clouzot, Charles Vanel, and Paul Meurisse.
- The movie *Rear Window*, directed by English filmmaker Alfred Hitchcock, is released in the United States, starring James Stewart and Grace Kelly.
- The movie *Sabrina*, directed by Billy Wilder, is released in the United States, starring Audrey Hepburn, Humphrey Bogart, and William Holden.
- The movie *Seven Samurai*, directed by Akira Kurosawa, is released in Japan, starring Toshiro Mifune, Takashi Shimura, and Kuninori Kodo.
- The movie *The Belles of St Trinians*, directed by Frank Launder and based on the drawings by Ronald Searle, is released in Britain, starring Alistair Sim, George Cole, Joyce Grenfell, and Hermione Baddeley.
- The movie *The Caine Mutiny*, directed by Edward Dmytryk, is released in the United States. Based on the novel by Herman Wouk, it stars Humphrey Bogart.
- The movie *The Divided Heart*, directed by Charles Crichton, is released in Britain, starring Cornell Borchers and Yvonne Mitchell.
- The movie *The Wild One*, directed by Hungarian filmmaker Laslo Benedek, is released in the United States, starring Marlon Brando, Lee Marvin, Mary Murphy, and Robert Keith.
- The movie *Them!*, directed by Gordon Douglas, is released in the United States. Featuring giant mutant ants that run amok in the southwest United States, it stars Edmund Gwenn, Joan Weldon, James Arness, and Onslow Stevens.
- The movie musical *Carmen Jones*, directed by the Austrian filmmaker Otto Preminger, is released in the United States. Based on Bizet's opera *Carmen*, it stars black stars and singers: Dorothy Dandridge, Harry Belafonte, and Pearl Bailey.
- The movie musical *Seven Brides for Seven Brothers*, directed by Stanley Donen, is released in the United States, starring Howard Keel and Jane Powell.
- The movie musical *A Star is Born*, directed by George Cukor, is released in the United States, starring Judy Garland and James Mason.
- The movie musical *White Christmas*, directed by Michael Curtiz, is released in the United States. A remake of *Holiday Inn*, it stars Bing Crosby, Danny Kaye, Rosemary Clooney, and Vera Ellen.

APRIL

12 The 1953 Academy Awards take place. Best Actor: William Holden, for *Stalag 17*; Best Supporting Actor: Frank Sinatra, for *From Here to Eternity*; Best Actress: Audrey Hepburn, for *Roman Holiday*; Best Supporting Actress: Donna Reed, for *From Here to Eternity*; Best Picture: *From Here to Eternity*, directed by Fred Zinnemann; Best Director: Fred Zinnemann, for *From Here to Eternity*.

Literature and Language

- The English writer C. S. Lewis publishes his novel *The Horse and His Boy*, the fifth volume of *The Chronicles of Narnia*.
- The English writer Doris Lessing publishes her novel *A Proper Marriage*.
- The English writer John Betjeman publishes his poetry collection *A Few Late Chrysanthemums*.
- The English writer John Masters publishes his novel *Bhowani Junction*.
- The English writer J. R. R. Tolkien publishes his novel *The Fellowship of the Ring*, the first volume of his *The Lord of the Rings* trilogy.
- The English writer Kingsley Amis publishes his novel *Lucky Jim*.
- The English writer William Golding publishes his novel *Lord of the Flies*, partly a reworking of the Victorian boys' tale *The Coral Island* (1858).
- The French writer and philosopher Simone de Beauvoir publishes her novel *Les Mandarins/The Mandarins*.
- The French writer Françoise Sagan publishes her novel *Bonjour Tristesse/Hello Sadness* at the age of 19.
- The French-born writer Anaïs Nin publishes her novel *A Spy in the House of Love* in English.
- The German writer Thomas Mann publishes his novel *Die Bekenntnisse des Hochstaplers Felix Krull/The Confessions of Felix Krull, Confidence Man*.
- The Irish-born English writer and philosopher Iris Murdoch publishes her novel *Under the Net*.
- The Nigerian writer Cyprian Ekwensi publishes his novel *People of the City*.
- The Nobel Prize for Literature is awarded to the U.S. novelist Ernest Hemingway.
- The Polish-born English historian Isaac Deutscher publishes *The Armed Prophet*, the first volume of his

three-volume biography of the Russian revolutionary leader Leon Trotsky.

- The Pulitzer Prize for Biography is awarded to Charles A. Lindbergh for *The Spirit of St Louis* and the Pulitzer Prize for Poetry is awarded to Theodore Roethke for *The Waking*. The Pulitzer Prize for Fiction is not awarded this year.
- The Swiss writer Max Frisch publishes his novel *Stiller/I'm Not Stiller*.
- The U.S. writer Eudora Welty publishes her novel *The Ponder Heart*.
- The U.S. writer Evan Hunter (who also writes detective fiction under the name Ed McBain) publishes his novel *The Blackboard Jungle*.
- The U.S. writer Peter De Vries publishes his novel *The Tunnel of Love*.
- The U.S. writer Randall Jarrell publishes his novel *Pictures from an Institution*.

Music

- Popular songs in the United States include "Stranger in Paradise," "Hernando's Hideaway," and "Young at Heart."
- The British trumpeter Eddie Calvert releases the single "Oh, Mein Papa"/"Oh, My Papa."
- The English musician and musicologist Thurston Dart publishes *The Interpretation of Music*.
- The French-born U.S. composer Edgard Varèse completes his orchestral work *Déserts*.
- The Greek composer Iannis Xenakis completes his orchestral work *Metastasis*.
- The Hungarian composer György Ligeti completes his String Quartet No. 1, *Métamorphoses nocturnes/ Nocturnal Metamorphoses*.
- The opera *Penelope*, by the Swiss composer Rolf Liebermann, is first performed, in Salzburg, Austria.
- The opera *The Turn of the Screw*, by the English composer Benjamin Britten, is first performed, in Venice, Italy. It is based on a story by the U.S. writer Henry James.
- The opera *Troilus and Cressida*, by the English composer William Walton, is first performed, in London, England.
- The Polish composer Witold Lutosławski completes his *Concerto for Orchestra*.
- The Russian composer Igor Stravinsky completes *In Memoriam Dylan Thomas* for voice and string quartet.
- The U.S. actress and singer Doris Day releases the single "Secret Love," from the soundtrack of the movie *Calamity Jane*.
- The U.S. composer George Crumb completes his *String Quartet*.
- The U.S. composer Quincey Porter completes his *Concerto Concertante* for two pianos and orchestra.
- The U.S. composer Samuel Barber completes his *Prayers of Kierkegaard* for voice and orchestra.
- The U.S. composer Vincent Persichetti completes his Symphony No. 4.
- The U.S. rock singer Elvis Presley releases the singles "That's All Right, Mama" and "Blue Moon of Kentucky."
- The U.S. singer Perry Como releases the single "Wanted."

FEBRUARY

6   Folkway Records releases a four-record set with 94 songs, including "Irene Good Night" and "Jailhouse Blue," by the U.S. folk singer Leadbelly.

JULY

18   The first jazz festival at Newport, Rhode Island, takes place.

Theater and Dance

- The New York Shakespeare Festival is founded by the U.S. producer and director Joseph Papp.
- The play *Amédée/Amadeus*, by the Romanian-born French dramatist Eugène Ionesco, is first performed in Paris, France.
- The play *Ladies of the Corridor*, by the U.S. writers Dorothy Parker and Arnaud d'Usseau, is first performed, in New York, New York.
- The play *Separate Tables* (comprising two linked plays) by the English writer Terence Rattigan, is first performed, at the St. James's Theatre in London, England.
- The play *The Bad Seed*, by the U.S. dramatist Maxwell Anderson, is first performed, in New York, New York. It is an adaptation of a novel by William March.
- The play *The Quare Fellow*, by the Irish writer Brendan Behan, is first performed, in Dublin, Ireland.
- The Pulitzer Prize for Drama is awarded to John Patrick for *The Teahouse of the August Moon*.

MARCH

28   The 1953–54 Tony Awards take place. Best Actor: David Wayne; Best Actress: Audrey Hepburn; Best Play: *The Teahouse of the August Moon*; Best Musical: *Kismet*.

AUGUST

5   The musical *Salad Days*, with music and lyrics by Julian Slade, is first performed, at the Vaudeville Theatre, London, England.

DECEMBER

27   The musical *The Saint of Bleecker Street* by the Italian-born U.S. composer Gian Carlo Menotti, is first performed, at the Broadway Theater in New York, New York.

Thought and Scholarship

- *History of Economic Analysis* by the Austrian-born U.S. economist Joseph Alois Schumpeter is published posthumously.
- English historian A. J. P. Taylor publishes *The Struggle for Mastery in Europe, 1848–1918*.
- English historian Asa Briggs publishes *Victorian People*.
- English historian of science Joseph Needham publishes the first volume of his 12-volume *Science and Civilization in China*. The final part appears in 1984.
- English philosopher Gilbert Ryle publishes *Dilemmas*.
- Martinique psychiatrist and social critic Frantz Fanon publishes *Les Damnés de la terre/The Wretched of the Earth*.
- Latvian-born English philosopher Isaiah Berlin publishes *Historical Inevitability*.

- The Pulitzer Prize for History is awarded to Bruce Catton for *A Stillness at Appomattox*.
- U.S. historian David M. Potter publishes *People of Plenty: Economic Abundance and the American Character*.
- U.S. journalist William F. Buckley publishes *McCarthy and His Enemies*.
- U.S. philosopher Max Black publishes *Problems of Analysis*.
- U.S. psychologist Abraham Harold Maslow publishes *Motivation and Personality*.

SOCIETY

Education

- New Hall college is founded at Cambridge University, England.
- The University of Alaska opens in Anchorage.

Everyday Life

- Publishers in the United States form the Comic Code Authority, a self-regulatory body, in response to complaints about the levels of violence and "lack of morality" in comics available to children. Its creation causes a split between mainstream comics and the emerging "underground" comics by such artists as Robert Crumb and Gilbert Shelton.
- Studies reveal that 90% of U.S. adults have at least three cups of coffee each day, and 45% smoke cigarettes, 60% of men and 30% of women.
- The Cha Cha Cha dance becomes popular in the United States.
- The Federation of British Sun Clubs is founded, to help promote nudism.
- The Northland shopping mall, designed by Victor Gruen Associates, opens north of Detroit, Michigan.

JANUARY

14   The U.S. actress Marilyn Monroe is married for a second time, to U.S. baseball star Joe DiMaggio; in October, she sues for divorce.

APRIL

- The International Longshoremen's Association halts a strike begun on March 3 in New York, New York, to settle questions of labor jurisdiction.

SEPTEMBER

- The United Steelworkers of America ban from their ranks communists, fascists, and Ku Klux Klan members.

11   The Miss America beauty competition, held in Atlantic City, New Jersey, is televised throughout the United States.

NOVEMBER

- Veterans Day becomes a U.S. holiday, replacing Armistice Day, which was inaugurated in 1928 specifically to honor veterans of World War I.

Media and Communication

- Twenty-nine million homes—60%—have television sets in the United States.
- Radio Corporation of America (RCA) produces the first color television sets in the United States.
- The Eurovision television network is formed, linking companies in eight countries. The first broadcast, made on June 6, features Pope Pius XII.
- The women's magazine *Marie-Claire* is launched, in France.

MARCH

7   The 1953–54 Emmy Awards for television are held. Best Dramatic Show: *US Steel Hour*; Best Actor: Danny Thomas; Best Actress: Loretta Young.

AUGUST

16   The first issue of the magazine *Sports Illustrated* is published by Time-Life, in the United States.

OCTOBER

3–September 17, 1962   The situation comedy *Father Knows Best* appears on U.S. television, starring Robert Young, Jane Wyatt, Elinor Donahue, Billy Gray, and Lauren Chapin.

25   A meeting of the U.S. cabinet is televised for the first time.

DECEMBER

15   The first episode of a three-part story about Davy Crockett is broadcast on the U.S. children's program *Disneyland*; it is followed by parts two and three on January 26, 1955 and February 23, 1955. Appearing on 163 television stations and seen by more than 40 million viewers, the program gives rise to major juvenile merchandising fads, including the coonskin cap.

Religion

- The Unification Church is founded by the Korean evangelist Sun Myung Moon.

Sports

- Joe Perry of the San Francisco 49ers becomes the first player in U.S. National Football League history to rush for 1,000 yards two seasons in a row.
- Soviet rowing crews enter the Henley Royal Regatta, England, for the first time and win three events, including the prestigious Grand Challenge Cup.
- The baseball team the St. Louis Browns of the American League move to Baltimore, Maryland, where they are renamed the Orioles.
- The Canadian ice-hockey player Gordie Howe of the Detroit Red Wings wins the Art Ross Trophy for the highest scorer in the National Hockey League (NHL) for the fourth successive year.
- The Grey Cup, formerly awarded to the winner of the Rugby Football Championship of Canada, is awarded to the winner of the Canadian Football Championship for the first time.

APRIL

12   The Minneapolis Lakers, led by George Mikam, win their third successive National Basketball Association title, their fifth in six years.

12 The U.S. golfer Sam Snead wins his third U.S. Masters title at Augusta, Georgia.

MAY

6 Roger Bannister of Great Britain, with a time of 3 min 59.4 sec, becomes the first person to run a mile in under four minutes, at the Iffley Road Sports Ground, Oxford, England.

30 The British runner Diane Leather becomes the first woman to run a mile in under five minutes, in Birmingham, England.

31 The U.S. driver Bill Vukovich wins his second successive Indianapolis 500 automobile race in a record 3 hrs 49 min 17.27 sec.

JUNE

16–July 4 The fifth soccer World Cup is held in Switzerland; West Germany beats Hungary 3–2 in the final in Bern before a crowd of 60,000 people.

JULY

2 The Czechoslovak-born tennis player Jaroslav Drobny defeats Ken Rosewall of Australia in four sets to become the first left-handed player to win a singles title at the Wimbledon tennis championships in London, England, since 1914.

3 The U.S. golfer Mildred "Babe" Zaharias wins her third U.S. Women's Open, at Salem, Massachusetts, by a record 12 strokes, just months after recovering from cancer treatment.

20 Two-and-a-half weeks after winning her third successive Wimbledon women's singles title in London, England, the playing career of the 19-year-old U.S. tennis star Maureen Connolly is ended by a riding accident.

AUGUST

7 In the final of the mile event at the British Empire and Commonwealth Games in Vancouver, Canada, the English runner Roger Bannister wins the title ahead of John Landy of Australia (who two months earlier broke the mile record set by Bannister in May, with a time of 3 min 57.9 sec). In the race, dubbed the "Miracle Mile," Bannister's time is 3 min 58.8 sec and Landy's 3 min 59.6 sec—the first race in which two runners complete the distance in under four minutes.

DECEMBER

26 The Cleveland Browns defeat the Detroit Tigers 56–10 in the U.S. National Football Championship Game at Cleveland, Ohio, to end a streak of three consecutive title game defeats.

BIRTHS & DEATHS

JANUARY
31 Edwin Howard Armstrong, U.S. inventor who developed the heterodyne circuit and frequency modulation (FM) for radio, dies in New York, New York (63).

FEBRUARY
18 John Travolta, U.S. actor, born in Englewood, New Jersey.

MARCH
9 Vagn Walfrid Ekman, Swedish oceanographer noted for his studies of ocean currents, dies in Gostad, near Stockaryd, Sweden (79).
28 Reba McEntire, U.S. country music singer, born in McAlester, Oklahoma.

APRIL
10 Auguste Lumière, French inventor who, with his brother Louis, developed the Cinématographe, the first practical film camera and projector, dies in Lyon, France (91).

MAY
19 Charles Ives, U.S. composer, dies in New York, New York (79).

JUNE
7 Alan Mathison Turing, English mathematician who pioneered computer theory and computer processes, dies in Wilmslow, Cheshire, England (41).

JULY
26 Vitas Gerulaitis, U.S. tennis player, born in Brooklyn, New York (–1994).

AUGUST
2 Elvis Costello (adopted name of Declan Patrick McManus), English singer and songwriter, born in London, England.
19 Alcide de Gasperi, prime minister of Italy 1945–53, who signed the peace treaty with the Allies after World War II, dies in Sella di Valsugana, Italy (73).

24 Getúlio Vargas, president of Brazil 1930–45, whose economic and social policies helped to modernize the country, dies in Rio de Janeiro, Brazil (71).

NOVEMBER
3 Henri Matisse, French painter, sculptor, illustrator, and designer, dies in Nice, France (84).
14 (Chryssomallis) Yanni, Greek-born U.S. composer and performer, born in Kalamata, Greece.
28 Enrico Fermi, Italian-born U.S. physicist who was responsible for overseeing the first nuclear chain reaction, dies in Chicago, Illinois (53).

DECEMBER
21 Chris(tine) Evert Lloyd, U.S. tennis player who dominated women's singles during the late 1970s and early 1980s, born in Fort Lauderdale, Florida.

1955

POLITICS, GOVERNMENT, AND ECONOMICS

Business and Economics

- U.S. tax accountants Henry Wohlman and Richard Bloch found the income tax preparation firm H & R. Block in Kansas City, Missouri.

JUNE
- The U.S. Postal Service grants postal workers an 8% pay raise.

JULY
31 The Pakistani rupee is devalued in response to the country's economic problems.

AUGUST
8 A barter agreement is made between Egypt, the USSR, and Romania (Egypt is to exchange cotton for oil and paraffin).

DECEMBER
- The Ford Foundation awards a record $500 million educational grant to private colleges, universities, and teaching hospitals.

Human Rights

- The civil-rights leader Martin Luther King, Jr., forms the Montgomery Improvement Association in Alabama. The organization launches a boycott of Montgomery buses, forcing them to desegregate the following year after a federal court judgment.
- The U.S. historian C. Vann Woodward publishes *The Strange Career of Jim Crow*.
- U.S. historian John Higham publishes *Strangers in the Land: Patterns of American Nativism, 1860–1925*.

MAY
31 In the case of *Brown II*, the U.S. Supreme Court orders the desegregation of state schools "with all deliberate speed." This follows delays in the implementation of its decision in *Brown v. Board of Education of Topeka, Kansas*, in May 1954.

NOVEMBER
- The U.S. Interstate Commerce Commission prohibits segregation on interstate trains and buses.
- The U.S. Supreme Court orders the desegregation of public parks and recreation facilities.

DECEMBER
- U.S. seamstress and social activist Rosa Parks is arrested after refusing to relinquish her seat to a white man on a bus in Montgomery, Alabama. Her arrest galvanizes the U.S. civil-rights movement.

Politics and Government

- A Universal Copyright Convention, signed by 16 countries at Geneva, Switzerland, in 1952, comes into force.
- Border raids between Israel and Jordan increase in intensity.
- Pakistan launches its Five-Year Plan to increase agricultural output and expand power generation and industry, thus addressing its economic weakness.
- President Dwight D. Eisenhower appoints jurist John M. Harlan to the U.S. Supreme Court.

JANUARY
- The Eisenhower administration reports that it dismissed 3,002 federal employees, between May 1953 and September 1954, who were believed to present a danger to national security because of supposed connections with communists.
- The U.S. Foreign Operations Administration provides economic assistance to South Vietnam, Cambodia, and Laos.
- The U.S. Senate pledges to defend Formosa (modern Taiwan) and the Pescadores Islands from Chinese incursion.
- The U.S. Senate votes unanimously to extend its investigation of U.S. communism.
15 The USSR agrees to extend full diplomatic recognition to West Germany, during a visit by the West German chancellor, Konrad Adenauer, to Moscow.
18 The governor of the British colony of Kenya proclaims an amnesty for Mau Mau nationalist rebels who surrender. About 1,000 rebels surrender by the end of the amnesty on July 10.
21 Following the retirement of the Norwegian Labor prime minister Oscar Torp, his Labor colleague Einar Gerhardsen resumes the premiership.
25 The Left Republican Jacques Soustelle is appointed governor-general of Algeria, with the task of restoring order in the French colony.

FEBRUARY
5 Pierre Mendès-France resigns as prime minister of France following the defeat of his government in a vote of confidence on its North Africa policy.
8 Georgi Malenkov, the prime minister of the USSR, resigns following opposition to his policy of reducing arms production. He is succeeded by Nikolai Bulganin.

23 The Radical Edgar Fauré forms a ministry in France.

23–25 The foreign ministers of the South-East Asia Treaty Organization (SEATO) countries confer at Bangkok, Thailand.

24 Turkey and Iraq sign a treaty of alliance, the Baghdad Pact, which provides for mutual support against communist militants.

MARCH

• The U.S. House of Representatives raises the salaries of congressmen and federal judges by 50%.

• The U.S. president Dwight D. Eisenhower issues a statement endorsing the use of atomic weapons in war.

2 Egypt and Syria establish a defensive alliance.

3 Greece, Yugoslavia, and Turkey set up a consultative parliamentary council, with 20 deputies from each country.

11 The Paris agreement of October 1954 is ratified by Italy, West Germany (on March 18), and France (on March 27), with a view to enlarging the Western European Union.

24 A new constitution comes into force in the British mandate of Tanganyika (now Tanzania), granting limited self-rule.

31 A purge of the Chinese Communist Party begins. Gao Gang, the former leader of the virtually autonomous Manchurian region and colleague of Mao Zedong, commits suicide following charges that he attempted to establish himself as dictator in Manchuria.

APRIL

• The U.S. president Dwight D. Eisenhower creates the Civil Defense Coordinating Board to oversee federal defense procedure.

1 The U.S. Senate ratifies the Paris agreement of October 1954 for enlarging the Western European Union.

5–24 Ministers of 29 states meet at the Bandung or Afro-Asian Conference held in Bandung, Indonesia, to form a "nonaligned bloc" of countries opposed to the "imperialism" and "colonialism" of the superpowers.

14 The Chinese prime minister and foreign minister Zhou Enlai visits Rangoon, Burma (now Yangon in Myanmar).

15 The USSR and Austria sign an economic agreement.

17 South Vietnam appeals to the United Nations (UN) over alleged breaches of the Geneva agreement by the Vietminh nationalists.

18 Imre Nagy is forced to resign as Hungarian prime minister, and Ándras Hegedüs becomes nominal prime minister, while Mátyás Rákosi returns to the post of secretary of the Hungarian Workers' Party.

28 Civil war begins in South Vietnam between supporters of Premier Ngo Dinh Diem and Prince Bo Dai.

29 The Christian Democrat Giovanni Gronchi is elected president of Italy.

MAY

5 The Allied occupation regime in West Germany, in existence since 1945, ends.

6 Britain submits its dispute with Argentina and Chile over ownership of the Falkland Islands to the International Court in The Hague, but Argentina and Chile refuse to present counterclaims.

7 The USSR annuls its wartime treaties of alliance with Britain and France in retaliation for the ratification of the Paris agreement, specifically the inclusion of West Germany in the Western European Union (WEU).

9 West Germany is admitted as a member of the North Atlantic Treaty Organization (NATO).

14 The Warsaw Treaty (of Friendship, Cooperation, and Mutual Assistance) is signed by the USSR, Albania, Bulgaria, Czechoslovakia, East Germany, Hungary, Poland, and Romania, establishing the "Warsaw Pact" and providing for a unified military command (with headquarters in Moscow) and stationing of Soviet military units in member countries.

15 The United States, USSR, Britain, and France sign a treaty in Vienna, Austria, restoring Austria's independence after its occupation since 1945.

26 In the British general election the ruling Conservatives win 345 seats over Labour with 277, the Liberals with 6, and United Ireland with 2. Anthony Eden is prime minister.

26 Nikolai Bulganin and Nikita Khrushchev of the USSR visit Yugoslavia (expelled from the Cominform, the Communist Information Bureau, in 1948) and, on June 2, sign a treaty of friendship.

JUNE

• The U.S. Congress extends the Selective Service Act to June 30, 1958. The act calls on men aged 18½ to register for the draft.

• The U.S. Congress extends the Reciprocal Trade Agreement Act to June 30, 1958. The act permits the president to negotiate individual trade agreements with other nations without Senate consent.

• The U.S. House of Representatives raises the pay of 1 million federal employees by 7.5%.

6 The Western powers propose a summit conference at Geneva, Switzerland, in order to ease tension and, on July 18, the USSR agrees to a meeting.

15 The United States and Britain sign an atomic energy agreement, providing for the exchange of information.

22 Mario Scelba's Italian coalition government resigns, and Antonio Segni, also a Christian Democrat, forms a coalition on June 26.

30 The United States and West Germany make a military aid agreement.

JULY

• The U.S. Congress appropriates over $3 billion for foreign aid.

• The U.S. Congress passes legislation that will bolster the nation's military reserves from 800,000 to nearly 3 million by 1960.

• The U.S. House of Representatives authorizes the construction of 45,000 public housing units over the course of the next year.

5 The assembly of the Western European Union holds its first meeting, at Strasbourg, France.

7 China agrees to provide communist North Vietnam with economic aid.

18–23 No agreements are reached at a summit conference of the United States, USSR, Britain, and France in Geneva, Switzerland; the USSR states that it will only agree to German reunification within the framework of a European collective security system.

21 Greece proposes that its claim to Cyprus be heard by the United Nations (UN) General Assembly.

24 Nikolai Bulganin and Nikita Khrushchev of the USSR visit East Germany.

30 Conscription is introduced in China.

AUGUST

- The U.S. Congress raises the minimum hourly wage from 75 cents to $1.

1 A Communist Youth Congress is held in Warsaw, Poland.

8–20 The International Conference on the Peaceful Uses of Atomic Energy is held in Geneva, Switzerland, attended by delegates from 73 countries and eight international agencies.

11 A Muslim-dominated right-wing ministry takes office in Indonesia under Burhanuddin Harahap.

15 An agreement is signed in Kampala, Uganda, which will permit the return of the exiled Bugandan kabaka.

15 Portuguese police fire on Indian demonstrators demanding the union of the Portuguese colony of Goa with India, killing 21 demonstrators.

19 India severs diplomatic relations with Portugal after clashes in the Portuguese enclave of Goa, on the west coast of India.

20 Anti-French riots take place in Morocco on the anniversary of Sultan Sidi Mohammed's deposition in 1953.

20 The nationalist Front for National Liberation (FLN) resume their series of attacks on French forces in Algeria, including a massacre near Philippeville.

30–September 7 The foreign ministers of Greece, Turkey, and Britain meet at a conference in London, England, to discuss the unrest in Cyprus over Greek Cypriot pressure for union with Greece, but fail to reach agreement.

SEPTEMBER

- News that President Dwight D. Eisenhower suffered a heart attack two days before sparks a massive sell-off at the New York Stock Exchange. Losses reach the highest ever at $14 billion.

6 Anti-Greek riots take place in Istanbul and Izmir, Turkey.

13 An announcement is made at the end of meetings between the West German chancellor Konrad Adenauer and Soviet leaders in Moscow, USSR, to the effect that diplomatic relations will be restored. On September 23 the German Bundestag (parliament) approves, and a Soviet ambassador is appointed on January 8, 1956.

20 The USSR signs a treaty with East Germany, establishing it as a sovereign state.

30 France withdraws from the United Nations (UN) General Assembly after it votes by 28 votes to 27 to debate nationalist opposition to French colonial rule in Algeria. The item is deleted from the agenda on November 25, after which the French delegation returns.

OCTOBER

11 China signs an agreement with the USSR for economic cooperation and the removal of Soviet forces from Port Arthur, China.

12 The British Royal Navy makes a goodwill visit to Leningrad (now St. Petersburg), USSR, and the Soviet Navy reciprocates with a visit to Portsmouth, England.

17 The exiled kabaka of Buganda, Mutesa II, the traditional ruler in Uganda, returns following the resolution of his disagreement with the government of the British colony over the granting of independence.

23 A plebiscite on a plan to place the Saar region under the control of the Western European Union is rejected by 423,434 votes to 201,973. In December, France agrees that the Saar can return to Germany.

23 A referendum in South Vietnam advocates the deposition of Emperor Bao Dai and, on October 26, a republic is proclaimed under Ngo Dinh Diem.

26 The South Vietnamese premier Ngo Dinh Diem declares Vietnam a republic.

27–November 16 A Geneva conference of the U.S., Soviet, British, and French foreign ministers fails to reach any agreement on German reunification.

NOVEMBER

2 David Ben-Gurion, the former Israeli prime minister, returns from retirement to form a coalition ministry.

3 Iran joins the Baghdad Pact (already signed by Iraq and Turkey).

6 The deposed sultan of Morocco, Sidi Mohammed, agrees conditions with France for his return, including the establishment of a constitutional government and the negotiation of terms for self-government. He returns on November 16.

9 South Africa withdraws from the United Nations (UN) General Assembly, because the UN decides to continue consideration of the Cruz Report of 1952 on "apartheid."

16 Sidi Mohammed, the deposed sultan of Morocco, returns to Morocco, and the first all-Moroccan government is formed on December 7.

26 The governor of Cyprus, John Harding, proclaims a state of emergency on the island following agitation for union with Greece.

DECEMBER

14 Albania, Austria, Bulgaria, Cambodia, Ceylon (now Sri Lanka), Finland, Hungary, Republic of Ireland, Italy, Jordan, Laos, Libya, Nepal, Portugal, Romania, and Spain are admitted to the United Nations (UN).

19 Sudan's parliament passes a resolution calling on Egypt and Britain to recognize Sudan as an independent state. Recognition is granted on January 1, 1956, and Sudan joins the Arab League on January 19.

SCIENCE, TECHNOLOGY, AND MEDICINE

Computing

- U.S. Bell Laboratories produces the first computer with transistors instead of vacuum tubes.
- U.S. electrical engineer Jack Gilmore builds the TX0, a computer that uses a cathode-ray tube display and function keys; it is the forerunner of the modern video terminal.

FEBRUARY

- IBM introduces the IBM 705 computer, the first commercially successful business computer to use magnetic core memory.

Ecology

- Explosive ammonium nitrate-fuel oil (ANFO) mixtures are developed in the United States for coal mining.

JANUARY
- The U.S. Atomic Energy Commission announces plans to privatize experimental nuclear power plants.

AUGUST
12–21 Hurricanes Connie (August 12) and Diane (August 21) cause $1.75 billion in property damage, leading to the establishment of the National Hurricane Center in Florida.

Exploration

SEPTEMBER
- The National Geographic Society, pointing to blue-green patches in photographs of the Martian surface, renews speculation that life exists on Mars.

Health and Medicine

- Prednisone is introduced in the United States for treating arthritis.
- The World Health Organization begins a global campaign to eradicate malaria.

APRIL
- Dr. Jonas E. Salk proclaims the success of his poliomyelitis vaccine, which has been tested in 44 states. It is released for general use in the United States on April 12.

Science

- English biochemist Dorothy Hodgkin elucidates the structure of vitamin B_{12}, a liver extract used in the treatment of pernicious anemia.
- French astronomer Audouin Dolfus ascends 7.2 km/4.5 mi above the earth in a balloon to make photoelectric observations of Mars.
- Russian-born Belgian physical chemist Ilya Prigogine describes the thermodynamics of irreversible processes.
- Swedish biochemist Axel Theorell receives the Nobel Prize for Physiology or Medicine for his discoveries concerning the nature and mode of action of oxidation enzymes.
- The French scientist and theologian Pierre Teilhard de Chardin publishes *Le Phénomène humain/The Phenomenon of Man.*
- U.S. anthropologist Julian Steward publishes *Theory of Culture Change: The Methodology of Multilinear Evolution,* in which he argues that there have been five lines of cultural evolution.
- U.S. biochemist Vincent Du Vigneaud receives the Nobel Prize for Chemistry for his investigations into sulfur compounds, and the first synthesis of a polypeptide hormone.
- U.S. chemist Albert Ghiorso and colleagues at the University of California, Berkeley, discover the radioactive element mendelevium (atomic no. 101), named for the Russian chemist Dmitry Mendeleyev. It is the first element to be discovered one atom at a time.
- U.S. geneticists Joshua Lederberg and Norton Zinder discover that some viruses carry part of the chromosome of one bacterium to another; called transduction it becomes an important tool in genetics research.
- U.S. physicists Willis Lamb and Polykarp Kusch share the Nobel Prize for Physics: Lamb for his discoveries concerning the structure of the hydrogen spectrum; and Kusch for his determination of the magnetic moment of the electron.

MAY
5 U.S. astronomer B. F. Burk announces the discovery that Jupiter emits radio waves.

Technology

- Both the United States and USSR announce they will attempt launching satellites during the International Geophysical Year (1957–58).
- British engineer Hiroshi Julian Goldsmid discovers that bismuth telluride is the material best suited for thermoelectric applications, achieving a temperature drop of 40°C/72°F below room temperature. It is used in generators and refrigerators.
- English radio astronomer Martin Ryle builds the first radio interferometer. Consisting of three antennae spaced 1.6 km/1 mi apart, it increases the resolution of radio telescopes, permitting the diameter of a radio source to be determined, or two closely spaced sources to be separated.
- Indian scientist Narinder Kapany discovers that light can be transmitted great distances along coated glass fibers.
- The first cesium atomic clock is installed at the National Physical Laboratory, Teddington, England.
- U.S. physicist Percy Bridgman, at General Electric, produces the first industrial quality artificial diamonds from carbon using extreme atmospheric pressure at 1,700°C/3,000°F.
- U.S. radiophysicists at the Massachusetts Institute of Technology develop the use of ultra high-frequency (UHF) waves for television broadcasting. With a 0.1–1 meter wavelength and a frequency of 3,000 and 300 megahertz they are used in the United States and Canada to carry channels 14 to 83.

APRIL
- U.S. communications engineer John Pierce analyzes various types of satellites and shows the potential of using the earth's gravity to control the altitude and orientation of satellites in geosynchronous orbit. It leads to the launch of the communications satellite *Echo I.*

JULY
18 The U.S. Navy develops a 5 megawatt nuclear power generator at Schenectady, New York. It is intended for submarines.

Transportation

- British aviator Walter Gibb sets a new altitude record of 20,000 m/65,876 ft, in a Canberra jet.

- Container ships begin to appear, revolutionizing the shipping industry by reducing the need for longshoremen. Their hulls are divided into compartments that accommodate truck containers, which can be loaded and unloaded far faster than traditional cargo ships. The first container ships are converted tankers.
- The first single-seat U.S. high-altitude jet reconnaissance and research aircraft, the U-2, is test flown. Its top speed is 795 kph/494 mph and it has a ceiling of 21,000 m/ 70,000 ft.
- The subway system in Rome, Italy, opens along an 11 km/7 mi route called the B line.
- U.S. firm IBM develops SABRE (Semi-Automated Business Related Environment) for American Airlines' passenger reservations. It consists of more than 1,000 teletypewriters connected to a central database—the first computer network.

MAY

27 The French Caravelle passenger jet makes its first flight. It creates a revolution in jet airplane design by placing the jets at the rear above the fuselage, thus improving aerodynamic efficiency. Regular scheduled flights begin in 1958.

SEPTEMBER

12 English engineer Christopher Cockerell patents the first hovercraft.

15 Soviet aircraft designer Andrey Tupolev's TU-104 jet inaugurates the world's first scheduled jet-airline passenger service.

OCTOBER

- The Soviet warship *Novorossiisk* sinks while on maneuvers in the Black Sea; 1,500 people die.

DECEMBER

27 Traffic fatalities over the Christmas weekend in the United States total 609 people.

ARTS AND IDEAS

Architecture

- English historian W. G. Hoskins publishes *The Making of the English Landscape*.
- The Church of Notre-Dame-du-Haut at Ronchamp, France, designed by the Swiss architect Le Corbusier, is completed.

Arts

- English art historian John Pope-Hennessy publishes *Italian Gothic Sculpture*.
- The Dutch artist Karel Appel paints *Amorous Dance*.
- The Dutch-born U.S. artist Willem de Kooning paints *Composition*.
- The English artist L. S. Lowry paints *Industrial Landscape*.
- The French-born U.S. artist Louise Bourgeois sculpts *One and Others*.

- The German-born U.S. artist Hans Hofmann paints *Radiant Space*.
- The German-born U.S. art historian Erwin Panofsky publishes *Meaning in the Visual Arts*.
- The Italian artist Alberto Burri creates his collage *Wood Combustion*.
- The Italian artist Pietro Annigoni paints *Portrait of HM Queen Elizabeth II*.
- The Museum of Modern Art in New York, New York, holds the exhibition "The Family of Man." Organized by the U.S. photographer Edward Steichen, it is one of the major photography exhibitions, bringing together over 500 photographs from around the world.
- The Spanish artist Pablo Picasso paints *The Women of Algiers*.
- The U.S. artist Cy Twombly paints *Free Wheeler (New York City)*.
- The U.S. artist Jasper Johns paints the first of his *Flag*, *Target*, and *Number* series, including *Target with Four Faces*.
- The U.S. artist Robert Rauschenberg creates his multimedia work *Bed*.
- U.S. photographer Minor White takes *Road with Poplar Trees*.

Film

- The documentary *Nuit et Brouillard/Night and Fog*, the story of the Auschwitz concentration camp, directed by French filmmaker Alain Resnais, is released in France.
- The movie *Bad Day at Black Rock*, directed by John Sturges, is released in the United States, starring Spencer Tracy and Robert Ryan.
- The movie *Le Monde du Silence/World of Silence*, an undersea documentary directed by French diver Jacques Cousteau and French filmmaker Louis Malle, is released in France.
- The movie *Marty*, directed by Delbert Mann, is released in the United States, based on the play by Paddy Chayevsky and starring Ernest Borgnine, Betsy Blair, Esther Minciotti, and Joe Mantell. It wins the Palme d'Or at the Cannes Film Festival in France.
- The movie *Pather Panchali/The Song of the Road*, directed by Satyajit Ray, is released in India. The first in a trilogy, it stars Kanu Bannerjee, Karuna Bannerjee, Uma Das Gupta, and Subir Bannerjee, and features music by Ravi Shankar.
- The movie *Rebel Without a Cause*, directed by Nicholas Ray, is released in the United States, starring James Dean, Natalie Wood, and Sal Mineo.
- The movie *Rififi*, directed by Jules Dassin, is released in France, starring Jean Servais, Carl Mohner, and Robert Manuel.
- The movie *The Blackboard Jungle*, directed by Richard Brooks, is released in the United States, starring Glenn Ford, Anne Francis, Sidney Poitier, and Rick Morrow.
- The movie *The Dam Busters*, directed by Michael Anderson, is released in Britain, starring Michael Redgrave and Richard Todd.
- The movie *The Fall of Lola Montes*, directed by Max Ophuls, is released in the United States, starring Martina Carol, Anton Walbrook, and Peter Ustinov.

- The movie *The Ladykillers*, directed by Alexander Mackendrick, is released in Britain, starring Alec Guinness, Katie Johnson, Peter Sellers, Cecil Parker, and Herbert Lom. It is the last of the Ealing comedies.
- The movie *The Night of the Hunter*, directed by Charles Laughton, is released in the United States, starring Robert Mitchum.
- The movie *The Seven Year Itch*, directed by Billy Wilder, is released in the United States, starring Marilyn Monroe and Tom Ewell.
- The movie *Voyage to Italy*, directed by Roberto Rossellini, is released, staring Ingrid Bergman and George Sanders.
- U.S. movie producer Walt Disney produces the first 360° movie projection at Disneyland, California.

APRIL

18 The 1954 Academy Awards take place. Best Actor: Marlon Brando, for *On the Waterfront*; Best Supporting Actor: Edmond O'Brien, for *The Barefoot Contessa*; Best Actress: Grace Kelly, for *The Country Girl*; Best Supporting Actress: Eve Marie Saint, for *On the Waterfront*; Best Picture: *On the Waterfront*, directed by Elia Kazan; Best Director: Elia Kazan, for *On the Waterfront*.

DECEMBER

26 The motion picture company RKO sells its entire movie library, including *Citizen Kane*, to C & C Super Corporation of New York, New York, for $15 million. C & C plans to sell the movie rights to television.

Literature and Language

- The *Guinness Book of World Records*, compiled by the English journalists Ross and Norris McWhirter (brothers), is published, appearing annually from now on.
- The Australian writer Patrick White publishes his novel *The Tree of Man*.
- The English historian E. P. Thompson publishes *William Morris: Romantic to Revolutionary*.
- The English writer Anthony Powell publishes *The Acceptance World*, the third novel of his 12-volume sequence *A Dance to the Music of Time*.
- The English writer and poet Robert Graves publishes *The Greek Myths*.
- The English writer C. S. Lewis publishes his novel *The Magician's Nephew*, the sixth volume of *The Chronicles of Narnia*.
- The English writer C. S. Lewis publishes his autobiography *Surprised by Joy: The Shape of My Early Life*.
- The English writer Graham Greene publishes his novel *The Quiet American*.
- The English writer Ivy Compton-Burnett publishes her novel *Mother and Son*.
- The English writer J. R. R. Tolkien publishes his novel *The Two Towers*, the second volume of his *The Lord of the Rings* trilogy.
- The English writer Philip Larkin publishes his second poetry collection *The Less Deceived*.
- The English writer William Golding publishes his novel *The Inheritors*.

- The French anthropologist Claude Lévi-Strauss publishes *Tristes Tropiques/Sad Tropics*, his intellectual autobiography.
- The French writer Alain Robbe-Grillet publishes his novel *Le Voyeur/The Voyeur*.
- The German physicist and philosopher Werner Heisenberg publishes *Das Naturbild der heutigen Physik/The Physicist's Conception of Nature*.
- The German writer Heinrich Böll publishes his novel *Das Brot der frühen Jahre/The Bread of Our Early Years*.
- The Irish-born English writer and philosopher Iris Murdoch publishes her novel *The Flight from the Enchanter*.
- The Nobel Prize for Literature is awarded to the Icelandic novelist Halldór Laxness.
- The Polish writer Czesław Miłosz publishes his novel *Dolina Issy/The Issa Valley*.
- The Pulitzer Prize for Biography is awarded to William S. White for *The Taft Story*, the Pulitzer Prize for Poetry is awarded to Wallace Stevens for *Collected Poems*, and the Pulitzer Prize for Fiction is awarded to William Faulkner for *A Fable*.
- The Russian-born U.S. writer Vladimir Nabokov publishes his novel *Lolita* in Paris, France, following rejection by U.S. publishers on grounds of obscenity. It is published in the United States in 1958.
- The Scottish writer Robin Jenkins publishes his novel *The Cone Gatherers*.
- The U.S. writer Eudora Welty publishes her short-story collection *The Bride of the Innisfallen*.
- The U.S. writer Flannery O'Connor publishes her short-story collection *A Good Man is Hard to Find*.
- The U.S. writer James Baldwin publishes *Notes of a Native Son*, a collection of essays.
- The U.S. writer Mary McCarthy publishes her novel *A Charmed Life*.
- The U.S. writer Norman Mailer publishes his novel *The Deer Park*.
- The U.S. writer Paul Bowles publishes his novel *The Spider's House*.
- The U.S. writer William Gaddis publishes his novel *The Recognitions*.
- The U.S.-born Irish writer J. P. Donleavy publishes his novel *The Ginger Man*, which runs into censorship problems.

Music

- English musicologist Jack Allan Westrup publishes *An Introduction to Musical History*.
- Popular songs in the United States include "Melody of Love," "The Yellow Rose of Texas," and "Let Me Go, Lover."
- The Czech composer Bohuslav Martinů completes his *Viola Sonata*.
- The English composer Edmund Rubbra completes his Symphony No. 6.
- The English composer Elisabeth Lutyens completes her *Music for Orchestra I*.
- The French composer Pierre Boulez completes his vocal work *Le Marteau sans maître/The Hammer Without a*

Master, settings of a poem by the French writer René Char.

- The Italian composer Goffredo Petrassi completes his *Concerto for Orchestra No. 5*.
- The Ivor Novello awards are founded in Britain, rewarding achievement in popular and light music. They are named for the late Welsh actor-manager, composer, and playwright Ivor Novello (adopted name of Ivor Novello Davies).
- The opera *Susannah*, by the U.S. composer Carlisle Floyd, is first performed, at the University of Houston, Texas.
- The opera *The Fiery Angel*, by the Russian composer Sergey Prokofiev, is first staged, in Venice, Italy. Written in 1923 and revised in 1927, it was first heard on French radio in 1954.
- The U.S. composer Alan Hovhaness completes his orchestral work *Mysterious Mountain*.
- The U.S. composer John Cage completes his *Speech* for five radios and a newsreader.
- The U.S. country singer Slim Whitman releases the single "Rose Marie." The song spends 11 consecutive weeks at number one in the UK singles charts, a record unbroken until 1991.
- The U.S. rock 'n' roll group Bill Haley and the Comets releases the single "Rock Around the Clock," also included in a controversial movie of this year, *The Blackboard Jungle*. Sales will exceed 17 million, making it second only to "White Christmas" as the best-selling single ever.
- The U.S. rock 'n' roll singer Chuck Berry releases the singles "Maybelline" and "Roll Over Beethoven" (the latter does not enter the charts until June 30, 1956).
- The U.S. singer Tennessee Ernie Ford releases the singles "Sixteen Tons" and "Give Me Your Word."

JANUARY

7   Marian Anderson becomes the first black singer to perform at the Metropolitan Opera House in New York, New York.

Theater and Dance

- The English playwright Ronald Duncan founds the English Stage Company in London, England, to perform the work of young and experimental playwrights and the best of foreign contemporary drama.
- The play *A View from the Bridge*, by the U.S. dramatist Arthur Miller, is first performed, at the Coronet Theater in New York, New York.
- The play *Bus Stop*, by the U.S. dramatist William Inge, is first performed, in New York, New York.
- The play *Cat on a Hot Tin Roof*, by the U.S. dramatist Tennessee Williams, is first performed, at the Morosco Theater in New York, New York.
- The play *The Diary of Anne Frank*, by the U.S. writers Frances Goodrich and Albert Hackett, is performed, in New York, New York. It is based on the journal of a Dutch Jewish girl who hid from the Nazis during the occupation of Amsterdam, in the Netherlands.
- The play *The Matchmaker*, by the U.S. writer Thornton Wilder, is first performed, at the Royale Theater in New York, New York. A revised version of his *The Merchant of Yonkers*, written in 1938, it forms the basis of the 1964 musical *Hello, Dolly!*

- The Pulitzer Prize for Drama is awarded to Tennessee Williams for *Cat on a Hot Tin Roof*.

MARCH

27   The 1954–55 Tony Awards take place. Best Actor: Alfred Lunt; Best Actress: Nancy Kelly; Best Play: *The Desperate Hours*; Best Musical: *The Pajama Game*.

APRIL

21   *Inherit the Wind*, by the U.S. dramatist Jerome Lawrence, a play based on the Scopes monkey trial in Tennessee (in which a teacher was accused of breaking the law by teaching Darwinian evolution), is first performed, at the National Theater in New York, New York.

MAY

5   The musical *Damn Yankees*, with music and lyrics by Richard Adler and Jerry Ross, is first performed, at 46th Street Theater, New York, New York. It features the song "Whatever Lola Wants."

Thought and Scholarship

- English historian A. J. P. Taylor publishes *Bismarck: The Man and the Statesman*.
- English historian G. R. Elton publishes *England under the Tudors*.
- English historian John Ernest Neale publishes the first volume of his *Elizabeth I and her Parliaments*. The second volume appears in 1957.
- English historian Stephen Runciman publishes *The Eastern Schism*.
- German-born U.S. political philosopher Herbert Marcuse publishes *Eros and Civilization: A Philosophical Inquiry into Freud*.
- The Canadian-born U.S. economist John Kenneth Galbraith publishes *The Great Crash*.
- The Pulitzer Prize for History is awarded to Paul Horgan for *Great River: The Rio Grande in North American History*.
- U.S. historian Philip D. Curtin publishes *Two Jamaicas*.
- U.S. philosopher C. I. Lewis publishes *The Ground and Nature of Right*.
- U.S. political journalist Walter Lippmann publishes *The Public Philosophy*.

SOCIETY

Education

- The International School of Nuclear Science and Engineering is established at Argonne National Laboratory, Illinois, to provide the first training in nuclear engineering.

Everyday Life

- A Columbia University study finds that more than 1 billion comic books are bought in the United States in a year.
- Tight jeans for both men and women are fashionable in North America and Western Europe.
- U.S. labor statistics state that 15 million people in the United States belong to unions.

FEBRUARY

- The American Federation of Labor (AFL) and the Congress of Industrial Organizations (CIO) report their merger to form the AFL-CIO.

JULY

18 Disneyland, created by Walt Disney, opens in Anaheim, California. It is the first theme park in the world.

Media and Communication

- The *Chicago Sun-Times* begins publication of the "Ann Landers Says" column, whose real author is Esther Pauline Friedman Lederer.
- The U.S. journalist William F. Buckley founds *National Review*, a review of politics and current affairs and a leading journal of U.S. conservatism.

JANUARY

19 Dwight D. Eisenhower is the first U.S. president to hold a televised news conference.

MARCH

7 The 1954–55 Emmy Awards for television take place. Best Actor in a Single Show: Robert Cummings; Best Actress in a Single Show: Judith Anderson; Best Actor in a Series: Art Carney; Best Actress in a Series: Audrey Meadows.

JUNE

7–November 9, 1958 *The $64,000 Question*, the first prime time TV quiz program offering big money prizes, appears on U.S. television; big winners include psychologist Joyce Brothers and actress Barbara Feldon.

JULY

July 1955–59 *Highway Patrol*, a U.S. crime series set in the world of the California Highway Patrol, begins, starring Broderick Crawford.

July 1955–82 The musical variety program *The Lawrence Welk Show*, featuring band leader and accordionist Welk, appears on U.S. television. Other performers include the Lennon Sisters, Norma Zimmer, and Bobby Burgess.

July 1955–89 *The Benny Hill Show*, a series of saucy caricatures and impersonations by the comedian Benny Hill, is shown on British television.

SEPTEMBER

10–September 1, 1975 The Western program *Gunsmoke* appears on U.S. television. Starring James Arness, Amanda Blake, Dennis Weaver, and Milburn Stone, it is the longest-running Western and the longest-running prime time series with continuing characters to date.

12–September 12, 1971 *Lassie*, U.S. children's series about the adventures of a collie, appears on U.S. television. Over the years, the cast includes Tommy Rettis, Jan Clayton, George Cleveland, John Provost, Chloris Leachman, June Lockhart, and Hugh Reilly.

20–September 11, 1959 *The Phil Silvers Show* (originally titled *You'll Never Get Rich*), a comedy set in the army about the adventures of the scheming Sergeant Ernest Bilko, appears on U.S. television, starring Phil Silvers, Harvey Lembeck, and Herbie Faye.

30–February 3, 1956 *The Adventures of Champion*, a U.S. Western children's series about a wild stallion, appears; it stars Barry Curtis, Jim Bannon, Francis Mcdonald, and Ewing Mitchell.

OCTOBER

2–September 6, 1965 *Alfred Hitchcock Presents*, a suspense series, appears on U.S. television.

BIRTHS & DEATHS

JANUARY
18 Kevin Costner, U.S. actor and director, born in Compton, California.

FEBRUARY
1 Margot Hemingway, U.S. actress and model, born in Ketchum, Idaho (–1996).

MARCH
2 Shoko Asahara, Japanese cult leader whose followers planted the nerve gas sarin in the Tokyo subway in 1995, is born in Kumamoto prefecture, Japan.
11 Alexander Fleming, Scottish bacteriologist who discovered penicillin, dies in London, England (73).
12 Charlie "Yardbird" or "Bird" Parker, U.S. jazz saxophonist, composer, and bandleader, dies in New York, New York (34).

APRIL
10 Pierre Teilhard de Chardin, French Jesuit priest, philosopher, and paleontologist, dies in New York, New York (73).
18 Albert Einstein, German-born U.S. physicist who developed the theory of relativity, dies in Princeton, New Jersey (76).

AUGUST
12 Thomas Mann, German novelist, dies near Zürich, Switzerland (80).
17 Fernand Léger, French painter who developed "machine art," dies in Gif-sur-Yvette, France (74).

OCTOBER
2 Cordell Hull, U.S. secretary of state 1933–44 who lowered tariffs to stimulate international trade and received the Nobel Peace Prize in 1944, dies in Bethesda, Maryland (84).
25 Alfred Reginald Radcliffe-Brown, English structural-functionalist anthropologist, dies in London, England (74).
28 Bill Gates, U.S. computer software executive who developed and marketed the Microsoft Disk Operating System (MS-DOS) which is standard on almost all IBM and IBM-compatible computers, born in Seattle, Washington.

NOVEMBER
4 Cy Young, U.S. professional baseball player, dies in Newcomerstown, Ohio (87).
13 Whoopi Goldberg, U.S. actress, born in New York, New York.
27 Arthur Honegger, Swiss composer, dies in Paris, France (63).

DECEMBER
13 António Egas Moniz, Portuguese neurologist who introduced the lobotomy as a means of treating certain psychoses, dies in Lisbon, Portugal (81).

3–September 24, 1959 *The Mickey Mouse Club*, a children's series (the second TV series from Walt Disney Studios), is shown on U.S. television. Starring as "Mouseketeers," are Annette Funicello, Carol "Cubby" O'Brien, Paul Petersen, Jimmie Dodd, and Roy Williams, among others.

3–December 8, 1984 *Captain Kangaroo*, a popular children's program, starring Robert James "Bob" Keeshan, is shown on children's television.

Religion

• French philosopher Etienne Gilson publishes *History of Christian Philosophy in the Middle Ages* (in English).

MAY

• The U.S. General Assembly of the Presbyterian Church authorizes the ordination of female ministers.

Sports

• The baseball team the Philadelphia Athletics of the American League move to Kansas City, Missouri.

MAY

7   The U.S. jockey Willie Shoemaker, on Swaps, wins his first Kentucky Derby.

JUNE

11 Eighty-three spectators and one driver are killed in an accident during the Le Mans 24-hour motor race in France.

29 Charles Dumas of the United States, aged 19, in winning the high jump at the U.S. Olympic Trials, becomes the first person to clear the 2.1 m/7 ft barrier with a jump of 2.11 m/7 ft ½ in.

JULY

23 The English car and speedboat enthusiast Donald Campbell, in a jet-propelled hydroplane, sets a new world water-speed record of 325.60 kph/202.32 mph, on Ullswater Lake, England.

30 Louison Bobet of France becomes the first cyclist to win the Tour de France three years in succession.

SEPTEMBER

16 The newly formed United States Auto Club (USAC) replaces the American Automobile Association (AAA) as the governing body for Indy-car racing in the United States.

28–October 4 The Brooklyn Dodgers become the first team to win the World Series after losing the first two games, eventually defeating the New York Yankees by four games to three.

DECEMBER

26 In their sixth consecutive U.S. National Football League (NFL) Championship Game, the Cleveland Browns defeat the Los Angeles Rams 38–14, in Los Angeles, California.

1956

POLITICS, GOVERNMENT, AND ECONOMICS

Business and Economics

• The U.S. journalist William Hollingsworth Whyte publishes *The Organization Man*.

MAY

30 Life insurance is nationalized in India.

Colonization

MARCH

2   France recognizes the independence of its former colony of Morocco, and Spain grants recognition on April 7.

20 France recognizes the independence of its protectorate of Tunisia. The bey of Tunis is head of state with Habib ben Ali Bourguiba as prime minister.

MAY

9   A plebiscite in the protectorate of British Togoland votes for integration with Gold Coast (soon to be independent as Ghana).

28 France formally cedes its former settlements in India to the Republic of India.

Human Rights

JANUARY

13 The South African government disenfranchises 60,000 Cape Coloureds (people of racially mixed parentage).

FEBRUARY

• Racial violence erupts at the University of Alabama, where white students try to prevent Autherine Lucy, the school's first black student, from enrolling there. Lucy is

suspended on March 1 for filing a suit against the university.
- The U.S. Supreme Court nullifies Louisiana state laws upholding segregation in public schools.

MAY

2   The general conference of the Methodist Church, meeting in Minneapolis, Minnesota, orders the abolishment of racial segregation in its churches.

AUGUST

25   The South African government orders 100,000 nonwhites to leave their homes in Johannesburg, to make room for whites.

Politics and Government

- British member of Parliament Robert Boothby calls for the banning of the movie *The Blackboard Jungle*, featuring the music of new rock 'n' roll acts such as Bill Haley and the Comets and Little Richard, following disturbances in movie theaters around the country.
- President Dwight D. Eisenhower appoints legal scholar William J. Brennan, Jr. to the U.S. Supreme Court.

JANUARY

- The Virginia legislature amends a state prohibition against public financing of private schools in order to circumvent the Supreme Court's Brown decision (1954) outlawing segregation in public schools.
2   Communists and "Poujadists" (members of the Union for the Defense of Traders and Artisans, named for their leader Pierre Poujade) gain seats in French elections, the communists winning 147 seats, compared with 97 in the 1951 elections, while the "Poujadists," contesting their first election, win 51.
23   Nikolai Bulganin, prime minister of the USSR, proposes a 20-year pact of friendship between the United States and the USSR.
24   The socialist Guy Mollet forms a government in France following electoral gains for the Left.
28   The National People's Army is founded in East Germany.

FEBRUARY

1   South Africa requests the USSR to close its consulates, on suspicion that the USSR is aiding black activists in southern Africa.
1   The U.S. president Dwight D. Eisenhower and the British prime minister Anthony Eden issue the "Declaration of Washington," reaffirming their joint policy in the Middle East.
2   A Sixth Five-Year Plan is adopted in the USSR at the 20th Communist Party Congress, aiming to achieve further increases in industrial and agricultural production. The plan is abandoned a year later and not replaced.
4   The USSR protests to the United States about its launching of balloons with photographic equipment over Soviet territory.
12   The USSR states that the dispatch of U.S. or British troops to the Middle East would violate the United Nations (UN) charter.
25   The general secretary of the Communist Party in the USSR, Nikita Khrushchev, denounces former leader Joseph Stalin and his policies, at a closed session of the 20th Conference of the Communist Party. The speech is made public on March 18.
28   India and Indonesia sign a mutual aid treaty.
29   The Pakistan parliament passes a bill containing a constitution for the new independent Islamic Republic of Pakistan. On March 2 it decides to stay in the British Commonwealth, and on March 23 it becomes independent, with Iskander Mirza, the governor-general, as provisional president.

MARCH

- The U.S. Supreme Court, in *Ullmann v. USA*, rules as constitutional a federal law that forces witnesses to testify in court cases in which the nation's security is at stake.
March–April   The U.S. Internal Revenue Service seizes the offices of the communist newspaper *Daily Worker* for overdue taxes. The offices are returned a week later after the newspaper posts a $4,500 bond.
2   King Hussein of Jordan dismisses the British commander of the Arab Legion, Lieutenant General John "Pasha" Glubb, in response to nationalist pressure.
5   Britain begins jamming Radio Athens broadcasts to Cyprus, which are encouraging terrorist activities. The jamming is continued until December.
8   West Germany amends its constitution to permit the introduction of conscription.
9   The British authorities in Cyprus deport Archbishop Mikhail Makarios and three others from Cyprus, sending them to the Seychelles, suspecting them of involvement with EOKA (Greek Cypriot nationalist) terrorists.
12   The Greek government again asks for the Cyprus question to be put before the United Nations (UN) General Assembly.

APRIL

April–September   New York labor columnist Victor Riesel is blinded by a man hired by mobster Johnny Dio. Dio is indicted for the crime, along with six others, on September 7.
10   A general election in Ceylon (now Sri Lanka) is won by the Sri Lanka Freedom Party, and Solomon Bandaranaike replaces Sir John Kotalawala as prime minister.
17   The USSR abolishes the Cominform (the Communist Information Bureau, established in 1947), in a move to help rapprochement with Yugoslavia and the West.
21   A military alliance is signed by Egypt, Saudi Arabia, and Yemen, at Jiddah, Saudi Arabia.
22   China appoints the religious leader the Dalai Lama as chairman of a committee to prepare Tibet for regional autonomy within the Chinese People's Republic.
29   The United Nations (UN) secretary-general Dag Hammarskjöld obtains the agreement of Israel and Jordan to respect a cease-fire. A similar agreement is obtained on May 1 from Lebanon and on May 2 from Syria.

MAY

- The U.S. Atomic Energy Commission tests the first airborne hydrogen bomb over the Pacific Ocean.
14   The USSR complains that U.S. planes have violated its air space.

27 India claims suzerainty over Chitral, a princely state which has been under Pakistani administration since 1947.

JUNE

1 Vyacheslav Molotov is dismissed as Soviet foreign minister, a position he has held since 1939, and is succeeded by Dmitri Shepilov.

2 President Tito of Yugoslavia visits Moscow, USSR, marking an improvement in relations between the countries since Yugoslavia was expelled from the Cominform (Communist Information Bureau) in 1948.

4 Egypt declares that it will not extend the (British) Suez Canal Company's concession to export oil after its expiry in 1968.

5 Chancellor Konrad Adenauer of West Germany and Prime Minister Mollet of France meet in Luxembourg to agree the future of the Saar region, which is to have political union with West Germany from January 1, 1957 and economic union in the longer term. A formal agreement is signed on October 27.

13 The last British troops leave their Suez Canal base in Egypt, in accordance with the British–Egyptian treaty of October 1954.

22 Following a general election in Austria on May 13, Julius Raab forms a new coalition of People's Party representatives and Socialists.

23 Colonel Gamal Abdel Nasser is elected president of Egypt, unopposed, in a popular vote which also approves a new constitution.

28 Riots in Poznań, Poland, demanding both bread and freedom, are put down with heavy loss of life, 74 workers and militiamen being killed.

30 The Leeward Islands federation is dissolved to enable the islands to enter the new Caribbean federation.

JULY

11 The separate Finno-Karelian Republic is abolished and incorporated as the Karelian Autonomous Republic within the Russian Federation.

17 Premier Kwame Nkrumah of the People's Party increases his majority in Gold Coast (now Ghana) elections.

19–20 The United States and Britain inform Egypt that they cannot, at present, participate in financing the proposed Aswan High Dam on the River Nile.

26 The Egyptian president Gamal Abdel Nasser announces the nationalization of the Suez Canal (owned partly by France and Britain) after the United States and Britain announce they will not help fund the Aswan Dam project. On July 31 Britain, France, and the United States retaliate with financial measures.

AUGUST

• Democrats nominate former Illinois governor Adlai E. Stevenson for president and Tennessee senator Estes Kefauver for vice president.

• Republicans renominate Dwight D. Eisenhower for president and Richard M. Nixon for vice president.

3 The Gold Coast League Assembly adopts Premier Kwame Nkrumah's resolution demanding independence (granted by Britain on September 18).

4 Indonesia, composed largely of former Dutch colonies, repudiates its debts to the Netherlands.

16–23 An international conference on the Suez Canal is held in London, England, with representatives from 22

countries, but not Egypt, who tried to nationalize it July 26. Eighteen countries support the U.S. Dulles Plan for an international Suez Canal Board, associated with the United Nations (UN), to manage the canal.

SEPTEMBER

9 President Gamal Abdel Nasser of Egypt rejects the Dulles Plan for international control of the Suez Canal.

19 A second conference on the Suez Canal is held in London, England, attended by delegates of 18 countries supporting the Dulles Plan for international control of the canal. On September 21 they establish a Canal Users Association, which first meets in London on October 18.

23 Britain and France refer the Suez dispute to the United Nations (UN) Security Council.

30–October 1 French and Israeli delegates (the Israelis led by foreign secretary Golda Meir) meet in secret in Montparnasse, Paris, France, to discuss possible coordination of military action against Egypt.

OCTOBER

8 Israel withdraws from the Israeli–Jordan Mixed Armistice Commission discussing their border dispute.

12 Britain informs Israel that it will assist Jordan, if it is attacked, under the 1948 treaty between the two countries.

13 The United Nations (UN) Security Council adopts the first part of a British–French resolution on the Suez Canal, but the USSR vetoes the second part requiring Egypt to comply with a set of principles guaranteeing Western access to the Canal.

16 The British prime minister Anthony Eden and the foreign secretary Selwyn Lloyd visit Paris, France, to discuss participation in action against Egypt with the French prime minister Guy Mollet and foreign minister Christian Pineau.

19 A Soviet–Japanese treaty ends an 11-year state of war dating from 1945, but the status of the disputed Kurile Islands remains unresolved.

21 The former political prisoner Władysław Gomułka returns to power in Poland when he is elected first secretary of the Communist Party instead of the Soviet candidate, Marshal Rokossovsky.

21–22 Representatives of the Israeli government (including the prime minister David Ben-Gurion), the French government (including the prime minister Guy Mollet), and the British government (including the foreign secretary Selwyn Lloyd) meet in secret at Sèvres, Paris, France, to discuss a coordinated action against Egypt during the Suez Crisis.

23 Demonstrators in Hungary call for democratic government, the return of Imre Nagy to power (granted October 24), the withdrawal of Soviet troops, and the release of Cardinal Mindszenty (granted October 30).

24 Imre Nagy is reappointed prime minister of Hungary after demonstrations, and promises reforms.

25 Egypt, Jordan, and Syria establish joint command of their armed forces during the Suez Crisis.

28 The primate of Poland Cardinal Stefan Wyszyński is released from prison by the communist authorities.

29 Israeli troops invade Egypt's Sinai Peninsula, triggering a new level of activity in the Suez Crisis.

29 János Kádár becomes leader of the Central Committee of the Hungarian Workers' Party, replacing its Stalinist head in the wake of demonstrations for reform.

30 Britain and France present an ultimatum to Egypt and Israel following Israel's invasion of the Sinai Peninsula on October 29, calling for a cease-fire and the withdrawal of forces 16 km/10 mi from the Suez Canal. Israel accepts, but not Egypt.

30 The Hungarian prime minister Imre Nagy promises free elections in Hungary, and Cardinal Mindszenty is released following eight years of captivity. The USSR responds by sending Soviet and satellite state troops to invade Hungary.

31 British and French planes bomb Egyptian airfields, causing a public outcry in Britain against this action in response to the Suez Crisis.

31 Roy Welensky succeeds Lord Malvern as prime minister of the Federation of Rhodesia and Nyasaland.

31 The United States suspends aid to Israel in protest at its invasion of Egypt in the Suez Crisis.

NOVEMBER

• Americans reelect Dwight D. Eisenhower president in a landslide. In the congressional elections, Democrats retain majorities in the House (233–200) and Senate (49–47).

1 Jordan prohibits the use of British air bases in Jordan for operations against Egypt during the Suez Crisis.

1 The Hungarian prime minister Imre Nagy forms a new government, which includes noncommunists, following the Soviet invasion on October 30.

1–2 An emergency session of the United Nations (UN) General Assembly is called to consider the Suez Crisis. John Foster Dulles, the U.S. secretary of state, attacks the British–French–Israeli action, and the Assembly votes for a cease-fire.

2 The Hungarian government renounces the Warsaw Treaty of 1955 and appeals to the United Nations (UN) and Western powers for assistance against the Soviet invasion.

2 The USSR vetoes the Western powers' request for the United Nations (UN) Security Council to consider its invasion of Hungary.

3 Britain and France agree to accept a Middle East cease-fire if a United Nations (UN) force will keep the peace.

4 Soviet forces attack Budapest, Hungary, and the Hungarian prime minister Imre Nagy takes refuge in the Yugoslavian embassy. János Kádár, the leader of the Central Committee of the Hungarian Workers' Party, cooperates with the USSR and forms a "revolutionary peasant-worker" government.

4 The United Nations (UN) General Assembly adopts a Canadian resolution to send an international force to the Middle East to respond to the Suez Crisis.

5 British paratroops land at Port Said, Egypt, at the northern end of the Suez Canal.

6 The USSR threatens to intervene in the Suez Crisis.

7 Britain and France accept a cease-fire in the Suez Crisis in Egypt, but Britain declares it will evacuate its troops only on the arrival of the United Nations (UN) emergency force.

8 The United Nations (UN) General Assembly demands the withdrawal of Soviet troops from Hungary.

12 The Hungarian leader János Kádár refuses entry to Hungary for United Nations (UN) observers, but accepts UN relief.

15 A United Nations (UN) emergency force arrives in Egypt to deal with the Suez Crisis.

17 A constituent assembly in Jammu and Kashmir, India, adopts a new constitution (to be in force from January 26, 1957) and reaffirms its accession to the Republic of India.

20 U.S. Air Force general Lauris Norstad succeeds Alfred Gruenther as Allied Supreme Commander of NATO forces in Europe.

21 The United Nations (UN) General Assembly formally censures the USSR over its invasion of Hungary.

DECEMBER

2 Fidel Castro and his followers land in Cuba and, after an initial setback, begin a campaign of guerrilla war, aiming to overthrow General Fulgencio Batista's government.

5 British and French forces begin their withdrawal from Egypt and the Suez Crisis there, completing their evacuation on December 22.

5 One hundred and fifty European, Asian, and black people are arrested in dawn raids in South Africa, and are charged with treason. A preliminary hearing is held between December 19 and January 9, though defendants are released on bail for Christmas.

18 Japan is admitted to the United Nations (UN).

27 A United Nations (UN) sponsored fleet begins clearance of the Suez Canal, which was blocked by Egypt during the Suez Crisis.

SCIENCE, TECHNOLOGY, AND MEDICINE

Computing

• IBM introduce RAMAC (Random Access Method of Accounting and Control), the first hard disk storage of data. Indexes are used to locate the data on the disk.

• IBM introduce the Model 305 Business Computer. It has a memory of 20 megabytes.

• Univac initiates the second generation of computers when it introduces the first commercially successful computer using transistors instead of vacuum tubes.

• U.S. computer programmer Jack Backus at IBM invents FORTRAN (formula translation), the first computer-programming language. It is used primarily by scientists and mathematicians.

Ecology

• The director of the U.S. National Parks, Conrad L. Wirth, announces "Mission 66," a plan to improve visitor facilities and undertake considerable restoration in the parks.

• The national park Ngorongoro Conservation Area is established in Tanganyika (modern Tanzania). It contains the crater of the extinct Ngorongoro volcano.

• The U.S. Congress creates the Virgin Islands National Park, on 15,150 acres bequeathed to the nation by Laurence Rockefeller.

Health and Medicine

- German physiologist Werner Forssmann and U.S. physiologists André Cournand and Dickinson Richards share the Nobel Prize for Physiology or Medicine for their discoveries concerning heart catheterization and pathological changes in the circulatory system.
- Ultrasonics are first used to sterilize surgical equipment. The instruments are placed in a small liquid tank where the sound waves cause cavitation (the creation of tiny bubbles) that results in turbulence, that in turn cleans the instruments.

JUNE

- In a meeting of the American Medical Association, U.S. physician Jonas E. Salk and U.S. surgeon general Leonard A. Scheele predict that poliomyelitis will be eliminated in three years.

AUGUST

1 Drug manufacturers in the United States begin to market the poliomyelitis vaccine developed by Dr. Jonas E. Salk.

Science

- English anthropologist E. E. Evans-Pritchard publishes *Nuer Religion*.
- English chemist Cyril Hinshelwood and Russian chemist Nikoly Semenov receive the Nobel Prize for Chemistry for their work on the kinetics of chemical reactions.
- Polish-born English scientist Jacob Bronowski publishes *Science and Human Values*.
- Romanian-born U.S. biologist George Palade discovers ribosomes, which contain RNA (ribonucleic acid).
- Spanish-born U.S. molecular biologist Severo Ochoa discovers polynucleotide phosphorylase, the enzyme responsible for the synthesis of RNA (ribonucleic acid).
- U.S. biochemist Arthur Kornberg, using radioactively-tagged nucleotides, discovers that the bacteria *Escherichia coli* uses an enzyme, now known as DNA polymerase, to replicate DNA (deoxyribonucleic acid). It allows him to synthesize DNA in the test tube.
- U.S. biologists Maklon Hoagland and Paul Zamecnik discover transfer RNA (ribonucleic acid) which transfers amino acids, the building blocks of proteins, to the correct site on the messenger RNA.
- U.S. geologists Bruce Heezen and William Ewing discover a global network of oceanic ridges and rifts 60,000 km/37,000 mi long that divide the earth's surface into "plates."
- U.S. physicists B. Cook, G. R. Lambertson, O. Piconi, and W. A. Wentzel discover the antineutron by passing an antiproton beam through matter.
- U.S. physicists Clyde Cowan and Fred Reines detect the existence of the neutrino, a particle with no electric charge and no mass, at the Los Alamos Laboratory, New Mexico.
- U.S. physicists William Shockley, John Bardeen, and Walter Brattain share the Nobel Prize for Physics for their work on semiconductors and their discovery of the transistor effect.

Technology

- German-born U.S. physicist Erwin Müller develops the field ion microscope, which enables individual atoms to be seen.
- Swiss engineer Pal Deriaz develops a mixed-flow turbine. Its blades have a variable pitch that can be adjusted to the load to improve efficiency.
- The Hassi R'Mel gas field, the largest in Africa, is discovered in Algeria; its reserves are estimated at 1.73 trillion cubic meters.
- The USSR launches its first intermediate-range ballistic missile (IRBM).

FEBRUARY

- U.S. engineers Charles Ginsburg and Ray Milton Dolby of Ampex Corporation demonstrate the first practical videotape recorder. It revolutionizes television broadcasting by permitting shows to be taped rather than shown live.

AUGUST

- The U.S. Bell Telephone Company develops the "visual telephone," which transmits pictures simultaneously with sound.

OCTOBER

17 The UK's first full-scale commercial nuclear power station, Calder Hall in northwestern England, is opened by Queen Elizabeth II. It produces 4.2 megawatts of electricity and also produces plutonium for nuclear weapons.

Transportation

- German engineer Felix Wankel invents the Wankel engine, an internal combustion engine that uses a triangular-shaped rotor instead of pistons.
- The port of Elizabeth opens in New Jersey. It is the first port especially designed for container ships.
- Twelve-volt ignition systems begin to replace six-volt systems in cars.
- U.S. automobile companies manufacture about 6 million cars and 1 million trucks. About one in every eight cars is a station wagon.
- U.S. car manufacturers begin to make two-door hardtops—cars where the pillar behind the front door has been eliminated.

JANUARY

31 The U.S. Air Force tests its first nuclear-powered jet engine. Radioactivity from its exhaust, however, prevents it from coming into use.

MARCH

10 British aviator Peter Twiss captures the air-speed record with a flight at 1,821 kph/1,132 mph, in a Fairey Delta research aircraft.

JUNE

29 The U.S. Congress passes the Federal Aid Highway Act, which provides for the construction of 68,000 km/42,500 mi of interstate highways to link major U.S. cities, based on a plan announced by President Dwight D. Eisenhower in June 1954. The Highway Revenue Act, which imposes a federal tax on gasoline to pay for the system, is also passed.

30 A DC-7 and a TWA flight collide over the Grand Canyon, Arizona, killing 128 people.

AUGUST

5–October 6 The U.S. nuclear submarine *Seawolf* remains submerged for a record 60 days and travels 22,146 km/ 13,761 mi.

23 A U.S. Army helicopter makes the first transcontinental nonstop flight for helicopters, 4,176 km/2,610 mi from San Diego, California, to Washington, D.C., in 31 hr 40 min.

SEPTEMBER

7 U.S. Air Force pilot Captain Iven Kincheloe sets a new altitude record of 38,466 m/126,200 ft, in a Bell X-2 rocket-powered aircraft.

27 U.S. Air Force pilot Milburn Apt achieves a record speed of 3,350 kph/2,094 mph, in an X-2 rocket-powered airplane launched from a B-50 bomber. He is the first person to exceed Mach 3 (Mach 3.196), but the plane crashes and Apt is killed.

NOVEMBER

8 Two U.S. Navy pilots establish a world balloon altitude record of 23,165 m/76,000 ft, in a plastic Stratolab balloon.

ARTS AND IDEAS

Architecture

- The auditorium and chapel at the Massachusetts Institute of Technology (MIT) in Boston, Massachusetts, designed by the Finnish architect Eero Saarinen, are completed.
- The Church of Madonna dei Poveri in Milan, Italy, designed by the Italian architects Luigi Figini and Gino Pollini, is completed.
- The English architect William Holford publishes his plan for the redevelopment of the area around St. Paul's Cathedral in London, England.
- The General Motors Technical Center in Warren, Michigan, designed by the Finnish architect Eero Saarinen, is completed.
- The High Court Building in Chandigarh, the Punjab, India, designed by the Swiss architect Le Corbusier, is completed. A new city, Chandigarh gave Le Corbusier opportunities to develop many of his ideas during the 1960s. Others who work there include the English architects Maxwell Fry and Jane Drew.
- The Mile High Center in Denver, Colorado, designed by the Chinese-born U.S. architect I. M. Pei, is completed.
- The Tappan Zee bridge is completed over the Hudson River, Tarrytown, New York, New York. It is the largest steel cantilever bridge in the world at 369 m/ 1,212 ft.

Arts

- The art exhibition "This is Tomorrow" at the Whitechapel Gallery in London, England, helps to launch pop art, an art that draws on consumer culture.
- The English artist Richard Hamilton creates the collage *What Is It That Makes Today's Homes So Different, So Appealing?*, one of the first works of British pop art.
- The French artist Yves Klein creates the first of his blue monochrome paintings. He patents the color in 1960 as YKB (Yves Klein Blue).
- The German-born English art historian Nikolaus Pevsner publishes *The Englishness of English Art*.
- The Spanish artist Antoni Tàpies paints *Earth + Paint*.
- The U.S. artist Franz Kline paints *Mahoning*.
- The U.S. artist Hans Hartung paints *10*.
- The U.S. artist Joan Mitchell paints *Hemlock*.

Film

- A movie of Shakespeare's play *Richard III*, directed by Laurence Olivier, is released in Britain. Olivier also stars in it, along with Claire Bloom, Ralph Richardson, and Cedric Hardwicke.
- At the Cannes Film Festival in France, the Palme d'Or is awarded to the documentary *Le Monde du Silence/ World of Silence*, directed by Jacques Cousteau and Louis Malle.
- The movie *A Town Like Alice*, directed by Jack Lee, is released in Britain. Based on the novel by Nevil Shute, it stars Virginia McKenna, Peter Finch, and Takagi.
- The movie *Anastasia*, directed by Russian filmmaker Anatole Litvak, is released in the United States, starring Ingrid Bergman.
- The movie *Aparajito/The Unvanquished*, directed by Satyajit Ray, is released in India. The second in a trilogy starting with *Pather Panchali* and concluding with *The World of Apu*, it stars Pinaki Sen Gupta, Karuna Bannerjee, and Kanu Bannerjee.
- The movie *Around the World in Eighty Days*, directed by Michael Anderson, is released in the United States. Based on the novel by Jules Verne, it stars David Niven, Cantinflas, Shirley MacLaine, and Robert Newton.
- The movie *Baby Doll*, directed by Elia Kazan, is released in the United States. Scripted by Tennessee Williams and based on his play *27 Wagonloads of Cotton*, it stars Karl Malden, Carroll Baker, and Eli Wallach.
- The movie *Bus Stop*, directed by Joshua Logan, is released in the United States, starring Marilyn Monroe, Don Murray, Arthur O'Connell, Betty Field, Hope Lange, and Hans Conried.
- The movie *Early Spring*, directed by Yasujiro Ozu, is released in Japan, starring Chikage Awajima, Ryo Ikebe, and Keiko Kishi.
- The movie *Friendly Persuasion*, directed by William Wyler, is released in the United States, starring Gary Cooper, Dorothy McGuire, and Anthony Perkins.
- The movie *Giant*, directed by George Stevens, is released in the United States, starring Rock Hudson, Elizabeth Taylor, and James Dean.
- The movie *Kanal/Canal*, directed by Andrzej Wajda, is released in Poland, starring Teresa Iżewska, Tadeusz Janczar, Emil Karewicz, and Wieńczysław Gliński.

- The movie *Lust for Life*, directed by Vincente Minnelli, is released in the United States. A fictionalized biography of the Dutch artist Vincent Van Gogh, based on the book by U.S. author Irving Stone, it stars Kirk Douglas.
- The movie *Mon Oncle/My Uncle*, directed by Jacques Tati, is released in France. Tati also stars in it.
- The movie *Reach for the Sky*, directed by Lewis Gilbert, is released in Britain, starring Kenneth More as the war hero Douglas Bader.
- The movie *The Bad Seed*, directed by Mervyn LeRoy, is released in the United States. Starring Nancy Kelly, Patty McCormack, Henry Jones, and William Hopper, it is based on the play by Maxwell Anderson.
- The movie musical *Carousel*, directed by Henry King, is released in the United States. With music and lyrics by Richard Rodgers and Oscar Hammerstein, it stars Gordon McRae, Shirley Jones, and Cameron Mitchell.
- The movie musical *The King and I*, directed by Walter Lang, is released in the United States. With music and lyrics by Richard Rodgers and Oscar Hammerstein, it stars Yul Brynner and Deborah Kerr, and features the songs "Getting to Know You" and "Shall We Dance?"
- The horror movie *Invasion of the Body Snatchers*, directed by Don Siegel, is released in the United States. Based on the novel *The Body Snatchers* by Jack Finney, it stars Kevin McCarthy, Dana Wynter, Larry Gates, King Donovan, Carolyn Jones, and Virginia Christine.
- The science fiction movie *Forbidden Planet*, directed by Fred McLeod Wilcox, is released in the United States. Based on *The Tempest*, it stars Walter Pidgeon, Anne Francis, Leslie Nielsen, and "Robby the Robot."

APRIL

16 The 1955 Academy Awards take place. Best Actor: Ernest Borgnine, for *Marty*; Best Supporting Actor: Jack Lemmon, for *Mister Roberts*; Best Actress: Anna Magnani, for *The Rose Tattoo*; Best Supporting Actress: Jo Van Fleet, for *East of Eden*; Best Picture: *Marty*, directed by Delbert Mann; Best Director: Delbert Mann, for *Marty*.

19 The U.S. movie star Grace Kelly marries Prince Rainier of Monaco. The screening of her movies in Monaco is subsequently banned.

Literature and Language

- The *Cahiers/Notebooks* of the French writer and mystic Simone Weil are published posthumously.
- The Algerian-born French writer Albert Camus publishes his novel *La Chute/The Fall*.
- The English writer Anthony Burgess publishes his novel *Time for a Tiger*.
- The English writer Angus Wilson publishes his short-story collection *Anglo-Saxon Attitudes*.
- The English writer C. S. Lewis publishes his novel *The Last Battle*, the final volume of *The Chronicles of Narnia*.
- The English writer J. R. R. Tolkien publishes his novel *The Return of the King*, the final novel of his *The Lord of the Rings* trilogy.
- The English writer Kathleen Raine publishes her *Collected Poems*.

- The English writer Laurie Lee publishes *Cider with Rosie*, recollections of his childhood in an English village.
- The English writer Rose Macaulay publishes her novel *The Towers of Trebizond*.
- The English writer William Golding publishes his novel *Pincher Martin*.
- The English zoologist Gerald Durrell publishes *My Family and Other Animals*.
- The Japanese writer Yukio Mishima publishes his novel *Kinkakuji/The Temple of the Golden Pavilion*.
- The Nobel Prize for Literature is awarded to the Spanish poet Juan Ramón Jiménez.
- The Pulitzer Prize for Biography is awarded to Talbot Faulkner Hamlin for *Benjamin Henry Latrobe*, the Pulitzer Prize for Poetry is awarded to Elizabeth Bishop for *Poems – North & South*, and the Pulitzer Prize for Fiction is awarded to MacKinlay Kantor for *Andersonville*.
- The Soviet writer Yevgeny Yevtushenko publishes his long poem "Stantsiya Zima"/"Zima Junction".
- The U.S. historian James Macgregor Burns publishes *Roosevelt: The Lion and the Fox*.
- The U.S. writer Allen Ginsberg publishes *Howl and Other Poems*, which becomes a classic of "Beat" literature.
- The U.S. writer and critic Edmund Wilson publishes *A Piece of My Mind: Reflections at Sixty*.
- The U.S. writer James Baldwin publishes his novel *Giovanni's Room*.
- The U.S. writer John Berryman publishes his poetry collection *Homage to Mistress Bradstreet*.
- The U.S. writer John Barth publishes his novel *The Floating Opera*.
- The U.S. writer John O'Hara publishes his novella *A Family Party*.
- The U.S. writer Nelson Algren publishes his novel *A Walk on the Wild Side*.
- The U.S. writer Patricia Highsmith publishes her novel *The Talented Mr Ripley*.
- The U.S. writer Richard Wilbur publishes his poetry collection *Things of This World*, which wins the Pulitzer Prize for Poetry in 1957.
- The U.S. writer Saul Bellow publishes his novel *Seize the Day*.
- The U.S. writer William Styron publishes his novella *The Long March*.
- U.S. statesman John F. Kennedy publishes *Profiles in Courage* (largely written by a ghostwriter), which wins a Pulitzer Prize for Biography in 1957.

April 1956–57 The Egyptian writer Naguib Mahfouz publishes his *Cairo Trilogy*, comprising *Bayn al-Qasrayn/Palace Walk*, *Qasr al-Shawq/Palace of Desire*, and *Al-Sukkari-yah/The Sukkariyah*.

Music

- Rock 'n' roll music dominates dance floors in the United States and Britain.
- The Eurovision Song Contest is launched. The first winner is Switzerland's Lys Assia with "Refrains."
- The French composer Olivier Messiaen completes his orchestral work *Oiseaux exotiques/Exotic Birds*.

- The German composer Karlheinz Stockhausen completes his electronic work *Gesang der Jünglinge/ Youthsong*.
- The opera *König Hirsch/King Stag*, by the German composer Hans Werner Henze, is first performed, in Berlin, Germany.
- The opera *The Ballad of Baby Doe*, by the U.S. composer Douglas Moore, is first performed, in Central City, Colorado.
- The popularity of singer Lonnie Donegan's "Rock Island Line" (recorded in 1954) triggers the skiffle craze in Britain. The sound is based on acoustic guitar and home-made percussion, including washboards. Its main significance is to make the British market more receptive to blues music.
- The Russian composer Dmitry Shostakovich completes his *String Quartet No. 6*.
- The U.S. actress and singer Doris Day releases the single "Que será, será"/"What Will Be, Will Be," from the movie *The Man Who Knew Too Much*. The song is written by Jay Livingston.
- The U.S. pop singer Pat Boone releases the single "I'll Be Home."
- The U.S. rhythm and blues guitarist Carl Perkins releases the single "Blue Suede Shoes."
- The U.S. rock 'n' roll singer Fats Domino releases the single "Blueberry Hill."
- The U.S. rock singer Elvis Presley releases the singles "Heartbreak Hotel," "Don't Be Cruel," "Love Me Tender," "Blue Suede Shoes," and "Hound Dog" which, with sales of over 3 million, is the top-selling single of the 1950s in the United States.
- The U.S. singer Harry Belafonte releases the single "Mary's Boy Child;" it enters the charts on December 22.

OCTOBER

29 The U.S. opera singer Maria Callas makes her debut at the New York Metropolitan Opera in New York, New York, singing the title role in the opera *Norma* by Vincenzo Bellini.

Theater and Dance

- The ballet *Spartak/Spartacus*, by the Armenian composer Aram Khachaturian, is first performed in Leningrad (now St. Petersburg), USSR. The choreography is by the Soviet choreographer Leonid Jakobson.
- The play *A Long Day's Journey into Night*, by the U.S. dramatist Eugene O'Neill, is first performed, at the Helen Hayes Theater in New York, New York.
- The play *Der Besuch der alten Dame/The Visit*, by the Swiss writer Friedrich Dürrenmatt, is first performed, in Zürich, Switzerland.
- The play *Le Balcon/The Balcony*, by the French writer Jean Genet, is first performed, in Paris, France.
- The play *Look Back in Anger*, by the English dramatist John Osborne, is first performed, at the Royal Court Theatre in London, England, a classic text of the "Angry Young Man" movement.
- The play *Romanoff and Juliet*, by the Russian-born English writer and actor Peter Ustinov, is first performed, in Manchester, England.

- The Pulitzer Prize for Drama is awarded to Albert Hackett and Frances Goodrich for *The Diary of Anne Frank*.

FEBRUARY

8 The play *Middle of the Night*, by U.S. playwright and screenwriter Paddy Chayefsky, starring Edward G. Robinson and Geena Rowlands, is first performed, at the ANTA Theater in New York, New York.

MARCH

15 The musical *My Fair Lady*, with lyrics by Alan Jay Lerner and music by Frederick Loewe, is first performed, at the Mark Hellinger Theater, New York, New York. It features the songs "I Could Have Danced All Night" and "I'm Getting Married in the Morning."

APRIL

1 The 1955–56 Tony Awards take place. Best Actor: Paul Muni; Best Actress: Julie Harris; Best Play: *Diary of Anne Frank*; Best Musical: *Damn Yankees*.

AUGUST

27 The English theater director Michael Croft founds the National Youth Theatre.

DECEMBER

1 The musical *Candide*, with music by Leonard Bernstein, is first performed, at the Martin Beck Theater in New York, New York. It is based on the philosophical novel by Voltaire.

31 The revue *At the Drop of a Hat*, starring Michael Flanders and Donald Swann, opens at the New Lindsey Theatre, London, England.

Thought and Scholarship

- Canadian-born newspaper owner Lord Beaverbrook publishes *Men and Power: 1917–18*.
- English philosopher A. J. Ayer publishes *The Problem of Knowledge*.
- English politician Anthony Crosland publishes *The Future of Socialism*.
- English statesman and writer Winston Churchill publishes the first volume of his *History of the English-Speaking Peoples*. The final volume appears in 1958.
- English writer Harold Acton publishes his historical study *The Bourbons of Naples*.
- German philosopher Martin Heidegger publishes *Was heisst Denken?/What is Called Thinking?*
- Polish-born U.S. philosopher Alfred Tarski publishes *Logic, Semantics, and Metamathematics*.
- The English scholars Michael Ventris and John Chadwick publish *Documents in Mycenaean Greek*. Several years before, Ventris had deciphered a form of Minoan writing called "Linear B."
- The Pulitzer Prize for History is awarded to Richard Hofstadter for *The Age of Reason*.
- U.S. historian Edmund S. Morgan publishes *The Puritan Family*.
- U.S. journalist William S. White publishes *Citadel: The Story of the US Senate*.
- U.S. political philosopher Eric Voegelin publishes *Order and History*.
- U.S. political scientist Clinton Rossiter publishes *The American Presidency*.

- U.S. sociologist C. Wright Mills publishes *The Power Elite*.

SOCIETY

Everyday Life

- Polaroid sells its one millionth instant camera.

MARCH

- Workers at Westinghouse Electric Corporation end a 156-day walkout after agreeing a new contract with company officials.

JUNE

29 The U.S. actress Marilyn Monroe marries the U.S. playwright Arthur Miller; this is her third marriage. They divorce in 1961.

SEPTEMBER

25 The first transatlantic telephone cable becomes operative. The twin cables, stretching 3,600 km/ 2,250 mi between Clarenville, Newfoundland, and Oban, Scotland, provide 36 telephone circuits—three times the capacity of shortwave radio-transmissions between Europe and the United States, which until now have been the main form of intercontinental communication.

DECEMBER

8 A call for a general strike in Hungary following the Soviet invasion leads to the proclamation of martial law and mass arrests by the new Soviet-backed regime.

Media and Communication

MARCH

17 The 1955–56 Emmy Awards for television take place. Best Drama Series: *Producers' Showcase*; Best Comedy Series: *The Phil Silvers Show*; Best Actor: Lloyd Nolan; Best Actress: Mary Martin. Edward R. Murrow receives the first award for Best News Commentator.

APRIL

2 *As the World Turns*, and *The Edge of Night*, the two first 30-minute daytime serials, or soap operas, on U.S. television, begin. The former is still in production.

SEPTEMBER

9 The appearance of U.S. rock singer Elvis Presley on Ed Sullivan's *Toast of the Town* earns ratings of 54 million, 83% of the television audience.

24–September 3, 1958 The situation comedy *The Donna Reed Show* appears on U.S. television, starring Donna Reed, Carl Betz, Shelly Fabares, and Paul Petersen.

Sports

- The first judo world championships take place in Tokyo, Japan. Shokichi Natsui of Japan wins the only event in the competition, the men's Open.
- The go-kart is invented in Los Angeles, California, by Californian motor-racing mechanic Art Ingels, using converted lawn-mower engines for power.
- The National Football League Players Association is founded in the United States.

BIRTHS & DEATHS

JANUARY

24 Alexander Korda, Hungarian-born British film director, dies in London, England (62).

29 H(enry) L(ouis) Mencken, U.S. humorist and critic, dies in Baltimore, Maryland (75).

31 A(lan) A(lexander) Milne, English author who created Winnie-the-Pooh, dies in Hartfield, Sussex, England (74).

MARCH

12 Bolesław Bierut, Polish communist leader, dies in Moscow, USSR (63).

17 Irène Joliot-Curie (born Irène Curie), French physicist who with her husband Jean-Frédéric Joliot-Curie created new radioactive elements artificially, dies in Paris, France (58).

JUNE

6 Björn Borg, Swedish tennis player who won the men's singles championship five successive years at Wimbledon in London, England (1976–80), born in Södertälge, Sweden.

JULY

9 Tom Hanks, U.S. actor, born in Concord, California.

AUGUST

1 Bertolt Brecht, German poet and playwright, dies in East Berlin, East Germany (now Berlin, Germany) (58).

25 Alfred Charles Kinsey, U.S. zoologist who reported on the sexual behavior of over 18,500 men and women, dies in Bloomington, Indiana (62).

SEPTEMBER

2 William E. Boeing, U.S. inventor whose Boeing Company is one of the world's largest manufacturers of airplanes, dies (74).

6 Michael Ventris, English cryptographer who deciphered the Minoan Linear B script, showing it to be an early form of Greek, is killed in a car accident near Hatfield, Hertfordshire, England (34).

22 Frederick Soddy, English chemist who developed the theory of isotopes, dies in Brighton, Sussex, England (79).

OCTOBER

1 Martina Navratilova, Czech-born U.S. tennis player who dominated women's singles tennis during the 1980s, born in Prague, Czechoslovakia.

7 Clarence Birdseye, U.S. businessman who invented a process for freezing packaged foods, dies in New York, New York (69).

25 Kornelia Ender, German swimmer, the first woman to win four gold medals at the Olympics in one year (1976), born in Plausen, East Germany.

NOVEMBER

1 Pietro Badoglio, Italian general who arranged Italy's armistice with the Allies during World War II, dies in Grazzano Badoglio, Italy (85).

2 Leo Baeck, Jewish rabbi and theologian who was the spiritual leader for German Jews under Nazi Germany, dies in London, England (83).

JANUARY

26–February 5 The 7th Winter Olympic Games take place at Cortina d'Ampezzo, Italy, attended by 820 competitors, of whom 132 are women, from 32 countries. The USSR, entering the Winter Olympics for the first time, heads the medal table with 7 golds, followed by Austria with 4, Finland and Switzerland with 3 each, and Sweden, Norway, and the United States with 2 each. Toni Sailor of Austria becomes the first skier to win all three Alpine events, the downhill, slalom, and giant slalom.

APRIL

27 The U.S. boxer Rocky Marciano retires as world heavyweight champion, undefeated. He has won all his 49 professional fights, including six defenses of his world title.

JUNE

29 Jacques Anquetil of France sets a new world one-hour cycling record of 46.159 km/28.683 mi, an improvement of 0.288 km/0.179 mi on the Italian racing cyclist Fausto Coppi's 1942 achievement of 45.871 km/28.504 mi.

OCTOBER

3–10 The New York Yankees defeat the Brooklyn Dodgers by four games to three to win the World Series. During the fifth game, Don Larsen of the Yankees pitches the first perfect game in World Series history.

NOVEMBER

22 The 16th Olympic Games, opening in Melbourne, Australia, are affected by political boycotts: Egypt, Lebanon, the Netherlands, Spain, and Switzerland refuse to take part following the French–British–Israeli action in Egypt and the Soviet invasion of Hungary. China also withdraws in protest at the participation of Formosa (Taiwan).

22–December 8 In the track and field events at the Olympic Games in Melbourne, Australia, Vladimir Kuts of the Soviet Union wins the 5,000 meters and 10,000 meters. Bobby-Joe Morrow of the United States and Betty Cuthbert of Australia win three gold medals each in the 100 meters, 200 meters, and 400 meter relay.

DECEMBER

• The New York Supreme Court approves a revision made by the New York Yacht Club to the 1857 deed of gift governing the America's Cup yacht race, making 12 m/39.4 ft class yachts eligible. Previously, the race was contested by much larger long-masted J-Class sloops, the prohibitively high cost of which had prevented any challenges being made for the cup since 1937.

8 The 16th Olympic Games close in Melbourne, Australia. The USSR wins 37 gold medals; the United States, 32; Australia, 13; Hungary, 9; Italy and Sweden, 8 each; Britain, 6; and West Germany, 5.

30 The New York Giants defeat the Chicago Bears 47–7 in New York, New York, to capture their first U.S. National Football League Championship since 1938.

1957

POLITICS, GOVERNMENT, AND ECONOMICS

Business and Economics

• Digital Equipment Corporation opens in Massachusetts.

Colonization

FEBRUARY

6 The Gold Coast (comprising the former colonies of the Gold Coast, Ashanti, the Northern Territories, and British Togoland) becomes an independent state within the British Commonwealth and is renamed Ghana, with Kwame Nkrumah as prime minister. On February 8 Ghana is admitted to the United Nations (UN).

AUGUST

31 The British protectorate over Malaya ends and the independent Malayan Federation comes into being.

Human Rights

• The civil-rights leader Martin Luther King, Jr., helps establish the Southern Christian Leadership Conference, an organization devoted to ending discrimination nonviolently.

• U.S. writer Norman Mailer publishes his essay "The White Negro."

JANUARY

• Alabama Ku Klux Klansmen accuse Willie Edwards, a black truck driver, of insulting a white woman. The Klansmen force Edwards, at gunpoint, to leap to his death from the Tyler Goodwin Bridge into the Alabama River.

SEPTEMBER

- The U.S. Congress creates a Civil Rights Commission to examine race relations and protect black American voting rights in the South.

Politics and Government

- President Dwight D. Eisenhower appoints Charles E. Whittaker to the U.S. Supreme Court.

JANUARY

- Speaking before a joint session of Congress, U.S. president Dwight D. Eisenhower delineates what becomes known as the Eisenhower Doctrine. It commits the United States to protect Middle East nations from Soviet aggression.
7   Zhou Enlai, prime minister of the communist Chinese People's Republic, visits Moscow, USSR.
8–February 26   Treason trials in Syria result in life sentences for ex-dictator Adib Shishkali and others.
9   Anthony Eden resigns as prime minister of Britain following criticism of his handling of the Suez Crisis.
10 The Conservative Harold Macmillan becomes British prime minister after the resignation of Anthony Eden and, on January 13, he forms a ministry with R. A. Butler as home secretary, Selwyn Lloyd as foreign secretary, and Peter Thorneycroft as chancellor of the Exchequer.
10 The United Nations (UN) General Assembly establishes a Special Committee on the Problems of Hungary following the Soviet invasion of 1956. The committee is denied entry into Hungary, but studies documents and takes evidence from over 100 refugees, publishing a report on June 20.
22 Israeli forces complete their withdrawal from the Sinai Peninsula of Egypt following their invasion of 1956, but remain in the "Gaza Strip" (Egyptian territory to the southwest of Israel).
30 The United Nations (UN) General Assembly calls on South Africa to reconsider its apartheid policies.

FEBRUARY

- A new constitution of the U.S. Communist Party repudiates activity designed to topple the U.S. government.
1   Japan protests to Britain over nuclear testing on Easter Island in the Pacific Ocean.
5   A general election is held in Ireland following the withdrawal of Clann na Poblachta from the Fine Gael-led coalition on January 28. Fianna Fáil, with 78 seats, wins a majority over all other parties (the others win 69 seats, of which 40 are won by Fine Gael), and, on March 20, Éamon de Valera becomes prime minister again, at the age of 75.
6   Israeli troops hand over the "Gaza Strip," Egyptian territory to the southwest of Israel seized in 1956, to a United Nations (UN) force.
11 A decree in the USSR rehabilitates five ethnic minorities that were deported to Central Asia and Siberia in the period 1944–45 by the then Soviet leader Joseph Stalin.
11–April 11   A Singapore Constitutional Conference held in London, England, agrees on internal self-government for the British colony to be introduced during 1958.
15 Andrey Gromyko replaces Dmitri Shepilov as foreign minister of the USSR.

MARCH

9   A military regime takes power following a coup in southern Sumatra, Indonesia.
13 An agreement between Britain and Jordan ends their 1948 treaty; British forces are to be withdrawn from Jordan by September 15 and Jordan is to purchase British military installations.
14 EOKA guerrillas in Cyprus offer to suspend terrorist activities on the release of Archbishop Makarios from detention.
14 Following unrest in Indonesia, President Ahmed Sukarno declares a state of siege and takes power into his own hands.
18 Japan protests to the United Nations (UN) about nuclear testing.
21 The United Nations (UN) secretary-general Dag Hammarskjöld visits President Gamal Abdel Nasser of Egypt to discuss the solution of the Suez Canal problem, which Egypt tried to nationalize; President Nasser insists that Egypt is to receive tolls for the use of the canal.
21–24   The U.S. president Dwight D. Eisenhower and the British prime minister Harold Macmillan hold the Bermuda Conference in order to reestablish their "special relationship" that has been strained by the Suez Crisis. The United States undertakes to make certain guided missiles available to Britain, though the warheads remain under U.S. control.
25 Belgium, France, West Germany, Italy, Luxembourg, and the Netherlands (the "Six") sign the Treaty of Rome establishing the European Economic Community (EEC) or "Common Market," and a second Rome Treaty establishing the European Atomic Energy Authority or "Euratom" (to take effect from January 1, 1958).

APRIL

- The U.S. Senate creates the Senate Hall of Fame. Robert M. Taft, Robert M. La Follette, John C. Calhoun, Daniel Webster, and Henry Clay are elected members.
4   The British government decides to build up British nuclear capability at the expense of its conventional forces.
9   King Hussein of Jordan dismisses the pro-Egyptian prime minister Sulaiman al-Nabulsi after Sulaiman declares his intention of establishing a republic in Jordan. On April 13, King Hussein foils a coup planned by General Abu Nuwar.
17 Jawaharlal Nehru forms a new Congress government in India, with Krishna Menon as minister of defense.
18 Japan instructs its population to boil drinking water and wash vegetables because of contamination caused by nuclear testing.
18 Representatives of Burma (now Myanmar), Ceylon (Sri Lanka), India, Indonesia, Iraq, Syria, and Japan attend the first meeting, in New Delhi, India, of an Asian Legal Consultative Committee.
20 The United States resumes its aid to Israel, suspended since October 1956 because of Israel's invasion of Egypt.
24 Ibrahim Hashem forms a conservative, pro-Western ministry in Jordan.
25 King Hussein proclaims martial law in Jordan following demonstrations. The United States dispatches the 6th Fleet to the eastern Mediterranean in order to support him.

28 King Hussein of Jordan visits King Saud of Saudi Arabia and, on April 29, Saudi Arabia pays the first installment of a subsidy to Jordan.

MAY

2 South Africa adopts *Die Stem Van Suid Afrika/The Voice of South Africa* as its national anthem.

6 The Italian government of Antonio Segni resigns on the withdrawal of the Social Democrats' support. On May 15 Adone Zoli, a Christian Democrat, forms a ministry.

10 The USSR appeals to the United States and Britain to cease nuclear testing.

15 Britain explodes its first hydrogen bomb, over Christmas Island in the Central Pacific Ocean.

21 The socialist Guy Mollet resigns as prime minister of France following the defeat of his government in the French Assembly.

JUNE

5 British and U.S. atomic authorities agree on a more wide-ranging exchange of information.

10 The Progressive Conservatives win the Canadian elections with 112 seats, while the Liberals win 105 seats, the Cooperative Commonwealth Federation wins 25, and others win 23. On June 17 Louis St. Laurent, Liberal, resigns, and on June 21 John Diefenbaker forms a Conservative ministry, ending 22 years of Liberal rule.

12 The Radical Maurice Bourgès-Manoury forms a ministry in France.

20 The report of the United Nations (UN) Special Committee on the Problems of Hungary finds that the Hungarian revolt of 1956 was spontaneous, resulting from grievances against the USSR and conditions in Hungary, and that the ruling Kádár regime has been imposed by the USSR.

JULY

4 Vyacheslav Molotov, Dmitri Shepilov, and Georgi Malenkov are expelled from the presidium of the Soviet Central Committee of the Communist Party as Nikita Khrushchev consolidates his power.

15 The Spanish dictator General Francisco Franco announces that the monarchy will be restored on his death or retirement.

19 The imam of Oman, Ghalib bin Ali, revolts against his ruler, the sultan of Oman, who requests British aid.

25 The Tunisian constituent assembly abolishes the monarchy, and Habib Bourguiba becomes president.

29 The International Atomic Energy Agency comes into being.

29 The United States, Britain, France, and West Germany issue a declaration on the principles for German reunification and call for free elections.

AUGUST

• South Carolina senator Strom Thurmond sets a new Senate filibuster record while opposing civil-rights legislation. Thurmond holds the floor for 24 hours, 27 minutes.

7 A purge of top-ranking officers in the Syrian army takes place. Turkey fears that the USSR is increasing its influence in Syria.

12 Following Britain's decision to restore self-government in British Guiana (now Guyana), an election is held for 14 seats on a new legislative council. Cheddi Jagan's

People's Progressive Party wins 9 seats and, on August 15, Jagan forms a government.

14 British troops end the revolt of Ghalib bin Ali, imam of Oman, against the sultan of Oman.

30 An All-African Federal Executive Council is formed in Nigeria, with Alhaji Abubakar Tafawa Balewa as prime minister.

SEPTEMBER

• President Dwight D. Eisenhower calls out 1,000 U.S. paratroops to enforce the desegregation of Central High School in Little Rock, Alabama.

4 Egypt and Syria agree to create an economic union.

10 A special session of the United Nations (UN) General Assembly, considering the report of the UN's Committee on Hungary, passes a resolution condemning the USSR for depriving the Hungarian people of their liberty.

11 The USSR complains to Turkey about concentrations of Turkish troops on Syrian borders.

15 Chancellor Konrad Adenauer's Christian Democratic Union wins the West German elections.

16–17 In a military coup in Thailand, Prime Minister Pibul Songgram flees and is replaced by Pote Sarasin, secretary-general of the Southeast Asia Treaty Organization (SEATO). An interim constitution is promulgated on January 28, 1958.

20 Sir Sidney Holland retires as prime minister of New Zealand and is succeeded by Keith Holyoake.

21 King Haakon VII of Norway dies and is succeeded by his son, Olaf V.

26 Dag Hammarskjöld of Sweden is reelected secretary-general of the United Nations (UN) for a further term of five years.

OCTOBER

2 Poland, with the support of Czechoslovakia and East Germany, outlines the Rapacki Plan for a denuclearized zone in central Europe to the United Nations (UN) General Assembly.

4 Milovan Djilas, the former vice president of Yugoslavia, is sentenced to a further term of imprisonment for spreading hostile propaganda.

12 Nikita Khrushchev, secretary-general of the Soviet Communist Party, sends letters to the Labour and Socialist Parties in Britain and Europe urging them to prevent aggression by the United States and Turkey in the Middle East.

16 Following incidents on its frontier with Turkey, Syria declares a state of emergency.

16 The U.S. secretary of state John Foster Dulles warns the USSR against attacking Turkey following incidents on the Turkish–Syrian border.

19 West Germany severs its relations with Yugoslavia, on the latter's recognition of East Germany.

26 The Soviet minister of defense Marshal Georgi Zhukov is relieved of his duties, as Nikita Khrushchev consolidates his hold on power in the USSR.

29 General Fulgencio Batistá suspends the Cuban constitution following the growth in strength of Fidel Castro's guerrillas.

30 The Radical Socialist Felix Gaillard forms a ministry in France.

NOVEMBER

• Nuclear scientist Edward Teller opens the U.S. Senate Preparedness Subcommittee hearings by exhorting senators to bolster the nation's air defense system in case of a Soviet attack.

11 Full internal self-government begins in the British colony of Jamaica.

14 Britain and the United States send token consignments of arms to Tunisia to forestall the supply of arms from the Soviet bloc, provoking the French delegation to leave the North Atlantic Treaty Organization (NATO) Conference on November 15 (France fears Tunisian support for Algerian nationalists).

26 The International Court of Justice in The Hague declares itself competent to adjudicate in a dispute between India and Portugal over the Portuguese enclave of Goa, off the west coast of India.

30 An attempt is made on the life of the Indonesian president Ahmed Sukarno, heightening tension during a time of crisis in relations with the Netherlands. Dutch nationals leave Indonesia and Dutch consulates close from December 5.

DECEMBER

1 Seventeen-year-old Charles Starkweather murders service station attendant Robert Colvert in Lincoln, Nebraska; this is the first of his 11 murders, crimes that many blame in part upon his admiration for the rebellious persona of actor James Dean.

8 Four small French left wing parties merge to form the Union de la Gauche Socialiste ("Union of the Socialist Left").

15 In the United Nations (UN) General Assembly, a Greek resolution that Cyprus is entitled to self-determination fails to gain the two-thirds majority required for adoption.

20 The European Nuclear Energy Agency is formed, to operate within the Organization for European Economic Cooperation.

21 The Supreme Soviet in the USSR passes a resolution supporting Nikita Khrushchev's call for a summit conference to be held to settle international problems.

SCIENCE, TECHNOLOGY, AND MEDICINE

Computing

- The U.S. Control Data Corporation markets the first supercomputer to use transistors. It is used by atomic energy and scientific laboratories.

Ecology

- African "killer" bees imported into Brazil escape and begin to migrate northward at about 320 km/200 mi per year.
- Australian meteorologists create artificial rain in New South Wales, Australia, increasing rainfall by 25%. In Queensland it saves crops.

FEBRUARY

4 An explosion in a coal mine near Bishop, Virginia, kills 39 miners.

17 A fire at a nursing home in Warrenton, Missouri, kills 72 people.

JUNE

27–28 Hurricane Audrey hits Texas and Louisiana, leaving 532 people dead or missing.

Exploration

- The United States launches the first Jupiter-C three-stage rocket. It has a recoverable nose cone and is used for the first flights to carry live animals.

JULY

1 International Geophysical Year begins. A cooperative international research program, it involves scientists from 70 nations in Antarctic exploration, oceanographic and meteorological research, geomagnetism, seismology, and the launching of satellites into space.

OCTOBER

4 The USSR launches the first artificial satellite, *Sputnik 1*, to study the cosmosphere. It weighs 84 kg/184 lb and circles the earth in 95 minutes, inaugurating the space age.

NOVEMBER

3–April 13, 1958 The Soviet spacecraft *Sputnik 2* is placed in orbit carrying a dog, Laika. It is the first vehicle to carry a living organism into orbit. Laika dies in space.

Health and Medicine

- Interferon, a natural protein that fights viruses, is discovered by Scottish virologist Alick Isaacs and Swiss virologist Jean Lindemann.
- Italian biochemist Daniel Bovet receives the Nobel Prize for Physiology or Medicine for his production of synthetic curare.
- U.S. dentist Robert Birden develops a high-speed (350,000 rpm) dental drill.
- Worcester Foundation scientist Gregory Pincus and Boston gynecologist John Rock begin a birth control pill trial in Puerto Rico.

JUNE

26 The British Medical Research Council reports that there is a strong relationship between smoking and lung cancer.

JULY

- U.S. surgeon general Leroy E. Burney announces that scientists have established a link between cigarette-smoking and lung cancer.

Science

- Chinese physicists Chen Ning Yang and Tsung-Dao Lee receive the Nobel Prize for Physics for their investigations of the violations of parity laws.
- English archeologist Kathleen Kenyon publishes *Digging up Jericho*.
- Experiments at Columbia University, New York, New York, confirm the theoretical predictions of Chinese physicists Chen Ning Yang and Tsung-Dao Lee that parity is not conserved in weak interactions.

- Japanese physicist Leo Esaki discovers tunneling, the ability of electrons to penetrate solids by acting as radiating waves.
- Scottish chemist Alexander Todd receives the Nobel Prize for Chemistry for his work on nucleotides and nucleotide coenzymes.
- U.S. physicists John Bardeen, Leon Cooper, and John Schrieffer formulate the theory of superconductivity, the characteristic of a solid material to lose its resistance to electric current when cooled below a certain extremely low temperature.

FEBRUARY

- The United States vows to assist the European Atomic Energy Community to develop an atomic energy industry.

AUGUST

19   U.S. astronomers, using a 33 cm/12 in telescope on board the uncrewed balloon-telescope *STRATO-SCOPE I*, take the first clear photographs of the sun from 24,384 m/80,000 ft.

SEPTEMBER

- The U.S. Atomic Energy Commission presides over the first underground atomic explosion, in the Nevada desert.

Technology

- Russian-born U.S. engineer Vladimir Zworykin patents an instrument for observing microscopic organisms on a television screen.
- The electron-beam method of welding metals in a vacuum is developed in France.
- The first portable electric typewriters are introduced in Syracuse, New York, by the U.S. corporation Smith Corona.
- The Jodrell Bank observatory, located near Manchester, England, and designed by English astronomer Bernard Lovell, begins operating. The first large radio telescope, it has a 76-m/250-ft diameter reflector, which can be rotated horizontally at 20° per minute and vertically at 24° per minute. Lovell uses it to track the Soviet satellite *Sputnik 1*, launched on October 4.
- The Mauvoisin Dam, Valais, is completed in Switzerland. It is the world's largest concrete arch dam to date, at 237 m/778 ft high.
- The Nistri periscope is developed. It is used to photograph the walls and contents of an Etruscan burial chamber.
- The USSR produces the short range (24 km/15 mi) "Frog 1" ballistic missile. It is 9.4 m/31 ft long, can be launched from an armored vehicle, and can deliver either a conventional or nuclear warhead.
- The USSR tests its first intercontinental ballistic missile (ICBM).

MARCH

- The electronics company Sony markets the first pocket-sized transistor radio, in Japan.
- The European Atomic Energy Community (Euratom) is established to promote the peaceful uses of atomic energy and to reduce Europe's dependency on oil. It comes into effect on January 1, 1958.

JULY

24   The Distant Early Warning (DEW) Line, extending from Alaska's northwest coast eastward to Baffin Island, becomes operational. It warns of incoming missiles from the USSR.

OCTOBER

10   A serious accident occurs at the reactor of the Atomic Energy Authority's plant at Windscale, northwest England. Some radiation escapes into the atmosphere, news of which is suppressed by the UK government.

DECEMBER

18   The first full-scale commercial nuclear power station in the United States opens at Shippingport, Pennsylvania. It produces 60,000 kilowatts of electricity.

Transportation

- Lotus introduces the first car with a fiberglass body: the Lotus Elite sports car.
- The Canadian ship *Labrador* discovers a new Northwest Passage (through to Baffin Bay), enabling ships supplying radar stations in the unfrozen Beaufort Sea to leave later for their home ports (previously they would be prevented from returning by ice).

JANUARY

16–18   The first nonstop jet flight around the world is completed by three U.S. Boeing B-52s in 45 hr 20 min.

MARCH

29   Ships of small draft begin using the Suez Canal following the partial clearance of ships sunk during the Suez Crisis. The canal is opened to ships of maximum draft on April 9.

JULY

- U.S. Navy pilot John H. Glenn, Jr., sets a transcontinental speed record of 3 hrs, 23 min, 8.4 sec, in a Navy F8U-1P jet.

AUGUST

19–20   U.S. Air Force pilot David Simons establishes a balloon altitude record of 30,942 m/101,516 ft, in *MAN HIGH II*.

26   After three years and $250 million spent on research and development, the U.S. automobile manufacturer Ford Motor Company reveals the Edsel, its new model, to consumers.

DECEMBER

- U.S. Air Force major Adrian E. Drew sets a jet speed record of 1932.2 kph/1207.6 mph, in an F-101 fighter plane.

19   A regular air service starts from London, England, to Moscow, USSR.

20   The Boeing 707 four-engine jet passenger aircraft makes its first commercial flights, from the United States.

28   U.S. pilot J. E. Bowman sets an altitude record of 9,346 m/30,335 ft for helicopters, in a Cessna YH41 Seneca.

ARTS AND IDEAS

Architecture

- The Connecticut General Life Insurance Building, in Hartford, Connecticut, designed by the U.S. architectural firm of Skidmore, Owings, and Merrill, is completed.

NOVEMBER
1 The Mackinac Bridge over the Mackinac Straits, Michigan is completed. Connecting the state's lower and upper peninsulas, it is the longest suspension bridge in the world at 1,125 m/3,691 ft long, and cost more than $100 million.

Arts

- The English artist Henry Moore sculpts *Reclining Figure* for the UNESCO building in Paris, France.
- The English artist Peter Blake paints *On the Balcony*.
- The French-born U.S. artist Louise Bourgeois sculpts *Sky City*.
- The Institute of Contemporary Art in London, England, exhibits and sells paintings by apes at London Zoo.
- The Irish-born British artist Francis Bacon paints *Screaming Nurse*.
- The Museum of Modern Art in New York, New York, holds a comprehensive Picasso exhibit to honor the artist's 75th birthday. More than 238,000 people visit the exhibit during the year.
- The Swiss artist Alberto Giacometti sculpts *Head with Large Eyes*.
- The U.S. artist Alexander Calder sculpts *Mobile* for the Idlewild (now JFK) Airport in New York, New York.
- The U.S. artist Clyfford Still paints *1957–D No 1*.
- The U.S. artist Franz Kline paints *August Day*.
- The U.S. artist Louise Nevelson sculpts *Tropical Garden II*.
- The U.S. artist Richard Diebenkorn paints *Girl and Three Coffee Cups*.
- The U.S.-born English artist Jacob Epstein sculpts *Christ in Majesty* for Llandaff Cathedral in south Wales.

November 1957–58 The Australian artist Sidney Nolan paints his *Gallipoli* series.

Film

- At the Cannes Film Festival in France, the Palme d'Or is awarded to *Friendly Persuasion*, directed by William Wyler.
- The movie *A King in New York*, directed by Charlie Chaplin, is released in Britain. Chaplin also stars in it.
- The movie *Bonjour Tristesse/Hello Sadness*, directed by Austrian filmmaker Otto Preminger, is released in the United States. Based on the novel by Françoise Sagan, it stars David Niven, Deborah Kerr, and Jean Seberg.
- The movie *Gunfight at the OK Corral*, directed by John Sturges, is released in the United States, starring Burt Lancaster, Kirk Douglas, and Jo Van Fleet.

- The movie *Kumonosu-Jo/Throne of Blood*, directed by Akira Kurosawa, is released in Japan. A version of Shakespeare's *Macbeth*, it stars Toshiro Mifune and Isuzu Yamada.
- The movie *Letyat Zhuravli/The Cranes are Flying*, directed by Mikhail Kalatozov, is released in the USSR, starring Tatiana Samoilova, Alexey Batalov, and Vasili Merkuriev.
- The movie *Love in the Afternoon*, directed by Billy Wilder, who also collaborated with his long-time screenwriter I. A. L. Diamond on the script, is released in the United States. It stars Audrey Hepburn and Gary Cooper.
- The movie *Paths of Glory*, directed by Stanley Kubrick, is released in the United States, starring Kirk Douglas, Adolphe Menjou, and George McCready.
- The movie *Porte des Lilas/Gate of Lilacs*, directed by René Clair, is released in France, starring Pierre Brasseur, George Brassens, and Henri Vidal.
- The movie *The Bridge on the River Kwai*, directed by David Lean, is released in Britain, starring Alec Guinness, William Holden, and Jack Hawkins.
- The movie *The Prince and the Showgirl*, directed by Laurence Olivier, is released in Britain. He also stars in it, along with Marilyn Monroe.
- The movie *The Seventh Seal*, directed by Ingmar Bergman, is released in Sweden, starring Max Von Sydow, Bengt Ekerot, Gunnar Bjornstrand, and Bibi Andersson. Bergman's movie *Wild Strawberries* is also released in Sweden, and stars Victor Sjöström, Ingrid Thulin, Gunnar Bjornstrand, and Bibi Andersson.
- The movie *Twelve Angry Men*, directed by Sidney Lumet, is released in the United States, starring Henry Fonda.
- The science fiction movie *The Incredible Shrinking Man*, directed by Jack Arnold, is released in the United States. Based on the novel by Richard Matheson, it stars Grant Williams, Randy Stuart, April Kent, and Paul Langton.
- The science fiction movie *The Amazing Colossal Man*, directed by Bert I. Gordon, is released in the United States. An army officer (played by Glenn Langan) who is exposed to an atomic explosion goes on a rampage after he reaches 20 m/60 ft in height.

APRIL
15 The 1956 Academy Awards take place. Best Actor: Yul Brynner, for *The King and I*; Best Supporting Actor: Anthony Quinn, for *Lust for Life*; Best Actress: Ingrid Bergman, for *Anastasia*; Best Supporting Actress: Dorothy Malone, for *Written on the Wind*; Best Picture: *Around the World in Eighty Days*, directed by Michael Anderson; Best Director: George Stevens, for *Giant*.

Literature and Language

- The Algerian-born French writer Albert Camus publishes his short-story collection *L'Exile et le royaume/Exile and the Kingdom*.
- The Australian writer Patrick White publishes his novel *Voss*.
- The English historian Herbert Butterfield publishes *George III and the Historians*.

- The English historian A. J. P. Taylor publishes *The Trouble Makers: Dissent over Foreign Policy, 1792–1939*.
- The English musicologists Alec Harman and Wilfrid Mellers publish the first volume of their four-volume *Man and his Music*. The final volume appears in 1959.
- The English poet Thom Gunn publishes his poetry collection *The Sense of Movement*, which includes "On the Move."
- The English scientist Fred Hoyle publishes *Man and Materialism*.
- The English writer Anthony Powell publishes *At Lady Molly's*, the fourth novel of his 12-volume sequence *A Dance to the Music of Time*.
- The English writer Colin MacInnes publishes his novel *City of Spades*, the first part of the so-called "London trilogy."
- The English writer Evelyn Waugh publishes his autobiographical novel *The Ordeal of Gilbert Pinfold*.
- The English writer Ian Fleming publishes *From Russia with Love*, a James Bond novel.
- The English writer John Braine publishes his novel *Room at the Top*.
- The English writer Lawrence Durrell publishes his novel *Justine*, the first volume of *The Alexandria Quartet*.
- The English writer Nevil Shute publishes his novel *On the Beach*.
- The English writer Ted Hughes publishes his poetry collection *The Hawk in the Rain*.
- The English-born U.S. writer Denise Levertov publishes her poetry collection *Here and Now*.
- The French cultural critic Roland Barthes publishes *Mythologies*.
- The French writer Alain Robbe-Grillet publishes his experimental novel *La Jalousie/Jealousy*.
- The French writer Claude Simon publishes his novel *Le vent/The Wind*.
- The illustrated children's books *How the Grinch Stole Christmas* and *The Cat in the Hat* are published by Dr. Seuss.
- The Indian politician Vengalil Krishnan Menon publishes *The Transfer of Power in India*.
- The Irish writer Rebecca West publishes her novel *The Fountain Overflows*.
- The Italian writer Elsa Morante publishes her novel *L'Isola di Arturo/Arturo's Island*.
- The Nobel Prize for Literature is awarded to the Algerian-born French novelist and dramatist Albert Camus.
- The novel *A Death in the Family* by the U.S. writer James Agee is published posthumously.
- The Polish-born U.S. writer Isaac Bashevis Singer publishes his short-story collection *Gimpel the Fool and Other Stories*.
- The Pulitzer Prize for Biography is awarded to John F. Kennedy for *Profiles in Courage* and the Pulitzer Prize for Poetry is awarded to Richard Wilbur for *Things of This World*. The Prize for Fiction is not awarded this year.
- The Russian writer Boris Pasternak publishes his novel *Doktor Zhivago/Dr. Zhivago* in Italy, permission having been refused in the USSR. An English translation appears in 1958. Its worldwide success causes Pasternak to be severely criticized in the USSR, and he declines the Nobel Prize for Literature in 1958 fearing that if he leaves the USSR he will not be allowed to return.
- The Swiss writer Max Frisch publishes his novel *Homo Faber*.
- The Trinidadian writer V. S. Naipaul publishes his novel *The Mystic Masseur*.
- The U.S. historian Arthur Meier Schlesinger publishes *The Crisis of the Old Order, 1919–33*.
- The U.S. journalist "Studs" Terkel publishes *Giants of Jazz*.
- The U.S. writer Bernard Malamud publishes his novel *The Assistant*.
- The U.S. writer Evan Connell publishes his short-story collection *The Anatomy Lesson*.
- The U.S. writer Jack Kerouac publishes his novel *On the Road*, one of the major works of the "Beat" movement of the 1950s and 1960s.
- The U.S. writer James Gould Cozzens publishes his novel *By Love Possessed*.
- The U.S. writer John Cheever publishes his novel *The Wapshot Chronicle*.
- The U.S. writer Mary McCarthy publishes her autobiographical *Memories of a Catholic Girlhood*.
- The U.S. writer Theodore Roethke publishes his poetry collection *Words for the Wind*.
- The U.S. writer William Faulkner publishes his novel *The Town*.

FEBRUARY

- The U.S. Supreme Court overturns the conviction of bookseller John Howard Griffin of Detroit, Michigan, for selling *The Devil Rides Outside*, a book thought to corrupt children.

Music

- The British singer Lonnie Donegan, known as the "King of Skiffle," releases the single "Cumberland Gap."
- The English composer Michael Tippett completes his Symphony No. 2.
- The French composer Jean Françaix completes his *Danses exotiques/Exotic Dances* for piano.
- The German composer Karlheinz Stockhausen completes his *Gruppen/Groups*, a work for three orchestras.
- The Italian composer Luciano Berio completes his orchestral work *Allelujah I*.
- The opera *Die Harmonie der Welt/The Harmony of the World*, by the German composer Paul Hindemith, is first performed, in Munich, Germany.
- The opera *Les Dialogues des Carmélites/The Carmelites' Dialogue*, by the French composer Francis Poulenc, is first performed, in Milan, Italy. It is based on a play by the French writer Georges Bernanos.
- The opera *Moses und Aaron/Moses and Aaron*, by the Austrian composer Arnold Schoenberg, is first performed, in Zürich, Switzerland. A concert version is performed in Hamburg, Germany, in 1964.
- The opera *Noye's Fludde/Noah's Flood*, a setting of a medieval miracle play composed by the English composer Benjamin Britten, is first performed, at the Aldeburgh Music Festival in England.

- The Russian composer Dmitry Shostakovich completes his Symphony No. 11 (the *1905*) and his Piano Concerto No. 2.
- The U.S. jazz pianist and composer Thelonius Monk forms his own band, after regaining the New York performer's license that he lost in 1951 as a result of a drug possession conviction.
- The U.S. pop duo the Everly Brothers release the singles "Bye Bye Love" and "Wake Up Little Susie."
- The U.S. pop singer Pat Boone releases the single "Love Letters in the Sand."
- The U.S. rock singer Elvis Presley releases the singles "All Shook Up"—his first number one in Britain—and "Jailhouse Rock."
- The U.S. rock singer/songwriter Buddy Holly releases the singles "Peggy Sue," "Rave On," and "That'll Be the Day."

Theater and Dance

- The ballet *Agon*, by the Russian composer Igor Stravinsky and the Russian choreographer George Balanchine, is first performed, in New York, New York.
- The ballet *The Prince of the Pagodas* is first performed, in London, England. The music is by English composer Benjamin Britten, the choreography by the English choreographer John Cranko, the costumes and sets by the English artist John Piper.
- The play *A Moon for the Misbegotten*, by the U.S. dramatist Eugene O'Neill, is first performed, in New York, New York.
- The play *Fin de Partie/Endgame*, by the Irish writer Samuel Beckett, is first performed (in French), in London, England. The English version is first performed in New York, New York, in 1958.
- The play *Orpheus Descending*, by the U.S. dramatist Tennessee Williams, is first performed, in New York, New York.
- The play *The Entertainer*, by the English dramatist John Osborne, is first performed.
- The play *The Hostage*, by the Irish writer Brendan Behan, is first performed, in Dublin, Ireland.
- The Pulitzer Prize for Drama is posthumously awarded to Eugene O'Neill for his autobiographical *Long Day's Journey into Night*.

JANUARY

16 The Sadlers Wells Ballet in the UK becomes the Royal Ballet.

APRIL

21 The 1956–57 Tony Awards are announced: Best Play: *Long Day's Journey Into Night*, by Eugene O'Neill; Best Musical: *My Fair Lady*, by Alan J. Lerner and Frederick Lowe; Best Actor: Fredric March; Best Actress: Margaret Leighton.

SEPTEMBER

13 *The Mousetrap*, by Agatha Christie, becomes Britain's longest-running play, with its 1,998th performance, in London, England.

26 The musical *West Side Story*, with lyrics by Stephen Sondheim and music by Leonard Bernstein, is first performed, at the Winter Garden Theater, New York,

New York. It features the songs "Tonight" and "Maria."

OCTOBER

19 The play *The Cave Dwellers*, by the U.S. writer William Saroyan, is first performed, at the Bijou Theater in New York, New York.

DECEMBER

19 The musical *The Music Man*, by Meredith Willson, is first performed, at the Majestic Theater in New York, New York; Robert Preston and Barbara Cook star.

Thought and Scholarship

- German-born U.S. social philosopher Erich Fromm publishes *The Art of Loving*.
- The Australian philosopher John Passmore publishes *A Hundred Years of Philosophy*.
- The Czech-born U.S. philosopher Ernest Nagel publishes *Logic Without Metaphysics*.
- The English art historian Kenneth Clark publishes *The Nude*.
- The Pulitzer Prize for History is awarded to George F. Kennan for *Russia Leaves the War: Soviet–American Relations, 1917–1920*.
- The U.S. journalist Vance Packard publishes *The Hidden Persuaders*.
- The U.S. linguist Noam Chomsky publishes *Syntactic Structures*, which establishes transformational-generative grammar as a linguistic theory.

APRIL

23 German physician and philanthropist Albert Schweitzer sends a letter to the Norwegian Nobel Committee urging a mobilization of world opinion against nuclear tests.

SOCIETY

Education

- The University of Waterloo opens in Ontario, Canada.

APRIL

- The National Education Association celebrates its centennial in Philadelphia, Pennsylvania.

SEPTEMBER

2 The National Defense Education Act in the United States provides for increased funding for education, especially in science and foreign languages, at both school and university levels.

Everyday Life

- Prince Philip, Duke of Edinburgh, grows a beard during the last stage of his world tour. The beard is much appreciated in St. Helena, where inhabitants grow beards in his honor.
- U.S. building inspector Walter F. Morrison develops and manufactures the Frisbee after seeing Yale University students throwing around Frisbee Pie Company tins.

FEBRUARY

8 Bruce Dern, a student at the University of Pennsylvania, resigns from the athletics team rather than shave his Elvis-style sideburns in accordance with the university sports teams' code of appearance.

JULY

12 A study estimates that 2.33 million people would die if New York, New York were hit during a nuclear attack.

SEPTEMBER

• The U.S. Labor Department announces that the average factory worker earns $2.08 per hour or $82.99 per week.

Media and Communication

• Self-help guru Norman Vincent Peale reaches an estimated 30 million people in the United States each week through his books, syndicated newspaper and magazine columns, and his radio and television shows.

• Sixty-seven ABC affiliates carry the U.S. dance show *American Bandstand*, featuring ex-radio disc jockey Dick Clark as the host.

September 1957–64 Nippon Hose Kyokai (NHK) broadcasts *The True Face of Japan* on Japanese television.

JANUARY

21 The U.S. president Dwight D. Eisenhower is inaugurated for a second term. The public ceremonies comprise the first nationally televised videotaped broadcast.

22 *Truth or Consequences* becomes the first U.S. television show to be videotaped for broadcast instead of being broadcast live.

MARCH

16 The 1956–57 Emmy Awards for television take place. Best Actor in a Single Show: Jack Palance; Best Actress in a Single Show: Claire Trevor; Best Actor in a Series: Robert Young; Best Actress in a Series: Loretta Young.

24 *Black Star Rising*, an account of U.S. vice president Richard M. Nixon's state trip to Africa, is shown on U.S. television.

MAY

27 Milbourne Christopher hosts the first nationally televised magic show in the United States, a 90-minute show called *The Festival of Magic*.

SEPTEMBER

14–September 21, 1963 The Western program *Have Gun, Will Travel* appears on U.S. television, starring Richard Boone and Kam Tong.

18–September 5, 1965 The Western program *Wagon Train* appears on U.S. television, starring Ward Bond, Robert

BIRTHS & DEATHS

JANUARY

10 Laura Ingalls Wilder, U.S. author known for her book *Little House on the Prairie*, dies in Mansfield, Missouri (89).

14 Humphrey Bogart, U.S. actor, dies in Hollywood, California (57).

16 Arturo Toscanini, Italian conductor, dies in New York, New York (89).

28 Nick Price, South African golfer, born in Durban, South Africa.

FEBRUARY

8 John von Neumann, Hungarian-born U.S. mathematician who worked in quantum physics, logic, and computer science, dies in Washington, D.C. (53).

9 Miklós Horthy (de Nagybánya), Hungarian general and head of state 1920–44, dies in Estoril, Portugal (88).

MARCH

11 Richard E. Byrd, U.S. pilot and polar explorer, dies in Boston, Massachusetts (68).

16 Constantin Brancusi, Romanian artist who pioneered abstract sculpture, dies in Paris, France (81).

20 C(harles) K(ay) Ogden, British writer and linguist, dies in London, England (67).

26 Edouard Herriot, French politician, leader of the Radical Party and

prime minister of France 1924–25, 1926, and 1932, dies in Lyon, France (84).

APRIL

9 Severiano ("Seve") Ballesteros, Spanish golfer, the youngest to win the British Open Championship (1979 at 22), born in Santander, Spain.

16 Johnny Torrio, U.S. gangster who with other crime bosses formed a national crime syndicate in about 1934, dies in New York, New York (75).

MAY

2 Joseph McCarthy, U.S. senator who, in the early 1950s, made unsubstantiated claims of communist subversion among high government officials, dies in Bethesda, Maryland (48).

7 Eliot Ness, U.S. law enforcement officer, head of the "Untouchables" (a special squad of apparently incorruptible officers), dies in Chicago, Illinois (54).

JUNE

12 Jimmy Dorsey, U.S. big-band leader and jazz musician, dies in New York, New York (53).

JULY

3 Frederick Lindemann Cherwell, Viscount Cherwell, English physicist who evolved a mathematical theory

of aircraft spin, dies in Oxford, England (71).

8 Nick Faldo, English golfer, born in Welwyn Garden City, Hertfordshire, England.

AUGUST

7 Oliver Hardy, U.S. comedian who, with his partner Stan Laurel, formed the first successful motion-picture comedy team, dies in North Hollywood, California (65).

SEPTEMBER

20 Jean Sibelius, Finnish composer, dies in Järvenpää, Finland (91).

OCTOBER

19 Vere Gordon Childe, Australian historian and archeologist who developed the study of preliterate European cultures, dies in Mt. Victoria, New South Wales, Australia (65).

24 Christian Dior, French fashion designer, dies in Montecatini, Italy (52).

29 Louis B. Mayer, U.S. film executive, head of Metro-Goldwyn-Mayer (MGM) 1924–48, dies in Los Angeles, California (72).

NOVEMBER

30 Beniamino Gigli, Italian operatic tenor, dies in Rome, Italy (67).

Horton, Frank McGrath, Terry Wilson, Denny Miller, and Michael Burns.

21–September 4, 1966 *Perry Mason*, a dramatic series about the cases of a criminal defense lawyer, appears on U.S. television. Based on a character created by Erle Stanley Gardner, it stars Raymond Burr, Barbara Hale, and William Hopper.

22–July 8, 1962 *Maverick*, a U.S. Western series starring James Garner as the antihero Bret Maverick, appears on U.S. television.

OCTOBER

4–September 12, 1963 The situation comedy *Leave It to Beaver* appears on U.S. television, starring Hugh Beaumont, Barbara Billingsley, Tony Dow, and Jerry Mathers.

Religion

- The English theologian Alan Watts publishes *The Way of Zen*.

SEPTEMBER

- U.S. evangelist Billy Graham concludes a whirlwind four-month religious tour of the United States in Times Square, New York, New York. Graham claims to have attracted 2 million listeners on his tour, and to have converted nearly 60,000 people in the city of New York alone.

Sports

- Bill Hartack of the United States becomes the first jockey to earn over $3 million in prize money in one year.
- Bobby Fischer, a 14-year-old from Brooklyn, New York, wins the U.S. chess championship in New York.
- Juan Manuel Fangio of Argentina, driving a Maserati, wins the German Grand Prix and the Nüburgring circuit to clinch the Formula One World Drivers' Championship for an unprecedented fourth successive year.
- The Admiral's Cup international yachting competition, created by the Admiral of the Royal Ocean Racing Club, Sir Miles Wyatt, is inaugurated in Britain.
- The first official go-kart race meetings are staged in the United States by the Go-Kart Club of America.

- The Swedish motorcyclist Bill Nilsson, riding an AJS, wins the inaugural 500-cc Motocross World Championship.
- The United States defeats Denmark 6–1 at Lytham St. Annes, Lancashire, England, to win the inaugural Uber Cup women's world badminton team championship.

FEBRUARY

11 The National Hockey League Players Association is founded in the United States.

MAY

12 The organizers of Italy's *Mille Miglia* ("Thousand Miles") motor race decide to discontinue the event after two drivers and eleven other people are killed when the Ferrari of the Spanish driver the Marquis de Portago crashes into a crowd of spectators.

JULY

6 Althea Gibson of the United States becomes the first black player to win a singles title at the Wimbledon lawn tennis championships in London, England.

19 The English runner Derek Ibbotson sets a new mile record of 3 min 57.2 sec at White City, London, England, improving on the Australian John Landy's 1954 time by 0.7 seconds.

AUGUST

23 Monterrey from Mexico become the first foreign winners of the Little League World Series in the United States.

OCTOBER

2–10 The Milwaukee Braves defeat the New York Yankees by four games to three in the World Series. During the season 2,215,404 fans, a National League record, watch Milwaukee's home games.

5 Great Britain's golfers, captained by Welsh golfer Dai Rees, achieve their first win in the Ryder Cup for 23 years, defeating the U.S. team 7½–4½ at Lindrick, Yorkshire, England.

NOVEMBER

16 Notre Dame end Oklahoma's 47-game college football winning streak with a 7–0 victory.

DECEMBER

29 In the fourth U.S. National Football League (NFL) Championship Game between the Detroit Tigers and the Cleveland Browns in six years, the Tigers triumph 59–14.

1958

POLITICS, GOVERNMENT, AND ECONOMICS

Business and Economics

- The Bank of America issues the first recognizable multipurpose credit card, the Bank Americard, later known as Visa; the American Express charge card is also launched.

JANUARY

- With the nation in the grip of recession, U.S. president Dwight D. Eisenhower warns Congress that significant wage or price increases would imperil the nation's economy. He also urges Congress to adopt legislation to combat labor racketeering as part of his wage-control program.

JUNE

20 Indonesia bans the operations of the Royal Dutch Shell Oil group.

Colonization

OCTOBER

2 Guinea becomes independent, having already rejected membership in the French Union.

Human Rights

SEPTEMBER

- Arkansas governor Orval E. Faubus flouts the U.S. Supreme Court by closing four Little Rock public high schools rather than desegregating them.

Politics and Government

- A conference on the law of the sea is held in Geneva, Switzerland.
- Communist China launches the "Great Leap Forward," aiming to increase industrial output at great speed, especially the production of steel. Communes become the basis of agricultural production.
- President Dwight D. Eisenhower appoints Potter Stewart to the U.S. Supreme Court.
- The international Atoms-for-Peace Conference is held in Geneva, Switzerland. Its aim is to further cooperation and to remove barriers of secrecy surrounding the peaceful use of atomic energy.

JANUARY

1 Some West German armed forces (including two armored divisions) are placed under North Atlantic Treaty Organization (NATO) command.
3 The British West Indies Federation comes into force.
20 The USSR threatens Greece with economic sanctions if Greece agrees to the installation of North Atlantic Treaty Organization (NATO) missile bases on its territory.
21 The 17-year-old Charles Starkweather kills the parents and baby sister of his 14-year-old girlfriend Caril Ann Fugate. He follows these crimes with seven more murders in Fugate's company in a week-long crime spree through Nebraska and Wyoming. In 1959, Starkweather is sentenced to death; Fugate is sentenced to life in prison.

FEBRUARY

- Former president Harry S. Truman publicly blames the United States's economic recession on the Eisenhower administration and accuses it of unintentionally promoting the fortunes of the USSR.
1 The presidents of Egypt and Syria sign documents to form the United Arab Republic, intended as the first step in the creation of a larger Arab state. On February 21 a plebiscite approves President Gamal Abdel Nasser of Egypt as head of state.
3 A treaty is signed at The Hague, Netherlands, by Belgium, Luxembourg, and the Netherlands, renewing the "Benelux" Economic Union for 50 years.
5 North Korea proposes the withdrawal of all foreign troops from North and South Korea. On February 7 China agrees to remove its troops from North Korea, but the United Nations (UN) refuses to withdraw its troops unless free elections are held throughout Korea. The withdrawal of Chinese troops is completed on October 28.
8 French forces bomb the Tunisian town of Sakiet Sidi Youssef in reprisal for alleged Tunisian complicity in an Algerian attack on a French patrol in Algeria on January 11. Tunisia confines French troops in Tunisia to barracks.
11 Tunisia informs France that French warships will no longer be allowed to use the port at Bizerte, Tunisia, following French military action in Tunisia.
14 The kingdoms of Iraq and Jordan unite in the Arab Federation, with King Faisal II of Iraq as head of state.
14 The Rapacki Plan for a denuclearized zone in central Europe (proposed by the Polish foreign minister Adam Rapacki) is delivered to foreign envoys in Warsaw, Poland, but is rejected by the United States on May 3, and by Britain on May 18.
15 A rebel government takes power in central Sumatra, Indonesia.

17 Following the ousting of the South Rhodesian prime minister Garfield Todd as leader of the United Federal Party, on February 8, Sir Edgar Whitehead forms a government.

17 France and Tunisia accept the mediation of the United States and Britain in their dispute over the alleged aiding of anti-French Algerian nationalists by Tunisia.

20 The Ghanaian president Kwame Nkrumah inaugurates the Foundation for Mutual Assistance in Africa South of the Sahara, in Accra, Ghana, supported by eight governments.

27–March 8 The Umma Party wins the largest number of seats in a general election in the Sudan, but lacks a majority.

MARCH

5 Syria accuses King Saud of Saudi Arabia of organizing a plot to overthrow the Syrian regime and destroy its union with Egypt.

27 Nikita Khrushchev ousts and replaces Nikolai Bulganin as Soviet prime minister (chairman of the Council of Ministers) and, on September 6, Bulganin is dismissed from the Communist Party Presidium, becoming chairman of the Soviet State Bank.

31 In a general election in Canada, the Progressive Conservatives increase their majority, winning 208 seats, while the Liberals take 49, and the Cooperative Commonwealth Federation 8. John Diefenbaker remains prime minister.

31–September 30 The USSR suspends testing of nuclear weapons.

APRIL

• Atomic scientist Edward Teller tells a U.S. Senate subcommittee that ending nuclear testing would subject the nation to grave peril.

• President Dwight D. Eisenhower signs housing legislation designed to jump-start the U.S. economy.

8 The U.S. president Dwight D. Eisenhower proposes mutual weapons inspection as a means of enforcing an atomic test ban.

15–22 The Ghanaian president Kwame Nkrumah hosts a conference of independent African states, in Accra, Ghana, attended by delegates from eight countries.

16 The French assembly defeats the government's proposals for restoring relations with Tunisia (following allegations that Tunisia has aided Algerian separatists), and Felix Gaillard's government resigns.

21 Dom Mintoff's Labour government in Malta finds Britain's terms for Malta's integration with Britain unacceptable and resigns. Failing to find an alternative government, the British governor Sir Robert Laycock assumes control, and following demonstrations in Valetta, Malta, he declares a state of emergency on April 30.

23 Garfield Todd and six other members of the United Federal Party of Southern Rhodesia (now Zimbabwe) leave and found a new United Rhodesia Party, committed to the establishment of majority rule.

MAY

• The U.S. Coast Guard arrests four nuclear weapons protestors as they attempt to set sail from Honolulu, Hawaii, toward the U.S. atomic testing facility in the Marshall Islands.

2 Following attacks by Yemeni tribesmen, a state of emergency is declared by Governor Sir William Luce in Britain's Aden colony.

8 The U.S. secretary of state John Foster Dulles declares in the Berlin House of Representatives that an attack on Berlin would be regarded as an attack on the Western Allies.

12 The United States and Canada establish a joint North American Air Defense Command.

13 French settlers in Algiers, Algeria, protest at the idea that the French government might negotiate with nationalist rebels, sparking a political crisis in France.

14 To resolve the political crisis caused by the protests of French settlers in Algiers, the French Popular Republican Pierre Pflimlin forms a government in France, which lasts until May 28.

15 Fearing concessions from the French government to Algerian nationalists, a committee of French settlers in Algeria declares its intention of taking power in the colony. The French parliament approves emergency powers for the government for a period of three months.

25 The Christian Democrats win the largest number of seats in the Italian general election, but lack an absolute majority.

27 Following floods, labor unrest, and ethnic conflict, a state of emergency is declared in Ceylon (now Sri Lanka).

JUNE

1 Following the resignation of the French government of Pierre Pflimlin on May 28, Charles de Gaulle forms a government. On June 2, de Gaulle is granted emergency powers for a further six months, and on June 3 is granted authorization to draw up a new constitution and to submit it to a popular referendum.

1 Iceland extends the limit reserved for its own fishing vessels to 19 km/12 mi from its coast.

16 The United States and Britain both sign ten-year agreements with Japan for cooperation on the development of atomic energy.

17 The former Hungarian prime minister Imre Nagy is executed after a secret trial.

19 Britain announces a new plan for its troubled colony of Cyprus, which involves representatives of the Greek and Turkish governments in the island's administration. Rejected by the Greek Cypriot leader Archbishop Mikhail Makarios and the Greek government, the plan is implemented on October 1 with Turkish participation.

25 The Christian Democrat Amintore Fanfani forms an Italian coalition to succeed the government of Adone Zoli, who resigned on June 19.

JULY

• The U.S. president Dwight D. Eisenhower signs legislation making Alaska the 49th state, pending ratification by voters of the territory.

1–August 21 An eight-power conference of experts at Geneva, Switzerland, agrees that the accurate detection of nuclear explosions is a viable way of enforcing a test-ban treaty.

3 The United States and Britain make an agreement for cooperation in the development of atomic weapons.

14 Brigadier Abdul Karim Kassem mounts a coup in Baghdad, Iraq, and King Faisal II, his heir, and the

prime minister Nuri-es-Said are murdered. King Hussein of Jordan assumes power as head of the Arab Federation.

15 Following the coup in Iraq, the United States dispatches forces to Lebanon at the request of the Lebanese president, Camille Chamoun.

15 South Africa resumes full membership in the United Nations (UN).

17 Following the coup in Iraq, British paratroops land in Jordan at the request of King Hussein, and remain until November 2.

19 Following the coup in Iraq, Iraq (nominally under the control of King Hussein of Jordan) and the United Arab Republic (UAR), formed of Egypt and Syria, sign a treaty of mutual defense, and on July 20 the UAR severs relations with Jordan.

19 The Soviet prime minister Nikita Khrushchev proposes a summit to discuss the situation in the Middle East, but the United States, Britain, and France suggest that the United Nations (UN) Security Council should consider the situation instead.

31–August 3 The Soviet prime minister Nikita Khrushchev visits Beijing, China, where he and the Chinese chairman Mao Zedong issue a statement calling for an end to nuclear tests and the closure of overseas missile bases.

AUGUST

• The U.S. president Dwight D. Eisenhower signs legislation granting a pension to former U.S. presidents.

1 King Hussein of Jordan dissolves the Federation of Jordan and Iraq following the coup in Iraq.

5 The Soviet prime minister Nikita Khrushchev withdraws his previous support for a United Nations (UN) Security Council meeting on the Middle East (given on July 28) and proposes a meeting of the UN General Assembly, which is accepted by the United States and Britain.

14 Britain, France, and other North Atlantic Treaty Organization (NATO) countries announce a relaxation of prohibitions on trade with the Soviet bloc and communist China, but the United States maintains its embargo on trade with China, North Korea, and North Vietnam.

23 The People's Republic of China begins bombarding Quemoy, an island near the Chinese mainland ruled by the Chinese Nationalist government on Formosa (now Taiwan).

24 The South African prime minister Johannes Strijdom dies and is succeeded by Hendrik Verwoerd on September 3.

29 The Chinese politburo approves the creation of a rural economy based on agricultural communes, the backbone of Maoist economic policy.

SEPTEMBER

1 Icelandic patrols board British fishing vessels found within the 19 km/12 mi fishing limit Iceland has claimed for itself.

7 In response to the tension over the bombardment of the Nationalist Chinese island of Quemoy by the People's Republic of China, the Soviet prime minister Nikita Khrushchev states that any U.S. attack on China will be regarded as an attack on the USSR.

19 The Algerian rebel leader Ferhat Abbas makes a proclamation in Cairo, Egypt, of the establishment of a Provisional Government of the Republic of Algeria.

19 The United Nations (UN) rejects an Indian proposal to consider the admission to the UN of the People's Republic of China, because the Nationalist government on Formosa (now Taiwan) is regarded as China's rightful representative.

28 A referendum held in France, Algeria, and other French overseas territories approves the constitution for the Fifth French Republic (promulgated on October 5), giving the president greater powers and strengthening the position of the government in the French assembly.

30 The USSR resumes nuclear testing following a self-imposed moratorium.

OCTOBER

7 Following unrest throughout Pakistan, President Iskander Mirza proclaims martial law and suspends the constitution.

20 Field Marshal Sarit Thanarat seizes power in Thailand in a military coup.

23 The USSR makes a loan to the United Arab Republic (UAR) for building the Aswan Dam on the River Nile. Delay in Western funding for the dam was the immediate cause of the Suez Crisis of 1956.

24 President Iskander Mirza of Pakistan forms a presidential cabinet, after declaring martial law and suspending the constitution on October 7, with General Ayub Khan as prime minister. President Mirza resigns on October 27, when Ayub Khan assumes the presidency and abolishes the post of prime minister.

24 The French prime minister Charles de Gaulle says he is willing to discuss a cease-fire with nationalist rebels in Algeria, but his proposal is rejected by the Algerian Provisional Government on October 25.

NOVEMBER

10–December 18 A ten-power Conference on Measures against Surprise Attack is held in Geneva, Switzerland, to try to reduce the risk of nuclear war. Representatives from the West and the Soviet bloc attend but fail to reach any agreement.

12 East Germany sends notes to 60 countries, requesting formal recognition of its existence.

12 The United Federal Party of Prime Minister Roy Welensky wins a general election in the Central African Federation.

17 The Sudanese army assumes power in Sudan, with General Ibrahim Aboud as head of state, prime minister, and commander of the armed forces.

23 The newly independent states of Ghana and Guinea announce they will form the nucleus of a union of West African states.

27 The USSR demands that troops be withdrawn from Berlin and that the city be established as a "free city." On December 14 the demands are rejected by a meeting of U.S., British, and French foreign ministers, and on December 16 by a North Atlantic Treaty Organization (NATO) council.

30 The Neo-Gaullist Union for a New Republic (UNR) wins the largest number of seats in the general election in France, taking 198 seats out of 465.

DECEMBER

3 Indonesia nationalizes Dutch businesses.

8–13 An All-Africa People's Conference is held in Accra, Ghana, with representatives from most countries, and establishes a permanent secretariat and resolves to work for freedom for Africa.

11 Following differences between coalition government members in the Netherlands on a tax issue, the Dutch Labor prime minister William Drees resigns, and is succeeded by Louis Beel of the Catholic People's Party on December 20.

12 Paul Delouvrier becomes delegate-general in Algeria, responsible only to the French prime minister Charles de Gaulle.

21 Charles de Gaulle is elected president of the French Republic with 78.5% of votes cast. The communist candidate wins 13.1% and the candidate of the Union of Democratic Forces 8.4%.

30 The French West African states of Chad, Congo, Gabon, Mali, Mauritania, and Senegal decide to form a federation within the French Community.

SCIENCE, TECHNOLOGY, AND MEDICINE

Computing

- One thousand electronic computers are in use in the United States, and 160 in Britain, at this time.

Ecology

DECEMBER

1 A fire at a parochial school in Chicago, Illinois, kills 87 children and three nuns.

Exploration

JANUARY

31 The U.S. Army launches *Explorer 1* into Earth orbit. The first U.S. satellite, it is used to study cosmic rays.

MARCH

17 The United States launches *Vanguard 1*. The second U.S. satellite, it tests solar cells and consists of a 1.47 kg/3.25 lb sphere equipped with two radio transmitters. It proves that the earth is slightly pear-shaped.

MAY

15 The USSR places *Sputnik 3* in orbit. It contains the first multipurpose space laboratory and transmits data about cosmic rays, the composition of the earth's atmosphere, and ion concentrations.

JULY

29 The U.S. National Aeronautics and Space Administration (NASA) is created for the research and development of vehicles and activities involved in space exploration.

AUGUST

27 The USSR launches the satellite *Sputnik 5*, which carries two dogs to a height of 450 km/279 mi.

NOVEMBER

- The United States launches *Atlas*, from Cape Canaveral, Florida. It is a one-half-stage rocket and has a range of 14,400 km/9,000 mi. It was originally designed as an intercontinental ballistic missile (ICBM).

3 Soviet astronomer Nikolai Kozyrev first observes a volcanic eruption on the moon, a gaseous eruption in the crater Alphonsus.

Health and Medicine

- U.S. geneticists George Beadle, Edward Tatum, and Joshua Lederberg share the Nobel Prize for Physiology or Medicine: Beadle and Tatum for their discovery that genes act by regulating definite chemical events; and Lederberg for his discoveries concerning genetic recombination.

- U.S. surgeon Clarence Walton Lillehei develops an external pacemaker.

- U.S. surgeon Norman Shumway performs the first successful heart transplant, in a dog.

JANUARY

January–July There is an epidemic of cholera and smallpox in East Pakistan (now Bangladesh); more than 75,000 people die.

APRIL

- Nobel prizewinning scientist Linus Pauling predicts that radioactive fallout from already detonated atomic bombs will cause 5 million birth defects and millions of outbreaks of cancer over the next 300 generations.

Science

- English biochemist Frederick Sanger receives the Nobel Prize for Chemistry for his determination of the structure of insulin.

- Radio astronomers receive the reflection of radio waves from Venus. Similar echoes from other objects in the solar system allow an accurate measurement of their distance.

- Russell Cave is discovered in Alabama; it contains 9,000 years of North American prehistory.

- Soviet physicists Pavel Cherenkov, Ilya Frank, and Igor Tamm are jointly awarded the Nobel Prize for Physics for their discovery and interpretation of the Cherenkov effect.

- The Equatorial Undercurrent is discovered in the equatorial Pacific Ocean. It has a width of 320–480 km/200–300 mi, a height of 200–300 m/650–1,000 ft, and flows 50–150 m/165–500 ft below the surface.

- The U.S. archeologists George R. Willey and Philip Phillips publish *Method and Theory in American Archaeology*.

- U.S. physicists Richard Feynman and Murray Gell-Mann formulate a theory that explains the phenomena associated with the weak interaction of subatomic particles.

FEBRUARY

10 The aurora borealis (northern lights) reach as far south as latitude 40° in the United States.

APRIL

- U.S. chemist Albert Ghiorso and colleagues at the University of California, Berkeley, discover the radioactive element nobelium (atomic no. 102), named for the Swedish chemist Alfred Nobel.

MAY

- Using data from the *Explorer* rockets, U.S. physicist James Van Allen discovers a belt of radiation around the earth. Now known as the Van Allen belts (additional belts were discovered later), they consist of charged particles from the sun trapped by the earth's magnetic field.

OCTOBER

11 The United States launches the space probe *Pioneer 1* into orbit.

Technology

- High explosive water gels or slurries are introduced. A mixture of ammonium nitrate, TNT (trinitrotoluene), and gelatinizing agent, they are safe and easy to use.
- The U.S. intercontinental guided missile *Snark* becomes operational. It compares the positions of stars with its guidance system to navigate.
- The U.S. telecommunications company Bell Laboratories invents the first modem, which allows telephone lines to transmit binary data.

JANUARY

- The U.S. Air Force announces it has formed two squadrons armed with intermediate-range ballistic missiles (IRBMs).
17 The Polaris intermediate-range ballistic missile (IRBM) is first launched. A solid-propellant missile, it can be fired underwater from a submarine.

AUGUST

27 The United States conducts the first Argus experiment, the explosion of three high-altitude nuclear bombs to study the effect of the earth's magnetic field on the charged particles released by the explosions.

SEPTEMBER

12 U.S. electrical engineer Jack Kilby demonstrates the first integrated circuit. It consists of transistors, resistors, and capacitors contained within a silicon substrate. It leads to the third generation of computers.

DECEMBER

18 The United States launches *PROJECT SCORE* (Signal Communications by Orbiting Relay Equipment), the first U.S. communications satellite. It functions for 13 days relaying messages stored on magnetic tape.

Transportation

- The People-to-People Health Foundation is formed in the United States to establish the first peacetime hospital ship *Hope*—a converted naval hospital ship. It makes its maiden voyage on September 22, 1960.
- The successful flight of the Rotocycle (Hiller XROE-1), a one-man helicopter, takes place, in the United States.
- The total number of transatlantic air passengers exceeds the number of sea passengers for the first time.

- The Union Tank Car Company, Baton Rouge, Illinois, is housed in a geodesic dome 117 m/284 ft in diameter and 35 m/116 ft high. It is the largest span-free structure in the world.
- The U.S. Navy decommissions the *Wisconsin*, the last battleship.

FEBRUARY

28 A school bus collides with a car and then veers off the road into the Big Sandy River, near Prestonburg, Kentucky; the crash kills the driver and 27 children.

MAY

- U.S. Air Force captain Walter Irwin establishes a new jet speed record of 2246.7 kph/1404.19 mph, in an F-104A Starfighter.
7 U.S. Air Force pilot Howard C. Johnson, flying a Lockheed F-104A Starfighter, sets an altitude record of 27,813 m/91,249 ft.

JUNE

- U.S. Air Force colonel Harry Burrell sets a new transatlantic air-speed record of 5 hrs, 27 min, 42.8 sec, in an Air Force KC-135.

AUGUST

- The USSR launches the nuclear-powered icebreaker *Lenin*. The world's largest icebreaker, it is 324 m/440 ft long and 27.5 m/90.5 ft in its beam.
1–5 The U.S. nuclear submarine *Nautilus* passes 2,945 km/ 1,830 mi under the ice cap at the North Pole from Point Barrow, Alaska, to the Greenland Sea, the first undersea crossing of a polar ice cap.

SEPTEMBER

- The U.S. nuclear submarine USS *Skate* establishes an underwater endurance record of 31 days.
5 A train wreck near Newark, New Jersey on the Jersey Central Railroad kills 40 people.

OCTOBER

- The first scheduled transatlantic jet services are launched, by British Overseas Airways Corporation flying a Comet IV between London, England, and New York, New York, followed by Pan-Am flying a Boeing 707 between Paris, France, and New York, New York.

DECEMBER

10 National Airlines begins the first domestic jet airline passenger service between New York, New York, and Miami, Florida.

ARTS AND IDEAS

Architecture

- The church at Imatra, Finland, designed by the Finnish architect Alvar Aalto, is completed.
- The Exhibition Hall on the Rond-Point de la Défense in Paris, France, designed by the Italian architect Pier Luigi Nervi and the French architect Jean Prouvé, is completed.
- The Kagawa Prefecture Office Building at Takamatsu, Japan, designed by the Japanese architect Kenzo Tange, is completed.

- The Los Manantiales Restaurant in Xochimilco, Mexico, designed by the Mexican architects Joaquín Alvares Ordonez and Félix Candela, is completed.
- The Palazzetto dello Sport, a sports stadium in Rome, Italy, designed by the Italian architect Pier Luigi Nervi, is completed.
- The Pirelli Skyscraper in Milan, Italy, designed by the Italian architects Pier Luigi Nervi and Gio Ponti, is completed.
- The President's Palace in Brasilia, Brazil, designed by the Brazilian architect Oscar Niemeyer, is completed.
- The Seagram Building in New York, New York, designed by the German architect Ludwig Mies van der Rohe and the U.S. architect Phillip Johnson, is completed.

Arts

- The English art historian John Pope-Hennessy publishes *Italian Renaissance Sculpture*.
- The French artist César creates *Compression*, scrap metal compressed into a cube.
- The Scottish artist Eduardo Paolozzi sculpts *Japanese War God*.
- The U.S. artist David Smith sculpts *8 planes and 7 bars*.
- The U.S. artist Jasper Johns sculpts *Light Bulb* and paints *Three Flags*.
- The U.S. artist Morris Louis paints *Tet*.
- The U.S. artist Sam Francis paints *Shining Black*.

APRIL
- Fire rips through the Museum of Modern Art (MOMA) in New York, New York, killing one person and causing an estimated $320,000 worth of damage.

Film

- At the Cannes Film Festival in France, the Palme d'Or is awarded to *Letyat Zhuravli/The Cranes are Flying*, directed by Mikhail Kalatozov.
- The movie *Auntie Mame*, directed by Morton DaCosta, is released in the United States. Based on the play by Jerome Lawrence and Robert E. Lee, it stars Rosalind Russell, Forrest Tucker, Coral Browne, Fred Clark, Roger Smith, Peggy Cass, Joanna Barnes, and Pippa Scott.
- The movie *Cat on a Hot Tin Roof*, directed by Richard Brooks, is released in the United States. Based on the play by Tennessee Williams, it stars Elizabeth Taylor, Paul Newman, Burl Ives, Jack Carson, Judith Anderson, Madeline Sherwood, and Larry Gates.
- The movie *Ivan the Terrible, Part II*, directed by the Latvian-born Russian filmmaker Sergey Eisenstein, is released in the USSR, ten years after Eisenstein's death, starring Nikolai Cherkassov, Ludmilla Tselitovskaya, and Serafima Birman, and featuring music by Russian composer Sergey Prokofiev. It was originally filmed in 1948, but banned by the then Soviet leader Joseph Stalin because it alluded to his dictatorial regime.
- The movie *Kakushi Toride No San-Akunin/The Hidden Fortress*, directed by Akira Kurosawa, is released in Japan, starring Toshiro Mifune, Misa Uehara, and Minoru Chiaki. The U.S. director George Lucas later

claims that this movie is the inspiration behind his film *Star Wars*.
- The movie *Les Tricheurs/Youthful Sinners*, directed by Marcel Carné, is released in France, starring Jacques Charrier, Pascale Petit, and Andréa Parisy, and featuring a jazz score from artists including Dizzy Gillespie and Stan Getz.
- The movie *Popiół i diament/Ashes and Diamonds*, directed by Andrzej Wajda, is released in Poland. Based on the novel by Jerzy Andrzejewski, it stars Zbigniew Cybulski, Ewa Krzyżanowska, and Adam Pawlikowski.
- The movie *Room at the Top*, directed by Jack Clayton, is released in Britain. Based on the novel by the English author John Braine, it stars Laurence Harvey and Simone Signoret.
- The movie *The Ballad of Narayama*, directed by Keisuke Kinoshita, is released in Japan.
- The movie *The Blob*, directed by Irvin S. Yeaworth, Jr., is released in the United States. Featuring Steve McQueen in his first starring role, it also stars Aneta Corseaut, Earl Rowe, and Olin Howlin.
- The movie *The Last Hurrah*, directed by John Ford, is released in the United States. Based on the novel by Edwin O'Connor, which was loosely based on the life of Boston mayor James Curley, it stars Spencer Tracy, Jeffrey Hunter, Basil Rathbone, Pat O'Brien, John Carradine, Jane Darwell, and Dianne Foster.
- The movie *The Wind Cannot Read*, directed by Ralph Thomas, is released in Britain, starring Dirk Bogarde and Yoko Tani.
- The movie *Touch of Evil*, directed by Orson Welles, is released in the United States. He also stars in it, along with Charlton Heston, Janet Leigh, and Marlene Dietrich.
- The movie *Vertigo*, directed by English filmmaker Alfred Hitchcock, is released in the United States, starring James Stewart and Kim Novak.
- The movie musical *Gigi*, directed by Vincente Minnelli, is released in the United States, starring Leslie Caron, Louis Jourdan, Maurice Chevalier, and Hermione Gingold. Based on a story by the French writer Colette, it features the songs "Thank Heaven for Little Girls" and "I Remember It Well."
- The movie musical *South Pacific*, based on *Tales of the South Pacific* by James Michener and directed by Joshua Logan, is released in the United States. With music and lyrics by Richard Rodgers and Oscar Hammerstein, it stars Mitzi Gaynor, Rossano Brazzi, Ray Walston, and John Kerr.

APRIL
14 The 1957 Academy Awards take place. Best Actor: Alec Guinness, for *The Bridge on the River Kwai*; Best Supporting Actor: Red Buttons, for *Sayonara*; Best Actress: Joanne Woodward, for *The Three Faces of Eve*; Best Supporting Actress: Miyoshi Umeki, for *Sayonara*; Best Picture: *The Bridge on the River Kwai*, directed by David Lean; Best Director: David Lean, for *The Bridge on the River Kwai*.

Literature and Language

- The English travel writer Eric Newby publishes *A Short Walk in the Hindu Kush*.

- The English writer Alan Sillitoe publishes his novel *Saturday Night and Sunday Morning*.
- The English writer Barbara Pym publishes her novel *A Glass of Blessings*.
- The English writer Doris Lessing publishes her novel *A Ripple from the Storm*.
- The English writer H. E. Bates publishes his novel *The Darling Buds of May*.
- The English writer Lawrence Durrell publishes his novel *Balthazar*, the second volume of his *The Alexandria Quartet*.
- The English writer T. H. White publishes his novel *The Candle in the Wind*, completing his quartet of novels on the Arthurian legends *The Once and Future King*, which is reissued as a single volume. Earlier versions of the first three books were published as follows: *The Sword in the Stone* (1939), *The Witch in the Wood* (1940) (now retitled *The Queen of Air and Darkness*), and *The Ill-Made Knight* (1941).
- The French writer and philosopher Simone de Beauvoir publishes her first volume of autobiography, *Mémoires d'une jeune fille rangée/Memoirs of a Dutiful Daughter*.
- The French writer Marguerite Duras publishes her novel *Moderato cantabile*.
- The Irish writer Brendan Behan publishes his autobiographical *Borstal Boy*.
- The Irish-born English writer and philosopher Iris Murdoch publishes her novel *The Bell*.
- The Italian poet Salvatore Quasimodo publishes his poetry collection *La terra impareggiabile/The Incomparable Earth*.
- The Italian writer Giuseppe Tomasi di Lampedusa publishes his novel *Il gattopardo/The Leopard*.
- The Kurdish writer Yashar Kemal publishes his novel *Ince Memed/Mehmed, My Hawk*.
- The Nigerian Ibo writer Chinua Achebe publishes his novel *Things Fall Apart*.
- The Pulitzer Prize for Biography is awarded to John Alexander Carroll, Mary Wells Ashworth, and (posthumously) Douglas Southall Freeman for *George Washington*, the Pulitzer Prize for Poetry is awarded to Robert Penn Warren for *Promises: Poems 1954–1956*, and the Pulitzer Prize for Fiction is awarded posthumously to James Agee for *A Death in the Family*.
- The South African writer and traveler Laurens van der Post publishes *The Lost World of the Kalahari*.
- The U.S. "Beat" writer Jack Kerouac publishes his novel *Dharma Bums*.
- The U.S. writer John Updike publishes his poetry collection *The Carpentered Hen and Other Tame Creatures*.
- The U.S. writer Leon Uris publishes his novel *Exodus*.
- The U.S. writer Truman Capote publishes his novella *Breakfast at Tiffany's*.
- The Welsh archeologist Glyn Daniel publishes *The Megalith Builders of Western Europe*.

MARCH

- Nobel prizewinning author William Faulkner laments the perceived erosion of the nation's institutions of higher learning in a speech at Princeton University, New Jersey. The schools are in danger of becoming "baby-sitting organizations," Faulkner tells his audience.

APRIL

- U.S. poet Robert Frost convinces a federal court in Washington, D.C., to drop treason charges against poet Ezra Pound. Pound had made radio broadcasts in support of Italy during World War II, but had been found unfit to stand trial on his return to the United States after the war.

Music

- The British folk group the Spinners is founded.
- The English composer Lennox Berkeley completes his Symphony No. 2.
- The English composer Benjamin Britten completes his *Nocturne* for voice and orchestra, settings of eight English poems about night, and his song cycle *Six Fragments from Hölderlin*, settings of texts by the German writer Friedrich Hölderlin.
- The French-born U.S. composer Edgard Varèse completes his electronic work *Poème électronique/Electronic Poems*.
- The Kingston Trio, a folk band popular on college campuses, release the single "Tom Dooley."
- The opera *Vanessa*, by the U.S. composer Samuel Barber, is first performed, in New York, New York.
- The Russian composer Igor Stravinsky completes his *Threni* for voices and orchestra, settings of biblical texts.
- The U.S. composer John Cage presents the first of his six *Variations*, performances, including diagrams drawn by Cage, in which any number of musicians could respond freely to the situation. The *Variations* are completed in 1966.
- The U.S. composer Morton Feldman completes his orchestral work *Atlantis*.
- The U.S. composer Norman Dello Joio completes *The Triumph of St Joan Symphony*, based on his opera *The Trial at Rouen* (1955).
- The U.S. country singer Jim Reeves releases the single "Anna Marie."
- The U.S. pop group the Teddy Bears releases the single "To Know Him Is To Love Him."
- The U.S. rhythm and blues musician Chuck Berry releases the singles "Sweet Little Sixteen" and "Johnny B Goode."
- The U.S. singer Connie Francis releases the singles "Stupid Cupid" and "Who's Sorry Now?"
- The U.S. singer Perry Como releases the single "Magic Moments," written by Burt Bacharach.

MARCH

11 The U.S. pianist Van Cliburn, a 23-year-old Texan, wins the Tchaikovsky International Piano and Violin Contest held in Moscow, USSR. He plays Sergei Rachmaninov's Piano Concerto No. 3.

24 The U.S. rock singer Elvis Presley reports for two years' compulsory military service.

Theater and Dance

- The play *Biedermann und die Brandstifter/The Fireraisers*, by the Swiss dramatist Max Frisch, is first performed, in Zürich, Switzerland.

- The play *Epitaph for George Dillon*, by the English dramatist John Osborne in collaboration with English writer Anthony Creighton, is first performed, in London, England.
- The play *Five Finger Exercise*, by the English writer Peter Shaffer, is first performed, in London, England.
- The play *Krapp's Last Tape*, by the Irish writer Samuel Beckett, is first performed, at the Royal Court Theatre in London, England.
- The play *The Birthday Party*, by the English dramatist Harold Pinter, is first performed, in Cambridge, England.
- The Pulitzer Prize for Drama is awarded to Ketti Frings for *Look Homeward, Angel*.

JANUARY

7 *Garden District*, a production of two short plays by the U.S. dramatist Tennessee Williams, opens at the York Playhouse in New York, New York.

APRIL

13 The 1957–58 Tony Awards take place. Best Actor: Ralph Bellamy; Best Actress: Helen Hayes; Best Play: *Sunrise at Campobello*: Best Musical: *The Music Man*.

OCTOBER

2 The play *A Touch of the Poet*, by the U.S. dramatist Eugene O'Neill, is first performed, at the Helen Hayes Theater in New York, New York.

DECEMBER

1 The musical *Flower Drum Song*, by Richard Rodgers and Oscar Hammerstein, is first performed, at the St. James Theater in New York, New York. Based on the novel by C. Y. Lee, it stars Miyoshi Umechi, Larry Blyden, Juanita Hill, Arabella Hong, and Pat Suzuki.

Thought and Scholarship

- Swiss philosopher Karl Jaspers publishes *Philosophie und Welt: Reden und Aufsätze/Philosophy and the World: Essays and Lectures*.
- The English historian Stephen Runciman publishes *Sicilian Vespers*.
- The German physicist and philosopher Werner Heisenberg publishes *Physics and Philosophy*.
- The German-born U.S. philosopher Hannah Arendt publishes *The Human Condition*.
- The Hungarian-born English philosopher Michael Polanyi publishes *Personal Knowledge*.
- The notebooks, *The Blue Book* and *The Brown Book*, of the Austrian philosopher Ludwig Wittgenstein are published posthumously.
- The Pulitzer Prize for History is awarded to Bray Hammond for *Banks and Politics in America: From the Revolution to the Civil War*.
- The Latvian-born English philosopher Isaiah Berlin publishes *Two Concepts of Liberty*.
- The U.S. historian Daniel J. Boorstin publishes the first volume of his three-volume *The Americans*. The final volume appears in 1973.
- The U.S. philosopher Monroe C. Beardsley publishes *Aesthetics: Problems in the Philosophy of Criticism*.
- The Victorian Society is founded in the UK to safeguard Victorian and Edwardian buildings threatened by demolition.

BIRTHS & DEATHS

JANUARY

30 Ernst Heinrich Heinkel, German aircraft designer who built the first rocket-powered aircraft, dies in Stuttgart, Germany (69).

FEBRUARY

1 Clinton Joseph Davisson, U.S. physicist who showed that electrons possess both wave and particle-like characteristics, dies in Charlottesville, Virginia (76).

APRIL

29 Michelle Pfeiffer, U.S. actress, born in Santa Ana, California.

MAY

29 Juan Ramón Jiménez, Spanish poet, dies in San Juan, Puerto Rico (76).

JUNE

17 Imre Nagy, independent communist and premier of Hungary 1953–55, who tried to gain Hungary's independence from the USSR, is executed in Budapest, Hungary (62).

AUGUST

14 Jean-Frédéric Joliot (after 1926 Joliot-Curie), French physicist who, with his wife Irène Curie, created new radioactive elements artificially, dies in Arcouest, France (58).

24 Johannes Gerhardus Strijdom, prime minister of South Africa 1954–58, who vigorously pursued a policy of apartheid, dies in Cape Town, South Africa (65).

27 Ernest Orlando Lawrence, U.S. physicist who invented the cyclotron particle accelerator, dies in Palo Alto, California (57).

28 Michael Jackson, U.S. rock singer, born in Gary, Indiana.

SEPTEMBER

11 Robert Service, British-born Canadian writer of popular verse who wrote "The Shooting of Dan McGrew," dies in Lancieux, France (84).

OCTOBER

• Pope Pius XII, Italian pope 1939–58, dies in Rome, Italy (82).

16 Robert Redfield, U.S. anthropologist who examined the relationship between folk and urban societies, dies in Chicago, Illinois (62).

24 G. E. Moore, British realist philosopher, dies in Cambridge, England (84).

NOVEMBER

15 Tyrone Power, U.S. actor known for his adventure roles, dies in Madrid, Spain (43).

DECEMBER

15 Wolfgang Pauli, Austrian-born U.S. physicist, who discovered the principle that no two electrons in the same atom can have the same energy, dies in Zürich, Switzerland (57).

SOCIETY

Everyday Life

- The hula hoop is developed by the Wham-O Manufacturing Co. of San Gabriel, California.

JANUARY
- A U.S. Gallup Poll finds Eleanor Roosevelt the nation's most admired woman.

AUGUST
4 First class postage for U.S. mail rises to 4 cents per ounce from 3 cents, the first increase since 1932.

Media and Communication

- In the United States, 45.6 million households have television sets.
- The "Quiz Show Scandal" emerges in the United States, when participants in the quiz show *Twenty-One* confess that they had been supplied with answers before the show. In response, the networks replace most quiz shows with lighter game shows.
- The Associated Press and International News Service merge to form United Press International in the United States.

APRIL
15 The 1957–58 Emmy Awards for television take place. Best Actor in a Single Show: Peter Ustinov; Best Actress in a Single Show: Polly Bergen; Best Actor in a Series: Robert Young; Best Actress in a Series: Jane Wyatt.

SEPTEMBER
30 The Western program *The Rifleman* appears on U.S. television, starring Chuck Connors, Johnny Crawford, Paul Fix, Bill Quinn, Hope Summers, and Joan Taylor.

OCTOBER
10 The detective program *77 Sunset Strip* appears on U.S. television, starring Efrem Zimbalist, Jr., Roger Smith, and Ed Byrnes.

Religion

APRIL
- The Vatican appoints Chicago archbishop Samuel Cardinal Stritch as proprefect of the Vatican's Sacred Congregation for the Propagation of the Faith, the highest post ever held by a U.S. citizen.

Sports

- ASK Riga of the USSR are the winners of the inaugural basketball European Cup for Champion Clubs, organized by the Fédération Internationale de Basketball Amateur in France.
- The National League baseball team the Brooklyn Dodgers moves to Los Angeles and the New York Giants to San Francisco, both in California.
- The Professional Bowlers' Association is founded in the United States.

MARCH
25 Sugar Ray Robinson of the United States outpoints fellow U.S. boxer Carmen Basilio over 15 rounds in Chicago, Illinois, to become the first boxer to win the world middleweight title five times.
26 Hashim Khan of Pakistan wins his seventh British Open men's squash title in eight years, at the Landsdowne Club, London, England.

JUNE
8–29 The sixth soccer World Cup tournament is held in Sweden. Brazil wins, beating the host nation 5–2 in the final in Stockholm. The 17-year-old Brazilian star Pelé scores two goals.
14 Great Britain wins the Wightman Cup women's team tennis competition, taking the trophy from the U.S. players for the first time since 1930, at Wimbledon, London, England.
15 At the Belgian Grand Prix at Spa-Francorchamps, Maria Teresa de Filippis becomes the first woman to drive in a Formula One world championship race. She finishes in tenth place.

SEPTEMBER
20–27 In the first America's Cup challenge since 1937, the U.S. yacht *Columbia* successfully defends the trophy from the British challenger *Sceptre*, winning all four races.

OCTOBER
1–9 The New York Yankees come back from three games to one down to defeat the Milwaukee Braves 4–3 in the World Series.

DECEMBER
28 The Baltimore Colts defeat the New York Giants 23–17 at Yankee Stadium, New York, New York, in the first U.S. National Football Championship Game to be decided by sudden death overtime.

1959

POLITICS, GOVERNMENT, AND ECONOMICS

Business and Economics

JULY
- U.S. steelworkers strike against 28 steel producers to win a more favorable contract.

Human Rights

- The Wolfenden Report calls for the decriminalization of homosexuality in Britain.

JANUARY
- The city of Atlanta, Georgia, integrates its buses, though the state governor calls for voluntary segregation.

MAY
- U.S. Air Force brigadier general Benjamin O. Davis, Jr., becomes the first black American to reach the rank of major general.

JULY
- The General Synod of the United Church of Christ repudiates segregation in the United States and proclaims the role of the church in mediating global social and political problems.

AUGUST
- Two integrated public high schools open in Little Rock, Arkansas, as police check demonstrators with fire hoses and clubs.

SEPTEMBER
- The U.S. Civil Rights Commission urges President Dwight D. Eisenhower to assign federal registrars to guarantee black Americans' right to vote.
1   A Swiss referendum rejects the granting of female suffrage.

Politics and Government

- A Martial Law Regulation in Pakistan implements land reform in West Pakistan. The maximum holding is fixed at 500 acres, the minimum at 50 acres, while subsistence holdings are fixed at 12.5 acres. Smaller areas cannot be sold or fragmented, and dispossessed landlords are to be compensated.

- An Intergovernmental Maritime Consultative Organization (since 1982 called the IMO) starts overseeing the law of the sea.
- The U.S. Eisenhower administration announces preliminary plans for a joint U.S.–USSR space venture.
- The U.S. historian Samuel Flagg Bemis publishes *A Short History of American Foreign Policy and Diplomacy*.

JANUARY
- Alaska becomes the 49th U.S. state.
1   The Cuban guerrilla campaign of the July 26 Movement forces General Fulgencio Batista to resign and flee to Dominica. A military junta appoints Carlos Piedra as provisional president.
2   The Cuban July 26 Movement ignores the military junta and proclaims Dr. Manuel Urratía provisional president. He announces a cabinet on January 3, with Fidel Castro as prime minister (takes oath on February 16).
4–5   Disturbances at Léopoldville in the Belgian Congo (now the Democratic Republic of Congo) force Belgium to grant reforms on January 13, guaranteeing eventual independence.
8   General Charles de Gaulle is proclaimed president of the Fifth Republic in France, and appoints Michel Debré as prime minister.
10   The USSR proposes a conference to draw up a German peace treaty, and the West replies on February 16 by suggesting a four-power foreign ministers' conference, which meets in Geneva, Switzerland, on May 11.
26   Amintore Fanfani resigns as prime minister of Italy and, on February 6, Antonio Segni, a Christian Democrat, forms a ministry supported by Liberals and Monarchists.

FEBRUARY
9   The United States begins supplying arms to Indonesia to aid in its suppression of communist insurgents.
11   Laos announces that it will recognize the United Nations (UN) as sole arbiter of disputes (ending its acceptance of the 1954 Geneva Agreement), following occupation of border territory by North Vietnamese forces.
14–15 In a two-day operation, police in New York, New York, smash a major drug ring when they collect heroin valued at $3.6 million and arrest 27 drug smugglers and distributors.
19   The prime ministers of Greece, Turkey, and Britain sign an agreement in London, England, granting Cyprus independence. As a republic, the president of Cyprus is to be Greek and the vice president Turkish, and the two communities are to be allowed considerable autonomy. Britain will retain two military bases on the island. Enosis (union with Greece) is ruled out.
20   Disturbances break out in the British protectorate of Nyasaland (now Malawi) and, on March 3, a state of

emergency is declared. Hastings Banda and other leaders of the Nyasaland African Congress are arrested.

23–28 The first meeting of the European Court of Human Rights is held, at Strasbourg, France.

26–May 20 The South Rhodesian prime minister Sir Edgar Whitehead declares a state of emergency and bans four African National Congress parties, fearing the spread of trouble from Nyasaland (now Malawi).

MARCH

- The U.S. president Dwight D. Eisenhower signs legislation that will make Hawaii the 50th state upon ratification by Hawaiian voters.
- The U.S. Supreme Court, in *Abbate v. USA* and *Bartkus v. Illinois*, upholds the principle of double jeopardy: an individual may be tried in both state and federal court.

1 The Greek nationalist leader Archbishop Makarios III returns to Cyprus from exile.

1–9 An unsuccessful army revolt takes place in Mosul, Iraq.

3 Eleven Mau Mau political prisoners are killed by Kenyan guards at the Hola detention camp in Kenya. News of the deaths on March 7 is followed by protests in Kenya and Britain.

9–23 The British prime minister Harold Macmillan and the British foreign secretary Selwyn Lloyd visit the French president Charles de Gaulle, the German chancellor Konrad Adenauer, the Canadian prime minister John Diefenbaker, and the U.S. president Dwight D. Eisenhower to report on their visit to the USSR.

12 The Zambia African National Congress is banned in the British protectorate of Northern Rhodesia for intimidating Africans planning to vote in forthcoming elections.

17 An uprising takes place in Tibet against the Chinese garrison there. The Dalai Lama is smuggled out of Lhasa, Tibet, and arrives in India on March 31. On September 9 the Dalai Lama appeals for United Nations (UN) intervention to help Tibet.

17 The USSR and Australia resume diplomatic relations (severed in April 1954).

20 The United Federal Party wins the elections in the British protectorate of Northern Rhodesia.

24 Iraq withdraws from the Baghdad Pact with Turkey. The 1956 British–Iraqi agreement, making Britain a signatory to the Pact, also lapses.

27 U.S. aircraft are "buzzed" by Soviet jet fighters in the Berlin air corridor connecting West Germany and West Berlin.

APRIL

- The state of Oklahoma repeals prohibition. Mississippi remains the last dry state.

4–May 30 The autonomous French West Africa colonies of Ivory Coast, Niger, Upper Volta (now Burkina Faso), and Dahomey (now Benin) sign a series of agreements to form the Sahel–Benin Union.

15 The Cuban leader Fidel Castro describes his government as "humanistic" rather than communist.

17 Malaya and Indonesia sign a treaty of friendship.

27 Liu Shaoqi is elected chairman of the People's Republic of China in succession to Mao Zedong, who remains head of the Communist Party.

MAY

- The U.S. president Dwight D. Eisenhower restores citizenship to Japanese-Americans interned during World War II.

2 The Afro-Asian Organization for Economic Cooperation meets in Cairo, Egypt, and announces the exclusion of the USSR from the organization.

4 The USSR sends a note to Japan urging the removal of U.S. bases from Japan, and offers to guarantee permanent neutrality for Japan.

7 An agreement between Britain and the United States enables Britain to purchase components of atomic weapons other than warheads from the United States.

11–August 5 A conference of foreign ministers is held in Geneva, Switzerland, to discuss divided Berlin and a German peace treaty.

19 Following an indecisive general election in the Netherlands on March 12, Jan Edward de Quay forms a four-party coalition ministry, and the Labor Party goes into opposition for the first time since 1945.

22 Canada and the United States make an agreement for cooperation in the use of atomic energy for mutual defense.

25–June 4 The Soviet prime minister Nikita Khrushchev visits Albania.

30 Iraq terminates its military assistance agreements with the United States because they conflict with its new policy of neutrality.

JUNE

- A U.S. federal court panel strikes down the Arkansas school law authorizing governor Orval Faubus to close the state's public schools rather than integrate them.
- The U.S. president Dwight D. Eisenhower signs legislation raising the nation's permanent debt ceiling to $285 billion.
- The U.S. Supreme Court upholds a 1957 congressional statute restricting defendants access to pretrial depositions.

June–September The U.S. Federal Communication Commission upholds a law requiring radio and television stations to provide equal time to opposing political candidates. The law is then overturned by Congress on September 14.

3 The British colony of Singapore becomes self-governing.

4 An Agrarian Reform Act in Cuba transfers land from large landowners to those who work it, provides land for the unemployed, and reduces the power of U.S.-owned sugar mills. The maximum personal holding is now 1,000 acres, and 3,300 acres for sugar, rice, and cattle farms.

6 Queen Elizabeth II of Great Britain and Northern Ireland opens the St. Lawrence Seaway, linking the Atlantic Ocean with Chicago and other ports on the Great Lakes of the United States.

14 The United States agrees to provide Greece with nuclear information and to supply ballistic missiles.

17 Éamon de Valera resigns as prime minister of Ireland to become its third president (in succession to Sean O'Kelly), and Sean Lemass becomes prime minister on June 23.

25 The USSR proposes a denuclearized zone in the Balkans and the Adriatic, in response to the United States's

decision to supply Greece with nuclear weapons. The proposal is rejected by the West between July 11–13.

JULY

- Vice President Richard M. Nixon, while visiting Moscow, holds the so-called "kitchen debate" with Soviet premier Nikita Khrushchev about the relative merits of capitalism and communism.
1 The Christian Democrat Heinrich Lübke is elected president of West Germany in succession to Dr. Theodor Heuss.
3 The Chinese government announces a program of land expropriation and redistribution in Tibet, following the Tibetan uprising and the flight of the Dalai Lama in March.
4 The first 49-star U.S. flag flies over the U.S. Capitol following the admission of Alaska in January.
5 Ghana begins a boycott of South African goods in protest at apartheid.
5 The incorporation of the Saar region into the West German economic system is completed.
5 The Indonesian president Achmed Sukarno dissolves the Indonesian constituent assembly (sitting since 1956) and issues a decree restoring the constitution of 1945, with its greater presidential powers.
17 Manuel Urratía is replaced as Cuban president by Osvaldo Dórticos in a dispute over communist influence in the government.
17 The Soviet prime minister Nikita Khrushchev reaffirms the USSR's guarantee of the Oder–Neisse frontier between East Germany and Poland and calls for a European denuclearized zone.
19 The presidents of Ghana, Guinea, and Liberia propose holding a conference of independent African states in 1960, to form a "Community of African States."
20 Cabinet government is introduced in the British colony of Trinidad and Tobago.
28 A party of Indian police is seized by communist Chinese forces in the disputed Jammu and Kashmir area.

AUGUST

- A U.S. Senate report accuses the Teamsters union president James R. Hoffa of racketeering.
- In an effort to encourage the USSR and Britain to curb nuclear testing, the United States extends a unilateral ban on testing to December 31.
- The U.S. president Dwight D. Eisenhower proclaims Hawaii the 50th state. Hawaiians had overwhelmingly endorsed statehood in a referendum on June 27.
- Vice President Richard M. Nixon, while visiting Moscow, warns the Soviet people that Premier Khrushchev imperilled his nation by trying to promote global communism.
7 Chinese forces make an incursion into the disputed border region of northeastern India, leading to minor clashes.
16 The United Arab Republic (UAR) of Egypt and Syria restores diplomatic relations with Jordan (severed on July 20, 1958).
21 Following the withdrawal of Iraq from the Baghdad Pact on March 24, the Pact changes its name to the Central Treaty Organization (CENTO) and moves its headquarters to Ankara, Turkey.
31 During the visit of U.S. president Dwight D. Eisenhower to Britain he appears with Prime Minister Harold

Macmillan on television, in discussion at 10 Downing Street, London, England.

SEPTEMBER

- The U.S. Congress passes legislation to distribute food stamps to needy Americans.
- The U.S. president Dwight D. Eisenhower signs legislation abolishing customs duty on modern works of art.
- The U.S. president Dwight D. Eisenhower welcomes Soviet premier Nikita Khrushchev to the United States. Khrushchev has come on a mission to promote good will between the two nations and to begin work toward nuclear disarmament.
4 The dispatch of a United Nations (UN) emergency force is requested by Laos, following alleged aggression by communist North Vietnamese forces.
7 The United States, USSR, Britain, and France issue statements announcing a proposal to establish a ten-power disarmament committee.
16 President Charles de Gaulle of France proposes a referendum offering Algerians a choice between secession or continued association with France, to be held within four years of the end of violence there.
22 The United Nations (UN) again votes against the admission of the People's Republic of China, viewing the Nationalist Chinese government based on Formosa (now Taiwan) as the official representatives of China.
25 Solomon Bandaranaike, prime minister of Ceylon (Sri Lanka), is assassinated by a Buddhist monk, and is succeeded by Wijayananda Dahanayake.
25 The Soviet leader Nikita Khrushchev visits Beijing, China.

OCTOBER

8 In the British general election, the Conservatives under Prime Minister Harold Macmillan win 365 seats, while Labour win 258, the Liberals 6, and others 1.
21 The United Nations (UN) General Assembly adopts a motion calling for the restoration of religious and civil liberties in Tibet, a stance which is denounced by the Chinese government on October 23.
26 A Basic Democracies Order is promulgated in Pakistan, providing for a four-tier hierarchy of councils, part elected, part nominated. Rawalpindi is provisionally chosen as capital.

NOVEMBER

- The U.S. president Dwight D. Eisenhower asks Congress to allocate $41 billion for defense for the fiscal year 1961.
- The U.S. Supreme Court upholds the Taft–Hartley Act of 1946, and orders striking steelworkers to return to work.
8 President Habib Bourguiba's Neo-Destour Party wins all seats in the elections to the Tunisian assembly.
8 The United Arab Republic (UAR) of Egypt and Syria signs an agreement with Sudan on sharing the waters of the River Nile.
10 The ending of the Mau Mau emergency in Kenya is officially announced by the government (a proclamation to this effect is signed by the governor of Kenya on January 12, 1960).
10 The United Nations (UN) General Assembly condemns apartheid in South Africa and racial discrimination in any part of the world.

13 The South African Progressive Party is founded at a conference in Johannesburg, South Africa.

15 Richard Hickock and Perry Smith rob the home of Herbert W. Clutter of Holcomb, Kansas; when they find less than $50 in the house, they murder all four residents: Herbert (48), Bonnie (45), Nancy (16), and Kenyon (15). Details of the crime, and the criminals' capture, trial, and execution will be recorded in 1966 by Truman Capote in his true-crime best seller *In Cold Blood*.

20–29 The finance ministers of Austria, Denmark, Great Britain, Norway, Portugal, Sweden, and Switzerland (the "Seven") meet at a conference in Stockholm, Sweden, and set in train a convention to establish the European Free Trade Association (EFTA).

DECEMBER

• U.S. secretary of defense Thomas S. Gates proclaims U.S. nuclear superiority over the USSR at a North Atlantic Treaty Organization (NATO) meeting in Paris, France.

3–23 The U.S. president Dwight D. Eisenhower makes a tour of European capitals.

6 The United Nations (UN) General Assembly resolves that the Togoland trusteeship territory (now Togo) should achieve independence in April 1960.

13 The United Nations (UN) decides not to intervene in the independence struggle in Algeria.

14 The Greek nationalist leader Archbishop Makarios III is elected president of Cyprus.

19 The Western powers meeting in Paris, France, invite the Soviet leader Nikita Khrushchev to attend a summit conference in April 1960.

25 The USSR agrees to give financial and technical aid to Syria.

SCIENCE, TECHNOLOGY, AND MEDICINE

Computing

• Several computer manufacturers announce that they are changing to producing computers with transistors rather than vacuum tubes. These second-generation computers are smaller, more reliable, consume less power, and are faster than those of the first-generation.

• U.S. computer programmer Grace Hopper invents COBOL (Common Business Oriented Language), a computer language for business use.

• U.S. computer programmer John McCarthy develops the List Processor (LISP) computer language which is used in artificial intelligence applications.

Ecology

FEBRUARY

• The U.S. Navy launches *Vanguard 2*, the first weather satellite.

10 A tornado touches down in St. Louis, Missouri, killing 22 people, injuring 350 more, and causing $12 million in property damage.

APRIL

• The U.S. Naval Research Laboratory reports a 300% increase in atmospheric radioactivity in the wake of Soviet resumption of nuclear testing in 1958, following a three-year self-imposed moratorium.

SEPTEMBER

17–19 The Japanese island of Honshu is devastated by Typhoon Vera, the worst in the country's history; 5,000 people are killed and 1.5 million left homeless.

DECEMBER

1 An Antarctic Treaty is signed, suspending territorial claims and aiming to prevent development in the region (valid June 23, 1961–December 1989).

Exploration

JANUARY

2 The USSR launches *Lunik 1*. The first spacecraft to escape Earth's gravity, it passes within 6,400 km/4,000 mi of the moon.

MARCH

3 The United States launches the moon probe *Pioneer 4*; it passes within 59,000 km/37,000 mi of the moon.

APRIL

• The U.S. National Aeronautics and Space Administration (NASA) selects a pool of nine military test pilots to compete to be the first U.S. astronaut to orbit the earth.

MAY

• The U.S. Army sends two monkeys 300 miles into space. They are recovered, unharmed, in the Caribbean Sea.

AUGUST

7 The U.S. National Aeronautics and Space Administration (NASA) launches the U.S. space probe *Explorer 6*. It investigates the Van Allen radiation belt discovered in 1958 by *Explorer 1* and takes the first television pictures of Earth's cloud cover. The United States launches ten other satellites during the year.

SEPTEMBER

14 The Soviet spacecraft *Luna 2* (launched on September 12) becomes the first spacecraft to strike the moon.

OCTOBER

7 The Soviet *Luna 3* (launched on October 4) takes the first photographs of the far side of the moon.

Health and Medicine

• British researchers first isolate 6-aminopenicillanic acid—the penicillin "nucleus." It forms the basis of over 2,000 semisynthetic penicillins, some of which have a clinical value as antibiotics.

• French researcher Jérôme Lejeune discovers that Down's syndrome is due to an extra chromosome 21. It is the first chromosomal disorder discovered.

• U.S. geneticists Severo Ochoa and Arthur Kornberg are jointly awarded the Nobel Prize for Physiology or

Medicine for their discovery of the mechanisms in the biological synthesis of ribonucleic acid (RNA) and deoxyribonucleic acid (DNA).

October 1959–62 Between 2,000 and 3,000 children in West Germany, and 500 in the UK, are born severely deformed to mothers who have taken the sedative thalidomide during the early stages of pregnancy.

OCTOBER

- New Jersey reports an outbreak of equine encephalitis, which has claimed the lives of 20 people.

NOVEMBER

9   The U.S. Secretary of Health, Education, and Welfare advises consumers not to buy cranberries grown in Oregon and Washington because a weedkiller used in those states has been found to cause cancer in laboratory rats.

Science

- Austrian-born British biochemist Max Perutz determines the structure of hemoglobin.
- Czech chemist Jaroslav Heyrovsky receives the Nobel Prize for Chemistry for his polarographic methods of chemical analysis.
- English anthropologist Mary Leakey discovers the 1.75-million-year-old remains of *Zinjanthropus boisei*, a fossil hominid now generally regarded as an australopithecine, at Olduvai Gorge in Tanganyika (now Tanzania) in Africa.
- English astronomer Martin Ryle and colleagues publish the *Third Cambridge Catalogue*, a catalog of radio sources that leads to the discovery of the first quasar.
- Soviet archeologist and linguist Tatiana Proskouriakov makes a major breakthrough in the decipherment of the Mayan hieroglyphics from Central America; she establishes that the majority of surviving inscriptions are records of historical events in the lives of the Mayan rulers.
- U.S. astronomer Harold Babcock discovers that the sun periodically reverses its magnetic polarity.
- U.S. geologists Marion Hubbert and William Rubey demonstrate that the overthrusting of large horizontal planes of rock that produces folded mountains is due to the reduction of friction caused by fluids in the rocks.
- U.S. physicist Luis Alvarez discovers the neutral xi-particle.
- U.S. physicists Emilio Segrè and Owen Chamberlain are jointly awarded the Nobel Prize for Physics for their discovery of the antiproton.

JUNE

- U.S., British, and Soviet scientists meet to devise methods for detecting atmospheric nuclear testing above a level of 50 kilometers.

DECEMBER

29 U.S. theoretical physicist Richard Feynman delivers a paper entitled "There's Plenty of Room at the Bottom" to the American Physical Society, in which he describes the manufacture of transistors and other electronic components one atom at a time. It marks the beginning of nanotechnology.

Technology

- The Dresden Nuclear Power Station at Morris, Illinois, becomes operative. It is the first "boiling water" nuclear generator.
- The electronics company Sony produces the first transistor black and white television, the Sony TV-8-301, in Japan. Color sets are produced the following year.
- The first breeder reactor (that produces more nuclear fuel than it consumes) is commissioned at Dounreay in Scotland.
- The G-2 nuclear reactor begins generating electricity in Marcoule, France, the first commercial reactor in the country. It has a capacity of 25 megawatts.
- The largest natural gas field in Europe, Groningen, is discovered off the Dutch coast. It has reserves estimated at 2.27 trillion cubic meters.
- U.S. engineer Jean Hoerni of Fairchild Semiconductor Corporation designs the planar or "flat" transistor and U.S. engineer Robert Noyce discovers a way to join the circuits by printing, eliminating hundreds of hours in their production. Their work leads to the creation of the first microchip, that stimulates the computer industry with its sharply reduced size and cost and leads to the third generation of computers.

FEBRUARY

6   The U.S. Titan I intercontinental ballistic missile (ICBM) is first tested. It has a range of 9,600 km/6,000 mi.
28 The U.S. Air Force launches *Discoverer 1* into a low polar orbit where it photographs the entire surface of the earth every 24 hours. The exposed film is returned to Earth in its ejectable capsule.

APRIL

- The United States launches *Discoverer 2*, a second military reconnaissance satellite.

Transportation

- The Pacific Great Eastern Railway in western Canada is the first railroad to introduce microwave radio communications. Other railroads turn to microwave in the 1970s.
- The U.S. Navy launches the cruiser *Long Beach*, the first nuclear-powered warship.
- The U.S. nuclear-powered submarine *Skate* is the first submarine to surface at the North Pole.

FEBRUARY

3   An American Airline airplane plunges into the East River, New York, New York, killing 66 people.

APRIL

- The St. Lawrence Seaway is completed. It provides the Great Lakes with access to the Atlantic Ocean.

JUNE

8   The U.S. X-15 rocket plane makes its first flight. Only three of the planes are built, but over the next ten years they achieve a speed of 7,200 kph/4,500 mph (Mach 6) and an altitude of 106,700 m/350,000 ft.
9   The U.S. nuclear-powered submarine *George Washington* is launched. The first of the Polaris submarines, it carries 16 Polaris A-1 missiles, each with a nuclear warhead and a range of 2,220 km/1,380 mi.

21 The U.S. Atomic Energy Commission launches the *Savannah*, the first atomic-powered passenger-cargo ship, to demonstrate the potential of nuclear power for civilian shipping.

25 English engineer Christopher Cockerell's hovercraft *SR.N1* crosses the English Channel in two hours.

ARTS AND IDEAS

Architecture

- The Banque Lambert in Brussels, Belgium, designed by the U.S. architectural firm of (Louis) Skidmore, (Nathaniel) Owings, and (John) Merrill, is completed.
- The Beth Sholom Synagogue in Elkin Park, Pennsylvania, designed by the U.S. architect Frank Lloyd Wright, is completed. In the same year, the Kalita Humphreys Theater in Dallas, Texas, is completed.
- The Yale University Hockey Rink in New Haven, Connecticut, designed by the Finnish architect Eero Saarinen, is completed.

Arts

- The English artist Elizabeth Frink sculpts *Winged Figure*.
- The English artist Peter Blake paints *Girly Door*.
- The exhibition "New American Painting" is held at the Tate Gallery in London, England.
- The Swiss-born U.S. photographer Robert Frank publishes his photography album *The Americans*.
- The U.S. artist Adolph Gottlieb paints *Black and Black*.
- The U.S. artist Allan Kaprow creates his first "happening"—*18 Happenings in 6 Parts*—in the Reuben Gallery in New York, New York. Typical of U.S. art in the 1960s and 1970s, happenings combine visual arts, music, and improvised theater, and often encourage audience participation.
- The U.S. artist Frank Stella paints *Die Fahne Hoch!/ Hoist the Flag!*
- The U.S. artist Robert Rauschenberg creates *Monogram*, a multimedia work (which he calls a "combine-painting") that includes a stuffed goat wearing an automobile tire. It becomes one of the most distinctive images of the 1960s.
- The U.S. photographer Richard Avedon publishes *Observations*, an album of his early photography.

July 1959–60 The U.S. artist David Smith sculpts his *Cubi* series.

21 The Solomon Guggenheim Museum, a modern art museum designed by U.S. architect Frank Lloyd Wright, opens in New York, New York.

Film

- *Notes of a Film Director*, a book on movie criticism and theory by the Soviet movie director Sergey Eisenstein, is published posthumously.

- The movie *Anatomy of a Murder*, directed by Austrian filmmaker Otto Preminger, is released in the United States, starring James Stewart, Ben Gazzara, Lee Remick, and George C. Scott.
- The movie *Apur Sansar/The World of Apu*, directed by Satyajit Ray, is released in India. The concluding part of a trilogy (following *Pather Panchali/The Song of the Road* and *Aparajito/Unvanquished*), it stars Soumitra Chatterjee, Sarmila Tagore, and Alok Chakravarti.
- The movie *Ben Hur*, directed by William Wyler, is released in the United States. Based on the novel by the U.S. author and diplomat Lew Wallace, it stars Charlton Heston.
- The movie *Compulsion*, directed by Richard Fleischer, is released in the United States. Based on the novel by Meyer Levin, it stars Dean Stockwell and Bradford Dillman.
- The movie *Foma Gordeyev/The Gordeyev Family*, directed by Mark Donskoi and starring Sergei Lukyanov, is released in the USSR.
- The movie *Hiroshima mon amour/Hiroshima My Love*, directed by Alain Resnais, is released in France, starring Emmanuelle Riva and Eiji Okada.
- The movie *Le Testament d'Orphée/Testament of Orpheus*, directed by Jean Cocteau, is released in France. He also stars in it, along with Edouard Dermithe and Maria Casarès.
- The movie *Look Back in Anger*, directed by Tony Richardson, is released in Britain. Based on the play by John Osborne, it stars Richard Burton, Mary Ure, Claire Blook, Edith Evans, and Gary Raymond.
- The movie *North by Northwest*, directed by Alfred Hitchcock, is released in the United States, starring Cary Grant, Eve Marie Saint, and James Mason.
- The movie *Ohayo/Good Morning*, directed by Yasujiro Ozu and starring Kuniko Miyake, is released in Japan.
- The movie *On the Beach*, directed by Stanley Kramer, is released in the United States. Based on the novel by Nevil Shute, it stars Gregory Peck, Ava Gardner, Fred Astaire, and Anthony Perkins.
- The movie *Orfeu Negro/Black Orpheus*, directed by Marcel Camus, is released in France, starring Breno Mello, Marpessa Dawn, Ademar da Silva, and Lourdes de Oliviera. It is awarded the Palme d'Or at the Cannes Film Festival in France, later in the year.
- The movie *Our Man in Havana*, directed by Carol Reed, is released in Britain. Based on the novel by Graham Greene, it stars Alec Guinness and Noël Coward.
- The movie *Peeping Tom*, directed by Michael Powell, is released in Britain, starring Carl Boehm, Moira Shearer, and Anna Massey.
- The movie *Pickpocket*, directed by Robert Bresson, is released in France, starring Martin Lasalle, Marika Green, and Pierre Leymarie.
- The movie *Plan 9 from Outer Space*, directed by Edward D. Wood, Jr., is released in the United States. Widely regarded as one of the worst movies ever made, it stars Tor Johnson, Lyle Talbot, Bela Lugosi, Vampira, and Criswell; it attains a wide cult following in the 1970s and 1980s.
- The movie *Rio Bravo*, directed by Howard Hawks, is released in the United States, starring John Wayne and Dean Martin.

- The movie *Shadows*, directed by John Cassavetes, is released in the United States. Featuring dialogue improvised by the cast, it stars Ben Carruthers, Leila Goldoni, Hugh Hurd, Rupert Crosse, and Anthony Ray.
- The movie *Some Like it Hot*, directed by Billy Wilder, is released in the United States, starring Marilyn Monroe, Jack Lemmon, and Tony Curtis.
- The movie *The Four Hundred Blows*, directed by François Truffaut, is released in France, starring Jean-Pierre Léaud, Claire Maurier, and Albert Rémy.

APRIL

13 The 1958 Academy Awards take place. Best Actor: David Niven, for *Separate Tables*; Best Supporting Actor: Burl Ives, for *The Big Country*; Best Actress: Susan Hayward, for *I Want to Live*; Best Supporting Actress: Wendy Hiller, for *Separate Tables*; Best Picture: *Gigi*, directed by Vincente Minelli; Best Director: Vincente Minelli, for *Gigi*.

Literature and Language

- The Canadian writer Al Purdy publishes his poetry collection *The Crafte So Longe To Lerne*.
- The Canadian writer Mordecai Richler publishes his novel *The Apprenticeship of Duddy Kravitz*.
- The English musicologist Deryck Cooke publishes *The Language of Music*.
- The English scholars Iona and Peter Opie publish *The Lore and Language of Schoolchildren*.
- The English travel writer Wilfred Thesiger publishes *Arabian Sands*.
- The English writer Alan Sillitoe publishes his short-story collection *The Loneliness of the Long Distance Runner*.
- The English writer Colin MacInnes publishes his novel *Absolute Beginners*.
- The English writer Ian Fleming publishes *Goldfinger*, a James Bond novel.
- The English writer Keith Waterhouse publishes his novel *Billy Liar*.
- The English writer Malcolm Bradbury publishes his novel *Eating People is Wrong*.
- The English writer Roald Dahl publishes his collection of short stories *Kiss, Kiss*.
- The English writer William Golding publishes his novel *Free Fall*.
- The French writer Alain Robbe-Grillet publishes his novel *Dans le labyrinthe/In the Labyrinth*.
- The French writer Raymond Queneau publishes his novel *Zazie dans le métro/Zazie in the Metro*.
- The German writer Günther Grass publishes his novel *Die Blechtrommel/The Tin Drum*.
- The German writer Heinrich Böll publishes *Billiard um halb zehn/Billiards at Half-Past Nine*.
- The Nobel Prize for Literature is awarded to the Italian poet Salvatore Quasimodo.
- The Polish writer Czesław Miłosz publishes his autobiography *Rodzinna Europa/Native Realm*.
- The Polish-born English historian Isaac Deutscher publishes *The Prophet Unarmed*, the second volume of his three-volume biography of the Russian revolutionary leader Leon Trotsky.
- The Pulitzer Prize for Biography is awarded to Arthur Walworth for *Woodrow Wilson*, the Pulitzer Prize for Poetry is awarded to Stanley Kunitz for *Selected Poems 1928–1958*, and the Pulitzer Prize for Fiction is awarded to Robert Lewis Taylor for *The Travels of Jamie McPheeters*.
- The Russian-born French writer Natalie Sarraute publishes her novel *Le Planétarium/The Planetarium*.
- The Scottish writer Muriel Spark publishes her novel *Memento Mori*.
- The Soviet writer Abram Tertz publishes his novel *Sud idyot/The Trial Begins*, for which he is persecuted by the Soviet authorities.
- The U.S. composer John Cage publishes *Virgil Thompson: His Life and Work*.
- The U.S. historian Stanley M. Elkins publishes *Slavery: A Problem in American Institutional and Intellectual Life*.
- The U.S. journalist Vance Packard publishes *The Wastemakers*.
- The U.S. writer Evan Connell publishes his novel *Mrs Bridge*.
- The U.S. writer James Purdy publishes his novel *Malcolm*.
- The U.S. writer Norman Mailer publishes *Advertisement for Myself*, a collection of autobiographical essays.
- The U.S. writer Philip Whalen publishes his poetry collection *Self-Portrait from Another Direction*.
- The U.S. writer Philip Roth publishes his short-story collection *Goodbye, Columbus*.
- The U.S. writer Robert Lowell publishes his poetry collection *Life Studies*, which includes "Skunk Hour."
- The U.S. writer Saul Bellow publishes his novel *Henderson the Rain King*.
- The U.S. writer W. D. Snodgrass publishes his poetry collection *Heart's Needle*, which wins the Pulitzer Prize for Poetry in 1960.
- The U.S. writer William Burroughs publishes his novel *The Naked Lunch*.
- The U.S. writer William Faulkner publishes his novel *The Mansion*.

JUNE

11 The U.S. Postmaster General bans the novel *Lady Chatterley's Lover* by D. H. Lawrence from the mail (meaning in effect that it cannot be distributed in the United States), citing its erotic passages.

JULY

21 A U.S. federal district court in New York, New York, lifts the ban that the Postmaster General had placed on *Lady Chatterley's Lover* by English author D. H. Lawrence, ruling that the novel, which was privately published in Florence in 1928, is not obscene. A complete edition is published.

Music

- Berry Gordy founds Motown Records in Detroit, Michigan, and launches the Tamla record label with "Come to Me," by Marv Johnson.
- Several folk tunes are among the most popular songs in the United States. They include "The Battle of New Orleans," "Stagger Lee," and "He's Got the Whole World in His Hands."
- The British jazz musician Ronnie Scott opens a jazz club at Gerrard Street, London, England.

- The British pop singer Cliff Richard releases the singles "Livin' Doll" and "Travellin' Light."
- The British singer Shirley Bassey releases the single "As I Love You."
- The English composer Alan Rawsthorne completes his Symphony No. 2, the *Pastoral*.
- The English composer Peter Maxwell Davies completes his orchestral work *Five Paul Klee Pictures*.
- The English composer Benjamin Britten completes his choral work *Cantata Academica/Academic Cantata*.
- The French composer Henri Dutilleux completes his Symphony No. 2.
- The French composer Jean Françaix completes his *L'Horloge de flore/The Floral Clock* for oboe and orchestra.
- The Italian composer Sylvano Bussotti completes his *Five Piano Pieces for David Tudor*.
- The Korean composer and artist Nam Paik devises *Hommage à Cage/Homage to John Cage*, during which two pianos have to be smashed.
- The opera *Aniara*, by the Swedish composer Karl-Birger Blomdahl, is first performed, in Stockholm, Sweden.
- The opera *La Voix humaine/The Human Voice*, by the French composer Francis Poulenc, is first performed, in Paris, France.
- The U.S. composer Ned Rorem completes his song settings *Two Poems of Theodore Roethke*.
- The U.S. pop group the Drifters release the single "There Goes my Baby."
- The U.S. rhythm and blues guitarist Bo Didley, originator of the Bo Didley beat, a stomping, primal pounding of guitar and drums, releases the album *Have Guitar Will Travel*.
- The U.S. singer Bobby Darin releases the single "Mack the Knife," from *The Threepenny Opera*.

MAY

4 The National Academy of Recording Arts and Sciences presents its first "Grammy Awards," for 1958. Winners include Best Album: *The Music from Peter Gunn*, composed by Henry Mancini; Best Record: "Volare," written by Dominico Mudugno, with English words by Mitchell Parish; Best Male Vocalist: Perry Como; Best Female Vocalist: Ella Fitzgerald.

NOVEMBER

29 The 1959 Grammy Awards take place. Best Album: *Come Dance with Me*, by Frank Sinatra; Best Male Vocalist: Frank Sinatra; Best Female Vocalist: Ella Fitzgerald; Best Group: the Mormon Tabernacle Choir.

Theater and Dance

- The play *A Taste of Honey*, by the English dramatist Shelagh Delaney, is first performed, at the Wyndham Theatre in London, England.
- The play *Becket*, by the French writer Jean Anouilh, is first performed, in Paris, France.
- The play *Les Nègres/The Blacks*, by the French writer Jean Genet, is first performed, in Paris, France.
- The play *Roots*, by the English dramatist Arnold Wesker, is first performed, in Coventry, England.
- The play *Sergeant Musgrave's Dance*, by the English dramatist John Arden, is first performed, at the Royal Court Theatre in London, England.

- The play *Sweet Bird of Youth*, by the U.S. dramatist Tennessee Williams, is first performed, in New York, New York.
- The play *The Andersonville Trial*, by the U.S. dramatist Saul Levitt, is first performed, in New York, New York.
- The play *The Connection*, by the U.S. dramatist Jack Gelber, is first performed, in New York, New York.
- The play *The Zoo Story*, by the U.S. dramatist Edward Albee, is first performed, in Berlin, West Germany.
- The Polish theater director Jerzy Grotowski creates the avant-garde Theater Laboratory (Laboratorium) in Wrocław, Poland.
- The Pulitzer Prize for Drama is awarded to Archibald MacLeish for *J B*.

MARCH

11 The play *A Raisin in the Sun*, by the U.S. writer Lorraine Hansberry, is first performed, at the Ethel Barrymore Theater in New York, New York. It stars Sidney Poitier and Claudia McNeil, and will win a New York Drama Critics Circle award.

APRIL

12 The 1958–59 Tony Awards take place. Best Actor: Jason Robards; Best Actress: Gertrude Berg; Best Play: *J B*; Best Musical: *Redhead*.

MAY

11 The musical comedy *Once Upon a Mattress*, by Jay Thompson, Marshall Barer, and Dean Fuller, is first performed, at the Phoenix Theater in New York, New York; Carol Burnett stars.

21 The musical *Gypsy*, with lyrics by Stephen Sondheim and music by Jule Styne, is first performed, at the Broadway Theater, New York, New York. It is based on the memoirs of Gypsy Rose Lee and features the song "Everything's Coming Up Roses."

NOVEMBER

16 The musical *The Sound of Music*, with lyrics by Oscar Hammerstein and music by Richard Rodgers, is first performed, at the Lunt-Fontanne Theater, New York, New York. It includes a range of hit songs such as "Edelweiss" and the title song.

Thought and Scholarship

- The English historian Asa Briggs publishes *The Age of Improvement*.
- The English philosopher Ernest Gellner publishes *Words and Things*.
- The English philosopher P. F. Strawson publishes *Individuals: An Essay in Descriptive Metaphysics*.
- The Pulitzer Prize for History is awarded to Leonard D. White, assisted by Jean Schneider, for *The Republican Era: 1869–1901*.
- The U.S. historian Garrett Mattingly publishes *The Armada*.
- The U.S. social scientist Seymour Martin Lipset publishes *Political Man*.
- The U.S. sociologist C. Wright Mills publishes *The Causes of World War III*.
- U.S. journalist James Burnham publishes *Congress and the American Tradition*.

- U.S. philosopher Sidney Hook publishes *Political Power and Personal Freedom: Critical Studies in Democracy, Communism, and Civil Rights*.
- U.S. political journalist Walter Lippmann publishes *The Communist World and Ours*.

SOCIETY

Education

- York University opens in North York, Ontario, Canada.

Everyday Life

- The Barbie doll, designed by Californian entrepreneurs Ruth and Eliot Handler, is launched in the United States.
- The hula hoop, launched the previous year, becomes a major craze in the United States when the price falls from $2.79 to 50 cents.
- The U.S. clothing manufacturer Glen Raven Mills develops fine nylon tights (pantyhose), originally marketed as Panti-Legs.

SEPTEMBER
20 While on a diplomatic visit to the United States, Nikita Khrushchev, premier of the USSR, is refused entry to the Disneyland amusement park for security reasons.

Media and Communication

- Many newspapers in Cuba close and others are later suppressed following Fidel Castro's assumption of power.
- Television is introduced in India, with sets in community centers in Delhi.
- The British Broadcasting Corporation (BBC) broadcasts the first transatlantic program, from London, England, to Montreal, Canada, showing the departure of the queen and Prince Philip for Canada.
- The U.S. comedian Tom Lehrer releases the album *An Evening Wasted with Tom Lehrer*.

JANUARY
- *New York Herald Tribune* journalist Marie Torre goes to jail for ten days for contempt of court; Torre had refused to divulge a source.
9–January 4, 1966 *Rawhide*, a Western series about cowboys on the long drive from Texas to Kansas, appears on U.S. television, starring Clint Eastwood and Eric Fleming.

MAY
6 The 1958–59 Emmy Awards for television take place. Best Drama Series: *Playhouse 90*; Best Comedy Series: *The Jack Benny Show*; Best Actor in a Series: Raymond Burr, for *Perry Mason*; Best Actress in a Series: Loretta Young, for *The Loretta Young Show*.

BIRTHS & DEATHS

JANUARY
21 Cecil B. De Mille, U.S. film director and producer known for his spectacular films such as *The Greatest Show on Earth*, dies in Hollywood, California (77).

FEBRUARY
3 Buddy Holly (adopted name of Charles Hardin Holley), U.S. rock star, dies in a plane crash after a concert in Clear Lake, Iowa (22).
7 Daniel F. Malan, South African politician who instituted apartheid, dies in Stellenbosch, South Africa (84).
16 John McEnroe, U.S. tennis player, born in Wiesbaden, West Germany.

MARCH
2 Raymond Chandler, U.S. author, creator of the private detective Philip Marlowe, dies in La Jolla, California (70).
3 Lou Costello (Louis Francis Cristillo), U.S. comedian, dies in Beverly Hills, California (50).

APRIL
9 Frank Lloyd Wright, U.S. architect and author who developed a "Prairie style" of architecture, dies in Phoenix, Arizona (91).
15 Kenneth Branagh, Irish actor, director, and producer, born in Belfast, Northern Ireland.

MAY
24 John Foster Dulles, U.S. secretary of state 1953–59, who was responsible for many of the Cold War policies with respect to the USSR, dies in Washington, D.C. (71).

JULY
6 George Grosz, German artist, dies in Berlin, Germany (65).
17 Billie Holiday (real name Eleanora Fagan), U.S. jazz singer, dies in New York, New York (44).

AUGUST
16 William F. Halsey, U.S. naval commander during World War II, dies in Fishers Island, New York (76).

SEPTEMBER
25 Solomon Bandaranaike, prime minister of Ceylon (now Sri Lanka) 1956–59, is assassinated in Colombo, Ceylon (60).

OCTOBER
5 Maya Lin, U.S. architect, born in Athens, Ohio.
14 Errol Flynn, Australian-born U.S. actor known for his swashbuckling films, dies in Vancouver, British Columbia, Canada (50).
16 George C. Marshall, U.S. general and Army chief of staff during World War II, and then secretary of state 1947–49, and secretary of defense 1950–51, dies in Washington, D.C. (78).

NOVEMBER
5 Bryan Adams, Canadian rock singer, born in Kingston, Ontario, Canada.
15 Charles Thomson Rees Wilson, Scottish physicist who invented the cloud chamber to study radioactivity, cosmic rays, and X-rays, dies in Carlops, Peeblesshire, Scotland (90).

DECEMBER
- Walter Williams, the last living veteran of the American Civil War, dies in Houston, Texas, at the age of 117.

September

12–January 16, 1973   The Western program *Bonanza* appears on U.S. television, starring Lorne Greene, Pernell Roberts, Dan Blocker, Michael Landon, Victor Sen Yung, and Ray Teal.

15–September 17, 1963   *Laramie*, a Western series set in Wyoming in the 1880s, is shown on U.S. television, starring John Smith, Bobby Crawford, Jr., Robert Fuller, Hoagy Carmichael, and Spring Byington.

29–September 18, 1963   The situation comedy *The Many Loves of Dobie Gillis* appears on U.S. television, starring Dwayne Hickman, Bob Denver, Frank Faylin, Florida Friebus, and Sheila James.

October

4–September 22, 1963   The situation comedy *Dennis the Menace* appears on U.S. television. Based on the cartoon character created by Henry King "Hank" Ketchum, it stars Jay North, Herbert Anderson, Gloria Henry, Joseph Kearns, and Jeannie Russell.

7–September 10, 1963   *Hawaiian Eye*, a police detective series set in Hawaii starring Anthony Eiseley, Robert Conrad, and Connie Stevens, is shown on U.S. television.

15–September 10, 1963   *The Untouchables*, an adventure series about the exploits of Treasury Department officials during Prohibition, appears on U.S. television. Based on the autobiography of Eliot Ness, it stars Robert Stack, Jerry Paris, Abel Fernandez, and Nick Georgiade.

31   At Ibadan in Nigeria, the first television service in Africa starts.

Religion

May

- The Unitarian and Universalist churches unite to form the Unitarian Universalist Church in the United States.

July

- Evangelical Lutherans join with United Evangelical Lutherans to form the American Lutheran Church.

Sports

- The U.S. golfer Jack Nicklaus wins the U.S. Amateur Golf Championship at Broadmoor, Colorado, at the age of 19.
- U.S. driver Lee Petty wins the National Association for Stock Car Auto Racing (NASCAR) Grand National Championship (known as the Winston Cup from 1970) for the second successive year. His son Richard Petty is the NASCAR Rookie of the Year.

January

28   The U.S. coach Vince Lombardi is appointed head coach of the Green Bay Packers football team from Green Bay, Michigan.

February

22   The U.S. driver Lee Petty, in a 1959 Oldsmobile 88, wins the inaugural Daytona 500 motor race at the new International Speedway, Daytona Beach, Florida.

May

25   The U.S. Supreme Court rules that a Louisiana state ban on boxing matches between white and black fighters is unconstitutional.

June

26   The Swedish boxer Ingemar Johansson beats the defending champion Floyd Patterson of the United States in three rounds in New York, New York, to win the world heavyweight boxing title; in the third round, Patterson is floored seven times.

August

1   Parry O'Brien of the United States sets a shot put world record of 19.30 m/63 ft 4 in at Albuquerque, New Mexico, his tenth world record at the event since 1953.

October

8   The Los Angeles Dodgers defeat the Chicago White Sox by four games to two in the World Series. It is Chicago's first appearance in the series since the "Black Sox" scandal of 1919.

1960

POLITICS, GOVERNMENT, AND ECONOMICS

Business and Economics

- The Austrian-born English economist Friedrich von Hayek publishes *The Constitution of Liberty*.

APRIL

- President Dwight D. Eisenhower's Cabinet Committee on Price Stability and Economic Growth predicts strong economic growth through the 1960s.
- Thor-Able-Star corporation launches Transit 1-B, a satellite expected to facilitate navigation.

JULY

- U.S. sugar imports plunge in response to Cuba's anti-Americanism.

SEPTEMBER

- Harcourt, Brace & Company merges with World Book Company to form Harcourt, Brace & World, one of the world's largest book publishers.

NOVEMBER

- Chrysler halts production of its popular model De Soto after 42 years.

Colonization

JANUARY

1 French Cameroon becomes the independent Republic of Cameroon.

20–February 20 A conference in Brussels, Belgium, agrees on independence for the Belgian Congo (now the Democratic Republic of Congo) from June 30. At that time, Joseph Kasavubu becomes president and Patrice Lumumba becomes prime minister.

APRIL

27 The French-governed part of Togoland becomes the independent Republic of Togo, Africa's smallest independent country.

27–May 4 A constitutional conference in London, England, on the future of the colony of Sierra Leone proposes independence from April 1961.

JUNE

26 British Somaliland becomes independent and, on June 27, unites with Somalia.

26 The French colony of Madagascar is proclaimed independent as the Malagasy Republic (but remains within the French Community). It is admitted to the United Nations (UN) on September 20.

JULY

1 Britain and Cyprus settle final terms for the independence of Cyprus and, on July 10, it is announced that power will be transferred on August 16.

11–12 France agrees to the independence of the colonies of French West Africa (now Benin), Niger, Upper Volta (now Burkina Faso), Ivory Coast, Chad, Central Africa (now the Central African Republic), and French Congo (from August).

OCTOBER

1 The Nigerian Federation becomes independent of Britain, with Nnamdi Azikiwe as governor-general.

11 The British government's Monckton Report on the constitution of Rhodesia and Nyasaland (Central African Federation, modern Malawi) recommends the continuation of the federation for economic reasons, but advocates a devolution of power, a broader franchise, greater participation of black Africans in politics, and the removal of discriminatory legislation.

NOVEMBER

28 The colony of Mauritania proclaims independence from France as an Islamic Republic.

Human Rights

JANUARY

- The radical organization Students for a Democratic Society (SDS) is founded in Michigan; its aim is to link white students with the black liberation movement in the southern states of the United States.

FEBRUARY

1 Black protestors begin a sit-in at a segregated Woolworth's lunch counter in Greensboro, North Carolina; within two months there are similar sit-ins in 54 cities in nine other southern states.

MARCH

1 A thousand black protesters pray and sing the national anthem at the foot of the statehouse in Montgomery, Alabama.

30 Following demonstrations, strikes, and marches by blacks demanding civil rights, the South African government proclaims a state of emergency (–August 31) and passes the Unlawful Organizations Act. On April 8 the African National Congress (ANC) and Pan-African Congress are banned, and Nelson Mandela and others form *Umkonto we Sizwe* ("Spear of the Nation"), as the guerrilla wing of the ANC.

APRIL

- Six years after the U.S. Supreme Court's Brown decision putting an end to school segregation, the periodical *Southern School News* announces that only 3% of southern schools are integrated.
- The Student Nonviolent Coordinating Committee (SNCC), a militant civil-rights organization, is formed in the United States by southern black college students active in voter registration drives and sit-ins.
- 27 The National Council of the Protestant Episcopal Church sanctions sit-ins.

JULY

- 25 Woolworth's desegregates its lunch counters in the United States, having lost $200,000 through sit-ins protesting against its policy of having separate counters for blacks and whites.

AUGUST

- 12 A cemetery in Troy, Michigan, denies burial to Winnebago Native American George V. Nash, a veteran of World War I. Offered burial in Arlington National Cemetery, Nash's family refuses in order to protest against the nation's history of discrimination. Nash is buried in Pontiac, Michigan.

Politics and Government

- Canada passes a Bill of Rights, a parliamentary declaration of traditional political liberties.
- The International Development Association, a lending agency under the World Bank, begins operating.
- The Organization of Petroleum Exporting Countries (OPEC) meets for the first time, in Baghdad, Iraq. It raises the price of oil.

JANUARY

- In his State of the Union address, U.S. president Dwight D. Eisenhower forecasts a $200 million budget surplus and predicts that 1960 will be the nation's "most prosperous year." He also notes a warming of U.S.–Soviet relations.
- Massachusetts senator John F. Kennedy announces his bid for the U.S. presidency.
- The U.S. ambassador to Cuba Philip W. Bonsal formally protests against the Cuban government's seizure of U.S. property. Cuban officials reject the protest the same day.
- Vice President Richard M. Nixon announces his candidacy for the U.S. presidency.
- 8 Kenneth Kaunda is released from prison (imprisoned in 1959) in Northern Rhodesia (now Zambia) and soon afterwards becomes president of the independence-seeking United National Independence Party.
- 16–18 A conference in London, England, on independence terms for Cyprus ends without agreement.
- 18–February 21 A Kenyan constitutional conference is held in London, England, and is boycotted at first by African elected members. They eventually take their places on January 25 and the conference agrees a new constitution.
- 19 A U.S.–Japanese Treaty of Mutual Cooperation and Security is signed in Washington, D.C.
- 24–February 1 French settlers in Algeria in favor of maintaining the country as a French colony riot in Algiers, Algeria, following the French president Charles

de Gaulle's offer of self-determination for Algeria (which they fear will lead to independence).

FEBRUARY

- Missouri senator Stuart Symington, a Democrat, accuses the Eisenhower administration of misleading the U.S. people about the USSR's alleged atomic weapons superiority.
- Repudiating the optimism of President Dwight D. Eisenhower's State of the Union address, the American Federation of Labor and the Congress of Industrial Organizations (AFL-CIO) predicts that the year 1961 will bring an economic recession.
- U.S. Air Force secretary Dudley C. Sharp warns the House Un-American Activities Committee that the nation's clergy has been infiltrated by communists.
- 5 Anastas Mikoyan, the deputy prime minister of the USSR, opens a Soviet exhibition in Havana, Cuba.
- 10–March 5 The Soviet leader Nikita Khrushchev visits India, Burma (now Myanmar), and Indonesia.
- 14 Military ruler Mohammad Ayub Khan is elected president of Pakistan.
- 17 The United States and Britain agree to build an early warning station for the detection of ballistic missiles, at Fylingdales, in northeastern England.
- 24 The Christian Democrat Antonio Segni resigns as prime minister of Italy after Liberals withdraw their support from his coalition. After a protracted deadlock, the Christian Democrat Amintore Fanfani succeeds in forming a ministry on July 22.

MARCH

- In response to a black American sit-down strike at the University of Texas, four men almost beat to death with a tire iron Felton Turner, a black resident of Houston, Texas. Turner is then hung upside down from a tree and the initials KKK are carved into his chest.
- President Dwight D. Eisenhower, back from a two-week tour of Latin American nations, proclaims the healthy status of U.S.–Latin relations.
- 5 The Indonesian President Achmed Sukarno suspends parliament and, on March 27, announces the formation of a "Mutual Cooperation" legislature, to comprise members nominated by himself.
- 15 A presidential election held in South Korea is won by the 85-year-old ruler Syngman Rhee, by fraudulent methods. Protest demonstrations spread throughout the country.
- 15 A ten-power disarmament committee meets in Geneva, Switzerland, until June 27, when Soviet and East European delegates walk out.
- 19 In a general election in Ceylon (now Sri Lanka) the two main parties win a similar number of seats. Dudley Senanayake of the United National Party forms a government on March 21, but it is defeated on a confidence vote on April 22, and new elections are called.
- 21 The "Sharpeville massacre" occurs in a township near Vereeniging (south of Johannesburg), South Africa, where members of the Pan-African Congress demonstrating against pass laws are fired on by police, killing 69 demonstrators and wounding 186 more.
- 29 The USSR and China sign a reciprocal trade agreement.

APRIL

1   The nationalist leader Dr. Hastings Banda is released from prison in the British protectorate of Nyasaland (now Malawi). On June 15 the state of emergency is lifted.

9   The South African prime minister Hendrik Verwoerd is shot and wounded by David Pratt, a wealthy European farmer and businessman who has been refused a visa to visit his second wife in the Netherlands.

13 Britain abandons the development of its ballistic missile "Bluestreak" in favor of the U.S. "Skybolt" missile.

14 The collectivization of East Germany's agriculture is completed.

28–May 25   Students demonstrate in Ankara and Istanbul, Turkey.

MAY

•   In response to U.S. infiltration of Soviet air space, after a U-2 spy aircraft was shot down over the USSR on May 1, Soviet premier Nikita Khrushchev cancels a scheduled summit with his U.S. counterpart in Paris, France, and rescinds an invitation for Eisenhower to visit Moscow, Russia.

•   President Dwight D. Eisenhower calls on the U.S. public to dissuade Congress from cutting foreign aid.

1   Soviet military forces shoot down a U.S. high-altitude U-2 spy aircraft over the Ural Mountains, USSR. On August 19, the pilot, Gary Powers, is sentenced to ten years' imprisonment for espionage.

2   Caryl Chessman is executed in San Quentin prison, California; convicted of rape, robbery, and kidnapping in 1948, he has conducted a 12-year campaign against capital punishment that has attracted nationwide support.

3   The European Free Trade Association (EFTA) comes into force, with 20% tariff cuts between members from July.

7   Leonid Brezhnev replaces Marshal Klement Voroshilov as president of the USSR.

13 Demonstrations against a House Un-American Activities Committee hearing in San Francisco City Hall, San Francisco, California, signal the beginning of radical action by students of the University of California, Berkeley.

16–19   A summit meeting takes place in Paris, France, between the Soviet leader Nikita Khrushchev, the British prime minister Harold Macmillan, the U.S. president Dwight D. Eisenhower, and the French president Charles de Gaulle. Khrushchev uses the U-2 incident to break up the summit, when President Dwight D. Eisenhower refuses to give a public apology for the incident and to pledge that there would be no further intrusions into Soviet air space.

23 Israel announces the arrest (following his abduction from Argentina) of Adolf Eichmann, who had been one of those responsible for organizing the mass extermination of Jews in World War II.

27 Following a period of unrest in Turkey, the military overthrows President Adnan Menderes, and General Cemal Gürsel assumes the presidency.

27 The United States ends aid to Cuba because of its government's increasingly left wing policies.

JUNE

•   U.S.–Cuban relations deteriorate, as U.S. officials accuse their Cuban counterparts of slandering the United States.

14 The French president Charles de Gaulle renews his offer to the Algerian provisional government to negotiate a cease-fire. The Front for National Liberation (FLN) agrees on June 20, but the talks break up on June 24.

15 Japanese students riot in protest against the Mutual Cooperation and Security Treaty, signed with the United States in January, and a planned visit by the U.S. president Dwight D. Eisenhower is postponed.

21 Britain, France, the Netherlands, and the United States sign an agreement to provide a Caribbean organization for economic and social cooperation; it replaces the Caribbean Commissions founded in 1949.

24 Greece, Yugoslavia, and Turkey dissolve the Balkan alliance of August 1954.

30 The Promotion of Bantu Self-Government Act comes into force in South Africa, establishing separate "homelands" for blacks.

JULY

•   Democrats nominate Massachusetts senator John F. Kennedy for president and Texas senator Lyndon B. Johnson for vice president.

•   Land expropriation continues in Cuba as the government seizes the Shell and Esso oil refineries. The United States suspends purchases of sugar from Cuba.

•   Republicans nominate vice president Richard M. Nixon for president and Massachusetts senator Henry Cabot Lodge for vice president.

1   Soviet forces shoot down a U.S. RB-47 survey aircraft over the Barents Sea, north of the Russian mainland. The United States threatens retaliation, but no action is forthcoming.

5–6 The army in the newly independent Congo Republic mutinies, and Europeans in the country flee from the Léopoldville (now Kinshasa) area to Brazzaville (French Congo).

8   Belgium sends troops to the newly independent Congo Republic following the army mutiny there, and Prime Minister Patrice Lumumba appeals to the United Nations (UN) for military assistance.

9   The Soviet leader Nikita Khrushchev threatens nuclear attack if the United States invades Cuba.

11 Moise Tshombe, prime minister of Katanga in the Congo Republic, proclaims the province's independence.

14 The government of the Congo Republic severs relations with Belgium.

15 A United Nations (UN) emergency force arrives in the Congo Republic following the outbreak of civil war there.

18 Following the cancellation of the U.S. president Dwight D. Eisenhower's visit to Japan in June after riots by Japanese students protesting against a U.S.–Japanese treaty, Nobusuke Kishi resigns as Japanese prime minister, and is succeeded by Hayato Ikeda.

19 The USSR protests at a U.S. proposal to equip the West German army with Polaris nuclear missiles.

20 A general election in Ceylon (now Sri Lanka) is won by the Sri Lanka Freedom Party and, on July 21, Mrs. Sirimavo Bandaranaike, widow of the prime minister assassinated in the previous September, is

appointed prime minister (the first woman prime minister of the Commonwealth).

20 Poland asks the North Atlantic Treaty Organization (NATO) powers to acknowledge the Oder–Neisse line, the border of Poland with East Germany. On August 12 Britain states that Germany's frontiers depend on negotiating a peace treaty, formally ending World War II.

25–August 4 A constitutional conference held in London, England, agrees on a new constitution for Nyasaland (now Malawi).

31 The official end of the "Malayan Emergency" (British and Mayalan operations against communist insurgents in Malaya, beginning in 1948) is announced.

AUGUST

• The American Federation of Labor and the Congress of Industrial Organizations (AFL-CIO) endorses Massachusetts senator John F. Kennedy for president.

8 The United Nations (UN) demands the evacuation of Belgian troops, put there following civil war in July, from the newly independent former Belgian colony the Congo Republic, and the last leave on September 2.

8–9 An army coup led by Captain Kong Le in Laos leads to the appointment of General Souvanna Phouma as head of government on August 15.

12 The United Nations (UN) secretary-general Dag Hammarskjöld and UN troops enter the rebellious Katanga province in the Congo Republic.

15 The Indonesian president Achmed Sukarno announces the nominated membership in a new People's Consultative Congress, intended as the highest authority in the state. It first meets on November 10.

16 Cyprus becomes an independent republic with Greek Cypriot Archbishop Makarios as president and Turkish Cypriot Dr. Fazil Kütchük as vice president.

25 The manifesto of the Soviet Communist Party condemns the teachings of Chinese leader Mao Zedong.

29 The Jordanian prime minister Hazza el-Majali is assassinated, by bombs thought to have been placed by Syrian intelligence agents.

30 East Germany imposes a partial blockade of West Berlin, and on September 8 imposes further restrictions.

SEPTEMBER

• Hoping to quash debate over his Catholicism, Massachusetts senator John F. Kennedy insists that his patriotic and religious allegiances are utterly compatible. Should they one day become incompatible, Kennedy vows, he would resign the presidency.

2 Cuba recognizes communist China and denounces its own 1952 military aid treaty with the United States.

2 The USSR provides aircraft to assist the government of Prime Minister Patrice Lumumba in the Congo Republic.

5 President Joseph Kasavubu of the Congo Republic dismisses Prime Minister Patrice Lumumba and replaces him with Joseph Ileo.

9 Representatives of Iran, Iraq, Kuwait, Saudi Arabia, and Venezuela meet in Baghdad, Iraq, and vote to establish the Organization of Petroleum-Exporting Countries (OPEC), a permanent organization to represent their interests. OPEC is finally formed in 1961.

10 Prince Boun Oum of Laos declares martial law following conflict between communist and anticommunist forces.

19 India and Pakistan sign a treaty on the use of the waters of the Indus River.

23 The Soviet leader Nikita Khrushchev addresses the United Nations (UN) General Assembly on colonial peoples and disarmament, attacking the Western world and especially the United States.

26 U.S. presidential candidates John F. Kennedy and Richard M. Nixon debate on television, establishing a precedent for several subsequent elections. Viewers consider the outcome to be a draw, but radio listeners believe Nixon to be the winner, indicating that style and appearance are as much a part of Kennedy's campaign as substance.

28 The North Atlantic Treaty Organization (NATO) introduces a unified air defense command.

OCTOBER

6 A referendum in South Africa favors the establishment of a republic (52.14% of votes in favor and 47.42% against).

12 The Japanese Socialist Party leader, Inajiro Asanuma, is assassinated by a nationalist for supporting the treaty with the United States of January 19.

15 Eight hundred members of former Turkish president Adnan Menderes' regime are put on trial, charged with corruption.

17 Police in New York, New York, arrest star contestant Charles Van Doren and 13 others for perjury in connection with their role in rigging the results of the popular television quiz show *Twenty-One*, a scandal which emerged in 1958.

19 The United States imposes an embargo on shipments to Cuba (excepting food and medicines) in response to the government's revolutionary political program.

NOVEMBER

• Americans elect John F. Kennedy president and Lyndon B. Johnson vice president in the closest popular vote in U.S. history (49.7% to 49.6%). In the Congressional elections, Democrats retain majorities in the House (263-174) and Senate (65-35).

• President Dwight D. Eisenhower tries to stem the flow of gold from U.S. coffers by urging Americans to reduce consumption of foreign goods.

• Some 200 people are arrested as an anti-integration riot erupts in New Orleans, Louisiana.

• The right-wing student organization Young Americans for Freedom is founded in the United States to take direct action against radical student groups.

1 The British prime minister Harold Macmillan announces a plan to provide facilities for U.S. Polaris-armed submarines at Holy Loch in Scotland.

25 After four months of unrest, the parliament of Southern Rhodesia (now Zimbabwe) passes a Law and Order Maintenance Act giving the police extra powers to deal with political campaigners. On November 1 the Chief Justice of the Central African Federation resigns in protest.

26 A general election in New Zealand is won by the National Party with 46 seats, over Labor with 34. Keith Holyoake is appointed prime minister and his government is sworn in on December 12.

DECEMBER

2 Britain refuses the Ugandan province of Buganda's request for independence.

9 General Souvanna Phouma and his ministers flee from Laos to Cambodia following the rebellion of General Phoumi and Prince Boun Oum. On December 16 the Laos assembly and king approve the prince as the new prime minister.

12 The creation of a National Front for the Liberation of South Vietnam is announced in communist North Vietnam, including a military arm, the National Liberation Army, known as the Vietcong. Its aim is to overthrow President Ngo Dinh Diem's South Vietnamese government.

14 A convention establishing the Organization for Economic Cooperation and Development (OECD) is signed in Paris, France, by the United States, Canada, and 18 member countries of the Organization for European Economic Cooperation (OEEC), which it replaces.

14 The Congo prime minister Patrice Lumumba's vice president, Antoine Gizenga, proclaims himself premier and establishes a procommunist government in Stanleyville (now Kisangani).

21 King Saud takes over the Saudi Arabian government on the resignation of its prime minister Emir Faisal.

SCIENCE, TECHNOLOGY, AND MEDICINE

Computing

- European and U.S. computer scientists agree on a set of standards for the programming language ALGOL (algorithmic language), in Paris, France.

NOVEMBER

- U.S. computer scientist Kenneth Olsen, at Digital Equipment Corporation, introduces the PDP-1 computer. It has a memory of 26 megabytes and is the first to use a monitor and keyboard. It is the forerunner of the minicomputer.

Ecology

c. 1960 Meteorologists begin to study storm systems using doppler radar, which can detect the speed and direction of moving storms because of the change in frequency of the reflected radar waves.

FEBRUARY

29 An earthquake that measures 5.8 on the Richter scale and its ensuing fire and tsunami destroy Agadir in Morocco, the worst earthquake recorded in Africa; 12,000 people are killed.

APRIL

6 The California legislature approves the United States's first state-sponsored antismog bill.

MAY

22 Concepción in Chile is destroyed by an earthquake that kills 5,700. A further 100 are killed in Japan and Hawaii by the ensuing tsunami.

OCTOBER

31 The east coast of Pakistan is hit by a cyclone and tidal wave that kill 10,000 and leave 900,000 homeless.

Exploration

- There are now 20 artificial satellites in orbit.

JANUARY

23 Swiss engineer Jacques Piccard and U.S. Navy lieutenant Don Walsh descend to the bottom of Challenger Deep (10,916 m/35,810 ft), off the Pacific island of Guam, in the bathyscaph *Trieste*, setting a new undersea record.

MARCH

11 The United States launches *Pioneer 5*, which relays the first measurements of deep space.

MAY

- The United States launches *Midas 2*, a satellite designed to provide early warning of a missile attack.

15 The USSR launches *Spacecraft I*. Weighing 4,540 kg/10,000 lb, it is the first vehicle large enough to contain a human passenger.

AUGUST

12 The U.S. National Aeronautics and Space Administration (NASA) launches *Echo I*, a 30-m/100-ft aluminum-coated balloon used as a passive communications satellite to reflect radio-waves. It remains in orbit for eight years and is a conspicuous object in the night sky. Its success leads to the development of the telecommunications satellite *Telstar*.

18 The U.S. satellite *Discoverer 14* is launched. A U.S. Air Force C-119 transport plane recovers its capsule in midair over the Pacific.

21 The USSR safely retrieves *Spacecraft II*, which has two dog passengers.

Health and Medicine

- A ten-year campaign to eradicate malaria begins in Indonesia. Mosquito-infested swamps are drained and houses are sprayed with DDT (dichlorodiphonyltrichloro ethane). Most of Java is free of the disease within four years.

- An oral poliomyelitis vaccine, using a weakened virus developed by Polish-born U.S. physician Albert Sabin, is approved for use in the United States.

- Australian physiologist Frank Macfarlane Burnet and British physiologist Peter Medawar are jointly awarded the Nobel Prize for Physiology or Medicine for their discovery of acquired immunological tolerance.

- British surgeon John Charnley performs a hip replacement operation, using a two-part joint replacement constructed of plastic and cobalt-chrome.

- Swedish surgeon Ake Senning implants the first internal pacemaker, which produces electrical impulses to regulate the heartbeat.

- U.S. physician Belding Scribner demonstrates the permanent Teflon arteriovenous shunt. Used by people with kidney disease, it uses tubes permanently inserted into the arm to facilitate treatment and avoid the need for repeated hemodialysis.

- U.S. surgeons Bradley Aust and Karel Absolon perform the first hemicorporectomy, the surgical removal of the lower half of the body.

MAY

31 The President's Joint Commission on Mental Illness and Health in the United States reports that 25% of Americans suffer from mental illness at some point in their lives.

JUNE

6 A study by the American Heart Association finds that men who smoke are 50% to 150% more likely to die from coronary disease than nonsmokers.

Science

- British chemist G. N. Robinson discovers the antibiotic methicillin.
- English anthropologist Jane Goodall discovers that chimpanzees can make tools, something only humans were thought capable of. She watches a chimpanzee fashion a blade of grass into a probe that can be poked into a termite mound to remove termites.
- English biochemist John Kendrew, using X-ray diffraction techniques, elucidates the three-dimensional structure of the muscle protein myoglobin.
- The National Center for Atmospheric Research is established at Boulder, Colorado.
- U.S. biochemist Robert Woodward and German biochemist Martin Strell independently synthesize chlorophyll.
- U.S. chemist Willard Libby receives the Nobel Prize for Chemistry for his development of radiocarbon dating.
- U.S. geophysicist Harry Hess develops the theory of sea-floor spreading, in which molten material wells up along the mid-oceanic ridges forcing the seafloor to spread out from the ridges. The flow is thought to be the cause of continental drift.

OCTOBER

- The 11th general Conference on Weights and Measures replaces the metric system with the International System (SI) of weights and measures. It redefines the seven basic units of measurement, from which all others are derived, in atomic terms. The meter, for instance is redefined as 1,650,763.73 wavelengths of the orange-red line in the krypton-86 spectrum.

Technology

- English astronomer Martin Ryle develops the synthesized aperture interferometer. Using two or more moveable antennae mounted on rails it greatly improves the resolution of radio telescopes, allowing the mapping of such distant radio sources as quasars.
- Laboratories can produce temperatures as low as 0.000001 K, a millionth of a degree above absolute zero (273.15°C/459.67°F).
- The halogen lamp is introduced. The halogen gas in the lamp regenerates the filament, permitting it to burn at higher temperatures, and thus burn brighter.

- The Rhine-Westphalia Power Company at Kahl-am-Main, West Germany, begins operation. It is the first boiling water nuclear power reactor in Europe.
- The U.S. photographer Ansel Adams publishes his photography album *This is the American Earth*.
- The U.S. Polaroid corporation introduces a high-speed film ten times faster than previous films.
- U.S. physicist Donald Glaser receives the Nobel Prize for Physics for the invention of the bubble chamber.
- U.S. physicist Theodore Maiman constructs the first laser (light amplification by stimulated emission of radiation), a device producing an intense beam of parallel or coherent light.

FEBRUARY

13 France explodes an atomic bomb over the Sahara Desert, thus becoming the fourth atomic power.

APRIL

1 The United States launches *TIROS 1* (Television and Infra-Red Observation Satellite). A weather satellite, it is equipped with television cameras, infrared detectors, and videotape recorders. It provides a worldwide weather observation system, along with subsequently launched *TIROS* satellites.

MAY

- A U.S. Atlas intercontinental ballistic missile travels 9,000 miles between Florida and Africa, a new world distance record.

JULY

20 The U.S. nuclear-powered submarine *George Washington* conducts the first subsurface firing of a ballistic missile.

OCTOBER

25 U.S. firm Bulova introduces the Accutron tuning-fork watch, the world's first electronic wristwatch.

NOVEMBER

- The U.S. navy develops the Communications Moon Relay (CMR) system, which uses the moon to reflect communication signals between Washington, D.C., and Hawaii.

Transportation

- Go-karting (driving and racing small motorized vehicles called go-karts, invented in 1956) becomes popular with children and adults in the United States.
- The U.S. Navy launches the first *Transit* satellite. Its purpose is to enable nuclear submarines to accurately determine their position regardless of weather conditions.

FEBRUARY

24–May 10 Following the route of Portuguese explorer Ferdinand Magellan, the U.S. nuclear-powered submarine *Triton* makes the first underwater circumnavigation of the globe, traveling 61,430 km/41,519 mi.

AUGUST

4 An X-15 rocket airplane, piloted by NASA test pilot Joseph Walker, establishes a world speed record of 3,514 kph/2,196 mph.

SEPTEMBER

24 The USS *Enterprise* is launched, the first nuclear-powered aircraft carrier.

DECEMBER

16 The worst airline disaster to date occurs when a United Airlines and a TWA plane collide in fog over New York, New York, killing 132 passengers and crew members.

ARTS AND IDEAS

Architecture

- The monastery of Ste. Marie de la Tourette at Eveaux-sur-l'Arbresle near Lyon, France, designed by the Swiss architect Le Corbusier, is completed.
- The Richards Medical Research Building in Philadelphia, Pennsylvania, designed by the U.S. architect Louis Kahn, is completed.
- The Tokyo Museum in Japan, designed by the Swiss architect Le Corbusier, is completed.

Arts

- The Austrian-born English art historian E. H. Gombrich publishes *Art and Illusion*.
- The English artist David Hockney paints *Adhesiveness*.
- The French artist Victor Vasarély paints *Orion MC*.
- The French artist Yves Klein stages the first of his *Anthropométries/Anthropometries* in Paris, France, during which he drags women covered in paint across a canvas spread on the ground.
- The German-born English artist Lucian Freud paints *Woman Smiling*.
- The Italian artist Renato Guttuso paints *Discussion*.
- The Swiss artist Jean Tinguely creates *Homage to New York*, a self-destructing sculpture.
- The U.S. artist Cy Twombly paints *School of Fontainebleau*.
- The U.S. artist Frank Stella paints *Six Mile Bottom* and *Avicenna*.
- The U.S. artist Mark Rothko paints *Black on Dark Sienna on Purple*.
- The U.S. artist Morris Louis paints *Gamma Zeta*.

Film

- About 46 million people attend movies each week in the United States; there are 13,200 indoor and 4,600 outdoor movie theaters.
- The movie *A Bout de Souffle/Breathless*, directed by Jean-Luc Godard, is released in France, starring Jean-Paul Belmondo and Jean Seberg.
- The movie *Butterfield 8*, directed by Daniel Mann, is released in the United States. Based on the novel by John O'Hara, it stars Elizabeth Taylor, Laurence Harvey, Eddie Fisher, and Dina Merrill.
- The movie *Exodus*, directed by Otto Preminger, is released in the United States. Based on the book by U.S.

author Leon Uris, it stars Paul Newman, Eve Marie Saint, and Ralph Richardson.
- The movie *I'm All Right Jack*, directed by John Boulting, is released in Britain, starring Ian Carmichael and Peter Sellers.
- The movie *L'Avventura/The Adventure*, directed by Michelangelo Antonioni, is released in Italy, starring Monica Vitti, Lea Massari, and Gabriele Ferzetti.
- The movie *La Dolce Vita/The Good Life*, directed by Federico Fellini, is released in Italy, starring Marcello Mastroianni.
- The movie *Never on Sunday*, directed by Jules Dassin, is released in Greece, starring Melina Mercouri.
- The movie *Psycho*, directed by English filmmaker Alfred Hitchcock, is released in the United States. Based on the book by Robert Bloch, it stars Anthony Perkins, Vera Miles, Janet Leigh, and John Gavin.
- The movie *Rocco and his Brothers*, directed by Luchino Visconti, is released in Italy, starring Alain Delon, Renato Salvatori, and Annie Girardot.
- The movie *Saturday Night and Sunday Morning*, directed by the Czechoslovakian filmmaker Karel Reisz, is released in Britain. Based on the novel by Alan Sillitoe, it stars Albert Finney, Shirley-Anne Field, and Rachel Roberts.
- The movie *Spartacus*, directed by Stanley Kubrick, is released in the United States, starring Kirk Douglas, Laurence Olivier, Peter Ustinov, Charles Laughton, Tony Curtis, and Jean Simmons.
- The movie *The Apartment*, directed by Billy Wilder, is released in the United States, starring Jack Lemmon, Shirley MacLaine, and Fred MacMurray.
- The movie *The Entertainer*, directed by Tony Richardson, is released in Britain. Based on the play by John Osborne, it stars Laurence Olivier.
- The movie *The Magnificent Seven*, directed by John Sturges, is released in the United States. Based on the Japanese movie *Seven Samurai*, it stars Yul Brynner, Steve McQueen, Robert Vaughn, James Coburn, Eli Wallach, Charles Bronson, and Horst Buchholz.

APRIL

18 The 1959 Academy Awards take place. Best Actor: Charlton Heston, for *Ben Hur*; Best Supporting Actor: Hugh Griffith, for *Ben Hur*; Best Actress: Simone Signoret, for *Room at the Top*; Best Supporting Actress: Shelley Winters, for *The Diary of Anne Frank*; Best Picture: *Ben Hur*, directed by William Wyler; Best Director: William Wyler, for *Ben Hur*.

Literature and Language

- The English philosopher A. J. Ayer publishes *Logical Positivism*.
- The English writer Anthony Powell publishes *Casanova's Chinese Restaurant*, the fifth novel of his 12-volume sequence *A Dance to the Music of Time*.
- The English writer David Storey publishes his novel *This Sporting Life*.
- The English writer John Betjeman publishes his autobiography *Summoned by Bells*.
- The English writer Lawrence Durrell publishes his novel *Clea*, the third volume of his *The Alexandria Quartet*.

- The English writer Lynne Reid Banks publishes her novel *The L-Shaped Room*.
- The English writer Stan Barstow publishes his novel *A Kind of Loving*.
- The French historian Philippe Ariès publishes *L'Enfant et la vie familiale sous l'ancien régime/The Child and the Family*.
- The French writer and philosopher Simone de Beauvoir publishes her second volume of autobiography *La Force de l'âge/The Prime of Life*.
- The French writer Claude Simon publishes his novel *La Route des Flandres/The Road to Flanders*.
- The Guyanese writer Wilson Harris publishes his novel *Palace of the Peacock*, the first part of his *The Guyana Quartet*.
- The Indian writer Raja Rao publishes his novel *The Serpent and the Rope*.
- The Irish writer Edna O'Brien publishes her novel *The Country Girls*.
- The Nobel Prize for Literature is awarded to the French poet Saint-John Perse.
- The Polish-born U.S. writer Isaac Bashevis Singer publishes his novel *The Magician of Lublin*.
- The Pulitzer Prize for Biography is awarded to Samuel Eliot Morison for *John Paul Jones*, the Pulitzer Prize for Poetry is awarded to William Snodgrass for *Heart's Needle*, and the Pulitzer Prize for Fiction is awarded to Allen Drury for *Advise and Consent*.
- The Swedish writer Gunner Ekelöf publishes his long poem "En Mölna-elegi"/"A Moelna Elegy".
- The U.S. writer Anne Sexton publishes her autobiographical poetry collection *To Bedlam and Part Way Back*.
- The U.S. writer Flannery O'Connor publishes her novel *The Violent Bear It Away*.
- The U.S. writer Gary Snyder publishes his poetry collection *Myths and Texts*.
- The U.S. writer Harper Lee publishes her novel *To Kill a Mockingbird*, which wins the Pulitzer Prize for Fiction in 1961.
- The U.S. writer John Barth publishes his novel *The Sot-Weed Factor*.
- The U.S. writer John Updike publishes his novel *Rabbit Run*, the first of four novels featuring the career of Harry "Rabbit" Armstrong.
- The U.S. writer Randall Jarrell publishes his poetry collection *The Woman at the Washington Zoo*.
- The U.S. writer Sylvia Plath publishes her poetry collection *The Colossus*.

MARCH

25 A U.S. Circuit Court of Appeals in New York, New York, rules that the novel *Lady Chatterley's Lover*, by the English writer D. H. Lawrence, is not obscene. A ban imposed by the Postmaster General had been overturned the previous year.

NOVEMBER

2 A court in the UK decides that the novel *Lady Chatterley's Lover*, by D. H. Lawrence, is not obscene. It soon becomes a best seller.

Music

- The British singer Lonnie Donegan, "King of Skiffle," releases the single "My Old Man's a Dustman."
- The English composer William Walton completes his Symphony No. 2.
- The first public performance by John Lennon, Paul McCartney, George Harrison, and Pete Best as the Beatles takes place, at Bruno Koschminder's Indra Club in Hamburg, West Germany.
- The French composer Jean Françaix completes his *Piano Sonata*.
- The French composer Olivier Messiaen completes his orchestral work *Chronochromie/Time-Color*.
- The French singer Edith Piaf releases the single "Non, je ne regrette rien"/"No Regrets."
- The German composer Karlheinz Stockhausen completes his electronic work *Kontakte/Contact*.
- The Italian composer Luciano Berio completes his *Circles* for voice and instruments.
- The opera *A Midsummer Night's Dream*, by the English composer Benjamin Britten, is first performed, at Aldeburgh, Suffolk, England. It is based on Shakespeare's play of the same title.
- The Polish composer Krzysztof Penderecki completes his orchestral work *Tren pamięci ofiarom Hiroszimy/Threnody for the Victims of Hiroshima*.
- The Russian composer Dmitry Shostakovich completes his String Quartets Nos. 7 and 8.
- The U.S. country singer Jim Reeves releases the single "He'll Have to Go."
- The U.S. girl group the Shirelles release the single "Will You Love Me Tomorrow;" it enters the charts on November 21.
- The U.S. orchestra leader Percy Faith releases the single "Theme from a Summer Place," the theme music from the movie *A Summer Place*.
- The U.S. rock 'n' roll singer Eddie Cochran releases the single "Three Steps to Heaven."
- The U.S. rock singer Elvis Presley releases the single "Are You Lonesome Tonight?" It enters the U.S. charts on November 14, 1960, and becomes the best-selling single of 1961 in Britain.
- The U.S. singer Johnny Mathis releases the single "The Shadow of Your Smile."
- The U.S. soul/rhythm and blues singer Ray Charles releases the single "Georgia On My Mind."

November 1960–69 Cliff Richard is the most successful singles artist in Britain in the 1960s, outselling even the Beatles.

November 1960–69 The Beatles' song "She Loves You" is the best-selling single of the 1960s in Britain. The Beatles are responsible for five out of the top six singles in Britain in the 1960s.

JANUARY

25 The U.S. National Association of Broadcasters suggests that any disc jockey guilty of "payola," illegally accepting money to play particular records, should pay a $500 fine and spend one year in jail.

MAY

19 U.S. radio disc jockey Alan Freed, who first popularized the term "rock 'n' roll," is arrested in Cleveland, Ohio,

The Beatles (1960–80)

1960

- The first public performance by John Lennon, Paul McCartney, George Harrison, and Pete Best as the Beatles takes place, at Bruno Koschminder's Indra Club in Hamburg, West Germany.

1961

March 21   The Beatles make their British debut at the Cavern Club in Liverpool, England.

1962

- The Beatles sign a management contract with Brian Epstein and a recording contract with the Parlophone record label.

1963

- The Beatles release the singles "Please Please Me," "She Loves You," and "Twist and Shout." They also release the single "I Want to Hold Your Hand," which sells more than 12 million copies worldwide and enters the U.S. charts at No. 1. The album *Please Please Me* is recorded in 12 hours at EMI's Abbey Road studios.

1964

- The Beatles have four hit singles and two hit albums in the first three months of the year in the United States, partly due to their North American tour which includes an appearance on the U.S. *Ed Sullivan Show*. Sales of Beatles' records represent 60% of all records sold in this period. Their success also marks the beginning of a period of domination by British groups of the U.S. charts.
- The Beatles release the single and album *A Hard Day's Night* from their film of the same name. They also release the single "Can't Buy Me Love," the best-selling single of the year in Britain.

February 7   The Beatles arrive at Kennedy Airport in New York, New York, to begin their second U.S. tour.

1965

- The Beatles release the singles "Help!," "Ticket to Ride," "Yesterday," and "Day Tripper," and the album *Help!*
- The film *Help!*, a sequel to *A Hard Day's Night*, is released in Britain, directed by Richard Lester.

1966

- The Beatles release the singles "Paperback Writer," "Eleanor Rigby," and "Yellow Submarine," and the album *Revolver*.

- The popularity of groups like the Beatles feeds through into youth fashion, with longer hair, collarless jackets, and cuban-heel boots becoming popular.

May 1   The Beatles play their final gig in Britain.

August 29   The Beatles play their last concert, at Candlestick Park in San Francisco, California.

1967

- The Beatles release *Sergeant Pepper's Lonely Hearts Club Band*, considered their most innovative album to date. They also release the singles "All You Need Is Love" and "Hello Goodbye."

May 27   The British Broadcasting Corporation (BBC) bans the Beatles' single "A Day in the Life," as it is seen to be encouraging drug-taking.

1968

- The Beatles launch their Apple record label.
- The Beatles release their animated film *Yellow Submarine*.
- The Beatles release the single "Hey Jude" and the album *The Beatles* (known as *The White Album*).

1969

- John Lennon and Yoko Ono release the single "Give Peace a Chance."
- Paul McCartney has to deny publicly rumors of his death: the speculation has resulted from alleged hidden messages in Beatles albums that he has been replaced by a double.
- The Beatles make their last ever public appearance on the roof of the Apple Records building in London. It is recorded as part of their film *Let It Be*. The police are called out by people in neighboring buildings who are disturbed by the noise. The group also releases the album *Abbey Road* and the single "Something" by George Harrison, the first Beatle hit not to have been written by John Lennon or Paul McCartney.

1970

- The Beatles release the single "Let It Be" and an album of the same name. The group officially splits up later in the year.

1980

December   John Lennon is shot dead by Mark David Chapman outside the Dakota, his apartment building in New York.

---

in a "payola" scandal, receiving bribes to play specific records. Nine others are also arrested in the sweep.

JULY

2   Local police make more than 100 arrests at the Newport Jazz Festival in Rhode Island, as people protest against the lack of tickets to the event.

Theater and Dance

- The absurdist play *Le Rhinocéros/The Rhinoceros*, by the Romanian-born French dramatist Eugène Ionesco, is first performed, in Paris, France.
- The play *A Man for All Seasons*, by the English dramatist Robert Bolt, based on the life of Sir Thomas

More, is first performed, at the Globe Theatre in London, England.

- The play *The Caretaker*, by the English dramatist Harold Pinter, is first performed, at the Arts Theatre in London, England.
- The play *The Dumb Waiter*, by the English dramatist Harold Pinter, is first performed, in London, England.
- The Pulitzer Prize for Drama is awarded to Jerome Weidman and George Abbot for *Fiorello!*
- The Royal Shakespeare Company is formed in the UK. In addition to its theater at Stratford-upon-Avon, it acquires the Aldwych Theatre for productions in London.

FEBRUARY

25   The play *Toys in the Attic*, by the U.S. dramatist Lillian Hellman, is first performed, in New York, New York.

APRIL

14   The musical comedy *Bye Bye Birdie*, by Charles Strouse and Lee Adams, opens at the Martin Beck Theater in New York, New York, featuring Dick Van Dyke, Kay Medford, and Chita Rivera.

24   The 1959–60 Tony Awards take place. Best Play: *The Miracle Worker*; Best Musical: *Firello!* and *The Sound of Music*; Best Actor: Melvyn Douglas; Best Actress: Anne Bancroft.

MAY

3   The musical *The Fantasticks* by Tom Jones and Harvey Schmidt opens at the Sullivan Street Playhouse, New York, New York.

JUNE

- An Actor's Equity guild strikes 22 Broadway theaters, in New York, New York, in the first strike in 41 years.

10   The musical *Oliver!*, with lyrics and music by Lionel Bart, is first performed, at the Wimbledon Theatre, London, England. Based on the novel by Charles Dickens, it features the songs "Food, Glorious Food" and "I'd Do Anything."

DECEMBER

3   The musical *Camelot*, with music by Frederick Loewe and lyrics by Alan Jay Lerner, is first performed, at the Majestic Theater, New York, New York.

Thought and Scholarship

- Scottish psychologist R. D. Laing publishes *The Divided Self: A Study in Sanity and Madness*.
- The German philosopher Hans-Georg Gadamer publishes *Wahrheit und Methode: Grundzüge einer philosophischen Hermeneutik/Truth and Method: Features of a Philosophical Hermeneutics*.
- The Pulitzer Prize for History is awarded to Margaret Leech for *In the Days of McKinley*.
- The U.S. economist Walt W. Rostow publishes *The Stages of Economic Growth: A Non-Communist Manifesto*.
- The U.S. historian Henry Steele Commager publishes *The Era of Reform*.
- The U.S. journalist William L. Shirer publishes *The Rise and Fall of the Third Reich*.
- The U.S. philosopher W. V. Quine publishes *Word and Object*.

- The U.S. political scientist Elmer Eric Schattschneider publishes *The Semi-Sovereign People*.

SOCIETY

Education

- Local government provides 56% of public school funding, state government provides 40%, and the federal government provides 4% in the United States.

JULY

- The Modern Language Association decries the qualification standards of foreign language teachers in U.S. public schools.

Everyday Life

- Ten percent of white males and 6% of white females have completed four or more years of college in the United States; the corresponding figure for blacks is 3.5%.
- Twenty-two percent of white males and 29% of white females have finished four years of high school in the United States; the corresponding numbers for black males and females are 12% and 15%.
- Six-hundred and seven independently owned restaurants make Howard Johnson the third largest food distributor in the United States, after the U.S. Army and Navy.
- Sixty-two percent of U.S. students, enrolled in the fifth grade eight years earlier, have graduated from high school.
- The lowest fifth of the population earns 4.8% of the total household income in the United States; the second fifth earns 11.9%; the third fifth earns 17.8%; the fourth fifth earns 24%; and the highest fifth earns 41.1%.
- The median income for families in the United States is $5,620, or $5,835 for white families and $3,233 for blacks and other minorities.
- The U.S. Xerox Corporation markets the Xerox 914 copier, which can make 23 × 35.5 cm/9 × 14 in copies on ordinary rather than coated paper. It begins a revolution in the office.
- There are 41 million Catholics, 9.8 million Methodists, 9.7 million Southern Baptists, 5.4 million Jews, 3.4 million Episcopalians, and 3.2 million Presbyterians in the United States.
- U.S. consumers spend $97 billion on food, beverages, and tobacco; $33 billion on clothes; $93 billion on housing and household operations; $19 billion on medical care; and $18 billion on recreation.
- U.S. writer Paul Goodman publishes *Growing Up Absurd: Problems for Youth in the Organized Society*.

JANUARY

- U.S. steel operators and the United Mine Workers Union agree on a new contract, thus ending the nation's lengthiest steel strike.

FEBRUARY

- The U.S. Census Bureau lists the nation's population at approximately 179,245,000, up from roughly 150,697,000 a decade ago.

APRIL

1   R. Griggs & Co. begin to produce Doc Martens boots under license in Britain.

MAY

6   Princess Margaret, sister of Elizabeth II, Queen of Great Britain and Northern Ireland, marries Antony Armstrong-Jones.

JULY

4   The 50-star U.S. flag, recognizing Hawaii's statehood of August 1959, becomes the official flag.

AUGUST

•   The Japan Stationery Company, in Tokyo, markets Pentel, the first felt-tip pens.

OCTOBER

•   Two thousand members of the American Federation of Labor and the Congress of Industrial Organizations (AFL-CIO) at the Union Carbide Nuclear Company strike for better wages. A settlement is reached on October 31.

DECEMBER

14   King Baudouin of Belgium marries the Spanish aristocrat Doña Fabiola de Mora y Aragòn.

Media and Communication

•   A television monitoring group in Los Angeles records in one week's viewing of U.S. television 144 murders and 143 attempted murders. The increase in portrayed violence has been caused by a ratings war between stations.

December 1960–64   Mark Wilson's magic show *The Magic Land of Allakazam* runs on Saturday mornings on national television in the United States, first on CBS and then ABC.

FEBRUARY

11–March 7   The U.S. comedian Jack Paar protests against the censorship by the network NBC of one of his jokes (about an American who does not understand the abbreviation "WC") by refusing to appear on his late-night television show.

JUNE

20   The 1959–60 Emmy Awards for television take place. Best Actor in a Single Show: Laurence Olivier, for *The Moon and Sixpence*; Best Actress in a Single Show: Ingrid Bergman, for *The Turn of the Screw*; Best Actor in a Series: Robert Stack, for *The Untouchables*; Best Actress in a Series: Jane Wyatt, for *Father Knows Best*.

SEPTEMBER

29–August 24, 1972   The situation comedy *My Three Sons* appears on U.S. television, starring Fred MacMurray, Tim Considine, Don Grady, Stanley Livingston, and William Frawley.

30–September 2, 1966   *The Flintstones*, an animated situation comedy about the lives of a suburban Stone Age family and their friends, appears on U.S. television; it is a Hanna-Barbera production.

OCTOBER

3–September 16, 1968   The situation comedy *The Andy Griffith Show* appears on U.S. television; Griffith stars as the sheriff of the small town of Mayberry, North Carolina; other stars include Don Knotts, Ronny Howard, Francis Bavier, Jim Nabors, Elinor Donahue, and Hal Smith.

7–September 18, 1964   The adventure series *Route 66* appears on U.S. television, starring Martin Milner and George Maharis.

Religion

JANUARY

9   Officials of the Protestant Episcopal Church in the United States endorse the use of limited measures of contraception in countries where overpopulation jeopardizes natural increase.

BIRTHS & DEATHS

JANUARY

4   Albert Camus, French novelist who received the Nobel Prize for Literature in 1957, dies in Sens, France (46).

7   Dorothea Lambert Chambers, English tennis player who dominated women's tennis prior to World War I, dies in London, England (81).

22   Michael Hutchins, Australian rock singer, leader of INXS, born in Sydney, Australia (–1997).

FEBRUARY

19   Prince Andrew, Duke of York, second son of Queen Elizabeth II of Great Britain and Northern Ireland, born.

MARCH

21   Ayrton Senna, Brazilian race-car driver, born in São Paulo, Brazil (–1994).

MAY

11   John D. Rockefeller, Jr., U.S. philanthropist who was instrumental in founding the United Nations in New York, New York, dies in Tucson, Arizona (86).

30   Boris Pasternak, Russian poet and novelist who wrote *Dr Zhivago*, dies near Moscow, USSR (70).

JULY

16   Albert Kesselring, German field marshal and Commander in Chief South, of the German armed forces, dies in Nauheim, West Germany (74).

AUGUST

4   Timothy John Winton, U.S. novelist, known for his book *The Riders*, born near Perth, Australia.

23   Oscar Hammerstein, U.S. lyricist and composer known for his work with Richard Rodgers, dies in Doylestown, Pennsylvania (65).

SEPTEMBER

25   Emily Post, U.S. expert on social graces, who wrote *Etiquette: The Blue Book of Social Usage*, dies in New York, New York (87).

OCTOBER

5   Alfred Louis Kroeber, U.S. anthropologist, dies in Paris, France (84).

NOVEMBER

5   Mack Sennett, U.S. film director and producer who created the Keystone Kops, dies in Hollywood, California (80).

16   Clark Gable, U.S. film star, dies in Hollywood, California (59).

MAY

- With reference to Massachusetts senator John F. Kennedy's presidential candidacy, the Southern Baptist Convention denounces the election of Roman Catholics to public office. Catholics, the Baptists alleged, could not help but put church before country.

Sports

c. 1960   Skateboarding is invented in California, United States, by surfers who fix roller-skate wheels to short surfboards. Soon afterwards the first skateboards are manufactured commercially, and over the decade the craze spreads east across the United States.
- The American Football League (AFL) is formed in the United States to challenge the National Football League (NFL).
- The Canadian team wins the inaugural world curling championship trophy, the Scotch Whiskey Cup.
- The Dallas Cowboys join the National Football League (NFL).

JANUARY

12   Dolph Schayes of the Syracuse Nationals becomes the first player in the history of the National Basketball Association (NBA) to score 15,000 career points.

FEBRUARY

1   The Australian tennis player Margaret Smith (later Court) wins the first of seven successive women's singles titles at the Australian tennis championships in Melbourne.

18–28   At the Winter Olympic Games in Squaw Valley, California, the United States wins its first hockey gold medal.

18–28   The 8th Winter Olympic Games take place in Squaw Valley, California, attended by 665 competitors, including 143 women, from 30 countries. The biathlon and women's speed skating events are introduced. The USSR wins 7 gold medals; West Germany, 4; and the United States, Norway, and Sweden, 3 each.

23   Crews begin to demolish Ebbets Field in Brooklyn, New York, the former home of the Brooklyn Dodgers who have moved to Los Angeles, California. A housing project will replace the field.

MARCH

27–April 9   The Boston Celtics beat the St. Louis Hawks by four games to three to win the National Basketball Association championship.

APRIL

7–14   The Montreal Canadiens defeat the Toronto Maple Leafs by four games to none to win the National Hockey League Stanley Cup for a record fifth sucessive year.

JUNE

12–19   The Uruguayan soccer team Peñarol defeats Olimpia from Paraguay 2–1 on aggregate over two legs to win the inaugural South American Champions' Club Cup (known from 1965 as the Copa Libertadores de América).

20   In beating Ingemar Johansson of Sweden in five rounds of their fight in New York, New York, U.S. boxer Floyd Patterson becomes the first boxer to regain the world heavyweight title.

21   The West German runner Armin Hary becomes the first person to run 100 meters in 10 seconds (by hand-held timing), in Zürich, Switzerland.

JULY

2   The Brazilian tennis player Maria Bueno wins the women's singles title at the Wimbledon championships, London, England, for the second year in succession.

21   The English yachtsman Francis Chichester, at the age of 58, wins the first single-handed transatlantic sailing race from Plymouth, southwest England, to Newport, Rhode Island, United States, in his yacht *Gipsy Moth III*.

23   Betsy Rawls of the United States becomes the first golfer to win the U.S. Women's Open four times.

AUGUST

25   The 17th Olympic Games open in Rome, Italy, with 84 nations competing. For the first time the number of competitors exceeds 5,000, around 600 of whom are women.

25–September 11   Cassius Clay of the United States (later known as Muhammad Ali) wins the light-heavyweight boxing gold medal at the Olympic Games in Rome, Italy.

25–September 11   The U.S. runner Wilma Rudolph, who suffered from polio as a child, wins gold medals in the 100 meters, 200 meters, and sprint relay at the Olympic Games in Rome, Italy.

SEPTEMBER

4   Real Madrid of Spain defeats Peñarol of Uruguay 5–1 on aggregate over two legs to win the inaugural soccer World Club Championship, played between the winners of the European and the South American Champions' Club cups.

6   At the Olympic Games in Rome, Italy, the Australian runner Herb Elliott sets a new world one-mile record of 3 min 54.5 secs, an improvement of 2.8 seconds on the previous best time.

9   A crowd of 21,597 watches the Denver Broncos defeat the Boston Patriots 13–10 in Boston, Massachusetts, in the first American Football League (AFL) regular season game. The AFL was formed earlier this year as a rival to the National Football League (NFL).

11   The 17th Olympic Games close in Rome, Italy. The Soviet Union has won 43 gold medals; the United States, 34; Italy, 13; West Germany, 10; Australia, 8; Turkey, 7; and Hungary, 6.

28   At Fenway Park in Boston, Massachusetts, Ted William, a Boston Red Sox since 1939, hits a home run in his last at-bat in the Major Leagues.

1961

POLITICS, GOVERNMENT, AND ECONOMICS

Business and Economics

- Green Giant launches its frozen food range in the United States.
- The H. W. Lay Co. of Atlanta, Georgia, merges with the Frito Co. of Dallas, Texas, to form Frito-Lay, Inc., the snack-food conglomerate.
- U.S. entrepreneur Ray Kroc consolidates his control of the McDonald's restaurant chain in the United States by buying out the McDonald brothers for $14 million and attaining exclusive rights to the "McDonald's" name. After embarking on a massive expansion program, Kroc's empire numbers 200 establishments by the end of the year.

FEBRUARY
14 South Africa introduces a new decimal coinage, the rand.

Colonization

APRIL
27 The British colony of Sierra Leone wins independence within the Commonwealth.

DECEMBER
9 Tanganyika (now Tanzania) becomes an independent state within the British Commonwealth.

Human Rights

DECEMBER
11 In the case of *Garner et al v. Louisiana*, the U.S. Supreme Court rules that sit-ins are legal and quashes the convictions of 16 black civil-rights protestors found guilty of breaking the peace by demanding service at a whites-only lunch counter in Baton Rouge, Louisiana.

Politics and Government

- Adolf Eichmann is tried in Israel and found guilty of crimes against the Jewish people during the Holocaust of World War II. He is executed on May 31, 1962.

- An eight-year development plan is launched in Indonesia, to achieve "Indonesian socialism."
- The British government imposes tighter immigration controls, requiring immigrants to have definite employment or to possess desired skills or qualifications.
- The English jurist H. L. A. Hart publishes *The Concept of Law*.
- The U.S. Office of Civil and Defense Mobilization publishes *The Family Fallout Shelter*, a 31-page guide that explains how to build a fallout shelter in case of nuclear war.

JANUARY
- John F. Kennedy is inaugurated the 35th president of the United States. Kennedy is the youngest man elected and the first Roman Catholic to hold the office.
- The State Department begins work on establishing the U.S. Peace Corps.
- In his first State of the Union address, President John F. Kennedy criticizes the nation's educational system. Too many teachers, the President maintains, are simply not qualified to teach.
3 After a period of deteriorating diplomatic relations the United States severs diplomatic relations with Cuba.
6 The United Nations (UN) secretary-general Dag Hammarskjöld, visits South Africa to discuss apartheid.
6–8 A referendum is held in Algeria, in which 69% of the voters support the French president Charles de Gaulle's policy of allowing Algeria to vote on self-determination and France to ratify the outcome of the vote. The Algerian nationalist Front de Libération Nationale (FLN) boycotts the referendum.
7 The Casablanca Conference of heads of state in Africa adopts an African Charter, which provides for the establishment of four permanent committees to coordinate policies.
17 Patrice Lumumba, the former prime minister of the Congo Republic, is killed near Elisabethville (now Lubumbashi) by agents of President Moise Tshombe's breakaway Katanga province.
22 *The Red and the Black*, a documentary on the Soviet influence in Africa, is broadcast on U.S. television.
26 Britain and the United Arab Republic (UAR) of Egypt and Syria resume full relations.
31–February 17 The constitutional conference on Northern Rhodesia (now Zambia) reconvenes in London, England, but two African parties boycott the talks and no agreement is reached.

FEBRUARY
- U.S. District Court judge J. Cullen Ganey finds 29 electrical manufacturers guilty of price fixing. Seven serve jail terms; together, the manufacturers pay nearly $2 million worth of fines.

4–5 Nationalist disturbances take place in Luanda, in the Portuguese colony of Angola, and on March 15 a revolt begins in the northern provinces.

9 President Joseph Kasavubu of the Congo Republic issues a decree making Joseph Ileo prime minister.

10 The United States relinquishes rights in many defense bases in the West Indies (acquired under a 1941 agreement with Britain).

11 A plebiscite is held in British-administered Cameroon under the supervision of the United Nations (UN). The north of the country votes to join Nigeria, while the south votes to join the Republic of Cameroon.

21 A British white paper (official government report) proposes majority rule for Northern Rhodesia.

21 The United Nations (UN) Security Council adopts a resolution authorizing UN forces to use force to prevent the outbreak of civil war in the Congo Republic.

22 The Soviet leader Nikita Khrushchev wages a campaign against the United Nations (UN) secretary-general Dag Hammarskjöld, and calls on the commission of African states to supervise the passage of the Congo Republic to independence.

27 Britain and Iceland settle their fisheries dispute: after three years, British ships will not fish within 19.2 km/ 12 mi of Iceland's coast.

MARCH

- The 23rd Amendment to the U.S. Constitution becomes law. It gives Washington, D.C., home rule and votes in presidential elections.

8–12 A conference of political leaders from the Congo Republic meets in Tananarive (now Antananarivo) in Madagascar and agrees on the formation of a confederation of 18 states.

8–17 At a meeting of Commonwealth prime ministers in London, England, South African prime minister Hendrik Verwoerd announces that South Africa will leave the Commonwealth on May 31.

9 The Dalai Lama appeals to the United Nations (UN) to restore the independence of Tibet (currently under Chinese rule).

26 In the Belgian elections, the Christian Socialists lose their overall majority and form a coalition government with the Socialists. Théodore Lefèvre succeeds Gaston Eyskens (both Christian Socialists) as prime minister.

26 The U.S. president John F. Kennedy meets the British prime minister Harold Macmillan at Key West, Florida, to discuss the situation in Southeast Asia.

29 Twenty-eight people (including Nelson Mandela) are tried for treason in South Africa, and are all acquitted.

APRIL

7 The United Nations (UN) General Assembly condemns South African racial policy in South West Africa (a UN mandate, now Namibia).

11 Nigeria imposes a boycott on trade with South Africa because of its system of apartheid.

13 The United Nations (UN) General Assembly condemns apartheid in South Africa.

17–20 One thousand five hundred Cuban exiles, trained by U.S. military instructors and supported by the CIA, land on Cuba in the "Bay of Pigs" invasion. An expected sympathetic uprising fails to occur and the invaders are killed or captured.

18 Following elections in Kenya, the Kenya African Democratic Union agrees to join the government. Their

leader Jomo Kenyatta is released by the governor on August 14.

21 A revolt in Algeria by members of the OAS (Secret Army Organization) under General Maurice Challe leads the French president Charles de Gaulle to declare a state of emergency on April 23. The coup collapses on April 26.

24 At a Coquilhatville conference of Congolese delegates, President Moise Tshombe of Katanga province denounces President Joseph Kasavubu's backing by the United Nations (UN) and is arrested after walking out of the conference.

MAY

- President John F. Kennedy visits Canada to spur Canadian officials to take more responsibility for the political stability of the Western hemisphere.

- President John F. Kennedy signs legislation creating the Alliance for Progress, a $600 million aid program for Latin America.

- White residents of Anniston and Birmingham, Alabama, attack two convoys of Northern "riders" on their way from Washington, D.C., to New Orleans to protest against racial segregation. When the freedom riders are attacked in Montgomery, Alabama, six days later, Attorney General Robert F. Kennedy calls out the National Guard.

May 1961–July 1962 A 14-nation conference on Laos, convenes in Geneva, Switzerland, but it soon becomes deadlocked.

1 The United Nations (UN) Trust Territory of Tanganyika (now Tanzania) achieves internal self-government, with Julius Nyerere as prime minister.

2 The warring factions in Laos agree to a cease-fire, and an International Control Commission arrives in the country on May 8.

5 President John F. Kennedy signs amendments to the Fair Labor Standards Act. The legislation raises the minimum wage to $1.15 and extends its coverage to an additional 3.6 million workers, effective on September 1.

9 Ali Amini, the new prime minister of Iran, dissolves parliament and bans political meetings following unrest.

16 A military junta led by General do Yong Chang overthrows the democratic government in South Korea.

24 Cyprus becomes the 16th member of the Council of Europe.

27 The Malayan prime minister Tunku Abdul Rahman proposes the formation of a Greater Malaysian Federation (including Singapore and, later, Sarawak and Sabah).

29 The Western European Union agrees that West Germany will be allowed to build destroyers equipped to fire nuclear weapons.

31 Ghana refuses to recognize the newly-independent South Africa because of opposition to its policy of apartheid.

31 South Africa becomes an independent republic outside the Commonwealth, with Charles Swart as president.

JUNE

- U.S. ambassador to the UN, Adlai Stevenson returns from a tour of South America and reports that political instability and popular discontent are widespread on the continent.

4 The U.S. president John F. Kennedy and Soviet premier Nikita Khrushchev meet in Vienna, Austria, to discuss the future of Laos, Berlin, Germany, and nuclear

disarmament. The Soviet leader Nikita Khrushchev proposes, to the U.S. president John F. Kennedy, a German peace conference to conclude a treaty and establish Berlin as a free city. He also proposes that disarmament discussions should proceed simultaneously with talks about a ban on nuclear tests, but this is rejected by the West on July 17.

9   The United Nations (UN) calls on Portugal to cease repressive measures in its colony of Angola.

13   Austria refuses the application of Archduke Otto von Habsburg, heir to the Habsburg throne, to return as a private individual.

19   By arrangement, Kuwait abrogates its agreement with Britain of 1899 and gains independence with the promise of British protection.

19   U.S. and Soviet representatives begin disarmament talks in Washington, D.C.

22   President Moise Tshombe of the Katanga province in the Congo Republic is freed, having been arrested on April 24.

23   The Antarctic Treaty (signed December 1, 1959) comes into effect. It pledges the 12 signatories to nonpolitical scientific investigation of the continent and bars any military activity.

25   General Abdul Karim Kassem, prime minister of Iraq, declares Kuwait an integral part of Iraq and calls upon Kuwait to surrender to Iraq.

30   Following Iraq's threat to Kuwait, Britain sends troops, but withdraws them by September 19 when they are replaced by Saudi-led troops of the Arab League.

JULY

- An Eastern Airlines passenger plane en route from Tampa to Miami is hijacked to Cuba. Cuban officials turn the matter over to the UN Security Council to avoid U.S. invasive action.
- In the face of mounting U.S.–Soviet tension, President John F. Kennedy orders Pentagon officials to appraise the nation's defense capability.
- President John F. Kennedy proclaims the week of July 14 to be Captive Nations Week, a symbolic gesture designed to bolster resistance movements in communist Eastern Europe.

10–25   The Ghanaian president Kwame Nkrumah visits the USSR.

20   Kuwait is admitted to the Arab League, but membership in the United Nations (UN) is vetoed by the USSR on November 30.

22   The United Nations (UN) orders a cease-fire in Tunisia, following clashes between French and Tunisian forces.

26   A referendum in Southern Rhodesia (now Zimbabwe) approves a new constitution, but the details of the British protectorate's progress to independence are left unresolved (the new constitution is approved in Britain by order in council on December 6).

26   Leaders of the attempted coup in Algeria are tried and, on August 11, eight of them are sentenced to death.

26   The parliament of the Congo Republic meets at Léopoldville (now Kinshasa) and confirms President Joseph Kasavubu's choice of prime minister, Cyrille Adoula.

AUGUST

- In a meeting with Republic of China premier Ch'en Ch'eng, President John F. Kennedy reaffirms U.S.

support for admitting the exiled Republic of China to the UN.

13   East Germany seals off the border between East and West Berlin, closing the Brandenburg Gate.

15   In a general election held in Nyasaland (now Malawi) under the constitution agreed in 1960, Dr. Hastings Banda's Malawi Congress Party (MCP) (representing the black majority) is victorious; the MCP demands an end to the Central African Federation.

17–18   East German building workers begin constructing the Berlin Wall, a near-impregnable physical barrier sealing off West Berlin and preventing the escape of East Germans to the West.

19   The U.S. president John F. Kennedy sends Vice President Lyndon Johnson to Berlin to assure Berliners that the United States guarantees their freedom.

21   In an election in British Guiana (now Guyana) Cheddi Jagan's People's Progressive Party retains power.

27   The more militant Ben Khedda replaces Ferhat Abbas as head of the Algerian Provisional Government.

SEPTEMBER

- Former vice president Richard M. Nixon announces that he will not run for president in the next election. Instead, he will campaign for governor of California.
- President John F. Kennedy signs the Foreign Assistance Act, which authorizes some $4.25 billion for foreign economic and military aid. He also signs legislation making hijacking a capital crime.

1   The United Nations (UN) breaks off relations with the government of secessionist Katanga province in the Congo Republic. Attempts by the UN to arrest members of the government lead to heavy fighting in Elisabethville and Jadotville.

1–6   Nonaligned powers (those neither pro-Western nor procommunist bloc) meet in Belgrade, Yugoslavia, under Jawaharlal Nehru of India and Kwame Nkrumah of Ghana.

17   The Christian Democratic Union and its allies lose their overall majority in West German elections.

18   André Muhirwa's antimonarchist Union and Progress National Party wins the elections in the central African territory of Rwanda-Urundi (divided since 1962 into Rwanda and Burundi).

18   The United Nations (UN) secretary-general Dag Hammarskjöld is killed in an airplane crash in the Congo Republic while traveling to see President Moise Tshombe of Katanga province. U Thant of Burma (now Myanmar) becomes acting secretary-general from November 3.

18–October 9   A Ugandan constitutional conference is held in London, England, ending with agreement for internal self-government from October 1962.

19   A referendum in the British colony of Jamaica votes for secession from the West Indies Federation.

28   An army coup in Damascus, Syria, overthrows the government there. On September 29, Syria secedes from the United Arab Republic and forms the Syrian Arab Republic.

28   The Ghanaian president Kwame Nkrumah imprisons leading members of the opposition, claiming a plot to assassinate him.

30   The Organization for Economic Cooperation and Development (OECD), established the previous year by an international convention, is founded. It is a successor

to the Organization for European Economic Cooperation (OEEC), but the OECD includes the United States and Canada among its founder members.

OCTOBER

- In a speech about the state of U.S. civil defenses, President John F. Kennedy urges U.S. families to build atomic fallout shelters.
11 The United States promises to support South Vietnam against communist aggression.
27 Mauritania and Mongolia are admitted to the United Nations (UN).
29 Constantine Karamanlis forms a new ministry in Greece after the victory of the National Radical Union in elections.

NOVEMBER

2 David Ben-Gurion forms a new coalition in Israel after long negotiations.

7 Konrad Adenauer is reappointed German chancellor.
19 The former prime minister of Southern Rhodesia (now Zimbabwe), Sir Garfield Todd, holds the inaugural meeting of the Rhodesian New African Party, which is committed to majority rule.
24 The United Nations (UN) General Assembly resolves to treat Africa as a denuclearized zone.

DECEMBER

4 In a general election in Barbados, the Labor Party led by Grantley Adams, prime minister of the West Indies Federation, loses to the Democratic Labor Party of Errol Barrow, further weakening the federation.
4 The People's National Movement led by Eric Williams returns to power in Trinidad and Tobago.
5 Following numerous attacks on United Nations (UN) personnel in Katanga province in the Congo Republic, Katangan forces attack UN positions, and fighting continues until a cease-fire on December 18.

Vietnam War (1961–75)

1961

December 11 The first U.S. troops arrive in South Vietnam.

1964

August The Tonkin Gulf incident moves the U.S. Congress to authorize President Lyndon B. Johnson to undertake "all necessary measures to repel any armed attack against forces of the United States and to prevent further aggression." This so-called Tonkin Gulf Resolution provides President Johnson with the de facto consent to wage an undeclared war on North Vietnam. On August 2, the U.S. destroyer *Maddox* is attacked off North Vietnam, in the Tonkin Gulf, by North Vietnamese torpedo boats; U.S. aircraft bomb naval bases in North Vietnam in reprisal. On August 4 the *Maddox* and the destroyer *C Turner Joy* are attacked.

1965

February 8 U.S. aircraft bomb North Vietnam following Vietcong attacks on U.S. areas in South Vietnam. This begins a pattern of regular U.S. bombing of North Vietnam known as Operation Rolling Thunder or Operation Flaming Dart.

March 8 Two battalions of U.S. Marines, 3,500 soldiers, land to defend Danang airbase in South Vietnam. They are the first U.S. combat troops to enter the war.

July In the face of South Vietnamese political and military collapse, U.S. general William Westmoreland beseeches President Johnson for 44 additional battalions, or 180,000 men.

July President Johnson announces that he will increase the number of U.S. troops in South Vietnam from 75,000 to 125,000. He also doubles the monthly draft quota from 17,000 to 35,000.

August 5 The CBS correspondant Morley Safer presents a story on the CBS evening news showing a company of U.S. marines setting fire to huts in the hamlet of Cam Ne, Vietnam, in retaliation for sniper fire. News reports like this are shocking the United States as the war is turned into a "living-room conflict."

October Opponents of the Vietnam War protest in concert across the United States. Some burn draft cards; one is arrested for doing so, under a new federal law.

1966

March U.S. secretary of defense Robert S. McNamara announces that 215,000 U.S. troops are now in South Vietnam. Some 20,000 more are scheduled to join them.

March 8 Australia triples its forces supporting the South Vietnamese government to 4,500 troops.

August 18 In their first major action in Vietnam, a single Australian company of 100 men inflicts more than 700 casualties on three Vietcong battalions near the village of Long Tan in Phuoc Tuy province, forcing them to retreat in disorder. When congratulated by General Westmoreland for winning, the Australian commander replies that battles on this scale mean that they are really losing.

September 23 The United States announces that it has been using defoliating agents in territory around the demilitarized zone between North and South Vietnam to deprive North Vietnamese infiltrators of protective cover.

October 14–15 In two days, U.S. bombers make 348 sorties into North Vietnam, the heaviest bombing raid to date.

October 24–25 A conference of Vietnam war allies is held in Manila, the Philippines, including South Vietnam, the United States, Australia, New Zealand, Philippines, South Korea, and Thailand.

1968

January Former Truman adviser Clark Clifford succeeds McNamara as secretary of defense. McNamara had alienated President Johnson by questioning the administration's escalation of the Vietnam War.

January 21–April 8 Five thousand U.S. marines and South Vietnamese soldiers are besieged by two North Vietnamese army divisions at Khe Sanh in the north of South Vietnam, in one of the fiercest battles of the entire Vietnam War.

January 30–February 29 The Vietcong launches the Tet offensive against South Vietnamese cities.

March A dispirited President Johnson appears on national television to say that he will not seek reelection. At the same time, he announces a partial bombing halt of North Vietnam and reports that he is ready to begin peace talks.

7   An economic agreement is announced between the European Economic Community (EEC) and 16 African states.

9   The National Democratic Party is banned in Southern Rhodesia (now Zimbabwe); within a week, its leader, Joshua Nkomo, founds the Zimbabwe African People's Union (ZAPU).

9   The USSR breaks off relations with Albania.

11 The first U.S. troops arrive in South Vietnam. The United States had promised to help the South Vietnamese against communist agression on October 10.

15 The United Nations (UN) General Assembly rejects a Soviet proposal for it to admit the People's Republic of China.

16 The United States agrees to make a loan to Ghana for the Volta River project (for the generation of hydroelectric power).

18 Indian forces invade the Portuguese territory of Goa on the east coast of India, claiming it as part of India. Goa surrenders on December 19.

21 President Moise Tshombe of Katanga province agrees to end its secession from the Congo Republic.

21–22 The U.S. president John F. Kennedy and the British prime minister Harold Macmillan meet in Bermuda to discuss relations with the USSR and nuclear weapons.

31 The Lebanese army prevents a coup by the Syrian Popular Party in Beirut, Lebanon.

March 16 U.S. soldiers massacre 450 men, women, and children at the village of My Lai, in South Vietnam. When news of the massacre emerges, some 20 months later, the troops will insist that they acted under the orders of lieutenant William L. Calley, Jr.

April U.S. Marines repel a three-month siege at a Special Forces camp in Khesanh, along the Mekong River in South Vietnam.

May 10 U.S. and North Vietnamese negotiators begin peace talks in Paris, France.

July 3 General William C. Westmoreland relinquishes command of U.S. forces in Vietnam, after losing President Johnson's confidence. Westmoreland is succeeded by General Creighton W. Abrams.

1969–75

1969

April U.S. B-52s drop an estimated 3,000 tons of bombs, a new record, on Vietcong positions near the Cambodian border in South Vietnam.

June 8 At a meeting with South Vietnamese president Nguyen Van Thieu on Midway Island, President Nixon announces that he will withdraw 25,000 U.S. troops from South Vietnam by the end of August. A further 35,000 troops are withdrawn on September 16.

1970

February U.S. national security adviser Henry Kissinger begins secret talks with his North Vietnamese counterpart Le Duc Tho.

April 30 U.S. and South Vietnamese forces attack communist enclaves in Cambodia following advances by communist forces under Pathet Lao.

May 1–4 Demonstrations begin at universities across the United States in protest at military intervention in Cambodia; the National Guard fire on a peaceful demonstration at Kent State University, Ohio, killing four students.

May 2 The United States bombs North Vietnam in the heaviest raids since November 1968.

1971

February 13 South Vietnamese troops invade Laos to close the Ho Chi Minh Trail to the North Vietnamese.

August 18 Australia and New Zealand announce the withdrawal of their forces from the Vietnam War.

November 12 President Nixon proclaims the end of the U.S. offensive role in the Vietnam War and withdraws 45,000 more troops.

1972

May 1 The South Vietnamese city of Quang Tri falls to North Vietnamese forces.

May 8 President Nixon orders the blockade and mining of North Vietnamese ports.

August 12 Heavy U.S. air raids on North Vietnam accompany the departure of U.S. combat infantry from South Vietnam.

September 7 South Korea withdraws its remaining 37,000 troops from South Vietnam.

September 15 South Vietnamese forces recapture the city of Quang Tri from the North Vietnamese.

December 18–30 U.S. forces carry out heavy bombing in North Vietnam.

1973

January 15 The U.S. president Richard M. Nixon orders a suspension of all military action against North Vietnam.

January 27 The United States, North and South Vietnam, and the Vietcong sign a Vietnam War cease-fire agreement in Paris.

1975

January 4 The province of Phuoc Binh in South Vietnam falls to invading North Vietnamese forces.

March 30 North Vietnamese forces capture Da Nang, South Vietnam's second largest city.

April 29 The last U.S. personnel flee Saigon, flying by helicopter from the U.S. embassy compound.

April 30 President Minh of South Vietnam surrenders Saigon to the North Vietnamese communist forces.

SCIENCE, TECHNOLOGY, AND MEDICINE

Computing

- IBM introduces the Selectric typewriter which has some basic word-processing capacity. Characters are arranged on a rotating sphere or "golf ball," rather than on individual arms. Because the sphere rotates there is no need for a moving carriage. It will account for over 70% of the electric typewriter market by the mid-1970s.

MAY
- The Atlas computer, the world's largest (with one megabyte of memory), is installed at Harwell, England, to aid atomic research and weather forecasting.

Ecology

- Chobe National Park, which contains a fossilized lake bed, and Gemsbok National Park, the largest national park in Africa, covering 24,305 sq km/9,384 sq mi, are established in Bechuanaland (now Botswana).
- Emission control devices are required on all new cars in California.
- The U.S. Congress creates Haleakala National Park on the Hawaiian island of Maui. The park consists of 26,403 acres on the site of the dormant Kaleakala Volcano.
- The World Wildlife Fund (now Worldwide Fund for Nature) is established to promote conservation.

May 1961–66 The northwest United States experiences the worst drought in U.S. history.

JANUARY
6 A fire at the Thomas Hotel in San Francisco, California, kills 20 people.

AUGUST
18–20 The U.S. Navy and the U.S. Environmental Sciences Service Administration initiate Project Stormfury, an attempt to modify hurricanes through seeding, by heavily seeding Hurricane Debbie with silver iodide. Wind speeds drop markedly.

SEPTEMBER
9 An international conference is held in Tanganyika (now Tanzania) for preserving African wildlife.

OCTOBER
10 A volcanic eruption takes place on the British dependency of Tristan da Cunha, and its inhabitants are evacuated (to return in 1963 and 1967).

NOVEMBER
6–9 A fire sweeps across the suburb of Bel Air in Los Angeles, California, destroying more than 400 homes.

Exploration

- The Soviet space probe *Venera 1* passes within 99,000 km/62,000 mi of Venus but fails to transmit data due to a telemetry failure.

- U.S. researchers establish Arctic Research Lab Ice Station II (Arliss II), a drifting sea ice station.

JANUARY
- The United States sends a second primate, this time a chimpanzee, 155 miles into space aboard a Project Mercury spacecraft. The chimp is successfully recovered.

APRIL
12 Soviet cosmonaut Yury Gagarin, in *Vostok 1*, is the first person to enter space. His flight lasts 108 minutes.

MAY
5 U.S. astronaut Alan Shepard in the Mercury capsule *Freedom 7* makes a 14.8-minute single suborbital flight. He is the first U.S. astronaut into space.
21 U.S. president John F. Kennedy commits the country to "landing a man on the moon and returning him safely to Earth before this decade is out." Following this he will ask Congress to allocate close to $2 billion for space exploration as part of his pledge.

AUGUST
7 Soviet cosmonaut Gherman Titov, the second cosmonaut to be launched into space, completes 17 orbits in 25.5 hours in *Vostok 2*, and becomes the first person to spend more than a day in space.

OCTOBER
27 The first two-stage *Saturn I* rocket is launched. The first rocket specifically designed for space flight, it is used to launch the Apollo spacecraft.

Health and Medicine

- Jean Nidetch founds Weight Watchers in New York, New York. Her system for losing weight is based on a low-protein diet and setting up networks of people to give mutual support at regular meetings. Weight Watchers is later bought by the food company Heinz.
- The U.S. pharmaceutical firm Johnson & Johnson introduces acetaminophen tablets as an alternative to aspirin; they market them as "Tylenol."
- U.S. physician Jack Lippes introduces the first intrauterine device (IUD) for birth control.

APRIL
- U.S. neurosurgeon Irving Cooper first uses cryosurgery to remove brain tumors. Cryogenic surgery is also first used to help patients with Parkinson's disease.

SEPTEMBER
8 A study published in the *Journal of the American Medical Association* reveals a statistical link between smoking tobacco and heart disease.

DECEMBER
- President John F. Kennedy urges Americans to adopt an exercise regime. Too many Army candidates, he remarks, are unfit for military service.

Math

- U.S. meteorologist Edward Lorenz discovers a mathematical system with chaotic behavior, leading to a new branch of mathematics known as chaos theory.

Science

- English molecular biologist Francis Crick and South African chemist Sydney Brenner discover that each base triplet on the DNA strand codes for a specific amino acid in a protein molecule.
- French biochemists François Jacob and Jacques Monod discover messenger ribonucleic acid (mRNA), which transfers genetic information to the ribosomes, where proteins are synthesized.
- Kenyan anthropologist Louis Leakey and English anthropologist Mary Leakey find the first fossilized remains of *Homo habilis* ("Handy Man") at Olduvai Gorge, Tanganyika (modern Tanzania). Makers of Oldowan stone tools—the oldest stone tools—they lived 1.15 to 1.7 million years ago.
- U.S. biochemist Melvin Calvin receives the Nobel Prize for Chemistry for his discoveries concerning the chemical processes of photosynthesis.
- U.S. chemist Albert Ghiorso and colleagues at the University of California, Berkeley, discover the radioactive element lawrencium (atomic no. 103), named for the U.S. physicist Ernest Lawrence.
- U.S. physicist Murray Gell-Mann and Israeli physicist Yuval Ne'eman independently propose a classification system for subatomic particles that comes to be known as the Eightfold Way.
- U.S. physicist Robert Hofstadter discovers that protons and neutrons have an internal structure.
- U.S. physicist Robert Hofstadter and German physicist Rudolf Ludwig Mössbauer share the Nobel Prize for Physics: Hofstadter for his work on electron scattering in atomic nuclei and his discoveries concerning the structure of nucleons; and Mössbauer for his discovery of the Mössbauer effect.
- U.S. physiologist Georg Von Békésy receives the Nobel Prize for Physiology or Medicine for his discoveries concerning the functioning of the inner ear.

Technology

- Maraging steel is invented in the United States. Containing 18% nickel plus cobalt, titanium, and molybdenum, it is ten times stronger than previous steel alloys.
- The first high-voltage submarine cables are laid under the English Channel from Dungeness, England, to Boulogne, France, a distance of 48 km/30 mi, in order to connect the national electricity grids of Britain and France. They carry 160,000 kilowatts of DC current at 200,000 volts.
- The U.S. Minuteman intercontinental ballistic missile (ICBM) is first launched. It uses a solid rocket fuel instead of liquid, making for a quicker response time. It is launched from underground concrete silos for maximum defense.
- The Vajont dam, Veneto, Italy is completed. It is the world's largest concrete arch dam to date at 262 m/858 ft high.
- U.S. firm Eastman Kodak introduces Kodachrome II color film, which is 2.5 times faster than Kodachrome.
- U.S. inventor George Devol and U.S. businessman Joseph Engelberger develop the first true robot, a programmable manipulator called "Programmed Article Transfer." Installed at General Motors by their company Unimation, it is used to unload parts from a die-casting operation.
- U.S. researcher Steven Hofstein designs the field-effect transistor used in integrated circuits.

Transportation

- A chartered plane crashes in the Shannon estuary in Ireland, killing 82 people.
- The French passenger liner *France* is launched. The longest ship in the world at 315 m/1,035 ft, it has an aluminum superstructure and fin stabilizers on its sides to reduce roll.
- The U.S. ship *Iwo Jima* is completed, the first ship designed and constructed for helicopters.
- Two U.S. Navy scientists establish a balloon altitude record of 35,000 m/113,500 ft, aboard *Stratolab No 5*.

December 1961–70   Increasing competition from the car and airplane results in a sharp decline in the number of railroad passengers.

MAY

1   Cuban exile Antulio Ramirez forces a National Airlines Convair, enroute from Miami to Key West, Florida, to land in Cuba. It is the world's first "skyjacking." Further skyjackings lead to the institution of searches at airports (1973).

28   The last journey of the "Orient Express," between Paris, France, and Bucharest, Romania, takes place after 78 years of service.

JULY

19   U.S. airline TWA is the first to introduce regular in-flight movies.

NOVEMBER

8   A plane carrying U.S. Army recruits crashes near Richmond, Virginia, killing 74 people.

ARTS AND IDEAS

Architecture

- The Amon Carter Museum in Fort Worth, Texas, designed by the U.S. architect Philip Johnson, is completed.
- The Upjohn Company Building, in Kalamazoo, Michigan, designed by the U.S. architectural firm of Skidmore, Owings, and Merrill, is completed.
- The U.S. Embassy in Athens, Greece, designed by the German architect Walter Gropius, is completed.

Arts

- The English photographer Bill Brandt publishes *Perspective of Nudes*, a photograph album.
- The English artist Anthony Caro sculpts *Sculpture Three*.
- The English artist David Hockney paints *Typhoo Tea*.
- The English artist Peter Phillips paints *For Men Only, MM and BB Starring*.

- The English artist Richard Hamilton creates the collage *She*.
- The French artist Niki de Saint-Phalle creates her first *Tir* paintings by shooting at bags filled with paint, which, on bursting, splash across a canvas.
- The Swedish-born U.S. artist Claes Oldenburg creates *Giant Hamburger with Pickle Attached*, a giant replica made of canvas.
- The U.S. artist Ellsworth Kelly paints *Orange White*.
- The U.S. artist George Segal sculpts *Gas Station*.
- The U.S. artist Roy Lichtenstein paints *Popeye*.
- The U.S. artist Tom Wesselman paints *Great American Nude No 1*, the first of a series.

MARCH

13 The Spanish painter Pablo Picasso, aged 79, marries Jacqueline Roque, aged 37.

Film

- The movie *A Soldier's Prayer*, directed by Masaki Kobayashi, is released in Japan. The third part of a trilogy entitled *The Human Condition*, it stars Tatsuya Nakadai and Michiyo Artama. The other parts are *No Greater Love* and *Road to Eternity*.
- The movie *A Taste of Honey*, directed by Tony Richardson, is released in Britain, starring Rita Tushingham, Dora Bryan, and Murray Melvin.
- The movie *Accatone*, directed by Pier Paolo Pasolini, is released in Italy, starring Franco Citti, Franca Pasut, and Silvana Corsini.
- The movie *Breakfast at Tiffany's*, directed by Blake Edwards, is released in the United States. Based on the novella by Truman Capote, it stars Audrey Hepburn and George Peppard.
- The movie *El Cid*, directed by Anthony Mann, is released in the United States, starring Charlton Heston and Sophia Loren.
- The movie *Jules et Jim*, directed by François Truffaut, is released in France, starring Jeanne Moreau, Oskar Werner, and Henri Serre.
- The movie *L'Année dernière à Marienbad/Last Year at Marienbad*, directed by Alain Resnais, is released in France, starring Delphine Seyrig, Giorgio Albertazzi, and Sacha Pitoeff.
- The movie *La Notte/The Night*, directed by Michelangelo Antonioni, is released in Italy, starring Marcello Mastroianni and Jeanne Moreau.
- The movie *The Guns of Navarone*, directed by J. Lee Thompson, is released in the United States, starring Gregory Peck and David Niven.
- The movie *The Hustler*, directed by Robert Rossen, is released in the United States, starring Paul Newman.
- The movie *The Misfits*, directed by John Huston, is released in the United States. Scripted by Arthur Miller, it stars Clark Gable, Marilyn Monroe, and Montgomery Clift.
- The movie *Through a Glass, Darkly*, directed by Ingmar Bergman, is released in Sweden, starring Harriet Andersson, Gunnar Bjornstrand, Max Von Sydow, and Lars Passgard.
- The movie *Two Women* or *La Ciociara*, directed by Vittorio De Sica, is released in Italy. Based on an Alberto Moravia story, it stars Sophia Loren.
- The movie *Une aussi longue absence/The Long Absence*, directed by Henri Colpi, is released in France, starring Alida Valli and Georges Wilson. It is awarded the Palme d'Or, with Buñuel's *Viridiana* at the French Cannes Film Festival later in the year.
- The movie *Victim*, directed by Basil Dearden, is released in Britain, starring Dirk Bogarde. It is one of the first mainstream movies to deal with homosexuality.
- The movie *Vie privée/A Very Private Affair*, directed by Louis Malle, is released in France, starring Marcello Mastroianni and Brigitte Bardot.
- The movie *Viridiana*, directed by Luis Buñuel, is released in Spain, starring Silvia Pinal and Fernando Rey. It tells the story of a novice about to take her vows who is debauched by an uncle with the complicity of the mother superior. The movie is criticized by the Spanish authorities and by the Vatican. It is the joint winner of the Palme d'Or, with Colpi's *The Long Absence* at the French Cannes Film Festival later in the year.
- The movie *Whistle down the Wind*, directed by Bryan Forbes, is released in Britain. Scripted by Keith Waterhouse, it stars Hayley Mills, Bernard Lee, and Alan Bates.
- The movie *Yojimbo*, directed by Akira Kurosawa, is released in Japan, starring Toshiro Mifune, Eijiro Tono, and Katamari Fujiwara.
- The movie version of Leonard Bernstein's musical *West Side Story*, directed by Robert Wise and Jerome Robbins, is released in the United States. A rewriting of Shakespeare's *Romeo and Juliet* set in New York, New York, it stars Natalie Wood, Richard Beymer, Rita Moreno, and George Chakiris.
- The Walt Disney animated cartoon *One Hundred and One Dalmatians*, based on the book by Dodie Smith, is released in the United States.

APRIL

17 The 1960 Academy Awards take place. Best Actor: Burt Lancaster, for *Elmer Gantry*; Best Supporting Actor: Peter Ustinov, for *Spartacus*; Best Actress: Elizabeth Taylor, for *Butterfield 8*; Best Supporting Actress: Shirley Jones, for *Elmer Gantry*; Best Picture: *The Apartment*, directed by Billy Wilder; Best Director: Billy Wilder, for *The Apartment*.

Literature and Language

- The Australian writer Patrick White publishes his novel *Riders in the Chariot*.
- The English writer Graham Greene publishes his novel *A Burnt Out Case*.
- The English writer Philip Toynbee publishes his novel *Pantaloon, or The Valediction*.
- The English writer Richard Hughes publishes his novel *The Fox in the Attic*.
- The French-born U.S. literary critic George Steiner publishes his critical work *The Death of Tragedy*.
- The German writer Günter Grass publishes his novel *Katz und Maus/Cat and Mouse*.
- The Guyanese writer Wilson Harris publishes his novel *The Far Journey*, the second part of his *The Guyana Quartet*.
- The Indian writer R. K. Narayan publishes his novel *The Man-eater of Malgudi*.

- The Irish writer Frank O'Connor publishes his autobiography *An Only Child*.
- The Irish-born English writer and philosopher Iris Murdoch publishes her novel *A Severed Head*.
- The Martinique writer Aimé Césaire publishes *Cadastre/Cadastre: Poems*.
- The Nobel Prize for Literature is awarded to the Yugoslav novelist Ivo Andrić.
- The Polish-born U.S. writer Isaac Bashevis Singer publishes his collection of short stories *The Spinoza of Market Street*, which first appeared in Yiddish in 1944.
- The Pulitzer Prize for Biography is awarded to David Donald for *Charles Sumner and the Coming of the Civil War*, the Pulitzer Prize for Poetry is awarded to Phyllis McGinley for *Times Three: Selected Verse From Three Decades*, and the Pulitzer Prize for Fiction is awarded to Harper Lee for *To Kill a Mockingbird*.
- The Russian writer Yevgeny Yevtushenko publishes his long poem "Babi Yar".
- The Scottish writer Muriel Spark publishes her novel *The Prime of Miss Jean Brodie*.
- The Trinidadian writer V. S. Naipaul publishes his novel *A House for Mr Biswas*.
- The U.S. writer Allen Ginsberg publishes his poetry collection *Kaddish*.
- The U.S. writer and critic Edmund Wilson publishes his poetry collection *Night Thoughts*.
- The U.S. writer Bernard Malamud publishes his novel *A New Life*.
- The U.S. writer Irving Stone publishes his *The Agony and the Ecstasy: A Biographical Novel of Michelangelo*.
- The U.S. writer J. D. Salinger publishes his story collection *Franny and Zooey*.
- The U.S. writer James Baldwin publishes *Nobody Knows My Name*, a collection of essays.
- The U.S. writer Joseph Heller publishes his novel *Catch 22*.
- The U.S. writer LeRoi Jones (from 1968 called Amiri Baraka) publishes his poetry collection *Preface to a Twenty Volume Suicide Note*.
- The U.S. writer Lewis Mumford publishes *The City in History*.
- The U.S. writer Robert Heinlein publishes his novel *Stranger in a Strange Land*.
- The U.S. writer Tillie Olsen publishes her story collection *Tell Me a Riddle*.

Music

- "Trad jazz," music based on traditional New Orleans-style jazz, becomes popular in Britain through the music of Acker Bilk, Kenny Ball, and Chris Barber.
- Soundtrack albums are very popular in the United States and Britain, with *South Pacific*, *Oklahoma!*, *The King and I*, and *Seven Brides for Seven Brothers* among those in the charts.
- The Beach Boys release their first single, "Surfin'." The group had formerly called itself the Pendletones, Kenny and the Cadets, and Carl and the Passions.
- The British cellist Jacqueline du Pré makes her debut as a soloist in London, England, aged 16.

- The British jazz clarinetist Acker Bilk (adapted from Bernard Stanley Bilk) releases the single "Stranger on the Shore." It is the most successful instrumental single ever in Britain, and debuts on U.S. charts March 16, 1962.
- The British pop singer Billy Fury releases the single "Halfway to Paradise."
- The British pop singer Helen Shapiro releases the single "Walking Back to Happiness."
- The British rock group the Rolling Stones is formed. Founder members include Mick Jagger, Keith Richard, Brian Jones, and Ian Stewart; the long-standing bassist Bill Wyman joins in late 1962, and drummer Charlie Watts in January 1963.
- The English composer Peter Maxwell Davies completes his String Quartet.
- The English composer Benjamin Britten completes his choral work *War Requiem* and his Cello Sonata No. 1.
- The English composer Michael Tippett completes his choral work *Magnificat and Nunc Dimittis*.
- The first elections to the Country Music Hall of Fame in Nashville, Tennessee, take place. They are held by and within the Country Music Association, and the first honorees are Jimmie Rodgers, Fred Rose, and Hank Williams (all deceased).
- The Hungarian-born Austrian composer György Ligeti completes his orchestral work *Atmosphères*.
- The Italian composer Luciano Berio completes his electronic work *Visage*.
- The Marvelettes' single "Please Mr. Postman" becomes the first chart number one from the Motown record label.
- The opera *Elegy for Young Lovers*, by the German composer Hans Werner Henze, is first performed, in Schwetzingen, Germany. The text is by the English-born U.S. writer W. H. Auden.
- The opera *Intolleranza 1960*, by the Italian composer Luigi Nono, is first performed in Venice, Italy.
- The opera *Recké pašije/The Greek Passion*, by the Czech composer Bohuslav Martinů, is first performed, posthumously, in Zürich, Switzerland.
- The Polish composer Witold Lutosławski completes his *Gry weneckie/Venetian Games*.
- The Russian composer Igor Stravinsky completes his cantata *A Sermon, A Narrative, A Prayer*.
- The Shadows become the first British rock group to top the UK album charts, with *The Shadows*.
- The twist dance craze takes off in the United States, inspired by Chubby Checker's song "The Twist." It will change the way young people dance, introducing a more freeform style.
- The U.S. composer Elliott Carter completes his Double Concerto for Harpsichord and Piano.
- The U.S. composer/conductor Henry Mancini and his orchestra release the single "Moon River," from the soundtrack to the movie *Breakfast at Tiffany's*.
- The U.S. country singer Patsy Cline releases the singles "I Fall to Pieces" and "Crazy." The latter will remain a major juke-box hit in the United States for decades.
- The U.S. female vocal group the Shirelles release the single "Mama Said."
- The U.S. pop singer Bobby Vee releases the single "Poetry in Motion."
- The U.S. pop singer Neil Sedaka releases the single "Happy Birthday, Sweet Sixteen."

- The U.S. record industry launches a series of 17.5 cm/7 in, six-track mini-LPs, but they do not catch on.
- The U.S. rock singer Elvis Presley's album *G I Blues*, the soundtrack from the movie, is this year's best-selling album in Britain.
- The U.S. singer Ben E. King releases the single "Stand By Me."
- The U.S. singer Bobby Lewis releases the single "Tossin' and Turnin'."
- The U.S. singer Frank Sinatra launches his own record label Reprise, in response to the increasing popularity of rock and roll music.
- The U.S. singer/songwriter Roy Orbison releases the singles "Running Scared" and "Crying."

April 1961–62 *Hootenanny*, a music show with folk singers that is broadcast from a different college campus each week, is shown on U.S. television.

MARCH

21 The British rock group the Beatles make their British debut at the Cavern Club in Liverpool, England.

APRIL

9 Police attempt to remove gathering folk singers from Washington Square Park in New York, New York, starting a short riot.

12 The 1959–60 Grammy Awards take place. Best Album: *Button Down Mind* by Bob Newhart; Best Record: "Theme from a Summer Place" by Henry Mancini; Best Male Vocalist: Ray Charles; Best Female Vocalist: Ella Fitzgerald; Best Group: Steve Lawrence and Eydie Gorme.

JUNE

2 The first successful prosecution of a record bootlegger (someone who makes and distributes illegal copies of sound recordings) takes place, in New Jersey.

JULY

6 The alternative music magazine *Mersey Beat* is launched in Liverpool, England. The first issue carries an article by local beat musician John Lennon.

SEPTEMBER

6 The U.S. folk/rock singer Bob Dylan makes his debut at the Gaslight Café in Greenwich Village, New York, New York, appearing with blues musician John Lee Hooker.

Theater and Dance

- The play *Andorra*, by the Swiss writer Max Frisch, is first performed, in Zürich, Switzerland.
- The play *Luther*, by the English dramatist John Osborne, is first performed, at the Theatre Royal in Nottingham, England.
- The play *The American Dream*, by the U.S. dramatist Edward Albee, is first performed, in New York, New York.
- The play *The Devils*, by the English dramatist John Whiting, is first performed in London, England.
- The play *The Night of the Iguana*, by the U.S. dramatist Tennessee Williams, is first performed at the Royale Theater in New York City.
- The Pulitzer Prize for Drama is awarded to Tad Mosel for *All the Way Home*.

MARCH

8 The play *Mary, Mary*, written by U.S. playwright Jean Kerr and starring Barbara Bel Geddes, is first performed, at the Helen Hayes Theater in New York, New York.

APRIL

13 The musical *Carnival*, with music and lyrics by Bob Merrill, is first performed at the Imperial Theater, New York, New York.

16 The 1960–61 Tony Awards take place. Best Play: *Beckett*; Best Musical: *Bye, Bye, Birdie*; Best Actor: Zero Mostel; Best Actress: Joan Plowright.

JUNE

16 The Soviet ballet star Rudolf Nureyev defects to the West while at Le Bourget airport in Paris, France.

OCTOBER

14 The musical comedy *How to Succeed in Business Without Really Trying*, by Abe Burrows, Jack Weinstock, Willie Gilbert, and Frank Loesser, based on the book by Sheperd Mead, opens at the 46th Street Theater in New York, New York.

NOVEMBER

30 The play *All the Way Home*, by Tad Mosel, based on the James Agee novel *A Death in the Family*, is first performed, at the Belasco Theater in New York, New York.

Thought and Scholarship

- The Czech-born U.S. philosopher Ernest Nagel publishes *The Structure of Science: Problems in the Logic of Scientific Explanation*.
- The English historian A. J. P. Taylor publishes *The Origins of the Second World War*, a revisionist study of Adolf Hitler's motives.
- The French philosopher Michel Foucault publishes *Folie et déraison: histoire de la folie à l'âge classique/History of Madness*.
- The German philosopher Martin Heidegger publishes *Nietzsche*.
- The Pulitzer Prize for History is awarded to Herbert Feis for *Between War and Peace: The Potsdam Conference*.
- The Scottish psychologist R. D. Laing publishes *The Self and Others*.
- U.S. psychologist Carl Rogers publishes *On Becoming a Person*.

SOCIETY

Education

- The President's Council on Youth Fitness publishes its Youth Physical Fitness booklet in the United States; it critiques the poor fitness of the country's youth and outlines a program for improvement in United States's schools.

Everyday Life

- Barbara Terry, the daughter of a hairdresser, invents the Afro hairstyle in the United States.
- Dr. William Scholl invents the Scholl sandal in the United States. The functional footwear will enjoy a revival as a fashion accessory in the mid-1990s.
- Julia Child publishes *Mastering the Art of French Cooking* in the United States, which becomes one of the best-selling cookbooks in the country.
- Kodak markets the first carousel slide projector, the Kodak 550, in the United States.
- Mattel Toys launches the Ken doll, a boyfriend for Barbie, in the United States.
- The British toy company Pedigree launches the Sindy doll, as a competitor to the very popular Barbie.
- The Carnation Co. launches Coffee-Mate, a nondairy whitener for coffee, in the United States.
- The Coca-Cola Company launches "Sprite," a lemon–lime flavoured carbonated soft drink, as a competitor to "7 Up" (produced by the company 7 Up).
- The popular doll Barbie abandons her ponytail and adopts a bubble hairdo, in the United States.
- The Squibb Co., New York, New York, manufactures the first electric toothbrush.
- The Swiss yogurt Ski goes on sale in Britain. It is the first fruit-flavored yogurt on the market.
- The U.S. ice-cream manufacturer Reuben Mattus creates a range of high-quality ice creams and invents a name which will suggest richness and a European origin—Häagen-Dazs.
- U.S. cigarette manufacturers spend over $110 million on television advertising, compared to $40 million in 1957.

FEBRUARY

22 The National Council of Churches, meeting in Syracuse, New York, endorses birth control as a means of family planning.

APRIL

- A recent poll reveals that 72% of U.S. secondary school teachers endorse the use of corporal punishment.
1 One study finds that 50,000 Cuban refugees live in Miami, Florida.

MAY

1 The Area Redevelopment Act provides funding for government programs to alleviate poverty and create jobs in depressed areas of the United States.
9 Federal Communications Commission chairman, Newton N. Minow, castigates TV programmers for rendering television a "vast wasteland." Rather than catering to the nation's "whims," they must serve the nation's "needs."

Media and Communication

- *The Old Man and the Hawk*, by Junichi Ushiyama, is broadcast in Japan.

BIRTHS & DEATHS

- Frank Bruno, English heavyweight boxer, world champion 1995–96, born in London, England.

JANUARY

1 Patrice Lumumba, first elected president of the Democratic Republic of the Congo 1960, is assassinated in Katanga, Congo (35).
4 Erwin Schrödinger, Austrian physicist who developed the wave theory of matter, dies in Vienna, Austria (73).
26 Wayne Gretzky, Canadian ice-hockey player, born in Brantford, Ontario, Canada.
31 Dorothy Thompson, U.S. feminist leader, broadcaster and journalist, dies in Lancaster, New York (66).

APRIL

6 Jules Bordet, Belgian bacteriologist who received the Nobel Prize for Physiology or Medicine in 1919 for his discovery of immune factors in the blood, dies in Brussels, Belgium (90).

MAY

4 Maurice Merleau-Ponty, French phenomenologist philosopher, dies in Paris, France (53).
13 Gary Cooper, U.S. actor, dies in Los Angeles, California (61).

JUNE

2 George S. Kaufman, U.S. playwright and stage director, dies in New York, New York (71).
6 Carl Jung, Swiss psychologist who founded analytic psychology, dies in Küsnacht, Switzerland (85).
30 Lee De Forest, U.S. physicist and inventor who invented the audion vacuum tube, a major component of early radios, telephones, televisions, and computers, dies in Hollywood, California (87).

JULY

1 Lady Diana Spencer, Princess of Wales, humanitarian, and charity worker, born at Park House, Sandringham, Norfolk (–1997).
2 Ernest Hemingway, U.S. novelist who wrote *A Farewell to Arms* (1929) and *For Whom the Bell Tolls* (1941), commits suicide in Ketchum, Idaho (61).
17 Ty Cobb (nicknamed "the Georgia Peach"), U.S. baseball player whose lifetime batting average (.367) remains unequaled, dies in Atlanta, Georgia (74).

AUGUST

20 Percy Williams Bridgman, U.S. physicist who was the first to experiment on materials at extremely high pressures, winner of the Nobel Prize for Physics in 1946, dies in Randolph, New Hampshire (79).

SEPTEMBER

1 Eero Saarinen, Finnish-born U.S. architect, dies in Ann Arbor, Michigan (51).
18 Dag Hammarskjöld, Swedish statesman and second secretary-general of the United Nations 1953–61, dies in an airplane crash near Ndola, Northern Rhodesia (now Zambia) (56).

OCTOBER

11 Steve Young, U.S. football player, born in Salt Lake City, Utah.
30 Luigi Einaudi, first president of the Republic of Italy (1948–55), dies in Rome, Italy (87).

NOVEMBER

2 James Thurber, U.S. writer and cartoonist, dies in New York, New York (66).
16 Sam Rayburn, U.S. Democratic Party leader and speaker of the House of Representatives 1937–54, dies in Bonham, Texas (79).

- FM radio stations begin broadcasting in stereo, in the United States.
- The news agency Novosti is founded in the USSR. It is set up to distribute material to foreign publications as well as to Soviet ones.
- The U.S. comedian Lenny Bruce is arrested for obscenity.

May 1961–63 *Yogi Bear*, a U.S. children's animated series about two bears living in Jellystone National Park, appears on U.S. television; it is a Hanna-Barbera production.

APRIL

9–March 7, 1966 *The Dick Van Dyke Show*, starring Dick Van Dyke as the comedy writer Robert Petrie and Mary Tyler Moore as his wife, is shown on U.S. television. The series is the first to integrate the characters' work with their home lives. Mory Amsterdam, Rose Marie, Richard Deacon, and Carl Reiner also star.

SEPTEMBER

16–September 9, 1965 *The Defenders*, a dramatic series about a father-and-son law firm, starring E. G. Marshall and Robert Reed, appears on U.S. television.

27–September 26, 1962 *Top Cat*, a Hanna-Barbera cartoon series about a gang of alley cats in New York, New York, appears on U.S. television.

28–August 30, 1966 *Dr Kildare*, a hospital drama, appears on U.S. television. Starring Richard Chamberlain and Raymond Massey, it is based on characters created by Max Brand.

OCTOBER

- The U.S. *Coronet Magazine* ceases publication after 25 years.

1 *Mister Ed*, a situation comedy about a talking horse, starring Alan Young, Connie Hines, and Larry Keating, starts on U.S. television; the voice of Mister Ed is supplied by Allan "Rocky" Lane.

2–March 21, 1966 The medical drama *Ben Casey* appears on U.S. television, starring Vince Edwards, Sam Jaffe, Bettye Ackerman, Harry Landers, Nick Dennis, and Franchot Tone.

DECEMBER

31 Radio Eireann launches a television service in Ireland.

Sports

- Anton Geesink of the Netherlands becomes the first non-Japanese winner of the World Judo Championships, in Paris, France.
- Janet Harman of the United States wins the inaugural Women's National Bowling Association Queen's Tournament.
- The Los Angeles Angels baseball team (from 1965 the California Angels) joins the American League.

JANUARY

1 The Houston Oilers defeat the Los Angeles Chargers 24–16 in the inaugural American Football League Championship Game before a crowd of 32,183 spectators in Houston, Texas.

FEBRUARY

3 The New Zealand runner Peter Snell sets a new 800 meters world record of 1 min 44.3 sec in Christchurch, New Zealand, an improvement of 1.4 seconds on the existing record set by Roger Moens of Belgium in 1955.

APRIL

2–11 For the second straight year, the Boston Celtics beat the St. Louis Hawks to win the National Basketball Association (NBA) championship.

6–16 The Chicago Black Hawks defeat the Detroit Red Wings by four games to two to win the National Hockey League Stanley Cup.

10 Gary Player of South Africa becomes the first non-U.S. citizen to win the U.S. Masters golf tournament, at Augusta, Georgia.

MAY

28 Mañuel Santana wins the men's singles at the French tennis championships to become the first Spaniard ever to hold a Grand Slam title.

JULY

16 Iolanda Balas of Romania sets her 14th women's high-jump world record. Since 1956 she has improved the record from 1.75 m/5.74 ft to 1.91 m/6.26 ft, including the first jump of 6 ft by a woman, in 1958.

SEPTEMBER

- Antonio Abertondo of Argentina becomes the first swimmer to achieve a double crossing of the English Channel, swimming from England to France and back in 43 hours and 5 minutes.

10 Phil Hill in a Ferrari becomes the first U.S. driver to win the Formula One World Drivers' Championship.

OCTOBER

1 The U.S. baseball player Roger Maris of the New York Yankees hits his 61st home run of the season to surpass fellow Yankee Babe Ruth's major league record of 60 home runs set in 1927. However, because Ruth's record came in a 154-game season, as against the 162-game season played by Maris, Ruth's achievement remains alongside that of Maris in the official record books.

4–9 The New York Yankees defeat the Cincinnati Reds by four games to win the World Series.

DECEMBER

31 The Green Bay Packers defeat the New York Giants 37–0 in Green Bay, Wisconsin, to capture their first National Football League (NFL) Championship for 17 years.

1962

POLITICS, GOVERNMENT, AND ECONOMICS

Business and Economics

- The S. S. Kregge Co. launches the chain of K. Mart discount stores in the United States, opening several stores at the same time. Their form now is "Kmart."
- The U.S. economist Milton Friedman publishes *Capitalism and Freedom*.
- The U.S. historian Alfred Chandler, Jr., publishes *Strategy and Structure: Chapters in the History of the American Industrial Enterprise*.

JANUARY

- Directors of American Airlines and Eastern Airlines announce plans to merge their companies. Stockholders authorize the merger on April 17.

APRIL

- As if to pit the U.S. public against the nation's steelworkers, United States Steel Company raises steel prices roughly 3.5% in the wake of a new union contract. After other steel companies follow suit, President John F. Kennedy castigates the companies' avarice. On April 13 the companies cancel the price hike after Inland Steel declines to raise its prices.

MAY

- The American Federation of Labor and the Congress of Industrial Organizations (AFL-CIO) begins a campaign for a 35-hour work week.
- The value of stocks on the New York stock exchange falls by $20.8 billion in a single day, the largest such loss since October 29, 1929. This time the market quickly recovers.

AUGUST

20 The U.S. national debts tops $300 billion for the first time.

Colonization

JULY

1 The Rwandan Republic and the Kingdom of Burundi (both former United Nations (UN) trusteeships) become independent.

AUGUST

6 Jamaica becomes independent within the British Commonwealth.

31 Trinidad and Tobago (previously members of the West Indies Federation) becomes an independent nation within the British Commonwealth.

OCTOBER

9 Uganda gains independence within the British Commonwealth.

Human Rights

MARCH

- Archbishop Joseph Francis Rummel orders all Roman Catholic schools in New Orleans, Louisiana, to desegregate.

APRIL

3 The U.S. Defense Department orders the desegregation of all National Guard units.

SEPTEMBER

20 Mississippi governor Ross R. Barnett defies a federal court order and refuses to admit black student James Meredith to the University of Mississippi.

30 A riot ensues after federal marshals escort black student James Meredith to register at the University of Mississippi; two people are killed in the mêlée.

NOVEMBER

20 The U.S. president John F. Kennedy signs an executive order banning discrimination by race in housing built with the aid of federal funds.

Politics and Government

- A new constitution is promulgated in Pakistan, establishing presidential government. The president is chief executive and appoints government ministers.
- President John F. Kennedy appoints the jurists Arthur J. Goldberg and Byron R. White to the U.S. Supreme Court.
- Press censorship is officially lifted in Spain, though this is not entirely fulfilled in practice.
- The European Economic Community (EEC) reaches agreement on a Common Agricultural Policy.
- The press in South Africa establishes the Press Board of Reference to deal with complaints of misreporting; it enables the press to escape direct state control.

JANUARY

- The U.S. State Department refuses passports to U.S. communists, thereby prohibiting them from traveling abroad.
- The U.S. withdraws its tanks from the Berlin Wall in an attempt to defuse U.S.–Soviet hostility.
- Trade representatives of the United States and the Common Market nations agree to reduce tariffs.

1 Western Samoa, previously administered by New Zealand, becomes the first sovereign independent Polynesian state.

6 The three rival princes of Laos are invited to Geneva, Switzerland, for joint negotiations; they accept on January 11.

9 A trade pact is agreed between Cuba and the USSR.

18 The central African territory of Rwanda-Urundi appeals to the United Nations (UN) to be granted independence.

22 Julius Nyerere resigns as prime minister of Tanganyika (now Tanzania) in order to devote himself to the Tanganyika African National Union; Rashidj Kawawa replaces him.

25 African heads of state of the Monrovia group (Liberia, Togo, Nigeria, and Cameroon) issue the Lagos Charter for Pan-African cooperation.

29 The three-power (United States, USSR, and Britain) Conference on the Discontinuance of Nuclear Weapon Tests, which has met 353 times at Geneva, Switzerland, since October 31, 1958, finally collapses.

FEBRUARY

- The U.S. Supreme Court rules unconstitutional segregated facilities in interstate travel enterprises.
- U-2 pilot Francis Gary Powers, imprisoned in the Soviet Union, is exchanged for Soviet spy Rudolf Abel.

7 An order by U.S. president John F. Kennedy banning virtually all U.S. trade with Cuba comes into effect.

8 A U.S. Military Assistance Command is established in South Vietnam to aid its fight against communist insurgents.

10 The Soviet leader Nikita Khrushchev proposes that an 18-nation disarmament committee should meet at summit level.

14 A constitutional conference on Kenya opens in London, England, where, on March 21, agreement is reached for the establishment of a two-chamber parliament and regional assemblies.

16 Antigovernment riots break out in Georgetown, British Guiana (now Guyana), in protest at austerity measures in the budget (announced January 31).

17–19 A general election in Malta is won by Dr. Borg Olivier's Nationalist Party with 25 seats, while Labour take 16 seats, and other parties take 9.

MARCH

- E. I. du Pont de Nemours & Company comes out on the losing end of the nation's biggest antitrust suit; a federal district court orders the company to discharge 63 million shares of General Motors stock.
- First Lady Jacqueline Kennedy begins a goodwill mission to Italy, the Vatican, India, and Pakistan.
- President John F. Kennedy informs Congress that the U.S., the European Economic Community, the UK, and 24 other nations have agreed to broad tariff reductions.
- The U.S. House of Representatives passes legislation to aid in the retraining of unemployed workers over the next three years.
- The U.S. Justice Department sues the Communist Party and four leading officials to recover $500,000 in back taxes.

1 The British protectorate of Uganda attains full internal self-government, with Benedicto Kiwanuka as prime minister.

2 A military coup in Burma (now Myanmar), led by General Ne Win, overthrows the government of Prime Minister U Nu.

8 U.S. president John F. Kennedy and Soviet premier Nikita Khrushchev agree to a two-year program of cultural and scientific exchange.

14 Seventeen foreign ministers attend a disarmament conference in Geneva, Switzerland, but France refuses to participate.

18 Following secret discussions (completed at Evian-les-Bains, France), the French government and the Provisional Government of Algeria make the "Evian agreements," under which a provisional Muslim–French government is to be installed in Algeria and a referendum is to be held on self-determination.

19 West Germany agrees to contribute to the costs of the British Army of the Rhine (BAOR).

21 The first of several parliamentary debates takes place in Britain on whether Nigerian opposition leader Chief Enahoro is a political refugee and deserves asylum status.

22 U.S. and South Vietnamese forces mount "Operation Sunrise" against communist guerrillas.

23 Denmark, Finland, Iceland, Norway, and Sweden sign the Helsinki Convention on mutual cooperation.

APRIL

- The U.S. Defense Department orders the integration of the nation's military reserves.
- The United States resumes atmospheric nuclear testing after a three-year moratorium.

April–May Renewed fighting breaks out in Laos between the forces of the rightist government of Prince Boun Owm and the communist Pathet Lao opposition, despite the cease-fire agreed in May 1961 and continuing negotiations between the three main political factions.

11 Following elections, the Labour politician Alexander Bustamante forms a ministry in Jamaica.

14 The Radical Michel Debré resigns as prime minister of France and is succeeded, on April 15, by the Gaullist Georges Pompidou.

18 Following Jamaica's vote (in September 1961) to leave the British West Indies Federation, the British Parliament passes the West Indies Act, dissolving the federation.

20 The rebel French leader in Algeria, Raoul Salan (who was tried in absentia in 1961), is captured in Algiers, Algeria.

25 Milton Obote's Congress Party wins the first elections held in Uganda.

27 The United Federal Party is returned to power in elections in the Central African Federation, which are boycotted by the European Opposition and all the African political parties.

MAY

- The U.S. Justice Department vows to prosecute federally-funded hospitals that maintain racial segregation.
- The United States detonates the first submarine-launched nuclear warhead off Christmas Island in the Pacific.

May–July The United States sends the first of several thousand soldiers to Thailand to prevent communist forces from overrunning Laos. The troops are withdrawn by July 27.

6   Antonio Segni is elected president of Italy on a ninth ballot.

12   A South African General Law Amendment Bill imposes the death penalty for sabotage in response to the growth of political terrorism.

12   Negotiations are held in Laos between the leaders of the three warring parties, who reach agreement. A Provisional Government of National Unity is established on May 22, with Prince Souvanna Phouma as president.

18   The Progressive Conservatives lose their overall majority in the Canadian elections, but John Diefenbaker remains prime minister. The Conservatives win 116 seats, the Liberals 100, and others 49.

24   Barbados, the Windward Islands, and the Leeward Islands meet at a conference in London, England, which ends with a proposal for the "Little Eight" to form a new West Indies federation without Jamaica and Trinidad and Tobago.

30   A new constitution for the British protectorate of Swaziland awards the resident white minority a permanent position in the government there.

JUNE

• President John F. Kennedy creates the Office of Science and Technology to spur U.S. research and development.

• The U.S. Supreme Court overturns a New York State law sanctioning official prayer in public schools.

14   The European Space Research Organization is established in Paris, France.

22   The Philippines claim sovereignty over part of British North Borneo (rejected by Britain, on August 7).

JULY

July–August   The United States suspends diplomatic relations with Peru after a military coup. Relations are reestablished on August 17, after civil rule is restored.

1   Robert Soblen, sentenced to life imprisonment in the United States for spying, arrives in London, England, following deportation from Jordan. The British home secretary refuses to grant asylum and Soblen commits suicide on September 11.

3   France proclaims the independence of Algeria following a referendum (first) showing 91% in favor; the provisional government in exile takes power.

16   The General Agreement on Tariffs and Trade (GATT) tariff conference, opened in September 1960, closes having negotiated substantial trade concessions.

23   A conference in Geneva, Switzerland, sitting since May 1961, guarantees the neutrality of Laos. The conference ends on July 23, and Laos reverts to civil war by early 1964.

31   The British and Malayan governments sign an agreement to establish a wider Malaysian Federation by August 31, including Malaya, Singapore, Sarawak, and North Borneo.

AUGUST

• At resumed nuclear disarmament talks in Geneva, the USSR rejects a U.S. and British proposal to ban nuclear tests and submit the issue of compliance to international inspection.

• President John F. Kennedy awards a gold medal for distinguished public service to Food and Drug administrator Dr. Frances O. Kelsey. Kelsey had worked doggedly to keep the teratogenic drug thalidomide off the U.S. market.

• President John F. Kennedy announces that two U.S. nuclear submarines achieved a successful rendezvous beneath the polar ice cap.

• The U.S. Congress appropriates $48 billion for defense for the next fiscal year.

• The U.S. Congress sends the 24th Amendment to the states. It prohibits poll taxes in federal elections.

7   The United Arab Republic (UAR) of Egypt signs an agreement for compensating British subjects whose property was seized after the Suez Crisis of 1956.

8   The leader of the South African organization *Umkonto we Sizwe* (" Spear of the Nation"), Nelson Mandela, is arrested when returning to Johannesburg, South Africa, from Natal. He is tried in November, and convicted of inciting workers to strike and of leaving the country without valid documents. He is sentenced to five years in prison.

15   Following mediation by the United Nations (UN), the Netherlands and Indonesia settle their dispute over West New Guinea. The UN is to administer the territory from October 1 to May 1, 1963, after which Indonesia is to assume sovereignty over the region.

16   An agreement is signed in London, England, for the British protectorate of Aden to enter the Federation of Saudi Arabia no later than March 1963.

16   The newly-independent state of Algeria is admitted to the Arab League.

SEPTEMBER

• A U.S. appellate court finds Mississippi governor Ross R. Barnett in contempt for his failure to desegregate the state university.

• In response to deteriorating East–West relations, the U.S. Congress summons 150,000 reservists to active duty and extends current enlistment terms.

• President John F. Kennedy signs legislation enacting the Area Development Act, allocating $900 million for domestic public works projects in impoverished communities.

• President John F. Kennedy signs the Food and Agricultural Act, establishing production quotas on surplus agricultural crops.

• To offset the United States's mounting trade deficit and halt the drainage of the nation's gold reserves, the Defense Department proposes selling U.S. military equipment to West Germany, France, and Italy.

1   The British colonies of Singapore and, on September 12, North Borneo vote to join the Malaysian Federation.

2   The USSR agrees to send arms to Cuba.

3   The government of the secessionist Katanga province of the Congo Republic accepts the plan of U Thant, the United Nations (UN) secretary-general, for reunification of the Congo.

7   Laos establishes diplomatic relations with the People's Republic of China and North Vietnam.

8   Chinese troops cross the "McMahon line" on India's northeastern border, in the border dispute between the two countries.

9–13   France resumes relations with Syria, Jordan, and Saudi Arabia.

20 The government of Southern Rhodesia (now Zimbabwe) declares the Zimbabwe African People's Union (agitating for black majority rule) an unlawful body.

25 The Cuban leader Fidel Castro states that the USSR intends to establish a base for its fishing fleet in Cuba.

26 The nationalist Ahmed Ben Bella is elected prime minister of Algeria.

27 A military coup in North Yemen overthrows Imam Mohammed. The coup is led by Colonel Abdullah al-Sallal and begins a civil war (–1965).

OCTOBER

• The U.S. Congress authorizes President John F. Kennedy to negotiate independently with foreign nations to lower tariffs and to relieve U.S. firms and individuals hurt by tariff reduction.

1 The United Nations (UN) takes over the administration of West New Guinea from Britain.

5 The French national assembly censures a proposed referendum for direct election of the president; the prime minister Georges Pompidou resigns, but President Charles de Gaulle asks him to continue in office.

10 The German newspaper *Der Spiegel* publishes an article on a North Atlantic Treaty Organization (NATO) exercise, criticizing the weakness of the West German army. The offices of the paper are occupied by the police on October 16.

16 A cease-fire is agreed, suspending fighting in the Congo Republic.

20–November 22 China launches a major offensive on Indian border positions in the frontier dispute between the two countries.

22 The Cuban Missile Crisis begins. The U.S. president John F. Kennedy announces that the USSR has installed a missile base in Cuba, and declares a naval blockade to prevent missile shipments.

26 In the Cuban Missile Crisis, the Soviet leader Nikita Khrushchev states that he is prepared to remove missiles from Cuba if the United States removes its missiles from Turkey. The U.S. president John F. Kennedy rejects the condition and states that work on the missile bases in Cuba must stop.

28 A referendum in France favors the election of the president by universal suffrage.

28 The Soviet leader Nikita Khrushchev announces that he has ordered the withdrawal of nuclear missiles from Cuba, and the U.S. president John F. Kennedy promises the United States will not invade Cuba, thus ending the Cuban Missile Crisis.

30 The United Nations (UN) General Assembly rejects a Soviet proposal to admit the People's Republic of China.

31 Following Chinese attacks on India's frontier, the Indian defense minister Krishna Menon is dismissed and Prime Minister Jawaharlal Nehru takes over his duties.

31 The United Nations (UN) General Assembly requests Britain to suspend the enforcement of a new constitution in Southern Rhodesia (now Zimbabwe) until majority rule is guaranteed, but the constitution comes into effect on November 1.

NOVEMBER

• In U.S. Congressional elections, Democrats retain majorities in the House (258–177) and Senate (67–33).

2 Julius Nyerere is elected president of Tanganyika (now Tanzania).

5 Saudi Arabia breaks off diplomatic relations with the United Arab Republic (UAR) of Egypt, following a period of unrest partly caused by the defection of several Saudi princes to Egypt.

5 The West German defense minister Franz Joseph Strauss is relieved of his duties over the *Spiegel* affair, because it is alleged that he was involved in police action against the magazine. On November 19, five Free Democrat ministers resign in protest at government involvement in the incident.

8 In a nationally televised address, President John F. Kennedy proclaims the Cuban Missile Crisis over. The United States declares it is satisfied that the USSR has dismantled its missile bases in Cuba.

9 A constitutional conference in London, England, on British Guiana (now Guyana) breaks down.

20 The USSR agrees to withdraw Ilyushin bombers from Cuba, and the United States announces the end of its blockade.

21 Following a threat of U.S. military aid for India, China agrees to a cease-fire on the Sino-Indian border and its forces subsequently withdraw.

27 Britain signs an agreement to provide India with arms to resist Chinese aggression.

27 Nigerian opposition leader Chief Enahoro is arrested in Britain for plotting against the Nigerian government.

29 A British–French agreement is signed to develop the *Concorde* supersonic airliner.

30 U Thant of Burma (now Myanmar) is elected United Nations (UN) secretary-general, having served as temporary secretary-general since the death of Swedish statesman Dag Hammarskjöld on September 18, 1961.

DECEMBER

• A federal jury convicts the U.S. Communist Party of failing to register as an agent of a foreign country (in this case, the Soviet Union). The party is fined $10,000.

• A group of private U.S. citizens negotiates the release of the Cuban exiles captured by Cuba in the Bay of Pigs fiasco in exchange for $50 million in food and medicine.

• Mississippi governor Ross R. Barnett is indicted for criminal contempt of court in the U.S. Fifth Circuit Court of Appeals in New Orleans, Louisiana. Barnett is charged with ignoring a court order to admit James H. Meredith (a black student) to the state university.

4 The Western European Union Assembly in Paris, France, calls for a single North Atlantic Treaty Organization (NATO) nuclear force.

5 The United States and the USSR sign an agreement on cooperation for the peaceful use of outer space.

9 Tanganyika (now Tanzania) becomes a republic within the Commonwealth, with Julius Nyerere as president.

11 A West German coalition government of Christian Democrats, Christian Socialists, and Free Democrats is formed following a cabinet crisis over the inclusion of right wing Bavarian Christian Social Union leader Franz Joseph Strauss, who is replaced by Kai-Uwe von Hassel.

14 In elections in Southern Rhodesia (now Zimbabwe), Winston Field's right-wing Rhodesian Front defeats Prime Minister Edgar Whitehead's United Federal Party.

14 The first African-dominated government in Northern Rhodesia (now Zambia) is formed under Kenneth Kaunda.

19 The U.S. president John F. Kennedy and the British prime minister Harold Macmillan meet at a conference in Nassau, the Bahamas, where the United States agrees to supply Britain with Polaris missiles instead of Skybolt. A crisis had occurred in the "special relationship" when the United States decided not to supply Skybolt as agreed.

27 India and Pakistan reopen talks on the disputed Kashmir province.

28 United Nations (UN) troops are engaged in heavy fighting with rebels in Katanga province, Congo Republic, and, on December 29, they occupy Elisabethville (now Lubumbashi).

SCIENCE, TECHNOLOGY, AND MEDICINE

Agriculture

- Gaines, a semidwarf variety of wheat, is introduced in the United States. Grown under irrigation and with heavy use of fertilizer, it dramatically increases crop yields.
- The Rockefeller and Ford Foundations found the Rice Research Institute in the Philippines and begin cross-breeding more than 10,000 different strains of rice.

Computing

- IBM builds the 7030 computer for the Los Alamos Laboratories, New Mexico. It contains 169,100 transistors and is 30 times faster than IBM's 704 mainframe computer.
- Magnetic discs begin to replace magnetic tape as the main means of storing computer data.

Ecology

- Part of the north summit of Mt Huascaran, Peru's highest mountain, breaks off during a thaw; 3,500 people are killed.
- The Petrified Forest National Park, Arizona, containing Native American ruins and a fossilized forest, is established.
- U.S. biologist Rachel Carson, in her book *Silent Spring*, draws attention to the dangers of chemical pesticides.
- Whaling has reduced the humpback whale population to an estimated 1,000.

FEBRUARY

16 Nearly half a million people flee their homes near Hamburg, Germany, when dikes burst.

SEPTEMBER

2 Over 10,000 die in an earthquake in northern Iran.

Exploration

- The United States launches the Orbiting Solar Observatory (OSO). The first of a series of solar observatories, it collects and transmits data on the sun's electromagnetic radiation.
- The USSR launches several probes to Mars. Only *Mars 1* flies in the right direction but it transmits no data because of a radio failure.
- U.S. spacecraft *Ranger 4* becomes the first U.S. spacecraft to hit the moon.

JANUARY

- The U.S. National Aeronautics and Space Administration (NASA) launches *Ranger 3*, a spacecraft designed to photograph and then explore the lunar surface. However, it misses its rendezvous with the moon and ends up in a solar orbit.

FEBRUARY

20 U.S. astronaut John Glenn, in the Mercury capsule *Friendship 7*, becomes the first U.S. astronaut to orbit the earth. He makes three orbits.

APRIL

- Like its predecessor, *Ranger 3*, the U.S. National Aeronautics and Space Administration's (NASA) lunar probe *Ranger 4* malfunctions. After careening into the moon, its transmitter goes dead.

26 The United States and UK launch the earth satellite *Ariel*. Designed to study the ionosphere, it is the first international cooperative launch.

AUGUST

26 The first UK satellite, *Aerial*, is launched to study cosmic radiation.

26 U.S. space probe *Mariner 2* is launched. It makes a flyby of Venus (December 14), passing within 34,000 km/21,600 mi of the planet's surface and takes measurements of temperature and atmospheric density.

Health and Medicine

- Czech ophthalmologist Otto Witcherle develops soft contact lenses.
- English biologist Francis Crick, New Zealand-born British molecular biologist Maurice Wilkins, and U.S. biologist James Watson are jointly awarded the Nobel Prize for Physiology or Medicine for their discovery of the structure of DNA.
- The West German-manufactured drug thalidomide, used as a sedative by pregnant women to alleviate morning sickness, is established as the cause of an increase in babies born with congenital malformations; the drug is banned in many countries.

Science

- Austrian-born British biochemist Max Perutz and English biochemist John Kendrew receive the Nobel Prize for Chemistry for determining the structure of globular proteins.
- English chemist Neil Bartlett prepares xenon hexafluoroplatinate, the first compound of an inert gas.

- Italian astronomers R. Giacconi, H. Gursky, F. R. Paolini, and Bruno Rossi discover the first astronomical X-ray source—in Scorpio.
- Radioactive cobalt-60 begins to be used as a catalyst between ethylene and bromine to produce bromoethane (ethyl bromide). It is the first time ionizing radiation has been used commercially to initiate a chemical reaction.
- Scottish-born U.S. anthropologist Victor Turner publishes *Forest of Symbols*, in which he initiates the symbolic study of cultures.
- Soviet physicist Lev Davidovich Landau receives the Nobel Prize for Physics for his theories concerning condensed matter, especially liquid helium.
- Soviet scientist K. Chudinov claims to have revived fossil algae approximately 250 million years old.
- The French anthropologist Claude Lévi-Strauss publishes *Le Pensée sauvage/The Savage Mind*.
- The U.S. anthropologist Michael D. Coe publishes *Mexico*.
- The U.S. philosopher of science Thomas S. Kuhn publishes *The Structure of Scientific Revolutions*.
- U.S. biochemist Robert Woodward synthesizes the antibiotic tetracycline.
- U.S. chemist Herbert Brown publishes *Hydroboration*, in which he outlines his discovery of organoboranes, involved in organic synthesis.
- Welsh physicist Brian Josephson discovers the Josephson effect, the high-frequency oscillation of a current between two superconductors across an insulating layer. Experimental computers built in the 1980s using the Josephson junction are 10–100 times faster than conventional ones.

Technology

- The Bell Telephone Co. introduces a commercial radio paging service in Seattle, Washington.
- The Canadian communications theorist Marshall McLuhan publishes *The Gutenberg Galaxy*.
- The Dow Corning Corporation (manufacturer of chemicals, glass, and other materials) of Detroit, Michigan, develops the silicon breast implant.
- The Dutch firm Philips introduces the audiocassette for recording sound on magnetic tape.
- The Grande Dixene Dam is completed in Valais, Switzerland. It is the world's largest concrete gravity dam at 285 m/935 ft.
- The U.S. Congress passes the Communications Satellite Act, which creates "Comsat" (Communications Satellite Corporation) to develop private commercial communications satellites.
- The U.S. Polaroid corporation introduces "Polacolor" film in its instant cameras. Color prints take 60 seconds.
- Twenty years after the beginning of the nuclear age, the United States has 200 atomic reactors in operation and Britain and the USSR have 39 each.

MARCH

- The U.S. Defense Department unveils the intercontinental ballistic missile *Titan 2*, which travels over 8,000 km/5,000 mi.

APRIL

- The United States tests Skybolt, the first airborne ballistic missile. The missile's booster rocket fails to fire and the missile misses its target.

JULY

10 The U.S. communications satellite *Telstar* is launched for the American Telephone and Telegraph company (AT&T) by the National Aeronautics Space Administration (NASA) from Cape Canaveral, Florida. Weighing 77 kg/170 lb and orbiting the earth every 157.8 minutes, it is designed to receive a signal from the ground, amplify it, and then relay it to another ground station. Live television pictures of the chairman of AT&T are transmitted from Andover, Maine, to Goonhilly Down, Cornwall, southwest England, and Brittany, France. Transmissions last only 15 minutes per orbit but they are the first to connect the television networks of Europe and North America.

DECEMBER

13 The Radio Corporation of America (RCA) launches the experimental telecommunications satellite *Relay 1*.

Transportation

- The first nuclear-powered destroyer, the *Bainbridge*, is launched by the United States.
- The Swedish warship *Wasa*, which sank in 1627, is raised at Stockholm.

JANUARY

- Directors of two of the nation's largest railroads, the New York and Pennsylvania, announce plans to merge their companies.

MAY

22 The (Simplon-) Orient Express luxury rail service makes its last trip from Paris, France, to Istanbul, Turkey, going out of service after nearly 80 years.

AUGUST

- Italian and French crews working on the Mont Blanc Tunnel meet. The 11.6 km-/7.2 mi-long tunnel has been dug under Europe's highest mountain and is the first large tunnel where the entire diameter of the tunnel has been drilled and blasted. The tunnel opens for vehicular traffic in 1965.

ARTS AND IDEAS

Architecture

- The rebuilding of Coventry Cathedral in England (damaged during World War II) is completed, following a design by the English architect Basil Spence. The U.S.-born English artist Jacob Epstein provides sculpture, the English artists John Hutton, Lawrence Lee, and John Piper the windows, and the English artist Graham Sutherland a tapestry.
- The Trans World Airlines Terminal at Idlewild (now John F. Kennedy) Airport, in New York, New York,

designed by the Finnish architect Eero Saarinen, is completed.

Arts

- The Colombian artist Fernando Botero paints *The Nuncio*.
- The English artist Richard Hamilton creates the collage *Towards a Definitive Statement on the Coming Trends in Men's Underwear and Accessories (c) Adonis in Y-fronts*.
- The Italian artist Michelangelo Pistoletto paints *Man Seen from the Back*.
- The Russian-born U.S. artist Jules Olitski paints *Green Jazz*.
- The Scottish artist Eduardo Paolozzi sculpts *Four Towers*.
- The Spanish artist Eduardo Chillida sculpts *The Anvil of Dreams XII*.
- The U.S. artist Ad Reinhardt paints *Abstract Painting No 5*.
- The U.S. artist Andy Warhol paints *210 Coca-Cola Bottles* and his *Campbell Soup Can* series. He also creates his silkscreen *Marilyn Monroe*, the first of many images of Marilyn Monroe used by him.
- The U.S. artist David Smith sculpts *Voltri IV* and *Voltri VII*.
- The U.S. artist Ellsworth Kelly paints *Red Blue Green*.
- The U.S. artist Kenneth Noland paints *Gift*.
- The U.S. artist R. B. Kitaj paints *Isaac Babel Riding with Budyonny*.
- The Venezuelan-born U.S. artist Marisol sculpts *The Family*.
- U.S. photographer Garry Winograd takes *Central Park Zoo*.

Film

- A special issue of *Cahiers du Cinéma/Cinema Notebooks* focuses on the French New Wave directors and what the movement has done to boost the French movie industry.
- The "Free Cinema," Britain's response to the French New Wave, is embodied in movies such as *A Kind of Loving* and *This Sporting Life*.
- The movie *A Kind of Loving*, directed by John Schlesinger, is released in Britain. Based on the novel by Stan Barstow, it stars Alan Bates and June Ritchie.
- The movie *Advise and Consent*, directed by Austrian filmmaker Otto Preminger, is released in the United States, starring Don Murray and Charles Laughton. It is based on the book by Allen Drury.
- The movie *Cape Fear*, directed by J. Lee Thompson, is released in the United States, starring Gregory Peck, Robert Mitchum, and Polly Bergen.
- The movie *Days of Wine and Roses*, directed by Blake Edwards, is released in the United States, starring Jack Lemmon and Lee Remick.
- The movie *Divorce, Italian Style*, directed by Pietro Germi, is released in Italy, starring Marcello Mastroianni and Daniela Rocca.
- The movie *Dr No*, directed by Terence Young, is released in Britain. The first in the highly successful series of James Bond movies, based on the novels by Ian Fleming, it stars Sean Connery and Ursula Andress.
- The movie *El ángel exterminador/The Exterminating Angel*, directed by Luis Buñuel, is released in Spain, starring Jacqueline Andere, Silvia Pinal, and Enrique Garcia Alvarez.
- The movie *How the West Was Won*, directed by John Ford, is released in the United States. A Western on an epic scale, it stars Debbie Reynolds and an extensive cast which includes Henry Fonda, Karl Malden, and Gregory Peck. Ford's movie *The Man Who Shot Liberty Valance* is also released in the United States. It stars James Stewart, John Wayne, Vera Miles, Lee Marvin, Edmond O'Brien, and Andy Devine.
- The movie *Ivan's Childhood*, directed by Andrei Tarkovsky, is released in the USSR, starring Kolya Burlyaev and Irma Takovskaya.
- The movie *Lawrence of Arabia*, directed by David Lean, is released in Britain. An epic biography of T. E. Lawrence, it stars Peter O'Toole, Omar Sharif, and Arthur Kennedy.
- The movie *Lolita*, directed by Stanley Kubrick, is released in the United States. Based on the novel by Vladimir Nabokov, it stars James Mason, Shelley Winters, Sue Lyon, and Peter Sellers.
- The movie *Mamma Roma/Mother Rome*, directed by Pier Paolo Pasolini, is released in Italy.
- The movie *My Life to Live*, directed by Jean-Luc Godard, is released in France, starring Anna Karina.
- The movie *Nattvärdsgasterna/Winter Light*, directed by Ingmar Bergman, is released in Sweden, starring Max Von Sydow and Ingrid Thulin.
- The movie *Phaedra*, directed by Jules Dassin, is released in the United States, starring Melina Mercouri and Anthony Perkins, and featuring music by Mikis Theodorakis.
- The movie *Ride the High Country*, directed by Sam Peckinpah, is released in the United States, starring Joel McCrea and Randolph Scott.
- The movie *The Loneliness of the Long Distance Runner*, directed by Tony Richardson, is released in Britain. Based on a story by Alan Sillitoe, it stars Tom Courtenay, Michael Redgrave, and James Bolam.
- The movie *The Longest Day*, directed by Andrew Marton, is released in the United States. An all-star cast includes John Wayne, Robert Mitchum, and Henry Fonda.
- The movie *The Manchurian Candidate*, directed by John Frankenheimer, is released in the United States, starring Laurence Harvey, Frank Sinatra, Janet Leigh, and Angela Lansbury. It is based on the novel by Richard Condon.
- The movie *The Trial*, directed by Orson Welles, is released in the United States. Based on the novel by Franz Kafka, it stars Orson Welles, Jeanne Moreau, and Anthony Perkins.
- The movie *To Kill a Mockingbird*, directed by Robert Mulligan, is released in the United States. Based on the novel by Harper Lee, it stars Gregory Peck, Mary Badham, and Brock Peters.
- The movie *Whatever Happened to Baby Jane?*, directed by Robert Aldrich, is released in the United States. Based on the novel by Henry Farrell, it stars Bette Davis, Joan Crawford, and Victor Buono.

APRIL

9 The 1961 Academy Awards take place. Best Actor: Maximilian Schell, for *Judgement at Nuremberg*; Best Supporting Actor: George Chakiris, for *West Side Story*; Best Actress: Sophia Loren, for *Two Women*; Best Supporting Actress: Rita Moreno, for *West Side Story*; Best Picture: *West Side Story*, directed by Robert Wise and Jerome Robbins; Best Director: Robert Wise and Jerome Robbins, for *West Side Story*.

MAY

25 At the Cannes Film Festival in France, the Palme d'Or is awarded to *The Given Word*, directed by Anselmo Duarte.

Literature and Language

- The Argentine writer Jorge Luis Borges publishes *Labyrinths*, a collection of his stories translated into English.
- The English writer Anthony Powell publishes *The Kindly Ones*, the sixth novel of his 12-volume sequence *A Dance to the Music of Time*.
- The English writer Anthony Burgess publishes his novel *A Clockwork Orange*, which becomes controversial because of its violence. An equally controversial movie adaptation by the director Stanley Kubrick is released in 1971 and soon withdrawn from general circulation in Britain.
- The English writer Doris Lessing publishes her novel *The Golden Notebook*.
- The Guyanese writer Wilson Harris publishes his novel *The Whole Armour*, the third part of his *The Guyana Quartet*.
- The Italian writer Giorgio Bassani publishes his novel *Il giardino dei Finzi-Contini/The Garden of the Finzi-Continis*.
- The Mexican writer Carlos Fuentes publishes his novel *La muerte de Artemio Criz/The Death of Artemio Criz*.
- The Nobel Prize for Literature is awarded to the U.S. novelist John Steinbeck.
- The Pulitzer Prize for Fiction is awarded to Edwin O'Connor for *The Edge of Sadness* and the Pulitzer Prize for Poetry is awarded to Alan Dugan for *Poems*. The Pulitzer Prize for Biography is not awarded this year.
- The Russian writer Alexander Solzhenitsyn publishes his novella *Odin den Ivana Denisovicha/One Day in the Life of Ivan Denisovich*, which wins international acclaim after being allowed into print by the Soviet authorities in the magazine *Novy Mir*.
- The Russian-born U.S. writer Vladimir Nabokov publishes his novel *Pale Fire*.
- The U.S. Black Mountain poet Robert Creeley publishes his poetry collection *For Love*.
- The U.S. writer Alison Lurie publishes her novel *Love and Friendship*.
- The U.S. writer and critic Edmund Wilson publishes his critical work *Patriotic Gore*, a study of American Civil War literature.
- The U.S. writer Anne Sexton publishes her poetry collection *All My Pretty Ones*.
- The U.S. writer James Baldwin publishes his novel *Another Country*.

- The U.S. writer John Steinbeck publishes his travel book *Travels with Charley in Search of America*.
- The U.S. writer Katherine Anne Porter publishes her novel *Ship of Fools*, which becomes the best-selling novel of the year in the United States.
- The U.S. writer Ken Kesey publishes his novel *One Flew Over the Cuckoo's Nest*.
- The U.S. writer Ray Bradbury publishes his novel *Something Wicked This Way Comes*.
- The U.S. writer Robert Bly publishes his poetry collection *Silence in the Snowy Fields*.
- The U.S. writer Robert Hayden publishes his poetry collection *A Ballad of Remembrance*, which includes "Middle Passage."
- U.S. author Mimi Sheraton publishes *The Seducer's Cookbook*, a satirical how-to guide for the single man.

MARCH

26 The U.S. poet Robert Frost publishes his first new collection of poems in 15 years, *In the Clearing*.

Music

- The Belgian composer Henri Pousseur completes his chamber work *Madrigal III*.
- The British instrumental group the Shadows releases the single "Wonderful Land."
- The British pop group the Tornadoes releases the single "Telstar," and becomes the first British group to top the U.S. charts.
- The British pop singer Frank Ifield releases the single "I Remember You," which becomes the most successful single of the year in Britain.
- The British pop singer Cliff Richard releases the single "The Young Ones."
- The British rock group the Beatles signs a management contract with Brian Epstein and a recording contract with the Parlophone record label.
- The English composer Elisabeth Lutyens completes her piano work *Five Bagatelles* and her *Music for Orchestra II*.
- The English composer Michael Tippett completes his Piano Sonata No. 2.
- The German composer Karl Hartmann completes his Symphony No. 8.
- The Hungarian-born Austrian composer György Ligeti completes his *Poème Symphonique/Symphonic Poem*, to be performed by 100 metronomes.
- The opera *King Priam*, by the English composer Michael Tippett, is first performed, in Coventry, England.
- The Polish composer Grażyna Bacewicz completes her Concerto for Orchestra.
- The Russian composer Dmitry Shostakovich completes his Symphony No. 13, *Babi Yar*, inspired by a poem by the Russian writer Yevgeny Yevtushenko.
- The U.S. artists Bobby "Boris" Pickett and the Crypt Kickers release the single "Monster Mash."
- The U.S. composer John Cage presents his piano work *4'33"*, which is to be "performed by anyone in any way."
- The U.S. folk singer Joan Baez releases the album *Joan Baez in Concert*, featuring the song "Pretty Boy Floyd."

- The U.S. folk trio Peter, Paul, and Mary releases the single "If I Had a Hammer," a workers' song from the 1940s.
- The U.S. folk/rock singer Bob Dylan releases the single "Blowin' in the Wind." Written in April 1962, it was released on the album *The Freewheelin' Bob Dylan* in May 1963.
- The U.S. girl group the Crystals releases the single "He's a Rebel."
- The U.S. group Booker T and the MGs releases the single "Green Onions."
- The U.S. pop group the Beach Boys releases the single "Surfin' Safari."
- The U.S. pop group the Four Seasons releases the single "Sherry."
- The U.S. pop singer Neil Sedaka releases the single "Breaking Up Is Hard to Do."
- The U.S. pop singer Pat Boone releases the single "Speedy Gonzalez."
- The U.S. rock singer Elvis Presley releases the singles "Return to Sender" and "Can't Help Falling in Love."
- The U.S. singer Chris Montez releases the single "Let's Dance."
- The U.S. singer Little Eva releases the single "Loco-Motion," and starts a dance craze.
- The U.S. singer Nat "King" Cole releases the single "Ramblin' Rose."
- The U.S. singer Tony Bennett releases the single "I Left My Heart in San Francisco."
- The U.S. soul/rhythm and blues singer Ray Charles releases the singles "I Can't Stop Loving You" and "You Don't Know Me."
- The U.S. trumpeter Herb Alpert releases the single "The Lonely Bull."
- The U.S. vocal group the Four Seasons releases the single "Big Girls Don't Cry."

MAY

29 The 1961–62 Grammy Awards take place. Best Album: *Judy at Carnegie Hall* by Judy Garland; Best Record: "Moon River" by Henry Mancini; Best Male Vocalist: Jack Jones; Best Female Vocalist: Judy Garland; Best Group: Lambert, Hendricks, and Ross.

OCTOBER

- The U.S. comedian Allan Sherman releases the album *My Son the Folksinger*, satirizing folk singers. It becomes a best seller.

Theater and Dance

- The play *Chips with Everything*, by the English dramatist Arnold Wesker, is first performed, in London, England.
- The play *Die Physiker/The Physicists*, by the Swiss writer Friedrich Dürrenmatt, is first performed, in Zürich, Switzerland.
- The play *Le Roi se meurt/Exit the King*, by the Romanian-born French dramatist Eugène Ionesco, is first performed, in Paris, France.
- The Pulitzer Prize for Drama is awarded to Frank Loesser and Abe Burrows for *How to Succeed in Business Without Really Trying*.

FEBRUARY

26 The play *Oh Dad, Poor Dad, Mamma's Hung You in the Closet and I'm Feeling So Sad*, by Arthur Kopit, is first performed, at the Phoenix Theater in New York, New York.

APRIL

29 The 1961–62 Tony Awards take place. Best Play: *A Man for All Season*; Best Musical: *How to Succeed in Business Without Really Trying*; Best Actor: Paul Scofield; Best Actress: Margaret Leighton.

MAY

8 The musical *A Funny Thing Happened on the Way to the Forum*, with music and lyrics by Stephen Sondheim, is first performed, starring Zero Mostel and Jack Guilford, at the Alvin Theater, New York, New York.

OCTOBER

27 The play *Who's Afraid of Virginia Woolf?*, by the U.S. dramatist Edward Albee, is first performed, at the Billy Rose Theater in New York, New York.

Thought and Scholarship

- *Sense and Sensibilia*, by the English philosopher J. L. Austin, is published posthumously.
- German philosopher Martin Heidegger publishes *Die Technik und die Kehre/The Question Concerning Technology*.
- Japanese philosopher D. T. Suzuki publishes *The Essentials of Zen Buddhism*.
- The Canadian writer George Woodcock publishes *Anarchism: A History of Libertarian Ideas and Movements*.
- The first Pulitzer Prize for General Nonfiction is awarded, to Theodor H. White for *The Making of the President 1960*.
- The Pulitzer Prize for History is awarded to Lawrence Gipson for *The Triumphant Empire: Thunder-Clouds Gather in the West*.
- U.S. philosopher Max Black publishes *Models and Metaphors*.
- U.S. philosopher Susanne Langer publishes *Philosophical Sketches*.
- U.S. psychologist A. H. Maslow publishes *Towards a Theory of Being*.

SOCIETY

Education

AUGUST

- The radical student organization, Students for a Democratic Society (SDS), established the previous year, issues The Port Huron Statement. Among other charges, the statement declares that "America rests in national stalemate, its goals ambiguous and tradition bound instead of informed and clear, its democratic system apathetic and manipulated."

Everyday Life

- Canaima Parque Nacional is established in Venezuela. Covering 30,000 sq km/11,583 sq mi, it is the largest national park in South America and second largest in the world. It contains the Salta Angel waterfall, the highest in the world.
- Iron City Beer in Pittsburgh, Pennsylvania, produces the first aluminum can with a ring-pull. These are not immediately popular because they add to the cost of the product and early designs are awkward.
- New U.S. dance crazes include the Mashed Potato and the Watusi.
- Royal Crown Cola launch Diet-Rite Cola in the United States, the first sugar-free soft drink on the market.
- The bossa nova dance, based on the jazz-samba musical style of Brazil, becomes very popular in the United States.
- The U.S. cigarette company Philip Morris introduces the cowboy motif to advertise Marlboro cigarettes. This will help them become the leading brand worldwide by the end of the decade.
- Yves St. Laurent founds his fashion house in France.

JANUARY
- Electrical workers in New York, New York, end a week-long strike after winning a new contract providing them with a 25-hour work week, and five hours overtime.
- The periodical *Harper's Bazaar* sparks cultural controversy by publishing a full-page nude advertisement.

FEBRUARY
19 The U.S. government establishes Abraham Lincoln's boyhood home in Indiana as a national monument.

DECEMBER
December 1962–April 1963   The International Typographical Union strikes against New York, New York, newspapers. The strike halts production of all nine of the city's daily newspapers. It lasts 114 days and costs the industry roughly $100 million.

Media and Communication

- *The Jetsons*, an animated television show based in the 21st century, begins on U.S. television.
- *Young Man* and *Bilbilly Sings*, two dramas by Katsumi Oyama, are broadcast in Japan.
- Helen Gurley Brown publishes her best-selling *Sex and the Single Girl*, a celebration of the opportunities outside marriage now available to young women. She will go on to become the editor of *Cosmopolitan* magazine.
- In the United States, 90% of households own at least one television, and around 13% own more than one.
- The *Los Angeles Times* is the first newspaper to be typeset on computer.
- The U.S. television quiz show contestant Charles Van Doren is convicted of perjury in connection with his role in rigging the popular quiz *Twenty-One*; he was given the answers by the program producers.
- The weekly news magazine *Panorama* is published in Italy.
- WNDT, the nation's first publicly-supported educational television and WNYC-TV, the nation's first municipally-owned television station, begin broadcasting in New York, New York.

FEBRUARY
- The satirical magazine *Private Eye* is launched in Britain. In April, it has to be saved from financial difficulties by comedian Peter Cook.
14 First Lady Jacqueline Kennedy, accompanied by commentator Charles Collingwood, leads NBC and ABC camera crews on a live tour of the White House, watched by about 46.5 million Americans.

BIRTHS & DEATHS

JANUARY
16 Richard Henry Tawney, English economic historian and social critic, dies in London, England (81).
26 "Lucky" Luciano (nickname of Charles Luciano), U.S. organized crime boss, dies in Capodicino Airport, Naples, Italy (64).

FEBRUARY
2 Garth Brooks, U.S. country music star, born in Tulsa, Oklahoma.

MAY
31 Adolf Eichmann, German Nazi war criminal, is hanged in Tel Aviv, Israel, for his part in exterminating Jews during World War II (56).

JULY
6 William Faulkner, U.S. novelist, author of a series of novels known as the Yoknapatawpha cycle and winner of the Nobel Prize for Literature in 1949, dies near Oxford, Mississippi (64).
21 George Macaulay Trevelyan, English historian, dies in Cambridge, Cambridgeshire, England (86).

AUGUST
5 Marilyn Monroe, U.S. actress and sex symbol, dies in Los Angeles, California, from an overdose of sleeping pills (36).
9 Hermann Hesse, German writer whose spiritual novels made him a cult figure, dies in Montagnola, Switzerland (85).

SEPTEMBER
3 e(dward) e(stlin) cummings, U.S. poet, dies in North Conway, New Hampshire (67).

NOVEMBER
7 Eleanor Roosevelt, United Nations diplomat and wife of U.S. president Franklin D. Roosevelt, dies in New York, New York (78).
18 Niels Bohr, Danish physicist who developed the science of quantum mechanics, dies in Copenhagen, Denmark (77).
19 Jodie Foster, U.S. actress, born in Los Angeles, California.
28 Wilhelmina, Queen of the Netherlands 1890–1962, dies in Het Loo, Netherlands (82).

DECEMBER
7 Kirsten Flagstad, Norwegian soprano, dies in Oslo, Norway (67).
15 Charles Laughton, English-born U.S. actor, dies in Hollywood, California (62).

MAY

22 The 1961–62 Emmy Awards for television take place. Best Drama Series: *The Defenders*; Best Actor in a Single Show: Peter Falk; Best Actress in a Single Show: Julie Harris; Best Actor in a Series: Don Knotts, for *The Andy Griffith Show*; Best Actress in a Series: Shirley Booth, for *Hazel*.

SEPTEMBER

19–September 9, 1970 *The Virginian*, a Western series based on a ranch in Wyoming, appears on U.S. television. Starring James Drury, Doug McClure, Gary Clarke, and Lee J. Cobb, it is loosely based on the novel by Owen Wister.

26–September 7, 1971 The situation comedy *The Beverly Hillbillies* appears on U.S. television, starring Buddy Ebsen, Irene Ryan, Donna Douglas, Max Baer, Jr., Raymond Bailey, and Nancy Kulp; the theme song is performed by Lester Flatt and Earl Scruggs.

OCTOBER

1–September 2, 1974 Lucille Ball returns to U.S. television in *The Lucy Show*, a situation comedy also starring Vivian Vance, Gale Gordon, and Lucie and Desi Arnaz, Jr.

2 Johnny Carson takes over *The Tonight Show* in the United States.

11–August 30, 1966 The situation comedy *McHale's Navy* appears on U.S. television, starring Ernest Borgnine, Joe Flynn, Tim Conway, Gavin MacLeod, and Yoshio Yoda.

22 During the Cuban Missile Crisis, President John F. Kennedy of the United States delivers his ultimatum to the USSR in a television address.

Religion

October 1962–65 The Second Vatican Council, a council of the Roman Catholic Church convened by Pope John XXIII, is held, its aim being to reform Catholic ministry and liturgy, and to seek reunion with other Christian denominations.

Sports

- Maury Wills, shortstop for the Los Angeles Dodgers, becomes the first player in major league baseball to steal 100 bases in a season. His tally of 104 bases stolen is eight more than the previous record of 96 set by Ty Cobb in 1915.

- More than 33 million fans bet about $2.6 billion on horse racing in the United States.
- The Australian tennis player Rod Laver achieves the Grand Slam, winning all four major tennis championships (the Australian Open, the French Open, Wimbledon, and the U.S. Open) in the same calendar year. He is the first person to do so since Don Budge of the United States in 1938.
- The New York Mets and the Houston Colt 45s (now the Astros) join the baseball National League in the United States.

MARCH

2 Wilt Chamberlain of the Philadelphia Warriors achieves a National Basketball Association single game record of 100 points against the New York Knicks.

APRIL

7–18 The Boston Celtics beat the Los Angeles Lakers by four games to three to win the National Basketball Association (NBA) championship for the fourth successive year.

10–27 The Toronto Maple Leafs defeat the Chicago Blackhawks by four games to two to win their first Stanley Cup for hockey since 1951.

MAY

21 The American Football League's two-and-a-half-year-old antitrust case against the National Football League is thrown out by a U.S. district court in Baltimore, Maryland.

30–June 17 The seventh soccer World Cup is held in Chile. The holders, Brazil, defeat Czechoslovakia 3–1 in the final in Santiago, before a crowd of 69,000.

JUNE

17 The U.S. golfer Jack Nicklaus wins the U.S. Open tournament, at Oakmont, Pennsylvania, just five months after turning professional.

JULY

27 The Australian swimmer Dawn Fraser becomes the first woman to swim 100 meters in less than one minute, at the Olympic Pool in Melbourne, Australia.

SEPTEMBER

25 The U.S. boxer Sonny Liston beats defending champion Floyd Patterson of the United States in the first round of their world heavyweight boxing fight in Chicago, Illinois.

OCTOBER

4–16 The New York Yankees defeat the San Francisco Giants in seven games to win the World Series for the nineteenth time.

1963

POLITICS, GOVERNMENT, AND ECONOMICS

Business and Economics

- The Coca-Cola Co. introduces the sugar-free soft drink Tab, in the United States.

JUNE
- The U.S. Supreme Court rules unconstitutional so-called shop agency labor contracts, by which nonunion workers are forced to pay dues equal to those of their unionized counterparts.

Colonization

FEBRUARY
1 Nyasaland (now Malawi) becomes self-governing, with Hastings Banda as prime minister.

AUGUST
1 Britain agrees to grant independence to the colony of Malta in 1964.

OCTOBER
1 Nigeria becomes a republic within the Commonwealth, with Nnamdi Azikiwe as president.
9 Mutesa II, the kabaka of Buganda, becomes the first president of Uganda on its becoming an independent state within the British Commonwealth.

DECEMBER
10 Zanzibar gains independence within the British Commonwealth (now part of Tanzania).
12 Kenya becomes independent within the British Commonwealth.

Human Rights

- U.S. housewife Betty Goldstein Friedan writes *The Feminine Mystique*, which expresses women's lack of fulfillment and their need for self-expression over and above motherhood.

JANUARY
28 Black student Harvey Gantt enrolls at Clemson University, desegregating the higher education system in South Carolina.

APRIL
12 Police in Birmingham, Alabama, arrest and jail civil-rights leader Martin Luther King, Jr., for his role in

desegregation protests in that city. While incarcerated, King pens his famous "Letter from a Birmingham Jail."

JUNE
- President John F. Kennedy signs legislation guaranteeing women equal pay for equal work, but the principle proves easier to mandate than to achieve.

JULY
- The United Brotherhood of Carpenters, the nation's largest building union, integrates its ranks.

AUGUST
28 Two hundred thousand black Americans take part in the March on Washington, a peaceful demonstration for civil rights in Washington, D.C. They are addressed by the civil-rights leader Martin Luther King, Jr., who proclaims, with the Lincoln Memorial as a backdrop, "I have a dream that my four little children will one day live in a nation where they will not be judged by the color of their skin but by the content of their character."

OCTOBER
22 About 225,000 schoolchildren in Chicago, Illinois, stay home as part of a one-day boycott to protest against segregation in the city's school system.

Politics and Government

JANUARY
- The Soviet Union walks away from informal nuclear test ban talks held in New York, New York, after two weeks of negotiations.
- The U.S. Congress sends President John F. Kennedy a budget of $98.8 billion, the largest to date.
2 U.S. Army general Lyman Lemnitzer succeeds General Lauris Norstad as NATO Supreme Allied Commander Europe.
3 A United Nations (UN) force captures Jadotville, in the secessionist province of Katanga in the Congo Republic.
14 The French president Charles de Gaulle rejects a U.S. offer of Polaris missiles for a putative North Atlantic Treaty Organization (NATO) nuclear force.
15 President Moise Tshombe of Katanga province in the Congo Republic formally ends Katanga's cession from Congo.
22 The French president Charles de Gaulle and the West German chancellor Konrad Adenauer sign a Franco-German treaty of cooperation.
24 Italy accepts a U.S. plan for a multilateral North Atlantic Treaty Organization (NATO) nuclear force.

FEBRUARY
- Following the Soviet Union's abandonment of informal nuclear test ban discussions a week earlier, the U.S. proceeds with underground nuclear testing.

- President John F. Kennedy asks Congress to pass legislation to help mentally handicapped Americans. Also this month he sends a Medicare proposal to Congress; the plan calls for tapping Social Security to fund medical insurance for the elderly.
- Two Cuban war planes attack a U.S. fishing boat adrift in Cuban waters, sparking international controversy.
5 John Diefenbaker's Canadian government is defeated in parliament, which is dissolved, and an election held on April 8.
8 Air force officers assassinate the Iraqi prime minister Abdel Karim Kassem in Baghdad, Iraq. He is succeeded by the pro-Egyptian Abdul Salam Arif.
14 The U.S. president John F. Kennedy proposes a youth program that includes a domestic version of the Peace Corps and a Youth Conservation Corps.
20 The United States recommends that surface ships should be used to carry Polaris missiles in a North Atlantic Treaty Organization (NATO) nuclear force.

MARCH

- Pope John XXIII canonizes Elizabeth Ann Seton, the first native-born American to be proclaimed a saint.
- President John F. Kennedy signs the Declaration of San José, committing Central American signatories to work toward creating a common market.
- The U.S. Supreme Court, in *Gideon v. Wainwright*, rules that defendants have a right to free counsel.
25 Terence O'Neill succeeds Lord Brookeborough as prime minister in Northern Ireland. Brooke had held the post since 1943.

APRIL

- A federal grand jury indicts seven major U.S. steel companies for illegal price-fixing.
6 Britain and the United States sign an agreement under which the United States supplies Polaris missiles to Britain.
8 The Liberals win the general election in Canada with 129 seats, while the Progressive Conservatives win 95 seats, and others 41.
12 Indonesian forces make an armed attack on Malaysia, pursuing territorial claims.
17 Syria, Iraq, and the United Arab Republic (UAR) of Egypt agree to federate.
17 The Canadian prime minister John Diefenbaker resigns following the defeat of the Progressive Conservatives in the general election and, on April 22, the Liberal Lester Pearson forms a government.
28 The Cuban prime minister Fidel Castro visits the USSR.

MAY

- Canada agrees to install U.S. nuclear warheads on its soil, as part of a joint U.S.–Canadian defense program.
- The U.S. Supreme Court overturns lower court convictions of individuals arrested in sit-in demonstrations against segregated Southern restaurants.
9 The governor of British Guiana declares a state of emergency at Prime Minister Cheddi Jagan's request, following civil disorder.
16 Talks between India and Pakistan on Kashmir break down.
16 The Geneva Conference on a General Agreement on Tariffs and Trade (GATT) begins the "Kennedy round" of negotiations for tariff cuts.

22–25 The Organization of African Unity (OAU) is founded at a conference of African leaders in Addis Ababa, Ethiopia; it aims to maintain solidarity between African leaders and remove colonialism from the African continent.

JUNE

- President John F. Kennedy signs legislation by which $1 and $2 bills will be backed by gold rather than silver.
- President John F. Kennedy challenges Congress to enact major civil-rights legislation, mandating, among other things, an end to the segregation of all public facilities—even those privately owned.
- U.S. civil-rights leader Medgar Evers is assassinated outside his home in Jackson, Mississippi. President John F. Kennedy condemns the killing. Evers is buried at Arlington National Cemetery.
11 After Alabama governor George C. Wallace refuses to permit two black students, Vivian Malone and James Hood, to enter the state university, the National Guard, summoned by President John F. Kennedy, ushers the students into the school buildings, desegregating the campus.
11 The Greek prime minister Constantine Karamanlis resigns in protest against King Paul's state visit to Britain.
20 The United States and USSR sign an agreement to establish a "hot line" from the White House, Washington, D.C., to the Kremlin, Moscow, USSR, to speed up communications in time of crisis.
21 France withdraws its naval Atlantic forces from the North Atlantic Treaty Organization (NATO), as it is not willing to be part of a joint NATO nuclear force.
25 President Moise Tshombe is forced to resign as prime minister of Katanga province in the Congo Republic.
26 During a tour of West Germany (June 23–27), the U.S. president John F. Kennedy visits West Berlin, and tells a crowd of 150,000 Berliners: "All free men ... are citizens of Berlin. And therefore, as a free man, I take pride in the words, 'Ich bin ein Berliner'" ("I am a Berliner").

JULY

- In an attempt to isolate the communist regime of Cuban president Fidel Castro, the U.S. government prohibits all financial commerce with Cuba.
- U.S. National Guard troops impose martial law in the town of Cambridge, Maryland, after racial violence erupts for the second time in one month.
11 The South African Security Police raid the headquarters of *Umkonto we Sizwe* ("Spear of the Nation") in the Johannesburg suburb of Rivonia; Walter Sisulu and others are captured, together with weapons and incriminating documents.
20 Soviet–Chinese ideological talks in Moscow, USSR, end. China denies that Nikita Khrushchev's policy of "Peaceful Coexistence" with the West can be sustained, widening the rift between the two countries.
26 An earthquake hits Skopje (now capital of Macedonia), Yugoslavia.

AUGUST

5 The United States, USSR, and Britain sign a nuclear test-ban treaty, which is subsequently signed by 96 states, but not France, before coming into force on October 1.

21 Many Buddhists, who have led domestic opposition to the South Vietnamese government, are arrested, and martial law is imposed.

30 The "hot line" direct link between the White House, Washington, D.C., and the Kremlin in Moscow, USSR, becomes operational.

SEPTEMBER

- President John F. Kennedy once more summons the National Guard, this time to Huntsville, Alabama, to force Alabama governor George C. Wallace to integrate the state's public schools.

7 Opposition leader Chief Enahoro is sentenced to 15 years' imprisonment by a Nigerian court, for plotting against the Nigerian government.

8 A new constitution in Algeria establishes presidential government; Ahmed ben Bella is president.

15 Four black girls are killed by a bomb explosion at the 16th Street Baptist Church in Birmingham, Alabama. A race riot ensues in which two more black youngsters are killed.

16 Malaya, North Borneo, Sarawak, and Singapore form the Federation of Malaysia which, on September 17, breaks off relations with Indonesia, following its increased hostility to the Federation's creation.

18 A United Nations (UN) Special Committee on apartheid in South Africa calls for the prohibition of arms and gasoline exports to South Africa.

19 A British–French report favors the building of a channel tunnel between the two countries.

21 The prime minister of Czechoslovakia Vilian Siroký is dismissed following failures in the development of agriculture.

OCTOBER

- President John F. Kennedy ratifies the recent nuclear test-ban treaty with the Soviet Union by authorizing the sale of 4 million metric tons of wheat to the USSR.

- The recent warming of U.S.–Soviet relations cools dramatically when Soviet troops halt a shipment of U.S. military supplies destined for West Berlin. The shipment is allowed to proceed after the United States protests vigorously.

- The United States demonstrates its rapid deployment capability in Operation Big Lift, by which the entire Second Army Division moves from Texas to West Germany in a meager 63 hours.

- The United States launches secretly two military satellites designed to monitor Soviet compliance with the nuclear test-ban treaty signed on October 7.

- U.S. scientist Linus C. Pauling wins the Nobel Peace Prize for his effort to combat nuclear proliferation.

4 Archbishop Beran of Prague, Czechoslovakia, is freed by the communist authorities after 14 years in prison.

7 The United Nations (UN) Trusteeship Committee calls on Britain not to transfer the armed forces of the Rhodesian Federation to Southern Rhodesia, because of its refusal to accept majority rule.

7 The United States and USSR sign a limited nuclear test-ban treaty, effective October 10.

10 The "Rivonia trial" of the leaders of the South African *Umkonto we Sizwe* (" Spear of the Nation"), including Nelson Mandela and Walter Sisulu, opens; they are charged with sabotage and conspiracy to overthrow the government (–June 1964).

11 The United Nations (UN) General Assembly condemns repression in South Africa by 106 votes to 1.

15 Ludwig Erhard becomes chancellor of West Germany on Konrad Adenauer's resignation.

18 The British prime minister Harold Macmillan resigns for reasons of health and, on October 19, is succeeded by the Scottish peer the Earl of Home, who later disclaims the peerage, is made a Knight of the Thistle, and becomes Sir Alec Douglas-Home. He is elected a member of the House of Commons, for Kinross, on November 8.

22–31 The constitutional conference on British Guiana (suspended in 1962) reopens in London, England, and ends without agreement.

26 The Soviet leader Nikita Khrushchev states that the USSR would not race the United States to place a person on the moon.

NOVEMBER

- For the second time in one month, Soviet troops stop U.S. military supplies from reaching West Berlin. Again, U.S. officials protest vigorously and, again, the supplies are permitted to proceed.

- John F. Kennedy is buried at Arlington National Cemetery.

- The so-called "chicken war" erupts between U.S. and Common Market poultry producers after a U.S. panel charges the European poultry industry with cheating U.S. producers out of some $26 million. In response, the United States raises tariffs on Common Market nations.

- The U.S. State Department prohibits diplomats of Warsaw Pact nations from visiting some 355 U.S. counties, for reasons of national security.

1 In an army coup in South Vietnam, President Ngo Dinh Diem is assassinated, as well as members of his family and Cabinet. He is succeeded by General Duong Van Minh, who has U.S. support for his coup.

22 The U.S. president John F. Kennedy is assassinated in Dallas, Texas, as he is driven to make a speech at the Dallas World Trade Center. The shots appear to come from the sixth floor of the Texas Book Depository on Elm Street. Former marine and procommunist Lee Harvey Oswald is arrested 80 minutes later on charges of killing a patrolman, and is subsequently identified as the assassin, although there is speculation as to whether he acted alone or as part of a conspiracy. Vice President Lyndon B. Johnson is sworn in as president later the same day.

24 U.S. nightclub owner Jack Ruby murders Lee Harvey Oswald, the alleged assassin of U.S. president John F. Kennedy two days previously, as police move Oswald from the city jail in Dallas, Texas. This adds fuel to speculations that Oswald acted as part of a much larger conspiracy. Millions of Americans watch the murder live on national television.

29 President Lyndon B. Johnson creates the so-called Warren Commission, named for its chairman, Chief Justice Earl Warren. The Commission is charged with investigating the events surrounding the assassination of President John F. Kennedy.

30 In a general election in Australia, the Liberal and Country Party coalition increases its majority; the Liberal Party wins 52 seats, the Country Party 20 seats, and the Labor Party 50 seats; Robert Menzies remains prime minister.

DECEMBER

4   The United Nations (UN) Security Council votes for a partial embargo on the sale and shipment of arms to South Africa.

8–11   Frank Sinatra, Jr., the son of the U.S. singer, is kidnapped in Lake Tahoe, Nevada, and later released unhurt in Los Angeles, California, after his father pays the kidnappers a $240,000 ransom.

22   Clashes in Cyprus between Greek and Turkish residents lead to a major breakdown in relations between the two communities. On December 30, a neutral zone is agreed.

22   The Greek liner *Lakonia* catches fire and sinks in the North Atlantic with the loss of 150 lives.

25   A state of emergency is declared in the Somali frontier region of Kenya because of a border dispute between the two countries.

31   The Central African Federation of Rhodesia and Nyasaland (now Zambia, Zimbabwe, and Malawi) is dissolved.

SCIENCE, TECHNOLOGY, AND MEDICINE

Ecology

JUNE

19   The U.S. satellite *TIROS 7* (Television and Infra-Red Observation Satellite) is launched. It is used by meteorologists to track, forecast, and analyze storms.

SEPTEMBER

30–October 9   The Caribbean is hit by hurricane Flora, which kills 6,000 people.

OCTOBER

31   A gas explosion at the Indiana State Fair kills 68 people and injures 340 more.

Exploration

•   The European Launcher Development Organization is formed to develop space-launch vehicles.

MAY

15–16   U.S. astronaut Gordon Cooper, in *Faith 7*, the last of the Mercury missions, completes a 22-orbit mission in 34 hr 20 min (a record) and then makes a manual landing when his automatic controls fail.

20   The United States launches a satellite containing a 20-kg/44-lb belt of copper wires into a 3,000 km/1,865 mi polar orbit. The wires are to serve as a reflective umbrella by which to test-relay radio and microwave signals from coast to coast.

JUNE

16   Soviet cosmonaut Valentina Tereshkova, the first woman in space, is launched into a three-day orbital flight aboard *Vostok 6*, to study the problem of weightlessness.

Health and Medicine

•   Australian physiologist John Eccles and English physiologists Alan Hodgkin and Andrew Huxley are jointly awarded the Nobel Prize for Physiology or Medicine for their discoveries concerning the transmission of impulses along nerves.

•   Queen Elizabeth Hospital, Hong Kong, the largest in the Commonwealth, is completed.

•   The measles vaccine is licensed in the United States.

•   U.S. physician Baruch Samuel Blumberg discovers the "Australian antigen" in an Australian aborigine. It causes the body to produce antibodies to the hepatitis B virus and permits the screening of blood donors for the disease. It also leads, in 1982, to the development of a vaccine.

•   U.S. surgeon James Hardy performs the first lung transplant.

•   U.S. surgeon Thomas Starlz performs the first liver transplant.

MARCH

17   A typhoid epidemic breaks out in Zermatt, Switzerland.

JUNE

8   The American Heart Association begins its first public campaign against smoking tobacco.

SEPTEMBER

•   The U.S. Food and Drug Administration debunks the drug Krebiozen, hailed as a miracle cure in the fight against cancer. Krebiozen, it turns out, is a common amino acid.

DECEMBER

•   The muscle relaxant and antidepressant Valium, developed by Roche Laboratories as a more potent alternative to Librium, appears on the market in the United States.

Science

•   Austrian zoologist Konrad Lorenz, in *On Aggression*, states that only humans intentionally kill their own species and that aggressive behavior is inborn but can be modified by the environment.

•   British geophysicists Fred Vine and Drummond Matthews analyze the magnetism of rocks in the Atlantic Ocean floor, which assume a magnetization aligned with the earth's magnetic field at the time of their creation. It provides concrete evidence of sea-floor spreading.

•   Dutch-born U.S. astronomer Maarten Schmidt discovers the first quasar (3C 273), an extraordinarily distant object brighter than the largest known galaxy yet with a star-like image.

•   French anthropologist Claude Lévi-Strauss publishes *Structural Anthropology*, in which he introduces the idea that social structures are reflections of mental structures.

•   German chemist Karl Ziegler shares the Nobel Prize for Chemistry with the Italian chemist Giulio Natta, for their work on the chemistry and technology of high polymers.

- U.S. biochemist Robert Woodward synthesizes the plant chemical colchicine.
- U.S. physicists Eugene Wigner and Maria Goeppert-Mayer and German physicist Hans Jensen receive the Nobel Prize for Physics: Wigner for his development of the shell theory of the atomic nucleus and Goeppert-Mayer and Jensen for their discoveries concerning nuclear shell structure.

APRIL

- The U.S. Atomic Energy Commission honors physicist J. Robert Oppenheimer, once blacklisted for alleged communist sympathy, with the prestigious Fermi Award.

Technology

- Emmett Leith and Juris Upatnieks of the University of Michigan develop the hologram.
- The Arecibo radio telescope in Puerto Rico begins operation; its 300-m/1,000-ft reflector is built into a naturally occurring parabola and is the largest single-reflector telescope in the world.
- The British lawnmower manufacturer Flymo develops the first hover lawnmower.
- The first CANDU (Canadian Deuterium Uranium) reactors begin operating in Canada. They use deuterium, uranium moderated by heavy water.
- The first geosynchronous satellite, *Syncom II*, is positioned over the Atlantic; it permits a regular transatlantic telecommunications service.
- The Polaroid Corporation develops color polaroid film in the United States.
- U.S. chemist Leslie Phillips and colleagues at the Royal Aircraft Establishment, Farnborough, develop carbon fiber. It is used for strength in bridges and turbine blades.
- U.S. firm Eastman Kodak introduces Instamatic cameras that take film cartridges instead of roll film.

NOVEMBER

18 The U.S. telecommunications firm AT&T introduces the first transistorized push-button telephones. Within a few years, this type of phone will dominate the U.S. market, almost completely replacing the dial phone.

Transportation

- The United States has 6% of the world population and 66% of the world's cars.
- U.S. electrical engineer William Powell Lear produces the first Lear jet, a small, low-priced jet aircraft for business executives.

APRIL

10 The U.S. Navy's nuclear submarine *Thresher* sinks in the Atlantic Ocean, killing all 129 crewmen, the world's worst submarine accident. Caused most likely by an electrical short, the incident mars what had been a string of remarkable successes in the nation's nuclear submarine program.

ARTS AND IDEAS

Architecture

- Dulles Airport in Washington, D.C., designed by the Finnish architect Eero Saarinen, is completed.
- The Apartment Block at Ramat Gan, in Israel, designed by Israeli architects Alfred Neumann and Zvi Hecker, is completed.
- The Assembly Hall of the University of Illinois in Urbana, Illinois, designed by the U.S. architects Max Abramovitz and Wallace Harrison, is completed.
- The Beinecke Library at Yale University in New Haven, Connecticut, a completely windowless building designed by the U.S. architect Gordon Bunshaft, is completed.
- The Engineering Department of Leicester University, England, designed by the English architects James Stirling and James Gowan, is completed.
- The Lafayette Towers in Detroit, Michigan, designed by the German architect Ludwig Mies van der Rohe, are completed.

Arts

- The English artist Allen Jones paints *Aphrodite*.
- The English artist Bridget Riley paints *Fall*.
- The English artist David Hockney paints *Domestic Scene, Los Angeles*.
- The English artist Peter Blake paints *The Lettermen*.
- The French artist Marcel Duchamp creates *Box in a Valise, Series E*.
- The U.S. artist Andy Warhol creates the silkscreen *Electric Chair* series.
- The U.S. artist Dan Flavin creates *The Diagonal of May 25, 1963 (To Constantin Brancusi)*, using a fluorescent light tube.
- The U.S. artist David Smith sculpts *Cubi I*.
- The U.S. artist Edward Ruscha paints *Standard Station, Amarillo, Texas*.
- The U.S. artist Roy Lichtenstein paints *I Know... Brad* and *Whaam!*.

Film

- *Beach Party*, the first of a series of beach movies featuring slapstick humor, rock 'n' roll music, and teenagers in bathing suits, is released in the United States. It stars Annette Funicello, Frankie Avalon, and Bob Cummings, and features songs by Dick Dale and the Del-Tones.
- The "spaghetti Western" genre, low-budget Westerns made in Italy, becomes very popular worldwide. Key figures of the genre include the U.S. actor Clint Eastwood and Italian movie director Sergio Leone.
- The movie *America, America*, directed by Elia Kazan, is released in the United States, starring Stathis Giallelis.
- The movie *Billy Liar*, directed by John Schlesinger, is released in Britain. Based on the novel by British journalist Keith Waterhouse, it stars Tom Courtenay and Julie Christie.

- The movie *Charade*, directed by Stanley Donen, is released in the United States, starring Cary Grant, Audrey Hepburn, and Walter Matthau.
- The movie *Cleopatra*, directed by Joseph L. Mankiewicz, is released in the United States, starring Elizabeth Taylor and Richard Burton. A historical epic on a grand scale, production costs a record £12 million/ U.S.$44 million.
- The movie *From Russia with Love*, directed by Terence Young, is released in Britain. Based on the novel by Ian Fleming, it stars Sean Connery as James Bond.
- The movie *Hud*, directed by Martin Ritt, is released in the United States, starring Paul Newman and Patricia Neal. It is based on the novel *Horseman, Pass By* by Larry McMurty.
- The movie *Irma La Douce*, directed by Billy Wilder, is released in the United States, starring Shirley MacLaine and Jack Lemmon.
- The movie *It's a Mad, Mad, Mad, Mad World*, directed by Stanley Kramer, is released in the United States, starring Spencer Tracy and a huge comic cast, including Sid Caesar, Phil Silvers, and Terry-Thomas.
- The movie *Le Mépris/Contempt*, directed by Jean-Luc Godard, is released in France.
- The movie *Muriel*, directed by Alain Resnais, is released in France, starring Delphine Seyrig and Jean-Pierre Kérien.
- The movie *The Birds*, directed by British filmmaker Alfred Hitchcock, is released in the United States, starring Tippi Hedren and Rod Taylor.
- The movie *The Cardinal*, directed by Austrian filmmaker Otto Preminger, is released in the United States, starring Tom Tryon and Carol Lynley.
- The movie *The Great Escape*, directed by John Sturges, is released in the United States. The star-filled cast includes Steve McQueen, James Garner, Richard Attenborough, and Charles Bronson.
- The movie *The Leopard*, directed by Luchino Visconti, is released in Italy. Based on the novel *Il Gattopardo* by Giuseppe de Lampedusa, it stars Burt Lancaster, Claudia Cardinale, and Alain Delon.
- The movie *The Nutty Professor*, directed by Jerry Lewis, is released in the United States. Lewis also stars in it with Stella Stevens.
- The movie *The Pink Panther*, directed by Blake Edwards, is released in the United States, starring Peter Sellers as the hapless Inspector Clouseau. The character proves very popular and five sequels are made with Sellers.
- The movie *The Running Man*, directed by Carol Reed, is released in Britain, starring Laurence Harvey, Alan Bates, and Lee Remick.
- The movie *The Servant*, scripted by the English dramatist Harold Pinter and directed by the U.S. filmmaker Joseph Losey, is released in Britain, starring Dirk Bogarde, James Fox, and Sarah Miles.
- The movie *This Sporting Life*, directed by Lindsay Anderson, is released in Britain. Based on the novel by David Storey, it stars Richard Harris and Rachel Roberts.
- The movie *Tom Jones*, directed by Tony Richardson, is released in Britain. Based on the novel by Henry Fielding, it stars Albert Finney and Susannah York.
- The movie *Tystnaden/The Silence*, directed by Ingmar Bergman, is released in Sweden. The final part of a trilogy which includes *Through a Glass, Darkly* and *Winter Light*, it stars Ingrid Thulin and Gunnel Lindblom.
- The movie *Yukinojo Henge/An Actor's Revenge*, directed by Kon Ichikawa, is released in Japan, starring Kazuo Hasegawa.

APRIL

8   The 1962 Academy Awards take place. Best Actor: Gregory Peck, for *To Kill a Mocking Bird*; Best Supporting Actor: Ed Begley, for *Sweet Bird of Youth*; Best Actress: Anne Bancroft, for *The Miracle Worker*; Best Supporting Actress: Patty Duke, for *The Miracle Worker*; Best Picture: *Lawrence of Arabia*, directed by David Lean; Best Director: David Lean, for *Lawrence of Arabia*.

Literature and Language

- *Meetings with Remarkable Men*, by the Russian-born mystic Georgei Ivanovich Gurdjieff, is published posthumously.
- A court in New York, New York, allows the publication of the 18th-century English novel *Fanny Hill*, by John Cleland, which some thought obscene. In England it is banned by London magistrates.
- The Argentine writer Julio Cortázar publishes his novel *Reyuela/Hopscotch*.
- The English writer John Fowles publishes his novel *The Collector*.
- The French writer and philosopher Simone de Beauvoir publishes her third volume of autobiography *La Force des choses/The Force of Circumstance*.
- The French writer Henry de Montherlant publishes his novel *Le Chaos et la nuit/Chaos and Night*.
- The French writer Louis-Ferdinand Céline publishes his novel *Nord/North*.
- The German writer Günther Grass publishes his novel *Hundejahre/Dog Years*.
- The German writer Heinrich Böll publishes *Ansichten eines Clowns/The Clown*.
- The German-born U.S. philosopher Hannah Arendt publishes *Eichmann in Jerusalem: A Report on the Banality of Evil*, and *On Revolution*.
- The Guyanese writer Wilson Harris publishes his novel *The Secret Ladder*, the final part of his *The Guyana Quartet*.
- The Japanese writer Yukio Mishima publishes his novel *Gogo no eiko/The Sailor Who Fell From Grace With the Sea*.
- The Nobel Prize for Literature is awarded to the Greek poet George Seferis.
- The Peruvian writer Mario Vargas Llosa publishes his novel *La ciudad y los perros/The City and the Dogs*.
- The Polish-born English historian Isaac Deutscher publishes *The Prophet Outcast*, the final volume of his three-volume biography of the Russian revolutionary leader Leon Trotsky.
- The Pulitzer Prize for Biography is awarded to Leon Edel for *Henry James*, the Pulitzer Prize for Poetry is awarded to William Carlos Williams for *Pictures from Breughel*, and the Pulitzer Prize for Fiction is

posthumously awarded to William Faulkner for *The Reivers*.

- The Scottish writer Muriel Spark publishes her novel *The Girls of Slender Means*.
- The Trinidadian writer V. S. Naipaul publishes his novel *Mr Stone and the Knights Companion*.
- The U.S. author Maurice Sendak writes and illustrates the children's classic *Where the Wild Things Are*.
- The U.S. economists Milton Friedman and Anna Schwartz publish *A Monetary History of the USA, 1867–1960*.
- The U.S. writer A. R. Ammons publishes his poetry collection *Expressions of Sea Level*.
- The U.S. writer Allen Ginsberg publishes his poetry collection *Reality Sandwiches*.
- The U.S. writer and critic Susan Sontag publishes her novel *The Benefactor*.
- The U.S. writer Charles Bukowski publishes his poetry collection *It Catches My Heart in its Hands*.
- The U.S. writer James Baldwin publishes *The Fire Next Time*, two essays warning of the threat of racial violence in the United States.
- The U.S. writer John Updike publishes his novel *The Centaur*.
- The U.S. writer Joyce Carol Oates publishes her short-story collection *By the North Gate*.
- The U.S. writer Kurt Vonnegut publishes his novel *Cat's Cradle*.
- The U.S. writer Mary McCarthy publishes her novel *The Group*.
- The U.S. writer Sylvia Plath publishes her novel *The Bell Jar*.
- The U.S. writer Thomas Pynchon publishes his novel *V.*

Music

- At Bell Laboratories, U.S. electrical engineer Max Mathews creates a computer that can synthesize music. The composer inputs mathematical functions that the computer translates into sound—the first musical synthesizer.
- English composer Harrison Birtwistle completes his choral work *Descriptions of the Passing of a Year*.
- Protest songs against conformity, consumerism, and war, such as Peter, Paul, and Mary's version of Bob Dylan's "Blowin' in the Wind," are popular in the United States.
- Rhythm and blues music becomes popular in Britain, with key acts including Chuck Berry and Bo Diddley.
- The *Daily Worker* defines Merseybeat and the Liverpool sound as "the voice of 80,000 crumbling houses and 30,000 people on the dole." It includes most notably the Beatles and Gerry and the Pacemakers, and soon extends to Manchester groups such as the Hollies and Billy J. Kramer and the Dakotas.
- The Australian entertainer Rolf Harris releases the single "Two Little Boys."
- The British pop group Gerry and the Pacemakers releases the single "You'll Never Walk Alone," from the musical *Carousel*.
- The British pop group the Searchers releases the single "Sweets For My Sweet."

- The British pop group Freddie and the Dreamers releases the single "You Were Made For Me."
- The British pop singer Cliff Richard releases the singles "Bachelor Boy" and "Summer Holiday," both from the soundtrack of his movie *Summer Holiday*.
- The British pop singer Dusty Springfield releases the single "I Only Want to Be With You."
- The British rock group the Beatles release the singles "Please Please Me," "She Loves You," "Twist and Shout," and "I Want to Hold Your Hand," which will sell more than 12 million copies worldwide, and enters the U.S. charts at No. 1. The album *Please Please Me* is also recorded in 12 hours at EMI's Abbey Road studios.
- The English composer John Tavener completes his Piano Concerto.
- The English composer Michael Tippett completes his Concerto for Orchestra.
- The English composer Benjamin Britten completes his piano work *Notturno/Night Piece*.
- The Estonian composer Arvo Pärt completes his Symphony No. 1.
- The Italian tenor Luciano Pavarotti makes his debut at Covent Garden, London, England, singing in the opera *La Bohème/The Bohemian Girl* by Puccini.
- The opera *Our Man in Havana*, by the Australian composer Malcolm Williamson, is first performed, in London, England.
- The Russian composer Igor Stravinsky completes *Abraham and Isaac* for voice and orchestra.
- The Scopitone video juke-box enjoys a short-lived popularity in the United States.
- The U.S. composer George Crumb completes his work *Night Music* for soprano, piano, celesta, and percussion.
- The U.S. composer Leonard Bernstein completes his Symphony No. 3, *Kaddish*.
- The U.S. composer Morton Feldman completes his vocal work *Journey to the End of Night*, based on a novel by the French writer Louis-Ferdinand Céline.
- The U.S. composer Morton Feldman completes his chamber work *De Kooning*.
- The U.S. girl group the Crystals releases the single "Da Doo Ron Ron."
- The U.S. girl group the Ronettes releases the single "Be My Baby."
- The U.S. girl group the Chiffons releases the singles "He's So Fine" and "One Fine Day."
- The U.S. pop group Jimmie Gilmer and the Fireballs releases the single "Sugar Shack."
- The U.S. pop group the Beach Boys releases the album *Surfin' USA*.
- The U.S. pop singer Lesley Gore releases the single "It's My Party."
- The U.S. rhythm and blues guitarist B. B. King releases the album *Mr Blues*.
- The U.S. singer Frank Sinatra releases the single "Fly Me to the Moon."
- The U.S. singer Gene Pitney releases the single "24 Hours from Tulsa."
- The U.S. soul/rhythm and blues singer Ray Charles releases the single "Take These Chains From My Heart."

MAY

15 The 1962–63 Grammy Awards take place. Best Album: *The First Family* by Vaughn Meader; Best Record: "I Left My Heart in San Francisco" by Tony Bennett; Best Male Vocalist: Tony Bennett; Best Female Vocalist: Ella Fitzgerald; Best Group: Peter, Paul, and Mary.

OCTOBER

2 The revue *At the Drop of Another Hat*, starring Michael Flanders and Donald Swann, opens at the Haymarket Theatre, in London, England.

NOVEMBER

- The single "Dominique", by the Belgian nun Soeur Sourire (Sister Luc-Gabrielle), is a surprise hit; she releases the album *The Singing Nun* in December.

Theater and Dance

- The musical *Oh, What a Lovely War!*, using songs of World War I, is first performed, at the Theatre Royal, in London, England. It is directed by Joan Littlewood.
- The play *Barefoot in the Park*, by the U.S. writer Neil Simon, is first performed, in New York, New York.
- The play *Der Stellvertreter/The Representative* (*The Deputy* in the United States), by the German dramatist Rolf Hochhuth, is first performed, in Berlin, Germany.
- The play *The Milk Train Doesn't Stop Here Anymore*, by the U.S. dramatist Tennessee Williams, is first performed, in New York, New York.
- The Pulitzer Prize for Drama is not awarded this year.

MARCH

21 The musical *Half a Sixpence*, inspired by H. G. Wells's novel *Kipps*, with lyrics and music by David Hendon, is first performed, at the Cambridge Theatre, in London, England.

APRIL

25 The 1962–63 Tony Awards take place. Best Play: *Who's Afraid of Virginia Woolf?*; Best Musical: *A Funny Thing Happened on the Way to the Forum*; Best Actor: Arthur Hill; Best Actress: Uta Hagen.

MAY

7 The Guthrie Theater in Minneapolis, Kansas, is opened. It is a specially designed theater planned by Tyrone Guthrie for presenting the classical repertory.

Thought and Scholarship

- The English historian Asa Briggs publishes *Victorian Cities*.
- The English philosopher R. M. Hare publishes *Freedom and Reason*.
- The English political philosopher John Plamenatz publishes *Man and Society: A Critical Examination of Some Important Social and Political Theories from Machiavelli to Marx*.
- The German philosopher Jürgen Habermas publishes *Theorie und Praxis/Theory and Practice*.
- The Pulitzer Prize for History is awarded to Constance McLaughlin Green for *Washington, Village and Capital, 1800–1878*.
- The Pulitzer Prize for General Nonfiction is awarded to Barbara W. Tuchman for *The Guns of August*.

- The U.S. historian William E. Leuchtenburg publishes *Franklin D Roosevelt and the New Deal*.

SOCIETY

Everyday Life

- In the U.S. charts, there are ten tribute albums to President John F. Kennedy, including *John Fitzgerald Kennedy – A Memorial Album*, a collection of radio broadcasts from the day of the assassination, which sells 4 million copies in a week.
- The General Electric Company develops the self-cleaning oven in the United States.
- The Monkey dance becomes popular in the United States.

JANUARY

- The International Longshoremen's Association concludes a strike against East Coast shippers begun on December 23, 1962. The strike is estimated to have cost the shipping industry over $800 million.
5 First class U.S. postage rises to 5 cents per ounce.
11 The first discotheque opens, the Whisky-A-Go-Go in Los Angeles, California, with the emphasis on youth and contemporary rock 'n' roll dance music.

APRIL

22–July 8 A general strike takes place in British Guiana (Guyana), with rioting and terrorism.

AUGUST

28–November 26 The U.S. Congress helps avert a rail strike by requiring labor and management to submit to federal arbitration. On November 26, a federal arbitration panel rules that 90% of diesel locomotive firemen's jobs are redundant. Railroad operators had originally aimed to abolish all such jobs.

Media and Communication

- *Doctor Who*, a science fiction series about a time-traveler, starts on British television. The original doctor is William Hartnell; the role is subsequently played by Patrick Troughton, Jon Pertwee, Tom Baker, Peter Davison, Colin Baker, Sylvester McCoy, and Paul McGann. The series also features the Doctor's infamous enemies, the Daleks.
- The Italian island of Capri bans transistor radios.
- The still-popular daytime soap opera *General Hospital* begins on ABC television in the United States.

MAY

26 The 1962–63 Emmy Awards for television take place. Best Actor in a Single Show: Trevor Howard; Best Actress in a Single Show: Kim Stanley; Best Actor in a Series: E. G. Marshall, for *The Defenders*; Best Actress in a Series: Shirley Booth, for *Hazel*.

JULY

1 The U.S. postal service introduces five-digit Zone Improvement Plan (ZIP) codes for addresses.

SEPTEMBER

17–August 29, 1967 *The Fugitive*, the story of Dr. Richard Kimble, wrongly convicted of murder, who is in pursuit of the one-armed man who killed his wife and is, in turn, pursued by the police, appears on U.S. television, starring David Janssen and Barry Morse.

18–August 31, 1966 The situation comedy *The Patty Duke Show* appears on U.S. television; Duke, who plays dual roles as a brash U.S. teenager and her "identical cousin," a reserved English girl, is the youngest person to date in U.S. television to have her own prime-time series.

29–September 4, 1966 The situation comedy *My Favorite Martian* appears on U.S. television, starring Ray Walston as a Martian who has crash-landed on Earth and Bill Bixby as the reporter who protects his secret.

OCTOBER

15 The *New York Mirror*, the nation's second largest circulation daily, ceases publication, despite its impressive daily sales. The paper's demise follows a 114-day-long strike.

DECEMBER

27 The British Broadcasting Corporation (BBC) ends the controversial satire program *That Was The Week That Was*.

Religion

JUNE

21 After the death of Pope John XXIII on June 3, the Italian clergyman Giovanni Battista Montini is elected Pope Paul VI.

OCTOBER

25 The Vatican Council approves the principle of a fixed Easter.

DECEMBER

• The Roman Catholic Ecumenical Council authorizes the use of English for portions of the mass and the sacraments in U.S. Catholic services.

Sports

• The U.S. golfer Arnold Palmer becomes the first player to win over $100,000 in a single season on the U.S. PGA Tour.

FEBRUARY

• The World Boxing Council (WBC) is formed in Mexico City, Mexico, a rival governing body for boxing to the World Boxing Association (WBA), based in New York, New York.

22 René Lacoste, the former French tennis great and sports apparel manufacturer, receives a patent for a steel frame tennis racket.

APRIL

9–18 The Toronto Maple Leafs defeat the Detroit Red Wings by four games to one to win the National Hockey League Stanley Cup.

14–24 The Boston Celtics again defeat the Los Angeles Lakers to win the National Basketball Association (NBA) championship. At the conclusion of the series, the Celtics' brilliant point guard Bob Cousy retires from professional competition.

BIRTHS & DEATHS

JANUARY

5 Roger Hornsby, U.S. baseball player, dies in Chicago, Illinois (66).

21 Hakeem "The Dream" Olajuwon, Nigerian-born U.S. basketball player, born in Lagos, Nigeria.

29 Robert Frost, U.S. poet known for his use of colloquial language, dies in Boston, Massachusetts (88).

30 Francis Poulenc, French composer, dies in Paris, France (64).

FEBRUARY

11 Sylvia Plath, U.S. poet and novelist, commits suicide in London, England (30).

APRIL

13 Gary Kasparov, Soviet chess master who dominated international chess from the mid-1980s, born in Baku, Azerbaijan, USSR.

MAY

6 Theodore von Kármán, Austrian-born U.S. engineer who pioneered the use of mathematics in aeronautics and astronautics, dies in Aachen, West Germany (81).

JUNE

3 John XXIII, Roman Catholic pope 1958–63 who convened the Second Vatican Council, dies in Rome, Italy (81).

19 Donald Forsha Jones, U.S. geneticist who produced the first high-yield hybrid corn, dies in Hamden, Connecticut (73).

JULY

17 Letsie III, king of Lesotho 1990–95 and from 1996, born.

AUGUST

2 W. E. B. Du Bois, U.S. sociologist and black leader, dies in Accra, Ghana (95).

2 William Morris (Lord Nuffield), British industrialist and philanthropist who manufactured Morris cars, dies near Henley-on-Thames, England (85).

3 Georges Braque, French painter who helped develop cubism, dies in Paris, France (81).

9 Whitney Houston, U.S. singer, born in Newark, New Jersey.

OCTOBER

11 Jean Cocteau, French writer, actor, and painter, dies in Milly-la-Forêt, France (74).

NOVEMBER

2 Aldous Huxley, English novelist best known for his science-fiction work *Brave New World* (1932), dies in Los Angeles, California (69).

22 C(live) S(taples) Lewis, British academic and writer, dies in Oxford, England (64).

22 John F. Kennedy, 35th president of the United States 1961–63, a Democrat, is assassinated in Dallas, Texas (46).

DECEMBER

28 Paul Hindemith, German composer and musical theorist, dies in Frankfurt am Main, Germany (68).

MAY

20 Tigran Petrosyan wins the world chess championship in Moscow, USSR, from fellow Soviet grandmaster Mikhail Botvinnik, who has held the world title for all but two years since 1948.

AUGUST

2–14 The first world netball championships take place at Eastbourne, in Sussex, England, with 11 nations competing; Australia are the first winners.

SEPTEMBER

7 The Pro Football Hall of Fame, established by the National Football League in honor of famous players, is dedicated in Canton, Ohio.

OCTOBER

2–6 The Los Angeles Dodgers defeat the New York Yankees in four straight games to win the World Series.

DECEMBER

26–29 The United States ends Australia's four-year reign as Davis Cup tennis champions, winning the challenge round in Australia by three matches to two.

29 The Chicago Bears defeat the New York Giants 14–10 in the National Football League (NFL) Championship Game to give the Bears' coach George Halas a record seventh NFL title.

1964

POLITICS, GOVERNMENT, AND ECONOMICS

Business and Economics

JANUARY

7 As part of its trade drive with Europe, Cuba orders 400 British buses.

FEBRUARY

20 The Balzan International Foundation makes a controversial award of a peace prize to the United Nations (UN). Switzerland (not a member of the UN) later blocks the Foundation's funds.

APRIL

- Texas Gulf Sulfur Company reports discovering a vast supply of zinc, copper, and silver ore, estimated at 25 million tons, outside Timmins, Ontario.

MAY

- The American Federation of Labor and the Congress of Industrial Organizations (AFL-CIO) repudiates federal wage guidelines designed to combat inflation.

Colonization

JULY

6 Britain's Nyasaland Protectorate, renamed Malawi, becomes independent within the Commonwealth.

SEPTEMBER

21 Malta gains independence within the British Commonwealth.

OCTOBER

24 Northern Rhodesia, renamed Zambia, becomes an independent republic within the Commonwealth, with Kenneth Kaunda as president (Southern Rhodesia is now known as just Rhodesia).

DECEMBER

12 Kenya becomes a republic within the Commonwealth, with Jomo Kenyatta as president.

Human Rights

- Civil-rights groups in the United States bring together white students and black protestors in the "Mississippi Freedom Summer" to demand black voting rights; six people die and a thousand are arrested in the ensuing violence.
- The U.S. author and publisher Helen Gurley Brown publishes *Sex and the Office* that argues that single women should pursue careers (at least until they get married).

APRIL

- The New York World's Fair opens to disappointing crowds amid controversy caused by, among other things, a threat by the Congress of Racial Equality (CORE) to impede the opening ceremonies in protest at the city's failure to combat racial discrimination.

JUNE

14 Eleven steel companies join with the United Steelworkers Union to end racial discrimination in the steel industry.

July

- A race riot erupts in Harlem, New York, after an off-duty white policeman shoots a black teenager.
- President Lyndon B. Johnson signs the Civil Rights Act of 1964. The act outlaws discrimination in federally-funded enterprises and in public facilities and accommodations. It also created an Equal Employment Opportunity Commission.
- The U.S. National Labor Relations Board labels racial discrimination within unions an unfair labor practice.

August

- Black civil-rights activists from the Mississippi Freedom Democratic Party disrupt the Democratic Party's convention in Chicago, Illinois. They unsuccessfully demand equality of representation with white delegates from Mississippi.
- Mississippi authorities discover the bodies of murdered white civil-rights workers James Chaney, Andrew Goodman, and Michael Schwerner at a farm near the city of Philadelphia, Pennsylvania. The three had been missing since June 21, after being arrested for speeding by Mississippi police.

Politics and Government

- INTELSAT (International Telecommunications Satellite Consortium) is founded by 18 countries to operate telecommunication satellites and establish a global commercial communications network.
- The English politician Randolph Churchill publishes *The Fight for the Leadership of the Conservative Party*.
- The United Nations (UN) establishes a Conference on Trade and Development (UNCTAD), to promote trade and trade agreements between countries.

January

- President Lyndon B. Johnson suspends diplomatic relations with Panama after violence erupts in the Canal Zone sparked by the flying of the U.S. flag.
- The 24th Amendment to the U.S. Constitution, prohibiting poll taxes, becomes law.
- 12 A rebellion takes place in Zanzibar (now part of Tanzania), which is declared a republic. The sultanate is abolished and the sultan banished, and Abdullah Kassim forms a procommunist government.
- 15 A constitutional conference on Cyprus opens in London, England, but fails to reach agreement.
- 20–24 An army mutiny in Tanzania (followed by similar troop mutinies in Uganda and Kenya) is suppressed by the government of Julius Nyerere only with the assistance of British military forces.
- 21–September 17 The sixth session of the 17-nation disarmament conference is held in Geneva, Switzerland.
- 22 Kenneth Kaunda, president of the United National Independence Party, becomes the first prime minister of Northern Rhodesia (now Zambia).
- 24–31 A referendum in Ghana supports giving the president the power to remove judges from the supreme and high court and establishes the Convention People's Party as the sole party. The results are announced on February 3.
- 27 France establishes diplomatic relations with the People's Republic of China.

30 In a coup in South Vietnam, General Duong Van Minh is replaced by General Nguyen Khanh.

February

- The U.S. Supreme Court, in *Reynolds v. Simms*, rules that congressional districts within a given state must be roughly proportional in order to fulfill the Constitutional principle of equal protection.
- The United States seizes four Cuban fishing vessels in U.S. waters. Four days later, Cuba responds by shutting off the water supply at the U.S. naval station at Guantanamo Bay.
- 6 A British–French agreement is signed for the creation of a rail channel tunnel.
- 11 Fighting breaks out between members of the Greek and Turkish communities at Limassol, Cyprus.
- 21 The attempted assassination of Ismet Inönü, prime minister (and former president) of Turkey, takes place.
- 23 Britain recognizes President Abdul Amari Karume's regime in Zanzibar (now part of Tanzania).

March

- A jury in Dallas, Texas, sentences Jack Ruby to death after convicting him of murdering Lee Harvey Oswald, the alleged assassin of John F. Kennedy.
- A jury in Tennessee convicts Teamsters president James ("Jimmy") R. Hoffa of jury tampering, sentencing him to eight years in prison. Hoffa will be convicted again in July, this time in Chicago, Illinois, of fraud and conspiracy.
- Massachusetts senator Henry Cabot Lodge, a write-in candidate, wins the Republican presidential primary in New Hampshire.
- President Lyndon B. Johnson declares a "war on poverty" and pledges to achieve "total victory."
- Soviet missiles down a U.S. reconnaissance plane after it strays inadvertently into East German airspace. The plane's crew is released after a vigorous U.S. protest.
- The U.S. Supreme Court, in *New York Times v. Sullivan*, rules that public officials may not recover libel damages in cases involving criticism of their performance while in office.
- 9 Further Greek–Turkish fighting takes place, in Ktima, Cyprus.
- 11 South Africa withdraws from the International Labor Organization, which oversees workers' rights.
- 25 Sakari Tuomioja of Finland is appointed United Nations (UN) mediator in the Cyprus dispute.
- 25 Violence spreads in British Guiana (now Guyana) after an eight-week strike of sugar-workers (the strike ends on July 26).
- 27 A United Nations (UN) peace force under General Gyani of India takes over from British troops in Cyprus.
- 28 British aircraft destroy a Yemeni fort in retaliation for raids into the British territory of South Arabia (later South Yemen).

April

- The U.S. Supreme Court endorses arbitration in labor disputes, upholding a lower court ruling that such panels are constitutional.
- The United States reopens diplomatic relations with Panama, after anti-American disturbances in the Canal Zone die down.
- 4 The Cypriot president Archbishop Mikhail Makarios abrogates the 1960 treaty between Greece, Turkey, and

Cyprus, and heavy fighting occurs in the north west of the island.

13 Winston Field resigns as prime minister of Southern Rhodesia (now Zimbabwe) on policy grounds, and Ian Smith forms a ministry.

16 Joshua Nkomo, leader of the Zimbabwe African People's Union, is detained by the government in Southern Rhodesia (now Zimbabwe).

27 Tanganyika and Zanzibar are united, with Julius Nyerere as president and, on October 29, the state is named the United Republic of Tanzania.

MAY

- The U.S. State Department reports that Soviet agents had infiltrated the U.S. embassy in Moscow, planting over 40 bugs.
- The U.S. Supreme Court rules unconstitutional a federal law divesting naturalized citizens of U.S. citizenship if they return to their country of origin for three years.
- The U.S. Supreme Court orders schools in Prince Edward County, Virginia, to be reopened and desegregated. The county school superintendent had closed the schools back in 1959 to prevent their integration.

5 The Palestine Liberation Organization (PLO) is founded in Jordan in an attempt to reconcile Palestinian factions.

19 The United States complains to the USSR about surveillance microphones found in its Moscow embassy.

22 A state of emergency is declared in British Guiana (now Guyana) following rioting.

JUNE

- A cloture (closure of a debate) vote ends a 75-day filibuster in the U.S. Senate by Southerners opposed to civil-rights legislation.
- The U.S. Supreme Court strikes down a clause in the 1950 Internal Security Act that denies passports to members of the U.S. Communist Party.
- U.S. Army deserter George Gessner is convicted of delivering U.S. nuclear secrets to the Soviet Union. He is sentenced to life in prison.

11 At the end of the "Rivonia trial" in South Africa (begun October 10, 1963), Nelson Mandela is sentenced to life imprisonment, while eight other defendants receive lesser sentences, and one is discharged.

11 Greece rejects direct talks with Turkey over Cyprus.

12 The USSR and East Germany sign a 20-year treaty of friendship.

19 Antigovernment rebels in the Congo Republic take Albertville (now Kalemi) in the north of the country.

20 A summit is held in Tokyo, Japan, between President Diosdado Macapagal of the Philippines, President Achmed Sukarno of Indonesia, and Tunku Abdul Rahman of Malaysia, to discuss friction between Indonesia and Malaysia. The talks break down on June 21.

30 United Nations (UN) military operations in the Congo Republic end.

JULY

- Alabama governor George C. Wallace withdraws from the 1964 presidential race, after his brand of southern populist conservatism, although popular with blue-collar workers in some urban areas of northern states such as Wisconsin or Maryland, is shown to be mostly rejected outside the South.

- Republicans nominate Arizona senator Barry Goldwater for president and New York representative William E. Miller for vice president.
- The U.S. Supreme Court orders a restaurant and hotel in Atlanta, Georgia, to admit black students, upholding the 1964 Civil Rights Act.

10 Moise Tshombe succeeds Cyrille Adoula as prime minister of the Congo Republic.

15 Anastas Mikoyan succeeds Leonid Brezhnev as president of the USSR.

16 Samuel H. ("Dr. Sam") Sheppard is released from prison, pending a retrial for the murder of his wife. The appeal that wins his freedom—based on the claims that publicity before and during the trial prejudiced the jury—is pursued by F. Lee Bailey, with the support of many prominent Americans, including mystery author Erle Stanley Gardner.

22–30 A constitutional conference in London, England, on the future of Gambia, agrees to independence in February 1965.

26 The strike of sugar-workers in British Guiana (now Guyana) is called off.

26 The USSR calls for a new 14-power meeting to discuss the civil war in Laos.

27–30 Disturbances take place in Northern Rhodesia (now Zambia), involving the extreme Lumpa Church, led by Alice Lenshina, which forbids its members to take part in political activity; the death toll rises to 491.

AUGUST

- Democrats nominate Lyndon B. Johnson for president and Minnesota senator Hubert M. Humphrey for vice president.
- President Lyndon B. Johnson signs the Economic Opportunity Act of 1964. It allocates nearly $950 million to promote economic development in hard-hit rural and urban areas.
- The Tonkin Gulf incident moves the U.S. Congress to authorize President Lyndon B. Johnson to undertake "all necessary measures to repel any armed attack against forces of the United States and to prevent further aggression." This so-called Tonkin Gulf Resolution provides President Johnson with the de facto consent to wage an undeclared war on North Vietnam.

2 The U.S. destroyer *Maddox* is attacked off North Vietnam, in the Tonkin Gulf, by North Vietnamese torpedo boats; U.S. aircraft bomb naval bases in North Vietnam in reprisal. On August 4, the *Maddox* and the destroyer C *Turner Joy* are attacked.

5 Antigovernment rebels in the Congo Republic capture Stanleyville (now Kisangani), and declare the foundation of a People's Republic of the Congo on August 7.

7 General Nguyen Khanh proclaims a state of emergency in South Vietnam and ousts President Duong Van Minh.

8 Turkish planes attack Cyprus and, on August 9, the United Nations (UN) orders a cease-fire.

11 The head of the Lumpa Church in Northern Rhodesia (now Zambia), Alice Lenshina, surrenders, but the violence in the country continues.

24 White mercenaries arrive in the Congo Republic to fight antigovernment rebels.

25 Following protests in South Vietnam, President Nguyen Khanh resigns and, on August 27, General Duong Van

Minh becomes chairman of a Provisional Leadership Council.

26 The Rhodesian nationalist movements the People's Caretaker Council and the Zimbabwe African National Union (ZANU) are banned.

28–30 A race riot erupts in Philadelphia, Pennsylvania, prompting mayor James H. J. Tate to cordon off 125 city blocks. Before the riot ends the next day, over 500 people are injured and 350 arrested.

SEPTEMBER

- President Lyndon B. Johnson signs legislation creating a 9.2 million acre wilderness system.
- The Warren Commission, charged with investigating the events surrounding the assassination of President John F. Kennedy, reports that assassin Lee Harvey Oswald acted alone.

2 The Indonesian army lands in Malaysia in support of territorial claims and, on September 4, Commonwealth troops move in to defend the federation.

24 A "Berlin Passes" agreement is signed between the authorities of West Berlin and East Germany, opening the Berlin Wall for a fortnight four times a year, so that West Berliners can visit relatives in the East.

OCTOBER

- The U.S. civil-rights leader Martin Luther King, Jr., wins the Nobel Peace Prize.

1 The U.S. Federal Communications Commission rules that radio and television stations transmitting a presidential press conference must provide other presidential candidates with equal time.

5–11 A conference is held in Cairo, United Arab Republic (Egypt), of 58 nonaligned states (those not aligned with either Western or communist blocs in world politics).

15 In the British general election, the Labour Party wins 317 seats, the Conservatives win 304, and the Liberals 9.

15 Nikita Khrushchev is replaced as first secretary of the Soviet Communist Party by Leonid Brezhnev and as prime minister by Alexey Kosygin, following foreign policy and agricultural failures.

16 Alec Douglas-Home resigns as British prime minister following elections, and Harold Wilson forms a Labour ministry, with Patrick Gordon Walker, defeated at Smethwick, as foreign secretary, George Brown as secretary of state for economic affairs, James Callaghan as chancellor of the Exchequer, and Lord Gardiner as lord chancellor.

16 China explodes an atomic bomb, and becomes a nuclear power.

20 A civilian government is established in South Vietnam, under Tran Van Huong.

29 Indonesian troops land on the west coast of Malaya, but Commonwealth troops capture the invaders.

NOVEMBER

- Americans reelect Lyndon B. Johnson president in a landslide. In the Congressional elections, Democrats retain majorities in the House (295–140) and Senate (68–32).

2 King Saud of Saudi Arabia is deposed and replaced by his brother Faisal.

5 In a referendum, conducted almost exclusively among whites, in Rhodesia (now Zimbabwe), 90% (of a 61% poll turnout) favor independence.

5 Zhou Enlai, prime minister of the People's Republic of China, visits Moscow, USSR, for summit talks of communist states.

8 A cease-fire comes into force in the civil war in Yemen (between Egyptian-supported procommunist rebels and the exiled Saudi-backed traditionalist government).

8 Eisaku Sato of the Liberal Democratic Party becomes prime minister of Japan following elections.

10 Kenya becomes a single-party state when members of parliament belonging to the Kenya African Democratic Union join the Kenya African National Union.

12 The high court in Rhodesia (now Zimbabwe) rules that black activist Joshua Nkomo's detention is illegal; he and other African leaders are released on November 16, but restrictions are placed on their movements.

16 The trial begins in Johannesburg, South Africa, under the Suppression of Communism Act, of 14 whites, including Abraham Fischer, who led the defense in the "Rivonia" trial.

17 Britain states its intention of banning exports of arms to South Africa because of its policy of apartheid.

24 Belgian paratroops, the Congolese army, and white mercenaries capture Stanleyville (now Kisangani) in the Congo Republic from antigovernment rebels, and rescue hostages.

DECEMBER

- FBI agents arrest 21 Mississippi residents for conspiring to violate the civil rights of the men found murdered on August 4. The charges are later dropped. Seven men are convicted in 1967.

6 The Italian president Antonio Segni resigns for health reasons, and is succeeded, on December 28, by Giuseppe Saragat.

7 Police in Berkeley, California, arrest about 730 members of the Free Speech Movement (FSM) at the University of California, including student leader Mario Savio, as he adresses a crowd of around 13,000 people. Students had created the FSM earlier in the fall after university officials had banned political activist groups from campus.

14 Following an election in British Guiana (now Guyana), in which Cheddi Jagan's People's Progressive Party lost its majority, the governor appoints Forbes Burnham of the People's National Congress as prime minister.

18 The United Nations (UN) extends its mandate for the peacekeeping force in Cyprus to March 1965.

SCIENCE, TECHNOLOGY, AND MEDICINE

Agriculture

APRIL

- President Lyndon B. Johnson signs the Agricultural Act of 1964. The legislation aims to stabilize agricultural prices, by rewarding farmers for scaling back production and adopting soil conservation methods.

Computing

- IBM introduces the system 2250 computer, the first CAD (computer aided design) computer.
- The IBM 360 computer is introduced. It is compatible with a host of peripheral equipment, which makes it a commercial success.

Ecology

- The U.S. Congress creates Canyonlands National Park from 257, 640 acres of Utah wilderness.
- The Wilderness Act, that establishes the National Wilderness Preservation System, is passed by the U.S. Congress.

JANUARY
- The United States and Canada commit to a joint flood control project in the Columbia River basin.

MARCH
27 An earthquake measuring between 8.3 and 8.5 (later amended upward) on the Richter scale strikes Anchorage in Alaska. Although the sparse population limits casualties to 131, it is the most severe earthquake ever recorded in North America. An area of 120,000 sq km/75,000 sq mi is tilted and in some places adjacent sections of land are separated by 25 m/82 ft.

DECEMBER
23 A cyclone in Ceylon and southern India leaves over 2,000 people dead.

Exploration

- Britain's *Blue Streak* rocket is launched.

JULY
28 The U.S. spacecraft *Ranger 7* is launched from Cape Kennedy; it succeeds in obtaining close-up photographs of the moon's surface before crashing (July 31).

OCTOBER
12–13 The Soviet *Voskhod 1* mission is the first spacecraft to have a crew of three.

NOVEMBER
28 The United States launches *Mariner 4* to Mars. Passing within 1,865 km/6,118 mi of the planet's surface (July 14, 1965), it relays the first close-up photographs of the planet's surface as well as information on the Martian atmosphere.

Health and Medicine

- The infant mortality rate in Britain is 20 per thousand, compared to 30 per thousand in 1951.
- The living brain of a rhesus monkey is isolated from its body by neurosurgeons at Cleveland General Hospital, Ohio.
- U.S. divers spend nine days, at a depth of 58.5 m/192 ft, off the coast of Bermuda, onboard *Sealab* to study the effects of depth on the human mind and body.
- U.S. physiologist Konrad Bloch and German physiologist Feodor Lynen are jointly awarded the Nobel Prize for Physiology or Medicine for their discoveries concerning the mechanism and regulation of the cholesterol and fatty acid metabolism.
- U.S. surgeon James Hardy transplants a chimpanzee's heart into a man at the University of Mississippi Medical Center. It beats for 90 minutes. The operation raises intense ethical, religious, and legal questions.

JANUARY
11 The U.S. surgeon general Luther Terry's report, *Smoking and Health*, confirms the links between cigarette smoking and lung cancer and heart disease. Within two years cigarette packets will carry a health warning.

JUNE
- The U.S. Federal Trade Commission announces that it will require tobacco companies to provide warning labels about the health risks of smoking on cigarette packages, effective from January 1, 1965.

Science

- English astronomer Fred Hoyle and Indian astronomer Jayant Narlikar propound a new theory of gravitation that solves the problem of inertia.
- English chemist Dorothy Hodgkin receives the Nobel Prize for Chemistry for her determination of the structures of biochemical compounds, notably penicillin and vitamin B_{12}, using X-ray crystallography (she is the third woman to win the prize).
- Scientists at the Brookhaven National Laboratory, Upton, Long Island, United States, discover the fundamental particle omega-minus using the "Nimrod" cyclotron.
- U.S. physicist Charles Townes shares the Nobel Prize for Physics with Soviet physicists Nicolay Basov and Aleksandr Prokhorov for their work in quantum electronics leading to the development of the maser.
- U.S. physicists James Cronin and Val Fitch discover an asymmetry in the behavior of elementary particles, which is termed CP (charge parity) nonconservation.
- U.S. physicists Murray Gell-Mann and George Zweig independently suggest the existence of the quark, a subatomic particle and the building block of hadrons, a subatomic particle that experiences the strong nuclear force.
- U.S. zoologist William Hamilton recognizes the importance of altruistic behavior in animals, paving the way for the development of sociobiology.

Technology

- A Swedish foundry is the first European company to install robots, which it uses to lift castings out of molds.
- The world's largest oil pipeline enters service. Capable of transporting 1 million barrels of oil a day, it runs between Houston, Texas, and New Jersey.

JANUARY
25 The passive radio communications satellite *Echo II* is launched from Vandenberg Air Force Base, California. The first joint space venture between the United States

and the USSR, radio signals are transmitted between Jodrell Bank Observatory, Manchester, England, reflected off *Echo II*, and received at the Zmenki Observatory, near Gorky, Russia.

MAY

14   The Soviet leader Nikita Khrushchev opens the Aswan Dam in the United Arab Republic (UAR) of Egypt.

JUNE

- The Dutch electronics company Philips launches the compact cassette in Britain. This is still the industry standard for analog audio cassettes.

AUGUST

28   The first *Nimbus 1* satellite is launched into a polar orbit. It replaces the U.S. *TIROS* satellites.

Transportation

- The 360 km/224 mi long Volga–Baltic waterway opens in the USSR, linking the Baltic Sea and the Caspian Sea via the River Volga.
- The U.S. Air Force introduces the F-111 fighter-bomber. It has swept-back wings and can achieve a speed of Mach 2.5.
- The U.S. historian Robert Fogel publishes *Railroads and American Growth*.
- Two notable suspension bridges open, the Forth Bridge in Scotland, and the Verrazano Narrows Bridge (the world's longest) at the entry to New York harbor.

FEBRUARY

- President Lyndon B. Johnson announces that he has authorized work on the A-11 fighter jet, which designers hope will be capable of exceeding 2,000 mph and achieving an altitude of 70,000 feet.

SEPTEMBER

28   The UK's advanced military fighter aircraft, the TSR-2, makes its first flight.

OCTOBER

1   The "New Tokaido Line" between Tokyo and Osaka opens. A 515-km/320-mi high-speed rail line, "bullet" trains travel at an average speed of 166 kph/103 mph.

DECEMBER

22   The USAF Lockheed SR-71 Blackbird reconnaissance jet, constructed mostly of titanium, makes its first flight. It has a ceiling of 30,000 m/100,000 ft and is the fastest jet made.

ARTS AND IDEAS

Architecture

- St. Catherine's College in Oxford, England, designed by the Danish architect Arne Jacobsen, is completed.
- The 28-km/17.5-mi Chesapeake Bay Bridge-Tunnel is completed. A complex of bridges and tunnels, the tunnels are entered through openings in artificial islands built in the bay.

- The Carpenter Center for the Visual Arts at Harvard University in Cambridge, Massachusetts, designed by the Swiss architect Le Corbusier, is completed.
- The City Hall in Toronto, Canada, designed by the Finnish architect Viljo Revell, is completed.

NOVEMBER

21   The Verrazano Narrows Bridge, linking Staten Island and Brooklyn, opens in New York, New York. It is the world's largest single span suspension bridge and has a span of 1,298 m/4,258 ft.

Arts

- The English artist Bridget Riley paints *Current*.
- The English writer and art critic Herbert Read publishes *Art and Education*.
- The Italian artist Michelangelo Pistoletto paints *He and She Talk*.
- The Scottish artist Eduardo Paolozzi sculpts *Wittgenstein at Casino*.
- The Swedish-born U.S. artist Claes Oldenburg creates *Giant Soft Toothpaste*, made of canvas.
- The U.S. art critic Harold Rosenberg publishes *The Anxious Object: Art Today and its Audience*.
- The U.S. artist Andy Warhol creates his *Brillo Boxes*, wooden boxes covered with silkscreen prints meant to imitate commercial cardboard boxes. He also creates the silkscreens *Jackie*, *Race Riots*, and *Flowers*.
- The U.S. artist Edward Kienholz creates *Back Seat Dodge–38*.
- The U.S. artist George Segal sculpts *Woman Standing in a Bathtub*.
- The U.S. artist Jasper Johns sculpts *Painted Bronze (Ale Cans)*.
- The U.S. artist Mel Ramos paints *Kar Kween*.
- The U.S. artist R. B. Kitaj paints *An Urban Old Man*.
- The U.S. artist Richard Linder paints *New York City IV*.
- The U.S. artist Robert Rauschenberg wins the Grand Prix at the art exhibition of the Venice Biennale. This is seen as marking the decline of European art and the U.S. domination of contemporary art.
- U.S. photographer Garry Winograd takes the photograph *Los Angeles*.
- U.S. photographer Lee Friedlander takes *New York City*.

Film

- *Cinema Novo* ("New Cinema"), the Brazilian equivalent of the French *Nouvelle Vague* ("New Wave"), is exemplified in *Barren Lives*, directed by Nelson Pereira Dos Santos, and the works of Glauber Rocha, such as *Black God, White Devil* and *Antonio das Mortes*.
- The movie *8½*, directed by Federico Fellini, is released in Italy, starring Marcello Mastroianni and Claudia Cardinale.
- The movie *Doctor Strangelove, or How I Learned to Stop Worrying and Love the Bomb*, directed by Stanley Kubrick, is released in the United States, starring Peter Sellers and George C. Scott.
- The movie *Goldfinger*, directed by Guy Hamilton, is released in the United States, starring Sean Connery as James Bond, and Honor Blackman.

- The movie *Hamlet*, directed by Grigory Kozintsev, is released in the USSR, starring Innokenti Smoktunovsky, Mikhail Nazvanov, Elsa Radzin, and Anastasia Vertinskaya. It is based on a translation by Boris Pasternak of William Shakespeare's play.
- The movie *King and Country*, directed by Joseph Losey, is released in Britain, starring Tom Courtenay, Dirk Bogarde, and Leo McKern.
- The movie *La Peau douce/Silken Skin*, directed by François Truffaut, is released in France, starring Jean Desailly, Françoise Dorléac, and Nelly Benedetti.
- The movie *Le Journal d'une femme de chambre/Diary of a Chambermaid*, directed by Spanish filmmaker Luis Buñuel, is released in France, starring Jeanne Moreau and Jean Ozenne.
- The movie *Lord of the Flies*, directed by Peter Brook, is released in Britain. Based on the novel by William Golding, it stars James Aubrey, Tom Chapin, and Hugh Edwards.
- The movie *Marnie*, directed by English filmmaker Alfred Hitchcock, is released in the United States, starring Tippi Hedren and Sean Connery.
- The movie *Per un pugno di dollari/A Fistful of Dollars*, a "spaghetti Western" directed by Sergio Leone, is released in the United States, starring Clint Eastwood.
- The movie *Red Desert*, directed by Michelangelo Antonioni, is released in Italy, starring Monica Vitti, Richard Harris, and Carlos Chionetti.
- The movie *Suna no Onna/Woman of the Dunes*, directed by Hiroshi Teshigahara, is released in Japan, starring Eiji Okada and Kyoko Kishoda.
- The movie *The Gospel According to St Matthew*, directed by Pier Paolo Pasolini, is released in Italy, starring Enrique Irazoqui, Susanna Pasolini, and Mario Socrate.
- The movie *The Passenger*, directed by Andrzej Munk, is released in Poland, based on the book *Pasażerka* by Zofia Posmysz-Piasecka, and starring Aleksandra Śląska and Anna Ciepielewska.
- The movie *The Pumpkin Eater*, directed by Jack Clayton, is released in Britain, starring Anne Bancroft, Peter Finch, and James Mason.
- The movie *Two Stage Sisters*, directed by Xie Jin, is released in China, starring Xie Fang and Cao Yindi.
- The movie *Zorba the Greek*, directed by Michael Cacoyannis, is released in Britain. Based on the novel by Nikos Kazantzakis, it stars Anthony Quinn, Alan Bates, and Lila Kedrova.
- The movie *Zulu*, directed by Cy Endfield, is released in Britain, starring Stanley Baker, Michael Caine, and Jack Hawkins, with narration by Richard Burton.
- The movie musical *Les Parapluies des Cherbourg/The Umbrellas of Cherbourg*, directed by Jacques Demy, is released in France, starring Catherine Deneuve, Anne Vernon, and Nino Castelnuovo. It is awarded the Palme d'Or at the Cannes Film Festival in France.
- The movie version of the musical *My Fair Lady*, directed by George Cukor, is released in the United States. Based on George Bernard Shaw's play *Pygmalion*, it stars Audrey Hepburn and Rex Harrison.
- The movie musical *Mary Poppins*, directed by Robert Stevenson, is released in the United States. Based on the P. L. Travers stories about a nanny with magic powers,

it stars Julie Andrews, David Tomlinson, Glynis Johns, and Dick Van Dyke.

APRIL

13 The 1963 Academy Awards take place. Best Actor: Sidney Poitier, for *Lilies of the Field*; Best Supporting Actor: Melvyn Douglas, for *Hud*; Best Actress: Patricia Neal, for *Hud*; Best Supporting Actress: Margaret Rutherford, for *The VIPs*; Best Picture: *Tom Jones*, directed by Tony Richardson; Best Director: Tony Richardson, for *Tom Jones*.

Literature and Language

- *A Moveable Feast*, a memoir of Paris, France, between the wars by the U.S. writer Ernest Hemingway, is published posthumously.
- Children's book *Harriet the Spy* is published by U.S. author Louise Fitzhugh.
- The English musicologist Wilfrid Mellers publishes *Music in a New Found Land*.
- The English politician Roy Jenkins publishes his biography *Asquith*.
- The English writer Anthony Powell publishes *The Valley of Bones*, the seventh novel of his 12-volume sequence *A Dance to the Music of Time*.
- The English writer John Le Carré publishes his novel *The Spy who Came in from the Cold*.
- The English writer Philip Larkin publishes his poetry collection *The Whitsun Weddings*.
- The English writer William Golding publishes his novel *The Spire*.
- The English-born U.S. writer Christopher Isherwood publishes his novel *A Single Man*.
- The French writer and philosopher Jean-Paul Sartre publishes his autobiography *Les Mots/Words*.
- The French writer Marguerite Duras publishes her novel *Le Ravissement de Lol V Stein/The Ravishment of Lol Stein*.
- The Nigerian Ibo writer Chinua Achebe publishes his novel *Arrow of God*.
- The Nobel Prize for Literature is awarded to the French writer and philosopher Jean-Paul Sartre, who refuses it.
- The Pulitzer Prize for Biography is awarded to Walter Jackson Bate for *John Keats* and the Pulitzer Prize for Poetry is awarded to Louis Simpson for *At the End of the Open Road*. The Pulitzer Prize for Fiction is not awarded this year.
- The Romanian-born German poet Paul Celan publishes his poetry collection *Die Niemandsrose/The No-One's Rose*.
- The U.S. writer Gore Vidal publishes his novel *Julian*.
- The U.S. writer Hubert Selby, Jr., publishes his short-story collection *Last Exit to Brooklyn*.
- The U.S. writer J. D. Salinger publishes his book of stories *Raise High the Roof Beam, Carpenters*; and *Seymour: An Introduction*.
- The U.S. writer John Berryman publishes his poetry collection *77 Dream Songs*.
- The U.S. writer Joyce Carol Oates publishes her novel *With Shuddering Fall*.
- The U.S. writer LeRoi Jones (from 1968 called Amiri Baraka) publishes his poetry collection *The Dead Lecturer*.

- The U.S. writer Richard Brautigan publishes his novel *A Confederate General from Big Sur.*
- The U.S. writer Robert Lowell publishes his poetry collection *For the Union Dead.*
- The U.S. writer Saul Bellow publishes his novel *Herzog.*
- U.S. writer Tom Wolfe publishes *The Kandy-Kolored Tangerine-Flake Streamline Baby*, a collection of essays. He is a pioneer of the "New Journalism" style, combining the techniques of reportage and fiction.

Music

- A number of British pop and rock groups belonging to the Musicians Union, including the Rolling Stones, cancel planned tours of South Africa in protest against the apartheid system.
- For the first time, the top ten of the UK singles chart contains only UK artists.
- Japan is the third biggest market for pop music, after the United States and the UK.
- Rumors emerge in the British press of animosity between beat groups from the north of England, including the Beatles, and London-based groups such as the Rolling Stones.
- The album *Apollo Saturday Night*, an anthology including songs by Wilson Pickett, Ben E. King, and Otis Redding, illustrates the strength of soul music in the United States.
- The Beatles have four hit singles and two hit albums in the first three months of the year in the United States, partly due to their North American tour which includes an appearance on the U.S. *Ed Sullivan Show.* Sales of Beatles' records represent 60% of all records sold in this period. Their success also marks the beginning of a period of domination by British groups of the U.S. charts.
- The British Broadcasting Corporation (BBC) restricts the number of pop records played on radio, because of fears that over-dependence on recorded music will lessen the importance of live performances.
- The British pop group Herman's Hermits releases the single "I'm Into Something Good."
- The British pop group the Dave Clark 5 releases the single "Glad All Over."
- The British pop group the Kinks releases the single "You Really Got Me."
- The British pop singer Cilla Black, formerly a cloakroom attendant at Liverpool's Cavern Club, releases the singles "Anyone Who Had a Heart" and "You're My World."
- The British pop singer Lulu releases the single "Shout."
- The British rock group the Animals releases the single "The House of the Rising Sun."
- The British rock group the Rolling Stones releases the single "Little Red Rooster," a cover of a U.S. rhythm and blues song, and the album *Rolling Stones.*
- The British rock group the Animals releases the album *The Animals.*
- The Danish composer Vagn Holmboe completes his *Requiem for Nietzsche.*
- The English composer Elisabeth Lutyens completes her *Music for Piano and Orchestra.*

- The English composer Benjamin Britten completes his Cello Suite No. 1.
- The movie *A Hard Day's Night*, directed by Richard Lester, is released in Britain. Starring the British rock group the Beatles, its mixture of music and comedy is very popular and it is a big commercial success.
- The British rock group the Beatles releases the single and album *A Hard Day's Night* from their movie of the same name. They also release the single "Can't Buy Me Love," the best-selling single of the year in Britain.
- The French composer Olivier Messiaen completes his orchestral work *Couleurs de la cité céleste/Colors of the Celestial City.*
- The Governor of Indiana asks radio stations to ban the Kingsmen's single "Louie, Louie" because the unintelligible lyrics are rumored to be obscene.
- The Irish singer Val Doonican releases the single "Walk Tall."
- The opera *Die Zerrissene/The Man Torn in Two*, by the Swiss composer Gottfried von Einem, is first performed, in Hamburg, Germany.
- The opera *Don Rodrigo*, by the Argentine composer Alberto Ginastera, is first performed, in Buenos Aires, Argentina.
- The Russian composer Igor Stravinsky completes his vocal work *Elegy for J F K.*
- The Russian composer Dmitry Shostakovich completes his String Quartets No. 9 and No. 10.
- The U.S. composer Milton Babbitt completes his electronic work *Philomel.*
- The U.S. folk singer Tom Paxton releases the album *Ramblin' Boy.*
- The U.S. girl group the Supremes releases the single "Baby Love."
- The U.S. girl group the Dixie Cups releases the single "Chapel of Love."
- The U.S. girl group the Supremes, the best-selling singles act in the 1960s in the United States, releases the album *Where Did Our Love Go*, which includes the single "Baby Love."
- The U.S. jazz saxophonist John Coltrane releases the single "A Love Supreme."
- The U.S. jazz singer and trumpeter Louis Armstrong releases the single "Hello, Dolly," from the soundtrack of the movie of the same name.
- The U.S. Motown label singer Mary Wells releases the single "My Guy."
- The U.S. pop group the Beach Boys releases the singles "Fun, Fun, Fun" and "I Get Around."
- The U.S. pop group the Drifters releases the single "Under the Boardwalk."
- The U.S. pop group the Righteous Brothers releases the single "You've Lost That Loving Feeling."
- The U.S. pop trio the Walker Brothers releases the single "Make It Easy on Yourself."
- The U.S. rock singer Elvis Presley releases the single "Blue Christmas."
- The U.S. saxophonist Stan Getz and Brazilian singer Astrud Gilberto release the single "The Girl from Ipanema," composed by the Brazilian Antonio Carlos Jobim. It will become one of the best-known tunes in the world.
- The U.S. singer/songwriter Roy Orbison releases the single "Pretty Woman."

FEBRUARY

7 The British rock group the Beatles arrive at Kennedy Airport in New York, New York, to begin their second U.S. tour.

MAY

12 The 1963–64 Grammy Awards take place. Best Album: *The Barbra Streisand Album* by Barbra Streisand; Best Record: "The Days of Wine and Roses" by Henry Mancini; Best Male Vocalist: Jack Jones; Best Female Vocalist: Barbra Streisand; Best Group: Peter, Paul, and Mary.

Theater and Dance

• The play *After the Fall*, by the U.S. writer Arthur Miller, is first performed in New York, New York. It deals indirectly with his marriage to Marilyn Monroe.
• The play *Der schwarze Schwan/The Black Swan*, by the German dramatist Martin Walser, is first performed, in Stuttgart, Germany.
• The play *Entertaining Mr Sloane*, by the English dramatist Joe Orton, is first performed, in London, England.
• The play *Inadmissible Evidence*, by the English dramatist John Osborne, is first performed, in London, England.
• The play *La Tragédie de Roi Christophe/The Tragedy of King Christophe*, by the Martinique writer Aimé Césaire, is first performed, in Salzburg, Austria. It was published in 1963.
• The play *Marat/Sade*, by the German dramatist Peter Weiss, is first performed, in Berlin, Germany. The full title is *Die Verfolgung und Ermordung Jean-Paul Marats, dargestellt durch die Schauspielgruppe des Hospizes zu Charenton unter Anleitung der Herrn de Sade/The Persecution and Assassination of Jean-Paul Marat, as Performed by the Inmates of the Asylum at Charenton Under the Direction of the Marquis de Sade*.
• The play *The Royal Hunt of the Sun*, by the English dramatist Peter Shaffer, is first performed, at the Old Vic Theatre in London, England.
• The plays *Dutchman* and *The Slave*, by the U.S. writer LeRoi Jones (from 1968 called Amiri Baraka), are first performed, in New York, New York.
• The Pulitzer Prize for Drama is not awarded this year.

JANUARY

16 The musical *Hello, Dolly!*, with lyrics and music by Jerry Herman, is first performed in a successful version at the St. James's Theater, New York, New York.
18 The play *Dylan*, by the U.S. playwright Sidney Michael, about the Welsh poet Dylan Thomas, is first performed, at the Plymouth Theater in New York, New York. It stars Alec Guinness.

MAY

24 The 1964–65 Tony Awards take place. Best Play: *Luther*; Best Musical: *Hello Dolly!*; Best Actor: Alec Guinness; Best Actress: Sandy Dennis.

SEPTEMBER

22 The musical *Fiddler on the Roof*, with lyrics by Sheldon Harnick and music by Jerry Bock, is first performed, at the Imperial Theater, New York, New York. Its run of eight years is the longest of any musical at this time. Songs from the show include "If I Were a Rich Man" and "Sunrise, Sunset."

Thought and Scholarship

• *Games People Play* is published by Eric Berne, which popularizes "transactional analysis."
• German-born English psychologist Hans Eysenck publishes *Crime and Personality*.
• The German-born U.S. political philosopher Herbert Marcuse publishes *One-Dimensional Man: Studies in the Ideology of Advanced Industrial Society*.
• The Pulitzer Prize for History is awarded to Sumner Chilton Powell for *Puritan Village: The Formation of a New England Town*.
• The Pulitzer Prize for General Nonfiction is awarded to Richard Hofstadter for *Anti-Intellectualism in American Life*.

SOCIETY

Education

AUGUST

14 Black students in Biloxi, Mississippi, attend a previously all-white elementary school, the first school desegregation below the college level in the state.

Everyday Life

• The American Tobacco Co. introduces Carlton, the first low-tar cigarette, in the United States.
• The Anglo-Dutch multinational corporation Unilever, a major manufacturer of oils, soaps, detergents, and processed foods, launches Flora margarine.
• The confectionery company Rowntrees of York launches After Eight mints in Britain.
• The Jiffy Packaging Co. introduces the Jiffy bag to the British market.
• The U.S. fashion designer Rudi Gernreich introduces the monokini, a topless swimsuit.
• The U.S. food company Kellogg introduces Pop-Tarts in the United States.
• The U.S. toy company Mattel produces the G. I. Joe action figure for boys, an early version of Action Man.
• The Verbands Mölkeri (United Dairy) company markets long-life milk in Switzerland.
• The Wonderbra is designed in Canada.

FEBRUARY

• The International Longshoremen's Association halts a nine-day loading stoppage on wheat bound for the USSR after U.S. trade officials assure union negotiators that half of all future shipments will travel on U.S. ships.

MARCH

15 The actors Elizabeth Taylor and Richard Burton are married in Montreal, Canada.

APRIL

1–18 A strike of Belgian doctors takes place over a new law on health insurance. A final settlement is reached on June 25.

MAY

28 The *Daily Telegraph* describes Carnaby Street as the center of the Swinging Sixties scene in London, England.

AUGUST

- California succeeds New York as the most populous state in the Union.

SEPTEMBER

September–November Chrysler Corporation and the United Auto Workers (UAW) Union agree to a three-year contract, just minutes before a strike is to begin. Ford Motor Company reaches a similar agreement with the UAW on September 18. On September 25, the UAW strikes General Motors Corporation, after union and company negotiators fail to reach a new contract. The strike at GM is resolved on November 7.

NOVEMBER

- Newspaper journalists in Detroit, Michigan, end a 132-day strike, the longest in industry history, after signing a new contract with the *Detroit News* and *Detroit Free Press*.

Media and Communication

- An intercity video-telephone system is provided by AT&T between Chicago, Illinois, New York, New York, and Washington, D.C.
- Chairman Mao announces tighter controls on the Chinese movie industry, in order to bring it into line with Party views.
- The "supermarket magazine" *Family Circle* is published in the United States and Britain.
- The Canadian communications theorist Marshall McLuhan publishes *Understanding Media*.
- To promote filmmaking in Algeria, the Center of Algerian Cinema is inaugurated.
- Xerox develops the first office fax in the United States. It can only operate on dedicated phone lines.

JANUARY

10–May 4, 1965 *That Was the Week that Was*, a program of satirical commentary, starring David Frost, Henry Morgan, Buck Henry, and Tom Lehrer, appears on U.S. television, based on the 1962–63 British program.

MAY

25 The 1963–64 Emmy Awards for television take place. Best Series: *The Dick Van Dyke Show*; Best Actor in a Single Show: Jack Klugman; Best Actress in a Single Show: Shelley Winters; Best Actor in a Series: Dick Van Dyke; Best Actress in a Series: Mary Tyler Moore, both for *The Dick Van Dyke Show*.

SEPTEMBER

15–June 2, 1969 The television series *Peyton Place* is broadcast in the United States. It is the first prime-time dramatic serial on U.S. television since the 1940s and stars Mia Farrow, Ryan O'Neal, Dorothy Malone, Dan Duryea, Ruby Dee, and Mariette Hartley.

17–July 1, 1972 *Bewitched*, a comedy series about a suburban witch trying to resist using her magic powers, appears on U.S. television. It stars Elizabeth Montgomery, Dick York (later Dick Sargent), and Agnes Moorehead.

18–September 2, 1966 *The Addams Family*, a comedy series based on cartoon characters created by Charles Addams, appears on U.S. television, starring Carolyn Jones, John Astin, Jackie Coogan, and Ted Cassidy.

19–September 2, 1967 *Flipper*, a children's adventure series about a boy and his dolphin friend on a Florida marine reserve, appears on U.S. television, starring Brian Kelly, Luke Halprin, and Tommy Nordon.

22–January 15, 1968 *The Man from U.N.C.L.E.*, a spy series starring Robert Vaughn, David McCallum, and Leo G. Carroll, is shown on U.S. television.

24–September 1, 1966 *The Munsters*, a comedy series about a family of vampires, werewolves, and other monsters, appears on U.S. television, starring Fred Gwynne, Yvonne de Carlo, and Al Lewis.

26–September 4, 1967 The situation comedy *Gilligan's Island* appears on U.S. television. Depicting the improbable adventures of seven people stranded on an uncharted island after their sightseeing boat sinks in a storm, it stars Bob Denver, Alan Hale, Jr., Jim Backus, Natalie Schafer, Tina Louise, Russell Johnson, and Dawn Wells.

OCTOBER

10 U.S. satellites *Syncom 3* (launched on August 19, 1964) in a synchronous orbit 37,000 km/23,000 mi above the Pacific Ocean, transmits the opening ceremonies of the Tokyo Olympics, the first transpacific television pictures.

Religion

- The French anthropologist Claude Lévi-Strauss publishes *Le cru et le cuit/The Raw and the Cooked*, the first volume of his *Mythologiques/Introduction to the Science of Mythology*. The final volume appears in 1971.

Sports

- The Australian tennis player Roy Emerson wins the men's singles titles at the Wimbledon, U.S., and Australian championships.
- The British racing driver and motorcyclist John Surtees wins the Formula One World Drivers' Championship to become the first driver to win world championships on two and four wheels, having been 350-cc and 500-cc world motorcycling champion between 1958 and 1960.
- The U.S. boxer Sugar Ray Robinson, five times world middleweight champion, retires from professional boxing with 174 victories in 201 bouts. He was never knocked out.
- The U.S. golfer Mickey Wright equals fellow U.S. golfer Betsy Rawls' record of four U.S. Women's Open golf titles.

JANUARY

29–February 9 The 9th Winter Olympic Games in Innsbruck, Austria, attract 1,091 competitors, including

200 women, from 36 countries. The Soviet Union wins 11 gold medals; Austria, 4; and Norway, Finland, France, Sweden, and West Germany, 3 each.

FEBRUARY

25 The U.S. boxer Cassius Clay beats Sonny Liston of the United States after six rounds of their fight in Miami, Florida, to win the world heavyweight boxing title. The same year, Clay announces his conversion to Islam, changing his name to Muhammad Ali.

MARCH

21 The UCLA Bruins conclude an unbeaten season by beating Duke University 98–93 to win the National Collegiate Athletic Association (NCAA) basketball championship.

APRIL

11–25 The Toronto Maple Leafs win their third straight National Hockey League (NHL) Stanley Cup, beating the Detroit Red Wings by four games to three.

12 Arnold Palmer of the United States becomes the first golfer to win the U.S. Masters at Augusta, Georgia, four times.

18–26 The Boston Celtics win their sixth straight National Basketball Association (NBA) championship, beating the San Francisco Warriors by four games to one.

MAY

• At the first world amateur surfing championships at Manly, Sydney, Australia, Bernard Farrelly of Australia wins the men's event and another Australian, Phyllis O'Donnell, wins the women's event.

2 The racehorse Northern Dancer, ridden by the U.S. jockey Bill Hartack, wins the U.S. Kentucky Derby in a record time of exactly two minutes.

JUNE

21 Jim Bunning of the Philadelphia Phillies pitches the first regular season perfect game (in which no opposing runners reach base) in the Major Leagues since 1922, against the New York Mets in Shea Stadium in New York, New York.

JULY

14 The French cyclist Jacques Anquetil becomes the first to win the Tour de France race five times, and also the first to win it for four successive years.

17–December 31 The British car and speedboat enthusiast Donald Campbell emulates his father Malcolm Campbell's achievement of holding the world land- and water-speed records simultaneously. He sets a new land-speed record of 648.77 kph/403.14 mph on Lake Eyre salt flats, Australia. Later in the year he reaches 444.615 kph/276.279 mph on Lake Dumbleyung, Australia, to break the water-speed record for the seventh time since 1955.

SEPTEMBER

2 Terje Pedersen of Norway achieves the first javelin throw in excess of 90 m/295 ft, in Oslo, Norway.

OCTOBER

• At the Olympic Games in Tokyo, Japan, Abebe Bikila of Ethiopia becomes the first athlete to regain the marathon title.

7–15 The St. Louis Cardinals defeat the New York Yankees in seven games to win the World Series. Cardinals pitcher Bob Gibson sets a World Series record by striking out 31 batters in three games.

10 The 18th Olympic Games open in Tokyo, Japan, attracting 5,140 competitors, including 683 women, from 93 countries. Judo and volleyball are introduced to the Games.

11 Arnold Palmer of the United States wins the inaugural World Matchplay golf championship at Wentworth, Surrey, England.

NOVEMBER

1 The U.S. football player Jim Brown, of the Cleveland Browns, becomes the first player in pro football to reach the 10,000 yards rushing mark.

BIRTHS & DEATHS

MARCH

6 King Paul I of Greece dies and is succeeded by his son Constantine II (63).

8 Norbert Weiner, U.S. mathematician who pioneered the field of cybernetics, dies in Stockholm, Sweden (69).

18 Bonnie Kathleen Blair, U.S. speed skater, is born in Cornwall, New York.

APRIL

5 Douglas MacArthur, U.S. general who commanded the allied forces in the South Pacific during World War II, dies in Washington, D.C. (83).

MAY

2 Nancy Witcher Langhorne, Lady Astor, British politician and the first woman to sit in the House of Commons, dies in Grimsthorpe Castle, Lincolnshire, England (84).

27 Jawaharlal Nehru, first prime minister of independent India 1947–64, dies in New Delhi, India (74).

JULY

16 Miguel Indurain, Spanish cyclist who won both the Tour of Italy and Tour de France in 1992, born in Villava, Spain.

AUGUST

12 Ian Fleming, English writer who created James Bond, secret agent 007, dies in Canterbury, Kent, England (56).

SEPTEMBER

1 Sean O'Casey, Irish playwright whose plays depict the reality of Dublin's slums, dies in Torquay, Devon, England (80).

OCTOBER

15 Cole Porter, U.S. composer and lyricist, dies in Santa Monica, California (73).

20 Herbert Hoover, 31st president of the United States 1929–33, a Republican, dies in New York, New York (90).

DECEMBER

1 J. B. S. Haldane, English geneticist who pioneered population genetics, dies in Bhubaneswar, India (72).

9 Edith Sitwell, English poet, dies in London, England (77).

1965

POLITICS, GOVERNMENT, AND ECONOMICS

Business and Economics

- Pepsi-Cola and Frito-Lay merge to form Pepsico, Inc.
- The Benetton clothing company is founded in Italy. Through its chain of franchises, it will attain commercial success worldwide.

FEBRUARY
- U.S. railroad unions and operators agree to reduce redundant workers via attrition.

APRIL
26 While contract negotiations continue, U.S. steel operators agree to increase wages for some 400,000 U.S. steel workers, thereby averting a nationwide strike.

SEPTEMBER
- Steel workers and operators agree to a new three-year contract, narrowly averting a nationwide strike.
- The U.S. Department of Housing and Urban Development (HUD) begins operations. It is charged with providing homes and promoting economic development in hard-pressed urban and rural areas.

NOVEMBER
10 Alcoa, the largest aluminum manufacturer in the United States, decides not to raise aluminum prices by 2%, after pressure had been brought to bear on it by the government, which threatened to divest part of the government's aluminum stockpile.

DECEMBER
- International Telephone and Telegraph (ITT) corporation announces plans to merge with American Broadcasting Company (ABC), a move that would make the new conglomerate worth over $1.8 billion.
- The U.S. Federal Reserve Board raises the discount rate from 4% to 4.5% to combat inflation.

Colonization

FEBRUARY
18 Gambia becomes independent within the British Commonwealth.

MARCH
3 The British protectorate of Bechuanaland (now Botswana) becomes self-governing, with Seretse Khama as prime minister.

Human Rights

JANUARY
18 Protest marches begin in Selma, Alabama; civil-rights campaigners led by Martin Luther King, Jr., of the Southern Christian Leadership Conference demand that blacks be allowed to register as voters.

FEBRUARY
18 In the town of Marion, near Selma, Alabama, black civil-rights activist Jimmie Lee Jackson is shot by police while taking part in a demonstration demanding that blacks be allowed to register as voters.
21 Radical black leader Malcolm X is shot dead at the Audubon Ballroom, New York, New York.

MARCH
7 In what becomes known as "Bloody Sunday," a march through Selma, Alabama, is broken up by police; white civil-rights protestor Reverend James Reeb is injured and dies of his wounds the next day. That same month, over 3,000 demonstrators depart Selma on a five-day civil-rights march to the state capital, Montgomery.
13 U.S. president Lyndon B. Johnson announces on television that he will submit a Voting Rights Bill to Congress to ensure that blacks are not prevented from registering as voters.

AUGUST
6 The Voting Rights Bill becomes law in the United States, making illegal the southern states' practice of disenfranchising black voters by imposing taxation, literacy, or other requirements on potential voters.
11–16 A race riot erupts in Watts, a neighborhood of Los Angeles, California, after policemen arrest a black driver for drunk driving. In five days of violence, 35 are killed, hundreds injured, and some $200 million of property is destroyed.

Politics and Government

- President Lyndon B. Johnson appoints jurist Abe Fortas to the U.S. Supreme Court.
- The Immigration Reform Act in the United States repeals the 1924 National Origins Act as of August 30, 1968; it reduces immigration from Europe and increases the number of Asian immigrants accepted.
- The U.S. journalist Arthur Schlesinger, Jr., publishes *A Thousand Days*, an account of the presidency of John F. Kennedy.

JANUARY
- Lyndon B. Johnson is inaugurated the 36th president of the United States.
- President Lyndon B. Johnson urges Congress to adopt a constitutional amendment providing for succession in

case of presidential disability, succession to the vice presidency, and reform of the electoral college system.

2   Indonesia withdraws from the United Nations (UN), the first member ever to do so, following Malaysia's admission to the UN Security Council.

2   The Pakistani president Ayub Khan defeats Fátima Jinnah in presidential elections.

8   In his State of the Union address, President Lyndon B. Johnson outlines a series of broad social and economic initiatives that he urges Congress to undertake. These initiatives will become known as Johnson's Great Society programs.

8   Indonesian troops, sent by their government because of its opposition to the newly-formed Federation of Malaysia, make further landings in mainland Malaysia; their incursions are contained by Malaysian, British, and British Commonwealth forces.

14 The prime ministers of Northern Ireland and of the Republic of Ireland meet for the first time in 43 years.

FEBRUARY

- U.S. security officers arrest four U.S. terrorists plotting to blow up the Statue of Liberty, Liberty Bell, and Washington Monument.

3   A cheating scandal rocks the U.S. Air Force Academy at Colorado Springs; 150 cadets resign.

8   U.S. aircraft bomb North Vietnam following Vietcong attacks on U.S. areas in South Vietnam. This begins a pattern of regular U.S. bombing of North Vietnam known as Operation Rolling Thunder or Operation Flaming Dart.

MARCH

- A U.S. spokesperson concedes that the United States's South Vietnamese allies have used poison gas in the war in Vietnam. The announcement provokes widespread criticism.

- Ku Klux Klansmen murder Michigan civil-rights worker Viola Gregg Liuzzo in Selma, Alabama. Three men are convicted of the murder and sentenced to ten years in jail, on December 3.

- The U.S. Supreme Court rules unconstitutional a Maryland law providing for movie censorship. A court hearing is required before a movie may be censored; the burden of proof lies with the censor.

8   The U.S. Supreme Court rules that individuals with unconventional religious beliefs may be eligible for conscientious objector status.

8   Two battalions of U.S. Marines, 3,500 soldiers, land to defend Danang airbase in South Vietnam. They are the first U.S. combat troops to enter the war.

9   The Appalachian Regional Development Act, providing economic assistance to the area, becomes law in the United States.

25 Dudley Senanayake forms a ministry in Ceylon (now Sri Lanka) following the defeat of Mrs. Sirimavo Bandaranaike in elections.

25 West Germany extends the time limit for holding trials of former Nazis, from May 1965 to December 1969.

APRIL

- President Lyndon B. Johnson orders U.S. Marines to the Dominican Republic after a military coup leads to civil war.

- The U.S. education commissioner sets Fall 1967 as the deadline by which all public schools are to be desegregated.

4   North Vietnamese MiG aircraft shoot down U.S. jets for the first time.

7   In an address at Johns Hopkins University, Baltimore, Maryland, U.S. president Lyndon B. Johnson offers North Vietnamese leader Ho Chi Minh participation in a southeast Asian development plan in return for an end to the war. The governments of North Vietnam and the People's Republic of China reject Johnson's overture the following day.

8   Members of the European Coal and Steel Community (ECSC), the European Economic Community (EEC), and Euratom sign a treaty providing for the merging of the Communities' superior institutions into a single Commission and Council of Ministers, to be known as the European Community (EC).

9   Clashes occur between Indian and Pakistani forces on the disputed Kutch–Sind border (between India and western Pakistan).

11 The Elementary and Secondary Education Act provides financial assistance for schools and educational programs in rundown areas of the United States.

21 The 114-nation Disarmament Commission resumes talks in New York, New York, after a five-year interval.

23 A large-scale raid is made over North Vietnam by U.S. aircraft.

29 Australia decides to send troops to assist South Vietnam in its war against communist insurgents.

MAY

- The U.S. Supreme Court nullifies a federal law authorizing the seizure of communist propaganda by the U.S. Postal Service.

7   In a general election in Rhodesia (now Zimbabwe), Ian Smith's Rhodesian Front Party wins a sweeping victory.

12 West Germany establishes diplomatic relations with Israel; Arab states respond by breaking off relations with West Germany.

JUNE

- Civil-rights protestors disrupt Chicago, Illinois, declaring the city's commitment to desegregation inadequate. In five days of protests, 350 people are arrested.

- The U.S. Supreme Court overturns the 1962 swindling conviction of Texas financier Billie Sol Estes, ruling that the presence of television cameras in the court room violated the due process clause of the 14th Amendment.

- The United States employs the B-52 bomber for the first time in a raid against Vietcong forces north of Saigon.

2   European hostages held by Congolese rebels in the Congo Republic are reported killed.

7   The U.S. Supreme Court, in *Griswold v. Connecticut,* overturns an 1879 Connecticut State law prohibiting the use of contraceptives.

8   U.S. forces in South Vietnam are authorized by the U.S. Congress to engage in offensive operations against communist Vietcong guerrillas.

19 The Algerian president Ahmed ben Bella is deposed; the army commander Houari Boumédienne heads a revolutionary council.

24 South Vietnam breaks off relations with France.

28 The Protection of the President Act in the United States makes assassination a federal offense, following the acknowledgment of the Warren Commission set up to investigate John F. Kennedy's death that it had no clearly defined legal jurisdiction.

30 India and Pakistan sign a cease-fire in the border dispute between the two countries.

JULY

- In the face of South Vietnamese political and military collapse, U.S. general William Westmoreland beseeches President Lyndon B. Johnson for 44 additional battalions, or 180,000 men.

- President Lyndon B. Johnson replaces U.S. ambassador to South Vietnam General Maxwell Taylor with former Massachusetts senator Henry Cabot Lodge. Taylor was too skeptical, from Johnson's perspective, of the United States' escalating participation in the war.

- President Lyndon B. Johnson announces that he will increase the number of U.S. troops in South Vietnam from 75,000 to 125,000. He also doubles the monthly draft quota from 17,000 to 35,000.

2 France announces a boycott of all European Economic Community (EEC) meetings other than those concerned with the day-to-day management of existing problems, following a dispute over Community agricultural policy and individual members' freedom of action.

15 King Constantine of Greece dismisses prime minister Andreas Papandreou. After weeks of unrest, Stephen C. Stefanopoulos becomes prime minister on September 17.

AUGUST

3 Preparatory talks for a constitutional conference on Aden and the South Arabian Federation open in London, England, but break down on August 7.

5 The CBS correspondant Morley Safer presents a story on the CBS evening news showing a company of U.S. marines setting fire to huts in the hamlet of Cam Ne, Vietnam, in retaliation for sniper fire. News reports like this are shocking the United States as the war is turned into a "living-room conflict."

9 Singapore secedes from Malaysia, and Yusof Bin Ishaq becomes president (with Lee Kuan Yew remaining prime minister).

17 With the war in southeast Asia escalating, Soviet negotiators ridicule a U.S. nuclear nonproliferation proposal before the UN Disarmament Committee in Geneva. The committee disbands two days later.

19 After a 20-month trial in West Germany of former officials of the Nazi death camp at Auschwitz, the court, sitting in Frankfurt, sentences six men to life imprisonment.

24 The United Arab Republic (Egypt) and Saudi Arabia sign a cease-fire agreement, suspending hostilities in the civil war in Yemen.

SEPTEMBER

- President Lyndon B. Johnson reports that he has accepted conditionally a new Panama Canal Treaty providing for joint U.S.–Panamanian control of the canal zone.

1 Left wing terrorists demanding independence for the British protectorate of Aden shoot the speaker of the legislative council. On September 26, Britain suspends the constitution.

1 Pakistani troops cross the Kashmir cease-fire line in the Pakistan–India border dispute.

6 India invades West Pakistan and bombs Lahore.

7–24 A constitutional conference in London, England, on the future of Mauritius ends with a promise of independence in 1966.

22 A cease-fire is agreed in the war between India and Pakistan, which is subsequently violated by both sides.

29 The USSR admits to supplying arms to communist North Vietnam.

30 The U.S. president Lyndon B. Johnson signs the Federal Aid to Arts Act, establishing the National Endowment for the Humanities and the National Endowment for the Arts.

OCTOBER

- Opponents of the Vietnam War protest in concert across the United States. Some burn draft cards; one is arrested for doing so, under a new federal law.

- The U.S. House Committee on Un-American activities launches an investigation into the activities of the Ku Klux Klan.

1 An attempted communist coup in Indonesia leads to widespread political violence.

4–11 The Rhodesian prime minister Ian Smith attends talks in London, England, on the future of Rhodesia (Zimbabwe).

13 President Joseph Kasavubu of the Congo Republic dismisses Moise Tshombe, the prime minister.

NOVEMBER

- The U.S. Supreme Court declares unconstitutional a law requiring U.S. communists to register with the federal government. Such a law violates the Constitution's protection against self-incrimination.

- Vietnam War opponents converge on Washington, D.C., to voice their displeasure to federal government officials.

8 In the Canadian elections, the prime minister Lester Pearson's Liberals are the largest party, but fail to win an overall majority (the Liberals win 131 seats, the Progressive Conservatives 97, and others 37).

11 The Rhodesian prime minister Ian Smith makes a Unilateral Declaration of Independence. Britain declares the regime illegal and introduces exchange and trade restrictions.

19 A constitutional congress on the future of British Guiana (now Guyana) ends with an agreement for independence in May 1966.

25 General Sese Seko Mobutu deposes President Joseph Kasavubu in a military coup in the Congo Republic.

DECEMBER

- By this month, 200,000 U.S. troops are stationed in Vietnam.

- President Lyndon B. Johnson suspends bombing raids of North Vietnam in an effort to compel the North Vietnamese to negotiate.

5 Charles de Gaulle wins the largest percentage of the vote in the first round of a French presidential election, but fails to obtain a clear majority.

9 Nikolai Podgorny replaces Anastas Mikoyan as president of the USSR.

17 Britain imposes an oil embargo on Rhodesia (now Zimbabwe) in response to its Unilateral Declaration of Independence.

18　Nine African states break off diplomatic relations with Britain for not using force against Rhodesia following its Unilateral Declaration of Independence.
19　Charles de Gaulle defeats François Mitterrand in the second round of the French presidential election.
29　President Ho Chi Minh of North Vietnam rejects unconditional peace talks offered by the United States.
29　The independence of the British protectorate of Bechuanaland (now Botswana) is announced for September 1966.
31　The executives of the European Economic Community (EEC), the European Coal and Steel Community (ECSC), and Euratom are merged into one executive authority.

SCIENCE, TECHNOLOGY, AND MEDICINE

Computing

- U.S. computer scientists John Kemeny and Thomas Kurtz develop BASIC (Beginners All-purpose Symbolic Instruction Code), a simplified computer programming language used in schools, businesses, and microcomputers.
- U.S. Digital Equipment Corporation (DEC) introduces the PDP-8 (Programmed Data Processor) computer. The first minicomputer, it has 4 kilobytes of memory, is easy to use, and costs $18,000. It stimulates the growth of computers in business and education.

Ecology

- It is estimated that the population of blue whales in the Antarctic is less than 2,000.
- The Gir Lion National Park is established in India. It is the last remaining natural habitat of the Asiatic lion.

FEBRUARY
5　After a drought that had begun the year before, the water storage reservoirs supplying New York, New York, dip to 25% of capacity, a record low.

MARCH
28　An earthquake in Chile kills about 400 people.

APRIL
11　A cluster of tornadoes kills 271 people, injures 5,000, and causes $300 million in property damage in Iowa, Illinois, Wisconsin, Indiana, Michigan, and Ohio.

Exploration

- French oceanographer Jacques Cousteau heads the Conshelf Saturation Dive Program, which sends six divers 100 m/328 ft down in the Mediterranean for 22 days.
- The U.S. launches *Pioneer 6* into solar orbit. It relays information about the solar wind and cosmic rays, and also data on the tail of comet Kohoutek.

MARCH
18　Soviet cosmonaut Alexey Leonov leaves spacecraft *Voskhod 2* and floats in space for 20 minutes—the first space walk.
23　U.S. astronauts Virgil Grissom and John Young are launched aboard *Gemini 3*. It is the first U.S. space mission with a crew of two.

JUNE
- The U.S. National Aeronautics and Space Administration (NASA) launches *Gemini 4*, whose four-day mission sees the first U.S. space walk by astronaut Edward White.
3–7　U.S. astronaut Edward White, during the *Gemini 4* space mission, demonstrates the ability of humans to function in outer space when he makes a 36-minute space walk, the first by a U.S. astronaut. He is also the first to use a personal propulsion pack during the walk.

JULY
- The Soviet spacecraft *Zond 3* relays close-up photographs of 7.8 million sq km/3 million sq mi of the moon's surface.

AUGUST
21–29　The U.S. spacecraft *Gemini 5* completes 120 orbits in eight days. It is the longest space flight taken to date and demonstrates the ability of humans to adapt to weightlessness.

DECEMBER
12　The U.S. spacecraft *Gemini 6* (launched on December 4) comes to within 0.3 m/1 ft of *Gemini 7* (launched on December 5). They are the first spacecraft to rendezvous with each other.

Health and Medicine

- French physiologists François Jacob, André Lwoff, and Jacques Monod are jointly awarded the Nobel Prize for Physiology or Medicine for their discoveries concerning genetic control of enzyme and virus synthesis.
- Kuru and Creutzfeld-Jakob disease are transmitted to primates by U.S. virologists Daniel Gajdusek and Clarence Gibbs.
- The first soft contact lenses are marketed in the United States.
- The U.S. Congress orders that cigarette packages carry a health warning in the United States.

AUGUST
1　Cigarette advertising is banned on British television.

Science

- Canadian geologist John Tuzo Wilson publishes *A New Class of Faults and Their Bearing on Continental Drift*, in which he formulates the theory of plate tectonics to explain continental drift and seafloor spreading.
- Japanese physicist Sin-Itiro Tomonaga and U.S. physicists Julian Schwinger and Richard Feynman are jointly awarded the Nobel Prize for Physics for their work in quantum electrodynamics.
- NASA launches *GEOS 1* (Geodynamics Experimental Ocean Satellite). Its aim is to provide a three-dimensional map of the world accurate to within 10 m/30 ft.

- U.S. astronomers Arno Penzias and Robert Wilson detect microwave background radiation in the universe and suggest that it is the residual radiation from the Big Bang.
- U.S. biochemist Robert Woodward synthesizes the antibiotic cephalosporin C.
- U.S. biochemist Robert Woodward receives the Nobel Prize for Chemistry for synthesis of organic substances, especially chlorophyll.

Technology

- A study estimates that the average family in the United States takes 52 photographs each year.
- The first Soviet *Molniya* communications satellite is launched.
- The Large Aperture Seismic Array is established in Montana. The signals from 525 seismometers, dispersed over an area of 30,000 sq km/11,600 sq mi, are combined to record seismic events with a high degree of sensitivity.
- The U.S. Postal Service begins experimenting with optical character readers to sort mail.

APRIL

5 The first international communication satellite, *Intelsat 1 (Early Bird)*, is launched into geostationary orbit over the Atlantic Ocean at the Equator. It provides 240 two-way telephone circuits or one television channel.

NOVEMBER

9 Power is blacked out in the northwest United States and Canada for 13 hours; 30 million people are affected.

26 The first French satellite, *A-1 Asterix*, is launched.

Transportation

- The last section of the Trans-Canada highway is completed in Newfoundland. Stretching from Victoria, British Columbia, to St. John's, Newfoundland, it is 7,821 km/4,860 mi long and is the world's longest national road.
- The Soviet Antonov AN-22 heavy transport aircraft makes its first passenger flight, with 720 passengers.
- The U.S. Congress passes the Highway Beautification Act, which requires all highway billboards to be removed by July 1, 1970.
- The U.S. Lockheed A-11 reconnaissance airplane is introduced. It achieves a speed of Mach 3.
- The Zeeland Bridge in the Netherlands is completed. It links Chouwen, Diuveland, and Noord Beveland, and at 5,022 m/16,472 ft long is the longest bridge in Europe.
- U.S. lawyer Ralph Nader publishes his book on road-safety, *Unsafe at any Speed*, an attack on the U.S. automobile industry.

ARTS AND IDEAS

Architecture

- The Roman Catholic Church of St. Mary in Tokyo, Japan, designed by the Japanese architect Kenzo Tange, is completed.
- The Salk Institute Laboratories, in La Jolla, California, designed by the U.S. architect Louis Kahn, are completed.
- The Shrine of the Book in Jerusalem, Israel, designed by the Austrian-born U.S. architect Frederick Kiesler, is completed.

OCTOBER

- The Gateway Arch in St. Louis, Missouri, designed by the Finnish architect Eero Saarinen, is completed. It spans the Mississippi River, commemorating the Louisiana Purchase of 1803 and symbolizing the city's role in the United States' western expansion of the previous century.

7 The Post Office Tower (now the Telecom Tower), is opened in London, England; it is the tallest building in Britain.

Arts

- The English artist Allen Jones paints *Curious Woman*.
- The English artist Peter Blake paints *Roxy, Roxy*.
- The French artist Martial Raysse paints *A Sweet and Simple Picture*.
- The German artist Joseph Beuys presents the performance work *How to Explain Pictures to a Dead Hare* in an art gallery in Düsseldorf, Germany.
- The German-born U.S. artist Richard Linder paints *Disneyland*.
- The Italian artist Michelangelo Pistoletto paints *Vietnam*.
- The U.S. artist Edward Kienholz sculpts *The Beanery*.
- The U.S. artist Joseph Kosuth creates *One and Three Chairs*.
- The U.S. artist Kenneth Noland paints *Transwest*.
- The U.S. artist Roy Lichtenstein paints *Red and Yellow Brushstrokes*.
- U.S. photographer Jerry Uelsmann takes *Poet's House*.

MARCH

30 Officials dedicate the Los Angeles County Art Museum, the United States' largest art museum west of the Mississippi River.

Film

- The movie *Alphaville*, directed by Jean-Luc Godard, is released in France, starring Eddie Constantine and Anna Karina.
- The movie *Doctor Who and the Daleks*, directed by Gordon Fleming is released in Britain. Based on the British television series, it stars Peter Cushing and Roy Castle.
- The movie *Doctor Zhivago*, directed by David Lean, is released in Britain. Based on the novel by Boris Pasternak, it stars Julie Christie and Omar Sharif.

- The movie *Obchod na Korze/The Shop on Main Street*, directed by Jan Kadar, is released in Czechoslovakia, starring Ida Kaminska.
- The movie *Pierrot-le-fou/Mad Pierrot*, directed by Jean-Luc Godard, is released in France. Based on the novel *Obsession* by Lionel White, it stars Jean-Paul Belmondo and Sylvie Vardan.
- The movie *Repulsion*, directed by the Polish-U.S. filmmaker Roman Polanski, is released in Britain, starring Catherine Deneuve, Ian Hendry, and John Fraser.
- The movie *Shakespeare Wallah*, directed by James Ivory, is released in Britain, starring Felicity Kendal and Shashi Kapoor.
- The movie *Simón de desierto/Simon of the Desert*, directed by Spanish filmmaker Luis Buñuel, is released in Spain, starring Claudio Brook and Silvia Pinal.
- The movie *The Battle of Algiers*, directed by the Italian filmmaker Gillo Pontecorvo, is released in France, starring Brahim Haggiag, Jean Martin, Yacef Saadi, and Tommaso Neri.
- The movie *The Birds, The Bees and the Italians*, directed by Pietro Germi, is released in Italy, starring Gastone Moschin and Virna Lisi. It is awarded the Palme d'Or, jointly with Lelouch's *Un Homme et une femme/A Man and a Woman*, at the Cannes Film Festival in France, later in the year.
- The movie *The Collector*, directed by William Wyler, is released in Britain. Based on the novel by John Fowles, it stars Samantha Eggar and Terence Stamp.
- The movie *The Knack – and How to Get It*, directed by Richard Lester, is released in Britain, starring Rita Tushingham, Michael Crawford, and Ray Brooks. It wins the Palme d'Or at the Cannes Film Festival in France, later in the year.
- The movie *Thunderball*, directed by Terence Young, is released in the United States, starring Sean Connery as James Bond.
- The movie *What's New, Pussycat?*, directed by Clive Donner, is released in the United States. Starring Peter Sellers, Peter O'Toole, Romy Schneider, Capucine, Paula Prentiss, and Woody Allen, it is Allen's first feature-length appearance as actor and writer.
- The movie musical *The Sound of Music*, directed by Robert Wise, is released in the United States, starring Julie Andrews and Christopher Plummer. It is a huge box-office success, becoming the most successful movie of the 1960s and even outperforming *Gone With the Wind*.
- The movie *Help!*, directed by Richard Lester, is released in Britain. A sequel to *A Hard Day's Night*, it also stars the British rock group the Beatles, but is less commercially successful.

APRIL

5 The 1964 Academy Awards take place. Best Actor: Rex Harrison, for *My Fair Lady*; Best Supporting Actor: Peter Ustinov, for *Topkapi*; Best Actress: Julie Andrews, for *Mary Poppins*; Best Supporting Actress: Lila Kedrova, for *Zorba the Greek*; Best Picture: *My Fair Lady*, directed by George Cukor; Best Director: George Cukor, for *My Fair Lady*.

Literature and Language

- Norman Mailer publishes his novel *An American Dream*.
- The English writer Basil Bunting publishes his poetry collection *Loquitur*.
- The English writer Doris Lessing publishes her novel *Landlocked*.
- The English writer Kathleen Raine publishes her poetry collection *The Hollow Hill*.
- The English writer Margaret Drabble publishes her novel *The Millstone*.
- The English writer Peter Matthiessen publishes his novel *At Play in the Fields of the Lord*.
- The English writer P. G. Wodehouse publishes his novel *Galahad at Blandings*.
- The Nigerian (Yoruba) writer Wole Soyinka publishes his novel *The Interpreters*.
- The Nigerian (Yoruba) writer Wole Soyinka publishes his poetry collection *Idanre and Other Poems*.
- The Nobel Prize for Literature is awarded to the Russian novelist Mikhail Sholokhov.
- The poetry collection *Ariel*, by the U.S. writer Sylvia Plath, is published posthumously.
- The Polish-born U.S. writer Jerzy Kosinski publishes his novel *The Painted Bird*.
- The Pulitzer Prize for Biography is awarded to Ernest Samuels for *Henry Adams*, the Pulitzer Prize for Poetry is awarded to John Berryman for *77 Dream Songs*, and the Pulitzer Prize for Fiction is awarded to Shirley Anne Grau for *The Keepers of the House*.
- The short-story collection, *Everything That Rises Must Converge*, by the U.S. writer Flannery O'Connor, is published posthumously.
- The U.S. writer Cormac McCarthy publishes his novel *The Orchard Keeper*.
- The U.S. writer John Updike publishes his novel *Of the Farm*.

Music

- In Chicago, Illinois, the Association for the Advancement of Creative Musicians, a collective to encourage self-employment by black jazz musicians, is formed.
- In the U.S. charts, nine of the top ten acts are British.
- The Australian pop group the Seekers releases the single "I'll Never Find Another You."
- The Beatles' concert at Shea Stadium, Queens, New York, New York, is televised in the United States.
- The British blues rock group the Yardbirds releases the single "For Your Love."
- The British pop group the Hollies releases the single "I'm Alive."
- The British pop group Gerry and the Pacemakers releases the single "Ferry Across the Mersey" (known in the United States as "Ferry Cross the Mersey").
- The British pop group Herman's Hermits releases the single "Mrs. Brown You've Got a Lovely Daughter."
- The British pop singer Petula Clark releases the single "Downtown."
- The British pop singer Tom Jones releases the single "It's Not Unusual."

- The British rock group the Beatles releases the singles "Help!," "Ticket to Ride," and "Day Tripper," and the album *Help!*
- The British rock group the Rolling Stones releases the single "(I Can't Get No) Satisfaction."
- The British rock group the Who releases the single "I Can't Explain."
- The British rock group the Beatles releases the single "Yesterday."
- The English composer John Tavener completes his Chamber Concerto.
- The English composer Peter Maxwell Davies completes his vocal work *Revelation and Fall* for soprano and chamber ensemble.
- The English composer Benjamin Britten completes his choral work *Voices for Today* and his song cycles *Songs and Proverbs of William Blake* and *Poet's Echo*, settings of Russian poems.
- The French composer Pierre Boulez completes his *Pli selon pli/Fold upon Fold* for voice and orchestra and his chamber work *Eclat/Brilliance*.
- The Hungarian composer György Ligeti completes his *Nouvelles Aventures/New Adventures* for small orchestra and three singers.
- The opera *Miss Julie*, by the U.S. composer Ned Rorem, is first performed, in New York, New York. It is based on a play of the same name by the Swedish writer August Strindberg.
- The Polish composer Witold Lutosławski completes his vocal work *Paroles tissées/Woven Words*.
- The U.S. broadcasting company CBS buys the Fender Guitar Company, the manufacturer of Stratocasters and Telecasters.
- The U.S. composer Leonard Bernstein completes his choral work *Chichester Psalms*.
- The U.S. composer Virgil Thomson completes his orchestral work *Ode to the Wonders of Nature*.
- The U.S. folk-rock musician Bob Dylan releases the single "Subterranean Homesick Blues" and the albums *The Times They Are A-Changin'* and *Bringing It All Back Home*.
- The U.S. folk-rock group the Byrds releases two albums, *Mr Tambourine Man* and *Turn!Turn!Turn!*, which includes singles by the same names.
- The U.S. girl group the Shangri-Las releases the single "Leader of the Pack." In Britain, it is termed "sick" by the British Broadcasting Corporation (BBC) and the pop television program *Ready, Steady, Go!*, and banned by both.
- The U.S. girl group the Supremes releases the single "Stop! In the Name of Love."
- The U.S. pop duo Sonny & Cher releases the single "I Got You Babe."
- The U.S. pop group Sam the Sham and the Pharaohs releases the single "Woolly Bully."
- The U.S. pop group the Beach Boys releases the single "California Girls."
- The U.S. pop group the Righteous Brothers releases the single "Unchained Melody."
- The U.S. pop group the Four Tops releases their eponymous first album, featuring the single "Baby, I Need Your Loving."
- The U.S. singer/songwriter Stevie Wonder releases the single "Uptight (Everything's Alright)."

- The U.S. soul singer James Brown releases the album *Grits and Soul*.
- The U.S. soul singer Wilson Pickett releases the single "In the Midnight Hour."
- The U.S. trumpeter Herb Alpert releases the single "A Taste of Honey."
- The U.S. vocal group the Temptations releases the single "My Girl."
- U.S. folk-rock musician Bob Dylan releases the album *Highway 61 Revisited*.

JANUARY

6   In an attempt to restrict the number of British pop and rock groups in the United States, the U.S. government announces that work permits for British bands will be restricted.

JULY

25   U.S. folk-rock musician Bob Dylan plays an electric guitar at the Newport Folk Festival, supported by the Butterfield Blues Band; his fans jeer, but he shows how folk music could merge with rock.

Theater and Dance

- The play *A Patriot for Me*, by the English dramatist John Osborne, is first performed, in London, England.
- The play *Loot*, by the English dramatist Joe Orton, is first performed, at the Cambridge Arts Theatre, England.
- The play *The Homecoming*, by the English dramatist Harold Pinter, is first performed, at the Aldwych Theatre in London, England.
- The play *The Odd Couple*, by the U.S. dramatist Neil Simon, is first performed, at the Plymouth Theater in New York, New York.
- The Pulitzer Prize for Drama is awarded to Frank D. Gilroy for *The Subject Was Roses*.
- The Vivian Beaumont Theatre opens at the Lincoln Center for Performing Arts in New York, New York.
- The watusi and the monkey become the latest dance crazes in the United States.

JUNE

13   The 1964–65 Tony Awards take place. Best Play: *The Subject Was Roses*; Best Musical: *Fiddler on the Roof*; Best Actor: Jack Albertson; Best Actress: Irene Worth.

NOVEMBER

27   The musical *Man of La Mancha*, with lyrics by Joe Darian and music by Mitch Leigh, is first performed, at the ANTA-Washington Square Theater, New York, New York. It is based on the work of the Spanish writer Miguel Cervantes, *Don Quijote de la Mancha*.

Thought and Scholarship

- The Algerian-born French political philosopher Louis Althusser publishes *Pour Marx/For Marx*.
- The English historians Grahame Clark and Stuart Piggott publish *Prehistoric Societies*.
- The English historian Christopher Hill publishes *Intellectual Origins of the English Revolution*.
- The Pulitzer Prize for History is awarded to Irwin Unger for *The Greenback Era*.
- The Pulitzer Prize for General Nonfiction is awarded to Howard Mumford Jones for *O Strange New World*.

- The U.S. philosopher Monroe Beardsley publishes *Philosophical Thinking*.
- U.S. historian Lawrence Stone publishes *The Crisis of Aristocracy, 1558–1641*.

SOCIETY

Education

- The Higher Education Act makes federal funds available to support underprivileged college and university students in the United States.
- The University of California opens new campuses in Irvine and Santa Cruz.

Everyday Life

- A study in the United States finds that 85% of airline stewardesses who leave their jobs resign to get married.
- An underwater telephone cable, 9,816 km/5,300 mi in length, is laid between Hawaii and Japan. It provides 128 telephone circuits. A similar cable is laid between the United States and France.
- Britain decides to adopt metric measurements.
- Ex-Harvard lecturer Timothy Leary writes *The Psychedelic Reader* and coins the phrase "Tune in, turn on, drop out" to describe the experience of using the hallucinogenic drug LSD.

- The artificial sweetener aspartame is launched in the United States, marketed under the name of Nutra-Sweet.
- The beat poet Allen Ginsberg coins the term "flower power" for the antiwar, alternative lifestyle attitudes of the 1960s.
- The British charity Oxfam extends its role to support family planning initiatives in the Third World as well as famine relief.
- The first miniskirts appear in Mary Quant's boutique, Bazaar, in the King's Road, Chelsea, London, England. Affordable and liberating, they rapidly become fashionable throughout the Western world.
- The lava lamp is launched in the United States.
- The Pepsi-Cola Co. launches Diet Pepsi in the United States.
- The rate of population growth in the United States stands at 1.2%, the lowest since 1945, the year before the baby boom.
- The world population is over 3 billion.
- U.S. authors Jinx Kragen and Judy Perry publish *Saucepans and the Single Girl*, a combination of cookbook and courting guide for single women.

SEPTEMBER

- The New York Newspaper Guild halts production of the city's daily newspapers. The stoppage lasts three weeks and costs the industry some $10 million.
- 6 The U.S. newspaper the *San Francisco Examiner* is the first to observe the birth of the hippie movement by noting that the Haight-Ashbury section of San Francisco, California has become "a hip hangout" for beatniks.

BIRTHS & DEATHS

JANUARY

4 T(homas) S(tearns) Eliot, U.S.-British modernist poet and playwright who had a strong influence on 20th-century poetry, dies in London, England (76).

24 Winston Churchill, British prime minister 1940–45 and 1951–55 who led Britain through World War II, dies in London, England (90).

FEBRUARY

15 Nat "King" Cole, U.S. jazz and popular singer, dies in Santa Monica, California (45).

21 Malcolm X, U.S. black militant leader, is assassinated in New York, New York (39).

23 Stan Laurel, U.S. comedian who, with Oliver Hardy, formed the most successful film comedy team, dies in Santa Monica, California (74).

MARCH

18 Farouk I, king of Egypt 1936–52, dies in Rome, Italy (45).

APRIL

21 Edward Victor Appleton, English physicist who received the Nobel Prize for Physics in 1947 for his discovery of the Appleton layer in the atmosphere which reflects radio waves, dies in Edinburgh, Scotland (72).

MAY

21 Geoffrey de Havilland, English aircraft designer who made some of the first jet airplanes, dies in Watford, Hertfordshire, England (82).

23 David Smith, U.S. sculptor known for his welded metal forms, dies in Albany, New York (59).

JUNE

2 Bernard Baruch, U.S. presidential advisor who helped draft the United Nations policy with regard to controlling atomic energy, dies in New York, New York (94).

13 Martin Buber, German Jewish religious philosopher, dies in Jerusalem, Israel (87).

22 David O. Selznick, U.S. film director, dies in Hollywood, California (63).

JULY

14 Adlai Ewing Stevenson, U.S. politician and diplomat, and Democratic presidential candidate 1952 and 1956, who helped found the United Nations, dies in London, England (65).

AUGUST

13 Ikeda Hayato, prime minister of Japan 1960–64, whose fiscal policies were responsible for Japan's rapid economic growth, dies in Tokyo, Japan (65).

27 Le Corbusier (assumed name of Charles Edouard Jeanneret), Swiss architect and city planner whose designs combined expressionism and Functionalism, dies in Cap Martin, France (77).

SEPTEMBER

4 Albert Schweitzer, German theologian, philosopher and doctor, dies in Lambaréné, Gabon (90).

27 Clara Bow, U.S. silent film star, dies in Los Angeles, California (60).

OCTOBER

22 Paul Tillich, German-born U.S. theologian and philosopher, dies in Chicago, Illinois (79).

NOVEMBER

21 Icelandic pop star Björk (Gudmundsdottir) is born in Reykjavik, Iceland.

DECEMBER

16 W. Somerset Maugham, English novelist and playwright, dies in Nice, France (91).

Media and Communication

- The Japanese electronic company Sony launches the Sony CV-2000, the first home video recorder, using Sony's Betamax format. The first color video recorder is available the following year.

JANUARY

30 The funeral of Winston Churchill in Britain is watched by more than 350 million people worldwide.

MAY

17 *Out of This World*, featuring the contributions of nine participating countries, is the first program to be broadcast across the Atlantic via the *Early Bird* satellite.

JUNE

28 A transatlantic telephone service is established via the *Early Bird* satellite.

SEPTEMBER

12 CBS withdraws from this year's Emmy Awards because of the inconsistency of the categories.

12 The 1964–65 Emmy Awards for television take place. Best Actor in a Single Show: Al Lunt; Best Actress in a Single Show: Lynn Fontaine, both for *The Magnificent Yankee*; Best Actor in a Series: Dick Van Dyke.

15–September 2, 1968 The espionage thriller *I Spy* appears on U.S. television. Starring Robert Culp and Bill Cosby, it is the first noncomedy program on U.S. television to star a black actor (Cosby).

17–September 19, 1969 The fantasy Western *The Wild, Wild West* appears on U.S. television. Combining elements of the traditional Western adventure with *The Man from U.N.C.L.E.* and the James Bond genre, it stars Robert Conrad and Ross Martin.

17–July 4, 1971 The situation comedy *Hogan's Heroes* appears on U.S. television. Set in a prisoner-of-war camp during World War II, it stars Bob Crane, Werner Klemperer, John Banner, Robert Clary, Ivan Dixon, and Sigrid Valdis.

18–September 1, 1970 *I Dream of Jeannie*, a comedy series about a NASA astronaut and the beautiful genie he frees from a bottle, appears on U.S. television. It stars Barbara Eden, Larry Hagman, and Bill Dailey.

NOVEMBER

29 Mary Whitehouse founds the National Viewers' and Listeners' Association in Britain to campaign against offensive and immoral broadcasting.

Religion

OCTOBER

4 On a papal visit to the United Nations in New York, New York, Pope Paul VI holds a mass in Yankee Stadium in the Bronx.

Sports

- Boston Celtics' center Bill Russell is voted the National Basketball Association's Most Valuable Player for the fifth time in eight years.
- Skateboarding becomes a popular pastime in the United States.

- The English rider Mike Hailwood wins his fourth successive 500-cc world motorcycle championship.

APRIL

9 The Harris County Sports Stadium, known as the Houston Astrodome, the largest indoor arena in the world, is opened in Houston, Texas. Its playing surface is the first to be covered in Astroturf, an artificial grass made of nylon.

17–May 1 The Montreal Canadiens win the National Hockey League Stanley Cup, beating the Chicago Black Hawks by four games to three.

18–25 The Boston Celtics win their seventh straight National Basketball Association championship, defeating the Los Angeles Lakers by four games to one.

MAY

31 The Scottish race-car driver Jim Clark, in a Lotus, becomes the first European since Gaston Chevrolet in 1920 to win the Indianapolis 500 motor race, in the United States.

JUNE

21 Gary Player of South Africa wins the U.S. Open golf championship to become only the third player after U.S. golfers Gene Sarazen and Ben Hogan to win all four major tournaments (the U.S. Masters, U.S. Professional Golfers Association Championship, British Open, and U.S. Open).

JULY

10 Peter Thomson of Australia wins his fifth British Open golf title at Royal Birkdale, England.

14 The Australian runner Ron Clarke sets a new 10,000 meters world record time of 27 min 39.4 sec, in Oslo, Norway, an improvement of 36.2 seconds on his existing record set in 1963.

18 The first All-African Games sports festival opens in Brazzaville, Congo, with 29 nations competing. Because of political problems the next games are not held until 1973.

SEPTEMBER

3–4 The Walker Cup amateurs golf match between Great Britain and Ireland and the United States in Baltimore, United States, ends in a tie, 12–12.

9 The U.S. baseball player Sandy Koufax of the Los Angeles Dodgers, in a game against the Chicago Cubs, achieves the eighth perfect pitching game in National League history, and the fourth of his career.

OCTOBER

6–14 The Los Angeles Dodgers beat the Minnesota Twins by four games to three to win the World Series.

NOVEMBER

1 Australia wins the inaugural women's softball world championships, hosted in Melbourne, Australia.

22 The U.S. boxer Muhammad Ali successfully defends his world heavyweight title, knocking out the former champion Floyd Patterson of the United States in the twelfth round in Las Vegas, Nevada.

DECEMBER

26 The Buffalo Bills defeat the San Diego Chargers in the American Football League Championship Game for the second successive year, winning 23–0.

1966

POLITICS, GOVERNMENT, AND ECONOMICS

Business and Economics

- According to Labor Department statistics, the United States has its highest rate of inflation since 1957.
- The U.S. historian Douglass C. North publishes *Growth and Welfare in the American Past: A New Economic History.*

FEBRUARY

14 Australia adopts decimal currency.

MARCH

22 General Motors (GM) president James Roche apologizes publicly to consumer advocate Ralph Nader after acknowledging that GM had spied on Nader's private life. GM had targeted Nader for criticizing the GM Corvair in his book, *Unsafe at Any Speed* (1965).

APRIL

- Pan American Airlines reports that it has contracted with the Boeing corporation for 25 747s. When operable in 1969, the new 747 will carry up to 500 passengers.
- The National Farm Workers Association (NFWA) scores its first major success, when the California grape producer Schenley Industries recognizes the NFWA as the grape-workers' bargaining agent.
- The U.S. Interstate Commerce Commission sanctions the merger of the Pennsylvania and New York Central railroads. Announced in January 1962, this is the largest corporate merger in U.S. history.

DECEMBER

- The Johnson administration chooses Boeing over Lockheed to contract the first Super Sonic Transport (SST). Meanwhile, Americans debate the environmental impact of a plane capable of exceeding the speed of sound.

Colonization

MAY

26 The colony of British Guiana gains independence as Guyana.

SEPTEMBER

30 The British protectorate of Bechuanaland becomes independent as Botswana, with Sir Seretse Khama as president.

OCTOBER

4 The British protectorate of Basutoland becomes independent as Lesotho, under King Moshoeshoe II.

NOVEMBER

30 Barbados becomes independent within the British Commonwealth.

Human Rights

- U.S. feminist Betty Friedan founds the National Organization for Women (NOW).

JANUARY

17 Robert Weaver, a Harvard-trained economist, becomes the first black American to hold a Cabinet position when President Lyndon B. Johnson names him as Secretary of the new Department of Housing and Urban Development.

MARCH

10 Three former members of the U.S. Black Muslim organization are convicted of the murder of Malcolm X in 1965.

MAY

- The U.S. education commissioner withholds federal funding from 12 southern school districts found to be in violation of the Civil Rights Act of 1964. The act requires federally-funded institutions to desegregate.

JUNE

- A sniper shoots James H. Meredith, the man who integrated the University of Mississippi in September 1962, as he marches between Memphis, Tennessee, and Jackson, Mississippi, to protest against racism in the United States. He later resumes his march, joined by civil-rights proponents from around the country.
- A White House Conference on Civil Rights in the United States provokes ridicule from leaders of the Congress of Racial Equality (CORE) and the Student Nonviolent Coordinating Committee (SNCC), who accuse conference organizers of grand-standing.

JULY

- Heat combines with racial hostility to ignite a race riot in Chicago, Illinois, after policemen shut off fire hydrants on the city's West Side. It takes the National Guard to restore order.

10 At a rally at Soldier Field in Chicago, Illinois, the civil-rights leader Martin Luther King, Jr., demands that the city end discrimination in housing, education, and

employment. The event marks King's effort to bring the civil-rights movement into the north.

Politics and Government

- The first conviction for burning the draft card is obtained in the United States.
- The hallucinogenic drug LSD is declared illegal in the United States.
- The U.S. Congress passes a "Truth in Packaging" law to protect U.S. consumers from deceptive marketing gimmicks.

JANUARY

1   Colonel Jean-Bedel Bokassa seizes power in the Central African Republic, and severs ties with the People's Republic of China, his predecessor David Dacko's patron.

1   Pope Paul VI appeals for peace in the Vietnam War.

8   A U.S. military offensive opens in the Vietcong-dominated Mekong Delta region of South Vietnam.

10   A peace agreement signed in Tashkent in Soviet Uzbekistan ends border fighting between India and Pakistan.

16   General Johnson Aguyi-Ironsi takes power in Nigeria after a military coup.

20   Robert Menzies retires as prime minister of Australia, and is succeeded by Harold Holt on January 25.

27–August 25   An 18-nation disarmament conference is held in Geneva, Switzerland.

30   France ends its boycott of European Economic Community (EEC) meetings (begun in July 1965).

31   Britain bans trade with Rhodesia following its Unilateral Declaration of Independence.

31   President Lyndon B. Johnson reports that the United States has resumed its bombing of North Vietnam after a 37-day Christmas cease-fire fails to advance peace negotiations.

FEBRUARY

- Operation White Wing, a U.S.-led campaign against the Vietcong in South Vietnam's Quang Ngai Province concludes after communist resistance in the area crumbles.
- President Lyndon B. Johnson and South Vietnamese premier Nguyen Cao Ky issue the Declaration of Honolulu, that outlines the imperative for pacification of communist influence in South Vietnam.
- The U.S. Congress holds six Ku Klux Klansmen in contempt of Congress for their failure to cooperate with a House Un-American Activities Committee investigation into Klan activity.

1   China protests to Britain about U.S. warships in Hong Kong, suggesting that Hong Kong is being used as a base for activities in Vietnam.

18   The U.S. secretary of state Dean Rusk states that the United States has exhausted every procedure for bringing peace to Vietnam.

21   The French president Charles de Gaulle calls for the withdrawal of U.S. forces from Vietnam.

23   A military junta under Salal Jedid seizes power in Syria from the moderate Ba'ath Party leader Salal al Bitar.

24   President Nkrumah of Ghana is overthrown by a military coup led by Colonel Joseph Ankrah, while the president is away on a tour of Asia.

MARCH

- Two-hundred U.S. and South Vietnamese troops perish when North Vietnamese forces ambush a U.S. Marine stronghold in South Vietnam's Ashau Valley.
- The U.S. Commerce Department imposes sanctions against Ian Smith's apartheid government in Rhodesia.
- The U.S. Supreme Court upholds the Voting Rights Act of 1965.
- The U.S. Supreme Court rules unconstitutional the poll tax, which makes voting contingent upon economic means.
- U.S. secretary of defense Robert S. McNamara announces that 215,000 U.S. troops are now in South Vietnam. Some 20,000 more are scheduled to join them.

2   Britain protests to Portugal about oil supplies reaching Rhodesia via Mozambique.

3   Ugandan prime minister Milton Obote deposes the Ugandan president and kabaka (king) of Buganda, Sir Edward Mutesa II.

5   The Organization of African Unity urges Britain to use force against Rhodesia following its Unilateral Declaration of Independence.

6–12   Food riots break out in West Bengal, India, spreading to Calcutta and Delhi.

8   Australia triples its forces supporting the South Vietnamese government, to 4,500 troops.

10   France announces that it will withdraw its troops from the North Atlantic Treaty Organization (NATO) following a row over the participation of the United States in the alliance.

11   Following anticommunist demonstrations, President Achmed Sukarno of Indonesia transfers all political powers to General Raden Suharto, and a purge of communists follows.

11   The Canadian government orders an inquiry into the involvement of former cabinet ministers with the East German spy Gerda Munsinger.

30   Prime Minister Henrik Verwoerd's National Party wins a sweeping victory in the South African general election.

31   In the British general election, the Labour Party wins 363 seats, the Conservatives win 253, and the Liberals 12. Labour receives 47.9% of votes cast, the Conservatives 41.9%, and the Liberals 8.5%. The Labour leader Harold Wilson remains prime minister.

APRIL

2   Unrest breaks out in Saigon, as protesters demand the end of military rule in South Vietnam, and, on April 14, the government promises elections within three to five months.

6–8   Increased ferry tolls spark riots in Hong Kong.

9   General Francisco Franco's dictatorial regime in Spain eases press censorship.

9   The United Nations (UN) authorizes Britain to prevent oil shipments to Rhodesia, by force.

15   A wave of anti-Chinese violence begins in Indonesia.

16   General Abdul Rahman Arif succeeds his brother Abdel Salim Arif as president of Iraq.

16   Rhodesia demands the departure of British diplomats from Salisbury, Rhodesia, following British measures against Rhodesia. On April 28, the demand is suspended.

18   Following elections in Austria, Joseph Klaus remains chancellor, but the People's Party replaces the Socialist Party as the party of government.

27–May 20   Clashes occur between police and students at Spanish universities.

MAY

- U.S. bombs rain down upon targets in North Vietnam, in the heaviest air raids to date.
3   In the Vietnam War, the United States admits to targeting communist troops in Cambodia for the first time, in a fracas along the Caibac River.
7   The Romanian statesman Nicolae Ceauşescu declares that Romania recognizes no supreme authority within the international communist movement.
9–20   Inconclusive talks are held between British and Rhodesian officials in London, England. A second round of talks is held in Salisbury, Rhodesia, in the period June 2–July 5.
18   Spain and Britain begin discussions on the future of Gibraltar, but the talks end without agreement on July 14.
23   South Vietnamese troops crush a Buddhist rebellion in Da Nang after a week of fighting.
24   The Ugandan army crushes a separatist rebellion in support of the deposed kabaka (king) of Buganda, Sir Edward Mutesa II, and the kingdom of Buganda is abolished on June 10.
28   Violent protests are held against the creation of a unitary state in the Federation of Nigeria.

JUNE

- The U.S. Supreme Court, in *Miranda v. Arizona*, interprets the Fifth Amendment's protection from self-incrimination to mean that individuals taken into police custody have to be advised of their right to remain silent and their right to counsel, subsequently known as "Miranda Rights."
- U.S. secretary of defense Robert S. McNamara announces that the United States will deploy 18,000 more troops to Vietnam, bringing the total to 285,000.
2   Éamon de Valera is reelected president of Ireland.
3   A purge of "rightists" in the Chinese communist leadership begins.
7   Demonstrators in East Pakistan (now Bangladesh) demand greater autonomy.
20–30   The French president Charles de Gaulle visits the USSR.
22   The South Vietnamese army moves into Quang Tri, the last stronghold of the Buddhist opposition.
29   The United States bombs oil depots near Hanoi and Haiphong in North Vietnam. Great Britain dissociates itself from the bombing of populated areas.

JULY

1   France withdraws its forces from the North Atlantic Treaty Organization (NATO) following a dispute over U.S. involvement in Europe's defense.
6   North Vietnam parades 50 captured U.S. airmen through the streets of Hanoi, North Vietnam.
11   The USSR announces further aid to North Vietnam in its war with South Vietnam.
13   Eight student nurses are murdered in Chicago, Illinois. Two weeks later police indict 24-year-old Richard Speck, who has served time in Texas for theft, forgery, and assault; he is convicted of the murders a year later.
14   Israeli jets raid Syria in retaliation for border incursions.
24   The European Economic Community (EEC) reaches agreement on its Common Agricultural Policy.

29   General Yakubu Gowon succeeds General Johnson Aguyi-Ironsi as ruler of Nigeria after an army mutiny.

AUGUST

- The 21st anniversary of the U.S. bombing of Hiroshima is the occasion of a nationwide demonstration against the Vietnam War. Opposition to the war hits President Lyndon B. Johnson close to home when protestors disrupt the wedding of his daughter, Luci.
- U.S. secretary of defense Robert S. McNamara summons 46,200 men to the draft, the highest draft call since the Korean War.
1   The student Charles Whitman locks himself in a tower on the University of Texas campus in Austin, Texas, and fatally shoots 13 students and wounds 31 others before police snipers kill him.
11   The three-year-old undeclared war between Indonesia and Malaysia ends with agreement to decide the status of Sarawak and Sabah by referendum.
13   The Central Committee of the Chinese Communist Party, in its first plenary session since 1962, endorses the "Great Proletarian Cultural Revolution," the movement to "purify" Chinese communism through a purge of the intelligentsia.
15   Israeli and Syrian forces clash around the Sea of Galilee.
18   Red Guards, the shock troops of the Cultural Revolution, make their first appearance in Beijing, China. Four days of anti-Western demonstrations follow.

SEPTEMBER

- Alabama governor George C. Wallace signs legislation prohibiting the state's public schools from upholding the U.S. Education Commission's desegregation guidelines.
- The U.S. Senate upholds a law banning voluntary prayer in public schools.
6   The South African prime minister Henrik Verwoerd is stabbed to death in parliament in Cape Town, South Africa, by a schizophrenic parliamentary messenger. He is succeeded by Johannes Vorster on September 13.
6–14   A Commonwealth conference in London, England, commits Britain to seeking United Nations (UN) mandatory sanctions against Rhodesia.
9   The Rhodesian High Court rules that Ian Smith's regime is unlawful, but is the only effective administration.
16   China accuses the United States of bombing Chinese territory near the North Vietnamese frontier.
23   The Minimum Wage Act in the United States raises the minimum hourly wage from $1.25 to $1.40, and extends the classes of workers it covers to include agricultural laborers, construction workers, and retail and catering employees.
23   The United States announces that it has been using defoliating agents in territory around the demilitarized zone between North and South Vietnam to deprive North Vietnamese infiltrators of protective cover.
30   Former German Nazi leaders Albert Speer and Baldur von Schirach are released from Spandau Prison in Berlin, West Germany, after serving 20 years for war crimes.

OCTOBER

- President Lyndon B. Johnson signs legislation expanding the nation's coastal fishing zone from 3 to 12 miles.

- President Lyndon B. Johnson signs a bill establishing the Department of Transportation, the 12th Cabinet department.
1 The Chinese defense minister Lin Biao accuses the USSR of plotting with the United States in the Vietnam War.
5 Spain closes its frontier with Gibraltar to all traffic except pedestrians, and refuses to accept Gibraltar passports from November 12.
7 The USSR expels all Chinese students as the Sino-Soviet rift widens.
14–15 In two days, U.S. bombers make 348 sorties into North Vietnam, the heaviest bombing raid to date.
24–25 A conference of Vietnam war allies is held in Manila, the Philippines, including South Vietnam, United States, Australia, New Zealand, Philippines, South Korea, and Thailand.
27 China announces the successful test-firing of a guided nuclear missile.
27 The United Nations (UN) Assembly ends South Africa's mandate over South West Africa because of its racial policies, but South Africa refuses to accept the decision.
28 Britain and France agree definite plans for a channel tunnel.

NOVEMBER

- In U.S. Congressional elections, Democrats retain majorities in the House (248–187) and Senate (64–36).
- Officials of the U.S. Catholic Archdiocese end the church's injunction against eating meat on Fridays, except during Lent.
2 The communist leader Enver Hoxha allies Albania with China and denounces the USSR.
13 Israeli forces attack the Hebron area of Jordan. On November 25 the United Nations (UN) censures Israel.
16 In his second trial for the 1954 murder of his wife Marilyn, Samuel H. ("Dr. Sam") Sheppard is found not guilty. The "bushy-haired man" who Sheppard claims was the real murderer is never found.
22 The Spanish cortes passes a new constitution proposed by General Francisco Franco, separating the offices of head of state and head of government and reintroducing direct elections to the cortes. In a referendum on December 14, 95% of the voters approve.
23 In the Chinese Cultural Revolution, Red Guards demand the dismissal of the head of state, Liu Shaoqi, and party secretary, Deng Xiaoping.

DECEMBER

- By this month, 400,000 U.S. troops are stationed in Vietnam.
1 Kurt Kiesinger becomes the chancellor of West Germany, following the resignation of Ludwig Erhard.
2 The United Nations (UN) unanimously elects U Thant for a second term as secretary-general.
2–4 The British prime minister Harold Wilson and the Rhodesian prime minister Ian Smith meet aboard HMS *Tiger* and prepare a plan for the settlement of the Rhodesian dispute. On December 5, Rhodesia rejects the plan.
7 An Arab Defense Council in Cairo, Egypt, decides that Saudi and Iraqi troops should be stationed along the Jordanian border in case of further Israeli attack.
13 A U.S. air raid on a Hanoi suburb kills over 100 North Vietnamese civilians.

16 The United Nations (UN) Security Council approves selective mandatory sanctions against Rhodesia.
20 Britain rules out legal independence for Rhodesia except under black majority rule.
22 The Rhodesian prime minister Ian Smith declares Rhodesia a republic following the failure of talks with Britain on its future.
30 Britain invites the United States, South Vietnam, and North Vietnam to meet on British territory to arrange a cease-fire in the Vietnam War.
31 Members of the European Free Trade Association (EFTA) abolish tariffs on industrial goods, creating a customs union.
31 Yugoslavia releases the communist dissident, Milovan Djilas, from prison.

SCIENCE, TECHNOLOGY, AND MEDICINE

Agriculture

- India is hit by the worst famine in 20 years and has to import 8 million tons of wheat from the United States.

Computing

- The seven-level American Standard Code for Information Interchange (ASCII) receives widespread acceptance as a means of transmitting the high volumes of data generated by business machines.

Ecology

- The city of Florence, Italy, suffers heavy flooding, which destroys many valuable Renaissance works of art. A fund-raising drive is immediately set up, to prevent the recurrence of such a disaster.
- The U.S. Department of the Interior issues the first rare and endangered species list; 78 species are included. Congress passes the Rare and Endangered Species Act to protect them.

JANUARY

29–31 As the century's worst blizzard pummels the eastern seaboard of the United States, 165 people are killed, and millions of dollars of property is damaged.

AUGUST

19 An earthquake in eastern Turkey kills 2,000 people.

OCTOBER

21 A landslide in the mining village of Aberfan, Glamorgan, Wales, caused by water soaking into coal-mine wastes, engulfs a school, killing 116 children and 28 adults.

NOVEMBER

4 Several days of extensive flooding in central and northern Italy begin.

Exploration

- A borehole drilled 1,390 m/4,560 ft into the Greenland ice sheet reveals that the bottom layers of ice are 150,000 years old.

FEBRUARY

- U.S. astronauts Elliot See, Jr., and Charles Basset, II, perish when their T-38 aircraft crashes near St. Louis, Missouri en route to a training session.

3 Soviet spacecraft *Luna 9* (launched January 31) makes the first soft landing on the moon and transmits photographs and soil data for three days.

MARCH

1 Soviet probe *Venera 3* (launched November 16, 1965) crash-lands on Venus, the first artificial object to land on another planet.

16 U.S. astronauts Neil Armstrong and David Scott, aboard *Gemini 8*, achieve the first linkup of a crewed spacecraft with another object, an *Agena* rocket.

JUNE

2 The U.S. National Aeronautics and Space Administration (NASA) spacecraft *Surveyor I* (launched on May 30) makes the first U.S. soft landing on the moon, and transmits over 10,000 photographs of the lunar surface.

AUGUST

10 The U.S. spacecraft *Lunar Orbiter 1* enters Moon orbit and transmits pictures of the dark side. It is the first of a series of five uncrewed spacecraft that photograph the moon to select sites for the Apollo missions and to make detailed lunar maps.

NOVEMBER

11 *Gemini 12*, the last of the *Gemini* two-person space missions, is launched. It makes the first fully automatically controlled reentry.

Health and Medicine

- Mao Zedong's Cultural Revolution has resulted in an increase in the birth rate in China, as the birth control campaign receives less attention.
- U.S. physiologists Peyton Rous and Charles Huggins share the Nobel Prize for Physiology or Medicine: Rous for his discovery of tumor-inducing viruses; and Huggins for his discoveries concerning hormonal treatment of prostate cancer.
- U.S. surgeon Richard Carlton Lillehei performs the first pancreas transplant.
- U.S. virologists Harry Meyer and Paul Parman develop a live virus vaccine for rubella (German measles), which reduces the incidence of the disease.

AUGUST

8 Heart surgeon Michael De Bakey installs the first artificial heart pump, a left ventricle bypass, into a patient at Methodist Hospital in Houston, Texas. The pump remains in operation for ten days.

Science

- Astronomers at the U.S. Naval Research Laboratory discover powerful X-rays emitted from within the constellation Cygnus.
- English molecular biologist Francis Crick publishes *Of Molecules and Men*, in which he discusses the revolution occurring in molecular biology and its implications.
- French physicist Alfred Kastler receives the Nobel Prize for Physics for his discovery of optical methods of studying Hertzian resonances in atoms.
- U.S. chemist Robert Mulliken receives the Nobel Prize for Chemistry for his molecular orbital theory of chemical bonds and structures.
- U.S. geologists Allan Cox, Richard Doell, and Brent Dalrymple publish a chronology of magnetic polarity reversals going back 3 million years. It is useful in dating fossils.

Technology

- A hydrogen bomb lost by the United States in 760 m/2,500 ft of water near Palomares, Spain, is recovered by the submersibles *Alvin, Aluminaut,* and *Cubmarine.*
- British engineers Charles Kao and Georges Hockman of Standard Telecommunications Laboratories show that data can be carried on light transmitted over long distances in glass fibers rather than on electric currents in copper wire, leading to the development of fiber-optic cables.
- The Urengoy natural gas field is discovered in western Siberia. The largest natural gas field in the world, its reserves are estimated at over 8 trillion cubic meters. Production begins in 1978.

August 1966–68 The U.S. Defense Department launches 26 Initial Defense Satellite Communication System (IDSCS) satellites. These communications satellites are launched eight at a time and placed in synchronous orbits over the equator.

Transportation

- A British Boeing 707 catches fire and crashes into Mt. Fuji, Japan, killing 124.

JANUARY

24 An Indian Boeing 707 crashes into Mont Blanc in France; 124 people are killed.

AUGUST

31 British Aerospace's *Harrier*, a vertical take off and landing (VTOL) jet, makes its first test flight.

ARTS AND IDEAS

Architecture

- Scarborough College at the University of Toronto, Canada, designed by the Australian architect John Andrews, is completed.

- The book *Inside the Endless House*, by the Austrian-born U.S. architect Frederick Kiesler, is published posthumously.
- The Guild House Apartments in Philadelphia, Pennsylvania, designed by the U.S. architects Robert Venturi and John Rauch, are completed.
- The Severn Bridge, linking England and Wales, is completed. It uses box girders to stiffen the trusses—a radical design for a suspension bridge.

Arts

- The new building for the Whitney Museum of American Art, designed by the Hungarian-born U.S. architect Marcel Breuer, is completed in New York, New York.
- The U.S. artist Allan Kaprow performs *Gas*, one of his best-known "happenings."
- The U.S. artist Robert Indiana paints *LOVE*.
- The U.S. artist Sol LeWitt creates *Open Modular Cube*.
- The U.S. conceptual artist Carl André sculpts *Equivalent 8*.
- The U.S. National Endowment for the Humanities is founded.
- U.S. photographer Diane Arbus takes *A Young Man in Curlers at Home on West Twentieth Street, New York City*.

Film

- The movie *A Man for All Seasons*, directed by U.S. filmmaker Fred Zinnemann, is released in Britain. It is based on the play by Robert Bolt, and stars Paul Scofield, Wendy Hillier, Susannah York, and Robert Shaw.
- The movie *Alfie*, directed by Lewis Gilbert, is released in Britain, starring Michael Caine in the lead role as a Cockney philanderer.
- The movie *Andrei Rublev*, directed by Andrei Tarkovsky, is released in the USSR, starring Anatoly Solonitsin and Ivan Lapikov.
- The movie *Blow-Up*, directed by Italian filmmaker Michelangelo Antonioni, is released in Britain, starring David Hemmings, Sarah Miles, and Vanessa Redgrave. It is awarded the Palme d'Or at the Cannes Film Festival in France, in the following year.
- The movie *Closely Observed Trains* (known in the United States as *Closely Watched Trains*), directed by Jiri Menzel, is released in Czechoslovakia, starring Vaclav Neckar and Jitka Bendova. Based on the novel by Bohumil Hrabal, it embodies the spirit of the coming Prague Spring of liberalization in 1968.
- The movie *Cul-de-sac*, directed by Polish-U.S. filmmaker Roman Polanski, is released in Britain, starring Lional Stander, Donald Pleasance, Jack MacGowran, and Françoise Dorléac.
- The movie *Georgy Girl*, directed by Canadian filmmaker Silvio Narizzano, is released in Britain, starring James Mason and Lynn Redgrave.
- The movie *La Religieuse/The Nun*, directed by Jacques Rivette, is released in France, starring Anna Karina. Despite criticism from the authorities and the church, its showing at the Cannes Film Festival is permitted. Its

notoriety leads to an increase in sales for the novel by Denis Diderot on which it is based.

- The movie *Persona*, directed by Ingmar Bergman, is released in Sweden, starring Liv Ullmann and Bibi Andersson.
- The movie *Teni Zabytykh Predkov/Shadows of Our Forgotten Ancestors*, directed by Sergo Paradjanov, is released in the USSR. A variation on Shakespeare's *Romeo and Juliet*, it stars Ivan Nikolaichuk and Larisa Kadochnikova.
- The movie *The Good, the Bad and the Ugly*, a "spaghetti Western" directed by Sergio Leone, is released in the United States, starring Clint Eastwood, Eli Wallach, and Lee Van Cleef.
- The movie *The Wild Angels*, directed by Roger Corman, is released in the United States, a movie that celebrates the Hells Angels motorcycle gangs.
- The movie *Un Homme et une femme/A Man and a Woman*, directed by Claude Lelouch, is released in France, starring Anouk Aimée and Jean-Louis Trintignant. It is awarded the Palme d'Or, jointly with Germi's *The Birds, the Bees and the Italians*, at the Cannes Film Festival in France, later in the year.
- The movie *Who's Afraid of Virginia Woolf?*, directed by Mike Nichols, is released in the United States, starring Elizabeth Taylor and Richard Burton. It is based on the play by Edward Albee.

APRIL

18 The 1965 Academy Awards take place. Best Actor: Lee Marvin, for *Cat Ballou*; Best Supporting Actor: Martin Balsam, for *A Thousand Clowns*; Best Actress: Julie Christie, for *Darling*; Best Supporting Actress: Shelley Winters, for *A Patch of Blue*; Best Picture: *The Sound of Music*, directed by Robert Wise; Best Director: Robert Wise, for *The Sound of Music*.

Literature and Language

- The Australian writer Patrick White publishes his novel *The Solid Mandala*.
- The English writer Anthony Powell publishes *The Soldier's Art*, the eighth novel of his 12-volume sequence *A Dance to the Music of Time*.
- The English writer Graham Greene publishes his novel *The Comedians*.
- The English writer John Fowles publishes his novel *The Magus*; Fowles publishes a revised version in 1977.
- The English writer Maureen Duffy publishes her novel *The Microcosm*.
- The French psychoanalyst Jacques Lacan publishes *Ecrits/Writings*.
- The French writer Anaïs Nin (who wrote in English) publishes the first volume of her seven-volume *The Diary of Anaïs Nin 1931–1966*. The final volume appears in 1980.
- The German writer Martin Walser publishes his novel *Das Einhorn/The Unicorn*.
- The Nobel Prize for Literature is awarded to the Israeli novelist Shmuel Yosef Agnon, and the German-born Swedish poet Nelly Sachs.
- The Pulitzer Prize for Biography is awarded to Arthur M. Schlesinger, Jr., for *A Thousand Days*, the Pulitzer Prize for Poetry is awarded to Richard Eberhart for

Selected Poems, and the Pulitzer Prize for Fiction is awarded to Katherine Anne Porter for *Collected Stories*.

- The South-African writer Nadine Gordimer publishes *The Late Bourgeois World*.
- The U.S. singer Leslie Uggams publishes *Beauty Book*, her guide for single living.
- The U.S. writer Adrienne Rich publishes her poetry collection *Necessities of Life*.
- The U.S. writer and critic Susan Sontag publishes *Against Interpretation*, a collection of essays.
- The U.S. writer Bernard Malamud publishes his novel *The Fixer*.
- The U.S. writer John Barth publishes his novel *Giles Goat-Boy*.
- The U.S. writer Paul Bowles publishes his novel *Up Above the World*.
- The U.S. writer Thomas Pynchon publishes his novel *The Crying of Lot 49*.
- The U.S.-born Irish writer J. P. Donleavy publishes his novel *The Saddest Summer of Samuel S.*
- The West Indian writer Jean Rhys publishes her novel *The Wide Sargasso Sea*, the story of the life of Rochester's wife from Charlotte Brontë's *Jane Eyre*.

FEBRUARY

7 The U.S. rock magazine *Crawdaddy* is launched in New York, New York.

Music

c. 1966 As tape cassettes and cartridges come on the market, sales of singles drop.
- The album *Supremes A Go-Go*, by the girl group the Supremes, is the first album by a female group to reach number one in the United States.
- The British pop group Dave Dee, Dozy, Beaky, Mick & Tich releases the single "Bend It."
- The British pop group the Small Faces releases the single "Itchycoo Park."
- The British pop singer Tom Jones releases the single "Green, Green Grass of Home," the best-selling single of the year in Britain.
- The British rock band the Troggs releases the single "Wild Thing."
- The British rock group the Beatles releases the singles "Paperback Writer," "Eleanor Rigby," and "Yellow Submarine." The album *Revolver* is released the same year.
- The British rock/blues trio Cream releases the album *Fresh Cream*.
- The British rock group the Rolling Stones releases the single "Paint It Black."
- The British rock group the Who releases the single "My Generation" and an album of the same name.
- The British rock group the Animals releases the album *The Best of the Animals*, featuring the single "Don't Bring Me Down."
- The Decca label's recording of Mahler's Second Symphony is the first record to be made using the Dolby system.
- The English composer Elizabeth Maconchy completes her String Quartet No. 8.
- The English composer John Tavener completes his cantata *The Whale*.

- The Estonian composer Arvo Pärt completes his Symphony No. 2.
- The Estonian composer Eduard Tubin completes his Symphony No. 8.
- The folk duo Simon and Garfunkel releases the single "Scarborough Fair."
- The new Metropolitan Opera House in New York, New York, is opened.
- The opera *Antony and Cleopatra*, by the U.S. composer Samuel Barber, is first performed, in New York, New York.
- The opera *The Bassarids*, by the German composer Hans Werner Henze, is first performed, in Salzburg, Austria.
- The Polish composer Krzysztof Penderecki completes his choral work *St Luke Passion*.
- The Russian composer Dmitry Shostakovich completes his String Quartet No. 11.
- The U.S. composer John Cage presents the last of his six *Variations*, performances in which any number of musicians could respond freely to the situation.
- The U.S. composer Norman Dello Joio completes his choral work *Songs of Walt Whitman*.
- The U.S. folk group the Mamas and the Papas releases two albums, *If You Can Believe Your Eyes and Ears* and *The Mamas and the Papas*, and the single "Monday, Monday."
- The U.S. folk/rock duo Simon and Garfunkel releases the singles "Sound of Silence" and "Homeward Bound."
- The U.S. folk/rock group the Byrds releases the singles "Fifth Dimension" and "Eight Miles High."
- The U.S. folk/rock singer Bob Dylan releases the album *Blonde on Blonde*.
- The U.S. girl group the Chiffons releases the single "Sweet Talkin' Guy."
- The U.S. girl group the Supremes releases the single "You Can't Hurry Love."
- The U.S. group Ray Conniff and the Singers releases the single "Somewhere, My Love," from the soundtrack to the movie *Doctor Zhivago*.
- The U.S. pop group the Beach Boys releases the singles "Good Vibrations" and "Barbara Ann," and the album *Pet Sounds*.
- The U.S. pop group the Walker Brothers releases the single "The Sun Ain't Gonna Shine Anymore."
- The U.S. psychedelic rock band the Lovin' Spoonful releases the album *Daydream*.
- The U.S. singer Frank Sinatra releases the single "Strangers in the Night."
- The U.S. singer Nancy Sinatra releases the single "These Boots Are Made for Walkin'."
- The U.S. singer Rick Nelson releases the album *Bright Lights and Country Music*, a mix of pop and country.
- The U.S. singer/songwriter Neil Diamond releases the single "Cherry, Cherry."
- The U.S. soul singer James Brown releases the singles "I Got You (I Feel Good)" and "It's a Man's, Man's, Man's World."
- The U.S. soul singer Percy Sledge releases the single "When a Man Loves a Woman."
- The U.S. vocal group the Four Tops releases the single "Reach Out, I'll Be There."

- The U.S. vocal group the Temptations releases the single "Ain't Too Proud to Beg."
- U.S. husband-and-wife rhythm and blues team Ike and Tina Turner release the single "River Deep Mountain High."
- U.S.-style open air music festivals become popular in Britain.

FEBRUARY

28 The Cavern Club in Liverpool, England, where the Beatles made their debut, closes down.

MARCH

4 John Lennon speculates that the Beatles are more popular than Jesus Christ; in response, Beatles records are burned in the U.S. Bible belt.

15 The 1965–66 Grammy Awards take place. Best Album: *September of My Years* by Frank Sinatra; Best Record: "A Touch of Honey" by Herb Alpert; Best Male Vocalist: Frank Sinatra; Best Female Vocalist: Barbra Streisand; Best Group: the Anita Kerr Singers.

MAY

1 The British rock group the Beatles play their final gig in Britain at a concert given by *New Musical Express* poll winners. The poll was of *New Musical Express* readers and a program of the concert was broadcast on May 15, 1966.

24 The musical *Mame*, with lyrics and music by Jerry Herman, is first performed, at the Winter Garden Theater, New York, New York.

JULY

23 The Cavern Club in Liverpool, England, reopens under new ownership, following a petition to the prime minister, Harold Wilson. It had been closed on February 28 by the official receiver as it was bankrupt and had debts exceeding £10,000.

AUGUST

29 The British rock group the Beatles give their last concert, at Candlestick Park in San Francisco, California.

SEPTEMBER

12–August 19, 1968 The U.S. pop group the Monkees is launched in its show on U.S. television, a situation comedy with tunes. The band members are Mickey Dolenz, Davy Jones, Mike Nesmith, and Peter Tork.

Theater and Dance

- The play *A Delicate Balance*, by the U.S. dramatist Edward Albee, is first performed, in New York, New York.
- The play *Publikumsbeschimpfung/Offending the Audience*, by the Austrian writer Peter Handke, is first performed, in Frankfurt, Germany.
- The play *Rosencrantz and Guildenstern are Dead*, by the Czech-born English dramatist Tom Stoppard, is first performed, at the Edinburgh Festival, Scotland. It opens the following year at the Old Vic Theatre in London, England.
- The play *Saved*, by the English dramatist Edward Bond, is first performed, in London, England.
- The play *The Lion in Winter*, by the U.S. dramatist James Goldman, is first performed, in New York, New York.

- The Pulitzer Prize for Drama is not awarded this year.

JANUARY

29 The musical *Sweet Charity*, with lyrics by Dorothy Fields and music by Cy Coleman, is first performed, at the Palace Theater, New York, New York. Songs featured in the show include "Big Spender" and "If My Friends Could See Me Now."

FEBRUARY

2 The play *Wait Until Dark*, by the U.S. dramatist Frederick Knott, is first performed, at the Ethel Barrymore Theater in New York, New York.

JUNE

16 The 1965–66 Tony Awards take place. Best Play: *Marat/Sade*; Best Musical: *Man of La Mancha*; Best Actor: Hal Holbrook; Best Actress: Rosemary Harris.

NOVEMBER

20 The musical *Cabaret*, by John Kander and Fred Ebb, is first performed, at the Broadhurst Theater, New York, New York.

Thought and Scholarship

- German philosopher Theodore Adorno publishes *Negative Dialektik/Negative Dialectic*.
- The Pulitzer Prize for History is awarded to Perry Miller for *The Life of the Mind in America*.
- The Pulitzer Prize for General Nonfiction is awarded to Edwin Way Teale for *Wandering Through Winter*.
- The U.S. historian Henry Steele Commager publishes *Freedom and Order: A Commentary on the American Political Scene*.
- The U.S. politician James William Fulbright publishes *The Arrogance of Power*.

SOCIETY

Everyday Life

- A craze for pin-back buttons with slogans starts in the United States.
- The miniskirt becomes fashionable in the United States.
- The popularity of groups like the Beatles feeds through into youth fashion, with longer hair, collarless jackets, and cuban-heel boots becoming popular.
- The U.S. manufacturer Procter and Gamble launches Pampers, the first disposable diapers. This product will go on to take nearly 50% of the worldwide market.
- U.S. gynecologist William Masters and U.S. psychologist Virginia Johnson write *Human Sexual Response*, the result of 11 years of research.

JANUARY

- A two-week-long transit strike begins in New York, New York, thoroughly disrupting city life.

MARCH

- The U.S. Supreme Court upholds the obscenity conviction of Eros publisher Ralph Ginzburg, basing its ruling not on the nature of Ginzburg's material itself, but on the lurid way it is marketed. In a related case, the Court upholds a 1957 ruling that protects material from censorship if it has a redeeming social value.

APRIL

- The New York City Newspaper Guild initiates the longest newspaper strike to date, after three city dailies—the *World-Telegram & Sun*, *Journal-American*, and *Herald-Tribune*—merge to form the *World-Journal-Tribune* news syndicate.

JULY

July, 1966–August The International Association of Machinists strikes in the United States, paralyzing airline traffic for the next month and a half.

Media and Communication

- Avant-garde rock band the Velvet Underground performs in a multimedia show, *The Exploding Plastic Inevitable*, created by artist Andy Warhol, in the United States.
- Former actor Ronald Reagan becomes the Republican Governor of California.
- Xerox develops the first desk-top fax machine, in the United States. It is able to operate on standard phone lines and takes six minutes to transmit a page.

JANUARY

11–January 15, 1969 *Daktari*, a children's series about the adventures of an animal doctor in Africa, appears on U.S. television, starring Marshall Thompson, Cheryl Miller, Yale Summers, and Hari Rhodes.

12–March 14, 1968 *Batman*, a children's series about Bruce Wayne and Dick Grayson who have double lives as superheroes fighting crime in Gotham City, appears on U.S. television. It stars Adam West as Batman and Burt Ward as Robin.

MAY

22 The 1965–66 Emmy Awards for television take place. Best Actor in a Single Show: Cliff Robertson; Best Actress in a Single Show: Simone Signoret; Best Actor in a Series: Bill Cosby, for *I Spy*; Best Actress in a Series: Barbara Stanwyck, for *The Big Valley*.

SEPTEMBER

8–September 13, 1968 *Tarzan*, children's adventure series, starring Ron Ely as the character created by Edgar Rice Burroughs, appears on U.S. television. Tarzan's famous yell is supplied from movies starring an earlier Tarzan, Johnny Weissmuller.

8–September 10, 1971 *That Girl*, starring Marlo Thomas as Anne Marie, an aspiring young actress living the single life in New York, New York, is shown on U.S. television. Ted Bessell costars.

9 The first episode of the science fiction program *Star Trek* is shown on U.S. television. Though its ratings are never very high, it quickly develops a cult following. It stars William Shatner, Leonard Nimoy, DeForrest Kelly, James Doohan, Walter Koenig, George Takei, and Nichelle Nichols.

12 The first issue of the *World-Journal and Tribune* appears; it is the result of the merger of three New York newspapers (the *New York Herald-Tribune*, *New York Journal-American*, and *New York World-Telegram & Sun*).

17–September 8, 1973 *Mission: Impossible*, an adventure series about an elite U.S. government spy agency, appears on U.S. television. Steven Hill (later Peter Graves), Martin Landau, Peter Lupus, Barbara Bain, and Greg Morris star.

BIRTHS & DEATHS

JANUARY

11 Alberto Giacometti, Swiss painter and sculptor, dies in Chur, Switzerland (64).

11 The Indian prime minister Lal Bahandra Shastri dies in Tashkent, Uzbekistan, USSR (62), and is succeeded by Indira Gandhi on January 19.

29 Romário, Brazilian soccer player, born in Villa Penna, Brazil.

FEBRUARY

1 Buster Keaton, U.S. silent-film actor and director, dies in Woodland Hills, California (70).

20 Chester W. Nimitz, U.S. commander in chief of the Pacific Fleet and all land and sea forces in the area during World War II, dies near San Francisco, California (80).

MARCH

5 Anna Akhmatova, Russian poet, dies in Domodedovo, near Moscow, Russia (76).

APRIL

10 Evelyn Waugh, English satirical novelist, dies in Combe Florey, near Taunton, Somerset, England (62).

JUNE

4 Cecilia Bartoli, Italian opera singer, born in Rome, Italy.

20 Georges Lemaître, Belgian astronomer who formulated the Big Bang theory of the origin of the universe, dies in Louvain, Belgium (71).

30 Margery Allingham, English writer who created the detective Albert Campion, dies in Colchester, Essex, England (62).

SEPTEMBER

6 Hendrik Frensch Verwoerd, prime minister of South Africa 1958–66, who created the Bantu Homelands and took South Africa out of the Commonwealth, is stabbed to death in the parliamentary chamber in Cape Town, South Africa (64).

6 Margaret Sanger, U.S. birth control advocate who opened the first birth control clinic in the United States, dies in Tucson, Arizona (82).

21 Paul Reynaud, French premier 1940, who opposed compromise with Hitler, dies in Paris, France (87).

OCTOBER

18 S. S. Kresge, U.S. businessman who established over 1,000 discount stores in the United States, dies in East Stroudsburg, Pennsylvania (99).

NOVEMBER

19 Gail Devers, U.S. track and field athlete, is born in Seattle, Washington.

DECEMBER

1 Walt Disney, U.S. motion-picture producer and creator of Mickey Mouse, Donald Duck, and other characters, dies in Los Angeles, California (65).

December

18 *How the Grinch Stole Christmas*, an animated cartoon based on the children's book by Dr. Seuss, debuts on U.S. television. Animation is by Chuck Jones, narration by Boris Karloff.

Sports

- Equestrian world championships are instituted for dressage and the three-day event.
- Giacomo Agostini of Italy, riding an MV Augusta, wins the first of seven consecutive 500-cc motorcycling world championships.
- The Chicago Bulls join the National Basketball Association (NBA) in the United States.
- The draft war between the National Football League and the American Football League reaches its peak.
- The first world orienteering championships are staged by the International Orienteering Federation in Finland, with Scandinavian runners dominating all the events.
- The inaugural Sports Car Club of America Trans-American Sedan Championship (now known as the Trans-Am Series) is won by Horst Kwech of Austria and Gaston Andrey of Switzerland in an Alfa Romeo.
- The U.S. baseball team the Milwaukee Braves of the National League move to Atlanta, Georgia.
- The U.S. drivers Ken Miles and Lloyd Ruby in a Ford Mk 2 win the inaugural 24-hour Daytona endurance auto race in Florida.

March

- The soccer World Cup, the Jules Rimet trophy, is stolen from an exhibition in Westminster, London, England. A week later a dog called Pickles finds the trophy by a footpath in Norwood, south London.
- The U.S. jockey Johnny Longden retires at the age of 59, having ridden a world record 6,032 winners in his 40-year career.
12 The Canadian hockey player Bobby Hull of the Chicago Black Hawks becomes the first player to score 50 goals in a National Hockey League season, in a game against the New York Rangers in Chicago, Illinois. He ends the season with 54 goals.
17 Arkle, ridden by the Irish jockey Pat Taaffe, wins the Cheltenham Gold Cup horse race in England for the third successive year.

April

11 The U.S. golfer Jack Nicklaus becomes the first player to win the U.S. Masters tournament at Augusta, Georgia, two years in succession.

24–May 5 The Montreal Canadiens win their second consecutive National Hockey League Stanley Cup, beating the Detroit Red Wings by four games to two.
28 The Boston Celtics win their eighth successive U.S. National Basketball Association (NBA) title. Their coach, Red Auerbach, retires to be replaced by Bill Russell (as player/coach), who becomes the first ever black American head coach.

June

8 The mounting rivalry between the American Football League and the National Football League in the United States is ended when the two bodies agree to merge. The merger will not be fully effective until 1970, but from 1967 a common draft of college players will take place and a Super Bowl game between the champions of each league will be inaugurated.

July

5 The Australian runner Ron Clarke sets a new 5,000 meters world record time of 13 min 16.6 sec in Stockholm, Sweden, an improvement of 9.6 seconds on the existing record and of 18.2 seconds on the first of his three previous world records at the distance, set in January 1965.
17 The U.S. runner Jim Ryun, a 19-year-old student, sets a new world record time of 3 min 51.3 sec for the mile at the U.S. Amateur Athletic Union championships at Berkeley, California.
30 The host nation, England, wins soccer's World Cup, beating West Germany in the final at Wembley, London, 4–2 after extra time. The England forward Geoff Hurst scores the first ever hat trick in a World Cup final.

August

- British soccer player Alan Ball is transferred from Blackpool to Everton for a fee of £110,000.

September

4 The Australian race-car driver Jack Brabham wins the Formula One World Drivers' Championship in a car manufactured by his own company.

October

5–9 The Baltimore Orioles defeat the Los Angeles Dodgers in four straight games to win the World Series.

November

14 Muhammad Ali of the United States beats fellow countryman Cleveland Williams to retain the heavyweight title before 34,420 in Houston's Astrodome, the largest indoor crowd in boxing history.
19 In college football, Notre Dame and Michigan State, both undefeated, fight a 10–10 tie at East Lansing, Michigan.

1967

POLITICS, GOVERNMENT, AND ECONOMICS

Business and Economics

- The U.S. restaurateur Craig Sams opens the first macrobiotic restaurant, in London, England. It serves dishes of brown rice and vegetables derived from the Zen Buddhist dietary system, intended to prolong life.

JUNE

27 Barclays Bank opens the world's first automatic cash machine at Enfield in London, England.

JULY

- United Rubber Workers win a new three-year contract from the nation's largest rubber producers.

AUGUST

- After the U.S. Republic Steel Corporation announces a 1.8% increase in the cost of steel bars, six other steel producers follow suit.

Colonization

SEPTEMBER

20 The mid-west of Nigeria proclaims itself independent as Dahomey (now Benin).

NOVEMBER

26 Aden becomes independent as the People's Republic of South Yemen, and the last British troops leave on November 29.

Human Rights

- The Sexual Offences Act (affecting England and Wales) permits homosexual acts in private between consenting adults over the age of 21.

JANUARY

- Former U.S. Army paratrooper Lucius Amerson becomes the first black sheriff to serve in the South since Reconstruction, taking office in Tuskegee, Alabama.

JUNE

- U.S. District Court judge J. Skelly Wright orders Washington, D.C., to end de facto segregation in the city's public schools by the beginning of the new school year.

12 The U.S. Supreme Court rules unconstitutional state laws prohibiting interracial marriage.

AUGUST

1 Stokely Carmichael, the former head of the Student Nonviolent Coordinating Committee, calls for a black revolution in the United States and suggests that black should replace Negro in the U.S. lexicon.

Politics and Government

- Indonesia, Malaysia, Singapore, Thailand, and the Philippines form the Association of Southeast Asian Nations (ASEAN) to promote regional growth and western security interests in Southeast Asia, and establish a secretariat in Jakarta, Indonesia.
- The "Kennedy round" of negotiations of the General Agreement on Tariffs and Trade (GATT) ends.
- The Outer Space Treaty that bans military activities in space is ratified by 63 members of the United Nations (UN).

JANUARY

- Former Atlanta restaurateur and avowed segregationist Lester Maddox is sworn in as governor of Georgia.
6 U.S. and South Vietnamese forces launch a major offensive in the Vietcong-controlled Mekong Delta region of southern South Vietnam.
26–February 12 Red Guards besiege the Soviet embassy in Beijing, China, alleging mistreatment of Chinese students in Moscow, USSR.
27 A treaty banning nuclear weapons from outer space is signed by 60 countries, including the United States and the USSR. It will be effective from October 10.
28 The USSR sends a note to the United States and Britain accusing West Germany of neo-Nazism and militarism.
30 France abolishes exchange controls and frees the gold market in an attempt to increase the importance of Paris, France, as a financial center.

FEBRUARY

- The 25th Amendment to the U.S. Constitution, providing for presidential succession, becomes law.
- The U.S. National Student Association acknowledges having received some $3 million from the CIA between 1952 and 1966 for covert operations abroad.
2 President Lyndon B. Johnson offers to halt the U.S. bombing of North Vietnam if the North Vietnamese cease infiltration of South Vietnam. The North Vietnamese leader Ho Chi Minh rejects the proposals on March 5.
6–13 The Soviet prime minister Alexey Kosygin visits Britain and discusses the Vietnam War with the British prime minister Harold Wilson.

10 A curfew is imposed in the British protectorate of Aden after nationalist riots.

11 The Chinese army takes over the public security ministry and places Beijing, China, under military rule during the Cultural Revolution.

15–21 The ruling Congress Party sustains heavy losses in an Indian general election, though Indira Ghandi remains prime minister.

21 The 18-nation disarmament conference reopens in Geneva, Switzerland.

22 U.S. and South Vietnamese forces begin Operation Junction City, their largest of the war so far, along the Cambodian border.

26 The Chinese premier Zhou Enlai calls for a return to order and discipline, in response to the anarchy of the Cultural Revolution.

MARCH

• A grand jury in New Orleans, Louisiana, indicts local businessman Clay Shaw for conspiring in the assassination of President John F. Kennedy.

• The U.S. Fifth Circuit Court of Appeals orders the states of Alabama, Florida, Georgia, Louisiana, Mississippi, and Texas to desegregate their schools by the start of the following school year.

• The U.S. House of Representatives denies a seat to New York Democrat Adam Clayton Powell, after Powell is found guilty of purposefully misusing government funds.

• The U.S. signs its first consular treaty with the Soviet Union.

2 The accidental U.S. bombing of Lang Vei kills 80 South Vietnamese civilians in the Vietnam War.

6 Svetlana Alliluyeva, Stalin's daughter, requests asylum at the U.S. embassy in Delhi, India.

12 A French general election reduces the Gaullist-led coalition government's majority in the French national assembly to one.

19 French Somaliland rejects independence in a referendum.

28 The United Nations (UN) secretary-general U Thant discloses his Vietnam peace plan, which is accepted by the United States, but rejected by North Vietnam.

31 The Supreme Headquarters of the North Atlantic Treaty Organization (NATO) is moved from France to Casteau in Belgium, following France's withdrawal of its forces from the organization.

APRIL

• Joseph Stalin's daughter Svetlana Aliluyeva arrives in the United States, having received political asylum at the U.S. embassy in New Delhi, India, on March 6.

• Nearly half a million people march from Central Park in New York, New York, to the United Nations headquarters to protest against the Vietnam War.

• President Lyndon B. Johnson attends a Pan-American conference in Punta del Este, Uruguay. The conferees call for a Latin American common market by 1970, along with infrastructure improvements.

• U.S. warplanes target the North Vietnamese port Haiphong, along with MIG aircraft installations.

1 President Nguyen Van Thieu of South Vietnam promulgates a new constitution, introducing a more democratic structure in response to U.S. pressure and popular discontent.

2–7 A United Nations (UN) diplomatic mission visits the troubled British protectorate of Aden. A general strike and terrorist campaign by Arab nationalists ensues.

7 Border clashes occur between Syria and Israel around Lake Tiberias.

8 Fighting resumes between Greek and Turkish Cypriots near Limassol, Cyprus.

21 A military coup in Athens, Greece, led by Colonel Georgios Papadopoulos, establishes the regime of the "Greek colonels."

27–October 29 The "Expo 67" exhibition in Montreal, Canada, marks the centenary of Canadian confederation.

MAY

• The National Guard is summoned to Jackson State College in Mississippi, after two black policemen arrest a man for speeding. One student dies and two are wounded in the mêlée.

2–10 The Bertrand Russell International War Crimes Tribunal in Stockholm, Sweden, finds the United States guilty of aggression in Vietnam.

6 An outbreak of rioting in Hong Kong begins three weeks of disturbances by Chinese workers opposed to British rule over the colony.

10 The Greek military junta takes control of the Greek Orthodox Church following its coup.

11 Britain, Denmark, and Ireland formally apply to join the European Economic Community (EEC).

13 Seventy thousand people parade in New York, New York, in support of U.S. soldiers serving in Vietnam.

16 The French president Charles de Gaulle, in a press conference, virtually vetoes British entry into the European Economic Community (EEC).

18 One hundred thousand Chinese people demonstrate in Beijing, China, against British possession of Hong Kong.

19 The United Nations (UN) withdraws its peacekeeping force from the Israeli–Egyptian border at the request of the United Arab Republic (UAR, or Egypt).

21–27 U.S. casualty figures in the Vietnam War reach a new single-week high: 313 dead, 2,626 wounded.

22 President Gamal Abdel Nasser of the United Arab Republic (UAR) closes the Gulf of Aqaba to Israeli shipping; Israel and the UAR call up their military reserves.

23 The United States tells the United Arab Republic (UAR) to respect the freedom of international waterways following its closing of the Gulf of Aqaba to Israeli shipping, and the USSR warns Israel against retaliatory aggression toward the UAR.

29 The U.S. Supreme Court rules unconstitutional a California law providing homeowners "absolute discretion" in renting or selling their property, on the grounds that such a principle violates the 14th Amendment.

30 The secession from Nigeria of the province of Biafra, under Colonel Chukwuemeka Odumegwu-Ojukwu, provokes civil war in Nigeria.

JUNE

• Israeli gunboats inadvertently attack the U.S. Navy vessel *Liberty* off the Sinai Peninsula, killing 34 and wounding 75.

• Mexican-American terrorists from a group known as the Political Confederation of Free City States seize the

Six Day War (1967)

JUNE

5   The Six Day War breaks out between Israel and the Arab states of the United Arab Republic (now Egypt), Syria, Jordan, Lebanon, and Iraq. In preemptive air strikes, Israel destroys over 300 enemy aircraft.

5–8   Three Israeli armoured divisions strike deep into the Sinai Peninsula, breaking the cohesion of seven Egyptian divisions. On June 8, as Israeli tanks reach the canal, the Egyptian commander in the Sinai commits suicide.

6   Egyptian president Gamal Abdel Nasser closes the Suez Canal and alleges that U.S. and British forces are aiding Israel.

7   Supported by tanks, Israeli paratroopers storm through the Lion Gate into Jerusalem, driving the Jordanian defenders down to Jericho and across the Jordan river.

9   Striking through the foothills of Mt. Hermon, Israeli paratroopers push onto the northern end of the Golan Heights in Syria, driving the Syrians north east toward Damascus.

10   The Six Day War ends with Israeli victory, and the USSR breaks off diplomatic relations with Israel.

JULY

4   The United Nations orders Israel to rescind its decision to unify the Arab and Israeli parts of Jerusalem following its victory in the Six Day War, but this is rejected by Israel on July 14.

---

county courthouse in Tiera Amarilla, New Mexico. They aim to recover 2,500 square miles of territory allegedly given to their forebears by the Spanish crown.

• President Lyndon B. Johnson meets his Soviet counterpart Alexey Kosygin for two days of talks in Glassboro, New Jersey.

• The U.S. Senate censures Connecticut Democrat Thomas J. Dodd for misusing federal funds.

5   The Six Day War breaks out between Israel and the Arab states of the United Arab Republic (UAR), Syria, Jordan, Lebanon, and Iraq. In preemptive air strikes, Israel destroys over 300 enemy aircraft.

6   In the Six Day War, the Egyptian president Gamal Abdel Nasser closes the Suez Canal and alleges that U.S. and British forces are aiding Israel.

8   In the Six Day War, Israel wins control of the Sinai Peninsula, and the United Arab Republic (UAR) and its allies agree to a cease-fire.

9   In the Six Day War, Israel attacks Syria after it violates the cease-fire.

10   The Six Day War ends with Israeli victory, and the USSR breaks off diplomatic relations with Israel.

17   China announces the explosion of its first hydrogen bomb, at Lop Nor, near Sinkiang.

20   Arab mutineers in Aden kill 22 British soldiers.

21   The Soviet president Nikolai Podgorny visits Cairo, Egypt, to discuss the rearmament of the United Arab Republic (UAR) following its defeat in the Six Day War.

30   Forty-six nations sign the Final Acts of the "Kennedy round" of the General Agreement on Tariffs and Trade (GATT).

JULY

• A race riot erupts in Newark, New Jersey, after police beat a black man stopped for a traffic violation. It takes the National Guard five days to restore order; 26 people die, 1,300 are injured, and millions of dollars worth of property is destroyed. Cambridge, Maryland, erupts in racial animosity, following a speech by H. Rap Brown, chairman of the Student Nonviolent Coordinating Committee. Brown is later arrested for inciting the violence. Detroit, Michigan, erupts in riots; the National Guard restores order, but not before 43 people die and an estimated $200 million worth of property is

destroyed, making this the worst race riot in U.S. history.

• Puerto Ricans vote 60.5% to 39.5% to retain their status as a U.S. commonwealth.

• The U.S. Defense Department announces plans to swell the number of U.S. troops in Vietnam to 525,000 by the end of next year.

1   The Commissions of the European Economic Community (EEC), European Coal and Steel Community (ECSC), and Euratom are merged in a unified administrative structure, the European Community (EC).

2   Fighting begins in eastern Congo between the army and white mercenaries supporting the ex-prime minister, Moise Tshombe.

4   The United Nations (UN) orders Israel to rescind its decision to unify the Arab and Israeli parts of Jerusalem following its victory in the Six Day War, but this is rejected by Israel on July 14.

16   The Hong Kong government arrests 600 communists following serious unrest and, on July 20, assumes emergency powers.

24   The French president Charles de Gaulle angers the Canadian government by shouting "Vive le Québec libre!" ("Long live free Quebec!") during a visit to Montreal.

AUGUST

• In the face of continuing racial injustice and widespread urban rioting, the civil-rights leader Martin Luther King, Jr., exhorts his followers to inaugurate a massive campaign of nonviolent civil disobedience.

22   During the Cultural Revolution in China, Red Guards set fire to the British embassy in Beijing.

24   The United States and the USSR present a draft nuclear nonproliferation treaty to the Geneva disarmament conference.

28   Belgium suspends all aid to the Congo following the renewal of fighting there.

SEPTEMBER

• The Pentagon announces plans to begin work on the Sentinel, an antiballistic missile system designed to intercept missiles launched from hostile communist regimes.

1   An Arab summit conference lifts the boycott on oil sales to Britain and the United States, imposed during the Six Day War.

5   Britain appeals for negotiations with the nationalist insurgents in its protectorate of Aden.

10 In a referendum in Gibraltar, 12,138 vote for retaining links with Britain, 44 for union with Spain.

12–15 Indian and Chinese troops clash on the Tibet–Sikkim frontier.

25 Aden nationalists call a cease-fire prior to talks with Britain.

OCTOBER

- A Mississippi jury convicts seven Ku Klux Klansmen of the 1964 murders of civil-rights workers James Chaney, Andrew Goodman, and Michael Schwerner.
- Antiwar protestors clash with police and riot troops outside the Pentagon during a demonstration in Washington, D.C. Over 600 protestors are detained.
- President Lyndon B. Johnson presides at a ceremony in which El Chamizal, a 437-acre territory along the Rio Grande River, is returned to Mexico. El Chamizal had been cut off from Mexico in the 1850s when the Rio Grande had changed course.
- The U.S. civil-rights lawyer Thurgood Marshall is sworn in as the nation's first black Supreme Court justice.
- The United States charges North Vietnam with mistreating U.S. prisoners of war, in violation of the 1949 Geneva protocol.
- U.S. Marines repel a month-long siege by North Vietnamese troops at their installation at Con Thien, near the Demilitarized Zone in South Vietnam.
- U.S. Selective Service director Lewis Hershey nullifies the draft deferments of students found to have interfered with recruitment.
- U.S. troops repel a five-day North Vietnamese assault on the U.S. Special Forces installation at Loc Ninh, along the Cambodian border.

13 Communists plant over 100 bombs in Hong Kong.

16 U.S. folk singer Joan Baez is among 119 arrested at an anti-Vietnam War protest rally in Oakland, California, one of dozens of antiwar protests across the nation this day as part of "Stop the Draft Week."

19 Arab nationalists kill a British high commission administrator in Aden.

21 Demonstrations against the Vietnam War take place in Washington, D.C., London, England, and other capitals.

21 The United Arab Republic (UAR) navy sinks an Israeli destroyer off Sinai and, on October 24, Israeli artillery destroys Suez oil refineries.

25 The Abortion Bill is passed in Britain, permitting abortion on medical and psychological grounds.

26 Mohammad Reza Pahlavi formally crowns himself shah of Iran at a ceremony in Tehran, Iran.

27 The United Nations (UN) Trusteeship Committee condemns British failure to overthrow Ian Smith's whites-only regime in Rhodesia.

28 Kenya and Somalia end their four-year border conflict.

NOVEMBER

2–7 Rival nationalist groups fight in the streets of Aden.

3   The Greek military government abolishes trial by jury for all political crimes.

4   Mercenaries supporting the former Congolese prime minister Moise Tshombe are driven out of Congo.

7   The USSR celebrates the 50th anniversary of the Bolshevik Revolution.

8   The British Commonwealth secretary George Thomson holds talks with Ian Smith in Salisbury, Rhodesia.

21–29 Negotiations take place in Geneva, Switzerland, between Britain and Arab nationalists over a transfer of power in South Arabia.

25 Cyprus asks the United Nations (UN) Security Council to prevent Turkish invasion. Turkey, Greece, and Cyprus agree a peace formula on December 3.

DECEMBER

7   The Romanian dictator Nicolae Ceauşescu becomes head of state as well as Communist Party general secretary.

8   Anti-Vietnam protesters organize a march in New York, New York. Paediatrician Benjamin Spock and Beat poet Allen Ginsberg are among the 250 people arrested.

13 King Constantine of Greece attempts to oust the ruling military junta, but fails and, on December 14, he flees to Rome, Italy.

16 The United Nations (UN) General Assembly demands South African withdrawal from South West Africa.

19 At a European Community (EC) Council, France vetoes negotiations for British entry to the EC, and Britain states that its application will not be withdrawn.

SCIENCE, TECHNOLOGY, AND MEDICINE

Agriculture

JUNE

- The U.S. National Academy of Sciences reports that traces of antibiotics added to animal feed may be found in meat, and that bacteria may be becoming more resistant because of this practice.

Computing

- U.S. scientist Gene Amdahl proposes the use of parallel processors in computers to produce faster processing speeds.

Ecology

- The International Whaling Commission prohibits hunting blue, right, gray, and humpback whales.
- U.S. scientists Syukuvo Manabe and R. T. Wetherald warn that the increase in carbon dioxide in the atmosphere, produced by human activities, is causing a "greenhouse effect," which will raise atmospheric temperatures and cause a rise in sea levels.

JANUARY

23 Hundreds of thousands are killed in Shantung province in China when flood tides, caused by heavy storms, inundate the province.

MAY

22   A fire in L'Innovation department store in Brussels, Belgium, kills 322 people.

Exploration

JANUARY

27   Three U.S. astronauts, Virgil ("Gus") I. Grissom, Edward H. White, II, and Roger B. Chaffee, die in a fire during a countdown rehearsal on the *Apollo 1* spacecraft at Cape Kennedy, Florida. They are the first human casualties of the U.S. space program.

APRIL

17   The U.S. spacecraft *Surveyor 3* is launched and soft lands on the moon, where it conducts sampling experiments on the lunar soil. It is subsequently visited by astronauts from the *Apollo 12* mission.

24   Soviet cosmonaut Vladimir Komarov dies during the descent of his *Soyuz 1* spacecraft when his parachute fails to open properly. He is the first fatality of the Soviet space program.

SEPTEMBER

8   U.S. spacecraft *Surveyor 5* is launched. It measures the proportions of chemicals in the lunar soil.

OCTOBER

18   The Soviet spacecraft *Venera 4* (launched on June 12) lands on Venus. The first soft landing on another planet, its instrument-laden capsule transmits information about Venus' atmosphere.

19   The U.S. spacecraft *Mariner 5* (launched on June 14) passes within 7,600 km/4,750 mi of the surface of Venus, transmitting data on the planet's atmosphere and magnetic field as it does so.

22–29   The Soviet spacecraft *Cosmos 186* and *Cosmos 188* complete the first automatic docking.

NOVEMBER

- The first three-stage *Saturn V* rocket is launched. Weighing nearly 2.3 million kg/5 million lb, it is used to lift the Apollo missions to the moon.

7   U.S. spacecraft *Surveyor 6* photographs one area of the moon then lifts off, repositions itself 2.4 m/8 ft away and resumes photographing. It is the first lift-off from an extraterrestrial body.

Health and Medicine

- A desalination plant, established at Key West, Florida, produces more than 2 million gallons of fresh water a day, supplying the city's entire water needs. Key West is the first U.S. city whose water is supplied solely by the sea.
- France legalizes birth control, but the means of contraception remain difficult to obtain.
- Greek-born U.S. neurologist George Cotzias begins to use L-dopa, a precursor of dopamine, to successfully treat patients with Parkinson's disease.
- Results of a 20-year fluoridation project, conducted in Evanston, Illinois, indicate that fluoride added to the water supply has reduced cavities by 58%.
- Swedish physiologist Ragnar Granit and U.S. physiologists Haldan Hartline and George Wald are jointly awarded the Nobel Prize for Physiology or Medicine for their discoveries concerning the physiological and chemical processes in the eye.
- The annual total number of cigarettes smoked in the United States is an average of 210 packs per person.
- U.S. surgeon Rene Favaloro develops the coronary bypass operation.

DECEMBER

3   South African surgeon Christiaan Barnard performs the first heart transplant operation. The patient, Louis Washkansky, survives for 18 days.

28   U.S. surgeon Adrian Kantrowitz performs the first heart transplant operation in the United States, and the second in the world.

Science

- A tank containing 100,000 gallons of cleaning fluid is installed in a former gold mine in South Dakota, United States, to detect neutrinos from the sun.
- Archeologists discover an obsidian blade at Tlapacoya outside Mexico City, Mexico. It is radiocarbon-dated at 21,000 BC, making it the oldest artifact found on the continent.
- British anthropologist Elwyn Simons discovers the skull of *Aegyptopithecus*, a 30-million-year-old ape believed to be the ancestor of the great apes, in the Fayum region of Egypt.
- German chemist Manfred Eigen and English chemists Ronald Norrish and George Porter receive the Nobel Prize for Chemistry for their investigation of rapid chemical reactions by means of very short pulses of energy.
- The 13th General Committee on Weights and Measures redefines the second in terms of the resonant frequency of the cesium atom.
- U.S. biochemist Marshall Nirenberg establishes that mammals, amphibians, and bacteria all share a common genetic code.
- U.S. chemist Charles Pedersen discovers crown ethers.
- U.S. nuclear physicists Sheldon Lee Glashow and Steven Weinberg and Pakistani nuclear physicist Abdus Salam separately develop the electroweak unification theory, which explains "electromagnetic" interactions and the "weak" nuclear force.
- U.S. physicist Hans Bethe receives the Nobel Prize for Physics for his discoveries concerning the energy production in stars.
- U.S. scientist Charles Caskey and associates demonstrate that identical forms of messenger RNA produce the same amino acids in a variety of living beings, showing that the genetic code is common to all life forms.

JULY

7   Irish astronomer Jocelyn Bell and English astronomer Anthony Hewish discover the first pulsar (announced in 1968). A new class of stars, they are later shown to be collapsed neutron stars emitting bursts of radio energy. The Crab Nebula supernova remnant is discovered to be a pulsar the following year.

Technology

- Amana Refrigeration markets the first microwave oven for home use in the United States.

- An experimental 750,000-volt electrical transmission line, the highest voltage transmission line in the world, is constructed in the USSR.
- Quartz watches are launched in the United States, costing from $550. They have been developed by a group of Swiss watch manufacturers.
- The *London Daily Express* is transmitted electronically, via telephone lines and satellite, to Puerto Rico. It is the first newspaper to be printed simultaneously in another part of the world.
- The Japanese car firm Mazda makes the first cars with a Wankel engine, a revolutionary new type of internal combustion engine that uses a triangular-shaped rotar instead of pistons.
- The Krasnoyarsk Dam on the Yenisey River, Russia, is completed. The world's largest hydroelectric power project, it generates 6,096 megawatts from the beginning of 1968.
- The U.S. Army introduces bullet-proof vests with titanium plates. They provide protection even against armor-piercing bullets.
- The world's first tidal power generating station is completed on the Rance River estuary, France. It has 24 reversible turbines, each of which can generate 10,000 kW.
- U.S. engineer Ray Milton Dolby invents the Dolby noise-reduction system, which reduces background noise. It becomes standard in tape recording and movies.

Transportation

MARCH

18 The Liberian-registered tanker *Torrey Canyon* strikes a submerged reef off the coast of Cornwall, England, and spills 860,000 barrels of crude oil into the sea. It is the biggest oil spill to date.

SEPTEMBER

3   Sweden changes to driving on the right.
20 The Cunard liner *Queen Elizabeth II* is launched from Clydebank, Glasgow, Scotland. It can accommodate 3,000 passengers, has a 531-seat movie theater and four swimming pools.

ARTS AND IDEAS

Architecture

- The History Faculty building at Cambridge University, England, designed by the English architect James Stirling, is completed.
- The Indian Institute of Management in Ahmedabad, India, designed by the U.S. architect Louis Kahn and the Indian architects B. V. Doshi and A. D. Raje, is completed.
- The Metropolitan Cathedral Church of Christ the King in Liverpool, England, designed by the English architect Frederick Gibberd, is completed.
- The Unitarian Church in Rochester, New York, designed by the U.S. architect Louis Kahn, is completed.

Arts

- The English artist Anthony Caro sculpts *Prairie*.
- The English artist David Hockney paints *Neat Lawn* and *A Bigger Splash*.
- The English artist Richard Long sculpts *A Line Made by Walking*.
- The U.S. artist Barnett Newman sculpts *Broken Obelisk*.
- The U.S. artist George Segal sculpts *Execution*.
- U.S. photographer Diane Arbus takes the photograph *Pro-War Parade*.

Film

- A movie of the U.S. folk/rock singer Bob Dylan's 1965 tour of Britain, *Don't Look Back*, is released in the United States.
- The movie *Accident*, directed by Joseph Losey, is released in Britain, starring Dirk Bogarde, Stanley Baker, Jacqueline Sassard, and Michael York.
- The movie *Barbarella*, directed by Roger Vadim, is released in France. Based on Jean-Claude Forest's science-fiction comic strip, it stars Jane Fonda.
- The movie *Belle de jour/Daytime Beauty*, directed by Spanish filmmaker Luis Buñuel, is released in France, starring Catherine Deneuve.
- The movie *Bonnie and Clyde*, directed by Arthur Penn, is released in the United States, starring Warren Beatty and Faye Dunaway.
- The movie *Deux ou trois choses que je sais d'elle/Two or Three Things I Know about Her*, directed by Jean-Luc Godard, is released in France. He also stars in the movie, along with Marina Vlady, Anny Duperey, and Roger Montsaret.
- The movie *Elvira Madigan*, directed by Bo Widerberg, is released in Sweden, starring Pia Degermark and Thommy Berggren.
- The movie *Far from the Madding Crowd*, directed by John Schlesinger, is released in Britain. Based on the novel by Thomas Hardy, it stars Julie Christie, Alan Bates, Peter Finch, and Terence Stamp.
- The movie *Guess Who's Coming to Dinner*, directed by Stanley Kramer, is released in the United States, starring Spencer Tracy, Katharine Hepburn, Sidney Poitier, and Katharine Houghton.
- The movie *In the Heat of the Night*, directed by Norman Jewison, is released in the United States, starring Sidney Poitier and Rod Steiger.
- The movie *La Collectionneuse/The Collector*, directed by French filmmaker Eric Rohmer and starring Patrick Bauchau, is released. The third of his *Six Contes Moraux/Six Moral Tales*, it is photographed by Nestor Almendros.
- The movie *Land in Anguish*, directed by Glauber Rocha, is released in Brazil.
- The movie *Le Voleur/The Thief of Paris*, directed by Louis Malle, is released in France, starring Jean-Paul Belmondo and Geneviève Bujold.
- The movie *Point Blank*, directed by British filmmaker John Boorman, is released in the United States, starring Lee Marvin and Angie Dickinson.
- The movie *The Dirty Dozen*, directed by Robert Aldrich, is released in the United States. The stars

include Lee Marvin, Ernest Borgnine, Charles Bronson, Jim Brown, and John Cassavetes.

- The movie *The Graduate*, directed by Mike Nichols, is released in the United States, starring Dustin Hoffman, Anne Bancroft, and Katherine Ross, and featuring the music of Simon and Garfunkel.
- The movie *The Producers*, directed by Mel Brooks, is released in the United States, starring Zero Mostel and Gene Wilder.
- The movie *The Valley of the Dolls*, directed by Mark Robson, is released in the United States. Based on the novel by best-selling author Jacqueline Susann, it stars Patty Duke, Sharon Tate, Susan Hayward, Barbara Parkins, Martin Milner, Joey Bishop, and George Jessel.
- The movie *You Only Live Twice*, directed by Lewis Gilbert, is released in the United States, starring Sean Connery as James Bond, and Akiko Wakabayashi.
- The semidocumentary movie *In Cold Blood*, directed by Richard Brooks, is released in the United States. Based on the true-crime best seller by Truman Capote, it stars Robert Blake, Scott Wilson, John Forsythe, and Will Geer.

APRIL

10 The 1966 Academy Awards take place. Best Actor: Paul Scofield, for *A Man for All Seasons*; Best Supporting Actor: Walter Matthau, for *The Fortune Cookie*; Best Actress: Elizabeth Taylor, for *Who's Afraid of Virginia Woolf?*; Best Supporting Actress: Sandy Dennis, for *Who's Afraid of Virginia Woolf?*; Best Picture: *A Man for All Seasons*, directed by Fred Zinnemann; Best Director: Fred Zinnemann, for *A Man For All Seasons*.

Literature and Language

- The Colombian writer Gabriel García Márquez publishes his novel *Cien años de soledad/One Hundred Years of Solitude*.
- The Egyptian writer Naguib Mahfouz publishes his novel *Miramar*.
- The English poet Ted Hughes publishes his poetry collection *Wodwo*.
- The English writer Angela Carter publishes her novel *The Magic Toyshop*.
- The English writer Alan Garner publishes his children's novel *The Owl Service*.
- The English writer Margaret Drabble publishes her novel *Jerusalem the Golden*.
- The English writer Paul Bailey publishes his novel *At the Jerusalem*.
- The French philosopher Jacques Derrida publishes *De la grammatologie/Of Grammatology*.
- The French writer Claude Simon publishes his novel *Histoire/History*.
- The French writer Michel Tournier publishes his novel *Vendredi, ou les limbes du Pacifique/Friday, or the Other Island*.
- The French-born U.S. literary critic George Steiner publishes his collection of essays *Language and Silence*.
- The Nobel Prize for Literature is awarded to the Guatemalan writer Miguel Ángel Asturias.
- The novel *The Third Policeman*, by the Irish writer Flann O'Brien, is published posthumously. It was written in 1940.

- The Pulitzer Prize for Biography is awarded to Justin Kaplan for *Mr Clemens and Mark Twain*, the Pulitzer Prize for Poetry is awarded to Anne Sexton for *Live or Die*, and the Pulitzer Prize for Fiction is awarded to *The Fixer*.
- The U.S. television and radio performer Virginia Graham publishes her beauty guide *Don't Blame the Mirror*, in which she advises women to wear false eyelashes to become more attractive.
- The U.S. writer Angus Wilson publishes his novel *No Laughing Matter*.
- The U.S. writer Donald Barthelme publishes his novel *Snow White*.
- The U.S. writer Gore Vidal publishes his novel *Washington, DC.*
- The U.S. writer Joyce Carol Oates publishes her novel *A Garden of Earthly Delights*.
- The U.S. writer Paul Goodman publishes his poetry collection *Hawkweed*.
- The U.S. writer Robert Lowell publishes his poetry collection *Near the Ocean*.
- The U.S. writer Thornton Wilder publishes his novel *The Eighth Day*.
- The U.S. writer William Styron publishes his novel *The Confessions of Nat Turner*, a novel about a 19th-century uprising by black slaves that is awarded the Pulitzer Prize for Fiction in 1968.

Music

- Albums are beginning to overtake singles in importance, both commercially and artistically.
- Elvis Presley marries Priscilla Beaulieu in the United States.
- The Australian pop group the Seekers releases the single "Georgy Girl."
- The Australian pop group the Bee Gees releases the single "(The Lights Went Out In) Massachusetts."
- The British pop group Herman's Hermits releases the single "There's a Kind of Hush."
- The British pop singer Sandie Shaw releases the single "Puppet on a String," Britain's winning entry for the Eurovision Song Contest.
- The British pop/folk singer Donovan releases the single "Mellow Yellow."
- The British rock band Procul Harum releases the single "A Whiter Shade of Pale."
- The British rock group the Beatles releases *Sergeant Pepper's Lonely Hearts Club Band*, considered their most innovative album to date. They also release the singles "All You Need Is Love" and "Hello Goodbye."
- The British rock group the Rolling Stones releases the single "Let's Spend the Night Together." When they perform this on the Ed Sullivan show on U.S. television, the lyrics are changed to "Let's Spend Some Time Together."
- The British singer Engelbert Humperdinck releases the single "The Last Waltz" and the single "Release Me," the best-selling single of the year in Britain.
- The English composer Elisabeth Lutyens completes her vocal work *And Suddenly It's Evening*.

- The English composer Peter Maxwell Davies completes his chamber work *Antechrist*.
- The English composer Benjamin Britten completes his Cello Suite No. 2.
- The German composer Karlheinz Stockhausen completes his electronic work *Hymnen/Hymns*.
- The Japanese composer Toru Takemitsu completes his orchestral work *November Steps*.
- The Northern Irish rock singer Van Morrison releases the single "Brown-Eyed Girl."
- The opera *A Penny for a Song*, by the English composer Richard Rodney Bennett, is first performed, in London, England.
- The opera *Arden muss sterben/Arden Must Die*, by the German-born English composer Alexander Goehr, is first performed, in Hamburg, Germany.
- The Polish composer Witold Lutosławski completes his Symphony No. 2.
- The Russian composer Dmitry Shostakovich completes his Violin Concerto No. 2.
- The U.S. avant-garde rock group Velvet Underground releases the album *The Velvet Underground and Nico*.
- The U.S. composer George Crumb completes his orchestral work *Echoes of Time and the River*.
- The U.S. country singer Glen Campbell releases the singles "Gentle On My Mind" and "By the Time I Get to Phoenix."
- The U.S. pop group Gladys Knight and the Pips releases the album *Everybody Needs Love*, featuring the single "I Heard it Through the Grapevine."
- The U.S. pop group the Monkees releases the singles "I'm a Believer," "Last Train to Clarksville," and "Daydream Believer." They achieve a record four hit albums in the United States in one year.
- The U.S. pop group the Fifth Dimension releases the album *Up, Up and Away*, featuring the single by the same name.
- The U.S. rock band Jefferson Airplane releases the singles "Somebody to Love" and "White Rabbit."
- The U.S. rock group the Doors releases the single "Light My Fire" and the album *The Doors*.
- The U.S. rock group the Jimi Hendrix Experience releases the albums *Are You Experienced?* and *Axis: Bold As Love*, and the single "Purple Haze."
- The U.S. rock group the Grateful Dead, who had become famous members of the psychedelic rock scene in San Francisco, California, releases the debut album *Grateful Dead*. It is a commercial and critical disappointment.
- The U.S. rock singer Janis Joplin and the U.S. rock band Big Brother and the Holding Company release the album *Big Brother and the Holding Company*. The album includes the single "Piece of My Heart," which enters the charts in August 1968.
- The U.S. singer Frank Sinatra and his daughter Nancy release the single "Somethin' Stupid."
- The U.S. singer Scott McKenzie releases the single "San Francisco (Be Sure to Wear Some Flowers in Your Hair)."
- The U.S. soul singer Aretha Franklin releases the singles "Respect," "Baby I Love You," and "(You Make Me Feel Like) A Natural Woman." She achieves five hit singles in one year.

- The U.S.-Canadian folk/rock group Buffalo Springfield releases the album *Buffalo Springfield Again*, which includes the protest song "For What It's Worth (Stop, Hey What's That Sound)."

MARCH

2 The 1966–67 Grammy Awards take place. Best Record: "Strangers in the Night" by Frank Sinatra; Best Male Vocalist: Frank Sinatra; Best Female Vocalist: Eydie Gorme; Best Group: the Anita Kerr Singers.

MAY

27 The British Broadcasting Corporation (BBC) bans the Beatles' single "A Day in the Life," as it is seen to be encouraging drug-taking.

JUNE

- The Summer of Love begins in San Francisco, California, with the Monterey Pop Festival. From this atmosphere emerge alternative lifestyles, that are established particularly in San Francisco. Acts include the Grateful Dead, Jefferson Airplane, and Janis Joplin.

Theater and Dance

- The play *A Day in the Death of Joe Egg*, by the English writer Peter Nichols, is first performed, in London, England.
- The play *Duck Hunting*, by the Russian writer Alexander Vampilov, is first performed, in Riga, Latvia, USSR.
- The play *Little Murders*, by the U.S. writer and cartoonist Jules Peiffer, is first performed, in New York, New York.
- The play *Soldaten/Soldiers*, by the German dramatist Rolf Hochhuth, is first performed, in Berlin, Germany.
- The play *Une saison au Congo/A Season in the Congo*, by the Martinique writer Aimé Césaire, is first performed, in Venice, Italy. It was published in 1966.
- The play *Zigger Zagger*, by the English dramatist Peter Terson, is first performed, in London, England. It is an important success for the National Youth Theatre.
- The Pulitzer Prize for Drama is awarded to Edward Albee for *A Delicate Balance*.

FEBRUARY

22 The play *MacBird*, a work by U.S. playwright Barbara Garson, loosely based on Shakespeare's *Macbeth* and parodying President Lyndon B. Johnson, is first performed, at the Village Gate in New York, New York.

MARCH

26 The 1966–67 Tony Awards take place. Best Play: *The Homecoming*, by English dramatist Harold Pinter; Best Musical: *Cabaret*; Best Actor: Paul Rogers; Best Actress: Beryl Reid.

OCTOBER

29 The rock musical *Hair*, with lyrics by Gerome Ragni and music by Galt MacDermot, is first performed, at the Public Theater, East Greenwich Village, New York, New York. Songs featured in the show include "Aquarius."

NOVEMBER

12 A revival of *Hello Dolly!*, with an all-black cast featuring Cab Calloway and Pearl Bailey, opens at the St. James Theater in New York, New York.

Thought and Scholarship

- The English historian Hugh Trevor-Roper publishes *Religion, the Reformation and Social Change*.
- The English historian Christopher Hill publishes *Reformation to Industrial Revolution*.
- The Pulitzer Prize for History is awarded to William Goetzmann for *Exploration and Empire: The Explorer and Scientist in the Winning of the American West*.
- The Pulitzer Prize for General Nonfiction is awarded to David Brion Davis for *The Problem of Slavery in Western Culture*.
- The U.S. historian Bernard Bailyn publishes *The Ideological Origins of the American Revolution*.
- U.S. jurist Lon L. Fuller publishes *Legal Fictions*.

SOCIETY

Everyday Life

- "Granny glasses," small glasses with thin wire frames, as worn by John Lennon, become popular.
- Hippie clothes, as sported at open-air rock festivals, influence mainstream fashion, with Afghan jackets, Paisley-patterned fabric and beads all becoming popular.
- Jane Fonda in the movie *Barbarella* promotes a fashion for knee-length white boots.
- Owen Finlay Maclaren develops the first lightweight baby buggy, the Maclaren Minor, in Britain.
- The Australian winemakers Tolley's are the first to sell wine in boxes.
- The British model Twiggy popularizes a waif-like look.
- The first Laura Ashley store opens in London, England.
- The Grey Line Bus Co. offers a "Hippie Hop" tour of San Francisco, California.
- The state of Wisconsin in the United States allows margarine to be colored yellow.
- The U.S. firm Raytheon introduces the first small and affordable microwave oven.
- Trudy Baker and Rachel Jones publish *Coffee, Tea, or Me*, an explicit memoir of their lives as stewardesses; the book sells over 1 million copies.
- U.S. cartoonist Robert Crumb publishes the first *Zap Comix* in San Francisco, California. Featuring characters like Fritz the Cat, Flakey Foont, and Mr. Natural, Crumb's work embodies the "underground" counterculture of the 1960s, mixing crude but finely drawn images of sex and drugs with incisive social commentary.

JANUARY
21 The girl's comic *Mandy* is launched in Britain.

MARCH
1 Direct dialing from New York, New York, to Paris, France, and London, England, is introduced.

APRIL
2 The Southern Education Reporting Service announces that 16% of black Americans in 11 southern states attend integrated schools.

JUNE
- Merchant marine deck officers serving on ships along the eastern seaboard of the United States strike, disrupting boat traffic and costing the industry hundreds of thousands of dollars.

JULY
5 The U.S. Federal Communications Commission orders AT&T to lower its long-distance and overseas telephone rates.

SEPTEMBER
- Public school teachers in New York, New York, conclude a three-week walk-out, after winning a new two-year contract worth more than $135 million.

OCTOBER
- United Auto Workers win a new three-year contract from Ford Motor Company, after a six-week strike.

NOVEMBER
- The U.S. population reaches 200 million.

Media and Communication

- Color television broadcasts begin in the UK, West Germany, France, and the USSR.
- Half of the world's telephones are in the United States.

MAY
5 The *New York World Journal*, an afternoon daily, ceases publication after only eight months. It has lost about $700,000 in each month.

JUNE
4 The 1966–67 Emmy Awards for television take place. Best Drama Series: *Mission: Impossible*; Best Actor in a Single Show: Peter Ustinov; Best Actress in a Single Show: Geraldine Page; Best Actor in a Series: Bill Cosby, for *I Spy*; Best Actress in a Series: Barbara Bains, for *Mission: Impossible*.
22 The Public Broadcasting Act in the United States establishes a corporation to spend funds, both federal and private, on noncommercial radio and television broadcasting.

SEPTEMBER
7–September 18, 1970 *The Flying Nun*, starring Sally Fields as Sister Bertrille, a novice who discovers that she can fly, is shown on U.S. television. The series also stars Madeline Sherwood and Alejandro Rey.
9–August 30, 1979 *Spider-Man*, an animated cartoon series about the adventures of Peter Parker, a reporter turned into a superhero after he is bitten by a radioactive spider, appears on U.S. television.
10–September 10, 1971 *The High Chaparral*, a Western series set on a ranch in the Arizona Territory in the 1870s, appears on U.S. television. Leif Erickson, Linda Crystal, Mark Slade, Henry Darrow, and Cameron Mitchell star.
11–August 9, 1978 The comedy variety program *The Carol Burnett Show* appears on U.S. television. Burnett stars with Harvey Korman, Tim Conway, Vicki Lawrence, and Lyle Waggoner.
14–January 16, 1973 *Ironside*, police drama starring Raymond Burr as paraplegic police chief, appears on U.S. television. It also stars Don Galloway, Barbara Anderson, and Dan Mitchell.

NOVEMBER

- The first national U.S. rock music magazine, *Rolling Stone*, is published by Jann Wenner in San Francisco, California.

Religion

MAY

- The U.S. Presbyterian Church adopts the Confession of 1967, its first since the Westminster Confession of 1647.

Sports

- Australia wins the Davis Cup for tennis for the fourth successive year, beating Spain 4–1 in the final.
- Carl Yaztremski of the Boston Red Sox achieves the baseball Triple Crown, leading the American League in home runs, runs batted in, and batting average.
- Football hooliganism is a growing problem in England.
- Geoff Hunt of Australia wins the inaugural World Amateur squash rackets championship staged by the newly-formed International Squash Rackets Federation. He also helps Australia to victory in the team event.
- The Australian tennis player John Newcombe wins the men's singles titles at the Wimbledon and U.S. tennis championships.
- The overall skiing champions of the inaugural Alpine World Cup are Jean-Claude Killy of France and Nancy Greene of Canada.
- U.S. Air Force Major William Knight sets an air speed record of 7,232 kph/4,520 mph, in an X-15A-2 rocket plane.

JANUARY

1   The Green Bay Packers defeat the Dallas Cowboys 34–27 to win their fourth National Football League (NFL) Championship title in five years, earning the right to represent the NFL in the inaugural American Football League–National Football League World Championship game or Super Bowl.

15 The first Super Bowl American football match is held (between the winners of the National Football League and the American Football League); the Green Bay Packers beat the Kansas City Chiefs 35–10 before 61,496 spectators in Los Angeles, California.

BIRTHS & DEATHS

JANUARY

16 Robert Jemison Van de Graaff, U.S. physicist who invented the high electric-voltage Van de Graaff generator, dies in Boston, Massachusetts (65).

FEBRUARY

2   Henry R. Luce, U.S. magazine publisher who published *Time*, *Life*, and *Fortune* magazines, dies in Phoenix, Arizona (68).

6   Henry Morgenthau, U.S. secretary of the treasury 1934–45, dies in Poughkeepsie, New York (75).

15 Frank Duryea, U.S. inventor who, with his brother Charles Duryea, built the first practical car powered by an internal combustion engine in the United States, dies in Saybrook, Connecticut (97).

18 J. Robert Oppenheimer, U.S. theoretical physicist and director of the Los Alamos laboratory which built the first atomic bomb, dies in Princeton, New Jersey (62).

20 Kurt Cobain, U.S. lead singer of the rock group Nirvana, born in Aberdeen, Washington (–1994).

APRIL

5   Hermann Joseph Muller, U.S. geneticist who demonstrated that X-rays speed up the mutation rate, dies in Bloomington, Indiana (76).

19 Konrad Adenauer, first chancellor 1949–63 of the Federal Republic of Germany (West Germany), dies in Rhöndorf, West Germany (91).

JUNE

7   Dorothy Parker, U.S. poet and writer of short stories, dies in New York, New York (73).

10 Spencer Tracey, U.S. actor, dies in Beverly Hills, California (67).

JULY

8   Vivien Leigh, English actress, dies in London, England (53).

21 Albert Lutuli, South African Zulu chief, president of the African National Congress 1952–60, and first African to be awarded the Nobel Peace Prize (1960), dies in Stanger, South Africa (about 69).

21 Jimmie Foxx, U.S. baseball player who became the second person to hit over 500 runs (after Babe Ruth), dies in Miami, Florida (59).

22 Carl Sandburg, U.S. poet, historian and novelist, dies in Flat Rock, North Carolina (89).

AUGUST

24 Henry Kaiser, U.S. industrialist, dies in Honolulu, Hawaii (85).

27 Brian Epstein, manager of the Beatles, dies from an overdose of sleeping pills in London, England (33).

31 Ilya Grigoryevich Ehrenburg, Russian writer, dies in Moscow, USSR (76).

SEPTEMBER

13 Michael Johnson, U.S. track and field athlete, born in Dallas, Texas.

18 John Douglas Cockcroft, English physicist who shared the Nobel Prize for Physics in 1951 for his pioneering use of particle accelerators, dies in Cambridge, England (70).

29 Leonard Colebrook, English physician who introduced the first sulfonamide drug (Prontosil) into the UK, dies (84).

OCTOBER

- Che (Ernesto) Guevara, Cuban and South American communist guerrilla, is shot dead in Bolivia by the Bolivian army (39).

3   Woody Guthrie, U.S. folk singer and songwriter, dies in New York, New York (55).

7   Norman Angell, English economist who won the Nobel Peace Prize in 1933, dies in Croydon, Surrey, England (93).

8   Clement Attlee, Earl Attlee, British prime minister 1945–51, a member of the Labour Party, dies in Westminster, London, England (84).

NOVEMBER

22 Boris Becker, German tennis player, the youngest to win the Wimbledon championships in London, England (1985 at 17), born in Leimen near Heidelberg, Germany.

DECEMBER

17 The Australian prime minister Harold Holt drowns near Portsea, Victoria, Australia.

29 Paul Whiteman, U.S. bandleader known as the "King of Jazz," dies in Doylestown, Pennsylvania (77).

FEBRUARY

2   League officials announce the formation of the American Basketball Association, an 11-team league that seeks to rival the National Basketball Association.

APRIL

14–24 The Philadelphia 76ers beat the San Francisco Warriors by four games to two to win the National Basketball Association championship, the first time in nine years that the Boston Celtics are not champions.

19   The U.S. runner Kathy Switzer, in defiance of the race organizers, becomes the first woman to run in the Boston Marathon in the United States since the race was inaugurated in 1897. Four years later women are allowed to enter.

20–May 2 The Toronto Maple Leafs beat the Montreal Canadiens by four games to two to win the National Hockey League Stanley Cup.

28   The World Boxing Association strips Muhammad Ali (formerly Cassius Clay) of his world heavyweight title for refusing to be drafted into the U.S. army.

MAY

14   New York Yankee centerfielder Mickey Mantle becomes the sixth player to hit 500 career home runs, at Yankee Stadium in the Bronx, New York, New York.

25   UCLA, coached by John Wooden, win the first of seven consecutive National Collegiate Athletic Association (NCAA) national basketball championships.

JULY

•   The U.S. runner Jim Ryun sets a new 1,500-meters world record of 3 min 33.1 sec, an improvement of 2.5 seconds on the existing record set by the Australian runner Herb Elliott in 1960.

July–September The U.S. tennis player Billie Jean King emulates fellow U.S. player Alice Marble's 1939 achievement of winning the singles, doubles, and mixed doubles at both the U.S. and Wimbledon tennis championships in the same year.

13   The English cyclist Tommy Simpson collapses and dies during the Tour de France cycle race. After large traces of illegal stimulants are found in his body, the Fédération Internationale de Cyclisme Professional introduces new antidrug regulations, many of which are also adopted by other sports.

OCTOBER

4–12 The St. Louis Cardinals defeat the Boston Red Sox by four games to three to win the World Series for the eighth time.

5   The British Lawn Tennis Association abolishes the distinction between amateurs and professionals, paving the way for open competition.

DECEMBER

12   After 226 days at sea, the English yachtsman Francis Chichester completes the first solo round-the-world voyage in his yacht *Gipsy Moth IV*.

◆

1968

POLITICS, GOVERNMENT, AND ECONOMICS

Business and Economics

•   The unemployment rate in the United States is 3.6%.
•   The U.S. fashion designer Calvin Klein founds the company that bears his name.
•   U.S. engineers Gordon Moore and Robert Noyce found Intel Corporation, which begins making integrated circuits for computers.

JANUARY

17   The U.S. media company Time, Inc. acquires Little, Brown and Company, a Boston publisher, for $17 million.

FEBRUARY

4   France is awarded extensive oil drilling rights in Iraq.

MARCH

1   A speculative flight from the U.S. dollar into gold starts to destabilize the international monetary system. The London, England, gold market closes from March 15 to April 1.

17   Following an international gold crisis, central banks agree a two-tier system for gold, official dealings at $35 per ounce, commercial dealings at a free price.

JUNE

•   On the New York Stock Exchange 2,350,000 shares change hands, a new record.

•   The United States Steelworkers Union signs a new three-year contract with the nation's steel producers, providing workers with a 6% annual increase.

JULY

•   The United Auto Workers (UAW) union withdraws from the American Federation of Labor and the Congress of Industrial Organizations (AFL-CIO), after years of enmity sparked by philosophical differences. The UAW will merge with the Teamsters to form the Alliance for Labor Action at the end of the month.

24 A conference of Spanish bishops proclaims workers' right to strike and to form independent labor unions.

NOVEMBER

20 The European exchange markets close after heavy speculation against the French franc. On November 23 the French president Charles de Gaulle refuses to devalue the currency.

Colonization

SEPTEMBER

6 The British protectorate of Swaziland becomes independent under King Sobhuza II.

OCTOBER

12 Equatorial Guinea wins independence from Spain.

Human Rights

- The U.S. historian Winthrop Jordan publishes *White Over Black: American Attitudes Toward the Negro, 1550-1812*.
- The U.S. social activist and Black Panther member Eldridge Cleaver publishes *Soul on Ice*, a book of essays on the personal effects of racism, that quickly acquires an international status.

FEBRUARY

5–8 Four days of rioting at historically black South Carolina State College in Orangeburg culminate in the shooting to death of three students. The protests begin because a local bowling alley excluded blacks.

MAY

- The Poor People's March on Washington, D.C., begins. Led by Reverend Ralph Abernathy, it was the brainchild of the late civil-rights leader Martin Luther King, Jr.

AUGUST

20 The Democratic Party's convention in Chicago, Illinois, votes not to recognize the official delegates, and to seat instead the Loyal Democrats, committed to the full participation of blacks in the Mississippi Democratic Party.

SEPTEMBER

7 About 200 female activists demonstrate against the Miss America pageant in Atlantic City, New Jersey.

NOVEMBER

6 Black students boycott classes at San Francisco State University, demanding the introduction of a black-studies curriculum.

Politics and Government

- After four years of negotiations, the U.S., USSR, Britain, and 58 other nations sign a nuclear nonproliferation treaty.
- Eighty thousand people march on the U.S. embassy in London, England, in protest at U.S. involvement in Vietnam.

JANUARY

- Former Truman adviser Clark Clifford succeeds Robert S. McNamara as secretary of defense. McNamara had alienated President Johnson by questioning the administration's escalation of the Vietnam War.
- In the State of the Union address, President Johnson identifies the federal budget deficit and inflation as the nation's most pressing domestic problems. He proposes raising income taxes by 10%.

5 The reformer Alexander Dubček becomes first secretary of the Czechoslovak Communist Party.

8 Israeli and Jordanian forces clash south of the Sea of Galilee.

10 John Grey Gorton becomes the 20th prime minister of Australia following Harold Holt's drowning in December 1967.

12 The Soviet dissidents Yuri Galanskov and Alexander Ginsburg are sentenced to hard labor in the USSR.

21 31 North Koreans raid Seoul, South Korea, in an unsuccessful attempt to assassinate President Pak Chung Hi of South Korea.

21–April 8 Five thousand U.S. marines and South Vietnamese soldiers are besieged by two North Vietnamese army divisions at Khe Sanh in the north of South Vietnam, in one of the fiercest battles of the entire Vietnam War.

23 U.S.–North Korean relations are strained after North Korean gunboats seize the crew of the U.S. Navy vessel USS *Pueblo* after it had allegedly strayed into North Korean waters. The North Koreans detain 83 U.S. crewmen until December 23.

30 Students in Warsaw, Poland, demonstrate against political censorship.

30–February 29 The Vietcong launches the Tet offensive against South Vietnamese cities.

31 The United Nations (UN) trust territory of Nauru becomes independent (population 6,000).

FEBRUARY

- Former Alabama governor George C. Wallace announces he is entering the 1968 U.S. presidential election on an independent ticket.
- Former vice president Richard M. Nixon announces plans to enter the Republican primaries for the 1968 U.S. presidential election.
- In the face of proliferating troop deployment in the Vietnam War, U.S. Selective Service director Lewis Hershey reduces the number of draft deferments for graduate school and other civilian occupations.
- The National Advisory Commission on Civil Disorders files a scathing report about the state of U.S. race relations. The so-called Kerner Commission Report, named for its chairman, Illinois governor Otto Kerner, attributes the recent spate of racial violence to lingering institutional prejudice, widespread complacency, and the economic degradation of the nation's inner cities.

7 A Flemish campaign against French-speakers at the University of Louvain, Belgium, brings down the Belgian government.

9 The Transvaal Supreme Court imprisons 30 men accused of terrorism in South West Africa.

25 President Makarios of Cyprus is reelected by a huge majority.

27 The Arab emirates of the Persian Gulf announce their intention to form a federation when British troops leave in 1971.

MARCH

- A dispirited President Lyndon B. Johnson appears on national television to say that he will not seek reelection. At the same time, he announces a partial bombing halt of North Vietnam and reports that he is ready to begin peace talks.
- Minnesota senator Eugene J. McCarthy scores a moral victory in the New Hampshire Democratic presidential primary, winning the state delegate count, despite losing the popular vote to the incumbent Lyndon B. Johnson, 42% to 48%.
- New York senator Robert F. Kennedy announces his candidacy for the 1968 presidential election.
- Racial violence erupts in Memphis, Tennessee, during a solidarity march for striking sanitation workers. One black marcher is killed and several wounded; the toll would probably have been higher, but for the calming influence of the civil-rights leader Martin Luther King, Jr.
- 11 A U.S. and South Vietnamese offensive begins in the Saigon area, South Vietnam.
- 16 U.S. soldiers massacre 450 men, women, and children at the village of My Lai, in South Vietnam. When news of the massacre emerges, some 20 months later, the troops will insist that they acted under the orders of lieutenant William L. Calley, Jr.
- 18 Heavy fighting breaks out in Zambia between government forces and African nationalists.
- 22 President Antonin Novotný of Czechoslovakia resigns and, on March 30, is succeeded by General Ludvik Svoboda, commander of Czech forces in World War II.

APRIL

- In an attempt to quell looting sparked by the assassination of the civil-rights leader Martin Luther King, Jr., Chicago mayor Richard J. Daley orders the city's police force to shoot to kill.
- Minnesota senator Eugene J. McCarthy wins the Wisconsin primary.
- New York governor Nelson A. Rockefeller, a Republican, announces his candidacy for president.
- U.S. Marines repel a three-month siege at a Special Forces camp in Khesanh, along the Mekong River in South Vietnam.
- Vice President Hubert H. Humphrey enters the 1968 race for president.
- 3 The United States and North Vietnam agree to establish direct contact as the first step toward a negotiated peace.
- 4 Black American civil-rights activist Martin Luther King, Jr., is assassinated in Memphis, Tennessee, by a sniper later identified as escaped convict James Earl Ray. King's assassination sparks a week of rioting in black ghettos throughout the nation. Ray is arrested in London, England, on June 8 and promptly extradited to the United States.
- 8 A new Czechoslovakian government takes office under Oldřich Černik.
- 8 The United States and its South Vietnamese allies launch Operation Complete Victory, involving some 100,000 U.S. troops, designed to put a definitive end to the Tet offensive.
- 9 East Germany adopts a new constitution, replacing the 1949 Basic Law which has been frequently amended.

- 11 Riots break out in Berlin following the attempted assassination of student leader Rudi Dutschke by right wingers.
- 19 Josef Smrkovský, chairman of the Czechoslovak national assembly, promises freedom of the press, assembly, and religion.
- 21 Following the resignation of Lester Pearson, Pierre Trudeau succeeds as prime minister of Canada.
- 25 The academic year at Columbia University in New York, New York, comes to an abrupt halt, as militant students take over five university buildings in a week-long sit-in to protest against a planned development. The university has planned the building of a new gymnasium in a neighboring black community without consultation, on land that some claim would be better used to build low-cost housing. Police storm the buildings on April 30, after destruction of property by the students; 150 people are injured and 628 arrests are made. Classes are formally suspended on May 5.

MAY

- The Vietcong begins a new offensive against U.S. and allied positions in South Vietnam.
- 2 Violent clashes begin between students and police, in the Latin Quarter of Paris, France.
- 5 Spain further restricts access to and from Gibraltar.
- 10 The "Night of the Barricades" sees violent demonstrations in Paris, France, and, on May 11, the French government makes concessions to student demands.
- 10 U.S. and North Vietnamese negotiators begin peace talks over the Vietnam War, in Paris, France.
- 14 The Czechoslovakian government announces a wide range of liberalizing reforms.
- 17 French students and strikers occupy factories and hold protest marches in various cities in France.
- 17 The Soviet premier Alexey Kosygin and the defense minister Marshal Andrey Grechko visit Prague, Czechoslovakia, following the Czech government's promise to introduce political reforms, announced without permission from Moscow.
- 24 Rioters set fire to the Bourse (stock exchange) in Paris, France. President Charles de Gaulle asks for a vote of confidence in a referendum.
- 26 The French government raises the minimum wage by 33.3% in response to the demands of rioters.
- 30 The French president Charles de Gaulle postpones his proposed referendum and calls a general election, as student riots continue.
- 31 Peace talks in the civil war between Nigeria and Biafra break down.

JUNE

- Chief justice Earl Warren announces that he will resign from the U.S. Supreme Court as soon as a replacement can be appointed.
- President Lyndon B. Johnson names associate justice Abe Fortas to succeed Earl Warren as chief justice of the U.S. Supreme Court.
- 3 Valerie Solanis, a part-time actor, shoots and wounds U.S. artist Andy Warhol.
- 6 New York senator Robert F. Kennedy is shot in Los Angeles, California, and dies the next day. Jordanian national Sirhan B. Sirhan is apprehended at the time of the shooting and indicted for murder on June 7.

11 East Germany announces that West Berliners will require visas to cross its territory.

12 The French government bans demonstrations and dissolves 11 student organizations in response to violent unrest.

19 India accuses Pakistan and China of aiding rebels in the dissident border areas of Nagaland and Mizo.

20 The total U.S. combat deaths in the Vietnam War now exceed 25,000.

24–July 25 Negotiations between Greek and Turkish Cypriots are held in Nicosia, Cyprus. A second round of talks takes place between August 29 and December 9.

25 Fifty thousand people march in Washington, D.C., in support of antipoverty legislation. The march, known as the Poor People's March, began in May, and had been planned by the civil-rights leader Martin Luther King, Jr., before his assassination.

27 The Czechoslovak national assembly passes laws abolishing censorship and rehabilitating political prisoners.

30 The Gaullists win a landslide victory in the second round of French general elections following left wing street violence.

July

- A riot erupts in Cleveland, Ohio, after a gunman attacks city police officers. Seven people are killed, scores are injured, and millions of dollars worth of property is destroyed.

1 Sixty-one nations, including Britain, the United States, and the USSR sign a nuclear nonproliferation treaty.

3 General William C. Westmoreland relinquishes command of U.S. forces in Vietnam, after losing the U.S. president Lyndon B. Johnson's confidence. Westmoreland is succeeded by General Creighton W. Abrams.

9 Couve de Murville succeeds Georges Pompidou as French premier following elections.

9 Czechoslovakia rejects a Soviet demand for a meeting of Communist Party leaders following its inception of a reform program.

14 The USSR halts the withdrawal of its troops from Czechoslovakia after Warsaw Pact exercises, after the Czechoslovakian governement rejects Soviet demands to halt its reform program.

15 Malaysia rejects the Philippines' claim to Sabah, North Borneo.

16 Soviet, East German, Hungarian, Polish, and Bulgarian Communist Party leaders declare recent Czechoslovak reforms unacceptable.

27 The first secretary of the Czechoslovak Communist Party Alexander Dubček states that Czechoslovakia will continue its reform program despite opposition from the leaders of other communist countries.

29–August 1 Czechoslovak and Soviet leaders hold talks at Cierna-nad-Tisou on Czechoslovakia's reform program.

31 The U.S. National Council of Catholic Bishops reiterates Pope Paul VI's condemnation of artificial forms of fertilization.

August

- A race riot errupts in Miami, Florida. The National Guard restores order, but not before three people are killed and hundreds wounded.

- Democrats nominate vice president Hubert H. Humphrey for president at a tumultuous national convention in Chicago, Illinois.

- Republicans nominate Richard M. Nixon for president and Maryland governor Spiro T. Agnew for vice president.

4 Israeli aircraft bomb Palestinian guerrilla bases in Jordan.

5 Spain declares a state of emergency in the province of Guipuzcoa, in the north of the country, after Basque separatists murder its police chief.

15 Nigeria, engaged in civil war, forbids the International Red Cross to fly relief supplies to starving Biafrans from a neutralized airstrip.

20 Soviet and other Warsaw Pact forces invade Czechoslovakia and arrest reform leaders, including Alexander Dubček.

21 A congress of the Czechoslovak Communist Party, meeting in secret, rejects collaboration with the USSR and reelects Alexander Dubček, currently imprisoned by the Soviets, as first secretary.

23 President Ludvik Svoboda of Czechoslovakia flies to Moscow, USSR, for talks following the Soviet invasion of Czechoslovakia. On August 25 he secures the release of the first secretary Alexander Dubček.

24 Yugoslavia and Romania jointly condemn the Soviet invasion of Czechoslovakia.

25 France explodes a hydrogen bomb in the South Pacific, thus becoming the fifth thermonuclear power.

26–29 The Democratic Party convention in Chicago, Illinois, attracts 3,000 Yippies (Youth International Party members) and anti-Vietnam War protestors; police break up a prayer vigil in Lincoln Park and arrest 667 people following violent clashes.

28 The Czechoslovak national assembly declares the Soviet occupation of the country illegal.

September

2 The USSR tells West Germany to stop trying to exert influence in Eastern Europe in favor of reform, and hints at a possible invasion. On September 17, the United States, Britain, and France warn the USSR against attacking West Germany.

12 Albania formally quits the Warsaw Pact.

15 The Organization of African Unity appeals to Biafra to abandon its struggle to become independent of Nigeria.

26 After 36 years in the position, Antonio Salazar resigns as prime minister of Portugal because of ill health, and is succeeded by Marcello Caetano.

27 The USSR postpones a World Communist Summit planned for November because of events in Czechoslovakia.

October

- U.S. Supreme Court justice Abe Fortas asks President Lyndon B. Johnson to withdraw him from consideration for the position of chief justice. Fortas has been accused of accepting money from the private foundation of convicted businessman Louis E. Wolfson.

4 Czechoslovak leaders visiting Moscow, USSR, agree to dismantle the remnants of their reform program.

5–6 Crowds in Londonderry, Northern Ireland, clash with police during a Catholic civil-rights march.

9–13 Talks about the future of Rhodesia take place between the British prime minister Harold Wilson and the Rhodesian leader Ian Smith aboard HMS *Fearless*, at Gibraltar.

16   The USSR and Czechoslovakia sign a treaty on the eventual withdrawal of Warsaw Pact forces from Czechoslovakia.

21   Anti-United States demonstrations take place in Tokyo, Japan.

28   The West German government initiates a security review after a spate of suicides of top secret service and military officials with access to secret information, but finds no evidence of espionage.

31   During the Cultural Revolution in China, the Communist Party expels President Liu Shaoqi after a protracted campaign against him by the Red Guard.

31   In a nationally televised address, the U.S. president Lyndon B. Johnson orders a complete halt to the bombing of North Vietnam and announces an agreement on the composition of Vietnamese delegations for peace talks.

NOVEMBER

- Americans elect Richard M. Nixon president and Maryland governor Spiro T. Agnew vice president. In the Congressional elections, Democrats retain majorities in the House (243–192) and Senate (58–42).

5   South Vietnam objects to the composition of the planned peace talks in Paris, France, on the Vietnam War but, on November 26, agrees to attend.

14   As the number of U.S. deaths in Vietnam exceeds 30,000, National 'Turn In Your Draft Card Day' is held, with widespread burning of cards.

15   The ruling military junta in Greece introduces a constitution with articles on personal freedom suspended.

16   Five thousand Catholic civil-rights marchers defy a ban on demonstrations in Londonderry, Northern Ireland.

17   Talks between the UK and Rhodesia in Salisbury, Rhodesia, on the future of Rhodesia, end in deadlock.

22   The British government proposes reforms in housing and the local election franchise in Northern Ireland in an attempt to allay Catholic grievances in the province.

29   Arab guerrillas attack an Israeli potash plant on the Dead Sea. On December 1, Israeli jets blow up two bridges in Jordan.

DECEMBER

- At year's end, 540,000 U.S. soldiers are deployed in Vietnam.

2   Iraqi artillery in Jordan shells Israeli villages. On December 4, Israel bombs Iraqi bases.

16   Spain annuls its decree of 1492 expelling the Jews.

18   The United Nations (UN) General Assembly declares British colonial rule in Gibraltar incompatible with the UN Charter.

23   The United States proposes to close, relocate, or share control of 50 military bases in Japan under U.S. control since 1945, following popular opposition in Japan.

26   Two Arab terrorists attack an Israeli airliner at Athens airport, Greece. On December 28, Israel bombs Beirut airport in Lebanon, wrecking 13 aircraft.

SCIENCE, TECHNOLOGY, AND MEDICINE

Agriculture

- Famine in Biafra caused by civil war results in the deaths of between 500,000 and 1 million people by starvation.

December 1968–74   Drought in the semidesert Sahel south of the Sahara results in famine and the deaths of 500,000 people and 5 million cattle.

Computing

- U.S. computer scientist Douglas Engelbart demonstrates the first computer mouse.
- U.S. Control Data Corporation launches the CDC 7600 supercomputer, designed by Seymour Cray. It is the world's most powerful computer.
- U.S. firms Control Data, NCR, and Burroughs introduce the first commercial computers that use integrated circuits. The first of the "third generation" of computers, they are faster and have a greater capacity than previous computers.
- U.S. scientist Edward Feigenbaum and U.S. geneticist Joshua Lederberg develop DENDRAL, an expert system (which duplicates human decision-making processes) for identifying chemical substances in compounds based on the results of mass-spectrographic results. Its success spurs the development of other expert systems, especially in medicine.

Ecology

- Kilimanjaro National Park is established in Tanzania, it contains Mt. Kilimanjaro, the highest mountain in Africa.
- Redwood National Park is established in California. It contains the giant redwood tree and the rare Roosevelt elk.

AUGUST

31   Earthquakes in northeastern Iran kill 12,000 people.

NOVEMBER

20   An explosion and subsequent fire at a coal mine in Farmington, West Virginia, kills 78 miners.

Exploration

- A borehole drilled 2,162 m/7,093 ft into the Antarctic ice at Byrd Station reveals that the bottom layers of ice are 100,000 years old.

SEPTEMBER

14–21   The Soviet spacecraft *Zond 5* flies around the moon and returns to Earth—the first spacecraft to do so.

OCTOBER

11–22   *Apollo 7*, the first U.S. Apollo space mission with a crew, tests the Command module used on subsequent flights to the moon, during 163 orbits of the earth. The crew make the first live transmission from space on October 13.

Health and Medicine

- U.S. and UK researchers report that oral contraceptives can cause blood clots in some women.
- U.S. geneticists Robert Holley and Marshall Nirenberg and Indian-born U.S. biochemist Har Gobind Khorana receive the Nobel Prize for Physiology or Medicine for their interpretation of the genetic code and its function in protein synthesis.

MARCH

- In Britain, figures show a drop of 23% in road deaths since the introduction of breath tests in 1967.

MAY

3 The first heart transplant in Britain takes place at the National Heart Hospital, London, England. The patient, Frederick West, survives for 45 days.

DECEMBER

- Evolution in the field of organ transplant spurs the American Medical Association to adopt a new standard for declaring a potential organ donor "dead:" when two independent physicians declare the donor's death irreversible.

Science

- U.S. chemist Lars Onsager receives the Nobel Prize for Chemistry for his discovery of the thermodynamics of irreversible processes.
- U.S. physicist Luis Alvarez receives the Nobel Prize for Physics for his work in elementary particle physics and the discovery of resonance states.
- U.S. scientist Elso Sterrenberg Barghorn and associates report the discovery of the remains of amino acids in rocks 3 billion years old.

JUNE

12 The first radar observations of an asteroid are made when the asteroid Icarus approaches within 6.8 million km/2.4 million mi of Earth.

OCTOBER

- U.S. geneticists Mark Ptashne and Walter Gilbert separately identify the first repressor genes.

Technology

- An 800-kilowatt tidal power station is opened near Murmansk in the USSR.
- Oil is discovered at Prudhoe Bay on Alaska's North Slope. It proves to be the largest oil field in North America.
- The U.S. survey ship *Glomar Challenger* starts drilling cores in the sea bed as part of the Deep Sea Drilling Project. Capable of drilling in water up to 6,000 m/ 20,000 ft deep, it can return core samples from 750 m/ 2,500 ft below the seafloor and is equipped with a gyroscopically-controlled roll-neutralizing system that allows it to maintain its stability in diverse weather conditions.

- USSR physicist Lev Andreevitch Artsimovich constructs the first experimental Toroidal Kamera Magnetic (Tokamak) fusion reactor. It uses a doughnut-shaped magnetic field to confine plasma to achieve fusion.

MARCH

7 The U.S. satellite *Explorer 36* is launched. It tests the feasibility of using lasers to communicate in space.

JULY

7 The French government tests its first thermonuclear fusion device (hydrogen bomb) on Mururoa atoll in the South Pacific.

Transportation

- Regular hovercraft services begin across the English Channel.
- The first "supertanker" for carrying oil goes into service.
- The U.S. government sets national standards for the emission of exhaust gases from cars.

MAY

21 The U.S. nuclear submarine *Scorpion* sinks off the Azores; 99 people die.

JULY

- Direct commercial airline traffic begins between the United States and the USSR.

DECEMBER

31 The world's first supersonic airliner, the Tupolev TU-144, designed by Soviet engineer Alexey Tupolev, makes its first flight.

ARTS AND IDEAS

Architecture

- The first phase of the University of East Anglia in Norwich, England, designed by the English architects Denys Lasdun and Partners, is completed.
- The John Hancock building in Chicago, Illinois, a 100-story structure with visible diagonal braces and tapered for stability, designed by the firm of Skidmore, Owings, and Merrill, is completed.

Arts

- The English artist Richard Hamilton paints *Swingeing London*.
- The German-born English artist Lucian Freud paints *Interior with Plant, Reflection Listening*.
- The Hayward Gallery in London, England, designed by the English architect Hubert Bennett and architects of Greater London Council, is completed.
- The Museum of Modern Art in New York, New York, holds the exhibition "Art of the Real."
- The New National Gallery in West Berlin, Germany, designed by the German architect Ludwig Mies van der Rohe, is completed.
- The U.S. artist Edward Ruscha paints *Burning Standard*.
- The U.S. artist Edward Kienholz creates *Portable War Memorial*.

- The U.S. artist Richard Serra creates *Splashing*, by throwing molten lead into a corner.

Film

- The American Film Institute launches a project to produce a catalog of every movie ever made in the United States.
- The British rock group the Beatles releases their animated movie *Yellow Submarine*.
- The movie *2001: A Space Odyssey*, directed by U.S. filmmaker Stanley Kubrick, is released in Britain. Based on Arthur C. Clarke's story, *The Sentinel*, it stars Gary Lockwood, Keir Dullea, and William Sylvester, with Douglas Rain as the voice of the computer HAL.
- The movie *Bullitt*, directed by Peter Yates, is released in the United States, starring Steve McQueen, Jacqueline Bisset, and Robert Vaughn.
- The movie *Faces*, directed by John Cassavetes, is released in the United States, starring John Marly and Gena Rowlands.
- The movie *If...*, directed by Lindsay Anderson, is released in Britain, starring Malcolm McDowell, David Wood, and Richard Warwick.
- The movie *Night of the Living Dead*, directed by George Romero, is released in the United States. A very significant influence on the development of the modern horror movie, it stars Judith O'Dea, Duane Jones, and Karl Hardman.
- The movie *Romeo and Juliet*, directed by Franco Zeffirelli, is released in Italy, starring Leonard Whiting and Olivia Hussey.
- The movie *Rosemary's Baby*, directed by Polish-U.S. filmmaker Roman Polanski, is released in the United States. Based on the book by Ira Levin, it stars Mia Farrow and John Cassavetes.
- The movie *Shame*, directed by Ingmar Bergman, is released in the United States, starring Liv Ullmann and Max Von Sydow.
- The movie *The Green Berets* is released in the United States. It stars John Wayne, who also codirects along with Ray Kellogg.
- The movie *The Lion in Winter*, directed by Anthony Harvey, is released in Britain. Adapted from the play by James Goldman, it stars Katharine Hepburn and Peter O'Toole.
- The movie musical *Funny Girl*, directed by William Wyler, is released in the United States. Based on the life of the U.S. comedienne Fanny Brice, it stars Barbra Streisand, Omar Sharif, and Walter Pidgeon.
- The movie musical *Oliver!*, directed by Carol Reed, is released in Britain. Based on the novel by Charles Dickens, it stars Ron Moody, Oliver Reed, and Mark Lester.

APRIL

10 The 1967 Academy Awards take place two days later than planned, because of the assassination of Martin Luther King, Jr., on April 4 and his funeral on April 9. Best Actor: Rod Steiger, for *In the Heat of the Night*; Best Supporting Actor: George Kennedy, for *Cool Hand Luke*; Best Actress: Katharine Hepburn, for *Guess Who's Coming to Dinner*; Best Supporting Actress: Estelle Parsons, for *Bonnie and Clyde*; Best Picture: *In the Heat of the Night*, directed by Norman Jewison; Best Director: Mike Nichols, for *The Graduate*.

Literature and Language

- Cecil Day Lewis becomes poet laureate in England, a position he holds until his death in 1972.
- The Belgian writer Marguerite Yourcenar publishes her novel *L'Oeuvre au noir/The Abyss*.
- The English writer Anthony Powell publishes *The Military Philosophers*, the ninth novel of his 12-volume sequence *A Dance to the Music of Time*.
- The English writer Anthony Burgess publishes his novel *Inside Mr Enderby*.
- The English writer Barry Hines publishes his novel *A Kestrel for a Knave*.
- The English writer Lawrence Durrell publishes his novel *Tunc*.
- The French journalist Jean-Jaques Servan-Schreiber publishes *Le Défi americain/The American Challenge*.
- The French writer Anaïs Nin (who wrote in English) publishes her critical study *The Novel of the Future*.
- The Israeli writer Amos Oz publishes his novel *Mikha'el sheli/My Michael*.
- The Nobel Prize for Literature is awarded to the Japanese novelist Yasunari Kawabata, the first Japanese writer to receive it.
- The Pulitzer Prize for Biography is awarded to George F. Kennan for *Memoirs, 1925–1950*, the Pulitzer Prize for Poetry is awarded to Anthony Hecht for *The Hard Hours*, and the Pulitzer Prize for Fiction is awarded to William Styron for *The Confessions of Nat Turner*.
- The Russian writer Alexander Solzhenitsyn publishes his novels *V kruge pervom/The First Circle* and *Rakovy korpus/Cancer Ward*.
- The U.S. writer Allen Ginsberg publishes his poetry collection *Planet News*.
- The U.S. writer Gore Vidal publishes his transvestite fantasy novel *Myra Breckinridge*.
- The U.S. writer Joan Didion publishes *Slouching Towards Bethlehem*, a collection of essays.
- The U.S. writer John Updike publishes his novel *Couples*, a study of sexual promiscuity in New England.
- The U.S. writer Kurt Vonnegut publishes his short-story collection *Welcome to the Monkey House*.
- The U.S. writer Philip K. Dick publishes his novel *Do Androids Dream of Electric Sheep?*
- The U.S. writer Richard Brautigan publishes his novel *Trout Fishing in America*.
- The U.S. writer Robert Creeley publishes his poetry collection *Pieces*.
- The U.S. writer Tom Wolfe publishes *The Electric Kool-Aid Acid Test*, an account of the 1960s' drugs culture.
- The U.S. writer Ursula Le Guin publishes her novel *A Wizard of Earthsea*.

Music

- "Bubblegum music," simple pop music tunes that people can dance to easily, emerges in reaction to progressive and psychedelic rock music. It is typified by the music played on the U.S. television cartoon show *The Archies*, such as "Sugar Sugar," and by groups such as Ohio Express with "Yummy yummy yummy" and the 1910 Fruitgum Co. with "Simon Says." It is short-lived but commercially successful.

- British guitarist Eric Clapton forms the first (short-lived) supergroup, Blind Faith.
- British rock group the Beatles launch their Apple record label.
- For the first time in Britain, albums are outselling singles.
- The British pop singer Cliff Richard releases the single "Congratulations."
- The British pop singer Tom Jones releases the single "Delilah."
- The British rock band Cream, founded by Eric Clapton, releases the album *Wheels of Fire*—the first album to sell 1 million copies—and the single "Sunshine of Your Love."
- The British rock group the Rolling Stones releases the album *Beggar's Banquet*.
- The British rock group the Beatles releases the single "Hey Jude," the best-selling single of the year in Britain, and the album *The Beatles* (known as *The White Album*).
- The British rock group the Rolling Stones releases the single "Jumpin' Jack Flash."
- The Northern Irish rock singer Van Morrison releases the album *Astral Weeks*.
- The British singer Mary Hopkin releases the single "Those Were the Days."
- The British/U.S. rock group Fleetwood Mac releases the instrumental single "Albatross."
- The Canadian folk singer Joni Mitchell releases the album *Songs To A Seagull*.
- The Candian singer/songwriter Leonard Cohen releases the album *The Songs of Leonard Cohen*.
- The English composer Edmund Rubbra completes his Symphony No. 8, *Homage á Teilhard de Chardin*.
- The movie *Head*, directed by Bob Rafelson, is released in the United States, starring the U.S. pop group the Monkees.
- The Hungarian composer György Ligeti completes his String Quartet No. 2.
- The Jeff Beck Group, with Rod Stewart on vocals and Jeff Beck on lead guitar, releases its only album, *Truth*.
- The newspaper *Sovetskaya Rossiya* denounces the actor/musician Vladimir Vysotsky for his "slangy songs about banal things and low morals," which are popularizing Western pop music in the USSR.
- The opera *Punch and Judy*, by the English composer Harrison Birtwistle, is first performed, at the Aldeburgh Festival in England.
- The opera *Ulisse/Ulysses*, by the Italian composer Luigi Dallapiccola, is first performed, in Berlin, Germany.
- The Russian composer Dmitry Shostakovich completes his String Quartet No. 12.
- The U.S. Bluegrass duo Flatt and Scruggs, with Earl Scruggs on the banjo and Lester Flatt singing, releases the album *Changin' Times*.
- The U.S. composer Samuel Barber completes his song settings *Despite and Still*.
- The U.S. country singer Glen Campbell releases "Wichita Lineman," the first country record to be a hit in the pop charts.

- The U.S. folk/rock duo Simon and Garfunkel releases the single "Mrs. Robinson," from the soundtrack of the movie *The Graduate*.
- The U.S. folk/rock singer Bob Dylan releases the album *John Wesley Harding*.
- The U.S. group Blood, Sweat, and Tears releases the album *The Child Is the Father Man*, an amalgam of jazz, blues, and rock that merges modern rock with the big band sound of an earlier era.
- The U.S. jazz singer and trumpeter Louis Armstrong releases the single "What a Wonderful World."
- The U.S. rock group The Band releases the album *Music from Big Pink*.
- The U.S. soul singer Aretha Franklin releases the single "I Say a Little Prayer."
- The U.S. soul singer James Brown releases the single "Say It Loud—I'm Black and I'm Proud."
- The U.S. soul singer Otis Redding releases the single "(Sittin' On) The Dock of the Bay."
- The U.S. soul singer/songwriter Marvin Gaye releases the single "I Heard It Through the Grapevine."

FEBRUARY

29   The 1967–68 Grammy Awards take place. Best Album: *Sergeant Pepper's Lonely Hearts Club Band* by the Beatles; Best Record: "Up, Up, and Away" by the Fifth Dimension; Best Male Vocalist: Glenn Campbell; Best Female Vocalist: Bobby Gentry; Best Group: the Fifth Dimension.

AUGUST

29–31   The second Isle of Wight pop festival takes place in Britain, with Bob Dylan starring. It attracts around 150,000 people.

Theater and Dance

- The play *Kaspar*, by the Austrian writer Peter Handke, is first performed, in Frankfurt, Germany.
- The play *The Price*, by the U.S. dramatist Arthur Miller, is first performed, in New York, New York.
- The Pulitzer Prize for Drama is not awarded this year.

MARCH

1   A "pop cantata" from the musical *Joseph and the Amazing Technicolour Dreamcoat*, with lyrics by Tim Rice and music by Andrew Lloyd Webber, is first performed, at Colet Court School in London, England. The first performance as a finished commercial product is on September 17, 1973.

APRIL

16   The play *The Boys in the Band*, by the U.S. writer Matt Crowley, is first performed, at Theater Four, New York, New York.

21   The 1967–68 Tony Awards take place. Best Play: *Rosencrantz and Guildenstern Are Dead*, by Czechoslovak-born British dramatist Tom Stoppard; Best Musical: *Hallelujah, Baby!*; Best Actor: Martin Balsam; Best Actress: Zoe Caldwell.

OCTOBER

3   The play *The Great White Hope*, by U.S. dramatist Howard Sackler, is first performed, at the Alvin Theater in New York, New York, a dramatization of the life of former heavyweight boxing champion Jack Johnson of the United States.

Thought and Scholarship

- Swiss psychologist Jean Piaget publishes *Le Structuralisme/Structuralism.*
- The German philosopher Jürgen Habermas publishes *Erkenntnis und Interesse/Knowledge and Human Interests.*
- The Pulitzer Prize for History is awarded to Bernard Bailyn for *The Ideological Origins of the American Revolution.*
- The Pulitzer Prize for General Nonfiction is awarded to Will Durant and Ariel Durant for *Rousseau and Revolution.*
- The U.S. historian Bernard Bailyn publishes *The Origin of American Politics.*
- The U.S. historian David M. Potter publishes *The South and Sectional Conflict.*
- The U.S. political and true-crime author Joe McGinniss publishes *The Selling of the President 1968*, which chronicles the importance of advertising and public relations in the modern political campaign.
- The U.S. writer Norman Mailer publishes *The Armies of the Night*, an account of the peace demonstrations in Washington, D.C., in October 1967.
- U.S. philosopher Max Black publishes *The Labyrinth of Language.*
- U.S. philosopher Nelson Goodman publishes *The Language of Art: An Approach to the Theory of Symbols.*
- U.S. psychologist Erik Erikson publishes *Identity: Youth and Crisis.*

SOCIETY

Everyday Life

- Designer Ralph Lauren launches his fashion house Ralph Lauren in the United States.
- Jacuzzi Brothers, makers of farm pumps in California, United States, introduce the Jacuzzi Whirlpool Bath.
- Russ Solomon opens the first Tower Record Store, in San Francisco, California.
- U.S. advertising executive Sinclair Baker publishes *The Permissible Lie: The Inside Truth about Advertising*, in which he purports to bare the manipulative secrets of his trade.
- Waterbeds are first brought onto the market in the United States.

JANUARY

7   U.S. first class postage rises to 6 cents per ounce.

FEBRUARY

19–March 8   Florida public school teachers launch the nation's first state-wide teachers' strike, demanding better pay and benefits.

APRIL

- HemisFair 68, a Pan-American exposition, opens in San Antonio, Texas, which is celebrating its bicentennial.

MAY

- The U.S. Communications Workers Union wins a landmark settlement from Bell Telephone after a three-week strike. Bell agrees to increase its workers' wages by 19.58% over the next three years.

SEPTEMBER

- A two-month-long teachers' strike begins in New York, New York, over questions of local school board control.

Media and Communication

- Sir William Carr sells a 51% stake in the British paper the *News of the World* to Rupert Murdoch of Australia, having rejected an offer from the British businessman Robert Maxwell.
- The *Doonesbury* comic strip, created by Garry Trudeau, is launched in the *Yale Daily News* in the United States. It develops into an increasingly political and satirical commentary, and in 1975 Trudeau wins a Pulitzer prize.
- The 911 emergency telephone system for police, fire, and ambulances is introduced in New York, New York. It is the first such system in the United States.
- The Algerian government nationalizes all movie companies in an attempt to expel the U.S. movie companies with interests in Algeria.
- The General Post Office introduces postcodes in the London, England, area.

JANUARY

22–May 14, 1973   *Rowan and Martin's Laugh-In*, comedy program starring Dan Rowan and Dick Martin, featuring Ruth Buzze, Judy Carne, Henry Gibson, Arte Johnson, Goldie Hawn, and Lily Tomlin, among others, appears on U.S. television.

MARCH

6   U.S. broadcaster Walter Cronkite delivers a personal and influential denunciation of the Vietnam War.

MAY

4   The *Saturday Evening Post* restricts its subscription list from 6.8 million to 3 million in an effort to save the magazine by only catering to high-income readers.

18   The Cannes Film Festival is abandoned halfway through, following disruption in support of the student protests in Paris, France.

19   The 1967–68 Emmy Awards for television take place. Best Drama Series: *Mission: Impossible*; Best Actor in a Single Show: Melvyn Douglas; Best Actress in a Single Show: Jean Stapleton; Best Actor in a Series: Bill Cosby, for *I Spy*; Best Actress in a Series: Barbara Bain, for *Mission: Impossible.*

SEPTEMBER

14   *60 Minutes*, a news program of commentary and investigative reporting, debuts on U.S. television. It features Dan Rather, Harry Reasoner, Morley Safer, and Mike Wallace, and is still in production after 30 years.

14–September 5, 1970   *Wacky Races*, an animated cartoon about a cross-country car race, featuring competitors such as Dick Dastardly and Penelope Pitstop, appears on U.S. television.

17–May 25, 1971   The situation comedy *Julia* appears on U.S. television. Diahann Carroll plays a widowed nurse whose husband was killed in Vietnam; it is the first U.S.

television program since 1953 to star a black woman. Marc Copage, Lloyd Nolan, Lurene Tuttle, and Betty Beaird also star.

23–September 2, 1974 Lucille Ball stars in her third U.S. television series, *Here's Lucy*, in which she portrays a secretary in an employment agency. The series also stars Gale Gordon, Mary Jane Croft, Luci Arnaz, and Desi Arnaz, Jr.

24–August 23, 1973 The crime drama *The Mod Squad* appears on U.S. television, starring Michael Cole, Clarence Williams, III, and Peggy Lipton as three young undercover police officers.

26–April 5, 1980 *Hawaii Five-O*, a police series set in Hawaii and starring Jack Lord, Kam Fong, Zulu, and James MacArthur, is broadcast in the United States.

Religion

- The Belgian theologian Edward Schillebeeckx publishes *God and the Future of Man*.
- The Methodist Church merges with the Evangelical United Brethren Church to form the United Methodist Church in the United States.

MARCH

- Pope Paul VI names Bishop Terence J. Cooke archbishop of New York, New York. Cooke succeeds the late Francis Cardinal Spellman.

JULY

29 Pope Paul VI issues an encyclical, *Humanae vitae/Of Human Life*, condemning artificial fertilization.

OCTOBER

- Boston cardinal Richard James Cushing announces that he will retire. The announcement follows intense criticism of Cushing's endorsement of Jacqueline Kennedy's marriage to Aristotle Onassis.

Sports

- The Houston Oilers of the American Football League move from Rice Stadium to the Houston Astrodome, Texas.
- The rebuilt Madison Square Garden sports arena and exhibition center is opened in New York, New York, with seating in the main arena for over 20,000 spectators.

JANUARY

- The United Soccer Association and the National Professional Soccer League, both instituted in 1967 in the United States, merge to form the North American Soccer League.

14 The Green Bay Packers defeat the Oakland Raiders 33–14 in Super Bowl II, in Miami, Florida. The crowd of 75,546 spectators generates the first $3 million gate in football history.

28 After leading the Green Bay Packers to victory in the first two Super Bowls and also to five National Football League Championship titles in six years, Vince Lombardi resigns as head coach, though he stays on as general manager.

FEBRUARY

6–18 The 10th Winter Olympic Games take place in Grenoble, France, attended by 1,158 competitors, including 211 women, from 37 countries. Norway wins 6 gold medals; the Soviet Union, 5; France and Italy, 4 each; and Austria and the Netherlands, 3 each. Jean-Claude Killy of France wins all three men's Alpine skiing events.

MARCH

30 The International Lawn Tennis Association abolishes the distinction between amateurs and professionals following the example of the British Lawn Tennis Association of October 15, 1967.

BIRTHS & DEATHS

FEBRUARY

21 Howard Florey, Australian pathologist who, with Ernst Boris Chain, purified penicillin for clinical use, dies in Oxford, England (69).

MARCH

27 Yuri Gagarin, Soviet cosmonaut and the first person to travel in space, is killed when his jet aircraft crashes near Moscow, USSR (34).

APRIL

1 Lev Davidovich Landau, Soviet physicist, dies in Moscow, USSR (60).

4 Martin Luther King, Jr., U.S. Baptist minister and civil-rights leader, is assassinated in Memphis, Tennessee (39).

7 Jim Clark, Scottish world champion racing driver, is killed in a racing accident in Hockenheim, West Germany (32).

19 Mswati III, monarch of Swaziland from 1986, born.

JUNE

1 Helen Keller, U.S. educator and writer who was deaf and blind, dies in Westport, Connecticut (87).

6 Robert Kennedy, U.S. attorney general and presidential advisor, is assassinated in Los Angeles, California, while campaigning for the Democrat presidential nomination (42).

JULY

23 Henry Dale, English physiologist who isolated acetylcholine and described its role in the transmission of nerve impulses, dies in Cambridge, England (93).

28 Otto Hahn, German chemist who, with Fritz Strassmann, discovered nuclear fission, dies in Göttingen, Germany (89).

SEPTEMBER

19 Chester F. Carlson, U.S. physicist who invented xerography, dies in New York, New York (62).

OCTOBER

2 Marcel Duchamp, French painter whose *Nude descending a Staircase, No 2* (1912) caused a sensation, dies in Neuilly, France (81).

29 Johann Olav Koss, world champion Norwegian speed skater, born in Norway.

NOVEMBER

28 Enid Blyton, English author of children's stories, dies in Hampstead, London, England (71).

DECEMBER

1 Karl Barth, Swiss theologian, dies in Basel, Switzerland (82).

20 John Steinbeck, U.S. novelist who wrote *The Grapes of Wrath*, dies in New York, New York (66).

30 Trygve Lie, Norwegian politician and first secretary-general of the United Nations 1946–52, dies in Geilo, Norway (72).

APRIL

18–May 4 The Pittsburgh Pipers defeat the New Orleans Buccaneers by four games to three to win the inaugural American Basketball Association championship title.

19 Amby Burfoot from Connecticut becomes the first U.S. winner of the Boston Marathon, Massachusetts, since 1957.

21–May 2 The Boston Celtics beat the Los Angeles Lakers by four games to two to win the National Basketball Association championship.

22–27 A month after the International Lawn Tennis Federation accepts open competition between amateurs and professionals, the world's first officially sanctioned open tennis tournament, the Hard Court Championships of Great Britain, is held in Bournemouth, England. The Australian player Ken Rosewall wins the men's singles and the English player Virginia Wade wins the women's singles.

27 Jimmy Ellis defeats fellow U.S. boxer Jerry Quarry on points at Oakland, California, in the final bout of a series of eliminators held by the World Boxing Association to find a new world heavyweight boxing champion, after Muhammad Ali has been stripped of his title for refusing to be drafted into the U.S. army.

MAY

- The American Basketball Association, a competitor for the National Basketball Association, ends its inaugural season with a $2.5 million operating loss.

5–11 The Montreal Canadiens defeat the St. Louis Blues in four straight games to win their eighth National Hockey League Stanley Cup in 13 years under coach Toe Blake.

8 The U.S. baseball player Jim "Catfish" Hunter of the Oakland A's, against the Minnesota Twins, pitches the first perfect game in the American League since 1922.

27 The U.S. football coach George Halas resigns as head coach of the Chicago Bears. Since joining the Bears in 1920 he has coached them for 40 seasons and won a record 324 games and seven National Football League titles.

JUNE

16 The U.S. player Lee Trevino wins the U.S. Open golf championship at Oak Hill, Rochester, New York.

24–July 6 At the first "open" Wimbledon tennis championships in London, England, the singles titles are won by Rod Laver of Australia and Billie Jean King of the United States, who win £2,000 and £750 respectively.

SEPTEMBER

9 Arthur Ashe wins both the inaugural Open and National (amateur) events at the U.S. tennis championships. As well as being the first black American male to win a Grand Slam tournament, he is also the first U.S. player to win the U.S. men's singles title since 1955.

14 The U.S. baseball player Denny McLain of the Detroit Tigers becomes the first pitcher to win 30 games in a season since Dizzy Dean of the St. Louis Cardinals in 1934.

OCTOBER

- At the Olympic Games in Mexico City, Mexico, the U.S. athletes Tommie Smith and John Carlos, who finished first and third in the 200 meters, stage a "black power" demonstration from the victory rostrum during the playing of the U.S. national anthem.

- The U.S. discus thrower Al Oerter becomes the first track and field athlete to win the same event at four successive Olympic Games, in Mexico City, Mexico.

2–10 The Detroit Tigers defeat the St. Louis Cardinals by four games to three to win their first World Series since 1945.

12–27 The 19th Olympic Games are held in Mexico City, Mexico, attended by 5,530 competitors, 781 of whom are women, from 112 countries. The United States wins 45 gold medals; the Soviet Union, 29; Japan, 11; East Germany, 9; France and Czechoslovakia, 7 each; and West Germany, Poland, and Britain, 5 each.

18 At the Olympic Games in Mexico City, Mexico, Bob Beamon of the United States smashes the long-jump world record with a leap of 8.90 m/29 ft 2.5 in. It is the first jump over 28 ft.

DECEMBER

26–28 The United States, led by Arthur Ashe, regains the Davis Cup in tennis, beating the defending champions Australia 4–1 in the challenge round. Australia has held the trophy for 15 of the previous 18 years.

1969

POLITICS, GOVERNMENT, AND ECONOMICS

Business and Economics

- Canadian-born U.S. academic Laurence J. Peter publishes *The Peter Principle* with U.S. author Raymond Hull, in which he describes the institution effect whereby individuals rise to the level of their incompetence.
- New York fashion designer Ralph Lauren establishes the clothing company of the same name.
- The drinks company Schweppes merges with the British confectionery company Cadbury Brothers to form Cadbury Schweppes.
- The first automatic teller machines (ATMs) are in use, in the United States.

FEBRUARY

26 General Motors recalls nearly 5 million cars and trucks, a new record, after alleged defects are identified.

MAY

9 A wave of currency speculation peaks with West German refusal to revalue the mark.

JULY

- The consumer price index has risen 6.4% since January 1, the highest jump in 18 years.

AUGUST

8 France devalues the franc by 12% following a European financial crisis.

Human Rights

JANUARY

- The U.S. education commissioner extends for 60 days the deadline by which time Southern schools receiving federal funds must be desegregated.

APRIL

- A manifesto proclaimed by the National Black Economic Development Conference demands that white churches and synagogues in the United States compensate black Americans with $500 million for years of institutional oppression.

JUNE

- The Gay Rights movement begins symbolically in Manhattan's Greenwich Village, when homosexuals assault police officers raiding the Stonewall Inn, a gay bar.

AUGUST

- Civil-rights lawyers in the U.S. Justice Department protest against the Nixon administration's attempt to extend a desegregation deadline for 33 Mississippi schools. In October, the U.S. Supreme Court denies the request and orders that the schools be desegregated immediately.

Politics and Government

- The Ninth Chinese Communist Party Congress ends the Cultural Revolution and reestablishes authority structures.

JANUARY

- In a breakthrough symbolizing the immensity of the task ahead, U.S. and North Vietnamese negotiators agree on the shape of the negotiating table.
- Richard Milhous Nixon is inaugurated 37th president of the United States. He assumes office in a fractious political and social climate.
- The U.S. House of Representatives votes to seat New York's Adam Clayton Powell, who had been unseated in the fall of 1967 for misusing federal funds.

1 Czechoslovakia becomes a two-state federation, under a new constitution giving Slovakia complete autonomy and equality with Bohemia-Moravia.

6 France bans the sale of military supplies to Israel following the use of French helicopters in Israel's attack on Beirut, Lebanon, on December 28, 1968.

10 Sweden becomes the first Western government to recognize the government of North Vietnam.

16 The Czech student Jan Palach publicly burns himself to death in Prague, Czechoslovakia, in protest at Soviet occupation.

18 The South Vietnamese and National Liberation Front (the political arm of the Vietcong antigovernment guerrillas in South Vietnam) join expanded peace talks in Paris, France, to discuss the Vietnam War.

24 General Francisco Franco imposes martial law in Spain in response to student disturbances.

27 Iraq executes 14 men accused of spying for Israel.

FEBRUARY

1 Yugoslavia and Romania jointly refute the "Brezhnev doctrine" of the Soviet leader Leonid Brezhnev on the supremacy of international communist interests (as defined by the USSR) over national Communist Party decisions.

3 The Palestine Liberation Organization (PLO) elects Yasser Arafat as chairman.

7 The British colony of Anguilla, the most northerly of the Leeward Islands, votes to break all ties with Britain.

12 Ndabaningi Sithole, leader of the Zimbabwe African National Union (ZANU), is convicted of incitement to murder the Rhodesian prime minister Ian Smith.

18 Palestinian terrorists attack an Israeli airliner at Zürich airport, Switzerland, wounding its pilots.

24 A general election for the Northern Ireland parliament reveals Unionists' divisions over reform. The Unionists win 36 seats (24 supporting the party leader and prime minister, Terence O'Neill, 12 against) against independents 3, Nationalists 6, Labour 2, others 5.

MARCH

- James Earl Ray is sentenced to 99 years in prison, after being convicted of assassinating the civil-rights leader Martin Luther King, Jr.
- New Orleans businessman Clay Shaw is acquitted of conspiring in the murder of president John F. Kennedy.
- With President Richard M. Nixon's authorization, the U.S. begins the secret bombing of Cambodia.

1 The communist Pathet Lao opposition in Laos rejects the government's offer of talks to end the civil war.

2–15 Soviet and Chinese forces clash on the Manchurian border, initiating an intensified period of violence along the disputed frontier.

12 On the Leeward Island of Anguilla, the British emissary is forced to leave, at gun-point, by rebels. On March 19, 250 British troops land and reestablish control.

25 A military government takes power in Pakistan amid escalating violence, and President Ayub Khan is replaced by General Yahya Khan.

28 Anti-Soviet demonstrations take place in Prague, Czechoslovakia.

APRIL

- Jordanian national Sirhan Sirhan is sentenced to death in California, after being convicted of murdering New York senator Robert F. Kennedy.
- Left wing students at Cornell University in Ithaca, New York, end a 36-hour sit-in, held to highlight the university's allegedly outdated curriculum. At Harvard University, 300 students occupy the campus administration building; 400 state and local police officials clear students from the premises.
- U.S. B-52s drop an estimated 3,000 tons of bombs, a new record, on Vietcong positions near the Cambodian border in South Vietnam.

3 U.S. combat deaths in Vietnam reach 33,641, a higher total than the Korean War.

4–July 1 United Nations (UN) representatives of the United States, USSR, Britain, and France hold talks on the Middle East in New York, New York.

8 Arab guerrillas attack Eilat in Israel; Israeli jets retaliate with an attack on Aqaba, Jordan.

10 King Hussein of Jordan proposes a six-point Middle East peace plan, but it is rejected by Palestinian organizations on April 16.

15 North Korea shoots down a U.S. naval intelligence plane; the U.S. threatens retaliation, but no action is taken.

17 Gustav Husak succeeds Alexander Dubček as first secretary of the Czechoslovak Communist Party.

20 British troops begin guarding public utilities after the main pipe carrying water to Belfast, Northern Ireland, is bombed.

22 Nigerian forces in the civil war capture Umuahia, the administrative capital of Biafra.

23 The government concedes universal adult suffrage in local elections in Northern Ireland, in response to Catholic civil-rights activists' demands.

24 Intensive U.S. air raids are made along the Cambodian border with South Vietnam, aimed at disrupting North Vietnamese supply routes along the Ho Chi Minh Trail.

27 A referendum in France narrowly rejects constitutional reforms, including administrative decentralization and a consultative senate.

28 The French president Charles de Gaulle resigns following rejection of his constitutional plans; Alain Poher becomes interim president.

MAY

- U.S. Supreme Court justice Abe Fortas resigns from the high court, amid continuing criticism of his ties to convicted businessman Louis E. Wolfson.
- Violence erupts at the University of California at Berkeley after students, faculty, and local residents refuse to leave the so-called People's Park, owned by the university. After five days of rioting, the park is finally cleared when National Guard helicopters drop chemical powder on the protesters.

1 James Chichester-Clark succeeds Terence O'Neill as premier of Northern Ireland on the latter's resignation. On May 6, he grants an amnesty to arrested rioters.

11 The Vietcong launch rocket and ground attacks throughout South Vietnam.

14 The U.S. president Richard M. Nixon suggests the mutual withdrawal of U.S., Allied, and North Vietnamese troops from South Vietnam.

15 Violence breaks out in Kuala Lumpur, Malaysia, between Malays and Chinese.

20 The government of Laos offers to halt U.S. bombing of the communist Pathet Lao opposition if North Vietnamese forces withdraw from Laos.

30 Gibraltar's constitution comes into effect, extending self-rule in the British colony. On July 30, a general election is held.

30 West Germany ends its policy of automatically severing relations with governments which recognize East Germany.

JUNE

- Jurist Warren E. Burger replaces Earl Warren as chief justice of the U.S. Supreme Court.

2 The Australian aircraft carrier *Melbourne* collides with the USS destroyer *Frank E Evans* during maneuvers in the China Sea; 24 sailors are killed.

5–17 Delegates from 75 countries attend the World Communist Conference in Moscow, USSR (postponed from the previous year).

8 At a meeting with South Vietnamese president Nguyen Van Thieu on Midway Island, President Richard M. Nixon announces that he will withdraw 25,000 U.S. troops from South Vietnam by the end of August. A further 35,000 troops are withdrawn on September 16.

8 Spain completely closes its land frontier with Gibraltar and, on June 27, suspends the ferry service from Algeciras, Spain.

15 Georges Pompidou is elected president of France and, on June 20, appoints Jacques Chaban-Delmas as prime minister.

20 Rhodesia votes to become a republic. On June 24, Britain cuts its last official links with Rhodesia.

JULY

- A U.S. appeals court overturns the convictions of Dr. Benjamin Spock and three others for encouraging draft evasion.

- In what becomes known as the Chappaquiddick incident, Massachusetts senator Edward M. Kennedy drives off a bridge at Chappaquiddick Island off the Massachusetts coast. Kennedy escapes the wreck, but his passenger Mary Jo Kopechne drowns. Unaccountably, Kennedy does not report the accident for ten hours, a failure he later characterizes as "indefensible."

- On a visit to Guam, President Richard M. Nixon proclaims the so-called Nixon Doctrine: countries receiving U.S. economic and military aid will hereafter be expected to furnish their own troops; they will no longer be able to rely on U.S. soldier power.

4   The Spanish leader General Francisco Franco offers Spanish citizenship to all Gibraltarians.

16–24 The U.S. moon-shot mission *Apollo 11* takes place. On July 20, U.S. astronaut Neil Armstrong becomes the first person to walk on the moon, famously saying "That's one small step for man, one giant leap for mankind." He and Buzz Aldrin also install and operate the first Moon seismograph at Tranquillity base, spending a total of 21 hours, 37 minutes on the moon's surface, while Michael Collins remains orbiting the moon in the command module.

19 The Indian prime minister Indira Gandhi issues an ordinance for the nationalization of 14 major Indian banks.

22 The Spanish dictator General Francisco Franco names Prince Juan Carlos as his eventual successor.

23–August 3 The U.S. president Richard M. Nixon visits southern Asia, Romania, and Britain.

24 Fighting breaks out between the United Arab Republic (UAR) and Israel, the heaviest since the Six Day War.

27 North Vietnam denies military intervention in the war between Pathet Lao insurgents and the U.S.-backed government in Laos.

AUGUST

- In a speech on welfare, President Richard M. Nixon proposes establishing a guaranteed minimum income for families with dependent children.

10 In what will become known as the Tate-La Bianca murders, members of the Charles Manson cult murder the actress Sharon Tate, the pregnant wife of the Polish-U.S. movie director Roman Polanski. Also murdered at the Polanski house in Bel Air, California, are Abigail Folger, Wojciech Frykowski, Jay Sebring, and Stephen Earl Parent; later the same day Leno and Rosemary La Bianca are murdered in Los Angeles. Lyrics from the Beatles' track "Helter Skelter" are found written in blood on the wall at the scene of the killings.

11 President Kenneth Kaunda of Zambia announces the nationalization of copper mines.

13 Soviet forces cross the Chinese border at Sinkiang in the continuing border dispute between the two countries.

17 Ulster Unionists in Northern Ireland rule out the idea of a coalition government with Republicans at Stormont (seat of the parliament).

19 The British army assumes full responsibility for security in Northern Ireland following civil unrest.

21 Fifty thousand protesters in Prague, Czechoslovakia, mark the anniversary of the Soviet invasion.

25 The Arab League meets in Cairo, Egypt, to plan a "holy war" against Israel.

28 The Irish Premier John Lynch proposes a federation of Ireland and Northern Ireland.

29 The British and Northern Irish governments agree on civil-rights reforms following violence in the province.

SEPTEMBER

- Eight radical activists (the Chicago Eight) are brought to trial in Chicago for allegedly inciting the violence at the 1968 Democratic convention. They are Rennie Davis, David Dellinger, John Froines, Tom Hayden, Abbie Hoffman, Jerry Rubin, Bobby Seale, and Lee Weiner.

- The U.S. launches Operation Intercept, an attempt to halt drug smuggling across the U.S.–Mexican border.

- U.S. labor secretary George Shultz orders adoption of the Philadelphia Plan, establishing guidelines for minority hiring in federally-funded projects.

1   Colonel Moamer al-Khaddhafi deposes King Idris of Libya in a military coup.

3   President Ho Chi Minh of North Vietnam dies and is succeeded, on September 23, by Ton Dac Thang.

7   Laos, with U.S. aid, begins an offensive against North Vietnamese forces on the Plain of Jars in Laos.

9   Israel attacks United Arab Republic (UAR) military bases south of Suez.

10 British troops start to dismantle barricades in Belfast and Londonderry, Northern Ireland.

11 The Soviet premier Alexey Kosygin makes a surprise visit to Beijing, China.

17 A week of violence between Hindus and Muslims breaks out in Gujarat, India.

27 President Ngyuen Van Thieu of South Vietnam says U.S. withdrawal from Vietnam will take "years and years" as his country has "no ambition" to take over the fighting.

27 Reformers in the Czechoslovakian government are purged.

28 In West German elections the Christian Democrats win 46% of votes, and the Social Democrats 43%.

OCTOBER

- Arkansas senator J. William Fulbright accuses the Nixon administration of waging a secret and illegal war in Cambodia.

- In the first of two Vietnam Moratorium days, U.S. antiwar protestors stage a massive rally in Washington, D.C. Elsewhere throughout the nation, protestors light candles, hold prayer vigils, and demonstrate.

- U.S. newspapers report a pattern of blacklisting at the U.S. Department of Health, Education, and Welfare (HEW)—part of a Nixon administration attempt to silence dissident scientists.

3   The Greek government restores freedom of the press, abolishes arbitrary arrest, and limits military powers.

10 The communist government of Czechoslovakia imposes drastic restrictions on foreign travel.

21 The Social Democrat Willy Brandt becomes chancellor of West Germany following elections on September 28.

26 The Portuguese government holds every seat in the first significantly contested elections since 1926. On November 8, opposition parties are dissolved.

28 The United States submits a new Middle East peace plan for international consideration, but it is rejected by Israel on December 22.

29 A new cabinet of young "technocrats" takes office in Spain.

30 The new military government of Libya requests the early closure of British bases in the country.

NOVEMBER

- President Richard M. Nixon appears on national television to defend his Vietnam War policy. He announces a willingness to compromise with his communist foes provided they recognize the South Vietnamese government. He appeals to the "silent majority" of Americans for support.

- President Richard M. Nixon pledges that the United States will not engage in biological warfare nor be the first to use chemicals in a war. Tear gas and defoliants such as Agent Orange, in use in Vietnam, are exempted from the pledge.

- President Richard M. Nixon signs legislation creating a lottery system for military draftees.

- The U.S. Senate rejects President Richard M. Nixon's nomination of South Carolina jurist Clement Haynsworth to the U.S. Supreme Court, the first such rejection in 39 years.

- This year's Veterans Day becomes the occasion for prowar demonstrations.

1 The Congress Party of India formally splits into two factions.

3 The U.S. president Richard M. Nixon promises the complete withdrawal of U.S. ground forces from Vietnam, on a secret timetable. A further 50,000 troops are withdrawn on December 15.

8 The United Arab Republic (UAR) navy shells Israeli positions in Sinai. On November 11, an air battle takes place over the Suez Canal.

11 The United Nations (UN) General Assembly rejects the admission of communist China for the 20th time.

14 In the second Vietnam Moratorium Day, 250,000 people protest in Washington, D.C., against the Vietnam War. Similar rallies occur throughout the nation's cities.

14 The Strategic Arms Limitation Talks (SALT) between the United States and USSR begin in Helsinki, Finland.

19 Ghana states that its 500,000 alien immigrants must leave the country within two weeks.

19 U.S. newspapers report that U.S. troops massacred 450 men, women, and children at the village of My Lai in South Vietnam on March 16, 1968.

21 The United States agrees to return the island of Okinawa (where it has had a military base since 1945) and the other Ryukyu Islands to Japan on January 1, 1972, and to remove all nuclear weapons from Japan.

24 The United States and USSR ratify a nuclear nonproliferation treaty.

29 The National Party wins its fourth successive victory in a New Zealand general election; Keith Holyoake remains prime minister.

DECEMBER

- The U.S. Congress passes legislation raising safety standards in the coal-mining industry and compensating coal workers who have contracted black lung disease.

- U.S. troop strength in Vietnam is reduced from 540,000 at the end of last year, to 480,000 by year's end.

2 A European Community (EC) summit agrees to prepare for negotiations on British entry.

9 The United States calls on Israel to withdraw from the occupied territories (land which it holds following the Six Day War of 1967) in return for a binding peace agreement in the Middle East.

12 Greece withdraws from the Council of Europe to preempt expulsion for its government's infringements of democratic freedoms.

13 Britain agrees to vacate its military bases in Libya by the end of March 1970.

15 Former prime minister Alexander Dubček becomes Czechoslovak ambassador to Turkey.

18 East Germany proposes that diplomatic relations with West Germany should be opened as between foreign states.

25 Israel launches a heavy attack on United Arab Republic (UAR) positions around Suez.

27 The United Arab Republic (UAR), Libya, and Sudan form a military, political, and economic alliance.

SCIENCE, TECHNOLOGY, AND MEDICINE

Computing

- The U.S. Department of Defense establishes a computer network that is the basis of the Internet.

Ecology

- James Fisher publishes *The Red Book*, which lists animals and plants in imminent danger of extinction.

- The U.S. Congress establishes the 505,000-acre North Cascades National Park in Washington State.

JANUARY

18–February 26 Heavy rains in southern California cause mud slides that kill more than 100 people in the region, destroy 10,000 homes, and contribute to $60 million in property damage.

25 An oilwell off California's Santa Barbara Channel has a blowout, releasing 1,477,479 l/325,000 gal of crude oil which covers 30 km/48 mi of shoreline.

JUNE

- Pesticides spilled into the Rhine by a chemical company in Frankfurt am Main kill millions of fish and contaminate the drinking water of the Netherlands.

AUGUST

17 The Mississippi Gulf coast and southern U.S. states are hit by hurricane Camille. The most severe hurricane in

Space Exploration (1957–98)

1957

October 4 The USSR launches the first artificial satellite, *Sputnik 1*, to study the cosmosphere. It weighs 84 kg/184 lb and circles the earth in 95 minutes, inaugurating the space age.

November 3–April 13 The Soviet spacecraft *Sputnik 2* is placed in orbit carrying a dog, Laika. It is the first vehicle to carry a living organism into orbit. Laika dies in space.

1958

July 29 The U.S. National Aeronautics and Space Administration (NASA) is created for the research and development of vehicles and activities involved in space exploration.

October 11 The United States launches the space probe *Pioneer 1* into orbit.

1959

- The Eisenhower administration announces preliminary plans for a joint U.S.–USSR space venture.

January 2 The USSR launches *Lunik 1*. The first spacecraft to escape Earth's gravity, it passes within 6,400 km/4,000 mi of the moon.

September 14 The Soviet spacecraft *Luna 2* (launched on September 12) becomes the first spacecraft to strike the moon.

October 7 The Soviet *Luna 3* (launched on October 4) takes the first photographs of the far side of the moon.

1961

April 12 Soviet cosmonaut Yuri Gagarin, in *Vostok 1*, is the first person to enter space. His flight lasts 108 minutes.

May 5 U.S. astronaut Alan Shepard, in the Mercury capsule *Freedom 7*, makes a 14.8-minute single suborbital flight. He is the first U.S. astronaut into space.

May 21 U.S. president John F. Kennedy commits the country to "landing a man on the moon and returning him safely to Earth before this decade is out." Following this, he will ask Congress to allocate close to $2 billion for space exploration as part of his pledge.

October 27 The first two-stage *Saturn I* rocket is launched. The first rocket specifically designed for space flight, it is used to launch the Apollo spacecraft.

1962

February 20 U.S. astronaut John Glenn, in the Mercury capsule *Friendship 7*, becomes the first U.S. astronaut to orbit the earth. He makes three orbits.

1964

November 28 The United States launches *Mariner 4* to Mars. Passing within 1,865 km/6,118 mi of the planet's surface (July 14, 1965), it relays the first close-up photographs of the planet's surface as well as information on the Martian atmosphere.

1965

March 18 Soviet cosmonaut Alexey Leonov leaves spacecraft *Voskhod 2* and floats in space for 20 minutes—the first space walk.

1966

February 3 Soviet spacecraft *Luna 9* (launched on January 31) makes the first soft landing on the moon and transmits photographs and soil data for three days.

1967

January 27 Three U.S. astronauts, Virgil I. Grissom, Edward H. White, II, and Roger B. Chaffee, die in a fire during a countdown rehearsal on the *Apollo 1* spacecraft at Cape Kennedy, Florida. They are the first human casualties of the U.S. space program.

November The first three-stage *Saturn V* rocket is launched. Weighing nearly 2.3 million kg/5 million lb, it is used to lift the Apollo missions to the moon.

1968

October 11–22 *Apollo 7*, the first U.S. Apollo space mission with a crew, tests the Command module used on subsequent flights to the moon, during 163 orbits of the earth. The crew make the first live transmission from space on October 13.

1969

July 16–24 The U.S. moon-shot mission *Apollo 11* takes place. On July 20, U.S. astronaut Neil Armstrong becomes the first person to walk on the moon, famously saying "That's one small step for man, one giant leap for mankind." He and Buzz Aldrin also install and operate the first moon seismograph at Tranquility base, spending a total of 21 hours, 37 minutes on the moon's surface, while Michael Collins remains orbiting the moon in the command module.

---

nearly 35 years, it kills 248, leaves 200,000 homeless, and causes $1.5 billion property damage. Winds exceed 301 kph/190 mph.

Exploration

- Norwegian ethnologist Thor Heyerdahl crosses the Atlantic Ocean, from Morocco to the Caribbean, on the papyrus raft *Ra*, in an attempt to prove that pre-Columbian cultures could have been influenced by Egyptian civilization.

- The Joint Oceanographic Institutions Deep Earth Sampling (JOIDES) project begins. It makes boreholes in the ocean floor and confirms the theory of seafloor spreading and that the oceanic crust everywhere is less than 200 million years old.

1970

April 13–17   NASA narrowly diverts a disaster aboard the moon-bound spaceship *Apollo 13*, after a canister of liquid oxygen explodes in the command module. The crew of James Lovell, John Swigert, and Fred Haise enter the lunar module, which they use as a "lifeboat" to return safely to earth.

1972

January 5   U.S. president Richard M. Nixon authorizes a $5.5 billion six-year program to develop plans for a spaceship capable of undertaking multiple missions, thereby launching the space shuttle program.

1973

May 14–February 8   The United States launches the first *Skylab* space station. It contains a workshop for carrying out experiments in weightlessness. It is visited by three three-person crews and astronauts make observations of the sun, manufacture superconductors, and conduct other scientific and medical experiments. The third mission lasts a record 84 days and gathers data about long space flights.

1975

July   The launch of the Soviet spaceship *Soyuz 19* signals the start of a joint U.S.–Soviet space mission. U.S. and Soviet astronauts meet in space on July 17 when *Soyuz 19* docks with its NASA counterpart, *Apollo 18*.

1981

April 12–14   The U.S. reusable space shuttle, using the orbiter *Columbia*, makes its first flight (second shuttle flight November 12–14). It is also the first landing of a U.S. spacecraft on land.

1983

June 18–24   A mission by the U.S. space shuttle *Challenger* includes Sally Ride, the first U.S. woman to go into space.

1986

January 28   The U.S. space shuttle *Challenger* explodes shortly after takeoff, killing the crew of seven and setting the U.S. space program back years.

February 19   The Soviet space station *Mir 1* is launched; it is intended to be permanently occupied.

1989

• Astronomers discover a river of gas at the center of the Milky Way, providing further evidence that a black hole, 4 million times as massive as the sun, exists at the center of our galaxy.

October 18   The U.S. space shuttle *Atlantis* launches the spacecraft *Galileo* to explore Jupiter. It reaches its destination in December 1995.

1990

February   The U.S. space probe *Voyager 1*, now near the edge of the solar system, turns and takes the first photograph of the entire solar system from space.

April 24   The space shuttle *Discovery* places the Hubble Space Telescope in Earth orbit; the main mirror proves to be defective.

December 2–12   The Soviet spacecraft *Soyuz TM-11* is launched, marking the first paying passenger space flight. Japanese newsman Toyuhiro Akiyama, the first Japanese cosmonaut, spends seven days onboard the spacecraft.

1996

December 3   U.S. astronomer Anthony Cook, using data from the satellite *Clementine*, announces the discovery of a frozen lake at the bottom of a crater on the dark side of the moon.

1997

June 25   During a manually guided docking maneuver the Russian space station *Mir* collides with its unmanned cargo supply vessel, causing the space station to lose power and oxygen and to tumble out of control. Repairs are subsequently made.

July 4   The U.S. spacecraft *Mars Pathfinder* lands on Mars. Two days later, the probe's rover, *Sojourner*, a six-wheeled vehicle that is controlled by an Earth-based operator, begins to explore the area around the spacecraft.

1998

January 16   NASA announces that John Glenn, a Democratic senator from Ohio who became the first American in orbit in 1962, will be part of the space shuttle *Discovery* team on a ten-day mission to study life sciences. Glenn, who will be 77, will become the oldest space traveler.

• The Soviet spacecraft *Soyuz 6*, *Soyuz 7*, and *Soyuz 8* are launched on successive days. The crews conduct welding experiments in space.

JANUARY

16   Two cosmonauts aboard Soviet spacecraft *Soyuz 5* (launched January 15) dock and transfer to *Soyuz 4* (launched January 14). Locked together for four hours they form the first experimental space station.

FEBRUARY

February–March   U.S. space probe *Mariner 6* (launched February 24) passes within 3,410 km/2,131 mi of the surface of Mars. *Mariner 7* (launched March 27) photographs the Martian landscape and makes thermal maps of the planet and analyzes its atmosphere.

MARCH

3–13   The U.S. *Apollo 9* mission tests the lunar module in Earth orbit.

MAY

22   Two astronauts aboard the U.S. *Apollo 10* spacecraft (launched May 18) transfer into the Lunar module and descend to within 15,250 m/50,000 ft of the moon's surface.

NOVEMBER

22   The lunar module from the U.S. spacecraft *Apollo 12* (launched November 14) lands on the moon in the Ocean of Storms. The crew collects 34 kg/75 lb of Moon rocks, inspects *Surveyor 3*, which landed nearby 2.5 years earlier, and uses a radioisotope-fueled generator to power experiments.

Health and Medicine

- The first effective artificial human heart is developed and implanted as a temporary device for patients requiring transplants.
- The Nobel Prize for Physiology or Medicine is awarded jointly to U.S. physiologists Max Delbrück, Alfred Hershey, and Salvador Luria for their discoveries concerning the replication mechanism and genetic structure of viruses.

JANUARY

21   A federal study reveals that millions of Americans live in a state of chronic hunger and malnutrition.

FEBRUARY

15   English physiologist Robert Edwards of the Cambridge Physiological Laboratory, Cambridge, England, completes the first in vitro fertilization of human egg cells.

APRIL

4   U.S. surgeon Dr. Denton Cooley implants the world's first completely artificial heart, a combination of Dacron and plastics, in Houston, Texas. The patient survives for four days.

JUNE

- Jacuzzi Bros. introduce the hot tub at the Orange County Fair in California.

SEPTEMBER

15   The world's first heart and lung transplant is performed at the Stanford Medical Center in California.

OCTOBER

October–December   The U.S. Department of Health, Education, and Welfare (HEW) bans use of cyclamates as an artificial sweetener; it sanctions limited use of cyclamates in December.

Science

- A multichannel spectrometer is installed at the Mt Palomar Observatory, California. It permits the rapid and accurate collection of data through the simultaneous observation of 32 wavelength bands.
- English chemist Derek Barton shares the Nobel Prize for Chemistry with Norwegian chemist Odd Hassel for the concept and applications of conformation.

- Human remains found at Lake Mungo, Australia, are dated at 26,000 years. They provide the earliest evidence of ritual cremation.
- The Sacramento Peak Observatory at Sunspot, New Mexico, becomes operational. All the air from its 76-cm/30-in diameter 54.9-m/180-ft long solar telescope has been evacuated to prevent it from overheating.
- U.S. chemist Albert Ghiorso and colleagues at the University of California, Berkeley, discover the radioactive element rutherfordium (atomic no. 104), named for the New Zealand-born British physicist Ernest Rutherford.
- U.S. geneticist Jonathan Beckwith and associates at the Harvard Medical School isolate a single gene for the first time.
- U.S. physicist Murray Gell-Mann receives the Nobel Prize for Physics for his discoveries and classification of elementary particles.

MARCH

- The Fermi National Accelerator Laboratory ("Fermilab") is established near Chicago, Illinois.

Technology

- A 765,000-volt power transmission line enters service in the United States. It is the highest voltage transmission line in the world.
- The U.S. Naval Laboratory develops an atomic clock based on the vibration of the ammonium atom; it is accurate to within one second in 1.7 million years.
- The U.S. Phillips Petroleum Company discovers a giant oil field in the North Sea off the coast of Norway.

MARCH

- The Pentagon reports that it is spending approximately $350 million a year on the production of chemical and biological weapons.

NOVEMBER

- The U.S. Congress appropriates money for the Safeguard antiballistic missile system.

Transportation

- High-speed passenger "turbo-trains" powered by aircraft-type turbines begin operating between Montreal and Toronto in Canada, and between New York, New York, and Boston, Massachusetts.
- Mexico City's subway system opens in Mexico. It has 36 km/22.5 mi of track.
- The U.S. Lockheed Galaxy C5A transport plane is introduced. The largest airplane in the world, it can carry a payload of 120,000 kg/265,000 lb and has a range of 8,800 km/5,500 mi.
- The U.S. ship *Acadia Forest* is launched. It is the first lighter-aboard-ship (LASH) and is designed to carry approximately 70 18-m/60-ft long by 9-m/30-ft wide steel lighters or barges, each of which can carry 500 tons of cargo.

MARCH

2   The prototype of the French–British supersonic airliner Concorde makes its first test flight. Its first supersonic flight takes place on October 1.

AUGUST

9   A DC-9 collides with a light aircraft that is piloted by a student, killing 83, near Indianapolis, Indiana.

24–September 14   The U.S. ship *Manhattan*, with the aid of two icebreakers, finds a route through the northwest passage to assess the economic feasibility of such a route.

DECEMBER

- The Boeing 747 joins the Pan Am airlines fleet and makes its first commercial flight, from Seattle, Washington, to New York, New York.

ARTS AND IDEAS

Architecture

- The terminal buildings at London Heathrow Airport, England, designed by the English architect Frederick Gibberd, are completed.

Arts

- English art historian Kenneth Clark publishes *Civilisation: A Personal View*, which accompanies a popular television series.
- The English artist Allen Jones sculpts *Hatstand, Table, and Chair*.
- The exhibition "When Attitude Becomes Form" is held at the Institute of Contemporary Art in London, England.
- The French artist Niki de Saint-Phalle sculpts *Black Nana*.
- The German-born English artist Frank Auerbach paints *Mornington Crescent, Winter*.
- The U.S. artist Donald Judd sculpts *Untitled*, a series of vertically arranged metal and glass boxes.

Film

- The comedy *Take the Money and Run*, by U.S. director Woody Allen, is released in the United States. Starring Janet Margolin, Marcell Hillaire, and Jacquelyn Hyde, it is Allen's first movie as director, writer, and actor.
- The epic Western *Once Upon a Time in the West*, directed by Italian filmmaker Sergio Leone, is released, starring Henry Fonda, Claudia Cardinale, Jason Robards, and Charles Bronson.
- The movie *Bob & Carol & Ted & Alice*, directed by Paul Mazursky, is released in the United States, starring Robert Culp, Natalie Wood, Elliott Gould, and Dyan Cannon.
- The movie *Butch Cassidy and the Sundance Kid*, directed by George Roy Hill, is released in the United States, starring Paul Newman and Robert Redford.
- The movie *Easy Rider*, directed by Dennis Hopper, is released in the United States. He also stars in it, with Peter Fonda and Jack Nicholson.
- The movie *Goodbye, Columbus*, directed by Larry Peerce, is released in the United States. Based on the title story of Philip Roth's short-story collection, it stars Richard Benjamin and Ali McGraw.
- The Western *True Grit*, directed by Henry Hathaway, is released in the United States, starring John Wayne.
- The movie *Il conformista/The Conformist*, directed by Bernardo Bertolucci, is released in Italy, starring Jean-Louis Trintignant and Stefania Sandrelli. A visually striking movie, it is photographed by Vittorio Storaro.
- The movie *Le Boucher/The Butcher*, directed by Claude Chabrol, is released in France, starring Jean Yanne and Stéphane Audran.
- The movie *Les Choses de la vie/The Things of Life*, directed by Claude Sautet, is released in France, starring Romy Schneider and Michel Piccoli.
- The movie *Midnight Cowboy*, directed by British filmmaker John Schlesinger, is released in the United States, starring Jon Voight and Dustin Hoffman.
- The movie *Oh! What a Lovely War*, directed by Richard Attenborough, is released in Britain. Based on the stage show of the same name, the stars include Ralph Richardson, Meriel Forbes, John Gielgud, and Kenneth More.
- The movie *On Her Majesty's Secret Service*, directed by Peter Hunt, is released in the United States. Based on the novel by Ian Fleming, it stars George Lazenby as James Bond, the only time he played the role.
- The movie *Satyricon*, directed by Federico Fellini, is released in Italy, starring Martin Potter, Hiram Keller, and Salvo Randone.
- The movie *The Prime of Miss Jean Brodie*, directed by Ronald Neame, is released in Britain. Based on the novel by Muriel Spark, it stars Maggie Smith, Robert Stephens, Pamela Franklin, and Gordon Jackson.
- The movie *The Wild Bunch*, directed by Sam Peckinpah, is released in the United States. The stars include William Holden, Ernest Borgnine, and Robert Ryan.
- The movie *They Shoot Horses, Don't They?*, directed by Sydney Pollack, is released in the United States. Based on the novel by Horace McCoy, it stars Gig Young and Jane Fonda.
- The movie *Women in Love*, directed by Ken Russell, is released in Britain. Based on the novel by D. H. Lawrence, it stars Glenda Jackson, Jennie Linden, Alan Bates, and Oliver Reed.
- The movie *Z*, directed by Greek filmmaker Constantin Costa-Gavras, is released in France, starring Jean-Louis Trintignant, Jacques Pérrin, and Yves Montand.
- The movie musical *Hello, Dolly!*, directed by Gene Kelly, is released in the United States. An adaptation of a long-running musical based on the play *The Matchmaker* by Thornton Wilder, it stars Barbra Streisand, Walter Matthau, and Michael Crawford.
- The Walt Disney movie *The Love Bug*, directed by Robert Stevenson, is released in the United States, the first in the series of movies about an animate Volkswagen Beetle called Herbie.

APRIL

14   The 1968 Academy Awards take place. Best Actor: Cliff Robertson, for *Charly*; Best Supporting Actor: Jack Albertson, for *The Subject was Roses*; Best Actress: Katharine Hepburn, for *The Lion in Winter* and Barbra Streisand, for *Funny Girl*; Best Supporting Actress: Ruth Gordon, for *Rosemary's Baby*; Best Picture: *Oliver!*,

directed by Carol Reed; Best Director: Carol Reed, for
Oliver!

MAY

23 At the Cannes Film Festival in France, the Palme d'Or is
    awarded to *If...* , directed by Lindsay Anderson.

Literature and Language

- The Canadian writer Margaret Atwood publishes her
  novel *The Edible Woman*.
- The English writer Doris Lessing publishes her novel
  The Four-Gated City.
- The English writer Graham Greene publishes his linked
  set of short stories *Travels with My Aunt*.
- The English writer John Fowles publishes his novel *The
  French Lieutenant's Woman*, set in Victorian England.
- The Irish writer Elizabeth Bowen publishes her novel
  Eva Trout.
- The Irish writer William Trevor publishes his novel
  Mrs Eckdorf in O'Neill's Hotel.
- The Nobel Prize for Literature is awarded to the Irish
  novelist and dramatist Samuel Beckett.
- The Pulitzer Prize for Biography is awarded to B. L.
  Reid for *The Man from New York*, the Pulitzer Prize for
  Poetry is awarded to George Oppen for *Of Being
  Numerous*, and the Pulitzer Prize for Fiction is awarded
  to N. Scott Momaday for *House Made of Dawn*.
- The Russian-born U.S. writer Vladimir Nabokov
  publishes his novel *Ada*.
- The U.S. writer Adrienne Rich publishes her poetry
  collection *Leaflets*.
- The U.S. writer Gwendolyn Brooks publishes her poetry
  collection *The Bean Eaters*.
- The U.S. writer John Cheever publishes his novel *Bullet
  Park*
- The U.S. writer Joyce Carol Oates publishes her novel
  them.
- The U.S. writer Kurt Vonnegut publishes his novel
  *Slaughterhouse Five, or The Children's Crusade: A
  Duty-Dance with Death*.
- The U.S. writer Mario Puzo publishes his novel *The
  Godfather*.
- The U.S. writer Philip Roth publishes his novel
  Portnoy's Complaint.
- The U.S. writer Robert Coover publishes his short-story
  collection *Pricksongs & Descants*.
- The U.S. writer Robert Penn Warren publishes his
  poetry collection *Audubon: A Vision*.
- The U.S. writer Thomas McGuane publishes his novel
  The Sporting Club.

Music

- *West Side Story*, the soundtrack from the movie, is the
  best-selling album of the 1960s in the United States.
- "Sugar Sugar" by the Archies (animated cartoon
  characters) is the best-selling single of the year in
  Britain. The voices are supplied by Ron Dante, Toni
  Wine, and Andy Kim.
- "The Ballad of John and Yoko," a single written by
  John Lennon and Paul McCartney and performed by
  The Beatles, is banned by the Australian Broadcasting
  Commission because it contains references to Christ and

the crucifixion. Some U.S. radio stations either "bleep"
the word Christ when the record is played, or refuse to
play it at all.
- Chubby Checker's song "The Twist" is the best-selling
  single of the 1960s in the United States.
- John Lennon and Yoko Ono release the single "Give
  Peace a Chance."
- Tape sales represent 40% of the music market in the
  United States. The total market is worth around $1
  billion and 75% comes from purchasers aged under 30.
- The Austrian composer Friedrich Cerha completes his
  chamber work *Catalogue des objets trouvées/Catalog of
  Found Objects*.
- The Beatle John Lennon returns his MBE to the queen in
  objection to Britain's political position on Vietnam,
  among other matters.
- The Beatle Paul McCartney has to publicly deny rumors
  of his death: the speculation has resulted from alleged
  hidden messages in Beatles albums that he has been
  replaced by a double.
- The British actress Jane Birkin and her husband, the
  French singer Serge Gainsbourg, release the single "Je
  t'aime ... moi non plus"/"I Love You ... Neither Do I,"
  which is banned by the British Broadcasting
  Corporation (BBC). Their record label Philips
  withdraws the single when it receives complaints from
  buyers about the simulated orgasm sounds, but the song
  become a hit when it is rereleased by Major-Minor.
- The British rock/blues trio Cream releases the album
  Goodbye.
- The British heavy metal/rock group Led Zeppelin
  releases the albums *Led Zeppelin* and *Led Zeppelin II*.
- The British pop group the Hollies releases the single "He
  Ain't Heavy, He's My Brother."
- The British pop singer Dusty Springfield releases the
  single "Son of a Preacher Man."
- The British pop singer David Bowie releases the single
  "Space Oddity."
- The British rock group the Who releases the single
  "Pinball Wizard" and the album *Tommy*, the
  soundtrack of their rock opera of the same name.
- The British rock group the Beatles make their last ever
  public appearance on the roof of the Apple Records
  building in London, England. It is recorded as part of
  their movie *Let It Be*. The police are called out by
  people in neighboring buildings who are disturbed by
  the noise. The group also releases the album *Abbey
  Road* and the single "Something" by George Harrison,
  the first Beatle hit not to have been written by John
  Lennon or Paul McCartney.
- The Canadian folk singer Joni Mitchell releases the
  album *Clouds*, featuring the singles "Chelsea Morning"
  and "Clouds."
- The Canadian singer/songwriter Leonard Cohen releases
  the album *Songs From A Room*.
- The English composer Harrison Birtwistle completes his
  dramatic composition *Down by the Greenwood Side*.
- The English composer John Tavener completes his *Celtic
  Requiem*.
- The English composer Peter Maxwell Davies completes
  his orchestral work *St. Thomas Wake*.
- The first Country Music Festival in Britain takes place.
  Tammy Wynette and Loretta Lynn feature among the
  stars.

- The French composer Olivier Messiaen completes his choral work *La Transfiguration de Notre Seigneur Jésus-Christ/The Transfiguration of Our Lord Jesus Christ*.
- The Italian composer Luciano Berio completes his *Sinfonia* for voices and orchestra.
- The Jamaican reggae singer Jimmy Cliff releases the single "Wonderful World, Beautiful People," one of the first reggae hits.
- The Jamaican reggae group Desmond Dekker and the Aces releases "The Israelites," the first reggae single to get to the top of the British charts.
- The opera *Diabły z Loudun/The Devils of Loudon*, by the Polish composer Krzysztof Penderecki, is first performed in Hamburg, Germany.
- The Polish composer Henryk Górecki completes his orchestral work *Old Polish Music*.
- The Russian composer Dmitry Shostakovich completes his Symphony No. 14.
- The U.S. band MC5 (originally named Motor City Five) releases the album *Kick Out the Jams*.
- The U.S. composer Morton Feldman completes his orchestral work *In Search of Orchestration*.
- The U.S. country singer Johnny Cash releases the single "A Boy Named Sue" and the album *Johnny Cash at San Quentin*.
- The U.S. folk/rock duo Simon and Garfunkel releases the single "The Boxer."
- The U.S. funk rock band Sly and the Family Stone releases the album *Stand!*
- The U.S. group Credence Clearwater Revival, known for its distinctive blues-inflected swamp rock sound, releases the albums *Green River* and *Willy and the Poorboys*. The group also has the album *Bayou Country* in the charts.
- The U.S. pop singer Roberta Flack releases "The First Time Ever I Saw Your Face." It is a hit in 1972 when included in the movie *Play Misty For Me*.
- The U.S. rock 'n' roll band Captain Beefheart and the Magic Band, led by Don Van Vliet, releases the album *Trout Mask Replica*.
- The U.S. rock band the Stooges, led by Iggy Pop, releases the album *The Stooges*.
- The U.S. rock group Santana releases an album by the same name. The band introduces a Latin flavor into rock.
- The U.S. rock group The Band releases the album *The Band*, which includes the group's most popular single, "Up on Cripple Creek."
- The U.S. rock singer Elvis Presley releases the single "Suspicious Minds."
- The U.S. singer Frank Sinatra releases the single "My Way."
- The U.S. singer/songwriter Stevie Wonder releases the single "My Cherie Amour."
- The U.S. singer/songwriter Neil Diamond releases the single "Sweet Caroline."
- The U.S. trumpeter Herb Alpert and his band Tijuana Brass have sold over 40 million albums throughout the 1960s.
- The vocal-harmony group Crosby, Stills, Nash, and Young releases the album *Crosby, Stills, Nash, and Young*.
- U.S. musician Frank Zappa releases the album *Hot Rats*.

MARCH
- Beatle John Lennon and his new wife Yoko Ono make their honeymoon, at the Hilton Hotel, Amsterdam, in the Netherlands, a "bed-in" for peace.
- 12 The 1968–69 Grammy Awards take place. Best Album: *By the Time I Get to Phoenix* by Glenn Campbell; Best Record: "Mrs. Robinson" by Simon and Garfunkel; Best Male Vocalist: José Feliciano; Best Female Vocalist: Dionne Warwick; Best Group: Simon and Garfunkel.

AUGUST
- 15–17 Half a million people attend the three-day Woodstock Music and Arts Fair on a farm in New York State. The line-up includes Jimi Hendrix, the Who, Janis Joplin, Jefferson Airplane, and Santana.

DECEMBER
- 6 During a Rolling Stones set at the Altamont Festival in Altamont, California, the teenage fan Meredith Hunter is killed by Hell's Angels acting as security guards.

Theater and Dance

- The English artists Gilbert and George (Gilbert Proesch and George Pasmore) present their performance work *Underneath the Arches*, in London, England.
- The play *Boesman and Lena*, by the South African dramatist Athol Fugard, is first performed, in Port Elizabeth, South Africa.
- The play *Last of the Red Hot Lovers*, by the U.S. dramatist Neil Simon, is first performed, at the Eugene O'Neill Theater in New York, New York.
- The play *Une tempête: Adaption pour un théâtre nègre/A Tempest: An Adaptation for Black Theater*, by the Martinique writer Aimé Césaire, is first performed, in Tunisia. It premieres in Martinique in 1972, having previously been published in 1968.
- The play *What the Butler Saw*, by the English dramatist Joe Orton, is first performed, in London, England.
- The Pulitzer Prize for Drama is awarded to Howard Sackler for *The Great White Hope*.

FEBRUARY
- 10 The short plays *Adaptation*, by the U.S. dramatist Elaine May and *Next*, by the U.S. dramatist Terence McNally, are first performed, at the Greenwich Mews Theater, off Broadway, in New York, New York.

APRIL
- 20 The 1968–69 Tony Awards take place. Best Play: *The Great White Hope*, by U.S. dramatist Howard Sackler; Best Musical: *1776*; Best Actor: James Earl Jones; Best Actress: Julie Harris.

Thought and Scholarship

- Bob Larson, U.S. rock 'n' roll musician turned minister, publishes *Hindus, Hippies, and Rock and Roll*, a book that defends Christianity and argues that the counterculture threatens traditional values.
- Latvian-born English philosopher Isaiah Berlin publishes *Four Essays on Liberty*.

- The French philosopher Michel Foucault publishes *L'Archéologie de savoir/The Archeology of Knowledge*.
- The German-born U.S. philosopher Herbert Marcuse publishes *An Essay on Liberation*.
- The Pulitzer Prize for History is awarded to Leonard Levy for *Origins of the Fifth Amendment*.
- The Pulitzer Prize for General Nonfiction is awarded to Norman Mailer for *The Armies of the Night*, and to René Jules Dubos for *So Human an Animal*.
- The Tanzanian statesman Julius Kambarage Nyerere publishes *Freedom and Socialism*.
- The U.S. historian Gordon Wood publishes *The Creation of the American Republic, 1776-1787*.
- The U.S. philosopher John Searle publishes *Speech Acts: An Essay in the Philosophy of Language*.
- The U.S. social historian Christopher Lasch publishes *The Agony of the American Left*.
- U.S. educator Arthur Jensen concludes that differences in IQ scores between black and white populations in the United States are due to genetic differences. His work is heavily criticized.
- U.S. political scientist E. E. Schattschneider publishes *Two Hundred Million Americans in Search of a Government*.

SOCIETY

Everyday Life

- In Paris, France, *Les Halles* food market is moved to Rungis, near Orly Airport.
- The mini dress fashion is followed by the ankle-length maxi.
- The Rip Off Press is founded in San Francisco, California, by Gilbert Shelton, Jack Jackson, Fred Todd, and Dave Moriaty. It publishes many of the "underground" counterculture comics including work by Robert Crumb and Shelton's own *Fabulous Furry Freak Brothers*.
- The U.S. clothes store The Gap is founded.
- The U.S. manufacturer of household products Procter and Gamble launches Ariel laundry detergent.
- U.S. psychiatrist David Reuben publishes *Everything You Always Wanted to Know About Sex (But Were Afraid to Ask)*.

FEBRUARY

- Dock workers in New York, New York, conclude a record 57-day strike, begun the preceding December, after reaching a new three-year contract.

MARCH

3 Japan's gross national product exceeds that of West Germany for the first time.

APRIL

7 The U.S. Supreme Court rules unconstitutional the laws prohibiting the private possession of obscene materials.

MAY

17 David Corn of Dallas bids $404,000 at an auction in New York, New York, to buy a copy of the first printing of the Declaration of Independence, one of 16 extant.

NOVEMBER

- The "Sex Fair" is held in Copenhagen in Denmark, an exposition featuring exhibitions of pornography and sexual aids.

Media and Communication

- The Australian businessman Rupert Murdoch buys the British paper the *Sun*, which is relaunched as a tabloid.
- The concert *Stones in the Park* is broadcast from New York, New York.
- There are now 81 million television sets in the United States.

November 1969–92 The comedy program *Hee Haw* appears on U.S. television, cohosted by Buck Owens and Roy Clark. Louis M. "Grandpa" Jones, Junior Samples, Jeannine Riley, Minnie Pearl, the Hagers, Irlene Mandrell, and Jeff Smith also appear regularly.

FEBRUARY

8 The *Saturday Evening Post*, based in Philadelphia, Pennsylvania, ceases publication after 148 years.

APRIL

4 CBS cancels the *Smothers Brothers Comedy Hour*, a popular comedy and variety show, because of disputes over the program's sharp and open criticism of President Lyndon B. Johnson's conduct of the Vietnam War.

JUNE

8 The 1968–69 Emmy Awards for television take place. Best Actor in a Single Show: Paul Scofield; Best Actress in a Single Show: Geraldine Page; Best Actor in a Series: Carl Betz, for *Judd for the Defense*; Best Actress in a Series: Barbara Bain, for *Mission: Impossible*.

JULY

20 Over 700 million people worldwide watch Neil Armstrong and Buzz Aldrin in the lander module from the U.S. spacecraft *Apollo 11* touch down on the moon.

SEPTEMBER

- The first U.S. issue of *Penthouse* is published in New York, New York, by Robert Guccione. It was first published in London, England, in 1965.

14–August 31, 1971 The situation comedy *The Bill Cosby Show* appears on U.S. television. Cosby, the first black man to star in a comedy program since 1953, plays a high school gym teacher; Lillian Randolph, Beah Richards, Lee Weaver, and Sid McCoy also star.

23–May 11, 1976 *Marcus Welby, MD*, a medical drama starring Robert Young, James Brolin, and Elena Verdugo, appears on U.S. television.

NOVEMBER

- *Sesame Street*, an educational program for children funded by the Ford Foundation, the Carnegie Corporation, and the U.S. Office of Education, first appears on U.S. television. The Muppet stars, created by Jim Henson, include Big Bird and Bert and Ernie.

DECEMBER

17 The U.S. singer and ukelele player Tiny Tim (best known for his falsetto rendition of "Tiptoe through the Tulips") and Miss Vicki (Victoria May Budinger) marry on Johnny Carson's television show *Tonight*.

Religion

- The U.S. Reverend David Wilkerson publishes *Purple Violet Squish*, a book that defends religion against attacks from the counterculture.

Sports

- In a significant expansion of major-league baseball in the United States, the Montreal Expos and the San Diego Padres join the National League, and the Kansas City Royals and the Seattle Pilots (from 1970 the Milwaukee Brewers) join the American League. The Expos are the first non-U.S. Major League team.
- Irina Rodnina of the Soviet Union wins the first of ten successive world pairs figure-skating titles. She is partnered by Alexey Ulanov 1969–72 and by her husband Alexander Zaitsev 1973–78.
- The Australian tennis player Rod Laver achieves his second Grand Slam, winning all four major tennis championships (the Australian Open, the French Open, Wimbledon, and the U.S. Open) in the same calendar year.
- The Brazilian soccer player Pelé, playing in his 909th first-class match (for the Santos club in São Paulo, Brazil), scores his 1,000th goal.
- The Ryder Cup golf tournament between the United States and Great Britain, at Royal Birkdale, Lancashire, England, results in a tie for the first time in its 42-year history, with both teams finishing on 16 points.

JANUARY
12   The New York Jets defeat the Baltimore Colts 16–7 in Miami, Florida, before 75,546 spectators, to become the first team from the American Football League to win the Super Bowl.

FEBRUARY
- Major league baseball players conclude a boycott of spring training after reaching a new three-year contract with team owners.
7   The U.S. football coach Vince Lombardi joins the Washington Redskins as head coach, part owner, and executive vice president.

APRIL
22   The English yachtsman Robin Knox-Johnston in his yacht *Suhaili* returns to Falmouth, England, to win the *Sunday Times* Golden Globe, the first single-handed round-the-world yacht race. In winning the race he becomes the first person to circumnavigate the world by sea without stopping.
27–May 4   For the second year running, the Montreal Canadiens defeat the St. Louis Blues in four straight games to win the National Hockey League Stanley Cup.

MAY
3   The U.S. jockey Bill Hartack, on Majestic Prince, equals fellow U.S. jockey Eddie Arcaro's record of five Kentucky Derby wins. Majestic Prince's trainer, Johnny Longden, becomes the first person to have both ridden and saddled a Kentucky Derby winner, having won the race as a jockey on Count Fleet in 1943.
5   Boston Celtics player/coach Bill Russell retires as a player after leading the Celtics to their tenth National Basketball Association title in the United States in 11 years.
18   The English race-car driver Graham Hill wins the Monaco Grand Prix for an unprecedented fifth time.

BIRTHS & DEATHS

FEBRUARY
3   Boris Karloff, British-born U.S. actor known for his horror films, dies in Midhurst, West Sussex, England (81).
26   Karl Jaspers, German existentialist philosopher, dies in Basel, Switzerland (86).

MARCH
28   Dwight David Eisenhower, 34th president of the United States 1953–61, a Republican, dies in Washington, D.C. (78).

MAY
2   Franz von Papen, German statesman who was instrumental in dissolving the Weimar Republic and bringing Hitler to power, dies in Obersasbach, West Germany (89).
8   Akebono (Chadwick Haheo Rowan), the first champion U.S. sumo wrestler, is born near Honolulu, Hawaii.

JUNE
21   Maureen Connolly, "Little Mo," U.S. tennis player who was the first woman to win Wimbledon, the U.S., Australian, and French singles championships in the same year (1953), dies in Dallas, Texas (34).
22   Judy Garland, U.S. singer and actress, dies in London, England (47).

JULY
5   Tom Mboya, Kenyan political leader, is assassinated in Nairobi, Kenya (38).
5   Walter Gropius, German architect, dies in Boston, Massachusetts (86).

AUGUST
17   Ludwig Mies van der Rohe, German-born U.S. architect who worked in the International Style, dies in Chicago, Illinois (82).
31   Rocky Marciano (Rocco Francis Marchegiano), U.S. world heavyweight boxer 1952–56, is killed in an airplane crash near Newton, Iowa (45).

SEPTEMBER
3   Ho Chi Minh, founder of the Indochina Communist Party (1930) and president of North Vietnam 1945–69, dies in Hanoi, North Vietnam (79).

OCTOBER
12   Sonja Henie, Norwegian-born U.S. figure skater who was the world amateur champion for ten successive years (1927–36), dies while traveling in an airplane to Oslo, Norway (57).
21   Jack Kerouac, U.S. poet, novelist, and leader of the Beat movement, dies in St. Petersburg, Florida (47).

NOVEMBER
12   Liu Shaoqi, chairman of the People's Republic of China 1959–68, dies in K'aifeng Province, China (about 71).

JUNE

17 The Soviet chess player Boris Spassky defeats fellow Soviet player Tigran Petrosyan 12.5–10.5 in Moscow, USSR, to become world chess champion.

24–25 In the longest match in the history of the Wimbledon tennis championships in London, England, the 41-year-old Pancho Gonzales defeats fellow U.S. player Charlie Pasarell after 112 games and 5 hours, 12 minutes of play. Gonzales lost the first set 22–20 and was two sets to love down when play was halted because of bad light.

JULY

4 Ann Jones of Great Britain defeats Billie Jean King of the United States in three sets in the final of the women's singles at the Wimbledon tennis championships, London, England; she is the first British winner of the title since Angela Mortimer in 1961.

12 The English golfer Tony Jacklin wins the British Open golf championship at Royal Lytham St. Anne's in Lancashire, England. He is the first Briton to win the tournament since Max Faulkner in 1951.

AUGUST

23 The Little League World Series is won by a team from Taiwan for the first time. Over the next 12 years the title will be won by Taiwanese teams on nine occasions.

SEPTEMBER

20 At the European athletics championships in Athens, Greece, Jaroslava Jehlichova of Czechoslovakia wins the first ever major international 1,500-meters women's track race in a world record time of 4 min 10.7 sec.

21 Dutch athlete Eduard de Noorlander, competing in the decathlon at the European Championships in Athens, Greece, becomes the first track and field athlete to be disqualified from a major championship for drug abuse.

22 The San Francisco Giants' baseball player Willie Mays becomes the first person since the U.S. player Babe Ruth to hit 600 home runs in major-league baseball.

OCTOBER

11–16 The New York Mets defeat the Baltimore Orioles by four games to one to become the first "expansion" side (added to the National League in 1962) to win baseball's World Series.

◆

1970

POLITICS, GOVERNMENT, AND ECONOMICS

Business and Economics

MARCH

23 The United States refuses to supply 25 Phantom fighter-bombers to Israel, but a sale of 18 is agreed on September 9.

Colonization

FEBRUARY

23 Guyana becomes a republic within the British Commonwealth.

APRIL

24 Gambia becomes a republic within the British Commonwealth.

OCTOBER

10 Fiji becomes independent within the British Commonwealth.

Human Rights

- The Australian-born English feminist Germaine Greer writes *The Female Eunuch*, a radical independent statement of feminism that argues that women should take responsibility for their lives rather than blaming men.
- U.S. artist and critic Kate Millett publishes *Sexual Politics*, a feminist analysis of gender inequities in English literature.

MAY

15 The International Olympic Committee expels South Africa because of its apartheid policies.

NOVEMBER

27 The Gay Liberation Front holds its first public demonstration in Britain.

Politics and Government

- Divorce is legalized in Italy.
- New York State liberalizes the abortion laws, virtually permitting "abortion on demand." Only two other states in the United States, Hawaii and Alaska, have this kind of legislation.
- The U.S. historian Eric Foner publishes *Free Soil, Free Labor, Free Men: The Ideology of the Republican Party before the Civil War*.

JANUARY

- In the State of the Union address, President Richard M. Nixon urges Congress to adopt legislation to protect the environment.
- The U.S. Supreme Court sets a deadline of February 1 for desegregating public schools in the states of Alabama, Florida, Georgia, Louisiana, Mississippi, and Tennessee.
- United Mine Workers (UMW) member and former UMW presidential candidate Joseph Yablonski is found murdered in his home, along with his wife and daughter.
1 The Chinese leader Mao Zedong accuses the USSR of "fascist dictatorship" and "moribund neocolonialism."
12 In the Nigerian civil war, the Biafran leader General Chukwuemeka Ojukwu flies into exile. On January 15, Nigeria accepts Biafra's unconditional surrender.
20 An abortive coup in Iraq is followed by the subsequent execution of 40 people for treason.
30 Serious fighting takes place between Israel and Syria in the Golan Heights.

FEBRUARY

- After receiving widespread criticism, the U.S. Army vows to halt surveillance of political activists and antiwar protestors.
- New York senator Daniel Patrick Moynihan becomes embroiled in controversy after a private memo is leaked to the press in which he suggests that "the issue of race could benefit from a period of benign neglect."
- Seven of the eight political activists (the Chicago Eight) charged with inciting the violence at the 1968 Democratic convention in Chicago, Illinois, are acquitted of conspiracy. Five of these seven are convicted of crossing a state line with intent to incite a riot; they are sentenced to five years in jail.
- U.S. national security adviser Henry Kissinger begins secret talks with his North Vietnamese counterpart Le Duc Tho.
2 A successful North Vietnamese offensive in northeastern Laos recaptures the Plain of Jars.
6 United Arab Republic (UAR) frogmen sink an Israeli supply ship at Eilat, Israel; Israeli jets sink UAR minesweepers in the Gulf of Suez in retaliation.
10 Jordan places tighter controls on the Palestinian guerrilla movement stationed within its borders, following clashes between it and the Jordanian army.
12 An Israeli air raid on factories near Cairo, Egypt, kills 70 civilians.
21 A Swiss airliner crashes near Baden, West Germany, killing 47 passengers; Palestinian terrorists claim responsibility.

MARCH

- In the face of a soaring federal budget deficit, U.S. defense secretary Melvin R. Laird proposes cutting 371 military bases at home and abroad for an estimated saving of $914 million.
1 The Socialist Party wins an unexpected victory in the Austrian general election and, on March 20, Bruno Kreisky becomes chancellor.
2 Rhodesia formally declares itself a republic, and Clifford Dupont becomes president on April 14.
8 A group of Greek Cypriots attempts to assassinate the Cypriot president Archbishop Mikhail Makarios and stage a coup.

10 The Israeli parliament, the Knesset, defines what constitutes a Jew under Israeli law, following a dispute between secular and religious factions.
11 Iraq recognizes Kurdish autonomy and gives Kurds a bigger say in central government, following a nine-year civil war.
19 The first meeting of East and West German heads of government takes place at Erfurt, East Germany. On May 21, East German leader Willi Stoph and West German leader Willy Brandt meet again at Kassel, West Germany.
30 Left wing Japanese students hijack a Boeing 727 and fly to North Korea.

APRIL

- The U.S. Senate rejects President Richard M. Nixon's nomination of G. Harrold Carswell to the U.S. Supreme Court. It is the Senate's second rejection of a Nixon nominee in less than a year.
- The United States and USSR begin a second round of Strategic Arms Limitation Talks (SALT) in Vienna, Austria.
1 France proposes an international conference on the conflict in Vietnam, Laos, and Cambodia.
1 The Vietcong launch major assaults throughout South Vietnam after a six-month lull.
8 In an Israeli air raid on Egypt, bombs land on a primary school in the Nile Delta, killing 30 children.
10 The Greek military government relaxes martial law and, on April 14, releases 332 political prisoners.
19 The communist Pathet Lao of Laos advances on the Cambodian capital, Phnom Penh, and, on April 20, the Cambodian government appeals for U.S. assistance.
20 The U.S. president Richard M. Nixon announces the withdrawal of a further 150,000 U.S. troops from Vietnam.
22 The USSR celebrates the centenary of the birth of the communist leader Vladimir Ilyich Lenin.
30 U.S. and South Vietnamese forces attack communist enclaves in Cambodia following advances by communist forces under Pathet Lao.

MAY

- Anti-Vietnam War protestors stage rallies in several U.S. cities. A rally in Washington, D.C., draws 100,000 protestors. Violence erupts on Wall Street in Manhattan, New York, as construction workers break up a rally.
- City and state police officers open fire on demonstrators at a rally at Jackson State College in Mississippi. Two students are killed in the incident.
- The U.S. Senate confirms President Richard M. Nixon's nomination of Minnesota judge Harry A. Blackmun to the U.S. Supreme Court.
1–4 Demonstrations begin at universities across the United States in protest at military intervention in Cambodia; the National Guard fire on a peaceful demonstration at Kent State University, Ohio, killing four students.
2 The United States bombs North Vietnam in the heaviest raids since November 1968.
13 The voting age in Britain is lowered from 21 to 18. Susan Wallace becomes the first person under 21 to vote, when she votes in the Bridgwater by-election.
22 Palestinian terrorists ambush a school bus and kill 12 people in Israel.

23 Government forces attack African guerrilla headquarters in the Portuguese colony of Angola.

27 The opposition Sri Lanka Freedom Party wins a general election in Ceylon and, on May 31, Mrs. Sirimavo Bandaranaike becomes prime minister.

JUNE

- President Richard M. Nixon creates a Commission on Campus Unrest, urging it to propose ways to prevent further episodes of violence.

- The U.S. Supreme Court, in *Welsh v. USA*, rules that conscientious objector status can be based on moral principle as well as on demonstrated religious commitment.

- The U.S. Supreme Court, in *Williams v. Florida*, rules constitutional juries of less than 12 persons.

5 France ends its 15-month boycott of the Western European Union (begun following a still-unresolved dispute over cooperation with the United States in European defense policy).

7 Fighting breaks out in Jordan between the Jordanian army and Palestinian guerrillas. On June 10, King Hussein of Jordan and the leader of the Palestine Liberation Organization (PLO) Yasser Arafat agree a cease-fire.

15 Twelve Russians, mainly Jews, attempt a hijack at Leningrad (now St. Petersburg) airport, USSR. On December 24, they are sentenced to death, though on December 31, this is commuted to life imprisonment.

19 The British prime minister Harold Wilson resigns following the general election and Edward Heath forms a Conservative ministry, with Sir Alec Douglas-Home as foreign secretary, Iain Macleod as chancellor of the Exchequer, and Reginald Maudling as home secretary.

25 The United States proposes the "Rogers Plan" for a cease-fire and United Nations (UN) mediation in the Middle East. The proposal is accepted by the United Arab Republic (UAR) on July 23 and by Israel on August 4.

26 The Czechoslovak Communist Party expels former reforming prime minister Alexander Dubček.

28 U.S. ground troops withdraw from Cambodia.

30 Britain, Denmark, Norway, and Ireland open negotiations in Luxembourg for European Community (EC) membership.

JULY

- Thousands of prowar demonstrators converge on Washington, D.C., to celebrate Honor America Day.

12 China agrees a loan to Tanzania and Zambia to build the "TanZam" railroad.

22 Tanzania, Uganda, and Zambia threaten to leave the Commonwealth if Britain sells arms to South Africa.

AUGUST

- FBI agents capture escaped convict Reverend Daniel J. Berrigan, a Jesuit priest, who had been convicted of destroying draft records in 1968.

- President Richard M. Nixon signs the Postal Reorganization Act, making the U.S. Postal Service an independent organization.

7 A 90-day truce begins between Israel, the United Arab Republic (UAR), and Jordan. On November 5, the truce is renewed for a further 90 days.

12 West Germany and the USSR sign a treaty in Moscow, USSR, renouncing the use of force.

25 The United Nations (UN) mediator Gunnar Jarring meets representatives of Israel, the United Arab Republic (UAR), and Jordan for talks in New York, New York.

SEPTEMBER

- President Richard M. Nixon signs legislation conferring on Washington, D.C., a nonvoting delegate to the U.S. House of Representatives.

- President Richard M. Nixon departs the United States for a whirlwind tour of Europe.

- The California Supreme Court rules unconstitutional a state law prohibiting abortion.

6 Palestinian terrorists hijack four aircraft, one to Cairo, Egypt (where it is blown up on September 7), two to Dawson's Field, Jordan (where it is blown up September 19 without loss of life), and one to Heathrow, London, England (where hijacker Leila Khaled is arrested).

7 An Indian presidential decree abolishes the titles and privileges of ruling princes, but on December 15 the decree is deemed unconstitutional by the courts.

9 Palestinian terrorists hijack a third BOAC airliner to Dawson's Field, Jordan.

16 King Hussein of Jordan orders the Jordanian army to disband the Palestinian militia. On September 17, house-to-house fighting begins in the Jordanian capital, Amman.

19 Palestinian hijackers blow up three aircraft (two hijacked on September 6, one on September 9) at Dawson's Field, Jordan. On September 30, the remaining hostages go free, after Britain, West Germany, and Switzerland release their Palestinian prisoners.

19 Syrian tanks invade Jordan in support of Palestinian guerrillas in conflict with the Jordanian army.

27 King Hussein of Jordan, the leader of the Palestine Liberation Organization (PLO) Yasser Arafat, and other Arab leaders sign an agreement in Cairo, Egypt, to end the civil war in Jordan.

28 President Gamal Abdel Nasser of Egypt dies, and is succeeded on September 29 by Anwar Sadat.

OCTOBER

- In a nationally televised address, President Richard M. Nixon proposes a "standstill cease-fire" in Vietnam. Both sides would remain in place while international arbitrators worked out an acceptable settlement. The North Vietnamese reject Nixon's proposal.

- Militant dissident Angela Davis is arrested in New York, New York, and charged with conspiracy in a court-house jail break on August 7 in San Raphael, California, in which four people died.

- President Richard M. Nixon signs the Organized Crime Control Act.

- President Richard M. Nixon signs the Legislative Reform Act, designed to simplify the convoluted legislative process.

- U.S. agronomist Norman E. Borlaug wins the Nobel Peace Prize. Borlaug has pioneered the development of high-yield grains for developing countries.

5 Quebec separatists kidnap Jasper Cross, the British trade commissioner, in Canada. He is released on December 3.

11 Quebec separatists kidnap Pierre Laporte, the minister of labor. His body is found on October 17.

13 The Peoples' Republic of China establishes diplomatic relations with Canada and, on November 6, with Italy.

23 The former Irish finance minister Charles Haughey is found not guilty of involvement in Irish Republican Army (IRA) gunrunning.

NOVEMBER

- FBI director J. Edgar Hoover informs Congress of an alleged plot to kidnap national security adviser Henry Kissinger and bomb federal buildings in Washington, D.C. The would-be perpetrators of these acts are reported to be Daniel and Philip Berrigan, both Jesuit priests.

- In U.S. Congressional elections, Democrats retain majorities in the House (255–180) and Senate (54–44).

- Lieutenant William L. Calley goes on trial at Fort Benning, Georgia, for his part in the My Lai massacre, where over 100 Vietnamese civilians were shot by U.S. troops under his command on March 16, 1968.

- The U.S. and Mexico sign a treaty designed to resolve years of border disputes.

- The United States and the USSR resume Strategic Arms Limitation Talks (SALT) in Helsinki, Finland. This is the third round of talks.

- Two senior U.S. Coast Guard officers are retired from duty following an incident where the captain of the U.S. Coast Guard vessel *Vigilant* permits Soviet sailors to board his ship and retrieve a Lithuanian sailor seeking asylum in the United States.

8 The United Arab Republic (UAR), Libya, and Sudan agree to form a federation and, on November 27, are joined by Syria.

9 Preliminary Anglo-Rhodesian talks begin in Pretoria, South Africa, to seek the basis for a settlement over the future of Rhodesia.

20 The United Nations (UN) General Assembly votes on whether to admit communist China, but the majority is less than the required two-thirds.

22 White mercenaries supported by the Portuguese government fail in an attempt to invade Guinea and overthrow its government, thus denying its territory to guerrillas operating against Portuguese colonial rule in neighboring Portuguese Guinea (now Guinea-Bissau).

DECEMBER

- President Richard M. Nixon vows to discontinue use of chemical defoliants in the war in Vietnam, after widespread criticism by environmental groups.

- The U.S. Atomic Energy Commission reports having conducted 24 underground nuclear tests beneath the Nevada desert during the past year.

- U.S. troop strength in Vietnam shrinks to 280,000.

2 Portugal grants a measure of autonomy to its colonies of Angola and Mozambique following guerrilla warfare in pursuit of independence.

3–28 A trial of Basque separatists in Burgos, Spain, prompts strikes and demonstrations.

7 The Awami League of Bengali nationalists wins the first free elections in East Pakistan (now Bangladesh) since 1948.

7 West Germany and Poland sign a treaty, formally recognizing the Oder–Neisse Line as the frontier between East Germany and Poland.

13 The Polish government sharply increases food, fuel, and clothing prices. On December 14, strikes, riots, and arson begin in Gdańsk, Poland, spreading to other Baltic ports.

20 Edward Gierek replaces Władysław Gomułka as first secretary of the Polish Communist Party.

30 Peace talks in Paris, France, attempting to find a solution to the Vietnam War, end their second full year, with all sides agreeing there has been no progress.

SCIENCE, TECHNOLOGY, AND MEDICINE

Computing

- The daisy wheel impact printer is introduced for use with computers.

- The U.S. firm IBM develops the floppy disc for storing computer data.

- U.S. computer programmers Kenneth Thomson and Dennis Ritchie develop the UNIX computer operating system. It becomes the standard operating system for computer systems with multiple tasking and multiple users.

- U.S. Control Data Corporation introduces the STAR 100 computer, the first to have a vectorial architecture, in which information is processed as vectors instead of numbers.

- U.S. firm Intel introduces the 1103 RAM (random access memory) chip which can store 1 kilobyte of information.

Ecology

- U.S. population biologists Paul Ralph and Anne Ehrlich publish *Population, Resources, and Experimental Issues in Human Ecology*, in which they predict famine in the 1970s through depletion of resources.

FEBRUARY

- President Richard M. Nixon sends Congress the blueprint for an environmental clean-up bill. Among other initiatives, the president proposes earmarking $10 billion for waste treatment.

APRIL

22 Millions of Americans participate in the first Earth Day, a landmark in the environmental movement.

MAY

21 Heavy floods cause extensive damage and loss of life in Romania.

30 Chimbote in Peru is rocked by an earthquake measuring 7.7 on the Richter scale. The most destructive earthquake so far this century, a huge chunk of Mt. Huascaran, Peru's highest mountain, collapses onto ten villages and completely buries the town of Yungay, killing 20,000 people. Nearly 70,000 are killed altogether.

NOVEMBER

12 A cyclone and tidal wave sweep low-lying islands near Chittagong, East Pakistan (now Bangladesh). Over 300,000 people are killed.

DECEMBER

- The U.S. Environmental Protection Agency is established to set and enforce the country's pollution standards.
- U.S. president Richard M. Nixon signs the Clean Air Act. The act imposes stricter air pollution standards and requires U.S. car manufacturers to reduce emissions of nitrogen dioxide, carbon monoxide, and hydrocarbons by 90% by the mid-1970s.

Exploration

- The Small Astronomy Satellite (SAS) is launched by the United States. It catalogs X-ray sources and leads to the development of the High Energy Astronomy Observatory (HEAO).
- The Soviet spacecraft *Venera 7* transmits information from the surface of Mars.

APRIL

13–17 The U.S. National Aeronautics and Space Administration (NASA) narrowly diverts a disaster aboard the moon-bound spaceship *Apollo 13*, after a canister of liquid oxygen explodes in the command module. The crew of James Lovell, John Swigert, and Fred Haise enter the lunar module, which they use as a "lifeboat" to return safely to earth.

JUNE

- The Soviet spacecraft *Soyuz 9* remains in orbit for 18 days establishing an endurance record.

SEPTEMBER

12–21 The Soviet uncrewed spacecraft *Luna 16* lands on the moon, collects soil samples in a sealed container, and returns to Earth.

NOVEMBER

- The Soviet spacecraft *Luna 17* (launched on November 10) lands on the moon and deploys the remotely-controlled roving Moon vehicle *Lunokhod 1*.

Health and Medicine

- Childproof safety caps for bottles and containers are developed in the United States.
- The Nobel Prize for Physiology or Medicine is awarded jointly to German-born British biochemist Bernard Katz, Swedish biochemist Ulf von Euler, and U.S. biochemist Julius Axelrod for their discoveries concerning the chemical nature of nerve transmission.
- U.S. biochemists Howard Temin and David Baltimore separately discover the enzyme reverse transcriptase, which allows some cancer viruses to transfer their RNA to the DNA of their hosts turning them cancerous—a reversal of the common pattern in which genetic information always passes from DNA to RNA.
- U.S. scientist Edward Shortlife develops MYCIN, a medical expert system used by physicians to diagnose bacterial blood infections and find a suitable treatment. It is formulated on the knowledge of leading authorities and is based on 500 "if-then" questions.

Science

- Argentinean biochemist Luis Leloir receives the Nobel Prize for Chemistry for his discovery of sugar nucleotides and their role in carbohydrate biosynthesis.
- French anthropologist Louis Dumont publishes *Homo Hierarchicus*, a detailed study of the Indian caste system.
- Swedish phycisist Hannes Alfvén shares the Nobel Prize for Physics with French physicist Louis Néel: Alfvén for his work in magneto-hydrodynamics and plasma physics; and Néel for his work in antiferromagnetism and ferrimagnetism and solid state physics.
- The *Orbiting Astronomical Observatory* and *Orbiting Geophysical Observatory* detect hydrogen in the tail of a comet.
- U.S. chemist Albert Ghiorso and colleagues at the University of California, Berkeley, discover the radioactive element hahnium (atomic no. 105), named for the discoverer of nuclear fission Otto Hahn.
- U.S. geneticist Hamilton Smith discovers type II restriction enzyme that breaks the DNA strand at predictable places, making it an invaluable tool in recombinant DNA technology.
- U.S. physicist Sheldon Glashow and associates postulate the existence of a fourth quark, which they name charm.

SEPTEMBER

- Indian-born U.S. biochemist Har Gobind Khorana assembles an artificial yeast gene from its chemical components.

Technology

- Carbon dioxide lasers are first used for industrial cutting and welding.
- The Dutch electronics company Philips launches the first car cassette player in Britain.
- The Effelsberg radio telescope near Bonn, Germany, begins operating; its 100 m/328 ft moveable dish is the largest fully steerable dish in the world.
- The U.S. firm RCA introduces the metal-oxide semiconductor (MOS). It permits integrated circuits to be made smaller and cheaper.
- The U.S. military initiates the Global Positioning System (GPS), consisting of 21 satellites. An individual can determine his or her position anywhere on the earth to within 23 m/75 ft by receiving the radio signals from a minimum of three satellites.
- The U.S. navy begins to rearm its Polaris submarines with Poseidon missiles, which have a range of about 4,500 km/2,800 mi.
- The U.S. survey ship *Glomar Challenger* discovers a huge oil field 3,660 m/12,000 ft under the Gulf of Mexico.
- The use of artificial fabrics such as polyester in clothing becomes increasingly popular.
- U.S. scientist Charles Burrus invents the light-emitting diode (LED).

FEBRUARY

11 Japan launches the satellite *Osumi*, making it the sixth country to place an artificial satellite into Earth's orbit.

APRIL

24 The People's Republic of China launches the satellite *Long March*, making it the seventh nation to place an artificial satellite into Earth's orbit.

Transportation

- The Automatic Car Identification (ACI) system is instituted in the United States. It is a nationwide computerized network for quickly locating railroad rolling stock.
- The National Railroad Passenger Corporation (Amtrak) is established to take over and improve the United States' intercity passenger services.

FEBRUARY

9 Pan Am begins scheduled flights with the Boeing 747 "jumbo jet" airliner, which can accommodate over 400 passengers.

MARCH

- The Indian–Pacific Express enters service between Sydney and Perth on the 3,936-km/2,460-mi Trans-Australian Railroad.

JUNE

- Federal regulators accept Penn Central Railroad's petition for reorganization under federal bankruptcy laws. Penn Central is the nation's largest railroad company.

JULY

5 An Air Canada DC-8 crashes near Toronto, killing 109 people, after two of its engines and part of a wing fall off.

OCTOBER

- President Richard M. Nixon signs legislation creating the National Railroad Passenger Corporation, a semiprivate corporation in charge of interstate passenger traffic.

ARTS AND IDEAS

Architecture

- The Aswan High Dam is completed on the River Nile in Egypt.

DECEMBER

- Work is completed on the north tower of the World Trade Center, New York, New York. At 412 m/ 1,350 ft, it is the tallest building in the world.

Arts

- The French artist Victor Vasarély paints *Orion Noir*.
- The German-born U.S. artist Eva Hesse creates *Untitled (Rope Piece)*, a sculpture made of latex-covered string.
- The U.S. artist Alice Neel paints *Andy Warhol*.
- The U.S. artist John De Andrea sculpts *Standing Man*.

- The U.S. artist Ralph Goings paints *Burger Chef*.
- The U.S. artist Robert Smithson creates *Spiral Jetty*. One of the best-known examples of "land art," it is a spiral walkway of earth and stones 460 m/1,500 ft long built on Great Salt Lake, Utah.

Film

- At the Cannes Film Festival in France, the Palme d'Or is awarded to *M*A*S*H*, based on the novel by Richard Hook and directed by Robert Altman. It is released in the United States and stars Donald Sutherland, Elliott Gould, Robert Duvall, and Sally Kellerman.
- The movie *Airport*, directed by George Seaton, is released in the United States. Based on the novel by Arthur Hailey, it stars Burt Lancaster, Dean Martin, Jean Seberg, and Helen Hayes.
- The movie *Borsalino*, directed by Jacques Deray, is released in France, starring Jean-Paul Belmondo and Alain Delon.
- The movie *Catch 22*, directed by Mike Nichols, is released in the United States. Based on the novel by Joseph Heller, it stars Alan Arkin, Martin Balsam, Richard Benjamin, and Art Garfunkel.
- The movie *Five Easy Pieces*, directed by Bob Rafelson, is released in the United States, starring Jack Nicholson, Karen Black, and Susan Anspach.
- The movie *Kes*, directed by Ken Loach, is released in Britain. Based on Barry Hines's novel *A Kestrel for a Knave*, it stars David Bradley, Lynne Perrie, Colin Welland, and Brian Glover.
- The movie *L'Aveu/The Confession*, directed by the Greek filmmaker Costa-Gavras, is released in France, starring Yves Montand.
- The movie *Le Genou de Claire/Claire's Knee*, directed by Eric Rohmer, is released in France. It is photographed by Nestor Almendros and stars Jean-Claude Brialy and Aurora Cornu.
- The movie *Love Story*, directed by Arthur Hiller, is released in the United States. Based on the novel by Erich Segal, it stars Ali McGraw and Ryan O'Neal.
- The movie *Patton*, directed by Franklin J. Schaffner, is released in the United States, starring George C. Scott and Karl Malden.
- The movie *Performance*, directed by Nicolas Roeg, is released in Britain, starring James Fox and Mick Jagger.
- The movie *The Railway Children*, directed by Lionel Jeffries, is released in Britain. Based on the novel by E. Nesbitt, it stars Jenny Agutter, Bernard Cribbens, and Dinah Sheridan.
- The movie *Woodstock*, a documentary account of the famous 1969 U.S. open-air concert, directed by Michael Wadleigh, is released in the United States. Joan Baez, Crosby, Stills, and Nash, Jefferson Airplane, Richie Havens, Jimi Hendrix, and others appear.
- The first drive-in movie theater in France opens in Paris.

APRIL

7 The 1969 Academy Awards take place. Best Actor: John Wayne, for *True Grit*; Best Supporting Actor: Gig Young, for *They Shoot Horses, Don't They?*; Best Actress: Maggie Smith, for *The Prime of Miss Jean Brodie*; Best Supporting Actress: Goldie Hawn, for *Cactus Flower*; Best Picture: *Midnight Cowboy*, directed

by John Schlesinger; Best Director: John Schlesinger, for *Midnight Cowboy*.

MAY

- Metro-Goldwyn-Mayer studios in Hollywood, Los Angeles, California, hold a large auction of movie props and costumes.

Literature and Language

- The Australian writer Patrick White publishes his novel *The Vivisector*.
- The black writer Gwendolyn Brooks publishes her poetry collection *Family Pictures*.
- The English poet Ted Hughes publishes his poetry collection *Crow*.
- The English-born U.S. writer Denise Levertov publishes her poetry collection *Relearning the Alphabet*.
- The French writer Michel Tournier publishes his novel *Le Roi des aulnes/The Erl King*.
- The Ghanaian writer Ama Ata Aidoo publishes her short-story collection *No Sweetness Here*.
- The Irish-born English writer Iris Murdoch publishes her novel *Bruno's Dream*.
- The Nobel Prize for Literature is awarded to the Russian novelist Alexander Solzhenitsyn.
- The Pulitzer Prize for Biography is awarded to T. Harry Williams for *Huey Long*, the Pulitzer Prize for Poetry is awarded to Richard Howard for *Untitled Subjects*, and the Pulitzer Prize for Fiction is awarded to Jean Stafford for *Collected Stories*.
- The Scottish psychologist R. D. Laing publishes his collection of poems *Knots*.
- The U.S. scholar Roland Bainton publishes *Erasmus of Christendom*.
- The U.S. writer Erich Segal publishes his novella *Love Story*.
- The U.S. writer Eudora Welty publishes her novel *Losing Battles*.
- The U.S. writer John Hawkes publishes his novel *The Blood Oranges*.
- The U.S. writer John Updike publishes his novel *Bech: A Book*.
- The U.S. writer Maya Angelou publishes the first volume of her autobiography, *I Know Why the Caged Bird Sings*. The title comes from a poem by U.S. poet Paul Laurence Dunbar.
- The U.S. writer Richard Bach publishes the allegorical novel *Jonathan Livingston Seagull*, the best-selling novel of the year in the United States.
- The U.S. writer Robert Hayden publishes his poetry collection *Words in the Mourning Time*.
- The U.S. writer Thomas Berger publishes his novel *Vital Part*.
- The U.S. writer W. S. Merwin publishes his poetry collection *The Carrier of Ladders*, which wins the Pulitzer Prize for Poetry.
- There are 36.1 million books published in the United States; 24.3 million copies of new books and 11.8 million copies of reprints.
- U.S. writer Saul Bellow publishes his novel *Mr Sammler's Planet*, for which he wins a National Book Award.

Music

- British pop singer Elton John releases the albums *Elton John* and *Tumbleweed Connection*.
- John Sebastian, the former lead singer of the influential band Lovin' Spoonful, releases his first solo album, *John B Sebastian*.
- Shortly after the deaths of Jimi Hendrix of inhalation asphyxia, associated with alcohol and drugs, and of Janis Joplin from a heroin overdose, the U.S. president Richard M. Nixon appeals for restrictions on pop music that promotes drug use.
- The British heavy metal/rock group Led Zeppelin releases the album *Led Zeppelin III*.
- The British pop group the Kinks releases the single "Lola."
- The British rock group the Beatles releases the single "Let It Be" and an album of the same name. The group officially splits up; all four members release solo albums.
- The British skiffle quartet Mungo Jerry releases the single "In the Summertime."
- The Canadian folk singer Joni Mitchell releases the album *Ladies of the Canyon*.
- The English composer Elisabeth Lutyens completes her choral work *The Roots of the World*.
- The former Beatle George Harrison releases the single "My Sweet Lord."
- The French singer Sacha Distel releases the single "Raindrops Keep Falling on my Head."
- The opera *The Knot Garden*, by the English composer Michael Tippett, is first performed, in London, England.
- The Polish composer Witold Lutosławski completes his Cello Concerto.
- The rock opera *Tommy*, by the British rock group the Who, opens at the Metropolitan Opera House in New York, New York.
- The Russian composer Dmitry Shostakovich completes his String Quartet No. 13.
- The underground music of the 1960s, typified by bands such as Velvet Underground, Pink Floyd, and the early Rolling Stones, has by the end of the decade been absorbed into mainstream culture.
- The U.S. composer George Crumb completes his *Black Angels* for amplified string quartet and his vocal work *Ancient Voices of Children*.
- The U.S. country singer Glen Campbell releases the single "It's Only Make Believe."
- The U.S. duo the Carpenters releases the singles "We've Only Just Begun," written by Burt Bacharach, and "(They Long to Be) Close to You."
- The U.S. folk/rock duo Simon and Garfunkel release the single "Bridge Over Troubled Water" and an album of the same name. It will be the best-selling album of the 1970s in Britain.
- The U.S. pop group the Jackson Five releases the single "I'll Be There."
- The U.S. rock group Bread releases the single "Make It With You."
- The U.S. rock group Creedence Clearwater Revival releases the album *Cosmo's Factory*.

- The U.S. rock group the Grateful Dead release the albums *Workingman's Dead* and *American Beauty*.
- The U.S. rock singer Elvis Presley releases the single "The Wonder of You," the best-selling single of the year in Britain. It reaches No. 9 in the U.S. charts.
- U.S. electronics engineer Robert Moog's synthesizer goes on the market in the United States.

MARCH

11 The pop group the Fifth Dimension wins the Grammy Award for Best Record for "Aquarius"/"Let the Sun Shine In" and the Grammy Award for Best Pop Group.

APRIL

26 The musical *Company*, with lyrics and music by Stephen Sondheim, is first performed, at the Alvin Theater, New York, New York.

Theater and Dance

- The play *Home*, by the English dramatist David Storey, is first performed, in London, England.
- The play *Morte accidentale di un anarchico/Accidental Death of an Anarchist*, by the Italian actor and dramatist Dario Fo, is first performed, in Milan, Italy.
- The play *The Philanthropist*, by the English dramatist Christopher Hampton, is first performed, in London, England.
- The Pulitzer Prize for Drama is awarded to Charles Gordone for *No Place to Be Somebody*.

NOVEMBER

- The Actors Equity Association goes on strike in New York, New York, closing 17 off-Broadway productions. The guild aims to make off-Broadway productions adhere to Broadway standards.

Thought and Scholarship

- The English historian Christopher Hill publishes *God's Englishman: Oliver Cromwell and the English Revolution*.
- The English political philosopher John Plamenatz publishes *Ideology*.
- The first volume of the *Cambridge Ancient History*, 3rd edition, is published, edited by Iorweth Edwards, Cyril Gadd, and Nicholas Hammond.
- The Pulitzer Prize for History is awarded to Dean Acheson for *Present at My Creation: My Years in the State Department*.
- The Pulitzer Prize for General Nonfiction is awarded to Eric H. Erikson for *Gandhi's Truth*.
- The U.S. historian Paul Kleppner publishes *The Cross of Culture: A Social Analysis of Mid-Western Politics, 1850–1900*.
- The U.S. journalist "Studs" Terkel publishes *Hard Times: An Oral History of the Great Depression*.
- The U.S. philosopher W. V. Quine publishes his *Philosophy of Logic* and *The Web of Belief*.
- U.S. academic Alvin Toffler publishes *Future Shock*, an analysis of the impact of technology on human society.

SOCIETY

Everyday Life

- Americans read from a selection of 9,573 different magazines and journals.
- Americans spend $75 billion on health care services, 7% of the Gross National Product, including $27 billion for hospital care.
- Canon Business Machines markets the first pocket calculator, in Japan.
- In the United States, 31% of white males and 39% of white females have completed four years of high school; the corresponding numbers for black males and females are 22% and 25% respectively.
- In the United States, 75% of the students enrolled in the fifth grade eight years earlier have graduated from high school.
- In the United States, the lowest-earning fifth of the population earns 5.4% of the total income; the second fifth earns 12.2%; the third fifth earns 17.6%; the fourth fifth earns 23.8%; and the highest-earning fifth earns 40.9%.
- Long hair for men, previously banned as a sign of Western decadence, is declared legal in the USSR.
- Queen Elizabeth II of England, accompanied by Prince Philip and Princess Anne, conducts the first royal walkabout (brief meeting with the general public on foot) during a tour of New Zealand.
- The median income for families in the United States is $9,867, or $10,236 for white families and $6,516 for blacks and other minorities.
- The midi style of skirt (mid-calf-length) is marketed in the United States and Europe but fails to catch on.
- The population of the world is *c.* 3.7 billion.
- There are 48 million Catholics, 11.6 million Southern Baptists, 10.7 million Methodists, 5.5 million Jews, 3.5 million Episcopalians, and 3 million Presbyterians in the United States.
- U.S. author William Hedgepeth publishes *The Alternative*, a study of commune life in the United States.
- U.S. consumers spend $141 billion on food, beverages, and tobacco; $62 billion on clothes; $178 billion on housing and household operations; and $40 billion on recreation.
- Women's median income in the United States is $5,440; that of men is $9,184.

November 1970–73 In the United States, 81,000 more blacks move from southern states to northern states than vice-versa.

November 1970–79 The number of one-parent families in the United States increases 79%, representing one in five of all families.

November 1970–79 There are over 4 million immigrants to the United States in the period 1970–79, coming mainly from Asia and the Americas.

November 1970–80 There is a 14% average increase in the literacy rate for women worldwide.

JANUARY

- Employees at General Electric end a three-month strike after reaching a new contract.

MARCH

- U.S. postal workers stage their first industry-wide strike in U.S. history. They return to work a week later, but not before the National Guard is summoned to tackle the backup.

APRIL

- The U.S. Census estimates the nation's population at 205,000,000.

SEPTEMBER

9 Ann Summers launches her chain of sex stores with the opening of the Ann Summers Sex Supermarket in London, England.

Media and Communication

- *Essence*, a magazine aimed at young urban black women, hits newsstands in U.S. cities.
- In Britain, *The Times* becomes the first newspaper in the world to use photo-typesetting, initially on its financial pages.
- Many Hollywood movie studios, including MCA and Fox, find themselves in financial trouble and have to make people redundant, when high-budget productions fail to make the anticipated profits.

- The 1969–70 Emmy Awards for television are held. Best Drama Series: *Marcus Welby, MD*; Best Comedy Series: *My World and Welcome To It*; Best Actor in a Drama: Robert Young, for *Marcus Welby, MD*; Best Actress in a Drama: Susan Hampshire, for *The Forsyte Saga*; Best Actor in a Comedy: Carroll O'Connor, for *All in the Family*; Best Actress in a Comedy: Hope Lange, for *The Ghost and Mrs Muir*.
- The British tabloid newspaper the *Sun* features its first topless woman on page three.
- The word "terrorism" first appears in the *New York Times* index.

APRIL

1 President Richard M. Nixon signs a bill banning cigarette advertising on U.S. radio and television. This takes effect the following year.

SEPTEMBER

17–June 27, 1974 *The Flip Wilson Show* appears on U.S. television and wins an Emmy award for outstanding variety series after its first year on air. Flip Wilson is the first black performer to succeed as the host of his own variety hour on U.S. television.

19–September 3, 1977 The *Mary Tyler Moore Show*, a television situation comedy, provides realistic insight into the lives of single career women in the United States in the 1970s. Mary Tyler Moore stars as Mary Richards, a single woman working at a television

BIRTHS & DEATHS

FEBRUARY

2 Bertrand Russell, British philosopher, dies near Penryhndeudraeth, Merioneth, Wales (97).

2 Marc Rothko, U.S. abstract expressionist painter, dies in New York, New York (66).

20 Noureddine Moreci, Algerian long-distance runner, born in Tenes, Algeria.

MARCH

11 Erle Stanley Gardner, U.S. lawyer and author who created the private detective Perry Mason, dies in Temecula, California (80).

APRIL

16 Richard Joseph Neutra, Austrian-born U.S. architect who introduced the International style into U.S. architecture, dies in Wuppertal, West Germany (78).

26 Gypsy Rose Lee, U.S. striptease artist and entertainer, dies in Los Angeles, California (56).

MAY

31 Terry Sawchuck, Canadian-U.S. ice-hockey goalkeeper, dies in New York, New York (50).

JUNE

4 Hjalmar Schacht, German financial advisor who ended Germany's

runaway inflation in the early 1920s, dies in Munich, Germany (93).

7 E(dward) M(organ) Forster, English novelist best known for *Howards End* (1910) and *A Passage to India* (1924), dies in Coventry, Warwickshire, England (91).

11 Alexander Kerensky, Russian revolutionary and head of the Russian provisional government July–October 1917, dies in New York, New York (89).

21 Achmed Sukarno, leader of Indonesia's independence movement and the country's first president 1949–66, dies in Jakarta, Indonesia (69).

JULY

27 Antonio Salazar, prime minister of Portugal 1932–68, dies in Lisbon, Portugal (81).

AUGUST

23 River Phoenix, U.S. actor, born in Madras, Ohio (–1993).

SEPTEMBER

1 François Mauriac, French novelist and playwright, dies in Paris, France (84).

3 Vince Lombardi, U.S. football coach who led the Green Bay Packers to five NFL championships, dies in Washington, D.C. (57).

14 Rudolf Carnap, U.S. philosopher of logical positivism, dies in Santa Monica, California (79).

18 Jimi Hendrix, U.S. rock singer and influential guitarist, dies as a result of mixing drugs and alcohol in London, England (27).

28 Gamal Abdel Nasser, prime minister of Egypt 1954–56 and then president 1956–70, dies in Cairo, Egypt (52).

OCTOBER

10 Edouard Daladier, French premier 1933, 1934, and 1938–40 who signed the Munich Agreement (1938) allowing Hitler to occupy Czechoslovakia unopposed, dies in Paris, France (86).

19 Lázaro Cárdenas, president of Mexico (1934–40) who redistributed vast amounts of land to Mexican peasants, dies in Mexico City, Mexico (75).

NOVEMBER

9 Charles de Gaulle, French general and president of France 1958–69, dies in Colombey-les-Deux-Eglises, France (79).

station; Ed Asner, Ted Knight, and Valerie Harper also star.

25–August 31, 1974 *The Partridge Family*, the story of a family rock group, is shown on U.S. television and launches the musical career of the pop rock singer David Cassidy. It also stars Shirley Jones, Susan Dey, and Danny Bonaduce.

Religion

JANUARY
- Joseph Fielding Smith becomes head of the Mormon Church. He succeeds David O. McKay, who died on January 18 at age 96.

MARCH
- The Old Testament and Apocrypha of the New English Bible, new translations of the original Hebrew and Greek texts, are published. Startlingly different from the King James Bible, they cause great controversy.

SEPTEMBER
- The unexpurgated New American Bible appears. It becomes the first Bible published by the Catholic Church to be written in English.

Sports

- For the third successive year, Louisiana State University's Pete Maravich sets an all-time college basketball season scoring record, with 1,381 points at an average of 44.5 points per game. In three years at LSU he scored a record 3,667 points at an average of 44.2 points per game.
- Professional American football is reorganized into two "conferences," the National Football Conference (NFC) and the American Football Conference (AFC), each with 13 teams and 3 divisions.
- Robert Young of Australia wins the inaugural World Professional Surfing Championships.
- The English World Cup soccer squad sets a trend for World Cup songs when it records the single "Back Home" as a prelude to participation in the 1970 World Cup in Mexico.
- The first multistyle karate world championships are staged in Tokyo, Japan, by the All-Japan Karate-do Organization (FAJKO).
- The U.S. jockey Bill Shoemaker surpasses fellow U.S. rider Johnny Longden's world record of 6,032 career wins.

JANUARY
January–September The Australian tennis player Margaret Court becomes only the second woman (after Maureen Connolly in 1953) to achieve the Grand Slam, winning all four major tennis tournaments (the Australian Open, the French Open, Wimbledon, and the U.S. Open) in the same calendar year.

11 The Kansas City Chiefs defeat the Minnesota Vikings 23–7 in Super Bowl IV, before a crowd of 80,562 at Tulane Stadium, New Orleans, Louisiana. The gate receipts of $3.8 million break the record for a one-day sporting event.

28 The black U.S. tennis player Arthur Ashe is unable to compete in the South African tennis championships after the apartheid South African government refuses him an entry visa.

FEBRUARY
16 The U.S. boxer Joe Frazier becomes the undisputed world heavyweight champion, stopping fellow U.S. fighter Jimmy Ellis in five rounds in New York, New York.

MAY
2 U.S. jockey Diane Crump is the first woman jockey to ride in the Kentucky Derby in the United States; she finishes 12th on Fathom.

JUNE
June–September Nijinsky, ridden by the English jockey Lester Piggott, is the first winner of the English Triple Crown (2,000 Guineas, Derby, and St. Leger) since Bahram in 1935. He also wins the King George VI and Queen Elizabeth Diamond Stakes and the Irish Derby in the same year.

21 Brazil defeats Italy 4–1 in the soccer World Cup final in Mexico City, Mexico, to become the first side to win the competition three times.

21 The English golfer Tony Jacklin wins the U.S. Open at Hazeltine Golf Club, Minnesota; he is the first Briton to win it since Ted Ray in 1920.

SEPTEMBER
13 Ken Rosewall of Australia wins the men's singles title at the U.S. Open tennis championships, 14 years after his last victory in the event.

24 A group of women tennis players led by the U.S. player Billie Jean King, unhappy at the disparity in prize money between men's and women's tournaments put on by the U.S. promoter Jack Kramer, sign up with the Phillip Morris tobacco company to form the lucrative Virginia Slims series.

OCTOBER
23 The U.S. driver Gary Gabelich sets a new world land-speed record of 1,001.639 kph/622.407 mph in a rocket-powered car at Bourneville Salt Flats, Utah.

1971

POLITICS, GOVERNMENT, AND ECONOMICS

Business and Economics

FEBRUARY

14 International oil companies accept the higher prices demanded by the Gulf States.

APRIL

19 British unemployment, at 3.4%, reaches its highest level since May 1940.

MAY

5 European currency markets close following their flight from the U.S. dollar into West German marks.

JUNE

7 Britain and the European Economic Community (Common Market) come to an agreement on Commonwealth sugar and the status of sterling.

AUGUST

27 Japan floats the yen.

DECEMBER

18 The United States devalues the dollar by 7.9% and lifts its import surcharge. Other major currencies are realigned accordingly.

Colonization

APRIL

19 Sierra Leone becomes a republic within the Commonwealth.

AUGUST

15 Bahrain declares its independence from Britain.

SEPTEMBER

1 Qatar declares its independence from Britain.

Human Rights

• Over 300 women in France announce they have had abortions and demand legalization of the procedure.

JANUARY

• The U.S. Supreme Court, in the case *Griggs v. Duke Power Company*, rules that businesses must apply the same hiring criteria to men and women alike, thereby upholding the hiring provisions of the 1964 Civil Rights Act.

Politics and Government

• The administration of Bantu areas in South Africa is vested in 16 (later 12) boards, reporting directly to the government in Pretoria, so removing the responsibility of town councils for their areas.

• The South Pacific Forum is formed on the initiative of New Zealand. It provides for occasional meetings of the heads of state of South Pacific countries.

JANUARY

• The U.S. president Richard M. Nixon signs the Omnibus Crime Control Act. The act allocates over $3.5 billion for state and local law enforcement.

January–April Charles Manson and three accomplices are convicted of murdering the U.S. actress Sharon Tate and six others in August 1969. The guilty are sentenced to death on April 19.

1 The Divorce Reform Act in Britain permits the dissolution of a marriage by consent after a two-year separation.

3 Sheikh Mujibur Rahman, the leader of the Awami League, which has a majority in the all-Pakistan National Assembly, pledges to seek full autonomy for East Pakistan in its proposed new constitution.

5 The Jewish state of Israel and the Arab states of Egypt and Jordan resume indirect peace talks under a United Nations mediator.

8 Left wing Tupamaros guerrillas kidnap Geoffrey Jackson, the British ambassador to Uruguay.

12 "Angry Brigade" anarchists in Britain bomb the Hertfordshire home of the employment minister Robert Carr.

25 General Idi Amin succeeds President Milton Obote of Uganda in a bloodless coup, accusing him of corruption and inegalitarian economic policies.

31 A telephone service between East and West Berlin, East and West Germany, is reestablished after 19 years.

FEBRUARY

• A race riot erupts in Wilmington, North Carolina, after a white policeman shoots a black youth. When an armed white man is killed in retaliation, police arrest Benjamin Chavis, field director of the United Church of Christ, and nine others for fire-bombing a local grocery store.

• The U.S. Supreme Court mitigates its decision in the 1966 *Miranda v. Arizona* case, ruling that a defendant's words, even if illegally obtained, may be used against the defendant's own testimony.

1　Robert Curtis becomes the first British soldier to be killed on duty in Northern Ireland during violent riots in Belfast.

4　In the Arab–Israeli wars, Egypt extends its cease-fire and offers to reopen the Suez Canal if Israel withdraws from the Egyptian peninsula of Sinai.

7　A referendum in Switzerland gives women the vote in national elections.

11　Forty nations, including the United States, the USSR, and Britain, sign a treaty banning atomic weapons from the seabed.

13　South Vietnamese troops invade Laos to close the Ho Chi Minh Trail to the North Vietnamese.

14　The USSR announces its ninth five-year plan, with a high priority for consumer goods.

15　Israel affirms a Jewish settlement policy in its occupied territories.

20　An emergency warning of nuclear attack is broadcast by mistake in the United States.

20　Spanish bishops call for the separation of church and state.

24　The British government publishes the Immigration Bill to restrict the rights of abode of Commonwealth citizens in the UK.

March

- President Tito of Yugoslavia becomes the first communist head of state to be received officially by the pope.

- The anarchist group Weather Underground bombs the U.S. Capitol in Washington, D.C., wreaking an estimated $300,000's worth of damage.

- The Bantu Homelands Constitution Act enables the South African state president to proclaim self-government for any of the eight African territorial authorities.

- The U.S. Supreme Court rules that only individuals opposed to all war, rather than to a given war, will be granted conscientious objector status.

1　A postponement of the establishment of the new Pakistani constituent assembly provokes a general strike in East Pakistan.

7　The Middle East cease-fire expires and is accompanied by the decision to withhold fire along the Suez Canal.

10　Indira Gandhi's Congress Party wins a landslide victory in the Indian general election.

10　Soviet Jews demanding emigration permits occupy the offices of the Supreme Soviet in Moscow, USSR.

10　Three off-duty British soldiers, two of them teenage brothers, are shot dead in a public house in a suburb of Belfast, Northern Ireland.

10　William MacMahon succeeds John Gorton as prime minister of Australia.

12　Demonstrators in Belfast, Northern Ireland, demand the internment of the Irish Republican Army (IRA) leaders.

23　The Unionist politician Brian Faulkner becomes prime minister of Northern Ireland.

26　Renewed conflict breaks out between the Jordanian army and Palestinians in Jordan.

26　Sheikh Mujibur Rahman, the leader of the Awami League, which has a majority in the all-Pakistan National Assembly, declares the independence of East Pakistan as Bangladesh ("Bengali country"). The split sparks a civil war.

31　The U.S. lieutenant William Calley is sentenced to life imprisonment for the My Lai massacre of 109 civilians in South Vietnam by U.S. troops in March 1968. On August 20, 1971, Lieutenant Calley's prison term is reduced to 20 years.

April

2　Pakistan protests against Indian support for East Pakistani separatism.

5–23　A violent left wing antigovernment rebellion erupts in Ceylon (now Sri Lanka), as a response to the sudden assumption of sweeping emergency powers.

7　The U.S. president Richard M. Nixon announces the withdrawal of 100,000 more troops from Vietnam by December 1.

13　Rioting breaks out in Belfast, Northern Ireland, after Irish Republican Army (IRA) gunmen fire on an Orangemen's (Protestant) parade.

15　Britain restores its telephone link with China, broken off in 1949 when the People's Republic of China was declared by Mao Zedong.

17　Egypt, Syria, and Libya sign the Benghazi Agreement to establish the Federation of Arab Republics that, based on democratic socialism, creates a joint defense policy and pursues a hard-line attitude toward Israel.

25　Two hundred thousand people demonstrate in Washington, D.C., against the Vietnam War. Twelve thousand protestors are arrested the following week.

29　U.S. combat deaths in the Vietnam War exceed 45,000.

May

3　Erich Honecker succeeds Walter Ulbricht as first secretary of the Socialist Unity Party of East Germany.

6　Greece and Albania resume diplomatic relations.

14　A plot to overthrow President Sadat of Egypt is foiled.

20　A court in Leningrad (now St. Petersburg), USSR, sentences nine Jews to hard labor for anti-Soviet activities.

20–21　The British prime minister Edward Heath and the French president Georges Pompidou, meeting in Paris, France, reach a general agreement on terms for British membership in the European Economic Community (Common Market).

27　Egypt signs a 15-year treaty of friendship with the USSR.

28　Chile and the USSR sign an agreement on economic cooperation.

31　India requests international aid for the millions of refugees from the civil war caused by the declaration of independence of East Pakistan as Bangladesh on March 26.

June

- The U.S. Federal Trade Commission informs manufacturers that they will be held liable for false or inflated advertising claims.

- The U.S. Supreme Court declares that states may not pay for nonreligious instruction in parochial schools.

- U.S. federal marshals end a 19-month occupation of Alcatraz Island in San Francisco Bay, California, by Native Americans who have claimed the site under the terms of a treaty promising to provide Native Americans with unused federal lands.

10　The United States ends its 21-year embargo on trade with China, which had been imposed by U.S. president Harry S. Truman during the Cold War.

21 The International Court of Justice in The Hague, the Netherlands, rules South Africa's administration of Namibia (South West Africa) to be illegal.

22 The prime minister of Malta Dom Mintoff demands the resignation of the British governor-general and a renegotiation of the British–Maltese defense agreement.

23 A final agreement on British entry to the European Economic Community (Common Market) is reached.

30 The 26th Amendment to the U.S. Constitution extends full voting rights to 18-year-olds.

30 The Yugoslav Federal Assembly passes 23 amendments to the 1963 constitution, devolving power to the constituent republics.

July

• The U.S. army announces that it will test all U.S. personnel serving in Vietnam for the drug heroin.

3 The Indonesian government wins a clear victory in the first general election for 16 years.

9 Two rioters are shot dead by troops in Londonderry, Northern Ireland.

10 Rebel soldiers in Morocco fail in a coup to depose King Hassan. Three days later, ten of their leaders are executed.

13–19 Heavy fighting takes place in Jordan between the Jordanian army and Palestinian guerrillas, with 1,500 guerrillas captured by July 19.

15 The U.S. president Richard M. Nixon announces that he will visit China in 1972.

18 Iraq closes its border with Jordan in protest at the Jordanian suppression of the Palestinian guerrilla movement.

23 Syria closes its border with Jordan in protest at the Jordanian suppression of the Palestinian guerrilla movement.

25 The East Caribbean states sign the Declaration of Grenada on political union.

August

• The U.S. Congress authorizes a payment of $250 million to bail out the struggling Lockheed Aircraft Corporation.

5 The United States and the USSR present a draft treaty at the Geneva Disarmament Conference for the banning of biological weapons.

9 The Northern Ireland government introduces internment and forbids processions.

9–11 Over 22 people in Northern Ireland die in fighting between British troops and the Irish Republican Army (IRA) in Belfast, Newry, and Londonderry. The Republic of Ireland opens a refugee camp for Catholics.

15 The U.S. president Richard M. Nixon introduces a "New Economic Policy," effectively ending the 1944 Bretton Woods system. The new policy suspends the conversion of dollars into gold and imposes a 90-day wage freeze and a 10% import surcharge, following the first U.S. trade deficit since 1894.

18 Australia and New Zealand announce the withdrawal of their forces from the Vietnam War.

19 NATO (the North Atlantic Treaty Organization) transfers its Mediterranean naval headquarters from Malta to Naples, Italy.

19 Sharp exchanges over Northern Ireland between the British prime minister Edward Heath and the Irish prime minister John Lynch bring Anglo-Irish relations close to breaking point.

24 Government changes in Greece strengthen the power of the prime minister, George Papadopoulos.

31 The British government orders an inquiry into the alleged ill-treatment of internees in Northern Ireland.

September

3 The United States, Britain, France, and the USSR sign the Berlin Agreement on communications between West Berlin and West Germany.

6 Over 100 Tupamaros Marxist urban guerrillas escape from prison in Bolivia.

9 Geoffrey Jackson, the British ambassador to Uruguay, is released by the Tupamaros guerrillas who had kidnapped him on January 8.

9–13 Four guards and 39 inmates die in a riot at Attica Correctional Facility in Attica, New York State. The riot erupted after inmates discovered apparent racial bias in sentencing and parole policy.

24 Britain requests the departure of 90 Soviet diplomats for alleged espionage.

27 The Roman Catholic cardinal József Mindszenty leaves Hungary after 15 years as a refugee from the communist government in the U.S. embassy and goes into exile in Austria.

27–28 The British, Irish, and Northern Ireland prime ministers, Edward Heath, John Lynch, and Brian Faulkner, meet to discuss Northern Ireland, but agree only to condemn violence.

October

1 Dutch foreign minister Joseph Luns succeeds Manlio Brosio as secretary-general of NATO (the North Atlantic Treaty Organization).

3 President Nguyen Van Thieu of South Vietnam retains office after all other candidates withdraw in protest at rigged elections.

5 Emperor Hirohito of Japan visits Britain for the first time since World War II.

7 Britain sends 1,500 more soldiers to Northern Ireland.

8 The USSR expels or bars 18 Britons in retaliation for Britain's requested departure of 90 Soviet diplomats on September 24.

12 Against growing resentment of his regime, the Shah of Iran gives a spectacular party to celebrate the 2,500th anniversary of the Persian Empire of Cyrus the Great.

20 The West German chancellor Willy Brandt is awarded the Nobel Peace Prize.

25 The United Nations General Assembly votes to admit communist China (the People's Republic of China) and expel Taiwan (the Republic of China).

27 President Mobutu of the Congo changes the name of his country to Zaire.

28 The British House of Commons votes 356–244 in favor of Britain's entry to the European Economic Community (Common Market). Sixty-nine Labour members of Parliament vote with the government, and 39 Conservative members with the opposition.

November

3 Britain annexes the small island of Rockall in the North Atlantic.

10–December 4 The communist prime minister of Cuba Fidel Castro visits Chile in order to demonstrate support for the embattled President Salvador Allende and to champion socialist revolution.

12 The U.S. president Richard M. Nixon proclaims the end of the U.S. offensive role in the Vietnam War and withdraws 45,000 more troops.

15 The British foreign secretary Alec Douglas-Home opens talks in Salisbury, Rhodesia (now Harare, Zimbabwe), with the Rhodesian prime minister Ian Smith, on a new Rhodesian constitution.

15 The representative of the People's Republic of China takes his seat in the United Nations General Assembly.

16 The Compton Report rejects allegations of brutality in internment camps in Northern Ireland.

17 The administration of Thailand is taken over by the National Executive Council following a military coup.

22 Pakistan accuses India of invading East Pakistan, which declared its independence on March 26.

24 An agreement is reached between the British foreign secretary Alec Douglas-Home and the Rhodesian prime minister Ian Smith on a new Rhodesian constitution.

25 Harold Wilson, the British Labour leader, proposes the unification of Ireland in 15 years' time.

28 Palestinian terrorists murder the Jordanian prime minister Wasfi Tell.

30 Iran occupies the Tunbs Islands in the Persian Gulf one day before the British protectorate expires. Iraq severs diplomatic relations with Iran and Britain, alleging collusion.

DECEMBER

• The U.S. Senate confirms the nomination of Lewis F. Powell to the Supreme Court. Four days later, the Senate confirms the nomination to the Supreme Court of William R. Rehnquist.

1 Following the murder of the Jordanian prime minister by Palestinian terrorists on November 28, King Hussein of Jordan rules out further talks with the Palestinian guerrillas.

1 President Tito of Yugoslavia purges the Croat leadership of nationalists.

2 The seven emirates of Abu Dhabi, Sharjah, Dubai, Umm al Qaiwain, Ras al Khaimah, Ajman, and Fujairah form the United Arab Emirates.

3 Pakistan bombs Indian airfields in retaliation for India's intervention in support of the independence of East Pakistan.

4 An Irish Republican Army (IRA) explosion in a Belfast public house, Northern Ireland, kills 15 civilians. Subsequent reprisals bring the annual death toll to 173, including 43 British troops.

6 India recognizes the independence of East Pakistan as Bangladesh. War breaks out along the border between India and West Pakistan.

16 East Pakistani forces surrender to India after its recognition of East Pakistan's independence as Bangladesh. India orders a cease-fire on the West Pakistan front and, on December 17, a cease-fire is declared in West Pakistan.

16 Leaders of the Zimbabwe African National Union (Patriotic Front (ZANU (PF)) and the Zimbabwe African People's Union (ZAPU) form the African National Council with the aim of rejecting the Anglo-Rhodesian independence settlement, which favors white majority rule.

20 Sheikh Mujibur Rahman, the leader of the Awami League, who declared the independence of East Pakistan as Bangladesh in March, is released from prison in West Pakistan and flown to London, England.

20 Zulfikar Ali Bhutto replaces Yahya Khan as president of Pakistan.

24 Malta makes an ultimatum to Britain, asking it to pay £18 million for the use of its naval bases or withdraw by the end of the year. On December 20, Malta extends its ultimatum.

31 The Austrian diplomat Kurt Waldheim takes office as secretary-general of the United Nations.

SCIENCE, TECHNOLOGY, AND MEDICINE

Computing

c. 1971 The programming language C is developed by Dennis Ritchie and Kenneth Thompson at Bell Laboratories; it is the preferred language of professional programmers and is widely used for writing software packages.

• Dot matrix printers are first introduced.

• U.S. programmer Raj Reddy develops a software program that allows computers to recognize human speech.

NOVEMBER

1 U.S. firm Intel introduces the 4-bit 0.1MHz 4004 microprocessor; devised by Ted Hoff, and containing 2,250 transistors, it is labeled a "micro-programmable computer on a chip." It can only process 4 bits (binary digits) of information at a time, but has about the same calculating power as ENIAC (Electronic Numerical Integrator, Analyzer, and Calculator) and allows the development of microcomputers.

Ecology

• Canada inaugurates the world's first nuclear power station cooled by ordinary water.

• Greenpeace, the environmental campaign organization, is founded to protest against U.S. nuclear testing at Amchitka Island, Alaska.

• Mt. Etna in Italy erupts and enters a phase of near continuous eruption for the next decade.

• The Arun natural gas field, the largest in Asia, is discovered in Indonesia; its reserves are estimated at 4.25 trillion cubic meters.

• The Bovanenkovskoye natural gas field is discovered in northwestern Siberia; the third largest field in the USSR, its reserves are estimated at 4.2 trillion cubic meters.

• The U.S. Department of the Interior and a consortium of utility companies propose strip-mining for coal in the northern midwest United States in order to supply power; their proposal is severely criticized by environmentalists.

- The United States bans the importation of all whale products.

JANUARY

- The U.S. political activist Ralph Nader founds the Earth Act Group, an environmental protection organization.

FEBRUARY

- An earthquake rocks southern California, killing 65 people and wreaking over $500 million worth of damage.
10 Los Angeles, California, is struck by an earthquake measuring 6.6 on the Richter scale; 51 people are killed and hundreds injured.
21 A series of tornadoes rips through Mississippi and Louisiana, killing 117 people.

AUGUST

- North Vietnam is inundated by severe flooding and more than 100,000 people die.

DECEMBER

25 A fire in a hotel in Seoul, South Korea, kills 162 people.

Exploration

- Anthropologists discover a stone-age tribe known as the Tasadays, living in caves on the island of Mindanao in the Philippines; they are subsequently revealed to be local villagers and their cultural identity a hoax perpetrated by politicians for publicity.

JANUARY

January–February The U.S. National Aeronautics and Space Administration (NASA) launches the U.S. spaceship *Apollo 14*. Under the command of the U.S. astronaut Alan B. Shepard, it reaches the moon on February 5 and returns to Earth four days later having collected 43 kg/95 lb of lunar rock.

APRIL

19 The USSR launches the 7.6-m/25-ft-long *Salyut 1* space station. Visited by a three-person crew on June 7–29, the cosmonauts die during their return to Earth when a faulty valve causes their capsule to lose pressure. The station reenters the earth's atmosphere six months later.

MAY

May–November The U.S. National Aeronautics and Space Administration (NASA) uncrewed spacecraft *Mariner 8* plummets into the Atlantic Ocean after the failure of a booster rocket.

JULY

26–August 7 The U.S. National Aeronautics and Space Administration (NASA) spaceship *Apollo 15*, commanded by the U.S. astronaut David R. Scott, is sent to the moon. It contains a lunar roving vehicle that enables Scott and his fellow crewman James B. Irwin to explore 27 km/17 mi of the lunar surface.

NOVEMBER

12 The U.S. space probe *Mariner 9* (launched in May) becomes the first artificial object to orbit another planet (Mars); it transmits 7,329 photographs of the planet and its two moons, Deimos and Phobos.
27 The Soviet craft *Mars 2* (launched in May) goes into orbit around Mars; a capsule from *Mars 3* lands on the planet, but its transmitters go dead after 20 seconds.

Health and Medicine

- A replacement knee joint is developed by Canadian surgeon Frank H. Gunston.
- An intrauterine contraceptive device (IUD) called the Dalkon Shield is introduced in the United States; 4 million are sold before infections, miscarriages, and birth defects are linked to the device and it is removed from the market.
- British physicians C. A. L. Bassett, R. J. Pawluk, and R. O. Becker discover that electric current speeds up the healing of fractures.
- Compulsory health insurance is extended to all Canadian provinces.
- Polish-born U.S. endocrinologist Andrew Schally isolates the luteinizing hormone-releasing hormone (LH-RH), essential to human ovulation.
- Surgeons develop the fibreoptic endoscope, making it possible to view inside the human body by inserting catheters into the arms or legs and manipulating them into organs, such as the heart.
- The anticancer drug Taxol is isolated by U.S. chemist Monroe Wall from the bark of the Pacific Yew tree (*Taxus brevifolia*).
- The Royal College of Surgeons in England reports that deaths due to cigarette smoking are comparable to the typhoid and cholera epidemics of the 19th century.
- U.S. biochemist Earl Sutherland receives the Nobel Prize for Physiology or Medicine for his discovery of cyclic AMP, a chemical messenger that plays a role in the action of many hormones.
c. 1971–c. 1980 Compressed air turbines begin to replace electric dental drills.

JANUARY

6 Choh Hao Li and associates at the University of California Medical Center announce the synthesis of the human growth hormone somatotrophin.

DECEMBER

24 President Richard M. Nixon authorizes the National Cancer Institute to spend $1.5 billion per year to fight cancer.

Science

- Canadian chemist Gerhard Herzberg receives the Nobel Prize for Chemistry for electron structure and geometry of molecules, particularly free radicals.
- English primatologist Jane Goodall publishes *In the Shadow of Man*, a study of chimpanzee behavior.
- English theoretical physicist Stephen Hawking suggests that after the Big Bang, mini black holes no bigger than a proton but containing more than a billion metric tons of mass were formed and that they were governed by both the laws of relativity and of quantum mechanics.
- The binary X-ray system Cygnus X-1 is discovered; the center is believed to contain a black hole.
- The Nobel Prize for Physics is awarded to Hungarian-born British physicist Dennis Gabor for the invention of holography.
- U.S. chemist R. B. Woodward and Swiss chemist A. Eschenmoser synthesize vitamin B_{12}.
- U.S. dendrochronologist Charles Ferguson of the University of Arizona establishes a tree-ring chronology dating back to c. 6000 BC.

December 1971–85   The optical parametric oscillator is developed by numerous physicists over a 15-year period; it uses photons to measure small movements of particles due to gravitational waves.

JULY

- In its report to Congress, *A Metric America: A Decision Whose Time has Come*, the U.S. National Bureau of Standards recommends that the United States change to the International Metric System over a period of ten years.

Technology

c. 1971   A technique known as large-scale integration (LSI) is developed in the United States which makes it possible to pack thousands of transistors, diodes, and resistors on a silicon chip less than 5 mm/0.2 in square; it makes possible the development of microprocessors and microcomputers.

- Swiss programmer Niklaus Wirth develops the computer language PASCAL. It is designed as a teaching tool for computer programming and allows errors to be discovered quickly.
- The "Poketronic" is launched in the United States by Texas Instruments; the first battery-powered pocket calculator it weighs more than 1 kg/2.2 lb, can only add, subtract, multiply, and divide and costs $150.
- The quadraphonic sound reproduction system is introduced.
- The U.S. telecommunications firm AT&T introduces the "picture-phone" in Chicago, Illinois, and Pittsburgh, Pennsylvania—its high cost makes it a commercial failure.

JANUARY

- *Intelsat 4* is launched; it can handle 3,000–9,000 telephone circuits or 12 color television channels simultaneously.
- 15 The Aswan High Dam in Egypt is officially opened. Its reservoir, Lake Nasser, is 300 km/186 mi long and necessitated the relocation of the Abu Simbel temple complex. The dam allows Egypt to control the annual flooding of the Nile but increases incidence of the disease schistosomiasis.

Transportation

- General Motors recalls 6.7 million vehicles in the United States to install restraint mounts; it is the largest recall of cars in history.
- Japan launches the world's largest supertanker, the *Nisseki Maru*; it weighs 372,000 metric tons/366,000 tons.
- The Soviet military transport plane *Ilyushin IL-76* makes its first test flight; it can carry loads of up to 40,000 kg/ 88,000 lb.

FEBRUARY

- The U.S. Federal Aviation Authority orders U.S. airline companies to screen all domestic and foreign passengers and luggage for weapons and explosives.
- 4 The prestigious Rolls Royce company, the manufacturer of luxury cars, goes bankrupt. To save face and to prevent job losses, the British government intervenes.

MAY

1 Amtrak (the National Railroad Passenger Corporation) takes over the running of passenger trains to improve passenger service in the United States.

JULY

30 A Japanese Boeing 727 collides in midair with a Japanese fighter over Morioka, Japan; 162 people die.

SEPTEMBER

4 An Alaskan Airlines Boeing 727 crashes in Tongass National Forest in Alaska; 119 people are killed.

ARTS AND IDEAS

Architecture

- The Audience Hall, designed by the Italian artist Pier Luigi Nervi, is completed in the Vatican.

Arts

- The Cleveland Museum of Art, designed by the architects Marcel Breuer and Hamilton Smith, is completed in Cleveland, Ohio.
- The English artist David Hockney paints *Rubber Ring Floating in a Swimming Pool* and *Mr and Mrs Ossie Clark and Percy*.
- The French-born U.S. sculptor Louise Bourgeois creates the sculpture *Trani Episode*.
- The German artist Anselm Kiefer paints *Mann im Wald/ Man in a Wood*.
- Three major art exhibitions are dominated by conceptual art: the Biennale in Paris, France; Prospect 71 in Düsseldorf, West Germany; and 6th Guggenheim International in New York.

Film

- The controversial movie *A Clockwork Orange* is released in the United States. Based on Anthony Burgess' novel, it is directed by Stanley Kubrick and stars Malcolm McDowell.
- The controversial movie *Straw Dogs*, which features a graphic rape scene and extended sequences of violence, is released in the United States. It is directed by Sam Peckinpah and stars Dustin Hoffman and Susan George.
- The movie *10 Rillington Place* is released in the UK. It is directed by the U.S. filmmaker Richard Fleischer and stars Richard Attenborough and Judy Geeson.
- The movie *Bananas*, directed by and starring Woody Allen, is released in the United States. It costars Louise Lasser.
- The movie *Carnal Knowledge* is released in the United States. It is directed by Mike Nichols and stars Jack Nicholson and Art Garfunkel.
- The movie *Death in Venice* is released in Italy. Based on a novella by German writer Thomas Mann, it is directed by Luchino Visconti and stars the English actor Dirk Bogarde.

- The movie *Die Angst des Tormanns beim Elfmeter/The Goalkeeper's Fear of the Penalty*, directed by Wim Wenders, is released in West Germany, based on the novel by Peter Handke and starring Arthur Brauss.
- The movie *Dirty Harry* is released in the United States. It is directed by Don Siegel and stars Clint Eastwood.
- The movie *Fiddler on the Roof* is released in the United States. An adaption of a long-running musical, it is directed by Norman Jewison and stars Chaim Topol.
- The movie *I Racconti di Canterbury/The Canterbury Tales*, directed by Pier Paolo Pasolini, is released in Italy. The director features as Chaucer in the movie. He also writes and directs the movie *Il Decamerone/The Decameron*, which is released in Italy. It is based on the medieval writer Giovanni Boccaccio's collection of stories.
- The movie *Il Giardino dei Finzi-Contini/The Garden of the Finzi-Continis*, directed by Vittorio De Sica, is released in Italy. It stars Dominique Sanda, Lino Capolicchio, and Helmut Berger.
- The movie *King Lear*, an adaptation of Shakespeare's play, is released in the USSR. It is directed by the Russian filmmaker Grigory Kozintsev and stars Yury Yarvet.
- The movie *Klute* is released in the United States. It is directed by Alan J. Pakula and stars Jane Fonda in an Academy Award-winning performance, and Donald Sutherland.
- The movie *La Soufle au coeur/Murmur of the Heart*, directed by Louis Malle and starring Lea Massari and Benoît Ferreux, is released in France.
- The movie *Play Misty for Me*, directed by Clint Eastwood, is released in the United States. Eastwood also costars, with Jessica Walter.
- The movie *Summer of '42*, directed by Richard Mulligan, is released in the United States, starring Jennifer O'Neill, Gary Grimes, and Jerry Houser.
- The movie *Sunday, Bloody Sunday* is released in the UK. It is directed by John Schlesinger and stars Glenda Jackson and Peter Finch.
- The movie *Taking Off* is released in the United States. It is directed by the Czech filmmaker Miloš Forman and stars Lynn Carlin, Buck Henry, and Linnea Heacock.
- The movie *The French Connection* is released in the United States. It is directed by William Friedkin and stars Gene Hackman and Fernando Rey. It will win several Academy Awards, including best picture, best director, and best actor.
- The movie *The Go-Between*, directed by U.S. filmmaker Joseph Losey, is released in the UK. Based on L. P. Hartley's novel, it stars Julie Christie and Alan Bates.
- The movie *The Last Picture Show* is released in the United States. It is directed by Peter Bogdanovich and features Timothy Bottoms, Jeff Bridges, and Cybill Shepherd.
- The movie *Two-Lane Blacktop*, directed by Monte Hellman, is released in the United States, starring James Taylor and Warren Oates.
- The movie *Walkabout*, directed by English filmmaker Nicolas Roeg, is released in Australia. Based on the novel by James Vance Marshall, it stars Jenny Agutter, Lucien John, and David Gulpilil.

- The movie *Willy Wonka and the Chocolate Factory* is released in the United States. Based on Roald Dahl's children's book, *Charlie and the Chocolate Factory*, it is directed by Mel Stuart and stars Gene Wilder and Jack Albertson.
- The movie *WR – Misterije Organizma/WR—Mysteries of the Organism*, directed by Dusan Makavejev, is released in Yugoslavia, starring Milena Dravić.
- The revisionist Western movie *McCabe and Mrs Miller*, directed by Robert Altman, is released in the United States, starring Warren Beatty and Julie Christie.
- The tough crime movie *Get Carter* is released in the UK. It stars Michael Caine and is directed by Mike Hodges.
- The U.S. release of *Sweet Sweetback's Baadasssss Song*, directed by Melvin Van Peebles, and *Shaft*, directed by Gordon Parks, signals the growing popularity of a cycle of "blaxploitation" movies written, starring, and directed by black Americans.

APRIL

5 French television refuses to broadcast Marcel Ophüls' 1970 documentary *The Sorrow and the Pity: A Chronicle of a French Town under the Occupation*, which exposes French wartime collaboration.

15 The 1970 Academy Awards take place. Best Actor: George C. Scott, for *Patton* (but he refuses it, criticizing the Oscars as a "meat market"); Best Supporting Actor: John Mills, for *Ryan's Daughter*; Best Actress: Glenda Jackson, for *Women in Love*; Best Supporting Actress: Helen Hayes, for *Airport*; Best Picture: *Patton*, directed by Franklin J. Schaffner; Best Director: Franklin J. Schaffner, for *Patton*.

MAY

27 The Cannes Film Festival holds its 25th anniversary awards, with the Palme d'Or going to the British movie *The Go-Between*, directed by U.S. filmmaker Joseph Losey. A special anniversary prize is awarded to the Italian Luchino Visconti, director of *Death in Venice*.

Literature and Language

- *The Waste Land: A Facsimile and Transcript of the Original Drafts* (of T. S. Eliot's poem *The Waste Land* from 1922), is published posthumously, edited by Valerie Eliot, his wife.
- Polish-born U.S. writer Jerzy Kosinski publishes his novel *Being There*.
- The Chilean poet Pablo Neruda is awarded the Nobel Prize for Literature.
- The English writer Anthony Powell publishes his novel *Books Do Furnish a Room*, the tenth volume in his 12-volume sequence *Dance to the Music of Time*, begun in 1951.
- The English writer Geoffrey Hill publishes his poetry collection *Mercian Hymns*. It wins the Whitbread Prize for Poetry.
- The English writer Jane Gardam publishes her novel *A Long Way from Verona*.
- The English writer Paul Scott publishes *The Towers of Silence*, the third volume of his *Raj Quartet*.
- The French-born U.S. literary critic George Steiner publishes his critical work *In Bluebeard's Castle: Some Notes Towards the Redefinition of Culture*.

- The German writer Heinrich Böll publishes his novel *Gruppenbild mit Dame/Group Portrait with Lady*.
- The Nobel Prize for Literature is awarded to the Chilean poet Pablo Neruda.
- The Pulitzer Prize for Biography is awarded to Lawrence Thompson for *Robert Frost* and the Pulitzer Prize for Poetry is awarded to William S. Merwin for *The Carrier of Ladders*. The Pulitzer Prize for Fiction is not awarded this year.
- The Russian writer Alexander Solzhenitsyn publishes his novel *Avgust chetyrnadtsatovo/August 1914* in the West (his works were banned in the USSR during the 1960s).
- The U.S. writer Anne Sexton publishes her poetry collection *Transformations*.
- The U.S. writer Bernard Malamud publishes his novel *The Tenants*.
- The U.S. writer E. L. Doctorow publishes his novel *The Book of Daniel*.
- The U.S. writer John Gardner publishes his novel *Grendel*.
- The U.S. writer John Updike publishes his novel *Rabbit Redux*, the second of his "Rabbit" novels. The first was published in 1960.
- The U.S. writer Philip Roth publishes his novel *Our Gang*.
- The U.S. writer Richard Brautigan publishes his novel *The Abortion: An Historical Romance, 1966*.
- The U.S. writer Thomas McGuane publishes his novel *The Bushwhacked Piano*.
- Two posthumous collections of poetry by the U.S. poet Sylvia Plath are published, *Crossing the Water* and *Winter Trees*.

Music

- The Argentine-born German composer Mauricio Kagel completes his orchestral work *Variations without Fugue*.
- Ex-Beatle George Harrison releases the triple album *All Things Must Pass*. His single "My Sweet Lord" is ruled in court to have "unconsciously plagiarized" the Chiffon's song "He's So Fine" and he pays more than $500,000 in damages.
- Ex-Beatle John Lennon releases the album *Imagine*.
- Canadian folk singer Joni Mitchell releases the album *Blue*.
- Glam rock emerges. A reaction against progressive rock, it is characterized by elaborate costumes, makeup, and stage posturing, as exemplified by British bands such as T Rex and the Sweet.
- The English composer Harrison Birtwistle completes his orchestral work *An Imaginary Landscape*.
- The English composer Benjamin Britten completes his Cello Suite No. 3.
- The Estonian composer Arvo Pärt completes his Symphony No. 3.
- The German composer Karlheinz Stockhausen completes his *Trans*, a work for orchestra, tape, and lights.
- The opera *Der Besuch der alten Dame/The Visit of the Old Lady*, by the Austrian composer Gottfried von Einem is first performed, in Vienna, Austria. It is based on a play by the Swiss writer Friedrich Dürrenmatt.

- The Polish composer Krzysztof Penderecki completes his choral work *Utrenja*.
- The Polish-born composer Andrzej Panufnik completes his Violin Concerto.
- The Russian composer Dmitry Shostakovich completes his Symphony No. 15, his last. It is first performed in Moscow in 1972, with his son Maxim conducting.
- The U.S. composer Elliott Carter completes his String Quartet No. 3 and his chamber work *Canon for Three: In Memoriam Igor Stravinsky*.
- The U.S. composer Steve Reich completes his *Drumming*, for percussion, voice, and piccolo.
- The U.S. rock and blues singer Janis Joplin releases the album *Pearl*.
- The U.S. songwriter and pop singer Carole King releases the albums *Tapestry* and *Music*. Around 15 million copies of *Tapestry* will be sold.
- U.S. musicologist and music educator Charles Rosen publishes *The Classical Style*.

MARCH

- Carole King wins three Grammy Awards: Best Record, "It's Too Late"; Best Album, *Tapestry*; and Best Female Pop Vocalist.
- Simon and Garfunkel win the Grammy Award for Best Album for *Bridge Over Troubled Water* and the Grammy for Best Record for the title song.
- 9   Alan Jay Lerner, Dorothy Fields, and Duke Ellington are among the first to be inducted into the Songwriter's Hall of Fame in the United States.

MAY

- 8   The British progressive rock band Yes releases *The Yes Album*.
- 12   Rock star Mick Jagger marries Bianca Perez Morena de Macias, daughter of a Nicaraguan diplomat.
- 15   The British rock group the Rolling Stones releases "Brown Sugar" and the album *Sticky Fingers*.
- 16   The opera *Owen Wingrave*, by the English composer Benjamin Britten, is first performed, on British television. It is based on a short story by Henry James. A revised version will open at Covent Garden, in London, England, in 1973.

JUNE

- 19   The British pop singer Rod Stewart releases the single "Maggie May" from the album *Every Picture Tells a Story*.
- 27   Rock concert halls Fillmore East, in New York, New York, and Fillmore West, in San Francisco, California, are closed by their founder Bill Graham for financial reasons.

AUGUST

- 1   George Harrison, joined by Ravi Shankar, Eric Clapton, Billy Preston, Leon Russell, Ringo Starr, and Bob Dylan, performs in the Benefit for Bangladesh in Madison Square Garden, New York, New York.

NOVEMBER

- 6   The British glam rock group T Rex releases "Hot Love" and the album *Electric Warrior*. TRexstasy is born and the group becomes the best-selling singles band in 1971 and 1972.
- 13   The U.S. singer/songwriter Don Maclean releases the single "American Pie," and an album of the same name.

27 The British heavy metal rock group Led Zeppelin releases the album *Led Zeppelin IV*, which features the classic "Stairway to Heaven."

DECEMBER

18 The U.S. pop singer Harry Nilsson releases "Without You" and the album *Son of Schmilsson*.

Theater and Dance

- The musical *Follies*, with lyrics and music by Stephen Sondheim, is first performed, at the Winter Gardens in New York, New York.
- The play *Madmen and Specialists*, by the Nigerian writer Wole Soyinka, is first performed, in Connecticut. The play deals with the Biafran War.
- The play *The Basic Training of Pavlo Hummel*, by the U.S. writer David Rabe, is first performed, at the Delacorte Theater in New York, New York. The play deals with the war in Vietnam.
- The play *The House of Blue Leaves*, by the U.S. writer John Guare, is first performed, in the Truck and Warehouse Theater, New York, New York.
- The play *The Prisoner of Second Avenue*, by the U.S. writer Neil Simon, is first performed, at the Eugene O'Neill Theater in New York, New York.
- The play *The Removalists*, by the Australian writer David Williamson, is first performed, in Sydney, Australia.
- The Pulitzer Prize for Drama is awarded to Paul Zindel for *The Effects of Gamma Rays on Man-in-the-Moon Marigolds*.
- The rock musical *Godspell*, with lyrics and music by Stephen Schwartz, opens at the Cherry Lane Theater in New York, New York.

JANUARY

19 A revival of *No, No, Nanette*, a 1925 musical by Otto Harbach, Frank Mandel, Vincent Youmans, and Irving Caesar, opens at the 46th Street Theater, New York, New York. Production is supervised by Busby Berkeley, and it stars Ruby Keeler.

SEPTEMBER

29 The play *Lear*, by the English writer Edward Bond, is first performed, in London, England.

Thought and Scholarship

- British historian Keith Thomas publishes *Religion and the Decline of Magic*.
- British historian Mark Girouard publishes *The Victorian Country House*.
- British historian Peter Brown publishes *The World of Late Antiquity*.
- British philosopher Alisdair MacIntyre publishes *Against the Self-Images of the Age*.
- French biochemist Jacques Monod publishes *Chance and Necessity*.
- German-born English psychologist Hans Eysenck publishes *Race, Intelligence, and Education*.
- Scottish psychologist R. D. Laing publishes *The Politics of the Family and Other Essays*.
- The Pulitzer Prize for History is awarded to James McGregor Burns for *Roosevelt: The Soldier of Freedom*.

- The Pulitzer Prize for General Nonfiction is awarded to John Toland for *The Rising Sun*.
- U.S. historian Dee Brown publishes *Bury My Heart at Wounded Knee: An Indian History of the American West*.
- U.S. philosopher John Rawls publishes *A Theory of Justice*.
- U.S. psychologist B. F. Skinner publishes *Beyond Freedom and Dignity*, a controversial defense of behaviorism.
- U.S. social scientists Frances Fox Piven and Richard Cloward publish *Regulating the Poor*.

MAY

22 The Lyndon Baines Johnson Presidential Library is dedicated, at the University of Texas.

SOCIETY

Education

- Austrian-born educator and social critic Ivan Illich publishes his polemic *Deschooling Society*.
- Britain's Open University (founded in 1969) is launched, using television and radio broadcasts among its teaching media.
- Universities are reopened in the People's Republic of China.

APRIL

- The U.S. Supreme Court, in the case *Swann v. Charlotte-Mecklenburg Board of Education*, upholds the policy of busing students to create racially integrated schools in order to achieve educational parity.

JUNE

25 The British education secretary, Margaret Thatcher, announces the end of free milk for primary school children.

Everyday Life

- "Hot pants"—very brief skin-tight shorts—become a popular fashion item for women in the West.
- A dance instructor holds the first aerobics class, in Malibu, California.
- Changes to the setup of the postal service in the United States, and consequent increases in charges, require many publications to reduce their formats.
- Populations (in millions): China 786.8; India 547.9; USSR 244.1; United States 205.1; Japan 106.0; Brazil 94.9; Bangladesh 63.3; Pakistan 62.1; West Germany 61.1; Nigeria 56.6; Great Britain and Northern Ireland 55.5; Italy 54.0; France 51.2; Mexico 50.6.
- Telephone direct-dialing between London, England, and New York, New York, is introduced.
- The American Postal Workers Union is created with nearly 300,000 members.
- There are 1,860 blacks in elective office in the United States.
- Voter registration in the United States South, at 59%, is 29% higher than in 1961.

- William Powell publishes *The Anarchist Cookbook* in the United States, a cult work that includes recipes for hash brownies and for bombs.

June 1971–1978   Immigration patterns in the United States: 38% from North America (Mexico, Caribbean); 35% from Asia; 19% from Europe; 6% from South America; and 2% from Africa.

JANUARY
20–March 8   British postal workers go on a nationwide strike in support of their claim for a 19% pay raise.

FEBRUARY
1–March 31   A strike halts Ford car production in Britain.

JUNE
13   Geraldine Boodrick gives birth to the world's first set of nonuplets, five boys and four girls, in Sydney, Australia. Only six of the babies survive.

OCTOBER
1   Disney World opens in Orlando, Florida: the development has cost an estimated $500 million.

NOVEMBER
11   Western members of the International Longshoremen's and Warehousemen's Union in the United States end a 134-day strike, begun on July 1, 1971.

Media and Communication

- *Masterpiece Theatre*, theatrical productions from British television introduced by Alistair Cooke, starts on U.S. television. Despite low ratings, the series wins Emmy awards and considerable critical acclaim.
- The 1970–71 Emmy Awards for television are held. Best Drama Series: *The Senator: The Bold Ones*; Best Comedy Series: *All in the Family*; Best Actor in a Drama: Hal Holbrook, for *The Senator: The Bold Ones*; Best Actress in a Drama: Susan Hampshire, for *The First Churchills*; Best Actor in a Comedy: Jack Klugman, for *The Odd Couple*; Best Actress in a Comedy: Jean Stapleton, for *All in the Family*.
- The television movie *Duel*, directed by Steven Spielberg and starring Dennis Weaver, is broadcast for the first time in the United States. It is Spielberg's first major production.

JANUARY
12–September 21, 1983   *All in the Family* (which becomes *Archie Bunker's Place* in 1979) wins the Emmy award for best comedy and for best new series. It runs for 13 seasons and is the fifth most popular television series of all time in the United States.

MAY
- The radio program *All Things Considered* is launched in the U.S.

JUNE
13   The *New York Times* publishes the first installment of *The History of the US Decision-making Process on Vietnam Policy*, popularly known as *The Pentagon Papers*. The newspaper received the classified text from former Defense Department official Daniel Ellsberg, who will be indicted for theft of the document. The U.S. Supreme Court upholds the paper's right to publish.

SEPTEMBER
15–September 1, 1978   *Columbo*, a detective series featuring Peter Falk as the scruffy inspector, is shown on U.S. television. It differs from other detective shows in concentrating on the process of discovering the identity of the criminal, which is known to the audience from the start.

OCTOBER
1   *The Electric Company*, a popular educational children's television show, debuts on public television.
19   Time, Inc. stops publication of the magazine *Look* after a 34-year run in the United States.

Religion
- The General Synod of the Church of England allows baptized members of other Christian denominations to receive communion in Anglican churches.
- The Swiss Catholic theologian Hans Küng publishes *Infallible? An Enquiry*, a challenge to papal infallibility.

NOVEMBER
- Two women, Joyce Bennett and Jane Hwang Hsien Yuen, are ordained priests by the Anglican bishop of Hong Kong.

Sports

JANUARY
1   Polls in the United States are split on college football's national champions for 1970; one poll picks Nebraska, the other poll picks Texas.
1   The Texas Longhorns' 30 game unbeaten run, the second longest in college American football history, is ended by Notre Dame, who beat them 24–11 in the Cotton Bowl.
17   The Baltimore Colts defeat the Dallas Cowboys 16–13 in Super Bowl V at Miami, Florida, with a field goal in the final minute by Jim O'Brien.
28–31   U.S. national figure skating champions are: Janet Lynn; John Metkevick; Jo Jo Starbuck and Kenneth Shelley, pairs; Judy Schwomeyer and James Sladky win the ice dancing competition.

FEBRUARY
4   Satchel Paige, who spent most of his playing career in the preintegration Negro leagues before joining the Cleveland Indians in 1948 at the age of 42, is inducted into the National Baseball Hall of Fame.

MARCH
8   U.S. boxer Joe Frazier beats Muhammad Ali of the United States over 15 rounds at Madison Square Garden, New York, New York, and retains the world heavyweight title. With takings from closed-circuit television the fight grosses almost $20 million.
25   The Boston Patriots change their name to the New England Patriots.

APRIL
10–14   An unprecedented visit to the People's Republic of China by the U.S. table tennis team to play a series of exhibition matches coincides with the relaxation of a 20-year U.S. embargo on trade with China.

30 The Milwaukee Bucks win the National Basketball Association (NBA) championship in a four-game sweep of the Baltimore Bullets.

MAY

4–18 The Montreal Canadiens win the Stanley Cup four games to three over the Chicago Black Hawks.

27 Britain and Ireland's amateur golfers defeat the United States 13–11 at St. Andrews, Scotland, to record their first Walker Cup victory since 1938.

29 Race-car driver Al Unser wins his second consecutive Indianapolis 500, with a record average speed of 253.7 kph/157.7 mph.

JUNE

21–July 10 Lee Trevino becomes the fourth U.S. golfer to win the U.S. and British Opens in the same year.

28 U.S. boxer Muhammad Ali wins a four-year legal battle when a U.S. court overturns his 1967 conviction for draft evasion.

BIRTHS & DEATHS

- U.S. surgeon John Gibbon, who performed the first successful open-heart operation in 1953, dies (68).

JANUARY

5 Sonny Liston (born Charles Liston), U.S. boxer and a former heavyweight champion, dies in Las Vegas, Nevada (38).

10 Coco (Gabrielle) Chanel, French couturier whose classic designs have been widely copied, dies in Paris, France (87).

FEBRUARY

12 James Cash Penney, U.S. founder of one of the largest chains of department stores, J. C. Penney, dies in New York, New York (85).

17 A. A. Berle, U.S. lawyer and diplomat to Latin America, dies in New York, New York (76).

MARCH

8 Harold Lloyd, U.S. film comedian who first gained popularity in the silent era, dies in Hollywood, California (77).

11 Whitney Young, U.S. civil-rights leader who fought for equal opportunities for blacks in industry and government service, dies in Lagos, Nigeria (48).

13 Rockwell Kent, U.S. painter of nature and adventure scenes, writer, illustrator, and social critic, dies in Plattsburgh, New York (88).

24 Arne Jacobsen, Danish architect and designer, dies in Copenhagen, Denmark (69).

27 M. C. Escher, Dutch artist known for his optical effects, dies in Laren, the Netherlands (72).

APRIL

3 Joseph Valachi, U.S. gangster who became the first person to reveal the history, membership, and inner workings of the Mafia crime organization, dies in La Tuna Correctional Institution, Texas (66).

6 Igor Stravinsky, Russian composer, dies in New York, New York (88).

8 Fritz von Opel, German automobile manufacturer who built the first rocket-propelled car, dies in St. Moritz, Switzerland (71).

21 François Duvalier (known as "Papa Doc"), president of Haiti 1957–71, who ruled through terror and corruption, dies in Port-au-Prince, Haiti (64).

21 George Fielding Eliot, U.S. author, columnist, and correspondent during World War II, dies in Torrington, Connecticut (76).

MAY

19 Ogden Nash, U.S. poet and editor, dies in Baltimore, Maryland (68).

28 Audie Murphy, U.S. soldier and actor, the most decorated soldier in World War II, dies in a plane crash in Roanoke, Virginia (56).

JUNE

1 Reinhold Neibuhr, U.S. theologian who persuaded Christian pacifists to oppose Hitler, dies in Stockbridge, Massachusetts (78).

4 György Lukács, Hungarian Marxist philosopher, writer, and literary critic who influenced European communism, dies in Budapest, Hungary (86).

JULY

1 (William) Lawrence Bragg, Australian-born British physicist and X-ray crystallographer, dies in Ipswich, England (81).

3 Jim Morrison, U.S. rock star as singer with The Doors, dies in Paris, France (27).

6 Louis Armstrong, U.S. jazz trumpeter, composer, and band leader, dies in New York (71).

23 W. V. S. Tubman, Liberian president 1943–71, who carried out many liberal reforms, dies in London, England (75).

AUGUST

12 Pete Sampras, U.S. tennis player who in 1990 became the youngest man to win the U.S. Open and was ranked number one 1993–96 and 1998, born in Washington, D.C.

27 Margaret Bourke-White, U.S. documentary photographer, dies in Stamford, Connecticut (67).

SEPTEMBER

11 Nikita Sergeyevich Khrushchev, first secretary of the Communist Party of the Soviet Union 1953–64 and premier 1958–64, dies in Moscow, USSR (77).

13 Lin Biao, Chinese field commander of the Red Army, dies in a plane crash in the Mongolian People's Republic while fleeing China after a failed attempt to depose Mao Zedong (63).

20 George Seferis, Greek poet, essayist, and diplomat, dies in Athens, Greece (71).

25 Hugo Lafayette Black, U.S. associate justice of the Supreme Court 1931–71 who championed the Bill of Rights, dies in Bethesda, Maryland (85).

OCTOBER

12 Dean Acheson, U.S. secretary of state, presidential advisor, and Pulitzer prizewinning author, dies in Sandy Spring, Maryland (78).

DECEMBER

9 Ralph Johnson Bunche, U.S. diplomat, an important member of the United Nations for over 20 years, dies in New York, New York (67).

12 David Sarnoff, U.S. radio broadcaster who promoted the sale of radios and formed the National Broadcasting Company (NBC), dies in New York, New York (79).

18 Bobby Jones, U.S. amateur golfer, the first man to win the Grand Slam—the British and U.S. Amateur and Open Championships—dies in Atlanta, Georgia (69).

JULY

2   The 19-year-old Australian tennis player Evonne Goolagong beats fellow Australian Margaret Court in the women's singles final at Wimbledon, London, England; while another Australian, John Newcombe, defeats Stan Smith of the United States in the men's final.

AUGUST

26 The New York Giants of the NFL announce that they will move to New Jersey after building an 80,000-seat stadium there; they will retain the New York part of their name.

SEPTEMBER

2   Seventeen-year-old Cheryl White on Jetolara is the first black American woman to win a thoroughbred race in the United States, at Waterford Park racetrack, West Virginia.

5–15 At the U.S. Open tennis championships, Stan Smith of the United States wins the men's singles and Billie Jean King of the United States wins the women's singles to give the United States its first clean sweep of the singles titles since 1956.

OCTOBER

3   U.S. tennis player Billie Jean King is the first female athlete to earn more than $100,000 in prize money in a year.

9–17 In baseball's World Series the Pittsburgh Pirates, led by Roberto Clemente and Manny Sanguillen, defeat the Baltimore Orioles by four games to three. The games are played at night under lights for the first time in World Series history.

DECEMBER

22–January 9, 1972 The Los Angeles Lakers establish a U.S. major league professional sports record with their 27th consecutive National Basketball Association (NBA) victory. Their run ends seven games later.

27 Arizona State defeat Florida State 45–38 in the inaugural Fiesta Bowl, at the Sun Devil Stadium, Tempe, Arizona.

1972

POLITICS, GOVERNMENT, AND ECONOMICS

Business and Economics

JANUARY

20 Juanita Kreps is appointed the first woman governor of the New York stock exchange.

20 The number of unemployed in Britain exceeds 1 million for the first time since 1947.

APRIL

17–June 12 British Rail services are disrupted in the UK by a work-to-rule in support of a 16% pay claim.

JULY

• The USSR starts making large-scale purchases of surplus U.S. grain.

8   The U.S. president Richard M. Nixon announces that the USSR will purchase $750 million worth of U.S. grain over three years.

NOVEMBER

• On the New York Stock Exchange, the Dow Jones Industrial Average closes above 1,000 points for the first time.

Human Rights

• Sociologists at Hebrew University, Israel, conduct a poll concluding that Israeli women reject women's liberation, believing their most admirable goals are to be good mothers and homemakers.

• The National Black Political Assembly in Gary, Indiana, United States, fails to reach agreement on founding a black political force.

• U.S. pharmacist Jan Hirsh founds Copley Pharmaceutical, Inc. with her brother so she can look after her baby in her office. She sells the business for $546 million in 1993.

MARCH

22 The U.S. Congress passes the Equal Rights Amendment (27th Amendment), that prohibits sex discrimination, but it fails to achieve ratification by the states.

JULY

• The former U.S. nun Susan Lynn Roley and former U.S. marine Joanne E. Pierce become the first female Federal Bureau of Investigation (FBI) agents.

OCTOBER

• A French teenager is tried for having an illegal abortion and is acquitted after outspoken support by influential figures, resulting in increased availability of free abortions in major cities.

DECEMBER

15 Australian law orders equal pay for women.

Politics and Government

- "Diplock Courts" without juries are introduced for some trials in Northern Ireland.
- In the case *Kleindienst v. Mandel*, the U.S. Supreme Court rules that freedom of expression implies the right to receive information as well as to disseminate it.
- Legislation is passed in the United States for the federal government to share its tax revenues with the states.
- The Center for National Policy is founded in Washington, D.C., and the Institute for Contemporary Studies is founded in San Francisco, California.
- The European Communities Act gives European institutions the power to override British law.
- The South African government abolishes colored representation on municipal councils in the Cape and substitutes nominated consultative committees.

JANUARY

- The U.S. Supreme Court rules that the one-year residency requirement for welfare recipients is unconstitutional.
- 9 In a conference call with reporters, billionaire recluse Howard Hughes states that his purported autobiography, being touted by Clifford Irving, is a fake. On March 13, Irving admits that the autobiography he had sold to publisher McGraw-Hill for an advance of $750,000 was a fake, and pleads guilty to federal conspiracy charges.
- 10 President Mujibur Rahman of Bangladesh arrives in Dacca, the Bangladeshi capital.
- 11–March 12 Lord Pearce heads a British commission to Rhodesia to assess opinion on the proposed new constitutional arrangements for independence.
- 12 Mujibur Rahman resigns the presidency of Bangladesh to become prime minister.
- 14 Talks are held in Rome, Italy, between the British defense secretary, Lord Carrington, and the Maltese premier, Dom Mintoff.
- 16 The withdrawal of British forces from Malta is suspended.
- 22 Britain, Denmark, Ireland, and Norway sign the Treaty of Accession to the European Economic Community (Common Market) in Brussels, Belgium.
- 25 The U.S. president Richard M. Nixon reveals that his national security adviser Henry Kissinger has been conducting secret peace negotiations with North Vietnam, during the Vietnam War, since 1969.
- 30 British troops shoot dead 13 civilians in Northern Ireland when violence erupts at a civil-rights march in the Bogside, Londonderry. The day is described as "Bloody Sunday" by Labour members of the British Parliament.
- 30 Pakistan leaves the Commonwealth in protest at Britain's plans to recognize Bangladesh as an independent nation.

FEBRUARY

- 2 Anti-British demonstrators burn down the British embassy in Dublin in the Republic of Ireland.
- 2 Keith Holyoake retires as prime minister of New Zealand.
- 4 Britain formally recognizes Bangladesh as an independent republic.

- 7 John Marshall succeeds Keith Holyoake as prime minister of New Zealand.
- 11 Greece demands that Cyprus surrender its secret armaments and accept a coalition government.
- 17 The British House of Commons approves the second reading of the European Communities Bill, giving European institutions the power to override British law, by 309 votes to 301.
- 21–27 The U.S. president Richard M. Nixon visits China to promote more congenial relations and foster scientific and cultural exchange.
- 22 An Irish Republican Army (IRA) bomb kills seven people at the paratroopers' headquarters in Aldershot, southern England.
- 27 Israel attacks southern Lebanon in reprisal for the Palestinian raids.
- 28 Japan acknowledges China's territorial rights over Taiwan.

MARCH

- The National Commission on Marijuana recommends decriminalizing private use of the drug in the U.S.
- The U.S. president Richard M. Nixon reduces the number of individuals and agencies authorized to classify political documents.
- The U.S. Senate sends the 27th Amendment to the states. Known as the Equal Rights Amendment, the legislation prohibits sex discrimination.
- The U.S. Supreme Court sanctions extends Federal Trade Commission authority to combat false advertising.
- The U.S. Supreme Court rules that the one-year state residency requirement to be eligible to vote is unconstitutional, and suggests a 30-day limit.
- 2 The British prime minister Edward Heath forbids the use of "intensive" interrogation techniques in Northern Ireland, following the Parker Report on the security forces.
- 4 A bomb explosion at a restaurant in Belfast, Northern Ireland, kills two and injures 136 people. The Irish Republican Army (IRA) claim responsibility.
- 13 Britain resumes ambassadorial relations with China and closes its consulate in Taiwan.
- 14 Following demands made by Greece on February 11, Cyprus yields its arms to United Nations peacekeepers but refuses ministerial changes.
- 15 King Hussein of Jordan proposes the creation of an autonomous Palestinian state on the West Bank.
- 19 India and Bangladesh sign a mutual defense pact.
- 20 Six people are killed in an Irish Republican Army (IRA) explosion in Donegall Street, Belfast, Northern Ireland.
- 29 The North Vietnamese launch a major offensive in the Vietnam War in Quang Tri, South Vietnam's northernmost city.
- 30 Britain assumes direct rule over Northern Ireland, with William Whitelaw as secretary of state.

APRIL

- The U.S. Federal Election Campaign Act limits advertising budgets and candidates' personal contributions to their own campaigns, and orders candidates to disclose all campaign contributions.
- 4 The USSR refuses a visa to the Swedish Academy official who is due to present the Nobel Prize for Literature to the Soviet novelist Alexander Solzhenitsyn.

6   Egypt breaks off relations with Jordan in protest at the latter's proposal of March 15 to create an autonomous Palestinian state on the West Bank.

6   President Salvador Allende of Chile vetoes the constitutional amendment that would have made the expropriation of property subject to congressional approval.

7   The British secretary of state for Northern Ireland William Whitelaw announces the immediate release of 73 internees in the province.

9   The USSR and Iraq sign a 15-year treaty of friendship and cooperation.

10 Britain, the United States, and the USSR sign a multilateral convention prohibiting the stockpiling of biological weapons.

19 North Vietnamese aircraft attack the U.S. 7th Fleet in the Gulf of Tonkin during the Vietnam War.

19 The Widgery Report on "Bloody Sunday" (January 30, 1972) in Northern Ireland concludes that the Irish Republican Army (IRA) fired the first shots.

23 In a French referendum, 67.7% vote in favor of admitting Britain and other countries to the European Economic Community (Common Market).

27 The British government lifts the ban on marches in Northern Ireland and declares an amnesty for 283 people convicted of participating in illegal marches.

27 The U.S. senator Edmund Muskie withdraws from the contest for the Democratic presidential nomination.

MAY

1   The South Vietnamese city of Quang Tri falls to North Vietnamese forces.

8   The U.S. president Richard M. Nixon orders the blockade and mining of North Vietnamese ports in the Vietnam War.

10 A referendum in the Republic of Ireland records 83% support for membership in the European Economic Community (Common Market).

14 The Ulster Defence Association (UDA) in Northern Ireland sets up the first Protestant "no go" areas in Belfast.

14–20 Demonstrators in the city of Kaunas, Lithuania, demand religious freedom for their Soviet republic.

15 The U.S. candidate for the Democratic presidential nomination, George Wallace, is shot and paralyzed at a rally in Maryland.

17 The West German Bundestag (legislative assembly) ratifies the 1970 treaties with the USSR and Poland, although the Christian Democrats abstain.

22 Ceylon ceases to be a British dominion and becomes a republic within the Commonwealth under the name of Sri Lanka.

22–30 Richard M. Nixon becomes the first U.S. president to visit the USSR. On May 26, he signs a treaty limiting antiballistic missile sites.

23 Britain abandons its Rhodesian settlement proposals when the Pearce Commission reports that black opinion is unfavorable.

30 Three pro-Palestinian Japanese terrorists kill 25 Israelis at Lod International Airport, Tel Aviv, Israel, in support of Palestinian territorial claims.

JUNE

•   The militant feminist Angela Davis is acquitted in the U.S. of aiding a courtroom escape that left four people dead, in 1970.

•   The U.S. Supreme Court rules that journalists may not withhold confidential information from grand juries.

1–15 West German police round up the Baader–Meinhof left wing urban guerrilla group.

11 A gun battle in Northern Ireland between troops, Catholics, and Protestants in Belfast leaves four people dead.

15 The Soviet president Nikolay Podgorny begins a four-day visit to North Vietnam.

17 U.S. police arrest five men planting electronic bugs at the Democratic Party headquarters in the Watergate apartment complex, Washington, D.C.

23 The British government temporarily floats the pound on the world currency markets to halt the drain on reserves, but the pound starts to sink.

27 The French socialist and communist parties agree on a common political program.

27–July 9 The Irish Republican Army (IRA) begins a cease-fire in Northern Ireland.

29 In the case *Furman v. Georgia*, the U.S. Supreme Court rules that the death penalty for three men condemned to death by the states of Georgia and Texas is unconstitutional as it constitutes cruel and unusual punishment.

JULY

1   The Iraqi government nationalizes the British-owned Iraq Petroleum Company's Kirkuk oil field operation.

2   India and Pakistan agree to renounce force in the settlement of their disputes.

5   Kakuei Tanaka succeeds Eisaku Sato as prime minister of Japan.

5   Pierre Messmer succeeds Jacques Chaban-Delmas as prime minister of France.

7   The British secretary of state for Northern Ireland, William Whitelaw, holds secret talks in London, England, with the Irish Republican Army (IRA).

12–14 The Democratic Party convention in Miami, Florida, nominates George McGovern as its presidential candidate. On July 14, it approves Thomas Eagleton for the vice presidency.

17–August 11 Trials of Czechoslovak dissidents begin in the capital, Prague, and Brno.

18 President Anwar Sadat of Egypt expels 20,000 Soviet advisers, accusing the USSR of failing to supply promised armaments.

21 The Irish Republican Army (IRA) in Northern Ireland launches bomb attacks on Belfast shopping centers and bus stations, killing 13 and injuring 130 people.

21–26 Five British dockers go to prison for contempt of court after refusing to stop the "blacking" of a container depot at Hackney, London, England. They are released on July 26.

31 Troops in Northern Ireland destroy the Catholic and Protestant barricades set up in "no go" areas in Belfast and Londonderry.

AUGUST

1   Egypt and Sudan announce plans for their federation by September 1973.

Watergate (1972–75)

1972

JUNE

17 U.S. police arrest five men planting electronic bugs at the Democratic Party headquarters in the Watergate apartment complex, Washington, D.C.

AUGUST

- *Washington Post* reporters Bob Woodward and Carl Bernstein implicate the Committee for the Reelection of the President (CREEP) in the Watergate burglary, leading to a series of revelations about the Nixon administration's complicity in the Watergate affair that contribute to the president's eventual downfall.

- The U.S. president Richard M. Nixon tells a skeptical public that White House investigators have absolved administration officials of complicity in the Watergate burglary.

SEPTEMBER

11 The U.S. Democratic Party accuses the Republican campaign finance chairman Maurice Stans of political espionage.

1973

- Former Nixon campaign officials James W. McCord and G. Gordon Liddy are convicted of burglary and wiretapping.

JANUARY

8 The trial opens in Washington, D.C., of seven men accused of attempting to bug the opposition Democratic Party headquarters in the Watergate apartment complex.

20 Richard M. Nixon is inaugurated as president of the United States for a second term.

APRIL

- President Nixon appears before the U.S. people to protest his innocence in the Watergate scandal. However, all those around him seem to have been involved, as the president reports that he has accepted the resignations of his chief of staff, H. R. Haldeman; domestic policy advisor, John Ehrlichman; legal counsel, John Dean; attorney general, Richard G. Kleindienst; and FBI director, L. Patrick Gray.

17 President Nixon drops the ban on White House staff appearing before a Senate committee to be questioned on the Watergate affair.

30 President Nixon accepts responsibility for the attempted bugging of the Watergate building, but denies any personal involvement.

MAY

17 A U.S. Senate committee begins hearings of White House staff evidence on the Watergate affair.

JUNE

25 Former White House counsel John Dean informs the U.S. Senate Committee of President Nixon's complicity in the cover-up of the Watergate affair.

OCTOBER

12 The U.S. Court of Appeals orders President Nixon to hand over the Watergate tapes.

23 The U.S. House of Representatives orders a judiciary committee to assess evidence for the impeachment of President Nixon.

1974

JANUARY

30 President Nixon famously stumbles in his State of the Union address, referring to the need "to replace the discredited president—er, present—system."

APRIL

30 President Nixon releases a 1,308-page edited transcript of the Watergate tapes to the Congressional Committee.

AUGUST

- U.S. journalists Bob Woodward and Carl Bernstein publish *All the President's Men*, an account of the Watergate Affair.

5 President Nixon admits complicity in the Watergate cover-up.

9 President Nixon resigns to avoid impeachment, and Gerald Ford becomes the 38th president of the United States.

SEPTEMBER

8 President Ford pardons former president Nixon for any offenses committed in office.

1975

JANUARY

1 H. R. Haldeman, John D. Ehrlichman, and John N. Mitchell, aides of former president Nixon, are found guilty of their Watergate offenses.

---

4 President Idi Amin of Uganda gives Asians holding foreign passports 90 days to leave the country on the grounds that they are "sabotaging the economy." His action prompts a flood of refugees into Britain.

5 Sargent Shriver becomes the Democratic vice-presidential candidate in the United States, when Thomas Eagleton withdraws following the disclosure that he has undergone psychiatric treatment.

12 Heavy U.S. air raids on North Vietnam accompany the departure of U.S. combat infantry from South Vietnam.

12 The Chinese Communist Party accuses the USSR of complicity in a plot to assassinate the party and government leader, Mao Zedong.

16–17 Moroccan air force officers fail in their attempt to shoot down an airliner carrying King Hassan II of Morocco. On August 17, the Moroccan defense minister commits suicide.

22–23 The Republican Party convention in Miami, United States, nominates President Richard M. Nixon for a second term. On August 23, it renominates Vice President Spiro Agnew.

25 China vetoes the admission of Bangladesh to the United Nations.

SEPTEMBER

- Federal prosecutors drop conspiracy charges against the Harrisburg Seven who had been accused of plotting to kidnap the U.S. national security adviser Henry Kissinger and bomb federal buildings in the U.S. Capitol, Washington, D.C.
1 Iceland unilaterally extends its fishing limit from 19 km/12 mi to 80 km/50 mi.
5 An Icelandic gunboat cuts the fishing gear of a British trawler fishing within the new unilaterally extended Icelandic territorial limit.
5 Eight members of the Palestinian Black September guerrilla group attack the Olympic village in Munich, West Germany, killing two Israeli athletes and taking nine hostage; they issue demands for the release of 200 Palestinians from Israeli jails. Five terrorists and all nine hostages are killed when West German police storm the compound the next day.
7 South Korea withdraws its remaining 37,000 troops from South Vietnam.
11 The U.S. Democratic Party accuses the Republican campaign finance chairman Maurice Stans of political espionage.
15 South Vietnamese forces recapture the city of Quang Tri from the North Vietnamese.
17 Ugandan exiles fail in their attempt to invade Uganda from Tanzania.
22 President Idi Amin orders 8,000 Asians to leave Uganda within 48 hours.
24 A referendum in Norway results in a 52.7% vote against entry into the European Economic Community (Common Market).
27–October 13 Border fighting breaks out between North and South Yemen.
29 Japan and China agree to end the legal state of war that has existed between them since 1937.
29 The Franks Committee in Britain recommends reform of the British Official Secrets Act in order to clarify the law on the leakage of official information.

OCTOBER

- A racial disturbance erupts on the U.S. aircraft carrier *Kitty Hawk*; 46 sailors are injured in the fracas.
- Advocates of the policy of busing students to create racially integrated schools delay antibusing legislation in the U.S. Senate.
- The U.S. president Richard M. Nixon signs legislation creating the Consumer Product Safety Commission.
1 A referendum in Denmark votes 2 to 1 in favor of entry into the European Economic Community (Common Market).
3 The United States and the USSR sign the final SALT (Strategic Arms Limitation Talks) accords limiting submarine-carried and land-based missiles.
21 The European Economic Community summit in Paris, France, approves the principle of economic and monetary union by 1980.
26 North Vietnam publishes a cease-fire agreement with the United States. President Richard M. Nixon's national security adviser, Henry Kissinger, says "peace is at hand" in Vietnam.
29 The Palestinian hijackers of a Lufthansa flight over Turkey secure the release of Arab terrorists held in West Germany since September 5.

30 A British Green Paper promises greater political power for Catholics in Northern Ireland.
30 Pierre Trudeau's Liberal Party wins a narrow victory in the Canadian general election.

NOVEMBER

- About 500 Native Americans march in Washington, D.C., and occupy the Bureau of Indian Affairs. They agree to leave after federal officials promise to review their grievances.
- Richard M. Nixon is reelected U.S. president in a landslide victory. In the congressional elections the Democrats retain majorities in the House of Representatives (255–179) and in the Senate (57–43).
- The U.S. State Department lifts a 22-year ban on travel to China.
1 President Thieu of South Vietnam rejects the U.S. Vietnam War cease-fire plan.
8 The deadline set by President Idi Amin for Asians to leave Uganda is reached. About 25,000 make their way to Britain by the end of the year.
9 Andrew Young becomes the first black American from the South to be elected to the U.S. Congress since the mid-19th century.
19 The Social Democrats are returned with an increased majority in the West German general election.
21 An eight-hour battle is fought between Israel and Syria on the Golan Heights.
22 Preparatory talks for the European Security Conference begin in Helsinki, Finland.
24 Finland formally recognizes East Germany as a separate country, the first Western nation to do so.
25 Norman Kirk becomes prime minister of New Zealand when the Labor Party wins a sweeping electoral victory.
28 Anglo-Icelandic talks on the dispute over fishing limits in waters off Iceland break down.

DECEMBER

2 The Labor Party wins the Australian general election.
5 Gough Whitlam, the leader of the Labor Party, becomes prime minister of Australia.
11 India and Pakistan agree on a truce line in Jammu and Kashmir.
18–30 U.S. forces carry out heavy bombing in North Vietnam in the Vietnam War.
20 The Diplock Commission in Britain recommends wider powers of arrest in Northern Ireland and suspension of trial by jury in certain cases.
21 West and East Germany sign a basic treaty to establish "neighborly relations on the basis of equality."
27 Britain ignores a Maltese ultimatum demanding a 10% increase in rent for the use of military bases in Malta.
31 The Northern Ireland Office reports a total of 467 killings in 1972.

SCIENCE, TECHNOLOGY, AND MEDICINE

Computing

- SMALLTALK, one of the first object-oriented computer languages, is developed by U.S. scientist Alan Kay. It is especially adapted to graphics and uses icons.
- The computer language PROLOG (Programming-in-Logic) is developed by French computer scientist Alain Colmeraurer; it has applications in artificial intelligence.
- U.S. company Telnet Communications Corporation establishes a worldwide computer network.
- U.S. computer scientist Nolan Bushnell invents "Pong," the first computer game.
- Wang laboratories introduces a word processing system using IBM electric typewriters as printers with text stored on magnetic tape.

Ecology

- Black sigatoka fungus attacks banana plants in Honduras; it quickly spreads throughout Central America.
- Dennis Meadows's *The Limits to Growth* is published by the Massachusetts Institute of Technology. Based on a Club of Rome report and computer simulation, it predicts environmental catastrophe if the depletion of the earth's resources, overpopulation, and pollution are not acted upon immediately.
- Drought in the USSR and China results in disastrous grain harvests; the USSR is forced to buy U.S. grain.
- Mt. Erebus in Antarctica erupts.
- The first section of the Transamazonia Highway is completed in Brazil; designed to assist settlement and exploitation of the underpopulated Amazon River Basin, when completed it will run 15,100 km/3,400 mi from Recife on the Atlantic coast to Cruzeiro do Sul near the Peruvian border.
- The UK and several other European countries sign an agreement prohibiting aircraft and ships from dumping toxic and plastic waste into the Atlantic; it is the first major international agreement governing pollution of the sea.
- The United Nations Environment Program (UNEP) is established; its aim is to advise and coordinate environmental activities within the United Nations.
- The United States restricts the use of DDT because it is discovered that it thins the eggshells of predatory birds, lowering their reproductive rates.

APRIL

- Under the auspices of the California Water Project, water from northern California begins to flow to central and southern Californian farms and communities.
2   A tornado in Bangladesh leaves 25,000 people homeless and kills 200.
10   Iran is hit by an earthquake measuring 6.9 on the Richter scale; 5,000 people are killed.

MAY

- The Chiapas-Tabasco oil field is discovered near Villahermosa, Mexico; it is the largest oil field in the western hemisphere.

JUNE

- The United Nations Conference on the Human Environment is held in Stockholm, Sweden; the first international conference on the state of the environment, its aim is to improve the world's environment through monitoring, resource management, and education.
6   A coal mine explosion at Wankee, Rhodesia (now Zimbabwe), kills 427 people.
10–20   The eastern United States is racked by Hurricane Agnes. Several states are declared disaster areas as thousands flee their homes following widespread flooding; 122 people die and nearly $2 billion property damage is caused.
23   The Susquehanna River bursts its banks, flooding the Wilkes-Barre area of Pennsylvania and causing widespread property damage.

OCTOBER

- The U.S. Congress passes the Water Pollution Control Act over President Richard M. Nixon's veto. The act establishes clean water standards for industry and commits federal funds to constructing and upgrading municipal sewage facilities.
18   The Water Pollution Control Act is passed by Congress in the United States; it requires the best available water pollution control equipment to be installed by municipalities by 1983.

DECEMBER

23   An earthquake measuring 6.2 on the Richter scale devastates Managua, the capital of Nicaragua; about 10,000 people are killed.

Exploration

JANUARY

5   U.S. president Richard M. Nixon authorizes a $5.5 billion six-year program to develop plans for a spaceship capable of undertaking multiple missions, thereby launching the space shuttle program.

MARCH

- The U.S. National Aeronautics and Space Administration (NASA) uncrewed spacecraft *Pioneer 10* takes off toward Jupiter.

APRIL

16–27   The United States launches the *Apollo 16* moon mission; astronauts Charles Duke and John Young return with 97 kg/214 lb of lunar soil and rock after spending a record 71 hr 2 min on the moon.

JULY

22   The Soviet craft *Venera 8* (launched March 27) makes a soft landing on Venus and transmits valuable data from the surface.
23   The United States launches *Landsat 1*, the first of a series of satellites for surveying the earth's resources from space.

DECEMBER

7–19   *Apollo 17* is launched, commanded by U.S. astronaut Eugene Cernan—the last crewed mission to the moon.

Health and Medicine

- Approximately 500 sex-change operations have been performed since Johns Hopkins University, Baltimore, Maryland, performed the first one in the United States in 1966.
- English engineer Godfrey Hounsfield performs the first successful CAT (computerized axial tomography) scan that provides cross-sectional X-rays of the human body.
- German researchers F. Eisenberger and C. Chaussy, in Munich, invent the lithotripter, a machine that disintegrates kidney stones using ultrasound (commercialized in 1980).
- Swiss researcher J.-F. Borel discovers the immunosuppressive properties of the drug cyclosporin-A.
- U.S. biochemist Gerald Edelman and English biochemist Rodney Porter share the Nobel Prize for Physiology or Medicine for their discoveries concerning the chemical structure of antibodies.
- U.S. microbiologist Daniel Nathans uses a restriction enzyme that splits DNA (deoxyribonucleic acid) molecules to produce a genetic map of the monkey virus (SV40), the simplest virus known to produce cancer; it is the first application of these enzymes to an understanding of the molecular basis of cancer.
- Venezuelan-born U.S. immunologist Baruj Benacerraf and U.S. microbiologist Hugh O'Neill McDevitt show immune response to be genetically determined.

JANUARY

10 The U.S. surgeon general reports that inhalation of cigarette smoke by nonsmokers is a severe health hazard; his report prompts calls to ban smoking in such public areas as restaurants, offices, and airplanes.

Math

- French mathematician René Frédéric Thom formulates catastrophe theory, an attempt to describe biological processes mathematically.

Science

- Kenyan anthropologist Richard Leakey discovers a fossil *Homo habilis* skull (Skull 1470) in Ethiopia, the most complete *H. habilis* skull known. It is believed to be more than 2 million years old and its cranial capacity is more than twice that of *Australopithecus*.
- The tomb of a Han dynasty prince is discovered south of Beijing, China, and includes jade suits.
- U.S. biochemists Christian Anfinsen, Stanford Moore, and William Stein receive the Nobel Prize for Chemistry for their work on amino-acid structure and biological activity of the enzyme ribonuclease.
- U.S. physicist Murray Gell-Mann presents the theory of quantum chromodynamics (QCD), that predicts that quarks interact according to their "color." Strongly interacting particles consist of quarks, which are bound together by gluons.
- U.S. physicists John Bardeen, Leon Cooper, and John Schrieffer receive the Nobel Prize for Physics for their theory of superconductivity.

Technology

- *c.* 1972   Highly accurate bombs equipped with guidance systems based on lasers and electro-optical systems are first used in Vietnam.
- Japanese researcher Hideki Shirakawa attempts to make the polymer polyacetylene but accidentally adds a thousand times too much catalyst and discovers electrically conductive plastics; they have a metallic appearance.
- The 400-GeV (gigaelectron volt) proton synchrotron at the Fermi National Accelerator Laboratory in Batavia, Illinois, goes into operation; 6 km/4 mi in circumference, it is the highest energy particle accelerator built to date.
- The 411-m/1,350-ft-high World Trade Center opens in New York, New York—it is the tallest building in the world, until 1973.
- The Dutch company Philips patents the Videodisk. Information is contained in 45,000 grooves, all of the same width and depth but varying in length and spacing, cut in a spiral onto the plastic disc, and reproduced by a laser.
- The Mica Dam on the Columbia River, British Columbia, Canada, is completed; at 242 m/794 ft tall, it is the highest earth-filled dam in the world.
- The National Geographical Institute in the United States "reinvents" photogrammetry (the art of making precise measurements using two different photographs of the same object) by developing very accurate instruments; the method is used to conduct topographical surveys of buildings and objects too delicate to be touched.

JANUARY

24 U.S. researcher William Dobelle announces the invention of the electronic eye; it consists of a pair of glasses with a miniature television camera connected to the visual cortex by a battery of electrodes.

APRIL

- U.S. firm Polaroid introduces SX-70 film; it produces single-sheet instant color photographs.

Transportation

- The A300B Airbus is introduced by the French company Groupement d'Intérêt Economique.
- The supertanker *Globtik Tokyo* is launched in Japan; weighing 431,755 metric tons/476,025 tons, it is nearly 30% larger than the *Nisseki Maru* launched the previous year.
- The U.S. Air Force introduces the F-15 fighter.
- Vietnam veteran Frederick W. Smith creates Federal Express, the overnight shipping company, in Memphis, Tennessee.

JANUARY

9 The luxury liner *Queen Elizabeth*, now used for marine research in Hong Kong harbor, is destroyed by fire.

APRIL

- The 160-km/100-mi San-Yo Shinkansen railroad opens in Japan, linking Osaka and Okayama; trains travel at speeds up to 249 kph/155 mph.

DECEMBER

8 A United Air Lines Boeing 737 crashes into houses near Midway Airport in Chicago, Illinois, killing 45 people.

29 An Eastern Airlines Lockheed Tri-Star jet crashes into the Florida Everglades, killing 101 people.

ARTS AND IDEAS

Architecture

- Construction of Sweden's Öland Island Bridge is completed; 6,070 m/19,882 ft in length, it is Europe's longest bridge.
- San Francisco's Transamerica Corporation building, the Transamerica Pyramid, is completed.
- The Florey Building for Queen's College, Oxford, England, designed by the English architect James Stirling, is completed.
- The Medical Faculty of the University of Louvain in Belgium, designed by the Belgian architect Lucien Kroll, is completed.
- The Nagakin Capsule Tower in Tokyo, Japan, designed by the Japanese architect Kisho Kurokawa, is completed.
- The North Jutland Museum at Aalborg in Denmark, designed by the Finnish architect Alvar Aalto, is completed.

MARCH
- The Pruitt Igoe public housing blocks (designed by U.S. architect Minoru Yamasaki) are destroyed, in St. Louis, Missouri. This is widely seen as symbolic of the end of modernist architecture.

Arts

- The English art historian Michael Baxandall publishes *Painting and Experience in Fifteenth-Century Italy*.
- The exhibition "Inquiry into Reality: Images of Today" is held at the 5th Documenta, in Kassel, West Germany.
- The German artist Joseph Beuys creates the gallery installation *Arens – Where Would I Have Got If I Hadn't Been Intelligent!*, in New York, New York.
- The Kimbell Art Museum in Fort Worth, Texas, designed by the U.S. architect Louis Kahn, is completed.
- The U.S. artist Edward Kienholz creates *Five Card Stud*.

Film

- Sears, Roebuck introduces the first video rental system in the United States, hiring out movies for $3–6 a night, to run on the Avco Cartavision video player.
- The controversial, sexually explicit movie *Last Tango in Paris*, directed by Bernardo Bertolucci, is released. It stars Marlon Brando and Maria Schneider.
- The epic gangster picture *The Godfather* is released in the United States. It is cowritten and directed by Francis Ford Coppola and stars Marlon Brando, Al Pacino, James Caan, Diane Keaton, and Robert Duvall.
- The movie *Aguirre: The Wrath of God*, directed by Werner Herzog, is released, starring Klaus Kinski.
- The movie *Deliverance*, based on the novel by James Dickey, is released in the United States. It is directed by

English filmmaker John Boorman, photographed by Vilmos Zsigmond, and stars Jon Voight and Burt Reynolds.
- The movie *Die Bitteren Tränen der Petra von Kant/The Bitter Tears of Petra Von Kant* is released in West Germany. It is directed by Rainer Werner Fassbinder and stars Margit Carstensen and Hanna Schygulla.
- The movie *Fellini's Roma*, directed by Federico Fellini, is released in Italy. It stars Peter Gonzales and Britta Barnes.
- The movie *Frenzy*, directed by Alfred Hitchcock, is released in the UK, starring Jon Finch, Alec McCowen, Barry Foster, and Billie Whitelaw.
- The movie *Harold and Maude* is released in the United States. It is directed by Hal Ashby and stars Bud Cort and Ruth Gordon.
- The movie *Lady Sings the Blues*, a biopic of blues singer Billie Holiday, is released in the United States. Directed by Sidney Furie, it stars Diana Ross, Billy Dee Williams, and Richard Pryor.
- The movie *Le Charme discret de la bourgeoisie/The Discreet Charm of the Bourgeoisie*, cowritten and directed by the Spanish-born filmmaker Luis Buñuel, is released in France. It stars Fernando Rey, Delphine Seyrig, Stéphane Audran, and Bulle Ogier.
- The movie *Ludwig*, directed by Luchino Visconti, is released in Italy, starring Helmut Berger and Romy Schneider.
- The movie *Macbeth*, an adaptation of Shakespeare's play, is released in the UK. It is directed by the Polish-born U.S. filmmaker Roman Polanski and stars Jon Finch.
- The movie *Pete 'n' Tillie*, directed by Martin Ritt, is released in the United States. Based on a novel by Peter de Vries, it stars Walter Matthau and Carol Burnett.
- The movie *Play It Again, Sam*, based on a play by Woody Allen, is released in the United States. It is directed by Herbert Ross and stars Allen, Diane Keaton, and Tony Roberts.
- The movie *Sleuth*, directed by Joseph Mankiewicz, is released in the UK, starring Laurence Olivier and Michael Caine.
- The movie *Sounder*, directed by Martin Ritt, is released in the United States, starring Paul Winfield, Cicely Tyson, Kevin Hooks, and James Best.
- The movie *Superfly*, directed by Gordon Parks, Jr., is released in the United States, starring Ron O'Neal, Carl Lee, and Sheila Frasier.
- The movie *The Poseidon Adventure* is released in the United States. It is directed by Ronald Neame and features an all-star cast including Gene Hackman. The movie is one of the first in a lucrative series of disaster movies.
- The movie *The Ruling Class*, directed by Peter Medak, is released in the UK. Adapted from the play by Peter Barnes, it stars Peter O'Toole, Alistair Sim, Arthur Lowe, and Harry Andrew.
- The movie *Tout va bien/All's Well*, directed by Jean-Luc Godard, is released in France, starring Jane Fonda and Yves Montand.
- The movie *Viskningar och Rop/Cries and Whispers*, written and directed by Swedish filmmaker Ingmar Bergman, is released in Sweden. It is photographed by Sven Nykvist and stars Harriet Andersson, Liv Ullmann, Ingrid Thulin, and Kari Sylwan.

- The musical movie *Cabaret*, directed by Bob Fosse, is released in the United States. It stars Liza Minnelli, Michael York, and Joel Grey. The movie wins a number of Academy Awards, including best director, best actress, and best supporting actor.
- The political satire *The Candidate* is released in the United States, directed by Michael Ritchie and starring Robert Redford.
- The satirical animated movie *Fritz the Cat* is released. Based on a comic strip by Robert Crum, it is written, directed, and animated by Ralph Bakshi. The animated format allows the movie to show obscenity and violence that would not have been allowed in a live-action feature.
- The screwball comedy *What's Up, Doc?* is released in the United States. It is directed by Peter Bogdanovich and stars Barbra Streisand and Ryan O'Neal.

MARCH

2 The Union of the Audiovisual Arts is created in Algeria, with a vision of a new politically motivated movie industry.
31 The Gaumont Palace, built in 1911 and the most famous movie theater in France, closes.

APRIL

9 The 1971 Academy Awards take place. Best Actor: Gene Hackman, for *The French Connection*; Best Supporting Actor: Ben Johnson, for *The Last Picture Show*; Best Actress: Jane Fonda, for *Klute*; Best Supporting Actress: Cloris Leachman, for *The Last Picture Show*; Best Picture: *The French Connection*, directed by William Friedkin; Best Director: William Friedkin, for *The French Connection*.
17 The movie *The Godfather* takes a record-breaking $26 million within a few days of opening, in the United States.

MAY

19 At the Cannes Film Festival in France the Palme d'Or is awarded to the Italian movie *Il Caso Mattei/The Mattei Affair*, directed by Francesco Rosi and Gian Maria Volonté.

OCTOBER

7 The Italian authorities impound Pier Paolo Pasolini's sexually explicit *I Racconti di Canterbury/The Canterbury Tales*.

Literature and Language

- *La Mort heureuse/A Happy Death*, an early novel by the Algerian-born French writer Albert Camus, is published posthumously.
- John Berger's novel *G* wins the Booker Prize in Britain. The author gives half the proceeds to the Black Panthers (a U.S. black revolutionary group) in protest at the involvement of Booker McConnell in the sugar industry in the Caribbean.
- Kathleen Woodiwiss begins a craze for historical novels with the publication of *The Flame and the Flower*.
- Pulitzer prizewinning *Up Country: Poems of New England* is published by Maxine Kumin.
- The Austrian writer Peter Handke publishes *Wunschloses Unglück/A Sorrow Beyond Dreams*, a memoir of his mother.

- The English poet John Betjeman is appointed poet laureate in Britain, a position he holds till his death in 1984.
- The English writer Frederick Forsyth publishes his novel *The Day of the Jackal*.
- The English writer Margaret Drabble publishes her novel *The Needle's Eye*.
- The English-born U.S. writer Denise Levertov publishes her poetry collection *Footprints*.
- The Finnish writer Tove Jansson publishes *Sommarboken/The Summer Book*.
- The French cultural critic Roland Barthes publishes *Le Plaisir du texte/Pleasure of the Text*.
- The French writer and philosopher Simone de Beauvoir publishes her fourth volume of autobiography *Tout compte fait/All Said and Done*.
- The Irish poet Seamus Heaney publishes his poetry collection *Wintering Out*.
- The Italian writer Italo Calvino publishes his novel *Le città invisibili/Invisible Cities*.
- The Nobel Prize for Literature is awarded to the German novelist Heinrich Böll.
- The Pulitzer Prize for Biography is awarded to Joseph P. Lash for *Eleanor and Franklin*, The Pulitzer Prize for Poetry is awarded to James Wright for *Collected Poems*, and the Pulitzer Prize for Fiction is awarded to Wallace Stegner for *Angels of Repose*.
- The Scottish poet Iain Crichton Smith publishes his poetry collection *Love Poems & Elegies*.
- The Trinidadian writer V. S. Naipaul publishes *In a Free State*, a collection of three novellas.
- The U.S. writer Anne Sexton publishes her poetry collection *The Book of Folly*.
- The U.S. writer Eudora Welty publishes her novel *The Optimist's Daughter*, which is awarded a Pulitzer prize.
- The U.S. writer Robert Hayden publishes his poetry collection *The Night-Blooming Cereus*.

Music

- George Harrison releases the triple album *The Concert for Bangladesh*, with artists featured including Eric Clapton, Bob Dylan, and Ringo Starr. It raises more than $8 million for UNICEF.
- Groups such as the Bay City Rollers, the Jackson Five, the Osmonds, and David Cassidy mark the era of "Teenybop," with the bands appealing particularly to teenage girls.
- Passion for the Osmond family is at its height in Britain. Little Jimmy (just nine years old) achieves the family's greatest chart success with his single "Long-Haired Lover from Liverpool."
- The British pop star and actor David Bowie releases the album *The Man Who Sold the World*.
- The British rock group Roxy Music releases *Roxy Music*, their first album.
- The English composer Harrison Birtwistle completes his orchestral work *The Triumph of Time*.
- The English composer Michael Tippett completes his Symphony No. 3.
- The first rock concert at Wembley Stadium in London, England, takes place. Artists appearing include Bill

Haley and Chuck Berry and a movie of the event, *The London Rock and Roll Show*, is released.

- The Italian composer Luciano Berio completes his vocal work *Recital I (for Cathy)* for mezzo-soprano and 17 instruments.
- The opera *Lorenzaccio*, by the Italian composer Sylvano Bussotti, is first performed, in Florence, Italy.
- The opera *Taverner*, by the English composer Peter Maxwell Davies, is first performed, at Covent Garden in London, England.
- The Scottish pop singer Ewan MacColl releases "The First Time Ever I Saw Your Face."
- The U.S. composer Aaron Copland completes his orchestral work *Three Latin-American Sketches*.
- The U.S. composer George Rochberg completes his String Quartet No. 3.
- The U.S. composer John Cage completes his orchestral work *Cheap Imitation*.
- The U.S. composer Morton Feldman completes his orchestral work *Cello and Orchestra*.
- The U.S. composer Ned Rorem completes his song cycle *Last Poems of Wallace Stevens*.
- The U.S. pop singer Donny Osmond releases "Puppy Love."
- The U.S. pop singer Johnny Nash releases the album *I Can See Clearly Now*.

MARCH

25 The U.S. pop singer Stevie Wonder releases the album *Music of My Mind*.

25 The U.S. rhythm and blues group Gladys Knight and the Pips releases the single "Help Me Make It Through the Night."

JUNE

3   The U.S. rock singer Alice Cooper releases the single "School's Out."

10 The British rock group the Rolling Stones releases the album *Exile on Main Street*.

17 The British pop star and actor David Bowie releases the album *The Rise and Fall of Ziggy Stardust and the Spiders from Mars*.

24 The Australian pop singer Helen Reddy releases "I Am Woman."

AUGUST

5   The U.S. rock and roll legend Chuck Berry has a hit with "My Ding-a-ling," despite an attempt by media campaigner Mary Whitehouse to have it banned in Britain.

Theater and Dance

- *Pippin*, a musical based on the life of Charlemagne, by Roger Hirson and Stephen Schwartz, opens in New York, New York, starring John Rubenstein, Ben Vereen, Eric Berry, and Irene Ryan.
- The ballet *Choral Dances*, by the U.S. choreographer Alvin Ailey, with music by Benjamin Britten, is first performed, in the United States.
- The monodrama *A Stretch of the Imagination*, by the Australian writer Jack Hibberd, is first performed, in Australia.
- The musical *Grease*, with lyrics and music by Jim Jacobs and Warren Casey, is first performed, at the Eden

Theater in New York, New York. Its better known songs include "Shakin'" and "At the High School Hop."

- The play *Head, Guts, Bones and Sound Bone Dance*, by the British-born Canadian writer Michael Cook, is first performed, in Halifax, Canada.
- The play *Jumpers*, by the Czechoslovak-born British dramatist Tom Stoppard, is first performed, at the Old Vic Theatre in London, England.
- The play *Leaving Home*, by the Canadian writer David French, is first performed, in Toronto, Canada.
- The play *Sizwe Banzi is Dead*, by the South African writer Athol Fugard, is first performed, in South Africa.
- The play *Stallerhof/Dairy Farm*, by the German writer Franz Kroetz, is first performed, in Germany.
- The play *The Chapel Perilous*, by the Australian writer Dorothy Hewett, is first performed in London, England.
- The play *The Sunshine Boys*, by the U.S. writer Neil Simon, is first performed, at the Broadhurst Theater in New York, New York.
- The play *The Tooth of Crime*, by the U.S. writer Sam Shepard, is first performed, in New York, New York.
- The Pulitzer Prize for Drama is not awarded this year.

Thought and Scholarship

- Austrian-born English philosopher Karl Popper publishes *Objective Knowledge*.
- C. Jencks and others publish *Inequality: A Reassessment of the Effect of Family and Schooling in America*.
- English historian Christopher Hill publishes *The World Turned Upside Down: Radical Ideas during the English Revolution*.
- English historian G. R. Elton publishes *Policy and Police: The Enforcement of the Reformation in the Age of Thomas Cromwell*.
- English philosopher Stephen Toulmin publishes *Human Understanding*.
- French philosopher Jacques Derrida publishes *Marges de la philosophie/On the Margins of Philosophy*.
- French sinologist Jacques Gernet publishes *A History of Chinese Civilization*.
- The Pulitzer Prize for History is awarded to Carl N. Degler for *Neither Black Nor White: Slavery and Race Relations in Brazil and the United States*.
- The Pulitzer Prize for General Nonfiction is awarded to Barbara W. Tuchman for *Stilwell and the American Experience in China*.
- U.S. paleontologists Stephen Jay Gould and Nils Eldridge propose the punctuated equilibrium model—the idea that evolution progresses in fits and starts rather than at a uniform rate.

SOCIETY

Education

- Financial support and additional holidays are granted to part-time adult learners following vocational courses in West Germany.

MARCH

15 A new education policy is launched in Pakistan, including the development of a People's Open University and the nationalization of most private elementary schools.

Everyday Life

- Magnavox develops *Odyssey*, the first video arcade game.
- Published in an atmosphere of increasing liberality, British gerontologist Alex Comfort's *The Joy of Sex: A Gourmet Guide to Lovemaking* encourages sexual experimentation.
- The dispute between the United Transportation Union and railroad companies, over the phase out of firemen's jobs on diesel freight locomotives ends, one of the longest labor disputes in U.S. history.
- The U.S. birth rate—15.8 per thousand of the population—is the lowest since records began in 1917.

JANUARY

9 Coal miners begin a national strike in Britain in support of their claim for pay increases of up to 47%.

28 During a performance at the White House by the Ray Conniff Singers, singer Carol Feraci unfolds a sign reading "Stop the Killing" and denounces President Nixon's Vietnam war policy.

FEBRUARY

9 One month after the start of the miners' strike in Britain, a state of emergency is declared.

19 The longest dock strike in U.S. history ends after 139 days.

MARCH

22 The Supreme Court in the United States rules that a Massachusetts law denying contraceptives to single people is unconstitutional.

JULY

28–August 16 A nationwide dock strike begins in Britain, when dockers' delegates reject the proposals of the Aldington–Jones Report to ease unemployment caused by "containerization."

DECEMBER

31 British inventor Clive Sinclair launches his pocket calculator, the first to be widely available. The "Sinclair Executive" weighs 70 g/12.5 oz and goes on sale for £79 in Britain and $195 in the United States.

Media and Communication

- *That Certain Summer*, starring Hal Holbrook and Martin Sheen, an early drama about male homosexuality, is shown on U.S. television.
- President Ferdinand Marcos closes down all broadcast channels in the Philippines apart from the state channel.
- The 1971–72 Emmy Awards for television are held. Best Drama Series: *Elizabeth R*; Best Comedy Series: *All in the Family*; Best Actor in a Drama: Peter Falk, for *Columbo*; Best Actress in a Drama: Glenda Jackson, for *Elizabeth R*; Best Actor in a Comedy: William Mindom, for *My World and Welcome To It*; Best Actress in a Comedy: Jean Stapleton, for *All in the Family*.

- The samurai series *Underground Executioner* is broadcast in Japan.
- The women's magazine *Cosmopolitan* begins monthly publication, promising to cover "life, love, sex, and money."
- When *The Washington Post* exposes the scandal underlying the Watergate break-ins, most other newspapers fail to pick up on the significance of the story.

JANUARY

- The U.S. surgeon general reports that television violence is unlikely to influence children not disposed to violent behavior.

2 Radio and television advertising of cigarettes ends as a result of legislation passed by the U.S. Congress.

14–September 2, 1977 The popular U.S. television comedy *Sanford and Son*, based on a British television show *Steptoe and Son*, airs for six seasons.

FEBRUARY

4 The U.S. Federal Communications Commission announces new rules regulating cable television, encouraging expansion into rural markets but restricting access to urban markets.

MARCH

March 1972–April 1973 The syndicated U.S. news columnist Jack Anderson charges International Telephone and Telegraph (ITT) and the Central Intelligence Agency (CIA) in the U.S. of colluding to topple the Marxist government of Salvador Allende in Chile. ITT admits the charges on April 2, 1973.

JUNE

- Publisher Rupert Murdoch purchases the newspapers *Sydney Daily Telegraph* and *Sunday Telegraph* in Australia.

JULY

1 *Ms*, the first mainstream feminist magazine, is launched in the United States, with U.S. journalist Gloria Steinem as editor: the first issue of 300,000 copies sells out in eight days.

AUGUST

- *Washington Post* reporters Bob Woodward and Carl Bernstein implicate the Committee for the Reelection of the President (CREEP) in the Watergate burglary, leading to a series of revelations about the Nixon administration's complicity in the Watergate affair that contribute to the president's eventual downfall.

SEPTEMBER

14–August 20, 1981 *The Waltons*, a television drama about a large southern family struggling against the odds during the Depression, starts on U.S. television.

17–September 19, 1983 *M*A*S*H*, a comedy about a mobile army surgical unit set during the Korean War, is shown on U.S. television. A spin-off from the movie directed by Robert Altman, it stars Alan Alda, Mike Farrel, Loretta Swit, Jamie Farr, David Ogden Stiers, and Harry Morgan.

DECEMBER

29 The magazine *Life* ceases circulation in the United States, after 36 years of weekly publication. It is relaunched in 1978.

Religion

- British canon John V. Taylor publishes *The Go-Between God*.
- Henry Mayr-Harting publishes *The Coming of Christianity to Anglo-Saxon England*.
- The Greek Orthodox leader Metropolitan Dimitrios of Imroz and Tenedos is elected as Ecumenical Patriarch of Constantinople.
- The United Reformed Church is formed in Britain through the union of the Congregational Church in England and Wales, and the Presbyterian Church in England.

JUNE

- Sally J. Priesand, of Cincinnati, Ohio, becomes the first woman to be ordained a rabbi.

SEPTEMBER

14 Pope Paul VI abolishes the requirement for those entering the priesthood or monastaries to have their head shaved in a tonsure.

Sports

- Off-track betting is legalized in the state of New York.
- The British Jockey Club allows women jockeys to compete in horseracing for the first time, though only on the flat.
- The Dallas Cowboys become the first U.S. American football team to introduce professional cheerleaders.
- U.S. runners Philip Knight and William Bowerman found Nike, Inc., under the name of Blue Ribbon Sports.

BIRTHS & DEATHS

- Philip Drinker, inventor of the iron lung, dies (78).

JANUARY

1 Maurice Chevalier, French musical comedy star of stage and film, dies in Paris, France (83).

7 John Berryman, U.S. poet, dies in Minneapolis, Minnesota (57).

14 Frederik IX, king of Denmark 1947–72, dies in Copenhagen, Denmark (71).

26 Mahalia Jackson, U.S. gospel singer, dies in Chicago, Illinois (60).

FEBRUARY

5 Marianne Moore, U.S. poet, critic, and translator, dies in New York (84).

20 Walter Winchell, U.S. newspaper gossip columnist, dies in Los Angeles, California (74).

28 Viktor Barna, Hungarian table-tennis player who later played for England, dies in Lima, Peru (60).

MARCH

6 Shaquille O'Neal, U.S. basketball player, born in Newark, New Jersey.

14 Howard Hathaway Aiken, U.S. mathematician who invented the Harvard Mark I computer, the forerunner of modern computers, dies in St. Louis, Missouri (73).

24 Cristobal Balenciaga, Spanish dress designer of elegant ball gowns and other classic clothing, dies in Valencia, Spain (77).

APRIL

3 Ferde Grofé, U.S. composer best known for his orchestral suites, dies in Santa Monica, California (80).

16 Yasunari Kawabata, Japanese novelist, dies in Zushi, Japan (72).

27 Kwame Nkrumah, West African nationalist politician, the first prime minister of independent Ghana,

then president 1957–66, dies in Bucharest, Romania (62).

MAY

2 J. Edgar Hoover, U.S. government official, director of the FBI 1924–72, dies in Washington, D.C. (77).

4 E. C. Kendall, U.S. chemist who isolated cortisone and used it to treat rheumatoid arthritis, dies in Princeton, New Jersey (86).

22 Cecil Day Lewis, Irish poet, British poet laureate from 1968, dies in Hadley Wood, Hertfordshire, England (68).

28 Edward VIII, king of Great Britain and Northern Ireland (January–December 1936) who abdicated to marry the U.S. divorcée Wallis Simpson, dies in Paris, France (77).

JUNE

12 Edmund Wilson, U.S. playwright, poet, essayist, critic, and influential editor, dies in Talcottville, New York (77).

JULY

31 Paul Spaak, Belgian statesman who played a major role in the formation of the EEC, NATO, and Benelux, dies in Brussels, Belgium (72).

AUGUST

11 Max Theiler, U.S. microbiologist who developed a vaccine for yellow fever, dies in New Haven, Connecticut (73).

14 Jules Romains, French novelist, dramatist, and poet, a founder of the literary movement *Unanimisme*, dies in Paris, France (86).

OCTOBER

1 Louis Leakey, Kenyan archeologist and anthropologist who discovered that the human species was much older than previously believed, dies in London, England (69).

11 Paul Ricca ("The Waiter"), Chicago gangster, dies in Chicago, Illinois (74).

24 Jackie Robinson, U.S. baseball player, the first black player in the major leagues, dies in Stamford, Connecticut (53).

26 Igor Sikorsky, Russian-born U.S. aircraft designer who successfully developed the helicopter, dies in Easton, California (83).

NOVEMBER

1 Ezra Pound, U.S. poet and literary critic, dies in Venice, Italy (87).

14 Martin Dies, Jr., U.S. conservative Democrat politician who investigated for communists in U.S. society, dies in Lufkin, Texas (72).

DECEMBER

10 Mark Van Doren, U.S. poet who won a Pulitzer prize for his poetry, dies in Torrington, Connecticut (78).

23 Andrey Nikolayevich Tupolev, Russian aircraft designer who helped to develop the world's first supersonic passenger airliner, dies in Moscow, USSR (84).

24 Charles Atlas, U.S. bodybuilder and promoter of bodybuilding by mail order, dies in Long Beach, New York (79).

26 Harry S. Truman, 33rd president of the United States 1945–53, a Democrat, dies in Kansas City, Missouri (88).

27 Lester Pearson, Canadian statesman and diplomat, prime minister of Canada 1963–68, dies in Ottawa, Canada (75).

31 Roberto Clemente, U.S. professional National League baseball player, dies in a plane crash en route to Nicaragua with relief supplies (38).

By 1990, Nike will be the leader in the training shoes market and Knight will be a billionaire.

JANUARY

1   Sportswriters select Nebraska as college football's national champions for the 1971 season.

14–16   U.S. national figure skating champions are: Janet Lynn; Ken Shelley; Jo Jo Starbuck and Ken Shelley, pairs; Judy Schwomeyer and James Sladky, dance.

FEBRUARY

3–13   The 11th Winter Olympic Games are held in Sapporo, Japan. The USSR wins 8 gold medals; East Germany, Switzerland and the Netherlands, 4 each; and the United States and West Germany, 3 each. Yukio Kasaya wins the 70 meters ski jump to give the host country its first-ever gold medal at the Winter Olympics.

MARCH

6   U.S. golfer Jack Nicklaus wins the Doral Eastern Open to become the leading money winner in golf history. His career earnings of $1,477,200 exceed those of fellow U.S. golfer Arnold Palmer.

31–April 13   A dispute about pension fund contributions leads to the first-ever major league baseball players' strike; 86 games in the new season are canceled before a settlement is reached.

APRIL

17   The Boston Marathon, the world's oldest annual marathon, officially includes women for the first time in its 75-year history.

30–May 11   The Boston Bruins beat the New York Rangers to win the National Hockey League Stanley Cup.

MAY

7   The Los Angeles Lakers beat the New York Knicks to win the National Basketball Association (NBA) championship.

27   Racing driver Mark Donohue wins the Indianapolis 500.

JUNE

11   The English race-car driver Graham Hill wins the Le Mans 24-hour race in France, becoming the first person to have won the Formula One World Drivers' championship, the Indianapolis 500, and Le Mans.

18   Jack Nicklaus wins his third U.S. Open and 13th "major," tying with Bobby Jones' record for the most majors.

JULY

•   Hawaiian-born Jesse Kuhaulua, also known as Takamiyama, is the first non-Japanese sumo wrestler to win an official top-division tournament.

1   Bobby Fischer of the United States beats Boris Spassky of the USSR 12.5–8.5 in the World Chess Championship in Reykjavik, Iceland.

18   Eddie Merckx of Belgium wins his fourth consecutive Tour de France cycling race.

AUGUST

22   The Rhodesian team is excluded from the Munich Olympic Games by the International Olympic Committee, under pressure from the black African nations protesting against white majority rule in Rhodesia under Ian Smith.

24   U.S. sport administrator Avery Brundage retires as president of the International Olympic Committee after 20 years in office.

26   The 20th Olympic Games open in Munich, West Germany, attended by 7,123 competitors, including 1,058 women, from 121 countries.

28–September 4   At the Olympic Games in Munich, West Germany, Mark Spitz of the United States wins an unprecedented seven gold medals in swimming, all in world record times.

SEPTEMBER

•   At the Olympic Games in Munich, West Germany, Valery Borzov of the USSR wins both the men's 100 and 200 meters.

•   The Association of Tennis Professionals (ATP) is founded in the United States by Jack Kramer, Arthur Ashe, and Stan Smith of the United States, and Cliff Drysdale of South Africa.

2–28   In the first ever encounter between the National Hockey League (NHL) and the USSR national team, the Team Canada NHL All-Stars defeat the USSR, sealing victory with a 6–5 win in Moscow in the final game of the eight-game series.

6   A memorial service is held at the Olympic stadium in Munich, West Germany, in honor of the 11 Israeli athletes murdered by Arab terrorists on September 5. Later the same day, with the support of the Israelis, competition recommences.

10   At the Olympic Games in Munich, West Germany, the U.S. basketball team suffer their first ever defeat in Olympic competition, losing the final 51–50 to the USSR in a disputed finish.

10   Emerson Fittipaldi becomes the first Brazilian race-car driver to win the Formula One World Drivers' Championship. At the age of 25, he is also the youngest-ever champion.

11   The 20th Olympic Games close in Munich, West Germany. The USSR wins 50 gold medals; the United States, 33; East Germany, 20; West Germany and Japan, 13 each; Australia, 8; Poland, 7; Hungary and Bulgaria, 6 each; Italy, 5; Sweden and Britain, 4 each.

OCTOBER

14–22   The Oakland Athletics beat the Cincinnati Reds to win the World Series.

NOVEMBER

8–February 4, 1973   In a state referendum, voters in Colorado, United States, decide that the environmental and financial cost of holding the Winter Olympics in 1976 is too great; the games are switched to Innsbruck, Austria.

DECEMBER

31   Roberto Clemente of the Pittsburgh Pirates baseball team is killed in a plane crash while flying to the aid of Nicaraguan earthquake victims.

1973

POLITICS, GOVERNMENT, AND ECONOMICS

Business and Economics

- Federal Express begins parcel delivery services in the United States.
- The first share options market opens in Chicago, United States.
- The U.S. company Timberland, which manufactures high-quality outdoor clothing, is founded.
- World economies undergo a simultaneous boom, with commodity prices increasing drastically. The rise in the price of oil and restriction of its supply after war breaks out in the Middle East disrupts Western economies.

JANUARY
- In the face of a fuel shortage, the U.S. president Richard M. Nixon lifts import quotas on crude oil.

FEBRUARY
- The European Trade Union Confederation, with 29 million members, is formed in the 14 countries belonging to the European Economic Community (Common Market) and the European Free Trade Association.
- 13 The United States devalues the dollar by 10% by raising the price of gold to $42.22 an ounce.

MARCH
- The U.S. Supreme Court upholds the use of local property taxes to support public education, despite the inequality the system engenders.
- 4–19 European exchange markets close in the face of a new currency crisis.
- 16 Finance ministers of the European Economic Community (Common Market) countries, meeting in Paris, France, agree to establish a floating exchange rate system.

APRIL
- The U.S. president Richard M. Nixon announces that he owes the Internal Revenue Service $465,000 in back taxes and interest accrued between 1969 and 1972.

MAY
- 1 The British Trades Union Congress calls a one-day strike in protest against the government's pay restraint policy.

SEPTEMBER
- The U.S. Securities and Exchange Commission abolishes fixed commission rates for brokers.

DECEMBER
- 12 An overtime ban by train drivers in Britain starts to disrupt rail services.
- 23 The shah of Iran announces that the Gulf States will increase the price of oil from $5.10 to $11.65 a barrel from January 1, 1974.

Colonization

JULY
- 10 The Bahamas achieve independence within the Commonwealth after almost 300 years of British colonial rule.

Human Rights

- *Our Bodies, Our Selves: A Course by and for Women* is published by the Boston Women's Health Collective.
- A physician in France is arrested for performing an illegal abortion; 10,000 protesters march to protest the abortion laws, resulting in the introduction of abortion rights legislation in parliament.
- British feminist Sheila Rowbotham publishes *Women's Consciousness in a Man's World*.
- The U.S. Supreme Court rules that advertisements for employment cannot specify gender.

FEBRUARY
- February–May Two-hundred members of the militant Native American Movement occupy Wounded Knee, South Dakota, to publicize their demand for the open election of tribal leaders, an investigation of the Bureau of Indian Affairs, and a review of Native American treaties. The siege ends after federal officers pledge to address the Native Americans' grievances.

MAY
- The U.S. Supreme Court rules that the spouses of women who serve in the armed forces are entitled to the same benefits as the spouses of male servicemen.

OCTOBER
- Maynard Jackson becomes the first black mayor of Atlanta, Georgia.

Politics and Government

- Cypriot Orthodox bishops call for Archbishop Makarios to resign.
- Pope Paul VI condemns "Christian fratricide" in Northern Ireland.
- The creation of a department of education in Australia subjects state policies to closer federal control.

- The French ministry of education is reorganized.
- The school-leaving age is raised to 16 in Britain.
- The state of Oregon, United States, decriminalizes the possession of small amounts of cannabis.
- The U.S. Supreme Court introduces the test of "redeeming social value" for obscenity cases.

JANUARY

- Golda Meir becomes the first prime minister of Israel to visit the Vatican in Rome, Italy.
- In the Watergate scandal, the former Nixon campaign officials James W. McCord and G. Gordon Liddy are convicted of burglary and wiretapping.
- The American Telephone and Telegraph company (AT&T) settles a discrimination suit filed on behalf of women and minorities. The company agrees to pay $15 million and establish hiring quotas and a job-training program.
- The U.S. defense secretary Melvin R. Laird announces the end of military conscription.
1 Britain, Ireland, and Denmark become members of the European Economic Community (Common Market).
4 Australia abandons the color bar in admitting new settlers.
6 Portuguese revolutionaries explode 12 bombs in Lisbon in protest at the colonial wars.
8 The trial opens in Washington, D.C., United States, of seven men accused of attempting to bug the opposition Democratic Party headquarters in the Watergate apartment complex.
9 Rhodesia closes its border with Zambia after terrorist attacks.
15 The U.S. president Richard M. Nixon orders a suspension of all military action against North Vietnam in the Vietnam War.
17 President Ferdinand Marcos of the Philippines proclaims a new constitution under which he will rule indefinitely.
20 Richard M. Nixon is inaugurated as president of the United States for a second term.
27 The United States, North and South Vietnam, and the Vietcong (armed forces of the National Front for the Liberation of South Vietnam) sign a Vietnam War cease-fire agreement in Paris, France.

FEBRUARY

7 Protest strikes, arson, and gun battles erupt in Northern Ireland following the first detention of Protestant terrorist suspects.
8 Archbishop Makarios is returned unopposed as president of Cyprus.
12 North Vietnam and the Vietcong (armed forces of the National Front for the Liberation of South Vietnam) release the first U.S. prisoners of war, following the signing on January 27 of a cease-fire agreement in the Vietnam War.
19 French right wing extremists steal the body of Marshal Pétain, head of the pro-Nazi Vichy government in World War II, from its tomb on the Ile d'Yeu, off the northeast coast of France.
21 The government of Laos and the communist resistance group, the Pathet Lao, sign a cease-fire agreement in the captial, Vientiane.
22 China and the United States agree to establish high-level liaison offices in Washington, D.C., United States, and Beijing, China.

MARCH

- In the face of consumer restiveness in the U.S., President Richard M. Nixon freezes prices on beef, pork, and lamb.
- U.S. federal officials seize the assets of the Equity Funding Corporation of America after prosecutors uncover evidence of insider-trading.
1 The National Coalition of the Fine Gael and Labour parties wins the general election in the Republic of Ireland.
2 Palestinian terrorists murder Cleo Noel, the U.S. ambassador to Sudan, after invading a reception at the Saudi Arabian embassy in Khartoum, Sudan.
8 In a Northern Ireland referendum, 591,820 people vote to remain in the United Kingdom and 6,463 to join the Republic of Ireland.
8 The Irish Republican Army (IRA) plants car bombs at Scotland Yard and the Old Bailey in London, England, killing one person and injuring 238.
10 Following a period of political tension, Richard Sharples, governor of Bermuda, is assassinated in the capital, Hamilton.
11 The Peronist candidate, Héctor Cámpora, wins the general election in Argentina.
14 Liam Cosgrave, leader of the Fine Gael party, becomes prime minister of the Republic of Ireland.
29 The last U.S. troops leave Vietnam and the last U.S. prisoners of war, captured during the Vietnam War, are released.

APRIL

- In the ongoing Watergate affair in the United States, the Federal Bureau of Investigation director L. Patrick Gray resigns after he is revealed to have destroyed White House records.
- The U.S. president Richard M. Nixon appears before the U.S. people to protest his innocence in the Watergate scandal. However, all those around him seem to have been involved, as the president reports that he has accepted the resignations of his chief of staff, H. R. Haldeman; domestic policy advisor, John Ehrlichman; legal counsel, John Dean; and attorney general, Richard G. Kleindienst.
9 Palestinian terrorists attack the home of the Israeli ambassador to Cyprus, in Nicosia, Cyprus.
11 In reprisal raids, Israeli commandos raid the Lebanese capital Beirut and kill three Palestinian guerrilla leaders.
16 Britain opens its embassy in East Germany.
17 The U.S. president Richard M. Nixon drops the ban on White House staff appearing before a Senate committee to be questioned on the Watergate affair (the attempted bugging of the campaign headquarters of the opposition Democratic Party).
23 In a major speech in New York, Henry Kissinger, head of the U.S. National Security Council, calls for a new "Atlantic Charter" governing relations between the United States, Europe, and Japan.
27 The Soviet foreign minister Andrey Gromyko and the chief of the KGB Yury Andropov are promoted to the Soviet Politburo in the first major reshuffle since 1964.
30 The U.S. president Richard M. Nixon accepts responsibility for the attempted bugging of the Watergate building in Washington, D.C. (the campaign headquarters of the opposition Democrats), but denies any personal involvement.

MAY

- Archibald Cox, a professor at Harvard Law School, becomes special Watergate prosecutor.
- The U.S. Senate Select Committee on Presidential Campaign Activities begins public hearings to investigate allegations of a cover-up in the Watergate scandal.
- 11 A U.S. federal judge dismisses all charges against Defense Department employee Daniel Ellsberg and Anthony Russo in the *Pentagon Papers* trial, following the leaking of top-secret information on the U.S. involvement in the Vietnam War, on the grounds of "improper government conduct."
- 11 Joop den Uyl becomes prime minister of the Netherlands after a record 164-day ministerial crisis.
- 17 A U.S. Senate committee begins hearings of White House staff evidence on the Watergate affair (the attempted bugging of the campaign headquarters of the opposition Democratic Party).
- 18–22 The Soviet leader Leonid Brezhnev visits West Germany.
- 22 Britain and the United States veto the United Nations resolution to extend the sanctions against Ian Smith's Rhodesia to South Africa and the Portuguese colonies for breaking the embargo.
- 23 The Greek government foils a naval mutiny.
- 26 An Icelandic gunboat shells and holes the British trawler *Everton*.
- 31 Erskine Childers succeeds Éamon de Valera as president of the Republic of Ireland.
- 31 The U.S. Senate votes to stop providing funds for the bombing of Cambodia and Laos.

JUNE

- The U.S. president Richard M. Nixon announces a retail price freeze on rents, wholesale farm prices, and interest and dividends in order to combat inflation.
- The U.S. president Richard M. Nixon establishes the Federal Energy Office to spur energy conservation and foster the development of alternative energy resources.
- The U.S. Supreme Court rules that juries may weigh the obscenity of given material according to local standards.
- The U.S. Supreme Court prohibits the involuntary confinement of mental patients capable of caring for themselves who do not pose a hazard to others.
- 1 British Honduras changes its name to Belize.
- 7 An Icelandic coastguard vessel rams a British warship in an escalation of the "Cod War."
- 8 The Spanish dictator General Franco appoints Admiral Luis Carrero Blanco as prime minister.
- 15 A second official cease-fire begins in Vietnam.
- 20 Thirty-five people die in Argentina during riots at Buenos Aires airport as Juan Perón returns from an 18-year exile.
- 24 The Soviet leader Leonid Brezhnev, during a visit to the United States, declares that the Cold War (tensions between the USSR and Eastern Europe and the United States and Western Europe) is over.
- 25 A former White House counsel, John Dean, informs the U.S. Senate Committee of President Richard M. Nixon's complicity in the cover-up of the Watergate affair (the attempted bugging of the campaign headquarters of the opposition Democrats).

- 26 The newly formed Ulster Freedom Fighters in Northern Ireland murder Senator Paddy Wilson of the Social Democratic and Labour Party (SDLP) in Belfast.
- 28 The election by proportional representation of the new Northern Ireland Assembly leaves the official Unionists dependent on the support of the Social Democratic and Labour Party (SDLP) and the Alliance Party.

JULY

- Inmates seize 21 guards in a riot at the Oklahoma State Prison in McAlester, Oklahoma. Several inmates are killed by the time order is reestablished.
- The U.S. president Richard M. Nixon signs a bill prohibiting military operations in Indochina unless approved by Congress.
- 3 The European Security Conference opens in Helsinki, Finland, with 35 foreign ministers in attendance.
- 5 Terrorists kidnap 273 people from a mission school in Rhodesia. On July 17, only eight are still unaccounted for.
- 7–16 The former White House aide Alexander P. Butterfield discloses the existence of the so-called "Watergate tapes," when he tells a U.S. Senate committee during the hearing on the Watergate affair that President Richard M. Nixon secretly tape-records all conversations in his office. Within a week, both the U.S. Senate and special prosecutor subpoena them.
- 14 The Argentine president, Héctor Cámpora, resigns to make way for Juan Perón.
- 17 A bloodless army-backed coup deposes King Mohammed Zahir Shah of Afghanistan and the country is proclaimed a republic.
- 21 France resumes nuclear tests at Mururoa Atoll in the Pacific, despite protests from Australia and New Zealand.
- 26 Terrorists belonging to the National Organization of Cypriot Combatants (EOKA) blow up Limassol police station in Cyprus in a continuing campaign for Enosis (union with Greece).
- 31 Militant Protestants, led by the Reverend Ian Paisley, disrupt the first sitting of the Northern Ireland Assembly.

AUGUST

- The U.S. vice president Spiro Agnew acknowledges that he is the subject of a Justice Department investigation into allegations that he received kickbacks when he was Baltimore county executive and governor of Maryland. He denies the allegations.
- 3–7 Race riots erupt at the University of Rhodesia.
- 5 An Arab terrorist attack at Athens airport kills three people and injures 55.
- 6–8 The accidental U.S. bombing of friendly Laotian villages causes hundreds of casualties.
- 10 Israeli fighter planes force down an Iraqi airliner in northern Israel, but a wanted Palestinian guerrilla is not on board.
- 14 A new Pakistani constitution takes effect, with Zulfikar Ali Bhutto as president.
- 15 U.S. bombing in Cambodia and Laos ends.
- 19 Following the formal abolition of the Greek monarchy, Georgios Papadopoulos becomes president.
- 29 Presidents Anwar Sadat of Egypt and Moamer al-Khaddhafi of Libya proclaim the unification of their two countries, with a plan for a joint constituent assembly.

SEPTEMBER

- New York State imposes mandatory sentencing for criminals convicted of selling hard drugs and for addicts who commit violent crimes.
- Nixon administration officials John Ehrlichman and G. Gordon Liddy are indicted for burglarizing the office of the psychiatrist Daniel Ellsberg, the former U.S. Defense Department official who made public the *Pentagon Papers* (top-secret Defense Department report on the history of the U.S. involvement in the Vietnam War).

3   Henry Kissinger becomes U.S. secretary of state.

7   Iceland threatens to break off diplomatic relations with Britain over the dispute concerning the Icelandic government's unilateral extension of the country's fishing limits from 12 to 15 miles.

11–12   A military junta headed by General Augusto Pinochet seizes power in Chile. Over 2,500 people die in fighting and President Allende reportedly commits suicide.

13   A major air battle is fought between Israel and Syria.

17   The British prime minister Edward Heath meets Prime Minister Liam Cosgrave of the Republic of Ireland at an airfield near Dublin for talks on Northern Ireland. It is the first official visit to the republic by a British prime minister.

18   East and West Germany are admitted to the United Nations.

23   Juan Perón and his wife Isabel are elected president and vice president of Argentina.

29   Austria closes a transit camp for emigrating Soviet Jews in response to the demands of Arab kidnappers.

OCTOBER

- In the so-called "Saturday Night Massacre," the U.S. attorney general, Elliot Richardson, resigns after refusing to heed President Richard M. Nixon's order to fire the Watergate special prosecutor, Archibald Cox.

Nixon fires Richardson's successor, Deputy Attorney General William Ruckelshaus, after Ruckelshaus likewise declines to fire Cox. The president's wish is finally granted when Solicitor General Robert Bork fires the special prosecutor.

- The U.S. secretary of state Henry Kissinger shares the Nobel Peace Prize with Le Duc Tho of North Vietnam for bringing the Vietnamese peace negotiations to a successful conclusion.

6   Full-scale war erupts in the Middle East, as Egypt and Syria attack Israel while Israelis are observing the Jewish holy day of Yom Kippur.

10   The U.S. vice president, Spiro Agnew, resigns after pleading guilty to tax evasion charges while governor of Maryland in 1967.

10–13   The USSR starts an airlift of military supplies to Arab states in the Middle East. Iraq joins the Yom Kippur War against Israel, followed by Saudi Arabia and Jordan on October 13, in an attempt to regain Israeli-occupied territory.

11   Counterattacking Israeli forces break through on the Golan Heights during the Yom Kippur War and invade Syria.

12   The U.S. Court of Appeals orders President Richard M. Nixon to hand over the Watergate tapes (evidence of his complicity in a cover-up of the attempted bugging of the opposition Democratic Party's campaign headquarters).

15   Britain and Iceland end the "Cod War" with an agreement on fishing rights.

16   Israeli forces cross the Suez Canal and invade Egypt in the Yom Kippur War.

17   Eleven Arab states agree to cut their oil production by 5% a month in protest against U.S. support for Israel in the Middle East Yom Kippur War.

19   The U.S. president Richard M. Nixon asks Congress to approve $2,000 million worth of military aid for Israel.

21–22   The U.S. secretary of state Henry Kissinger and the general secretary of the Soviet Communist Party Leonid

Yom Kippur War (1973)

OCTOBER

6   Full-scale war erupts in the Middle East, as Egypt and Syria attack Israel while Israelis are observing the Jewish holy day of Yom Kippur.

7–8   Counterattacking Egyptian bridgeheads on the eastern side of the canal, Israeli armoured formations suffer heavy losses and are forced to pull back into the central Sinai. Meanwhile, Syrian forces, pushing across the Golan Heights toward the Jordan Valley, suffer huge casualties in the Wadi Harridan, which becomes known as the "Vale of Tears."

10–13   The USSR starts an airlift of military supplies to Arab states in the Middle East. Iraq joins the Yom Kippur War against Israel, followed by Saudi Arabia and Jordan on October 13, in an attempt to regain Israeli-occupied territory.

11   Counterattacking Israeli forces stop the Syrian advance on the Golan Heights and drive east into Syria.

14   In an armoured battle second in size only to Kursk, USSR (1943), Israeli tanks defeat an Egyptian offensive into

central Sinai, and drive it back to the bridgehead on the Suez Canal.

16   Israeli forces cross the Suez Canal and invade Egypt.

17   Eleven Arab states agree to cut their oil production by 5% a month in protest against U.S. support for Israel.

19   U.S. president Richard M. Nixon asks Congress to approve $2,000 million worth of military aid for Israel.

21–22   U.S. secretary of state Henry Kissinger and the general secretary of the Soviet Communist Party Leonid Brezhnev, meeting in Moscow, agree a plan to stop the Yom Kippur War in the Middle East. Egypt and Israel accept a United Nations cease-fire on October 22, but fighting continues.

24   Syria accepts a cease-fire in the Yom Kippur War against Israel and fighting halts on both fronts.

NOVEMBER

11   Israel and Egypt accept the U.S. plan for cease-fire observance and prisoner exchange.

Brezhnev meeting in Moscow, agree a plan to stop the Yom Kippur War in the Middle East. Egypt and Israel accept a United Nations cease-fire on October 22, but fighting continues.

23 The U.S. House of Representatives orders a judiciary committee to assess evidence for the impeachment of President Richard M. Nixon.

24 Syria accepts a cease-fire in the Yom Kippur War against Israel and fighting halts on both fronts.

25 The United States puts its forces on precautionary alert in response to fears of Soviet intervention in the Middle East.

NOVEMBER

- Executives of the U.S. Gulf and Ashland oil companies plead guilty to making illegal contributions to President Richard M. Nixon's reelection campaign committee.
- Rose Mary Woods, secretary to the U.S. president Richard M. Nixon, claims before the court hearing of Judge John Sirica that she accidentally erased five or so minutes of a crucial Watergate tape, from which 18.5 minutes are missing; the rest goes unaccounted for.
- The U.S. Congress authorizes the construction of a trans-Alaska oil pipeline.
- The U.S. president Richard M. Nixon appoints Leon A. Jaworski as Watergate special prosecutor.

5–9 The U.S. secretary of state Henry Kissinger tours Arab capitals on a peace mission.

7 The U.S. Congress overrides President Richard M. Nixon's veto and passes the War Powers Act, restricting the ability of the president to maintain troops overseas without congressional approval.

11 Israel and Egypt accept the U.S. plan for cease-fire observance and prisoner exchange.

13 The energy crisis in Britain prompts the government to declare a state of emergency.

25 Following weeks of unrest, armed forces in Greece oust the president, Georgios Papadopoulos.

DECEMBER

9 Talks at Sunningdale, England, between the Irish and British governments and the Northern Ireland Executive-designate agree on the formation of a Council of Ireland with representatives from all three parties.

11 West Germany and Czechoslovakia agree to invalidate the 1938 Munich Agreement, compelling Czechoslovakia to surrender the Sudetenland to Germany, and establish diplomatic relations.

13 The British prime minister Edward Heath orders industry to work a three-day week from December 31 to save energy.

17 Arab terrorists kill 32 people in an attack on Rome airport, Italy.

18 The Irish Republican Army (IRA), seeking to achieve a united and independent Ireland by force, launches a Christmas bombing campaign in London, England.

20 The Spanish prime minister Luis Carrero Blanco is assassinated by a bomb in the capital, Madrid.

21–22 A Middle East peace conference in Geneva, Switzerland, sets up a working party to discuss the disengagement of troops on the Egypt–Israel front.

29 Carlos Arias Navarro becomes prime minister of Spain.

SCIENCE, TECHNOLOGY, AND MEDICINE

Agriculture

- The first calf is produced from a frozen embryo.

Computing

- U.S. computer scientists T. B. Martins and R. B. Cox develop the first voice-operated computer.

Ecology

- An international conference on the environment held in Lebanon warns that the Mediterranean is being turned into a "dead sea" by the sewage and industrial waste being dumped into it.
- Fearing the extinction of kangaroos, Australia bans the sale and export of live animals and hides.
- Hohe Tauern Naturschutzpark national park in Austria is established; it is the largest national park in Europe, covering 1,000 sq km/2,589 sq mi.
- Petroleum is discovered in the Ross Sea, Antarctica.
- Representatives from 80 nations sign the Convention on International Trade in Endangered Species (CITES) that prohibits trade in 375 endangered species of plants and· animals and the products derived from them, such as ivory; the United States does not sign.
- The pipeline for transmission of natural gas from the Ukraine in the USSR to West Germany opens.
- The U.S. Fish and Wildlife Bureau issues the first Endangered and Threatened Species List.
- The U.S. National League of Cities reports that garbage levels are reaching dangerous levels and recommends widespread recycling.
- U.S. engineer Joseph Lindmayer invents a photovoltaic cell that is 50% more efficient than other solar cells in converting solar energy into electricity.

JANUARY

10 A tornado in San Justo, Argentina, levels nearly every building in the city.

FEBRUARY

10 The world's largest liquefied-gas storage tank explodes in Staten Island, New York, killing 40 people.

APRIL

- Spring run-off combines with torrential rain to lift the Mississippi River to its highest flood level in 30 years: 15.3 m/50.3 ft. The flooding kills 11 people, displaces 35,000, and wreaks an estimated half a billion dollars' worth of damage.

AUGUST

30 Kenya bans hunting elephants and trading in ivory.

SEPTEMBER

24 An accident at the Windscale power station in Cumberland (now Cumbria), northwest England,

releases radiation into the surrounding area and raises concern about the safety of nuclear power; the station subsequently changes its name to Sellafield.

Exploration

APRIL

- The uncrewed U.S. spacecraft *Pioneer 11* rockets toward Jupiter.

MAY

- The U.S. National Aeronautics and Space Administration (NASA) launches *Skylab*, the first U.S. space station. It contains a workshop for carrying out experiments in weightlessness, an observatory for monitoring the sun, and cameras for photographing the earth's surface.
- The U.S. National Aeronautics and Space Administration (NASA) *Skylab 2* transports a team of astronauts on a repair mission to the original U.S. space station *Skylab*, damaged during its launch on May 14.
14–February 8, 1974   The United States launches the first *Skylab* space station. It is visited by three three-person crews and astronauts make observations of the sun, manufacture superconductors, and conduct other scientific and medical experiments. The third mission lasts a record 84 days and gathers data about long space flights.

JULY

- *Skylab 3* conveys a team of U.S. astronauts to the original *Skylab* space station, launched on May 14, to make further repairs and conduct experiments.

NOVEMBER

- The U.S. National Aeronautics and Space Administration (NASA) launches the uncrewed spacecraft *Mariner 10*, bound for the planet Mercury via Venus.

DECEMBER

- The U.S. probe *Pioneer 10* (launched March 2, 1972) passes within 130,000 km/81,000 mi of Jupiter, taking hundreds of photographs. It is destined to travel beyond the solar system, leaving it on June 13, 1983.

Health and Medicine

- Denmark extends free medical aid to all residents.
- Some 20 years after the first appearance of Minamata disease, the Japanese courts find the Chisso Corporation to have been responsible by its dumping of mercury waste.
- The U.S. firm 3M makes the first cochlear implant.
- The U.S. Food and Drug Administration standardizes the nutritional information on food packaging.
- U.S. biochemists Stanley Cohen and Herbert Boyer develop the technique of recombinant DNA (deoxyribonucleic acid). Strands of DNA are cut by restriction enzymes from one species and then inserted into the DNA of another; this marks the beginning of genetic engineering.
- U.S. chemist and medical information scientist Paul Lauterbur obtains the first NMR (nuclear magnetic

resonance) image, in Britain. Radio waves are beamed through a patient's body while subjected to a powerful magnetic field; an image is generated because different atoms absorb radio waves at different frequencies under the influence of a magnetic field.

MARCH

- The U.S. National Commission on Marijuana and Drug Abuse recommends treatment for drug users and the classification of alcoholism as a drug problem.

MAY

- Arizona bans smoking in public places; other states enact similar laws over the next few years.

Science

- Comet Kohoutek is first observed by Czech astronomer Lubos Kohoutek.
- German chemist Ernst Fischer and English chemist Geoffrey Wilkinson receive the Nobel Prize for Chemistry for their work on organometallic sandwich compounds.
- Japanese physicist Leo Esaki, Norwegian-born U.S. physicist Ivar Giaever, and Welsh physicist Brian Josephson receive the Nobel Prize for Physics for their work on tunneling in semiconductors and superconductors.
- Polish-born English scientist Jacob Bronowski publishes *The Ascent of Man*, which accompanies a popular television series.
- Researchers at the European Center for Particle Research (CERN) find some confirmation for the electroweak force—one of the four fundamental forces—when they discover neutral currents in neutrino reactions.
- The *Interpretation of Cultures* by U.S. anthropologist Clifford Geertz is published. Geertz argues that culture is embedded in symbols and that their value derives from their use and interpretation in social interaction; it has a profound influence on British and U.S. anthropology.
- The Nobel Prize for Physiology or Medicine is awarded jointly to Austrian zoologists Karl von Frisch and Konrad Lorenz, and Dutch-born British zoologist Nikolaas Tinbergen for their discoveries concerning individual and social behavior patterns in animals.
- Two fossil skulls, both about 1.85 million years old, are discovered at Koobi Fora, Kenya; they have features typical of *Australopithecus boisei* as well as *Homo habilis*, confounding classification of early hominid species.
- U.S. anthropologist Donald Johanson at Hadar, Ethiopia, discovers portions of both legs, including a complete knee, of an australopithecine dated to about 3.4 million years ago; the knee provides valuable information about the evolution of bipedalism.

Technology

- German physicists Hans Dehmelt, Philip Ekstron, and David Wineland invent the Penning trap; an electron-capturing device that can hold a single electron in place for months at a time.

- The continuous-wave tunable laser is developed in the United States; it can be tuned to various frequencies and provides a continuous, rather than a pulsed, beam of laser light.
- The Nicholas Mayall Telescope begins operation on Kitt Peak, Arizona, United States; its 4-m/13-ft dish makes it the second largest optical telescope in the world.
- The Organization of Petroleum Exporting Countries (OPEC) raises oil prices dramatically, causing a worldwide energy crisis. People drive less and turn to more fuel-efficient cars, airlines reduce services, offices turn the heating down, the U.S. president Richard M. Nixon proposes tax incentives to encourage oil exploration, demand for nuclear power increases, and coal prices rise, giving a boost to the ailing industry.

APRIL

1   A committee of grocers and manufacturers recommends the use of Universal Product Codes (UPC) (bar codes) on items sold in grocery stores. The codes will permit electronic scanning of items, reduce cashier error, and improve stock control; a few stores use it from 1974 and it comes into general use in the United States in 1980.

NOVEMBER

- The U.S. president Richard M. Nixon responds to the Arab oil embargo by calling on the U.S. to achieve energy self-sufficiency by the year 1980. The president asks Congress to extend Daylight Saving Time, reduce highway speed limits to 88 kph/55 mph, and establish heating oil quotas for households, schools, and industry.
29   The distribution of gasoline rationing coupons begins in Britain during the energy crisis caused by the oil embargo.

Transportation

- Private vehicles are banned from part of the ancient city of Rome, Italy, in an effort to relieve congestion and reduce noise and air pollution.
- The supertanker *Brooklyn* is launched; weighing 234,000 metric tons/230,000 tons and 333.5 m/1,094 ft long, it is the largest U.S. merchant ship.
- Tokyo International Airport located at Narita, 60 km/37 mi outside Tokyo, Japan, is completed; political disputes prevent it from opening until 1978.

FEBRUARY

1   More than 200 people die in Rangoon harbor, Burma (now Myanmar), when a Japanese freighter collides with a Burmese ferry.
21   A Libyan airliner crashes in the Egyptian peninsula of Sinai after being intercepted by Israeli jets, killing 106 people.

APRIL

10   A British European Airways jet crashes while attempting a landing at Basel, Switzerland; 104 people die.

AUGUST

- In growing recognition of the current energy crisis, the U.S. Congress lifts restrictions on the financing of mass transit systems applied through the Highway Trust Fund.

ARTS AND IDEAS

Architecture

- The 1,074-m/3,524-ft Bosporus Bridge at Istanbul, Turkey, opens. It spans the Bosporus, linking Asia and Europe, and is the fourth longest suspension bridge in the world.
- The Modena Cemetery in Italy, designed by the Italian architect Aldo Rossi, is completed.
- The Sears Tower opens in Chicago, Illinois; with 110 stories and standing 443 m/1,454 ft high, it is the world's tallest building, until 1996.
- The Sydney Opera House, designed by the Danish architect Jørn Utzon, is completed in Australia. His highly original design—perhaps the best-known building in Australia—was controversial, and he left the project before building had finished.
- The World Trade Center in New York, New York, designed by the Japanese architect Minoru Yamasaki, is completed.

Arts

- The German-born English artist Lucian Freud paints *Large Interior, W 9*.
- The U.S. artist Duane Hanson sculpts *Florida Shopper*, a work of Superrealist sculpture.
- The U.S. artist Helen Frankenthaler paints *Moveable Feast*.
- The U.S. artist Mirian Schapiro creates *Pandora's Box*, a feminist collage.
- The U.S. artist Philip Pearlstein paints *Female Nude on Chair with Red Rugs*.
- The U.S. artist Richard Estes paints *Paris Street Scene*. The works of Estes mark the emergence of superrealism (photorealism).

Film

- The British heavy metal rock group Led Zeppelin releases *The Song Remains the Same*, a movie of their concert at Madison Square Garden, New York, New York. It is directed by Peter Clifton and Joe Massot.
- The movie *A Touch of Class*, directed by Melvin Frank, is released in the United States. It stars Glenda Jackson and George Segal.
- The movie *American Graffiti*, cowritten and directed by George Lucas, is released in the United States, starring Richard Dreyfuss, Ron Howard, and Cindy Williams.
- The movie *Badlands*, written and directed by Terrence Malick, is released in the United States. It stars Martin Sheen and Sissy Spacek.
- The movie *Bang the Drum Slowly*, directed by John Hancock, is released in the United States, starring Michael Moriarty, Robert De Niro, and Vincent Gardenia.
- The movie *Blume in Love*, directed by Paul Mazursky, is released in the United States, starring George Segal, Susan Anspach, and Kris Kristofferson.

- The movie *Don't Look Now*, directed by Nicolas Roeg and starring Julie Christie and Donald Sutherland, is released in the UK. It is based on a short story by Daphne du Maurier.
- The movie *El espíritu de la colmena/The Spirit of the Beehive*, written and directed by Victor Erice, is released in Spain. It stars Fernando Fernán Gómez and Teresa Gimpera, and the child actresses Ana Torrent and Isabel Tellería.
- The movie *High Plains Drifter*, directed by and starring Clint Eastwood, is released.
- The movie *L'Horloger de St Paul/The Clockmaker* is released in France. It is directed by Bertrand Tavernier and stars Philippe Noiret.
- The movie *La Maman et la putain/The Mother and the Whore*, directed by Jean Eustache, is released in France. It stars Jean-Pierre Léaud, Bernadette Lafont, and Françoise Lebrun.
- The movie *La Nuit Américaine/Day for Night*, directed by François Truffaut, is released in France, starring Jacqueline Bisset and Jean-Pierre Aumont.
- The movie *Mean Streets* is released in the United States. It is cowritten and directed by Martin Scorsese and stars Harvey Keitel and Robert De Niro.
- The movie *O Lucky Man*, directed by Lindsay Anderson, is released in the UK. It stars Malcolm McDowell and Rachel Roberts.
- The movie *Paper Moon*, directed by Peter Bogdanovich, is released in the United States. It stars Ryan O'Neal and his ten-year-old daughter Tatum, who will win an Academy Award for her performance.
- The movie *Papillon/Butterfly*, based on the novel by Henri Charrière, is released in the United States. It is directed by Franklin J. Schaffner and stars Steve McQueen and Dustin Hoffman.
- The movie *Save the Tiger*, directed by John Avildsen, is released in the United States, starring Jack Lemmon, Jack Gilford, and Laurie Heinemann.
- The movie *Scener ur ett äktenskap/Scenes from a Marriage*, written and directed by the Swedish filmmaker Ingmar Bergman, is released. Edited from six television episodes, the feature-length movie stars Liv Ullmann, Erland Josephson, and Bibi Andersson.
- The movie *Serpico*, directed by Sidney Lumet, is released in the United States, starring Al Pacino.
- The movie *Sleeper*, directed by Woody Allen, is released in the United States. He also stars in it, along with Diane Keaton.
- The movie *The Day of the Jackal*, based on the novel by Frederick Forsyth, is released in the UK. It is directed by Fred Zinnemann and stars Edward Fox.
- The movie *The Last Detail* is released in the United States. It is directed by Hal Ashby and stars Jack Nicholson, Otis Young, and Randy Quaid.
- The movie *The Long Goodbye*, based on the novel by Raymond Chandler, is released in the United States. It is directed by Robert Altman and stars Elliot Gould as private investigator Philip Marlowe.
- The movie *The Sting*, directed by George Roy Hill, is released in the United States. It stars Robert Redford and Paul Newman. The movie will win seven Academy Awards, including best picture, best director, and best music score.

- The movie *The Way We Were*, directed by Sydney Pollack, is released in the United States. It stars Barbra Streisand and Robert Redford.
- The movie *Westworld*, directed by Michael Crichton, is released in the United States, starring Richard Benjamin and Yul Brynner.
- The horror movie *The Exorcist* is released in the United States. Based on the best-selling novel by William Peter Blatty, it is directed by William Friedkin and stars Ellen Burstyn, Max Von Sydow, and Linda Blair.
- The Italian–French coproduction *La Grande Bouffe/Blow-Out*, directed by Marco Ferreri, is released. It stars Marcello Mastroianni, Ugo Tognazzi, Michel Piccoli, and Philippe Noiret. Portraying four men's attempts to commit suicide by eating themselves to death, the movie provokes an outcry when it is featured at the Cannes Film Festival.
- The Kung Fu movie *Enter the Dragon* is released in the United States. It is directed by Robert Clouse and stars Bruce Lee.
- The musical *Jesus Christ Superstar* is filmed in the United States by Norman Jewison.
- The spoof Western *Blazing Saddles*, cowritten and directed by Mel Brooks, is released in the United States. It stars Gene Wilder, Clevon Little, and Madeline Kahn.
- The Western *Pat Garrett and Billy the Kid*, directed by Sam Peckinpah, is released in the United States. It stars James Coburn and Kris Kristofferson, and features a soundtrack by Bob Dylan, who also has a minor part in the movie.

FEBRUARY

2   The director and stars of the movie *Last Tango in Paris*, Bernardo Bertolucci, Marlon Brando, and Maria Schneider, are cleared of obscenity charges in Italy. The movie had been withdrawn from exhibition throughout Italy on December 21, 1972.

MARCH

27 The 1972 Academy Awards take place. Best Actor: Marlon Brando, for *The Godfather*; Best Supporting Actor: Joel Grey, for *Cabaret*; Best Actress: Liza Minelli, for *Cabaret*; Best Supporting Actress: Eileen Heckart, for *Butterflies are Free*; Best Picture: *The Godfather*, directed by Francis Ford Coppola; Best Director: Bob Fosse, for *Cabaret*.

MAY

25 At the Cannes Film Festival, the Palme d'Or is awarded jointly to Jerry Schatzberg for the U.S. movie *Scarecrow* and Alan Bridges for the British movie *The Hireling*.

Literature and Language

- The Australian writer Patrick White publishes his novel *The Eye of the Storm*.
- The Caribbean writer Derek Walcott publishes his autobiographical poetry collection *Another Life*.
- The English writer Anthony Burgess publishes his critical work *Joysprick: An Introduction to the Language of James Joyce*.

- The English writer Anthony Powell publishes *Temporary Kings*, the eleventh novel of his 12-volume sequence *A Dance to the Music of Time*.
- The English writer Graham Greene publishes his novel *The Honorary Consul*.
- The English writer Martin Amis publishes his novel *The Rachel Papers*.
- The English writer Richard Hughes publishes his novel *The Wooden Shepherdess*.
- The first volume of *Byron's Letters and Journals* edited by L. A. Marchand is published. The last volume will be published in 1982.
- The Irish-born British writer Iris Murdoch publishes her novel *The Black Prince*.
- The Nobel Prize for Literature is awarded to the Australian novelist Patrick White.
- The Pulitzer Prize for Fiction is awarded to Eudora Welty for *The Optimist's Daughter*, the Pulitzer Prize for Poetry is awarded to Maxine Winokur Kumin for *Up Country*, and the Pulitzer Prize for Biography is awarded to W. A. Swanberg for *Luce and His Empire*.
- The Russian writer Alexander Solzhenitsyn publishes *Arkhipelag Gulag/The Gulag Archipelago* in Paris, France, a detailed account of the Soviet prison camps.
- The U.S. literary critic Harold Bloom publishes *The Anxiety of Influence*.
- The U.S. writer Adrienne Rich publishes her poetry collection *Diving into the Wreck*.
- The U.S. writer Bernard Malamud publishes his short-story collection *Rembrandt's Hat*.
- The U.S. writer Denise Levertov publishes her poetry collection *The Poet in the World*.
- The U.S. writer Erica Jong publishes her novel *Fear of Flying*. Controversial because of its explicit sexuality, it becomes a best seller.
- The U.S. writer Gore Vidal publishes his novel *Burr*.
- The U.S. writer Norman Mailer publishes his controversial biography of Marilyn Monroe *Marilyn*.
- The U.S. writer Philip Roth publishes *The Great American Novel*.
- The U.S. writer Robert Lowell publishes his poetry collection *The Dolphin*.
- The U.S. writer Thomas Pynchon publishes his novel *Gravity's Rainbow*.

NOVEMBER
- Citizens of Drake, North Dakota, burn 36 copies of the U.S. writer Kurt Vonnegut's *Slaughterhouse-Five*; the books are described as "tools of the devil."

Music

- The British pop singer Gary Glitter releases "I'm the Leader of the Gang (I Am)."
- The British pop star Elton John releases the albums *Goodbye Yellow Brick Road* and *Don't Shoot Me, I'm Only the Piano Player*. The *Los Angeles Times* calls him "the first superstar of the Seventies."
- The English composer Elisabeth Lutyens completes her *Plenum III* for string quartet.
- The English composer Malcolm Arnold completes his Symphony No. 7.

- The English composer Michael Tippett completes his Piano Sonata No. 3.
- The English composer Edmund Rubbra completes his Symphony No. 9, *Sinfonia sacra/Sacred Symphony*.
- The German composer Hans Werner Henze completes *Tristan*, preludes for piano, orchestra, and tape.
- The Hungarian-born Austrian composer György Ligeti completes his choral work *Clocks and Clouds*.
- The Italian composer Luciano Berio completes his orchestral work *Still*.
- The Italian composer Bruno Maderna completes his theater piece *Satyricon*.
- The New York music venue CBGB's, which will help to launch the careers of the Ramones, Talking Heads, and Blondie, opens.
- The opera *Death in Venice*, by the English composer Benjamin Britten, is first performed, at Aldeburgh in England. It is based on the novella *Death in Venice* by the German writer Thomas Mann.
- The Russian composer Dmitry Shostakovich completes his String Quartet No. 14 and his song cycle *Poems of Maria Tsvetayeva*.
- The U.S. composer Steve Reich completes his *Music for Pieces of Wood*.
- The U.S. pop group Bobby "Boris" Pickett and the Crypt Kickers has a hit with its rereleased single "Monster Mash."
- The U.S. pop singer Jim Croce releases "Bad, Bad, Leroy Brown" and the album *Life and Times*.
- U.S. rock and roll star Elvis Presley divorces his wife Priscilla after six years of marriage, giving her a $750,000 settlement.

FEBRUARY
17 The U.S. pop group Dawn releases the single "Tie a Yellow Ribbon Round the Old Oak Tree."

MARCH
17 The British progressive rock band Pink Floyd releases the album *The Dark Side of the Moon*. It will sell 20 million copies worldwide and remain in the U.S. top 200 albums for 17 years.

APRIL
14 The British heavy metal rock group Led Zeppelin releases the album *Houses of the Holy*.

MAY
12 The British pop star and actor David Bowie releases the album *Aladdin Sane*.
26 The British pop group Slade releases "Cum On Feel The Noize" and "Skweeze Me Pleeze Me."

AUGUST
18 The U.S. pop singer Stevie Wonder releases the album *Innervisions*.

SEPTEMBER
1 The U.S. new wave band the New York Dolls releases *New York Dolls*, their first album.
1 The U.S. rhythm and blues singer Roberta Flack releases the album *Killing Me Softly With His Song*.
29 The British rock group the Rolling Stones releases "Angie" and the album *Goat's Head Soup*.

OCTOBER
20 The U.S. rock singer Lou Reed releases the album *Berlin* and his classic single "Walk on the Wild Side."

November

10 The British rock musician Mike Oldfield releases the album *Tubular Bells*. It is the first album to be released on Richard Branson's Virgin label.

24 The U.S. singer and actress Barbra Streisand releases "The Way We Were."

Theater and Dance

- *Chicago*, a Bob Fosse musical, opens in New York, New York.
- The English literary historian Allardyce Nicoll publishes *English Drama 1900–1930: The Beginnings of the Modern Period*. It is a companion to his six-volume *History of the English Drama, 1660–1900*.
- The musical *A Little Night Music*, with lyrics and music by Stephen Sondheim, is first performed, at the Shubert Theater in New York, New York. Based on the movie *Smiles of a Summer Night* by Ingmar Bergman, it includes the song "Send in the Clowns."
- The play *Absurd Person Singular*, by the English writer Alan Ayckbourn, is first performed, at the Criterion Theatre in London, England.
- The play *Bingo*, by the English writer Edward Bond, is first performed, in Exeter, England.
- The play *Da*, by the Irish writer Hugh Leonard, is first performed, in Dublin, Ireland.
- The play *Equus*, by the English writer Peter Shaffer, is first performed, at the Old Vic Theatre in London, England.
- The play *The Hotel Baltimore*, by the U.S. writer Lanford Wilson, is first performed, at the Circle in the Square Theater in New York, New York.
- The Pulitzer Prize for Drama is awarded to Jason Miller for *The Championship Season*.

April

- The play *The Cheviot, The Stag, and the Black, Black Oil*, by the British writer John McGrath, is first performed, in Scotland.

September

17 The musical *Joseph and the Amazing Technicolor Dreamcoat*, with lyrics by Tim Rice and music by Andrew Lloyd Webber, is first performed, at the Albery Theatre in London, England, with Gary Bond as Joseph.

Thought and Scholarship

- *The Victorian City: Images and Realities*, edited by British economic historian H. J. Dyos and U.S. literary historian M. Wolff, is published.
- British historian G. R. Elton publishes *Reform and Renewal: Thomas Cromwell and the Common Weal*.
- British historian M. I. Finley publishes *The Ancient Economy*.
- English psychologist John Bowlby publishes *Attachment and Loss*.
- German economist E. F. Schumacher publishes *Small is Beautiful: A Study of Economics as if People Mattered*, an influential book that expresses a growing concern with the disparity between the economies of the West and the Third World.

- German psychoanalyst and social philosopher Erich Fromm publishes *The Anatomy of Human Destructiveness*.
- Sam B. Warner, Jr., publishes *The Urban Wilderness: A History of the American City*.
- The English philosopher Michael Dummett publishes *Frege: Philosophy of Language*.
- The first volume of *The Cambridge History of China* is published.
- The Pulitzer Prize for History is awarded to Michael Kammen for *People of Paradox: An Inquiry Concerning the Origin of American Civilization*.
- The Pulitzer Prize for General Nonfiction is awarded to Frances Fitzgerald for *Fire in the Lake*.
- U.S. educator James Wilson publishes *Political Organizations*.
- U.S. historian David M. Potter publishes *History and American Society*.
- U.S. linguist and social critic Noam Chomsky publishes *For Reasons of State*.
- U.S. philosopher Saul Kripke publishes *Naming and Necessity*.
- U.S. political scientist James Lloyd Sundquist publishes *Dynamics of the Party System: Alignment and Realignment of Political Parties in the United States*.

September 1973–77 English historian Theodore Zeldin publishes his two-volume *France, 1848–1948*.

SOCIETY

Education

- The Carnegie Commission in the United States devises a classification to facilitate the comparison and analysis of diverse institutions of higher education.
- Tsukuba University is founded in Japan.

Everyday Life

- "Pet rocks" become a major consumer fad in the United States. By 1975, over a million are sold.
- Bic introduces the disposable cigarette lighter, in France.
- Blacks holding U.S. elective office number 2,621. Most are in the states of Michigan, New York, Mississippi, Alabama, and Arkansas.
- Israeli postal worker Mordecai Meirovitch invents the board game Mastermind, which is launched in the United States and UK by Invicta Plastics.
- Women account for 44.7% of the U.S. work force. Salaries differ by as much as 20% between men and women performing the same job.

September 1973–79 The value of a typical single-family home in the United States increases by 95% over a six-year period; the monthly cost of owning a home rises by 61% over the same period.

January

21 In the case *Roe v. Wade*, the U.S. Supreme Court rules that state restrictions on abortion are unconstitutional and that a woman has the right to an abortion within

the first six months of pregnancy. This provokes militant antiabortion protests.

FEBRUARY

13–March 23   A strike by British gas workers cuts off supplies in some areas.

27   British civil servants stage a one-day strike in support of pay claims by their three unions.

MARCH

1–April 14   Hospital ancillary workers in Britain strike for higher pay.

APRIL

- The United Farm Workers Union, headed by the U.S. labor organizer Cesar Chavez, goes on strike in California after the state's grape growers announce a contract with the International Brotherhood of Teamsters (transport workers union).

SEPTEMBER

- The United Auto Workers Union initiates a strike against the Chrysler Corporation in the U.S. The union wants members to be able to decline certain overtime work and seeks full pensions for those who have labored for 30 years.

OCTOBER

19   While on tour in Australia, Queen Elizabeth assents to a change in her title there to Queen of Australia.

28   The United Nations reports that drought and famine have caused up to 100,000 deaths in Ethiopia.

NOVEMBER

12   British coal miners and power workers begin an overtime ban in protest at the pay offer made to them.

14   Princess Anne, the queen's only daughter, marries Mark Phillips in Westminster Abbey, London, England.

21   The National Union of Mineworkers in Britain rejects any pay deal under Phase Three of the government's anti-inflation program.

29   A fire in a department store in Kumamoto, Japan, kills 107 people.

Media and Communication

- The 1972–73 Emmy Awards for television are held. Best Drama Series: *The Waltons*; Best Comedy Series: *All in the Family*; Best Actor in a Drama: Richard Thomas, for *The Waltons*; Best Actress in a Drama: Michael Learned, for *The Waltons*; Best Actor in a Comedy: Jack Klugman, for *The Odd Couple*; Best Actress in a Comedy: Mary Tyler Moore, for *The Mary Tyler Moore Show*.
- November 1973–74   *The World at War*, a documentary about World War II, using contemporary footage, is shown on British television.

MARCH

6   *The Young and the Restless*, a soap opera still in production, starts on U.S. television.

MAY

- The U.S. Supreme Court rules that radio and television stations do not have to sell equal airtime for political issues.
- 5–July 28   *The Ascent of Man*, a series on the evolution of human thought presented by Jacob Bronowski, is shown on British television.

JULY

10   The British newspaper *The Times* alleges that Portuguese troops massacred 400 people in Mozambique in 1972.

AUGUST

16   The Soviet government refuses to allow the U.S. children's television program *Sesame Street* to be broadcast in the USSR.

SEPTEMBER

8–August 30, 1975   *Star Trek*, an animated cartoon program based on the popular live-action series, appears on U.S. television.

OCTOBER

8   The London Broadcasting Company (LBC) becomes the first commercial radio station in mainland Britain, ending the 50-year British Broadcasting Corporation (BBC) monopoly of radio. The first channel, funded by advertising, broadcasts only news.

20–March 6, 1978   *The Six Million Dollar Man*, an adventure series about a NASA pilot rebuilt after an accident as a bionic superhuman, is shown on U.S. television. It stars Lee Majors.

24–April 15, 1978   *Kojak*, starring Telly Savalas as the lollipop-sucking detective, is shown on U.S. television. It also stars Dan Frazer, Kevin Dobson, and George Savalas.

DECEMBER

17   Emergency measures introduced by the Conservative government in Britain during the energy crisis include a television blackout after 10.30 at night.

Religion

- British Judaic scholar Geza Vermes publishes *Jesus the Jew*.
- Mother Teresa of Calcutta receives the first Templeton Prize for Progress in Religion.

Sports

- Skateboarding, a land recreation for surfers, becomes widely popular in the United States.
- The Yomiuri Giants win their ninth consecutive Japanese baseball championship.
- Women tennis professionals led by Billie Jean King force the U.S. Lawn Tennis Association to award equal prize money to men and women in the U.S. Open Championships.

JANUARY

1   Sportswriters vote the University of Southern California as college football's national champions for the 1972 season.

7–18   The 2nd African Games are held at Lagos, Nigeria.

11   In baseball, the American League introduces the designated hitter rule, which allows another player to bat instead of the pitcher in a team's lineup.

14   The Miami Dolphins defeat the Washington Redskins 14–7 in Super Bowl VII in Los Angeles, California, to become the first team in NFL history to win all their regular and post-season games.

BIRTHS & DEATHS

JANUARY

22 Lyndon Baines Johnson, 36th president of the United States 1963–69, a Democrat, dies in Texas (64).

26 Edward G. Robinson, U.S. film actor famous for his gangster roles, dies (80).

FEBRUARY

18 Frank Costello, U.S. gangster, dies in New York, New York (82).

22 Winthrop Rockefeller, U.S. politician, governor of Arkansas, dies in Palm Springs, California (60).

28 Eric Lindros, Canadian hockey star, born in London, Ontario.

MARCH

6 Pearl S. Buck, U.S. novelist whose books concerned life in China, dies in Danby, Vermont (80).

8 Eugene "Bull" Connor, U.S. politician, infamous racist who supported segregation, dies in Birmingham, Alabama (75).

25 Edward Steichen, U.S. pioneer photographer known for his portraits of celebrities in the 1930s and 1940s, dies in West Redding, Connecticut (92).

25 Noël Coward, English playwright, composer, actor, director, and producer of theatrical comedy, dies in St. Mary, Jamaica (73).

APRIL

8 Pablo Picasso, Spanish painter and sculptor who, along with Georges Braque, founded cubism, dies in Mougins, France (91).

28 Jacques Maritain, French Roman Catholic philosopher, dies in Toulouse, France (90).

MAY

18 Jeanette Rankin, U.S. feminist, the first woman member of Congress 1917–19, dies in Carmel, California (92).

26 Jacques Lipchitz, Russian-born French sculptor whose style was based on cubism, and who was one of the originators of nonrepresentational sculpture, dies on Capri, Italy (81).

JUNE

1 Harvey Firestone, Jr., U.S. tire manufacturer, dies in Akron, Ohio (75).

1 Helen Parkhurst, U.S. educator and author who established a system of assessed work instead of examinations, dies in New Milford, Connecticut (86).

21 Frank Leahy, U.S. football coach who led Notre Dame to three national championships, dies in Portland, Oregon (64).

JULY

2 Betty Grable, U.S. actress, dies in Santa Monica, California (66).

6 Otto Klemperer, German conductor and composer, dies in Zürich, Switzerland (88).

11 Robert Ryan, U.S. film and theater actor, dies (63).

12 Lon Chaney, Jr., U.S. silent film star and master of makeup, dies (67).

23 Edward Rickenbacker, U.S. flying ace of World War I, later an airline executive, dies in Zürich, Switzerland (82).

AUGUST

1 Francesco Malipiero, Italian composer who combined modern techniques with the stylistic quality of early music, dies in Treviso, Italy (91).

1 Walter Ulbricht, head of state of the German Democratic Republic 1960–73, who had the Berlin Wall erected, dies in East Berlin, Germany (80).

6 Fulgencio Batistá y Zaldívar, Cuban soldier and ruler 1933–44 and 1952–59, dies in Marbella, Spain (72).

16 Selman Abraham Waksman, Ukranian-born U.S. microbiologist who discovered the antibiotic streptomycin, dies in Hyannis, Massachusetts (84).

17 Conrad Aiken, U.S. novelist, short-story writer, poet, and critic, dies in Savannah, Georgia (84).

31 John Ford (adopted name of Sean O'Feeney), U.S. film director best known for his Westerns, dies in Palm Desert, California (78).

SEPTEMBER

2 J(ohn) R(onald) R(euel) Tolkien, South African-born English novelist, known for his *Lord of the Rings* trilogy, dies in Bournemouth, Hampshire, England (81).

11 Evans Edward Evans-Pritchard, English anthropologist known for his studies of religion among African peoples, dies in Oxford, England (71).

11 Salvador Allende (Gossens), Chilean politician and first Marxist president, dies in Santiago, Chile (65).

15 Gustaf VI Adolf, king of Sweden 1950–73, dies in Hälsingborg, Sweden (90).

23 Pablo Neruda, Chilean poet, diplomat, and Marxist, dies in Santiago, Chile (69).

28 W(ystan) H(ugh) Auden, English-born poet who later became a U.S. citizen, dies in Vienna, Austria (66).

OCTOBER

8 Gabriel Marcel, French existentialist philosopher, dies in Paris, France (83).

20 Paavo Nurmi, Finnish track athlete who dominated long-distance running in the 1920s, dies in Helsinki, Finland (76).

21 Alan Cobham, British pioneer long-distance aviator who developed in-flight refueling, dies in Tortola, British Virgin Islands (79).

22 Pablo Casals, Spanish cellist and conductor, dies in Rio Piedras, Puerto Rico (96).

25 Abebe Bikila, Ethiopian marathon runner, the first man to win a second successive Olympic marathon, dies (46).

NOVEMBER

5 Alfred Sherwood Romer, U.S. paleontologist, dies in Cambridge, Massachusetts (78).

13 Elsa Schiaparelli, Italian-born French dress designer who combined simplicity with flamboyant colors, dies in Paris, France (77).

DECEMBER

1 David Ben-Gurion, Zionist statesman and first prime minister of the newly formed state of Israel 1948–53 and 1955–63, dies in Tel Aviv, Israel (87).

2 Monica Seles, Serbian-born U.S. tennis player, youngest ever winner of the French Open in 1990, seeded number one by 1992, is born in Novi Sad, Yugoslavia.

5 Robert Watson-Watt, Scottish physicist who developed radar in England, dies in Inverness, Scotland (81).

25 Ismet Inönü, Turkish statesman, president of Turkey 1939–46 and in three coalition governments 1961–65, dies in Ankara, Turkey (84).

30 Henri Busser, French composer, conductor, and teacher, dies in Paris, France (101).

22 U.S. boxer George Foreman knocks out Joe Frazier of the United States in the second round of their bout to win the world heavyweight title in Kingston, Jamaica.

24–27 U.S. national figure skating champions are: Janet Lynn; Gordon McKellen; Melissa and Mark Militano, pairs; Mary Campbell and Johhny Johns, dance.

27 UCLA defeats Notre Dame 82–63 to break the University of San Francisco's all-time college basketball record of 60 consecutive wins, set in 1956.

MARCH

• The inaugural Idiatrod Trail Sled Race is won by Alaskan Dick Wilmarth, who covers the 1,864 km/1,158 mi course from Anchorage to Nome, Alaska, in 20 days 49 min 41 sec.

3 Robyn Smith is the first woman jockey to win a stakes race in the United States when she wins at Aqueduct Raceway in New York, New York.

APRIL

15 The $25,000-Colgate–Dinah Shore Winners Circle Tournament at Palm Springs, California, United States, the richest golf tournament ever held for women, is won by U.S. golfer Mickey Wright.

29–May 10 The Montreal Canadiens beat the Chicago Blackhawks to win the Stanley Cup.

MAY

5–June 9 Secretariat, ridden by U.S. jockey Ron Turcotte, wins the Kentucky Derby, the Preakness Stakes, and the Belmont Stakes to become the first horse to win the U.S. Triple Crown since Citation, ridden by Eddie Arcaro, in 1948.

10 The New York Knicks beat the Los Angeles Lakers to win the National Basketball Association (NBA) championship.

JUNE

17 U.S. golfer Johnny Miller wins the U.S. Open at Oakmont, Pennsylvania, with a 63 in the final round.

20–22 The United States defeats Great Britain and Ireland 16–10 in the Ryder Cup golf competition at Muirfield; this is the first time the competition is held in Scotland.

25–July 7 The men's events at the Wimbledon tennis championships in London, England, are boycotted by around 80 members of the Association of Tennis Professionals because of a dispute with the International Lawn Tennis Federation over the latter's suspension of Nikki Pilic for refusing to play in Yugoslavia's Davis Cup team.

JULY

• The 71-year-old U.S. golfer Gene Sarazen and 19-year-old English amateur David Russell both make holes in one at the 8th hole in the British Open at Royal Troon, Scotland.

11 The U.S. athlete Dwight Stones breaks the world high-jump record with a leap of 2.30 m/7 ft 6½ in, in Munich, West Germany.

28 The host country England defeats Australia by 92 runs at Edgbaston, Birmingham, England, in the final of the inaugural women's cricket World Cup.

AUGUST

10 Lynne Cox, a 16-year-old Californian, swims the English Channel in 9 hours 36 minutes to set a new women's world record.

13 The U.S. golfer Jack Nicklaus wins the U.S. Professional Golfers Association (PGA) championship at Canterbury, Cleveland, Ohio, to surpass U.S. golfer Bobby Jones's 1930 record of 13 major championship victories. He also becomes the first golfer to earn more than $2 million in winnings.

SEPTEMBER

9 The Scottish race-car driver Jackie Stewart announces his retirement from racing after winning the Formula One Drivers' World Championship for the third time in five years, driving a Tyrrell-Ford.

21 The U.S. tennis player Billie Jean King beats 55-year-old Bobby Riggs of the United States in a match at the Houston Astrodome, Texas, United States, before an estimated television audience of 40 million people. Riggs, the 1939 Wimbledon singles champion, had challenged King to a $100,000 winner-takes-all contest to prove that men at any age are tougher than women.

OCTOBER

13 The Oakland As capture the World Series for the second consecutive season; they beat the New York Mets.

13 The South African golfer Gary Player wins the Piccadilly World Matchplay Championship at Wentworth, Surrey, England, for a record fifth time.

NOVEMBER

12 FIFA (the Fédération International de Football Association) disqualifies the USSR from the World Cup after their refusal to play the second leg of their play-off with Chile in Santiago because the national stadium had been used to detain political prisoners in the recent military coup.

DECEMBER

1 The black American world light-heavyweight champion Bob Foster beats Pierre Fourie of South Africa on points, before a racially segregated crowd of 40,000 people in Johannesburg in the first bout between "black" and "white" opponents to be held in South Africa.

16 O. J. Simpson of the Buffalo Bills becomes the first professional American football player to rush for more than 2,000 yards in a season.

1974

POLITICS, GOVERNMENT, AND ECONOMICS

Business and Economics

- Electricity rates rise 30% in the United States.
- The U.S. economy weakens as inflation reaches 10.3% and automobile sales and housing start to decline by 20% and 40% respectively. Unemployment reaches 7.2% by the end of the year.
- The U.S. firm Hewlett Packard introduces the first programmable pocket calculator.

APRIL
1   British Airways is formed from a merger of the British Overseas Airways Corporation (BOAC) and British European Airways (BEA).

OCTOBER
- The U.S. Congress creates the Commodity Futures Trading Commission to police the finance industry.

Colonization

FEBRUARY
7   The Caribbean island of Grenada becomes independent within the Commonwealth.

SEPTEMBER
10 Portuguese Guinea gains its independence from Portugal under the name Guinea-Bissau.

Human Rights

- The U.S. Equal Opportunity Act forbids discrimination on the grounds of marital status or sex.
- U.S. historians Robert Fogel and Stanley Engerman publish *Time on the Cross: The Economics of American Negro Slavery*.

JULY
- The U.S. Supreme Court strikes down a busing policy designed to racially integrate Detroit public schools (by transporting pupils from further afield to the schools).

SEPTEMBER
September–December White pupils in Boston, Massachusetts, riot over the use of busing (transporting children by bus from their home districts to schools in other districts) to enforce the desegregation of schooling. Renewed violence prompts the state governor, Francis Sargent, to call out the National Guard on October 15.

Politics and Government

- Karen Silkwood, a laboratory technician at the Kerr-McGee nuclear plant in Oklahoma, United States, dies in mysterious circumstances after expressing concern about safety at the plant.
- The Atomic Energy Commission is disbanded. The following year its functions are taken over by the Energy Research and Development Administration (replaced by the Department of Energy in 1977) and the Nuclear Regulatory Commission.
- The Global Atmospheric Research Program (GARP) is launched. An international project, its aim is to provide a greater understanding of the mechanisms of the world's weather by using satellites and by developing a mathematical model of the earth's atmosphere.
- The United Nations calls for a New International Economic Order, in which the development of the Third World is a priority.
- The U.S. journalists Bob Woodward and Carl Bernstein publish *All the President's Men*, an account of the Watergate Affair.
- The World Health Organization launches its Expanded Program on Immunization, to immunize children in developing countries against a variety of diseases.

JANUARY
- An audio expert testifies that the 18.5-minute gap in a crucial White House "Watergate" tape is the product of deliberate erasure.
- The U.S. Supreme Court rules that schools must teach English to students for whom English is a second language.
1   The Unionist politician Brian Faulkner takes office as chief executive of Northern Ireland.
3   An amendment to the Social Security Act in the United States provides for the payment of a cost-of-living allowance.
15 Protestors in Jakarta, Indonesia, demonstrate against the visit of the Japanese premier, Kakeui Tanaka, to show anti-Japanese feeling.
18 Israel and Egypt agree on the disengagement of forces along the Suez Canal.
25 Britain offers industrial goods worth £110 million to Iran in exchange for 5 million extra tons of oil, to boost short supplies during the energy crisis,
30 President Richard M. Nixon famously stumbles in his State of the Union address, referring to the need "to replace the discredited president—er, present—system."

FEBRUARY

- Patricia Hearst, daughter of the U.S. publisher Randolph Hearst, is kidnapped from her home in Berkeley, California, by members of the self-styled Symbionese Liberation Army (SLA).
4 An Irish Republican Army (IRA) bomb kills 12 people—servicemen and members of their families—on a bus from Manchester to Catterick in North Yorkshire, England.
13 The USSR expels the dissident author Alexander Solzhenitsyn and deprives him of his Soviet citizenship.
22 Pakistan recognizes Bangladesh as an independent nation at the start of the Islamic summit conference in Lahore, Pakistan.
27 A new constitution is introduced in Sweden, stripping the monarchy of all its remaining powers.
28 The British general election produces no overall majority. Labour wins 301 seats, the Conservatives 297, the Liberals 14, and others 9.

MARCH

- Arab states lift their oil embargo against the United States.
4 The British prime minister Edward Heath resigns when the Liberals refuse to form a coalition with the Conservatives following the election results of February 28.
4 The European Economic Community (Common Market) proposes economic cooperation with 20 Arab countries.
5 Harold Wilson forms a minority Labour government in Britain, with James Callaghan as foreign secretary, Denis Healey as chancellor of the Exchequer, Roy Jenkins as home secretary, and Michael Foot as employment secretary.
14 Heavy fighting breaks out between Kurdish rebels and Iraqi forces on the Iraqi–Turkish border.
20 Princess Anne of Britain escapes a kidnap attempt by Ian Ball, an unemployed van driver, while driving down the Mall in London, England. Ball is subsequently sent to a psychiatric hospital.

APRIL

- Patricia Hearst, the daughter of the U.S. publisher Randolph Hearst, after being kidnapped by members of the Symbionese Liberation Army (SLA) on February 5, announces via tape that she has joined the SLA. She later participates with her Symbionese Liberation Army kidnappers in the robbery of a bank in San Francisco, California.
- The U.S. president Richard M. Nixon signs legislation raising the minimum wage to $2.30 per hour and extending it to 8 million workers.
2 Alain Poher becomes interim president of France on the death of Georges Pompidou.
3 The U.S. president Richard M. Nixon agrees to pay $432,787 owed in back income tax.
11 Palestinian terrorists kill 18 Israelis, mostly women and children, in a raid on the village of Kiryat Shemona.
19 An Israeli–Syrian air battle is fought over the Golan Heights.
25–26 General António Ribeiro de Spínola leads a successful coup in Portugal. On April 26, the junta vows to dismantle the authoritarian state and end the wars in Angola, Mozambique, and Portuguese Guinea (now Guinea-Bissau).

28 Political prisoners are released in Portugal and censorship is ended, following the coup by General António Ribeiro de Spínola on April 25.
30 The U.S. president Richard M. Nixon releases a 1,308-page edited transcript of the Watergate tapes to the Congressional Committee.

MAY

- The Maryland State Bar Association disbars the former U.S. vice president Spiro Agnew (deprives him of his professional legal status) because of tax evasion.
6 Willy Brandt resigns as West German chancellor after a close aide, Günter Guillaume, admits to spying for East Germany.
13 A referendum in Italy upholds the liberalization of the laws relating to divorce.
16 Sixteen children die when Israeli troops storm a school occupied by Palestinian terrorists at Ma'alot near the Lebanese border.
17 Three bomb explosions in Dublin, the capital of the Republic of Ireland, and Monaghan, also in the Republic, kill 32 people. The bombs are set by Loyalist terrorists.
18 An atomic bomb test makes India the world's sixth nuclear power.
19 The conservative politician Valéry Giscard d'Estaing wins the second round of the French presidential election with 50.8% of votes, against the socialist François Mitterrand's 49.2%.
24–April 4 The British Conservative leader Edward Heath visits China.
27 The conservative politician Jacques Chirac is appointed prime minister of France.
28 The Northern Ireland Executive collapses when all the Unionist members resign. On May 29, Britain reimposes direct rule and the general strike ends.
31 The U.S. secretary of state Henry Kissinger secures an agreement between Syria and Israel to disengage forces on the Golan Heights.

JUNE

- The U.S. federal judge W. Arthur Garrity orders the Boston School Committee to racially integrate Boston public schools.
- The U.S. Supreme Court rules unconstitutional a Florida law requiring newspapers to publish the responses of political candidates to unfavorable editorials.
3 An Irish Republican Army (IRA) hunger striker, Michael Gaughan, dies in Parkhurst prison on the Isle of Wight, England.
4 Yitzhak Rabin succeeds Golda Meir as prime minister of Israel.
12–19 The U.S. president Richard M. Nixon tours the Middle East.
17 An Irish Republican Army (IRA) bomb explodes outside Westminster Hall, in London, England, injuring 11 people.
20 The British House of Commons rejects plans for greater state control over industry. The rejection is one of over 20 government defeats between March and October.
27–July 3 The U.S. president Richard M. Nixon visits the USSR.
28 President Makarios of Cyprus asks Greek officers to leave the Cypriot National Guard, wanting only Greek Cypriots in the army.

28 The Ethiopian armed forces take control of government buildings and broadcasting.

JULY

- The U.S. Congress creates an independent legal services bureau to furnish legal counsel to the poor.
- The U.S. president Richard M. Nixon signs the National Research Act, creating guidelines for scientific research on humans.

1 Isabel Perón becomes president of Argentina on the death of her husband, Juan Perón.

14 A left wing government takes office in Portugal under Colonel Vasco Gonçalves.

15 The Cypriot National Guard, with Greek support, overthrows President Makarios of Cyprus and installs Nicos Sampson, a former National Organization of Cypriot Combatants (EOKA) terrorist, in his place.

17 An Irish Republican Army (IRA) bomb at the Tower of London in England kills one person and injures 37.

20–22 Turkey invades Cyprus, claiming right of intervention under the 1960 treaty which sets Turkey as a guarantor, along with Greece and Britain, of the Cypriot constitution. A cease-fire follows on July 22.

23–24 The Greek military government resigns. On July 24, the former prime minister Konstantinos Karamanlis returns from exile in France to form a civilian administration.

24–30 The U.S. Supreme Court, in the case *USA v. Richard M. Nixon*, orders President Nixon to surrender the remaining tapes subpoenaed by the special prosecutor. The Court rules that presidential privilege does not extend to evidence in the Watergate criminal investigation.

25–30 The foreign ministers of Britain, Turkey, and Greece meet in Geneva, Switzerland, to discuss the future of Cyprus.

AUGUST

1 The 1952 constitution is restored in Greece.

5 The U.S. president Richard M. Nixon admits complicity in the Watergate cover-up (concerning the attempted bugging of the opposition Democratic Party's campaign headquarters).

9 The U.S. president Richard M. Nixon resigns to avoid impeachment because of his involvement in the Watergate affair, and Gerald Ford becomes the 38th president of the United States.

10 The U.S. president Gerald Ford nominates the former New York governor Nelson A. Rockefeller for vice president.

12–14 Turkey issues a 24-hour ultimatum demanding the creation of autonomous Turkish cantons in Cyprus. On August 14, Turkish forces resume their offensive having turned down appeals by Greek foreign minister George Manos and Cypriot president Nicos Sampson to consult their governments.

14 Greece withdraws its armed forces from the North Atlantic Treaty Organization (NATO) in protest at its failure to oppose the Turkish "menace to world peace" following the Turkish invasion of Cyprus.

16 A second cease-fire following the Turkish invasion of Cyprus leaves 40% of the island under Turkish control.

18 Nineteen Irish Republican Army (IRA) terrorists use explosives to escape from Portlaoise prison in the Republic of Ireland.

SEPTEMBER

- The U.S. president Gerald Ford offers clemency to Vietnam War draft dodgers who have only to swear allegiance to the country and perform two years' service.

4 The United States and East Germany establish diplomatic relations.

6 The Labour finance minister Wallace ("Bill") Rowling succeeds the late Norman Kirk as prime minister of New Zealand.

8 The U.S. president Gerald Ford pardons the former president Richard M. Nixon for any offenses committed in office.

12 A military coup in Ethiopia deposes Emperor Haile Selassie.

13–17 Japanese "Red Army" terrorists in the Netherlands take French diplomats hostage in The Hague. On September 17, France and the Netherlands pay a ransom for their release.

20 A nationalist government under Joaquim Chissano takes office in Mozambique.

30 General Francisco Costa Gomes succeeds General Spínola as president of Portugal.

OCTOBER

- As a consequence of the Watergate scandal, the U.S. Congress limits private contributions to federal election campaigns and establishes a public campaign fund.

5 Irish Republican Army (IRA) bombs in Britain kill five and injure 65 in two public houses in Guildford, Surrey.

8 The U.S. president Gerald Ford launches the "Whip Inflation Now" economic program.

10 The British general election gives Labour an overall majority of 3 with 316 seats. The Conservatives have 276, Liberals 13, Scottish Nationalists 11, and others 16.

15 Riots and arson attacks erupt at the Maze prison, near Belfast, in Northern Ireland.

28 Twenty Arab nations recognize the Palestine Liberation Organization (PLO) as the sole legitimate representative of the Palestinian people.

28–30 Chancellor Helmut Schmidt of West Germany holds talks with the general secretary of the Soviet Communist Party, Leonid Brezhnev, in Moscow, USSR.

30 Britain, France, and the United States veto a motion to expel South Africa from the United Nations because of its apartheid policies.

NOVEMBER

- In the U.S. congressional elections the Democrats retain majorities in the House of Representatives (291–144) and in the Senate (61–37).

5 Democrat Ella Grasso becomes governor of the state of Connecticut, and the first woman governor of a U.S. state who is not the wife or widow of a former governor.

5 The U.S. Congress grants "home rule" to the District of Columbia, Washington, which now has its own council, mayor, and congressional observer delegates.

13 Yasser Arafat, the leader of the Palestine Liberation Organization, addresses the United Nations General Assembly in New York, New York.

14 The U.S. secretary of state Henry Kissinger proposes international cooperation to reduce the price of oil.

21 Irish Republican Army (IRA) bombs in Britain explode in two Birmingham public houses, killing 21 and injuring 120 people.

21 The U.S. Congress passes the Freedom of Information Act over President Gerald Ford's veto. It prohibits the government from denying access to documents without good cause and requires federal agencies to supply documents without delay.

23–25 The U.S. president Gerald Ford and the general secretary of the Soviet Communist Party Leonid Brezhnev meet in Vladivostok, USSR, to discuss arms control.

24 The Ethiopian military government executes 60 politicians and nobles without trial.

26 Kakuei Tanaka resigns as prime minister of Japan amid allegations of corruption.

29 The Prevention of Terrorism Act is passed in Britain following a spate of Irish Republican Army (IRA) outrages. Police are given power to hold terrorist suspects for five days without charge and suspects can be banned from the British mainland or deported to Northern Ireland.

DECEMBER

• Nelson A. Rockefeller takes the oath of office as vice president of the United States.

2 Israel announces that it possesses the means to manufacture nuclear weapons.

7 President Makarios of Cyprus returns to the island after five months in exile.

8 A referendum in Greece results in a 62% vote against the restoration of the monarchy.

9 Takeo Miki succeeds Kakuei Tanaka as prime minister of Japan.

11 The Rhodesian prime minister Ian Smith calls a constitutional conference to end the guerrilla war in the country.

SCIENCE, TECHNOLOGY, AND MEDICINE

Agriculture

• Hundreds of thousands of people die in Bangladesh as a result of famine.

MARCH

19 Riots occur over food shortages in Bihar, India.

Computing

• IBM introduces a typewriter that can store up to 50 pages of type on magnetic tape and replay it at 150 words per minute.

• The first word processors are introduced by the Xerox corporation.

• U.S. technician David Ahl develops the first microcomputer; it includes a central processing unit, television screen, and keyboard. It arouses little interest.

APRIL

• Intel introduces the 8-bit 8080 microprocessor; it has 5,000 transistors.

Ecology

• Drought in Somalia kills thousands of people. The following year, the USSR airlifts 120,000 nomads to collective farms on the coast.

• Mexican chemist Mario Molina and U.S. chemist F. Sherwood Rowland warn that the chlorofluorocarbons (CFCs) used in refrigerators and as aerosol propellants may be damaging the atmosphere's ozone layer that filters out much of the sun's ultraviolet radiation.

• The Brazilian government begins a $5-billion program to replace gasoline for cars with an alcohol and gasoline mixture; by 1980, 750,000 cars run on "gasohol."

• The national maximum speed limit in the United States is reduced to 88 kph/55 mph, saving nearly 18,000 lives over the next five years, as well as 3.4 billion gallons of fuel per year.

• The Parque Nacional da Amazonia is established in Brazil; with an area of 10,000 sq km/4,000 sq mi, it preserves a large area of tropical rainforest.

FEBRUARY

1 Between 170 and 190 people die in a fire in a high-rise bank building in São Paulo, Brazil.

APRIL

3 Half the town of Xenia, Ohio, is destroyed by tornadoes; $500 million damage is caused and 34 people are killed; a dozen more tornadoes touch down elsewhere and a total of 315 people are killed.

MAY

• Expo '74 opens in Spokane, Washington, with emphasis on the global environment.

JUNE

30 Twenty-four people die in a fire in a nightclub in Port Chester, New York.

AUGUST

11 Severe flooding in Bangladesh covers nearly half the country and kills over 2,000 people.

SEPTEMBER

• The National Coal Board in the UK increases the price of coal by 28%.

19–20 Hurricane Fifi causes over $1 billion in damage and kills over 8,000 people in Honduras.

DECEMBER

25 Cyclone Tracey destroys nearly the entire city of Darwin, Australia; two-thirds of the population are evacuated, $1 billion in damage is caused, and 65 people are killed.

28 An earthquake in Pakistan measuring 6.3 on the Richter scale kills over 5,200 people.

Exploration

• The UK X-ray satellite *Ariel 5* is launched.

• The U.S. probe *Mariner 10* (launched November 3, 1973) photographs the upper atmosphere of Venus

(February) and then takes the first photographs of the surface of Mercury (March and September), flying within 740 km/460 mi of the planet's surface.

December 1974–75   *Symphonie* satellites are launched by France and West Germany. Placed in geosynchronous orbit over West Africa, they provide Africa with telecommunications services to western Europe and the Americas.

MAY

- The U.S. launches the world's first *Synchronous Meteorological Satellite* (SMS).

DECEMBER

- U.S. probe *Pioneer 11* flies to within 42,000 km/ 26,000 mi of Jupiter and photographs its polar regions.

Health and Medicine

- British-born Danish immunologist Niels Jerne proposes a network theory of the immune system.
- The CAT (computerized axial tomography) scanner comes into wide-scale use, revolutionizing diagnostic medicine.
- U.S. chemist Albert Claude, British-born Belgian biochemist Christian de Duve, and Romanian cell biologist George Palade share the Nobel Prize for Physiology or Medicine for their discoveries concerning the structural and functional organization of the cell.

JANUARY

January–June   Between 20,000 and 30,000 people die in a smallpox epidemic in India.

JUNE

- U.S. surgeon Jay Heimlich describes a method for saving people from choking on food. Quick upward thrusts of the heel of the hand placed in the person's abdomen dislodges the food. This becomes known as the "Heimlich maneuver."

JULY

- The National Academy of Sciences advises a worldwide ban on recombinant DNA (deoxyribonucleic acid) experiments on the bacterium *Escherichia coli* for fear that a more virulent form may be created.

Science

- English archeologist Colin Renfrew publishes *Before Civilization: The Radiocarbon Revolution and Prehistoric Europe.*
- English biochemist Leslie Orgel shows that RNA-replicase is not necessary for RNA (ribonucleic acid) to replicate, but that zinc aids this replication. It is a reaction that could have played a role in the evolution of DNA.
- English physicist Stephen Hawking suggests that black holes emit subatomic particles until their energy is diminished to the point where they explode.
- English radio astronomers Martin Ryle and Antony Hewish receive the Nobel Prize for Physics for their work in radio astronomy.
- German chemists Manfred Eigen and Manfred Sumper demonstrate that RNA-replicase mixed with nucleotide

monomers produce molecules that replicate, mutate, and evolve.

- U.S. anthropologists Donald Johanson and Maurice Taieb discover the 3.2-million-years-old remains of "Lucy," an adult female hominid classified as *Australopithecus afarensis*, at Hadar in Ethiopia. About 40% of her skeleton is found and it indicates that she was bipedal.
- U.S. chemist Paul Flory receives the Nobel Prize for Chemistry for his work on the physical chemistry of macromolecules.
- U.S. physicist Kenneth Geddes Wilson develops a technique for improving theories concerning transformations of matter called phase transitions.
- U.S. theoretical physicist Sheldon Glashow proposes the first grand unified theory that envisions the strong, weak, and electromagnetic forces as variants of a single superforce.

MARCH

- A "terracotta army" consisting of over 6,000 life-size model soldiers is discovered in the Qin dynasty tomb near Xian in central China; they guard the tomb of China's first emperor, Shi Huangdi.

JUNE

- Soviet physicist Georgy Flerov and his associates announce the discovery of seaborgium (atomic no. 106).

SEPTEMBER

- U.S. astronomer Charles T. Kowal announces the discovery and naming of Leda, the 13th moon of Jupiter.

NOVEMBER

16   U.S. physicists Burton Richter and Samuel Chao Chung Ting announce they have separately discovered the fourth quark, the J/ψ particle. It confirms the theory of charm in elementary particles.

Technology

- German cartographer Arno Peters develops a cartographic projection that improves on Mercator's projection by establishing the correct proportions of land masses, although it distorts the outlines of land masses.
- High-definition television (HDTV) with 1,125 lines is introduced by Panasonic.
- The energy crisis induced by the oil embargo in the Middle East means that Daylight Savings Time is observed all year round in the United States to save fuel.
- The Soviet main battle tank, the T-72, enters service; it carries a 120-mm gun and can travel at 56 kph/35 mph.
- The transmission time for faxes is six minutes per page.
- U.S. physicist Samuel Hurst applies for a patent for a method of counting individual atoms using a laser.

APRIL

April–May   U.S. oil companies report sharp first-quarter profits. Occidental Petroleum boasts an increase of 748%.

MAY

- The U.S. Congress authorizes the creation of a Federal Energy Administration, effective from 1975, to manage the nation's energy policy and police the oil industry.

JUNE
26 The first product barcode (on a pack of Wrigley's chewing gum) is scanned at the checkout of the Marsh Supermarket in Troy, Ohio.

Transportation

- Charles de Gaulle airport opens at Roissy, 19 km/12 mi north of Paris, France.

MARCH

3 A Turkish DC-10 crashes near Paris, France; 346 people are killed. It is the worst airplane crash to date.

SEPTEMBER

26 Over 275 people die when a Soviet destroyer catches fire and sinks in the Black Sea.

DECEMBER

1 A TWA 727 crashes near Upperville, Virginia; 92 people are killed.

ARTS AND IDEAS

Architecture

- The Canadian National Tower in Toronto, Canada, designed by the architects John Andrews and Webb Zerata, is completed. At 553 m/1,815 ft, it is the world's highest freestanding structure.

Arts

- The Gunma Prefectural Museum of Fine Arts in Takasaki, Japan, designed by the Japanese architect Arata Isozaki, is completed.
- The new wing of the Minneapolis Institute of Art in Minnesota, designed by the Japanese architect Kenzo Tange, is completed.
- The U.S. artist Bruce Nauman creates the sculpture *Double Steel Cage*.
- The U.S. artist Cy Twombly paints *Turn and Coda*.
- The U.S. artist John de Andrea sculpts *Freckled Woman*.
- The U.S. artist R. B. Kitaj paints *Arcades (after Walter Benjamin)*.

Film

- *Trollflöjten/The Magic Flute*, a movie of Mozart's opera, directed by Ingmar Bergman, is released in Sweden.
- The disaster movie *The Towering Inferno*, directed by John Guillermin and Irwin Allen, is released in the United States. It features an all-star cast including Paul Newman and Steve McQueen.
- The movie *A Woman Under the Influence*, directed by John Cassavetes, is released in the United States, starring Peter Falk and Gena Rowlands.
- The movie *Alice Doesn't Live Here Anymore* is released in the United States. It is directed by Martin Scorsese and stars Kris Kristofferson and Ellen Burstyn.

- The movie *Alice in den Städten/Alice in the Cities* is released in West Germany. It is directed by Wim Wenders and stars Rudiger Vogler.
- The movie *Amarcord*, cowritten and directed by the Italian filmmaker Federico Fellini, is released, starring Magali Nöel and Bruno Zanin.
- The movie *Angst essen Seele auf/Fear Eats the Soul* is released in West Germany. It is directed by Rainer Werner Fassbinder and stars Brigitte Mira and El Hedi Ben Salem. The movie is a remake of U.S.-based filmmaker Douglas Sirk's movie *All That Heaven Allows*.
- The movie *Bring Me the Head of Alfredo Garcia*, directed by Sam Peckinpah, is released in the United States, starring Warren Oates.
- The movie *Emmanuelle*, directed by Just Jaeckin, is released in France, at the Triomphe movie theater on the Champs-Elysées in Paris. A very successful soft-porn movie, it stars Sylvia Kristel, Marika Green, and Daniel Sarky. It will run for a record-breaking 11 years.
- The movie *Godfather Part II* is released in the United States. It is directed by Francis Ford Coppola and stars Al Pacino and Robert De Niro. The movie will win a number of Academy Awards, including best picture, best directing, best adapted screenplay, and best musical score.
- The movie *Harry and Tonto*, directed by Paul Mazursky, is released in the United States, starring Art Carney.
- The movie *Il Fiore delle mille e una notte/The Arabian Nights*, directed by Pier Paolo Pasolini, is released in Italy, starring Ninetto Davoli and Ines Pellegrini.
- The movie *Lacombe, Lucien* is released in France. It is directed by Louis Malle and stars Pierre Blaise, Aurore Clément, and Holger Löwenadler.
- The movie *Lenny*, directed by Bob Fosse, is released in the United States. Based on the life of comedian Lenny Bruce, it stars Dustin Hoffman.
- The movie *Les Valseuses/Going Places*, cowritten and directed by Bertrand Blier, is released in France. It stars Gérard Depardieu, Patrick Dewaere, and Miou-Miou.
- The movie *Murder on the Orient Express*, directed by U.S. filmmaker Sidney Lumet, is released in the UK. Based on the novel by Agatha Christie, it stars Albert Finney as Hercule Poirot, and an all-star cast includes Ingrid Bergman, John Gielgud, Sean Connery, Anthony Perkins, and Lauren Bacall.
- The movie *Stavisky*, directed by Alain Resnais, is released in France, starring Jean-Paul Belmondo.
- The movie *The Great Gatsby*, directed by Francis Ford Coppola, is released in the United States. Based on the book by F. Scott Fitzgerald, it stars Robert Redford and Mia Farrow.
- The movie *The Parallax View* is released in the United States. It is directed by Alan J. Pakula and stars Warren Beatty.
- The movie *The Taking of Pelham One, Two, Three*, directed by Joseph Sargent, is released in the United States. It stars Walter Matthau, Robert Shaw, Martin Balsam, and Hector Elizondo.
- The movie *The Texas Chainsaw Massacre* is released in the United States. It is directed by Tobe Hooper and stars Marilyn Burns and Gunnar Hansen.

- The movie *Thunderbolt and Lightfoot* is released in the United States, directed by Michael Cimino and starring Clint Eastwood and Jeff Bridges.
- The movie *Young Frankenstein*, directed by Mel Brooks, is released in the United States, starring Gene Wilder.
- The neonoir movie *Chinatown* is released in the United States. It is written by Robert Towne, directed by Roman Polanski, and stars Jack Nicholson, Faye Dunaway, and John Huston.
- There are 700 million videocassettes rented in the United States.

JANUARY

10 The Communist Party in France complains about the paucity of government funding to the movie industry: the subsidy is less than 0.05%.

APRIL

2 The 1973 Academy Awards take place. Best Actor: Jack Lemon, for *Save the Tiger*; Best Supporting Actor: John Houseman, for *The Paper Chase*; Best Actress: Glenda Jackson, for *A Touch of Class*; Best Supporting Actress: Tatum O'Neal, for *Paper Moon*; Best Picture: *The Sting*, directed by George Roy Hill; Best Director: George Roy Hill, for *The Sting*.

MAY

- The movie *Callan* is released, premiering at the Cannes Film Festival, France, directed by Don Sharp and starring Edward Woodward. It is the first movie to have Dolby sound.
24 At the Cannes Film Festival, the Palme d'Or is awarded to Francis Ford Coppola for the U.S. movie *The Conversation*.

AUGUST

27 As the number of soft-porn movies made in France increases, the French government announces changes that remove most movie censorship.

NOVEMBER

15 The movie *Earthquake*, directed by Mark Robson, is released in the United States, the first to be made in Sensurround, which uses deep sound to give the sensation of earth tremors.

Literature and Language

- English writer Anthony Burgess publishes his novel *The Napoleon Symphony*.
- English writer Kingsley Amis publishes his novel *Ending Up*.
- English writer Richard Adams publishes his novel *Shardik*.
- The *New Cambridge Bibliography of English Literature*, edited by George Watson, is published in four volumes.
- The Cuban writer Alejo Carpentier publishes his novel *El recurso del método/Reasons of State*.
- The English poet Ted Hughes publishes a collection of poetry, *Season Songs*.
- The English writer Beryl Bainbridge publishes her novel *The Bottle Factory Outing*.
- The English writer John Le Carré publishes his novel *Tinker, Tailor, Soldier, Spy*.
- The English writer John Fowles publishes his novel *The Ebony Tower*.

- The English writer Philip Larkin publishes his poetry collection *High Windows*.
- The Irish-born British writer Iris Murdoch publishes her novel *The Sacred and Profane Love Machine*.
- The Italian writer Elsa Morante publishes her novel *La storia/History*.
- The Nobel Prize for Literature is awarded to the Swedish novelist Eyvind Johnson and the Swedish novelist and poet Harry Martinson.
- The Pulitzer Prize for Biography is awarded to Louis Sheaffer for *O'Neill, Son and Artist* and the Pulitzer Prize for Poetry is awarded to Robert Lowell for *The Dolphin*. The Pulitzer Prize for Fiction is not awarded this year.
- The Russian writer Alexander Solzhenitsyn is expelled from the USSR for political dissidence after publication of *Arkhipelag Gulag/The Gulag Archipelago* in Paris, France, in 1973.
- The U.S. historian Bernard Bailyn publishes *The Ordeal of Thomas Hutchinson*.
- The U.S. writer Alison Lurie publishes her novel *The War Between the Tates*.
- The U.S. writer Elmore Leonard publishes his novel *52 Pick-Up*.
- The U.S. writer Gary Snyder publishes his poetry collection *Turtle Island*, which wins the Pulitzer Prize for Poetry.
- The U.S. writer Tillie Olsen publishes her novel *Yonnondio: From the Thirties*.
- U.S. writer Robert M. Pirsig publishes his philosophical work *Zen and the Art of Motorcycle Maintenance*.

NOVEMBER

2 U.S. author J. D. Salinger breaks a 21-year silence to announce a lawsuit against a publisher and several major bookstore chains for unauthorized publication and distribution of short stories written early in his career.

Music

- The British pop group Status Quo releases "Down, Down" and the album *Quo*.
- The English composer Elisabeth Lutyens completes her orchestral work *Winter of the World*.
- The ex-Beatle Paul McCartney (with his band Wings) releases "Jet" and the album *Band on the Run*.
- The French composer Olivier Messiaen completes his orchestral work *Des Canyons aux étoiles/From Canyons to the Stars* for piano, horn, and orchestra.
- The German composer Karlheinz Stockhausen completes his orchestral work *Inori/Adorations*.
- The German pop group Can releases the album *Soon Over Babaluma*.
- The Hungarian-born Austrian composer György Ligeti completes his orchestral work *San Francisco Polyphony*. It will be premiered in 1975 in San Francisco, California.
- The opera *Ratsumies/The Horseman*, by the Finnish composer Aulis Sallinen is first performed, in Savonlinna, Finland.
- The Russian composer Dmitry Shostakovich completes his String Quartet No. 15.

- The Swedish pop group Abba wins the Eurovision Song Contest with "Waterloo" and shoots to international stardom.
- The U.S. composer Jacob Druckman completes his *Lamia* for voice and orchestra.
- The U.S. rock singer Bob Dylan and the Canadian group The Band undertake the classic Rolling Thunder Revue tour in the United States, giving 39 shows.

APRIL

13 The U.S. pop singer Ray Stevens releases "The Streak."

JUNE

15 The British pop star and actor David Bowie releases the album *Diamond Dogs*.

JULY

20 The British rock singer Eric Clapton releases the album *461 Ocean Boulevard*.

OCTOBER

12 The Jamaican-born pop singer Carl Douglas releases "Kung Fu Fighting."

Theater and Dance

- *The Churchill Play*, by the English writer Howard Brenton, is first performed, in London, England.
- English writer Alan Ayckbourn publishes his play *The Norman Conquests*.
- The German artist Joseph Beuys presents his performance work *I Like America and America Likes Me* in New York, New York.
- The play *Bad Habits*, by the U.S. writer Terrence McNally, is first performed, at the Booth Theater in New York, New York.
- The play *Coralie Lansdowne Says No*, by the Australian writer Alexander Buzo, is first performed, in Melbourne, Australia.
- The play *Die Macht der Gewöhnheit/The Force of Habit*, by the Austrian writer Thomas Bernhard, is first performed, in Austria.
- The play *Non si page! Non si page!/Can't Pay, Won't Pay*, by the Italian writer and actor Dario Fo, is first performed, in Italy. Fo soon gains an international reputation.
- The play *Travesties*, by the Czechoslovak-born English dramatist Tom Stoppard, is first performed, at the Aldwych Theatre in London, England.
- The Pulitzer Prize for Drama is not awarded this year.
- The Russian ballet dancer Mikhail Baryshnikov defects to the United States.

Thought and Scholarship

- Australian-born British moral philosopher J. L. Mackie publishes *The Cement of the Universe*.
- English philosopher P. F. Strawson publishes *Freedom and Resentment*.
- French philosopher Louis Althusser publishes *Eléments d'autocritique/Essays in Self-Criticism*.
- The 15th edition of the *Encyclopaedia Britannica* is published. It has three main sections: the Propaedia (a thematic guide), the Micropaedia (which contains the bulk of the entries), and the Macropaedia (which contains longer, more detailed entries).

- The Pulitzer Prize for History is awarded to Daniel J. Boorstin for *The Americans: The Democratic Experience*.
- The Pulitzer Prize for General Nonfiction is awarded to Ernest Becker for *The Denial of Death*.
- The U.S. historian Forrest McDonald publishes *The Presidency of George Washington*.
- U.S. historian Arthur Schlesinger, Jr., publishes *The Imperial Presidency*.
- U.S. philosopher Robert Nozick publishes *Anarchy, State, and Utopia*.
- U.S. political scientist David Mayhew publishes *Congress: the Electoral Connection*.

SOCIETY

Education

- Kenya abolishes tuition fees for basic education.

MAY

- Nine-hundred cadets are implicated in a cheating scandal at the U.S. Naval Academy. All are required to retake an examination.

OCTOBER

- Five male colleges at Oxford University in Britain—Brasenose, Jesus, Wadham, Hertford, and St. Catherine's—admit women for the first time.

Everyday Life

- Beverly Johnson becomes the first black model on the cover of a major fashion magazine when she appears on *Vogue*.
- Starting among university students in the United States, streaking becomes a more public phenomenon at sporting events in the United States and Britain.
- The U.S. Census Bureau reports 19,440,000 families classified as poor, with nearly 11 million households headed by males and nearly 9 million headed by females.

JANUARY

11 Sue Rosenkowitz becomes the first woman to give birth to surviving sextuplets, three boys and three girls, in Cape Town, South Africa.

FEBRUARY

10 British mineworkers begin an all-out strike in support of their pay claim of 30–40%.

APRIL

11–13 A strike by 6 million Japanese workers wanting more pay in response to global inflation, beings; the strike ends with a generous settlement.

MAY

8–28 A national rail strike is held in India over pay and price rises due to inflation.

19 A Protestant general strike begins in Northern Ireland against the power-sharing executive created by the Sunningdale Agreement of December 9, 1973.

OCTOBER

1   The first McDonald's hamburger restaurant in the UK opens.

5   David Kunst successfully completes the first verified around-the-world walk: it has taken him 4 years, 3 months, and 15 days.

NOVEMBER

15 The price of sugar in the United States jumps to $0.65 a pound, up from $0.18 in January.

Media and Communication

- ORTF in France is abolished and replaced by three "commercial" stations, but the state is the only stockholder.

- The 1973–74 Emmy Awards for television are held. Best Drama Series: *Upstairs, Downstairs*; Best Comedy Series: *M*A*S*H*; Best Actor in a Drama: Telly Savalas, for *Kojak*; Best Actress in a Drama: Michael Learned, for *The Waltons*; Best Actor in a Comedy: Alan Alda, for *M*A*S*H*; Best Actress in a Comedy: Mary Tyler Moore, for *The Mary Tyler Moore Show*.

- There is a worldwide shortage of newsprint.

- Time, Inc. begins publication of the magazine *People* in the United States as a successor to *Life*.

JANUARY

15–July 12, 1984 The situation comedy *Happy Days*, about family life in the 1950s, premiers on U.S. television and runs for 11 seasons.

SEPTEMBER

11–March 21, 1983 *Little House on the Prairie*, a popular television drama based on the classic series of books by Laura Ingalls Wilder, starts on U.S. televison. It chronicles the Ingalls family's struggles in the American West in the 1870s.

DECEMBER

- The *New York Times* accuses the Central Intelligence Agency (CIA) of illegally investigating over 10,000 U.S. dissenters. The CIA director William Colby acknowledges the wrongdoing in a letter to the U.S. president Gerald Ford on December 26.

Religion

- Roman Catholics are permitted to become Freemasons in countries where this does not involve anticlericalism.

- The monk, Brother Roger Schutz of Taizé, is awarded the Templeton Prize for Progress in Religion.

JANUARY

13 A public opinion poll in the United States reveals that fewer Catholics and Protestants attend church than ten years ago, but that the number of Jews going to weekly services has increased.

JULY

29–October 7 Eleven women are ordained Episcopal ministers in the U.S. The ordinations are invalidated by the Episcopal House of Bishops on August 15, though the body endorses the principle of ordaining women on October 17.

DECEMBER

24 Pope Paul VI inaugurates a Holy Year of pilgrimage.

Sports

- *Pumping Iron* by U.S. authors Charles Gaines and George Butler, a portrayal of the world of competitive bodybuilding, is published. The success of the book and a movie three years later, starring the Austrian bodybuilder Arnold Schwarzenegger, give competitive bodybuilding a great boost.

- Teofilo Stevenson of Cuba wins the heavyweight title at the inaugural World Amateur Boxing Championships in Havana, Cuba.

- The International Olympic Committee, based in Switzerland, relaxes its strict amateur code to allow future Olympic competitors to receive financial compensation for loss of earnings while in training or during the games themselves.

- Zaire becomes the first black African nation to qualify for the World Cup soccer finals.

JANUARY

1   Polls in the United States are split on college football's national champions for the year; one poll picks Alabama and another picks Notre Dame.

1–September 9 The U.S. tennis player Jimmy Connors wins the men's singles titles at the Australian, U.S., and Wimbledon championships.

APRIL

- The black American baseball slugger Henry (Hank) Aaron of the Atlanta Braves surpasses Babe Ruth's home run record of 714. Along the way, Aaron has endured race-baiting and numerous threats on his life from American bigots.

25 The introduction of sudden-death overtime in preseason and regular season games is one of several changes made by the National Football League (NFL) to make the game more exciting.

28–May 12 The Boston Celtics are the National Basketball Association (NBA) champions for the 12th time in 18 years.

MAY

4   Cannonade, ridden by U.S. jockey Angelo Cordero of the United States, wins the 100th Kentucky Derby, at Churchill Downs, Louisville, United States.

7   In hockey, the Philadelphia Flyers beat the Boston Bruins by four games to two, to become the first of the six new teams which joined the National Hockey League (NHL) in 1967 to win the Stanley Cup.

26 Race-car driver Johhny Rutherford wins the Indianapolis 500.

JUNE

June–October The Belgian cyclist Eddie Merckx becomes the first rider to win the Tour de France, the Giro d'Italia, and the world professional road race in the same season.

4   The U.S. baseball player Hank Aaron of the Atlanta Braves breaks Babe Ruth's record of 714 home runs in all major league competition.

12 Little League baseball announces that girls will be allowed to play in its teams for the first time in the United States.

JULY

- Hank Aaron of the Atlanta Braves surpasses Ty Cobb's all-time major league baseball record of 3,033 games.
- 7 The host nation, West Germany, wins the soccer World Cup, defeating the Netherlands 2–1 in the final in Munich.

SEPTEMBER

10–17 *Courageous*, captained by Ted Turner, beats its Australian rival *Southern Cross* and keeps the America's Cup.

OCTOBER

1 The English boxer John Conteh defeats Jorge Ahumada of Argentina on points in London, England, to win the World Boxing Council light-heavyweight world title.
3 Frank Robinson is named manager of the Cleveland Indians, becoming the first black American to take charge of a major league baseball team.

BIRTHS & DEATHS

JANUARY

2 Charles Bohlen, U.S. diplomat and Russian affairs expert, dies in Washington, D.C. (69).

2 Errett Cobban Cord, U.S. car manufacturer who produced the Cord, the first popular front-wheel drive car, dies in Reno, Nevada (79).

25 U Thant, Burmese educator and civil servant, secretary-general of the United Nations 1961–71, dies in New York (65).

29 H(erbert) E(rnest) Bates, English novelist and short-story writer who gained his reputation during World War II, dies in Canterbury, Kent, England (68).

31 Samuel Goldwyn, U.S. pioneer Hollywood filmmaker and producer, one of the founders of Metro-Goldwyn-Mayer (MGM), dies in Los Angeles, California (91).

FEBRUARY

11 J. Hans D. Jenson, German physicist who, with Maria Goeppert-Mayer and Eugene P. Wagner, proposed the shell theory of the atom, dies in Heidelberg, Germany (66).

MARCH

17 Louis Isadore Kahn, Estonian-born U.S. architect, dies in New York (73).

19 Ann Klein, U.S. fashion designer best known for casual sportswear, dies in New York, New York (60).

20 Chet Huntley, U.S. television news anchor, dies in Bozeman, Montana (62).

26 Edward U. Condon, U.S. physicist who used quantum mechanics to understand the atom and its nucleus, dies in Boulder, Colorado (72).

28 Dorothy Fields, U.S. lyricist who wrote songs for musical revues and films, dies in New York, New York (69).

APRIL

2 Georges Pompidou, French statesman, premier of the Fifth French Republic 1962–68 and president of France 1968–74, dies in Paris, France (62).

12 Josephine Baker, U.S. singer and dancer who took Paris, France, by storm in the 1920s, dies there (67).

19 Mohammed Ayub Khan, president of Pakistan 1958–69, dies near Islamabad, Pakistan (66).

24 Bud Abbott, U.S. comedian, half of the comedy duo Abbott and Costello, dies in Woodland Hills, California (73).

MAY

24 Duke Ellington, U.S. jazz composer, pianist, and big-band leader, dies in New York (75).

26 Stewart Alsop, influential U.S. newspaper columnist, dies in Washington, D.C. (60).

JUNE

18 Georgi K. Zhukov, Russian marshal, one of the USSR's most important military leaders in World War II, dies (77).

22 Darius Milhàud, French composer, dies in Geneva, Switzerland (81).

JULY

1 Juan Perón, Argentinean soldier and statesman, president of Argentina 1946–55 and 1973–74, dies in Buenos Aires, Argentina (78).

9 Earl Warren, U.S. chief justice 1953–69 and chairman of the committee that investigated Kennedy's assassination, dies in Washington, D.C. (83).

13 Patrick M(aynard) S(tuart) Blackett, British physicist working in the field of cosmic radiation, dies in London, England (76).

17 "Dizzy" Dean, U.S. professional baseball player and baseball commentator, dies in Reno, Nevada (63).

24 James Chadwick, English physicist who discovered the neutron, dies in Cambridge, England (82).

29 Erich Kästner, German novelist, poet, satirist, and author of children's books, dies in Munich, West Germany (75).

AUGUST

22 Jacob Bronowski, Polish-born English mathematician and writer, dies in New York (66).

26 Charles Lindbergh, U.S. aviator, the first person to fly solo nonstop across the Atlantic, dies in Maui, Hawaii (72).

31 Norman E. Kirk, New Zealand prime minister 1972–74 who opposed French nuclear testing in the Pacific, dies in Wellington, New Zealand (51).

OCTOBER

4 Anne Sexton, U.S. poet known for her confessional poetry, commits suicide (46).

13 Ed Sullivan, U.S. journalist and gossip columnist, best known as the host of the television variety show *The Ed Sullivan Show*, dies.

NOVEMBER

7 Eric Linklater, Scottish novelist, poet, and historical writer known for his satirical wit, dies in Aberdeen, Scotland (75).

21 Frank Martin, Swiss composer, pianist, harpsichordist, and teacher, dies in Naarden, the Netherlands (84).

29 H. L. Hunt, U.S. oil billionaire, dies in Dallas, Texas (85).

DECEMBER

14 Walter Lippmann, U.S. political columnist and author, dies in New York (85).

26 Jack Benny, U.S. radio and television comedian for more than 30 years, dies in Beverly Hills, California (80).

27 Amy Vanderbilt, U.S. author of *Amy Vanderbilt's Complete Book of Etiquette*, dies in New York, New York (68).

12–17 In baseball, the Oakland Athletics defeat the Los Angeles Dodgers by four games to one to win the World Series for the third successive year, the first team in 21 years to do so.
29 South Africa wins the Davis Cup for tennis by default when India refuses to play in the final because of the South African government's apartheid policies.
29 U.S. boxer Muhammad Ali, employing his famous "rope-a-dope" tactics, knocks out George Foreman of the United States in the eighth round of their bout to

regain the world heavyweight boxing title in Kinshasa, Zaire.

NOVEMBER
30 The South African golfer Gary Player hits a 10 under par round of 59 in the second round of the Brazilian Open in Rio de Janeiro to equal the world record for the lowest score in a tournament round of golf.

◆

1975

POLITICS, GOVERNMENT, AND ECONOMICS

Business and Economics

- Bill Gates, aged 19, and friend Paul Allen Gardiner, found Microsoft. It becomes the biggest seller of computer software in the world and makes Gates a billionaire before he is 30.
- The Worldwatch Institute is founded in the United States to research the interdependence of the world economy and the environment.

FEBRUARY
- The U.S. Social Security Advisory Council reports that the nation's $46-billion Social Security fund will dry up by 1981 unless replenished.

MAY
- *Fortune* magazine reports that General Motors' 40-year run as the wealthiest U.S. company has ended; the Exxon Corporation now boasts that distinction.

JUNE
10 The Municipal Assistance Corporation is formed in the United States to help New York, New York, avoid bankruptcy.

OCTOBER
21 Unemployment in Britain passes the 1 million mark for the first time since the 1940s.

Colonization

JANUARY
15 Portugal agrees to grant independence to Angola.

JUNE
25 Mozambique achieves independence from Portugal, with Samora Machel as president.

JULY
5 The Cape Verde Islands gain their independence from Portugal.
6 The Comoros Islands gain their independence from France.
12 São Tomé e Príncipe gains its independence from Portugal.

SEPTEMBER
16 Papua New Guinea gains its independence from Australia and joins the Commonwealth.

NOVEMBER
10 Angola gains its independence from Portugal with Agostinho Neto as president, but civil war breaks out between the Popular Movement for the Liberation of Angola (MPLA) and the National Union for the Total Independence of Angola (UNITA).
25 Suriname, formerly Dutch Guiana, gains its independence from the Netherlands.

Human Rights

- U.S. historian Edmund S. Morgan publishes *American Slavery, American Freedom*.

MARCH
- The U.S. Commission on Civil Rights reports that northern schools are more segregated than southern schools.

SEPTEMBER
- The U.S. Congress directs the nation's military academies to admit women into their ranks by the fall of 1976.

OCTOBER
- The decorated Vietnam War veteran Sgt. Leonard Matlovich is given a general discharge from the U.S. army after announcing his homosexuality.

NOVEMBER

- The U.S. states of New York and New Jersey defeat the 27th, or Equal Rights, Amendment, prohibiting sexual discrimination.
- 28 The Age Discrimination in Employment Act in the United States strengthens the law against age discrimination in the workplace.

Politics and Government

- French philosopher Michel Foucault publishes *Surveiller et punir/Discipline and Punishment*.
- New Democratic members of the U.S. Congress overturn the seniority system and disperse the power of committee chairs to subcommittees and members.
- The Indian Self-Determination Act is passed in the United States.
- The Internal Security Committee of the U.S. House of Representatives, formerly known as the Un-American Activities Committee, is abolished.
- The Metric Conversion Act to change the United States over to the metric system is enacted but it has little effect.
- The seven largest capitalist economic powers (the United States, Canada, Japan, West Germany, France, Italy, and Britain, the "Group of Seven") hold their first meeting, in Bonn, West Germany.
- The United Nations declares 1975 International Women's Year.

JANUARY

- The U.S. president Gerald Ford extends his offer of clemency to Vietnam War draft dodgers to March 1.
- January–November The U.S. president Gerald Ford appoints Vice President Nelson Rockefeller head of a committee to determine whether the Central Intelligence Agency has overstepped its mandate in investigating U.S. dissenters. Rockefeller's committee reports in the affirmative on June 10. The Idaho senator Frank Church leads a U.S. Senate investigation of Federal Bureau of Investigation (FBI) and Central Intelligence Agency (CIA) activity undertaken during the Nixon administration. On November 20, the committee accuses both agencies of illegally monitoring U.S. citizens and the CIA of plotting to assassinate foreign leaders, including Fidel Castro of Cuba and Patrice Lumumba of the Congo.
- 1 H. R. Haldeman, John D. Ehrlichman, and John N. Mitchell, aides of the former U.S. president Richard M. Nixon, are found guilty of their Watergate offenses.
- 4 The province of Phuoc Binh in South Vietnam falls to invading North Vietnamese forces.
- 20 The British government abandons the Channel Tunnel project because of escalating costs.
- 23 The British government decides to hold a referendum on the revised terms for British membership in the European Economic Community (Common Market).
- 31 The Industry Bill is published in Britain, establishing a National Enterprise Board to facilitate state intervention in industry.

FEBRUARY

- The U.S. Defense Department grants a security clearance to Otis Francis Taber, an avowed homosexual.

1 The Lomé Convention is signed, giving 46 developing countries preferential access to European Economic Community markets.
6 Five hundred Spanish civil servants sign a prodemocracy manifesto.
9 The Irish Republican Army (IRA) announces in Dublin, in the Republic of Ireland, that it will call a cease-fire from February 10.
11 Margaret Thatcher is elected leader of Britain's Conservative Party in the second ballot of the leadership election, with 146 votes. William Whitelaw wins 79 votes, and three other challengers 49 between them.
13 Northern Cyprus declares its separate existence as the Turkish Federated State of Cyprus.
21 H. R. Haldeman, John D. Ehrlichman, and John N. Mitchell, aides of the former U.S. president Richard M. Nixon, are sentenced to 2½–8 years in prison for their Watergate offenses.
24 Bangladesh introduces a presidential government and becomes a one-party state under Sheik Mujibur Rahman.
27 Peter Lorenz, chair of the West Berlin Christian Democratic Union, is kidnapped by terrorists.

MARCH

2 Iran becomes a one-party state.
5 Peter Lorenz, the chair of the West Berlin Christian Democratic Union who was kidnapped on February 27, is released after his captors' demands are met.
30 North Vietnamese forces capture Da Nang, South Vietnam's second largest city.

APRIL

9 The British House of Commons votes by 396 to 170 to confirm Britain's membership in the European Economic Community (Common Market).
13 Civil war erupts in Lebanon when clashes between Palestinians and Christian Phalangists outside a church in the capital, Beirut, leave 30 people dead.
17 Communist Khmer Rouge revolutionaries in Cambodia capture the capital, Phnom Penh, in the civil war between the right wing government of the Khmer Republic and the National United Front of Cambodia (the former leader Prince Sihanouk and the Khmer Rouge).
25 The first free elections in Portugal since the 1920s fail to produce an overall majority. The Socialists, under Mario Soares, emerge as the largest party.
25 The South African government decides to abolish many measures of "petty apartheid."
29 The last U.S. personnel flee the South Vietnamese capital, Saigon (now Ho Chi Minh City), flying by helicopter from the U.S. embassy compound.
30 President Minh of South Vietnam surrenders the capital, Saigon (now Ho Chi Minh City), to the North Korean communist forces.

MAY

12–15 The Cambodian navy seizes the U.S. merchant ship *Mayaguez*. It is recaptured by U.S. forces on May 15.
27 The Supreme Court of Alaska, United States, rules that the personal possession and cultivation of marijuana is protected by the state constitution.

JUNE

- The U.S. Supreme Court rules that standard minimum legal fees violate the nation's antitrust laws.
- 5 A referendum in Britain approves British membership in the European Economic Community (Common Market) by 67.2%.
- 5 The Suez Canal is reopened by the Egyptian president, Anwar Sadat, following its eight-year closure because of Arab–Israeli hostilities.
- 9–August 15 The trial is held in Lancaster, England, of the "Birmingham Six" charged with the 1974 pub bombings in Birmingham. All are found guilty and sentenced to life imprisonment. They are released on March 14, 1991, following a successful appeal.
- 10 The report of the Rockefeller Commission into Central Intelligence Agency (CIA) activities in the United States reveals illegal domestic operations and an extensive mail-opening program.
- 12 Indira Gandhi is found guilty of electoral corruption in India, but she remains prime minister pending appeals.
- 26 The Indian prime minister Indira Gandhi declares a state of emergency pending her appeal against the charge of electoral corruption. Censorship is imposed and opposition leaders, including Morarji Desai, the leader of the Janata Party, are imprisoned.
- 30 The U.S. Supreme Court rules that defendants in criminal cases can conduct their own defense rather than accept the services of a court-appointed lawyer.

JULY

- "Jimmy" R. Hoffa, former president of the International Brotherhood of Teamsters (transport workers), disappears in the U.S. and is presumed to have been murdered by the mob.
- 29 A bloodless coup in Nigeria replaces General Yakubu Gowon with Brig Murtala Mohammad.
- 29 The Organization of American States lifts the ban on relations with Cuba.

AUGUST

- The U.S. Congress eradicates literacy requirements for voting and extends the protection of the Voting Rights Act of 1965 to new linguistic minorities.
- 1 The Helsinki Conference on Security and Cooperation in Europe issues a "Final Act" signed by 30 states. The states are to respect one another's equality and individuality, avoid the use of force in disputes, and respect human rights.
- 15 President Mujibur Rahman of Bangladesh is killed in a coup. His civilian successor is Khandakar Mushtaq Ahmed.
- 23–25 The leaders of the Greek military junta are found guilty of treason and sentenced to death. The sentence is commuted on August 25.
- 31 The International Monetary Fund (IMF) abandons the remaining role of gold in world monetary affairs.

SEPTEMBER

- 4 Riots follow the introduction of school busing (transporting children by bus from their home districts to schools in other districts) for desegregation purposes in Louisville, Kentucky, United States.
- 5 Lynette "Squeaky" Fromme, a follower of the U.S. murderer Charles Manson, attempts to assassinate President Gerald Ford in Sacramento, California.

- 18 The kidnapped U.S. heiress Patricia Hearst is arrested for armed bank robbery, having joined her captors in crime.
- 22 Fifteen people die in bombings in nine Northern Ireland towns.
- 22 Sara Jane Moore attempts to assassinate the U.S. president Gerald Ford in San Francisco, California.
- 23 Israel and Egypt reach an agreement on an Israeli withdrawal from the Egyptian Sinai peninsula, which has been occupied by Israel since 1967.

OCTOBER

- The U.S. Supreme Court upholds corporal punishment where students have been made aware of its use for certain behavior, stating that to be forewarned is to be forearmed.
- 8 Over 50 people are killed when fighting resumes in the Lebanese civil war between Christians and Muslims.
- 10 Part of Israeli-occupied Sinai is returned to Egypt, following the agreement reached on September 23.
- 22 Three Irish Republican Army (IRA) members and a young woman (the "Guildford Four") are found guilty of bombing a public house in Guildford, England, and sentenced to life imprisonment.

NOVEMBER

- President Gerald Ford backs a U.S. federal loan of over $2 billion to help New York, New York, stave off bankruptcy.
- The Maryland governor, Marvin Mandel, is indicted by a U.S. federal grand jury on charges of bribery, mail and income tax fraud, and racketeering.
- William O. Douglas announces his retirement from the U.S. Supreme Court at the age of 77, after serving 36 years. His remains the longest Supreme Court tenure in U.S. history.
- November 1975–March 1976 The New Jersey Superior Court denies the request of the parents of Karen Anne Quinlan, who lies comatose from a drug overdose, for their daughter to be taken off the respirator. The Court grants the request the following March, but Karen lives on without the respirator.
- 1–December 29 The British doctor Sheila Cassidy is imprisoned and tortured in Chile. On December 30, the British ambassador in Santiago, the Chilean capital, is recalled in protest.
- 3 Queen Elizabeth II of Great Britain and Northern Ireland formally opens the North Sea oil pumps, marking the official start of Britain's exploitation of North Sea oil reserves.
- 3 The government in Bangladesh imposes martial law.
- 6–9 Unarmed Moroccans invade Spanish Sahara (now the disputed Western Sahara area of Morocco).
- 7 The verdict of electoral corruption on the Indian prime minister, Indira Gandhi, is quashed by the Supreme Court.
- 14 Spain agrees with Morocco and Mauritania to pull out of the Sahara by February 1976 and to organize consultations about the region's future.
- 25 The British government sends three frigates to protect trawlers in Icelandic fishing grounds during the "Cod War."
- 26 An attempted coup by left wing paratroops in Portugal is defeated.

Angolan Civil War (1975–89)

1975

November 10 Angola gains its independence from Portugal with Agostinho Neto as president, but civil war breaks out between the Popular Movement for the Liberation of Angola (MPLA) and the National Union for the Total Independence of Angola (UNITA).

December The U.S. Senate cuts off covert aid to anticommunist forces in the Angolan civil war following that country's independence.

1976

February 17 MPLA forces secure control over most Angolan territory.

1980

July 2 South African troops withdraw from Angola after a three-week raid on guerrilla bases.

1984

November 2 Angola offers to reduce the number of Cuban troops in the country if South Africa agrees to relinquish control of Namibia.

1985

April 15 The president of South Africa P. W. Botha announces that South African military forces in Angola will leave by April 18.

1988

January 29 Talks in Luanda reach agreement on the withdrawal of Cuban military personnel from Angola.

1989

January 10 Cuban troops begin to withdraw from Angola.

June 23 President José Eduardo dos Santos of Angola and Jonas Savimbi, leader of the UNITA rebels, sign a declaration ending the 14-year civil war in Angola.

---

27 The Irish Republican Army (IRA) murders the publisher and right wing activist Ross McWhirter at his home in Enfield, Greater London, England.

28 The Revolutionary Front for the Independence of East Timor (FRETILIN) unilaterally declares East Timor independent from Portugal.

29 The Education for All Handicapped Children Act in the United States requires public schools to provide appropriate education for every school-age handicapped child, irrespective of his or her disability.

29 The New Zealand National Party defeats the Labor government, and Robert Muldoon, leader of the National Party, becomes prime minister.

DECEMBER

• The U.S. Senate cuts off covert aid to anticommunist forces in the Angolan civil war following that country's independence.

• The year ends on a portentous note in the U.S. when a bomb explodes in the main terminal at New York's La Guardia airport. Eleven people die, 70 are injured, and holiday air traffic is thoroughly disrupted.

2–14 A train in the Netherlands is hijacked by South Moluccan terrorists.

3 Communist forces take control of Laos. King Savang Vatthana abdicates and the country is proclaimed a "People's Democratic Republic" under the presidency of Prince Souphanouvong.

6–12 Four Irish Republican Army (IRA) gunmen hold a couple hostage in Balcombe Street, London, England. They surrender when the siege ends suddenly.

7 Indonesian forces invade the newly independent East Timor and commit numerous atrocities.

11 The first shots are fired in the "Cod War" around Iceland.

13 The general election in Australia gives a large majority to the newly installed Liberal government of Malcolm Fraser.

21 Palestinian terrorists take 60 hostages, including 11 oil ministers, at the Organization of Petroleum-Exporting Countries (OPEC) summit in Vienna, Austria.

22 The U.S. Energy Policy and Conservation Act establishes strategic reserves of petroleum and requires cars to meet gasoline mileage standards.

23 Richard Welch, the Central Intelligence Agency (CIA) head of operations in Greece, is shot dead in Athens following his exposure by a newspaper as a spy.

27 The Indian general election is postponed until 1977.

30 The former Greek dictator Georgios Papadopoulos is imprisoned for a further 25 years for shootings at the Athens Polytechnic in November 1973.

SCIENCE, TECHNOLOGY, AND MEDICINE

Agriculture

December 1975–79 One million people die from famine caused by Khmer Rouge policies in Kampuchea.

Computing

• A computer equipped with an array processor is produced by the U.S. firm Floating Point Systems; it is used for making scientific calculations.

• Steve Wozniak, later a cofounder (with Steven Jobs) of Apple Computers, develops a prototype microcomputer; it has no commercial success.

• The first "personal computer," the Altair 8800, is marketed in the United States; it has no keyboard or

screen but uses toggle switches to input data and flashing lights for output.
- The U.S. firm IBM introduces the laser printer.
- U.S. computer programmer Michael Shrayer develops the "Electric Pencil," the first word processing software package for a personal computer.

Ecology

- A huge gas and oil field is discovered in Utah near the Wyoming border; its reserves of natural gas are estimated at 275 billion cu m/360 cu yd, and its reserves of oil at 1 billion barrels.
- A tornado in Omaha, Nebraska, causes $100 million of damage, but Weather Service alerts limit the death toll to three.
- Atlantic salmon return to spawn in the Connecticut River, United States after an absence of nearly a hundred years; the river was restocked in 1973 after efforts were made to end pollution.
- Mauna Loa volcano erupts in Hawaii for the first time since 1950.
- Morne Trois Oitons National Park is established in Dominica in the West Indies; it is a tropical mountain wilderness.
- The Banqiao and Shimantan dams in Henan Province, China, burst; about 230,000 people are killed in the worst accident of its kind.
- The Ecology Party is founded in Britain (known since 1985 as the Green Party).

SEPTEMBER
6 An earthquake measuring 6.8 on the Richter scale hits the town of Lice in eastern Turkey, killing over 2,000 people.

DECEMBER
12 A fire in a tent city in Mina, Saudi Arabia, kills 138 people.
27 A mine explosion at Chasnala, India, kills 431 people.

Exploration

- The U.S. firm RCA's *Satcom* communication satellite is launched; it is the first U.S. satellite to be body-stabilized—all three axes of the satellite's body are stabilized with respect to the earth by means of spinning inertia wheels.
- The United States launches *Landsat 2*; located 180° away from *Landsat 1*, the two together provide a view of the same geographic area with the same Sun angle every nine days.

MARCH
15 The U.S.–German space probe *Helios 1* (launched December 10, 1974) passes the sun at a distance of 45 million km/28 million mi and returns information about the sun's magnetic field and solar wind.

JULY
- The launch of the Soviet spaceship *Soyuz 19* signals the start of a joint U.S.–Soviet space mission. U.S. and Soviet astronauts meet in space on July 17 when *Soyuz 19* docks with its NASA counterpart, *Apollo 18*.

AUGUST
1 The European Space Agency is founded in Paris, France, to undertake research and develop technologies for use in space.

OCTOBER
- The United States launches the first *Geostationary Operational Environmental Satellite* (GOES); it provides 24-hour coverage of U.S. weather.
22–25 The Soviet spacecraft *Venera 9* and *10* land on Venus and transmit the first pictures from the surface of another planet.

Health and Medicine

- An outbreak of animal encephalitis spreads across 16 U.S. states.
- Argentine immunologist César Milstein and German immunologist Georges Köhler develop the first monoclonal antibodies—lymphocyte and myeloma tumor cell hybrids that are cloned to secrete unlimited amounts of specific antibodies—in Cambridge, England.
- Birth control becomes a priority in India; abortion is legalized and the government launches campaigns advocating sterilization for both sexes.
- Swiss scientists publish details of the first chemically directed synthesis of insulin.
- U.S. virologists David Baltimore and Howard Martin Temin and Italian biologist Renato Dulbecco share the Nobel Prize for Physiology or Medicine for their discoveries concerning the interaction between tumor viruses and the genetic material of the cell.

JANUARY
- High medical malpractice settlements spur several U.S. insurance companies to stop offering doctors malpractice insurance.

MARCH
- Some 2,000 interns and residents strike in New York, New York, hospitals to win shorter working hours. The strike ends three days later when the doctors' hours are reduced.

APRIL
15 Karen Ann Quinlan enters a coma in the United States after drinking an alcohol and tranquilizer mixture; fed through a nasal tube, she is kept alive for eight years. Her highly publicized case spurs debate about an individual's right to die.

JULY
- The U.S. National Center for Health Statistics lists the death rate from cancer at 176.3 per 100,000.

OCTOBER
12 The Toxic Substances Control Act is passed by the U.S. Congress; it requires that the production of PCBs (polychlorinated biphenyls) be phased out within three years as they have been associated with birth defects and cancer.

Math

- U.S. mathematician Mitchell Fingelbaum discovers a new fundamental constant (approximately 4.6692016) that plays an important part in chaos theory.

Science

- "U" subatomic particles are produced at the accelerator at Stanford University, California.
- Australian chemist John Cornforth and Swiss chemist Vladimir Prelog receive the Nobel Prize for Chemistry for their work in stereochemistry.
- British scientist Derek Brownhall produces the first clone of a rabbit, in Oxford, England.
- Danish physicist Aage Bohr, U.S.-born Danish physicist Ben Mottelson, and U.S. physicist James Rainwater receive the Nobel Prize for Physics for their work toward understanding the atomic nucleus.
- Italian archeologist Paolo Matthiae discovers 15,000 clay tablets with cuneiform texts at Tell Mardikh (ancient Ebla) in Syria; they date to 3000 BC and are discovered in the order in which they were stored.
- Kenyan field worler Bernard Ngeneo discovers a *Homo erectus* skull at Koobi Fora, Kenya, that is estimated to be 1.7 million years old; discovered in the same stratum as *Australopithecus boisei*, it puts an end to the single species hypothesis, the idea that there has never been more than one hominid species at any point in history.
- The gel-transfer hybridization technique for the detection of specific DNA (deoxyribonucleic acid) sequences is developed; it is a key development in genetic engineering.
- U.S. anthropologist Donald Johanson and his team at Hadar in Ethiopia discover the "first family"—the remains of at least 13 *Australopithecus afarensis* individuals of varying ages, estimated to be 3.2 million years old.
- U.S. physicist Samuel Hurst's machine identifies a single cesium atom in a sample of 1019 argon atoms.
- U.S. physiologist John Hughes discovers endorphins (morphine-like chemicals) in the brain.
- U.S. radio astronomers Russell Hulse and Joseph Taylor identify PSR1913+16 as a binary pulsar; it loses energy at a rate which the theory of general relativity predicts for the emission of gravitational waves.

AUGUST
- U.S. physicist Martin Perl discovers the tau lepton (or tauon) atomic particle.

OCTOBER
3 English archeologist Mary Leakey announces her discovery in Tanzania of the jaws and teeth of 11 skeletons with identifiable human characteristics, dating back over 2 million years.

DECEMBER
11 The U.S. Congress passes legislation calling for the voluntary conversion to the metric system in ten years.

Technology

c. 1975 Color photocopiers begin to appear.
c. 1975 Soviet scientist B. V. Deryaguin develops thin sheets of polycrystalline diamond, using a vapor deposition technique, that are used as semiconductors and as very hard coatings.
c. 1975 The USSR and the United States simultaneously develop beam weapons that produce beams of protons which destroy solid targets such as satellites.
c. 1975 U.S. steel manufacturers increase the strength of steel by blowing powdered lime into the molten metal during the basic oxygenation process.
- French researcher Antoine Labeyrie develops an interferometer (a device using the interference of waves to make precise measurements) that can distinguish between two objects 1 m/3.3 ft apart at a distance of 60,000 km/37,284 mi; it leads to even more powerful interferometers which prove useful in making precise measurements of celestial bodies.
- Liquid crystals are first used for display purposes in electronic devices such as watches and calculators.
- The Anglo-Australian Telescope begins operation in Siding Spring Mountain, New South Wales, Australia; its 3.9-m/12.8-ft reflector makes it the third largest optical telescope in the world and the largest in the southern hemisphere.
- The British firm EMI makes the first computer capable of understanding human speech and answering in a synthetic voice.
- The Chirkeyskaya Dam across the Sulak River in Daghestan, USSR, is completed; at 233 m/765 ft high it is the highest double curvature arch dam in the world.
- The first computerized checkouts appear in supermarkets in the United States.

Transportation

- Mirabel International Airport, the world's largest, opens in Montreal, Canada.
- The Great Uhuru Railroad linking Zambia's copper district with the Tanzanian port of Dar es Salaam is completed; 1,705 km/1,060 mi long, it has been built with Chinese funds and expertise through some of Africa's most rugged country.
- The United States launches the nuclear powered aircraft carrier *Nimitz*, the largest warship afloat.

FEBRUARY
28 A subway train crashes at Moorgate station, London, England; 43 people are killed and 90 injured.

APRIL
4 A U.S. Air Force Galaxy C-58 crashes shortly after taking off from Saigon during an airlift of 2,000 Vietnamese children; 172 passengers, mostly children, are killed.

JUNE
24 An Eastern Airlines Boeing 747 crashes on arrival during an electrical storm at Kennedy Airport, New York; 113 people are killed in the worst U.S. domestic airplane crash to date.

AUGUST
3 Nearly 400 people die when two Chinese excursion boats collide off Guangzhou (Canton), China.

NOVEMBER
10 The ore carrier *Edmund Fitzgerald* sinks during a storm on Lake Superior, North America; 29 people die.

December

26 The USSR's Tupolev-144 begins regular scheduled services carrying mail and freight; it is the first supersonic commercial transport to do so.

ARTS AND IDEAS

Architecture

- The 82-km/52-mi-long Orange–Great Fish River irrigation tunnel in South Africa is completed; it is the longest irrigation tunnel in the world.
- The John Hancock Tower in Boston, Massachusetts, designed by the Chinese-born architect I. M. Pei, is completed.
- The Walden 7 apartment block in Barcelona, Spain, designed by the Spanish architect Ricardo Bofill, is completed.
- The Wills, Faber & Dumas Insurance Building in Ipswich, England, designed by the English architect Norman Foster, is completed.

Arts

- The English artist Leon Kossoff paints *Portrait of George Thompson*.
- The Lehman Pavilion in the Museum of Modern Art (MOMA) in New York, New York, is completed. It was designed by the architects Kevin Roche and John Dinkeloo.
- The U.S. artist Alex Katz paints *Trio*.
- The U.S. artist Dan Flavin creates the gallery exhibited work of art *Untitled (For Ellen)*.
- The U.S. artist Isamu Noguchi creates *Dodge Memorial Fountain*, a steel fountain set up in Hart Plaza, Detroit, Michigan.

Film

- Moviegoers pay more than $2 billion to see movies in the United States.
- The blockbuster movie *Jaws*, directed by Steven Spielberg, is released in the United States. It stars Roy Scheider, Robert Shaw, and Richard Dreyfuss.
- The movie *Ansikte mot ansikte/Face to Face*, directed by Ingmar Bergman, is released in Sweden. Edited from a four-part television series, it stars Liv Ullmann and Erland Josephson.
- The movie *Barry Lyndon*, directed by Stanley Kubrick, is released in the United States. Based on the novel by William Thackeray, it stars Ryan O'Neal.
- The movie *Cousin, Cousine*, directed by Jean-Charles Tacchella, is released in France. It stars Marie-Christine Barrault and Victor Lanoux.
- The movie *Dersu Uzala*, directed by Japanese filmmaker Akira Kurosawa, is filmed in the USSR and released in Japan. It stars Maxim Munzuk and Yury Solomine.
- The movie *Die grosse Ekstase des Bildschnitzers Steiner, Jeder für sich und Gott gegen alle/The Enigma of*

Kaspar Hauser is released in West Germany (U.S. title *Every Man for Himself and God Against All*). It is written and directed by Werner Herzog and stars Bruno S.

- The movie *Die Verlorene Ehre der Katharina Blum/The Lost Honor of Katharina Blum*, directed by Volker Schlöndorff and Margarethe von Trotta, is released in West Germany. It is based on the novel by Heinrich Böll.
- The movie *Dog Day Afternoon*, directed by Sidney Lumet, is released in the United States. It stars Al Pacino and John Cazale.
- The movie *L'Histoire d'Adèle H/The Story of Adèle H*, directed by François Truffaut, is released in France. Based on the life of Victor Hugo's daughter, it stars Isabelle Adjani.
- The movie *Le vieux fusil/The Old Gun*, directed by Robert Enrico, is released in France.
- The movie *Love and Death*, written and directed by Woody Allen, is released in the United States. Allen costars with Diane Keaton.
- The movie *Monty Python and the Holy Grail*, directed by Terry Gilliam and Terry Jones, is released in the UK. It stars the directors as well as the rest of the Monty Python team, John Cleese, Michael Palin, Eric Idle, and Graham Chapman.
- The movie *Nashville*, directed by Robert Altman, is released in the United States. The movie features an all-star cast, including Keith Carradine, Lily Tomlin, and Shelley Duvall.
- The movie *Night Moves*, directed by Arthur Penn, is released in the United States, starring Gene Hackman.
- The movie *One Flew Over the Cuckoo's Nest* is released in the United States. It is directed by the Czech-born filmmaker Miloš Forman and stars Jack Nicholson. The movie will be only the second in Academy Award history, after Frank Capra's 1934 comedy *It Happened One Night*, to win Oscars in all the major categories: best picture, best director, best actor, best actress, and best screenplay.
- The movie *Picnic at Hanging Rock*, directed by Peter Weir, is released in Australia, starring Anne Lambert, Rachel Roberts, and Helen Morse, and based on the novel by Joan Lindsay.
- The movie *Salo o le 120 Giornate di Sodoma/Salo, or the 120 Days of Sodom*, directed by Pier Paolo Pasolini, is released in Italy, a controversial adaptation of the novel by the Marquis de Sade. It is the last movie Pasolini directs before he is murdered.
- The movie *Shampoo* is released in the United States. It is directed by Hal Ashby and stars Warren Beatty, Julie Christie, and Goldie Hawn.
- The movie *The Day of the Locust* is released in the United States. Based on the novel by Nathanael West, it is directed by John Schlesinger and stars Donald Sutherland and Karen Black.
- The movie *The Godfather Part II*, directed by Francis Ford Coppola is released in the United States, starring Al Pacino, Diane Keaton, Andy Garcia, Eli Wallach, and Bridget Fonda.
- The movie *The Man Who Would Be King*, based on the story by Rudyard Kipling, is released in the United States. It is directed by John Huston and stars Sean Connery and Michael Caine.

- The movie *The Passenger*, directed by the Italian filmmaker Michelangelo Antonioni, is released. It stars Jack Nicholson and Maria Schneider.
- The movie *The Rocky Horror Picture Show* is released in the UK. Based on Richard O'Brien's stage hit, it is directed by Jim Sharman and stars Tim Curry, Susan Sarandon, and Barry Bostwick.
- The movie *The Wiz* by U.S. director Sidney Lumet is released in the United States. Based on a musical version of Frank L. Baum's *The Wizard of Oz*, and with an all-black cast, it stars Diana Ross, Michael Jackson, Richard Pryor, and Nipsey Russell.
- The movie *The Yakuza* is released in the United States. It is directed by Sydney Pollack, scripted by Paul Schrader and Robert Towne, and stars Robert Mitchum. Pollack's movie *Three Days of the Condor*, starring Robert Redford and Faye Dunaway, is also released in the United States.
- The rock opera movie *Tommy*, directed by Ken Russell, is released in the UK. It stars Roger Daltrey and features the music of The Who, Elton John, Eric Clapton, and Tina Turner.

APRIL

8 The 1974 Academy Awards take place. Best Actor: Art Carney, for *Harry and Tonto*; Best Supporting Actor: Robert De Niro, for *The Godfather Part II*; Best Actress: Ellen Burstyn, for *Alice Doesn't Live Here Anymore*; Best Supporting Actress: Ingrid Bergman, for *Murder on the Orient Express*; Best Picture: *The Godfather Part II*, directed by Francis Ford Coppola; Best Director: Francis Ford Coppola, for *The Godfather Part II*.

MAY

23 At the Cannes Film Festival, the Palme d'Or is awarded to the Algerian director Mohammed Lakhdar-Hamina for *Chronicle of the Burning Years*.

NOVEMBER

21 Publication of the movie sex magazine *L'Organe* is banned, in France.

Literature and Language

- The Argentine writer Jorge Luis Borges publishes his story collection *El libro de arena/The Book of Sand*.
- The Colombian writer Gabriel García Márquez publishes his novel *El otoño del patriarca*. An English translation, *The Autumn of the Patriarch*, is published in 1977.
- The English writer Anthony Powell publishes *Hearing Secret Harmonies*, the final novel of his 12-volume sequence *A Dance to the Music of Time*.
- The English writer Ian McEwan publishes his novel *First Love, Last Rites*.
- The English writer Malcolm Bradbury publishes his novel *The History Man*.
- The English writer Martin Amis publishes his novel *Dead Babies*.
- The English writer Paul Scott publishes his novel *A Division of the Spoils*, the last volume of his *Raj Quartet*.

- The French social and literary critic Roland Barthes publishes his autobiographical *Roland Barthes par Roland Barthes/Roland Barthes by Roland Barthes*.
- The French writer Michel Tournier publishes his novel *Les Météores/Gemini*.
- The French-born U.S. literary critic George Steiner publishes his critical work *After Babel: Aspects of Language and Translation*.
- The German-born Indian writer Ruth Prawer Jhabvala publishes her novel *Heat and Dust*.
- The Irish writer Seamus Heaney publishes his poetry collection *North*.
- The Italian writer Primo Levi publishes his collection of meditations and recollections *Il sistema periodico/The Periodic Table*.
- The Mexican writer Carlos Fuentes publishes his novel *Terra Nostra/Our Land*.
- The Nobel Prize for Literature is awarded to the Italian poet Eugenio Montale.
- The poetry collection, *The Awful Rowing Toward God*, by the U.S. writer Anne Sexton is published posthumously.
- The Pulitzer Prize for Biography is awarded to Robert A. Caro for *The Power Broker: Robert Moses and the Fall of New York*, the Pulitzer Prize for Poetry is awarded to Gary Snyder for *Turtle Island*, and the Pulitzer Prize for Fiction is awarded to Michael Shaara for *The Killer Angels*.
- The U.S. linguist and social critic Noam Chomsky publishes *Reflections on Language*.
- The U.S. writer Joyce Carol Oates publishes her novel *Assassins*.
- The U.S. writer Paul Theroux publishes his travel book *The Great Railway Bazaar*.
- The U.S. writer Saul Bellow publishes his novel *Humboldt's Gift*.
- The U.S. writer William Gaddis publishes his novel *JR*.
- The writer P. G. Wodehouse is knighted in Britain, just before his death.
- U.S. author Judith Rossner publishes her novel *Looking for Mr Goodbar*.

Music

- The British pop star Elton John releases the albums *Captain Fantastic and the Brown Dirt Cowboy* and *Rock of the Westies*.
- The English composer Benjamin Britten completes his String Quartet No. 3 and his cantata *Phaedra*, settings of selections from the play *Phèdra* by the French dramatist Jean Racine as translated by the U.S. writer Robert Lowell.
- The English pop group 10cc releases "I'm Not in Love."
- The French composer Pierre Boulez completes his orchestral work *Rituel in memoriam Bruno Maderna*.
- The Jamaican pop group Bob Marley and the Wailers releases "No Woman No Cry" and the album *Natty Dread*, one of the classics of reggae.
- The opera *Al gran sole carico d'amore/To the Great Sun Charged with Love* by the Italian composer Luigi Nono, is first performed, in Milan, Italy. It is revised in 1977.

- The opera *The Last Temptation*, by the Finnish composer Joonas Kokkonen, is first performed, in Helsinki, Finland.
- The Polish composer Witold Lutosławski completes his work for voice (baritone) and orchestra *Les Espaces du sommeil/To the Edge of a Dream*.
- The Polish composer Henryk Górecki completes his *Symphony No. 3* ("Symphony of Sorrowful Songs").
- The Russian composer Alfred Schnittke completes his *Requiem*.
- The U.S. composer Elliott Carter completes his vocal work *A Mirror on Which to Dwell*, based on poems by the U.S. writer Elizabeth Bishop.
- The U.S. conductor James Levine becomes musical director of the Metropolitan Opera, New York, New York.
- The U.S. pop singer Bruce Springsteen releases "Born to Run" and an album of the same name.
- The U.S. pop singer Janis Ian releases "At Seventeen."

FEBRUARY

8   The German pop group Kraftwerk releases the album *Autobahn*.
8   The U.S. folk/rock singer Bob Dylan releases the album *Blood on the Tracks*.

MARCH

1   The 1974–75 Grammy Awards take place. Best Album: *Fullfillingess' First Finale* by Stevie Wonder; Best Male Pop Vocalist: Stevie Wonder; Best Female Pop Vocalist: Olivia Newton-John; Best Record: "I Honestly Love You" by Olivia Newton-John.
15 The British heavy metal rock group Led Zeppelin releases the album *Physical Graffiti* and becomes the first band ever to have six albums in the U.S. chart simultaneously.

SEPTEMBER

6   The British pop singer Rod Stewart releases the single "Sailing" and the album *Atlantic Crossing*. "Sailing" becomes the best-selling single of the 1970s in Britain.

DECEMBER

12 The U.S. pop group Frankie Valli and the Four Seasons release "December 1963 (Oh What a Night)."
13 The U.S. pop singer Patti Smith releases the album *Horses*.
20 The British pop group Queen promotes its song "Bohemian Rhapsody," from the album *A Night at the Opera*, with the first pop video. The video, produced by Bruce Gowers on a £4,500 budget, debuts on the television program *Top of the Pops*.

Theater and Dance

- *The Fool*, by the English writer Edward Bond, is first performed, in London, England.
- The musical *A Chorus Line*, with lyrics by Edward Kleban and music by Marvin Hamlisch, is first performed, at the Public Theater in New York, New York.
- The play *Absent Friends*, by the English writer Alan Ayckbourn, is first performed, at the Garrick Theatre in London, England.
- The play *American Buffalo*, by the U.S. writer David Mamet, is first performed, in Chicago, Illinois.

- The play *Białe małżeństwo/Mariage Blanc*, by the Polish writer Tadeusz Różewicz, is first performed, in Poland.
- The play *Death and the King's Horseman*, by the Nigerian writer Wole Soyinka, is first performed, in Cambridge, England.
- The play *East*, by the English writer Steven Berkoff, is first performed, at the Edinburgh Festival, Scotland.
- The play *No Man's Land*, by the English writer Harold Pinter, is first performed, at the Old Vic Theatre in London, England.
- The play *Same Time Next Year*, by the Canadian writer Bernard Slade, is first performed, at the Brooks Atkinson Theater in New York, New York.
- The play *Seascape*, by the U.S. writer Edward Albee, is first performed, at the Shubert Theater in New York, New York.
- The play *Statements after an Arrest Under the Immorality Act*, by the South African writer Athol Fugard, is first performed, in South Africa.
- The play *The Ritz*, by the U.S. writer Terence McNally, is first performed, at the Longacre Theater in New York, New York.
- The Pulitzer Prize for Drama is awarded to Edward Albee for *Seascapes*.

Thought and Scholarship

- British historian Paul Addison publishes *The Road to 1945*.
- English historian A. J. P. Taylor publishes *The Second World War: An Illustrated History*.
- English historian E. P. Thompson publishes *Whigs and Hunters*.
- The first volume of *The Cambridge History of Africa* is published, edited by Richard Gray. The last volume will appear in 1986.
- The Pulitzer Prize for History is awarded to Dumas Malone for *Jefferson and His Time*.
- The Pulitzer Prize for General Nonfiction is awarded to Annie Dillard for *The Pilgrim at Tinker Creek*.
- U.S. historian Carl Bridenbaugh publishes *The Spirit of '76: The Growth of American Patriotism Before Independence, 1607–1776*.
- U.S. historian Willard B. Gatewood, Jr., publishes *Black Americans and the White Man's Burden, 1898–1903*.
- U.S. philosopher of science Paul Feyerabend publishes *Against Method*.
- U.S. political historian Theodore White publishes *Breach of Faith*.
- U.S. writer Paul Fussell publishes *The Great War and Modern Memory*.

SOCIETY

Education

- Legislation in New Zealand facilitates the integration of private schools into the state system.
- The New School Act in Denmark legislates for primary and secondary comprehensive "folk" schools.

JANUARY

- The Educational Testing Service of Princeton, New Jersey, reports that women with advanced degrees earn less than their male counterparts and are promoted less readily.

Everyday Life

- Countries with the highest populations (in millions): China 843; India 615; Japan 112; United States 213; USSR 255.
- General Mills produces the first cereal bars, Nature Valley Granola Bars, in the United States.
- Gillette of Boston, Massachusetts, launches the first disposable razors, made of plastic.
- Out of 34,083 doctors' degrees awarded in the United States, 7,266 are to women.
- Over 725,000 hysterectomies are performed in the United States, usually on women who fear pregnancy or uterine or ovarian cancer. This rate is up 25% in five years, and it is almost three times the rate in England and four times that in Sweden.
- Philip Morris launches Miller Lite, the first light beer, in the United States.
- The average female worker in the United States earns 57% of what the average male earns. Average annual salaries of female faculty members in universities are about $4,000 lower than those of men at the same institution.
- The first "drive-thru" McDonald's hamburger restaurant is opened.
- The percentage of government seats held by women is 4% in Africa; 13% in Asia; 3.4% in Latin America; 3.6% in North America; 13% in Europe; and 32% in the USSR.
- The U.S. Department of Commerce and the Bureau of the Census publish *Historical Statistics of the United States: Colonial Times to 1970*.
- Unemployment among blacks is 15% during this year's recession, while the rate for whites is 9%.
- Women outnumber men in the United States for the first time due to longer life spans for women, who live an average of eight years longer than men.

January 1975–80   There is a 4.2% average increase in female enrolment in early education programs worldwide. For the world, excluding China, the increase is 20.3%.

JANUARY

2   British hospital consultants begin a work-to-rule over their new contracts.

FEBRUARY

3   Auto industry layoffs reach 274,000 workers.
19   The British government sends troops to Glasgow, Scotland, to clear rubbish heaps after a nine-week strike by refuse collectors.

APRIL

18   National Health Service employees in Britain end strike action after being granted pay rises of up to 38%.

MAY

30   Unemployment in the United States reaches 9.2%, the highest rate since 1941.

OCTOBER

24   Women in Iceland stage a one-day general strike.

Media and Communication

- The 1974–75 Emmy Awards for television are held. Best Drama Series: *Upstairs, Downstairs*; Best Comedy Series: *The Mary Tyler Moore Show*; Best Actor in a Drama: Robert Blake, for *Baretta*; Best Actress in a Drama: Jean Marsh, for *Upstairs, Downstairs*; Best Actor in a Comedy: Tony Randall, for *The Odd Couple*; Best Actress in a Comedy: Valerie Harper, for *Rhoda*.

JANUARY

18–July 23, 1985   *The Jeffersons*, a popular situation comedy about a black family in New York, New York, is shown on U.S. television.

APRIL

- The U.S. National Association of Broadcasters pledges not to broadcast violent or profane television programs during what becomes known as family viewing time.

OCTOBER

11   *Saturday Night Live* hits U.S. television: with performers such as Chevy Chase, John Belushi, and Dan Ackroyd, and later Bill Murray and Eddie Murphy, it is an immediate success and has a significant influence on U.S. comedy.

DECEMBER

16–September 2, 1984   The U.S. television comedy *One Day at a Time* deals with the lives of a divorced woman raising her two teenage daughters.

Religion

FEBRUARY

- Elijah Muhammad, founder of the religious group the Nation of Islam (Black Muslims), dies in Chicago, Illinois. He is succeeded by his son Wallace the next day.

SEPTEMBER

- Mother Elizabeth Ann Bayley Seton (1774–1821) becomes America's first native-born saint, having been canonized by Pope Paul VI.

Sports

- An all-time high 9.2 million tennis rackets are sold in the United States.
- The University of California at Los Angeles (UCLA) spends $2.8 million on men's sports and $.2 million on women's sports.

JANUARY

1   Oklahoma and USC share the college football national championship.
12   The Pittsburgh Steelers beat the Minnesota Vikings 16–6 in Super Bowl X at New Orleans, Louisiana, to win their first championship since joining the National Football League (NFL) in 1933.

MARCH

16   Northern Ireland defeats Yugoslavia 1–0 in the first international soccer match to take place in Belfast, Northern Ireland, since 1971. Northern Ireland has been

forced to play its "home" games in England because of security concerns.

31 The University of California at Los Angeles (UCLA) wins its tenth college basketball championship in 12 years.

APRIL

3 The Cold War heats up on the chessboard as the U.S. world champion Bobby Fisher surrenders his title by default to the Soviet challenger, Anatoly Karpov, after

Fisher refuses a Karpov challenge by failing to turn up for the match in Manila, in the Philippines.

10–13 Jack Nicklaus of the United States wins the Masters golf tournament for a record fifth time.

27 Four people are killed at the Spanish motor-racing Grand Prix in Barcelona when a car flies into the crowd after hitting a safety barrier. Two days earlier, the drivers had refused to practice because of concern about the safety barriers, but agreed to let the race go ahead under pressure from the Spanish authorities.

BIRTHS & DEATHS

• Ida Fuller, U.S. reformer and the first woman to receive a social security check, dies in Brattleboro, Vermont (99).

JANUARY
4 Carlo Levi, Italian writer and painter who began a trend toward social realism in Italian literature, dies in Rome, Italy (72).

19 Thomas Hart Benton, U.S. painter and muralist, dies in Kansas City, Missouri (75).

28 Antonin Novotný, Czechoslovakian president 1957–68, deposed because of his Stalinist beliefs and policies, dies in Prague, Czechoslovakia (70).

FEBRUARY
3 William D. Coolidge, U.S. physical chemist, inventor of the X-ray tube, dies in Schenectady, New York (91).

8 Robert Robinson, English chemist whose research into plant biology and alkaloids was important in the discovery of penicillin, dies in Great Missenden, Buckinghamshire, England (88).

14 Julian Huxley, English biologist, philosopher, and author, influential in the development of embryology, dies in London, England (87).

14 P(elham) G(renville) Wodehouse, English novelist, short-story writer, playwright, and lyricist, creator of Jeeves, the archetypal gentleman's gentleman, dies in Southampton, Long Island, New York (93).

19 Luigi Dallapiccola, Italian composer of atonal choral and orchestral works, dies in Florence, Italy (71).

24 Nikolay Bulganin, Soviet statesman, premier of the Soviet Union 1955–58, dies in Moscow, USSR (79).

MARCH
8 George Stevens, U.S. film director of the early Laurel and Hardy films and later of such films as *Giant* and *Shane*, dies in Lancaster, California (70).

15 Aristotle Onassis, Greek shipping magnate and international businessman whose second wife was Jacqueline Kennedy, dies in Paris, France (69).

25 Faisal, Saudi Arabian king 1964–75, is assassinated by his nephew in Riyadh, Saudi Arabia (68). He is succeeded by a younger brother, Crown Prince Khalid.

APRIL
5 Jiang Jie Shi (Chiang Kai-shek), Chinese statesman, leader of the Nationalist government 1928–49, and then of the Chinese Nationalist government in exile on Taiwan, dies in Taipei, Taiwan (87).

10 Walker Evans, U.S. photographer best known for his photographs of rural U.S. southerners during the depression, dies in New Haven, Connecticut (70).

16 Sarvepalli Radhakrishnan, Indian scholar, philosopher, and prime minister of India 1962–67, dies in Madras, India (86).

MAY
8 Avery Brundage, U.S. sports administrator, controversial president of the International Olympic Committee 1952–72, dies in Garmisch-Partenkirchen, West Germany (87).

20 Barbara Hepworth, English abstract sculptor, dies in St. Ives, Cornwall, England (72).

JUNE
3 Eisaku Sato, Japanese prime minister 1964–72, dies in Tokyo, Japan (74).

3 Ozzie Nelson, U.S. television actor, dies in Hollywood, California (69).

6 Alvin H. Hansen, U.S. economist and the principal U.S. exponent of Keynesian economics in the 1930s and 1940s, dies in Alexandria, Virginia (87).

AUGUST
9 Dmitry Shostakovich, Russian composer, dies in Moscow, USSR (68).

27 Haile Selassie, Ethiopian emperor 1930–74, who modernized the country but was deposed, dies a prisoner in his palace in Addis Ababa, Ethiopia (83).

29 Éamon de Valera, Irish politician and revolutionary, president 1959–73, who took Ireland out of the British Commonwealth, dies in Dublin, Ireland (92).

SEPTEMBER
10 George Thomson, English physicist who worked on the diffraction of electrons, dies in Cambridge, England (83).

29 Casey Stengel, U.S. baseball manager known for his colorful personality, dies in Glendale, California (84).

OCTOBER
22 Arnold Toynbee, English historian whose 12-volume *A Study of History* provoked much debate, dies in York, England (86).

NOVEMBER
5 Edward L. Tatum, U.S. biochemist in the field of molecular genetics, dies in New York (65).

5 Lionel Trilling, U.S. author and critic, dies in New York, New York (70).

20 Francisco Franco, Spanish leader of the right wing nationalist forces in the Spanish Civil War 1936–39, then dictator for life, dies in Madrid, Spain (82).

29 Graham Hill, British race-car driver, winner of the Grand Prix World Championship in 1962 and 1968, dies near London, England (46).

DECEMBER
7 Thornton Wilder, U.S. novelist and playwright, dies in Hamden, Connecticut (78).

18 Theodosius Dobzhansky, Russian-born U.S. geneticist who combined evolutionary theory with genetics, dies in Davis, California (75).

MAY

5 Bob Watson of the Houston Astros drives in the millionth run in major league baseball in San Francisco, California, in the United States, 99 years and 12 days after the first run.

15–27 The Philadelphia Flyers win their second consecutive Stanley Cup.

16 Junko Tabei of Japan becomes the first woman to climb Mt. Everest, the world's highest mountain.

18 The Golden State Warriors win the National Basketball Association (NBA) title.

JUNE

3 The Brazilian soccer player Pelé comes out of retirement to play for New York Cosmos in the North American Soccer League. His $7 million three-year contract makes him the highest-paid sportsman in the world.

29 Independiente of Argentina defeat Union Española of Chile 2–0 in a play-off in Asunción, Paraguay, to win the Copa Libertadores de América, the South American club soccer championship, for the fourth successive year.

JULY

4 The U.S. tennis player Billie Jean King wins her sixth women's singles title at the Wimbledon championships, London, England, in nine years.

5 Arthur Ashe of the United States becomes the first black American men's singles champion at the Wimbledon tennis championships, London, England.

AUGUST

12 John Walker of New Zealand becomes the first man to run a mile in under 3 min 50 sec, in Gothenburg, Sweden.

SEPTEMBER

24 Douglas Haston and Doug Scott become the first British climbers to make a successful ascent of Mt. Everest, the world's highest mountain. They reach the summit via the previously unconquered steep southwest face.

30 U.S. boxer Muhammad Ali beats Joe Frazier of the United States on points in Manila, the Philippines, to retain the world heavyweight boxing title.

OCTOBER

5 Star Appeal, ridden by English jockey Greville Starkey, wins the Prix de l'Arc de Triomphe at Longchamp, France, at odds of 119–1, the longest in the 54-year history of the race.

9 João Oliveira of Brazil sets a new world triple-jump record of 17.89 m/58.69 ft in Mexico City, an improvement of 45 cm/18 in on the existing record.

11 A U.S. television audience of over 70 million watch the Cincinnati Reds defeat the Boston Red Sox in the deciding seventh game of baseball's World Series. It gives the Reds their first World Series since 1940.

22 The World Football League, formed in 1974 as a rival to the National Football League (NFL), folds.

28 Peru defeats Colombia 1–0 in a soccer play-off in Venezuela to decide the winner of the first South American Championship (Copa America) to be held since 1967.

◆

1976

POLITICS, GOVERNMENT, AND ECONOMICS

JANUARY

1 The Venezuelan government nationalizes its oil industry.

MARCH

5 The British pound falls below U.S.$2 for the first time ever.

15 The French franc is forced out of the European currency "snake" (system of exchange rates).

Business and Economics

- The German company Keuffel und Esser makes its last slide rule.
- The median price for a single-family home in the United States reaches $38,100.
- With $1,500, Stephen Jobs and Stephen Wozniak begin making computer prototypes in a California garage—the start of Apple Computers.

Colonization

JUNE

28 The Seychelles gain their independence within the Commonwealth.

AUGUST

1 Trinidad and Tobago, having achieved independence from Britain in 1962, gain the status of republic within the Commonwealth.

Human Rights

- Four U.S. military academies admit their first women.
- U.S. feminist Betty Friedan publishes *It Changed My Life: Writings on the Women's Movement.*

MARCH

29 The U.S. Supreme Court rules that states have the right to enforce laws banning homosexual acts.

OCTOBER

8 The South African government rules that its new policy permitting multiracial sport at club level, introduced on October 2, does not permit blacks and whites to play together in the same team; it only allows black and white teams to play against each other. On October 10, four leading white South African rugby union players defy the government by turning out for a racially integrated team in Port Elizabeth.

Politics and Government

- Iceland breaks off diplomatic relations with Britain over the "Cod War."
- Mairead Corrigan, Betty Williams, and Ciaran McKeaun found the Northern Ireland Peace Movement; Corrigan and Williams share the 1976 Nobel Peace Prize.
- The Organization of Petroleum-Exporting Countries (OPEC) establishes a special fund for international development to recycle cash surpluses generated by the energy crisis.
- The U.S. Supreme Court rules against "gag" orders whereby courts restrict the press coverage of criminal trials.
- West Germany legalizes abortion.

JANUARY

4–6 Fifteen people die in sectarian murders in South Armagh, Northern Ireland, on January 4–5. On January 6, the Special Air Service (SAS) is sent in to control the situation.
7 The government of the Christian Democrat Aldo Moro in Italy resigns after the Socialist Party withdraws its support.
9 Hua Guofeng succeeds the late Zhou Enlai as premier of China.
13 Argentina suspends its diplomatic ties with Britain in the dispute over sovereignty of the Falkland Islands in the south Atlantic.
18 The British Labour members of Parliament Jim Sillars and John Robertson launch the Scottish Labour Party (SLP) to campaign for greater devolution for Scotland.
23 The Soviet newspaper *Red Star* dubs the British Conservative leader, Margaret Thatcher, the "Iron Lady" following an anticommunist speech by her.
28 The Spanish prime minister Carlos Navarro proposes lifting the ban on political parties.
30 In the case *Buckley v. Valeo*, the U.S. Supreme Court rejects the placing of limits on spending for political campaigns.

FEBRUARY

8 The Dutch government begins an inquiry into the claim of the U.S. aircraft-manufacturing company Lockheed that it bribed Prince Bernhard of the Netherlands.

11 Aldo Moro forms a minority Christian Democratic government in Italy.
13 The Nigerian head of state General Murtala Mohammad is killed during an unsuccessful coup. He is succeeded by General Olusegun Obasanjo.
17 Forces of the Popular Movement for the Liberation of Angola (MPLA) secure control over most Angolan territory.
24 Jimmy Carter, the governor of Georgia, United States, emerges as the surprise winner of the New Hampshire Democratic primary election.
24–March 5 The 25th Congress of the Communist Party of the Soviet Union is held.
27 The Polisario nationalist front declares the independence of Western Sahara, in northwest Africa, but an assembly of tribal chiefs votes for union with Morocco.

MARCH

9 The British prime minister Harold Wilson claims that there had been "South African participation" in allegations made against the Liberal leader, Jeremy Thorpe.
12 Lebanese army leaders set up an interim military council until political control of the country is restored.
16 Harold Wilson announces that he will resign as prime minister of Britain.
20 The U.S. heiress Patricia Hearst is found guilty of armed bank robbery.
24 A military coup deposes President Isabel Perón of Argentina, and all political parties and unions are "suspended."
27 The Italian Communist Party leader Enrico Berlinguer announces that a communist Italy would stay in the North Atlantic Treaty Organization (NATO) and remain pluralist.

APRIL

2 A new Portuguese constitution with a commitment to socialism is promulgated.
4 Prince Sihanouk retires as Cambodian head of state, to be succeeded by Khieu Samphan of the Khmer Rouge.
4 The government of Thailand is defeated in the general election.
5 Riots erupt in China over the removal by "ultra-leftists" of wreaths laid in memory of Zhou Enlai, the former premier.
5 The Labour Party leader James Callaghan becomes prime minister of Britain.
9 Peter Hain, the leader of Britain's Young Liberals, is acquitted of bank robbery. Evidence emerges that South Africans had tried to frame him.
14 Western Sahara is divided between Morocco and Mauritania.
16 A new coalition government is formed in Thailand.
16 India and Pakistan normalize diplomatic relations for the first time since the 1971 war over the independence of East Pakistan as Bangladesh.
30 The Christian Democratic government of Aldo Moro in Italy collapses and an election is called.

MAY

9 Ulrike Meinhof, the German terrorist leader and member of the Baader–Meinhof gang, commits suicide in prison.
12 An Icelandic gunboat attacks a British trawler in the ongoing "Cod War."

31 Syrian soldiers and tanks enter Lebanon.

JUNE

1 The "Cod War" between Iceland and Britain ends after mediation by Norway, and a 200-mile fishing limit is agreed.

8–12 The Polish leader Edward Gierek decides to normalize relations between Poland and West Germany and visits Bonn, the West German capital.

10 Arab countries meeting in Cairo, Egypt, call for a Syrian withdrawal from Lebanon, following Syria's invasion on May 31.

16 The U.S. ambassador to Lebanon Francis Meloy is kidnapped and murdered by unidentified terrorists.

16–25 South African police kill 76 students in Soweto and other townships during protests and riots about teaching in Afrikaans.

20 The Italian general election produces a major advance for the Communist Party.

21 Arab Protection Force troops under the aegis of the Arab League arrive in Lebanon to take control from the Syrian invaders.

24 The Polish government announces large price rises, causing rioting in factory areas.

25 Idi Amin declares himself Uganda's president for life.

27–July 3 Palestinian terrorists hijack an Air France plane and force it to fly to Entebbe, Uganda. On July 1, 100 passengers are released at Entebbe airport and Israeli commandos free 106 hostages two days later.

JULY

1 Adolfo Suárez becomes prime minister of Spain.

2 North and South Vietnam are formally reunified.

2 The U.S. Supreme Court rules that capital punishment is not unconstitutional.

14 Canada abolishes the death penalty.

14 Jimmy Carter, the governor of Georgia, is nominated as candidate for the U.S. presidency at the Democratic convention in New York, New York.

14 The ban on political parties in Spain is lifted.

14 The Drought Bill is published in Britain to deal with water shortages, with fines for excessive use of water.

21 The Irish Republican Army (IRA) assassinates Christopher Ewart-Biggs, the British ambassador to Ireland in Dublin.

27 The former Japanese prime minister Kakuei Tanaka is charged with accepting bribes from the U.S. aircraft-manufacturing company Lockheed.

28 Britain breaks off diplomatic relations with Uganda over the disappearance of a former Entebbe hostage.

29 A new Italian government is formed, led by the Christian Democrat Giulio Andreotti, dependent on Communist Party acquiescence.

30 An amnesty for political prisoners in Spain is announced.

AUGUST

4–September 13 Further riots break out in Soweto and Port Elizabeth, South Africa.

19 Gerald Ford narrowly wins renomination for the U.S. presidency against a challenge from Ronald Reagan at the Republican convention in Kansas City.

25 Jacques Chirac resigns suddenly as prime minister of France and is succeeded by Raymond Barre.

28 Peace marches are held all over Ireland, with 25,000 people marching in Belfast, Northern Ireland.

SEPTEMBER

• The U.S. House of Representatives approves the Hyde Amendment to the Health, Education, and Welfare appropriations bill. It prohibits the use of federal funds for abortion except in cases where the life of the mother is in jeopardy.

9 The price rises announced in Poland on June 24 are suspended.

16 The Episcopalian Church in the United States approves the ordination of women to the priesthood.

19 Ian Smith, the prime minister of Rhodesia (now Zimbabwe), accepts the principle of majority rule in his country.

19 The Swedish general election ends 40 years of government by the Social Democrats.

OCTOBER

3 Helmut Schmidt's Social Democrat-led coalition returns to power in West Germany with a reduced majority.

4 The U.S. agriculture secretary Earl Butz resigns after making racist comments.

6 A military coup in Thailand seizes control from Prime Minister Seni Pramoj.

6 The U.S. president Gerald Ford declares "there is no Soviet domination of Eastern Europe."

7 Hua Guofeng succeeds Mao Zedong as Chinese premier. The "Gang of Four," including Mao's widow, are arrested and denounced for plotting to take power.

7 Thorbjörn Fälldin becomes Conservative prime minister of Sweden.

17 A summit of Arab countries in Riyadh, Saudi Arabia, produces a cease-fire plan for Lebanon, which was invaded by Syria on May 31.

21 A cease-fire plan for Lebanon, produced at a summit of Arab countries in Riyadh, Saudi Arabia, on October 17, is implemented.

25 The black homeland of Transkei, South Africa, becomes nominally independent.

28–December 12 At a conference on Rhodesia in Geneva, Switzerland, the parties led by Joshua Nkomo and Robert Mugabe form the Patriotic Front.

NOVEMBER

2 In the U.S. presidential election, the Democratic candidate, Jimmy Carter, defeats the Republican, President Gerald Ford, with 297 electoral college votes to 241. Democrats retain majorities in the House (292-143) and Senate (68-31).

11 Political parties are legalized in Egypt.

15 Syrian troops take control of the Lebanese capital, Beirut.

15 The Parti Québecois wins a large victory in the Quebec provincial elections in Canada and the new premier, René Lévesque, promises a vote on independence by 1980.

DECEMBER

4 Swiss voters reject a proposal to cut the working week to 40 hours.

5 Japan's ruling Liberal Democratic Party suffers losses in the general election.

5 Jean-Bédel Bokassa, head of state of the Central African Republic, proclaims his country an empire and himself its emperor.

5   The former French prime minister Jacques Chirac refounds the Gaullist party as the Rassemblement pour la République (RPR).

15   A referendum in Spain approves the transition to a democracy.

20   The Israeli prime minister Yitzhak Rabin dissolves his coalition government and calls an election.

24   Takeo Fukuda succeeds Takeo Miki as prime minister of Japan.

SCIENCE, TECHNOLOGY, AND MEDICINE

Computing

- Computer networking begins in offices when Wang Laboratories introduces a word processor located on a central computer that can be shared by various terminals.
- Daisywheel printers are introduced; they can print between 30 and 55 characters per second.
- IBM computers are built with chips with 16 kilobits (16,384 bits) of memory.
- IBM develops the ink-jet printer.

Ecology

- The American Panel on Atmospheric Chemistry warns that the earth's ozone layer may be being destroyed by chloroflurocarbons (CFCs) from spray cans and refrigeration systems.
- U.S. scientists experiment with algae and microorganisms that consume crude oil as a means of clearing up oil spills.

December 1976–79   The International Magnetosphere Study conducts a three-year observation of the earth's magnetosphere and its effects on the lower stratosphere including the disruptive effects of magnetic storms on communications.

FEBRUARY

1   California's worst drought to date results in compulsory water rationing in Marin county; the drought continues the next year.

4   An earthquake in Guatemala measuring 7.5 on the Richter scale kills nearly 23,000 people.

JUNE

26   Nearly 3,000 people are killed and 3,000 are missing after an earthquake and landslides in Indonesia.

JULY

26   A massive release of poisonous dioxin gas from a pesticide plant near Seveso in Italy kills thousands of domestic and farm animals in the surrounding region.

28   An earthquake in Tangshan, China, measuring 8.2 on the Richter scale levels nearly every building and kills 242,000 people. It is the worst earthquake in modern history.

AUGUST

17   An earthquake measuring 7.8 on the Richter scale, and a tsunami 30 m/98 ft high, hit Mindanao in the Philippines; 3,000 people are killed by the earthquake and nearly 5,000 by the tsunami.

NOVEMBER

24   An earthquake in eastern Turkey, measuring 7.9 on the Richter scale, kills 4,000 people.

DECEMBER

17   More than 180,000 barrels of crude oil are spilled into the Atlantic off Nantucket Island when the Liberian tanker *Argo Merchant* breaks in two after running aground the previous day.

Exploration

- The U.S. *Lageos* (Laser Geodynamic Satellite) is launched; it uses laser beams to make precise measurements of the earth's movements in an attempt to improve the prediction of earthquakes. Placed in an orbit 9,321 km/5,793 mi high, it is expected to remain in orbit for 8 million years.
- The U.S. spacecraft *Viking 1* and *Viking 2* (launched in 1975) soft-land on Mars (July 20, September 3). They make meteorological readings of the Martian atmosphere and search for traces of bacterial life which prove inconclusive.
- Three *Marisat* (Maritime Satellite Systems) satellites are launched; they improve ship-to-shore communications.

JANUARY

15   The U.S.-German space probe *Helios 2* is launched; able to withstand extremely high temperatures, it passes within 43.4 million km/27.0 million mi of the sun and relays data about cosmic rays, the sun's magnetic field, and the solar wind.

Health and Medicine

- A mystery disease afflicts 182 people who attend the meeting of the American Legion in Philadelphia, United States; 29 die within a month and the disease becomes known as legionnaire's disease. It is caused by the bacterium *Legionella pneumophilia*.
- The first oncogene (cancer-inducing gene) is discovered by U.S. scientists Harold E. Varmus and J. Michael Bishop.
- The first prenatal diagnosis using a gene-specific probe in amniotic fluid is performed.
- The U.S. Food and Drug Administration bans the use of chloroform as an anesthetic because it is a suspected carcinogen.
- U.S. virologist Carleton Gajdusek and U.S. physician Baruch Blumberg are jointly awarded the Nobel Prize for Physiology or Medicine for their discoveries concerning new mechanisms for the origin and transmission of infectious diseases.

APRIL

- Fearing a "swine flu" epidemic, the U.S. government spends $135 million on a vaccination program; only six cases of the flu are reported but over 500 of those inoculated develop Guillain-Barré syndrome, a rare disease that causes paralysis; hundreds sue the government.

Math

- U.S. mathematicians Kenneth Appel and Wolfgang Haken use a computer to prove the four-color problem—that the minimum number of colors needed to color a map such that no two adjacent sections have the same color is four. The proof takes 1,000 hours of computer time and hundreds of pages.

Science

- Astronomers at Harvard College Laboratory in the United States discover bursts of X-rays coming from a star cluster 30,000 light-years from Earth.
- Footprints of three hominids, attributed to *Australopithecus afarensis* and made 3.7 million years ago, are found near Laetoli, Tanzania; analysis indicates that their bipedal locomotion was almost identical to that of modern humans.
- Japanese molecular biologist Susumu Tonegawa demonstrates that antibodies are produced by large numbers of genes working in combination.
- The "gypsy" subparticle is discovered.
- The synthesis of unnilseptium (atomic no. 107) is announced by Soviet scientists at the Joint Institute for Nuclear Research in Dubna, USSR.
- U.S. biochemist Herbert Boyer and venture capitalist Robert Swanson found Genentech in San Francisco, California, the world's first genetic engineering company.
- U.S. chemist William Lipscomb receives the Nobel Prize for Chemistry for his work on the structure and chemical bonding of boranes of compounds of boron and hydrogen.
- U.S. paleoanthropoligist Alun Hughes discovers the remains of several *Homo habilis* individuals at Sterkfontein, South Africa, along with many stone tools; their estimated age is 1.5 to 2 million years.
- U.S. physicists Burton Richter and Samuel Chao Chung Ting receive the Nobel Prize for Physics for their discovery of a new class of particles (ψ, or J).

AUGUST

28 Indian-born U.S. biochemist Har Gobind Khorana and his colleagues announce the construction of the first artificial gene to function naturally when inserted into a bacterial cell. This is a major breakthrough in genetic engineering.

OCTOBER

14 A committee to create standard regulations governing recombinant DNA (deoxyribonucleic acid) research is established by the International Council of Scientific Unions.

Technology

- French researcher Jean-Marie Lehn invents "cryptands" (also known as crown ether), synthetic crystalline materials that can capture electrons which, once captured, act with unique chemical and electrical properties; they are used in medicine as tracers and in the production of polymers in industry.
- Konica introduces the first camera with automatic focus in Japan.
- The 6-m/19.7-ft UTR-Z telescope is completed at Zelenchukskaya, USSR; it is the largest reflecting telescope in the world.
- The Chivor Dam across the Batá River in Colombia is completed; at 237 m/778 ft high, it is the world's highest rock-fill dam with a clay core.
- The transmission time for faxes drops from six minutes to three minutes per page; sales increase as prices fall.
- U.S. chemist Stephanie Kwolek develops Kevlar, a plastic fiber as strong as steel; it is used to make bulletproof vests, boat-shells, and tires.

Transportation

- The South Bay Diversion Channel linking the Churchill and Nelson rivers in Manitoba, Canada, is completed; it is the final link in the world's longest waterway, from Tuktoyaktuk on the Mackenzie River to Port Eads on the Mississippi river delta—a total of 10,682 km/ 6,637 mi.
- The U.S. Air Force introduces the F-16 Fighting Falcon, a multipurpose fighter aircraft capable of speeds of more than Mach 2 (twice the speed of sound) and carrying 6,893 kg/15,200 lb of bombs.

JANUARY

21 The British–French supersonic airliner Concorde begins a regular passenger service across the Atlantic; it is the world's first scheduled supersonic passenger service.

21 Two Concorde aircraft make their first commercial flights, from London, England, to Bahrain and from Paris, France, to Rio de Janeiro, Brazil.

FEBRUARY

5 The U.S. Railroad Revitalization and Reform Bill is signed, providing $6.4 billion to revitalize the nation's railroads.

MARCH

27 The Washington, D.C., underground system opens; it costs $5 billion and soon has 121 km/75 mi of track.

30 An injection of $2.14 billion is made to improve the railroad lines between Boston, Massachusetts, New York, New York, and Washington, D.C.

JULY

28 A USAF Lockheed SR-71 Blackbird reconnaissance jet sets a speed record for jets when it flies at 3,529.56 kph/ 2,193.167 mph at Beale Air Force Base, California.

SEPTEMBER

10 The world's worst mid-air collision occurs when a British Airways Trident and a Yugoslav DC-9 collide in the air near Zagreb; 176 people are killed.

11 The Bay Area Rapid Transit (BART) system in the San Francisco Bay Area, California, is completed; the first entirely automatic rapid transit system, it controls the speed of trains and ensures a safe distance between them.

20 The subway opens in Brussels, Belgium.

ARTS AND IDEAS

Architecture

- The Kaijima House, Kichijoji in Musashino City, Japan, designed by the Japanese architect Arata Isozaki, is completed.
- The Row House Sumiyoshi in Osaka, Japan, designed by the Japanese architect Tadao Ando, is completed.

Arts

- An extension to the Metropolitan Museum in New York, New York, designed by the architects Kevin Roche and John Dinkeloo, is completed.
- The Bulgarian-born U.S. artist Christo creates *Running Fence*, 40 km of fabric stretched across a valley in California.
- The display of *Equivalents VIII*—an arrangement of building bricks at the Tate Gallery in London, England, by the U.S. artist Carl André—causes a controversy. The work was created in 1966.
- The French artist César (Baldaccini) creates the sculpture *Le Pouce*.
- The U.S. artist Chuck Close paints *Linda*.
- The U.S. artist Frank Stella paints *Bermuda Petrel*.
- The U.S. artist Nam June Paik creates *Fish Flew in the Sky*, a video installation.
- The U.S. artist Susan Rothenberg paints *Butterfly*.
- The U.S. photographer Richard Avedon publishes *Portraits*, which contains some of his best-known images of U.S. celebrities.
- The Venice Biennale art exhibition in Italy is rehabilitated after a lapse of four years.

Film

- The controversial and sexually explicit movie *Ai no Corrida/In the Realm of the Senses*, directed by Nagisa Oshima, is released in Japan.
- The epic movie *Novecento/1900*, directed by Italian filmmaker Bernardo Bertolucci, is released. It stars Robert De Niro, Gérard Depardieu, Donald Sutherland, Burt Lancaster, Dominique Sanda, Stefania Sandrelli, and Sterling Hayden.
- The movie *A Star is Born*, directed by Frank Pierson, is released in the United States. It stars Barbra Streisand and Kris Kristofferson.
- The movie *All the President's Men*, directed by Alan J. Pakula, is released in the United States. The story of journalists' exposé of Watergate, it stars Robert Redford and Dustin Hoffman.
- The movie *Assault on Precinct 13*, directed by John Carpenter, is released in the United States. It stars Austin Stoker and Darwin Joston.
- The movie *Carrie*, directed by Brian De Palma, is released in the United States. Based on Stephen King's first novel, it stars Sissy Spacek.
- The movie *Fellini's Casanova*, directed by Federico Fellini, is released in Italy. It stars Donald Sutherland.

- The movie *Im Lauf der Zeit/Kings of the Road*, directed by Wim Wenders, is released in West Germany. It stars Rudiger Vogler and Hanns Zischler.
- The movie *L'Innocente/The Innocent*, directed by Luchino Visconti, is released in Italy. It stars Giancarlo Giannini, Laura Antonelli, and Jennifer O'Neill.
- The movie *Maîtresse/Mistress*, directed by Barbet Schroeder, is released in France, starring Gérard Depardieu and Bulle Ogier.
- The movie *Marathon Man*, directed by John Schlesinger, is released in the United States. It stars Dustin Hoffman, Laurence Olivier, and Roy Scheider.
- The movie *Network*, directed by Sidney Lumet, is released in the United States. It stars Peter Finch, Faye Dunaway, and William Holden.
- The movie *Robin and Marian* is released in the UK. It is directed by Richard Lester and stars Sean Connery and Audrey Hepburn.
- The movie *Rocky*, directed by John G. Avildsen, is released in the United States. It is written by and stars Sylvester Stallone. Made in 28 days, with a budget of less than $1 million, it goes on to gross over $100 million in the United States alone.
- The movie *Sebastiane*, directed by Derek Jarman, is released in the UK. Filmed in Latin with English subtitles, it stars Leonardo Treviglio.
- The movie *Silent Movie*, directed by Mel Brooks, is released in the United States. It stars Mel Brooks, Marty Feldman, Dom de Luise, Bernadette Peters, Sid Caesar, and the French mime Marcel Marceau, who utters the only word in the movie, "*Non.*"
- The movie *Taxi Driver*, directed by Martin Scorsese, is released in the United States. It stars Robert De Niro, Cybill Shepherd, Harvey Keitel, and Jodie Foster. At the Cannes Film Festival in France, it is awarded the Palme d'Or.
- The movie *The Front*, directed by Martin Ritt, is released in the United States. It stars Woody Allen and Zero Mostel.
- The movie *The Killing of a Chinese Bookie* is released in the United States. It is directed by John Cassavetes and stars Ben Gazzara.
- The movie *The Last Tycoon*, directed by Elia Kazan, is released in the United States. Based on the novel by F. Scott Fitzgerald, it stars Robert De Niro.
- The movie *The Man Who Fell to Earth*, directed by Nicholas Roeg, is released in the UK. It stars David Bowie.
- The movie *The Outlaw–Josey Wales*, directed by and starring Clint Eastwood, is released in the United States.
- The movie *The Omen*, directed by Richard Donner, is released in the United States. It stars Gregory Peck and Lee Remick.
- The movie *The Sunshine Boys*, directed by Herbert Ross, is released in the United States. Based on a play by Neil Simon, it stars Walter Matthau and George Burns.
- The German–French coproduction *Die Marquise von O/The Marquise of O*, directed by French filmmaker Eric Rohmer, is released.
- The home videocassette recorder is introduced into the U.S. market, with two incompatible models. The Japanese electronics company Sony markets the Betamax system, released in 1975, and fellow Japanese electronics company Japanese Matsushita Corporation

(JVC) markets the Video Home System (or VHS), that eventually dominates the trade.

- The musical gangster movie *Bugsy Malone* is released in the UK. It is written and directed by Alan Parker and features an all-child cast, including the U.S. actress Jodie Foster.

MARCH

29 The 1975 Academy Awards take place. Best Actor: Jack Nicholson, for *One Flew over the Cuckoo's Nest*; Best Supporting Actor: George Burns, for *The Sunshine Boys*; Best Actress: Louise Fletcher, for *One Flew over the Cuckoo's Nest*; Best Supporting Actress: Lee Grant, for *Shampoo*; Best Picture: *One Flew over the Cuckoo's Nest*, directed by Miloš Forman; Best Director: Miloš Forman, for *One Flew over the Cuckoo's Nest*.

APRIL

3 The Césars, the French equivalent of the Academy Awards, are launched.

NOVEMBER

11 Universal and Walt Disney take the video manufacturers Sony-Betamax to court in the United States for infringement of copyright legislation.

14 The televising of *Gone With the Wind* attracts the highest audience for a movie ever in the United States, with more than 33 million viewers.

Literature and Language

- *The Diaries of Evelyn Waugh* are published posthumously, edited by Michael Davie.
- The *Collected Poems of W H Auden* are published.
- The Argentine writer Manuel Puig publishes his novel *El beso de la mujer araña/Kiss of the Spider Woman*.
- The Australian writer Patrick White publishes his novel *A Fringe of Leaves*.
- The Chinese-U.S. writer Maxine Hong Kingston publishes her autobiographical novel *The Woman Warrior*.
- The English writer David Storey publishes his novel *Saville*.
- The first volume of *The Correspondence of John Locke*, edited by E. S. de Beer, is published. The final volume will appear in 1989.
- The French writer Alain Robbe-Grillet publishes his novel *Topologie d'une cité famtôme/Topology of a Phantom City*.
- The Pulitzer Prize for Biography is awarded to Richard W. B. Lewis for *Edith Wharton: A Biography*, the Pulitzer Prize for Fiction is awarded to Saul Bellow for *Humboldt's Gift*, and the Pulitzer Prize for Poetry is awarded to John Asbery for *Self-Portrait in a Convex Mirror*.
- The U.S. novelist Lisa Alther publishes her novel *Kinflicks*.
- The U.S. novelist Saul Bellow is awarded the Nobel Prize for Literature.
- The U.S. poet Richard Wilbur publishes his poetry collection *The Mind-Reader*.
- The U.S. writer Alex Haley publishes his novel *Roots*. Documenting the history of a family of black Americans of African origin through seven generations, it becomes a phenomenal success as a book and a TV series. It will win a Pulitzer prize in 1977.

- The U.S. writer Gore Vidal publishes his novel *1876*.
- The U.S. writer James Merrill publishes his poetry collection *Divine Comedies*, which wins the Pulitzer Prize for Poetry in 1977.
- The U.S. writer Philip Roth publishes his novel *The Professor of Desire*.
- The U.S. writer Raymond Carver publishes his collection of short stories *Will You Please be Quiet, Please*.

Music

- The Dutch composer Louis Andriessen completes his opera *De Staat/The State*.
- The Greek singer Demis Roussos releases the hit single "When Forever Has Gone."
- The Italian composer Luciano Berio completes his vocal work *Coro*.
- The Japanese composer Toru Takemitsu completes his orchestral work *Marginalia*.
- The opera *Einstein on the Beach*, by the U.S. composer Philip Glass, is first performed, in Avignon, France. The text is by Robert Wilson.
- The opera *The Voyage of Edgar Allan Poe*, by the U.S. composer Dominick Argento, is first performed, in Minneapolis, Minnesota.
- The opera *We Come to the River*, by the German composer Hans Werner Henze, is first performed, in London, England. The text is by the English writer Edward Bond.
- The pop group Abba becomes Sweden's biggest export earner after Volvo.
- The South African composer John Joubert completes his choral work *The Magus*.
- The U.S. composer David Del Tredici completes *Final Alice*, for voice, folk group, and orchestra.
- The U.S. composer Norman Dello Joio completes his orchestral work *Colonial Variations*.

JANUARY

31 The British rock singer Peter Frampton releases the album *Frampton Comes Alive*.

APRIL

24 The British heavy metal rock group Led Zeppelin releases the album *Presence*.

MAY

8 The British rock group the Rolling Stones releases the album *Black and Blue*.

JUNE

5 The U.S. new wave group the Ramones releases the album *The Ramones*.

JULY

4 The pop singers Elton John and Kiki Dee release "Don't Go Breaking My Heart."

10 The U.S. pop duo the Carpenters releases the album *A Kind of Hush*.

OCTOBER

2 The British pop singer Rod Stewart releases the single "Tonight's the Night."

NOVEMBER

6   The U.S. singer-songwriter Tom Waits releases the album *Small Change*.

DECEMBER

11 The Swedish pop group Abba releases the disco hit "Dancing Queen."

11 The U.S. pop singer and actress Barbra Streisand has a hit with "Evergreen," written for the 1976 movie *A Star is Born*, in which she costarred with Kris Kristofferson.

12 The U.S. pop group the Eagles releases the album *Hotel California*, and the single of the same name.

Theater and Dance

- The National Theatre, part of the South Bank Centre in London, England, is completed. It was designed by the English architect Denys Lasdun.
- The play *Audience*, by the Czech writer and politician Václav Havel, is first performed, in Vienna, Austria.
- The play *California Suite*, by the U.S. writer Neil Simon, is first performed, at the Eugene O'Neill Theater in New York, New York.
- The play *For Colored Girls who have Considered Suicide when the Rainbow was Enuf*, by the black American writer Shange Ntozake, is first performed, at the Booth Theater in New York, New York.
- The play *Knock Knock*, by the U.S. writer Jules Feiffer, is first performed, at the Biltmore Theater in New York, New York.
- The Pulitzer Prize for Drama is awarded to Michael Bennett, James Kirkwood, Nicholas Dante, Marvin Hamlisch, and Edward Kieben for the musical *A Chorus Line*.

JANUARY

11 *Pacific Overtures*, a musical by John Weidman, Stephen Sondheim, and Hugh Wheeler based on an 1853 expedition by Commodore Matthew C. Perry to Japan, opens in New York, New York.

MARCH

2   *Bubblin' Brown Sugar*, a musical revue by Loften Mitchel featuring the music of Eubie Blake, Cab Calloway, Duke Ellington, and others, opens in New York, New York.

DECEMBER

22 The musical *Your Arms Too Short to Box With God*, written by Alex Bradford and Micki Grant, and based on the biblical Book of Matthew, opens in New York, New York.

Thought and Scholarship

- *Early Modern Ireland, 1534–1691*, the first volume in *A New History of Ireland*, is published, edited by T. W. Moody, F. X. Martin, and F. J. Byrne.
- British historian J. M. Roberts publishes *The Hutchinson History of the World*.
- English historian Arnold Toynbee publishes *Mankind and the Mother Earth: A Narrative History of the World*.
- French statesman Valéry Giscard d'Estaing publishes *La Démocratie française/French Democracy*.

- Hungarian philosopher of science and mathematics Imre Lakatos publishes *Proofs and Refutations*.
- The Pulitzer Prize for History is awarded to Paul Horgan for *Lamy of Santa Fe*.
- The Pulitzer Prize for General Nonfiction is awarded to Robert N. Butler for *Why Survive?*
- U.S. cultural historian Shere Hite publishes *The Hite Report: A Nationwide Study of Female Sexuality*.
- U.S. historian Ernest May publishes *The Making of the Monroe Doctrine*.
- U.S. historian Herbert George Gutman publishes *The Black Family in Slavery and Freedom, 1750–1925*.
- U.S. writer Adrienne Rich publishes her critical work *Of Woman Born: Motherhood as Experience and Institution*.

SOCIETY

Everyday Life

- Perrier water is introduced in the United States.
- Soft drinks pass milk in popularity in the United States.
- The *Statistical History of the United States* is published by the United States Bureau of the Census. It is a revised version of the one published in 1965.
- The case *Virginia State Board of Pharmacy v. Virginia Consumer Council* establishes that commercial speech is protected by the First Amendment to the U.S. Constitution.
- The Ethics and Public Policy Center and the Rockford Institute, dealing with family and religious issues, is founded in the United States.

JANUARY

31 The population of the world reaches 4 billion.

JULY

4   The bicentenary of the Declaration of Independence is marked by nationwide celebrations in the United States.

SEPTEMBER

20 In a *Playboy* interview U.S. presidential candidate Jimmy Carter says, "I have committed adultery in my heart many times."

Media and Communication

- Barbara Walters becomes the first woman to cohost a national evening news program in the United States. Her salary is reported to be $1 million per year.
- The 1975–76 Emmy Awards for television are held. Best Drama Series: *Police Story*; Best Comedy Series: *The Mary Tyler Moore Show*; Best Actor in a Drama: Peter Falk, for *Columbo*; Best Actress in a Drama: Michael Learned, for *The Waltons*; Best Actor in a Comedy: Jack Albertson, for *Chico and The Man*; Best Actress in a Comedy: Mary Tyler Moore, for *The Mary Tyler Moore Show*.
- The Monotype company in Britain introduces laser typesetting.
- The popularity of CB (citizens-band) radio in the United States leads to a record 656,000 license applications a

month; CB code phrases also filter through to everyday life.

- With the launch of videocassette recorders on the market by Sony and JVC, television advertising rates are hit, as viewers can now choose not to view commercials.

September 1976–85 *Alice*, a situation comedy about a widow (who wants to be a singer) and her 12-year-old son, is shown on U.S. television.

JANUARY

27–May 10, 1983 *Laverne & Shirley*, a slapstick television comedy about two women living and working in Milwaukee, Minnesota, is shown on U.S. television.

SEPTEMBER

22–August 19, 1981 *Charlie's Angels*, a popular detective drama starring three sexy and tough female detectives, is shown on U.S. television, making stars of Kate Jackson, Farrah Fawcett, Jaclyn Smith, and, later, Cheryl Ladd.

Religion

- The Catholic Cardinal Suenens of Belgium is awarded the Templeton Prize for Progress in Religion.

OCTOBER

1 The Roman Catholic bishop of Umtali, Rhodesia (now Zimbabwe), is sentenced to ten years' imprisonment for antigovernment activities.

NOVEMBER

26 Catholicism ceases to be the state religion of Italy.

Sports

- The final cost of the 1976 Olympic Games in Montreal, Canada, is calculated at $1,400 million, compared to the budgeted cost of $310 million. Debt repayments from Montreal and the province of Quebec continue into the 1990s.
- The first British Women's Open Championship is won at Fulford, Yorkshire, England, by British golfer Jenny Lee-Smith.

JANUARY

1 Oklahoma wins the college football championship for the 1975 season.

10 The U.S. national figure skating champions are Dorothy Hammill and Terry Kubicka. Tai Babilonia and Randy Gardner win the pairs competition and Colleen O'Connor and John Millns win the ice dancing competition.

FEBRUARY

4–15 The 12th Winter Olympic games are held at Innsbruck, Austria. The Soviet Union wins 13 gold medals; East Germany, 7; United States and Norway, 3 each. Austria's Franz Klammer wins the men's alpine downhill. Rosi Mittermaier of West Germany wins gold medals in the women's downhill and slalom, and a silver in the giant slalom. Alex Gorhkov and Ludmila Pakhomova of the USSR win the inaugural ice dance event.

7 Diane Thorne becomes the first female jockey to win a National Hunt race, at Stratford-upon-Avon, England, since the Jockey Club's decision in January to permit women to ride against men in hurdle races and steeplechases as well as on the flat.

MARCH

6 Light-welterweight Wilfred Benitez of Puerto Rico defeats Antonio Cervantes of Colombia on points in San Juan, Puerto Rico, to win the World Boxing Association (WBA) light-welterweight world title, and so become at 17 years, 176 days, the youngest ever boxing world champion.

MAY

9 The Montreal Canadiens win their franchise's 19th Stanley Cup.

30 Janet Guthrie is the first woman to compete in the Indianapolis 500 motor race.

30 Race-car driver Johnny Rutherford wins the Indianapolis 500, shortened to 410 km/255 mi because of rain.

JUNE

- Sue Barker becomes the first British tennis player to win the women's singles title in the French Open Championships since Ann Jones in 1966.

2 The English jockey Lester Piggott, riding Empery, becomes the first jockey to win the English Derby seven times.

4 The Boston Celtics defeat the Phoenix Suns 128–126 in triple overtime in the National Basketball Association (NBA) finals; two days later they clinch their 13th title.

17 The American Basketball Association (ABA) merges with the National Basketball Association (NBA), increasing the number of NBA teams by four to 22.

JULY

- At the Montreal Olympics, the Romanian gymnast Nadia Comaneci scores the first ever maximum 10.00 marks at the Olympics, and then gets four more on the way to winning three gold medals and one silver.
- At the Olympic Games in Montreal, all the men's swimming titles are won by U.S. swimmers except the 200 meters breaststroke which is won by David Wilkie of Great Britain.

July–August At the Montreal Olympic Games, Polish athlete Danuta Rosani is the first track and field athlete to test positive for anabolic steroids since the drugs were banned in 1975.

1 The 21st Olympic Games open in Montreal, Canada, boycotted by 20 African nations, Iraq, and Guyana following New Zealand's rugby tour of South Africa; Taiwan withdraws after the Canadian government refuses to recognize it as the Republic of China.

1–7 The United States withdraws from the Davis Cup tennis organization and tournament after a proposal to impose a ban on countries that refuse to play matches for political reasons is turned down. The United States then rejoins.

25–29 In the track events at the Montreal Olympic Games, in Canada, Lasse Viren of Finland retains his 5,000 and 10,000 meters titles, while Alberto Juantorena of Cuba wins both the 400 and 800 meters events.

AUGUST

1 The 21st Olympic Games close in Montreal, Canada. The USSR wins 49 gold medals; East Germany, 40; the United States, 34; West Germany, 10; Japan, 9; Poland, 7; Bulgaria and Cuba, 6 each; Romania, Hungary, Finland, and Sweden, 4 each.

16 The St. Louis Cardinals play a preseason game against the San Diego Chargers in Tokyo, Japan; the first NFL game to take place outside North America.

27 The U.S. tennis player Renee Richards, who in 1975 underwent a sex change, is denied entry to the U.S. Open women's championships when she refuses to take a chromosome gender test.

SEPTEMBER

12 The Austrian race-car driver Niki Lauda, in a McClaren, finishes fourth in the Italian Grand Prix, a month after suffering serious facial injuries when his car crashed in flames at the German Grand Prix.

OCTOBER

• The Australians Geoff Hunt and Heather McKay win the men's and women's singles titles at the inaugural World Open squash championships.

BIRTHS & DEATHS

JANUARY

5 John A. Costello, prime minister of Ireland 1948–51 and 1954–57, dies in Dublin, Ireland (84).

8 Zhou Enlai, Chinese diplomat and communist premier 1949–76, dies in Beijing, China (77).

12 Agatha Christie, English playwright and author of detective novels, dies in Wallingford, Oxfordshire, England (85).

23 Paul Robeson, U.S. singer, film actor, and civil-rights activist, dies in Philadelphia, Pennsylvania (77).

FEBRUARY

1 George Hoyt Whipple, U.S. pathologist whose research into the liver led to a successful treatment for anemia, dies in Rochester, New York (97).

1 Werner Heisenberg, German physicist and philosopher who introduced the uncertainty principle into quantum mechanics, dies in Munich, Germany (74).

MARCH

14 Busby Berkeley, U.S. choreographer and film director who used elaborate sets and teams of female dancers to create kaleidoscopic patterns when filmed from above, dies in Palm Springs, California (80).

17 Luchino Visconti, Italian film director, a forerunner of neorealism who also directed theater and opera, dies in Rome, Italy (69).

21 Vladimir Spider Sabich, U.S. athlete, two-time world champion skier, dies in Aspen, Colorado (33).

24 Bernard L. Montgomery ("Monty"), British field marshal and commander during World War II, dies near Alton, Hampshire, England (88).

25 Josef Albers, German-born U.S. painter, poet, teacher, and theoretician of art, dies in New Haven, Connecticut (88).

APRIL

1 Max Ernst, German painter and sculptor, one of the founders of surrealism, dies in Paris, France (84).

2 Henrik Dam, Danish biochemist who discovered vitamin K, dies in Copenhagen, Denmark (81).

5 Howard Hughes, reclusive U.S. manufacturer, aviator, and film producer, dies in an airplane over Texas (70).

24 Mark Tobey, U.S. abstract painter who often used white on a dark background, dies in Basel, Switzerland (85).

MAY

11 Alvar Aalto, Finnish architect, furniture designer, and city planner, dies in Helsinki, Finland (78).

26 Martin Heidegger, German existentialist philosopher, dies in Messkirch, West Germany (86).

31 Jacques L. Monod, French biochemist who worked on genes and cell metabolism, dies in Cannes, France (66).

JUNE

6 J. Paul Getty, U.S. oil billionaire, dies in Sutton Place, Surrey, England (83).

JULY

6 Zhu De, Chinese communist military leader, founder and commander in chief of the Red Army in the fight against the nationalists and the Japanese, dies in Beijing, China (90).

9 Fred Savage, U.S. television actor, born in Chicago, Illinois.

AUGUST

2 Fritz Lang, Austrian-born U.S. film director who made *Metropolis*, dies in Los Angeles, California (85).

4 Roy Herbert Thomson, Canadian-born British publisher, owner of *The Times* and several other newspapers, dies in London, England (82).

26 Lotte Lehmann, German-born U.S. soprano particularly associated with the songs of Robert Schumann, dies in Santa Barbara, California (88).

SEPTEMBER

9 Mao Zedong, Chinese Marxist theorist who was chairman of the People's Republic of China 1949–59 and chairman of the Chinese Communist Party 1949–76, dies in Beijing, China (83).

OCTOBER

5 Lars Onsager, Norwegian-born U.S. chemist who developed a general theory of irreversible processes, dies in Coral Gables, Florida (72).

6 Gilbert Ryle, English philosopher, a leading figure in the "Oxford Philosophy" movement, dies in Whitby, North Yorkshire, England (76).

15 Carlo Gambino, U.S. Mafia chief, dies in Massapequa, New York (74).

NOVEMBER

11 Alexander Calder, U.S. sculptor and inventor of the mobile, dies in New York, New York (78).

12 Walter Piston, U.S. neoclassical composer of symphonies and chamber music, dies in Belmont, Massachusetts (82).

18 Man Ray, U.S. dada and surrealist photographer, painter, and filmmaker, dies in Paris, France (86).

20 Trofim Denisovich Lysenko, Soviet biologist and agronomist who rejected conventional genetics, dies in Kiev, USSR (c. 78).

23 André Malraux, French novelist, art historian and statesman, dies in Paris, France (75).

DECEMBER

4 Benjamin Britten, English composer, pianist, and conductor, dies in Aldeburgh, Suffolk, England (63).

20 Richard Daley, U.S. mayor of Chicago since 1955, dies in Chicago, Illinois (74).

22 Martín Luis Guzmán, Mexican novelist during the revolution, dies in Mexico City, Mexico (89).

15 Glasgow Rangers soccer club in Scotland announces that it is ending sectarian and religious bias both on and off the pitch, indicating that it is now willing to sign Roman Catholic players for the first time.
16 The Cincinnati Reds beat the New York Yankees four games to zero to win the World Series.
24 For the first time in its history the New York City Marathon covers all five of the city's boroughs (previously it had been held in Central Park).
U.S. runners Bill Rodgers and Miki Gorman respectively win the men's competition and women's competition.

24 The English race-car driver James Hunt, in a McLaren, wins the Formula One World Drivers' Championship by one point from Austria's Niki Lauda.

NOVEMBER
4 Baseball's first ever free agent reentry draft takes place in New York, New York.

1977

POLITICS, GOVERNMENT, AND ECONOMICS

Business and Economics

- Political scientist Charles Lindblom publishes *Politics and Markets*.
- The Canadian-born U.S. economist J. K. Galbraith publishes *The Age of Uncertainty*.
- West Germany's per capita gross national product exceeds that of the United States, for the first time.

JULY
1 The European Economic Community (EEC) and the European Free Trade Association (EFTA) agree to free trade in industrial goods.

Colonization

JUNE
27 Djibouti gains its independence from France.

DECEMBER
4 The black homeland of Bophuthatswana, South Africa, becomes nominally independent.

Human Rights

JANUARY
1 California allows the terminally ill to authorize the removal of life-support equipment.

1 Jacqueline Means becomes the first woman officially ordained as a priest by the U.S. Episcopal Church.
7 Human-rights supporters in Czechoslovakia publish the manifesto "Charter 77," pressing for implementation of the 1975 Helsinki human-rights guarantees given at the 1975 Helsinki conference in Finland.

NOVEMBER
18 A National Women's Conference in Houston, Texas, is attended by 442 delegates, to urge passage of the Equal Rights Amendment and an end to discrimination in the workplace.

Politics and Government

- A European Economic Community directive unifies the organization of value-added tax (VAT) throughout the Common Market.
- A Supreme Court ruling in the United States means that Medicaid funding will only be used for abortions where medical necessity, rape, or incest is involved.
- Following riots in South Africa, urban Bantu councils are replaced by community councils.
- Polish-born U.S. movie director Roman Polanski pleads guilty to having sex with a thirteen-year-old in the United States, but flees the country before he can be sentenced.
- Roger H. Davidson and Walter J. Oleszek publish *Congress against Itself*.
- The Panama Canal Treaty is signed; it provides for a joint Panamanian–U.S. operation of the Panama Canal until the year 2000, when Panama is to assume full control.
- The United States signs the Convention on International Trade in Endangered Species (CITES).
- U.S. singer Connie Francis is awarded $1,475,000 in a lawsuit brought against the Howard Johnson hotel chain: she filed suit after she had been raped, claiming that the hotel had failed to provide a safe and secure room.

JANUARY

3 The International Monetary Fund lends Britain $3.9 billion.

6 The former British home secretary Roy Jenkins takes office as president of the European Economic Community Commission.

17 The murderer Gary Gilmore is executed by firing squad in Utah, the first execution in the United States since 1967.

18 The Indian prime minister Indira Gandhi calls a general election and releases her political rival, Morarji Desai, from prison.

20 Jimmy Carter is inaugurated as the 39th president of the United States. In an effort to show his informality, Carter and wife Rosalyn break with tradition and walk to the White House after the inaugural ceremony.

21 The U.S. president Jimmy Carter pardons draft dodgers during the Vietnam War.

24 The prime minister of Rhodesia Ian Smith rejects British proposals on Rhodesia.

FEBRUARY

1 An incursion by Khmer Rouge forces into Thailand kills 30 people.

3 Colonel Mengistu Haile Mariam becomes leader of Ethiopia after killing the existing head of state, General Teferi Bante, and six other leading members of the ruling military council.

9 The Irish Republican Army (IRA) gang who set up the Balcombe Street siege in London, England, in December 1975 are sent to prison for at least 30 years.

16 The archbishop of Uganda, Janani Luwum, a human-rights advocate who had denounced abuse of power by security forces, is killed by forces of President Idi Amin.

MARCH

2 Communist leaders from France, Italy, and Spain meet in Madrid, Spain.

7 Zulfikar Ali Bhutto claims a massive victory in Pakistan's general election.

9–11 Hanafi Muslim gunmen seize three buildings in Washington, D.C.

11–23 Violent protests throughout Pakistan allege that Zulfikar Ali Bhutto's election victory is fraudulent.

12 Political parties are banned in Chile and censorship is tightened under General Augusto Pinochet.

16 The leader of the Progressive Socialist Party in Lebanon Kamal Jumblatt is assassinated.

20 The Congress Party is defeated in the Indian general election and the prime minister Indira Gandhi loses her seat.

20 The left makes large gains in the French local elections. In Paris, however, the Gaullist leader Jacques Chirac is elected to the office of mayor, reestablished for the first time since 1871.

24 Morarji Desai becomes prime minister of the Janata Party government in India.

APRIL

7 The Baader–Meinhof terrorists assassinate West Germany's chief prosecutor Siegfried Buback.

7 Yitzhak Rabin withdraws as prime ministerial candidate in Israel after being investigated for banking violations.

9 The Communist Party is legalized in Spain.

19 The U.S. Supreme Court rules that spanking schoolchildren is not unconstitutional.

20 The U.S. president Jimmy Carter proposes a radical energy conservation plan to reduce U.S. dependency on imported oil; it involves tax on imported oil, and incentives for purchasing fuel-efficient cars and the discovery of new resources. Congress greatly modifies the program.

21 Zia ur-Rahman is inaugurated as president of Bangladesh.

24 Andreas Baader and two other members of the Baader–Meinhof terrorist gang are imprisoned in West Germany.

MAY

• The former U.S. president Richard M. Nixon gives a series of lengthy television interviews on Watergate (the attempted bugging of the opposition Democrats' campaign headquarters) in his first major public appearance since his resignation.

17 The Likud party led by Menachem Begin wins the Israeli general elections.

21 Menachem Begin, the leader of the Likud party, becomes prime minister of Israel.

23–June 11 South Moluccan terrorists hijack a train in the Netherlands.

25 Labor wins the general election in the Netherlands.

30 The United States and Cuba agree that they will exchange diplomats on September 1.

JUNE

June–August The U.S. Senate votes to bar federal funding of elective abortions except in cases of rape, incest, or where the life of the mother is in jeopardy, by rejecting a challenge to the Hyde Amendment.

4 A fourth constitution of the USSR is published, making explicit the leading role of the Communist Party.

5 The president of the Seychelles James Mancham is deposed in a coup. He is succeeded by France-Albert René.

8 Uganda is excluded from the Commonwealth conference for its human-rights abuses.

15 Prime Minister Adolfo Suárez wins a small majority in Spain's first general election since 1936.

16 Leonid Brezhnev combines the post of Soviet president with that of Communist Party secretary.

16 The Fianna Fáil party wins a large victory over the governing coalition in the Republic of Ireland.

30 The Southeast Asia Treaty Organization (SEATO), a collective military system, is dissolved.

JULY

5 A coup ousts Zulfikar Ali Bhutto as prime minister of Pakistan. He is replaced by General Zia ul-Haq, Bhutto's former army Chief of Staff.

11 The British antiobscenity campaigner Mary Whitehouse secures the conviction of the newspaper *Gay News* for blasphemy.

14 John Kerr announces his resignation as Australian governor-general with effect from December.

21 Junius Jayawardene, leader of the United National Party, defeats Mrs. Sirimavo Bandaranaike's government in the Sri Lankan general election.

21–25 Libya and Egypt fight a border war.

22 The Chinese Communist Party expels the "Gang of Four," who had tried to seize power after the death of

Mao Zedong. Deng Xiaoping is reinstated as deputy premier.

23   Somali forces invade the Ogaden area of Ethiopia.

31   Tamil separatist members of parliament in Sri Lanka begin to draft a new constitution.

AUGUST

4   The U.S. president Jimmy Carter signs legislation establishing the Department of Energy, aiming to develop a plan for energy conservation and development after the "oil shock." Energy becomes the 12th cabinet department and the first instituted since 1966.

18   The 11th Chinese Communist Party Congress indicates a swing away from hard-line Maoism toward economic improvement.

26   French is made the only official language of Quebec, Canada.

31   Ian Smith's Rhodesian Front wins all 50 white seats in the 66-seat parliament.

SEPTEMBER

1   The U.S. secretary of state Cyrus Vance and the British foreign secretary David Owen propose a peace plan for Rhodesia, recommending a large role for Nkomo and Mugabe's Patriotic Front.

5   The West German industrialist Hans-Martin Schleyer is kidnapped.

7   The United States and Panama sign the Panama Canal Treaty that returns the canal zone to Panama.

13   Burt Lance resigns as director of the Office of Management and Budget after being accused of financial impropriety while a banker in Georgia.

16   The "Hyde Amendment" in the United States limits federal funds for abortion.

21   The alliance between the Socialist and Communist parties in France breaks up.

OCTOBER

1   General Zia of Pakistan cancels the general election due on October 18.

7   The USSR adopts its fourth constitution, which was published on June 4.

18   Andreas Baader and two other members of the West German Baader–Meinhof terrorist gang commit suicide in prison.

18   West German commandos storm a hijacked Ethiopian airliner in the Somali capital, Mogadishu.

19   The West German industrialist Hans-Martin Schleyer, who was kidnapped on September 5, is found dead in France.

20   A military coup in Thailand overthrows the civilian government of Tanin Kraivixien.

NOVEMBER

1   The United States quits the International Labor Organization, that formulates standards for labor conditions, but President Jimmy Carter raises the minimum wage to $2.65 an hour.

4   The United Nations imposes a strict arms embargo on South Africa.

8   Ed Koch wins the mayoral election in New York, New York.

9   President Anwar Sadat of Egypt makes peace overtures to Israel. He alienates other Arab states and his own foreign minister but wins acceptance from the Israeli prime minister Menachem Begin.

11   An Anti-Nazi League is set up in Britain to combat the growth of the National Front.

19–21   The Egyptian president Anwar Sadat visits Israel and addresses the Israeli parliament, the Knesset.

24   The prime minister of Rhodesia Ian Smith proposes a new constitution with equal votes.

30   The ruling National Party wins a record majority in the South African general election.

DECEMBER

2–4   A conference of Arab states in Tripoli, Libya, condemns Egypt for making peace overtures toward the Jewish state of Israel.

4   Jean-Bédel Bokassa is crowned emperor of the Central African Empire.

10   The government of Liberal prime minister Malcolm Fraser wins another large majority in the Australian federal elections.

24–25   The Israeli prime minister Menachem Begin visits Egypt as part of negotiations for peace in the Middle East.

31   The number of violent deaths in Northern Ireland falls sharply in 1977, with 111 killed compared to 297 in 1976.

SCIENCE, TECHNOLOGY, AND MEDICINE

Computing

- Apple Computers launches the Apple II personal computer; owners must use their own television screens and store data on audiocassette tapes. It is the first mass-produced personal computer in assembled form.
- The U.S. firms Commodore Business Machines and Tandy Corporation introduce computers with built-in monitors, although data and programs are still stored on tape cassettes; other computers use separate television screens.
- U.S. computer programmers Joe Condon and Ken Thompson build a computer dedicated to playing chess; it contains 325 chips and can evaluate 5,000 chess positions a second.

Ecology

- Dutch scientists discover that the wastes from incinerators are contaminated by dioxins—chemicals thought to cause cancer.
- U.S. futurist Peter E. Glaser proposes that energy is beamed to Earth by a solar collector placed in geostationary orbit; with an area of 100 sq km/40 sq mi, it could supply about 10 gigawatts of electricity.

MARCH

4   A severe earthquake in Romania wrecks much of Bucharest; over 1,500 people are killed and 11,000 injured.

APRIL
- A Norwegian oil well in the North Sea blows out of control for eight days, spilling about 8.2 million gallons of crude oil into the sea and creating an oil slick 32 km/20 mi long.

MAY
28 A fire in a nightclub in Southgate, Kentucky, kills 164 people.

JUNE
20 The 1,300-km/800-mi trans-Alaska oil pipeline bringing crude oil from the North Slope oil field to the port of Valdez is inaugurated; it has cost $9.7 billion.

JULY
21 The U.S. Surface Mining and Reclamation Act is passed; it requires coal companies to restore strip-mined land to its original state.

NOVEMBER
19 A cyclone and flood kill an estimated 7,000–10,000 people in the state of Andhra Pradesh, India.

Exploration

- Norwegian ethnologist Thor Heyerdahl sails his reed raft *Tigris* down the Tigris River to Pakistan in an attempt to prove that the ancient Sumerians could have spread their culture through southwest Asia by such means.
- Scientists discover chemosynthetically-based animal communities around sulfurous thermal springs deep under the sea near the Galápagos Islands, Ecuador.
- The *High Energy Astronomy Observatory 1* (HEAO 1) is launched by the U.S. National Aeronautics and Space Administration (NASA). It generates a catalog of X-ray sources.

Health and Medicine

- French-born U.S. endocrinologist Roger Guillemin and U.S. endocrinologist Andrew V. Schally share the Nobel Prize for Physiology or Medicine for their discovery of peptide hormone production by the hypothalamus region of the brain, with U.S. scientist Rosalyn Yalow for the development of radioimmunoassays of peptide hormones.
- German physician Andreas Gruentzig invents balloon angioplasty, a method of unclogging diseased arteries by guiding a catheter to the blocked area of the artery. A second catheter with a small balloon on the tip is passed through the first, and then inflated to widen the artery for blood flow. The balloon is then deflated and removed.
- In-vitro fertilization (IVF) is developed by the British gynecologist and obstetrician Patrick Steptoe. The first IVF baby is born in 1978.
- India's family planning campaign, initiated as an emergency measure by Indira Gandhi, fails when it is revealed that 500 women have been forcibly sterilized and 1,500 men have died from poorly performed vasectomies. The relaxation of measures will result in millions more pregnancies.
- Moscow and several other Soviet cities ban cigarette smoking in restaurants and other public places.

- The first major scientific account of legionnaire's disease is given by U.S. epidemiologist David William Fraser.

JULY
12 U.S. medical researcher Raymond Damadian produces the first images of human tissues using an NMR (nuclear magnetic resonance) scanner; used to detect cancer and other diseases without the need for X-rays, the scanner is based on the fact that electromagnetic fields cause some atomic nuclei to align themselves. The scanners become commercially available in the United States in 1984.

AUGUST
1   A total ban on alcohol by 1981 is proposed in India.
23 The revolutionary new ulcer-treatment drug cimetidine wins Federal Drug Administration approval and is marketed as Tagamet in the United States.

SEPTEMBER
10 Several Arab states report outbreaks of cholera.

OCTOBER
26 The last known case of smallpox is reported, in Somalia.

Science

- A baby mammoth, 40,000 years old, is found frozen in ice in the USSR.
- English biochemist Frederick Sanger describes the full sequence of 5,386 bases in the DNA (deoxyribonucleic acid) of virus ΦX174 in Cambridge, England; the first sequencing of an entire genome.
- German-born U.S. physicist Leon Lederman discovers the fifth ("beauty" or "bottom") quark, upsilon meson.
- Soviet-born Belgian chemist Ilya Prigogine receives the Nobel Prize for Chemistry for his contributions to the thermodynamics of irreversible processes, particularly to the theory of dissipative structures.
- Swedish neurologist Tomas Hökfelt discovers that most neurons contain not one but several neurotransmitters.
- The interplanetary body Chiron is discovered by U.S. astronomer Charles Kowal; 182 km/113 mi in diameter, it is initially thought to be an asteroid but is later identified as a giant planetary nucleus.
- The tomb of Philip of Macedon (died 336 BC) is discovered at Verghina in northern Greece.
- UK biochemists Frederick Sanger and Alan Coulson and U.S. molecular biologists Walter Gilbert and Allan Maxam develop a rapid gene-sequencing technique which uses gel electrophoresis.
- U.S. physicists Philip Anderson, John Van Vleck, and English physicist Neville Mott receive the Nobel Prize for Physics for their contributions to understanding the behavior of electrons in magnetic, noncrystalline solids.
- U.S. scientist Herbert Boyer, of the firm Genentech, fuses a segment of human DNA (deoxyribonucleic acid) into the bacterium *Escherichia coli* which begins to produce the human protein somatostatin; this is the first commercially produced genetically engineered product.

MARCH
- U.S. astronomer James Elliot, with several groups of other U.S. astronomers, discover rings around Uranus when the planet occludes a relatively bright star.

Technology

- Japanese researcher Hideki Shirakawa and U.S. researchers Alan McDiarmid and Alan Heeger add iodine to one of the new electrically conductive plastics, vastly improving its conductive characteristics.
- The Bell Telephone Company in the United States transmits television signals over a distance of 2.4 km/1.5 mi using fibreoptics.
- The U.S. cultural critic Susan Sontag publishes *On Photography* and *Illness as Metaphor*.
- The U.S. Polaroid Corporation introduces an instant print 8-mm color film.

JUNE

- The U.S. Air Force builds a ramp and platform 38 m/125 ft high to test the effects of electromagnetic pulses caused by nuclear explosions. Because metal parts would be affected and interfere with the tests it is constructed entirely of wood glued together; it is the world's largest wooden structure.

JULY

13 Electricity goes out for 25 hours in New York, New York due to a short in neighboring Westchester County; 776 looters are arrested, 100 policemen are injured, nearly 500 fires are reported, and $135 million worth of property is damaged or destroyed.

OCTOBER

- The U.S. treasury department levies a 32% duty on five Japanese steel companies accused of dumping below-cost steel plate on the U.S. steel market.

Transportation

- California enforces strict antipollution legislation compelling car manufacturers to install catalytic converters that reduce exhaust emissions by 90%.
- The Soviet icebreaker *Arktika* becomes the first surface ship to reach the North Pole.
- U.S. inventor Paul MacCready's aircraft *Gossamer Condor* makes the first human-powered flight and wins the £50,000 Kremer Prize.

JANUARY

18 A train derails outside Sydney, Australia, killing 82 people.

FEBRUARY

4 An elevated train is hit from behind by another train in Chicago, Illinois, crashing onto an intersection below and killing 11 passengers and pedestrians and injuring 189 people.

MARCH

27 A KLM Boeing 747 collides during takeoff with a Pan Am 747 still on the ground at Tenerife in the Canary Islands; a total of 582 people are killed on board both planes. It is the world's worst air disaster to date.

APRIL

29 British Aerospace is formed to run Britain's nationalized aviation industry.

SEPTEMBER

26 The first Laker "Skytrain" flies from London, England to New York, New York, for $102 a ticket, launching Laker Airways' no frill, low cost service.

NOVEMBER

20 Australian Kenneth Warby sets a record for the highest speed achieved on water, 555 kph/300 knots, in his hydroplane *Spirit of Australia*, on the Blowering Dam Lake, New South Wales, Australia.

DECEMBER

16 The London Underground extension to Heathrow Airport, London, England, opens, making Heathrow the first airport in the world to be connected to a city rail system.

ARTS AND IDEAS

Architecture

- The English architectural historian Mark Girouard publishes *Sweetness and Light: The 'Queen Anne' Movement, 1860–1900*.
- The New River Gorge Bridge is completed at Fayetteville, West Virginia; with a span of 518.2 m/1,700 ft, it is the world's longest steel arch bridge.
- The Paul Mellon Center for British Studies, at Yale University in New Haven, Connecticut, is completed. It was designed by the U.S. architect Louis Kahn.

Arts

- An exhibition of the work of French artist Marcel Duchamp is held at the Pompidou Center in Paris, France.
- An exhibition of unofficial Soviet art is held at the Institute of Contemporary Art in London, England.
- The Centre National d'Art et de Culture Georges Pompidou (Pompidou Center) in Paris, France, designed by Renzo Piano and Richard Rogers, is completed.
- The English artist Richard Long creates and performs *Throwing a Stone Around MacGillycuddy's Rocks*.
- The extra Venice Biennale is held in Italy, devoted to art of dissent and dissidents, especially in Eastern Europe and the USSR.
- The German-born English artist Frank Auerbach paints *Camden Theatre in the Rain*.
- The U.S. artist Walter De Maria creates the sculpture *Lightning Field*.

Film

- André Blay of Michigan-based Magnetic Video obtains from Fox the rights to sell videos of such movies as *M*A*S*H* and *The Sound of Music*; he sells them by mail order for $50 each. A year after buying the rights cheaply, he sells them back to Fox for $7.2 million.
- Following a poll of its members, the American Film Institute names *Gone With the Wind* as the all-time greatest movie.
- Professor Victor Komar of the Cinema and Photo Research Unit in the USSR demonstrates the first movie

made using holography: depicting a girl putting away jewelry, it lasts just 30 seconds.

- The disco movie *Saturday Night Fever*, directed by John Badham, is released in the United States. It stars John Travolta and features music by the Bee Gees.
- The movie *Annie Hall*, directed by Woody Allen, is released in the United States. Allen costars with Diane Keaton. The movie will win Academy Awards for best picture, best director, best actress, and best original screenplay.
- The movie *Cet Obscur Objet du désir/That Obscure Object of Desire*, cowritten and directed by Spanish filmmaker Luis Buñuel, is released in France. It stars Fernando Rey, Carole Bouquet, and Angela Molina.
- The movie *Close Encounters of the Third Kind*, directed by Steven Spielberg, is released in the United States. It stars Richard Dreyfuss, François Truffaut, and Teri Garr. A reedited special edition will be released in 1980.
- The movie *Człowiek z marmuru/Man of Marble*, directed by Andrzej Wajda, is released in Poland. It stars Jerzy Radziwiłowicz and Krystyna Janda.
- The movie *Der Amerikanische Freund/The American Friend*, directed by Wim Wenders, is released in West Germany. Based on Patricia Highsmith's thriller *Ripley's Game*, it stars Dennis Hopper and Bruno Ganz.
- The movie *Julia*, directed by Fred Zinnemann, is released in the United States. Based on the book by Lillian Hellman, it stars Jane Fonda, Vanessa Redgrave, Jason Robards, Jr., Maximillian Schnell, and Meryl Streep.
- The movie *La Dentellière/The Lacemaker*, directed by Swiss filmmaker Claude Goretta, is released in France. It stars Isabelle Huppert.
- The movie *Looking for Mr Goodbar*, directed by Richard Brooks, is released in the United States. It stars Diane Keaton and Richard Gere.
- The movie *Mr Klein*, directed by U.S. filmmaker Joseph Losey, is released in France. It stars Alain Delon and Jeanne Moreau.
- The movie *Opening Night*, directed by John Cassavetes, is released in the United States. Cassavetes costars with his wife Gena Rowlands.
- The movie *Padre Padrone*, directed by the brothers Paolo and Vittorio Taviani, is released in Italy.
- The movie *Providence*, directed by French filmmaker Alain Resnais, is released in the UK. It stars Dirk Bogarde, John Gielgud, and Ellen Burstyn.
- The movie *Star Wars*, directed by George Lucas, is released in the United States. It stars Mark Hamill, Harrison Ford, Carrie Fisher, and Alec Guinness.
- The movie *Stroszek*, directed by Werner Herzog, is released in West Germany, starring Bruno S, Eva Mattes, and Clemens Scheitz.
- The movie *The Goodbye Girl*, directed by Herbert Ross and scripted by Neil Simon, is released in the United States. It stars Richard Dreyfuss and Marsha Mason.
- The movie *The Last Wave*, directed by Peter Weir, is released in Australia, starring Richard Chamberlain.
- The musical *New York, New York*, directed by Martin Scorsese, is released in the United States. It stars Robert De Niro and Liza Minnelli.

MARCH

28 The 1976 Academy Awards take place. Best Actor: Peter Finch, for *Network*; Best Supporting Actor: Jason Robards, for *All the President's Men*; Best Actress: Faye Dunaway, for *Network*; Best Supporting Actress: Beatrice Straight, for *Network*; Best Picture: *Rocky*, directed by John G. Avildsen; Best Director: John G. Avildsen, for *Rocky*.

AUGUST

4 The movie *The Spy Who Loved Me*, directed by Lewis Gilbert, is released in the United States. It stars Roger Moore as James Bond.

SEPTEMBER

22 French director Claude Autant-Lara blames the decline in movie attendance in France on Jean-Luc Godard and the other directors of the New Wave.

NOVEMBER

5 Misr Studios in Cairo, Egypt, celebrates the 50th anniversary of Egyptian filmmaking.

11 A royal decree is passed in Spain ending movie censorship and permitting the importing of foreign movies.

Literature and Language

- *Johnny Panic and the Bible of Dreams*, a collection of short stories by the U.S. writer Sylvia Plath, is published posthumously.
- *Sunset at Blandings* by the English comic writer P. G. Wodehouse is published posthumously.
- English writer John Fowles publishes his novel *Daniel Martin*.
- English writer John le Carré publishes his novel *The Honourable Schoolboy*.
- English writer Margaret Drabble publishes her novel *The Ice Age*.
- English writer Richard Adams publishes his novel *The Plague Dogs*.
- The Chinese government lifts the ban on Shakespeare and Beethoven.
- The English historian José Harris publishes *William Beveridge: A Biography*.
- The English writer Bruce Chatwin publishes his travel book *In Patagonia*.
- The English writer Olivia Manning publishes her novel *The Danger Tree*, the first part of her *Levant Trilogy*.
- The English writer Patrick Leigh Fermor publishes his travel book *A Time of Gifts*.
- The English writer Paul Scott publishes his novel *Staying On*, which wins the Booker Prize.
- The French social and literary critic Roland Barthes publishes *Fragments d'un discours amoureux/A Lover's Discourse*.
- The French writer Hélène Cixous publishes her novel *Angst*.
- The German writer Günter Grass publishes his novel *Der Butt/The Flounder*.
- The Indian writer R. K. Narayan publishes his novel *The Painter of Signs*.
- The Irish writer Edna O'Brien publishes her novel *Johnny I Hardly Knew You*.

- The Irish writer Samuel Beckett publishes *Four Novellas*.
- The Italian writer Leonardo Sciascia publishes his novel *Candido*.
- The Japanese writer Kobo Abe publishes his novel *Mikkai/Secret Rendezvous*.
- The Kenyan writer Ngugi wa Thiong'o publishes his novel *Petals of Blood*.
- The Nobel Prize for Literature is awarded to the Spanish poet Vincent Aleixandre.
- The novel *Silmarillion* by the English writer J. R. R. Tolkien is published posthumously, a "prequel" to his *The Lord of the Rings* cycle.
- The Peruvian writer Mario Vargas Llosa publishes his novel *La tía Julia y el escribidor/Aunt Julia and the Scriptwriter*.
- The Pulitzer Prize for Biography is awarded to John E. Nack for *A Prince of Our Disorder: The Life of T E Lawrence* and the Pulitzer Prize for Poetry is awarded to James Merrill for *Divine Comedies*. The Pulitzer Prize for Fiction is not awarded this year.
- The U.S. writer Andre Dubus publishes his short-story collection *Adultery and Other Choices*.
- The U.S. writer Joan Didion publishes her novel *A Book of Common Prayer*.
- The U.S. writer John Cheever publishes his novel *Falconer*.
- The U.S. writer Peter Taylor publishes his short-story collection *In the Miro District and Other Stories*.
- The U.S. writer Toni Morrison publishes her novel *The Song of Solomon*.
- The U.S. writer W. S. Merwin publishes his poetry collection *The Compass Flower*.
- The women's publishing house Virago is founded in Britain.

Music

- Ex-Beatle Paul McCartney and his band Wings have a hit with "Mull of Kintyre," cowritten by McCartney and band-member Denny Laine. Over 2.5 million copies are sold.
- Punk music comes to prominence in the UK, with the emergence of bands such as the Sex Pistols, the Clash, the Buzzcocks, the Damned, and the Stranglers.
- The Anglo-American rock group Fleetwood Mac releases the albums *Rumours*, one of the best-selling pop albums to date, and *Albatross*.
- The British pop group the Clash releases *The Clash*, their first album.
- The British punk band the Damned releases the album *Damned Damned Damned*, the first punk LP to make it into the album charts.
- The English composer Elisabeth Lutyens completes her song cycle *Variations: Winter series – Spring Sowing*.
- The Estonian composer Arvo Pärt completes his orchestral work *Tabula rasa* and his *Cantus in Memory of Benjamin Britten*.

- The Institut de recherche et de coordination acoustique–musique (IRCAM), is opened in the Pompidou Center in Paris, France. A complex of laboratories and electronic studios, its purpose is to experiment with modern compositional methods. Its director is the French composer and conductor Pierre Boulez.
- The Jamaican pop group Bob Marley and the Wailers releases the album *Exodus*.
- The Japanese composer Toru Takemitsu completes his orchestral work *A Flock Descends into the Pentagonal Garden*.
- The opera *Mary Queen of Scots*, by the Scottish composer Thea Musgrave, is first performed, in Edinburgh, Scotland. It is based on the play *Moray* by Amalia Elguera.
- The opera *The Ice Break*, by the English composer Michael Tippett, is first performed, at Covent Garden, in London, England. It was completed in 1976.
- The opera *The Martyrdom of St Magnus*, by the English composer Peter Maxwell Davies, is first performed, in Orkney, Scotland. The text is from *Magnus* by the Scottish poet George Mackay Brown.
- The U.S. composer Elliott Carter completes *A Symphony for Three Orchestras*.
- The U.S. composer Gardner Read completes his Piano Concerto.
- The U.S. composer George Crumb completes his work *Star-Child* for voices, bell ringers, and orchestra.
- The U.S. composer John Cage completes his *Freeman Etudes* for solo violin.
- The U.S. composer Leon Kirchner completes his opera *Lily*.
- The U.S. composer Ned Rorem completes his symphonic suite *Sunday Morning*.
- The U.S. pop group Television releases the album *Marquee Moon*.

JANUARY

22 The Swedish pop group Abba releases the single "Knowing Me Knowing You" and the album *Arrival*.

FEBRUARY

19 The 1976–77 Grammy Awards take place. Best Pop Male Vocalist: Stevie Wonder; Best Album: *Songs in the Key of Life* by Stevie Wonder; Best Record: "This Masquerade" by George Benson; Best Female Pop Vocalist: Linda Ronstadt.

AUGUST

6 The U.S. pop star Donna Summer releases the single "I Feel Love." Her music reflects the rise of disco music and the development of techno-pop.

16–17 Around 2 million Elvis Presley records sell within one day of his death.

SEPTEMBER

17 The U.S. pop singer Iggy Pop releases the album *Lust for Life*.

OCTOBER

29 The U.S. rock group Meat Loaf releases the album *Bat Out of Hell*; it will sell more than 25 million copies worldwide.

DECEMBER

3 The British pop singer Elvis Costello releases the album *My Aim is True*.

10 The British punk group the Sex Pistols releases the album *Never Mind the Bollocks Here's the Sex Pistols*. The British Broadcasting Corporation (BBC) ban their single "God Save the Queen," released earlier in the year, but it is top of the charts during the queen's silver jubilee celebrations in June.

Theater and Dance

- The musical *Annie*, with lyrics by Martin Charnin and music by Charles Strouse, is first performed, at the Alvin Theater in New York, New York. It is based on the cartoon character Little Orphan Annie.
- The play *A Life in the Theatre*, by the U.S. writer David Mamet, is first performed, at the Theater de Lys in New York, New York.
- The play *Gemini*, by the U.S. writer Albert Innaurato, is first performed, at the Little Theater in New York, New York.
- The play *Privates on Parade*, by the English writer Peter Nichols, is first performed, in London, England.
- The play *The Elephant Man*, by the U.S. writer Bernard Pomerance, is first performed, at the Hampstead Theatre in London, England.
- The play *Waiting for the Parade*, by the Canadian writer John Murrell, is first performed.
- The Pulitzer Prize for Drama is awarded to Michael Cristofer for *The Shadow Box*.

Thought and Scholarship

- *The Myth of God Incarnate* is published, edited by British theologian John Hick.
- English historian H. C. Darby publishes *Domesday England*.
- English historian Lawrence Stone publishes *The Family, Sex and Marriage, 1500–1800*.
- English historian Simon Schama publishes *Patriots and Liberators*.
- English political historian David Marquand publishes *Ramsay MacDonald*.
- French historian Philippe Ariès publishes *The Hour of Our Death*.
- Scottish historian Fergus Millar publishes *The Emperor in the Roman World, 31 BC–AD 337*.
- The Pulitzer Prize for History is posthumously awarded to David M. Potter for *The Impending Crisis: 1841–1861*.
- The Pulitzer Prize for General Nonfiction is awarded to William H. Warner for *Beautiful Swimmers*.
- U.S. philosopher Thomas Kuhn publishes *The Essential Tension*.

SOCIETY

Education

- Competitive higher education entrance examinations are reinstated in China.

- Latin is abolished as a compulsory subject in Italian middle schools.

Everyday Life

- In the United States, George Anderson opens the first video rental store, charging $50 to join and $10 per movie a night.
- Over 500 million pairs of denim jeans are sold in the United States, with Levi Strauss the largest producer. This represents a huge increase over a decade: sales in 1967 were around 200 million.
- There are 4,311 black elected officials in the United States, up from 1,469 in 1970.
- Two homosexual men in New York, New York, are diagnosed as having the rare cancer Kaposi's sarcoma. They are later thought to be the first victims of AIDS.
- U.S. historian Alfred D. Chandler, Jr., publishes *The Visible Hand: The Managerial Revolution in American Business*.

SEPTEMBER
10–20 Bakery workers in Britain stage a national strike.

OCTOBER
- Nearly half a million Longshoremen strike container ports in Atlantic and Gulf coast cities. The strike ends on November 29 after the union wins a three-year contract promising job security and a 30.5% pay hike.
27–November 11 Unofficial strike action by British power station workers causes sporadic blackouts.

NOVEMBER
14–January 12, 1978 British firefighters go on strike.

DECEMBER
6–March 24, 1978 One of the longest strikes in the history of the U.S. coal industry ends when miners receive higher wages and more generous benefits.
8 Violent clashes erupt in Ohio and Utah, United States, during the coal miners' strike.

Media and Communication

- *A Wandering Life* is shown on Japanese television.
- Eighty-four percent of all travel in the United States is by private vehicle; 9% of the population walk to their destination, and only 2.4% use public transportation.
- The 1976–77 Emmy Awards for television are held. Best Drama Series: *Upstairs, Downstairs*; Best Comedy Series: *The Mary Tyler Moore Show*; Best Actor in a Drama: James Garner, for *The Rockford Files*; Best Actress in a Drama: Lindsay Wagner, for *The Bionic Woman*; Best Actor in a Comedy: Carroll O'Connor, for *All in the Family*; Best Actress in a Comedy: Beatrice Arthur, for *Maude*.
December 1977–78 An antiviolence campaign in the United States launched by churches and the Parent Teachers Association has a significant effect on the content of shows such as *Starsky and Hutch*, with less violence portrayed and more sentimental storylines developed.

JANUARY
25–February 1 *Roots*, a mini-series based on the book by Alex Haley, is shown over eight nights on U.S.

television. It stars LeVar Burton, Cicely Tyson, and John Amos; the final episode is seen by 80 million people.

MARCH

15–September 18, 1985 The television comedy *Three's Company*, in which two women and a man are roommates, is shown on U.S. television, making actors John Ritter and Suzanne Somers famous.

SEPTEMBER

13–April 20, 1981 *Soap*, a spoof of the world of soap opera, starts on U.S. television. The stars include Katherine Helmond, Robert Guillame, Billy Crystal, and Robert Urich.

24–September 5, 1986 *The Love Boat*, a situation comedy set on a luxury cruise ship, featuring famous guest stars in romantic stories, is shown on U.S. television.

BIRTHS & DEATHS

JANUARY

14 Anaïs Nin, French-born U.S. novelist and diarist influenced by the surrealists and psychology, dies in Los Angeles, California (73).

14 Anthony Eden, British foreign secretary and prime minister 1955–57, dies in Alvedision, Wiltshire, England (79).

APRIL

11 Jacques Prévert, French poet and screenwriter, dies in Omonville-la-Petite, France (77).

12 Philip K. Wrigley, businessman and owner of the Chicago Cubs baseball team, dies.

MAY

5 Ludwig Erhard, German statesman and economist responsible for Germany's postwar recovery, chancellor of the Federal Republic of Germany 1963–66, dies in Bonn, Germany (80).

9 James Jones, U.S. author who wrote the novel *From Here to Eternity*, dies in Southampton, New York (55).

10 Joan Crawford, U.S. film actress with a glamorous screen image, dies in New York (69).

JUNE

3 Archibald Vivian Hill, English physiologist who studied muscle action and especially the amount of heat produced by muscle activity, dies (91).

3 Roberto Rossellini, Italian film director, dies in Rome, Italy (71).

16 Werner von Braun, German rocket engineer who was also involved in the exploration of space in Germany and the United States, dies in Alexandria, Virginia (65).

JULY

2 Vladimir Nabokov, Russian-born U.S. author and critic, best known for his novel *Lolita*, dies in Montreux, Switzerland (78).

9 Alice Paul, U.S. suffragist and women's rights activist, dies in Moorestown, New Jersey (82).

AUGUST

3 Makarios III, Cypriot archbishop, leader in the struggle for union with Greece and president of the Independent Republic of Cyprus 1959–77, dies in Nicosia, Cyprus (63).

4 Edgar Douglas Adrian (Edgar Baron), English physiologist who won the Nobel Prize for Physiology or Medicine in 1932 for his discoveries concerning nerve impulses, dies in London, England (87).

4 Ernst Bloch, German Marxist philosopher who developed the "philosophy of hope," dies in Stuttgart, Germany (92).

16 Elvis Presley, U.S. rock and roll singer, whose great success changed U.S. popular culture, dies of heart failure (probably associated with drug abuse) at his home, Graceland, in Memphis, Tennessee (42).

19 Groucho (real name Julius) Marx, U.S. comedian of stage, film, radio, and television along with two of his brothers, Harpo and Chico, dies in Los Angeles, California (86).

23 Naum Gabo, Russian-born pioneering sculptor in constructivist art, dies in Waterbury, Connecticut (87).

26 Hans Rey, German-born U.S. illustrator best known for his Curious George children's books, dies in Boston, Massachusetts (78).

SEPTEMBER

8 Zero Mostel, U.S. theater and film actor, dies in Philadelphia, Pennsylvania (62).

12 Robert Lowell, U.S. poet, dies in New York, New York (60).

12 Steven Biko, South African black leader, dies from head injuries in police custody in Pretoria, South Africa (30).

13 Leopold Stokowski, U.S. conductor and composer who promoted contemporary music and was involved in new music technology in the 1930s, dies in Nether Wallop, Hampshire, England (95).

16 Maria Callas, Greek-born U.S. soprano opera singer, dies in Paris, France (53).

23 John N. Nash, British official World War I artist, also an illustrator and teacher, dies in Colchester, Essex, England (84).

OCTOBER

14 Bing Crosby, U.S. popular singer and songwriter, dies near Madrid, Spain (73).

27 James M. Cain, U.S. "hard-boiled" fiction writer of the 1930s and 40s whose major novels such as *The Postman Always Rings Twice* were made into some of the most famous *films noirs* of the 1940s, dies at University Park, Maryland (85).

NOVEMBER

5 Guy Lombardo, Canadian-born U.S. dance band leader known for hosting New Year's Eve celebrations on radio and television, dies in Houston, Texas (74).

18 Kurt von Schuschnigg, Austrian chancellor 1934–38 who tried to prevent Austria's takeover by Nazi Germany in 1938, dies near Innsbruck, Austria (79).

DECEMBER

7 Peter C. Goldmark, U.S. inventor of the long-playing record and the first practical color television, dies in Westchester County, New York (71).

10 Adolph Rupp, U.S. college basketball coach at the University of Kentucky, dies in Lexington, Kentucky (76).

12 Frank Boucher, Canadian ice hockey player for the New York Rangers, dies in Kemptville, Ontario, Canada (76).

25 Charlie Chaplin, British-born U.S. actor and director of the silent film era, who gained fame playing a pathetic but humorous character, dies in Corsier-sur-Vevey, Switzerland (88).

26 Howard Hawks, U.S. director of films starring the major actors of the time, dies in Palm Springs, California (81).

NOVEMBER

- Australian publisher Rupert Murdoch acquires *The New York Post*. His worldwide business now includes more than 80 newspapers.

Religion

- Religious Denominations in the United States (in millions): Roman Catholics, 49.8; Baptists, 24.9; Methodists, 12.8; Lutherans, 8.0; Presbyterians, 3.4; Episcopalians, 2.8; Mormons, 2.5; Greek Orthodox, 1.9; Jews, 5.8.
- Ten thousand copies of the Torah are shipped from the United States to the Moscow synagogue in the Soviet Union for the first time since 1917.
- The Anglican–Roman Catholic Commission in Britain advises that the Anglican Communion should recognize the primacy of the pope.
- The German Protestant theologian Jürgen Moltmann publishes *The Church in the Power of the Spirit*.

MAY

2–13 An unsuccessful Protestant general strike is held in Northern Ireland.

JUNE

6 Joseph Lason, the Roman Catholic bishop of Biloxi, Mississippi, becomes the first black bishop in the United States since the 19th century.

SEPTEMBER

16 Following the 1976 decision of the Episcopalian Church in the United States to ordain women, a breakaway group founds the Anglican Church in North America, claiming to be true heirs to the Anglican tradition.

Sports

- In baseball, the American League is expanded to include the Seattle Mariners and the Toronto Blue Jays.
- Sandro Munari of Italy wins the inaugural FIA Cup for Drivers, the precursor of the World Drivers' Championship for rally drivers.
- Skateboarding becomes popular among U.S. children.
- The 17-year-old U.S. jockey Steve Cauthen rides 487 winners and earns a record $6,151,750 in prize money in his first full season on the U.S. racing circuit.
- The first official skateboarding world championships are held at Long Beach, California.
- The Mayor Daley Marathon, later the Chicago Marathon, is run for the first time.

JANUARY

1 Sportswriters vote the University of Pittsburgh as college football's top team for the 1976 season.
9 The Oakland Raiders defeat the Minnesota Vikings 32–14 in Super Bowl XI before a crowd of 100,421 at Pasadena, California.

FEBRUARY

3 U.S. national figure skating champions are: Linda Fratianne; Charles Tickner; Randy Gardner and Tai Babilonia, pairs; Judi Genovese and Kent Weigle, dance.

MAY

3–8 The inaugural individual World Badminton Championships are held in Malmoe, Sweden.
7 The Montreal Canadiens win the Stanley Cup, beating the Boston Bruins.
21–June 11 In horse racing, Seattle Slew ridden by Jean Cruguet wins the Kentucky Derby, the Preakness Stakes, and the Belmont Stakes to win U.S. Triple Crown.
22 The Portland Trail Blazers win the National Basketball Association (NBA) championship, becoming the first team to rally after losing the first two games of the series. They defeat the Philadelphia 76ers.
26 George Willing, a toy designer, scales the south tower of the World Trade Center in New York, New York. He is fined $1.10, one cent for each of the 110 stories.
29 The U.S. race-car driver A. J. Foyt becomes the first person to win the Indianapolis 500 four times.

JUNE

10 U.S. golfer Al Geiberger hits 59 in the Memphis Classic to record the lowest ever round in U.S. professional golf.

JULY

1 British tennis player Virginia Wade wins the women's singles and Bjorn Borg of Sweden wins the men's singles title at the Centenary Wimbledon Tennis Championships in London, England.
9 The British Open golf tournament at Turnberry, Scotland, is won by the U.S. golfer Tom Watson.
30 The Argentine boxer Carlos Monzon retires after the fourteenth successful defense of his world middleweight title, against Rodrigo Valdez of Colombia in Monte Carlo, Monaco.

SEPTEMBER

2–4 The first International Amateur Athletics Federation (IAAF) World Cup is held in Düsseldorf, West Germany.

OCTOBER

1 At Giants stadium, New Jersey, New York Cosmos play Santos FC to mark the retirement of the Brazilian soccer player Pelé who, since making his debut in 1956, has scored 1,281 goals in 1,363 competitive matches.
11–18 Reggie Jackson of the New York Yankees hits home runs in three consecutive bats against the Los Angeles Dodgers, to help the Yankees clinch their first World Series since 1958.

NOVEMBER

20 Walter Payton of the Chicago Bears breaks the National Football League (NFL) single game rushing record with 275 yards against the Minnesota Vikings.

1978

POLITICS, GOVERNMENT, AND ECONOMICS

Business and Economics

MAY

5 The first Ben and Jerry's ice-cream store is opened by Ben Cohen and Jerry Greenfield in Burlington, Vermont. They specialize in "superpremium" ice-cream and attempt to pursue a progressive social agenda as part of their business practice.

JUNE

6 Californians vote overwhelmingly (65%–35%) in favor of Proposition 13, which reduces property taxes by 57%. Opponents argue that the tax cut will hurt public education.

NOVEMBER

1 The dollar rises sharply after the U.S. president Jimmy Carter announces a major support plan, including higher interest rates.

18 British oil tanker drivers start an overtime ban.

DECEMBER

15 Cleveland, Ohio, defaults on its debts, the first U.S. city to do so since the 1930s depression.

Colonization

JULY

7 The Solomon Islands gain their independence from Britain.

Human Rights

- Selling young girls is outlawed in Afghanistan.
- The Pregnancy Discrimination Act is passed in the United States, protecting women from being denied employment because of pregnancy.

JANUARY

18 The European Court of Human Rights clears the British government of torture, but finds it guilty of inhuman and degrading treatment of prisoners in Northern Ireland.

MAY

18 Yuri Orlov, a Soviet human-rights campaigner, is sentenced to seven years in a labor camp.

JUNE

9 The Church of Jesus Christ of Latter-Day Saints (Mormons) in the United States ends a ban on the ordination of black priests.

Politics and Government

- A new constitution in China declares that education should be developed to raise the cultural and scientific level of the whole nation.
- Increasing populations in the Middle East aggravate tension between warring countries, as land and resources become more scarce.
- Pedro Joaquin Chamorro, publisher of the newspaper *La Prensa*, is murdered in Nicaragua. His death increases support for the Sandinista rebels against the dictator Anastasio Somoza.
- The European Court affirms the superiority of European Economic Community (EEC) law over the national law of member states.
- The Manhattan Institute for Policy Research is founded in the United States.
- The Microprocessor Industry Support Scheme is launched by the UK government to promote the development of microprocessors in the UK.
- The president of Pakistan, Zia ul-Haq, orders that education should place greater emphasis on loyalty to Islam.

JANUARY

3 Indira Gandhi is expelled from the Congress Party in India.

12 Giulio Andreotti's Christian Democratic government collapses in Italy.

16–18 Egypt and Israel hold talks in Jerusalem.

24 In Canada, the basic part of Quebec's language law enforcing the use of French is declared unconstitutional by the province's Superior Court.

FEBRUARY

1 "Muldergate" begins in South Africa when parliament learns that the Information Department, headed by Connie Mulder, had made unauthorized expenditure in an attempt to counter the country's negative image abroad.

3 The European Economic Community and China conclude their first trade agreement.

7 The Ford Motor Company in the United States is fined $125 million for fitting faulty fuel tanks.

14 The U.S. president Jimmy Carter proposes the sale of 50 jet fighters to Egypt.

25 Indira Gandhi takes up leadership of the splinter Congress (I) Party.

MARCH

3   The Rhodesian prime minister, Ian Smith, and three black leaders sign an agreement for a power-sharing government and eventual majority rule, but exclude Robert Mugabe's and Joshua Nkomo's Patriotic Front.

5   A new Chinese constitution affirms the rule of law, in contrast to the policies under the Cultural Revolution.

11   A new government led by Giulio Andreotti is installed in Italy with the support of the Communist Party.

12   The general election in France returns the right to power with a reduced majority.

14   Israel invades southern Lebanon.

16   Red Brigade terrorists in Italy kidnap the former prime minister Aldo Moro.

18   The former Pakistani prime minister Zulfikar Ali Bhutto is sentenced to death for ordering the murder of one of his opponents in 1974.

22   The first United Nations "UNIFIL" (United Nations Interim Force in Lebanon) troops arrive in Lebanon.

APRIL

6   The mandatory retirement age in the United States is raised from 65 to 70.

7   The West German chancellor Helmut Schmidt proposes a European currency stabilization plan. It is later enacted as the European Monetary System (EMS).

18   The U.S. Senate ratifies the second Panama Canal Treaty, which sets conditions for the canal's operation until Panama assumes control of it in 1999.

27   Communist and Islamic forces take power in Afghanistan from the government of President Mohammed Doud.

MAY

8   The South African prime minister B. J. Vorster accepts responsibility for the unauthorized expenditure of the Information Department.

9   The body of Aldo Moro, the former Italian prime minister kidnapped by Red Brigade terrorists on March 16, is found in Rome, Italy, after the government refuses to make concessions to his captors.

10   Nine people die in Islamic fundamentalist riots in Qom, Iran.

16   Fifty tribespeople die and 24 are wounded in a gun battle between guerrillas and troops in Rhodesia.

JUNE

13   The Israelis pull out of southern Lebanon but fighting erupts in the north.

15   President Giovanni Leone of Italy resigns following allegations of corruption and tax evasion. He is succeeded by Alessandro Pertini.

15   The South African prime minister B. J. Vorster abolishes the Information Department.

24   A South Yemeni parcel bomb kills President Ahmed al-Ghashmi of North Yemen.

26   The president of South Yemen Salem Ruba Ali is assassinated by the faction that murdered the North Yemeni president Ahmed al-Ghashmi.

28   The U.S. Supreme Court, in *Bakke v. the Regents of the University of California*, challenges California's racial quota system, ordering the University of California to admit Allan P. Bakke, a qualified white student, to its medical school.

JULY

5   A coup in Ghana replaces Col I. K. Acheampong with his deputy, Fred Akuffo.

14   The Soviet dissident Anatoly Shcharansky is sentenced to 13 years in jail.

AUGUST

8   The Rhodesian government announces its intention to abolish racial discrimination in public places.

12   Japan and China sign a treaty of peace and friendship.

22–24   Sandinista guerrillas in Nicaragua seize the parliament building in the capital, Managua, in an attempt to overthrow President Somoza.

25   Spain abolishes the death penalty in peacetime.

27   The new Iranian government of Jaafar Sharif-Emami lifts the ban on political parties.

SEPTEMBER

5–17   A summit at Camp David, Maryland, United States, between the U.S. president Jimmy Carter, the Egyptian president Anwar Sadat, and the Israeli prime minister Menachem Begin concludes with a "framework" peace treaty ending 30 years of hostility between Israel and Egypt.

8   Demonstrations in the Iranian capital, Tehran, lead to 95 deaths.

15   The Spanish parliament recognizes the demand of the Basques for autonomy.

16   The Rhodesian executive council starts conscripting blacks to fight the Patriotic Front led by Robert Mugabe and Joshua Nkomo.

20   B. J. Vorster resigns as prime minister of South Africa on grounds of ill health.

21   The outgoing military regime in Nigeria promulgates a new constitution based on that of the United States.

28   The Israeli parliament, the Knesset, approves the Camp David peace accord between Israel and Egypt.

29   P. W. Botha becomes prime minister of South Africa.

OCTOBER

4   An estimated 500 people are killed or wounded in heavy battles in the civil war in Beirut, Lebanon.

5   The Swedish center-right government collapses over its policy on nuclear power.

10   B. J. Vorster becomes president of South Africa.

12   Border clashes between Uganda and Tanzania are caused by President Idi Amin's expansionist claims on Tanzanian territory.

13   A minority Liberal government is established in Sweden under Ola Ullsten.

26   The Government Ethics Law in the United States provides absolute protection for civil servants bringing evidence of corruption or mismanagement to the attention of Congress or the people.

29   The late Mao Zedong's collection of thoughts, known as the *Little Red Book*, is denounced in China.

NOVEMBER

2   The South African lawyer Anton Mostert, despite a request from Prime Minister P. J. Botha for confidentiality, releases evidence from his inquiry into the former Information Department.

5   A referendum in Austria stops the Zwentersdorf nuclear power station from being switched on.

6   A military government is appointed in Iran.

7   Midterm elections in the United States produce small Democratic losses in Congress.
7   The former South African information minister Connie Mulder resigns.
8   Indira Gandhi returns to the Indian parliament following her victory in a by-election.
8   Uganda drops its territorial claim on Tanzania.
25 Robert Muldoon returns to power in New Zealand with a much reduced majority for the National Party.
27 Tanzanian troops move into the Ugandan border areas.
27 The Japanese prime minister Takeo Fukuda resigns.

DECEMBER

5   The Erasmus Commission in South Africa issues its report on the Information Department scandal ("Muldergate"), but ignores allegations that President B. J. Vorster knew about the unauthorized expenditure to attempt to counter the country's negative image abroad.
6   The British prime minister James Callaghan announces that Britain will not join the new European Monetary System.
7   Masayoshi Ohira becomes prime minister of Japan.
15 The United States and China normalize diplomatic relations with effect from January 1, 1979.
17 The Organization of Petroleum-Exporting Countries (OPEC) decides to raise oil prices by 14.5% by the end of 1979.
19–26 Indira Gandhi is expelled from the Indian parliament following her prosecution on charges of political misconduct and is imprisoned.
25 Vietnam begins a full-scale invasion of Cambodia.
27 A U.S. man is found not guilty of raping his wife in what is seen as a test case on relations between the sexes.

SCIENCE, TECHNOLOGY, AND MEDICINE

Computing

- Apple Computers introduces personal computers with disc drives.
- Intel introduce the 16-bit 8086 microprocessor, starting the x86 line of microprocessors. It has 29,000 transistors and runs at 10 MHz.
- The Italian company Olivetti and the Japanese company Casio both produce the first electronic typewriters with a memory capable of storing text.
- The U.S. company DEC introduces the VAX (virtual address extension) computer; able to run very large programs, it becomes an industry standard for scientific and technical applications.
- U.S. computer programmer John Barnaby develops the word processing program "Wordstar;" it becomes the most popular word processor in the early 1980s.
- U.S. librarian Alicia Page designs a computerized system for interlibrary loans; by 1985 her company makes $6 million a year.

Ecology

- The United States bans the use of chlorofluorocarbons (CFCs) as spray propellants in order to reduce damage to the ozone layer.

JANUARY

23 Sweden bans aerosol sprays because of their damaging effect on the environment. It is the first country to do so.

MARCH

27 When the offshore oil rig *Alexander Kielland* capsizes off Stravanger, Norway, 147 workers drown.

APRIL

16 A tornado kills 600 people in Orissa state, India.

AUGUST

- Toxic chemicals (PCBs, dioxins, and pesticides) leak into the basements of houses in the Love Canal neighborhood of Niagara Falls, New York. The site, an abandoned canal, was used as a chemical waste dump by the Hooker Chemicals and Plastics Corporation 1947–53. Residents are evacuated but their long-term exposure results in high rates of chromosomal damage and birth defects. It is the worst environmental disaster involving chemical waste in U.S. history.

SEPTEMBER

16 An earthquake at Tabas in Iran measuring 7.7 on the Richter scale kills 25,000 people.

Exploration

c. 1978 Satellite data begin to be useful in the discovery of new oil deposits.
- *Landsat 3* is launched, completing the initial series of land surveying satellites.
- Miniature nuclear reactors begin to be made to power radar satellites in the USSR.
- The *International Ultraviolet Explorer* is launched into geostationary orbit; it provides data on ultraviolet sources in outer space.

JUNE

15–November 2 Two Soviet cosmonauts spend a record 139 days and 14 hours in space.
27 The U.S. satellite *Seasat 1* is launched to measure the temperature of sea surfaces, wind and wave movements, ocean currents, and icebergs; it operates for 99 days before its power fails.

DECEMBER

- The Soviet spacecraft *Venera 11* and *12* soft-land on Venus and collect data on the lower atmosphere.
- The U.S. space probes *Pioneer Venus 1* (launched on May 20) and *2* (launched on August 8) go into orbit around Venus, the first relaying information about the atmosphere, the second taking radar photographs of the surface that reveal huge mountains and basins.

Health and Medicine

- Cyclosporin A is introduced as an immunosuppressant drug in organ transplant surgery; it is given Federal Drug Administration approval in 1983.

- Swiss biochemist Werner Arber and U.S. microbiologists Daniel Nathans and Hamilton Smith are jointly awarded the Nobel Prize for Physiology or Medicine for the discovery of restriction enzymes and their application to problems of molecular genetics.
- The French surgeon Gabriel Coscas is the first to make medical use of an argon laser—in ophthamology.

MAY

18 Despite intense Vatican opposition, Italy votes to make abortion legal in the first 90 days of pregnancy.

JULY

25 Louise Brown is born at Oldham Hospital, London, England; she is the first "test tube" baby. Having been unable to remove a blockage from her mother's Fallopian tube, gynecologist Patrick Steptoe and physiologist Robert Edwards removed an egg from her ovary, fertilized it with her husband's sperm, and reimplanted it in her uterus.

Science

- English anthropologist Alan Macfarlane publishes *The Origins of English Individualism*.
- English chemist Peter Mitchell receives the Nobel Prize for Chemistry for his studies of biological energy transfer and chemiosmotic theory.
- For his invention and application of the helium liquefier, Soviet physicist Pyotr Kapitza shares the Nobel Prize for Physics with U.S. physicists Arno Penzias and Robert Wilson for their discovery of microwave background radiation, which supports the Big Bang theory.
- The existence of Pluto's satellite Charon is established by U.S. astronomers James Christy and Robert Harrington.
- The foundations of the Aztec great temple under the center of Mexico City are discovered.

JUNE

22 U.S. astronomer James W. Christy discovers Charon, a moon orbiting Pluto.

Technology

- Japanese firm Nippon Electricity Company (NEC) introduce the Voice Data Input Terminal that can process 120 words spoken in groups of up to five words.
- The first optical-fiber telephone link in Europe is established between Martlesham and Ipswich in the UK.
- The Japanese company Konica introduces the first automatic-focus camera.
- The Swiss firm Pozel invents the self-heating flask; when the top is unscrewed the fluid inside is heated by a chemical reaction in a coil at the base.

JULY

4 Scientists at the Princeton Large Torus test reactor achieve a temperature of 60 million degrees Fahrenheit, and maintain it for one-twentieth of a second. It is hailed as a breakthrough for nuclear fusion.

Transportation

- Californian motorcyclist Donald Vesco sets a motorcycle speed record of 512.624 kph/318.598 mph, on his streamlined motorcycle *Lightning Bolt*.
- Core samples from the seabed are collected by the U.S. research vessel *Glomar Challenger* from a record depth of 7,042 m/23,104 ft.
- The Canadian government creates Via Rail, a crown corporation which takes over the passenger services of the Canadian Pacific Railway and Canadian National Railway.
- The Karakorum Highway through the Kunjerab Pass between Pakistan and China opens; it is the world's highest cross-border highway (4.6 km/2.8 mi).
- The Swedish company Saab mass-produces the Saab turbo—the first mass-produced car to have a turbo adapter.
- The U.S. Air Force introduces the F/A-18 Hornet, a single seat, carrier-based, all-weather fighter.
- The world's longest floating bridge, 1,850 m/6,074 ft, opens across the Demerara River in Guyana.

JANUARY

1 An Air India plane explodes and falls into the sea near Bombay killing 213 people in India's worst air disaster.

19 The last Volkswagen "Beetle" is produced at Emden, West Germany; 19.2 million of them have been manufactured since 1949. Production continues on a smaller scale in some countries, such as Brazil and Mexico.

MARCH

16 The U.S. oil tanker *Amoco Cadiz* runs aground off Brittany, France, spilling 1.62 million barrels of oil into the sea and contaminating 177 km/110 mi of coastline.

APRIL

4 During a violent storm several cargo ships in the Bay of Bengal sink and at least 1,000 people perish.

SEPTEMBER

25 A Pacific Southwest Boeing 727 collides with a Cessna while landing at Lindbergh Field, San Diego, California; all 135 people on board are killed, plus two in the Cessna and four on the ground; it is the worst mid-air collision in U.S. history.

OCTOBER

24 The U.S. Airline Deregulation Act provides for the phasing out of government control of the airline industry; routes are to be deregulated by 1982 and prices by January 1, 1985. The airlines respond by abandoning the less profitable shorter routes and competing on the longer, more profitable ones by cutting fares.

NOVEMBER

22 Two-hundred Vietnamese refugees die when their overcrowded fishing boat sinks off the coast of Malaysia.

ARTS AND IDEAS

Architecture

- The Sainsbury Centre at the University of East Anglia in England, designed by the English architect Norman Foster, is completed.

MAY

- Narita International Airport opens outside Tokyo, Japan.

Arts

- The "Paris–Berlin" exhibition is held at the Pompidou Center in Paris, France.
- The English artist Barry Flanagan creates the sculpture *As Night*.
- The extension to the National Gallery in Washington, D.C., designed by the Chinese-born architect I. M. Pei, is completed.
- The German neo-expressionist painter Anselm Keifer creates *Untitled*.
- The Italian artist Sandro Chia paints *Perpetual Motion*.

Film

- *Watership Down*, an animated feature-length adaptation of the novel about a community of rabbits by English writer Richard Adams, is released in the UK.
- *Poitin*, directed by Robert Quinn and starring Cyril Cusack, is released.
- *Time* declares the German movie industry "the liveliest in Europe," lionizing directors such as Rainer Werner Fassbinder, Werner Herzog, and Wim Wenders.
- The *film noir*, *The Driver*, directed by Walter Hill, is released in the United States, starring Ryan O'Neal, Bruce Dern, and Isabelle Adjani.
- The comedy *National Lampoon's Animal House*, directed by John Landis, is released in the United States. It stars John Belushi and Tim Matheson and becomes a cult classic.
- The comic movie *La Cage aux Folles* is released in France. It is directed by Edouard Molinaro and stars Ugo Tognazzi and Michel Serrault.
- The movie *California Suite*, directed by Herbert Ross, is released in the United States. It features an all-star cast including Jane Fonda, Alan Alda, Walter Matthau, Maggie Smith, Richard Pryor, Bill Cosby, and Michael Caine.
- The movie *Coma*, written and directed by Michael Crichton, is released in the United States, starring Geneviève Bujold and Michael Douglas, and based on the novel by Robin Cook.
- The movie *Coming Home*, directed by Hal Ashby, is released in the United States. About the experiences of Vietnam veterans, it stars Jane Fonda and Jon Voight, both of them in Academy Award-winning performances.
- The movie *Days of Heaven*, directed by Terrence Malick and photographed by Nestor Almendros, is released in the United States. It stars Richard Gere and Brooke Adams.
- The movie *Die Ehe der Maria Braun/The Marriage of Maria Braun* is released in West Germany. It is directed by Rainer Werner Fassbinder and stars Hanna Schygulla.
- The movie *Eraserhead*, directed by David Lynch, is released in the United States. It stars John Nance.
- The movie *Get Out Your Handkerchiefs*, directed by Bertrand Blier, is released in France, starring Gérard Depardieu, Patrick Dewaere, and Carole Laure.
- The movie *Heaven Can Wait*, starring Warren Beatty, is released in the United States. It is also produced, cowritten, and codirected by Beatty, and is a remake of the movie *Here Comes Mr Jordan*.
- The movie *Hostsonaten/Autumn Sonata*, directed by Ingmar Bergman, is released in Sweden. It stars Ingrid Bergman and Liv Ullmann.
- The movie *Interiors*, directed by Woody Allen, is released in the United States, starring Kristin Griffith, Marybeth Hurt, Richard Jordan, and Diane Keaton.
- The movie *Midnight Express*, directed by English filmmaker Alan Parker, is released in the United States. It stars Brad Davis.
- The movie *Pretty Baby*, directed by French filmmaker Louis Malle, is released in the United States. It stars Brooke Shields, Susan Sarandon, and Keith Carradine.
- The movie *Superman*, directed by Richard Donner, is released in the United States. It stars Christopher Reeve and Margot Kidder.
- The movie *The Chant of Jimmie Blacksmith*, directed by Fred Schepisi, is released in Australia. It stars Tommy Lewis.
- The movie *The Deer Hunter*, directed by Michael Cimino, is released in the United States. A harrowing account of the impact of the Vietnam War on a small Pennsylvanian community, it features an all-star cast including Robert De Niro, Christopher Walken, and Meryl Streep.
- The movie *Violette Nozière/Violette*, directed by Claude Chabrol, is released In France. It stars Isabelle Huppert and Stéphane Audran.
- The horror movie *Halloween*, directed by John Carpenter, is released in the United States. It stars Donald Pleasance and Jamie Lee Curtis.
- The musical movie *Grease* is filmed in the United States by Randal Kleiser, based on the stage musical and starring John Travolta and Olivia Newton-John. It spawns the best-selling singles "You're The One That I Want" and "Summer Nights."

APRIL

3 The 1977 Academy Awards take place. Best Actor: Richard Dreyfuss, for *The Goodbye Girl*; Best Supporting Actor: Jason Robards, for *Julia*; Best Actress: Diane Keaton, for *Annie Hall*; Best Supporting Actress: Vanessa Redgrave, for *Julia*; Best Picture: *Annie Hall*, directed by Woody Allen; Best Director: Woody Allen, for *Annie Hall*.

Literature and Language

- Chapman Pincher publishes *Inside Story*, an exposé of counterintelligence activities in the UK.

- English writer A. S. Byatt publishes her novel *The Virgin in the Garden.*
- English writer Anthony Burgess publishes his novel *1985.*
- English writer Ian McEwan publishes his novel *The Cement Garden.*
- English writer Martin Amis publishes his novel *Success.*
- The *Encyclopedia of American Foreign Policy* is published, edited by Alexander De Conde.
- The Irish-born British novelist Iris Murdoch publishes her novel *The Sea, The Sea,* which wins the Booker Prize.
- The Australian writer David Malouf publishes his novel *An Imaginary Life*
- The English writer Graham Greene publishes his novel *The Human Factor.*
- The English writer J. G. Farrell publishes his novel *The Singapore Grip.*
- The German writer Hans Enzensberger publishes his poetry collection *Der Untergang des Titanic/The Sinking of the Titanic.*
- The Polish-born U.S. poet Czesław Miłosz publishes his poetry collection *Bells in Winter.*
- The Polish-born U.S. novelist Isaac Bashevis Singer is awarded the Nobel Prize for Literature. In the same year he publishes his novel *Shosha.*
- The Pulitzer Prize for Biography is awarded to Walter Jackson Bate for *Samuel Johnson,* the Pulitzer Prize for Poetry is awarded to Howard Nemerov for *Collected Poems,* and the Pulitzer Prize for Fiction is awarded to James A. McPherson for *Elbow Room.*
- The U.S. writer Adrienne Rich publishes her poetry collection *The Dream of a Common Language.*
- The U.S. writer James Merrill publishes his poetry collection *Mirabell: Books of Number.*
- The U.S. writer John Cheever publishes *The Stories of John Cheever,* which wins a Pulitzer prize.
- The U.S. writer John Irving publishes his novel *The World According to Garp.*
- The U.S. writer Robert Hayden publishes his poetry collection *American Journal,* which includes "Elegies for Paradise Valley."

Music

- As punk declines, new wave music emerges into the mainstream, influenced particularly by U.S. bands such as Talking Heads, Blondie, and the Ramones. An early influence on punk, new wave's roots are in New York, New York, especially venues such as the club CBGB's.
- Disco music predominates, as the soundtrack to the movie *Saturday Night Fever* tops the album charts for six months.
- English punk rocker Sid Vicious is arrested in New York, New York, in connection with the fatal stabbing of his girlfriend, Nancy Spungen. He dies before going to trial, of a heroin overdose, on February 2.
- The British pop singer Kate Bush releases "Wuthering Heights" and the album *The Kick Inside.*
- The British pop singer Elvis Costello releases the album *This Year's Model.*
- The English artist David Hockney designs the settings for a production of Mozart's opera *The Marriage of Figaro* at Glyndebourne in England.

- The Estonian composer Arvo Pärt completes his orchestral work *Wenn Bach Bienen gezüchtet hätte/If Bach Had Kept Bees* (revised in 1980).
- The German-born U.S. composer Lukas Foss completes his *13 Ways of Looking at a Blackbird* for soprano, flute, piano, and orchestra, a setting of a poem by the U.S. writer Wallace Stevens.
- The Jamaican pop group Bob Marley and the Wailers releases the album *Kaya.*
- The opera *Le Grand Macabre/The Great Macabre* by the Hungarian-born Austrian composer György Ligeti is first performed, in Stockholm, Sweden. It was completed in 1972.
- The opera *Lear,* by the German composer Aribert Reimann, is first performed, in Munich, Germany. The German singer Dietrich Fischer-Dieskau is Lear. The opera is based on William Shakespeare's *King Lear.*
- The opera *Paradise Lost* by the Polish composer Krzysztof Penderecki is first performed, in Chicago, Illinois. The text, by Christopher Fry, is based on John Milton's epic poem.
- The Polish-born composer Andrzej Panufnik completes his orchestral work *Metasinfonia.*
- The U.S. composer Morton Feldman completes his orchestral work *Flute and Orchestra.*
- The U.S. pop group Village People releases the singles "YMCA" and "In the Navy," which the U.S. Navy considers adopting until it becomes aware of the band's homosexual associations.
- The U.S. pop singer Donna Summer releases "McArthur Park."

FEBRUARY
18 The Swedish pop group Abba releases *The Album.*
23 The 1977–78 Grammy Awards take place. Best Album: Fleetwood Mac's *Rumours*; Best Record: The Eagles' "Hotel California;" Best Male Pop Vocalist: James Taylor; Best Female Pop Vocalist: Barbra Streisand.

AUGUST
12 The U.S. pop group Talking Heads releases the album *More Songs About Buildings and Food.*

SEPTEMBER
23 The U.S. new wave group Blondie releases the album *Parallel Lines.*

DECEMBER
2 The U.S. pop group Chic releases "Le Freak" and the album *C'est Chic.*

Theater and Dance

- The ballet *Orpheus and Eurydice,* by the German choreographer Pina Bausch, to music by the 18th-century composer Christoph Gluck, is first performed, in Germany.
- The musical *Evita,* with text by Tim Rice and music by Andrew Lloyd Webber, receives its first performance, at the Prince Edward Theatre, in London, England. The song "Don't Cry for Me Argentina" becomes well known.
- The play *Betrayal,* by the English writer Harold Pinter, is first performed, at the National Theatre in London, England.

- The play *Buried Child*, by the U.S. writer Sam Shepard, is first performed, at the Theater de Lys in New York, New York.
- The play *Night and Day*, by the Czechoslovak-born English dramatist Tom Stoppard is first performed, at the Phoenix Theatre in London, England.
- The play *Plenty*, by the English writer David Hare, is first performed, at the National Theatre in London, England.
- The Pulitzer Prize for Drama is awarded to Donald L. Coburn for *The Gin Game*.

MAY

9 *Ain't Misbehavin'*, a musical that proves to be the year's most popular play, opens on Broadway in New York, New York.

Thought and Scholarship

- *The Times Atlas of World History* is published, edited by British historian Geoffrey Barraclough.
- British social historian Paul Thompson publishes *The Voice of the Past: Oral History*.
- English historian John M. Roberts publishes *The French Revolution*.
- French philosopher Jacques Derrida publishes *Eperons: les styles de Nietzsche/Spurs: Nietzsche's Styles*.
- The Pulitzer Prize for History is awarded to Alfred Chandler, Jr., for *The Invisible Hand: The Managerial Revolution in American Business*.
- The Pulitzer Prize for General Nonfiction is awarded to Carl Sagan for *The Dragons of Eden*.
- The U.S. historian Arthur Schlesinger, Jr., publishes *Robert Kennedy and his Times*.
- U.S. philosopher Daniel Dennett publishes *Brainstorms*.
- U.S. philosopher Nelson Goodman publishes *Ways of Worldmaking*.

SOCIETY

Education

MAY

2 A new core curriculum at Harvard University in Cambridge, Massachusetts, is designed to ensure "literacy in the major forms of intellectual discourse."

OCTOBER

6 Hannah Gray is inaugurated as the first woman president of a U.S. university, at the University of Chicago, in Chicago, Illinois.

Everyday Life

- *c.* 1978 Designer jeans, by designers such as Calvin Klein, become popular.
- While 4.2 million men earn more than $25,000 per year, just 140,000 women earn that much.
- About 45 legal and 500,000 illegal abortions are performed in Greece this year.

- Garfield the cat, the creation of U.S. cartoonist Jim Davis, appears in syndicated newspapers for the first time.
- In the United States, 49% of all women work, up from 31% in 1950; 48% of married women work, double the percentage in 1950.
- Kimberly-Clark launches Huggies, a range of fitted disposable diapers, to compete with Procter and Gamble's product Pampers.
- Life expectancy in the United States is 70.2 years for men and 77.8 years for women, up from 64.4 and 69.5 in 1945.
- Of companies in Japan, 91% have jobs inaccessible to women; 73% start males and females in the same positions at different salaries; 52% do not promote women; 77% have different retirement plans for men and women; and only 1.7% of companies provide childcare facilities.
- Texas Instruments launches "Speak and Spell," the first electronic toy with digital speech synthesis.
- The birth rate in the United States is 15.3 per 1,000 population, a decline from 24.1 in 1950.
- The Hispanic population in the United States reaches 19 million. Nearly half are of Mexican origin and half live in California or Texas.
- The queen's sister Princess Margaret obtains a divorce from her husband, the Earl of Snowdon, in the UK.
- Total legal immigration to the United States is 601,442, a jump of 200,000 people since 1975.
- Women as a percentage of university students: Iran, 33%; Kenya, 22%; Austria, 39%; Sri Lanka, almost 40%.

JANUARY

6 A picketer is killed in the United States in violent incidents during the coal miners' dispute.

MAY

26 Resorts International opens a casino on the boardwalk at Atlantic City, New Jersey, where voters approved casino gambling last year. This becomes the first U.S. casino outside the state of Nevada.

AUGUST

9–November 6 A newspaper strike in New York, New York, closes down the *New York Times*, the *New York Daily News* and the *New York Post*, in protest against layoffs.

OCTOBER

31 Iranian oil workers commence strike action.

NOVEMBER

24 Public lavatories for dogs are installed, with flush toilets, in Paris, France.

DECEMBER

31 The government of Iran admits that nearly all production and export of oil has been halted after the shah puts Iran under military control and oil workers have gone on strike, with foreign technicians leaving the country.

Media and Communication

- *Self*, a women's health and beauty magazine, begins publication.

- In the United States, 98% of households own television sets; 78% of these are color.
- The 1977–78 Emmy Awards for television are held. Best Drama Series: *The Rockford Files*; Best Comedy Series: *All in the Family*; Best Actor in a Drama: Ed Asner, for *Lou Grant*; Best Actress in a Drama: Sada Thompson, for *Family*; Best Actor in a Comedy: Carroll O'Connor, for *All in the Family*; Best Actress in a Comedy: Jean Stapleton, for *All in the Family*.
- The U.S. writer Armistead Maupin publishes *Tales of the City*, a series of stories that appeared in the *San Francisco Chronicle* from 1976 to 1977.

MARCH

16   Larry Flynt, owner and publisher of the U.S. sex magazine *Hustler*, is shot and wounded during his trial on an obscenity charge.

APRIL

2–May 3, 1991   *Dallas*, the first night-time soap opera, runs for 14 seasons and spawns many similar shows such as *Dynasty*.

SEPTEMBER

12–June 10, 1983   *Taxi*, a sitcom about a taxi company set in New York, New York, starts on U.S. television. It stars Judd Hirsch, Danny De Vito, Marilu Henner, and Christopher Lloyd.

14–August 12, 1982   *Mork and Mindy*, a spin-off from the comedy series *Happy Days*, starts on U.S. television. It stars Robin Williams as a bizarre alien trying to fit in on earth.

OCTOBER

29   It is revealed that the former Information Department funded *The Citizen*, a progovernment English-language newspaper, in South Africa.

Religion

- In Britain, the General Synod of the Church of England rejects the ordination of women to the priesthood and episcopate.

BIRTHS & DEATHS

JANUARY
13   Hubert Humphrey, Democrat politician, 38th vice president of the United States 1963–69 and senator from Minnesota, dies in Waverly, Minnesota (66).
14   Kurt Gödel, Austrian-born U.S. mathematician and logician, dies in Princeton, New Jersey (71).

FEBRUARY
11   James B. Conant, U.S. scientist and president of Harvard University, and U.S. High Commissioner for West Germany after World War II, dies in Hanover, New Hampshire (84).

MARCH
1   Paul Scott, English novelist most of whose novels, including the *Raj Quartet*, were set in India, dies in London, England (57).
19   Faith Baldwin, U.S. romantic novelist, dies in Stamford, Connecticut (84).
31   Charles Herbert Best, Canadian physiologist whose work contributed to the discovery of insulin, dies in Toronto, Canada (79).

MAY
1   Aram Khachaturian, Georgian-born Soviet composer, dies in Moscow, USSR (74).
14   William P. Lear, U.S. industrialist, known for his Lear business jets, dies in Reno, Nevada (75).
16   Robert Menzies, Australian prime minister 1939–41 and 1949–66, dies in Melbourne, Australia (83).

26   Tamara Karsavina, Anglo-Russian ballerina who partnered Nijinsky in Michel Fokine's avant-garde ballets, dies in Beaconsfield, Buckinghamshire, England (93).

AUGUST
2   Carlos Chávez, Mexican composer and conductor who combined elements of folk songs with modern techniques, dies in Mexico City, Mexico (79).
6   Edward Durell Stone, U.S. head of a large architectural company who designed modern buildings around the world, dies in New York, New York (76).
6   Pope Paul VI, pope 1963–78, dies in Castel Gandolfo, Italy (80).
21   Charles Eames, U.S. furniture designer and architect, dies in St.-Louis, Missouri (71).
22   Jomo Kenyatta, African nationalist statesman, first prime minister 1963–64, then president of independent Kenya 1964–78, dies in Mombassa, Kenya (89).
26   Charles Boyer, French-born stage and screen actor usually cast as the typical Gallic lover, dies in Phoenix, Arizona (80).

SEPTEMBER
9   Jack L. Warner, U.S. film producer who in 1923 established Warner Brothers with his three brothers, which pioneered talking pictures and produced such classics as *Casablanca*, *A Streetcar Named Desire*, and *My Fair Lady*, dies (86).

17   Willy Messerschmitt, German aircraft designer and engineer, dies in Munich, Germany (80).
19   Etienne Gilson, French Christian philosopher and international scholar of medieval thought, dies in Cravant, France (94).
28   Pope John Paul I, pope for 38 days in 1978, dies in Rome, Italy (65).

NOVEMBER
7   Gene Tunney, U.S. boxer who defeated Jack Dempsey to become world heavyweight champion, dies in Greenwich, Connecticut (80).
8   Norman Rockwell, U.S. popular artist and illustrator of covers for the *Saturday Evening Post*, dies in Stockbridge, Massachusetts (84).
15   Margaret Mead, U.S. anthropologist who studied the nonliterate peoples of Oceania, dies in New York, New York (76).
19   Giorgio de Chirico, Greek-born Italian painter, one of the founders of the Metaphysical Style, dies in Rome, Italy (90).

DECEMBER
8   Golda Meir, Israeli politician, a founder and fourth prime minister 1969–74 of the state of Israel, dies in Jerusalem, Israel (80).
14   Salvador de Madariaga, Spanish author, historian, and diplomat involved in the League of Nations, dies in Locarno, Switzerland (92).

AUGUST

26 Albino Luciani, Patriarch of Venice, is elected pope. He takes the name John Paul I.

OCTOBER

16 Following the deaths of Pope Paul VI on August 6 and his successor John Paul I on September 28, Karol Wojtyła, archbishop of Kraków, Poland, is elected as John Paul II, the first non-Italian pope since 1522.

NOVEMBER

18 U.S. cult leader Jim Jones leads 913 followers, most of them Americans, and including 276 children, in a mass suicide at the so-called People's Temple in Jonestown, Guyana. The slaughter is precipitated by the murder of U.S. representative Leo J. Ryan and four associates, who had visited Jonestown to investigate charges of religious coercion.

Sports

- Americans buy 55 million pairs of running shoes.
- It is agreed that golfers from continental Europe will be allowed to compete alongside British and Irish players in Ryder Cup matches against the United States, in an attempt to produce a more even contest. Since the competition was launched in 1927, the United States had only lost three times.
- James Fixx's book *The Complete Book of Running* captures and intensifies the national enthusiasm for getting fit through jogging in the United States.
- Roger Penske and U. E. "Pat" Patrick form CART (Championship Auto Racing Teams, Inc.) as a rival organization to the United States Auto Club. The following year they inaugurate what is now known as the PPG Indy Car Series.

JANUARY

1 Sportswriters pick Notre Dame as college football's national champions for the 1977 season.

15 The Dallas Cowboys beat the Denver Broncos 27–10 in Super Bowl XII at the Louisiana Superdome in New Orleans, Louisiana; it is the first time the Super Bowl has been held indoors.

FEBRUARY

10 U.S. national figure skating champions are: Linda Fratianne; Charles Tickner; Tai Babilonia and Randy Gardner, pairs; Stacey Smith and John Summers, dance.

15 U.S. boxer Leon Spinks beats Muhammad Ali on points in Las Vegas, Nevada, to win the undisputed world heavyweight boxing title.

18 The first Hawaii Ironman triathlon competition is held at Oahu, Hawaii.

APRIL

8–June 27 The Kenyan athlete Henry Rono sets world records in the men's 10,000 meters, 5,000 meters, 3,000 meters, and 3,000-meters steeplechase at separate events.

MAY

- It is reported that the Soviet president Leonid Brezhnev has given permission for the first golf course to be built in Russia.

8 Reinhold Messner of Italy and Peter Habeler of Austria become the first climbers to reach the summit of Mt. Everest, the world's highest mountain, without bottled oxygen.

13 The Montreal Canadiens beat the Boston Bruins at ice hockey to win the Stanley Cup.

21 The Washington Bullets beat the Seattle SuperSonics to win the National Basketball Association (NBA) championship.

29–September 3 Al Unser is the first driver to win the United States Auto Club "Triple Crown," comprising of the Indianapolis 500, the Schaefer 500, and the California 500.

JUNE

June 6 Affirmed, ridden by U.S. jockey Steve Cauthen, wins the Kentucky Derby, Preakness Stakes, and Belmont Stakes to become the 11th horse to capture the U.S. Triple Crown.

8 The New Zealand-born British yachtswoman Naomi James arrives in Dartmouth, England, on her yacht *Express Crusader*, completing the first solo nonstop round-the-world voyage via Cape Horn by a woman.

10 Larry Holmes of the United States beats fellow countryman Ken Norton on points in Las Vegas, Nevada, in the United States, and wins the World Boxing Council heavyweight title.

25 The host nation, Argentina, wins the soccer World Cup, beating the Netherlands 3–1 in the final in Buenos Aires.

JULY

29 Penny Dean, a 23-year-old Californian, swims the English Channel in a new world record time of 7 hours 42 minutes.

SEPTEMBER

10 Mario Andretti becomes the first U.S. driver to win the Formula One Drivers' World Championship since Phil Hill in 1961.

10 The U.S. tennis player Jimmy Connors defeats Björn Borg of Sweden in the final of the men's singles at the U.S. Open championships, held for the first time at Flushing Meadows, New York. Chris Evert of the United States wins the women's singles title for the fourth successive year.

17 Muhammad Ali beats fellow U.S. boxer Leon Spinks on points in a World Boxing Association world heavyweight title bout in New Orleans, Louisiana, becoming the first boxer to regain a world heavyweight title twice.

20 The Republic of Ireland plays Northern Ireland in a soccer international for the first time. The match, in Dublin, Ireland, finishes scoreless.

OCTOBER

- For the second year running the New York Yankees beat the Los Angeles Dodgers in baseball's World Series.

10–11 The U.S. men's tennis team retains the Davis Cup by beating Great Britain 4–1 in the final. It is Great Britain's first appearance in the final since 1937.

DECEMBER

22 In college American football, the U.S. Naval Academy defeats Brigham Young University (BYU) 23–16 in the inaugural Holiday Bowl, at the Jack Murphy stadium, San Diego, California.

1979

POLITICS, GOVERNMENT, AND ECONOMICS

Business and Economics

- Oil prices double under the impact of the Iranian revolution.
- The Dutch company Philips and the Japanese company Sony work collaboratively to develop the compact disc (CD); tiny pits on the plastic are read by laser to reproduce sound or other information. CDs are first marketed in 1982.
- The European Monetary System (EMS) and its Exchange Rate Mechanism (ERM) are established to regulate European currency fluctuations.

JANUARY
- Coca-Cola is marketed for the first time in the People's Republic of China.

MARCH
13 The European Monetary System (EMS) becomes operational.

AUGUST
8 The U.S. federal government offers to save the Chrysler motor company from bankruptcy, but its proposed loan is far less than the $1.5 billion requested.

SEPTEMBER
10 The British Leyland motor company announces 25,000 redundancies in Britain.

OCTOBER
- The Federal Reserve Board inspires panic among investors by raising the discount rate from 11% to 12% while tightening the money supply. Over the next few days, stock and bond prices plunge and banks raise their prime interest rates to 14.5%.
14 France imposes a prohibitive tariff on British lamb exports in defiance of the European Court.

DECEMBER
31 World oil prices are 88% higher at the end of 1979 than at the beginning of the year.

Colonization

FEBRUARY
22 St. Lucia, in the West Indies, gains its independence from Britain.

JULY
11 The Gilbert Islands, in the Pacific, gain their independence from Britain with the new name Kiribati.

OCTOBER
27 St. Vincent and the Grenadines, in the West Indies, gain their independence from Britain.

Human Rights

- Abortion is legalized in France.
- Egyptian feminist Nawal El Saadawi publishes *The Hidden Face of Eve: Women in the Arab World*, which reveals female genital mutilation and discusses the traditional emphasis on virginity and family honor.
- New laws in Pakistan called the Hadood Ordinances ban women's testimony in serious criminal trials and require four adult males as witnesses to prove rape charges. If the accused is not convicted, under the Qazf Ordinance a woman may receive 80 lashes for false testimony.
- Portuguese journalist Maria Antonia Palla produces a documentary on abortion and is tried for "outrage against public morals" and for inciting women to crime.
- The women's movement is launched in Japan to campaign for equal women's rights to government housing, bank loans, benefits, and tax reductions.
- Woman march in protest in Teheran, Iran, against Ayatollah Khomeini's legislation that impinges on women's rights and obliges them to wear the *chador*, a heavy veil over the face, in public.

SEPTEMBER
- Karen Stevenson, of the University of North Carolina, becomes the first black American woman to be awarded a Rhodes scholarship.

OCTOBER
- In a reprise of the Boston busing violence of 1974, white students attack buses carrying black students to integrated public schools.

Politics and Government

- In the case *United Steelworkers of America v. Weber*, the U.S. Supreme Court rules that companies can run voluntary training courses for black Americans even if white workers are excluded.
- The first International Agreement dealing with transnational air pollution is signed by European members of the United Nations.
- U.S. law student Ted Bundy is convicted on several charges, including the murder of a 12-year-old girl, but

he is believed to have killed at least 36 females, both adult and children. Bundy is sentenced to death, with the sentence being carried out in 1989.

JANUARY

1 The United States and China open full diplomatic relations.

4 The shah of Iran appoints Shakpur Bakhtiar prime minister as a concession to popular discontent.

7 Vietnamese troops and Cambodian rebels capture the Cambodian capital, Phnom Penh, and oust the Khmer Rouge regime.

16 The shah of Iran and his family flee to Egypt, driven into exile by supporters of the Shiite Muslim leader Ayatollah Khomeini.

20 Tanzanian troops invade Uganda after border clashes.

26–29 Islamic revolutionary violence erupts in the Iranian capital, Tehran.

31 Giulio Andreotti's government resigns in Italy, ending the "historic compromise" between Christian Democrats and communists.

FEBRUARY

1 The Shiite Muslim leader Ayatollah Khomeini returns to Iran from Paris, France, where he has been in exile since 1964.

8 U.S. President Jimmy Carter announces that he has suspended military aid to Nicaragua in an effort to compel Nicaraguan president Anastasio Somoza to negotiate with the Sandinista rebels.

12 Prime Minister Shakpur Bakhtiar of Iran flees the country. A Revolutionary Council loyal to the Shiite Muslim leader Ayatollah Khomeini is created, with Mehdi Bazargan as premier designate.

14 Protesters seize the U.S. embassy in the Iranian capital, Tehran.

17–March 5 China makes punitive incursions into Vietnam.

19 President Zia ur-Rahman's Bangladesh Nationalist Party wins the general election in Bangladesh.

20 Eleven members of a loyalist gang known as the "Shankill butchers" are sentenced for 19 sectarian murders in the Northern Ireland capital, Belfast, following a sensational trial.

23 Rhodesian aircraft attack rebel camps in neighboring Zambia.

23–March 16 North and South Yemen wage war; the former is supported by the USSR, the latter by the West.

MARCH

12 The left wing New Jewel Movement under Maurice Bishop seizes power from Prime Minister Eric Gairy in Grenada.

15 A civilian government committed to democratization takes office in Brazil.

15 The Central Treaty Organization (CENTO) defense pact collapses when Turkey withdraws, following the withdrawal of Iran and Pakistan on March 12.

22 The Irish Republican Army (IRA) assassinates the British ambassador to the Netherlands Richard Sykes in The Hague.

26 Egypt and Israel sign a peace treaty at the White House in Washington, D.C.

27 Hafizullah Amin is appointed prime minister of Afghanistan.

28 The British Labour government loses a House of Commons motion of no confidence by 310–311. The prime minister James Callaghan calls a general election.

30 A bomb planted by the Irish National Liberation Army kills Airey Neave, the Conservative spokesman on Northern Ireland, in the House of Commons parking garage, London, England.

31 Malta cuts its military ties with Britain.

APRIL

1 Following a referendum, Iran is declared an Islamic Republic by the Shiite Muslim leader Ayatollah Khomeini.

2 The publication of the interim Erasmus Report on the scandal of unauthorized expenditure by the former Information Department in South Africa clears serving politicians.

7 The former Iranian prime minister Amir Hovaida is executed in a purge of the shah's former officials in Iran.

10–20 Multiracial elections are held in Rhodesia.

11 The Ugandan capital, Kampala, falls to Tanzanian and rebel forces and the president Idi Amin flees the country.

13 Yusufu Lule succeeds Idi Amin as president of Uganda.

16 Connie Mulder, former head of the Information Department, is expelled from the National Party in South Africa following the "Muldergate" scandal over unauthorized expenditure by the department.

18 Over 100 children are killed in a demonstration against school uniforms in Bangui, Central African Empire (now Central African Republic).

MAY

2 Riots break out in Longwy, France, over the proposed closure of steel plants.

3 The Conservatives under Margaret Thatcher win the British general election with 339 seats. Labour has 269, the Liberals 11, and other parties 16.

4 The British Conservative leader Margaret Thatcher becomes Britain's first woman prime minister.

5 Rebel guerrillas in El Salvador capture the French, Venezuelan, and Costa Rican embassies.

10 Congress rejects President Jimmy Carter's plan for gasoline rationing in the United States.

22 Pierre Trudeau's Liberal government loses the Canadian general election. Joe Clark is appointed prime minister of a Progressive Conservative minority government.

28 Greece signs the Treaty of Accession to the European Economic Community (Common Market), for entry in 1981.

JUNE

1 Bishop Abel Muzorewa is appointed prime minister of the renamed Zimbabwe Rhodesia (formerly Southern Rhodesia).

3–4 The communists lose ground in the Italian general election.

4 Fred Akuffo is deposed as president of Ghana in a military coup led by Flight-Lieutenant Jerry Rawlings.

4 President B. J. Vorster of South Africa resigns after the final Erasmus Report shows that he knew about illegal activities at the Information Department under Connie Mulder.

7 The first direct elections for the European Parliament are held, with a low turnout. In Britain, the Conservatives win 60 seats, Labour 17, and the Liberals none.

14–26   Sandinista rebels in Nicaragua close in on the capital, Managua.

15–18   A summit meeting in Vienna, Austria, between the U.S. and Soviet presidents Jimmy Carter and Leonid Brezhnev ends with the signing of the SALT II treaty limiting nuclear weapons between the two countries.

20   President Yusufu Lule of Uganda loses a confidence vote in parliament and is replaced by Godfrey Binaisa.

JULY

2   The Bavarian Christian Social Union leader Franz Josef Strauss is designated opposition candidate for the post of West German chancellor in the 1980 general election.

5   Iran nationalizes its industries.

9   Hilla Limann is elected president of Ghana.

11   The Janata Party in India loses overall control of the government through defections.

13   Palestinian guerrillas attack the Egyptian embassy in the Turkish capital, Ankara, killing three people.

15   Morarji Desai, the leader of the Janata Party, resigns as prime minister of India.

16   Saddam Hussein becomes president of Iraq.

16   The U.S. president Jimmy Carter proposes radical measures to deal with the energy crisis, speaking of "a crisis of confidence that strikes at the very heart, soul, and spirit of our national will."

17   The Nicaraguan dictator Anastasio Somoza flees to the United States, to escape Sandinista rebels and other opponents of his government.

19   In an effort to revitalize his administration, U.S. president Jimmy Carter shakes up his Cabinet, accepting the resignations of five cabinet officers.

19   Left wing Sandinista rebels take the Nicaraguan capital, Managua, and set up a new government.

28   Charan Singh becomes prime minister of India.

29   Argentina and Britain reestablish diplomatic relations.

AUGUST

1–8   The Commonwealth Conference in Lusaka, Zambia, proposes a conference to settle the Zimbabwe Rhodesia problem.

3   A military coup in Equatorial Guinea deposes President Francisco Macias Nguema.

3   Supporters of the Shiite Muslim leader Ayatollah Khomeini dominate the new constituent assembly in Iran.

5   Mauritania renounces its claims to Western Sahara and makes peace with the Polisario nationalist guerrillas of the region.

15   Andrew Young, the U.S. ambassador to the United Nations, resigns when it is revealed that he has had unauthorized contact with the Palestine Liberation Organization (PLO).

27   Eighteen soldiers and a civilian are killed in an Irish Republican Army (IRA) attack at Warrenpoint in Northern Ireland.

SEPTEMBER

6   Thirty thousand refugee "boat people" from Vietnam are allowed to settle in the United States.

16   Non-Socialist parties retain power with a majority of one in the Swedish general election.

16   President Nur Muhammad Taraki of Afghanistan is overthrown in a coup, to be replaced by Hafizullah Amin.

20   The former president of the Central African Empire (now Central African Republic) David Dacko overthrows his uncle, Emperor Jean-Bédel Bokassa, and the country reverts to republic status.

24–29   Francisco Macias Nguema, former president of Equatorial Guinea, is found guilty of genocide and executed.

OCTOBER

- A civilian government takes power in Nigeria after 13 years of military rule.

- The U.S. government approves the sale of 25 million metric tons of wheat and corn–a new record–to the USSR over the next year.

- U.S. president Jimmy Carter signs legislation creating the Department of Education, the 13th Cabinet office. The law transforms the Department of Health, Education, and Welfare into the Department of Health and Human Service.

7   The Liberal Democrats win a narrow victory in Japan's general election.

8   Eschel Rhoodie of South Africa's former Information Department is sentenced to six years' imprisonment for fraud.

14   The Israeli foreign minister General Moshe Dayan resigns in protest against Israel's stand on Palestinian autonomy.

15   The offices of *The Times of Malta* are fire-bombed by demonstrators celebrating Dom Mintoff's 30 years as Labour leader and prime minister.

16   President Zia ul-Haq of Pakistan cancels the general election and bans political activity.

23   The Czech dramatist and human-rights activist Václav Havel and five other Czech dissidents are convicted of subversion.

25   Referendums in Spain approve the devolution of power to Catalonia and the Basque provinces.

26   The president of South Korea Park Chung Hee is assassinated by his secret service.

30   The French labor minister Robert Boulin commits suicide following accusations of a scandal over property purchases.

NOVEMBER

- The "Tokyo Round" of negotiations of the General Agreement on Tariffs and Trade (GATT) is successfully completed.

4   Iranian students seize the U.S. embassy in Tehran, taking 63 U.S. citizens and 40 others hostage. They demand the return of the shah from the United States for trial.

6   Ayatollah Khomeini's Islamic Revolutionary Council takes power from the provisional government in Iran.

7   Senator Edward Kennedy announces his challenge to the U.S. president Jimmy Carter for the Democratic nomination in the 1980 presidential election.

12   The U.S. president Jimmy Carter imposes an embargo on Iranian oil in response to the seizure of U.S. hostages in Iran.

13   Ronald Reagan, former governor of California, declares his candidacy for the Republican nomination in the 1980 U.S. presidential election.

19   The U.S. House of Representatives votes to provide $1.56 billion aid to the Chrysler motor company.

20–23 Around 200 armed militants seize the Grand Mosque in Mecca, Saudi Arabia, apparently in protest at the corruption of the Saudi regime. The siege is ended by Saudi Arabian troops.

28 The Syrian ambassador to the United Nations Hammoud El-Choufi resigns from his post, accusing Hafez al-Assad's government of corruption, repression, and opportunism.

29–30 The British prime minister Margaret Thatcher at the European Economic Community summit in Dublin, in the Republic of Ireland, demands a rebate of British contributions to the Community.

DECEMBER

2 A mob burns the U.S. embassy in the Libyan capital, Tripoli.

5 Jack Lynch resigns as prime minister of the Republic of Ireland.

7 Charles Haughey becomes prime minister of the Republic of Ireland.

10 Mother Teresa of Calcutta is awarded the Nobel Peace Prize for her work with abandoned children and the dying.

10 The rebel parliament in Zimbabwe Rhodesia concludes, ending Rhodesia's unilateral declaration of independence (UDI).

12 Lord Soames, a former British Conservative minister, arrives in Zimbabwe Rhodesia to oversee the formal end of British rule.

13 Joe Clark's Progressive Conservative government in Canada is defeated in a confidence debate. Clark calls a general election.

18 The Canadian Liberal leader Pierre Trudeau reverses his decision to retire from the party leadership.

21 The Lancaster House Agreement is signed in London, England, providing for an end to the civil war in Zimbabwe Rhodesia and the introduction of majority rule.

25 Soviet troops invade Afghanistan in a bid to halt the civil war and protect Soviet interests.

27 President Hafizullah Amin of Afghanistan is killed in a coup d'état and replaced by the communist leader Babrak Karmal.

28 A cease-fire in the civil war, provided for in the Lancaster House Agreement of December 21, comes into force in Zimbabwe Rhodesia.

SCIENCE, TECHNOLOGY, AND MEDICINE

Computing

- Motorola introduces the 8 MHz 68000 microprocessor; the first with a 32-bit register, it becomes the basis of the Macintosh computer.
- The first spreadsheet program for personal computers, VisiCalc, leads to the expansion in business use of PCs.

Ecology

- Indonesia is hit by a tsunami 10 m/32 ft high; nearly 200 people are killed.

JANUARY

16 In eastern Iran an earthquake kills an estimated 1,000 people.

APRIL

10 About 8,000 homes are destroyed and more than 60 people are killed in Wichita Falls, Texas, when a tornado with six vortices rips through the town.

JULY

11 The International Whaling Commission bans the hunting of sperm whales.

19 Over 1 million barrels of crude oil are estimated to spill into the Caribbean when the oil tankers *Atlantic Express* and *Aegean Captain* collide off Trinidad and Tobago.

AUGUST

29–September 7 Hurricane David ravages the Caribbean and the southern United States. On the island of Dominica 60,000 people (three-quarters of the population) are left homeless and 60% of agricultural production is destroyed; in the Dominican Republic between 600 and 1,000 people are killed and 150,000 are left homeless.

SEPTEMBER

12–15 Alabama and Florida are hit by Hurricane Frederick, only days after Hurricane David; it is the most expensive U.S. hurricane to date, with damages estimated to exceed $2.3 billion. Early forecasting and warnings, however, lead to extensive evacuation, and only five people die.

NOVEMBER

1 After an accident in Galveston Bay, Texas, the *Burmah Agate* catches fire and spills 62,000 barrels of oil into the bay.

Exploration

- The satellite *HEAO 2* (High Energy Astronomy Observatory; later renamed the Einstein Observatory) discovers numerous X-ray sources.
- The Soviet space station *Salyut 6* (launched September 29, 1977) is the first to be docked by two other spacecraft.
- The U.S. space probe *Pioneer 11* (launched in 1973) travels through the rings of Saturn to within 20,900 km/13,000 mi. The rings are found to be made of ice-covered rocks. Two additional rings and high-energy particles within Saturn's magnetosphere are also discovered.
- U.S. space probes *Voyager 1* (March) and 2 (July) fly past Jupiter; *Voyager 1* discovers a ring around Jupiter and two moons (the 15th and 16th).

FEBRUARY

25–August 19 Soviet cosmonauts Vladimir Lyakhov and Valery Ryumin set a new record for time spent in space of 175 days, 36 min.

JULY

- The U.S. space station *Skylab 1* falls back to Earth after traveling 140 million km/87 million mi in orbit since 1973.

DECEMBER

4   The European Space Agency's first *Ariane* rocket is launched from the Guiana Space Center in Kourou, French Guiana; it is designed to deploy satellites into orbit.

Health and Medicine

- British obstetrician Ian Donald is the first to use ultrasound to examine a fetus.
- H. Goodman and J. Baxter of the University of California, Berkeley, together with D. V. Goeddel of Genentech, announce the biosynthetic production of a human growth hormone.
- Japanese researcher Ryochi Naito carries out the first experiment on a human being using artificial blood—he injects himself with the milky-looking fluid.
- Portugal extends free medical aid to all residents.
- Researchers at Edinburgh University, Scotland, successfully clone the hepatitis B viral antigen, opening the way for a successful vaccine.
- South African-born U.S. physicist Allen Cormack and English engineer Godfrey Hounsfield are jointly awarded the Nobel Prize for Physiology or Medicine for the development of computerized axial tomography (CAT), an improved method of obtaining X-ray images of internal bodily organs.
- The Center for Disease Control in Atlanta, Georgia, reports the first cases of the disease later known as AIDS.
- The U.S. surgeon general publishes a 1,200-page report confirming that cigarette smoking causes cancer and is linked with numerous other diseases.

MARCH

- U.S. scientist Herbert Needleman publishes an influential study indicating that high levels of lead in children's blood and teeth are associated with lower IQ scores.

APRIL

- Anthrax spores are accidentally released at the Microbiology and Virology Institute in Sverdlovsk, Russia, USSR. Tight censorship is imposed but a 30-sq-km/12-sq-mi area is believed to be contaminated and several hundred people die after inhaling the spores.

Science

- French anthropologist François Lévêque discovers a badly crushed Neanderthal skeleton near the village of St.-Césaire in France. Dated at about 35,000 years old, it is one of the latest Neanderthals known and is of special interest because it is found with tools previously assumed to belong to the Cro-Magnon culture.
- Physicists in Hamburg at DESY (Deutsches Elektron Synchroton) observe gluons—particles that carry the strong nuclear force which holds quarks together.
- The European Molecular Biology Laboratory in Heidelberg, West Germany, opens.

- The IRAM array telescope begins operation at Plateau de Bruce, France; its four 15-m/19.2-ft dishes make it the largest millimeter telescope in the world.
- The Multiple Mirror Telescope begins operation on Mt. Hopkins, Arizona; it focuses the light from six 180-cm/70-in telescopes to form one image, giving the light-gathering power of a single 4.5-m/15.7-ft telescope; it becomes the prototype for larger optical telescopes.
- U.S. astronomers John Eddy and Aram Boornazian announce that the sun is shrinking at a rate of 1.5 m/5 ft per hour.
- U.S. chemist Herbert Brown and German chemist Georg Wittig receive the Nobel Prize for Chemistry for use of boron and phosphorus compounds, respectively, in organic syntheses.
- U.S. physicist Arthur Ruoff subjects the gas xenon to a pressure of 320,000 atmospheres and obtains metallic xenon; it opens the way to the production of metallic hydrogen used in superconductivity research.
- U.S. physicists Sheldon Glashow and Steven Weinberg and Pakistani physicist Abdus Salam receive the Nobel Prize for Physics for their unification of the weak and electromagnetic interaction.

Technology

- Broadcasts via satellite begin in Canada.
- In a controlled chemical explosion, U.S. steel manufacturers weld glass to steel to prevent it from corroding.
- Matsushita in Japan develops and patents the first pocket-sized flat-screen television set.
- Philips/MCA launches the LaserVision video disc system in the United States.
- The 3 m/9.8 ft NASA Infrared Telescope Facility (IRTF) telescope and the 3.8 m/12.5 ft UK Infrared Telescope both begin operation on Mauna Kea, Hawaii.
- The 3M Corporation of St. Paul, Minnesota, launches Post-It notes; the special adhesive that allows the notes to stick temporarily and without marking was invented by accident.
- The Ideal Toy Co. in New York, New York, begins manufacturing the Rubik cube, invented by a Hungarian lecturer in architectural design, Professor Erno Rubik.
- The UK General Post Office installs the first digital telephone exchange in the UK at Glenkindle near Aberdeen, Scotland.
- The United States' 72 nuclear power reactors generate 12% of the nation's power supply.
- The Xerox Corporation introduces the Ethernet, an office communications network.
- U.S. astronomers D. Walsh, R. Carswell, and R. Weymann discover the first gravitational lens—a massive foreground object that bends the light from background objects.
- U.S. sports-equipment distributor Paul Fireman obtains the U.S. license to manufacture British Reebok training shoes. Reebok will go on to challenge Nike's market lead.

FEBRUARY

13   IBM introduces teletext, in the United States, a system that enables word processors to communicate over a great distance.

MARCH

29 Radioactive material escapes from the nuclear power station at Three Mile Island, Pennsylvania, when the reactor overheats. Fearing a meltdown and the release of radioactive cesium, 144,000 people are evacuated from the immediate area. The accident halts the growing trend toward reliance on nuclear energy in the United States; 11 orders for new reactors are immediately canceled, with more canceled the following year.

JUNE

3 Pemex Oil's offshore oil-well *Ixtoc 1* blows up, releasing an estimated 3 million barrels of crude oil into the Gulf of Mexico. The largest oil spill ever recorded, the slick spreads 965 km/600 mi to Texas, contaminating Gulf fisheries and beaches. The well defies capping efforts and it continues to disgorge oil until March 24, 1980.

JULY

1 Akio Morita, chairman of Sony, launches the Walkman, a small portable, personal tape recorder, at a price of $165; he is reputed to have invented the product because his own children were fond of loud music.

SEPTEMBER

23 A rally protesting against nuclear weapons draws 200,000 people to Central Park in New York, New York.

Transportation

- A maglev (magnetic levitation) train sets a speed record of 517 kph/321 mph, in Japan.
- Tachographs, instruments which monitor and regulate distance and speed traveled by long-distance truck drivers, are first introduced on heavy trucks in the UK. They are used as a safety measure to help prevent accidents by prohibiting drivers from driving too far without breaks.
- The Dai-shimizu rail tunnel is completed at Honshu, Japan; 22 km/14 mi long, it is the longest rail tunnel in the world.

MAY

25 A DC-10 aircraft crashes at Chicago, Illinois, after an engine falls off; 273 people are killed in the worst airplane crash in U.S. history to date. It results in the grounding of all DC-10s in the United States between May 29 and July 13.

JUNE

13 U.S. cyclist Brian Allen's human-powered carbon-fiber aircraft *Gossamer Albatross* crosses the English Channel in 2 hours and 49 minutes.

NOVEMBER

28 An Air New Zealand DC-10 crashes into Mt. Erebus, Antarctica, killing 257 sightseers.

ARTS AND IDEAS

Architecture

- The Nurek Dam across the Vakhsh River in Tajikistan, USSR, is completed; at 300 m/984 ft high, it is the highest earth-filled dam in the world.
- The Overseas Chinese Banking Corporation Headquarters in Singapore, designed by B. E. P. Akitek, with I. M. Pei as consultant, is completed.
- The Piazza d'Italia, designed by the U.S. architect Charles Moore, is completed in New Orleans, Louisiana. The flamboyant use of a range of classical styles heralds the confident arrival of postmodernist architecture.

Arts

- The Austrian-born English art critic E. H. Gombrich publishes *The Sense of Order: A Study in the Psychology of Decorative Art*.
- The exhibition "Paris–Moscou" is held at the Pompidou Center in Paris, France. It features works of Russian avant garde.
- The French government accepts a large gift of works from the Picasso estate, that will form the basis of a Picasso museum to be established in Paris, France.
- The Italian art critic Achille Bonito Olivia coins the term "Transavanguardia" for a style of Italian art in the 1970s that seeks a return to figurative and expressive painting. Artists in this movement include Sandro Chia and Francesco Clemente.
- The portrait *Juan de Pareja*, by the 17th-century Spanish artist Velázquez, is sold at Christie's for $5.5 million, the most expensive painting bought at an auction to date.
- The Swiss artist Jean Tinguely sculpts *Klamauk*.
- The U.S. artist Judy Chicago completes the book *The Dinner Party*, one of the leading expressions of feminist art.
- The U.S. artist Philip Guston paints *The Coat*.

Film

- *Don Giovanni*, a movie of Mozart's opera, is released. It is directed by U.S. filmmaker Joseph Losey.
- *The Warriors*, a U.S. movie directed by Walter Hill about teenage gangs in New York, New York, provokes violent outbursts in movie theaters and takes more than $2 million in its first two weeks.
- The movie '10', by U.S. director Blake Edwards, is released, starring Dudley Moore, Julie Andrews, and Bo Derek.
- The movie *Alien*, directed by British filmmaker Ridley Scott, is released in the United States. It stars Sigourney Weaver.
- The movie *All that Jazz*, directed by Bob Fosse, is released in the United States. It stars Roy Scheider and Jessica Lange.
- The movie *Apocalypse Now*, directed by Francis Ford Coppola, is released in the United States. Based on

Joseph Conrad's *Heart of Darkness*, it stars Martin Sheen, Marlon Brando, and Robert Duvall.
- The movie *Being There*, directed by Hal Ashby, is released in the United States. Based on the novel by Jerzy Kosinski, it stars Peter Sellers and Shirley MacLaine.
- The movie *Breaking Away*, directed by Peter Yates, is released in the United States. It stars Dennis Christopher, Dennis Quaid, Daniel Stern, and Jackie Earle Haley.
- The movie *Breaker Morant*, directed by Bruce Beresford, is released in Britain, starring Edward Woodward and based on a controversial court martial incident during the Boer War.
- The movie *Buffet Froid/Cold Buffet*, directed by Bertrand Blier, is released in France, featuring his father, Bernard Blier, and Gérard Depardieu.
- The movie *Cristo si e Fermato a Eboli/Christ Stopped at Eboli*, directed by Francesco Rosi, is released in Italy. It is based on the novel by Carlo Levi and stars Gian Maria Volonté.
- The movie *Die Blechtrommel/The Tin Drum*, directed by Volker Schlöndorff, is released in West Germany. Based on the novel by Günter Grass, it stars David Bennent.
- The movie *Kramer vs Kramer*, directed by Robert Benton, is released in the United States. It stars Dustin Hoffman and Meryl Streep.
- The movie *Mad Max*, directed by George Miller, is released in Australia. It stars Mel Gibson.
- The movie *Manhattan*, cowritten, directed by, and starring Woody Allen, is released in the United States. Diane Keaton, Michael Murphy, Meryl Streep, and Mariel Hemingway costar.
- The movie *Monty Python's Life of Brian*, directed by Terry Jones, is released in the United States and the UK. It stars the Monty Python team Graham Chapman, John Cleese, Terry Gilliam, Eric Idle, Terry Jones, and Michael Palin. In the United States, criticism from religious quarters causes the movie to be withdrawn. This leads to further unrest, as citizen groups protest that the move constitutes censorship.
- The movie *Moonraker*, directed by Lewis Gilbert, is released in the United States. It stars Roger Moore as James Bond.
- The movie *My Brilliant Career*, directed by Gillian Armstrong, is released in Australia. It stars Judy Davis and Sam Neill.
- The movie *Norma Rae*, directed by Martin Ritt, is released in the United States, starring Sally Field.
- The movie *Nosferatu, Phantom der Nacht/Nosferatu the Vampyre* is released in West Germany. It is directed by Werner Herzog and stars Klaus Kinski, Isabelle Adjani, and Bruno Ganz. Herzog's movie *Woyzeck* is also released in West Germany. Based on the play by Georg Büchner, it stars Klaus Kinski and Eva Mattes.
- The movie *Quadrophenia*, directed by Franc Roddam, is released in the UK. It stars Phil Daniels, Mark Wingett, and Sting.
- The movie *Star Trek: The Motion Picture*, directed by Robert Wise, is released in the United States. It stars Leonard Nimoy and William Shatner.

- The movie *Tess*, directed by Polish-born U.S. filmmaker Roman Polanski, is released. Based on the novel by Thomas Hardy, it stars Nastassja Kinski and Peter Firth.
- The movie *The China Syndrome* is released in the United States. Directed by James Bridges, it stars Jane Fonda, Jack Lemmon, and Michael Douglas.
- The movie *The Muppet Movie*, directed by James Frawley, is released in the United States, starring the Muppets—including Kermit the Frog, Miss Piggy, Gonzo, and Fozzie—as well as a host of guest stars.
- The movie *The Rose*, directed by Mark Rydell, is released in the United States. Based on the life of singer Janis Joplin, it stars Bette Midler and Alan Bates.
- The movie *Wise Blood*, directed by John Huston, is released in the United States, starring Brad Dourif. It is based on the novel by Flannery O'Connor.
- The movie version of the musical *Hair*, directed by Czech-born U.S. filmmaker Miloš Forman, is released in the United States. It stars John Savage, Trent Williams, and Beverly D'Angelo.

FEBRUARY

22 At the West Berlin Film Festival, the Soviet Union and its communist allies protest against the showing of *The Deer Hunter*, about the war in Vietnam, by withdrawing from the festival.

APRIL

4 The 1978 Academy Awards take place. Best Actor: Jon Voight, for *Coming Home*; Best Supporting Actor: Christopher Walken, for *The Deer Hunter*; Best Actress: Jane Fonda, for *Coming Home*; Best Supporting Actress: Maggie Smith, for *California Suite*; Best Picture: *The Deer Hunter*, directed by Michael Cimino; Best Director: Michael Cimino, for *The Deer Hunter*.

MAY

24 At the Cannes Film Festival, the Palme d'Or is awarded jointly to Volker Schlöndorff for the German movie *Die Blechtrommel/The Tin Drum* and to Francis Ford Coppola for the U.S. movie *Apocalypse Now*.

OCTOBER

2 Universal and Walt Disney lose their court case against Sony-Betamax when personal home use of video recording equipment is ruled legal.

Literature and Language

- *The Collected Poems of Kingsley Amis* are published.
- English novelist Alan Sillitoe publishes *The Storyteller*.
- The Rhodesian-born English writer Doris Lessing publishes her novel *Shikasta*.
- English writer Frederick Forsyth publishes his novel *The Devil's Alternative*.
- English writer Kingsley Amis publishes his novel *Jake's Thing*.
- English writer Piers Paul Read publishes his novel *A Married Man*.
- English writer Tom Sharpe publishes his novel *The Wilt Alternative*.
- English writer William Golding publishes his novel *Darkness Visible*.
- Irish writer Seamus Heaney publishes his *Field Work*.
- South African novelist André Brink publishes his novel *A Dry White Season*.

- The Barbadan writer Edward Kamau Braithwaite publishes his poetry collection *Mother Poem*.
- The Czech writer Milan Kundera publishes his work *The Book of Laughter and Forgetting*, in Paris, France. Kundera is stripped of his citizenship by the Czech government in his absence, for his support of liberalization.
- The English writer Craig Raine publishes his poetry collection *A Martian Sends a Postcard Home*.
- The English writer J. G. Ballard publishes his novel *The Unlimited Dream Company*.
- The Italian writer Italo Calvino publishes *Se una notte d'inverno un viaggiatore/If on a Winter's Night a Traveler*.
- The Nobel Prize for Literature is awarded to the Greek poet Odysseus Elytis.
- The Pulitzer Prize for Biography is awarded to Leonard Baker for *Days of Sorrow and Pain: Leo Baeck and the Berlin Jews*, the Pulitzer Prize for Poetry is awarded to Robert Penn Warren for *Now and Then: Poems 1976–1978*, and the Pulitzer Prize for Fiction is awarded to John Cheever for *The Stories of John Cheever*.
- The Scottish writer Muriel Spark publishes her novel *Territorial Rights*.
- The South African writer Nadine Gordimer publishes her novel *Burger's Daughter*.
- The Swiss writer Max Frisch publishes his novel *Der Mensch erscheint im Holozän/Man in the Holocene*.
- The Trinidadian writer V. S. Naipaul publishes his novel *A Bend in the River*.
- The U.S. writer Amiri Baraka (before 1968 called LeRoi Jones) publishes his poetry collection *AM/TRAK*.
- The U.S. writer Bernard Malamud publishes his novel *Dubin's Lives*.
- The U.S. writer Joan Didion publishes *The White Album*, a collection of essays.
- The U.S. writer Louis Zukofsky publishes his poetry collection *A*.
- The U.S. writer Norman Mailer publishes his "nonfiction" novel *The Executioner's Song*, based on the execution of the murderer Gary Gilmore.
- The U.S. writer Paul Theroux publishes his travel book *The Old Patagonian Express*.
- The U.S. writer Peter Matthiessen publishes *The Snow Leopard*, describing his travels through Nepal. It is awarded a National Book Award.
- The U.S. writer Philip Roth publishes his novel *The Ghost Writer*.
- The U.S. writer Robert Bly publishes his poetry collection *Visiting Emily Dickinson's Grave and Other Poems*.
- The U.S. writer Tobias Wolff publishes his collection of short stories *In the Garden of the North American Martyrs*.
- The U.S. writer William Styron publishes his novel *Sophie's Choice*.
- U.S. writer John Updike publishes his novel *The Coup*.

- As a reaction against the ubiquitous disco music, rap is created by urban black musicians.
- Digital recording starts, with Stephen Stills the first artist to be recorded digitally.
- Record companies introduce innovative marketing techniques to boost sales of singles, such as the limited edition 12-inch colored vinyl disk.
- The English composer Michael Tippett completes his String Quartet No. 4.
- The English pop singer Rod Stewart releases "Do Ya Think I'm Sexy?"
- The final version of the opera *Lulu*, by the Austrian composer Alban Berg, is first performed, at the Opéra in Paris, France. Its earlier version (with Act 3 incomplete) dates from 1935. In this 1979 version the score of Act 3 was orchestrated by the Austrian composer Friedrich Cerha.
- The French composer Maurice Ohana completes his opera *Livres de Prodiges/Books of Miracles*.
- The German composer Wolfgang Rihm completes his opera *Jacob Lenz*.
- The U.S. composer Jacob Druckman completes his orchestral work *Aureole*.
- The U.S. composer Morton Feldman completes his orchestral work *Violin and Orchestra*.

JANUARY

27 The British pop singer Elvis Costello releases the album *Armed Forces*.

FEBRUARY

16 The 1978–79 Grammy Awards take place. Best Pop Group: The Bee Gees; Best Album: *Saturday Night Fever*; Best Male Pop Vocalist: Barry Manilow; Best Female Pop Vocalist: Anne Murray.

MAY

12 The U.S. disco singer Donna Summer releases the album *Bad Girls*.
31 The British pop group Supertramp releases the album *Breakfast in America*.

JULY

21 The Canadian pop singer Neil Young releases the album *Rust Never Sleeps*.

SEPTEMBER

1 The Swedish pop group Abba releases "Voulez-Vous."

NOVEMBER

3 The British pop group the Police releases "Message in a Bottle" and "Walking on the Moon" and the album *Regatta de Blanc*.

DECEMBER

3 At a concert given by the British pop group The Who in Cincinnati, Ohio, 11 people are crushed to death and 28 injured.
15 The British progressive rock group Pink Floyd releases the concept album *The Wall*. A movie is later made by the British director Alan Parker, starring Bob Geldof.
16 The U.S. disco music star Gloria Gaynor releases "I Will Survive."

Music

- Album sales drop for the first time in 25 years in the United States.

Theater and Dance

- The musical *Sweeney Todd*, with lyrics and music by the U.S. composer Stephen Sondheim, receives its first

performance, at the Uris Theater, New York, New York.
- The play *Amadeus*, by the English writer Peter Shaffer, is first performed, at the Olivier Theatre in London, England, directed by Peter Hall. It is based on the life of the composer Mozart.
- The play *Bent*, by the U.S. writer Martin Sherman, is first performed, at the Royal Court Theatre in London, England.
- The play *Cloud Nine*, by the English writer Caryl Churchill, is first performed, at the Royal Court Theatre in London, England.
- The play *On Golden Pond*, by the U.S. writer Ernest Thompson, is first performed, at the Apollo Theater in New York, New York.
- The play *The Man from Muckinupin*, by the Australian writer Dorothy Hewett, is first performed.
- The play *Travelling North*, by the Australian writer David Williamson, is first performed.
- The play *Wings*, by the U.S. writer Arthur Kopit, is first performed, at the Lyceum Theater in New York, New York.
- The Pulitzer Prize for Drama is awarded to Sam Shepard for *Buried Child*.

Thought and Scholarship

- British psychologist Michael Rutter and others publish *Fifteen Thousand Hours*.
- English historian Charles Phythian-Adams publishes *Desolation of a City: Coventry and the Urban Crisis of the Late Middle Ages*.
- French philosopher Jean-François Lyotard publishes *The Postmodern Condition*.
- Palestinian-American critic Edward Said publishes *The Question of Palestine*.
- The Pulitzer Prize for History is awarded to Don E. Fehrenbacher for *The Dred Scott Case: Its Significance in Law and Politics*.
- The Pulitzer Prize for General Nonfiction is awarded to Edward O. Wilson for *On Human Nature*.
- U.S. historian Christopher Lasch publishes *The Culture of Narcissism*.
- U.S. philosopher Richard Rorty publishes *Philosophy and the Mirror of Nature*.
- U.S. philosopher Thomas Nagel publishes *Mortal Questions*.
- U.S. writer Adrienne Rich publishes her critical work *On Lies, Secrets, and Silence*.

SOCIETY

Education

SEPTEMBER
18 The Inner London Education Authority (ILEA) in the UK votes to ban corporal punishment from London's schools by February 1981.

NOVEMBER
- Former Coca-Cola president Robert W. Woodruff donates $100 million to Emory University in Atlanta, Georgia.

Everyday Life

- Of women aged over 64 in Canada, almost 60% live at or below the poverty level.
- The British House of Lords has 51 women out of 1,107 members, and the House of Commons has 19 women out of 635 members.
- The Danish parliament has 49 women out of 179 members.
- The U.S. Family Planning Association announces that the Pill is the most frequently used method of birth control.

MARCH
10 A general strike begins in Nicaragua.

APRIL
19 Michelle Triola is awarded $104,000 in her palimony suit against actor Lee Marvin.

AUGUST
10 Workers in the British engineering industry impose a four-day week.
27 British engineering workers step up industrial action by imposing a three-day week. The strike ends on October 4 with a compromise pay agreement.

NOVEMBER
19–28 Strikes at some British Leyland car plants in Britain follow the dismissal of Derek Robinson ("Red Robbo"), a union shop steward.

DECEMBER
15 Canadian journalists Chris Haney and Scott Abbott invent the board game Trivial Pursuit; after initial commercial reluctance, a breakthrough comes when they sign a deal in 1982 with Selchow & Richter, the developers of Scrabble. This earns them an estimated $200 million.

Media and Communication

- Argentine Jacobo Timerman, publisher of the newspaper *La Opinion*, is deported following his criticism of the ruling junta.
- The 1978–79 Emmy Awards for television are held. Best Drama Series: *Lou Grant*; Best Comedy Series: *Taxi*; Best Actor in a Drama: Ron Leibman, for *Kaz*; Best Actress in a Drama: Mariette Hartley, for *The Incredible Hulk*; Best Actor in a Comedy: Carroll O'Connor, for *All in the Family*; Best Actress in a Comedy: Ruth Gordon, for *Taxi*.
- The British Post Office initiates a "Prestel" system whereby subscribers, using telephones, computers, and televisions, can make airline, hotel, and theater reservations as well obtain rail, flight, and stock information.
- There are now 150 million television sets in the United States.

JANUARY

26–August 16, 1985 *The Dukes of Hazzard*, about Southern outlaws Bo and Luke Duke, and their efforts to outwit lawman "Boss" Hogg, starts on U.S. television. It stars Tom Wopat, John Schneider, and Sorrell Brooke.

FEBRUARY

11 *Elvis*, a television movie about Elvis Presley, starring Kurt Russell, is shown on U.S. television.

APRIL

28 *I Know Why the Caged Bird Sings*, an adaption of Maya Angelou's autobiography starring Constance Good and Esther Rolle, is shown on U.S. television.

SEPTEMBER

22–July 31, 1984 *Hart to Hart*, a crime series featuring a millionaire husband-and-wife detective team, starts on U.S. television. It stars Robert Wagner and Stephanie Powers.

BIRTHS & DEATHS

JANUARY

3 Conrad Hilton, U.S. entrepreneur and founder of the Hilton Hotel Corporation, dies in Santa Monica, California (91).

5 Charlie Mingus, U.S. jazz composer, bassist, pianist, and bandleader, dies in Cuernavaca, Mexico (56).

5 Max Born, German physicist who worked in the field of subatomic particles, dies in Göttingen, Germany (96).

9 Pier Luigi Nervi, Italian engineer and architect, dies in Rome, Italy (87).

26 Nelson Rockefeller, 41st vice president of the United States and governor of New York 1959–73, dies in New York, New York (70).

FEBRUARY

2 Sid Vicious (born John Simon Ritchie), British punk rocker who played with the Sex Pistols, dies of a drug overdose in New York, New York (22).

7 Josef Mengele, the "Angel of Death," Nazi doctor who managed the gas chambers at Auschwitz extermination camp and conducted experiments on inmates, dies near São Paulo, Brazil (67).

8 Dennis Gabor, Hungarian-born British electrical engineer, the inventor of holography, dies in London, England (78).

12 Jean Renoir, French film director of both the silent and sound eras, son of the impressionist painter Pierre-Auguste Renoir, dies in Los Angeles, California (84).

MARCH

15 Léonide Massine, Russian ballet dancer and innovative choreographer, dies in Cologne, West Germany (82).

16 Jean Monnet, French political economist and diplomat who rebuilt France's economy after World War II, dies in France (90).

APRIL

4 Zulfikar Ali Bhutto, Pakistani former president and prime minister, overthrown in a coup and sentenced to death, is hanged in Rawalpindi, Pakistan (51).

MAY

8 Talcott Parsons, U.S. sociologist, dies in Munich, Germany (76).

22 Kurt Jooss, German dancer, choreographer, and teacher who worked in England during the Hitler era, dies in Herlbronn, Germany (78).

28 Mary Pickford, Canadian-born U.S. film actress of the silent era, known as "America's Sweetheart," dies in Santa Monica, California (86).

JUNE

1 Werner Forssmann, German heart surgeon who invented the technique of heart catheterization, dies in Schopfheim, West Germany (75).

11 John Wayne, U.S. film actor who usually starred in westerns and war films, dies in Los Angeles, California (72).

JULY

8 Robert Burns Woodward, U.S. chemist who first synthesized chlorophyll, tetracycline, cholesterol, cortisone, vitamin B12, and other complex organic substances, dies in Cambridge, Massachusetts (62).

10 Arthur Fiedler, conductor of the Boston Pops orchestra for 50 years, dies in Brookline, Massachusetts (84).

12 Carmine Galante, leader of organized crime in New York, New York, for over 30 years, is assassinated there (69).

29 Herbert Marcuse, German-born U.S. political philosopher, dies in Starnberg, West Germany (81).

AUGUST

2 Thurman Munson, U.S. baseball player, catcher for the New York Yankees, dies in a plane crash in Canton, Ohio (38).

12 Ernst Boris Chain, German-born British biochemist who worked on the isolation and purification of penicillin, dies in Ireland (73).

16 John Diefenbaker, Canadian prime minister 1957–63, a member of the Progressive Conservative Party, dies in Ottawa, Canada (83).

22 James T. Farrell, U.S. novelist, short-story writer, and critic, dies in New York, New York (75).

27 Lord Louis Mountbatten, British statesman, naval commander, and last viceroy of India, is murdered by an Irish Republican Army terrorist bomb in his boat in Donegal Bay, off the coast of Ireland (79).

SEPTEMBER

10 Agostinho Neto, Angolan poet, physician, and first president of the People's Republic of Angola 1975–79, dies in Moscow, USSR (56).

22 Otto Frisch, Austrian-born physicist who named the process of nuclear fission, dies in Cambridge, England (74).

OCTOBER

6 Elizabeth Bishop, U.S. poet, dies in Boston, Massachusetts (68).

17 S(idney) J(oseph) Perelman, U.S. humorist who wrote film scripts for the Marx Brothers and shared an Academy Award for the script of *Around the World in Eighty Days*, dies in New York, New York (75).

26 Park Chung Hee, president of South Korea 1963–79, whose policies were responsible for South Korea's rapid economic expansion, dies in Seoul, South Korea (61).

30 Barnes Wallis, British military aeronautical designer and engineer who invented the "dambuster" bomb, dies in Leatherhead, Surrey, England (92).

DECEMBER

30 Richard Rodgers, U.S. composer and songwriter of musical comedy who had a long partnership with Oscar Hammerstein, dies in New York, New York (77).

25 One of Canada's most important newspapers, the 111-year-old *Montreal Star*, ceases publication eight months after a lengthy strike over the introduction of new technology and staffing practices.

Religion

• The General Synod of the Church of England refuses to allow female priests ordained abroad to celebrate holy communion.

SEPTEMBER

7 Robert Runcie is appointed to replace Donald Coggan as archbishop of Canterbury. He is enthroned on March 25, 1980.

29–October 1 Pope John Paul II makes the first ever papal visit to Ireland.

Sports

• In auto racing, Rick Mears wins the inaugural CART (later PPG Indy Car) World Series.
• The National Basketball Association (NBA) in the United States adopts the three-point field goal for the first time.
• The Panamanian-born U.S. jockey Laffit Pincay Junior is the first jockey to win $8 million in prize money in a season in the United States.
• The U.S. sports goods company Nike introduces the first air-cushioned trainer, the Nike Tailwind; the technology for the product was developed from aerospace research into lunar landings.
• Tom Ferguson is the Professional Rodeo Cowboys Association All-Around World Champion Cowboy for a record sixth successive year.

JANUARY

1 Sportswriters select Alabama and the University of Southern California as champions of the 1978 college football season.

21 The Pittsburgh Steelers beat the Dallas Cowboys 35–31 in Super Bowl XIII to become the first team to win three Super Bowls.

FEBRUARY

2 U.S. figure skating champions are: Linda Fratianne; Charles Tickner; Tai Babilonia and Randy Gardner, pairs; Stacey Smith and John Summers, dance.

MARCH

22 The World Hockey League, set up in 1972 as a rival to the National Hockey League, folds. However, four of its teams, the Edmonton Oilers, Québec Nordiques, New England (later Hartford) Whalers, and Winnipeg Jets join the National Hockey League (NHL).

APRIL

12 U.S. golfer Fuzzy Zoeller becomes the first player to win the Masters golf tournament in his first appearance.

MAY

13–21 The Montreal Canadiens beat the New York Rangers by four games to one to win the Stanley Cup for the fourth successive year.

20–June 1 The Seattle SuperSonics, in a reverse of the previous year's results, beat the Washington Bullets to win the National Basketball Association (NBA) championship.

JUNE

6 Troy, ridden by the Scottish jockey Willie Carson, wins the 200th English Derby at Epsom, Surrey, England.

17 Hale Irwin wins his second of three U.S. Open golf championships; he also wins in 1974 and 1990.

JULY

7 The U.S. tennis player Billie Jean King wins a record 20th Wimbledon championship title when she partners the U.S. player Martina Navratilova to victory in the ladies' doubles.

22 The Spanish golfer Severiano Ballesteros wins the British Open at Royal Lytham St. Anne's, becoming the first golfer from continental Europe to win the championship since Arnaud Massy of France in 1907.

AUGUST

14 Seventeen people die in the south Irish Sea when a hurricane hits boats participating in the Fastnet yacht race.

15 The English runner Sebastian Coe becomes the first person to hold the outdoor world records for the 800 meters, the mile, and the 1,500 meters simultaneously.

SEPTEMBER

• Lee Elder becomes the first black American professional golfer to represent the United States in the Ryder Cup.

9 At 20 years, 205 days old, the U.S. tennis player John McEnroe becomes the youngest winner of the men's singles at the U.S. Open championships since Pancho Gonzales of the United States in 1948; and at 16 years, 271 days, fellow U.S. player Tracey Austin becomes the youngest-ever winner of the women's singles.

OCTOBER

10–17 The Pittsburgh Pirates beat the Baltimore Orioles four games to three to win the World Series, just the second team in baseball history to rally from a three to one deficit.

20 The black U.S. boxer John Tate wins the World Boxing Association heavyweight title in Pretoria, South Africa; defeating the white South African Gerrie Coetzee on points over 15 rounds before 80,000 spectators, the largest-ever live audience for a heavyweight title fight.

NOVEMBER

24 The first random drug tests of professional soccer players at club matches take place in England.

1980

POLITICS, GOVERNMENT, AND ECONOMICS

Business and Economics

- General Motors in the United States announces its first annual loss since 1921.
- The *Encyclopedia of American Economic History* is published.
- The U.S. businesswoman Michaela Walsh founds Women's World Banking, which provides loans to women with no credit or collateral. By 1991, the organization helps over 500,000 women entrepreneurs worldwide.

JUNE
- Britain becomes a net exporter of oil with its own North Sea operations.

Colonization

APRIL
18 Zimbabwe Rhodesia gains its independence from Britain, and is renamed "Zimbabwe." Its first president is the Reverend Canaan Banana.

JULY
30 The New Hebrides, in the Pacific, become independent from Britain and France within the Commonwealth as Vanuatu.

Human Rights

- Women in Iraq earn the right to vote and hold office.

MARCH
6 Novelist Marguerite Yourcenar becomes the first female member of the Académie Française.

JUNE
17–21 Over 30 people die in South Africa in clashes with police in black townships around Cape Town.

Politics and Government

- Government regulations in France reduce university autonomy, placing restrictions on the number and type of courses.

- The "Abscam" ("Arab Scam") investigation in the United States, in which Federal Bureau of Investigation agents pose as Arab oilmen, finds several members of Congress willing to take bribes.
- The trucking industry is deregulated in the United States.

JANUARY
- In his State of the Union address, U.S. president Jimmy Carter pledges to safeguard oil lanes in the Persian Gulf, by force if necessary.
- U.S. president Jimmy Carter responds to the Soviet invasion of Afghanistan by enacting a series of punitive measures. Principal among these are the cancellation of an expected shipment of 17 million metric tons of grain to the Soviet Union.
1 The United Nations secretary-general Kurt Waldheim visits the Iranian capital Tehran to seek release of the U.S. hostages.
3 The Congress (I) Party, led by Indira Gandhi, wins a sweeping victory in the Indian general election.
6 The total death toll in Northern Ireland since 1969 exceeds 2,000.
8 The U.S. president Jimmy Carter describes the Soviet invasion of Afghanistan in December 1979 as the greatest threat to peace since World War II.
22 The Soviet Union sends the dissident physicist Andrey Sakharov into internal exile at Gorky (now Nizhny Novgorod).
23 Israel completes its withdrawal from 18,130 sq km/ 7,000 sq mi of the Egyptian Sinai peninsula.
25 Abolhassan Bani-Sadr becomes president of Iran.
29 Canada announces the escape of four U.S. diplomats from Iran on Canadian passports.

FEBRUARY
12 The Brandt report, *North–South: A Programme for Survival*, advocates a fundamental change in the relations between the industrial northern hemisphere of the world and the poor southern hemisphere.
14 Polling begins in Zimbabwe Rhodesia for 20 white seats in the new parliament, in accordance with the Lancaster House Agreement of December 21, 1979.
18 The Liberals defeat the Progressive Conservatives in the Canadian general election. The Liberal leader, Pierre Trudeau, becomes prime minister.
22 Martial law is proclaimed in the Afghan capital Kabul, as resistance to the Soviet invaders continues.
24–March 11 A United Nations commission visits Iran but fails to see the U.S. hostages.
26 Israel and Egypt exchange ambassadors for the first time.
27 Polling begins in Zimbabwe Rhodesia for 80 black seats in the new parliament, in accordance with the Lancaster House Agreement of December 21, 1979.

MARCH

4 Robert Mugabe's Zimbabwe African National Union (ZANU) wins the Zimbabwe Rhodesian general election.

11 President Zia ul-Haq crushes an attempted military coup in Pakistan.

11 Robert Mugabe, leader of the Zimbabwe African National Union (ZANU), forms a coalition government in Zimbabwe Rhodesia, with Joshua Nkomo, leader of the Zimbabwe African People's Union (ZAPU), as minister of home affairs.

16 Martial law is proclaimed in the city of Aleppo as political violence sweeps Syria.

18 The United States bans the sale of high technology equipment to the USSR.

19 The British government declares that a private consortium may construct the Channel Tunnel, but that no public money will be forthcoming.

24 Archbishop Oscar Romero of El Salvador is shot dead while celebrating mass in the capital, San Salvador.

31 A Basque regional parliament opens in Guernica, northern Spain.

APRIL

6 Ten thousand Cubans seek political asylum in the Peruvian embassy in Havana, Cuba.

7 Iraqi artillery bombards the Iranian border town of Oweisa.

7 The United States bans trade with Iran, breaks off relations, and expels Iranian diplomats in the face of the continuing hostage crisis.

9 The Israelis carry out a major raid on Palestinian positions in southern Lebanon.

10 Spain agrees to reopen the border with the British dependency of Gibraltar, closed since 1969 because of the dispute over sovereignty.

14 Israel and Egypt decide to hold negotiations on Palestinian autonomy.

24 The Republican congressman John Anderson announces his independent candidature for the U.S. presidency.

Iran–Iraq War (1980–90)

1980

April 7 Iraqi artillery bombards the Iranian border town of Oweisa.

September 22 Iraq invades Iran in an attempt to gain control of the Shatt al-Arab waterway.

1981

June 7 Taking advantage of the conflict, Israeli warplanes destroy a nuclear installation near Baghdad.

1982

July 13 Iranian troops enter Iraq, aiming to take the city of Basra at the head of the Persian Gulf. The offensive is repulsed by Iraqi forces.

1984

February 11 Iraq commences the bombing of nonmilitary targets in Iran.

February 27 Iraq announces a blockade of the main Iranian oil terminal at Kharg Island and threatens to attack all oil tankers loading there.

March 4 The speaker of the Iranian parliament claims that 400 Iranian soldiers have been killed by Iraqi chemical weapons in the course of the Iran–Iraq war.

May 24 Iranian war planes attack oil tankers off the coast of Saudi Arabia, in an apparent effort to widen the Iran–Iraq war. On May 27, the United States sends Stinger antiaircraft missiles to Saudi Arabia in case of Iranian attack.

June 10 Iraq seeks United Nations supervision of its agreement with Iran to stop attacks on civilian areas.

1985

October 5 In the first major consignment of the arms-for-hostages deal, Iran receives 508 U.S.-made TOW missiles.

1986

February 19 Iran temporarily captures the Iraqi oil port of Faw, giving it control of the mouth of the Shatt al-Arab waterway.

1987

February 5 Iran launches a missile attack on Baghdad. On February 19, a truce is agreed in the "war of cities," in which both sides have inflicted damage on heavily populated areas.

May 17 Two Iraqi Exocet missiles hit USS *Stark* in the Gulf and kill 37 crewmembers.

July 20 The United Nations Security Council adopts Resolution 598 calling on Iran and Iraq to implement an immediate cease-fire in their long-running war.

September 11 The United Nations secretary-general Javier Pérez de Cuellar begins a peace mission to end the war.

November 8–11 At an Arab summit meeting in Jordan, Syria's president Hafez al-Assad agrees to end his country's political and military support of Iran in its conflict with Iraq.

1988

March 16 The Iraqi air force drops chemical bombs on Halabja, killing at least 4,000 people.

July 3 USS *Vincennes* shoots down an Iran Air airbus with 290 people on board.

August 8 Iraq and Iran announce a cease-fire in their prolonged war.

1990

August 15 Iraq makes peace with Iran, accepting all Iranian terms for a formal end to the war.

25 A U.S. commando mission to rescue U.S. hostages in Iran fails, with the loss of eight lives.

27 A young girl named Naheed leads a group of children protesting against the Soviet occupation of Afghanistan; 70 children are killed.

28 The European Economic Community summit in Luxembourg fails to reach agreement on Britain's demand for a rebate payment against contributions.

30 Crown Princess Beatrix of the Netherlands succeeds her mother, Juliana, as queen.

30 Iranian terrorists seize the Iranian embassy in London, England, demanding the release of political prisoners in Iran.

May

1 The Soviet Union's traditional May Day parade is boycotted by the ambassadors of 15 countries because of the Soviet invasion of Afghanistan.

5 Britain's Special Air Service (SAS) storms the Iranian embassy in London, England, retaking it from the terrorists who seized the building on April 30.

8 The Schlebusch Commission in South Africa publishes its report introducing constitutional changes. The Senate is abolished, the president is empowered to nominate 20 members of the House of Assembly, and an advisory president's council is formed.

10 A Franco-African agreement is signed to form a 30-nation French-speaking commonwealth.

14 President Anwar Sadat of Egypt discontinues talks with Israel on Palestinian autonomy.

18 China successfully conducts its first long-range missile test.

18 The European Economic Community imposes trade sanctions against Iran.

24 Foreign ministers of the European Economic Community agree on a rebate to Britain of £710 million.

26 George Bush abandons his bid for the Republican nomination for the U.S. presidency.

26 The South African government arrests 52 clergymen, including Timothy Bavin, bishop of Johannesburg, and Desmond Tutu, General Secretary of the South African Council of Churches.

28 The first Islamic parliament, the Majlis, opens in Iran.

30 The New Hebrides (now Vanuatu), in the Pacific, appeal for British and French help to suppress a rebellion by French settlers and plantation workers on the island of Espíritu Santo.

June

3 A nuclear alert is given in the United States when a computer error indicates a missile attack by the Soviet Union.

11 The Libyan head of state Colonel Moamer al-Khaddhafi halts the "liquidation" of Libyan exiles, except those collaborating with the United States, Israel, or Egypt.

22 About 1,000 people die in ethnic violence in Tripura, northeast India.

25 Basque terrorists explode bombs on the Costa Blanca to disrupt the Spanish tourist trade.

26 The French president Valéery Giscard d'Estaing discloses France's capability to produce the neutron bomb.

July

1 An increase in meat prices prompts industrial unrest in Poland.

2 South African troops withdraw from Angola after a three-week raid on guerrilla bases.

17 The Republican Party convention in Detroit nominates Ronald Reagan as U.S. presidential candidate. He chooses George Bush as running mate for vice president.

24 An Anglo-French force occupies the island of Espíritu Santo in the New Hebrides (now Vanuatu) to help suppress a local rebellion.

27 The inauguration of Fernando Belaúnde Terry as president of Peru ends 12 years of military rule.

30 The Israeli Knesset (parliament) proclaims unified Jerusalem the capital of Israel.

August

2 Right wing Italian terrorists kill 82 people with a bomb at Bologna railroad station.

5 The Belgian parliament passes a bill dividing the country into three autonomous linguistic regions.

13–28 French fishermen blockade English Channel ports in their campaign for government aid.

14 The Democratic Party convention in New York, New York, nominates President Jimmy Carter and Vice President Walter Mondale for a second term in office.

26 Leadership changes in China consolidate the power of the pragmatic reformers led by Deng Xiaoping.

31 Lech Wałęsa, leader of the Gdańsk shipyard strikers, signs an agreement with the Polish government allowing the formation of independent labor unions and granting the release of political prisoners.

September

5 Stanisław Kania succeeds Edward Gierek as first secretary of the Polish Communist Party.

9 Britain closes its embassy in the Iranian capital, Tehran.

10 Libya and Syria proclaim themselves a single state.

11 A referendum in Chile approves an eight-year extension of Augusto Pinochet's military government.

12 Ayatollah Khomeini of Iran sets out conditions for the release of the U.S. hostages held since November 4, 1979.

12 General Kenan Evren heads a military takeover in Turkey.

22 Iraq invades Iran in an attempt to gain control of the Shatt al-Arab waterway.

22 The Indian government assumes emergency powers to combat violence in southern India.

28 President Zia ul-Haq of Pakistan visits the Iranian and Iraqi capitals, Tehran and Baghdad, in an attempt to mediate in the Iran–Iraq War.

October

• The U.S. House of Representatives expels Democrat Michael Joseph Myers of Pennsylvania, who had been convicted of bribery and conspiracy in the FBI Abscam investigation. Myers becomes the first member to be expelled since 1861.

5 West Germany reelects Chancellor Helmut Schmidt's coalition with an increased majority.

23 Nikolai Tikhonov succeeds Alexei Kosygin as Soviet prime minister.

24 The Polish authorities register a new independent labor union, named "Solidarność"/"Solidarity."

27–December 18 Seven Irish Republican Army (IRA) prisoners in the Maze prison near Belfast, Northern Ireland, go on hunger strike in their demand for "political status."

NOVEMBER

4   In the U.S. presidential election, the Republican candidate Ronald Reagan wins a sweeping victory over President Jimmy Carter, with 489 electoral votes against Carter's 49. The Republicans win control of the Senate and gain 33 seats in the House of Representatives.

20 The treason trial of the former Chinese leaders, the "Gang of Four," opens in the capital, Beijing.

27 Four Welsh nationalist extremists are jailed for arson attacks on holiday homes in Wales.

27 The British government announces its aim to cut 100,000 jobs in the civil service.

30 Syria masses its troops on the Jordanian border. Jordan calls up reserves in response.

DECEMBER

2   The European Economic Community warns the Soviet Union against military intervention in Poland.

3   The USSR begins a major offensive against Afghan resistance fighters in an attempt to keep the Kabul-based communist government in power in the face of resistance.

8   The British and Irish prime ministers Margaret Thatcher and Charles Haughey, meeting in Dublin, in the Irish Republic, agree to establish a commission to examine Anglo-Irish links respecting Northern Ireland.

10 The Soviet president Leonid Brezhnev calls on the West and China to make the Persian Gulf and Indian Ocean "a zone of peace."

15 Milton Obote becomes president of Uganda after the first general election in 18 years.

16 A memorial to workers killed in the riots of December 1970 is unveiled in Gdańsk, Poland.

16 The Organization of Petroleum-Exporting Countries (OPEC) increases crude oil prices by 10%.

21 Iran demands a "deposit" of $24,000 million for the release of the U.S. hostages held since November 4, 1979.

27 Violent anti-Soviet demonstrations erupt in the Iranian capital, Tehran, on the anniversary of the Soviet invasion of Afghanistan.

29 The United States rejects Iran's demand for $24,000 million for the release of the U.S. hostages held since November 4, 1979.

SCIENCE, TECHNOLOGY, AND MEDICINE

Computing

- IBM develops a voice-recognition system which can display spoken words on a screen at a normal speaking rate; it can recognize 1,000 words with 91% accuracy.
- The database software package dBase II is developed by U.S. computer scientist Wayne Ratliffe; later versions of it become the principal filing system for personal computers.
- U.S. firm Votrax develops the SC-01 single-chip voice synthesizer; by storing phonemes (the smallest unit of speech that distinguishes one utterance from another) as 6-bit words and then combining them to make words, it has an unlimited vocabulary.

Ecology

- A ten-year World Climate Research Program is launched to study and predict climate changes and human influence on climate change.
- Over 1,000 people are killed on the island of Mindanao in the Philippines when two cyclones hit.
- Over 1,000 people die during a severe summer heat wave in the southern United States.
- The Comprehensive Environmental Responses, Compensation, and Liability Act (commonly called "Superfund") is passed in the United States.
- The midwest United States is hit by a severe drought.

MAY

18 Mt. St. Helens volcano in Washington state, United States, erupts explosively in a blast 500 times more powerful than the Hiroshima bomb, causing an outbreak of fires, mudslides, and floods; 34 people die in the largest eruption in U.S. history. Ash from the volcano blankets the surrounding area and affects global temperature readings for months to come.

AUGUST

4–11 Hurricane Allen hits southern Texas and several Caribbean islands, killing 235 people.

OCTOBER

10 An earthquake measuring 6.5 on the Richter scale at El Asnam, Algeria, kills over 3,500 people and leaves 33,000 people homeless.

NOVEMBER

21 A fire in the MGM Grand Hotel at Las Vegas, Nevada, traps 3,500 people. Helicopters rescue more than 1,000 from the roof, but 84 people die.

23 Southern Italy is struck by an earthquake measuring 7.2 on the Richter scale; 4,500 people are killed.

DECEMBER

4   A fire kills 26 people at the Stouffer Inn in Harrison, New York, New York.

Exploration

- The U.S. *Magsat* satellite completes its mapping of the earth's magnetic field.

JULY

18 India launches its *Rohini* satellite and becomes the eighth country to launch a satellite.

OCTOBER

11 The Soviet cosmonauts Valery V. Ryumin and Leonid I. Popov return to Earth after a record 185 days in space aboard *Salyut 6*.

NOVEMBER

12 The U.S. space probe *Voyager 1* flies past Saturn within 124,000 km/77,000 mi; it discovers the planet's 13th, 14th, and 15th moons and transmits information about the planet, its moons, and its rings.

Health and Medicine

- A new vaccine for the prevention of hepatitis B is tested in the United States. It is the first genetically engineered vaccine and has a success rate of 92%. It wins Federal Drug Administration approval in 1986.

- A team at the Washington University School of Medicine in St. Louis, Missouri, transplants insulin-producing pancreatic islets from a rat to a mouse, creating the possibility of making similar transplants from animals to humans.
- French endocrinologist Etienne-Emile Baulieu develops the abortion-inducing drug RU486.
- French physician Yves Leroy develops short-wave thermography for analyzing breast cancers using heat radiation.
- Italy extends free medical aid to all citizens.
- Paints containing lead are banned by the U.S. government.
- The Swiss firm Biogen produces human interferon in bacteria for the treatment of viral diseases.
- The United Nations launches the International Drinking and Water Supply and Sanitation Decade to advance safe drinking water supplies and proper sanitation.
- U.S. molecular biologist Paul Berg receives the Nobel Prize for Chemistry for his studies on the biochemistry of nucleic acids, especially recombinant DNA (deoxyribonucleic acid); U.S. molecular biologist Walter Gilbert and English biochemist Frederick Sanger receive the Nobel Prize for Chemistry for determining base sequences in nucleic acids.
- U.S. researcher Richard Dobelle improves his electronic eye; six patients are able to identify simple geometric shapes and letters of the alphabet.
- Venezuelan-born U.S. immunologist Baruj Benacerraf, French immunologist Jean Dausset, and U.S. geneticist George Snell share the Nobel Prize for Physiology or Medicine for their discoveries concerning genetically determined structures on the cell surface that regulate immunological reactions.

MAY
- The World Health Organization announces the eradication of smallpox.

JUNE
9   Philadelphia's Wistar Institute introduces a rabies vaccine that requires only four shots in the arm instead of at least 16 in the abdomen. The new vaccine is known as human diploid cell vaccine (HDCV) because it is prepared from viruses grown in human diploid cells.

SEPTEMBER
22   The U.S. company Procter and Gamble recalls tampons after government studies demonstrate that Toxic Shock Syndrome, caused by a bacterial toxin that grows in the tampons, has killed 25 women.

Math

- Mathematicians worldwide complete the classification of all finite and simple groups, a task that has taken over 100 mathematicians more than 35 years to complete. The results take up more than 14,000 pages in mathematical journals.
- Polish-born French mathematician Benoit Mandelbrot discovers fractals. The Mandelbrot set is a spectacular shape with a fractal boundary (a boundary of infinite length enclosing a finite area).

Science

- A gene is transferred from one mouse to another by U.S. geneticist Martin Cline and colleagues.
- A thin layer of iridium-rich clay, about 65 million years old, is found around the world. U.S. physicist Luis Alvarez suggests that it was caused by the impact of a large asteroid or comet that threw enough dust into the sky to obscure the sun and cause the extinction of the dinosaurs.
- German physicist Hans Dehmelt and colleagues at the University of Heidelberg, Germany, succeed in photographing a single barium atom.
- The Very Large Array (VLA) radio telescope at Socorro, New Mexico, enters service; its 27 25-m/81-ft diameter dishes are steerable and moveable on railroad tracks and are equivalent to one dish 27 km/17 mi in diameter; together they provide high resolution radio images.
- U.S. astronomer Carl Sagan publishes *Cosmos*.
- U.S. astronomer Uwe Fink and associates report the discovery of a thin atmosphere on Pluto.
- U.S. particle physicist Alan Guth proposes the theory of the inflationary universe—that the universe expanded very rapidly for a short time after the Big Bang.
- U.S. physicists James Cronin and Val Fitch receive the Nobel Prize for Physics for demonstrating the simultaneous violation of both charge-conjugation and parity-inversion symmetries.
- Warren's Shaft, a vertical well that formed part of Jerusalem's waterworks before King David's time, is rediscovered by the City of David Archeological Project (it was originally discovered by Charles Warren in 1867 but its location was lost). When it is cleaned out it provides access to the entire ancient waterworks system.

Technology

c. 1980   The United States begins to manufacture cruise missiles with a speed of about 885 kph/550 mph, and an extremely accurate navigational system (Tercom) that uses contour maps stored in its computerized memory; they fly low to the ground to escape detection by radar.
- *Intelsat 5* communication satellite is launched; it can relay 12,000 telephone calls and two color television channels.
- An experimental telephone inquiry system called "Minitel" is introduced in France; computer terminals are placed in homes and callers are offered a large number of on-line information services.
- Faxes take one minute per page to send.
- M. Ikeya and T. Liki of Yamaguchi University, Japan, announce a new method of dating fossil remains: electron spin resonance spectroscopy, which measures the amount of natural radiation received by such remains.
- The Multi-Element Radio-Linked Interferometer Network (MERLIN) radio telescope begins operation in the UK. It has five dishes measuring 25 m/82 ft, one measuring 32 m/105 ft, and one measuring 76 m/249 ft, making it the largest radio telescope in the world.
- The Tevatron at Fermilab located at the Fermi National Accelerator Laboratory in Batavia, Illinois, United

States, is completed; the most powerful proton synchrotron in the world, it is designed to operate at 1,000 GeV or 1 TeV (teraelectron volt).

- U.S. firm Hughes Aircraft Corporation develops the laser scissor for cutting textiles with a laser beam.

SEPTEMBER

24   Japan's leading newspaper *Asahi Shimbun* is produced by new technology, "untouched by human hands."

Transportation

c. 1980   Electronic antilock braking systems to prevent cars from skidding are introduced in the United States.

- Japanese oceanologists discover traces of Kublai Khan's Chinese invasion fleet which was sunk by a hurricane or "divine wind" in 1274 on its way to Japan.
- The average U.S. citizen travels 14.7 km/9.2 mi in 22 minutes each way to get to work.
- The BAM (Baikal–Amur Magistral) railroad from Lake Baikal to the Amur River in Siberia, USSR, is completed; covering a distance of nearly 3,200 km/2,000 mi, it provides access to coal, oil, and mineral deposits for exploitation.

FEBRUARY

16   The second subway line in Rome, Italy, the "A" line, begins operations.

APRIL

20   A ferry sinks near Dacca, Bangladesh, and at least 230 people die.

22   The overcrowded passenger ferry *Don Juan* crashes into the oil tanker *Talcloban City* in the Philippines; 113 people are confirmed dead and 200 are missing and presumed dead.

MAY

8–12   Max Leroy "Maxie" Anderson and his son Kristian complete the first nonstop transcontinental balloon flight, from Fort Baker, California to Ste.-Félicité, Quebec, Canada.

AUGUST

9   The butane gas stove of a Muslim pilgrim to Mecca sets a Saudi-Arabian Lockheed 1011 Tristar jet on fire shortly after takeoff from Riyadh; 301 people are killed.

19   A freight train overruns a stop signal in Poland, goes down the wrong track, and hits a crowded passenger train; 62 people are killed and 50 injured.

SEPTEMBER

21   The Hartsfield-Atlanta International Airport in Atlanta, Georgia, is completed; costing $750 million, it has more passenger gates than Chicago's O'Hare Airport.

ARTS AND IDEAS

Architecture

SEPTEMBER

25   The new, 16.3-km/10.1-mi-long St. Gotthard Road Tunnel is completed at St. Gotthard Pass in Switzerland;

it is the longest road tunnel in the world and can accommodate up to 1,500 vehicles per hour.

Arts

- A Picasso exhibition is held at the Museum of Modern Art (MOMA) in New York, New York.
- The English art historian Norbert Lynton publishes *The Story of Modern Art*.
- The English artist Barry Flanagan sculpts *Leaping Hare*.
- The German artist Georg Baselitz creates *Model For a Sculpture*.
- The Italian artist Sandro Chia paints *Excited Pastoral*.
- The Polish artist Magdalena Abakanowicz creates the group sculpture *80 Backs*.
- The U.S. artist Richard Diebenkorn paints *Ocean Park No. 122*.
- The U.S. photographer Cindy Sherman publishes her photograph *Untitled no. 66*.
- The U.S. photographer Robert Mapplethorpe publishes his photograph *Ajitto*.

JULY

July–September   The exhibition "The Avant-garde in Russia 1910–30" is held at the Los Angeles County Museum in California.

Film

- The 15½-hour epic movie, *Berlin Alexanderplatz*, directed by Rainer Werner Fassbinder, is released in West Germany. It stars Gunter Lamprecht and Hanna Schygulla.
- The movie *9 to 5*, directed by Colin Higgins, is released in the United States. It stars Lily Tomlin, Dolly Parton, and Jane Fonda.
- The movie *Airplane*, directed by Jim Abrahams and David and Jerry Zucker, is released in the United States, starring Robert Stack, Lloyd Bridges, Robert Hays, Julie Hagarty, and Leslie Nielson.
- The movie *American Gigolo*, directed by Paul Schrader, is released in the United States. It stars Richard Gere.
- The movie *Coal Miner's Daughter*, directed by British filmmaker Michael Apted, is released in the United States. It stars Sissy Spacek and Tommy Lee Jones.
- The movie *Dressed to Kill* is released in the United States. It is directed by Brian De Palma and stars Michael Caine, Angie Dickinson, and Nancy Allen.
- The movie *Dyrygent/The Orchestra Conductor*, directed by Andrzej Wajda, is released in Poland. It stars English actor John Gielgud.
- The movie *Gloria*, directed by John Cassavetes, is released in the United States. It stars Gena Rowlands and Buck Henry.
- The movie *Heaven's Gate*, directed by Michael Cimino, is released in the United States, starring Kris Kristofferson, Christopher Walken, and Isabelle Huppert. It is a commercial disaster, costing a record $36 million to produce.
- The movie *Kagemusha*, directed by Akira Kurosawa, is released in Japan, starring Tatsuya Nakadai.
- The movie *La Città delle Donne/The City of Women*, directed by Federico Fellini, is released in Italy. It stars Marcello Mastroianni.

- The movie *Le Dernier Métro/The Last Metro* is released in France. It is directed by François Truffaut and stars Catherine Deneuve and Gérard Depardieu.
- The movie *Loulou*, directed by Maurice Pialat, is released in France, starring Isabelle Huppert and Gérard Depardieu.
- The movie *Megalexandros/Alexander the Great*, directed by Theo Angelopoulos, is released in Greece.
- The movie *Melvin and Howard*, directed by Jonathan Demme, is released in the United States. It stars Paul Le Mat and Jason Robards.
- The movie *Moscow Does Not Believe in Tears*, directed by Vladimir Menshov, is released in the USSR, starring Vera Alentova, Irina Muravyova, and Raisa Ryazanova.
- The movie *Ordinary People*, directed by Robert Redford, is released in the United States. Based on the novel by Judith Guest, it stars Mary Tyler Moore, Donald Sutherland, and Timothy Hutton.
- The movie *Popeye*, directed by Robert Altman, is released in the United States. It stars Robin Williams and Shelley Duvall.
- The movie *Raging Bull*, directed by Martin Scorsese, is released in the United States. It stars Robert De Niro.
- The movie *Stardust Memories*, directed by Woody Allen, is released in the United States, starring Allen, Charlotte Rampling, and Jessica Harper.
- The movie *The Blues Brothers*, directed by John Landis, is released in the United States. It stars John Belushi and Dan Ackroyd, and features music personalities such as Aretha Franklin, James Brown, and Ray Charles.
- The movie *The Big Red One*, directed by Sam Fuller, is released in the United States, starring Lee Marvin, Mark Hamill, and Robert Carradine.
- The movie *The Elephant Man*, directed by David Lynch, is released in the United States. It stars John Hurt and Anthony Hopkins.
- The movie *The Empire Strikes Back*, directed by Irvin Kershner, is released in the United States. The second installment in the *Star Wars* trilogy, it stars Mark Hamill, Harrison Ford, and Carrie Fisher.
- The movie *The Long Good Friday*, directed by John Mackenzie, is released in the UK. It stars Bob Hoskins and Helen Mirren.
- The movie *The Long Riders* is released in the United States. Directed by Walter Hill, it features the Carradine brothers (David, Keith, and Robert), the Keach brothers (Stacy and James), the Quaid brothers (Randy and Dennis), and the Guest brothers (Nicholas and Christopher).
- The movie *The Shining*, directed by Stanley Kubrick, is released in the United States. Based on the novel by Stephen King, it stars Jack Nicholson and Shelley Duvall.
- The Iranian government merges the private and public sectors of the film industry to form the Babylone production company.
- The low-budget independent movie *The Return of the Secaucus Seven*, written, directed by, and starring John Sayles, is released in the United States.
- The National Film Development Corporation is formed in India, to promote Indian movies.
- The Zaire government nationalizes the movie distribution company Cofilmex.

MARCH

11 Francis Ford Coppola buys the Hollywood General Studios, which he renames Zoetrope.

APRIL

14 The 1979 Academy Awards take place. Best Actor: Dustin Hoffman, for *Kramer vs Kramer*; Best Supporting Actor: Melvyn Douglas, for *Being There*; Best Actress: Sally Field, for *Norma Rae*; Best Supporting Actress: Meryl Streep, for *Kramer vs Kramer*; Best Picture: *Kramer vs Kramer*, directed by Robert Benton; Best Director: Robert Benton, for *Kramer vs Kramer*.

MAY

23 At the Cannes Film Festival, the Palme d'Or is awarded jointly to Akira Kurosawa for the Japanese movie *Kagemusha* and Bob Fosse for the U.S. movie *All That Jazz*.

AUGUST

3 A fire at the Cinémathéque Française in Paris, France, results in the loss of several thousand reels of film.

SEPTEMBER

1 The legal fixing of movie theater prices in France comes to an end.

Literature and Language

- Australian novelist Peter Carey publishes his novel *The Fat Man in History*.
- British writer Robert McCrum publishes his novel *In the Secret State*.
- English novelist Julian Barnes publishes his novel *Metroland*.
- English writer Margaret Drabble publishes her novel *Middle Ground*.
- The *Harvard Encyclopedia of American Ethnic Groups* is published, edited by Stephan Thernstrom.
- The Australian writer Patrick White publishes his novel *The Twyborn Affair*.
- The English novelist John Le Carré publishes his novel *Smiley's People*.
- The English writer Anthony Burgess publishes his novel *Earthly Powers*.
- The English writer William Golding publishes his novel *Rites of Passage*, which wins the Booker Prize.
- The Indian writer Anita Desai publishes her novel *Clear Light of Day*.
- The Irish writer Samuel Beckett publishes *Company*.
- The Irish writer Sean O'Faolain publishes *Midsummer Night Madness and Other Stories*.
- The Italian writer and scholar Umberto Eco publishes his novel *Il nome della rosa/The Name of the Rose*. Though littered with scholarly allusions and Latin quotations, the novel—a detective story set in the Middle Ages—is an unexpected bestseller.
- The Kenyan writer Ngugi wa Thiong'o publishes his novel *Caitaani Mutharaba-ini/Devil on the Cross*. Written in Kikuyu and drawing heavily on traditional oral literature, the novel expresses a growing sense of African cultural identity.
- The Nobel Prize for Literature is awarded to the Polish-born U.S. poet Czesław Miłosz.

- The novel *A Confederacy of Dunces* by the U.S. writer John Kennedy Toole is published 11 years after its author commits suicide. He is posthumously awarded a Pulitzer prize.
- The Pulitzer Prize for Biography is awarded to Edmund Morris for *The Rise of Theodore Roosevelt*, the Pulitzer Prize for Poetry is awarded to Donald Justice for *Selected Poems*, and the Pulitzer Prize for Fiction is awarded to Norman Mailer for *The Executioner's Song*.
- The Russian writer Joseph Brodsky publishes his poetry collection *A Part of Speech*.
- The U.S. journalist Tom Wolfe publishes *The Right Stuff*, a fictionalized history of the U.S. space program.
- The U.S. writer Joyce Carol Oates publishes her novel *Bellefleur*.
- The U.S. writer Russell Hoban publishes his novel *Riddley Walker*.
- The U.S. writer Truman Capote publishes *Music for Chameleons*, a selection of fiction and nonfiction.

Music

- *The New Grove Dictionary of Music and Musicians* edited by Stanley Sadie is published.
- A new wave of heavy metal music begins with groups like Iron Maiden emerging in the wake of heavy metal giants of the 1970s.
- Audio cassettes represent almost 40% of album sales in the music market.
- Digitally recorded LP records are widely marketed for the first time.
- The British pop group UB40 releases *Signing Off*.
- The British rock group Joy Division releases the album *Closer*.
- The English composer Elisabeth Lutyens completes her orchestral work *Wild Decembers*.
- The French composer Pierre Boulez completes his orchestral work *Notations*.
- The Georgian composer Ghiya Kancheli completes his Symphony No. 6.
- The German composer Karlheinz Stockhausen completes his opera *Donnerstag aus Licht/Thursday from Light*. This is the first part of a seven-opera cycle.
- The Hungarian composer György Kurtág completes his *Messages of the Late Miss R V Troussova* for voice and chamber ensemble.
- The opera *Satyagraha*, by the U.S. composer Philip Glass, is first performed, in Rotterdam, in the Netherlands. The text is drawn from ancient Hindu scripts.
- The Polish composer Krzysztof Penderecki completes his Symphony No. 2 (Christmas).
- The U.S. composer Elliott Carter completes his piano work *Night Fantasies*.
- The U.S. composer John Cage completes his vocal work *Roaratorio, an Irish Circus on Finnegan's Wake*.
- The U.S. pop group Captain Beefheart and the Magic Band releases the album *Doc at the Radar Station*.

FEBRUARY
2 The Irish rock group the Boomtown Rats releases the single "I Don't Like Mondays."

9 The British pop group the Clash releases the album *London's Calling*.
27 The 1979 Grammy Awards are held. Best Album: *52nd Street* by Billy Joel; Best Record: "What a Fool Believes" by the Doobie Brothers; Best Male Pop Vocalist: Billy Joel for *52nd Street*; Best Female Pop Vocalist: Dionne Warwick for "I'll Never Love This Way Again"; Best Pop Group: The Doobie Brothers for "Minute by Minute."

MARCH
22 The British pop singer Elvis Costello releases the album *Get Happy*.

OCTOBER
4 The British pop star and actor David Bowie releases the album *Scary Monsters (and Super Creeps)*.

NOVEMBER
1 The U.S. rock singer Bruce Springsteen releases the album *The River*.

DECEMBER
13 The U.S. new wave pop group Blondie releases the album *Autoamerican*.

Theater and Dance

- A stage version of Charles Dickens's novel *Nicholas Nickleby*, adapted for stage by David Edgar, is first performed, at the Aldwych Theatre in London, England. The play runs for over eight hours.
- The Centre International de Créations Théâtrales, founded by the English director Peter Brook, receives the New York Drama Critics' Circle Award.
- The musical *Barnum*, with lyrics by Michael Stewart and music by Cy Coleman, is first performed, at the St. James Theater in New York, New York.
- The musical *Les Misérables*, with lyrics by Herbert Kretzmer and Alain Boubil, and music by Claude-Michel Schönberg, is first performed, at the Palais des Sports in Paris, France. Its first English performance will be in 1985 in London, England.
- The play *Children of a Lesser God*, by the U.S. writer Mark Medoff, is first performed, at the Longacre Theater in New York, New York.
- The play *Piaf!*, by the English writer Pam Gems, is first performed, at Wyndham's Theatre in London, England. It is based on the life of the French singer Edith Piaf.
- The play *The Fifth of July*, by the U.S. writer Lanford Kingston, is first performed, at the New Apollo Theater in New York, New York.
- The play *Translations*, by the Irish writer Brian Friel, is first performed, in Derry, Northern Ireland.
- The play *True West*, by the U.S. writer Sam Shepard, is first performed, at the Public Theater in New York, New York.
- The Pulitzer Prize for Drama is awarded to Lanford Wilson for *Talley's Folly*.
- The Teatro del Mondo in Venice, Italy, designed by the Italian architect Aldo Rossi, is completed.
- The Tony Awards for theater are presented to Mark Medoff for Best Play, *Children of a Lesser God*, and to Andrew Lloyd Webber and Tim Rice for Best Musical, *Evita*.

Thought and Scholarship

- British historian William A. McCutcheon publishes *The Industrial Archaeology of Northern Ireland*.
- English Egyptologist John Baines and Egyptian Egyptologist Jaromír Málek publish the *Atlas of Ancient Egypt*.
- English philosopher Janet Radcliffe Richards publishes *The Sceptical Feminist: A Philosophical Enquiry*.
- The Pulitzer Prize for History is awarded to Leon F. Litwack for *Been in the Storm So Long*.
- The Pulitzer Prize for General Nonfiction is awarded to Douglas R. Hofstadter for *Gödel, Escher, Bach*.
- Trinidadian writer Shiva Naipaul publishes *Black and White*, a study of subcultures in the United States.
- U.S. philosopher Donald Davidson publishes *Essays on Action and Events*.
- U.S. philosopher Richard Rorty publishes *Philosophy and the Mirror of Nature*.

SOCIETY

Education

- A new curriculum for elementary schools is introduced in Japan.

MAY

28 The U.S. service academies graduate their first classes of women: 61 from West Point, 55 from Annapolis, and 97 from the Air Force Academy.

Everyday Life

- Bulky full-length down coats are popular winter-wear in the United States.
- Divorce rates (divorces per 1,000 of the population): France 1.50; Germany 2.68; Great Britain and Northern Ireland 3.08; United States 5.19; USSR 3.50.
- For the first time since World War II, Poland introduces meat rationing; meat is being exported to raise hard currency to pay off foreign debts.
- Jewish population (main centers): United States 5,750,000; Israel 3,283,000; USSR 1,811,000; France 600,000; Great Britain 350,000; Canada 308,000; Argentina 242,000; Brazil 110,000; South Africa; 108,000.
- Life expectancy for females: world average, 64 years; Ethiopia, 43; Nepal, 44; Somalia, 45; United States, 77.
- Over 18% of births in the United States are to unmarried mothers; over 40% of births are to women under 20.
- Over 1.5 million abortions are performed in the United States; there are 3 million illegal abortions in Brazil and 280,000 in Columbia; in Egypt, a quarter of all pregnancies are aborted.
- Populations of cities (in millions): Tokyo 11.6; Shanghai 10.0; Buenos Aires 9.7; Mexico City 8.9; Beijing 8.7; Seoul 8.4; Cairo 8.1; Moscow 8.0; New York 7.1; Tientsin 7.0.

- The New Romantic look, inspired by glam rock, starts to appear, sported by bands such as Spandau Ballet and Duran Duran.
- The population of the world is 4.45 billion.
- The population of the United States is 226.5 million compared to 76 million in 1900.
- The world average illiteracy rate for women is 34%.

JANUARY

- Public school teachers in Cleveland, Ohio, end an 11-week strike after winning a 20% salary increase over the ensuing 15 months.
2–April 2 A national steel strike is held in Britain.
30 The British Department of Employment reports that more working days were lost through strikes in 1979 than in any year since 1926.

MAY

1 Sweden is practically at a standstill as pay negotiations crumble amid strikes and lockouts.
20 A fire in a nursing home in Kingston, Jamaica, kills 157 people.

JUNE

10 U.S. comedian Richard Pryor suffers extensive burns while "freebasing"—smoking an explosive mixture of ether and cocaine.

AUGUST

14 Polish strikers occupy the Lenin shipyard in Gdańsk.

NOVEMBER

10–December 11 British firefighters work to rule in a pay dispute.

Media and Communication

- Intelpost, the first public international electronic facsimile service, is launched.
- The 1979–80 Emmy Awards for television are held. Best Drama Series: *Lou Grant*; Best Comedy Series: *Taxi*; Best Actor in a Drama: Ed Asner, for *Lou Grant*; Best Actress in a Drama: Barbara Bel Geddes, for *Dallas*; Best Actor in a Comedy: Richard Mulligan, for *Soap*; Best Actress in a Comedy: Cathryn Damon, for *Soap*.
- There are now 35 television stations broadcasting mainly religious programs in the United States.

JANUARY

27–29 *The Martian Chronicles*, a mini-series based on the book by Ray Bradbury, is shown on U.S. television, starring Rock Hudson, Gayle Hunnicutt, and Darren McGavin.

APRIL

23 Saudi Arabia expels the British ambassador in protest at a British television program *Death of a Princess* about the execution of a Saudi princess and her lover for adultery.
30 *Gideon's Trumpet*, a documentary style drama about the U.S. Supreme Court guaranteeing defendants the right to counsel, is shown on U.S. television. It stars Henry Fonda and John Housemann.

JUNE

1 U.S. entrepreneur Ted Turner launches the Cable News Network (CNN), the first 24-hour network in the world to focus solely on news.

AUGUST

20 The USSR jams Western radio broadcasts for the first time in seven years to prevent news of widespread strikes in Poland.

NOVEMBER

21 *Dallas* breaks existing television rating records when more than half the population of the United States watches the episode *Who Shot JR?*

DECEMBER

11–September 12, 1988 *Magnum, P. I.*, starring Tom Selleck as a former naval intelligence officer turned detective living on Oahu, Hawaii, is shown on U.S. television.

Sports

- Canadian ice-hockey player Scott Olsen and his brother create rollerblades, high-speed roller-skates, and found Rollerblade Inc. in Minneapolis, Minnesota, to manufacture them.
- In cycling, the women's world road race is won by Beth Heiden of the United States, who a year earlier won the world overall speed skating title.

BIRTHS & DEATHS

JANUARY

8 John Mauchly, U.S. physicist and engineer who, with John P. Eckert, built ENIAC, the first electronic computer, dies in Ambler, Pennsylvania (72).

10 George Meany, U.S. labor leader who headed the American Federation of Labor and Congress of Industrial Organizations (AFL–CIO), dies in Washington, D.C. (84).

18 Cecil Beaton, English photographer specializing in portraits of famous people, dies in Broadchalke, Wiltshire, England (76).

19 William Orville Douglas, U.S. associate justice of the Supreme Court for 36 years, the longest period in history, dies in Washington, D.C. (81).

29 Jimmy Durante, U.S. comedian, dies in Santa Monica, California (86).

FEBRUARY

17 Graham Sutherland, English painter known for his surrealist landscapes and his portraits, dies in London, England (76).

20 Alice Roosevelt Longworth, U.S. author and socialite, daughter of Theodore Roosevelt, dies in Washington, D.C. (96).

22 Oskar Kokoschka, Austrian expressionist painter, writer, poet, and dramatist, dies in Villeneuve, Switzerland (93).

MARCH

18 Erich Fromm, German-born U.S. psychoanalyst and philosopher, dies in Muralto, Switzerland (79).

26 Roland Barthes, French scholar and critic working in the field of semiotics (the study of signs and symbols), dies in Paris, France (64).

31 Jesse Owens, black U.S. track and field athlete who won four gold medals at the 1936 Olympics in Berlin, dies in Phoenix, Arizona (66).

APRIL

15 Jean-Paul Sartre, French existentialist philosopher, novelist, and playwright, dies in Paris, France (74).

29 Alfred Hitchcock, British film director best known for his films of suspense, dies in Bel Air, California (80).

MAY

4 Josip Broz Tito, Yugoslavian communist leader from 1943, elected president 1953–80, dies in Ljubljana (now in Slovenia), Yugoslavia (87).

JUNE

3 A. C. Nielsen, businessman and market researcher who founded the A. C. Nielsen Co. in 1923 to research radio and then television program ratings, dies in Chicago, Illinois (82).

7 Henry Miller, U.S. novelist, dies in Pacific Palisades, California (88).

12 Masayoshi Ohira, Japanese prime minister 1978–80, dies in Tokyo, Japan (70).

JULY

23 Peter Sellers, British television and film comedian who became famous in *The Goon Show*, and as Inspector Clouseau in the Pink Panther films, dies in London, England (54).

27 Muhammad Reza Shah Pahlavi, shah of Iran 1941–79, overthrown by the revolution of the Ayatollah Khomeini, dies in Cairo, Egypt (60).

AUGUST

6 Marino Marini, Italian portrait sculptor, dies in Viareggio, Italy (79).

SEPTEMBER

8 Willard Frank Libby, U.S. chemist who discovered the technique of radioactive carbon dating, dies in Los Angeles, California (71).

17 Anastasio Somoza, Nicaraguan dictator, dies in Ascuncion, Paraguay (64).

17 Jean Piaget, Swiss psychologist who originated the field of developmental psychology, dies in Geneva, Switzerland (84).

18 Katherine Anne Porter, U.S. Pulitzer prizewinning writer and teacher whose 1962 novel *Ship of Fools* was filmed in 1965, dies in Silver Springs, Maryland (90).

OCTOBER

26 Marcello Caetano, premier of Portugal from 1968 until the revolution of 1974, dies in Rio de Janeiro, Brazil (74).

NOVEMBER

22 Mae West, U.S. stage and film actress and sex symbol, dies in Los Angeles, California (88).

DECEMBER

- John Lennon, English pop singer and songwriter, one of the Beatles, is shot dead by Mark David Chapman outside the Dakota, his apartment building in New York, New York (40).

4 Francisco Sá Carneiro, Portuguese prime minister January–December 1980, dies in an airplane crash.

16 Harland "Colonel" Sanders, U.S. businessman, founder of the Kentucky Fried Chicken fast-food restaurants, dies in Shelbyville, Kentucky (90).

18 Alexey Nikolaievich Kosygin, Soviet statesman and premier of the Soviet Union 1964–80, dies in Moscow, USSR (76).

22 Karl Doenitz, German naval officer who created the German U-boat fleet in World War II, dies in Aumühle, West Germany (89).

31 Marshall McLuhan, Canadian communications scholar who was convinced of the power of television and electronic media over the written word, dies in Toronto, Canada (69).

- The inaugural Miss Olympia (later Ms. Olympia) competition for female bodybuilders is held in the United States.

JANUARY

1 Sportswriters pick Alabama as the United States' number-one college football team for the 1979 season.

11 Fourteen-year-old Nigel Short from Bolton, Greater Manchester, England, becomes the youngest International Master in the history of chess.

18–20 U.S. national figure skating champions are: Linda Fratianne; Charles Tickner; Tai Babilonia and Randy Gardner, pairs; Stacey Smith and John Summers, dance.

20 The Pittsburgh Steelers defeat the Los Angeles Rams 31–19 in Super Bowl XIV before a record crowd of 103,985 in Pasadena, California, to become the first team to win four Super Bowls.

FEBRUARY

12 In the wake of the USSR's invasion of Afghanistan, the International Olympic Committee rejects a U.S. demand for the cancellation or relocation of the 1980 Moscow Olympics.

13–24 The 13th Winter Olympic Games are held in Lake Placid, New York. The USSR wins 10 gold medals; East Germany, 9; United States, 6; Austria and Sweden, 3 each. Eric Heiden of the United States wins all five men's speed skating gold medals. In the ski events, Ingemar Stenmark of Sweden wins the men's slalom and giant slalom titles. In ice hockey the United States inflicts a shock defeat on the USSR on the way to winning the gold medal.

MARCH

16 Alan Minter becomes the first British boxer to win a world title in the United States since Ted "Kid" Lewis in 1917, when he wins the world middleweight title, beating Vito Antuofermo of Italy in Las Vegas, Nevada.

25 The British Olympic Association decides to send a team to the Moscow Olympics a week after the House of Commons approves the British government's appeal to boycott the games.

APRIL

10–13 At age 23, Spanish golfer Seve (Severiano) Ballesteros becomes the youngest winner and the first European winner of the U.S. Masters golf tournament at Augusta, Georgia.

MAY

3 Genuine Risk, ridden by Jacinto Vasquez, is only the second filly ever to win the Kentucky Derby and the first since Regret in 1915.

4 The Los Angeles Lakers beat the Philadelphia 76ers to win the National Basketball Association (NBA) championship.

13–24 The New York Islanders beat the Philadelphia Flyers and win the first of their four straight Stanley Cups.

25 Racing driver Johnny Rutherford wins his third Indianapolis 500.

JUNE

15 U.S. golfer Jack Nicklaus wins his fourth U.S. Open golf tournament.

JULY

5 The Swedish tennis player Björn Borg wins his fifth consecutive men's singles title at the Wimbledon championships in London, England.

19 The 22nd Olympic Games open in Moscow, USSR. Following the Soviet invasion of Afghanistan in 1979, the games are boycotted by 65 countries, most notably the United States, West Germany, Japan, and Kenya.

19–August 3 At the Olympic Games in Moscow, Teofilo Stevenson of Cuba wins an unprecedented third successive heavyweight boxing gold medal.

AUGUST

- U.S. golfer Jack Nicklaus wins the U.S. PGA Championship to take his record of victories in the Majors to 17.

3 The 22nd Olympic Games close in Moscow, USSR. The USSR wins 80 gold medals; East Germany, 47; Bulgaria, Cuba, and Italy, 8 each; Hungary, 7; Romania and France, 6 each; Great Britain, 5.

20 Reinhold Messner of Italy completes the first entirely solo ascent of Mt. Everest, the world's highest mountain.

OCTOBER

- Geoff Hunt of Australia is World Open squash champion for the fourth consecutive year.

14–21 The Philadelphia Phillies baseball team, who joined the National League in 1883, defeat the Kansas City Royals by four games to two to win their first-ever World Series.

1981

POLITICS, GOVERNMENT, AND ECONOMICS

Business and Economics

JANUARY

28 U.S. president Ronald Reagan ends oil price controls introduced in 1971, leaving prices free to move according to market forces.

FEBRUARY

22 The U.S. government loans the troubled Chrysler Corporation $400 million.

AUGUST

16 The USSR reschedules Polish debt repayments and increases supplies of raw materials and consumer goods to Poland.

NOVEMBER

20 The USSR contracts to supply Siberian natural gas to West Germany.

Colonization

SEPTEMBER

21 Belize becomes an independent state within the Commonwealth.

NOVEMBER

1 The Caribbean islands of Antigua and Barbuda become independent states within the Commonwealth.

Human Rights

- Pirjo Haggman of Finland and Flor Isava-Fonseca of Venezuela are the first two women ever to serve on the International Olympic Committee, based in Switzerland.
- The Civil Rights Commission urges the U.S. government to settle Native American land claims in the east.
- Two Indonesian women are jailed for lesbian acts; one is subjected to surgical and medical treatment designed to "cure" her. In Iran, lesbians are subject to execution after three warnings.
- U.S. feminist Andrea Dworkin publishes *Pornography*.

APRIL

4 The first Mexican-American mayor of a major U.S. city, Henry Gabriel Cisneros, is elected in San Antonio, Texas.

Politics and Government

- Legislation in Japan permits the establishment of a "University of the Air."
- Strict population controls in China that limit families to one child lead to an increase in female infanticide.
- The Education Consolidation and Improvement Act in the United States reduces federal spending on education.
- The European Court rules that dismissal for refusing to join a union "closed shop" is a violation of human rights.
- The United Nations Education, Scientific and Cultural Organization publishes *General History of Africa*.

JANUARY

1 Greece becomes the tenth member of the European Community.

4 The U.S. Congress convenes; the House of Representatives remains Democrat-controlled, but the Senate is Republican.

6 Gaston Thorn succeeds Roy Jenkins as president of the European Commission.

13 The Namibian peace conference breaks up without agreement in Geneva, Switzerland.

14 U.S. president Jimmy Carter delivers his farewell speech, stressing his concerns about the environment and civil rights.

15 Pope John Paul II receives an official delegation from the Polish labor union Solidarity, led by Lech Wałęsa.

20 Iran releases all 52 U.S. hostages, held since November 4, 1979, after an agreement is signed in Algiers releasing Iranian financial assets in the United States.

20 Ronald Reagan is inaugurated as 40th president of the United States.

25 A show trial in Beijing, China convicts the "Gang of Four" prominent former political leaders of treason. Jiang Qing, widow of Chairman Mao Zedong, receives a suspended death sentence.

27 The U.S. hostages released by Iran attend a White House reception after a celebratory motorcade through Washington, D.C.

29 Adolfo Suárez resigns as Spanish prime minister, to be succeeded on February 10 by Leopoldo Calvo Sotelo.

FEBRUARY

3 Labor politician Gro Harlem Brundtland becomes the first woman prime minister of Norway.

6 The Reverend Ian Paisley leads a midnight parade of 500 Protestants with firearm certificates during his "Carson trail" demonstrations in Northern Ireland.

11 General Wojciech Jaruzelski replaces Józef Pińkowski as communist prime minister of Poland.

12 Fighting breaks out between rival ZANU–PF (Zimbabwe African National Union—Popular Front)

and ZAPU (Zimbabwe African Peoples Union) ex-guerrilla forces in Zimbabwe. On February 16, Joshua Nkomo, the ZAPU leader, persuades his supporters to lay down their arms.

18 U.S. president Ronald Reagan proposes spending cuts of $49,000 million and a 30% reduction in taxation over three years.

20 The United States accuses the USSR and Cuba of attempting to subvert El Salvador through support for the left wing FMLN guerrilla movement.

23 Two hundred Civil Guards storm the Spanish parliament and hold members at gunpoint in an attempted coup. The Guards surrender after King Juan Carlos denounces the coup on February 24.

MARCH

2 The U.S. State Department announces $25 million in military aid and $225 million in economic aid for El Salvador.

22 The USSR extends Warsaw Pact military maneuvers in Poland until April 7 following political unrest in the country.

22 U.S. secretary of state Alexander Haig states that the main objective of U.S. foreign policy is to contain Soviet expansion.

26 U.S. actress Carol Burnett wins $1,600,000 in a libel suit against the magazine the *National Enquirer*.

27 The USSR brands the Polish labor union Solidarity as "counterrevolutionary."

30 John Hinckley attempts to assassinate U.S. president Ronald Reagan; he wounds the president and press secretary James Brady.

APRIL

1 Food rationing is introduced in Poland.

1 Heavy fighting breaks out in Beirut, Lebanon, between the Arab peacekeeping force and Christian militias.

7 A referendum in the Philippines grants sweeping new powers to President Ferdinand Marcos.

11 Bobby Sands, an imprisoned Irish Republican Army (IRA) hunger striker, wins a British by-election for the Northern Ireland constituency of Fermanagh and South Tyrone.

17 Polish farmers win the right to form an independent labor union.

24 U.S. president Ronald Reagan lifts the embargo on grain sales to the USSR imposed by President Jimmy Carter in 1979.

28 Conflict intensifies in Lebanon between rival militias supporting Syria and Israel.

30 The Central Committee of the Polish United Workers' Party approves a program of moderate economic and political reforms.

MAY

• States in the Persian Gulf (Abu Dhabi, Bahrain, Kuwait, Oman, Qatar, and Saudi Arabia) establish the Gulf Cooperation Council.

5 Riots break out in Northern Ireland following the death of the Irish Republican Army (IRA) hunger striker and successful parliamentary candidate Bobby Sands in the Maze prison.

6 The United States expels all Libyan diplomats after allegations that Libya is actively supporting international terrorism.

8–27 U.S. peace envoy Philip Habib tours the Middle East, attempting to establish a peace process between Israel and its Arab neighbors.

10 François Mitterrand becomes the first Socialist president of France, winning 51.7 percent of the vote to Valéry Giscard d'Estaing's 48.3 percent.

13 A Turkish gunman, Mehmet Ali Agca, seriously wounds Pope John Paul II in an assassination attempt in St. Peter's Square, Rome. He is jailed for life on July 22.

21 President François Mitterrand appoints the Socialist Party leader Pierre Mauroy as French premier.

26 The Italian government falls after revelations of infiltration by members of the illegal masonic lodge "P2." Italy bans secret societies on July 24.

JUNE

7 The Israeli air force bombs the Osirak nuclear reactor under construction near Baghdad, Iraq. On June 19, the United Nations Security Council condemns the attack after Iraq denies that the reactor was for military use.

11 The governing Fianna Fáil party loses the general election in Ireland. On June 30, Garret FitzGerald becomes Taoiseach (prime minister) at the head of a Fine Gael–Labour coalition.

12 General Wojciech Jaruzelski reorganizes the Polish communist government to tackle the growing economic crisis in the country.

21 The Socialist Party wins a landslide victory in the second round of elections to the French National Assembly. A new government is formed on June 23, including three communist ministers.

22 In the United States' largest ever naturalization ceremony in Los Angeles, California, 9,700 immigrants become citizens.

22 Ayatollah Ruhollah Khomeini denounces President Abolhassan Bani-Sadr of Iran, who flees to France on June 29.

28 A bomb attack on the offices of the Islamic Republican Party kills 72 people in Tehran, Iran, including Chief Justice Ayatollah Mohammad Hossein Beheshti.

JULY

5–6 Arson and riots break out in the Toxteth district of Liverpool, England. Disturbances follow in Manchester, the Brixton district of London, Hull, and elsewhere.

17 Israeli military aircraft attack Palestinian areas of Beirut. Israel and the Palestine Liberation Organization agree a cease-fire on July 29 after two weeks of fighting in southern Lebanon.

23 The Polish government announces plans to increase food rationing and quadruple food prices.

24 Muhammad Ali Rajai is elected president of Iran.

AUGUST

4 The Economic Recovery Tax Act, reducing both income tax and federal spending, comes into force in the United States.

9 U.S. president Ronald Reagan announces his administration's decision to proceed with the manufacture of the so-called "neutron" bomb.

13 East Germany officially celebrates the 20th anniversary of the construction of the Berlin Wall.

13 President Ronald Reagan succeeds in getting a large tax-cut package through the U.S. Congress.

19   U.S. military aircraft shoot down two Libyan fighters during U.S. naval exercises in the Gulf of Sirte off the coast of Libya.

26   The South African premier P. W. Botha confirms that his country's troops are actively involved in the civil war in neighboring Angola.

30   A bomb in Tehran kills the Iranian president Muhammad Ali Rajai and the prime minister Mohammed Javed Bahonar.

SEPTEMBER

4   The French ambassador to Lebanon is assassinated in Beirut.

4   The Warsaw Pact begins its largest program of military exercises in the Baltic since World War II.

5–10   The Polish labor union Solidarity holds its first national congress in Gdańsk.

9   The French Socialist government announces the nationalization of 36 banks and 11 industrial groups.

16   The British Liberal Party conference at Llandudno, Wales, votes for an electoral alliance with the Social Democratic Party (SDP).

30   The French National Assembly abolishes the death penalty, and thus the use of the guillotine.

OCTOBER

2   Hojatolislam Ali Khamenei is elected president of Iran and, on October 29, Hosein Musavi becomes prime minister.

3   The Irish Republican Army (IRA) hunger strike at the Maze prison in Northern Ireland ends after seven months and ten deaths.

4   The grave of Kennedy assassin Lee Harvey Oswald is dug up to dispel rumors that another man was buried in his place.

18   Andreas Papandreou's Panhellenic Socialist Movement (Pasok) wins the Greek general election and, on October 21, he forms Greece's first Socialist government.

18   General Wojciech Jaruzelski, prime minister of Poland, succeeds Stanisław Kania as first secretary of the Polish Communist Party.

22–23   An International Meeting on Cooperation and Development, attended by representatives of 22 countries, is held at Cancún, Mexico, to discuss economic problems facing developing countries.

23   The Presbyterian Church of South Africa begins to conduct mixed-race marriages, in defiance of the country's apartheid laws.

NOVEMBER

1   The ruling Tunisian government wins all seats in the country's first multiparty elections since 1959.

4   Crisis talks begin in Poland between prime minister Wojciech Jaruzelski, Solidarity leader Lech Wałęsa, and the Polish Roman Catholic primate Cardinal Józef Glemp.

6   The British prime minister Margaret Thatcher and the Irish Taoiseach (prime minister) Garret FitzGerald agree to establish an Anglo-Irish intergovernmental Council. Protest strikes break out in Northern Ireland on November 23.

6   U.S. president Ronald Reagan publicly abandons his goal of a balanced budget by the fiscal year 1984.

14   The West African states of Gambia and Senegal agree to form the confederation of Senegambia.

18   U.S. president Ronald Reagan offers to cancel the deployment of cruise and Pershing missiles in Europe if the USSR dismantles medium-range nuclear missiles targeted on Western Europe.

18   U.S. president Ronald Reagan proposes arms spending of $180 billion over six years, primarily on new intercontinental missiles and bombers.

25   An Arab summit conference in Fez, Morocco, quickly reaches deadlock over a Saudi Arabian peace plan for the Middle East.

28   The center-right National Party wins a very narrow victory in the New Zealand general election.

29   A terrorist bomb kills 64 people in Damascus, Syria.

DECEMBER

1   U.S.–Soviet arms limitation talks open in Geneva, Switzerland.

4   U.S. president Ronald Reagan lifts curbs on the CIA's domestic covert activities, providing the intelligence to be gathered is "pertinent."

9   The Soviet physicist Andrei Sakharov and his wife, Yelena Bonner, end their 17-day hunger strike when their daughter-in-law, Lisa Alekseeva, is given a visa to join her husband in the United States.

13   Martial law is imposed in Poland, leading to mass detentions and imposing curbs on civil liberties and labor union activities.

14   Israel formally annexes the Golan Heights, taken from Syria in the 1967 Yom Kippur War.

18   Mehmet Shehu, the Albanian prime minister, is reported to have committed suicide. He is later denounced as a U.S.–Soviet–Yugoslav spy, and his death as authorized by the communist government.

22   General Leopoldo Galtieri becomes president of Argentina.

29   Responding to perceived Soviet political pressure on Poland to adopt martial law, President Ronald Reagan introduces U.S. economic sanctions against the USSR.

31   Flight Lieutenant Jerry Rawlings stages his second military coup in Ghana.

SCIENCE, TECHNOLOGY, AND MEDICINE

Computing

- Dutch company Philips and the Laboratoires d'Electronique et Physique Appliquée, France, together develop smart cards.
- The electronics company Commodore launch the VIC-20, which will become the first microcomputer to sell over 1 million units.
- The IBM personal computer is introduced.
- The Japanese introduce computer chips with 64 kilobytes of memory.
- U.S. artist Nancy Burson copatents a computer process to alter and age pictures of faces, which is used by plastic surgeons as well as law enforcement agencies.
- U.S. firm 3M develops the erasable optical disc, enabling discs to be reused.

August

12 IBM launches its personal computer, using the Microsoft disc-operating system (MS-DOS).

Ecology

- The roof of the Hyatt Hotel in Kansas City, Missouri, collapses, killing 111 people and injuring 180.
- The U.S. Committee on the Atmosphere and Biosphere reports evidence linking acid rain to sulfur emissions from power plants.
- The U.S. government-commissioned *Global 2000 Report to the President* is published; it predicts global environmental catastrophe if pollution, industrial expansion, and population are not brought under control.
- The world's largest solar power generating station, Solar One, is completed in California; it has a capacity of 10 megawatts.

February

12 A fire in a discotheque in Dublin, Ireland, kills 44 people.

May

10–12 Fires burn out of control for two days in Mandalay, Burma (now Myanmar), leaving 35,000 people homeless.

June

11 Over 2,000 people in southeastern Iran are killed when an earthquake measuring 6.6 on the Richter scale strikes.

July

24 Severe flooding in Sichuan province, China, makes up to 1.5 million people homeless.

Exploration

August

- The U.S. probe *Voyager 2* records data on the atmospheres of Saturn and its moon Titan.

Health and Medicine

- *Jane Fonda's Workout Book*, a diet and exercise program, is a best seller in the United States. The increasing interest in fitness spawns a whole get-fit book and video market.
- The genetic code for the hepatitis B surface antigen is discovered, creating the possibility of a bioengineered vaccine.
- The Nobel Prize for Physiology or Medicine is awarded to U.S. neurologist Roger Sperry for his discoveries concerning the functional specialization of the cerebral hemispheres, and to U.S. neurophysiologist David Hubel and Swedish neuroscientist Torsten Wiesel for their discoveries concerning information processing in visual perception.
- The U.S. Center for Disease Control in Atlanta, Georgia, first conclusively identifies AIDS; doctors realize that they have previously seen similar cases among drug users and homosexuals.

- The U.S. Food and Drug Administration grants permission to Eli Lilley and Co. to market insulin produced by bacteria, the first genetically engineered product to go on sale.

August 1981–86 The survival rate for all cancers in U.S. women is 60%; for breast cancer, the rate is almost 77%.

May

- Over 600 people in Spain die from eating contaminated cooking oil.

October

22 The artificial sweetener Aspartame is given approval by the Federal Drug Administration for use in soft drinks and for tabletop use; it is marketed as "Nutrasweet."

Science

- A new family of deep-water stingray is named when a specimen of *Hexatrygon bickelli* is washed up on a South African beach.
- Chinese scientists make the first clone of a fish (a golden carp).
- Dutch-born U.S. physicist Nicolaas Bloembergen, U.S. physicist Arthur Schawlow, and Swedish physicist Kai Siegbahn receive the Nobel Prize for Physics for their work on electron and laser spectroscopy.
- Japanese industrial chemist Kenichi Fukui and Polish-born U.S. chemist Roald Hoffmann receive the Nobel Prize for Chemistry for their progress on theories concerning chemical reactions.
- The most massive star in the universe, R136, is discovered; it is 2,500 times more massive than our Sun and ten times as bright.
- U.S. and Spanish archeologists discover a paleolithic limestone altar with the remains of burned offerings in a cave in northern Spain; it suggests that the Neanderthals had some form of ritual worship.
- U.S. geneticists J. W. Gordon and F. H. Ruddle of the University of Ohio inject genes from one animal into the fertilized egg of a mouse that develop into mice with the foreign gene in many of the cells; the gene is then passed on to their offspring creating permanently altered (transgenic) animals; it is the first transfer of a gene from one animal species to another.
- U.S. geneticists Robert Weinberg, Geoffrey Cooper, and Michael Wigler discover that oncogenes (genes that cause cancer) are integrated into the genome of normal cells.

Technology

- Chemists devise a way of giving polymers some of the properties of metals, including the ability to conduct electricity; this enables scientists at the University of Pennsylvania, United States, to construct the first plastic battery.
- French researchers Claude Michel and Bernard Reveau synthesize some metallic oxides that have excellent conducting properties; the materials prove invaluable in achieving superconductivity at relatively high temperatures.
- New "glassy" metal alloys, with high strength combined with lightness, are created by a new technique whereby

rapidly cooling the molten metal prevents the normal crystallization that takes place during cooling.
- The first working high-definition television (HDTV) is demonstrated in Japan.
- The two-dimensional fluorescent lamp is introduced.
- U.S. scientists Adam Heller and Ferdinand Thiel develop a liquid junction cell that converts 11.5% of solar energy into electricity.

OCTOBER

24 One hundred and fifty thousand people attend a CND (Campaign for Nuclear Disarmament) rally in London, England.

Transportation

- Car air conditioning, cruising speed, radio, and engine performance begin to be monitored and controlled by computer.
- Only 6.2 million automobiles are manufactured in the United States, the lowest figure for 20 years.
- U.S. pilot Stephen Ptacek crosses the English Channel from Paris, France, to Manston, Kent, England (368 km/ 180 mi), at a height of 3,353 m/11,000 ft, in 5.5 hours in *Solar Challenger*, the first solar-powered aircraft; it uses 16,000 solar cells.

JANUARY

6   The Brazilian steamer *Novo Amapa* sinks in the Amazon River near Macapá, Brazil, killing 260 people.
27 The Indonesian vessel *Sobral Santos* catches fire and then sinks in the Java Sea, killing 580 passengers and crew.

APRIL

12–14 The U.S. reusable space shuttle, using the orbiter *Columbia*, makes its first flight (second shuttle flight between November 12–14). It is also the first landing of a U.S. spacecraft on land.

JUNE

6   A train is swept off a bridge into the Bagmati River in India and more than 800 people are killed in the world's worst train wreck.

AUGUST

2   U.S. air-traffic controllers begin a national strike, grounding commercial aviation for several days. They are dismissed on August 6 for failing to comply with a presidential order to return to work.

SEPTEMBER

19 The riverboat *Sobral Santos* sinks in the Amazon River, Brazil, killing at least 300 people.
22 French railroads introduce the TGV (*train à grande vitesse*, "high-speed train"); electrically powered and capable of cruising at 290 kph/180 mph, it is Europe's first super high-speed passenger train. Later in the year it achieves a record speed of 380 kph/236 mph.

ARTS AND IDEAS

Architecture

- The U.S. journalist Tom Wolfe publishes *From Bauhaus to Our House*, a satire on modern architecture.

Arts

- c. 1981 The Figuration Libre movement in art, based on the use of comic strips and graffiti, comes to prominence in France.
- Ettore Sottsass's Milan-based design consortium Memphis launches its wildly bright and playful furniture at the Milan Salone Internazionale del Mobile, in Italy.
- Following the restoration of democracy in Spain, Picasso's painting *Guernica* is taken from the Museum of Modern Art in New York, New York, to the Prado in Madrid.
- The German-born English artist Lucian Freud paints *Naked Girl with Dog*.
- The Italian artist Francesco Clemente paints *Toothache*.
- The U.S. artist Carl André sculpts *Niner*.
- The U.S. artist David Salle paints *An Illustrator Was There*.
- The U.S. artist Eric Fischl paints *Bad Boy*.
- The U.S. artist Jon Borofsky sculpts *Hammering Man*.
- The U.S. artist Julian Schnabel paints *Prehistory: Glory, Honor, Privilege, Poverty*.
- The U.S. artist Leon Golub paints *Interrogation II*.
- The U.S. artist Richard Serra completes his sculpture *Tilted Arc*, which is set up in Foley Square, New York, New York.
- The U.S. artist Sherrie Levine publishes her photograph *After Walker Evans: 7*.

Film

- The movie *An American Werewolf in London*, directed by John Landis, is released in the United States. It stars David Naughton, Jenny Agutter, and Griffin Dunne.
- The movie *Arthur*, directed by Steve Gordon, is released in the United States, starring Dudley Moore, Liza Minnelli, and John Gielgud.
- The movie *Atlantic City*, directed by Louis Malle, is released in the United States. It stars Burt Lancaster and Susan Sarandon.
- The movie *Blow Out* is released in the United States. It is directed by Brian De Palma and stars John Travolta and Nancy Allen.
- The movie *Bodas de sangre/Blood Wedding*, directed by Carlos Saura, a flamenco ballet adaptation of the play by Federico García Lorca (1933), is released in Spain. It is choreographed by and stars Antonio Gades.
- The movie *Body Heat*, written and directed by Lawrence Kasdan, is released in the United States. It stars William Hurt and Kathleen Turner.
- The movie *Chariots of Fire*, directed by Hugh Hudson, is released in the UK. It stars Ian Charleson and Ben Cross.
- The movie *Coup de Torchon/Clean Slate*, directed by Bertrand Tavernier, is released in France, an adaptation of the Jim Thompson crime novel *Pop. 1280*. It stars Philippe Noiret and Isabelle Huppert.
- The movie *Cutter's Way*, directed by Czech-born U.S. filmmaker Ivan Passer, is released in the United States, starring Jeff Bridges and John Heard. It is based on Newton Thornburg's novel *Cutter and Bone*.

- The movie *Człowiek z Żelaza/Man of Iron*, directed by Andrzej Wajda, is released in Poland. It stars Jerzy Radziwiłłowicz and Krystyna Janda. It is awarded the Palme d'Or at the French Cannes Film Festival on May 27 this year.
- The movie *Das Boot/The Boat*, directed by Wolfgang Petersen, is released in West Germany. It stars Jürgen Prochnow.
- The movie *Diva*, directed by Jean-Jacques Beineix, is released in France. It stars Frédéric Andrei, Wilhelmenia Wiggins Fernandez, and Richard Bohringer.
- The movie *Excalibur*, directed by John Boorman, is released in the UK. It stars Nicol Williamson, Nigel Terry, and Helen Mirren.
- The movie *For Your Eyes Only*, directed by John Glen, is released in the United States. It stars Roger Moore as James Bond.
- The movie *Gregory's Girl*, directed by Bill Forsyth, is released in the UK. It stars Gordon John Sinclair and Dee Hepburn.
- The movie *La Femme de l'aviateur/The Aviator's Wife*, directed by Erich Rohmer, is released in France.
- The movie *Mephisto*, directed by István Szabó, is released in Hungary. It stars Klaus Maria Brandauer.
- The movie *My Dinner with André*, directed by Louis Malle, is released in the United States. It stars Wallace Shawn and André Gregory.
- The movie *On Golden Pond*, directed by Mark Rydell, is released in the United States. It stars Katharine Hepburn, Henry Fonda (in his last movie), and Jane Fonda.
- The movie *Pixote*, directed by the Argentinean-born filmmaker Hector Babenco, is released in Brazil. It stars Fernando Ramos da Silva and Marilia Pera.
- The movie *Raiders of the Lost Ark*, the first movie in Steven Spielberg's *Indiana Jones* trilogy, is released in the United States. It stars Harrison Ford and Karen Allen.
- The movie *Reds*, directed by and starring Warren Beatty, is released in the United States. Diane Keaton costars.
- The movie *The French Lieutenant's Woman*, directed by the Czech filmmaker Karel Reisz, is released in the UK. Based on the book by John Fowles, it stars Meryl Streep and Jeremy Irons.
- The movie *The Postman Always Rings Twice*, an adaptation of James M. Cain's novel, is released in the United States. It is directed by Bob Rafelson and stars Jack Nicholson and Jessica Lange.
- The movie *Thief*, starring James Caan and written and directed by Michael Mann, is released in the United States.
- The movie *Time Bandits*, directed by Terry Gilliam, is released in the UK. It features an all-star cast including Sean Connery, Shelley Duvall, John Cleese, Ian Holm, and Ralph Richardson.
- The movie *True Confessions*, directed by Belgian filmmaker Ulu Grosbard, is released in the United States, starring Robert De Niro and Robert Duvall.
- The war movie *Gallipoli*, directed by Peter Weir, is released in Australia. It stars Mark Lee and Mel Gibson.

MARCH

31 The 1980 Academy Awards take place. Best Actor: Robert De Niro, for *Raging Bull*; Best Supporting Actor: Timothy Hutton, for *Ordinary People*; Best Actress: Sissy Spacek, for *Coal Miner's Daughter*; Best Supporting Actress: Mary Steenburgen, for *Melvin and Howard*; Best Picture: *Ordinary People*, directed by Robert Redford; Best Director: Robert Redford, for *Ordinary People*.

Literature and Language

- Australian novelist Peter Carey publishes his novel *Bliss*.
- British poet John Betjeman publishes his *Church Poems*.
- English novelist Martin Amis publishes his novel *Other People*.
- English writer Ian McEwan publishes his novel *The Comfort of Strangers*.
- Terence Kilmartin publishes a reworking of Scott Moncrieff's translation of Marcel Proust's novel *Remembrance of Things Past*.
- The Caribbean writer Derek Walcott publishes his poetry book *The Fortunate Traveller*.
- The Chinese writer Zhang Jie publishes her novel *Leaden Wings*.
- The Colombian writer Gabriel García Márquez publishes *Crónica de una muerte nunciada/Chronicle of a Death Foretold*.
- The English writer D. M. Thomas publishes his novel *The White Hotel*.
- The Indian-born English writer Salman Rushdie publishes his novel *Midnight's Children*, which wins the Booker Prize.
- The Nigerian writer Wole Soyinka publishes his autobiography *Aké: The Years of Childhood*.
- The Nobel Prize for Literature is awarded to the Bulgarian novelist and essayist Elias Canetti.
- The Peruvian writer Mario Vargas Llosa publishes his novel *La guerra del fin del mundo/The War of the End of the World*.
- The Pulitzer Prize for Biography is awarded to Robert K. Massie for *Peter the Great*, the Pulitzer Prize for Poetry is awarded to James Schuyler for *The Morning of the Poem*, and the Pulitzer Prize for Fiction is awarded posthumously to John Kennedy Toole for *A Confederacy of Dunces*.
- The Scottish novelist Alasdair Gray publishes his novel *Lanark*.
- The U.S. writer A. R. Ammons publishes his poetry collection *A Coast of Trees*.
- The U.S. writer John Updike publishes his novel *Rabbit is Rich*, which wins the Pulitzer Prize for Fiction.
- The U.S. writer Martin Cruz Smith publishes his novel *Gorky Park*.
- The U.S. writer Maya Angelou publishes her novel *The Heart of a Woman*.
- The U.S. writer Paul Theroux publishes his novel *The Mosquito Coast*.
- The U.S. writer Raymond Carver publishes his short-story collection *What We Talk About When We Talk About Love*.
- The U.S. writer Toni Morrison publishes her novel *Tar Baby*.

Music

- The Belgian composer Henri Pousseur completes his orchestral work *Le Second apothéose de Rameau/The Second Apotheosis of Rameau*.
- The British pop singer Phil Collins releases "In The Air Tonight."
- The Estonian composer Arvo Pärt completes his *Passio Domini nostri Jesu Christi secundum Joannem/The Passion of our Lord Jesus Christ according to John* (or *St John Passion*), for voices and chamber ensemble.
- The French composer Pierre Boulez completes his work *Répons* for 24 players, six soloists, and computerized electronics.
- The French musician Jean-Michel Jarre becomes the first western pop star to give a concert in China.
- The German-born U.S. composer Lukas Foss completes his orchestral work *Night Music for John Lennon*.
- The Japanese composer Toru Takemitsu completes his orchestral work *Dreamtime*.
- The Russian composer Alfred Schnittke completes his Symphony No. 3.
- The U.S. composer John Cage completes his orchestral work *Thirty Pieces for Five Orchestras*.

FEBRUARY

7 The British new wave group the Jam releases the album *Sound Affects*.
25 The 1980–81 Grammy Awards are held. Best Album: *Sailing* by Christopher Cross; Best Record: "Sailing" by Christopher Cross; Best Female Pop Vocalist: Bette Midler for "The Rose"; Best Rock Group: Bob Seger and the Silver Bullet Band for "Against the Wind."

MARCH

21 The British rock musician Brian Eno and Talking Heads lead singer David Byrne release the album *My Life in the Bush of Ghosts*.

APRIL

- The classical music conductor Herbert von Karajan demonstrates the first compact discs, developed by the Dutch company Philips, at the Salzburg Festival, in Austria.

JULY

11 The U.S. pop singers Diana Ross and Lionel Richie release "Endless Love."

AUGUST

1 With a target audience aged 12–34, and an estimated 2.5 million subscribers, the MTV (music television) channel is launched, with the video of the Buggles' single "Video Killed the Radio Star."

SEPTEMBER

19 A free concert by the reunited Simon and Garfunkel in Central Park, New York, New York, is attended by 400,000 people.

OCTOBER

24 The British pop group the Police releases "Every Little Thing She Does Is Magic" and the album *Ghost In The Machine*.
24 The British pop group Ultravox releases the album *Rage in Eden*.

NOVEMBER

7 The U.S. pop group the J. Geils Band releases the single "Centerfold."

Theater and Dance

- *A Soldier's Play*, by the U.S. writer Charles Fuller, is first performed, at the Theater Four in New York, New York.
- *Torch Song Trilogy*, by the U.S. writer Harvey Fierstein is first performed, at the Richard Allen Center in New York, New York.
- The ancient Greek play trilogy the *Oresteia*, by Aeschylus, is performed at the National Theatre in London, England. The acclaimed translation is by the English poet Tony Harrison.
- The musical *Cats* is first performed, in London, England. Written by Tim Rice and Andrew Lloyd Webber, it is based on T. S. Eliot's book of poems for children *Old Possum's Book of Practical Cats*. One of its best-known songs is "Memories."
- The play *Another Country*, by the English writer Julian Mitchell, is first performed, in London, England.
- The play *Caritas*, by the English writer Arnold Wesker, is first performed, in London, England.
- The play *Goose Pimples*, by the English writer and director Mike Leigh, is first performed, in London, England.
- The play *Mass Appeal*, by the U.S. writer Bill C. Davis, is first performed, at the Booth Theater in New York, New York.
- The play *Restoration*, by the English writer Edward Bond, is first performed, in London, England.
- The play *Steaming*, by the English writer Nell Dunn, is first performed, at the Theatre Royal in London, England.
- The Pulitzer Prize for Drama is awarded to Beth Henley for *Crimes of the Heart*.

Thought and Scholarship

- British historian Stephen Koss publishes the first volume of *The Rise and Fall of the Political Press*. The second volume will follow in 1984.
- British philosopher Alisdair MacIntyre publishes *After Virtue*.
- English philosopher R. M. Hare publishes *Moral Thinking*.
- German social scientist Jürgen Habermas publishes *Theorie des kommunikatives Handelns/The Theory of Communicative Action*.
- The Pulitzer Prize for History is awarded to Lawrence A. Cremin for *American Education: The National Experience, 1783–1876*.
- The Pulitzer Prize for General Nonfiction is awarded to Carl E. Schorske for *Fin-de-siècle Vienna*.
- The U.S. feminist Betty Friedan publishes *The Second Stage*.
- U.S. economist Milton Friedman publishes *Monetary Trends in the United States and the United Kingdom*.
- U.S. historian James M. McPherson publishes *Ordeal by Fire: The Civil War and Reconstruction*.

- U.S. historian Joel Garreau publishes *The Nine Nations of North America*.
- U.S. historian Martin Joel Wiener publishes *English Culture and the Decline of the Industrial Spirit, 1850–1980*.
- U.S. historian Thomas C. Cochran publishes *Frontiers of Change: Early Industrialization of America*.
- U.S. political scientist James Lloyd Sundquist publishes *The Decline and Resurgence of Congress*.

SOCIETY

Education

- Japan introduces a new curriculum for lower secondary schools.
- The first university degrees at bachelor level are awarded in China.

Everyday Life

- Divorce becomes legal in Spain.
- Divorces in the United States reach their highest to date at 1,210,000 this year.
- In fashion, U.S. women want a fresher and more plain, but sexy, style.
- It is estimated that the average woman in India has eight pregnancies in her lifetime; 3.5 million Indian women are sterilized each year.
- Japanese fashion designer Rei Kawakubo, of Comme des Garçons, shows her collection in Paris, France for the first time.
- Japanese fashion has a significant influence on the West, with the loose-fitting designs of Issey Miyake, Yohji Yamamoto, Mitsuhiro Matsuda, and Rei Kawakubo gaining popularity.
- Populations (in millions): China 991.3; India 690.2; USSR 268.0; U.S. 229.8; Indonesia 149.5; Brazil 120.5; Japan 117.6; Bangladesh 90.7; Nigeria 87.6; Pakistan 84.5; Mexico 71.2; West Germany 61.7; Italy 56.2; Great Britain and Northern Ireland 56.0; France 54.0.
- The sale of video cassette recorders exceeds 1 million a year for the first time in the United States.
- The world population stands at 4.5 billion, up 2 billion since 1950.
- Women in the United States spend 30.5 hours a week doing housework; men spend 14.
- Women's pay as a percentage of men's pay: Denmark, 84.5%; New Zealand, 75%; Finland, 61%; West Germany, 72.5%; UK, 69.5%; Italy, 85%; United States, 59%.

August

3–5 The Solidarity labor union movement blockades Warsaw city center in Poland in protest at food shortages.

Media and Communication

- The government of Indonesia bans television commercials.
- There are now regular television transmissions in 137 countries worldwide.
- Veteran news anchorman and journalist Walter Cronkite retires.

January

12–May 11, 1989 *Dynasty*, a soap opera about the lives of a Colorado oil family, is shown on U.S. television. Stars include John Forsythe, Linda Evans, and Joan Collins, and there are cameo appearances from former U.S. president Gerald Ford and former secretary of state Henry Kissinger.

14 The Federal Communication Commission (FCC) significantly eases regulations restricting the time radio stations can allot to commercials.

15–May 19, 1987 *Hill Street Blues*, a police series with a strong soap opera flavor, starts on U.S. television. It stars Daniel J. Travanti, Veronica Hamel, Michael Conrad, and Michael Warren.

27 *The Bunker*, a documentary drama about the last days of Adolf Hitler, is shown on U.S. television, starring Anthony Hopkins, Susan Blakely, and Richard Jordan.

February

8 *Kent State*, a documentary drama about the 1970 killing of four students by the Ohio National Guard at Kent State University, is shown on U.S. television. It stars Jane Fleiss, Talia Balsam, and Keith Gordon.

March

10 Disney Pictures decides to launch the Disney Channel, their own subscription channel, on cable television in the United States.

July

29 Charles, Prince of Wales, marries Lady Diana Spencer in St. Paul's Cathedral in London, England. Television coverage attracts 39 million people, the largest British audience to date.

August

8 The *Washington Star* ceases publication after 128 years.

September

13 The 1980–81 Emmy Awards for television are held. Best Drama Series: *Hill Street Blues*; Best Comedy Series: *Taxi*; Best Actor in a Drama: Daniel J. Travanti, for *Hill Street Blues*; Best Actress in a Drama: Barbara Babcock, for *Hill Street Blues*; Best Actor in a Comedy: Judd Hirsh, for *Taxi*; Best Actress in a Comedy: Isabel Sanford, for *The Jeffersons*.

October

14 The television biography *Jacqueline Bouvier Kennedy*, starring Jaclyn Smith and James Franciscus, is shown on U.S. television.

November

7 *Skokie*, a documentary drama about the attempt by U.S. Nazis to march in Skokie, Illinois, is shown on U.S. television, starring Danny Kaye, Eli Wallach, and Kim Hunter.

December

4–May 17, 1990   The night-time television soap opera *Falcon Crest*, about rich and powerful winery owners in a fictitious valley near San Francisco, is shown on U.S. television.

November

12   The General Synod of the Church of England votes to recognize the sacraments of the Free Churches and their women ministers and to allow women to be ordained as deacons.

Religion

August

24   The Salvation Army withdraws from the World Council of Churches because of its financial support for African guerrilla movements.

Sports

- Mairzy Dotes, ridden by the U.S. jockey Cash Asmussen, wins the inaugural Japan Cup at Fuchu racecourse, Tokyo, Japan.
- The Australian Institute of Sport, a coaching academy for the country's top sportsmen and sportswomen, is established at Canberra.

BIRTHS & DEATHS

January

5   Harold Clayton Urey, U.S. chemist who discovered the heavy form of hydrogen known as deuterium, dies in La Jolla, California (87).

6   A(rchibald) J(oseph) Cronin, Scottish physician and novelist who combined realism, romance, and social criticism, dies in Montreux, Switzerland (84).

10   Fawn Brodie, U.S. author and biographer, dies in Santa Monica, California (64).

14   David Lilienthal, U.S. lawyer and government official, the first head of the Atomic Energy Commission, dies in New York, New York (81).

15   Emmanuel Celler, U.S. Democrat politician who fought for national civil-rights legislation, dies in New York, New York (92).

23   Samuel Barber, U.S. lyric and romantic composer, dies in New York, New York (70).

February

1   Donald Douglas, U.S. aircraft designer who founded the Douglas Aircraft Company, dies in Palm Springs, California (88).

5   Ella Grasso, U.S. politician, the first woman governor not married to a former governor, dies in Hartford, Connecticut (61).

19   John Knudson Northrop, U.S. aircraft designer who designed many commercial and military aircraft, dies in Glendale, California (85).

26   Howard Hanson, U.S. romantic composer, conductor, and teacher, dies in Rochester, New York (84).

March

23   Mike Hailwood, English motorcycle racer, the youngest ever 250cc world champion, dies in Birmingham, England (40).

30   DeWitt Wallace, U.S. publisher who started *Reader's Digest* magazine, dies in Mt Kisco, New York (91).

April

8   Omar Bradley, U.S. army commander of the 12th Army Group in World War II, later the first chairman of the U.S. joint chiefs of staff, dies in New York, New York (88).

12   Joe Louis, U.S. world heavyweight champion boxer 1937–49, dies in Las Vegas, Nevada (66).

May

9   Nelson Algren, U.S. novelist and travel writer whose best-known novel *The Man with the Golden Arm* won the National Book Award and was filmed in 1956, dies (71).

11   Bob Marley, Jamaican reggae singer and songwriter whose topical songs popularized reggae music throughout the world in the 1970s, dies in Miami, Florida (36).

18   William Saroyan, U.S. Pulitzer prizewinning playwright and novelist, dies in Fresno, California (72).

30   Zia ur-Rahman, president of Bangladesh 1976–81, is killed in an attempted coup (45).

July

1   Marcel Lajos Breuer, Hungarian-born U.S. architect and designer, an exponent of the International Style, dies in New York, New York (79).

30   Kazuo Taoka, Japanese crime boss who headed the 10,000-member Yamaguchi-gumi crime organization, dies in Amagasaki, Japan (69).

August

18   Anita Loos, U.S. writer and screenwriter best known for her fictitious diary *Gentlemen Prefer Blonds*, dies in New York, New York (88).

29   Lowell Thomas, U.S. explorer, journalist, and radio commentator, dies in Pawling, New York (89).

31   Joseph Hirshhorn, U.S. businessman, art collector, and philanthropist, dies in Washington, D.C. (82).

September

12   Eugenio Montale, Italian poet, author, translator, and editor, dies in Milan, Italy (84).

27   Robert Montgomery, U.S. film and television actor, director, and Republican politician, dies (77).

October

6   Anwar Sadat, Egyptian president 1970–81, is assassinated by Muslim extremists at a military parade in Cairo, Egypt (62).

16   Moshe Dayan, Israeli commander and statesman who led Israel's victories against the Arabs and was one of the founders of the Camp David agreements, dies in Tel Aviv, Israel (66).

November

10   Abel Gance, French film director, dies in Paris, France (92).

12   William Holden, U.S. actor who won an Adademy Award for *Stalag 17*, dies in Santa Monica, California (63).

22   Hans Krebs, German-born British biochemist working in the field of cell metabolism, dies in Oxford, England (81).

28   Natalie Wood, U.S. film actress whose best-known films include *Miracle on 34th Street* and *Rebel without a Cause*, dies in a yachting accident (43).

December

27   Hoagy Carmichael, Academy Award-winning U.S. composer, pianist, singer, and actor, dies in Palm Springs, California (82).

- The International Olympic Committee, based in Switzerland, paves the way for professional participation in the games by passing on to individual international Olympic federations the responsibility for determining Olympic eligibility.

JANUARY

1   Sportswriters pick the University of Georgia as college football's best team for the 1980 season.
25 The Oakland Raiders are the first wild card team to win a Super Bowl, defeating the Philadelphia Eagles 27–10 in Super Bowl XV in New Orleans, Louisiana.

FEBRUARY

3–8   U.S. national figure skating champions are: Elaine Zayak; Scott Hamilton; Kitty and Peter Carruthers, pairs; Judy Blumberg and Michael Seibert, dance.
15   Richard Petty wins the Daytona 500 Grand National stock car race at Daytona Beach, Florida, for the seventh time.

MAY

5–14   The Boston Celtics beat the Houston Rockets to take the National Basketball Association (NBA) crown.
12   The New York Islanders win the Stanley Cup, beating the Minnesota North Stars four games to one.
25   Errol Tobias is the first nonwhite player to be selected to represent South Africa in a rugby union international.
25   U.S. race-car driver Bobby Unser wins the Indianapolis 500.
27   At the age of 49, U.S. jockey Bill Shoemaker rides his 8,000th winner.

JUNE

12–July 31   All 650 major league baseball players walk out in a dispute over free agent compensation; 712 games are lost during the 49-day strike before a settlement is reached.

AUGUST

13   Jon Erikson from Chicago, Illinois, becomes the first person to swim the English Channel three times nonstop, in a time of 38 hr 27 min.
19   The U.S. athlete Renaldo Nehemiah sets a new world record time for the 110-meter hurdles of 12.93 seconds, in Zürich, Switzerland.
19–28   In nine days, the English runners Steve Ovett and Sebastian Coe establish three new world records for the mile; the record is cut by over 1 second to 3 min 47.53 sec. Coe runs 3 min 48.53 sec in Zürich, Switzerland. Ovett then runs 3 min 48.40 sec in Koblenz, West Germany, before Coe regains the record with a run of 3 min 47.33 sec in Brussels, Belgium.
30   John Henry, ridden by Bill Shoemaker, wins the first Arlington Million horse race, at Arlington Park, Illinois.

SEPTEMBER

13   In tennis, John McEnroe of the United States is the first player since Bill Tilden in 1922 to win three successive men's singles titles at the U.S. Championships.

OCTOBER

20–28   In baseball, the Los Angeles Dodgers win their first World Series since 1965, overcoming a two-game deficit to beat the New York Yankees four games to two.

1982

POLITICS, GOVERNMENT, AND ECONOMICS

Business and Economics

- In the second half of 1982, unemployment in the United States reaches its highest level since the recession of the 1930s, with 12 million out of work, representing a rate of 10.4 percent.
- International commodity prices reach their lowest level since World War II.
- Mexico defaults on a loan payment, leading to general concern about the ability of Third World countries to meet their international debts and about the consequences of defaults for lending nations. The International Monetary Fund (IMF) intervenes with debt rescheduling and imposes austerity measures on debtor countries.
- The deregulation of savings and loan institutions in the United States leads to an upsurge in bad loans and fraud.
- The U.S. trade deficit reaches $110.7 billion.
- U.S. company Apple Computer becomes the first personal computer manufacturer to achieve sales of $1 billion.

JANUARY

8   The American Telephone and Telegraph company (AT&T) is forced to sell 22 of its local companies, effectively ending its monopoly of telephone services.

19 The Polish authorities announce increases in food prices of between 200 percent and 400 percent from February 1.

FEBRUARY

19 The British government-supported De Lorean car company in Northern Ireland is put into receivership.

28 Auto workers at the Ford plant in Detroit, Michigan, agree to give up regular pay rises in exchange for greater job security.

MAY

13 Braniff International becomes the first U.S. airline to file for bankruptcy.

SEPTEMBER

13 A report prepared by Lord Shackleton in Britain on the scope for the economic development of the Falkland Islands recommends the investment of £100 million.

OCTOBER

7 The day's trading on the New York Stock Exchange passes a new record, with 147,070,000 shares changing hands.

19 The British government announces the closure of the De Lorean car plant in Northern Ireland with the loss of 1,500 jobs. John De Lorean is arrested in Los Angeles on drugs charges.

Human Rights

• The Chinese writer Zhang Jie publishes her novella *Ark*, widely seen as the first genuinely feminist work to come from modern China.

JUNE

30 The 1972 Equal Rights Amendment in the United States, prohibiting discrimination on the basis of sex, fails to secure ratification of a sufficient number of states to ensure inclusion in the Constitution.

Politics and Government

• A U.S. federal court in Little Rock, Arkansas, declares it unconstitutional to teach creationism on a par with evolutionary theory.

• New constitutions in China of the Communist Party and the state transfer power back to the bureaucracy and the leadership, serving the interests of leader Deng Xiaoping.

• The British Criminal Justice Act creates a new system of custodial offenses for young offenders, but abolishes imprisonment and Borstal (youth) detention as punishments.

• U.S. president Ronald Reagan announces "New Federalism," by which the responsibility for funding several welfare measures is left to the states.

JANUARY

8 Spain agrees to end its 12-year blockade of the British Crown colony Gibraltar, but the frontier is not opened until December 15.

16 Britain and the Vatican resume full diplomatic relations after a break of over 400 years.

24 The Egyptian president Hosni Mubarak announces a policy of nonalignment and seeks assistance from the USSR on industrial projects.

29 The U.S. government agrees to cover Poland's debt payments.

31 A curfew is imposed in Gdańsk, Poland, following riots over price increases.

31 Israel agrees to accept a U.S. peacekeeping force in Sinai.

FEBRUARY

1 U.S. president Ronald Reagan announces emergency aid for the government of El Salvador.

6 U.S. president Ronald Reagan asks Congress to approve a huge cut in domestic spending.

9 The European Community and the United States announce an end to East–West talks in Madrid, Spain, until martial law in Poland is lifted.

17 The prime minister of Zimbabwe Robert Mugabe dismisses the ZAPU (Zimbabwe African Peoples Union) leader, Joshua Nkomo, from the government.

19 The court martial opens in Spain of 32 officers charged with involvement in the 1981 attempted coup. On June 3, they are sentenced to 30 years' imprisonment.

23 Forces of the Ugandan Freedom Movement attack the country's capital Kampala.

27 Wayne Williams is convicted of murdering 23 children and five adults in a two-year killing spree in Atlanta, Georgia.

MARCH

1 General Wojciech Jaruzelski, the Polish premier, visits Moscow, USSR for talks on the economic and political crisis in Poland.

10 The United States imposes an embargo on Libyan oil imports and on exports of high-technology goods to Libya.

11 The British government announces its intention to purchase the Trident II submarine-launched missile system to replace Britain's existing Polaris nuclear weapons.

15 The Sandinista leader Daniel Ortega suspends the Nicaraguan constitution and declares a one-month state of emergency throughout the country.

19 An Argentine scrap-metal dealer lands on the island of South Georgia in the South Atlantic and raises the Argentine flag.

23 An army coup topples the government of Guatemala and installs a junta headed by General Ríos Montt.

24 A military coup brings General Hossain Mohammad Ershad to power in Bangladesh.

APRIL

2 Argentina invades and occupies the British-held Falkland Islands in the South Atlantic. Britain breaks diplomatic relations with Argentina.

3 United Nations Security Council Resolution 502 demands the withdrawal of Argentine forces from the Falklands.

4 The British government proposes new political institutions in Northern Ireland in the White Paper "A Framework for Devolution," including a new elected Northern Ireland Assembly.

4 The first ships of a Royal Navy task force set sail from Britain for the Falklands.

7 The U.S. secretary of state Alexander Haig offers to mediate in the Falklands dispute between Britain and Argentina.

Falklands War (1982)

MARCH

19 An Argentine scrap-metal dealer lands on the island of South Georgia in the South Atlantic and raises the Argentine flag.

APRIL

2 Argentina invades and occupies the British-held Falkland Islands in the South Atlantic. Britain breaks diplomatic relations with Argentina.

3 United Nations Security Council Resolution 502 demands the withdrawal of Argentine forces from the Falklands.

4 The first ships of a Royal Navy task force set sail from Britain for the Falklands.

7 The U.S. secretary of state Alexander Haig offers to mediate in the Falklands dispute between Britain and Argentina.

11 The European Community imposes economic sanctions on Argentina in response to the Argentine occupation of the Falklands.

12 Britain declares a 200-mile maritime exclusion zone around the Falkland Islands.

19 The British government rejects the Haig plan to resolve the Falklands conflict. On April 29, the Argentine government also rejects it.

25 British commandos recapture South Georgia from the small Argentine force occupying the island.

30 The Reagan administration in the United States imposes economic sanctions on Argentina over the Falklands crisis, and offers to supply war materials to Britain.

MAY

1 British warplanes bomb Port Stanley airport in the Falkland Islands.

2 The British submarine HMS *Conqueror* sinks the Argentine cruiser *General Belgrano* off the Falkland Islands, killing 368 officers and crewmen.

4 Argentine air-launched missiles sink the British destroyer HMS *Sheffield* in the Falkland Islands, killing 21 Royal Navy sailors.

21 British troops land on the island of East Falkland and establish a bridgehead at Port San Carlos.

28 British troops recapture Port Darwin and Goose Green in the Falkland Islands, taking 1,400 Argentine prisoners.

JUNE

8 The British landing ships *Sir Tristram* and *Sir Galahad* are hit by Argentine air-launched missiles at Bluff Cove in the Falkland Islands. Both ships are severely damaged, and 40 soldiers and crewmen are killed.

14 Argentine forces surrender at Port Stanley, ending the Falklands War; 255 Britons and 652 Argentines have died in the conflict.

JULY

11 Argentina recognizes a de facto cessation of hostilities with Britain, and the following day the British government declares an end to hostilities.

---

11 The European Community imposes economic sanctions on Argentina in response to the Argentine occupation of the Falklands.

12 Britain declares a 200-mile maritime exclusion zone around the Falkland Islands.

15 Five Muslim fundamentalists are executed in Cairo for involvement in the October 1981 assassination of President Anwar Sadat.

17 Repatriation of the Canadian constitution (its removal from British law to place it entirely under Canadian control) breaks Canada's last link with the British government.

19 The British government rejects the Haig plan to resolve the Falklands conflict. On April 29, the Argentine government also rejects it.

19 The U.S. government bans tourist travel to Cuba.

25 British commandos recapture South Georgia from the small Argentine force occupying the island.

30 The Reagan administration in the United States imposes economic sanctions on Argentina over the Falklands crisis, and offers to supply war materials to Britain.

MAY

1 Fifty thousand supporters of the Polish labor union movement Solidarity demonstrate against martial law. Military controls are tightened on May 4 in response.

1 British warplanes bomb Port Stanley airport in the Falkland Islands.

2 The British submarine HMS *Conqueror* sinks the Argentine cruiser *General Belgrano* off the Falkland Islands, killing 368 officers and crewmen.

3 The Israeli prime minister Menachem Begin announces that Israel will assert its sovereignty over the occupied West Bank.

4 Argentine air-launched missiles sink the British destroyer HMS *Sheffield* in the Falkland Islands, killing 21 Royal Navy sailors.

6 The Conservative Party makes large gains in British local elections.

21 British troops land on the island of East Falkland and establish a bridgehead at Port San Carlos.

22 Pope John Paul II celebrates a "Mass for Peace" in Rome with English and Argentine cardinals.

28 British troops recapture Port Darwin and Goose Green in the Falkland Islands, taking 1,400 Argentine prisoners.

JUNE

3 Israel's ambassador to Britain, Shlomo Argov, is shot and wounded in the street in London, England.

4 Israeli jets bomb guerrilla targets in Lebanon in retaliation for the shooting of the Israeli ambassador, Shlomo Argov, in London, England.

5 Israeli armed forces invade Lebanon. On June 6, Israeli and Syrian forces clash in southern Lebanon, and the United Nations Security Council calls for a halt to the fighting.

5   Italian actress Sophia Loren is released from jail after serving 17 days of a 30-day sentence for tax fraud.

5   The Israeli invasion of Lebanon produces mixed reactions in both Israel and in the world Jewish community.

7   Rebel forces in Chad capture the capital, Ndjamene, overthrowing the regime of President Goukouni Oueddei.

8   The British landing ships *Sir Tristram* and *Sir Galahad* are hit by Argentine air-launched missiles at Bluff Cove in the Falkland Islands. Both ships are severely damaged, and 40 soldiers and crewmen are killed.

11 Israeli forces defeat Syrian armor in a pitched battle around Lake Karoun, Lebanon.

12 Approximately 550,000 protesters against nuclear arms march though New York, New York.

13 The French government announces a freeze of prices and incomes until October 31, following devaluation of the franc.

14 Argentine forces surrender at Port Stanley, ending the Falklands War; 255 Britons and 652 Argentines have died in the conflict.

14 Israeli forces surround 6,000 Palestine Liberation Organization guerrillas in West Beirut, Lebanon.

15 The U.S. Supreme Court rules that children of illegal immigrants have the right to free education.

17 President Leopoldo Galtieri of Argentina resigns.

21 John Hinckley, failed assassin of U.S. president Ronald Reagan, is found not guilty of attempted murder, by reason of insanity.

22 The leaders of the three main Kampuchean opposition factions meet in Kuala Lumpur, Malaysia, to form a united front against the Vietnamese-supported government of their country.

22 The U.S. government extends its prohibition on supplying materials for the USSR's Euro-Siberian gas pipeline to overseas companies manufacturing materials under license.

25 The U.S. secretary of state Alexander Haig resigns, to be succeeded by George Shultz.

27 Israel demands the surrender of PLO guerrillas in West Beirut and, on June 29, offers to allow them to leave Beirut with their arms.

28 The city of San Francisco, California, bans the private possession of handguns.

July

1   The Argentine air force and navy commanders resign from the ruling military junta on the appointment of General Reynaldo Bignone as president.

2   The U.S. Supreme Court overturns a judgment making the National Association for the Advancement of Colored People liable for damages arising from business boycotts.

7   An intruder, Michael Fagan, breaks into Buckingham Palace in London, England, steals a bottle of wine from a cellar, and enters the queen's bedroom. The queen only manages to summon help when he asks for a cigarette.

11 Argentina recognizes a de facto cessation of hostilities with Britain in the South Atlantic, and the following day the British government declares an end to hostilities.

13 Iranian troops enter Iraq, aiming to take the city of Basra at the head of the Persian Gulf. The offensive is repulsed by Iraqi forces.

17 The Israeli prime minister Menachem Begin gives Palestine Liberation Organization guerrillas in West Beirut 30 days to leave the city.

20 The Palestine Liberation Organization (PLO) offers to accept United Nations Security Council Resolution 242, recognizing Israel's right to exist, in return for U.S. recognition of the PLO. On July 25, the Palestinian leader Yassir Arafat signs a document accepting the resolution, but the following day the U.S. refuses to recognize the PLO.

29 The Arab League announces the Palestine Liberation Organization's intention to leave West Beirut.

31 The U.S. Congress cuts $35.2 billion from public spending, including deep cuts in funding for education, health, housing, urban aid, and food stamp programs, as a counterpart to the Reagan administration's 1981 tax-cutting Economic Recovery Tax Act.

August

6   The Italian authorities order the liquidation of the country's largest privately owned bank, the Banco Ambrosiano of Milan.

17 China and the United States agree to a gradual reduction in U.S. arms sales to Taiwan.

19 The Israeli cabinet accepts a U.S. plan to evacuate Palestine Liberation Organization guerrillas and Syrian troops from Beirut. The first convoys of guerrillas leave for Cyprus on August 21, and Yassir Arafat leaves for Tunisia on August 30.

19 The U.S. Congress passes a tax-raising package to fight the growing budget deficit.

23 The Lebanese Chamber of Deputies elects the leader of the Christian Phalangists Bashir Gemayel as president, despite Muslim opposition.

26 The Argentine government lifts its ban on political parties.

31 Demonstrations take place in many Polish cities on the second anniversary of the founding of the labor union movement Solidarity.

September

1   After European protests, the United States lifts sanctions on non-U.S. companies working on the Trans-Siberian oil pipeline.

1   The U.S. government announces new Middle East peace proposals, but the following day they are rejected by Israel.

1–12 The Chinese Communist Party holds its 12th Congress in Beijing. Hua Guofeng, who had succeeded Mao Zedong as chairman, is removed from the Politburo.

6   Polish dissidents occupy the Polish embassy in Bern, Switzerland, taking 13 hostages and demanding an end to martial law in Poland. The siege is finally ended by Swiss police on September 9.

6   Troops in El Salvador are accused of killing 300 unarmed civilians during an antiguerrilla campaign in San Vicente province.

10 Argentine senior navy and air force officers agree to rejoin the ruling military junta.

14 The president-elect of Lebanon, Bashir Gemayel, is killed in a Beirut bomb explosion. His brother Amin is sworn in as president on September 23.

17 The West German Social Democrat–Free Democrat government collapses following the withdrawal of Free Democrat ministers. On October 1, a new Christian Democrat–Free Democrat government is formed under Christian Democrat Leader Helmut Kohl.

18 Over 800 Palestinians are killed after Christian Phalangist militiamen enter the West Beirut refugee camps Sabra and Chatila. On September 25, there are protests in Israel over the massacre, and on September 28, the Israeli prime minister Menachem Begin agrees to an independent board of inquiry.

19 Eight hundred U.S. marines join the multinational peacekeeping forces in Beirut.

19 The Social Democratic Labor Party, led by Olof Palme, regains power in the Swedish general election, replacing the center-right coalition of Thorbjörn Fälldin.

26 Israeli troops withdraw from West Beirut, and are replaced by a peacekeeping force of French, Italian, and U.S. troops.

OCTOBER

6 The Commonwealth Games Federation votes to ban from future Commonwealth Games any sportsman or sportswoman who has broken the Gleneagles Agreement of 1977 prohibiting sporting links with South Africa while that country continues to enforce the apartheid system.

8 Poland's communist-controlled parliament bans the Solidarity union and forbids the setting up of new labor unions.

10 The United States imposes trade sanctions on Poland.

11 Sikhs besiege the Indian parliament in New Delhi following the murders of Sikhs in Punjab state.

12 Yassir Arafat, leader of the Palestine Liberation Organization, holds talks with King Hussein of Jordan over the proposed establishment of a Palestinian state confederated with Jordan.

13 Strikes in Polish shipyards end when military law is enforced.

20 Sinn Féin wins five seats in elections to the new Northern Ireland Assembly.

28 The Socialist Workers' Party (PSOE), led by Felipe González, wins a landslide victory in the Spanish general election.

30 A new Portuguese constitution comes into force, ending military influence in government.

NOVEMBER

2 The Democrats make large gains in the U.S. mid-term elections, but the Republicans retain control of the Senate.

3 George Wallace wins a fourth term as governor of Alabama.

7 Major Jean-Baptiste Ouedraogo seizes power in a military coup in Upper Volta (now Burkina Faso), with Captain Thomas Sankara as prime minister.

11 A bomb destroys the Israeli military headquarters in Tyre, Lebanon, with 100 people killed.

12 The Polish Solidarity leader Lech Wałęsa is released from detention.

13 The Vietnam War Memorial, on the Mall in Washington, D.C., designed by Maya Ling Lin, is

completed. The names of 58,156 dead and missing U.S. soldiers are inscribed on a long wall of polished black granite.

16 Sino-Soviet talks open in Moscow, the first since 1969.

22 Ramiz Alia becomes the new Albanian head of state, replacing Haxhi Lleshi.

DECEMBER

2 The Canadian parliament approves a Charter of Rights and Freedoms.

6 Seventeen people are killed in a bomb explosion at a public house in Ballykelly, County Londonderry, Northern Ireland.

7 The U.S. House of Representatives rejects President Ronald Reagan's request for $988 million to build and deploy the first five of 100 MX missiles.

12 Thieves in New York, New York, steal $9,800,000 from an armored truck company, the largest cash robbery in U.S. history.

14 Garret FitzGerald is elected Taoiseach (prime minister) at the head of a Fine Gael–Labour coalition government in Ireland.

15 The International Monetary Fund (IMF) agrees credits of $4.5 billion to Brazil to enable it to service its foreign debts.

19 Poland's Council of State announces the suspension of martial law, effective from December 31.

SCIENCE, TECHNOLOGY, AND MEDICINE

Agriculture

- Crops fail for the fourth consecutive year in the USSR, forcing the country to draw on its reserves and to import grain to maintain its livestock herds.

December 1982–84 Civil war and drought cause a major famine in Ethiopia; at least 800,000 people die and 1.5 million flee the country before foreign grain is received the following year.

Computing

- IBM introduces its 3084 computer, which is twice as powerful as the previous model.

Ecology

- The Convention on Conservation of Antarctic Marine Living Organisms comes into effect, establishing a protective oceanic zone around the continent.
- The U.S. Congress passes the Endangered Species Act Amendments.

MARCH

March–April El Chichón volcano in Mexico erupts violently, sending dust and gases into the stratosphere.

APRIL

30 Agreement is reached at the United Nations' Law of the Sea Conference on an international convention

governing the use and exploitation of the sea and seabed; the United States and UK do not sign.

DECEMBER

13 An earthquake in North Yemen, measuring 6.0 on the Richter scale, kills nearly 3,000 people.

Exploration

- The U.S. rocket *Conestoga 1* makes a suborbital flight; it is the first private space craft.

NOVEMBER

11 The orbiter *Columbia* makes the first deployment of a satellite from the U.S. space shuttle.

Health and Medicine

c. 1982 Cholera spreads among refugee camps in Ethiopia and the Sudan.

- Liposuction becomes available in the United States.
- Many low-income women in the United States with unwanted pregnancies are sterilized; 33% of couples nationally are sterilized; 41% of Native American women have been sterilized, often without their consent.
- The Swedish firm Kabivitrum manufactures human growth hormone using genetically engineered bacteria.
- The U.S. firm Eli Lilly and Company is the first to market a drug produced by recombinant DNA—human insulin.
- U.S. geneticist Ralph Brinster of the University of Pennsylvania transfers the rat gene controlling the growth hormone somatotrophin into a mouse; the mouse grows to double its normal size.
- U.S. researcher Stanley Prusiner discovers prions (proteinaceous infectious particles); they are responsible for several neurological diseases including BSE ("mad cow disease", first identified in 1986).

FEBRUARY

26 The National Academy of Sciences notes widespread use of marijuana in the United States and warns of its harmful effects.

DECEMBER

2 At the University of Utah Medical Center an artificial heart, designed by Robert Jarvik, is implanted into heart patient Barney Clark who lives for 112 days.

Science

- Astronomers at Villanova University in Pennsylvania, United States, announce the discovery of rings around Neptune.
- Astrophysicists at Groningen University in the Netherlands postulate the existence of a black hole at the center of the Milky Way.
- Dolphins are discovered to possess magnetized tissues that aid in navigation; they are the first mammals discovered to have such tissues.
- South African molecular biologist Aaron Klug receives the Nobel Prize for Chemistry for his development of crystallographic methods for determining the structure of biologically important nucleic acid protein complexes.

- The naturally occurring chemical tribulin is discovered in the brain; it stimulates alertness.
- The Nobel Prize for Physiology or Medicine is awarded jointly to Swedish biochemists Sune Bergström and Bengt Samuelson, and British pharmacologist John Vane for their discovery of prostaglandins and related biologically active substances.
- U.S. physicist Kenneth Wilson receives the Nobel Prize for Physics for his theory of phase transitions and critical phenomena.

AUGUST

29 Scientists at Darmstadt, West Germany, announce the production of the element unnilenium (atomic no. 109, now called Meitnerium) by fusing bismuth and iron nuclei.

Technology

- Astronomy student Martine Kempf designs a voice-recognition system that is used for voice-controlled wheelchairs within four years.
- Kodak launches the digital camera and digital film.
- Sony launches the first pocket television set, the Sony Flat TV, in Japan, with a screen size of 5 cm/2 in. It costs $239.
- The transmission time for faxes is reduced from one minute to 20 seconds per page, making it far cheaper to send fax messages and increasing their popularity.
- U.S. company Intel introduces the 16-bit 80286 microprocessor; it has 130,000 transistors and runs at speeds up to 12 MHz.
- U.S. company Procter and Gamble launches Vizir, the first liquid detergent for washing machines.
- U.S. firm Applied Biosystems markets an automated gene sequencer that can sequence 18,000 DNA bases a day, compared with a few hundred a year by hand in the 1970s.
- U.S. firm Polaroid introduces a transparency film that is "instantly" processed outside the camera.
- U.S. firms Columbia Data Products and Compaq produce the first "clones" of an IBM personal computer; they use the same operating system as the IBM personal computer.

OCTOBER

- Japanese company Sony launches the first compact disc (CD) players in Japan, working with Philips, the Dutch manufacturer of the compact disc.

DECEMBER

12 More than 20,000 women encircle the Greenham Common air base in Berkshire, England, in protest against the proposed siting of U.S. cruise missiles there.

Transportation

- Japanese car manufacturers control 22.6% of the market in the United States, compared to 3.7% in 1970.
- Length of railroad track in operation: United States, 270,312 km/168,000 mi; USSR, 143,268 km/89,042 mi; France, 34,375 km/21,364 mi; West Germany, 28,410 km/17,657 mi; Great Britain, 17,871 km/11,107 mi; Italy, 16,153 km/10,039 mi; Spain, 13,540 km/

8,415 mi; Sweden, 11,337 km/7,046 mi; Turkey, 8,190 km/5,090 mi; Finland, 6,090 km/3,785 mi; Austria, 5,808 km/3,610 mi; Norway, 4,240 km/ 2,635 mi.

JANUARY

13 A build-up of ice causes a Boeing 737 to crash into 14th Street Bridge, Washington, D.C., shortly after takeoff; only 5 of the 79 people on board are rescued, and 4 others are killed on the bridge or attempting to rescue survivors from the Potomac River.

FEBRUARY

9 Psychologically disturbed airline pilot Seji Katagiru throws two of his Japan Air Lines DC-8's four engines into reverse, causing it to plunge into Tokyo Bay, killing 24 of its 174 passengers and crew.

19 The Boeing 757 airliner makes its first flight.

JULY

9 A Pan Am 727 crashes while attempting to take off in a rainstorm at Moisant Airport, New Orleans, Louisiana; 153 people are killed.

23 Actor Vic Morrow and two child actors are killed in a helicopter accident while filming a motion picture version of the television program *The Twilight Zone*.

ARTS AND IDEAS

Architecture

- The Humana Building in Louisville, Kentucky, designed by the U.S. architect Michael Graves, is completed.
- The Inmos Microprocessor Factory in Gwent, South Wales, designed by the English architect Richard Rogers, is completed.
- The Public Services Building in Portland, Oregon, designed by the U.S. architect Michael Graves, is completed. It is quickly seen as a major work of postmodernist design.

JUNE

7 Elvis Presley's home "Graceland" in Memphis, Tennessee, opens to the public.

Arts

- English artist David Hockney creates the photo-collage *The Grand Canyon Looking North, September 1982*.
- The art exhibition "Zeitgeist" is held at the Martin Gropius Bau in Berlin, West Germany.
- The French artist Daniel Buren creates *Installation* for the exhibition "Documenta 7" in Kassel, West Germany.
- The German artist Anselm Kiefer paints *Wayland's Song (With Wing)*.
- The German artist Georg Baselitz paints *Last Supper in Dresden*.
- The Indian artist Anish Kapoor creates the sculpture *White Sand, Red Millet, Many Flowers*.

- The Saitama Prefectural Museum of Art in Japan, designed by the Japanese architect Kisho Kurokawa, is completed.
- The U.S. artist Eric Fischl paints *The Old Man's Boat and the Old Man's Dog*.
- The U.S. artist Jenny Holzer creates *Times Square*, in which a series of messages are flashed across a Spectacolor board in Times Square, New York, New York. The messages become known as Holzerisms and include "Abuse of Power Comes as No Surprise" and "A Little Knowledge Can Go a Long Way."
- The U.S. artist Julian Schnabel paints *Humanity Asleep*.
- The U.S. graffiti artist Jean-Michel Basquiat holds eight one-man shows in the United States.

Film

- At the Cannes Film Festival, the Palme d'Or is awarded jointly to Constantin Costa-Gavras for the U.S. film *Missing* and to Serif Gören for the Turkish movie *Yol*. A special 25th anniversary prize is awarded to Michelangelo Antonioni for the Italian movie *Identificazione di una donna/Identification of a Woman*.
- The movie *An Officer and a Gentleman*, directed by Taylor Hackford, is released in the United States. It stars Richard Gere and Deborah Winger.
- The movie *Blade Runner*, directed by Ridley Scott, is released in the United States. Based on Philip K. Dick's science fiction novel *Do Androids Dream of Electric Sheep?*, it stars Harrison Ford and Rutger Hauer. A "director's cut" of the movie is released in 1993.
- The movie *Conan the Barbarian*, directed by John Milius, is released in the United States. It stars Arnold Schwarzenegger.
- The movie *Danton*, directed by Polish filmmaker Andrzej Wajda, is released in France. It stars Gérard Depardieu and Wojciech Pszoniak.
- The movie *Diner*, directed by Barry Levinson, is released in the United States. It stars Steve Guttenberg, Daniel Stern, Mickey Rourke, Kevin Bacon, Timothy Daly, Paul Reiser, and Ellen Barkin.
- The movie *ET: The Extra-Terrestrial*, directed by Steven Spielberg, is released in the United States. It stars child actors Henry Thomas and Drew Barrymore.
- The movie *Fanny och Alexander/Fanny and Alexander*, written and directed by Ingmar Bergman, is released in Sweden. Edited from a television series, it stars Pernilla Allwin and Bertil Guve.
- The movie *Fitzcarraldo*, directed by German filmmaker Werner Herzog, is released in the United States. It stars Klaus Kinski and Claudia Cardinale.
- The movie *La Balance/Scales of Justice*, directed by U.S. filmmaker Bob Swaim, is released in France, starring Nathalie Baye and Philippe Léotard.
- The movie *Le Retour de Martin Guerre/The Return of Martin Guerre*, directed by Daniel Vigne, is released in France. Based on the book by Natalie Zimon Davis, it stars Gérard Depardieu and Nathalie Baye.
- The movie *Lola* is released in West Germany. It is directed by Rainer Werner Fassbinder and stars Barbara Sukowa and Armin Mueller-Stahl.
- The movie *Missing*, directed by Greek filmmaker Costa-Gavras, is released in the United States. It stars Jack Lemmon and Sissy Spacek.

- The movie *My Favourite Year*, directed by Richard Benjamin, is released in the United States, starring Peter O'Toole.
- The movie *One From the Heart*, directed by Francis Ford Coppola, is released in the United States. It stars Frederic Forrest, Teri Garr, Raul Julia, and Nastassja Kinski. Despite a $26 million budget, the film is a flop and Coppola is forced to sell his Zoetrope studios.
- The movie *Poltergeist*, directed by Tobe Hooper, is released in the United States. It stars Craig T. Nelson and JoBeth Williams.
- The movie *Sophie's Choice*, directed by Alan J. Pakula, is released in the United States. It stars Meryl Streep, Kevin Kline, and Peter MacNichol.
- The movie *The King of Comedy*, directed by Martin Scorsese, is released in the United States. It stars Robert De Niro and Jerry Lewis.
- The movie *The Verdict*, directed by Sidney Lumet, is released in the United States. It stars Paul Newman, Charlotte Rampling, Jack Warden, and James Mason.
- The movie *The World According to Garp*, directed by George Roy Hill, is released in the United States. Based on the novel by John Irving, it stars Robin Williams, Mary Beth Hurt, and Glenn Close.
- The movie *Tootsie*, directed by Syndey Pollack, is released in the United States. It stars Dustin Hoffman and Jessica Lange.
- The movie *Victor/Victoria*, directed by U.S. filmmaker Blake Edwards, is released in the UK, starring Julie Andrews and James Garner.
- The movie *Yol*, directed by Serif Gören on behalf of the imprisoned writer-director Yilmaz Güney, is released in Turkey. It stars Tarik Akan, Serif Sezer, and Halil Ergün.
- The Indian–British coproduction *Gandhi*, directed by Richard Attenborough, sets a world record for the largest number of extras. It stars Ben Kingsley, and wins eight Academy Awards, including best picture, best director, and best actor.
- The Swiss–French coproduction *Passion*, directed by Jean-Luc Godard, is released. It stars Isabelle Huppert, Hanna Schygulla, and Michel Piccoli.
- The teen comedy movie *Fast Times at Ridgemont High* is released in the United States. It is written by Cameron Crowe, based on his own novel, and directed by Amy Heckerling.

MARCH

19 The Coca-Cola Company buys the Hollywood studio Columbia Pictures in the United States.
29 The 1981 Academy Awards take place. Best Actor: Henry Fonda, for *On Golden Pond*; Best Supporting Actor: John Gielgud, for *Arthur*; Best Actress: Katharine Hepburn, for *On Golden Pond*; Best Supporting Actress: Maureen Stapleton, for *Reds*; Best Picture: *Chariots of Fire*, directed by Hugh Hudson; Best Director: Warren Beatty, for *Reds*.

Literature and Language

- English novelist Julian Barnes publishes his novel *Before She Met Me*.
- English writer Anthony Burgess publishes his novel *End of the World News*.
- English writer Graham Greene publishes his novel *Monsignor Quixote*.
- German novelist Heinrich Böll publishes his novel *The Safety Net*.
- Irish writer Samuel Beckett publishes his novel *Ill Seen, Ill Said*.
- The Australian writer Thomas Keneally publishes his novel *Schindler's Ark*.
- The black American writer Gwendolyn Brooks publishes her poetry collection *To Disembark*.
- The Chilean writer Isabel Allende publishes her novel *La casa de los espíritus/The House of the Spirits*.
- The Colombian novelist Gabriel García Márquez is awarded the Nobel Prize for Literature.
- The Dutch writer Harry Mulisch publishes his novel *De aanslag/The Assault*, which wins him an international reputation.
- The English writer Timothy Mo publishes his novel *Sour Sweet*.
- The Italian writer Primo Levi publishes *Se non ora, quando?/If Not Now, When?*
- The Japanese-born English writer Kazuo Ishiguro publishes his novel *A Pale View of Hills*.
- The Mexican writer Carlos Fuentes publishes his novel *Una familia lejana/Distant Relations*.
- The Pulitzer Prize for Biography is awarded to William S. McFeely for *Grant: A Biography*, the Pulitzer Prize for Poetry is posthumously awarded to Sylvia Plath for *The Collected Poems*, and the Pulitzer Prize for Fiction is awarded to John Updike for *Rabbit is Rich*.
- The South African writer André Brink publishes his novel *A Chain of Voices*.
- The U.S. novelist Anne Tyler publishes her novel *Dinner at the Homesick Restaurant*.
- The U.S. novelist Charles Bukowski publishes his novel *Ham on Rye*.
- The U.S. novelist Edmund White publishes his novel *A Boy's Own Story*.
- The U.S. novelist Joyce Carol Oates publishes her novel *A Bloodsmoor Romance*
- The U.S. writer Alice Walker publishes her novel *The Color Purple*. It wins the Pulitzer Prize for Fiction in 1983.
- The U.S. writer Denise Levertov publishes her poetry collection *Candles in Babylon*.
- The U.S. writer Saul Bellow publishes his novel *The Dean's December*.
- U.S. writer Bernard Malamud publishes his novel *God's Game*.

Music

- The Argentinean composer Mauricio Kagel completes the jazz composition *Rrrrrr...*
- The British folk-rock duo Richard and Linda Thompson releases the album *Shoot Out the Lights*.
- The British pop group Madness releases the single "House of Fun."
- The English composer Elisabeth Lutyens completes her String Quartet No. 12.
- The German pop group Kraftwerk releases the single "The Model."

- The opera *La vera storia/The True History*, by the Italian composer Luciano Berio, is first performed, in Milan, Italy.
- The Russian composer Edison Denisov completes his orchestral work *Death is a Long Sleep*, variations on a theme by the Austrian composer Franz Joseph Haydn.
- The Russian composer Boris Tishchenko completes his Second Violin Concerto.
- The U.S. composer Virgil Thomsom completes his orchestral work *A Love Scene*.

JANUARY

9   The Swedish pop group Abba releases the album *The Visitors*.

16   The British pop group Soft Cell releases "Tainted Love."

FEBRUARY

24   The 1981–82 Grammies are held. Best Album: *Double Fantasy* by John Lennon and Yoko Ono; Best Record "Bette Davis Eyes" by Kim Carnes; Best Male Pop Vocalist: Al Jareau; Best Female Pop Vocalist: Lena Horne; Best Pop Group: Manhattan Transfer for "Boy from New York City."

28   The English pop group the Human League releases the album *Dare*.

APRIL

10   The English pop singer Paul McCartney and the U.S. pop singer Stevie Wonder release "Ebony and Ivory."

MAY

29   The U.S. performance artist and singer Laurie Anderson releases the album *Big Science*.

JUNE

12   The British pop group the Clash releases the album *Combat Rock*.

OCTOBER

16   The British pop group Dire Straits releases the album *Love Over Gold*.

16   The U.S. pop group duo and vocal group Grandmaster Flash and the Furious Five release *The Message*, a seminal hip-hop album.

30   The U.S. soul singer Marvin Gaye releases the single "Sexual Healing."

NOVEMBER

6   The British pop singer Phil Collins releases "You Can't Hurry Love."

20   The U.S. rock singer Prince releases the album *1999*.

DECEMBER

4   The British pop group Culture Club releases the single "Do You Really Want To Hurt Me?"

25   Michael Jackson's *Thriller* confirms his status as a pop icon. Within ten years, 40 million copies will have been sold, making it the best-selling album of all time.

Theater and Dance

- The play *Edmond*, by the U.S. writer David Mamet, is first performed, in New York, New York.
- The play *Noises Off*, by the English writer Michael Frayn, is first performed, at the Lyric Theatre in London, England.
- The play *The Real Thing*, by the Czechoslovak-born English dramatist Tom Stoppard, is first performed, at the Strand Theatre in London, England.

- The play *Whodunnit*, by the English writer Anthony Shaffer, is first performed, at the Biltmore Theater in New York, New York.
- The Pulitzer Prize for Drama is awarded to Charles Fuller for *A Soldier's Play*.

MAY

29   *A Little Shop of Horrors*, a play later turned into a movie that achieves a cult following, opens in New York, New York.

Thought and Scholarship

- British philosopher A. J. Ayer publishes *Philosophy in the Twentieth Century*.
- The Pulitzer Prize for History is awarded to C. Vann Woodward (editor) for *Mary Chestnut's Civil War*.
- The Pulitzer Prize for General Nonfiction is awarded to Tracy Kidder for *The Soul of the New Machine*.
- U.S. philosopher Richard Rorty publishes *The Consequences of Pragmatism*.

SOCIETY

Education

- Japan introduces a new upper secondary school curriculum and standardized textbooks.
- UNESCO sets 2000 as the target year for the eradication of illiteracy in Africa.

Everyday Life

- *Time* magazine's "Man of the Year" is "Pac-Man," a character from a computer game that sweeps the United States in 1982.
- Infant mortality rates, female/male: developed countries 18/24; developing countries 104/116; Africa 129/151; North America 12/16; Europe 19/25; Asia 99/108.
- The Coca-Cola Company launches Diet Coke.
- The population of China rises to over 1 billion.
- U.S. wholefood enthusiast Gregory Sams develops the vegeburger, which contains sesame seeds, cereals, soy, and vegetables.
- U.S. winter fashions include ponchos.
- Women as a percentage of the work force: Spain 29%; Sweden 46%; China 36%; East Germany 50%; UK 42%; United States 43%.

JULY

19   The Census Bureau announces that 14 percent of U.S. citizens have incomes below the official poverty line.

SEPTEMBER

29–October 1   Seven Americans die when cyanide is placed in bottles of Tylenol. The makers of the drug, Johnson and Johnson, recall 264,000 bottles, and new tamper-proof packaging for pharmaceuticals and other products is developed.

OCTOBER

1   The Disney Corporation opens a new theme park: the EPCOT Center at Lake Buena Vista, Florida.

Media and Communication

- British, U.S., German, and French television stations begin experimental broadcasts of movies that can be seen in three dimensions provided the viewer wears special stereoscopic glasses.
- Madonna is one of the first stars launched by the MTV music channel, highlighting her dancing and the quality of her video production, and she becomes a pop icon of the 1980s.

MARCH

25–August 25, 1988 *Cagney and Lacey*, a U.S. detective series starring Tyne Daly and Meg Foster (later replaced by Sharon Gless) as two policewomen, is shown on U.S. and British television.

JUNE

7 *Sister, Sister*, a drama written by Maya Angelou and starring Diahann Carroll, Rosalind Cash, Irene Cara, and Paul Winfield, is shown on U.S. television.

SEPTEMBER

15 *USA Today* begins publication in the United States; one of very few national papers, it uses an all-color format.

19 The 1981–82 Emmy Awards for television are held. Best Drama Series: *Hill Street Blues*; Best Comedy Series: *Barney Miller*; Best Actor in a Drama: Daniel J. Travanti, for *Hill Street Blues*; Best Actress in a Drama: Michael Learned, for *Nurse*; Best Actor in a Comedy: Alan Alda, for *M*A*S*H*; Best Actress in a Comedy: Carol Kane, for *Taxi*.

22–September 17, 1989 *Family Ties*, a situation comedy starring Michael J. Fox, reflecting the conflicting values of the members of a typical 1980s family, is shown on U.S. television.

30 *Cheers*, a popular situation comedy about several characters who hang out in a bar in Boston, is shown on U.S. television.

OCTOBER

26–May 25, 1988 *St Elsewhere*, a hospital drama series, is shown on U.S. television.

NOVEMBER

- *The Blue and the Grey*, a drama series set during the American Civil War, is shown on U.S. television. It stars John Hammond, Stacy Keach, Sterling Hayden, Gregory Peck, Lloyd Bridges, Colleen Dewhurst, Paul Winfield, and Robert Vaughn.
- 23 Television commercials are deregulated in the United States, removing restrictions on content and length.

Religion

- The Anglican–Roman Catholic International Commission (ARCIC) publishes *The Final Report*.

MAY

28–June 2 Pope John Paul II makes the first papal visit to Britain since 1531.

JUNE

- Assemblies of the Presbyterian Church and the United Presbyterian Church in the United States agree to merge, ending a split dating from the American Civil War.

Sports

- Around 1,300 athletes participate in the inaugural Gay Games at San Francisco, California.
- It is estimated that 19 million people took part in aerobics classes in the United States during this year.
- Rickey Henderson of the Oakland Athletics sets a major league baseball record of 130 stolen bases in a season.
- Wayne Gretsky of the Edmonton Oilers is the first player in the history of the National Hockey League to score 200 points in a season.

JANUARY

1 Clemson wins college football's national championship for the 1981 season.

24 The San Francisco 49ers win their first Super Bowl, defeating the Cincinnati Bengals 26-21 in Super Bowl XVI in Miami, Florida.

28–31 U.S. national figure skating champions are: Rosalynn Sumners; Scott Hamilton; Kitty and Peter Carruthers, pairs; Judy Blumberg and Michael Seibert, dance.

MARCH

11–13 Scott Hamilton and Elaine Zayak of the United States win titles at the World Figure Skating Championships.

19 Fifteen England cricketers, led by Graham Gooch, are banned from Test cricket for three years for participating in a cricket tour of South Africa, breaking an international ban on sporting links with that country because of its policy of apartheid.

MAY

7 The National Football League (NFL) fails to stop the Oakland Raiders from moving to Los Angeles, California, when a federal court rules that the NFL had violated antitrust laws. Later the Raiders and their new home, the Los Angeles Coliseum, receive nearly $50 million in damages.

8 The Canadian race-car driver Gilles Villeneuve is killed during practice for the Belgian Grand Prix at Zolder, Belgium.

8–16 The New York Islanders beat the Vancouver Canucks to win the Stanley Cup.

15 In the closest finish to date in the Indianapolis 500 motor race, the winner, Gordon Johncock, beats Rick Mears by only 0.16 seconds.

27–June 8 The Los Angeles Lakers beat the Philadelphia 76ers in the National Basketball Association (NBA) finals.

JUNE

5 Swedish tennis player Mats Wilander is, at 17 years old, the youngest winner of the men's singles at the French Open championships.

19–20 The Belgian race-car driver Jacky Ickx wins the Le Mans 24-hour race for a record sixth time.

JULY

4 In the longest men's singles final ever at the Wimbledon tennis championships in London, England, the U.S. player Jimmy Connors takes 4 hours and 16 minutes to beat fellow U.S. player John McEnroe.

7 At the Bislett Games in Oslo, Norway, the English athlete Dave Moorcroft sets a new 5,000 meters world record of 13 min 0.41 sec, 6 seconds inside the previous best.

11 Soccer's World Cup is won by Italy, who beat West Germany 3–1 in the final before a crowd of 90,000 in Madrid, Spain.

18 Tom Watson of the United States wins the British Open at Royal Troon, Scotland, becoming the fifth golfer to win the U.S. and British Opens in the same season.

AUGUST

4–13 The inaugural Race Across America bicycle race (then known as the Great American Bike Race) is won by Lon Haldeman of the United States, who completes the 4,791-km/2,976-mi course from Santa Monica, California to New York, New York, in 9 days, 20 hours, 2 minutes.

SEPTEMBER

8 The English athlete Daley Thompson wins the European decathlon title in Athens, Greece, setting a new world record of 8,743 points; he simultaneously holds the Olympic, Commonwealth, and European decathlon titles.

12 At the European Championships in Athens, Greece, Rosa Mota of Portugal wins the first-ever women's marathon at an international championship contest. It follows the historic course from the village of Marathon run by the messenger Phaedippides in 490 BC.

20–November 22 The professional American football season is interrupted in the United States by a players' strike lasting 57 days. The dispute is settled by a Collective Bargaining Agreement that establishes a minimum salary for players and introduces severance pay to help those moving to other careers.

BIRTHS & DEATHS

- Anna Freud, Austrian-born child psychoanalyst dies (87).
- René Jules Dubos, French-U.S. microbiologist who studied soil microorganisms and their antibacterial qualities, dies (81).

JANUARY

15 Red Smith, U.S. newspaperman and sports columnist, dies in Stamford, Connecticut (76).

FEBRUARY

17 Lee Strasberg, U.S. actor and artistic director of the Actors Studio from 1948, dies in New York, New York (80).

17 Thelonius Monk, U.S. jazz pianist and composer, dies in Englewood, New Jersey (61).

MARCH

5 John Belushi, U.S. comedy television and film actor and part of the Blues Brothers duo with Dan Ackroyd, dies from a drug overdose in Beverly Hills, California (33).

6 Ayn Rand, Russian-born U.S. novelist best known for her anticommunist novels *The Fountainhead* and *Atlas Shrugged*, dies in New York, New York (76).

8 R. A. Butler, British politician prominent during World War II and the start of the Cold War, dies in Great Yeldham, Essex, England (79).

29 Carl Orff, German composer also known for his innovations in musical education, dies in Munich, Germany (86).

APRIL

20 Archibald MacLeish, U.S. poet, professor, and assistant secretary of state 1944–45, dies in Boston, Massachusetts (89).

MAY

29 Romy Schneider, Austrian film actress, dies (43).

JUNE

10 Rainer Werner Fassbinder, German film and theater director, writer, and actor, dies in Munich, Germany (36).

12 Karl von Frisch, German zoologist who discovered how bees communicate, dies in Munich, Germany (95).

13 Khalid ibn Abdel Aziz Al Saud, Saudi Arabian king 1975–82, dies at Ta'if, Saudi Arabia (69).

18 John Cheever, Pulitzer prizewinning U.S. novelist and short-story writer, dies in Ossining, New York (70).

21 Prince William of Wales, son of Prince Charles and Diana, Princess of Wales, and second in line to the British throne, born in London, England.

29 Pierre Balmain, French couturier and founder of the House of Balmain fashion house, dies in Paris, France (68).

JULY

29 Vladimir Zworykin, Russian-born U.S. electronic engineer who furthered the development of television, dies in Princeton, New Jersey (92).

AUGUST

5 John Charnley, British orthopedic surgeon who developed the technique of hip replacement, dies in Manchester, England (70).

12 Henry Fonda, U.S. actor of stage and film, dies in Los Angeles, California (77).

29 Ingrid Bergman, Swedish star of U.S. and international films, dies in London, England (67).

SEPTEMBER

1 Władysław Gomulka, Polish leader 1956–70, a communist, dies in Warsaw, Poland (77).

4 Douglas Bader, British pilot who lost both legs in a flying accident, and went on to become an ace pilot in World War II, dies in London, England (72).

9 Grace Kelly, U.S. film and television actress who married Prince Rainier of Monaco in 1956, dies in Monte Carlo, Monaco (53).

OCTOBER

4 Glenn Gould, Canadian pianist known as one of the greatest interpreters of Bach, dies in Toronto, Canada (50).

4 Leroy Grumman, U.S. aircraft executive and designer, dies in Manhasset, New York (87).

18 Pierre Mendès-France, French socialist politician, premier 1954–55, dies in Paris, France (75).

NOVEMBER

1 King Vidor, U.S. film director who was a key Hollywood figure in the 1930s, dies (88).

5 Jacques Tati, French film actor and director known for his comic pantomime acting, dies in Paris, France (74).

10 Leonid Brezhnev, Soviet statesman, First Secretary of the Soviet Communist Party 1964–82, dies in Moscow, USSR (75).

DECEMBER

20 Artur Rubinstein, Polish-born U.S. virtuoso pianist, dies in Geneva, Switzerland (95).

OCTOBER

- Wheelchair-bound Neoli Fairhall of New Zealand wins the women's archery title in Brisbane, Australia, becoming the first paraplegic to win a Commonwealth Games gold medal.

12–20 The St. Louis Cardinals win the World Series, beating the Milwaukee Brewers in seven games.

13 The International Olympic Committee posthumously restores the two gold medals won by U.S. athlete Jim Thorpe at the 1912 Olympic Games but forfeited a year later when it was discovered that he had once played professional minor league baseball.

DECEMBER

9 The World Boxing Council in Mexico votes in favor of reducing the 15-round limit for world title fights to 12 from January 1, 1983, to reduce the chances of a boxer suffering serious injuries in a bout.

12 The English tennis player Virginia Wade becomes the first woman to be elected to the All England Lawn Tennis Club.

1983

POLITICS, GOVERNMENT, AND ECONOMICS

Business and Economics

- The London, England, auctioneers Sotheby's is bought by the U.S. Alfred Taubman.

JANUARY

18 The Group of Ten economically dominant countries agree to an increase in funding of the "General Arrangements to Borrow" unit of the International Monetary Fund (IMF) from $7.1 billion to $19 billion.

FEBRUARY

24 Western banks underwrite a $5 billion loan to Mexico, also approving a short-term loan of $433 million.

MAY

25 The United States agrees to export high technology goods to China.

Colonization

SEPTEMBER

19 The Caribbean islands of St. Kitts and Nevis achieve independence from Britain.

Human Rights

- Women in Iran cannot serve in the judiciary, the military, or the police force under the Islamic cultural revolution. Laws regulate women's clothing and forbid their use of public transportation, theaters, and beaches.

MAY

24 Civil-rights activist Jesse Jackson becomes the first black person to address the Alabama State Legislature in Montgomery.

AUGUST

19 Forty thousand Argentines protest at a proposed amnesty for military personnel involved in human-rights violations during the 1970s.

NOVEMBER

2 The U.S. Congress votes to make the birthday of the black American civil-rights leader Martin Luther King, Jr., (January 15) a federal holiday from 1986.

Politics and Government

- A new law in France allows the repayment of 75% of abortion costs by the government.
- A referendum in the Republic of Ireland results in a two-to-one majority for enshrining the existing legal ban on abortion in the national constitution.
- Over 1 million illegal immigrants, mostly Hispanic, are caught trying to enter the United States.
- The Iranian religious leader Ayatollah Khomeini declares that Islam is a "religion of the sword" and sends armed pilgrims to Mecca.
- The U.S. Supreme Court's ruling in the case *INS v. Chadha* invalidates the legislative veto of delegated powers.

JANUARY

7 The United States lifts its arms embargo on Guatemala.

13 Saudi Arabia reestablishes diplomatic links with Libya.

17 Nigeria orders the expulsion of 2 million illegal immigrants.

19 South Africa reimposes direct rule on Namibia (South West Africa).

24 Thirty-two Italian Red Brigade terrorists are jailed for the kidnap and murder of former premier Aldo Moro in 1978.

27 U.S.–Soviet arms reduction talks resume in Geneva, Switzerland, with the USSR proposing a nuclear-free zone for central Europe.

FEBRUARY

8 The Japanese electronics manufacturer Hitachi pleads guilty in a U.S. federal court to charges of conspiracy to obtain classified information on IBM computers.

8 The Kahane Commission on the Beirut massacre of September 18, 1982, condemns the Israeli government and recommends the dismissal of the defense minister, Ariel Sharon. He resigns on February 11.

15 The Christian Phalangist militia withdraws from Beirut, giving the Lebanese government control over the city.

19 Joshua Nkomo, the former guerrilla commander and leader of the ZAPU (Zimbabwe African People's Union) political party, is detained by the police in Zimbabwe.

24 A U.S. congressional committee condemns the internment of Japanese Americans during World War II.

24 One thousand five hundred people are reported dead following violent clashes during local elections in the state of Assam in India.

28 The International Monetary Fund (IMF) grants Brazil a loan of $5.4 billion.

MARCH

5 Bob Hawke's Labor Party wins the Australian general election, retaking power from the Liberal–Country Party caretaker administration of Malcolm Fraser.

6 Chancellor Helmut Kohl's ruling Christian Democratic Union wins the general election in West Germany, with the Green Party gaining its first seats in the Bundestag.

8 Speaking in Orlando, Florida, U.S. president Ronald Reagan condemns the USSR as an "evil empire."

9 The leader of the ZAPU (Zimbabwe African People's Union) party, Joshua Nkomo, flees Zimbabwe, but returns on August 15.

14 The Organization of Petroleum-Exporting Countries (OPEC) agrees to cut oil prices for the first time since its formation in 1961.

17 Chad seeks the assistance of the United Nations in its border dispute with Libya.

31 U.S. president Ronald Reagan halts the sale of F-16 fighter aircraft to Israel until its troops are fully withdrawn from Lebanon.

APRIL

10 A U.S. peace plan for the Middle East collapses when Jordan withdraws from the talks.

12 Vietnam claims victory over the Kampuchean rebels opposed to the pro-Vietnamese Heng Samrin government in Phnom Penh.

18 The U.S. embassy in Beirut, Lebanon, is badly damaged and many people are killed by a suicide bomber.

24 Bruno Kreisky's Socialist Party loses its majority in the Austrian general election. A new coalition government is formed under Chancellor Fred Sinowatz on May 11.

24 Turkey's military government permits the formation of political parties, but its ban on political activity remains in force for 150 leading politicians.

27 U.S. president Ronald Reagan asks congress to support increased aid to the government of El Salvador.

MAY

4 The Iranian government outlaws Tudeh, the Iranian Communist Party, and expels 18 Soviet diplomats.

4 The U.S. president Ronald Reagan declares his support for the aim of the Nicaraguan Contras to overthrow the country's Sandinista government.

17 Israel and Lebanon sign an agreement providing for the withdrawal of Israeli troops from Lebanon within three months.

JUNE

1 Civilian members of the Palestinian Al Fatah faction declare their opposition to Yassir Arafat's leadership of the Palestine Liberation Organization.

9 A new center-left coalition government under Mário Soares takes office in Portugal, ending 60 years of army rule.

9 The Conservatives under Margaret Thatcher win an overall majority of 144 seats in the British general election, with 397 seats against Labour's 209 and the Liberal–SDP Alliance's 23.

15 The U.S. Supreme Court curbs the power of state and local governments to limit access to legal abortions.

16 Pope John Paul II begins an eight-day visit to Poland and has talks with Premier Wojciech Jaruzelski and Lech Wałęsa. On June 19, the Polish government warns the church to stay out of politics.

24 The Palestine Liberation Organization (PLO) leader Yassir Arafat is ordered out of Syria, and Syrian tanks besiege PLO guerrilla bases in Lebanon.

JULY

12 China and Britain hold talks in Beijing on the future of Hong Kong.

16 The nine-nation committee of the Organization of African Unity calls on foreign countries to end all involvement in the long-running civil war in Chad.

20 The Israeli cabinet agrees on a partial withdrawal of troops from Lebanon, redeploying them south of the Chouf Mountains.

21 The Polish government announces an end to martial law and an amnesty for political prisoners.

25 The Sri Lankan government imposes a curfew following attacks on the Tamil community. On July 28, a ban is imposed on political parties advocating partition of the country between Tamils and the majority Sinhalese.

26 The USSR announces economic reforms allowing factory managers greater autonomy over wages, bonuses, and technical innovations.

28 The U.S. House of Representatives votes to end covert aid to the Nicaraguan Contra guerrillas by September 30.

AUGUST

• The multiracial United Democratic Front is formed under Allan Boesak in South Africa. Opposed to apartheid, it attracts 2 million members in affiliated clubs, societies, and churches.

2 Libyan warplanes bomb the town of Faya-Largeau in Chad. France sends paratroops on August 7 to supplement its 500 "military instructors" in Chad.

8 General Ríos Montt's junta is overthrown in a military coup in Guatemala. The new ruler, General Mejía Victores, declares an amnesty for guerrillas.

11 The town of Faya-Largeau in Chad falls to invading Libyan troops. A further 3,500 French troops are sent to assist President Hissene Habré of Chad on August 19.

12 President Zia ul-Haq of Pakistan announces elections for March 1985 and the lifting of martial law.

14 French police seize a large consignment of arms bound for the Irish Republican Army (IRA).

20 U.S. president Ronald Reagan lifts the country's ban on the export of pipe-laying equipment to the USSR.

21 The Philippines' opposition leader Benigno Aquino is assassinated at Manila airport.

28 The Israeli prime minister Menachem Begin announces his intention to resign. He is succeeded on September 15 by Yitzhak Shamir.

SEPTEMBER

1 A South Korean Boeing 747 airliner is shot down by a Soviet fighter, killing 269 people, after straying into Soviet air space near Sakhalin Island. On September 5, western European nations impose a 14-day ban on flights by the Soviet airline Aeroflot.

4 Civil war breaks out in Lebanon's Chouf mountains following the withdrawal of Israeli troops from the region.

6 A final document of the European Conference on Security and Cooperation is adopted in Madrid, pledging governments to continue the "Helsinki process" of peaceful settlement of disputes and increased respect for human rights.

6 The USSR admits that its military chiefs ordered fighter aircraft to stop the flight of the stray South Korean airliner on September 1. On September 8, the U.S. secretary of state George Shultz describes the Soviet response to the airliner disaster as inadequate.

11 Violent protests in Chile mark the tenth anniversary of the military coup of General Augusto Pinochet as opposition grows to his repressive regime.

16 The U.S. Central Intelligence Agency (CIA) issues a denial that the South Korean airliner shot down by Soviet aircraft on September 1 was engaged in spying.

21 Demonstrators in the Philippines demand the resignation of President Ferdinand Marcos. On September 29, Marcos orders the closure of any newspaper alleging the involvement of army officers in the murder of his political opponent Benigno Aquino.

26 A cease-fire is agreed in the civil war in southern Lebanon, and the Lebanese government agrees to a conference of national reconciliation.

OCTOBER

6 The Indian government takes over direct control of Punjab state in response to growing violence between the Sikh and Hindu communities there.

10 The commission in the Philippines investigating the murder of Benigno Aquino resigns. President Ferdinand Marcos appoints a new commission on October 22.

12 The Chinese Communist Party commences the biggest purge of its membership since the Cultural Revolution. The qualifications of 40 million party members are to be reviewed.

12 U.S. president Ronald Reagan orders U.S. marines to remain in Beirut, Lebanon, for a further 18 months.

19 Maurice Bishop's left wing government in the Caribbean island state of Grenada is overthrown in a coup by extreme left opponents, and Bishop and three colleagues are executed.

22 Antinuclear protests are held across Europe against the deployment of U.S. Pershing II and cruise missiles.

23 Attacks by suicide bombers kill 241 U.S. and 58 French troops of the peacekeeping force in a military compound in Beirut, Lebanon.

25 U.S. marines invade Grenada to depose the new military government. On October 28, the United States vetoes a United Nations resolution deploring the invasion.

30 Raúl Alfonsín's Radical Party gains an absolute majority in the Argentine general election.

31 The British governor-general of Grenada, Paul Scoon, confirms that he requested assistance from East Caribbean forces, and indirectly from the United States, prior to the U.S. invasion of October 25.

NOVEMBER

2 The South African government holds a referendum of white voters on the Constitution Act that provides for parliament to be reconstituted as three chambers (one each for whites, coloreds, and Indians) and for parliament to elect the state president. Two-thirds of voters support the plan.

3 U.S. politician Jesse Jackson announces his candidacy for the Democratic presidential nomination.

4 The British governor-general of Grenada, Paul Scoon, declares a state of emergency amid continuing unrest after the U.S. invasion of October 25.

9 China's foreign ministry announces its intention to declare a unilateral policy on Hong Kong in September 1984 if no agreement has been reached with Britain by that time.

14 The Turkish Cypriot leader Rauf Denktaş declares unilaterally an independent Turkish Republic of Cyprus.

15 At Greenham Common airbase in England, hundreds of women protest against the arrival of U.S. cruise missiles.

22 The West German Bundestag votes for deployment of U.S. Pershing II missiles in West Germany.

23 The USSR delegation walks out of the arms limitation talks in Geneva following the deployment of U.S. missiles in Europe. The next day, President Yuri Andropov announces that the USSR will increase the number of its submarine missiles targeted at the United States.

DECEMBER

4 U.S. planes attack Syrian positions in Lebanon, and Syrian troops kill eight U.S. marines in Beirut.

6 Turkey's National Security Council is dissolved, ending three years of military rule.

10 Raúl Alfonsín is installed as president of Argentina, ending eight years of military rule.

17 An Irish Republican Army (IRA) car bomb explodes outside Harrods department store in London, England, killing six people.

20 The Palestine Liberation Organization (PLO) leader Yassir Arafat is forced to evacuate his forces from Lebanon after talks between Lebanon and Israel.

25 Egypt and Jordan sign an accord restoring economic relations.

29 The United States announces its intention of withdrawing from the United Nations Educational, Scientific, and Cultural Organization (UNESCO) at the end of 1984, alleging that the organization "exhibited hostility toward the basic installations of a free society."

31 A military coup in Nigeria led by Major General Mohammed Buhari ousts the government of President Shehu Shagari.

SCIENCE, TECHNOLOGY, AND MEDICINE

Computing

- British computer company Inmos develops a computer capable of parallel processing: several operations such as memory, logic, and control are processed simultaneously, considerably speeding up overall processing speed.
- Japan launches the "fifth generation" computer project, aimed at producing a machine capable of 1 billion computations per second.
- U.S. computer manufacturer Apple introduces the "Lisa," the first computer to use a mouse and pull-down menus.

FEBRUARY

- IBM introduces the PC-XT personal computer, the first to have a built-in hard disc drive. The hard disc can store 10 megabytes of information even when the machine is turned off. It is supplied with DOS 2 that allows an unlimited number of files and subdirectories to be created.

MARCH

29 The Tandy Corporation markets the first laptop computer in the United States. The TRS-80 Model 100 weighs less than 2 kg/4 lb and runs on four small batteries; prices range from $799 to $999.

AUGUST

21 A group of Milwaukee teenagers, aged between 17 and 22, successfully hack (break into) 60 computers across the United States.

Ecology

- A four-month eruption on Mt. Etna in Italy prompts authorities to use dynamite to divert lava flows.
- An exceptionally warm El Niño (warm ocean surge) off the coasts of Ecuador and Peru drives the huge schools of anchovies, which thrive in the cold water, further offshore, resulting in the deaths of millions of larger fish and the birds which feed on them and seriously disrupting commercial fishing.
- Hurricane Alicia hits northern Texas, causing $2 billion in damage.
- Japan and Korea are hit by a tsunami 15 m/49 ft high; over 100 people are killed.

JANUARY

- Kilauea volcano in Hawaii, United States, erupts and spews lava flows for months.

Exploration

- Studies from the *Lageos* satellite (launched in 1976) indicate that the earth's gravitational field is changing.
- The Search for Extraterrestrial Intelligence (SETI) program is established at NASA's Ames Research Center, Mountain View, California.

- The Soviet space probes *Venera 15* and 16, launched on June 2 and 7, enter orbit around Venus on October 10 and 14 respectively.

JANUARY

25 The *Infrared Astronomical Satellite* (IRAS), an orbiting observatory, is launched; it is designed to detect infrared radiation from objects in space and makes the most complete (96%) survey of the infrared sky. It also finds the first evidence of planetary material around the star Vega outside our solar system.

JUNE

13 The U.S. space probe *Pioneer 10* becomes the first artificial object to leave the solar system.

18 Astronauts on board the space shuttle *Challenger* first use the Remote Manipulating Structure ("arm") to deploy and retrieve a satellite.

18–24 A mission by the U.S. space shuttle *Challenger* includes Sally Ride, the first U.S. woman to go into space.

JULY

21 Vostock station, Antarctica, records a temperature of −89.2°C/−128.6°F—the lowest on record.

SEPTEMBER

30 Guion Bluford becomes the first black American to go into space, aboard the U.S. space shuttle.

Health and Medicine

- French pediatrician Fernand Daffos diagnoses disease in a fetus by extracting and analyzing blood from the umbilical cord.
- John Buster and Maria Bustillo perform the first successful transfer of a human embryo, in the United States.
- The U.S. Food and Drug Administration permits the irradiation of spices because they are subject to insect infestation from tropical countries. The irradiation of pork is permitted the following year and fruit and vegetables in 1986.
- U.S. geneticist James Gusella identifies the gene for Huntington's disease.
- U.S. medical researcher Robert Gallo at the U.S. National Cancer Institute, Maryland, and French medical researcher Luc Montagnier at the Pasteur Institute in Paris, France, isolate the virus thought to cause AIDS; it becomes known as the HIV virus (human immunodeficiency virus).

Science

- Canadian-born U.S. chemist Henry Taube receives the Nobel Prize for Chemistry for his work on electron-transfer reactions in inorganic chemical reactions.
- Kenyan anthropologist Meave Leakey discovers a 16-million-year-old jawbone of *Sivapithecus* in Kenya, which is believed to be an ancestor of present-day apes.
- The American Chemical Society reports that it has recorded 6 million known chemicals.
- The first discovery of a fossil land mammal (a marsupial) in Antarctica is made.
- The first experiments are conducted with the Joint European Torus (JET) equipment at Culham, England,

in an attempt to generate electricity by means of nuclear fusion.

- The Nobel Prize for Physiology or Medicine is awarded to U.S. geneticist Barbara McClintock for her discovery of mobile genetic elements.
- The Nobel Prize for Physics is awarded jointly to Indian-born U.S. astrophysicist Subrahmanyan Chandrasekhar and U.S. astrophysicist William Fowler for their studies on the importance of nuclear reactions for the formation of chemical elements in the universe.
- The Roman Temple of Sulis Minerva in Bath, England, is excavated.
- The skull of a creature called *Pakicetus* is discovered in Pakistan; estimated to be 50 million years old, it is intermediate in evolution between whales and land animals.
- The U.S. anthropologist Clifford Geertz publishes *Local Knowledge: Further Essays in Interpretive Anthropology*.
- U.S. biologist Lynn Margulis discovers that cells with nuclei form by the synthesis of nonnucleated cells.
- U.S. biologists Andrew Murray and Jack Szostak create the first artificial chromosome; it is grafted onto a yeast cell.

APRIL

- U.S. biochemist Kary Mullis invents the polymerase chain reaction (PCR); a method of multiplying genes or known sections of the DNA molecule a million times without the need for the living cell.

JUNE

- The W and Z subatomic particles are detected in experiments at the European Center for Nuclear Research (CERN), Switzerland, by Italian physicist Carlo Rubbia and Dutch physicist Somin van der Meer; the existence of these particles had been predicted as carriers of the weak nuclear force.

OCTOBER

20 The General Conference on Weights and Measures at Sèvres, France, redefines the meter as the distance that light travels through a vacuum in $1/299{,}792{,}458$ seconds.

Technology

- An optical character reader that prints a machine-readable bar code on letters is inaugurated by the U.S. Postal Service. Used by major post offices throughout the country, readers permit high-speed automatic processing to individual carrier routes.
- Car drivers in Chicago, Illinois, try out cellular phones when Motorola introduce a test system of low-power transmitters across the city.
- Soviet engineers drill a borehole to a depth of 12.3 km/7.6 mi at Zapolarny in the Kola peninsula, USSR—the deepest ever drilled.

MARCH

23 The U.S. president Ronald Reagan proposes a "Star Wars" defense system for the United States, using satellites to detect and destroy incoming missiles.

APRIL

19 France tests its neutron bomb on Mururoa atoll in the South Pacific.

Transportation

- Ninety Soviet sailors are killed when their nuclear-powered submarine sinks in the North Pacific.
- Showing very little change since 1977, 82% of the U.S. population use a private vehicle to reach a destination, 2.2% use public transportation, and 8.5% walk.

MAY

25 The Egyptian riverboat *10th of Ramadan* sinks in Lake Nasser; 357 people die.

AUGUST

6 The tanker *Castillo de Bellver* catches fire off Cape Town, South Africa, spilling 250,000 tons of crude oil into the sea.

ARTS AND IDEAS

Architecture

- The AT&T (American Telephone and Telegraph) Building in New York, New York, designed by the U.S. architects Philip Johnson and John Burgee, is completed.
- The Norton House in Venice, California, designed by the U.S. architect Frank Gehry, is completed.
- The Rokko Housing complex in Hyogo, Japan, designed by the Japanese architect Tadao Ando, is completed.

Arts

- The Bulgarian-born U.S. artist Christo creates *Surrounded Islands, Biscayne Bay, Greater Miami, Florida*, which involves skirting islands with sheets of flaming flamingo pink plastic.
- The German artist Joseph Beuys creates the sculpture *Untitled Vitrine*.
- The German artist Jorg Immendorf paints *Café Deutschland Hörerwunsch*.
- The Indian artist Anish Kapoor sculpts *Six Secret Places*.
- The Russian artists Vitaly Komar and Aleksandr Melamid paint *The Origin of Socialist Realism*.
- The temporary exhibition "The Temporary Contemporary" is held at the Museum of Contemporary Art, Los Angeles, California, while the main museum is being built. It proves so popular that it remains open (as "The Permanent Temporary Contemporary") after the permanent MOCA opens.
- The U.S. artist Barbara Kruger creates her photomontage *You Are Not Yourself*.
- The U.S. photographer Cindy Sherman publishes the photograph *Untitled* No. 131.
- U.S. photographer Joanne Leonard creates *Julia and the Window of Vulnerability*, using a photograph and chalk drawing.

Film

- *Gandhi* becomes the most popular foreign movie at the Indian box office.

- During the year, 741 movies are made in 27 languages in India.
- East German television buys U.S. movies starring Robert Redford to schedule against competition from West German television.
- The comedy movie *Trading Places* is released in the United States. It is directed by John Landis and stars Eddie Murphy and Dan Ackroyd.
- The movie *48 Hours*, directed by Walter Hill, is released in the United States. It stars Eddie Murphy and Nick Nolte.
- The movie *Carmen*, directed by Carlos Saura, is released in Spain, starring Laura del Sol and Antonio Gades.
- The movie *Educating Rita*, directed by Lewis Gilbert, is released in the UK. Based on the play by Willy Russell, it stars Michael Caine and Julie Walters.
- The movie *El Norte*, directed by Gregory Nava, is released in the United States, starring Zaide Silvia Gutiérrez and David Villalpando.
- The movie *Flashdance*, directed by Adrian Lyne, is released in the United States. It stars Jennifer Beals.
- The movie *Hammett* is released in the United States, directed by German filmmaker Wim Wenders and starring U.S. actor Frederic Forrest.
- The movie *L'Argent/Money*, directed by Robert Bresson, is released in France. It stars Christian Patey and Sylvie van den Elsen.
- The movie *La Vie est un roman/Life is a Bed of Roses*, directed by Alain Resnais, is released in France. It stars Vittorio Gassman, Ruggero Raimondi, and Geraldine Chaplin.
- The movie *Lianna*, directed by John Sayles, is released in the United States, starring Linda Griffiths and Jane Hallaren.
- The movie *Local Hero*, directed by Bill Forsyth, is released in the UK. It stars Peter Riegert and Burt Lancaster.
- The movie *Never Say Never Again*, directed by Irvin Kershner, is released in the United States. It stars Sean Connery as James Bond.
- The movie *Nostalghia/Nostalgia*, directed by Andrei Tarkovsky, is released in the USSR, starring Oleg Yankovsky.
- The movie *Octopussy*, directed by John Glen, is released in the United States. It stars Roger Moore as James Bond.
- The movie *Pauline à la plage/Pauline on the Beach*, directed by Eric Rohmer, is released in France, starring Amanda Langlet and Arielle Dombasle.
- The movie *Prénom Carmen/First Name: Carmen*, directed by Jean-Luc Godard, is released in France, starring Maruschka Detmars and Jacques Bonnaffe.
- The movie *Risky Business*, directed by Paul Brickman, is released in the United States. It stars Tom Cruise and Rebecca De Mornay.
- The movie *Rumble Fish*, directed by Francis Ford Coppola, is released in the United States. It stars Mickey Rourke and Matt Dillon.
- The movie *Silkwood*, directed by Mike Nichols, is released in the United States. It stars Meryl Streep, Kurt Russell, and Cher.
- The movie *Terms of Endearment*, directed by James L. Brooks, is released in the United States. It stars Shirley MacLaine, Debra Winger, and Jack Nicholson.

- The movie *The Big Chill*, cowritten and directed by Lawrence Kasdan, is released in the United States. It stars Tom Berenger, Glenn Close, Jeff Goldblum, William Hurt, Kevin Kline, Meg Tilly, and JoBeth Williams.
- The movie *The Dresser*, directed by Peter Yates, is released in the UK. It stars Albert Finney and Tom Courtenay.
- The movie *The Right Stuff*, directed by Philip Kaufman, is released in the United States. Based on the book by Tom Wolfe, it stars Sam Shepard and Scott Glenn.
- The movie *The Return of the Jedi*, directed by Richard Marquand, is released in the United States. The final installment of the Star Wars trilogy, it stars Mark Hamill, Harrison Ford, and Carrie Fisher.
- The movie *The Year of Living Dangerously*, directed by Peter Weir, is released in Australia. It stars Mel Gibson, Sigourney Weaver, and Linda Hunt.
- The movie *Yentl* is released in the United States, produced, written, directed by, and starring Barbra Streisand.
- The movie *Zelig*, written, directed by, and starring Woody Allen, is released in the United States. Mia Farrow costars.
- The vampire movie *The Hunger*, directed by Tony Scott, is released in the United States. It stars Catherine Deneuve, Susan Sarandon, and David Bowie.

APRIL

11 The 1982 Academy Awards take place. Best Actor: Ben Kingsley, for *Gandhi*; Best Supporting Actor: Lou Gosset, Jr., for *An Officer and a Gentleman*; Best Actress: Meryl Streep, for *Sophie's Choice*; Best Supporting Actress: Jessica Lange, for *Tootsie*; Best Picture: *Gandhi*, directed by Richard Attenborough; Best Director: Richard Attenborough, for *Gandhi*.

MAY

19 At the Cannes Film Festival in France, the Palme d'Or is awarded to Japanese director Shohei Imamura for the film *Narayama Bushiko/The Ballad of Narayama*. It stars Ken Ogata and Sumiko and was released in Japan earlier in the year.

Literature and Language

- German historian Paul Ratchnevsky publishes *Genghis Khan: His Life and Legacy*.
- The Antigua-born U.S. writer Jamaica Kincaid publishes her collection of short stories *At the Bottom of the River*.
- The Indian novelist R. K. Narayan publishes his novel *A Tiger for Malgudi*.
- The Indian-born English writer Salman Rushdie publishes his novel *Shame*.
- The Irish writer William Trevor publishes his novel *Fools of Fortune*.
- The Nobel Prize for Literature is awarded to the English novelist William Golding.
- The Pulitzer Prize for Biography is awarded to Russell Baker for *Growing Up*, the Pulitzer Prize for Poetry is awarded to Galway Kinnell for *Selected Poems*, and the Pulitzer Prize for Fiction is awarded to Alice Walker for *The Color Purple*.

- The Russian-born U.S. writer Isaac Asimov publishes his science fiction novel *Foundation's Edge*.
- The South African writer J. M. Coetzee publishes his novel *The Life and Times of Michael K*, which wins the Booker Prize.
- The U.S. novelist John Updike publishes *Hugging the Shore*, a collection of essays.
- The U.S. novelist Kurt Vonnegut publishes his novel *Deadeye Dick*.
- The U.S. novelist Norman Mailer publishes his novel *Ancient Evenings*.
- The U.S. novelist Philip Roth publishes his novel *The Anatomy Lesson*.

December

6   The most expensive book ever sold is auctioned at Sotheby's in London, England. *The Gospels of Henry the Lion* sells for £7.4 million.

Music

- For the first time, cassettes outsell vinyl LPs in the United States.
- The British pop duo Wham! releases the album *Fantastic*.
- The English pop group Culture Club releases "Karma Chameleon."
- The French composer Olivier Messiaen completes his opera *St. François d'Assise/St. Francis of Assissi*.
- The Italian composer Luciano Berio completes his vocal work *Un Re in ascolto*. It is first performed in Salzburg, Austria, in 1984.
- The opera *A Quiet Place*, by the U.S. composer Leonard Bernstein, is first performed, in Houston, Texas. It is revised the following year.
- The opera *Akhnaten*, by the U.S. composer Philip Glass, is first performed, in Stuttgart, Germany.
- The Polish composer Witold Lutosławski completes his Symphony No. 3.
- The U.S. composer Ned Rorem completes his choral work *Whitman Cantata* and publishes *Setting the Tone: Essays and a Diary*.
- The U.S. pop singer Billy Joel releases the album *An Innocent Man*.
- The U.S. pop singer Michael Jackson releases "Beat It" and "Billy Jean."
- U.S. performance artist Laurie Anderson has a hit with her single "O Superman" and stages a visual/music six-hour show *United States Parts I–IV*. Critics label her "an electronic Cassandra."

January

22   The British pop group Dexy's Midnight Runners releases the single "Come On Eileen."

February

23   The 1982–83 Grammy Awards are held. Best Album: *Toto IV* by Toto; Best Record: "Rosanna" by Toto; Best Female Pop Vocalist: Melissa Manchester for "You Should Hear How She Talks About You;" Best Male Pop Vocalist: Lionel Ritchie for "Truly;" Best Pop Group: Joe Cocker and Jennifer Warnes for "Up Where We Belong."

April

2   The Irish rock group U2 releases the single "New Year's Day."
23   The U.S. rock band ZZ Top releases its breakthrough album *Eliminator*. It will be one of the best-selling groups of the 1980s.
30   The English pop star and actor David Bowie releases the single "Let's Dance," and an album of the same name.

May

14   The U.S. rock group REM releases the album *Murmur*.
16   *Motown 25*, a musical celebration of the 25th anniversary of Motown Records, is shown on U.S. television, featuring Diana Ross and the Supremes, Smokey Robinson and the Miracles, Michael Jackson, the Four Tops, the Temptations, and Stevie Wonder.
28   The British pop duo the Eurythmics releases the album *Sweet Dreams (Are Made of This)*.

July

2   The British pop group the Police releases "Every Breath You Take," and the album *Synchronicity*.
4   The British pop group Duran Duran releases "Is There Something I Should Know?"

September

3   The U.S. pop singer Madonna releases the album *Madonna*.

October

15   The pop singers Michael Jackson and Paul McCartney release "Say, Say, Say."

December

24   The U.S. pop singer Cyndi Lauper releases the album *She's So Unusual*.

Theater and Dance

- The dance pieces *Quartets*, by the U.S. choreographer Merce Cunningham, are first performed, in the United States.
- The musical *La Cage aux Folles*, by Jerry Herman and Harvey Fierstein, is first performed, at the Palace Theater in New York, New York.
- The play *'Night Mother*, by the U.S. writer Marsha Norman, is first performed, at the Golden Theater in New York, New York.
- The play *A Map of the World*, by the English writer David Hare, is first performed, in London, England.
- The play *Brighton Beach Memoirs*, by the U.S. writer Neil Simon, is first performed, at the Alvin Theater in New York, New York.
- The play *Fool for Love*, by the U.S. writer Sam Shepard, is first performed, at the Douglas Fairbanks Theater in New York, New York.
- The play *Glengarry Glen Ross*, by the U.S. writer David Mamet, is first performed, in London, England.
- The play *The Genius*, by the English writer Howard Brenton, is first performed, in London, England.
- The Pulitzer Prize for Drama is awarded to Marsha Norman for *'Night Mother*.

October

22   The Metropolitan Opera in New York, New York, celebrates its 100th anniversary with a special television program, *Live from the Met*.

Thought and Scholarship

- Austrian-born English philosopher Karl Popper publishes *Realism and the Aim of Science*.
- English philosopher Ernest Gellner publishes *Nations and Nationalism*.
- Palestinian-American critic Edward Said publishes *The World, the Text, and the Critic*.
- The 48th and final volume of *Horace Walpole's Correspondence* is published, edited by U.S. scholar W. S. Lewis.
- The Pulitzer Prize for History is awarded to Rhys L. Isaac for *The Transformation of Virginia, 1740–1790*.
- The Pulitzer Prize for General Nonfiction is awarded to Susan Sheehan for *Is There No Place on Earth for Me?*
- U.S. historian Daniel J. Boorstin publishes *The Discoverers*.
- U.S. historian Maldwyn A. Jones publishes *The Limits of Liberty: American History 1607–1980*.

SOCIETY

Education

- The Gulbenkian Foundation for Modern Art in Lisbon, Portugal, designed by the English architect Leslie Martin, is completed.
- The school-leaving age is raised to 18 in Belgium.

APRIL

26 The National Commission on Excellence in Education's report, "A Nation at Risk," is sharply critical of declining standards in the United States.

Everyday Life

- In 1983, 4.1 million video recorders are sold in the United States.
- Because of campaigns against drunk driving and greater use of safety belts, U.S. auto accident deaths drop to 43,028, the lowest rate in 20 years.
- Black clothing becomes fashionable in the United States. Leg warmers are popular winter-wear.
- Illiteracy levels in selected countries (percentage of adult population): Afghanistan 81.8; Angola 59.0; Argentina 6.1; Bangladesh 70.8; Brazil 22.2; China 34.5; Egypt 61.8; Ethiopia 37.6; India 59.2; Indonesia 32.7; Iran 45.2; Israel 8.2; Malaysia 30.4; Mexico 17.0; Pakistan 73.8; Peru 18.1; Saudi Arabia 48.9; Sri Lanka 13.2; Sudan 68.6; Tunisia 49.3.
- In Switzerland, the Swatch timepiece is created.
- The popularity of Cabbage Patch Dolls in the United States is so great that a black market emerges. Sales will peak in 1985 at about $600 million.
- The U.S. Census Bureau reports the highest level of persons living in poverty in the United States in 18 years (35,300,000).
- Top fashion designers plan to market their styles at discount prices in the United States. Halston signs a deal with the department store J. C. Penny to design clothes to sell for between $20 and $200.

- Women make up 42% of higher education students in Romania, 34% in Ecuador, and 33% in the Netherlands.

FEBRUARY

22 The U.S. Supreme Court rules that games company Parker Brothers cannot sue for copyright infringement the producers of a game called "Anti-Monopoly."

APRIL

20 The U.S. Congress approves social security reforms, including a phased reduction of welfare benefits.

22 The leader of the Polish Solidarity labor union, Lech Wałęsa, returns to work at the Lenin Shipyard in Gdańsk.

OCTOBER

- UK and U.S. studies indicate that long-term use of oral contraceptives may increase the risk of breast and cervical cancer.

5 The Nobel Peace Prize is awarded to Lech Wałęsa, the Polish union leader and subsequently president of Poland.

Media and Communication

- Australian-born U.S. media tycoon Rupert Murdoch purchases the *Chicago Sun-Times* for $90 million.
- The number of cable television subscribers in the United States reaches 25 million.
- Two popular mini-series on U.S. television are *The Thorn Birds* and *The Winds of War*.

JANUARY

23–June 14, 1987 *The A-Team* is a popular drama about a group of Vietnam veterans, falsely accused of bank robbery, who manage to elude their pursuers and champion worthy causes, leading to exciting chase scenes and showdowns.

MARCH

- Condé Nast Publications relaunches *Vanity Fair* in the United States, 46 years after the last issue.

MAY

- *Stern* magazine in Germany publishes extracts from *The Hitler Diaries*, which are considered authentic by English historian Hugh Trevor-Roper, but later exposed on May 11 as a fake produced by a dealer in Nazi memorabilia.

29 *Big Bird in China*, a children's variety show special, taped on location in China, with the Sesame Street character Big Bird, is shown on U.S. television.

SEPTEMBER

19 The final episode of the television series *M*A*S*H* receives by far the largest audience for a nonsports program to date, 125,000,000 viewers.

25 The 1982–83 Emmy Awards for television are held. Best Drama Series: *Hill Street Blues*; Best Comedy Series: *Cheers*; Best Actor in a Drama: Ed Flanders, for *St Elsewhere*; Best Actress in a Drama: Tyne Daly, for *Cagney and Lacey*; Best Actor in a Comedy: Judd Hirsh, for *Taxi*; Best Actress in a Comedy: Shelley Long, for *Cheers*.

DECEMBER

18 Former U.S. president Gerald Ford appears in an episode of the prime time television soap opera *Dynasty*.

Sports

- In the United States 78.1 million fans attend baseball games, more than in any other sport.
- In harness racing, the prize purse in the Hambletonian Stakes tops 1 million dollars for the first time.
- The United States fails to win the America's Cup yacht race for the first time since the race series began in 1870; the winner is the Australian yacht *Australia II*, skippered by John Bertrand, which defeats *Liberty*, skippered by Dennis Conner, by four races to three.

JANUARY

1   Sportswriters pick Penn State as college football's best team for the 1982 season.

FEBRUARY

3–4   U.S. national figure skating champions are: Rosalynn Sumners; Scott Hamilton; Kitty and Peter Carruthers, pairs; Judy Blumberg and Michael Seibert, dance.

8   The 1981 English Derby winner, Shergar, is kidnapped from the Aga Khan's stud farm in County Kildare in the Republic of Ireland by five armed men. A £2 million ransom demand is made, but the Aga Khan refuses on principle to pay, and the horse is never seen again.

MAY

10–17   The New York Islanders win their fourth straight Stanley Cup, beating the Edmonton Oilers.

22–31   The Philadelphia 76ers defeat the Los Angeles Lakers in four straight games to win the National Basketball Association (NBA) title.

29   U.S. racing driver Tom Sneva wins the Indianapolis 500.

JUNE

5   Yannick Noah becomes the first Frenchman to win the men's singles title at the French Open tennis championships since Marcel Bernard in 1946.

JULY

2   The Czech-born U.S. tennis player Martina Navratilova wins her fourth successive singles title at the Wimbledon tennis championships in London, England.

6   In baseball, the American League defeats the National League in the All Star Game for the first time since 1971 and only the second time since 1962.

17   The Michigan Panthers defeat the Philadelphia Stars 24–22 in Denver, Colorado, to win the inaugural United States Football League (USFL) championship, set up as a rival to the National Football League (NFL).

17   The U.S. golfer Tom Watson wins the British Open for the fifth time, at Royal Birkdale, in Lancashire, England.

AUGUST

6   The first professional American football match to take place in Britain is played at Wembley Stadium, London, between the Minnesota Vikings and the St. Louis Cardinals.

7–14   The first International Amateur Athletics Federation World Athletics Championships are held in Helsinki, Finland, with 157 nations competing. The United States

BIRTHS & DEATHS

JANUARY

15   Meyer Lansky, Russian-born U.S. crime syndicate boss, dies in Miami Beach, Florida (80).

24   George Cukor, U.S. film and theater director who won an Academy Award for the direction of *My Fair Lady* in 1964, dies (83).

26   Paul "Bear" Bryant, U.S. football coach at the University of Alabama, with the most career victories (323) for a major college team, dies in Tuscaloosa, Alabama (69).

FEBRUARY

25   Tennessee Williams (Thomas Lanier Williams), U.S. dramatist, most of whose plays are set in the Deep South, dies in New York, New York (71).

MARCH

11   Donald Maclean, British diplomat and member of the Foreign Office who spied for the USSR during World War II and the Cold War, dies in Moscow, USSR (69).

13   Louis Bobet, French cyclist and the first man to win the Tour de France three consecutive times, dies in Biarritz, France (58).

APRIL

4   Gloria Swanson, U.S. silent film star and glamor girl of the 1920s, dies in New York, New York (86).

22   Earl "Fatha" Hines, U.S. bandleader known as "the father of modern jazz piano," dies in Oakland, California (77).

30   George Melitonovich Balanchine, Russian-born U.S. choreographer and a founder of the New York Ballet, dies in New York, New York (79).

MAY

20   Clair Bee, U.S. basketball coach and author, dies in Cleveland, Ohio (83).

31   Jack Dempsey, U.S. world heavyweight boxing champion 1919–26, dies in New York, New York (87).

JULY

1   R. Buckminster Fuller, U.S. architect and engineer who developed the geodesic dome, dies in Los Angeles, California (87).

23   Georges Auric, French composer of film scores and ballets, dies in Paris, France (84).

27   David Niven, English film actor, novelist, and author of popular anecdotal memoirs, dies in Château d'Oex, Switzerland (73).

29   Luis Buñuel, Spanish surrealist filmmaker, dies in Mexico City, Mexico (83).

AUGUST

17   Ira Gershwin, U.S. songwriter who worked both independently and with his younger brother George to produce hit shows and songs, dies in Hollywood, California (86).

SEPTEMBER

10   John Vorster, prime minister of South Africa 1966–78, and president 1978–79, dies in Cape Town, South Africa (67).

OCTOBER

3   Earl Tupper, U.S. inventor of Tupperware, dies in San José, California (76).

31   George Halas, U.S. founder, owner, and influential coach of the Chicago Bears in the National Football League, dies in Chicago, Illinois (88).

DECEMBER

25   Joan Miró, Catalan surrealist and abstract artist, dies in Palma, Majorca, Spain (90).

leads the gold medal table with eight medals. Mary Decker and Carl Lewis of the United States win two and three gold medals respectively. Grete Waitz of Norway wins the first-ever world championship women's marathon.

SEPTEMBER

28 The National Basketball Association (NBA) announces that any player convicted of taking illegal drugs, or admitting to having taken them, will be banned from the league for life.

OCTOBER

4 British driver Richard Noble breaks the world one-mile land speed record in the Black Rock Desert, Nevada, in his *Thrust 2* jet car, averaging a speed of 1,019.44 kph/ 633.468 mph over the required two runs.

11 The Baltimore Orioles win the World Series, beating the Philadelphia Phillies.

1984

POLITICS, GOVERNMENT, AND ECONOMICS

Business and Economics

- Seventy-nine U.S. banks fail in the course of the year, the largest number since 1933. A further 817 are said to have financial problems.
- The West German firm Bosch develops the platinum spark plug.
- Trading on the New York Stock Exchange reaches a new record, with 200 million shares changing hands.

JANUARY

5 Texaco, Inc. moves to acquire the Getty Oil Company in the largest business merger in U.S. history.

JUNE

15 In the largest ever corporate merger, U.S. oil company Standard Oil buys the Gulf Corporation for $13.2 billion.

Colonization

JANUARY

1 The sultanate of Brunei becomes independent after 95 years as a British protectorate.

Human Rights

- Christine Craft, a U.S. newsreader who was demoted to reporter because she was considered "too old, unattractive, and not deferential enough to men," is awarded damages of $325,000.

JANUARY

17 The Commission on Civil Rights in the United States votes to discontinue the use of numerical quotas in the promotion of black Americans.

Politics and Government

- The 1929 concordat between the Vatican City State and Italy is revised, with Roman Catholicism losing its status as official state religion of Italy.

JANUARY

1 A supreme military council under General Mohammed Buhari assumes power in Nigeria.

7 El Salvador, Costa Rica, Honduras, and Guatemala agree a peace plan for their troubled region.

10 "Amity talks" are convened in Sri Lanka between Tamil and Sinhalese representatives.

12 Former U.S. secretary of state Henry Kissinger issues a policy document on Central America, proposing a doubling of U.S. aid to the region.

17 A 35-nation conference on disarmament in Europe opens in Stockholm, Sweden.

18 The president of the American University in Beirut Malcolm Kerr is shot dead by a militant pro-Iranian group.

19 The Islamic Conference Organization votes to readmit Egypt following the suspension of its membership since the Camp David accord with Israel.

19 The United States partly lifts trade sanctions on Poland.

29 U.S. president Ronald Reagan announces his intention to seek reelection.

FEBRUARY

6 President Amin Gemayel of Lebanon orders a 24-hour curfew as Shiite Muslim and Druze militias overrun West Beirut.

7 U.S. president Ronald Reagan orders U.S. marines to withdraw from Beirut. The last marines leave on February 26.

11 Iraq commences the bombing of nonmilitary targets in Iran in a new escalation of the war between the two countries.

13 Konstantin Chernenko is named first secretary of the Soviet Communist Party following the death of Yuri Andropov.

27 Iraq announces a blockade of the main Iranian oil terminal at Kharg Island and threatens to attack all oil tankers loading there.

MARCH

1 A joint South African–Angolan monitoring commission begins the supervision of South African troop withdrawal from southern Angola.

4 The speaker of the Iranian parliament claims that 400 Iranian soldiers have been killed by Iraqi chemical weapons in the course of the Iran–Iraq war.

5 The U.S. Supreme Court rules that the public financing of nativity scenes does not violate the principle of separation of church and state.

12–20 A new conference aimed at reconciling opposed political and social groups in Lebanon is held in Lausanne, Switzerland.

27 Colorado senator Gary Hart wins the Connecticut primary, becoming the frontrunner for the Democratic presidential nomination.

31 The Indian government agrees to amend the Punjabi constitution to acknowledge Sikhism as a religion distinct from Hinduism.

APRIL

3 The Indian state of Punjab is declared a "dangerously disturbed area." On April 5, the government allows detention without trial in the state.

10 The U.S. Senate votes against mining Nicaraguan ports.

17 Yvonne Fletcher, a policewoman in London, England, is killed and 11 others injured when gunmen fire on demonstrators outside the Libyan People's Bureau. On April 22, Britain breaks diplomatic relations with Libya and, on April 27, the siege of the building ends.

20 Widespread demonstrations are held in West Germany against the deployment of U.S. cruise and Pershing missiles in Europe.

26–May 1 U.S. president Ronald Reagan visits China and negotiates several new trade agreements, including export deals for U.S. nuclear technology.

MAY

2 The dissident Soviet physicist Andrei Sakharov begins a hunger strike when authorities refuse to allow his wife, Yelena Bonner, to travel abroad for medical treatment. His protest ends on August 6.

7 Chemical companies agree $180 million compensation for U.S. Vietnam veterans alleging health problems resulting from exposure to Agent Orange.

10 The Danish parliament votes to halt payments to NATO for the deployment of Pershing II and cruise missiles in Europe.

10 The International Court of Justice at The Hague, the Netherlands, rules that the United States should cease its blockade of Nicaraguan ports.

14 The opposition makes gains in elections in the Philippines.

24 Five former El Salvador soldiers are found guilty of the murder of three U.S. nuns and a female missionary in El Salvador in 1980.

24 Iranian war planes attack oil tankers off the coast of Saudi Arabia, in an apparent effort to widen the Iran–Iraq war. On May 27, the United States sends Stinger antiaircraft missiles to Saudi Arabia in case of Iranian attack.

24 The U.S. House of Representatives votes to continue military aid to El Salvador, but against further aid to the Nicaraguan Contra guerrillas.

JUNE

1 The U.S. secretary of state George Shultz calls on the Nicaraguan government to end its support for rebels in El Salvador.

5 The U.S. Supreme Court rules that political asylum seekers must prove a "clear probability" of persecution if they return home.

6 Indian troops storm the Golden Temple complex at Amritsar in Punjab state, killing 250 Sikh extremists. On June 11, Sikh soldiers mutiny at eight army bases in protest at the attack.

10 Iraq seeks United Nations supervision of its agreement with Iran to stop attacks on civilian areas as the war between the two countries continues.

14 The Netherlands parliament approves a cabinet decision to delay a final decision on the deployment of U.S. cruise missiles in the Netherlands.

29 The Indian prime minister Indira Gandhi dismisses the governor and police chief of the state of Punjab.

JULY

4 Lebanese army units take over positions in Beirut from the Shiite, Christian, and Druze militias.

11 It becomes compulsory to wear seat belts when driving in the state of New York.

14 The Labor Party, led by David Lange, defeats the ruling National Party of Robert Muldoon in the New Zealand general election.

18 A lone gunman, Oliver Huberty, shoots 20 people dead and wounds 16 in a McDonald's restaurant in San Diego, California.

18 The U.S. Democratic Party convention in San Francisco selects Walter Mondale and Geraldine Ferraro as presidential and vice presidential candidates in the forthcoming elections. Ferraro is the first woman chosen to run for vice president.

AUGUST

3 The Upper Volta head of state, Captain Thomas Sankara, renames his country Burkina Faso ("land of incorruptible people").

4 Violent clashes erupt between the Tamil and Sinhalese communities in Sri Lanka.

6–13 The United Nations holds its second conference on world population, in Mexico. Representatives of 149 countries adopt 88 recommendations.

8 Premier Mugabe of Zimbabwe announces a plan for the conversion of Zimbabwe to a one-party state.

13 Libya and Morocco agree to a political federation.

16 The British entrepreneur John De Lorean is acquitted in the United States of eight charges of drug trafficking.

22 The U.S. Republican Party convention in Dallas, Texas, nominates President Ronald Reagan and Vice President George Bush as the party's candidates for the November election.

23 Yelena Bonner, wife of the dissident Soviet physicist Andrei Sakharov, is sentenced to five years' internal exile for slandering the USSR.

31 Israel's Likud party leader Yitzhak Shamir and the Labor Party leader Shimon Peres agree to form a government of national unity and to alternate in the post of prime minister.

SEPTEMBER

3 Fourteen people die in rioting in Sharpeville and other black townships around Johannesburg, South Africa. Overnight, the death toll rises to 29.

4 The Progressive Conservatives, led by Brian Mulroney, defeat John Turner's ruling Liberals in the Canadian general election.

14 The South African prime minister P. W. Botha is sworn in as the country's first executive president. On September 17, the first 19-member multiracial cabinet is sworn in.

17 France reaches an agreement with Libya for the withdrawal of both countries' armed forces from Chad by mid-November.

20 A suicide bomber of the Shiite organization Islamic Jihad attacks the U.S. embassy in Beirut in an explosion that kills 40 people.

25 Jordan restores full diplomatic relations with Egypt.

26 A draft agreement for the return of Hong Kong to China in 1997 is signed by British and Chinese representatives at a ceremony in Beijing.

OCTOBER

12 An Irish Republican Army (IRA) bomb explodes at the Grand Hotel, in Brighton, England, during the Conservative Party conference, killing 4, injuring 32, and narrowly missing the British prime minister Margaret Thatcher. A fifth victim dies on November 13.

20 The Central Committee of the Chinese Communist Party agrees a program of economic reforms, giving factory managers greater autonomy.

23 An official report in the Philippines into the murder on August 21, 1983, of the opposition leader Benigno Aquino declares that 26 people, including top military officials, were involved.

27 The Polish authorities admit that the pro-Solidarity priest, Father Jerzy Popiełuszko, kidnapped on October 19, has been murdered by a member of the security police. His body is found in a reservoir on October 30 and, on October 31, three officers are charged.

31 Indian prime minister Indira Gandhi is assassinated in New Delhi by extremist Sikhs among her bodyguards, apparently in response to the storming of the Sikh Golden Temple at Amritsar by Indian government troops.

31 Rajiv Gandhi is sworn in as prime minister of India amid communal violence between Sikhs and Hindus after the assasination of his mother Indira by her Sikh bodyguards.

NOVEMBER

2 Angola offers to reduce the number of Cuban troops in the country if South Africa agrees to relinquish control of Namibia.

4 The Sandinista Front wins the Nicaraguan elections, and Daniel Ortega is elected president with 63% of the popular vote.

6 In the U.S. presidential election, the Republican president Ronald Reagan, with 525 electoral college votes, wins a landslide victory over the Democrat candidate Walter Mondale, with 13 college votes.

12–15 An Organization of African Unity summit in Addis Ababa, Ethiopia, calls for massive international aid for Africa.

16 The French president François Mitterrand acknowledges that Libyan troops are still in Chad in defiance of the withdrawal agreement between France and Libya.

26 The United States restores full diplomatic relations with Iraq following their severance in 1967.

DECEMBER

1 King Hussein of Jordan and the Egyptian president Hosni Mubarak hold talks in Cairo on peace initiatives for the West Bank.

7 Tamil terrorists attack a Sri Lankan army convoy, killing over 100 people.

15 Cuba agrees to take back 2,746 criminals and mental patients who entered the United States in 1980.

15 The Soviet Politburo member Mikhail Gorbachev visits London, England, and states that the USSR is willing to negotiate large reductions in nuclear weapons. The British prime minister Margaret Thatcher declares "I like Mr. Gorbachev. We can do business together."

22 Dom Mintoff resigns as prime minister of Malta, to be succeeded by Carmello Mifsud Bonnici.

22 Vigilante Bernhard Goetz shoots four youths, paralyzing one, on the New York subway. He claims he was threatened.

24 Rajiv Gandhi's Congress (I) Party wins a large majority in the Indian general election.

31 The United States withdraws from the United Nations Educational, Scientific, and Cultural Organization, alleging that it is too critical of U.S. policy. It had announced its intention December 29, 1983, saying that the organization "exhibited hostility toward the basic installations of a free society."

SCIENCE, TECHNOLOGY, AND MEDICINE

Computing

c. 1984 Computer "viruses" such as "Friday 13th," "Trojan Horse," "Holland Girl," and "Christmas Tree" begin to appear.

c. 1984 Computers begin to monitor and control the flow of oil through pipelines.

• Computers are used to generate the 25 minutes of space-battle scenes in the movie *The Last Starfighter*; it is the first film to make extensive use of computers.

• Japanese firm NEC produces computer chips with 256 kilobits of memory; similar ones are manufactured in the United States the following year.

• U.S. computer manufacturer Apple launches the Macintosh personal computer in the United States; it is the first successful graphic-based microcomputer using icons and a mouse.

DECEMBER

20 The development of a 1 MB random access memory (RAM) chip is announced by Bell Laboratories; it is capable of storing four times as much data as any currently available.

Ecology

- Over 500 people are killed and a million left homeless when a typhoon hits the Philippines.

MARCH

- Mauna Loa in Hawaii, the world's largest active volcano, erupts.

JUNE

9 Tornadoes in the USSR kill over 400 people.

DECEMBER

3 A leak of toxic methyl isocyanate gas from the Union Carbide pesticide plant near Bhopal, India, kills 2,600 people and injures 300,000. In February 1989, India's Supreme Court orders Union Carbide to pay $470 million in damages.

Exploration

- The United States launches the earth resource satellite *Landsat 4*; it uses cameras to view the earth in several bands of the infrared spectrum.

JULY

18 Soviet cosmonaut Svetlana Savitskaya becomes the first woman to walk in space.

NOVEMBER

- The U.S. National Aeronautics and Space Administration (NASA) astronauts use a Manned Maneuvering Unit (MMU) to retrieve two communications satellites.

Health and Medicine

- Bath houses are closed in San Francisco, California, to slow the spread of the AIDS virus.
- The American Cancer Society sponsors the "Great Smoke-Out"; over 5 million smokers quit and 15 million cut back their smoking.
- The Nobel Prize for Physiology or Medicine is awarded jointly to British-born Danish immunologist Niels Jerne, German immunologist Georges Köhler, and Argentine-born British molecular biologist César Milstein for their work on immunity and the discovery of a technique for producing highly specific, monoclonal antibodies.
- The Reagan administration in the United States withdraws funds to worldwide family-planning programs that perform or offer information about abortions; 67 nations are unable to offer help without this funding, and 200,000 women die of botched abortions as a result.
- The U.S. Environmental Protection Agency identifies nearly 540 abandoned hazardous-waste dumps in the United States that present a threat to public health.
- UK researchers develop the first vaccine against leprosy.

- William Clewall of the University of Colorado, United States, performs the first successful operation on an unborn fetus.

JANUARY

- An Australian woman gives birth to a child created by in vitro fertilization using her husband's sperm and another woman's egg.

OCTOBER

- Ethical questions are raised when surgeons at Loma Linda University Medical Center in California, United States, transplant the heart of a baboon into a two-week-old girl, "Baby Fae." The patient survives for 20 days.

Science

- A team of international physicists at the European Center for Nuclear Research (CERN) in Geneva, Switzerland, discovers the sixth (top) quark; its discovery completes the theoretical classification of subatomic building blocks.
- Allan Wilson and Russell Higuchi of the University of California, Berkeley, United States, clone genes from an extinct animal, the quagga.
- An international team of scientists at Deutsche Elektronen-Synchrotron (DESY) near Hamburg, West Germay, discovers the "zeta" subatomic particle, a massive particle with neutral charge.
- Archeologists discover the remains of an 8,000-year-old settlement, known as Altit-Yam, at an underwater site off the coast of Israel.
- Astronomers at Cornell University, New York, report the discovery of eight infrared galaxies—thought to resemble primeval galaxies—located by the *Infrared Astronomical Satellite*.
- At Nariokotome near Lake Turkana in Kenya, the Kenyan paleoarcheologist Kamoya Kimeu discovers the nearly complete skeleton of an 11- or 12-year-old *Homo erectus* boy; the most complete specimen of *Homo erectus* known, it is also one of the oldest, at 1.6 million years old.
- Australian geologists Bod Pidgeon and Simon Wilde discover zircon crystals in the Jack Hills north of Perth, Australia, that are estimated to be 4.276 million years old—the oldest rocks ever discovered.
- British geneticist Alec Jeffreys discovers that a core sequence of DNA (deoxyribonucleic acid) is almost unique to each person; this examination of DNA, known as "genetic fingerprinting," can be used in criminal investigations and to establish family relationships.
- From studies of DNA (deoxyribonucleic acid), U.S. scientists Charles Sibley and Jon Ahlquist argue that humans are more closely related to chimpanzees than to other great apes, differing in their DNA by only 1%, and that humans and apes diverged approximately 5–6 million years ago.
- Robert Sinsheimer, the chancellor of the University of California at Santa Cruz, California, proposes that all human genes be mapped; the proposal eventually leads to the development of the Human Genome Project.
- Sheep are successfully cloned.

- The element unniloctium (atomic no. 108, now called Hassium) is synthesized by a team of chemists in Darmstadt, West Germany.
- The naturally mummified body of a man ("Lindow Man") is found in an English peat bog. He had been ritually sacrificed by Druid priests.
- The Nobel Prize for Physics is awarded jointly to Italian physicist Carlo Rubbia and Dutch physicist Simon van der Meer for their basic studies on particle physics.
- U.S. astronomers working in Chile photograph a partial ring system around Neptune.
- U.S. chemist Bruce Merrifield receives the Nobel Prize for Chemistry for chemical syntheses of peptides and proteins on a solid matrix.

Technology

- The Dutch company Philips and Japanese firm Sony introduce the CD-ROM, a laser-read, read-only disk.
- The Itaipu power plant on the Paraná River on the border between Brazil and Paraguay starts operating; the largest generating station in the world, it produces 13,200 megawatts of electricity.
- The U.S. military make the first midair direct hit of one missile by another—a major step in antiballistic missile (ABM) technology.
- U.S. physicist Dennis Matthews builds the first X-ray laser.
- Visa International launches holographic 3D credit cards.

FEBRUARY

7 Two U.S. shuttle astronauts make untethered space walks, using jet-propelled backpacks to move in space.

MAY

- The first domestic robot, Hubot the Robot, is advertised in the *New York Times*, at a price of $3,495.

NOVEMBER

19 At least 500 people are killed and 300 homes destroyed in Mexico City when 50,000 barrels of gas explode at a depot owned by the state oil company Pemex.

Transportation

- The U.S. B-1 long-range bomber crashes during its test flight.

JUNE

22 Virgin Atlantic Airlines makes its first flight from London, England, to New York, New York.

ARTS AND IDEAS

Architecture

- The English architect Denys Lasdun publishes *Architecture in the Age of Scepticism*.
- The Mediathèque in Villeurbane, Lyons, France, designed by the Swiss architect Mario Botta, is completed.

- The Neue Staatsgalerie (an art gallery) in Stuttgart, West Germany, designed by the English architect James Stirling, is completed. It is one of the leading works of postmodernism.

Arts

- The English artist Gillian Ayers paints *Scilla*.
- The exhibition "Primitivism in the Twentieth Century" is held at the Museum of Modern Art (MOMA) in New York, New York.
- The German artist Hans Haacke paints *Taking Stock (unfinished)*.
- The U.S. artist Frank Stella becomes the first visual artist to hold the post of Charles Eliot Norton Professor of Poetry at Harvard University, in Cambridge, Massachusetts.

Film

- Movie audiences in France have fallen since 1983, but the number of French-made movies has increased.
- Edgar Reitz films the 16-hour epic *Heimat/Home* in West Germany.
- The movie *A Passage to India*, directed by David Lean, is released in the UK. Based on the novel by E. M. Forster, it stars Judy Davis, Victor Banerjee, Peggy Ashcroft, James Fox, and Alec Guinness.
- The movie *Amadeus*, directed by Miloš Forman, is released in the United States. Based on Peter Shaffer's play about Salieri and Mozart, it stars F. Murray Abraham and Tom Hulce.
- The movie *Beverly Hills Cop*, directed by Martin Brest, is released in the United States, starring Eddie Murphy, Judge Reinhold, John Ashton, and Steven Berkoff.
- The movie *Broadway Danny Rose*, written and directed by Woody Allen, is released in the United States. It stars Allen and Mia Farrow.
- The movie *Choose Me*, directed by Alan Rudolph, is released in the United States, starring Keith Carradine, Lesley Ann Warren, and Geneviève Bujold.
- The movie *Ghostbusters*, directed by Ivan Reitman, is released in the United States. It stars Dan Ackroyd, Harold Ramis, and Bill Murray.
- The movie *Greystoke: The Legend of Tarzan, Lord of the Apes*, directed by Hugh Hudson, is released in the United States. It stars Christopher Lambert, Andie MacDowell, Ralph Richardson, and Ian Holm.
- The movie *Huang Tudi/Yellow Earth* is released in China. It is directed by Chen Kaige and photographed by Zhang Yimou.
- The movie *Indiana Jones and the Temple of Doom*, the second movie in Steven Spielberg's *Indiana Jones* trilogy, is released in the United States, starring Harrison Ford. It makes over $42 million in six days, breaking almost every box office record.
- The movie *Man of Flowers*, directed by the Dutch-born filmmaker Paul Cox, is released in Australia. It stars Norman Kaye and Alyson Best.
- The movie *Once Upon a Time in America*, directed by Italian filmmaker Sergio Leone, is released in the United States. It stars James Woods and Robert De Niro.

- The movie *Paris, Texas*, directed by German filmmaker Wim Wenders, is released in the United States. It stars Harry Dean Stanton and Nastassja Kinski. It is awarded the Palme d'Or at the Cannes Film Festival in France.
- The movie *Qué he hecho yo para merecer esto?/What Have I Done to Deserve This?* is released in Spain. It is written and directed by Pedro Almodóvar and stars Carmen Maura.
- The movie *Repo Man*, directed by Alex Cox, is released in the United States, starring Emilio Estevez and Harry Dean Stanton.
- The movie *Romancing the Stone*, directed by Robert Zemeckis, is released in the United States. It stars Kathleen Turner and Michael Douglas.
- The movie *Rue Cases Nègres/Black Shack Alley*, directed by Martinique-born filmmaker Euzhan Palcy, is released in France. It stars Garry Cadenat and Darling Legitimus.
- The movie *Stop Making Sense*, directed by Jonathan Demme, is released in the United States, featuring the new wave band Talking Heads in concert.
- The movie *The Gods Must Be Crazy*, directed by James Uys, is released in South Africa, starring N'xau, Marius Weyers, Sandra Prinsloo, and Nic de Jager.
- The movie *The Killing Fields*, directed by Roland Joffé, is released in the UK. It stars Sam Waterstone and Haing S. Ngor.
- The movie *Un Amour de Swann/Swann in Love*, directed by German filmmaker Volker Schlöndorff, is released in France. Based on part of Marcel Proust's *A la recherche du temps perdu/Remembrance of Things Past*, it stars Jeremy Irons.
- The movie *Un Dimanche à la campagne/A Sunday in the Country*, directed by Bertrand Tavernier, is released in France. It stars Sabine Azéma and Louis Ducreux.
- The horror movie *A Nightmare on Elm Street*, directed by Wes Craven, is released in the United States. It stars Robert Englund.
- The landmark independent movie *Stranger Than Paradise*, directed by Jim Jarmusch, is released in the United States.
- The low-budget, independent movie *Blood Simple*, written, directed, and produced by Joel and Ethan Coen, is released in the United States. It stars Frances McDormand and John Getz.
- The science fiction movie *The Terminator*, directed by James Cameron, is released in the United States. It stars Arnold Schwarzenegger, Linda Hamilton, and Michael Biehn.
- The spoof rock documentary *This is Spinal Tap*, directed by Rob Reiner, is released in the United States, starring Christopher Guest, Michael Mckern, and Harry Shearer.

APRIL

9   The 1983 Academy Awards take place. Best Actor: Robert Duvall, for *Tender Mercies*; Best Supporting Actor: Jack Nicholson, for *Terms of Endearment*; Best Actress: Shirley MacLaine, for *Terms of Endearment*; Best Supporting Actress: Linda Hunt, for *The Year of Living Dangerously*; Best Picture: *Terms of Endearment*, directed by James L. Brooks; Best Director: James L. Brooks, for *Terms of Endearment*.

JUNE

- The Screen Actors' Guild in the United States awards Disney cartoon character Donald Duck membership in recognition of his 50th birthday.

Literature and Language

- A new edition of James Joyce's novel *Ulysses* is published, correcting 5,000 errors. It is edited by Hans Gabler.
- Irish poet Seamus Heaney publishes his poetry collection *Station Island*.
- The Antigua-born U.S. writer Jamaica Kincaid publishes her novel *Annie John*.
- The Australian writer David Malouf publishes his novel *Harland's Half Acre*.
- The Czech writer Milan Kundera publishes his novel *Nesnesitelná lehkost bytí/The Unbearable Lightness of Being*.
- The English novelist Martin Amis publishes his novel *Money*.
- The English writer Anita Brookner publishes her novel *Hotel du Lac*, which wins the Booker Prize.
- The English writer Angela Carter publishes her novel *Nights at the Circus*.
- The English writer J. G. Ballard publishes his autobiographical novel *The Empire of the Sun*.
- The English writer Julian Barnes publishes his novel *Flaubert's Parrot*.
- The French writer Marguerite Duras publishes her novel *L'Amant/The Lover*.
- The New Zealand writer Keri Hulme publishes her novel *The Bone People*, which wins the Booker Prize.
- The Nobel Prize for Literature is awarded to the Czech poet Jaroslav Seifert.
- The novel *Arcadio* by the U.S. writer William Goyen is published posthumously.
- The Pulitzer Prize for Biography is awarded to Louis R. Harlan for *Booker T Washington*, the Pulitzer Prize for Poetry is awarded to Mary Oliver for *American Primitive*, and the Pulitzer Prize for Fiction is awarded to William Kennedy for *Ironweed*.
- The U.S. novelist Alison Lurie publishes her novel *Foreign Affairs*, which wins a Pulitzer prize in 1985.
- The U.S. poet John Ashbery publishes his poetry collection *A Wave*.
- The U.S. writer Amiri Baraka (before 1968 called LeRoi Jones) publishes his *Autobiography of LeRoy Jones/Amiri Baraka*.
- The U.S. writer Gore Vidal publishes his novel *Lincoln*.
- The U.S. writer Saul Bellow publishes *Him with His Foot in His Mouth and Other Short Stories*.
- U.S. author Joseph Heller publishes his novel *God Knows*.
- U.S. novelist Norman Mailer publishes his novel *Tough Guys Don't Dance*.
- U.S. writer John Updike publishes his novel *The Witches of Eastwick*.
- U.S. writer William Gibson's science fiction novel *Neuromancer* popularizes the concept of cyberspace.

DECEMBER

18 U.S. publisher Rea Hederman buys the *New York Review of Books* for $5 million.

Music

- Rap, a music style developed by inner-city black and Latino teenagers in the 1970s in New York, New York, becomes popular worldwide. Breakdancing, a highly energetic and athletic form of dancing often done on the street, develops from the rap scene.
- The "gender-bending" trend in pop music is featured in *Newsweek* when Culture Club's Boy George appears on the front cover.
- The British pop singer Elvis Costello releases the album *Goodbye Cruel World*.
- The English composer Michael Tippett completes his choral work *The Mask of Time*.
- The English composer Andrew Lloyd Webber completes his *Requiem*.
- The German pop group Einsturtzende Neubauten releases the album *Strategien gegen Architekturen/ Strategies against Architecture*.
- The Japanese composer Toru Takemitsu completes his orchestral work *riverrun*.
- The Polish composer Krzysztof Penderecki completes *Polish Requiem*.
- The Polish composer Witold Lutosławski completes his work for voice and orchestra *Chain II*.
- The Russian composer Alfred Schnittke completes his String Quartet No. 3.
- The Russian composer Elena Firsova completes her vocal work *Earthly Life*.
- The U.S. composer Elliott Carter completes his chamber work *Canon for Four: Homage to William*.
- The U.S. composer John Cage completes his chamber work *Thirty Pieces for String Quartet*.
- The U.S. composer Ned Rorem completes his choral work *An American Oratorio*.
- The U.S. composer Robert Ashley completes his two video operas *Atalanta Strategy* and *Foreign Experiences*.
- The U.S. rock band Van Halen sells 6 million copies of its single "Jump."

FEBRUARY

25 The British pop singer Phil Collins releases "Against All Odds (Take A Look At Me Now)."

28 The 1983–84 Grammy Awards are held. Best Album: *Thriller* by Michael Jackson; Best Record: "Beat It" by Michael Jackson; Best Male Vocalist: Michael Jackson; Best Female Pop Vocalist: Irene Cara for "Flashdance;" Best Pop Group: The Police for "Every Breath You Take."

MAY

5 The British pop group the Smiths releases the album *The Smiths*, featuring the single "Heaven Knows I'm Miserable Now."

JUNE

23 An auction of John Lennon's possessions, as well as some belonging to his widow Yoko Ono, raises $430,000.

23 The U.S. rock singer Bruce Springsteen releases the album *Born in the USA*.

OCTOBER

20 The Irish rock group U2 releases the album *The Unforgettable Fire*.

NOVEMBER

17 The U.S. pop singer Madonna releases "Like a Virgin."

Theater and Dance

- The musical *Sunday in the Park with George* is first performed, at the Booth Theater in New York, New York. Written by Stephen Sondheim, it is based on the works of the French painter Georges Seurat.
- The musical *Starlight Express*, with lyrics by Richard Stilgoe and music by Andrew Lloyd Webber, is first performed, at the Apollo Theatre in London, England. The show features performers on roller skates.
- The play *Breaking the Silence*, by the English writer Stephen Poliakoff, is first performed, in London, England.
- The play *Ghetto*, by the Israeli writer Joshua Sobol, is first performed, in Israel.
- The play *Hurlyburly*, by the U.S. writer David Rabe, is first performed, at the Ethel Barrymore Theater in New York, New York.
- The play *Ma Rainey's Black Bottom*, by the U.S. writer August Wilson, is first performed, at the Cort Theater in New York, New York.
- The Pulitzer Prize for Drama is awarded to David Mamet for *Glengarry Glen Ross*.

JUNE

3 *The Real Thing* starring Glenn Close wins three Tony Awards.

Thought and Scholarship

- *The Oxford Illustrated History of Britain* is published, edited by Welsh historian Kenneth O. Morgan.
- The first volume of *The Cambridge History of Latin America* is published, edited by Leslie Bethell. The last volume will appear in 1991.
- The Pulitzer Prize for History is not awarded this year.
- The Pulitzer Prize for General Nonfiction is awarded to Paul Starr for *Social Transformation of American Medicine*.
- The U.S. social historian Christopher Lasch publishes *The Minimal Self: Psychic Survival in Troubled Times*.
- U.S. philosopher Donald Davidson publishes *Inquiries into Truth and Interpretation*.
- U.S. philosopher Nelson Goodman publishes *Of Mind and Other Matters*.

SOCIETY

Education

- School reforms in the USSR include the lengthening of compulsory schooling to 11 years, and to 12 years in the Baltic republics of Estonia, Latvia, and Lithuania.
- The Perkins Vocational Education Act in the United States provides financial incentives for state

developments to encourage vocational education and links between school and industry.

APRIL

14   The Texas Board of Education in the United States repeals a rule requiring evolution to be taught in schools as one of several possible theories of human origins, rather than as fact.

Everyday Life

- *The Yuppie Handbook* confirms "Yuppie" (standing for "young urban (or upwardly mobile) professional") as a label for the attitudes and lifestyle of an affluent social group with an aspirational lifestyle, and as an icon of the 1980s in Britain and the United States.
- France is selected as the venue for the new European Disney theme park.
- Oversized men's clothing is popular in women's fashion in the United States, and used clothing stores experience a boom in sales.
- Stonewashed denim jeans appear on the market in the United States.
- The Filofax, a portable looseleaf filing system, emerges as the indispensable yuppie accessory.
- The Illinois State Lottery prize of $40 million is won by a 28-year-old printer.
- The U.S. Census Bureau estimates the population of the United States at 236,158,000.
- The U.S. Census Bureau indicates that there are 454,136 people in prison in the United States, double the number ten years before.
- The U.S. cosmetics industry sells $10 billion in products.

JANUARY

1   The American Telephone and Telegraph company (AT&T) is broken up into regional telephone systems, a research company, and a residual corporation dealing with long-distance connections.

DECEMBER

31   The cover story of *Newsweek* is devoted to "the year of the yuppie."

Media and Communication

- British editor Tina Brown is brought in to edit the U.S. magazine *Vanity Fair* and turns it into a lifestyle manual for the 1980s.
- Oprah Winfrey becomes the host of the talk show *AM Chicago*, later called *The Oprah Winfrey Show*. By the 1990s, she is one of the wealthiest women in the world.
- The Reuters news agency is floated on the stock market.

JANUARY

17   Home video-taping is ruled legal by the U.S. Supreme Court.

MARCH

4   The Television Hall of Fame is established, with inductees including Lucille Ball and Milton Berle.

JULY

23   Miss America, Vanessa Williams, relinquishes her title following the publication of explicit pictures of her in *Penthouse*.

SEPTEMBER

16–July 26, 1989   *Miami Vice*, a crime series set in Florida, starts on U.S. television. It stars Don Johnson and Philip Michael Thomas, and its popularity soon leads to a number of celebrities, including James Brown and Phil Collins, playing cameo roles.

20   *The Cosby Show*, a situation comedy about a middle-class black family, begins on U.S. television. It is the top-rated U.S. television show during the 1980s.

23   The 1983–84 Emmy Awards for television are held. Best Drama Series: *Hill Street Blues*; Best Comedy Series: *Cheers*; Best Actor in a Drama: Tom Selleck, for *Magnum, PI*; Best Actress in a Drama: Tyne Daly, for *Cagney and Lacey*; Best Actor in a Comedy: John Ritter, for *Three's Company*; Best Actress in a Comedy: Jane Curtin, for *Kate & Allie*.

OCTOBER

8   *The Burning Bed*, a documentary drama about a woman who killed her abusive husband, starring Farrah Fawcett, is shown on U.S. television. It receives the highest rating of any single program during the 1984–85 season.

NOVEMBER

4   The first French television subscription channel Canal Plus begins broadcasting, with around 200,000 viewers.

20   CBS, Inc. acquires 12 publications in the United States owned by Ziff-Davis, including *Photography*, *Modern Bride*, and *Car & Driver* in the biggest magazine acquisition in history.

DECEMBER

7   A front-page article in China's *People's Daily* argues that Marxism is not the solution to all the country's economic problems. A "correction" on December 10 criticizes the article for its failure to emphasize the continued importance of Marxist principles.

Religion

- The Roman Catholic Church in Chile officially backs demonstrations against violations of human rights for the first time under the regime of General Augusto Pinochet.
- The U.S. evangelists Billy Graham and Luis Palau hold a series of missions in Britain.

MARCH

7   Students stage a sit-in at Stanisław Staszic College in Mietne, Poland, to demand the restoration of crucifixes in classrooms.

APRIL

6   The Polish government and the Roman Catholic Church agree to a compromise on the display of crucifixes in state schools and other public places.

JUNE

14   The Southern Baptist Convention resolves to oppose the ordination of women.

26   Thirty-two Hebrew manuscripts thought to have been destroyed by the Nazis are auctioned in New York, New York, for $1,450,000. After a controversy over rightful ownership, the collection is recalled in 1985 and donated to institutions where the books could be available to scholars and the public.

SOCIETY

SEPTEMBER

3 The Roman Catholic Sacred Congregation for the Doctrine of the Faith publishes *An Instruction on Certain Aspects of the Theology of Liberation*, warning against acceptance of Marxist ideology.

7 Father Leonardo Boff of Brazil, a leading Franciscan proponent of liberation theology, appears before the Doctrinal Office of the Vatican, accompanied by two Brazilian cardinals. His book *The Church: Charisma and Danger* is condemned by church authorities as dangerous.

NOVEMBER

11 U.S. bishops condemn the growing inequalities in U.S. society.

Sports

- Among a number of National Football League (NFL) records to fall, Miami Dolphins quarterback Dan Marino sets new marks of yards gained in a season of 5,084 yards and 48 touchdown passes. Walter of the Chicago Bears breaks Jim Brown's career rushing record of 12,312 yards, while Los Angeles Rams running back Eric Dickerson breaks O. J. Simpson's 1973 season mark of 2,003 yards.

- In three competitions, the Winter Olympics, the European Championships, and the World Championships, the British ice dancers Jayne Torvill and Christopher Dean are awarded an unprecedented 59 maximum scores of 6.

- Steve Cauthen becomes the first U.S. jockey to become champion flat-race jockey in Britain since Danny Maher in 1913.

- There is over $1 million in sales of home exercise equipment in the United States.

JANUARY

19 Francesco Moser of Italy becomes the first cyclist to take the world one-hour record past 50 km/31 mi, in Mexico City, Mexico.

20–21 U.S. national figure skating champions are: Rosalynn Sumners; Scott Hamilton; Kitty and Peter Carruthers, pairs; Judy Blumberg and Michael Seibert, dance.

22 The Raiders football team, in their second season since moving to Los Angeles from Oakland, defeat the Washington Redskins 38–9 in Super Bowl XVIII in Stanford, California.

FEBRUARY

8–19 The 14th Winter Olympic Games are held in Sarajevo, Yugoslavia. East Germany wins 9 gold medals; the USSR, 6; United States, Finland, and Sweden, 4 each. Jayne Torvill and Christopher Dean of Great Britain win the ice dance gold medal. Bill Johnson is the first U.S. skier to win the men's downhill. Twins Phil and Steve Mahre of the United States finish first and second in the slalom.

MARCH

28 In American football, the Colts move from Baltimore, Maryland, to Indianapolis, Indiana.

APRIL

5 The U.S. basketball player Kareem Abdul-Jabbar of the Los Angeles Lakers becomes the leading scorer in National Basketball Association history when he overtakes U.S. player Wilt Chamberlain's career total of 31,419 points.

6 The South African runner Zola Budd is granted British citizenship, enabling her to compete in the Los Angeles Olympics.

MAY

10–19 The Edmonton Oilers end the New York Islanders' reign as National Hockey League (NHL) champions by beating them four games to one to win the Stanley Cup.

27 The Boston Celtics beat the Los Angeles Lakers to win the National Basketball Association (NBA) championship.

27 U.S. race-car driver Rick Mears wins the Indianapolis 500.

JULY

7 Georgina Clark becomes the first woman to umpire a final on the Centre Court at the Wimbledon tennis championships, London, England.

22 The French cyclist Laurent Fignon wins the Tour de France for the second successive year.

28 The 23rd Olympic Games open in Los Angeles, California, and are boycotted by the Soviet bloc, with

BIRTHS & DEATHS

JANUARY

13 (Justin) Brooks Atkinson, U.S. theater critic for the *New York Times*, dies in Huntsville, Alabama (89).

14 Maurice Bellonte, French aviator who made the first nonstop flight from Paris, France, to New York with Dieudonné Costes in 1930, dies in Paris (87).

14 Ray Kroc, U.S. restaurateur who founded McDonald's fast-food hamburger restaurants, dies in San Diego, California (81).

19 Max Bentley, Canadian hockey player, dies in Saskatoon, Saskatchewan, Canada (63).

20 Johnny Weissmuller, U.S. freestyle Olympic swimmer and film actor best known for his role as Tarzan, dies in Acapulco, Mexico (79).

21 Jackie Wilson, U.S. rhythm and blues musician who recorded with Motown Records, dies in Mt. Holly, New Jersey (51).

FEBRUARY

6 Jorge Guillén, Spanish poet and critic who belonged to the so-called "Generation of 1927," dies in Málaga, Spain (91).

6 Waite Charles Hoyt, U.S. baseball player with Babe Ruth and Lou Gehrig on the New York Yankees, dies in Cincinnati, Ohio (84).

9 Yuri Andropov, Soviet politician and First Secretary of the Soviet Communist Party 1982–84, dies in Moscow, USSR (69).

12 Julio Cortazar, Argentine writer, dies in Paris, France (69).

14 Ethel Merman, U.S. performer and star of Broadway musicals, dies in New York, New York (75).

21 Mikhail Sholokov, Russian novelist and short-story writer, dies in Veshenskaya, USSR (78).

26 Richmond Alexander Lattimore, U.S. poet and classical scholar, and translator of Homer's *Iliad* and *Odyssey*, dies in Rosemont, Pennsylvania (77).

MARCH

1 Jackie Coogan, U.S. silent film and television actor who was Hollywood's first major child star, dies in Santa Monica, California (69).

5 Tito Gobbi, Italian baritone opera singer, dies in Rome, Italy (68).

5 William Powell, U.S. film actor best known for his role in the six "Thin Man" films with Myrna Loy, dies in Palm Springs, California (91).

6 Martin Niemöller, German anti-Nazi theologian and clergyman, dies in Wiesbaden, Germany (92).

26 Sékou Touré, first president of the Republic of Guinea 1958–84, dies in Cleveland, Ohio (62).

31 Karl Rahner, German Jesuit priest, Roman Catholic theologian, and philosopher, dies in Innsbruck, Austria (80).

APRIL

1 Marvin Gaye, U.S. motown singer and songwriter, dies in Los Angeles, California (44).

5 Arthur ("Bomber") Harris, British air officer who originated "saturation bombing" by the RAF in World War II, dies in Goring-on-Thames, Oxfordshire, England (91).

8 Pyotr Leonidovich Kapitsa, Soviet physicist who discovered superfluidity in helium, dies in Moscow, USSR (89).

22 Ansel Adams, U.S. landscape photographer and technical innovator, dies in Carmel, California (82).

26 "Count" Basie (William Basie), U.S. jazz pianist, composer, and big-band organizer, dies in Hollywood, Florida (79).

MAY

16 Irwin Shaw, U.S. novelist, short-story writer, and playwright, dies in Davos, Switzerland (71).

19 John Betjeman, English poet and poet laureate from 1972, dies in Trebetherick, Cornwall, England (76).

JUNE

13 Nathaniel Alexander Owings, U.S. architect and cofounder of a firm that specializes in skyscrapers including Sears Tower, Chicago, dies in Santa Fe, New Mexico (81).

15 Grace Tully, U.S. memoirist and personal secretary to President Franklin D. Roosevelt, dies in Washington, D.C. (83).

15 Meredith Wilson, U.S. composer, conductor, and lyricist of musical comedies, dies in Santa Monica, California (82).

22 Joseph Losey, U.S. film director, dies in London, England (75).

25 Michel Foucault, French philosopher, dies in Paris, France (57).

30 Lillian Hellman, U.S. dramatist, screenwriter and political activist, dies in Martha's Vineyard, Massachusetts (77).

JULY

8 Brassai, Hungarian-born French photographer who recorded life in the streets, theaters, and bars of Paris, dies in Nice, France (84).

9 Peter Hurd, U.S. artist and book illustrator whose work includes the *Last of the Mohicans*, dies in Roswell, New Mexico (80).

21 James F. Fixx, U.S. marathon runner and author of *The Complete Guide to Running*, the "joggers' Bible," dies of a heart attack while jogging in Hardwick, Utah (52).

25 Willie Mae Thornton, U.S. cabaret singer best known for "Have Mercy Baby" and "Ball and Chain," dies in Los Angeles, California (57).

26 G. H. Gallup, U.S. organizer of public opinion polls, dies in Tschingel, Switzerland (82).

AUGUST

• Viktor Ivanovich Chukarin, Soviet gymnast who won 11 gold medals in the 1952 and 1956 Olympics, dies in Moscow, USSR (62).

5 Richard Burton, British stage and film actor twice married to actress Elizabeth Taylor, dies in Geneva, Switzerland (58).

11 Alfred A. Knopf, U.S. publisher who founded the prestigious publishing house under his own name (which became a subsidiary of Random House in 1966), dies in Purchase, New York (91).

14 J(ohn) B(oynton) Priestley, English novelist, playwright, and essayist, dies in Alveston, Warwickshire, England (89).

25 Truman Capote, U.S. novelist, short-story writer, and playwright who pioneered a new genre with the "nonfiction novel," *In Cold Blood*, dies in Los Angeles, California (59).

30 Sawako Ariyoshi, Japanese author of murder mysteries and historical novels whose works examine social problems in Japan, dies in Tokyo, Japan (53).

SEPTEMBER

7 Joseph Edward Cronin, U.S. baseball player, dies in Osterville, Massachusetts (77).

14 Janet Gaynor, U.S. film actress who in 1927 won the first Academy Award for best actress for her portrayal of a prostitute in *Seventh Heaven*, dies (77).

15 Prince Henry (known as Harry), the second son of Prince Charles and Princess Diana, and third in line to the British throne, is born in London, England.

OCTOBER

6 George Gaylord Simpson, U.S. paleontologist who contributed to evolutionary theory, dies in Tucson, Arizona (82).

14 Martin Ryle, English radio astronomer who developed a revolutionary radio telescope system, dies in Cambridge, England (66).

19 Jerzy Aleksander Popiełuszko, Polish Roman Catholic priest, a supporter of Solidarity, is kidnapped and killed by the Polish secret police in Włocławek, Poland (37).

20 Carl Ferdinand Cori, U.S. biochemist whose research led to a greater understanding of diabetes, dies in Cambridge, Massachusetts (87).

20 Paul Adrien Maurice Dirac, English physicist, author of the complete theoretical formulation of quantum mechanics, dies in Tallahassee, Florida (82).

21 François Truffaut, French film producer and critic, dies in Neuilly-sur-Seine, France (52).

31 Indira Gandhi, prime minister of India 1966–77 and 1980–84 is assassinated in New Dehli, India (66).

NOVEMBER

20 Ahmed Faiz, Pakistani poet and political activist, dies in Lahore, Pakistan (73).

DECEMBER

4 John Rock, U.S. gynecologist and obstetrician and one of the developers in the 1950s of the first oral contraceptive, dies in Peterborough, New Hampshire (94).

14 Vicente Aleixandre, Spanish poet, dies in Madrid, Spain (86).

28 Sam Peckinpah, U.S. film director and screenwriter known for his violent Westerns, dies in Inglewood, California (59).

the exception of Romania, and by Iran and Libya, in retaliation for the U.S. boycott of the Moscow Olympics in 1980. The People's Republic of China, however, competes for the first time.

AUGUST

- At the Los Angeles Olympics, Carl Lewis of the United States equals Jesse Owens's feat in the 1936 games by winning golds in the 100 meters, 200 meters, 4 × 100 meters relay, and the long jump.
- At the Los Angeles Olympics, Nawal El Moutawakel of Morocco wins the inaugural women's marathon to become the first Arab woman to win an Olympic track title. Her compatriot, Said Aouita, becomes the first Arab man to win a track title when he wins the 5,000 meters.
- 10 In the women's 3,000 meters final at the Los Angeles Olympics, Britain's South African runner Zola Budd and the favorite, Mary Decker of the United States, crash out of the race after colliding with each other.
- 12 The 23rd Olympic Games close in Los Angeles, United States. The United States wins 83 gold medals; Romania, 20; West Germany, 17; China, 15; Italy, 14; Canada and Japan, 10 each; New Zealand, 8; Yugoslavia, 7; South Korea, 6; Britain, France, and the Netherlands, 5 each.

SEPTEMBER

- Czech-born U.S. tennis player Martina Navratilova wins the women's singles at the U.S. Open tennis championships to become only the third woman after Maureen Connolly and Margaret Court to win six consecutive Grand Slam singles titles.

OCTOBER

- 9 The Detroit Tigers win the World Series, beating the San Diego Padres four games to one.
- 21 The Austrian race-car driver Niki Lauda wins the Formula One World Drivers' Championship for the third time.

NOVEMBER

- 9 In the first heavyweight world championship fight sanctioned by the International Boxing Federation (IBF), Larry Holmes stops fellow U.S. fighter James "Bonecrusher" Smith in the 12th round, in Las Vegas, Nevada.
- 10 The first Breeders' Cup series of thoroughbred horse races is held at Hollywood Park, California, before a crowd of 64,254.

DECEMBER

- Eric Dickerson of the Los Angeles Rams sets new game and season professional records for rushing 215 yards and 2,105 yards respectively.
- 18 Sweden wins the Davis Cup in tennis, beating the United States 4–1 in the final in Gothenburg, Sweden.

1985

POLITICS, GOVERNMENT, AND ECONOMICS

Business and Economics

- Consumer credit in the United States reaches $525 billion.
- Homelessness becomes a serious problem in the United States, with between 350,000 and 3 million people believed homeless.
- The U.S. companies R. J. Reynolds and Nabisco merge in a deal that pioneers the use of "junk bonds."
- The World Bank sets up a Fund for Africa.

APRIL

22 The Japanese car company Nissan negotiates a single-union deal with the Amalgamated Union of Engineering Workers (AUEW) for employees at a new car construction plant at Washington in northeast England.

MAY

2 U.S. steel companies U.S. Steel, LTV Steel, Bethlehem Steel, and Inland Steel Armco abandon coordinated wage negotiations.

AUGUST

7 Broadcaster Ted Turner bids $1.5 billion to buy MGM/United Artists Entertainment Company.

Human Rights

- Conservative Judaism accepts women as rabbis.
- The International Women's Development Agency is founded, and the United Nations holds a 12-day "Decade of Women" conference in Nairobi, Kenya.

MAY

17 The Japanese diet (parliament) approves a bill to remove restrictions on women's work.

AUGUST

10 Allan Boesak, president of the World Alliance of Reformed Churches, is arrested during a demonstration in Cape Town, South Africa.

DECEMBER

9 Five former members of Argentina's military junta are found guilty of human-rights violations.

Politics and Government

- An act of parliament in South Africa provides for the introduction of regional services councils, with indirectly elected representatives of white, colored, and African councils from 1987.
- In the case *Garcia v. San Antonio MTA*, the U.S. Supreme Court rules that it has no concern in the application of the principles of federalism.
- The U.S. Congress passes the Safe Drinking Water Act Amendments.

JANUARY

7–8 The U.S. secretary of state George Shultz and the Soviet foreign minister Andrei Gromyko hold talks in Geneva, Switzerland, on the resumption of arms control negotiations.

14 Hun Sen is elected prime minister of Kampuchea, in succession to the late Chan Sy.

14 The Israeli cabinet agrees to a three-stage withdrawal from occupied Lebanon, commencing in February.

17–20 A summit conference at the UN between President Spyros Kyprianu of Cyprus and the Turkish Cypriot leader Rauf Denktaş fails to resolve differences between their communities.

18 A panel of prosecutors in the Philippines announces that they have enough evidence to charge 26 people with involvement in the murder of the opposition leader Benigno Aquino. The trial opens on February 1.

25 A grand jury announces that vigilante Bernhard Goetz should face only illegal weapons charges for his 1984 New York subway attack.

25 The South African president P. W. Botha opens the country's new three-chamber parliament for whites, Indians, and coloreds.

FEBRUARY

4 The Reagan administration's U.S. defense budget calls for the tripling of expenditure on the Star Wars research program.

5 Spain reopens its frontier with Gibraltar, ending the 16-year-long siege imposed by General Francisco Franco on the British territory.

10 The imprisoned African National Congress (ANC) leader Nelson Mandela refuses the South African government's offer of freedom, conditional on his renunciation of violence as a means to political change in the country.

19 The Irish Dáil (parliament) passes an emergency law enabling the government to seize up to IR £10 million from Provisional IRA bank accounts.

20 The Irish Dáil legalizes the sale of contraceptives in stores.

MARCH

1 Julio Sanguinetti takes office as Uruguay's first elected president for 12 years.

11 Mikhail Gorbachev is named first secretary of the Soviet Communist Party. He calls for more *glasnost* ("openness") in Soviet life and later pursues a policy of *perestroika* ("reconstruction").

12–23 A further round of arms talks between the United States and the USSR is held in Geneva, Switzerland.

15 Twenty-one years of military rule in Brazil ends after increasing popular discontent during 1984, with the election of Tancredo Neves as president. When he dies on April 21, Vice President José Sarney is elected in his place.

18 The U.S. Supreme Court rules restrictions on spending by political action committees to be invalid.

20 The Belgian parliament approves the deployment of U.S. cruise missiles on Belgian territory.

21 South African police fire on crowds at Uitenhage on the 25th anniversary of the Sharpeville massacre, killing 17 blacks. A judicial commission of inquiry is announced into the shootings the following day.

29–30 A summit of European Community heads of government in Brussels agrees terms for the admission of Spain and Portugal to the Community on January 1, 1986.

APRIL

2 The Israeli army moves 1,100 Lebanese prisoners from detention camps in southern Lebanon to Israel.

6 A bloodless coup in Sudan, led by General Siwar ad-Dahab, ends the 16-year rule of Colonel Gaafar Mohamed el-Nimeiri.

7 The Soviet leader Mikhail Gorbachev announces a moratorium on Soviet missile deployments in Europe until November, and offers to hold summit talks with the U.S. president Ronald Reagan.

8 The Indian government sues the U.S. Union Carbide Corporation for damages caused by the 1984 Bhopal gas leak.

11 Ramiz Alia succeeds Enver Hoxha, Albania's first communist chief of state, and national leader for over 40 years, following his death.

15 South Africa accepts the recommendations of a parliamentary committee to abolish laws forbidding marriage and sexual intercourse between races.

15 The president of South Africa P. W. Botha announces that South African military forces in Angola will leave by April 18.

17 The antidiscrimination section of Canada's federal constitution, the Charter of Rights and Freedoms, is incorporated into law.

22 The trial opens in Argentina of nine former military leaders, including General Leopoldo Galtieri, for political crimes.

26 Warsaw Pact leaders agree to renew their military alliance for a further 30 years.

MAY

1 Ten thousand supporters of the labor union Solidarity clash with police during May Day demonstrations in Gdańsk, Poland.

1 The United States imposes financial and trade sanctions on Nicaragua.

5 U.S. president Ronald Reagan arouses anger by visiting the Bitburg military cemetery in West Germany, where 49 SS men are buried.

10–13 Sikh extremists plant bombs in three Indian cities, with 84 reported dead.

13 Philadelphia police kill 11 people and make 200 homeless when they bomb a house occupied by gunmen.

14 Tamil guerrillas attack the city of Anuradhapura, Sri Lanka, and 146 people are killed.

19 The Shiite Muslim militia attempts to drive Palestinians from the refugee camps of Sabra, Shatila, and Bourj-el-Barajneh in Beirut, Lebanon.

20 Israel releases 1,150 prisoners under the supervision of the International Red Cross, in exchange for the last three Israeli soldiers held by Palestinian groups.

28 U.S. president Ronald Reagan introduces a radical tax reform package designed to achieve "fairness, growth, and simplicity."

JUNE

2 President Junius Jayawardene of Sri Lanka discusses communal violence in his country with the Indian prime minister Rajiv Gandhi.

6 A skeleton thought to be that of the fugitive Auschwitz doctor Josef Mengele is exhumed in Brazil. On June 21, the identity of the remains is confirmed by a team of forensic experts.

10 Israel completes its withdrawal from all occupied territories in southern Lebanon with the exception of a "security zone."

12 Spain and Portugal sign the treaty of accession to the European Community.

14 Two Shiite Muslim gunmen hijack a TWA jet with 145 U.S. passengers and a crew of eight, demanding the release of over 700 prisoners held by Israel. One passenger is shot dead. On June 17, the hostages are removed from the jet and held in south Beirut, Lebanon.

15 South Africa appoints a multiracial administration for Namibia but retains control of the territory's foreign policy and defense.

30 The 39 U.S. hostages from the TWA jet hijacked on June 14 are taken from Beirut to Damascus, then released following Syrian intervention.

JULY

1 An explosion badly damages the Greenpeace ship *Rainbow Warrior* in Auckland harbor, New Zealand, killing one man. The ship was in the South Pacific to disrupt French nuclear tests at Mururoa atoll.

2 Andrei Gromyko is named president of the USSR, while Eduard Shevardnadze becomes foreign minister.

8 U.S. president Ronald Reagan brands Iran, Libya, Cuba, Nicaragua, and North Korea as terrorist states.

13 Surgeons remove a cancerous growth from U.S. president Ronald Reagan's colon.

18–20 An Organization of African Unity conference in Addis Ababa, Ethiopia, declares that most African countries are on the verge of economic collapse.

20 The South African government declares a state of emergency in 36 districts in response to increased violence.

24 The Indian prime minister Rajiv Gandhi announces an agreement with Sant Harchand Singh Longowal, leader of the Sikh community in Punjab, aimed at reducing tension in the state.

27 A bloodless coup in Uganda, led by Brigadier Tito Okello, ousts President Milton Obote.

AUGUST

15 President P. W. Botha of South Africa restates his administration's commitment to apartheid and rules out parliamentary representation for blacks.

23 A West German counterespionage official Hans Joachim Tiedge seeks asylum in East Germany. On August 28, the head of the West German secret service is fired.

26 An official report exonerates the French government of involvement in the sinking of the Greenpeace ship *Rainbow Warrior*. The findings are rejected by the New Zealand government and, on August 27, the French prime minister Laurent Fabius orders further investigations.

27 A bloodless military coup in Nigeria, led by Major General Ibrahim Babangida, ends the rule of Major General Mohammed Buhari.

27 The South African civil-rights activist Allan Boesak is again arrested on the eve of leading a march to the prison where Nelson Mandela is held. Violence breaks out on August 28 when police seek to prevent the march.

SEPTEMBER

2 Pol Pot resigns as commander in chief of the Khmer Rouge army opposed to the pro-Vietnamese government in Kampuchea, to be replaced by a former premier, Son Sann.

9 The United States announces selective economic sanctions against South Africa.

10 European Community foreign ministers approve sanctions against South Africa, although Britain delays a decision until September 25.

13 Britain expels 25 Soviet diplomats and officials for alleged espionage activities, and the following day the USSR expels 25 Britons in return.

16 Ten Politburo members and 64 members of the Central Committee of the Chinese Communist Party resign to make way for younger members.

16 The Commerce Department predicts that the U.S. deficit will reach $130 billion this year, the world's largest deficit figure.

17 A secretary in the office of Chancellor Helmut Kohl of West Germany defects to East Germany.

20 The French defense minister Charles Hernu resigns and Admiral Pierre Lacoste, head of the Foreign Service, is dismissed over the *Rainbow Warrior* affair.

21–22 A meeting in New York of the "Group of Five" industrial nations (the United States, Japan, West Germany, Britain, and France) reaches the Plaza Accord, an agreement to cooperate in order to maintain the stability of exchange rates.

22 The French prime minister Laurent Fabius admits that the Greenpeace ship *Rainbow Warrior* was sunk by French secret service agents.

26 Elections are held for Hong Kong's Legislative Council, the first in 100 years of colonial rule.

OCTOBER

1 Israeli warplanes attack the Palestine Liberation Organization headquarters in Tunis, killing 60, in a revenge attack for the murder of three Israelis in Cyprus.

7 Four Palestinian guerrillas hijack the Italian cruise liner *Achille Lauro* with 450 people on board in the Mediterranean. On October 9, the hijackers surrender

to the Egyptian authorities after killing one passenger, an elderly U.S. citizen.

10 U.S. jets intercept a plane carrying the *Achille Lauro* hijackers from Egypt to Tunis and force it to land in Sicily. The Egyptian president Hosni Mubarak accuses the United States of "piracy."

12 The United States protests when the Italian authorities release Mohammed Abbas, a terrorist alleged to have masterminded the *Achille Lauro* hijack.

27 Julius Nyerere retires as president of Tanzania after 24 years, to be succeeded by Ali Hassan Mwinyi.

NOVEMBER

4 Two French secret service agents plead guilty to manslaughter and sabotage in relation to the sinking of the Greenpeace ship *Rainbow Warrior* in Auckland, New Zealand. On November 21, they are sentenced to ten years in prison.

6 General Wojciech Jaruzelski resigns as prime minister of Poland to become president of the Council of State. He is succeeded by Zbigniew Messner.

15 The Anglo-Irish Agreement is signed at Hillsborough Castle, giving the Irish Republic a consultative role in the affairs of Northern Ireland. The British treasury minister Ian Gow resigns in protest.

19–21 U.S. president Ronald Reagan and Soviet leader Mikhail Gorbachev agree to open negotiations on arms reductions at the Geneva summit, in Switzerland.

24 Egyptian commandos at Malta airport storm an Egyptian airliner hijacked by Palestinian gunmen, with the deaths of 59 people.

DECEMBER

2 A court in the Philippines acquits the 26 people accused of complicity in the murder of the opposition leader, Benigno Aquino. Aquino's widow, Cory (Corazón) Aquino, announces that she will run for the presidency against Ferdinand Marcos.

11 Police and Loyalist demonstrators clash as the first conference under the Anglo-Irish Agreement is held in Belfast, Northern Ireland.

12 The Gramm–Rudman–Hollings Act, requiring the U.S. government to meet targeted budget deficits, becomes law. It is abandoned a year later.

17 All Britain's Ulster Unionist MPs resign from the House of Commons in protest at the Anglo-Irish Agreement.

17 The Ugandan head of state General Tito Okello and Yoweri Museveni, leader of the National Resistance Army, sign a peace accord.

21 Haitians demonstrate against the government of Jean-Claude ("Baby Doc") Duvalier, dictator since 1971.

21 South African police forcibly remove Winnie Mandela, wife of the jailed African National Congress leader Nelson Mandela, from her home in Soweto.

25 Fighting breaks out on the border between Mali and Burkina Faso, in West Africa.

30 General Zia ul-Haq ends martial law in Pakistan.

31 King Hussein of Jordan meets President Hafez al-Assad of Syria in their first meeting for six years.

SCIENCE, TECHNOLOGY, AND MEDICINE

Agriculture

- Agriculture legislation in the United States provides for crop insurance and low-cost, long-term loans to farmers.

DECEMBER

23 U.S. president Ronald Reagan approves $169 billion in aid to the United States' troubled agricultural sector.

Computing

- Five national supercomputing centers are established by the U.S. National Science Foundation—in San Diego, California; Pittsburgh, Pennsylvania; Princeton, New Jersey; Ithaca, New York; and Champaign-Urbana, Illinois.

- The U.S. Internal Revenue Service begins using a computer system to automate the processing of 1984 tax returns.

- U.S. computer chip manufacturer Intel launches the 32-bit 20MHz 80386 microprocessor; it has 275,000 transistors.

- U.S. firm Microsoft develops Windows for the IBM PC.

Ecology

- The International Whaling Commission bans commercial whaling, in order to prevent the extinction of whales.

- The U.S. Congress passes the Superfund Improvement Act, tightening environmental protection law.

- U.S. zoologist Dian Fossey, who tried to protect endangered gorillas in Rwanda, is murdered. Poachers are suspected.

MARCH

- The British Antarctic Survey detects a hole in the ozone layer which opens each year in the spring over Antarctica.

MAY

25 A cyclone and tsunami hit southern Bangladesh; over 10,000 people die.

31 Over 30 tornadoes strike Ohio, Pennsylvania, and New York, killing 76 people.

JULY

13 Citizens of western countries are spurred to action against famine in Africa by such events as the Live Aid concerts.

SEPTEMBER

19 Over 7,000 people die in Mexico City in an earthquake which measures 7.8 on the Richter scale.

NOVEMBER

13 An estimated 25,000 people are killed when Nevado del Ruiz volcano in Colombia erupts.

Exploration

- European, Japanese, and Soviet probes are launched to rendezvous with Halley's comet in 1986.
- The crew of the shuttle *Atlantis* undertake construction exercises to develop skills for building a large orbiting space station.
- The U.S. space shuttle *Discovery* (launched on August 27) deploys three satellites; the crew also retrieves, repairs, and redeploys an orbiting satellite.

- The United States launches the earth resource *Landsat 5*; like *Landsat 4*, it uses cameras to view the earth in several bands of the infrared spectrum.

APRIL
- NASA invites aerospace firms to compete for the design of an orbiting space station.

The Personal Computer (1930–97)

1930
- U.S. electrical engineer Vannevar Bush builds the differential analyzer. The first analog computer, it is used to solve differential equations. It is the forerunner of modern computers.

1938
- German inventor Konrad Zuse constructs the first binary calculator using a binary code (Boolean algebra); it is the first working computer.

1943
- Colossus, the first electronic computer and code-breaker, is developed at Bletchley Park, England, to break German codes. Designed by Thomas Flowers, M. H. A. Newman, and English mathematician Alan Turing, it has 1,500 vacuum tubes and is the first all-electronic calculating device.

1944
- U.S. mathematician Howard Aitken builds the Harvard University Mark I, or Automatic Sequence Controlled Calculator. The first program-controlled computer, it is 15 m/50 ft long and 2.4 m/8 ft high, and its operations are controlled by a sequence of instruction codes on punched paper that operate electromechanical switches. Simple multiplication takes 4 seconds and division 11 seconds.

1950
- Dr. Yoshiro Nakamata of the Imperial University, Tokyo, Japan, develops the floppy disk and licenses it to International Business Machines (IBM).

1951
June   U.S. engineers John Mauchly and John Eckert build UNIVAC 1 (Universal Automated Computer), the first commercially available electronic digital computer, in Philadelphia, Pennsylvania.

1956
- IBM introduces RAMAC (Random Access Method of Accounting and Control), the first hard disk storage of data. Indexes are used to locate the data on the disk.
- Univac initiates the second generation of computers when it introduces the first commercially successful computer using transistors instead of vacuum tubes.
- U.S. computer programmer Jack Backus at IBM invents FORTRAN (formula translation), the first computer programming language.

1960
November   U.S. computer scientist Kenneth Olsen, at Digital Equipment Corporation, introduces the PDP-1 computer. It has a memory of 26 megabytes and is the first to use a

monitor and keyboard. It is the forerunner of the minicomputer.

1962
- Magnetic disks begin to replace magnetic tape as the main means of storing computer data.

1965
- U.S. computer scientists John Kemeny and Thomas Kurtz develop BASIC (Beginners All-purpose Symbolic Instruction Code), a simplified computer programming language used in schools, businesses, and microcomputers.

1966
- The seven-level American Standard Code for Information Interchange (ASCII) receives widespread acceptance as a means of transmitting the high volumes of data generated by business machines.

1968
- U.S. computer scientist Douglas Engelbart demonstrates the first computer mouse.
- U.S. firms Control Data, NCR, and Burroughs introduce the first commercial computers that use integrated circuits. The first of the "third generation" of computers, they are faster and have a greater capacity than previous computers.

1969
- The U.S. Department of Defense establishes a computer network that is the basis of the Internet.

1970–97

1970
- U.S. computer programmers Kenneth Thomson and Dennis Ritchie develop the UNIX computer operating system. It becomes the standard operating system for computer systems with multiple tasking and multiple users.

1971
- Dot matrix printers are first introduced.
- Swiss programmer Niklaus Wirth develops the computer language PASCAL. It is designed as a teaching tool for computer programming and allows errors to be discovered quickly.

1972
- U.S. computer scientist Nolan Bushnell invents "Pong," the first computer game.

1974
- The first word processors are introduced by the Xerox Corporation.

Health and Medicine

- An epidemic of bovine spongiform encephalopathy (BSE) is reported in beef cattle in Britain; it is later traced to cattle feed containing sheep carcasses infected with scrapie; in following years there are fears that beef consumption could lead to Creutzfeld-Jakob disease in humans.
- Lasers are first used to clean out clogged arteries, in the United States.

- Researchers at the Massachusetts Eye and Ear Infirmary and the Whitehead Institute, Massachusetts, United States, isolate the first human cancer gene, retinoblastoma.
- Researchers locate gene markers on chromosomes for cystic fibrosis and polycystic kidney disease.
- The Nobel Prize for Physiology or Medicine is awarded jointly to U.S. geneticists Michael Brown and Joseph Goldstein for their discoveries concerning the regulation of cholesterol metabolism.

- U.S. technician David Ahl develops the first microcomputer; it includes a central processing unit, television screen, and keyboard. It arouses little interest.

1975
- Bill Gates, aged 19, and friend Paul Allen Gardiner, found Microsoft. It becomes the biggest seller of computer software in the world and makes Gates a billionaire before he is 30.
- The first "personal computer," the Altair 8800, is marketed in the United States; it has no keyboard or screen but uses toggle switches to input data and flashing lights for output.
- IBM introduces the laser printer. The following year the company develops the ink-jet printer.

1977
- Apple Computers launches the Apple II personal computer; owners must use their own television screens and store data on audiocassette tapes. It is the first mass-produced personal computer in assembled form.

1981
August 12   IBM launches its personal computer, using the Microsoft disc-operating system (MS-DOS).

1982
- *Time* magazine's "Man of the Year" is "Pac-Man," a character from a computer game that sweeps the United States in 1982.
- U.S. firms Columbia Data Products and Compaq produce the first "clones" of an IBM personal computer; they use the same operating system as the IBM personal computer.

1983
February   IBM introduces the PC-XT personal computer, the first to have a built-in hard disc drive.

March 29   The Tandy Corporation markets the first laptop computer in the United States. The TRS-80 Model 100 weighs less than 2 kg/4 lb and runs on four small batteries; prices range from $799 to $999.

1984
c. 1984   Computer viruses begin to appear.
- The Dutch company Philips and Japanese firm Sony introduce the CD-ROM.
- U.S. computer manufacturer Apple launches the Macintosh personal computer in the United States; it is the first successful graphic-based microcomputer using icons and a mouse.

December 20   The development of a 1 MB random access memory (RAM) chip is announced by Bell Laboratories; it is capable of storing four times as much data as any currently available.

1985
- Microsoft develops Windows for the IBM PC.

1987
- Japanese firm Sega Electronics introduces a three-dimensional video game, requiring special liquid crystal glasses to view the images.

1988
- The first computer "vaccines" against computer viruses are developed in the United States.

1989
c. 1989   Developments in desktop publishing make high-quality print production more generally accessible.
- U.S. computer microchip manufacturer Intel launches the 25MHz 80486 microprocessor. It has 1.2 million transistors and includes a math coprocessor and cache memory.
- U.S. computing innovator Jaron Lanier makes the experience of virtual reality possible with his design of a headset and special gloves, that will allow a user to experience and manipulate a computer-generated world.

1991
- Several U.S. companies introduce local area networks (LANs), which use nondirectional microwaves to transmit data as fast as fiber optic cables.

1993
- Personal computers based on the first 64-bit processor, the Intel Pentium chip, go on sale in the United States.

1994
- The World Wide Web, a computer network that allows users to utilize graphical interfaces through Web "browsers," makes the Internet much more accessible to general users and permits a freedom of information distribution not previously possible.

1995
August   Microsoft launches Windows 95, a new computer operating system.

1997
- U.S. company Dragon Systems releases "Naturally Speaking," the world's first voice-recognition software program that recognizes and creates text from normal continuous speech. Spoken words are transcribed immediately onto the computer screen at up to 160 words per minute or higher, with over 95% accuracy.

- U.S. researcher Steven Rosenberg discovers interleukin 2, a crucial protein in the immune system involved in the activation of lymphocytes; researchers soon begin experimenting on its anticancer properties.

MAY

- A woman in the United States treated for infertility gives birth to septuplets; three survive, but with medical problems.

Science

- A well-preserved amphibian skeleton dated 340 million years old is discovered in Scottish oil shale. It is the earliest amphibian found.
- French-born U.S. endocrinologist Roger Guillemin discovers inhibin, which suppresses follicle-stimulating hormone secretion involved in male testicular function.
- German researcher Bert Vallee and associates discover angiogenin, the factor that stimulates the growth of new blood vessels.
- Harold Kroto and David Walton at the University of Sussex, England, discover a new unusually stable elemental form of solid carbon made up of closed cages of 60 carbon atoms shaped liked soccer balls; they call them buckminsterfullerines or "buckyballs."
- The Nobel Prize for Physics is awarded to German physicist Klaus von Klitzing for his discovery of the quantum Hall effect.
- U.S. anthropologist Alan Walker discovers an almost complete australopithecine skull at Lake Turkana, Kenya, dated at 2.5 million years old. It has a puzzling mixture of primitive and advanced features.
- U.S. chemists Herbert Hauptman and Jerome Karle receive the Nobel Prize for Chemistry for their methods of determining crystal structures.
- West German physicist Gerd Binnig and Swiss physicist Heinrich Rohrer invent the atomic-force microscope, which explores surfaces by the force of atomic interaction, at the IBM laboratory in Zürich, Switzerland. Individual atoms can be traced and it has the advantage over the scanning tunneling microscope in that it can be used to image biological molecules.

Technology

- A chip that operates on fuzzy logic is developed at AT&T Bell Laboratories by Masaki Togai and Hiroyuki Watanabe.
- A lead–iron phosphate glass is developed in the United States; it is used to build durable containers for storing nuclear waste.
- Japanese firm Mitsubishi invents the spiral escalator.
- The Japanese firm Seiko-Epson develops a television with a 6-cm/2-in screen that is a liquid crystal display (LCD).
- The Los Alamos National Laboratory in New Mexico, United States, invents solar paint—a type of paint that contains metallic particles making it 10–20% more effective at capturing solar energy than black paint.
- The U.S. Bell Laboratories develops an optical fiber capable of simultaneously sending 300,000 telephone conversations or 200 high-resolution television channels.

- The U.S. Department of Defense declassifies information about lanxides—ceramic and metal composites.
- The U.S. National Bureau of Standards begins marketing latex microspheres which are used in biomedical research. Manufactured aboard the space shuttle, they are the first commercially available product that is "made in space."
- The world's largest fast-breeder reactor, the Superphénix, begins operating at Creys-Malville, France; it produces 1,200 megawatts of electricity, but continuous technical problems close it down for most of the time before the French government decommissions it in 1992.
- U.S. firm Cray Research introduces the Cray 2, a supercomputer with four processors and a 2 billion-byte memory that can perform 1 billion floating point operations per second.
- U.S. inventor Alan Adler, makes the "aerobie," a flexible toy ring, the shape of which has been determined by computer and which can glide about 100 m/328 ft—further than any other object.

Transportation

- *c.* 1985 Bike couriers are much in evidence, especially in U.S. cities. The job is high-risk and pays little, and opportunities will decline with the development of electronic communications.
- *c.* 1985 Bulk cargo containers begin to be transported across the United States on "doublestack" freight trains; it is cheaper than by sea.
- In a record year for the U.S. auto industry, 15.6 million automobiles are sold.
- Americans purchase 15.6 million cars and trucks, the highest number to date.
- Catalytic converters that require lead-free fuel are made mandatory in Switzerland for private cars. Switzerland is the first country to pass such a law.
- U.S. and European firms develop automatic car guidance systems that provide information on the best route to follow to a given destination considering road conditions and distance; information is relayed by radio.
- U.S. diver Andy Matroci discovers the wreck of the Spanish galleon *Nuestra Señora de Atocha*, which sank off Florida in 1622; its cargo of bullion is estimated to be worth $400 million.

JANUARY

13 Africa's worst train accident—the world's third worst—occurs when a train bound for Addis Ababa, Ethiopia, derails and plummets into a ravine killing 392 people and injuring 370.

JUNE

23 An Air India Boeing 747 flying from Canada crashes into the Atlantic off the Irish coast, killing all 329 people on board. A terrorist bomb is suspected as the cause of the disaster.

AUGUST

2 A Delta L-1011 attempts an emergency landing at Dallas-Fort Worth airport, Texas during a violent thunderstorm; 140 of the 161 people on board are killed.

12   A Japan Airlines Boeing 747 crashes into a mountain near Tokyo, killing 520 people; it is the world's worst crash involving a single plane.

SEPTEMBER

1   The wreck of the *Titanic*, which sank in 1912, is discovered by U.S. entrepreneur Robert Ballard using the *Argo*, a remote-controlled robot equipped with video cameras.

ARTS AND IDEAS

Architecture

- The Hong Kong and Shanghai Bank Headquarters in Hong Kong, designed by the English architect Norman Foster, is completed.
- The Lloyds Building in London, England, designed by the English architect Richard Rogers, is completed.

Arts

- The German neo-expressionist artist Anselm Kiefer creates *The High Priestess*.
- The German-born English artist Lucian Freud paints *Self-Portrait*.
- The Museum für Kunsthandwerk (the Museum of Applied Arts) in Frankfurt am Main, West Germany, designed by the U.S. architect Richard Meier, is completed.
- The Saatchi Collection in London, England, opens, a collection specializing in contemporary art.
- The U.S. artist Andrew Wyeth paints *Field Hand*.
- The U.S. artist Susan Rothenberg paints *Holding the Floor*.
- The U.S. photographer Cindy Sherman publishes *Untitled* No. 140.

SEPTEMBER

- The Bulgarian-born U.S. artist Christo wraps the Pont Neuf Bridge in Paris, France, in glistening golden plastic. This is one of several major structures Christo will turn into "package art."
- The Picasso Museum is opened in Paris, France.

Film

- Disney's 1940 classic *Fantasia* is released in a specially recorded digital version, the first movie with digital sound.
- MGM-UA decides to add color to around 20 black-and-white movies by a process known as colorization, beginning with the 1942 movie *Yankee Doodle Dandy*, released on July 4.
- The Argentinean movie *La historia official/The Official Story*, directed by Luis Puenzo, is released. Concerned with the plight of Argentina's "disappeared," it stars Norma Aleandro and Hector Alterio.
- The epic Holocaust documentary *Shoah*, directed by Claude Lanzmann, is released in France.

- The movie *A Private Function*, directed by Malcolm Mowbray, is released in the UK. It stars Michael Palin and Maggie Smith.
- The movie *A Room with a View*, directed by James Ivory, is released in the UK. Based on the novel by E. M. Forster, it stars Maggie Smith, Helena Bonham Carter, Denholm Elliott, and Julian Sands.
- The movie *A View to a Kill*, directed by John Glen, is released in the United States. It stars Roger Moore as James Bond.
- The movie *After Hours*, directed by Martin Scorsese, is released in the United States. It stars Griffin Dunne and Rosanna Arquette.
- The movie *Back to the Future*, directed by Robert Zemeckis, is released in the United States. It stars Michael J. Fox and Christopher Lloyd.
- The movie *Birdy*, directed by British filmmaker Alan Parker, is released in the United States. It stars Matthew Modine and Nicolas Cage.
- The movie *Brazil*, directed by Terry Gilliam, is released in the United States. It stars Jonathan Pryce.
- The movie *Cocoon*, directed by Ron Howard, is released in the United States, starring Steve Guttenberg, Don Ameche, Wilford Brimly, Jessica Tandy, and Gwen Verdon.
- The movie *Desperately Seeking Susan*, directed by Susan Seidelman and starring Madonna and Rosanna Arquette, is released in the United States.
- The movie *Jagged Edge*, directed by Richard Marquand, is released in the United States, starring Jeff Bridges, Glenn Close, Robert Loggia, and Peter Coyote.
- The movie *Kiss of the Spider Woman*, directed by Hector Babenco, is released in the United States. It stars William Hurt, Raul Julia, and Sonia Braga.
- The movie *Letter to Brezhnev*, directed by Chris Bernard, is released in the UK, starring Alfred Molina and Margi Clarke.
- The movie *My Beautiful Laundrette*, directed by Stephen Frears, is released in the UK. It stars Daniel Day Lewis and Gordon Warnecke.
- The movie *Out of Africa*, directed by Sydney Pollack, is released in the United States. It stars Meryl Streep and Robert Redford.
- The movie *Prizzi's Honor*, directed by John Huston, is released in the United States. It stars Jack Nicholson and Kathleen Turner.
- The movie *Ran*, directed by Akira Kurosawa, is released in Japan. A version of Shakespeare's *King Lear*, it stars Tatsuya Nakadai.
- The movie *Redl Ezredes/Colonel Redl*, directed by István Szabó, is released in Hungary. It stars Klaus Maria Brandauer and Armin Mueller-Stahl.
- The movie *St Elmo's Fire*, directed by Joel Schumacher, is released in the United States. It stars members of the "brat pack," including Rob Lowe, Demi Moore, Emilio Estevez, and Andrew McCarthy.
- The movie *Subway*, directed by Luc Besson, is released in France, starring Isabelle Adjani, Christopher Lambert, and Richard Bohringer.
- The movie *The Color Purple*, directed by Steven Spielberg, is released in the United States. Based on the novel by Alice Walker, it stars Whoopi Goldberg and Danny Glover.

- The movie *The Purple Rose of Cairo*, directed by Woody Allen, is released in the United States. It stars Mia Farrow and Jeff Daniels.
- The movie *The Trip to Bountiful*, directed by Peter Masterson, is released in the United States, based on the play by Horton Foote and starring Geraldine Page, Robert Redford, and Rebecca de Mornay.
- The movie *Trouble in Mind* is released in the United States. It is written and directed by Alan Rudolph and stars Kris Kristofferson and Keith Carradine.
- The movie *Witness*, directed by Peter Weir, is released in the United States. It stars Harrison Ford, Kelly McGillis, and Lukas Haas.
- The number of adolescents visiting the cinema in the United States drops by 20%, while video rental by this group increases 200%.

MARCH

25 The 1984 Academy Awards take place. Best Actor: F. Murray Abraham, for *Amadeus*; Best Supporting Actor: Haing S. Ngor, for *The Killing Fields*; Best Actress: Sally Field, for *Places in the Heart*; Best Supporting Actress: Peggy Ashcroft, for *A Passage to India*; Best Picture: *Amadeus*, directed by Miloš Forman; Best Director: Miloš Forman, for *Amadeus*.

APRIL

8 Australian businessman Rupert Murdoch buys 50% of the Twentieth-Century Fox movie company in the United States.

MAY

20 At the Cannes Film Festival in France, the Palme d'Or is awarded to Yugoslavian director Emir Kusturica for *Otac Na Sluzbenom Putu/When Father Was Away on Business*.

OCTOBER

7 The Catholic League for Civil and Religious Rights protests in New York, New York, against Jean-Luc Godard's movie *Je vous salue, Marie/Hail Mary*, which is perceived as blasphemous.

Literature and Language

- Australian writer Peter Carey publishes his novel *Illywacker*.
- English writer A. S. Byatt publishes her novel *Still Life*.
- The Irish-born British writer Iris Murdoch publishes her novel *The Good Apprentice*.
- The Canadian writer Robertson Davies publishes his novel *What's Bred in the Bone*.
- The Canadian writer Margaret Atwood publishes her novel *The Handmaid's Tale*.
- The Czech writer Ivan Klíma publishes his collection of short stories *Moje první lásky/My First Loves*.
- The English poet Tony Harrison publishes his long poem "V."
- The English writer Brian Aldiss publishes *Helliconia Winter*, the last volume of *The Helliconia Trilogy*.
- The English writer Peter Ackroyd publishes his novel *Hawksmoor*.
- The fifth edition of *The Oxford Companion to English Literature* is published, edited by Margaret Drabble.
- The German writer Patrick Süskind publishes his novel *Perfume*.

- The Nobel Prize for Literature is awarded to the French novelist Claude Simon.
- The Pulitzer Prize for Biography is awarded to Kenneth Silverman for *The Life and Times of Cotton Mather*, the Pulitzer Prize for Poetry is awarded to Carolyn Kizer for *Yin*, and the Pulitzer Prize for Fiction is awarded to Alison Lurie for *Foreign Affairs*.
- The Rhodesian-born English writer Doris Lessing publishes her novel *The Good Terrorist*.
- The Russian writer Alexander Kaletski publishes *Metro, A Novel of the Moscow Underground*.
- The U.S. novelist Anne Tyler publishes her novel *The Accidental Tourist*.
- The U.S. novelist Kurt Vonnegut publishes his novel *Galápagos*.
- The U.S. novelist Philip Roth publishes *Zuckerman Bound*, a volume containing the three novels of his Zuckerman trilogy (*The Ghost Writer*, *Zuckerman Unbound*, and *The Anatomy Lesson*) and a newly written epilogue.
- The U.S. poet Amy Clampitt publishes her poetry collection *What the Light Was Like*.
- The U.S. writer Grace Paley publishes her short-story collection *Later the Same Day*.
- The U.S. writer Harold Brodkey publishes his short-story collection *Women and Angels*.
- The U.S. writer Peter Taylor publishes his short-story collection *The Old Forrest and Other Short Stories*.
- The U.S. writer Tobias Wolff publishes his collection of short stories *Back in the World*.

NOVEMBER

26 Random House purchases the rights to Ronald Reagan's autobiography for $3 million, the highest amount to date for a single book.

Music

- As part of the Band Aid campaign, British pop stars David Bowie and Mick Jagger record a version of Martha Reeves and the Vandellas' "Dancing in the Streets."
- Demand for CDs and CD players exceeds supply in the United States; manufacturers predict the decline of the LP record.
- The English pop group Wham! releases "I'm Your Man."
- The Estonian composer Arvo Pärt completes his *Stabat Mater*.
- The Irish pop group the Pogues releases the album *Rum, Sodomy and the Lash*.
- The Parents' Music Resource Center, formed by Tipper Gore and Susan Baker in the United States, moves to make recording companies print warnings on records with explicit lyrics.
- The Russian composer Alfred Schnittke completes his orchestral work *(K)ein Sommernachtstraum/(Not) A Midsummer Night's Dream*.
- The Russian-born U.S. composer Benjamin Lees completes his Symphony No. 4 (*Memorial Candles*).
- The U.S. composer and conductor André Previn completes his Piano Concerto.
- The U.S. composer Joan Towers completes her Piano Concerto.

- The U.S. composer Norman Dello Joio completes his orchestral work *Variations on a Bach Chorale*.
- The U.S. composer Steve Reich completes his work *New York Counterpoint* for clarinet and (electronic) tape.
- The U.S. pop group Sonic Youth releases the album *Bad Moon Rising*.

FEBRUARY

9 The U.S. pop singer Madonna releases the singles "Into the Groove" and "Material Girl."

23 The British rock group Simple Minds releases the single "Don't You Forget About Me."

26 The 1984–85 Grammy Awards are held. Best Album: *Can't Slow Down* by Lionel Richie; Best Record: "What's Love Got to Do With It?" by Tina Turner; Best Male Pop Vocalist: Phil Collins for "Against All Odds;" Best Female Pop Vocalist: Tina Turner; Best Pop Group: the Pointer Sisters for "Jump."

MARCH

2 The British pop group the Smiths releases the album *Meat is Murder*.

9 The British pop singer Phil Collins releases the album *No Jacket Required*.

23 The United States For Africa single "We Are the World," is released, written by Michael Jackson and Lionel Ritchie and recorded by an all-star group of U.S. singers.

30 The British pop duo Tears for Fears releases the album *Songs From the Big Chair* and the single "Everybody Wants to Rule the World."

JUNE

8 The British pop group Dire Straits releases the album *Brothers in Arms*. It becomes the first CD to sell 1 million copies.

27 The U.S. pop singer Whitney Houston releases "Saving All My Love For You" and the album *Whitney*, which becomes the best-selling album by a female artist to date.

29 The most expensive piece of pop memorabilia to date is sold at Sotheby's in New York, New York, when John Lennon's Rolls Royce fetches over £1.75 million.

JULY

13 Live Aid, organized by Band Aid to raise funds for famine-relief in Africa, is a day-long concert held simultaneously at Wembley Stadium in London, England, and JFK Stadium in Philadelphia, Pennsylvania. Over $70 million is raised worldwide.

AUGUST

16 Pop star Madonna marries actor Sean Penn in New York, New York.

OCTOBER

23 The British pop singer Kate Bush releases the album *Hounds of Love*.

Theater and Dance

- *Les Liaisons dangereuses/Dangerous Liaisons*, a stage adaptation by Christopher Hampton of a 1782 classic French novel by Pierre Choderlos de Laclos, is first performed, in England.
- *The Mahabharata*, a nine-hour stage adaptation by Jean-Claude Carrière and Peter Brook of an ancient Indian religious epic, is first performed, in Avignon, France.
- The musical *Les Misérables* is first performed in English, at the Palace Theatre in London, England. The music is by Claude-Michel Schönberg and the lyrics by Herbert Kretzmer and Alain Boubil. The original French version was first performed in Paris, France, in 1980.
- The musical *The Mystery of Edwin Drood*, with music and lyrics by Rupert Holmes, is first performed, at the Imperial Theater in New York, New York. It is based on an unfinished novel by Charles Dickens.
- The play *A Lie of the Mind*, by the U.S. writer Sam Shepard, is first performed, at the Promenade Theater in New York, New York.
- The play *As Is*, by the U.S. writer William M. Hoffman, is first performed, at the Lyceum Theater in New York, New York.
- The play *Biloxi Blues*, by the U.S. writer Neil Simon, is first performed, at the Neil Simon Theater in New York, New York.
- The play *Largo desolato*, by the Czech writer and politician Václav Havel, is first performed.
- The play *Pravda*, by Howard Brenton and David Hare, is first performed, in London, England.
- The Pulitzer Prize for Drama is awarded to Stephen Sondheim and James Lapine for the musical *Sunday in the Park with George*.

Thought and Scholarship

- British historian Judith M. Brown publishes *Modern India: The Origins of an Asian Democracy*.
- German social scientist Jürgen Habermas publishes *The Philosophical Discourse of Modernity*.
- The Pulitzer Prize for History is awarded to Thomas K. McCraw for *The Prophets of Regulation*.
- The Pulitzer Prize for General Nonfiction is awarded to Louis "Studs" Terkel for *The Good War: An Oral History of World War II*.
- British-born neurologist U.S. Oliver Sachs publishes his collection of essays *The Man Who Mistook his Wife for a Hat*.

SOCIETY

Education

JUNE

4 An Alabama law allowing a minute of prayer in public schools is declared unconstitutional by the Supreme Court.

Everyday Life

- Divorce rates (divorces per 1,000 of the population): France 1.95; Germany 2.10; Great Britain and Northern Ireland 3.08; United States 5.0; USSR 3.36.
- Electronics manufacturer Sony launches the first 8-mm compact camcorder, the Sony CCDM8, in Japan.

- It continues to be fashionable for professional women to wear suits, but brighter colors are introduced.
- Of 46 million working women in the United States, half hold jobs in only 20 of 441 possible professions; 80% are in jobs traditionally held by women.
- Percentage of population living in towns and cities: Australia 86; Bangladesh 18; Brazil 73; Chile 83; China 22; Denmark 86; Egypt 46; France 73; West Germany 86; Great Britain 92; Netherlands 88; India 25; Iran 54; Israel 90; Italy 67; Japan 76; Kenya 20; Mexico 69; Nigeria 30; Pakistan 29; South Africa 56; Sweden 86; United States 74; USSR 66; Zambia 48.
- Pictures of missing children first begin to be shown on milk cartons in the United States.
- Social statistics reveal that in 1985 U.S. women spend an average of 27 hours a week doing housework; U.S. men spend 12.
- The average literacy rate of women worldwide is 97%. In developing countries, however, only 55% of women are literate.
- The Barbie doll is given a business suit and briefcase as well as a French-designed wardrobe.
- The U.S. Secretary of the Army rejects the suggestion (put forward as part of a plan to redesign uniforms) that male officers be allowed to carry umbrellas as they are considered unmilitary and would contribute to slovenly saluting.

MARCH

3   A National Union of Mineworkers (NUM) delegates' conference in Britain votes to return to work without a formal settlement of the pit strike.

APRIL

23 The Coca-Cola Company replaces its established recipe with a sweeter version, called New Coke, aimed at younger consumers, in the United States. Following protests, it has to reinstate the old formula under the Classic name.

AUGUST

4   Black miners in South Africa's gold and coal mines go on indefinite strike, demanding an end to the state of emergency.

NOVEMBER

29 Black union leaders in South Africa form a new union, the Congress of South African Labor Unions, covering 500,000 workers.

Media and Communication

- *Billboard* magazine begins a "Top 40 VC" list for best-selling videocassettes in the United States.
- The world's largest television set, the 24 m/80 ft by 46 m/150 ft Sony JumboTron, is demonstrated in Japan.

MARCH

8   Samuel I. Newhouse, Jr., buys *New Yorker* magazine for $142 million.

17 Capital Cities Communications buys the American Broadcasting Company (ABC) for $3.5 billion in the United States.

MAY

6   Australian publisher Rupert Murdoch purchases most of Metromedia's television stations in the United States.

AUGUST

2   The first mail order catalog in the United States, the Montgomery Ward & Company catalog, which began in 1872, is discontinued due to increasing costs.

SEPTEMBER

4   Australian publisher Rupert Murdoch becomes a U.S. citizen in order to comply with U.S. law prohibiting aliens from owning television stations in the United States.

14 *The Golden Girls* starring Bea Arthur, Betty White, Rue McClanahan, and Estelle Getty, a situation comedy about four mature single retired women, is first shown on U.S. television.

15 A television version of Arthur Miller's play *Death of a Salesman*, starring Dustin Hoffman, is shown on U.S. televison.

18–September 7, 1989   *The Equalizer*, a crime series starring Edward Woodward as a British ex-intelligence officer working as a vigilante in New York, starts on U.S. television.

22 The 1984–85 Emmy Awards for television are held. Best Drama Series: *Cagney and Lacey*; Best Comedy Series: *The Cosby Show*; Best Actor in a Drama: William Daniels, for *St Elsewhere*; Best Actress in a Drama: Tyne Daly, for *Cagney and Lacey*; Best Actor in a Comedy: Robert Guillaume, for *Benson*; Best Actress in a Comedy: Jane Curtin, for *Kate & Allie*.

NOVEMBER

2   The South African government imposes emergency restrictions on the reporting of unrest.

11 *An Early Frost*, the first television drama about AIDS, is shown on U.S. television, starring Aidan Quinn, Gena Rowlands, and Ben Gazzara.

Religion

MAY

8   The Doctrinal Office of the Vatican imposes one year's silence on Father Leonardo Boff of Brazil, a leading exponent of "liberation theology."

NOVEMBER

24 A synod in the Vatican is held to assess the impact of the reforms introduced by the Second Vatican Council.

Sports

- Alain Prost becomes the first French driver to win the Formula One World Drivers' Championship.
- The North American Soccer League, instituted in 1968, folds.
- U.S. national figure skating champions are: Tiffany Chin; Brian Boitano; Jill Watson and Peter Oppegard, pairs; Judy Blumberg and Michael Seibert, dance.

JANUARY

1   Brigham Young University win college football's national championship for the 1984 season.

19–20   The first World Indoor Games for track and field events are held at Bercy, Paris, France.

BIRTHS & DEATHS

- Frank Macfarlane Burnet, Australian physician, an authority on immunology and viral diseases, dies (86).

FEBRUARY

8 William Lyons, British industrialist, inventor and producer of Jaguar cars, dies in Wappenbury, Warwickshire, England (83).

11 Ben Abruzzo, U.S. balloonist, the first to cross the Atlantic in a balloon, dies in Albuquerque, New Mexico (54).

20 Clarence Nash, U.S. vocal impressionist who was the voice of Donald Duck in several languages for more than 50 years, dies in Burbank, California (80).

27 Henry Cabot Lodge, U.S. Republican politician and U.S. delegate to the United Nations (UN), dies in Beverly, Massachusetts (82).

MARCH

8 Ralph McAllister Ingersoll, U.S. managing editor of the *New Yorker* and *Fortune* magazines and founder of *Life* magazine, dies in Miami Beach, Florida (84).

10 Konstantin Chernenko, Soviet premier 1984–85, dies in Moscow, USSR (73).

16 Roger Sessions, U.S. composer and author of several books on music, dies in Princeton, New Jersey (88).

23 "Zoot" Sims, U.S. saxophonist with the big bands in the Swing era, dies in New York, New York (59).

28 Marc Chagall, Russian-born French painter and designer, dies in St. Paul de Venne, France (97).

APRIL

11 Enver Hoxha, Albanian prime minister 1946–54 and First Secretary of the Albanian Communist Party 1954–85, dies in Tiranë, Albania (76).

13 Oscar Nemon, Croatian-born British sculptor of portraits including Churchill and the royal family, dies in Oxford, England (79).

23 Samuel James Ervin, Jr., U.S. Democrat senator, chairman of the Senate Select Committee on Presidential Campaign Activities (the Watergate Committee), dies in Winston-Salem, North Carolina (88).

MAY

11 Chester Gould, U.S. cartoonist, the creator of Dick Tracy, dies in Woodstock, Illinois (84).

12 Jean Dubuffet, French painter and sculptor, the founder of Art Brut ("raw art"), dies in Paris, France (83).

19 John Joseph Martin, U.S. dance critic for the *New York Times* who encouraged modern dance in the United States, dies in Saratoga, New York (91).

31 Louis Robert, French archeologist, an expert in Greek inscriptions, dies in Paris, France (81).

JUNE

21 Tage Erlander, prime minister of Sweden 1946–68, responsible for turning Sweden into a welfare state, dies in Huddinge, near Stockholm, Sweden (84).

JULY

4 Willem Visser 't Hooft, Dutch clergyman, secretary of the World Council of Churches 1938–66, dies in Geneva, Switzerland (84).

9 Charlotte, Grand Duchess of Luxembourg 1919–64, who guarded Luxembourg's independence, dies in Fischbach Castle, Luxembourg (89).

16 Heinrich Böll, West German poet, novelist, short-story writer, and translator, dies in Hütgenwald-Grosshau, West Germany (67).

17 Susanne Langer, U.S. educator and philosopher of linguistic analysis and aesthetics, dies in Old Lyme, Connecticut (89).

AUGUST

8 Louise Brooks, U.S. film star of the silent era, dies in Rochester, New York (78).

12 Marcel Mihalovici, Romanian-born composer best known for his chamber music, dies in Paris, France (86).

28 Ruth Gordon, U.S. actress who appeared in films over a span of 40 years, dies (88).

30 Taylor Caldwell, U.S. novelist, dies in Greenwich, Connecticut (84).

SEPTEMBER

3 Johnny Marks, U.S. popular composer and songwriter, best known for "Rudolph the Red-Nosed Reindeer," dies in New York (75).

8 John Franklin Envers, U.S. microbiologist who, along with two colleagues, developed a vaccine for poliomyelitis, dies in Waterford, Connecticut (88).

17 Laura Ashley, Welsh designer of fabrics and clothes characterized by floral patterns, frills, and lace, dies in Coventry, Warwickshire, England (60).

27 André Kertész, Hungarian-born U.S. photographer and photojournalist, dies in New York, New York (91).

30 Charles Francis Richter, U.S. seismologist who developed the Richter scale of earthquake magnitude, dies in Pasadena, California (85).

30 Helen Clark McInnes, U.S. author of spy novels, dies in New York (77).

30 Simone Signoret, French dramatic actress of stage and film, dies in Eure, France (64).

OCTOBER

1 E(lwyn) B(rooks) White, U.S. essayist for the *New Yorker* magazine and author of the children's classic *Charlotte's Web*, dies in Brookline, Maine (86).

2 Rock Hudson, U.S. film actor, the first celebrity to have announced publicly that he had AIDS, dies in Beverly Hills, California (59).

10 Orson Welles, U.S. film actor, director, producer, and writer, best known for *Citizen Kane*, dies in Los Angeles, California (70).

10 Yul Brynner, Academy Award-winning U.S. stage and screen actor, dies in New York, New York (65).

15 Jacques Oudin, French immunologist, one of the founders of the science, dies in Paris, France (77).

27 Walter Segal, Swiss-born architect, a pioneer of low-cost self-assembled housing, dies in London, England (78).

NOVEMBER

1 Phil Silvers, U.S. comedian who played Sergeant Bilko for many years on television, dies in Los Angeles, California (73).

17 Stuart Chase, U.S. economist and adviser to President Franklin D. Roosevelt, who coined the phrase the "New Deal," dies in Redding, Connecticut (97).

19 Stepin Fetchit (born Lincoln Theodore Perry), the first well-known black Hollywood actor, dies (93).

28 Fernand Braudel, French historian, educator, and historiographer, dies in Paris, France (83).

DECEMBER

6 Burleigh Grimes, U.S. professional baseball player, dies in Clear Lake, Wisconsin (92).

7 Robert Graves, English poet, novelist, and critic, dies in Deyá, Majorca, Spain (90).

14 Roger Maris, U.S. baseball player who broke Babe Ruth's record of home runs for a single season, dies in Houston, Texas (51).

MAY

21–30 The Edmonton Oilers are once again the Stanley Cup champions, beating the Philadelphia Flyers in five games.

26 U.S. racing driver Danny Sullivan wins the Indianapolis 500.

29 Thirty-nine people are killed at the Heysel stadium in Brussels, Belgium, following a riot by Liverpool fans before the European Cup Final between Liverpool and Juventus of Italy; as a consequence, English soccer clubs are banned from all European competitions for five years.

JUNE

5 The U.S. jockey Steve Cauthen wins the English Derby at Epsom, Surrey, on Slip Anchor, becoming the first jockey to have won both the Epsom and Kentucky Derbys.

8 The Irish boxer Barry McGuigan outpoints Eusebio Pedroza of Panama in London, England, to win the world featherweight championship.

9 The Los Angeles Lakers defeat the Boston Celtics by four games to two to end their run of eight consecutive National Basketball Association (NBA) finals defeats to the Celtics going back to 1959.

JULY

7 The West German tennis player Boris Becker, at 17 years and 227 days, wins the men's singles title in the Wimbledon championships, London, England. He is the youngest, the first West German, and the first unseeded player to win the title.

11 Nolan Ryan of the Houston Astros becomes the first Major League baseball player to strike out 4,000 batters.

13 The Soviet pole vaulter Sergey Bubka makes the first ever 6-m/19.7-ft jump, in Paris, France.

21 The French cyclist Bernard Hinault wins the Tour de France for the fifth time, a feat only previously achieved by Jaques Anquetil of France and Eddie Merckx of Belgium.

27 British runner Steve Cram sets a new world mile record of 3 min 46.31 sec in Oslo, Norway.

SEPTEMBER

September–November Garry Kasparov of the USSR defeats Anatoly Karpov of the USSR 13-11 in Moscow to win the World Chess Championship. At 22 years, 210 days he is the youngest ever world champion.

11 In baseball, Pete Rose of the Cincinnati Reds breaks Ty Cobb's major league career record of 4,191 hits.

15 Europe's golfers, captained by the English golfer Tony Jacklin, defeat the United States 16.5–11.5 in the Ryder Cup at The Belfry, Sutton Coldfield in England. It is the first time the United States has lost the trophy since 1957.

21 Larry Holmes of the United States loses his International Boxing Federation (IBF) world heavyweight boxing crown to fellow U.S. fighter Michael Spinks on points in Las Vegas, Nevada. It is Holmes's first defeat in 48 professional fights, 22 of which were world title bouts.

OCTOBER

19–27 The Kansas City Royals beat the St. Louis Cardinals four games to three to win baseball's World Series.

◆

1986

POLITICS, GOVERNMENT, AND ECONOMICS

Business and Economics

- Oil oversupply leads to a slump in prices, to $6 a barrel compared to over $30 in the early 1980s. This in turn leads to an increase in prosperity in industrial countries and states not dependent on oil revenues.
- The final volume of *The Collected Works of Walter Bagehot*, edited by Norman St. John-Stevas, is published.

- The Singer company in the United States announces it is withdrawing from the manufacture of sewing machines to concentrate on aerospace products.

APRIL

1 The price of North Sea oil falls below $10 a barrel for the first time.

27 The world's largest advertising agency, BBDO International, is formed in a merger of Madison Avenue agencies.

28 General Motors overtakes the Exxon Corporation as the largest company in the United States.

JUNE

6 The U.S. national debt for the year reaches $2 trillion, its highest level to date.

AUGUST

22 U.S. nuclear processing firm Kerr-McGee agrees to pay $1.3 million to the estate of murdered antinuclear protester Karen Silkwood.

OCTOBER

27 The "Big Bang" deregulation of the stock exchange in London, England, introduces computerized dealing and abolishes the distinctions between various types of trader.

DECEMBER

30 The Esso oil company announces its withdrawal from operations in South Africa.

Human Rights

• Liechtenstein allows women to vote for the first time in elections to the national diet (parliament).
• Takako Doi becomes head of the Japanese Socialist party. She is the first woman head of a major political party in Japan.

JANUARY

20 Martin Luther King Day is observed for the first time.

MAY

25 Thirty thousand blacks are expelled from their homes in the Crossroads squatter camp near Cape Town, South Africa.

Politics and Government

• A repeal of the Urban Areas Act in South Africa includes the removal of the pass laws.
• A Tax Reform Act is passed in the United States to simplify the federal tax system.
• The Dutch Reformed Church in South Africa declares that racism is a sin.

JANUARY

1 One hundred and fifty four Tamil refugees from Sri Lanka are rescued from lifeboats off Canada's Newfoundland coast.

1 Spain and Portugal become the 11th and 12th members of the European Community.

7 The United States imposes sanctions on Libya for its alleged involvement in international terrorism.

9 Michael Heseltine resigns as British defense secretary following cabinet disagreement over the future of the ailing Westland helicopter company. He is succeeded by George Younger. On January 24, the trade secretary Leon Brittan also resigns, over the leak of a letter connected with the affair. He is replaced by Paul Channon.

22 Three Sikhs are sentenced to death in India for the murder in 1984 of Indira Gandhi, the prime minister.

25 The National Resistance Army in Uganda occupies the capital, Kampala. On January 29, the army leader Yuweri Museveni is sworn in as Uganda's president.

25 The Soviet head of state Mikhail Gorbachev proposes a 15-year timetable for the elimination of all nuclear weapons.

FEBRUARY

7 A presidential election is held in the Philippines. On February 9, computer operators from the Commission on Elections protest, claiming that they have evidence of widespread vote rigging.

7 President Jean-Claude ("Baby Doc") Duvalier of Haiti flees to France, following antigovernment demonstrations. General Henri Namphy forms a new government.

11 The Soviet Jewish dissident Anatoly Shcharansky and three others are freed to emigrate, in exchange for five East Europeans held on spying charges in the West.

15 Opposition members walk out of the parliament of the Philippines when President Ferdinand Marcos declares himself victor in the presidential election.

19 After 37 years, the U.S. Senate ratifies the United Nations Convention on the Prevention and Punishment of the Crime of Genocide.

19 Iran temporarily captures the Iraqi oil port of Faw, giving it control of the mouth of the strategic Shatt al-Arab waterway.

22 The defense minister of the Philippines Juan Ponce Enrile and the deputy chief of staff Fidel Ramos take over the headquarters of the defense ministry, declaring their opposition to President Ferdinand Marcos and their support for the opposition leader Cory (Corazón) Aquino.

25 President Ferdinand Marcos flees the Philippines, and the opposition leader Cory (Corazón) Aquino is sworn in as president.

27 Despite Ferdinand Marcos's protests, the United States recognizes election victor Cory Aquino as president of the Philippines.

28 Sweden's prime minister Olof Palme is assassinated by a gunman in a Stockholm street.

MARCH

2 Queen Elizabeth of Great Britain and Northern Ireland signs the Australia Bill in Canberra, severing Australia's last constitutional ties with Britain.

6 The Soviet Communist Party Congress agrees sweeping changes in the membership in the Central Committee and the Politburo.

7 The South African government lifts the state of emergency imposed in July 1985.

12 Spain votes in a referendum to remain in NATO, but for its military forces to remain separate from the NATO command structure.

16 The opposition parties win a narrow majority in the French general election, ending five years of Socialist rule. On March 20, Jacques Chirac, the Gaullist leader, is appointed prime minister.

APRIL

4–7 The Contadora group of Central American countries, meeting in Panama, fails to reach an agreement on ending the fighting in Nicaragua and El Salvador.

5 A bomb attack on the La Belle discotheque in West Berlin, frequented by U.S. servicemen, kills two and injures scores more. Libyan terrorist involvement is suspected.

11 Brian Keenan, a lecturer at the American University of Beirut, is taken hostage by Muslim extremists.

15 Bombers from U.S. warships and bases in Britain attack targets in Libya: 100 people are killed, and one airplane is shot down.

17 John McCarthy, the acting bureau chief for Worldwide Television in Beirut, is taken hostage by Muslim extremists.

17 The bodies of two kidnapped Britons and one U.S. citizen are found near Beirut. They had been murdered after the U.S. raid on Libya earlier that year.

18 A bomb is discovered in an El Al passenger's luggage at Heathrow airport. A Jordanian, Nezar Hindawi, is arrested for the attempted bombing.

18 President P. W. Botha of South Africa announces an end to pass laws imposing restrictions on the movement of nonwhite citizens within the country.

29 An arson attack causes the worst library fire in the United States to date; 800,000 books are damaged or destroyed at the Los Angeles Central Library, Los Angeles, California.

30 In India, 2,000 police and paramilitary commandos enter the Sikh Golden Temple at Amritsar in Punjab, to expel militants who had proclaimed an independent Sikh state of Khalistan.

MAY

4 Babrak Karmal resigns as general secretary of the People's Democratic (Communist) Party of Afghanistan, to be replaced by Mohammad Najibullah, former head of the Afghan secret police.

10 Britain expels three Syrian diplomats for their alleged involvement in terrorism. On May 11, Syria expels three British diplomats in retaliation.

18 Sri Lankan forces seek to establish control over the Jaffna peninsula in the north of the country, held by Tamil insurgents.

24–26 The presidents of Nicaragua, Guatemala, El Salvador, Honduras, and Costa Rica sign the Declaration of Esquipulas at a summit in Guatemala, endorsing the Contadora peace treaty and calling for an end to U.S. military intervention in the region.

JUNE

2 One thousand Sikhs are arrested during protests on the second anniversary of the Indian army's attack on the Sikh Golden Temple at Amritsar, in Punjab, India.

8 The former United Nations secretary-general Kurt Waldheim is elected president of Austria.

10 Patrick Magee is convicted of the murder of five people by his involvement in the IRA bombing of the Grand Hotel in Brighton, England, in October 1984. On June 23, he is jailed for life.

12 A report of the Commonwealth Eminent Persons Group is published, calling for economic sanctions against South Africa.

12 The South African president P. W. Botha announces a countrywide state of emergency in response to increasing popular unrest; 1,000 black activists are arrested.

17 U.S. chief justice Warren Burger retires, and is succeeded by William Rehnquist.

20 A conference of 120 nations in Paris, France, organized by the United Nations Special Committee against Apartheid, the Organization of African Unity, and the Non-Aligned Movement, calls for sanctions against South Africa.

26–27 A European Community summit conference at The Hague appoints Britain's Geoffrey Howe to lead a peace mission to South Africa.

27 A referendum in the Republic of Ireland rejects a proposal to allow divorce.

30 The U.S. Supreme Court rules that Georgia's law prohibiting oral and anal intercourse is not unconstitutional.

JULY

2 The U.S. Supreme Court supports the use of preferential quotas in the hiring of employees.

5 The leader of the Turkish Cypriots Rauf Denktaş refuses a United Nations request for talks on the reopening of the border dividing Cyprus.

7 The French agents jailed in New Zealand for the sinking of the Greenpeace ship *Rainbow Warrior* in Auckland harbor are released into French custody.

17 The U.S. Senate approves a treaty allowing the extradition of suspected IRA terrorists to Britain.

23 Prince Andrew, the third child of Queen Elizabeth II and Prince Philip, marries Sarah Ferguson, in London, England.

29 A United Nations mission to South Africa, led by British foreign secretary Geoffrey Howe, fails to secure the release of Nelson Mandela or the lifting of the ban on the African National Congress.

AUGUST

3–5 A special conference is held in London, England, of seven Commonwealth leaders to consider policy on South Africa. Britain is the only country to oppose a sanctions program.

12 The United States suspends its defense obligations to New Zealand following the New Zealand Labor government's espousal of an antinuclear policy, and denial of access to New Zealand for U.S. warships and military aircraft capable of carrying nuclear weapons.

18 Israel and the USSR hold talks in Helsinki on the social and political conditions of Jews in the Soviet Union, the first such talks for 19 years.

23 Gennady Zakharov, a Soviet diplomat accredited to the United Nations, is arrested in the United States and charged with spying. On August 30, a U.S. newspaper correspondent, Nicholas Daniloff, is arrested in Moscow and charged with spying.

SEPTEMBER

6 President Augusto Pinochet of Chile survives an assassination attempt. A nationwide state of siege is declared.

7 The Right Reverend Desmond Tutu is enthroned as the first black archbishop of Cape Town, South Africa.

11 Share prices on Wall Street register their biggest fall since 1929, due to renewed fears of inflation.

16 European Community foreign ministers agree to prohibit new European investment in South Africa.

17 The U.S. State Department orders 25 members of the Soviet mission to the United Nations out of the country by October.

22 French actresses Catherine Deneuve and Brigitte Bardot sue filmmaker Roger Vadim for his revelations about them in his best-selling autobiography.

29 The USSR releases U.S. journalist and alleged spy Nicholas Daniloff.

30 The British Labour Party leader Neil Kinnock pledges that a future Labour government will close all U.S. nuclear bases in Britain.

OCTOBER

2   The Indian prime minister Rajiv Gandhi survives an assassination attempt in New Delhi.

2   The U.S. Senate votes to impose economic sanctions on South Africa, overturning a presidential veto.

3   A comprehensive Anti-Apartheid Act in the United States imposes strict sanctions on South Africa and causes many multinational firms to disinvest.

5   The Soviet human-rights campaigner Yuri Orlov is released from Siberian exile and flown to the United States.

11–12   A U.S.–USSR mini-summit in Reykjavik, Iceland, fails to reach an agreement on arms control after the U.S. president Ronald Reagan refuses to abandon his commitment to the Strategic Defense Initiative (Star Wars) program.

20   An Israeli nuclear technician, Mordechai Vanunu, is kidnapped in London, England, after revealing details of Israel's nuclear resources. On November 9, Israel admits that Vanunu is in Israeli custody.

20   Yitzhak Shamir of the Likud Party succeeds Labor's Shimon Peres as Israeli prime minister under the terms of their 1984 rotation agreement.

24   Britain breaks off diplomatic relations with Syria after allegations of Syrian involvement in the failed plot to bomb an El Al jet at Heathrow airport in London, England, in April.

NOVEMBER

2   The U.S. hostage David Jacobsen is freed by his Muslim captors in Beirut following the intervention of the Church of England envoy Terry Waite.

3   Details of a U.S. arms deal with Iran to secure the release of western hostages held by pro-Iranian Muslim groups in Beirut appear in a Lebanese magazine.

3   Joaquim Chissano becomes president of Mozambique following the death of President Samora Machel in an airplane crash in South Africa.

4   In U.S. Congressional elections, the Republican Party loses control of the Senate to the Democrats, 55–45.

7   The Simpson–Mazzoli immigration law in the United States gives legal status to many illegal immigrants, but makes employers who knowingly hire illegal aliens subject to civil fines.

10   President Hossain Mohammad Ershad announces an end to martial law in Bangladesh.

13   The U.S. president Ronald Reagan admits to a secret arms deal with Iran, but denies that it has any connection with the possible release of western hostages in Beirut.

14   A U.S. securities dealer, Ivan Boesky, is fined $100 million for illegal insider dealing.

25   U.S. president Ronald Reagan's national security adviser Admiral John Poindexter resigns, and his aide Lieutenant Colonel Oliver North is dismissed from the National Security Council (NSC) in the United States after the revelation that money from arms sales to Iran was illegally channeled to Contra rebels in Central America. On November 26, Reagan appoints former senator John Tower to head an inquiry into the role of the NSC in the Iran–Contra Affair.

27   French high school and university students protest at government education reforms. The reform bill is withdrawn on December 8.

DECEMBER

19   Lawrence Walsh is appointed special prosecutor in the United States to investigate the Iran–Contra Affair.

23   The Soviet authorities announce that the dissident physicist Andrey Sakharov and his wife Yelena Bonner can return to Moscow after seven years' internal exile.

SCIENCE, TECHNOLOGY, AND MEDICINE

Agriculture

- The U.S. Department of Agriculture permits the Biological Corporation of Omaha to market a virus produced by genetic engineering; it is the first living genetically altered organism to be sold. The virus is used against a form of swine herpes.
- The U.S. Department of Agriculture permits the first outdoor test of genetically altered high-yield plants (tobacco plants).

DECEMBER

8–11   Food riots force the Zambian government to reverse its decision to double the price of corn flour.

Computing

- U.S. neurologist Terry Sejnowski develops a neural network computer that learns to read text out loud at Johns Hopkins University, Baltimore, Maryland.

Ecology

- Two wells 4 km/2.5 mi deep and connected at the bottom are used to generate 4 megawatts of geothermal power at the Los Alamos National Laboratory in New Mexico, United States. Water introduced in one well emerges from the other at a temperature of 190°C/375° F.

JANUARY

8   The United States and Canada issue a joint report on acid rain; it recommends that the U.S. government assist industries to burn coal more cleanly.

APRIL

26   A major accident at the Chernobyl nuclear power station near Kiev, Ukraine, USSR, is announced after abnormally high levels of radiation are reported in Sweden, Denmark, and Finland. Shortly after the accident more than 30 fire fighters and plant workers die from radiation exposure and over the next few years an estimated 6,500 to 45,000 people die from cancer. High rates of genetic defects are also reported, and a vast area of land will be uninhabitable for thousands of years.

AUGUST

26   Over 1,700 people die in Cameroon when toxic carbon dioxide gas erupts from volcanic Lake Nyas.

SEPTEMBER

24 Mt. Etna in Italy erupts violently. Volcanic activity continues into early 1987.

NOVEMBER

1 Water supplies along the Rhine are contaminated and millions of fish are killed when a fire at the Sandoz pharmaceutical company near Basel, Switzerland, results in 1,000 metric tons of toxic chemicals being discharged into the river.

Exploration

- The U.S. space probe *Giotto* (launched July 2, 1985) reveals that the nucleus of Halley's comet measures 15 km/24 mi by 10 km/16 mi and consists of ices (chiefly water), various gases, and dust particles.

JANUARY

- The U.S. space probe *Voyager 2* passes within 81,000 km/50,600 mi of Uranus; photographs taken by the probe reveal ten unknown satellites and two new rings.

28 The U.S. space shuttle *Challenger* explodes shortly after takeoff, killing the crew of seven and setting the U.S. space program back years.

FEBRUARY

19 The Soviet space station *Mir 1* is launched; it is intended to be permanently occupied.

Health and Medicine

- Scientists at the Massachusetts Institute of Technology, Boston, Massachusetts, discover the first gene that inhibits growth; it inhibits the cancer retinoblastoma.
- Surgeons develop an operation for removing tissue from the cornea by laser.
- The approximate location of a gene causing Duchenne muscular dystrophy is announced; it makes it possible to screen for carriers of the gene.
- The Nobel Prize for Physiology or Medicine is awarded jointly to U.S. biochemist Stanley Cohen and Italian neurologist Rita Levi-Montalcini for their discovery of factors that promote the growth of nerve and epidermal cells.
- The Swedish company Pharmacia Les Therapeutics AB develops Nicoret, a nicotine chewing gum to help people give up smoking.
- The U.S. Food and Drug Administration approves the Caridex system for treating tooth decay which uses a mild acid instead of drilling to remove decay.
- There are 25,000 diagnosed cases of AIDS in the United States.
- U.S. gay activist Cleve Jones conceives the idea of a patchwork quilt to commemorate the victims of AIDS.
- U.S. inventor Tony Hodges patents a split computer keyboard to prevent repetitive stress syndrome.

APRIL

- The first large plant to irradiate food is set up in New Jersey, United States, to process fruits and vegetables arriving from tropical countries; other plants soon open in the Netherlands, Japan, Canada, and other countries.

AUGUST

- It becomes illegal in the United States for hospitals to discharge patients who are unable to pay.

OCTOBER

22 The U.S. surgeon general urges education, abstinence, and greater use of condoms in the fight against AIDS.

DECEMBER

17 British surgeons John Wallwork and Roy Calne perform the first triple transplant—heart, lung, and liver—at Papworth Hospital, Cambridge, England.

Science

- Archeologists in Egypt discover the undisturbed tomb of Maya, Tutankhamen's treasurer; it is 3,500 years old.
- Argentine paleontologists report the discovery of the first fossil dinosaur to be found in Antarctica.
- At Olduvai Gorge in Tanzania, the U.S. paleoanthropologist Tim White discovers portions of a skull, arm, leg bones, and teeth belonging to a *Homo habilis* individual estimated to be 1.8 million years old. It is the only fossil in which limb bones have been securely assigned to *H. habilis*, and while all the features of the skull resemble *H. habilis*, the arm and leg bones display australopithecine traits.
- By analyzing the yearly growth patterns of 850-million-year-old stromatolites (pillars of rock composed of layers of dead photosynthetic organisms which grow by minute amounts each day), researchers at the University of California, Berkeley, United States, discover that 850 million years ago the year was 435 days long.
- French archeologists Nie de Guidon and G. Delibrias report the discovery of a hearth at Boqueirão do Sito da Pedra Furada, a rock shelter in eastern Brazil, which is radiocarbon-dated at about 32,000 years old. It is the oldest archeological site in the New World and suggests that human beings entered the Americas much earlier than 12,000 years ago, as currently believed. The site also contains the oldest rock art in the Americas, dated at 17,000 years ago.
- Paleontologists discover the fossil remains of two crow-sized birds in Texas which are about 225 million years old. Named *Protoavis*, the birds predate *Archaeopteryx* by about 75 million years; they are capable of true flight but also have many saurian features.
- Researchers from Florida State University discover the remains of over 40 individuals at the 8,000-year-old Windover burial site in Florida, with soft tissue—including brains—still intact.
- Scientists at Arizona State University conduct computer simulations that strongly suggest that a Mars-sized object struck the earth a glancing blow about 4.6 billion years ago and was then captured by the earth; by the end of the year the impact theory is the leading hypothesis about the moon's origin.
- Scientists at the Brookhaven National Laboratory in Upton, New York, discover that the number of brain cells involved in a cat's memory of where to find food is between 5 and 100 million, or about one-tenth of the brain, thus challenging the idea that single memories are localized.
- Scientists use ten laser beams, which deliver a total energy of 100 trillion watts during one-billionth of a second, to convert a small part of the hydrogen nuclei contained in a glass sphere to helium at the Lawrence

Livermore National Laboratory in California; it is the first fusion reaction induced by a laser.

- U.S. archeologist Diane Chase discovers the tomb of a Mayan woman of very high status, challenging the current theory that women were held in low esteem in Mayan culture.
- U.S. chemist Dudley Herschbach, Taiwanese-born U.S. chemist Yuan Lee, and German-born Canadian chemist John Polanyi receive the Nobel Prize for Chemistry for their work on the dynamics of chemical elementary processes.
- U.S. researchers Steven Clark and Yu Chang Yang discover the immune system chemical known as interleukin 3.

Technology

- Canadian firm Alcan Aluminum develops the aluminum-air battery in which an electric current is produced by the dissolution of aluminum in salt water.
- German physicist Johannes Bednorz and Swiss physicist Karl Alex Müller announce the discovery of a superconducting ceramic material in which superconductivity occurs at a much higher temperature (30 K) than hitherto known, increasing the potential for use of superconductivity for more energy-efficient motors and computers. They receive the Nobel Prize for Physics—in record time—for their discovery.
- The California Submillimeter Observatory telescope begins operation on Mauna Kea, Hawaii; its 10.4-m/ 34-ft disc makes it the largest submillimeter telescope in the world.
- The first laptop computer is introduced in the United States.
- The Japanese company Fuji launches the disposable camera, designed so that the whole unit is handed over for processing.
- The Nobel Prize for Physics is awarded jointly to German physicist Ernst Ruska for developing the electron microscope, and to German physicist Gerd Binnig and Swiss physicist Heinrich Rohrer for the development of the scanning tunneling microscope.

Transportation

- A riverboat capsizes in the Dhaleshwar River in Bangladesh; over 600 people die.
- The 20-m/65-ft motorboat *Virgin Atlantic Challenger II* crosses the Atlantic from west to east in 3 days, 8 hours, 31 minutes, setting the world's record for the fastest Atlantic crossing by any vessel.
- The Annacis Island Crossing Bridge (renamed Alex Fraser) at Vancouver, Canada, is completed; at 465 m/ 1,525 ft long, it is the world's longest cable-stayed bridge.
- The Aston Martin driven by James Bond in the movie *Goldfinger* is sold at a sale of movie memorabilia at Sotheby's in New York, New York, for almost £180,000.
- The city of Los Angeles in California begins construction of a subway system.
- The Danube–Black Sea Canal from Cernavoda to Constanza in Romania is completed; linking the Danube

to the Black Sea, it has been built using political prisoners and army conscripts.
- The European A320 Airbus is the first commercial aircraft to use a "fly-by-wire" system.
- The M25, the world's longest ring road at 195 km/ 121 mi, is completed around London, England.
- The subway system in Sendai, Japan, starts operating; it is controlled by computers using fuzzy logic.
- The wind-powered ship *Wind Star* is launched; it is 134 m/440 ft long and the sails on its four 62-m/204-ft masts are computer-controlled.
- The world's largest cargo ship, the Dutch ore carrier *Berge Stahl*, is launched; it is 439 m/1,125 ft long.

AUGUST

31 The Soviet liner *Admiral Nakhimov* collides with the freighter *Pyotr Vasev* in the Black Sea, killing 398 people.

OCTOBER

3–6 A Soviet nuclear submarine, crippled by an explosion and fire, sinks off Bermuda; it carries 16 ballistic missiles each with two nuclear warheads.

DECEMBER

14–23 U.S. pilots Dick Rutan and Jeanna Yeager make the first round-the-world, nonstop flight without refueling in the lightweight airplane *Voyager*; it flies 40,269 km/ 25,012 mi, at an average speed of 115.8 kph/ 186.4 mph and carries 4,500 l/1,200 gal of fuel.

ARTS AND IDEAS

Architecture

MARCH

31 Hampton Court Palace, near London, England, is severely damaged by fire.

JULY

4 The Statue of Liberty in New York, New York, is reopened by U.S. president Ronald Reagan in the presence of President François Mitterrand of France, following refurbishment in celebration of its 100th birthday.

Arts

- The French-born U.S. artist Louise Bourgeois creates the sculpture *Articulated Lair*.
- The German-born English artist Frank Auerbach paints *Head of Catherine Lampert*.
- The German-born English artist Lucien Freud paints *Painter and Model*.
- The Musée d'Orsay in Paris, France, designed by Gae Aulenti and an international team of architects, is completed.
- The Museum of Contemporary Art in Los Angeles, California, designed by Japanese architect Arata Isozaki, is completed.
- The Palazzo Grassi gallery in Venice, Italy, opens. Its first exhibition is "Futurism and Futurisms."

- The U.S. artist David Salle paints *Landscape with Two Nudes and Three Eyes*.
- The U.S. artist Jeff Koons creates *Rabbit*.

APRIL

2   Curators in New Orleans, Louisiana, discover 12th-century Chinese manuscripts, hidden for 800 years, inside a donated Buddhist sculpture.

Film

- French movie theater audiences number 1.6 million for the year; U.S. audiences equal 10.3 million.
- The movie *37.2° le Matin/Betty Blue*, directed by Jean-Jacques Beineix, is released in France. It stars Béatrice Dalle and Jean-Hugues Anglade.
- The movie *9½ Weeks*, directed by Adrian Lyne, is released in the United States. It stars Mickey Rourke and Kim Basinger.
- The movie *A Better Tomorrow*, directed by John Woo, is released in Hong Kong. It stars Chow Yun-Fat and Leslie Cheung.
- The movie *Aliens*, directed by James Cameron, is released in the United States, starring Sigourney Weaver.
- The movie *Blue Velvet*, directed by David Lynch, is released in the United States. It stars Kyle MacLachlan, Isabella Rossellini, Dennis Hopper, and Laura Dern.
- The movie *Caravaggio*, directed by Derek Jarman, is released in the UK. It stars Nigel Terry and Sean Bean.
- The movie *Children of a Lesser God*, directed by Randa Haines, is released in the United States, starring William Hurt and Marlee Matlin.
- The movie *Crocodile Dundee*, directed by Peter Faiman, is released in Australia. It stars Paul Hogan.
- The movie *Doña Herlinda y su hijo/Doña Herlinda and her Son*, directed by Jaime Humberto Hermosillo, is released in Mexico. It stars Arturo Meza, Marco Antonio Treviño, and Leticia Lupersio.
- The movie *Down and Out in Beverly Hills*, directed by Paul Mazursky, is released in the United States, starring Nick Nolte, Richard Dreyfuss, and Bette Midler.
- The movie *Ginger e Fred/Ginger and Fred*, directed by Federico Fellini, is released in Italy. It stars Marcello Mastroianni and Giulietta Massina.
- The movie *Hannah and her Sisters*, written and directed by Woody Allen, is released in the United States. It features an all-star cast including Allen, Mia Farrow, Dianne Wiest, Barbara Hershey, Max von Sydow, and Michael Caine.
- The movie *Jean de Florette*, directed by Claude Berri, is released in France. Based on the book by Marcel Pagnol, it stars Gérard Depardieu, Daniel Auteuil, and Yves Montand.
- The movie *Le Declin de l'empire américain/The Decline of the American Empire* is released in Canada. It is written and directed by Denys Arcand.
- The movie *Le Rayon vert/The Green Ray* (*Summer* in the United States), directed by Eric Rohmer, is released in France.
- The movie *Manhunter*, directed by Michael Mann, is released in the United States. Based on the novel *Red Dragon* by Thomas Harris, it stars William L. Petersen.

- The movie *Manon des Sources/Manon of the Springs*, directed by Claude Berri, is released in France. Based on the book by Marcel Pagnol, it stars Daniel Auteuil, Yves Montand, and Emmanuelle Béart.
- The movie *Matador*, directed by Pedro Almodóvar, is released in Spain, starring Assumpta Serna and Antonio Banderas.
- The movie *Mona Lisa*, directed by Neil Jordan, is released in the UK. It stars Bob Hoskins and Cathy Tyson.
- The movie *Platoon*, directed by Oliver Stone, is released in the United States. It stars Charlie Sheen, Tom Berenger, and Willem Dafoe.
- The movie *Round Midnight*, directed by Bertrand Tavernier, is released in France. It stars saxophonist Dexter Gordon.
- The movie *Sid and Nancy*, directed by Alex Cox, is released in the United States, starring Gary Oldman and Chloe Webb.
- The movie *Something Wild*, directed by Jonathan Demme, is released in the United States. It stars Jeff Daniels, Melanie Griffith, and Ray Liotta.
- The movie *Stand By Me*, directed by Rob Reiner, is released in the United States. Based on a Stephen King story, it stars Wil Wheaton and River Phoenix.
- The movie *Tampopo*, directed by Juzo Itami, is released in Japan. It stars Ken Watanabe and Tsutomu Yamakazi.
- The movie *Tenue de Soirée/Evening Dress* (also known as *Menage* in the United States) directed by Bertrand Blier, is released in France. It stars Gérard Depardieu, Michel Blanc, and Miou-Miou.
- The movie *The Color of Money*, directed by Martin Scorsese, is released in the United States. It stars Paul Newman and Tom Cruise.
- The movie *The Fly*, directed by David Cronenberg, is released in the United States. A remake of the 1958 movie, it stars Jeff Goldblum and Geena Davis.
- The movie *The Mission*, directed by Roland Joffé, is released in the UK. It stars Robert De Niro and Jeremy Irons. It is awarded the Palme d'Or at the French Cannes Film Festival on May 19.
- The movie *The Name of the Rose*, directed by French filmmaker Jean-Jacques Annaud, is released. Based on the novel by Umberto Eco, it stars Sean Connery and Christian Slater.
- The movie *The River's Edge* is released in the United States. It is directed by Tim Hunter and features a teenage cast including Crispin Glover, Keanu Reeves, and Ione Skye Leitch.
- The movie *Top Gun*, directed by Tony Scott, is released in the United States. It stars Tom Cruise and Kelly McGillis.
- The movie *True Stories*, directed by and starring Talking Heads vocalist David Byrne, is released in the United States. Talking Heads also release an album of the same name featuring songs from the movie.
- The Franco-Swedish coproduction *Offret-Sacrificatio/The Sacrifice*, the last movie to be directed by Andrei Tarkovsky, is released. It stars Erland Josephson, Susan Fleetwood, and Valerie Mairesse.
- The low-budget independent movie *She's Gotta Have It*, written and directed by Spike Lee, is released in the United States. It stars Tracy Camilla Johns.

- The low-budget independent movie *Down By Law* is released in the United States. It is directed by Jim Jarmusch and stars Tom Waits, John Lurie, and Roberto Benigni.

MARCH

24 The 1985 Academy Awards take place. Best Actor: William Hurt, for *Kiss of the Spider Woman*; Best Supporting Actor: Don Ameche, for *Cocoon*; Best Actress: Geraldine Page, for *The Trip to Bountiful*; Best Supporting Actress: Anjelica Huston, for *Prizzi's Honor*; Best Picture: *Out of Africa*, directed by Sydney Pollack; Best Director: Sydney Pollack, for *Out of Africa*.

25 CNN's Ted Turner buys MGM-UA, gaining the right to show the studio's pictures on his cable network.

MAY

19 At the Cannes Film Festival in France, the Palme d'Or is awarded to Roland Joffé's British movie, *The Mission*. Alain Cavalier's *Thérèse* wins the Jury Prize.

SEPTEMBER

1 David Puttnam becomes the first British producer to hold a senior position in a major U.S. movie studio when he becomes chief of production for Columbia Pictures.

Literature and Language

- *William Shakespeare: The Complete Works*, edited by Stanley Wells and Gary Taylor, is published.
- English novelist Fay Weldon publishes her novel *The Shrapnel Academy*.
- The English writer John Le Carré publishes his novel *A Perfect Spy*.
- The English writer Kingsley Amis publishes his novel *The Old Devils*, which wins the Booker Prize.
- The final volume of the *Supplement to the Oxford English Dictionary* is published.
- The German writer Günter Grass publishes his novel *Die Rättin/The Rat*.
- The Indian writer Vikram Seth publishes *The Golden Gate*, a novel in verse.
- The Japanese writer Endo Shusaku publishes his novel *Scandal*.
- The Japanese-born English writer Kazuo Ishiguro publishes his novel *An Artist of the Floating World*.
- The New Zealand writer Fleur Adcock publishes her poetry collection *The Incident Book*.
- The Nobel Prize for Literature is awarded to the Nigerian (Yoruba) poet and dramatist Wole Soyinka.
- The Pulitzer Prize for Biography is awarded to Elizabeth Frank for *Louise Bogan: A Portrait*, the Pulitzer Prize for Poetry is awarded to Henry Taylor for *The Flying Change*, and the Pulitzer Prize for Fiction is awarded to Larry McMurty for *Lonesome Dove*.
- The U.S. writer Garrison Keillor publishes his radio monologues *Lake Wobegon Days*.
- The U.S. writer Louise Erdrich publishes her novel *The Beet Queen*.
- The U.S. writer Paul Auster publishes his novel sequence *New York Trilogy*.

- The U.S. writer Peter Taylor publishes his novel *A Summons to Memphis*, which wins a Pulitzer prize.
- The U.S. writer Richard Ford publishes his novel *The Sportswriter*.
- The U.S. writer William Gaddis publishes his novel *Carpenter's Gothic*.
- U.S. writer John Updike publishes his novel *Roger's Version*.
- *Answered Prayers*, a novel by U.S. writer Truman Capote, is published posthumously.

FEBRUARY

26 In the United States, the poet Robert Penn Warren is named the first official poet laureate by the Librarian of Congress, Daniel Boorstin.

Music

- As sales of singles decline by more than 25%, album sales are on the increase.
- The British pop singer Elvis Costello releases the albums *Blood and Chocolate* and *King of America*.
- The English pop singer Elton John releases "Nikita."
- The first digital audio tape (DAT) recorders are demonstrated in Japan.
- The German composer Udo Zimmermann completes the second version of his opera *Die Weisse Rose/The White Rose*. The original version was completed in 1967.
- The Japanese composer Toru Takemitsu completes his chamber work *Rain Dreaming*.
- The opera *Die schwarze Maske/The Black Mask*, by the Polish composer Krzysztof Penderecki, is first performed, in Salzburg, Austria.
- The opera *The Mask of Orpheus*, by the English composer Harrison Birtwistle, is first performed, at the Coliseum in London, England.
- The opera *Yan Tan Tethera*, by the English composer Harrison Birtwistle, is first performed, on television in Britain.
- The Russian composer Sofia Gubaidulina completes her symphony in 12 movements *Stimmen... Verstummen.../ Silent Voices*.
- The South African composer Kevin Volans completes his String Quartet No. 1 (*White Man Sleeps*).
- The U.S. composer Elliott Carter completes his String Quartet No. 4 and his orchestral work *A Celebration of 100 x 150 Notes*, the first of his *Three Celebrations*.
- The U.S. composer John Harbison completes *The Flight into Egypt*. It is a vocal work for four-part chorus of mixed voices and orchestra accompaniment.
- The U.S. composer John Cage completes his *But what about the noise of crumpling paper ...* for percussion instruments.

FEBRUARY

25 The 1985–86 Grammy Awards are held. Best Album: *No Jacket Required* by Phil Collins; Best Record: "We Are the World" by United States for Africa; Best Male Pop Vocalist: Phil Collins; Best Female Pop Vocalist: Whitney Houston for "Saving All My Love for You;" Best Pop Group: United States for Africa for "We Are the World."

MARCH

12 The U.S. pop group Hüsker Dü releases the album *Candy Apple Grey*.

APRIL

19 The British pop group the Pet Shop Boys releases the single "West End Girls" and the album *Please*.

19 The British pop group Simply Red releases the album *Picture Book*.

19 The U.S. rock singer Prince releases "Kiss" and the album *Parade – Music from 'Under The Cherry Moon.'*

JUNE

14 The British rock singer Peter Gabriel releases the album *So*. His single "Sledgehammer" wins awards for its innovative video.

14 The U.S. pop group Run DMC releases the album *Raisin' Hell*.

28 The English pop group Genesis releases the album *Invisible Touch*.

JULY

19 The British pop group the Smiths releases the album *The Queen is Dead*.

19 The U.S. pop singer Madonna releases the album *True Blue*, the best-selling album of 1986.

SEPTEMBER

13 U.S. musician Paul Simon's album *Graceland*, with its cross-cultural mix of Creole, Mexican, and African elements, is released to great critical acclaim.

NOVEMBER

29 The U.S. rock singer Bruce Springsteen releases the album *Live, 1975–1985*.

Theater and Dance

• The musical *Chess*, with lyrics by Tim Rice and music by Bjorn Ulvaeus and Benny Anderson, is first performed, in London, England.

• The play *Breaking the Code*, by the English writer Hugh Whitemore, is first performed, at the Haymarket Theatre in London, England,

• The play *Fences*, by the U.S. writer August Wilson, is first performed, at the James Earl Jones Theater in New York, New York.

• The Pulitzer Prize for Drama is not awarded this year.

• The U.S. writer Larry Kramer completes *The Normal Heart*, a play dealing with the issue of AIDS.

OCTOBER

• The musical *Phantom of the Opera*, with lyrics by Charles Hart and music by Andrew Lloyd Webber, is first performed, at Her Majesty's Theatre in London, England. Despite critical reservations that the show is lightweight, it is very popular and will run in London and on tour for more than ten years.

Thought and Scholarship

• French sociologist Jean Baudrillard publishes *America*.

• The Pulitzer Prize for History is awarded to Walter A. McDougall for *Space Voyage*.

• The Pulitzer Prize for General Nonfiction is awarded to Joseph Lelyveld for *Move Your Shadow: South Africa, Black and White*, and to J. Anthony Lukas for *Common Ground: A Turbulent Decade in the Lives of Three American Families*.

• U.S. former official and congressman David Stockman publishes *The Triumph of Politics: How the Reagan Revolution Failed*.

• U.S. historian Arthur M. Schlesinger, Jr., publishes *The Cycles of American History*.

• U.S. historian Bernard Bailyn publishes *The Peopling of British North America*.

• U.S. philosopher D. K. Lewis publishes *On the Plurality of Worlds*.

• U.S. philosopher Thomas Nagel publishes *The View from Nowhere*.

BIRTHS & DEATHS

JANUARY

2 Bill Veeck, U.S. entrepreneur and baseball team owner famous for his promotions that lured fans to games, dies in Chicago, Illinois (71).

4 Christopher Isherwood, Anglo-U.S. novelist and playwright, dies in Santa Monica, California (81).

7 Juan Pérez Rulfo, Mexican writer, a founder of the "magic realism" school of writing, dies in Mexico City, Mexico (67).

8 Pierre Léon Marie Fournier, French cellist, dies in Geneva, Switzerland (79).

14 Donna Reed, U.S. film and television actress, dies in Beverly Hills, California (74).

15 James H. Crowley, U.S. football player and coach who played halfback and was one of the famous "Four Horsemen" of Notre Dame, dies in Saranton, Pennsylvania (83).

23 Joseph Beuys, German avant garde sculptor and performance artist, dies in Düsseldorf, Germany (64).

24 L(afayette) Ron(ald) Hubbard, U.S. author and religious leader, founder of the controversial Church of Scientology, dies in San Luis Obispo, California (74).

28 Christa McAuliffe, U.S. schoolteacher and the first civilian to participate in the U.S. space program, dies in the explosion of the space shuttle *Challenger* at Cape Canaveral, Florida (37).

FEBRUARY

6 Minoru Yamasaki, U.S. architect, designer of New York's World Trade Center, dies in Detroit, Michigan (73).

11 Frank Herbert, U.S. science fiction writer whose books include the "Dune" series, dies in Madison, Wisconsin (65).

17 Red Ruffing, U.S. baseball player, right-handed pitcher for the New York Yankees, dies in Mayfield, Ohio (81).

26 Jacques Plante, Canadian hockey player, a goalkeeper for 19 years, dies in Geneva, Switzerland (57).

28 Olof Palme, Swedish prime minister 1969–76 and 1982–86, is assassinated in Stockholm, Sweden (59).

MARCH

6 Georgia O'Keeffe, U.S. artist who painted semiabstract forms of color and light and many large flower paintings, dies in Santa Fe, New Mexico (98).

8 Hubert Fichte, German realist writer, dies in Hamburg, West Germany (50).

10 Ray Milland, British actor who appeared in films in both the United States and the UK and won an Academy Award in 1945 for his portrayal of an alcoholic in *The Lost Weekend*, dies (79).

18 Bernard Malamud, U.S. author who won a Pulitzer prize for *The Fixer*, dies in New York, New York (71).

23 Moses Feinstein, U.S. religious leader and Jewish Orthodox rabbi, dies in New York, New York (91).

30 James Cagney, U.S. film actor who often played gangsters or criminals, dies in Millbrook, New York (86).

30 John Anthony Ciardi, U.S. poet, critic, translator, and author of *How Does a Poem Mean?*, dies in Edison, New Jersey (69).

APRIL

7 Leonid Vitalyvich Kantorovich, Soviet economist who applied the technique of linear programming to improve economic forecasting, dies in Moscow, USSR (74).

14 Simone de Beauvoir, French existentialist writer, philosopher, and feminist, dies in Paris, France (78).

22 Mircea Eliade, U.S. religious scholar who attempted to relate religious beliefs to primordial myths, dies in Chicago, Illinois (84).

23 Harold Arlen, U.S. popular composer and songwriter, dies in New York, New York (81).

23 Otto Preminger, Austrian-born U.S. film actor, director, and producer, dies (80).

26 Broderick Crawford, U.S. actor in films and television who won an Academy Award for *All the King's Men*, dies (74).

27 J(osef) Allen Hynek, U.S. astrophysicist who studied UFOs and gave some respectability to the subject, dies in Scottsdale, Arizona (75).

MAY

9 Tenzing Norgay, Nepalese sherpa who, with Edmund Hillary, was the first person to reach the summit of Mt. Everest, dies in Darjeeling, India (72).

11 Fritz Pollard, U.S. football player and coach who encouraged black players into the sport, dies in Silver Springs, Maryland (92).

20 Helen Brook Taussig, U.S. cardiologist, developer of an operation to treat babies with congenital heart defects, dies in West Chester, Pennsylvania (87).

31 (Leo) James Rainwater, U.S. physicist whose work concerned atomic nuclei, dies in Yonkers, New York (68).

JUNE

13 Benny Goodman, U.S. jazz and classical clarinettist and orchestra leader in the Swing era, dies in New York, New York (77).

14 Alan Jay Lerner, U.S. lyricist who collaborated with Frederick Loewe for many years writing Broadway musicals, dies in New York, New York (68).

14 Jorge Luis Borges, Argentine poet, short-story writer, and essayist, who established the modernist Ultraist movement in South America, dies in Geneva, Switzerland (86).

17 Kate Smith, U.S. singer known for singing "God Bless America," dies in Raleigh, North Carolina (77).

26 Moses Finley, U.S.-born British historian who specialized in the society, economy, and political processes of ancient Greece, dies in Cambridge, England (74).

JULY

3 Rudy Vallee, U.S. singer popular in the 1920s and 1930s, dies in Hollywood, California (84).

8 Hyman George Rickover, U.S. naval officer who developed the USS *Nautilus*, the world's first nuclear-powered submarine, dies in Arlington, Virginia (86).

14 Raymond Loewy, French-born U.S. industrial designer, dies in Monte Carlo, Monaco (92).

24 Fritz Albert Lipmann, German-born U.S. biochemist in the field of cellular metabolism, dies in Poughkeepsie, New York (87).

26 Averell Harriman, U.S. diplomat, a negotiator in the Nuclear Test Ban Treaty of 1963, dies in Yorktown Heights, New York (94).

AUGUST

2 Roy Marcus Cohn, U.S. lawyer, examiner during Senator McCarthy's witch-hunt for supposed communists during the 1950s, dies in New York, New York. (59).

3 Beryl Markham, British aviator and the first woman to fly solo west across the Atlantic, dies in Nairobi, Kenya (83).

31 Henry Moore, English sculptor of abstract bronze and stone figures, dies in Much Hadham, Hertfordshire, England (88).

31 Urhokaleua Kekkonen, Finnish president 1956–81 who was determined to retain Finland's independence from the USSR, dies in Helsinki, Finland (85).

OCTOBER

5 Hal B. Wallis, U.S. producer of films including *Casablanca* and *True Grit*, dies in Rancho Mirage, California (88).

19 Samora Moisès Machel, Mozambique's president from 1975 until his death, dies in an airplane crash in South Africa (53).

22 Albert Szent-Györgyi, Hungarian biochemist who isolated vitamin C, dies in Woods Hole, Massachusetts (93).

23 Edward Albert Doisy, U.S. biochemist who discovered vitamin K, dies in St. Louis, Missouri (92).

31 Robert Sanderson Mulliken, U.S. chemist and physicist who worked on the electronic structure of molecules, dies in Arlington, Virginia (90).

NOVEMBER

8 Vyacheslav Molotov, Russian diplomat who negotiated at the international conferences following World War II, dies near Moscow, USSR (96).

29 Cary Grant, British-born U.S. film actor, dies in Davenport, Iowa (82).

DECEMBER

8 Anatoly Marchenko, Soviet dissident, author of *My Testimony* describing his time in a labor camp, dies in Chistopol, USSR (48).

15 Serge Lifar, Russian-born French dancer and choreographer, ballet master of the Paris Opéra Ballet, dies in Lausanne, Switzerland (81).

21 Nikolaas Tinbergen, Dutch zoologist and ethologist, dies in Oxford, England (79).

27 Dumas Malone, U.S. historian, author of *Jefferson and his Time*, dies in Charlottesville, Virginia (94).

29 Harold Macmillan, British politician, Conservative prime minister 1957–63, dies in Birch Grove, Sussex, England (92).

SOCIETY

Everyday Life

- Asians account for the first time for half of all legal immigrants to the United States.
- For the first time, the number of women in the United States holding professional jobs is greater than that of men, by 29,000.
- Nintendo video games, including *Super Mario Brothers*, are launched and quickly gain worldwide popularity. Sophisticated programming and graphics ensure their success and by 1990 sales exceed $3 billion.
- Over this year, fitness foods account for 10% of the $300 billion U.S. retail food industry.
- Popsicle Industries, makers of the Popsicle, 100 million of which are sold each year, announces it will use only one stick.
- The number of videocassette recorders sold in the United States exceeds $13 million.
- The tuxedo, first worn in New York, New York, in 1886, has its 100th anniversary.
- The U.S. Census Bureau reports 2,220,000 unwed couples.
- U.S. CD sales are over $930 million this year.

MAY
20 U.S. actor Clint Eastwood is elected mayor of his hometown, Carmel, California.
25 An estimated 30 million people take part in Sportaid's "Race Against Time," a series of fun runs held around the world to raise money for the starving people of Africa.
25 To draw attention to the plight of the homeless, approximately 6 million people form a human chain— Hands Across America—most of the way from New York to California.

JUNE
19 Two Americans die from cyanide poisoning after taking Excedrin capsules that had been tampered with. The manufacturer, Bristol-Myers, Inc., recalls its capsules.

SEPTEMBER
12 A new wage offer ends a bitter year-long strike at the Hormel meatpacking plant in Minnesota, United States.
21 Britain's Prince of Wales admits that he talks to plants.

DECEMBER
31 A fire in the Dupont Plaza Hotel, Puerto Rico, kills 193 New Year's revelers.

Media and Communication

- *Cosmopolitan* is the favored magazine of U.S. college students.
- Twenty-six U.S. newspapers discontinue their evening editions in favor of morning editions.

FEBRUARY
9–10 *Dress Gray*, a fact-based movie adaption by Gore Vidal about a murder at the West Point military academy, is shown on U.S. television. It stars Hal Holbrook, Lloyd Bridges, and Alec Baldwin.

APRIL
27 A "video pirate" interrupts transmissions on the Home Box Office cable service in New York, New York, with a message announcing that he is not prepared to pay for cable service.

JUNE
1 The U.S. Senate allows its proceedings to be televised but discontinues in July.

AUGUST
1 Sylvester Stallone is named the best-paid actor by *Company* magazine, getting around $12 million a movie. The top actress (Barbra Streisand) gets $5 million.

SEPTEMBER
- Oprah Winfrey's Chicago-based talk show is syndicated on national television in the United States, dominating daytime ratings.
21 The 1985–86 Emmy Awards for television are held. Best Drama Series: *Cagney and Lacey*; Best Comedy Series: *The Golden Girls*; Best Actor in a Drama: William Daniels, for *St Elsewhere*; Best Actress in a Drama: Sharon Gless, for *Cagney and Lacey*; Best Actor in a Comedy: Michael J. Fox, for *Family Ties*; Best Actress in a Comedy: Betty White, for *The Golden Girls*.
26–June 18, 1990 *A.L.F*, a sitcom about an alien living with a suburban family on Earth, is shown on U.S. televison.

OCTOBER
3 *LA Law*, a TV drama that follows the lives of attorneys employed by a high-powered Los Angeles law firm, first appears on U.S. television.

NOVEMBER
21 *On Trial: Lee Harvey Oswald*, an imaginary trial of the alleged assassin of John F. Kennedy, is shown on U.S. television, with Vincent Bugliosi as the prosecutor and Gerry Spence as the defense attorney.

Religion

- A major Vatican document, "Instruction on Christian Freedom and Liberation," recommends passive resistance against injustice and accepts armed struggle as "a last resort to put an end to obvious and prolonged tyranny."
- Religious denominations in the United States (in millions): Roman Catholics 52.9; Baptists 23.7; Methodists 12.6; Lutherans 7.8; Mormons 3.8; Presbyterians 3.6; Episcopalians 2.5; Greek Orthodox 1.9; Jews 5.8.
- The Vatican declares Father Charles Curran of the United States unfit to teach Catholic theology because of his writings on divorce, contraception, abortion, and homosexuality.

Sports

- Susan Butcher becomes the first woman to win the Iditarod Trail Dog Sled Race from Anchorage to Nome, Alaska.
- The average salary of a major league baseball player is $412,000, with 58 players earning over $1 million a year.

- The Japanese cyclist Koichi Nakano wins the World Professional Sprint Championship for the tenth successive year.

JANUARY

1   Sportswriters pick Oklahoma as college football's best team for the 1985 season.

14 The National Collegiate Athletic Association vote in favor of drug testing, both for championship events and as an entrance requirement for student athletes.

16 The Popplewell inquiry into crowd safety and control at sports grounds, commissioned after the Bradford City disaster of May 11, 1985, is published in Britain. Among its recommendations is the implementation of a national identity card program for supporters.

26 The Chicago Bears defeat the New England Patriots 46–10 in New Orleans to win Super Bowl XX. The game attracts an estimated U.S. television audience of 127 million, the largest in U.S. television history.

FEBRUARY

8   U.S. national figure skating champions are: Debi Thomas (the first black person to win a singles title); Brian Boitano; Gillian Waschsman and Todd Waggoner, pairs; Renee Roca and Donald Adair, dance.

28 Baseball Commissioner Peter Ueberroth announces the suspension of 11 major league players for illegal drug use. Most of the players had been involved in widely publicized federal trials of drug dealers in Pittsburgh, Pennsylvania.

APRIL

13 The U.S. golfer Jack Nicklaus, aged 46, wins his sixth U.S. Masters tournament at Augusta, Georgia.

29 Boston Redsox pitcher Roger Clemens achieves a major league baseball record of 20 strikeouts in a single game, against the Seattle Mariners.

MAY

3   Bill Shoemaker, on Ferdinand, is at 54 the oldest jockey to win the Kentucky Derby.

16–24 The Montreal Canadiens beat the Calgary Flames to win the Stanley Cup.

24 Canadian Hervé Filion becomes the first driver in harness racing in the United States to achieve 10,000 wins, at Yonkers Raceway, New York.

26–June 8 The Boston Celtics win their 16th National Basketball Association (NBA) title, beating the Houston Rockets four games to two.

31 U.S. race-car driver Bobby Rahal wins the Indianapolis 500.

JUNE

15 The U.S. golfer Ray Floyd, at the age of 43, becomes the oldest winner of the U.S. Open, in Shinnecock Hills, New York.

29 In the soccer World Cup held in Mexico, Argentina beats West Germany 3–2 in the final in Mexico City, before a crowd of 114,000.

JULY

5–20 The first Goodwill Games are held in Moscow, USSR, conceived by U.S. entrepreneur Ted Turner to promote goodwill between the United States and the USSR following the boycotts of the 1980 and 1984 Olympic Games. Over 3,000 athletes from 79 countries compete in 18 different sports.

20 The Australian golfer Greg Norman wins the British Open at Turnberry, Scotland, the first Australian to do so for 21 years.

27 Greg LeMond becomes the first U.S. cyclist to win the Tour de France bicycle race.

AUGUST

- The women golfers of Britain and Ireland win the Curtis Cup at Prairie Dunes, Kansas; this is their first victory in the United States and their first in the series since 1956.

4   The United States Football League, formed as a rival to the NFL in 1983, announces that it is canceling its 1986 season, six days after winning just one dollar in a $1.69 billion antitrust law suit against the NFL.

SEPTEMBER

- At the U.S. Open tennis championships all four semifinalists in the men's and women's singles are Czechoslovaks or Czech born: Ivan Lendl, Miloslav Mecir, Martina Navratilova, and Helena Sukova. Lendl and Navratilova win.

7   Instant video replays operated by an extra official are used for the first time in the National Football League (NFL) in the United States to decide disputed plays in certain situations.

27 The British boxer Lloyd Honeyghan becomes the undisputed welterweight world champion when he stops the holder, Don Curry of the United States, in the sixth round of their title fight in Atlantic City, New Jersey, in the United States.

OCTOBER

18–27 In baseball's World Series, the New York Mets come back from the brink of defeat in the sixth game to defeat the Boston Red Sox by four games to three.

NOVEMBER

- In the final of the World Open squash championships in Toulouse, France, Ross Norman of New Zealand becomes the first person to beat Pakistan's Jahangir Khan since April 1981.

22 George Branhamm III wins the Professional Bowlers Association Brunswick Memorial Open to become the first black American to win a major professional bowling event.

22 Mike Tyson of the United States beats Trevor Berbick of Canada in two rounds to win the World Boxing Council World Heavyweight title in Las Vegas, Nevada, in the United States; at 20 years old, he is the youngest champion ever.

DECEMBER

9   The British greyhound Ballyregan Bob is retired after winning a world record 32 consecutive races.

1987

POLITICS, GOVERNMENT, AND ECONOMICS

Business and Economics

- The Global Fund for Women is founded.

MARCH

25 The Belgian government mints ECU coins: these are legal tender in Belgium.

JULY

22 The U.S. General Electric Company announces the sale of its consumer electronics division to French electronics company Thomson.

OCTOBER

19 The New York Dow Jones Industrial Average falls 508.32 points (23%) on "Black Monday," precipitating large falls in stock prices across the world.

DECEMBER

19 U.S. oil company Texaco agrees to pay $3 billion to its rival Pennzoil in compensation for interference with a Pennzoil bid for the Getty Oil Company.

31 The U.S. dollar reaches an all-time low against major currencies.

Human Rights

- The U.S. Supreme Court rules in the case of *McCleskey v. Kemp* that the statistical demonstration of racism in the application of the death penalty is not sufficient to make it a cruel and unusual punishment, and thus unconstitutional.

Politics and Government

- Family clinics in the United States that give counsel on abortion are denied federal aid.
- The U.S. Supreme Court decrees invalid state laws requiring schools to give equal time to "creationist science," since they violate the Constitution's separation of church and state.

JANUARY

6 The Portuguese Council of State agrees to restore Macao to China before 2000. On April 13, Portugal signs an agreement to return Macao in 1999.

9 The South African government bans all reporting of the activities of the African National Congress (ANC).

13 The U.S. Supreme Court upholds a California law obliging employers to grant pregnant women up to four months' unpaid leave.

15 Arms control talks between the United States and the USSR resume in Geneva, Switzerland.

20 The archbishop of Canterbury's envoy Terry Waite disappears in Beirut, while on a mission to obtain the release of Western hostages. On February 2, he is reported to be held "under arrest" in the city.

21 A new coalition government takes office in Austria under Franz Vranitzky.

27 The Soviet leader Mikhail Gorbachev proposes reforms in the USSR's political system, including secret ballots for the election of party officials.

27 U.S. president Ronald Reagan issues a public statement that he "regrets" the Iran–Contra arms deals.

FEBRUARY

- The finance ministers of six Western countries agree on the Louvre Accord, proposing measures to stabilize the dollar.

5 Iran launches a missile attack on Baghdad, capital of its opponent in the Iran–Iraq war. On February 19, a truce is agreed in the "war of cities," in which both sides have inflicted damage on heavily populated areas.

9 Sino-Soviet talks on the historical border dispute between the two countries are held in Moscow, USSR— the first since 1979.

10 Robert McFarlane, the former head of the National Security Council in the United States, attempts suicide after he is implicated in the Iran–Contra Affair.

10 The Soviet government announces the release of 140 political dissidents.

17 The Fianna Fáil party, led by Charles Haughey, is returned as the largest party in the Irish general election.

20 Congress votes to cut off U.S. aid to the Nicaraguan Contra rebels.

22 Syrian forces numbering 4,000 enter West Beirut in an effort to end fighting between Shiite Muslim and Druze militias.

26 The report in the United States of the Tower Commission, which investigated the management of the White House during the period of the Iran–Contra Affair, is critical of the White House chief of staff, Donald Regan. On February 27, Regan is replaced by former senator Howard Baker.

28 The Soviet leader Mikhail Gorbachev proposes a separate agreement abolishing intermediate-range nuclear weapons in Europe and drops the USSR's insistence on the curtailment of the U.S. Star Wars program.

MARCH

2–4 Proposals from both the United States and the USSR on the limitation or abolition of medium-range nuclear missiles in Europe are tabled at the Geneva arms talks in Switzerland.

4 The U.S. president Ronald Reagan accepts full responsibility for the Iran–Contra Affair.

10 Charles Haughey of the Fianna Fáil party is elected Taoiseach (prime minister) of Ireland for the third time.

16 Massachusetts governor and Democrat Michael Dukakis enters the 1988 U.S. presidential race.

18 The U.S. Congress votes to raise the rural freeway speed limit from 55 to 65 miles per hour.

19 The Czechoslovak leader Gustav Husák announces political and economic reforms.

31 The Superior Court judgment in the "Baby M" case in the United States denies parental rights to a surrogate mother.

APRIL

1 Japan privatizes its national railroads by transferring the system to seven private companies.

7–8 Syrian forces relieve the Palestinian refugee camps of Shatila and Bourj-el-Barajneh, south of Beirut, after a five-month siege by the Shiite Amal militia.

8 The state of siege in Paraguay, in force since 1947, is finally allowed to lapse by the administration of General Alfredo Stroessner.

10 The Soviet leader Mikhail Gorbachev announces that the USSR is prepared to negotiate on short- as well as intermediate-range nuclear missiles.

12 The general election in Fiji is won by an Indian-dominated coalition led by Timoci Bavadra.

17 Tamil terrorists ambush several buses near Trincomalee in Sri Lanka, killing 129 people.

17–19 Argentine army officers mutiny in an unsuccessful attempt to overthrow the government of President Raúl Alfonsín.

20–26 The Palestinian National Council, meeting in Algiers, reelects Yassir Arafat as its leader but reduces his authority.

25 An Irish Republican Army (IRA) car bomb in Northern Ireland kills the senior Ulster judge Sir Maurice Gibson and his wife.

27 The U.S. Justice Department bars the Austrian president Kurt Waldheim from entering the United States because of his alleged involvement in Nazi atrocities during World War II.

MAY

1 Quebec agrees to sign an amended Canadian constitution recognizing the state as a "distinct society."

6 The ruling National Party wins a sweeping victory in the South African general election, with the far right Conservatives becoming the second largest party.

8 Nine Irish Republican Army (IRA) men are killed in a battle with police and troops after an attempted bomb attack on a police station in Loughgall, County Armagh, Northern Ireland.

10 The Nationalist Party, led by Edward Fenech Adami, defeats the ruling Malta Labour Party of Mifsud Bonnici in the Maltese general election.

11 The Indian government imposes direct rule on the state of Punjab in the face of continuing unrest between the Sikh and Hindu communities.

14 A military coup in Fiji, led by Colonel Sitiveni Rabuka, overthrows the elected government of Timoci Bavadra.

14 Egypt breaks off diplomatic relations with Iran over its financing of Islamic fundamentalism.

17 An Iraqi Exocet missile hits USS *Stark* in the Persian Gulf, killing 37 U.S. naval personnel. Iraq subsequently explains that the missile was launched accidentally.

28 A 19-year-old West German, Mathias Rust, lands a small plane in Moscow's Red Square. The following day, the commander in chief of the USSR's air defenses is dismissed.

JUNE

1 Rashid Karami, the Lebanese prime minister, is assassinated by a bomb explosion that destroys the helicopter in which he is traveling.

4 The West German Bundestag (parliament) endorses the U.S.–Soviet plan to eliminate medium-range nuclear missiles from Europe.

11 Margaret Thatcher leads the Conservative Party to a third consecutive win in the British general elections.

14 The Socialist Party makes large gains in the Italian general election.

21 Multicandidate lists are introduced in 5% of constituencies in local elections in the USSR.

25 Károly Grósz, a conservative, becomes Hungary's prime minister and later introduces an austerity program to deal with economic problems.

JULY

1 Members of the European Community complete ratification of the Single European Act. It comes into force on July 1, with the aim of starting the creation of a single market in Europe by 1993. It also introduces qualified majority voting in the European Council of Ministers.

1 U.S. president Ronald Reagan nominates conservative judge Robert Bork as replacement for Supreme Court Justice Lewis Powell.

7 In evidence before the Iran–Contra hearings in the United States, Lieutenant Colonel Oliver North claims his actions were sanctioned by his superiors.

14 Opposition parties become legal in Taiwan. The Democratic Progressive Party, formed in 1986, emerges as the main opposition to the ruling Kuomintang government under Chiang Ching-Kuo.

17 In the Iran–Contra hearings in the United States, Rear Admiral John Poindexter, President Reagan's National Security Adviser, states that he authorized the diversion of funds to Contra rebels.

20 The United Nations Security Council adopts Resolution 598 calling on Iran and Iraq to implement an immediate cease-fire in their long-running war.

21 The United States offers naval protection to Kuwaiti tankers in the Persian Gulf.

22 The Soviet leader Mikhail Gorbachev offers to dismantle all short- and medium-range nuclear missiles in the USSR.

29 Sri Lankan president Junius Jayawardene and Indian prime minister Rajiv Gandhi sign an agreement aimed at ending communal violence in Sri Lanka.

AUGUST

4 Tamil rebels in Sri Lanka agree to surrender their arms to an Indian peacekeeping force.

4 The U.S. Federal Communications Commission scraps the law requiring broadcasters to air both sides of controversial issues.

8 The Arias Plan for peace in Central America is signed by the presidents of Guatemala, El Salvador, Honduras, Nicaragua, and Costa Rica.

12 U.S. president Ronald Reagan insists that he was not told of the diversion of funds from arms sales to the Nicaraguan Contras.

19 A gunman, Michael Ryan, kills 14 people in Hungerford, England, before shooting himself. On September 22, the British government bans automatic weapons of the kind used by Ryan.

19 The United States announces the restoration of full diplomatic relations with Syria.

19 Zimbabwe's House of Assembly agrees a change to the constitution, abolishing the 20 seats reserved for whites under the 1979 Lancaster House Agreement.

SEPTEMBER

3 A coup in Burundi ends the rule of Colonel Jean-Baptiste Bagaza, and a new Military Council for National Redemption is formed under the leadership of Major Pierre Buyoya.

6 The Radical Civic Union Party of President Raúl Alfonsín loses its majority in Argentina's Chamber of Deputies.

7 The East German leader Erich Honecker begins a five-day official visit to West Germany, the first by an East German leader.

11 The United Nations secretary-general Javier Pérez de Cuellar begins a peace mission to end the Iran–Iraq War.

15 Diplomatic relations are established between Albania and West Germany.

15–17 The U.S. secretary of state George Shultz and the Soviet foreign minister Eduard Shevardnadze reach agreement in principle on the elimination of intermediate-range nuclear weapons.

17 A constitutional affairs committee of the President's Council in South Africa recommends repeal of the 1953 Separate Amenities Act and relaxation of the 1950 Group Areas Act.

25 Colonel Sitiveni Rabuka leads the second coup within a year against the government of Fiji.

OCTOBER

1 Violent demonstrations take place against Chinese rule in the Tibetan capital, Lhasa.

3 Canada and the United States agree on moves to reduce tariffs and economic barriers in North America.

6 Colonel Sitiveni Rabuka declares Fiji a republic, formally severing its legal ties with Britain.

8 An inquest jury in Britain returns a verdict of unlawful killing on the 187 victims of the Zeebrugge *Herald of Free Enterprise* ferry disaster.

13–17 A Commonwealth Conference is held in Vancouver, Canada. Britain dissents from the conference declaration on South Africa.

15 Captain Blaise Compaoré leads a military coup in Burkina Faso. Prime Minister Thomas Sankara and eight others die.

15 Queen Elizabeth II of Great Britain and Northern Ireland accepts the resignation of Ratu Sir Penaia Ganilau as governor-general of Fiji, acknowledging the end of a 113-year colonial link.

19 U.S. destroyers and commandos attack Iranian oil installations in the Persian Gulf.

23 A U.S. Senate committee rejects Robert Bork, nominated by President Ronald Reagan, as a justice of the Supreme Court.

24 After 30 years' exclusion, the Teamsters Union is readmitted to the AFL-CIO (American Federation of Labor and Congress of Industrial Organizations).

25–November 1 At the 13th Communist Party Congress in Beijing, Deng Xiaoping retires as general secretary and as a Politburo member.

NOVEMBER

1 French authorities uncover an arms haul on the trawler *Eksund*, thought to be destined for the Irish Republican Army (IRA).

2 The Soviet leader Mikhail Gorbachev, in a speech to mark the 70th anniversary of the Russian Revolution, criticizes Stalin for political errors.

7 Douglas Ginsburg, second Reagan nominee for U.S. Supreme Court justice, withdraws his name after allegations of previous drug abuse.

8 Irish Republican Army (IRA) bombs explode in Northern Ireland at a Remembrance Day service in Enniskillen, County Fermanagh, killing 11 people. On November 15, the Roman Catholic bishops in Northern Ireland and the Irish Republic denounce IRA violence.

8–11 At an Arab summit meeting in Jordan, Syria's president Hafez al-Assad agrees to end his country's political and military support of Iran in its conflict with Iraq.

12 Boris Yeltsin is dismissed as chief of the Moscow Communist Party after he criticizes the slow pace of reforms.

18 A report of the joint U.S. Senate/House of Representatives Iran–Contra Committee blames President Ronald Reagan for the administration's illegal activities. Eight Republicans refuse to sign the report.

23–24 U.S. secretary of state George Shultz and Soviet foreign minister Eduard Shevardnadze agree on a treaty to eliminate all intermediate-range nuclear weapons.

24 Li Peng succeeds Zhao Ziyang as prime minister of China.

24 The Irish government agrees new extradition arrangements with Britain, removing the right of terrorist suspects to claim exemption on the grounds of legitimate political motivation.

24–December 4 Cuban inmates of Atlanta federal prison riot in protest at plans to deport them to Cuba.

DECEMBER

7–10 At a U.S.–Soviet summit in Washington, D.C., U.S. president Ronald Reagan and Soviet leader Mikhail Gorbachev agree to eliminate intermediate-range nuclear forces.

17 Gustav Husák resigns as general secretary of the Czechoslovak Communist Party, to be succeeded by Miloš Jakeš.

17 The U.S. Congress bans Japanese construction firms from bidding for public building works in the United States.

22 The United Nations Security Council criticizes Israeli action against Palestinians protesting on the West Bank and in the Gaza Strip.
22 Zimbabwe's prime minister Robert Mugabe and the opposition leader Joshua Nkomo agree to unite their ZANU (Zimbabwe African National Union) and ZAPU (Zimbabwe African People's Union) parties under the name ZANU–PF (ZANU–Popular Front).
28 Tunisia and Libya restore diplomatic relations.

SCIENCE, TECHNOLOGY, AND MEDICINE

Agriculture

- Chinese scientists insert genes controlling human growth hormones into goldfish and loach; they grow to four times the normal size.
- The development of the first bio-insecticides is announced in the United States; they eliminate insects without harming the environment.
- The first genetically altered bacteria are released into the environment in the United States; they protect crops against frost.

APRIL
24 Tests are carried out on gene-altered bacteria to aid agriculture, despite scientists' fears that loss of control is inevitable.

NOVEMBER
18 The Ethiopian government announces that 5 million people are facing starvation in its northern provinces.

Computing

- Japanese firm Sega Electronics introduces a three-dimensional video game, requiring special liquid crystal glasses to view the images.
- U.S. firm 3 D Systems invents stereolithography—a process of quickly making plastic prototypes of various objects. The prototype is first drawn by a computer, then an ultraviolet laser etches the object in a reservoir of transparent liquid plastic, instantly polymerizing it; the prototype can then simply be removed from the reservoir.
- U.S. researcher David Miller invents the Symmetric Self-Electro-Optic Effect Device (S-Seed); it alters its reflectivity to light when irradiated by a laser and will later be used in the first optical computers.

MARCH
9 An advanced supercomputer, the Numerical Aerodynamic Simulation Facility, enters service; it is able to make 1,720,000,000 computations per second.

Ecology

- At a conference in Montreal, Canada, an international agreement, the Montreal Protocol, is reached to limit the use of ozone-depleting chlorofluorocarbons (CFCs) by 50% by the end of the century; the agreement is later condemned by environmentalists as "too little, too late."
- The EEC (European Economic Community) declares 1987 European Year of the Environment.
- The last remaining wild Californian condor is captured and transferred to a local zoo for breeding.
- U.S. researchers prove that thunderstorm systems can propel pollutants into the lower stratosphere when they observe high levels of carbon monoxide and nitric acid at high altitude during a thunderstorm.

MARCH
5–6 An earthquake in northeastern Ecuador measuring 7.3 on the Richter scale kills more than 4,000 people.

MAY
6–June 2 Northern China is swept by forest fires in which 193 people die.

JULY
15–October 2 Tax incentives in Brazil encouraging conversion of jungle into ranch land result in an average of over 25,920 sq km/10,000 sq mi of Amazon rainforest being burned each day during a 79-day period.

Exploration

- Radio waves are observed from 3C326—believed to be a galaxy in the process of formation.
- The Soviet satellite *Cosmos* is launched; it is the 2,000th satellite.
- The USSR's *Energiya* superbooster is launched—the world's most powerful space launcher with a thrust of 3 million kg/6.6 million lb.

FEBRUARY
8–December 29 The Soviet cosmonaut Yuri Romanenko spends a record 326 days in the *Mir* space station.

Health and Medicine

- A South African woman gives birth to triplets formed from her daughter's transplanted embryos.
- A three-year-old girl in the United States receives a new liver, pancreas, small intestine, and parts of the stomach and colon; this is the first successful five-organ transplant.
- Canadian surgeons use a laser to clear a blocked coronary artery.
- German-born British geneticist Walter Bodmer and associates announce the discovery of a marker for a gene that causes cancer of the colon.
- Ignacio Navarro Madrazo discovers that the symptoms of Parkinson's disease can be alleviated by implanting cells from the adrenal gland into the brain.
- Surgeons at the University of Pennsylvania Hospital, United States, transplant an entire human knee.
- The French firm Agrotechnic invents the mechanical cow. It uses soy beans to produce a liquid similar to milk that can by digested by people allergic to milk.
- The Nobel Prize for Physiology or Medicine is awarded to Japanese molecular biologist Susumu Tonegawa for his discovery of the process by which genes alter to produce a range of different antibodies.

- The U.S. Food and Drug Administration licenses the antidepressant drug Prozac.
- U.S. researcher Hari Reddi, and his team at the National Institute of Health, discover bone morphogenetic protein—a protein that encourages bone growth. It is expected to speed up healing of fractures and bone damage done during surgery.

March

20 The AIDS treatment drug AZT is given approval by the U.S. Federal Drug Administration. Treatment costs $10,000 per year per patient and does not cure the disease, although it relieves some symptoms and does extend victims' lives.

September

- The cholesterol-lowering drug Lovastatin wins Federal Drug Administration approval.
1 Belgium becomes the first country to introduce a national smoking ban in all public buildings.

October

10 The *New York Times* announces Dr. Helen Donis-Keller's mapping of all 23 pairs of human chromosomes, allowing the location of specific genes for the prevention and treatment of genetic disorders.

Science

- A nest of fossilized dinosaur eggs is discovered in Alberta, Canada; it is the second such nest to be found.
- Archeologists discover spear points at a site in Washington, United States, from the Clovis culture complex dated to about 11,500 years ago; it is one of the oldest occupied sites in North America.
- David Page and associates announce the discovery of a gene that initiates the development of male features in mammals.
- Foxes in Belgium are immunized against rabies by using bait containing a genetically engineered vaccine, dropped from helicopters. The success of the experiment leads to a large-scale vaccination program.
- Harvey Butcher, director of the Westerbrook Synthesis Telescope in Groningen, the Netherlands, estimates that the universe is younger than 10 billion years.
- Objects the size of planets are found orbiting the stars Gamma Cephei and Epsilon Eridani.
- The James Clerk Maxwell Telescope, operated by the Royal Observatory, based in Edinburgh, Scotland, begins operation on Mauna Kea, Hawaii; its 15-m/49-ft dish makes it the largest submillimeter telescope in the world.
- The Nobel Prize for Physics is awarded jointly to German physicist Georg Bednorz and Swiss physicist Alex Müller for their discovery of high-temperature superconductors.
- U.S. chemists Donald Cram and Charles Pedersen and French chemist Jean-Marie Lehn receive the Nobel Prize for Chemistry for the development of molecules with highly selective structure-specific interactions.

February

23 Astronomers around the world observe a spectacular supernova in the Large Magellanic Cloud, the galaxy closest to ours, when a star (SN1987A) suddenly becomes a thousand times brighter than our own Sun. It is the first supernova visible to the naked eye since 1604.

April

- The U.S. Patent and Trademark Office announces its intention to allow the patenting of animals produced by genetic engineering.

Technology

c. 1987 The American Telephone and Telegraph company (AT&T) digitizes all its long-distance facilities; sounds are converted into digital form for more efficient transmission through the lines and then reconverted at the receiving end.

- A ferrofluidic paint, which contains microscopic grains of magnetic material as small as a nanometer, is developed in the United States. The paint stops the reflection of radar waves and the U.S. airforce uses it to make airplanes "invisible" to radar.
- As prices drop and the technology develops to improve the speed of transmission, fax machines become an established feature in offices.
- At a conference in Kyoto, Japan, it is announced that superconductivity has been observed at temperatures of 65 K.
- Consumer electronics companies Seiko and Ferguson jointly launch a color pocket television in the UK; it has a 6.25-cm/2.5-in LCD screen and costs £250.
- Digital audio tape cassettes, producing high-quality sound, go on sale.
- Japanese firm Nippon Zeon discovers memory plastics—plastics that change their shape at one temperature and then return to their original shape at another. Applications are envisioned in the auto industry.
- The Japanese company Citizen launches the talking watch, Voice master VX-2, which answers when asked the time.
- The world's most powerful wind-powered generator begins operating in the Orkney Islands, Scotland; it produces 3 megawatts of electricity.
- U.S. firm Diamond Sensor Systems develops the rapid blood analyzer; it can analyze the oxygen, carbon dioxide, pH, potassium, calcium, and hematocrit of the blood automatically in about two minutes.
- U.S. firm Ometron develops the vibration analyzer; based on laser interferometry, it can record vibrations as small as a fraction of the wavelength of light.
- U.S. researchers James Van House and Arthur Rich invent the positron microscope; it uses positrons instead of electrons to give an image of the material being studied.

February

12 Chinese physicist Paul Ching-Wu Chu and associates at the University of Huston, Texas, make a material that is superconducting at the temperature of liquid nitrogen—77K or –196°C/–321°F.

June

- The William Herschel telescope, set up at the Los Muchachos Observatory in the Canary Islands, begins operating: its 4.2-m/13.8-ft reflector makes it the largest British telescope.

Transportation

- Frustration on Los Angeles' freeways leads to some motorists using guns against others.
- The Canadian Communication Research Center tests an airplane with an electric motor that is powered by microwaves from the ground; it can fly indefinitely.

MARCH

6   The Townsend Thoresen cross-channel ferry *Herald of Free Enterprise* capsizes off Zeebrugge, Belgium, killing 187 people.

AUGUST

16 A Northwest Airlines McDonnel Douglas MD-30 disintegrates in a fireball on a busy highway in Detroit, Michigan: 153 people are killed.

NOVEMBER

- Construction of the Channel Tunnel between England and France begins; there are to be two tunnels, each 7.6 m/25 ft wide and 49.4 km/30.7 mi long.
29 A Korean Air Boeing 747 is blown up by a North Korean terrorist bomb; the plane falls into the sea off Burma (now Myanmar), killing all 115 people aboard.

DECEMBER

20 The Philippine passenger ferry *Doña Paz* collides with a tanker off Mindoro Island in the Philippines; nearly 2,000 people drown.
21 A ferry disaster in the Philippines kills 2,000 people.

ARTS AND IDEAS

Architecture

- A retrospective exhibition of the works of the architect Le Corbusier is held at the Hayward Gallery in London, England.

APRIL

23 A building being constructed by the lift-slab method, by which flooring slabs are poured on the ground and then raised to the desired level, collapses in Bridgeport, Connecticut; 28 workers are killed and the method comes into question.

Arts

- The auction house Christie's sells Vincent van Gogh's *Irises* for £30 million ($53.9 million), a world record sale price for art of any kind. Earlier in the year they had sold his *Sunflowers* for £24 million ($39.9 million).
- The de Menil Museum in Houston, Texas, designed by the Italian architect Renzo Piano, is completed.
- The French artist Christian Boltanski creates the installation *Chases High School: Graduating Class of 1931*.
- The German artist Georg Baselitz paints *Double Portrait*.
- The U.S. artist Barbara Kruger creates *I Shop Therefore I Am*, a photographically produced graphic art piece.

Film

- *Rhosyn A Rhith/Coming Up Roses*, directed by Stephen Bayly, is the first feature-length movie in Welsh to go on general release.
- British movie producer David Puttnam resigns as chief of production of Columbia Pictures in the United States, following its merger with Tristar.
- Income from video rental in the United States reaches twice the level of box-office receipts.
- Richard Attenborough's UK-funded movie *Cry Freedom*, starring Kevin Kline and Denzel Washington, is banned by the South African government for its antiapartheid message.
- The Academy Award-winning documentary *Hotel Terminus: The Life and Times of Klaus Barbie* is released in the United States. A profile of a Nazi war criminal brought to trial in France in the 1980s, it is directed by Marcel Ophüls.
- The animated movie *Akira*, directed by Katsuhiro Otomo, is released in Japan.
- The comedy *Raising Arizona*, written, produced, and directed by Joel and Ethan Coen, is released in the United States. It stars Nicolas Cage and Holly Hunter.
- The movie *84 Charing Cross Road*, directed by David Jones, is released in the UK. It is adapted from the novel by Helene Hanff, and stars Anne Bancroft and Anthony Hopkins.
- The movie *Babette's Gastebud/Babette's Feast*, written and directed by Gabriel Axel, is released in Denmark. Based on a short story by Isak Dinesen, it stars French actress Stéphane Audran.
- The movie *Broadcast News*, directed by James Brooks, is released in the United States, starring William Hurt, Albert Brooks, and Holly Hunter.
- The movie *Der Himmel über Berlin/Wings of Desire*, directed by Wim Wenders, is released in West Germany. It stars Bruno Ganz, Solveig Dommartin, and Peter Falk.
- The movie *Dirty Dancing*, directed by Emile Ardolino, is released in the United States. It stars Patrick Swayze and Jennifer Grey.
- The movie *Drowning by Numbers*, directed by Peter Greenaway, is released in the UK. It stars Bernard Hill, Joan Plowright, Juliet Stevenson, and Joely Richardson.
- The movie *Full Metal Jacket*, a harrowing account of troops preparing for and fighting in the Vietnam War directed by Stanley Kubrick, is released in the United States. It stars Matthew Modine, Adam Baldwin, and Vincent D'Onofrio.
- The movie *Good Morning, Vietnam*, directed by Barry Levinson, is released in the United States, starring Robin Williams.
- The movie *Hong Gaoliang/Red Sorghum*, directed by Zhang Yimou, is released in China, starring Gong Li and Jiang Wen.
- The movie *Hope and Glory*, written and directed by John Boorman, is released in the UK. It stars Sarah Miles and David Hayman.
- The movie *House of Games*, directed by U.S. writer David Mamet, is released in the United States. It stars Lindsay Crouse and Joe Mantegna, and is Mamet's directorial debut.

- The movie *La ley del deseo/Law of Desire*, directed by Pedro Almodóvar, is released in Spain.
- The movie *Lethal Weapon*, directed by Richard Donner, is released in the United States. It stars Mel Gibson and Danny Glover.
- The movie *Matewan* is released in the United States. It is written and directed by John Sayles and photographed by Haskell Wexler.
- The movie *Mitt liv som Hund/My Life as a Dog*, directed by Lasse Hallström, is released in Sweden. It stars Anton Glanzelius.
- The movie *Moonstruck*, directed by Norman Jewison, is released in the United States. It stars Cher and Nicolas Cage.
- The movie *Radio Days*, directed by Woody Allen, is released in the United States.
- The movie *Robocop*, directed by the Dutch filmmaker Paul Verhoeven, is released in the United States. It stars Peter Weller.
- The movie *The Big Easy*, directed by Jim McBride, is released in the United States. It stars Dennis Quaid and Ellen Barkin.
- The movie *The Dead*, filmed by veteran writer-director John Huston, is released in the United States. Based on a story from James Joyce's *Dubliners*, it stars Huston's daughter, Anjelica, and Donal McCann. It is Huston's final movie as a director.
- The movie *The Empire of the Sun*, directed by Steven Spielberg, is released in the United States. It is based on the novel by J. G. Ballard and stars Christian Bale.
- The movie *The Last Emperor*, directed by Bernardo Bertolucci, is released. It stars John Lone, Joan Chen, and Peter O'Toole.
- The movie *The Living Daylights*, directed by John Glen, is released in the UK. It stars Timothy Dalton as James Bond.
- The movie *The Untouchables*, directed by Brian De Palma, is released in the United States. It stars Sean Connery, Kevin Costner, and Robert De Niro.
- The movie *The Year My Voice Broke*, directed by John Duigan, is released in Australia, starring Noah Taylor.
- The movie *Three Men and a Baby*, directed by Leonard Nimoy, is released in the United States. A remake of Coline Serreau's 1985 French hit *Trois hommes et un couffin*, it stars Ted Danson, Steve Guttenberg, and Tom Selleck.
- The movie *Wall Street*, directed by Oliver Stone, is released in the United States. It stars Michael Douglas and Charlie Sheen.
- The movie *Withnail & I*, written and directed by Bruce Robinson, is released in the UK. It stars Richard E. Grant and Paul McGann.
- The Italian government finally lifts its ban on Bernardo Bertolucci's movie *Last Tango in Paris*.
- The mock documentary *Intervista*, directed by Federico Fellini, is released in Italy.
- The thriller *Fatal Attraction*, directed by Adrian Lyne, is released in the United States. It stars Michael Douglas and Glenn Close.

FEBRUARY

27 Hollywood celebrates its centenary, dating its beginning back to the first land register entry to mention the name.

MARCH

31 The 1986 Academy Awards take place. Best Actor: Paul Newman, for *The Color of Money*; Best Supporting Actor: Michael Caine, for *Hannah and her Sisters*; Best Actress: Marlee Matlin, for *Children of a Lesser God*; Best Supporting Actress: Dianne Wiest, for *Hannah and her Sisters*; Best Picture: *Platoon*, directed by Oliver Stone; Best Director: Oliver Stone, for *Platoon*.

MAY

19 At the Cannes Film Festival in France, the Palme d'Or is awarded to Maurice Pialat for *Sous le soleil de Satan/Under Satan's Sun*, the first French movie to win in 20 years. It stars Gérard Depardieu and Sandrine Bonnaire. At the same award ceremony, a 40th-anniversary prize is awarded to Italian filmmaker Federico Fellini for *Intervista*. For the first time the awards are broadcast live worldwide.

JUNE

- The U.S. Copyright Office decides that it will register colorized versions of black-and-white movies.

OCTOBER

19 The major movie studios are badly affected by the stockmarket crash in the United States, suffering losses of around 20%. More than 7% of French movie theaters close during the year. In Denmark, a movie theater closes, on average, every two weeks.

Literature and Language

- *Oscar Wilde* by the U.S. biographer Richard Ellmann is published posthumously.
- English explorer Wilfred Thesiger publishes his autobiography *The Life of My Choice*.
- The Australian novelist Louis Nowra publishes his novel *Palu*.
- The English writer Bruce Chatwin publishes his travel book *Songlines*.
- The first volume of the graphic novel *Maus: A Survivor's Tale* by Art Spiegelman is published.
- The Irish-born Canadian writer Brian Moore publishes his novel *The Colour of Blood*.
- The Nigerian writer Chinua Achebe publishes his novel *Anthills of the Savannah*.
- The Nobel Prize for Literature is awarded to the Russian-born U.S. poet Joseph Brodsky.
- The Pulitzer Prize for Biography is awarded to David J. Garrow for *Bearing the Cross: Martin Luther King, Jr*, the Pulitzer Prize for Poetry is awarded to Rita Dove for *Thomas and Beulah*, and the Pulitzer Prize for Fiction is awarded to Peter Taylor for *A Summons to Memphis*.
- The Russian writer Anatoly Rybakov publishes his novel *Deti Arbata/Children of the Arbat*. A depiction of the brutalities of the Stalinist era, it had been banned by the Soviet authorities for 20 years.
- The South African writer Nadine Gordimer publishes her novel *A Sport of Nature*.
- The Sri Lankan-born Canadian writer Michael Ondaatje publishes his novel *In the Skin of a Lion*.
- The U.S. journalist Tom Wolfe publishes his novel *Bonfire of the Vanities*.
- The U.S. novelist George Higgins publishes his novel *Outlaws*.

- The U.S. novelist Paul Auster publishes his novel *In the Country of Last Things*.
- The U.S. writer Gore Vidal publishes his novel *Empire*.
- The U.S. writer Saul Bellow publishes his novel *More Die of Heartbreak*.
- The U.S. writer Toni Morrison publishes her novel *Beloved*, which wins the Pulitzer Prize for Fiction in 1988.
- U.S. writer Arthur Miller publishes his autobiography *Timebends*.
- U.S. writer Maya Angelou publishes her autobiographical work *All God's Children Need Travelling Shoes*.

Music

- Satellite television channel MTV is launched in Europe, with the video of Dire Straits' "Money For Nothing."
- The English composer Malcolm Arnold completes his Symphony No. 9.
- The English composer Michael Nyman completes his opera *The Man who Mistook his Wife for a Hat*.
- The English composer John Tavener completes his work for cello and strings *The Protecting Veil*.
- The Greek composer Iannis Xenakis completes his orchestral work *Tracées*.
- The Icelandic pop group the Sugarcubes releases their debut single "Birthday."
- The Japanese composer Toru Takemitsu completes his *Nostalghia (in memory of Andrey Tarkovsky)* for violins.
- The opera *Nixon in China* by the U.S. composer John Adams is first performed, in Houston, Texas.
- The U.S. composer Elliot Carter completes his Oboe Concerto.
- The U.S. composer Steve Reich completes his electronic work *Electronic Counterpoint*.
- The U.S. folk singer/songwriter Suzanne Vega releases her second album *Solitude Standing*.
- The U.S. pop group Los Lobos releases the album *La Bamba*.
- The U.S. pop singer Bruce Springsteen releases the album *Tunnel of Love*.

FEBRUARY

24 The 1986–97 Grammy Awards are held. Best Album: *Graceland* by Paul Simon; Best Record and Best Pop Vocalist: "Higher Love" by Steve Winwood; Best Female Pop Vocalist: Barbra Streisand for *The Broadway Album*; Best Female Rock Vocalist: Tina Turner for "Back Where You Started."

APRIL

4   The Irish rock group U2 releases the album *The Joshua Tree*.

18 The U.S. rock singer Prince releases the album *Sign O' The Times*.

JUNE

27 The U.S. pop singer Whitney Houston releases "I Wanna Dance with Somebody," and the album *Whitney Houston*, which becomes the first record album by a female singer to go straight to number one in the UK and U.S. album charts simultaneously.

AUGUST

16 Fifty thousand people gather in Memphis, Tennessee, to commemorate the tenth anniversary of the death of Elvis Presley.

22 The British heavy metal group Def Leppard releases the album *Hysteria*, the best-selling album to date by a UK band in the United States.

29 The U.S. pop group Guns 'n' Roses releases the album *Appetite For Destruction*.

SEPTEMBER

5   The British pop group New Order releases the album *Substance*.

26 The U.S. pop singer Michael Jackson releases the album *Bad*, the best-selling album of 1987.

OCTOBER

5   The opera *The Electrification of the Soviet Union*, by the English composer Nigel Osborne, is first performed, at Glyndebourne, England. The text, based on Boris Pasternak's story "The Last Summer," was written by the poet Craig Raine.

31 Ex-Police lead singer Sting releases the album *Nothing Like the Sun*.

NOVEMBER

21 British pop singer George Michael, ex-lead singer of Wham!, releases the album *Faith*.

DECEMBER

20 The U.S. white rap group the Beastie Boys releases "Fight For Your Right to Party" and the album *Licensed To Kill*, which becomes the first rap album to top the chart.

Theater and Dance

- The musical *Into the Woods*, with music by Stephen Sondheim and lyrics by James Lapine, is first performed, at the Martin Beck Theater in New York, New York.
- The play *Burn This*, by the U.S. writer Lanford Wilson, is first performed, at the Plymouth Theater in New York, New York.
- The play *Driving Miss Daisy*, by the U.S. writer Alfred Uhry is first performed, at the Playwrights Horizon Theater in New York, New York.
- The Pulitzer Prize for Drama is awarded to August Wilson for *Fences*.

JUNE

7   *Les Misérables* wins the Tony Award for Best Musical; *Fences* wins for Best Play and Best Actor (James Earl Jones); and *Me and My Girl* wins Best Actress (Maryann Plunkett).

Thought and Scholarship

- British historian David Cressy publishes *Coming Over: Migration and Communication between England and New England in the Seventeenth Century*.
- British historian Paul Kennedy publishes *The Rise and Fall of the Great Powers*.
- British historian Simon Schama publishes *The Embarrassment of Riches*, a social history of the Netherlands.
- The English historian Paul Johnson publishes *A History of the Jews*.

- The Pulitzer Prize for History is awarded to Bernard Bailyn for *Voyagers to the West: A Passage in the Peopling of American on the Eve of the Revolution.*
- The Pulitzer Prize for General Nonfiction is awarded to David K. Shipler for *Arab and Jew: Wounded Spirits in a Promised Land.*
- U.S. journalist Randy Shilts publishes *And the Band Played On: Politics, People and the AIDS Epidemic.*
- U.S. philosopher Hilary Putnam publishes *The Many Faces of Realism.*
- U.S. political scientist Allan Bloom publishes *The Closing of the American Mind.*

SOCIETY

Everyday Life

- A U.S. toy manufacturer who mass-produces dolls of Marine Lieutenant Colonel Oliver North, regarded in some circles as a hero for his illegal activities in support of the Nicaraguan Contras, suffers severe losses.
- About half of all U.S. households now have cable TV.
- Pat Anthony of Northern Transvaal in South Africa becomes the first surrogate grandmother, giving birth to her daughter's triplets.
- Surveys show that one-third of all blacks in the United States are now middle class—the figure has doubled since 1969.
- The average monthly income spent on childcare in the United States is 6.6%. Those living in poverty spend 25% of their income on childcare.
- The case of 'Baby M', the child of a surrogate birth agreement in the United States, raises ethical issues when her custody is contested by her natural mother Mary Beth Whitehead and the couple who paid for the surrogacy, William and Elizabeth Stern. On March 31, the New Jersey judge rules that Whitehead has no parental rights. Surrogacy, not covered by existing laws, is becoming increasingly common. Full custody of the baby is given to William Stern.
- The miniskirt reappears in the fashion world.
- The number of divorces (as percentage of marriages contracted): Australia 34; Belgium 31; Canada 43; Czechoslovakia 32; Denmark 44; Finland 38; France 31; West Germany 30; Great Britain and Northern Ireland 41; Greece 13; Netherlands 28; Italy 8; Japan 22; Norway 40; Sweden 44; United States 48.
- The U.S. Census Bureau reports the Hispanic population of the United States to be nearly 19 million.
- The year is shortened by one second to adjust it to the Gregorian calendar.
- Women own 30% of U.S. businesses.

January

16 KRON television in San Francisco, California, shows the first advertisements promoting the use of condoms for safe sex.

March

19 Popular TV evangelist Reverend Jim Bakker admits to an extramarital sexual escapade, beginning the decline of his successful ministry.

July

11 The world population reaches 5 billion—double that of 1950.

Media and Communication

- *USA Today* is the most-read newspaper in the United States, with a circulation of 1.6 million.
- Australian-born U.S. media tycoon Rupert Murdoch acquires U.S. publisher Harper & Row for $300 million.
- Sonic Solutions, Inc., develops "NoNoise" in the United States; independently in the UK, the National Sound Archive develops "CEDAR" (computer-enhanced digital audio restoration)—two different methods of digitally restoring old sound recordings.
- The first singing press advertisement appears in *New York* magazine and the *New Yorker*—an advertisement for Absolut vodka plays "Jingle Bells."
- The Institut für Rundfunktechnik in Germany develops a new technique for projecting three-dimensional television images. It consists of two images, each of 625 lines, even lines for one color and odd lines for the other, that are combined to form a three-dimensional image; special glasses are required to view it.

January

18–19 *Out on a Limb*, starring Shirley MacLaine in an adaptation of her book, appears on U.S. television.

July

1 Wendy Henry becomes the first woman to edit a national newspaper in Britain when she takes over the *News of the World*.

August

16 *Elvis '56*, examining Elvis Presley's break-through year, appears on U.S. television.

September

14 The U.S. A. C. Nielsen Company begins to track TV audience ratings with "people meters," which are more accurate than the diaries previously used.

20 The 1986–87 Emmy Awards for television are held. Best Drama Series: *LA Law*; Best Comedy Series: *The Golden Girls*; Best Actor in a Drama: Bruce Willis, for *Moonlighting*; Best Actress in a Drama: Sharon Gless, for *Cagney and Lacey*; Best Actor in a Comedy: Michael J. Fox, for *Family Ties*; Best Actress in a Comedy: Rue McClanahan, for *The Golden Girls*.

24–July 9, 1989 *A Different World*, a spinoff from *The Cosby Show*, is broadcast on U.S. television.

Religion

- The Greek Orthodox leader Patriarch Demetrios I of Constantinople joins Pope John Paul II in blessing crowds in St. Peter's Square in Rome, Italy.
- The Vatican announces plans to renew contact with the dissident French archbishop Marcel Lefèbvre, who had opposed the reforms of the Second Vatican Council (1962–65).

August

17 Believers in "new age" spirituality celebrate a "harmonic convergence," the alignment of all nine planets, at several "power points" around the world, including Mt. Olympus in Greece, Machu Picchu in Peru, and Glastonbury in England.

Sports

- Former British Olympic 400 meter silver medallist David Jenkins pleads guilty in San Diego, California, to illegally manufacturing and selling anabolic steroids.
- Hervé Filion becomes the first driver in U.S. harness racing to earn $10 million in winnings.
- Omar Henry becomes the first black player to be chosen by the South African cricket selectors for the national team.
- Stephen Roche of Ireland becomes only the second cyclist after Eddy Merckx of Belgium to win the Tour de France, the Giro d'Italia, and the world professional road race in the same year.
- The French cyclist Jeannie Longo wins every race she enters, including the women's Tour de France and World Road Race Championship.
- The U.S. basketball player Michael Jordan of the Chicago Bulls becomes only the second player in National Basketball Association history to score 3,000 points in a season.

JANUARY

1   Sportswriters and coaches pick Penn State as college football's national champion for the 1986 season.

25   The New York Giants defeat the Denver Broncos 39–20 in Super Bowl XXI in Pasadena, California, to win their first National Football League (NFL) title since 1956.

31–February 4   The U.S. boat *Stars and Stripes*, skippered by Dennis Conner, completes a 4–0 victory over the Australian yacht *Kookaburrra III* at Freemantle, Australia, to bring the America's Cup back to the United States.

FEBRUARY

7–8   U.S. national figure skating champions: Jill Trenary; Brian Boitano; Jill Watson and Peter Oppegard, pairs; Suzanne Semanick and Scott Gregory win the ice dancing competition.

MAY

10–18   The Canadian ice hockey team the Edmonton Oilers win their third Stanley Cup in four years; this time they beat the Philadelphia Flyers four games to three.

BIRTHS & DEATHS

FEBRUARY

4   Liberace, U.S. entertainer known for his extravagant performances and sequinned costumes, dies of AIDS in Palm Springs, California (67).

23   Andy Warhol, U.S. artist and filmmaker, a leading exponent of pop art in the 1960s, dies in New York, New York (59).

MARCH

3   Danny Kaye, U.S. comic actor who contributed his talents to UNICEF for 30 years, dies in Los Angeles, California (74).

12   Woody Hayes, U.S. football coach who won two national championships at Ohio State, dies in Upper Arlington, Ohio (74).

19   Duc Louis de Broglie, French physicist who discovered the wave nature of electrons, dies in Paris, France (94).

APRIL

11   Erskine Caldwell, U.S. author whose works depicted the poverty of farmers during the Depression, dies in Paradise Valley, Arizona (83).

11   Primo Levi, Italian Jewish writer and chemist who wrote an account of his survival in a Nazi concentration camp, dies in Turin, Italy (67).

MAY

14   Rita Hayworth, U.S. actress and sex symbol during World War II, dies in New York, New York (68).

29   Jean Delay, French psychiatrist who pioneered the successful use of drugs for schizophrenia, dies in Paris, France (79).

JUNE

1   Errol Walton Barrow, Barbadian premier 1961–66 and prime minister 1966–76 and 1986–87, dies in Bridgetown, Barbados (67).

1   Rashid Karami, Lebanese prime minister from 1984, dies near Beirut, Lebanon (55).

3   Andrés Segovia, Spanish musician and concert guitarist, dies in Madrid, Spain (93).

22   Fred Astaire, U.S. dancer who starred in many musical comedies with Ginger Rogers, dies in Los Angeles, California (88).

JULY

25   Charles Stark Draper, U.S. aeronautical engineer who developed inertial navigation, dies in Cambridge, Massachusetts (85).

AUGUST

9   Leon Keyserling, U.S. economist and adviser to Democrat presidents, dies in Washington, D.C. (79).

17   Rudolf Hess, German Nazi leader and deputy of Adolf Hitler, dies in Spandau prison in West Berlin, West Germany, where he had remained imprisoned since World War II (93).

SEPTEMBER

1   Arnoldo Momigliano, Italian-born British ancient historian who specialized in early and late Rome and historiography, dies in London, England (78).

11   Peter Tosh, Jamaican singer and leading reggae performer, dies in Kingston, Jamaica (42).

OCTOBER

2   Peter Brian Medawar, British immunologist who worked on acquired immunological tolerance and transplant rejection, dies (72).

3   Jean Anouilh, French playwright, dies in Lausanne, Switzerland (77).

13   Walter Houser Brattain, U.S. scientist, one of three whose work with semiconductors led to the development of the transistor, dies in Seattle, Washington (85).

20   Andrey Nikolayevich Kolmogorov, Russian mathematician who developed some basic postulates of probability theory, dies in Moscow, USSR (84).

29   Woody Herman, U.S. clarinettist, saxophonist, band leader, and vocalist, dies in Los Angeles, California (74).

NOVEMBER

1   James Baldwin, U.S. novelist, playwright, and essayist who wrote about race issues, dies in St.-Paul, France (63).

DECEMBER

1   Alvin Ailey, U.S. dancer and choreographer who established the Alvin Ailey American Dance Theater, dies in New York, New York (56).

24 Al Unser, Sr., is the second driver to win the Indianapolis 500 four times; and at 47 years, 11 months, he is the oldest-ever winner.

JUNE

2–14 The Los Angeles Lakers beat the Boston Celtics for the National Basketball Association (NBA) crown.
4 The U.S. athlete Edwin Moses's unbeaten run of 122 successive wins in the 400-meters hurdles, stretching back to August 26, 1977, ends in Madrid, Spain, when he is beaten by Danny Harris of the United States.

JULY

4 Czech-born U.S. tennis player Martina Navratilova wins her sixth straight Wimbledon women's singles title.

26 Stephen Roche becomes the first Irishman and the second cyclist from beyond continental Europe to win the Tour de France.

SEPTEMBER

12 The Czech-born U.S. tennis player Ivan Lendl wins the men's singles at the U.S. Open championships for the third year in succession.
20 The French race-car driver Alain Prost wins a world record 28th Grand Prix victory in Portugal.
27 European golfers retain the Ryder Cup at Muirfield Village, Ohio; this is the U.S. team's first home defeat in the competition.

OCTOBER

17–25 The Minnesota Twins win the World Series, beating the St. Louis Cardinals in seven games.

1988

POLITICS, GOVERNMENT, AND ECONOMICS

Business and Economics

- British cosmetics entrepreneur Anita Roddick's Body Shop now has 300 stores in 34 countries.
- English economist Henry Phelps Brown publishes *Egalitarianism and the Generation of Inequality*.
- The Financial Corporation of America becomes the largest bankruptcy in U.S. history, with losses of $33.9 billion.
- The first successful plastic money is introduced in Australia: a $10 bill commemorating the Australian bicentennial.
- The U.S. national debt reaches $1.2 trillion.
- U.S. fast-food company McDonald's opens its 10,000th store.

JANUARY

8 The New York stock market registers its third largest one-day fall in history, with the Dow Jones Industrial Average closing 140.58 points down on the day.

OCTOBER

31 British Airways introduces the air miles program, offering points toward free flights for specified purchases.

Human Rights

- U.S. historians Bonnie Anderson and Judith Zinsser publish *A History of Their Own*, a two-volume women's world history survey.

Politics and Government

- Opposition political parties are legalized in Hungary by the government of Károly Grósz.
- The legal right of criminal suspects in Northern Ireland to remain silent under police questioning is abolished.

JANUARY

2 Canada and the United States sign a free trade agreement.
17 Presidential elections are held in Haiti amidst allegations of voting irregularities.
22 The United States submits a draft space defense treaty at the U.S.–Soviet disarmament talks in Geneva, Switzerland.
25 Ramsewak Shankar is inaugurated as president of Suriname, bringing an end to eight years of military rule.
29 Talks in Luanda reach agreement on the withdrawal of Cuban military personnel from Angola.

FEBRUARY

4 The Supreme Court of the USSR approves the posthumous judicial rehabilitation of Nikolai Bukharin and nine other Soviet leaders executed or imprisoned after the 1938 show trial.
5 The United States indicts Panama's leader General Manuel Noriega on drug-smuggling charges.
5 U.S. president Ronald Reagan and Soviet leader Mikhail Gorbachev are nominated for the Nobel Peace Prize.

7   Leslie Manigat is inaugurated as president in Haiti, ending two years of military rule.

8   An international commission finds that Austrian president Kurt Waldheim knew about wartime atrocities in the Balkans, but clears him of war crimes.

8   In the U.S. presidential election primaries, Bob Dole comes first in the Iowa Republican caucus, Pat Robertson comes second, and Vice President George Bush third.

8   The Soviet leader Mikhail Gorbachev announces that Soviet troops will begin to withdraw from Afghanistan on May 15.

10   Eighty people die in violence during local elections in Bangladesh.

18   Anthony Kennedy, the third candidate for the U.S. Supreme Court justice vacancy left by Lewis Powell, is sworn in.

20   The Regional Soviet in Nagorno-Karabakh votes for the region to be transferred from Azerbaijan to Armenia.

23   The U.S. secretary of state George Shultz arrives in Israel at the start of a Middle East peace mission.

26   The Soviet leader Mikhail Gorbachev makes an unprecedented television appeal for calm after a week of nationalist demonstrations in Armenia.

MARCH

1   Soviet troops enforce a curfew in Sumgait, Azerbaijan, following deaths in ethnic violence.

6   Three suspected Irish Republican Army (IRA) terrorists are shot dead by a British SAS (Special Air Service) team in Gibraltar.

14–16 China and Vietnam clash during a period of three days over the disputed Spratly Islands in the South China Sea.

18   Panama declares a state of emergency in response to "undeclared war" being waged by the United States.

19   In a move designed to unnerve the Sandinista government of neighboring Nicaragua, 3,000 U.S. troops are airlifted to Honduras.

20   Elections to the National Assembly in El Salvador are won by the right wing Nationalist Republican Alliance (ARENA).

23   Contra commanders and Sandinista government officials sign a 60-day cease-fire agreement in Nicaragua.

24   U.S. marine lieutenant colonel Oliver North, former deputy director of the National Security Council, pleads not guilty to criminal charges arising from the Iran–Contra affair.

APRIL

3   A peace agreement between Ethiopia and Somalia ends 11 years of border conflict.

3   Indian forces seal the border with Pakistan against the infiltration of Sikh extremists after 120 deaths in a week of violence in Punjab.

4   Evan Mecham, found guilty of diverting campaign funds during the governorship election, is removed from the governorship of Arizona.

5   Shiite Muslim extremists hijack a Kuwait Airways Boeing 747 airliner, forcing it to fly to Iran and to Cyprus, where two hostages are shot dead. The hijack ends in Algiers on April 20.

10   Hundreds of deaths result from an explosion at an army ammunition dump near Islamabad in Pakistan, for which Afghan agents are believed responsible.

16   The military commander of the Palestine Liberation Organization (PLO) Abu Jihad is assassinated in Tunis, Tunisia. Israeli secret service agents are believed to be responsible.

18   U.S. airplanes and warships destroy two Iranian oil platforms and attack ships in the Persian Gulf in retaliation for damage to a U.S. frigate.

22   France flies in military reinforcements when three gendarmes are killed and others captured by Kanak separatists in New Caledonia.

25   John Demjanjuk (believed to be the former prison-camp guard known as "Ivan the Terrible") is sentenced to death in Israel for war crimes in the gas chambers in the Treblinka concentration camp during World War II.

30   A Census Bureau report reveals a growing "wealth gap" between rich and poor Americans.

MAY

2   Thousands of shipyard workers go on strike in Poland and seven leaders of the Solidarity labor union are detained.

3   Donald Regan, a former aide to U.S. president Ronald Reagan, reveals that the president consults an astrologer before making important decisions.

3   The militant group Islamic Jihad frees three French hostages in Lebanon amidst allegations that France has done a deal with Iran.

8   The Socialist president of France François Mitterrand defeats the Gaullist candidate Jacques Chirac in the presidential elections, winning over 54% of votes.

10   Jacques Chirac resigns as prime minister of France and is succeeded by the Socialist Michel Rocard.

15   Soviet troops begin withdrawing from Afghanistan after eight-and-a-half years.

19   Sikh rebels surrender to Indian government forces after occupying the Golden Temple complex in Amritsar, Punjab.

JUNE

1   U.S. president Ronald Reagan and Soviet leader Mikhail Gorbachev sign an intermediate-range nuclear forces treaty in Moscow.

13   U.S. tobacco company the Liggett Group is found liable for the cancer death of a smoker, the first case in which a tobacco company is found guilty. When an appeals court rules for a retrial, the plaintiff drops the case.

19   The civilian president of Haiti, Leslie Manigat, is deposed in a military coup and replaced by Lieutenant General Henri Namphy.

23   Soviet troops move into parts of Armenia, Azerbaijan, and the disputed region of Nagorno-Karabakh, as ethnic violence enters its fifth month.

28–July 1 At the 19th Communist Party conference in Moscow, Soviet leader Mikhail Gorbachev outlines plans for changes in the administrative structure of the USSR, intended to make the Party more democratic and businesses more autonomous.

JULY

6   The presidential elections in Mexico are won by Carlos Salinas de Gortari, of the ruling Institutional Revolutionary Party (PRI).

11   Nicaragua expels the U.S. ambassador and seven of his colleagues on a charge of inciting violent antigovernment incidents.

14 Howard Baker, the White House Chief of Staff, resigns from the U.S. administration.

18 The 70th birthday of Nelson Mandela, the African National Congress leader, is marked by worldwide protests calling for his release from prison in South Africa.

21 The Democratic Party nominates Michael Dukakis as its candidate in the U.S. presidential elections.

28 An Israeli representative makes the first official visit to the USSR since the breaking of diplomatic relations between the two countries in 1967.

31 King Hussein of Jordan announces plans to cut Jordan's legal and administrative ties with the occupied West Bank.

AUGUST

8 Iraq and Iran announce a cease-fire in their prolonged war.

17 President Zia ul-Haq of Pakistan and the U.S. ambassador to Pakistan are killed when the plane carrying them explodes in mid-air. A state of emergency is declared.

17 The Republican Party nominates George Bush as its candidate in the U.S. presidential elections.

23 The Trade Bill, to protect U.S. industries threatened by foreign imports, becomes law.

SEPTEMBER

4 Serbs and Montenegrins demonstrate in Yugoslavia, calling for martial law in Kosovo province and protection from Albanian separatists.

17 Lieutenant General Henri Namphy is deposed as president of Haiti in a military coup led by Lieutenant General Prosper Avril.

21 A state of emergency is declared in the Nagorno-Karabakh region of the USSR, disputed between Armenia and Azerbaijan.

22 Brazil concludes an agreement with its creditor banks, rescheduling debts of U.S.$62,100 million.

24 The abortion-inducing drug RU486 is authorized for use in France and China; antiabortion groups protest.

29 The Nobel Peace Prize is awarded to United Nations peacekeeping forces.

30 Major changes are made in the Soviet Politburo, including the retirement of President Andrey Gromyko and the dismissal of several leading figures.

OCTOBER

1 Mikhail Gorbachev is elected president of the USSR by the Supreme Soviet.

2 The Estonian Popular Front is established to campaign for greater democracy in the republic.

3 Chad and Libya end their long-running war and establish diplomatic relations.

6 The Algerian government introduces emergency measures following rioting against rising prices and unemployment.

11 Ladislav Adamec replaces Lubomír Štrougal as prime minister of Czechoslovakia in the course of major changes in the government and Communist Party.

26 Simultaneous elections to white, black, "colored," and Indian local councils are held for the first time in South Africa.

31 The Polish government announces the closure of the Gdańsk shipyard, birthplace of the Solidarity labor union movement.

NOVEMBER

1 The general election in Israel results in a hung parliament, and Prime Minister Yitzhak Shamir forms a coalition with the Labor Party under Shimon Peres.

8 Republican candidate George Bush, with 426 electoral college votes, defeats Democrat Michael Dukakis, with 112 votes, in the U.S. presidential elections, but the Democratic Party increases its majority in the Senate and House of Representatives.

15 The Palestine Liberation Organization (PLO) parliament in exile proclaims an independent state of Palestine.

16 Benazir Bhutto's Pakistan People's Party wins 94 seats in the general election. On December 2, she is sworn in as prime minister of Pakistan.

16 The Supreme Soviet in Estonia votes to give itself the right to veto laws from Moscow.

21 The general election in Canada is won by the Progressive Conservative Party, led by Prime Minister Brian Mulroney.

23 Two regions of Azerbaijan, in the USSR, are placed under a state of emergency following ethnic clashes.

24 Egypt and Algeria restore diplomatic relations.

DECEMBER

7 The president of the USSR Mikhail Gorbachev, in the course of a visit to New York, announces plans to reduce Soviet armed forces and conventional weapons.

15 The United States resumes official contact with the Palestine Liberation Organization (PLO) after a 13-year boycott.

21 A terrorist bomb explodes on a Pan Am Boeing 747 airliner flying over Lockerbie in Scotland, killing all 259 passengers on board and 11 people on the ground.

22 A United Nations agreement is reached on Namibian independence, with the phased withdrawal of Cuban forces supporting the South West Africa People's Organization (SWAPO).

24 Canada approves a free-trade treaty that will eventually abolish all tariffs and trade barriers between Canada and the United States.

30 The government of Yugoslavia, led by Branko Mikulic, resigns as parliament blocks an economic reform package.

SCIENCE, TECHNOLOGY, AND MEDICINE

Agriculture

c. 1988 Irrigation of crops in the United States begins to be monitored and controlled by computer systems.

- By altering battery-hen feed, U.S. researcher Paul May produces a low cholesterol egg; it has 125 mg of cholesterol compared with 280 mg for normal eggs.

- In a bid to reduce over-production of foodstuffs, the European Community agrees the set-aside agriculture policy, by which farmers are subsidized for taking land out of production.

- The first dairy cattle are produced by cloning embryos.

- The first fruit-picking robots are used in the United States.
- The number of farms in the United States reaches its lowest level since before the Civil War.

Computing

- At Fujitsu laboratories in Japan, T. Kotani and coworkers develop a microprocessor which incorporates a Josephson junction; it works hundreds of times faster than conventional computer chips.
- The first computer "vaccines" against computer viruses are developed in the United States.
- U.S. computer scientists John Gustafson, Gary Montry, and Robert Benner develop a method of parallel processing that speeds up the processing of complex problems by a factor of 1,000; 100 times was thought to be the limit of this method.
- U.S. firm Motorola introduces a RISC (Reduced Instruction Set Computing) microprocessor; it processes fewer instructions and can operate much faster—processing up to 17 million instructions per second—than other processors.
- U.S. firm Scriptel develops the "Pen Writer" that allows handwriting to be input into computer memory by writing on the screen.
- U.S. researcher Dana Anderson invents a holographic computer, capable of generating three-dimensional images.

NOVEMBER

2 Serious damage is done to more than 6,000 computer systems worldwide when the "Internet worm" computer virus, developed by Cornell University graduate student Robert Morris, is implanted in the Internet computer network.

Ecology

- A United Nations Environment Program (UNEP) report claims that two-thirds of the world's urban population breathe "disturbingly high levels" of sulfur dioxide and dust.
- Fires burn 35,640 ha/88,000 acres of Yellowstone National Park, Wyoming.
- The UN's Global Environment Monitoring System reports that levels of pesticides, industrial chemicals, and natural toxins are within established health criteria.
- The United States experiences its worst drought since 1934, forcing it to import grain for the first time ever.

November 1988–94 The amount of chlorofluorocarbons released into the air in the United States is reduced by 52%.

FEBRUARY

23 Torrential rain in Brazil leaves 275 people reported dead and 25,000 homeless.

APRIL

14 Hailstones weighing a record 1 kg /2.2 lb kill 92 people in the Gopalganji region of Bangladesh.

JULY

6 An explosion and fire on Occidental Petroleum's North Sea oil rig *Piper Alpha* kills 167 people.

6 Six miles of beach on Long Island, New York, are closed following contamination by medical waste, including needles and dressings.

AUGUST

- Thousands of people are killed and hundreds of thousands left homeless as floods inundate the eastern coast of China.

7 Over 1 million people in Sudan are left homeless after widespread flooding in Khartoum and the surrounding provinces.

25 The center of Lisbon, Portugal, is gutted by fire.

31 Widespread flooding in Bangladesh kills 1,000 people and leaves 25 million homeless.

SEPTEMBER

10–18 Hurricane Gilbert, the most powerful hurricane recorded, kills 300 people and causes an estimated $5 billion in damages from the Caribbean to Mexico.

DECEMBER

7 At least 25,000 people are killed in Armenia, in the USSR, by an earthquake measuring 6.9 on the Richter scale.

Exploration

JULY

- Two Soviet *Phobos* space probes are launched (July 7 and 12) to study Phobos, one of the moons of Mars; *Phobos 1* is accidentally sent a "suicide" instruction.

SEPTEMBER

19 *Horizon*, Israel's first satellite, is launched; it is used for geophysical studies.

29–October 3 The U.S. space shuttle *Discovery* makes the first shuttle mission since the *Challenger* disaster three years previously.

NOVEMBER

15 The Soviet uncrewed space shuttle *Buran* ("Blizzard") makes its inaugural flight, under radio control.

Health and Medicine

- A French company markets the abortion-inducing drug RU486, developed by Etienne Baulieu; it induces an abortion up to seven weeks after fertilization by blocking receptors for the production of the hormone progesterone; antiabortion groups protest.
- A U.S. survey indicates that the risk of a heart attack can be halved by taking aspirin daily.
- One in 60 babies born in New York, New York, in the course of the year is HIV-positive.
- Researchers at the Agency of Industrial Science and Technology of Japan develop a contractile synthetic material that contracts in acetone and expands in water, giving it the potential to be used in artificial limbs with muscular functions.
- Several U.S. and European firms develop microcapsule reservoirs only 250 nanometers in diameter and made of a biodegradable polymer. They contain insulin that is delivered when the microcapsule dissolves; it constitutes a fundamentally new method of treating diabetes.

- Surgeons implant the first plutonium-powered pacemaker in a human heart, in the United States.
- Surgeons in Britain perform the first brain cell transplants.
- The Nobel Prize for Physiology or Medicine is awarded jointly to British physiologist James Black, U.S. biochemist Gertrude Elion, and U.S. pharmacologist George Hitchings for their discoveries of important principles for drug treatment.
- The U.S. Federal Drug Administration approves Minoxidil, the first successful baldness remedy.
- The U.S. firm 3M and the Australian firm Nucleus improve cochlear implants by transmitting the received sounds to the auditory nerve according to their frequencies.
- The U.S. firm Drug Delivery succeeds in injecting insulin into an animal without the use of a needle. Delivery is achieved by electro-osmosis: a weak electric current is applied to an adhesive patch containing the insulin, modifying the permeability of the skin and allowing the drug to enter the body. Several U.S. and European pharmaceutical firms begin manufacturing medicines that can be similarly administered.
- U.S. researchers graft tissues from the bone marrow, spleen, thymus, and lymph nodes of human fetuses into mice lacking an immune system; the mice then develop an immune system identical to that of humans—a valuable tool in the development of vaccines.

Science

- At the Michigan Institute of Technology, German-born U.S. biomedical researcher Rudolf Jaenisch and associates implant a human gene, connected with a hereditary disorder, into a mouse.
- Fossil remains of a modern *Homo sapiens* are discovered in Israel, dated about 92,000 years old; they suggest modern humans appeared twice as early as previously thought.
- German chemists Johann Deisenhofer, Robert Huber, and Hartmut Michel receive the Nobel Prize for Chemistry for their determination of the three-dimensional structure of the reaction center of photosynthesis.
- Researchers at IBM's Almaden Research Center in San José, California, using a scanning tunneling microscope, produce the first image of the ring structure of benzene, the simplest aromatic hydrocarbon. The image confirms the structure of the molecule envisioned by Frederick Kekulé in 1865.
- Simon Lilly of the University of Hawaii, United States, reports the location of a galaxy about 12 billion light-years from Earth, adding to evidence about the date of the universe's formation.
- The Human Genome Organization (HUGO) is established in Washington, D.C., United States; scientists announce a project to compile a complete "map" of human genes.
- The tomb of a Moche leader, dating from about AD 300, is found near Sipan in Peru.
- U.S. cartographer Arthur Robinson improves on the Mercator projection method of making maps by developing a map with the continents in the correct

proportions and outlines, although it still contains distortions.

APRIL

- The U.S. Patent and Trademark Office grants Harvard University a patent for a mouse developed by genetic engineering.

OCTOBER

19 The Nobel Prize for Physics is awarded to U.S. physicists Leon Max Lederman, Melvin Schwartz, and Jack Steinberger for creating a stream of neutrinos in a particle accelerator (the neutrino-beam method), and for demonstrating, by their discovery of the muon neutrino, that there are two types of neutrino.

Technology

- An almost frictionless high-speed bearing is made by U.S. aerospace engineer Francis Moon and Indian-born U.S. engineer Rishi Raj, using a high temperature superconductor.
- British chemist Richard Friend develops a molecular transistor constructed of polyacetylene. Its active elements are carbon based rather than the usual gallium arsenide, which make it far more efficient than classical transistors.
- Dutch firm CCA Biochem develops the biodegradable polymer polyactide; capable of being broken down by human metabolism, it is ideal for use in suturing threads, bone platelets, and artificial skin.
- Fujitsu laboratories in Japan develop monocrystalline superconductors—crystal superconductors only one layer of crystal thick. They retain heat better than several layers and thus allow the construction of large integrated circuits with little energy loss and unequaled speed.
- Israeli inventor Herman Branover and the U.S.–Israeli Solmecs firm develop a prototype of a magnetohydrodynamic (MHD) generator that uses molten lead fluid and coal as a fuel, making it suitable for countries that do not have petroleum resources.
- The American Telephone and Telegraph company (AT&T) develops the mono-electronic transistor, in which an electric current can be induced by the passage of a single electron.
- The first glass-fibreoptic cable is laid across the Atlantic Ocean and can carry 37,800 voice channels.
- The French Center for Studies in Telecommunications demonstrates the first voice-operated telephone booth. Callers insert a card in a slot, press a button for a dial tone, and then state the telephone number; with no visible telephone, vandalism is reduced.
- The U.S. National Academy of Engineering creates the Draper Prize—the highest prize for engineering, worth $375,000. It is engineering's equivalent of a Nobel prize.
- The world's largest wind-powered generator, the Boeing Mod-5B, with rotors 97.5 m/320 ft long, is installed in Oahu, Hawaii; it produces 3.2 megawatts of electricity.
- U.S. chemist J. Wayne Rabelais and Indian chemist Srinandan Kasi develop diamond film—layers of pure carbon which adhere tightly to surfaces. It is used as an insulator and for industrial grinding.
- U.S. metallurgical engineer Frank Filisko invents "Filisko fluid"—a hydraulic fluid that changes its

viscosity according to the strength of an applied electric current; viscosity can be changed within a millisecond and controlled by a computer permitting hydraulics to operate over a range of temperatures and pressures.

JANUARY

- Researchers at the National Institute for Metals, in Japan, develop a high-temperature bismuth-based superconductor—the third type of high-temperature superconductor.

MARCH

- Researchers at the University of Arkansas, United States, develop a high-temperature superconductor based on thallium; it is the fourth type of high-temperature superconductor.

AUGUST

- Japanese electronics manufacturer Sony launches the Video Walkman, which has a 7.5-cm/3-in color television and an 8-mm/0.3-in VCR. It weighs 1.5 kg/ 3 lb in total.

NOVEMBER

9   The Pentagon reveals the existence of its radar-evading F-117A stealth fighter.

Transportation

- The Seikan Tunnel under Tsugaru Strait between Honshu and Hokkaido islands, Japan, is completed; 54 km/86.9 mi long, it is the longest undersea railroad tunnel in the world.
- The Seto-Ohashi double-deck suspension bridge, linking Kojima on Honshu Island with Sakaide on Shikoku Island, Japan, opens; at 12.3 km/7.6 mi long, it is the longest road and rail bridge in the world, and with a span of 2,131 m/6,496 ft it is also the longest suspension bridge.
- Three Italian jets collide and crash into spectators during an air show in Ramstein, West Germany, killing at least 50 people and injuring 500.
- U.S. airline Northwest Airlines introduces personal television sets (in the seatback) on its Detroit–Tokyo route.

APRIL

15   A modified Soviet Tupolev TU-155 aircraft makes its test flight; it runs on liquid hydrogen rather than conventional fuels.
20   The Pentagon releases artist's sketches of its hitherto secret B-2 stealth bomber.
23   The lightweight aircraft *Daedalus 88*, piloted by the Greek-born U.S. student Kanellos Kanellopoulos, sets a new record for human-powered flight, covering 119 km/ 74 mi from Heraklion, Greece to the island of Santorini, in 3 hours, 54 minutes.

JULY

3   The U.S. guided missile cruiser USS *Vincennes* shoots down an Iranian civilian airliner in error in the Persian Gulf, killing all 286 people on board.

AUGUST

6   A ferryboat sinks in the Ganges River, India, killing 400 people.

ARTS AND IDEAS

Architecture

- The exhibition "Deconstructivist Architecture" is held at the Museum of Modern Art (MOMA) in New York, New York.

Arts

- The Indian artist Anish Kapoor creates *Mother as Void*.
- The Italian artist Francesco Clemente paints *Paradigm*.
- The painting *False Start* by the U.S. artist Jasper Johns is sold for $17,050,000, a world record for contemporary art and for a work by a living artist.
- The Portuguese-born English artist Paula Rego paints *The Cadet and His Sister*.
- The U.S. artist Peter Halley paints *Red Cell*.

Film

- French subscription television channel Canal Plus signs an agreement with movie theaters not to broadcast movies before 11 pm.
- Hollywood scriptwriters strike for five months; estimated losses to the industry are $150 million.
- Ron Howard's U.S. movie *Willow* employs newly developed morphing technology, the computerized manipulation of an image from one form into another.
- The Australian-U.S. coproduction *A Cry in the Dark* (also known as *Evil Angels* in Australia), directed by Fred Schepisi, is released. Based on the true-life Australian case in which a baby was allegedly eaten by a dingo, it stars Meryl Streep and Sam Neill.
- The controversial movie *The Last Temptation of Christ*, directed by Martin Scorsese, is released in the United States. Based on the novel by Nikos Kazantzakis, it stars Willem Dafoe.
- The movie *A Fish Called Wanda*, directed by Charles Crichton, is released in the UK. It stars John Cleese, Jamie Lee Curtis, Kevin Kline, and Michael Palin.
- The movie *A World Apart*, directed by Chris Menges, is released in the United States. It stars Barbara Hershey, David Suchet, Jeroen Krabbé, and Jodhi May.
- The movie *Another Woman*, written and directed by Woody Allen, is released in the United States. It features Gena Rowlands, Mia Farrow, Ian Holm, Blythe Danner, and Gene Hackman.
- The movie *Au revoir, les enfants/Goodbye Children*, directed by Louis Malle, is released in France. It stars Gaspard Manesse and Raphael Fejto.
- The movie *Big*, directed by Penny Marshall, is released in the United States. It stars Tom Hanks.
- The movie *Bird*, directed by Clint Eastwood, is released in the United States. Based on the life of Charlie Parker, it stars Forest Whitaker.
- The movie *Bull Durham*, written and directed by Ron Shelton, and starring Kevin Costner, Susan Sarandon, and Tim Robbins, is released in the United States.

- The movie *Camille Claudel*, directed by former cinematographer Bruno Nuytten, is released in France. It stars Isabelle Adjani and Gérard Depardieu.
- The movie *Cinema Paradiso*, directed by Giuseppe Tornatore, is released in Italy. It stars Philippe Noiret and Salvatore Cascio.
- The movie *Colors*, an exploration of gang culture in Los Angeles directed by Dennis Hopper, is released in the United States, starring Hopper and Penn.
- The movie *Dangerous Liaisons*, directed by Steven Frears, is released in the United States. It stars Glenn Close, John Malkovich, and Michelle Pfeiffer.
- The movie *Dead Ringers*, directed by David Cronenberg, is released in Canada. It stars Jeremy Irons and Geneviève Bujold.
- The movie *Die Hard*, directed by John McTiernan, is released in the United States. It stars Bruce Willis and Alan Rickman.
- The movie *Distant Voices, Still Lives*, directed by Terence Davies, is released in the UK. It stars Freda Dowie, Pete Postlethwaite, and Angela Walsh.
- The movie *Eight Men Out* is released in the United States, written and directed by John Sayles and starring John Cusack and Charlie Sheen.
- The movie *Gorillas in the Mist* is released in the United States. Based on the real-life experiences of anthropologist Dian Fossey, it is directed by British filmmaker Michael Apted and stars Sigourney Weaver and Bryan Brown.
- The movie *Hairspray*, written and directed by John Waters, is released in the United States. It stars Ricki Lake, Divine, Debbie Harry, and Sonny Bono.
- The movie *Mississippi Burning*, directed by British filmmaker Alan Parker, is released in the United States. It stars Gene Hackman and Willem Dafoe.
- The movie *Mujeres al borde de un ataque de nervios/ Women on the Verge of a Nervous Breakdown*, written and directed by Pedro Almodóvar, is released in Spain. It stars Carmen Maura.
- The movie *Pelle Erobreren/Pelle the Conqueror*, directed by Bille August and starring Max von Sydow and Pelle Hvenegaard, is released. It wins the Palme d'Or at the Cannes Film Festival in France, on May 23.
- The movie *Rain Man*, directed by Barry Levinson, is released in the United States. It stars Dustin Hoffman, in an Academy Award-winning performance, and Tom Cruise. It also wins Oscars for best picture and best director.
- The movie *Running on Empty*, directed by Sidney Lumet, is released in the United States. It stars River Phoenix, Christine Lahti, Judd Hirsch, and Martha Plimpton.
- The movie *Salaam Bombay!*, directed by Mira Nair, is released in the UK. It stars Shafiq Syed.
- The movie *Spoorloos/The Vanishing*, directed by George Sluizer, is released in the Netherlands.
- The movie *The Accidental Tourist*, cowritten and directed by Lawrence Kasdan, is released in the United States. Based on the novel by Anne Tyler, it stars William Hurt, Kathleen Turner, and Geena Davis.
- The movie *The Accused*, directed by Jonathan Kaplan, is released in the United States. It stars Jodie Foster and Kelly McGillis.
- The movie *The Moderns*, directed by Alan Rudolph, is released in the United States, starring Keith Carradine, Linda Fiorentino, and John Lone.
- The movie *The Unbearable Lightness of Being*, directed by Philip Kaufman, is released in the United States. Based on the novel by Milan Kundera, it stars Daniel Day Lewis, Juliette Binoche, and Lena Olin.
- The movie *Torch Song Trilogy*, directed by Paul Bogart, is released in the United States. It stars Anne Bancroft, Matthew Broderick, and Harvey Fierstein.
- The movie *Who Framed Roger Rabbit?*, directed by Robert Zemeckis, is released in the United States. Featuring the interaction of live performers with animated characters, it stars Bob Hoskins.
- The movie *Working Girl*, directed by Mike Nichols, is released in the United States. It stars Melanie Griffith, Harrison Ford, Sigourney Weaver, Alec Baldwin, and Joan Cusack.
- The Polish director Krzysztof Kieślowski releases *Dekalog/Decalogue*, a movie series made for television based on the Ten Commandments. Extended versions of *Krótki film o miłości/A Short Movie about Love* and *Krótki film o zabijaniu/A Short Movie about Killing* are also released.
- The ruby slippers worn by Judy Garland for the filming of *The Wizard of Oz* are auctioned for $165,000.

APRIL

11 The 1987 Academy Awards take place. Best Actor: Michael Douglas, for *Wall Street*; Best Supporting Actor: Sean Connery, for *The Untouchables*; Best Actress: Cher, for *Moonstruck*; Best Supporting Actress: Olympia Dukakis, for *Moonstruck*; Best Picture: *The Last Emperor*, directed by Bernardo Bertolucci; Best Director: Bernardo Bertolucci, for *The Last Emperor* (that wins all nine Academy Awards for which it is nominated).

NOVEMBER

28 The first European Academy Awards, in Berlin, West Germany, are televised to an estimated audience of 300 million.

Literature and Language

- Canadian novelist Margaret Atwood publishes her novel *Cat's Eye*.
- English novelist Doris Lessing publishes her novel *The Fifth Child*.
- English poet Philip Larkin's *Collected Poems* are published.
- English writer Graham Greene publishes his novel *The Captain and the Enemy*.
- The Australian writer Peter Carey publishes his novel *Oscar and Lucinda*, which wins the Booker Prize.
- The Colombian writer Gabriel García Márquez publishes his novel *El amor en los tiempos del cólera/ Love in the Time of Cholera*.
- The English novelist David Lodge publishes his novel *Nice Work*.
- The English writer Bruce Chatwin publishes his novel *Utz*.
- The Indian writer Anita Desai publishes her novel *Baumgartner's Bombay*.

- The Indian-born English writer Salman Rushdie publishes his novel *The Satanic Verses*.
- The Indian-born writer Adam Zameenzad publishes his novel *My Friend Matt and Hena the Whore*.
- The Italian writer and scholar Umberto Eco publishes his novel *Il pendolo di Foucault/Foucault's Pendulum*.
- The New Zealand novelist Janet Frame publishes her novel *The Carpathians*.
- The Nobel Prize for Literature is awarded to the Egyptian novelist Naguib Mahfouz.
- The Pulitzer Prize for Biography is awarded to David Herbert Donald for *Look Homeward: A Life of Thomas Wolfe*, the Pulitzer Prize for Poetry is awarded to William Meredith for *Partial Accounts: New and Selected Poems*, and the Pulitzer Prize for Fiction is awarded to Toni Morrison for *Beloved*.
- The U.S. poet W. S. Merwin publishes his poetry collection *The Rain in the Trees*.
- The U.S. writer Elmore Leonard publishes his novel *Freaky Deaky*.
- The U.S. writer Neil Sheehan publishes *A Bright Shining Lie: John Paul Vann and America in Vietnam*.
- The U.S. writer Stephen Dobyns publishes his novel *The Two Deaths of Seora Puccini*.
- The U.S. writer Thomas Harris publishes his novel *The Silence of the Lambs*.
- The U.S. writer W. S. Merwin publishes his poetry collection *The Rain in the Trees*.
- The Yugoslav writer Milorad Pavić publishes his novel *Dictionary of the Khazars*.
- U.S. writer Raymond Carver publishes his *Elephant and Other Stories*.

Music

- Rap music and hip-hop culture gain wider acceptance in mainstream U.S. culture with Run-D.M.C.'s album, *Tougher Than Leather*.
- Rock stars make a worldwide tour to give concerts in aid of Amnesty International.
- The Finnish composer Kalevi Aho completes Symphony No. 7.
- The German composer Karlheinz Stockhausen completes his opera *Montag aus Licht/Monday from Light*. This is the second part of his seven-opera cycle.
- The Hungarian-born Austrian composer György Ligeti completes his *Concerto for Piano and Orchestra*.
- The Irish pop group My Bloody Valentine releases the album *Isn't Anything*.
- The opera *The Making of the Representative for Planet 8*, by the U.S. composer Philip Glass, is first performed, in Houston, Texas. It is based on the novel sequence *Canopus in Argos* by the Rhodesian-born English novelist Doris Lessing.
- The Peruvian-born U.S. composer Meredith Monk completes his vocal work *Cat Song*.
- The Polish composer Witold Lutosławski completes his *Piano Concerto*.
- The U.S. composer Elliott Carter completes his chamber work *Birthday Flourish* and his orchestral work *Remembrance*, the second of his *Three Celebrations*.
- The U.S. composer Ned Rorem completes his orchestral work *A Quaker Reading*.

- The U.S. pop group Sonic Youth releases the album *Daydream Nation*.
- The U.S. pop group the Pixies releases the album *Surfer Rosa*.
- The U.S. pop singer Tracy Chapman releases the album *Tracy Chapman*.
- The U.S.-born Mexican composer Conlon Nancarrow completes his String Quartet No. 3.

MARCH

2   The 1987–88 Grammy Awards are held. Best Album: *The Joshua Tree* by U2; Best Record: "Graceland" by Paul Simon; Best Male Pop Vocalist: Sting for "Bring on the Night;" Best Female Pop Vocalist: Whitney Houston for "I Wanna Dance with Somebody;" Best Male Rock Vocalist: Bruce Springsteen for "Tunnel of Love."

MAY

7   The Australian pop singer and actress Kylie Minogue releases "I Should Be So Lucky" and the album *Kylie*.

28 The Canadian pop singer k d lang releases the album *Shadowland*.

JUNE

11 A 70th Birthday Tribute concert for South African dissident political leader Nelson Mandela takes place at Wembley Stadium in London, England. Featuring acts such as Peter Gabriel, Simple Minds, George Michael, Annie Lennox, Miriam Makeba, and Youssou N'Dour, it represents a significant protest against the apartheid regime in South Africa.

OCTOBER

29 The Irish rock group U2 releases the album *Rattle and Hum*. A movie of the same name featuring U2 live in performance is also released.

NOVEMBER

12 The U.S. rock group the Traveling Wilburys, consisting of George Harrison, Jeff Lynne, Roy Orbison, Bob Dylan, and Tom Petty, releases *Volume I*.

DECEMBER

19 The British pop singer Rick Astley releases "Never Gonna Give You Up."

Theater and Dance

- The play *M Butterfly*, by the Hong Kong-born U.S. writer David Henry Hwang, is first performed, at the Eugene O'Neill Theater in New York, New York.
- The play *Our Country's Good*, by the U.S. writer Timberlake Wertenbaker, is first performed, at the Royal Court Theatre in London, England. It is an adaptation of Thomas Keneally's novel *The Playmaker*.
- The play *Rumors*, by the U.S. writer Neil Simon, is first performed, at the Broadhurst Theater in New York, New York.
- The play *Speed-the-Plow*, by the U.S. writer David Mamet, is first performed, at the Royale Theater in New York, New York.
- The Pulitzer Prize for Drama is awarded to Alfred Uhry for *Driving Miss Daisy*.

JUNE

5   *Phantom of the Opera*, by Andrew Lloyd Webber, wins two Tony Awards for theater.

Thought and Scholarship

- Scottish philosopher Alisdair MacIntyre publishes *Whose Justice? Which Rationality?*
- The English historian Martin Gilbert publishes the eighth and final volume of the official biography of Winston Churchill, *Never Despair, 1945–65.*
- The Pulitzer Prize for History is awarded to Robert V. Bruce for *The Launching of Modern American Science, 1846–1876.*
- The Pulitzer Prize for General Nonfiction is awarded to Richard Rhodes for *The Making of the Atomic Bomb.*
- U.S. historian Eric Foner publishes *Reconstruction: America's Unfinished Revolution.*
- U.S. historian James McPherson publishes *Battle Cry of Freedom*, a study of the United States in the 19th century.
- U.S. philosopher Ted Honderich publishes *The Consequences of Determinism.*

SOCIETY

Education

- U.S. entertainer Bill Cosby donates $20 million to Spelman College, the largest gift made to date to a black college.

Everyday Life

- Australian butcher Dallas Chapman develops fatless meat; similar in appearance to sausages, its fat content is reduced by 96%, cholesterol by 30%, and calories by 85%.
- Book sales in the United States increase by more than 3% over the year; children's book sales reach double the level of sales in 1983.
- English physicist Stephen Hawking publishes *A Brief History of Time*, which becomes an unexpected worldwide bestseller.
- The British magazine *Deadline* introduces the Tank Girl comic strip.
- The number of births in the United States in 1988 is 3,829,000, the highest in 25 years.
- The U.S. Census Bureau reports that the median age in the United States exceeds 32 for the first time.
- U.S. advertising appears on Soviet television for the first time.
- U.S. cultural critic Susan Sontag publishes *AIDS and its Metaphors.*

JANUARY

26 Celebrations in Sydney mark the bicentenary of the arrival of European settlers in Australia.
28 Family planning clinics in the United States are barred from providing abortion assistance if they receive federal funds.
28 The Canadian Supreme Court overturns a law restricting abortion as unconstitutional.

APRIL

23 The U.S. government bans smoking on all internal passenger airline flights of under two hours' duration.

JUNE

15 The U.S. Census Bureau reports that for the first time over half of all new mothers remain in the job market.

AUGUST

31 The Solidarity leader Lech Wałęsa holds his first talks with the Polish authorities since the banning of the labor union in 1981.

SEPTEMBER

6 The U.S. Census Bureau reports a 34% increase since 1980 in the number of Hispanics; over 8% of the U.S. population.

DECEMBER

4 Workers in Spain mount a 24-hour general strike, the first such for 50 years.

Media and Communication

- Daytime television soap operas in the United States are replaced by the live broadcast of the trial of Hedda Nussbaum and Joel Steinberg, accused of beating their daughter, Lisa, age six, to death.
- Network television viewing in the United States drops as almost 53% of homes subscribe to cable and 56% of homes have videocassette recorders.
- U.S. television journalist Geraldo Rivera's nose is broken during an on-air altercation between white supremacists and critics.

JANUARY

24–26 The U.S. television special *The Murder of Mary Phagan*, starring Jack Lemmon, Peter Gallagher, and Richard Jordan, is broadcast.
30–April 23 *Voices and Visions* a 13-week documentary about the lives and work of U.S. poets, including Robert Frost, Walt Whitman, Emily Dickinson, and Sylvia Plath, is shown on U.S. television.

FEBRUARY

5 *The Main Event*, the first prime-time network wrestling broadcast since 1955, appears on U.S. television.
6 *The World According to Me*, a television adaptation of Jackie Mason's one-man Broadway show, appears on U.S. television.
7 The Paris Video Library opens in France, making a database of images and movies about Paris available to the public.

MARCH

3 The U.S. television special *Dear America: Letters Home From Vietnam* is broadcast.
27–28 The U.S. television special *Gore Vidal's Lincoln*, starring Mary Tyler Moore and Sam Waterston, is broadcast.

AUGUST

28 The 1987–88 Emmy Awards for television are held. Best Drama Series: *thirtysomething*; Best Comedy Series: *The Wonder Years*; Best Actor in a Drama: Richard Kiley, for *A Year in the Life*; Best Actress in a Drama: Tyne Daly, for *Cagney and Lacey*; Best Actor in a Comedy: Michael J. Fox, for *Family Ties*; Best Actress in a Comedy: Beatrice Arthur, for *The Golden Girls.*

OCTOBER

18 The situation comedy *Roseanne* begins broadcasting on U.S. television, starring comic actress Roseanne Barr and following the struggles of a not-so-typical blue collar family.

NOVEMBER

13–23 *War and Remembrance*, a sequel to the 1983 miniseries *The Winds of War*, is broadcast on U.S. television.

14 The U.S. television comedy *Murphy Brown* begins broadcasting. It stars U.S. actress Candice Bergen.

Religion

• The Holy Shroud of Turin, claimed by some to be Christ's mortuary cloth, is shown by carbon dating to date from about 1330.

FEBRUARY

29 Archbishop Desmond Tutu and 100 clergy are detained in Cape Town while protesting at curbs on antiapartheid organizations, imposed on February 24.

APRIL

8 U.S. television evangelist Jimmy Swaggart confesses to committing lewd acts with a prostitute and is ejected from his church.

MAY

5 Eugene Antonio Marino is installed as archbishop of Atlanta, the first black Roman Catholic archbishop in the United States.

6 Pope John Paul II begins a 13-day tour of Uruguay, Bolivia, Peru, and Paraguay.

JUNE

• The Lambeth Conference of Anglican Bishops is held in Canterbury, England.

5 In Moscow, USSR, World Christian church leaders celebrate 1,000 years of Christianity in Russia.

30 Dissident Catholic French archbishop Marcel Lefèbvre consecrates four bishops in his traditionalist movement and is automatically excommunicated by the Catholic Church.

SEPTEMBER

• Pope John Paul II reiterates his opposition to women priests in the Catholic Church in his Apostolic Letter "Mulieris Dignitatem"/"The Dignity of Woman."

25 Barbara Harris, a divorcée, is elected the first female bishop in the Anglican communion, to serve as suffragan bishop of Massachusetts. She is consecrated on February 11, 1989.

BIRTHS & DEATHS

• André Frédéric Cournand, French-born U.S. physician who shared a Nobel prize for his work on a method of catheterizing the heart, dies (93).

• Sewall Wright, U.S. geneticist and statistician who synthesized Charles Darwin's theory of evolution with genetics, dies (99).

FEBRUARY

15 Richard Feynman, U.S. theoretical physicist in the field of quantum electrodynamics, dies in Los Angeles, California (69).

MARCH

3 Sewall Wright, U.S. geneticist, one of the founders of population genetics, dies in Madison, Wisconsin (98).

21 Patrick Christopher Steptoe, English obstetrician who pioneered in vitro fertilization, dies (75).

APRIL

12 Alan Paton, South African novelist who publicized the problems of apartheid in *Cry, the Beloved Country*, dies near Durban, South Africa (85).

17 Louise Nevelson, U.S. sculptor whose works are large, abstract, often monochromatic pieces, dies in New York, New York (88).

MAY

8 Robert Heinlein, U.S. science fiction writer whose books did much to gain wider acceptance of the genre, dies in Carmel, California (80).

JULY

27 Frank Zamboni, U.S. inventor of the Zamboni machine that resurfaces ice, dies in Long Beach, California (87).

AUGUST

2 Raymond Carver, U.S. author and short-story writer, dies in Port Angeles, Washington (50).

13 Edward Bennett Williams, U.S. defense lawyer and sports team owner, dies in Washington, D.C. (68).

14 Enzo Ferrari, Italian race-car designer and sports car manufacturer, dies in Modena, Italy (90).

17 Mohammad Zia-ul-Haq, president of Pakistan 1978–88, who had his predecessor, Lulfiqar Ali Bhutto, executed, is killed in Bahawalpur, Pakistan, when his plane is blown up by an assassin's bomb (64).

SEPTEMBER

1 Luis W. Alvarez, U.S. physicist who received the Nobel Prize for Physics in 1968 for his discovery of several subatomic particles, dies in Berkeley, California (77).

29 Charles Samuel Addams, U.S. cartoonist whose cartoons inspired the TV series *The Addams Family*, dies in New York, New York (76).

OCTOBER

2 Pietro Annigoni, Italian artist who painted mainly in tempera, dies in Florence, Italy (78).

9 Felix Wankel, German engineer who designed a revolutionary rotary internal combustion engine known as the Wankel engine, dies in Lindau, Germany (86).

22 Henry Armstrong, U.S. boxer who simultaneously held the featherweight, welterweight, and lightweight championships 1937–39, dies in Los Angeles, California (75).

DECEMBER

21 Nikolaas Tinbergen, Dutch-born British zoologist who specialized in the study of instinctive behavior in animals, dies (81).

30 Isamu Noguchi, U.S. sculptor of organic abstract shapes, dies in New York, New York (84).

Sports

- Runner Grete Waitz of Norway wins her ninth New York Marathon in 11 years.
- The U.S. yacht *Stars and Stripes*, skippered by Dennis Conner, successfully defends the America's Cup against the New Zealand challenger, *New Zealand*, skippered by David Barnes.
- U.S. golfer Curtis Strange is the first golfer to earn a million dollars in prize money in a season.

JANUARY

January–September The West German tennis player Steffi Graf becomes the third woman to win the "Grand Slam" of all four major tournaments (the Australian Open, French Open, Wimbledon, and U.S. Open). She also wins an Olympic gold medal, following the restoration of tennis to the Olympic Games in Seoul, South Korea.

1 Coaches and sportswriters pick Miami as college football's national champions for the 1987 season.

8–9 U.S. national figure skating champions are: Debi Thomas; Brian Boitano; Jill Watson and Peter Oppegard, pairs; Suzanne Semanick and Scott Gregory, dance.

31 The Washington Redskins defeat the Denver Broncos 42–10 in Super Bowl XXII.

FEBRUARY

13–28 The 15th Winter Olympics are held in Calgary, Canada. The USSR wins 11 gold medals; East Germany, 9; and Switzerland and Finland, 4 each. Katerina Witt of East Germany retains her figure-skating title. In the ski-jumping, Matti Nykänen of Finland wins three gold medals, but the novice British jumper Eddie Edwards attracts more publicity for finishing last.

APRIL

2–28 The Baltimore Orioles set a Major League record by losing their first 21 games of the season.

10 Sandy Lyle becomes the first British golfer to win the U.S. Masters, in Augusta, Georgia.

MAY

6 Andy Hampsten becomes the first U.S. rider to win the Giro d'Italia (Tour of Italy) cycle race.

20 The Canadian ice hockey team the Edmonton Oilers beat the Boston Bruins to win the Stanley Cup, their fourth in five years.

29 U.S. race-car driver Rick Mears wins the Indianapolis 500.

JUNE

7–21 The Los Angeles Lakers beat the Detroit Pistons to repeat as National Basketball Association (NBA) champions.

AUGUST

17 Butch Reynolds breaks fellow U.S. athlete Lee Evans's 20-year-old 400 meters world record of 43.86 seconds with a time of 43.29 seconds, at a meeting in Zürich, Switzerland.

SEPTEMBER

17 The 24th Olympic Games open in Seoul, South Korea, attended by 8,465 competitors from 159 countries.

17–October 2 At the Olympic Games in Seoul, South Korea, Florence Griffith-Joyner of the United States wins gold medals in the women's 100 meters, 200 meters, and 4 × 100 meter relay. She also wins a silver in the 4 × 400 meter relay.

23 At the Seoul Olympic Games in South Korea, the Canadian runner Ben Johnson wins the 100 meters in a world record time of 9.79 seconds; he is then stripped of the title three days later when drug tests reveal traces of an anabolic steroid, stanozol.

25 At the Olympic Games in Seoul, South Korea, Kristin Otto of East Germany wins six gold medals for swimming, a record for a woman at one year's games.

OCTOBER

2 The 24th Olympic Games close in Seoul, South Korea. The USSR wins 55 gold medals; East Germany, 37; the United States, 36; South Korea, 12; West Germany and Hungary, 11 each; Bulgaria, 10; Romania, 7; France and Italy, 6 each; China, Great Britain, and Kenya, 5 each.

15–20 The Los Angeles Dodgers beat the Oakland As to win the World Series.

15–24 Over 4,000 athletes from 60 countries participate in the 11th Paralympics for the disabled and partially disabled in Seoul, South Korea. For the first time, Olympic competition sites and facilities are used.

NOVEMBER

4 The U.S. boxer Thomas Hearns defeats James Kinchen of the United States in Las Vegas, Nevada, to win the vacant World Boxing Organization super-middleweight title, becoming the first boxer to win world titles in five different weight divisions. Three days later Sugar Ray Leonard captures his fifth title, winning the World Boxing Council Light-heavyweight crown.

1989

POLITICS, GOVERNMENT, AND ECONOMICS

Business and Economics

MARCH

5   Time, Inc. and Warner Communications announce a planned merger that will create the world's largest media company, Time Warner.

9   U.S. airline company Eastern Airlines files for Chapter 11 bankruptcy.

SEPTEMBER

28   Japanese electronics hardware company Sony buys Columbia Pictures for $3.4 billion.

OCTOBER

13   In Wall Street's second largest one-day fall, the Dow Jones index plunges by 190 points.

31   The Japanese conglomerate Mitsubishi buys the Rockefeller Center in New York City.

Human Rights

JUNE

5   In the case *Wards Cove Packing v. Antonio*, the U.S. Supreme Court overturns a decision of 1971 and transfers the responsibility from employers to employees for deciding whether women and minorities should receive special treatment in employment.

12   In the case *Martin v. Wilks*, the U.S. Supreme Court rules that white workers can use civil-rights legislation to challenge unfair treatment resulting from affirmative action.

Politics and Government

• Hungarian-born U.S. actress Zsa Zsa Gabor is sentenced to three days in jail after she slaps a Beverley Hills policeman who gave her a traffic ticket.

• Japanese Americans interned during World War II are awarded $20,000 compensation each.

• The United Nations Environment Program (UNEP) reports that the number of species, and the amount of genetic variation within individual species, is decreasing due to the rapid destruction of natural environments.

JANUARY

2   The former prime minister of Sri Lanka Ranasinghe Premadasa is sworn in as president after his election in 1988. Dingiri Banda Wijetunga becomes prime minister.

5   The serious conspiracy charges against U.S. marine lieutenant colonel Oliver North in respect of the Iran–Contra affair are dropped.

5   U.S. navy jets shoot down two Libyan MiG fighters off the Libyan coast.

6   The USSR announces the mass rehabilitation of thousands of citizens who were victims of Stalin's purges in the 1930s–50s.

7   Emperor Hirohito of Japan dies after a 62-year reign, to be succeeded by his son, Crown Prince Akihito.

10   Cuban troops begin to withdraw from Angola.

11   The Hungarian parliament passes a law allowing the formation of political parties.

11   U.S. president Ronald Reagan makes his farewell speech, acclaiming the economic "miracle" achieved by the United States under his presidency.

12   A gunman fires into a school playground in Stockton, California, killing five children and wounding 30.

15   Riot police in Prague break up a demonstration marking the 25th anniversary of student Jan Palach's suicide in protest at the 1968 Soviet invasion of Czechoslovakia.

19   Ante Marković is named prime minister of Yugoslavia.

20   George Bush is inaugurated as 41st president of the United States.

31   The trial begins in the United States of Lieutenant Colonel Oliver North, the marines officer at the center of the Iran–Contra Affair. He is charged with lying to Congress, tax violations, illegally shredding documents, and nine other offenses.

FEBRUARY

2   Carlos Andrés Pérez is sworn in as president of Venezuela, following his election victory in 1988.

2   President P. W. Botha resigns as leader of the ruling National Party in South Africa, after suffering a stroke. He is succeeded by F. W. de Klerk.

3   The 35-year dictatorial regime of Alfredo Stroessner in Paraguay is overthrown by a military coup led by General Andrés Rodríguez, who replaces him as president. On May 1, Rodríguez gains a landslide victory in elections won by his right-of-center Colorado Party.

9   In the Jamaican general election, Michael Manley's People's National Party wins a landslide victory over the ruling Jamaica Labour Party of Edward Seaga.

14   Ayatollah Khomeini of Iran issues a *fatwa* against the British author Salman Rushdie, calling for his death for blasphemy against Islam in his book *The Satanic Verses*. Rushdie goes into hiding.

17 The leaders of Morocco, Libya, Algeria, Tunisia, and Mauritania agree to form a new economic bloc called the Arab Maghreb Union.

18 President Mohammad Najibullah imposes a state of emergency in Afghanistan to bolster his authority.

21 Václav Havel, the dissident Czech playwright, is imprisoned for inciting public disorder in Prague in January.

26 U.S. president George Bush, on a state visit to China, holds talks with premier Deng Xiaoping.

MARCH

5 The Sudanese cabinet resigns. Prime Minister Sadiq al-Mahdi agrees to form a coalition government and introduce a peace plan to end the country's civil war.

7 China imposes martial law in Lhasa, Tibet, following public unrest over Chinese rule.

7 Iran formally breaks off diplomatic relations with Britain over the Rushdie affair.

9 The Senate rejects President George Bush's appointment of John Tower as U.S. defense secretary because of allegations that he has received treatment for alcoholism.

10 U.S. president George Bush nominates Dick Cheney as U.S. defense secretary. The Senate later approves this choice.

11 A South African law commission publishes a working paper calling for the abolition of apartheid and the introduction of a universal franchise.

15 A large rally in Budapest calls for democracy and national independence for Hungary.

19 Alfredo Cristiani, of the ARENA party, gains an outright victory over Fidel Chavez Mena, of the Christian Democrats, in the presidential election in El Salvador. The voting is widely believed to have been rigged.

23 U.S. representatives hold talks with Palestine Liberation Organization officials in Tunis, Tunisia. PLO leader Yassir Arafat describes the outcome as "positive."

24 The U.S. Congress approves $41 million in aid for Nicaragua's Contra rebels.

26 Voters are offered a choice of candidates for the first time in elections for the Congress of People's Deputies in the USSR. Boris Yeltsin, dismissed from the Politburo 17 months before, gains 89% of the vote in his Moscow constituency, while many senior Party officials fail to get elected.

28 Solomon Mamaloni, leader of the People's Action Party and new prime minister of the Solomon Islands, announces his intention of turning the Islands into a republic, ending the 100-year link with Britain.

APRIL

5 The Solidarity leader Lech Wałęsa and the Polish government sign an agreement for political and economic reforms.

6 U.S. marine lieutenant colonel Oliver North claims during his trial that he acted on orders in arranging arms deals with Iran and diverting the profits to the Nicaraguan Contras.

7 U.S. marine lieutenant colonel Oliver North admits lying to Congress in order to cover up his role in the Iran–Contra scandal.

9 A new U.S. law protects whistleblowers—government employees who expose fraud or waste.

17 Students march on Beijing's Tiananmen Square to call for increased democracy in China.

17 The Polish Solidarity labor union is legalized and allowed to participate in parliamentary elections.

20 Multiparty elections are held in Czechoslovakia for the first time since 1946.

25 The Japanese prime minister Noboru Takeshita resigns over a bribery scandal, to be replaced by Sosuke Uno.

26 Anti-Senegalese violence erupts in Mauritius, leaving 400 dead. On April 28, revenge killings occur in Senegal.

MAY

2 Hungarian troops start to dismantle the 218-mile-long security fence along Hungary's border with Austria.

2 The center-right coalition under Ruud Lubbers in the Netherlands becomes the first European government to resign over an environmental issue, when the Liberal Democrats refuse to support proposals for financing antipollution measures.

4 U.S. marine lieutenant colonel Oliver North is found guilty on three minor charges for his role in the Iran–Contra affair.

6 Elections in Panama are won by the opposition, and are subsequently annulled by the country's effective dictator, General Manuel Noriega.

11 President George Bush orders the U.S. military presence in Panama to be boosted by 2,000 extra troops.

11 The CIA (Central Intelligence Agency) accuses Iran of complicity in the bombing of Pan Am flight 103.

14 Carlos Menem, leader of the rightist reformed Peronist party, defeats Eduardo Angeloz of the ruling Radical party in Argentina's presidential elections. On July 8, Menem takes over as president on the resignation of Raúl Alfonsín.

19 Italy's Christian Democrat prime minister Ciriaco de Mita announces the resignation of his center-left government. On July 23, Giulio Andreotti becomes prime minister, leading a similar coalition.

20 Thirteen people are convicted in Spain for their part in distributing contaminated cooking oil in 1981, an incident that killed more than 600 people.

29 Speaking at a NATO summit in Bonn, West Germany, U.S. president George Bush proposes a major military withdrawal from Europe.

JUNE

3 People's Liberation Army tanks in China move into Tiananmen Square in Beijing, killing 2,000 prodemocracy protesters.

4 The former Polish labor union Solidarity achieves a landslide victory in elections to the Sejm (parliament).

12 Soviet president Mikhail Gorbachev and West German chancellor Helmut Kohl sign the "Bonn Document," affirming the right of European states to determine their own political systems.

18 Andreas Papandreou's Pasok government loses its overall majority in the general election in Greece. On July 2, an interim government coalition of the New Democracy and Communist parties, led by Tzannis Tzannetakis, is sworn in.

21 The U.S. Supreme Court rules that the Constitution's guarantee of free speech includes the act of trampling or burning the national flag. President George Bush and the House of Representatives express dismay at the ruling.

23 President José Eduardo dos Santos of Angola and Jonas Savimbi, leader of the UNITA rebels, sign a declaration ending the 14-year civil war in Angola.

28 The Tamil Tiger guerrillas in Sri Lanka agree to a cease-fire in their war against government forces. It lasts until November 5.

29 It is alleged that some White House officials are involved in a gay prostitution ring.

30 The government of Sadiq al-Mahdi in Sudan is overthrown when a Revolutionary Command Council for National Salvation under Lieutenant General Omar Hassan Ahmed el-Bashir seizes power.

July

2 An Irish Republican Army (IRA) car bomb explodes in Hanover, killing a British soldier; it is the first of a series of attacks on British army personnel stationed in West Germany.

3 Britain states that there will be no automatic right of abode in Britain for Hong Kong residents worried about the colony's future under Chinese rule.

3 In the case *Webster v. Reproductive Health Services*, the U.S. Supreme Court upholds a Missouri state law that prohibits public hospitals and clinics from performing abortions except where the mother's life is in danger.

5 U.S. marine lieutenant colonel Oliver North is given a suspended sentence and fined $150,000 for his role in the Iran–Contra affair.

19 By just one vote, the Polish Sejm (parliament) elects the sole candidate, General Wojciech Jaruzelski, to the new post of executive president.

23 Elections for the Upper House in Japan end the 34-year Liberal Democrat majority.

28 Hashemi Rafsanjani is elected the first executive president of Iran.

31 Islamic terrorists claim to have hanged U.S. lieutenant colonel William Higgins, taken hostage in Beirut, Lebanon, in 1987.

August

1 State price controls are abolished in Poland, and food prices rise by up to 500%.

1 U.S. president George Bush holds urgent talks with Syria and Iran in an effort to resolve the hostage crisis in Lebanon.

3 Lebanese captors reprieve U.S. hostage Joseph Cicippio from a "death sentence" issued earlier in the week.

7 New Zealand prime minister David Lange resigns and is succeeded as both prime minister and Labor Party leader by Geoffrey Palmer.

8 The Japanese prime minister Sosuke Uno resigns when he is implicated in a sex scandal. He is succeeded by Toshiki Kaifu.

8 The United States rejects Iran's offer to help free hostages held by pro-Iran militants in the Middle East in exchange for the unfreezing of U.S.-held Iranian assets.

9 The Financial Institutions Rescue, Recovery, and Enforcement Act, a bailout package for troubled savings and loan institutions in the United States, goes into operation.

19 The Polish United Workers' Party agrees to join a Solidarity-led coalition government.

23 Over 2 million people in the Soviet Baltic republics form a 290-km/180-mile human chain to mark the 50th anniversary of the Soviet–German nonaggression pact that led to the incorporation of the republics into the USSR.

24 The Solidarity candidate Tadeusz Mazowiecki is elected Poland's new prime minister.

30 New York hotelier Leona Helmsley is found guilty of evading more than $1 million in taxes.

31 U.S. president George Bush sends $65 million to help the Colombian government's battle against the Medellín cocaine barons.

September

1 The United States breaks off diplomatic relations with Panama in an attempt to increase pressure for the overthrow of its dictator, General Manuel Noriega.

6 In a whites-only election in South Africa, the National Party is returned with a reduced majority, and F. W. de Klerk is elected president.

6 President George Bush launches a $7.9-billion plan to halve drug use in the United States.

6 The Christian Democrat Party led by Ruud Lubbers remains the largest party after the Dutch general election. On September 7, the Christian Democrats form a coalition government with the Labor Party.

10 Hungary begins to allow East Germans within its frontiers to cross freely to the West.

11 An opposition political movement ("New Forum") emerges in East Germany.

11 Norwegian elections take place under a new system that favors the smaller parties. On October 16, a Conservative-led coalition takes office under Jan Peder Syse.

12 A Solidarity-dominated cabinet is formed in Poland under Tadeusz Mazowiecki, the first noncommunist government in Eastern Europe since 1948.

14 Sam Najoma, president of the South West Africa People's Organization (SWAPO), returns to Namibia after nearly 30 years of exile.

20 An estimated 250,000 trees, covering 10% of Israel's 20,000-acre Carmel National Park, are burned by Arab militants.

24 An Arab League cease-fire enables civilians to return to their homes in Beirut after six months of fighting between Shiite and Druze militias.

26 Vietnamese troops begin to withdraw from Cambodia (formerly Kampuchea).

27 The national parliament of Slovenia approves constitutional amendments that give the country the right to secede from the Federation of Yugoslavia.

October

4 A mass demonstration in Leipzig demands political reform in East Germany.

6 An attempted army coup fails to topple President Manuel Noriega of Panama.

7 The Hungarian Socialist Workers' Party votes for its own dissolution.

8 The Latvian Popular Front announces its intention to seek Latvian independence from the USSR.

9 Rezsó Nyers is elected president of the new Hungarian Socialist Party, formed out of the old Hungarian Socialist Workers' Party.

11 Poland opens its borders with East Germany and declares that it will accept refugees from the political unrest there.

18 Erich Honecker resigns from the leadership of the Communist Party and the state in East Germany, to be succeeded by Egon Krenz, a reformist communist.

19 The alleged terrorists known as the "Guildford Four" are cleared on appeal in Britain of Irish Republican Army (IRA) bombing convictions after serving 14 years of their life sentences.

23 A new Hungarian Republic is declared, with a constitution allowing multiparty democracy.

31 Turgut Özal, prime minister since 1983, succeeds General Kenan Evren as Turkey's first civilian president for 30 years. He is succeeded as prime minister by Yildirim Akbulut.

NOVEMBER

1 President Daniel Ortega's Sandinista regime in Nicaragua ends its 19-month cease-fire with the Contra rebels as rebel-sponsored terrorist activity increases throughout the country.

5 Greece holds its second general election of the year after the collapse of the ruling coalition. On November 23, a new coalition government is sworn in, led by Professor Xenophon Zolatas.

6–7 Members of the Association of Southeast Asian Nations (ASEAN) join Canada, Australia, New Zealand, Japan, and South Korea in forming the Council for Asia–Pacific Economic Cooperation.

7 Namibia begins five days of polling to elect the first independent government of Africa's last colony.

7 The entire East German government led by Willi Stoph resigns amid continuing proreform demonstrations.

8 Jordan holds its first parliamentary election since 1967 after the resignation of Prime Minister Zaid al-Rifai and riots over price increases. The Muslim Brotherhood wins 25 seats out of 80, but is banned from government.

9 China's senior statesman Deng Xiaoping resigns as chairman of the Central Military Commission.

9 East Germany announces the opening of its border with West Germany as unrest continues and refugees continue to reach the West through the neighboring countries. The authorities begin demolishing sections of the Berlin Wall the following day.

10 Petar Mladenov replaces Todor Zhivkov as general secretary of the Communist Party in Bulgaria, ending Zhivkov's 35-year dictatorship.

12 Seventy-eight people die in battles between left wing guerrillas and government soldiers in El Salvador.

13 The reformer Hans Modrow is elected prime minister of East Germany.

16 President F. W. de Klerk announces the end of the Separate Amenities Act in South Africa, further weakening the legal basis of apartheid.

16 Six Jesuit priests, their housekeeper, and her 15-year-old daughter are tortured and murdered in El Salvador, at the University of Central America in San Salvador.

17 Fighting breaks out in San Salvador as rebel guerrillas win over parts of the city after rigged presidential elections are won by Alfredo Cristiani of the ARENA party.

17 The Czech police break up a rally for political reform in Prague.

17 The minimum U.S. wage is set at $4.25 per hour, starting from April 1991.

22 President René Muhawad of Lebanon, elected on November 5, dies in a terrorist bomb explosion after announcing his support for a peace plan. On November 24, he is succeeded by Elias Hrawi, amid continuing friction between the Christian leader General Michel Aoun and occupying Syrian troops.

22 The Congress (I) Party led by Rajiv Gandhi loses its parliamentary majority in the Indian general election. On December 2, a new multiparty government is sworn in under V. P. Singh of the new Janata Dal ("People's Party").

27 A general strike in Czechoslovakia supports calls for an end to communist rule.

28 The Czechoslovak prime minister Ladislav Adamec formally renounces the communist monopoly on power.

DECEMBER

2 The U.S. president George Bush and the Soviet president Mikhail Gorbachev formally declare the Cold War to be at an end.

3 The Politburo and Communist Party Central Committee resign in East Germany after revelations of widespread corruption. On December 8, the former leader Erich Honecker is charged with abuse of office.

6 Forty people are killed in a bomb attack on police headquarters in Bogotá, Colombia.

10 A majority noncommunist coalition government takes power in Czechoslovakia, led by Marian Calfa.

11 The forcible repatriation of Vietnamese "boat people" (refugees) from Hong Kong begins.

14 The Christian Democrat candidate Patricio Aylwin wins an overwhelming victory in the Chilean presidential elections.

15 Panama declares war on the United States. The next day, a U.S. soldier is shot dead in Panama.

16–17 Violent antigovernment demonstrations erupt in Timişoara, Romania, following the arrest of the Protestant pastor Lázlo Tökes.

17 Fernando Collor de Mello of the conservative National Reconstruction Party (PRN) narrowly wins the presidential election in Brazil, taking office on March 15, 1990.

17 The Romanian army fires on a demonstration in the city of Timişoara, killing about 100 people, but rumors report a far higher figure. On December 20, President Nicolae Ceauşescu declares a state of emergency as protests spread.

19 U.S. troops invade Panama to overthrow the regime of General Manuel Noriega.

22 The army joins forces with antigovernment demonstrators in Romania and overthrows President Nicolae Ceauşescu. On December 25, Nicolae and Elena Ceauşescu are captured, given a summary trial, and executed by the army.

22 The Brandenburg Gate in Berlin, a symbol of the city and of the division of Germany, is ceremonially opened to mark the fall of the Berlin Wall.

26 An interim government is formed in Romania by the National Salvation Front. It announces constitutional changes, guarantees rights of national minorities, allows for freedom of worship and a free market economy, and promises free elections.

26 Panamanian president General Manuel Noriega takes refuge in the papal nunciature in Panama City.

27 Egypt and Syria resume full diplomatic relations.
29 The former dissident Václav Havel attends a thanksgiving mass in St. Vitus' Cathedral, Prague, after his inauguration as the first noncommunist president of Czechoslovakia for 41 years.
30 Nicaragua expels 30 U.S. diplomats.

SCIENCE, TECHNOLOGY, AND MEDICINE

Computing

c. 1989 Developments in desktop publishing make high-quality print production more generally accessible.
• U.S. computer microchip manufacturer Intel launches the 25MHz 80486 microprocessor; it has 1.2 million transistors and includes a math coprocessor and cache memory.
• U.S. computing innovator Jaron Lanier makes the experience of virtual reality possible with his design of a headset and special gloves, that will allow a user to experience and manipulate a computer-generated world.

Ecology

• Worldwide, 1989 is the warmest year on record; environmentalists suggest this is due to the "greenhouse effect."
• A lemur, *Allocebus tricholis*, previously thought to be extinct, is discovered in Madagascar.
• Brazil suspends tax incentives favoring burning in the Amazon jungle in response to worldwide environmentalist opinion; land clearance continues, however.
• New Californian laws ban gas-powered lawnmowers and outdoor barbecues and require many vehicles to run on alternative fuels.

JANUARY
11 A declaration outlawing the use of poison gas and toxic and bacteriological weapons is agreed by 149 countries.

MARCH
24 The *Exxon Valdez* oil tanker runs aground in Prince William Sound, Alaska, spilling an estimated 40,504,000 l/8,910,880 gal of oil. It is the largest oil spill in U.S. history. Over 4,800 km/3,000 mi of shoreline are polluted.

APRIL
19 An explosion in the gun turret aboard the USS *Iowa* kills 47 marines.

SEPTEMBER
17 The northeast Caribbean is hit by Hurricane Hugo; more than 70 people are killed, hundreds of thousands left homeless, and $4 billion damage is caused.

OCTOBER
16 The Convention on International Trade in Endangered Species (CITES) agrees to a total ban on trading in ivory.

17 An earthquake measuring 7.1 on the Richter scale hits San Francisco, California, killing at least 273 people, many of whom die when the upper level of the Nimitz Highway collapses. It is North America's most destructive earthquake since 1906, causing at least $6 billion in property damage.
17 The third game of baseball's World Series at Candlestick Park, San Francisco, between the San Francisco Giants and the Oakland As is disrupted by an earthquake.

DECEMBER
19 Nearly 19 million l/4.2 million gal of crude oil spill into the Atlantic from the Iranian tanker *Khark 5* following an explosion and fire.

Exploration

• The European Space Agency's *Hipparcos* satellite is launched; it carries two telescopes for measuring the distance of stars.
• The U.S. Cosmic Background Explorer (COBE) satellite is launched to study microwave background radiation, thought to be a vestige of the Big Bang.
• The U.S. Delta Star "Star Wars" satellite is launched; it successfully detects and tracks test missiles shortly after they are launched.

MAY
4 The U.S. space shuttle launches the probe *Magellan* to map the surface of Venus using radar.

AUGUST
25 The U.S. space probe *Voyager* 2 reaches Neptune and transmits pictures; it discovers a great dark spot on the planet and six new moons.

OCTOBER
18 The U.S. space shuttle *Atlantis* launches the spacecraft *Galileo* to explore Jupiter. It reaches its destination in December 1995.

Health and Medicine

• Abortion becomes legal in Romania after the downfall of the Ceauşescu regime.
• At the Fetal Treatment Center in San Francisco, California., U.S. pediatric surgeon Michael R. Harrison and colleagues remove a fetus from its mother's womb, operate on its lungs, and return it to the womb. It is the first operation of its kind.
• Researchers in Toronto, Canada, identify a gene responsible for cystic fibrosis.
• Scientists in Britain introduce genetically engineered white blood cells into cancer patients, to attack tumors.
• The Nobel Prize for Physiology or Medicine is awarded jointly to U.S. virologist Michael Bishop and U.S. molecular biologist Harold Varmus for their discovery of oncogenes—genes carried by viruses that can trigger cancerous growth in normal cells.
October 1989–90 The failure of the U.S. immunization program is highlighted when more than 100 children die from a measles epidemic that sweeps through several large U.S. cities; three-quarters of the children had not been vaccinated.

DECEMBER

31 Since 1981, 10,611 women in the United States have reported having AIDS. Between 1984 and 1988, the proportion of U.S. AIDS sufferers who are women has increased from 6.4% to 10.4%.

Science

- Astronomers discover a river of gas at the center of the Milky Way, providing further evidence that a black hole, 4 million times as massive as the sun, exists at the center of our galaxy.
- Star HD 114762 is discovered to have a planet-like body circling it.
- The Australia Telescope is completed; it has seven 22-m/72-ft dishes and one 64-m/210-ft dish, which are spread throughout New South Wales, Australia, making it one of the largest radio telescopes in the world.
- The Australian Research Council is established to provide advice on national research priorities, to coordinate research, and to recommend allocation of resources.
- The first visual image of a DNA (deoxyribonucleic acid) molecule is obtained by U.S. scientists.
- The Nobel Prize for Physics is awarded jointly to German nuclear physicist Wolfgang Paul and German-born U.S. physicist Hans Dehmelt for their ion-trap method for isolating single atoms, and to U.S. physicist Norman Ramsey for his measurement techniques leading to the discovery of the cesium atomic clock.
- U.S. archeologists discover the site of the Assyrian city of Mashkan-shapir in Iraq. Built in about 1850 BC, it is one of the oldest cities in the world and has remained undisturbed until this time.
- U.S. astronomers J. P. Huchra and M. J. Geller discover a large, thin sheet of galaxies, which they name the "Great Wall"; no current astronomical theory can explain its distinctive form. It is the largest known structure in the universe and is 500 million lightyear long and 200 wide.
- U.S. biochemists Sidney Altman and Thomas Cech receive the Nobel Prize for Chemistry for their discovery of the catalytic properties of RNA (ribonucleic acid).

MARCH

- U.S. physicist Stanley Pons and English physicist Martin Fleischmann announce that they have achieved nuclear fusion at room temperature (cold fusion); other scientists fail to replicate their experiment.
28 The Laboratory for International Fuzzy Engineering Research is established In Yokohama, Japan, by the Japanese Ministry of International Trade and Industry to develop "fuzzy theory."

Technology

- A pipeline-corrosion "pig" is introduced in the U.S. oil industry; it travels down oil pipelines using sensors to locate areas of corrosion.
- Researchers at Boeing's High Technology Center develop a solar voltaic cell consisting of two layers, one that converts blue light and the other red light into electricity; together they convert 37% of solar radiation into electricity, nearly twice that of other solar voltaic cells.
- The Sayano-Shushensk Dam across the Yenisey River in Siberia is completed; 245 m/804 ft high, it is the tallest composite arch and gravity dam in the world.
- The Shippingport Atomic Power Station, Pennsylvania (the first full-scale nuclear power station in the United States), becomes the first U.S. power station to be decommissioned, after 32 years of operation.

JANUARY

- The Austrian Post Office launches the first holographic postage stamps.

JUNE

3 Daily broadcasts of high definition television (HDTV) begin in Japan.

JULY

14 The LEP (Large Electron Positron Collider) is inaugurated at the CERN research center in Switzerland; the new accelerator has a circumference of 27 km/16.8 mi and is the largest scientific apparatus in the world.

Transportation

- An anticollision device is introduced on corporate jets in the United States; it monitors up to 30 nearby aircraft and issues voiced instructions to avoid imminent collisions.
- The 450-m/1,476-ft Chao Phraya Bridge in Bangkok, Thailand, is completed. It is the longest single-plane cable stay bridge in the world.
- The Roger's Pass tunnel in British Columbia, Canada, is completed; at 35 km/21.9 mi long, it is the longest road tunnel in the world.
- The U.S. military tests a "vortex flap" on its swept-wing supersonic fighter jets; it greatly improves maneuverability.
- The wreck of the German battleship *Bismarck*, sunk by Britain's Royal Navy in 1941, is discovered by U.S. entrepreneur Robert Ballard 4.8 km/3 mi under the surface of the North Atlantic.
- Two trains collide head-on in Bangladesh, killing 170 people and injuring 1,000 others.

FEBRUARY

24 Nine people on board a United Airlines Boeing 747, en route from Honolulu, are sucked out of the plane when a cargo door is torn open.

MARCH

27 As the oil spill from the tanker *Exxon Valdez*, aground in Prince William Sound, Alaska, spreads over 100 sq mi/260 sq km, a state of emergency is declared in the area affected.

JULY

- The U.S. Air Force's Stealth Bomber (B-2) makes its first flight. Its profile, and the material used in its construction, are intended to reduce radar reflection.
19 A United Airlines DC-10 crashes into a cornfield near Sioux City, Iowa; 112 of the 296 people on board are killed.

19 A French DC-10, en route from Chad to Paris, France, is blown up by a terrorist bomb; it crashes in Niger, killing all 171 people on board.

20 The TGV Atlantique (*train à grande vitesse*, "high-speed train") between Paris and Le Mans, France, makes its first run; it travels at speeds up to 299 kph/186 mph.

21 A U.S. Air Boeing 737 falls into the East River after an abortive takeoff from La Guardia airport, New York.

ARTS AND IDEAS

Architecture

- Britain's Prince of Wales publishes *A Vision of Britain: A Personal View of Architecture*. An attack on much of contemporary architecture, the book stimulates a lively debate about architecture and urban renewal in the UK.
- La Grande Arche at La Défense, designed by the architects Johann Otto von Spreckelsen and Paul Andreu, is completed in Paris, France.
- The Basilica of Our Lady of Peace is completed in Yamoussoukro, Ivory Coast; modeled after St. Peter's basilica in Rome, its dome is 160 m/525 ft high, making it the tallest church in the world.

Arts

- A controversial glass pyramid entrance to the Louvre museum, designed by the Chinese-born U.S. architect I. M. Pei, is completed in Paris, France.
- The English artist David Hockney sends a picture by a series of faxes from his home in California to the UK, where the pieces are reassembled.
- The English sculptor Richard Deacon creates *Kiss and Tell*.
- The sculpture *Tilted Arc*, by Richard Serra, set in Foley Square, New York, New York, is dismantled and removed by government officials after years of complaints that it is ugly and expensive. The controversy sharpens opinion in the United States about the relationship between government and the arts.
- The U.S. artist Jennifer Bartlett paints *An Ordinary Evening in New Haven*.

OCTOBER

28 The U.S. Congress bans the National Endowment for the Arts from funding "obscene" works such as Robert Mapplethorpe's sexually explicit photographs.

Film

- The animated feature movie *The Little Mermaid* is released in the United States by the Disney studio.
- The black comedy *Heathers*, directed by Michael Lehmann and starring Winona Ryder and Christian Slater, is released in the United States.
- The dramatic comedy movie *Enemies, A Love Story*, adapted from a novel by Isaac Bashevis Singer, is released in the United States. It is directed by Paul Mazursky and stars Anjelica Huston, Ron Silver, Margaret Sophie Stein, and Lena Olin.
- The movie *Batman*, directed by Tim Burton, is released in the United States. Based on the comic strip created by Bob Kane, it stars Michael Keaton, Jack Nicholson, and Kim Basinger.
- The movie *Beiqing Chengshi/A City of Sadness*, directed by Hou Hsiao-Hsien, is released in Taiwan, starring Li Tianlu and Chen Songyong.
- The movie *Born on the Fourth of July*, directed by Oliver Stone, is released in the United States. It is based on the book by Ron Kovic, and stars Tom Cruise.
- The movie *Crimes and Misdemeanors*, written and directed by Woody Allen, is released in the United States. It stars Allen, Mia Farrow, Alan Alda, Anjelica Huston, and Martin Landau.
- The movie *Dead Poets Society*, directed by Australian filmmaker Peter Weir, is released in the United States. It stars Robin Williams, Robert Sean Leonard, Ethan Hawke, and Josh Charles.
- The movie *Do the Right Thing*, written and directed by Spike Lee, is released the United States. It features an all-star cast including Lee, Danny Aiello, Ossie Davis, Ruby Dee, and John Turturro.
- The movie *Driving Miss Daisy*, directed by Bruce Beresford, is released in the United States. Based on the play by Alfred Uhry, it stars Jessica Tandy and Morgan Freeman.
- The movie *Drugstore Cowboy*, directed by Gus Van Sant, is released in the United States. It stars Matt Dillon and Kelly Lynch.
- The movie *Eat a Bowl of Tea*, directed by Wayne Wang, is released in the United States.
- The movie *Glory*, directed by Edward Zwick, is released in the United States. It stars Matthew Broderick, Denzel Washington, Cary Elwes, and Morgan Freeman.
- The movie *Indiana Jones and the Last Crusade*, the final movie in Steven Spielberg's *Indiana Jones* trilogy, is released in the United States. It features Harrison Ford, Sean Connery, and Denholm Elliott.
- The movie *Jésus de Montréal/Jesus of Montreal*, directed by Denys Arcand, is released in Canada. It stars Lothaire Bluteau, Catherine Wilkening, and Johanne-Marie Tremblay.
- The movie *Monsieur Hire*, directed by Patrice Leconte, is released in France. Based on a novel by Georges Simenon, it stars Michel Blanc and Sandrine Bonnaire.
- The movie *My Left Foot*, directed by Jim Sheridan, is released in Ireland. It stars Daniel Day Lewis and Brenda Fricker.
- The movie *Rikyu*, directed by Hiroshi Teshigahara, is released in Japan. It stars Rentaro Mikuni and Tsutomo Yamazaki.
- The movie *sex, lies, and videotape*, directed by Steven Soderbergh, is released in the United States. It is awarded the Palme d'Or at the Cannes Film Festival in France, on May 23.
- The movie *Sweetie*, directed by New Zealand filmmaker Jane Campion, is released in Australia.
- The movie *The Killer*, directed by John Woo, is released in Hong Kong, starring Chow Yun-Fat, Sally Yeh, and Danny Lee.
- The movie *The War of the Roses*, based on a novel by Warren Adler, is released in the United States. It stars

Michael Douglas, Kathleen Turner, Danny De Vito, who also directs, and Marianne Sägebrecht.

- The movie *When Harry Met Sally*, directed by Rob Reiner, is released in the United States. It stars Billy Crystal and Meg Ryan.
- The movie *Henry V*, an adaption of Shakespeare's play directed by and starring Kenneth Branagh, is released in Britain.
- The humorous documentary *Roger & Me*, directed by Michael Moore, is released in the United States. It features journalist Michael Moore's attempts to interview the chairman of General Motors about factory closure.
- The thriller *Sea of Love*, directed by Harold Becker, is released in the United States. Scripted by Richard Price, it stars Al Pacino and Ellen Barkin.

MARCH

29 The 1988 Academy Awards take place. Best Actor: Dustin Hoffman, for *Rain Man*; Best Supporting Actor: Kevin Kline, for *A Fish Called Wanda*; Best Actress: Jodie Foster, for *The Accused*; Best Supporting Actress: Geena Davis, for *The Accidental Tourist*; Best Picture: *Rain Man*, directed by Barry Levinson; Best Director: Barry Levinson, for *Rain Man*.

NOVEMBER

9 The first French Film Festival to be held in the United States is opened by Audrey Hepburn.

Literature and Language

- Australian writer Germaine Greer publishes her autobiographical *Daddy, We Hardly Knew You*.
- English novelist Julian Barnes publishes his novel *A History of the World in 10½ Chapters*.
- The English journalist Hugo Young publishes *One of Us: A Biography of Margaret Thatcher*.
- The English poet Ted Hughes publishes his poetry collection *Wolfwatching*.
- The English writer Martin Amis publishes his novel *London Fields*.
- The French-born U.S. literary critic George Steiner publishes his critical work *Real Presences*.
- The Indian-born U.S. writer Bharati Mukherjee publishes her novel *Jasmine*.
- The Israeli writer David Grossman publishes his novel *See Under: Love*.
- The Japanese-born English writer Kazuo Ishiguro publishes his novel *Remains of the Day*, which wins the Booker Prize.
- The Nobel Prize for Literature is awarded to the Spanish novelist Camilo José Cela.
- The Pulitzer Prize for Biography is awarded to Richard Ellmann for *Oscar Wilde*, the Pulitzer Prize for Poetry is awarded to Richard Wilbur for *New and Collected Poems*, and the Pulitzer Prize for Fiction is awarded to Anne Tyler for *Breathing Lessons*.
- The second edition of *The Oxford English Dictionary*, edited by J. A. Simpson and E. S. C. Weiner, is published.
- The South African writer Breyten Breytenbach publishes his novel *Memory of Snow and Dust*.

- The U.S. novelist Amy Tan publishes her novel *The Joy Luck Club*.
- The U.S. novelist David Leavitt publishes his novel *Equal Affections*.
- The U.S. novelist E. L. Doctorow publishes his novel *Billy Bathgate*.
- The U.S. novelist John Irving publishes his novel *A Prayer for Owen Meany*.
- The U.S. novelist Paul Auster publishes his novel *Moon Palace*.
- The U.S. writer Annie Dillard publishes her critical work *The Writing Life*.
- The U.S. writer Tobias Wolff publishes his autobiography *This Boy's Life*.
- The West Indian poet Derek Walcott publishes his long poem "Omeros."
- U.S. biographer Anne Stevenson publishes *Bitter Fame*, her biography of the U.S. poet Sylvia Plath.
- U.S. travel writer Bill Bryson publishes his *Lost Continent: Travels in Small Town America*.

Music

- The Finnish composer Magnus Lindberg completes *Kinetics*, an orchestral piece.
- The Italian pop group Black Box releases "Ride On Time."
- The opera *New Year* by the English composer Michael Tippett is first performed, in Houston, Texas.
- The U.S. composer Elliott Carter completes his orchestral work *Anniversary*, the last of his *Three Celebrations*.
- The U.S. composer John Cage completes his vocal works *Europera III* and *Europera IV*.
- The U.S. pop group New Kids on the Block releases the album *Hangin' Tough*.
- The U.S. pop group the Neville Brothers releases the album *Yellow Moon*.

JANUARY

28 The U.S. rock singer Lou Reed releases the album *New York*.

FEBRUARY

22 The 1988–89 Grammy Awards are held. Best Album: *Faith* by George Michael; Best New Artist and Female Vocalist: Tracy Chapman for "Fast Car;" Best Female Rock Vocalist: Tina Turner for *Tina Live in Europe*. "Don't Worry, Be Happy" by Bobby Mcferrin wins Best Song and Best Record.

MARCH

11 The British pop group Fine Young Cannibals releases the album *The Raw And The Cooked*.

APRIL

8 The U.S. pop singer Madonna releases the single "Like A Prayer." She loses her Pepsi sponsorship when religious groups complain that the video is blasphemous.

JULY

8 The U.S. rock singer Prince releases *Batman*, the soundtrack to the movie of the same name.

13 The Bastille Opera, in Paris, France, opens, for two performances only. It does not open fully till 1990.

23 The U.S. pop group Public Enemy releases the album *It takes a Nation of Millions to Hold Us Back*.

NOVEMBER

26 Singer-songwriter Jules Shear perfoms in the first MTV "Unplugged" session. This feature will develop into a successful range of albums, featuring artists such as Nirvana, Rod Stewart, and k d lang.

DECEMBER

17 The U.S. heavy rock group Guns 'n' Roses releases the album *G 'n' R Lies*.

Theater and Dance

- Archeologists uncover the remains in London, England, of the Rose and Globe theaters—16th-century theaters where many of Shakespeare's plays were originally performed.
- The musical *Aspects of Love* is first performed, at the Prince of Wales Theatre in London, England. The lyrics are by Don Black and Charles Hart and the music by Andrew Lloyd Webber.
- The musical *Buddy*, based on the life of the pop singer Buddy Holly, is first performed, at the Victoria Palace Theatre in London, England.
- The musical *City of Angels*, with music by Cy Coleman and lyrics by David Zippel, is first performed, at the Virginia Theater in New York, New York.
- The musical *Miss Saigon*, with music by Alain Boubil and Claude-Michel Schönberg and lyrics by Richard Maltby, is first performed, at the Theatre Royal Drury Lane, in London, England.
- The play *A Few Good Men*, by the U.S. writer Aaron Sorkin, is first performed, at the Music Box Theater in New York, New York.
- The play *Shadowlands*, by the English writer William Nicholson, is first performed, at the Queen's Theatre in London, England. It is based on the life of the English writer C. S. Lewis.
- The Pulitzer Prize for Drama is awarded to Wendy Wasserstein for *The Heidi Chronicles*.

Thought and Scholarship

- Australian philosopher David Armstrong publishes *A Combinatorial Theory of Possibility*.
- English historian Christopher Brooke publishes *The Medieval Idea of Marriage*.
- English historian Paul Langford publishes *A Polite and Commercial People: England 1727–1783*, which is a volume in the *New Oxford History of England* series.
- English historian Peter Brown publishes *The Body and Society: Men, Women, and Sexual Renunciation in Early Christianity*.
- English historian Simon Schama publishes *Citizens: A Chronicle of the French Revolution*.
- The first volume of *The Cambridge History of Japan* is published, edited by John Hall and others.
- The Pulitzer Prize for History is awarded to Taylor Branch for *Parting the Waters*, and to James M. McPherson for *Battle Cry of Freedom*.
- The Pulitzer Prize for General Nonfiction is awarded to Neil Sheehan for *A Bright and Shining Lie*.
- U.S. historian Drew R. McCoy publishes *The Last of the Founding Fathers: James Madison and the Republican Legacy*.

- U.S. historian Nathan O. Hatch publishes *The Democratization of American Christianity*.
- U.S. historian Paul Fussell publishes *Wartime: Understanding and Behavior in the Second World War*.
- U.S. philosopher Gilbert Harman publishes *Skepticism and the Definition of Knowledge*.
- U.S. philosopher Willard V. Quine publishes *Pursuit of Truth*.

SOCIETY

Education

- The School Achievement Indicators Program begins in Canada.

Everyday Life

c. 1989 Telephone sex lines take off in the United States, when phone companies begin to bill for these services separately.

- A U.S. Supreme Court case undermines women's right to legal abortions by restricting abortions at facilities that receive federal funding.
- Illicit drugs are being used at least once a month by 14.5 million Americans.
- In fashion, U.S. women prefer softer, more feminine clothes to the masculine style of the early 1980s, and black is favored over bright colors. Men turn to the double-breasted suit.
- Of women executives in the United States, 52% are single with no children, 39% have children and are married or divorced, and 9% are married without children.
- The largest religious denomination in the United States is the Roman Catholic Church, with the Southern Baptist Convention taking second place and the United Methodist Church third.
- The percentages of women in elective office in the United States in 1989 are: Congress 5%, state legislatures 17%, county governing boards 9%.
- The ubiquity worldwide of the Teenage Mutant Ninja Turtles characters indicates the growing size of the world licensed merchandising market.
- The U.S. president George Bush expresses his distaste for broccoli and declares his liberty as leader of the free world never to have to eat the vegetable again; broccoli growers protest and deliver a consignment to the White House.
- There are over 6 million immigrants to the United States in the period 1980–9, coming mainly from Asia and the Americas. This compares with over 4 million in the period 1970–79.

JANUARY

21 The birth of Christopher Bollig in the United States makes Augusta Bunge of Wisconsin a great-great-great-great grandmother and creates a seven-generation family.

APRIL

9　About 300,000 proabortion activists march in Washington, D.C., to protest against U.S. government plans to tighten up abortion laws.

JULY

14　Celebrations to mark the 200th anniversary of the start of the French Revolution are held in France.

NOVEMBER

- Sportswear manufacturer Reebok launches the Reebok Pump, the first inflatable training shoe.

Media and Communication

- Eight of ten new magazines in the United States fail as advertising revenue in magazines drops, while book publishing prospers.

FEBRUARY

5–8　*Lonesome Dove*, an adaptation of Larry McMurty's novel, starring Robert Duvall, Tommy Lee Jones, Robert Urich, Danny Glover, and Anjelica Huston, is shown on U.S. television.

APRIL

23　*Murderers Among Us: The Simon Wiesenthal Story*, a biography of Nazi hunter Wiesenthal starring Ben Kingsley, is shown on U.S. television.

BIRTHS & DEATHS

JANUARY

7　Hirohito, Emperor of Japan 1927–89, dies in Tokyo, Japan (87).

23　Salvador Dalí, Spanish surrealist painter who also designed furniture, jewelry, and stage and film sets, dies in Figueras, Spain (84).

FEBRUARY

19　Eric Goldman, U.S. historian and adviser to President Lyndon B. Johnson, dies in Princeton, New Jersey (73).

26　Roy Eldridge, U.S. jazz trumpeter popular in the 1940s, dies in Valley Stream, New York (78).

MARCH

3　Richard Brandon Morris, U.S. historian of the colonial period and the American Revolution, dies in New York, New York (84).

9　Robert Mapplethorpe, U.S. black-and-white photographer known for his celebrity portraits, male nudes, and flower photos, dies in Boston, Massachusetts (42).

27　Malcolm Cowley, U.S. author and critic, dies in New Milford, Connecticut (91).

APRIL

12　Sugar Ray Robinson, U.S. professional boxer, six times world champion, dies in Culver City, California (69).

19　Daphne du Maurier, English gothic novelist whose works include *Rebecca* and "The Birds," dies in Par, Cornwall, England (81).

22　Emilio Segré, Italian physicist who discovered the antiproton, dies in Lafayette, California (84).

30　Sergio Leone, Italian film director known for his "spaghetti Westerns," dies in Rome, Italy (60).

MAY

20　Gilda Radner, U.S. actress and comedian best known for sketches on the television show *Saturday Night Live*, dies in Los Angeles, California (42).

JUNE

3　Ruhollah Khomeini, Iranian Shiite Muslim Ayatollah and organizer of the 1979 revolution that made him political and religious leader of Iran for life, dies in Tehran, Iran (89).

9　George Wells Beadle, U.S. biochemist who received the Nobel Prize for Physiology or Medicine in 1958 for demonstrating that genes control enzyme structure, dies in Pomona, California (85).

27　A(lfred) J(ules) Ayer, English philosopher and teacher, a proponent of logical positivism, dies in London, England (78).

JULY

2　Andrey Gromyko, Soviet foreign minister 1957–85 and president 1985–88, dies (79).

10　Mel Blanc, U.S. actor most famous for being the voice of Bugs Bunny and Daffy Duck, dies in Los Angeles, California (81).

11　Laurence Olivier, English stage and film actor, director, and producer, dies near London, England (82).

AUGUST

11　William B. Shockley, U.S. physicist who was instrumental in the development of the transistor, dies in San Francisco, California (79).

26　Irving Stone, U.S. author of biographical novels including *The Agony and the Ecstasy* about Michelangelo, dies in Los Angeles, California (86).

29　Peter Scott, British artist, ornithologist, and broadcaster, founder of the World Wildlife Fund (now the Worldwide Fund for Nature), dies in Bristol, England (79).

SEPTEMBER

15　Robert Penn Warren, U.S. novelist and poet, the only U.S. writer to win Pulitzer prizes for both fiction and poetry, dies in Stratton, Vermont (84).

22　Irving Berlin, U.S. songwriter and popular composer for stage and film, dies in New York, New York (101).

28　Ferdinand Marcos, Philippine head of state 1966–86, dies in Honolulu, Hawaii (72).

30　Virgil Thomson, U.S. composer, music critic, and conductor, dies in New York, New York (92).

OCTOBER

6　Bette Davis, U.S. film actress who frequently played sensitive or neurotic women, dies in Neuilly-sur-Seine, France (81).

25　Mary McCarthy, U.S. author and social critic, dies in New York, New York (77).

NOVEMBER

5　Vladimir Horowitz, Russian-born U.S. pianist, dies in New York, New York (85).

22　René Muhawad, Lebanese president for less than a month, dies in Beirut, Lebanon (64).

DECEMBER

14　Andrey Dimitriyevich Sakharov, Soviet nuclear physicist and outspoken supporter of human rights and civil liberties, dies in Moscow, USSR (68).

22　Samuel Beckett, Irish writer and winner of the Nobel Prize for Literature in 1969, dies in Paris, France (83).

25　Nicolae Ceauşescu, president of the Socialist Republic of Romania 1967–89, is executed near Bucharest, Romania (71).

MAY

15 *Roe v. Wade*, a docu-drama about the U.S. Supreme Court's 1973 abortion decision, starring Holly Hunter, is shown on U.S. television.

SEPTEMBER

12–August 29, 1993 *Life Goes On*, the first primetime series to feature a regular character with Down's syndrome, is shown on U.S. television.

17 The 1988–89 Emmy Awards for television are held. Best Drama Series: *LA Law*; Best Comedy Series: *Cheers*; Best Actor in a Drama: Carroll O'Connor, for *In the Heat of the Night*; Best Actress in a Drama: Dana Delany, for *China Beach*; Best Actor in a Comedy: Richard Mulligan, for *Empty Nest*; Best Actress in a Comedy: Candice Bergen, for *Murphy Brown*.

Religion

- British historian Lyndal Roper publishes *The Holy Household: Women and Morals in Reformation Augsburg*.

MAY

17 The Roman Catholic Church in Poland is given a status unparalleled in postwar Eastern Europe, with the restoration of property confiscated in the 1950s and the right to run schools.

DECEMBER

1 Mikhail Gorbachev becomes the first leader of the USSR to visit the Vatican. He and Pope John Paul II agree to reestablish diplomatic relations between their states.

Sports

- Eddie Lawson of the United States, on a Honda, wins his fourth 500 cc world motorcycling championship.
- Soccer hooliganism is a growing problem in Europe. In the Netherlands, 25 games are postponed because of threats of violence.
- The first cycling World Cup series is won by Sean Kelly of the Republic of Ireland.
- The franchise for the Dallas Cowboys football team is sold for $140 million. It had been bought for $600,000 in 1970.
- With 598 winners from 2,312 rides, the 19-year-old U.S. jockey Kent Desormeaux breaks the record for the most wins by a jockey in a year in the United States.

JANUARY

1 Notre Dame is college football champion for the 1988 season.

FEBRUARY

11–12 U.S. national figure skating champions are: Jill Trenary; Christopher Bowman; Kristi Yamaguchi and Rudi Galindo, pairs; Susan Wynne and Joseph Dunbar, dance.

APRIL

15 Ninety-six Liverpool fans die in a crush during the Football Association (FA) Cup semifinal against Nottingham Forest at Hillsborough, Sheffield, England.

23 Kareem Abdul-Jabbar of the Los Angeles Lakers retires as the leading career scorer in National Basketball Association history, with 38,387 points in 1,560 games.

MAY

5–14 The inaugural international cycle stage race the Tour de Trump (later renamed the Tour DuPont) in the United States, is won by Dag Otto Lauritzen of Norway.

25 The Calgary Flames defeat the Montreal Canadiens to win the Stanley Cup.

28 Brazilian race-car driver Emerson Fittipaldi wins the Indianapolis 500; his average speed is 269 kph/167 mph.

JUNE

13 The Detroit Pistons reverse the results of the previous year by beating the Los Angeles Lakers to win the National Basketball Association (NBA) championship.

15–18 U.S. golfer Curtis Strange wins his second straight U.S. Open golf championship, the first repeat champion since Ben Hogan in 1950 and 1951.

JULY

23 The U.S. cyclist Greg Lemond wins the Tour de France by the closest margin of victory in the history of the race, just eight seconds ahead of Laurent Fignon of France.

AUGUST

6 Mark Allen of the United States wins the men's title at the first official world triathlon championships in Avignon, France.

17 Britain and Ireland's amateur golfers win the Walker Cup against the United States for the first time since 1971; this is their first victory in the United States.

OCTOBER

- The Canadian ice-hockey player Wayne Gretsky of the Los Angeles Kings surpasses Gordie Howe's National Hockey League scoring record with a new record of 1,850 points.

3 Art Shell is appointed head coach of the Los Angeles Raiders. He is the first black American professional head coach in football since Fritz Pollard in 1921.

14–28 The Oakland Athletics defeat their neighbors the San Francisco Giants in four straight games in baseball's World Series.

NOVEMBER

19 The United States qualifies for the World Cup soccer finals for the first time since 1950.

22 Kirby Puckett, an outfielder for the Minnesota Twins, becomes the first baseball player to sign a contract for $3 million a season.

1990

POLITICS, GOVERNMENT, AND ECONOMICS

Business and Economics

JANUARY

31 U.S. fast-food company McDonald's opens its first branch in the USSR, in Pushkin Square, Moscow.

FEBRUARY

13 The U.S. "junk bond" brokers Drexel Burnham Lambert file for bankruptcy following the indictment in 1989 of leading bond dealer Michael Milken.

Human Rights

JUNE

4 Janet Adkinson of Portland, Oregon, commits suicide using the "suicide machine," invented earlier in the year by U.S. pathologist Jack Kevorkian, who becomes known as "Dr. Death."

25 Active homosexuals are admitted to the rabbinate by the Central Conference of American Rabbis, but the Evangelical Lutheran Church suspends two churches that have ordained homosexuals.

SEPTEMBER

29 The World Summit for Children is held in New York, New York. Sponsored by UNICEF, it aims to bring governments together to save children from disease, illiteracy, and to guarantee better prenatal care, although no extra money is allocated for these tasks. It is the largest gathering of political leaders ever on any issue.

OCTOBER

19 The ruling South African National Party formally opens its membership to all races.

Politics and Government

• A law forbidding religious propaganda in Albania is repealed.
• Drug possession is criminalized in Italy.

JANUARY

1 Poland introduces the harshest transitional austerity program of economic reforms in Eastern Europe.

3 General Manuel Noriega of Panama surrenders to the U.S. authorities and is taken to Florida to face charges of drug smuggling.

15 Soviet troops are sent into the Caucasian region of Nagorno-Karabakh to quell continuing ethnic violence between Armenians and Azeris.

15 The Bulgarian National Assembly votes to end the communist monopoly on power.

18 Azerbaijan declares war on Armenia.

19 Soviet troops fire on demonstrators in Baku, the capital of Azerbaijan.

19 The Mayor of Washington, D.C., Marion Barry, is arrested after being filmed smoking crack cocaine in a hotel room.

22 Yugoslavia's Communist Party votes to abolish its monopoly on power.

26 Indian troops bring the state of Kashmir under direct rule and enforce a curfew, following deaths in separatist violence and the resignation of the state government.

FEBRUARY

1 The Bulgarian government resigns. On February 8, a new all-communist government is formed, dominated by the reformed Bulgarian Socialist Party.

1 The Yugoslav government sends troops to the Serbian province of Kosovo in an attempt to end clashes between ethnic Albanians and the Serbian authorities.

2 The South African president F. W. de Klerk ends a 30-year ban on the African National Congress (ANC).

7 The Soviet Communist Party votes to end its monopoly on political power.

11 The African National Congress (ANC) leader, Nelson Mandela, is released in South Africa after almost 26 years in prison.

15 The Social Democratic Labor Party government in Sweden resigns. On February 26, the party's leader Ingvar Carlsson is reappointed prime minister of a new Social Democratic government.

16 The SWAPO leader Sam Nujoma is elected the first president of independent Namibia. On February 21, the Republic of Namibia becomes an independent sovereign state.

21 The Kenyan authorities ban demonstrations after public calls for President Daniel arap Moi's resignation and demands for an inquiry into the murder of the foreign minister.

24 The opposition *Sajudis* ("Movement") party in Lithuania defeats the rival pro-Moscow and nationalist Communist parties in the USSR's first multiparty elections since 1917.

25 The U.S.-backed coalition under Violeta Chamorro defeats Daniel Ortega's Sandinista government in Nicaragua's first free elections since 1979.

26 The USSR agrees to withdraw its troops from Czechoslovakia by July 1991.

27 The Exxon Corporation is indicted on five criminal charges relating to the 1989 Alaskan oil spill.

MARCH

6 President Mohammad Najibullah's government in Afghanistan puts down an attempted coup.

10 General Prosper Avril resigns as president of Haiti. On March 12, Ertha Pascal-Trouillot succeeds him as acting president.

11 General Augusto Pinochet, dictator of Chile since 1973, hands over power to elected president Patricio Aylwin.

11 Lithuania declares its independence from the USSR.

11 Vytautas Landsbergis is elected president of Lithuania.

13 Israel's national unity coalition government collapses after the dismissal of the Labor leader Shimon Peres from the government by Prime Minister Yitzhak Shamir, as a result of differences over the peace process.

13 The United States lifts economic sanctions against Nicaragua.

15 Mikhail Gorbachev is sworn in as the first executive president of the USSR.

18 In East Germany's first free elections since 1933, the Alliance for Germany, a coalition led by the right wing Christian Democratic counterpart of West Germany's ruling party, wins 48% of the vote.

24 The ruling Labor Party, led by Prime Minister Bob Hawke, is returned for a fourth term in the Australian general election.

25 Eighty-seven people die in a fire, suspected arson, at the illegal Happy Land social club in the Bronx, New York. It is the city's worst fire since 1911.

25 The Soviet authorities send tanks to Vilnius, the capital of Lithuania, to discourage proponents of secession.

30 Estonia suspends the Soviet constitution on its territory.

APRIL

1 Robert Mugabe gains a decisive victory in the presidential elections in Zimbabwe, and his ruling ZANU–PF party wins 117 of the 120 seats.

3 King Baudouin of Belgium steps down from the throne temporarily to allow the passing of a new law legalizing abortion, which he has hitherto refused to sign on principle.

4 A Chinese People's Congress approves the Basic Law, a mini-constitution proposed for Hong Kong after the 1997 Chinese takeover.

8 The conservative New Democracy Party gains a narrow majority in the Greek general election. On April 11, Constantine Mitsotakis takes office as prime minister.

8 The traditionalist Hungarian Democratic Forum and its allies win a landslide victory in the Hungarian general election after the reputation of the ruling Hungarian Socialist Party is damaged by a bugging scandal.

11 Parts for a "supergun" destined for Iraq are detained by customs officers on Teesside, England.

11 Three Western hostages are released in Lebanon after a French arms deal with Libya, in contravention of a European Community embargo.

12 Lothar de Maizière is sworn in as prime minister of a coalition government in East Germany.

18 The USSR cuts off all oil supplies to Lithuania in response to the Lithuanian declaration of independence.

22 U.S. hostage Robert Polhill is freed in Beirut, Lebanon.

30 U.S. hostage Frank Reed is freed in Beirut, Lebanon.

MAY

1 Opposition demonstrations disrupt the traditional Soviet May Day parade in Red Square, Moscow.

4 Constantine Karamanlis is reelected president of Greece.

4 Latvia declares itself an independent sovereign state.

8 Estonia declares its independence from the USSR.

20 Romania holds its first free elections since 1937. The National Salvation Front wins two-thirds of the seats and its leader, Ion Iliescu, wins a landslide victory in the presidential elections.

22 The traditionally antagonistic North and South Yemen merge to form the Yemen Republic.

27 César Gaviria Trujillo of the ruling Liberal Party is chosen as president-elect in the elections in Colombia.

27 The National League for Democracy wins multiparty elections in Myanmar (formerly Burma), though the army later refuses to hand over power.

29 In the Russian parliament, Boris Yeltsin is elected president of the Russian Federation, narrowly defeating the candidate favored by the president of the USSR Mikhail Gorbachev.

30 Contra rebels in Nicaragua agree to lay down their arms.

JUNE

5 A communist hard-liner, Vladimir Ivashko, is elected president of Ukraine.

7 President F. W. de Klerk lifts the four-year state of emergency from all parts of South Africa except Natal province.

8 The Civic Forum triumphs in the first free elections in Czechoslovakia since 1946.

8 The Russian parliament votes that its laws should take precedence over those of the USSR; on June 12, the Russian Federation formally declares itself a sovereign state.

11 Alberto Fujimori of the Change 90 Movement defeats the novelist Mario Vargas Llosa of the Democratic Front Movement in the presidential elections in Peru.

12 The fundamentalist Islamic Salvation Front wins control of most municipal and provincial assemblies in the Algerian elections.

12 The Likud Party leader Yitzhak Shamir forms a new right wing coalition government in Israel.

14 Mobs of miners patrol the streets of Bucharest, Romania, attacking antigovernment demonstrators.

22 The Canadian provinces of Manitoba and Newfoundland refuse to ratify the Meech Lake Accord recognizing Quebec as a "distinct society."

26 U.S. president George Bush reneges on his central campaign pledge: "Read my lips: no new taxes."

29 Lithuania suspends its declaration of independence for 100 days during negotiations with the Soviet government.

JULY

1 East Germany cedes sovereignty over economic, monetary, and social policy to the West German government and the Bundesbank, with the Deutschmark becoming its official currency.

2 Imelda Marcos, the wife of the former dictator Ferdinand Marcos, is acquitted of plotting to steal funds from the Philippines for private use.

6   Petar Mladenov resigns as president of Bulgaria, to be succeeded in August by Zhelyu Zhelev.

8   The Indian army takes direct control of the province of Kashmir after outbreaks of separatist violence.

12 The Russian president Boris Yeltsin and other reformers resign from the Communist Party of the USSR.

16 The Ukrainian parliament votes for sovereignty, and the former Communist Party leader Leonid Kravchuk is indirectly elected president.

19 Iraqi troops begin massing on the border with Kuwait, following Iraqi threats over disputed territory.

26 The Americans With Disabilities Act, protecting disabled people from discrimination in employment and public access, comes into force. It gives rights of access to public facilities and employment equality to disabled people in the United States.

29 Free elections are held in Mongolia, with the communist-reformist Mongolian People's Revolutionary Party, led by Punsalmaagiyn Ochirbat, winning a majority.

29 Troops loyal to President Samuel Doe in Liberia massacre at least 600 refugees sheltering in a church in the capital, Monrovia. On August 5, the United States sends marines to evacuate U.S. citizens from the city.

AUGUST

2   Iraqi forces invade Kuwait, and the emir, Sheikh Jaber al-Sabah, flees to Saudi Arabia.

3   Árpád Göncz is sworn in as president of Hungary, following the electoral victory in April–May of a center-right coalition led by the Hungarian Democratic Forum of József Antall.

4   Iraqi troops and tanks, having occupied Kuwait, mass on the Kuwaiti border with Saudi Arabia.

6   The United Nations Security Council imposes sanctions against Iraq, including an embargo on Iraqi oil sales, in an effort to persuade Iraqi forces to withdraw from Kuwait.

7   President George Bush sends U.S. military forces to Saudi Arabia to prevent an Iraqi invasion.

Gulf War (1990–91)

1990

JULY

19 Iraqi troops begin massing on the border with Kuwait, following Iraqi threats over disputed territory.

AUGUST

2   Iraqi forces invade Kuwait, and the emir, Sheikh Jaber al-Sabah, flees to Saudi Arabia.

4   Iraqi troops and tanks, having occupied Kuwait, mass on the Kuwaiti border with Saudi Arabia.

6   The United Nations Security Council imposes sanctions against Iraq, including an embargo on Iraqi oil sales, in an effort to persuade Iraqi forces to withdraw from Kuwait.

7   President George Bush sends U.S. military forces to Saudi Arabia to prevent an Iraqi invasion.

9   Iraq announces its formal annexation of Kuwait.

16 As part of the continuing military buildup in the Gulf, over 20 U.S. stealth fighters fly to Saudi Arabia.

19 Iraq rounds up Western nationals in Kuwait and deports them to Iraq to serve as "human shields" at military installations.

22 President George Bush calls up military reservists in the United States as the crisis in the Gulf deepens.

SEPTEMBER

9   In a snap summit held in Helsinki, Finland, President Bush and Soviet president Mikhail Gorbachev agree a united stand against Iraqi military aggression in the Gulf.

18 Michael Dugan, the U.S. Air Force Chief of Staff, is fired for revealing plans to bomb Baghdad.

DECEMBER

21 Defense Secretary Dick Cheney promises "absolute, total victory" to U.S. troops in the Gulf.

1991

JANUARY

15 Iraq fails to meet the United Nations deadline of midnight U.S. time for withdrawal from Kuwait.

16 A U.S.-led coalition commences air offensive "Operation Desert Storm" to liberate Kuwait from Iraqi occupation, beginning the Gulf War.

18 Iraq launches Scud missiles against Israel during the Gulf War.

21 Iraq threatens to use Western nationals taken hostage during its invasion of Kuwait as "human shields" against air attacks during the Gulf War.

24 Iraq begins to pump Kuwaiti oil into the Persian Gulf, creating the world's largest oil spill. About 6–8 million barrels of oil are spilled, polluting 675 km/420 mi of coastline.

FEBRUARY

22–November 3 Hundreds of Kuwaiti oil wells are set alight by Iraqi soldiers; the last fire is extinguished on November 3.

24 The U.S.-led coalition launches a ground offensive against Iraqi forces.

27 Coalition forces enter the capital Kuwait City and declare Kuwait liberated from the Iraqis.

MARCH

•   Veterans of the Gulf War complain of headaches, memory loss, listlessness, depression, respiratory problems, lethargy, muscle weakness, nausea, and pain. Known as Gulf War Syndrome, these symptoms may be caused by the cocktail effect of a combination of vaccinations against tropical diseases and diseases likely to be used in biological weapons, nerve gas, antinerve gas drugs, and organophosphate (OP) insecticides.

3   An armistice is signed by leaders of the international coalition and the Iraqi army, ending the Gulf War (in force from April 11).

8   The president of Pakistan Gulam Ishaq Khan dismisses the Pakistan People's Party government of Benazir Bhutto on charges of corruption and ineptitude.

8   West African states send a multinational peacekeeping force to end the civil war in Liberia.

9   Iraq announces its formal annexation of Kuwait.

14 The Soviet president Mikhail Gorbachev issues decrees rehabilitating all those Soviet citizens who were victims of Stalin-era repression and restoring Soviet citizenship to exiled dissidents, including the writer Alexander Solzhenitsyn.

15 Iraq makes peace with Iran, accepting all Iranian terms for a formal end to the war between the two countries.

16 As part of the continuing military buildup in the Gulf, over 20 U.S. stealth fighters fly to Saudi Arabia.

19 Iraq rounds up Western nationals in Kuwait and deports them to Iraq to serve as "human shields" at military installations.

19 The center-right coalition government in East Germany collapses amid increasing popular pressure for full unification with West Germany.

21 Four hundred people die in South Africa in clashes between the African National Congress and the Zulu Inkatha movement in townships in Transvaal.

22 President George Bush calls up military reservists in the United States as the crisis in the Gulf deepens.

24 The Irish hostage Brian Keenan, held by an Islamic militant group in Lebanon since 1986, is released.

31 East and West Germany sign a reunification treaty.

31 The former Soviet republic of Uzbekistan declares its independence, with the former Uzbek Communist Party leader Islam Karimov as president.

SEPTEMBER

3   Ethnic Albanians in Kosovo province, Yugoslavia, stage a 24-hour strike following the imprisonment of the Albanian labor union leader Hajrullah Gorani by the Serbian authorities.

4   Geoffrey Palmer resigns as Labor prime minister of New Zealand. Michael Moore replaces him as both Labor leader and prime minister.

9   In a snap summit held in Helsinki, Finland, U.S. president George Bush and Soviet president Mikhail Gorbachev agree a united stand against Iraqi military aggression in the Gulf.

10 Political and military groups in Cambodia, including the pro-Vietnamese government and the Khmer Rouge, agree on a peace formula to end the country's civil war.

10 President Samuel Doe of Liberia is captured and assassinated by rebel forces. Prince Johnson takes over the government.

18 In South Africa, the African National Congress (ANC) official Winnie Mandela, wife of the ANC leader Nelson Mandela, is charged with kidnapping and assault.

18 Michael Dugan, the U.S. Air Force Chief of Staff, is fired for revealing plans to bomb Baghdad, Iraq.

27 Britain and Iran resume diplomatic relations broken over the Rushdie affair.

28 The Serbian parliament in Yugoslavia adopts a new constitution, stripping the province of Kosovo of its autonomy.

OCTOBER

2   At Guangzhou airport, China, a hijacked Chinese Boeing 737 crashes into another 737, killing a total of 120 people.

2   The German Democratic Republic (East Germany) ceases to exist at midnight and, on October 3, East and West Germany are formally reunited.

4   France and Belgium send troops to Rwanda to guarantee the safety of their nationals during an invasion from Uganda.

5   The U.S. House of Representatives rejects the administration's federal budget. Nonessential federal services begin to close down after President George Bush initially refuses to grant emergency funding. The necessary emergency bill is signed on October 9 and, on October 27 and 28, a revised budget is passed by both Houses.

8   Israeli police fire on Palestinian demonstrators at Temple Mount, Jerusalem. Israel later refuses to cooperate with United Nations' attempts to carry out an inquiry into the incident.

15 The Nobel Peace Prize is awarded to the Soviet president Mikhail Gorbachev, architect of the policies of *glasnost* (openness) and *perestroika* (restructuring).

24 Benazir Bhutto's Pakistan People's Party suffers an overwhelming defeat by the conservative Islamic Democratic Alliance (IDA) in the Pakistan general election. On November 6, the IDA leader Nawaz Sharif is sworn in as prime minister.

26 The Mayor of Washington, D.C., Marion Barry is sentenced to six months in jail for possessing cocaine.

27 A European Community summit opens in Rome, Italy. With the exception of Britain, all members vote to begin the second stage of economic and monetary union by 1994 and to achieve a single European currency by 2000.

27 The National Party, led by James Bolger, defeats the ruling Labor Party in the New Zealand elections.

28 Noncommunist parties triumph in elections in the Soviet republic of Georgia, with calls for independence and a market economy.

29 The coalition government in Norway resigns. On October 30, Gro Harlem Brundtland forms a minority Labor government.

NOVEMBER

3–10 As the U.S. military buildup in the Gulf continues, Secretary of State James Baker tours Middle Eastern states allied with the United States.

6   The Democrats gain seats in both the House and Congress in U.S. Congressional elections.

7   Mary Robinson wins the Irish presidential election to become the country's first woman president.

7   The Janata Dal minority government of V. P. Singh resigns in India.

12 Emperor Akihito of Japan is formally enthroned.

18 The Socialist Party of Labor, a recreated Communist Party, is founded in Romania.

20 An election is held in Britain for the leadership of the Conservative Party, with Michael Heseltine as challenger to the prime minister, Margaret Thatcher. Thatcher fails to secure the margin needed for reelection in a single ballot, with 204 votes against Heseltine's 152. On November 22, Thatcher removes her name from the second ballot.

20 The Hungarian prime minister József Antall announces that the Warsaw Pact will be scrapped by 1992.

23 The Soviet parliament grants the president Mikhail Gorbachev emergency powers to maintain order in the USSR.

25 Christian militias withdraw from East Beirut, following an agreement to create a reunified city policed by government troops and Syrian soldiers.

26 Lee Kuan Yew resigns as Singapore's leader after 31 years as prime minister.

27 John Major wins the second ballot in Britain for the leadership of the Conservative Party with 185 votes, against 131 for Michael Heseltine and 56 for Douglas Hurd. Heseltine and Hurd withdraw from the third ballot, and Major becomes leader.

28 Margaret Thatcher resigns as British prime minister, to be succeeded by John Major.

DECEMBER

2 West German Christian Democratic chancellor Helmut Kohl is elected chancellor in the first elections of a reunited Germany.

9 Slobodan Milošević of the Serbian Socialist Party is elected president in Serbia's first free elections for 50 years.

9 The former Solidarity leader Lech Wałęsa wins a landslide victory in the Polish presidential election.

12 The Zimbabwean parliament passes legislation to nationalize white-owned farms at a fixed rate of compensation.

13 U.S. pathologist Jack Kervorkian, known as "Dr. Death," is acquitted of murder charges that were filed after he assisted the suicide of a patient on June 4. The judge rules that physician-assisted suicide is not against the law in the state of Michigan. Kervorkian will be tried for murder and acquitted three more times by 1997.

14 The Polish government of Tadeusz Mazowiecki resigns. On December 29, President Lech Wałęsa nominates Jan Krzysztof Bielicki as prime minister.

16 Father Jean-Bertrand Aristide, a left wing Roman Catholic priest, becomes president of Haiti in the country's first fully free elections.

17 Lothar de Maizière resigns from the German government after allegations that he worked for the Stasi (the former East German secret police).

20 Eduard Shevardnadze resigns as Soviet foreign minister, declaring that the USSR is heading for dictatorship.

21 Defense Secretary Dick Cheney promises "absolute, total victory" to U.S. troops in the Gulf.

23 A referendum in Slovenia favors independence from Yugoslavia.

SCIENCE, TECHNOLOGY, AND MEDICINE

Agriculture

• The United States, China, and the USSR all have bumper wheat crops, forcing prices down from $3.72 per bushel to $2.20. However, political and economic wrangles in the USSR cause Moscow and Leningrad (now St. Petersburg) stores to run out of bread, and food supplies to fall so low as to threaten famine.

NOVEMBER

29 The United States begins an airlift of food supplies to the USSR as the economic crisis there continues to deepen.

Ecology

• More than 1,400 Muslim pilgrims are crushed to death in Saudi Arabia, in a stampede in an overcrowded tunnel leading from Mecca to the hill outside.

APRIL

22 The 20th anniversary of Earth Day is celebrated around the world.

MAY

• In Germany, Wella Shampoo is the first product packaged in Biopal, the first fully biodegradable plastic.

JUNE

7 A vaccine against rabies is introduced in northeastern Pennsylvania where it is intended to immunize racoons. It is the first genetically-engineered live virus to be introduced into the U.S. environment.

21–24 Two major earthquakes in northwest Iran, measuring approximately 7.5 on the Richter scale, kill an estimated 50,000 people, injure 200,000, and leave 500,000 homeless.

JULY

16 An earthquake measuring 7.7 on the Richter scale kills over 1,600 people in the Philippines.

NOVEMBER

15 A Clean Air Act in the United States raises standards for emissions made by utilities and industrial concerns.

Exploration

• U.S. astronomer Mark Showalter discovers an 18th moon of Saturn when analyzing pictures transmitted by *Voyager 2*.

JANUARY

24–April 21 Japan launches *Muses-A*, the first probe to be sent to the moon since 1976; it places a small satellite in lunar orbit (March).

FEBRUARY

• The U.S. space probe *Voyager 1*, now near the edge of the solar system, turns and takes the first photograph of the entire solar system from space.

APRIL

24 The space shuttle *Discovery* places the Hubble Space Telescope in Earth orbit; the main mirror proves to be defective.

JUNE

1 The German-built Earth-orbiting X-ray observatory *Röntgensatellite* is launched; its mission is to study X-rays given off by the coronae of stars.

AUGUST

10 The U.S. *Magellan* radar mapper arrives in orbit around Venus; it transmits the most detailed pictures of the planet's surface yet produced.

DECEMBER

2–12 The Soviet spacecraft *Soyuz TM-11* is launched, marking the first paying passenger space flight. Japanese newsman Toyuhiro Akiyama, the first Japanese cosmonaut, spends seven days onboard the spacecraft.

Health and Medicine

- A four-year-old girl in the United States has the gene for adenosine deaminase inserted into her DNA (deoxyribonucleic acid); she is the first human to receive gene therapy.
- Bowel and liver grafts are transplanted at the University of Western Ontario, Canada, enabling the patient to resume a normal diet after the operation for the first time in surgical history.
- French geneticist Pierre Chambon and associates announce the discovery of a gene that may be important in the development of breast cancer.
- The Nobel Prize for Physiology or Medicine is awarded jointly to U.S. surgeons Joseph Murray and Donnall Thomas for their pioneering work in organ and cell transplants.

Science

- Canadian scientists discover fossils of the oldest known multicellular animals, dating from 600 million years ago.
- Chemists at the Louis Pasteur University, Strasbourg, France, announce the creation of nucleohelicates— compounds that mimic the double helix structure of DNA (deoxyribonucleic acid).
- Researchers at IBM's Almaden Research Center in California, United States, are the first to manipulate individual atoms on a surface; they use a scanning tunneling microscope and spell out the initials "IBM."
- Six institutions are selected to participate in the project for mapping the genes of selected human chromosomes.
- The Nobel Prize for Physics is awarded to U.S. physicists Jerome Friedman and Henry Kendall and Canadian physicist Richard Taylor for their experiments demonstrating that protons and neutrons are made up of quarks.
- U.S. chemist Elias James Corey receives the Nobel Prize for Chemistry for developing novel methods for the synthesis of complex natural compounds.

JANUARY

1 The volt, which measures electrical potential, and the ohm, which measures electrical resistance, are redefined in atomic terms.

JULY

- U.S. astronomers Juan Uson, Stephen Boughin, and Jeffrey Kuhn announce the discovery of the largest known galaxy; over 1 billion light-years away, it has a diameter of 5.6 million light-years—80 times that of the Milky Way—and contains about 2 trillion stars.

Technology

- A transistor that can operate at 75 billion cycles per second is developed by the U.S. firm IBM.
- Japanese chemist Fumihiro Wakai and his associates develop a stretchable ceramic, made from a silicon nitride compound; one potential use envisioned is for precision engine parts that can withstand high temperatures.
- The British company Imperial Chemical Industries (ICI) develops the first practical biodegradable plastic, Biopal.
- The Rogun earth-fill dam is completed on the Vakhsh River in Tajikistan, USSR; 335 m/1,099 ft high, it is the tallest dam in the world.
- The U.S. telecommunications equipment company PhoneMate launches the digital answering machine ADAM, the first with messages stored on a silicon chip rather than tape.
- U.S. electronics company Dragon Systems launches the first voice-controlled typewriter, the Dragon Dictate Voice-Typewriter; it costs $9,000.

JANUARY

29 U.S. scientist Alan Huang and his colleagues at Bell Laboratories demonstrate the first all-optical processor; calculations are performed optically using lasers, lenses, and fast light switches.

SEPTEMBER

- The Japanese company Sony launches the first DAT recorder for domestic use, the Sony DTC 55ES.

NOVEMBER

- The Keck 1 Telescope on Mauna Kea volcano, Hawaii, is erected; its 10-m/32.8-ft reflector, composed of 36 segments, makes it the largest optical telescope in the world.

Transportation

- A new computerized railroad car, the X-2000, is introduced in Sweden on the Stockholm–Gothenburg line; its computerized steering and suspension permit it to take curves 30–40% faster than conventional railroad cars.
- A new radar system that detects wind shear is tested at Stapleton International Airport, Denver, Colorado.

MAY

17 A U.S. presidential commission investigating the bombing of Pan Am flight 103 deplores lax security at Frankfurt airport, West Germany.

18 A French TGV (*train à grande vitesse*, "high-speed train") between Courtalain and Tours sets a world speed record for trains when it travels at 515.3 kph/ 320.2 mph.

JULY

14 U.S. motorcyclist Dave Campos sets a world motorcycle speed record of 519.609 kph/322.87 mph on his streamlined *Easyriders* at Bonneville Salt Flats, Utah.

ARTS AND IDEAS

Architecture

- The world's largest cathedral is consecrated by Pope John Paul II in Yamoussoukro, Ivory Coast.
- Two-thirds of U.S. families own their own homes, about double the home ownership rate in Germany, France, Britain, and Japan.

DECEMBER

1 British and French tunneling engineers, working from opposite sides of the English Channel to build the Channel Tunnel, break through the last few yards of ground separating their excavations.

Arts

- The 14-year-old Chinese artist Wang Yani is the first to have a one-woman show at the Smithsonian Institute, Washington, D.C.
- The English artist Damian Hirst creates *My Way*.
- The U.S. artist Donald Sultan paints *Polish Landscape II, January 5, 1990*.
- The U.S. artist Jeff Koons creates the porcelain sculpture *Jeff and Ilona (Made in Heaven)*.
- The U.S. artist Jenny Holzer becomes the first woman to represent the United States at the Venice Biennale (a major international art exhibition held every two years) in Italy.
- The U.S. National Endowment for the Arts introduces new regulations requiring artists to return their grants if their work is later judged to be obscene.
- Vincent Van Gogh's painting *Portrait of Dr Gachet* sells for $83 million, making it the most expensive work of 20th-century art to date.

Film

- The movie *¡Atame!/Tie Me Up! Tie Me Down!*, written and directed by Pedro Almodóvar, is released in Spain. It stars Victoria Abril and Antonio Banderas.
- The movie *Akira Kurosawa's Dreams*, directed by Akira Kurosawa, is released in Japan. It stars Akira Terao and Mitsuko Baisho.
- The movie *An Angel at My Table*, directed by New Zealand filmmaker Jane Campion, is released, a biographical account of the life of the New Zealand writer Janet Frame.
- The movie *Awakenings*, inspired by the writings and work of British-born U.S. neurologist Oliver Sacks, is released in the United States. It is directed by Penny Marshall and stars Robert De Niro and Robin Williams.
- The movie *Cry Baby*, directed by John Waters, is released in the United States, starring Johnny Depp.
- The movie *Cyrano de Bergerac*, directed by Jean-Paul Rappeneau, is released in France. It stars Gérard Depardieu.
- The movie *Dances With Wolves*, directed by and starring Kevin Costner, is released in the United States.

- The movie *Das Schreckliche Mädchen/The Nasty Girl*, directed by Michael Verhoeven, is released in Germany. It stars Lena Stolze.
- The movie *Delicatessen*, directed by Jean-Pierre Jeunet and Marc Caro, is released in France. It stars Dominique Pinon and Marie-Laure Dougnac.
- The movie *Dick Tracy*, directed by and starring Warren Beatty, is released in the United States.
- The movie *Edward Scissorhands* is released in the United States. It is directed by Tim Burton and stars Johnny Depp and Winona Ryder.
- The movie *Ghost*, directed by Jerry Zucker, is released in the United States. It stars Demi Moore, Patrick Swayze, and Whoopi Goldberg.
- The movie *Henry and June*, based on the diaries of Anaïs Nin, is released in the United States. It is directed by Philip Kaufman and stars Fred Ward, Uma Thurman, Maria de Medeiros, and Richard E. Grant.
- The movie *Home Alone*, directed by Chris Columbus, is released in the United States. It stars Macaulay Culkin, Joe Pesci, and Daniel Stern. It is the biggest grossing comedy in U.S. movie history.
- The movie *Ju Dou* is released in China, where it is subsequently banned. It is directed by Zhang Yimou and stars Li Wei, Gong Li, Li Baotian, and Zhang Yi.
- The movie *Miller's Crossing*, directed and produced by Joel and Ethan Coen, is released in the United States, starring Albert Finney and Gabriel Byrne.
- The movie *Postcards from the Edge*, adapted from the novel by Carrie Fisher, is released in the United States. It is directed by Mike Nichols and stars Meryl Streep and Shirley MacLaine.
- The movie *Presumed Innocent*, directed by Alan J. Pakula, is released in the United States. It stars Harrison Ford, Brian Dennehy, Raul Julia, Bonnie Bedelia, Paul Winfield, and Greta Scacchi.
- The movie *Reversal of Fortune*, directed by Iranian-born U.S. filmmaker Barbet Schroeder, is released in the United States. Based on a celebrated legal case, it stars Jeremy Irons, Glenn Close, Ron Silver, and Annabella Sciorra.
- The movie *Teenage Mutant Ninja Turtles*, directed by Steve Barron, is released in the United States.
- The movie *The Grifters*, directed by British filmmaker Stephen Frears, is released in the United States. It stars Anjelica Huston, John Cusack, and Annette Bening.
- The movie *Truly, Madly, Deeply*, directed by Anthony Minghella, is released in the UK, starring Juliet Stevenson and Alan Rickman.
- The movie *Wild at Heart*, directed by David Lynch, is released in the United States. It stars Nicolas Cage and Laura Dern.
- The gangster movie *GoodFellas*, cowritten and directed by Martin Scorsese, is released in the United States. It stars Ray Liotta, Robert de Niro, Joe Pesci, Lorraine Bracco, and Paul Sorvino.
- The Motion Picture Association of America attempts to introduce a No Children Under 17 rating as a guideline in the United States. However, movie theaters refuse to show such movies, so the rating is dropped for major movies.
- The romantic comedy *Pretty Woman*, directed by Garry Marshall, is released in the United States. It stars Julia Roberts and Richard Gere.

- The science-fiction movie *Total Recall*, directed by Dutch filmmaker Paul Verhoeven, is released in the United States. It stars Arnold Schwarzenegger.
- The U.S. movie director Francis Ford Coppola is declared bankrupt.

MARCH

28 The 1989 Academy Awards take place. Best Actor: Daniel Day Lewis, for *My Left Foot*; Best Supporting Actor: Denzel Washington, for *Glory*; Best Actress: Jessica Tandy, for *Driving Miss Daisy*; Best Supporting Actress: Brenda Fricker, for *My Left Foot*; Best Picture: *Driving Miss Daisy*, directed by Bruce Beresford; Best Director: Oliver Stone, for *Born on the Fourth of July*.

MAY

21 At the Cannes Film Festival in France, the Palme d'Or is awarded to U.S. filmmaker David Lynch for *Wild at Heart*.

Literature and Language

- English novelist Anita Brookner publishes her novel *Brief Lives*.
- English novelist William Boyd publishes his novel *Brazzaville Beach*.
- Irish novelist John McGahern publishes his novel *Amongst Women*.
- South African writer J. M. Coetzee publishes his novel *Age of Iron*.
- The Canadian writer Mordechai Richler publishes his novel *Solomon Gursky Was Here*.
- The Chilean writer Isabel Allende publishes her short-story collection *Cuentos de Eva Luna/The Stories of Eva Luna*.
- The English writer A. S. Byatt publishes her novel *Possession: A Romance*, which wins the Booker Prize.
- The English writer Peter Ackroyd publishes his biography *Dickens*.
- The English writer Penelope Fitzgerald publishes her novel *The Gate of Angels*.
- The English writer Piers Paul Read publishes his novel *On the Third Day*.
- The Indian-born writer Adam Zameenzad publishes his novel *Cyrus Cyrus*.
- The Irish poet Paul Muldoon publishes his collection *Madoc: A Mystery*.
- The Nobel Prize for Literature is awarded to the Mexican poet and essayist Octavio Paz.
- The Pulitzer Prize for Biography is awarded to Sebastian de Grazia for *Machiavelli in Hell*, the Pulitzer Prize for Poetry is awarded to Charles Simic for *The World Doesn't End*, and the Pulitzer Prize for Fiction is awarded to Oscar Hijuelos for *The Mambo Kings Play Songs of Love*.
- The Russian writer Alexander Solzhenitsyn is awarded the Russia State Literature Prize for *Arkhipelag Gulag/The Gulag Archipelago*.
- The U.S. cultural critic Camille Paglia publishes *Sexual Personae: Art and Decadence from Nefertiti to Emily Dickinson*. Paglia's spirited attack on many feminist principles causes a heated debate.

- The U.S. novelist John Updike publishes his novel *Rabbit at Rest*, the last in his *Rabbit* series. The first, *Run, Rabbit*, appeared in 1960.
- The U.S. novelist Kurt Vonnegut publishes his novel *Hocus Pocus*.
- The U.S. novelist Larry McMurty publishes his novel *Buffalo Girls*.
- The U.S. novelist Nicholson Baker publishes his novel *Room Temperature*.
- The U.S. novelist Richard Ford publishes his novel *Wildlife*.
- The U.S. novelist Thomas Pynchon publishes his novel *Vineland*.
- The U.S. poet Amy Clampitt publishes her poetry collection *Westward*.
- U.S. poet John Berryman publishes his *Collected Poems 1937–71* and *The Dream Songs*.

Music

- Popular music groups such as Orb and the Grid emerge in the United States, playing a new kind of music, ambient techno.
- The Bastille Opera, in Paris, France, is formally opened.
- The British pop group Pink Floyd performs music from their album *The Wall* in Berlin, Germany.
- The French composer Pierre Boulez completes a revised version of his vocal work *Don/Gift*, for soprano and orchestra. The first version (for piano and voice) was written in 1960.
- The French composer Jean Françaix completes his *Elégie/Elegy* for wind instruments.
- The Greek composer Iannis Xenakis completes his orchestral work *Tuorakemsu*.
- The Hungarian-born Austrian composer György Ligeti completes his Concerto for Violin and Orchestra.
- The opera *Das verratene Meer/The Revealed Sea* by the German composer Hans Werner Henze is first performed, in Berlin, Germany. Based on a novel by the Japanese novelist Yukio Mishima, it was completed in 1989.
- The opera *Hydrogen Jukebox*, by the U.S. composer Philip Glass, is first performed, in Charleston, South Carolina.
- The opera *The Vanishing Bridegroom*, by the Scottish composer Judith Weir, is first performed, in Glasgow, Scotland.
- The Polish-born English composer Andrzej Panufnik completes his String Quartet No. 3.
- The U.S. pop band New Kids on the Block are the first of a series of boy bands that attract a huge female adolescent following.
- The U.S. pop group Babes in Toyland releases *Spanking Machine*, their first album.
- The U.S. pop group Sonic Youth releases the album *Goo*.

FEBRUARY

21 The 1989–90 Grammy Awards are held. Best Album and Best Female Pop and Rock Vocalist: Bonnie Raitt for *Nick of Time*; Best Song: Bette Midler for "Wind Beneath My Wings;" Best Male Vocalist: Michael Bolton for "How Am I Supposed to Live Without You?"

March

10 The U.S. rap singer MC Hammer dominates charts in the United States with the album *Please Hammer Don't Hurt 'Em*; more than 10 million copies will be sold.

17 The British rock singer Chris Rea releases the album *Road to Hell* and the single of the same name.

17 The Irish pop singer Sinead O'Connor releases "Nothing Compares 2 U" and the album *I Do Not Want What I Haven't Got*.

29 U.S. record companies agree to print a warning label on recordings with offensive lyrics.

Theater and Dance

- The musical *Once on this Island*, with lyrics by Lynn Ahrens and music by Stephen Flaherty, is first performed, at the Booth Theater in New York, New York.
- The play *Dancing at Lughnasa*, by the Irish writer Brian Friel, is first performed, at the Abbey Theatre in Dublin, Ireland.
- The play *Prelude to a Kiss*, by the U.S. writer Craig Lucas, is first performed, at the Helen Hayes Theater in New York, New York.
- The Pulitzer Prize for Drama is awarded to August Wilson for *The Piano Lesson*.
- The revue *Five Guys Named Moe* is first performed, at the Lyric Theatre in London, England. Its best-known song is "There Ain't Nobody Here But Us Chickens."

Thought and Scholarship

- Austrian-born English philosopher Karl Popper publishes *A World of Propensities*.
- British theologian John MacQuarrie publishes *Jesus Christ in Modern Thought*.
- The Pulitzer Prize for History is awarded to Stanley Karnow for *In Our Image: America's Empire in the Philippines*.
- The Pulitzer Prize for General Nonfiction is awarded to Dale Maharidge and Michael Williamson for *And Their Children After Them*.
- Trinidadian writer V. S. Naipaul publishes *India: A Wounded Civilization*.
- U.S. critic Harold Bloom publishes *The Book of J*.
- U.S. feminist writer Naomi Wolf publishes *The Beauty Myth: How Images of Beauty are Used Against Women*.
- U.S. historian Laurel Thatcher Ulrich publishes *A Midwife's Tale: The Life of Martha Ballard, Based on Her Diary 1785–1812*.
- U.S. philosopher Donald Davidson publishes *Structure and Content of Truth*.
- U.S. political historian James Rosenau publishes *Turbulence in World Politics*.
- U.S. social historian Kevin Phillips publishes *The Politics of Rich and Poor*.
- U.S. social historian Mike Davis publishes *City of Quartz: Excavating the Future in Los Angeles*.

SOCIETY

Everyday Life

- In the United States, 113 million people have credit cards; Americans have $236.4 billion in credit card debt.
- A third of Chinese college graduates are women.
- About 120 million Americans, or 40% of the population, live in suburbs.
- According to a Gallup survey, 37% of U.S. homes have a vegetable garden and 9% have an herb garden.
- According to the U.S. Census Bureau, 32 million Americans speak a language besides English while at home, and about 18 million of those people speak Spanish.
- According to the U.S. Census Bureau, 28% of Americans are obese, including 30% of women and 38% of black Americans.
- After ten years in development, the Gillette Sensor razor is launched in the United States.
- Americans make 5,942,000 automatic teller machine (ATM) transactions.
- Divorce rates (divorces per 1,000 of the population) in selected countries in 1990 are: France 1.87; Germany 1.94; Great Britain and Northern Ireland 2.88; United States 4.7 (rate for 1988); USSR 3.94 (rate for 1989).
- For the first time, the majority of the U.S. population lives in metropolitan areas.
- Households in the United States headed by a single woman total 16.7%, compared to 9.3% in 1950.
- In the United States, 21% of citizens have completed at least four years of college (whites 22%; blacks 11%; Hispanics 9%), up from 8% in 1960.
- In the United States, 78% of citizens have completed at least four years of high school (whites 79%; blacks 66%; Hispanics 51%), up from 41% in 1960. Mississippi has the largest population of citizens that have not completed high school, 36%; while Utah has the lowest, 15%.
- It is estimated that between 3 and 4 million women are battered each year in the United States.
- Life expectation at birth for men/women in selected countries in 1990 is: Australia 74/80; Brazil 62/68; Canada 73/80; China 68/71; France 73/78; Ghana 42/43; Great Britain and Northern Ireland 73/78; India 55/56; Japan 76/82; Kenya 55/60; Mexico 70/75; United States 72/79; USSR 65/74; West Germany 72/78
- Out of 34,400 doctors' degrees awarded in the United States, 12,900 are to women.
- Populations of some major world cities (in millions) in 1990 are: Mexico City, Mexico 18.7; Cairo, Egypt 14.0; Shanghai, China 12.8; Tokyo, Japan 11.9; Beijing, China 10.4; São Paulo, Brazil 10.1; Seoul, South Korea 10.0; Calcutta, India 9.2; Paris, France 9.1; Moscow, Russia 8.9.
- The crime rate against women in the United States is significantly higher than in other countries. The United States has a rape rate 13 times that in England—every hour, 16 women in the United States confront rapists and a woman is raped every six minutes—4 times that in Germany, and 20 times that in Japan.

- The homicide rate among U.S. black men between the ages of 15 and 24 has risen by two-thirds between 1985 and 1988.
- The number of fast-food stores in the United States grows to 119,000 from only 67,290 in 1980.
- The number of U.S. book stores increases to 17,620 from 10,200 in 1980.
- The population of the United States is 249,632,692.
- The United States' colleges and universities confer 482,000 associate degrees, 1.1 million bachelor degrees, 337,000 master degrees, 72,000 professional degrees, and 39,000 doctorates.
- There are 188,798,000 cars, trucks, and buses in the United States.
- There are 1.5 billion pairs of tights and stockings sold in 1990 in the United States.
- There are two women out of 986 chief executives working for 1,000 of the largest U.S. public corporations. In another survey of 799 major companies ranked by *Fortune* magazine, there are 19 women among 3,993 directors and executives. Of those 19 women, 18 are white.
- U.S. consumers buy 205 billion books.
- U.S. consumers spend $7.5 billion on CDs, cassettes, and albums.
- Women comprise 11% of U.S. military troops, the highest percentage to date.
- World population distribution by continents, in percentages of the total world population (compared with percentages in 1950) is as follows: Asia 58.8 (54.7); Europe 9.4 (15.6); Africa 12.1 (8.8); USSR 5.4 (7.2); Latin America 8.5 (6.6); North America 5.2 (6.6).

FEBRUARY

25 The U.S. Congress extends its ban on smoking to all domestic airline flights.

DECEMBER

10 The U.S. Food and Drug Administration approves the highly effective Norplant contraceptive invented by Rockefeller Foundation researcher Sheldon Segal. Already in use in 14 other countries, it is implanted under the skin of the arm and slowly releases progesterone over a 15-year period.

27 San Francisco, California, passes laws limiting the use of video display terminals, requiring 15-minute breaks for each two hours of work in front of a terminal.

Media and Communication

- *Twin Peaks* and *The Simpsons* are the two new hits of the year on U.S. television.
- The success of the television cartoon series *The Simpsons*, featuring Bart Simpson and family, significantly boosts the ratings for Rupert Murdoch's Fox channel in the United States.

MARCH

26 A 30-second television advertising slot during coverage of the Oscars ceremony costs U.S. advertisers $3.5 million.

MAY

31 The comedy *Seinfeld* is first broadcast on U.S. television, starring Larry Seinfeld, Julia Louise-Dreyfus, Michael Richards, and Jason Alexander.

JULY

- Japanese electronics manufacturer Sony launches the Data Discman, an electronic book player that runs 8.8-cm/3.5-in discs, capable of storing up to 2,500 pages of text.

SEPTEMBER

16 The 1989–90 Emmy Awards for television are held. Best Drama Series: *LA Law*; Best Comedy Series: *Murphy Brown*; Best Actor in a Drama: Peter Falk, for *Columbo*; Best Actress in a Drama: Patricia Wettig, for *thirtysomething*; Best Actor in a Comedy: Ted Danson, for *Cheers*; Best Actress in a Comedy: Candice Bergen, for *Murphy Brown*.

23–27 The U.S. television special *The Civil War*, directed by Ken Burns, is broadcast.

Religion

JULY

25 English churchman George Carey, bishop of Bath and Wells, is named as successor to Robert Runcie as archbishop of Canterbury.

Sports

- After the United States women's tennis team had inflicted four 7–0 "whitewashes" over their British opponents in five years (1985–89), the British and U.S. tennis federations decide to suspend competition in the Wightman Cup.
- Magic Johnson of the Los Angeles Lakers wins the National Basketball Association's Most Valuable Player award for the third time in four years.
- The first mountain bike world championships are held in Durango, California.

JANUARY

1 Coaches and sportswriters vote Miami as college football's national champion for the 1989 season.

21 The U.S. tennis player John McEnroe is disqualified from the Australian Open in Melbourne for abusing officials during a match.

28 The San Francisco 49ers defeat the Denver Broncos 55–10 in Super Bowl XXIV in New Orleans, Louisiana, to match the Pittsburgh Steelers' achievement of four Super Bowls. It is the first time that a football team has scored over 50 points in the Super Bowl.

FEBRUARY

3 U.S. jockey Bill Shoemaker retires, having ridden a world record 8,833 winners from 40,350 mounts since making his racing debut on March 19, 1949.

10–11 U.S. national figure skating champions are: Jill Trenary; Todd Eldredge; Kristi Yamaguchi and Rudi Galindo, pairs; Suzanne Wynne and Joseph Dunbar, dance.

11 U.S. boxer James "Buster" Douglas wins the undisputed world heavyweight title, knocking out the champion Mike Tyson of the United States in the tenth round of their fight in Tokyo, Japan.

13 Antiapartheid campaigners persuade the South African cricket authorities to cut short an unofficial tour by a team of England cricketers, led by Mike Gatting.

APRIL

4 The English golfer Nick Faldo wins the U.S. Masters at Augusta, Georgia, for the second successive year.

26 The San Diego Yacht Club's *Stars and Stripes* is reinstated as the winner of the 1988 America's Cup after a New York judge reverses a ruling made in 1989 that San Diego's use of a catamaran against the New Zealand challenger's monohull broke the rules of the race.

MAY

24 Canadian ice-hockey team Edmonton Oilers win their fifth Stanley Cup in seven years.

27 Dutch racing driver Arie Luyendyk wins the Indianapolis 500; his average speed is 297 kph/185 mph, a new record.

JUNE

14 The Detroit Pistons repeat as National Basketball Association (NBA) champions, beating the Portland Trail Blazers.

23 Cameroon defeats Colombia 2–1 in Naples, Italy, to become the first African nation to reach the quarter finals of the soccer World Cup.

JULY

7 The U.S. tennis player Martina Navratilova wins her ninth women's singles title at the Wimbledon championships, in London, England, beating the former record of eight set by the U.S. player Helen Wills Moody between 1927 and 1938.

8 In the soccer World Cup, held in Italy, West Germany beats Argentina 1–0 in the final in Rome before a crowd of 73,000.

10 The European Football Association (UEFA) lifts its ban on English clubs playing in European competitions, imposed in 1985 after the Heysel Stadium disaster in Belgium, with the exception of Liverpool, which remains suspended for another year.

22 Greg Lemond of the United States becomes only the sixth cyclist to win the Tour de France three times.

OCTOBER

16–20 The Cincinnati Reds beat the Oakland As in four straight games to win the World Series.

BIRTHS & DEATHS

JANUARY

19 Arthur Goldberg, U.S. lawyer, Supreme Court justice, and ambassador to the United Nations (UN), dies in Washington, D.C. (81).

25 Ava Gardner, U.S. actress and sex symbol, dies in London, England (77).

26 Lewis Mumford, U.S. architectural critic and historian of urbanization, dies in Amenia, New York (94).

MARCH

21 Lev Yashin, Soviet soccer player who played goalkeeper for the USSR throughout the 1950s and 1960s, dies in Moscow, USSR (60).

APRIL

8 Ryan White, U.S. AIDS patient who waged a public battle against the disease and helped reverse prejudiced public opinion, dies in Indianapolis, Indiana (18).

15 Greta Garbo, Swedish-born film star of the 1920s and 1930s, then a legendary recluse after 1941, dies in New York, New York (84).

17 Ralph David Abernathy, U.S. civil-rights leader who worked with Martin Luther King, Jr., dies in Atlanta, Georgia (64).

21 Erté (adopted name of Romain de Tirtoff), Russian-born fashion illustrator and designer particularly associated with the art deco movement of the 1920s and 1930s, dies in Paris, France (97).

MAY

22 Rocky Graziano, U.S. heavyweight boxing champion who then became a comic actor, dies in New York, New York (68).

JUNE

2 Steen Rasmussen, Danish architect and city planner, dies (92).

AUGUST

6 Gordon Bunshaft, U.S. architect who introduced the International Style to corporate architecture, dies in New York, New York (81).

17 Pearl Bailey, U.S. singer in Broadway musicals and in films, dies in Philadelphia, Pennsylvania (72).

18 B(urrhus) F(rederic) Skinner, U.S. psychologist who developed behaviorist psychology, dies in Cambridge, Massachusetts (86).

SEPTEMBER

7 A(lan) J(ohn) P(ercival) Taylor, British historian, journalist, and lecturer, dies in London, England (84).

10 Samuel Doe, Liberian president 1985–90, dies in Monrovia, Liberia (38).

26 Alberto Moravia, Italian existentialist novelist and short-story writer, dies in Rome, Italy (82).

30 Patrick White, Australian novelist and playwright, winner of the Nobel Prize for Literature in 1973, dies in Sydney, Australia (78).

OCTOBER

14 Leonard Bernstein, U.S. conductor and composer of popular and classical music, dies in New York, New York (72).

27 Xavier Cugat, Spanish bandleader and actor who introduced the Rumba to the United States, dies in Barcelona, Spain (90).

NOVEMBER

2 Eliot Furness Porter, U.S. nature photographer whose bird photographs are collected in *Birds of North America*, dies in Santa Fe, New Mexico (88).

17 Robert Hofstadter, U.S. physicist who discovered the structure of protons and neutrons, dies in Stanford, California (75).

23 Roald Dahl, British writer of macabre short stories and children's novels, dies in Oxford, England (74).

DECEMBER

2 Aaron Copland, U.S. composer, conductor, and teacher, who mixed elements of jazz and folk, dies in Westchester, New York (90).

10 Armand Hammer, U.S. petroleum executive who maintained economic ties with the USSR, dies in Los Angeles, California (92).

13 Alice Marble, U.S. tennis player who dominated women's singles and doubles tennis during the late 1930s, dies in Palm Springs, California (77).

25 U.S. boxer Evander Holyfield defeats James "Buster" Douglas of the United States in three rounds in Las Vegas, Nevada, to become the undisputed world heavyweight champion.

NOVEMBER

16–18 The inaugural Solheim Cup competition between the women professional golfers of the United States and Europe is played at Lake Nona Golf Club, Florida. The United States wins 11.5–4.5.

1991

POLITICS, GOVERNMENT, AND ECONOMICS

Business and Economics

- The sale of new homes in the United States is down 6% from the previous year.

JANUARY

8   The Pan Am airline (founded in 1927), burdened with massive debts, files for bankruptcy (it is closed down on December 4).

18 Eastern Airlines, the sixth largest in the United States, goes into liquidation.

APRIL

5   The European Bank of Reconstruction and Development (EBRD), established to assist economic development in Eastern Europe and the USSR, is opened in London, England.

JULY

5   The Bank of Credit and Commerce International (BCCI) collapses after the discovery of massive fraud and involvement in organized crime, arms dealing, and the drug trade.

8   Children's Bonus Bonds, a special tax-free savings opportunity for children under 16, are issued in Britain.

AUGUST

- The Bank America Corporation of San Francisco and the Security Pacific Corporation of Los Angeles, California, merge to form the largest bank in U.S. history.

Human Rights

- A nationwide poll in the United States indicates that 61% of women feel that they have been subjected to sexual harassment while at work; only 4% report the incidents.

AUGUST

31 A civil-rights museum honoring Martin Luther King, Jr., opens in Memphis, Tennessee, at the Lorraine Motel, the site of King's assassination.

Politics and Government

- The Antarctic Treaty is signed by the 39 nations. It imposes a 50-year ban on mineral exploitation of the continent.
- The Gulf War is the first war in which laser weapons are used extensively.
- The U.S. president George Bush makes the controversial nomination of the conservative black judge Clarence Thomas to the U.S. Supreme Court; during the televised Senate confirmation hearing, Professor Anita Hill accuses Thomas of sexual harassment; the Senate narrowly approves the nomination.
- The U.S. Supreme Court rules that nude dancing in Las Vegas, Nevada, is not protected by the First Amendment (the "clear and present danger" test).
- There are 695,000 inmates in U.S. state prisons and 60,000 more in federal prisons, an 80,000 increase in the prison population over the previous year.

JANUARY

6   Jorge Serrano Elias of the Solidarity Action Movement is elected as the successor to President Vinicio Cerezo in Guatemala.

7   Five thousand ethnic Greek Albanians flee to Greece following rumors that border guards are no longer turning back refugees.

7   Soviet paratroopers are despatched to the Baltic republics following independence demonstrations.

8   The government of Kazimiera Prunskiene in Lithuania resigns over price increases.

10 Albertas Shiminas becomes prime minister of Lithuania.

13 Former socialist prime minister Mario Soares is reelected president of Portugal.

13 Soviet troops storm the television station in Vilnius, Lithuania, killing 13 independence campaigners.

15 Iraq fails to meet the United Nations deadline of midnight U.S. time for withdrawal from Kuwait.

15 The U.S. Supreme Court rules that Oklahoma City, Oklahoma, has taken steps to end school segregation and releases it from court-imposed busing.

16 A U.S.-led coalition commences air offensive "Operation Desert Storm" to liberate Kuwait from Iraqi occupation, beginning the Gulf War.

17 King Olav of Norway dies, aged 87; his son succeeds as Harald V.

18 Iraq launches Scud missiles against Israel during the Gulf War.

18 Soviet troops attack the Interior Ministry in Riga, Latvia, killing four independence protesters.

20 A hundred thousand people march through Moscow, capital of the USSR, in protest at the action of Soviet troops in the Baltic republics.

21 Iraq threatens to use Western nationals taken hostage during its invasion of Kuwait as "human shields" against air attacks during the Gulf War.

24 Iraq begins to pump Kuwaiti oil into the Persian Gulf during the Gulf War, creating the world's largest oil spill. About 6–8 million barrels of oil are spilled, polluting 675 km/420 mi of coastline.

26 Rebels in Somalia take the capital Mogadishu; President Siad Barre flees to Kenya.

29–31 The Palestine Liberation Organization (PLO) launches missiles at Israel during the Gulf War.

FEBRUARY

1 President F. W. de Klerk announces plans to repeal the laws underpinning apartheid in South Africa.

4 The U.S. president George Bush announces a budget significantly reducing defense spending and welfare payments (it is approved by the Senate on April 25).

5 A constituent assembly convenes in Colombia to draft a new constitution; left wing guerrillas begin a nationwide terror campaign.

9 A Lithuanian referendum votes for independence from the USSR.

14 The government of Juan Carlos Furtado resigns because of disagreement over how to handle Peru's economic crisis.

16 A bomb planted by a drugs cartel member kills 22 people and injures 135 others in Medellín, Colombia.

22–November 3 Hundreds of Kuwaiti oil wells are set alight by Iraqi soldiers during the Gulf War; the last fire is extinguished on November 3.

23 Martial law is declared in Thailand, following the military's overthrow of the government of Chatichai Choonhavan.

24 The U.S.-led coalition launches a ground offensive against Iraqi forces in the Gulf War.

27 Coalition forces enter the capital Kuwait City and declare Kuwait liberated from the Iraqis.

MARCH

1 A popular revolt against the government of Saddam Hussein begins in Basra, Iraq, and spreads to other Shiite cities; at the same time a separate Kurdish revolt starts in the north.

1–7 Twenty thousand Albanian refugees land at Italian ports, despite attempts by the Italian authorities to stop them.

2 Nicaragua announces an austerity package involving devaluation of the cordoba following the disclosure that in 1990 inflation ran at 13,000%.

3 A nationwide outcry follows the televising in the United States of video footage showing the black motorist Rodney King being beaten by four white policemen in Los Angeles, California.

3 An armistice is signed by leaders of the international coalition and the Iraqi army, ending the Gulf War (in force from April 11).

3 Latvia and Estonia vote for independence from the USSR in referenda.

6 Chandra Shekhar resigns as prime minister of a minority government in India.

11 The trial begins of the former Greek prime minister Andreas Papandreou, on charges of corruption.

14 The "Birmingham Six" are released in Britain after the Appeal Court finds their 1974 conviction for Irish Republican Army (IRA) pub bombings in Birmingham, England, "unsafe and unsatisfactory."

17 A referendum in the USSR approves President Mikhail Gorbachev's proposal for a renewed federation of the socialist republics, giving them greater autonomy.

17 The Yugoslav republic of Serbia suspends the constitution of the predominantly Albanian province of Kosovo, and the use of the Albanian language for official purposes is declared illegal.

24 In Benin's first democratic elections for 20 years, the socialist president Mathieu Ahmed Kerekou is defeated by Nicéphore Soglo, supported by the Union for the Triumph of Democratic Renewal (UTRD).

25 Iraqi government forces bomb the city of Kirkuk in northeast Iraq, held by Kurdish rebels; by March 30, the Iraqi government has recovered most of the country.

31 The military structure of the Warsaw Pact (formed in 1955 between the USSR and East European communist states) is formally dissolved.

31 The ruling Communist Party wins a majority in elections in Albania, amid claims of electoral corruption.

APRIL

5 Turkey and Iran admit Kurdish refugees fleeing persecution in Iraq; soon over 1 million leave the country.

6 The left wing Sendero Luminoso (Shining Path) guerrilla organization in Peru cuts off the electricity supply to the capital, Lima, and mounts attacks on foreign embassies, causing extensive damage.

9 The Soviet republic of Georgia votes for independence from the USSR.

11 Iraqi forces attack Kurdish refugees within the U.S. exclusion zone north of the 36th parallel.

13 Giulio Andreotti forms a new government in Italy, the 50th since 1945.

16 The U.S. president George Bush announces the establishment of "safe havens" for Kurdish refugees in northern Iraq, where they will be protected by U.S., French, and British forces.

17 British, French, and U.S. troops start to enter northern Iraq to establish camps for Kurdish rebels.

20 A conference of South American health ministers meets in Sucre, Bolivia, to discuss the region's worst cholera epidemic of the 20th century (which broke out in Peru in January).

22 Agreement is reached by 39 countries on a 50-year moratorium on mineral exploration in Antarctica.

30   Major General Justin Lekhanya, military leader of Lesotho, is deposed in a coup by Colonel Elias Ramaema.

MAY

5   The United Nations demands that Iraq cease its persecution of the Kurds; the United States begins sending humanitarian relief to refugees.

9   The U.S. president George Bush is diagnosed as suffering from Graves' disorder, a thyroid disorder, after concern over his development of an irregular heartbeat.

9   Yugoslavia's collective state presidency grants special powers for the predominantly Serb Yugoslav national army for operations in Croatia, freeing it from effective government control, following Serb–Croat clashes in Krajina.

12   The Congress Party is victorious in the first multiparty elections in Nepal for 32 years; G. P. Koirala becomes prime minister on May 26.

14   Winnie Mandela, wife of the African National Congress (ANC) leader Nelson Mandela, is sentenced in South Africa to six years' imprisonment for kidnap and accessory to assault.

15   A cease-fire begins in Angola, suspending fighting between the communist People's Movement for the Liberation of Angola (MPLA) and the U.S.-backed National Union for the Total Independence of Angola (UNITA).

15   The socialist politician Edith Cresson becomes the first woman prime minister of France, following the resignation of Michel Rocard.

16   Karl Otto Pöhl, president of the German Bundesbank, resigns over differences with the German government over monetary policy.

17   The Somali National Movement declares northern Somalia independent.

19   The Yugoslav republic of Croatia votes in favor of independence in a referendum.

21   President Haile Mengistu of Ethiopia flees to Zimbabwe as rebel troops advance on the capital, Addis Ababa.

21   The former Indian prime minister Rajiv Gandhi is assassinated by a Tamil suicide bomber during India's general election campaign.

24   Israel flies 14,000 Ethiopian Jews to Israel amid mounting instability in Ethiopia.

26   The Georgian nationalist Zviad Gamsakhurdia is elected president of the republic of Georgia.

28   The Ethiopian People's Revolutionary Democratic Front (EPRDF) captures the Ethiopian capital Addis Ababa, overthrowing the established Marxist government.

31   The Angolan president José dos Santos of the People's Movement for the Liberation of Angola (MPLA) and Jonas Savimbi, leader of the National Union for the Total Independence of Angola (UNITA), sign a peace agreement in Lisbon, Portugal, to end the civil war in Angola that has been fought since independence in 1975.

JUNE

4   The Algerian prime minister Mouloud Hamrouche resigns after security forces fire on Islamic Salvation Front rioters in Algiers.

5   South Africa ends discriminatory land legislation, dismantling the legal framework of apartheid.

7   The Islamic Salvation Front ends protests in exchange for the promise of elections in Algeria.

12   The Russian reformer Boris Yeltsin is elected leader of the Russian Federation.

17   South Africa repeals the Population Registration Act, dismantling the legal framework of apartheid.

19   The leading Colombian drugs baron Pablo Escobar García gives himself up to police after the constituent assembly repeals legislation governing extradition of criminals to the United States.

20   The Congress (I) leader P. V. Narasimha Rao is appointed Indian prime minister at the head of a minority government, following elections.

20   The German parliament votes to move the seat of government from Bonn to Berlin.

20   The U.S. Supreme Court holds it legal for police to board long-distance buses without a warrant and search passengers for drugs.

21   Federal agents in San Francisco, California, seize 1,080 pounds of heroin, the largest heroin find in history.

25   The republics of Croatia and Slovenia declare independence from Yugoslavia.

JULY

1   A law passed by Congress extending the employment rights of mentally ill Americans goes into effect. Among other provisions, employers cannot ask job applicants if they have a history of mental illness.

1   A protocol signed in Prague, Czechoslovakia (now the Czech Republic), dissolves the political structure of the Warsaw Pact (formed in 1955 between the USSR and East European communist states).

1   European Community ministers order an embargo on the export of arms to Yugoslavia following the outbreak of inter-ethnic violence there.

8   Slovenia's independence is recognized by the federal government of Yugoslavia.

24   The Indian government abandons centralized planning and introduces reforms to liberalize the economy.

25   Police in Milwaukee, Wisconsin, arrest Jeffrey L. Dahmer and charge him with the serial murder of 17 victims. Dahmer later confesses to the crimes and on February 17, 1992, is sentenced to 15 consecutive life terms in prison.

31   The U.S. president George Bush and the Soviet leader Mikhail Gorbachev sign the Strategic Arms Reduction Treaty (START) to reduce their arsenals of long-range nuclear weapons by a third.

AUGUST

•   Two thousand six hundred people are arrested at blockades of abortion clinics in Wichita, Kansas, by antiabortion campaigners.

6   Bangladesh abandons the presidential system of government and returns to parliamentary rule.

8   John McCarthy, the British journalist held hostage in Lebanon, is released after 1,943 days in captivity.

15   The United Nations (UN) Security Council condemns Iraq for hindering the work of UN inspectors by denying access to nuclear facilities.

18   The remains of King Frederick II the Great of Prussia, buried in Austria since 1945, are reinterred at Sans Souci Palace in Potsdam, Germany, in accordance with his wishes.

19   Reactionary communists led by Gennady Yanayev stage a coup against the Soviet president Mikhail Gorbachev, who is placed under house arrest in the Crimea; radio and television stations are shut down and military rule imposed in many cities.

20   The Soviet republic of Estonia declares its independence from the USSR.

21   The coup in the USSR against President Mikhail Gorbachev fails; Gorbachev returns to Moscow the following day.

21   The Soviet republic of Latvia declares its independence from the USSR.

24   The Soviet president Mikhail Gorbachev resigns as general secretary of the Communist Party of the USSR, criticizing its role in the coup of August 19–21.

26   The Serb-dominated Yugoslav national army begins a siege of the Croatian town of Vukovar.

28   President Mikhail Gorbachev dismisses the Soviet government and disbands the leadership of the KGB (the secret police of the USSR).

30   The Soviet republic of Azerbaijan declares its independence from the USSR.

SEPTEMBER

2   The governmental system of the USSR is suspended prior to the establishment of a new constitution.

6   The Soviet authorities make formal grants of independence to Latvia, Lithuania, and Estonia.

7   A European Community-sponsored peace conference on Yugoslavia opens in The Hague, the Netherlands, chaired by the British statesman Lord Carrington.

11   President Mikhail Gorbachev of the USSR announces the withdrawal of Soviet troops from Cuba.

15   The ruling Social Democrats lose a general election in Sweden; Prime Minister Ingvar Carlsson resigns and Carl Bildt subsequently forms a right wing coalition.

16   Legal charges against Colonel Oliver North over the Iran-Contra affair are dropped.

17   A cease-fire negotiated between Croats and Serbs in Yugoslavia is quickly broken.

22   The Soviet republic of Armenia declares its independence from the USSR.

25   The United Nations imposes a mandatory arms embargo on Yugoslavia following the outbreak of serious ethnic clashes.

26–October 1   Troops are deployed in Romania after two days of riots by miners demanding higher wages; the government led by Petre Roman resigns and Teodor Stolojan is named prime minister on October 1.

30   President Jean Bertrand Aristide is overthrown in a military coup in Haiti.

OCTOBER

1   The Russian city of Leningrad reverts to its prerevolution name of St. Petersburg.

1   The Serb-dominated Yugoslav national army begins a siege of the Croatian port of Dubrovnik; federal jets attack the Croatian capital, Zagreb, on October 7.

3   The Arkansas governor Bill Clinton announces his candidacy for the 1992 U.S. presidential elections.

4   Carl Bildt forms a right wing coalition government in Sweden.

6   Prime Minister Cavaco Silva's ruling Social Democratic Party gains an outright majority in the general elections in Portugal.

8   Having overthrown President Jean Bertrand Aristide on September 30, the military install Judge Joseph Norette as provisional president of Haiti.

13   The Bulgarian Socialist Party is defeated in elections; a noncommunist government under Filip Dimitrov is formed in November.

15   The parliament in the Yugoslav republic of Bosnia-Herzegovina votes to declare independence.

16   George Hennard, using two semiautomatic pistols, kills 22 people at a restaurant in Killeen, Texas, the worst gun massacre in U.S. history.

17   The U.S. House of Representatives votes to remove legislation banning semiautomatic weapons from a Democratic anticrime bill.

18   A peace agreement is signed in Rome, Italy, to end civil war in Mozambique between the government and Mozambique National Resistance (MNR) rebels.

20   Suleyman Demirel's True Path Party wins the general elections in Turkey.

21–31   President Mobutu of Zaire dismisses Prime Minister Etienne Tshisekedi, provoking violent rioting; the opposition movement forms a rival government on October 31.

23   The four factions engaged in the civil war in Cambodia sign a peace accord in Paris, France.

27   Poland holds its first free parliamentary elections since World War II but the result is inconclusive, with no party polling more than 12%.

31   President Kenneth Kaunda is defeated in Zambian elections and succeeded by Frederick Chiluba, leader of the Movement for Multi-Party Democracy (MMD).

NOVEMBER

8   Filip Dimitrov of the Union of Democratic Forces (UDF) becomes the first noncommunist prime minister of Bulgaria since 1944.

8–December 2   European Community foreign ministers decide to impose immediate economic and trade sanctions against Yugoslavia in response to the sieges of Vukovar and Dubrovnik in Croatia by the Serb-dominated Yugoslav national army; on December 2, the sanctions are dropped against all republics except Serbia and Montenegro.

12   Indonesian troops kill 115 people at an independence demonstration in Dili, East Timor.

13   Hundreds of civilians are evacuated from the Croatian port of Dubrovnik, Yugoslavia, during a cease-fire arranged by the United Nations.

14   Prince Norodom Sihanouk returns to Cambodia after 13 years' exile as president of a multifaction Supreme National Council.

17   The Croatian town of Vukovar is taken by Serb forces after an 86-day siege.

18   Terry Waite, envoy to the archbishop of Canterbury and the last British hostage in Lebanon, is freed after 1,763 days in captivity.

24   A general election in Belgium produces gains for Flemish extremists and the Green Party.

DECEMBER

1   The Soviet republic of Ukraine votes to secede from the USSR.

2–4   Joseph Cicipio, U.S. hostage in Lebanon is released, followed by Alan Steen (December 3) and Terry Anderson (December 4).

3   The Kenyan general assembly votes to reintroduce multiparty politics.

5   Canada introduces strict gun controls, banning automatics, sawn-off rifles and shotguns, and other classes of weapon.

5   Leonid Kravchuk becomes president of Ukraine on its formal accession to independence from the USSR.

8   The leaders of the Soviet republics of Russia, Belarus, and Ukraine agree to the formation of a Commonwealth of Independent States (CIS) to replace the USSR.

9–10   A summit of European Community heads of government in Maastricht, the Netherlands, agrees the Maastricht Treaty on closer economic and political union (Britain obtains the right to abstain from social legislation and a single currency).

12   William Kennedy Smith, nephew of the Massachusetts senator Edward Kennedy, is acquitted of rape after a ten-day trial.

13   The United Nations ends its ban on sporting, scientific, and academic links with South Africa following the repeal of apartheid.

19   Paul Keating replaces Bob Hawke as prime minister and leader of the Australian Labor Party.

20   Ante Marković, a Croat, resigns as federal prime minister of Yugoslavia in protest at the funding of the Serb-dominated Yugoslav national army by the federal budget.

21   Following the lead of Russia, Belarus, and Ukraine (on December 8), eight other republics of the USSR sign the agreement to form a Commonwealth of Independent States (CIS).

25   Mikhail Gorbachev resigns as president of the USSR, which officially ceased to exist on December 9.

26   The Islamic Salvation Front defeats the ruling National Liberation Front in the first round of the Algerian elections.

SCIENCE, TECHNOLOGY, AND MEDICINE

Computing

c. 1991   Computer viruses, programs deliberately constructed and disseminated to damage existing data, become more destructive. The development of "disinfection" programs takes off as a result.

- Americans spend $53.6 billion on computers and video products, $17 billion on books and maps, $33 billion on toys, and $23 billion on magazines and newspapers.

- British firm Virtuality launches its first commercial virtual reality products: games machines in arcades where players wear head-mounted displays.

- The British Science Museum constructs Charles Babbage's second difference engine, demonstrating that it would have worked had the materials then been available. It evaluates polynomials up to the seventh power, with 30-figure accuracy.

- U.S. computer manufacturer Apple introduces "System 7," an intuitive, easy-to-use interface, with icons, windows, and a mouse.

- U.S. firm Cray Research introduces the Cray Y-MP 90 computer, which is capable of 16 billion calculations a second.

Ecology

c. 1991   Ecotourism, an attempt to make tourist travel environmentally-aware and constructive, goes mainstream with the development of eco package tours. Ecotourism features visits to scenic, "natural," or endangered environmental sites, with emphasis on balancing the needs of the local economy and the desires of the tourist with environmental needs. Favorite sites are rain forests, African game reserves, and the Galapagos islands.

c. 1991   Manufacturers begin to introduce more recyclable materials into their packaging.

- "Biosphere 2," an experiment that attempts to reproduce the world's biosphere in miniature within a sealed glasshouse, is launched in Arizona, United States. Eight people remain sealed inside for two years.

FEBRUARY

9   Radioactive water leaks out of the Mihama nuclear power plant in Japan, contaminating the water in the steam generator. It is Japan's worst nuclear accident.

APRIL

4   The U.S. Environmental Protection Agency announces ozone layer depletion at twice the speed previously predicted.

16   Tornadoes strike seven midwestern and southwestern states in the United States, killing 23 people.

22   An earthquake on the Panama–Costa Rica border kills 80 people.

29   Around 200,000 people are killed by a cyclone in Bangladesh.

MAY

- A storm surge inundates the Chittagong delta in Bangladesh, killing 125,000 people.

JUNE

- Mt. Pinatubo on Luzon, in the Philippines, erupts in the third largest eruption this century. Clouds of ash are sent 20 km/12 mi into the atmosphere, along with the greatest volume of sulfur dioxide ever measured. Timely warnings lead to the evacuation of 56,000 people and there are only a few deaths.

SEPTEMBER

3   A fire at a chicken processing plant in Hamlet, North Carolina, kills 25 people and injures 45 others.

OCTOBER

20–23   Twenty-three people die and 2,777 homes and 433 apartment units are destroyed by fire in Oakland, California. The property damage is valued at more than $5 billion.

NOVEMBER

6   The Philippines are hit by severe floods and landslides.

Exploration

- A borehole in the Kola Peninsula in Arctic Russia, begun in the 1970s, reaches a record depth of 12,261 m/ 40,240 ft.

- The Space Life Sciences-1 laboratory is launched by the U.S. shuttle *Columbia*. Astronauts conduct experiments on themselves, rats, and jellyfish polyps.

APRIL

7   The U.S. space shuttle *Atlantis* launches the *Compton Gamma Ray Observatory* into Earth orbit to study gamma-rays and their sources. It weighs 16.7 metric tons/17 tons and is the heaviest payload ever carried by a space shuttle.

MAY

18–26   English chemist Helen Sharman becomes the first Briton to go into space, as a participant in a Soviet space mission launched in *Soyuz TM-12*. She spends six days with Soviet cosmonauts aboard the *Mir* space station.

OCTOBER

29   The U.S. spacecraft *Galileo* takes the closest ever picture of an asteroid—Gaspra—at a distance of 26,071 km/ 16,200 mi.

Health and Medicine

c. 1991   The medication Ritalin is widely used to treat children whose poor performance at school is interpreted as a symptom of the psychiatric condition Attention Deficit Hyperactivity Disorder (ADHD), consisting of hyperactivity, disruptive behavior, and short attention span, which was first identified in 1987.

- Australian and British studies show that passive smoking is a significant cause of lung cancer. Children whose parents smoke suffer an increased risk of asthma and respiratory infections.
- German physiologists Erwin Neher and Bert Sakmann are jointly awarded the Nobel Prize for Physiology or Medicine for their discoveries concerning the function of single ion channels in cells.
- Heart surgeons develop a way of repairing damaged hearts using muscles from the patient's body.
- Nicotine patches become available on prescription in the United States as an aid to giving up smoking.
- The realization that all people with Down's syndrome will eventually develop early-onset Alzheimer's disease if they live long enough, leads to the discovery that some forms of Alzheimer's disease are caused by a gene defect on chromosome 21.
- The U.S. Center for Disease Control estimates that 400,000 people die each year from smoking.
- U.S. pathologist Jack Kervorkian, known as "Dr. Death," publishes *Prescription: Medicide: The Goodness of Planned Death*, a book advocating physician-assisted suicide.
- Veterans of the Gulf War complain of headaches, memory loss, listlessness, depression, respiratory problems, lethargy, muscle weakness, nausea, and pain. Known as Gulf War Syndrome, these symptoms may be caused by the cocktail effect of a combination of vaccinations against tropical diseases and diseases likely to be used in biological weapons, nerve gas, antinerve gas drugs, and organophosphate (OP) insecticides.

JANUARY

23   The worst cholera epidemic this century strikes Peru. Nearly 100,000 are affected and more than 700 people die. It is believed to have spread by the consumption of seafood contaminated by untreated sewage.

MAY

31   Health Care Financing Administration (HCFA) officials in the United States announce a new fee schedule for doctors treating Medicare patients. HCFA hopes to lessen healthcare inflation.

OCTOBER

9   The U.S. Food and Drug Administration approves DDI, a drug to combat AIDS that is much cheaper than AZT, and which can be taken by those who cannot tolerate AZT.

NOVEMBER

7   Basketball star Earvin "Magic" Johnson retires on discovering that he is infected with the HIV virus that causes AIDS.

Science

- British geneticists Peter Goodfellow and Robin Lovell-Badge discover the gene on the Y chromosome that determines sex.
- Drawings done in charcoal on the walls of the Cosquer Cave near Marseille, France, are discovered and are radiocarbon-dated to 27,110 years old.
- Experiments at the CERN research center in Switzerland demonstrate the existence of three generations of elementary particles, each with two quarks and two leptons.
- French physicist Pierre-Gilles de Gennes receives the Nobel Prize for Physics for generalizing methods of studying simple systems to more complex forms of matter, in particular to liquid crystals and polymers.
- Swiss chemist Richard Ernst receives the Nobel Prize for Chemistry for improvements in the technology of nuclear magnetic resonance.
- The body of a man, complete with clothing, bow, arrows, a copper ax, and other implements, is found preserved in a glacier in the Italian Alps. Known as the "iceman," he is estimated to be 5,300 years old. The discovery leads to a reappraisal of the boundary between the Bronze and the Stone Age.
- The European Space Agency's first remote-sensing satellite (*ERS-1*) is launched into polar orbit to monitor the earth's temperature from space.
- The Jodrell Bank radio astronomy center near Manchester, England, reports the possible discovery of a planet orbiting pulsar star PSR 1829–10.
- The remains of an ancient civilization are discovered at Taperinha on the Amazon River, East of Santarem, Brazil. Believed to have existed 6,000–8,000 years ago, it predates the ancient New World civilizations of Mexico and the Andes.
- The World Ocean Experiment (WOCE) program is set up to monitor ocean temperatures, circulation, and other parameters.

JANUARY

- An asteroid 16 km/10 mi in diameter passes between the moon and the earth, scoring a near miss.

NOVEMBER

9   The Joint European Torus (JET) at Culham, near Oxford, England, produces a 1.7 megawatt pulse of

power in an experiment that lasts two seconds. It is the first time that a substantial amount of fusion power has been produced in a controlled experiment, as opposed to an atomic bomb.

Technology

- British Telecom begins offering Integrated Services Digital Network (ISDN) to businesses in the UK. Introduced in Japan in 1988, it provides the fast transfer of computerized information. New services include computer conferencing, teleshopping, home banking, and services where both voice and computer communications take place simultaneously.
- Dutch company Philips introduces an electromagnetic induction light with no parts that can wear out and which lasts for 60,000 hours.
- Several U.S. companies introduce local area networks (LANs) that use nondirectional microwaves to transmit data as fast as fiber optic cables.
- The New Technology Telescope, an optical telescope that is part of the European Southern Observatory at La Silla, Chile, comes into operation. Its thin lightweight mirror, 3.38 m/141 in across, is kept in shape by computer-adjustable supports to produce a sharper image than is possible with conventional mirrors.
- The U.S. General Instrument Corporation develops the first digital high-definition television (HDTV) prototype.
- The U.S. Taliq Corporation introduces Taliq Liquid Crystal glass, which is normally opaque but turns clear when an electric current is applied. It is used primarily for office dividers.
- The world's first solar power station connected to a national grid goes on line at Adrano, Sicily. Giant mirrors follow the sun throughout the day, focusing the rays onto a steam boiler that drives a conventional turbine. The plant generates up to one megawatt.

FEBRUARY

1   Dutch company Philips demonstrates its digital tape cassette at the electronics fair in Las Vegas, Nevada.

Transportation

- The first magnetohydrodynamic passenger boat, the *Yamato 1*, is tested in Japan. Electric current passes through electrodes, which accelerates water through two cylindrical thrusters propelling the boat forward at 8 knots.

JANUARY

17   English businessman Richard Branson and U.S. balloonist Per Lindstrand complete the first hot-air balloon crossing of the Pacific Ocean, covering 10,818 km/6,761 mi in 46 hours.

MAY

26   A Boeing 767, en route to Vienna from Bangkok, explodes shortly after takeoff; 223 people are killed.

ARTS AND IDEAS

Architecture

- The Sainsbury Wing of the National Gallery in London, England, designed by the U.S. architect Robert Venturi and the English architect Denise Scott Brown, is completed.
- The Skarnsundet Bridge is completed in Norway; it is the longest cable-stayed bridge in the world, with a main span of 527 m/1,729 ft.
- The Terminal at Stansted airport in Essex, England, designed by the English architect Norman Foster, is completed.

NOVEMBER

4   Five former presidents, George Bush, Ronald Reagan, Jimmy Carter, Gerald Ford, and Richard M. Nixon, gather for the dedication of the Ronald Reagan Presidential Library in Simi Valley, California, which contains more than 47 million documents relating to his presidency.

Arts

- The exhibition "High and Low" is held at the Museum of Modern Art in New York, New York.
- The exhibition "Pop Art" is held at the Royal Academy in London, England.

MARCH

11   Publisher and philanthropist Walter Annenberg bequeaths his $1 billion art collection to the Metropolitan Museum of Art in New York, New York.

Film

- At the César awards in Paris, France, *Cyrano de Bergerac* wins a record ten Césars, including best picture, best director (Jean-Paul Rappeneau), and best actor (Gérard Depardieu).
- The documentary *Paris is Burning*, about gay black men who compete in drag competitions, is released. It is directed by U.S. filmmaker Jennie Livingston.
- The movie *Barton Fink*, directed by Joel Coen, is released in the United States, starring John Turturro and John Goodman.
- The movie *Boyz N the Hood*, directed by John Singleton, is released in the United States, starring Ice Cube, Larry Fishburne, and Cuba Gooding, Jr. Singleton, at the age of 23, becomes the youngest director to receive an Oscar nomination.
- The movie *City Slickers*, directed by Ron Underwood, is released in the United States, starring Billy Crystal, Daniel Stern, Bruno Kirby, and Jack Palance.
- The movie *Edward II*, directed by Derek Jarman, is released in Britain. Based on the play by Christopher Marlowe, it stars Steven Waddington, Kevin Collins, and Tilda Swinton.
- The movie *Europa, Europa*, directed by Polish filmmaker Agnieszka Holland, is released in France, starring Marco Hofschneider, Julie Delpy, and André Wilms.

- The movie *JFK*, directed by Oliver Stone, is released in the United States, starring Kevin Costner, Sissy Spacek, Joe Pesci, Tommy Lee Jones, and Gary Oldman.
- The movie *Korczak*, directed by Andrzej Wajda, is released in Poland, starring Wojciech Pszoniak.
- The movie *La Belle Noiseuse*, directed by Jacques Rivette, is released in France, starring Michel Piccoli, Jane Birkin, and Emmanuelle Béart.
- The movie *La Double Vie de Véronique/The Double Life of Véronique*, directed by Krzysztof Kieślowski, is released in Poland, starring Irène Jacob, Halina Gryglaszewska, and Kalina Jędrusik.
- The movie *Les Amants du Pont-Neuf/The Lovers on the Pont-Neuf*, directed by Leos Carax, is released in France, starring Juliette Binoche and Denis Lavant.
- The movie *Let Him Have It*, directed by Peter Medak, is released in Britain. It stars Christopher Eccleston as Derek Bentley, who was hanged through a miscarriage of justice.
- The movie *My Own Private Idaho*, directed by Gus Van Sant, is released in the United States, starring River Phoenix and Keanu Reeves.
- The movie *Naked Lunch*, directed by David Cronenberg, is released in Britain. Based on the novel by William S. Burroughs, it stars Peter Weller, Judy Davis, Ian Holm, and Julian Sands.
- The movie *Prospero's Books*, directed by Peter Greenaway, is released in Britain, starring John Gielgud, Michael Clark, Michel Blanc, Erland Josephson, and Isabelle Pasco.
- The movie *Raise the Red Lantern*, directed by Zhang Yimou, is released in China, starring Gong Li, Ma Jingwu, He Caifei, Cao Cuifeng, and Jin Shuyan.
- The movie *Reservoir Dogs*, directed by Quentin Tarantino, is released in the United States, starring Harvey Keitel, Tim Roth, Michael Madsen, and Steve Buscemi.
- The movie *Robin Hood: Prince of Thieves*, directed by Kevin Reynolds, is released in the United States, starring Kevin Costner, Morgan Freeman, Mary Elizabeth Mastroantonio, and Alan Rickman.
- The movie *Terminator 2: Judgement Day*, directed by James Cameron, is released in the United States, starring Arnold Schwarzenegger. With its use of spectacular innovative computer-generated effects, its budget is a record $100 million.
- The movie *The Addams Family*, directed by Barry Sonnenfeld, is released in the United States, starring Anjelica Huston, Raul Julia, and Christopher Lloyd.
- The movie *The Commitments*, directed by Alan Parker, is released in Britain. Based on the novel by Irish author Roddy Doyle, it stars Robert Arkins, Michael Aherne, Bronagh Gallagher, and Andrew Strong.
- The movie *The Doors*, directed by Oliver Stone, is released in the United States, starring Val Kilmer as Jim Morrison, Meg Ryan, Kevin Dillon, and Kyle MacLachlan.
- The movie *The Fisher King*, directed by Terry Gilliam, is released in the United States, starring Jeff Bridges, Robin Williams, Amanda Plummer, and Mercedes Ruehl.
- The movie *The Last Days of Chez Nous*, directed by Gillian Armstrong, is released in Australia, starring Bruno Ganz and Lisa Harrow.

- The movie *The Silence of the Lambs*, directed by Jonathan Demme, is released in the United States. Based on the novel by Thomas Harris, it stars Jodie Foster and Anthony Hopkins.
- The movie *The Vanishing*, directed by Dutch filmmaker George Sluizer, is released in the Netherlands, starring Bernard-Pierre Donnadieu, Gene Bervoets, and Johanna Ter Steege.
- The movie *Thelma and Louise*, directed by English filmmaker Ridley Scott, is released in the United States, starring Susan Sarandon and Geena Davis.
- The movie *Toto the Hero*, directed by Jaco Van Dormael, is released in Belgium, starring Michel Bouquet and Jo de Backer.
- The Walt Disney animated movie *Beauty and the Beast* is released. Its success revives interest in feature-length animation.

MARCH

20 The 1990 Academy Awards are held. Best Actor: Jeremy Irons, for *Reversal of Fortune*; Best Supporting Actor: Joe Pesci, for *GoodFellas*; Best Actress: Kathy Bates, for *Misery*; Best Supporting Actress: Whoopi Goldberg, for *Ghost*; Best Director: Kevin Costner, for *Dances with Wolves*; Best Picture: *Dances with Wolves*, directed by Kevin Costner.

Literature and Language

- Andrew Morton writes *Diana: Her True Story*, a biography of the Princess of Wales, with the collaboration of her friends.
- Douglas Coupland's novel, *Generation X*, identifies a generation of disillusioned twentysomethings with little hope for the future. It uses the term "McJob" to denote a low-wage, low-skill job, especially in the fast-food industry.
- Norman J. Schwarzkopf, the U.S. general who led the victorious allied forces in the Gulf War, signs a $5 million advance for the rights to his memoir.
- Simon and Schuster cancel the publication of Bret Easton Ellis's novel *American Psycho*, because of controversy over its ruthless, amoral, psychopathic main character.
- The Chilean writer Isabel Allende publishes her novel *El plan infinito/The Infinite Plain*.
- The English writer Angela Carter publishes her last novel *Wise Children*.
- The English writer Pat Barker publishes her novel *Regeneration*, the first part of her *Regeneration* trilogy.
- The Nigerian writer Ben Okri publishes his novel *The Famished Road*, which wins the Booker Prize.
- The Nobel Prize for Literature is awarded to the South African novelist Nadine Gordimer.
- The Pulitzer Prize for Biography is awarded to Steven Naifeh and George White Smith for *Jackson Pollock: An American Saga*, the Pulitzer Prize for Poetry is awarded to Mona Van Duyn for *Near Changes*, and the Pulitzer Prize for Fiction is awarded to John Updike for *Rabbit at Rest*.
- The sale of books in the United States increases by 9.1%.
- The U.S. journalist Robert Dallek publishes *Lone Star Rising: Lyndon Johnson and His Times, 1908–60*.

- The U.S. writer Adrienne Rich publishes her poetry collection *An Atlas of the Difficult World*.
- The U.S. writer Amy Tan publishes her novel *The Kitchen-God's Wife*.
- The U.S. writer Garrison Keillor publishes his novel *A Radio Romance*.
- The U.S. writer Harold Brodkey publishes his novel *The Runaway Soul*.
- The U.S. writer James Broughton publishes his poetry collection *The Androgyne Journal*.
- The U.S. writer John Ashbery publishes his long poem "Flow Chart."
- The U.S. writer John Barth publishes his novel *The Last Voyage of Somebody the Sailor*.
- The U.S. writer Mary Gaitskill publishes her novel *Two Girls, Fat and Thin*.
- The U.S. writer Norman Mailer publishes his novel *Harlot's Ghost*.
- The U.S. writer Philip Roth publishes his memoir *Patrimony*.
- The U.S. writer Richard Condon publishes his novel *The Final Addition*.
- The U.S. writer Russell Banks publishes his novel *The Sweet Hereafter*.

Music

- Following the death from AIDS of British rock group Queen's lead singer Freddie Mercury, the single "Bohemian Rhapsody" is rereleased and goes to number one in the UK charts for the second time.
- The Australian pop singer Kylie Minogue sets a record when her first 13 singles make the Top 10 in the British charts.
- The British pop group Primal Scream releases the album *Screamadelica*.
- The British pop group Simply Red releases the album *Stars*.
- The British punk group the Clash rereleases the single "Should I Stay or Should I Go?"
- The British rock singer Elvis Costello releases the album *Mighty Like a Rose*.
- The English composer Michael Tippett completes his String Quartet No. 5.
- The English composer Harrison Birtwistle completes his orchestral work *Gawain's Journey*.
- The English composer John Tavener completes his choral work *Icon of the Nativity* and his chamber work *The Last Sleep of the Virgin*.
- The Estonian composer Arvo Pärt completes his *Berlin Mass*.
- The German composer York Georg Höller completes his work for piano, orchestra, and tape *Pensées/Thoughts*.
- The Irish rock group U2 releases the album *Achtung Baby*.
- The Japanese electronics company Sony launches the mini disk in Japan and the United States. It holds 74 minutes of music and is 6.4 cm/2.5 in in diameter.
- The opera *Sir Gawain and the Green Knight*, by the English composer Harrison Birtwistle and based on the 14th-century English poem, is first performed, in London, England.

- The opera *The Ghosts of Versailles*, by the U.S. composer John Corigliano, is first performed, in New York, New York.
- The resurgence in use of the hallucinogenic drug LSD in the United States and the UK is accompanied by the development of ambient techno music.
- The Russian composer Alfred Schnittke completes his *Concerto Grosso* No. 5.
- The Russian composer Dmitri Smirnov completes his *Song of Liberty* for voices and orchestra.
- The Scottish composer Judith Weir completes her chamber work *I Broke off a Golden Branch*.
- The U.S. heavy rock group Guns 'n' Roses releases the album *Use Your Illusion II*.
- The U.S. pop singer Michael Jackson releases the album *Dangerous*.
- The U.S. rap group Public Enemy releases the single "Apocalypse '91: The Empire Strikes Back."
- The U.S. rock group Nirvana releases the album *Nevermind*; it marks the advent of grunge music, much of it coming from Seattle, Washington.
- The U.S. rock group REM releases the single "Losing My Religion" and the album *Out of Time*.
- U.S. grunge bands, such as Nirvana, Pearl Jam, and Soundgarden, provide the music for Generation X, or the "slacker" generation, the disaffected youth of the United States who see no hopeful future for themselves. The term Generation X is derived from U.S. writer Douglas Coupland's novel of the same name.

FEBRUARY

20 The 1990–91 Grammy Awards are held. Best Album: *Back on the Block* by Quincy Jones; Best Single: "Another Day in Paradise" by Phil Collins; Best Male Pop Vocalist: Roy Orbison; Best Female Pop Vocalist: Mariah Carey.

23 The British pop group Happy Mondays releases the album *Pills 'n' Thrills and Bellyaches*.

NOVEMBER

- The records of the rapper Ice Cube provoke controversy in the United States, as they are described as promoting violence against racial minorities. The Simon Wiesenthal Center in Los Angeles, California, an international center promoting Holocaust remembrance, asks record stores to stop selling the album *Death Certificate*.

DECEMBER

16 Gilbert O'Sullivan, composer of the 1970s hit "Alone Again (Naturally)," wins a multimillion dollar lawsuit in the United States against rapper Biz Markie for sampling his work, and the judge also recommends criminal prosecution. The popularity of sampling—the incorporation of segments of other songs, especially featured in rap music—results in debates over copyright protection.

Theater and Dance

- Broadway theater in New York, New York, suffers from the overall economic malaise; the number of productions falls by two to 28, attendance falls from 8 million to 7.4 million, and box office receipts fall from $283 million to $267 million.

- One of the most talked about shows of the year on Broadway, New York, New York, is *Miss Saigon*. Controversies surround the show's $100 ticket prices and its attempts to use the cast from the London, England, show on Broadway.
- The play *Kvetch*, by the English dramatist Steven Berkoff, is first performed, in London, England.
- The play *Lost in Yonkers*, by the U.S. dramatist Neil Simon, is first performed, in New York, New York. It wins him the Pulitzer Prize for Drama.
- The play *Silly Cow*, by the English writer and performer Ben Elton, is first performed, in London, England.
- The play *The Madness of George III*, by the English writer Alan Bennett, is first performed, in London, England.
- The Pulitzer Prize for Drama is awarded to Neil Simon for *Lost in Yonkers*.

JUNE

2   The 1990–91 Tony Awards are held. Best Play: *Lost in Yonkers*; Best Musical: *The Will Rogers Follies*; Best Actor in a Play: Nigel Hawthorne; Best Actress in a Play: Mercedes Ruehl.

Thought and Scholarship

- The English philosopher Michael Dummett publishes *The Logical Basis of Metaphysics*.
- The Pulitzer Prize for History is awarded to Laurel Thatcher Ulrich for *A Midwife's Tale: The Life of Martha Ballard, Based on Her Diary 1785–1812*.
- The Pulitzer Prize for General Nonfiction is awarded to Edward O. Wilson and Burt Holldobler for *The Ants*.
- The U.S. journalist E. J. Dionne publishes *Why Americans Hate Politics*.
- The U.S. journalist Nicholas Lemann publishes *The Promised Land: The Great Black Migration and How It Changed America*.
- The U.S. philosopher Thomas Nagel publishes *Equality and Partiality*.
- U.S. linguist Noam Chomsky publishes *Deterring Democracy*.
- U.S. politician Robert B. Reich publishes *The Work of Nations: Preparing Ourselves for the the 21st Century*.

- U.S. writer Paul Auster publishes his essay collection *The Art of Hunger*.

SOCIETY

Education

- Distance learning programs continue to expand worldwide.

Everyday Life

c. 1991   As cheaper phone charges make telemarketing more viable, "infomercials"—advertisements styled as informative programs—proliferate on U.S. television.

c. 1991   Baby-doll dresses—frilly with high waists—become popular as part of a trend for infantile fashions. This is exemplified by the U.S. singer Courtney Love, who labels it her "kinderwhore" look.

c. 1991   The Caesar haircut—very short and brushed forward—starts to become popular with men.

- Thirty-seven million state and federal fishing licenses and 31 million hunting licenses are issued in the United States.
- In the United States, 5.5 million children live in poverty.
- In the United States this year, 6.2 million parents receive child support payments.
- A study in the United States reveals that women hold 45% of all government jobs, but just 31% of upper-level positions in government agencies.
- A U.S. government study finds that on average black Americans die six years earlier than white Americans.
- A U.S. government survey finds that among the nation's ethnic groups, Hispanics have the highest rates of diabetes, high blood pressure, kidney disease, and some cancers.
- Americans spend $728.6 billion on healthcare, 13% of the total GDP. Private business spends $205.4 billion, households spend $247 billion, the government spends $254.5 billion, and $21.7 billion comes from nonpatient revenues and endowments.

BIRTHS & DEATHS

- Austin Bradford Hill, English epidemiologist and statistician, who was one of the first to demonstrate the link between cigarette smoking and lung cancer, dies in Cumbria, England (94).

JANUARY

11   Carl David Anderson, U.S. physicist who discovered the positron, the first particle of antimatter, dies in San Marino, California (85).

15   Leona Baumgartner, U.S. doctor and government official noted for her promotion of healthcare, dies in Chicago, Illinois (88).

17   Giacomo Manzù, Italian sculptor, dies in Ardeu, near Rome, Italy (82).

17   Olaf V of Norway, Norwegian monarch 1957–91, dies in Oslo, Norway (87).

22   Northrup Frye, Canadian literary critic, dies in Toronto, Ontario, Canada (78).

24   Jack Schaeffer, U.S. novelist best known for his book *Shane*, dies in Santa Fe, New Mexico (83).

28   Harold Edward ("Red ") Grange, U.S. football player, dies in Lake Wales, Florida (87).

30   John Bardeen, U.S. physicist who shared two Nobel Prizes for Physics, one for inventing the transistor (1956) and one for developing a theory of superconductivity (1972), dies in Boston, Massachusetts (82).

FEBRUARY

6   Danny Thomas, U.S. comedian, dies in Los Angeles, California (79).

6   Salvador Edward Luria, Italian-born U.S. physician who received the Nobel Prize for Physiology or Medicine in 1969 for his work on bacteriophages, dies in Lexington, Massachusetts (78).

14   John Alex McCone, U.S. industrialist and head of the Central Intelligence Agency (CIA) 1961–65, dies in Pebble Beach, California (89).

- Americans spend $450.5 billion on education at all levels.
- Americans take 177 million business trips and 692 million vacation or pleasure trips this year.
- Automatic number identification or "Caller-ID" is introduced in the United States. The caller's number is displayed on the receiver's telephone before it is answered.
- British-manufactured miniature Polly Pocket dolls become the most popular toy in Japan.
- Derek Humphry publishes *Final Exit*, a how-to book for suicides.

- Economic recession causes a decline in the number of bottles of champagne purchased in Britain, previously the top champagne importer in the world.
- In the grip of the longest recession since the 1930s, unemployment in Britain stands at 2.5 million and house repossessions at 80,000 for the year.
- In the United States, 21% of prison inmates are aged between 18 and 24, 46% between 25 and 34, and 23% between 35 and 44.
- In the United States, 66% of single women over 16 and 58% of married women hold jobs.

MARCH

1 Edwin Herbert Land, U.S. physicist who developed the Polaroid camera, an instantaneous one-step process for developing and printing photographs, dies in Cambridge, Massachusetts (81).

3 Arthur Murray, U.S. dance teacher, dies in Honolulu, Hawaii (95).

3 William George Penny, British physicist who developed Britain's first atomic bomb, dies in East Hendred, Oxfordshire, England (81).

APRIL

1 Martha Graham, U.S. choreographer of modern dance, dies in New York, New York (96).

3 Charles Goren, U.S. bridge player and columnist, dies in Encino, California (90).

3 Graham Greene, English novelist, dies in Vevey, Switzerland (86).

16 David Lean, English film director who directed *The Bridge on the River Kwai* (1957), *Lawrence of Arabia* (1962), and *Dr Zhivago* (1965), dies in London, England (83).

20 Donald Siegel, U.S. film director, dies in Nipomo, California (78).

20 Sean O'Faolain (born John Whelan), Irish novelist, short-story writer, critic, and biographer, dies in Dublin, Ireland (91).

23 Johnny Thunders, U.S. rock guitarist, singer, and songwriter, dies in New Orleans, Louisiana, from a drug overdose (38).

MAY

6 Wilfred Hyde White, English actor, dies in Woodland Hills, California (87).

14 Jiang Qing, third wife of the Chinese leader Mao Zedong, a member of the Gang of Four and influential in promoting China's Cultural Revolution, commits suicide in Beijing, China (about 77).

21 Rajiv Gandhi, prime minister of India 1984–89, is assassinated in Sriperumpudur, Tamil Nadu, India (46).

JUNE

1 Charles Sutherland Elton, English ecologist who defined the concept of food chains, dies in Oxford, England (91).

JULY

1 Michael Landon, U.S. actor and director known for his roles in *Little House on the Prairie* and *Bonanza*, dies in Malibu, California (54).

2 Lee Remick, U.S. film and television actress, dies in Los Angeles, California (55).

16 Robert Motherwell, U.S. abstract expressionist painter, dies in Provincetown, Massachusetts (76).

AUGUST

6 Harry Reasoner, U.S. broadcast journalist, dies in Norwalk, Connecticut (68).

6 Shahpur Bakhtiar, who became the last prime minister of Iran (1979) after Shah Pahlavi left the country during the Iranian Revolution, is stabbed to death in Suresnes, France (77).

SEPTEMBER

2 Laura Riding, U.S. prose writer and poet and a member of the Fugitive Group of poets, dies in Sebastian, Florida (90).

3 Frank Capra, Italian-born U.S. film director who directed *It's a Wonderful Life* and *Mr Smith Goes to Washington*, dies in La Quinta, California (94).

7 Edwin McMillan, U.S. nuclear physicist who discovered neptunium and plutonium, dies in La Jolla, California (70).

13 Joseph Pasternak, U.S. film producer, dies in Beverly Hills, California (90).

24 Dr. Seuss (pseudonym of Theodore Seuss Geisel), U.S. writer of children's books, dies in La Jolla, California (87).

25 Klaus Barbie, German Nazi war criminal known as the "Butcher of Lyon," dies in Lyon, France (77).

28 Miles Davis, U.S. jazz trumpeter and bandleader, dies in Santa Monica, California (65).

OCTOBER

17 Tennessee Ernie Ford, U.S. country and western singer, dies in Reston, Virginia (72).

24 Gene Roddenberry, U.S. writer and film and television producer who created *Star Trek*, dies in Santa Monica, California (70).

NOVEMBER

5 Fred MacMurray, U.S. actor, dies in Santa Monica, California (61).

9 Yves Montand, Italian-born French singer and actor, dies in Senlis, France (70).

11 (Clarence) Leo Fender, U.S. guitar-maker who created the solid-body electric guitar, dies in Fullerton, California (81).

14 Tony (Cecil Antonio) Richardson, English director and producer who helped establish the English Stage Company 1955 at the Royal Court Theatre in London, England, dies in Los Angeles, California (63).

18 Gustáv Husák, communist leader of Czechoslovakia 1969–75 and president of Czechoslovakia (now the Czech and Slovak Republics) 1975–89, dies in Bratislava, Czechoslovakia (now capital of the Slovak Republic) (78).

23 Klaus Kinski, German actor, dies in Lagunitas, California (65).

24 Freddie Mercury, lead singer and songwriter of the British rock group Queen, dies of AIDS in London, England (45).

29 Louis Finkelstein, U.S. religious leader, dies in New York, New York (96).

DECEMBER

5 Roy (Roland) Welensky, Rhodesian politician instrumental in the creation of the Federation of Rhodesia and Nyasaland (1953), and prime minister 1956–63, dies in Blandford Forum, Dorset, England (84).

- In the United States, 7.6 million people subscribe to cellular phone services.
- Japanese electronics companies Sega and Nintendo compete for the lucrative console games market. Sega's "Sonic the Hedgehog" is matched against Nintendo's "Super Mario Brothers."
- Life expectancy in the United States: 75.4 years average, 79.3 years for white females, 74.5 years for white males, 72.6 for black females, and 66 for black males.
- Religious affiliation in the United States: Protestants 60.2%; Catholics 26.2%; non-Christian faiths 3.7%; atheists 7.5%.
- Studies reveal that one in four babies in the United States is born out of wedlock.
- The "coffee culture" emerges in Seattle, Washington, personified, in part, by the national success of the Seattle-based purveyors of gourmet coffee, Starbuck's.
- The antiprogesterone abortion pill introduced in France in 1989 under the name RU486 is licensed in the UK as mifepristone. It must be used in the first nine weeks of pregnancy and can only be given in hospitals or recognized clinics. It has a success rate of 95%.
- The first Toys 'Я' Us superstore opens in Tokyo, Japan.
- The number of Asians in the United States increases by 108% since 1980, while the number of Hispanics increases by 53% in the same period.
- The number of black–white marriages in the United States has tripled since 1970.
- The number of people who identify themselves as Native Americans reaches 1.8 million, triple the number in 1960.
- The red ribbon signifying AIDS awareness is designed for the Tony Awards in New York, New York.
- The U.S. Border Patrol arrests 1.1 million people trying to enter the United States illegally.
- The U.S. Census Bureau reports that from 1984 to 1988 the income of the richest 20% grew by 14%, but that nationwide the median income dropped from $37,012 to $35,752.
- The U.S. civilian labor force is 126.3 million people.
- The U.S. toy manufacturer Larami introduces the Super Soaker water gun which can shoot jets of water 90 ft/ 25 m, and Tiger Toys launches the action figure Captain Planet, based on the U.S. television series.
- The world population is 5.5 billion, compared with 3.63 billion in 1970.
- There are 24,700 murders, 106,600 rapes, 688,000 robberies, 1.1 million aggravated assaults, and 1.6 million car thefts in the United States.
- There are 40 major labor strikes in the United States this year, involving 392,000 workers.
- There are 805,872 lawyers in the United States, up from 285,933 in 1960 and 542,205 in 1980.
- Unemployment in the United States reaches 7.1%, the highest level in six years.
- U.S. girls become more active in sports. In the nation's high schools, 36% of girls play a sport, compared with just 7% in 1972, the year Congress passed Title IX of the Educational Amendments Act.
- Women's fashions in the United States include longer hemlines for skirts, often reaching to mid-calf.

JANUARY

25 U.S. federal health officials announce that 100,777 people have died from AIDS since the discovery of the disease in 1981.
27 The American Civil Liberties Union elects its first female president, Nadine Stroessner, a law professor at New York University.

FEBRUARY

3   The U.S. Post Office announces an increase in the cost of a first class stamp, from 25 cents to 29 cents.

MARCH

13 McDonald's announce a new lower fat hamburger; the McLean DeLuxe has half the fat grams of a regular hamburger.

OCTOBER

23 The first of the Planet Hollywood theme restaurants, owned by movie stars Arnold Schwartzenegger, Bruce Willis, and Sylvester Stallone, and movie director John Hughes, opens in New York, New York.
24 One of Yale University's secret societies, Skull and Bones, votes to admit the first women since the club's founding in 1832.

Media and Communication

- A consortium led by Canadian businessman Conrad Black takes over the Fairfax Group of newspapers in Australia.
- PBS (Public Broadcasting System) broadcasts a six-and-a-half-hour epic documentary about Sanskrit, *The Mahabharata*, in the United States.
- The Canadian rock singer Bryan Adams releases the single "(Everything I Do) I Do It for You." Its stay at the number one position on the British charts for 16 weeks is the second longest ever.
- The Dutch electronics company Philips launches the Compact Disc Interactive (CD-I) in the United States, a multimedia technology that is viewed using a special player on a television set.
- The Japanese electronics company Sharp launches a flat wall-mounted television, which is 7.7 cm/3 in deep and 22 cm/8.6 in high.
- The new NBC comedy *Brooklyn Bridge*, about Jewish family life in the 1950s, receives critical acclaim but fails to win a large enough viewership to last past its first season.
- Videoplus, a system using codes to allow automatic video programming, is launched in the UK.

MARCH

- The British version of the U.S. men's magazine *Esquire* is launched.
13 The British newspaper publisher and businessman Robert Maxwell purchases the *New York Daily News*.

MAY

20 At the Cannes Film Festival in France, the Golden Palm is awarded to *Barton Fink*, directed by Joel Coen. The movie also takes the prize for best director and best actor.

AUGUST

5   The 1990–91 Emmy Awards for television are held. Best Drama Series: *LA Law*; Best Comedy Series: *Cheers*;

Best Actor in a Drama: James Earl Jones, for *Gabriel's Fire*; Best Actress in a Drama: Patricia Wettig, for *thirtysomething*; Best Actor in a Comedy: Burt Reynolds, for *Evening Shade*; Best Actress in a Comedy: Kirstie Alley, for *Cheers*.

Religion

JANUARY

14 The United Church of Christ issues a proclamation declaring that racist attitudes permeate most aspects of life in the United States.

JUNE

6 The Greek Orthodox Church suspends its membership in the National Council of Churches, the United States' largest ecumenical organization, citing the council's liberalism on matters of abortion and homosexuality.

JULY

19 The General Convention of the Episcopal Church issues a compromise statement on homosexuality, affirming that sexual relations should be limited to marriage but noting that not all church members agree with the statement.

Sports

c. 1991 Extreme sports, such as bungee jumping, snowboarding, and sky-surfing, are becoming increasingly popular.

- The Pittsburgh Penguins defeat the Minnesota North Stars by four games to two to win the National Hockey League (NHL) Stanley Cup for the first time.

JANUARY

26 In the closest game in the history of the Super Bowl, the New York Giants defeat the Buffalo Bills 20–19 at Miami, Florida.

FEBRUARY

16 The U.S. driver Jeff Gordon, in a Chevrolet, wins the Daytona 500 motor race at Daytona Beach, Florida.

APRIL

- Welsh golfer Ian Woosnam wins the U.S. Masters golf tournament at Augusta, Georgia. It is the fourth

successive year that the tournament has been won by a British golfer.

14 The United States defeats England 19–16 in the final of the inaugural women's Rugby Union World Cup in Cardiff, Wales.

MAY

26 U.S. driver Rick Mears becomes the third driver to win the Indianapolis 500 motor race four times, after fellow U.S. drivers A. J. Foyt and Al Unser.

JUNE

9 The London Monarchs defeat the Barcelona Dragons 21–0 in the inaugural American football World Bowl at Wembley Stadium, London, England.

12 The Chicago Bulls win their first ever U.S. National Basketball Association (NBA) title. Michael Jordan of the Bulls is the top NBA scorer for the fifth succcessive year.

JULY

9–10 Following the final dismantling of apartheid, South Africa is readmitted to the International Olympic Committee and to the International Cricket Council.

AUGUST

11 The U.S. golfer John Daly, a virtually unknown 25-year-old, is the surprise winner of the U.S. PGA (Professional Golfers' Association) Championship at Crooked Stick Golf Club, Carmel, Indiana.

30 In the third World Athletics Championships in Tokyo, Japan, Mike Powell of the United States sets a new world record for the long jump of 8.95 m/29 ft 4.5 in, beating the record set by Bob Beamon of the United States in 1968—the oldest in track and field athletics.

SEPTEMBER

29 The United States regains the Ryder Cup in golf, defeating Europe 14½–13½ at Kiwah Island, South Carolina.

30 U.S. Peter Morris wins the first World Scrabble Championship, with a score of 371.

DECEMBER

1 France defeats the United States by three matches to one to win the Davis Cup tennis competition for the first time since 1932, in Lyon, France.

1992

POLITICS, GOVERNMENT, AND ECONOMICS

Business and Economics

- The Lloyds insurance market in London, England, reveals losses of £2 billion, the first in a series of severe losses.

JANUARY

2 Price controls are lifted in Russia, Ukraine, and many other republics of the Commonwealth of Independent States (CIS), leading to huge rises in the cost of food.

SEPTEMBER

13 The Italian lira is devalued by 7% following a crisis in the European Exchange Rate Mechanism (ERM).

17 The Italian lira is suspended from the European Exchange Rate Mechanism (ERM) and the Spanish peseta is devalued by 5%.

Colonization

MARCH

12 Mauritius becomes a republic within the British Commonwealth.

Politics and Government

- The 27th Amendment to the U.S. Constitution is finally ratified after 200 years; first proposed in 1789, it prevents Congress from voting itself pay rises while in session.
- The Rock the Vote campaign, involving groups such as REM, the Red Hot Chili Peppers, and Pearl Jam, is set up in the United States to encourage young people to vote. The MTV channel is a major supporter of the campaign, running frequent public service advertisements.
- U.S. president George Bush vomits and collapses at a Japanese state dinner.

JANUARY

- A succession of opinion polls in the United States suggests that President George Bush's margin over Pat Buchanan, his right wing isolationist rival as Republican presidential candidate, has fallen by 10% from its November 1991 level of 36%.

1 Serbia and Croatia agree a United Nations plan for the deployment of peacekeeping forces in Yugoslavia.

1 The Egyptian deputy prime minister Boutros Boutros-Ghali becomes secretary-general of the United Nations on the retirement of Javier Pérez de Cuéllar.

2 An opposition Democratic Party forms in Kenya under Mwai Kibaki following the ending of one-party rule in 1991.

6 President Zviad Gamsakhurdia of Georgia flees to Armenia at the end of a two-week siege of government buildings in the capital Tbilisi by rebel forces.

8 Laurent Fabius replaces Pierre Mauroy as leader of the French Socialist Party.

11–12 President Chadli Benjedid of Algeria resigns as armed forces take control to thwart electoral victory by the Islamic Salvation Front. The High Security Council cancels the second round of elections on January 12.

15 The European Community recognizes the former Yugoslav republics of Croatia and Slovenia as independent.

16 A United Nations-guaranteed peace agreement between the government of El Salvador and the opposition Farabundo Marti National Liberation Front (FMLN) is signed in Mexico City, Mexico.

16 President Zviad Gamsakhurdia of Georgia declares war on the rebel forces who caused his flight to Armenia on January 6.

17 The former Greek prime minister Andreas Papandreou is found not guilty of corruption charges.

19 Zhelyu Zhelev is reelected president in Bulgaria's first free elections.

23 Edgar Savisaar's government in Estonia resigns following its inability to deal with fuel and food shortages.

23 The United Nations imposes an arms embargo on Somalia in an attempt to end its civil war.

26 The European Community lifts economic sanctions on South Africa.

27 Democratic presidential candidate Bill Clinton, the former governor of Arkansas, appears on U.S. prime time television with his wife Hillary to deny allegations of an intermittent affair from 1977 to 1989 with Gennifer Flowers, an Arkansas state employee.

30 Charles Haughey, prime minister of the Republic of Ireland, resigns after allegations of the tapping of journalists' telephones.

FEBRUARY

6 Albert Reynolds succeeds Charles Haughey as prime minister of the Republic of Ireland.

6 An article in the *Wall Street Journal* suggests that Democratic presidential candidate Bill Clinton, the former governor of Arkansas, had received preferential

deferment of his draft obligations during the Vietnam War in the late 1960s.

9   The Algerian government declares a state of emergency after two days of clashes between Islamic fundamentalists and security forces; the Islamic Salvation Front is banned.

9   The first democratic local elections in Romania for 45 years bring an end to one-party rule.

11   The former world U.S. heavyweight boxing champion Mike Tyson is found guilty of rape; on March 26, he is sentenced to six years' imprisonment.

13   Prime Minister Carl Bildt announces the end of Sweden's policy of neutrality in foreign affairs.

18   Sikh militants murder 17 people in the Punjab, India, in an attempt to enforce a boycott of state elections.

18   The New Hampshire primaries give the Republican incumbent George Bush victory by 53% to 37% over his right-wing presidential rival Pat Buchanan, but the level of support for Buchanan indicates Bush's vulnerability. For the Democrats, former Arkansas governor Bill Clinton trails Senator Paul Tsongas by 26% to 35%, but his strong showing makes him the perceived frontrunner.

22   Edward Adami's ruling Nationalist Party wins a general election in Malta.

23   A cease-fire is agreed in Somalia between President Ali Mahdi Muhammad and General Muhammad Farah Aydid.

26   The U.S. Supreme Court rules that students can sue colleges for sexual harassment and other forms of sex discrimination.

28   The European Court rules that almost all European Community legislation adopted since 1957 could be invalid because of technical problems concerning signatures on documents.

29   A referendum in the Yugoslav republic of Bosnia-Herzegovina, boycotted by Bosnian Serbs, decides in favor of becoming an independent sovereign state.

March

1   King Fahd of Saudi Arabia grants a "Basic Law," giving his subjects new constitutional rights.

2   Violent clashes take place in Sarajevo, the capital of Bosnia-Herzegovina, between militant Serbs, Croats, and Muslims.

3   Troops of the former USSR begin their withdrawal from Lithuania following its independence.

4   A Virginia court convicts a physician, Cecil Jacobson, who inseminated several of his infertility patients with his own sperm without their knowledge or consent.

5   A Council of Baltic Sea States is founded to aid economic development and strengthen links with the European Community.

5   The Christian Democrat leader Jean-Luc Dehaene forms a coalition government in Belgium after a three-month political crisis.

10   The Republican incumbent George Bush wins all eight states in the "Super Tuesday" primaries of the U.S. presidential election, effectively ending the challenge of his right wing isolationist rival Pat Buchanan. A leading opinion poll on the same day shows him trailing both the Democratic frontrunners, Bill Clinton and Paul Tsongas, for the first time.

17   The white electorate in South Africa votes for constitutional and political reform in a referendum (68.6% vote in favor).

22   The opposition Democrat Party in Albania wins an absolute majority in general elections, ending 45 years of communist rule.

22   The Socialist Party in France suffers a heavy defeat in regional elections; the National Front takes 13.9% of the vote.

31   The United Nations votes to impose sanctions on Libya after its refusal to hand over for trial two men suspected of involvement in the Lockerbie bombing (sanctions come into effect on April 15).

April

2   Edith Cresson resigns as prime minister of France and is replaced by Pierre Bérégovoy following the Socialist Party's poor showing in regional elections.

2   John Gotti, head of New York's largest Mafia family, is convicted of murder and racketeering (he is sentenced to life imprisonment on June 23).

5   President Alberto Fujimori of Peru suspends the constitution and, with military backing, dissolves Congress.

6   Established parties suffer losses in Italy's general election to the Lombard League, the Greens, and the anti-Mafia La Rete Party.

7   The European Community (EC) formally recognizes the independence of the former Yugoslav republic of Bosnia-Herzegovina; fighting escalates as the Yugoslav federal air force aids Serb forces.

8   Serb and Yugoslav federal army forces begin a bombardment of Sarajevo, the capital of Bosnia-Herzegovina.

9   A British general election confounds the predictions of opinion pollsters by returning the Conservatives for a fourth term in government, though with a reduced majority of 21. The Conservatives win 336 seats, Labour 271, and the Liberal Democrats 20 (the Conservatives receive 41.9% of votes cast, Labour 34.4%, and the Liberal Democrats 17.8%).

9   A federal court in Miami, Florida, finds former Panamanian dictator Manuel Noriega guilty of several charges of cocaine trafficking and money laundering. On July 10, he receives a 40-year jail sentence.

9   Sali Berisha becomes president of Albania following the resignation of Ramiz Alia.

13   The South African president Nelson Mandela announces he is separating from his wife Winnie, whose alleged involvement in criminal activity is damaging the reputation of the African National Congress (ANC).

16   President Najibullah of Afghanistan is overthrown by the army as Mujaheddin rebels approach the capital, Kabul.

21   Fighting breaks out in Sarajevo, the capital of Bosnia-Herzegovina, between Serb forces and Muslims and Croats; two days later peace talks, chaired by United Nations mediator Lord Carrington, take place.

22   After international criticism of his suspension of the constitution and dissolution of Congress on April 5, President Alberto Fujimori of Peru promises to return the country to democracy within 12 months.

22 Over 200 people die in Guadalajara, Mexico, after gasoline leaking from a ruptured pipe into the sewers ignites.

23 The Colombian government introduces a state of emergency to cope with the worst drought in the country's history.

24 Giuliano Amato resigns as Italian prime minister following electoral losses; the next day President Francesco Cossiga also resigns.

25–28 Fighting takes place in Kabul between Mujaheddin groups prior to their takeover of power in Afghanistan.

29 Four white policemen in Los Angeles, California, are acquitted of beating the black motorist Rodney King; between April 30 and May 3, 58 people die in riots and looting which break out in protest at the acquittals.

MAY

• A series of opinion polls show the Texas billionaire Ross Perot leading both the Republican incumbent George Bush and the Democratic frontrunner Bill Clinton in the U.S. presidential election.

6 The government of Omar Karami resigns over the worsening economic situation in Lebanon.

8 Riot police clash with demonstrators in Bangkok, Thailand, as they call for the resignation of the unelected prime minister General Suchinda Kraprayaon.

16 Rashid al-Solh takes office as prime minister of Lebanon.

20 The government of Papua New Guinea reaches a peace agreement with secessionists on Bougainville Island.

20 The king of Thailand promises constitutional amendments in return for an end to the popular demonstrations calling for the resignation of the unelected prime minister General Suchinda Kraprayaon.

24 General Suchinda Kraprayaon steps down as Thailand's prime minister following protests demanding reform; the following day a reform bill is introduced into the House of Representatives.

25 Oscar Scalfaro is elected president of Italy.

26 In an intensification of the Angolan civil war, National Union for the Total Independence of Angola (UNITA) forces take the key northern town of Soyo.

30 The United Nations imposes a ban on trade, air, and sporting links and an oil embargo on the new Yugoslav state (comprising Serbia and Montenegro) because of continuing Serbian aggression in Bosnia-Herzegovina.

JUNE

1 A Tennessee court rules that a divorced man can stop his ex-wife from using a frozen embryo that has been fertilized with his sperm.

2 A Danish referendum votes against ratification of the Maastricht Treaty on European union (50.2% of the population vote against it).

2 Bill Clinton, the governor of Arkansas, formally receives the Democratic Party's nomination for the 1992 U.S. presidential elections at its convention in New York, New York.

3–14 The United Nations Conference on Environment and Development is held in Rio de Janeiro, Brazil. It is attended by delegates from 178 countries, most of whom sign binding conventions to combat global warming and to preserve biodiversity (the latter is not signed by the United States).

5 The Polish government is voted out of office by parliament following conflict with President Lech Wałęsa over relations with Russia; Waldemar Pawlak replaces Jan Olszewski as prime minister.

6 Elections in Czechoslovakia (now the Czech and Slovak republics) result in victory for proindependence parties in Slovakia and for profederal parties in the Czech lands.

16 Fidel Ramos wins the Philippines presidential election.

16 The former U.S. defense secretary Caspar Weinberger is indicted to face charges that he lied to Congress during the Iran–Contra affair.

18 A referendum in the Republic of Ireland endorses ratification of the Maastricht Treaty on European union, as agreed in the Netherlands on December 10, 1991 (57.3% vote in favor).

18 The U.S. Supreme Court rules that defense lawyers cannot remove potential jurors on the basis of race.

18 Thirty-nine people are killed in the "Boipatong massacre" in South Africa, allegedly by Inkatha supporters. Two days later police fire on black residents in Boipatong.

22 The U.S. Supreme Court rules that laws criminalizing hate speech are an unconstitutional violation of the First Amendment.

23 The African National Congress (ANC) withdraws from constitutional discussions in protest at recent violence in South Africa.

23 The Labor Party wins a convincing victory over the ruling Likud Party in the general elections in Israel.

24 The U.S. Supreme Court opens the way for damage suits by cigarette smokers against the tobacco companies when it rules that the warning labels on cigarette packages do not exempt the manufacturers from lawsuits.

29 President Muhammad Boudiaf of Algeria is assassinated by Islamic fundamentalists.

29 United Nations forces take over control of Sarajevo airport, Bosnia-Herzegovina, from Serbs to facilitate the airlift of supplies to the besieged population (flights begin on July 2).

JULY

2 Ali Kafi becomes president of Algeria, following the assassination of President Mohammed Boudiaf on June 29.

5 United Nations (UN) military observers arrive in the war-torn Somali capital, Mogadishu, to help distribute food aid.

6 The right wing Sixto Durán Ballén is elected president of Ecuador with a mandate to introduce an economic austerity program.

7 Abdul Sabbur Fareed becomes prime minister of an interim government in Afghanistan.

9 Chris Patten is sworn in as the 28th governor of the British colony of Hong Kong, replacing Lord Wilson of Tillyorn.

13 The Labor Party leader Yitzhak Rabin forms a government in Israel.

15 The president and vice president of the Islamic Salvation Front in Algeria are sentenced to 12 years' imprisonment for conspiracy against the state.

16 A car bomb planted by the left wing Sendero Luminoso (Shining Path) guerrilla organization kills 20 people in the Peruvian capital, Lima.

16 The Taiwanese parliament gives the government the right to lift its ban on trade and social links with communist China, after two years of debate.

16 The Texas billionaire Ross Perot announces the abandonment of his campaign for the U.S. presidency after a series of errors of political judgment, including a reference to "you people" at a meeting of the National Association for the Advancement of Colored People.

17 President Václav Havel of Czechoslovakia (now the Czech and Slovak republics) resigns after Slovak deputies vote to declare their republic a sovereign state.

25 A court in Orlando, Florida, grants 12-year-old Gregory Kingsley a legal separation from his mother on grounds of neglect.

28 The Italian government forces through emergency legislation to cut the federal budget and prevent bankruptcy.

29 The former East German leader Erich Honecker is forced to leave the Chilean embassy in Moscow, Russia, to face trial in Germany on manslaughter charges for the killing of people who tried to escape over the Berlin Wall during the Cold War.

AUGUST

3 The African National Congress (ANC) begins a "mass action" protest campaign in South Africa.

7 An agreement is reached in Rome, Italy, in an attempt to end the civil war in Mozambique.

13 The United Nations (UN) condemns the "ethnic cleansing" program (forced removal of Bosnian Muslims and Croats from areas regarded as ethnically Serbian) undertaken by Serbians in Bosnia-Herzegovina as a war crime.

14 The United Nations Security Council approves the use of force in support of the humanitarian effort in the former Yugoslavia.

19 Lynden Pindling loses a general election to Hubert Ingraham's Free National Movement and resigns as president of the Bahamas after 25 years.

22–26 Five nights of serious rioting at a reception center for asylum seekers in Rostock marks a resurgence of antiforeigner violence in eastern Germany.

27 The British statesman Lord Owen replaces Lord Carrington as the European Community's chief mediator in the Yugoslav crisis.

27 The United States, Britain, and France impose an air exclusion zone in southern Iraq to protect Shiite Muslims from air attacks by the forces of the Iraqi president Saddam Hussein.

29 A cease-fire begins in Afghanistan after three weeks of heavy fighting between progovernment forces and the Mujaheddin faction.

SEPTEMBER

1 John Bannon, Prime Minister of South Australia, resigns after acknowledging responsibility for huge losses by the State Bank of South Australia.

3 A conference opens in Geneva, Switzerland, to try to bring peace to the former Yugoslavia; it is jointly chaired by the European Community mediator Lord Carrington and the United Nations negotiator Cyrus Vance.

7 President Rakhmon Nabiyev of Tajikistan is forced to resign following domestic unrest.

7 The U.S. presidential election campaign formally opens, with the Democratic challenger Bill Clinton showing opinion poll leads of up to 30% over the Republican incumbent George Bush.

12 Police in Colombia capture Abimael Guzmán, the leader of the left wing guerrilla group Sendero Luminoso (Shining Path).

12 Ramiz Alia, former president of Albania, is arrested on charges of misuse of state funds and abuse of power.

15 Britain announces that it will send troops to assist in the humanitarian mission in the former Yugoslavia.

16 In a European monetary crisis, the British chancellor of the Exchequer, Norman Lamont, increases the base rate from 10% to 12%, then to 15% in an attempt to defend the pound against speculative selling; sterling, the lira, and the peseta all fall below their Exchange Rate Mechanism (ERM) floors; sterling is withdrawn from the ERM and allowed to "float," and the base rate returns to 12% (cut to 9% on September 22).

19 A cease-fire is agreed between Azerbaijan and Armenia over the disputed region of Nagorno-Karabakh (but each side accuses the other of breaking it before the end of September).

20 A French referendum produces a vote narrowly (51.04%) in favor of ratification of the Maastricht Treaty on European Union, as agreed in the Netherlands on December 10, 1991.

20 Right wing parties win a strong position in parliament in Estonia's first post-independence elections.

24 Thousands of citizens flee northwestern Liberia as battles rage between rebel forces following the breakdown of African peacekeeping.

29–30 Angola's first multiparty elections are held; the results, announced on October 17, give victory for José dos Santos's ruling Popular Movement for the Liberation of Angola–Workers' Party (MPLA–PT).

OCTOBER

1 The Texas billionaire Ross Perot formally declares his independent candidacy for the U.S. presidency again, after claiming that both main parties have failed to address the need to reduce the federal deficit.

5 The Peoples' Progressive Party leader Cheddi Jaggan is elected president of Guyana.

11 President Paul Biya wins a slim majority in Cameroon's first multiparty elections, the results of which are disputed.

12–18 The 14th Congress of the Chinese Communist Party (the first since the Tiananmen Square massacre of 1989) endorses leader Deng Xiaoping's continuing economic reforms.

14 An article in the *Washington Post* reveals that President George Bush has ordered the State Department to search the passport files of Bill Clinton, his Democratic opponent in the presidential election, and files held in the U.S. embassies in London, England, and Oslo, Norway, for evidence of misconduct in connection with Clinton's alleged Vietnam draft avoidance.

15 Tamil Tigers independence fighters massacre 140 Muslims in the north of Sri Lanka.

24   Gunmen kill 20 people at an Inkatha leader's homestead south of Durban, South Africa, in an intensification of African National Congress–Inkatha violence.

26   A Canadian referendum rejects the Charlottetown reform agreement that would grant concessions to French-speaking Quebec.

NOVEMBER

7   Bill Clinton (Democrat), the governor of Arkansas, wins the U.S. presidential election with 370 electoral college votes. President George Bush (Republican) gains 168 electoral votes and H. Ross Perot (Independent) fails to win any, although he takes 19% of the popular vote. In the Congressional elections the Democrats retain control of both chambers.

12   Results of a referendum (November 3–5) among Inuit people in northern Canada endorse the creation of Nunavut, a semiautonomous Inuit territory.

16   The Goldstone Commission in South Africa exposes evidence of a state "dirty tricks" campaign against the African National Congress (ANC).

18   The Pakistan opposition leader Benazir Bhutto is teargassed by government forces as she leads a march to Islamabad calling for fresh elections.

22   In legislative elections in Peru, parties supporting President Alberto Fujimori win an absolute majority in the new Democratic Constituent Congress, despite obtaining only 38% of the vote; the elections are boycotted by the main opposition parties.

27   President José dos Santos and Jonas Savimbi, leader of the National Union for the Total Independence of Angola (UNITA), issue a Namibia Declaration committing themselves to acceptance of the Bicesse Peace Accord and continuing United Nations presence in Angola.

30–December 4   The South West Africa People's Organization (SWAPO) wins a landslide victory in elections in Namibia.

DECEMBER

2   The prime minister of Greece, Constantine Mitsotakis, dismisses his entire cabinet after facing dissent over austerity measures and his moderate position over Macedonia. A new cabinet is appointed the following day.

6   Hindu extremists demolish a 16th-century mosque at Ayodhya, provoking sectarian violence throughout India which claims over 1,200 lives.

9   The separation of Charles and Diana, Prince and Princess of Wales, is announced in Britain.

9   U.S. troops arrive in Mogadishu, Somalia, to oversee the delivery of international food aid in operation "Restore Hope."

11–12   A summit of European Community heads of state in Edinburgh, Scotland, deals with Danish objections to the Maastricht Treaty on European union.

16   The Czech National Council adopts a constitution for the new, separate, Czech Republic to come into being on January 1, 1993.

16   The Israeli cabinet approves an order to deport 415 Palestinians to Lebanon; Lebanon refuses to accept the deportees, who are forced to set up camp in "no man's land" in a security zone in southern Lebanon.

20   Slobodan Milošević is reelected to the Serbian presidency and his Socialist Party of Serbia wins gains in legislative elections.

24   The former U.S. defense secretary Caspar Weinberger and five others are pardoned by the U.S. president George Bush for their involvement in the Iran–Contra affair.

29   Fernando Collor de Mello resigns as president of Brazil as impeachment proceedings begin against him in the Senate. The following day he is found guilty of corruption and official misconduct, and banned from public office for eight years.

29   President Daniel Arap Moi of Kenya wins a fourth term in office in disputed elections.

SCIENCE, TECHNOLOGY, AND MEDICINE

Agriculture

- The town of Cgungungo in the Atacama Desert, Argentina, is supplied by water from fog. The system uses large sheets of plastic mesh suspended on a hilltop, and supplies 11,000 l/2,400 gal of water per day.

Computing

- Active matrix displays began to appear on laptop computers, replacing cathode-ray technology.
- The Japanese firm Fujitsu announces the launch of the first computer capable of performing 300 billion calculations a second.

MARCH

6   The Michelangelo computer virus (so-called because it is activated on the anniversary of the birth of the Italian artist Michelangelo) erases hard discs on computers worldwide.

SEPTEMBER

5   Warner Brothers make a $100 million recording contract with the U.S. pop artist Prince.

Ecology

FEBRUARY

11   The U.S. president George Bush announces that the United States will phase out CFCs (chlorofluorocarbons) by 1995, five years earlier than planned; British secretary of state for the environment Michael Heseltine makes a similar announcement for Britain three days later.

APRIL

13   The Chicago River surges into tunnels beneath the buildings in Chicago's downtown district, called the Loop, causing a power cut in a 12-block area and forcing offices and businesses to close.

JUNE

28 The area's most powerful earthquake in forty years, measuring 7.4 on the Richter scale, rocks the Yucca Valley, east of Los Angeles. It kills one person.

AUGUST

24 Hurricane Andrew strikes the coast of south Florida, killing 38 people, leaving about 250,000 people without homes, and causing $30 billion of property damage. Insurance claims make this the most expensive natural disaster in U.S. history.

28 Typhoon Omar strikes Guam, a U.S. territory in the Pacific, damaging about one-eighth of the island's 32,000 homes.

SEPTEMBER

23–24 Over 80 people are killed in flash floods in southeastern France.

Exploration

- The Cosmic Background Explorer (COBE) satellite detects ripples in the microwave background radiation, thought to originate from the formation of galaxies.
- The U.S. space probe *Magellan* maps 99% of the surface of Venus to a resolution of 100 m/330 ft.

FEBRUARY

8 The U.S. space probe *Ulysses* flies over the north and south poles of Jupiter to enter a trajectory for reaching the south pole of the sun; it transmits data about Jupiter's magnetosphere.

MAY

5 The U.S. National Aeronautics and Space Administration (NASA) launches the new shuttle craft *Endeavour*, named for the 18th-century vessel captained by the English explorer James Cook.

14 Astronauts on the U.S. space shuttle fit a new motor to the *Intelsat-6* satellite and fire it into a new orbit.

JULY

10 The European Space Agency's *Giotto* space probe is diverted to encounter the comet Grigg-Skjellerup.

Health and Medicine

- A vaccine for hepatitis A becomes available.
- British researchers introduce a healthy version of the cystic fibrosis gene into the lungs of mice with artificially induced cystic fibrosis, restoring normal function.
- Epibatidine, a chemical extracted from the skin of an Ecuadorian frog, is identified as a member of an entirely new class of alkaloid. It is an organochlorine compound and is a powerful painkiller, about 200 times as effective as morphine.
- In Sydney, Australia, Liesel Scholem becomes the first person to be awarded damages in compensation for passive smoking suffered in the workplace.
- Medicaid, the U.S. federal-state health insurance program for nursing home care and the nation's indigent, accounts for 15% of the average state's budget.
- Smoking in the United States falls to its lowest level in 37 years, about one in four adults.
- The Nobel Prize for Physiology or Medicine is awarded jointly to U.S. physicians Edmond Henri Fischer and Edwin Gerhard Krebs for their discovery of protein phosphorylation (the chemical bonding of a phosphate molecule to a protein) as a control mechanism in the metabolic activity of mammalian cells.
- The Swiss medical company Ciba-Geigy Pharmaceuticals launches Nicotinell, a nicotine patch for people who want to give up smoking, available over the counter.
- U.S. biologist Philip Leder receives a patent for the first genetically engineered animal, the oncomouse, which is sensitive to carcinogens.

APRIL

16 The U.S. Food and Drug Administration introduces new limitations on the use of silicone gel breast implants.

JUNE

28 The first transplant of a baboon liver into a human is performed by surgeons at the University of Pittsburgh Medical Center, Pennsylvania.

OCTOBER

7 The U.S. Department of Agriculture reports that oils used in the manufacture of margarine may increase the chance of heart disease.

NOVEMBER

1 Smoking is banned in all public places in France. The ban is generally ignored.

Science

- An individual honey fungus (*Armallaria ostoyae*) is identified as the world's largest living thing. Discovered in Washington State and estimated to be between 500 and 1,000 years old, it has an underground network of hyphae covering 600 hectares/1,480 acres.
- Sperm cells are discovered by U.S. physician David Garbers of the University of Texas to have odor receptors and may therefore reach eggs by detecting scent.
- The largest Bronze Age hill fort in the British Isles is discovered on a hill near Baltinglass, County Wicklow, in the Republic of Ireland. It covers an area of 130 hectares/320 acres.
- The tooth of a 55-million-year-old mammal is discovered at Murgon, Australia, indicating that mammals arrived in Australia at about the same time as marsupials.
- The world's oldest sea-going vessel, dating from about 1400 BC, is discovered at Dover, England.
- The world's oldest surviving wooden structure, a well 15 m/49 ft deep, made of huge oak timbers, is discovered at Kückhoven, Germany. It is tree-ring dated to 5090 BC.
- Two Japanese researchers develop a material that becomes superconducting at around $-103°C/-153°F$.
- U.S. astronomers Jeffrey McClintock, Ronald Remillard, and Charles Bailyn identify Nova Muscae as a black hole approximately 18,000 light-years from Earth.
- U.S. chemist Rudolph Marcus receives the Nobel Prize for Chemistry for his theoretical discoveries relating to reduction and oxidation reactions.

Technology

- French physicist Georges Charpak receives the Nobel Prize for Physics for his invention of the multiwire proportional chamber particle accelerator.
- In Ohio, U.S. scientists Don Hollister and Don Pelazzo develop a light bulb which will last for 14 years, compared to the 12-month life-span of an ordinary bulb.
- The first commercial wind farm in the UK, near Camelford, Cornwall, begins to generate electricity.
- The Hadron Electron Ring Accelerator (HERA) particle accelerator is built under the streets of Hamburg, Germany. Occupying a tunnel 6.3 km/3.9 mi in length, it is the world's most powerful particle accelerator, accelerating protons to energies of 820 GeV (billion electron volts) and electrons to 30 GeV.
- The U.S. biotechnology company Agracetus patents transgenic cotton, which has had a foreign gene added to it by genetic engineering.

APRIL

14 The Keck I telescope on Mauna Kea is completed. The most powerful optical telescope in the world, its mirror is made of 36 computer-controlled hexagonal segments. Scientific observations begin in May 1993.

NOVEMBER

- The U.S. national on-line information service Delphi becomes the first national U.S. service to open a gateway to the Internet.

ARTS AND IDEAS

Arts

- The "Matisse" exhibition is held at the Museum of Modern Art (MOMA) in New York, New York.
- The "Russian Utopia" exhibition is held at the Guggenheim Museum in New York, New York.
- The English artist Damian Hirst creates *The Physical Impossibility of Death in the Mind of Someone Living*, a shark preserved in a tank of formaldehyde.

Film

- *I'm Your Man* is the first interactive movie to appear in a movie theater, in New York, New York. Viewers vote on the outcome of the narrative by using the "choice mechanism" on each seat.
- The movie *1492: Conquest of Paradise*, directed by Ridley Scott, is released, starring Gérard Depardieu as Christopher Columbus. It is out of touch with public sentiment and is among the year's biggest movie flops.
- The movie *A Few Good Men*, directed by Rob Reiner, is released in the United States, starring Tom Cruise, Jack Nicholson, and Demi Moore.
- The movie *A River Runs Through It*, directed by Robert Redford, is released in the United States, starring Brad Pitt, Craig Sheffer, and Tom Skerritt.

- The movie *Basic Instinct*, directed by Paul Verhoeven, is released in the United States, starring Michael Douglas and Sharon Stone.
- The movie *Batman Returns*, directed by Tim Burton, is released in the United States, starring Michael Keaton, Michelle Pfeiffer, Danny De Vito, and Christopher Walken.
- The movie *Bob Roberts*, directed by Tim Robbins, is released in the United States. He also stars in it.
- The movie *Bram Stoker's Dracula*, directed by Francis Ford Coppola, is released in the United States, starring Gary Oldman, Winona Ryder, and Anthony Hopkins.
- The movie *Candyman*, directed by Bernard Rose, is released in the United States, starring Virginia Madsen and Tony Todd.
- The movie *Chaplin*, directed by British filmmaker Richard Attenborough, is released in the United States, starring Robert Downey, Jr., as Charlie Chaplin.
- The movie *Cronos*, directed by Guillermo del Toro, is released in Mexico, starring Federico Luppi and Ron Perlman.
- The movie *Glengarry Glen Ross*, directed by James Foley, is released in the United States. Based on the play by David Mamet, it stars Al Pacino, Jack Lemmon, Ed Harris, and Alec Baldwin.
- The movie *Howards End*, directed by James Ivory, is released in Britain. Based on the novel by E. M. Forster, it stars Anthony Hopkins, Emma Thompson, and Vanessa Redgrave.
- The movie *Husbands and Wives*, directed by Woody Allen, is released in the United States. He also stars in it, along with Mia Farrow, Judy Davis, and Sydney Pollack.
- The movie *Indochine*, directed by Régis Wargnier, is released in France, starring Catherine Deneuve and Vincent Perez.
- The movie *Jamón Jamón*, directed by Juan José Bigas Luna, is released in Spain, starring Stefania Sandrelli, Anna Galiena, and Juan Diego Penélope.
- The movie *L'Amant/The Lover*, directed by Jean-Jacques Annaud, is released in France, starring Jane March, Tony Leung, and Frédéric Meininger.
- The movie *Malcolm X*, directed by Spike Lee, is released in the United States. Based on the life of the assassinated black American nationalist, it stars Denzel Washington.
- The movie *Man Bites Dog*, directed by Rémy Belvaux, André Bonzel, and Benoît Poelvoorde, is released in Belgium. It stars Benoît Poelvoorde, Jacqueline Poelvoorde-Pappaert, Nelly Pappaert, and Jenny Drye.
- The movie *My Cousin Vinny*, directed by Jonathan Lynn, is released in the United States, starring Joe Pesci and Marisa Tomei.
- The movie *One False Move*, directed by Carl Franklin, is released in the United States, starring Bill Paxton, Cyndia Williams, Billy Bob Thornton, and Michael Beach.
- The movie *Orlando*, directed by Sally Potter, is released in Britain. Based on the novel by Virginia Woolf, it stars Tilda Swinton, Billy Zane, Quentin Crisp, and Lothaire Bluteau.
- The movie *Patriot Games*, directed by Phillip Noyce, is released in the United States, based on the novel by Tom Clancy and starring Harrison Ford and Anne Archer.

- The movie *Peter's Friends*, directed by Kenneth Branagh, is released in Britain. He also stars in it with Stephen Fry, Emma Thompson, Alphonsia Emmanuel, Hugh Laurie, Rita Rudner, Imelda Staunton, Tony Slattery, and Phyllida Law.
- The movie *Red Rock West*, directed by John Dahl, is released in the United States, starring Nicolas Cage, Lara Flynn Boyle, and Dennis Hopper.
- The movie *Scent of a Woman*, directed by Martin Brest, is released in the United States, starring Al Pacino.
- The movie *Simple Men*, directed by Hal Hartley, is released in the United States, starring Robert Burke, William Sage, Karen Sillas, and Elina Lowensohn.
- The movie *Strictly Ballroom*, directed by Baz Luhrmann, is released in Australia, starring Paul Mercurio and Tara Morice.
- The movie *Sweet Emma, Dear Böbe*, directed by Istvan Szabo, is released in Hungary, starring Johanna Ter Steege, Eniko Börcsök, and Peter Andorai.
- The movie *The Best Intentions*, directed by Danish filmmaker Bille August, is released in Sweden. Based on Swedish director Ingmar Bergman's semibiographical account of his parents' early lives, it stars Samuel Fröler, Pernilla August, and Max Von Sydow. It is awarded the Palme d'Or at the Cannes Film Festival in France.
- The movie *The Crying Game*, directed by Neil Jordan, is released in Britain, starring Stephen Rea, Miranda Richardson, Forest Whittaker, Jim Broadbent, and Jaye Davidson.
- The movie *The Last of the Mohicans*, directed by Michael Mann, is released in the United States. Based on the novel by James Fenimore Cooper, it stars Daniel Day Lewis and Madeline Stowe.
- The movie *The Player*, directed by Robert Altman, is released in the United States, starring Tim Robbins, and featuring many Hollywood stars in cameo roles.
- The movie *The Stolen Children*, directed by Gianni Amelio, is released in Italy, starring Enrico Lo Verso, Valentina Scalici, and Giuseppe Ieracitano.
- The movie *The Story of Qui Ju*, directed by Zhang Yimou, is released in China, starring Gong Li and Lei Laosheng.
- The movie *Tous les Matins du Monde/All the Mornings of the World*, directed by Alain Corneau, is released in France, starring Gérard Depardieu, Jean-Pierre Marielle, Anne Brochet, and Guillaume Depardieu.
- The movie *Un Coeur en hiver/A Heart in Winter*, directed by Claude Sautet, is released in France, starring Daniel Auteuil and Emmanuelle Béart.
- The movie *Unforgiven*, directed by Clint Eastwood, is released in the United States. He also stars in it, along with Gene Hackman, Morgan Freeman, and Richard Harris.
- The movie *Wayne's World*, directed by Penelope Spheeris, is released in the United States, starring Mike Myers and Dana Carvey and based on their regular routine on the U.S. television program *Saturday Night Live*.
- The movie *White Badge*, directed by Chung Ji-Yiong, is released in South Korea. It is the first openly antiwar movie to be approved by the South Korean censors.
- The movie *White Men Can't Jump*, directed by Ron Shelton, is released in the United States, starring Woody Harrelson and Wesley Snipes.

- The Walt Disney animated movie *Aladdin* is released in the United States, featuring the voice of Robin Williams as the genie.

MARCH

30 The 1991 Academy Awards are held. Best Actor: Anthony Hopkins, for *The Silence of the Lambs*; Best Supporting Actor: Jack Palance, for *City Slickers*; Best Actress: Jodie Foster, for *The Silence of the Lambs*; Best Supporting Actress: Mercedes Ruehl, for *The Fisher King*; Best Director: Jonathan Demme, for *The Silence of the Lambs*; Best Picture: *The Silence of the Lambs*, directed by Jonathan Demme.

Literature and Language

- Barbara Taylor Bradford, U.S. romance novelist, receives a $24 million contract to write three novels.
- The Belgian-born U.S. writer May Sarton publishes her memoirs, *Endgame: A Journal of the Seventy-Ninth Year*.
- The Canadian writer Robertson Davies publishes his novel *Murther and Walking Spirits*.
- The Chinese writer Jung Chang publishes her memoir *Wild Swans: Three Daughters of China*.
- The English writer Barry Unsworth publishes his novel *Sacred Hunger*, which wins the Booker Prize.
- The English writer Ian McEwan publishes his novel *Black Dogs*.
- The graphic novel *Maus: A Survivor's Tale, Vol 2: And Here My Trouble Began* by Art Spiegelman is published.
- The Nobel Prize for Literature is awarded to the West Indian (St. Lucian) poet Derek Walcott.
- The Pulitzer Prize for Biography is awarded to Lewis B. Puller, Jr., for *Fortunate Man: The Healing of a Vietnam Vet*, the Pulitzer Prize for Poetry is awarded to James Tait for *Selected Poems*, and the Pulitzer Prize for Fiction is awarded to Jane Smiley for *A Thousand Acres*.
- The Scottish writer Jeff Torrington publishes his novel *Swing Hammer Swing!*
- The Sri Lankan-born Canadian writer Michael Ondaatje publishes his novel *The English Patient*.
- The U.S. writer Denise Levertov publishes her poetry collection *The Evening Train*.
- The U.S. writer Donna Tartt publishes her novel *The Secret History*.
- The U.S. writer Gary Snyder publishes his poetry collection *No Nature: New and Selected Poems*.
- The U.S. writer Janet Hobhouse publishes her novel *The Furies*.
- The U.S. writer Joan Didion publishes her collection of biographical essays *After Henry*.
- The U.S. writer Mona Van Duyn publishes *If It Be Not I: Collected Poems 1959–1982*.
- The U.S. writer Toni Morrison publishes her novel *Jazz*.

Music

- An AIDS awareness benefit concert, in memory of the British rock group Queen's lead singer, Freddie Mercury, is held at Wembley Arena in London, England.
- Country music is enjoying a revival in the United States, particularly through the records of U.S. country singer Garth Brooks, who is outselling even Michael Jackson.

- Music compact discs begin to outsell cassettes in the United States.
- The British dance band the Orb releases the album *U F Orb*, a core example of ambient house music.
- The British pop group The Shamen releases the single "Ebeneezer Goode," which arouses controversy because it allegedly celebrates the use of the drug ecstasy.
- The British rock group Genesis releases the single "We Can't Dance."
- The British rock guitarist Eric Clapton releases the album *Unplugged*.
- The British rock singer P. J. Harvey releases the album *Dry*.
- The British rock singer Morrissey releases the album *Your Arsenal*.
- The Canadian acoustic duo the Indigo Girls releases the album *Rites of Passage*.
- The Canadian singer/songwriter Leonard Cohen releases the album *The Future*.
- The English composer Peter Maxwell Davies completes his orchestral work *Sir Charles: His Pavan*.
- The English composer Harrison Birtwistle completes his vocal works *Night* and *Tenabrae/Darkness*, settings of poems by the Romanian-born German writer Paul Celan.
- The English composer Jonathan Harvey completes his chamber work *Lotuses*.
- The English composer George Lloyd completes his *Symphonic Mass*.
- The English composer John Tavener completes his work for cello and ensemble *Eternal Memory*.
- The German composer York Georg Höller completes his orchestral work *Aura*.
- The German/U.S. pop group Snap releases the single "Rhythm is a Dancer."
- The German-born English composer Alexander Goehr completes his orchestral work *Colossus or Panic*.
- The Jamaican ragga star Buju Banton is not allowed to appear at the WOMAD (World of Music, Arts, and Dance) Festival in Brighton, England, because his song "Boom By By" is said to advocate violence against homosexuals.
- The opera *Desert of Roses*, by the U.S. composer Robert Moran, is first performed, in Houston, Texas.
- The opera *Kullervo*, by the Finnish composer Aulis Sallinen, is first performed, in Los Angeles, California.
- The opera *The Voyage*, by the U.S. composer Philip Glass, is first performed, at the Metropolitan Opera House in New York, New York.
- The U.S. composer Elliott Carter completes his work for oboe and harp *Trilogy*.
- The U.S. grunge band Pearl Jam releases the album *Ten*.
- The U.S. pop group Boyz II Men releases the single "End of the Road."
- The U.S. pop singer Whitney Houston releases the single "I Will Always Love You" and the album *The Bodyguard*, the soundtrack from the movie of the same name.
- The U.S. pop star Madonna publishes *Sex*, a collection of explicit photographs, and the album *Erotica*.
- The U.S. rock group REM releases the album *Automatic for the People*.

FEBRUARY

19 The musical *Crazy for You*, based on songs by U.S. composer George Gershwin and U.S. lyricist Ira Gershwin, is performed for the first time, at the Shubert Theater, New York, New York.

26 The 1991–92 Grammy Awards are held. Best Album: *Unforgettable* by Natalie Cole; Best Single: "Unforgettable" by Natalie Cole; Best Male Pop Vocalist: Michael Bolton; Best Female Pop Vocalist: Bonnie Raitt.

JULY

- The U.S. rap group Body Count have to withdraw the single "Cop Killer" from their album in the face of protests led by U.S. president George Bush.

OCTOBER

3 The Irish singer Sinead O'Connor arouses controversy when she tears up a picture of the Pope during her appearance on the U.S. television program *Saturday Night Live*.

Theater and Dance

- Broadway, New York, New York, has its best theater season ever, with receipts topping $292 million.
- The English acting company Théâtre de Complicité create *Street of Crocodiles*, a play based on the stories of the Polish writer Bruno Schulz.
- The play *Oleanna*, by the U.S. writer David Mamet, is first performed, in New York, New York.
- The play *Six Degrees of Separation*, by the U.S. writer John Guare, is first performed, in New York, New York.
- The play *The Rise and Fall of Little Voice*, by the British dramatist Jim Cartwright, is first performed, in London, England.
- The Pulitzer Prize for Drama is awarded to Robert Schenkan for *The Kentucky Cycle*.

JUNE

1 The 1991–92 Tony Awards are held. Best Play: *Dancing at Lughnasa*; Best Musical: *Crazy for You*; Best Actor in a Play: Judd Hirsch; Best Actress in a Play: Glenn Close.

Thought and Scholarship

- Francis Fukayama publishes *The End of History and the Last Man*, which argues that the triumph of capitalism over communism means the end of history.
- Presidential candidate Bill Clinton, governor of Arkansas, publishes *Putting People First*, which outlines his political beliefs.
- The Pulitzer Prize for History is awarded to Mark E. Neely, Jr., for *The Fate of Liberty: Abraham Lincoln and Civil Liberties*.
- The Pulitzer Prize for General Nonfiction is awarded to Daniel Yergin for *The Prize: The Epic Quest for Oil*.
- The U.S. journalist Donald Barlett and James B. Steele publish *America: What Went Wrong?*

SOCIETY

Education

- The cost of tuition rises on average 10% in U.S. colleges and universities.

Everyday Life

c. 1992   Companies worldwide begin to market "clear products"—color- and often additive-free—to meet a trend for greater simplicity after the excesses of the 1980s.

c. 1992   The Belgian fashion designers Dries Van Noten, Ann Demeulemeester, and Martin Margiela "deconstruct" fashion, producing a range of clothes in drab colors and often unfinished in appearance, in reaction against the over-designed fashions of the 1980s.

- Of U.S. families, 73.3% hold debts: 38.7% hold mortgages, 40% have credit card debts, and 7% have real estate debts.
- This year, 973,977 people immigrate to and settle in the United States.
- A study finds that Americans work 140 more hours a year than in 1970 and that vacation, sick leave, and days off have declined by 15% in the same period.
- A survey finds Americans are giving less of their income to charity; in 1979 Americans donated 7% of their after-tax incomes to charity as opposed to just 4% in 1992.
- A survey finds that more than one-third of the 100 largest charities in the United States pay their chief executives more than $200,000 a year.
- A U.S. government survey finds that 13 million Americans attended a classical musical recital, 5 million attended a ballet, 27 million attended an art museum, and 54 million read at least one book during this year.
- A U.S. survey finds that men are more likely than women to die in the week before their birthdays, while women are more likely than men to die in the week after their birthdays.
- About 61 million people in the United States attend movies, 55 million go to amusement parks, and about 42 million go to sports events.
- Actor and director Woody Allen and his partner, actress Mia Farrow, go to court in the United States to fight over the custody of their children.
- Americans make 274.7 million visits to national parks, monuments, recreation areas, and similar locations this year.
- Retail customers in the United States redeem more than 4.1 billion discount coupons during the year.
- The Dutch drinks company Bavarian Breweries launches drinks cans which open using push buttons on the top.
- The Gross Domestic Product in the United States increases by 3.9%.
- The Mall of America in Bloomington, Minnesota, is opened. Covering 78 acres, it is the biggest shopping mall in the world.

- The percentage of Americans living in poverty rises for the second consecutive year, reaching 14.2% of the population.
- The U.S. company Pharmacal launches Femidom, a female condom originally developed for use in the Third World.
- The U.S. cultural critic Camille Paglia publishes *Sex, Art, and American Culture.*
- The use of the drug ecstasy becomes increasingly popular at clubs and raves in the United States and the UK.
- There are 23,800 murders, 109,100 rapes, 672,000 robberies, 1.12 million aggravated assaults, and 1.6 million car thefts in the United States.
- There are 604,000 police officers serving in the United States.
- While school dropout rates continue to decrease for white and black students in the United States, they increase for Hispanic students.

FEBRUARY
24   The automobile manufacturer General Motors announces losses for 1991 of $7.2 billion, a world record, and that it will close 12 plants in Canada and the United States over the next few years as a result.

MARCH
19   The British royal family announces the separation of the Duke and Duchess of York, who were married in 1986.

APRIL
5   An abortion rights march in Washington, D.C., draws 500,000 supporters.
12   The theme park EuroDisney (later Disneyland Paris) opens at Marne-la-Vallée, just outside Paris, France. Development has cost $4.5 billion.
23   Princess Anne, the Princess Royal of Britain, is granted a divorce from Captain Mark Phillips.
23–May 7   A public service strike causes disruption in Germany as unions seek higher pay to compensate for economic conditions arising from reunification. The dispute ends with agreement on a 5.4% increase.

SEPTEMBER
24   A U.S. Navy inquiry finds that high-ranking officers covered up a sexual assault scandal at the annual Tailhook convention, a meeting of past and present naval aviators, in 1991.
25   A court in Orlando, Florida allows a 12-year-old boy to divorce his parents, permitting him to be adopted by his foster parents as he wishes. His natural parents had demanded custody.

OCTOBER
8   The U.S. Post Office announces a new postage stamp series featuring music stars, such as Elvis Presley, Patsy Cline, and Buddy Holly.

NOVEMBER
7   Fifty-five percent of eligible voters vote in the U.S. presidential election, an increase of the 50% turnout in the 1988 election.

DECEMBER
- A talking Barbie doll that says "Math class is tough," released in October, is withdrawn after protests about the bad example it sets to girls.

Media and Communication

- A U.S. survey finds that football is the favorite sport to watch on television, with 38% of the public favoring it, as compared to 16% for baseball and 12% for basketball.
- British newspaper owners David and Frederick Barclay purchase the *European*, formerly owned by Robert Maxwell, and relaunch the paper.
- In the United States, 60% of households receive cable television.
- Legislation is passed in the United States levying a tax on digital audio tape, digital compact cassette, and mini disk recorders and the blank cassettes they use, in order to create a pool of money for copyright holders, allegedly deprived of revenue by home-recording.
- The American Telephone and Telegraph company (AT&T) launches a system of personal telephone numbers in the United States. Subscribers can get a number for life, including numbers created from words, such as 700-FLOWERS.
- The American Telephone and Telegraph company (AT&T) launches a personal color videophone. The 7.5 cm/3 in model was developed by Compression Laboratories in California.
- The electronics companies Matsushita and Philips launch the digital compact cassette.
- The first digital FM radio transmitter begins broadcasting in Paris, France.
- The four major U.S. television networks grab a decreasing share of the market. While in 1991, the networks' Saturday evening shows captured 66% of the market, in 1992 they capture 56% of viewers.
- The French electronics company Micromega, licensed by the Dutch company Philips, launches a recordable compact disc player (at a price of £4,500). Recordable discs cost £13.

FEBRUARY

28 At the Smithsonian Institute's National Air and Space Museum in Washington, D.C., a new exhibit features the 1960s cult television show *Star Trek*.

MARCH

29 The comedy *Ellen* (called *These Friends of Mine* in the first season) begins on U.S. television, starring Ellen DeGeneres.

APRIL

8 The British comic magazine *Punch*, first published in 1841, closes down.

JUNE

3 U.S. presidential candidate Bill Clinton plays the saxophone on the U.S. television program *The Arsenio Hall Show*.

AUGUST

20 The British newspaper the *Daily Mirror* publishes compromising photographs of the Duchess of York on holiday in France with U.S. businessman John Bryan.

30 The 1991–92 Emmy Awards for television are held. Best Drama Series: *Northern Exposure*; Best Comedy Series: *Murphy Brown*; Best Actor in a Drama: Christopher Lloyd, for *Avonlea*; Best Actress in a Drama: Dana Delany, for *China Beach*; Best Actor in a

Comedy: Craig T. Nelson, for *Coach*; Best Actress in a Comedy: Candice Bergen, for *Murphy Brown*.

SEPTEMBER

18 *Picket Fences* is first broadcast on U.S. television. Set in the fictional small town of Rome, Wisconsin, it stars Kathy Baker and Tom Skerritt, and deals with a range of issues from the topical, such as drunk driving or rape, to the bizarre, such as spontaneous human combustion.

23 The comedy *Mad About You* begins on U.S. television. Based around the lives of a young married couple in New York, New York, it stars Paul Reiser and Helen Hunt.

Religion

MAY

12 The General Conference of the United Methodist Church declares that homosexual behavior conflicts with Christian teachings.

JULY

1 The Roman Catholic Church orders its U.S. bishops to oppose any laws that promote the public acceptance of homosexuality.

NOVEMBER

- After 359 years, the Roman Catholic Church officially accepts that Galileo was right: the earth does go around the sun.

Sports

- A U.S. government survey finds that 60% of adults participate in a regular or semiregular exercise program, and that better educated adults take the most exercise.
- Following the dismantling of apartheid, South Africa plays its first official Test cricket match since 1970 and participates in its first Olympic Games since 1960.
- Michael Jordan of the Chicago Bulls is voted the National Basketball Association's (NBA) Most Valuable Player for the second successive year.
- Monica Seles of Yugoslavia wins the women's singles titles at the Australian, French, and U.S. Open tennis championships for the second successive year.

FEBRUARY

8–23 The 16th Winter Olympic Games are held in Albertville, France, with 1,801 competitors, including 488 women, from 64 countries, competing in 57 events. Germany wins 10 gold medals; the Unified Team (Russia, Belarus, Ukraine, Kazakhstan, and Uzbekistan from the former Soviet Union) and Norway, 9 each; Austria, 6; the United States, 5; and Italy, 4. Alberto Tomba of Italy wins the Giant Slalom to become the first skier to retain an Olympic Alpine title.

MAY

10 The U.S. golfer Tom Kite wins the U.S. Open at Pebble Beach, California, at the age of 42. It is his first victory in a major tournament.

JULY

5 André Agassi of the United States wins the men's singles at the Wimbledon tennis championships, London, England—his first victory in a Grand Slam singles event.

19 At Muirfield, Scotland, Nick Faldo becomes the first British golfer since Henry Cotton in 1948 to win the British Open three times.

25 The 25th Olympic Games open in Barcelona, Spain, with 9,364 competitors, including 2,707 women, from 169 countries, competing in a record 259 medal events. South Africa appears at its first Games since 1960. Following the collapse of the Soviet Union, the Baltic states Lithuania, Estonia, and Latvia compete independently, and Russia and the other nations of the Commonwealth of Independent States and Georgia compete as the Unified Team. Germany competes as one team.

25–August 9 At the Olympic Games in Barcelona, Spain, the U.S. men's basketball team is a major new attraction. Dubbed the "Dream Team," it comprises leading U.S. professionals from the National Basketball Association including Michael Jordan, Magic Johnson, and Larry Bird. They win the gold medal with ease, scoring an average of 117.25 points per game.

BIRTHS & DEATHS

JANUARY
1 Grace Hopper, U.S. computer scientist who created the first compiler and helped invent the computer language COBOL, dies in Arlington, Virginia (85).

FEBRUARY
10 Alex Palmer Haley, U.S. author best known for his Pulitzer prizewinning book *Roots: The Saga of an American Family* (1976), dies in Seattle, Washington (70).
16 Angela Carter, English writer, author of *The Magic Toyshop* (1967), *Nights at the Circus* (1984), and *Wise Children* (1991), dies (51).

MARCH
9 Menachem Begin, prime minister of Israel 1977–83, dies in Tel Aviv, Israel (78).
23 Friedrich August von Hayek, Austrian-born British economist who was opposed to Keynesian economics and the intervention of government in the economy, dies in Freiburg-im-Breisgau, Germany (92).

APRIL
1 Konstantin Mikhailovich, Russian ballet dancer, dies in St. Petersburg, Russia (82).
6 Isaac Asimov, U.S. science fiction writer, dies in New York, New York (72).
8 Daniel Bovet, Swiss physiologist who pioneered research into antihistamine drugs, dies in Rome, Italy (85).
10 Peter Dennis Mitchell, English chemist who received the Nobel Prize for Chemistry in 1978 for work on the conservation of energy by plants during respiration and photosynthesis, dies in Bodmin, Cornwall, England (71).
23 Satyajit Ray, Indian film director, dies in Calcutta, India (70).
27 Gerard Kitchen O'Neill, U.S. physicist who developed the colliding beam storage-ring particle accelerator, dies in Redwood, California (65).
27 Olivier Messiaen, French composer and organist, dies in Clichy, near Paris, France (83).
28 Francis Bacon, Irish-born British artist known for his macabre paintings, dies in Madrid, Spain (82).

MAY
6 Marlene Dietrich, German-born U.S. motion-picture actress, dies in Paris, France (90).
17 Lawrence Welk, U.S. bandleader and accordion player, dies in Santa Monica, California (89).

JUNE
3 Robert Morley, English actor and playwright, dies in Reading, Berkshire, England (84).
29 John Egerton Christmas Piper, English painter, printmaker, and designer known for his dramatic views of landscape and architecture, dies in Fawley, Oxfordshire, England (88).

JULY
9 Eric Sevareid, U.S. radio and television newscaster, dies in Washington, D.C. (80).

AUGUST
5 Robert David Muldoon, New Zealand prime minister 1975–84, dies in Auckland, New Zealand (70).
12 John Cage, U.S. composer, dies in New York, New York (79).
29 Mary Norton, English writer of children's stories who created the Borrowers, dies in Hartland, Devonshire, England (88).

SEPTEMBER
2 Barbara McClintock, U.S. geneticist who discovered the phenomena of crossing over of segments of chromosomes during meiosis, dies in Huntington, New York (90).
12 Anthony Perkins, U.S. actor, dies in Hollywood, California (59).

OCTOBER
6 Denholm Elliott, English actor, dies in Ibiza, Spain (70).
7 Joseph Mitsuo Kitagawa, Japanese-born U.S. theologian, dies in Chicago, Illinois (77).
10 Willy Brandt, chancellor of the Federal Republic of Germany (West Germany) 1969–74, dies in Unkel, Germany (78).
19 Petra Kelly, German political activist, cofounder of the Green Party, dies in Bonn, Germany (44).

NOVEMBER
2 Hal Roach, early Hollywood film director who directed the Laurel and Hardy films, dies in Bel Air, California (100).
12 Jan Hendrik Oort, Dutch astronomer who discovered that the Milky Way galaxy rotates, and determined the sun's position in the galaxy, dies in Leiden, Netherlands (92).
23 Roy Acuff, U.S. country and western singer, dies in Nashville, Tennessee (89).
27 Alexander Dubček, Czechoslovak communist leader 1968–69 whose liberal policies led to the Soviet occupation of Czechoslovakia (now the Czech and Slovak republics), dies in Prague, Czechoslovakia (now the Czech Republic) (70).
27 Sidney Robert Nolan, Australian artist known particularly for his paintings of the Australian outback and Australian folklore, dies in London, England (75).
29 Marchese di Barsento Pucci, Italian fashion designer whose brightly colored designs were popular in the mid-1950s to mid-1960s, dies in Florence, Italy (78).

DECEMBER
21 Albert King, influential U.S. blues guitarist and singer, dies in Memphis, Tennessee (69).
25 Monica (Enid) Dickens, English novelist, dies in Reading, England (77).

29 At the Olympic Games in Barcelona, Spain, the English cyclist Chris Boardman, in the 4,000-meters individual pursuit, becomes the first Briton to win an Olympic cycling gold medal since 1908.

AUGUST

1 At the Olympic Games in Barcelona, Spain, the Jamaican-born English sprinter Linford Christie wins the men's 100-meters title. At the age of 32, he is the oldest-ever winner of the event by four years.

6 At the Olympic Games in Barcelona, Spain, Kevin Young of the United States becomes the first person ever to run the 400-meters hurdles in under 47 seconds.

9 The 25th Olympic Games close in Barcelona, Spain. The unified Russian team (comprising the 11 nations of the Commonwealth of Independent States and Georgia) wins 45 gold medals; the United States, 37; Germany, 33; China, 16; Cuba, 14; Spain, 13; South Korea, 12; Hungary, 11; France, 8; Australia, 7; and Italy and Canada, 6 each.

16 Nigel Mansell of Britain, driving a Williams–Renault, wins the Formula One World Drivers' Championship, setting a new record of nine Grand Prix victories in one season.

SEPTEMBER

3–14 A record 1.3 million spectators watch 3,500 athletes from 82 countries compete in the Paralympics sports festival for athletes with disabilities, in Barcelona, Spain.

The United States wins 76 gold medals; Germany, 61; Britain, 40; France, 36; and Spain, 34.

4–5 Dan O'Brien of the United States breaks the English athlete Daley Thompson's eight-year old decathlon world record with a score of 8,891 at a meeting in Talence, France. Earlier in the year, O'Brien, the 1991 world champion, surprisingly failed to qualify for the Olympic Games.

6 Wayne Rainey of the United States, on a Yamaha, wins his third successive 500-cc world motorcycle championship.

OCTOBER

24 The Toronto Blue Jays from Canada defeat the Atlanta Braves of the United States by four games to two to become the first team from outside the United States to win baseball's World Series.

NOVEMBER

13 The U.S. boxer Riddick Bowe wins the world heavyweight title, outpointing the holder, fellow U.S. boxer Evander Holyfield, in Las Vegas, Nevada.

DECEMBER

14 Lennox Lewis becomes the first British-born world heavyweight boxing champion in the 20th century when he is awarded the World Boxing Council version of the title after it is vacated by Riddick Bowe of the United States, who retains his World Boxing Association and International Boxing Federation crowns.

◆

1993

POLITICS, GOVERNMENT, AND ECONOMICS

Business and Economics

• The English historian R. H. Britnell publishes *The Commercialisation of English Society, 1000–1500*.

Human Rights

• Several U.S. newspapers refuse to publish cartoons by Lynn Johnston in his series *For Better or Worse* because a teenage boy reveals to his friends and family that he is gay.

• The Supreme Court in Hawaii rules that the refusal to allow same-sex marriages is unconstitutional.

Politics and Government

• In the U.S. federal government's fiscal year 1994 budget, .46 of every dollar will go for benefit payments to individuals while .18 will go for defense, and .15 will be granted to state and local governments.

• The "First Republic" in Italy is ended as a referendum supports a change in the electoral system, replacing proportional representation with majority voting.

JANUARY

1 Government troops in Angola launch an offensive against the headquarters of Jonas Savimbi, leader of the National Union for the Total Independence of Angola (UNITA), in Huambo.

1 The Czech and Slovak republics become separate sovereign countries.

1 The European Community's single market comes into force, establishing the free movement of goods, capital, and services across national borders, with some restrictions.

3 The U.S. president George Bush and the Russian president Boris Yeltsin sign the second Strategic Arms

Reduction Treaty (START II), committing the United States and Russia to dismantle two-thirds of their nuclear warheads.

6   President Alberto Fujimori formally reestablishes constitutional government in Peru.

13 Allied forces carry out air strikes against targets in southern Iraq following Iraq's refusal to remove missiles stationed south of the 32nd parallel (the Shiite exclusion zone).

13 Erich Honecker, the former leader of East Germany, is released from prison in Berlin and allowed to join his wife in Chile. (He returns for the final session of his trial on February 8.)

14 The U.S. president Bill Clinton's choice for post of Attorney General, Zoë Baird, is revealed to be under FBI investigation for employing illegal immigrants (on February 5, the second choice, Kimba Wood, withdraws on the same grounds).

18 Elections in Haiti following the military's seizure of power are boycotted by most electors.

19 Legislation permitting contact between Israeli citizens and the Palestine Liberation Organization (PLO) passes its final reading in the Israeli parliament; the PLO leader Yassir Arafat is interviewed for the first time on Israeli television, on January 21.

20 Bill Clinton (Democrat) is inaugurated as the 42nd president of the United States; the following day he appoints his wife Hillary to head a task force on health reforms.

29 The U.S. president Bill Clinton orders the suspension of the ban on homosexuals serving in the armed forces.

31 Car bombs in the Colombian capital Bogotá kill 25 people; reprisal attacks against the families and associates of drugs cartel leaders in Medellín leave 30 dead.

FEBRUARY

10 The first of a series of ministerial resignations takes place in Italy as a corruption scandal shakes the government.

11 Janet Reno is appointed U.S. attorney general following controversy over two previous candidates for the post.

14 The former communist Democratic Labor Party wins elections in Lithuania, defeating the Lithuanian Reform Movement, which had played a major role in the 1991 campaign for independence.

22 The United Nations Security Council decides to create a war crimes tribunal relating to the former Yugoslavia—the first such tribunal since the Nuremberg trials following World War II (1945–46).

24 Brian Mulroney resigns as Canadian prime minister following economic difficulties and problems over the status of Quebec.

25 Algirdas Brazauskas is sworn in as president of Lithuania, following the Democratic Labor Party's victory in the elections of February 14.

25 The first direct elections to the national assembly are held in Cuba, with an official turn-out of 99.6%.

26 A terrorist bomb explosion kills five people and badly damages the World Trade Center in New York, New York.

MARCH

1   U.S. forces carry out an air-drop of relief supplies to areas in eastern Bosnia-Herzegovina cut off from United Nations operations.

7   A 56-day siege of Huambo ends as Angolan armed forces withdraw before a National Union for the Total Independence of Angola (UNITA) bombardment.

10 Fighting breaks out in the Italian senate as Prime Minister Giuliano Amato is heckled over corruption allegations.

10 The U.S. gynecologist Dr. David Gunn is shot dead by an antiabortion activist in Pensacola, Florida, in a wave of violent attacks on abortion clinics by the prolife group "Rescue America."

12 An emergency session of the Russian Congress votes to restrict the powers of President Boris Yeltsin and defeats his constitutional amendments.

12 North Korea withdraws from the Nuclear Nonproliferation Treaty, having refused to allow inspection of its facilities.

12 Prime Minister Paul Keating's Labor Party wins a fifth consecutive victory in the general elections in Australia.

12 Two hundred and fifty people are killed in a car bomb explosion in Bombay, India, believed to have been planted by Islamic extremists; there is a further explosion in Calcutta on March 16.

19 A United Nations relief convoy led by the French general Philippe Morillon reaches the besieged Muslim enclave of Srebrenica in Bosnia.

20 The Russian president Boris Yeltsin announces "special rule" and sets a date for a referendum on the constitution.

20 The United Nations supervises the evacuation of civilians from the Muslim enclave of Srebrenica in Bosnia-Herzegovina, besieged for almost a year (the siege ends on April 18).

22 One hundred thousand people demonstrate in the Algerian capital Algiers against an upsurge in Islamic terrorism.

24 Ezer Weizman is elected president of Israel (he is sworn in on May 13); Binyamin Netanyahu replaces Yitzhak Shamir as leader of the Likud Party.

27 Jiang Zemin becomes state president of China.

28 Attempts to dismiss President Boris Yeltsin are defeated in the Russian Congress.

29 Edouard Balladur becomes prime minister of France after victory for the right wing Rally for the Republic–Union for French Democracy (RPR–UDF) alliance in elections; the ruling Socialist Party retains only 54 of its 252 seats.

APRIL

3–4 A summit between the U.S. president Bill Clinton and the Russian president Boris Yeltsin produces an agreement for $1,600 million of aid to Russia.

10 Chris Hani, a leading figure in the African National Congress (ANC), is assassinated in South Africa by a member of the right-wing Afrikaner Resistance Movement.

11 Inhabitants of the occupied territories in Israel are prevented from leaving them in an attempt to stem an upsurge in violence.

17 Two of the policemen in the Rodney King case (concerning the beating of the black motorist by four

white policemen in 1991) are convicted of assault; on August 4, they are sentenced to 30 months' imprisonment.

19 The U.S. Federal Bureau of Investigation (FBI) storms the compound of the Branch Davidian cult in Waco, Texas (under siege since February 28); over 80 people die when cult members set fire to the compound.

19 In South Africa, 4 million people strike on the day of the funeral of the murdered African National Congress (ANC) activist Chris Hani.

21 A plebiscite in Brazil rejects the reestablishment of the monarchy.

21 The former Bolivian dictator General Luis García Meza is sentenced to 30 years in jail for murder and corruption.

21 The U.S. president Bill Clinton's package of legislation designed to stimulate the economy is defeated in the House of Representatives.

23 A U.S. Defense Department report on the "Tailhook affair" of September 1991 (when a dinner for active and retired naval airmen resulted in claims of sexual harassment and assault from women attending) states that 117 senior officers indulged in "offensive and possibly criminal behavior."

25 A Russian referendum produces a vote of confidence in President Boris Yeltsin and his policy of liberalization.

29 Brazil's Supreme Court rules that the former president Fernando Collor de Mello be indicted on criminal charges for passive corruption and criminal association.

MAY

1 Ranasinghe Premadasa, president of Sri Lanka, is assassinated during a parade in the capital Colombo.

3 The Social Democratic Party (SPD) chair Bjöorn Engholm resigns in the first of a series of political corruption scandals in Germany.

4 The Turkish Cypriot entrepreneur Asil Nadir, awaiting trial in Britain for theft and false accounting after the collapse of the Polly Peck company, jumps bail and flees to northern Cyprus.

4 The United Nations takes over the military and humanitarian effort in Somalia from a U.S.-led task force.

6 The United Nations Security Council declares "safe areas" in Sarajevo, Tuzla, Zepa, Goradze, Bihać, and Srebrenica in Bosnia-Herzegovina; in spite of this, Bosnian Serbs attack Goradze and Srebrenica on May 30.

7 Multiparty talks in Johannesburg, South Africa, reach agreement for the holding of nonracial elections by April 1994.

13 The United States formally abandons the Strategic Defense Initiative (SDI), its attempt to build a laser defense system against ballistic missile attack.

16 German troops are sent to Somalia as part of the United Nations peacekeeping force; this is the first time since their incorporation into NATO (the North Atlantic Treaty Organization) that they have served outside Europe.

18 In a second referendum, Denmark approves the Maastricht Treaty on European union by a narrow majority, following the granting of concessions on its implementation.

19 The United States recognizes the People's Movement for the Liberation of Angola (MPLA) government in Angola, having previously supported its rivals, the National Union for the Total Independence of Angola (UNITA).

24 Demonstrations are held in Lhasa, Tibet, after the arrest of dissidents; Western observers investigating human-rights abuses cut short their visit.

24 Eritrea formally becomes independent from Ethiopia, after a 30-year civil war.

25 President Jorge Serrano Elias stages a coup in Guatemala.

26 A General Agreement on Tariffs and Trade (GATT) arbitration rules that European Community import restrictions on bananas unfairly limit Latin American imports.

27 The U.S. House of Representatives narrowly votes to approve President Bill Clinton's program of tax increases and spending cuts.

29 Five Turkish women are killed in a neo-Nazi arson attack in Solingen, Germany (Turkish demonstrations and rioting throughout Germany in response to this attack continue until June 1).

JUNE

1 President Jorge Serrano Elias of Guatemala is deposed.

3 The U.S. president Bill Clinton withdraws his nomination of black law professor Lani Guinier for head of the Justice Department's Civil Rights Division after reading her work on positive discrimination and the empowerment of minorities.

4 A rebellion begins among the army in Azerbaijan (President Abulfaz Elchibey is forced to leave Baku on June 18).

5 Somali national forces attack Pakistani troops serving with the United Nations force overseeing the relief effort, killing 24 people.

6 Guerrillas, believed to be from the NPFL, attack a refugee camp near Harbel in Liberia and massacre over 450 people.

6 Ramiro de Léon is elected by Congress to replace Jorge Serrano Elias, deposed on June 1, as president of Guatemala.

7 Gonzalo Sánchez de Lozada of the ruling Nationalist Resistance Movement (MNR) is elected president of Bolivia.

11 President Ali Akbar Rafsanjani of Iran is reelected for a second term.

14 U.S. president Bill Clinton nominates the moderate judge Ruth Ginsburg to the Supreme Court, despite opposition from women's groups, labor unions, and homosexual groups seeking a more radical appointment. Earlier nominees, including the moderate Massachusetts judge Stephen Breyer, had been dropped by Clinton after allegations from their political opponents of possible financial impropriety.

15 The last Russian troops leave Cuba following the dissolution of the USSR.

17 The United Nations issues a warrant for the arrest of the warlord General Muhammad Farah Aydid in an attempt to end the civil war in Somalia.

23 International sanctions are imposed on Haiti following the military's seizure of power.

23 Presidential elections in Nigeria are annulled by the ruling military government (protests persist into July).

25 Armed supporters of the Afrikaner Volksfront storm the Johannesburg World Trade Center, the scene of talks on the constitutional future of South Africa.

25 Kim Campbell, Progressive Conservative, becomes the first woman prime minister of Canada, following the resignation of Brian Mulroney.

26 The United States launches a missile attack on Iraqi intelligence headquarters in Baghdad, in retaliation for an alleged plot to kill the former U.S. president George Bush.

JULY

3 A peace agreement is signed between the exiled president of Haiti, Jean-Bertrand Aristide, and General Raoul Cédras, leader of the 1991 military coup.

10 The water supply is cut off in Sarajevo, the capital of Bosnia-Herzegovina, when fuel supplies fail to get through besieging Serb forces.

16 Jacques Attali of France resigns as president of the European Bank of Reconstruction, after it is revealed that in its first period of operation it spent twice as much on refurbishment of its London, England, headquarters as on loans to Eastern Europe.

18 Having governed Japan since 1955, the Liberal Democrats lose their overall majority in the general elections.

18 President Ghulam Ishaq Khan and Prime Minister Nawaz Sharif of Pakistan both resign following conflict between them, prior to fresh elections.

19 William S. Sessions is the first director of the U.S. Federal Bureau of Investigation (FBI) to be dismissed, following allegations of improper use of resources.

21 Nicaraguan troops put down a revolt by ex-Sandinista rebels, who have seized the northern town of Estelí; 45 people are killed.

29 John Demjanjuk, sentenced to death in 1988 for war crimes committed during World War II as death-camp guard "Ivan the Terrible," is cleared by the Supreme Court in Israel after his identification is doubted.

AUGUST

2 Following speculative pressure on currencies in the European Exchange Rate Mechanism (ERM), the mechanism collapses and currencies are allowed to fluctuate within a broad band of 15% on either side of central rates.

4 President Juvénal Habyarimana and the Rwandan Patriotic Front sign a peace accord, ending a revolt begun in October 1990; elections are set for June 1995.

5 The government of Sudan launches a major offensive against the Sudan People's Liberation Army (SPLA), displacing 100,000 people and threatening famine.

9 Albert of Liège, brother of the late King Baudouin, is sworn in as the new king of Belgium.

10 A seven-party coalition under Morihiro Hosokawa takes up the government of Japan, following the defeat of the Liberal Democrats in the general elections last month.

10 The U.S. president Bill Clinton signs a budget deficit reduction plan.

15 Juan Carlos Wasmosy becomes the first elected president of Paraguay since the country's foundation in 1811.

21 A United Nations relief convoy arrives in the besieged enclave of Mostar, Bosnia-Herzegovina.

27 General Ibrahim Babangida steps down as president of Nigeria, handing power to a nonelected interim government.

SEPTEMBER

7 The body of the former president Ferdinand Marcos, who died in 1989, is returned to the Philippines for burial.

7 U.S. vice president Al Gore presents the report "From Red Tape to Results: Creating a Government that Works Better and Costs Less" (popularly known as the "Reinventing Government" initiative), aiming to reduce federal spending by $108,000 million over five years. The estimated loss of 252,000 federal jobs prompts strident labor union opposition to almost all the proposals.

9 Two hundred civilians are killed when a U.S. helicopter on United Nations peacekeeping duty fires on a crowd in Mogadishu, Somalia.

17 The last Russian troops withdraw from Poland following the ending of the Warsaw Pact (formed in 1955 between the USSR and East European communist states).

17 The remains of General Władysław Sikorski, leader of the Polish government in exile during World War II, are reinterred in his home country, having been buried in Britain since 1943.

19 A Polish general election gives victory to former communists.

19 Prime Minister Paul Keating of Australia announces that the country will become a republic by the year 2001.

21 The Russian president Boris Yeltsin suspends the Russian parliament and calls elections; the Supreme Soviet defies this action and swears in Alexander Rutskoi as president.

24 A failed assassination attempt on President Saddam Hussein of Iraq leads to the execution of 120 army officers.

24 Imelda Marcos, the widow of the former president of the Philippines, Ferdinand Marcos, is sentenced to imprisonment for corruption.

27 The White House in Moscow, seat of the Russian parliament, is sealed off by troops (telephone links and water and electricity supplies have already been cut off).

OCTOBER

4 Rebels holding out in the Moscow parliament building surrender after attacks by pro-Yeltsin forces; a state of emergency remains in force in Russia until October 18.

6 A general election in Pakistan produces a hung parliament.

8 The international community lifts sanctions against South Africa in response to African National Congress (ANC) leader Nelson Mandela's speech of September 24 requesting this.

9 General Muhammad Farah Aydid, leader of a warring faction in Somalia, announces a unilateral cease-fire.

11 Georgia joins the Commonwealth of Independent States (CIS), the last of the former Soviet republics to do so.

15 The Nobel Peace Prize is awarded jointly to the South African president F. W. de Klerk and Nelson Mandela, leader of the African National Congress (ANC), for their work to reform the apartheid system.

19 Benazir Bhutto of the opposition Pakistan Peoples' Party is sworn in as prime minister of Pakistan.

20 Emergency measures are imposed in Kenya after renewed ethnic violence in the Rift Valley between the majority Kikuyu and minority tribes.

21 President Melchior Ndadaye (Burundi's first Hutu president) and other senior ministers are killed during an attempted coup by the Tutsi-dominated army.

25 The Liberal Party wins a decisive victory in the Canadian general elections; the Progressive Conservative Party, in office since 1984, retains only two seats, while the Bloc Québecois becomes the second largest party.

26 Waldemar Pawlak becomes prime minister of a coalition government in Poland.

31 A referendum in Peru approves President Alberto Fujimori's draft constitution, allowing the president to stand for a further term of office and reintroducing the death penalty for terrorism.

NOVEMBER

1 The Maastricht Treaty on European union comes into force; the European Community becomes the European Union (EU).

4 The Liberal Party leader Jean Chrétien is sworn in as prime minister of Canada, following the party's victory in last month's general elections.

6 Jim Bolger's National Party retains office following a general election in New Zealand.

14 Farooq Ahmed Leghari becomes president of Pakistan following elections on November 13.

17 A military coup ends a brief period of civilian rule in Nigeria; defense minister General Sanni Abacha takes over as head of state.

17 The U.S. House of Representatives approves the North American Free Trade Agreement negotiated with Canada and Mexico.

18 The World Food Program launches a relief program for around 1 million refugees from genocide in Burundi.

26 Iraq accepts United Nations supervision of its weapons program.

30 The Brady Act (named for the former White House press secretary James Brady, who was wounded during the attempted assassination of President Ronald Reagan in 1981) introduces some controls on the acquisition of firearms in the United States.

DECEMBER

1 Oil is discovered off the Falkland Islands, a British possession in the South Atlantic.

2 Pablo Escobar Gaviria, head of the Medellín drug-trafficking cartel, is shot dead by police in Colombia.

7 A multiracial Transitional Executive Council takes over government in South Africa to prepare for elections.

11 Eduardo Frei Ruíz-Tagle, of the Coalition for Democracy, is elected president of Chile.

12 In legislative elections in Russia, the largest share of the vote (22.8%) goes to the ultra-nationalist Liberal Democratic Party of Russia led by Vladimir Zhirinovsky; voters approve President Boris Yeltsin's draft constitution in a simultaneous referendum.

15 The "Uruguay Round" of negotiations for a revised General Agreement on Tariffs and Trade (GATT, started in September 1986) end in Geneva, Switzerland; 117 nations agree the GATT Final Act.

15 The prime ministers of Britain and the Republic of Ireland, John Major and Albert Reynolds, make the "Downing Street Declaration," stating the basis for talks

on peace for Northern Ireland; constitutional change will require the majority agreement of the populations of Northern Ireland and the Republic of Ireland.

SCIENCE, TECHNOLOGY, AND MEDICINE

Agriculture

- The German government requires all chicks to be immunized against salmonella by adding a live weakened strain of *Salmonella enteriditis* to their drinking water.

Computing

- Japanese Fujitsu Corporation announces the development of a 256-megabit memory chip.
- Mosaic, the first graphical browser that allows pictures from the Internet to be seen, is developed at the National Center for Supercomputing Applications at the University of Illinois, United States.
- Personal computers based on the first 64-bit processor, the Intel Pentium chip, go on sale in the United States.
- The adventure game *Myst* is the first CD-ROM to be commercially successful, selling more than 1 million copies by the end of 1994.

Ecology

- An ice core drilled in Greenland, providing evidence of climate change over 250,000 years, suggests that sudden fluctuations have been common and that the recent stable climate is unusual.
- German stores are obliged to take back the packaging of many of the products they sell for recycling and it becomes illegal to throw away packaging from most large electronic items.

JULY

12 Following two months of heavy rain in the United States, many Midwestern states suffer severe flooding as rivers burst their banks; 29 people die.

OCTOBER

28 Brush fires break out in southern California and reach the suburbs of Los Angeles, leaving many homeless and causing damage worth over $1,000 million.

Exploration

FEBRUARY

11 Sir Ranulph Fiennes and Dr. Michael Stroud of Britain complete the first unsupported crossing of Antarctica on foot, having covered 2,160 km/1,350 mi in 95 days.

JUNE

- NASA loses contact with its *Mars Observer* space probe (cost $980 million).

AUGUST

- The U.S. spacecraft *Galileo* discovers the first asteroid moon. About 1.5 km/0.95 mi across and named Dactyl (in 1994), it orbits the asteroid Ida.

DECEMBER

7 The Hubble Space Telescope (placed in Earth orbit in 1990) is repaired and reboosted into a nearly circular orbit by five U.S. astronauts operating from the U.S. space shuttle *Endeavour*—at a cost of $360 million.

Health and Medicine

- AIDS becomes the leading cause of death among men aged between 25 and 44 in the United States.
- An artificial form of factor VIII, used in the treatment of hemophilia, goes on sale in Germany and Sweden, and in the UK in 1994.
- Around £1.2 billion is spent on nonprescription medicine in Britain.
- Interferon beta 1b became the first drug to be approved in the United States for treating multiple sclerosis. It significantly slows the progress of the disease.
- Legislation is introduced in the Netherlands to protect doctors involved in cases of euthanasia, effectively legalizing the practice.
- Researchers isolate the first gene that predisposes individuals to cancer. About 1 in 200 people carry the gene.
- The gene responsible for Huntington's chorea is identified. It makes it easier to test individuals for the disease and increases the chances of developing a cure.
- The Nobel Prize for Physiology or Medicine is awarded jointly to British molecular biologist Richard John Roberts and English-born U.S. molecular biologist Phillip Allen Sharp for their discovery of split genes.
- Trials using gene therapy to treat people with cystic fibrosis begin in the United States; gene therapy is administered in the form of a nasal spray.
- U.S. researchers discover that the gene coding for apolipoprotein (APOE) is implicated in the cause of Alzheimer's disease. It is estimated that 1 person in 30 carries this protein mutation.

Science

- Genetic material from the Duke of Edinburgh and other relatives of the Romanov royal family of Russia are compared, using genetic fingerprinting, with the supposed remains of Czar Nicholas II and his family: it is proved that the remains are genuine.
- It is discovered that Russia possesses the "Schliemann Gold"—objects found by the German archeologist Heinrich Schliemann at Troy in 1873, which disappeared from Berlin at the end of World War II.
- Physicists at Lancaster University, England, achieve a temperature of 2.8 × 10–10 K (0.28 millionths of a degree above absolute zero).
- The first pictures of individual atoms, obtained by the use of a scanning tunneling microscope, are published.
- U.S. and Pakistani paleontologists discover in Pakistan a fossil whale which is about the size of an adult male sea lion and has legs. Called *Ambulocetus*, it is 50 million

years old and was able to walk on land but spent most of its time in the sea.
- U.S. astronomers identify part of the dark matter in the universe as stray planets and brown dwarfs. Known as MACHOs (massive astrophysical compact halo objects), they may constitute approximately half of the dark matter in the Milky Way's halo.
- U.S. astronomers Jane Luu and David Jewitt discover four large ice objects in the solar system, beyond Pluto. They are the first members of the Kuiper belt (a ring of small, icy bodies orbiting the sun beyond the planets and thought to be the source of comets) to be observed.
- U.S. astronomers Russell Hulse and Joseph Taylor, Jr., are jointly awarded the Nobel Prize for Physics for their discovery of a new type of pulsar.
- U.S. biochemist Kary Mullis and Canadian biochemist Michael Smith share the Nobel Prize for Chemistry: Mullis for his invention of the polymerase chain reaction technique for amplifying DNA (deoxyribonucleic acid), and Smith for developing techniques for splicing foreign gene segments into an organism's DNA in order to modify the proteins produced.
- U.S. geneticist Dean Hammer and colleagues at the U.S. National Cancer Institute publish the approximate location of a gene that could predispose human males to homosexuality.
- U.S. physicists achieve the most successful nuclear fusion experiment to date when hydrogen isotopes are heated to 300 million degrees, creating 3 million watts of power.

MARCH

- A star in the galaxy M81, about 11 million light-years away, erupts into a supernova. Archival photographs allow astronomers to study the behavior of the star before it exploded.

Technology

- Chemists at the University of Cambridge, England, develop light-emitting polymers (LEPs) from the semiconducting polymer poly(p-phenylenevinyl) (PPV) that emit as much light as conventional LEDs and in a variety of colors.
- French and Russian chemists create a superhard material by crystallizing buckminsterfullerenes at very high pressure. The material is able to scratch diamond.
- The U.S. Congress cancels the proposed Superconducting Super Collider particle accelerator.
- The U.S. Global Positioning System is completed. Using 24 *Navstar* satellites, it enables users, including hikers and motorists, to locate their position to within 100 m/ 328 ft.
- The world's largest array of photovoltaic cells, at Davis, California, is plugged into the local electricity system, producing 479 kilowatts, enough for 125 homes.
- U.S. scientist Albert Bradley develops the Autonomous Benthic Explorer (ABE), a robotic submersible that can descend to depths of 6.4 km/4 mi and remain at such depths for up to one year.
- Using holography, 10,000 pages (100 megabytes) of digital data are stored in an iron-doped lithium nobate crystal measuring 1 cm^3.

SEPTEMBER

15 *The National Information Infrastructure: Agenda for Action* is published in the United States. It proposes a framework for the creation of a national "information highway."

Transportation

- Japanese engineers construct a ceramic engine powered by methanol. It is lighter and has a cleaner exhaust than comparable metal engines powered by gasoline.
- The Third River Canal in Iraq is completed. Running between Mahmudiya near Baghdad and Basra on the Persian Gulf, its purpose is to drain the marshes near Basra.

FEBRUARY

18 One thousand people die in a ferry disaster off the coast of Haiti.

SEPTEMBER

22 A train is derailed and catches fire north of Mobile, Alabama; 47 people are killed.

ARTS AND IDEAS

Architecture

- The English historian Simon Thurley publishes *The Royal Palaces of Tudor England: Architecture and Court Life, 1460–1547.*
- The exhibition "Arata Isozaki: Works in Architecture" is held at the Brooklyn Museum in New York, New York.
- The Fire Station in Weil An Rhein, Germany, designed by the English architect Zaha Hadid, is completed.

Arts

- The English artist Rachel Whiteread is awarded the Turner Prize for *House*, the plaster cast of the inside of a house in the East End of London, England. She also receives a spoof prize from the "K Foundation" for the "worst artist of the year."
- The exhibition "From Cézanne to Matisse—the Barnes Collection" is held at the Musée d'Orsay in Paris, France. This is the first time that items from the Barnes Collection have left Pennsylvania.
- The German-born English artist Lucian Freud paints *Painter Working, Reflection.*

Film

- At the Cannes Film Festival in France, the Palme d'Or is awarded jointly to *Farewell My Concubine*, directed by Chen Kaige, the first movie from China to win the award, and to *The Piano*, directed by Jane Campion. *Farewell My Concubine* stars Leslie Cheung

and Zhang Fengy; *The Piano*, released in Australia, stars Holly Hunter, Harvey Keitel, Sam Neill, and Anna Paquin.

- The movie *A Bronx Tale*, directed by Robert De Niro, is released in the United States. He also stars in it, along with Chazz Palminteri, Lillo Brancato, and Francis Capro.
- The movie *A Perfect Life*, directed by Clint Eastwood, is released in the United States, starring Kevin Costner.
- The movie *Accidental Hero*, directed by British filmmaker Stephen Frears, is released in the United States, starring Dustin Hoffman, Geena Davis, and Andy Garcia.
- The movie *Carlito's Way*, directed by Brian de Palma, is released in the United States, starring Al Pacino and Sean Penn.
- The movie *Demolition Man*, directed by Marco Brambilla, is released in the United States, starring Sylvester Stallone, Wesley Snipes, and Sandra Bullock.
- The movie *El Mariachi*, directed by Robert Rodriguez, is released in Mexico, starring Carlos Gallardo. Made on a budget of only $7,000, it grosses $1.8 million in the United States alone.
- The movie *Falling Down*, directed by Joel Schumacher, is released in the United States, starring Michael Douglas. The movie gives rise to accusations that it has provoked copy-cat crimes in the style of the main character.
- The movie *Flight of the Innocent*, directed by Carlo Carlei, is released in Italy.
- The movie *Germinal*, directed by Claude Berri, is released in France, starring Gérard Depardieu and Miou-Miou. Based on the novel by Emile Zola, it is one of the most expensive French movies to be made, with a budget of $25 million.
- The movie *Groundhog Day*, directed by Harold Ramis, is released in the United States, starring Bill Murray and Andie MacDowell.
- The movie *In the Name of the Father*, directed by Jim Sheridan, is released in Britain. Telling the story of the wrongful imprisonment of the Guildford Four, it stars Daniel Day Lewis, Pete Postlethwaite, and Emma Thompson.
- The movie *In the Line of Fire*, directed by Wolfgang Petersen, is released in the United States, starring Clint Eastwood and John Malkovich.
- The movie *Indecent Proposal*, directed by British filmmaker Adrian Lyne, is released in the United States, starring Robert Redford, Woody Harrelson, and Demi Moore.
- The movie *Jurassic Park*, directed by Steven Spielberg, is released in the United States. Based on the novel by Michael Crichton, it stars Sam Neill, Laura Dern, Jeff Goldblum, Richard Attenborough, and Bob Peck.
- The movie *La Scorta/The Escort*, directed by Ricky Tognazzi, is released in Italy, starring Claudio Amendola, Enrico Lo Verso, Carlo Cecchi, and Ricky Memphis.
- The movie *Les Nuits Fauves/Savage Nights*, directed by Cyril Collard, is released in France. It is based on Collard's book and he also stars in it, along with Romane Bohringer.
- The movie *Les Visiteurs/The Visitors*, directed by Jean-Marie Poiré, is released in France, starring Christian

Clavier and Jean Reno. It is the most successful movie of the year at the box office in France, making twice as much money as *Jurassic Park*.

- The movie *Like Water for Chocolate*, directed by Alfonso Arau, is released in Mexico. Based on the novel by Laura Esquival, it stars Marco Leonardi and Lumi Cavazos.
- The movie *Malice*, directed by Harold Becker, is released in the United States, starring Alec Baldwin, Nicole Kidman, and Bill Pullman.
- The movie *Mrs Doubtfire*, directed by Chris Columbus, is released in the United States. Based on Anne Fine's novel *Alias Madame Doubtfire*, it stars Robin Williams and Sally Field.
- The movie *Much Ado About Nothing*, directed by Kenneth Branagh, is released in Britain. He also stars in it with an all-star cast including Emma Thompson.
- The movie *Naked*, directed by Mike Leigh, is released in Britain, starring David Thewlis.
- The movie *Olivier, Olivier*, directed by Polish filmmaker Agnieszka Holland, is released in France, starring Françoise Cluzet, Brigitte Rouan, and Jean-François Stévenin.
- The movie *Philadelphia*, directed by Jonathan Demme, is released in the United States. The first mainstream Hollywood movie to deal with the subject of AIDS, it stars Tom Hanks.
- The movie *Schindler's List*, directed by Steven Spielberg, is released in the United States. Based on Thomas Keneally's book *Schindler's Ark*, it stars Liam Neeson, Ben Kingsley, and Ralph Fiennes.
- The movie *Shadowlands*, directed by Richard Attenborough, is released in Britain. Based on the life of C. S. Lewis, it stars Anthony Hopkins and Debra Winger.
- The movie *Short Cuts*, directed by Robert Altman, is released in the United States. Based on short stories by Raymond Carver, it has an all-star cast, which includes Tim Robbins, Andie MacDowell, Anne Archer, and Jack Lemmon.
- The movie *Sleepless in Seattle*, directed by Nora Ephron, is released in the United States, starring Tom Hanks and Meg Ryan.
- The movie *Sommersby*, directed by British filmmaker John Amiel, is released in the United States. An adaptation of the French movie *The Return of Martin Guerre*, it stars Richard Gere and Jodie Foster.
- The movie *Sonatine*, directed by Takeshi Kitano, is released in Japan, starring "Beat" Takeshi (Takeshi Kitano), Aya Kokumai, and Tetsu Watanabe.
- The movie *Strawberry and Chocolate*, directed by Tomás Gutiérez Alea and Juan Carlos Tabio, is released in Cuba, starring Jorge Perugorria and Vladimir Cruz.
- The movie *The Age of Innocence*, directed by Martin Scorsese, is released in the United States. Based on the novel by Edith Wharton, it stars Daniel Day Lewis, Michelle Pfeiffer, and Winona Ryder.
- The movie *The Firm*, directed by Sydney Pollack, is released in the United States. Based on the novel by John Grisham, it stars Tom Cruise.
- The movie *The Fugitive*, directed by Andrew Davis, is released in the United States. Based on the original television series, it stars Harrison Ford and Tommy Lee Jones.

- The movie *The Remains of the Day*, directed by James Ivory, is released in Britain. Based on the novel by Kazuo Ishiguro, it stars Anthony Hopkins and Emma Thompson.
- The movie *The Scent of Green Papaya*, directed by Tran Anh Hung, is released in Vietnam, starring Yên-Khê Tran Nu, Man San Lu, and Thi Lôc Truong.
- The movie *The Wedding Banquet*, directed by Ang Lee, is released in Taiwan, starring Mitchell Lichtenstein, Winston Chao, and May Chin.
- The movie *This Boy's Life*, directed by British filmmaker Michael Caton-Jones, is released in the United States. Based on the book by Tobias Wolff, it stars Robert De Niro, Ellen Barkin, and Leonardo DiCaprio.
- The movie *Trois Coleurs: Bleu/Three Colors Blue*, directed by Polish filmmaker Krzysztof Kieślowski, is released in France, starring Juliette Binoche. It is the first in a trilogy of movies, and is followed by *Trois Coleurs: Blanc/Three Colors White* (1994) and *Trois Coleurs: Rouge/Three Colors Red* (1994).
- The movie *True Romance*, directed by Tony Scott and scripted by Quentin Tarantino, is released in the United States, starring Christian Slater, Patricia Arquette, Dennis Hopper, and Christopher Walken.
- The movie *Under Siege*, directed by Andrew Davies, is released in the United States, starring Stephen Seagal and Tommy Lee Jones.
- The movie *What's Eating Gilbert Grape?*, directed by Swedish filmmaker Lasse Hallström, is released in the United States, starring Johnny Depp and Leonardo DiCaprio.

MARCH

28 The 1992 Academy Awards are held. Best Actor: Al Pacino, for *Scent of a Woman*; Best Supporting Actor: Gene Hackman, for *Unforgiven*; Best Actress: Emma Thompson, for *Howards End*; Best Supporting Actress: Marisa Tomei, for *My Cousin Vinny*; Best Director: Clint Eastwood, for *Unforgiven*; Best Picture: *Unforgiven*, directed by Clint Eastwood.

Literature and Language

- Margaret Thatcher publishes memoirs of her time as British prime minister in *The Downing Street Years*.
- The Australian writer David Malouf publishes his novel *Remembering Babylon*.
- The Canadian writer Carol Shields publishes her novel *The Stone Diaries*.
- The English historian Peter Preston publishes his biography *Franco*.
- The English writer Andrew Motion publishes the authorized biography *Philip Larkin: A Writer's Life*.
- The English writer Pat Barker publishes her novel *The Eye in the Door*, the second part of her *Regeneration* trilogy.
- The Indian writer Vikram Seth publishes his novel *A Suitable Boy* in India.
- The Irish writer Roddy Doyle publishes his novel *Paddy Clarke Ha Ha Ha*.
- The Nobel Prize for Literature is awarded to the U.S. writer Toni Morrison.
- The Pulitzer Prize for Biography is awarded to David McCullough for *Truman*.

- The Pulitzer Prize for Fiction is awarded to Robert Olen Butler for *A Good Scent from a Strange Mountain*.
- The Pulitzer Prize for Poetry is awarded to Louise Gluck for *The Wild Iris*.
- The U.S. writer A. R. Ammons publishes his poetry collection *Garbage*.
- The U.S. writer Adrienne Rich publishes her critical work *What is Found There: Notebooks on Poetry and Politics*.
- The U.S. writer Donald Hall publishes his poetry collection *The Museum of Clear Ideas*.
- The U.S. writer James Merrill publishes his memoir *A Different Person Memoir*.
- The U.S. writer Joan Brady publishes her novel *Theory of War*.
- The U.S. writer John Ashbery publishes his poetry collection *Hotel Lautréamont*.
- The U.S. writer M. F. K. Fisher publishes *Stay Me, Oh Comfort Me: Journals and Stories*.
- The U.S. writer Octavia E. Butler publishes her novel *Parable of the Sower*.
- The West Indian-born English writer Caryl Phillips publishes his novel *Crossing the River*.

Music

- Music compact discs are outselling cassettes in Britain.
- Ragga, a form of reggae music played on digital instruments, becomes popular, with groups such as Shabba Ranks, Chaka Demus & Pliers, and Apache Indian releasing records.
- Rap music becomes more popular, with groups such as Arrested Development, and Positive K, and rappers such as Ice Cube, releasing records which are bought by an increasingly mainstream audience.
- The British pop group Take That releases the singles "Pray" and "Everything Changes," and the album *Take That and Party*.
- The British pop group the Pet Shop Boys releases the album *Very*.
- The British pop singer Phil Collins releases the album *Both Sides*.
- The British pop singer Annie Lennox releases the album *Diva*.
- The British rock group Suede releases the album *Suede*.
- The British rock group Radiohead releases the album *The Bends*.
- The British rock singer Morrissey releases the album *Vauxhall and I*.
- The British rock singer Elvis Costello collaborates with the Brodsky Quartet on the album *The Juliet Letters*.
- The Danish composer Poul Ruders completes his orchestral work *Zenith*.
- The English composer Peter Maxwell Davies completes his *Strathclyde Concerto* No. 8 for bassoon and his orchestral work *Chat Moss*.
- The English composer Jonathan Lloyd completes his orchestral work *Tolerance*.
- The English composer Michael Berkeley completes his *Elegy* for strings.
- The English composer George Benjamin completes his orchestral work *Sudden Time*.
- The English composer Benedict Mason completes his electronic work *Colour and Information*.

- The English composer Michael Tippett completes his orchestral work *The Rose Lake*.
- The Icelandic singer Björk releases the album *Debut*.
- The Irish rock group U2 releases the album *Zooropa*.
- The Swedish pop group Ace of Base releases the single "All She Wants."
- The U.S. composer Elliott Carter completes his orchestral work *Partita*.
- The U.S. composer Philip Glass completes his String Quartet No. 5.
- The U.S. grunge group Pearl Jam releases the album *V*.
- The U.S. grunge group Nirvana releases the album *In Utero*.
- The U.S. pop singer Tina Turner releases the album *What's Love Got to Do with It?*
- The U.S. rock group REM releases the single "Everybody Hurts."
- The U.S. rock singer Meat Loaf releases the single "I'd Do Anything for Love (But I Won't Do That)" and the album *Bat Out of Hell II – Back to Hell*.
- The U.S. rock singer Sheryl Crow releases the album *Tuesday Night Music Club*.
- The U.S. singer/songwriter Tom Waits releases the album *The Black Rider*.

FEBRUARY

10 U.S. pop star Michael Jackson appears on *The Oprah Winfrey Show*, his first television interview in 14 years.

MAY

3 The musical *Kiss of the Spiderwoman*, with lyrics and music by John Kander and Fred Ebb, is first performed, at the Broadhurst Theater, New York, New York.

AUGUST

25 U.S. rapper Snoop Doggy Dogg is charged with being an accomplice to the murder of a man killed by one of his bodyguards. He is acquitted on February 20, 1996.

26 U.S. pop singer Michael Jackson, in the face of allegations of child abuse made on August 17, withdraws from part of his world tour, and loses his sponsorship from Pepsi on November 13. He later makes an out-of-court settlement with the boy involved, Jordy Chandler.

Theater and Dance

- The play *Arcadia*, by the Czechoslovak-born English dramatist Tom Stoppard, is first performed, in London, England.
- The play *Moonlight*, by the English dramatist Harold Pinter, is first performed, in London, England.
- The Pulitzer Prize for Drama is awarded to Tony Kushner for *Angels in America*.

JUNE

4 The 1992–93 Tony Awards are held. Best Play: *Angels in America: Millenium Approaches*; Best Musical: *Kiss of the Spider Woman*; Best Actor: Ron Leibman; Best Actress: Madeline Kahn.

DECEMBER

12 *Sunset Boulevard*, with lyrics by Christopher Hampton and Don Black and music by Sir Andrew Lloyd Webber,

and based on the movie by Billy Wilder, is first performed, at the Adelphi Theatre in London, England.

Thought and Scholarship

- The Canadian historians Margaret Conrad and Alvin Finkel publish volume one of *History of the Canadian Peoples: Beginnings to 1867*.
- The English philosopher Michael Dummett publishes *Origins of Analytical Philosophy*.
- The Pulitzer Prize for History is awarded to Gordon S. Wood for *The Radicalism of the American Revolution*.
- The Pulitzer Prize for General Nonfiction is awarded to Garry Wills for *Lincoln at Gettysburg*.
- The U.S. historians Stanley Elkins and Eric McKitrick publish *The Age of Federalism*.
- The U.S. philosopher Larry S. Temkin publishes *Inequality*.
- The U.S. writer Gore Vidal publishes *United States, Essays 1952–1992*.

SOCIETY

Everyday Life

c. 1993　Theme restaurants such as the Harley Davidson Café, Planet Hollywood, and the Hard Rock Café are popular in the United States.
- Twenty-eight percent of Hispanic families in the United States are in the lowest fifth of family income, while 10% of Hispanic families are in the highest fifth.
- Thirty-seven percent of black households in the United States fall into the lowest fifth of the population for household income, while 9% of black households fall into the highest fifth.
- A U.S. survey reveals that 51.1 million workers, or 46% of the labor force, use computers for their work; the most popular application is word processing.
- According to a U.S. government survey, 48% of Americans volunteer; the average volunteer commitment is four hours per week.
- Australian student and lifeguard Damian Taylor is the first man to win a beauty contest in competition against women when he becomes Miss Wintersun Queen.
- In Britain, the government attempts to counter the growth of raves and house parties by placing restrictions on freedom of movement and gatherings in the form of curfews.
- In the United States, 12% of white babies, 22% of black babies, and 21% of Native American babies are born to teenage mothers.
- In the United States, 68% of black babies and 24% of white babies are born to unmarried mothers.
- Major labor strikes in the United States this year total 40, involving 182,000 workers.
- Men in the United States are 18% more likely to be involved in an accident than women.
- Of the 23,180 murders in the United States this year, 20% occur during other felony crimes, 31% occur as

a result of arguments, and 28% occur for reasons unknown; 43,547,000 people are victims of crimes; about three-quarters are victims of property crimes.
- Of the 44.4 million trips by Americans to foreign countries, 12 million are to Canada, 15.2 million are to Mexico, and 17.1 million are overseas.
- The average U.S. family donates $880, or 2% of total income, a year to charity, up from $790 in 1987.
- The infant mortality rate in the United States is 8.4 per 1,000 live births, down from 12.6 in 1980. The rate is 16.5 for black babies and 6.8 for white babies.
- The popularity of grunge music establishes a fashion trend for checked shirts, ripped jeans, and combat boots, the latter often worn with feminine dresses.
- There are 37,571 educational, religious, or philanthropic foundations in the United States with assets of more than $189.2 billion. They grant more than $11.3 billion.
- There are 8,929,000 public libraries in the United States.
- U.S. business firms give $162 billion to charity, a 3.6% increase over the previous year.
- U.S. religious groups launch True Love Waits, an organization aiming to make premarital celibacy attractive to young people. Its effectiveness is unknown, although it garners a lot of publicity.

December 1993–94　The U.S. Census Bureau estimates that 17% of U.S. families move house in this period, more than half within the same county.

MARCH
31　The U.S. unemployment rate is 7%, down from 7.3% the previous year.

MAY
22　The runways at Los Angeles airport in California are closed for about 40 minutes while Christophe, a fashionable Beverly Hills hairdresser, cuts President Bill Clinton's hair on board his official plane, Air Force One. In addition to the cost of disrupting air traffic, the cut costs $200 and the incident becomes known as "Hairgate."

JUNE
9　Crown Prince Naruhito of Japan marries Masako Owada, a member of the Japanese diplomatic corps.

AUGUST
6　The royal family opens Buckingham Palace, London, England, to the general public. Vistors pay £8 a head.

Media and Communication

- *Mighty Morphin Power Rangers*, suburban Californians turned superheroes, first appears on television, leading to a massive merchandising business worldwide.
- Personal digital assistants, the Amstrad PenPad and the Apple Newton MessagePad, are launched. These are electronic personal organizers with the facility to convert handwriting to typed text.
- U.S. businessman Rupert Murdoch purchases Star TV, a five-channel satellite station based in Hong Kong and broadcasting to an estimated 40 million viewers in Asia.

JANUARY
- The science fiction program *Star Trek: Deep Space Nine* is broadcast on U.S. television. A further *Star Trek*

spin-off, it stars Avery Brooks, Rene Auberjonois, Nana Visitor, Terry Ternell, Colm Meaney, and Siddig El Fadi.

FEBRUARY

- The science fiction television program *Babylon 5* is broadcast on U.S. television. Created by J. Michael Straczynski, it stars Michael O'Hare (later replaced by Bruce Boxleitner), Jerry Doyle, and Claudia Christiansen.

SEPTEMBER

10 The television program the *X-Files* is first broadcast in the United States. Created by Chris Carter, it stars David Duchovny and Gillian Anderson as FBI agents investigating strange phenomena.

11 The 1992–93 Emmy Awards for television are held. Best Drama Series: *Picket Fences*; Best Comedy Series: *Seinfeld*; Best Actor in a Drama: Tom Skerritt, for *Picket Fences*; Best Actress in a Drama: Kathy Baker, for *Picket Fences*; Best Actor in a Comedy: Ted Danson, for *Cheers*; Best Actress in a Comedy: Roseanne Barr, for *Roseanne*.

16 The comedy program *Frasier* begins on U.S. television. A spin-off from *Cheers*, it stars Kelsey Grammer as Dr. Frasier Crane, with David Hyde Pierce, John Mahoney, Peri Gilpen, and Jane Leeves.

Sports

- Alain Prost of France retires from automobile racing after winning his fourth Formula One World Drivers' Championship.
- Canadian hockey player Mario Lemieux of the Pittsburgh Penguins scores 160 points to win the Art Ross Trophy and the Hart Trophy as the National Hockey League's Most Valuable Player, despite missing 24 games while undergoing radiation treatment for Hodgkin's disease.
- The Montréal Canadiens defeat the Los Angeles Kings by four games to one to extend their all-time record of victories in the National Hockey League (NHL) Stanley Cup to 24.
- The world chess champion Garry Kasparov of Azerbaijan and the number one challenger for his title, the English player Nigel Short, break away from the International Chess Federation (FIDE), the established governing body for the game, to form the Professional Chess Association (PCA). Kasparov was stripped of his FIDE title, which was regained by the former champion Anatoly Karpov of Russia. However, Kasparov, who defeated Short 12.5–7.5 in London, England, for the PCA title, remains widely accepted as the world's number one player.

JANUARY

31 The Dallas Cowboys defeat the Buffalo Bills 52–17 in Pasadena, California, in Super Bowl XXVII, to win their first Super Bowl since 1978.

JUNE

5 U.S. jockey Julia Krone rides Colonial Affair to victory in the Belmont Stakes, New York, to become the first woman jockey to win a U.S. Triple Crown race.

20 The U.S. golfer Lee Janzen wins the U.S. Open at Baltusrol, New Jersey, equaling the U.S. golfer Jack Nicklaus's championship record aggregate score of 272 set on the same course in 1980.

21–July 4 Prize money at the Wimbledon tennis championships in London, England, reaches the £5 million mark for the first time. When the tournament first went open to professionals as well as amateurs in 1968 the total prize money was £26,500.

JULY

3 Steffi Graf of Germany wins her third successive women's singles title at the Wimbledon tennis championships, London, England. She also wins this year's French and U.S. Opens.

AUGUST

21 At the World Championships in Stuttgart, Germany, the U.S. men's 4 × 100-meters relay team equals its world

BIRTHS & DEATHS

JANUARY

6 John Birks "Dizzy" Gillespie, U.S. trumpet player and bandleader who originated the "bebop" style of jazz, dies in Englewood, New Jersey (75).

6 Rudolf Hametovich Nureyev, Russian ballet dancer, dies in Paris, France (54).

20 Audrey Hepburn, U.S. film actress, dies in Tolochenaz, Switzerland (63).

24 Thurgood Marshall, first black member of the U.S. Supreme Court, dies in Bethesda, Maryland (84).

30 Takichiro Mori, Japanese real estate tycoon who transformed Tokyo by replacing wooden frame buildings with steel-frame structures, dies in Tokyo, Japan (about 88).

FEBRUARY

2 Pablo Gaviria Escobar, Colombian drug dealer, racketeer, and politician, is killed by police while resisting arrest in Medellín, Colombia (44).

5 Joseph L(eo) Mankiewicz, U.S. filmmaker, dies in Bedford Hills, California (83).

6 Arthur Ashe, U.S. tennis player and the first black man to win a major men's singles championship, dies in New York, New York (49).

20 Ferruccio Lamborghini, Italian automobile manufacturer noted for his luxury sports cars, dies in Perugia, Italy (76).

21 Harvey Kuntzman, U.S. cartoonist who created Alfred E. Neuman and *Mad* magazine, dies in Mt. Vernon, New York (69).

27 Lilian Gish, U.S. silent film actress, dies in New York, New York (99).

MARCH

1 Luis Kutner, U.S. human rights activist who created Amnesty International, dies in Chicago, Illinois (84).

3 Albert Bruce Sabin, Polish-born U.S. physician who developed an oral vaccine for poliomyelitis, dies in Washington, D.C. (86).

3 Carlos García Montoya, Spanish guitarist noted for his flamenco music, dies in Wainscott, New York (89).

8 Billy (William Clarence) Eckstine (originally Eckstein), U.S. jazz singer, bandleader, and trumpet player, dies in Pittsburgh, Pennsylvania (78).

17 Helen Hayes, U.S. film and theater actress, dies in Nyack, New York (92).

23 Denis Parsons Burkitt, British surgeon who first described the childhood tumor named for him, Burkitt's lymphoma, dies (82).

APRIL

1 Solly Zuckerman, South African-born British zoologist who did extensive research on primates, dies in London, England (88).

8 Marian Anderson, U.S. contralto, dies in Portland, Oregon (91).

10 Chris (Martin Thembisile) Hani, South African communist and antiapartheid activist, leader of the military wing of the African National Congress (ANC) 1987–93, is assassinated by a right wing extremist in Boksburg, Transvaal, South Africa (50).

15 Leslie Charteris, British-born U.S. author who created Simon Templar ("the Saint"), dies in Windsor, Berkshire, England (85).

15 Tuzo Wilson, Canadian geophysicist who developed the science of plate tectonics, dies in Toronto, Ontario, Canada (84).

17 Turgut Özal, prime minister of Turkey 1983–89 and president 1989–93, dies in Ankara, Turkey (65).

18 Elisabeth Frink, English sculptor known for her rugged, naturalistic bronzes based on human and animal forms, dies in Woolland, Dorset, England (62).

23 Cesar Estrada Chavez, U.S. migrant farm worker who established the National Farm Workers Association (1962), dies in San Luis, Arizona (66).

24 Oliver Tambo, president of the African National Congress (ANC) 1969–91, dies in Johannesburg, South Africa (75).

MAY

1 Pierre (Eugène) Bérégovoy, prime minister of France 1992–93, commits suicide in Nievers, France (67).

JUNE

3 John Presper Eckert, Jr., U.S. engineer who, with John W. Mauchley, invented ENIAC, the first electronic digital computer, dies in Bryn Mawr, Pennsylvania (74).

5 Conway Twitty, U.S. country music singer, dies in Springfield, Missouri (59).

15 James Simon Wallis Hunt, English race-car driver, winner of the 1976 Formula 1 Grand Prix, dies in London, England (45).

19 William Golding, English novelist whose works include *Lord of the Flies* (1954), dies in Perranarworthal, Cornwall, England (81).

28 Boris Christoff, Bulgarian bass singer known for his interpretation of Verdi and Russian operas, dies in Rome, Italy (79).

JULY

3 Donald Scott Drysdale, U.S. baseball player and sports broadcaster, dies in Montreal, Quebec, Canada (56).

6 Wolfgang Paul, German nuclear physicist who developed the ion trap, or "Paul trap," used to store single atoms long enough to make accurate spectroscopic measurements on single atoms, dies in Bonn, Germany (79).

10 Masuji Ibuse, Japanese novelist and poet, author of *Kuroi ame/Black Rain*, dies in Tokyo, Japan (95).

31 Baudouin I, King of the Belgians 1951–93, dies in Mutril, Spain (62).

AUGUST

16 Stewart Granger (born James Lablache), English-U.S. film actor, dies in Santa Monica, California (80).

SEPTEMBER

9 Freya Madeline Stark, English traveler, mountaineer, and writer, dies in Asolo, Italy (100).

12 Raymond Burr, U.S. actor known for his roles as the detectives Perry Mason and Ironside, dies near Healdsburg, California (76).

OCTOBER

7 Agnes George DeMille, U.S. choreographer, dies in New York, New York (88).

25 Vincent Price, U.S. actor noted for his horror thrillers, dies in Los Angeles, California (82).

31 Federico Fellini, Italian film director, dies in Rome, Italy (73).

31 River Phoenix, U.S. actor, dies from a drug overdose in Los Angeles, California (23).

NOVEMBER

1 Severo Ochoa, Spanish biologist who first synthesized RNA, dies in Madrid, Spain (88).

12 H(arry) R(obbins) Haldeman, U.S. businessman and chief of staff to Richard M. Nixon 1969–73, crucially involved in the Watergate cover-up, dies in Santa Monica, California (67).

19 Kenneth Burke, U.S. philosopher and literary critic, dies in Andover, New Jersey (96).

22 Anthony Burgess (pen name of Anthony John Burgess Wilson), English novelist and critic, dies in London, England (76).

29 Gary Moore, U.S. television quiz show host and entertainer, dies in Hilton Head Island, South Carolina (78).

DECEMBER

• Félix Houphouët-Boigny, first president of the independent Republic of Ivory Coast 1960–93, dies in Yamoussoukro, Ivory Coast (88).

• Zviad Gamsakhurdia, anticommunist prime minister 1989–91 and then president of Georgia 1991–92, either commits suicide or is killed by Russian troops in western Georgia (54).

4 Frank (Francis Vincent) Zappa, U.S. rock musician and composer, dies in Los Angeles, California (52).

6 Don Ameche, U.S. actor, dies in Scottsdale, Arizona (85).

14 Myrna Loy, U.S. actress, dies in New York, New York (88).

16 Kakuei Tanaka, Japanese businessman and prime minister of Japan 1972–74, dies in Tokyo, Japan (75).

24 Norman Vincent Peale, U.S. religious leader, dies in Pawling, New York (95).

28 William L(awrence) Shirer, U.S. journalist and historian, commentator for the Columbia Broadcasting System (CBS), and author of *The Rise and Fall of the Third Reich: A History of Nazi Germany*, dies in Boston, Massachusetts (89).

record time of 37.40 seconds set a year earlier at the Barcelona Olympics in Spain.

SEPTEMBER

5 The Algerian runner Noureddine Morceli sets a new world mile record of 3 min 44.39 sec at Rieti, Italy.

19 The English race-car driver Nigel Mansell wins the PPG Indycar series in the United States at his first attempt.

24–26 The United States retains the golf Ryder Cup, defeating Europe 15–13 at The Belfry, Sutton Coldfield, England.

OCTOBER

6 The Chicago Bulls basketball star Michael Jordan retires from professional basketball at the age of 30, having led the U.S. National Basketball Association (NBA) in scoring for seven successive seasons.

NOVEMBER

6 Evander Holyfield of the United States defeats fellow U.S. boxer Riddick Bowe on points to win the World Boxing Association and International Boxing Federation versions of the world heavyweight title.

14 Don Shula of the Miami Dolphins surpasses George Halas's all-time National Football League coaching record of 324 wins.

♦

1994

POLITICS, GOVERNMENT, AND ECONOMICS

Business and Economics

• The Japanese company Ricoh produces a prototype of a "recycle copier" that removes the toner from paper allowing the paper to be reused.

JUNE

14 Private banks are established in Iran for the first time since the nationalization of banking following the Islamic revolution of 1979.

JULY

1 A new currency, the real, is introduced in Brazil in an attempt to stabilize the economy.

Human Rights

APRIL

19 In the case of *J E B v. Alabama Ex Rel T B*, the U.S. Supreme Court rules that sexual discrimination in the selection of juries is a violation of the equal protection guarantee in the 14th Amendment to the Constitution.

Politics and Government

• The U.S. diplomat Henry Kissinger publishes *Diplomacy*.

JANUARY

1 The North American Free Trade Agreement (NAFTA), between Mexico, the United States, and Canada, comes into effect.

1 The second stage of economic and monetary union in Europe comes into force with the establishment of the European Economic Area, incorporating European Free Trade Association (EFTA) members (excepting Switzerland and Liechtenstein) into the European Union free market.

1 The Zapatista National Liberation Army leads a rebellion of Native American groups which begins in the state of Chiapas, Mexico.

3 One hundred and twenty two people die in a prison riot in Maracaibo, Venezuela, after violence breaks out between Native American and non-Native American prisoners.

10–11 A NATO (North Atlantic Treaty Organization) summit in Brussels, Belgium, launches the "partnership for peace" program to encourage cooperation with former members of the Warsaw Pact.

13 The national assembly in Burundi elects Cyprien Ntaryamira (a Hutu) as president, following the death of Melchior Ndadaye in October 1993.

16 The radical Yegor Gaidar resigns from the Russian cabinet in protest at the conservatism of government policy; four days later Viktor Chernomyrdin reforms the cabinet, including mainly centrists.

19 Proposed reforms against political corruption are defeated in the upper house in Japan; a compromise is reached ten days later, removing the weighting given to rural votes and limiting, rather than prohibiting, corporate donations to politicians.

21 Lorena Bobbitt of Virginia is cleared of maliciously wounding her husband after she cut off his penis in June 1993; it is accepted that she became temporarily insane.

31 Gerry Adams, the president of the Irish republican party Sinn Féin, is granted a visa to visit the United States.

FEBRUARY

2   José Maria Figueres of the opposition National Liberal Party (PLN) wins the presidential elections in Costa Rica.

5   A Serb mortar attack on the market place in Sarajevo, Bosnia-Herzegovina, kills at least 68 civilians.

9   NATO (the North Atlantic Treaty Organization) demands that the Serbs withdraw their artillery from around the Bosnian capital Sarajevo or face airstrikes (the demands are largely met by February 17).

16 Greece imposes a trade ban on Macedonia in the ongoing dispute over Macedonia's status.

17 Libya extends the application of Islamic law, the sharia.

20 The United Arab Emirates extend the application of Islamic law, the sharia.

21 The former head of the U.S. Central Intelligence Agency (CIA) Soviet counterintelligence, Aldrich Hazen Ames, is arrested with his wife on charges of having spied for the USSR.

23 Bosnian and Croat forces in Bosnia-Herzegovina agree a cease-fire.

25 Over 50 Palestinians are massacred in a gun attack by an Israeli settler on a mosque in Hebron, on the West Bank, Israel; the following day the Israeli government seals off the West Bank and the Gaza Strip.

26 An amnesty for political prisoners is announced in Russia, including leaders of the attempted coup in 1991; Aleksander Rutskoi and Ruslan Khasbulatov are both released.

28 A Virginia judge releases Lorena Bobbitt from a mental hospital. The previous month she had been acquitted by reason of insanity of cutting off the penis of her husband, John Bobbitt.

MARCH

1   An International Atomic Energy Agency inspection team enters North Korea, but is not given access to certain key sites.

1   Negotiations are concluded on the enlargement of the European Union to include Sweden, Finland, and Austria.

11 Government forces rout armed right wing Afrikaaners attempting to maintain an independent white homeland in Bophuthatswana, South Africa.

16 Negotiations are concluded on the inclusion of Norway in the European Union, subject to approval in a national referendum.

18 Bosnia-Herzegovina and Croatia sign an accord on the creation of a federation of Bosnian Muslims and Croats.

20 President Zine al-Abidine Ben Ali of Tunisia and the Constitutional Democratic Rally (RCD) win elections, but new legislation ensures the presence of an opposition in the legislature.

22 South Korea places its forces on full alert after the breakdown of talks with North Korea.

23 Luis Donaldo Colosio, presidential candidate of the ruling Institutional Revolutionary Party (PRI), is assassinated in Mexico.

24 Allegations are made in the U.S. Congress that President Bill Clinton and his wife Hillary may have used their part-ownership of the Whitewater Development Corporation in Arkansas for improper purposes, especially in connection with the failed Madison Guaranty Savings Bank. (The affair, known as

"Whitewatergate," is already being looked into by a special investigator.)

24 The warring factions of General Muhammad Farah Aydid and President Ali Mahdi Muhammad in Somalia sign a peace agreement following United Nations-sponsored negotiations; U.S. troops withdraw the following day.

26–27 The right wing Freedom Alliance led by the businessman Silvio Berlusconi wins the parliamentary elections in Italy; Berlusconi becomes prime minister in May.

31 Serb troops bombard United Nations "safe areas" in Goradze and Srebrenica, Bosnia-Herzegovina.

31 The South African president F. W. de Klerk imposes a state of emergency in KwaZulu–Natal after 31 people die at an antielection demonstration by the Inkatha Freedom Party on March 28.

APRIL

8   Elections in Hungary result in a clear majority for the former communist Socialist Party led by Gyula Horn.

8   Morihiro Hosokawa resigns as prime minister of Japan after the weakening of his coalition and accusations of financial misconduct.

10 The Inkatha Freedom Party agrees to take part in multiparty general elections in South Africa, having received guarantees about the position of the Zulu monarchy in KwaZulu–Natal.

10–11 NATO (the North Atlantic Treaty Organization) makes air strikes on Serbian posts near the United Nations "safe area" of Goradze in Bosnia-Herzegovina, but subsequently (April 17) Goradze falls to Serb forces.

14 Greece deprives its former king, Constantine II, of his Greek citizenship.

20 The Popular Movement for the Liberation of Angola (MPLA) government of Angola and the National Union for the Total Independence of Angola (UNITA) reach agreement over principles for new elections.

23–27 A series of terrorist attacks are mounted in South Africa by white right wing groups attempting to disrupt elections.

26–29 The first nonracial general election in South Africa results in an overwhelming victory for the African National Congress (ANC).

MAY

6   Paula Jones files a case against the U.S. president Bill Clinton alleging sexual harassment when he was governor of Arkansas; a federal judge rules (July 21) that the case can be held pending until it has been determined whether an incumbent president is immune from civil law suits that predate his presidential term.

8   Ernesto Pérez Ballandares is elected president of Panama in the first election since the deposition of the dictator Manuel Noriega in 1989.

9   A cease-fire is established in Nagorno-Karabakh (an Armenian-populated enclave in Azerbaijan), with the support of an international peace-keeping force.

10 Nelson Mandela is sworn in as the first black president of South Africa. A new cabinet is formed the following day, including representatives from all four racial groups into which the population had been divided under the apartheid system.

11 Silvio Berlusconi, leader of the right wing Freedom Alliance, becomes prime minister of Italy.

13 Israel withdraws its military forces from the Jericho area of the occupied West Bank to make way for self-rule by the Palestinian National Authority, as agreed in Washington, D.C., in September 1993; five days later, on May 18, Israeli military forces are withdrawn from the Gaza Strip.

14 The government of Georgia and rebels in the breakaway region of Abkhazia agree a cease-fire, to be monitored by Russian peacekeepers.

18–21 European gypsies hold their first conference in Seville, Spain.

22 The Tutsi Rwandan Patriotic Front takes control of the capital Kigali after heavy fighting in the Rwandan civil war.

23 The United States tightens trade sanctions on Haiti, allowing only the import of essentials and upheld by a blockade searching incoming vessels.

26 The U.S. president Bill Clinton renews the "most favored nation" status granted to China, despite previous insistence that economic concessions be linked to improvements in China's human rights record.

27 Russian writer Alexander Solzhenitsyn returns to Russia after 20 years in exile.

30 The Democrat Dan Rostenkowski, chairman of the influential U.S. House of Representatives' Ways and Means Committee, is indicted on corruption charges.

JUNE

1 Armando Calderón Sol of the ruling Arena party is inaugurated as president of El Salvador following elections.

1 South Africa rejoins the British Commonwealth.

8 A cease-fire is signed in Bosnia-Herzegovina by leaders of the Bosnian Serbs and the Bosnian Federation, but it is soon broken by violations.

8 The U.S. president, Bill Clinton, who studied at Oxford University, England, from 1968 to 1970 but left without taking a degree, returns to Oxford for the award of an honorary doctorate of civil law.

12 The U.S. president Bill Clinton and his wife Hillary testify under oath about their involvement in the Whitewater financial scandal. (A Congressional committee begins a hearing on the affair on July 26.)

Nelson Mandela (1918–98)

1918

July 18 Nelson Mandela, South African nationalist, political prisoner, and president from 1994, born in Umtata, Cape of Good Hope, South Africa.

1960

March 30 Following demonstrations, strikes, and marches by blacks demanding civil rights, the South African government proclaims a state of emergency and passes the Unlawful Organizations Act. On April 8, the African National Congress (ANC) and Pan-African Congress are banned, and Mandela and others form Umkonto we Sizwe ("Spear of the Nation"), as the guerrilla wing of the ANC.

1961

March 29 Twenty-eight people, including Mandela, are tried for treason in South Africa. They are all acquitted.

1962

August 8 Mandela, is arrested when returning to Johannesburg from Natal. He is tried in November, and convicted of inciting workers to strike and of leaving the country without valid documents. He is sentenced to five years in prison.

1963

October 10 The "Rivonia trial" of the leaders of the Spear of the Nation, including Mandela and Walter Sisulu, opens; they are charged with sabotage and conspiracy to overthrow the government. Mandela is sentenced to life imprisonment, while eight other defendants receive lesser sentences, and one is discharged.

1985

February 10 Mandela refuses the South African government's offer of freedom, conditional on his renunciation of violence as a means to political change in the country.

1986

July 29 A United Nations mission to South Africa, led by British foreign secretary Geoffrey Howe, fails to secure the release of Mandela or the lifting of the ban on the ANC.

1988

June 11 A 70th Birthday Tribute concert for South African dissident political leader Nelson Mandela takes place at Wembley Stadium in London, England. Featuring acts such as Peter Gabriel, Simple Minds, George Michael, Annie Lennox, Miriam Makeba, and Youssou N'Dour, it represents a significant protest against the apartheid regime in South Africa.

July 18 The 70th birthday of Nelson Mandela, the African National Congress leader, is marked by worldwide protests calling for his release.

1990

February 11 Mandela is released after almost 26 years in prison.

1993

October 8 The international community lifts sanctions against South Africa in response to Mandela's speech of September 24 requesting this.

October 15 The Nobel Peace Prize is awarded jointly to the South African president F. W. de Klerk and Mandela for their work to reform the apartheid system.

1994

May 10 Mandela is sworn in as the first black president of South Africa. A new cabinet is formed the following day, including representatives from all four racial groups into which the population had been divided under the apartheid system.

1996

March 19 Mandela divorces his wife, Winnie, who has been linked with the murder of police informers during the apartheid years.

1998

February 6 Mandela opens the 1998 session of parliament in Pretoria, South Africa. He stresses employment and anticorruption measures in his state-of-the-nation speech.

14 Representatives of 25 European countries and Canada sign a United Nations protocol in Oslo, Norway, to reduce sulfur emissions, a cause of acid rain.

14 The United Nations completes a program to destroy Iraq's chemical weapons, in accordance with peace terms agreed after the Gulf War.

15–18 Jimmy Carter, former president of the United States, visits North Korea and helps defuse the crisis over inspection of nuclear facilities.

21 Legislation in Latvia imposes a language test for, and excludes former military personnel from, citizenship in a move aimed at disadvantaging Russian inhabitants.

23 France sends troops into Rwanda to protect refugees and support the humanitarian effort, following difficulties in establishing an international force.

23 The Land Development Law is suspended in Ecuador after widespread protests by the indigenous population, who claim that it has removed their grazing and watering rights.

24–25 A summit of European Union heads of government meets on the island of Corfu, at which (June 25) Prime Minister John Major of Britain vetoes the nomination of Jean-Luc Dehaene, prime minister of Belgium, as president of the European Commission (on July 15, Jacques Santer, prime minister of Luxembourg, is chosen as president).

29 Following the collapse of the previous coalition government, Tomiichi Murayama of the Social Democratic Party becomes prime minister of Japan.

JULY

1 Yassir Arafat, chairman of the Palestine Liberation Organization (PLO), enters Gaza, setting foot on Palestinian territory for the first time in 25 years; on July 5, he visits Jericho.

4–September 4 Oil workers in Nigeria strike in sympathy with the opposition presidential candidate Moshood Abiola, who is currently being tried for treason.

8 The leader of North Korea, Kim Il Sung, dies at the age of 82, prompting a struggle for the succession.

9 The government of the People's Republic of China announces that the British colony of Hong Kong's legislative council will be terminated on China's resumption of sovereignty in 1997; it rejects the reform package approved in the colony on June 30.

12 A federal constitutional court in Germany approves the principle that Germany's armed forces can be deployed outside the NATO (North Atlantic Treaty Organization) area in collective security operations (as has already happened in Somalia).

15 Jacques Santer, prime minister of Luxembourg, is elected president of the European Commission.

18 Over 2 million refugees are reported to have left Rwanda following the outbreak of ethnic violence.

18 The Tutsi-dominated Rwandan Patriotic Front claims victory in the Rwandan civil war; the following day, Pasteur Bizimungu assumes the presidency, with Hutu Faustin Twogiramunga as prime minister.

23 A military coup in the Gambia deposes President Sir Dawda Kairaba Jawara; on July 26, the 29-year-old coup leader Yahya Jammeh names himself president and promises elections.

25 King Hussein of Jordan and Yitzhak Rabin, prime minister of Israel, sign a joint declaration in

Washington, D.C., formally ending conflict between them (on October 26, a peace treaty is signed in a desert ceremony on the border between Jordan and Israel).

29 Dr. John Britton and his escort are shot dead by a prominent antiabortionist, Paul Hill, in Pensacola, Florida.

31 The United Nations Security Council authorizes "all necessary means" to remove the military regime in Haiti.

AUGUST

7 Ernesto Samper Pizano of the ruling Liberal Party is inaugurated as president of Colombia.

11 President Fidel Castro of Cuba lifts restrictions on those wishing to leave Cuba, provoking a major exodus from the island; by the end of August, 20,000 people have left. On August 19, the U.S. president Bill Clinton removes automatic refugee status for Cubans fleeing to the United States (and on September 9, restrictions on departures are reintroduced after agreement is reached between Cuba and the United States).

14 The international terrorist Ilich Ramírez Sánchez, known as "Carlos the Jackal," is arrested in Khartoum, Sudan.

16 The Sri Lankan ruling party, the United National Party, is defeated in legislative elections and replaced by the "People's Alliance," a left wing coalition led by Chandrika Kumaratunga.

21 Serb forces take the Muslim enclave of Bihać in Bosnia-Herzegovina.

22 Ernesto Zedillo becomes president of Mexico after an election victory for the center-right Institutional Revolutionary Party (PRI).

29–30 Russian troops finally withdraw from Estonia and (August 30) from Latvia, following the dissolution of the USSR.

31 The Irish Republican Army (IRA) in Northern Ireland announces its complete cessation of violence (the British government lifts its broadcasting ban on representatives of Sinn Féin on September 16).

SEPTEMBER

6 The Labour Party wins a landslide victory in Barbados; Owen Arthur becomes prime minister.

8 The last Russian troops leave Poland following the dissolution of the Warsaw Pact; U.S., British, and French troops make their formal departure from Berlin, Germany.

12 The separatist Parti Québecois wins an overall majority in the provincial legislature in Quebec, Canada.

19 U.S. troops invade Haiti to overthrow the military junta, encountering no resistance; on September 26, the United States lifts sanctions.

26 The U.S. president Bill Clinton's attempts to introduce health care reforms collapse in the face of opposition from Congress.

29 The former Belgian foreign minister Willy Claes is appointed secretary-general of NATO (the North Atlantic Treaty Organization).

30 The Russian president Boris Yeltsin lands at Shannon airport in the Republic of Ireland on his way back from a tour of the United States, but remains on board his plane, failing to meet the prime minister of Ireland, Albert Reynolds, who was waiting for him on the runway.

OCTOBER

3 Fernando Henrique Cardoso of the Social Democratic Party wins the presidential elections in Brazil.

13 Raoul Cédras, leader of the deposed junta in Haiti, takes exile in Panama.

15 President Jean-Bertrand Aristide returns to Haiti after three years in exile; on October 17, he agrees to leave the Roman Catholic priesthood in an attempt to mend his relationship with the Vatican, which opposes his liberation theology and is the only sovereign state to have recognized Raoul Cédras's military regime.

15 The Nobel Peace Prize is awarded to the Palestinian leader Yassir Arafat, and to the former prime minister and foreign minister Shimon Peres and the current prime minister Yitzhak Rabin of Israel.

16 The ruling center-right coalition led by Helmut Kohl retains office in Germany after a general election, but with a reduced majority.

20 Israel closes its borders with the West Bank and Gaza after attacks by the Palestinian organization Hamas, including the suicide bombing of a bus in Tel Aviv.

21 The United States reaches an agreement with North Korea over its nuclear program; North Korea agrees to submit to regular inspections, while the United States agrees to finance the modernization of North Korea's domestic nuclear industry and give it diplomatic recognition.

26 A peace treaty is signed in a desert ceremony on the border between Jordan and Israel, confirming the declaration signed by King Hussein of Jordan and Prime Minister Yitzhak Rabin of Israel in Washington, D.C., on July 25.

27 Mozambique holds multiparty elections; on November 19, the results give victory to President Joaquim Chissano of the Mozambique National Resistance (MNR).

31 The Lusaka Protocol is signed in a further attempt to end the Angolan civil war; the National Union for the Total Independence of Angola (UNITA) is given seats in government in return for the merging of its units with the regular army.

NOVEMBER

2 A rising in northern Pakistan begins, calling for the introduction of Islamic law.

7 South Korea lifts its ban on direct trade with North Korea.

7 The South African government dismisses 2,000 army trainees who had gone absent without leave in protest at camp conditions during the integration of the military wing of the African National Congress (ANC) into a new National Defense Force.

8 The Democrats suffer a heavy defeat in the U.S. midterm elections; the Republicans gain control of the House of Representatives and achieve a majority in the Senate, controlling both houses for the first time in 40 years.

8 The United Nations Security Council sets up an international criminal tribunal to prosecute those responsible for genocide in Rwanda and Burundi.

9 Prime Minister Chandrika Kumoratunga becomes the first woman president of Sri Lanka; her mother, Sirima Bandaranaike Kumaratunga, takes over as prime minister.

10 Iraq recognizes the independence of Kuwait.

10 The town of Huambo in Angola, the main stronghold of the National Union for the Total Independence of Angola (UNITA), falls to the People's Movement for the Liberation of Angola (MPLA) government forces.

12–13 Riots and demonstrations in East Timor during the arrival of delegates to an Asia–Pacific Cooperation meeting draws attention to oppression by Indonesian authorities.

17 Albert Reynolds resigns as prime minister of the Republic of Ireland after the collapse of his coalition government.

18 Violent clashes occur in the Gaza Strip between the Palestinian police force and supporters of the Palestinian organization Hamas and Islamic jihad.

21–25 NATO (the North Atlantic Treaty Organization) launches airstrikes on Serb positions in Bosnia-Herzegovina in response to the bombing of the United Nations safe area of Bihać.

22 The Italian prime minister Silvio Berlusconi is revealed to be under investigation for bribery.

25–26 In the breakaway Russian republic of Chechnya, opposition forces with Russian backing launch an unsuccessful attack on the capital Grozny; on November 29, the Russian president Boris Yeltsin issues an ultimatum, requiring both sides to lay down their arms.

27 Julio María Sanguinetti of the opposition Colorado Party is elected president of Uruguay.

27–28 A Norwegian referendum rejects European Union membership (52.4% vote against it).

28 Jeffrey Dahmer, the "Milwaukee Cannibal," imprisoned in 1992 for the murder of 17 men and boys, is murdered at Portage Prison, Wisconsin.

DECEMBER

11 Russian forces invade the breakaway republic of Chechnya.

12 The former Brazilian president Fernando de Collor is acquitted of corruption charges.

14 President Boris Yeltsin of Russia issues an ultimatum to the leader of the Chechen rebels, Dzhokhar Dudayev, to surrender or face invasion of the capital Grozny; it is rejected.

15 Following the resignation of Albert Reynolds as prime minister of the Republic of Ireland, John Bruton of the Fine Gael party forms a new coalition and becomes prime minister.

17 The presidents of Argentina, Brazil, Paraguay, and Uruguay sign a pact in Ouro Preto, Brazil, creating the Southern Common Market (Mercosur), in force from January 1, 1995.

21 The warring factions in Liberia sign a peace agreement in Ghana, ending civil war.

22 Silvio Berlusconi, the new prime minister of Italy, resigns to avoid probable defeat in a no-confidence vote in parliament.

30 Two women are killed and 15 others injured in a shooting at an abortion clinic in Brookline, Boston, Massachusetts.

31 Russian forces launch an offensive against Grozny, the capital of the breakaway republic of Chechnya.

31 The warring parties in Bosnia-Herzegovina sign a cease-fire with effect from January 1, 1995, to last for four months (until April 30).

SCIENCE, TECHNOLOGY, AND MEDICINE

Agriculture

FEBRUARY
- The U.S. Food and Drug Administration approves the use of genetically engineered bovine somatotropin (BST), that increases a cow's milk yield by 10–40%. It is banned in Europe.

OCTOBER
- The International Rice Research Institute introduces a new variety of rice that produces 200 rice grains per head, compared with the present 100. The plant is also more compact, enabling it to be planted more densely.

Computing

- Americans spend $89 billion on computers and video products, $19 billion on books and maps, $39 billion on toys and sport supplies, and $23 billion on newspapers and magazines.
- The World Wide Web, a computer network that allows users to utilize graphical interfaces through Web "browsers," makes the Internet much more accessible to general users and permits a freedom of information distribution not previously possible.

DECEMBER
20 U.S. microchip manufacturer Intel agrees to replace free of charge flawed Pentium chips that have been installed in more than four million computers in the United States.

Ecology

- One of the world's biggest oil spills occurs in the Komi region of northern Russia, when a broken pipeline leaks into the Pechora River.
- The International Whaling Commission establishes a whale sanctuary in Antarctica.
- The United Nations Basel Convention bans the transport of hazardous waste, from the 25 industrialized nations that make up the Organization for Economic Cooperation and Development (OECD), across international boundaries.

JANUARY
17 An earthquake hits southern California, killing 57 people.

Exploration

JANUARY
8 The Russian space mission *Soyuz-TM 18* is launched to the *Mir* space station. Russian cosmonaut Valery Polyakov plans to spend 14 months at the space station to study the effect on the human body of being in space for the time required to travel to Mars.

25 The U.S. spacecraft *Clementine* is launched. The objective of the mission is to make scientific observations of the moon and the near-Earth asteroid 1620 Geographos. The *Clementine* discovers an enormous crater on the far side of the moon. The South Pole-Aitken crater is 2,500 km/1,563 mi across and 13 km/8 mi deep, making it the largest crater in the solar system discovered so far. It also reveals the possibility of a permanent frozen water-ice deposit in a crater near the south pole of the moon. On May 7, a malfunction in one of the onboard computers causes the spacecraft to burn up all its fuel and go out of control, making the flyby of Geographos impossible.

FEBRUARY
- Russian cosmonaut Sergey Krikalev flies with U.S. astronauts Charles Bolden and Kenneth Reightler in the Space Shuttle *Discovery*. He is the first cosmonaut to fly on a U.S. mission in space.

DECEMBER
6 Pictures taken by the Hubble Space Telescope of galaxies in their infancy are published.

Health and Medicine

- An epidemic of diphtheria in Russia results in 47,802 cases and 1,746 deaths.
- The Nobel Prize for Physiology or Medicine is awarded jointly to the U.S. pharmacologist Alfred G. Gilman and the U.S. molecular biochemist Martin Rodbell for their discovery of a family of proteins that translate messages from outside a cell into action inside cells.
- Trials using transfusions of artificial blood begin in the United States. The blood contains genetically engineered hemoglobin.
- U.S. surgeons use lasers to successfully eliminate bullae (air blisters in the lungs caused by damage from disease) in a procedure called lung-reduction pneumenoplasty (LRP).

SEPTEMBER
- A gene that triggers breast cancer is identified and is found to be responsible for almost half the cases of inherited breast cancer and most cases of ovarian cancer.

OCTOBER
- The Pan American Health Organization declares the Americas to be free of polio.

NOVEMBER
27 RJ Reynolds Tobacco Company in the United States announces that it plans to test market next year a smokeless cigarette, called Eclipse, for those concerned about passive smoking.

DECEMBER
31 The number of AIDS cases worldwide exceeds 1 million for the first time, when the World Health Organization reports that there are 1,025,073 officially reported AIDS cases.

Math

- U.S. mathematician Andrew Wiles proves Fermat's last theorem, a problem that had remained unsolved since 1637.

Science

- A network of hundreds of Paleolithic cave drawings, rivaling those of Lascaux and Altamira, are discovered in the Grotte Chauvet cave in southeast France. They are dated the following year to between 30,340 and 32,410 years old, making them the world's oldest known paintings.
- A new species of kangaroo is discovered in Papua New Guinea. Known locally as the bondegezou, it weighs 15 kg/7 lb and is 1.2 m/3.9 ft in height.
- Bones of the earliest known human ancestor, a hominid named *Australopithecus ramidus*, are found in Ethiopia and dated at 4.4 million years old.
- Canadian physicist Bertram Brockhouse and U.S. physicist Clifford Shull share the Nobel Prize for Physics: Brockhouse for the development of neutron spectroscopy, and Shull for the development of neutron diffraction techniques.
- The closest pulsar to the earth (PSR J0108–1431) is discovered; it is 280 light-years away.
- The oldest surviving fungi are found as dormant spores in the hay lining the boots of the "iceman" who died 5,300 years ago and whose body was preserved in a glacier in the Alps (found in 1991).
- U.S. chemist George Olah receives the Nobel Prize for Chemistry for developing a technique for examining hydrocarbon molecules.

JULY

4 Electrical flashes known as "Sprites"—upper atmosphere optical phenomena associated with thunderstorms—are first examined by plane, by a team from the University of Alaska Statewide System, Fairbanks, Alaska, United States.

16–22 Fragments of the comet Shoemaker-Levy 9 collide with Jupiter.

SEPTEMBER

- The European Synchrotron Radiation Facility (ESRF) opens in Grenoble, France.

OCTOBER

- Ununnilium (atomic no. 110) is discovered by researchers at the heavy-ion cyclotron based at Darmstadt, Germany. It lasts for a millisecond.

NOVEMBER

26 Short stretches of dinosaur DNA are extracted by a team from the University of Provo, Utah, from unfossilized bone retrieved from coal deposits approximately 80 million years old.

DECEMBER

- The Apollo asteroid (an asteroid with an orbit that crosses that of Earth) 1994 XM1 passes within 100,000 km/60,000 mi of Earth, the closest observed approach of any asteroid.

Technology

- A nuclear reprocessing plant at Sellafield, Cumbria, England, begins operating. It reprocesses spent fuel from nuclear reactors from around the world and produces plutonium as the end product.

DECEMBER

- The Three Gorges Dam on the Chang Jiang River in China is officially opened. It is the world's largest hydroelectric project.

Transportation

- A scale model scramjet (supersonic combustion ramjet) is tested and produces speeds of 9,000 kph/5,590 mph (Mach 8.2). The scramjet uses oxygen from the atmosphere to burn its fuel.
- The U.S. Federal Aviation Administration requires all airliners to be equipped with an onboard radar called Traffic Alert and Collision Avoidance System, which warns pilots of an impending collision.

APRIL

6 The presidents of Rwanda and Burundi, Juvénal Habyarimana and Cyprien Ntaryamira, are killed in an airplane crash; interethnic violence erupts on a huge scale.

MAY

6 The Channel Tunnel between Britain and France is officially opened by Queen Elizabeth II of Britain and the French president François Mitterrand.

JUNE

12 The U.S. Boeing 777 airliner makes its first flight.

SEPTEMBER

28 The car ferry *Estonia* sinks in the Baltic off Finland; an estimated 900 people die.

DECEMBER

2 In a settlement with U.S. government investigators, General Motors agrees to pay $51.3 million to fund various motor safety programs. The deal ends an investigation into safety hazards associated with GM trucks.

ARTS AND IDEAS

Architecture

- The Groninger Museum in Groninger, Netherlands, designed by the Italian architect Alessandro Mendini and others, is completed.

JUNE

16 The Swedish government approves the "Öresund link" project to connect Sweden with Denmark by bridge and tunnel.

Arts

- The controversial cleaning of Michelangelo's paintings in the Sistine Chapel in the Vatican is completed.

- The English artist Damian Hirst creates *Away from the Flock*.
- The exhibition "Some Went Mad: Some Ran Away" is held at the Serpentine Gallery in London, England.
- The Tate Gallery in London, England, selects Bankside Power Station on the south bank of the Thames as the future home for London's first Museum of Modern Art.

Film

- The documentary *Crumb*, directed by Terry Zwigoff, is released in the United States, based on the life and work of U.S. cartoonist Robert Crumb.
- The movie *Ace Ventura: Pet Detective*, directed by Tom Shadyac, is released in the United States, starring Jim Carrey and Courteney Cox.
- The movie *Amateur*, directed by Hal Hartley, is released in the United States, starring Isabelle Huppert, Martin Donovan, Elina Lowensohn, and Damian Young.
- The movie *Amnesia*, directed by Gonzalo Justiniano, is released in Chile, starring Julio Jung, Pedro Vicuña, and Nelson Villagra.
- The movie *Bandit Queen*, directed by Shekhar Kapur, is released in India. Based on the life of Phoolan Devi, who led a gang in Uttar Pradesh, it stars Seema Biswas.
- The movie *Blue Sky*, directed by English filmmaker Tony Richardson, is released in the United States, starring Jessica Lange and Tommy Lee Jones.
- The movie *Bullets over Broadway*, directed by Woody Allen, is released in the United States, starring John Cusack, Jennifer Tilly, Dianne Wiest, and Chazz Palminteri.
- The movie *Clear and Present Danger*, directed by Phillip Noyce, is released in the United States, based on the novel by Tom Clancy and starring Harrison Ford, Willem Dafoe, and Anne Archer.
- The movie *Death and the Maiden*, directed by Roman Polanski, is released in the United States. Based on the play by Ariel Dorfman, it stars Sigourney Weaver and Ben Kingsley.
- The movie *Disclosure*, directed by Barry Levinson, is released in the United States, based on the novel by Michael Crichton and starring Michael Douglas and Demi Moore.
- The movie *Eat Drink Man Woman*, directed by Ang Lee, is released in Taiwan, starring Sihung Lung, Kuei-Mei Yang, Chien-Lien Wu, Yu-Wen Wang, and Winston Chao.
- The movie *Ed Wood*, directed by Tim Burton, is released in the United States, starring Johnny Depp and Martin Landau.
- The movie *Faraway, So Close*, directed by Wim Wenders, is released in Germany. A sequel to *Wings of Desire*, it stars Otto Sander, Peter Falk, and Bruno Ganz and has cameo appearances from Lou Reed and Mikhail Gorbachev.
- The movie *Forrest Gump*, directed by Robert Zemeckis, is released in the United States, based on the book by Winston Groom and starring Tom Hanks.
- The movie *Four Weddings and a Funeral*, directed by Mike Newell, is released in Britain, starring Hugh Grant and Andie MacDowell.

- The movie *Geronimo*, directed by Walter Hill, is released in the United States, starring Wes Studi.
- The movie *L'Enfer/Torment*, directed by Claude Chabrol, is released in France, starring Emmanuelle Béart and François Cluzet.
- The movie *La reine Margot/Queen Margot*, directed by Patrice Chereau, is released in France, starring Isabelle Adjani, Daniel Auteuil, and Jean-Hughes Anglade.
- The movie *Léon*, directed by French filmmaker Luc Besson, is released in the United States, starring Jean Reno, Natalie Portman, and Gary Oldman.
- The movie *Legends of the Fall*, directed by Edward Zwick, is released in the United States, starring Anthony Hopkins, Brad Pitt, Aidan Quinn, and Henry Thomas.
- The movie *Mary Shelley's Frankenstein*, directed by Kenneth Branagh, is released in the United States. He also stars in it along with Robert De Niro, Tom Hulce, and Helena Bonham-Carter.
- The movie *Natural Born Killers*, directed by Oliver Stone, is released in the United States, starring Woody Harrelson and Juliette Lewis. It proves to be controversial, with its proclaimed message of the dangers of media glorification of violence lost in what looks like a celebration of the violence it denounces.
- The movie *Nobody's Fool*, directed by Robert Benton, is released in the United States. Based on the novel by Richard Russo, it stars Paul Newman, Jessica Tandy, and Melanie Griffith.
- The movie *Once Were Warriors*, directed by Lee Tamahori, is released in New Zealand, starring Rem Owen, Temuera Morrison, and Mamaengaroa Kerr-Bell.
- The movie *Prêt-à-Porter*, directed by Robert Altman, is released in the United States. A satire of the fashion world, it has a huge star cast, including Anouk Aimeé, Lauren Bacall, Richard E. Grant, Marcello Mastroianni, Tim Robbins, and Julia Roberts.
- The movie *Pulp Fiction*, directed by Quentin Tarantino, is released in the United States, starring John Travolta, Samuel L. Jackson, Uma Thurman, Tim Roth, and Harvey Keitel. It is awarded the Palme d'Or at the Cannes Film Festival in France.
- The movie *Quiz Show*, directed by Robert Redford, is released in the United States, starring John Turturro and Ralph Fiennes.
- The movie *Sirens*, directed by John Duigan, is released in Australia, starring Hugh Grant, Tara Fitzgerald, and Sam Neill.
- The movie *Speed*, directed by Dutch filmmaker Jan de Bont, is released in the United States, starring Keanu Reeves, Dennis Hopper, and Sandra Bullock.
- The movie *Star Trek: Generations*, directed by David Carson, is released in the United States. Marking the end of the series of movies based on the original television program *Star Trek* and the beginning of a new series based on *Star Trek: The Next Generation*, it stars Patrick Stewart, William Shatner, Malcolm McDowell, and many members of the cast of both programs.
- The movie *The Adventures of Priscilla, Queen of the Desert*, directed by Stephan Elliot, is released in Australia, starring Terence Stamp.
- The movie *The Client*, directed by Joel Schumacher, is released in the United States. Based on the novel by John

Grisham, it stars Susan Sarandon and Tommy Lee Jones.

- The movie *The Flintstones*, directed by Brian Levant, is released in the United States, based on the television animation series, and starring John Goodman, Elizabeth Perkins, Rick Moranis, and Rosie O'Donnell.
- The movie *The Last Seduction*, directed by John Dahl, is released in the United States, starring Linda Fiorentino.
- The movie *The Mask*, directed by Charles Russell, is released in the United States, starring Jim Carrey and Cameron Diaz.
- The movie *The Pelican Brief*, directed by Alan J. Pakula, is released in the United States. Based on the novel by John Grisham, it stars Julia Roberts and Denzel Washington.
- The movie *The Paper*, directed by Ron Howard, is released in the United States, starring Michael Keaton, Glenn Close, Robert Duvall, and Marisa Tomei.
- The movie *The Shawshank Redemption*, directed by Frank Darabont, is released in the United States. Based on the novel by Stephen King, it stars Tim Robbins and Morgan Freeman.
- The movie *To Live*, directed by Zhang Yimou, is released in China, starring Ge You and Gong Li.
- The movie *Vanya on 42nd Street*, directed by French filmmaker Louis Malle, is released in the United States. Constructed around a rehearsal by André Gregory of Chekhov's *Uncle Vanya*, it stars Wallace Shawn.
- The movie *Wolf*, directed by Mike Nichols, is released in the United States, starring Jack Nicholson and Michelle Pfeiffer.
- The movies *Trois Couleurs: Blanc/Three Colors White*, starring Julie Delpy and Zbigniew Zamachowski, and *Trois Couleurs: Rouge/Three Colors Red*, starring Irène Jacob, Jean-Louis Trintignant, Jean-Pierre Lorit, and Juliette Binoche, are released in France. They are the second and third of a trilogy of movies by the Polish filmmaker Krzystof Kieślowski. They have been preceded by *Trois Couleurs: Blue/Three Colors Blue* (1993).
- The Walt Disney animated movie *The Lion King* is released in the United States.

MARCH

21 The 1993 Academy Awards are held. Best Actor: Tom Hanks, for *Philadelphia*; Best Supporting Actor: Tommy Lee Jones, for *The Fugitive*; Best Actress: Holly Hunter, for *The Piano*; Best Supporting Actress: Anna Paquin, for *The Piano*; Best Director: Steven Spielberg, for *Schindler's List*; Best Picture: *Schindler's List*, directed by Steven Spielberg.

OCTOBER

October, 1994–January 1995   French dubbing actors go on strike, in a claim for "residual fees," alleging that 90% of the movie-going public prefer dubbed to subtitled movies.

DECEMBER

27 The year's top ten grossing movies in the United States are *Forrest Gump*, *The Lion King*, *True Lies*, *The Flintstones*, *Santa Clause*, *Clear and Present Danger*, *Speed*, *The Mask*, *Maverick*, and *Interview with a Vampire*.

Literature and Language

c. 1994   The term "himbo" is coined for brainless but good-looking men, the male equivalent of "bimbo."

- *One Art*, the collected letters of the U.S. writer Elizabeth Bishop, is published posthumously, edited by Robert Giroux.
- The Australian writer Peter Carey publishes his novel *The Unusual Life of Tristan Smith*.
- The British writer Louis de Bernières publishes his novel *Captain Corelli's Mandolin*.
- The English poet James Fenton publishes his poetry collection *Out of Danger*.
- The Irish writer Paul Durcan publishes his poetry collection *Give Me Your Hand*.
- The Nobel Prize for Literature is awarded to the Japanese novelist Kenzaburo Oe.
- The Pulitzer Prize for Biography is awarded to David Levering Lewis for *W E B DuBois: The Biography of a Race*, the Pulitzer Prize for Poetry is awarded to Yusef Komunyakaa for *Neon Vernacular*, and the Pulitzer Prize for Fiction is awarded to E. Annie Proulx for *The Shipping News*.
- The U.S. cultural critic Camille Paglia publishes *Vamps and Tramps: New Essays*.
- The U.S. journalist and writer John Berendt publishes his "nonfiction novel" *Midnight in the Garden of Good and Evil*.
- The U.S. writer Amy Clampitt publishes her poetry collection *A Silence Opens*.
- The U.S. writer Coraghessan T. Boyle publishes his short-story collection *Without A Here*.
- The U.S. writer E. L. Doctorow publishes his novel *The Waterworks*.
- The U.S. writer James Broughton publishes his poetry collection *Little Sermons on the Big Joy*.
- The U.S. writer John Irving publishes his novel *A Son of the Circus*.
- The U.S. writer John Updike publishes *The After Life and Other Stories*.
- The U.S. writer Joseph Heller publishes his novel *Closing Time*.
- The U.S. writer Philip Levine publishes *The Bread of Time: Towards an Autobiography*.
- The U.S. writer William Gaddis publishes his novel *A Frolic of his Own*.

Music

c. 1994   Punk enjoys a revival in fashion and music, with both old and new bands emerging.

- The British dance group m people releases the album *Elegant Slumming*.
- The British pop group D: Ream releases the single "Things Can Only Get Better."
- The British pop group Take That is the first pop group to have four successive singles go into the British charts at number one.
- The British progressive rock group Pink Floyd releases the album *The Division Bell*.
- The British rock group Blur releases the album *Parklife*.
- The British rock group Oasis releases the album *Definitely Maybe*.

- The British rock group the Rolling Stones releases the album *Voodoo Lounge*.
- The British rock singer Elvis Costello releases the album *Brutal Youth*.
- The British singer George Michael takes his record label Sony to court in an attempt to extract himself from a contract which he claims restricts his creativity. He loses the case.
- The Danish singer Whigfield releases the single "Saturday Night."
- The English composer Peter Maxwell Davies completes his Symphony No. 5.
- The English composer John Tavener completes his choral work *The Apocalypse*.
- The Swedish pop group Ace of Base releases the single "Don't Turn Around" and the album *The Sign aka Happy Nation*.
- The U.S. performance artist Laurie Anderson releases the album *Bright Red*.
- The U.S. pop group All-4-One releases the single "I Swear."
- The U.S. pop singer Mariah Carey releases the album *Music Box*.
- The U.S. pop singer Prince releases the album *Come*.
- The U.S. rap group the Beastie Boys releases the album *Ill Communication*.
- The U.S. rap singer Snoop Doggy Dogg releases the album *Doggy Style*.
- The U.S. rock group REM releases the album *Monster*.
- The U.S. folk/rock singer Bob Dylan allows the accounting firm Coopers & Lybrand to use his song "The Times They Are A-Changin'" in an advertisement.
- The U.S. rock singer/songwriter Prince changes his name to a symbol, a stylized elaboration of the male and female symbols, and from now on is known as "the Artist formerly known as Prince."
- The U.S. singer David Byrne releases the album *David Byrne*.
- Woodstock 94 takes place in New York State. A commemoration of the original Woodstock concert 25 years before, it features acts such as the Red Hot Chili Peppers, Metallica, and Joe Cocker.

MARCH

1   The 1993–94 Grammy Awards are held. Best Song: "A Whole New World," from the film *Aladdin*; Best Album: *The Bodyguard*, by Whitney Houston; Best Male Pop Vocalist: Sting; Best Female Pop Vocalist: Whitney Houston; Best Pop Duo: Peabo Bryson and Regina Belle.

DECEMBER

30 In Rome, Italy, a judge rules that U.S. pop star Michael Jackson plagiarized a song by Italian singer Al Bano and bans the sale of Jackson's album *Dangerous* on which the song, "Will You Be There?," appears.

Theater and Dance

- The play *Pentecost*, by the English dramatist David Edgar, is first performed, in Stratford-upon-Avon, England.
- The play *Skylight*, by the English dramatist David Hare, is first performed, in London, England.

- The play *The Cryptogram*, by the U.S. writer David Mamet, is first performed, in New York, New York.
- The play *Three Tall Women*, by the U.S. dramatist Edward Albee, is first performed, in New York, New York.
- The Pulitzer Prize for Drama is awarded to Edward Albee for *Three Tall Women*.

JUNE

5   The 1993–94 Tony Awards are held. Best Play (awarded jointly): *Angels in America: Perestroika: Millenium Approaches*; Best Musical: *Passion*; Best Actor: Stephen Spinella; Best Actress: Diana Rigg.

Thought and Scholarship

- *The Oxford History of the American West* is published, edited by Clyde A. Smith and others.
- Palestinian-American critic Edward Said publishes *The Politics of Dispossession*.
- The English historian Eric Hobsbawm publishes *Age of Extremes: The Short Twentieth Century, 1914–1991*.
- The Pulitzer Prize for History is not awarded this year.
- The Pulitzer Prize for General Nonfiction is awarded to David Remnick for *For Lenin's Tomb*.

SOCIETY

Everyday Life

- In the United States, 124 million people have credit cards, holding 1.1 billion cards in all, and a total of $366.4 billion in credit card debt.
- Twenty-four million people play golf in the United States, up from 13 million in 1975.
- In the United States, 37.9 million state and federal fishing licenses and 31.6 million hunting licenses are issued.
- Approximately one in six (42,359) Americans are crime victims; about three-quarters are victims of property crimes. There are 23,300 murders, 102,100 rapes, 619 robberies, 1.12 million aggravated assaults, and 1.54 million car thefts in the United States.
- Fifty-nine per cent of U.S. households have basic cable and 74% have VCRs.
- In the United States, 681,457,000 visits are made to physician's offices; women make 60% of these visits.
- A U.S. Census Bureau survey finds that 53% of employees are provided with a group health plan and 41% of employees participate in a company pension plan.
- About 40 million Americans, one in six, lack health insurance.
- According to a Gallup survey, 30% of U.S. homes have a vegetable garden and 10% have an herb garden.
- According to the U.S. Census Bureau, 12.4% of Americans live in cities with populations of more than 1 million, 15% live in cities with populations between 50,000 and 99,999, and 18% live in towns of less than 10,000 people.

- Americans make 8,135,000 ATM transactions.
- Americans save $192 billion, down from $272 billion in 1992.
- Americans take 221 million business trips and 801 million vacation or pleasure trips this year.
- An estimated 33.4 million people in the United States suffer from some form of arthritis.
- An estimated 4 million undocumented aliens enter the United States, nearly half of that total into California.
- Beef is the most popular meat in the United States, followed by chicken, pork, turkey, and fish.
- Blacks are 20% more likely than whites to be victims of crime in the United States, and a member of a household with an income of less than $15,000 is more than twice as likely to be a victim of crime as a member of a household with an income of more than $75,000.
- California has the largest number of immigrants of all U.S. states, about 208,000 people; New York is next with 144,000.
- In the United States, 11,912,000 people are arrested, the most common charge being theft and the next most common being drug-related.
- In the United States this year, 138 police officers are killed while on duty.
- In the United States' public schools (kindergarten through high school), there are 4.4 million computers in use in classrooms, or one computer for every 11 students.
- In the United States, 38.1 million people, or 14.5% of the population, live below the government-defined poverty level.
- In the United States, 94% of households have a telephone, 98% have a radio, and 98% have a television.
- In the United States, Levi's introduces a custom-fit service for their mass-produced jeans.
- Mini-backpacks are a popular accessory.
- Of the $919.2 billion (13.7% of the Gross Domestic Product) spent on health care services in the United States, an increase of 6.4%, far lower than the 15% increase in 1980 and 12% increase in 1990, private business pays $241.3 billion, households pay $310.3 billion, the federal government pays $190.6 billion, state and local government pays $151.3 billion, and other nonpatient revenues total $25.9 billion. The average cost per American for health care is $3,510.
- Of the 804,000 people who immigrate to the United States, 161,000 come from Europe, 293,000 come from Asia, and 47,000 come from South America.
- Piercing of noses, navels, tongues, lips, and even nipples, becomes increasingly popular in the United States and Europe.
- The average person in the United States drinks 131 gallons of nonalcoholic beverages (including 25 gallons of milk and 52 gallons of soft drinks) and 36 gallons of alcoholic beverages a year.
- The average U.S. citizen spends $3,500 on personal health care, an increase from $500 in 1970 and $1,800 in 1983.
- The average U.S. consumer spends $110 on basic cable, $79 on books, $73 for home videos, $56 for recorded music, $49 for daily newspapers, $36 for magazines, and $7 for Internet access per year.
- The average vacation in the United States is 3.4 nights, down from 5.6 nights in 1985.
- The median household income in the United States is $32,264—for whites, $34,028; for blacks, $21,027; and for Hispanics, $23,421.
- The U.S. Border Patrol arrests 1.04 million people trying to enter the United States illegally.
- The U.S. Census Bureau estimates that accidental injuries cause productivity loss and wage and property losses of more than $440 billion.
- The United States' prisons hold 1,054,000 inmates, an all-time record. Of these, 2,890 are on death row.
- There are 1,512 commercial television stations in the United States.
- There are 198,045,000 cars, trucks, and buses in the United States.

BIRTHS & DEATHS

- Jan Tinbergen, Dutch economist who, with Ragnar Frisch, received the first Nobel Prize for Economics for developing econometrics, dies in The Hague, the Netherlands (90).

JANUARY

1 Cesar Romero, U.S. actor, dies in Santa Monica, California (86).

2 Dixie Lee Ray, U.S. zoologist who popularized science, dies in Fox Island, Washington (79).

5 "Tip" (Thomas Philip) O'Neill, U.S. speaker of the U.S. House of Representatives 1977–86, dies in Boston, Massachusetts (81).

22 Aristoteles ("Telly") Savalas, U.S. actor known for his role as New York City police lieutenant Kojak, dies in Universal City, California (70).

28 William Jaird Levitt, U.S. architect who pioneered the use of mass-produced single-dwelling houses for U.S. servicemen returning from World War II, dies in Manhasset, New York (86).

FEBRUARY

6 Jack Kirby, U.S. comic book artist who created over 400 characters including Spiderman, the Incredible Hulk, and Captain America, dies in Thousand Oaks, California (76).

9 Howard Martin Temin, U.S. virologist who, with Renato Dulbecco and David Baltimore, discovered reverse transcriptase, dies in Madison, Wisconsin (59).

19 Derek Jarman, English filmmaker of innovative and controversial films, dies in London, England (52).

24 Frances Rose ("Dinah") Shore, U.S. singer, dies in Los Angeles, California (73).

24 Jean Sablon, French singer popular in the United States and Europe during the 1930s, dies in Cannes-la-Bocca, France (87).

MARCH

4 John (Franklin) Candy, Canadian comedian, dies in Durango, Mexico (43).

6 Melina Mercouri, Greek actress and politician, dies in New York, New York (68).

9 Fernando Rey, Spanish actor, dies in Madrid, Spain (76).

9 Lawrence Edmund Spivak, U.S. journalist who founded the radio program *Meet the Press*, dies in Washington, D.C. (93).

22   Walter Lantz, U.S. animator who created Woody Woodpecker, dies in Burbank, California (93).

28   Eugène Ionescu, Romanian-born French dramatist whose play *La Cantatrice chauve/The Bald Prima Donna* (1950) inspired the Theater of the Absurd, dies in Paris, France (81).

APRIL

3   Jérôme-Jean-Louis-Marie Lejeune, French geneticist who discovered the first chromosomal abnormality (trisomy 21, responsible for Down's syndrome), dies in Paris, France (67).

8   Kurt Cobain, U.S. lead singer of the rock group Nirvana, commits suicide in Seattle, Washington (27).

16   Ralph Waldo Ellison, black U.S. novelist known for his novel *Invisible Man* (1952), dies in New York, New York (80).

17   Roger Wolcott Sperry, U.S. neurologist who elucidated the functions of different parts of the human brain, dies in Pasadena, California (80).

22   Richard M(ilhous) Nixon, 37th president of the United States 1969–74, a Republican, the first president to resign, dies in New York, New York (81).

MAY

1   Ayrton Senna, Brazilian race-car driver, is killed at Imola, Italy, when his car crashes during the San Marino Grand Prix (34).

8   George Peppard, U.S. film actor, dies in Los Angeles, California (65).

12   Erik (Homburger) Erikson, German-born U.S. psychoanalytic theorist who coined the phrase "identity crisis," dies in Harwich, Massachusetts (91).

19   Jacqueline Bouvier Kennedy Onassis, wife of President John F. Kennedy, dies in New York, New York (64).

24   John (Barrington) Wain, English poet and novelist, one of the "Angry Young Men," dies in Oxford, England (69).

25   Eric Honecker, German communist politician, leader of East Germany 1971–89, dies in Santiago, Chile (81).

JUNE

12   Menachem Mendel Schneerson, Russian-born U.S. rabbi, leader in 1950 of the Lubavitch right wing orthodox Judaic movement, dies in New York, New York (92).

14   Henry Mancini, U.S. composer noted for his film scores, dies in Los Angeles, California (70).

21   William Wilson Morgan, U.S. astronomer who discovered the spiral structure of the Milky Way, dies in Williams Bay, Wisconsin (88).

JULY

8   Kim Il Sung, Korean dictator 1948–94, dies in Pyongyang, North Korea (82).

16   Julian Seymour Schwinger, U.S. quantum physicist whose research concerned the behavior of charged particles in electrical fields, winner of the Nobel Prize for Physics in 1965, dies in Los Angeles, California (76).

20   Paul Delvaux, Belgian surrealist renowned for his unearthly canvases portraying female nudes in settings of ruined, classical architecture, dies in Veurne, Belgium (96).

28   Colin Macmillan Turnbull, British anthropologist known for his work among the pygmies, dies in Harrow, England (69).

29   Dorothy Hodgkin (born Dorothy Crowfoot), English chemist who determined the structure of vitamin B_{12} and won the Nobel Prize for Chemistry in 1964, dies in Shipton-on-Stour, Warwickshire, England (84).

AUGUST

11   Peter Cushing, English actor known for his roles of Dracula, Frankenstein, and Dr Who, dies in Canterbury, Kent, England (81).

13   Elias Canetti, Bulgarian-born English novelist and playwright, winner of the Nobel Prize for Literature in 1981, dies in Zürich, Switzerland (89).

13   Manfred Wörner, German defense minister who was secretary-general of NATO 1988–94, dies in Brussels, Belgium (59).

18   Richard Laurence Millington Synge, English biochemist who, with Archer J. P. Martin, developed partition chromatography, dies in Norwich, Norfolk, England (79).

19   Linus Pauling, U.S. chemist who won the Nobel Prize for Chemistry in 1954 for his discoveries concerning chemical bonding, and the Nobel Peace Prize in 1962 for crusading against the use of nuclear weapons, dies in Big Sur, California (93).

SEPTEMBER

6   James Clavell, U.S. novelist, dies in Vevel, Switzerland (69).

11   Jessica Tandy, British-born U.S. actress, dies in Easton, Connecticut (84).

17   Karl Raimund Popper, Austrian-born English philosopher who argued that only one exception was needed to prove a hypothesis false, dies in Croydon, Surrey, England (92).

18   Vitas Gerulaitis, U.S. tennis player, dies in Southampton, New York (40).

20   Jule (Julius Kerwin) Styne, English-born U.S. composer of songs, mainly for musicals and films, dies in New York, New York (89).

OCTOBER

7   Niels Kaj Jerne, British-Danish immunologist who theorized that the body has an immense variety of antibodies that are activated when needed, dies in Castillon-du-Gard, France (82).

20   Burt Lancaster, U.S. film actor, dies in Los Angeles, California (80).

22   Rollo Reece May, U.S. psychologist who pioneered existential psychology, dies in Tiburon, California (85).

24   Raul Julia, U.S. film actor, dies in New York, New York (54).

29   Pearl Primus, U.S. dancer, choreographer, and dance teacher who pioneered an awareness and understanding of the black American tradition in dance, dies in New Rochelle, New York (74).

NOVEMBER

12   Wilma Glodean Rudolph, U.S. track and field athlete who, at the 1960 Olympics, became the first U.S. woman to win three gold medals at a single Olympics, dies in Brentwood, Tennessee (54).

18   Cab Calloway, U.S. entertainer and big band leader known for his recording "Minnie the Moocher," dies in Hockessin, Delaware (86).

28   Jerry Rubin, U.S. political activist during the Vietnam era, dies in Los Angeles, California (56).

DECEMBER

13   Antoine Pinay, French finance minister and premier of France 1952 who brought inflation in France under control after World War II and who introduced a new franc by devaluing the old one, dies in Saint-Chamond, France (102).

20   Dean Rusk, U.S. secretary of state under Kennedy and Johnson, dies in Athens, Georgia (85).

- There are 267.6 million visits to national parks, monuments, recreation areas, and the like in the United States this year.
- There are 4,913 AM radio stations and 5,109 FM stations in the United States.
- There are 55,364 students enrolled in public schools in the United States (kindergarten through high school) and 8,741 in private schools.
- There are 5.4 million Boy Scouts and 3.4 million Girl Scouts in the United States.
- There are 5.88 million people of the Jewish faith in the United States, accounting for 2.3% of the nation's population. New York State has the largest Jewish population, 1.6 million people or 9% of the state's population.
- There are 845,257 filings for bankruptcies in the United States; of these 7% are business and 93% are personal. The number of bankruptcies declines 8% from the previous year.
- U.S. businesses spend $11.9 billion advertising on television.
- U.S. consumers buy 212.7 billion books.
- U.S. consumers spend $10 billion on CDs, cassettes, and albums.

JANUARY

- German designer Karl Lagerfeld stirs up controversy when he creates a dress decorated with phrases from the Koran. The design is quickly withdrawn.
27 A 24-hour general strike takes place in Spain, in protest against reforms of the labor market.

MAY

- The first genetically engineered food goes on sale in California and Chicago, Illinois. The "Flavr Savr" tomato is produced by the U.S. biotechnology company Calgene.

SEPTEMBER

12 Frank Corder, a truck-driver from Maryland, commits suicide by crashing a two-seater Cessna aircraft on the south lawn of the White House.
17 For the first time, contestants in the bathing suit round of the Miss America beauty pageant, held in Atlantic City, New Jersey, go barefoot rather than wearing high heels.

NOVEMBER

19 The National Lottery, the first regular British national lottery, is launched, under government control and run by Camelot. It is the largest lottery in the world.

Media and Communication

- A Gallup poll claims that 80% of U.S. citizens have watched an "infomercial" or other direct response advertisement, and 20% have ordered from them.
- Iconoclastic television journalist Michael Moore produces his *TV Nation* program for U.S. and British television.
- Prodigy Services Co., a partnership of IBM and Sears, introduces Prodigy PC Via Cable, an interactive television system for the home, which uses a home computer to deliver supplementary material on television programs.

MAY

- The British men's magazine *Loaded* is launched.

JUNE

- The Dutch electronics company Philips launches movies on digital video disc, using technology developed jointly by Philips and Japanese electronics company Sony.

SEPTEMBER

11 The 1993–94 Emmy Awards for television are held. Best Drama Series: *Picket Fences*; Best Comedy Series: *Frasier*; Best Actor in a Drama: Dennis Franz, for *NYPD Blue*; Best Actress in a Drama: Sela Ward, for *Sisters*; Best Actor in a Comedy: Kelsey Grammer, for *Frasier*; Best Actress in a Comedy: Candice Bergen, for *Murphy Brown*.
22 The comedy *Friends* begins on U.S. television. Based on the lives of six young friends in New York, New York, it stars Courteney Cox, Jennifer Aniston, Lisa Kudrow, Matt Perry, Matt Le Blanc, and David Schwimmer.
22 The medical drama *ER* begins on U.S. television, starring George Clooney, Anthony Edwards, Noah Wyle, Eriq La Salle, and Julianna Margulies.

Sports

- For the first time, all the major U.S. golf tournaments are won by foreign players: José Maria Olazábal of Spain wins the U.S. Masters; Ernie Els of South Africa, the U.S. Open; and Nick Price of Zimbabwe, the U.S. PGA (Professional Golfers Association) Championship.
- The Houston Rockets defeat the New York Knicks by four games to three to win their first National Basketball Association (NBA) title.
- The New York Rangers defeat the Vancouver Canucks by four games to three to win their first National Hockey League (NHL) Stanley Cup since 1940.
- The ten most popular sports activities in the United States (by percentage of participants) are exercise walking, swimming, biking, exercising with equipment, camping, fishing, bowling, basketball, hiking, and golf.
- The U.S. golfer Tiger Woods, aged 18, becomes the youngest winner of the U.S. Amateur Championship, at Ponte Vedra Beach, Florida.
- Twenty-one years after losing the undisputed world heavyweight boxing title, George Foreman knocks out fellow U.S. boxer Michael Moorer in Las Vegas, Nevada, to win the World Boxing Association and International Boxing Federation versions of the crown. At 45 years old, he is the oldest ever world heavyweight champion.

JANUARY

30 The Dallas Cowboys defeat the Buffalo Bills 30–3 in Super Bowl XXVIII. It is the second win in a row for the Cowboys and the Bills' fourth consecutive defeat in the Super Bowl.
30 The Hungarian chess player Peter Leko, aged 14, becomes the world's youngest-ever grand master.

FEBRUARY

12–27 The 17th Winter Olympic Games are held in Lillehammer, Norway. For the first time the winter games are not held in the same year as the summer games. Competitors number 1,737, from 67 countries compete in 61 medal events. Russia wins 11 golds; Norway, 10; Germany, 9; Italy, 7; and the United States, 6. Alberto Tomba of Italy becomes the first skiier to win golds in Alpine events at three successive Olympics. The Swiss skiier Vreni Schneider wins a record five Alpine medals, including three golds. In speed skating, Bonnie Blair of the United States wins her third consecutive women's title at 500 meters and her second consecutive one at 1,000 meters, while Johann Olav-Koss of Norway wins three of the men's titles.

APRIL

27–November 6   The world one-hour cycling record is broken four times during the year, all at Bordeaux, France. In April, the Scottish cyclist Graham Obree regains the record he lost to the English rider Chris Boardman nine months earlier with a distance of 52.713 km/32.755 mi. In September, Miguel Induráin of Spain extends the record to 53.040 km/32.959 mi, only for Tony Rominger of Switzerland to set a new mark of 53.832 km/33.451 mi a month later. Finally, on November 6, Rominger adds another 1.459 km/0.907 mi to take the record beyond 55 km/34 mi.

JUNE

June–July   The 15th soccer World Cup is held in the United States. Brazil wins for a record fourth time, defeating Italy 3–2 on penalties after the game ends scoreless after extra time. The match is watched by a crowd of 94,000 at the Pasadena Rose Bowl, California.

JULY

2   Conchita Martínez becomes the first Spanish player to win the women's singles at the Wimbledon tennis championships, London, England, defeating Martina Navratilova in her last Wimbledon singles match.

2   Two weeks after scoring the own goal that eliminated Colombia from the soccer World Cup finals in the United States, Andrés Escobar is murdered in the Colombian city of Medellín.

6   The U.S. sprinter Leroy Burrell sets a new 100-meters world record of 9.85 seconds, in Lausanne, Switzerland.

6–7   Two stages of the Tour de France cycle race are held in southern England, partly to commemorate the 50th anniversary of the D-Day landings but also to celebrate the opening of the Channel Tunnel. The Tour has come to Britain once before, in 1974, to publicize a new ferry route.

31   Sergey Bubka of the Ukraine sets his 17th outdoor pole vault world record with a jump of 6.14 m/20.14 ft at Sestriere in Italy.

AUGUST

12   The English track and field athlete Sally Gunnell wins the 400-meter hurdles at the European Championships in Helsinki, Finland, and thereby becomes the first woman to hold the Olympic, European, and Commonwealth titles and the world record at the same time.

12–April 2, 1995   The proposed capping of major-league baseball players' salaries results in a 232-day strike in the United States and the first ever cancellation of the World Series.

SEPTEMBER

25   The British boxer Lennox Lewis loses his World Boxing Council world heavyweight title to Oliver McCall of the United States, who stops him in the second round of their bout in London, England.

OCTOBER

16   Michael Schumacher, in a Benetton Ford, becomes the first German to win the Formula One World Drivers' Championship.

DECEMBER

4   The English golfer Nick Faldo wins the "Million Dollar Challenge" held at Sun City, South Africa; his prize of $1 million is the largest prize ever awarded in the sport.

1995

POLITICS, GOVERNMENT, AND ECONOMICS

Business and Economics

- Britain's oldest merchant bank, Barings, collapses (in administration January 26) after Nicholas Leeson, a futures trader based in Singapore, accumulates losses of 625 million Greek drachmas; Barings' main operating sections and liabilities for Far East losses are sold to the Netherlands-based Internationale Nederlanden Groep NV for 1 Greek drachma (March 6); Leeson is arrested at Frankfurt airport, Germany (March 2), and eventually agrees to return to Singapore (October 29), where he pleads guilty to two charges of deception (he is sentenced to six-and-a-half years in prison on December 2).

MARCH
7 The U.S. dollar reaches its lowest ever exchange rates against the German mark and Japanese yen.
17 The French bank Crédit Lyonnais is bailed out by the government following heavy losses.

MAY
16 The Polish currency, the złoty, is floated on the international currency markets.

AUGUST
28 A stock exchange opens in the capital of Mongolia, Ulan Bator.

SEPTEMBER
26 The Japanese bond trader Toshihide Iguchi of the Daiwa Bank is charged with incurring losses of U.S.$1.1 billion through unauthorized dealing, the largest ever loss made by a Japanese bank.

Human Rights

JUNE
29 In the case of *Miller v. Johnson*, the U.S. Supreme Court rules that it is unconstitutional for race to be used as a "predominant factor" in drawing boundaries for electoral districts.

Politics and Government

- Legislation passed under the Republicans' "Contract with America" includes the Unfunded Mandates Bill (signed March 22), that prohibits the federal government from imposing unfunded tasks on states, and the Stockholder Lawsuits Bill (vetoed by President Bill Clinton on December 19; veto overridden on December 22); three bills to impose term limits on Congress members are defeated; a fourth bill is passed (March 29), but by a majority insufficient for that required for a constitutional amendment.

JANUARY
1 Austria, Finland, and Sweden join the European Union, increasing the Union's population from 345 million to 368 million.
1 The Southern Common Market or Mercosur, the world's fourth largest free-trade grouping, comprising Argentina, Brazil, Paraguay, and Uruguay, comes into existence.
1 The World Trade Organization is inaugurated, the successor organization to the General Agreement on Tariffs and Trade (GATT), to regulate commercial relations between the signatories of the GATT international trade agreement.
2 Chechen fighters repel the Russian offensive against Grozny, capital of the breakaway republic of Chechnya (started 31 December 1994); the Russian army resumes its offensive the following day.
3 A financial crisis occurs in Mexico as the value of the peso falls; President Ernesto Zedillo announces spending cuts, and negotiates agreements with unions on wages and over the granting of international credit facilities.
4 The 104th Congress is inaugurated in the U.S.; Newt Gingrich is elected Speaker of the House of Representatives, the first Republican Speaker since 1955. The Republican-dominated House immediately abolishes three minor committees and many subcommittees, and sets a six-year term limit for chairpersons and maximum tenure of eight years for the Speaker.
5 Hastings Banda, former president of Malawi, is arrested on murder charges.
5 Newt Gingrich, Speaker of the U.S. House of Representatives, embarks on the "Contract with America," the program of legislation proposed by the Republicans in the November 1994 elections which they intend to implement in the first 100 days of Congress.
6 The Sri Lankan government and Tamil Tiger independence fighters sign a cease-fire.
10 Japan and the United States finalize a financial services agreement, permitting greater access to Japan's corporate bond markets for foreign firms.
10 The imam of the main Paris mosque, Dalil Boubakeur, presents a "Muslim Charter" and announces the foundation of a representative council of Muslims.

13 As the financial crisis in Mexico worsens, President Bill Clinton of the United States authorizes loan guarantees of $40 billion to stabilize the peso and prevent Mexico from defaulting on short-term debts (on January 31 the guarantees are increased to $50.76 billion).

13 Following the resignation of Silvio Berlusconi as prime minister of Italy (December 22, 1994), President Oscar Scalfaro invites Lamberto Dini, an independent, to form a government (the new government is sworn in on January 18).

17 Quibilah Shabazz, the daughter of the assassinated U.S. black nationalist leader Malcolm X, is indicted on charges of hiring an assassin to kill his rival in the Nation of Islam movement, Louis Farrakhan.

19 In Grozny, capital of the breakaway republic of Chechnya, Russian troops capture the presidential palace, the main center of Chechen resistance.

24 The trial opens of the U.S. former football star O. J. Simpson for the murder of his former wife Nicole Brown Simpson and her friend Ronald Goldman (on June 12, 1994); Simpson is acquitted on October 3 after claims of racial bias in the investigating police force.

26 Heavy fighting breaks out along the disputed border between Peru and Ecuador.

26 The U.S. House of Representatives approves a constitutional amendment requiring a balanced budget by the year 2002, as proposed in the Republicans' "Contract with America." (The amendment fails to secure the necessary two-thirds support in the Senate by one vote on March 2.)

28 The United States and Vietnam agree to open liaison offices in each other's capitals and exchange diplomats.

30 A car bomb planted in the Algerian capital Algiers by Islamic fundamentalists kills 41 people.

FEBRUARY

8 Five hundred thousand miners from 200 of Russia's 228 coal mines hold a day-long "warning strike," demanding payment of wage arrears.

8 The president of the breakaway Russian republic of Chechnya, Dzhokhar Dudayev, announces that he and his military units are leaving the capital Grozny, conceding its loss; fighting continues to the south and east of the city.

17 Following heavy fighting in January on the Peru–Ecuador border, a peace treaty is signed.

21 The Inkatha Freedom Party led by Chief Gatsha Buthelezi, representing Zulu interests, walks out of the South African parliament (on March 5, it agrees to return).

22 At a press conference in Belfast, Northern Ireland, the prime ministers of the Republic of Ireland and Britain, John Bruton and John Major, present a 37-page framework document for all-party peace negotiations over the future of Northern Ireland.

26 China makes an agreement with the United States for the protection of intellectual property rights in China (the United States is concerned to limit Chinese pirating of U.S. material).

28 President Lee Teng-hui of Taiwan unveils a plaque commemorating the native Taiwanese massacred by Nationalist troops from the Chinese mainland on February 28, 1947 (on March 23, Taiwan's parliament

approves the payment of compensation to victims' relatives).

28 United Nations troops withdraw from Somalia, having been unable to end its civil war.

MARCH

2 Giulio Andreotti, former prime minister of Italy, is sent for trial charged with membership in the Mafia (the trial opens on September 26 in Palermo, Sicily).

5 All members of the British colony of Hong Kong's regional and urban councils are elected for the first time; "prodemocracy" parties do well.

5 General elections in Estonia are won by a Coalition Party of former communists and the Rural People's Union, ousting the reformist Fatherland Party.

6 The European Union and Turkey agree to form a trade alliance.

6 The Russian army claims complete control of Grozny, capital of the rebel republic of Chechnya.

9 Canadian patrol boats seize a Spanish trawler just outside Canada's territorial waters in a dispute over fishing rights (the crew is released on March 15).

9 President Ernesto Zedillo of Mexico announces further austerity measures in an attempt to stem his country's financial crisis and the fall in value of the peso.

10 The U.S. president Bill Clinton's nominee for director of the Central Intelligence Agency (CIA), General Michael Carns, withdraws after it is revealed that he has violated immigration and labor laws in his employment of a Filipino man.

11 Ernest Kabushemeye, minister of mines and energy and Hutu leader of the Rally of the Burundian People, is murdered in Burundi, sparking off ethnic clashes, the flight of refugees, and fears of genocide similar to the 1994 massacres in Rwanda.

13 Argentina agrees an international financing package in an attempt to stabilize its economy.

16 The U.S. president Bill Clinton meets Gerry Adams, leader of the Irish Sinn Féin party, at the White House, Washington, D.C., and permits him to raise funds in the United States.

20 A release of nerve gas on the underground railroad in Tokyo, Japan, kills 12 people, injures about 5,000, and paralyzes the rail system; two days later police raid the offices of the Aum Shinrikyo religious sect (founded in 1987) in Kamikuishiki, Honshu.

20 The cease-fire in Bosnia-Herzegovina agreed in December 1994 is broken when the Bosnian army attacks Serb positions; Serbs respond with attacks on government forces and Muslim towns (–March 30).

26 Seven members of the European Union (Belgium, France, Germany, Luxembourg, the Netherlands, Portugal, and Spain) remove internal border controls in line with the 1985 Schengen Agreement.

27 Jim Bolger, Prime Minister of New Zealand, meets the U.S. president Bill Clinton during the first visit to the United States of a New Zealand prime minister since 1984 (in December 1994 the U.S. government recognized New Zealand's ban on ships carrying nuclear weapons).

27 The South African president Nelson Mandela dismisses his wife Winnie from her cabinet position for insubordination. (She is reinstated on April 11 because Mandela fails to undertake the required consultations

with political leaders, but is dismissed again on April 14.)

APRIL

- The British police establish the world's first national DNA (deoxyribonucleic acid) database. Those convicted or suspected of sex offenses, serious assaults, or burglaries in England and Wales must provide a sample of saliva or hair for DNA analysis.

4   Tutsi soldiers massacre 400 Hutu women and children in Burundi.

6   The U.S. House of Representatives passes the tenth and final item in the Republicans' "Contract with America" program, a tax-cutting measure, having failed to pass only one item.

9   Alberto Fujimori is reelected president of Peru, the first person to be elected for a second consecutive term in Peru's history; he is sworn in on July 28.

16   Canada and the European Union make an agreement ending their long-running dispute over fishing in the northwest Atlantic and providing for the conservation of fish stocks.

19   A bomb explodes in a parking garage underneath a federal office block in Oklahoma City, Oklahoma, killing 166 people (including 19 children) and injuring over 400, the worst terrorist attack in U.S. history. Later in the day, Timothy McVeigh is stopped for speeding and subsequently recognized as a suspect bomber.

19   Poisonous phosgene gas is released in a crowded train at the main railroad station in Yokohama, Japan; about 370 people are treated in hospital. Two days later gas is released in a department store in Yokohama.

22   Special prosecutor Kenneth Starr interviews the U.S. president Bill Clinton and his wife Hillary about their involvement in the Whitewater Development Corporation and related matters.

22   Two thousand Hutus are killed at a refugee camp in Rwanda.

23   The socialist Lionel Jospin is the surprise victor in the first round of the French presidential elections with 23.3% of the vote; Jacques Chirac (Gaullist) is second with 20.8%.

30   The cease-fire in Bosnia-Herzegovina expires; violence escalates during May.

MAY

7   Jacques Chirac (Gaullist) wins the second round of the French presidential elections with 52.6% of the vote; Lionel Jospin (Socialist) achieves 47.4%.

7   The British conservationist and paleontologist Richard Leakey announces a plan to found a new political party in Kenya and accuses President Daniel arap Moi of mismanagement and corruption; the new party's name, Safina, meaning "Noah's Ark," is announced on June 13.

12   A Review and Extension Conference of Parties to the 1968 Treaty on Nonproliferation of Nuclear Weapons, in New York, New York, ends with agreement to extend the treaty indefinitely.

14   Carlos Menem (Peronist) is reelected as president of Argentina with 49.8% of the vote (he is sworn in on July 8).

16   Serbs resume the shelling of the besieged Bosnian capital, Sarajevo.

16   Shoko Asahara, leader of the Aum Shinrikyo religious sect (believed to be responsible for the gas attack on the Tokyo subway on March 20), is arrested in Japan.

17   President François Mitterrand of France transfers power to Jacques Chirac (Gaullist) following his victory in the presidential elections; Chirac appoints Alain Juppé as prime minister.

22   The U.S. Supreme Court rules, in the case of *U.S. Term Limits, Inc. v. Thornton*, that state legislation to limit the number of terms served by representatives in the federal Congress is unconstitutional.

25   NATO (the North Atlantic Treaty Organization) launches airstrikes against the Serbs following their refusal to surrender artillery; in response, Serbs kill 67 people in attacks on the United Nations safe haven of Tuzla, Bosnia-Herzegovina.

26   A judge in Baltimore, Maryland, refuses a request to exhume the body of John Wilkes Booth, who assassinated President Lincoln in 1865. Some historians believe the authorities captured and killed the wrong man, but the judge notes that without dental records the exhumation would be inconclusive.

26   Bosnian Serbs begin seizure of United Nations troops as hostages, in response to the threat of NATO (North Atlantic Treaty Organization) air strikes; by June over 377 troops have been taken (they are released between June 2–18).

28   In local elections in Spain, the conservative Popular Party wins the largest share of the vote (43% against 29% for the socialists), taking control of most cities.

31   Lord Owen resigns as European Union mediator in the former Yugoslavia.

JUNE

3   NATO (North Atlantic Treaty Organization) defense ministers agree the creation of a Mobile Theater Reserve (known as the "rapid reaction force") for use in Bosnia-Herzegovina, to be operational by mid-July.

6   The South African Constitutional Court rules that the death penalty is incompatible with the Bill of Rights included in the interim constitution.

7   In a televised address to parliament, Prime Minister Paul Keating of Australia announces a timetable for turning Australia into a republic by the year 2001.

9   The Japanese parliament adopts a resolution expressing regret at the country's acts during World War II, but is criticized abroad for failure to apologize.

9   The presidents of Ukraine and Russia, Leonid Kuchma and Boris Yeltsin, meeting at Sochi in Russia, reach an agreement to end their dispute over the former Soviet Black Sea fleet: the fleet is to be divided equally, with Russia then purchasing part of the Ukrainian fleet.

10–20   The Shell oil company begins towing its disused North Sea oil platform Brent Spa to a dumping site in the Atlantic; on June 16, Greenpeace activists occupy the platform and, on June 20, following a boycott of Shell gasoline stations in Germany and the Netherlands, the company cancels the dumping.

12   Carl Bildt, former prime minister of Sweden, succeeds Lord Owen as European Union mediator in the former Yugoslavia.

13 President Jacques Chirac of France announces a series of eight nuclear tests at Mururoa Atoll in the Pacific (breaking France's self-imposed halt in testing of April 1992).

14 Bosnian government forces launch a major offensive against Bosnian Serb forces; in response, Bosnian Serbs renew their bombardment of Sarajevo, the capital of Bosnia-Herzegovina.

14–19 A rebel Chechen unit seizes hostages in the Russian town of Budennovsk and holds them in the town hospital; five days later most hostages are freed and the Chechens are allowed to return to the breakaway republic of Chechnya.

23 Rebel Chechen fighters and Russian officials make a preliminary peace agreement: Chechen fighters are to disarm and all but 8,000 Russian troops are to leave the breakaway Russian republic of Chechnya; elections are to be held in the republic in September.

28 Security forces kill 17 people in a massacre at Guerro, southwest Mexico.

JULY

6 A special prosecutor is appointed to investigate the personal financial affairs of the U.S. commerce secretary Ron Brown.

10 The opposition leader Aung San Suu Kyi is unexpectedly released from house arrest in Myanmar (she was arrested in July 1989).

11 Serbs capture the United Nations-designated safe area of Srebrenica in eastern Bosnia-Herzegovina; Muslim women and children are moved to Tuzla, while men are held back and massacred.

11 The U.S. president Bill Clinton announces the intention of the United States to establish full diplomatic relations with Vietnam.

11–August 7 The Russian president Boris Yeltsin is rushed to hospital; on July 18, in an interview from hospital, he admits to having had a heart attack. He returns to work on August 7.

14–25 Serbs attack the United Nations safe haven of Zepa in eastern Bosnia-Herzegovina, which falls on July 25.

18 A U.S. Senate panel begins hearings into the Whitewater affair.

20 Serbs and allies attack the United Nations safe haven of Bihać in northwestern Bosnia-Herzegovina; on July 27, Croat troops enter Bosnia to relieve pressure on Bihać.

22 Kenneth Starr, the special prosecutor investigating the Whitewater affair, again interviews the U.S. president Bill Clinton and his wife Hillary under oath.

26–August 11 The U.S. Senate passes a bill enabling the United States unilaterally to lift the embargo on supply of arms to forces in Bosnia-Herzegovina; it is subsequently passed by the House of Representatives on August 1, but vetoed by President Bill Clinton on August 11.

28 The name of Bombay, India, is changed to Mumbai (Bambai in Hindi) following a decision taken by the Maharashtra state government.

28 Vietnam is the first communist state to be admitted to the Association of South-East Asian Nations (ASEAN).

30 Chechen and Russian representatives sign a peace agreement in Grozny, the capital of the breakaway republic of Chechnya.

AUGUST

4–9 Croat armed forces invade and occupy the Serb-inhabited region of Krajina in Croatia; Serb refugees pour into Serb areas of Bosnia-Herzegovina and Serbia.

9 As many as 40 people are killed when Brazilian police evict landless families squatting in Rondonia state, northwest Brazil.

9 The U.S. government announces a new initiative to seek peace in Bosnia-Herzegovina.

10 Several close relatives of President Saddam Hussein of Iraq who hold positions in the government defect to Jordan in protest at his despotic rule.

15 On the 50th anniversary of the end of World War II, Prime Minister Tomiichi Murayama of Japan expresses a "feeling of deep remorse" and offers a "heartfelt apology" for Japan's actions in the war.

19 The six main factions in the Liberian civil war sign a peace accord in Abuja, Nigeria.

28 Serb troops in Bosnia-Herzegovina bombard Sarajevo market place, killing 37 people.

30 NATO (North Atlantic Treaty Organization) aircraft begin large-scale attacks on Serbian positions in Bosnia; 300 sorties are flown in the first 12 hours, and by September 13 over 800 missions have been completed.

SEPTEMBER

1 A six-member Council of State is inaugurated in Liberia; two days later, the Council announces the formation of a new transitional government.

4 The 4th United Nations Women's World Conference opens in Beijing, China.

4 Three U.S. servicemen allegedly rape a 12-year-old girl in Okinawa, Japan, causing protests against U.S. military forces in Japan.

5 The first in a series of French nuclear test explosions at Mururoa Atoll in the south Pacific is followed by large-scale riots on Tahiti and protests elsewhere in the Pacific region.

8 Representatives of the "Contact Group" (Britain, France, Germany, Russia, and the United States) and the foreign ministers of Bosnia-Herzegovina, Croatia, and Yugoslavia, meeting in Geneva, Switzerland, agree basic principles for a peace accord between the warring parties in Bosnia (their foreign ministers reach a further agreement in New York, New York, on September 26).

11 Bosnian government forces launch an offensive in western and central Bosnia-Herzegovina, that reduces Serb-controlled territory from 70% to 50%.

11 Prime Minister Vladimir Meciar of the Slovak Republic announces the convertibility of the Slovak crown from October 1.

11 The Mexican government and the Zapatista National Liberation Army sign an accord establishing procedures for dealing with the grievances of Zapatista rebels, following nine months of fighting.

12 General Jean-Louis Mourut, head of the army historical service in France, admits that the Dreyfus affair of 1894 was a "military conspiracy... partly founded on false documents."

15 The president of Kazakhstan decrees the transfer of the country's capital from Alma Ata in the south to Akmola in the north.

17 In the final elections to the Legislative Council ("Legco") in Hong Kong before the restoration of the British colony to China, the Democratic Party wins 19 of 60 seats.

19 The *Washington Post* includes a 35,000-word manifesto insert written by the terrorist bomber known as the "Unabomber," who has waged a 17-year campaign against users of modern technology.

26 The Czech Republic makes the koruna widely convertible from October 1.

OCTOBER

1 Nigeria's head of state General Sanni Abacha announces that military government will continue until October 1, 1998.

4 French troops free President Djohar of the Comoros Islands following his deposition by the French mercenary Colonel Bob Denard (Denard surrenders the following day).

5 President Bill Clinton announces the agreement of a 60-day cease-fire in Bosnia-Herzegovina from October 10 (to come into effect on October 12).

10 The opposition leader Aung San Suu Kyi is reinstated as general secretary of the National League for Democracy in Myanmar.

11 Ecuador's vice president Alberto Dahik Garzani flees to Costa Rica facing charges of embezzlement.

15 Silvio Berlusconi, former prime minister of Italy, and his brother Paolo are committed for trial on corruption charges.

16 A "Million Man March" is held in Washington, D.C., organized by Louis Farrakhan, leader of the Nation of Islam; an estimated 837,000 black American men attend.

17 Armed forces in Sri Lanka launch the *Rivirasa* ("Sunshine") offensive against the Tamil rebels' stronghold of Jaffna.

20 Willy Claes, secretary-general of NATO (the North Atlantic Treaty Organization), resigns after the Belgian parliament votes to lift his immunity from prosecution so that he can be tried for alleged corruption.

26 President Boris Yeltsin of Russia is again rushed to hospital; on November 27, he moves to a sanatorium where he stays until December 26.

30 In a referendum held in Quebec, voters narrowly defeat the proposal that the province should leave the Canadian federation (50.56% against, 49.44% in favor).

NOVEMBER

1 Peace talks between the warring parties in Bosnia-Herzegovina are held at the Wright-Paterson airforce base near Dayton, Ohio, United States; the delegations are headed by President Alija Izetbegović of Bosnia-Herzegovina, President Franjo Tudjman of Croatia, and President Slobodan Milošević of Yugoslavia, acting also for the Bosnian Serbs.

1 The former French colony of Cameroon is admitted to the British Commonwealth.

3 Queen Elizabeth II of Britain gives the royal assent in Wellington, New Zealand, to legislation returning land and granting compensation to the Tainui Maori tribe and apologizing for the consequences of British aggression in the late 1860s.

4 Prime Minister Yitzhak Rabin of Israel is assassinated at a peace rally in Tel Aviv by a Jewish law student, Yigal Amir, protesting against the cession of land to Palestinians.

5 Javier Solana Madariaga, who as foreign secretary of Spain has a history of opposition to NATO (the North Atlantic Treaty Organization), is appointed its secretary-general.

10 Nigerian authorities hang the writer Ken Saro-Wiwa and eight others who campaigned against environmental damage in the Ogoni region; the following day Nigeria is suspended from the British Commonwealth.

12 The Croatian government and Serb leaders sign an agreement for the reintegration of Eastern Slavonia, the last Serb-held part of Croatia.

13 In a dispute with Republicans in Congress over the 1996 U.S. budget, President Bill Clinton blocks two temporary funding measures, resulting in the closure of nonessential government services from November 14; on November 19, a resolution provides funding to December 15. A further closure occurs on December 16 and lasts into the new year.

13 The British Commonwealth admits Mozambique, a former Portuguese colony.

15 Prime Minister Alain Juppé of France announces reforms to the social security system to reduce expenditure, leading to protest strikes.

19 The former communist Aleksander Kwaśniewski defeats President Lech Wałęsa in presidential elections in Poland, winning 51.7% of the votes against Wałęsa's 48.3%; he is sworn in on December 23.

20 Andreas Papandreou, the 76-year-old prime minister of Greece, is rushed to hospital, suffering from pneumonia.

20–24 Sri Lankan government forces enter the Tamil stronghold of Jaffna, sealing off the town on November 24.

24 A referendum in the Republic of Ireland votes in favor of maintaining the illegality of divorce.

27 An international criminal tribunal opens in Arusha, Tanzania, to handle charges arising from the genocidal conflict in Rwanda.

30–December 1 The U.S. president Bill Clinton visits Northern Ireland; the following day he visits Dublin in the Republic of Ireland.

DECEMBER

14 The formal signing of the peace plan for Bosnia-Herzegovina takes place at the Elysée Palace, Paris, France; it creates two entities within Bosnia-Herzegovina, a Muslim–Croat federation with 51% of territory and a Serb republic with 49%; a United Nations peacekeeping force will be replaced by a NATO (North Atlantic Treaty Organization) implementation force.

16 Many U.S. government functions are again closed as the temporary finance provision agreed on November 19 expires and the budget dispute between President Bill Clinton and Republicans in Congress continues.

23 The bodies of 16 members of the Solar Temple religious sect are found in a clearing near Grenoble, France; 14 were probably shot by two others, who then committed suicide.

23 The former Malawian prime minister Hastings Banda is acquitted of murder charges.

SCIENCE, TECHNOLOGY, AND MEDICINE

Agriculture

- A genetically engineered potato is developed in the United States that contains the gene for Bt toxin, a natural pesticide produced by the soil bacterium *Bacillus thuringiensis* (Bt). The potato plant produces Bt within its leaves. By 1997, over a quarter of a million acres of the potatoes are planted.
- Australian geneticists produce a genetically engineered variety of cotton, containing a gene from a soil bacteria that kills the cotton bollworm and native budworm.

AUGUST

- The U.S. Environmental Protection Agency approves the sale of genetically modified corn, which contains a gene from a soil bacterium that produces a toxin fatal to the European corn borer—a pest that causes approximately $1 billion damages annually.

OCTOBER

- A deadly rabbit virus being tested on Wardang Island, off the coast of south Australia, escapes to the mainland where it begins to kill rabbits in the thousands. It is deliberately released throughout Australia in September 1996.

Computing

- U.S. firm Sun Microsystems develops the computer programming language "Java," which is used to construct World Wide Web sites.

AUGUST

- Microsoft launches Windows 95, a new computer operating system.

NOVEMBER

- The Pentium Pro is launched by Intel. It is a 64-bit microprocessor containing 5.5 million transistors, compared with Pentium's 3.1 million, and can execute 166 million instructions per second.

Ecology

- At the international climate conference held in Melbourne, Australia, it is reported that periodic disruptions of surface currents (which may cause climate changes) have been discovered in the Atlantic and Indian Oceans.
- The Prince Gustav Ice Shelf and the northern Larsen Ice Shelf in Antarctica begin to disintegrate—a result of global warming.
- U.S. chemist F. Sherwood Roland, Mexican chemist Mario Molina, and Dutch chemist Paul Crutzen receive the Nobel Prize for Chemistry for explaining the chemical process of the ozone layer.

JANUARY

17 An earthquake in the Kansai region of Japan devastates the city of Kobe, kills over 5,000 people, and leaves 310,000 homeless.

30–February 1 Following heavy rain in northwest Europe, 250,000 people in the Netherlands leave their homes in the country's largest peacetime evacuation when major rivers threaten to burst their banks.

JUNE

23 A department store collapses in Seoul, South Korea, killing 521 people.

SEPTEMBER

27 Britain and Argentina make an agreement for oil and gas exploration in the South Atlantic southwest of the Falkland Islands, with a joint commission overseeing the exploration.

Exploration

JANUARY

9 Russian cosmonaut Valery Poliakov, on board the *Mir* space station, spends his 366th day in space, breaking the record for the longest stay in space. He returns to Earth on March 22, after 439 days.

FEBRUARY

3–11 NASA's space shuttle *Discovery* is piloted by Eileen Collins, the first woman to do so.

MARCH

22 Russian cosmonaut Yelena Kondakova, on the *Mir* space station, sets a new record for time spent in space by a woman. She returns to Earth after 170 days.

APRIL

- The European Space Agency's Earth-sensing satellite *ERS-2* is launched successfully. It will work in tandem with *ERS-1*, launched in 1991, to take measurements of global ozone.

JUNE

29–July 4 The U.S. space shuttle *Atlantis* docks with the Russian *Mir* space station in the first superpower linkup in space since 1975.

JULY

- The Hubble Space Telescope discovers a 320-km/200-mi yellow spot on the surface of Jupiter's moon, Io. Although volcanic in origin, its exact cause is unknown.
- The U.S. spacecraft *Galileo* enters an unexpected dust storm 55 million km/34 million mi from Jupiter. It detects 20,000 particles a day, whereas previously the maximum detected was 200.

NOVEMBER

- The Infrared Space Observatory (ISO) is launched. Its aim is to discover brown dwarfs (cool masses of gas smaller than the sun) that make up much of the dark matter of the galaxy.

DECEMBER

7 The U.S. spacecraft *Galileo*'s probe enters Jupiter's atmosphere while *Galileo* continues to orbit the planet. The probe radios information back about the chemical composition of the atmosphere to the orbiter for 57 minutes before being destroyed by atmospheric pressure.

Health and Medicine

c. 1995 In the context of increasing numbers of charges about childhood abuse, the controversial phenomenon of False Memory Syndrome is identified by psychologists who believe that traumatic events in childhood can be forgotten by the memory, resulting in psychological problems in adult life. Many other experts believe that there is no such syndrome, and that it is the psychologist who creates these false memories.

- Less than 25% of people in the United States smoke, compared to around 40% in the 1960s.
- The diphtheria epidemic in Russia results in 1,500 deaths.
- The French pharmaceutical company Rhône-Poulenc patents an anticoagulant drug based on a protein isolated from the saliva of vampire bats. It is marketed as Draculin.
- Trials begin in the United States to treat breast cancer by gene therapy. The women are injected with a virus genetically engineered to destroy their tumors.
- U.S. embryologists Edward Lewis and Eric Wieschaus and German embryologist Christiane Nüsslein-Volhard are jointly awarded the Nobel Prize for Physiology or Medicine for their discoveries concerning the genetic control of early embryonic development.
- U.S. researchers estimate that HIV reproduces at a rate of a billion viruses a day, even in otherwise healthy individuals, but is held at bay by the immune system producing enough white blood cells to destroy them. Gradually, the virus mutates so much that the immune system is overwhelmed and the victim develops AIDS.

MARCH

- The U.S. Food and Drug Administration approves a vaccine for chickenpox.

APRIL

4 U.S. surgeons report the successful transplant of genetically altered hearts of pigs into baboons, a notable advance in trans-species operations.

MAY

- An outbreak of the deadly Ebola virus occurs in Kikwit, Zaire, killing 244 of the 315 people who contract it.

JULY

- The U.S. government approves experimentation of genetically altered animal organs in humans.

OCTOBER

23 British surgeon Stephen Westaby of the John Radcliffe Hospital, Oxford, England, makes the first implant of a battery-operated heart.

Science

- A burial ground of the hundreds of laborers who constructed the Great Pyramid in Egypt is discovered. The bones display the signs of constant heavy labor.
- A fossil chordate *Yunnanozoon lividum* is discovered in Chengjiang, China. It is the first chordate recorded from the early Cambrian period and is 525 million years old.
- A vast underground tomb believed to be the burial site of 50 of the sons of Ramses II is discovered in the Valley of the Kings in Egypt.

- Australian physicists incorporate the world's largest niobium ingot (1.5 metric tons in weight and 3 m/9.8 ft long) into a gravity wave detector in an attempt to detect gravity waves.
- Kenyan paleoanthropologist Meave Leakey announces the discovery of the bones of *Australopithecus anamensis*, an upright hominid from about 4 million years ago.
- Physicists at the CERN research center in Switzerland detect "glueballs," gluons that stick together and behave as single particles.
- Researchers in Spain find human remains in a cave at Gran Dolina in northern Spain, dating back more than 780,000 years. Previously, it was thought humans reached Europe around 300,000 years later than this.
- The first comet-sized objects in the Kuiper belt are discovered; previously the only objects found had diameters of at least 100 km/62.5 mi, whereas comets generally have diameters of less than 10 km/6.2 mi.
- The largest carnivorous dinosaur *Giganotosaurus carolinii* is discovered in Patagonia. It lived about 97 million years ago, was 12.5 m/41 ft in length, and weighed 6–8 metric tons.
- The Los Alamos National Laboratory, New Mexico, United States, produces a flexible superconducting film that is superconducting at the relatively high temperature of 77 K (–196°C/–320°F).
- U.S. and French geophysicists discover that the Indo-Australian plate split in two in the middle of the Indian Ocean about 8 million years ago.
- U.S. astronomers discover the first brown dwarf, an object larger than a planet but not massive enough to ignite into a star, in the constellation Lepus. It is about 20–40 times as massive as Jupiter. Four other brown dwarfs are discovered in 1996. Also U.S. astronomers discover water in the sun—in the form of superheated steam—in two sunspots where the temperature is only 3,000°C/5.400°F.
- U.S. physicists Martin Perl and Frederick Reines share the Nobel Prize for Physics: Perl for the discovery of the tau lepton, and Reines for the detection of the neutrino.
- U.S. scientists at Fermilab, near Chicago, Illinois, announce the discovery of the top quark, an elementary particle almost as heavy as a gold atom.
- U.S. scientists successfully germinate bacterial spores extracted from the gut of a bee fossilized in amber 40 million years ago.

JUNE

- U.S. physicists announce the discovery of a new form of matter, called a Bose–Einstein condensate (because its existence had been predicted by Albert Einstein and Indian physicist Satyendra Bose), created by cooling rubidium atoms to just above absolute zero.

JULY

- U.S. astronomers Alan Hale and Thomas Bopp discover the Hale-Bopp comet. The brightest periodic comet, its icy core is estimated to be 40 km/25 mi wide.

DECEMBER

- Unununium (atomic no. 111) is discovered by researchers at the heavy-ion cyclotron based in Darmstadt, Germany.

Technology

- The largest liquid-mirror telescope (3 m/9.8 ft across) (a reflecting telescope constructed with a rotating mercury mirror) is completed for NASA's Orbital Debris Observatory in New Mexico.
- The Omega laser is developed at the University of Rochester, New York State. It generates 60 trillion watts of ultraviolet light in pulses that last for 0.65 billionths of a second, and is used in researching the civil applications of nuclear fusion.
- U.S. company Ultralife introduces the first rechargeable battery made from lightweight solid materials.

JUNE
- Sizewell B, the UK's first pressurized-water nuclear reactor and the most advanced nuclear power station in the world, begins operating in Suffolk, England.

AUGUST
- The world's first commercial wave-powered electricity generator begins operating on the River Clyde, Scotland. Known as "Osprey," it generates 2 megawatts of electricity.

Transportation

c. 1995 Skateboarding enjoys a revival in the United States and Britain.

JULY
25 A bomb explodes on a train in St. Michel underground station, Paris, France, killing seven people and injuring 84.

OCTOBER
28 Fire in the underground railroad system in Baku, Azerbaijan, kills over 300 people.

ARTS AND IDEAS

Architecture

JANUARY
- The 2,200-m/7,216-ft Pont de Normandie bridge, which spans the Seine estuary, France, becomes the world's longest cable-stayed bridge.

Arts

- The first modern art museum in Russia, the Museum of Modern Russian Art, opens at Vladivostok.
- The Korean-born U.S. artist Nam June Paik creates *Cybertown*, a global community connected through the Internet.
- The Swiss architects Jacques Herzog and Pierre de Meuron win the competition to design the Tate Gallery of Modern Art at Bankside, London, England.
- The U.S. artist Delmas Howe paints *Liberty, Equality, and Fraternity*.

Film

- The movie *Apollo 13*, directed by Ron Howard, is released in the United States, based on the book *Lost Moon* by Jim Lovell, and starring Tom Hanks as Lovell, along with Bill Paxton, Kevin Bacon, Ed Harris, and Gary Sinise.
- The movie *Babe*, directed by Chris Noonan, is released in Australia. It is based on the children's story by Dick King-Smith.
- The movie *Batman Forever*, directed by Joel Schumacher, is released in the United States, starring Val Kilmer, Chris O'Donnell, Tommy Lee Jones, Nicole Kidman, and Jim Carrey.
- The movie *Braveheart*, directed by Mel Gibson, is released in the United States. He also stars in it, as William Wallace the Scottish rebel, along with Patrick McGoohan and Sophie Marceau.
- The movie *The Bridges of Madison County*, directed by Clint Eastwood, is released. Based on the novel by Robert Waller, it stars Clint Eastwood and Meryl Streep.
- The movie *Carrington*, directed by Christopher Hampton, is released in Britain, starring Emma Thompson and Jonathan Pryce.
- The movie *Casino*, directed by Martin Scorsese, is released in the United States, starring Robert De Niro and Sharon Stone.
- The movie *Circle of Friends*, directed by Pat O'Connor, is released in Ireland, starring Minnie Driver, Geraldine O'Rawe, and Saffron Burrows.
- The movie *Dumb and Dumber*, directed by Peter Farrelly, is released in the United States, starring Jim Carrey and Jeff Daniels.
- The movie *Goldeneye*, directed by Martin Campbell, is released in the United States, starring Pierce Brosnan as James Bond and Judi Dench as "M."
- The movie *Heat*, directed by Michael Mann, is released in the United States, starring Robert De Niro and Al Pacino.
- The movie *Il Postino/The Postman*, directed by British filmmaker Michael Radford, is released in Italy, starring Massimo Troisi, who dies 12 hours after filming was completed.
- The movie *In the Heat of the Sun*, directed by Jiang Wen, is released in China, starring Geng Le and Xia Yu.
- The movie *Interview with a Vampire*, directed by Neil Jordan, is released in the United States. Based on the novel by Anne Rice, it stars Tom Cruise and Brad Pitt.
- The movie *La cérémonie/The Ceremony*, directed by Claude Chabrol, is released in France, starring Isabelle Huppert.
- The movie *Land and Freedom*, directed by Ken Loach, is released in Britain, starring Ian Hart and Rosana Pastor.
- The movie *Nelly and M Arnaud*, directed by Claude Sautet, is released in France, starring Emmanuelle Béart and Michel Serreau.
- The movie *Nixon*, directed by Oliver Stone, is released in the United States, starring Anthony Hopkins, Joan Allen, Powers Boothe, Bob Hoskins, and Ed Harris.

- The movie *Sense and Sensibility*, directed by Taiwanese filmmaker Ang Lee, is released in Britain, starring Emma Thompson and Kate Winslet.
- The movie *Shallow Grave*, directed by Danny Boyle, is released in Britain, starring Ewan McGregor, Christopher Eccleston, and Kerry Fox.
- The movie *Shanghai Triad*, directed by Zhang Yimou, is released in China, starring Gong Li.
- The movie *Small Faces*, directed by Gillies MacKinnon, is released in Britain, starring Clare Higgins, Iain Robertson, Ian McElhinney, and J. S. Duffy.
- The movie *The American President*, directed by Rob Reiner, is released in the United States, starring Michael Douglas and Annette Bening.
- The movie *The Madness of King George*, directed by Nicholas Hytner, is released in Britain. Scripted by Alan Bennett, it stars Nigel Hawthorne.
- The movie *The Usual Suspects*, directed by Bryan Singer, is released in the United States, starring Gabriel Byrne, Stephen Baldwin, Chazz Palminteri, Kevin Pollak, Pete Postlethwaite, and Kevin Spacey.
- The movie *Ulysses' Gaze*, directed by Theo Angelopoulos, is released in Greece, starring Harvey Keitel.
- The movie *Underground*, directed by Emir Kusturica, is released in France, starring Miki Manojlovic and Lazar Ristovki. It is awarded the Palme d'Or at the Cannes Film Festival in France.
- The movie *Waterworld*, directed by Kevin Reynolds, is released in the United States, starring Kevin Costner. Costing $175 million, making it the most expensive movie ever, it is not a big enough success to justify its budget.
- The movie *While You Were Sleeping*, directed by John Turteltaub, is released in the United States, starring Sandra Bullock and Bill Pullman.
- The United States' top grossing movies are *Batman Forever* ($184 million), *Apollo 13*, *Toy Story*, *Pocahontas*, *Ace Ventura: When Nature Calls*, *Casper*, *Die Hard with a Vengeance*, *Crimson Tide*, *Goldeneye*, and *Waterworld*.
- The Walt Disney animated movie *Pocahontas* is released in the United States.
- U.S. director, writer, and producer Steven Spielberg joins with motion picture executives Jeffrey Katzenberg and David Geffen to found Dreamworks SKG, the first major Hollywood studio to be founded since 1935.

MARCH

27 The 1994 Academy Awards are held. Best Actor: Tom Hanks, for *Forrest Gump*; Best Supporting Actor: Martin Landau, for *Ed Wood*; Best Actress: Jessica Lange, for *Blue Sky*; Best Supporting Actress: Dianne Wiest, for *Bullets over Broadway*; Best Director: Robert Zemeckis, for *Forrest Gump*; Best Picture: *Forrest Gump*, directed by Robert Zemeckis.

SEPTEMBER

22 The movie *Showgirls*, directed by Paul Verhoeven, is released in the United States, starring Elizabeth Berkeley and Kyle MacLachlan. A movie about Las Vegas strippers, it is the first major studio release with the restrictive NC-17 rating that allows no viewers under 17.

Literature and Language

- The English politician and writer Roy Jenkins publishes his biography *Gladstone*.
- The English writer Kate Atkinson publishes her novel *Behind the Scenes at the Museum*, which is the Whitbread Book of the Year.
- The English writer Martin Amis publishes his novel *The Information*.
- The English writer Nick Hornby publishes his comic novel *High Fidelity*.
- The English writer Pat Barker publishes her novel *The Ghost Road*, the final part of her *Regeneration* trilogy; it wins the Booker Prize.
- The English writer Sean O'Brien publishes his poetry collection *The Ghost Train*.
- The Indian-born English writer Salman Rushdie publishes his novel *The Moor's Last Sigh*.
- The Nobel Prize for Literature is awarded to the Irish poet Seamus Heaney.
- The Pulitzer Prize for Biography is awarded to Joan D. Hedrick for *Harriet Beecher Stowe: A Life*, the Pulitzer Prize for Poetry is awarded to Philip Levine for *Simple Truth*, and the Pulitzer Prize for Fiction is awarded to Carol Shields for *The Stone Diaries*.
- The U.S. writer Anne Tyler publishes her novel *Ladder of Years*.
- The U.S. writer Norman Mailer publishes *Oswald's Tale: An American Mystery*, a personal reflection on the life and death of Lee Harvey Oswald.
- The U.S. writer Philip Roth publishes his novel *Sabbath's Theater*.

Music

- "Britpop" comes to the fore in Britain—white, guitar-based bands, such as Blur, Oasis and Pulp, playing song-based pop-rock, often influenced by the Beatles and 1960s British pop.
- The British pop group Simply Red releases the album *Life*.
- The British pop group Wet Wet Wet releases the album *Picture This*.
- The British pop singer Annie Lennox releases the album *Medusa*.
- The British progressive rock group Pink Floyd releases the album *Pulse*.
- The British rock group the Beatles releases the album *Anthology 1* and the single "Free as a Bird," the first new Beatles single for 25 years.
- The British rock group Blur releases the single "Country House" and the album *The Great Escape*.
- The British rock group Oasis releases the singles "Some Might Say" and "Roll With It" and the album *(What's the Story?) Morning Glory*.
- The British rock group Pulp releases the album *Different Class*.
- The British rock group the Rolling Stones releases the album *Stripped*.
- The British rock group Queen releases the album *Made in Heaven*.
- The British rock group Supergrass releases the album *I Should Coco*.

- The British rock singer Paul Weller releases the album *Stanley Road*.
- The Canadian rock singer Neil Young, with the U.S. rock group Pearl Jam, releases the album *Mirrorball*.
- The Canadian singer Alanis Morissette releases the album *Jagged Little Pill*.
- The Canadian singer Celine Dion releases the single "Think Twice."
- The English composer Peter Maxwell Davies completes his *Strathclyde Concerto* No. 10.
- The ex-lead singer of U.S. rock group 10,000 Maniacs, Natalie Merchant, releases the solo album *Tiger Lily*.
- The first consumer CD Plus titles—a combination of the features of CD-ROMs and high sound quality audio CDs—are released.
- The U.S. composer Steve Reich completes his *City Life*, which employs sounds taken from everyday life such as boat horns, street noises, and so on.
- The U.S. pop singer Coolio releases "Gangsta's Paradise," the best-selling single of the year in the United States.
- The U.S. pop singer Madonna releases the single "Take a Bow."
- The U.S. pop singer Michael Jackson releases the album *HIStory – Past Present and Future Book 1*.
- The U.S. rock group Bon Jovi releases the album *These Days*.
- The U.S. rock group Garbage releases the album *Garbage*.
- The U.S. rock singer Bruce Springsteen releases the album *The Ghost of Tom Joad*.
- U.S. pop singer Michael Jackson's "You Are Not Alone" is the first single to enter the U.S. charts at number one.

MARCH

1   The 1994–95 Grammy Awards are held. Best Record: "All I Wanna Do" by Sheryl Crow; Best Song: "Streets of Philadelphia" by Bruce Springsteen; Best Album: *MTV Unplugged* by Tony Bennett; Best Male Pop Vocalist: Elton John; Best Female Pop Vocalist: Sheryl Crow; Best Pop Group: All-4-One.

APRIL

3   The rock group Pearl Jam announces that it will start a summer rock tour without using Ticketmaster, the popular ticket-selling agency, which they say has a national monopoly in the United States and has created inflated ticket prices.

AUGUST

6   Scholars meet at the University of Mississippi in Oxford, Mississippi, for the first annual International Conference on Elvis Presley.

Theater and Dance

- The play *Break of Day*, by the U.S. writer Timberlake Wertenbaker, is first performed, in New York, New York.
- The Pulitzer Prize for Drama is awarded to Horton Foote for *The Young Man from Atlanta*.

JUNE

4   The 1994–95 Tony Awards are held. Best Play: *Love! Valour! Compassion!*; Best Musical: *Sunset Boulevard*; Best Actor: Ralph Fiennes; Best Actress: Cherry Jones.

Thought and Scholarship

- *The New Cambridge Medieval History: 700–900* is published, edited by Rosamund McKitterick.
- The Pulitzer Prize for History is awarded to Doris Kearns Goodwin for *No Ordinary Time: Franklin and Eleanor Roosevelt: The Home Front in World War II*.
- The Pulitzer Prize for General Nonfiction is awarded to Jonathan Weiner for *The Beak of the Finch: A Story of Evolution in Our Time*.
- The U.S. historian Jonathan Israel publishes *The Dutch Republic: Its Rise, Greatness and Fall, 1477–1806*.
- The U.S. politician Newt Gingrich publishes *To Renew America*.
- The U.S. social historian Christopher Lasch publishes *The Revolt of the Elites and the Betrayal of Democracy*.
- The U.S. writer Michael Kazin publishes *The Populist Persuasion: An American History*.

SOCIETY

Everyday Life

- Twelve percent of Americans aged 25 to 34 live with their parents, a similar percentage to that of 1990.
- In the United States, 46.1 million people belong to health maintenance organizations, an increase from 9.1 million in 1980.
- Sixty-seven percent of single women over 16 and 61% of married women hold jobs in the United States.
- Of the U.S. labor force, 7,693,000 people, or 6.2%, hold more than one job.
- According to the U.S. Census Bureau, 13% of the U.S. population is older than 65; Florida, with 18.6% of its population older than 65, has the largest concentration of senior citizens.
- According to the U.S. Census Bureau, the average size of a U.S. household is 2.65 people, down from 3.33 people in 1960.
- According to the U.S. Census Bureau, two-thirds of U.S. families with televisions have cable TV.
- Americans make 10,464,000 ATM transactions.
- Americans spend $1.1 billion on word-processing software.
- In the United States, 23% of people older than 25 have a college degree, up from 11% in 1970.
- In the United States, 23% of citizens have completed at least four years of college (whites 24%; blacks 13%; Hispanics 9.3%).
- In the United States, 33.7 million people subscribe to cellular phone services.
- In the United States, 64% of married women with children under six work, as opposed to 45% in 1980 and 19% in 1960.

- In the United States, 82% of citizens have completed at least four years of high school (whites 83%; blacks 74%; Hispanics 53%).
- It is estimated that 25% of people aged over 18 in the United States smoke cigarettes, a similar percentage as in 1990 but down from 42% in 1965.
- More than 54% of all Americans over 65 live at home with their spouse.
- Of the U.S. over-18 population, 27% of U.S. men and 19% of U.S. women have never married.
- The average per capita income in the United States is $22,788, up from $18,666 in 1990.
- The average U.S. employee works 39.2 hours each week; the average U.S. agricultural worker works 41 hours each week.
- The price of apples in the United States is $.83 per pound, up from $.57 per pound in 1989, and the price of chicken breast is $1.95 per pound, down from $2.01 per pound in 1989.
- The state with the highest per capita income in the United States is Connecticut; the lowest is Mississippi.
- The U.S. civilian labor force is 132.3 million people, of which 124.9 million hold jobs.
- The U.S. government spends $73.8 billion on education, or 5% of its total budget.
- The United States' colleges and universities confer 1.2 million bachelor degrees, 534,000 associate degrees, 409,000 master degrees, 78,000 professional degrees, and 43,000 doctorates.
- The Walt Disney movie *Toy Story*, the first full-length movie made entirely with computer animation, is released in the United States. The Buzz Lightyear toy featured in the movie is a huge commercial success.
- There are 1,533 daily newspapers in the United States, with 58.2 million subscribers, and 888 Sunday newspapers, with circulation totaling 61.2 million.
- There are 31 major labor strikes in the United States this year, involving 192,000 workers.

- U.S. electronics companies CyberMaxx and Virtual 10 launch virtual reality headsets for home use in the United States.

JANUARY
- Customs officers in Sweden catch a woman entering the country with 65 baby snakes hidden in her bra; she claimed that she planned to start a reptile farm.

SEPTEMBER
8 The U.S. Justice Department announces that it has begun an investigation into possible violation of U.S. pornography laws by Calvin Klein underwear advertisements.
22 A survey finds that 33% of U.S. obstetrician-gynecologists perform abortions, down from 42% in a 1983 survey.

OCTOBER
30 A survey finds that 17% of adults in the United States and Canada have access to the Internet and that 11% of adults have used the Internet in the previous three months. The survey also finds that two-thirds of Internet users are men.

NOVEMBER
9 Bill Watterson, creator of the popular comic strip *Calvin and Hobbes*, which chronicles the antics of a six-year-old boy and his toy tiger, Hobbes, announces that he will cease drafting the strip that he started in 1986.
23 French railroad workers begin a three-week strike following the announcement of money-saving cuts in the railroad system.

Media and Communication

- The centenary of cinema is celebrated throughout the world.

JANUARY
16 The science fiction program *Star Trek: Voyager* begins on U.S. television. A further *Star Trek* spin-off, it stars

BIRTHS & DEATHS

JANUARY
1 Eugene Paul Wigner, Hungarian-born U.S. physicist who introduced the notion of parity, or symmetry theory, into nuclear physics, dies in Princeton, New Jersey (92).
4 Sol Tax, U.S. anthropologist, dies in Chicago, Illinois (87).
6 Joe (Yoseel Masheel) Slovo, South African lawyer and politician, general secretary of the South African Communist Party 1987–91 and one of the most influential figures in the African National Congress (ANC), dies in Johannesburg, South Africa (68).
9 Prince Souphanouvong, leader of the Laotian guerrilla organization Pathet Lao (Land of the Lao) and first president of the Republic of Laos, 1975–86, dies in Laos (85).

18 Adolf Butenandt, German biochemist who discovered the sex hormones estrone, androsterone, and progesterone, dies in Munich, Germany (91).
30 Gerald (Malcolm) Durrell, English naturalist, writer, and zoo curator, dies in St. Helier, Jersey (70).
31 George (Francis) Abbott, U.S. playwright, theater director, and producer, dies in Miami Beach, Florida (107).
31 George Robert Stibitz, U.S. mathematician who developed the first binary calculator (one of the first digital computers), dies in Hanover, New Hampshire (90).

FEBRUARY
2 Donald Pleasance, British actor, dies in St.-Paul-de-Venice, France (76).

2 Fred (Frederick John) Perry, English lawn-tennis player who dominated men's singles tennis in the mid-1930s and was the last Briton to win the men's singles at Wimbledon (1936), dies in Melbourne, Australia (85).
4 Patricia Highsmith, U.S. crime novelist, creator of the psychopathic murderer Tom Ripley, dies in Locarno, Switzerland (74).
5 Doug McClure, U.S. actor, dies in Sherman Oaks, California (59).
9 J(ames) William Fulbright, U.S. Democrat politician responsible for the Fulbright Scholarships, which provide grants for thousands of Americans to study abroad and for overseas students to study in the United States, dies in Washington, D.C. (89).

14   U Nu, prime minister of the Union of Burma 1948–58, and 1960–62, dies in Yangon (Rangoon), Myanmar (87).

20   Robert (Oxton) Bolt, English historical dramatist and screenwriter who wrote *A Man for All Seasons* (1960), *Lawrence of Arabia* (1962), and *Dr Zhivago* (1965), dies near Petersfield, England (70).

25   Jack Clayton, English film director known especially for his films *Room at the Top* and *The Innocents*, dies in Slough, England (73).

March

1   Georges Jean Franz Köhler, German immunologist who helped revolutionize medical research through the development of monoclonal antibodies, dies in Freiburg-im-Breisgau, Germany (48).

14   William Alfred Fowler, U.S. astrophysicist who worked on the life cycle of stars and shared the Nobel Prize for Physics in 1983 with Subrahmanyan Chandrasekhar for his work on the origin of chemical elements, dies in Pasadena, California (83).

15   Florence Chadwick, U.S. swimmer and the first woman to swim the English Channel in both directions, dies in San Diego, California (76).

24   Joseph Needham, English biochemist and historian of Chinese science, dies in Cambridge, England (94).

April

2   Hannes Olof Gösta Alfvén, Swedish astrophysicist who made fundamental contributions to the field of magnetohydrodynamics (MHD) and helped found plasma physics, dies in Djorsholnr, Sweden (86).

10   Morarji Ranchhodji Desai, independent India's first non-Congress Party prime minister 1977–79, as leader of the Janata party, dies in Bombay, India (99).

14   Burl Ives, U.S. actor and folk singer, dies in Anacortes, Washington (85).

25   Ginger Rogers, U.S. dancer and actress, partner of Fred Astaire, dies in Rancho Mirage, California (83).

27   Peter (Maurice) Wright, English secret intelligence agent, author of *Spycatcher: The Candid Autobiography of a Senior Intelligence Officer*, dies in Tasmania, Australia (78).

May

5   Mikhail Botvinnik, Russian chess player, world champion 1948–57, 1958–60, and 1961–63, dies in Moscow, Russia (83).

18   Elizabeth Montgomery, U.S. actress known for her role in the television program *Bewitched*, dies in Beverly Hills, California (62).

24   Harold Wilson, Labour prime minister of Britain 1964–70 and 1974–76, dies in London, England (79).

25   Ernest Thomas Sinton Walton, Irish physicist who with John Cockcroft developed the first particle accelerator and shared the Nobel Prize for Physics in 1951, dies in Belfast, Northern Ireland (91).

26   Friz Freleng, U.S. animator best known for the characters Bugs Bunny, Daffy Duck, and the Pink Panther, dies in Los Angeles, California (89).

June

23   Jonas Salk, U.S. physician who developed the first effective vaccine against poliomyelitis, dies in La Jolla, California (80).

25   Warren Burger, Chief Justice of the U.S. Supreme Court 1969–86, dies in Washington, D.C. (87).

29   Lana Turner, U.S. actress, dies in Los Angeles, California (74).

July

1   Wolfman Jack (Robert Westo Smith), U.S. radio disc jockey, dies (57).

3   Pancho Gonzales, U.S. tennis player who dominated U.S. singles tennis during the 1950s, dies in Las Vegas, Nevada (67).

4   Eva Gabor, Hungarian-born U.S. actress, dies in Bel Air, Los Angeles, California (76).

17   Juan Manuel Fangio, Argentine race-car driver who won the Drivers' World Championship a record five times 1951–57, dies in Buenos Aires, Argentina (84).

25   Charlie Rich, U.S. country singer, dies in Hammond, Louisiana (62).

August

3   Ida Lupino, U.S. actress, director and screenwriter, dies in Burbank, California (77).

13   Mickey Mantle, U.S. baseball player, dies in Dallas, Texas (64).

21   Subrahmanyan Chandrasekhar, Indian-born U.S. astrophysicist who made pioneering studies of the structure and evolution of stars and shared the Nobel Prize for Physics

in 1983 with U.S. astrophysicist William Alfred Fowler for his work on the origin of chemical elements, dies in Chicago, Illinois (84).

23   Alfred Eisenstaedt, German-born U.S. photographer known for his war photographs, dies in Martha's Vineyard, Massachusetts (96).

September

4   William Moses Kunstler, U.S. criminal lawyer, known for representing radical groups including the Black Panthers and the Chicago Seven, dies in New York, New York (76).

October

9   Alec Douglas-Home, Baron Home of the Hirsel, prime minister of Britain 1963–64, a Conservative, dies in Coldstream, Berwickshire, Scotland (92).

22   Kingsley Amis, English writer, dies in London, England (73).

25   Robert ("Bobby") Riggs, U.S. tennis player, dies in Leucadia, California (77).

November

4   Yitzhak Rabin, prime minister of Israel 1974–77 and 1992–95 is assassinated in Tel Aviv, Israel (73).

10   Kenule ("Ken") Saro-Wiwa, Nigerian author and environmental activist, is executed in Port Harcourt, Nigeria (54).

23   Louis Malle, French film director, dies in Beverly Hills, California (63).

December

2   (William) Robertson Davies, Canadian novelist known for his Deptford trilogy, dies in Orangeville, Ontario, Canada (82).

5   Stanley Keith Runcorn, British geophysicist who discovered that the earth's magnetic field undergoes periodic reversals, dies in San Diego, California (73).

18   Conrad Zuse, German engineer who built Z3, the first program-controlled binary digital computer, dies in Berlin, Germany (85).

22   James Edward Meade, English Keynesian economist who shared the Nobel Prize for Economics in 1977 for his work on trade and capital movements and published the four-volume *Principles of Political Economy* (1965–76), dies in Cambridge, England (88).

25   Dean Martin, U.S. singer and actor, dies in Beverly Hills, California (78).

Kate Mulgrew, Robert Belhan, Robert Duncan McNeill, Tim Russ, and Roxann Biggs-Rawson.

FEBRUARY

15   The Iranian parliament passes a law banning the import, distribution, and private use of satellite reception dishes.

APRIL

• The British men's magazine *Maxim* is launched.

SEPTEMBER

9   The 1994–95 Emmy Awards for television are held. Best Drama Series: *NYPD Blue*; Best Comedy Series: *Frasier*; Best Actor in a Drama: Mandy Patinkin, for *Chicago Hope*; Best Actress in a Drama: Kathy Baker, for *Picket Fences*; Best Actor in a Comedy: Kelsey Grammer, for *Frasier*; Best Actress in a Comedy: Candice Bergen, for *Murphy Brown*.

13   *Forbes* magazine's annual list of entertainers who earned the most over the past two years includes Steven Spielberg ($285 million), Oprah Winfrey ($146 million), The Beatles ($130 million), and magician David Copperfield ($81 million).

OCTOBER

28   In Canada, radio presenter Pierre Brassard, imitating prime minister Jean Chrétien, phones Queen Elizabeth II in London, England, and broadcasts their discussion.

NOVEMBER

17   The last edition of the British newspaper *Today*, launched in 1986, is published. Its owner, News International, blames its demise on continuing losses (£11 million in its final year).

DECEMBER

25   *Time* magazine names Newt Gingrich, Republican representative for Georgia, who is speaker of the House, as its "man of the year."

Sports

• Emmitt Smith of the Dallas Cowboys scores 25 touchdowns, surpassing the National Football League all-time season record of 24 set by John Riggins of the Washington Redskins in 1983.

• The Canadian driver Jacques Villeneuve wins both the Indianapolis 500 and the PPG Indy Car Championship.

• The Carolina Panthers join the National Football Conference (NFC) and the Jacksonville Jaguars the American Football Conference (AFC), in the first National Football League expansion since 1976.

• The Los Angeles Rams football team move to St. Louis, Missouri, and the Los Angeles Raiders move back to Oakland, California, which they left in 1982.

• The Miami Dolphins quarterback Dan Marino breaks Minnesota Viking quarterback Fran Tarkenton's all-time National Football League career passing records for attempts, completions, yardage, and touchdowns, all in this year.

• The University of California at Los Angeles (UCLA) wins its 11th National College Athletic Association (NCAA) men's basketball championship, its first for 20 years.

JANUARY

• The World Alpine Skiing Championships in the Sierra Nevada, Spain, are canceled due to lack of snow.

13–April 26   The yacht *Mighty Mary*, with the first all-woman crew in the history of the America's Cup yacht race series, narrowly fails in its attempt to overcome Dennis Conner's *Stars and Stripes* in the defender trials.

28   The U.S. tennis player André Agassi wins the Australian Open men's singles title, in Melbourne, Australia, at his first attempt.

29   The San Francisco 49ers defeat the San Diego Chargers 49–26 in Miami, Florida, to win an unprecedented fifth Super Bowl. The 49ers' quarterback Steve Young throws a record six Super Bowl touchdown passes.

FEBRUARY

1   The Utah Jazz guard John Stockton breaks fellow U.S. player Magic Johnson's all-time National Basketball Association career assists record of 9,921.

MARCH

• The Italian skier Alberto Tomba wins the overall, slalom, and giant slalom World Cup titles.

11   Picabo Street becomes the first U.S. skier to win a World Cup downhill title.

17   The U.S. basketball player Michael Jordan announces that he is ending his 17-month retirement and will rejoin the Chicago Bulls immediately. Ten days later he confirms that he has not lost his touch with 55 points in the Bulls' victory over the New York Knicks at Madison Square Garden, New York, New York.

25   The former world heavyweight boxing champion Mike Tyson is released from jail in the United States after serving three years of a six-year sentence for rape.

31   After 232 days, the major-league baseball strike in the United States over the proposed capping of players' salaries is officially called off.

MAY

13   In the America's Cup yacht race series the New Zealand challenger *Black Magic*, skippered by Russell Coutts, beats Dennis Conner's *Young America* 5–0 in a best-of-nine race series to inflict on the United States only its second defeat in the 144-year history of the race.

JUNE

5   The Ethiopian runner Haile Gebrselassie breaks the world 10,000-meters record by nearly 9 seconds with a run of 26 min 43.53 sec, at Hengelo in the Netherlands.

10   Lammtarra, ridden by Irish jockey Walter Swinburn, wins the Epsom Derby, England, in a record time of 2 min 32.31 sec. Later in the season, with the Italian jockey Frankie Dettori in the saddle, he wins both the King George VI and Queen Elizabeth Diamond Stakes in England and the Prix de l'Arc de Triomphe in France on October 1.

24   The Rugby World Cup is held in South Africa. In the final, in Johannesburg, the host nation defeats New Zealand 15–12 after extra time.

JULY

23   The Spanish cyclist Miguel Induráin becomes the first person to win the Tour de France race in five successive years.

AUGUST

7   At the fifth International Amateur Athletics Federation (IAAF) World Championships in Gothenburg, Sweden, Jonathan Edwards of Britain becomes the first person to jump over 18 m/59 ft in the triple jump. He sets

two new world records of 18.16 m/59.58 ft and 18.29 m/60 ft.

9–11 At the fifth International Amateur Athletics Federation (IAAF) World Championships in Gothenburg, Sweden, U.S. runner Michael Johnson becomes the world champion at both the men's 200 meters and 400 meters. He wins a third gold medal in the 4 × 400 relay.

20 The Yugoslavian-born U.S. tennis player Monica Seles marks her comeback to competitive tennis 16 months after being stabbed in the back by an obsessed fan of her German rival Steffi Graf, by winning the women's singles at the Canadian Open.

27 The governing body of Rugby Union, the International Rugby Football Board, votes to end the game's "amateur only" status, to "put an end to hypocrisy."

SEPTEMBER

2 The English boxer Frank Bruno wins a world heavyweight boxing title at his fourth attempt, defeating the World Boxing Council champion Oliver McCall of the United States on points before 30,000 spectators at Wembley Stadium, London, England.

6 Cal Ripken, Jr., of the Baltimore Orioles breaks New York Yankee Lou Gehrig's record of playing 2,130 consecutive major league baseball games, which has stood since 1939.

10 The U.S. tennis player Pete Sampras wins his third U.S. Open singles title, beating top seed André Agassi of the U.S. in the final.

10–24 The amateur golfers of Britain and Ireland defeat the United States in the Walker Cup, held at Porthcawl, Wales. The final score of 14–10 is the largest margin of

victory over the United States ever achieved in the competition. Shortly afterwards, Europe's professional golfers regain the Ryder Cup, defeating the United States 14½–13½ at Oak Hill Country Club, Rochester, New York.

13 The Harlem Globetrotters basketball team suffer their first defeat for 24 years, losing 91–85 in Vienna, Austria, to a team led by ex-LA Lakers star Kareem Abdul-Jabaar. Before this, they had won 8,829 games in succession.

OCTOBER

21–28 The Atlanta Braves defeat the Cleveland Indians by four games to two to win their first World Series since 1957, when they were the Milwaukee Braves.

28 Cigar, ridden by U.S. jockey Jerry Bailey, wins the Breeders' Cup Classic horse race at Belmont Park, New York, New York.

NOVEMBER

10 Jansher Khan of Pakistan wins the men's World Open squash title for a record seventh time, defeating Britain's Del Harris in the final in Cyprus.

13 The Atlanta Braves baseball pitcher Greg Maddux wins the Cy Young National League award for a record fourth successive year.

19 The Baltimore Stallions defeat Calgary 37–20 in Regina, Saskatchewan, Canada, to become the first ever U.S. team to win the Canadian Football League's Grey Cup.

DECEMBER

12 The U.S. National Broadcasting Company (NBC) attains the rights to televise the 2004 and 2008 Summer Olympic Games and the 2006 Winter Olympic Games for $2.3 billion.

1996

POLITICS, GOVERNMENT, AND ECONOMICS

Business and Economics

MARCH
15 The Dutch Fokker aviation company goes bankrupt.

SEPTEMBER
10 British Foreign and Commonwealth Office documents show that $500 million worth of gold ($6 billion in today's prices) from unknown sources was deposited in

Swiss banks during World War II; there is speculation that some belonged to Holocaust victims.

NOVEMBER
15 The petroleum giant Texaco makes an out-of-court settlement in the United States of $175 million with former employees claiming racial discrimination.

Human Rights

APRIL
23 A meeting of the foreign ministers of the Commonwealth countries votes to impose sanctions on Nigeria in protest at its human rights abuses.

MAY
• Southern Black churches in the United States begin to be targeted by arsonists. There are nearly 200 incidents by the end of the year.

NOVEMBER

8 At an army training base in Maryland, United States, 30 female recruits complain of sexual abuse, reigniting the debate over the military's treatment of women.

Politics and Government

- "Soccer moms," suburban working women with children, are reckoned to be a powerful interest group in the U.S. presidential elections.

JANUARY

5 The Russian foreign minister Andrei Kozyrev, a reformer, resigns following electoral gains by extreme nationalists.

8 Seven Europeans and 19 Indonesians from a scientific research team are kidnapped on Irian Jaya, Indonesia, by the separatist Papua Independence Organization.

9 Rebels from the breakaway Russian republic of Chechnya take 3,000 people hostage in the Russian town of Kizlar, demanding withdrawal of Russian troops from Chechnya. The following day 2,870 hostages are released, and the remainder transported toward Chechnya.

11 Ryutaro Hashimoto becomes prime minister of Japan, following the resignation of Tomiichi Murayama on January 5.

14 Alvaro Arzú Irigoyen is inaugurated as president of Guatemala following elections.

15 Russian government troops attempt to end the Chechen hostage crisis by force; over 60 people are killed and some rebels escape with their hostages from the attack on the village of Pervomaiskoye; nine days later, on January 24, 46 remaining hostages are freed.

18 Kostas Simitis becomes Greek prime minister following the resignation on January 15 of Andreas Papandreou because of ill-health.

18 Ten people are killed when neo-Nazis gasoline-bomb a hostel for foreign asylum seekers in the town of Lübeck, Germany.

21 In the first Palestinian general elections, the Palestine Liberation Organization (PLO) leader Yassir Arafat is chosen as president.

22–29 A general strike organized by prodemocracy activists paralyzes Swaziland; King Mswati III promises reforms.

24 Prime Minister Józef Oleksy of Poland resigns following charges that he spied for the KGB (secret police of the former USSR).

26 Hillary Clinton testifies before a grand jury investigating the Whitewater affair in the United States.

27 A military coup in Niger led by Colonel Ibrahim Barre Mainassara deposes President Mahamane Ousmane.

29 Fourteen people are killed in an attack near Johannesburg, South Africa; the "Third Force," made up of Inkatha militants and disaffected security personnel, is believed to be responsible.

29 France proclaims an end to its controversial Pacific nuclear testing program.

31 A truck bomb planted by the separatist organization the Tamil Tigers kills 55 people in Colombo, Sri Lanka.

FEBRUARY

1 The United States announces that it will assist the United Nations (UN) food assistance program for North Korea, established to prevent famine following floods in 1995.

7 Following the resignation of Prime Minister Józef Oleksy on January 24, a coalition government is formed in Poland under Włodzimíerz Cimoszewicz (February 7).

9 The Irish Republican Army (IRA) explodes a bomb on the Isle of Dogs, east London, England, breaking its cease-fire which has been in force since August 1994; two people die.

15 Suicide bombers from the Palestinian group Hammas attack the Israeli cities of Jerusalem and Ashkelon, killing 25 people.

15 The Bangladeshi prime minister Begum Khaleda Zia is reelected in general elections.

19 One million people demonstrate in Madrid, Spain, against the violence of the Basque separatist group ETA (Euskadi ta Askatasuna, "Basque Nation and Liberty").

21 The legislative assembly of Northern Territory, Australia, legalizes euthanasia for the terminally ill.

23 The sons-in-law of President Saddam Hussein of Iraq who defected to Jordan in August 1995, return to Iraq and are immediately executed by their relatives.

24 Cuban forces shoot down two light aircraft from the organization "Brothers to the Rescue," formed by expatriate Cubans to assist those attempting to escape to the United States; the action provokes strong U.S. condemnation.

27 Martial law is declared in Lebanon following a general strike for higher public sector pay.

MARCH

2 Australian general elections result in victory for the opposition Liberal–National coalition led by John Howard, who becomes prime minister on March 11.

3 José Maria Aznar's Popular Party gains most votes in a general election in Spain but does not secure an overall majority.

3–4 Attacks on the city of Tel Aviv, Israel, by Hezbollah (extremist Muslim) suicide bombers claim 34 lives.

7 Three servicemen from the U.S. base on Okinawa Island, Japan, are given jail terms in Japan for the rape of a Japanese girl in September 1995.

8 Reformist politicians unexpectedly gain votes in parliamentary elections in Iran at the expense of extremists.

8–25 China stages military exercises in the Taiwan Strait in an attempt to intimidate voters in Taiwan's first free presidential elections.

9 The Socialist Jorge Sampaio is inaugurated as president of Portugal, following elections.

13 Gunman Thomas Hamilton opens fire in a classroom in Dunblane, Scotland, killing 16 primary school children and their teacher before he shoots himself dead.

17 Göran Persson succeeds Ingvar Carlsson as head of a minority Swedish Social Democrat and Labor Party government.

18 Riots accompany the burial of the independence activist Thomas Wapai Wainggai on Irian Jaya, Indonesia; four people die.

19 The South African president Nelson Mandela divorces his wife Winnie, who has been linked with the murder of police informers during the apartheid years.

19 The veteran politician Bob Dole's victory in the Midwestern primaries assures him of his nomination as

the Republican Party's candidate for the 1996 U.S. presidential election.

23 The proindependence candidate Lee Teng-hui is elected president of Taiwan.

25 The European Union bans the export of British beef abroad following anxiety over the potential for transmission of the BSE infection to humans as CJD (Creutzfeldt-Jakob disease).

28 The former Polish leader Wojciech Jaruzelski goes on trial for the murder of 44 demonstrators killed in 1971, while he was defense minister (the trial is indefinitely suspended on April 25 because of doubts over the court's jurisdiction in the case).

29 An Intergovernmental Conference (IGC) to plan the development of the European Union (EU) is inaugurated at the Turin Conference of the EU countries.

29 Following elections in Sierra Leone, Ahmad Tejan Kabbah becomes president, ending military control of the country.

29 Three British soldiers are given life sentences on the island of Cyprus for the abduction, rape, and murder of the Danish tour guide Louise Jensen.

APRIL

3 Theodore J. Kaczynski, suspected of being the "Unabomber" responsible for nationwide bomb attacks against users of modern technology, is arrested at his cabin in Montana.

4 The former dictator Mathieu Kérékou is sworn in as president of Benin, following the failure of his opponents to prove electoral fraud.

10 The United States deploys warships off the coast of Liberia to facilitate the evacuation of U.S. citizens and other foreign nationals caught up in the Liberian civil war.

11 The ruling president Kim Young Sam's New Korea Party is returned to power in elections in South Korea.

11–12 Israeli helicopters attack Beirut, the capital of Lebanon, following Hezbollah (extremist Muslim) rocket attacks on Israel.

14 A bomb kills 14 people at a cancer hospital in Lahore, Pakistan, founded by the cricketer turned politician Imran Khan.

15 The Truth and Justice Commission, set up to investigate political crimes committed by all sides during the apartheid era, opens in Johannesburg, South Africa; it is chaired by Archbishop Desmond Tutu.

15 The United States signs an agreement for the return of some military bases to Japan and undertakes to make the presence of its troops more acceptable, following complaints about their behavior.

17 Erik and Lyle Menendez are given life sentences in California for the murder of their parents in 1989.

17 Troops kill 23 members of the Landless Workers Movement at a demonstration in the northern state of Pará, Brazil.

18 Islamic extremists kill 17 Greek holiday-makers in a gun attack in Cairo, Egypt.

18 Israeli aircraft attack a United Nations (UN) refugee camp at Qana in Lebanon and kill 97 people, beginning Operation "Grapes of Wrath," a major Israeli offensive against the extremist Muslim organization Hezbollah.

21 The rebel Chechen leader Dzhokhar Dudayev is killed during an attack by Russian aircraft on his headquarters south of the Chechen capital, Grozny.

27 A cease-fire suspends fighting between Israeli forces and Hezbollah (extremist Muslim) terrorists based in Lebanon.

28 Gunman Martin Bryant kills 35 people at the holiday resort of Port Arthur, Tasmania, Australia.

28 The U.S. president Bill Clinton testifies for the defense in the trial of his former business partners Jim and Susan McDougal and former Arkansas governor Guy Tucker on charges arising from the dealings of the Whitewater property company.

29 A United Nations (UN) war crimes tribunal opens in The Hague, the Netherlands, to investigate allegations of crimes against humanity committed during the Yugoslavian civil war.

MAY

10 Australia introduces strict gun controls in response to the massacre at Port Arthur of April 28.

10 Three thousand Vietnamese boat people riot in Hong Kong in protest at plans to repatriate them, injuring 50 prison officers.

15 The Republican presidential candidate Bob Dole resigns from the U.S. Senate, effectively ending his involvement in politics should he fail to win the presidency, in an attempt to boost his campaign.

16 Admiral Jeremy "Mike" Boorda shoots himself dead in the United States following charges that he has worn combat decorations to which he is not entitled.

16 Atal Vajpayee, leader of the Bharatiya Janata Party, becomes head of a coalition government in India following inconclusive elections.

17 Romano Prodi forms a center-left coalition government in Italy, following elections.

20 Jim and Susan McDougal and Guy Tucker, former governor of Arkansas, are found guilty of fraud and conspiracy in relation to the failure of the Whitewater property company.

JUNE

1 H. D. Deve Gowda becomes prime minister of a center-left coalition in India, following the resignation of Atal Vajpayee on May 28.

5 It is revealed that the Clinton administration in the U.S. has used Federal Bureau of Investigation (FBI) files to obtain information on political opponents.

5 The ruling prime minister Václav Klaus reforms his coalition following elections in the Czech Republic.

10 All-party talks on the future of Northern Ireland begin at Stormont Castle, Belfast, Northern Ireland; Sinn Féin, the political wing of the Irish Republican Army (IRA), is not admitted because of the IRA's cease-fire violations.

15 An Irish Republican Army (IRA) bomb explodes in the Arndale Centre in Manchester, England, injuring 220 people and devastating the shopping precinct.

16 Boris Yeltsin gains most votes in the first round of the Russian presidential elections (35.3%); the communist Gennady Zyuganov comes second with 32% of the votes.

18 A U.S. Senate report strongly criticizes First Lady Hillary Clinton for her role in the Whitewater affair.

18 Binyamin Netanyahu of the Likud Party forms a government in Israel, following the defeat of the Labor Party in elections.

18 In a political trade-off, the Russian president Boris Yeltsin appoints his rival presidential candidate Alexander Lebed as his national security advisor in an attempt to win over Lebed's supporters before the second round of voting in presidential elections.

20 The government of Papua New Guinea launches a fresh offensive against separatists on the island of Bougainville.

21 At a European Union (EU) summit in Florence, Italy, a deal is made for the lifting of the export ban on British beef (involving the slaughter of 147,000 at-risk cattle); in return, Britain ends its obstruction of EU business.

23 Shaikh Hasina Wajed of the Awami League becomes prime minister of a coalition government in Bangladesh, following elections.

25 An Islamic fundamentalist group, Hezbollah-Gulf, bombs a U.S. military base at Dharan, Saudi Arabia, killing 19 people.

27 Irish journalist Veronica Guerin is murdered while she is investigating drug dealing in Dublin, Ireland.

28 A new constitution is adopted in Ukraine, giving President Leonid Kravchuk greater powers.

28 The Irish Republican Army (IRA) mounts a mortar attack on a British base in Osnabrück, Germany; there are no casualties.

30 The Democratic Union wins elections in Mongolia, defeating the ruling communist Mongolian Revolutionary People's Party.

July

3 The Hungarian government establishes a fund to compensate Jewish victims of the Holocaust, the first Eastern European country to do so.

7–13 The Royal Ulster Constabulary (RUC) bans a controversial Loyalist apprentice boys' march in Londonderry, Northern Ireland; the decision is reversed on July 11 and the march takes place; violence continues until July 13.

9 Around 50 people are killed in Libya when police fire on a demonstration staged by opponents of the Libyan leader Moamer al-Khaddhafi at a soccer match in the capital, Tripoli.

9 Boris Yeltsin is inaugurated as Russian president, having defeated his communist challenger Gennady Zyuganov in the second round of the presidential elections.

9–13 President Nelson Mandela of South Africa makes a state visit to Britain; he addresses both houses of Parliament (July 11) and receives honorary degrees from eight universities.

18–20 In a meeting with the "Paris Club" of creditor nations, Peru renegotiates its debts in an attempt to alleviate its financial difficulties.

19 Radovan Karadžić, the president of the independent Serb region of Bosnia-Herzegovina, resigns following his indictment on war crime charges.

24 A bomb planted by Tamil Tiger separatists explodes in Colombo, Sri Lanka, killing 70 people.

24 The Hutu president of Burundi, Sylvestre Ntibantunganya, seeks refuge in the U.S. embassy in Bujumbura, having been attacked while attending the funeral of Tutsi victims of a massacre.

24 The leading Somali warlord General Muhammad Farah Aydid is fatally wounded in a gun battle in Mogadishu; he dies on August 1.

25 The Tutsi-dominated Burundi army stages a coup, making Major Pierre Buyoya head of state; political parties are banned and freedom of movement is restricted.

27 A bomb explodes in the Centennial Olympic Park, Atlanta, Georgia, killing two people; suspicion falls on the security guard who discovered the device.

31 Fifteen people are crushed to death at a railroad station in Johannesburg, South Africa, after private security guards use electric cattle prods to control crowds, causing a stampede.

August

6–8 Chechen rebels launch a major offensive on Grozny, capturing key points in the capital of the disputed Russian republic.

7 Ibrahim Barre Mainassara wins presidential elections in Niger, amid allegations of vote rigging.

8 A general strike in Argentina in protest at President Carlos Menem's austerity measures paralyzes the country (a second strike takes place on September 26).

10 Abdalá Bucaram Ortiź of the Rodolsista Party is inaugurated as president of Ecuador following elections.

11–14 Fierce inter-ethnic fighting flares up in Cyprus between the Greek and Turkish communities.

14 Japan makes compensation payments to 20,000 "comfort women" from countries occupied during World War II; they were forced to become soldiers' concubines.

16 A peace agreement establishing a program for ending the civil war in Liberia is signed in Ajuba, Nigeria; elections are scheduled for May 31, 1997.

17 The discovery of the bodies of two young girls, victims of pedophile Marc Dutroux, causes a public outcry in Belgium.

22 The Russian negotiator Aleksander Lebed and the rebel Chechen leader Aslan Maskhadov negotiate a cease-fire in the breakaway Russian republic.

23 French police storm the Church of St. Bernard in Paris, France, which is sheltering 300 asylum seekers and is at the center of a national controversy over immigration policy.

27 Seven Iraqi dissidents hijack a Sudan Airways airliner and force it to fly to Stansted airport, England, where they surrender; on August 31, they are charged with air piracy.

28 In Britain, the marriage of Charles and Diana, Prince and Princess of Wales, is formally ended.

28 The People's Revolutionary Army (ERP) in Mexico launches a series of attacks across the country, killing 14 people.

29 A peace deal ending the war in the Russian breakaway republic of Chechnya postpones a decision on the question of sovereignty until the year 2001.

30–31 Left wing guerrillas kill over 100 people in attacks on police and military targets in Colombia.

31 Iraqi aircraft violate the no-fly zone in the north of the country to attack Kurdish targets.

SEPTEMBER

2   The government of the Philippines signs a peace agreement with Muslim separatists on the island of Mindanao, ending 24 years of conflict.

3   The United States responds to Iraqi air attacks on Kurds in northern Iraq by launching cruise missiles against southern Iraq.

14   Bosnia-Herzegovina elects a new legislature reflecting its ethnic complexity; Republika Srpska has its own separate assembly and president, while Alia Izetbegović becomes president of the collective presidency.

22   The Pan-Hellenic Socialist Movement government of Kostas Simitis is reelected in Greece.

25–29   Fighting breaks out in Israel over the unblocking of an ancient tunnel under the Old City of Jerusalem; 57 Palestinians and 15 policemen are killed.

26   The former South African police colonel Eugene De Kock claims that South African security forces were responsible for assassinating the Swedish prime minister Olaf Palme in 1986.

27   The Taleban Islamic fundamentalist movement takes over the Afghan capital, Kabul, and imposes Islamic law.

OCTOBER

10   The former Indian prime minister P. V. Narasimha Rao is charged with corruption and fraud.

17   Eighty-two people are crushed to death in Guatemala during a soccer World Cup qualifying match with Costa Rica.

20   Arnoldo Alemán Lacayo of the Liberal Democratic Alliance is elected president of Nicaragua.

20   In Brussels, Belguim, 250,000 Belgians demonstrate in protest at lack of progress in the investigation into organized pedophilia.

21   The United Nations High Commissioner for Refugees (UNHCR) reports that 250,000 Hutu refugees have fled northeastern Zaire following fighting between ethnic Tutsi Banyamulenge and Zairean armed forces.

25   Gro Harlem Brundtland resigns as Norwegian prime minister and is succeeded by Thorbjoen Jagland.

28   The ruling Zimbabwe African National Union–Popular Front officially renounces Marxism–Leninism.

30   Eugene De Kock, the former South African police colonel at the center of investigations into covert government operations in the apartheid era, is sentenced to life imprisonment for gun-running and murder.

NOVEMBER

4   Prime Minister Benazir Bhutto of Pakistan is dismissed by President Farooq Ahmed Leghari following corruption allegations.

5   Bill Clinton is reelected president of the United States, defeating Republican nominee Bob Dole with 379 electoral college votes to 159. The popular vote is Clinton 45,590,703; Dole 37,816,307; Reform candidate Ross Perot 7,866,284. The Republicans retain control of the House of Representatives and the Senate.

5   The Russian president Boris Yeltsin successfully undergoes a quadruple heart by-pass operation.

15   The refugee crisis in Zaire and Rwanda is defused without the need for outside help after Tutsi rebels defeat extremist Hutu militiamen, allowing 700,000 Hutus under their control to return to Rwanda.

23   Unidentified hijackers seize control of an Ethiopian Boeing 767 airliner; the plane runs out of fuel and crashes into the Indian Ocean off the Comoros Islands, killing 127 people.

27   The Swiss Council of State votes unanimously for an independent investigation into allegations of collaboration by Swiss banks with the Nazis during World War II.

28   A referendum in Algeria endorses government plans to change the constitution in order to prevent Islamic fundamentalists coming to power.

28   General Radko Mladić steps down as army commander in Republika Srpska, having been indicted by the international tribunal in The Hague, the Netherlands, to stand trial for war crimes.

29   General Chavalit Yongchaiyut forms a government in Thailand following the New Aspiration Party's victory in elections.

29   The anticommunist Emil Constantinescu is inaugurated as president of Romania following elections.

DECEMBER

3   A bomb planted by Algerian Islamic fundamentalists explodes in the Paris Metro, France, killing four people and injuring over 100.

5   Madeleine Albright becomes the first female U.S. secretary of state.

10   Jim Bolger (National Party) forms a coalition with the New Zealand First Party led by Winston Peters following inconclusive elections in New Zealand.

12   Uday Hussein, the eldest son of President Saddam Hussein of Iraq, is shot in an assassination attempt; he is left permanently paralyzed.

13–14   A European Union (EU) summit in Dublin, Ireland, makes significant progress toward the introduction of a single currency.

15   In the Yugoslavian capital, Belgrade, 250,000 people demonstrate in protest at the government's refusal to recognize the opposition's victory in November's municipal elections.

17   Left wing guerrillas from the Tupac Amarú organization take hostage 575 diplomats attending a reception given by the Japanese ambassador in Lima, Peru.

17   The Transitional National Council passes legislation in Algeria to make Arabic the official language by July 5, 1998.

18–31   Tupac Amarú guerrillas release over 200 hostages taken when they seized the Japanese embassy in Lima, Peru, the previous day. There are further releases on December 23; by December 31, 81 hostages are still held.

19   After being charged with corruption and fraud in October, the former Indian prime minister P. V. Narasimha Rao resigns as leader of the Congress Party.

21   Loyalist terrorists in Northern Ireland break their cease-fire, in force since August 1994, with a car-bomb attack in Belfast.

26   Jo-Benet Ramsey, a six-year-old beauty-pageant queen, is found strangled in the basement of her parents' home in Boulder, Colorado. The search for the killer draws the country's attention throughout the following year. Her parents remain under suspicion.

29   The Guatemalan government signs an agreement ending its civil war with the Guatemalan National

Revolutionary Unity Movement; waged since 1961, the war has claimed 100,000 lives, while 40,000 people have "disappeared."

SCIENCE, TECHNOLOGY, AND MEDICINE

Agriculture

JANUARY

- The first genetically engineered salmon are hatched, at Loch Fyne in Scotland. The salmon contain genes from the ocean pout as well as a salmon growth hormone gene that causes them to grow five times as fast as other salmon.

DECEMBER

6 Cosmonauts aboard the *Mir* spaceship successfully harvest a small wheat crop, the first plants to be successfully cultivated from seed in space.

Computing

- IBM's Deep Blue computer beats Russian grand master Gary Kasparov at chess, the first computer to defeat a grand master.
- Japanese researchers construct a computer able to perform 1.08 trillion floating-point operations per second.
- Virtual casinos proliferate on the Internet. By 1997, there are over 50 sites, based mostly in the Caribbean. Concerns are raised over regulation.

MARCH

25 The 1995 Academy Awards are transmitted over the World Wide Web by U.S. computer company Microsoft as a "webcast."

Ecology

- More than half the households in the United States are required by law to recycle their waste, especially paper.

MARCH

25–April 2 The flood gates of the Glen Canyon Dam on the Colorado River are opened, releasing 532 billion liters/ 117 billion gallons of water into the Grand Canyon. The aim is to revive natural habitats by imitating the regular spring floods that used to occur before the dam was built in 1963.

JUNE

2 U.S. scientists at the National Oceanic and Atmospheric Administration in Washington, D.C., announce the first decline in levels of ozone-depleting chemicals in the air.

JULY

7 A flash flood in the French Pyrenees kills over 100 people at a holiday campsite.

AUGUST

7 Eighty-four people die when floods sweep through a campsite at Biescas, northern Spain.

SEPTEMBER

18 U.S. president Bill Clinton signs the act creating the Grand Staircase Escalante National Monument in southern Utah. The new park covers 688,000 hectares/ 1.7 million acres and is one of the largest in the United States.

OCTOBER

October–November Badhabunga volcano, 200 km/ 130 mi east of Reykjavik, Iceland, erupts underneath Europe's largest glacier, the Vatnajökull, which covers one-tenth of the country. The glacier is pierced on October 3. There are fears that much of the glacier will melt, flooding large areas. The eruptions stop on October 12 and flooding does not occur until November 5, when bridges and roads are washed out.

4 The World Conservation Union (IUCN) publishes the latest Red List of endangered species. Over 1,000 mammals are listed, far more than on previous lists. The organization believes it has underestimated the risks of habitats from pollution and that the number of endangered species is greater than previously thought.

Exploration

JANUARY

- The U.S. spacecraft *Galileo* shows less helium on the planet Jupiter than expected. The ratio of helium to hydrogen is similar to that of the sun, suggesting that the composition of Jupiter has remained unchanged since its formation. The probe also records 700-kph/435-mph winds below one of the cloud layers, suggesting internal heating.

FEBRUARY

17 NASA launches the *Near Earth Asteroid Rendezvous* (NEAR) space craft toward the asteroid Eros. It will reach the asteroid in February 1999 and will then go into orbit around it and study its size, shape, mass, magnetic field, composition, and surface and internal structure.

26 A $442-million satellite is lost in space when its 20 km-/ 12-mi-long tether, which links the satellite to the shuttle *Columbia*, snaps. The tethered satellite is designed to generate electricity as it is pulled across the earth's magnetic field by the shuttle.

MARCH

- The U.S. spacecraft *Galileo* detects a magnetic field around Ganymede, suggesting it has a molten core. It also detects molecules containing both carbon and nitrogen, suggesting that life may have existed on the moon.

25 The Russian space station *Mir* and the U.S. space shuttle *Atlantis* dock. U.S. astronaut Shannon Lucid begins a five-month stay aboard *Mir*.

JUNE

4 The European Space Agency's Arianespace launches the new *Ariane 5* rocket from French Guiana, after ten years of development work. It veers off course immediately after takeoff on its maiden flight and disintegrates (it is

blown up for safety reasons), setting the European space program back years.

JULY

2   The U.S. aerospace company Lockheed Martin unveils plans for the X-33, a $1-billion wedge-shaped rocket ship. Called the *Venture Star*, it will be built and operated by Lockheed Martin and will replace the U.S. space shuttle fleet by the year 2012.

AUGUST

13   NASA scientists report that new images taken by the spacecraft *Galileo* of Europa, one of Jupiter's moons, show that icy floes on its surface may contain evidence of life.

SEPTEMBER

26   U.S. astronaut Shannon Lucid ends her 188-day stay in space. It is the longest stay for a U.S. astronaut and the longest for a woman. She has spent most of the time aboard the Russian space station *Mir*.

NOVEMBER

7   The U.S. National Aeronautics and Space Administration (NASA) launches the *Mars Global Surveyor* probe. The objectives of the probe are to study the magnetic field, climate, and composition of the atmosphere of Mars.

15–January 18, 1997   Norwegian polar explorer Borge Ousland becomes the first person to walk alone across Antarctica. He uses skis and is aided by a "para-wing" sail which gives wind assistance to his sled.

16   The Russian spacecraft *Mars-96* is launched from a site in Kazakhstan, but the booster rockets fail to fire and it falls back to Earth and crashes into the Pacific two days later.

DECEMBER

3   U.S. astronomer Anthony Cook, using data from the satellite *Clementine*, announces the discovery of a frozen lake at the bottom of a crater on the dark side of the moon. It would be important for a future Moon colony.

4   The U.S. National Aeronautics and Space Administration (NASA) launches the *Mars Pathfinder*. Its main goal is to demonstrate the feasibility of low-cost landings on, and exploration of, Mars. The spacecraft carries a roving machine to explore the surface.

19   The U.S. *Galileo* spacecraft flies within 692 km/430 mi of the cracked and icy surface of Jupiter's moon Europa. The detailed pictures suggest that Europa has the water and warmth necessary to support life. However, as yet, no life has been found, nor has the spacecraft found any sign of the subterranean ocean that some researchers speculate lies beneath the icy crust. Based on data received from the spacecraft *Galileo*, U.S. astronomers also conclude that Jupiter's moon Io has a metallic core. A 10-megawatt beam of electrons flowing between Jupiter and Io is also detected.

Health and Medicine

• Australian biologist Peter Doherty and Swiss biologist Rolf Zinkernagel are jointly awarded the Nobel Prize for Physiology or Medicine for their discoveries concerning the specificity of cell mediated immune defense.

• Redux becomes the first appetite suppressant to be made available in the United States for more than 20 years and is the only drug prescribed for long-term maintenance of weight loss.

• Synthetic aspirins without side effects, known as "superaspirins," are marketed.

• The death rate from AIDS in the United States falls from 15.6 per 100,000 people to 11.6, a 26% decline. It is the first decline in the 15 years since the pandemic began. AIDS is no longer the main killer of adults between the ages of 25 and 44 but it remains so for African Americans in that age group. The number of AIDS cases in Europe, Australia, and New Zealand also reaches a plateau or decreases.

• Two U.S. dentists discover a new muscle running from the jaw to just behind the eye socket. About 3 cm/1 in long, it helps to support and raise the jaw.

FEBRUARY

21   U.S. researcher Joanna Fowler and her colleagues at the Brookhaven National Laboratory in Upton, New York, report that smoking reduces the enzyme monamine oxidase B in the brain, which leads to an increase in the amount of dopamine, a chemical that helps regulate mood, movement, and the reinforcement of behavior patterns. It is the first identification of a mechanism of cigarette addiction. High levels of dopamine are also found in other addictive drugs.

MARCH

12   The World Health Organization (WHO) publicly launches an obesity task force in Barcelona, Spain, to combat a worldwide epidemic of obesity.

APRIL

3   The U.S. Defense Department announces that there is no evidence for the existence of Gulf War Syndrome, which afflicts many soldiers who took part in the Gulf War, 1990–91.

3   The World Health Organization (WHO) announces the development, by an international team of scientists, of a weekly injection that reduces sperm production to a negligible level, while leaving sexual performance unimpaired.

MAY

9   Scientists at the National Institute of Allergy and Infectious Disease in Bethesda, Maryland, discover a protein, "fusin," which allows the HIV virus to fuse with a human immune system cell's outer membrane and inject genetic material. Its presence is necessary for the AIDS virus to enter the cell.

20   The U.S. biotechnology company Biogen's product Avonex (Interferon beta-1a) is approved for the treatment of multiple sclerosis in the United States. It is approved by the European Union in March 1997.

OCTOBER

17   U.S. researchers from the University of Texas and the Beckman Research Institute based in Hope, California, announce the discovery that cigarette smoke alters a gene that suppresses the uncontrolled growth of cells that cause tumors. It is the first direct evidence for the statistical link between cigarette smoking and cancer.

Science

- Astronomers announce the discovery of a galaxy in the constellation Virgo, estimated to be 14 billion light-years away—the most distant galaxy ever detected. In the same year, astronomers from the Leiden Observatory in the Netherlands and from Johns Hopkins University in Baltimore, Maryland, United States, using data from the Hubble Space Telescope, discover a black hole in the galaxy in the constellation Virgo.
- British paleontologists discover the world's oldest flowering plant, *Bevhalstia pebja*, in southern England. It is a wetland herb about 25 cm/10 in high and it is about 130 million years old.
- Construction of the world's largest neutrino detector, the Antarctic Muon and Neutrino Detector Array (AMANDA), begins at the South Pole.
- Japanese chemists produce the first synthetic cellulose.
- Paleontologists from the Institute of Vertebrate Paleontology and Paleoanthropology in Beijing, China, discover the remains of a 135-million-year-old fossil bird in northeast China. Called the "Confucius bird" (*Confusciusornis sactus*), it had a modern-looking beak with no teeth, unlike Archeopteryx.
- Researchers from the University of California discover anemones in the Bahamas that have been alive for 1500 to 2000 years—longer than any other known marine creature.
- The shrimp *Synalpheus regalis*, which lives in sponges in the coral reefs of Belize, is discovered to live in social colonies like those of ants. All the shrimps are the offspring of a single reproductive female, care of young is cooperative, and larger individuals act to defend the colony.
- Two new objects about 500 km/300 mi in diameter are discovered in the Kuiper belt, four to six times further from the sun than Neptune.
- U.S. geophysicists discover that the earth's core spins slightly faster than the rest of the planet.
- U.S. physicists David Lee, Douglas Osheroff, and Robert Richardson are jointly awarded the Nobel Prize for Physics for their discovery of superfluidity in helium-3.

JANUARY

- At a meeting of the American Astronomical Society, U.S. astronomers announce the discovery of three new planets orbiting stars, all within 50 light-years of Earth. By July 1996 the total number of new planets discovered since October 1995 has risen to ten.
4 A team of European physicists at the CERN research center in Switzerland create the first atoms of antimatter: nine atoms of antihydrogen survive for 40 nanoseconds.
18 New Zealand ornithologist Gavin Hunt reveals that crows on the island of New Caledonia in the South Pacific make tools out of leaves and twigs which they use to reach insects in dead wood—something only chimpanzees and humans were thought capable of.
30 The comet Hyakutake is discovered by Japanese amateur astronomer Yuji Hyakutake.

FEBRUARY

- Element no. 112 is discovered at the GSI heavy-ion research center, Darmstadt, Germany. A single atom is created, which lasts for a third of a millisecond.

MARCH

- The Near Earth Asteroid Tracking (NEAT) system, in its first full month in operation, detects about 200 new asteroids.
20 UK archeologists announce at the Royal Society in London, England, that recent carbon dating of bone fragments found at Stonehenge in Wiltshire indicates that the site may be 5,000 years old—1,000 years older than previously thought.
24 Comet Hyakutake makes its closest approach, passing within 15.4 million km/9.5 million mi of Earth. It is the brightest comet for decades, with a tail extending over 12 degrees of the sky.
27 The ROSAT X-ray astronomy satellite records the emission of X-rays from Comet Hyakutake, which are usually associated with a much hotter source.

APRIL

- UK archeologist David Keys reports the discovery of London, England's first Anglo-Saxon purpose-built port. Constructed in the 880s near present-day Southwark Bridge on the north bank of the River Thames, London, it consists of two quays 15 m/50 ft apart which extend 6 m/20 ft into the river to create a small harbor.
19 U.S. archeologist Anna Roosevelt discovers 11,200- to 10,000-year-old paintings of fish, birds, deer, and humans in the heart of the Amazon jungle at Caverna da Pedra Pintada, Brazil. The oldest paintings in the Americas, they indicate that the Amazon basin was inhabited earlier than previously thought.

MAY

16 Paleontologists from the University of Chicago discover, in Morocco, the remains of the largest carnivorous dinosaur known: *Carcharodontosaurus saharicus* ("shark-toothed reptile from the Sahara"). It lived 90 million years ago, weighed 7.8 metric tons/8 tons, ran at a speed of 32 kph/20 mph, and at 13.5 m/44 ft in length was 1 m/3.3 ft longer than *Tyrannosaurus rex*.

AUGUST

- U.S. geneticists clone two rhesus monkeys from embryo cells.
1 The UK Central Veterinary Laboratory publishes a report indicating that BSE (bovine spongiform encephalopathy, or "mad cow disease") can be transmitted from cow to calf.
6 U.S. NASA scientist Daniel Goldwin's report on a meteorite discovered in Antarctica in 1984 claims that it is 4.5 billion years old and is believed to have been ejected from Mars millions of years ago, hitting Antarctica 13,000 years ago. The meteorite is found to contain fossil microorganisms, suggesting that life once existed on Mars. Critics claim the meteorite was contaminated.

SEPTEMBER

21 Australian archeologists claim to have discovered rock carvings 76,000 years old and stone tools 176,000 years old in Australia. If correctly dated, they suggest that *Homo sapiens* reached Australia far earlier than the 60,000 years ago currently believed.

OCTOBER

3   British scientists announce meteorite evidence of life on Mars, supporting claims made by NASA and U.S. scientists in August.

NOVEMBER

3   French archeologist Frank Giddo announces the discovery of the royal district of Alexandria, Egypt, where the Egyptian queen Cleopatra VII lived; it sank beneath the Mediterranean after an earthquake and tidal wave in AD 335.

23   British paleontologist Peter Ward announces the discovery, in South Africa, of the fossil remains of a lystrosaur, a pig-like early mammal which lived during the Permian era about 250 million years ago. The discovery overturns the existing theory that the first mammals were therapsids—small shrew-like creatures which emerged millions of years later during the age of the dinosaurs.

30   The 5-km/13-mi-long close-approach asteroid Toutates passes within 5 million km/3 million mi of Earth. Traveling at 140,000 kph/85,0000 mph, it comes close to Earth every 4–5 years.

Technology

-   Scientists from the Scott Polar Institute, using data from the European Space Agency's *ERS-1* satellite, discover a 14,000-sq-km/5,400-sq-mi, 125-m/410-ft-deep lake, 4 km/2.5 mi under the Antarctic ice sheet. Called Lake Vostok after the Russian ice-drilling station it lies beneath, the ice sheet, which acts as a blanket, and a pressure of 300–400 atmospheres allow the water to remain liquid.

MARCH

-   The first solar power plant capable of storing heat, "Solar 2," becomes operational. Located in California's Mohave Desert, it consists of 2,000 motorized mirrors that focus the sun's rays on to a tower containing molten nitrate salt, which retains its heat for up to 12 hours. The molten salt is used to boil water to drive a 10-megawatt steam turbine.

MAY

-   The Lawrence Livermore National Laboratory, California, produces a laser of 1.3 petawatts (130 trillion watts).

JULY

-   U.S. engineers Theodore O. Poehler and Peter C. Searson announce the invention of the first all-plastic battery. It uses polymers instead of conventional electrode materials and has implications for military and space applications, as well as its use in consumer devices such as hearing aids and wristwatches.

29   China conducts an underground nuclear explosion test. The next day in Geneva, Switzerland, at a meeting of 61 countries to complete a global test ban agreement, China declares a moratorium on future tests.

NOVEMBER

-   The first gas pipeline between North Africa and Europe enters service. The 1,400-km/875-mi pipeline brings natural gas from Algeria via Morocco and the Strait of Gibraltar to Córdoba in southern Spain.

Transportation

-   Fifty-four million cars in the United States have airbags, including 24.1 million with driver and passenger side airbags.

-   Japan tests the first fire-fighting helicopter. It is designed to reach skyscrapers beyond the reach of fire-engine ladders.

JANUARY

9   An Antonov 32 cargo aircraft crashes on a market in Kinshasa, Zaire, killing over 300 people.

19   A ferry capsizes off the north coast of Indonesia; 200 people die.

FEBRUARY

10   A road tunnel collapses on Hokkaido Island, Japan, killing 20 people.

15   The Liberian-registered *Sea Empress* supertanker runs aground at the entrance to Milford Haven Harbour, south Wales, UK. Salvage attempts fail and over 70,000 metric tons of oil are spilled into the sea.

APRIL

3   A plane carrying a trade delegation to the former Yugoslavia crashes at Dubrovnik, Croatia, killing 32 people; among the dead is the U.S. secretary of commerce Ron Brown.

MAY

11   A fire in the cargo hold of a 27-year-old DC-9, en route from Miami, Florida, to Atlanta, Georgia, and operated by ValuJet, a small U.S. regional airline offering deeply discounted fares, causes it to crash into the Everglades 32 km/20 mi north of Miami International Airport, killing 110 people. Rescue operations are hampered by the presence of alligators and poisonous snakes, and there are calls for the investigation of the safety of discount airlines which use old planes.

21   The overcrowded Tanzanian-owned ferry *Bukoba* capsizes in Lake Victoria, Tanzania; 500 to 600 people drown.

JULY

17   A TWA jumbo jet, en route from New York, New York, to Paris, France, explodes over the Atlantic soon after takeoff from John F. Kennedy airport; 230 people are killed. A terrorist bomb is suspected, although later investigation suggests this is probably not the cause.

OCTOBER

31   A Brazilian airliner crashes into a residential neighborhood in Saõ Paolo, Brazil; 95 people are killed.

NOVEMBER

12   A Saudi Arabian Boeing 747 collides with a Kazakh Airways Illyushin 76 about 95 km/60 mi outside of Delhi, India. It is the world's worst ever mid-air collision, and world's third worst air disaster; 312 passengers on board the Boeing and 38 on the Illyushin are killed.

18   Fire breaks out on a Eurostar freight train traveling through the Channel Tunnel between Britain and France; the tunnel is closed for repairs and a safety inquiry is established.

5 General Motors launches the Saturn EV1 in California and Arizona. The first mass-market electric car, it has two seats, can accelerate from 0 to 60 mph in 8.5 seconds, has a top speed of 80 mph, and takes two hours to recharge. It requires no starter and no key: drivers enter a five-digit personal ID number and press "run." Sales are slow due to lack of recharging centers. In May 1997, Honda launches the EV plus which uses nickel-metal hydride batteries.

ARTS AND IDEAS

Architecture

- Poundbury, England, a new town sponsored by Prince Charles and designed by Luxembourg architect Leon Krier, opens its first 250 homes.
- The Center for Visual Arts in Toledo, Ohio, designed by U.S. architect Frank Gehry, wins an Honor Award from the American Institute of Architects.
- The first section of the Getty Center, an arts center and museum in Los Angeles, California, designed by the U.S. architect Richard Meier, is opened. The entire center officially opens in December 1997.
- The new town of Celebration, created by the Walt Disney Company and designed by a large group of architects, opens near Orlando, Florida. The town is expected to reach a population of around 20,000.
- The Spanish architect José Rafael Moneo is chosen to design a Roman Catholic cathedral to replace the building damaged by the 1994 earthquake in Los Angeles, California.

MARCH

9 The Petronas Towers, under construction in Kuala Lumpur, Malaysia, become the tallest buildings in the world. The two identical towers are 451.89 m/ 1,482.61 ft tall, 8.83 m/29 ft higher than the Chicago Sears Tower.

JUNE

- The Spanish architect José Rafel Moneo wins the Pritzker Architecture Prize, for lifetime achievement.

Arts

- "Mysteries of Ancient China," an exhibition of artifacts from 4500 BC to AD 220, is held at the British Museum in London, England.
- "Rings: Five Passions in World Art," an exhibition of more than 125 works of art at the High Museum in Atlanta, Georgia, marks the 100th anniversary of the modern Olympics.
- "Splendors of Imperial China: Treasures from the National Palace Museum, Taipei," a comprehensive exhibition of paintings, drawings, bronzes, jades, and ceramics, opens at the Metropolitan Museum of Art in New York, New York.

- A design by German architect Daniel Libeskind is chosen for a new wing of the Victoria and Albert Museum in London, England.
- The Edinburgh International Festival celebrates its 50th anniversary in Edinburgh, Scotland.
- The Museum of Modern Art (MOMA) in New York, New York, holds an exhibition of 50 years of photographs by the U.S. photographer Roy DeCarava, who documented the U.S. civil-rights movement and black cultural life in the United States.

Film

- The movie *101 Dalmatians*, directed by Stephen Herek, is released in the United States, staring Glenn Close, Jeff Daniels, and Joely Richardson. It is a remake of the 1961 animated movie.
- The movie *A Time to Kill*, directed by Joel Schumacher and based on the book by John Grisham, is released in the United States, starring Matthew McConaughey, Samuel L. Johnson, and Sandra Bullock.
- The movie *Al Massui/The Destiny*, directed by Youssef Chahine, is released in Egypt, starring Nour el Sherif, Mahmoud Nemida, and Mohamed Mounir.
- The movie *Brassed Off*, directed by Mike Herman, is released in Britain, starring Pete Postlethwaite, Tara Fitzgerald, Ewan McGregor, and Jim Carter.
- The movie *Breaking the Waves*, directed by Danish filmmaker Lars von Trier, is released in Britain, starring Emily Watson and Stellan Skarsgard.
- The movie *Dead Man Walking*, directed by Tim Robbins and Susan Sarandon, is released in the United States. It also stars Susan Sarandon with Sean Penn.
- The movie *Emma*, directed by Douglas McGrath, is released in the United States. Based on the book by Jane Austen, it stars Gwyneth Paltrow, Toni Collette, Ewan McGregor, and Alan Cumming.
- The movie *Eraser*, directed by Chuck Russel, is released in the United States, starring Arnold Schwarzenegger, Vanessa Williams, and Robert Pastorelli.
- The movie *Evita*, directed by English filmmaker Alan Parker, is released in the United States, based on the Andrew Lloyd Webber musical, starring Madonna, Antonio Banderas, and Jonathan Pryce.
- The movie *Fargo*, directed by Joel Coen, is released in the United States, starring Frances McDormand, William H. Macy, Steve Buscemi, and Peter Stormare.
- The movie *Fierce Creatures*, directed by Robert Young, is released in Britain, starring John Cleese, Jamie Lee Curtis, Kevin Kline, and Michael Palin.
- The movie *Gabbeh*, directed by Mohsen Makhmalbaf, is released in Iran, starring Shaghayeh Djodat and Hossein Moharami.
- The movie *Get on the Bus*, directed by Spike Lee, is released in the United States. Based around the "Million Man March" of 1995, it stars Ossie Davis, Charles S. Dalton, Andre Braugher, DeAudre Bonds, Albert Hall, Thomas Jefferson Byrd, Richard Belzer, and Gabriel Casseus.
- The movie *Happy Together*, directed by Kar-wai Wong, is released in the United States, starring Tony Leung Chiu-Wai, Leslie Cheung Kwok-Wong, and Chang Chen.

- The movie *In the Bleak Midwinter*, directed by Kenneth Branagh, is released in Britain. He also stars in it, with Richard Briers, Joan Collins, Michael Maloney, John Sessions, and Julia Sawalha.
- The movie *Independence Day*, directed by Roland Emmerich, is released in the United States, starring Will Smith, Bill Pullman, Jeff Goldblum, and Judd Hirsch.
- The movie *Jane Eyre*, directed by Italian filmmaker Franco Zeffirelli, is released, starring William Hurt and Charlotte Gainsbourg.
- The movie *Jerry Maguire*, directed by Cameron Crowe, is released in the United States, starring Tom Cruise, Cuba Gooding, Jr., and Renée Zellweger.
- The movie *Kansas City*, directed by Robert Altman, is released in the United States, starring Jennifer Jason Leigh, Miranda Richardson, Harry Belafonte, and Steve Buscemi.
- The movie *Le Hussard sur le toit/The Horseman on the Roof*, directed by Jean-Paul Rappeneau, is released in France. Based on the novel by Jean Giono, it stars Juliette Binoche.
- The movie *Leaving Las Vegas*, directed by Mike Figgis, is released in the United States, starring Nicolas Cage and Elizabeth Shue.
- The movie *Lone Star*, directed by Joe Morton, is released in the United States, starring Kris Kristofferson, Chris Cooper, Matthew McConaughey, and Elizabeth Peña.
- The movie *Marvin's Room*, directed by Terry Zaks, is released in the United States, starring Diane Keaton, Meryl Streep, and Leonardo DiCaprio.
- The movie *Matilda*, directed by Danny DeVito, is released in the United States. Based on the children's book by Roald Dahl, it stars Danny DeVito, Mara Wilson, Rhea Perlman, and Pam Ferris.
- The movie *Michael Collins*, directed by Neil Jordan, is released in the United States, starring Liam Neeson, Aidan Quinn, and Julia Roberts.
- The movie *Mission Impossible*, directed by Brian De Palma, is released in the United States, based on the 1966–73 television series and starring Tom Cruise, Kirsten Scott-Thomas, John Voight, and Henry Czerny.
- The movie *Secrets and Lies*, directed by Mike Leigh, is released in Britain, starring Brenda Blethyn, Timothy Spall, Phyllis Logan, and Marianne Jean-Baptiste. It wins the Palme d'Or at the Cannes Film Festival in France.
- The movie *Seven*, directed by David Fincher, is released in the United States, starring Morgan Freeman, Brad Pitt, Kevin Spacey, and Gwyneth Paltrow.
- The movie *Shine*, directed by Scott Hicks, is released in Australia, starring Geoffrey Rush and Armin Mueller-Stahl.
- The movie *Sling Blade*, directed by Billy Bob Thornton, is released in the United States. Thornton also stars in it, with Dwight Yoakam, Lucas Black II, and Natalie Canerday.
- The movie *Star Trek: First Contact*, directed by Jonathan Frakes, is released in the United States, starring Patrick Stewart, Jonathan Frakes, James Cromwell, and Alice Krige.
- The movie *Surviving Picasso*, directed by James Ivory, is released in Britain, starring Anthony Hopkins as Picasso.

- The movie *The Birdcage*, directed by Mike Nichols, is released in the United States, starring Nathan Lane and Robin Williams.
- The movie *The Crucible*, directed by British filmmaker Nicholas Hytner, is released in the United States. Based on the play by Arthur Miller, it stars Daniel Day Lewis, Winona Ryder, Paul Scofield, and Joan Allen.
- The movie *The English Patient*, directed by English filmmaker Anthony Minghella, is released in the United States. Based on the novel by Michael Ondaatje, it stars Ralph Fiennes, Kristin Scott Thomas, Juliette Binoche, Willem Dafoe, and Colin Firth.
- The movie *The Nutty Professor*, directed by Tom Shadyac, is released in the United States, starring Eddy Murphy. It is based on the 1963 Jerry Lewis comedy.
- The movie *The Pillow Book*, directed by Peter Greenaway, is released in Britain, starring Ewan McGregor and Vivian Wu.
- The movie *The People vs Larry Flynt*, directed by Miloš Forman, is released in the United States. Based on the biography of the founder of the pornographic magazine *Hustler*, it stars Woody Harrelson and Courtney Love.
- The movie *The Portrait of a Lady*, directed by New Zealand filmmaker Jane Campion, is released in the United States. Based on the novel by Henry James, it stars Nicole Kidman, John Malkovich, Richard E. Grant, Shelley Winters, Shelley Duval, and John Gielgud.
- The movie *The Rock*, directed by Michael Bay, is released in the United States, starring Sean Connery, Nicolas Cage, and Ed Harris.
- The movie *The Sweet Hereafter*, directed by Atom Egoyam, is released in Canada, starring Ian Holm, Maury Chaykin, Sarah Pulley, and Tom McCamus.
- The movie *Trainspotting*, directed by Danny Boyle, is released in Britain. Based on the novel by Irvine Welsh, it stars Ewan McGregor, Ewen Bremner, Johnny Lee Miller, and Robert Carlyle.
- The movie *Twister*, directed by Dutch filmmaker Jan de Bont, is released in the United States, starring Helen Hunt and Bill Paxton.
- The movie *Unagi/The Eel*, directed by Shohei Imamura, is released in Japan, starring Kosi Yakusho, Misa Shimizu, and Fujio Tsuneda.
- The movie *William Shakespeare's Romeo and Juliet*, directed by Australian filmmaker Baz Luhrmann, is released in the United States, starring Leonardo DiCaprio and Claire Danes.
- The movie musical *Everyone Says I Love You*, directed by Woody Allen, is released in the United States, starring Goldie Hawn, Alan Alda, Woody Allen, Tim Roth, and Julia Roberts.
- The United States's top grossing movies are *Independence Day* ($306 million), *Twister*, *Mission Impossible*, *The Rock*, *The Nutty Professor*, *The Birdcage*, *Ransom*, *A Time to Kill*, *Phenomenon*, and *The First Wives Club*.

MARCH

25 The 1995 Academy Awards are held. Best Actor: Nicolas Cage, for *Leaving Las Vegas*; Best Supporting Actor: Kevin Spacey, for *The Usual Suspects*; Best Actress: Susan Sarandon, for *Dead Man Walking*; Best Supporting Actress: Mira Sorvino, for *Mighty*

Aphrodite; Best Director: Mel Gibson, for *Braveheart*; Best Picture: *Braveheart*, directed by Mel Gibson.

DECEMBER

4 U.S. filmmaker Spike Lee completes a deal with the advertising agency DDB Needham to start a new advertising firm, called DDB/Spike.

Literature and Language

- *This Wild Darkness*, U.S. writer Harold Brodkey's journal about his experience of AIDS, is published posthumously.
- A collection of poems by the English-born U.S. writer T. S. Eliot, *Inventions of the March Hare: Poems 1909–1917*, is published posthumously, edited by Christopher Ricks.
- New Zealand linguist Steven Fischer deciphers a script found on Easter Island known as rongorongo. Written in Rapanui, the island's Polynesian tongue, it tells the story of creation.
- The Australian writer David Malouf publishes his novel *The Conversations at Curlow Creek*.
- The Canadian writer Margaret Atwood publishes her novel *Alias Grace*, based on the 19th-century case of a 16-year-old girl convicted of murder.
- The Dominican-born U.S. writer Junot Díaz publishes *Drown*, a collection of his short stories.
- The Egyptian writer Naguib Mahfouz publishes *Asda as-sirah ad-dhatiyyah/Echoes of the Autobiography*.
- The English writer Beryl Bainbridge publishes her novel *Every Man for Himself*, based on the doomed voyage of the *Titanic*.
- The Rhodesian-born English writer Doris Lessing publishes her novel *Love, Again*.
- The English writer Graham Swift publishes his novel *Last Orders*, which wins the Booker Prize.
- The English writer Julian Barnes publishes his short-story collection *Cross Channel*.
- The English writer John Le Carré publishes his novel *The Tailor of Panama*.
- The English writer James Knowlson publishes *The Life of Samuel Beckett*.
- The English writer Margaret Drabble publishes her novel *The Witch of Exmoor*.
- The Irish poet Seamus Heaney publishes his poetry collection *The Spirit Level*.
- The Irish politician Gerry Adams publishes his autobiography *Before the Dawn*.
- The Irish writer Roddy Doyle publishes his novel *The Woman who Walked into Doors*.
- The Irish writer Seamus Deane publishes his autobiographical first novel, *Reading in the Dark*.
- The Nigerian writer Ben Okri publishes his novel *Dangerous Love*.
- The Nobel Prize for Literature is awarded to the Polish poet Wisława Szymborska.
- The Pulitzer Prize for Poetry is awarded to Jorie Graham for *The Dream of the Unified Field* and the Pulitzer Prize for Fiction is awarded to Richard Ford for *Independence Day*.
- The U.S. classicist Robert Fagle publishes his new English translation of Homer's *Odyssey*.

- The U.S. poet Gary Snyder publishes his poetry collection *Mountains and Rivers Without End*.
- The U.S. poet Hayden Carruth wins the National Book Award for Poetry for his collection *Scrambled Eggs and Whiskey: Poems 1991–1995*.
- The U.S. poet Robert Hass publishes his poetry collection *Sun under Wood*.
- The U.S. scholar Hershel Parker publishes the first volume of his biography *Herman Melville*.
- The U.S. writer Andrea Barrett wins the National Book Award for Fiction for *Ship Fever*, a collection of short stories.
- The U.S. writer David Markson publishes his novel *Reader's Block*.
- The U.S. writer David Foster Wallace publishes his novel *Infinite Jest*.
- The U.S. writer Elizabeth McCracken publishes her novel *The Giant's House*.
- The U.S. writer George Garrett publishes his novel *The King of Babylon Shall Not Come Against You*.
- The U.S. writer Joyce Carol Oates publishes her novel *We Were the Mulvaneys*.
- The U.S. writer Ralph Ellison's short-story collection *Flying Home* is published posthumously, edited by the U.S. scholar John F. Callahan.
- The U.S. writer Ron Hansen publishes his novel *Atticus*.
- The U.S. writer Tobias Wolff publishes *The Night in Question*, a collection of short stories.

MAY

- The English writer Helen Dunmore wins the inaugural Orange Prize for the best novel in English written by a woman for *A Spell of Winter*.

Music

- *The Smurfs Go Pop!*, an album of cover versions by the children's cartoon characters the Smurfs, is released.
- *Brain Opera*, an electronic interactive opera by U.S. composer Tod Machover, is first performed, at the inaugural Lincoln Center Festival, in New York, New York. It is also accessible via the Internet.
- *Outis*, an opera by Italian composer Luciano Berio, is first performed, at La Scala in Milan, Italy.
- At the Brit music awards, Jarvis Cocker, the lead singer of the British group Pulp, makes fun of U.S. pop singer Michael Jackson during a song in which Jackson adopts a Christ-like posture.
- The British dance group the Prodigy releases the single "Firestarter."
- The British pop group the Spice Girls releases the album *Spice*.
- The British pop group Take That releases "How Deep Is Your Love," the final single before the group split up.
- The British pop group Jamiroquai releases the album *Travelling Without Money*.
- The British pop singer George Michael releases the single "Jesus to a Child" and the album *Older*.
- The British punk band the Sex Pistols reforms.
- The British rock group the Manic Street Preachers releases the single "Design for Life" and the album *Everything Must Go*.

- The British rock group Ocean Colour Scene releases the single "The Day We Caught the Train" and the album *Moseley Shoals*.
- The English singer Sting releases the album *Mercury Falling*.
- The Irish pop group Boyzone releases the album *A Different Beat*.
- The Italian-born U.S. artist Robert Miles releases the single "Children." A dance instrumental, it is the most frequently broadcast track on U.S. radio and television during 1996, and sells more than 4.5 million copies by the end of 1997.
- The rock singer Sheryl Crow releases the album *Sheryl Crow*.
- The U.S. composer George Walker becomes the first black person to be awarded the Pulitzer Prize for Music, for his *Lilacs*.
- The U.S. country and Western singer George Strait releases the album *Blue Clear Sky*.
- The U.S. pop group the Fugees releases the album *The Score*.
- The Canadian pop singer Celine Dion releases the album *Falling into You*.
- The U.S. rock group The Dave Matthews Band releases the album *Crash*.
- The U.S. rock group No Doubt releases the album *Tragic Kingdom*.
- The U.S. rock group REM releases the album *New Adventures in Hi-Fi*.
- The U.S. rock singer Bonnies Raitt releases the album *Road Tested*.
- The U.S. rock singer Jakob Dylan releases the song "6th Avenue Heartbreak."
- The U.S. rock singer Neil Young with Crazy Horse releases the album *Broken Arrow*.
- U.S. singer Shawn Colvin releases the album *A Few Small Repairs*.
- U.S. singer Toni Braxton releases the album *Secrets*. The American Music Awards vote it the best rhythm and blues album of the year.
- U.S. singer Tracy Chapman releases the album *New Beginning* and the single "Give Me One Reason."

Theater and Dance

- A new international theater festival is launched at the Lincoln Center in New York, New York, with a performance of the complete works of Samuel Beckett by the Gate Theatre of Dublin, Ireland.
- The comedy *Art*, written by the French playwright Yasmina Reza and translated by Christopher Hampton, opens at the Wyndham Theatre in London, England, starring Albert Finney, Tom Courtenay, and Ken Stott.
- The Lyceum Theatre in Covent Garden, London, England, reopens as a theater for the first time since 1939, with a production of *Jesus Christ Superstar*, written by Andrew Lloyd Webber and Tim Rice, directed by Gale Edwards, and starring Zubin Varla.
- The musical *Passion*, by the U.S. composer and lyricist Stephen Sondheim, opens in London, England, starring Maria Friedman and Michael Ball.
- The play *Ashes to Ashes*, by the English playwright Harold Pinter opens at the Ambassador Theatre in London, England.

- The play *Portia Coughlan*, by the Irish playwright Marina Carr, is first performed, at the Abbey Theatre in Dublin, Ireland.
- The play *Stanley*, by English playwright Pam Gem, opens at the Royal National Theatre in London, England, starring Antony Sher, Deborah Findlay, and Anna Chancellor.
- The Pulitzer Prize for Drama is awarded posthumously to Jonathan Larson for *Rent*.

FEBRUARY
- The rock musical *Rent*, by U.S. composer and writer Jonathan Larson, based on Italian composer Giacomo Puccini's *La Bohème/The Bohemian Girl*, opens at the New York Theater Workshop, New York, New York. Its creator dies suddenly of an aneurysm on the night of the final dress rehearsal in January.

JUNE
2 The 1995–96 Tony Awards are held. Best Play: *Master Class*; Best Musical: *Bring in 'Da Noise, Bring in 'Da Funk*; Best Actor: George Grizzard; Best Actress: Zoe Caldwell.

JULY
- The musical *Martin Guerre*, directed by Declan Donnellan and based on *The Return of Martin Guerre* by Natalie Zemon Davis, opens in London, England. It is withdrawn after a poor reception and reopens in November to improved reviews.

AUGUST
- The restored Globe Theatre opens on the South Bank, London, England, with a production of William Shakespeare's *The Two Gentlemen of Verona*.

OCTOBER
- The musical *Big* closes in New York, New York, after only six months on Broadway. With production costs of more than $10 million, it is one of Broadway's most expensive failures to date.
4 The Circle Repertory Company is dissolved in New York, New York. It was started in 1969.

Thought and Scholarship

- The Pulitzer Prize for History is awarded to Alan Taylor for *William Cowper's Town: Power and Persuasion on the Frontier of the Early American Republic*.
- The Pulitzer Prize for General Nonfiction is awarded to Tina Rosenberg for *The Haunted Land: Facing Europe's Ghosts after Communism*.
- U.S. historian Daniel Jonah Goldhagen publishes his controversial work *Hitler's Willing Executioners: Ordinary Germans and the Holocaust*.

SOCIETY

Everyday Life

- According to the American Automobile Association (AAA), it costs 42.6 cents per mile (approximately $6,389 per year) to own and drive a new car.
- Attack dogs become the most popular pets in Russia. Increased security measures are necessary after the

BIRTHS & DEATHS

JANUARY

1 Arthur Randolph, German-born U.S. rocket scientist, chief coordinator of the Saturn project which sent man to the moon, dies in Hamburg, Germany (89).

5 Lincoln Kirstein, founder and general director of the New York City Ballet, dies in New York, New York (88).

7 Károly Grósy, prime minister of Hungary 1987–90, dies (65).

8 François Mitterrand, Socialist president of France 1981–95, dies in Paris, France (79).

11 Eric Hebborn, English art forger, dies in Rome, Italy (61).

15 Moshoeshoe II, King of Lesotho 1966–96 who led the country to independence, dies in a car crash in Lesotho (57).

17 Barbara Jordan, U.S. Democratic congresswoman, first black woman from the South to be elected to Congress (1971), dies in Austin, Texas (59).

17 Charles Madge, British sociologist who organized the Mass Observation project which utilized 2,000 observers throughout the UK to measure public opinion, dies in London, England (83).

18 Lé Fini, French surrealist painter, dies in Paris, France (87).

18 Minnesota Fats (adopted name of Rudolf Walter Wanderone), U.S. pool player, dies in Nashville, Tennessee (82).

18 N(andamuri) T(arako) Rama Roa, Indian politician and film star who portrayed mythological characters, dies (72).

20 Gerry (Gerald) Mulligan, U.S. jazz saxophonist, arranger, and composer, dies in Darien, Connecticut (68).

28 Jerry Siegel, creator of Superman and other comic book characters, dies in Los Angeles, California (81).

28 Joseph Brodsky, Russian poet, winner of the Nobel Prize for Literature in 1987, dies in New York, New York (55).

28 Julian Hill, U.S. chemist who discovered nylon, dies in Hockessin, Delaware (91).

28 Terence Reese, English bridge player and author, dies in Hove, England (82).

FEBRUARY

2 Gene Kelly, U.S. dancer and actor, dies in Beverly Hills, California (83).

9 Adolf Galland, German air ace of World War II who claimed 100 enemy aircraft and commanded the German Luftwaffe (air force), dies in Oberwinter, Germany (83).

17 Evelyn Laye, English theater actress and singer, dies in London, England (95).

20 Toru Takemitsu, Japanese composer, dies in Tokyo, Japan (65).

27 Pat(ricia) Rosemary Koechilin-Smythe, UK international showjumper, dies (67).

MARCH

3 Marguerite Duras, French writer, dramatist, and filmmaker, dies in Paris, France (81).

9 George Burns (originally Nathan Birnbaum), U.S. comedian, dies in Beverly Hills, California (100).

10 Ross Hunter (originally Martin Fuss), U.S. film producer who produced *Pillow Talk* (1959), and *Airport* (1970), dies near Los Angeles, California (79).

11 Vince Edwards (originally Vincent Edward Zoino), U.S. television and film actor known for his role as Dr. Ben Casey, dies in Los Angeles, California (67).

12 Krzysztof Kieślowski, Polish film director and screenwriter, dies in Warsaw, Poland (54).

18 Odysseus Elytis (pen name of Odysseus Alepoudhelis), Greek poet, winner of the Nobel Prize for Literature in 1979, dies in Athens, Greece (84).

27 Edmund S(ixtus) Muskie, U.S. Democrat politician, dies in Washington, D.C. (81).

31 Dante Giacosa, Italian car designer who created the Fiat 500 or "Topolino" ("Little Mouse"), which sold over four million between 1936 and 1975, dies in Turin, Italy (91).

APRIL

4 Barney Ewell, U.S. sprinter who dominated the sport in the mid-1940s, dies in Lancaster, Pennsylvania (78).

6 Greer Garson, U.S. actress, dies in Dallas, Texas (92).

9 Richard Condon, U.S. thriller writer, author of *The Manchurian Candidate* (1959) and *Prizzi's Honor* (1982), dies in Dallas, Texas (81).

13 George Mackay Brown, Scottish poet, dies in Kirkwall, Orkney Islands, Scotland (74).

23 P(amela) L(yndon) Travers, English author, creator of Mary Poppins, dies in London, England (96).

26 John (Norris) McArthur, English malariologist and microscopist who developed the McArthur microscope, a cigarette pack-size light microscope, dies (94).

MAY

5 Ai Qing, Chinese poet, dies in Beijing, China (86).

5 Beryl Burton, English cyclist, five-time world 3,000 meters pursuit champion and two-time road racing champion, dies after a fall from her bicycle in Harrowgate, England (59).

6 William Colby, director of the Central Intelligence Agency (CIA) 1973–76, is found dead in the Wicomico River, Maryland (76).

8 Serge Chermayeff (originally Sergey Ivanovitch Issakovitch), Russian-born English architect, dies in Wellfleet, Massachusetts (96).

11 Nnamdi Azikiwe, first president of Nigeria 1963–66, dies in Lagos, Nigeria (91).

23 Dorothy Hyson, U.S. film and stage actress, dies in London, England (81).

30 Timothy Leary, U.S. writer and psychologist who advised the world to "turn on, tune in, drop out," dies in Beverly Hills, California (75).

JUNE

1 N(eelam) Sanjiva Reddy, president of India 1977–82, dies (83).

6 George Snell, U.S. immunologist who discovered the histocompatibility gene complex, making tissue transplant more feasible, dies in Bar Harbor, Maine (92).

6 Jean Sinclair, South African activist, founder of the antiapartheid Black Sash movement, dies in Johannesburg, South Africa (87).

10 Uno Chiyo, Japanese novelist and kimono designer, dies in Tokyo, Japan (98).

15 Ella Fitzgerald, U.S. jazz singer, dies in Beverly Hills, California (78).

23 Andreas Papandreou, premier of Greece 1981–89 and 1993–96, dies in Athens, Greece (77).

27 Albert R. "Cubby" Broccoli, U.S. film producer who produced the James Bond films, dies in Beverly Hills, California (87).

29 Pamela Mason, English-born U.S. author and actress, dies in Beverly Hills, California (80).

JULY

1 Margot Hemingway, U.S. actress and model, dies in Santa Monica, California (41).

9 Melvin Belli, U.S. trial lawyer known for defending the common people against large corporations, dies in San Francisco, California (88).

12 John Chancellor, U.S. television journalist, dies in Princeton, New Jersey (68).

13 Pandro (Samuel) Berman, U.S. film producer, known especially for films starring Ginger Rogers and Fred Astaire, dies in Beverly Hills, California (91).

16 Geoffrey (Alan) Jellico, English landscape architect, dies in Highgate, England (95).

17 Chas Chendley, bass guitarist with the rock group The Animals, dies in Newcastle, England (57).

17 Paul Touvier, French war criminal known as the "Hangman of Lyon," who escaped custody for 40 years, dies in Fresnes prison, Paris, France (81).

23 Jean Muir, U.S. actress, known for her role in the 1940s television series *The Aldrich Family*, dies in Mesa, Arizona (85).

28 Roger Tory Peterson, U.S. ornithologist, known in Britain as the author of *A Field Guide to the Birds of Britain and Europe*, dies in Old Lyme, Connecticut (87).

30 Claudette Colbert, U.S. actress, dies in Barbados (92).

AUGUST

1 Muhammad Farah Aidid, Somali soldier and politician who drove the Somali president Siad Barre from office in 1991, is killed in faction fighting in Mogadishu, Somalia (59).

2 Michel Debré, prime minister of France 1959–62, dies in Montlouis-sur-Loire, France (84).

7 Ossie Clark (originally Raymond Clarke), English fashion designer, is stabbed to death in London, England (54).

8 Frank Whittle, British engineer who patented the basic design for the jet engine, dies in Columbia, Maryland (89).

8 Nevill Francis Mott, English physicist who researched the electronic properties of metals, semiconductors, and noncrystalline materials, winner of the Nobel Prize

for Physics in 1977, dies in Milton Keynes, England (90).

13 Antonio de Spínola, president of Portugal whose book *Portugal and the Future* (1974) sparked the revolution against the dictatorship which brought him to power and eventually restored democracy, dies in Lisbon, Portugal (86).

14 Uzo Egonu, Nigerian painter and printmaker, dies (64).

SEPTEMBER

9 Bill Monroe, U.S. bluegrass musician, dies in Springfield, Tennessee (84).

10 Gerard Ernest Geisel, president of Brazil 1974–79, dies in Rio de Janeiro, Brazil (89).

13 Jane Baxter (originally Feodora Katherine Alice Forde), English film and stage actress, dies in Wimbledon, London, England (87).

17 Spiro T(heodore) Agnew, the first U.S. vice president (1969–73) to resign under duress, dies in Berlin, Maryland (77).

20 Paul Erdös, Hungarian mathematician, dies in Warsaw, Poland (83).

22 Dorothy Lamour (originally Mary Leta Kaumeyer), U.S. actress, dies in Hollywood, California (81).

26 Geoffrey Wilkinson, English inorganic chemist who conducted pioneering work on the organometallic compounds of the transition metals, winner of the Nobel Prize for Chemistry in 1973, dies (75).

26 Nicu Ceauşescu, son of Romanian dictator Nicolae Ceauşescu, noted for his sadistic practices and his excesses of alcohol, drugs, and sex, dies in Vienna, Austria (45).

27 Ahmadzai Najibullah, communist president of Afghanistan 1986–92, is executed by the Talibaan (Islamic student army) in Kabul, Afghanistan (49).

29 Shusaku Endo, Japanese novelist, dies in Tokyo, Japan (73).

OCTOBER

5 Seymour Cray, U.S. computer designer who built the first super computers, dies in Colorado Springs, Colorado (71).

12 René Lacoste, French tennis player and sports equipment manufacturer, dies in St. Jean-de-Lux, France (92).

14 Laura La Plante, U.S. silent film actress, dies in Los Angeles, California (91).

NOVEMBER

1 Junius Richard Jayawardene, prime minister of Sri Lanka in 1977 and first president 1978–88, dies (90).

3 Jean-Bédel Bokassa, ruler of the Central African Republic 1965–79, dies in Bangui, Central African Republic (75).

5 Paula Hinton, English ballerina, dies in Birkenhead, England (72).

12 Gwen Catley, English soprano, dies in Hove, England (90).

14 Abdus Salam, Pakistani theoretical physicist, joint winner of the Nobel Prize for Physics in 1979 for his work on unified theory, dies in Oxford, England (70).

17 Alger Hiss, U.S. diplomat and liberal Democrat, convicted in 1950 of being a Soviet spy, dies in New York, New York (91).

30 Tiny Tim (originally Herbert Kauhry), U.S. singer known for his song "Tiptoe Through the Tulips," dies in Minneapolis, Minnesota (74).

DECEMBER

1 Babrak Karmal, prime minister and then president of Afghanistan 1979–86, who was installed as the new head of state with Soviet support, dies in Moscow, Russia (67).

9 Mary Leakey, English anthropologist, dies in Nairobi, Kenya (83).

15 Laurens van der Post, South African-born English author and explorer, dies in London, England (90).

17 Irving Caesar, U.S. lyricist who wrote songs for Al Jolson, Shirley Temple, Frank Sinatra, Doris Day, and others, dies in New York, New York (101).

19 Marcello Mastroianni, Italian film star, dies in Paris, France (71).

20 Carl Sagan, U.S. astronomer and author, who popularized science and designed the plaque on the Pioneer space probe, dies in Seattle, Washington (62).

30 Lew Ayres, U.S. actor best known for *All Quiet on the Western Front*, dies in Los Angeles, California (88).

collapse of communism, and the dogs are used for protection. In Moscow, attacks by dogs increase by more than 50% during the year. Owners are the most frequent victims.

- Following complaints about injuries resulting from popping corks, the champagne industry in France moves to make champagne corks safer.
- In the United States, 9.4% of households have access to the Internet.
- The rate of growth in world population declines for the first time since the flu epidemic at the end of the World War I, and includes all African countries for the first time. The decline is due to the greater availability of contraceptives, more family planning centers, better education of girls, and a growing recognition that children cost money.

APRIL

1   The U.S. population is estimated at 264.6 million; 26% are under 18, and 13% are over 65.

NOVEMBER

18–29   French truck drivers blockade roads and ports until a dispute over pay and conditions is resolved in their favor.

Media and Communication

- Ninety-eight percent of U.S. households have a color television.

JANUARY

9   The comedy *3rd Rock from the Sun* begins on U.S. television. It stars John Lithgow as the leader of a group of aliens studying the customs of Earth, and also stars Kirsten Johnston, French Stewart, Joseph Gordon-Levitt, and Jane Curtin.

MARCH

- The miniseries *Rasputin*, starring Alan Rickman, Ian McKellen, and Greta Scacchi, is shown on U.S. television.

MAY

19   The last episode of *Murder She Wrote* starring Angela Lansbury is aired in the United States. It is the longest uninterrupted run of any detective series and has run for 264 episodes.

SEPTEMBER

8   The 1995–96 Emmy Awards for television are held. Best Drama Series: *ER*; Best Comedy Series: *Frasier*; Best Actor in a Drama: Dennis Franz, for *NYPD Blue*; Best Actress in a Drama: Kathy Baker, for *Picket Fences*; Best Actor in a Comedy: John Lithgow, for *3rd Rock from the Sun*; Best Actress in a Comedy: Helen Hunt, for *Mad About You*.

NOVEMBER

- The British men's magazine *Stuff* is launched.

Sports

- In the National Football League, the Cleveland Browns move to Baltimore, Maryland, where they are renamed the Ravens.
- The Colorado Avalanche, the former Québec Nordiques, defeat the Florida Panthers in four straight games to win the National Hockey League (NHL) Stanley Cup, in their first season since moving to Denver, Colorado.
- The Spanish bullfighter Christina Sanchez becomes the first female matador in Europe.

JANUARY

5   The Miami Dolphins coach Don Shula, who leads the all-time National Football League career list with 347 wins, announces his retirement.
8   The Liberian soccer player George Weah of A. C. Milan, Italy, becomes the first African to be voted FIFA (Fédération Internationale de Football Association) World Footballer of the Year. He was also the 1995 European and African Footballer of the Year.
27   The Yugoslavian-born U.S. tennis player Monica Seles wins the women's singles at the Australian Open tennis championship in Melbourne.
28   The Dallas Cowboys defeat the Pittsburgh Steelers 27–17 at Tempe, Arizona, to win their third Super Bowl in four years. The game is watched on U.S. television by an estimated 138.5 million people, the largest-ever U.S. television audience.

FEBRUARY

12   The former world heavyweight boxing champion Tommy Morrison of the United States reveals that he is HIV-positive.

MARCH

16   The U.S. boxer Mike Tyson regains the World Boxing Council world heavyweight title, stopping the defending champion, the English fighter Frank Bruno, in the third round of their fight in Las Vegas, United States. Shortly afterwards Bruno announces his retirement.
18   The U.S. basketball player Dennis Rodman of the Chicago Bulls is fined $20,000 and suspended for six games for assaulting a referee during a National Basketball Association game.

APRIL

14   The English golfer Nick Faldo becomes the first European to win the U.S. Masters three times, at Augusta, Georgia. He is also the first British golfer to win six major tournaments since Harry Vardon won his sixth British Open in 1914.

JUNE

10   Yevgeny Kafelnikov wins the men's singles at the French Open tennis championships, becoming the first Russian to win a Grand Slam tennis title.
16   The Chicago Bulls led by Michael Jordan win their fourth U.S. National Basketball Association title in six years.
24–July 7   At the Wimbledon tennis championships in London, England, Steffi Graf of Germany wins her seventh women's singles title in nine years. Martina Hingis of Switzerland becomes the youngest-ever winner of a Wimbledon title, winning the women's doubles with Helena Sukova at the age of 15 years, 282 days, just three days younger than the 1887 women's singles winner, Lottie Dod.
29   The English boxer Henry Akinwande stops Jeremy Williams of the United States in the third round of their bout in Indio, California, to win the World Boxing Organization world heavyweight title.

JULY

14 Cigar, ridden by U.S. jockey Jerry Bailey, wins the Arlington Citation Challenge horse race at Arlington Park, Chicago, Illinois, to equal Citation's record of 16 consecutive wins between 1948 and 1950. Cigar's winning streak subsequently ends on August 10 when he loses the Pacific Classic.

18 The Orlando Magic basketball star Shaquille O'Neal joins the Los Angeles Lakers in a record seven-year deal worth $121 million.

19 The 26th Olympic Games open in Atlanta, Georgia, attended by over 10,000 athletes, representing a record 197 countries in 29 sports. Among the new sports to be introduced is women's softball.

23 At the Olympic Games in Atlanta, Georgia, the U.S. gymnast Kerri Strug overcomes a badly sprained ankle to complete her final vault to ensure that the United States wins its first-ever women's team gold medal. As it turns out, this last jump makes no difference to the final result but her bravery wins the hearts of the U.S. public.

27 At the Olympic Games in Atlanta, Georgia, Donovan Bailey of Canada wins the men's 100 meters in a new world record time of 9.84 seconds. He wins a second gold medal in the 4 × 100-meters relay.

27 At the Olympic Games in Atlanta, Georgia, the English oarsman Steven Redgrave wins the coxless pairs rowing title to become the first oarsman to win four consecutive Olympic gold medals. Only four other people have won gold medals at four or more consecutive Games.

AUGUST

• At the Olympic Games in Atlanta, Georgia, Carl Lewis of the United States wins the men's long jump to become only the second track and field athlete after U.S. discus thrower Al Oerter to win gold medals at four consecutive Games. His career total of nine gold medals puts him on a par with Paavo Nurmi of Finland and just one short of U.S. athlete Ray Ewry's haul of ten golds, achieved in the discontinued standing jump events between 1900 and 1908.

1 At the Olympic Games in Atlanta, Georgia, Michael Johnson of the United States becomes the first man to win both the 200 meters and 400 meters titles at the same Games. In the 200 meters final he sets a new 200 meters world record time of 19.32 sec, breaking his own old record by .34 sec. On the same day, Marie-José Pérec of France becomes only the second woman to achieve the women's 200 meters and 400 meters double.

4 The 26th Olympic Games close in Atlanta, Georgia, United States. The United States wins 44 gold medals; Russia, 26; Germany, 20; China, 16; France, 15; Italy, 13; and Australia, Cuba, and Ukraine, 9 each.

14 Svetlana Masterkova of Russia reduces the women's world mile record by over 3 seconds with a run of 4 min 12.56 sec in Zürich, Switzerland.

25 The U.S. golfer Tiger Woods becomes the first player to win the U.S. Amateur Championship three years in a row. Two days later he turns professional, backed by endorsement deals involving Nike and Titleist, reported to exceed $40 million.

SEPTEMBER

6 The English cyclist Chris Boardman breaks the world one-hour record at the Manchester Velodrome, England, reaching 56.376 km/35.032 mi, an improvement of 1.085 km/0.674 mi on the existing record set by Tony Rominger of Switzerland in November 1994.

7 Six months after regaining the World Boxing Council world heavyweight title, Mike Tyson of the United States wins back the World Boxing Association crown, knocking out fellow U.S. boxer Bruce Seldon in the first round.

14 The United States defeats Canada 5–2 to win the inaugural World Cup of Hockey, which, unlike the long-established Ice Hockey World Championships, includes players from the North American National Hockey League.

22 The United States' women golfers regain the Solheim Cup, defeating Europe 17–11 at Chepstow, Wales.

27 The Italian jockey Frankie Dettori rides all seven winners in one day at the Ascot race course, Berkshire, England, at accumulative odds of 25,095 to 1.

29–30 The U.S. women's tennis team, led by the Yugoslavian-born player Monica Seles, wins its first Federation Cup since 1990, defeating Spain, which has won the event for the preceding three years.

OCTOBER

13 The English race-car driver Damon Hill, in a Williams–Renault, wins the Formula One World Drivers' Championship.

20 Washington's D.C. United defeats the Los Angeles Galaxy 3–2 in sudden death overtime at Foxboro Stadium, Boston, Massachusetts, before 34,000 spectators, to win the inaugural Major League Soccer (MLS) Cup.

20–26 The New York Yankees defeat the Atlanta Braves by four games to two to win their 23rd World Series, their first since 1978.

NOVEMBER

9 The U.S. boxer Evander Holyfield stops defending champion Mike Tyson of the United States to regain the World Boxing Association world heavyweight title in Las Vegas, Nevada. It is only the second defeat of Tyson's career, while Holyfield emulates Muhammad Ali's achievement of regaining the world title twice.

9 Women's amateur boxing is recognized by the British Boxing Board of Control.

10 The Miami Dolphins quarterback Dan Marino becomes the first player in the history of the U.S. National Football League to reach a career passing mark of 50,000 yards.

Religion

• The Pulitzer Prize for Biography is awarded to Jack Miles for *God: A Biography*.

1997

POLITICS, GOVERNMENT, AND ECONOMICS

Business and Economics

- Apple computer sales fall to about 3% of the market; down from 20% ten years earlier.

JULY

9 The chief executive of U.S. computer company Apple Computer Inc., Gilbert Amelio, resigns as sales hit a downturn. He was only in the job for 18 months. The resignation signals the ongoing financial difficulties of the company.

23 The European Commission accepts the $14 billion merger of the U.S. aerospace companies Boeing Co. and McDonnell Dougles Corp. The merger, which would result in annual revenues of $40 billion, is the largest-ever in aerospace history.

AUGUST

6 U.S. computer company Apple Computer, Inc. announce that their rival Microsoft Corp would invest $150 million in Apple and pay the company $100 million for cross-licensing.

SEPTEMBER

1 Wisconsin introduces a welfare program called "Wisconsin Works" or "W2." The program assumes that every welfare claimant is capable of some type of work and eliminates automatic welfare entitlement. Wisconsin is the first state to do so.

8 The online company Compuserve, 80% of which is owned by H. & R. Block, announces that it will be sold to America Online (AOL) and WorldCom, Inc.

18 "Big Six" accounting firms Coopers & Lybrand and Price Waterhouse announce a merger which would make them the world's largest accounting and consulting firm, with 8,600 partners and around $12 billion in annual revenues.

23–25 The World Bank and the International Monetary Fund (IMF) hold their annual plenary session of their boards of governors in Hong Kong. They address such issues as corruption and liberalization of global markets.

OCTOBER

- The Hang Seng, Hong Kong's share index, falls 20% because of currency speculation against the Hong Kong dollar. On October 24, it recovers to rise 7%.

1 U.S. telecommunications firm WorldCom, Inc. makes an unsolicited $30 billion offer for MCI Communications Corp, which outbids a previous offer by British Telecom by $11 billion. If successful, it would be the largest takeover in history.

15 The U.S. Telecommunications company GTE joins the bidding for the takeover of MCI Communications Corp with a cash offer of $28 billion. If successful, it would be the largest cash takeover in history.

20 "Big Six" accounting firms KPMG Peat Marwick and Ernst & Young announce a merger to create the world's largest consulting and accounting firm, one month after the merger of Coopers & Lybrand and Price Waterhouse.

22 The South Korean government announces that it will take over Kia Motors Corp, which declared bankruptcy earlier in the year. Kia is South Korea's third-largest automobile manufacturer.

27 The Dow Jones index makes its biggest drop in history–554 points–triggering the first ever automatic trading cut-off.

NOVEMBER

10 U.S. telecommunications giant MCI agrees to accept a $37 billion takeover bid from WorldCom, Inc. WorldCom increased its offer from October by $7 billion, outbidding British Telecom and GTE. The merger will be the largest in U.S. history to date.

17 Hokkaido Takushoku, Japan's tenth largest commercial bank, ceases operations; on November 24, Yamaichi Securities, the fourth largest securities house, becomes Japan's biggest ever corporate failure.

18 Chief Operating Officer David Hoare replaces Ann Iverson as chief executive of UK textiles and clothing company Laura Ashley Holdings PLC.

24 The Japanese Yamaichi Securities Co. announces that it will cease business after a serious liquidity crisis. The failure of the 100-year-old company causes concern about the health of Japanese business.

25 Leaders of the Asia–Pacific Economic Cooperation (APEC) issue a bulletin at the close of their annual trade meeting in Vancouver, Canada, in which they outline plans for reducing tariffs and liberalizing trade restrictions in an effort to stabilize the floundering Southeast Asian economies. They also agreed that the International Monetary Fund (IMF) would be in charge of the bailout.

DECEMBER

8 Swiss Bank Corp and Union Bank of Switzerland confirm plans of a merger, which will make them the largest bank in Switzerland and the second-largest financial institution in the world, after the Bank of Tokyo-Mitsubishi in Japan.

Human Rights

- The Chinese political dissident Jingsheng Wei publishes *The Courage to Stand Alone: Letters from Prison and Other Writings*.

MAY

22 Kelly Flinn, a lieutenant in the U.S. Air Force, the first woman to fly the B-52 bomber, is discharged for having an adulterous relationship, prompting claims of sexism in the military's treatment of her.

JUNE

18 At its annual meeting in Dallas, Texas, the Southern Baptist Convention passes a resolution approving a boycott of Disney products in protest at the corporation's alleged promotion of homosexuality.

AUGUST

28 A controversial antiaffirmative action measure goes into effect in the state of California. School admissions policies must not include race or gender biases.

SEPTEMBER

26 Russian president Boris Yeltsin signs a bill that curbs religious freedom, reversing many measures granted in 1990 by the Soviet Union. Activities of religious groups that have not been registered for at least 15 years will be restricted. The Vatican and the United States condemn the bill.

Politics and Government

JANUARY

1 The Ghanaian diplomat Kofi Annan replaces Boutros Boutros-Ghali as secretary-general of the United Nations.

5 A procession of slow-moving cars brings the Yugoslavian capital, Belgrade, to a standstill in protest at the government's refusal to recognize opposition victories in municipal elections (November, 1996); there are further massive demonstrations on January 7.

6 The former Canadian prime minister Brian Mulroney accepts $1 million in an out-of-court settlement with the federal government and police, having been wrongly accused of corruption.

7 Despite allegations of ethics violations, members of the U.S. House of Representatives elect Newt Gingrich as speaker, the first Republican for 68 years to be reelected for a second term.

10 President Arnaldo Alemán Lacayo of the right wing Liberal Alliance (AL) takes office in Nicaragua.

15 Israel and the Palestine Liberation Organization (PLO) sign an agreement in Washington, D.C., reaffirming Israeli withdrawal from the West Bank town of Hebron; troops are withdrawn on January 17.

15 Petra Luschini is sworn in as Moldovan president following elections.

17 The trial in Britain of 86-year-old Szymon Serafinowicz on war crimes charges relating to the killing of Jews in Belarus during World War II collapses when he is declared senile.

19 Franz Vranitsky retires as Austrian chancellor, nominating fellow Social Democratic Party member Viktor Klima as his successor.

20 Bill Clinton (Democrat) is inaugurated as president of the United States for a second term, with Al Gore as vice president.

21 An article in the Swedish newspaper *Dagens Nyheter* accuses the state bank of accepting looted Nazi gold during World War II.

21 The U.S. House of Representatives formally reprimands the House speaker, the outspoken Republican Newt Gingrich, and fines him $300,000, for bringing discredit on the House by using tax-exempt donations for political purposes and for submitting false evidence to the House Ethics Committee.

23 Switzerland establishes a fund to compensate victims of the Holocaust and their families following the discovery of Nazi gold in Swiss banks.

26 Serious violence breaks out in southern Albania in protest at the collapse of pyramid savings programs.

27 The trial of John Du Pont, the richest man to be tried for murder in the United States, begins in Media, Pennsylvania; he is accused of killing former Olympic wrestling champion David Schultz and is convicted on February 25.

FEBRUARY

4 In a civil trial in Santa Monica, California, the U.S. former football star O. J. Simpson is found guilty of causing the death of his wife Nicole Brown Simpson and her friend Ronald Goldman; the jury awards total damages of $33.5 million to the victims' families.

4 Serious rioting follows the collapse of the "Gjallica" pyramid saving program based in the southern Albanian port of Vlore; police lose control of the town to rioters a week later, on February 11.

6 The Ecuadorian legislature dismisses President Abdalá Bucaram Ortíz on grounds of mental incapacity and appoints Fabián Alarcón acting president. Bucaram's vice president, Rosalia Arteaga, challenges Alarcón's constitutional right to the post but Alarcón is sworn in as interim president on February 12.

9 Twenty-two-year-old Stephen Anderson shoots six people dead, including his father, at the ski resort of Raumira, North Island, New Zealand.

13 Hwang Jang Kop, chair of the legislature's foreign-relations committee and within the top 25 of the nation's political hierarchy, becomes the highest-ranking North Korean official to defect to South Korea.

17 Kenneth Starr, the Whitewater special prosecutor investigating allegations of business irregularities involving U.S. president Bill Clinton while governor of Arkansas, announces his resignation in order to become dean of Pepperdine University law school in California. He retracts his resignation on February 21.

17 Mian Muhammad Nawaz Sharif becomes prime minister of Pakistan following electoral victory for the Pakistan Muslim League.

19 Deng Xiaoping, China's "paramount leader" since 1978, dies aged 92.

21 Reports indicate the replacement of Kang Song San as prime minister of North Korea; the acting premier is Hong Song Nam.

23 The Egyptian government renews for a further three years the state of emergency imposed in 1981 to counter the threat posed by Islamic extremists.

23 The Palestinian gunman Ali Abu Kamak shoots seven people, killing one, on the observation deck of the Empire State Building, New York, New York. He then shoots and kills himself.

25 The Estonian prime minister Tiit Vahi resigns following a corruption scandal; he is replaced on February 27 by Mart Siiman, deputy chairman of the Coalition Party.

27 The former U.S. army paratrooper James N. Burmeister is found guilty of murdering a black couple in a neo-Nazi initiation ceremony, raising concern over neo-Nazism in the armed forces; he is given two life terms on March 8.

MARCH

1 The Albanian president Sadi Berisha declares a state of emergency following continued rioting.

3 Koh Kun of the ruling New Korea Party (NKP) replaces Lee Soo Sung as prime minister of South Korea following the collapse of the Hanbo industrial conglomerate.

4 A proposed Republican amendment to the U.S. Constitution requiring the government to produce a balanced budget fails by one vote to gain the necessary two-thirds majority in the Senate.

4 The Algerian government announces elections for June 5; thousands die in prepolling violence.

5 The first talks for 25 years between North Korea and South Korea are held in New York, New York, together with U.S. officials. The question of talks between the three countries and China is discussed.

6 President Cheddi Jagan of Guyana dies of a heart attack. His interim replacement is Samuel Hinds.

6 Protests in Poland follow an announcement that the Gdańsk shipyard, birthplace of the labor union Solidarity, is to close.

7 German miners strike over plans to cut government coal subsidies; four days later (March 11), they bring the city of Bonn to a standstill with massive demonstrations before (March 12) a review of the proposals is promised.

9 Heavy clashes occur between Ugandan and Sudanese forces along their common border.

11 Radiation is discharged into the atmosphere from Tokaimura nuclear reactor in Japan. (On April 8, officials from the state power corporation Domen admit that the accident was the country's worst ever.)

11 The Albanian president Sadi Berisha appoints Bashkim Fino of the opposition Socialist Party prime minister.

12 A Jordanian soldier shoots seven Israeli schoolgirls dead at Nayarayim, on the Israel–Lebanon border.

15 Rebel Tutsi forces under Laurent Kabila take the key town of Kisangani, Zaire, from troops loyal to President Mobutu Sese Seko.

17 The late Guyanan president Cheddi Jagan's wife, Janet, becomes prime minister of Guyana.

17 The U.S. president Bill Clinton's nomination for director of the Central Intelligence Agency (CIA), Anthony Lake, withdraws his candidacy following hostile questioning by Republicans on the Senate intelligence committee.

18 The Israeli government orders work to begin on the Har Homa settlement in east Jerusalem despite the objections of Palestinians, sparking a political crisis in the Middle East.

22 I. K. Gujral, of the United Front Party, becomes prime minister of India following the fall of H. D. Dewe Gowda's coalition government.

24 The Australian federal Senate overturns legislation permitting euthanasia in Northern Territory.

26 Julius Chan resigns as prime minister of Papua New Guinea following controversy over the use of British mercenaries against secessionists on the island of Bougainville.

31 The trial of Timothy McVeigh, charged with the Oklahoma City bombing of April 19, 1995, opens in Denver, Colorado; on June 2, McVeigh is found guilty and, on June 13, he is sentenced to death.

APRIL

2 The Polish Sejm (parliament) approves a new constitution as a replacement for the communist charter of 1952 (suspended in 1992).

9 Lubumbashi, capital of Zaire's economically vital Shaba province, falls to antigovernment rebels under Laurent Kabila.

11 The first troops of a European Union "advisory force" arrive in Albania; the force remains in the relatively stable north of the country.

14 After being found guilty of fraud in May 1996, Jim McDougal, a former business associate of U.S. president Bill Clinton, is sentenced to three years in jail.

15 The report of an all-party committee in Belgium investigating pedophile murders is strongly critical of police and government incompetence but rejects allegations of a high-level conspiracy.

22 Troops storm the Japanese ambassador's residence in Lima, Peru, ending the hostage crisis which began on December 17, 1996; all 14 Tupac Amarú guerrillas are killed.

27–May 3 A standoff in the Davis Mountains, Texas, between federal officials and the self-declared "Republic of Texas" group ends peacefully. On November 3, the group leader Richard McLaren is found guilty of kidnapping and conspiracy to kidnap, and sentenced to 99 years in prison.

28 The Russian president Boris Yeltsin decrees far-reaching economic reforms designed to combat price-fixing and corruption in the state-owned monopolies.

MAY

1 The Labour Party led by Tony Blair wins the general election in Britain; Labour wins 418 seats, the Conservatives 165, and the Liberal Democrats 46; the following day John Major resigns as leader of the Conservative Party.

14 Fifty thousand Turkish troops begin a major offensive against bases of the Workers' Party of Kurdistan (PKK, a Kurdish guerrilla organization) established in northern Turkey.

16 A formal agreement between President Bill Clinton and Republican Congressmen is announced in the United States, promising a balanced budget by the year 2002.

16 The U.S. president Bill Clinton formally apologizes to 399 black men in Alabama left untreated for syphilis between 1932 and 1972 as part of a government experiment.

16–17 Antigovernment Tutsi rebels take Kinshasa, the capital of Zaire, and President Mobutu Sese Seko flees.

The country is renamed the Democratic Republic of Congo.

18   Natsagiyn Bagabandi of the Mongolian People's Revolutionary Party (the former Communist Party) defeats the ruling president Punsalmoagiyn Ochirbat in elections.

19   President Bill Clinton of the United States renews China's "most favored nation" status (granting it trade concessions), despite doubts over its human-rights record.

23   A Union Charter linking Belarus and Russia and aiming at eventual unification of the two countries is signed by presidents Alexander Lukashenko and Boris Yeltsin.

25   Major Johnny Paul Koruma leads a military coup that deposes President Ahmed Tejan Kebbah of Sierra Leone.

27   The Supreme Court of the United States rules that a president cannot claim immunity from a civil lawsuit unrelated to his official duties; Paula Corbin Jones is therefore able to pursue her sexual harassment case against President Bill Clinton.

29   The antigovernment Tutsi rebel leader Laurent Kabila is sworn in as president of the Democratic Republic of Congo (Zaire).

29   The Peruvian legislature dismisses three Constitutional Tribunal judges who opposed a law allowing President Alberto Fujimori to run for a third term in 2000.

JUNE

1   Bulgaria establishes a Currency Control Board, pegging the value of the lev to the dollar, in compliance with the conditions of an International Monetary Fund (IMF) aid package.

1   The Socialist Party wins the general election in France.

2   In the Canadian general election, the ruling prime minister Jean Chrétien's Liberal Party is reelected with a majority of four.

3   Germany abandons plans to use its gold reserves in meeting the financial criteria set by the European Union for joining a single currency, following domestic and international criticism of the measure.

3   The Socialist Party leader Lionel Jospin becomes prime minister of France following the general election, replacing Alain Juppé, the Rally for the Republic (RPR) leader who had led the previous center–right coalition government.

5   Algerian elections return the ruling National Democratic Rally party of President Liamine Zeroual to government; however, widespread vote-rigging is alleged.

5   Kim Hyun Chul, son of the South Korean president Kim Young Sam, is charged with bribery and corruption relating to the awarding of government contracts.

6   Henry Francis Hays, a member of the Ku Klux Klan, becomes the first white person to be executed in the state of Alabama for the murder of a black person since 1913.

6   Sinn Féin, the political arm of the Irish Republican Army (IRA), wins its first seat in the Daíl Eireann (house of representatives) in inconclusive Irish elections. Bertie Ahern of Fianna Fáil becomes prime minister on June 26, forming a minority coalition government with the right-of-center Progressive Democrats.

9   The Haitian prime minister Rosny Smarth steps down after months of unrest on the island, precipitating a lengthy cabinet crisis.

10   The former Black Panther Elmer "Geronimo" Pratt is released from prison in the United States after new evidence makes his conviction for the killing of a white schoolmistress in 1972 unsafe.

10   The notorious Khmer Rouge leader Son Sen and his family are killed in Cambodia by a supporter of Sen's rival, Pol Pot.

11   The British House of Commons votes for a total ban on handguns in a free vote.

16   A European Union (EU) heads of government meeting in Amsterdam, the Netherlands, fails to agree on expansion of the EU or extension of the system of majority voting.

17   Eugene Terreblanche, leader of the white Afrikaaner Resistance Movement (AWB) in South Africa, is sentenced to six years in jail for the attempted murder of a black farm hand.

17   Five men commit suicide following raids by French police on the homes of suspected pedophiles; 600 people are arrested.

19   The U.S. fast-food chain McDonald's wins a two-year libel case in Britain against two environmental campaigners who claimed that the company caused environmental damage and exploited workers in the Third World and that its products were linked with disease.

19   William Hague, aged 36, succeeds John Major as leader of the British Conservative Party. In the third round of the ballot of Conservative members of parliament, Hague defeats his rival Kenneth Clarke by 92 to 70 votes.

20   In a landmark agreement, U.S. tobacco companies agree to settle claims made against them by former smokers by paying $368.5 billion into a compensation fund over the next 25 years. This is in exchange for the industry's immunity from legal action.

20–22   The world's main industrialized countries meet at Denver, Colorado. Russia joins the Group of Seven (G-7)—Canada, France, Germany, Italy, Japan, the UK, and the United States. The gathering is now known as the Summit of the Eight.

23   After four days of talks in Islamabad, Pakistan, representatives of Pakistan and India agree to negotiate the future of Kashmir.

JULY

1   The British crown colony of Hong Kong reverts to Chinese control, ending 156 years of colonial rule. Hong Kong becomes a Special Administrative Region within China.

2   British chancellor of the Exchequer Gordon Brown presents the first budget plan of the new Labour Party government. The plan features a reduction in taxes on business profits and an increase in social spending, as well as a plan for an overhaul of the benefit system.

2   The Bank of Thailand abandons its attempt to support the baht, which loses 17% of its value, beginning a Southeast Asian economic crisis.

5   Second Prime Minister Hun Sen of the Cambodian People's Party overthrows First Prime Minister Norodom Ranariddh of the royalist United Front for an

Independent, Neutral, Peaceful, and Cooperative Cambodia (FUNCINPEC) in a coup in Cambodia.

6   The ruling Institutional Revolutionary Party, suffering its worst electoral defeats in 70 years, loses control of the lower house in legislative elections in Mexico.

8   At a summit meeting in Madrid, Spain, leaders of the North Atlantic Treaty Organization (NATO) formally invite the Czech Republic, Hungary, and Poland to join their military alliance in 1999.

10   During a raid in Prijedor, Bosnia-Herzegovina, British troops in the command of the North Atlantic Treaty Organization (NATO) kill a Bosnian-Serb, Simo Drljaca, who was accused of committing war crimes. Drljaca is shot after resisting arrest and firing at and wounding a British soldier.

10   The U.S. Senate confirms the appointment of George J. Tenet as director of the Central Intelligence Agency. His nomination was approved unanimously after the Justice Department decided not to investigate Tenet's personal finances.

12   A crowd of 500,000 people demonstrate in Bilbao, Spain, for the release of Miguel Angel Blanco, a government official held hostage by ETA (Euskadi ta Askatasuna, "Basque Nation and Liberty") Basque separatist terrorists demanding the relocation of ETA prisoners to the Basque country; Blanco is found dead the following day.

12   The recently discovered remains of the Latin American revolutionary activist Che Guevara are returned to Cuba from Bolivia, where he was killed in 1967.

14   Kocheril Raman Narayanan is elected president of India. He is the first president to be from India's lowest, "untouchable" caste.

15–23   One of the largest manhunts in U.S. history takes place for the serial killer Andrew Cunanan, wanted for murdering world-famous fashion designer Gianni Versace in Florida. The search ends when his body is found in a Miami Beach apartment in Florida after an apparent suicide.

19   The warlord Charles Taylor is elected president of Liberia; his National People's Party wins legislative elections.

20   The anti-Talibaan United Islamic Front for the Salvation of Afghanistan captures the town of Charikar, and subsequently advances to within 32 km/20 mi of the Afghan capital, Kabul.

20   The Irish Republican Army (IRA) restores its cease-fire (broken on February 9, 1996) in order to participate in talks on the future of Northern Ireland.

23   Sadi Berisha resigns as president of Albania following months of unrest over the collapse of pyramid investment programs.

23   Slobodan Milošević is sworn in as president of Yugoslavia, a federation of Serbia and Montenegro. He was nearing the end of his second five-year term as president of Serbia, and ran unopposed for the new position.

25   Brendan Smyth, a Roman Catholic priest in Ireland, is sentenced to 12 years in prison for sexually abusing children 74 times over a 36-year period. He recently completed a four-year prison sentence in Northern Ireland for similar crimes.

25   The socialist Fatos Nano becomes prime minister of Albania, following elections.

28   The White House and the U.S. Congress agree on a final version of a plan to balance the budget by 2002. The plan comprises a balanced budget bill and a tax cuts bill.

30   Two suicide bombers set off explosives in a crowded market in west Jerusalem, killing at least 13 other people and injuring at least 150 others. The extremist Palestinian Islamic organization Hamas claims responsibility.

31   The U.S. government lifts a ten-year-old ban on travel by American tourists to Lebanon. The ban was initiated in 1987 during the hostage crisis.

AUGUST

•   The largest sex scandal in U.S. Army history is uncovered at Aberdeen Proving Ground in Maryland, involving sexual assault and abuse. It prompts an investigation at army installations worldwide. The ensuing report discovers that sexual harassment and discrimination are pervasive in the army.

5   Hugo Bánzer Suárez is elected president by the Bolivian Congress.

11   For the first time, U.S. president Bill Clinton uses the line-item veto (a power granted by Congress to the president in April 1996) to deal with taxation and expenditure bills.

13   The Russian deputy prime minister Alfred Kokh resigns following allegations of corruption in his handling of the privatization of the state nickel mining group.

19   After a week of ethnic violence in Mombasa, Kenya, the country suffers a decline in tourism, its most profitable industry.

25   The former Cambodian prime minister and Khmer Rouge leader Pol Pot is found guilty by a Khmer Rouge court in Cambodia of ordering the murder of his rival Son Sen and given a life sentence.

25   The government of Andris Skele in Latvia resigns; Guntar Krasts forms a coalition three days later.

27   The governments of Sweden and Norway admit to sterilizing thousands of people deemed "substandard" (including those of low intelligence and the mentally or physically disabled) between 1934 and 1976.

28   The United Nations Security Council passes a resolution that imposes air and travel sanctions against the National Union for Total Liberation of Angola (UNITA), an armed rebel group that controls some parts of Angola.

29   Britain's Northern Ireland Secretary Mo Mowlam invites Sinn Féin, the political arm of the Irish Republican Army (IRA), to all-party talks on Northern Ireland.

31   Diana, Princess of Wales, her companion Dodi Fayed, and their driver are killed in a car crash in the Place de l'Alma underpass in Paris, France. Blame for the crash is initially laid with photographers chasing the car, but it is revealed on September 1 that the driver, Henri Paul, had been drinking and was taking prescription drugs.

SEPTEMBER

2   A court in Denmark sentences three neo-Nazis to jail terms for sending letter bombs to mixed-race couples and other targets in Britain.

4   Three suicide bombers from an offshoot of the Palestinian Hamas organization kill three Israelis and injure 190 others in attacks on west Jerusalem.

6 The funeral service for Diana, Princess of Wales, is held in Westminster Abbey, London, England; her body is subsequently taken to Althorp, the Spencer family estate in Northamptonshire, for burial. An estimated 2 billion people worldwide watch the service on television.

10 The U.S. secretary of state Madeleine Albright visits the Middle East; on September 11, she calls on Israel to stop its settlement building program.

11 In a referendum, 74.3% of Scottish voters approve the creation of their own parliament, with 63.5% voting in favor of giving it tax-raising powers. The parliament is to have some control over local interest rates, and will have the power to raise or lower tax rates by up to three percentage points.

12 The 15th Congress of the Chinese Communist Party confirms Jiang Zemin as general secretary and endorses the continuation of the late Deng Xiaoping's liberal economic policies.

14 After discussions in Calgary, Alberta, the premiers of nine out of Canada's ten provinces and the commissioners of its two territories agree to recognize the unique character of Quebec's culture and society. Quebec's separatist premier, Lucien Bouchard, boycotts the meeting.

15 William Weld, U.S. president Bill Clinton's nominee for ambassador to Mexico, withdraws his candidacy after the refusal by Jesse Helms, chairman of the U.S. Senate foreign-relations committee, to schedule a hearing for his nomination.

18 A ruling Socialist Party member of the Albanian parliament shoots and wounds an opposition delegate in the People's Assembly in Tirana, triggering widespread riots.

18 Welsh voters narrowly approve the establishment of a representative assembly for Wales (50.3% in favor).

21 The right wing Solidarity Electoral Alliance wins the legislative elections in Poland.

23 Turkish troops conduct large-scale attacks on bases of the Workers' Party of Kurdistan (PKK, a Kurdish guerrilla organization) in northern Iraq.

24 The military wing of the main Islamic opposition group in Algeria instructs its members to lay down their arms for the first time in six years of civil war.

OCTOBER

• The U.S. Congress votes in favor of legislation requiring young foreign au pairs to be trained in childcare and child safety and to take a minimum number of educational courses during the year they spend in the United States. The vote is prompted by the case of the British au pair Louise Woodward, who was accused of murdering a baby boy in her care.

1 Fiji formally rejoins the British Commonwealth, having repealed legislation discriminating against Fijian Indians which had led to its expulsion in 1987.

2 North Atlantic Treaty Organization (NATO) officials report that the Muslim-led Bosnian government is secretly rearming and training its military to attack the Bosnian Serbs.

3 The U.S. attorney general Janet Reno orders the Justice Department to investigate allegations of illegal campaign financing involving Vice President Al Gore; the investigation is extended to President Bill Clinton on October 15.

8 The European Commission rejects U.S. proposals for global rules permitting law enforcement officials to unscramble coded messages transmitted over telephone lines and computer networks, characterizing the rules as an invasion of privacy.

10 Four major U.S. tobacco companies, Brown & Williamson, Lorillard, Philip Morris, and R. J. Reynolds, announce a $349 million settlement with flight attendants who claimed health problems resulting from secondhand smoke in the workplace. This is the first class-action suit involving liability for secondhand smoke.

12 Forty thousand Zapatista National Liberation Army guerrillas and their supporters march through Mexico City, Mexico, demanding greater rights for Native Americans.

12 Ramzi Ahmed Yousef and Eyad Ismoil are convicted in the United States of the 1993 World Trade Center bombing in New York, New York.

13 Kjell Magne Bondevik of the Christian People's Party becomes prime minister of a minority coalition government in Norway following elections.

13 The legislators of Nevis vote to secede from the federation of St. Kitts and Nevis. The initiative will be decided by a referendum within six months.

14 Vietnam devalues its currency, the dong, in response to the Southeast Asian economic crisis.

17 France opens official archives relating to the killing of Algerian demonstrators by police in 1961; the number of dead, previously put at two, is now estimated at over 90.

23 The rebel "Cobra" militiamen leader Denis Sassau-Nguesso arrives in Brazzaville, the capital of Congo, following victory in his war with President Pascal Lissouba.

25 An estimated 1.5 million black women participate in the Million Woman March in Philadelphia, Pennsylvania, to protest against the notion of blacks as victims.

26 Italy joins the Schengen group, a zone with open borders in the European Union with seven other member countries.

27 In a speech before parliament, British chancellor of the Exchequer Gordon Brown says that the government does not plan to join the European Union's economic and monetary union (EMU) until at least 2002. The EMU plans to launch the new European currency, the euro, in 1999.

29 Iraq threatens to end cooperation with the United Nations Special Commission (UNSCOM), responsible for ensuring Iraq's nuclear, chemical, and biological disarmament, unless UNSCOM's U.S. personnel are withdrawn. UNSCOM suspends operations in Iraq.

30 The British nanny Louise Woodward is found guilty of the murder of baby Matthew Eappen by a court in Cambridge, Massachusetts; the following day she is sentenced to life imprisonment.

31 After Indonesian president Suharto agreed to major economic reforms and anticorruption measures in the banking industry, including the closure of 16 banks, the International Monetary Fund (IMF) announces a $33 billion loan package to stabilize Indonesia's economy.

31 Jerzy Buzek of the right wing Solidarity Electoral Alliance (AWS) forms a coalition government with the probusiness Freedom Union (UW) in Poland.

NOVEMBER

- The U.S. Justice Department sees Microsoft's coercion of computer manufacturers to bundle its Web browser, Internet Explorer, with its operating system, Windows 95, as unfair trading and an attempt to dominate the market, and orders the company to pay $1,000,000 a day. The fine is waived in December.

1 Conservative shadow agriculture minister David Curry resigns in protest at party leader William Hague's firm opposition to Britain joining the European monetary union. The move marks a growing dispute within the Conservative party between those who are for and against joining the union.

4–7 French truck drivers blockade roads and ports until a negotiated settlement ends their dispute over pay and conditions.

5 The British Labour government confirms that they are exempting Formula One automobile racing from a ban on tobacco advertising in sports events. A scandal erupts after links are revealed between the government and high level Formula One officials.

10 In a significant defeat, the U.S. president Bill Clinton is forced to withdraw "fast track" legislation, giving him greater power to negotiate trade treaties, because of Republican opposition in Congress and lack of support from his own party.

10 U.S. Judge Hiller Zobel reduces the second degree murder charge against the British nanny Louise Woodward to involuntary manslaughter and frees her, deeming the 279 days she has spent in jail awaiting trial sufficient punishment; Woodward must remain in the United States pending an appeal by the prosecution. Zobel also publishes his ruling on the Internet—he is the first judge to do so.

17 Richard Hu, finance minister of Singapore, announces measures to liberalize the financial sector in anticipation of the deregulation of the country's economy in 1998.

17 Up to 68 people are killed when Islamic terrorists attack two tourist buses near Luxor, Egypt.

20 British home secretary Jack Straw announces plans to increase the electronic tagging of convicts to help reduce the prison population. The plan would enable criminals serving short sentences to be released up to two months ahead of schedule, fitted with electronic bracelets to record their movements.

21 South Korea, the world's tenth largest economy, seeks International Monetary Fund (IMF) assistance in response to financial crisis and a fall in value of its currency, the won.

24 The Truth and Reconciliation Committee in South Africa begins hearing allegations of involvement in political murder against Winnie Madikizela-Mandela, former wife of President Nelson Mandela.

25 Britain's chancellor of the Exchequer Gordon Brown announces in a pre-budget report that the British welfare system is to be radically revised; he also allocates extra money for out-of-school work clubs and pensioners' heating bills. He announces plans to reduce Britain's corporate tax rate from 31% to 30%, to take effect in April 1999, which would result in a £2 billion tax cut for business over the next few years.

28 In India, I. K. Gujral's minority United Front government collapses when Congress (I) withdraws support. An early general election is called for December 4.

30 Carlos Roberto Flores Facussé is reelected president of Honduras; his Liberal Party wins legislative elections.

DECEMBER

1 The British government establishes an independent commission to recommend alternative voting systems, promising a referendum on the issue before the next election.

2 Attorney General Janet Reno announces that she will not recommend the appointment of a special prosecutor into possible violations of campaign finance law by U.S. president Bill Clinton and vice president Al Gore.

3 The International Monetary Fund (IMF) and the South Korean government formally agree to terms of a $57 billion bailout to help recover the country's failing economy.

4 More than 125 countries sign an international treaty in Ottawa, Canada, banning landmines.

8 Jenny Shipley of the National Party becomes New Zealand's first woman prime minister, replacing Jim Bolger, who announced on November 3 that he would resign the leadership of the National Party and the premiership.

9 North Korea, South Korea, the United States, and China meet in Geneva, Switzerland, to start talks about a permanent peace agreement in place of the armistice that ended the Korean War in 1953.

10 The Chinese government announces that Australia is an "approved destination" for Chinese tourists; Australia is the first non-Asian country to achieve the status.

12 Mouaouia Ould Sidi Mohammed Taya is reelected president of Mauritania. The election is boycotted by the main opposition parties.

12 The U.S. Justice Department orders Microsoft to sell its Internet browser separately from its Windows operating system to prevent it from building a monopoly of Web access programs.

13 At a meeting in Luxembourg, European Union (EU) heads of government invite Cyprus, the Czech Republic, Estonia, Hungary, Poland, and Slovenia to start talks in March 1998 on joining the EU.

15 The U.S. Federal Trade Commission (FTC) approves the £23.8 billion merger of Guinness and Grand Met. This enables the new company, Diageo, to be traded on the London Stock Exchange.

16 The Japanese government announces measures to prevent further financial crises and to stimulate the economy. The measures include issuing government bonds worth 10 trillion yen and tax cuts of 850 billion yen.

17 Thabo Mbeki becomes president of the ruling African National Congress (ANC) during the party's 50th national conference at Mafikeng, South Africa. Mbeki replaces Nelson Mandela, who steps down as party leader while remaining president of South Africa.

18 Kim Dae Jung of the opposition National Congress for New Politics wins presidential elections in South Korea.

19 In the first case of its kind in Australia, a primary school principal in Victoria is charged with failing to report a claim by a five-year-old boy that he was being sexually abused by his father.

23 Venezuelan terrorist Ilich Ramírez Sánchez, known as Carlos the Jackal, is sentenced to life imprisonment in Paris, France, for the murder in 1975 of two French secret service agents and a Lebanese informer.

27 Billy Wright, presumed leader of the Loyalist Volunteer Force, a militant Protestant group in Northern Ireland, is shot and killed by Roman Catholic inmates at the Maze prison near Lisburn, Northern Ireland. The killers are members of the Irish National Liberation Army (INLA), a guerrilla group that had broken off from the Irish Republican Army (IRA). The incident escalates concerns for the future of the Northern Ireland peace process.

29 Presidential and legislative elections in Kenya are disrupted by violence (in which at least ten people are killed), allegations of polling irregularities, and floods. Because of these disruptions, polling is extended by an extra day. President Daniel arap Moi, already in power for 19 years, is sworn in for a further five-year term on January 5, 1998.

29 The number of recorded murders for the year (1997) in New York, New York, is the lowest since 1967. The total is 756; in 1992 it was 2,262.

SCIENCE, TECHNOLOGY, AND MEDICINE

Computing

- About 39% of U.S. households have personal computers.
- An attempt in the United States to bring in legislation to control the Internet, intended to prevent access to sexual material, is rejected as unconstitutional.
- Multimedia personal computers fall below $1,000 for the first time. Nearly one-third of all new PCs sold in the year are sold below this figure.
- There are between 100 and 150 million Web pages on the World Wide Web.
- U.S. company Dragon Systems releases "Naturally Speaking," the world's first voice-recognition software program that recognizes and creates text from normal continuous speech. Spoken words are transcribed immediately onto the computer screen at up to 160 words per minute or higher, with over 95% accuracy.
- U.S. software company Microsoft's stock more than doubles during the year as the company becomes the major player on the Internet.

JANUARY
- U.S. firm Texas Instruments introduces a digital-signal microprocessor chip that can process 1.6 billion instructions a second—about 40 times more powerful than current chips.

MARCH
6 The queen of England gets a web site. It is entitled the British Monarchy, and its address is http://www.royal.gov.uk/

JUNE
3 U.S. computer scientists announce the construction of logic gates from DNA (deoxyribonucleic acid) which simulate the functions of an **OR** gate and an **AND** gate. Rather than responding to an electronic signal, the DNA gates respond to nucleotide sequences.

AUGUST
4 Using computer models, British meteorologist Alan O'Neill demonstrates a connection between the collapse of anchovy fishing in Peru, drought in Australia, and the late arrival of India's monsoons and El Niño, the warm ocean surge off South America's west coast.

Ecology

- Outside Mecca in Saudi Arabia, more than 200 Muslim pilgrims are killed when a fire breaks out among the tents where they are staying during the religious celebrations.

FEBRUARY
- U.S. zoologists Bill Detrich and Kirk Malloy show that the increased ultraviolet radiation caused by the hole in the ozone layer above Antarctica kills large numbers of fish in the Southern Ocean. Because their transparent eggs and larvae stay near the surface for up to a year, they are exposed to the full force of the ultraviolet rays. It is the first time ozone depletion in the Antarctic has been shown to harm organisms larger than one-celled marine plants.

MARCH
26 German ecologist Venugopalan Ittekkot shows that dams on the River Danube keep back silicate sediments and thus starve the Black Sea of food for many marine plants, and create ideal conditions for the growth of toxic competitors, altering the sea's ecosystem. Silicate-loving sea grasses have been replaced by nitrate-loving species such as dinoflagellates which cause poisonous red tides. It raises concern that the world's thousands of dams may be slowly killing the world's seas.

APRIL
15 At least 217 Muslim pilgrims are killed and 1,300 others injured as fire sweeps through a tent city near Mecca, Saudi Arabia.

MAY
10 An earthquake in northern Iran, measuring 7.2 on the Richter scale, kills more than 1,600 people, and makes a further 50,000 people homeless.

JUNE
June–November Plantation owners in Indonesia, burning forests to clear land, cause the worst forest fires in Southeast Asian history. Smoke blankets most parts of Southeast Asia, including Malaysia, Singapore, Brunei, and Indonesia, closing airports, offices, and schools. World record levels of atmospheric pollution reach life-threatening levels; up to 20 million people in Indonesia are affected with throat and respiratory inflammations and diarrhea, and in October in the state of Sarawak, Malaysia, over 10,000 people in one week seek medical help for respiratory complaints. More than 50,000 Indonesian soldiers and civilians along with over 1,000 fire-fighters from Indonesia and Malaysia and specialists from other countries are used to combat the

fires which by September have consumed between 300,000–600,000 hectares/740,300–1,480,000 acres.

9–29   At the tenth Convention on International Trade in Endangered Species (CITES) convention in Harare, Zimbabwe, the elephant is downlisted to CITES Appendix II (vulnerable) and the ban on ivory exportation in Botswana, Namibia, and Zimbabwe is lifted.

11   French meteorologist Cyril Moulin shows that up to a billion metric tons of dust a year are blown off the arid drought-prone lands surrounding the Sahara Desert in north Africa and carried as far as the UK and the Caribbean. The amount has more than doubled in the past 30 years.

25   A volcanic eruption in the Soufrière Hills on the British dependency of Montserrat in the Leeward Islands, West Indies, kills 23 people and prompts pleas to Britain for assistance.

26   The second Earth Summit takes place in New York, New York. Delegates report on progress since the 1992 Rio Summit and note that progress on the Rio biodiversity convention has been slower than on the convention on climate. The delegates fail to agree on a deal to address the world's escalating environmental crisis. Dramatic falls in aid to the so-called Third World countries, which the 1992 summit promised to increase, are at the heart of the breakdown.

July

• Flooding in central Europe causes more than 100 deaths in Poland and the Czech Republic and forces hundreds of thousands of people to evacuate. The flood, caused by the overflow of the Oder River, is the worst to hit the area in 200 years.

7   The Chilean government grants permission to U.S. businessman and conservationist Douglas Tompkins, to create a national park on a 677,000 acre/274,000 ha area of land he owns in southern Chile.

25   The U.S. Senate votes unanimously to pass a resolution that urges President Clinton not to agree to an international treaty that limits emissions of greenhouse gases by industrialized countries, warning that such a pact could pose a threat to the U.S. economy.

August

3–8   Soufrière Hills volcano on the Caribbean island of Montserrat, after nearly two years of constant eruption, enters a phase of violent eruption and major pyroclastic flow which, over the next few months, virtually destroys the capital city of Plymouth. The British government considers permanently relocating all of Montserrat's citizens off the island.

26   At the World Climate Research Program meeting in Geneva, Switzerland, weather experts predict that El Niño could cause extreme weather conditions during the first six months of 1998 in Asia, Africa, and the United States.

27   The voluntary evacuation of Montserrat begins because of the threat of further volcanic activity.

September

• Forest fires in Indonesia cause dense smog throughout the region; a state of emergency is declared in eastern Malaysia on September 19.

7   Australian researcher William de la Mare, using old whaling records which record data on every whale caught since the 1930s, including the ship's latitude, announces the discovery that Antarctic sea-ice could have decreased by up to a quarter between the mid-1950s and the 1970s. The finding has major implications, both for global climate conditions as well as for whaling.

26   Two earthquakes strike central Italy, killing at least 11 people and injuring more than 120. The worst in Italy since 1980, the earthquakes also damage priceless frescoes at the Basilica of St. Francis in Assisi.

October

8–9   Hurricane Pauline hits Mexico's southern coast, killing at least 230 people and leaving around 20,000 homeless. The strength of the storm, which causes extensive damage to the tourist resort of Acapulco, is blamed on El Niño.

22   U.S. president Bill Clinton announces a proposal to fight global warming by introducing $5 billion in tax breaks to companies who agree to reduce their greenhouse emissions.

November

• Three weeks of rain causes severe flooding in Somalia, killing over 2,000 people and leaving 250,000 people homeless. A cholera outbreak follows the floods.

3   Typhoon Linda hits the southern coast of Vietnam, killing more than 100 people and destroying around 13,000 homes in Ca Mau and the neighboring province of Ben Tre.

25   The Federal Energy Regulatory Commission orders the U.S. company Edwards Manufacturing to demolish the 160-year-old Edwards Dam on the Kennebec River, Maine, to give sturgeon and salmon a chance to reach their spawning grounds. It is the first time a working hydroelectric dam has been ordered to be removed.

Exploration

• The *Solar Heliospheric Observatory* satellite (SOHO) reveals that Venus's ion-packed tail is 45 million km/ 27,963,000 mi in length. Discovered in the late 1970s, it stretches away from the sun and is caused by the bombardment of the ions in Venus's upper atmosphere by the solar wind.

January

• The U.S. Universal Lunarian Society begins offering one-acre sites in the lunar crater Copernicus for $50 with the idea of colonizing the moon. The lunar colony, to be called The City of Lunaria, will consist of 61 zones, each one mile in diameter, covered by elliptical domes containing a controlled atmosphere.

February

• The U.S. spacecraft *Galileo* begins orbiting Jupiter's moon Europa. It takes photographs of the moon for a potential future landing site.

28   The Italian–Dutch satellite *BeppoSAX* observes the first visible-light image of a cosmic gamma-ray burst (GRB)—powerful flashes of gamma rays which occur daily, and randomly, and which outshine all other gamma rays combined. The bursts release more energy in 10 seconds than the sun will emit in its entire 10-billion-year lifetime, yet no source has ever been observed. Dutch astronomer Jan van Paradijs and his Italian–Dutch team observe a light source in a distant

galaxy that quickly fades after the burst. The bursts were previously thought to be relatively nearby in space.

MARCH

- U.S. astronomers announce that the spacecraft *Galileo* has detected molecules containing carbon and nitrogen on Jupiter's moon Callisto, suggesting that life once existed there.

APRIL

8   English astronomer Alan Penny announces the European Space Agency's project Darwin, a collection of six infrared telescopes 40 times more powerful than the Hubble Space Telescope. Planned to be launched in the year 2015, Darwin's telescopes would have to be stationed between Mars and Jupiter to avoid the light reflected by dust in the inner solar system, and would have to be positioned relative to one another to an accuracy of millionths of a meter. Together they would make a telescope 100 m/328 ft across and would be sensitive enough to detect water or air, and thus life, on a planet 40 or 50 light-years away.

JUNE

25   During a manually guided docking maneuver the Russian space station *Mir* collides with its unmanned cargo supply vessel, causing the space station to lose power and oxygen and to tumble out of control. Repairs are subsequently made.

27   The U.S. *Near Earth Asteroid Rendezvous* (NEAR) spacecraft flies within 1,200 km/746 mi of the asteroid Mathilde, taking high-resolution photographs and revealing a 25-km/15.5-mi crater covering the 53-km/33-mi asteroid.

JULY

4   The U.S. spacecraft *Mars Pathfinder* lands on Mars. Two days later the probe's rover *Sojourner*, a six-wheeled vehicle which is controlled by an Earth-based operator, begins to explore the area around the spacecraft.

AUGUST

7   The space shuttle *Discovery* blasts off from Cape Canaveral, Florida, on a 12-day ozone research mission to gather environmental data and test new equipment to be used on a future international space station.

SEPTEMBER

12   The U.S. *Mars Global Surveyor* spacecraft goes into orbit around Mars to conduct a detailed photographic survey of the planet, commencing in March 1998, and reports the discovery of bacteria there. The spacecraft uses a previously untried technique called "aerobraking" to turn its initially highly elongated orbit into a 400-km/249-mi circular orbit by dipping into the outer atmosphere of the planet.

NOVEMBER

25   U.S. astronaut Winston Scott and Japanese astronaut Takao Doi, on board the U.S. space shuttle *Columbia*, succeed in retrieving the *Spartan* satellite which had gone out of control the previous week when it was hit by *Columbia*'s robotic arm as it was being released into space. They retrieve it by hand.

Health and Medicine

- Alternative medicines such as acupuncture, herbal remedies, osteopathy and chiropractice gain increasing acceptance in the United States from both the public and medical communities. Over $15 billion a year is spent on alternative medicine.
- Health Maintenance Organizations (HMOs) in the United States cover 75% of privately insured patients, up from only 13% in 1993. The HMOs, however, are criticized for denying essential care in their efforts to cut costs.
- The Nobel Prize for Physiology or Medicine is awarded to the U.S. physiologist Stanley B. Prusiner for his discovery of prions—a new type of disease-causing agent.
- U.S. physician Andrew Weil's book *8 Weeks to Optimum Health* tops the best-seller list.

JANUARY

- The World Health Organization (WHO) estimates that 22.6 million men, women, and children have to date been infected by HIV, the virus responsible for causing AIDS. Approximately 42% of adult sufferers are female, with the proportion of women infected steadily increasing.

10   Ten "right-to-die" charges against U.S. physician Jack Kevorkian are dropped, ruled a waste of taxpayers' money, ending official attempts to stop Kevorkian, known as "Dr. Death," from helping terminally ill patients to die. To date he has assisted at least 45 patients.

31   An international team of scientists reports the discovery of the gene for a type of glaucoma (open angle glaucoma, one of the commonest forms of blindness) that threatens up to one person in 50 in later life. The gene, on human chromosome number 1, codes for a protein called TIGR which could be linked to the destruction of nerve cells in the eye.

FEBRUARY

- The Centers for Disease Control and Prevention in Atlanta, Georgia, report that deaths among people with AIDS declined 13% during the first six months of 1996 over the same period the year before.

MARCH

- Over 260 Michigan schoolteachers and children become ill after eating strawberries tainted with the hepatitis A virus. The strawberries were grown in Mexico in a field next to an open unlined privy.

6   The National Center for Health Statistics finds that 35% of U.S. adults are overweight enough to be unhealthy, an increase of 15% since 1980. It notes that 36% of women, 33% of men, 14% of children aged 6–11, and 12% of adolescents aged 12–17 are obese.

APRIL

30   U.S. researchers at the University of Pennsylvania Medical Center report that chimpanzees immunized with a new kind of DNA-based vaccine and then infected with 250 times the HIV needed to cause infection, had no trace of the virus after 48 weeks. The report again raises hopes for a vaccine.

MAY

8   U.S. AIDS researcher David D. Ho and colleagues show how aggressive treatment of HIV-1 infection with a cocktail of three antiviral drugs can drive the virus to below the limits of conventional clinical detection within eight weeks.

17–20   At a meeting of the American Society of Clinical Oncology, researchers announce the development of vaccines that cause the immune system to shrink certain cancers, such as those attacking the skin, breast, prostate, and ovaries. Unlike the normal preventative vaccines, the new vaccines fight tumors that already exist. They use components of the cancer to provoke white blood cells to attack the invader.

JUNE

26   UK physiologist Stephen O'Rahilly and colleagues show that human obesity can be caused by a mutation in the gene that produces the hormone leptin. The brain uses leptin as a measure of the amount of body fat; an increase in fat means an increase in leptin which suppresses the appetite and increases the burning of excess calories. A deficiency of leptin, caused by a malfunction in its gene, means that the brain receives no signal of body fat levels which, as far as the brain is concerned, means no fat. Pharmaceutical companies compete for the rights to develop dieting products based on this knowledge.

27   U.S. scientists at the National Human Genome Research Institute in Bethesda, Maryland, announce the discovery of a gene that causes Parkinson's disease. The gene produces a protein called alpha synuclein. When the instructions of the gene go wrong, the protein's structure is affected and this causes the buildup of deposits on brain cells that is usually seen in Parkinson's sufferers.

AUGUST

4   U.S. researchers Sidney Altman, Cecilia Guerreir-Takada, and Reza Salavati discover a gene-transfer method of disabling the genes in disease organisms that allow them to neutralize common antibiotics. This makes the bacteria vulnerable, once again, to treatment with antibiotics and combats the growing problem of bacterial drug-resistance. The biomedical company Innovir Laboratories works on developing the process to combat viruses such as those responsible for hepatitis B and C.

12   Nebraska's Hudson Meats Ltd. recalls 25 million pounds of ground beef, the biggest such recall in history, after the meat is found to be contaminated with *E. coli* bacteria.

28   Researchers at the University of Utah report the development of a nontoxic, temperature-sensitive hydrogel (a drug-delivering sac) which can be injected into the body to deliver the required dose of a medicine at an appointed time, for a specified duration, and which is biodegradable. It will revolutionize the administration of complicated drugs such as insulin.

SEPTEMBER

•   The fen/phen fad diet, popular in the United States, ends when doctors discover that taking a mixture of the appetite suppressants fenfluramine and phentermine can cause permanent heart damage.

18   U.S. geneticist Bert Vogelstein and colleagues demonstrate that the p53 gene, which is activated by the presence of carcinogens, induces cells to commit suicide by stimulating them to produce large quantities of poisonous chemicals, called "reactive oxygen species" (ROS). The cells literally poison themselves. It is perhaps the human body's most effective way of combating cancer. Many cancers consist of cells with a malfunctioning p53 gene.

OCTOBER

2   UK scientists Moira Bruce and, independently, John Collinge and their colleagues show that the new variant form of the brain-wasting Creutzfeldt-Jakob disease (CJD) is the same disease as bovine spongiform encephalopathy (BSE or "mad cow disease") in cows.

NOVEMBER

•   The U.S. Food and Drug Administration (FDA) approves Regaine Extra Strength For Men, an over-the-counter baldness cure which promises to cause the growth of 45% more hair than the previous version. The FDA also approves Propecia, the first pill to treat prostate problems that is also found to prevent hair loss and generate hair growth. It becomes the second scientifically proven treatment for hair loss.

•   The U.S. Food and Drug Administration (FDA) approves Rituxan, the first anticancer monoclonal antibody made from genetically engineered mouse antibodies. The antibody binds itself to non-Hodgkin's lymphoma (a cancer of the lymph system) cancer cells and triggers the immune system to kill the cells. It has few side effects.

4   Oregon becomes the first state to permit doctors to prescribe lethal drug doses for terminally ill patients when 60% of Oregon voters vote to uphold a law passed in 1994 (but not implemented) on euthanasia.

19   The first septuplets to be successfully delivered alive are born in Des Moines, Iowa, to Kenny and Bobbi McCaughey, who had been taking fertility drugs.

DECEMBER

2   The U.S. Food and Drug Administration (FDA) approves the irradiation of pork, beef, and lamb following cases of contaminated hamburger meat from Nebraska.

29   Hong Kong begins killing 1.25 million chickens—the entire population—for fear of a pandemic of "bird flu." To date 12 people have contracted the disease and four have died.

Math

JUNE

26   U.S. mathematician Andrew Wiles is awarded the Wolfskehl Prize for solving Fermat's Last Theorem. The most notorious problem in mathematics, the Last Theorem was created in the 17th century by the French judge Pierre de Fermat, who studied mathematics in his spare time. In 1908, German industrialist Paul Wolfskehl bequeathed DM100,000 (£1 million by today's value) to be given to the first person to solve it.

Science

•   "Sakurai's object," a new star named for the amateur Japanese astronomer who discovered it in 1996 in the constellation of Sagittarius, has expanded since its discovery from an Earth-sized hot dwarf, with a surface temperature of 50,000°C/90,032°F, to a bright yellow supergiant about 80 times wider than the sun and no hotter than 6,000°C/10,832°F. "Sakurai's object" may be a red giant star that had previously shrunk, the contraction of its core triggering nuclear reactions and subsequent reinflation.

- The Nobel Prize for Physics is awarded to U.S. physicists Steven Chu and William D. Phillips and French physicist Claude Cohen-Tannoudji for development of methods to cool and trap atoms with laser light.
- The Nobel Prize for Chemistry is awarded to U.S. molecular biologist Paul D. Boyer and UK molecular biologist John E. Walker for their elucidation of the enzymatic mechanism underlying the synthesis of adenosine triphosphate (ATP), and also to Danish biologist Jens C. Skou for the first discovery of an ion-transporting enzyme, Na+, K+-ATPase.
- U.S. microbiologists bring to life a previously unknown *Staphylococcus* bacterium species from spores preserved in amber.

JANUARY

30　In a coal mine in southern Thailand, Thai researchers discover fragments of lower and upper jaws and teeth of a medium-sized monkey-like creature that lived about 40 million years ago. Known as *Siamopithecus eocaenus* ("dawn ape from Thailand"), it weighed 6–7 kg/ 13–15 lb and provides some of the earliest evidence for the evolution of monkeys, apes, and humans.

FEBRUARY

- U.S. genetic scientist Don Wolf announces the production of monkeys cloned from embryos. It is a step closer to cloning humans and raises acute philosophical issues.

20　U.S. researchers Jin Meng and André R. Wyss describe impressions and casts of fossilized hair recovered from 60-million-year-old rocks in Inner Mongolia, China. The casts show that hair is an extremely ancient feature of mammals, going right back to their origin.

24　The U.S. president Bill Clinton announces a ban on using federal funds to support human cloning research, and calls for a moratorium on this type of scientific research. He also asks the National Bioethics Advisory Commission to review and issue a report on the ramifications that cloning would have on humans.

27　Canadian astronomer David Gray reports that the star 51 Pegasi, thought to have a planet orbiting it, pulsates in precisely the way needed to mimic the signature of a planet in orbit around it. It casts doubt over the presence of other extra-solar planets discovered in the past 18 months.

27　German archeologist Hartmut Thieme describes three wooden spears recovered from a lignite mine at Schöningen, about 100 km/62 mi east of Hannover, Germany. About 2 m/6.5 ft long, shaped and balanced for throwing in the manner of modern javelins, and carved from a single trunk of spruce, they are 400,000 years old and are the oldest wooden hunting weapons ever found.

27　Scottish researcher Ian Wilmut of the Roslin Institute in Edinburgh, Scotland, announces that British geneticists have cloned an adult sheep. A cell was taken from the udder of the mother sheep and its DNA

(deoxyribonucleic acid) combined with an unfertilized egg that had had its DNA removed. The fused cells were grown in the laboratory and then implanted into the uterus of a surrogate mother sheep. The resulting lamb, Dolly, came from an animal that was six years old. This is the first time cloning has been achieved using cells other than reproductive cells. The news is met with international calls to prevent the cloning of humans.

MARCH

23　The comet Hale-Bopp comes to within 196 million km/ 122 million mi of Earth, the closest since 2000 BC. NASA launches rockets to study the comet. Its icy nucleus is estimated to be 40 km/25 mi wide, making it at least ten times larger than that of Comet Hyakutake and twice the size of Comet Halley.

APRIL

28　U.S. astronomer William Purcell announces the discovery of a huge stream of antimatter at the heart of the Milky Way galaxy. The jet, the source of which is a mystery, extends for 3,000 light-years above the center of the galaxy.

MAY

8　English zoologists Gareth Jones and Elizabeth Barratt announce the discovery of a new British mammal—a pipistrelle, or bat. Almost identical to the European pipistrelle and living in the same habitat, the two use different echolocation and courting frequencies and are genetically different, having experienced 5–10 million years of separate evolution.

16　U.S. geneticists identify a gene *clock* in chromosome 5 in mice that regulates the circadian rhythm.

30　Spanish paleoanthropologist Bermúdez de Castro and his team discover the fossilized remains of six individuals belonging to a new human species in a cave in Spain's Atepuerca Mountains. Named *Homo antecessor*, and about 780,000 years old (the only human fossils found in Europe of that age), they possess a face like *Homo sapiens* and a jaw and brow similar to the Neanderthals, and are believed to be the ancestors of both modern humans and Neanderthals. The bones also exhibit signs of cannibalism—the earliest known example of such practice.

JUNE

3　U.S. geneticist Huntington F. Wilard constructs the first artificial human chromosome. He inserts telomeres (which consist of DNA (deoxyribonucleic acid) and protein on the tips of chromosomes) and centromeres (specialized regions of DNA within a chromosome) removed from white blood cells into human cancer cells which are then assembled into chromosomes which are about one-tenth the size of normal chromosomes. The artificial chromosome is successfully passed on to all daughter cells.

5　U.S. astronomer Jane Luu and colleagues report the discovery of a new type of object within the solar system—a "worldlet," known by its catalog number 1996TL66, which has a diameter of 490 km/305 mi and which never gets closer to the sun than about 35 Astronomical Units (AU, where one AU is equivalent to about 150 million km/93 million mi, the distance between the earth and sun). They suggest it represents a new class of object belonging to a population of possibly several thousand orbiting between the Kuiper belt and the Oort cloud.

JULY

10   Japanese astronomer Makoto Hattori and colleagues report the discovery of a knot of mass, which they call a "dark cluster." It has the chemical and gravitational properties of a cluster of galaxies, but is optically invisible. A new type of cosmic entity, it helps explain how light from a particular quasar has been distorted and challenges the theories of galaxy formation.

11   Teams of researchers from Germany and the United States use mitochondrial DNA (deoxyribonucleic acid) extracted from the original fossils of Neanderthal Man, discovered in the Neander Valley near Düsseldorf, Germany, in 1856, to confirm that Neanderthal Man and modern humans diverged evolutionarily about 600,000 years ago. It supports the theory that modern humans arose recently in Africa as a distinct species and replaced Neanderthals with little or no interbreeding, the Neanderthals becoming extinct without evolving into modern humans.

18   Japanese scientist Yoshinori Kuwabara announces that his team has successfully grown goat embryos in an acrylic tank. The embryos, removed from their mother at 17 weeks into pregnancy, are placed in the tank filled with liquid which simulates amniotic fluid. The placenta is replaced by a machine to pump oxygen and nutrients into the embryo's blood. At 20 weeks' gestation the goat is "born." At present the procedure can only be done late in development.

24   Canadian researcher Richard Bottomley and colleagues date the 100-km/62-mi-wide Popigai impact crater in Siberia, thought to be the fifth largest impact crater on Earth, to 35.7 million years old. They suggest that the meteorite that created it may be responsible for the mass extinction that occurred at the end of the Eocene and the start of the Oligocene geological periods, which is dated to about the same time.

25   U.S. researcher Joseph L. Kirschvink and colleagues, by examining the record of remnant magnetism in very ancient rocks, discover that the outer layers of the earth shifted by 90 degrees relative to the core between about 535 and 520 million years ago. This major reorganization of the continents they suggest may have led to the Cambrian Explosion—the rapid appearance of abundant fossils in the geological record in the Cambrian Period, which began 540 million years ago.

AUGUST

- U.S. geneticist Craig Venter and colleagues publish the genome of the bacterium *Helicobacter pylori*, a bacterium that infects half the world's population and which is the leading cause of stomach ulcers. It is the sixth bacterium to have its genome published, but is clinically the most important. It has 1,603 putative genes, encoded in a single circular chromosome that is 1,667,867 nucleotide base-pairs of DNA long. Complete genomes are increasingly being published as gene-sequencing techniques improve.

1   A study presented at the Division of Planetary Sciences of the American Astronomical Society in Cambridge, Massachusetts, says that the moon was created early in Earth's history by debris thrown off from Earth after a collision with a planet three times as large as Mars.

7   Canadian researcher Suzanne W. Simard and colleagues announce the discovery that trees use the thread-like growths of fungi called mycorrhizae which infest their roots and connect the trees together underground to exchange food resources. It suggests that forest trees succeed as cooperative communities rather than competing individuals.

22   Scientists from the Worldwide Fund for Nature (WWF) announce the discovery of a new species of muntjac deer in Vietnam. A dwarf species weighing only about 16 kg/35 lb, it has antlers the length of a thumbnail and lives at altitudes of 457–914 m/1,500–3,000 ft.

SEPTEMBER

11   Israeli physicist Rafi de-Picciotto demonstrates the formation, within semiconductor materials, of "quasiparticles," which have a charge one-third that of an electron. Quasiparticles are not true particles in the sense that an electron, or proton, is but a stable association between particles that behaves as if it were a separate entity. They challenge the idea that charge always comes in discrete units based on the charge of a single electron.

OCTOBER

9   U.S. scientist Richard Superfine and colleagues, using atomic force microscopy, demonstrate that carbon nanotubes, sheets of carbon atoms rolled into concentric tubes a few millionths of a millimeter in diameter, are the stiffest and strongest materials known. The nanotubes which are bent almost double without breaking, return to their original shapes when the bending force is removed.

NOVEMBER

13   Chinese paleontologists Zhexi Luo and Chuankui Li describe the fossil skeleton of *Zhangheotherium*, a 145-million-year-old rat-sized creature discovered in northern China. Belonging to an extinct group of mammals called the symmetrodonts which lived in the shadow of the dinosaurs, it possesses both monotreme and mammalian features and represents one of the first steps toward modern mammals.

Technology

- A credit card-sized version of the plastic battery is introduced by its U.S. inventors in Baltimore, Maryland. It produces 2.5 volts of electricity.

- Most camera makers release quality digital cameras that shoot pixels instead of film, making them a low-cost alternative to 35 mm cameras. Sales nearly double from the previous year when 1.7 million cameras were sold worldwide.

- There are 300 active artificial satellites in orbit around Earth, the majority of which are used for communications purposes.

- U.S. physicists display the first atomic laser. It emits atoms that act like lightwaves.

FEBRUARY

- Two new instruments are added to the Hubble Space Telescope: the Near Infrared Camera and Multi-Object Spectrometer (NICMOS), which will enable Hubble to see things further away (and therefore older) then ever before, and the Space Telescope Imaging Spectrograph which works 30 times faster than its predecessor.

APRIL

29 The Chemical Weapons Convention of 1993 comes into force, banning the development, production, stockpiling, transfer, and use of chemical weapons. It has been ratified by 81 countries.

JULY

31 Japanese researcher Akira Fujishima and colleagues describe a self-cleaning and antifogging coating for glass and other hard surfaces. The coating, a thin layer of titanium dioxide, causes water, in the presence of ultraviolet light, to form a film instead of a droplet on the surface and allows the water to wash away oil and dirt.

DECEMBER

22 After three years of delays, the defense ministers of Britain, Germany, Italy, and Spain sign an agreement to begin producing a new military airplane, the "Eurofighter."

Transportation

FEBRUARY

4 In a collision between two Israeli army helicopters near the Israel–Lebanon border 65 soldiers and eight aircrew die.

AUGUST

6 A Korean Airlines Boeing 747 crashes on the island of Guam, killing more than 225 people.

14 The U.S. Congress general accounting office announces that the B-2 Stealth bomber's special coating of radar-absorbent paint deteriorates when the plane is left out in the rain or exposed to heat or humidity, making the plane no longer invisible to radar.

SEPTEMBER

8 The ferry *Fierte Gonaivience* capsizes off Port-au-Prince, Haiti; around 600 people are killed.

14 A train derails on a bridge in Madyah Pradesh, India, killing more than 80 people and injuring hundreds more.

26 An A300 B-4 Airbus crashes at Medan in southern Sumatra, killing 234 people; smog from forest fires is blamed as the probable cause.

30 A Federal Bureau of Investigation/Central Intelligence Agency (FBI/CIA) investigation into the explosion aboard TWA Flight 800 in July 1996 concludes it was caused by a buildup of pressure in a fuel tank.

OCTOBER

10 A DC-9 airliner from Argentina crashes in Uruguay, killing all of the 75 people on board.

NOVEMBER

22 Australian scientists demonstrate a 5-mm/0.2-in-long car—the world's smallest—by having it circle some Australian 10-cent coins. The car drives itself and travels at 0.36 kph/0.22 mph.

DECEMBER

6 A Russian Antonov 124 military transport plows into a residential area in Irkutsk, Russia, shortly after takeoff, killing 70 people.

15 A Tajik charter airliner crashes in the United Arab Emirates, killing 85 passengers.

ARTS AND IDEAS

Architecture

- The Japanese architect Yoshio Taniguchi is chosen to design plans to double the size of the Museum of Modern Art in New York, New York.
- The Miho Museum, designed by Chinese-born U.S. architect I. M. Pei, opens in the hills of a nature preserve near Kyoto, Japan.
- The U.S. architect Richard Meier wins the Gold Medal of the American Institute of Architects, for career achievement.
- The U.S. architects Tod Williams and Billie Tsien are chosen to design a new Museum of American Folk Art on West 53rd Street in New York, New York, planned to open in 2000.

JULY

- Building begins on the Millennium Dome, a temporary structure to house a millennium exhibition, designed by British architect Richard Rogers, in Greenwich, London, England.

AUGUST

29 An entrance fee for visitors to Westminster Abbey, London, England, will be charged for the first time. Previously, visitors were only charged for viewing certain parts of the Cathedral, such as the Royal chapels. The fee is set at £4.

DECEMBER

- The completed Getty Center, a $1-billion arts center and museum designed by the U.S. architect Richard Meier, opens in Los Angeles, California.

Arts

- The exhibition "Glory of Byzantium" is held at the Metropolitan Museum of Art in New York, New York.

SEPTEMBER

- A three-part retrospective of the U.S. artist Robert Rauschenberg opens at the Guggenheim Museum in New York, New York.

26 An earthquake in Assisi, Italy, seriously damages some frescoes in the St. Francis Basilica.

OCTOBER

- The U.S. actress Jane Alexander resigns after four years as chairwoman of the National Endowment for the Arts, complaining of the lack of federal support.

19 The widely acclaimed futuristic branch of New York's Guggenheim Museum, designed by the U.S. architect Frank Gehry, opens in Bilbao, Spain.

Film

- A movie of Shakespeare's *Hamlet*, by the British director Kenneth Branagh, is released. He also stars in it, with an all-star cast including Derek Jacobi, Julie Christie, Kate Winslet, and Richard Briers.
- The *Star Wars* movie trilogy is relaunched with enhanced special effects and new scenes, as a prelude to a new 3-part "prequel" by U.S. director George Lucas.

- The movie *Air Force One*, directed by Wolfgang Petersen, is released in the United States, starring Harrison Ford, Gary Oldman, Glenn Close, and Wendy Crewson.
- The movie *Basquiat*, directed by Julian Schnabel, is released in the United States, starring Jeffrey Wright, Michael Wincott, Benicio Del Toro, Claire Forlani, and David Bowie.
- The movie *Batman & Robin*, directed by Joel Schumacher, is released in the United States, starring Arnold Schwarzenegger, George Clooney, Uma Thurman, Alicia Silverstone, and Chris O'Donnell.
- The movie *Bean*, directed by Mel Smith, is released in Britain, starring Rowan Atkinson and Peter MacNicol.
- The movie *Chasing Amy*, directed by Kevin Smith, is released in the United States, starring Ben Affleck, Joey Lauren Adams, and Jason Lee.
- The movie *Con Air*, directed by Simon West, is released in the United States, starring Nicolas Cage, John Cusack, John Malkovich, and Steve Buscemi.
- The movie *Eve's Bayou*, directed by Kasi Lemmons, is released in the United States, starring Samuel L. Jackson and Debbi Morgan.
- The movie *Face Off*, directed by Hong Kong filmmaker John Woo, is released in the United States, starring John Travolta and Nicolas Cage.
- The movie *George of the Jungle*, directed by Sam Weisman, is released in the United States, starring Brendon Fraser, Leslie Mann, Thomas Haden Church, Holand Taylor, and John Cleese as the voice of the ape named "Ape."
- The movie *I Know what you did Last Summer*, directed by Jim Gillespie, is released in the United States, starring Jennifer Love Hewitt, Ryan Phillipe, Freddie Prinze, Jr., and Anne Hetch.
- The movie *In the Company of Men*, directed by Neil LaBute, is released in the United States, starring Aaron Eckhart, Matt Malloy, and Stacey Edwards.
- The movie *Knockin' On Heaven's Door*, directed by English filmmaker Thomas Jahn is released, starring Til Schweiger and Jan Josef Liefers.
- The movie *Liar Liar*, directed by Tom Shadyac, is released in the United States, starring Jim Carrey, Maura Tierney, and Justin Cooper.
- The movie *Lost Highway*, directed by David Lynch, is released in the United States, starring Bill Pullman and Patricia Arquette.
- The movie *My Best Friend's Wedding*, directed by Australian filmmaker P. J. Hogan, is released in the United States, starring Julia Roberts, Dermot Mulroney, Cameron Diaz, and Rupert Everett.
- The movie *Ponette*, directed by Jacques Doillon, is released in France, starring four-year-old Victoire Thivisol and Xavier Beavois.
- The movie *Rosewood*, directed by John Singleton, is released in the United States, starring Jon Voight, Ving Rhames, and Don Cheadle.
- The movie *Scream*, directed by Wes Craven, is released in the United States, starring Neve Campbell, Skeet Ulrich, Drew Barrymore, Courteney Cox, and David Arquette.
- The movie *Selena*, directed by Gregory Nava, is released in the United States, starring Jennifer Lopez, Edward James Olmos, and Jon Seda.

- The movie *The Borrowers*, directed by Peter Hewitt, is released in Britain, starring John Goodman and Jim Broadbent.
- The movie *The Fifth Element*, directed by French filmmaker Luc Besson, is released in the United States, starring Bruce Willis, Gary Oldman, Ian Holm, and Milla Jovovich.
- The movie *The Lost World*, directed by Steven Spielberg, is released in the United States, starring Jeff Goldblum, Julianne Moore, Pete Postlethwaite, Arliss Howard, and Richard Attenborough.
- The movie *Total Eclipse*, directed by the Polish filmmaker Agnieszka Holland, is released in France. The story of the relationship between French poets Rimbaud and Verlaine, it stars David Thewlis and Leonardo DiCaprio.
- The movie *Welcome to Sarajevo*, directed by Michael Winterbottom, is released in Britain, starring Stephen Dillane and Woody Harrelson.
- The movie *Wild America*, directed by William Dear, is released in the United States, starring Jonathan Taylor Thomas, Devon Sawa, Scott Bairstow, Frances Fisher, and Jamey Sheridan.
- The Walt Disney animated movie *Hercules*, directed by Ron Clements and John Musker, is released in the United States, starring the voices of Tate Donovan, Danny DeVito, and James Woods.

MARCH

24 The 1996 Academy Awards are held. Best Actor: Geoffrey Rush, for *Shine*; Best Supporting Actor: Cuba Gooding, Jr., for *Jerry Maguire*; Best Actress: Frances McDormand, for *Fargo*; Best Supporting Actress: Juliette Binoche, for *The English Patient*; Best Director: Anthony Minghella, for *The English Patient*; Best Picture: *The English Patient*, directed by Anthony Minghella.

MAY

18 The 50th Cannes Film Festival is held at Cannes, France. The Japanese director Shahei Imamura receives the Palme d'Or for his movie *Unagi/The Eel*.

JULY

- The movie *Contact*, directed by Robert Zemeckis, is released in the United States, starring Jodie Foster, Matthew McConaughey, and Tom Skerritt.
- The movie *Men in Black*, directed by Barry Sonnenfeld, is released in the United States, starring Tommy Lee Jones and Will Smith.

SEPTEMBER

- The movie *LA Confidential*, directed by Curtis Hanson, is released in the United States, starring Kevin Spacey, Russell Crowe, Guy James, Cromwell Pearce, Kim Basinger, and Danny DeVito.
- The movie *The Full Monty*, directed by Peter Cattaneo, is released in Britain, starring Robert Carlyle, Tom Wilkinson, Mark Addy, Paul Barber, and Steve Huison.

OCTOBER

- The movie *The Ice Storm*, directed by Taiwanese filmmaker Ang Lee, is released in the United States, starring Kevin Kline, Joan Allen, James Schamus, Sigourney Weaver, and Christina Ricci.

November

- The movie *Alien Resurrection*, directed by Jean-Pierre Jeunet, is released in the United States, starring Sigourney Weaver, Winona Ryder, Ron Perlman, and Dan Heydaya.
- The movie *Good Will Hunting* is released in the United States, directed by Gus Van Sant and starring Matt Damon, Ben Affleck, Robin Williams, and Minnie Driver.

December

- The 18th James Bond movie, *Tomorrow Never Dies*, directed by Roger Spottiswoode, is released in the United States, starring Pierce Brosnan, Jonathan Pryce, Michele Yeoh, and Teri Hatcher.
- The movie *Amistad*, directed by Steven Spielberg, is released in the United States, starring Matthew McConaughey, Anthony Hopkins, and Djimon Hounsou.
- The movie *As Good As It Gets* is released in the United States, directed by James Brooks and starring Jack Nicholson and Helen Hunt.
- The movie *Jackie Brown*, directed by Quentin Tarantino, is released in the United States, starring Pam Grier, Samuel L. Jackson, Robert De Niro, Bridget Fonda, and Robert Forster.
- The movie *Oscar and Lucinda*, directed by Gillian Armstrong, is released in the United States, starring Ralph Fiennes and Cate Blanchett.
- The movie *The Apostle* is released in the United States, directed by Robert Duvall and starring Duvall and Farrah Fawcett.
- The movie *Titanic*, directed by James Cameron, is released in the United States, starring Kate Winslet, Leonardo DiCaprio, Billy Zane, and Gloria Stuart. Costing over $200 million, it is the most expensive movie made to date. In the last two weekends of the year it grosses over $88 million.

Literature and Language

- An anthology of Indian literature, *Mirrorwork: 50 Years of Indian Writing (1947–1997)*, is published, coedited by the Indian-born English writer Salman Rushdie and Elizabeth West.
- One-third of Europeans speak English in addition to their mother tongue, making English the lingua franca of Europe.
- The Antiguan-born U.S. writer Jamaica Kincaid publishes her family memoir *My Brother*.
- The British writer Phillip Kerr publishes his novel *Esau*.
- The Colombian-born writer Gabriel García Márquez publishes his novel *News of a Kidnapping*.
- The English writer Graham Robb publishes the biography *Victor Hugo*, which wins a Whitbread Literary award.
- The English writer Ian McEwan publishes his novel *Enduring Love*.
- The English writer Jim Crace publishes his novel *Quarantine*, a retelling of Christ's 40 days in the wilderness. It wins a Whitbread Literary award.
- The English writer Ted Hughes publishes *Tales from Ovid*, which wins a Whitbread Literary award. It is a loose translation of the Roman poet Ovid's *Metamorphoses*.
- The Guyana-born British writer Pauline Melville publishes her novel *The Ventriloquist's Tale*, which wins a Whitbread award.
- The Indian writer Arundhati Roy publishes her novel *The God of Small Things*, which wins the Booker Prize.
- The Irish writer Bernard MacLaverty publishes his novel *Grace Notes*.
- The Irish writer Edna O'Brien publishes her novel *Down the River*.
- The Pulitzer Prize for Biography is awarded to Frank McCourt for *Angela's Ashes: A Memoir*, the Pulitzer Prize for Poetry is awarded to Lisel Mueller for *Alive Together: New and Selected Poems*, and the Pulitzer Prize for Fiction is awarded to Steven Millhauser for *Martin Dressler: The Tale of an American Dreamer*.
- The South African writer J. M. Coetzee publishes his memoir *Boyhood: Scenes from Provincial Life*.
- The U.S. climber and writer Jon Krakauer publishes *Into Thin Air* about his 1996 expedition up Mt. Everest in which 11 members of the party died in a storm.
- The U.S. writer Alex Shoumatoff publishes *Legends of the American Desert*, a nonfiction work about the U.S. Southwest.
- The U.S. writer Charles Frazier publishes his Civil War novel *Cold Mountain*.
- The U.S. writer Jonathan Kwitny publishes *Man of the Century: The Life and Times of Pope John Paul II*.
- The U.S. writer Laurence Bergreen publishes his biography *Louis Armstrong: An Extravagant Life*.
- The U.S. writer Philip Roth publishes his novel *American Pastoral*.
- The U.S. writer Thomas Pynchon publishes his historical novel *Mason and Dixon*.

September

- The U.S. writer Don DeLillo publishes his novel *Underworld*.

December

10   The Italian actor, director, and playwright Dario Fo wins the Nobel Prize for Literature.

Music

- A piano designed in 1884 by the artist Sir Lawrence Alma-Tadema sells at Christie's in London, England, for $1,210,885, the highest price paid for a piano to date.
- Haitian-born U.S. pop singer Wyclef Jean releases the album *The Carnival*.
- Rock group Reprazent featuring Roni Size releases the album *New Forms*.
- The British pop group the Spice Girls releases the single "Too Much." They become the first group ever to have their first four singles go to number one in the British charts.
- The Icelandic singer Björk releases the album *Homogenic*.
- The Jamaican reggae singer Luciano releases the album *Messenger*.
- The pop group Wham! releases the album *The Best of Wham*.
- The singer Enya releases the album *Paint the Sky with Stars–The Best of Enya*.
- The Spanish singer Marc Anthony releases the album *Contra la corriente/Against the Current*.

- The U.S. R&B singer Mary J. Blige releases the album *Share My World*.
- The U.S. composer and trumpeter Wynton Marsalis wins the Pulitzer Prize for Music for his oratorio about slavery, *Blood in the Fields*. This is the first Pulitzer awarded to a jazz musician.
- The U.S. country singer Matraca Berg releases the album *Sunday Morning to Saturday Night*.
- The U.S. singer songwriter Alana Davis releases the album *Blame It on Me*.
- Various artists release the album *Diana, Princess of Wales–Tribute*.

FEBRUARY

- Harpist Anna Lelkes becomes the first female member of the Vienna Philharmonic in Austria.
- 1 The rock group Bush releases the album *Razorblade Suitcase*.
- 15 The rock group Texas releases the album *White On Blonde*.
- 22 The English rock group Blur releases the album *Blur*.
- 25 The 1996–97 Grammy Awards are held. Best Song: "Change the World" written by Gordon Kennedy, Wayne Kirkpatrick, and Tommy Sims; Best Record: *Change the World* by Eric Clapton; Best Album: *Falling into You* by Celine Dion; Best Male Pop Vocalist: Eric Clapton; Best Female Pop Vocalist: Toni Braxton.

MARCH

- 1 The U.S. pop and rhythm and blues singer Erykah Badu releases the album *Erykah Badu: Baduizm*.
- 15 The English pop group the Spice Girls releases the single "Mama"/"Who Do You Think You Are?"
- 15 The Irish rock group U2 releases the album *Pop*.

APRIL

- 19 The English pop group Chemical Brothers releases the album *Dig Your Own Hole*.
- 19 The English rock group Blur releases the song "Song 2."

MAY

- 3 The English rock group Supergrass releases the album *In It for the Money*.

JUNE

- The English rock group Radiohead releases the single "Paranoid Android" and the album *OK Computer*, which sells over 2 million copies by the end of the year.
- 28 The English rock group The Verve releases the single "Bitter Sweet Symphony."

JULY

- The Royal Opera House in London, England, closes for two years for £214 million of redevelopment work.
- 19 The English rock group Oasis releases the single "D'You Know What I Mean."

AUGUST

- 30 The English rock group Oasis releases the album *Be Here Now*.

SEPTEMBER

- U.S. rock singer Bob Dylan releases the album *Time Out of Mind*.
- 13 The pop singer Shola Ama releases the album *Much Love*.
- 20 The English pop star Elton John releases the single "Candle in the Wind '97'" as a tribute to Diana,

Princess of Wales. It goes immediately to number one and becomes the best-selling single of all time.

OCTOBER

- The Italian mezzo-soprano Cecilia Bartoli stars in the Italian composer Gioacchino Rossini's *La Cenerentola* at the Metropolitan Opera in New York, New York.
- 11 The British rock group Portishead releases the album *Portishead*.
- 11 The English rock group The Verve releases the album *Urban Hymns*.
- 25 The Danish pop group Aqua releases the single "Barbie Girl."

NOVEMBER

- 15 The English pop group the Spice Girls releases the album *Spiceworld*.

DECEMBER

- U.S. country singer Garth Brooks releases the album *Sevens*.

Theater and Dance

- The ballet *Prince of the Pagodas*, starring the English dancer Darcey Bussell, is performed by the Royal Ballet at the Lincoln Center Festival in New York, New York.
- The Broadway musical *The Lion King*, produced by the Walt Disney Company, is first performed, in New York, New York, directed by Julie Taymor and starring Jason Raize.
- The Pulitzer Prize for Drama is not awarded this year.

JANUARY

- The ballet *Brandenburg*, a set of three dances by U.S. choreographer Jerome Robbins to music by the German composer Johann Sebastian Bach, is first performed, by the New York City Ballet in New York, New York.

MARCH

- *Lord of the Dance*, by Irish-American dancer Michael Flatley, opens as a rival to the Irish folk dance performance *Riverdance*.
- English dancer Maina Gielgud, the former director of the Australian Ballet, becomes artistic director of the Royal Danish Ballet in Copenhagen, Denmark.

APRIL

- 23 The Broadway musical *Titanic* opens at the Lunt-Fontanne Theater in New York, New York.

MAY

- The 1,800-seat New Amsterdam Theater on West 42nd Street in New York, New York, built in 1903, reopens after a lavish $34 million restoration sponsored by the Walt Disney Company and designed by Spanish-born U.S. architect Hugh Hardy.

JUNE

- William Shakespeare's *Henry V* is performed at the new Globe Theatre in London, England, directed by Richard Olivier and starring the Globe's artistic director, Mark Rylance.
- 1 The 1996–97 Tony Awards are held. Best Play: *Skylight*; Best Musical: *Juan Darien, A Carnival Mass*; Best Actor: Brian Bedford; Best Actress: Julie Harris.

SEPTEMBER

- The English director Trevor Nunn, formerly of the Royal Shakespeare Company, succeeds Richard Eyre as artistic director of the Royal National Theatre in London, England.

Thought and Scholarship

- English historian Orlando Figes publishes *A People's Tragedy*, a history of the Russian Revolution.
- The Pulitzer Prize for History is awarded to Jack N. Rakove for *Original Meanings: Politics and Ideas in the Making of the Constitution.*
- The Pulitzer Prize for General Nonfiction is awarded to Richard Kluger for *Ashes to Ashes: America's Hundred-Year Cigarette War, the Public Health, and the Unabashed Triumph of Philip Morris.*
- U.S. writer Stephen E. Ambrose publishes *Citizen Soldiers*, about the soldiers who fought in World War II.

SOCIETY

Education

JUNE

11 English behavioral scientist David Skuse claims that boys and girls differ genetically in the way they acquire social skills. Girls acquire social skills intuitively and are "preprogrammed," while boys have to be taught. This has important implications for education.

JULY

23 The British government announces a plan to start charging university students a tuition fee of £1,000 and to scrap grants in favor of student loans. Students and some lawmakers oppose the plan, viewing it as a violation of students' rights to attend university regardless of their ability to pay.

AUGUST

16 The Turkish government passes a law that requires children to attend a secular school for at least eight years, three years longer than stipulated in the previous law, in an attempt to limit the influence of Muslim schools.

SEPTEMBER

3 A vote in Newfoundland, Canada, ends church control of state schools. Local Roman Catholic groups are expected to appeal.

5 The National University of Samoa opens in Apia, the national capital.

30 In his keynote speech at the Labour Party conference, British prime minister Tony Blair says that parliament will appropriate £2 billion for school equipment and repairs, £700 million more than was originally promised. He also announces a new initiative in which the government and private business would cooperate to provide all schools with computers and Internet access by 2002.

NOVEMBER

27 Tens of thousands of students in Bonn, Germany, protest against declining standards, including overcrowding in classrooms and outdated textbooks, in Germany's university system.

DECEMBER

4 The British Labour government announces plans to limit the size of infant classes.

Everyday Life

- The Tamagotchi toy, a pocket-sized electronic (or virtual) pet that requires daily attention from its owner to continue to function, is launched in Japan. It quickly becomes very popular worldwide, both with children and adults.

FEBRUARY

6 Official figures show the number of people out of work in Germany to be the highest since 1933.

JUNE

25 An auction of some of Princess Diana's dresses in New York, New York, raises over $5 million for cancer and AIDS research.

JULY

9–12 British Airways flight attendants go on strike in protest of planned changes in the company's work policy. The disruption leads to widespread delays and cancellations of flights.

15 Italian fashion designer Gianni Versace is shot and killed outside his house in Miami Beach, Florida. Police later identify Andrew Cunanan, who is wanted in connection with four other murders, as the killer.

AUGUST

3 Union workers for United Parcel Service (UPS) go on a 16-day strike over the issue of part-time work, paralyzing the world's largest parcel delivery company, creating havoc for those who rely on the service, and causing ripple effects throughout the business community. Nearly 185,000 Teamster members go on strike–the biggest strike in more than a decade. On August 19, the Teamsters Union reaches a five-year contract agreement with UPS, ending the strike. The contract includes wage increases and the creation of more full-time work.

SEPTEMBER

- There is an unprecedented massive outporing of public grief at the death of Diana, Princess of Wales. Thousands of floral tributes are laid in her memory at Kensington Palace in London, England, and at other locations worldwide.

19 Ted Turner, billionaire founder of the television news network Cable News Network (CNN), announces that he will donate $100 million to the United Nations (UN) every year for ten years.

OCTOBER

- U.S. unemployment reaches a record low of 4.7%.

10 French prime minister Lionel Jospin pledges to introduce legislation to cut the maximum length of the working week from 39 to 35 hours by 2000.

NOVEMBER

10 Schools in Ontario, Canada, reopen after unions representing half of Ontario's 126,000 striking teachers decided to end a ten-day walk-out, which kept 2.1

million elementary and high-school students out of class. The strike, the largest of its kind to date in North America, was in protest at major education reforms.

DECEMBER

7 The Histadrut labor union in Israel agrees to terms with the Treasury to end a four-day nationwide strike that involved around 700,000 workers, mostly civil servants. The strike, mainly over pensions and privatization issues, was one of the largest and longest in Israel's history and shut down many public services.

28 Swisscom, the Swiss national telecommunications company, reveals that it can use mobile phones to track people, locating them to within a few hundred meters. The Swiss police view the service as an efficient investigative tool.

Media and Communication

MARCH

• Two-way TV is launched in Britain, an interactive system that enables viewers to participate in programs such as game shows.

30 The U.S. comedian Ellen DeGeneres comes out in an episode of her sitcom *Ellen*. Many advertisers remove their sponsorship and some local television stations refuse to broadcast it. Other people host parties in DeGeneres' honor, seeing the event as a landmark in gay rights as she is the first openly gay lead character on mainstream U.S. television.

MAY

31 The 1996–97 Emmy Awards for television are held. Best Drama Series: *Law and Order*; Best Comedy Series: *Frasier*; Best Actor in a Drama: Dennis Franz, for *NYPD Blue*; Best Actress in a Drama: Gillian Anderson, for *The X-Files*; Best Actor in a Comedy: John Lithgow, for *3rd Rock from the Sun*; Best Actress in a Comedy: Helen Hunt, for *Mad About You*.

SEPTEMBER

25 The opening episode of the fourth season of the U.S. medical program *ER* is performed live, twice, for broadcast to four different time zones in the United States. It stars Anthony Edwards, George Clooney, Julianna Margulies, and Laura Innes.

OCTOBER

26 The Golden Globe awards are held in Beverly Hills, California. The series *X-Files* takes best drama, best actress (Gillian Anderson), and best actor (David Duchovny).

DECEMBER

29 Intel Corp's chairman and chief executive officer Andrew Grove is named *Time* magazine's 1997 "Man of the Year" for his contribution in developing microchips.

Religion

• A group of Poor Clare nuns in Italy releases the album *Songs for Mary*. A compilation of religious songs, it becomes a Christmas hit in Italy.

MARCH

26 Thirty-nine members of the Heaven's Gate religious cult, who believe they will board a spaceship following the comet Hale-Bopp, are found dead in a mansion in Rancho Santa Fe, California. They committed suicide by taking a cocktail of drugs and alcohol.

AUGUST

29 The Roman Catholic Church in Rome, Italy, issues new guidelines for handling doctrinal differences within the Church.

31 A celebration to mark the 100th anniversary of the Zionist movement ends in Basel, Switzerland. Theodor Herzl convened the first Zionist conference there 100 years ago to work toward a Jewish homeland.

SEPTEMBER

13 A state funeral is held in Calcutta, India, for Mother Theresa, the Nobel Peace prizewinning Catholic nun who served the poor in Calcutta for nearly 70 years. Hundreds of thousands of mourners from a range of cultures and religions visited Calcutta to pay their respects since her death on September 5 from heart failure.

30 The Roman Catholic church issues a statement, called the "Declaration of Repentance," in which it formally apologizes for its silence when the French government deported Jews to Nazi death camps in Germany and Poland during World War II. The statement is considered the most direct apology for the silence of the Roman Catholic church during the Holocaust.

OCTOBER

4–5 The Promise Keepers, a U.S. right wing all-male Christian organization with a massive national following, hold an assembly on the Mall in Washington, D.C. Feminist opponents of the group object to their tenet of unquestioned male authority in the family.

31 Pope John Paul II condemns the failure of Christians to speak out against the genocide of the Jews at the hands of the Nazis during World War II. Although the pope acknowledges that the church was responsible for antisemitism in the past, he does not apologise directly to the Jews on behalf of the Roman Catholic Church.

NOVEMBER

1 Martin Luther King III, the eldest son of Martin Luther King, Jr., is elected president of the Southern Christian Leadership Conference in the United States.

27 Around 28,000 couples are married by the Reverend Sun Myung Moon of the Unification Church in Washington, D.C., in a ceremony broadcast around the world via satellite.

DECEMBER

14 President Fidel Castro of Cuba, in anticipation of a visit from Pope John Paul II, announces that Christmas will be an official holiday in Cuba for the first time in 30 years.

25 In his annual Christmas message, Pope John Paul II calls for action against poverty and freedom from political and ethnic violence.

Sports

JANUARY

26 In Super Bowl XXXI in New Orleans, Louisiana, the Green Bay Packers defeat the New England Patriots 35–21. It is the Packers' first Super Bowl since they won the first two Super Bowls in 1967 and 1968.

26 The Swiss tennis player Martina Hingis wins the women's singles title at the Australian Open in Melbourne to become (at 16 years, 92 days) the youngest winner of a Grand Slam championship title since the English player Lottie Dod won Wimbledon in London, England, in 1887 at the age of 15.

MARCH

22 Tara Lipinski of the United States wins the women's title at the World Figure Skating Championships in Lausanne, Switzerland. At 14 years, 9 months and 12 days she is the youngest-ever world champion, 32 days younger than Sonja Henie of Norway when she won the event in 1927.

APRIL

5 The Grand National horse race at Aintree, Liverpool, England, is postponed less than an hour before it is due to start after a coded IRA (Irish Republican Army) bomb warning is received. Two days later, Lord Gyllene, ridden by Northern Ireland's Tony Dobbin, wins the rescheduled race.

13 Tiger Woods of the United States, aged 21, becomes the youngest-ever winner of the U.S. Masters golf tournament at Augusta, Georgia. As well as setting a new record lowest aggregate score of 270 for the championship, his 12-stroke margin of victory is the highest ever in any of the four major tournaments over 72 holes.

MAY

3–June 7 After winning the Kentucky Derby and Preakness Stakes, Silver Charm, ridden by U.S. jockey Gary Stevens, narrowly fails to become the first horse since Affirmed in 1978 to win the U.S. Triple Crown when he finishes second to Touch Gold in the Belmont Stakes.

11 The IBM super computer Deep Blue defeats the world chess champion Gary Kasparov of Azerbaijan 3.5–2.5 in New York, New York. A year earlier in Philadelphia, Pennsylvania, Kasparov had beaten an earlier version of Deep Blue, 4–2.

27 The Dutch driver Arie Luyendyk, in an Oldsmobile G-Force-Aurora, wins the Indianapolis 500 motor race, which has twice been postponed because of bad weather.

31–June 7 The Detroit Red Wings, with a team featuring five Russians, defeat the Philadelphia Flyers by four games to two to win their first National Hockey League (NHL) Stanley Cup for hockey for 42 years.

JUNE

2 The Maldives lose 17–0 to Iran in a soccer World Cup qualifying match in Damascus, Syria, to record the worst ever defeat in the history of the competition. They eventually finish bottom of their group, having conceded a record 59 goals to their opponents in six games.

8 Gustavo Kuerten wins the men's singles at the French Open tennis championships in Paris, France, to become the first Brazilian to win a men's Grand Slam singles tournament.

12 For the first time in the 126-year history of major league baseball, regular season interleague play is introduced with Texas Rangers of the American League playing the San Francisco Giants of the National League at Arlington, Texas, in the inaugural interleague game. The Rangers win by four games to three.

13 The Chicago Bulls defeat the Utah Jazz by four games to two to win their fifth National Basketball Association (NBA) championship in seven years. Chicago's Michael Jordan is voted Most Valuable Player in the Playoffs for a record fifth time.

28 Evander Holyfield of the United States retains his World Boxing Association (WBA) world heavyweight title in Las Vegas, Nevada, when the challenger Mike Tyson of the United States is disqualified in the third round for biting Holyfield's ear. Tyson is subsequently fined $3 million and banned from fighting, but he is allowed to keep his $30-million purse.

JULY

5–6 Martina Hingis of Switzerland, aged 16 years, 279 days, becomes the youngest winner of the women's singles at the Wimbledon tennis championships in London, England, since 1887 when Lottie Dod of England won at the age of 15 years, 285 days. Pete Sampras of the United States wins his fourth men's singles title in five years, while Australia's Mark Woodforde and Todd Woodbridge win a record fifth consecutive men's doubles title.

9 The Nevada State Athletic Commission revokes the license of U.S. boxer Mike Tyson and fines him $3 million for biting off the ear of U.S. boxer Evander Holyfield in the June 28 World Boxing Association (WBA) world heavyweight title fight in Las Vegas, Nevada.

11 The Japanese baseball pitcher Hideki Irabu makes his major league debut for the New York Yankees against Detroit, after signing a $12.8-million four-year contract. He strikes out nine batters and concedes only five hits in the Yankees' 10–3 victory.

13 English golfer Alison Nicholas becomes only the second Briton after Laura Davies in 1987 to win the U.S. Women's Open, at North Plains, Oregon.

20 U.S. golfer and former U.S. amateur champion Justin Leonard wins the British Open at Royal Troon, Scotland.

27 Jan Ullrich becomes the first German cyclist to win the Tour de France.

AUGUST

3 U.S. sprinter Maurice Greene wins the men's 100-meters event at the International Amateur Athletics Federation (IAAF) World Championships in Athens, Greece. Marion Jones, also of the United States, wins the women's event.

4 Cathy Freeman of Australia wins the women's 400-meters final at the International Amateur Athletics Federation (IAAF) World Championships in Athens, Greece, becoming the first Aboriginal to win a world title.

10 Sergey Bubka of the Ukraine wins an unprecedented sixth successive pole vault title at the International

BIRTHS & DEATHS

- James Callaghan, British prime minister 1976–79, a Labour politician, dies in London, England (85).

JANUARY

4 Harry Helmsley, New York property tycoon who bought the Empire State Building in 1961, dies in New York, New York (87).

5 Burton Lane, Broadway and Hollywood composer, dies in New York, New York (84).

8 Melvin Calvin, U.S. chemist, winner of the Nobel Prize for Chemistry in 1961 for discovering the chemical nature of photosynthesis, dies in Berkeley, California (85).

10 Alexander Robertus Todd, English organic chemist, winner of the Nobel Prize for Chemistry in 1957 for synthesizing nucleotides, which make up DNA and RNA, dies in Cambridge, England (89).

10 Mary Bancroft, U.S. spy during World War II, dies in New York, New York (93).

17 Clyde William Tombaugh, U.S. astronomer who discovered Pluto, dies in Las Cruces, New Mexico (90).

18 Paul Tsongas, U.S. Democratic presidential candidate in 1992, dies in Boston, Massachusetts (55).

20 Tuzo Itami, Japanese movie director, commits suicide in Tokyo, Japan (64).

FEBRUARY

2 Fela Anikulapo Kuti, Nigerian singer, songwriter, and musician, proponent of African nationalism and ethnic identity, dies in Lagos, Nigeria (58).

5 Pamela Harriman, U.S. ambassador to France 1993–97, fundraiser for President Bill Clinton, and daughter-in-law of Winston Churchill, dies in Paris, France (76).

10 Brian Connolly, British singer with the pop group Sweet, dies (47).

19 Deng Xiaoping, leader of China 1980–97, chief architect of China's social reform, dies in Beijing, China (93).

23 Oscar Lowenstein, English theatrical and film producer, dies (80).

25 Andrey Sinyavsky, Russian novelist and dissident, dies in Paris, France (51).

MARCH

1 Michael Manly, prime minister of Jamaica 1972–80 and 1989–92, dies in Kingston, Jamaica (72).

3 V(ictor) S(audon) Pritchett, English short-story writer and novelist, dies in London, England (96).

7 Norman de Bruyne, English inventor and aircraft designer, designer of the Snark monoplane, dies in Cambridge, England (92).

8 Alexander Salking, U.S. film producer of *Superman*, dies in Neuilly, France (75).

14 Fred Zinnemann, Austrian-born U.S. film producer, who produced *High Noon*, *From Here to Eternity*, and *Oklahoma*, dies in London, England (89).

19 Willem de Kooning, Dutch-born U.S. abstract expressionist painter, dies in Long Island, New York (92).

20 Tony Zale (originally Anton Florian Zaleski), U.S. world middleweight boxing champion 1940–48, dies in Portage, Indiana (83).

24 Harold Melvin, lead singer of the 1950s group the Blue Notes, dies in Philadelphia, Pennsylvania (57).

26 Otto John, German secret agent who was involved in the plot to kill Hitler, dies in Innsbruck, Austria (88).

APRIL

2 Tomoyuki Tanaki, Japanese film producer, creator of the movie monster Godzilla, dies in Tokyo, Japan (86).

5 (Irwin) Allen Ginsberg, U.S. poet and political activist, dies in New York, New York (70).

17 Chaim Herzog, president of Israel 1983–93, dies in Tel Aviv, Israel (79).

21 General Andres Rodriguez, president of Paraguay 1989–93 who overthrew the Paraguayan dictator Alfredo Stroessner and restored the country to democracy, dies in New York, New York (72).

24 Edward Purcell, U.S. physicist who shared the Nobel Prize for Physics with Felix Bloch in 1952 for his work on nuclear magnetic resonance (NMR), dies in Cambridge, Massachusetts (84).

27 Peter Winch, English philosopher, author of *The Idea of a Social Science* (1958), dies in Champaign, Illinois (71).

MAY

2 John Carew Eccles, Australian physiologist who shared (with Alan Hodgkin and Andrew Huxley) the Nobel Prize for Physiology or Medicine in 1963 for work on conduction in the central nervous system, dies in Lugano, Switzerland (94).

13 Laurie Lee, English writer, author of *Cider with Rosie*, dies in Gloucestershire, England (83).

26 Manfred von Ardenne, German scientist and inventor of the high definition electron microscope, dies in Dresden, Germany (90).

JUNE

1 Nikolay Aleksandrovich Tikhonov, Soviet prime minister (chair of the Council of Ministers) 1980–85, dies in Moscow, Russia (92).

2 Adolphus "Doc" Cheatham, U.S. jazz trumpeter, dies in Washington, D.C. (91).

5 Ronnie Lene, English pop singer, songwriter, and founder of the Small Faces, dies in Trinidad, Colorado (51).

6 Prudence Napier, English primatologist, dies (81).

8 Amus Tutola, Nigerian novelist, author of *The Palm-Wine Drinkard* (1952), dies in Ibadan, Nigeria (77).

15 Kim Casali, English cartoonist and creator of the series "Love is...," and also the first woman in England to conceive her husband's baby by artificial insemination after his death, dies in Surrey, England (55).

21 John Akii-Bua, Ugandan Olympic hurdler, dies in Kampala, Uganda (47).

25 Jacques Cousteau, French oceanographer who invented the aqualung, dies in Paris, France (87).

JULY

1 Robert (Charles Duran) Mitchum, U.S. film actor, dies in Santa Barbara, California (79).

2 James Stewart, U.S. actor, dies in Beverly Hills, California (89).

9 J(ohn) Z(achary) Young, English zoologist who contributed to knowledge of nerve structure and function through his discovery and study of the giant nerve fibers in squids, dies (89).

31 Bao Dai, last emperor of Vietnam 1927–55, dies in exile in Paris, France (83).

AUGUST

1 Sviatoslav, Richter Russian concert pianist, one of the 20th century's greatest pianists, dies in Moscow, Russia (82).

AUGUST

2 William S(eward) Burroughs, U.S. writer noted for his experimental methods, black humor, explicit homo-eroticism, and apocalyptic vision, author of *Naked Lunch*, dies in Lawrence, Kansas (83).

5 Clarence M. Kelley, U.S. director of the Federal Bureau of Investigation (FBI) 1973–77, dies in Kansas City, Missouri (85).

12 Luther Allison, U.S. guitarist, singer and composer, dies in Madison, Wisconsin (57).

23 John Kendrew, English biochemist who, with Max Perutz, received the Nobel Prize for Chemistry in 1962 for determining the structure of myoglobin, dies in Cambridge, England (80).

24 Luigi Viloresi, Italian race-car driver, dies in Modena, Italy (88).

31 Diana Spencer, Princess of Wales, humanitarian, and charity worker, is killed in a car crash in Paris, France (36).

SEPTEMBER

3 Viktor Frankl, Austrian psychiatrist and psychotherapist, author of *Man's Search for Meaning* based on his experience in a Nazi concentration camp, dies in Vienna, Austria (92).

4 Aldo Rossi, Italian architect, dies in a car crash in Milan, Italy (66).

4 Hans Jürgen Eysenck, German-born British psychologist whose theory that intelligence is almost entirely inherited and can be only slightly modified by education aroused controversy, dies in London, England (81).

5 Georg Solti, Hungarian-born British conductor, music director at the Royal Opera House, Covent Garden, London, England 1961–71, and director of the Chicago Symphony Orchestra 1969–91, dies in Antibes, France (84).

6 Mother Teresa (Agnes Gonxha Bojaxhiu), Albanian-born Indian ascetic who founded the Order of the Missionaries of Charity, devoted to helping the poor, dies in Calcutta, India (87).

7 Mobutu Sese Seko, president of Zaire 1965–97, dies in exile in Rabat, Morocco (66).

9 Burgess Meredith, U.S. actor, dies in Malibu, California (89).

12 Janet Leach, English potter, dies in St. Ives, England (79).

12 Stikkan "Stig" Anderson, Swedish manager and producer of the pop group Abba, dies (66).

17 Richard Bernard ("Red") Skelton, U.S. comedian, dies in Rancho Mirage, California (84).

18 Jimmy Witherspoon, U.S. blues singer, dies in Los Angeles, California (64).

22 Bryan Ingham, English painter and sculptor, dies (61).

29 Roy Lichtenstein, U.S. artist, known for his use of commercial images and cartoon-style paintings, dies in New York, New York (73).

OCTOBER

3 A(lfred) L(eslie) Rowse, British historian, dies in St. Austell, Cornwall, England (93).

5 Otto Ernst Remer, German Nazi security chief during World War II, dies in Marbella, Spain (85).

6 Arthur Tracy, royal biographer who wrote biographies of the queen, queen mother, prince of Wales, and others, under the pen name Helen Cathcart, dies in Midhurst, Sussex, England (88).

11 Maurice Griffiths, English yacht designer and author, editor of *Yachting Monthly* 1927–67, dies (95).

12 John Denver (born John Deutschendorf), U.S. country singer and songwriter, dies when his plane crashes into Monterey Bay near San Francisco, California (53).

14 Harold Robbins, U.S. author of popular novels including *The Carpetbaggers*, *Stiletto*, and *The Betsy*, dies in Palm Springs, California (81).

16 James Michener, U.S. author of *Tales of the South Pacific* and *Hawaii*, dies in Austin, Texas (90).

19 Kenneth Wood, English electrical engineer, inventor of the Kenwood electric mixer, dies (81).

24 Michael Balfour, U.S.-born English actor, known for roles in *The Belles of St Trinians* and *Sink the Bismarck!*, dies (79).

30 Samuel Fuller, U.S. film director, dies in Los Angeles, California (86).

NOVEMBER

6 Isaiah Berlin, Latvian-born British philosopher and historian of ideas, dies in London, England (88).

9 Bob Jones, Jr., U.S. fundamentalist preacher and president of Bob Jones University, dies.

9 Carl G. Hempel, German philosopher of science, a member of the Vienna circle of logical positivists, dies in Princeton, New Jersey (92).

16 Georges Marchais, French politician, secretary-general of the French Communist Party 1972–94, dies in Paris, France (77).

18 Joyce Wethered, English golfer who dominated English ladies golf in the early 1920s, dies (96).

21 Robert Simpson, English composer, dies (76).

22 Michael Hutchence, Australian rock singer, leader of INXS, dies in Sydney, Australia (37).

25 Hastings Kamuzu Banda, prime minister of Nyasaland (Malawi) 1964–66, first president of Malawi 1966–94, dies in Johannesburg, South Africa (92).

27 Eric Laithwaite, English electrical engineer who built the first magnetically-levitating high-speed train, dies (76).

DECEMBER

1 Stéphane Grappelli, French jazz musician and violinist, dies in Paris, France (89).

4 Richard Vernon, English actor, dies (82).

11 Eddie Chapman, English safecracker and double agent who carried out sabotage missions for the Germans during World War II, dies (83).

22 Bruce Woodcock, British heavyweight boxing champion 1945–50, dies in Doncaster, England (76).

Amateur Athletics Federation (IAAF) World Championships in Athens, Greece.

14 Denmark's Kenyan-born runner Wilson Kipketer breaks the English athlete Sebastian Coe's 16-year-old 800-meters world record of 1 min 41.73 sec when he runs a time of 1 min 41.24 sec in Zürich, Switzerland. Ten days later in Brussels, Belgium, he reduces the record to 1 min 41.11 sec.

17 Australian golfer Karrie Webb wins her second British Women's Open Championship in three years, at Sunningdale, England.

17 Michael Doohan of Australia, riding a Honda, wins the British Grand Prix at Donington Park, Castle Donington, Leicestershire, England, to capture his fourth successive 500-cc world motorcycle racing championship.

17 U.S. golfer Davis Love III wins the U.S. Professional Golfers Association (PGA) Championship at Winged Foot Golf Club, Mamaroneck, New York, to record his first victory in a major tournament.

26 U.S. runner Carl Lewis runs in what he announces is the last race of his 15-year, nine Olympic gold medal career, at the Istaf Grand Prix in Berlin, Germany.

30 The Houston Comets defeat the New York Liberty 65–51 in Houston, Texas, to win the inaugural Women's National Basketball Association (WNBA) championship.

SEPTEMBER

6 Martina Hingis of Switzerland wins the women's singles tournament at the U.S. Open tennis championships, her third Grand Slam singles title of the year after winning the Australian Open and Wimbledon tournaments.

7 Patrick Rafter of Australia defeats Britain's Greg Rusedski in the final of the men's singles tournament at the U.S. Open tennis championships. Rafter is the first Australian to win the title since John Newcombe in 1973, and Rusedski is the first Briton to reach a Grand Slam final since 1936.

21 Patrice Martin of France wins an unprecedented fifth successive men's overall world water ski title at the Water Ski World Championships in Colombia.

25 British driver Andy Green in the jet-powered *Thrust SSC*, sets a new land speed world record of 1,149.272 kph/714.144 mph at Black Rock Desert, Nevada. The previous record of 1,019.467 kph/633.468 mph had been set in 1983 by the Thrust SSC's project leader, British driver Richard Noble.

28 Europe's golfers retain the Ryder Cup, defeating the United States 14½–13½ at Valderrama, in southern Spain. It is the first time that Europe has hosted the competition at a non-British venue.

OCTOBER

4 British boxer Lennox Lewis defends his World Boxing Council (WBC) heavyweight title when he defeats Polish boxer Andrzej Gołota with a first round knockout in Atlantic City, New Jersey. The fight lasts for only 1 min 35 sec.

15 British driver Andy Green, driving the 13.7 m-/45 ft-long jet car *Thrust SSC*, sets a new land speed record

and breaks the sound barrier with two runs of 1,214.933 kph/759.333 mph (Mach 1.015) and 1,26.574 kph/766.609 mph (Mach 1.020) at Black Rock Desert, Nevada. Similar speeds set two days earlier were unofficial because the second run occurred over an hour later.

26 Jacques Villeneuve, driving a Williams–Renault, becomes the first Canadian to win the Formula 1 World Drivers' Championship.

26 The Florida Marlins, a 1993 National League expansion team, win their first World Series, defeating the Cleveland Indians by four games to three.

NOVEMBER

• U.S. golfer Tiger Woods is the first player to win over $2 million in prize money in a season on the U.S. PGA Tour. At the age of 22, he is also the youngest player ever to finish top of the money list.

2 Kenyan runner John Kagwe wins the New York City Marathon with a time of 2 hr 8 min 12 sec, the second-fastest time ever on the course.

3 Australian and U.S. swimming officials protest against the results of the Chinese national swimming championships held in Shanghai in October in which two low-ranked Chinese female swimmers broke world records in the 200 and 400 meter relays. The officials allege that the Chinese swimmers were using performance-enhancing drugs.

8 Skip Away, ridden by U.S. jockey Mike Smith, wins the one-and-a-quarter-mile-long Breeders' Cup Classic horse race at Hollywood Park, California, in a record time of 1 min 59 sec.

8 U.S. boxer Evander Holyfield defeats compatriot and International Boxing Federation (IBF) champion Michael Moorer with a technical knockout in the eighth round of the IBF heavyweight championship in Las Vegas, Nevada, making Holyfield both the World Boxing Association (WBA) and the IBF champion.

22 New Zealand rowers Robert Hamill and Phil Stubbs break the record for crossing the Atlantic when they win a trans-Atlantic rowing race of 2,757 nautical miles from the Canary Islands to Barbados in a time of 41 days, 1 hour, 55 minutes. The previous record, set in 1986 by British rowers Sean Crowley and Mike Nestor, was 73 days.

30 Sweden wins the Davis Cup in tennis, defeating the United States 5–0 in Gothenburg, Sweden.

DECEMBER

9 British entrepreneur and balloonist Richard Branson is forced to abandon his effort to become the first person to travel around the world in a balloon when his balloon is blown away before the planned launch in Marrakesh, Morocco.

23 Talks between promoters for U.S. boxer Evander Holyfield, British boxer Lennox Lewis, and Time Warner sports, which televises boxing on its cable stations, break down when Holyfield's promoter, Don King, demands a fee of around $8 million to arrange a bout between the two heavyweight champions.

1998

POLITICS, GOVERNMENT, AND ECONOMICS

Business and Economics

JANUARY

1   The Russian government revalues the ruble, making it 1,000 times its previous value.

4   The U.S. Secretary of the Treasury announces that the 12-month figures to the end of November 1997 showed a government surplus in taxes. It is the first time the U.S. budget has been balanced in 30 years.

5   The British venture-capital company Cinven and other investors announce that they will buy the IPC consumer magazine group, Britain's largest, from British publisher Reed Elsevier.

5   The German car manufacturer Volkswagen introduces its New Beetle, an up-to-date version of its original Beetle, the most popular car in history.

6   The credit card company Visa International reports that personal bankruptcy in the United States rose by 19.5% in 1997.

12 The largest investment bank in Hong Kong, Peregrine Investments Holdings Ltd., collapses following an unsuccessful sale of shares to Zurich Group of Switzerland and formally files for liquidation the following day.

23 The Royal Bank of Canada, Canada's largest bank, and the Bank of Montreal, the country's third largest bank, announce plans of a merger, that will create the second largest bank in North America.

FEBRUARY

25 British insurance companies Commercial Union and General Accident announce plans to merge.

MARCH

5   The German medical supplier Fresenius Medical Care announces that it will withdraw from a deal to provide dialysis equipment to a military hospital in Guangzhou, China, because of evidence that the hospital was selling kidneys removed from executed prisoners.

9   Publishers Reed Elsevier and Wolters Kluwer abandon plans to merge after U.S. and European regulators imply that they would require the companies to sell off many of their assets.

23 The German media company Bertelsmann AG announces that it will buy Random House, Inc. from the U.S. publisher Advance Publications for $1.5 billion. Bertelsmann is already the world's third largest media company, behind Walt Disney and Time Warner.

30 British liquor company Bacardi Ltd., based in Bermuda, agrees to buy the Bombay gin and Dewar's whiskey brands from British liquor company Diageo PLC, the company that was created in 1997 from the merger between Guinness and Grand Metropolitan.

APRIL

6   U.S. consumer bank Citicorp and U.S. investment bank and insurance firm Travelers Group announce plans to merge. The deal is estimated at $83 billion, which is the world's largest merger deal to date.

8   The South Korean government sells $4 billion worth of government bonds to international investors. Analysts view the high demand for the bonds as increased confidence in the South Korean economy after the country's financial crisis in 1997.

13 U.S. bank BankAmerica announces plans to take over NationsBank in a deal valued at $60 billion, the second largest proposed deal to date after the merger plans announced in April between U.S. banks Citicorp and Travelers Group.

15 The South Korean car manufacturer Kia Motors Corp is put in court receivership, where it is protected from creditors until it develops a plan for financial recovery. Workers strike between April 16–20 in protest of the court-appointed administrator of the plan, Yoo Chong Yul, whom they fear will sell the company.

17 British cable television company Telewest Communications announces that it will take over its rival General Cable for £635 million.

24 British mail-order company Great Universal Stores clinches a deal to buy its rival Argos for £1.6 billion, to form one of Britain's largest retail companies.

MAY

7   British company Vickers announces that it will sell its luxury car manufacturer, Rolls-Royce Motor Cars, to German car manufacturer Volkswagen AG for £430 million. Vickers agreed to sell Rolls-Royce to Bayerische Motoren Werke (BMW) in April, but Volkswagen outbid BMW by £90 million.

7   German manufacturer Daimler-Benz, makers of Mercedes-Benz cars, announces plans to merge with U.S. car manufacturer Chrysler Corp to form a new company, Daimler-Chrysler. The deal is valued at $38.3 billion.

11 U.S. telephone service provider SBC Communications, Inc. announces plans to take over another telecommunications firm, Ameritech Corp, in a deal worth $56.18 billion. The merger would be the largest ever in the telecommunications industry.

18 French businessman and art collector Francois Pinault announces that he will buy British auction house Christie's.

18 The U.S. federal government and 20 states file lawsuits in Washington, D.C., against U.S. computer software company Microsoft for violating antitrust laws by using its Windows operating system to try to monopolize sales of other kinds of software.

JUNE

9 Air France pilots, rail workers, and police strike on the opening day of the World Cup soccer tournament in Paris. They resume work the following day.

17 The New York-based investment bank Goldman Sachs announces plans to float on the stock market, which will award the executive committee the biggest bonus in Wall Street history. The six committee members will likely own shares worth some $4 billion in total.

JULY

7 The London Stock Exchange and the German stock exchange, Deutsche Börse, agree to create a pan-European stock exchange, with a capital of £2,000 billion.

9 A hundred traders on the NASDAQ stock exchange, the second biggest exchange in the United States, and the world's largest electronic stock market, are charged with manipulating the exchange by widening the spread between bid and offer prices.

Human Rights

JANUARY

12 The German government announces the establishment of a DM 200 million pension fund that will compensate Jewish Holocaust survivors from Eastern and Central Europe.

APRIL

12 British gay rights campaigner Peter Tatchell is arrested after climbing the pulpit and disrupting the traditional Easter sermon of the Archbishop of Canterbury, at Canterbury Cathedral, England. Tatchell, a leader of the gay rights group Outrage!, is protesting against the Archbishop's position toward homosexuals.

JUNE

• The human rights group Amnesty International reports that as many as 141 countries are not adhering to the Universal Declaration of Human Rights, which is 50 years old, citing cases of executions without trial, torture, prisoners of conscience, and poverty.

7 Three white men, two with white supremacist tattoos, are arrested in Texas, accused of murdering a black man, James Byrd, Jr., by dragging him behind their truck for two miles.

JULY

20 An inquiry into the murder of Stephen Lawrence, who was stabbed to death in London, England, on April 22, 1993, concludes that he was killed by racist thugs and that police investigations were incompetent and plagued by racism.

Politics and Government

JANUARY

1 Mohammed Rafiq Tarar, is elected president of Pakistan in a landslide victory.

1 The Pakistani government's anticorruption commission brings corruption charges against former prime minister Benazir Bhutto, her husband, and her mother, for accumulating wealth through kickbacks while she had been prime minister.

2 A new caretaker government takes office in the Czech Republic, headed by Josef Tosovsky, a former governor of the Czech National Bank.

3 Swedish police arrest 314 youths at a rock concert outside Stockholm organized by a white supremacist group linked to the neo-Nazi organization Nordland.

5 Daniel arap Moi, who was reelected president of Kenya in December, 1997, is sworn in for a fifth term. Moi has been president since 1978.

5 Lithuanian-American Valdus Adamkus is elected president of Lithuania. He pledges to develop Lithuania's integration with Western Europe and to deepen its links with the United States.

5 U.S. president Bill Clinton announces that he will propose a balanced budget for 1999, three years earlier than planned.

6 The United Nations World Food Program launches an appeal for $378 million to provide food for North Korea. It is the largest such appeal in the program's history.

7 Terry Nichols, who was convicted in December 1997 of conspiracy and involuntary manslaughter in the 1995 bombing of the Alfred P. Murrah federal building in Oklahoma City, escapes the death penalty after the jury sentencing him could not reach a consensus.

8 At a meeting in New York, New York, a group of 16 banks from around the world agree to extend South Korea's debt repayment deadline until March 31.

9 French premier Lionel Jospin announces plans for an emergency one billion franc fund for poor people, prompted by weeks of demonstrations by unemployed workers.

9 Marlene Corrigan is convicted of misdemeanor child abuse after her 13-year-old daughter Christina, who weighed 310 kg/680 lb, died of heart failure caused by obesity.

11 Sonia Gandhi, the wife of the former Indian prime minister Rajiv Gandhi who was assassinated in 1991, begins a campaign to restore support for the Congress (I), the party founded by her husband's former family.

12 During a five-day meeting in Tokyo, Japan, Japanese premier Ryutaro Hashimoto apologizes on behalf of his country to British prime minister Tony Blair for the Japanese treatment of British prisoners of war during World War II.

13 Iraq prevents a team of United Nations inspectors, led by the United States, from continuing their search for weapons depots. Iraq banned U.S. members of an inspection team the previous November. The United States warns that it is likely to take military action against Iraq.

14 The European Commission recommends relaxing the ban on beef exports from the UK by allowing exports

from Northern Ireland. The ban was instituted in March 1996 after reports of a high incidence of "mad cow" disease in British herds.

15 Indonesian president Suharto signs a pact with the International Monetary Fund (IMF) promising major economic reforms and anticorruption measures to help save his country's floundering economy.

16 In the largest tobacco industry legal payout to date, eight tobacco companies and three trade groups agree to a $15.3 billion settlement in a suit brought by the state of Texas which sought compensation for money spent on treating smoking-related illnesses. The companies are required to pay the settlement to the state over the next 25 years.

18 Moderate Serb Milorad Dodik of the Independent Social Democrat party is elected premier of Bosnia-Herzegovina.

20 Václav Havel is reelected president of the Czech Republic, to serve another five-year term.

21 An investigation is launched into whether U.S. president Bill Clinton urged Monica Lewinsky, a 24-year-old trainee, to lie under oath and deny that she had an affair with him. Investigations continue until the end March amid further accusations and denials.

21 John Gotti, Jr., son of Mafia crime boss John J. Gotti, is arrested in New York, New York, on charges of extortion, fraud, money laundering, and racketeering. The arrest follows a five-year federal investigation.

22 The U.S. computer company Microsoft makes an initial out-of-court settlement with the U.S. government, who sued the company to prevent it from attaining a monopoly on Internet browsing software. Microsoft agrees to make the companion browser to its Windows 95 system more difficult to install.

26 A law banning the possession of all handguns goes into effect in Britain.

26 U.S. and British naval forces begin to assemble in the Persian Gulf and to draw up plans for a bombing campaign against Iraq because Iraqi president Saddam Hussein continues to hinder the work of UN weapons inspectors.

26 U.S. federal judge Stanley Sporkin rules that the U.S. Navy is forbidden to discharge senior chief petty officer Timothy McVeigh (not related to the man who was convicted of the 1995 bombing of a federal building in Oklahoma) because he is homosexual. Although McVeigh did not reveal his sexual orientation to the Navy, officers discovered his homosexuality through a listing on the Internet service America Online.

28 A court in Poonamallee, Tamil Nadu, India, condemns 26 people to death by hanging for their roles in the assassination of former Prime Minister Rajiv Gandhi in 1991. The sentencing ends India's longest ever assassination trial.

28 The Turkish government releases a report confirming that some government officials did participate in mid-1990s death-squad attacks, mostly aimed at Kurdish rebels.

29 A bomb explodes outside an abortion clinic in Birmingham, Alabama, killing one person and seriously injuring another. This is the first time that a bombing of a clinic causes a death. A religious antiabortion group called the Army of God takes responsibility.

29 British prime minister Tony Blair announces that the government will launch a new investigation into "Bloody Sunday," the 1972 killing of 14 unarmed Catholic protesters by British troops in Londonderry, Northern Ireland.

FEBRUARY

1 Businessman and economist Miguel Rodriguez of the Social Christian Unity Party is elected president of Costa Rica, replacing President Jose Figueres Olsen of the National Liberation Party.

2 Guy Snowdon, head of lottery firm Gtech Holdings Corp, is found guilty by a jury in London, England, of libeling British entrepreneur Richard Branson. Snowdon is fined £100,000 and ordered to pay Branson's legal fees, estimated at more than £1,000,000.

2 U.S. president Bill Clinton presents the 1999 $1.73 trillion budget, balanced for the first time since 1969, to Congress.

3 The British government announces that it is changing its method of recording unemployment figures to be in line with international labor-monitoring groups. The current method only categorizes people receiving benefit as unemployed.

4–7 British prime minister Tony Blair makes his first official visit to the United States as leader of the British government. Many comparisons are made between Blair and the American president Bill Clinton.

6 South African president Nelson Mandela opens the 1998 session of parliament in Pretoria, South Africa. He stresses employment and anticorruption measures in his state of the nation speech.

6 Thirty-five-year-old former primary school teacher Mary Kay Letourneau is sentenced to seven-and-a-half years in prison after she violated a court order to stay away from a 14-year-old boy with whom she had sexual relations.

8–11 A European Union delegation visits Algeria on a four-day peace mission amid ongoing bloodshed in the country's civil war, instigated by militant Islamic rebels.

9 Around 24 gunmen open fire on Georgian president Eduard Shevardnadze's motorcade in Tbilisi, Georgia, in the second assassination attempt on the president. Shevardnadze is unharmed, but three people die and four people suffer injuries in the attack.

9–April 23 Nigeria launches an artillery attack against Sierra Leone's military junta in Freetown, Sierra Leone. Fighting continues for several weeks until ousted president Ahmad Tejan Kabbah returns.

10 For the first time in nearly 30 years, Australia commits armed ground forces to a foreign military endeavor. Prime Minister John Howard pledges military support to the United States if it attacks Iraq for hindering U.S.-led United Nations arms inspections.

11 A U.S. district judge in Eugene, Oregon, rules that U.S. disabled golfer Casey Martin is allowed to use a golf cart in Professional Golfers Association (PGA) competitions.

12 The Cuban government announces that it will free more than 200 prisoners, including some political prisoners, on "humanitarian grounds." The release was sparked by Pope John Paul II's plea during his visit to the island the previous month.

13 Nigerian-led troops under an alliance of West African countries ousts Johnny Paul Koromah's military

government of Sierra Leone. Koromah seized power from democratically-elected president Ahmad Kabbah in May 1997.

13 The Australian Constitutional Convention votes to replace the queen as head of state with a president chosen by a bipartisan parliamentary majority. A public referendum in 1999 will decide whether the country should become a republic.

15 Glafkos John Clerides is reelected president of Cyprus and in March begins talks with the European Union on the country's possible accession.

17 Former U.S. Naval Academy midshipman Diane Zamora is convicted of capital murder by a jury in Fort Worth, Texas. She had been accused of helping her boyfriend, David Graham, kill a 16-year-old girl, Adrianne Jones, with whom he had a sexual encounter.

18 The first budget of Hong Kong since its return to Chinese sovereignty includes tax cuts of HK$100 billion, the largest in Hong Kong's history.

19 An armed gang demanding the release of seven suspects being held for an assassination attempt on Georgian president Eduard Shevardnadze attack a United Nations office in western Georgia, taking ten hostages. One of the hostages is released on February 22 and the rest are released three days later.

20 In a trade deal with the United States, the government of Taiwan agrees to reduce import taxes on a range of U.S. goods and services.

20 Indonesian president Suharto abandons plans to link his country's currency to the U.S. dollar. The plans were opposed by the International Monetary Fund (IMF), who promised a loan package to help stabilize the country's economy.

23 Iraqi prime minister Tariq Aziz and Kofi Annan, the UN secretary-general, sign a breakthrough peacekeeping deal to avert war and permit UN weapons inspectors to continue their work.

24 Canadian finance minister Paul Martin presents the country's first balanced budget since 1969.

24 Cuba's National Assembly reelects Fidel Castro and his brother Raul Castro as president and first vice president of Cuba. Castro has ruled the country as a communist, one-party state since 1959.

24–27 Demonstrations are held in Istanbul, Turkey, to protest against a government ban on religious clothing in state schools and universities that includes the traditional Muslim long beards and head scarfs. The government relaxes the ban as a result.

25 National Congress for New Politics leader Kim Dae Jung is inaugurated president of South Korea. A dissident under the country's past military governments, he was elected in December 1997.

26 British health secretary Frank Dobson announces a ban on the use of British plasma in blood products for medical procedures because of the threat of Creutzfeldt-Jakob disease, the human disease linked to the bovine "mad cow" disease.

26 U.S. chat show host Oprah Winfrey is cleared of slander charges by a federal grand jury in Amarillo, Texas. A group of cattle ranchers had sued her for $12 million, claiming that her negative comments about beef, in reference to "mad cow" disease during an April 1996 broadcast of *The Oprah Winfrey Show*, caused U.S. beef prices to plummet.

27 U.S. vice president Al Gore announces that the United States is ending its 35-year ban on the sale of weapons to South Africa. The ban started as a sanction against the white minority government during apartheid.

MARCH

1 Serbia sends troops into the southern province of Kosovo to flush out ethnic Albanian secessionist paramilitaries. Hundreds of men, women, and children are killed over the next few weeks. It is the worst bloodshed to date in Kosovo's nine-year campaign by its Albanian majority to regain their autonomy.

6 The Ontario government agrees to pay C$4 million to the Dionne sisters, the three living siblings of the world's first surviving quintuplets. The government had taken custody of the girls soon after their birth and put them on display for more than nine years at a theme park called "Quintland," which generated more than C$500 million.

9 Britain, France, Germany, Italy, Russia, and the United States announce that they will impose sanctions on Yugoslavia in an effort to stem Serbian violence against ethnic Albanians in the Southern province of Kosovo. The Yugoslav president Slobodan Milošević is given ten days to withdraw troops from Kosovo.

9 British home secretary Jack Straw announces that Britain will not extradite Roisin McAliskey, a suspect in an IRA bombing at a British military base in Osnabrück, Germany, in June 1996. McAliskey was suffering from health problems, including serious postnatal depression.

9 U.S. prosecutors and defense attorneys appeal the 1997 manslaughter conviction of British nanny Louise Woodward, who was initially sentenced after eight-month-old Matthew Eappen died in her care.

10 President Ahmad Kabbah returns to power as Sierra Leone's president, after Nigerian-led West African peacekeeping forces ousted Johnny Paul Koromah's military government in February. Koromah had seized power from Kabbah in May 1997.

10 Thojib Suharto is "reelected" president of Indonesia despite his deteriorating health and an economy weakened by a sharp decline in value of Indonesian currency. He remains opposed to economic reforms demanded by the International Monetary Fund (IMF) which has arranged a $43 billion/£27 billion economic bail-out program.

10 U.S. president Bill Clinton lifts a trade restriction, the Jackson–Vanik Amendment, that prohibits U.S. companies doing business in Vietnam in order to get U.S. Export–Import Bank financing.

11 Ten police officers who were accused of torturing and sexually abusing 14 teenagers in December 1995 are acquitted by a court in Manisa, Turkey. The judges in the case claim that the prosecution has not produced indisputable evidence.

11 The center-left coalition leader Poul Rasmussen is reelected premier of Denmark by a narrow margin.

12 Amidst mounting corruption scandals in Japanese financial institutions, the central bank of Japan is raided and the head of its capital markets division, Yasuyuki Yoshizawa, is arrested for accepting bribes, prompting Yasuo Matsushita, the bank's governor, to resign.

13 A military jury at Fort Belvoir, Virginia, acquits army sergeant major Gene McKinney of all charges of sexual misconduct brought by six female colleagues, but he is demoted for obstructing justice by trying to tell one of the accusers what to say to investigators.

15 Australian prime minister John Howard announces plans to sell the government's majority shares in Telstra Corp, the country's largest telecommunications company, if his Liberal–National coalition government is reelected. Proceeds would go to repay around 40% of Australia's national debt.

15 Kathleen Willey, a former campaign volunteer and part-time White House staffer, appears on the Central Broadcasting Service (CBS) program *60 Minutes* to discuss an incident in 1993 in which U.S. president Bill Clinton allegedly kissed and fondled her. Her testimony is a key part of the lawsuit of Paula Jones, who is suing the president for sexual harassment while he was governor of Arkansas in 1991.

16 European Union agriculture ministers approve plans to export beef from Northern Ireland. This will be the first export of beef from the UK since the ban imposed in March 1996 because of the threat of "mad cow" disease.

17 Zhu Rongji is elected prime minister of China. He quickly announces that he is axing half of its 8 million civil servant jobs to combat budget deficits. Many believe his reforms will mark a new era in Chinese politics.

19 Atal Behari Vajpayee, Nationalist BJP party leader, is elected prime minister of India. He calls for national "reconciliation and accord," but also threatens that India might install and deploy nuclear weapons.

23 Russian president Boris Yeltsin dismisses all 29 of his ministers including two of its pivotal figures—Viktor Chernomyrdin, the prime minister, and his most aggressive free-marketeer, Anatoly Chubais, the first deputy prime minister. The government crisis lasts until April 24, when the state Duma bows to president Yeltsin's will and endorses Sergey Kiriyenko as prime minister.

24 Mitchell Johnson, 13, and Andrew Golden, 11, students at Westside Middle School in Jonesboro, Arkansas, open fire on the school playground from nearby woods, killing four students and one teacher and injuring ten others.

25 Britain, France, Germany, Italy, Russia, and the United States agree to delay imposing economic sanctions on Yugoslavia for one month. The countries threatened sanctions on Yugoslavia earlier in the month in an effort to stem Serbian violence against ethnic Albanians in the southern province of Kosovo. The countries still, however, plan to seek a United Nations arms embargo against Yugoslavia.

25 The British House of Commons approves, by a vote of 211–15, a ban on corporal punishment in privately-funded schools. Corporal punishment was banned in state schools in 1986.

25 The European Commission officially recommends 11 European Union countries—Austria, Belgium, Finland, France, Germany, Ireland, Italy, Luxembourg, the Netherlands, Portugal, and Spain—to join the European economic and monetary union (EMU), for the launch of the European currency, the euro, in 1999. Of the other

four European Union countries, Greece would not meet the economic criteria, and Britain, Denmark, and Sweden already chose not to participate in the euro launch.

30 Premier Robert Kocharyan is elected president of Armenia.

31 The Organization of Petroleum-Exporting Countries (OPEC) agrees to reduce its oil production by 1,250,000 barrels a day to help stop plunging oil prices.

31 The United Nations Security Council votes unanimously to impose an arms embargo on Yugoslavia in an effort to stem Serbian violence against ethnic Albanians in the southern province of Kosovo.

APRIL

1 U.S. federal judge Susan Wright dismisses the four-year-old civil lawsuit of Paula Jones against U.S. president Bill Clinton, in which Jones charged Clinton with sexual harassment in 1991 when he was governor of Arkansas.

3 During a summit in Brussels, Belgium, European Union government ministers settle a long-standing dispute that threatened to delay the launch of the new European currency, the euro, over who will head the new European Central Bank. The job goes to Wim Duisenberg, former president of the Dutch central bank.

6 At a United Nations ceremony Britain and France ratify the Comprehensive Test Ban Treaty (CTBT), that prohibits all testing of nuclear weapons; they are the first countries with nuclear capabilities to ratify the ban.

8 The Indonesian government announces that it has reached a new financial agreement with the International Monetary Fund (IMF), the third such agreement in six months. The IMF had postponed any payment of loans after Indonesian president Suharto failed to stick to terms mapped out in previous agreements.

10 The Republic of Ireland, Britain, and the political parties in Northern Ireland reach a peace agreement over the latter involving the devolution of a wide range of executive and legislative powers to a Northern Ireland Assembly.

10 The central bank of Japan announces that it disciplined 98 bank employees for accepting gifts from commercial banks. The move was part of an internal corruption investigation, started in April when a senior bank official was arrested for accepting bribes.

15 Cambodian Khmer Rouge leader Pol Pot, who was responsible for the deaths of 1.7 million Cambodians, dies, reportedly of heart failure, near the border of Cambodia and Thailand, escaping international efforts to capture him and try him for genocide.

15 On the opening day of their annual meeting in Washington, D.C., finance officials from the Group of Seven (G-7), industrialized nations, comprising Britain, Canada, Germany, France, Italy, Japan, and the United States, call on Japan to take strong financial measures and make structural reforms to boost their floundering economy.

17–19 Thousands of workers demonstrating in Seoul, South Korea, clash with riot police. The workers are protesting against massive job cuts since the country's economic crisis began in 1997.

19 Austrian president Thomas Klestil is reelected for a second six-year term.

19 Wang Dan, a leader of the 1989 Tiananmen Square demonstrations in Beijing, China, who has been imprisoned for almost nine years, is released on medical parole and sent to Detroit, Michigan, for treatment.

20 British prime minister Tony Blair announces that the United States will invite Israeli prime minister Benjamin Netanyahu and Palestine Liberation Organization (PLO) leader Yassir Arafat to Middle East peace talks in London, England.

23 Belgian interior minister Johan Lanotte and justice minister Stefaan De Clerck resign over the brief escape of suspected child killer Marc Dutroux, who was charged with five murders and the rape of several young girls. Dutroux was captured after four hours.

23 The Mongolia parliament elects former journalist Tsakhiagiin Elbegdorj premier of the country. Elbegdorj, the 35-year-old leader of the National Democratic Party, becomes the youngest ever premier of Mongolia.

24 The largest public execution in recent history takes place in a soccer field in Kigali, Rwanda, when 22 people are shot for their part in the massacre of 500,000 Hutus in 1994.

29 Britain, France, Germany, Italy, Russia, and the United States declare an international freeze on all of the Yugoslav government's foreign assets, in a move to try to stem Serbian violence against ethnic Albanians in the southern province of Kosovo.

30 The United States Senate votes to admit Poland, Hungary, and the Czech Republic into the North Atlantic Treaty Organization (NATO). The last country admitted was Spain in 1982.

MAY

1 Jean Kambanda, the former premier of Rwanda, pleads guilty to six counts of genocide during the country's civil war in 1994, before the International Criminal Tribunal for Rwanda, in Arusha, Tanzania.

4 U.S. dictrict judge Garland Burrell, Jr., sentences Theodore Kaczynski, the "Unabomber," to four life sentences, plus 30 years for four bombings that killed three people and wounded 11 others. Authorities suspected that Kaczynski was responsible for 16 bombings over 17 years.

7 The U.S. Senate votes unanimously to pass a reform bill for the Internal Revenue Service (IRS), after hearings that cited corruption, abuse of power, and poor customer service.

8 Tobacco companies agree to pay the state of Minnesota and Blue Cross and Blue Shield of Minnesota $6.6 billion to settle a law suit filed to compensate for the cost of treating smoking-related illnesses.

15 The U.S. House of Representatives passes a Religious Persecution Bill by a vote of 375–41. The bill imposes sanctions on nations guilty of extreme acts of persecution such as enslavement and murder.

18 The United States and the European Union (EU) reach a compromise in their dispute over U.S. sanctions against foreign companies doing business with Cuba, Iran, and Libya. The U.S. agrees to relax sanctions against energy companies, and the EU agrees to tighten controls over the export of weapons to Iran.

21 A 15-year-old student opens fire with a semiautomatic rifle in the cafeteria of his secondary school in Springfield, Oregon, killing two students and injuring 22 others.

21 Indonesian president Suharto resigns after a week of riots in Jakarta in which much of the city is burned. He is replaced by his vice president Bucharuddin Jusuf Habibie.

24 In Hong Kong's first legislative elections since it reverted to Chinese sovereignty, prodemocracy parties win more than 60% of the popular vote.

JUNE

• Hundreds of thousands of refugees flee the capital city of Bissau in the West African country of Guinea-Bissau after a coup attempt. Senegal and Guinea send troops to support loyalist forces.

• The European Commission recommends that the two-year-old export ban on British beef, costing Britain some £1.5 billion, be lifted. The ban was put in place after the discovery of "mad cow" disease in British herds.

10 In part of Scotland Yard's biggest anticorruption campaign in the UK for 25 years, detectives raid the homes of suspected officers.

15 Australian politician Pauline Hanson, One Nation Party candidate who is opposed to immigration and seeks welfare cuts for Aborigines, wins 30% of votes in Queensland state elections.

16 The Supreme Court of Massachusetts votes 4–3 to uphold the trial judge's decision to reduce the sentence of British nanny Louise Woodward, who was accused of murdering Matthew Eappen, an 18-month-old baby in her care, from second-degree murder to manslaughter.

18 The British government announces that the new UK minimum wage will be set at £3.60 per hour, to go into effect in April 1999.

22 The Hong Kong government announces an emergency £2.5 billion rescue package in an effort to prevent the country's failing economy from affecting the rest of the world.

25 U.S. president Bill Clinton arrives in China for a nine-day visit, the first by a U.S. president since the Tiananmen Square massacre in 1989.

JULY

• By early July, approximately a third of the 200,000 Serbs living in the former Yugoslavian state of Kosovo have left the province, while ethnic Albanians have returned to fight Serbian forces.

6 In the largest military operation in Northern Ireland for 30 years, 28,000 British troops and police block the biggest annual Orangemen's parade in its 191-year history when they prevent the 6,000 marchers from returning to Portadown after leaving Drumcree church. The Orangemen vow to remain.

8 The Australian government passes the Native Title Bill, giving greater protection to farmers and miners who fear Aboriginal land claims would destroy their livelihoods. Aboriginal leaders condemn it.

8 The UK Ministry of Defence announces the sale of £2.3 billion worth of assets to pay for the modernization of the armed forces.

8 U.S. women claiming to have been injured by silicone breast implants win a $3.2 billion/£2 billion settlement, ending ten years of legal battles and 170,000 lawsuits.

12 The UK minister for welfare reform announces wide-ranging measures to prevent benefit fraud, after he

reveals that £7 billion is stolen by benefit cheats per year.

12   Three young boys are killed in an arson attack in the Drumcree siege—the latest in eight days of violence. The Orangemen continue their standoff despite a loss of sympathy created by the deaths.

14   The UK chancellor of the Exchequer Gordon Brown announces an extra £40 billion for health and education over the next three years.

15   The standoff between Orangemen and British and RUC forces at Drumcree, Northern Ireland, ends when security forces forcibly remove the remaining protestors in a dawn raid.

17   The last czar of Russia, Czar Nicholas II, and his family are buried in St. Petersburg, Russia, 80 years after their murder at Yekaterinburg, Russia. Russian president Boris Yeltsin makes a public apology after initially refusing to attend the ceremony.

29   After four days of fighting, Serb forces overrun the former Yugoslavian province of Kosovo, routing the Kosovo Liberation Army (KLA). Over 100,000 Albanians are displaced.

30   The court of appeal overturns the guilty verdict of British convict Derek Bentley, who was controversially convicted and hanged in 1953 for the murder of a policeman.

SCIENCE, TECHNOLOGY, AND MEDICINE

Agriculture

JANUARY

- The German Red Cross estimates that 10,000 children a month are dying from malnutrition in North Korea and that 2 million died in 1997. The famine has been caused by poor agricultural practices that have brought environmental catastrophe.

20   Veterinarians in Dubai, United Arab Emirates, announce the birth of Rama the "cama," the first cross between a camel and a llama. It has the long fleece of a llama and the strength of a camel; it has no hump.

MARCH

4   Around 25,000 people march through central London to promote understanding of the issues facing rural Britain, including the 1997 bill to ban hunting with dogs, and government policies on farming.

18   The European Commission embarks on a path of historic reform by announcing the phasing out of price supports for agricultural products, the bedrock of the Common Agricultural Policy (CAP) since its creation in 1962.

Computing

JANUARY

26   U.S. company Compaq Computer Corporation announces that it will take over its rival, Digital Equipment Corporation, for $9.6 billion, which will make it the world's second largest computer company after IBM.

APRIL

- A U.S. study of six major search engines for finding information on the Internet concludes that the best (HotBot) only accesses 34% of relevant pages, whilst the worst (Lycos) finds only 3%.

JUNE

16   Some 10,000 people log on to watch the first birth recorded live on the Internet. The baby, Sean, is born in Arnold Palmer Hospital, Orlando, Florida.

25   The U.S. software company Microsoft releases its operating system Windows 98.

Ecology

JANUARY

10   An earthquake measuring 6.2 on the Richter scale erupts in Hebei, a northeastern province of China, killing 50 people and injuring more than 11,000. It shakes some buildings in the capital, Beijing, which is 225 km/140 mi away, and cracks the Great Wall.

12   The Australian deputy prime minister Tim Fischer sends military troops to assist rescue efforts in Queensland, which suffered severe four-day flooding.

22   The Australian government bans Japanese fishing boats from its waters after Japan refuses to limit its fishing of bluefin tuna, a probable endangered species.

FEBRUARY

February–March   Hundreds of fires in Sumatra and Kalimantan, the Indonesian portion of Borneo, blanket the islands in smoke. Singapore asks for international aid.

4   Nearly 4,000 are killed and 30,000 people lose their homes when an earthquake measuring 6.1 on the Richter scale hits the mountainous province of Takhar in northern Afghanistan.

MARCH

March–April   A series of tornadoes hit the southeastern United States, killing more than 60 people, spurred by the warmed ocean currents of El Niño.

23–April 1   Forest fires in Brazil destroy 51,800 sq km/ 20,000 sq mi of highland savannah and rainforest. Heavy rains finally quench the fires.

24   A tornado carrying winds of 185 kph/115 mph strikes the eastern states of Orissa and West Bengal in India, killing at least 105 people and injuring some 1,100.

APRIL

8   The International Union for the Conservation of Nature (IUCN), based in Switzerland, publishes a survey which reports that one in every eight known plant species in the world is in danger of becoming extinct.

14   Toxic algae in the waters off Hong Kong kill fish and result in beaches being closed. Environmentalists claim this "red tide" is at least partly caused by pollution from southern China, but the Hong Kong government claims it developed naturally.

17 An iceberg 40 km/25 mi long and 4.8 km/3 mi wide breaks off from the Larson B ice shelf in Antarctica. Global warming is thought to be the cause.

JUNE

- Scientists report the discovery of at least 300 never before documented species of insects and spiders in the rainforest in British Columbia, Canada. The results of the report will influence policy on the preservation of the area, which is being considered for logging.
5 British deputy prime minister John Prescott announces proposals to protect Britain's national parks following concern about traffic congestion, pollution, and soil erosion. Traffic free-zones, bicycle lanes, and cheap bus fares are being considered for the park areas.

JULY

5–25 Temperatures in Texas and Oklahoma remain above 38° C/100° F for 20 consecutive days in the worst drought in the area since 1980. Over 100 people die and $4.6 billion/£2.8 billion damage is done to the Texas economy. El Niño is blamed for the high temperatures, which continue into August.
17 A 10-m/30-ft tidal wave hits the north coast of Papua New Guinea, inundating several villages and killing an estimated 6,000 people. Of the survivors, 70% are adults; a generation of children is wiped out.

Exploration

JANUARY

6 The U.S. spacecraft *Lunar Prospector* is launched to gather information on the moon's resources, structure, and origin.
16 The National Aeronautics and Space Administration (NASA) announces that John Glenn, a Democratic senator from Ohio who became the first American in orbit in 1962, will be part of the space shuttle *Discovery* team on a ten-day mission to study life sciences. Glenn, who will be 77, will become the oldest space traveler.
24 The U.S. space shuttle *Endeavor* successfully docks with the Russian space station *Mir*. U.S. astronaut S. W. Thomas replaces U.S. astronaut David Wolf on the space station.
26 Analysis of high resolution images from the *Galileo* spacecraft suggests that the icy crust of Europa, Jupiter's fourth largest moon, may hide a vast ocean that might be warm enough to support life.

MARCH

5 U.S. scientists announce that the *Lunar Prospector* satellite has detected 11 million metric tons of water on the moon. It is in the form of ice.
11 U.S. astronomer Brian Marsden predicts that an asteroid will pass within 48,000 km/30,000 mi of the earth in the year 2028, raising the possibility that it could hit the earth. The following day, however, scientists from the U.S. National Aeronautics and Space Administration (NASA) refute his theory, saying that the asteroid is not likely to come closer than 960,000 km/600,000 mi to the earth.

APRIL

6 The U.S. National Aeronautics and Space Administration (NASA) releases a new picture of a rock formation on Mars. A previous picture made the formation look like a face, fueling the theory that the formation was constructed by a Martian civilization. The new picture, which does not look like a face, refutes this theory.

JULY

2 U.S. scientists report that the spacecraft *Galileo* has discovered 12 different vents on Jupiter's moon Io which spew lava at temperatures greater than any planetary body in the solar system—up to 1,175° C/3,100° F. The temperatures are caused by changes in the moon's shape as it orbits Jupiter.
7 A Russian nuclear submarine in the Barents Sea launches a commercial satellite into space. The first launch of its kind, it allows launches from any latitude and increases the range of orbit.
7 Two Japanese satellites, using sensors and lasers, perform the first automatic docking of any space vehicles.

Health and Medicine

JANUARY

16 The World Health Organization announces an outbreak of Rift Valley fever in northeast Kenya. Thousands are affected and more than 300 die. The outbreak is triggered by flooding and a subsequent explosion in the mosquito population.

FEBRUARY

9 U.S. scientist David Ho reports the discovery of the AIDS virus in a 1959 blood sample and suggests that the transfer from ape to human occurred in the late 1940s or early 1950s.
16 "Billy," weighing 4 kg/8.8 lb, is born in Tarzana, California, seven-and-a-half years after being conceived. It is the longest time a human embryo has been frozen and later implanted in a woman's uterus.
17 U.S. manufacturer Dow Corning Corp agrees to pay a total of $3 billion in compensation to around 177,000 women who claimed that their silicone breast implants, made by the company, had caused them some injury.

MARCH

13 Mary Morgan, the wife of child care expert and author of *Baby and Child Care* Benjamin Spock, makes a public plea for funds to help pay for her 94-year-old husband's health care costs, which include 24-hour nursing, special food, yoga, massage, and other therapies.
15 *Psychology Today* magazine reports that 5 million Americans are addicted to the Internet.
27 The U.S. manufacturing company Pfizer gains approval from the U.S. Food and Drug Administration (FDA) for its pill Viagra, which can cure male impotence. It becomes the fastest-selling prescription drug in U.S. history.

APRIL

- U.S. doctor Judah Folkman of Children's Hospital in Boston, Massachusetts, discovers that a combination of two drugs, angiostatin and endostatin, completely eliminates cancerous tumors in mice. The National Cancer Institute plans to begin trials on humans by the end of the year.

6   A report from the U.S. National Cancer Institute reveals that a study has shown that tamoxifen, a synthetic hormone, could prevent breast cancer, but might have serious side effects, including uterine cancer and blood clots, in women over 50.

10   The U.S. National Cancer Institute issues a report that claims that cigar smoking, which is on the increase, could be as harmful as cigarette smoking, increasing the risk of mouth, throat, and lung cancer.

13   Dolly, the sheep who was cloned in 1996, gives birth to a female lamb at the Roslin Institute in Edinburgh, Scotland.

20   The American Society of Clinical Oncology reports that two studies show that Raloxifene, a drug used to prevent osteoporosis, might prevent breast cancer, without the risks associated with tamoxifen, another drug recently discovered to prevent the disease.

22   Scientists at the Public Health Laboratory Service in London, England, report the discovery of a bacterium, *Pseudonas aeruginosa*, that is resistant to all known antibiotics. It causes a wide range of infections in people with impaired immune systems.

28   UK researchers at Guy's Hospital in London, England, announce the development of a vaccine against *Streptococcus mutans*, the bacterium that causes tooth decay. They hope it will be incorporated into toothpaste to eradicate decay.

JULY

3   Researchers at the Institute of Animal Health in Berkshire, England, announce the discovery of the gene that gives chickens immunity to salmonella, one of the most intractable health problems in England.

14   In Montreal, Canada, UK physician Roy Calne announces that a drug derived from a fungal growth discovered in the soil of Easter Island reduces the risk of rejection among kidney transplant patients by 60%, with few side effects. It is the first major transplant advance in 15 years. The drug is called rapamune after the native name for the island.

Science

JANUARY

7   Doctors meeting at the World Medical Association's conference in Hamburg, Germany, call for a worldwide ban on human cloning. U.S. president Bill Clinton calls for legislation banning cloning, the following day.

8   U.S. astronomers present evidence that the universe will never stop expanding and that it is about 15 billion years old, much older than previous estimates, at a meeting of the American Astronomical Society in Washington, D.C.

27   Al Schultz of the Space Science Institute in Baltimore, Maryland, using the Hubble Space Telescope, announces the discovery of a giant planet, larger than the sun, orbiting Proxima Centauri, the closest star to Earth. It is the first planet outside the solar system to be directly observed.

30   After five years of DNA testing, the Russian government affirms that the human remains excavated at Yekaterinburg, Russia, in 1991, are those of Czar Nicholas.

30   U.S. scientist Angela Christiano of Columbia University, New York, New York, publishes a study that identifies a "hairless" gene that causes severe hair loss.

FEBRUARY

5   Paleontologists led by Shuhai Xiao of Harvard University, Cambridge, Massachusetts, and Li Chia-wei of Tsing Hua University, Taiwan, discover animal and plant fossils that could be up to 580 million years old, in Guizhou province, China.

12   British archeologist Elizabeth Moore of the University of London, England, announces that radar surveys of Angkor, Cambodia, reveal remains of temples from 8th–13th centuries AD, much older than other ruins previously found on the site. The radar pictures also show ancient canals, dikes, and reservoirs.

20   Researchers at the University of Texas, in conjunction with the British company SmithKline Beecham, publish a study in which they identify a hormone that triggers hunger in humans. Scientists hope the discovery will lead to potential treatments of appetite disorders.

MARCH

2   U.S. scientist Dennis McFadden and his team of researchers from the University of Texas in Austin report a physiological difference between lesbians and heterosexual women that could influence sexual orientation. Echoes produced in the ears of lesbians in response to clicking sounds were weaker than those of their heterosexual counterparts.

11   Australian paleontologists announce the discovery of 800,000–900,000-year-old stone tools made by *Homo erectus* on the Indonesian island of Flores. They suggest that *H. erectus* were seafarers and had the language abilities and social structure to organize the movements of large groups to colonize new islands.

12   Astronomers in Mauna Kea, Hawaii, announce the sighting of a new galaxy, named 0140+326RD1, which is around 90 million light-years farther away than the previously known furthest galaxy from Earth.

26   Italian scientists Cristiano del Sasso and Marco Signore report their research on a 113-million-year-old baby dinosaur fossil of an unknown species, complete with several organs including the intestines, liver, and windpipe. The fossil was found in the Matese mountains, north of Naples, Italy.

29   Israeli archeologists announce that they have discovered the oldest ruins ever found of a Jewish synagogue, dating from around 70 BC, near Jericho in the West Bank.

JULY

4   Astronomers from the University of Hawaii discover the first asteroid entirely within the earth's orbit; it is 40 m/ 130 ft in diameter.

4   Japanese biotechnicians announce the successful freeze-drying of mouse sperm. The sperm are reconstituted and can successfully fertilize eggs. Unlike ordinary freezing methods the freeze-dried sperm can be kept at room temperature.

4   U.S. ornithologists announce the discovery of a new species of bird in Ecuador belonging to the genus *Antpitta*; this is claimed to be the most important species of bird discovered in 50 years.

5   The Egyptian Antiquities Department reports the discovery of a well-preserved ancient river port in the

northern Sinai Peninsula. It served as a trading port with Phoenicia, Crete, and Cyprus, 367–283 BC.

8 U.S. archeologists in Aqaba, Jordan, announce the discovery of the world's oldest Christian church, built by the Christian community of Ayla in the late 3rd century.

11 British astronomers in Hawaii discover what they believe to be a solar system forming around the star Epsilon Eridan, ten light-years away.

11 Researchers at the Fermi National Accelerator laboratory in Batavia, Illinois, announce the discovery of the tau neutrino.

24 One of the oldest churches in Britain, built shortly after the Roman legions left in AD 410, is uncovered in the ruins of Vindolanda, on Hadrian's Wall.

Technology

MARCH

• The U.S. armed forces begin trials to replace metal dog tags with smartcards. The plastic cards have computer chips embedded in them which contain information on the enlisted person's blood group, allergies, and so on, which medical personnel can read with a hand-held computer.

• There is a growing trend in U.S. courts for the use of computer-generated evidence. Lawyers use it, for example, to simulate complicated genetic techniques or to help juries visualize injuries.

APRIL

2 U.S. software company Knowledge Adventure introduce a product called "JumpStart Baby" which is designed for nine-month-old babies to play on their parents' laps. "Lapware" is the fastest-growing sector in the software market.

14 U.S. vice president Al Gore announces plans for Internet2, a high-speed data communications network which will serve the main U.S. research universities, and bypass the congestion on the Internet. It should be operational by 1999.

16 U.S. scientists at the National Renewable Energy Laboratory develop a solar cell that can split water into hydrogen and oxygen. It is seen as a breakthrough in the generation of alternative fuels.

23 The first cash machines to use "iris recognition technology" to identify the user and dispense money enter service in Swindon, England.

MAY

13 The government of India detonates five nuclear weapons in the Thar Desert, Rajasthan. The international community condemns the action, fearing a South Asian arms race.

28 Pakistan conducts five underground nuclear tests, two weeks after a similar action by India, escalating the nuclear arms race in South Asia. Afterwards, president Rafiq Tarar suspends the country's constitution and declares a state of emergency. President Bill Clinton announces wide-ranging economic sanctions.

30 Two days after it detonated five underground nuclear devices, Pakistan detonates another, despite appeals for restraint from the international community.

JULY

22 Iran tests a new medium-range missile capable of hitting Israel; the United States, Israel, and Saudi Arabia protest.

Transportation

JANUARY

4–6 U.S. car manufacturers exhibit several new cars with advanced fuel efficient technology that would reduce polluting emissions, at the North American International Auto Show in Detroit, Michigan.

FEBRUARY

2 A Cebu Pacific DC-9 crashes in the southern Philippines, killing all 104 people aboard.

3 A U.S. military aircraft flying low severs a ski lift cable at a ski resort in Italy's Dolomite mountains, killing 20 people in a cable car that falls 90 m/300 ft to the ground.

4 The Federal Aviation Administration (FAA) admits that it is behind in its effort to sort out computer glitches before 2000. If computers are not adjusted before the millennium, air-traffic control systems could be inoperable, threatening airline safety.

7 Swiss balloonist Bertrand Piccard, in the balloon *Breitling Orbiter*, sets a record for the longest nonstop, nonrefueled flight by an aircraft: 9 days, 17 hours, 55 minutes.

16 A China Airways jet crashes near Taipei, Taiwan, killing all 196 people on board, as well as 7 people on the ground. One of the victims was the head of Taiwan's central bank, Sheu Yuan-dong, who was returning from an economic conference in Bali.

JULY

1 The London Research Centre reports that between 1981 and 1991 the number of women drivers in London increased by 50%, while the number of male drivers remained the same. Reasons for the increase include driving children to school, shopping, and fear of going out after dark. The number of accidents involving women also passed that of men.

2 Hong Kong's Chek Lap Tok airport, which has the largest passenger terminal in the world, is officially opened. U.S. president Bill Clinton is one of the first to land there. The airport operates in chaos for the first few weeks.

3 The British powerboat *Adventurer* lands in Gibraltar after voyaging around the world in 74 days, 20 hours, 58 minutes, breaking the 38-year-old record by eight days.

6 Hong Kong's Kai Tak airport, in the center of the city, closes.

21 British financial journalist Brian Milton lands in Surrey, England, after circumnavigating the globe in a microlight in 120 days, beating the 175-day record set in 1924 for the round-the-world flight in an open-cockpit, single-engine aircraft.

28 The British Defence and Evaluation Research Agency unveils plans for a revolutionary trimaran hull to replace the long, thin hulls of the navy's present warships. The new style ships will have a 40% larger deck area than

current frigates, and will be capable of speeds up to 40 knots compared to the present 28 knots.

31 The UK government announces that sections of the M25 between the M3 and the M4 will become Britain's first 12-lane highway.

ARTS AND IDEAS

Architecture

FEBRUARY

24 British prime minister Tony Blair unveils plans for the inside of the Millennium Dome in Greenwich, London, England. Organizers expect 12 million visitors to the Dome, which will contain 13 exhibitions, a piazza for live performances, restaurants, and stores.

MARCH

29 The Vasco da Gama bridge across the Tagus River north of Lisbon, Portugal, is officially opened. It is the longest bridge in Europe: 18 km/11.25 mi long with 12 km/7.5 mi of bridges and viaducts.

APRIL

5 The world's largest suspension bridge, linking Kobe and Awaji Island in Japan, opens to traffic. It cost £2.2 billion and is 3.9 km/2.4 mi long.

JUNE

• The corporate logo for the Millennium Dome in Greenwich, London, England, is announced. It is the "New Britannia" woman, who is basically androgenous. The logo will appear on promotional material and an 18-m/60-ft version will be inside the dome.

Arts

MARCH

5 The world's most expensive sculpture, Antonio Canova's *Three Graces*, is permanently disfigured by a hairline crack thought to have occurred when it was last moved.

MAY

13 A portrait is uncovered on the wall of a chapel in Domremy, France, believed to be the only surviving likeness of the French heroine Joan of Arc.

JULY

2–October 4 Over 60 paintings by the Russian-born French painter Marc Chagall are shown at the Royal Academy of Art in London.

8 The world's largest work of art, a 4-km/2.5-mi outline of an Aboriginal man, is plowed in the desert in southern Australia; no one claims responsibility.

9 Statues of ten 20th-century Christian martyrs are unveiled at Westminster Abbey, London, England.

Film

MARCH

• The movie *Primary Colors* opens in the United States, directed by Mike Nichols and starring John Travolta and Emma Thompson.

• The movie *The Big Lebowski* opens in the United States, directed by Joel Coen and starring Jeff Bridges, John Goodman, Julianne Moore, Steve Buscemi, and John Turturro.

23 The 1997 Academy Awards are held. Best picture: *Titanic*; best director: James Cameron for *Titanic*; best actress: Helen Hunt, for *As Good as it Gets*; best actor: Jack Nicholson, for *As Good as it Gets*.

MAY

• The movie *Deep Impact* opens, directed by Mimi Leder and starring Robert Duval, Tea Leoni, Elija Wood, Morgan Freeman, and Leelee Sobienski.

• The movie *Godzilla* opens, directed by Roland Emmerich, starring Mathew Broderick, Jean Reno, and Harry Shearer.

• The movie *The Horse Whisperer* opens in the United States, directed by and starring Robert Redford.

JUNE

• The movie *The Truman Show* opens in the United States, directed by Peter Weir and starring Jim Carrey.

• The movie *X-Files* opens in the United States, directed by Rob Bowman and starring David Duchovny and Gillian Anderson.

JULY

• The movie *Austin Powers: International Man of Mystery*, released in the United States in 1997, and starring U.S. comedian Mike Myers and British actress Elizabeth Hurley, achieves cult status and sparks a retro-fad in fashion for men's ruffled shirts.

1 The movie *Armageddon*, directed by Michael Bay and starring Bruce Willis, Ben Affleck, and Liv Tyler, opens in the United States.

24 The movie *Saving Private Ryan*, directed by Stephen Spielberg and starring Tom Hanks, opens in the United States.

31 The movie *Dr Dolittle*, directed by Betty Thomas and starring Eddy Murphy and Ossie Davis, is released in the UK.

31 The movie *Lost in Space*, directed by Stephen Hopkins and starring Gary Oldman, William Hurt, and Matt LeBlanc, opens in the UK.

Literature and Language

JANUARY

• U.S. writer Toni Morrison publishes her novel *Paradise*.

1 The *Times* of London, England, begins serializing a group of previously unpublished poems by British poet Ted Hughes about his late wife, U.S. poet Sylvia Plath, who committed suicide in 1963.

APRIL

• The Pulitzer Prize for Fiction is awarded to U.S. writer Philip Roth for his novel *American Pastoral*.

• U.S. writer John Irving publishes his novel *A Widow for One Year*.

JULY

• English author William Blake's illuminated books are published in paperback for the first time in the UK.

8 The first edition of the *Canterbury Tales*, printed by William Caxton in 1476 or 1477, is bought by Sir Paul Getty for $7.6 million/£4.6 million.

Music

FEBRUARY

26 The Grammy Awards are held in New York, New York: Bob Dylan, best album *Time out of Mind*; Elton John, best male vocalist "Candle in the Wind;" Dylan Thomas, Jr., best composer and best rock performance "One Headlight."

MARCH

• U.S. pop singer Madonna releases a new album, *Ray of Light*, her first album of original songs since *Bedtime stories* in 1994.

APRIL

• The Pulitzer Prize for Music is awarded to Aaron Jay Kernis for his String Quartet No. 2, *Musica Instrumentalis*.
• The Pulitzer Special Award goes posthumously to the U.S. composer George Gershwin for his contributions to music in the United States.

MAY

15 U.S. singer and actor Frank Sinatra, considered by many critics to be the preeminent singer of this century, dies in Beverly Hills, California. He made some 1,800 recordings and gathered nine Grammys. An Academy Award-winning actor, he appeared in at least 60 movies.

31 British singer Geri Halliwell, "Ginger Spice" of the pop group the Spice Girls, announces she is leaving the group. The four other members say they will keep on singing without her.

Theater and Dance

APRIL

• The play *The Iceman Cometh*, by U.S. writer Eugene O'Neill, opens at the Almeida Theatre in London, England, directed by Howard Davies and starring Kevin Spacey.

MAY

12–July 12 To combat the rise of expensive, technologically sophisticated stages, the Battersea Arts Centre in London, England, stages all its performances in the dark.

JULY

2 The Old Vic Theatre in London, England, which opened in 1818, is saved from redevelopment when a new charitable trust buys it.

SOCIETY

Education

FEBRUARY

25 An international test of education standards finds U.S. high-school students among the worst in math and science in the industrialized world.

APRIL

17 A controversial report on Australia's higher education system recommends a more businesslike approach to running universities, whereby they would have to compete for federal funds using a student voucher system.

Everyday Life

JANUARY

26 The National Education Association and the American Federation of Teachers announce plans to merge, which will create the largest labor union in the United States to date.

FEBRUARY

5 The German government announces that the unemployment rate has risen to 12.6%, with the highest number of people unemployed in more than 50 years, which prompts unemployed workers to demonstrate.

10 The U.S. food company Frito-Lay begins selling fat-free crisps made with olestra, a synthetic fat substitute produced by U.S. company Proctor and Gamble.

24 The Scandinavian countries score the highest in an international study of achievement in mathematics and science by the U.S. Department of Education.

25 Switzerland's first legal brothel opens in Zürich.

APRIL

12 The U.S. Census Bureau reports that 26 million Americans, nearly one in ten, is an immigrant. Most come from Central or South America.

22 Animal Kingdom, one of the world's largest live-animal theme parks, opens in Disneyland, California.

MAY

13 The European parliament approves a ban on all tobacco advertising and sponsorship.

JULY

• Hiking-style boots replace trainers as the footwear of choice for U.S. teenagers.

29 Thirteen factory workers in Ohio win the world's largest lottery prize, $161 million/£108 million. The Powerball lottery is played in 21 U.S. states.

Media and Communication

JANUARY

12 A UK study, conducted on the Atlantic island of St. Helena where television was introduced only in 1995, shows that TV violence has had little effect on children.

MARCH

• A new genre of magazines sweep the United States. Known as "microniche" magazines, they cater to small markets such as interracial couples or women suffering breast cancer.

3 An Independent Television Commission report in the UK finds that young children prefer factual and live-action drama to cartoons and slapstick cartoons to action cartoons. All the children involved distinguished between "good" and "bad" action cartoons based on the amounts of danger and violence in them.

MAY

15 An estimated 76 million viewers tune in to the last episode of the U.S. sitcom *Seinfeld*, starring Jerry Seinfeld with Julia Louise-Dreyfus, Michael Richards, and Jason Alexander.

Religion

JANUARY

1–14 At least 1,700 men, women, and children are massacred in Algeria by Islamic fundamentalists.

16 The Constitutional Court in Turkey bans the Islamist Refah (Welfare) Party, the country's largest political party, because it violates a constitutional mandate for a secular government.

21 Pope John Paul II visits Cuba for the first time, where he criticizes the repression of personal and religious freedoms under the communist government of President Fidel Castro.

MARCH

4 Roman Catholic priests are outraged when the European Union requires that Communion wafers have a sell-by date.

30 Thousands of Buddhists gather at Taiwan's Chang Kai-shek airport in Taipei to welcome the arrival from India of a tooth believed to have been from Buddha.

APRIL

• The 1998 John M. Templeton Prize for Progress in Religion is awarded to British businessman and philanthropist Sigmund Sternburg.

MAY

30 The Global March for Jesus, an international Christian movement involving an estimated 10 million people around the world, opens. The focus of the march is religious persecution.

JUNE

10 The Southern Baptist Church, the largest Protestant group in the United States, add an amendment to their basic code of beliefs that says a wife must "submit graciously" to the leadership of her husband.

Sports

JANUARY

2–9 The FIDE World Chess Championships are decided on a knockout basis for the first time, with reigning champion Anatoly Karpov of Russia winning the tournament.

12 Chinese swimmer Yuan Yuan and her coach Zhou Zhewen are sent home from the World Swimming Championships in Perth, Australia, a week after being caught in possession of phials of the human growth hormone somatotrophin, a banned performance-enhancing substance used to build muscle bulk. Four other Chinese swimmers failed precompetition drug tests.

14 Russian swimmer Alexander Popov sets a new world record for the 100 m freestyle of 48.93 seconds.

25 Ethiopian runner Haile Gebrselassie reduces his own 3,000 m world record of 7 min 30.72 sec, set in

Stuttgart on February 4, 1996, by over four-and-a-half seconds, with a new time of 7min 26.14 sec, in Karlsruhe, Germany.

25 The Denver Broncos defeat the Green Packers 31–24 at the Super Bowl in San Diego. It is their first National Football League (NFL) championship in 38 years.

31 Martina Hingis of Switzerland beats Conchita Martinez of Spain 6–3, 6–3 to win the women's title at the Australian Open in Melbourne for the second successive year.

FEBRUARY

1 Petr Korda of the Czech Republic defeats Marcelo Rios of Chile 6–2, 6–2, 6–2 in the men's final of the Australian Open in Melbourne.

7–22 The 18th Winter Olympic Games are held at Nagano, Japan. They are the largest to date, with over 2,400 athletes from 72 countries taking part. Snowboarding, curling, and women's ice hockey are included as medal sports for the first time. Tara Lipinski of the United States, aged 15 years, 255 days, wins the women's figure skating title to become the youngest ever individual Winter Olympic gold medallist.

21 England records the highest ever score in the history of the International Championship in rugby union when they defeat Wales 60–26 at Twickenham in London, England.

MARCH

5 U.S. boxer Mike Tyson sues his former promoter Don King for more than $100 million for embezzling at least half of his $127 million in purse money.

12 Australian businessman Rupert Murdoch buys the Los Angeles Dodgers baseball team for a record $350 million. The sale includes Dodger Stadium.

19 Cool Dawn, ridden by British jockey Tony McCoy, wins the Cheltenham Tote Gold Cup horse race in Cheltenham, England.

22–23 At the World Cross Country Championships in Marrakesh, Morocco, Paul Tergat of Kenya wins the men's 12 km event for the fourth year in succession. Sonia O'Sullivan of Ireland wins both the women's 4 km and 8 km races.

28 Cambridge beats Oxford by three lengths in the University Boat Race on the river Thames in London, England.

30 The University of Kentucky Wildcats defeat the University of Utah Runnin' Utes 78–69 to win the National Collegiate Athletic Association (NCAA) championship in San Antonio, Texas.

APRIL

4 British jockey Carl Llewellyn, riding Earth Summit, wins the Grand National at Aintree, Liverpool, England.

5 France defeats Wales 51–0 at Wembley Stadium in London, England, to complete its second Five Nations rugby union championship grand slam in a row.

5 Scottish squash player Peter Nicol wins the British Open in squash.

12 Mark O'Meara of the United States, aged 41, wins the U.S. Masters golf tournament at Augusta, Georgia. Fellow U.S. golfer Jack Nicklaus, aged 58 and competing in the event for the 40th consecutive year, finishes in sixth place.

20 The Boston marathon takes place in Boston, Massachusetts. Kenyan runner Moses Tanui is the

fastest man, with a time of 2 hr 7 min 44 sec, and Ethiopian runner Fatuma Roba is the fastest woman, with a time of 2 hr 23 min 21 sec.

26 The London marathon takes place in London, England. Abel Anton is the fastest man, with a time of 2 hr 7 min 57 sec, and Irish runner Catherina McKiernan, in her first marathon, is the fastest woman, with a time of 2 hr 26 min 26 sec.

MAY

4 John Higgins of Scotland beats Ken Doherty of Ireland 18–12 in the world snooker championship final in Sheffield, England.

7 The International Amateur Athletic Federation (IAAF) launches its Year of the Woman Athlete by staging the first ever mixed athletics meeting in the Gulf State of Qatar where strict adherence to Muslim doctrine has hitherto prevented women from taking part in sport except in segregated, closed arenas.

16 A fortnight after becoming the first foreign manager to win the English league championship, Frenchman Arsène Wenger leads his Arsenal side to a 2–0 victory over Newcastle United at Wembley Stadium in London, England, in the FA Cup final. Arsenal become only the second club after Manchester United to win two league and cup "doubles," having previously performed this feat in 1971.

20 Real Madrid of Spain defeats Juventus of Italy 1–0 in Amsterdam, the Netherlands, to win the European Cup for a record seventh time.

24 The Swedish-registered *EF Language* wins the Whitbread round-the-world yacht race.

24 U.S. driver Eddie Cheever wins the Indianapolis 500 auto race at the Indianapolis Motor Speedway in Indiana.

JUNE

• The Detroit Red Wings defeat the Washington Capitals by four games to 0 to win the National Hockey League (NHL) Stanley Cup for the second straight year.

1 Holland beats Spain 3–2 in the hockey World Cup final in Utrecht, the Netherlands.

6 High-Rise, ridden by French jockey Olivier Peslier, wins the English Derby horse race at Epsom, Surrey, England.

6 Victory Gallop, ridden by U.S. jockey Gary Stevens, wins the 130th Belmont Stakes horse race in Elmont, New York.

10 In the opening game of soccer's World Cup finals, Brazil beat Scotland 2–1 in front of 80,000 people, at St. Denis stadium, Paris, France.

14 English soccer supporters in Marseille, France, for their World Cup game against Tunisia, clash with French supporters of North African descent, sparking concern over security for future matches.

14 The Chicago Bulls, led by U.S. basketball player Michael Jordan, defeat the Utah Jazz for the second year in a row to win their sixth National Basketball Association (NBA) championship. The score was 87–86.

21 Following Germany's soccer World Cup match against Yugoslavia, in Lens, France, German fans riot, targeting the French police. In one incident, a French policeman is beaten with a metal bar and suffers brain damage.

BIRTHS & DEATHS

JANUARY

5 Sonny Bono, U.S. singer, songwriter, and politician, is killed in a skiing accident in Lake Tahoe, California (62).

26 Shinichi Suzuki, Japanese violinist and teacher of the Suzuki method, dies in Matsumoto, Japan (99).

FEBRUARY

8 (John) Enoch Powell, charismatic British Conservative politician known for his controversial views on immigration, dies in London, England (85).

MARCH

10 Lloyd Bridges, U.S. actor, dies in Los Angeles, United States (85).

15 Benjamin McLane Spock, U.S. pediatrician and child psychologist whose book *Common Sense Book of Baby and Child Care* (1946) revolutionized attitudes toward rearing children, dies in San Diego, California (94).

APRIL

7 Tammy Wynette, U.S. country singer, dies in Nashville, Tennessee (55).

15 Pol Pot, Cambodian dictator and leader of the Khmer Rouge communist movement who was responsible for the deaths of 1.7 million Cambodians, dies in a Khmer Rouge camp near the Thai border (73).

19 Linda McCartney, U.S.-born British businesswoman and photographer, dies near Tucson, Arizona (56).

23 James Earl Ray, U.S. gunman who pleaded guilty to the 1968 assassination of black civil-rights leader Martin Luther King, Jr., dies in prison in Nashville, Tennessee (70).

MAY

15 Frank (Francis Albert) Sinatra, U.S. singer and actor known for his love ballads, dies in Beverly Hills, California (82).

29 Barry Goldwater, U.S. senator 1953–64 and 1969–87, and Republican presidential candidate in 1964, dies in Phoenix, Arizona (89).

JULY

6 Roy Rogers, U.S. cowboy movie star, dies in Victorville, California (86).

7 Moshood Abiola, Nigerian opposition leader detained since 1993 by the military dictator, dies from an apparent heart attack in Abuja, Nigeria, at a meeting with U.S. officials trying to negotiate his release (60). Violence lasting for a week erupts in Lagos at the news.

21 U.S. actor Robert Young, known for his roles in the television programs *Marcus Welby MD* and *Father Knows Best*, dies in Westlake, California (91).

21 U.S. astronaut Alan Shepard, the first U.S. astronaut to fly in space, dies in California (74).

24 R. W. (Tiny) Rowland, controversial UK businessman who built the Lonrho Corporation, dies in London (80).

German politicians suggest that their team should withdraw from the tournament, but the French and soccer authorities reject the offer.

21 U.S. golfer Lee Janzen wins the U.S. Open by one stroke over U.S. golfer Payne Stewart, in San Francisco, California.

22 The Wimbledon tennis championships open in London, England.

25 German tennis player Tommy Haas defeats U.S. player Andre Agassi 4-6, 6-1, 7-6, 6-4 in the Wimbledon tennis championships in London, England.

JULY

5 U.S. tennis player Pete Sampras wins the men's singles championship at Wimbledon, London, England. Czech tennis player Jana Novotna wins the women's singles title.

12 German race-car driver Michael Schumacher wins the British Grand Prix.

12 France wins the soccer World Cup, defeating Brazil 3–0. The following day 500,000 people march down the Champs Elyseés.

19 U.S. golfer Mark O'Mear wins the British Open golf tournament.

INDEX

The Handmaid's Tale 764
au pairs 909
Auberjonois, Rene 858
Aubers Ridge, Battle of 102
Auchinleck, Sir Claude 334
Auckland 759
Auden, W.H. 46, 228, 245, 270, 279, 289,
    297, 329, 362, 380, 389, 407, 416,
    511, 643, 672
    The Age of Anxiety 380, 389
    The Ascent of F6 289
    The Dog Beneath the Skin 270
    The Double Man 329
    For the Time Being 362
    The Orators 245
Audience Research Institute 322
audio cassettes 520, 540, 602, 713, 743
audion tubes 43, 76
Audran, Stéphane 593, 626, 690, 785
Audubon Society 30
Auerbach, Frank 680, 773
    Camden Theatre in the Rain 680
    Lampert, Catherine, head of 773
    Mornington Crescent Winter 593
Auerbach, Charlotte 387
Auerbach, Red 564
Auffenberg, Moritz von, General 91
August, Bille 796, 843
    The Best Intentions 843
    Pelle the Conqueror 796
August 1914 (Solzhenitsyn, Alexander) 615
August Day (Kline, Franz) 467
Augusta 325
Aulén, Gustaf Emmanuel Hildebrand 239
Aulenti, Gae 773
Aum Shinrikyo sect 875, 876
Aung San Suu Kyi 877, 878
aureomycin 387
Auric, Georges 150, 191, 745
Auriol, Vincent 376
Aurobindo, Sri 407
    Savitri 407
aurora borealis 475
Auschwitz 308, 356, 548
Aust, Bradley 496
Auster, Paul 775, 787, 808, 832
    The Art of Hunger 832
    In the Country of Last Things 787
    Moon Palace 808
    New York Trilogy 775
Austin, J.L. 524
    Sense and Sensibilia 523
Austin, Mary 17
    The Land of Little Rain 17
Austin, Tracey 705
Austin Seven 165
Australia 1, 48, 49, 66, 96, 153, 187, 217,
    437, 506, 507, 547, 556, 610, 633,
    769, 851, 888, 894 895, 930
Australia II 745
Australia Telescope 806
Australian antigen 529
Australian Broadcasting Commission 594
Australian Institute of Sport 725
Australian Research Council 806
australopithecine skulls 181, 649, 660, 670,
    762, 866, 880
Austria 41, 67, 137, 138, 147, 241, 275,
    293, 367, 419, 434, 446, 599, 861, 874
Austrian War Dog Association 117
Austro-Daimler company 23
Autant-Lara, Claude 379, 681
    Devil in the Flesh 379
Auteuil, Daniel 774, 843, 867
L'Auto 20
autobahns 140

Autochrome system 44
autogyros 235
Automatic Car Identification (ACI) system
    603
automatic pilots 113, 243
automatic teller machines (ATMs) 565, 586,
    820, 870, 883
automation 366
automobiles
    accidents 157
    antifreeze 151
    antilock braking 711
    automatic guidance systems 762
    automatic transmission 287
    bumpers 31
    car stickers 363
    catalytic converters 762
    computer-controlled facilities 721
    cost of owning and driving 899
    exhaust emissions 508, 580, 602, 680
    fiberglass bodies 466
    flashing indicator lights 440
    front-wheel drive 260
    fuel efficiency 936
    fuel gauges 219
    fuel injection 406, 440
    headlights 189
    high-compression engines 414
    hydraulic braking 165
    ignition systems 457
    license plates 16
    platinum spark plugs 746
    power steering 197, 414
    radial tyres 388, 431
    radios 165
    starter motors 76
    tubeless tyres 378
    world's smallest 917
Autonomous Benthic Explorer (ABE) 853
Avanti 79
Avedon, Richard 485, 670
Aventine Secession 172
Averescu, Alexandru, General 112
Avery, Oswald 351
Avery, Sewell 348
Avezzano earthquake 104
Avildsen, John 639, 671, 681
    Rocky 671, 681
    Save the Tiger 639
Avonex 893
Avril, Gine 166
Avril, Prosper, President of Haiti 792, 813
Awaji Island bridge 937
Awami League 601
Axel, Gabriel 785
    Babette's Feast 785
Axelrod, George 425
    The Seven Year Itch 425
Axelrod, Julius 80, 602
Ayckbourn, Alan 641, 652, 663
    Absent Friends 663
    Absurd Person Singular 641
    The Norman Conquests 652
Aydid, Muhammad Farah 281, 837, 850,
    851, 861, 890, 901
Ayer, A.J. 65, 114, 280, 322, 460, 497, 734,
    810
    Language, Truth, and Logic 280
    Logical Positivism 497
    Philosophy in the Twentieth Century 734
    The Problem of Knowledge 460
Ayers, Gillian 750
    Scilla 750
Aylmer, Felix 388
Aylwin, Patricio, President of Chile 804, 813

Ayodhya mosque 840
Ayora, Isidro 217
Ayres, Agnes 158
Ayres, Lew 53
Ayub Khan, President of Pakistan 474, 547,
    587
Azaña, Manuel, President of Spain 234, 273,
    275
Azerbaijan 162, 360, 791, 792, 812, 826,
    839, 850
Azikiwe, Nnamdi 25, 491, 526, 900
Aziz, Tariq 930
Aznar, José Maria 888
Aznar-Cabañas, Juan Bautista, Admiral 232
Azores, the 368
AZT 784, 828
B-1 bomber 750
B-2 bomber 795, 806, 917
B-9 bomber 235
B-36 bomber 388
B-52 bomber 547
Baade, Walter 148, 251, 396
Baader, Andreas 677, 678
Baader-Meinhof gang 621, 667, 677, 678
Babangida, Ibrahim, General 759, 851
Babbage, Charles 827
Babbitt, Milton 542
    Philomel 542
Babcock, Barbara 724
Babcock, Harold 422, 485
Babcock, Horace 422
Babel, Isaak 198
    Red Cavalry 198
Babenco, Hector 722
    Kiss of the Spider Woman 763
    Pixote 722
Babes in Toyland (pop group) 819
    Spanking Machine 819
Babilonia, Tai 674, 685, 694, 705, 716
baby buggies 573
Baby Doc . *See* Duvalier, Jean-Claude
Baby-doll dresses 832
Baby Fae 749
Baby M 781, 788
Baby Ruth candy bar 144
Babylon 96
Babylon 5 858
Bacall, Lauren 184, 352, 371, 389, 650, 867
Bacardi Ltd. 927
Bacchini, Romolo 38
Bacewicz, Grazyna 522
Bach, Richard 604
    Jonathan Livingston Seagul 604
Bachelard, Gaston 298, 322
    Philosophy of No 322
    The Psychoanalysis of Fire 298
Bachrach, Howard L. 151
Backus, Jack 456, 760
Bacon, Francis 59, 351, 432, 440, 467, 847
    Head Surrounded by Sides of Beef 434
    Screaming Nurse 467
    Study After Velàzquez 432
    Three Studies for Figures at the Base of a
        Crucifixion 351
Bacon, Henry 165
Bacon, Leonard 329
    Sunderland Capture 329
Bacon, Lloyd 213, 253
    42nd Street 252 253
    Footlight Parade 252 253
    The Singing Fool 213
Bacon, Robert 36
bacteria, isolation of 3
bacteriological weapons 805
bacteriophages 156
Bad Godesberg 294

TITLES INDEX